# CRIME IN THE UNITED STATES

*2023*

*SEVENTEENTH EDITION*

*EDITED BY SHANA HERTZ HATTIS*

**Bernan** Press

*Lanham • Boulder • New York • London*

Published by Bernan Press
An imprint of The Rowman & Littlefield Publishing Group, Inc.
4501 Forbes Boulevard, Suite 200, Lanham, Maryland 20706
www.rowman.com

86-90 Paul Street, London EC2A 4NE

British Library Cataloguing in Publication Information available

**Library of Congress Cataloging-in-Publication Data**

ISBN 13: 978-163671-391-5
e-ISBN: 978-1-63671-392-2

# CONTENTS

## LIST OF FIGURES

# SECTION I

# SUMMARY OF THE UNIFORM CRIME REPORTING (UCR) PROGRAM

# SUMMARY OF THE UNIFORM CRIME REPORTING (UCR) PROGRAM

Bernan Press is proud to present its seventeenth edition of *Crime in the United States*. This title was formerly published by the Federal Bureau of Investigation (FBI), but is no longer available in printed form from the government. This edition contains final data from 2020 and 2021, the most current years for which data is available.

## Transition to NIBRS

As of January 1, 2021, the FBI's National Incident-Based Reporting System (NIBRS) became the national standard for law enforcement crime data reporting in the United States. The 2021 data year will mark the first time that the FBI and BJS estimate reported crime in the United States based solely on NIBRS data.

As of June 2022, all 50 U.S. states and the District of Columbia were certified to report crime data to NIBRS. Just under two-thirds of the U.S. population is covered by NIBRS-reporting law enforcement agencies, and 62 NIBRS-certified agencies serve cities with a population of 250,000 or more; these agencies cover a total population of more than 37 million. However, data is extremely limited for several large states in 2021, including California (7 percent of the population represented), the District of Columbia (47 percent of the population represented), Florida (0 percent of the population represented), Maryland (47 percent of the population represented), New Jersey (42 percent of the population represented), New York (19 percent of the population represented), and Pennsylvania (17 percent of the population represented). Of the 18,806 NIBRS-eligible law enforcement agencies, 11,333 (60.3 percent) reported data for 2021. (Eligibility is determined by the agency submitting a minimum of 3 months of data.)

The absence of these large segments of population, an issue that is expected to be alleviated in future years, makes the 2021 data not comparable to previous years. Consequently, 5-year and 10-year trend tables do not include the 2021 data. The FBI has provided limited analysis of year-over-year trends, and these are included where possible in this edition.

Some data has been suppressed by NIBRS. This occurs as a result of high uncertainty for a generated estimate. This uncertainty then requires is the application of suppression rules found within the NIBRS estimation methodologies. Suppression refers to the withholding of estimates from release due to high levels of uncertainty to ensure an unbiased view of the available NIBRS data.

In most instances, differences in the comparison of 2021 data to 2020 do not meet the criteria for statistical significance. However, it should be noted that the main contributor to that finding is the large amount of variation—both random and systematic—that is measured in the 2020 data due to low coverage of participating agencies. As coverage increases, the FBI will be able to improve its ability to measure these critical metrics for the nation.

The FBI has provided some estimates for 2021 trends based on this limited data; more information, including a detailed breakdown on how the values were extrapolated through the use of a confidence interval, can be found at <https://cde.ucr.cjis.gov> in the *Transition to the National Incident-Based Reporting System (NIBRS): A Comparison of 2020 and 2021 NIBRS Estimates* report.

Due to a system upgrade in 2019, the FBI now calculates rates for each offense based on the individual offenses and population published for each agency in tables 8-11. (Previous to 2019, when agencies were published in tables 8-11, but they had one or two offenses removed from publication due to not meeting UCR publication guidelines, the agency's data was not used to calculate rates for this table.) The FBI derived the offense rates by dividing the individual offense counts by the individual populations covered by contributing agencies for which 12 months of publishable data were supplied and then multiplying the resulting figure by 100,000. See Appendix V for the agency and population counts.

## About the UCR Program

The UCR program's primary objective is to generate reliable information for use in law enforcement administration, operation, and management; however, over the course of the program, its data has stood out as one of the country's leading social indicators.

The UCR program is a nationwide, cooperative statistical effort of (typically) more than 18,000 city, university and college, county, state, tribal, and federal law enforcement agencies voluntarily reporting data on crimes brought to their attention. However, for 2021, and due to the NIBRS migration, this number is much lower and covers only 64 percent of the population. Since 1930, the FBI has administered the UCR program and continued to assess and monitor the nature and type of crime in the nation. Criminologists, sociologists, legislators, municipal planners, the media, and other students of criminal justice use the data for varied research and planning purposes.

## Note for Users

To ensure that data are uniformly reported, the FBI provides contributing law enforcement agencies with guidelines that explain how to classify and score offenses and provides uniform crime offense definitions. Acknowledging that offense definitions may vary from state to state, the FBI cautions agencies to report offenses according to the guidelines provided in the handbook, rather than by local or state statutes. Most agencies make a good faith effort to comply with established guidelines.

The UCR program publishes the statistics most commonly requested by data users.

### Considering Other Characteristics of a Jurisdiction

To assess criminality and law enforcement's response from jurisdiction to jurisdiction, data users must consider many variables, some of which (despite having significant impact on crime) are not readily measurable or applicable among all locales. Geographic and demographic factors specific to each jurisdiction must be considered and applied in order to make an accurate and complete assessment of crime in that jurisdiction. Several sources of information are available to help the researcher explore the variables that affect crime in a particular locale. The U.S. Census Bureau data, for example, can help the user better understand the makeup of a locale's population. The transience of the population, its racial and ethnic makeup, and its composition by age and gender, educational levels, and prevalent family structures are all key factors in assessing and understanding crime.

Local chambers of commerce, planning offices, and similar entities provide information regarding the economic and cultural makeup of cities and counties. Understanding a jurisdiction's industrial/economic base, its dependence upon neighboring jurisdictions, its transportation system, its economic dependence on nonresidents (such as tourists and convention attendees), and its proximity to military installations, correctional institutions, and other types of facilities all contribute to accurately gauging and interpreting the crime known to and reported by law enforcement.

The strength (including personnel and other resources) and aggressiveness of a jurisdiction's law enforcement agency are also key factors in understanding the nature and extent of crime occurring in that area. Although information pertaining to the number of sworn and civilian employees can be found in this publication, it cannot be used alone as an assessment of the emphasis that a community places on enforcing the law. For example, one city may report more crime than another comparable city because its law enforcement agency identifies more offenses. Attitudes of citizens toward crime and their crime reporting practices—especially for minor offenses—also have an impact on the volume of crimes known to police.

### Making Valid Crime Assessments

It is essential for all data users to become as well educated as possible about understanding and quantifying the nature and extent of crime in the United States and in the jurisdictions represented by law enforcement contributors to the UCR program. Valid assessments are possible only with careful study and analysis of the various unique conditions that affect each local law enforcement jurisdiction.

Some factors that are known to affect the volume and type of crime occurring from place to place are:

- Population density and degree of urbanization

- Variations in composition of population, particularly in the concentration of youth

- Stability of the population with respect to residents' mobility, commuting patterns, and transient factors

- Modes of transportation and highway systems

- Economic conditions, including median income, poverty level, and job availability

- Cultural factors and educational, recreational, and religious characteristics

- Family conditions, with respect to divorce and family cohesiveness

- Climate

- Effective strength of law enforcement agencies

- Administrative and investigative emphases of law enforcement

- Policies of other components of the criminal justice system (that is, prosecutorial, judicial, correctional, and probational policies)

- Residents' attitudes toward crime

- Crime reporting practices of residents

Although many of the listed factors equally affect the crime of a particular area, the UCR program makes no attempt to relate them to the data presented. **The data user is therefore cautioned against comparing statistical data of individual reporting units from cities, counties, metropolitan areas, states, or colleges or universities solely on the basis on their population coverage or student enrollment.** Until data users examine all the variables that affect crime in a town, city, county, state, region, or college or university, they can make no meaningful comparisons.

### Historical Background

Since 1930, the FBI has administered the UCR program; the agency continues to assess and monitor the nature and type of crime in the nation. Data users look to the UCR program for various research and planning purposes.

Recognizing a need for national crime statistics, the International Association of Chiefs of Police (IACP) formed the Committee on Uniform Crime Records in the 1920s to develop a system of uniform crime statistics. After studying state criminal codes and making an evaluation of the record-keeping practices in use, the committee completed a plan for crime reporting that became the foundation of the UCR program in 1929. The plan included standardized offense definitions for seven main offense classifications known as Part I crimes to gauge fluctuations in the overall volume and rate of crime. Developers also instituted the Hierarchy Rule as the main reporting procedure for what is now known as the Summary Reporting System of the UCR program.

Seven main offense classifications, known as Part I crimes, were chosen to gauge the state of crime in the nation. These seven offense classifications included the violent crimes of murder and nonnegligent manslaughter, rape, robbery, and aggravated assault; also included were the property crimes of burglary, larceny-theft, and motor vehicle theft. By congressional mandate, arson was added as the eighth Part I offense category. Data collection for arson began in 1979.

During the early planning of the program, it was recognized that the differences among criminal codes precluded a mere aggregation of state statistics to arrive at a national total. Also, because of the variances in punishment for the same offenses in different states, no distinction between felony and misdemeanor crimes was possible. To avoid these problems and provide nationwide uniformity in crime reporting, standardized offense definitions were developed. Law enforcement agencies use these to submit data without regard for local statutes. UCR program offense definitions can be found in Appendix I.

In January 1930, 400 cities (representing 20 million inhabitants in 43 states) began participating in the UCR program. Congress enacted Title 28, Section 534, of the *United States Code* that same year, which authorized the attorney general to gather crime information. The attorney general, in turn, designated the FBI to serve as the national clearinghouse for the collected crime data. Since then, data based on uniform classifications and procedures for reporting have been obtained annually from the nation's law enforcement agencies.

### Advisory Groups

Providing vital links between local law enforcement and the FBI for the UCR program are the Criminal Justice Information Systems Committees of the IACP and the National Sheriffs' Association (NSA). The IACP represents the thousands of police departments nationwide, as it has since the program began. The NSA encourages sheriffs throughout the country to participate fully in the program. Both committees serve the program in advisory capacities.

In 1988, a Data Providers' Advisory Policy Board was established. This board operated until 1993, when it combined with the National Crime Information Center Advisory Policy Board to form a single Advisory Policy Board (APB) to address all FBI criminal justice information services. The current APB works to ensure continuing emphasis on UCR-related issues. The Association of State Uniform Crime Reporting Programs (ASUCRP) focuses on UCR issues within individual state law enforcement associations and also promotes interest in the UCR program. These organizations foster widespread and responsible use of uniform crime statistics and lend assistance to data contributors.

### Redesign of UCR

Although UCR data collection was originally conceived as a tool for law enforcement administration, the data were widely used by other entities involved in various forms of social planning by the 1980s. Recognizing the need for more detailed crime statistics, law enforcement called for a thorough evaluative study to modernize the UCR program. The FBI formulated a comprehensive three-phase redesign effort. The Bureau of Justice Statistics (BJS) agency in the Department of Justice responsible for funding criminal justice information projects, agreed to underwrite the first two phases. These phases were conducted by an independent contractor and structured to determine what, if any, changes should be made to the current program. The third phase would involve implementation of the changes identified.

The final report, the *Blueprint for the Future of the Uniform Crime Reporting Program,* was released in the summer of 1985. It specifically outlined recommendations for an expanded, improved UCR program to meet future informational needs. There were three recommended areas of enhancement to the UCR program:

- Offenses and arrests would be reported using an incident-based system

- Data would be collected on two levels. Agencies in level one would report important details about those offenses comprising the Part I crimes, their victims, and arrestees. Level two would consist of law enforcement agencies covering populations of more than 100,000 and a sampling of smaller agencies that would collect expanded detail on all significant offenses

- A quality assurance program would be introduced

In January 1986, Phase III of the redesign effort began, guided by the general recommendations set forth in the *Blueprint*.

The FBI selected an experimental site to implement the redesigned program, while contractors developed new data guidelines and system specifications. Upon selecting the South Carolina Law Enforcement Division (SLED), which enlisted the cooperation of nine local law enforcement agencies, the FBI developed automated data capture specifications to adapt the SLED's state system to the national UCR program's standards, and the BJS funded the revisions. The pilot demonstration ran from March 1 through September 30, 1987, and resulted in further refinement of the guidelines and specifications.

From March 1 through March 3, 1988, the FBI held a national UCR conference to present the new system to law enforcement and to obtain feedback on its acceptability. Attendees of the conference passed three overall recommendations without dissent: first, that there be established a new, incident-based national crime reporting system; second, that the FBI manage this program, and third, that an Advisory Policy Board composed of law enforcement executives be formed to assist in directing and implementing the new program. Furthermore, attendees recommended that the implementation of national incident-based reporting proceed at a pace commensurate with the resources and limitations of contributing law enforcement agencies.

**Establishing the NIBRS**

From March 1988 through January 1989, the FBI developed and assumed management of the UCR program's National Incident-Based Reporting System (NIBRS), and by April 1989, the first test of NIBRS data was submitted to the national UCR program. Over the next few years, the national IUCR program published information about the rdesigned program in five documents:

- *Uniform Crime Reporting Handbook*, NIBRS Edition (1992) provides a nontechnical program overview focusing on definitions, policies, and procedures of the IBRS

- *Data Submission Specifications* (May 1992) is used by local and state systems personnel, who are responsible for preparing magnetic media for submission to the FBI

- *Approaches to Implementing an Incident-Based System* (July 1992) is a guide for system designers

- *Error Message Manual* (revised December 1999) contains designations of mandatory and optional data elements, data element edits, and error messages

- *Data Collection Guidelines* (revised August 2000) contains a system overview and descriptions of the offense codes, reports, data elements, and data values used in the system

As more agencies inquired about the NIBRS, the FBI, in May 2002, made the *Handbook for Acquiring a Records Management System (RMS) That Is Compatible with the NIBRS* available to agencies considering or developing automated incident-based records management systems. The handbook, developed under the sponsorship of the FBI and the BJS, provides instructions for planning and conducting a system acquisition and offers guidelines on preparing an agency for conversion to the new system and to the NIBRS.

Originally designed with 52 data elements, the redesigned NIBRS captures up to 57 data elements via 6 types of data segments: administrative, offense, victim property, offender, and arrestee. Although, in the late 1980s, the FBI committed to hold all changes to the NIBRS in abeyance until a substantial amount of contributors implemented the system, modifications have been necessary. The system's flexibility has allowed the collection of four additional pieces of information to be captured within an incident: bias-motivated offenses (1990), the presence of gang activity (1997), data for law enforcement officers killed and assaulted (2003), and data on cargo theft (2005). The system has also allowed the addition of new codes to further specify location types and property types (2010).

The FBI began accepting NIBRS data from a handful of agencies in January 1989. As more contributing law enforcement agencies become educated about the rich data available through incident-based reporting and as resources permit, more agencies are implementing the NIBRS. Based on the 2012 data submissions, 15 states submit all their data via the NIBRS and 32 state UCR Programs are certified for NIBRS participation.

**Suspension of the *Crime Index* and the *Modified Crime Index***

In June 2004, the CJIS APB approved discontinuing the use of the *Crime Index* in the UCR program and its publications and directed the FBI to publish a violent crime total and a property crime total. The *Crime Index*, first published in *Crime in the United States* in 1960, was the title used for a simple aggregation of the seven main offense classifications (Part I offenses) in the Summary Reporting System. The Modified Crime Index was the number of Crime Index offenses plus arson.

For several years, the CJIS Division studied the appropriateness and usefulness of these indices and brought the matter before many advisory groups including the UCR Subcommittee of the CJIS APB, the ASUCRP, and a meeting of leading criminologists and sociologists hosted by the BJS. In short, the *Crime Index* and the *Modified Crime Index* were not true indicators of the degrees of criminality because they were always driven upward by the offense with the highest number, typically larceny-theft. The sheer volume of those offenses overshadowed more serious but less frequently committed offenses, creating a bias against a jurisdiction with a high number of larceny-thefts but a low number of other serious crimes such as murder and rape.

**Recent Developments in UCR Program**

In the fall of 2011, the APB recommended, and FBI Director Robert Mueller III approved, changing the definition of rape. Since 1929, in the SRS, rape had been defined as "the carnal knowledge of a female forcibly and against her will," (*UCR Handbook*, 2004, p.19). Beginning with the 2013 data collection, the SRS definition for the violent crime of rape will be: "Penetration, no matter how slight, of the vagina or anus with any body part or object, or oral penetration by a sex organ of another person, without the consent of the victim." This definition can be found in the *Summary Reporting System [SRS] User Manual*, Version 1.0, dated June 20, 2013. The FBI is developing reporting options for law enforcement agencies to meet this requirement, which will be built into the redeveloped data collection system.

In addition to approving the new definition of rape for the SRS, the APB and Director Mueller approved removing the word "forcible" from the name of the offense and also replacing the phrase "against the person's will" with "without the consent of the victim" in other sex-related offenses in the SRS, the NIBRS, the Hate Crime Statistics Program, and Cargo Theft.

In response to a directive by the U.S. Government's Office of Management and Budget, the national UCR Program has expanded its data collection categories for race from four (White, Black, American Indian or Alaska Native, and Asian or Other Pacific Islander) to five (White, Black or African American, American Indian or Alaska Native, Asian, and Native Hawaiian or Other Pacific Islander). Also, the ethnicity categories have changed from "Hispanic" to "Hispanic or Latino" and from "Non-Hispanic" to "Not Hispanic or Latino." These changes are reflected in data presented from 2012.

The national UCR Program staff continues to develop data collection methods to comply with both the William Wilberforce Trafficking Victims Protection Reauthorization Act of 2008 and the Matthew Shepard and James Byrd, Jr. Hate Crime Prevention Act of 2009. As a result, the FBI began accepting data on human trafficking as well as data on crimes motivated by "gender and gender identity" bias and "crimes committed by, and crimes directed against, juveniles" from contributors in January 2013.

**Uniform Crime Reporting Program Changes Definition of Rape**

For the first time in the more than 80-year history of the Uniform Crime Reporting (UCR) Program, the FBI has changed the definition of a Part 1 offense. In December 2011, then FBI Director Robert S. Mueller, III, approved revisions to the UCR Program's definition of rape as recommended by the FBI's Criminal Justice Information Services (CJIS) Division Advisory Policy Board (APB), which is made up of representatives from all facets of law enforcement.

Beginning in 2013, rape is defined for Summary UCR purposes as, "Penetration, no matter how slight, of the vagina or anus with any body part or object, or oral penetration by a sex organ of another person, without the consent of the victim." The new definition updated the 80-year-old historical definition of rape which was "carnal knowledge of a female forcibly and against her will." Effectively, the revised definition expands rape to include both male and female victims and offenders, and reflects the various forms of sexual penetration understood to be rape, especially nonconsenting acts of sodomy, and sexual assaults with objects. Beginning in 2017, only this revised definition of rape was used.

"This new, more inclusive definition will provide us with a more accurate understanding of the scope and volume of these crimes," said Attorney General Eric Holder. Proponents of the new definition and of the omission of the term "forcible" say that the changes broaden the scope of the previously narrow definitions by capturing (1) data without regard to gender, (2) the penetration of any bodily orifice, penetration by any object or body part, and (3) offenses in which physical force is not involved. Now, for example, instances in which offenders use drugs or alcohol or incidents in which offenders sodomize victims of the same gender will be counted as rape for statistical purposes.

It has long been the UCR Program's mission to collect and publish data regarding the scope and nature of crime in the nation, including those for rape. Since the FBI began collecting data using the revised definition of rape in January 2013, program officials expected that the number of reported rapes would rise. According to David Cuthbertson, former FBI Assistant Director of the CJIS Division, "As we implement this change, the FBI is confident that the number of victims of this heinous crime will be more accurately reflected in national crime statistics."

**About the Editor**

Shana Hertz Hattis is a consulting writer-editor for Bernan Press. She holds a master of science in education degree in from Northwestern University and a bachelor's degree in journalism from the same university. She has previously edited *Vital Statistics of the United States: Births, Life Expectancy, Deaths, and Selected Health Data* and several volumes of *Crime in the United States* for Bernan.

# SECTION II

# OFFENSES KNOWN TO POLICE

**VIOLENT CRIME**

- MURDER

- RAPE

- ROBBERY

- AGGRAVATED ASSAULT

**PROPERTY CRIME**

- BURGLARY

- LARCENY-THEFT

- MOTOR VEHICLE THEFT

- ARSON

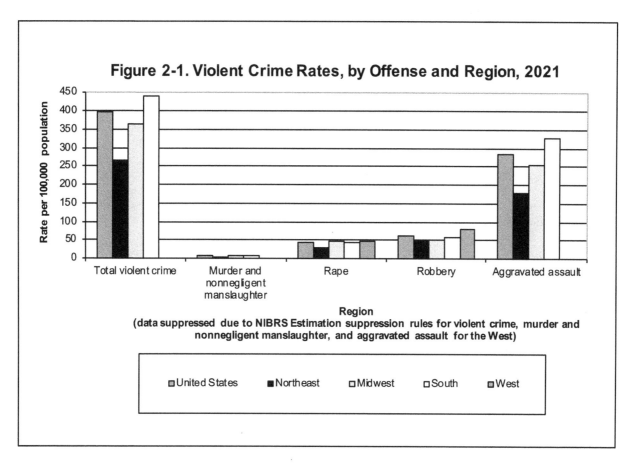

Figure 2-1. Violent Crime Rates, by Offense and Region, 2021

Region
(data suppressed due to NIBRS Estimation suppression rules for violent crime, murder and nonnegligent manslaughter, and aggravated assault for the West)

□ United States ■ Northeast □ Midwest □ South □ West

**Definition**

Violent crime consists of four offenses: murder and nonnegligent manslaughter, rape, robbery, and aggravated assault. According to the Uniform Crime Reporting (UCR) program, run by the Federal Bureau of Investigation (FBI), violent crimes involve either the use of force or the threat of force.

**Data Collection**

The data presented in *Crime in the United States* reflect the Hierarchy Rule, which counts only the most serious offense in a multiple-offense criminal incident. In descending order of severity, the violent crimes are murder and nonnegligent manslaughter, rape, robbery, and aggravated assault; these are followed by the property crimes of burglary, larceny-theft, and motor vehicle theft. Arson is also considered a property crime, but the Hierarchy Rule does not apply to the arson offense. In cases in which arson occurs in conjunction with another violent or property crime, the arson and the additional crime are reported. More information on the expanded violent crime tables (which are available online but not included in this publication) can be found in Section I.

**Important Note: Transition to NIBRS**

As of January 1, 2021, the FBI's National Incident-Based Reporting System (NIBRS) became the national standard for law enforcement crime data reporting in the United States. The 2021 data year will mark the first time that the FBI and BJS estimate reported crime in the United States based solely on NIBRS data.

As of June 2022, all 50 U.S. states and the District of Columbia were certified to report crime data to NIBRS. Just under two-thirds of the U.S. population is covered by NIBRS-reporting law enforcement agencies, and 62 NIBRS-certified agencies serve cities with a population of 250,000 or more; these agencies cover a total population of more than 37 million. However, data is extremely limited for several large states in 2021, including California (7 percent of the population represented), the District of Columbia (47 percent of the population represented), Florida (0 percent of the population represented), Maryland (47 percent of the population represented), New Jersey (42 percent of the population represented), New York (19 percent of the population represented), and Pennsylvania (17 percent of the population represented). Of the 18,806

NIBRS-eligible law enforcement agencies, 11,333 (60.3 percent) reported data for 2021. (Eligibility is determined by the agency submitting a minimum of 3 months of data.)

The absence of these large segments of population, an issue that is expected to be alleviated in future years, makes the 2021 data not comparable to previous years. Consequently, 5-year and 10-year trend tables do not include the 2021 data. The FBI has provided limited analysis of year-over-year trends, and these are included where possible in this edition.

Some data has been suppressed by NIBRS. This occurs as a result of high uncertainty for a generated estimate. This uncertainty then requires is the application of suppression rules found within the NIBRS estimation methodologies. Suppression refers to the withholding of estimates from release due to high levels of uncertainty to ensure an unbiased view of the available NIBRS data.

In most instances, differences in the comparison of 2021 data to 2020 do not meet the criteria for statistical significance. However, it should be noted that the main contributor to that finding is the large amount of variation—both random and systematic—that is measured in the 2020 data due to low coverage of participating agencies. As coverage increases, the FBI will be able to improve its ability to measure these critical metrics for the nation.

The FBI has provided some estimates for 2021 trends based on this limited data; more information, including a detailed breakdown on how the values were extrapolated through the use of a confidence interval, can be found at <https://cde.ucr.cjis.gov> in the *Transition to the National Incident-Based Reporting System (NIBRS): A Comparison of 2020 and 2021 NIBRS Estimates* report.

Due to a system upgrade in 2019, the FBI now calculates rates for each offense based on the individual offenses and population published for each agency in tables 8-11. (Previous to 2019, when agencies were published in tables 8-11, but they had one or two offenses removed from publication due to not meeting UCR publication guidelines, the agency's data was not used to calculate rates for this table.) The FBI derived the offense rates by dividing the individual offense counts by the individual populations covered by contributing agencies for which 12 months of publishable data were supplied and then multiplying the resulting figure by 100,000. See Appendix V for the agency and population counts.

### National Volume, Trends, and Rate

In 2021, an estimated 1,313,200 violent crimes occurred in the United States, a decrease of 1.0 percent from the 2020 estimate. An estimated 395.7 violent crimes were committed per 100,000 inhabitants in 2021, a decrease of 1.7 percent from 2020. Aggravated assaults accounted for 71.9 percent

of violent crimes, the highest percentage of violent crimes reported to law enforcement. Robbery accounted for 15.4 percent of violent crimes, rape accounted for 11.0 percent of violent crimes, and murder accounted for 1.7 percent of violent crimes. (Table 1 and *Transition to the National Incident-Based Reporting System (NIBRS): A Comparison of 2020 and 2021 NIBRS Estimates* report)

Occurrences of robbery and aggravated assault incidents decreased from 2020 to 2021, with robbery decreasing by 8.2 percent and aggravated assault by 0.1 percent. Murder and nonnegligent manslaughter occurrences increased 4.3 percent and rape occurrences increased 3.4 percent. (Table 1 and *Transition to the National Incident-Based Reporting System (NIBRS): A Comparison of 2020 and 2021 NIBRS Estimates* report)

In 2021, offenders used firearms in 79.9 percent of the nation's murders, 43.8 percent of robberies, and 41.3 percent of aggravated assaults. (Weapons data are not collected for rape offenses.) (Expanded Homicide data and *Transition to the National Incident-Based Reporting System (NIBRS): A Comparison of 2020 and 2021 NIBRS Estimates* report)

Many violent crimes are committed by people in known relationships. Figure 2 shows the number of murder victims who knew their offender. In the figure, the relationship categories of husband and wife include common-law spouses and ex-spouses. The categories of mother, father, sister, brother, son, and daughter include stepparents, stepchildren, and stepsiblings. The category of "acquaintance" includes homosexual relationships and the composite category of other known-to-victim offenders.

### Regional Offense Trends and Rate

The UCR program divides the United States into four regions: the Northeast, the South, the Midwest, and the West. (More details concerning geographic regions are provided in Appendix IV.) The population distribution of the regions can be found in Table 3, and the estimated volume and rate of violent crime by region are provided in Table 4.

NORTHEAST

The Northeast accounted for an estimated 17.2 percent of the nation's population in 2021 and an estimated 11.6 percent of its violent crimes. The estimated number of violent crimes increased 6.0 percent from 2020 to 2021. Murders increased 27.3 percent in the Northeast. Rapes decreased 1.1 percent. Robberies rose by 21.9 percent, while aggravated assaults rose 2.7 percent from 2020. In 2021, there were an estimated 267.2 violent crimes per 100,000 inhabitants, a 3.6 percent increase from 2020. (Tables 3 and 4 and *Transition to the National Incident-Based Reporting System (NIBRS): A Comparison of 2020 and 2021 NIBRS Estimates* report)

## MIDWEST

With an estimated 20.7 percent of the total population of the United States, the Midwest accounted for 19.1 percent of the nation's estimated number of violent crimes in 2021. The region had a 3.8 percent decrease in violent crime from 2020 to 2021. The estimated number of aggravated assaults decreased 5.7 percent, while the estimated number of robberies fell 3/2 percent. The estimated number of murders rose 7.1 percent. The estimated number of rapes increased 4.3 percent. The rate of violent crime per 100,000 inhabitants in the Midwest was 364.1, a decrease of 4.6 percent from 2020 to 2021. (Tables 3 and 4 and *Transition to the National Incident-Based Reporting System (NIBRS): A Comparison of 2020 and 2021 NIBRS Estimates* report)

## SOUTH

The South, the nation's most populous region, accounted for 38.4 percent of the nation's population in 2021. Approximately 42.7 percent of violent crimes in 2021 occurred in the South. Violent crime decreased 0.7 percent from 2020 to 2021, while the estimated number of murders rose 6.9 percent and the estimated number of aggravated assaults rose 2.8 percent. Robberies dropped 17.9 percent, while rapes increased 0.5 percent. The estimated rate of violent crime in the South was 440.5 incidents per 100,000 inhabitants in 2021, a 1.1 percent decrease from 2020. (Tables 3 and 4 and *Transition to the National Incident-Based Reporting System (NIBRS): A Comparison of 2020 and 2021 NIBRS Estimates* report)

## WEST

With 23.7 percent of the nation's population in 2021, the West accounted for less than a quarter of the nation's population. Data for violent crime, murder and nonnegligent manslaughter, and aggravated assault in the West were suppressed based on NIBRS Estimation suppression rules. Rapes and robberies rose by 4.9 percent and 11.4 percent, respectively, between 2020 and 2021. (Tables 3 and 4 and *Transition to the National Incident-Based Reporting System (NIBRS): A Comparison of 2020 and 2021 NIBRS Estimates* report)

**Community Types**

The UCR program typically aggregates data for three community types: metropolitan statistical areas (MSAs), cities outside MSAs, and nonmetropolitan counties outside MSAs. MSAs include a central city or urbanized area with at least 50,000 inhabitants, as well as the county that contains the principal city and other adjacent counties that have a high degree of social and economic integration as measured through commuting. Cities outside MSAs are mostly incorporated areas, and nonmetropolitan counties are made up of mostly unincorporated areas. (For additional information about community types, see Appendix IV.) Due to the NIBRS migration, this data was not available for the 2021 data year.

**MURDER AND NONNEGLIGENT MANSLAUGHTER**

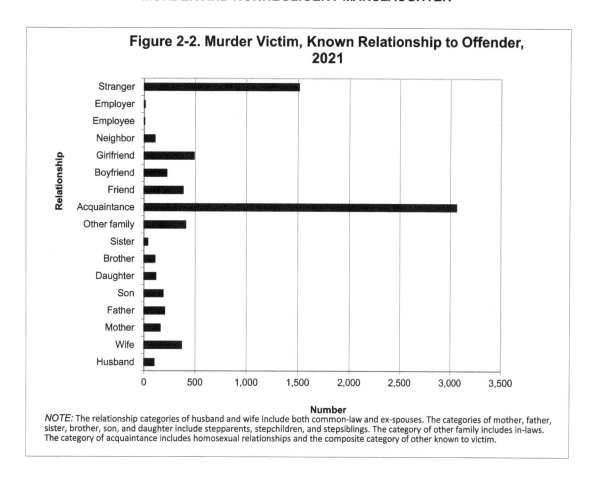

Figure 2-2. Murder Victim, Known Relationship to Offender, 2021

NOTE: The relationship categories of husband and wife include both common-law and ex-spouses. The categories of mother, father, sister, brother, son, and daughter include stepparents, stepchildren, and stepsiblings. The category of other family includes in-laws. The category of acquaintance includes homosexual relationships and the composite category of other known to victim.

### Definition

The UCR program defines murder and non-negligent manslaughter as the willful (non-negligent) killing of one human being by another. The classification of this offense is based solely on police investigation, rather than on the determination of a court, medical examiner, coroner, jury, or other judicial body. The UCR program does not include the following situations under this offense classification: deaths caused by negligence, suicide, or accident; justifiable homicides; and attempts to murder or assaults to murder, which are considered aggravated assaults.

### Data Collection/Supplementary Homicide Data

The UCR provides supplementary information about murder victims and offenders by age, sex, and race; the types of weapons used in the murders; the relationships of the victims to the offenders; and the circumstances surrounding the incident. Law enforcement agencies are asked to provide this data for each murder reported to the UCR program. Data can be

viewed in the Expanded Homicide Data section on the FBI's Crime Explorer data page: https://crime-data-explorer.app. cloud.gov/pages/home. Some highlights from these tables have been included below.

Please refer to the note about the limited data for 2021 at the beginning of this analysis for information about the transition to NIBRS and how it has affected comparisons and the examination of trends.

### National Volume, Trends, and Rates

An estimated 22,900 persons were murdered nationwide in 2021. This number was a 4.3 percent increase from the 2020 estimate. The 2021 murder rate, 6.9 offenses per 100,000 inhabitants, was a 3.5 percent increase from the 2020 rate. Murder accounted for 1.7 percent of the overall estimated number of violent crimes in 2020. (Table 1 and *Transition to the National Incident-Based Reporting System (NIBRS): A Comparison of 2020 and 2021 NIBRS Estimates* report)

## Regional Offense Trends and Rates

The UCR program divides the United States into four regions: the Northeast, the South, the Midwest, and the West. (More details concerning geographic regions are provided in Appendix IV.) In 2021, 42.1 percent of murders were reported in the South, the country's most populous region. The Midwest reported 19.1 percent of all murders, while the Northeast reported 11.6 percent of murders. Data for murder and non-negligent manslaughter in the West was suppressed based on NIBRS Estimation suppression rules. (Table 3)

NORTHEAST

In 2021, the Northeast accounted for an estimated 17.2 percent of the nation's population and 11.6 percent of its estimated number of murders. With an estimated 2,800 murders, the Northeast saw a 27.3 percent increase from its 2020 figure. The offense rate for the Northeast was 4.9 murders per 100,000 inhabitants in 2021, a 25.6 percent rise from 2020. (Tables 3 and 4 and Transition to the National Incident-Based Reporting System (NIBRS): A Comparison of 2020 and 2021 NIBRS Estimates report)

MIDWEST

The Midwest accounted for an estimated 20.7 percent of the nation's total population and 19.1 percent of the country's estimated number of murders in 2021. The Midwest reported an estimated 4,500 murders in 2021, up 7.1 percent from 2020. The region experienced a rate of 6.6 murders per 100,000 inhabitants in 2021, above its 2020 rate of 6.1. (Tables 3 and 4 and Transition to the National Incident-Based Reporting System (NIBRS): A Comparison of 2020 and 2021 NIBRS Estimates report)

SOUTH

The South accounted for an estimated 38.4 percent of the nation's population in 2021 and 42.7 percent of the nation's murders, the highest proportion among the four regions. The estimated 10,800 murders represented a 6.9 percent increase from the 2020 figure. The region's estimated rate of 8.5 murders per 100,000 inhabitants represented an increase of 7.6 percent from the estimated rate for 2020. (Tables 3 and 4 and Transition to the National Incident-Based Reporting System (NIBRS): A Comparison of 2020 and 2021 NIBRS Estimates report)

WEST

The West accounted for an estimated 23.7 percent of the nation's population in 2021. Data for murder and nonnegligent manslaughter in the West was suppressed based on NIBRS Estimation suppression rules. (Tables 3 and 4 and *Transition to the National Incident-Based Reporting System (NIBRS): A Comparison of 2020 and 2021 NIBRS Estimates* report)

## Community Types

The UCR program typically aggregates data for three community types: metropolitan statistical areas (MSAs), cities outside MSAs, and nonmetropolitan counties outside MSAs. MSAs include a central city or urbanized area with at least 50,000 inhabitants, as well as the county that contains the principal city and other adjacent counties that have a high degree of social and economic integration as measured through commuting. Cities outside MSAs are mostly incorporated areas, and nonmetropolitan counties are made up of mostly unincorporated areas. (For additional information about community types, see Appendix IV.) Due to the NIBRS migration, this data was not available for the 2021 data year.

## Supplementary Homicide Reports Data

VICTIMS/OFFENDERS

Based on 2021 supplemental homicide data (where the ages, sexes, or races of the murder victims were identified), 83.8 percent of the victims were 20 years of age or over, 14.9 percent were 19 years of age or less, and the age of 1.3 percent of the victims was unknown. Of the 14,677 murder victims represented in the 2021 expanded data whose gender was identified, 78.1 percent were male. Concerning race, 37.4 percent of victims were White, 58.1 percent were Black or African American, and 4.4 percent were of other races. Approximately 11.6 percent of victims were of Hispanic or Latino origin. For murders in which the gender of the offender was identified, 79.6 percent were males; the sex of offenders for 10.8 percent of homicides was unknown. For the offenders for whom race was identified, 53.6 percent were Black or African American, 33.3 percent were White, and 1.8 percent were other races; 13.2 percent were of unknown race. Approximately 10.0 percent of offenders were of Hispanic origin. (Expanded Homicide Data)

VICTIM-OFFENDER RELATIONSHIPS

For the 15,449 incidents in which the victim-offender relationship was specified (including the designation of "unknown") in 2021, 10.7 percent of victims were slain by family members, 9.8 percent were murdered by strangers, and 27.7 percent were killed by someone they knew other than family members (acquaintances, neighbors, friends, employers, romantic partners, employees, etc.). The victim-offender relationship was unknown in 51.9 percent of incidents. (Expanded Homicide Data)

## CIRCUMSTANCES/WEAPONS

Available circumstances have changed with the 2021 data year due to the migration to NIBRS. Concerning the known circumstances surrounding murders in 2021, and including murders with unknown circumstances, 1.4 percent of victims were murdered during gang killings in 2021. Circumstances of rape, robbery, burglary, larceny-theft, motor vehicle theft, and arson accounted for 3.7 percent of murders. Circumstances where the facts provided did not permit determination of circumstances accounted for 50.4 percent of reported homicides. Of the homicides for which the type of weapon was specified, 79.2 percent involved the use of firearms. Of the identified firearms used, handguns comprised 51.7 percent of the total. (Expanded Homicide Data)

**RAPE**

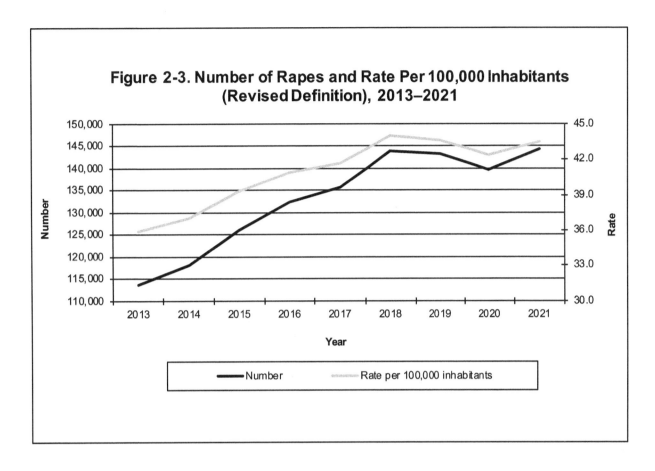

**Figure 2-3. Number of Rapes and Rate Per 100,000 Inhabitants (Revised Definition), 2013–2021**

### Definition

In 2013, the FBI UCR Program began collecting rape data under a revised definition within the Summary Reporting System. Previously, offense data for forcible rape were collected under the legacy UCR definition: the carnal knowledge of a female forcibly and against her will. Beginning with the 2013 data year, the term "forcible" was removed from the offense title, and the definition was changed. The revised UCR definition of rape is penetration, no matter how slight, of the vagina or anus with any body part or object, or oral penetration by a sex organ of another person, without the consent of the victim. Attempts or assaults to commit rape are also included in the statistics presented here; however, statutory rape and incest are excluded.

In 2016, the FBI Director approved the recommendation to discontinue the reporting of rape data using the UCR legacy definition beginning in 2017. However, to maintain the 20-year trend in Table 1, national estimates for rape under the legacy definition were provided along with estimates under the revised definition until 2020.

The UCR Program counts one offense for each victim of a rape, attempted rape, or assault with intent to rape, regardless of the victim's age. Non-consensual sexual relations involving a familial member is considered rape, not incest. All other crimes of a sexual nature are considered to be Part II offenses; as such, the UCR Program collects only arrest data for those crimes. The offense of statutory rape, in which no force is used but the female victim is under the age of consent, is included in the arrest total for the sex offenses category.

Please refer to the note about the limited data for 2021 at the beginning of this analysis for information about the transition to NIBRS and how it has affected comparisons and the examination of trends.

### National Volume, Trends, and Rates

In 2021, the estimated number of rapes, 144,300, increased 3.4 percent from the 2020 estimate. (Table 1 and *Transition to the National Incident-Based Reporting System (NIBRS): A Comparison of 2020 and 2021 NIBRS Estimates* report)

**Regional Offense Trends and Rates**

The UCR program divides the United States into four regions: the Northeast, the South, the Midwest, and the West. (More details concerning geographic regions are provided in Appendix IV) Regional analysis offers estimates of the volume of female rapes, the percent change from the previous year's estimate, and the rate of rape per 100,000 female inhabitants in each region.

NORTHEAST

The Northeast made up 17.2 percent of the U.S. population in 2021. An estimated 12.1 percent of the national total occurred in the Northeast. The region's rate of rape occurrences – 30.5 per 100,000 inhabitants – was a 2.9 percent drop from 2020. (Tables 3 and 4 and Transition to the National Incident-Based Reporting System (NIBRS): A Comparison of 2020 and 2021 NIBRS Estimates report)

MIDWEST

The Midwest accounted for 23.4 percent of the U.S. population in 2021. Of all the rapes in the nation, 23.4 percent occurred in the Midwest in 2021. The 2021 estimate (32,400 rapes) represented an increase of 4.3 percent from the 2020 estimate. The region's rate of rape occurrences – 49.2 per 100,000 inhabitants – was a 3.8 percent increase from 2020. (Tables 3 and 4 and Transition to the National Incident-Based Reporting System (NIBRS): A Comparison of 2020 and 2021 NIBRS Estimates report)

SOUTH

The South, the nation's most populous region, accounted for an estimated 38.4 percent of the nation's population in 2021; the region also accounted for an estimated 38.7 percent of the nation's estimated number of rapes. An estimated 55,900 victims reported rape in the South in 2021, up 0.5 percent from 2020. The region's rate of rape occurrences – 43.9 per 100,000 inhabitants – was unchanged from 2020. (Tables 3 and 4 and Transition to the National Incident-Based Reporting System (NIBRS): A Comparison of 2020 and 2021 NIBRS Estimates report)

WEST

The West accounted for 23.7 percent of the nation's population in 2021. The region also accounted for 20.1 percent of the nation's total number of estimated rapes with an estimated 32,900 offenses. The West saw a 4.9 percent decrease in rapes from 2020 to 2021. The region's rate of rape occurrences – 49.4 per 100,000 inhabitants – was a 4.9 percent drop from 2020. (Tables 3 and 4 and Transition to the National Incident-Based Reporting System (NIBRS): A Comparison of 2020 and 2021 NIBRS Estimates report)

**Community Types**

The UCR program typically aggregates data for three community types: metropolitan statistical areas (MSAs), cities outside MSAs, and nonmetropolitan counties outside MSAs. MSAs include a central city or urbanized area with at least 50,000 inhabitants, as well as the county that contains the principal city and other adjacent counties that have a high degree of social and economic integration as measured through commuting. Cities outside MSAs are mostly incorporated areas, and nonmetropolitan counties are made up of mostly unincorporated areas. (For additional information about community types, see Appendix IV.) Due to the NIBRS migration, this data was not available for the 2021 data year.

**ROBBERY**

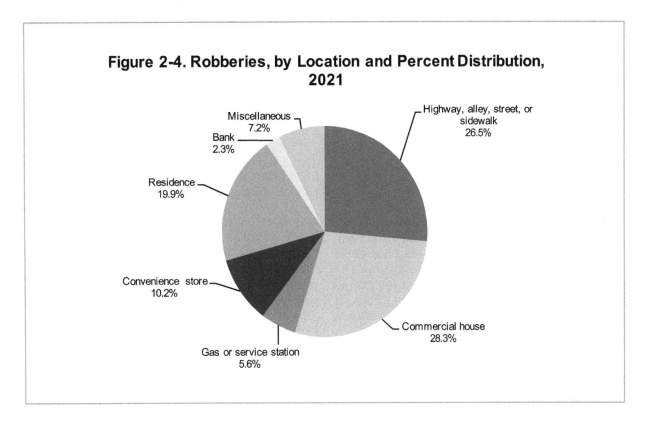

## Figure 2-4. Robberies, by Location and Percent Distribution, 2021

Miscellaneous 7.2%

Bank 2.3%

Residence 19.9%

Convenience store 10.2%

Gas or service station 5.6%

Commercial house 28.3%

Highway, alley, street, or sidewalk 26.5%

### Definition

The UCR program defines robbery as the taking or attempt to take anything of value from the care, custody, or control of a person or persons by force or threat of force or violence and/or by putting the victim in fear.

Please refer to the note about the limited data for 2021 at the beginning of this analysis for information about the transition to NIBRS and how it has affected comparisons and the examination of trends.

### National Volume, Trends, and Rates

In 2021, the estimated robbery total (202,200) decreased 8.2 percent from the 2020 estimate. The 2021 estimated robbery rate (60.9 per 100,000 inhabitants) showed a decrease of 8.8 percent when compared with the 2020 rate. (Table 1 and *Transition to the National Incident-Based Reporting System (NIBRS): A Comparison of 2020 and 2021 NIBRS Estimates* report)

### Regional Offense Trends and Rates

The UCR program divides the United States into four regions: the Northeast, the South, the Midwest, and the West. (More details concerning geographic regions are provided in Appendix IV.)

NORTHEAST

The Northeast, with an estimated 17.2 percent of the nation's population in 2021, accounted for 14.9 percent of the nation's estimated number of robberies. The estimated number of robberies increased 21.9 percent from 2020. The rate for this region was 52.6 robberies per 100,000 inhabitants, up from 44.2 robberies per 100,000 inhabitants in 2020. (Tables 3 and 4 and Transition to the National Incident-Based Reporting System (NIBRS): A Comparison of 2020 and 2021 NIBRS Estimates report)

MIDWEST

The Midwest accounted for 20.7 percent of the total population of the United States and 17.8 percent of its estimated number of robberies in 2021. An estimated 35,900 robberies occurred in the Midwest in 2021, a 3.2 percent decrease from the estimated figure from 2020. The region's robbery rate was 52.2 robberies per 100,000 inhabitants in 2020, down 3.9 percent from 2020. (Tables 3 and 4 and Transition to the National Incident-Based Reporting System (NIBRS): A Comparison of 2020 and 2021 NIBRS Estimates report)

## SOUTH

The South, the nation's most highly populated region, accounted for an estimated 38.4 percent of the nation's population and 37.2 percent of the nation's estimated number of robberies in 2021. Robberies accounted for an estimated 75,300 violent crimes in this region in 2021, representing a 17.4 percent decrease from the 2020 figure. The 2021 robbery rate in the South was 59.2 per 100,000 inhabitants, down 18.2 percent from 2020. (Tables 3 and 4 and Transition to the National Incident-Based Reporting System (NIBRS): A Comparison of 2020 and 2021 NIBRS Estimates report)

## WEST

The West was home to an estimated 23.7 percent of the nation's population and accounted for 30.9 percent of the nation's estimated number of robberies in 2020. The estimated number of robberies (62,500) in the region in 2021 represented an 11.4 percent increase from the 2020 figure. The rate of robberies per 100,000 inhabitants in the West was 79.5, an 11.5 percent decrease from the 2020 rate. (Tables 3 and 4 and Transition to the National Incident-Based Reporting System (NIBRS): A Comparison of 2020 and 2021 NIBRS Estimates report)

### Community Types

The UCR program typically aggregates data for three community types: metropolitan statistical areas (MSAs), cities outside MSAs, and nonmetropolitan counties outside MSAs. MSAs include a central city or urbanized area with at least 50,000 inhabitants, as well as the county that contains the principal city and other adjacent counties that have a high degree of social and economic integration as measured through commuting. Cities outside MSAs are mostly incorporated areas, and nonmetropolitan counties are made up of mostly unincorporated areas. (For additional information about community types, see Appendix IV.) Due to the NIBRS migration, this data was not available for the 2021 data year.

### Offense Analysis

The UCR program collects supplemental data about robberies to document the use of weapons, the dollar loss associated with the offense, and the location types.

## ROBBERY BY WEAPON

Firearms were used in 42.1 percent of robberies in 2021. Offenders used knives or cutting instruments in 7.8 percent of these crimes, blunt objects in 3.0 percent of incidents, and poison in 0.1 percent of offenses. (Expanded Robbery Data)

## ROBBERY TRENDS BY LOCATION

By location type, the greatest proportion of robberies in 2021 occurred in commercial houses (19.9 percent) and on highways/alleys/sidewalks/streets (18.7 percent). Robbers struck residences in 14.0 percent of offenses. Convenience stores accounted for 7.2 percent of robberies, followed by gas and service stations (3.9 percent) and banks (1.7 percent). (Table 23)

**AGGRAVATED ASSAULT**

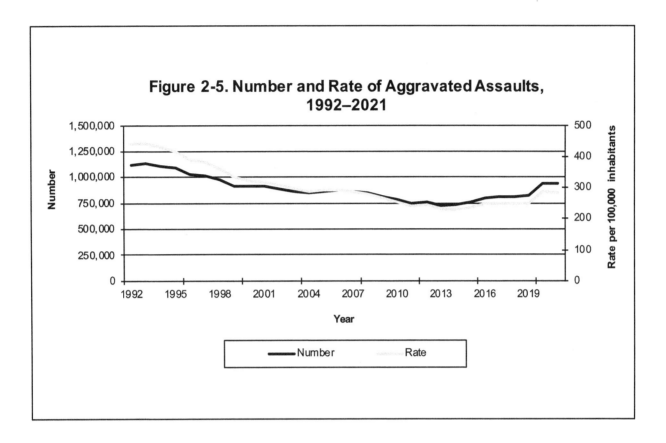

Figure 2-5. Number and Rate of Aggravated Assaults, 1992–2021

## Definition

The UCR program defines aggravated assault as an unlawful attack by one person upon another for the purpose of inflicting severe or aggravated bodily injury. This type of assault is usually accompanied by the use of a weapon or by other means likely to produce death or great bodily harm. Attempted aggravated assaults that involve the display or threat of a gun, knife, or other weapon are included in this crime category because serious personal injury would likely result if these assaults were completed. When aggravated assault and larceny-theft occur together, the offense falls under the category of robbery.

Please refer to the note about the limited data for 2021 at the beginning of this analysis for information about the transition to NIBRS and how it has affected comparisons and the examination of trends.

## National Volume, Trends, and Rates

In 2021, estimated occurrences of aggravated assaults totaled 943,800, a 0.1 percent decrease from the 2020 figure. The estimated rate of aggravated assault in 2021 was 284.4 per 100,000 inhabitants, a 0.8 percent decrease from 2020. (Table 1 and *Transition to the National Incident-Based Reporting System (NIBRS): A Comparison of 2020 and 2021 NIBRS Estimates* report)

Among the four types of violent crime offenses (murder, rape, robbery, and aggravated assault), aggravated assault typically has the highest rate of occurrence. This trend continued in 2021. (Table 1)

## Regional Offense Trends and Rates

The UCR program divides the United States into four regions: the Northeast, the South, the Midwest, and the West. (More details concerning geographic regions are provided in Appendix IV.)

NORTHEAST

The region with the smallest proportion of the nation's population (an estimated 17.2 percent in 2021) also accounted for the smallest proportion of the nation's estimated number of aggravated assaults (10.8 percent). Occurrences of aggravated assault increased 2.7 percent from 2020 to 2021, rising to an estimated 102,400 incidents. The region continued to have the lowest aggravated assault rate in the nation, at 179.2 incidents per 100,000 inhabitants, although this represented a 0.4

percent increase from the rate in 2020. (Tables 3 and 4 and Transition to the National Incident-Based Reporting System (NIBRS): A Comparison of 2020 and 2021 NIBRS Estimates report)

## MIDWEST

With 20.7 percent of the nation's total population in 2021, the Midwest accounted for approximately 18.7 percent of the nation's estimated number of aggravated assaults. Occurrences of this offense dropped 5.7 percent from the estimated total for 2020, decreasing to an estimated 176,300 incidents. The region's aggravated assault rate, at 256.2 incidents per 100,000 inhabitants, represented a 6.4 percent decrease from the 2020 rate. (Tables 3 and 4 and Transition to the National Incident-Based Reporting System (NIBRS): A Comparison of 2020 and 2021 NIBRS Estimates report)

## SOUTH

The South, the nation's most highly populated region, accounted for an estimated 38.4 percent of the nation's population in 2021 and the largest amount of the nation's estimated number of aggravated assaults (44.3 percent). From 2020 to 2021, the estimated number of aggravated assaults increased 2.8 percent to a total of 418,500 incidents. The rate of aggravated assaults rose 2.3 percent to 328.9 incidents per 100,000 inhabitants. (Tables 3 and 4 and Transition to the National Incident-Based Reporting System (NIBRS): A Comparison of 2020 and 2021 NIBRS Estimates report)

## WEST

In 2021, the West was home to an estimated 23.7 percent of the nation's population. Data for aggravated assault in the West was suppressed based on NIBRS Estimation suppression rules (Tables 3 and 4 and Transition to the National Incident-Based Reporting System (NIBRS): A Comparison of 2020 and 2021 NIBRS Estimates report)

### Community Types

The UCR program typically aggregates data for three community types: metropolitan statistical areas (MSAs), cities outside MSAs, and nonmetropolitan counties outside MSAs. MSAs include a central city or urbanized area with at least 50,000 inhabitants, as well as the county that contains the principal city and other adjacent counties that have a high degree of social and economic integration as measured through commuting. Cities outside MSAs are mostly incorporated areas, and nonmetropolitan counties are made up of mostly unincorporated areas. (For additional information about community types, see Appendix IV.) Due to the NIBRS migration, this data was not available for the 2021 data year.

### Offense Analysis

AGGRAVATED ASSAULT BY WEAPON

Of the aggravated assault offenses for which law enforcement agencies provided expanded data in 2021, 34.8 percent were committed with firearms, 16.5 percent involved knives or other cutting instruments, 10.2 percent involved blunt objects, and 2.2 percent involved unknown weapons. (Expanded Aggravated Assault Data)

**PROPERTY CRIME**

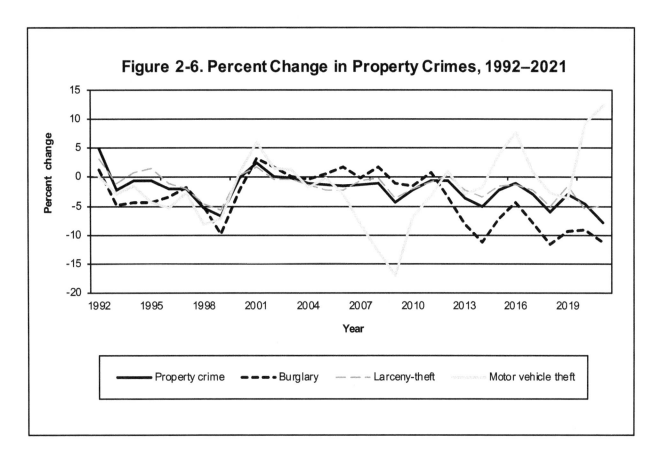

Figure 2-6. Percent Change in Property Crimes, 1992–2021

**Definition**

The UCR program's definition of property crime includes the offenses of burglary, larceny-theft, motor vehicle theft, and arson. The object of theft-type offenses is the taking of money or property without the use of force or threat of force against the victims. Property crime includes arson because the offense involves the destruction of property; however, arson victims may be subjected to force. Because of limited participation and the varying collection procedures conducted by local law enforcement agencies, only limited data are available for arson. More information on the expanded arson tables (which are available online but not included in this publication) can be found in Section I.

**Data Collection**

The data presented in *Crime in the United States* reflect the Hierarchy Rule, which counts only the most serious offense in a multiple-offense criminal incident. In descending order of severity, the violent crimes are murder and nonnegligent manslaughter, rape, robbery, and aggravated assault; these are followed by the property crimes of burglary, larceny-theft, and motor vehicle theft. The Hierarchy Rule does not apply to the offense of arson.

**Important Note: Transition to NIBRS**

As of January 1, 2021, the FBI's National Incident-Based Reporting System (NIBRS) became the national standard for law enforcement crime data reporting in the United States. The 2021 data year will mark the first time that the FBI and BJS estimate reported crime in the United States based solely on NIBRS data.

As of June 2022, all 50 U.S. states and the District of Columbia were certified to report crime data to NIBRS. Just under two-thirds of the U.S. population is covered by NIBRS-reporting law enforcement agencies, and 62 NIBRS-certified agencies serve cities with a population of 250,000 or more; these agencies cover a total population of more than 37 million. However, data is extremely limited for several large states in 2021, including California (7 percent of the population represented), the District of Columbia (47 percent of the population represented), Florida (0 percent of the population represented), Maryland (47 percent of the population represented), New Jersey (42 percent of the population represented), New York (19 percent of the population represented), and Pennsylvania (17 percent of the population represented). Of the 18,806 NIBRS-eligible law enforcement agencies, 11,333 (60.3 percent) reported data for 2021. (Eligibility is determined by the agency submitting a minimum of 3 months of data.)

The absence of these large segments of population, an issue that is expected to be alleviated in future years, makes the 2021 data not comparable to previous years. Consequently, 5-year and 10-year trend tables do not include the 2021 data. The FBI has provided limited analysis of year-over-year trends, and these are included where possible in this edition.

Some data has been suppressed by NIBRS. This occurs as a result of high uncertainty for a generated estimate. This uncertainty then requires is the application of suppression rules found within the NIBRS estimation methodologies. Suppression refers to the withholding of estimates from release due to high levels of uncertainty to ensure an unbiased view of the available NIBRS data.

In most instances, differences in the comparison of 2021 data to 2020 do not meet the criteria for statistical significance. However, it should be noted that the main contributor to that finding is the large amount of variation—both random and systematic—that is measured in the 2020 data due to low coverage of participating agencies. As coverage increases, the FBI will be able to improve its ability to measure these critical metrics for the nation.

The FBI has provided some estimates for 2021 trends based on this limited data; more information, including a detailed breakdown on how the values were extrapolated through the use of a confidence interval, can be found at <https://cde.ucr. cjis.gov> in the *Transition to the National Incident-Based Reporting System (NIBRS): A Comparison of 2020 and 2021 NIBRS Estimates* report.

Due to a system upgrade in 2019, the FBI now calculates rates for each offense based on the individual offenses and population published for each agency in tables 8-11. (Previous to 2019, when agencies were published in tables 8-11, but they had one or two offenses removed from publication due to not meeting UCR publication guidelines, the agency's data was not used to calculate rates for this table.) The FBI derived the offense rates by dividing the individual offense counts by the individual populations covered by contributing agencies for which 12 months of publishable data were supplied and then multiplying the resulting figure by 100,000. See Appendix V for the agency and population counts.

### National Volume, Trends, and Rates

An estimated 6,416,800 property crimes were committed in the United States in 2021, representing a 3.8 percent decrease from the 2020 estimate. The 2021 estimated property crime rate of 1,524.3 per 100,000 population represented a 4.5 percent decrease from the 2020 estimate. From 2020 to 2021, motor vehicle theft increased 12.3 percent to an estimated 890,200 occurrences; larceny-theft decreased 4.9 percent to 4,627,000 estimated incidents from 2020 to 2021; and

burglary decreased 11.4 percent in the same timeframe to an estimated 899,700 occurrences. While the rate per 100,000 population increased 11.5 percent to 268.8 for motor vehicle theft from 2020 to 2021, the burglary rate decreased 12.0 percent to 271.1 and the larceny-theft rate decreased 5.6 percent to 1,394.1. (Table 1 and *Transition to the National Incident-Based Reporting System (NIBRS): A Comparison of 2020 and 2021 NIBRS Estimates* report)

### Regional Offense Trends and Rates

The UCR program separates the United States into four regions: the Northeast, the Midwest, the South, and the West. (Geographic breakdowns can be found in Appendix IV.) Property crime data collected by the UCR program and aggregated by region reflected the following results.

NORTHEAST

The Northeast region accounted for 17.2 percent of the nation's population in 2021. The region also accounted for 10.8 percent of the nation's estimated number of property crimes in 2021. Law enforcement in the Northeast saw a 0.2 percent decrease in the estimated number of property crimes from 2020 to 2021. The property crime rate for the Northeast, estimated at 1,316.5 incidents per 100,000 inhabitants, was 2.5 percent less than the 2020 rate. (Tables 3 and 4 and Transition to the National Incident-Based Reporting System (NIBRS): A Comparison of 2020 and 2021 NIBRS Estimates report)

MIDWEST

The Midwest, with 20.7 percent of the U.S. population in 2021, accounted for 18.2 percent of the nation's estimated number of property crimes. Law enforcement in the Midwest saw the number of property crimes decrease 4.8 percent from 2020 to 2021. The rate of property crime in the Midwest in 2021, estimated at 1,700.6 incidents per 100,000 inhabitants, represented a 5.5 percent decrease from the 2020 rate. (Tables 3 and 4 and Transition to the National Incident-Based Reporting System (NIBRS): A Comparison of 2020 and 2021 NIBRS Estimates report)

SOUTH

The South, the nation's most populous region, accounted for 38.4 percent of the U.S. population in 2021. The region also accounted for an estimated 44.3 percent of the nation's property crimes. The South experienced a 6.8 percent decrease in its estimated number of property crimes from 2020 to 2021. The 2021 property crime rate, an estimated 2,074.1 incidents per 100,000 inhabitants, dropped 7.2 percent from the 2020 rate. (Tables 3 and 4 and Transition to the National Incident-Based Reporting System (NIBRS): A Comparison of 2020 and 2021 NIBRS Estimates report)

WEST

In 2021, the West accounted for 23.7 percent of the nation's population. From 2020 to 2021, the estimated number of property crimes in this region increased 1.9 percent. The estimated property crime rate in the West in 2021, 2,509.7 incidents per 100,000 inhabitants, was a 1.8 percent increase from the 2020 rate. (Tables 3 and 4 and Transition to the National Incident-Based Reporting System (NIBRS): A Comparison of 2020 and 2021 NIBRS Estimates report)

### Community Types

The UCR program typically aggregates data for three community types: metropolitan statistical areas (MSAs), cities outside MSAs, and nonmetropolitan counties outside MSAs. MSAs include a central city or urbanized area with at least 50,000 inhabitants, as well as the county that contains the principal city and other adjacent counties that have a high degree of social and economic integration as measured through commuting. Cities outside MSAs are mostly incorporated areas, and nonmetropolitan counties are made up of mostly unincorporated areas. (For additional information about community types, see Appendix IV.) Due to the NIBRS migration, this data was not available for the 2021 data year.

**BURGLARY/BREAKING & ENTERING**

## Figure 2-7. Burglary, by Location and Time, 2021

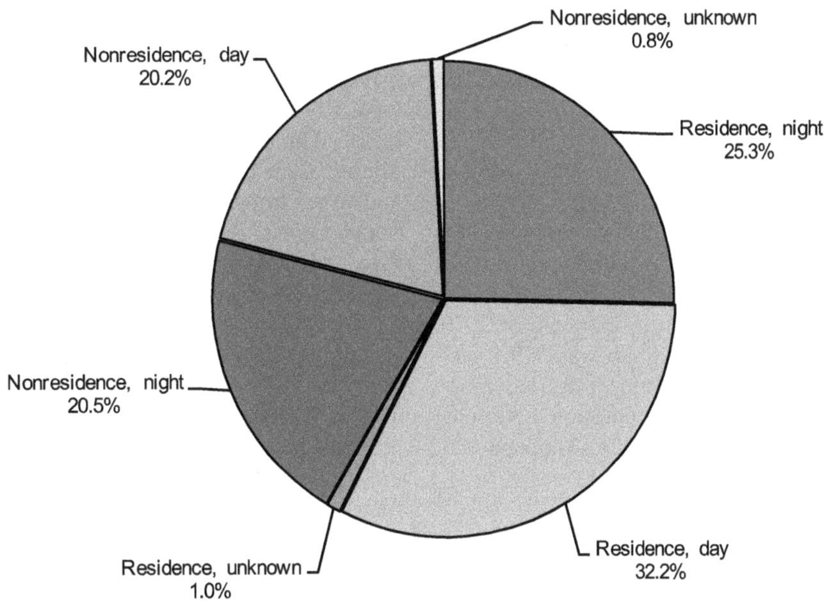

Nonresidence, unknown
0.8%

Residence, night
25.3%

Nonresidence, day
20.2%

Nonresidence, night
20.5%

Residence, day
32.2%

Residence, unknown
1.0%

### Definition

The UCR program defines burglary as the unlawful entry of a structure to commit a felony or theft. To classify an offense as a burglary, the use of force to gain entry need not have occurred. The program has three subclassifications for burglary: forcible entry, unlawful entry where no force is used, and attempted forcible entry. The UCR definition of "structure" includes, but is not limited to, apartments, barns, house trailers or houseboats (when used as permanent dwellings), offices, railroad cars (but not automobiles), stables, and vessels (such as ships).

Please refer to the note about the limited data for 2021 at the beginning of this analysis for information about the transition to NIBRS and how it has affected comparisons and the examination of trends.

### National Volume, Trends, and Rate

In 2021, there were an estimated 899,700 burglaries—a decrease of 11.4 percent when compared with 2020 data. Burglary accounted for 14.0 percent of the estimated number of property crimes committed in 2021. The burglary rate for the United States in 2021 was 271.1 incidents per 100,000

inhabitants, a 4.5 percent decrease from the 2020 rate. (Table 1 and *Transition to the National Incident-Based Reporting System (NIBRS): A Comparison of 2020 and 2021 NIBRS Estimates* report)

### Regional Offense Trends and Rates

The UCR program divides the United States into four regions: the Northeast, the Midwest, the South, and the West. (Details regarding these regions can be found in Appendix IV.) An analysis of burglary data by region showed the following details.

NORTHEAST

In 2021, 17.2 percent of the nation's population lived in the Northeast. This region accounted for 9.2 percent of the estimated total number of burglary offenses in the nation in 2021. The region's burglary rate, an estimated 145.3 offenses per 100,000 inhabitants, represented a decrease of 18.0 percent from the 2010 rate. The number of incidents dropped 16.0 percent to 83,100 from 2020 to 2021. (Tables 3 and 4 and Transition to the National Incident-Based Reporting System (NIBRS): A Comparison of 2020 and 2021 NIBRS Estimates report)

## MIDWEST

The Midwest accounted for 20.7 percent of the nation's population in 2021. This region accounted for 18.2 percent of the nation's estimated number of burglaries. In this region, the estimated number of burglaries dropped 14.2 percent to 163,700 from 2020 to 2021. The Midwest had a burglary rate of 237.8 offenses per 100,000 inhabitants, a 14.9 percent decrease from the 2020 rate. (Tables 3 and 4 and Transition to the National Incident-Based Reporting System (NIBRS): A Comparison of 2020 and 2021 NIBRS Estimates report)

## SOUTH

The South, the nation's most highly populated region (38.4 percent of all inhabitants), had the most burglaries in 2021 (an estimated 43.7 percent of the nation's total); however, this represented an 11.2 percent drop from its estimate in 2020. The estimated rate of burglary in the South was 309.1 incidents per 100,000 inhabitants, an 11.6 percent decrease from the 2020 rate. (Tables 3 and 4 and Transition to the National Incident-Based Reporting System (NIBRS): A Comparison of 2020 and 2021 NIBRS Estimates report)

## WEST

The West accounted for 23.7 percent of the nation's population in 2021. This region accounted for an estimated 32.3 percent of the nation's burglaries. The region's burglary rate was 69.7, a 6.2 percent decrease from the 2020 rate. The total number of burglaries (290,800) also represented a 6.2 percent decrease from the 2020 estimate. (Tables 3 and 4 and Transition to the National Incident-Based Reporting System (NIBRS): A Comparison of 2020 and 2021 NIBRS Estimates report)

### Community Types

The UCR program typically aggregates data for three community types: metropolitan statistical areas (MSAs), cities outside MSAs, and nonmetropolitan counties outside MSAs. MSAs include a central city or urbanized area with at least 50,000 inhabitants, as well as the county that contains the principal city and other adjacent counties that have a high degree of social and economic integration as measured through commuting. Cities outside MSAs are mostly incorporated areas, and nonmetropolitan counties are made up of mostly unincorporated areas. (For additional information about community types, see Appendix IV.) Due to the NIBRS migration, this data was not available for the 2021 data year.

### Offense Analysis

The UCR program requests that participating law enforcement agencies provide details regarding the nature of burglaries in their jurisdictions, such as type of entry, type of structure, time of day, and dollar loss associated with each offense.

As in the past, burglars targeted residences more often than nonresidential structures. In 2021, burglaries of residential properties accounted for 57.6 percent of all burglary offenses. Of the burglaries for which time of day could be established, most burglaries of residences (55.1 percent of all reported residential burglaries) occurred during the day, while most burglaries of nonresidential structures (47.7 percent of all reported nonresidential burglaries) occurred at night. (Table 23)

**LARCENY-THEFT**

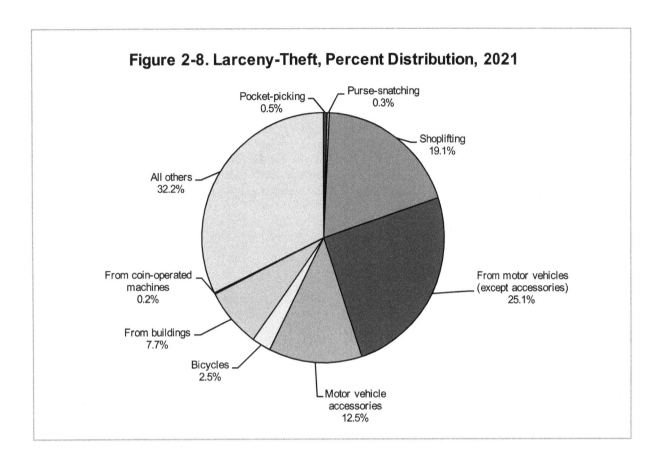

### Figure 2-8. Larceny-Theft, Percent Distribution, 2021

Pocket-picking
0.5%

Purse-snatching
0.3%

Shoplifting
19.1%

All others
32.2%

From motor vehicles
(except accessories)
25.1%

From coin-operated
machines
0.2%

From buildings
7.7%

Bicycles
2.5%

Motor vehicle
accessories
12.5%

### Definition

The UCR program defines larceny-theft as the unlawful taking, carrying, leading, or riding away of property from the possession or constructive possession of another. Examples are thefts of bicycles, motor vehicle parts and accessories, shoplifting, pocket picking, or the stealing of any property or article not taken by force and violence or by fraud. Attempted larcenies are included. Embezzlement, confidence games, forgery, check fraud, and so on, are excluded from this category.

Please refer to the note about the limited data for 2021 at the beginning of this analysis for information about the transition to NIBRS and how it has affected comparisons and the examination of trends.

### National Volume, Trends, and Rates

Larceny-thefts accounted for an estimated 72.1 percent of property crimes in 2021, with an estimated 4,627,00 larceny-thefts nationwide. The estimated number of larceny-thefts declined 4.9 percent from 2020 to 2021. The rate of larceny-thefts (1,394.1 per 100,000 inhabitants in 2021) declined 5.6 percent from 2020 to 2021. (Table 1 and *Transition to the National Incident-Based Reporting System (NIBRS): A Comparison of 2020 and 2021 NIBRS Estimates* report)

### Regional Offense Trends and Rates

The UCR program defines four regions within the United States: the Northeast, the Midwest, the South, and the West. (See Appendix IV for a geographical description of each region.)

NORTHEAST

The Northeast was the region with the smallest proportion (17.2 percent) of the U.S. population in 2021. The region also experienced the fewest larceny-thefts in the country, accounting for only 12.6 percent of all larceny-thefts. The estimated number of offenses in 2021 (584,000) represented a 0.4 percent increase from 2020, although the estimated rate—1,021.7 incidents per 100,000 inhabitants—represented a 1.9 percent decline. (Tables 3 and 4 and Transition to the National Incident-Based Reporting System (NIBRS): A Comparison of 2020 and 2021 NIBRS Estimates report)

MIDWEST

With 20.7 percent of the U.S. population in 2021, the Midwest accounted for an estimated 18.3 percent of the nation's larceny-thefts. The estimated number of offenses (848,300) declined 5.2 percent from the 2020 total, and the estimated rate of occurrence (1,232.5 incidents per 100,000 inhabitants) declined 5.9 percent. (Tables 3 and 4 and Transition to the National Incident-Based Reporting System (NIBRS): A Comparison of 2020 and 2021 NIBRS Estimates report)

SOUTH

With nearly two-fifths of the U.S. population in 2021 (38.4 percent), the South had the nation's highest proportion of larceny-theft offenses: an estimated 41.7 percent. Estimated offenses in this region in 2020 totaled 1,929,000, a 7.0 percent decrease from the 2020 estimate. The South's larceny-theft rate—estimated at 1,516.9 offenses per 100,000 inhabitants—decreased 7.5 percent from the 2020 estimate. (Tables 3 and 4 and Transition to the National Incident-Based Reporting System (NIBRS): A Comparison of 2020 and 2021 NIBRS Estimates report)

WEST

In 2021, an estimated 23.7 percent of the U.S. population lived in the West. This region was also where 28.9 percent of the nation's estimated number of larceny-thefts took place. Occurrences of larceny-theft did not change in a statistically significant way from 2020 to 2021, nor did the rate of larceny-theft per 100,000 inhabitants. (Tables 3 and 4 and Transition to the National Incident-Based Reporting System (NIBRS): A Comparison of 2020 and 2021 NIBRS Estimates report)

**Community Types**

The UCR program typically aggregates data for three community types: metropolitan statistical areas (MSAs), cities outside MSAs, and nonmetropolitan counties outside MSAs. MSAs include a central city or urbanized area with at least 50,000 inhabitants, as well as the county that contains the principal city and other adjacent counties that have a high degree of social and economic integration as measured through commuting. Cities outside MSAs are mostly incorporated areas, and nonmetropolitan counties are made up of mostly unincorporated areas. (For additional information about community types, see Appendix IV.) Due to the NIBRS migration, this data was not available for the 2021 data year.

**Offense Analysis**

Table 23 provides a further breakdown of larceny-theft offenses, including shoplifting, thefts from buildings, thefts of motor vehicle accessories, thefts of bicycles, thefts from coin-operated machines, purse snatching, and pocket picking. The "all other" category, which includes the less-defined types of larceny-theft, accounted for 20.0 percent of all offenses in 2021.

Offenses in which the stolen property was valued at more than $200 accounted for 38.2 percent of all larceny-thefts in 2021, while larceny-thefts of under $50 represented 18.1 percent and larceny-thefts of $50 to $200 represented 11.4 percent of all larceny-thefts. (Table 23)

**MOTOR VEHICLE THEFT**

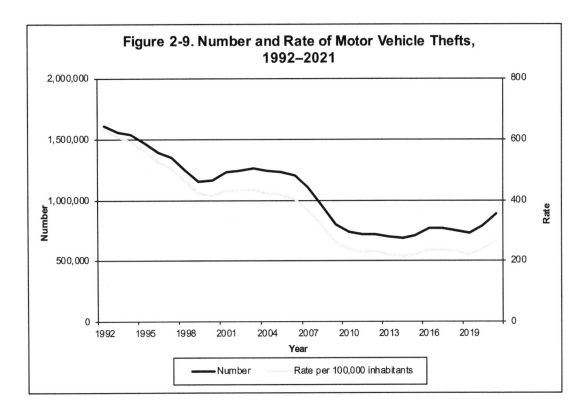

Figure 2-9. Number and Rate of Motor Vehicle Thefts, 1992–2021

---

### Definition

The UCR program defines motor vehicle theft as the theft or attempted theft of a motor vehicle. The offense includes the stealing of automobiles, trucks, buses, motorcycles, snowmobiles, etc. The taking of a motor vehicle for temporary use by a person or persons with lawful access is excluded.

Please refer to the note about the limited data for 2021 at the beginning of this analysis for information about the transition to NIBRS and how it has affected comparisons and the examination of trends.

### National Volume, Trends, and Rates

In 2021, an estimated 890,200 motor vehicle thefts took place in the United States, a 12.3 percent increase from 2020. The rate of motor vehicle theft, 268.2 per 100,000 population, represented an 11.5 percent increase from the 2020 estimate. (Table 1 and *Transition to the National Incident-Based Reporting System (NIBRS): A Comparison of 2020 and 2021 NIBRS Estimates* report)

### Regional Offense Trends and Rates

In order to analyze crime by geographic area, the UCR program divides the United States into four regions: the Northeast, the Midwest, the South, and the West. (Appendix IV provides a map delineating the regions.) This section provides a regional overview of motor vehicle theft.

NORTHEAST

The Northeast accounted for an estimated 17.2 percent of the nation's population in 2021. The region also accounted for an estimated 9.6 percent of its motor vehicle thefts. An estimated 85,500 motor vehicle thefts occurred in the Northeast in 2021, a 16.2 percent rise in occurrences from 2020. The estimated rate of 149.5 motor vehicle thefts per 100,000 inhabitants in the Northeast in 2021 represented a 13.4 percent increase from the 2020 rate. (Tables 3 and 4 and Transition to the National Incident-Based Reporting System (NIBRS): A Comparison of 2020 and 2021 NIBRS Estimates report)

MIDWEST

An estimated 20.7 percent of the country's population resided in the Midwest in 2021. The region accounted for 17.8 percent of the nation's motor vehicle thefts. The Midwest had an estimated 158,500 motor vehicle thefts in 2021, an increase of 10.7 percent from the previous year's total. The motor vehicle theft rate was estimated at 230.3 motor vehicles stolen per 100,000 inhabitants, an increase of 9.9 percent from the 2020 rate. (Tables 3 and 4 and Transition to the National

Incident-Based Reporting System (NIBRS): A Comparison of 2020 and 2021 NIBRS Estimates report)

## SOUTH

The South, the nation's most populous region, was home to an estimated 38.4 percent of the U.S. population in 2021 and accounted for 35.6 percent of the nation's motor vehicle thefts. The estimated 316,800 motor vehicle thefts in the South represented a 0.7 percent increase from the 2020 estimate. Motor vehicles in the South were stolen at an estimated rate of 249.0 offenses per 100,000 inhabitants in 2021, a rate that was up 0.3 percent from the 2020 rate. (Tables 3 and 4 and Transition to the National Incident-Based Reporting System (NIBRS): A Comparison of 2020 and 2021 NIBRS Estimates report)

## WEST

With approximately 23.7 percent of the U.S. population in 2021, the West accounted for 39.0 percent of all motor vehicle thefts in the nation. An estimated 347,100 motor vehicle thefts occurred in this region, the most of any region. This number represented a 19.1 percent increase from the previous year's estimate. The region's 2021 rate of 441.2 motor vehicles stolen per 100,000 inhabitants was 19.1 percent higher than the 2020 rate. (Tables 3 and 4 and Transition to the National Incident-Based Reporting System (NIBRS): A Comparison of 2020 and 2021 NIBRS Estimates report)

### Community Types

The UCR program typically aggregates data for three community types: metropolitan statistical areas (MSAs), cities outside MSAs, and nonmetropolitan counties outside MSAs. MSAs include a central city or urbanized area with at least 50,000 inhabitants, as well as the county that contains the principal city and other adjacent counties that have a high degree of social and economic integration as measured through commuting. Cities outside MSAs are mostly incorporated areas, and nonmetropolitan counties are made up of mostly unincorporated areas. (For additional information about community types, see Appendix IV.) Due to the NIBRS migration, this data was not available for the 2021 data year.

**ARSON**

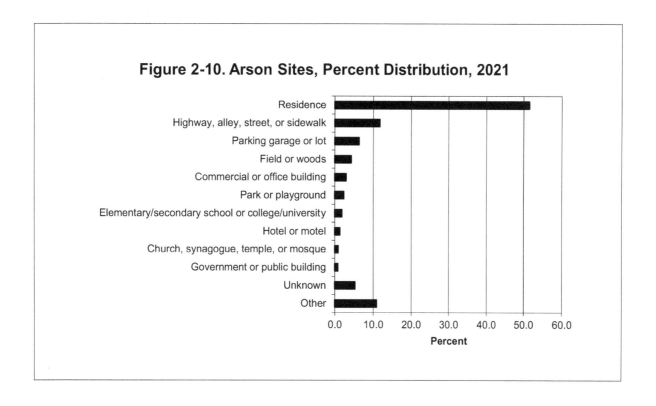

**Figure 2-10. Arson Sites, Percent Distribution, 2021**

#### Definition

The UCR program defines arson as any willful or malicious burning or attempt to burn (with or without intent to defraud) a dwelling house, public building, motor vehicle, aircraft, or personal property of another, etc.

Please refer to the note about the limited data for 2021 at the beginning of this analysis for information about the transition to NIBRS and how it has affected comparisons and the examination of trends.

#### Data Collection

Only fires that investigators determined were willfully set (not fires labeled as "suspicious" or "of unknown origin") are included in this arson data collection. Points to consider regarding arson statistics include:

National offense rates per 100,000 inhabitants (found in Tables 1, 2, and 4) do not include arson data; the FBI presents rates for arson separately. Arson rates are calculated based upon data received from all law enforcement agencies that provide the UCR program with data for 12 complete months. However, for 2021, the FBI estimated that 40,900 arsons occurred, a 3.2 percent decrease from 2020. The arson rate, 12.3 per 100,000 population, represented a 3.9 percent decrease from the 2020 estimate. (*Transition to the National Incident-Based Reporting System (NIBRS): A Comparison of 2020 and 2021 NIBRS Estimates* report)

#### Population Groups: Trends and Rates

The number of arsons reported in cities 2020 was 24.5 percent higher than the number reported in 2019. Among the population groups labeled *city,* the group with 100,000 to 249,999 inhabitants reported the largest increase (30.7 percent). Cities with under 10,000 inhabitants showed the smallest increase (12.7 percent). Agencies in the nation's metropolitan counties reported a 17.0 percent increase in the number of arsons, while those in nonmetropolitan counties reported a 20.9 percent increase from 2019 to 2020. Agencies in suburban areas reported an 18.2 percent rise in arsons. (Table 12)

#### Offense Analysis

The UCR program breaks down arson offenses into three property categories: structural, mobile, and other. In addition, the structural property type is broken down into seven types of structures, and the mobile property type consists of two subgroupings. The program also collects information on the estimated dollar value of the damaged property. Arson rates were based on information received from 11,794 agencies that provided 12 months of complete arson data to the UCR program.

**Property Type**

Of the 32,360 arsons where location was known, 51.5 percent occurred at residences; 11.6 percent occurred on highways, alleys, streets, or sidewalks; and 6.3 percent of arsons occurred in parking garages and lots. Approximately 0.9 percent of arsons occurred at religious buildings, such as synagogues, churches, temples, or mosques. (Expanded Arson Data)

## Table 1. Crime in the United States, by Volume and Rate Per 100,000 Inhabitants, 2001–2021

(Number, rate per 100,000 population.)

| Year | Population[1] | Violent crime[2] | | Murder and nonnegligent manslaughter | | Rape (revised definition)[3] | | Rape (legacy definition)[4] | | Robbery | | Aggravated assault | |
|---|---|---|---|---|---|---|---|---|---|---|---|---|---|
| | | Number | Rate | Number | Rate | Number | Rate | Number | Rate | Number | Rate | Number | Rate |
| 2001[5] | 285,317,559 | 1,439,480 | 504.5 | 16,037 | 5.6 | X | X | 90,863 | 31.8 | 423,557 | 148.5 | 909,023 | 318.6 |
| 2002 | 287,973,924 | 1,423,677 | 494.4 | 16,229 | 5.6 | X | X | 95,235 | 33.1 | 420,806 | 146.1 | 891,407 | 309.5 |
| 2003 | 290,788,976 | 1,383,676 | 475.8 | 16,528 | 5.7 | X | X | 93,883 | 32.3 | 414,235 | 142.5 | 859,030 | 295.4 |
| 2004 | 293,656,842 | 1,360,088 | 463.2 | 16,148 | 5.5 | X | X | 95,089 | 32.4 | 401,470 | 136.7 | 847,381 | 288.6 |
| 2005 | 296,507,061 | 1,390,745 | 469.0 | 16,740 | 5.6 | X | X | 94,347 | 31.8 | 417,438 | 140.8 | 862,220 | 290.8 |
| 2006 | 299,398,484 | 1,435,123 | 479.3 | 17,309 | 5.8 | X | X | 94,472 | 31.6 | 449,246 | 150.0 | 874,096 | 292.0 |
| 2007 | 301,621,157 | 1,422,970 | 471.8 | 17,128 | 5.7 | X | X | 92,160 | 30.6 | 447,324 | 148.3 | 866,358 | 287.2 |
| 2008 | 304,059,724 | 1,394,461 | 458.6 | 16,465 | 5.4 | X | X | 90,750 | 29.8 | 443,563 | 145.9 | 843,683 | 277.5 |
| 2009 | 307,006,550 | 1,325,896 | 431.9 | 15,399 | 5.0 | X | X | 89,241 | 29.1 | 408,742 | 133.1 | 812,514 | 264.7 |
| 2010 | 309,330,219 | 1,251,248 | 404.5 | 14,722 | 4.8 | X | X | 85,593 | 27.7 | 369,089 | 119.3 | 781,844 | 252.8 |
| 2011 | 311,587,816 | 1,206,005 | 387.1 | 14,661 | 4.7 | X | X | 84,175 | 27.0 | 354,746 | 113.9 | 752,423 | 241.5 |
| 2012 | 313,873,685 | 1,217,057 | 387.8 | 14,856 | 4.7 | X | X | 85,141 | 27.1 | 355,051 | 113.1 | 762,009 | 242.8 |
| 2013 | 316,497,531 | 1,168,298 | 369.1 | 14,319 | 4.5 | 113,695 | 36 | 82,109 | 25.9 | 345,093 | 109.0 | 726,777 | 229.6 |
| 2014 | 318,907,401 | 1,153,022 | 361.6 | 14,164 | 4.4 | 118,027 | 37.0 | 84,864 | 26.6 | 322,905 | 101.3 | 731,089 | 229.2 |
| 2015 | 320,896,618 | 1,199,310 | 373.7 | 15,883 | 4.9 | 126,134 | 39.3 | 91,261 | 28.4 | 328,109 | 102.2 | 764,057 | 238.1 |
| 2016 | 323,405,935 | 1,250,162 | 386.6 | 17,413 | 5.4 | 132,414 | 40.9 | 96,970 | 30.0 | 332,797 | 102.9 | 802,982 | 248.3 |
| 2017 | 325,147,121 | 1,247,917 | 383.8 | 17,294 | 5.3 | 135,666 | 41.7 | 99,708 | 30.7 | 320,596 | 98.6 | 810,319 | 249.2 |
| 2018 | 326,687,501 | 1,209,997 | 370.4 | 16,374 | 5.0 | 143,765 | 44.0 | 101,363 | 31.0 | 281,278 | 86.1 | 810,982 | 248.2 |
| 2019[6] | 328,329,953 | 1,210,229 | 368.6 | 16,669 | 5.1 | 143,224 | 43.6 | 103,060 | 31.4 | 268,483 | 81.8 | 822,017 | 250.4 |
| 2020 | 329,484,123 | 1,326,600 | 402.6 | 20,000 | 6.7 | 139,500 | 44.6 | X | X | 220,200 | 66.8 | 944,800 | 286.7 |
| 2021[7] | 331,900,098 | 1,313,200 | 395.7 | 22,900 | 6.9 | 144,300 | 43.5 | X | X | 202,200 | 60.9 | 943,800 | 284.4 |

## Table 1. Crime in the United States, by Volume and Rate Per 100,000 Inhabitants, 2001–2021—Continued

(Number, rate per 100,000 population.)

| Year | Property crime Number | Property crime Rate | Burglary Number | Burglary Rate | Larceny-theft Number | Larceny-theft Rate | Motor vehicle theft Number | Motor vehicle theft Rate |
|---|---|---|---|---|---|---|---|---|
| 2001[5] | 10,437,189 | 3,658.1 | 2,116,531 | 741.8 | 7,092,267 | 2,485.7 | 1,228,391 | 430.5 |
| 2002 | 10,455,277 | 3,630.6 | 2,151,252 | 747.0 | 7,057,379 | 2,450.7 | 1,246,646 | 432.9 |
| 2003 | 10,442,862 | 3,591.2 | 2,154,834 | 741.0 | 7,026,802 | 2,416.5 | 1,261,226 | 433.7 |
| 2004 | 10,319,386 | 3,514.1 | 2,144,446 | 730.3 | 6,937,089 | 2,362.3 | 1,237,851 | 421.5 |
| 2005 | 10,174,754 | 3,431.5 | 2,155,448 | 726.9 | 6,783,447 | 2,287.8 | 1,235,859 | 416.8 |
| 2006 | 10,019,601 | 3,346.6 | 2,194,993 | 733.1 | 6,626,363 | 2,213.2 | 1,198,245 | 400.2 |
| 2007 | 9,882,212 | 3,276.4 | 2,190,198 | 726.1 | 6,591,542 | 2,185.4 | 1,100,472 | 364.9 |
| 2008 | 9,774,152 | 3,214.6 | 2,228,887 | 733.0 | 6,586,206 | 2,166.1 | 959,059 | 315.4 |
| 2009 | 9,337,060 | 3,041.3 | 2,203,313 | 717.7 | 6,338,095 | 2,064.5 | 795,652 | 259.2 |
| 2010 | 9,112,625 | 2,945.9 | 2,168,459 | 701.0 | 6,204,601 | 2,005.8 | 739,565 | 239.1 |
| 2011 | 9,052,743 | 2,905.4 | 2,185,140 | 701.3 | 6,151,095 | 1,974.1 | 716,508 | 230.0 |
| 2012 | 9,001,992 | 2,868.0 | 2,109,932 | 672.2 | 6,168,874 | 1,965.4 | 723,186 | 230.4 |
| 2013 | 8,651,892 | 2,733.6 | 1,932,139 | 610.5 | 6,019,465 | 1,901.9 | 700,288 | 221.3 |
| 2014 | 8,209,010 | 2,574.1 | 1,713,153 | 537.2 | 5,809,054 | 1,821.5 | 686,803 | 215.4 |
| 2015 | 8,024,115 | 2,500.5 | 1,587,564 | 494.7 | 5,723,488 | 1,783.6 | 713,063 | 222.2 |
| 2016 | 7,928,530 | 2,451.6 | 1,516,405 | 468.9 | 5,644,835 | 1,745.4 | 767,290 | 237.3 |
| 2017 | 7,682,988 | 2,362.9 | 1,397,045 | 429.7 | 5,513,000 | 1,695.5 | 772,943 | 237.7 |
| 2018 | 7,219,084 | 2,209.8 | 1,235,013 | 378.0 | 5,232,167 | 1,601.6 | 751,904 | 230.2 |
| 2019[6] | 6,995,235 | 2,130.6 | 1,118,096 | 340.5 | 5,152,267 | 1,569.2 | 724,872 | 220.8 |
| 2020 | 6,672,500 | 2,025.0 | 1,015,000 | 308.0 | 4,865,100 | 1,476.5 | 792,400 | 240.5 |
| 2021[7] | 6,416,800 | 1,933.4 | 899,700 | 271.1 | 4,627,000 | 1,394.1 | 890,200 | 268.2 |

NOTE: Although arson data are included in the trend and clearance tables, sufficient data are not available to estimate totals for this offense. Therefore, no arson data are published in this table.

NA = Not available.

X = Not applicable.

1 Populations through 2020 are U.S. Census Bureau provisional estimates as of July 1 for each year except 2000 and 2010, which are decennial census counts.   2 The violent crime figures include the offenses of murder, rape (legacy definition), robbery, and aggravated assault.   3 The figures shown in this column for the offense of rape were estimated using the revised UCR definition of rape.   4 The figures shown in this column for the offense of rape were estimated using the legacy UCR definition of rape.   5 The murder and nonnegligent homicides that occurred as a result of the events of September 11, 2001, are not included in this table.   6 The crime figures have been adjusted.   7 The 2021 data includes 11,794 agencies, covering approximately 65 percent of the total population, due to the NIBRS migration; rates for 2021 are not considered by the FBI to be statistically significant and comparisons with other years cannot be made. Limited data for 2021 were available for California, the District of Columbia, Florida, Illinois, Maryland, New Jersey, New Mexico, New York, and Pennsylvania.

## Table 2. Crime, by Community Type, 2020

(Number, rate per 100,000 population, percent.)

| Area | Population[1] | Violent crime[2] | Murder and nonnegligent manslaughter | Rape[3] | Robbery | Aggravated assault | Property crime | Burglary | Larceny-theft | Motor vehicle theft |
|---|---|---|---|---|---|---|---|---|---|---|
| **United States** | 329,484,123 | 1,313,105 | 21,570 | 126,430 | 243,600 | 921,505 | 6,452,038 | 1,035,314 | 4,606,324 | 810,400 |
| Rate per 100,000 inhabitants | | 398.5 | 6.5 | 38.4 | 73.9 | 279.7 | 1,958.2 | 314.2 | 1,398.0 | 246.0 |
| **Metropolitan Statistical Area** | 283,601,617 | | | | | | | | | |
| Area actually reporting[4] | 97.1% | 1,127,195 | 18,499 | 102,090 | 225,756 | 780,850 | 5,463,031 | 837,142 | 3,908,491 | 717,398 |
| Estimated total | 100.0% | 1,175,523 | 19,230 | 107,098 | 234,032 | 815,163 | 5,741,726 | 882,846 | 4,115,100 | 743,780 |
| Rate per 100,000 inhabitants | | 414.5 | 6.8 | 37.8 | 82.5 | 287.4 | 2,024.6 | 311.3 | 1,451.0 | 262.3 |
| **Cities Outside Metropolitan Areas** | 18,709,511 | | | | | | | | | |
| Area actually reporting[4] | 91.9% | 67,798 | 967 | 8,824 | 5,335 | 52,672 | 380,070 | 67,989 | 282,672 | 29,409 |
| Estimated total | 100.0% | 75,504 | 1,042 | 9,540 | 6,185 | 58,737 | 431,657 | 78,030 | 320,428 | 33,199 |
| Rate per 100,000 inhabitants | | 403.6 | 5.6 | 51.0 | 33.1 | 313.9 | 2,307.2 | 417.1 | 1,712.6 | 177.4 |
| **Nonmetropolitan counties** | 27,172,995 | | | | | | | | | |
| Area actually reporting[4] | 91.0% | 53,176 | 1,100 | 8,688 | 2,330 | 41,058 | 232,681 | 63,708 | 140,227 | 28,746 |
| Estimated total | 100.0% | 62,078 | 1,298 | 9,792 | 3,383 | 47,605 | 278,655 | 74,438 | 170,796 | 33,421 |
| Rate per 100,000 inhabitants | | 228.5 | 4.8 | 36.0 | 12.4 | 175.2 | 1,025.5 | 273.9 | 628.6 | 123.0 |

Note: Although arson data are included in the trend and clearance tables, sufficient data are not available to estimate totals for this offense. Therefore, no arson data are published in this table.
Data for 2021 were not available for this table due to the NIBRS data migration.
1 Population figures are U.S. Census Bureau provisional estimates as of July 1, 2019.    2 The violent crime figures include the offenses of murder, rape (revised definition), robbery, and aggravated assault.    3 The figures shown in this column for the offense of rape were estimated using the revised Uniform Crime Reporting definition of rape.    4 The percentage reported under "Area actually reporting" is based upon the population covered by agencies providing 3 months or more of crime reports to the FBI.

## Table 3. Crime in the United States, Population and Offense Distribution, by Region, 2021

(Percent distribution.)

| Region | Population | Violent crime | Murder and nonnegligent manslaughter | Rape (revised definition)[1] | Robbery | Aggravated assault | Property crime | Burglary | Larceny-theft | Motor vehicle theft |
|---|---|---|---|---|---|---|---|---|---|---|
| United States[2] | 100.0 | 100.0 | 100.0 | 100.0 | 100.0 | 100.0 | 100.0 | 100.0 | 100.0 | 100.0 |
| Northeast | 17.2 | 11.6 | 12.2 | 12.1 | 14.9 | 10.8 | 11.7 | 9.2 | 12.6 | 9.6 |
| Midwest | 20.7 | 19.1 | 19.7 | 23.4 | 17.8 | 18.7 | 18.2 | 18.2 | 18.3 | 17.8 |
| South | 38.4 | 42.7 | 47.2 | 38.7 | 37.2 | 44.3 | 41.1 | 43.7 | 41.7 | 35.6 |
| West | 23.7 | * | * | 20.1 | 30.9 | * | 30.8 | 32.3 | 28.9 | 39.0 |

*Note:* Although arson data are included in the trend and clearance tables, sufficient data are not available to estimate totals for this offense. Therefore, no arson data are published in this table.
* = Data was suppressed based on NIBRS Estimation suppression rules.
1 The figures shown in the rape column were calculated using the revised Uniform Crime Reporting (UCR) definition of rape.    2 Because of rounding, percentages may not sum to 100.0.

# Table 4. Crime in the United States,[1] by Region, 2020–2021

(Number, rate per 100,000 population, percent.)

| Area | Population[2] | Violent crime[3] | | Murder and nonnegligent manslaughter | | Rape (revised definition)[4] | | Robbery | |
|---|---|---|---|---|---|---|---|---|---|
| | | Number | Rate | Number | Rate | Number | Rate | Number | Rate |
| **UNITED STATES** | | | | | | | | | |
| 2020 | 329,484,123 | 1,326,600 | 402.6 | 22,000 | 6.7 | 139,500 | 42.3 | 220,200 | 66.8 |
| 2021 | 331,900,098 | 1,313,200 | 395.7 | 22,900 | 6.9 | 144,300 | 43.5 | 202,200 | 60.9 |
| Percent change | | -1.0 | -1.7 | +4.1 | +3.0 | +3.4 | +2.8 | -8.2 | -8.8 |
| **NORTHEAST** | | | | | | | | | |
| 2020 | 57,609,156 | 144,100 | 258.0 | 2,200 | 3.9 | 17,600 | 31.4 | 24,700 | 44.2 |
| 2021 | 57,259,256 | 152,700 | 267.2 | 2,800 | 4.9 | 17,400 | 30.5 | 30,100 | 52.6 |
| Percent change | | +6.0 | +3.6 | +27.3 | +25.6 | -1.1 | -2.9 | +21.9 | +19.0 |
| **MIDWEST** | | | | | | | | | |
| 2020 | 68,985,505 | 260,600 | 381.6 | 4,200 | 6.1 | 32,400 | 47.4 | 37,100 | 54.3 |
| 2021 | 68,836,505 | 250,600 | 364.1 | 4,500 | 6.6 | 33,800 | 49.2 | 35,900 | 52.2 |
| Percent change | | -3.8 | -4.6 | +7.1 | +8.2 | +4.3 | +3.8 | -3.2 | -3.9 |
| **SOUTH** | | | | | | | | | |
| 2020 | 126,266,262 | 564,600 | 445.6 | 10,100 | 7.9 | 55,600 | 43.9 | 91,700 | 72.4 |
| 2021 | 127,346,029 | 560,500 | 440.5 | 10,800 | 8.5 | 55,900 | 43.9 | 75,300 | 59.2 |
| Percent change | | -0.7 | -1.1 | +6.9 | +7.6 | +0.5 | +0.0 | -17.9 | -18.2 |
| **WEST** | | | | | | | | | |
| 2020 | 78,588,565 | ** | ** | ** | ** | 37,000 | 47.1 | 56,100 | 89.8 |
| 2021 | 78,589,763 | ** | ** | ** | ** | 38,800 | 49.4 | 62,500 | 79.5 |
| Percent change | | NA | NA | NA | NA | +4.9 | +4.9 | +11.4 | -11.5 |

## Table 4. Crime in the United States,[1] by Region, 2020–2021—Continued

(Number, rate per 100,000 population, percent.)

| Area | Aggravated assault | | Property crime | | Burglary | | Larceny-theft | | Motor vehicle theft | |
|---|---|---|---|---|---|---|---|---|---|---|
| | Number | Rate | Number | Rate | Number | Rate | Number | Rate | Number | Rate |
| **UNITED STATES** | | | | | | | | | | |
| 2020 | 944,800 | 286.7 | 6,672,500 | 2,025.0 | 1,015,000 | 308.0 | 4,865,100 | 1,476.5 | 792,400 | 240.5 |
| 2021 | 943,800 | 284.4 | 6,146,800 | 1,524.3 | 899,700 | 271.1 | 4,627,000 | 1,394.1 | 890,200 | 268.2 |
| Percent change | -0.1 | -0.8 | -7.9 | -24.7 | -11.4 | -12.0 | -4.9 | -5.6 | +12.3 | +11.5 |
| **NORTHEAST** | | | | | | | | | | |
| 2020 | 99,700 | 178.4 | 753,900 | 1,349.9 | 98,900 | 177.2 | 581,400 | 1,041.0 | 73,600 | 131.8 |
| 2021 | 102,400 | 179.2 | 752,500 | 1,316.5 | 83,100 | 145.3 | 584,000 | 1,021.7 | 85,500 | 149.5 |
| Percent change | +2.7 | +0.4 | -0.2 | -2.5 | -16.0 | -18.0 | +0.4 | -1.9 | +16.2 | +13.4 |
| **MIDWEST** | | | | | | | | | | |
| 2020 | 187,000 | 273.7 | 1,229,200 | 1,799.5 | 190,900 | 279.5 | 895,100 | 1,310.4 | 143,200 | 209.6 |
| 2021 | 176,300 | 256.2 | 1,170,500 | 1,700.6 | 163,700 | 237.8 | 848,300 | 1,232.5 | 158,500 | 230.3 |
| Percent change | -5.7 | -6.4 | -4.8 | -5.5 | -14.2 | -14.9 | -5.2 | -5.9 | +10.7 | +9.9 |
| **SOUTH** | | | | | | | | | | |
| 2020 | 407,200 | 321.4 | 2,832,900 | 2,236.1 | 443,000 | 349.6 | 2,075,300 | 1,638.2 | 314,500 | 248.3 |
| 2021 | 418,500 | 328.9 | 2,639,000 | 2,074.1 | 393,200 | 309.1 | 1,929,000 | 1,516.1 | 316,800 | 249.0 |
| Percent change | +2.8 | +2.3 | -6.8 | -7.2 | -11.2 | -11.6 | -7.0 | -7.5 | +0.7 | +0.3 |
| **WEST** | | | | | | | | | | |
| 2020 | ** | ** | 1,938,200 | 2,464.3 | 310,100 | 394.3 | 1,336,400 | 1,699.4 | 291,500 | 370.6 |
| 2021 | ** | ** | 1,974,300 | 2,509.7 | 290,800 | 369.7 | 1,336,600 | 1,698.8 | 347,100 | 441.2 |
| Percent change | NA | NA | +1.9 | +1.8 | -6.2 | -6.2 | +0.0 | -0.0 | +19.1 | +19.1 |

NOTE: Although arson data are included in the trend and clearance tables, sufficient data are not available to estimate totals for this offense. Therefore, no arson data are published in this table. Totals are rounded to the nearest 100 due to uncertainty in the estimates.

** = Data was suppressed based on NIBRS Estimation suppression rules.

1 The previous year's crime figures have been adjusted.　2 Population figures are U.S. Census Bureau provisional estimates as of April 1, 2020, and July 1, 2021.　3 The violent crime figures include the offenses of murder, rape (revised definition), robbery, and aggravated assault.　4 The figures shown in this column for the offense of rape were estimated using the revised Uniform Crime Reporting (UCR) definition of rape.

## Table 5. Crime in the United States, by State and Area, 2020

(Number, percent, rate per 100,000 population.)

| Area | Population[1] | Violent crime[2] | Murder and nonnegligent manslaughter | Rape (revised definition)[3] | Robbery | Aggravated assault | Property crime | Burglary | Larceny-theft | Motor vehicle theft |
|---|---|---|---|---|---|---|---|---|---|---|
| **Alabama[4]** | | | | | | | | | | |
| Metropolitan statistical area | 3,750,044 | | | | | | | | | |
| Area actually reporting | 86.6% | 16,638 | 319 | 1,147 | 2,260 | 12,912 | 75,971 | 13,921 | 53,997 | 8,053 |
| Estimated total | 100.0% | 17,789 | 336 | 1,243 | 2,374 | 13,836 | 84,113 | 15,452 | 59,871 | 8,790 |
| Cities outside metropolitan areas | 527,001 | | | | | | | | | |
| Area actually reporting | 87.4% | 2,834 | 73 | 188 | 204 | 2,369 | 13,407 | 2,276 | 10,061 | 1,070 |
| Estimated total | 100.0% | 3,174 | 81 | 210 | 242 | 2,641 | 15,217 | 2,673 | 11,313 | 1,231 |
| Nonmetropolitan counties | 644,487 | | | | | | | | | |
| Area actually reporting | 71.5% | 798 | 18 | 89 | 29 | 662 | 3,863 | 953 | 2,358 | 552 |
| Estimated total | 100.0% | 1,359 | 54 | 155 | 50 | 1,100 | 5,831 | 1,535 | 3,391 | 905 |
| State total | 4,921,532 | 22,322 | 471 | 1,608 | 2,666 | 17,577 | 105,161 | 19,660 | 74,575 | 10,926 |
| Rate per 100,000 inhabitants | | 453.6 | 9.6 | 32.7 | 54.2 | 357.1 | 2,136.8 | 399.5 | 1,515.3 | 222.0 |
| **Alaska** | | | | | | | | | | |
| Metropolitan statistical area | 338,179 | | | | | | | | | |
| Area actually reporting | 100.0% | 3,853 | 21 | 596 | 608 | 2,628 | 11,760 | 1,668 | 8,678 | 1,414 |
| Cities outside metropolitan areas | 127,563 | | | | | | | | | |
| Area actually reporting | 90.6% | 900 | 8 | 266 | 55 | 571 | 2,147 | 315 | 1,685 | 147 |
| Estimated total | 100.0% | 946 | 9 | 269 | 64 | 604 | 2,391 | 355 | 1,860 | 176 |
| Nonmetropolitan counties | 265,416 | | | | | | | | | |
| Area actually reporting | 100.0% | 1,327 | 19 | 267 | 40 | 1,001 | 2,377 | 752 | 1,246 | 379 |
| State total | 731,158 | 6,126 | 49 | 1,132 | 712 | 4,233 | 16,528 | 2,775 | 11,784 | 1,969 |
| Rate per 100,000 inhabitants | | 837.8 | 6.7 | 154.8 | 97.4 | 578.9 | 2,260.5 | 379.5 | 1,611.7 | 269.3 |
| **Arizona** | | | | | | | | | | |
| Metropolitan statistical area | 7,066,114 | | | | | | | | | |
| Area actually reporting | 93.0% | 30,068 | 431 | 2,971 | 6,094 | 20,572 | 152,680 | 21,627 | 114,824 | 16,229 |
| Estimated total | 100.0% | 31,245 | 457 | 3,083 | 6,134 | 21,571 | 158,648 | 22,997 | 118,727 | 16,924 |
| Cities outside metropolitan areas | 126,679 | | | | | | | | | |
| Area actually reporting | 85.2% | 4,000 | 37 | 158 | 57 | 3,748 | 4,253 | 1,012 | 2,625 | 616 |
| Estimated total | 100.0% | 4,207 | 39 | 168 | 67 | 3,933 | 4,929 | 1,092 | 3,170 | 667 |
| Nonmetropolitan counties | 228,608 | | | | | | | | | |
| Area actually reporting | 73.0% | 314 | 10 | 9 | 8 | 287 | 1,204 | 321 | 655 | 228 |
| Estimated total | 100.0% | 528 | 17 | 12 | 10 | 489 | 1,746 | 399 | 1,001 | 346 |
| State total | 7,421,401 | 35,980 | 513 | 3,263 | 6,211 | 25,993 | 165,323 | 24,488 | 122,898 | 17,937 |
| Rate per 100,000 inhabitants | | 484.8 | 6.9 | 44.0 | 83.7 | 350.2 | 2,227.7 | 330.0 | 1,656.0 | 241.7 |
| **Arkansas** | | | | | | | | | | |
| Metropolitan statistical area | 1,927,318 | | | | | | | | | |
| Area actually reporting | 95.0% | 13,909 | 184 | 1,353 | 1,153 | 11,219 | 53,598 | 10,190 | 37,829 | 5,579 |
| Estimated total | 100.0% | 14,275 | 189 | 1,390 | 1,216 | 11,480 | 55,526 | 10,497 | 39,220 | 5,809 |
| Cities outside metropolitan areas | 494,464 | | | | | | | | | |
| Area actually reporting | 97.9% | 3,637 | 91 | 449 | 228 | 2,869 | 15,072 | 3,329 | 10,673 | 1,070 |
| Estimated total | 100.0% | 3,674 | 91 | 451 | 237 | 2,895 | 15,277 | 3,362 | 10,820 | 1,095 |
| Nonmetropolitan counties | 608,740 | | | | | | | | | |
| Area actually reporting | 79.8% | 1,957 | 33 | 338 | 48 | 1,538 | 5,998 | 1,608 | 3,648 | 742 |
| Estimated total | 100.0% | 2,414 | 41 | 385 | 124 | 1,864 | 8,397 | 1,995 | 5,373 | 1,029 |
| State total | 3,030,522 | 20,363 | 321 | 2,226 | 1,577 | 16,239 | 79,200 | 15,854 | 55,413 | 7,933 |
| Rate per 100,000 inhabitants | | 671.9 | 10.6 | 73.5 | 52.0 | 535.8 | 2,613.4 | 523.1 | 1,828.5 | 261.8 |
| **California** | | | | | | | | | | |
| Metropolitan statistical area | 38,539,958 | | | | | | | | | |
| Area actually reporting | 99.9% | 170,104 | 2,158 | 12,997 | 44,286 | 110,663 | 827,403 | 141,667 | 519,418 | 166,318 |
| Estimated total | 100.0% | 170,131 | 2,158 | 13,000 | 44,291 | 110,682 | 827,545 | 141,689 | 519,521 | 166,335 |
| Cities outside metropolitan areas | 268,242 | | | | | | | | | |
| Area actually reporting | 100.0% | 1,583 | 9 | 149 | 281 | 1,144 | 6,887 | 1,501 | 4,407 | 979 |
| Nonmetropolitan counties | 559,878 | | | | | | | | | |
| Area actually reporting | 100.0% | 2,312 | 36 | 300 | 156 | 1,820 | 7,622 | 2,339 | 4,274 | 1,009 |
| State total | 39,368,078 | 174,026 | 2,203 | 13,449 | 44,728 | 113,646 | 842,054 | 145,529 | 528,202 | 168,323 |
| Rate per 100,000 inhabitants | | 442.0 | 5.6 | 34.2 | 113.6 | 288.7 | 2,138.9 | 369.7 | 1,341.7 | 427.6 |
| **Colorado** | | | | | | | | | | |
| Metropolitan statistical area | 5,093,407 | | | | | | | | | |
| Area actually reporting | 99.5% | 22,960 | 277 | 3,289 | 3,862 | 15,532 | 151,647 | 21,038 | 101,466 | 29,143 |
| Estimated total | 100.0% | 23,015 | 277 | 3,297 | 3,872 | 15,569 | 152,467 | 21,104 | 102,105 | 29,258 |
| Cities outside metropolitan areas | 345,449 | | | | | | | | | |
| Area actually reporting | 96.4% | 963 | 10 | 223 | 74 | 656 | 8,425 | 1,151 | 6,610 | 664 |
| Estimated total | 100.0% | 989 | 10 | 228 | 75 | 676 | 8,696 | 1,184 | 6,819 | 693 |
| Nonmetropolitan counties | 368,863 | | | | | | | | | |
| Area actually reporting | 91.5% | 523 | 7 | 118 | 16 | 382 | 3,103 | 872 | 1,775 | 456 |
| Estimated total | 100.0% | 566 | 7 | 127 | 17 | 415 | 3,419 | 958 | 1,960 | 501 |
| State total | 5,807,719 | 24,570 | 294 | 3,652 | 3,964 | 16,660 | 164,582 | 23,246 | 110,884 | 30,452 |
| Rate per 100,000 inhabitants | | 423.1 | 5.1 | 62.9 | 68.3 | 286.9 | 2,833.8 | 400.3 | 1,909.3 | 524.3 |
| **Connecticut** | | | | | | | | | | |
| Metropolitan statistical area | 2,958,732 | | | | | | | | | |
| Area actually reporting | 100.0% | 6,159 | 130 | 530 | 1,982 | 3,517 | 52,571 | 6,158 | 38,631 | 7,782 |
| Cities outside metropolitan areas | 111,501 | | | | | | | | | |
| Area actually reporting | 100.0% | 87 | 1 | 13 | 24 | 49 | 1,225 | 124 | 952 | 149 |
| Nonmetropolitan counties | 486,773 | | | | | | | | | |
| Area actually reporting | 100.0% | 213 | 9 | 51 | 27 | 126 | 1,874 | 374 | 1,009 | 491 |
| State total | 3,557,006 | 6,459 | 140 | 594 | 2,033 | 3,692 | 55,670 | 6,656 | 40,592 | 8,422 |
| Rate per 100,000 inhabitants | | 181.6 | 3.9 | 16.7 | 57.2 | 103.8 | 1,565.1 | 187.1 | 1,141.2 | 236.8 |

## Table 5. Crime in the United States, by State and Area, 2020—Continued

(Number, percent, rate per 100,000 population.)

| Area | Population[1] | Violent crime[2] | Murder and nonnegligent manslaughter | Rape (revised definition)[3] | Robbery | Aggravated assault | Property crime | Burglary | Larceny-theft | Motor vehicle theft |
|---|---|---|---|---|---|---|---|---|---|---|
| **Delaware** | | | | | | | | | | |
| Metropolitan statistical area | 986,809 | | | | | | | | | |
|   Area actually reporting | 100.0% | 4,262 | 73 | 261 | 700 | 3,228 | 19,355 | 2,508 | 15,182 | 1,665 |
| Cities outside metropolitan areas | None | | | | | | | | | |
| Nonmetropolitan counties | None | | | | | | | | | |
| State total | 986,809 | 4,262 | 73 | 261 | 700 | 3,228 | 19,355 | 2,508 | 15,182 | 1,665 |
|   Rate per 100,000 inhabitants | | 431.9 | 7.4 | 26.4 | 70.9 | 327.1 | 1,961.4 | 254.2 | 1,538.5 | 168.7 |
| **District of Columbia**[5] | | | | | | | | | | |
| Metropolitan statistical area | 712,816 | | | | | | | | | |
|   Area actually reporting | 100.0% | 7,127 | 201 | 311 | 2,373 | 4,242 | 24,899 | 1,964 | 19,536 | 3,399 |
| Cities outside metropolitan areas | None | | | | | | | | | |
| Nonmetropolitan counties | None | | | | | | | | | |
| District total | 712,816 | 7,127 | 201 | 311 | 2,373 | 4,242 | 24,899 | 1,964 | 19,536 | 3,399 |
|   Rate per 100,000 inhabitants | | 999.8 | 28.2 | 43.6 | 332.9 | 595.1 | 3,493.0 | 275.5 | 2,740.7 | 476.8 |
| **Florida** | | | | | | | | | | |
| Metropolitan statistical area | 21,043,573 | | | | | | | | | |
|   Area actually reporting | 99.8% | 80,320 | 1,238 | 7,441 | 13,205 | 58,436 | 371,991 | 49,202 | 285,586 | 37,203 |
|   Estimated total | 100.0% | 80,538 | 1,240 | 7,456 | 13,241 | 58,601 | 373,436 | 49,404 | 286,718 | 37,314 |
| Cities outside metropolitan areas | 140,051 | | | | | | | | | |
|   Area actually reporting | 92.0% | 843 | 18 | 50 | 102 | 673 | 3,756 | 839 | 2,607 | 310 |
|   Estimated total | 100.0% | 885 | 18 | 54 | 111 | 702 | 3,983 | 876 | 2,769 | 338 |
| Nonmetropolitan counties | 549,688 | | | | | | | | | |
|   Area actually reporting | 93.5% | 1,810 | 30 | 163 | 145 | 1,472 | 6,423 | 1,900 | 3,989 | 534 |
|   Estimated total | 100.0% | 1,945 | 32 | 176 | 169 | 1,568 | 7,137 | 2,013 | 4,505 | 619 |
| State total | 21,733,312 | 83,368 | 1,290 | 7,686 | 13,521 | 60,871 | 384,556 | 52,293 | 293,992 | 38,271 |
|   Rate per 100,000 inhabitants | | 383.6 | 5.9 | 35.4 | 62.2 | 280.1 | 1,769.4 | 240.6 | 1,352.7 | 176.1 |
| **Georgia**[6] | | | | | | | | | | |
| Metropolitan statistical area | 8,903,595 | | | | | | | | | |
|   Area actually reporting | 70.7% | 27,159 | 615 | 2,092 | 4,533 | 19,919 | 129,465 | 16,813 | 95,500 | 17,152 |
|   Estimated total | 100.0% | 37,571 | 855 | 2,843 | 6,496 | 27,377 | 182,131 | 24,901 | 134,357 | 22,873 |
| Cities outside metropolitan areas | 641,416 | | | | | | | | | |
|   Area actually reporting | 61.6% | 1,842 | 38 | 180 | 234 | 1,390 | 12,023 | 1,767 | 9,555 | 701 |
|   Estimated total | 100.0% | 2,700 | 47 | 274 | 353 | 2,026 | 18,207 | 2,740 | 14,355 | 1,112 |
| Nonmetropolitan counties | 1,165,006 | | | | | | | | | |
|   Area actually reporting | 75.9% | 1,905 | 28 | 244 | 105 | 1,528 | 10,588 | 2,403 | 7,078 | 1,107 |
|   Estimated total | 100.0% | 2,579 | 41 | 303 | 167 | 2,068 | 14,650 | 3,498 | 9,631 | 1,521 |
| State total | 10,710,017 | 42,850 | 943 | 3,420 | 7,016 | 31,471 | 214,988 | 31,139 | 158,343 | 25,506 |
|   Rate per 100,000 inhabitants | | 400.1 | 8.8 | 31.9 | 65.5 | 293.8 | 2,007.4 | 290.7 | 1,478.5 | 238.2 |
| **Hawaii** | | | | | | | | | | |
| Metropolitan statistical area | 1,133,616 | | | | | | | | | |
|   Area actually reporting | 14.7% | 379 | 5 | 71 | 59 | 244 | 3,537 | 496 | 2,612 | 429 |
|   Estimated total | 100.0% | 2,769 | 27 | 401 | 798 | 1,543 | 28,815 | 3,791 | 20,438 | 4,586 |
| Cities outside metropolitan areas | None | | | | | | | | | |
| Nonmetropolitan counties | 273,390 | | | | | | | | | |
|   Area actually reporting | 100.0% | 807 | 14 | 168 | 69 | 556 | 5,113 | 839 | 3,516 | 758 |
| State total | 1,407,006 | 3,576 | 41 | 569 | 867 | 2,099 | 33,928 | 4,630 | 23,954 | 5,344 |
|   Rate per 100,000 inhabitants | | 254.2 | 2.9 | 40.4 | 61.6 | 149.2 | 2,411.4 | 329.1 | 1,702.5 | 379.8 |
| **Idaho** | | | | | | | | | | |
| Metropolitan statistical area | 1,361,287 | | | | | | | | | |
|   Estimated total | 99.9% | 3,582 | 26 | 693 | 159 | 2,704 | 16,647 | 2,974 | 12,205 | 1,468 |
|   Area actually reporting | 100.0% | 3,583 | 26 | 693 | 159 | 2,705 | 16,653 | 2,975 | 12,210 | 1,468 |
| Cities outside metropolitan areas | 186,575 | | | | | | | | | |
|   Area actually reporting | 96.3% | 366 | 3 | 49 | 10 | 304 | 2,052 | 362 | 1,543 | 147 |
|   Estimated total | 100.0% | 380 | 3 | 51 | 10 | 316 | 2,135 | 380 | 1,603 | 152 |
| Nonmetropolitan counties | 279,051 | | | | | | | | | |
|   Area actually reporting | 100.0% | 469 | 12 | 88 | 5 | 364 | 1,525 | 376 | 1,002 | 147 |
| State total | 1,826,913 | 4,432 | 41 | 832 | 174 | 3,385 | 20,313 | 3,731 | 14,815 | 1,767 |
|   Rate per 100,000 inhabitants | | 242.6 | 2.2 | 45.5 | 9.5 | 185.3 | 1,111.9 | 204.2 | 810.9 | 96.7 |
| **Illinois**[7] | | | | | | | | | | |
| Metropolitan statistical area | 11,178,842 | | | | | | | | | |
|   Area actually reporting | 94.3% | 48,707 | 1,086 | 4,258 | 11,829 | 31,534 | 170,797 | 25,705 | 125,469 | 19,623 |
|   Estimated total | 100.0% | 49,959 | 1,105 | 4,438 | 12,019 | 32,397 | 178,768 | 27,076 | 131,388 | 20,304 |
| Cities outside metropolitan areas | 800,198 | | | | | | | | | |
|   Area actually reporting | 81.3% | 2,047 | 13 | 380 | 157 | 1,497 | 11,607 | 2,131 | 8,870 | 606 |
|   Estimated total | 100.0% | 2,324 | 13 | 402 | 168 | 1,741 | 13,375 | 2,564 | 10,139 | 672 |
| Nonmetropolitan counties | 608,490 | | | | | | | | | |
|   Area actually reporting | 88.9% | 1,268 | 33 | 239 | 74 | 922 | 3,639 | 1,208 | 2,115 | 316 |
|   Estimated total | 100.0% | 1,329 | 33 | 250 | 74 | 972 | 4,144 | 1,380 | 2,408 | 356 |
| State total | 12,587,530 | 53,612 | 1,151 | 5,090 | 12,261 | 35,110 | 196,287 | 31,020 | 143,935 | 21,332 |
|   Rate per 100,000 inhabitants | | 425.9 | 9.1 | 40.4 | 97.4 | 278.9 | 1,559.4 | 246.4 | 1,143.5 | 169.5 |
| **Indiana** | | | | | | | | | | |
| Metropolitan statistical area | 5,294,758 | | | | | | | | | |
|   Area actually reporting | 88.2% | 20,174 | 458 | 1,692 | 3,998 | 14,026 | 95,762 | 14,562 | 68,534 | 12,666 |
|   Estimated total | 100.0% | 21,151 | 464 | 1,812 | 4,104 | 14,771 | 102,523 | 16,051 | 73,029 | 13,443 |
| Cities outside metropolitan areas | 560,706 | | | | | | | | | |
|   Area actually reporting | 55.8% | 726 | 8 | 88 | 33 | 597 | 5,881 | 705 | 4,756 | 420 |
|   Estimated total | 100.0% | 1,345 | 11 | 176 | 60 | 1,098 | 11,226 | 1,398 | 9,016 | 812 |

## Table 5. Crime in the United States, by State and Area, 2020—Continued

(Number, percent, rate per 100,000 population.)

| Area | Population[1] | Violent crime[2] | Murder and nonnegligent manslaughter | Rape (revised definition)[3] | Robbery | Aggravated assault | Property crime | Burglary | Larceny-theft | Motor vehicle theft |
|---|---|---|---|---|---|---|---|---|---|---|
| **Nonmetropolitan counties** | 899,489 | | | | | | | | | |
| Area actually reporting | 52.0% | 1,133 | 27 | 211 | 35 | 860 | 3,491 | 723 | 2,154 | 614 |
| Estimated total | 100.0% | 1,665 | 30 | 360 | 51 | 1,224 | 6,704 | 1,489 | 4,035 | 1,180 |
| **State total** | 6,754,953 | 24,161 | 505 | 2,348 | 4,215 | 17,093 | 120,453 | 18,938 | 86,080 | 15,435 |
| Rate per 100,000 inhabitants | | 357.7 | 7.5 | 34.8 | 62.4 | 253.0 | 1,783.2 | 280.4 | 1,274.3 | 228.5 |
| **Iowa** | | | | | | | | | | |
| **Metropolitan statistical area** | 1,947,544 | | | | | | | | | |
| Area actually reporting | 97.4% | 6,581 | 90 | 774 | 813 | 4,904 | 39,132 | 8,154 | 26,184 | 4,794 |
| Estimated total | 100.0% | 6,721 | 90 | 801 | 825 | 5,005 | 39,935 | 8,334 | 26,736 | 4,865 |
| **Cities outside metropolitan areas** | 568,224 | | | | | | | | | |
| Area actually reporting | 96.3% | 1,922 | 14 | 308 | 100 | 1,500 | 10,086 | 2,145 | 7,080 | 861 |
| Estimated total | 100.0% | 1,992 | 14 | 317 | 102 | 1,559 | 10,450 | 2,222 | 7,337 | 891 |
| **Nonmetropolitan counties** | 647,793 | | | | | | | | | |
| Area actually reporting | 98.0% | 859 | 7 | 169 | 8 | 675 | 3,151 | 1,118 | 1,591 | 442 |
| Estimated total | 100.0% | 888 | 7 | 171 | 16 | 694 | 3,340 | 1,183 | 1,678 | 479 |
| **State total** | 3,163,561 | 9,601 | 111 | 1,289 | 943 | 7,258 | 53,725 | 11,739 | 35,751 | 6,235 |
| Rate per 100,000 inhabitants | | 303.5 | 3.5 | 40.7 | 29.8 | 229.4 | 1,698.2 | 371.1 | 1,130.1 | 197.1 |
| **Kansas** | | | | | | | | | | |
| **Metropolitan statistical area** | 2,032,826 | | | | | | | | | |
| Area actually reporting | 79.5% | 8,485 | 76 | 773 | 697 | 6,939 | 40,181 | 5,580 | 29,847 | 4,754 |
| Estimated total | 100.0% | 9,430 | 83 | 881 | 774 | 7,692 | 47,379 | 6,354 | 35,268 | 5,757 |
| **Cities outside metropolitan areas** | 561,423 | | | | | | | | | |
| Area actually reporting | 92.4% | 2,017 | 8 | 291 | 125 | 1,593 | 12,770 | 2,028 | 9,782 | 960 |
| Estimated total | 100.0% | 2,205 | 9 | 310 | 131 | 1,755 | 13,453 | 2,226 | 10,180 | 1,047 |
| **Nonmetropolitan counties** | 319,556 | | | | | | | | | |
| Area actually reporting | 96.1% | 722 | 8 | 68 | 23 | 623 | 3,089 | 1,003 | 1,679 | 407 |
| Estimated total | 100.0% | 750 | 8 | 72 | 23 | 647 | 3,245 | 1,075 | 1,745 | 425 |
| **State total** | 2,913,805 | 12,385 | 100 | 1,263 | 928 | 10,094 | 64,077 | 9,655 | 47,193 | 7,229 |
| Rate per 100,000 inhabitants | | 425.0 | 3.4 | 43.3 | 31.8 | 346.4 | 2,199.1 | 331.4 | 1,619.6 | 248.1 |
| **Kentucky** | | | | | | | | | | |
| **Metropolitan statistical area** | 2,672,178 | | | | | | | | | |
| Area actually reporting | 99.9% | 9,441 | 241 | 809 | 2,117 | 6,274 | 60,950 | 10,833 | 41,376 | 8,741 |
| Estimated total | 100.0% | 9,446 | 241 | 809 | 2,119 | 6,277 | 61,003 | 10,841 | 41,415 | 8,747 |
| **Cities outside metropolitan areas** | 528,590 | | | | | | | | | |
| Area actually reporting | 99.5% | 846 | 15 | 180 | 157 | 494 | 10,407 | 1,957 | 7,336 | 1,114 |
| Estimated total | 100.0% | 849 | 15 | 180 | 157 | 497 | 10,475 | 1,970 | 7,384 | 1,121 |
| **Nonmetropolitan counties** | 1,276,483 | | | | | | | | | |
| Area actually reporting | 100.0% | 1,305 | 67 | 382 | 93 | 763 | 8,195 | 2,596 | 3,970 | 1,629 |
| **State total** | 4,477,251 | 11,600 | 323 | 1,371 | 2,369 | 7,537 | 79,673 | 15,407 | 52,769 | 11,497 |
| Rate per 100,000 inhabitants | | 259.1 | 7.2 | 30.6 | 52.9 | 168.3 | 1,779.5 | 344.1 | 1,178.6 | 256.8 |
| **Louisiana** | | | | | | | | | | |
| **Metropolitan statistical area** | 3,917,340 | | | | | | | | | |
| Area actually reporting | 94.3% | 24,966 | 626 | 1,774 | 3,312 | 19,254 | 114,133 | 19,428 | 84,040 | 10,665 |
| Estimated total | 100.0% | 25,881 | 638 | 1,857 | 3,459 | 19,927 | 119,029 | 20,211 | 87,609 | 11,209 |
| **Cities outside metropolitan areas** | 264,144 | | | | | | | | | |
| Area actually reporting | 76.6% | 1,757 | 51 | 68 | 164 | 1,474 | 7,688 | 1,793 | 5,494 | 401 |
| Estimated total | 100.0% | 1,985 | 51 | 92 | 202 | 1,640 | 8,934 | 1,991 | 6,394 | 549 |
| **Nonmetropolitan counties** | 463,834 | | | | | | | | | |
| Area actually reporting | 91.1% | 1,677 | 42 | 172 | 56 | 1,407 | 5,184 | 1,361 | 3,292 | 531 |
| Estimated total | 100.0% | 1,838 | 45 | 187 | 86 | 1,520 | 6,026 | 1,496 | 3,888 | 642 |
| **State total** | 4,645,318 | 29,704 | 734 | 2,136 | 3,747 | 23,087 | 133,989 | 23,698 | 97,891 | 12,400 |
| Rate per 100,000 inhabitants | | 639.4 | 15.8 | 46.0 | 80.7 | 497.0 | 2,884.4 | 510.1 | 2,107.3 | 266.9 |
| **Maine** | | | | | | | | | | |
| **Metropolitan statistical area** | 803,976 | | | | | | | | | |
| Area actually reporting | 100.0% | 797 | 11 | 236 | 119 | 431 | 9,312 | 1,011 | 7,795 | 506 |
| **Cities outside metropolitan areas** | 254,490 | | | | | | | | | |
| Area actually reporting | 100.0% | 353 | 4 | 111 | 42 | 196 | 3,917 | 501 | 3,242 | 174 |
| **Nonmetropolitan counties** | 291,675 | | | | | | | | | |
| Area actually reporting | 100.0% | 316 | 7 | 139 | 9 | 161 | 2,381 | 497 | 1,702 | 182 |
| **State total** | 1,350,141 | 1,466 | 22 | 486 | 170 | 788 | 15,610 | 2,009 | 12,739 | 862 |
| Rate per 100,000 inhabitants | | 108.6 | 1.6 | 36.0 | 12.6 | 58.4 | 1,156.2 | 148.8 | 943.5 | 63.8 |
| **Maryland[4]** | | | | | | | | | | |
| **Metropolitan statistical area** | 5,905,671 | | | | | | | | | |
| Area actually reporting | 100.0% | 23,755 | 548 | 1,700 | 7,114 | 14,393 | 95,548 | 14,906 | 70,271 | 10,371 |
| **Cities outside metropolitan areas** | 51,424 | | | | | | | | | |
| Area actually reporting | 100.0% | 349 | 4 | 18 | 53 | 274 | 1,323 | 203 | 1,051 | 69 |
| **Nonmetropolitan counties** | 98,707 | | | | | | | | | |
| Area actually reporting | 100.0% | 111 | 1 | 14 | 7 | 89 | 616 | 152 | 435 | 29 |
| **State total** | 6,055,802 | 24,215 | 553 | 1,732 | 7,174 | 14,756 | 97,487 | 15,261 | 71,757 | 10,469 |
| Rate per 100,000 inhabitants | | 399.9 | 9.1 | 28.6 | 118.5 | 243.7 | 1,609.8 | 252.0 | 1,184.9 | 172.9 |
| **Massachusetts** | | | | | | | | | | |
| **Metropolitan statistical area** | 6,864,763 | | | | | | | | | |
| Area actually reporting | 99.2% | 21,064 | 160 | 1,818 | 2,995 | 16,091 | 71,962 | 10,234 | 54,919 | 6,809 |
| Estimated total | 100.0% | 21,186 | 160 | 1,837 | 3,012 | 16,177 | 72,225 | 10,289 | 55,107 | 6,829 |
| **Cities outside metropolitan areas** | 28,811 | | | | | | | | | |
| Area actually reporting | 100.0% | 102 | 0 | 14 | 3 | 85 | 377 | 34 | 337 | 6 |

## Table 5. Crime in the United States, by State and Area, 2020—Continued

(Number, percent, rate per 100,000 population.)

| Area | Population[1] | Violent crime[2] | Murder and nonnegligent manslaughter | Rape (revised definition)[3] | Robbery | Aggravated assault | Property crime | Burglary | Larceny-theft | Motor vehicle theft |
|---|---|---|---|---|---|---|---|---|---|---|
| **Nonmetropolitan counties** | | | | | | | | | | |
| Area actually reporting | 100.0% | 0 | 0 | 0 | 0 | 0 | 0 | 0 | 0 | 0 |
| **State total** | 6,893,574 | 21,288 | 160 | 1,851 | 3,015 | 16,262 | 72,602 | 10,323 | 55,444 | 6,835 |
| Rate per 100,000 inhabitants | | 308.8 | 2.3 | 26.9 | 43.7 | 235.9 | 1,053.2 | 149.7 | 804.3 | 99.2 |
| **Michigan** | | | | | | | | | | |
| **Metropolitan statistical area** | 8,171,665 | | | | | | | | | |
| Area actually reporting | 97.7% | 42,329 | 712 | 4,587 | 4,283 | 32,747 | 116,391 | 19,432 | 80,101 | 16,858 |
| Estimated total | 100.0% | 42,773 | 715 | 4,669 | 4,315 | 33,074 | 118,153 | 19,707 | 81,403 | 17,043 |
| **Cities outside metropolitan areas** | 574,930 | | | | | | | | | |
| Area actually reporting | 99.9% | 1,702 | 14 | 437 | 83 | 1,168 | 7,910 | 894 | 6,533 | 483 |
| Estimated total | 100.0% | 1,703 | 14 | 437 | 83 | 1,169 | 7,921 | 895 | 6,542 | 484 |
| **Nonmetropolitan counties** | 1,219,960 | | | | | | | | | |
| Area actually reporting | 99.0% | 3,146 | 25 | 955 | 40 | 2,126 | 9,493 | 2,616 | 6,023 | 854 |
| Estimated total | 100.0% | 3,165 | 25 | 959 | 40 | 2,141 | 9,559 | 2,629 | 6,072 | 858 |
| **State total** | 9,966,555 | 47,641 | 754 | 6,065 | 4,438 | 36,384 | 135,633 | 23,231 | 94,017 | 18,385 |
| Rate per 100,000 inhabitants | | 478.0 | 7.6 | 60.9 | 44.5 | 365.1 | 1,360.9 | 233.1 | 943.3 | 184.5 |
| **Minnesota** | | | | | | | | | | |
| **Metropolitan statistical area** | 4,414,276 | | | | | | | | | |
| Area actually reporting | 99.9% | 13,564 | 170 | 1,792 | 3,773 | 7,829 | 103,367 | 14,521 | 76,020 | 12,826 |
| Estimated total | 100.0% | 13,568 | 170 | 1,793 | 3,773 | 7,832 | 103,424 | 14,527 | 76,068 | 12,829 |
| **Cities outside metropolitan areas** | 575,358 | | | | | | | | | |
| Area actually reporting | 99.2% | 1,385 | 11 | 270 | 83 | 1,021 | 11,045 | 1,389 | 8,933 | 723 |
| Estimated total | 100.0% | 1,392 | 11 | 270 | 83 | 1,028 | 11,145 | 1,403 | 9,013 | 729 |
| **Nonmetropolitan counties** | 667,708 | | | | | | | | | |
| Area actually reporting | 100.0% | 738 | 9 | 148 | 21 | 560 | 5,643 | 1,440 | 3,615 | 588 |
| **State total** | 5,657,342 | 15,698 | 190 | 2,211 | 3,877 | 9,420 | 120,212 | 17,370 | 88,696 | 14,146 |
| Rate per 100,000 inhabitants | | 277.5 | 3.4 | 39.1 | 68.5 | 166.5 | 2,124.9 | 307.0 | 1,567.8 | 250.0 |
| **Mississippi** | | | | | | | | | | |
| **Metropolitan statistical area** | 1,441,468 | | | | | | | | | |
| Area actually reporting | 77.5% | 3,692 | 177 | 410 | 885 | 2,220 | 28,621 | 5,026 | 20,558 | 3,037 |
| Estimated total | 100.0% | 4,412 | 186 | 628 | 938 | 2,660 | 33,213 | 5,817 | 23,818 | 3,578 |
| **Cities outside metropolitan areas** | 555,942 | | | | | | | | | |
| Area actually reporting | 49.0% | 1,305 | 49 | 119 | 174 | 963 | 9,620 | 2,583 | 6,416 | 621 |
| Estimated total | 100.0% | 2,370 | 73 | 213 | 310 | 1,774 | 18,048 | 5,038 | 11,866 | 1,144 |
| **Nonmetropolitan counties** | 969,376 | | | | | | | | | |
| Area actually reporting | 46.9% | 925 | 32 | 132 | 94 | 667 | 5,085 | 1,838 | 2,691 | 556 |
| Estimated total | 100.0% | 1,856 | 56 | 307 | 171 | 1,322 | 11,090 | 3,633 | 6,096 | 1,361 |
| **State total** | 2,966,786 | 8,638 | 315 | 1,148 | 1,419 | 5,756 | 62,351 | 14,488 | 41,780 | 6,083 |
| Rate per 100,000 inhabitants | | 291.2 | 10.6 | 38.7 | 47.8 | 194.0 | 2,101.6 | 488.3 | 1,408.3 | 205.0 |
| **Missouri** | | | | | | | | | | |
| **Metropolitan statistical area** | 4,621,557 | | | | | | | | | |
| Area actually reporting | 99.3% | 28,401 | 656 | 2,102 | 4,317 | 21,326 | 125,871 | 17,644 | 87,324 | 20,903 |
| Estimated total | 100.0% | 28,614 | 656 | 2,112 | 4,346 | 21,500 | 126,817 | 17,778 | 87,968 | 21,071 |
| **Cities outside metropolitan areas** | 635,377 | | | | | | | | | |
| Area actually reporting | 95.9% | 2,573 | 35 | 315 | 146 | 2,077 | 18,815 | 2,949 | 14,378 | 1,488 |
| Estimated total | 100.0% | 2,654 | 35 | 321 | 147 | 2,151 | 19,564 | 3,070 | 14,941 | 1,553 |
| **Nonmetropolitan counties** | 894,614 | | | | | | | | | |
| Area actually reporting | 95.9% | 2,027 | 31 | 223 | 80 | 1,693 | 8,914 | 2,347 | 5,061 | 1,506 |
| Estimated total | 100.0% | 2,117 | 32 | 228 | 82 | 1,775 | 9,317 | 2,452 | 5,300 | 1,565 |
| **State total** | 6,151,548 | 33,385 | 723 | 2,661 | 4,575 | 25,426 | 155,698 | 23,300 | 108,209 | 24,189 |
| Rate per 100,000 inhabitants | | 542.7 | 11.8 | 43.3 | 74.4 | 413.3 | 2,531.0 | 378.8 | 1,759.1 | 393.2 |
| **Montana** | | | | | | | | | | |
| **Metropolitan statistical area** | 386,281 | | | | | | | | | |
| Area actually reporting | 100.0% | 2,000 | 21 | 235 | 194 | 1,550 | 12,719 | 1,597 | 9,723 | 1,399 |
| **Cities outside metropolitan areas** | 235,155 | | | | | | | | | |
| Area actually reporting | 98.7% | 1,729 | 13 | 191 | 47 | 1,478 | 5,019 | 540 | 3,971 | 508 |
| Estimated total | 100.0% | 1,747 | 13 | 194 | 47 | 1,493 | 5,089 | 547 | 4,027 | 515 |
| **Nonmetropolitan counties** | 459,141 | | | | | | | | | |
| Area actually reporting | 99.4% | 1,323 | 20 | 169 | 38 | 1,096 | 5,081 | 770 | 3,552 | 759 |
| Estimated total | 100.0% | 1,330 | 20 | 169 | 38 | 1,103 | 5,109 | 775 | 3,572 | 762 |
| **State total** | 1,080,577 | 5,077 | 54 | 598 | 279 | 4,146 | 22,917 | 2,919 | 17,322 | 2,676 |
| Rate per 100,000 inhabitants | | 469.8 | 5.0 | 55.3 | 25.8 | 383.7 | 2,120.8 | 270.1 | 1,603.0 | 247.6 |
| **Nebraska** | | | | | | | | | | |
| **Metropolitan statistical area** | 1,272,351 | | | | | | | | | |
| Area actually reporting | 99.0% | 5,058 | 51 | 840 | 689 | 3,478 | 28,674 | 3,136 | 21,292 | 4,246 |
| Estimated total | 100.0% | 5,102 | 51 | 846 | 695 | 3,510 | 28,866 | 3,165 | 21,422 | 4,279 |
| **Cities outside metropolitan areas** | 341,322 | | | | | | | | | |
| Area actually reporting | 93.1% | 812 | 10 | 224 | 55 | 523 | 5,428 | 774 | 4,203 | 451 |
| Estimated total | 100.0% | 910 | 10 | 237 | 71 | 592 | 5,869 | 855 | 4,542 | 472 |
| **Nonmetropolitan counties** | 323,879 | | | | | | | | | |
| Area actually reporting | 86.1% | 295 | 8 | 63 | 5 | 219 | 1,347 | 293 | 868 | 186 |
| Estimated total | 100.0% | 461 | 8 | 80 | 33 | 340 | 2,256 | 435 | 1,524 | 297 |
| **State total** | 1,937,552 | 6,473 | 69 | 1,163 | 799 | 4,442 | 36,991 | 4,455 | 27,488 | 5,048 |
| Rate per 100,000 inhabitants | | 334.1 | 3.6 | 60.0 | 41.2 | 229.3 | 1,909.2 | 229.9 | 1,418.7 | 260.5 |
| **Nevada** | | | | | | | | | | |
| **Metropolitan statistical area** | 2,853,689 | | | | | | | | | |
| Area actually reporting | 100.0% | 13,540 | 155 | 1,741 | 2,709 | 8,935 | 56,841 | 10,635 | 36,142 | 10,064 |

## Table 5. Crime in the United States, by State and Area, 2020—Continued

(Number, percent, rate per 100,000 population.)

| Area | Population[1] | Violent crime[2] | Murder and nonnegligent manslaughter | Rape (revised definition)[3] | Robbery | Aggravated assault | Property crime | Burglary | Larceny-theft | Motor vehicle theft |
|---|---|---|---|---|---|---|---|---|---|---|
| **Cities outside metropolitan areas** | 48,735 | | | | | | | | | |
| Area actually reporting | 100.0% | 217 | 11 | 30 | 29 | 147 | 1,155 | 273 | 748 | 134 |
| **Nonmetropolitan counties** | 235,835 | | | | | | | | | |
| Area actually reporting | 100.0% | 688 | 14 | 80 | 47 | 547 | 2,466 | 666 | 1,442 | 358 |
| **State total** | 3,138,259 | 14,445 | 180 | 1,851 | 2,785 | 9,629 | 60,462 | 11,574 | 38,332 | 10,556 |
| Rate per 100,000 inhabitants | | 460.3 | 5.7 | 59.0 | 88.7 | 306.8 | 1,926.6 | 368.8 | 1,221.4 | 336.4 |
| | | | | | | | | | | |
| **New Hampshire** | | | | | | | | | | |
| **Metropolitan statistical area** | 862,794 | | | | | | | | | |
| Area actually reporting | 99.2% | 1,274 | 9 | 306 | 203 | 756 | 8,897 | 774 | 7,500 | 623 |
| Estimated total | 100.0% | 1,301 | 9 | 310 | 207 | 775 | 9,038 | 797 | 7,602 | 639 |
| **Cities outside metropolitan areas** | 467,654 | | | | | | | | | |
| Area actually reporting | 95.6% | 568 | 1 | 206 | 57 | 304 | 5,264 | 497 | 4,444 | 323 |
| Estimated total | 100.0% | 646 | 1 | 214 | 71 | 360 | 5,682 | 563 | 4,745 | 374 |
| **Nonmetropolitan counties** | 35,827 | | | | | | | | | |
| Area actually reporting | 92.2% | 42 | 2 | 17 | 0 | 23 | 238 | 43 | 171 | 24 |
| Estimated total | 100.0% | 53 | 2 | 18 | 2 | 31 | 294 | 52 | 211 | 31 |
| **State total** | 1,366,275 | 2,000 | 12 | 542 | 280 | 1,166 | 15,014 | 1,412 | 12,558 | 1,044 |
| Rate per 100,000 inhabitants | | 146.4 | 0.9 | 39.7 | 20.5 | 85.3 | 1,098.9 | 103.3 | 919.1 | 76.4 |
| | | | | | | | | | | |
| **New Jersey** | | | | | | | | | | |
| **Metropolitan statistical area** | 8,882,371 | | | | | | | | | |
| Area actually reporting | 100.0% | 17,353 | 329 | 1,277 | 4,384 | 11,363 | 102,875 | 12,983 | 79,614 | 10,278 |
| **Cities outside metropolitan areas** | None | | | | | | | | | |
| **Nonmetropolitan counties** | None | | | | | | | | | |
| **State total** | 8,882,371 | 17,353 | 329 | 1,277 | 4,384 | 11,363 | 102,875 | 12,983 | 79,614 | 10,278 |
| Rate per 100,000 inhabitants | | 195.4 | 3.7 | 14.4 | 49.4 | 127.9 | 1,158.2 | 146.2 | 896.3 | 115.7 |
| | | | | | | | | | | |
| **New Mexico** | | | | | | | | | | |
| **Metropolitan statistical area** | 1,418,447 | | | | | | | | | |
| Area actually reporting | 100.0% | 11,598 | 109 | 809 | 1,768 | 8,912 | 44,460 | 9,501 | 27,801 | 7,158 |
| **Cities outside metropolitan areas** | 395,987 | | | | | | | | | |
| Area actually reporting | 94.0% | 2,753 | 29 | 216 | 262 | 2,246 | 11,207 | 2,802 | 7,250 | 1,155 |
| Estimated total | 100.0% | 2,896 | 32 | 229 | 270 | 2,365 | 11,968 | 2,939 | 7,758 | 1,271 |
| **Nonmetropolitan counties** | 291,885 | | | | | | | | | |
| Area actually reporting | 96.0% | 1,881 | 23 | 131 | 46 | 1,681 | 3,307 | 1,148 | 1,592 | 567 |
| Estimated total | 100.0% | 1,899 | 23 | 132 | 48 | 1,696 | 3,431 | 1,225 | 1,629 | 577 |
| **State total** | 2,106,319 | 16,393 | 164 | 1,170 | 2,086 | 12,973 | 59,859 | 13,665 | 37,188 | 9,006 |
| Rate per 100,000 inhabitants | | 778.3 | 7.8 | 55.5 | 99.0 | 615.9 | 2,841.9 | 648.8 | 1,765.5 | 427.6 |
| | | | | | | | | | | |
| **New York** | | | | | | | | | | |
| **Metropolitan statistical area** | 17,993,042 | | | | | | | | | |
| Area actually reporting | 99.3% | 67,582 | 783 | 4,604 | 17,267 | 44,928 | 255,315 | 29,045 | 207,497 | 18,773 |
| Estimated total | 100.0% | 67,805 | 783 | 4,632 | 17,310 | 45,080 | 257,063 | 29,270 | 208,938 | 18,855 |
| **Cities outside metropolitan areas** | 492,133 | | | | | | | | | |
| Area actually reporting | 95.3% | 1,060 | 7 | 208 | 117 | 728 | 7,862 | 1,192 | 6,402 | 268 |
| Estimated total | 100.0% | 1,098 | 7 | 218 | 119 | 754 | 8,404 | 1,263 | 6,858 | 283 |
| **Nonmetropolitan counties** | 851,601 | | | | | | | | | |
| Area actually reporting | 92.9% | 1,361 | 14 | 595 | 56 | 696 | 7,158 | 1,466 | 5,318 | 374 |
| Estimated total | 100.0% | 1,436 | 18 | 618 | 96 | 704 | 7,321 | 1,470 | 5,333 | 518 |
| **State total** | 19,336,776 | 70,339 | 808 | 5,468 | 17,525 | 46,538 | 272,788 | 32,003 | 221,129 | 19,656 |
| Rate per 100,000 inhabitants | | 363.8 | 4.2 | 28.3 | 90.6 | 240.7 | 1,410.7 | 165.5 | 1,143.6 | 101.7 |
| | | | | | | | | | | |
| **North Carolina** | | | | | | | | | | |
| **Metropolitan statistical area** | 8,612,057 | | | | | | | | | |
| Area actually reporting | 88.8% | 32,769 | 561 | 1,966 | 5,855 | 24,387 | 170,639 | 31,200 | 124,252 | 15,187 |
| Estimated total | 100.0% | 36,136 | 615 | 2,248 | 6,444 | 26,829 | 191,181 | 35,707 | 138,329 | 17,145 |
| **Cities outside metropolitan areas** | 588,746 | | | | | | | | | |
| Area actually reporting | 78.1% | 3,290 | 81 | 207 | 431 | 2,571 | 18,779 | 4,953 | 12,715 | 1,111 |
| Estimated total | 100.0% | 4,113 | 97 | 245 | 564 | 3,207 | 23,894 | 6,564 | 15,955 | 1,375 |
| **Nonmetropolitan counties** | 1,400,020 | | | | | | | | | |
| Area actually reporting | 84.9% | 3,378 | 113 | 359 | 267 | 2,639 | 17,352 | 6,346 | 9,329 | 1,677 |
| Estimated total | 100.0% | 4,202 | 140 | 429 | 332 | 3,301 | 20,951 | 7,681 | 11,270 | 2,000 |
| **State total** | 10,600,823 | 44,451 | 852 | 2,922 | 7,340 | 33,337 | 236,026 | 49,952 | 165,554 | 20,520 |
| Rate per 100,000 inhabitants | | 419.3 | 8.0 | 27.6 | 69.2 | 314.5 | 2,226.5 | 471.2 | 1,561.7 | 193.6 |
| | | | | | | | | | | |
| **North Dakota** | | | | | | | | | | |
| **Metropolitan statistical area** | 382,437 | | | | | | | | | |
| Area actually reporting | 100.0% | 1,273 | 18 | 237 | 110 | 908 | 10,531 | 2,121 | 7,318 | 1,092 |
| **Cities outside metropolitan areas** | 193,373 | | | | | | | | | |
| Area actually reporting | 100.0% | 1,045 | 12 | 113 | 32 | 888 | 4,261 | 734 | 2,818 | 709 |
| **Nonmetropolitan counties** | 189,499 | | | | | | | | | |
| Area actually reporting | 100.0% | 200 | 2 | 46 | 9 | 143 | 1,464 | 341 | 850 | 273 |
| **State total** | 765,309 | 2,518 | 32 | 396 | 151 | 1,939 | 16,256 | 3,196 | 10,986 | 2,074 |
| Rate per 100,000 inhabitants | | 329.0 | 4.2 | 51.7 | 19.7 | 253.4 | 2,124.1 | 417.6 | 1,435.5 | 271.0 |
| | | | | | | | | | | |
| **Ohio[8]** | | | | | | | | | | |
| **Metropolitan statistical area** | 9,394,238 | | | | | | | | | |
| Area actually reporting | 90.3% | 31,161 | 764 | 3,932 | 7,216 | 19,249 | 167,695 | 29,577 | 121,075 | 17,043 |
| Estimated total | 100.0% | 32,797 | 774 | 4,237 | 7,522 | 20,264 | 183,497 | 31,741 | 133,675 | 18,081 |
| **Cities outside metropolitan areas** | 1,012,995 | | | | | | | | | |
| Area actually reporting | 76.4% | 1,350 | 12 | 338 | 166 | 834 | 14,656 | 1,943 | 12,103 | 610 |
| Estimated total | 100.0% | 1,739 | 13 | 414 | 225 | 1,087 | 20,824 | 2,627 | 17,319 | 878 |

## Table 5. Crime in the United States, by State and Area, 2020—Continued

(Number, percent, rate per 100,000 population.)

| Area | Population[1] | Violent crime[2] | Murder and nonnegligent manslaughter | Rape (revised definition)[3] | Robbery | Aggravated assault | Property crime | Burglary | Larceny-theft | Motor vehicle theft |
|---|---|---|---|---|---|---|---|---|---|---|
| **Nonmetropolitan counties** | 1,285,984 | | | | | | | | | |
| Area actually reporting | 85.0% | 1,349 | 27 | 342 | 64 | 916 | 10,102 | 2,441 | 6,742 | 919 |
| Estimated total | 100.0% | 1,568 | 33 | 401 | 79 | 1,055 | 12,042 | 2,911 | 8,013 | 1,118 |
| State total | 11,693,217 | 36,104 | 820 | 5,052 | 7,826 | 22,406 | 216,363 | 37,279 | 159,007 | 20,077 |
| Rate per 100,000 inhabitants | | 308.8 | 7.0 | 43.2 | 66.9 | 191.6 | 1,850.3 | 318.8 | 1,359.8 | 171.7 |
| **Oklahoma** | | | | | | | | | | |
| **Metropolitan statistical area** | 2,660,978 | | | | | | | | | |
| Area actually reporting | 100.0% | 13,795 | 225 | 1,554 | 2,028 | 9,988 | 77,442 | 16,896 | 49,075 | 11,471 |
| **Cities outside metropolitan areas** | 731,657 | | | | | | | | | |
| Area actually reporting | 99.9% | 3,247 | 38 | 382 | 289 | 2,538 | 22,973 | 5,121 | 15,474 | 2,378 |
| Estimated total | 100.0% | 3,250 | 38 | 382 | 289 | 2,541 | 22,999 | 5,128 | 15,490 | 2,381 |
| **Nonmetropolitan counties** | 588,148 | | | | | | | | | |
| Area actually reporting | 98.0% | 1,185 | 33 | 162 | 33 | 957 | 7,110 | 2,338 | 3,603 | 1,169 |
| Estimated total | 100.0% | 1,210 | 33 | 166 | 34 | 977 | 7,264 | 2,391 | 3,678 | 1,195 |
| State total | 3,980,783 | 18,255 | 296 | 2,102 | 2,351 | 13,506 | 107,705 | 24,415 | 68,243 | 15,047 |
| Rate per 100,000 inhabitants | | 458.6 | 7.4 | 52.8 | 59.1 | 339.3 | 2,705.6 | 613.3 | 1,714.3 | 378.0 |
| **Oregon[8]** | | | | | | | | | | |
| **Metropolitan statistical area** | 3,560,965 | | | | | | | | | |
| Area actually reporting | 96.3% | 10,123 | 96 | 1,227 | 1,975 | 6,825 | 94,922 | 11,466 | 68,855 | 14,601 |
| Estimated total | 100.0% | 10,389 | 96 | 1,287 | 2,018 | 6,988 | 97,297 | 11,799 | 70,580 | 14,918 |
| **Cities outside metropolitan areas** | 315,863 | | | | | | | | | |
| Area actually reporting | 97.4% | 1,020 | 12 | 174 | 134 | 700 | 10,030 | 1,399 | 7,802 | 829 |
| Estimated total | 100.0% | 1,040 | 12 | 178 | 137 | 713 | 10,233 | 1,438 | 7,957 | 838 |
| **Nonmetropolitan counties** | 364,679 | | | | | | | | | |
| Area actually reporting | 90.3% | 884 | 15 | 90 | 22 | 757 | 4,748 | 1,040 | 2,945 | 763 |
| Estimated total | 100.0% | 951 | 17 | 100 | 25 | 809 | 5,252 | 1,149 | 3,274 | 829 |
| State total | 4,241,507 | 12,380 | 125 | 1,565 | 2,180 | 8,510 | 112,782 | 14,386 | 81,811 | 16,585 |
| Rate per 100,000 inhabitants | | 291.9 | 2.9 | 36.9 | 51.4 | 200.6 | 2,659.0 | 339.2 | 1,928.8 | 391.0 |
| **Pennsylvania[4]** | | | | | | | | | | |
| **Metropolitan statistical area** | 11,346,468 | | | | | | | | | |
| Area actually reporting | 56.3% | 26,424 | 672 | 1,887 | 6,619 | 17,246 | 93,715 | 12,118 | 72,972 | 8,625 |
| Estimated total | 100.0% | 45,360 | 943 | 3,753 | 9,972 | 30,692 | 187,212 | 27,994 | 144,943 | 14,275 |
| **Cities outside metropolitan areas** | 638,381 | | | | | | | | | |
| Area actually reporting | 63.9% | 522 | 12 | 91 | 68 | 351 | 3,649 | 503 | 3,025 | 121 |
| Estimated total | 100.0% | 1,397 | 16 | 174 | 226 | 981 | 8,237 | 1,239 | 6,364 | 634 |
| **Nonmetropolitan counties** | 798,405 | | | | | | | | | |
| Area actually reporting | 0.1% | 4 | 0 | 1 | 0 | 3 | 10 | 0 | 10 | 0 |
| Estimated total | 100.0% | 3,036 | 50 | 301 | 530 | 2,155 | 14,718 | 2,541 | 11,612 | 565 |
| State total | 12,783,254 | 49,793 | 1,009 | 4,228 | 10,728 | 33,828 | 210,167 | 31,774 | 162,919 | 15,474 |
| Rate per 100,000 inhabitants | | 389.5 | 7.9 | 33.1 | 83.9 | 264.6 | 1,644.1 | 248.6 | 1,274.5 | 121.0 |
| **Puerto Rico** | | | | | | | | | | |
| **Metropolitan statistical area** | 3,159,343 | | | | | | | | | |
| Area actually reporting | 100.0% | 4,939 | 508 | 142 | 1,153 | 3,136 | 12,937 | 2,831 | 8,151 | 1,955 |
| **Cities outside metropolitan areas** | | | | | | | | | | |
| Area actually reporting | 100.0% | 257 | 21 | 6 | 24 | 206 | 304 | 121 | 160 | 23 |
| Total | 3,159,343 | 5,196 | 529 | 148 | 1,177 | 3,342 | 13,241 | 2,952 | 8,311 | 1,978 |
| Rate per 100,000 inhabitants | | 164.5 | 16.7 | 4.7 | 37.3 | 105.8 | 419.1 | 93.4 | 263.1 | 62.6 |
| **Rhode Island** | | | | | | | | | | |
| **Metropolitan statistical area** | 1,057,125 | | | | | | | | | |
| Area actually reporting | 100.0% | 2,440 | 32 | 407 | 336 | 1,665 | 13,166 | 1,763 | 9,894 | 1,509 |
| **Cities outside metropolitan areas** | None | | | | | | | | | |
| **Nonmetropolitan counties** | None | | | | | | | | | |
| State total | 1,057,125 | 2,440 | 32 | 407 | 336 | 1,665 | 13,166 | 1,763 | 9,894 | 1,509 |
| Rate per 100,000 inhabitants | | 230.8 | 3.0 | 38.5 | 31.8 | 157.5 | 1,245.5 | 166.8 | 935.9 | 142.7 |
| **South Carolina** | | | | | | | | | | |
| **Metropolitan statistical area** | 4,482,389 | | | | | | | | | |
| Area actually reporting | 98.9% | 22,153 | 412 | 1,782 | 2,722 | 17,237 | 119,049 | 18,299 | 88,013 | 12,737 |
| Estimated total | 100.0% | 22,439 | 423 | 1,799 | 2,751 | 17,466 | 120,444 | 18,534 | 89,047 | 12,863 |
| **Cities outside metropolitan areas** | 202,374 | | | | | | | | | |
| Area actually reporting | 95.3% | 2,073 | 56 | 92 | 189 | 1,736 | 9,021 | 1,804 | 6,683 | 534 |
| Estimated total | 100.0% | 2,146 | 59 | 95 | 196 | 1,796 | 9,391 | 1,873 | 6,958 | 560 |
| **Nonmetropolitan counties** | 533,277 | | | | | | | | | |
| Area actually reporting | 95.2% | 2,965 | 65 | 184 | 167 | 2,549 | 11,580 | 2,831 | 7,514 | 1,235 |
| Estimated total | 100.0% | 3,106 | 67 | 192 | 175 | 2,672 | 12,152 | 2,970 | 7,887 | 1,295 |
| State total | 5,218,040 | 27,691 | 549 | 2,086 | 3,122 | 21,934 | 141,987 | 23,377 | 103,892 | 14,718 |
| Rate per 100,000 inhabitants | | 530.7 | 10.5 | 40.0 | 59.8 | 420.3 | 2,721.1 | 448.0 | 1,991.0 | 282.1 |
| **South Dakota** | | | | | | | | | | |
| **Metropolitan statistical area** | 432,981 | | | | | | | | | |
| Area actually reporting | 99.4% | 2,270 | 30 | 336 | 223 | 1,681 | 11,251 | 1,970 | 7,647 | 1,634 |
| Estimated total | 100.0% | 2,279 | 30 | 336 | 225 | 1,688 | 11,301 | 1,977 | 7,684 | 1,640 |
| **Cities outside metropolitan areas** | 220,585 | | | | | | | | | |
| Area actually reporting | 96.2% | 1,807 | 7 | 206 | 21 | 1,573 | 4,399 | 665 | 3,278 | 456 |
| Estimated total | 100.0% | 1,836 | 7 | 209 | 25 | 1,595 | 4,567 | 691 | 3,401 | 475 |
| **Nonmetropolitan counties** | 239,151 | | | | | | | | | |
| Area actually reporting | 85.9% | 236 | 2 | 43 | 1 | 190 | 921 | 261 | 541 | 119 |
| Estimated total | 100.0% | 361 | 3 | 54 | 24 | 280 | 1,600 | 368 | 1,032 | 200 |

## Table 5. Crime in the United States, by State and Area, 2020—Continued

(Number, percent, rate per 100,000 population.)

| Area | Population[1] | Violent crime[2] | Murder and nonnegligent manslaughter | Rape (revised definition)[3] | Robbery | Aggravated assault | Property crime | Burglary | Larceny-theft | Motor vehicle theft |
|---|---|---|---|---|---|---|---|---|---|---|
| **State total** | 892,717 | 4,476 | 40 | 599 | 274 | 3,563 | 17,468 | 3,036 | 12,117 | 2,315 |
| Rate per 100,000 inhabitants | | 501.4 | 4.5 | 67.1 | 30.7 | 399.1 | 1,956.7 | 340.1 | 1,357.3 | 259.3 |
| **Tennessee** | | | | | | | | | | |
| **Metropolitan statistical area** | 5,395,999 | | | | | | | | | |
| Area actually reporting | 100.0% | 40,585 | 602 | 2,198 | 5,346 | 32,439 | 145,547 | 21,208 | 106,428 | 17,911 |
| **Cities outside metropolitan areas** | 487,422 | | | | | | | | | |
| Area actually reporting | 100.0% | 2,780 | 27 | 200 | 159 | 2,394 | 14,532 | 2,231 | 11,025 | 1,276 |
| **Nonmetropolitan counties** | 1,003,413 | | | | | | | | | |
| Area actually reporting | 100.0% | 2,963 | 34 | 280 | 70 | 2,579 | 11,596 | 3,040 | 6,645 | 1,911 |
| **State total** | 6,886,834 | 46,328 | 663 | 2,678 | 5,575 | 37,412 | 171,675 | 26,479 | 124,098 | 21,098 |
| Rate per 100,000 inhabitants | | 672.7 | 9.6 | 38.9 | 81.0 | 543.2 | 2,492.8 | 384.5 | 1,802.0 | 306.4 |
| **Texas** | | | | | | | | | | |
| **Metropolitan statistical area** | 26,246,546 | | | | | | | | | |
| Area actually reporting | 99.8% | 122,935 | 1,809 | 12,239 | 26,282 | 82,605 | 613,723 | 96,741 | 437,257 | 79,725 |
| Estimated total | 100.0% | 123,092 | 1,809 | 12,258 | 26,293 | 82,732 | 614,731 | 96,947 | 437,942 | 79,842 |
| **Cities outside metropolitan areas** | 1,450,340 | | | | | | | | | |
| Area actually reporting | 96.3% | 4,930 | 65 | 683 | 430 | 3,752 | 28,072 | 6,515 | 19,073 | 2,484 |
| Estimated total | 100.0% | 5,023 | 65 | 685 | 432 | 3,841 | 28,809 | 6,732 | 19,494 | 2,583 |
| **Nonmetropolitan counties** | 1,663,873 | | | | | | | | | |
| Area actually reporting | 98.8% | 2,934 | 57 | 561 | 109 | 2,207 | 15,400 | 5,101 | 8,476 | 1,823 |
| Estimated total | 100.0% | 2,969 | 57 | 566 | 109 | 2,237 | 15,620 | 5,172 | 8,597 | 1,851 |
| **State total** | 29,360,759 | 131,084 | 1,931 | 13,509 | 26,834 | 88,810 | 659,160 | 108,851 | 466,033 | 84,276 |
| Rate per 100,000 inhabitants | | 446.5 | 6.6 | 46.0 | 91.4 | 302.5 | 2,245.0 | 370.7 | 1,587.3 | 287.0 |
| **Utah** | | | | | | | | | | |
| **Metropolitan statistical area** | 2,911,284 | | | | | | | | | |
| Area actually reporting | 92.9% | 6,761 | 82 | 1,423 | 1,155 | 4,101 | 67,990 | 7,892 | 51,407 | 8,691 |
| Estimated total | 100.0% | 7,667 | 91 | 1,575 | 1,337 | 4,664 | 75,331 | 8,749 | 56,842 | 9,740 |
| **Cities outside metropolitan areas** | 156,076 | | | | | | | | | |
| Area actually reporting | 80.7% | 311 | 5 | 110 | 13 | 183 | 2,097 | 233 | 1,654 | 210 |
| Estimated total | 100.0% | 390 | 5 | 138 | 16 | 231 | 2,592 | 280 | 2,041 | 271 |
| **Nonmetropolitan counties** | 182,519 | | | | | | | | | |
| Area actually reporting | 91.0% | 376 | 6 | 84 | 9 | 277 | 1,953 | 362 | 1,339 | 252 |
| Estimated total | 100.0% | 414 | 6 | 96 | 9 | 303 | 2,168 | 415 | 1,476 | 277 |
| **State total** | 3,249,879 | 8,471 | 102 | 1,809 | 1,362 | 5,198 | 80,091 | 9,444 | 60,359 | 10,288 |
| Rate per 100,000 inhabitants | | 260.7 | 3.1 | 55.7 | 41.9 | 159.9 | 2,464.4 | 290.6 | 1,857.3 | 316.6 |
| **Vermont** | | | | | | | | | | |
| **Metropolitan statistical area** | 221,248 | | | | | | | | | |
| Area actually reporting | 100.0% | 439 | 5 | 115 | 32 | 287 | 3,561 | 362 | 3,116 | 83 |
| **Cities outside metropolitan areas** | 190,219 | | | | | | | | | |
| Area actually reporting | 100.0% | 384 | 3 | 64 | 24 | 293 | 2,846 | 341 | 2,409 | 96 |
| **Nonmetropolitan counties** | 211,880 | | | | | | | | | |
| Area actually reporting | 100.0% | 258 | 6 | 34 | 8 | 210 | 1,179 | 258 | 836 | 85 |
| **State total** | 623,347 | 1,081 | 14 | 213 | 64 | 790 | 7,586 | 961 | 6,361 | 264 |
| Rate per 100,000 inhabitants | | 173.4 | 2.2 | 34.2 | 10.3 | 126.7 | 1,217.0 | 154.2 | 1,020.5 | 42.4 |
| **Virginia** | | | | | | | | | | |
| **Metropolitan statistical area** | 7,542,652 | | | | | | | | | |
| Area actually reporting | 99.9% | 15,961 | 438 | 1,905 | 2,814 | 10,804 | 112,733 | 9,615 | 93,273 | 9,845 |
| Estimated total | 100.0% | 15,963 | 438 | 1,906 | 2,814 | 10,805 | 112,764 | 9,621 | 93,297 | 9,846 |
| **Cities outside metropolitan areas** | 242,932 | | | | | | | | | |
| Area actually reporting | 99.6% | 538 | 22 | 94 | 45 | 377 | 5,265 | 581 | 4,384 | 300 |
| Estimated total | 100.0% | 540 | 22 | 94 | 45 | 379 | 5,282 | 584 | 4,397 | 301 |
| **Nonmetropolitan counties** | 804,979 | | | | | | | | | |
| Area actually reporting | 100.0% | 1,422 | 64 | 279 | 88 | 991 | 7,068 | 1,260 | 5,102 | 706 |
| **State total** | 8,590,563 | 17,925 | 524 | 2,279 | 2,947 | 12,175 | 125,114 | 11,465 | 102,796 | 10,853 |
| Rate per 100,000 inhabitants | | 208.7 | 6.1 | 26.5 | 34.3 | 141.7 | 1,456.4 | 133.5 | 1,196.6 | 126.3 |
| **Washington** | 6,908,760 | | | | | | | | | |
| **Metropolitan statistical area** | | 21,080 | 269 | 2,395 | 5,037 | 13,379 | 195,996 | 36,804 | 133,204 | 25,988 |
| Area actually reporting | 99.8% | 21,102 | 269 | 2,398 | 5,041 | 13,394 | 196,238 | 36,852 | 133,377 | 26,009 |
| Estimated total | 100.0% | | | | | | | | | |
| **Cities outside metropolitan areas** | 316,271 | | | | | | | | | |
| Area actually reporting | 93.5% | 859 | 11 | 160 | 103 | 585 | 8,375 | 1,539 | 6,061 | 775 |
| Estimated total | 100.0% | 902 | 11 | 169 | 105 | 617 | 8,951 | 1,699 | 6,415 | 837 |
| **Nonmetropolitan counties** | 468,581 | | | | | | | | | |
| Area actually reporting | 100.0% | 592 | 21 | 110 | 37 | 424 | 5,034 | 1,616 | 2,865 | 553 |
| **State total** | 7,693,612 | 22,596 | 301 | 2,677 | 5,183 | 14,435 | 210,223 | 40,167 | 142,657 | 27,399 |
| Rate per 100,000 inhabitants | | 293.7 | 3.9 | 34.8 | 67.4 | 187.6 | 2,732.4 | 522.1 | 1,854.2 | 356.1 |
| **West Virginia** | 1,152,948 | | | | | | | | | |
| **Metropolitan statistical area** | | 3,276 | 61 | 543 | 261 | 2,411 | 16,207 | 3,282 | 11,446 | 1,479 |
| Area actually reporting | 83.1% | 4,091 | 68 | 598 | 313 | 3,112 | 18,269 | 3,640 | 13,024 | 1,605 |
| Estimated total | 100.0% | | | | | | | | | |
| **Cities outside metropolitan areas** | 172,139 | | | | | | | | | |
| Area actually reporting | 61.5% | 414 | 3 | 48 | 13 | 350 | 1,798 | 197 | 1,505 | 96 |
| Estimated total | 100.0% | 1,094 | 3 | 59 | 15 | 1,017 | 3,596 | 365 | 3,018 | 213 |
| **Nonmetropolitan counties** | 459,700 | | | | | | | | | |
| Area actually reporting | 90.5% | 1,094 | 40 | 166 | 40 | 848 | 2,939 | 820 | 1,688 | 431 |
| Estimated total | 100.0% | 1,167 | 46 | 175 | 41 | 905 | 3,111 | 872 | 1,786 | 453 |
| | 1,784,787 | 6,352 | 117 | 832 | 369 | 5,034 | 24,976 | 4,877 | 17,828 | 2,271 |

## Table 5. Crime in the United States, by State and Area, 2020—Continued

(Number, percent, rate per 100,000 population.)

| Area | Population[1] | Violent crime[2] | Murder and nonnegligent manslaughter | Rape (revised definition)[3] | Robbery | Aggravated assault | Property crime | Burglary | Larceny-theft | Motor vehicle theft |
|---|---|---|---|---|---|---|---|---|---|---|
| **State total** | | 355.9 | 6.6 | 46.6 | 20.7 | 282.1 | 1,399.4 | 273.3 | 998.9 | 127.2 |
| Rate per 100,000 inhabitants | | | | | | | | | | |
| | | | | | | | | | | |
| **Wisconsin** | 4,359,969 | | | | | | | | | |
| Metropolitan statistical area | 99.3% | 16,356 | 270 | 1,541 | 2,960 | 11,585 | 70,961 | 10,348 | 52,276 | 8,337 |
| Area actually reporting | 100.0% | 16,454 | 271 | 1,551 | 2,977 | 11,655 | 71,533 | 10,430 | 52,706 | 8,397 |
| Estimated total | 642,656 | | | | | | | | | |
| **Cities outside metropolitan areas** | 96.3% | 1,359 | 11 | 297 | 50 | 1,001 | 9,127 | 743 | 7,900 | 484 |
| Area actually reporting | 100.0% | 1,442 | 11 | 304 | 65 | 1,062 | 9,585 | 813 | 8,235 | 537 |
| Estimated total | 830,030 | | | | | | | | | |
| **Nonmetropolitan counties** | 97.2% | 874 | 24 | 156 | 23 | 671 | 5,062 | 1,426 | 3,233 | 403 |
| Area actually reporting | 100.0% | 965 | 26 | 165 | 39 | 735 | 5,536 | 1,501 | 3,576 | 459 |
| **State total** | 5,832,655 | 18,861 | 308 | 2,020 | 3,081 | 13,452 | 86,654 | 12,744 | 64,517 | 9,393 |
| Rate per 100,000 inhabitants | | 323.4 | 5.3 | 34.6 | 52.8 | 230.6 | 1,485.7 | 218.5 | 1,106.1 | 161.0 |
| | | | | | | | | | | |
| **Wyoming** | | | | | | | | | | |
| **Metropolitan statistical area** | 181,286 | | | | | | | | | |
| Area actually reporting | 100.0% | 513 | 7 | 114 | 45 | 347 | 4,571 | 547 | 3,512 | 512 |
| **Cities outside metropolitan areas** | 237,938 | | | | | | | | | |
| Area actually reporting | 96.4% | 591 | 5 | 166 | 12 | 408 | 3,562 | 421 | 2,819 | 322 |
| Estimated total | 100.0% | 621 | 5 | 167 | 18 | 431 | 3,736 | 449 | 2,944 | 343 |
| **Nonmetropolitan counties** | 163,104 | | | | | | | | | |
| Area actually reporting | 92.0% | 210 | 5 | 49 | 3 | 153 | 995 | 205 | 688 | 102 |
| Estimated total | 100.0% | 230 | 6 | 52 | 3 | 169 | 1,072 | 229 | 734 | 109 |
| **State total** | 582,328 | 1,364 | 18 | 333 | 66 | 947 | 9,379 | 1,225 | 7,190 | 964 |
| Rate per 100,000 inhabitants | | 234.2 | 3.1 | 57.2 | 11.3 | 162.6 | 1,610.6 | 210.4 | 1,234.7 | 165.5 |

NOTE: Although arson data are included in the trend and clearance tables, sufficient data are not available to estimate totals for this offense. Therefore, no arson data are published in this table.
1 Population figures are U.S. Census Bureau provisional estimates as of July 1, 2020.  2 The violent crime figures include the offenses of murder, rape (revised definition), robbery, and aggravated assault.  3 The figures shown in this column for the offense of rape (revised definition) were estimated using the revised Uniform Crime Reporting (UCR) definition of rape. See chapter notes for further explanation.  4 Limited data for 2020 were available for Alabama, Maryland, and Pennsylvania.
5 Includes offenses reported by the Metro Transit Police and the Arson Investigation Unit of the District of Columbia Fire and Emergency Medical Services.  6 Because of changes in the state/local agency's reporting practices, figures are not comparable to previous years' data.  7 The FBI determined that the state did not follow national UCR Program guidelines for reporting an offense. Consequently, those figures are not included in this table. The agency of Rockford submits independently and therefore includes all offenses.  8 This state's agencies submitted rape data according to the legacy UCR definition of rape.

## Table 6. Crime in the United States, by Selected Metropolitan Statistical Area, 2020

(Number, percent, rate per 100,000 population.)

| Area | Population | Violent crime | Murder and nonnegligent manslaughter | Rape[1] | Robbery | Aggravated assault | Property crime | Burglary | Larceny-theft | Motor vehicle theft |
|---|---|---|---|---|---|---|---|---|---|---|
| **Abilene, TX M.S.A.** | 172,211 | | | | | | | | | |
| Includes Callahan, Jones, and Taylor Counties | | | | | | | | | | |
| City of Abilene | 124,061 | 514 | 3 | 117 | 63 | 331 | 2,649 | 435 | 2,013 | 201 |
| Total area actually reporting | 100.0% | 611 | 6 | 142 | 64 | 399 | 3,088 | 568 | 2,269 | 251 |
| Rate per 100,000 inhabitants | | 354.8 | 3.5 | 82.5 | 37.2 | 231.7 | 1,793.1 | 329.8 | 1,317.6 | 145.8 |
| **Akron, OH M.S.A.** | 702,634 | | | | | | | | | |
| Includes Portage and Summit Counties | | | | | | | | | | |
| City of Akron | 197,433 | 1,797 | 47 | 215 | 268 | 1,267 | 6,971 | 1,288 | 4,855 | 828 |
| Total area actually reporting | 95.9% | 2,599 | 55 | 330 | 347 | 1,867 | 14,557 | 2,315 | 10,999 | 1,243 |
| Estimated total | 100.0% | 2,659 | 55 | 359 | 354 | 1,891 | 15,032 | 2,375 | 11,389 | 1,268 |
| Rate per 100,000 inhabitants | | 378.4 | 7.8 | 51.1 | 50.4 | 269.1 | 2,139.4 | 338.0 | 1,620.9 | 180.5 |
| **Albany, GA M.S.A.[2]** | 145,715 | | | | | | | | | |
| Includes Dougherty,[2] Lee,[2] Terrell, and Worth[2] Counties | | | | | | | | | | |
| City of Albany[2] | 71,567 | 1,234 | 19 | 40 | 132 | 1,043 | 3,148 | 575 | 2,234 | 339 |
| Total area actually reporting | 96.2% | 1,451 | 23 | 68 | 147 | 1,213 | 4,200 | 821 | 2,897 | 482 |
| Estimated total | 100.0% | 1,469 | 23 | 70 | 151 | 1,225 | 4,281 | 837 | 2,953 | 491 |
| Rate per 100,000 inhabitants | | 1,008.1 | 15.8 | 48.0 | 103.6 | 840.7 | 2,937.9 | 574.4 | 2,026.6 | 337.0 |
| **Albany-Lebanon, OR M.S.A.** | 130,611 | | | | | | | | | |
| Includes Linn County | | | | | | | | | | |
| City of Albany | 48,329 | 72 | 2 | 12 | 24 | 34 | 1,336 | 97 | 1,134 | 105 |
| City of Lebanon | 17,635 | 23 | 0 | 4 | 1 | 18 | 297 | 23 | 251 | 23 |
| Total area actually reporting | 100.0% | 195 | 7 | 34 | 31 | 123 | 2,821 | 345 | 2,212 | 264 |
| Rate per 100,000 inhabitants | | 149.3 | 5.4 | 26.0 | 23.7 | 94.2 | 2,159.8 | 264.1 | 1,693.6 | 202.1 |
| **Albany-Schenectady-Troy, NY M.S.A.** | 875,848 | | | | | | | | | |
| Includes Albany, Rensselaer, Saratoga, Schenectady, and Schoharie Counties | | | | | | | | | | |
| City of Albany | 96,318 | 869 | 16 | 61 | 161 | 631 | 2,650 | 422 | 1,945 | 283 |
| City of Schenectady | 65,176 | 468 | 5 | 26 | 90 | 347 | 1,622 | 266 | 1,187 | 169 |
| City of Troy | 49,052 | 330 | 9 | 16 | 68 | 237 | 1,411 | 263 | 1,026 | 122 |
| Total area actually reporting | 99.7% | 2,382 | 34 | 306 | 432 | 1,610 | 14,535 | 1,782 | 11,839 | 914 |
| Estimated total | 100.0% | 2,386 | 34 | 307 | 433 | 1,612 | 14,552 | 1,785 | 11,852 | 915 |
| Rate per 100,000 inhabitants | | 272.4 | 3.9 | 35.1 | 49.4 | 184.1 | 1,661.5 | 203.8 | 1,353.2 | 104.5 |
| **Albuquerque, NM M.S.A.** | 923,729 | | | | | | | | | |
| Includes Bernalillo, Sandoval, Torrance, and Valencia Counties | | | | | | | | | | |
| City of Albuquerque | 562,065 | 7,552 | 80 | 441 | 1,439 | 5,592 | 28,171 | 5,075 | 18,131 | 4,965 |
| Total area actually reporting | 100.0% | 9,296 | 87 | 566 | 1,585 | 7,058 | 33,754 | 6,356 | 21,278 | 6,120 |
| Rate per 100,000 inhabitants | | 1,006.4 | 9.4 | 61.3 | 171.6 | 764.1 | 3,654.1 | 688.1 | 2,303.5 | 662.5 |
| **Alexandria, LA M.S.A.** | 151,268 | | | | | | | | | |
| Includes Grant and Rapides Parishes | | | | | | | | | | |
| City of Alexandria | 45,986 | 850 | 19 | 15 | 145 | 671 | 3,317 | 754 | 2,300 | 263 |
| Total area actually reporting | 82.1% | 1,363 | 21 | 53 | 172 | 1,117 | 5,534 | 1,455 | 3,610 | 469 |
| Estimated total | 100.0% | 1,464 | 22 | 62 | 190 | 1,190 | 6,079 | 1,541 | 4,004 | 534 |
| Rate per 100,000 inhabitants | | 967.8 | 14.5 | 41.0 | 125.6 | 786.7 | 4,018.7 | 1,018.7 | 2,647.0 | 353.0 |
| **Amarillo, TX M.S.A.[2]** | 265,667 | | | | | | | | | |
| Includes Armstrong, Carson, Oldham,[2] Potter, and Randall Counties | | | | | | | | | | |
| City of Amarillo | 200,296 | 1,676 | 15 | 141 | 241 | 1,279 | 7,369 | 1,400 | 4,903 | 1,066 |
| Total area actually reporting | 99.9% | 1,787 | 18 | 168 | 249 | 1,352 | 8,082 | 1,561 | 5,353 | 1,168 |
| Estimated total | 100.0% | 1,787 | 18 | 168 | 249 | 1,352 | 8,083 | 1,561 | 5,354 | 1,168 |
| Rate per 100,000 inhabitants | | 672.6 | 6.8 | 63.2 | 93.7 | 508.9 | 3,042.5 | 587.6 | 2,015.3 | 439.6 |
| **Ames, IA M.S.A.[3]** | 124,033 | | | | | | | | | |
| Includes Boone[3] and Story Counties | | | | | | | | | | |
| City of Ames | 67,109 | 122 | 0 | 54 | 15 | 53 | 1,189 | 218 | 903 | 68 |
| Total area actually reporting | 94.6% | 201 | 1 | 64 | 15 | 121 | | | 1,183 | 117 |
| Estimated total | 100.0% | 228 | 1 | 67 | 19 | 141 | | | 1,386 | 128 |
| Rate per 100,000 inhabitants | | 183.8 | 0.8 | 54.0 | 15.3 | 113.7 | | | 1,117.4 | 103.2 |
| **Anchorage, AK M.S.A.** | 305,257 | | | | | | | | | |
| Includes Anchorage Municipality and Matanuska-Susitna Borough | | | | | | | | | | |
| City of Anchorage | 286,388 | 3,472 | 18 | 558 | 558 | 2,338 | 9,872 | 1,444 | 7,279 | 1,149 |
| Total area actually reporting | 100.0% | 3,576 | 18 | 570 | 566 | 2,422 | 10,393 | 1,488 | 7,703 | 1,202 |
| Rate per 100,000 inhabitants | | 1,171.5 | 5.9 | 186.7 | 185.4 | 793.4 | 3,404.7 | 487.5 | 2,523.4 | 393.8 |
| **Ann Arbor, MI M.S.A.** | 368,868 | | | | | | | | | |
| Includes Washtenaw County | | | | | | | | | | |
| City of Ann Arbor | 120,647 | 294 | 1 | 49 | 38 | 206 | 1,592 | 153 | 1,358 | 81 |
| Total area actually reporting | 100.0% | 1,521 | 9 | 233 | 134 | 1,145 | 4,670 | 569 | 3,698 | 403 |
| Rate per 100,000 inhabitants | | 412.3 | 2.4 | 63.2 | 36.3 | 310.4 | 1,266.0 | 154.3 | 1,002.5 | 109.3 |
| **Appleton, WI M.S.A.** | 239,143 | | | | | | | | | |
| Includes Calumet and Outagamie Counties | | | | | | | | | | |
| City of Appleton | 72,570 | 194 | 1 | 35 | 19 | 139 | 1,129 | 125 | 942 | 62 |
| Total area actually reporting | 97.4% | 385 | 3 | 83 | 28 | 271 | 2,672 | 299 | 2,228 | 145 |
| Estimated total | 100.0% | 408 | 3 | 85 | 32 | 288 | 2,798 | 319 | 2,319 | 160 |
| Rate per 100,000 inhabitants | | 170.6 | 1.3 | 35.5 | 13.4 | 120.4 | 1,170.0 | 133.4 | 969.7 | 66.9 |

## Table 6. Crime in the United States, by Selected Metropolitan Statistical Area, 2020—Continued

(Number, percent, rate per 100,000 population.)

| Area | Population | Violent crime | Murder and nonnegligent manslaughter | Rape[1] | Robbery | Aggravated assault | Property crime | Burglary | Larceny-theft | Motor vehicle theft |
|---|---|---|---|---|---|---|---|---|---|---|
| **Asheville, NC M.S.A.** | 467,076 | | | | | | | | | |
| Includes Buncombe, Haywood, Henderson, and Madison Counties | | | | | | | | | | |
| City of Asheville | 93,980 | 761 | 11 | 54 | 153 | 543 | 5,395 | 730 | 4,142 | 523 |
| Total area actually reporting | 77.1% | 1,240 | 20 | 105 | 207 | 908 | 10,540 | 2,170 | 7,312 | 1,058 |
| Estimated total | 100.0% | 1,481 | 24 | 135 | 234 | 1,088 | 12,301 | 2,638 | 8,439 | 1,224 |
| Rate per 100,000 inhabitants | | 317.1 | 5.1 | 28.9 | 50.1 | 232.9 | 2,633.6 | 564.8 | 1,806.8 | 262.1 |
| **Athens-Clarke County, GA M.S.A.[2]** | 215,827 | | | | | | | | | |
| Includes Clarke, Madison,[2] Oconee, and Oglethorpe[2] Counties | | | | | | | | | | |
| City of Athens-Clarke County[2] | 128,152 | 654 | 4 | 105 | 102 | 443 | 3,785 | 597 | 2,837 | 351 |
| Total area actually reporting | 80.4% | 777 | 4 | 117 | 105 | 551 | 4,368 | 732 | 3,221 | 415 |
| Estimated total | 100.0% | 834 | 6 | 123 | 112 | 593 | 4,719 | 789 | 3,482 | 448 |
| Rate per 100,000 inhabitants | | 386.4 | 2.8 | 57.0 | 51.9 | 274.8 | 2,186.5 | 365.6 | 1,613.3 | 207.6 |
| **Atlantic City-Hammonton, NJ M.S.A.** | 262,199 | | | | | | | | | |
| Includes Atlantic County | | | | | | | | | | |
| City of Atlantic City | 37,550 | 309 | 9 | 28 | 116 | 156 | 1,013 | 139 | 785 | 89 |
| City of Hammonton | 13,845 | 23 | 0 | 0 | 0 | 23 | 189 | 37 | 145 | 7 |
| Total area actually reporting | 100.0% | 665 | 17 | 55 | 183 | 410 | 5,054 | 793 | 3,978 | 283 |
| Rate per 100,000 inhabitants | | 253.6 | 6.5 | 21.0 | 69.8 | 156.4 | 1,927.5 | 302.4 | 1,517.2 | 107.9 |
| **Austin-Round Rock-Georgetown, TX M.S.A.[2]** | 2,283,668 | | | | | | | | | |
| Includes Bastrop, Caldwell,[2] Hays,[2] Travis,[2] and Williamson Counties | | | | | | | | | | |
| City of Austin | 1,000,276 | 4,671 | 44 | 478 | 1,101 | 3,048 | 36,322 | 4,774 | 27,481 | 4,067 |
| City of Round Rock[2] | 137,593 | 185 | 3 | 25 | 55 | 102 | 2,282 | 235 | 1,954 | 93 |
| City of Georgetown | 84,210 | 123 | 4 | 50 | 16 | 53 | 1,077 | 148 | 836 | 93 |
| City of San Marcos | 67,432 | 283 | 2 | 99 | 32 | 150 | 1,419 | 260 | 1,017 | 142 |
| Total area actually reporting | 100.0% | 7,207 | 74 | 995 | 1,424 | 4,714 | 54,045 | 7,687 | 40,683 | 5,675 |
| Rate per 100,000 inhabitants | | 315.6 | 3.2 | 43.6 | 62.4 | 206.4 | 2,366.6 | 336.6 | 1,781.5 | 248.5 |
| **Bakersfield, CA M.S.A.** | 897,941 | | | | | | | | | |
| Includes Kern County | | | | | | | | | | |
| City of Bakersfield | 388,265 | 2,007 | 44 | 106 | 604 | 1,253 | 15,619 | 3,134 | 8,656 | 3,829 |
| Total area actually reporting | 100.0% | 6,216 | 116 | 331 | 1,190 | 4,579 | 27,890 | 6,358 | 13,995 | 7,537 |
| Rate per 100,000 inhabitants | | 692.3 | 12.9 | 36.9 | 132.5 | 509.9 | 3,106.0 | 708.1 | 1,558.6 | 839.4 |
| **Bangor, ME M.S.A.** | 152,409 | | | | | | | | | |
| Includes Penobscot County | | | | | | | | | | |
| City of Bangor | 32,179 | 51 | 2 | 7 | 13 | 29 | 1,207 | 100 | 1,044 | 63 |
| Total area actually reporting | 100.0% | 88 | 6 | 12 | 16 | 54 | 2,339 | 260 | 1,950 | 129 |
| Rate per 100,000 inhabitants | | 57.7 | 3.9 | 7.9 | 10.5 | 35.4 | 1,534.7 | 170.6 | 1,279.5 | 84.6 |
| **Barnstable Town, MA M.S.A.** | 211,545 | | | | | | | | | |
| Includes Barnstable County | | | | | | | | | | |
| City of Barnstable | 44,169 | 188 | 0 | 30 | 12 | 146 | 350 | 52 | 281 | 17 |
| Total area actually reporting | 100.0% | 635 | 3 | 92 | 28 | 512 | 1,730 | 374 | 1,288 | 68 |
| Rate per 100,000 inhabitants | | 300.2 | 1.4 | 43.5 | 13.2 | 242.0 | 817.8 | 176.8 | 608.9 | 32.1 |
| **Baton Rouge, LA M.S.A.[2]** | 855,151 | | | | | | | | | |
| Includes Ascension, Assumption, East Baton Rouge, East Feliciana, Iberville,[2] Livingston, Pointe Coupee, St. Helena, West Baton Rouge, and West Feliciana Parishes | | | | | | | | | | |
| City of Baton Rouge | 219,245 | 2,087 | 102 | 55 | 457 | 1,473 | 10,580 | 1,898 | 7,854 | 828 |
| Total area actually reporting | 97.8% | 4,734 | 143 | 218 | 653 | 3,720 | 26,001 | 3,884 | 20,343 | 1,774 |
| Estimated total | 100.0% | 4,839 | 144 | 223 | 662 | 3,810 | 26,433 | 3,977 | 20,637 | 1,819 |
| Rate per 100,000 inhabitants | | 565.9 | 16.8 | 26.1 | 77.4 | 445.5 | 3,091.0 | 465.1 | 2,413.3 | 212.7 |
| **Battle Creek, MI M.S.A** | 133,509 | | | | | | | | | |
| Includes Calhoun County | | | | | | | | | | |
| City of Battle Creek | 60,479 | 540 | 8 | 38 | 30 | 464 | 1,569 | 335 | 1,066 | 168 |
| Total area actually reporting | 100.0% | 886 | 14 | 101 | 48 | 723 | 3,170 | 574 | 2,326 | 270 |
| Rate per 100,000 inhabitants | | 663.6 | 10.5 | 75.7 | 36.0 | 541.5 | 2,374.4 | 429.9 | 1,742.2 | 202.2 |
| **Bay City, MI M.S.A.** | 102,285 | | | | | | | | | |
| Includes Bay County | | | | | | | | | | |
| City of Bay City | 32,485 | 276 | 0 | 48 | 25 | 203 | 500 | 104 | 331 | 65 |
| Total area actually reporting | 100.0% | 384 | 3 | 90 | 32 | 259 | 1,084 | 206 | 760 | 118 |
| Rate per 100,000 inhabitants | | 375.4 | 2.9 | 88.0 | 31.3 | 253.2 | 1,059.8 | 201.4 | 743.0 | 115.4 |
| **Beaumont-Port Arthur, TX M.S.A.[2]** | 391,609 | | | | | | | | | |
| Includes Hardin,[2] Jefferson, and Orange[2] Counties | | | | | | | | | | |
| City of Beaumont[2] | 116,766 | 1,431 | 20 | 79 | 300 | 1,032 | 3,863 | 955 | 2,546 | 362 |
| City of Port Arthur[2] | 54,257 | 422 | 7 | 42 | 76 | 297 | 1,253 | 346 | 775 | 132 |
| Total area actually reporting | 99.9% | 2,371 | 35 | 181 | 432 | 1,723 | 8,028 | 2,000 | 5,102 | 926 |
| Estimated total | 100.0% | 2,372 | 35 | 181 | 432 | 1,724 | 8,036 | 2,002 | 5,107 | 927 |
| Rate per 100,000 inhabitants | | 605.7 | 8.9 | 46.2 | 110.3 | 440.2 | 2,052.0 | 511.2 | 1,304.1 | 236.7 |
| **Beckley, WV M.S.A** | 114,718 | | | | | | | | | |
| Includes Fayette and Raleigh Counties | | | | | | | | | | |
| City of Beckley | 15,762 | 137 | 2 | 8 | 11 | 116 | 905 | 149 | 708 | 48 |
| Total area actually reporting | 95.3% | 355 | 7 | 40 | 18 | 290 | 2,248 | 467 | 1,635 | 146 |
| Estimated total | 100.0% | 433 | 7 | 44 | 22 | 360 | 2,269 | 474 | 1,645 | 150 |
| Rate per 100,000 inhabitants | | 377.4 | 6.1 | 38.4 | 19.2 | 313.8 | 1,977.9 | 413.2 | 1,434.0 | 130.8 |

## Table 6. Crime in the United States, by Selected Metropolitan Statistical Area, 2020—Continued

(Number, percent, rate per 100,000 population.)

| Area | Population | Violent crime | Murder and nonnegligent manslaughter | Rape[1] | Robbery | Aggravated assault | Property crime | Burglary | Larceny-theft | Motor vehicle theft |
|---|---|---|---|---|---|---|---|---|---|---|
| **Bellingham, WA M.S.A** | 231,784 | | | | | | | | | |
| Includes Whatcom County | | | | | | | | | | |
| City of Bellingham | 93,629 | 240 | 0 | 29 | 80 | 131 | 4,306 | 610 | 3,320 | 376 |
| Total area actually reporting | 100.0% | 428 | 5 | 72 | 90 | 261 | 5,459 | 885 | 4,129 | 445 |
| Rate per 100,000 inhabitants | | 184.7 | 2.2 | 31.1 | 38.8 | 112.6 | 2,355.2 | 381.8 | 1,781.4 | 192.0 |
| **Bend, OR M.S.A.** | 201,709 | | | | | | | | | |
| Includes Deschutes County | | | | | | | | | | |
| City of Bend | 103,485 | 174 | 0 | 28 | 31 | 115 | 1,959 | 201 | 1,593 | 165 |
| Total area actually reporting | 100.0% | 360 | 0 | 57 | 50 | 253 | 3,664 | 397 | 2,919 | 348 |
| Rate per 100,000 inhabitants | | 178.5 | 0.0 | 28.3 | 24.8 | 125.4 | 1,816.5 | 196.8 | 1,447.1 | 172.5 |
| **Billings, MT M.S.A.** | 183,705 | | | | | | | | | |
| Includes Carbon, Stillwater, and Yellowstone Counties | | | | | | | | | | |
| City of Billings | 110,157 | 939 | 14 | 85 | 125 | 715 | 5,249 | 717 | 3,715 | 817 |
| Total area actually reporting | 100.0% | 1,152 | 15 | 103 | 133 | 901 | 6,378 | 868 | 4,512 | 998 |
| Rate per 100,000 inhabitants | | 627.1 | 8.2 | 56.1 | 72.4 | 490.5 | 3,471.9 | 472.5 | 2,456.1 | 543.3 |
| **Binghamton, NY M.S.A.[2]** | 235,803 | | | | | | | | | |
| Includes Broome[2] and Tioga Counties | | | | | | | | | | |
| City of Binghamton[2] | 44,083 | 372 | 1 | 28 | 50 | 293 | 1,775 | 294 | 1,380 | 101 |
| Total area actually reporting | 99.0% | 669 | 4 | 111 | 79 | 475 | 4,818 | 711 | 3,875 | 232 |
| Estimated total | 100.0% | 673 | 4 | 111 | 80 | 478 | 4,857 | 715 | 3,909 | 233 |
| Rate per 100,000 inhabitants | | 285.4 | 1.7 | 47.1 | 33.9 | 202.7 | 2,059.8 | 303.2 | 1,657.7 | 98.8 |
| **Bismarck, ND M.S.A.** | 129,675 | | | | | | | | | |
| Includes Burleigh, Morton, and Oliver Counties | | | | | | | | | | |
| City of Bismarck | 74,997 | 260 | 0 | 49 | 26 | 185 | 2,471 | 343 | 1,876 | 252 |
| Total area actually reporting | 100.0% | 433 | 4 | 74 | 30 | 325 | 3,692 | 610 | 2,677 | 405 |
| Rate per 100,000 inhabitants | | 333.9 | 3.1 | 57.1 | 23.1 | 250.6 | 2,847.1 | 470.4 | 2,064.4 | 312.3 |
| **Blacksburg-Christiansburg, VA M.S.A.** | 167,909 | | | | | | | | | |
| Includes Giles, Montgomery, and Pulaski Counties and Radford City | | | | | | | | | | |
| City of Blacksburg | 44,422 | 29 | 0 | 13 | 2 | 14 | 310 | 29 | 266 | 15 |
| City of Christiansburg | 22,643 | 37 | 0 | 13 | 2 | 22 | 479 | 44 | 424 | 11 |
| Total area actually reporting | 100.0% | 313 | 5 | 99 | 20 | 189 | 2,476 | 336 | 2,013 | 127 |
| Rate per 100,000 inhabitants | | 186.4 | 3.0 | 59.0 | 11.9 | 112.6 | 1,474.6 | 200.1 | 1,198.9 | 75.6 |
| **Bloomington, IL M.S.A.[4]** | 170,810 | | | | | | | | | |
| Includes McLean County[4] | | | | | | | | | | |
| City of Bloomington[4] | 77,386 | 314 | 1 | 64 | 23 | 226 | | 144 | | 70 |
| Total area actually reporting | 97.1% | 475 | 1 | 105 | 44 | 325 | | 289 | | 123 |
| Estimated total | 100.0% | 483 | 1 | 106 | 45 | 331 | | 299 | | 129 |
| Rate per 100,000 inhabitants | | 282.8 | 0.6 | 62.1 | 26.3 | 193.8 | | 175.0 | | 75.5 |
| **Bloomington, IN M.S.A.[2]** | 170,127 | | | | | | | | | |
| Includes Monroe[2] and Owen Counties | | | | | | | | | | |
| City of Bloomington[2] | 86,347 | 480 | 7 | 52 | 67 | 354 | 2,079 | 346 | 1,595 | 138 |
| Total area actually reporting | 83.8% | 547 | 8 | 86 | 77 | 376 | 2,792 | 410 | 2,180 | 202 |
| Estimated total | 100.0% | 586 | 8 | 91 | 79 | 408 | 3,072 | 467 | 2,372 | 233 |
| Rate per 100,000 inhabitants | | 344.4 | 4.7 | 53.5 | 46.4 | 239.8 | 1,805.7 | 274.5 | 1,394.3 | 137.0 |
| **Boise City, ID M.S.A.** | 771,135 | | | | | | | | | |
| Includes Ada, Boise, Canyon, Gem, and Owyhee Counties | | | | | | | | | | |
| City of Boise | 231,223 | 677 | 4 | 170 | 55 | 448 | 3,793 | 479 | 3,035 | 279 |
| Total area actually reporting | 99.9% | 2,025 | 14 | 451 | 92 | 1,468 | 8,952 | 1,441 | 6,669 | 842 |
| Estimated total | 100.0% | 2,026 | 14 | 451 | 92 | 1,469 | 8,958 | 1,442 | 6,674 | 842 |
| Rate per 100,000 inhabitants | | 262.7 | 1.8 | 58.5 | 11.9 | 190.5 | 1,161.7 | 187.0 | 865.5 | 109.2 |
| **Boston-Cambridge-Newton, MA-NH M.S.A.[2]** | 4,885,414 | | | | | | | | | |
| Includes the Metropolitan Divisions of Boston, MA; Cambridge-Newton-Framingham, MA; and Rockingham County-Strafford County, NH | | | | | | | | | | |
| City of Boston, MA[2] | 697,323 | 4,354 | 58 | 184 | 919 | 3,193 | 13,015 | 1,698 | 10,037 | 1,280 |
| City of Cambridge, MA | 119,938 | 341 | 1 | 25 | 67 | 248 | 2,200 | 202 | 1,917 | 81 |
| City of Newton, MA | 88,281 | 48 | 0 | 4 | 8 | 36 | 486 | 51 | 420 | 15 |
| City of Framingham, MA | 74,680 | 264 | 2 | 13 | 20 | 229 | 862 | 110 | 625 | 127 |
| City of Waltham, MA | 62,339 | 85 | 1 | 10 | 3 | 71 | 385 | 51 | 310 | 24 |
| Total area actually reporting | 99.9% | 12,392 | 109 | 1,062 | 1,865 | 9,356 | 48,632 | 5,737 | 38,398 | 4,497 |
| Estimated total | 100.0% | 12,399 | 109 | 1,063 | 1,865 | 9,362 | 48,653 | 5,740 | 38,415 | 4,498 |
| Rate per 100,000 inhabitants | | 253.8 | 2.2 | 21.8 | 38.2 | 191.6 | 995.9 | 117.5 | 786.3 | 92.1 |
| **Boston, MA M.D.[2]** | 2,037,005 | | | | | | | | | |
| Includes Norfolk, Plymouth, and Suffolk Counties | | | | | | | | | | |
| Total area actually reporting | 99.7% | 7,583 | 73 | 528 | 1,285 | 5,697 | 24,436 | 3,062 | 18,980 | 2,394 |
| Estimated total | 100.0% | 7,590 | 73 | 529 | 1,285 | 5,703 | 24,457 | 3,065 | 18,997 | 2,395 |
| Rate per 100,000 inhabitants | | 372.6 | 3.6 | 26.0 | 63.1 | 280.0 | 1,200.6 | 150.5 | 932.6 | 117.6 |
| **Cambridge-Newton-Framingham, MA M.D.** | 2,404,962 | | | | | | | | | |
| Includes Essex and Middlesex Counties | | | | | | | | | | |
| Total area actually reporting | 100.0% | 4,421 | 32 | 401 | 510 | 3,478 | 19,930 | 2,362 | 15,778 | 1,790 |
| Rate per 100,000 inhabitants | | 183.8 | 1.3 | 16.7 | 21.2 | 144.6 | 828.7 | 98.2 | 656.1 | 74.4 |

## Table 6. Crime in the United States, by Selected Metropolitan Statistical Area, 2020—Continued

(Number, percent, rate per 100,000 population.)

| Area | Population | Violent crime | Murder and nonnegligent manslaughter | Rape[1] | Robbery | Aggravated assault | Property crime | Burglary | Larceny-theft | Motor vehicle theft |
|---|---|---|---|---|---|---|---|---|---|---|
| **Rockingham County-Strafford County, NH M.D.** | 443,447 | | | | | | | | | |
| Includes Rockingham and Strafford Counties | | | | | | | | | | |
| Total area actually reporting | 100.0% | 388 | 4 | 133 | 70 | 181 | 4,266 | 313 | 3,640 | 313 |
| Rate per 100,000 inhabitants | | 87.5 | 0.9 | 30.0 | 15.8 | 40.8 | 962.0 | 70.6 | 820.8 | 70.6 |
| **Boulder, CO M.S.A.** | 327,747 | | | | | | | | | |
| Includes Boulder County | | | | | | | | | | |
| City of Boulder | 106,598 | 343 | 2 | 31 | 72 | 238 | 4,019 | 654 | 2,994 | 371 |
| Total area actually reporting | 100.0% | 961 | 4 | 177 | 140 | 640 | 9,046 | 1,328 | 6,723 | 995 |
| Rate per 100,000 inhabitants | | 293.2 | 1.2 | 54.0 | 42.7 | 195.3 | 2,760.1 | 405.2 | 2,051.3 | 303.6 |
| **Bowling Green, KY M.S.A.** | 181,430 | | | | | | | | | |
| Includes Allen, Butler, Edmonson, and Warren Counties | | | | | | | | | | |
| City of Bowling Green | 71,861 | 247 | 9 | 56 | 71 | 111 | 3,195 | 560 | 2,318 | 317 |
| Total area actually reporting | 100.0% | 341 | 11 | 80 | 83 | 167 | 4,163 | 763 | 2,933 | 467 |
| Rate per 100,000 inhabitants | | 188.0 | 6.1 | 44.1 | 45.7 | 92.0 | 2,294.5 | 420.5 | 1,616.6 | 257.4 |
| **Bremerton-Silverdale-Port Orchard, WA M.S.A.** | 272,867 | | | | | | | | | |
| Includes Kitsap County | | | | | | | | | | |
| City of Bremerton | 41,817 | 143 | 1 | 16 | 23 | 103 | 1,342 | 224 | 945 | 173 |
| City of Port Orchard | 14,886 | 61 | 0 | 9 | 8 | 44 | 550 | 100 | 380 | 70 |
| Total area actually reporting | 100.0% | 597 | 5 | 133 | 57 | 402 | 4,887 | 873 | 3,496 | 518 |
| Rate per 100,000 inhabitants | | 218.8 | 1.8 | 48.7 | 20.9 | 147.3 | 1,791.0 | 319.9 | 1,281.2 | 189.8 |
| **Bridgeport-Stamford-Norwalk, CT M.S.A.[3]** | 928,567 | | | | | | | | | |
| Includes Fairfield County | | | | | | | | | | |
| City of Bridgeport | 144,350 | 829 | 24 | 47 | 340 | 418 | 2,514 | 675 | 1,196 | 643 |
| City of Stamford[3] | 130,425 | 284 | 6 | 26 | 85 | 167 | | | 1,206 | 234 |
| City of Norwalk | 89,140 | 143 | 2 | 12 | 21 | 108 | 1,222 | 148 | 930 | 144 |
| City of Danbury | 85,080 | 98 | 4 | 9 | 40 | 45 | 806 | 81 | 643 | 82 |
| City of Stratford | 51,895 | 53 | 2 | 2 | 31 | 18 | 923 | 105 | 651 | 167 |
| Total area actually reporting | 100.0% | 1,522 | 40 | 122 | 550 | 810 | | | 8,017 | 1,923 |
| Rate per 100,000 inhabitants | | 163.9 | 4.3 | 13.1 | 59.2 | 87.2 | | | 863.4 | 207.1 |
| **Brownsville-Harlingen, TX M.S.A.** | 423,478 | | | | | | | | | |
| Includes Cameron County | | | | | | | | | | |
| City of Brownsville | 183,627 | 738 | 7 | 83 | 153 | 495 | 3,394 | 403 | 2,870 | 121 |
| City of Harlingen | 65,014 | 269 | 3 | 21 | 67 | 178 | 2,437 | 315 | 1,999 | 123 |
| Total area actually reporting | 99.7% | 1,526 | 13 | 176 | 247 | 1,090 | 8,241 | 1,161 | 6,692 | 388 |
| Estimated total | 100.0% | 1,528 | 13 | 176 | 247 | 1,092 | 8,261 | 1,165 | 6,705 | 391 |
| Rate per 100,000 inhabitants | | 360.8 | 3.1 | 41.6 | 58.3 | 257.9 | 1,950.8 | 275.1 | 1,583.3 | 92.3 |
| **Buffalo-Cheektowaga, NY M.S.A.[2]** | 1,119,988 | | | | | | | | | |
| Includes Erie and Niagara[2] Counties | | | | | | | | | | |
| City of Buffalo[2] | 254,627 | 2,592 | 61 | 53 | 680 | 1,798 | 7,844 | 1,146 | 5,508 | 1,190 |
| City of Cheektowaga Town | 76,536 | 216 | 1 | 22 | 51 | 142 | 2,226 | 273 | 1,782 | 171 |
| Total area actually reporting | 100.0% | 4,237 | 79 | 257 | 1,030 | 2,871 | 21,574 | 2,844 | 16,547 | 2,183 |
| Rate per 100,000 inhabitants | | 378.3 | 7.1 | 22.9 | 92.0 | 256.3 | 1,926.3 | 253.9 | 1,477.4 | 194.9 |
| **Burlington, NC M.S.A.** | 171,665 | | | | | | | | | |
| Includes Alamance County | | | | | | | | | | |
| City of Burlington | 55,003 | 527 | 3 | 43 | 56 | 425 | 2,391 | 419 | 1,782 | 190 |
| Total area actually reporting | 100.0% | 820 | 12 | 65 | 80 | 663 | 4,070 | 738 | 2,992 | 340 |
| Rate per 100,000 inhabitants | | 477.7 | 7.0 | 37.9 | 46.6 | 386.2 | 2,370.9 | 429.9 | 1,742.9 | 198.1 |
| **Burlington-South Burlington, VT M.S.A.** | 221,248 | | | | | | | | | |
| Includes Chittenden, Franklin, and Grand Isle Counties | | | | | | | | | | |
| City of Burlington | 42,862 | 151 | 1 | 36 | 16 | 98 | 1,032 | 109 | 906 | 17 |
| City of South Burlington | 19,690 | 33 | 0 | 5 | 6 | 22 | 608 | 33 | 557 | 18 |
| Total area actually reporting | 100.0% | 439 | 5 | 115 | 32 | 287 | 3,561 | 362 | 3,116 | 83 |
| Rate per 100,000 inhabitants | | 198.4 | 2.3 | 52.0 | 14.5 | 129.7 | 1,609.5 | 163.6 | 1,408.4 | 37.5 |
| **California-Lexington Park, MD M.S.A.** | 114,031 | | | | | | | | | |
| Includes St. Mary's County | | | | | | | | | | |
| Total area actually reporting | 100.0% | 224 | 8 | 27 | 38 | 151 | 1,556 | 255 | 1,214 | 87 |
| Rate per 100,000 inhabitants | | 196.4 | 7.0 | 23.7 | 33.3 | 132.4 | 1,364.5 | 223.6 | 1,064.6 | 76.3 |
| **Canton-Massillon, OH M.S.A.** | 396,284 | | | | | | | | | |
| Includes Carroll and Stark Counties | | | | | | | | | | |
| City of Canton | 70,124 | 1,002 | 14 | 115 | 154 | 719 | 3,411 | 708 | 2,350 | 353 |
| City of Massillon | 32,617 | 56 | 0 | 20 | 10 | 26 | 759 | 95 | 624 | 40 |
| Total area actually reporting | 98.0% | 1,441 | 19 | 223 | 214 | 985 | 8,414 | 1,575 | 6,157 | 682 |
| Estimated total | 100.0% | 1,451 | 19 | 225 | 216 | 991 | 8,546 | 1,591 | 6,266 | 689 |
| Rate per 100,000 inhabitants | | 366.2 | 4.8 | 56.8 | 54.5 | 250.1 | 2,156.5 | 401.5 | 1,581.2 | 173.9 |
| **Cape Coral-Fort Myers, FL M.S.A.** | 787,016 | | | | | | | | | |
| Includes Lee County | | | | | | | | | | |
| City of Cape Coral | 199,503 | 255 | 1 | 18 | 20 | 216 | 2,130 | 305 | 1,692 | 133 |
| City of Fort Myers | 90,380 | 467 | 9 | 39 | 67 | 352 | 1,699 | 193 | 1,359 | 147 |
| Total area actually reporting | 100.0% | 2,100 | 32 | 239 | 304 | 1,525 | 8,118 | 1,180 | 6,167 | 771 |
| Rate per 100,000 inhabitants | | 266.8 | 4.1 | 30.4 | 38.6 | 193.8 | 1,031.5 | 149.9 | 783.6 | 98.0 |

## Table 6. Crime in the United States, by Selected Metropolitan Statistical Area, 2020—Continued

(Number, percent, rate per 100,000 population.)

| Area | Population | Violent crime | Murder and nonnegligent manslaughter | Rape[1] | Robbery | Aggravated assault | Property crime | Burglary | Larceny-theft | Motor vehicle theft |
|---|---|---|---|---|---|---|---|---|---|---|
| **Cape Girardeau, MO-IL M.S.A.[2]** Includes Alexander County,[4] IL and Bollinger and Cape Girardeau Counties, MO[2] | 96,785 | | | | | | | | | |
| City of Cape Girardeau, MO[2] | 40,845 | 362 | 4 | 42 | 35 | 281 | 1,204 | 179 | 892 | 133 |
| Total area actually reporting | 97.9% | 530 | 5 | 59 | 38 | 428 | 1,785 | 339 | 1,284 | 162 |
| Estimated total | 100.0% | 532 | 5 | 59 | 38 | 430 | 1,811 | 342 | 1,305 | 164 |
| Rate per 100,000 inhabitants | | 549.7 | 5.2 | 61.0 | 39.3 | 444.3 | 1,871.2 | 353.4 | 1,348.3 | 169.4 |
| **Carson City, NV M.S.A.[2]** Includes Carson City[2] | 56,250 | | | | | | | | | |
| Total area actually reporting | 100.0% | 225 | 1 | 62 | 13 | 149 | 643 | 165 | 396 | 82 |
| Rate per 100,000 inhabitants | | 400.0 | 1.8 | 110.2 | 23.1 | 264.9 | 1,143.1 | 293.3 | 704.0 | 145.8 |
| **Casper, WY M.S.A.[2]** Includes Natrona County[2] | 80,625 | | | | | | | | | |
| City of Casper | 58,244 | 124 | 2 | 59 | 14 | 49 | 1,659 | 222 | 1,270 | 167 |
| Total area actually reporting | 100.0% | 183 | 4 | 71 | 16 | 92 | 1,954 | 274 | 1,467 | 213 |
| Rate per 100,000 inhabitants | | 227.0 | 5.0 | 88.1 | 19.8 | 114.1 | 2,423.6 | 339.8 | 1,819.5 | 264.2 |
| **Cedar Rapids, IA M.S.A.** Includes Benton, Jones, and Linn Counties | 274,312 | | | | | | | | | |
| City of Cedar Rapids | 134,330 | 432 | 11 | 16 | 102 | 303 | 4,254 | 832 | 2,865 | 557 |
| Total area actually reporting | 85.6% | 593 | 12 | 48 | 111 | 422 | 5,303 | 1,133 | 3,486 | 684 |
| Estimated total | 100.0% | 691 | 12 | 71 | 116 | 492 | 5,803 | 1,278 | 3,789 | 736 |
| Rate per 100,000 inhabitants | | 251.9 | 4.4 | 25.9 | 42.3 | 179.4 | 2,115.5 | 465.9 | 1,381.3 | 268.3 |
| **Champaign-Urbana, IL M.S.A.[3,4]** Includes Champaign and Piatt Counties[4] | 225,728 | | | | | | | | | |
| City of Champaign[4] | 89,785 | 827 | 9 | 60 | 88 | 670 | | 281 | | 191 |
| City of Urbana[3,4] | 42,211 | | 2 | 41 | 36 | | | 137 | | 42 |
| Total area actually reporting | 99.0% | | 12 | 139 | 147 | | | 613 | | 324 |
| Estimated total | 100.0% | | 12 | 139 | 147 | | | 616 | | 325 |
| Rate per 100,000 inhabitants | | | 5.3 | 61.6 | 65.1 | | | 272.9 | | 144.0 |
| **Charleston, WV M.S.A.** Includes Boone, Clay, Jackson, Kanawha, and Lincoln Counties | 254,717 | | | | | | | | | |
| City of Charleston | 46,038 | 424 | 11 | 37 | 51 | 325 | 2,122 | 506 | 1,423 | 193 |
| Total area actually reporting | 85.3% | 1,191 | 30 | 137 | 88 | 936 | 5,775 | 1,297 | 3,859 | 619 |
| Estimated total | 100.0% | 1,366 | 30 | 149 | 95 | 1,092 | 5,873 | 1,332 | 3,910 | 631 |
| Rate per 100,000 inhabitants | | 536.3 | 11.8 | 58.5 | 37.3 | 428.7 | 2,305.7 | 522.9 | 1,535.0 | 247.7 |
| **Charleston-North Charleston, SC M.S.A.** Includes Berkeley, Charleston, and Dorchester Counties | 819,676 | | | | | | | | | |
| City of Charleston | 139,582 | 650 | 17 | 54 | 100 | 479 | 3,218 | 326 | 2,439 | 453 |
| City of North Charleston | 117,503 | 1,345 | 38 | 90 | 318 | 899 | 5,998 | 651 | 4,667 | 680 |
| Total area actually reporting | 99.0% | 3,607 | 91 | 293 | 648 | 2,575 | 20,056 | 2,492 | 15,247 | 2,317 |
| Estimated total | 100.0% | 3,657 | 93 | 296 | 654 | 2,614 | 20,333 | 2,533 | 15,461 | 2,339 |
| Rate per 100,000 inhabitants | | 446.2 | 11.3 | 36.1 | 79.8 | 318.9 | 2,480.6 | 309.0 | 1,886.2 | 285.4 |
| **Charlottesville, VA M.S.A.** Includes Albemarle, Buckingham, Fluvanna, Greene, and Nelson Counties and Charlottesville City | 220,388 | | | | | | | | | |
| City of Charlottesville | 47,671 | 189 | 5 | 25 | 28 | 131 | 916 | 79 | 765 | 72 |
| Total area actually reporting | 100.0% | 415 | 13 | 83 | 47 | 272 | 2,849 | 280 | 2,376 | 193 |
| Rate per 100,000 inhabitants | | 188.3 | 5.9 | 37.7 | 21.3 | 123.4 | 1,292.7 | 127.0 | 1,078.1 | 87.6 |
| **Chattanooga, TN-GA M.S.A.[2]** Includes Catoosa,[2] Dade, and Walker Counties, GA and Hamilton, Marion, and Sequatchie Counties, TN | 569,147 | | | | | | | | | |
| City of Chattanooga, TN | 184,211 | 2,504 | 33 | 182 | 268 | 2,021 | 11,709 | 1,173 | 8,435 | 2,101 |
| Total area actually reporting | 86.0% | 3,329 | 40 | 255 | 322 | 2,712 | 16,606 | 1,994 | 11,791 | 2,821 |
| Estimated total | 100.0% | 3,487 | 45 | 270 | 343 | 2,829 | 17,474 | 2,137 | 12,414 | 2,923 |
| Rate per 100,000 inhabitants | | 612.7 | 7.9 | 47.4 | 60.3 | 497.1 | 3,070.2 | 375.5 | 2,181.2 | 513.6 |
| **Cheyenne, WY M.S.A.** Includes Laramie County | 100,661 | | | | | | | | | |
| City of Cheyenne | 64,751 | 244 | 2 | 35 | 27 | 180 | 2,186 | 172 | 1,768 | 246 |
| Total area actually reporting | 100.0% | 330 | 3 | 43 | 29 | 255 | 2,617 | 273 | 2,045 | 299 |
| Rate per 100,000 inhabitants | | 327.8 | 3.0 | 42.7 | 28.8 | 253.3 | 2,599.8 | 271.2 | 2,031.6 | 297.0 |
| **Chico, CA M.S.A.** Includes Butte County | 216,938 | | | | | | | | | |
| City of Chico | 105,355 | 540 | 3 | 56 | 80 | 401 | 2,113 | 246 | 1,551 | 316 |
| Total area actually reporting | 100.0% | 1,069 | 12 | 128 | 143 | 786 | 4,328 | 833 | 2,832 | 663 |
| Rate per 100,000 inhabitants | | 492.8 | 5.5 | 59.0 | 65.9 | 362.3 | 1,995.0 | 384.0 | 1,305.4 | 305.6 |
| **Cincinnati, OH-KY-IN M.S.A.** Includes Dearborn, Franklin, Ohio, and Union Counties, IN; Boone, Bracken, Campbell, Gallatin, Grant, Kenton, and Pendleton Counties, KY; and Brown, Butler, Clermont, Hamilton, and Warren Counties, OH | 2,227,744 | | | | | | | | | |
| City of Cincinnati, OH | 304,724 | 2,721 | 92 | 215 | 750 | 1,664 | 11,224 | 2,322 | 7,396 | 1,506 |
| Total area actually reporting | 89.1% | 4,733 | 123 | 656 | 1,132 | 2,822 | 32,917 | 5,080 | 24,525 | 3,312 |
| Estimated total | 100.0% | 5,250 | 128 | 735 | 1,217 | 3,170 | 36,953 | 5,737 | 27,573 | 3,643 |
| Rate per 100,000 inhabitants | | 235.7 | 5.7 | 33.0 | 54.6 | 142.3 | 1,658.8 | 257.5 | 1,237.7 | 163.5 |

## Table 6. Crime in the United States, by Selected Metropolitan Statistical Area, 2020—Continued

(Number, percent, rate per 100,000 population.)

| Area | Population | Violent crime | Murder and nonnegligent manslaughter | Rape[1] | Robbery | Aggravated assault | Property crime | Burglary | Larceny-theft | Motor vehicle theft |
|---|---|---|---|---|---|---|---|---|---|---|
| **Clarksville, TN-KY M.S.A.** | 311,846 | | | | | | | | | |
| Includes Christian and Trigg Counties, KY and Montgomery and Stewart Counties, TN | | | | | | | | | | |
| City of Clarksville, TN | 161,167 | 983 | 15 | 84 | 78 | 806 | 3,615 | 441 | 2,765 | 409 |
| Total area actually reporting | 100.0% | 1,321 | 21 | 133 | 117 | 1,050 | 5,777 | 893 | 4,254 | 630 |
| Rate per 100,000 inhabitants | | 423.6 | 6.7 | 42.6 | 37.5 | 336.7 | 1,852.5 | 286.4 | 1,364.1 | 202.0 |
| **Cleveland, TN M.S.A.** | 125,999 | | | | | | | | | |
| Includes Bradley and Polk Counties | | | | | | | | | | |
| City of Cleveland | 45,994 | 454 | 2 | 21 | 62 | 369 | 2,312 | 374 | 1,734 | 204 |
| Total area actually reporting | 100.0% | 710 | 5 | 39 | 71 | 595 | 3,398 | 612 | 2,422 | 364 |
| Rate per 100,000 inhabitants | | 563.5 | 4.0 | 31.0 | 56.3 | 472.2 | 2,696.8 | 485.7 | 1,922.2 | 288.9 |
| **Cleveland-Elyria, OH M.S.A.** | 2,042,966 | | | | | | | | | |
| Includes Cuyahoga, Geauga, Lake, Lorain, and Medina Counties | | | | | | | | | | |
| City of Cleveland | 379,121 | 6,281 | 160 | 393 | 1,593 | 4,135 | 15,433 | 3,692 | 8,800 | 2,941 |
| City of Elyria | 53,677 | 136 | 7 | 21 | 26 | 82 | 785 | 178 | 546 | 61 |
| Total area actually reporting | 87.6% | 8,616 | 207 | 664 | 2,100 | 5,645 | 30,659 | 5,749 | 20,511 | 4,399 |
| Estimated total | 100.0% | 9,002 | 210 | 740 | 2,175 | 5,877 | 34,823 | 6,261 | 23,896 | 4,666 |
| Rate per 100,000 inhabitants | | 440.6 | 10.3 | 36.2 | 106.5 | 287.7 | 1,704.5 | 306.5 | 1,169.7 | 228.4 |
| **Coeur d'Alene, ID M.S.A.** | 170,237 | | | | | | | | | |
| Includes Kootenai County | | | | | | | | | | |
| City of Coeur d'Alene | 53,405 | 209 | 1 | 66 | 8 | 134 | 835 | 92 | 701 | 42 |
| Total area actually reporting | 100.0% | 343 | 2 | 81 | 16 | 244 | 1,807 | 308 | 1,403 | 96 |
| Rate per 100,000 inhabitants | | 201.5 | 1.2 | 47.6 | 9.4 | 143.3 | 1,061.5 | 180.9 | 824.1 | 56.4 |
| **College Station-Bryan, TX M.S.A.[2]** | 268,082 | | | | | | | | | |
| Includes Brazos,[2] Burleson,[2] and Robertson Counties | | | | | | | | | | |
| City of College Station | 120,831 | 217 | 2 | 55 | 27 | 133 | 2,299 | 321 | 1,768 | 210 |
| City of Bryan[2] | 87,435 | 463 | 7 | 104 | 49 | 303 | 1,718 | 280 | 1,302 | 136 |
| Total area actually reporting | 100.0% | 799 | 10 | 182 | 88 | 519 | 4,970 | 835 | 3,698 | 437 |
| Rate per 100,000 inhabitants | | 298.0 | 3.7 | 67.9 | 32.8 | 193.6 | 1,853.9 | 311.5 | 1,379.4 | 163.0 |
| **Colorado Springs, CO M.S.A.** | 752,364 | | | | | | | | | |
| Includes El Paso and Teller Counties | | | | | | | | | | |
| City of Colorado Springs | 485,083 | 2,896 | 36 | 400 | 376 | 2,084 | 16,394 | 2,588 | 11,374 | 2,432 |
| Total area actually reporting | 99.6% | 3,655 | 47 | 577 | 440 | 2,591 | 19,859 | 3,100 | 13,880 | 2,879 |
| Estimated total | 100.0% | 3,661 | 47 | 578 | 441 | 2,595 | 19,960 | 3,106 | 13,958 | 2,896 |
| Rate per 100,000 inhabitants | | 486.6 | 6.2 | 76.8 | 58.6 | 344.9 | 2,653.0 | 412.8 | 1,855.2 | 384.9 |
| **Columbia, MO M.S.A.[2]** | 210,096 | | | | | | | | | |
| Includes Boone,[2] Cooper, and Howard[2] Counties | | | | | | | | | | |
| City of Columbia[2] | 124,829 | 552 | 13 | 89 | 58 | 392 | 3,326 | 404 | 2,478 | 444 |
| Total area actually reporting | 98.2 | 739 | 15 | 132 | 71 | 521 | 4,522 | 573 | 3,366 | 583 |
| Estimated total | 100.0% | 769 | 15 | 134 | 75 | 545 | 4,635 | 590 | 3,440 | 605 |
| Rate per 100,000 inhabitants | | 366.0 | 7.1 | 63.8 | 35.7 | 259.4 | 2,206.1 | 280.8 | 1,637.3 | 288.0 |
| **Columbia, SC M.S.A.** | 847,504 | | | | | | | | | |
| Includes Calhoun, Fairfield, Kershaw, Lexington, Richland, and Saluda Counties | | | | | | | | | | |
| City of Columbia | 131,777 | 991 | 19 | 86 | 206 | 680 | 5,898 | 728 | 4,536 | 634 |
| Total area actually reporting | 100.0% | 4,729 | 78 | 355 | 644 | 3,652 | 27,730 | 4,335 | 20,161 | 3,234 |
| Rate per 100,000 inhabitants | | 558.0 | 9.2 | 41.9 | 76.0 | 430.9 | 3,272.0 | 511.5 | 2,378.9 | 381.6 |
| **Columbus, OH M.S.A.** | 2,145,231 | | | | | | | | | |
| Includes Delaware, Fairfield, Franklin, Hocking, Licking, Madison, Morrow, Perry, Pickaway, and Union Counties | | | | | | | | | | |
| City of Columbus | 911,383 | 5,064 | 174 | 816 | 1,796 | 2,278 | 28,530 | 5,551 | 19,874 | 3,105 |
| Total area actually reporting | 93.8% | 6,534 | 191 | 1,128 | 2,097 | 3,118 | 45,217 | 7,810 | 33,179 | 4,228 |
| Estimated total | 100.0% | 6,718 | 192 | 1,164 | 2,131 | 3,231 | 47,407 | 8,082 | 34,972 | 4,353 |
| Rate per 100,000 inhabitants | | 313.2 | 9.0 | 54.3 | 99.3 | 150.6 | 2,209.9 | 376.7 | 1,630.2 | 202.9 |
| **Corpus Christi, TX M.S.A.[2]** | 430,354 | | | | | | | | | |
| Includes Nueces and San Patricio Counties | | | | | | | | | | |
| City of Corpus Christi[2] | 329,050 | 2,772 | 34 | 232 | 478 | 2,028 | 10,747 | 2,042 | 7,824 | 881 |
| Total area actually reporting | 99.9% | 3,175 | 43 | 278 | 509 | 2,345 | 12,659 | 2,428 | 9,202 | 1,029 |
| Estimated total | 100.0% | 3,176 | 43 | 278 | 509 | 2,346 | 12,668 | 2,430 | 9,208 | 1,030 |
| Rate per 100,000 inhabitants | | 738.0 | 10.0 | 64.6 | 118.3 | 545.1 | 2,943.6 | 564.7 | 2,139.6 | 239.3 |
| **Crestview-Fort Walton Beach-Destin, FL M.S.A.** | 290,040 | | | | | | | | | |
| Includes Okaloosa and Walton Counties | | | | | | | | | | |
| City of Crestview | 25,787 | 93 | 4 | 18 | 13 | 58 | 602 | 72 | 457 | 73 |
| City of Fort Walton Beach | 22,871 | 74 | 2 | 13 | 4 | 55 | 462 | 89 | 324 | 49 |
| Total area actually reporting | 100.0% | 780 | 10 | 117 | 50 | 603 | 3,927 | 601 | 2,947 | 379 |
| Rate per 100,000 inhabitants | | 268.9 | 3.4 | 40.3 | 17.2 | 207.9 | 1,354.0 | 207.2 | 1,016.1 | 130.7 |
| **Danville, IL M.S.A.[4]** | 74,737 | | | | | | | | | |
| Includes Vermilion County[4] | | | | | | | | | | |
| City of Danville[4] | 30,208 | 505 | 8 | 10 | 59 | 428 | | 399 | | 48 |
| Total area actually reporting | 100.0% | 785 | 13 | 70 | 87 | 615 | | 658 | | 170 |
| Rate per 100,000 inhabitants | | 1,050.3 | 17.4 | 93.7 | 116.4 | 822.9 | | 880.4 | | 227.5 |

## Table 6. Crime in the United States, by Selected Metropolitan Statistical Area, 2020—Continued

(Number, percent, rate per 100,000 population.)

| Area | Population | Violent crime | Murder and nonnegligent manslaughter | Rape[1] | Robbery | Aggravated assault | Property crime | Burglary | Larceny-theft | Motor vehicle theft |
|---|---|---|---|---|---|---|---|---|---|---|
| **Davenport-Moline-Rock Island, IA-IL M.S.A.[4]** | 377,817 | | | | | | | | | |
| Includes Henry, Mercer, and Rock Island Counties, IL4 and Scott County, IA | | | | | | | | | | |
| City of Davenport, IA | 101,806 | 750 | 10 | 67 | 136 | 537 | 3,996 | 912 | 2,615 | 469 |
| City of Moline, IL[4] | 41,128 | 204 | 1 | 32 | 25 | 146 | | 225 | | 76 |
| City of Rock Island, IL[4] | 36,981 | 213 | 7 | 8 | 50 | 148 | | 139 | | 124 |
| Total area actually reporting | 96.5% | 1,770 | 26 | 221 | 265 | 1,258 | | 1,833 | | 934 |
| Estimated total | 100.0% | 1,798 | 26 | 225 | 269 | 1,278 | | 1,866 | | 950 |
| Rate per 100,000 inhabitants | | 475.9 | 6.9 | 59.6 | 71.2 | 338.3 | | 493.9 | | 251.4 |
| **Decatur, IL M.S.A.[4]** | 102,740 | | | | | | | | | |
| Includes Macon County[4] | | | | | | | | | | |
| City of Decatur[4] | 70,175 | 489 | 13 | 41 | 83 | 352 | | 621 | | 196 |
| Total area actually reporting | 100.0% | 540 | 13 | 49 | 84 | 394 | | 677 | | 214 |
| Rate per 100,000 inhabitants | | 525.6 | 12.7 | 47.7 | 81.8 | 383.5 | | 658.9 | | 208.3 |
| **Deltona-Daytona Beach-Ormond Beach, FL M.S.A.** | 675,651 | | | | | | | | | |
| Includes Flagler and Volusia Counties | | | | | | | | | | |
| City of Daytona Beach | 70,084 | 725 | 14 | 25 | 77 | 609 | 2,145 | 274 | 1,668 | 203 |
| City of Ormond Beach | 44,271 | 161 | 1 | 26 | 23 | 111 | 1,035 | 166 | 773 | 96 |
| City of DeLand | 35,874 | 188 | 1 | 8 | 16 | 163 | 870 | 111 | 697 | 62 |
| Total area actually reporting | 100.0% | 2,280 | 26 | 192 | 274 | 1,788 | 9,815 | 1,528 | 7,452 | 835 |
| Rate per 100,000 inhabitants | | 337.5 | 3.8 | 28.4 | 40.6 | 264.6 | 1,452.7 | 226.2 | 1,102.9 | 123.6 |
| **Denver-Aurora-Lakewood, CO M.S.A.** | 2,998,046 | | | | | | | | | |
| Includes Adams, Arapahoe, Broomfield, Clear Creek, Denver, Douglas, Elbert, Gilpin, Jefferson, and Park Counties | | | | | | | | | | |
| City of Denver | 737,709 | 6,329 | 97 | 670 | 1,218 | 4,344 | 34,294 | 5,223 | 20,662 | 8,409 |
| City of Aurora | 385,720 | 3,473 | 39 | 397 | 775 | 2,262 | 13,079 | 1,760 | 7,390 | 3,929 |
| City of Lakewood | 159,719 | 903 | 8 | 110 | 219 | 566 | 8,050 | 1,076 | 5,580 | 1,394 |
| City of Centennial | 112,104 | 144 | 1 | 6 | 26 | 111 | 1,979 | 317 | 1,360 | 302 |
| City of Broomfield | 71,795 | 76 | 0 | 15 | 13 | 48 | 2,145 | 222 | 1,654 | 269 |
| City of Commerce City | 62,164 | 298 | 6 | 73 | 38 | 181 | 2,051 | 238 | 1,241 | 572 |
| Total area actually reporting | 99.6% | 14,675 | 183 | 1,970 | 2,811 | 9,711 | 98,712 | 13,268 | 63,475 | 21,969 |
| Estimated total | 100.0% | 14,701 | 183 | 1,974 | 2,816 | 9,728 | 99,017 | 13,307 | 63,699 | 22,011 |
| Rate per 100,000 inhabitants | | 490.4 | 6.1 | 65.8 | 93.9 | 324.5 | 3,302.7 | 443.9 | 2,124.7 | 734.2 |
| **Des Moines-West Des Moines, IA M.S.A.** | 709,374 | | | | | | | | | |
| Includes Dallas, Guthrie, Jasper, Madison, Polk, and Warren Counties | | | | | | | | | | |
| City of Des Moines | 215,290 | 1,517 | 33 | 119 | 246 | 1,119 | 8,400 | 1,925 | 5,053 | 1,422 |
| City of West Des Moines | 69,252 | 93 | 1 | 27 | 7 | 58 | 1,140 | 129 | 893 | 118 |
| Total area actually reporting | 100.0% | 2,402 | 44 | 247 | 295 | 1,816 | 14,354 | 3,006 | 9,299 | 2,049 |
| Rate per 100,000 inhabitants | | 338.6 | 6.2 | 34.8 | 41.6 | 256.0 | 2,023.5 | 423.8 | 1,310.9 | 288.8 |
| **Detroit-Warren-Dearborn, MI M.S.A.** | 4,308,550 | | | | | | | | | |
| Includes the Metropolitan Divisions of Detroit-Dearborn-Livonia and Warren-Troy-Farmington Hills | | | | | | | | | | |
| City of Detroit | 659,616 | 14,370 | 328 | 676 | 1,848 | 11,518 | 21,178 | 4,361 | 11,239 | 5,578 |
| City of Warren | 133,928 | 672 | 12 | 93 | 91 | 476 | 1,938 | 348 | 1,169 | 421 |
| City of Dearborn | 93,507 | 277 | 5 | 25 | 31 | 216 | 1,662 | 194 | 1,215 | 253 |
| City of Livonia | 93,342 | 209 | 0 | 26 | 12 | 171 | 1,196 | 115 | 979 | 102 |
| City of Troy | 84,441 | 86 | 1 | 9 | 15 | 61 | 732 | 46 | 635 | 51 |
| City of Farmington Hills | 80,708 | 84 | 0 | 11 | 9 | 64 | 558 | 65 | 439 | 54 |
| City of Southfield | 72,794 | 288 | 3 | 33 | 35 | 217 | 1,309 | 190 | 759 | 360 |
| City of Taylor | 60,698 | 371 | 1 | 25 | 35 | 310 | 1,108 | 182 | 790 | 136 |
| City of Pontiac | 59,411 | 840 | 13 | 50 | 88 | 689 | 1,096 | 240 | 743 | 113 |
| City of Novi | 61,554 | 60 | 1 | 15 | 3 | 41 | 429 | 21 | 372 | 36 |
| Total area actually reporting | 100.0% | 24,568 | 452 | 1,989 | 2,791 | 19,336 | 57,445 | 9,472 | 37,647 | 10,326 |
| Rate per 100,000 inhabitants | | 570.2 | 10.5 | 46.2 | 64.8 | 448.8 | 1,333.3 | 219.8 | 873.8 | 239.7 |
| **Detroit-Warren-Dearborn, MI M.S.A.** | 1,736,289 | | | | | | | | | |
| Includes Wayne County | | | | | | | | | | |
| Total area actually reporting | 100.0% | 18,894 | 387 | 1,136 | 2,247 | 15,124 | 35,699 | 6,526 | 21,529 | 7,644 |
| Rate per 100,000 inhabitants | | 1,088.2 | 22.3 | 65.4 | 129.4 | 871.1 | 2,056.1 | 375.9 | 1,239.9 | 440.2 |
| **Warren-Troy-Farmington Hills, MI M.D.** | 2,572,261 | | | | | | | | | |
| Includes Lapeer, Livingston, Macomb, Oakland, and St. Clair Counties | | | | | | | | | | |
| Total area actually reporting | 100.0% | 5,674 | 65 | 853 | 544 | 4,212 | 21,746 | 2,946 | 16,118 | 2,682 |
| Rate per 100,000 inhabitants | | 220.6 | 2.5 | 33.2 | 21.1 | 163.7 | 845.4 | 114.5 | 626.6 | 104.3 |
| **Dover, DE M.S.A.** | 183,675 | | | | | | | | | |
| Includes Kent County | | | | | | | | | | |
| City of Dover | 38,428 | 329 | 9 | 22 | 24 | 274 | 1,549 | 57 | 1,412 | 80 |
| Total area actually reporting | 100.0% | 813 | 13 | 79 | 58 | 663 | 3,404 | 372 | 2,829 | 203 |
| Rate per 100,000 inhabitants | | 442.6 | 7.1 | 43.0 | 31.6 | 361.0 | 1,853.3 | 202.5 | 1,540.2 | 110.5 |
| **Dubuque, IA M.S.A.** | 97,551 | | | | | | | | | |
| Includes Dubuque County | | | | | | | | | | |
| City of Dubuque | 57,904 | 231 | 1 | 54 | 26 | 150 | 1,165 | 208 | 885 | 72 |
| Total area actually reporting | 100.0% | 262 | 1 | 62 | 26 | 173 | 1,363 | 267 | 1,004 | 92 |
| Rate per 100,000 inhabitants | | 268.6 | 1.0 | 63.6 | 26.7 | 177.3 | 1,397.2 | 273.7 | 1,029.2 | 94.3 |

## Table 6. Crime in the United States, by Selected Metropolitan Statistical Area, 2020—Continued

(Number, percent, rate per 100,000 population.)

| Area | Population | Violent crime | Murder and nonnegligent manslaughter | Rape[1] | Robbery | Aggravated assault | Property crime | Burglary | Larceny-theft | Motor vehicle theft |
|---|---|---|---|---|---|---|---|---|---|---|
| **Duluth, MN-WI M.S.A.[2]** | 287,596 | | | | | | | | | |
| Includes Carlton,[2] Lake,[2] and St. Louis Counties, MN and Douglas County, WI[2] | | | | | | | | | | |
| City of Duluth, MN | 85,555 | 257 | 1 | 33 | 44 | 179 | 3,224 | 326 | 2,677 | 221 |
| Total area actually reporting | 100.0% | 607 | 5 | 93 | 67 | 442 | 6,924 | 982 | 5,455 | 487 |
| Rate per 100,000 inhabitants | | 211.1 | 1.7 | 32.3 | 23.3 | 153.7 | 2,407.5 | 341.5 | 1,896.8 | 169.3 |
| **Durham-Chapel Hill, NC M.S.A.** | 653,860 | | | | | | | | | |
| Includes Chatham, Durham, Granville, Orange and Person Counties | | | | | | | | | | |
| City of Durham | 284,925 | 2,447 | 36 | 125 | 626 | 1,660 | 10,650 | 1,906 | 7,779 | 965 |
| City of Chapel Hill | 64,853 | 93 | 0 | 7 | 22 | 64 | 1,140 | 198 | 885 | 57 |
| Total area actually reporting | 100.0% | 3,272 | 53 | 190 | 745 | 2,284 | 16,350 | 3,085 | 11,888 | 1,377 |
| Rate per 100,000 inhabitants | | 500.4 | 8.1 | 29.1 | 113.9 | 349.3 | 2,500.5 | 471.8 | 1,818.1 | 210.6 |
| **Eau Claire, WI M.S.A.** | 170,028 | | | | | | | | | |
| Includes Chippewa and Eau Claire Counties | | | | | | | | | | |
| City of Eau Claire | 69,086 | 191 | 2 | 41 | 38 | 110 | 1,927 | 334 | 1,494 | 99 |
| Total area actually reporting | 100.0% | 326 | 3 | 72 | 42 | 209 | 2,951 | 558 | 2,227 | 166 |
| Rate per 100,000 inhabitants | | 191.7 | 1.8 | 42.3 | 24.7 | 122.9 | 1,735.6 | 328.2 | 1,309.8 | 97.6 |
| **El Centro, CA M.S.A.** | 180,129 | | | | | | | | | |
| Includes Imperial County | | | | | | | | | | |
| City of El Centro | 44,238 | 158 | 1 | 10 | 30 | 117 | 1,003 | 213 | 679 | 111 |
| Total area actually reporting | 96.1% | 582 | 7 | 32 | 80 | 463 | 3,384 | 851 | 2,085 | 448 |
| Estimated total | 100.0% | 609 | 7 | 35 | 85 | 482 | 3,526 | 873 | 2,188 | 465 |
| Rate per 100,000 inhabitants | | 338.1 | 3.9 | 19.4 | 47.2 | 267.6 | 1,957.5 | 484.7 | 1,214.7 | 258.1 |
| **Elizabethtown-Fort Knox, KY M.S.A.** | 154,232 | | | | | | | | | |
| Includes Hardin, Larue, and Meade Counties | | | | | | | | | | |
| City of Elizabethtown | 30,505 | 44 | 3 | 8 | 9 | 24 | 286 | 68 | 182 | 36 |
| Total area actually reporting | 100.0% | 155 | 5 | 26 | 25 | 99 | 1,286 | 279 | 836 | 171 |
| Rate per 100,000 inhabitants | | 100.5 | 3.2 | 16.9 | 16.2 | 64.2 | 833.8 | 180.9 | 542.0 | 110.9 |
| **Elmira, NY M.S.A.** | 82,347 | | | | | | | | | |
| Includes Chemung County | | | | | | | | | | |
| City of Elmira | 26,820 | 59 | 2 | 0 | 25 | 32 | 812 | 87 | 684 | 41 |
| Total area actually reporting | 100.0% | 173 | 3 | 32 | 28 | 110 | 1,329 | 131 | 1,131 | 67 |
| Rate per 100,000 inhabitants | | 210.1 | 3.6 | 38.9 | 34.0 | 133.6 | 1,613.9 | 159.1 | 1,373.5 | 81.4 |
| **El Paso, TX M.S.A.[2]** | 845,510 | | | | | | | | | |
| Includes El Paso[2] and Hudspeth Counties | | | | | | | | | | |
| City of El Paso[2] | 685,288 | 2,167 | 28 | 261 | 289 | 1,589 | 8,507 | 847 | 7,245 | 415 |
| Total area actually reporting | 100.0% | 2,611 | 33 | 319 | 321 | 1,938 | 9,708 | 1,042 | 8,134 | 532 |
| Rate per 100,000 inhabitants | | 308.8 | 3.9 | 37.7 | 38.0 | 229.2 | 1,148.2 | 123.2 | 962.0 | 62.9 |
| **Enid, OK M.S.A.** | 61,092 | | | | | | | | | |
| Includes Garfield County | | | | | | | | | | |
| City of Enid | 49,708 | 233 | 4 | 35 | 15 | 179 | 1,420 | 375 | 948 | 97 |
| Total area actually reporting | 100.0% | 254 | 4 | 38 | 15 | 197 | 1,576 | 430 | 1,039 | 107 |
| Rate per 100,000 inhabitants | | 415.8 | 6.5 | 62.2 | 24.6 | 322.5 | 2,579.7 | 703.9 | 1,700.7 | 175.1 |
| **Evansville, IN-KY M.S.A.[2]** | 315,160 | | | | | | | | | |
| Includes Posey, Vanderburgh, and Warrick Counties, IN and Henderson County, KY | | | | | | | | | | |
| City of Evansville[2] | 117,747 | 1,185 | 10 | 77 | 115 | 983 | 4,252 | 626 | 3,188 | 438 |
| Total area actually reporting | 92.0% | 1,563 | 14 | 119 | 140 | 1,290 | 6,292 | 1,011 | 4,636 | 645 |
| Estimated total | 100.0% | 1,601 | 14 | 123 | 143 | 1,321 | 6,557 | 1,067 | 4,817 | 673 |
| Rate per 100,000 inhabitants | | 508.0 | 4.4 | 39.0 | 45.4 | 419.2 | 2,080.5 | 338.6 | 1,528.4 | 213.5 |
| **Fairbanks, AK M.S.A.** | 32,922 | | | | | | | | | |
| Includes Fairbanks North Star Borough | | | | | | | | | | |
| City of Fairbanks | 30,832 | 260 | 3 | 24 | 41 | 192 | 1,276 | 171 | 908 | 197 |
| Total area actually reporting | 100.0% | 277 | 3 | 26 | 42 | 206 | 1,367 | 180 | 975 | 212 |
| Rate per 100,000 inhabitants | | 841.4 | 9.1 | 79.0 | 127.6 | 625.7 | 4,152.2 | 546.7 | 2,961.5 | 643.9 |
| **Fargo, ND-MN M.S.A.** | 248,368 | | | | | | | | | |
| Includes Clay County, MN and Cass County, ND | | | | | | | | | | |
| City of Fargo, ND | 126,927 | 584 | 7 | 107 | 61 | 409 | 4,403 | 1,016 | 2,922 | 465 |
| Total area actually reporting | 100.0% | 871 | 14 | 172 | 82 | 603 | 7,027 | 1,611 | 4,690 | 726 |
| Rate per 100,000 inhabitants | | 350.7 | 5.6 | 69.3 | 33.0 | 242.8 | 2,829.3 | 648.6 | 1,888.3 | 292.3 |
| **Farmington, NM M.S.A.[2]** | 123,608 | | | | | | | | | |
| Includes San Juan County | | | | | | | | | | |
| City of Farmington[2] | 44,191 | 529 | 1 | 78 | 40 | 410 | 1,447 | 295 | 1,010 | 142 |
| Total area actually reporting | 100.0% | 817 | 4 | 122 | 51 | 640 | 2,026 | 447 | 1,373 | 206 |
| Rate per 100,000 inhabitants | | 661.0 | 3.2 | 98.7 | 41.3 | 517.8 | 1,639.1 | 361.6 | 1,110.8 | 166.7 |
| **Fayetteville, NC M.S.A.[2]** | 531,101 | | | | | | | | | |
| Includes Cumberland, Harnett,[2] and Hoke Counties | | | | | | | | | | |
| City of Fayetteville | 212,033 | 2,074 | 30 | 87 | 262 | 1,695 | 7,210 | 1,327 | 5,418 | 465 |
| Total area actually reporting | 89.3% | 2,811 | 44 | 145 | 345 | 2,277 | 11,555 | 2,516 | 8,219 | 820 |
| Estimated total | 100.0% | 2,938 | 46 | 160 | 360 | 2,372 | 12,396 | 2,752 | 8,737 | 907 |
| Rate per 100,000 inhabitants | | 553.2 | 8.7 | 30.1 | 67.8 | 446.6 | 2,334.0 | 518.2 | 1,645.1 | 170.8 |

## Table 6. Crime in the United States, by Selected Metropolitan Statistical Area, 2020—Continued

(Number, percent, rate per 100,000 population.)

| Area | Population | Violent crime | Murder and nonnegligent manslaughter | Rape[1] | Robbery | Aggravated assault | Property crime | Burglary | Larceny-theft | Motor vehicle theft |
|---|---|---|---|---|---|---|---|---|---|---|
| **Flint, MI M.S.A.** | 402,374 | | | | | | | | | |
| Includes Genesee County | | | | | | | | | | |
| City of Flint | 94,842 | 996 | 44 | 67 | 83 | 802 | 1,614 | 406 | 1,004 | 204 |
| Total area actually reporting | 100.0% | 2,324 | 75 | 260 | 177 | 1,812 | 5,823 | 1,281 | 3,882 | 660 |
| Rate per 100,000 inhabitants | | 577.6 | 18.6 | 64.6 | 44.0 | 450.3 | 1,447.2 | 318.4 | 964.8 | 164.0 |
| **Florence, SC M.S.A.** | 205,067 | | | | | | | | | |
| Includes Darlington and Florence Counties | | | | | | | | | | |
| City of Florence | 38,597 | 562 | 12 | 15 | 72 | 463 | 2,390 | 322 | 1,812 | 256 |
| Total area actually reporting | 95.7% | 1,708 | 38 | 96 | 174 | 1,400 | 7,081 | 1,335 | 4,942 | 804 |
| Estimated total | 100.0% | 1,764 | 39 | 100 | 181 | 1,444 | 7,384 | 1,379 | 5,177 | 828 |
| Rate per 100,000 inhabitants | | 860.2 | 19.0 | 48.8 | 88.3 | 704.2 | 3,600.8 | 672.5 | 2,524.5 | 403.8 |
| **Fond du Lac, WI M.S.A.** | 103,517 | | | | | | | | | |
| Includes Fond du Lac County | | | | | | | | | | |
| City of Fond du Lac | 43,295 | 134 | 1 | 25 | 9 | 99 | 878 | 66 | 776 | 36 |
| Total area actually reporting | 100.0% | 181 | 2 | 44 | 10 | 125 | 1,187 | 130 | 1,003 | 54 |
| Rate per 100,000 inhabitants | | 174.9 | 1.9 | 42.5 | 9.7 | 120.8 | 1,146.7 | 125.6 | 968.9 | 52.2 |
| **Fort Smith, AR-OK M.S.A.** | 250,603 | | | | | | | | | |
| Includes Crawford, Franklin, and Sebastian Counties, AR and Sequoyah County, OK | | | | | | | | | | |
| City of Fort Smith, AR | 88,071 | 1,031 | 7 | 96 | 106 | 822 | 4,871 | 637 | 3,716 | 518 |
| Total area actually reporting | 99.1% | 1,530 | 11 | 188 | 114 | 1,217 | 7,176 | 1,294 | 5,166 | 716 |
| Estimated total | 100.0% | 1,541 | 11 | 190 | 115 | 1,225 | 7,224 | 1,303 | 5,199 | 722 |
| Rate per 100,000 inhabitants | | 614.9 | 4.4 | 75.8 | 45.9 | 488.8 | 2,882.6 | 519.9 | 2,074.6 | 288.1 |
| **Fort Wayne, IN M.S.A.** | 415,629 | | | | | | | | | |
| Includes Allen and Whitley Counties | | | | | | | | | | |
| City of Fort Wayne | 272,270 | 1,124 | 39 | 97 | 245 | 743 | 6,117 | 655 | 4,952 | 510 |
| Total area actually reporting | 94.5% | 1,369 | 41 | 125 | 267 | 936 | 7,067 | 800 | 5,662 | 605 |
| Estimated total | 100.0% | 1,392 | 41 | 129 | 269 | 953 | 7,266 | 851 | 5,782 | 633 |
| Rate per 100,000 inhabitants | | 334.9 | 9.9 | 31.0 | 64.7 | 229.3 | 1,748.2 | 204.7 | 1,391.1 | 152.3 |
| **Fresno, CA M.S.A.** | 996,752 | | | | | | | | | |
| Includes Fresno County | | | | | | | | | | |
| City of Fresno | 535,472 | 3,560 | 77 | 148 | 889 | 2,446 | 16,475 | 3,036 | 10,789 | 2,650 |
| Total area actually reporting | 100.0% | 5,948 | 94 | 302 | 1,169 | 4,383 | 24,724 | 4,955 | 15,697 | 4,072 |
| Rate per 100,000 inhabitants | | 596.7 | 9.4 | 30.3 | 117.3 | 439.7 | 2,480.5 | 497.1 | 1,574.8 | 408.5 |
| **Gainesville, FL M.S.A.** | 330,910 | | | | | | | | | |
| Includes Alachua, Gilchrist, and Levy Counties | | | | | | | | | | |
| City of Gainesville | 135,076 | 1,042 | 10 | 128 | 209 | 695 | 4,297 | 411 | 3,400 | 486 |
| Total area actually reporting | 100.0% | 2,516 | 17 | 271 | 356 | 1,872 | 7,414 | 1,120 | 5,513 | 781 |
| Rate per 100,000 inhabitants | | 760.3 | 5.1 | 81.9 | 107.6 | 565.7 | 2,240.5 | 338.5 | 1,666.0 | 236.0 |
| **Gainesville, GA M.S.A.[2]** | 207,015 | | | | | | | | | |
| Includes Hall County | | | | | | | | | | |
| City of Gainesville[2] | 44,398 | 184 | 0 | 12 | 38 | 134 | 1,116 | 140 | 887 | 89 |
| Total area actually reporting | 100.0% | 479 | 7 | 58 | 60 | 354 | 2,631 | 369 | 2,003 | 259 |
| Rate per 100,000 inhabitants | | 231.4 | 3.4 | 28.0 | 29.0 | 171.0 | 1,270.9 | 178.2 | 967.6 | 125.1 |
| **Glens Falls, NY M.S.A.[2]** | 123,934 | | | | | | | | | |
| Includes Warren and Washington Counties | | | | | | | | | | |
| City of Glens Falls[2] | 14,215 | 10 | 0 | 2 | 0 | 8 | 105 | 7 | 95 | 3 |
| Total area actually reporting | 98.0% | 152 | 0 | 94 | 7 | 51 | 898 | 121 | 739 | 38 |
| Estimated total | 100.0% | 156 | 0 | 95 | 8 | 53 | 914 | 124 | 751 | 39 |
| Rate per 100,000 inhabitants | | 125.9 | 0.0 | 76.7 | 6.5 | 42.8 | 737.5 | 100.1 | 606.0 | 31.5 |
| **Goldsboro, NC M.S.A.** | 123,171 | | | | | | | | | |
| Includes Wayne County | | | | | | | | | | |
| City of Goldsboro | 34,051 | 397 | 2 | 11 | 46 | 338 | 1,709 | 349 | 1,272 | 88 |
| Total area actually reporting | 97.7% | 585 | 7 | 18 | 65 | 495 | 2,959 | 733 | 1,941 | 285 |
| Estimated total | 100.0% | 593 | 7 | 19 | 65 | 502 | 3,094 | 758 | 2,045 | 291 |
| Rate per 100,000 inhabitants | | 481.4 | 5.7 | 15.4 | 52.8 | 407.6 | 2,512.0 | 615.4 | 1,660.3 | 236.3 |
| **Grand Forks, ND-MN M.S.A.[2]** | 100,189 | | | | | | | | | |
| Includes Polk County, MN[2] and Grand Forks County, ND | | | | | | | | | | |
| City of Grand Forks, ND | 56,163 | 164 | 4 | 34 | 14 | 112 | 1,315 | 210 | 988 | 117 |
| Total area actually reporting | 100.0% | 233 | 6 | 47 | 15 | 165 | 1,762 | 313 | 1,299 | 150 |
| Rate per 100,000 inhabitants | | 232.6 | 6.0 | 46.9 | 15.0 | 164.7 | 1,758.7 | 312.4 | 1,296.5 | 149.7 |
| **Grand Island, NE M.S.A.** | 75,484 | | | | | | | | | |
| Includes Hall, Howard, and Merrick Counties | | | | | | | | | | |
| City of Grand Island | 51,547 | 216 | 0 | 50 | 17 | 149 | 1,258 | 149 | 1,015 | 94 |
| Total area actually reporting | 100.0% | 257 | 0 | 59 | 17 | 181 | 1,383 | 178 | 1,091 | 114 |
| Rate per 100,000 inhabitants | | 340.5 | 0.0 | 78.2 | 22.5 | 239.8 | 1,832.2 | 235.8 | 1,445.3 | 151.0 |
| **Grand Junction, CO M.S.A.** | 154,127 | | | | | | | | | |
| Includes Mesa County | | | | | | | | | | |
| City of Grand Junction | 64,149 | 348 | 3 | 43 | 40 | 262 | 2,966 | 385 | 2,298 | 283 |
| Total area actually reporting | 99.7% | 563 | 3 | 89 | 56 | 415 | 4,546 | 749 | 3,319 | 478 |
| Estimated total | 100.0% | 565 | 3 | 89 | 56 | 417 | 4,594 | 751 | 3,361 | 482 |
| Rate per 100,000 inhabitants | | 366.6 | 1.9 | 57.7 | 36.3 | 270.6 | 2,980.7 | 487.3 | 2,180.7 | 312.7 |

## Table 6. Crime in the United States, by Selected Metropolitan Statistical Area, 2020—Continued

(Number, percent, rate per 100,000 population.)

| Area | Population | Violent crime | Murder and nonnegligent manslaughter | Rape[1] | Robbery | Aggravated assault | Property crime | Burglary | Larceny-theft | Motor vehicle theft |
|---|---|---|---|---|---|---|---|---|---|---|
| **Grand Rapids-Kentwood, MI M.S.A.** | 1,083,395 | | | | | | | | | |
| Includes Ionia, Kent, Montcalm, and Ottawa Counties | | | | | | | | | | |
| City of Grand Rapids | 202,513 | 1,443 | 28 | 121 | 192 | 1,102 | 3,956 | 463 | 2,912 | 581 |
| City of Kentwood | 52,263 | 229 | 4 | 28 | 26 | 171 | 1,207 | 166 | 837 | 204 |
| Total area actually reporting | 99.9% | 3,789 | 50 | 744 | 380 | 2,615 | 13,834 | 1,780 | 10,278 | 1,776 |
| Estimated total | 100.0% | 3,793 | 50 | 745 | 380 | 2,618 | 13,853 | 1,783 | 10,293 | 1,777 |
| Rate per 100,000 inhabitants | | 350.1 | 4.6 | 68.8 | 35.1 | 241.6 | 1,278.7 | 164.6 | 950.1 | 164.0 |
| **Grants Pass, OR M.S.A.** | 87,577 | | | | | | | | | |
| Includes Josephine County | | | | | | | | | | |
| City of Grants Pass | 38,420 | 133 | 0 | 27 | 25 | 81 | 1,160 | 131 | 901 | 128 |
| Total area actually reporting | 100.0% | 252 | 9 | 40 | 34 | 169 | 1,500 | 171 | 1,045 | 284 |
| Rate per 100,000 inhabitants | | 287.7 | 10.3 | 45.7 | 38.8 | 193.0 | 1,712.8 | 195.3 | 1,193.2 | 324.3 |
| **Great Falls, MT M.S.A.** | 81,529 | | | | | | | | | |
| Includes Cascade County | | | | | | | | | | |
| City of Great Falls | 58,345 | 266 | 0 | 43 | 28 | 195 | 2,999 | 293 | 2,535 | 171 |
| Total area actually reporting | 100.0% | 359 | 0 | 55 | 28 | 276 | 3,261 | 355 | 2,719 | 187 |
| Rate per 100,000 inhabitants | | 440.3 | 0.0 | 67.5 | 34.3 | 338.5 | 3,999.8 | 435.4 | 3,335.0 | 229.4 |
| **Greeley, CO M.S.A.** | 331,283 | | | | | | | | | |
| Includes Weld County | | | | | | | | | | |
| City of Greeley | 110,505 | 470 | 9 | 53 | 78 | 330 | 2,722 | 369 | 1,961 | 392 |
| Total area actually reporting | 97.3% | 1,053 | 16 | 174 | 130 | 733 | 6,799 | 819 | 4,781 | 1,199 |
| Estimated total | 100.0% | 1,074 | 16 | 177 | 134 | 747 | 7,165 | 838 | 5,076 | 1,251 |
| Rate per 100,000 inhabitants | | 324.2 | 4.8 | 53.4 | 40.4 | 225.5 | 2,162.8 | 253.0 | 1,532.2 | 377.6 |
| **Green Bay, WI M.S.A.** | 324,478 | | | | | | | | | |
| Includes Brown, Kewaunee, and Oconto Counties | | | | | | | | | | |
| City of Green Bay | 104,649 | 552 | 6 | 71 | 45 | 430 | 1,600 | 206 | 1,279 | 115 |
| Total area actually reporting | 100.0% | 730 | 8 | 121 | 52 | 549 | 3,216 | 475 | 2,554 | 187 |
| Rate per 100,000 inhabitants | | 225.0 | 2.5 | 37.3 | 16.0 | 169.2 | 991.1 | 146.4 | 787.1 | 57.6 |
| **Greensboro-High Point, NC M.S.A.** | 777,379 | | | | | | | | | |
| Includes Guilford, Randolph, and Rockingham Counties | | | | | | | | | | |
| City of Greensboro | 299,887 | 2,704 | 59 | 95 | 581 | 1,969 | 10,830 | 2,212 | 7,503 | 1,115 |
| City of High Point | 108,114 | 734 | 13 | 27 | 117 | 577 | 3,246 | 489 | 2442 | 315 |
| Total area actually reporting | 83.0% | 4,124 | 88 | 195 | 790 | 3,051 | 18,395 | 3,617 | 12,962 | 1,816 |
| Estimated total | 100.0% | 4,479 | 95 | 230 | 837 | 3,317 | 20,792 | 4,194 | 14,558 | 2,040 |
| Rate per 100,000 inhabitants | | 576.2 | 12.2 | 29.6 | 107.7 | 426.7 | 2,674.6 | 539.5 | 1,872.7 | 262.4 |
| **Greenville, NC M.S.A.** | 182,129 | | | | | | | | | |
| Includes Pitt County | | | | | | | | | | |
| City of Greenville | 94,372 | 415 | 13 | 26 | 71 | 305 | 2,481 | 360 | 2,006 | 115 |
| Total area actually reporting | 99.1% | 659 | 21 | 33 | 110 | 495 | 3,588 | 624 | 2,780 | 184 |
| Estimated total | 100.0% | 664 | 21 | 34 | 110 | 499 | 3,665 | 638 | 2,840 | 187 |
| Rate per 100,000 inhabitants | | 364.6 | 11.5 | 18.7 | 60.4 | 274.0 | 2,012.3 | 350.3 | 1,559.3 | 102.7 |
| **Hanford-Corcoran, CA M.S.A.** | 151,473 | | | | | | | | | |
| Includes Kings County | | | | | | | | | | |
| City of Hanford | 58,075 | 321 | 5 | 17 | 45 | 254 | 1,119 | 155 | 755 | 209 |
| City of Corcoran | 21,700 | 112 | 2 | 11 | 12 | 87 | 392 | 82 | 199 | 111 |
| Total area actually reporting | 100.0% | 777 | 11 | 63 | 91 | 612 | 2,506 | 451 | 1,498 | 557 |
| Rate per 100,000 inhabitants | | 513.0 | 7.3 | 41.6 | 60.1 | 404.0 | 1,654.4 | 297.7 | 989.0 | 367.7 |
| **Harrisonburg, VA M.S.A.** | 135,962 | | | | | | | | | |
| Includes Rockingham County and Harrisonburg City | | | | | | | | | | |
| City of Harrisonburg | 53,442 | 117 | 1 | 15 | 14 | 87 | 811 | 74 | 688 | 49 |
| Total area actually reporting | 100.0% | 207 | 5 | 41 | 16 | 145 | 1,335 | 177 | 1,065 | 93 |
| Rate per 100,000 inhabitants | | 152.2 | 3.7 | 30.2 | 11.8 | 106.6 | 981.9 | 130.2 | 783.3 | 68.4 |
| **Hartford-East Hartford-Middletown, CT M.S.A.** | 1,014,700 | | | | | | | | | |
| Includes Hartford, Middlesex, and Tolland Counties | | | | | | | | | | |
| City of Hartford | 121,749 | 1,208 | 23 | 31 | 280 | 874 | 3,787 | 430 | 2,708 | 649 |
| City of East Hartford | 49,720 | 77 | 0 | 12 | 37 | 28 | 1,208 | 101 | 886 | 221 |
| City of Middletown | 46,106 | 38 | 3 | 4 | 7 | 24 | 597 | 62 | 477 | 58 |
| Total area actually reporting | 100.0% | 2,211 | 37 | 175 | 614 | 1,385 | 21,196 | 2,381 | 16,043 | 2,772 |
| Rate per 100,000 inhabitants | | 217.9 | 3.6 | 17.2 | 60.5 | 136.5 | 2,088.9 | 234.7 | 1,581.1 | 273.2 |
| **Hattiesburg, MS M.S.A.** | 168,941 | | | | | | | | | |
| Includes Covington, Forrest, Lamar, and Perry Counties | | | | | | | | | | |
| City of Hattiesburg | 45,870 | 171 | 7 | 31 | 27 | 106 | 2,418 | 342 | 1,904 | 172 |
| Total area actually reporting | 80.6% | 306 | 10 | 62 | 41 | 193 | 3,377 | 639 | 2,480 | 258 |
| Estimated total | 100.0% | 422 | 10 | 102 | 43 | 267 | 3,743 | 720 | 2,705 | 318 |
| Rate per 100,000 inhabitants | | 249.8 | 5.9 | 60.4 | 25.5 | 158.0 | 2,215.6 | 426.2 | 1,601.2 | 188.2 |
| **Hilton Head Island-Bluffton, SC M.S.A.** | 226,652 | | | | | | | | | |
| Includes Beaufort and Jasper Counties | | | | | | | | | | |
| City of Bluffton | 27,549 | 25 | 0 | 7 | 2 | 16 | 199 | 38 | 145 | 16 |
| Total area actually reporting | 91.6% | 642 | 16 | 60 | 61 | 505 | 3,009 | 435 | 2,356 | 218 |
| Estimated total | 100.0% | 741 | 22 | 65 | 67 | 587 | 3,354 | 516 | 2,580 | 258 |
| Rate per 100,000 inhabitants | | 326.9 | 9.7 | 28.7 | 29.6 | 259.0 | 1,479.8 | 227.7 | 1,138.3 | 113.8 |

## Table 6. Crime in the United States, by Selected Metropolitan Statistical Area, 2020—Continued

(Number, percent, rate per 100,000 population.)

| Area | Population | Violent crime | Murder and nonnegligent manslaughter | Rape[1] | Robbery | Aggravated assault | Property crime | Burglary | Larceny-theft | Motor vehicle theft |
|---|---|---|---|---|---|---|---|---|---|---|
| **Homosassa Springs, FL M.S.A.** | 150,189 | | | | | | | | | |
| Includes Citrus County | | | | | | | | | | |
| Total area actually reporting | 100.0% | 405 | 7 | 25 | 38 | 335 | 1,928 | 334 | 1,403 | 191 |
| Rate per 100,000 inhabitants | | 269.7 | 4.7 | 16.6 | 25.3 | 223.1 | 1,283.7 | 222.4 | 934.2 | 127.2 |
| **Hot Springs, AR M.S.A.** | 99,763 | | | | | | | | | |
| Includes Garland County | | | | | | | | | | |
| City of Hot Springs | 38,893 | 287 | 9 | 39 | 43 | 196 | 2,276 | 656 | 1,431 | 189 |
| Total area actually reporting | 100.0% | 582 | 9 | 77 | 53 | 443 | 3,575 | 1,200 | 2,052 | 323 |
| Rate per 100,000 inhabitants | | 583.4 | 9.0 | 77.2 | 53.1 | 444.1 | 3,583.5 | 1,202.9 | 2,056.9 | 323.8 |
| **Houston-The Woodlands-Sugar Land, TX M.S.A.[2]** | 7,180,258 | | | | | | | | | |
| Includes Austin, Brazoria, Chambers, Fort Bend, Galveston, Harris, | | | | | | | | | | |
|   Liberty, Montgomery, and Waller Counties | | | | | | | | | | |
| City of Houston | 2,346,155 | 29,474 | 400 | 1,137 | 8,757 | 19,180 | 98,043 | 15,788 | 67,474 | 14,781 |
| City of Sugar Land[2] | 119,671 | 68 | 4 | 8 | 20 | 36 | 1,277 | 111 | 1,077 | 89 |
| City of Baytown[2] | 77,823 | 338 | 9 | 43 | 85 | 201 | 2,917 | 390 | 2,106 | 421 |
| City of Conroe | 94,451 | 175 | 2 | 35 | 47 | 91 | 2,336 | 246 | 1,914 | 176 |
| City of Galveston[2] | 50,751 | 327 | 6 | 80 | 65 | 176 | 1,694 | 225 | 1,217 | 252 |
| Total area actually reporting | 99.9% | 45,358 | 662 | 3,206 | 12,057 | 29,433 | 187,868 | 28,857 | 132,143 | 26,868 |
| Estimated total | 100.0% | 45,368 | 662 | 3,208 | 12,057 | 29,441 | 187,935 | 28,871 | 132,187 | 26,877 |
| Rate per 100,000 inhabitants | | 631.8 | 9.2 | 44.7 | 167.9 | 410.0 | 2,617.4 | 402.1 | 1,841.0 | 374.3 |
| **Huntington-Ashland, WV-KY-OH M.S.A.** | 353,926 | | | | | | | | | |
| Includes Boyd, Carter, and Greenup Counties, KY; Lawrence County OH; | | | | | | | | | | |
|   and Cabell, Putnam, and Wayne Counties, WV | | | | | | | | | | |
| City of Huntington, WV | 44,684 | 368 | 7 | 35 | 69 | 257 | 1,642 | 378 | 1,083 | 181 |
| City of Ashland, KY | 19,979 | 41 | 1 | 7 | 7 | 26 | 642 | 105 | 490 | 47 |
| Total area actually reporting | 87.3% | 719 | 12 | 153 | 89 | 465 | 4,704 | 933 | 3,299 | 472 |
| Estimated total | 100.0% | 850 | 14 | 164 | 101 | 571 | 5,213 | 1,015 | 3,697 | 501 |
| Rate per 100,000 inhabitants | | 240.2 | 4.0 | 46.3 | 28.5 | 161.3 | 1,472.9 | 286.8 | 1,044.6 | 141.6 |
| **Idaho Falls, ID M.S.A.** | 154,789 | | | | | | | | | |
| Includes Bonneville, Butte, and Jefferson Counties | | | | | | | | | | |
| City of Idaho Falls | 63,457 | 291 | 2 | 35 | 18 | 236 | 1,152 | 325 | 704 | 123 |
| Total area actually reporting | 100.0% | 439 | 4 | 57 | 25 | 353 | 1,994 | 534 | 1,241 | 219 |
| Rate per 100,000 inhabitants | | 283.6 | 2.6 | 36.8 | 16.2 | 228.1 | 1,288.2 | 345.0 | 801.7 | 141.5 |
| **Iowa City, IA M.S.A.** | 175,256 | | | | | | | | | |
| Includes Johnson and Washington Counties | | | | | | | | | | |
| City of Iowa City | 75,964 | 151 | 2 | 21 | 16 | 112 | 1,335 | 261 | 934 | 140 |
| Total area actually reporting | 99.4% | 471 | 3 | 80 | 26 | 362 | 2,599 | 501 | 1,880 | 218 |
| Estimated total | 100.0% | 475 | 3 | 80 | 27 | 365 | 2,623 | 506 | 1,896 | 221 |
| Rate per 100,000 inhabitants | | 271.0 | 1.7 | 45.6 | 15.4 | 208.3 | 1,496.7 | 288.7 | 1,081.8 | 126.1 |
| **Ithaca, NY M.S.A** | 101,580 | | | | | | | | | |
| Includes Tompkins County | | | | | | | | | | |
| City of Ithaca | 30,927 | 98 | 0 | 14 | 31 | 53 | 1,157 | 141 | 1,000 | 16 |
| Total area actually reporting | 100.0% | 163 | 0 | 45 | 35 | 83 | 1,924 | 224 | 1,660 | 40 |
| Rate per 100,000 inhabitants | | 160.5 | 0.0 | 44.3 | 34.5 | 81.7 | 1,894.1 | 220.5 | 1,634.2 | 39.4 |
| **Jackson, MI M.S.A.** | 157,798 | | | | | | | | | |
| Includes Jackson County | | | | | | | | | | |
| City of Jackson | 32,332 | 350 | 7 | 47 | 32 | 264 | 1,001 | 173 | 722 | 106 |
| Total area actually reporting | 100.0% | 881 | 14 | 170 | 44 | 653 | 2,641 | 392 | 1,984 | 265 |
| Rate per 100,000 inhabitants | | 558.3 | 8.9 | 107.7 | 27.9 | 413.8 | 1,673.7 | 248.4 | 1,257.3 | 167.9 |
| **Jackson, TN M.S.A.** | 178,525 | | | | | | | | | |
| Includes Chester, Crockett, Gibson, and Madison Counties | | | | | | | | | | |
| City of Jackson | 67,234 | 703 | 12 | 21 | 87 | 583 | 2,414 | 361 | 1,814 | 239 |
| Total area actually reporting | 100.0% | 1,115 | 17 | 46 | 106 | 946 | 3,840 | 701 | 2,750 | 389 |
| Rate per 100,000 inhabitants | | 624.6 | 9.5 | 25.8 | 59.4 | 529.9 | 2,151.0 | 392.7 | 1,540.4 | 217.9 |
| **Jacksonville, FL M.S.A.** | 1,580,803 | | | | | | | | | |
| Includes Baker, Clay, Duval, Nassau, and St. Johns Counties | | | | | | | | | | |
| City of Jacksonville | 920,508 | 6,424 | 140 | 456 | 928 | 4,900 | 26,432 | 3,860 | 19,602 | 2,970 |
| Total area actually reporting | 100.0% | 7,901 | 156 | 641 | 1,085 | 6,019 | 34,037 | 4,996 | 25,414 | 3,627 |
| Rate per 100,000 inhabitants | | 499.8 | 9.9 | 40.5 | 68.6 | 380.8 | 2,153.1 | 316.0 | 1,607.7 | 229.4 |
| **Jacksonville, NC M.S.A.** | 199,234 | | | | | | | | | |
| Includes Onslow County | | | | | | | | | | |
| City of Jacksonville | 71,842 | 245 | 3 | 24 | 23 | 195 | 1,481 | 263 | 1,153 | 65 |
| Total area actually reporting | 100.0% | 419 | 4 | 40 | 40 | 335 | 3,151 | 720 | 2,236 | 195 |
| Rate per 100,000 inhabitants | | 210.3 | 2.0 | 20.1 | 20.1 | 168.1 | 1,581.6 | 361.4 | 1,122.3 | 97.9 |
| **Janesville-Beloit, WI M.S.A.** | 163,558 | | | | | | | | | |
| Includes Rock County | | | | | | | | | | |
| City of Janesville | 64,682 | 145 | 4 | 31 | 36 | 74 | 1,392 | 136 | 1,200 | 56 |
| City of Beloit | 36,921 | 179 | 2 | 23 | 34 | 120 | 1,069 | 117 | 878 | 74 |
| Total area actually reporting | 100.0% | 381 | 6 | 63 | 75 | 237 | 2,916 | 324 | 2,427 | 165 |
| Rate per 100,000 inhabitants | | 232.9 | 3.7 | 38.5 | 45.9 | 144.9 | 1,782.9 | 198.1 | 1,483.9 | 100.9 |

## Table 6. Crime in the United States, by Selected Metropolitan Statistical Area, 2020—Continued

(Number, percent, rate per 100,000 population.)

| Area | Population | Violent crime | Murder and nonnegligent manslaughter | Rape[1] | Robbery | Aggravated assault | Property crime | Burglary | Larceny-theft | Motor vehicle theft |
|---|---|---|---|---|---|---|---|---|---|---|
| **Jefferson City, MO M.S.A.[2]** | 151,302 | | | | | | | | | |
| Includes Callaway,[2] Cole,[2] Moniteau, and Osage Counties | | | | | | | | | | |
| City of Jefferson City | 42,653 | 109 | 2 | 17 | 16 | 74 | 821 | 70 | 658 | 93 |
| Total area actually reporting | 97.8% | 238 | 4 | 44 | 19 | 171 | 2,367 | 425 | 1,702 | 240 |
| Estimated total | 100.0% | 251 | 4 | 45 | 20 | 182 | 2,465 | 436 | 1,775 | 254 |
| Rate per 100,000 inhabitants | | 165.9 | 2.6 | 29.7 | 13.2 | 120.3 | 1,629.2 | 288.2 | 1,173.2 | 167.9 |
| **Johnson City, TN M.S.A.** | 204,189 | | | | | | | | | |
| Includes Carter, Unicoi, and Washington Counties | | | | | | | | | | |
| City of Johnson City | 66,917 | 295 | 3 | 29 | 38 | 225 | 2,701 | 285 | 2,173 | 243 |
| Total area actually reporting | 100.0% | 625 | 6 | 56 | 51 | 512 | 4,371 | 567 | 3,231 | 573 |
| Rate per 100,000 inhabitants | | 306.1 | 2.9 | 27.4 | 25.0 | 250.7 | 2,140.7 | 277.7 | 1,582.4 | 280.6 |
| **Jonesboro, AR M.S.A.** | 135,377 | | | | | | | | | |
| Includes Craighead and Poinsett Counties | | | | | | | | | | |
| City of Jonesboro | 79,702 | 642 | 12 | 78 | 55 | 497 | 2,825 | 1,038 | 1,576 | 211 |
| Total area actually reporting | 95.8% | 871 | 13 | 130 | 63 | 665 | 3,847 | 1,339 | 2,193 | 315 |
| Estimated total | 100.0% | 893 | 13 | 132 | 67 | 681 | 3,964 | 1,358 | 2,276 | 330 |
| Rate per 100,000 inhabitants | | 659.6 | 9.6 | 97.5 | 49.5 | 503.0 | 2,928.1 | 1,003.1 | 1,681.2 | 243.8 |
| **Joplin, MO M.S.A.[2]** | 179,903 | | | | | | | | | |
| Includes Jasper and Newton[2] Counties | | | | | | | | | | |
| City of Joplin | 50,935 | 338 | 9 | 49 | 67 | 213 | 3,276 | 379 | 2,528 | 369 |
| Total area actually reporting | 100.0% | 655 | 11 | 98 | 91 | 455 | 6,354 | 868 | 4,761 | 725 |
| Rate per 100,000 inhabitants | | 364.1 | 6.1 | 54.5 | 50.6 | 252.9 | 3,531.9 | 482.5 | 2,646.4 | 403.0 |
| **Kahului-Wailuku-Lahaina, HI M.S.A.** | 167,178 | | | | | | | | | |
| Includes Maui County | | | | | | | | | | |
| Total area actually reporting | 100.0% | 379 | 5 | 71 | 59 | 244 | 3,537 | 496 | 2,612 | 429 |
| Rate per 100,000 inhabitants | | 226.7 | 3.0 | 42.5 | 35.3 | 146.0 | 2,115.7 | 296.7 | 1,562.4 | 256.6 |
| **Kalamazoo-Portage, MI M.S.A.** | 265,804 | | | | | | | | | |
| Includes Kalamazoo County | | | | | | | | | | |
| City of Kalamazoo | 76,411 | 1,094 | 14 | 77 | 136 | 867 | 3,670 | 737 | 2,445 | 488 |
| City of Portage | 49,798 | 111 | 2 | 15 | 10 | 84 | 1,340 | 153 | 1,098 | 89 |
| Total area actually reporting | 100.0% | 1,763 | 20 | 175 | 199 | 1,369 | 8,789 | 1,571 | 6,144 | 1,074 |
| Rate per 100,000 inhabitants | | 663.3 | 7.5 | 65.8 | 74.9 | 515.0 | 3,306.6 | 591.0 | 2,311.5 | 404.1 |
| **Kankakee, IL M.S.A.[4]** | 108,899 | | | | | | | | | |
| Includes Kankakee County[4] | | | | | | | | | | |
| City of Kankakee[4] | 25,863 | 244 | 8 | 23 | 33 | 180 | | 112 | | 52 |
| Total area actually reporting | 75.7% | 340 | 9 | 50 | 41 | 240 | | 203 | | 93 |
| Estimated total | 100.0% | 387 | 10 | 57 | 52 | 268 | | 250 | | 120 |
| Rate per 100,000 inhabitants | | 355.4 | 9.2 | 52.3 | 47.8 | 246.1 | | 229.6 | | 110.2 |
| **Kennewick-Richland, WA M.S.A.** | 303,959 | | | | | | | | | |
| Includes Benton and Franklin Counties | | | | | | | | | | |
| City of Kennewick | 85,526 | 215 | 1 | 38 | 46 | 130 | 2,836 | 521 | 2,097 | 218 |
| City of Richland | 59,370 | 164 | 3 | 33 | 18 | 110 | 1,553 | 267 | 1,216 | 70 |
| Total area actually reporting | 100.0% | 718 | 9 | 116 | 133 | 460 | 6,869 | 1,323 | 5,010 | 536 |
| Rate per 100,000 inhabitants | | 236.2 | 3.0 | 38.2 | 43.8 | 151.3 | 2,259.8 | 435.3 | 1,648.2 | 176.3 |
| **Killeen-Temple, TX M.S.A.[2,3]** | 464,991 | | | | | | | | | |
| Includes Bell, Coryell, and Lampasas Counties[2] | | | | | | | | | | |
| City of Killeen[2,3] | 154,417 | 1,033 | 26 | 87 | 159 | 761 | | | 1,851 | 436 |
| City of Temple | 79,878 | 297 | 8 | 64 | 29 | 196 | 2,098 | 302 | 1,460 | 336 |
| Total area actually reporting | 99.6% | 1,750 | 48 | 216 | 228 | 1,258 | | | 5,641 | 1,047 |
| Estimated total | 100.0% | 1,754 | 48 | 216 | 228 | 1,262 | | | 5,663 | 1,052 |
| Rate per 100,000 inhabitants | | 377.2 | 10.3 | 46.5 | 49.0 | 271.4 | | | 1,217.9 | 226.2 |
| **Kingsport-Bristol, TN-VA M.S.A.** | 306,891 | | | | | | | | | |
| Includes Hawkins and Sullivan Counties, TN and Scott and Washington Counties and Bristol City, VA | | | | | | | | | | |
| City of Kingsport, TN | 54,260 | 372 | 5 | 40 | 28 | 299 | 2,426 | 271 | 1,856 | 299 |
| City of Bristol, TN | 27,013 | 155 | 3 | 19 | 10 | 123 | 774 | 73 | 617 | 84 |
| Total area actually reporting | 100.0% | 1,116 | 20 | 144 | 59 | 893 | 6,466 | 919 | 4,679 | 868 |
| Rate per 100,000 inhabitants | | 363.6 | 6.5 | 46.9 | 19.2 | 291.0 | 2,106.9 | 299.5 | 1,524.6 | 282.8 |
| **Kingston, NY M.S.A.** | 175,918 | | | | | | | | | |
| Includes Ulster County | | | | | | | | | | |
| City of Kingston | 22,682 | 85 | 3 | 12 | 17 | 53 | 455 | 55 | 378 | 22 |
| Total area actually reporting | 92.0% | 224 | 5 | 64 | 25 | 130 | 1,550 | 178 | 1,303 | 69 |
| Estimated total | 100.0% | 246 | 5 | 67 | 29 | 145 | 1,846 | 208 | 1,561 | 77 |
| Rate per 100,000 inhabitants | | 139.8 | 2.8 | 38.1 | 16.5 | 82.4 | 1,049.4 | 118.2 | 887.3 | 43.8 |
| **Knoxville, TN M.S.A.** | 875,248 | | | | | | | | | |
| Includes Anderson, Blount, Campbell, Knox, Loudon, Morgan, Roane, and Union Counties | | | | | | | | | | |
| City of Knoxville | 188,672 | 1,528 | 38 | 124 | 241 | 1,125 | 7,977 | 1,080 | 5,775 | 1,122 |
| Total area actually reporting | 100.0% | 3,343 | 56 | 326 | 328 | 2,633 | 17,024 | 2,674 | 11,953 | 2,397 |
| Rate per 100,000 inhabitants | | 381.9 | 6.4 | 37.2 | 37.5 | 300.8 | 1,945.0 | 305.5 | 1,365.7 | 273.9 |

## Table 6. Crime in the United States, by Selected Metropolitan Statistical Area, 2020—Continued

(Number, percent, rate per 100,000 population.)

| Area | Population | Violent crime | Murder and nonnegligent manslaughter | Rape[1] | Robbery | Aggravated assault | Property crime | Burglary | Larceny-theft | Motor vehicle theft |
|---|---|---|---|---|---|---|---|---|---|---|
| **Kokomo, IN M.S.A.[2]** | 82,444 | | | | | | | | | |
| Includes Howard County[2] | | | | | | | | | | |
| City of Kokomo[2] | 58,001 | 437 | 8 | 25 | 38 | 366 | 1,152 | 225 | 838 | 89 |
| Total area actually reporting | 98.6% | 490 | 8 | 28 | 40 | 414 | 1,291 | 267 | 921 | 103 |
| Estimated total | 100.0% | 498 | 8 | 29 | 42 | 419 | 1,313 | 276 | 933 | 104 |
| Rate per 100,000 inhabitants | | 604.0 | 9.7 | 35.2 | 50.9 | 508.2 | 1,592.6 | 334.8 | 1,131.7 | 126.1 |
| **La Crosse-Onalaska, WI-MN M.S.A.[2]** | 136,752 | | | | | | | | | |
| Includes Houston County, MN[2] and La Crosse County, WI | | | | | | | | | | |
| City of La Crosse, WI | 51,211 | 131 | 1 | 34 | 26 | 70 | 2,236 | 170 | 1,958 | 108 |
| City of Onalaska, WI | 19,072 | 19 | 0 | 1 | 5 | 13 | 715 | 44 | 655 | 16 |
| Total area actually reporting | 100.0% | 213 | 1 | 46 | 31 | 135 | 3,421 | 293 | 2,975 | 153 |
| Rate per 100,000 inhabitants | | 155.8 | 0.7 | 33.6 | 22.7 | 98.7 | 2,501.6 | 214.3 | 2,175.5 | 111.9 |
| **Lafayette, LA M.S.A.** | 489,998 | | | | | | | | | |
| Includes Acadia, Iberia, Lafayette, St. Martin, and Vermilion Parishes | | | | | | | | | | |
| City of Lafayette | 126,679 | 712 | 14 | 17 | 147 | 534 | 5,725 | 1,069 | 4,247 | 409 |
| Total area actually reporting | 84.7% | 1,919 | 37 | 75 | 227 | 1,580 | 10,679 | 2,284 | 7,553 | 842 |
| Estimated total | 100.0% | 2,205 | 41 | 104 | 276 | 1,784 | 12,188 | 2,523 | 8,644 | 1,021 |
| Rate per 100,000 inhabitants | | 450.0 | 8.4 | 21.2 | 56.3 | 364.1 | 2,487.4 | 514.9 | 1,764.1 | 208.4 |
| **Lake Charles, LA M.S.A.[2]** | 210,851 | | | | | | | | | |
| Includes Calcasieu and Cameron Parishes | | | | | | | | | | |
| City of Lake Charles[2] | 79,077 | 409 | 7 | 31 | 49 | 322 | 2,511 | 849 | 1,424 | 238 |
| Total area actually reporting | 95.2% | 1,625 | 19 | 123 | 87 | 1,396 | 7,839 | 2,215 | 4,924 | 700 |
| Estimated total | 100.0% | 1,663 | 19 | 127 | 94 | 1,423 | 8,041 | 2,247 | 5,070 | 724 |
| Rate per 100,000 inhabitants | | 788.7 | 9.0 | 60.2 | 44.6 | 674.9 | 3,813.6 | 1,065.7 | 2,404.5 | 343.4 |
| **Lake Havasu City-Kingman, AZ M.S.A.[2]** | 214,625 | | | | | | | | | |
| Includes Mohave County | | | | | | | | | | |
| City of Lake Havasu City[2] | 56,243 | 105 | 0 | 27 | 3 | 75 | 790 | 115 | 619 | 56 |
| City of Kingman | 31,351 | 124 | 2 | 9 | 17 | 96 | 1,106 | 136 | 868 | 102 |
| Total area actually reporting | 100.0% | 490 | 14 | 50 | 47 | 379 | 4,643 | 889 | 3,324 | 430 |
| Rate per 100,000 inhabitants | | 228.3 | 6.5 | 23.3 | 21.9 | 176.6 | 2,163.3 | 414.2 | 1,548.7 | 200.3 |
| **Lakeland-Winter Haven, FL M.S.A.** | 737,548 | | | | | | | | | |
| Includes Polk County | | | | | | | | | | |
| City of Lakeland | 113,876 | 404 | 12 | 58 | 80 | 254 | 2,813 | 320 | 2,275 | 218 |
| City of Winter Haven | 46,275 | 171 | 4 | 19 | 12 | 136 | 920 | 125 | 724 | 71 |
| Total area actually reporting | 100.0% | 2,115 | 40 | 171 | 209 | 1,695 | 10,002 | 1,576 | 7,471 | 955 |
| Rate per 100,000 inhabitants | | 286.8 | 5.4 | 23.2 | 28.3 | 229.8 | 1,356.1 | 213.7 | 1,013.0 | 129.5 |
| **Lansing-East Lansing, MI M.S.A.** | 550,296 | | | | | | | | | |
| Includes Clinton, Eaton, Ingham, and Shiawassee Counties | | | | | | | | | | |
| City of Lansing | 118,651 | 1,699 | 16 | 121 | 195 | 1,367 | 3,565 | 1,002 | 1,993 | 570 |
| City of East Lansing | 48,098 | 74 | 0 | 17 | 13 | 44 | 817 | 86 | 568 | 163 |
| Total area actually reporting | 100.0% | 2,741 | 23 | 385 | 259 | 2,074 | 9,020 | 1,795 | 6,111 | 1,114 |
| Rate per 100,000 inhabitants | | 498.1 | 4.2 | 70.0 | 47.1 | 376.9 | 1,639.1 | 326.2 | 1,110.5 | 202.4 |
| **Laredo, TX M.S.A.[2]** | 278,663 | | | | | | | | | |
| Includes Webb County[2] | | | | | | | | | | |
| City of Laredo | 265,515 | 859 | 12 | 90 | 156 | 601 | 3,836 | 626 | 2,994 | 216 |
| Total area actually reporting | 98.3% | 924 | 12 | 95 | 158 | 659 | 4,093 | 705 | 3,146 | 242 |
| Estimated total | 100.0% | 936 | 12 | 96 | 159 | 669 | 4,175 | 719 | 3,207 | 249 |
| Rate per 100,000 inhabitants | | 335.9 | 4.3 | 34.5 | 57.1 | 240.1 | 1,498.2 | 258.0 | 1,150.9 | 89.4 |
| **Las Vegas-Henderson-Paradise, NV M.S.A.[2]** | 2,313,970 | | | | | | | | | |
| Includes Clark County | | | | | | | | | | |
| City of Las Vegas Metropolitan Police Department[2] | 1,693,061 | 8,934 | 96 | 1,068 | 1,707 | 6,063 | 37,426 | 7,057 | 23,546 | 6,823 |
| City of Henderson[2] | 328,056 | 682 | 13 | 104 | 177 | 388 | 4,679 | 619 | 3,516 | 544 |
| Total area actually reporting | 100.0% | 11,077 | 127 | 1,264 | 2,322 | 7,364 | 47,356 | 8,683 | 30,109 | 8,564 |
| Rate per 100,000 inhabitants | | 478.7 | 5.5 | 54.6 | 100.3 | 318.2 | 2,046.5 | 375.2 | 1,301.2 | 370.1 |
| **Lawton, OK M.S.A.** | 125,862 | | | | | | | | | |
| Includes Comanche and Cotton Counties | | | | | | | | | | |
| City of Lawton | 92,507 | 727 | 14 | 79 | 102 | 532 | 2,071 | 632 | 1,166 | 273 |
| Total area actually reporting | 100.0% | 759 | 16 | 85 | 106 | 552 | 2,343 | 723 | 1,305 | 315 |
| Rate per 100,000 inhabitants | | 603.0 | 12.7 | 67.5 | 84.2 | 438.6 | 1,861.6 | 574.4 | 1,036.8 | 250.3 |
| **Lewiston, ID-WA M.S.A.** | 63,436 | | | | | | | | | |
| Includes Nez Perce County, ID and Asotin County, WA | | | | | | | | | | |
| City of Lewiston, ID | 32,886 | 61 | 1 | 15 | 4 | 41 | 767 | 135 | 582 | 50 |
| Total area actually reporting | 100.0% | 117 | 3 | 27 | 7 | 80 | 1,307 | 254 | 968 | 85 |
| Rate per 100,000 inhabitants | | 184.4 | 4.7 | 42.6 | 11.0 | 126.1 | 2,060.3 | 400.4 | 1,525.9 | 134.0 |
| **Lewiston-Auburn, ME M.S.A.[2]** | 108,661 | | | | | | | | | |
| Includes Androscoggin County[2] | | | | | | | | | | |
| City of Lewiston | 36,186 | 97 | 2 | 26 | 16 | 53 | 639 | 81 | 519 | 39 |
| City of Auburn | 23,455 | 46 | 2 | 18 | 6 | 20 | 518 | 41 | 455 | 22 |
| Total area actually reporting | 100.0% | 193 | 4 | 61 | 23 | 105 | 1,449 | 169 | 1,204 | 76 |
| Rate per 100,000 inhabitants | | 177.6 | 3.7 | 56.1 | 21.2 | 96.6 | 1,333.5 | 155.5 | 1,108.0 | 69.9 |

## Table 6. Crime in the United States, by Selected Metropolitan Statistical Area, 2020—Continued

(Number, percent, rate per 100,000 population.)

| Area | Population | Violent crime | Murder and nonnegligent manslaughter | Rape[1] | Robbery | Aggravated assault | Property crime | Burglary | Larceny-theft | Motor vehicle theft |
|---|---|---|---|---|---|---|---|---|---|---|
| **Lexington-Fayette, KY M.S.A.** | 521,623 | | | | | | | | | |
| Includes Bourbon, Clark, Fayette, Jessamine, Scott, and Woodford Counties | | | | | | | | | | |
| City of Lexington | 325,851 | 1,043 | 28 | 178 | 335 | 502 | 9,357 | 1,450 | 6,870 | 1,037 |
| Total area actually reporting | 100.0% | 1,308 | 31 | 236 | 391 | 650 | 13,357 | 2,072 | 9,824 | 1,461 |
| Rate per 100,000 inhabitants | | 250.8 | 5.9 | 45.2 | 75.0 | 124.6 | 2,560.7 | 397.2 | 1,883.4 | 280.1 |
| **Little Rock-North Little Rock-Conway, AR M.S.A.** | 747,089 | | | | | | | | | |
| Includes Faulkner, Grant, Lonoke, Perry, Pulaski, and Saline Counties | | | | | | | | | | |
| City of Little Rock | 197,688 | 3,657 | 49 | 196 | 376 | 3,036 | 9,602 | 1,527 | 7,062 | 1,013 |
| City of North Little Rock | 66,303 | 665 | 20 | 12 | 110 | 523 | 2,433 | 366 | 1,750 | 317 |
| City of Conway | 68,599 | 359 | 3 | 45 | 29 | 282 | 1,915 | 159 | 1,628 | 128 |
| Total area actually reporting | 100.0% | 7,014 | 98 | 504 | 664 | 5,748 | 23,746 | 4,039 | 17,116 | 2,591 |
| Rate per 100,000 inhabitants | | 938.8 | 13.1 | 67.5 | 88.9 | 769.4 | 3,178.5 | 540.6 | 2,291.0 | 346.8 |
| **Logan, UT-ID M.S.A.[2]** | 143,828 | | | | | | | | | |
| Includes Franklin County, ID and Cache County, UT[2] | | | | | | | | | | |
| City of Logan, UT | 51,899 | 100 | 0 | 41 | 6 | 53 | 592 | 82 | 472 | 38 |
| Total area actually reporting | 91.4% | 156 | 1 | 73 | 6 | 76 | 993 | 134 | 756 | 103 |
| Estimated total | 100.0% | 170 | 1 | 78 | 7 | 84 | 1,148 | 158 | 871 | 119 |
| Rate per 100,000 inhabitants | | 118.2 | 0.7 | 54.2 | 4.9 | 58.4 | 798.2 | 109.9 | 605.6 | 82.7 |
| **Longview, TX M.S.A.[2]** | 286,379 | | | | | | | | | |
| Includes Gregg, Harrison, Rusk, and Upshur[2] Counties | | | | | | | | | | |
| City of Longview | 81,751 | 276 | 10 | 62 | 47 | 157 | 2,362 | 461 | 1,729 | 172 |
| Total area actually reporting | 99.7% | 891 | 23 | 142 | 97 | 629 | 5,916 | 1,258 | 4,062 | 596 |
| Estimated total | 100.0% | 893 | 23 | 142 | 97 | 631 | 5,930 | 1,261 | 4,071 | 598 |
| Rate per 100,000 inhabitants | | 311.8 | 8.0 | 49.6 | 33.9 | 220.3 | 2,070.7 | 440.3 | 1,421.5 | 208.8 |
| **Longview, WA M.S.A.** | 111,183 | | | | | | | | | |
| Includes Cowlitz County | | | | | | | | | | |
| City of Longview | 38,629 | 99 | 0 | 25 | 20 | 54 | 1,196 | 214 | 846 | 136 |
| Total area actually reporting | 100.0% | 208 | 2 | 60 | 26 | 120 | 2,224 | 436 | 1,527 | 261 |
| Rate per 100,000 inhabitants | | 187.1 | 1.8 | 54.0 | 23.4 | 107.9 | 2,000.3 | 392.1 | 1,373.4 | 234.7 |
| **Los Angeles-Long Beach-Anaheim, CA M.S.A.** | 13,124,616 | | | | | | | | | |
| Includes the Metropolitan Divisions of Anaheim-Santa Ana-Irvine and Los Angeles-Long Beach-Glendale | | | | | | | | | | |
| City of Los Angeles | 4,000,587 | 28,882 | 351 | 1,983 | 8,013 | 18,535 | 85,932 | 13,773 | 50,990 | 21,169 |
| City of Long Beach | 462,654 | 2,343 | 36 | 242 | 721 | 1,344 | 12,707 | 2,554 | 7,373 | 2,780 |
| City of Anaheim | 351,913 | 1,241 | 16 | 133 | 412 | 680 | 8,865 | 1,229 | 5,897 | 1,739 |
| City of Santa Ana | 333,107 | 1,429 | 15 | 145 | 401 | 868 | 6,926 | 1,136 | 4,078 | 1,712 |
| City of Irvine | 297,069 | 152 | 1 | 36 | 49 | 66 | 4,452 | 828 | 3,336 | 288 |
| City of Glendale | 200,168 | 206 | 3 | 14 | 87 | 102 | 3,197 | 407 | 2,357 | 433 |
| City of Torrance | 143,421 | 274 | 3 | 44 | 105 | 122 | 2,935 | 378 | 2,060 | 497 |
| City of Pasadena | 141,473 | 414 | 7 | 51 | 118 | 238 | 3,021 | 654 | 2,015 | 352 |
| City of Orange | 138,846 | 180 | 4 | 14 | 54 | 108 | 2,396 | 504 | 1,468 | 424 |
| City of Costa Mesa | 113,317 | 488 | 2 | 64 | 116 | 306 | 3,581 | 513 | 2,699 | 369 |
| City of Burbank | 102,419 | 174 | 1 | 12 | 48 | 113 | 2,474 | 293 | 1,880 | 301 |
| City of Carson | 91,372 | 392 | 8 | 21 | 98 | 265 | 2,044 | 253 | 1,262 | 529 |
| City of Santa Monica | 90,474 | 541 | 1 | 38 | 167 | 335 | 3,852 | 931 | 2,530 | 391 |
| City of Newport Beach | 84,448 | 141 | 1 | 29 | 43 | 68 | 1,785 | 321 | 1,312 | 152 |
| City of Tustin | 79,795 | 148 | 0 | 13 | 76 | 59 | 2,131 | 283 | 1,586 | 262 |
| City of Gardena | 59,385 | 269 | 5 | 18 | 104 | 142 | 1,324 | 168 | 686 | 470 |
| City of Arcadia | 58,122 | 87 | 2 | 6 | 20 | 59 | 1,034 | 265 | 696 | 73 |
| City of Fountain Valley | 55,345 | 67 | 0 | 6 | 6 | 23 | 38 | 1,338 | 199 | 998 | 141 |
| Total area actually reporting | 100.0% | 62,030 | 737 | 4,538 | 17,385 | 39,370 | 274,976 | 46,244 | 169,909 | 58,823 |
| Rate per 100,000 inhabitants | | 472.6 | 5.6 | 34.6 | 132.5 | 300.0 | 2,095.1 | 352.3 | 1,294.6 | 448.2 |
| **Anaheim-Santa Ana-Irvine, CA M.D.** | 3,162,050 | | | | | | | | | |
| Includes Orange County | | | | | | | | | | |
| Total area actually reporting | 100.0% | 7,340 | 59 | 777 | 2,134 | 4,370 | 61,066 | 9,427 | 42,599 | 9,040 |
| Rate per 100,000 inhabitants | | 232.1 | 1.9 | 24.6 | 67.5 | 138.2 | 1,931.2 | 298.1 | 1,347.2 | 285.9 |
| **Los Angeles-Long Beach-Glendale, CA M.D.** | 9,962,566 | | | | | | | | | |
| Includes Los Angeles County | | | | | | | | | | |
| Total area actually reporting | 100.0% | 54,690 | 678 | 3,761 | 15,251 | 35,000 | 213,910 | 36,817 | 127,310 | 49,783 |
| Rate per 100,000 inhabitants | | 549.0 | 6.8 | 37.8 | 153.1 | 351.3 | 2,147.1 | 369.6 | 1,277.9 | 499.7 |
| **Lubbock, TX M.S.A.[2]** | 324,679 | | | | | | | | | |
| Includes Crosby, Lubbock, and Lynn[2] Counties | | | | | | | | | | |
| City of Lubbock | 262,146 | 2,852 | 28 | 225 | 431 | 2,168 | 10,770 | 2,296 | 7,316 | 1,158 |
| Total area actually reporting | 98.3% | 2,973 | 31 | 251 | 442 | 2,249 | 11,862 | 2,564 | 8,015 | 1,283 |
| Estimated total | 100.0% | 2,985 | 31 | 252 | 443 | 2,259 | 11,956 | 2,584 | 8,075 | 1,297 |
| Rate per 100,000 inhabitants | | 919.4 | 9.5 | 77.6 | 136.4 | 695.8 | 3,682.4 | 795.9 | 2,487.1 | 399.5 |
| **Lynchburg, VA M.S.A.** | 264,579 | | | | | | | | | |
| Includes Amherst, Appomattox, Bedford, and Campbell Counties and Lynchburg City | | | | | | | | | | |
| City of Lynchburg | 82,871 | 367 | 3 | 36 | 51 | 277 | 1,350 | 177 | 1,047 | 126 |
| Total area actually reporting | 100.0% | 646 | 9 | 84 | 64 | 489 | 3,103 | 378 | 2,446 | 279 |
| Rate per 100,000 inhabitants | | 244.2 | 3.4 | 31.7 | 24.2 | 184.8 | 1,172.8 | 142.9 | 924.5 | 105.5 |

## Table 6. Crime in the United States, by Selected Metropolitan Statistical Area, 2020—Continued

(Number, percent, rate per 100,000 population.)

| Area | Population | Violent crime | Murder and nonnegligent manslaughter | Rape[1] | Robbery | Aggravated assault | Property crime | Burglary | Larceny-theft | Motor vehicle theft |
|---|---|---|---|---|---|---|---|---|---|---|
| **Macon-Bibb County, GA M.S.A.[2]** | 229,395 | | | | | | | | | |
| Includes Bibb,[2] Crawford,[2] Jones,[2] Monroe, and Twiggs[2] Counties | | | | | | | | | | |
| Total area actually reporting | 87.5% | 1,529 | 42 | 69 | 212 | 1,206 | 5,863 | 1,008 | 4,084 | 771 |
| Estimated total | 100.0% | 1,624 | 44 | 78 | 222 | 1,280 | 6,299 | 1,088 | 4,369 | 842 |
| Rate per 100,000 inhabitants | | 707.9 | 19.2 | 34.0 | 96.8 | 558.0 | 2,745.9 | 474.3 | 1,904.6 | 367.1 |
| **Madera, CA M.S.A.** | 156,466 | | | | | | | | | |
| Includes Madera County | | | | | | | | | | |
| City of Madera | 66,351 | 310 | 4 | 35 | 69 | 202 | 1,141 | 200 | 691 | 250 |
| Total area actually reporting | 100.0% | 578 | 9 | 61 | 105 | 403 | 2,132 | 353 | 1,329 | 450 |
| Rate per 100,000 inhabitants | | 369.4 | 5.8 | 39.0 | 67.1 | 257.6 | 1,362.6 | 225.6 | 849.4 | 287.6 |
| **Madison, WI M.S.A.** | 671,149 | | | | | | | | | |
| Includes Columbia, Dane, Green, and Iowa Counties | | | | | | | | | | |
| City of Madison | 262,736 | 842 | 10 | 74 | 165 | 593 | 7,301 | 1,307 | 5,346 | 648 |
| Total area actually reporting | 98.3% | 1,310 | 16 | 157 | 228 | 909 | 11,885 | 1,914 | 8,980 | 991 |
| Estimated total | 100.0% | 1,354 | 17 | 161 | 236 | 940 | 12,117 | 1,951 | 9,148 | 1,018 |
| Rate per 100,000 inhabitants | | 201.7 | 2.5 | 24.0 | 35.2 | 140.1 | 1,805.4 | 290.7 | 1,363.0 | 151.7 |
| **Manchester-Nashua, NH M.S.A.** | 419,347 | | | | | | | | | |
| Includes Hillsborough County | | | | | | | | | | |
| City of Manchester | 113,018 | 670 | 5 | 73 | 110 | 482 | 2,560 | 287 | 2,096 | 177 |
| City of Nashua | 89,671 | 107 | 0 | 54 | 12 | 41 | 818 | 54 | 710 | 54 |
| Total area actually reporting | 98.3% | 886 | 5 | 173 | 133 | 575 | 4,631 | 461 | 3,860 | 310 |
| Estimated total | 100.0% | 913 | 5 | 177 | 137 | 594 | 4,772 | 484 | 3,962 | 326 |
| Rate per 100,000 inhabitants | | 217.7 | 1.2 | 42.2 | 32.7 | 141.6 | 1,138.0 | 115.4 | 944.8 | 77.7 |
| **Manhattan, KS M.S.A.[3]** | 130,281 | | | | | | | | | |
| Includes Geary, Pottawatomie,[3] and Riley Counties | | | | | | | | | | |
| Total area actually reporting | 96.3% | 478 | 6 | 65 | 20 | 387 | | | 1,573 | 151 |
| Estimated total | 100.0% | 490 | 6 | 67 | 21 | 396 | | | 1,658 | 163 |
| Rate per 100,000 inhabitants | | 376.1 | 4.6 | 51.4 | 16.1 | 304.0 | | | 1,272.6 | 125.1 |
| **Mankato, MN M.S.A.[2]** | 102,134 | | | | | | | | | |
| Includes Blue Earth and Nicollet[2] Counties | | | | | | | | | | |
| City of Mankato | 43,276 | 108 | 1 | 30 | 11 | 66 | 1,033 | 115 | 855 | 63 |
| Total area actually reporting | 100.0% | 191 | 1 | 49 | 15 | 126 | 1,479 | 196 | 1,187 | 96 |
| Rate per 100,000 inhabitants | | 187.0 | 1.0 | 48.0 | 14.7 | 123.4 | 1,448.1 | 191.9 | 1,162.2 | 94.0 |
| **McAllen-Edinburg-Mission, TX M.S.A.[2]** | 876,280 | | | | | | | | | |
| Includes Hidalgo County[2] | | | | | | | | | | |
| City of McAllen | 144,569 | 123 | 3 | 43 | 23 | 54 | 2,791 | 139 | 2,603 | 49 |
| City of Edinburg | 103,491 | 325 | 6 | 79 | 36 | 204 | 2,310 | 281 | 1,966 | 63 |
| City of Mission | 85,052 | 132 | 1 | 27 | 14 | 90 | 1,304 | 133 | 1,096 | 75 |
| Total area actually reporting | 98.1% | 2,363 | 35 | 419 | 271 | 1,638 | 15,559 | 2,055 | 12,658 | 846 |
| Estimated total | 100.0% | 2,408 | 35 | 424 | 276 | 1,673 | 15,851 | 2,104 | 12,877 | 870 |
| Rate per 100,000 inhabitants | | 274.8 | 4.0 | 48.4 | 31.5 | 190.9 | 1,808.9 | 240.1 | 1,469.5 | 99.3 |
| **Medford, OR M.S.A.** | 221,880 | | | | | | | | | |
| Includes Jackson County | | | | | | | | | | |
| City of Medford | 84,016 | 388 | 2 | 36 | 94 | 256 | 3,615 | 296 | 3,012 | 307 |
| Total area actually reporting | 100.0% | 663 | 3 | 67 | 122 | 471 | 6,289 | 698 | 5,058 | 533 |
| Rate per 100,000 inhabitants | | 298.8 | 1.4 | 30.2 | 55.0 | 212.3 | 2,834.4 | 314.6 | 2,279.6 | 240.2 |
| **Memphis, TN-MS-AR M.S.A.[2]** | 1,348,509 | | | | | | | | | |
| Includes Crittenden County, AR; DeSoto, Marshall, Tate, and Tunica[2] Counties, MS; and Fayette, Shelby, and Tipton Counties, TN | | | | | | | | | | |
| City of Memphis, TN | 650,937 | 15,310 | 289 | 411 | 2,131 | 12,479 | 36,197 | 5,831 | 25,924 | 4,442 |
| Total area actually reporting | 95.3% | 18,195 | 324 | 605 | 2,375 | 14,891 | 49,358 | 7,664 | 35,783 | 5,911 |
| Estimated total | 100.0% | 18,324 | 327 | 648 | 2,384 | 14,965 | 50,144 | 7,822 | 36,321 | 6,001 |
| Rate per 100,000 inhabitants | | 1,358.8 | 24.2 | 48.1 | 176.8 | 1,109.7 | 3,718.5 | 580.0 | 2,693.4 | 445.0 |
| **Merced, CA M.S.A.** | 277,305 | | | | | | | | | |
| Includes Merced County | | | | | | | | | | |
| City of Merced | 84,197 | 672 | 7 | 40 | 133 | 492 | 1,949 | 390 | 1,132 | 427 |
| Total area actually reporting | 100.0% | 1,660 | 24 | 84 | 252 | 1,300 | 5,951 | 1,285 | 3,320 | 1,346 |
| Rate per 100,000 inhabitants | | 598.6 | 8.7 | 30.3 | 90.9 | 468.8 | 2,146.0 | 463.4 | 1,197.2 | 485.4 |
| **Miami-Fort Lauderdale-Pompano Beach, FL M.S.A.** | 6,216,543 | | | | | | | | | |
| Includes the Metropolitan Divisions of Fort Lauderdale-Pompano Beach-Sunrise, Miami-Miami Beach-Kendall, and West Palm Beach-Boca Raton-Boynton Beach | | | | | | | | | | |
| City of Miami | 476,102 | 2,645 | 61 | 94 | 610 | 1,880 | 13,092 | 1,453 | 10,017 | 1,622 |
| City of Fort Lauderdale | 184,347 | 1,158 | 37 | 91 | 321 | 709 | 7,662 | 1,074 | 5,681 | 907 |
| City of Pompano Beach | 113,545 | 837 | 19 | 62 | 244 | 512 | 3,142 | 434 | 2,237 | 471 |
| City of West Palm Beach | 113,268 | 863 | 18 | 76 | 231 | 538 | 3,862 | 452 | 2,967 | 443 |
| City of Boca Raton | 101,583 | 206 | 2 | 35 | 67 | 102 | 1,996 | 191 | 1,573 | 232 |
| City of Sunrise | 96,428 | 195 | 3 | 21 | 60 | 111 | 1,324 | 96 | 1,031 | 197 |
| City of Miami Beach | 89,017 | 668 | 5 | 62 | 200 | 401 | 5,109 | 444 | 4,244 | 421 |
| City of Deerfield Beach | 81,749 | 285 | 3 | 20 | 59 | 203 | 1,603 | 135 | 1,273 | 195 |
| City of Boynton Beach | 79,913 | 523 | 9 | 20 | 105 | 389 | 1,794 | 153 | 1,468 | 173 |
| City of Delray Beach | 70,487 | 401 | 5 | 31 | 67 | 298 | 2,412 | 245 | 1,929 | 238 |
| City of Jupiter | 67,054 | 83 | 1 | 10 | 13 | 59 | 701 | 99 | 552 | 50 |

## Table 6. Crime in the United States, by Selected Metropolitan Statistical Area, 2020—Continued

(Number, percent, rate per 100,000 population.)

| Area | Population | Violent crime | Murder and nonnegligent manslaughter | Rape[1] | Robbery | Aggravated assault | Property crime | Burglary | Larceny-theft | Motor vehicle theft |
|---|---|---|---|---|---|---|---|---|---|---|
| City of Doral | 68,425 | 63 | 0 | 9 | 8 | 46 | 1,238 | 103 | 986 | 149 |
| City of Palm Beach Gardens | 58,629 | 65 | 1 | 8 | 14 | 42 | 999 | 86 | 871 | 42 |
| City of Coral Gables | 50,017 | 51 | 0 | 7 | 13 | 31 | 1,167 | 127 | 959 | 81 |
| Total area actually reporting | 99.4% | 25,744 | 463 | 1,909 | 5,499 | 17,873 | 135,122 | 13,941 | 106,055 | 15,126 |
| Estimated total | 100.0% | 25,920 | 465 | 1,921 | 5,529 | 18,005 | 136,292 | 14,095 | 106,985 | 15,212 |
| Rate per 100,000 inhabitants | | 417.0 | 7.5 | 30.9 | 88.9 | 289.6 | 2,192.4 | 226.7 | 1,721.0 | 244.7 |
| **Fort Lauderdale-Pompano Beach-Deerfield Beach, FL M.D.** | 1,970,496 | | | | | | | | | |
| Includes Broward County | | | | | | | | | | |
| Total area actually reporting | 100.0% | 7,058 | 150 | 596 | 1,716 | 4,596 | 40,341 | 4,385 | 30,940 | 5,016 |
| Rate per 100,000 inhabitants | | 358.2 | 7.6 | 30.2 | 87.1 | 233.2 | 2,047.3 | 222.5 | 1,570.2 | 254.6 |
| **Miami-Miami Beach-Kendall, FL M.D.** | 2,733,199 | | | | | | | | | |
| Includes Miami-Dade County | | | | | | | | | | |
| Total area actually reporting | 98.6% | 13,125 | 224 | 776 | 2,687 | 9,438 | 66,623 | 6,400 | 52,888 | 7,335 |
| Estimated total | 100.0% | 13,301 | 226 | 788 | 2,717 | 9,570 | 67,793 | 6,554 | 53,818 | 7,421 |
| Rate per 100,000 inhabitants | | 486.6 | 8.3 | 28.8 | 99.4 | 350.1 | 2,480.4 | 239.8 | 1,969.0 | 271.5 |
| **West Palm Beach-Boca Raton-Boynton Beach, FL M.D.** | 1,512,848 | | | | | | | | | |
| Includes Palm Beach County | | | | | | | | | | |
| Total area actually reporting | 100.0% | 5,561 | 89 | 537 | 1,096 | 3,839 | 28,158 | 3,156 | 22,227 | 2,775 |
| Rate per 100,000 inhabitants | | 367.6 | 5.9 | 35.5 | 72.4 | 253.8 | 1,861.3 | 208.6 | 1,469.2 | 183.4 |
| **Midland, MI M.S.A.** | 82,820 | | | | | | | | | |
| Includes Midland County | | | | | | | | | | |
| City of Midland | 41,526 | 62 | 0 | 18 | 1 | 43 | 328 | 40 | 282 | 6 |
| Total area actually reporting | 100.0% | 120 | 1 | 43 | 1 | 75 | 580 | 93 | 461 | 26 |
| Rate per 100,000 inhabitants | | 144.9 | 1.2 | 51.9 | 1.2 | 90.6 | 700.3 | 112.3 | 556.6 | 31.4 |
| **Midland, TX M.S.A.** | 187,186 | | | | | | | | | |
| Includes Martin and Midland Counties | | | | | | | | | | |
| City of Midland | 150,529 | 549 | 10 | 81 | 50 | 408 | 3,119 | 404 | 2,249 | 466 |
| Total area actually reporting | 100.0% | 700 | 13 | 92 | 55 | 540 | 4,058 | 532 | 2,838 | 688 |
| Rate per 100,000 inhabitants | | 374.0 | 6.9 | 49.1 | 29.4 | 288.5 | 2,167.9 | 284.2 | 1,516.1 | 367.5 |
| **Milwaukee-Waukesha, WI M.S.A.[2]** | 1,575,891 | | | | | | | | | |
| Includes Milwaukee, Ozaukee, Washington, and Waukesha[2] Counties | | | | | | | | | | |
| City of Milwaukee | 589,105 | 9,407 | 191 | 431 | 1,925 | 6,860 | 16,074 | 3,408 | 8,178 | 4,488 |
| City of Waukesha | 72,421 | 123 | 1 | 17 | 21 | 84 | 595 | 62 | 477 | 56 |
| Total area actually reporting | 99.5% | 10,678 | 206 | 629 | 2,218 | 7,625 | 30,716 | 4,532 | 20,659 | 5,525 |
| Estimated total | 100.0% | 10,688 | 206 | 631 | 2,219 | 7,632 | 30,821 | 4,540 | 20,751 | 5,530 |
| Rate per 100,000 inhabitants | | 678.2 | 13.1 | 40.0 | 140.8 | 484.3 | 1,955.8 | 288.1 | 1,316.8 | 350.9 |
| **Missoula, MT M.S.A.** | 121,047 | | | | | | | | | |
| Includes Missoula County | | | | | | | | | | |
| City of Missoula | 76,468 | 376 | 4 | 60 | 32 | 280 | 2,745 | 273 | 2,285 | 187 |
| Total area actually reporting | 100.0% | 489 | 6 | 77 | 33 | 373 | 3,080 | 374 | 2,492 | 214 |
| Rate per 100,000 inhabitants | | 404.0 | 5.0 | 63.6 | 27.3 | 308.1 | 2,544.5 | 309.0 | 2,058.7 | 176.8 |
| **Modesto, CA M.S.A.** | 549,195 | | | | | | | | | |
| Includes Stanislaus County | | | | | | | | | | |
| City of Modesto | 216,560 | 1,603 | 16 | 106 | 281 | 1,200 | 5,340 | 706 | 3,533 | 1,101 |
| Total area actually reporting | 100.0% | 2,823 | 33 | 185 | 587 | 2,018 | 10,843 | 1,825 | 6,927 | 2,091 |
| Rate per 100,000 inhabitants | | 514.0 | 6.0 | 33.7 | 106.9 | 367.4 | 1,974.3 | 332.3 | 1,261.3 | 380.7 |
| **Monroe, LA M.S.A.** | 199,081 | | | | | | | | | |
| Includes Morehouse, Ouachita, and Union Parishes | | | | | | | | | | |
| City of Monroe | 47,119 | 1,399 | 19 | 9 | 154 | 1,217 | 2,883 | 649 | 2,042 | 192 |
| Total area actually reporting | 91.4% | 2,540 | 22 | 107 | 221 | 2,190 | 6,930 | 1,611 | 4,799 | 520 |
| Estimated total | 100.0% | 2,605 | 23 | 113 | 233 | 2,236 | 7,275 | 1,665 | 5,049 | 561 |
| Rate per 100,000 inhabitants | | 1,308.5 | 11.6 | 56.8 | 117.0 | 1,123.2 | 3,654.3 | 836.3 | 2,536.2 | 281.8 |
| **Morristown, TN M.S.A.** | 143,413 | | | | | | | | | |
| Includes Grainger, Hamblen, and Jefferson Counties | | | | | | | | | | |
| City of Morristown | 30,330 | 258 | 1 | 12 | 22 | 223 | 1,290 | 177 | 998 | 115 |
| Total area actually reporting | 100.0% | 519 | 2 | 39 | 30 | 448 | 2,686 | 473 | 1,900 | 313 |
| Rate per 100,000 inhabitants | | 361.9 | 1.4 | 27.2 | 20.9 | 312.4 | 1,872.9 | 329.8 | 1,324.8 | 218.3 |
| **Mount Vernon-Anacortes, WA M.S.A.** | 130,213 | | | | | | | | | |
| Includes Skagit County | | | | | | | | | | |
| City of Mount Vernon | 36,513 | 70 | 1 | 9 | 13 | 47 | 1,109 | 142 | 857 | 110 |
| City of Anacortes | 17,735 | 15 | 0 | 2 | 7 | 6 | 398 | 43 | 327 | 28 |
| Total area actually reporting | 100.0% | 192 | 2 | 20 | 36 | 134 | 3,153 | 467 | 2,436 | 250 |
| Rate per 100,000 inhabitants | | 147.5 | 1.5 | 15.4 | 27.6 | 102.9 | 2,421.4 | 358.6 | 1,870.8 | 192.0 |
| **Muskegon, MI M.S.A.** | 173,165 | | | | | | | | | |
| Includes Muskegon County | | | | | | | | | | |
| City of Muskegon | 36,391 | 254 | 5 | 8 | 20 | 221 | 1,004 | 174 | 740 | 90 |
| Total area actually reporting | 100.0% | 714 | 10 | 97 | 58 | 549 | 3,581 | 486 | 2,841 | 254 |
| Rate per 100,000 inhabitants | | 412.3 | 5.8 | 56.0 | 33.5 | 317.0 | 2,068.0 | 280.7 | 1,640.6 | 146.7 |

## Table 6. Crime in the United States, by Selected Metropolitan Statistical Area, 2020—Continued

(Number, percent, rate per 100,000 population.)

| Area | Population | Violent crime | Murder and nonnegligent manslaughter | Rape[1] | Robbery | Aggravated assault | Property crime | Burglary | Larceny-theft | Motor vehicle theft |
|---|---|---|---|---|---|---|---|---|---|---|
| **Napa, CA M.S.A.** | 136,475 | | | | | | | | | |
| Includes Napa County | | | | | | | | | | |
| City of Napa | 78,237 | 267 | 0 | 44 | 36 | 187 | 1,320 | 272 | 883 | 165 |
| Total area actually reporting | 100.0% | 539 | 1 | 65 | 59 | 414 | 2,306 | 522 | 1,511 | 273 |
| Rate per 100,000 inhabitants | | 394.9 | 0.7 | 47.6 | 43.2 | 303.4 | 1,689.7 | 382.5 | 1,107.2 | 200.0 |
| **Naples-Marco Island, FL M.S.A.** | 391,365 | | | | | | | | | |
| Includes Collier County | | | | | | | | | | |
| City of Naples | 22,388 | 21 | 1 | 4 | 1 | 15 | 276 | 26 | 223 | 27 |
| City of Marco Island | 18,121 | 15 | 0 | 3 | 1 | 11 | 103 | 13 | 75 | 15 |
| Total area actually reporting | 100.0% | 876 | 6 | 68 | 122 | 680 | 3,806 | 416 | 3,039 | 351 |
| Rate per 100,000 inhabitants | | 223.8 | 1.5 | 17.4 | 31.2 | 173.8 | 972.5 | 106.3 | 776.5 | 89.7 |
| **Nashville-Davidson–Murfreesboro–Franklin, TN M.S.A.** | 1,969,367 | | | | | | | | | |
| Includes Cannon, Cheatham, Davidson, Dickson, Macon, Maury, Robertson, Rutherford, Smith, Sumner, Trousdale, Williamson, and Wilson Counties | | | | | | | | | | |
| City of Metropolitan Nashville Police Department | 688,013 | 7,951 | 113 | 385 | 1,742 | 5,711 | 28,023 | 3,745 | 21,238 | 3,040 |
| City of Murfreesboro | 151,769 | 740 | 11 | 91 | 101 | 537 | 3,772 | 362 | 3,113 | 297 |
| City of Franklin | 85,722 | 195 | 1 | 17 | 14 | 163 | 792 | 58 | 685 | 49 |
| Total area actually reporting | 100.0% | 12,137 | 152 | 757 | 2,097 | 9,131 | 46,329 | 6,307 | 35,206 | 4,816 |
| Rate per 100,000 inhabitants | | 616.3 | 7.7 | 38.4 | 106.5 | 463.7 | 2,352.5 | 320.3 | 1,787.7 | 244.5 |
| **New Bern, NC M.S.A.** | 123,955 | | | | | | | | | |
| Includes Craven, Jones, and Pamlico Counties | | | | | | | | | | |
| City of New Bern | 30,047 | 190 | 4 | 11 | 21 | 154 | 930 | 199 | 701 | 30 |
| Total area actually reporting | 89.0% | 421 | 11 | 32 | 39 | 339 | 2,366 | 589 | 1,640 | 137 |
| Estimated total | 100.0% | 451 | 11 | 35 | 42 | 363 | 2,666 | 657 | 1,850 | 159 |
| Rate per 100,000 inhabitants | | 363.8 | 8.9 | 28.2 | 33.9 | 292.8 | 2,150.8 | 530.0 | 1,492.5 | 128.3 |
| **New Haven-Milford, CT M.S.A.[2]** | 799,461 | | | | | | | | | |
| Includes New Haven County | | | | | | | | | | |
| City of New Haven | 130,299 | 922 | 21 | 29 | 336 | 536 | 4,575 | 547 | 3,267 | 761 |
| City of Milford[2] | 54,968 | 33 | 0 | 3 | 25 | 5 | 1,107 | 109 | 884 | 114 |
| Total area actually reporting | 100.0% | 2,049 | 49 | 164 | 745 | 1,091 | 17,342 | 1,843 | 12,726 | 2,773 |
| Rate per 100,000 inhabitants | | 256.3 | 6.1 | 20.5 | 93.2 | 136.5 | 2,169.2 | 230.5 | 1,591.8 | 346.9 |
| **New Orleans-Metairie, LA M.S.A.[2]** | 1,275,017 | | | | | | | | | |
| Includes Jefferson, Orleans, Plaquemines, St. Bernard, St. Charles,[2] St. James, St. John the Baptist, and St. Tammany Parishes | | | | | | | | | | |
| City of New Orleans | 393,779 | 5,215 | 201 | 712 | 1,106 | 3,196 | 17,876 | 1,994 | 12,358 | 3,524 |
| Total area actually reporting | 95.3% | 7,698 | 272 | 899 | 1,464 | 5,063 | 33,569 | 3,915 | 25,120 | 4,534 |
| Estimated total | 100.0% | 7,960 | 277 | 924 | 1,504 | 5,255 | 35,121 | 4,145 | 26,290 | 4,686 |
| Rate per 100,000 inhabitants | | 624.3 | 21.7 | 72.5 | 118.0 | 412.2 | 2,754.6 | 325.1 | 2,061.9 | 367.5 |
| **Niles, MI M.S.A.** | 152,517 | | | | | | | | | |
| Includes Berrien County | | | | | | | | | | |
| City of Niles | 11,102 | 74 | 0 | 16 | 11 | 47 | 328 | 42 | 225 | 61 |
| Total area actually reporting | 100.0% | 1,013 | 8 | 130 | 58 | 817 | 2,882 | 566 | 2,030 | 286 |
| Rate per 100,000 inhabitants | | 664.2 | 5.2 | 85.2 | 38.0 | 535.7 | 1,889.6 | 371.1 | 1,331.0 | 187.5 |
| **North Port-Sarasota-Bradenton, FL M.S.A.** | 850,904 | | | | | | | | | |
| Includes Manatee and Sarasota Counties | | | | | | | | | | |
| City of North Port | 72,389 | 117 | 3 | 27 | 6 | 81 | 743 | 88 | 634 | 21 |
| City of Sarasota | 59,002 | 349 | 1 | 32 | 59 | 257 | 1,622 | 227 | 1,271 | 124 |
| City of Bradenton | 60,688 | 306 | 4 | 25 | 46 | 231 | 1,322 | 108 | 1,115 | 99 |
| City of Venice | 24,366 | 16 | 0 | 2 | 5 | 9 | 346 | 56 | 274 | 16 |
| Total area actually reporting | 100.0% | 2,854 | 22 | 321 | 373 | 2,138 | 12,831 | 1,711 | 10,194 | 926 |
| Rate per 100,000 inhabitants | | 335.4 | 2.6 | 37.7 | 43.8 | 251.3 | 1,507.9 | 201.1 | 1,198.0 | 108.8 |
| **Norwich-New London, CT M.S.A.** | 173,802 | | | | | | | | | |
| Includes New London County | | | | | | | | | | |
| City of Norwich | 38,576 | 134 | 3 | 14 | 28 | 89 | 542 | 114 | 350 | 78 |
| City of New London | 26,776 | 67 | 0 | 7 | 24 | 36 | 500 | 79 | 333 | 88 |
| Total area actually reporting | 100.0% | 313 | 4 | 42 | 66 | 201 | 2,210 | 302 | 1,635 | 273 |
| Rate per 100,000 inhabitants | | 180.1 | 2.3 | 24.2 | 38.0 | 115.6 | 1,271.6 | 173.8 | 940.7 | 157.1 |
| **Ocala, FL M.S.A.** | 368,501 | | | | | | | | | |
| Includes Marion County | | | | | | | | | | |
| City of Ocala | 61,275 | 413 | 3 | 55 | 61 | 294 | 1,936 | 161 | 1,663 | 112 |
| Total area actually reporting | 100.0% | 1,557 | 19 | 184 | 136 | 1,218 | 6,012 | 1,141 | 4,289 | 582 |
| Rate per 100,000 inhabitants | | 422.5 | 5.2 | 49.9 | 36.9 | 330.5 | 1,631.5 | 309.6 | 1,163.9 | 157.9 |
| **Ocean City, NJ M.S.A.** | 91,384 | | | | | | | | | |
| Includes Cape May County | | | | | | | | | | |
| City of Ocean City | 10,893 | 8 | 0 | 1 | 2 | 5 | 334 | 39 | 287 | 8 |
| Total area actually reporting | 100.0% | 154 | 0 | 19 | 25 | 110 | 1,856 | 237 | 1,559 | 60 |
| Rate per 100,000 inhabitants | | 168.5 | 0.0 | 20.8 | 27.4 | 120.4 | 2,031.0 | 259.3 | 1,706.0 | 65.7 |
| **Odessa, TX M.S.A.[2]** | 169,268 | | | | | | | | | |
| Includes Ector County | | | | | | | | | | |
| City of Odessa[2] | 126,288 | 1,020 | 13 | 107 | 106 | 794 | 3,163 | 586 | 2,113 | 464 |
| Total area actually reporting | 100.0% | 1,180 | 19 | 109 | 160 | 892 | 5,005 | 859 | 3,270 | 876 |
| Rate per 100,000 inhabitants | | 697.1 | 11.2 | 64.4 | 94.5 | 527.0 | 2,956.8 | 507.5 | 1,931.8 | 517.5 |

## Table 6. Crime in the United States, by Selected Metropolitan Statistical Area, 2020—Continued

(Number, percent, rate per 100,000 population.)

| Area | Population | Violent crime | Murder and nonnegligent manslaughter | Rape[1] | Robbery | Aggravated assault | Property crime | Burglary | Larceny-theft | Motor vehicle theft |
|---|---|---|---|---|---|---|---|---|---|---|
| **Ogden-Clearfield, UT M.S.A.[2]** | 692,112 | | | | | | | | | |
| Includes Box Elder,[2] Davis, Morgan, and Weber Counties | | | | | | | | | | |
| City of Ogden | 88,309 | 446 | 4 | 79 | 75 | 288 | 2,915 | 375 | 2,151 | 389 |
| City of Clearfield | 32,358 | 69 | 1 | 13 | 10 | 45 | 525 | 60 | 413 | 52 |
| Total area actually reporting | 100.0% | 1,197 | 14 | 354 | 140 | 689 | 11,454 | 1,580 | 8,686 | 1,188 |
| Rate per 100,000 inhabitants | | 172.9 | 2.0 | 51.1 | 20.2 | 99.6 | 1,654.9 | 228.3 | 1,255.0 | 171.6 |
| **Oklahoma City, OK M.S.A.[2]** | 1,427,075 | | | | | | | | | |
| Includes Canadian, Cleveland, Grady, Lincoln, Logan, McClain, and Oklahoma Counties | | | | | | | | | | |
| City of Oklahoma City[2] | 663,661 | 4,818 | 63 | 559 | 817 | 3,379 | 25,853 | 5,849 | 16,222 | 3,782 |
| Total area actually reporting | 100.0% | 6,719 | 111 | 842 | 1,032 | 4,734 | 41,616 | 8,847 | 27,156 | 5,613 |
| Rate per 100,000 inhabitants | | 470.8 | 7.8 | 59.0 | 72.3 | 331.7 | 2,916.2 | 619.9 | 1,902.9 | 393.3 |
| **Olympia-Lacey-Tumwater, WA M.S.A.** | 294,061 | | | | | | | | | |
| Includes Thurston County | | | | | | | | | | |
| City of Olympia | 53,571 | 268 | 1 | 24 | 69 | 174 | 1,753 | 271 | 1,284 | 198 |
| City of Lacey | 53,826 | 83 | 0 | 13 | 21 | 49 | 1,386 | 160 | 1,099 | 127 |
| City of Tumwater | 24,493 | 63 | 0 | 10 | 13 | 40 | 613 | 94 | 453 | 66 |
| Total area actually reporting | 100.0% | 657 | 3 | 73 | 127 | 454 | 5,636 | 990 | 4,029 | 617 |
| Rate per 100,000 inhabitants | | 223.4 | 1.0 | 24.8 | 43.2 | 154.4 | 1,916.6 | 336.7 | 1,370.1 | 209.8 |
| **Omaha-Council Bluffs, NE-IA M.S.A.** | 954,892 | | | | | | | | | |
| Includes Harrison, Mills, and Pottawattamie Counties, IA and Cass, Douglas, Sarpy, Saunders, and Washington Counties, NE | | | | | | | | | | |
| City of Omaha, NE | 480,297 | 3,032 | 37 | 351 | 464 | 2,180 | 15,247 | 1,521 | 10,697 | 3,029 |
| City of Council Bluffs, IA | 62,144 | 574 | 0 | 36 | 68 | 470 | 2,976 | 408 | 2,127 | 441 |
| Total area actually reporting | 99.6% | 4,093 | 44 | 526 | 570 | 2,953 | 21,718 | 2,423 | 15,293 | 4,002 |
| Estimated total | 100.0% | 4,103 | 44 | 527 | 574 | 2,958 | 21,780 | 2,431 | 15,337 | 4,012 |
| Rate per 100,000 inhabitants | | 429.7 | 4.6 | 55.2 | 60.1 | 309.8 | 2,280.9 | 254.6 | 1,606.2 | 420.2 |
| **Orlando-Kissimmee-Sanford, FL M.S.A.** | 2,658,987 | | | | | | | | | |
| Includes Lake, Orange, Osceola, and Seminole Counties | | | | | | | | | | |
| City of Orlando | 293,363 | 2,524 | 31 | 169 | 507 | 1,817 | 11,158 | 1,198 | 8,812 | 1,148 |
| City of Kissimmee | 74,337 | 318 | 4 | 29 | 32 | 253 | 1,707 | 206 | 1,359 | 142 |
| City of Sanford | 62,342 | 511 | 3 | 38 | 84 | 386 | 1,396 | 210 | 1,084 | 102 |
| Total area actually reporting | 100.0% | 11,347 | 158 | 1,118 | 1,919 | 8,152 | 49,514 | 7,138 | 37,606 | 4,770 |
| Rate per 100,000 inhabitants | | 426.7 | 5.9 | 42.0 | 72.2 | 306.6 | 1,862.1 | 268.4 | 1,414.3 | 179.4 |
| **Oshkosh-Neenah, WI M.S.A.** | 172,301 | | | | | | | | | |
| Includes Winnebago County | | | | | | | | | | |
| City of Oshkosh | 67,080 | 187 | 4 | 48 | 12 | 123 | 1,239 | 138 | 1,036 | 65 |
| City of Neenah | 26,390 | 57 | 1 | 12 | 5 | 39 | 315 | 21 | 282 | 12 |
| Total area actually reporting | 98.6% | 322 | 6 | 75 | 21 | 220 | 2,233 | 360 | 1,772 | 101 |
| Estimated total | 100.0% | 332 | 6 | 76 | 23 | 227 | 2,283 | 368 | 1,808 | 107 |
| Rate per 100,000 inhabitants | | 192.7 | 3.5 | 44.1 | 13.3 | 131.7 | 1,325.0 | 213.6 | 1,049.3 | 62.1 |
| **Owensboro, KY M.S.A.** | 119,839 | | | | | | | | | |
| Includes Daviess, Hancock, and McLean Counties | | | | | | | | | | |
| City of Owensboro | 60,430 | 161 | 5 | 41 | 45 | 70 | 2,326 | 404 | 1,638 | 284 |
| Total area actually reporting | 100.0% | 197 | 6 | 53 | 51 | 87 | 2,793 | 539 | 1,903 | 351 |
| Rate per 100,000 inhabitants | | 164.4 | 5.0 | 44.2 | 42.6 | 72.6 | 2,330.6 | 449.8 | 1,588.0 | 292.9 |
| **Oxnard-Thousand Oaks-Ventura, CA M.S.A.** | 839,861 | | | | | | | | | |
| Includes Ventura County | | | | | | | | | | |
| City of Oxnard | 210,064 | 743 | 8 | 81 | 274 | 380 | 4,323 | 638 | 2,907 | 778 |
| City of Thousand Oaks | 126,823 | 76 | 1 | 21 | 23 | 31 | 1,315 | 189 | 1,027 | 99 |
| City of Ventura | 109,295 | 328 | 2 | 31 | 94 | 201 | 3,086 | 460 | 2,354 | 272 |
| City of Camarillo | 70,424 | 53 | 0 | 16 | 17 | 20 | 817 | 100 | 661 | 56 |
| Total area actually reporting | 100.0% | 1,686 | 20 | 224 | 494 | 948 | 13,083 | 1,909 | 9,616 | 1,558 |
| Rate per 100,000 inhabitants | | 200.7 | 2.4 | 26.7 | 58.8 | 112.9 | 1,557.8 | 227.3 | 1,145.0 | 185.5 |
| **Palm Bay-Melbourne-Titusville, FL M.S.A.** | 606,953 | | | | | | | | | |
| Includes Brevard County | | | | | | | | | | |
| City of Palm Bay | 116,897 | 328 | 3 | 59 | 39 | 227 | 1,770 | 241 | 1,380 | 149 |
| City of Melbourne | 83,806 | 757 | 8 | 74 | 86 | 589 | 2,531 | 393 | 1,987 | 151 |
| City of Titusville | 46,919 | 295 | 5 | 24 | 51 | 215 | 1,081 | 199 | 764 | 118 |
| Total area actually reporting | 100.0% | 2,288 | 30 | 225 | 298 | 1,735 | 10,662 | 1,629 | 8,161 | 872 |
| Rate per 100,000 inhabitants | | 377.0 | 4.9 | 37.1 | 49.1 | 285.9 | 1,756.6 | 268.4 | 1,344.6 | 143.7 |
| **Panama City, FL M.S.A.** | 174,857 | | | | | | | | | |
| Includes Bay County | | | | | | | | | | |
| City of Panama City | 34,672 | 303 | 4 | 38 | 29 | 232 | 1,453 | 252 | 1,059 | 142 |
| Total area actually reporting | 99.4% | 843 | 11 | 93 | 67 | 672 | 4,603 | 771 | 3,451 | 381 |
| Estimated total | 100.0% | 847 | 11 | 93 | 68 | 675 | 4,626 | 775 | 3,467 | 384 |
| Rate per 100,000 inhabitants | | 484.4 | 6.3 | 53.2 | 38.9 | 386.0 | 2,645.6 | 443.2 | 1,982.8 | 219.6 |
| **Parkersburg-Vienna, WV M.S.A.** | 88,918 | | | | | | | | | |
| Includes Wirt and Wood Counties | | | | | | | | | | |
| City of Parkersburg | 29,096 | 106 | 2 | 29 | 23 | 52 | 1,269 | 265 | 911 | 93 |
| City of Vienna | 10,049 | 9 | 0 | 1 | 1 | 7 | 348 | 10 | 331 | 7 |
| Total area actually reporting | 100.0% | 257 | 2 | 56 | 25 | 174 | 2,013 | 380 | 1,476 | 157 |
| Rate per 100,000 inhabitants | | 289.0 | 2.2 | 63.0 | 28.1 | 195.7 | 2,263.9 | 427.4 | 1,660.0 | 176.6 |

## Table 6. Crime in the United States, by Selected Metropolitan Statistical Area, 2020—Continued

(Number, percent, rate per 100,000 population.)

| Area | Population | Violent crime | Murder and nonnegligent manslaughter | Rape[1] | Robbery | Aggravated assault | Property crime | Burglary | Larceny-theft | Motor vehicle theft |
|---|---|---|---|---|---|---|---|---|---|---|
| **Pensacola-Ferry Pass-Brent, FL M.S.A.** | 507,320 | | | | | | | | | |
| Includes Escambia and Santa Rosa Counties | | | | | | | | | | |
| City of Pensacola | 53,083 | 327 | 5 | 26 | 52 | 244 | 1,543 | 191 | 1,272 | 80 |
| Total area actually reporting | 100.0% | 2,180 | 38 | 271 | 395 | 1,476 | 9,849 | 1,911 | 7,084 | 854 |
| Rate per 100,000 inhabitants | | 429.7 | 7.5 | 53.4 | 77.9 | 290.9 | 1,941.4 | 376.7 | 1,396.4 | 168.3 |
| **Peoria, IL M.S.A.[4]** | 396,798 | | | | | | | | | |
| Includes Fulton,[4] Marshall,[4] Peoria,[4] Stark,[4] Tazewell,[4] and Woodford Counties | | | | | | | | | | |
| City of Peoria[4] | 109,924 | 1,084 | 14 | 72 | 196 | 802 | | 652 | | 430 |
| Total area actually reporting | 91.7% | 1,633 | 22 | 191 | 227 | 1,193 | | 1,380 | | 685 |
| Estimated total | 100.0% | 1,689 | 23 | 200 | 237 | 1,229 | | 1,439 | | 719 |
| Rate per 100,000 inhabitants | | 425.7 | 5.8 | 50.4 | 59.7 | 309.7 | | 362.7 | | 181.2 |
| **Phoenix-Mesa-Chandler, AZ M.S.A.[2]** | 5,064,185 | | | | | | | | | |
| Includes Maricopa and Pinal Counties | | | | | | | | | | |
| City of Phoenix | 1,708,960 | 13,646 | 187 | 1,068 | 3,278 | 9,113 | 51,089 | 7,406 | 36,254 | 7,429 |
| City of Mesa[2] | 527,361 | 1,960 | 19 | 235 | 380 | 1,326 | 9,737 | 1,597 | 7,124 | 1,016 |
| City of Chandler | 264,071 | 543 | 9 | 123 | 104 | 307 | 4,898 | 505 | 3,956 | 437 |
| City of Scottsdale | 263,006 | 470 | 7 | 109 | 97 | 257 | 4,945 | 683 | 3,963 | 299 |
| City of Tempe | 199,935 | 1,100 | 8 | 155 | 248 | 689 | 7,124 | 960 | 5,464 | 700 |
| City of Casa Grande[2] | 59,822 | 338 | 1 | 23 | 38 | 276 | 1,200 | 150 | 947 | 103 |
| Total area actually reporting | 90.5% | 22,455 | 288 | 2,145 | 4,722 | 15,300 | 107,047 | 15,453 | 79,187 | 12,407 |
| Estimated total | 100.0% | 23,512 | 314 | 2,250 | 4,749 | 16,199 | 112,293 | 16,684 | 82,568 | 13,041 |
| Rate per 100,000 inhabitants | | 464.3 | 6.2 | 44.4 | 93.8 | 319.9 | 2,217.4 | 329.5 | 1,630.4 | 257.5 |
| **Pine Bluff, AR M.S.A** | 86,540 | | | | | | | | | |
| Includes Cleveland, Jefferson, and Lincoln Counties | | | | | | | | | | |
| City of Pine Bluff | 40,718 | 746 | 23 | 27 | 59 | 637 | 1,990 | 414 | 1,323 | 253 |
| Total area actually reporting | 100.0% | 950 | 24 | 55 | 70 | 801 | 2,638 | 578 | 1,710 | 350 |
| Rate per 100,000 inhabitants | | 1,097.8 | 27.7 | 63.6 | 80.9 | 925.6 | 3,048.3 | 667.9 | 1,976.0 | 404.4 |
| **Pittsfield, MA M.S.A.** | 123,599 | | | | | | | | | |
| Includes Berkshire County | | | | | | | | | | |
| City of Pittsfield | 41,865 | 341 | 1 | 35 | 34 | 271 | 664 | 232 | 369 | 63 |
| Total area actually reporting | 91.7% | 509 | 1 | 56 | 49 | 403 | 1,350 | 369 | 884 | 97 |
| Estimated total | 100.0% | 533 | 1 | 60 | 53 | 419 | 1,401 | 380 | 919 | 102 |
| Rate per 100,000 inhabitants | | 431.2 | 0.8 | 48.5 | 42.9 | 339.0 | 1,133.5 | 307.4 | 743.5 | 82.5 |
| **Pocatello, ID M.S.A.** | 96,729 | | | | | | | | | |
| Includes Bannock and Power Counties | | | | | | | | | | |
| City of Pocatello | 56,900 | 206 | 0 | 12 | 11 | 183 | 1,223 | 291 | 822 | 110 |
| Total area actually reporting | 100.0% | 260 | 0 | 14 | 11 | 235 | 1,747 | 349 | 1,233 | 165 |
| Rate per 100,000 inhabitants | | 268.8 | 0.0 | 14.5 | 11.4 | 242.9 | 1,806.1 | 360.8 | 1,274.7 | 170.6 |
| **Portland-South Portland, ME M.S.A.[2]** | 542,906 | | | | | | | | | |
| Includes Cumberland, Sagadahoc, and York Counties[2] | | | | | | | | | | |
| City of Portland | 66,229 | 129 | 0 | 28 | 34 | 67 | 1,143 | 94 | 991 | 58 |
| City of South Portland | 25,593 | 32 | 1 | 4 | 10 | 17 | 402 | 24 | 346 | 32 |
| Total area actually reporting | 100.0% | 516 | 1 | 163 | 80 | 272 | 5,524 | 582 | 4,641 | 301 |
| Rate per 100,000 inhabitants | | 95.0 | 0.2 | 30.0 | 14.7 | 50.1 | 1,017.5 | 107.2 | 854.8 | 55.4 |
| **Portland-Vancouver-Hillsboro, OR-WA M.S.A.[3]** | 2,511,480 | | | | | | | | | |
| Includes Clackamas, Columbia, Multnomah,[3] Washington, and Yamhill Counties, OR and Clark and Skamania Counties, WA | | | | | | | | | | |
| City of Portland, OR | 662,941 | 3,465 | 53 | 262 | 807 | 2,343 | 31,416 | 3,759 | 21,287 | 6,370 |
| City of Vancouver, WA | 186,440 | 884 | 5 | 137 | 167 | 575 | 6,709 | 1,065 | 4,448 | 1,196 |
| City of Hillsboro, OR | 111,146 | 257 | 2 | 55 | 46 | 154 | 2,147 | 212 | 1,695 | 240 |
| City of Beaverton, OR | 100,085 | 235 | 1 | 38 | 47 | 149 | 2,197 | 255 | 1,693 | 249 |
| City of Tigard, OR | 56,377 | 107 | 1 | 14 | 24 | 68 | 1,472 | 161 | 1,170 | 141 |
| Total area actually reporting | 99.5% | | | 1,029 | 1,505 | 5,104 | 67,067 | 8,584 | 46,657 | 11,826 |
| Estimated total | 100.0% | | | 1,032 | 1,507 | 5,116 | 67,267 | 8,607 | 46,815 | 11,845 |
| Rate per 100,000 inhabitants | | | | 41.1 | 60.0 | 203.7 | 2,678.4 | 342.7 | 1,864.0 | 471.6 |
| **Port St. Lucie, FL M.S.A.** | 495,563 | | | | | | | | | |
| Includes Martin and St. Lucie Counties | | | | | | | | | | |
| City of Port St. Lucie | 206,450 | 264 | 5 | 35 | 40 | 184 | 1,666 | 189 | 1,381 | 96 |
| Total area actually reporting | 100.0% | 1,170 | 23 | 170 | 167 | 810 | 5,459 | 679 | 4,362 | 418 |
| Rate per 100,000 inhabitants | | 236.1 | 4.6 | 34.3 | 33.7 | 163.5 | 1,101.6 | 137.0 | 880.2 | 84.3 |
| **Prescott Valley-Prescott, AZ M.S.A.** | 239,151 | | | | | | | | | |
| Includes Yavapai County | | | | | | | | | | |
| City of Prescott Valley | 47,459 | 80 | 0 | 21 | 10 | 49 | 374 | 39 | 317 | 18 |
| City of Prescott | 44,835 | 168 | 0 | 31 | 3 | 134 | 657 | 129 | 494 | 34 |
| Total area actually reporting | 100.0% | 581 | 8 | 72 | 24 | 477 | 2,910 | 490 | 2,195 | 225 |
| Rate per 100,000 inhabitants | | 242.9 | 3.3 | 30.1 | 10.0 | 199.5 | 1,216.8 | 204.9 | 917.8 | 94.1 |
| **Providence-Warwick, RI-MA M.S.A.** | 1,621,159 | | | | | | | | | |
| Includes Bristol County, MA and Bristol, Kent, Newport, Providence, and Washington Counties, RI | | | | | | | | | | |
| City of Providence, RI | 179,603 | 873 | 17 | 66 | 183 | 607 | 4,337 | 602 | 3,191 | 544 |
| City of Warwick, RI | 80,605 | 66 | 0 | 21 | 7 | 38 | 993 | 92 | 823 | 78 |
| Total area actually reporting | 99.5% | 4,620 | 41 | 644 | 610 | 3,325 | 18,780 | 2,756 | 13,972 | 2,052 |
| Estimated total | 100.0% | 4,630 | 41 | 645 | 611 | 3,333 | 18,808 | 2,760 | 13,995 | 2,053 |
| Rate per 100,000 inhabitants | | 285.6 | 2.5 | 39.8 | 37.7 | 205.6 | 1,160.2 | 170.2 | 863.3 | 126.6 |

## Table 6. Crime in the United States, by Selected Metropolitan Statistical Area, 2020—Continued

(Number, percent, rate per 100,000 population.)

| Area | Population | Violent crime | Murder and nonnegligent manslaughter | Rape[1] | Robbery | Aggravated assault | Property crime | Burglary | Larceny-theft | Motor vehicle theft |
|---|---|---|---|---|---|---|---|---|---|---|
| **Pueblo, CO M.S.A.[5]** | 168,374 | | | | | | | | | |
| Includes Pueblo County[5] | | | | | | | | | | |
| City of Pueblo | 113,002 | 1,181 | 16 | 199 | 198 | 768 | 5,233 | 896 | 3,399 | 938 |
| Total area actually reporting | 100.0% | 1,216 | 18 | 199 | 208 | 791 | | 1,112 | | 1,078 |
| Rate per 100,000 inhabitants | | 722.2 | 10.7 | 118.2 | 123.5 | 469.8 | | 660.4 | | 640.2 |
| **Punta Gorda, FL M.S.A.** | 191,879 | | | | | | | | | |
| Includes Charlotte County | | | | | | | | | | |
| City of Punta Gorda | 20,766 | 14 | 0 | 0 | 2 | 12 | 272 | 14 | 241 | 17 |
| Total area actually reporting | 100.0% | 292 | 1 | 32 | 21 | 238 | 1,651 | 221 | 1,302 | 128 |
| Rate per 100,000 inhabitants | | 152.2 | 0.5 | 16.7 | 10.9 | 124.0 | 860.4 | 115.2 | 678.6 | 66.7 |
| **Racine, WI M.S.A.[2]** | 196,239 | | | | | | | | | |
| Includes Racine County[2] | | | | | | | | | | |
| City of Racine | 76,573 | 414 | 2 | 36 | 86 | 290 | 1,381 | 321 | 916 | 144 |
| Total area actually reporting | 100.0% | 540 | 3 | 54 | 101 | 382 | 2,437 | 444 | 1,788 | 205 |
| Rate per 100,000 inhabitants | | 275.2 | 1.5 | 27.5 | 51.5 | 194.7 | 1,241.9 | 226.3 | 911.1 | 104.5 |
| **Raleigh-Cary, NC M.S.A.** | 1,422,373 | | | | | | | | | |
| Includes Franklin, Johnston, and Wake Counties | | | | | | | | | | |
| City of Raleigh | 480,964 | 1,886 | 21 | 165 | 467 | 1,233 | 9,716 | 1,298 | 7,060 | 1,358 |
| City of Cary | 172,079 | 115 | 1 | 13 | 25 | 76 | 1,627 | 194 | 1,323 | 110 |
| Total area actually reporting | 99.3% | 3,144 | 47 | 276 | 668 | 2,153 | 21,023 | 3,118 | 15,791 | 2,114 |
| Estimated total | 100.0% | 3,180 | 47 | 280 | 673 | 2,180 | 21,397 | 3,194 | 16,068 | 2,135 |
| Rate per 100,000 inhabitants | | 223.6 | 3.3 | 19.7 | 47.3 | 153.3 | 1,504.3 | 224.6 | 1,129.7 | 150.1 |
| **Rapid City, SD M.S.A.** | 143,884 | | | | | | | | | |
| Includes Meade and Pennington Counties | | | | | | | | | | |
| City of Rapid City | 78,492 | 673 | 13 | 108 | 104 | 448 | 3,137 | 657 | 2,014 | 466 |
| Total area actually reporting | 100.0% | 957 | 15 | 211 | 115 | 616 | 4,275 | 887 | 2,804 | 584 |
| Rate per 100,000 inhabitants | | 665.1 | 10.4 | 146.6 | 79.9 | 428.1 | 2,971.1 | 616.5 | 1,948.8 | 405.9 |
| **Redding, CA M.S.A.** | 178,587 | | | | | | | | | |
| Includes Shasta County | | | | | | | | | | |
| City of Redding | 92,895 | 513 | 5 | 67 | 94 | 347 | 2,323 | 596 | 1,529 | 198 |
| Total area actually reporting | 100.0% | 977 | 12 | 99 | 126 | 740 | 3,430 | 936 | 2,028 | 466 |
| Rate per 100,000 inhabitants | | 547.1 | 6.7 | 55.4 | 70.6 | 414.4 | 1,920.6 | 524.1 | 1,135.6 | 260.9 |
| **Reno, NV M.S.A.[2]** | 483,469 | | | | | | | | | |
| Includes Storey and Washoe Counties | | | | | | | | | | |
| City of Reno[2] | 259,168 | 1,460 | 17 | 281 | 286 | 876 | 5,564 | 1,105 | 3,486 | 973 |
| Total area actually reporting | 100.0% | 2,238 | 27 | 415 | 374 | 1,422 | 8,842 | 1,787 | 5,637 | 1,418 |
| Rate per 100,000 inhabitants | | 462.9 | 5.6 | 85.8 | 77.4 | 294.1 | 1,828.9 | 369.6 | 1,165.9 | 293.3 |
| **Richmond, VA M.S.A.** | 1,303,052 | | | | | | | | | |
| Includes Amelia, Charles City, Chesterfield, Dinwiddie, Goochland, Hanover, Henrico, King and Queen, King William, New Kent, Powhatan, Prince George, and Sussex Counties and Colonial Heights, Hopewell, Petersburg, and Richmond Cities | | | | | | | | | | |
| City of Richmond | 233,350 | 814 | 66 | 20 | 274 | 454 | 6,816 | 771 | 5,434 | 611 |
| Total area actually reporting | 100.0% | 2,811 | 129 | 268 | 605 | 1,809 | 23,905 | 2,229 | 19,789 | 1,887 |
| Rate per 100,000 inhabitants | | 215.7 | 9.9 | 20.6 | 46.4 | 138.8 | 1,834.5 | 171.1 | 1,518.7 | 144.8 |
| **Riverside-San Bernardino-Ontario, CA M.S.A.** | 4,651,426 | | | | | | | | | |
| Includes Riverside and San Bernardino Counties | | | | | | | | | | |
| City of Riverside | 334,370 | 1,491 | 20 | 152 | 394 | 925 | 9,980 | 1,639 | 6,456 | 1,885 |
| City of San Bernardino | 216,365 | 3,033 | 68 | 134 | 730 | 2,101 | 6,059 | 1,201 | 3,149 | 1,709 |
| City of Ontario | 187,464 | 686 | 10 | 83 | 195 | 398 | 3,994 | 641 | 2,296 | 1,057 |
| City of Corona | 171,848 | 240 | 1 | 36 | 86 | 117 | 3,610 | 677 | 2,160 | 773 |
| City of Temecula | 116,442 | 148 | 0 | 12 | 67 | 69 | 2,262 | 368 | 1,537 | 357 |
| City of Chino | 96,309 | 335 | 3 | 31 | 77 | 224 | 2,075 | 274 | 1,493 | 308 |
| City of Redlands | 71,820 | 238 | 6 | 51 | 69 | 112 | 1,865 | 323 | 1,289 | 253 |
| City of Palm Desert | 53,811 | 125 | 0 | 5 | 28 | 92 | 1,564 | 278 | 1,105 | 181 |
| Total area actually reporting | 100.0% | 20,054 | 335 | 1,296 | 4,281 | 14,142 | 92,307 | 17,140 | 54,945 | 20,222 |
| Rate per 100,000 inhabitants | | 431.1 | 7.2 | 27.9 | 92.0 | 304.0 | 1,984.5 | 368.5 | 1,181.3 | 434.7 |
| **Roanoke, VA M.S.A.** | 313,488 | | | | | | | | | |
| Includes Botetourt, Craig, Franklin, and Roanoke Counties and Roanoke and Salem Cities | | | | | | | | | | |
| City of Roanoke | 99,335 | 448 | 15 | 38 | 90 | 305 | 3,809 | 412 | 3,048 | 349 |
| Total area actually reporting | 100.0% | 821 | 25 | 79 | 130 | 587 | 6,607 | 656 | 5,357 | 594 |
| Rate per 100,000 inhabitants | | 261.9 | 8.0 | 25.2 | 41.5 | 187.2 | 2,107.6 | 209.3 | 1,708.8 | 189.5 |
| **Rochester, MN M.S.A.[2]** | 222,817 | | | | | | | | | |
| Includes Dodge,[2] Fillmore,[2] Olmsted, and Wabasha Counties | | | | | | | | | | |
| City of Rochester | 120,336 | 300 | 5 | 74 | 44 | 177 | 2,314 | 332 | 1,828 | 154 |
| Total area actually reporting | 98.7% | 414 | 6 | 110 | 47 | 251 | 2,984 | 522 | 2,248 | 214 |
| Estimated total | 100.0% | 418 | 6 | 111 | 47 | 254 | 3,041 | 528 | 2,296 | 217 |
| Rate per 100,000 inhabitants | | 187.6 | 2.7 | 49.8 | 21.1 | 114.0 | 1,364.8 | 237.0 | 1,030.4 | 97.4 |
| **Rochester, NY M.S.A.[2]** | 1,061,736 | | | | | | | | | |
| Includes Livingston, Monroe,[2] Ontario, Orleans, Wayne, and Yates Counties | | | | | | | | | | |
| City of Rochester | 205,199 | 1,680 | 48 | 86 | 418 | 1,128 | 6,887 | 1,389 | 4,583 | 915 |

## Table 6. Crime in the United States, by Selected Metropolitan Statistical Area, 2020—Continued

(Number, percent, rate per 100,000 population.)

| Area | Population | Violent crime | Murder and nonnegligent manslaughter | Rape[1] | Robbery | Aggravated assault | Property crime | Burglary | Larceny-theft | Motor vehicle theft |
|---|---|---|---|---|---|---|---|---|---|---|
| Total area actually reporting | 94.0% | 2,644 | 54 | 374 | 562 | 1,654 | 16,302 | 2,594 | 12,284 | 1,424 |
| Estimated total | 100.0% | 2,782 | 54 | 388 | 587 | 1,753 | 17,338 | 2,725 | 13,135 | 1,478 |
| Rate per 100,000 inhabitants | | 262.0 | 5.1 | 36.5 | 55.3 | 165.1 | 1,633.0 | 256.7 | 1,237.1 | 139.2 |
| **Rockford, IL M.S.A.[4]** | 332,940 | | | | | | | | | |
| Includes Boone and Winnebago[4] Counties | | | | | | | | | | |
| City of Rockford | 144,795 | 2,101 | 30 | 102 | 238 | 1,731 | 4,104 | 742 | 2,968 | 394 |
| Total area actually reporting | 84.0% | 2,432 | 34 | 180 | 280 | 1,938 | | 1,000 | | 510 |
| Estimated total | 100.0% | 2,566 | 36 | 199 | 297 | 2,034 | | 1,132 | | 578 |
| Rate per 100,000 inhabitants | | 770.7 | 10.8 | 59.8 | 89.2 | 610.9 | | 340.0 | | 173.6 |
| **Sacramento-Roseville-Folsom, CA M.S.A.** | 2,364,420 | | | | | | | | | |
| Includes El Dorado, Placer, Sacramento, and Yolo Counties | | | | | | | | | | |
| City of Sacramento | 519,050 | 3,547 | 42 | 125 | 879 | 2,501 | 14,248 | 2,834 | 8,903 | 2,511 |
| City of Roseville | 144,128 | 277 | 4 | 18 | 87 | 168 | 2,843 | 318 | 2,245 | 280 |
| City of Folsom | 82,427 | 83 | 0 | 13 | 21 | 49 | 1,198 | 223 | 911 | 64 |
| City of Rancho Cordova | 76,292 | 322 | 6 | 13 | 73 | 230 | 1,555 | 302 | 1,107 | 146 |
| City of West Sacramento | 54,068 | 211 | 3 | 22 | 82 | 104 | 1,505 | 209 | 1,083 | 213 |
| Total area actually reporting | 100.0% | 8,945 | 113 | 639 | 2,069 | 6,124 | 47,650 | 8,796 | 32,420 | 6,434 |
| Rate per 100,000 inhabitants | | 378.3 | 4.8 | 27.0 | 87.5 | 259.0 | 2,015.3 | 372.0 | 1,371.2 | 272.1 |
| **Saginaw, MI M.S.A.** | 188,889 | | | | | | | | | |
| Includes Saginaw County | | | | | | | | | | |
| City of Saginaw | 47,767 | 1,029 | 24 | 57 | 62 | 886 | 720 | 225 | 388 | 107 |
| Total area actually reporting | 100.0% | 1,501 | 33 | 141 | 93 | 1,234 | 2,410 | 512 | 1,671 | 227 |
| Rate per 100,000 inhabitants | | 794.6 | 17.5 | 74.6 | 49.2 | 653.3 | 1,275.9 | 271.1 | 884.6 | 120.2 |
| **Salem, OR M.S.A.** | 436,715 | | | | | | | | | |
| Includes Marion and Polk Counties | | | | | | | | | | |
| City of Salem | 176,632 | 698 | 2 | 28 | 148 | 520 | 6,698 | 678 | 4,911 | 1,109 |
| Total area actually reporting | 99.0% | 1,139 | 7 | 74 | 224 | 834 | 12,365 | 1,341 | 8,935 | 2,089 |
| Estimated total | 100.0% | 1,177 | 7 | 104 | 225 | 841 | 12,462 | 1,349 | 9,015 | 2,098 |
| Rate per 100,000 inhabitants | | 269.5 | 1.6 | 23.8 | 51.5 | 192.6 | 2,853.6 | 308.9 | 2,064.3 | 480.4 |
| **Salinas, CA M.S.A.** | 431,704 | | | | | | | | | |
| Includes Monterey County | | | | | | | | | | |
| City of Salinas | 155,984 | 866 | 8 | 69 | 233 | 556 | 3,481 | 790 | 1,779 | 912 |
| Total area actually reporting | 100.0% | 1,480 | 14 | 175 | 342 | 949 | 7,728 | 1,463 | 4,736 | 1,529 |
| Rate per 100,000 inhabitants | | 342.8 | 3.2 | 40.5 | 79.2 | 219.8 | 1,790.1 | 338.9 | 1,097.0 | 354.2 |
| **Salt Lake City, UT M.S.A.[2]** | 1,246,234 | | | | | | | | | |
| Includes Salt Lake and Tooele[2] Counties | | | | | | | | | | |
| City of Salt Lake City | 202,187 | 1,865 | 17 | 277 | 487 | 1,084 | 14,865 | 1,545 | 11,128 | 2,192 |
| Total area actually reporting | 99.9% | 4,784 | 60 | 835 | 961 | 2,928 | 47,548 | 5,350 | 35,415 | 6,783 |
| Estimated total | 100.0% | 4,785 | 60 | 835 | 961 | 2,929 | 47,566 | 5,352 | 35,429 | 6,785 |
| Rate per 100,000 inhabitants | | 384.0 | 4.8 | 67.0 | 77.1 | 235.0 | 3,816.8 | 429.5 | 2,842.9 | 544.4 |
| **San Angelo, TX M.S.A.[2]** | 122,608 | | | | | | | | | |
| Includes Irion, Sterling, and Tom Green[2] Counties | | | | | | | | | | |
| City of San Angelo | 101,860 | 357 | 7 | 65 | 41 | 244 | 3,039 | 475 | 2,242 | 322 |
| Total area actually reporting | 100.0% | 397 | 8 | 80 | 41 | 268 | 3,259 | 542 | 2,365 | 352 |
| Rate per 100,000 inhabitants | | 323.8 | 6.5 | 65.2 | 33.4 | 218.6 | 2,658.1 | 442.1 | 1,928.9 | 287.1 |
| **San Antonio-New Braunfels, TX M.S.A.[2]** | 2,591,157 | | | | | | | | | |
| Includes Atascosa, Bandera, Bexar,[2] Comal, Guadalupe, Kendall, Medina,[2] and Wilson[2] Counties | | | | | | | | | | |
| City of San Antonio[2] | 1,573,189 | 11,569 | 130 | 1,187 | 2,163 | 8,089 | 57,057 | 7,919 | 42,158 | 6,980 |
| City of New Braunfels | 78,610 | 219 | 6 | 10 | 25 | 178 | 1,230 | 206 | 866 | 158 |
| Total area actually reporting | 99.9% | 13,741 | 170 | 1,555 | 2,391 | 9,625 | 72,724 | 10,939 | 53,056 | 8,729 |
| Estimated total | 100.0% | 13,749 | 170 | 1,556 | 2,392 | 9,631 | 72,783 | 10,951 | 53,095 | 8,737 |
| Rate per 100,000 inhabitants | | 530.6 | 6.6 | 60.1 | 92.3 | 371.7 | 2,808.9 | 422.6 | 2,049.1 | 337.2 |
| **San Diego-Chula Vista-Carlsbad, CA M.S.A.** | 3,331,816 | | | | | | | | | |
| Includes San Diego County | | | | | | | | | | |
| City of San Diego | 1,437,608 | 5,303 | 56 | 485 | 1,207 | 3,555 | 24,321 | 3,324 | 16,044 | 4,953 |
| City of Chula Vista | 278,027 | 916 | 10 | 63 | 302 | 541 | 3,257 | 476 | 2,021 | 760 |
| City of Carlsbad | 116,516 | 224 | 3 | 24 | 35 | 162 | 1,841 | 256 | 1,428 | 157 |
| City of Poway | 49,479 | 53 | 0 | 4 | 16 | 33 | 366 | 84 | 245 | 37 |
| Total area actually reporting | 100.0% | 11,517 | 114 | 967 | 2,527 | 7,909 | 49,471 | 7,301 | 32,863 | 9,307 |
| Rate per 100,000 inhabitants | | 345.7 | 3.4 | 29.0 | 75.8 | 237.4 | 1,484.8 | 219.1 | 986.3 | 279.3 |
| **San Francisco-Oakland-Berkeley, CA M.S.A.** | 4,729,308 | | | | | | | | | |
| Includes the Metropolitan Divisions of Oakland-Berkeley-Livermore, San Francisco-San Mateo-Redwood City, and San Rafael | | | | | | | | | | |
| City of San Francisco | 881,514 | 4,796 | 48 | 198 | 2,388 | 2,162 | 38,737 | 7,452 | 25,319 | 5,966 |
| City of Oakland | 437,923 | 5,653 | 102 | 362 | 2,479 | 2,710 | 22,622 | 2,537 | 13,373 | 6,712 |
| City of Berkeley | 122,346 | 537 | 6 | 47 | 274 | 210 | 5,535 | 797 | 3,933 | 805 |
| City of San Mateo | 105,246 | 274 | 4 | 41 | 71 | 158 | 2,306 | 523 | 1,493 | 290 |
| City of Livermore | 91,200 | 164 | 1 | 38 | 47 | 78 | 1,526 | 164 | 1,166 | 196 |
| City of Redwood City | 86,983 | 187 | 1 | 38 | 58 | 90 | 1,489 | 240 | 970 | 279 |
| City of Pleasanton | 83,164 | 94 | 1 | 11 | 40 | 42 | 1,188 | 161 | 937 | 90 |
| City of San Ramon | 76,502 | 54 | 0 | 11 | 22 | 21 | 796 | 104 | 636 | 56 |
| City of Walnut Creek | 70,849 | 91 | 0 | 3 | 27 | 61 | 2,063 | 264 | 1,582 | 217 |

## Table 6. Crime in the United States, by Selected Metropolitan Statistical Area, 2020—Continued

(Number, percent, rate per 100,000 population.)

| Area | Population | Violent crime | Murder and nonnegligent manslaughter | Rape[1] | Robbery | Aggravated assault | Property crime | Burglary | Larceny-theft | Motor vehicle theft |
|---|---|---|---|---|---|---|---|---|---|---|
| City of South San Francisco | 68,260 | 155 | 1 | 15 | 58 | 81 | 1,560 | 157 | 1,155 | 248 |
| City of San Rafael | 58,512 | 229 | 0 | 26 | 67 | 136 | 1,912 | 260 | 1,152 | 500 |
| Total area actually reporting | 100.0% | 20,814 | 253 | 1,504 | 8,440 | 10,617 | 142,267 | 20,761 | 92,931 | 28,575 |
| Rate per 100,000 inhabitants | | 440.1 | 5.3 | 31.8 | 178.5 | 224.5 | 3,008.2 | 439.0 | 1,965.0 | 604.2 |
| **Oakland-Berkeley-Livermore, CA M.D.** | 2,826,657 | | | | | | | | | |
| Includes Alameda and Contra Costa Counties | | | | | | | | | | |
| Total area actually reporting | 100.0% | 13,515 | 187 | 967 | 5,307 | 7,054 | 81,991 | 10,295 | 52,093 | 19,603 |
| Rate per 100,000 inhabitants | | 478.1 | 6.6 | 34.2 | 187.7 | 249.6 | 2,900.6 | 364.2 | 1,842.9 | 693.5 |
| **San Francisco-San Mateo-Redwood City, CA M.D.** | 1,645,756 | | | | | | | | | |
| Includes San Francisco and San Mateo Counties | | | | | | | | | | |
| Total area actually reporting | 100.0% | 6,676 | 65 | 485 | 3,010 | 3,116 | 55,003 | 9,668 | 37,150 | 8,185 |
| Rate per 100,000 inhabitants | | 405.6 | 3.9 | 29.5 | 182.9 | 189.3 | 3,342.1 | 587.5 | 2,257.3 | 497.3 |
| **San Rafael, CA M.D.** | 256,895 | | | | | | | | | |
| Includes Marin County | | | | | | | | | | |
| Total area actually reporting | 100.0% | 623 | 1 | 52 | 123 | 447 | 5,273 | 798 | 3,688 | 787 |
| Rate per 100,000 inhabitants | | 242.5 | 0.4 | 20.2 | 47.9 | 174.0 | 2,052.6 | 310.6 | 1,435.6 | 306.4 |
| **San Jose-Sunnyvale-Santa Clara, CA M.S.A.** | 1,987,878 | | | | | | | | | |
| Includes San Benito and Santa Clara Counties | | | | | | | | | | |
| City of San Jose | 1,029,542 | 4,375 | 40 | 566 | 1,185 | 2,584 | 23,847 | 4,045 | 12,737 | 7,065 |
| City of Sunnyvale | 154,133 | 229 | 2 | 32 | 61 | 134 | 3,178 | 516 | 2,276 | 386 |
| City of Santa Clara | 131,976 | 206 | 1 | 39 | 85 | 81 | 3,301 | 432 | 2,314 | 555 |
| City of Mountain View | 83,745 | 144 | 0 | 9 | 52 | 83 | 2,177 | 422 | 1,566 | 189 |
| City of Milpitas | 86,416 | 111 | 2 | 16 | 40 | 53 | 2,103 | 277 | 1,516 | 310 |
| City of Palo Alto | 65,459 | 81 | 1 | 12 | 39 | 29 | 1,931 | 242 | 1,570 | 119 |
| City of Cupertino | 59,343 | 69 | 0 | 9 | 26 | 34 | 830 | 196 | 581 | 53 |
| Total area actually reporting | 100.0% | 6,306 | 56 | 826 | 1,723 | 3,701 | 44,263 | 7,338 | 26,867 | 10,058 |
| Rate per 100,000 inhabitants | | 317.2 | 2.8 | 41.6 | 86.7 | 186.2 | 2,226.6 | 369.1 | 1,351.5 | 506.0 |
| **San Luis Obispo-Paso Robles, CA M.S.A.** | 281,778 | | | | | | | | | |
| Includes San Luis Obispo County | | | | | | | | | | |
| City of San Luis Obispo | 47,722 | 207 | 1 | 39 | 28 | 139 | 1,620 | 284 | 1,219 | 117 |
| City of Paso Robles | 32,428 | 53 | 3 | 2 | 8 | 40 | 363 | 35 | 295 | 33 |
| Total area actually reporting | 100.0% | 816 | 7 | 93 | 79 | 637 | 4,610 | 868 | 3,381 | 361 |
| Rate per 100,000 inhabitants | | 289.6 | 2.5 | 33.0 | 28.0 | 226.1 | 1,636.0 | 308.0 | 1,199.9 | 128.1 |
| **Santa Cruz-Watsonville, CA M.S.A.** | 271,608 | | | | | | | | | |
| Includes Santa Cruz County | | | | | | | | | | |
| City of Santa Cruz | 65,073 | 309 | 2 | 33 | 76 | 198 | 2,237 | 267 | 1,734 | 236 |
| City of Watsonville | 54,151 | 299 | 4 | 27 | 44 | 224 | 1,132 | 167 | 655 | 310 |
| Total area actually reporting | 100.0% | 970 | 12 | 104 | 172 | 682 | 6,155 | 905 | 4,252 | 998 |
| Rate per 100,000 inhabitants | | 357.1 | 4.4 | 38.3 | 63.3 | 251.1 | 2,266.1 | 333.2 | 1,565.5 | 367.4 |
| | 444,547 | | | | | | | | | |
| **Includes Santa Barbara County** | | | | | | | | | | |
| City of Santa Maria | 108,140 | 834 | 2 | 81 | 179 | 572 | 2,472 | 328 | 1,114 | 1,030 |
| City of Santa Barbara | 91,692 | 389 | 2 | 60 | 84 | 243 | 2,188 | 217 | 1,748 | 223 |
| Total area actually reporting | 100.0% | 1,824 | 8 | 227 | 341 | 1,248 | 8,827 | 1,178 | 5,812 | 1,837 |
| Rate per 100,000 inhabitants | | 410.3 | 1.8 | 51.1 | 76.7 | 280.7 | 1,985.6 | 265.0 | 1,307.4 | 413.2 |
| **Santa Rosa-Petaluma, CA M.S.A.** | 490,455 | | | | | | | | | |
| Includes Sonoma County | | | | | | | | | | |
| City of Santa Rosa | 176,932 | 913 | 4 | 110 | 135 | 664 | 2,838 | 542 | 1,875 | 421 |
| City of Petaluma | 60,806 | 255 | 2 | 25 | 33 | 195 | 756 | 90 | 597 | 69 |
| Total area actually reporting | 100.0% | 2,212 | 10 | 239 | 266 | 1,697 | 6,412 | 1,272 | 4,408 | 732 |
| Rate per 100,000 inhabitants | | 451.0 | 2.0 | 48.7 | 54.2 | 346.0 | 1,307.4 | 259.4 | 898.8 | 149.2 |
| **Seattle-Tacoma-Bellevue, WA M.S.A.** | 4,030,255 | | | | | | | | | |
| Includes the Metropolitan Divisions of Seattle-Bellevue-Kent and Tacoma-Lakewood | | | | | | | | | | |
| City of Seattle | 771,517 | 4,832 | 52 | 301 | 1,471 | 3,008 | 37,593 | 10,427 | 22,255 | 4,911 |
| City of Tacoma | 220,123 | 1,856 | 28 | 127 | 435 | 1,266 | 12,123 | 1,987 | 7,967 | 2,169 |
| City of Bellevue | 150,548 | 175 | 4 | 19 | 68 | 84 | 4,526 | 597 | 3,641 | 288 |
| City of Kent | 133,883 | 470 | 8 | 78 | 184 | 200 | 5,393 | 1,054 | 3,378 | 961 |
| City of Everett | 112,439 | 379 | 4 | 37 | 98 | 240 | 3,654 | 515 | 2,436 | 703 |
| City of Renton | 102,856 | 348 | 6 | 37 | 108 | 197 | 4,342 | 498 | 3,063 | 781 |
| City of Auburn | 82,779 | 362 | 10 | 40 | 121 | 191 | 3,394 | 584 | 2,150 | 660 |
| City of Redmond | 74,154 | 74 | 0 | 12 | 19 | 43 | 1,742 | 207 | 1,443 | 92 |
| City of Lakewood | 61,432 | 381 | 4 | 32 | 72 | 273 | 2,620 | 445 | 1,721 | 454 |
| Total area actually reporting | 100.0% | 13,692 | 181 | 1,253 | 3,767 | 8,491 | 127,233 | 24,849 | 83,956 | 18,428 |
| Rate per 100,000 inhabitants | | 339.7 | 4.5 | 31.1 | 93.5 | 210.7 | 3,156.9 | 616.6 | 2,083.1 | 457.2 |
| **Seattle-Bellevue-Kent, WA M.D.** | 3,115,239 | | | | | | | | | |
| Includes King and Snohomish Counties | | | | | | | | | | |
| Total area actually reporting | 100.0% | 9,720 | 128 | 943 | 2,934 | 5,715 | 97,577 | 19,512 | 64,595 | 13,470 |
| Rate per 100,000 inhabitants | | 312.0 | 4.1 | 30.3 | 94.2 | 183.5 | 3,132.2 | 626.3 | 2,073.5 | 432.4 |
| **Tacoma-Lakewood, WA M.D.** | 915,016 | | | | | | | | | |
| Includes Pierce County | | | | | | | | | | |
| Total area actually reporting | 100.0% | 3,972 | 53 | 310 | 833 | 2,776 | 29,656 | 5,337 | 19,361 | 4,958 |
| Rate per 100,000 inhabitants | | 434.1 | 5.8 | 33.9 | 91.0 | 303.4 | 3,241.0 | 583.3 | 2,115.9 | 541.8 |

# Table 6. Crime in the United States, by Selected Metropolitan Statistical Area, 2020—Continued

(Number, percent, rate per 100,000 population.)

| Area | Population | Violent crime | Murder and nonnegligent manslaughter | Rape[1] | Robbery | Aggravated assault | Property crime | Burglary | Larceny-theft | Motor vehicle theft |
|---|---|---|---|---|---|---|---|---|---|---|
| **Sebastian-Vero Beach, FL M.S.A.** | 162,048 | | | | | | | | | |
| Includes Indian River County | | | | | | | | | | |
| City of Sebastian | 26,626 | 21 | 0 | 4 | 3 | 14 | 155 | 12 | 132 | 11 |
| City of Vero Beach | 17,776 | 34 | 0 | 1 | 6 | 27 | 250 | 37 | 190 | 23 |
| Total area actually reporting | 100.0% | 219 | 3 | 14 | 28 | 174 | 1,880 | 187 | 1,513 | 180 |
| Rate per 100,000 inhabitants | | 135.1 | 1.9 | 8.6 | 17.3 | 107.4 | 1,160.2 | 115.4 | 933.7 | 111.1 |
| **Sebring-Avon Park, FL M.S.A.** | 106,784 | | | | | | | | | |
| Includes Highlands County | | | | | | | | | | |
| City of Sebring | 10,664 | 79 | 3 | 8 | 15 | 53 | 389 | 69 | 302 | 18 |
| Total area actually reporting | 100.0% | 296 | 8 | 29 | 39 | 220 | 1,889 | 333 | 1,405 | 151 |
| Rate per 100,000 inhabitants | | 277.2 | 7.5 | 27.2 | 36.5 | 206.0 | 1,769.0 | 311.8 | 1,315.7 | 141.4 |
| **Sheboygan, WI M.S.A.[2]** | 115,218 | | | | | | | | | |
| Includes Sheboygan County[2] | | | | | | | | | | |
| City of Sheboygan | 47,814 | 157 | 1 | 33 | 15 | 108 | 832 | 97 | 702 | 33 |
| Total area actually reporting | 100.0% | 209 | 1 | 55 | 15 | 138 | 1,364 | 134 | 1,169 | 61 |
| Rate per 100,000 inhabitants | | 181.4 | 0.9 | 47.7 | 13.0 | 119.8 | 1,183.8 | 116.3 | 1,014.6 | 52.9 |
| **Sherman-Denison, TX M.S.A.[2]** | 137,545 | | | | | | | | | |
| Includes Grayson County[2] | | | | | | | | | | |
| City of Sherman[2] | 44,611 | 197 | 6 | 34 | 24 | 133 | 1,095 | 222 | 769 | 104 |
| City of Denison[2] | 25,858 | 113 | 1 | 23 | 9 | 80 | 484 | 124 | 276 | 84 |
| Total area actually reporting | 98.4% | 388 | 9 | 74 | 40 | 265 | 2,027 | 445 | 1,331 | 251 |
| Estimated total | 100.0% | 392 | 9 | 74 | 40 | 269 | 2,064 | 453 | 1,355 | 256 |
| Rate per 100,000 inhabitants | | 285.0 | 6.5 | 53.8 | 29.1 | 195.6 | 1,500.6 | 329.3 | 985.1 | 186.1 |
| **Shreveport-Bossier City, LA M.S.A.[2]** | 392,827 | | | | | | | | | |
| Includes Bossier, Caddo, and De Soto Parishes | | | | | | | | | | |
| City of Shreveport | 185,588 | 1,713 | 69 | 125 | 235 | 1,284 | 8,907 | 1,516 | 6,690 | 701 |
| City of Bossier City[2] | 68,869 | 609 | 8 | 52 | 77 | 472 | 3,201 | 400 | 2,472 | 329 |
| Total area actually reporting | 99.5% | 2,675 | 85 | 196 | 336 | 2,058 | 14,056 | 2,363 | 10,505 | 1,188 |
| Estimated total | 100.0% | 2,683 | 85 | 196 | 338 | 2,064 | 14,095 | 2,369 | 10,533 | 1,193 |
| Rate per 100,000 inhabitants | | 683.0 | 21.6 | 49.9 | 86.0 | 525.4 | 3,588.1 | 603.1 | 2,681.3 | 303.7 |
| **Sierra Vista-Douglas, AZ M.S.A.** | 125,923 | | | | | | | | | |
| Includes Cochise County | | | | | | | | | | |
| City of Sierra Vista | 42,800 | 82 | 1 | 4 | 12 | 65 | 888 | 85 | 764 | 39 |
| City of Douglas | 16,044 | 17 | 0 | 1 | 1 | 15 | 395 | 67 | 311 | 17 |
| Total area actually reporting | 91.0% | 190 | 8 | 8 | 20 | 154 | 1,876 | 340 | 1,403 | 133 |
| Estimated total | 100.0% | 310 | 8 | 15 | 33 | 254 | 2,598 | 479 | 1,925 | 194 |
| Rate per 100,000 inhabitants | | 246.2 | 6.4 | 11.9 | 26.2 | 201.7 | 2,063.2 | 380.4 | 1,528.7 | 154.1 |
| **Sioux City, IA-NE-SD M.S.A.** | 144,522 | | | | | | | | | |
| Includes Woodbury County, IA; Dakota and Dixon Counties, NE; and Union County, SD | | | | | | | | | | |
| City of Sioux City, IA | 82,628 | 477 | 9 | 61 | 75 | 332 | 2,682 | 479 | 1,933 | 270 |
| Total area actually reporting | 94.8% | 595 | 9 | 72 | 79 | 435 | 3,245 | 552 | 2,357 | 336 |
| Estimated total | 100.0% | 619 | 9 | 76 | 79 | 455 | 3,326 | 569 | 2,409 | 348 |
| Rate per 100,000 inhabitants | | 428.3 | 6.2 | 52.6 | 54.7 | 314.8 | 2,301.4 | 393.7 | 1,666.9 | 240.8 |
| **Sioux Falls, SD M.S.A.** | 273,001 | | | | | | | | | |
| Includes Lincoln, McCook, Minnehaha, and Turner Counties | | | | | | | | | | |
| City of Sioux Falls | 187,370 | 1,120 | 13 | 97 | 102 | 908 | 5,867 | 684 | 4,259 | 924 |
| Total area actually reporting | 99.3% | 1,297 | 15 | 124 | 107 | 1,051 | 6,856 | 1,075 | 4,745 | 1,036 |
| Estimated total | 100.0% | 1,304 | 15 | 124 | 109 | 1,056 | 6,891 | 1,080 | 4,771 | 1,040 |
| Rate per 100,000 inhabitants | | 477.7 | 5.5 | 45.4 | 39.9 | 386.8 | 2,524.2 | 395.6 | 1,747.6 | 381.0 |
| **South Bend-Mishawaka, IN-MI M.S.A.[2]** | 323,697 | | | | | | | | | |
| Includes St. Joseph County, IN and Cass County, MI | | | | | | | | | | |
| City of South Bend, IN | 102,119 | 1,765 | 28 | 78 | 238 | 1,421 | 3,741 | 659 | 2,511 | 571 |
| City of Mishawaka, IN[2] | 50,610 | 80 | 0 | 15 | 6 | 59 | 1,207 | 131 | 935 | 141 |
| Total area actually reporting | 87.1% | 2,031 | 29 | 132 | 266 | 1,604 | 6,675 | 1,221 | 4,527 | 927 |
| Estimated total | 100.0% | 2,121 | 30 | 149 | 274 | 1,668 | 7,031 | 1,302 | 4,773 | 956 |
| Rate per 100,000 inhabitants | | 655.2 | 9.3 | 46.0 | 84.6 | 515.3 | 2,172.1 | 402.2 | 1,474.5 | 295.3 |
| **Spartanburg, SC M.S.A.** | 324,314 | | | | | | | | | |
| Includes Spartanburg and Union Counties | | | | | | | | | | |
| City of Spartanburg | 37,469 | 536 | 4 | 29 | 94 | 409 | 2,286 | 434 | 1,595 | 257 |
| Total area actually reporting | 99.8% | 1,642 | 9 | 90 | 173 | 1,370 | 7,919 | 1,700 | 5,275 | 944 |
| Estimated total | 100.0% | 1,643 | 9 | 90 | 173 | 1,371 | 7,935 | 1,703 | 5,286 | 946 |
| Rate per 100,000 inhabitants | | 506.6 | 2.8 | 27.8 | 53.3 | 422.7 | 2,446.7 | 525.1 | 1,629.9 | 291.7 |
| **Spokane-Spokane Valley, WA M.S.A.** | 572,842 | | | | | | | | | |
| Includes Spokane and Stevens Counties | | | | | | | | | | |
| City of Spokane | 223,524 | 1,341 | 19 | 187 | 280 | 855 | 11,514 | 1,745 | 8,666 | 1,103 |
| City of Spokane Valley | 102,366 | 342 | 3 | 28 | 77 | 234 | 4,370 | 691 | 3,339 | 340 |
| Total area actually reporting | 100.0% | 2,005 | 30 | 282 | 393 | 1,300 | 19,927 | 3,277 | 14,863 | 1,787 |
| Rate per 100,000 inhabitants | | 350.0 | 5.2 | 49.2 | 68.6 | 226.9 | 3,478.6 | 572.1 | 2,594.6 | 312.0 |
| **Springfield, IL M.S.A.[4]** | 205,389 | | | | | | | | | |
| Includes Menard and Sangamon[4] Counties | | | | | | | | | | |
| City of Springfield[4] | 113,912 | 1,078 | 11 | 101 | 195 | 771 | | 937 | | 254 |

## Table 6. Crime in the United States, by Selected Metropolitan Statistical Area, 2020—Continued

(Number, percent, rate per 100,000 population.)

| Area | Population | Violent crime | Murder and nonnegligent manslaughter | Rape[1] | Robbery | Aggravated assault | Property crime | Burglary | Larceny-theft | Motor vehicle theft |
|---|---|---|---|---|---|---|---|---|---|---|
| Total area actually reporting | 94.1% | 1,357 | 12 | 133 | 215 | 997 | | 1,223 | | 357 |
| Estimated total | 100.0% | 1,369 | 12 | 134 | 215 | 1,008 | | 1,257 | | 366 |
| Rate per 100,000 inhabitants | | 666.5 | 5.8 | 65.2 | 104.7 | 490.8 | | 612.0 | | 178.2 |
| **Springfield, MA M.S.A.** | 693,972 | | | | | | | | | |
| Includes Franklin, Hampden and Hampshire Counties | | | | | | | | | | |
| City of Springfield | 153,084 | 1,480 | 18 | 70 | 350 | 1,042 | 3,730 | 618 | 2,616 | 496 |
| Total area actually reporting | 97.5% | 3,163 | 28 | 272 | 536 | 2,327 | 10,694 | 1,671 | 7,988 | 1,035 |
| Estimated total | 100.0% | 3,216 | 28 | 280 | 546 | 2,362 | 10,788 | 1,695 | 8,050 | 1,043 |
| Rate per 100,000 inhabitants | | 463.4 | 4.0 | 40.3 | 78.7 | 340.4 | 1,554.5 | 244.2 | 1,160.0 | 150.3 |
| **Springfield, MO M.S.A.**[2] | 473,913 | | | | | | | | | |
| Includes Christian, Dallas, Greene, Polk, and Webster Counties | | | | | | | | | | |
| City of Springfield[2] | 168,856 | 2,545 | 22 | 178 | 375 | 1,970 | 11,738 | 1,795 | 8,639 | 1,304 |
| Total area actually reporting | 97.9% | 2,943 | 26 | 230 | 398 | 2,289 | 15,370 | 2,496 | 11,237 | 1,637 |
| Estimated total | 100.0% | 2,993 | 26 | 232 | 405 | 2,330 | 15,647 | 2,533 | 11,433 | 1,681 |
| Rate per 100,000 inhabitants | | 631.6 | 5.5 | 49.0 | 85.5 | 491.7 | 3,301.7 | 534.5 | 2,412.5 | 354.7 |
| **Springfield, OH M.S.A.** | 133,456 | | | | | | | | | |
| Includes Clark County | | | | | | | | | | |
| City of Springfield | 58,696 | 338 | 8 | 52 | 107 | 171 | 3,014 | 619 | 2,060 | 335 |
| Total area actually reporting | 94.1% | 391 | 9 | 57 | 110 | 215 | 3,741 | 767 | 2,611 | 363 |
| Estimated total | 100.0% | 401 | 9 | 59 | 112 | 221 | 3,872 | 784 | 2,719 | 369 |
| Rate per 100,000 inhabitants | | 300.5 | 6.7 | 44.2 | 83.9 | 165.6 | 2,901.3 | 587.5 | 2,037.4 | 276.5 |
| **Staunton, VA M.S.A.** | 123,568 | | | | | | | | | |
| Includes Augusta County and Staunton and Waynesboro Cities | | | | | | | | | | |
| City of Staunton | 25,048 | 45 | 2 | 10 | 6 | 27 | 549 | 54 | 469 | 26 |
| Total area actually reporting | 100.0% | 231 | 4 | 63 | 15 | 149 | 1,812 | 256 | 1,438 | 118 |
| Rate per 100,000 inhabitants | | 186.9 | 3.2 | 51.0 | 12.1 | 120.6 | 1,466.4 | 207.2 | 1,163.7 | 95.5 |
| **St. George, UT M.S.A.** | 182,066 | | | | | | | | | |
| Includes Washington County | | | | | | | | | | |
| City of St. George | 91,673 | 148 | 3 | 42 | 10 | 93 | 1,025 | 148 | 772 | 105 |
| Total area actually reporting | 98.4% | 290 | 5 | 73 | 13 | 199 | 2,038 | 268 | 1,583 | 187 |
| Estimated total | 100.0% | 294 | 5 | 74 | 13 | 202 | 2,118 | 273 | 1,652 | 193 |
| Rate per 100,000 inhabitants | | 161.5 | 2.7 | 40.6 | 7.1 | 110.9 | 1,163.3 | 149.9 | 907.4 | 106.0 |
| **St. Joseph, MO-KS M.S.A.** | 124,927 | | | | | | | | | |
| Includes Doniphan County, KS and Andrew, Buchanan, and DeKalb Counties, MO | | | | | | | | | | |
| City of St. Joseph, MO | 74,680 | 414 | 3 | 122 | 47 | 242 | 3,843 | 576 | 2,711 | 556 |
| Total area actually reporting | 99.4% | 518 | 4 | 143 | 48 | 323 | 4,407 | 695 | 3,052 | 660 |
| Estimated total | 100.0% | 521 | 4 | 143 | 48 | 326 | 4,424 | 698 | 3,063 | 663 |
| Rate per 100,000 inhabitants | | 417.0 | 3.2 | 114.5 | 38.4 | 261.0 | 3,541.3 | 558.7 | 2,451.8 | 530.7 |
| **St. Louis, MO-IL M.S.A.2,**[4] | 2,802,055 | | | | | | | | | |
| Includes Bond, Calhoun, Clinton,[4] Jersey,[4] Macoupin,[4] Madison,[4] Monroe,[4] and St. Clair Counties, IL and Franklin, Jefferson,[2] Lincoln,[2] St. Charles,[2] St. Louis,[2] and Warren Counties and St. Louis City, MO | | | | | | | | | | |
| City of St. Louis, MO | 298,422 | 6,017 | 263 | 234 | 1,242 | 4,278 | 17,399 | 2,552 | 11,626 | 3,221 |
| City of St. Charles, MO | 71,563 | 192 | 3 | 19 | 27 | 143 | 1,368 | 145 | 1,022 | 201 |
| Total area actually reporting | 95.2% | 13,647 | 399 | 937 | 2,183 | 10,128 | | 8,827 | | 10,171 |
| Estimated total | 100.0% | 13,925 | 402 | 974 | 2,218 | 10,331 | | 9,130 | | 10,327 |
| Rate per 100,000 inhabitants | | 497.0 | 14.3 | 34.8 | 79.2 | 368.7 | | 325.8 | | 368.6 |
| **Stockton, CA M.S.A.** | 763,250 | | | | | | | | | |
| Includes San Joaquin County | | | | | | | | | | |
| City of Stockton | 314,981 | 4,023 | 56 | 189 | 909 | 2,869 | 9,391 | 1,533 | 6,362 | 1,496 |
| Total area actually reporting | 100.0% | 5,517 | 84 | 264 | 1,281 | 3,888 | 17,805 | 2,817 | 12,091 | 2,897 |
| Rate per 100,000 inhabitants | | 722.8 | 11.0 | 34.6 | 167.8 | 509.4 | 2,332.8 | 369.1 | 1,584.1 | 379.6 |
| **Sumter, SC M.S.A.** | 140,399 | | | | | | | | | |
| Includes Clarendon and Sumter Counties | | | | | | | | | | |
| City of Sumter | 39,542 | 491 | 10 | 9 | 45 | 427 | 1,459 | 211 | 1,179 | 69 |
| Total area actually reporting | 99.4% | 1,138 | 28 | 49 | 88 | 973 | 3,831 | 738 | 2,809 | 284 |
| Estimated total | 100.0% | 1,140 | 28 | 49 | 89 | 974 | 3,852 | 742 | 2,824 | 286 |
| Rate per 100,000 inhabitants | | 812.0 | 19.9 | 34.9 | 63.4 | 693.7 | 2,743.6 | 528.5 | 2,011.4 | 203.7 |
| **Syracuse, NY M.S.A.** | 642,895 | | | | | | | | | |
| Includes Madison, Onondaga, and Oswego Counties | | | | | | | | | | |
| City of Syracuse | 142,011 | 1,192 | 32 | 96 | 222 | 842 | 4,009 | 1,032 | 2,463 | 514 |
| Total area actually reporting | 100.0% | 1,953 | 35 | 297 | 315 | 1,306 | 10,985 | 1,874 | 8,039 | 1,072 |
| Rate per 100,000 inhabitants | | 303.8 | 5.4 | 46.2 | 49.0 | 203.1 | 1,708.7 | 291.5 | 1,250.4 | 166.7 |
| **Tallahassee, FL M.S.A.** | 388,159 | | | | | | | | | |
| Includes Gadsden, Jefferson, Leon, and Wakulla Counties | | | | | | | | | | |
| City of Tallahassee | 196,012 | 1,516 | 24 | 196 | 238 | 1,058 | 5,786 | 1,067 | 4,159 | 560 |
| Total area actually reporting | 97.8% | 2,119 | 35 | 253 | 280 | 1,551 | 8,391 | 1,684 | 5,889 | 818 |
| Estimated total | 100.0% | 2,157 | 35 | 256 | 285 | 1,581 | 8,643 | 1,728 | 6,075 | 840 |
| Rate per 100,000 inhabitants | | 555.7 | 9.0 | 66.0 | 73.4 | 407.3 | 2,226.7 | 445.2 | 1,565.1 | 216.4 |

## Table 6. Crime in the United States, by Selected Metropolitan Statistical Area, 2020—Continued

(Number, percent, rate per 100,000 population.)

| Area | Population | Violent crime | Murder and nonnegligent manslaughter | Rape[1] | Robbery | Aggravated assault | Property crime | Burglary | Larceny-theft | Motor vehicle theft |
|---|---|---|---|---|---|---|---|---|---|---|
| **Tampa-St. Petersburg-Clearwater, FL M.S.A.** | 3,234,443 | | | | | | | | | |
| Includes Hernando, Hillsborough, Pasco, and Pinellas Counties | | | | | | | | | | |
| City of Tampa | 407,350 | 2,119 | 41 | 101 | 325 | 1,652 | 5,561 | 925 | 3,993 | 643 |
| City of St. Petersburg | 267,690 | 1,772 | 15 | 110 | 275 | 1,372 | 6,841 | 887 | 5,315 | 639 |
| City of Clearwater | 117,859 | 460 | 0 | 92 | 87 | 281 | 2,232 | 249 | 1,850 | 133 |
| City of Largo | 85,594 | 332 | 4 | 38 | 60 | 230 | 1,810 | 154 | 1,505 | 151 |
| City of Pinellas Park | 54,114 | 187 | 0 | 32 | 47 | 108 | 1,788 | 185 | 1,484 | 119 |
| Total area actually reporting | 100.0% | 10,159 | 130 | 1,076 | 1,525 | 7,428 | 44,114 | 5,914 | 34,203 | 3,997 |
| Rate per 100,000 inhabitants | | 314.1 | 4.0 | 33.3 | 47.1 | 229.7 | 1,363.9 | 182.8 | 1,057.5 | 123.6 |
| **The Villages, FL M.S.A.** | 137,110 | | | | | | | | | |
| Includes Sumter County | | | | | | | | | | |
| Total area actually reporting | 100.0% | 279 | 3 | 22 | 20 | 234 | 967 | 191 | 666 | 110 |
| Rate per 100,000 inhabitants | | 203.5 | 2.2 | 16.0 | 14.6 | 170.7 | 705.3 | 139.3 | 485.7 | 80.2 |
| **Toledo, OH M.S.A.** | 639,977 | | | | | | | | | |
| Includes Fulton, Lucas, Ottawa, and Wood Counties | | | | | | | | | | |
| City of Toledo | 271,237 | 2,729 | 53 | 213 | 493 | 1,970 | 7,849 | 1,777 | 5,064 | 1,008 |
| Total area actually reporting | 92.0% | 3,052 | 56 | 296 | 542 | 2,158 | 12,195 | 2,219 | 8,783 | 1,193 |
| Estimated total | 100.0% | 3,108 | 56 | 306 | 552 | 2,194 | 12,956 | 2,337 | 9,383 | 1,236 |
| Rate per 100,000 inhabitants | | 485.6 | 8.8 | 47.8 | 86.3 | 342.8 | 2,024.4 | 365.2 | 1,466.1 | 193.1 |
| **Trenton-Princeton, NJ M.S.A.** | 367,006 | | | | | | | | | |
| Includes Mercer County | | | | | | | | | | |
| City of Trenton | 82,909 | 969 | 40 | 50 | 262 | 617 | 1,733 | 412 | 1,038 | 283 |
| City of Princeton | 31,458 | 11 | 0 | 0 | 3 | 8 | 196 | 19 | 161 | 16 |
| Total area actually reporting | 100.0% | 1,316 | 41 | 101 | 343 | 831 | 4,910 | 846 | 3,587 | 477 |
| Rate per 100,000 inhabitants | | 358.6 | 11.2 | 27.5 | 93.5 | 226.4 | 1,337.9 | 230.5 | 977.4 | 130.0 |
| **Tucson, AZ M.S.A.[2]** | 1,060,180 | | | | | | | | | |
| Includes Pima County[2] | | | | | | | | | | |
| City of Tucson | 550,448 | 3,843 | 61 | 463 | 978 | 2,341 | 19,931 | 2,097 | 15,956 | 1,878 |
| Total area actually reporting | 100.0% | 5,020 | 86 | 545 | 1,169 | 3,220 | 29,948 | 3,407 | 24,023 | 2,518 |
| Rate per 100,000 inhabitants | | 473.5 | 8.1 | 51.4 | 110.3 | 303.7 | 2,824.8 | 321.4 | 2,265.9 | 237.5 |
| **Tulsa, OK M.S.A.[2]** | 1,005,482 | | | | | | | | | |
| Includes Creek, Okmulgee, Osage, Pawnee, Rogers,[2] Tulsa, and Wag- oner Counties | | | | | | | | | | |
| City of Tulsa | 402,166 | 4,555 | 72 | 378 | 741 | 3,364 | 20,557 | 4,407 | 12,246 | 3,904 |
| Total area actually reporting | 100.0% | 5,947 | 94 | 565 | 873 | 4,415 | 31,267 | 6,704 | 19,185 | 5,378 |
| Rate per 100,000 inhabitants | | 591.5 | 9.3 | 56.2 | 86.8 | 439.1 | 3,109.7 | 666.7 | 1,908.0 | 534.9 |
| **Twin Falls, ID M.S.A.[3]** | 113,458 | | | | | | | | | |
| Includes Jerome and Twin Falls[3] Counties | | | | | | | | | | |
| City of Twin Falls | 50,872 | 259 | 2 | 36 | 7 | 214 | 892 | 100 | 754 | 38 |
| Total area actually reporting | 100.0% | 435 | 3 | 71 | 11 | 350 | | | 994 | 90 |
| Rate per 100,000 inhabitants | | 383.4 | 2.6 | 62.6 | 9.7 | 308.5 | | | 876.1 | 79.3 |
| **Tyler, TX M.S.A.** | 234,573 | | | | | | | | | |
| Includes Smith County | | | | | | | | | | |
| City of Tyler | 108,139 | 472 | 6 | 53 | 69 | 344 | 3,296 | 523 | 2,563 | 210 |
| Total area actually reporting | 100.0% | 869 | 18 | 104 | 94 | 653 | 5,092 | 994 | 3,632 | 466 |
| Rate per 100,000 inhabitants | | 370.5 | 7.7 | 44.3 | 40.1 | 278.4 | 2,170.8 | 423.7 | 1,548.3 | 198.7 |
| **Utica-Rome, NY M.S.A.[2]** | 287,148 | | | | | | | | | |
| Includes Herkimer and Oneida Counties | | | | | | | | | | |
| City of Utica[2] | 59,483 | 298 | 1 | 23 | 70 | 204 | 2,017 | 267 | 1,636 | 114 |
| City of Rome[2] | 31,978 | 65 | 0 | 8 | 7 | 50 | 570 | 70 | 457 | 43 |
| Total area actually reporting | 95.0% | 625 | 4 | 138 | 95 | 388 | 4,594 | 598 | 3,768 | 228 |
| Estimated total | 100.0% | 644 | 4 | 142 | 99 | 399 | 4,684 | 615 | 3,837 | 232 |
| Rate per 100,000 inhabitants | | 224.3 | 1.4 | 49.5 | 34.5 | 139.0 | 1,631.2 | 214.2 | 1,336.2 | 80.8 |
| **Valdosta, GA M.S.A.[2]** | 147,899 | | | | | | | | | |
| Includes Brooks,[2] Echols, Lanier,[2] and Lowndes[2] Counties | | | | | | | | | | |
| City of Valdosta[2] | 56,628 | 220 | 6 | 13 | 43 | 158 | 1,848 | 222 | 1,530 | 96 |
| Total area actually reporting | 96.2% | 433 | 8 | 57 | 62 | 306 | 3,201 | 477 | 2,475 | 249 |
| Estimated total | 100.0% | 472 | 9 | 60 | 68 | 335 | 3,380 | 503 | 2,608 | 269 |
| Rate per 100,000 inhabitants | | 319.1 | 6.1 | 40.6 | 46.0 | 226.5 | 2,285.3 | 340.1 | 1,763.4 | 181.9 |
| **Vallejo, CA M.S.A.** | 447,025 | | | | | | | | | |
| Includes Solano County | | | | | | | | | | |
| City of Vallejo | 122,326 | 1,212 | 27 | 134 | 315 | 736 | 4,078 | 1,811 | 1,200 | 1,067 |
| Total area actually reporting | 100.0% | 2,350 | 40 | 275 | 589 | 1,446 | 10,689 | 2,751 | 5,695 | 2,243 |
| Rate per 100,000 inhabitants | | 525.7 | 8.9 | 61.5 | 131.8 | 323.5 | 2,391.1 | 615.4 | 1,274.0 | 501.8 |
| **Victoria, TX M.S.A.** | 100,050 | | | | | | | | | |
| Includes Goliad and Victoria Counties | | | | | | | | | | |
| City of Victoria | 67,407 | 311 | 2 | 34 | 42 | 233 | 1,823 | 354 | 1,345 | 124 |
| Total area actually reporting | 100.0% | 449 | 6 | 58 | 54 | 331 | 2,205 | 491 | 1,552 | 162 |
| Rate per 100,000 inhabitants | | 448.8 | 6.0 | 58.0 | 54.0 | 330.8 | 2,203.9 | 490.8 | 1,551.2 | 161.9 |
| **Vineland-Bridgeton, NJ M.S.A.** | 148,593 | | | | | | | | | |
| Includes Cumberland County | | | | | | | | | | |
| City of Vineland | 59,288 | 227 | 3 | 17 | 34 | 173 | 1,239 | 198 | 1,000 | 41 |

## Table 6. Crime in the United States, by Selected Metropolitan Statistical Area, 2020—Continued

(Number, percent, rate per 100,000 population.)

| Area | Population | Violent crime | Murder and nonnegligent manslaughter | Rape[1] | Robbery | Aggravated assault | Property crime | Burglary | Larceny- theft | Motor vehicle theft |
|---|---|---|---|---|---|---|---|---|---|---|
| City of Bridgeton | 24,032 | 234 | 2 | 11 | 82 | 139 | 737 | 158 | 534 | 45 |
| Total area actually reporting | 100.0% | 669 | 8 | 39 | 154 | 468 | 3,192 | 593 | 2,446 | 153 |
| Rate per 100,000 inhabitants | | 450.2 | 5.4 | 26.2 | 103.6 | 315.0 | 2,148.1 | 399.1 | 1,646.1 | 103.0 |
| **Virginia Beach-Norfolk-Newport News, VA-NC M.S.A.[2]** | 1,773,594 | | | | | | | | | |
| Includes Camden, Currituck and Gates[2] Counties, NC and Gloucester, Isle of Wight, James City, Mathews, Southampton, and York Counties and Chesapeake, Franklin, Hampton, Newport News, Norfolk, Poquoson, Portsmouth, Suffolk, Virginia Beach, and Williamsburg Cities, VA | | | | | | | | | | |
| City of Virginia Beach, VA | 450,858 | 445 | 17 | 60 | 124 | 244 | 6,816 | 499 | 5,693 | 624 |
| City of Norfolk, VA | 242,516 | 1,543 | 49 | 103 | 259 | 1,132 | 6,591 | 519 | 5,282 | 790 |
| City of Newport News, VA | 178,896 | 1,119 | 25 | 67 | 104 | 923 | 3,648 | 416 | 2,896 | 336 |
| City of Hampton, VA | 134,082 | 357 | 24 | 33 | 95 | 205 | 3,338 | 301 | 2,765 | 272 |
| City of Portsmouth, VA | 94,205 | 867 | 34 | 26 | 222 | 585 | 4,277 | 465 | 3,314 | 498 |
| Total area actually reporting | 100.0% | 6,239 | 183 | 465 | 1,014 | 4,577 | 34,571 | 3,117 | 28,200 | 3,254 |
| Rate per 100,000 inhabitants | | 351.8 | 10.3 | 26.2 | 57.2 | 258.1 | 1,949.2 | 175.7 | 1,590.0 | 183.5 |
| **Visalia, CA M.S.A.** | 464,150 | | | | | | | | | |
| Includes Tulare County | | | | | | | | | | |
| City of Visalia | 135,733 | 555 | 8 | 106 | 142 | 299 | 3,077 | 610 | 2,049 | 418 |
| Total area actually reporting | 100.0% | 1,699 | 29 | 206 | 356 | 1,108 | 9,400 | 1,828 | 5,770 | 1,802 |
| Rate per 100,000 inhabitants | | 366.0 | 6.2 | 44.4 | 76.7 | 238.7 | 2,025.2 | 393.8 | 1,243.1 | 388.2 |
| **Waco, TX M.S.A.** | 275,324 | | | | | | | | | |
| Includes Falls and McLennan Counties | | | | | | | | | | |
| City of Waco | 140,870 | 905 | 14 | 80 | 142 | 669 | 4,854 | 870 | 3,568 | 416 |
| Total area actually reporting | 98.5% | 1,264 | 16 | 156 | 178 | 914 | 7,013 | 1,319 | 5,084 | 610 |
| Estimated total | 100.0% | 1,274 | 16 | 158 | 179 | 921 | 7,078 | 1,332 | 5,127 | 619 |
| Rate per 100,000 inhabitants | | 462.7 | 5.8 | 57.4 | 65.0 | 334.5 | 2,570.8 | 483.8 | 1,862.2 | 224.8 |
| **Walla Walla, WA M.S.A.** | 60,767 | | | | | | | | | |
| Includes Walla Walla County | | | | | | | | | | |
| City of Walla Walla | 32,944 | 83 | 0 | 21 | 11 | 51 | 749 | 126 | 573 | 50 |
| Total area actually reporting | 100.0% | 129 | 1 | 26 | 14 | 88 | 1,267 | 255 | 920 | 92 |
| Rate per 100,000 inhabitants | | 212.3 | 1.6 | 42.8 | 23.0 | 144.8 | 2,085.0 | 419.6 | 1,514.0 | 151.4 |
| **Watertown-Fort Drum, NY M.S.A.[2]** | 108,426 | | | | | | | | | |
| Includes Jefferson County[2] | | | | | | | | | | |
| City of Watertown | 24,624 | 181 | 0 | 40 | 21 | 120 | 967 | 158 | 766 | 43 |
| Total area actually reporting | 100.0% | 271 | 0 | 73 | 22 | 176 | 1,749 | 254 | 1,432 | 63 |
| Rate per 100,000 inhabitants | | 249.9 | 0.0 | 67.3 | 20.3 | 162.3 | 1,613.1 | 234.3 | 1,320.7 | 58.1 |
| **Wausau-Weston, WI M.S.A.** | 163,196 | | | | | | | | | |
| Includes Lincoln and Marathon Counties | | | | | | | | | | |
| City of Wausau | 38,492 | 174 | 0 | 26 | 14 | 134 | 560 | 66 | 435 | 59 |
| Total area actually reporting | 100.0% | 399 | 3 | 74 | 20 | 302 | 1,487 | 227 | 1,144 | 116 |
| Rate per 100,000 inhabitants | | 244.5 | 1.8 | 45.3 | 12.3 | 185.1 | 911.2 | 139.1 | 701.0 | 71.1 |
| **Wenatchee, WA M.S.A.** | 121,320 | | | | | | | | | |
| Includes Chelan and Douglas Counties | | | | | | | | | | |
| City of Wenatchee | 34,525 | 67 | 0 | 16 | 6 | 45 | 570 | 72 | 448 | 50 |
| Total area actually reporting | 100.0% | 141 | 1 | 30 | 16 | 94 | 1,392 | 239 | 1,029 | 124 |
| Rate per 100,000 inhabitants | | 116.2 | 0.8 | 24.7 | 13.2 | 77.5 | 1,147.4 | 197.0 | 848.2 | 102.2 |
| **Wheeling, WV-OH M.S.A.** | 137,859 | | | | | | | | | |
| Includes Belmont County, OH and Marshall and Ohio Counties, WV | | | | | | | | | | |
| City of Wheeling, WV | 26,222 | 330 | 1 | 31 | 28 | 270 | 582 | 180 | 361 | 41 |
| Total area actually reporting | 86.0% | 525 | 2 | 82 | 31 | 410 | 1,140 | 279 | 782 | 79 |
| Estimated total | 100.0% | 585 | 2 | 86 | 36 | 461 | 1,423 | 317 | 1,011 | 95 |
| Rate per 100,000 inhabitants | | 424.3 | 1.5 | 62.4 | 26.1 | 334.4 | 1,032.2 | 229.9 | 733.4 | 68.9 |
| **Wichita Falls, TX M.S.A.[2]** | 150,700 | | | | | | | | | |
| Includes Archer, Clay, and Wichita Counties | | | | | | | | | | |
| City of Wichita Falls[2] | 104,673 | 405 | 9 | 83 | 76 | 237 | 3,222 | 626 | 2,318 | 278 |
| Total area actually reporting | 95.5% | 512 | 9 | 91 | 82 | 330 | 3,721 | 768 | 2,618 | 335 |
| Estimated total | 100.0% | 544 | 9 | 95 | 83 | 357 | 3,864 | 809 | 2,702 | 353 |
| Rate per 100,000 inhabitants | | 361.0 | 6.0 | 63.0 | 55.1 | 236.9 | 2,564.0 | 536.8 | 1,793.0 | 234.2 |
| **Wilmington, NC M.S.A.** | 302,620 | | | | | | | | | |
| Includes New Hanover and Pender Counties | | | | | | | | | | |
| City of Wilmington | 125,794 | 791 | 22 | 66 | 143 | 560 | 3,204 | 595 | 2,410 | 199 |
| Total area actually reporting | 80.1% | 1,001 | 24 | 100 | 172 | 705 | 5,181 | 881 | 4,026 | 274 |
| Estimated total | 100.0% | 1,126 | 26 | 115 | 186 | 799 | 6,058 | 1,127 | 4,568 | 363 |
| Rate per 100,000 inhabitants | | 372.1 | 8.6 | 38.0 | 61.5 | 264.0 | 2,001.9 | 372.4 | 1,509.5 | 120.0 |
| **Winchester, VA-WV M.S.A.** | 141,877 | | | | | | | | | |
| Includes Frederick County and Winchester City, VA and Hampshire County, WV | | | | | | | | | | |
| City of Winchester, VA | 28,279 | 72 | 2 | 21 | 10 | 39 | 586 | 56 | 495 | 35 |
| Total area actually reporting | 99.7% | 209 | 5 | 44 | 16 | 144 | 1,628 | 185 | 1,316 | 127 |
| Estimated total | 100.0% | 214 | 5 | 44 | 16 | 149 | 1,629 | 185 | 1,317 | 127 |
| Rate per 100,000 inhabitants | | 150.8 | 3.5 | 31.0 | 11.3 | 105.0 | 1,148.2 | 130.4 | 928.3 | 89.5 |

## Table 6. Crime in the United States, by Selected Metropolitan Statistical Area, 2020—Continued

(Number, percent, rate per 100,000 population.)

| Area | Population | Violent crime | Murder and nonnegligent manslaughter | Rape[1] | Robbery | Aggravated assault | Property crime | Burglary | Larceny-theft | Motor vehicle theft |
|---|---|---|---|---|---|---|---|---|---|---|
| **Worcester, MA-CT M.S.A.** | 871,848 | | | | | | | | | |
| Includes Windham County, CT and Worcester County, MA | | | | | | | | | | |
| City of Worcester, MA | 184,850 | 1,169 | 10 | 40 | 210 | 909 | 3,695 | 667 | 2,581 | 447 |
| Total area actually reporting | 98.1% | 2,620 | 13 | 257 | 320 | 2,030 | 8,486 | 1,447 | 6,118 | 921 |
| Estimated total | 100.0% | 2,648 | 13 | 262 | 322 | 2,051 | 8,555 | 1,460 | 6,169 | 926 |
| Rate per 100,000 inhabitants | | 303.7 | 1.5 | 30.1 | 36.9 | 235.2 | 981.2 | 167.5 | 707.6 | 106.2 |
| **Yakima, WA M.S.A.** | 250,785 | | | | | | | | | |
| Includes Yakima County | | | | | | | | | | |
| City of Yakima | 93,862 | 639 | 9 | 22 | 100 | 508 | 3,220 | 599 | 2,115 | 506 |
| Total area actually reporting | 95.5% | 944 | 21 | 69 | 161 | 693 | 6,593 | 1,372 | 4,175 | 1,046 |
| Estimated total | 100.0% | 966 | 21 | 72 | 165 | 708 | 6,835 | 1,420 | 4,348 | 1,067 |
| Rate per 100,000 inhabitants | | 385.2 | 8.4 | 28.7 | 65.8 | 282.3 | 2,725.4 | 566.2 | 1,733.8 | 425.5 |
| **Yuba City, CA M.S.A.** | 174,855 | | | | | | | | | |
| Includes Sutter and Yuba Counties | | | | | | | | | | |
| City of Yuba City | 67,165 | 242 | 4 | 29 | 70 | 139 | 1,850 | 264 | 1,275 | 311 |
| Total area actually reporting | 100.0% | 715 | 7 | 70 | 139 | 499 | 4,266 | 727 | 2,500 | 1,039 |
| Rate per 100,000 inhabitants | | 408.9 | 4.0 | 40.0 | 79.5 | 285.4 | 2,439.7 | 415.8 | 1,429.8 | 594.2 |
| **Yuma, AZ M.S.A.** | 216,821 | | | | | | | | | |
| Includes Yuma County | | | | | | | | | | |
| City of Yuma | 99,096 | 498 | 11 | 39 | 43 | 405 | 1,927 | 330 | 1,412 | 185 |
| Total area actually reporting | 100.0% | 717 | 20 | 68 | 54 | 575 | 3,235 | 653 | 2,184 | 398 |
| Rate per 100,000 inhabitants | | 330.7 | 9.2 | 31.4 | 24.9 | 265.2 | 1,492.0 | 301.2 | 1,007.3 | 183.6 |
| **Aguadilla-Isabela, Puerto Rico M.S.A.** | 286,064 | | | | | | | | | |
| Includes Aguada, Aguadilla, Anasco, Isabela, Lares, Moca, Rincon, San Sebastian, and Utuado Municipios | | | | | | | | | | |
| Total area actually reporting | 100.0% | 372 | 20 | 16 | 31 | 305 | 802 | 234 | 509 | 59 |
| Rate per 100,000 inhabitants | | 130.0 | 7.0 | 5.6 | 10.8 | 106.6 | 280.4 | 81.8 | 177.9 | 20.6 |
| **Arecibo, Puerto Rico M.S.A.** | 173,218 | | | | | | | | | |
| Includes Arecibo, Camuy, Hatillo, and Quebradillas Municipios | | | | | | | | | | |
| Total area actually reporting | 100.0% | 249 | 24 | 6 | 31 | 188 | 470 | 150 | 274 | 46 |
| Rate per 100,000 inhabitants | | 143.7 | 13.9 | 3.5 | 17.9 | 108.5 | 271.3 | 86.6 | 158.2 | 26.6 |
| **Guayama, Puerto Rico M.S.A.** | 72,240 | | | | | | | | | |
| Includes Arroyo, Guayama, and Patillas Municipios | | | | | | | | | | |
| Total area actually reporting | 100.0% | 178 | 11 | 9 | 29 | 129 | 235 | 82 | 148 | 5 |
| Rate per 100,000 inhabitants | | 246.4 | 15.2 | 12.5 | 40.1 | 178.6 | 325.3 | 113.5 | 204.9 | 6.9 |
| **Mayagüez, Puerto Rico M.S.A.** | 93,412 | | | | | | | | | |
| Includes Hormigueros, Las Marias, and Mayaguez Municipios | | | | | | | | | | |
| Total area actually reporting | 100.0% | 105 | 16 | 7 | 9 | 73 | 214 | 64 | 134 | 16 |
| Rate per 100,000 inhabitants | | 112.4 | 17.1 | 7.5 | 9.6 | 78.1 | 229.1 | 68.5 | 143.5 | 17.1 |
| **Ponce, Puerto Rico M.S.A.** | 211,465 | | | | | | | | | |
| Includes Adjuntas, Juana Diaz, Ponce, and Villalba Municipios | | | | | | | | | | |
| Total area actually reporting | 100.0% | 287 | 20 | 8 | 91 | 168 | 743 | 166 | 509 | 68 |
| Rate per 100,000 inhabitants | | 135.7 | 9.5 | 3.8 | 43.0 | 79.4 | 351.4 | 78.5 | 240.7 | 32.2 |
| **San Germán, Puerto Rico M.S.A.** | 120,280 | | | | | | | | | |
| Includes Cabo Rojo, Lajas, Sabana Grande, and San German Municipios | | | | | | | | | | |
| Total area actually reporting | 100.0% | 100 | 9 | 3 | 10 | 78 | 185 | 63 | 109 | 13 |
| Rate per 100,000 inhabitants | | 83.1 | 7.5 | 2.5 | 8.3 | 64.8 | 153.8 | 52.4 | 90.6 | 10.8 |
| **San Juan-Bayamón-Caguas, Puerto Rico M.S.A.** | 2,002,906 | | | | | | | | | |
| Includes Aguas Buenas, Aibonito, Barceloneta, Barranquitas, Bayamon, Caguas, Canovanas, Carolina, Catano, Cayey, Ceiba, Ciales, Cidra, Comerio, Corozal, Dorado, Fajardo, Florida, Guaynabo, Gurabo, Humacao, Juncos, Las Piedras, Loiza, Luquillo, Manati, Maunabo, Morovis, Naguabo, Naranjito, Orocovis, Rio Grande, San Juan, San Lorenzo, Toa Alta, Toa Baja, Trujillo Alto, Vega Alta, Vega Baja, and Yabucoa Municipios | | | | | | | | | | |
| Total area actually reporting | 100.0% | 3,510 | 400 | 91 | 934 | 2,085 | 10,114 | 2,011 | 6,362 | 1,741 |
| Rate per 100,000 inhabitants | | 175.2 | 20.0 | 4.5 | 46.6 | 104.1 | 505.0 | 100.4 | 317.6 | 86.9 |
| **Yauco, Puerto Rico M.S.A.** | 84,112 | | | | | | | | | |
| Includes Guanica, Guayanilla, Penuelas, and Yauco Municipios | | | | | | | | | | |
| Total area actually reporting | 100.0% | 138 | 8 | 2 | 18 | 110 | 174 | 61 | 106 | 7 |
| Rate per 100,000 inhabitants | | 164.1 | 9.5 | 2.4 | 21.4 | 130.8 | 206.9 | 72.5 | 126.0 | 8.3 |

1 The figures shown in this column for the offense of rape were reported using only the revised Uniform Crime Reporting (UCR) definition of rape. See the chapter notes for further explanation.   2 Because of changes in the state/local agency's reporting practices, figures are not comparable to previous years' data.   3 The FBI determined that the agency's data were overreported. Consequently, those data are not included in this table.   4 The FBI determined that the state did not follow national UCR Program guidelines for reporting an offense. Consequently, those figures are not included in this table.   5 The FBI determined that the agency's data were underreported. Consequently, those data are not included in this table.

## Table 7. Offense Analysis, United States, 2016–2021

(Number.)

| Classification | 2016 | 2017 | 2018 | 2019[1] | 2020 | 2021 |
|---|---|---|---|---|---|---|
| **Murder** | 17,413 | 17,294 | 16,374 | 16,669 | 21,570 | 22,900 |
| **Rape**[2] | 132,414 | 135,666 | 143,765 | 143,224 | 126,430 | 144,300 |
| **Robbery**[3] | 332,797 | 320,596 | 281,278 | 268,483 | 243,600 | 202,200 |
| By location | | | | | | |
| Highway/alley/street/sidewalk | 129,337 | 119,180 | 102,149 | 94,263 | 77,984 | 37,852 |
| Commercial house | 50,785 | 49,654 | 45,148 | 44,210 | 41,139 | 40,337 |
| Gas or service station | 9,708 | 9,603 | 8,863 | 8,570 | 8,804 | 7,964 |
| Convenience store | 20,656 | 21,048 | 19,647 | 18,346 | 18,039 | 14,529 |
| Residence | 55,102 | 51,260 | 45,408 | 42,885 | 42,637 | 28,375 |
| Bank | 5,914 | 5,441 | 4,461 | 3,841 | 2,669 | 3,353 |
| Miscellaneous | 61,296 | 64,410 | 55,602 | 56,368 | 52,328 | 10,339 |
| **Burglary**[3] | 1,516,405 | 1,397,045 | 1,235,013 | 1,118,096 | 1,035,314 | 899,700 |
| By location | | | | | | |
| Residence (dwelling) | 1,054,470 | 939,509 | 808,611 | 702,700 | 575,049 | 357,270 |
| Residence, night | 311,805 | 285,358 | 257,085 | 238,720 | 220,533 | 154,723 |
| Residence, day | 543,930 | 474,495 | 408,349 | 354,525 | 280,183 | 196,684 |
| Residence, unknown | 198,735 | 179,656 | 143,178 | 109,455 | 74,333 | 5,863 |
| Nonresidence (store, office, etc.) | 461,935 | 457,536 | 426,402 | 415,396 | 460,265 | 262,541 |
| Nonresidence, night | 199,741 | 200,859 | 190,817 | 191,731 | 221,126 | 125,253 |
| Nonresidence, day | 159,630 | 157,375 | 151,091 | 153,010 | 175,367 | 132,232 |
| Nonresidence, unknown | 102,564 | 99,302 | 84,493 | 70,654 | 63,772 | 5,056 |
| **Larceny-theft (except motor vehicle theft)**[3] | 5,644,835 | 5,513,000 | 5,232,167 | 5,152,267 | 4,606,324 | 4,627,000 |
| By type | | | | | | |
| Pocket-picking | 27,648 | 31,026 | 27,326 | 29,865 | 18,910 | 14,439 |
| Purse-snatching | 22,671 | 21,961 | 20,113 | 18,810 | 14,101 | 8,728 |
| Shoplifting | 1,179,137 | 1,144,948 | 1,116,664 | 1,128,275 | 964,196 | 548,591 |
| From motor vehicles (except accessories) | 1,477,587 | 1,477,684 | 1,410,567 | 1,397,708 | 1,268,031 | 721,752 |
| Motor vehicle accessories | 415,590 | 407,017 | 324,298 | 330,039 | 393,091 | 359,670 |
| Bicycles | 184,546 | 174,803 | 157,042 | 156,013 | 158,157 | 72,419 |
| From buildings | 605,765 | 586,612 | 534,418 | 504,601 | 390,286 | 221,407 |
| From coin-operated machines | 12,349 | 12,014 | 11,511 | 11,475 | 8,809 | 4,763 |
| All others | 1,719,542 | 1,656,937 | 1,630,232 | 1,575,481 | 1,390,743 | 927,255 |
| By value | | | | | | |
| Over $200 | 2,561,619 | 2,529,654 | 2,445,915 | 2,439,300 | 2,219,999 | 1,516,357 |
| $50 to $200 | 1,221,246 | 1,169,612 | 1,120,011 | 1,093,554 | 931,647 | 525,376 |
| Under $50 | 1,861,970 | 1,813,734 | 1,666,185 | 1,619,413 | 1,454,678 | 837,291 |
| **Motor vehicle theft** | 767,290 | 772,943 | 751,904 | 724,872 | 810,400 | 890,200 |

NOTE: Totals are rounded to the nearest 100 due to uncertainty in the estimates.
1 The crime figures have been adjusted.   2 The figures shown for this offense of rape were estimated using the revised Uniform Crime Reporting (UCR) definition of rape. See chapter notes for more detail.   3 Because of rounding, the number of offenses may not add to the total.

## Table 8. Offenses Known to Law Enforcement, by Selected State and City, 2021

(Number.)

| State/city | Population | Violent crime | Murder and nonnegligent manslaughter | Rape | Robbery | Aggravated assault | Property crime | Burglary | Larceny-theft | Motor vehicle theft | Arson |
|---|---|---|---|---|---|---|---|---|---|---|---|
| **ALABAMA** | | | | | | | | | | | |
| Abbeville | 2,539 | 4 | 1 | 0 | 0 | 3 | 53 | 11 | 37 | 5 | 0 |
| Alabaster | 33,963 | 25 | 1 | 4 | 0 | 20 | 282 | 13 | 253 | 16 | 1 |
| Alexander City | 14,066 | 40 | 0 | 0 | 7 | 33 | 283 | 178 | 87 | 18 | 1 |
| Altoona | 913 | 4 | 0 | 0 | 0 | 4 | 7 | 1 | 6 | 0 | 0 |
| Andalusia | 8,643 | 44 | 1 | 6 | 1 | 36 | 254 | 45 | 198 | 11 | 0 |
| Anniston | 20,913 | 162 | 7 | 7 | 30 | 118 | 1,094 | 229 | 708 | 157 | 3 |
| Arab | 8,437 | 38 | 0 | 6 | 2 | 30 | 293 | 78 | 175 | 40 | 0 |
| Argo | 4,306 | 9 | 0 | 0 | 1 | 8 | 24 | 5 | 13 | 6 | 1 |
| Arley | 338 | 1 | 0 | 0 | 0 | 1 | 11 | 3 | 6 | 2 | 0 |
| Ashville | 2,412 | 11 | 0 | 0 | 0 | 11 | 50 | 14 | 30 | 6 | 0 |
| Athens | 29,411 | 18 | 0 | 0 | 1 | 17 | 315 | 43 | 255 | 17 | 0 |
| Attalla | 5,804 | 16 | 0 | 1 | 2 | 13 | 207 | 39 | 149 | 19 | 1 |
| Auburn | 70,003 | 81 | 0 | 13 | 11 | 57 | 896 | 68 | 764 | 64 | 0 |
| Bay Minette | 9,647 | 38 | 1 | 3 | 2 | 32 | 88 | 14 | 61 | 13 | 0 |
| Bayou La Batre | 2,444 | 25 | 1 | 0 | 2 | 22 | 185 | 43 | 125 | 17 | 0 |
| Bear Creek | 1,061 | 6 | 0 | 2 | 0 | 4 | 20 | 4 | 14 | 2 | 1 |
| Blountsville | 1,654 | 1 | 0 | 1 | 0 | 0 | 19 | 3 | 11 | 5 | 1 |
| Brent | 4,663 | 23 | 0 | 2 | 0 | 21 | 51 | 9 | 41 | 1 | 0 |
| Bridgeport | 2,258 | 13 | 0 | 2 | 0 | 11 | 37 | 5 | 29 | 3 | 0 |
| Brilliant | 859 | 7 | 0 | 1 | 0 | 6 | 15 | 3 | 8 | 4 | 1 |
| Brookside | 1,318 | 2 | 0 | 1 | 0 | 1 | 10 | 1 | 7 | 2 | 0 |
| Butler | 1,670 | 8 | 0 | 0 | 1 | 7 | 18 | 4 | 13 | 1 | 0 |
| Carrollton | 927 | 1 | 0 | 0 | 0 | 1 | 8 | 1 | 5 | 2 | 0 |
| Cedar Bluff | 1,830 | 3 | 0 | 0 | 0 | 3 | 44 | 7 | 31 | 6 | 0 |
| Centre | 3,624 | 9 | 0 | 0 | 0 | 9 | 118 | 10 | 102 | 6 | 0 |
| Centreville | 2,538 | 10 | 0 | 0 | 0 | 10 | 33 | 9 | 20 | 4 | 2 |
| Chatom | 1,157 | 2 | 0 | 0 | 0 | 2 | 8 | 2 | 5 | 1 | 0 |
| Cherokee | 994 | 8 | 0 | 0 | 0 | 8 | 42 | 10 | 30 | 2 | 1 |
| Chickasaw | 5,618 | 23 | 0 | 5 | 1 | 17 | 106 | 13 | 82 | 11 | 0 |
| Citronelle | 3,867 | 8 | 0 | 1 | 0 | 7 | 62 | 14 | 41 | 7 | 0 |
| Collinsville | 1,939 | 5 | 0 | 0 | 1 | 4 | 24 | 2 | 18 | 4 | 0 |
| Coosada | 1,325 | 2 | 0 | 0 | 0 | 2 | 19 | 8 | 9 | 2 | 2 |
| Creola | 2,043 | 3 | 0 | 0 | 1 | 2 | 38 | 7 | 25 | 6 | 0 |
| Cullman | 16,696 | 29 | 0 | 4 | 4 | 21 | 600 | 47 | 509 | 44 | 2 |
| Dadeville | 2,988 | 20 | 0 | 1 | 0 | 19 | 57 | 6 | 47 | 4 | 0 |
| Daleville | 5,075 | 16 | 1 | 2 | 0 | 13 | 106 | 17 | 77 | 12 | 0 |
| Daphne | 28,387 | 6 | 0 | 1 | 1 | 4 | 281 | 43 | 224 | 14 | 0 |
| Dauphin Island | 1,380 | 6 | 0 | 0 | 0 | 6 | 35 | 5 | 27 | 3 | 0 |
| Dora | 1,963 | 14 | 0 | 0 | 1 | 13 | 74 | 8 | 50 | 16 | 0 |
| Dothan | 69,747 | 68 | 1 | 4 | 4 | 59 | 280 | 188 | 78 | 14 | 2 |
| Douglas | 784 | 2 | 0 | 0 | 0 | 2 | 46 | 16 | 23 | 7 | 0 |
| Eufaula | 11,489 | 102 | 1 | 3 | 9 | 89 | 466 | 77 | 278 | 111 | 1 |
| Evergreen | 3,422 | 20 | 0 | 1 | 2 | 17 | 76 | 15 | 46 | 15 | 1 |
| Excel | 610 | 2 | 1 | 0 | 0 | 1 | 19 | 5 | 12 | 2 | 1 |
| Fairhope | 24,467 | 13 | 0 | 4 | 1 | 8 | 109 | 3 | 99 | 7 | 1 |
| Fayette | 4,214 | 6 | 0 | 1 | 0 | 5 | 45 | 6 | 32 | 7 | 0 |
| Florence | 41,325 | 151 | 2 | 21 | 11 | 117 | 1,302 | 209 | 972 | 121 | 2 |
| Foley | 22,166 | 33 | 0 | 1 | 2 | 30 | 351 | 74 | 236 | 41 | 0 |
| Frisco City | 1,107 | 4 | 0 | 0 | 0 | 4 | 13 | 5 | 8 | 0 | 0 |
| Fultondale | 9,365 | 27 | 2 | 3 | 2 | 20 | 260 | 90 | 143 | 27 | 0 |
| Gadsden | 34,613 | 536 | 5 | 44 | 45 | 442 | 2,627 | 363 | 1,810 | 454 | 15 |
| Geneva | 4,246 | 16 | 1 | 2 | 2 | 11 | 177 | 35 | 125 | 17 | 2 |
| Georgiana | 1,601 | 3 | 0 | 0 | 0 | 3 | 17 | 4 | 13 | 0 | 0 |
| Geraldine | 895 | 2 | 0 | 0 | 0 | 2 | 14 | 3 | 8 | 3 | 0 |
| Glencoe | 5,074 | 4 | 0 | 1 | 0 | 3 | 31 | 9 | 22 | 0 | 0 |
| Gordo | 1,580 | 0 | 0 | 0 | 0 | 0 | 12 | 2 | 8 | 2 | 0 |
| Guin | 2,238 | 6 | 0 | 0 | 0 | 6 | 26 | 8 | 12 | 6 | 0 |
| Hackleburg | 1,227 | 8 | 0 | 1 | 0 | 7 | 22 | 8 | 13 | 1 | 0 |
| Hamilton | 6,621 | 1 | 0 | 0 | 0 | 1 | 25 | 6 | 14 | 5 | 0 |
| Harpersville | 1,757 | 8 | 0 | 1 | 0 | 7 | 46 | 13 | 27 | 6 | 0 |
| Hayden | 1,359 | 1 | 0 | 0 | 0 | 1 | 19 | 2 | 13 | 4 | 0 |
| Headland | 4,770 | 9 | 0 | 1 | 2 | 6 | 73 | 17 | 48 | 8 | 0 |
| Heflin | 3,400 | 5 | 0 | 0 | 1 | 4 | 45 | 14 | 25 | 6 | 0 |
| Hokes Bluff | 4,237 | 5 | 0 | 0 | 0 | 5 | 39 | 5 | 27 | 7 | 0 |
| Ider | 737 | 4 | 0 | 2 | 0 | 2 | 9 | 0 | 6 | 3 | 0 |
| Jackson | 4,523 | 26 | 1 | 0 | 4 | 21 | 65 | 11 | 50 | 4 | 0 |
| Jasper | 13,177 | 45 | 0 | 6 | 4 | 35 | 422 | 120 | 266 | 36 | 1 |
| Killen | 958 | 2 | 0 | 0 | 0 | 2 | 15 | 3 | 11 | 1 | 0 |
| Kimberly | 3,688 | 0 | 0 | 0 | 0 | 0 | 14 | 3 | 8 | 3 | 0 |
| Kinston | 553 | 8 | 0 | 0 | 0 | 8 | 16 | 4 | 8 | 4 | 1 |
| Lanett | 6,014 | 24 | 2 | 0 | 3 | 19 | 211 | 39 | 144 | 28 | 0 |
| Leesburg | 1,017 | 1 | 0 | 0 | 0 | 1 | 10 | 1 | 6 | 3 | 0 |
| Leighton | 752 | 15 | 0 | 1 | 2 | 12 | 30 | 5 | 20 | 5 | 0 |
| Level Plains | 1,944 | 4 | 0 | 0 | 0 | 4 | 42 | 6 | 28 | 8 | 0 |
| Lexington | 709 | 0 | 0 | 0 | 0 | 0 | 9 | 2 | 5 | 2 | 0 |
| Lincoln | 7,058 | 24 | 0 | 5 | 4 | 15 | 191 | 29 | 124 | 38 | 3 |
| Linden | 1,829 | 14 | 0 | 0 | 0 | 14 | 43 | 8 | 27 | 8 | 0 |
| Luverne | 2,694 | 18 | 0 | 0 | 0 | 18 | 72 | 12 | 49 | 11 | 0 |
| Lynn | 630 | 0 | 0 | 0 | 0 | 0 | 10 | 4 | 3 | 3 | 0 |
| Margaret | 5,388 | 7 | 1 | 0 | 0 | 6 | 26 | 6 | 12 | 8 | 0 |
| McIntosh | 207 | 3 | 0 | 0 | 0 | 3 | 25 | 3 | 14 | 8 | 0 |
| Midfield | 4,918 | 59 | 2 | 3 | 8 | 46 | 124 | 33 | 69 | 22 | 4 |

## Table 8. Offenses Known to Law Enforcement, by Selected State and City, 2021—Continued

(Number.)

| State/city | Population | Violent crime | Murder and nonnegligent manslaughter | Rape | Robbery | Aggravated assault | Property crime | Burglary | Larceny-theft | Motor vehicle theft | Arson |
|---|---|---|---|---|---|---|---|---|---|---|---|
| Midland City | 2,396 | 10 | 0 | 2 | 0 | 8 | 28 | 4 | 18 | 6 | 0 |
| Millport | 963 | 0 | 0 | 0 | 0 | 0 | 7 | 2 | 4 | 1 | 0 |
| Mobile | 242,894 | 6,770 | 111 | 485 | 516 | 5,658 | 27,430 | 4,815 | 19,423 | 3,192 | 39 |
| Montevallo | 7,179 | 12 | 0 | 1 | 0 | 11 | 88 | 13 | 67 | 8 | 0 |
| Morris | 2,210 | 2 | 0 | 0 | 0 | 2 | 18 | 1 | 14 | 3 | 0 |
| Mountain Brook | 20,006 | 15 | 0 | 2 | 1 | 12 | 212 | 36 | 158 | 18 | 1 |
| Mount Vernon | 1,498 | 7 | 0 | 0 | 1 | 6 | 28 | 8 | 20 | 0 | 0 |
| Muscle Shoals | 15,051 | 34 | 1 | 5 | 2 | 26 | 415 | 61 | 316 | 38 | 1 |
| New Hope | 2,939 | 3 | 0 | 0 | 0 | 3 | 16 | 1 | 9 | 6 | 0 |
| Newton | 1,446 | 3 | 0 | 0 | 0 | 3 | 31 | 6 | 17 | 8 | 0 |
| Northport | 26,309 | 72 | 0 | 5 | 8 | 59 | 311 | 51 | 230 | 30 | 0 |
| Notasulga | 804 | 3 | 0 | 0 | 1 | 2 | 20 | 2 | 16 | 2 | 1 |
| Odenville | 3,907 | 15 | 0 | 2 | 2 | 11 | 22 | 4 | 16 | 2 | 0 |
| Oneonta | 6,603 | 18 | 0 | 3 | 3 | 12 | 307 | 33 | 249 | 25 | 1 |
| Opelika | 31,644 | 215 | 1 | 15 | 17 | 182 | 948 | 116 | 742 | 90 | 2 |
| Opp | 6,279 | 34 | 0 | 2 | 3 | 29 | 155 | 36 | 105 | 14 | 1 |
| Orange Beach | 6,440 | 14 | 0 | 3 | 0 | 11 | 182 | 21 | 154 | 7 | 0 |
| Owens Crossroads | 2,316 | 6 | 0 | 0 | 1 | 5 | 27 | 1 | 22 | 4 | 0 |
| Ozark | 14,065 | 42 | 2 | 4 | 2 | 34 | 325 | 39 | 265 | 21 | 2 |
| Parrish | 923 | 3 | 0 | 0 | 0 | 3 | 44 | 17 | 24 | 3 | 0 |
| Phenix City | 36,744 | 265 | 7 | 33 | 41 | 184 | 1,592 | 227 | 1,105 | 260 | 5 |
| Piedmont | 4,436 | 10 | 0 | 0 | 1 | 9 | 35 | 8 | 18 | 9 | 0 |
| Pine Hill | 822 | 7 | 0 | 1 | 1 | 5 | 5 | 2 | 2 | 1 | 0 |
| Priceville | 4,137 | 2 | 0 | 0 | 1 | 1 | 17 | 3 | 11 | 3 | 0 |
| Prichard | 21,170 | 202 | 12 | 6 | 24 | 160 | 376 | 81 | 204 | 91 | 9 |
| Rainbow City | 9,602 | 7 | 0 | 0 | 1 | 6 | 111 | 26 | 73 | 12 | 1 |
| Rainsville | 5,168 | 3 | 1 | 0 | 1 | 1 | 32 | 10 | 19 | 3 | 0 |
| Red Bay | 3,103 | 9 | 0 | 1 | 0 | 8 | 42 | 8 | 30 | 4 | 0 |
| Reform | 1,531 | 10 | 0 | 0 | 0 | 10 | 15 | 6 | 6 | 3 | 0 |
| Riverside | 2,393 | 3 | 0 | 1 | 0 | 2 | 38 | 7 | 24 | 7 | 0 |
| Rogersville | 1,296 | 4 | 0 | 1 | 0 | 3 | 39 | 8 | 26 | 5 | 0 |
| Samson | 1,845 | 13 | 0 | 0 | 0 | 13 | 24 | 3 | 16 | 5 | 1 |
| Saraland | 14,764 | 29 | 0 | 1 | 3 | 25 | 229 | 15 | 181 | 33 | 0 |
| Sardis City | 1,782 | 4 | 0 | 0 | 0 | 4 | 13 | 8 | 5 | 0 | 1 |
| Satsuma | 6,214 | 10 | 0 | 0 | 0 | 10 | 45 | 5 | 32 | 8 | 1 |
| Slocomb | 1,924 | 0 | 0 | 0 | 0 | 0 | 15 | 0 | 13 | 2 | 0 |
| Somerville | 783 | 0 | 0 | 0 | 0 | 0 | 17 | 2 | 10 | 5 | 0 |
| Southside | 9,108 | 1 | 0 | 0 | 0 | 1 | 33 | 4 | 27 | 2 | 0 |
| Stevenson | 1,886 | 15 | 0 | 0 | 0 | 15 | 47 | 7 | 31 | 9 | 0 |
| St. Florian | 818 | 0 | 0 | 0 | 0 | 0 | 21 | 4 | 15 | 2 | 0 |
| Sulligent | 1,826 | 3 | 0 | 0 | 1 | 2 | 31 | 6 | 23 | 2 | 1 |
| Sumiton | 2,311 | 3 | 0 | 1 | 0 | 2 | 85 | 11 | 68 | 6 | 0 |
| Sylacauga | 11,859 | 87 | 5 | 11 | 10 | 61 | 465 | 100 | 325 | 40 | 4 |
| Sylvania | 1,863 | 6 | 0 | 1 | 0 | 5 | 19 | 3 | 9 | 7 | 0 |
| Thomasville | 3,726 | 13 | 0 | 0 | 0 | 13 | 63 | 5 | 54 | 4 | 0 |
| Triana | 1,477 | 2 | 0 | 0 | 0 | 2 | 23 | 7 | 16 | 0 | 0 |
| Trinity | 2,477 | 6 | 0 | 0 | 0 | 6 | 37 | 7 | 25 | 5 | 3 |
| Troy | 18,822 | 69 | 2 | 8 | 4 | 55 | 320 | 32 | 270 | 18 | 1 |
| Trussville | 23,379 | 23 | 0 | 5 | 3 | 15 | 405 | 14 | 372 | 19 | 0 |
| Tuscumbia | 8,449 | 9 | 0 | 0 | 1 | 8 | 108 | 9 | 43 | 56 | 0 |
| Tuskegee | 7,864 | 54 | 1 | 2 | 5 | 46 | 99 | 19 | 66 | 14 | 0 |
| Valley | 9,038 | 42 | 1 | 3 | 1 | 37 | 349 | 54 | 247 | 48 | 3 |
| Vernon | 1,828 | 10 | 0 | 2 | 0 | 8 | 44 | 10 | 26 | 8 | 1 |
| Vestavia Hills | 34,369 | 24 | 0 | 6 | 3 | 15 | 290 | 29 | 218 | 43 | 0 |
| Wadley | 706 | 2 | 0 | 0 | 0 | 2 | 9 | 0 | 9 | 0 | 0 |
| Warrior | 3,192 | 2 | 1 | 0 | 0 | 1 | 4 | 0 | 3 | 1 | 0 |
| Weaver | 3,027 | 17 | 1 | 1 | 0 | 15 | 81 | 9 | 58 | 14 | 0 |
| Wedowee | 800 | 1 | 0 | 0 | 0 | 1 | 35 | 7 | 18 | 10 | 0 |
| Wetumpka | 8,617 | 10 | 0 | 1 | 1 | 8 | 160 | 35 | 114 | 11 | 0 |
| Winfield | 4,544 | 8 | 0 | 0 | 0 | 8 | 119 | 15 | 67 | 37 | 2 |
| Woodstock | 1,653 | 14 | 0 | 3 | 1 | 10 | 69 | 8 | 45 | 16 | 0 |
| **ALASKA** | | | | | | | | | | | |
| Bethel | 6,717 | 83 | 3 | 17 | 4 | 59 | 51 | 11 | 24 | 16 | 1 |
| Bristol Bay Borough | 769 | 6 | 0 | 0 | 0 | 6 | 18 | 9 | 5 | 4 | 0 |
| Cordova | 2,162 | 7 | 0 | 2 | 0 | 5 | 7 | 2 | 4 | 1 | 0 |
| Craig | 1,273 | 0 | 0 | 0 | 0 | 0 | 1 | 0 | 1 | 0 | 0 |
| Dillingham | 2,324 | 10 | 0 | 1 | 0 | 9 | 3 | 0 | 2 | 1 | 0 |
| Haines | 2,624 | 3 | 0 | 2 | 0 | 1 | 15 | 7 | 5 | 3 | 0 |
| Homer | 6,143 | 23 | 0 | 4 | 1 | 18 | 80 | 9 | 67 | 4 | 0 |
| Kenai | 7,970 | 34 | 0 | 17 | 1 | 16 | 135 | 14 | 110 | 11 | 0 |
| Ketchikan | 8,198 | 25 | 0 | 9 | 0 | 16 | 105 | 4 | 101 | 0 | 0 |
| Kodiak | 5,776 | 52 | 0 | 11 | 4 | 37 | 71 | 7 | 53 | 11 | 0 |
| Kotzebue | 3,264 | 34 | 0 | 7 | 0 | 27 | 27 | 12 | 12 | 3 | 0 |
| Nome | 3,871 | 76 | 0 | 45 | 0 | 31 | 45 | 9 | 23 | 13 | 1 |
| North Pole | 2,106 | 14 | 0 | 3 | 1 | 10 | 61 | 2 | 52 | 7 | 0 |
| North Slope Borough | 9,310 | 91 | 2 | 30 | 1 | 58 | 58 | 13 | 30 | 15 | 2 |
| Palmer | 7,972 | 13 | 0 | 2 | 3 | 8 | 86 | 3 | 71 | 12 | 1 |
| Petersburg | 3,302 | 9 | 0 | 5 | 0 | 4 | 55 | 7 | 47 | 1 | 0 |
| Seward | 2,950 | 16 | 0 | 5 | 0 | 11 | 44 | 4 | 33 | 7 | 0 |
| Skagway | 1,202 | 0 | 0 | 0 | 0 | 0 | 0 | 0 | 0 | 0 | 0 |
| Soldotna | 4,855 | 39 | 0 | 7 | 2 | 30 | 99 | 11 | 84 | 4 | 2 |
| Unalaska | 4,484 | 15 | 0 | 4 | 1 | 10 | 28 | 3 | 17 | 8 | 0 |

## Table 8. Offenses Known to Law Enforcement, by Selected State and City, 2021—Continued

(Number.)

| State/city | Population | Violent crime | Murder and nonnegligent manslaughter | Rape | Robbery | Aggravated assault | Property crime | Burglary | Larceny-theft | Motor vehicle theft | Arson |
|---|---|---|---|---|---|---|---|---|---|---|---|
| Valdez | 3,842 | 8 | 0 | 1 | 0 | 7 | 29 | 7 | 20 | 2 | 0 |
| Wasilla | 11,485 | 63 | 0 | 6 | 5 | 52 | 270 | 22 | 219 | 29 | 0 |
| Wrangell | 2,522 | 4 | 0 | 0 | 0 | 4 | 8 | 1 | 6 | 1 | 0 |
| **ARIZONA** | | | | | | | | | | | |
| Apache Junction | 44,607 | 125 | 1 | 15 | 9 | 100 | 643 | 93 | 445 | 105 | 4 |
| Avondale | 91,009 | 347 | 7 | 19 | 73 | 248 | 3,336 | 290 | 2,803 | 243 | 13 |
| Bisbee | 5,111 | 16 | 5 | 0 | 1 | 10 | 82 | 18 | 62 | 2 | 1 |
| Buckeye | 93,218 | 171 | 3 | 46 | 9 | 113 | 1,048 | 138 | 819 | 91 | 10 |
| Camp Verde | 11,299 | 23 | 0 | 1 | 1 | 21 | 169 | 34 | 107 | 28 | 0 |
| Casa Grande | 62,566 | 314 | 4 | 49 | 41 | 220 | 1,363 | 136 | 1,076 | 151 | 16 |
| Chandler | 281,162 | 529 | 7 | 78 | 84 | 360 | 4,786 | 542 | 3,853 | 391 | 22 |
| Chino Valley | 13,039 | 18 | 1 | 1 | 0 | 16 | 82 | 7 | 67 | 8 | 0 |
| Clarkdale | 4,577 | 12 | 0 | 0 | 0 | 12 | 19 | 7 | 12 | 0 | 0 |
| Coolidge | 13,973 | 65 | 0 | 4 | 6 | 55 | 348 | 40 | 268 | 40 | 3 |
| Douglas | 16,349 | 24 | 1 | 2 | 3 | 18 | 315 | 37 | 257 | 21 | 0 |
| Eagar | 4,960 | 10 | 0 | 1 | 0 | 9 | 12 | 4 | 6 | 2 | 0 |
| El Mirage | 36,476 | 134 | 1 | 14 | 13 | 106 | 604 | 69 | 462 | 73 | 4 |
| Gilbert | 272,941 | 324 | 3 | 71 | 36 | 214 | 2,920 | 383 | 2,358 | 179 | 8 |
| Huachuca City | 1,722 | 3 | 0 | 1 | 0 | 2 | 17 | 4 | 11 | 2 | 0 |
| Lake Havasu City | 57,735 | 132 | 2 | 38 | 4 | 88 | 746 | 99 | 572 | 75 | 13 |
| Marana | 53,347 | 63 | 2 | 5 | 13 | 43 | 1,186 | 47 | 1,112 | 27 | 5 |
| Maricopa | 55,768 | 141 | 2 | 5 | 7 | 127 | 442 | 53 | 349 | 40 | 0 |
| Mesa | 513,713 | 2,080 | 25 | 277 | 325 | 1,453 | 10,074 | 1,374 | 7,622 | 1,078 | 36 |
| Oro Valley | 47,282 | 27 | 1 | 6 | 2 | 18 | 623 | 40 | 559 | 24 | 0 |
| Page | 7,530 | 52 | 0 | 6 | 2 | 44 | 224 | 38 | 169 | 17 | 4 |
| Paradise Valley | 12,895 | 8 | 0 | 1 | 0 | 7 | 186 | 41 | 135 | 10 | 0 |
| Payson | 16,011 | 89 | 0 | 2 | 1 | 86 | 284 | 83 | 177 | 24 | 3 |
| Peoria | 194,566 | 495 | 8 | 74 | 60 | 353 | 2,847 | 418 | 2,155 | 274 | 6 |
| Pinetop-Lakeside | 4,540 | 25 | 0 | 3 | 2 | 20 | 123 | 17 | 97 | 9 | 0 |
| Prescott | 45,391 | 207 | 1 | 34 | 8 | 164 | 594 | 153 | 416 | 25 | 6 |
| Prescott Valley | 48,921 | 132 | 2 | 15 | 6 | 109 | 395 | 17 | 351 | 27 | 3 |
| Quartzsite | 3,827 | 14 | 0 | 3 | 2 | 9 | 74 | 11 | 46 | 17 | 0 |
| Sahuarita | 33,005 | 49 | 1 | 9 | 0 | 39 | 282 | 48 | 215 | 19 | 0 |
| San Luis | 37,140 | 31 | 0 | 1 | 1 | 29 | 242 | 40 | 144 | 58 | 1 |
| Scottsdale | 245,886 | 527 | 5 | 98 | 102 | 322 | 5,792 | 688 | 4,686 | 418 | 18 |
| Show Low | 11,670 | 31 | 0 | 6 | 1 | 24 | 261 | 19 | 235 | 7 | 3 |
| Sierra Vista | 43,814 | 104 | 4 | 21 | 12 | 67 | 616 | 93 | 496 | 27 | 1 |
| Somerton | 16,976 | 18 | 0 | 2 | 1 | 15 | 97 | 18 | 68 | 11 | 0 |
| Springerville | 1,987 | 10 | 0 | 0 | 0 | 10 | 4 | 1 | 2 | 1 | 0 |
| Superior | 3,270 | 16 | 0 | 1 | 1 | 14 | 56 | 15 | 37 | 4 | 0 |
| Surprise | 145,832 | 193 | 1 | 46 | 19 | 127 | 2,153 | 202 | 1,807 | 144 | 16 |
| Tolleson | 7,351 | 76 | 1 | 9 | 11 | 55 | 806 | 73 | 637 | 96 | 6 |
| Tombstone | 1,302 | 3 | 0 | 0 | 0 | 3 | 47 | 10 | 33 | 4 | 0 |
| Wellton | 3,187 | 7 | 2 | 1 | 0 | 4 | 31 | 3 | 25 | 3 | 0 |
| Williams | 3,349 | 24 | 1 | 2 | 0 | 21 | 79 | 10 | 63 | 6 | 0 |
| Yuma | 100,710 | 468 | 21 | 25 | 45 | 377 | 1,931 | 336 | 1,362 | 233 | 20 |
| **ARKANSAS** | | | | | | | | | | | |
| Alexander | 3,701 | 31 | 0 | 5 | 1 | 25 | 82 | 29 | 46 | 7 | 3 |
| Alma | 5,925 | 39 | 0 | 14 | 1 | 24 | 158 | 36 | 115 | 7 | 0 |
| Amity | 670 | 3 | 0 | 0 | 1 | 2 | 9 | 2 | 3 | 4 | 0 |
| Arkadelphia | 10,624 | 30 | 1 | 0 | 3 | 26 | 176 | 46 | 128 | 2 | 2 |
| Ashdown | 4,326 | 17 | 1 | 4 | 2 | 10 | 84 | 18 | 60 | 6 | 0 |
| Ash Flat | 1,101 | 11 | 0 | 0 | 0 | 11 | 47 | 4 | 43 | 0 | 0 |
| Augusta | 1,900 | 3 | 0 | 1 | 0 | 2 | 8 | 1 | 6 | 1 | 0 |
| Austin | 4,874 | 2 | 0 | 0 | 0 | 2 | 29 | 24 | 3 | 2 | 0 |
| Bald Knob | 2,864 | 12 | 0 | 6 | 0 | 6 | 70 | 9 | 58 | 3 | 0 |
| Barling | 5,103 | 30 | 0 | 5 | 0 | 25 | 69 | 9 | 56 | 4 | 0 |
| Batesville | 10,880 | 36 | 0 | 16 | 2 | 18 | 228 | 49 | 149 | 30 | 0 |
| Beebe | 8,299 | 20 | 0 | 5 | 1 | 14 | 149 | 16 | 124 | 9 | 1 |
| Bella Vista | 29,723 | 59 | 0 | 12 | 0 | 47 | 174 | 20 | 147 | 7 | 0 |
| Benton | 37,911 | 193 | 1 | 29 | 16 | 147 | 1,110 | 163 | 847 | 100 | 8 |
| Bentonville | 60,329 | 166 | 2 | 25 | 6 | 133 | 722 | 91 | 597 | 34 | 2 |
| Berryville | 5,537 | 14 | 0 | 3 | 0 | 11 | 126 | 26 | 85 | 15 | 4 |
| Blytheville | 13,003 | 158 | 2 | 6 | 8 | 142 | 560 | 81 | 455 | 24 | 2 |
| Bono | 2,637 | 5 | 0 | 4 | 0 | 1 | 16 | 0 | 14 | 2 | 0 |
| Booneville | 3,744 | 27 | 0 | 7 | 0 | 20 | 76 | 10 | 61 | 5 | 1 |
| Bradford | 735 | 3 | 0 | 0 | 0 | 3 | 11 | 2 | 8 | 1 | 0 |
| Brinkley | 2,480 | 20 | 1 | 3 | 0 | 16 | 64 | 16 | 38 | 10 | 5 |
| Brookland | 4,136 | 4 | 0 | 1 | 0 | 3 | 29 | 2 | 23 | 4 | 0 |
| Bryant | 21,902 | 34 | 0 | 6 | 3 | 25 | 752 | 50 | 643 | 59 | 1 |
| Bull Shoals | 1,951 | 2 | 0 | 0 | 0 | 2 | 12 | 1 | 10 | 1 | 0 |
| Cabot | 26,696 | 93 | 0 | 37 | 0 | 56 | 442 | 71 | 306 | 65 | 2 |
| Caddo Valley | 630 | 10 | 0 | 3 | 0 | 7 | 35 | 4 | 30 | 1 | 0 |
| Camden | 10,499 | 145 | 1 | 11 | 11 | 122 | 373 | 99 | 246 | 28 | 4 |
| Cammack Village | 706 | 0 | 0 | 0 | 0 | 0 | 11 | 1 | 8 | 2 | 0 |
| Carlisle | 2,147 | 18 | 0 | 4 | 1 | 13 | 66 | 11 | 53 | 2 | 2 |
| Charleston | 2,499 | 13 | 0 | 0 | 0 | 13 | 35 | 11 | 22 | 2 | 0 |
| Cherokee Village | 4,650 | 2 | 0 | 2 | 0 | 0 | 66 | 22 | 38 | 6 | 0 |
| Cherry Valley | 565 | 1 | 0 | 0 | 0 | 1 | 3 | 1 | 2 | 0 | 1 |
| Clarendon | 1,303 | 14 | 0 | 1 | 1 | 12 | 57 | 20 | 35 | 2 | 0 |
| Clarksville | 9,775 | 35 | 2 | 13 | 0 | 20 | 198 | 38 | 149 | 11 | 0 |

## Table 8. Offenses Known to Law Enforcement, by Selected State and City, 2021—Continued

(Number.)

| State/city | Population | Violent crime | Murder and nonnegligent manslaughter | Rape | Robbery | Aggravated assault | Property crime | Burglary | Larceny-theft | Motor vehicle theft | Arson |
|---|---|---|---|---|---|---|---|---|---|---|---|
| Clinton | 2,492 | 4 | 0 | 4 | 0 | 0 | 57 | 9 | 39 | 9 | 0 |
| Conway | 69,018 | 339 | 0 | 45 | 33 | 261 | 1,930 | 177 | 1,591 | 162 | 5 |
| Corning | 2,982 | 11 | 0 | 0 | 0 | 11 | 35 | 3 | 27 | 5 | 1 |
| Cotter | 956 | 2 | 0 | 2 | 0 | 0 | 10 | 2 | 8 | 0 | 0 |
| Crossett | 4,629 | 37 | 2 | 4 | 7 | 24 | 115 | 34 | 79 | 2 | 1 |
| Damascus | 383 | 0 | 0 | 0 | 0 | 0 | 2 | 0 | 1 | 1 | 0 |
| Danville | 2,361 | 8 | 0 | 2 | 0 | 6 | 14 | 1 | 10 | 3 | 0 |
| Dardanelle | 4,475 | 19 | 0 | 13 | 0 | 6 | 46 | 13 | 28 | 5 | 1 |
| Decatur | 1,800 | 15 | 0 | 3 | 0 | 12 | 40 | 5 | 31 | 4 | 0 |
| De Queen | 6,387 | 15 | 2 | 2 | 0 | 11 | 134 | 48 | 78 | 8 | 3 |
| Des Arc | 1,553 | 3 | 0 | 0 | 0 | 3 | 17 | 6 | 9 | 2 | 0 |
| DeWitt | 2,941 | 21 | 0 | 3 | 1 | 17 | 46 | 14 | 30 | 2 | 2 |
| Diamond City | 803 | 1 | 0 | 0 | 0 | 1 | 8 | 2 | 5 | 1 | 0 |
| Dover | 1,451 | 4 | 0 | 2 | 1 | 1 | 21 | 7 | 13 | 1 | 0 |
| Dumas | 3,897 | 27 | 2 | 2 | 0 | 23 | 57 | 11 | 43 | 3 | 0 |
| El Dorado | 17,263 | 286 | 8 | 9 | 13 | 256 | 536 | 196 | 305 | 35 | 5 |
| Elkins | 3,778 | 9 | 0 | 4 | 0 | 5 | 19 | 2 | 17 | 0 | 0 |
| England | 2,643 | 13 | 0 | 1 | 1 | 11 | 49 | 17 | 27 | 5 | 4 |
| Etowah | 308 | 0 | 0 | 0 | 0 | 0 | 5 | 1 | 3 | 1 | 0 |
| Eudora | 1,833 | 12 | 0 | 0 | 2 | 10 | 23 | 6 | 16 | 1 | 1 |
| Fairfield Bay | 2,164 | 4 | 0 | 2 | 0 | 2 | 41 | 7 | 33 | 1 | 0 |
| Farmington | 7,748 | 20 | 0 | 8 | 1 | 11 | 65 | 19 | 39 | 7 | 1 |
| Fayetteville | 91,309 | 556 | 4 | 62 | 65 | 425 | 4,389 | 375 | 3,419 | 595 | 8 |
| Flippin | 1,313 | 9 | 0 | 1 | 0 | 8 | 37 | 4 | 33 | 0 | 0 |
| Fordyce | 3,527 | 55 | 0 | 6 | 1 | 48 | 167 | 30 | 128 | 9 | 0 |
| Forrest City | 13,496 | 249 | 11 | 9 | 14 | 215 | 652 | 79 | 443 | 130 | 7 |
| Fort Smith | 87,912 | 996 | 9 | 95 | 71 | 821 | 4,916 | 668 | 3,675 | 573 | 16 |
| Gassville | 2,183 | 4 | 0 | 1 | 0 | 3 | 50 | 4 | 46 | 0 | 0 |
| Gentry | 4,323 | 20 | 1 | 6 | 0 | 13 | 11 | 0 | 8 | 3 | 0 |
| Gillett | 690 | 0 | 0 | 0 | 0 | 0 | 3 | 1 | 2 | 0 | 0 |
| Glenwood | 2,092 | 6 | 0 | 1 | 0 | 5 | 30 | 12 | 18 | 0 | 0 |
| Gravette | 3,660 | 16 | 0 | 5 | 0 | 11 | 32 | 3 | 24 | 5 | 0 |
| Green Forest | 2,955 | 36 | 1 | 10 | 1 | 24 | 49 | 17 | 27 | 5 | 2 |
| Greenland | 1,408 | 9 | 0 | 2 | 0 | 7 | 16 | 4 | 11 | 1 | 0 |
| Greenwood | 9,426 | 12 | 0 | 1 | 0 | 11 | 48 | 7 | 38 | 3 | 0 |
| Greers Ferry | 857 | 0 | 0 | 0 | 0 | 0 | 6 | 0 | 6 | 0 | 0 |
| Gurdon | 2,050 | 21 | 0 | 2 | 0 | 19 | 18 | 9 | 8 | 1 | 1 |
| Guy | 796 | 1 | 0 | 0 | 0 | 1 | 2 | 0 | 2 | 0 | 0 |
| Hackett | 842 | 1 | 0 | 1 | 0 | 0 | 1 | 1 | 0 | 0 | 0 |
| Hamburg | 2,514 | 9 | 0 | 0 | 0 | 9 | 38 | 14 | 24 | 0 | 0 |
| Hampton | 1,230 | 5 | 0 | 0 | 1 | 4 | 19 | 6 | 11 | 2 | 0 |
| Hardy | 761 | 2 | 0 | 1 | 0 | 1 | 14 | 3 | 8 | 3 | 0 |
| Harrisburg | 2,287 | 15 | 1 | 0 | 0 | 14 | 17 | 2 | 11 | 4 | 0 |
| Harrison | 13,160 | 32 | 0 | 7 | 2 | 23 | 262 | 34 | 212 | 16 | 1 |
| Haskell | 4,700 | 12 | 0 | 2 | 0 | 10 | 51 | 21 | 28 | 2 | 1 |
| Hazen | 1,317 | 6 | 0 | 1 | 1 | 4 | 13 | 4 | 7 | 2 | 0 |
| Heber Springs | 6,872 | 33 | 0 | 10 | 0 | 23 | 217 | 37 | 158 | 22 | 1 |
| Helena-West Helena | 9,820 | 241 | 6 | 17 | 12 | 206 | 435 | 139 | 256 | 40 | 15 |
| Higginson | 749 | 0 | 0 | 0 | 0 | 0 | 3 | 0 | 3 | 0 | 0 |
| Highfill | 965 | 2 | 0 | 0 | 0 | 2 | 2 | 0 | 2 | 0 | 0 |
| Highland | 1,111 | 0 | 0 | 0 | 0 | 0 | 22 | 10 | 12 | 0 | 0 |
| Hope | 9,373 | 113 | 0 | 6 | 8 | 99 | 303 | 55 | 216 | 32 | 2 |
| Hot Springs | 39,040 | 169 | 5 | 15 | 27 | 122 | 1,966 | 298 | 1,481 | 187 | 8 |
| Hoxie | 2,559 | 12 | 0 | 1 | 0 | 11 | 17 | 5 | 11 | 1 | 0 |
| Hughes | 1,178 | 5 | 0 | 0 | 0 | 5 | 13 | 3 | 8 | 2 | 1 |
| Jacksonville | 28,356 | 357 | 3 | 35 | 31 | 288 | 1,348 | 258 | 916 | 174 | 8 |
| Johnson | 3,809 | 11 | 0 | 0 | 0 | 11 | 97 | 29 | 30 | 38 | 1 |
| Jonesboro | 81,208 | 588 | 11 | 63 | 54 | 460 | 2,448 | 845 | 1,392 | 211 | 14 |
| Lake City | 2,810 | 2 | 0 | 1 | 0 | 1 | 23 | 3 | 17 | 3 | 0 |
| Lamar | 1,741 | 6 | 1 | 1 | 0 | 4 | 6 | 0 | 6 | 0 | 0 |
| Lavaca | 2,453 | 3 | 0 | 3 | 0 | 0 | 22 | 6 | 14 | 2 | 0 |
| Leachville | 1,816 | 12 | 0 | 1 | 0 | 11 | 60 | 21 | 37 | 2 | 0 |
| Lincoln | 2,492 | 8 | 0 | 1 | 0 | 7 | 52 | 11 | 36 | 5 | 0 |
| Little Flock | 2,842 | 5 | 1 | 0 | 0 | 4 | 35 | 14 | 16 | 5 | 0 |
| Little Rock | 198,260 | 4,091 | 62 | 252 | 397 | 3,380 | 10,635 | 1,970 | 7,609 | 1,056 | 93 |
| Lonoke | 4,152 | 44 | 0 | 4 | 1 | 39 | 145 | 34 | 104 | 7 | 0 |
| Lowell | 10,171 | 28 | 0 | 4 | 1 | 23 | 129 | 46 | 72 | 11 | 0 |
| Luxora | 991 | 0 | 0 | 0 | 0 | 0 | 6 | 1 | 2 | 3 | 0 |
| Magnolia | 11,410 | 68 | 1 | 3 | 15 | 49 | 346 | 184 | 151 | 11 | 0 |
| Malvern | 10,805 | 107 | 0 | 13 | 9 | 85 | 511 | 189 | 288 | 34 | 5 |
| Mammoth Spring | 938 | 0 | 0 | 0 | 0 | 0 | 2 | 1 | 1 | 0 | 0 |
| Mansfield | 1,083 | 1 | 0 | 0 | 0 | 1 | 11 | 2 | 6 | 3 | 1 |
| Marianna | 3,219 | 27 | 0 | 3 | 0 | 24 | 114 | 31 | 74 | 9 | 0 |
| Marion | 12,266 | 137 | 7 | 6 | 4 | 120 | 350 | 60 | 271 | 19 | 1 |
| Marked Tree | 2,366 | 26 | 0 | 2 | 0 | 24 | 26 | 7 | 13 | 6 | 0 |
| Marmaduke | 1,262 | 13 | 0 | 8 | 0 | 5 | 19 | 3 | 16 | 0 | 0 |
| Marshall | 1,321 | 8 | 0 | 4 | 1 | 3 | 11 | 3 | 7 | 1 | 0 |
| Maumelle | 18,343 | 26 | 0 | 5 | 3 | 18 | 287 | 47 | 229 | 11 | 1 |
| Mayflower | 2,437 | 15 | 0 | 0 | 1 | 14 | 92 | 22 | 62 | 8 | 0 |
| McCrory | 1,473 | 2 | 0 | 2 | 0 | 0 | 30 | 3 | 24 | 3 | 0 |
| McGehee | 3,545 | 27 | 0 | 3 | 2 | 22 | 87 | 31 | 48 | 8 | 0 |
| McRae | 670 | 0 | 0 | 0 | 0 | 0 | 2 | 0 | 2 | 0 | 0 |
| Mena | 5,377 | 8 | 0 | 2 | 1 | 5 | 186 | 23 | 157 | 6 | 0 |

# Table 8. Offenses Known to Law Enforcement, by Selected State and City, 2021—Continued

(Number.)

| State/city | Population | Violent crime | Murder and nonnegligent manslaughter | Rape | Robbery | Aggravated assault | Property crime | Burglary | Larceny-theft | Motor vehicle theft | Arson |
|---|---|---|---|---|---|---|---|---|---|---|---|
| Menifee | 323 | 3 | 0 | 0 | 0 | 3 | 6 | 1 | 5 | 0 | 0 |
| Mineral Springs | 1,133 | 5 | 1 | 1 | 0 | 3 | 6 | 1 | 5 | 0 | 0 |
| Monette | 1,639 | 2 | 0 | 1 | 0 | 1 | 22 | 5 | 17 | 0 | 0 |
| Monticello | 9,145 | 43 | 4 | 8 | 2 | 29 | 237 | 39 | 178 | 20 | 2 |
| Morrilton | 6,672 | 30 | 0 | 8 | 0 | 22 | 312 | 23 | 276 | 13 | 3 |
| Mountain Home | 12,657 | 25 | 0 | 11 | 0 | 14 | 359 | 34 | 309 | 16 | 0 |
| Mountain View | 2,917 | 9 | 0 | 1 | 0 | 8 | 46 | 11 | 34 | 1 | 0 |
| Mulberry | 1,699 | 2 | 0 | 2 | 0 | 0 | 44 | 2 | 34 | 8 | 0 |
| Murfreesboro | 1,565 | 4 | 0 | 1 | 0 | 3 | 10 | 2 | 8 | 0 | 0 |
| Nashville | 4,263 | 26 | 0 | 6 | 1 | 19 | 120 | 18 | 101 | 1 | 0 |
| Newport | 7,335 | 119 | 0 | 12 | 5 | 102 | 380 | 98 | 267 | 15 | 1 |
| Norfork | 543 | 0 | 0 | 0 | 0 | 0 | 0 | 0 | 0 | 0 | 0 |
| North Little Rock | 66,677 | 762 | 20 | 16 | 97 | 629 | 2,465 | 369 | 1,734 | 362 | 10 |
| Ola | 1,190 | 3 | 0 | 1 | 0 | 2 | 7 | 1 | 5 | 1 | 0 |
| Osceola | 6,472 | 172 | 0 | 7 | 5 | 160 | 225 | 88 | 102 | 35 | 5 |
| Ozark | 3,618 | 14 | 0 | 5 | 0 | 9 | 62 | 26 | 33 | 3 | 0 |
| Paragould | 29,559 | 362 | 0 | 26 | 8 | 328 | 1,107 | 143 | 856 | 108 | 1 |
| Paris | 3,352 | 15 | 1 | 5 | 0 | 9 | 83 | 20 | 49 | 14 | 0 |
| Pea Ridge | 6,652 | 13 | 0 | 5 | 0 | 8 | 68 | 14 | 51 | 3 | 0 |
| Perryville | 1,438 | 4 | 0 | 0 | 0 | 4 | 22 | 5 | 16 | 1 | 0 |
| Piggott | 3,464 | 3 | 0 | 1 | 0 | 2 | 17 | 4 | 13 | 0 | 0 |
| Pine Bluff | 39,670 | 820 | 23 | 35 | 55 | 707 | 2,326 | 444 | 1,532 | 350 | 41 |
| Plumerville | 773 | 0 | 0 | 0 | 0 | 0 | 10 | 1 | 9 | 0 | 0 |
| Pottsville | 3,423 | 2 | 0 | 0 | 0 | 2 | 19 | 6 | 13 | 0 | 0 |
| Prairie Grove | 7,380 | 19 | 0 | 8 | 0 | 11 | 59 | 6 | 50 | 3 | 0 |
| Prescott | 2,892 | 4 | 0 | 1 | 0 | 3 | 48 | 5 | 35 | 8 | 0 |
| Quitman | 705 | 0 | 0 | 0 | 0 | 0 | 20 | 2 | 17 | 1 | 0 |
| Ravenden | 443 | 2 | 0 | 1 | 0 | 1 | 7 | 2 | 3 | 2 | 0 |
| Redfield | 1,513 | 1 | 0 | 0 | 0 | 1 | 27 | 11 | 14 | 2 | 0 |
| Rogers | 72,122 | 274 | 3 | 98 | 14 | 159 | 1,562 | 115 | 1,335 | 112 | 7 |
| Rose Bud | 493 | 1 | 0 | 0 | 0 | 1 | 4 | 0 | 4 | 0 | 0 |
| Russellville | 29,465 | 188 | 0 | 22 | 4 | 162 | 826 | 91 | 661 | 74 | 1 |
| Salem | 1,657 | 2 | 0 | 2 | 0 | 0 | 14 | 3 | 9 | 2 | 0 |
| Searcy | 23,604 | 155 | 2 | 26 | 10 | 117 | 970 | 88 | 788 | 94 | 1 |
| Shannon Hills | 4,196 | 26 | 0 | 6 | 2 | 18 | 46 | 17 | 26 | 3 | 2 |
| Sheridan | 5,075 | 16 | 0 | 6 | 1 | 9 | 122 | 19 | 94 | 9 | 1 |
| Sherwood | 31,857 | 221 | 0 | 19 | 12 | 190 | 844 | 235 | 548 | 61 | 2 |
| Siloam Springs | 17,877 | 80 | 4 | 10 | 1 | 65 | 493 | 84 | 362 | 47 | 1 |
| Springdale | 85,234 | 405 | 2 | 60 | 29 | 314 | 2,568 | 292 | 1,918 | 358 | 11 |
| Stamps | 1,446 | 2 | 0 | 1 | 0 | 1 | 16 | 3 | 11 | 2 | 0 |
| Star City | 1,989 | 25 | 0 | 6 | 2 | 17 | 44 | 10 | 29 | 5 | 1 |
| St. Charles | 210 | 1 | 0 | 0 | 0 | 1 | 2 | 0 | 2 | 0 | 0 |
| Stuttgart | 8,312 | 141 | 4 | 8 | 3 | 126 | 263 | 57 | 190 | 16 | 0 |
| Swifton | 726 | 2 | 0 | 1 | 0 | 1 | 4 | 0 | 1 | 3 | 0 |
| Texarkana | 29,516 | 278 | 4 | 15 | 22 | 237 | 843 | 111 | 655 | 77 | 6 |
| Trumann | 6,869 | 49 | 1 | 7 | 4 | 37 | 253 | 38 | 194 | 21 | 2 |
| Tuckerman | 1,670 | 2 | 0 | 1 | 0 | 1 | 18 | 3 | 12 | 3 | 0 |
| Turrell | 543 | 1 | 0 | 0 | 0 | 1 | 0 | 0 | 0 | 0 | 0 |
| Van Buren | 23,912 | 98 | 0 | 20 | 2 | 76 | 659 | 194 | 411 | 54 | 0 |
| Vilonia | 4,824 | 5 | 0 | 0 | 0 | 5 | 50 | 8 | 38 | 4 | 0 |
| Waldron | 3,303 | 6 | 0 | 0 | 0 | 6 | 100 | 46 | 50 | 4 | 0 |
| Ward | 5,649 | 48 | 1 | 7 | 1 | 39 | 89 | 22 | 57 | 10 | 1 |
| Warren | 5,458 | 35 | 1 | 4 | 4 | 26 | 139 | 45 | 81 | 13 | 2 |
| West Fork | 2,649 | 1 | 0 | 1 | 0 | 0 | 51 | 7 | 42 | 2 | 0 |
| West Memphis | 23,959 | 648 | 7 | 33 | 50 | 558 | 953 | 199 | 588 | 166 | 6 |
| White Hall | 4,830 | 13 | 0 | 1 | 0 | 12 | 53 | 15 | 31 | 7 | 0 |
| Wilson | 793 | 3 | 0 | 2 | 0 | 1 | 7 | 2 | 4 | 1 | 0 |
| Wynne | 7,546 | 86 | 2 | 5 | 4 | 75 | 321 | 59 | 240 | 22 | 5 |
| **CALIFORNIA**[1] | | | | | | | | | | | |
| Carlsbad | 116,633 | 235 | 2 | 26 | 40 | 167 | 2,032 | 280 | 1,544 | 208 | 18 |
| Chula Vista | 275,978 | 871 | 6 | 41 | 249 | 575 | 3,334 | 400 | 1,989 | 945 | 50 |
| El Cajon | 102,665 | 525 | 2 | 43 | 113 | 367 | 1,860 | 261 | 1,179 | 420 | 26 |
| Escondido | 150,507 | 545 | 3 | 27 | 140 | 375 | 2,644 | 333 | 1,741 | 570 | 30 |
| La Mesa | 59,968 | 157 | 2 | 12 | 42 | 101 | 1,145 | 181 | 751 | 213 | 15 |
| National City | 61,171 | 402 | 4 | 19 | 91 | 288 | 1,291 | 132 | 831 | 328 | 16 |
| Oceanside | 175,335 | 771 | 6 | 83 | 163 | 519 | 3,346 | 426 | 2,433 | 487 | 40 |
| San Diego | 1,434,673 | 5,404 | 63 | 444 | 1,040 | 3,857 | 26,348 | 3,286 | 16,601 | 6,461 | 150 |
| **COLORADO** | | | | | | | | | | | |
| Alamosa | 9,414 | 77 | 2 | 13 | 10 | 52 | 495 | 83 | 379 | 33 | 17 |
| Arvada | 123,548 | 345 | 3 | 33 | 87 | 222 | 4,261 | 438 | 2,964 | 859 | 17 |
| Aspen | 7,750 | 4 | 0 | 2 | 0 | 2 | 169 | 7 | 156 | 6 | 0 |
| Ault | 2,197 | 2 | 0 | 0 | 0 | 2 | 2 | 2 | 0 | 0 | 0 |
| Aurora | 393,897 | 3,963 | 42 | 408 | 771 | 2,742 | 15,282 | 1,900 | 7,847 | 5,535 | 154 |
| Avon | 7,012 | 17 | 0 | 5 | 0 | 12 | 75 | 3 | 61 | 11 | 0 |
| Basalt | 4,226 | 17 | 0 | 16 | 0 | 1 | 36 | 3 | 32 | 1 | 0 |
| Bayfield | 2,614 | 6 | 1 | 0 | 1 | 4 | 43 | 6 | 30 | 7 | 1 |
| Black Hawk | 132 | 7 | 0 | 0 | 2 | 5 | 320 | 3 | 293 | 24 | 0 |
| Boulder | 108,698 | 407 | 3 | 46 | 71 | 287 | 3,750 | 565 | 2,783 | 402 | 31 |
| Breckenridge | 4,996 | 10 | 0 | 4 | 0 | 6 | 159 | 7 | 138 | 14 | 0 |
| Brighton | 41,535 | 111 | 0 | 21 | 10 | 80 | 1,181 | 104 | 845 | 232 | 8 |
| Broomfield | 73,077 | 85 | 2 | 13 | 32 | 38 | 2,360 | 254 | 1,737 | 369 | 6 |

## Table 8. Offenses Known to Law Enforcement, by Selected State and City, 2021—Continued

(Number.)

| State/city | Population | Violent crime | Murder and nonnegligent manslaughter | Rape | Robbery | Aggravated assault | Property crime | Burglary | Larceny-theft | Motor vehicle theft | Arson |
|---|---|---|---|---|---|---|---|---|---|---|---|
| Buena Vista | 3,175 | 1 | 0 | 0 | 1 | 0 | 13 | 3 | 9 | 1 | 0 |
| Burlington | 3,038 | 7 | 0 | 0 | 0 | 7 | 36 | 4 | 28 | 4 | 0 |
| Calhan | 831 | 7 | 0 | 0 | 0 | 7 | 9 | 4 | 4 | 1 | 3 |
| Canon City | 16,552 | 114 | 3 | 25 | 10 | 76 | 704 | 88 | 559 | 57 | 7 |
| Carbondale | 6,761 | 15 | 0 | 5 | 1 | 9 | 47 | 0 | 45 | 2 | 0 |
| Castle Rock | 73,221 | 40 | 0 | 14 | 9 | 17 | 1,188 | 102 | 1,008 | 78 | 1 |
| Cedaredge | 2,320 | 4 | 0 | 1 | 0 | 3 | 4 | 0 | 4 | 0 | 0 |
| Centennial | 111,199 | 194 | 6 | 15 | 27 | 146 | 2,134 | 263 | 1,416 | 455 | 21 |
| Center | 2,399 | 10 | 0 | 9 | 0 | 1 | 38 | 7 | 27 | 4 | 0 |
| Cherry Hills Village | 6,685 | 0 | 0 | 0 | 0 | 0 | 72 | 19 | 41 | 12 | 0 |
| Colorado Springs | 488,747 | 2,806 | 38 | 402 | 359 | 2,007 | 15,703 | 2,416 | 10,729 | 2,558 | 182 |
| Commerce City | 60,845 | 395 | 5 | 82 | 42 | 266 | 2,600 | 220 | 1,631 | 749 | 16 |
| Cortez | 8,760 | 44 | 0 | 13 | 7 | 24 | 257 | 35 | 196 | 26 | 2 |
| Craig | 8,905 | 37 | 0 | 7 | 0 | 30 | 195 | 32 | 153 | 10 | 2 |
| Crested Butte | 1,703 | 2 | 0 | 0 | 0 | 2 | 10 | 2 | 8 | 0 | 0 |
| Cripple Creek | 1,270 | 6 | 0 | 1 | 0 | 5 | 59 | 0 | 54 | 5 | 1 |
| Dacono | 6,877 | 5 | 0 | 5 | 0 | 0 | 101 | 5 | 55 | 41 | 0 |
| Del Norte | 1,528 | 2 | 0 | 2 | 0 | 0 | 27 | 8 | 19 | 0 | 0 |
| Delta | 9,047 | 19 | 0 | 8 | 1 | 10 | 402 | 61 | 303 | 38 | 6 |
| Denver | 740,209 | 6,897 | 100 | 742 | 1,326 | 4,729 | 42,781 | 5,839 | 24,214 | 12,728 | 194 |
| Dillon | 973 | 3 | 0 | 1 | 0 | 2 | 22 | 1 | 18 | 3 | 0 |
| Dinosaur | 334 | 3 | 0 | 1 | 1 | 1 | 3 | 2 | 1 | 0 | 0 |
| Durango | 19,995 | 46 | 0 | 9 | 5 | 32 | 604 | 59 | 511 | 34 | 3 |
| Eagle | 6,954 | 12 | 0 | 2 | 0 | 10 | 74 | 9 | 57 | 8 | 1 |
| Eaton | 6,191 | 6 | 0 | 1 | 0 | 5 | 23 | 4 | 15 | 4 | 0 |
| Edgewater | 5,415 | 21 | 0 | 6 | 6 | 9 | 365 | 27 | 261 | 77 | 1 |
| Elizabeth | 1,928 | 6 | 0 | 0 | 0 | 6 | 21 | 0 | 18 | 3 | 0 |
| Empire | 304 | 2 | 1 | 0 | 0 | 1 | 23 | 3 | 13 | 7 | 0 |
| Englewood | 35,630 | 245 | 2 | 18 | 44 | 181 | 2,443 | 284 | 1,579 | 580 | 17 |
| Erie | 31,873 | 17 | 0 | 4 | 2 | 11 | 310 | 30 | 232 | 48 | 3 |
| Estes Park | 6,617 | 12 | 0 | 1 | 0 | 11 | 41 | 15 | 24 | 2 | 0 |
| Evans | 23,698 | 52 | 1 | 5 | 12 | 34 | 480 | 71 | 291 | 118 | 10 |
| Fairplay | 814 | 2 | 0 | 1 | 0 | 1 | 11 | 0 | 11 | 0 | 0 |
| Firestone | 15,932 | 8 | 0 | 0 | 0 | 8 | 195 | 10 | 131 | 54 | 1 |
| Florence | 3,993 | 21 | 0 | 3 | 0 | 18 | 47 | 5 | 32 | 10 | 1 |
| Fort Collins | 170,744 | 515 | 3 | 94 | 45 | 373 | 3,509 | 337 | 2,817 | 355 | 18 |
| Fort Lupton | 8,800 | 27 | 0 | 8 | 3 | 16 | 155 | 20 | 100 | 35 | 0 |
| Fort Morgan | 11,234 | 63 | 2 | 19 | 1 | 41 | 328 | 60 | 236 | 32 | 7 |
| Fountain | 31,557 | 116 | 0 | 23 | 15 | 78 | 639 | 71 | 469 | 99 | 3 |
| Fraser/Winter Park | 2,478 | 8 | 0 | 2 | 2 | 4 | 75 | 14 | 53 | 8 | 0 |
| Frederick | 11,844 | 7 | 0 | 4 | 0 | 3 | 42 | 3 | 28 | 11 | 0 |
| Frisco | 2,892 | 9 | 0 | 1 | 0 | 8 | 110 | 4 | 76 | 30 | 0 |
| Fruita | 14,465 | 27 | 0 | 4 | 2 | 21 | 148 | 14 | 124 | 10 | 4 |
| Garden City | 282 | 2 | 0 | 0 | 0 | 2 | 22 | 3 | 16 | 3 | 0 |
| Georgetown | 1,109 | 4 | 0 | 2 | 0 | 2 | 20 | 0 | 12 | 8 | 0 |
| Glendale | 5,192 | 95 | 0 | 11 | 30 | 54 | 836 | 76 | 504 | 256 | 2 |
| Glenwood Springs | 10,297 | 44 | 2 | 20 | 1 | 21 | 347 | 23 | 291 | 33 | 2 |
| Golden | 20,498 | 47 | 0 | 2 | 2 | 43 | 721 | 85 | 516 | 120 | 8 |
| Granada | 508 | 2 | 0 | 0 | 0 | 2 | 7 | 0 | 5 | 2 | 0 |
| Granby | 2,209 | 1 | 0 | 0 | 0 | 1 | 35 | 2 | 26 | 7 | 0 |
| Grand Junction | 63,928 | 378 | 3 | 69 | 33 | 273 | 2,900 | 347 | 2,272 | 281 | 21 |
| Greeley | 110,660 | 590 | 9 | 52 | 88 | 441 | 3,054 | 356 | 2,132 | 566 | 14 |
| Green Mountain Falls | 737 | 0 | 0 | 0 | 0 | 0 | 1 | 1 | 0 | 0 | 0 |
| Gunnison | 6,950 | 29 | 0 | 6 | 0 | 23 | 109 | 7 | 94 | 8 | 0 |
| Gypsum | 7,391 | 9 | 0 | 3 | 0 | 6 | 26 | 2 | 21 | 3 | 0 |
| Haxtun | 936 | 0 | 0 | 0 | 0 | 0 | 7 | 0 | 6 | 1 | 0 |
| Hayden | 1,995 | 1 | 0 | 0 | 0 | 1 | 27 | 6 | 20 | 1 | 1 |
| Holyoke | 2,230 | 3 | 0 | 1 | 0 | 2 | 3 | 0 | 1 | 2 | 0 |
| Hotchkiss | 929 | 1 | 0 | 0 | 0 | 1 | 19 | 3 | 16 | 0 | 0 |
| Hudson | 2,812 | 9 | 0 | 1 | 1 | 7 | 48 | 1 | 33 | 14 | 1 |
| Hugo | 787 | 0 | 0 | 0 | 0 | 0 | 7 | 1 | 3 | 3 | 0 |
| Idaho Springs | 1,871 | 12 | 0 | 0 | 1 | 11 | 79 | 6 | 58 | 15 | 0 |
| Johnstown | 14,413 | 22 | 0 | 7 | 2 | 13 | 423 | 27 | 347 | 49 | 2 |
| Lafayette | 29,027 | 85 | 2 | 22 | 8 | 53 | 817 | 97 | 606 | 114 | 7 |
| La Junta | 6,831 | 37 | 4 | 9 | 3 | 21 | 321 | 44 | 242 | 35 | 2 |
| Lakeside | 8 | 0 | 0 | 0 | 0 | 0 | 157 | 1 | 154 | 2 | 0 |
| Lakewood | 158,977 | 1,088 | 12 | 118 | 286 | 672 | 8,554 | 1,130 | 5,491 | 1,933 | 50 |
| Lamar | 7,612 | 8 | 2 | 1 | 0 | 5 | 94 | 18 | 74 | 2 | 2 |
| La Salle | 2,524 | 1 | 0 | 1 | 0 | 0 | 47 | 8 | 21 | 18 | 0 |
| Leadville | 2,796 | 6 | 1 | 1 | 0 | 4 | 36 | 10 | 22 | 4 | 0 |
| Limon | 1,951 | 4 | 0 | 1 | 0 | 3 | 3 | 1 | 0 | 2 | 0 |
| Littleton | 46,466 | 74 | 0 | 15 | 19 | 40 | 1,443 | 280 | 818 | 345 | 5 |
| Lone Tree | 14,007 | 65 | 0 | 9 | 10 | 46 | 1,246 | 55 | 1,084 | 107 | 5 |
| Longmont | 99,714 | 477 | 2 | 141 | 50 | 284 | 2,674 | 268 | 2,001 | 405 | 31 |
| Louisville | 19,127 | 64 | 0 | 15 | 2 | 47 | 573 | 79 | 420 | 74 | 3 |
| Loveland | 85,349 | 237 | 2 | 61 | 16 | 158 | 1,651 | 167 | 1,307 | 177 | 6 |
| Mancos | 1,404 | 4 | 0 | 3 | 0 | 1 | 20 | 2 | 14 | 4 | 0 |
| Manitou Springs | 5,509 | 21 | 0 | 3 | 1 | 17 | 126 | 28 | 64 | 34 | 7 |
| Meeker | 2,305 | 1 | 0 | 0 | 0 | 1 | 31 | 0 | 25 | 6 | 0 |
| Milliken | 9,074 | 0 | 0 | 0 | 0 | 0 | 27 | 1 | 19 | 7 | 0 |
| Monte Vista | 4,030 | 19 | 0 | 3 | 1 | 15 | 115 | 20 | 91 | 4 | 0 |
| Montrose | 19,984 | 55 | 0 | 4 | 4 | 47 | 796 | 69 | 674 | 53 | 3 |
| Monument | 8,397 | 22 | 0 | 4 | 5 | 13 | 180 | 32 | 134 | 14 | 1 |

## Table 8. Offenses Known to Law Enforcement, by Selected State and City, 2021—Continued

(Number.)

| State/city | Population | Violent crime | Murder and nonnegligent manslaughter | Rape | Robbery | Aggravated assault | Property crime | Burglary | Larceny-theft | Motor vehicle theft | Arson |
|---|---|---|---|---|---|---|---|---|---|---|---|
| Mountain View | 553 | 1 | 0 | 0 | 1 | 0 | 10 | 0 | 7 | 3 | 0 |
| Mountain Village | 1,486 | 1 | 0 | 0 | 0 | 1 | 16 | 1 | 14 | 1 | 0 |
| Mount Crested Butte | 901 | 1 | 0 | 0 | 0 | 1 | 6 | 0 | 6 | 0 | 0 |
| Nederland | 1,569 | 0 | 0 | 0 | 0 | 0 | 3 | 0 | 2 | 1 | 0 |
| New Castle | 5,012 | 5 | 0 | 0 | 0 | 5 | 27 | 1 | 17 | 9 | 0 |
| Northglenn | 39,162 | 248 | 2 | 35 | 31 | 180 | 1,562 | 129 | 983 | 450 | 14 |
| Oak Creek | 966 | 6 | 1 | 0 | 1 | 4 | 1 | 0 | 1 | 0 | 0 |
| Pagosa Springs | 2,178 | 6 | 0 | 0 | 0 | 6 | 40 | 3 | 35 | 2 | 0 |
| Palisade | 2,812 | 5 | 0 | 1 | 0 | 4 | 53 | 3 | 46 | 4 | 0 |
| Parachute | 1,118 | 9 | 0 | 2 | 0 | 7 | 24 | 4 | 15 | 5 | 0 |
| Parker | 60,178 | 88 | 0 | 23 | 4 | 61 | 1,069 | 102 | 824 | 143 | 12 |
| Platteville | 4,239 | 5 | 0 | 2 | 0 | 3 | 65 | 8 | 42 | 15 | 0 |
| Pueblo | 113,371 | 1,421 | 27 | 193 | 250 | 951 | 6,452 | 1,376 | 3,690 | 1,386 | 89 |
| Rangely | 2,295 | 15 | 0 | 5 | 0 | 10 | 0 | 0 | 0 | 0 | 0 |
| Rifle | 9,819 | 40 | 0 | 18 | 4 | 18 | 262 | 24 | 199 | 39 | 1 |
| Rocky Ford | 3,790 | 2 | 0 | 0 | 0 | 2 | 16 | 8 | 5 | 3 | 0 |
| Salida | 5,735 | 12 | 0 | 2 | 0 | 10 | 121 | 12 | 102 | 7 | 0 |
| Severance | 8,343 | 0 | 0 | 0 | 0 | 0 | 23 | 4 | 16 | 3 | 0 |
| Sheridan | 6,070 | 71 | 0 | 5 | 15 | 51 | 605 | 41 | 405 | 159 | 6 |
| Silt | 3,129 | 3 | 0 | 1 | 1 | 1 | 14 | 0 | 8 | 6 | 0 |
| Silverthorne | 5,019 | 8 | 0 | 4 | 1 | 3 | 126 | 20 | 81 | 25 | 0 |
| Simla | 698 | 1 | 0 | 0 | 0 | 1 | 6 | 2 | 1 | 3 | 0 |
| South Fork | 422 | 0 | 0 | 0 | 0 | 0 | 7 | 2 | 5 | 0 | 0 |
| Springfield | 1,355 | 5 | 0 | 0 | 0 | 5 | 13 | 6 | 6 | 1 | 0 |
| Steamboat Springs | 13,282 | 41 | 0 | 10 | 2 | 29 | 184 | 17 | 150 | 17 | 2 |
| Sterling | 14,006 | 57 | 1 | 20 | 4 | 32 | 466 | 86 | 350 | 30 | 4 |
| Telluride | 2,436 | 4 | 0 | 0 | 1 | 3 | 31 | 1 | 30 | 0 | 0 |
| Thornton | 151,324 | 460 | 5 | 156 | 80 | 219 | 4,970 | 422 | 3,374 | 1,174 | 17 |
| Timnath | 3,801 | 6 | 0 | 0 | 1 | 5 | 102 | 17 | 80 | 5 | 0 |
| Trinidad | 8,045 | 33 | 1 | 6 | 7 | 19 | 339 | 101 | 202 | 36 | 4 |
| Vail | 5,507 | 25 | 0 | 3 | 3 | 19 | 223 | 27 | 184 | 12 | 0 |
| Walsh | 510 | 0 | 0 | 0 | 0 | 0 | 0 | 0 | 0 | 0 | 0 |
| Westminster | 115,942 | 454 | 12 | 60 | 103 | 279 | 5,167 | 438 | 3,238 | 1,491 | 33 |
| Wheat Ridge | 32,027 | 173 | 0 | 28 | 40 | 105 | 1,960 | 229 | 1,286 | 445 | 16 |
| Windsor | 28,756 | 16 | 0 | 0 | 0 | 16 | 148 | 21 | 115 | 12 | 0 |
| Woodland Park | 8,257 | 15 | 0 | 5 | 0 | 10 | 121 | 5 | 109 | 7 | 1 |
| **CONNECTICUT** | | | | | | | | | | | |
| Ansonia | 18,452 | 24 | 1 | 3 | 12 | 8 | 385 | 25 | 293 | 67 | 0 |
| Avon | 18,226 | 6 | 0 | 0 | 4 | 2 | 200 | 19 | 158 | 23 | 0 |
| Berlin | 20,440 | 18 | 0 | 1 | 9 | 8 | 480 | 60 | 377 | 43 | 4 |
| Bethel | 20,066 | 9 | 0 | 3 | 1 | 5 | 97 | 12 | 76 | 9 | 0 |
| Bloomfield | 21,254 | 41 | 2 | 5 | 11 | 23 | 552 | 25 | 474 | 53 | 2 |
| Branford | 27,707 | 19 | 0 | 3 | 7 | 9 | 399 | 22 | 328 | 49 | 0 |
| Bridgeport | 143,394 | 800 | 20 | 58 | 417 | 305 | 2,176 | 429 | 1,028 | 719 | 3 |
| Bristol | 59,659 | 49 | 0 | 6 | 26 | 17 | 775 | 113 | 561 | 101 | 2 |
| Brookfield | 16,944 | 8 | 0 | 1 | 1 | 6 | 131 | 6 | 113 | 12 | 0 |
| Canton | 10,223 | 4 | 0 | 1 | 1 | 2 | 63 | 4 | 51 | 8 | 0 |
| Cheshire | 28,755 | 4 | 0 | 1 | 1 | 2 | 209 | 14 | 159 | 36 | 0 |
| Clinton | 12,846 | 10 | 0 | 2 | 7 | 1 | 332 | 18 | 290 | 24 | 1 |
| Coventry | 12,384 | 3 | 0 | 1 | 1 | 1 | 55 | 11 | 38 | 6 | 0 |
| Cromwell | 13,750 | 5 | 0 | 0 | 4 | 1 | 304 | 23 | 257 | 24 | 1 |
| Danbury | 84,631 | 92 | 2 | 28 | 38 | 24 | 944 | 111 | 710 | 123 | 5 |
| Darien | 21,790 | 9 | 0 | 1 | 3 | 5 | 365 | 28 | 285 | 52 | 0 |
| Derby | 12,197 | 45 | 0 | 3 | 12 | 30 | 345 | 33 | 257 | 55 | 1 |
| East Hampton | 12,726 | 0 | 0 | 0 | 0 | 0 | 85 | 8 | 74 | 3 | 0 |
| East Hartford | 49,470 | 80 | 2 | 18 | 27 | 33 | 1,637 | 170 | 1,245 | 222 | 2 |
| East Haven | 28,377 | 42 | 0 | 5 | 9 | 28 | 669 | 46 | 546 | 77 | 0 |
| East Lyme | 18,467 | 6 | 0 | 1 | 0 | 5 | 76 | 2 | 61 | 13 | 1 |
| Easton | 7,462 | 0 | 0 | 0 | 0 | 0 | 84 | 4 | 65 | 15 | 0 |
| East Windsor | 11,702 | 16 | 0 | 2 | 9 | 5 | 402 | 103 | 272 | 27 | 0 |
| Enfield | 43,452 | 65 | 2 | 9 | 13 | 41 | 662 | 53 | 549 | 60 | 0 |
| Fairfield | 62,473 | 33 | 0 | 3 | 12 | 18 | 1,020 | 66 | 846 | 108 | 1 |
| Farmington | 25,510 | 14 | 0 | 5 | 6 | 3 | 405 | 35 | 334 | 36 | 0 |
| Glastonbury | 34,424 | 17 | 0 | 0 | 11 | 6 | 478 | 51 | 393 | 34 | 1 |
| Granby | 11,585 | 2 | 0 | 1 | 1 | 0 | 96 | 5 | 86 | 5 | 1 |
| Greenwich | 62,917 | 13 | 0 | 5 | 4 | 4 | 495 | 41 | 361 | 93 | 0 |
| Groton | 8,823 | 21 | 0 | 7 | 0 | 14 | 78 | 14 | 52 | 12 | 0 |
| Groton Long Point | 504 | 0 | 0 | 0 | 0 | 0 | 4 | 0 | 4 | 0 | 0 |
| Groton Town | 28,753 | 40 | 0 | 10 | 5 | 25 | 288 | 22 | 238 | 28 | 0 |
| Guilford | 22,009 | 12 | 1 | 1 | 6 | 4 | 233 | 15 | 198 | 20 | 1 |
| Hamden | 60,165 | 237 | 3 | 8 | 59 | 167 | 1,434 | 111 | 1,124 | 199 | 1 |
| Hartford | 121,160 | 579 | 34 | 31 | 109 | 405 | 2,608 | 235 | 1,910 | 463 | 20 |
| Ledyard | 14,534 | 7 | 1 | 1 | 1 | 4 | 47 | 9 | 30 | 8 | 1 |
| Madison | 17,890 | 2 | 0 | 1 | 1 | 0 | 70 | 1 | 58 | 11 | 1 |
| Manchester | 57,274 | 89 | 2 | 21 | 26 | 40 | 1,788 | 111 | 1,503 | 174 | 2 |
| Meriden | 58,799 | 217 | 3 | 32 | 65 | 117 | 1,276 | 238 | 875 | 163 | 3 |
| Middlebury | 7,851 | 4 | 0 | 1 | 1 | 2 | 76 | 9 | 53 | 14 | 0 |
| Middletown | 45,852 | 50 | 3 | 9 | 16 | 22 | 600 | 43 | 477 | 80 | 1 |
| Milford | 54,984 | 57 | 1 | 13 | 29 | 14 | 1,096 | 56 | 940 | 100 | 2 |
| Monroe | 19,311 | 1 | 0 | 0 | 1 | 0 | 95 | 14 | 65 | 16 | 0 |
| Naugatuck | 30,810 | 34 | 0 | 9 | 7 | 18 | 432 | 41 | 325 | 66 | 0 |
| New Britain | 72,093 | 299 | 2 | 49 | 73 | 175 | 1,918 | 181 | 1,456 | 281 | 11 |

## Table 8. Offenses Known to Law Enforcement, by Selected State and City, 2021—Continued

(Number.)

| State/city | Population | Violent crime | Murder and nonnegligent manslaughter | Rape | Robbery | Aggravated assault | Property crime | Burglary | Larceny-theft | Motor vehicle theft | Arson |
|---|---|---|---|---|---|---|---|---|---|---|---|
| New Canaan | 20,147 | 3 | 1 | 1 | 0 | 1 | 160 | 9 | 112 | 39 | 1 |
| New Haven | 130,903 | 813 | 25 | 50 | 237 | 501 | 4,265 | 484 | 3,081 | 700 | 27 |
| Newington | 29,803 | 35 | 0 | 6 | 12 | 17 | 1,074 | 179 | 824 | 71 | 0 |
| New London | 26,797 | 74 | 2 | 16 | 30 | 26 | 468 | 62 | 332 | 74 | 8 |
| New Milford | 26,548 | 13 | 0 | 7 | 2 | 4 | 217 | 8 | 188 | 21 | 0 |
| Newtown | 27,858 | 4 | 0 | 1 | 1 | 2 | 112 | 6 | 89 | 17 | 0 |
| North Branford | 14,031 | 9 | 0 | 5 | 0 | 4 | 107 | 12 | 84 | 11 | 0 |
| North Haven | 23,504 | 13 | 2 | 0 | 9 | 2 | 492 | 48 | 391 | 53 | 1 |
| Norwalk | 88,930 | 53 | 2 | 7 | 14 | 30 | 1,173 | 94 | 930 | 149 | 1 |
| Norwich | 38,431 | 120 | 1 | 13 | 26 | 80 | 577 | 133 | 399 | 45 | 6 |
| Old Saybrook | 10,007 | 6 | 0 | 0 | 0 | 6 | 57 | 5 | 49 | 3 | 0 |
| Orange | 13,874 | 11 | 0 | 0 | 11 | 0 | 469 | 30 | 403 | 36 | 0 |
| Plainfield | 15,053 | 24 | 0 | 14 | 2 | 8 | 62 | 5 | 41 | 16 | 1 |
| Plainville | 17,466 | 27 | 0 | 5 | 11 | 11 | 446 | 22 | 383 | 41 | 1 |
| Plymouth | 11,486 | 3 | 0 | 3 | 0 | 0 | 108 | 6 | 89 | 13 | 1 |
| Portland | 9,185 | 3 | 0 | 0 | 1 | 2 | 79 | 11 | 64 | 4 | 1 |
| Putnam | 9,354 | 23 | 0 | 14 | 1 | 8 | 91 | 12 | 73 | 6 | 2 |
| Redding | 9,042 | 2 | 0 | 1 | 1 | 0 | 29 | 4 | 22 | 3 | 0 |
| Ridgefield | 24,919 | 7 | 0 | 2 | 1 | 4 | 42 | 3 | 30 | 9 | 0 |
| Rocky Hill | 20,069 | 21 | 0 | 5 | 7 | 9 | 325 | 25 | 267 | 33 | 0 |
| Seymour | 16,306 | 11 | 0 | 1 | 1 | 9 | 111 | 6 | 87 | 18 | 1 |
| Shelton | 41,095 | 21 | 1 | 3 | 10 | 7 | 373 | 60 | 245 | 68 | 0 |
| Simsbury | 25,639 | 2 | 1 | 0 | 1 | 0 | 112 | 6 | 97 | 9 | 1 |
| Southington | 43,897 | 37 | 0 | 11 | 19 | 7 | 805 | 64 | 663 | 78 | 0 |
| South Windsor | 26,142 | 10 | 1 | 2 | 1 | 6 | 540 | 62 | 445 | 33 | 1 |
| Stamford | 132,292 | 264 | 6 | 26 | 92 | 140 | 1,756 | 133 | 1,430 | 193 | 4 |
| Stonington | 18,571 | 13 | 0 | 4 | 0 | 9 | 149 | 17 | 121 | 11 | 0 |
| Stratford | 51,683 | 78 | 1 | 13 | 38 | 26 | 913 | 79 | 704 | 130 | 2 |
| Suffield | 15,817 | 5 | 0 | 1 | 0 | 4 | 68 | 13 | 45 | 10 | 1 |
| Thomaston | 7,468 | 4 | 0 | 1 | 1 | 2 | 73 | 10 | 51 | 12 | 0 |
| Torrington | 33,631 | 27 | 0 | 10 | 5 | 12 | 431 | 35 | 369 | 27 | 2 |
| Trumbull | 35,378 | 28 | 0 | 5 | 14 | 9 | 633 | 53 | 525 | 55 | 5 |
| Vernon | 29,423 | 22 | 1 | 1 | 4 | 16 | 354 | 54 | 273 | 27 | 0 |
| Wallingford | 43,969 | 20 | 1 | 3 | 7 | 9 | 281 | 39 | 224 | 18 | 0 |
| Waterbury | 106,480 | 345 | 9 | 39 | 132 | 165 | 3,333 | 276 | 2,410 | 647 | 9 |
| Waterford | 18,803 | 10 | 0 | 0 | 2 | 8 | 196 | 14 | 177 | 5 | 1 |
| Watertown | 21,418 | 9 | 0 | 0 | 0 | 9 | 315 | 27 | 252 | 36 | 1 |
| West Hartford | 62,809 | 47 | 1 | 0 | 41 | 5 | 1,584 | 141 | 1,354 | 89 | 0 |
| West Haven | 54,248 | 112 | 2 | 24 | 47 | 39 | 1,267 | 94 | 954 | 219 | 4 |
| Weston | 10,204 | 0 | 0 | 0 | 0 | 0 | 13 | 1 | 8 | 4 | 0 |
| Westport | 28,652 | 6 | 1 | 1 | 2 | 2 | 365 | 37 | 233 | 95 | 0 |
| Wethersfield | 25,807 | 26 | 0 | 5 | 13 | 8 | 480 | 85 | 345 | 50 | 0 |
| Willimantic | 17,763 | 22 | 0 | 3 | 6 | 13 | 103 | 11 | 75 | 17 | 1 |
| Wilton | 18,236 | 3 | 0 | 0 | 2 | 1 | 120 | 4 | 102 | 14 | 0 |
| Winchester | 10,481 | 3 | 0 | 1 | 1 | 1 | 80 | 5 | 65 | 10 | 0 |
| Windsor | 28,601 | 31 | 0 | 9 | 10 | 12 | 595 | 28 | 491 | 76 | 0 |
| Windsor Locks | 12,828 | 13 | 2 | 4 | 4 | 3 | 160 | 8 | 122 | 30 | 0 |
| Wolcott | 16,550 | 11 | 0 | 4 | 5 | 2 | 267 | 30 | 205 | 32 | 0 |
| Woodbridge | 8,676 | 3 | 1 | 0 | 2 | 0 | 102 | 12 | 70 | 20 | 2 |
| **DELAWARE** | | | | | | | | | | | |
| Blades | 1,526 | 4 | 1 | 0 | 1 | 2 | 10 | 1 | 9 | 0 | 0 |
| Bridgeville | 2,487 | 4 | 1 | 0 | 0 | 3 | 30 | 1 | 27 | 2 | 0 |
| Camden | 3,660 | 17 | 0 | 4 | 2 | 11 | 173 | 5 | 161 | 7 | 0 |
| Cheswold | 1,787 | 8 | 0 | 1 | 1 | 6 | 32 | 5 | 26 | 1 | 0 |
| Clayton | 3,707 | 7 | 1 | 2 | 0 | 4 | 21 | 2 | 19 | 0 | 0 |
| Dagsboro | 973 | 1 | 0 | 0 | 0 | 1 | 19 | 1 | 18 | 0 | 0 |
| Delaware City | 1,852 | 7 | 0 | 1 | 2 | 4 | 26 | 4 | 22 | 0 | 1 |
| Delmar | 1,911 | 7 | 0 | 1 | 0 | 6 | 40 | 7 | 33 | 0 | 0 |
| Dewey Beach | 419 | 20 | 0 | 2 | 1 | 17 | 37 | 4 | 29 | 4 | 0 |
| Dover | 38,439 | 358 | 4 | 27 | 24 | 303 | 1,517 | 42 | 1,394 | 81 | 2 |
| Ellendale | 457 | 2 | 0 | 0 | 0 | 2 | 11 | 1 | 10 | 0 | 0 |
| Elsmere | 5,741 | 34 | 1 | 0 | 9 | 24 | 101 | 18 | 69 | 14 | 0 |
| Felton | 1,447 | 4 | 0 | 0 | 1 | 3 | 8 | 1 | 6 | 1 | 0 |
| Fenwick Island | 468 | 1 | 0 | 0 | 0 | 1 | 14 | 2 | 12 | 0 | 0 |
| Frankford | 1,039 | 3 | 1 | 0 | 1 | 1 | 8 | 2 | 4 | 2 | 0 |
| Frederica | 869 | 1 | 0 | 0 | 1 | 0 | 3 | 1 | 2 | 0 | 0 |
| Georgetown | 7,945 | 54 | 0 | 3 | 12 | 39 | 263 | 31 | 222 | 10 | 1 |
| Greenwood | 1,197 | 7 | 0 | 0 | 1 | 6 | 8 | 0 | 8 | 0 | 0 |
| Harrington | 3,672 | 31 | 0 | 1 | 0 | 30 | 82 | 20 | 54 | 8 | 0 |
| Laurel | 4,595 | 60 | 0 | 8 | 3 | 49 | 151 | 15 | 125 | 11 | 0 |
| Lewes | 3,479 | 10 | 0 | 3 | 0 | 7 | 39 | 3 | 35 | 1 | 0 |
| Middletown | 24,307 | 61 | 0 | 0 | 5 | 56 | 449 | 18 | 399 | 32 | 0 |
| Milford | 12,582 | 88 | 0 | 6 | 14 | 68 | 384 | 33 | 342 | 9 | 1 |
| Millsboro | 4,753 | 20 | 0 | 3 | 4 | 13 | 178 | 26 | 146 | 6 | 0 |
| Milton | 3,189 | 8 | 0 | 0 | 1 | 7 | 35 | 2 | 27 | 6 | 0 |
| Newark | 34,064 | 96 | 1 | 7 | 26 | 62 | 633 | 44 | 551 | 38 | 1 |
| New Castle | 5,419 | 18 | 1 | 1 | 6 | 10 | 171 | 10 | 148 | 13 | 0 |
| Newport | 871 | 10 | 0 | 0 | 1 | 9 | 21 | 6 | 13 | 2 | 0 |
| Ocean View | 2,290 | 3 | 0 | 1 | 0 | 2 | 20 | 2 | 18 | 0 | 0 |
| Rehoboth Beach | 1,622 | 10 | 0 | 2 | 0 | 8 | 101 | 2 | 94 | 5 | 0 |
| Seaford | 8,392 | 81 | 0 | 1 | 13 | 67 | 416 | 55 | 341 | 20 | 1 |
| Selbyville | 2,667 | 9 | 0 | 0 | 3 | 6 | 69 | 19 | 44 | 6 | 0 |

## Table 8. Offenses Known to Law Enforcement, by Selected State and City, 2021—Continued

(Number.)

| State/city | Population | Violent crime | Murder and nonnegligent manslaughter | Rape | Robbery | Aggravated assault | Property crime | Burglary | Larceny-theft | Motor vehicle theft | Arson |
|---|---|---|---|---|---|---|---|---|---|---|---|
| Smyrna | 12,383 | 61 | 2 | 11 | 2 | 46 | 295 | 19 | 256 | 20 | 0 |
| South Bethany | 557 | 0 | 0 | 0 | 0 | 0 | 4 | 0 | 4 | 0 | 0 |
| Wilmington | 70,331 | 1,004 | 39 | 4 | 220 | 741 | 2,555 | 468 | 1,652 | 435 | 3 |
| Wyoming | 1,695 | 8 | 0 | 1 | 0 | 7 | 21 | 3 | 14 | 4 | 0 |
| **DISTRICT OF COLUMBIA**[1] | | | | | | | | | | | |
| **FLORIDA**[1] | | | | | | | | | | | |
| **GEORGIA**[1] | | | | | | | | | | | |
| Acworth | 22,956 | 24 | 1 | 1 | 2 | 20 | 320 | 29 | 269 | 22 | 1 |
| Adairsville | 5,094 | 12 | 0 | 3 | 0 | 9 | 102 | 10 | 78 | 14 | 0 |
| Alapaha | 673 | 0 | 0 | 0 | 0 | 0 | 5 | 1 | 4 | 0 | 0 |
| Albany | 70,214 | 1,114 | 15 | 55 | 98 | 946 | 2,978 | 446 | 2,186 | 346 | 18 |
| Alma | 3,322 | 9 | 0 | 0 | 2 | 7 | 91 | 20 | 59 | 12 | 0 |
| Alpharetta | 68,954 | 165 | 3 | 23 | 11 | 128 | 749 | 47 | 657 | 45 | 1 |
| Americus | 14,798 | 186 | 5 | 8 | 8 | 165 | 614 | 52 | 529 | 33 | 2 |
| Arcade | 2,064 | 2 | 1 | 0 | 0 | 1 | 44 | 6 | 34 | 4 | 0 |
| Athens-Clarke County | 127,410 | 736 | 4 | 104 | 94 | 534 | 3,535 | 398 | 2,702 | 435 | 23 |
| Atlanta | 521,274 | 4,609 | 159 | 150 | 835 | 3,465 | 19,154 | 1,689 | 14,272 | 3,193 | 13 |
| Bainbridge | 12,074 | 90 | 0 | 11 | 6 | 73 | 558 | 82 | 452 | 24 | 2 |
| Ball Ground | 2,414 | 1 | 0 | 0 | 0 | 1 | 9 | 3 | 6 | 0 | 0 |
| Barnesville | 6,660 | 5 | 0 | 0 | 0 | 5 | 22 | 0 | 20 | 2 | 0 |
| Bartow | 246 | 0 | 0 | 0 | 0 | 0 | 0 | 0 | 0 | 0 | 0 |
| Baxley | 4,646 | 59 | 0 | 11 | 1 | 47 | 208 | 43 | 147 | 18 | 2 |
| Blackshear | 3,529 | 12 | 0 | 4 | 0 | 8 | 130 | 20 | 103 | 7 | 3 |
| Blairsville | 660 | 1 | 0 | 0 | 0 | 1 | 20 | 0 | 20 | 0 | 0 |
| Blakely | 4,439 | 47 | 0 | 2 | 2 | 43 | 91 | 15 | 73 | 3 | 0 |
| Bloomingdale | 3,194 | 3 | 0 | 0 | 0 | 3 | 32 | 6 | 23 | 3 | 0 |
| Blythe | 698 | 0 | 0 | 0 | 0 | 0 | 0 | 0 | 0 | 0 | 0 |
| Boston | 1,313 | 1 | 0 | 0 | 0 | 1 | 13 | 2 | 11 | 0 | 0 |
| Bowdon | 2,096 | 8 | 0 | 0 | 1 | 7 | 30 | 3 | 25 | 2 | 1 |
| Braselton | 14,568 | 15 | 0 | 1 | 5 | 9 | 105 | 19 | 75 | 11 | 0 |
| Braswell | 387 | 0 | 0 | 0 | 0 | 0 | 0 | 0 | 0 | 0 | 0 |
| Bremen | 6,880 | 13 | 0 | 2 | 1 | 10 | 136 | 13 | 113 | 10 | 0 |
| Brookhaven | 56,770 | 245 | 4 | 22 | 47 | 172 | 1,441 | 172 | 1,125 | 144 | 5 |
| Broxton | 1,198 | 2 | 0 | 0 | 1 | 1 | 4 | 1 | 2 | 1 | 0 |
| Byron | 5,350 | 8 | 0 | 1 | 2 | 5 | 120 | 12 | 95 | 13 | 0 |
| Cairo | 9,269 | 38 | 0 | 2 | 9 | 27 | 230 | 41 | 174 | 15 | 0 |
| Calhoun | 17,719 | 57 | 0 | 8 | 3 | 46 | 350 | 26 | 313 | 11 | 0 |
| Camilla | 4,907 | 22 | 1 | 0 | 7 | 14 | 92 | 17 | 67 | 8 | 0 |
| Canton | 33,386 | 36 | 0 | 3 | 2 | 31 | 275 | 12 | 247 | 16 | 0 |
| Carrollton | 27,786 | 138 | 1 | 26 | 14 | 97 | 943 | 63 | 808 | 72 | 4 |
| Cartersville | 22,276 | 122 | 0 | 30 | 16 | 76 | 643 | 62 | 531 | 50 | 8 |
| Cave Spring | 1,065 | 1 | 0 | 0 | 0 | 1 | 15 | 3 | 10 | 2 | 0 |
| Cedartown | 9,999 | 75 | 1 | 10 | 7 | 57 | 313 | 32 | 252 | 29 | 2 |
| Centerville | 8,082 | 11 | 1 | 0 | 1 | 9 | 98 | 6 | 76 | 16 | 0 |
| Chamblee | 31,254 | 279 | 3 | 15 | 40 | 221 | 1,105 | 107 | 857 | 141 | 3 |
| Chatsworth | 4,246 | 12 | 0 | 0 | 0 | 12 | 29 | 0 | 25 | 4 | 0 |
| Chickamauga | 3,235 | 2 | 0 | 0 | 0 | 2 | 26 | 10 | 15 | 1 | 0 |
| Clarkston | 12,677 | 57 | 2 | 3 | 27 | 25 | 271 | 69 | 162 | 40 | 1 |
| Claxton | 2,200 | 22 | 1 | 2 | 7 | 12 | 82 | 26 | 51 | 5 | 0 |
| Clayton | 2,122 | 7 | 0 | 4 | 1 | 2 | 41 | 7 | 33 | 1 | 0 |
| Cleveland | 4,246 | 6 | 0 | 2 | 1 | 3 | 91 | 14 | 76 | 1 | 0 |
| Cochran | 5,013 | 23 | 1 | 1 | 0 | 21 | 65 | 10 | 49 | 6 | 1 |
| Cohutta | 644 | 0 | 0 | 0 | 0 | 0 | 10 | 1 | 9 | 0 | 0 |
| College Park | 15,241 | 297 | 10 | 5 | 60 | 222 | 777 | 109 | 488 | 180 | 2 |
| Coolidge | 523 | 1 | 0 | 0 | 0 | 1 | 8 | 0 | 8 | 0 | 0 |
| Cordele | 10,223 | 102 | 0 | 2 | 15 | 85 | 398 | 53 | 324 | 21 | 4 |
| Covington | 14,517 | 70 | 0 | 7 | 6 | 57 | 429 | 50 | 330 | 49 | 2 |
| Dallas | 14,704 | 20 | 1 | 4 | 2 | 13 | 141 | 15 | 116 | 10 | 3 |
| Dalton | 33,389 | 122 | 1 | 20 | 10 | 91 | 652 | 79 | 505 | 68 | 3 |
| Danielsville | 605 | 1 | 0 | 0 | 1 | 0 | 12 | 3 | 7 | 2 | 0 |
| Darien | 1,848 | 12 | 0 | 0 | 0 | 12 | 66 | 18 | 42 | 6 | 0 |
| Dawson | 4,076 | 25 | 2 | 0 | 1 | 22 | 57 | 10 | 43 | 4 | 1 |
| Decatur | 26,350 | 58 | 2 | 3 | 19 | 34 | 593 | 46 | 509 | 38 | 1 |
| Doerun | 726 | 0 | 0 | 0 | 0 | 0 | 9 | 3 | 5 | 1 | 0 |
| Donalsonville | 2,471 | 4 | 0 | 1 | 0 | 3 | 22 | 2 | 20 | 0 | 0 |
| Doraville | 10,322 | 56 | 3 | 5 | 16 | 32 | 406 | 23 | 304 | 79 | 1 |
| Douglas | 11,606 | 10 | 1 | 1 | 0 | 8 | 72 | 2 | 70 | 0 | 0 |
| Douglasville | 34,475 | 221 | 6 | 19 | 22 | 174 | 1,596 | 97 | 1,405 | 94 | 0 |
| Duluth | 29,986 | 44 | 0 | 6 | 9 | 29 | 362 | 34 | 295 | 33 | 0 |
| Dunwoody | 49,621 | 103 | 2 | 12 | 30 | 59 | 1,396 | 90 | 1,219 | 87 | 0 |
| East Ellijay | 573 | 1 | 0 | 0 | 0 | 1 | 47 | 1 | 44 | 2 | 0 |
| Eastman | 5,054 | 51 | 0 | 2 | 12 | 37 | 252 | 36 | 208 | 8 | 2 |
| Edison | 1,394 | 2 | 1 | 0 | 0 | 1 | 2 | 1 | 0 | 1 | 1 |
| Elberton | 4,328 | 42 | 0 | 6 | 2 | 34 | 157 | 29 | 118 | 10 | 2 |
| Ellaville | 1,835 | 1 | 0 | 1 | 0 | 0 | 27 | 4 | 18 | 5 | 0 |
| Ellijay | 1,736 | 4 | 0 | 0 | 0 | 4 | 23 | 4 | 17 | 2 | 0 |
| Emerson | 1,602 | 3 | 0 | 1 | 0 | 2 | 23 | 0 | 19 | 4 | 0 |
| Enigma | 1,354 | 1 | 0 | 1 | 0 | 0 | 23 | 9 | 14 | 0 | 0 |
| Eton | 890 | 0 | 0 | 0 | 0 | 0 | 3 | 0 | 2 | 1 | 0 |
| Euharlee | 4,450 | 5 | 0 | 2 | 0 | 3 | 18 | 2 | 14 | 2 | 1 |

## Table 8. Offenses Known to Law Enforcement, by Selected State and City, 2021—Continued

(Number.)

| State/city | Population | Violent crime | Murder and nonnegligent manslaughter | Rape | Robbery | Aggravated assault | Property crime | Burglary | Larceny-theft | Motor vehicle theft | Arson |
|---|---|---|---|---|---|---|---|---|---|---|---|
| Fairburn | 17,583 | 47 | 1 | 2 | 6 | 38 | 244 | 36 | 169 | 39 | 1 |
| Fayetteville | 18,554 | 28 | 0 | 6 | 6 | 16 | 323 | 24 | 280 | 19 | 1 |
| Fitzgerald | 8,563 | 80 | 0 | 2 | 7 | 71 | 356 | 46 | 276 | 34 | 1 |
| Flowery Branch | 9,155 | 6 | 0 | 2 | 0 | 4 | 106 | 20 | 86 | 0 | 0 |
| Folkston | 5,074 | 3 | 0 | 0 | 1 | 2 | 55 | 11 | 44 | 0 | 0 |
| Forest Park | 20,015 | 214 | 7 | 13 | 37 | 157 | 960 | 132 | 684 | 144 | 3 |
| Fort Valley | 8,906 | 73 | 1 | 6 | 10 | 56 | 260 | 42 | 194 | 24 | 0 |
| Franklin | 956 | 4 | 0 | 1 | 0 | 3 | 15 | 0 | 14 | 1 | 1 |
| Franklin Springs | 1,214 | 0 | 0 | 0 | 0 | 0 | 1 | 1 | 0 | 0 | 0 |
| Gainesville | 45,385 | 178 | 4 | 21 | 28 | 125 | 1,183 | 138 | 929 | 116 | 6 |
| Garden City | 9,268 | 149 | 2 | 10 | 16 | 121 | 401 | 51 | 277 | 73 | 2 |
| Gordon | 1,801 | 5 | 0 | 0 | 0 | 5 | 15 | 4 | 10 | 1 | 0 |
| Grantville | 3,369 | 27 | 0 | 4 | 0 | 23 | 23 | 4 | 16 | 3 | 0 |
| Gray | 3,240 | 1 | 0 | 0 | 0 | 1 | 34 | 3 | 30 | 1 | 0 |
| Greensboro | 3,262 | 4 | 1 | 1 | 1 | 1 | 106 | 11 | 86 | 9 | 1 |
| Griffin | 22,617 | 298 | 2 | 19 | 26 | 251 | 992 | 136 | 754 | 102 | 10 |
| Grovetown | 17,293 | 24 | 0 | 0 | 5 | 19 | 120 | 19 | 91 | 10 | 1 |
| Guyton | 2,455 | 4 | 0 | 1 | 0 | 3 | 12 | 2 | 7 | 3 | 0 |
| Hahira | 3,080 | 2 | 0 | 0 | 0 | 2 | 30 | 5 | 23 | 2 | 0 |
| Hampton | 8,313 | 5 | 0 | 0 | 0 | 5 | 23 | 2 | 19 | 2 | 0 |
| Harlem | 3,648 | 1 | 0 | 1 | 0 | 0 | 13 | 0 | 13 | 0 | 0 |
| Hartwell | 4,453 | 12 | 1 | 0 | 0 | 11 | 242 | 10 | 224 | 8 | 1 |
| Hazlehurst | 4,072 | 22 | 1 | 0 | 0 | 21 | 129 | 19 | 97 | 13 | 0 |
| Helen | 564 | 7 | 0 | 2 | 1 | 4 | 48 | 10 | 36 | 2 | 0 |
| Hiawassee | 923 | 1 | 0 | 0 | 0 | 1 | 12 | 1 | 11 | 0 | 0 |
| Hiram | 4,315 | 39 | 0 | 3 | 2 | 34 | 390 | 16 | 355 | 19 | 1 |
| Hoboken | 542 | 0 | 0 | 0 | 0 | 0 | 0 | 0 | 0 | 0 | 0 |
| Hogansville | 3,155 | 11 | 0 | 0 | 0 | 11 | 41 | 7 | 31 | 3 | 1 |
| Holly Springs | 17,484 | 0 | 0 | 0 | 0 | 0 | 48 | 4 | 38 | 6 | 0 |
| Homerville | 2,335 | 4 | 0 | 2 | 1 | 1 | 26 | 3 | 21 | 2 | 1 |
| Jackson | 5,361 | 12 | 1 | 0 | 1 | 10 | 97 | 14 | 76 | 7 | 1 |
| Jasper | 4,074 | 9 | 0 | 1 | 0 | 8 | 122 | 17 | 99 | 6 | 0 |
| Jefferson | 12,833 | 11 | 1 | 2 | 2 | 6 | 141 | 15 | 115 | 11 | 1 |
| Johns Creek | 85,974 | 20 | 1 | 3 | 3 | 13 | 360 | 55 | 274 | 31 | 1 |
| Kennesaw | 35,145 | 48 | 0 | 4 | 4 | 40 | 414 | 34 | 354 | 26 | 0 |
| Kingsland | 18,556 | 4 | 0 | 0 | 1 | 3 | 42 | 2 | 37 | 3 | 0 |
| LaGrange | 30,874 | 186 | 6 | 21 | 36 | 123 | 1,269 | 173 | 1,017 | 79 | 4 |
| Lake City | 2,818 | 9 | 0 | 1 | 5 | 3 | 39 | 3 | 30 | 6 | 0 |
| Lake Park | 1,464 | 2 | 0 | 1 | 0 | 1 | 9 | 0 | 9 | 0 | 0 |
| Lavonia | 2,191 | 3 | 0 | 1 | 1 | 1 | 64 | 4 | 52 | 8 | 0 |
| Lawrenceville | 31,223 | 110 | 3 | 9 | 11 | 87 | 642 | 57 | 516 | 69 | 2 |
| Leesburg | 3,098 | 2 | 0 | 1 | 0 | 1 | 38 | 8 | 28 | 2 | 0 |
| Lilburn | 13,199 | 26 | 0 | 3 | 9 | 14 | 343 | 27 | 299 | 17 | 0 |
| Locust Grove | 9,513 | 22 | 0 | 7 | 1 | 14 | 383 | 16 | 346 | 21 | 0 |
| Loganville | 13,633 | 19 | 0 | 2 | 2 | 15 | 117 | 6 | 106 | 5 | 0 |
| Lookout Mountain | 1,566 | 0 | 0 | 0 | 0 | 0 | 9 | 1 | 5 | 3 | 0 |
| Louisville | 2,162 | 2 | 0 | 0 | 0 | 2 | 30 | 5 | 19 | 6 | 0 |
| Madison | 4,286 | 14 | 2 | 1 | 4 | 7 | 99 | 10 | 81 | 8 | 0 |
| Manchester | 3,890 | 13 | 1 | 0 | 2 | 10 | 92 | 16 | 70 | 6 | 2 |
| Marietta | 61,223 | 285 | 3 | 28 | 55 | 199 | 1,562 | 161 | 1,235 | 166 | 6 |
| Maysville | 2,212 | 0 | 0 | 0 | 0 | 0 | 4 | 0 | 2 | 2 | 0 |
| McDonough | 28,222 | 106 | 5 | 9 | 12 | 80 | 659 | 65 | 516 | 78 | 2 |
| McRae-Helena | 8,250 | 11 | 0 | 0 | 2 | 9 | 43 | 14 | 23 | 6 | 1 |
| Metter | 4,000 | 7 | 0 | 3 | 0 | 4 | 92 | 21 | 56 | 15 | 0 |
| Milledgeville | 18,551 | 142 | 5 | 9 | 12 | 116 | 768 | 68 | 646 | 54 | 1 |
| Millen | 2,730 | 10 | 0 | 1 | 3 | 6 | 72 | 10 | 57 | 5 | 2 |
| Milton | 40,781 | 31 | 0 | 4 | 3 | 24 | 204 | 27 | 170 | 7 | 1 |
| Monroe | 14,091 | 86 | 1 | 7 | 11 | 67 | 465 | 54 | 388 | 23 | 2 |
| Montezuma | 2,870 | 12 | 0 | 0 | 0 | 12 | 36 | 6 | 28 | 2 | 1 |
| Morrow | 7,254 | 38 | 1 | 5 | 21 | 11 | 453 | 21 | 384 | 48 | 2 |
| Moultrie | 14,133 | 91 | 3 | 9 | 8 | 71 | 556 | 54 | 464 | 38 | 2 |
| Mount Zion | 1,907 | 1 | 0 | 0 | 0 | 1 | 12 | 4 | 6 | 2 | 0 |
| Nahunta | 1,178 | 0 | 0 | 0 | 0 | 0 | 0 | 0 | 0 | 0 | 0 |
| Nashville | 4,797 | 28 | 1 | 2 | 1 | 24 | 163 | 21 | 134 | 8 | 0 |
| Newington | 263 | 4 | 0 | 0 | 0 | 4 | 6 | 1 | 5 | 0 | 0 |
| Newnan | 44,023 | 508 | 2 | 22 | 18 | 466 | 751 | 83 | 608 | 60 | 3 |
| Newton | 549 | 0 | 0 | 0 | 0 | 0 | 0 | 0 | 0 | 0 | 0 |
| Norcross | 18,337 | 85 | 0 | 8 | 19 | 58 | 447 | 57 | 363 | 27 | 2 |
| Ocilla | 3,746 | 25 | 1 | 2 | 1 | 21 | 76 | 14 | 59 | 3 | 3 |
| Oglethorpe | 1,109 | 1 | 0 | 0 | 0 | 1 | 4 | 2 | 1 | 1 | 0 |
| Omega | 1,222 | 4 | 0 | 0 | 1 | 3 | 24 | 2 | 22 | 0 | 0 |
| Palmetto | 5,010 | 4 | 0 | 0 | 1 | 3 | 35 | 3 | 25 | 7 | 0 |
| Peachtree City | 36,994 | 15 | 0 | 4 | 2 | 9 | 356 | 22 | 293 | 41 | 0 |
| Pelham | 3,362 | 18 | 1 | 1 | 2 | 14 | 80 | 9 | 62 | 9 | 0 |
| Pembroke | 2,743 | 7 | 0 | 1 | 0 | 6 | 44 | 7 | 34 | 3 | 0 |
| Pendergrass | 593 | 0 | 0 | 0 | 0 | 0 | 3 | 0 | 1 | 2 | 0 |
| Perry | 19,469 | 46 | 1 | 3 | 6 | 36 | 485 | 46 | 411 | 28 | 1 |
| Pine Mountain | 1,468 | 3 | 0 | 0 | 0 | 3 | 27 | 3 | 23 | 1 | 0 |
| Pooler | 26,911 | 38 | 0 | 10 | 5 | 23 | 712 | 67 | 605 | 40 | 4 |
| Port Wentworth | 10,416 | 15 | 1 | 1 | 1 | 12 | 164 | 17 | 117 | 30 | 0 |
| Remerton | 1,054 | 10 | 2 | 1 | 2 | 5 | 25 | 4 | 18 | 3 | 0 |
| Reynolds | 942 | 1 | 0 | 0 | 0 | 1 | 5 | 2 | 3 | 0 | 0 |
| Richmond Hill | 15,025 | 37 | 1 | 10 | 3 | 23 | 197 | 21 | 150 | 26 | 0 |

# Table 8. Offenses Known to Law Enforcement, by Selected State and City, 2021—Continued

(Number.)

| State/city | Population | Violent crime | Murder and nonnegligent manslaughter | Rape | Robbery | Aggravated assault | Property crime | Burglary | Larceny-theft | Motor vehicle theft | Arson |
|---|---|---|---|---|---|---|---|---|---|---|---|
| Rincon | 10,836 | 13 | 0 | 1 | 2 | 10 | 144 | 41 | 91 | 12 | 3 |
| Ringgold | 3,508 | 17 | 0 | 0 | 0 | 17 | 117 | 19 | 89 | 9 | 1 |
| Rockmart | 4,520 | 22 | 0 | 2 | 3 | 17 | 267 | 45 | 210 | 12 | 2 |
| Rome | 36,792 | 250 | 1 | 20 | 24 | 205 | 1,370 | 143 | 1,086 | 141 | 6 |
| Rossville | 3,986 | 15 | 0 | 2 | 0 | 13 | 132 | 17 | 102 | 13 | 0 |
| Roswell | 96,041 | 306 | 5 | 23 | 23 | 255 | 1,332 | 129 | 1,062 | 141 | 1 |
| Sandersville | 5,215 | 14 | 0 | 2 | 0 | 12 | 51 | 3 | 42 | 6 | 1 |
| Sandy Springs | 111,533 | 209 | 7 | 24 | 33 | 145 | 1,639 | 193 | 1,292 | 154 | 5 |
| Shiloh | 501 | 0 | 0 | 0 | 0 | 0 | 2 | 0 | 2 | 0 | 0 |
| Smyrna | 57,024 | 187 | 2 | 23 | 34 | 128 | 987 | 123 | 763 | 101 | 2 |
| Snellville | 20,382 | 49 | 0 | 6 | 8 | 35 | 379 | 14 | 347 | 18 | 0 |
| Social Circle | 4,674 | 9 | 0 | 1 | 0 | 8 | 39 | 6 | 27 | 6 | 1 |
| South Fulton | 104,282 | 977 | 24 | 21 | 58 | 874 | 2,088 | 166 | 1,421 | 501 | 8 |
| Sparta | 1,205 | 3 | 0 | 0 | 1 | 2 | 10 | 0 | 9 | 1 | 0 |
| Springfield | 4,237 | 5 | 0 | 1 | 0 | 4 | 33 | 7 | 25 | 1 | 0 |
| Stapleton | 389 | 0 | 0 | 0 | 0 | 0 | 0 | 0 | 0 | 0 | 0 |
| Statesboro | 33,722 | 143 | 3 | 31 | 29 | 80 | 764 | 100 | 630 | 34 | 8 |
| Stone Mountain | 6,357 | 29 | 3 | 3 | 1 | 22 | 102 | 8 | 83 | 11 | 1 |
| Swainsboro | 7,517 | 34 | 1 | 2 | 1 | 30 | 148 | 27 | 118 | 3 | 0 |
| Sylvania | 2,438 | 5 | 0 | 0 | 1 | 4 | 38 | 2 | 33 | 3 | 0 |
| Sylvester | 5,642 | 31 | 0 | 4 | 1 | 26 | 86 | 9 | 72 | 5 | 0 |
| Tallapoosa | 3,237 | 6 | 0 | 0 | 1 | 5 | 70 | 9 | 53 | 8 | 0 |
| Temple | 5,104 | 12 | 0 | 2 | 2 | 8 | 111 | 14 | 88 | 9 | 0 |
| Thomasville | 18,485 | 100 | 1 | 7 | 14 | 78 | 640 | 81 | 499 | 60 | 2 |
| Thunderbolt | 2,609 | 3 | 0 | 0 | 0 | 3 | 46 | 4 | 40 | 2 | 0 |
| Toccoa | 8,283 | 19 | 1 | 2 | 4 | 12 | 331 | 23 | 281 | 27 | 2 |
| Tunnel Hill | 892 | 0 | 0 | 0 | 0 | 0 | 10 | 0 | 10 | 0 | 0 |
| Twin City | 1,693 | 5 | 0 | 0 | 0 | 5 | 16 | 2 | 11 | 3 | 0 |
| Tybee Island | 3,057 | 22 | 0 | 1 | 2 | 19 | 136 | 15 | 108 | 13 | 0 |
| Tyrone | 7,803 | 7 | 0 | 0 | 1 | 6 | 48 | 4 | 36 | 8 | 0 |
| Valdosta | 56,844 | 207 | 8 | 26 | 38 | 135 | 1,265 | 101 | 1,055 | 109 | 1 |
| Vidalia | 10,452 | 92 | 0 | 6 | 8 | 78 | 475 | 84 | 361 | 30 | 2 |
| Villa Rica | 17,094 | 46 | 1 | 10 | 6 | 29 | 418 | 59 | 322 | 37 | 2 |
| Warner Robins | 79,483 | 506 | 7 | 24 | 80 | 395 | 3,139 | 509 | 2,402 | 228 | 11 |
| Warwick | 381 | 0 | 0 | 0 | 0 | 0 | 3 | 1 | 2 | 0 | 0 |
| Waycross | 13,359 | 127 | 2 | 21 | 15 | 89 | 612 | 110 | 454 | 48 | 9 |
| Waynesboro | 5,340 | 28 | 2 | 1 | 1 | 24 | 200 | 36 | 136 | 28 | 2 |
| Whitesburg | 617 | 5 | 0 | 0 | 0 | 5 | 10 | 1 | 8 | 1 | 0 |
| Winder | 18,709 | 63 | 1 | 5 | 12 | 45 | 397 | 33 | 340 | 24 | 2 |
| Woodstock | 34,798 | 44 | 1 | 6 | 0 | 37 | 345 | 14 | 319 | 12 | 2 |
| **HAWAII** | | | | | | | | | | | |
| Honolulu | 985,138 | 2,234 | 6 | 250 | 718 | 1,260 | 27,090 | 3,225 | 19,067 | 4,798 | 271 |
| **IDAHO** | | | | | | | | | | | |
| American Falls | 4,280 | 6 | 0 | 0 | 1 | 5 | 39 | 2 | 27 | 10 | 1 |
| Bellevue | 2,519 | 4 | 0 | 1 | 0 | 3 | 4 | 2 | 2 | 0 | 0 |
| Blackfoot | 12,026 | 35 | 0 | 7 | 1 | 27 | 194 | 34 | 134 | 26 | 6 |
| Boise | 231,902 | 689 | 4 | 208 | 59 | 418 | 3,116 | 350 | 2,506 | 260 | 27 |
| Bonners Ferry | 2,712 | 13 | 0 | 6 | 0 | 7 | 14 | 3 | 10 | 1 | 0 |
| Buhl | 4,560 | 15 | 1 | 5 | 3 | 6 | 47 | 8 | 37 | 2 | 1 |
| Chubbuck | 16,168 | 46 | 0 | 6 | 5 | 35 | 365 | 48 | 291 | 26 | 2 |
| Coeur d'Alene | 54,358 | 172 | 1 | 47 | 9 | 115 | 651 | 77 | 519 | 55 | 4 |
| Emmett | 7,346 | 38 | 0 | 9 | 0 | 29 | 58 | 14 | 39 | 5 | 0 |
| Filer | 2,984 | 5 | 0 | 0 | 0 | 5 | 12 | 3 | 8 | 1 | 0 |
| Fruitland | 5,655 | 11 | 0 | 4 | 0 | 7 | 42 | 16 | 18 | 8 | 0 |
| Garden City | 12,018 | 94 | 1 | 7 | 2 | 84 | 226 | 43 | 154 | 29 | 2 |
| Gooding | 3,537 | 16 | 0 | 2 | 0 | 14 | 25 | 5 | 16 | 4 | 0 |
| Hailey | 8,988 | 12 | 0 | 2 | 1 | 9 | 19 | 5 | 13 | 1 | 1 |
| Heyburn | 3,496 | 4 | 0 | 0 | 1 | 3 | 21 | 8 | 13 | 0 | 1 |
| Idaho Falls | 64,792 | 232 | 0 | 55 | 7 | 170 | 993 | 276 | 590 | 127 | 7 |
| Jerome | 12,231 | 41 | 0 | 18 | 1 | 22 | 120 | 19 | 81 | 20 | 3 |
| Ketchum | 2,932 | 10 | 0 | 0 | 0 | 10 | 24 | 1 | 22 | 1 | 0 |
| Kimberly | 4,257 | 7 | 0 | 1 | 0 | 6 | 30 | 15 | 15 | 0 | 0 |
| Lewiston | 33,153 | 62 | 4 | 22 | 2 | 34 | 741 | 157 | 545 | 39 | 1 |
| McCall | 3,847 | 5 | 0 | 3 | 0 | 2 | 310 | 267 | 42 | 1 | 1 |
| Meridian | 126,744 | 217 | 0 | 46 | 10 | 161 | 921 | 98 | 792 | 31 | 8 |
| Middleton | 9,359 | 9 | 0 | 2 | 0 | 7 | 51 | 17 | 27 | 7 | 0 |
| Montpelier | 2,523 | 5 | 0 | 2 | 0 | 3 | 26 | 6 | 20 | 0 | 0 |
| Moscow | 26,368 | 10 | 0 | 0 | 0 | 10 | 432 | 78 | 341 | 13 | 3 |
| Nampa | 105,619 | 359 | 2 | 115 | 12 | 230 | 1,484 | 202 | 1,128 | 154 | 12 |
| Payette | 8,065 | 37 | 0 | 6 | 1 | 30 | 113 | 16 | 88 | 9 | 0 |
| Pocatello | 57,306 | 186 | 4 | 24 | 10 | 148 | 1,077 | 179 | 776 | 122 | 3 |
| Ponderay | 1,195 | 3 | 0 | 0 | 0 | 3 | 25 | 1 | 23 | 1 | 0 |
| Preston | 5,724 | 4 | 0 | 2 | 1 | 1 | 41 | 4 | 35 | 2 | 0 |
| Priest River | 1,950 | 1 | 0 | 0 | 0 | 1 | 21 | 1 | 19 | 1 | 0 |
| Rexburg | 30,105 | 12 | 0 | 3 | 0 | 9 | 127 | 15 | 108 | 4 | 2 |
| Rigby | 4,482 | 5 | 1 | 1 | 0 | 3 | 44 | 3 | 38 | 3 | 0 |
| Rupert | 5,981 | 16 | 0 | 4 | 0 | 12 | 63 | 18 | 38 | 7 | 0 |
| Sandpoint | 9,476 | 8 | 0 | 0 | 0 | 8 | 122 | 31 | 79 | 12 | 0 |
| Shelley | 4,674 | 5 | 0 | 3 | 1 | 1 | 33 | 4 | 26 | 3 | 0 |
| Soda Springs | 2,998 | 15 | 0 | 0 | 0 | 15 | 14 | 4 | 10 | 0 | 0 |
| Spirit Lake | 2,632 | 8 | 0 | 1 | 0 | 7 | 42 | 10 | 30 | 2 | 1 |

## Table 8. Offenses Known to Law Enforcement, by Selected State and City, 2021—Continued

(Number.)

| State/city | Population | Violent crime | Murder and nonnegligent manslaughter | Rape | Robbery | Aggravated assault | Property crime | Burglary | Larceny-theft | Motor vehicle theft | Arson |
|---|---|---|---|---|---|---|---|---|---|---|---|
| St. Anthony | 3,601 | 2 | 0 | 0 | 0 | 2 | 26 | 3 | 22 | 1 | 0 |
| Sun Valley | 1,513 | 1 | 0 | 0 | 0 | 1 | 4 | 0 | 3 | 1 | 0 |
| Twin Falls | 52,158 | 271 | 0 | 61 | 8 | 202 | 816 | 77 | 671 | 68 | 5 |
| Weiser | 5,461 | 9 | 0 | 1 | 0 | 8 | 7 | 5 | 2 | 0 | 0 |
| **ILLINOIS**[1] | | | | | | | | | | | |
| Algonquin | 30,796 | 26 | 2 | 11 | 0 | 13 | 191 | 11 | 175 | 5 | 2 |
| Altamont | 2,351 | 4 | 0 | 2 | 0 | 2 | 18 | 5 | 13 | 0 | 0 |
| Alton | 25,871 | 144 | 2 | 22 | 18 | 102 | 812 | 120 | 595 | 97 | 9 |
| Arthur | 2,183 | 1 | 0 | 0 | 0 | 1 | 18 | 4 | 12 | 2 | 0 |
| Barrington | 10,163 | 13 | 0 | 0 | 2 | 11 | 43 | 4 | 30 | 9 | 0 |
| Barrington Hills | 4,144 | 0 | 0 | 0 | 0 | 0 | 19 | 5 | 12 | 2 | 0 |
| Batavia | 26,460 | 26 | 0 | 13 | 3 | 10 | 227 | 25 | 188 | 14 | 0 |
| Bethalto | 9,170 | 19 | 0 | 8 | 1 | 10 | 51 | 7 | 36 | 8 | 1 |
| Bloomington | 77,166 | 238 | 4 | 63 | 19 | 152 | 812 | 139 | 611 | 62 | 9 |
| Carlyle | 3,133 | 6 | 0 | 1 | 1 | 4 | 43 | 4 | 37 | 2 | 0 |
| Champaign | 90,231 | 627 | 8 | 70 | 66 | 483 | 1,365 | 286 | 1,009 | 70 | 15 |
| Cherry Valley | 2,842 | 11 | 0 | 1 | 3 | 7 | 191 | 11 | 175 | 5 | 0 |
| Chicago Ridge | 13,722 | 23 | 0 | 4 | 3 | 16 | 211 | 22 | 162 | 27 | 1 |
| Cicero | 79,288 | 334 | 0 | 28 | 127 | 179 | 901 | 224 | 481 | 196 | 10 |
| Coal City | 5,317 | 3 | 0 | 3 | 0 | 0 | 21 | 2 | 19 | 0 | 2 |
| Coal Valley | 3,717 | 5 | 0 | 1 | 0 | 4 | 27 | 7 | 19 | 1 | 0 |
| Colona | 5,039 | 6 | 0 | 2 | 0 | 4 | 59 | 10 | 40 | 9 | 1 |
| Deerfield | 18,562 | 8 | 0 | 4 | 0 | 4 | 110 | 10 | 97 | 3 | 0 |
| DeKalb | 42,475 | 240 | 1 | 41 | 24 | 174 | 998 | 103 | 825 | 70 | 9 |
| East Hazel Crest | 1,472 | 0 | 0 | 0 | 0 | 0 | 20 | 4 | 9 | 7 | 0 |
| East Peoria | 22,235 | 62 | 0 | 18 | 4 | 40 | 427 | 48 | 361 | 18 | 0 |
| Edwardsville | 25,269 | 10 | 0 | 4 | 0 | 6 | 131 | 12 | 112 | 7 | 2 |
| Elwood | 2,200 | 5 | 1 | 2 | 1 | 1 | 16 | 1 | 14 | 1 | 0 |
| Evanston | 72,497 | 130 | 6 | 16 | 70 | 38 | 1,654 | 196 | 1,345 | 113 | 8 |
| Fairview Heights | 16,034 | 44 | 1 | 5 | 5 | 33 | 474 | 24 | 423 | 27 | 2 |
| Flossmoor | 8,979 | 11 | 0 | 2 | 2 | 7 | 83 | 5 | 69 | 9 | 0 |
| Fox Lake | 10,386 | 41 | 0 | 12 | 1 | 28 | 198 | 37 | 133 | 28 | 1 |
| Franklin Park | 17,313 | 27 | 0 | 8 | 8 | 11 | 222 | 26 | 159 | 37 | 1 |
| Fulton | 3,266 | 3 | 0 | 0 | 0 | 3 | 28 | 9 | 15 | 4 | 0 |
| Geneva | 21,680 | 13 | 1 | 6 | 1 | 5 | 123 | 7 | 111 | 5 | 3 |
| Glencoe | 8,749 | 2 | 0 | 1 | 0 | 1 | 39 | 3 | 35 | 1 | 0 |
| Glenwood | 8,580 | 15 | 0 | 1 | 6 | 8 | 113 | 10 | 76 | 27 | 0 |
| Granite City | 27,787 | 156 | 2 | 42 | 17 | 95 | 672 | 124 | 415 | 133 | 17 |
| Grayslake | 24,076 | 34 | 0 | 22 | 1 | 11 | 215 | 24 | 163 | 28 | 1 |
| Grayville | 1,532 | 4 | 0 | 1 | 0 | 3 | 20 | 7 | 12 | 1 | 0 |
| Harvard | 8,935 | 22 | 0 | 5 | 0 | 17 | 46 | 2 | 34 | 10 | 0 |
| Highland Park | 29,392 | 20 | 0 | 8 | 0 | 12 | 194 | 34 | 144 | 16 | 3 |
| Homewood | 18,393 | 36 | 1 | 5 | 18 | 12 | 536 | 15 | 478 | 43 | 0 |
| Jacksonville | 18,398 | 30 | 0 | 3 | 2 | 25 | 92 | 2 | 77 | 13 | 1 |
| Johnsburg | 6,298 | 1 | 0 | 1 | 0 | 0 | 62 | 0 | 62 | 0 | 0 |
| Kildeer | 4,002 | 0 | 0 | 0 | 0 | 0 | 23 | 4 | 19 | 0 | 0 |
| La Grange | 15,253 | 22 | 0 | 14 | 5 | 3 | 97 | 3 | 92 | 2 | 1 |
| La Grange Park | 12,808 | 5 | 0 | 2 | 0 | 3 | 73 | 5 | 62 | 6 | 1 |
| Lake in the Hills | 28,284 | 16 | 0 | 9 | 1 | 6 | 74 | 4 | 65 | 5 | 2 |
| Lakemoor | 5,896 | 0 | 0 | 0 | 0 | 0 | 95 | 4 | 89 | 2 | 0 |
| Lake Zurich | 19,764 | 20 | 0 | 10 | 0 | 10 | 178 | 18 | 157 | 3 | 0 |
| Lemont | 17,470 | 12 | 0 | 9 | 0 | 3 | 70 | 18 | 41 | 11 | 0 |
| Loves Park | 23,323 | 65 | 1 | 13 | 4 | 47 | 305 | 42 | 240 | 23 | 3 |
| Mackinaw | 1,853 | 2 | 0 | 2 | 0 | 0 | 17 | 6 | 11 | 0 | 0 |
| Manito | 1,450 | 3 | 0 | 0 | 0 | 3 | 7 | 1 | 5 | 1 | 0 |
| Maryville | 7,997 | 8 | 0 | 1 | 0 | 7 | 38 | 4 | 30 | 4 | 0 |
| Mason City | 2,064 | 8 | 0 | 3 | 1 | 4 | 9 | 3 | 5 | 1 | 0 |
| McHenry | 27,106 | 22 | 0 | 8 | 0 | 14 | 158 | 13 | 139 | 6 | 2 |
| Metropolis | 5,821 | 18 | 0 | 4 | 2 | 12 | 143 | 29 | 101 | 13 | 1 |
| Midlothian | 14,116 | 26 | 3 | 10 | 9 | 4 | 195 | 12 | 155 | 28 | 1 |
| Milan | 4,922 | 5 | 1 | 2 | 0 | 2 | 112 | 20 | 79 | 13 | 1 |
| Millstadt | 3,803 | 3 | 0 | 1 | 0 | 2 | 24 | 2 | 16 | 6 | 0 |
| Moline | 40,832 | 254 | 0 | 68 | 16 | 170 | 1,177 | 162 | 857 | 158 | 7 |
| Montgomery | 20,371 | 39 | 2 | 24 | 2 | 11 | 205 | 13 | 185 | 7 | 2 |
| Morris | 15,321 | 26 | 0 | 14 | 4 | 8 | 163 | 13 | 141 | 9 | 1 |
| Morton | 16,218 | 20 | 0 | 6 | 0 | 14 | 137 | 20 | 110 | 7 | 0 |
| Mount Zion | 5,753 | 12 | 0 | 6 | 0 | 6 | 35 | 3 | 30 | 2 | 0 |
| Mundelein | 30,936 | 20 | 0 | 5 | 0 | 15 | 148 | 25 | 113 | 10 | 0 |
| Normal | 54,636 | 104 | 3 | 34 | 9 | 58 | 685 | 48 | 596 | 41 | 2 |
| Northfield | 5,380 | 4 | 0 | 1 | 2 | 1 | 46 | 7 | 39 | 0 | 0 |
| O'Fallon | 29,688 | 39 | 1 | 8 | 2 | 28 | 291 | 17 | 239 | 35 | 0 |
| Oswego | 37,362 | 24 | 0 | 15 | 1 | 8 | 124 | 9 | 103 | 12 | 2 |
| Palos Heights | 12,361 | 15 | 0 | 5 | 3 | 7 | 64 | 7 | 52 | 5 | 0 |
| Palos Park | 4,704 | 1 | 0 | 0 | 0 | 1 | 14 | 0 | 12 | 2 | 0 |
| Pekin | 31,593 | 104 | 4 | 27 | 5 | 68 | 576 | 108 | 421 | 47 | 3 |
| Pingree Grove | 10,801 | 0 | 0 | 0 | 0 | 0 | 24 | 1 | 22 | 1 | 0 |
| Rantoul | 12,241 | 48 | 0 | 12 | 6 | 30 | 217 | 43 | 162 | 12 | 2 |
| River Forest | 10,647 | 8 | 0 | 0 | 8 | 0 | 153 | 19 | 133 | 1 | 0 |
| River Grove | 9,724 | 11 | 0 | 1 | 3 | 7 | 92 | 10 | 68 | 14 | 0 |
| Riverwoods | 3,520 | 2 | 0 | 1 | 0 | 1 | 16 | 7 | 9 | 0 | 0 |
| Rochester | 3,714 | 3 | 0 | 1 | 0 | 2 | 33 | 5 | 24 | 4 | 0 |
| Rockford | 144,027 | 2,210 | 19 | 140 | 210 | 1,841 | 3,573 | 626 | 2,490 | 457 | 35 |

## Table 8. Offenses Known to Law Enforcement, by Selected State and City, 2021—Continued

(Number.)

| State/city | Population | Violent crime | Murder and nonnegligent manslaughter | Rape | Robbery | Aggravated assault | Property crime | Burglary | Larceny-theft | Motor vehicle theft | Arson |
|---|---|---|---|---|---|---|---|---|---|---|---|
| Rock Island | 36,666 | 239 | 2 | 10 | 21 | 206 | 907 | 120 | 631 | 156 | 15 |
| Rosemont | 4,128 | 34 | 0 | 5 | 6 | 23 | 242 | 9 | 213 | 20 | 1 |
| Salem | 6,904 | 14 | 0 | 7 | 1 | 6 | 100 | 27 | 66 | 7 | 1 |
| Sandwich | 7,381 | 16 | 0 | 5 | 0 | 11 | 30 | 5 | 24 | 1 | 1 |
| Shiloh | 13,760 | 13 | 2 | 1 | 2 | 8 | 92 | 11 | 70 | 11 | 0 |
| Silvis | 7,467 | 25 | 1 | 8 | 3 | 13 | 260 | 47 | 186 | 27 | 0 |
| Skokie | 62,163 | 123 | 1 | 17 | 35 | 70 | 1,282 | 126 | 1,065 | 91 | 3 |
| South Beloit | 7,509 | 24 | 1 | 7 | 1 | 15 | 65 | 13 | 42 | 10 | 1 |
| Springfield | 113,331 | 950 | 11 | 84 | 161 | 694 | 4,323 | 822 | 3,171 | 330 | 38 |
| Stickney | 6,462 | 6 | 0 | 1 | 3 | 2 | 54 | 10 | 41 | 3 | 1 |
| Stone Park | 4,746 | 10 | 0 | 0 | 2 | 8 | 31 | 6 | 13 | 12 | 0 |
| Swansea | 13,245 | 8 | 0 | 2 | 0 | 6 | 130 | 5 | 113 | 12 | 0 |
| Sycamore | 18,399 | 22 | 1 | 7 | 1 | 13 | 213 | 12 | 194 | 7 | 1 |
| Tinley Park | 55,058 | 56 | 0 | 11 | 10 | 35 | 472 | 44 | 361 | 67 | 3 |
| Tolono | 3,337 | 5 | 0 | 1 | 0 | 4 | 33 | 13 | 20 | 0 | 0 |
| Troy | 10,447 | 8 | 0 | 3 | 0 | 5 | 61 | 3 | 54 | 4 | 0 |
| Urbana | 41,673 | 208 | 9 | 23 | 21 | 155 | 824 | 145 | 653 | 26 | 6 |
| Wauconda | 13,410 | 5 | 0 | 1 | 0 | 4 | 25 | 6 | 14 | 5 | 0 |
| Wheeling | 39,087 | 16 | 3 | 5 | 1 | 7 | 380 | 18 | 353 | 9 | 2 |
| Willow Springs | 5,543 | 2 | 0 | 0 | 1 | 1 | 17 | 2 | 12 | 3 | 0 |
| Wilmette | 26,793 | 10 | 0 | 5 | 2 | 3 | 214 | 26 | 183 | 5 | 0 |
| Winfield | 9,625 | 11 | 0 | 1 | 1 | 9 | 35 | 1 | 29 | 5 | 0 |
| Winnebago | 2,957 | 4 | 0 | 0 | 1 | 3 | 14 | 1 | 13 | 0 | 0 |
| Worth | 10,289 | 15 | 0 | 2 | 2 | 11 | 92 | 15 | 69 | 8 | 1 |
| **INDIANA** | | | | | | | | | | | |
| Albion | 2,372 | 3 | 0 | 1 | 0 | 2 | 12 | 2 | 7 | 3 | 0 |
| Anderson | 54,490 | 221 | 6 | 34 | 29 | 152 | 1,359 | 195 | 987 | 177 | 10 |
| Angola | 8,851 | 9 | 0 | 2 | 1 | 6 | 174 | 7 | 148 | 19 | 0 |
| Auburn | 13,700 | 11 | 0 | 1 | 1 | 9 | 113 | 10 | 89 | 14 | 1 |
| Avon | 20,055 | 20 | 0 | 6 | 6 | 8 | 477 | 25 | 401 | 51 | 1 |
| Bargersville | 8,933 | 1 | 0 | 1 | 0 | 0 | 48 | 2 | 42 | 4 | 0 |
| Bedford | 13,217 | 12 | 0 | 1 | 0 | 11 | 220 | 13 | 199 | 8 | 0 |
| Beech Grove | 14,966 | 39 | 0 | 7 | 15 | 17 | 447 | 73 | 276 | 98 | 3 |
| Bloomington | 86,118 | 480 | 3 | 44 | 69 | 364 | 1,872 | 261 | 1,485 | 126 | 19 |
| Bluffton | 10,113 | 6 | 0 | 1 | 0 | 5 | 79 | 4 | 67 | 8 | 0 |
| Bristol | 1,707 | 6 | 0 | 0 | 0 | 6 | 48 | 9 | 33 | 6 | 0 |
| Brookville | 2,522 | 3 | 0 | 1 | 0 | 2 | 11 | 0 | 10 | 1 | 0 |
| Brownsburg | 28,227 | 19 | 1 | 9 | 3 | 6 | 225 | 16 | 182 | 27 | 0 |
| Butler | 2,723 | 4 | 0 | 0 | 0 | 4 | 32 | 9 | 21 | 2 | 0 |
| Carmel | 103,540 | 50 | 1 | 13 | 6 | 30 | 678 | 38 | 576 | 64 | 2 |
| Cedar Lake | 13,806 | 15 | 0 | 2 | 1 | 12 | 77 | 9 | 66 | 2 | 0 |
| Charlestown | 8,645 | 14 | 0 | 0 | 0 | 14 | 70 | 12 | 45 | 13 | 2 |
| Chesterton | 14,351 | 16 | 0 | 0 | 1 | 15 | 60 | 6 | 47 | 7 | 1 |
| Cicero | 5,016 | 10 | 0 | 1 | 0 | 9 | 12 | 1 | 10 | 1 | 0 |
| Clarksville | 21,434 | 54 | 2 | 1 | 9 | 42 | 1,018 | 49 | 858 | 111 | 2 |
| Claypool | 430 | 0 | 0 | 0 | 0 | 0 | 11 | 2 | 6 | 3 | 0 |
| Columbia City | 9,479 | 26 | 0 | 3 | 1 | 22 | 123 | 18 | 99 | 6 | 0 |
| Cumberland | 6,197 | 17 | 0 | 1 | 5 | 11 | 188 | 11 | 152 | 25 | 3 |
| Danville | 10,364 | 6 | 0 | 2 | 0 | 4 | 112 | 9 | 96 | 7 | 0 |
| Dyer | 15,914 | 3 | 0 | 0 | 0 | 3 | 80 | 7 | 63 | 10 | 0 |
| East Chicago | 27,554 | 284 | 11 | 10 | 27 | 236 | 603 | 66 | 430 | 107 | 5 |
| Edinburgh | 4,629 | 6 | 0 | 1 | 1 | 4 | 71 | 7 | 49 | 15 | 0 |
| Elkhart | 52,205 | 693 | 9 | 83 | 55 | 546 | 1,694 | 218 | 1,219 | 257 | 19 |
| Evansville | 118,240 | 867 | 19 | 87 | 79 | 682 | 4,276 | 663 | 3,163 | 450 | 42 |
| Fishers | 99,184 | 77 | 0 | 11 | 9 | 57 | 667 | 48 | 565 | 54 | 0 |
| Fort Wayne | 274,295 | 703 | 41 | 130 | 164 | 368 | 6,151 | 613 | 4,946 | 592 | 89 |
| Franklin | 26,091 | 18 | 0 | 5 | 3 | 10 | 298 | 16 | 258 | 24 | 2 |
| Goshen | 34,336 | 77 | 1 | 14 | 12 | 50 | 733 | 69 | 590 | 74 | 7 |
| Greenfield | 23,650 | 21 | 0 | 5 | 3 | 13 | 218 | 18 | 168 | 32 | 1 |
| Greenwood | 61,277 | 67 | 0 | 13 | 20 | 34 | 1,168 | 72 | 963 | 133 | 2 |
| Hammond | 74,824 | 590 | 15 | 37 | 101 | 437 | 2,095 | 218 | 1,662 | 215 | 17 |
| Hartford City | 5,620 | 30 | 0 | 0 | 0 | 30 | 17 | 8 | 7 | 2 | 0 |
| Highland | 22,144 | 18 | 0 | 0 | 7 | 11 | 304 | 22 | 264 | 18 | 1 |
| Hobart | 27,777 | 55 | 2 | 7 | 13 | 33 | 616 | 28 | 553 | 35 | 4 |
| Huntington | 17,006 | 8 | 0 | 3 | 0 | 5 | 180 | 28 | 141 | 11 | 0 |
| Indianapolis | 895,826 | 6,430 | 239 | 588 | 1,726 | 3,877 | 30,831 | 4,411 | 20,598 | 5,822 | 319 |
| Jasper | 15,720 | 32 | 0 | 3 | 1 | 28 | 114 | 6 | 105 | 3 | 0 |
| Kendallville | 9,895 | 17 | 0 | 11 | 1 | 5 | 104 | 8 | 82 | 14 | 0 |
| Knox | 3,538 | 40 | 0 | 2 | 1 | 37 | 34 | 10 | 16 | 8 | 0 |
| Kokomo | 58,248 | 364 | 4 | 37 | 19 | 304 | 878 | 178 | 602 | 98 | 3 |
| La Porte | 21,391 | 52 | 1 | 5 | 10 | 36 | 425 | 61 | 314 | 50 | 1 |
| Lawrence | 49,916 | 150 | 5 | 38 | 54 | 53 | 960 | 115 | 676 | 169 | 1 |
| Lebanon | 16,155 | 57 | 0 | 7 | 2 | 48 | 216 | 25 | 165 | 26 | 2 |
| Linton | 5,286 | 12 | 0 | 8 | 0 | 4 | 173 | 6 | 152 | 15 | 1 |
| Logansport | 17,371 | 11 | 1 | 6 | 2 | 2 | 306 | 30 | 248 | 28 | 1 |
| Lowell | 10,223 | 3 | 0 | 0 | 0 | 3 | 22 | 2 | 19 | 1 | 0 |
| McCordsville | 8,078 | 10 | 0 | 1 | 0 | 9 | 155 | 0 | 132 | 23 | 0 |
| Michigan City | 31,008 | 179 | 3 | 19 | 31 | 126 | 1,297 | 252 | 948 | 97 | 12 |
| Mishawaka | 50,523 | 131 | 2 | 30 | 26 | 73 | 1,464 | 118 | 1,149 | 197 | 6 |
| Mount Vernon | 6,391 | 13 | 0 | 3 | 0 | 10 | 103 | 12 | 80 | 11 | 1 |
| Muncie | 67,262 | 298 | 7 | 30 | 33 | 228 | 1,678 | 347 | 1,113 | 218 | 8 |
| Munster | 22,377 | 27 | 0 | 3 | 9 | 15 | 199 | 19 | 169 | 11 | 0 |

## Table 8. Offenses Known to Law Enforcement, by Selected State and City, 2021—Continued

(Number.)

| State/city | Population | Violent crime | Murder and nonnegligent manslaughter | Rape | Robbery | Aggravated assault | Property crime | Burglary | Larceny-theft | Motor vehicle theft | Arson |
|---|---|---|---|---|---|---|---|---|---|---|---|
| Nappanee | 6,864 | 17 | 0 | 3 | 0 | 14 | 40 | 4 | 27 | 9 | 0 |
| New Albany | 36,921 | 160 | 0 | 9 | 19 | 132 | 1,062 | 146 | 755 | 161 | 2 |
| New Haven | 16,088 | 39 | 0 | 7 | 4 | 28 | 176 | 26 | 135 | 15 | 1 |
| New Whiteland | 6,443 | 0 | 0 | 0 | 0 | 0 | 26 | 6 | 16 | 4 | 0 |
| North Vernon | 6,594 | 24 | 1 | 3 | 1 | 19 | 116 | 3 | 103 | 10 | 1 |
| North Webster | 1,162 | 4 | 0 | 0 | 0 | 4 | 47 | 7 | 37 | 3 | 0 |
| Osceola | 2,488 | 5 | 0 | 2 | 0 | 3 | 31 | 3 | 22 | 6 | 0 |
| Pittsboro | 3,913 | 3 | 0 | 2 | 0 | 1 | 8 | 2 | 6 | 0 | 0 |
| Plainfield | 37,257 | 48 | 0 | 9 | 6 | 33 | 648 | 62 | 518 | 68 | 0 |
| Portage | 37,166 | 100 | 0 | 23 | 5 | 72 | 337 | 18 | 291 | 28 | 2 |
| Porter | 4,839 | 3 | 0 | 0 | 0 | 3 | 23 | 1 | 14 | 8 | 0 |
| Seymour | 20,302 | 25 | 2 | 11 | 3 | 9 | 360 | 28 | 295 | 37 | 2 |
| Shelbyville | 19,557 | 129 | 1 | 5 | 6 | 117 | 374 | 149 | 194 | 31 | 2 |
| Sheridan | 3,085 | 8 | 0 | 1 | 0 | 7 | 29 | 4 | 21 | 4 | 1 |
| Silver Lake | 916 | 1 | 0 | 0 | 0 | 1 | 22 | 1 | 15 | 6 | 0 |
| Speedway | 12,264 | 50 | 1 | 2 | 26 | 21 | 386 | 28 | 304 | 54 | 1 |
| St. John | 20,168 | 1 | 0 | 0 | 1 | 0 | 41 | 2 | 36 | 3 | 0 |
| Terre Haute | 60,372 | 814 | 1 | 30 | 65 | 718 | 3,204 | 901 | 1,806 | 497 | 31 |
| Valparaiso | 34,167 | 58 | 3 | 18 | 3 | 34 | 349 | 21 | 314 | 14 | 2 |
| Vincennes | 16,650 | 20 | 0 | 3 | 3 | 14 | 526 | 68 | 397 | 61 | 1 |
| Walkerton | 2,261 | 5 | 0 | 0 | 0 | 5 | 16 | 3 | 10 | 3 | 0 |
| Warsaw | 15,353 | 57 | 0 | 10 | 3 | 44 | 442 | 59 | 335 | 48 | 3 |
| Washington | 12,722 | 15 | 0 | 4 | 0 | 11 | 152 | 7 | 139 | 6 | 1 |
| Westfield | 48,140 | 39 | 0 | 9 | 6 | 24 | 361 | 30 | 314 | 17 | 1 |
| West Lafayette | 52,675 | 39 | 0 | 13 | 4 | 22 | 422 | 21 | 392 | 9 | 2 |
| Whiteland | 4,753 | 1 | 0 | 0 | 1 | 0 | 59 | 3 | 46 | 10 | 0 |
| Whitestown | 10,738 | 12 | 0 | 1 | 0 | 11 | 150 | 4 | 125 | 21 | 0 |
| Winona Lake | 4,888 | 4 | 0 | 0 | 0 | 4 | 30 | 5 | 25 | 0 | 0 |
| Zionsville | 29,876 | 8 | 0 | 1 | 2 | 5 | 107 | 7 | 93 | 7 | 0 |
| **IOWA** | | | | | | | | | | | |
| Adel | 5,845 | 6 | 0 | 2 | 0 | 4 | 128 | 20 | 95 | 13 | 0 |
| Albia | 3,706 | 8 | 0 | 2 | 1 | 5 | 44 | 5 | 34 | 5 | 0 |
| Algona | 5,340 | 23 | 0 | 2 | 0 | 21 | 15 | 3 | 12 | 0 | 0 |
| Altoona | 20,064 | 54 | 0 | 2 | 6 | 46 | 378 | 22 | 329 | 27 | 1 |
| Ames | 67,886 | 123 | 4 | 57 | 8 | 54 | 885 | 128 | 687 | 70 | 5 |
| Ankeny | 73,109 | 97 | 0 | 21 | 2 | 74 | 714 | 52 | 591 | 71 | 5 |
| Asbury | 5,999 | 1 | 0 | 0 | 0 | 1 | 24 | 4 | 16 | 4 | 1 |
| Atlantic | 6,457 | 16 | 0 | 2 | 0 | 14 | 94 | 13 | 76 | 5 | 2 |
| Audubon | 1,852 | 3 | 0 | 1 | 0 | 2 | 34 | 10 | 19 | 5 | 0 |
| Belle Plaine | 2,406 | 12 | 0 | 1 | 0 | 11 | 35 | 16 | 16 | 3 | 0 |
| Bettendorf | 37,022 | 47 | 0 | 13 | 3 | 31 | 608 | 104 | 440 | 64 | 2 |
| Buffalo | 1,256 | 0 | 0 | 0 | 0 | 0 | 9 | 4 | 4 | 1 | 0 |
| Burlington | 24,417 | 137 | 0 | 19 | 7 | 111 | 763 | 144 | 528 | 91 | 5 |
| Camanche | 4,360 | 11 | 0 | 1 | 0 | 10 | 33 | 9 | 23 | 1 | 0 |
| Carroll | 9,651 | 3 | 0 | 0 | 0 | 3 | 112 | 21 | 86 | 5 | 1 |
| Carter Lake | 3,793 | 32 | 0 | 4 | 0 | 28 | 129 | 16 | 94 | 19 | 2 |
| Cedar Falls | 40,321 | 80 | 0 | 17 | 6 | 57 | 750 | 116 | 587 | 47 | 1 |
| Cedar Rapids | 134,763 | 465 | 10 | 9 | 64 | 382 | 3,654 | 511 | 2,711 | 432 | 25 |
| Centerville | 5,394 | 12 | 0 | 2 | 0 | 10 | 100 | 17 | 68 | 15 | 1 |
| Charles City | 7,174 | 22 | 1 | 8 | 1 | 12 | 107 | 38 | 66 | 3 | 1 |
| Cherokee | 4,800 | 19 | 0 | 0 | 0 | 19 | 23 | 6 | 13 | 4 | 0 |
| Clarinda | 5,346 | 11 | 0 | 2 | 0 | 9 | 52 | 12 | 36 | 4 | 1 |
| Clarion | 2,662 | 5 | 0 | 0 | 0 | 5 | 9 | 0 | 9 | 0 | 0 |
| Clear Lake | 7,492 | 21 | 0 | 5 | 0 | 16 | 173 | 36 | 108 | 29 | 1 |
| Clinton | 24,865 | 143 | 1 | 17 | 11 | 114 | 803 | 167 | 562 | 74 | 8 |
| Clive | 17,652 | 16 | 0 | 1 | 1 | 14 | 226 | 27 | 163 | 36 | 4 |
| Coralville | 22,874 | 65 | 0 | 7 | 4 | 54 | 402 | 38 | 344 | 20 | 0 |
| Council Bluffs | 62,202 | 224 | 0 | 26 | 28 | 170 | 2,127 | 404 | 1,372 | 351 | 15 |
| Creston | 7,644 | 37 | 0 | 6 | 1 | 30 | 113 | 23 | 72 | 18 | 1 |
| Davenport | 102,014 | 670 | 10 | 96 | 98 | 466 | 3,652 | 636 | 2,559 | 457 | 24 |
| Decorah | 7,422 | 7 | 0 | 0 | 0 | 7 | 29 | 1 | 27 | 1 | 0 |
| Denison | 8,241 | 13 | 0 | 2 | 0 | 11 | 72 | 14 | 48 | 10 | 1 |
| Des Moines | 213,060 | 1,340 | 2 | 109 | 165 | 1,064 | 6,762 | 738 | 4,580 | 1,444 | 27 |
| DeWitt | 5,212 | 20 | 0 | 3 | 1 | 16 | 73 | 21 | 48 | 4 | 0 |
| Dubuque | 57,790 | 252 | 3 | 47 | 22 | 180 | 1,184 | 190 | 898 | 96 | 17 |
| Dyersville | 4,478 | 7 | 0 | 1 | 1 | 5 | 13 | 2 | 9 | 2 | 0 |
| Eldridge | 6,998 | 4 | 0 | 1 | 0 | 3 | 60 | 4 | 43 | 13 | 0 |
| Emmetsburg | 3,645 | 14 | 0 | 1 | 0 | 13 | 22 | 2 | 17 | 3 | 0 |
| Estherville | 5,516 | 23 | 0 | 4 | 0 | 19 | 43 | 10 | 24 | 9 | 0 |
| Evansdale | 4,732 | 2 | 0 | 0 | 1 | 1 | 43 | 12 | 25 | 6 | 0 |
| Fairfield | 10,608 | 15 | 1 | 5 | 1 | 8 | 128 | 23 | 94 | 11 | 0 |
| Fort Dodge | 23,788 | 117 | 0 | 23 | 10 | 84 | 596 | 86 | 445 | 65 | 5 |
| Fort Madison | 10,185 | 71 | 2 | 15 | 3 | 51 | 277 | 83 | 174 | 20 | 4 |
| Glenwood | 5,260 | 11 | 0 | 2 | 0 | 9 | 48 | 8 | 36 | 4 | 1 |
| Grinnell | 9,084 | 48 | 0 | 6 | 1 | 41 | 162 | 27 | 127 | 8 | 3 |
| Grundy Center | 2,666 | 10 | 0 | 1 | 0 | 9 | 17 | 8 | 3 | 6 | 0 |
| Harlan | 4,767 | 7 | 0 | 1 | 0 | 6 | 9 | 3 | 3 | 3 | 0 |
| Hiawatha | 7,512 | 26 | 0 | 2 | 0 | 24 | 59 | 9 | 36 | 14 | 0 |
| Huxley | 4,379 | 2 | 0 | 2 | 0 | 0 | 62 | 6 | 52 | 4 | 0 |
| Independence | 6,227 | 18 | 0 | 5 | 0 | 13 | 52 | 12 | 38 | 2 | 0 |
| Indianola | 16,203 | 75 | 0 | 12 | 0 | 63 | 275 | 32 | 226 | 17 | 3 |
| Iowa City | 77,522 | 238 | 2 | 28 | 24 | 184 | 1,249 | 215 | 925 | 109 | 4 |

## Table 8. Offenses Known to Law Enforcement, by Selected State and City, 2021—Continued

(Number.)

| State/city | Population | Violent crime | Murder and nonnegligent manslaughter | Rape | Robbery | Aggravated assault | Property crime | Burglary | Larceny-theft | Motor vehicle theft | Arson |
|---|---|---|---|---|---|---|---|---|---|---|---|
| Johnston | 23,759 | 35 | 0 | 11 | 1 | 23 | 199 | 22 | 156 | 21 | 1 |
| Keokuk | 10,025 | 87 | 0 | 10 | 3 | 74 | 281 | 44 | 202 | 35 | 3 |
| Lansing | 926 | 2 | 0 | 2 | 0 | 0 | 3 | 0 | 3 | 0 | 0 |
| Le Mars | 10,233 | 30 | 0 | 7 | 0 | 23 | 109 | 8 | 93 | 8 | 5 |
| Manchester | 4,987 | 14 | 0 | 1 | 1 | 12 | 57 | 7 | 43 | 7 | 0 |
| Maquoketa | 5,894 | 26 | 0 | 9 | 1 | 16 | 144 | 37 | 90 | 17 | 2 |
| Marengo | 2,460 | 9 | 0 | 2 | 0 | 7 | 43 | 4 | 35 | 4 | 0 |
| Marion | 41,370 | 102 | 1 | 23 | 2 | 76 | 460 | 76 | 334 | 50 | 3 |
| Marshalltown | 26,651 | 110 | 1 | 18 | 5 | 86 | 483 | 101 | 335 | 47 | 4 |
| Mason City | 26,550 | 108 | 3 | 13 | 10 | 82 | 752 | 161 | 528 | 63 | 8 |
| Monticello | 3,882 | 18 | 0 | 0 | 0 | 18 | 40 | 11 | 25 | 4 | 1 |
| Mount Pleasant | 8,494 | 22 | 0 | 5 | 1 | 16 | 86 | 29 | 44 | 13 | 0 |
| Mount Vernon-Lisbon | 6,794 | 21 | 0 | 8 | 1 | 12 | 27 | 0 | 24 | 3 | 0 |
| Muscatine | 23,499 | 83 | 0 | 20 | 3 | 60 | 395 | 89 | 283 | 23 | 3 |
| Newton | 15,116 | 56 | 1 | 12 | 0 | 43 | 251 | 55 | 171 | 25 | 2 |
| North Liberty | 20,482 | 48 | 0 | 14 | 1 | 33 | 82 | 10 | 66 | 6 | 0 |
| Oelwein | 5,731 | 17 | 0 | 0 | 0 | 17 | 71 | 23 | 41 | 7 | 1 |
| Osage | 3,541 | 6 | 0 | 0 | 0 | 6 | 20 | 11 | 9 | 0 | 0 |
| Osceola | 5,320 | 15 | 0 | 2 | 1 | 12 | 92 | 20 | 66 | 6 | 4 |
| Oskaloosa | 11,832 | 28 | 0 | 4 | 2 | 22 | 171 | 21 | 135 | 15 | 4 |
| Ottumwa | 24,308 | 211 | 3 | 47 | 11 | 150 | 786 | 124 | 580 | 82 | 3 |
| Pella | 10,260 | 9 | 0 | 4 | 0 | 5 | 60 | 8 | 48 | 4 | 1 |
| Pleasant Hill | 10,153 | 19 | 0 | 4 | 0 | 15 | 213 | 59 | 136 | 18 | 0 |
| Polk City | 5,350 | 1 | 0 | 1 | 0 | 0 | 5 | 1 | 4 | 0 | 0 |
| Red Oak | 5,229 | 15 | 1 | 5 | 0 | 9 | 72 | 22 | 43 | 7 | 2 |
| Sheldon | 5,058 | 7 | 0 | 1 | 1 | 5 | 47 | 13 | 31 | 3 | 0 |
| Shenandoah | 4,749 | 15 | 0 | 3 | 1 | 11 | 53 | 10 | 38 | 5 | 1 |
| Sioux Center | 7,729 | 9 | 0 | 4 | 0 | 5 | 9 | 0 | 9 | 0 | 0 |
| Sioux City | 82,750 | 477 | 2 | 83 | 52 | 340 | 2,518 | 403 | 1,883 | 232 | 25 |
| Spencer | 10,966 | 11 | 0 | 9 | 1 | 1 | 137 | 28 | 104 | 5 | 0 |
| Spirit Lake | 5,292 | 7 | 0 | 2 | 0 | 5 | 83 | 20 | 50 | 13 | 1 |
| Storm Lake | 10,414 | 29 | 0 | 2 | 1 | 26 | 142 | 30 | 100 | 12 | 2 |
| Story City | 3,320 | 4 | 0 | 2 | 0 | 2 | 82 | 27 | 52 | 3 | 0 |
| Tipton | 3,174 | 15 | 0 | 4 | 0 | 11 | 21 | 5 | 15 | 1 | 0 |
| Urbandale | 45,201 | 52 | 0 | 5 | 10 | 37 | 407 | 62 | 279 | 66 | 2 |
| Vinton | 4,996 | 2 | 0 | 1 | 0 | 1 | 28 | 7 | 18 | 3 | 0 |
| Walcott | 1,628 | 5 | 0 | 1 | 0 | 4 | 19 | 7 | 9 | 3 | 0 |
| Washington | 7,201 | 32 | 0 | 11 | 0 | 21 | 182 | 24 | 144 | 14 | 1 |
| Waterloo | 67,174 | 356 | 5 | 35 | 51 | 265 | 1,741 | 413 | 1,109 | 219 | 13 |
| Waukee | 27,858 | 25 | 0 | 5 | 1 | 19 | 184 | 16 | 139 | 29 | 0 |
| Waukon | 3,570 | 2 | 0 | 0 | 0 | 2 | 56 | 4 | 52 | 0 | 0 |
| Waverly | 10,340 | 43 | 0 | 7 | 0 | 36 | 104 | 16 | 80 | 8 | 0 |
| Webster City | 7,608 | 22 | 0 | 4 | 3 | 15 | 73 | 16 | 50 | 7 | 1 |
| West Branch | 2,539 | 5 | 0 | 2 | 0 | 3 | 11 | 3 | 8 | 0 | 0 |
| West Burlington | 2,863 | 18 | 1 | 1 | 0 | 16 | 176 | 12 | 152 | 12 | 0 |
| West Des Moines | 70,414 | 102 | 0 | 23 | 17 | 62 | 1,225 | 151 | 987 | 87 | 5 |
| Williamsburg | 3,191 | 2 | 0 | 0 | 0 | 2 | 12 | 2 | 9 | 1 | 0 |
| Windsor Heights | 4,717 | 10 | 0 | 0 | 1 | 9 | 150 | 4 | 142 | 4 | 0 |
| **KANSAS** | | | | | | | | | | | |
| Abilene | 6,055 | 9 | 0 | 1 | 0 | 8 | 51 | 7 | 41 | 3 | 3 |
| Anthony | 2,011 | 4 | 0 | 2 | 0 | 2 | 24 | 6 | 17 | 1 | 0 |
| Arma | 1,405 | 4 | 0 | 0 | 0 | 4 | 37 | 5 | 28 | 4 | 1 |
| Atchison | 10,374 | 41 | 0 | 7 | 1 | 33 | 197 | 1 | 181 | 15 | 0 |
| Atwood | 1,210 | 5 | 0 | 2 | 0 | 3 | 14 | 2 | 11 | 1 | 0 |
| Augusta | 9,290 | 22 | 1 | 6 | 2 | 13 | 207 | 36 | 163 | 8 | 0 |
| Baldwin City | 4,706 | 21 | 0 | 3 | 0 | 18 | 29 | 9 | 18 | 2 | 0 |
| Baxter Springs | 3,859 | 19 | 0 | 0 | 0 | 19 | 114 | 33 | 70 | 11 | 1 |
| Bel Aire | 8,660 | 4 | 0 | 0 | 0 | 4 | 116 | 13 | 87 | 16 | 0 |
| Belleville | 1,828 | 4 | 1 | 1 | 1 | 1 | 31 | 8 | 23 | 0 | 1 |
| Beloit | 3,540 | 9 | 0 | 4 | 0 | 5 | 31 | 7 | 23 | 1 | 0 |
| Bonner Springs | 8,072 | 18 | 0 | 2 | 2 | 14 | 200 | 16 | 153 | 31 | 1 |
| Burlington | 2,533 | 6 | 0 | 1 | 0 | 5 | 26 | 4 | 21 | 1 | 0 |
| Caney | 1,924 | 1 | 0 | 0 | 0 | 1 | 31 | 2 | 25 | 4 | 0 |
| Cheney | 2,180 | 1 | 0 | 0 | 0 | 1 | 42 | 3 | 38 | 1 | 0 |
| Cherryvale | 2,098 | 9 | 0 | 1 | 0 | 8 | 30 | 9 | 18 | 3 | 1 |
| Clay Center | 3,957 | 13 | 0 | 1 | 0 | 12 | 94 | 20 | 70 | 4 | 0 |
| Clearwater | 2,589 | 7 | 0 | 2 | 0 | 5 | 24 | 3 | 13 | 8 | 0 |
| Coffeyville | 9,066 | 62 | 2 | 6 | 5 | 49 | 288 | 44 | 220 | 24 | 1 |
| Colby | 5,305 | 21 | 0 | 0 | 1 | 20 | 70 | 17 | 47 | 6 | 0 |
| Columbus | 2,978 | 12 | 0 | 1 | 0 | 11 | 60 | 13 | 38 | 9 | 0 |
| Concordia | 4,860 | 13 | 0 | 2 | 0 | 11 | 149 | 31 | 109 | 9 | 1 |
| Council Grove | 2,090 | 7 | 0 | 0 | 0 | 7 | 20 | 3 | 17 | 0 | 0 |
| Derby | 25,425 | 42 | 1 | 4 | 2 | 35 | 509 | 34 | 453 | 22 | 2 |
| Dodge City | 26,612 | 124 | 1 | 14 | 11 | 98 | 441 | 52 | 351 | 38 | 3 |
| Edwardsville | 4,540 | 24 | 0 | 7 | 1 | 16 | 92 | 11 | 63 | 18 | 4 |
| El Dorado | 12,819 | 24 | 0 | 3 | 1 | 20 | 589 | 363 | 189 | 37 | 2 |
| Elkhart | 1,685 | 4 | 0 | 0 | 0 | 4 | 14 | 3 | 11 | 0 | 0 |
| Ellis | 2,013 | 5 | 0 | 1 | 1 | 3 | 17 | 4 | 12 | 1 | 0 |
| Ellsworth | 2,917 | 1 | 0 | 0 | 0 | 1 | 12 | 3 | 8 | 1 | 2 |
| Eudora | 6,418 | 8 | 0 | 1 | 1 | 6 | 26 | 3 | 21 | 2 | 0 |
| Fairway | 3,972 | 6 | 0 | 2 | 0 | 4 | 32 | 4 | 18 | 10 | 1 |
| Fort Scott | 7,607 | 23 | 2 | 2 | 0 | 19 | 171 | 10 | 144 | 17 | 7 |

## Table 8. Offenses Known to Law Enforcement, by Selected State and City, 2021—Continued

(Number.)

| State/city | Population | Violent crime | Murder and nonnegligent manslaughter | Rape | Robbery | Aggravated assault | Property crime | Burglary | Larceny-theft | Motor vehicle theft | Arson |
|---|---|---|---|---|---|---|---|---|---|---|---|
| Frontenac | 3,387 | 4 | 0 | 1 | 0 | 3 | 59 | 9 | 46 | 4 | 0 |
| Galena | 2,798 | 15 | 0 | 0 | 0 | 15 | 48 | 4 | 32 | 12 | 1 |
| Garden City | 25,920 | 144 | 4 | 25 | 9 | 106 | 903 | 145 | 654 | 104 | 8 |
| Gardner | 22,714 | 44 | 0 | 6 | 2 | 36 | 245 | 21 | 196 | 28 | 4 |
| Garnett | 3,243 | 14 | 0 | 1 | 2 | 11 | 30 | 4 | 19 | 7 | 1 |
| Girard | 2,644 | 9 | 0 | 1 | 2 | 6 | 55 | 5 | 40 | 10 | 1 |
| Goddard | 5,020 | 8 | 0 | 1 | 1 | 6 | 45 | 4 | 40 | 1 | 0 |
| Goodland | 4,283 | 8 | 0 | 0 | 1 | 7 | 48 | 5 | 39 | 4 | 0 |
| Grandview Plaza | 1,532 | 8 | 0 | 1 | 0 | 7 | 32 | 8 | 22 | 2 | 0 |
| Great Bend | 14,795 | 59 | 1 | 12 | 2 | 44 | 374 | 85 | 260 | 29 | 1 |
| Halstead | 2,022 | 11 | 0 | 0 | 0 | 11 | 17 | 5 | 11 | 1 | 0 |
| Hays | 20,861 | 88 | 1 | 12 | 8 | 67 | 394 | 43 | 334 | 17 | 4 |
| Haysville | 11,445 | 18 | 0 | 4 | 1 | 13 | 219 | 43 | 155 | 21 | 0 |
| Hesston | 3,738 | 1 | 0 | 1 | 0 | 0 | 31 | 13 | 15 | 3 | 0 |
| Hiawatha | 3,075 | 12 | 0 | 3 | 0 | 9 | 113 | 8 | 98 | 7 | 0 |
| Hillsboro | 2,739 | 0 | 0 | 0 | 0 | 0 | 21 | 5 | 15 | 1 | 0 |
| Hoisington | 2,429 | 12 | 1 | 3 | 0 | 8 | 27 | 9 | 16 | 2 | 1 |
| Holton | 3,193 | 4 | 0 | 0 | 1 | 3 | 41 | 5 | 35 | 1 | 0 |
| Horton | 1,659 | 11 | 0 | 0 | 0 | 11 | 13 | 6 | 6 | 1 | 0 |
| Hugoton | 3,653 | 11 | 0 | 1 | 0 | 10 | 29 | 2 | 27 | 0 | 0 |
| Hutchinson | 40,015 | 110 | 0 | 15 | 6 | 89 | 731 | 135 | 544 | 52 | 7 |
| Independence | 8,326 | 65 | 0 | 10 | 9 | 46 | 377 | 88 | 263 | 26 | 5 |
| Iola | 5,222 | 33 | 0 | 10 | 0 | 23 | 176 | 43 | 123 | 10 | 1 |
| Kechi | 2,129 | 5 | 0 | 0 | 0 | 5 | 22 | 4 | 15 | 3 | 0 |
| Kingman | 2,727 | 3 | 0 | 1 | 0 | 2 | 41 | 6 | 31 | 4 | 0 |
| Lansing | 12,021 | 23 | 0 | 5 | 0 | 18 | 94 | 7 | 72 | 15 | 0 |
| Larned | 3,591 | 11 | 1 | 2 | 2 | 6 | 87 | 23 | 58 | 6 | 4 |
| Leavenworth | 35,990 | 316 | 5 | 40 | 27 | 244 | 865 | 147 | 573 | 145 | 15 |
| Leawood | 34,957 | 23 | 0 | 2 | 3 | 18 | 516 | 51 | 425 | 40 | 0 |
| Lenexa | 57,012 | 110 | 0 | 12 | 10 | 88 | 919 | 88 | 694 | 137 | 0 |
| Liberal | 18,658 | 86 | 0 | 18 | 5 | 63 | 247 | 42 | 187 | 18 | 7 |
| Louisburg | 4,619 | 9 | 0 | 2 | 0 | 7 | 78 | 40 | 36 | 2 | 0 |
| Lyons | 3,403 | 16 | 0 | 2 | 0 | 14 | 39 | 6 | 29 | 4 | 2 |
| Maize | 5,491 | 19 | 0 | 2 | 1 | 16 | 126 | 59 | 61 | 6 | 0 |
| Marion | 1,721 | 2 | 0 | 0 | 0 | 2 | 8 | 3 | 5 | 0 | 0 |
| McPherson | 13,002 | 55 | 0 | 9 | 2 | 44 | 260 | 40 | 203 | 17 | 3 |
| Medicine Lodge | 1,784 | 2 | 0 | 1 | 0 | 1 | 18 | 5 | 13 | 0 | 0 |
| Merriam | 11,138 | 76 | 0 | 6 | 9 | 61 | 658 | 36 | 494 | 128 | 1 |
| Mission | 9,931 | 45 | 0 | 2 | 4 | 39 | 373 | 22 | 283 | 68 | 0 |
| Mission Hills | 3,539 | 9 | 0 | 0 | 0 | 9 | 74 | 25 | 39 | 10 | 0 |
| Mulberry | 521 | 4 | 0 | 1 | 0 | 3 | 6 | 2 | 4 | 0 | 0 |
| Mulvane | 6,610 | 9 | 0 | 2 | 0 | 7 | 199 | 60 | 131 | 8 | 0 |
| Neodesha | 2,186 | 12 | 0 | 3 | 0 | 9 | 24 | 2 | 17 | 5 | 0 |
| Newton | 18,705 | 122 | 2 | 26 | 6 | 88 | 466 | 60 | 372 | 34 | 6 |
| Olathe | 143,307 | 352 | 2 | 58 | 17 | 275 | 1,818 | 146 | 1,427 | 245 | 9 |
| Osage City | 2,748 | 13 | 0 | 2 | 0 | 11 | 28 | 5 | 20 | 3 | 0 |
| Oswego | 1,668 | 1 | 0 | 0 | 0 | 1 | 22 | 6 | 15 | 1 | 1 |
| Ottawa | 12,303 | 38 | 0 | 9 | 0 | 29 | 158 | 20 | 120 | 18 | 3 |
| Overland Park | 199,881 | 471 | 1 | 45 | 43 | 382 | 4,339 | 366 | 3,416 | 557 | 12 |
| Paola | 5,668 | 10 | 0 | 2 | 0 | 8 | 80 | 5 | 70 | 5 | 0 |
| Park City | 8,006 | 16 | 0 | 5 | 1 | 10 | 271 | 26 | 200 | 45 | 0 |
| Parsons | 9,368 | 68 | 1 | 5 | 11 | 51 | 317 | 57 | 237 | 23 | 5 |
| Pittsburg | 19,939 | 144 | 1 | 17 | 17 | 109 | 1,228 | 119 | 959 | 150 | 9 |
| Plainville | 1,755 | 2 | 0 | 0 | 1 | 1 | 13 | 1 | 9 | 3 | 0 |
| Prairie Village | 22,402 | 29 | 0 | 5 | 3 | 21 | 285 | 41 | 194 | 50 | 0 |
| Roeland Park | 6,644 | 17 | 0 | 1 | 5 | 11 | 173 | 6 | 133 | 34 | 1 |
| Rose Hill | 3,983 | 10 | 0 | 1 | 0 | 9 | 18 | 5 | 12 | 1 | 0 |
| Russell | 4,369 | 14 | 0 | 5 | 0 | 9 | 45 | 11 | 28 | 6 | 1 |
| Sabetha | 2,552 | 8 | 0 | 4 | 0 | 4 | 11 | 1 | 9 | 1 | 0 |
| Salina | 46,112 | 232 | 2 | 43 | 17 | 170 | 1,656 | 232 | 1,265 | 159 | 18 |
| Scott City | 3,726 | 14 | 0 | 0 | 0 | 14 | 25 | 7 | 15 | 3 | 0 |
| Seneca | 2,087 | 1 | 0 | 0 | 0 | 1 | 18 | 1 | 17 | 0 | 0 |
| Shawnee | 66,710 | 188 | 0 | 13 | 22 | 153 | 1,176 | 226 | 770 | 180 | 6 |
| Spring Hill | 8,167 | 9 | 0 | 2 | 0 | 7 | 113 | 18 | 88 | 7 | 1 |
| St. Marys | 2,649 | 3 | 0 | 1 | 0 | 2 | 21 | 2 | 19 | 0 | 0 |
| Tonganoxie | 5,761 | 6 | 0 | 1 | 0 | 5 | 28 | 0 | 21 | 7 | 0 |
| Ulysses | 5,489 | 13 | 0 | 0 | 0 | 13 | 15 | 5 | 9 | 1 | 0 |
| Valley Center | 7,443 | 4 | 0 | 0 | 0 | 4 | 54 | 6 | 44 | 4 | 0 |
| Valley Falls | 1,149 | 1 | 0 | 0 | 0 | 1 | 8 | 2 | 6 | 0 | 0 |
| Wellington | 7,491 | 24 | 0 | 3 | 1 | 20 | 207 | 28 | 164 | 15 | 3 |
| Wellsville | 1,777 | 2 | 0 | 1 | 0 | 1 | 13 | 2 | 8 | 3 | 0 |
| Westwood | 1,657 | 3 | 0 | 0 | 2 | 1 | 56 | 11 | 42 | 3 | 0 |
| Winfield | 11,756 | 39 | 0 | 6 | 0 | 33 | 333 | 89 | 226 | 18 | 2 |
| **KENTUCKY** | | | | | | | | | | | |
| Adairville | 893 | 0 | 0 | 0 | 0 | 0 | 0 | 0 | 0 | 0 | 0 |
| Albany | 1,974 | 0 | 0 | 0 | 0 | 0 | 0 | 0 | 0 | 0 | 0 |
| Alexandria | 9,949 | 5 | 0 | 0 | 1 | 4 | 138 | 5 | 121 | 12 | 0 |
| Anchorage | 2,435 | 0 | 0 | 0 | 0 | 0 | 10 | 3 | 7 | 0 | 0 |
| Ashland | 19,913 | 38 | 2 | 10 | 5 | 21 | 576 | 96 | 439 | 41 | 3 |
| Auburn | 1,409 | 0 | 0 | 0 | 0 | 0 | 1 | 0 | 1 | 0 | 1 |
| Audubon Park | 1,489 | 0 | 0 | 0 | 0 | 0 | 17 | 4 | 8 | 5 | 0 |
| Augusta | 1,137 | 3 | 0 | 0 | 1 | 2 | 10 | 0 | 8 | 2 | 0 |

# Table 8. Offenses Known to Law Enforcement, by Selected State and City, 2021—Continued

(Number.)

| State/city | Population | Violent crime | Murder and nonnegligent manslaughter | Rape | Robbery | Aggravated assault | Property crime | Burglary | Larceny-theft | Motor vehicle theft | Arson |
|---|---|---|---|---|---|---|---|---|---|---|---|
| Bancroft | 513 | 0 | 0 | 0 | 0 | 0 | 1 | 0 | 1 | 0 | 0 |
| Barbourville | 2,955 | 10 | 0 | 0 | 4 | 6 | 51 | 18 | 20 | 13 | 0 |
| Bardstown | 13,378 | 15 | 1 | 2 | 7 | 5 | 324 | 43 | 231 | 50 | 3 |
| Bardwell | 655 | 0 | 0 | 0 | 0 | 0 | 2 | 0 | 1 | 1 | 0 |
| Beattyville | 1,451 | 7 | 0 | 1 | 0 | 6 | 10 | 2 | 4 | 4 | 0 |
| Beaver Dam | 3,558 | 2 | 0 | 0 | 1 | 1 | 24 | 2 | 16 | 6 | 0 |
| Bellefonte | 803 | 0 | 0 | 0 | 0 | 0 | 0 | 0 | 0 | 0 | 0 |
| Bellevue | 5,748 | 2 | 0 | 0 | 1 | 1 | 48 | 7 | 36 | 5 | 0 |
| Benton | 4,461 | 1 | 0 | 0 | 0 | 1 | 72 | 12 | 55 | 5 | 0 |
| Berea | 16,576 | 12 | 0 | 4 | 2 | 6 | 240 | 36 | 159 | 45 | 0 |
| Bloomfield | 1,088 | 0 | 0 | 0 | 0 | 0 | 8 | 2 | 6 | 0 | 0 |
| Booneville | 153 | 0 | 0 | 0 | 0 | 0 | 4 | 1 | 2 | 1 | 0 |
| Bowling Green | 71,826 | 237 | 6 | 66 | 53 | 112 | 2,704 | 388 | 1,983 | 333 | 9 |
| Brandenburg | 2,897 | 2 | 1 | 0 | 1 | 0 | 28 | 0 | 22 | 6 | 0 |
| Brodhead | 1,182 | 0 | 0 | 0 | 0 | 0 | 1 | 1 | 0 | 0 | 0 |
| Brooksville | 649 | 0 | 0 | 0 | 0 | 0 | 4 | 1 | 3 | 0 | 0 |
| Brownsville | 839 | 3 | 0 | 1 | 0 | 2 | 9 | 1 | 7 | 1 | 0 |
| Burgin | 997 | 0 | 0 | 0 | 0 | 0 | 3 | 0 | 3 | 0 | 0 |
| Burkesville | 1,427 | 1 | 0 | 0 | 0 | 1 | 4 | 2 | 0 | 2 | 0 |
| Burnside | 792 | 0 | 0 | 0 | 0 | 0 | 19 | 5 | 12 | 2 | 0 |
| Cadiz | 2,725 | 7 | 0 | 0 | 1 | 6 | 64 | 21 | 37 | 6 | 0 |
| Calvert City | 2,502 | 3 | 0 | 0 | 0 | 3 | 28 | 3 | 22 | 3 | 0 |
| Campbellsville | 11,500 | 19 | 1 | 5 | 4 | 9 | 240 | 73 | 147 | 20 | 7 |
| Carlisle | 2,056 | 0 | 0 | 0 | 0 | 0 | 10 | 4 | 5 | 1 | 0 |
| Carrollton | 3,794 | 4 | 0 | 0 | 1 | 3 | 41 | 5 | 23 | 13 | 0 |
| Catlettsburg | 1,724 | 5 | 0 | 1 | 1 | 3 | 23 | 3 | 16 | 4 | 0 |
| Cave City | 2,437 | 5 | 0 | 1 | 0 | 4 | 23 | 9 | 11 | 3 | 1 |
| Centertown | 429 | 0 | 0 | 0 | 0 | 0 | 0 | 0 | 0 | 0 | 0 |
| Central City | 5,664 | 2 | 0 | 0 | 2 | 0 | 83 | 12 | 65 | 6 | 0 |
| Clarkson | 889 | 0 | 0 | 0 | 0 | 0 | 0 | 0 | 0 | 0 | 0 |
| Clay | 1,083 | 0 | 0 | 0 | 0 | 0 | 2 | 0 | 2 | 0 | 0 |
| Clay City | 1,083 | 0 | 0 | 0 | 0 | 0 | 15 | 3 | 8 | 4 | 0 |
| Clinton | 1,231 | 2 | 0 | 0 | 1 | 1 | 2 | 1 | 0 | 1 | 0 |
| Cloverport | 1,151 | 1 | 0 | 0 | 0 | 1 | 0 | 0 | 0 | 0 | 0 |
| Coal Run Village | 1,475 | 0 | 0 | 0 | 0 | 0 | 14 | 2 | 10 | 2 | 0 |
| Cold Spring | 6,697 | 0 | 0 | 0 | 0 | 0 | 73 | 6 | 60 | 7 | 0 |
| Columbia | 4,937 | 2 | 0 | 0 | 0 | 2 | 15 | 4 | 9 | 2 | 0 |
| Corbin | 7,126 | 10 | 1 | 2 | 1 | 6 | 134 | 38 | 85 | 11 | 0 |
| Covington | 40,298 | 136 | 2 | 22 | 41 | 71 | 729 | 114 | 500 | 115 | 7 |
| Crab Orchard | 820 | 0 | 0 | 0 | 0 | 0 | 0 | 0 | 0 | 0 | 0 |
| Cumberland | 1,824 | 0 | 0 | 0 | 0 | 0 | 1 | 1 | 0 | 0 | 2 |
| Cynthiana | 6,294 | 6 | 0 | 1 | 0 | 5 | 88 | 18 | 56 | 14 | 2 |
| Danville | 17,042 | 18 | 0 | 7 | 2 | 9 | 279 | 60 | 193 | 26 | 4 |
| Dawson Springs | 2,616 | 2 | 0 | 0 | 0 | 2 | 30 | 13 | 15 | 2 | 0 |
| Dayton | 5,678 | 8 | 0 | 3 | 3 | 2 | 43 | 8 | 31 | 4 | 0 |
| Dry Ridge | 2,209 | 1 | 0 | 0 | 0 | 1 | 19 | 0 | 17 | 2 | 0 |
| Eddyville | 2,549 | 0 | 0 | 0 | 0 | 0 | 19 | 6 | 12 | 1 | 0 |
| Edgewood | 8,796 | 2 | 0 | 1 | 1 | 0 | 41 | 1 | 35 | 5 | 0 |
| Edmonton | 1,595 | 2 | 0 | 0 | 0 | 2 | 17 | 7 | 7 | 3 | 0 |
| Elizabethtown | 30,530 | 56 | 1 | 15 | 18 | 22 | 364 | 97 | 210 | 57 | 2 |
| Elkhorn City | 862 | 0 | 0 | 0 | 0 | 0 | 1 | 0 | 0 | 1 | 0 |
| Elkton | 2,158 | 2 | 0 | 0 | 0 | 2 | 31 | 4 | 22 | 5 | 0 |
| Elsmere | 8,672 | 11 | 0 | 3 | 3 | 5 | 89 | 20 | 53 | 16 | 0 |
| Eminence | 2,574 | 2 | 0 | 1 | 0 | 1 | 45 | 8 | 35 | 2 | 1 |
| Erlanger | 23,678 | 17 | 0 | 5 | 2 | 10 | 93 | 15 | 61 | 17 | 0 |
| Eubank | 335 | 0 | 0 | 0 | 0 | 0 | 0 | 0 | 0 | 0 | 0 |
| Evarts | 783 | 1 | 0 | 0 | 0 | 1 | 2 | 0 | 1 | 1 | 0 |
| Falmouth | 2,074 | 6 | 0 | 0 | 2 | 4 | 31 | 2 | 24 | 5 | 0 |
| Ferguson | 945 | 0 | 0 | 0 | 0 | 0 | 3 | 2 | 1 | 0 | 0 |
| Flatwoods | 7,019 | 5 | 1 | 1 | 0 | 3 | 33 | 7 | 20 | 6 | 0 |
| Fleming-Neon | 601 | 0 | 0 | 0 | 0 | 0 | 0 | 0 | 0 | 0 | 0 |
| Flemingsburg | 2,800 | 2 | 0 | 1 | 0 | 1 | 43 | 7 | 33 | 3 | 0 |
| Florence | 33,824 | 62 | 1 | 20 | 21 | 20 | 1,213 | 57 | 1,082 | 74 | 2 |
| Fort Mitchell | 8,273 | 4 | 0 | 3 | 0 | 1 | 92 | 3 | 74 | 15 | 0 |
| Fort Thomas | 16,269 | 6 | 0 | 4 | 0 | 2 | 64 | 9 | 46 | 9 | 0 |
| Fort Wright | 5,787 | 2 | 0 | 0 | 2 | 0 | 36 | 1 | 32 | 3 | 0 |
| Fountain Run | 207 | 0 | 0 | 0 | 0 | 0 | 0 | 0 | 0 | 0 | 0 |
| Frankfort | 27,753 | 56 | 2 | 18 | 8 | 28 | 760 | 127 | 527 | 106 | 1 |
| Franklin | 9,105 | 29 | 0 | 7 | 8 | 14 | 240 | 49 | 167 | 24 | 1 |
| Fulton | 2,077 | 0 | 0 | 0 | 0 | 0 | 13 | 2 | 8 | 3 | 0 |
| Georgetown | 36,590 | 61 | 0 | 15 | 16 | 30 | 647 | 85 | 494 | 68 | 1 |
| Glasgow | 14,452 | 32 | 3 | 5 | 5 | 19 | 354 | 70 | 253 | 31 | 1 |
| Graymoor-Devondale | 3,098 | 6 | 0 | 1 | 4 | 1 | 92 | 24 | 50 | 18 | 0 |
| Grayson | 3,808 | 11 | 0 | 0 | 3 | 8 | 56 | 7 | 39 | 10 | 0 |
| Greensburg | 2,048 | 7 | 0 | 1 | 0 | 6 | 25 | 2 | 20 | 3 | 0 |
| Greenup | 1,092 | 1 | 0 | 0 | 0 | 1 | 7 | 1 | 6 | 0 | 0 |
| Greenville | 4,122 | 8 | 0 | 0 | 1 | 7 | 19 | 4 | 13 | 2 | 1 |
| Guthrie | 1,427 | 1 | 0 | 0 | 0 | 1 | 2 | 0 | 1 | 1 | 0 |
| Hardinsburg | 2,346 | 3 | 1 | 1 | 0 | 1 | 7 | 1 | 4 | 2 | 0 |
| Harlan | 1,447 | 0 | 0 | 0 | 0 | 0 | 22 | 4 | 13 | 5 | 0 |
| Harrodsburg | 8,560 | 10 | 0 | 1 | 3 | 6 | 94 | 16 | 65 | 13 | 2 |
| Hartford | 2,719 | 3 | 0 | 0 | 0 | 3 | 4 | 2 | 1 | 1 | 0 |
| Hawesville | 979 | 1 | 0 | 1 | 0 | 0 | 6 | 1 | 5 | 0 | 0 |

## Table 8. Offenses Known to Law Enforcement, by Selected State and City, 2021—Continued

(Number.)

| State/city | Population | Violent crime | Murder and nonnegligent manslaughter | Rape | Robbery | Aggravated assault | Property crime | Burglary | Larceny-theft | Motor vehicle theft | Arson |
|---|---|---|---|---|---|---|---|---|---|---|---|
| Hazard | 4,721 | 6 | 0 | 2 | 1 | 3 | 75 | 10 | 51 | 14 | 1 |
| Henderson | 27,878 | 65 | 0 | 16 | 15 | 34 | 690 | 162 | 448 | 80 | 0 |
| Heritage Creek | 1,146 | 0 | 0 | 0 | 0 | 0 | 11 | 3 | 8 | 0 | 0 |
| Hickman | 2,078 | 2 | 0 | 0 | 0 | 2 | 1 | 0 | 1 | 0 | 1 |
| Highland Heights | 7,023 | 6 | 0 | 2 | 0 | 4 | 79 | 5 | 66 | 8 | 0 |
| Hillview | 9,274 | 12 | 0 | 3 | 6 | 3 | 166 | 18 | 112 | 36 | 0 |
| Hodgenville | 3,257 | 6 | 0 | 3 | 1 | 2 | 24 | 2 | 16 | 6 | 0 |
| Hopkinsville | 30,787 | 118 | 9 | 16 | 19 | 74 | 1,149 | 167 | 894 | 88 | 4 |
| Horse Cave | 2,422 | 0 | 0 | 0 | 0 | 0 | 7 | 1 | 3 | 3 | 0 |
| Hurstbourne Acres | 1,902 | 1 | 0 | 0 | 1 | 0 | 19 | 1 | 15 | 3 | 0 |
| Hustonville | 367 | 0 | 0 | 0 | 0 | 0 | 0 | 0 | 0 | 0 | 0 |
| Hyden | 319 | 0 | 0 | 0 | 0 | 0 | 0 | 0 | 0 | 0 | 0 |
| Independence | 29,339 | 23 | 0 | 9 | 0 | 14 | 91 | 12 | 69 | 10 | 1 |
| Indian Hills | 2,980 | 0 | 0 | 0 | 0 | 0 | 26 | 5 | 15 | 6 | 0 |
| Irvine | 2,271 | 4 | 0 | 0 | 0 | 4 | 20 | 5 | 8 | 7 | 0 |
| Irvington | 1,194 | 0 | 0 | 0 | 0 | 0 | 3 | 0 | 2 | 1 | 0 |
| Jackson | 1,892 | 1 | 0 | 0 | 0 | 1 | 26 | 6 | 18 | 2 | 0 |
| Jamestown | 1,802 | 3 | 0 | 0 | 0 | 3 | 13 | 1 | 10 | 2 | 0 |
| Jeffersontown | 27,533 | 42 | 0 | 6 | 19 | 17 | 774 | 68 | 586 | 120 | 0 |
| Jenkins | 1,865 | 1 | 0 | 0 | 0 | 1 | 2 | 0 | 0 | 2 | 0 |
| Junction City | 2,347 | 0 | 0 | 0 | 0 | 0 | 3 | 1 | 1 | 1 | 0 |
| La Center | 936 | 0 | 0 | 0 | 0 | 0 | 0 | 0 | 0 | 0 | 0 |
| La Grange | 9,186 | 11 | 0 | 0 | 2 | 9 | 155 | 16 | 120 | 19 | 0 |
| Lakeside Park-Crestview Hills | 6,110 | 1 | 0 | 0 | 1 | 0 | 35 | 2 | 27 | 6 | 0 |
| Lancaster | 3,845 | 15 | 0 | 4 | 1 | 10 | 114 | 45 | 53 | 16 | 1 |
| Lawrenceburg | 11,581 | 6 | 0 | 2 | 0 | 4 | 48 | 7 | 32 | 9 | 0 |
| Lebanon | 5,751 | 9 | 2 | 0 | 1 | 6 | 73 | 13 | 49 | 11 | 0 |
| Lebanon Junction | 1,986 | 2 | 0 | 0 | 2 | 0 | 10 | 2 | 7 | 1 | 0 |
| Leitchfield | 6,838 | 9 | 0 | 3 | 0 | 6 | 152 | 27 | 114 | 11 | 0 |
| Lewisburg | 807 | 0 | 0 | 0 | 0 | 0 | 2 | 0 | 1 | 1 | 0 |
| Lewisport | 1,683 | 0 | 0 | 0 | 0 | 0 | 0 | 0 | 0 | 0 | 0 |
| Lexington | 328,965 | 947 | 31 | 186 | 279 | 451 | 8,940 | 1,181 | 6,769 | 990 | 14 |
| Liberty | 2,136 | 1 | 0 | 0 | 0 | 1 | 1 | 0 | 1 | 0 | 0 |
| Livingston | 212 | 0 | 0 | 0 | 0 | 0 | 0 | 0 | 0 | 0 | 0 |
| London | 8,080 | 9 | 0 | 0 | 3 | 6 | 351 | 85 | 233 | 33 | 1 |
| Louisa | 2,313 | 2 | 0 | 0 | 1 | 1 | 26 | 8 | 10 | 8 | 0 |
| Louisville Metro | 678,236 | 6,655 | 192 | 235 | 1,276 | 4,952 | 22,447 | 4,028 | 14,299 | 4,120 | 173 |
| Loyall | 576 | 0 | 0 | 0 | 0 | 0 | 3 | 0 | 3 | 0 | 0 |
| Ludlow | 4,502 | 7 | 1 | 2 | 1 | 3 | 40 | 5 | 30 | 5 | 0 |
| Madisonville | 18,546 | 28 | 0 | 5 | 6 | 17 | 172 | 51 | 92 | 29 | 2 |
| Manchester | 1,261 | 2 | 0 | 0 | 1 | 1 | 22 | 4 | 15 | 3 | 1 |
| Marion | 2,833 | 5 | 0 | 4 | 0 | 1 | 25 | 5 | 18 | 2 | 0 |
| Martin | 533 | 0 | 0 | 0 | 0 | 0 | 0 | 0 | 0 | 0 | 0 |
| Mayfield | 9,648 | 28 | 1 | 7 | 6 | 14 | 319 | 79 | 217 | 23 | 0 |
| Maysville | 8,650 | 18 | 1 | 5 | 6 | 6 | 281 | 72 | 187 | 22 | 0 |
| McKee | 770 | 1 | 0 | 0 | 1 | 0 | 3 | 0 | 2 | 1 | 0 |
| Meadow Vale | 765 | 0 | 0 | 0 | 0 | 0 | 3 | 0 | 3 | 0 | 0 |
| Middlesboro | 8,762 | 22 | 0 | 6 | 0 | 16 | 279 | 41 | 221 | 17 | 4 |
| Middletown | 7,930 | 9 | 0 | 1 | 4 | 4 | 261 | 26 | 211 | 24 | 0 |
| Millersburg | 785 | 0 | 0 | 0 | 0 | 0 | 7 | 1 | 5 | 1 | 0 |
| Monticello | 5,880 | 9 | 0 | 1 | 1 | 7 | 75 | 17 | 44 | 14 | 0 |
| Morehead | 7,673 | 11 | 1 | 6 | 0 | 4 | 175 | 12 | 149 | 14 | 1 |
| Morganfield | 3,371 | 1 | 0 | 0 | 1 | 0 | 23 | 5 | 13 | 5 | 0 |
| Morgantown | 2,366 | 2 | 0 | 1 | 1 | 0 | 10 | 2 | 2 | 6 | 0 |
| Mount Sterling | 7,281 | 6 | 0 | 1 | 0 | 5 | 146 | 21 | 111 | 14 | 0 |
| Mount Vernon | 2,366 | 13 | 0 | 3 | 3 | 7 | 16 | 5 | 9 | 2 | 1 |
| Mount Washington | 15,048 | 5 | 0 | 0 | 2 | 3 | 114 | 9 | 86 | 19 | 0 |
| Muldraugh | 985 | 1 | 0 | 1 | 0 | 0 | 15 | 3 | 7 | 5 | 0 |
| Munfordville | 1,665 | 5 | 0 | 0 | 0 | 5 | 7 | 2 | 3 | 2 | 0 |
| Murray | 19,605 | 26 | 1 | 7 | 5 | 13 | 325 | 53 | 254 | 18 | 1 |
| New Haven | 904 | 0 | 0 | 0 | 0 | 0 | 0 | 0 | 0 | 0 | 0 |
| Newport | 14,851 | 36 | 0 | 10 | 14 | 12 | 351 | 38 | 276 | 37 | 1 |
| Nicholasville | 31,184 | 35 | 0 | 10 | 8 | 17 | 652 | 90 | 513 | 49 | 0 |
| Northfield | 1,055 | 0 | 0 | 0 | 0 | 0 | 10 | 2 | 8 | 0 | 0 |
| Oak Grove | 7,355 | 27 | 1 | 6 | 10 | 10 | 222 | 24 | 175 | 23 | 1 |
| Olive Hill | 1,524 | 0 | 0 | 0 | 0 | 0 | 12 | 3 | 6 | 3 | 1 |
| Owensboro | 60,636 | 147 | 1 | 39 | 34 | 73 | 2,259 | 355 | 1,621 | 283 | 10 |
| Owenton | 1,546 | 0 | 0 | 0 | 0 | 0 | 4 | 2 | 2 | 0 | 0 |
| Owingsville | 1,569 | 1 | 0 | 0 | 0 | 1 | 3 | 2 | 0 | 1 | 0 |
| Paducah | 24,873 | 79 | 4 | 25 | 9 | 41 | 776 | 69 | 627 | 80 | 5 |
| Paintsville | 3,897 | 2 | 0 | 0 | 1 | 1 | 12 | 4 | 3 | 5 | 0 |
| Paris | 9,710 | 15 | 0 | 2 | 2 | 11 | 164 | 23 | 132 | 9 | 0 |
| Park Hills | 2,996 | 1 | 0 | 0 | 0 | 1 | 23 | 3 | 16 | 4 | 1 |
| Pembroke | 892 | 0 | 0 | 0 | 0 | 0 | 4 | 0 | 3 | 1 | 1 |
| Perryville | 763 | 0 | 0 | 0 | 0 | 0 | 0 | 0 | 0 | 0 | 0 |
| Pewee Valley | 1,588 | 2 | 0 | 0 | 0 | 2 | 1 | 1 | 0 | 0 | 0 |
| Pikeville | 6,378 | 11 | 0 | 1 | 1 | 9 | 192 | 63 | 116 | 13 | 0 |
| Pineville | 1,670 | 0 | 0 | 0 | 0 | 0 | 23 | 8 | 14 | 1 | 0 |
| Pioneer Village | 3,003 | 0 | 0 | 0 | 0 | 0 | 9 | 4 | 3 | 2 | 0 |
| Pippa Passes | 611 | 0 | 0 | 0 | 0 | 0 | 1 | 0 | 0 | 1 | 0 |
| Prestonsburg | 3,424 | 5 | 0 | 0 | 1 | 4 | 38 | 8 | 21 | 9 | 1 |
| Princeton | 6,036 | 10 | 0 | 1 | 1 | 8 | 121 | 27 | 81 | 13 | 0 |
| Prospect | 4,941 | 0 | 0 | 0 | 0 | 0 | 23 | 3 | 17 | 3 | 0 |

# Table 8. Offenses Known to Law Enforcement, by Selected State and City, 2021—Continued

(Number.)

| State/city | Population | Violent crime | Murder and nonnegligent manslaughter | Rape | Robbery | Aggravated assault | Property crime | Burglary | Larceny-theft | Motor vehicle theft | Arson |
|---|---|---|---|---|---|---|---|---|---|---|---|
| Providence | 2,967 | 2 | 0 | 0 | 0 | 2 | 9 | 4 | 3 | 2 | 0 |
| Raceland | 2,331 | 0 | 0 | 0 | 0 | 0 | 2 | 0 | 2 | 0 | 0 |
| Radcliff | 22,957 | 65 | 5 | 11 | 16 | 33 | 487 | 100 | 319 | 68 | 3 |
| Ravenna | 552 | 0 | 0 | 0 | 0 | 0 | 3 | 0 | 2 | 1 | 0 |
| Richmond | 37,354 | 56 | 4 | 11 | 14 | 27 | 780 | 133 | 544 | 103 | 7 |
| Russell | 3,183 | 0 | 0 | 0 | 0 | 0 | 32 | 9 | 22 | 1 | 0 |
| Russell Springs | 2,671 | 5 | 0 | 2 | 0 | 3 | 35 | 8 | 21 | 6 | 0 |
| Russellville | 7,190 | 20 | 0 | 5 | 1 | 14 | 219 | 33 | 166 | 20 | 1 |
| Sadieville | 378 | 0 | 0 | 0 | 0 | 0 | 2 | 1 | 1 | 0 | 0 |
| Salyersville | 1,617 | 1 | 0 | 0 | 0 | 1 | 3 | 0 | 2 | 1 | 0 |
| Science Hill | 693 | 0 | 0 | 0 | 0 | 0 | 1 | 0 | 1 | 0 | 0 |
| Scottsville | 4,579 | 11 | 0 | 0 | 2 | 9 | 122 | 29 | 76 | 17 | 3 |
| Sebree | 1,516 | 0 | 0 | 0 | 0 | 0 | 3 | 0 | 3 | 0 | 0 |
| Shelbyville | 17,065 | 20 | 2 | 2 | 5 | 11 | 225 | 40 | 160 | 25 | 0 |
| Shepherdsville | 12,416 | 25 | 0 | 7 | 4 | 14 | 249 | 42 | 160 | 47 | 3 |
| Shively | 15,732 | 72 | 9 | 1 | 37 | 25 | 481 | 68 | 267 | 146 | 0 |
| Simpsonville | 3,014 | 6 | 0 | 1 | 4 | 1 | 71 | 6 | 55 | 10 | 0 |
| Smiths Grove | 827 | 1 | 0 | 0 | 0 | 1 | 19 | 2 | 15 | 2 | 0 |
| Somerset | 11,889 | 22 | 0 | 4 | 3 | 15 | 242 | 63 | 138 | 41 | 1 |
| Southgate | 4,073 | 4 | 0 | 1 | 0 | 3 | 18 | 2 | 14 | 2 | 0 |
| South Shore | 1,042 | 0 | 0 | 0 | 0 | 0 | 4 | 0 | 4 | 0 | 0 |
| Springfield | 3,006 | 5 | 0 | 0 | 1 | 4 | 22 | 8 | 11 | 3 | 0 |
| Stamping Ground | 840 | 0 | 0 | 0 | 0 | 0 | 2 | 2 | 0 | 0 | 0 |
| Stanford | 3,634 | 0 | 0 | 0 | 0 | 0 | 22 | 2 | 14 | 6 | 0 |
| Stanton | 2,660 | 2 | 0 | 0 | 1 | 1 | 27 | 4 | 15 | 8 | 1 |
| St. Matthews | 18,038 | 34 | 1 | 5 | 17 | 11 | 813 | 50 | 698 | 65 | 0 |
| Strathmoor Village | 662 | 0 | 0 | 0 | 0 | 0 | 3 | 1 | 1 | 1 | 0 |
| Sturgis | 1,782 | 0 | 0 | 0 | 0 | 0 | 6 | 0 | 6 | 0 | 0 |
| Taylor Mill | 6,837 | 4 | 0 | 0 | 0 | 4 | 19 | 3 | 11 | 5 | 0 |
| Taylorsville | 1,335 | 2 | 0 | 0 | 0 | 2 | 12 | 5 | 6 | 1 | 1 |
| Tompkinsville | 2,217 | 3 | 0 | 0 | 0 | 3 | 10 | 3 | 1 | 6 | 0 |
| Trenton | 377 | 0 | 0 | 0 | 0 | 0 | 0 | 0 | 0 | 0 | 0 |
| Uniontown | 923 | 0 | 0 | 0 | 0 | 0 | 0 | 0 | 0 | 0 | 0 |
| Vanceburg | 1,392 | 0 | 0 | 0 | 0 | 0 | 3 | 1 | 0 | 2 | 0 |
| Versailles | 27,051 | 12 | 0 | 4 | 4 | 4 | 244 | 45 | 171 | 28 | 1 |
| Villa Hills | 7,498 | 7 | 0 | 2 | 1 | 4 | 72 | 7 | 56 | 9 | 0 |
| Vine Grove | 6,712 | 9 | 0 | 4 | 1 | 4 | 42 | 11 | 25 | 6 | 0 |
| Warsaw | 1,677 | 7 | 0 | 1 | 2 | 4 | 24 | 6 | 18 | 0 | 1 |
| Wayland | 368 | 0 | 0 | 0 | 0 | 0 | 1 | 1 | 0 | 0 | 0 |
| West Buechel | 1,277 | 9 | 0 | 1 | 5 | 3 | 86 | 8 | 57 | 21 | 0 |
| West Liberty | 3,418 | 1 | 0 | 1 | 0 | 0 | 6 | 2 | 3 | 1 | 0 |
| West Point | 870 | 1 | 0 | 0 | 0 | 1 | 7 | 0 | 3 | 4 | 0 |
| Wheelwright | 450 | 0 | 0 | 0 | 0 | 0 | 0 | 0 | 0 | 0 | 0 |
| Whitesburg | 1,784 | 0 | 0 | 0 | 0 | 0 | 0 | 0 | 0 | 0 | 0 |
| Wilder | 3,063 | 2 | 0 | 0 | 0 | 2 | 41 | 7 | 31 | 3 | 0 |
| Williamsburg | 5,408 | 16 | 1 | 2 | 3 | 10 | 45 | 12 | 28 | 5 | 0 |
| Williamstown | 3,941 | 1 | 0 | 1 | 0 | 0 | 30 | 6 | 22 | 2 | 0 |
| Wilmore | 6,388 | 2 | 0 | 2 | 0 | 0 | 47 | 14 | 30 | 3 | 0 |
| Winchester | 18,689 | 22 | 2 | 6 | 2 | 12 | 624 | 107 | 448 | 69 | 1 |
| Windy Hills | 2,469 | 0 | 0 | 0 | 0 | 0 | 0 | 0 | 0 | 0 | 0 |
| Woodburn | 377 | 0 | 0 | 0 | 0 | 0 | 0 | 0 | 0 | 0 | 0 |
| Woodlawn Park | 970 | 0 | 0 | 0 | 0 | 0 | 2 | 0 | 2 | 0 | 0 |
| Worthington | 1,477 | 0 | 0 | 0 | 0 | 0 | 0 | 0 | 0 | 0 | 0 |
| **LOUISIANA** | | | | | | | | | | | |
| Abbeville | 11,898 | 101 | 2 | 2 | 6 | 91 | 254 | 36 | 189 | 29 | 0 |
| Alexandria | 45,343 | 842 | 21 | 55 | 91 | 675 | 3,271 | 1,022 | 1,962 | 287 | 3 |
| Arnaudville | 1,040 | 2 | 0 | 0 | 0 | 2 | 5 | 1 | 4 | 0 | 0 |
| Baker | 12,931 | 0 | 0 | 0 | 0 | 0 | 0 | 0 | 0 | 0 | 0 |
| Basile | 1,788 | 9 | 0 | 0 | 0 | 9 | 0 | 0 | 0 | 0 | 0 |
| Bastrop | 9,543 | 130 | 8 | 1 | 7 | 114 | 609 | 135 | 442 | 32 | 7 |
| Baton Rouge | 218,060 | 2,642 | 88 | 116 | 309 | 2,129 | 9,610 | 2,994 | 5,367 | 1,249 | 12 |
| Bernice | 1,580 | 3 | 0 | 0 | 0 | 3 | 6 | 2 | 4 | 0 | 0 |
| Blanchard | 3,137 | 0 | 0 | 0 | 0 | 0 | 18 | 2 | 13 | 3 | 0 |
| Bogalusa | 11,334 | 154 | 5 | 9 | 8 | 132 | 395 | 86 | 269 | 40 | 2 |
| Bossier City | 68,879 | 659 | 5 | 38 | 73 | 543 | 2,999 | 349 | 2,391 | 259 | 4 |
| Broussard | 13,667 | 27 | 2 | 1 | 2 | 22 | 252 | 47 | 193 | 12 | 1 |
| Church Point | 4,344 | 6 | 0 | 0 | 1 | 5 | 26 | 4 | 16 | 6 | 0 |
| Clinton | 1,472 | 11 | 0 | 0 | 0 | 11 | 3 | 0 | 3 | 0 | 0 |
| De Ridder | 10,512 | 40 | 0 | 1 | 1 | 38 | 168 | 26 | 133 | 9 | 1 |
| Dixie Inn | 265 | 6 | 0 | 0 | 0 | 6 | 4 | 0 | 3 | 1 | 0 |
| Erath | 2,022 | 9 | 0 | 3 | 0 | 6 | 15 | 1 | 11 | 3 | 0 |
| Fisher | 215 | 0 | 0 | 0 | 0 | 0 | 0 | 0 | 0 | 0 | 0 |
| Golden Meadow | 1,919 | 9 | 0 | 0 | 0 | 9 | 72 | 19 | 51 | 2 | 0 |
| Gonzales | 11,399 | 65 | 1 | 1 | 4 | 59 | 851 | 38 | 778 | 35 | 1 |
| Gramercy | 3,160 | 12 | 0 | 0 | 0 | 12 | 61 | 7 | 49 | 5 | 0 |
| Greenwood | 3,074 | 9 | 0 | 0 | 3 | 6 | 47 | 1 | 40 | 6 | 0 |
| Gretna | 17,603 | 119 | 1 | 5 | 13 | 100 | 508 | 65 | 393 | 50 | 1 |
| Hammond | 21,544 | 269 | 5 | 9 | 16 | 239 | 1,214 | 157 | 947 | 110 | 1 |
| Harahan | 9,243 | 30 | 1 | 2 | 3 | 24 | 59 | 12 | 39 | 8 | 0 |
| Heflin | 222 | 0 | 0 | 0 | 0 | 0 | 0 | 0 | 0 | 0 | 0 |
| Houma | 32,351 | 282 | 20 | 0 | 17 | 245 | 1,262 | 227 | 959 | 76 | 5 |
| Iowa | 3,121 | 52 | 0 | 0 | 1 | 51 | 72 | 12 | 54 | 6 | 0 |

## Table 8. Offenses Known to Law Enforcement, by Selected State and City, 2021—Continued

(Number.)

| State/city | Population | Violent crime | Murder and nonnegligent manslaughter | Rape | Robbery | Aggravated assault | Property crime | Burglary | Larceny-theft | Motor vehicle theft | Arson |
|---|---|---|---|---|---|---|---|---|---|---|---|
| Jennings | 9,592 | 2 | 0 | 0 | 0 | 2 | 0 | 0 | 0 | 0 | 0 |
| Kenner | 66,250 | 273 | 8 | 11 | 31 | 223 | 1,478 | 142 | 1,184 | 152 | 4 |
| Krotz Springs | 1,153 | 11 | 1 | 1 | 1 | 8 | 20 | 4 | 15 | 1 | 1 |
| Lake Charles | 79,053 | 380 | 9 | 28 | 36 | 307 | 1,958 | 405 | 1,355 | 198 | 4 |
| Lutcher | 3,088 | 4 | 0 | 0 | 0 | 4 | 19 | 1 | 18 | 0 | 0 |
| Mansfield | 4,544 | 24 | 1 | 0 | 0 | 23 | 3 | 1 | 2 | 0 | 0 |
| Marion | 737 | 0 | 0 | 0 | 0 | 0 | 1 | 0 | 1 | 0 | 0 |
| Marksville | 5,230 | 79 | 1 | 3 | 2 | 73 | 275 | 44 | 219 | 12 | 0 |
| Monroe | 46,808 | 1,244 | 19 | 9 | 111 | 1,105 | 2,655 | 524 | 1,939 | 192 | 3 |
| Morgan City | 10,343 | 125 | 0 | 9 | 6 | 110 | 353 | 91 | 237 | 25 | 4 |
| Opelousas | 15,457 | 291 | 5 | 5 | 17 | 264 | 1,012 | 236 | 704 | 72 | 4 |
| Patterson | 5,616 | 41 | 0 | 2 | 0 | 39 | 53 | 17 | 31 | 5 | 2 |
| Pearl River | 2,638 | 12 | 0 | 1 | 0 | 11 | 32 | 6 | 22 | 4 | 0 |
| Plain Dealing | 927 | 0 | 0 | 0 | 0 | 0 | 0 | 0 | 0 | 0 | 0 |
| Ponchatoula | 7,648 | 40 | 0 | 3 | 1 | 36 | 207 | 21 | 170 | 16 | 0 |
| Port Allen | 4,676 | 45 | 0 | 2 | 4 | 39 | 89 | 11 | 74 | 4 | 0 |
| Rayne | 7,987 | 5 | 0 | 0 | 0 | 5 | 39 | 2 | 34 | 3 | 0 |
| Rayville | 3,411 | 8 | 0 | 2 | 0 | 6 | 19 | 2 | 13 | 4 | 0 |
| Ruston | 21,888 | 129 | 4 | 8 | 10 | 107 | 684 | 132 | 509 | 43 | 2 |
| Sibley | 1,149 | 0 | 0 | 0 | 0 | 0 | 2 | 1 | 0 | 1 | 0 |
| Slidell | 27,561 | 81 | 4 | 2 | 10 | 65 | 681 | 65 | 563 | 53 | 0 |
| Sulphur | 20,097 | 58 | 1 | 8 | 5 | 44 | 736 | 144 | 533 | 59 | 1 |
| Tallulah | 6,382 | 52 | 3 | 0 | 3 | 46 | 45 | 7 | 31 | 7 | 0 |
| Thibodaux | 14,402 | 71 | 1 | 3 | 3 | 64 | 378 | 44 | 309 | 25 | 3 |
| Vidalia | 3,611 | 18 | 1 | 0 | 3 | 14 | 75 | 11 | 60 | 4 | 0 |
| Vinton | 3,192 | 30 | 0 | 3 | 3 | 24 | 97 | 23 | 64 | 10 | 0 |
| Walker | 6,325 | 31 | 0 | 6 | 2 | 23 | 244 | 25 | 209 | 10 | 1 |
| Westlake | 4,906 | 12 | 0 | 1 | 1 | 10 | 101 | 25 | 72 | 4 | 0 |
| West Monroe | 11,989 | 236 | 2 | 19 | 15 | 200 | 803 | 170 | 589 | 44 | 2 |
| Westwego | 8,274 | 58 | 3 | 0 | 2 | 53 | 127 | 24 | 82 | 21 | 2 |
| Zachary | 18,774 | 101 | 4 | 8 | 5 | 84 | 537 | 85 | 402 | 50 | 4 |
| **MAINE** | | | | | | | | | | | |
| Ashland | 1,206 | 2 | 0 | 0 | 0 | 2 | 2 | 0 | 2 | 0 | 0 |
| Auburn | 23,446 | 51 | 0 | 13 | 9 | 29 | 652 | 61 | 563 | 28 | 3 |
| Augusta | 18,713 | 58 | 1 | 18 | 10 | 29 | 564 | 61 | 471 | 32 | 1 |
| Baileyville | 1,450 | 3 | 0 | 1 | 0 | 2 | 3 | 2 | 1 | 0 | 0 |
| Bangor | 31,898 | 64 | 0 | 8 | 24 | 32 | 1,450 | 134 | 1,262 | 54 | 7 |
| Bar Harbor | 7,752 | 8 | 0 | 4 | 0 | 4 | 29 | 0 | 28 | 1 | 0 |
| Bath | 8,320 | 10 | 0 | 1 | 1 | 8 | 67 | 2 | 62 | 3 | 0 |
| Belfast | 6,712 | 0 | 0 | 0 | 0 | 0 | 47 | 4 | 42 | 1 | 0 |
| Berwick | 8,074 | 5 | 0 | 2 | 0 | 3 | 70 | 4 | 53 | 13 | 0 |
| Biddeford | 21,523 | 91 | 1 | 23 | 7 | 60 | 517 | 44 | 452 | 21 | 4 |
| Boothbay Harbor | 2,232 | 1 | 0 | 1 | 0 | 0 | 8 | 1 | 7 | 0 | 0 |
| Brewer | 8,897 | 9 | 0 | 1 | 4 | 4 | 256 | 10 | 238 | 8 | 0 |
| Bridgton | 5,539 | 5 | 0 | 2 | 2 | 1 | 49 | 8 | 35 | 6 | 0 |
| Brunswick | 20,656 | 18 | 0 | 5 | 1 | 12 | 156 | 8 | 142 | 6 | 0 |
| Bucksport | 4,917 | 4 | 0 | 1 | 0 | 3 | 40 | 8 | 29 | 3 | 0 |
| Buxton | 8,402 | 10 | 0 | 2 | 0 | 8 | 75 | 13 | 58 | 4 | 0 |
| Calais | 3,017 | 4 | 0 | 1 | 0 | 3 | 25 | 3 | 21 | 1 | 0 |
| Camden | 4,802 | 1 | 0 | 1 | 0 | 0 | 24 | 5 | 18 | 1 | 0 |
| Cape Elizabeth | 9,356 | 4 | 0 | 1 | 0 | 3 | 6 | 0 | 6 | 0 | 0 |
| Caribou | 7,570 | 3 | 0 | 1 | 0 | 2 | 53 | 4 | 43 | 6 | 1 |
| Carrabassett Valley | 789 | 1 | 0 | 1 | 0 | 0 | 5 | 0 | 4 | 1 | 0 |
| Clinton | 3,358 | 0 | 0 | 0 | 0 | 0 | 13 | 2 | 11 | 0 | 0 |
| Cumberland | 8,415 | 3 | 0 | 2 | 0 | 1 | 25 | 3 | 20 | 2 | 1 |
| Damariscotta | 2,153 | 1 | 0 | 0 | 0 | 1 | 23 | 1 | 20 | 2 | 0 |
| Dexter | 3,685 | 2 | 0 | 0 | 0 | 2 | 26 | 3 | 22 | 1 | 0 |
| Dover-Foxcroft | 4,073 | 2 | 0 | 1 | 1 | 0 | 28 | 3 | 23 | 2 | 0 |
| East Millinocket | 7,139 | 3 | 0 | 0 | 0 | 3 | 94 | 14 | 74 | 6 | 1 |
| Eliot | 7,212 | 1 | 0 | 0 | 0 | 1 | 22 | 1 | 19 | 2 | 0 |
| Ellsworth | 8,302 | 7 | 0 | 5 | 0 | 2 | 154 | 9 | 132 | 13 | 1 |
| Fairfield | 6,534 | 11 | 0 | 3 | 1 | 7 | 134 | 22 | 107 | 5 | 1 |
| Falmouth | 12,573 | 1 | 0 | 0 | 1 | 0 | 68 | 4 | 60 | 4 | 2 |
| Farmington | 7,621 | 10 | 0 | 5 | 0 | 5 | 68 | 4 | 61 | 3 | 0 |
| Fort Fairfield | 3,258 | 2 | 0 | 0 | 0 | 2 | 22 | 2 | 14 | 6 | 0 |
| Fort Kent | 3,778 | 0 | 0 | 0 | 0 | 0 | 12 | 2 | 8 | 2 | 0 |
| Freeport | 8,713 | 1 | 0 | 0 | 0 | 1 | 74 | 2 | 71 | 1 | 1 |
| Fryeburg | 3,435 | 6 | 1 | 3 | 0 | 2 | 35 | 3 | 31 | 1 | 0 |
| Gardiner | 5,675 | 4 | 0 | 3 | 1 | 0 | 52 | 4 | 42 | 6 | 0 |
| Gorham | 18,130 | 5 | 0 | 3 | 0 | 2 | 70 | 9 | 58 | 3 | 2 |
| Gouldsboro | 1,744 | 0 | 0 | 0 | 0 | 0 | 0 | 0 | 0 | 0 | 0 |
| Greenville | 1,626 | 0 | 0 | 0 | 0 | 0 | 30 | 0 | 29 | 1 | 0 |
| Hallowell | 2,386 | 0 | 0 | 0 | 0 | 0 | 11 | 0 | 11 | 0 | 0 |
| Hampden | 7,537 | 0 | 0 | 0 | 0 | 0 | 48 | 9 | 38 | 1 | 0 |
| Holden | 3,124 | 0 | 0 | 0 | 0 | 0 | 24 | 2 | 21 | 1 | 0 |
| Houlton | 5,732 | 10 | 0 | 3 | 0 | 7 | 199 | 16 | 172 | 11 | 0 |
| Islesboro | 562 | 0 | 0 | 0 | 0 | 0 | 0 | 0 | 0 | 0 | 0 |
| Jay | 4,575 | 6 | 0 | 1 | 0 | 5 | 36 | 2 | 32 | 2 | 0 |
| Kennebunk | 11,799 | 6 | 0 | 5 | 0 | 1 | 53 | 1 | 51 | 1 | 0 |
| Kennebunkport | 3,692 | 2 | 0 | 1 | 0 | 1 | 17 | 2 | 15 | 0 | 0 |
| Kittery | 9,915 | 7 | 0 | 3 | 2 | 2 | 93 | 2 | 88 | 3 | 0 |
| Lewiston | 36,191 | 95 | 0 | 27 | 15 | 53 | 592 | 78 | 480 | 34 | 3 |

# Table 8. Offenses Known to Law Enforcement, by Selected State and City, 2021—Continued

(Number.)

| State/city | Population | Violent crime | Murder and nonnegligent manslaughter | Rape | Robbery | Aggravated assault | Property crime | Burglary | Larceny-theft | Motor vehicle theft | Arson |
|---|---|---|---|---|---|---|---|---|---|---|---|
| Limestone | 2,150 | 1 | 0 | 0 | 0 | 1 | 6 | 2 | 2 | 2 | 0 |
| Lincoln | 4,862 | 6 | 1 | 1 | 1 | 3 | 122 | 17 | 104 | 1 | 0 |
| Lisbon | 9,057 | 5 | 0 | 1 | 0 | 4 | 54 | 10 | 43 | 1 | 0 |
| Livermore Falls | 3,178 | 2 | 0 | 0 | 0 | 2 | 23 | 3 | 15 | 5 | 0 |
| Machias | 1,811 | 1 | 0 | 1 | 0 | 0 | 3 | 0 | 3 | 0 | 0 |
| Madawaska | 3,686 | 3 | 0 | 1 | 0 | 2 | 65 | 5 | 58 | 2 | 0 |
| Mechanic Falls | 2,977 | 2 | 0 | 2 | 0 | 0 | 17 | 6 | 10 | 1 | 0 |
| Mexico | 2,631 | 5 | 0 | 2 | 0 | 3 | 83 | 12 | 69 | 2 | 0 |
| Milbridge | 1,296 | 0 | 0 | 0 | 0 | 0 | 0 | 0 | 0 | 0 | 0 |
| Milo | 2,311 | 1 | 0 | 0 | 0 | 1 | 39 | 12 | 26 | 1 | 0 |
| Newport | 3,245 | 0 | 0 | 0 | 0 | 0 | 61 | 2 | 56 | 3 | 0 |
| North Berwick | 4,762 | 2 | 0 | 2 | 0 | 0 | 21 | 3 | 16 | 2 | 0 |
| Norway | 4,988 | 1 | 0 | 0 | 0 | 1 | 56 | 4 | 48 | 4 | 0 |
| Oakland | 6,351 | 3 | 0 | 2 | 0 | 1 | 42 | 6 | 32 | 4 | 0 |
| Ogunquit | 938 | 2 | 0 | 1 | 0 | 1 | 21 | 0 | 19 | 2 | 0 |
| Old Orchard Beach | 9,145 | 20 | 0 | 7 | 1 | 12 | 125 | 13 | 105 | 7 | 1 |
| Old Town | 7,362 | 3 | 1 | 0 | 0 | 2 | 103 | 15 | 87 | 1 | 0 |
| Orono | 10,666 | 3 | 0 | 1 | 0 | 2 | 66 | 8 | 56 | 2 | 0 |
| Oxford | 4,102 | 1 | 0 | 1 | 0 | 0 | 57 | 9 | 47 | 1 | 0 |
| Paris | 5,161 | 3 | 0 | 0 | 0 | 3 | 35 | 7 | 25 | 3 | 0 |
| Phippsburg | 2,281 | 0 | 0 | 0 | 0 | 0 | 3 | 1 | 1 | 1 | 0 |
| Pittsfield | 3,982 | 5 | 0 | 1 | 1 | 3 | 18 | 4 | 13 | 1 | 0 |
| Portland | 66,875 | 152 | 0 | 24 | 20 | 108 | 1,200 | 86 | 1,035 | 79 | 11 |
| Presque Isle | 8,882 | 17 | 0 | 8 | 0 | 9 | 139 | 15 | 112 | 12 | 0 |
| Rangeley | 1,149 | 0 | 0 | 0 | 0 | 0 | 5 | 0 | 5 | 0 | 0 |
| Rockland | 7,172 | 6 | 0 | 3 | 0 | 3 | 81 | 3 | 75 | 3 | 0 |
| Rockport | 3,395 | 0 | 0 | 0 | 0 | 0 | 18 | 3 | 14 | 1 | 0 |
| Rumford | 5,726 | 8 | 0 | 4 | 1 | 3 | 66 | 6 | 59 | 1 | 2 |
| Sabattus | 5,077 | 2 | 0 | 1 | 0 | 1 | 8 | 2 | 5 | 1 | 0 |
| Saco | 20,290 | 32 | 0 | 12 | 3 | 17 | 223 | 24 | 189 | 10 | 3 |
| Sanford | 21,300 | 40 | 0 | 16 | 1 | 23 | 511 | 37 | 446 | 28 | 2 |
| Scarborough | 21,810 | 7 | 0 | 2 | 0 | 5 | 342 | 20 | 319 | 3 | 0 |
| Skowhegan | 8,205 | 13 | 0 | 3 | 6 | 4 | 221 | 16 | 197 | 8 | 0 |
| South Berwick | 7,654 | 5 | 0 | 2 | 1 | 2 | 35 | 6 | 27 | 2 | 0 |
| South Portland | 26,048 | 56 | 0 | 15 | 6 | 35 | 352 | 20 | 302 | 30 | 1 |
| Southwest Harbor | 1,796 | 0 | 0 | 0 | 0 | 0 | 5 | 1 | 4 | 0 | 0 |
| Thomaston | 2,761 | 1 | 0 | 0 | 0 | 1 | 37 | 1 | 34 | 2 | 0 |
| Topsham | 8,960 | 10 | 0 | 0 | 2 | 8 | 75 | 4 | 66 | 5 | 0 |
| Veazie | 1,815 | 0 | 0 | 0 | 0 | 0 | 13 | 2 | 9 | 2 | 0 |
| Waldoboro | 5,079 | 2 | 0 | 1 | 0 | 1 | 32 | 12 | 20 | 0 | 1 |
| Washburn | 1,519 | 2 | 0 | 0 | 0 | 2 | 4 | 1 | 2 | 1 | 0 |
| Waterville | 16,667 | 35 | 0 | 10 | 9 | 16 | 657 | 58 | 582 | 17 | 0 |
| Wells | 10,950 | 12 | 0 | 5 | 1 | 6 | 107 | 10 | 90 | 7 | 0 |
| Westbrook | 19,451 | 29 | 0 | 5 | 6 | 18 | 208 | 19 | 170 | 19 | 0 |
| Wilton | 3,912 | 8 | 0 | 0 | 0 | 8 | 28 | 3 | 24 | 1 | 0 |
| Windham | 19,118 | 18 | 0 | 7 | 2 | 9 | 104 | 13 | 83 | 8 | 1 |
| Winslow | 7,641 | 13 | 0 | 7 | 0 | 6 | 82 | 8 | 69 | 5 | 1 |
| Winter Harbor | 510 | 1 | 0 | 0 | 0 | 1 | 4 | 0 | 4 | 0 | 0 |
| Winthrop | 6,023 | 6 | 0 | 1 | 1 | 4 | 43 | 7 | 30 | 6 | 0 |
| Wiscasset | 3,750 | 4 | 0 | 1 | 0 | 3 | 22 | 2 | 20 | 0 | 0 |
| Yarmouth | 8,628 | 3 | 0 | 2 | 1 | 0 | 36 | 2 | 34 | 0 | 0 |
| York | 13,413 | 6 | 1 | 1 | 1 | 3 | 98 | 8 | 89 | 1 | 1 |
| **MARYLAND[1]** | | | | | | | | | | | |
| Boonsboro | 3,676 | 5 | 1 | 0 | 0 | 4 | 10 | 3 | 7 | 0 | 0 |
| Bowie | 58,546 | 72 | 1 | 3 | 17 | 51 | 630 | 41 | 537 | 52 | 0 |
| Cumberland | 18,971 | 136 | 4 | 21 | 22 | 89 | 548 | 133 | 386 | 29 | 3 |
| Frostburg | 8,413 | 5 | 0 | 1 | 1 | 3 | 17 | 4 | 12 | 1 | 0 |
| Hagerstown | 39,942 | 293 | 4 | 27 | 90 | 172 | 985 | 271 | 601 | 113 | 2 |
| Oakland | 1,794 | 2 | 0 | 0 | 0 | 2 | 33 | 1 | 31 | 1 | 0 |
| **MASSACHUSETTS** | | | | | | | | | | | |
| Abington | 17,623 | 29 | 0 | 2 | 1 | 26 | 139 | 12 | 111 | 16 | 1 |
| Acton | 23,853 | 8 | 0 | 4 | 0 | 4 | 119 | 16 | 97 | 6 | 1 |
| Acushnet | 10,798 | 11 | 0 | 4 | 1 | 6 | 30 | 3 | 22 | 5 | 1 |
| Adams | 7,904 | 48 | 1 | 6 | 1 | 40 | 89 | 19 | 65 | 5 | 0 |
| Agawam | 28,757 | 97 | 0 | 10 | 6 | 81 | 265 | 69 | 175 | 21 | 3 |
| Amesbury | 17,809 | 20 | 0 | 2 | 3 | 15 | 56 | 6 | 46 | 4 | 0 |
| Amherst | 40,843 | 68 | 0 | 27 | 1 | 40 | 139 | 29 | 99 | 11 | 1 |
| Andover | 37,216 | 7 | 0 | 0 | 0 | 7 | 192 | 37 | 146 | 9 | 1 |
| Aquinnah | 328 | 0 | 0 | 0 | 0 | 0 | 2 | 0 | 2 | 0 | 0 |
| Arlington | 45,767 | 19 | 0 | 1 | 4 | 14 | 135 | 31 | 99 | 5 | 0 |
| Ashburnham | 6,429 | 4 | 0 | 2 | 0 | 2 | 23 | 6 | 16 | 1 | 0 |
| Ashby | 3,242 | 5 | 0 | 3 | 0 | 2 | 20 | 4 | 15 | 1 | 0 |
| Ashfield | 1,718 | 1 | 0 | 0 | 0 | 1 | 10 | 1 | 8 | 1 | 0 |
| Ashland | 18,160 | 14 | 0 | 1 | 2 | 11 | 62 | 10 | 45 | 7 | 0 |
| Athol | 11,802 | 45 | 0 | 7 | 3 | 35 | 109 | 13 | 83 | 13 | 0 |
| Attleboro | 46,007 | 132 | 0 | 15 | 14 | 103 | 583 | 51 | 479 | 53 | 3 |
| Auburn | 16,885 | 25 | 0 | 3 | 3 | 19 | 265 | 24 | 231 | 10 | 2 |
| Avon | 4,631 | 9 | 0 | 0 | 1 | 8 | 122 | 6 | 109 | 7 | 1 |
| Ayer | 8,357 | 16 | 0 | 8 | 0 | 8 | 50 | 9 | 36 | 5 | 0 |
| Barnstable | 44,841 | 197 | 1 | 32 | 10 | 154 | 331 | 65 | 246 | 20 | 3 |
| Barre | 5,637 | 15 | 0 | 2 | 0 | 13 | 17 | 2 | 12 | 3 | 1 |

## Table 8. Offenses Known to Law Enforcement, by Selected State and City, 2021—Continued

(Number.)

| State/city | Population | Violent crime | Murder and nonnegligent manslaughter | Rape | Robbery | Aggravated assault | Property crime | Burglary | Larceny-theft | Motor vehicle theft | Arson |
|---|---|---|---|---|---|---|---|---|---|---|---|
| Becket | 1,700 | 2 | 0 | 1 | 0 | 1 | 5 | 2 | 3 | 0 | 0 |
| Bedford | 14,241 | 4 | 0 | 2 | 0 | 2 | 61 | 10 | 49 | 2 | 0 |
| Belchertown | 15,148 | 21 | 0 | 7 | 1 | 13 | 67 | 12 | 49 | 6 | 0 |
| Bellingham | 17,634 | 32 | 1 | 2 | 1 | 28 | 168 | 8 | 153 | 7 | 1 |
| Belmont | 26,206 | 13 | 1 | 1 | 1 | 10 | 172 | 57 | 110 | 5 | 1 |
| Berkley | 7,007 | 5 | 0 | 2 | 0 | 3 | 11 | 3 | 7 | 1 | 0 |
| Berlin | 3,864 | 2 | 0 | 0 | 0 | 2 | 16 | 1 | 15 | 0 | 0 |
| Bernardston | 2,085 | 3 | 0 | 1 | 0 | 2 | 23 | 4 | 13 | 6 | 0 |
| Beverly | 42,851 | 47 | 0 | 6 | 3 | 38 | 206 | 13 | 178 | 15 | 2 |
| Billerica | 43,644 | 32 | 0 | 3 | 2 | 27 | 178 | 24 | 131 | 23 | 2 |
| Blackstone | 9,304 | 8 | 0 | 2 | 0 | 6 | 15 | 4 | 10 | 1 | 0 |
| Bolton | 5,579 | 1 | 0 | 0 | 0 | 1 | 27 | 8 | 18 | 1 | 1 |
| Boston | 704,758 | 3,885 | 36 | 223 | 771 | 2,855 | 11,614 | 1,342 | 9,118 | 1,154 | 26 |
| Bourne | 19,904 | 46 | 0 | 6 | 2 | 38 | 176 | 44 | 113 | 19 | 0 |
| Boxborough | 5,880 | 4 | 0 | 1 | 0 | 3 | 15 | 3 | 12 | 0 | 0 |
| Boxford | 8,436 | 0 | 0 | 0 | 0 | 0 | 13 | 0 | 11 | 2 | 0 |
| Boylston | 4,806 | 1 | 0 | 0 | 0 | 1 | 19 | 5 | 14 | 0 | 0 |
| Braintree | 37,643 | 59 | 0 | 3 | 2 | 54 | 341 | 17 | 290 | 34 | 0 |
| Brewster | 9,843 | 11 | 0 | 3 | 2 | 6 | 55 | 16 | 38 | 1 | 0 |
| Bridgewater | 8,446 | 26 | 0 | 7 | 1 | 18 | 54 | 9 | 39 | 6 | 0 |
| Brimfield | 3,722 | 1 | 0 | 0 | 0 | 1 | 12 | 1 | 7 | 4 | 1 |
| Brockton | 100,516 | 675 | 8 | 63 | 96 | 508 | 1,666 | 160 | 1,037 | 469 | 14 |
| Brookfield | 3,473 | 5 | 0 | 0 | 0 | 5 | 11 | 0 | 9 | 2 | 1 |
| Brookline | 59,748 | 39 | 0 | 1 | 14 | 24 | 564 | 61 | 474 | 29 | 0 |
| Burlington | 29,087 | 35 | 0 | 12 | 1 | 22 | 277 | 18 | 246 | 13 | 2 |
| Cambridge | 121,699 | 372 | 1 | 34 | 64 | 273 | 2,364 | 205 | 2,040 | 119 | 5 |
| Canton | 24,570 | 75 | 0 | 8 | 3 | 64 | 141 | 11 | 120 | 10 | 0 |
| Carlisle | 5,312 | 2 | 0 | 1 | 0 | 1 | 25 | 2 | 22 | 1 | 0 |
| Carver | 12,347 | 11 | 0 | 3 | 0 | 8 | 63 | 9 | 51 | 3 | 0 |
| Charlton | 13,881 | 8 | 1 | 1 | 0 | 6 | 37 | 6 | 28 | 3 | 0 |
| Chatham | 6,031 | 4 | 0 | 2 | 0 | 2 | 51 | 5 | 46 | 0 | 0 |
| Chelmsford | 35,985 | 36 | 0 | 7 | 2 | 27 | 238 | 19 | 211 | 8 | 0 |
| Chelsea | 39,971 | 291 | 2 | 31 | 68 | 190 | 659 | 81 | 522 | 56 | 4 |
| Cheshire | 3,093 | 0 | 0 | 0 | 0 | 0 | 2 | 1 | 1 | 0 | 0 |
| Chicopee | 55,332 | 267 | 3 | 32 | 30 | 202 | 1,009 | 125 | 768 | 116 | 2 |
| Chilmark | 948 | 3 | 0 | 1 | 0 | 2 | 4 | 0 | 4 | 0 | 0 |
| Clinton | 14,099 | 4 | 0 | 0 | 0 | 4 | 7 | 0 | 6 | 1 | 0 |
| Cohasset | 8,738 | 5 | 0 | 1 | 0 | 4 | 43 | 9 | 34 | 0 | 0 |
| Concord | 19,025 | 12 | 0 | 2 | 0 | 10 | 82 | 10 | 72 | 0 | 0 |
| Dalton | 6,452 | 20 | 0 | 3 | 1 | 16 | 27 | 9 | 15 | 3 | 1 |
| Danvers | 27,904 | 48 | 0 | 2 | 4 | 42 | 253 | 19 | 218 | 16 | 1 |
| Dartmouth | 34,158 | 57 | 0 | 6 | 8 | 43 | 408 | 39 | 359 | 10 | 0 |
| Dedham | 25,699 | 17 | 0 | 0 | 4 | 13 | 298 | 15 | 265 | 18 | 0 |
| Deerfield | 5,041 | 11 | 0 | 1 | 0 | 10 | 28 | 8 | 20 | 0 | 0 |
| Dennis | 13,971 | 62 | 0 | 14 | 1 | 47 | 172 | 43 | 126 | 3 | 1 |
| Douglas | 9,259 | 8 | 0 | 3 | 0 | 5 | 18 | 6 | 7 | 5 | 0 |
| Dover | 6,246 | 0 | 0 | 0 | 0 | 0 | 8 | 0 | 8 | 0 | 0 |
| Dracut | 31,879 | 58 | 0 | 6 | 3 | 49 | 147 | 22 | 118 | 7 | 4 |
| Dudley | 11,778 | 24 | 0 | 2 | 0 | 22 | 31 | 15 | 16 | 0 | 1 |
| Dunstable | 3,454 | 1 | 0 | 0 | 0 | 1 | 4 | 0 | 4 | 0 | 1 |
| Duxbury | 16,780 | 10 | 0 | 3 | 0 | 7 | 35 | 3 | 30 | 2 | 0 |
| East Bridgewater | 15,324 | 28 | 1 | 1 | 0 | 26 | 55 | 8 | 39 | 8 | 1 |
| East Brookfield | 2,215 | 3 | 0 | 0 | 0 | 3 | 6 | 0 | 3 | 3 | 0 |
| Eastham | 4,937 | 14 | 0 | 2 | 0 | 12 | 69 | 5 | 61 | 3 | 0 |
| Easthampton | 15,720 | 21 | 0 | 5 | 0 | 16 | 110 | 6 | 96 | 8 | 0 |
| East Longmeadow | 16,286 | 29 | 0 | 11 | 3 | 15 | 174 | 36 | 117 | 21 | 0 |
| Easton | 25,509 | 36 | 0 | 6 | 4 | 26 | 131 | 12 | 107 | 12 | 0 |
| Edgartown | 4,470 | 26 | 0 | 1 | 0 | 25 | 39 | 2 | 35 | 2 | 0 |
| Erving | 1,744 | 4 | 0 | 1 | 0 | 3 | 11 | 2 | 8 | 1 | 0 |
| Essex | 3,888 | 2 | 0 | 1 | 0 | 1 | 9 | 1 | 8 | 0 | 0 |
| Everett | 46,959 | 142 | 1 | 24 | 12 | 105 | 570 | 68 | 416 | 86 | 0 |
| Fairhaven | 16,257 | 42 | 0 | 7 | 4 | 31 | 136 | 7 | 113 | 16 | 0 |
| Fall River | 90,618 | 853 | 3 | 53 | 90 | 707 | 926 | 340 | 464 | 122 | 13 |
| Falmouth | 31,320 | 101 | 1 | 12 | 6 | 82 | 304 | 112 | 176 | 16 | 3 |
| Fitchburg | 40,626 | 188 | 0 | 19 | 12 | 157 | 399 | 55 | 293 | 51 | 3 |
| Foxborough | 18,774 | 43 | 0 | 10 | 2 | 31 | 124 | 7 | 102 | 15 | 0 |
| Framingham | 75,042 | 221 | 1 | 5 | 11 | 204 | 820 | 91 | 652 | 77 | 0 |
| Franklin | 35,425 | 29 | 1 | 0 | 0 | 28 | 60 | 16 | 41 | 3 | 1 |
| Freetown | 9,567 | 16 | 0 | 4 | 0 | 12 | 39 | 10 | 26 | 3 | 0 |
| Gardner | 20,795 | 64 | 0 | 14 | 7 | 43 | 204 | 26 | 164 | 14 | 1 |
| Georgetown | 8,920 | 6 | 0 | 2 | 0 | 4 | 24 | 6 | 17 | 1 | 0 |
| Gill | 1,473 | 2 | 0 | 0 | 0 | 2 | 9 | 0 | 9 | 0 | 0 |
| Gloucester | 30,963 | 50 | 0 | 4 | 2 | 44 | 182 | 22 | 139 | 21 | 1 |
| Goshen | 1,057 | 0 | 0 | 0 | 0 | 0 | 0 | 0 | 0 | 0 | 0 |
| Grafton | 19,347 | 9 | 0 | 0 | 0 | 9 | 26 | 3 | 15 | 8 | 0 |
| Granby | 6,264 | 6 | 0 | 2 | 0 | 4 | 20 | 5 | 14 | 1 | 1 |
| Granville | 1,626 | 2 | 0 | 0 | 0 | 2 | 0 | 0 | 0 | 0 | 0 |
| Great Barrington | 6,964 | 17 | 0 | 5 | 1 | 11 | 54 | 8 | 45 | 1 | 1 |
| Greenfield | 17,222 | 65 | 0 | 17 | 1 | 47 | 334 | 84 | 232 | 18 | 4 |
| Groton | 11,407 | 6 | 0 | 3 | 0 | 3 | 36 | 7 | 26 | 3 | 1 |
| Groveland | 6,967 | 1 | 0 | 0 | 0 | 1 | 10 | 2 | 6 | 2 | 0 |
| Hadley | 5,335 | 30 | 0 | 7 | 1 | 22 | 88 | 3 | 82 | 3 | 0 |
| Halifax | 8,275 | 9 | 0 | 0 | 0 | 9 | 44 | 1 | 41 | 2 | 0 |

# Table 8. Offenses Known to Law Enforcement, by Selected State and City, 2021—Continued

(Number.)

| State/city | Population | Violent crime | Murder and nonnegligent manslaughter | Rape | Robbery | Aggravated assault | Property crime | Burglary | Larceny-theft | Motor vehicle theft | Arson |
|---|---|---|---|---|---|---|---|---|---|---|---|
| Hamilton | 8,165 | 4 | 0 | 0 | 0 | 4 | 23 | 6 | 16 | 1 | 0 |
| Hanover | 15,396 | 5 | 0 | 2 | 0 | 3 | 50 | 7 | 39 | 4 | 0 |
| Hanson | 11,550 | 10 | 0 | 3 | 0 | 7 | 26 | 4 | 20 | 2 | 1 |
| Hardwick | 3,077 | 8 | 0 | 0 | 0 | 8 | 4 | 1 | 3 | 0 | 0 |
| Harvard | 6,681 | 8 | 0 | 5 | 0 | 3 | 19 | 6 | 12 | 1 | 0 |
| Harwich | 12,235 | 19 | 0 | 3 | 0 | 16 | 87 | 23 | 61 | 3 | 1 |
| Hatfield | 3,241 | 8 | 0 | 0 | 0 | 8 | 10 | 1 | 9 | 0 | 0 |
| Haverhill | 64,944 | 376 | 1 | 19 | 12 | 344 | 545 | 127 | 363 | 55 | 3 |
| Hingham | 26,172 | 19 | 0 | 2 | 0 | 17 | 111 | 24 | 83 | 4 | 0 |
| Hinsdale | 1,890 | 6 | 0 | 0 | 0 | 6 | 0 | 0 | 0 | 0 | 0 |
| Holbrook | 11,163 | 44 | 0 | 8 | 5 | 31 | 132 | 18 | 99 | 15 | 1 |
| Holden | 19,605 | 11 | 0 | 2 | 1 | 8 | 29 | 5 | 23 | 1 | 0 |
| Holland | 2,493 | 1 | 0 | 0 | 0 | 1 | 7 | 1 | 5 | 1 | 1 |
| Holliston | 15,138 | 10 | 0 | 3 | 1 | 6 | 57 | 12 | 43 | 2 | 0 |
| Holyoke | 40,326 | 367 | 2 | 17 | 63 | 285 | 1,299 | 156 | 1,041 | 102 | 10 |
| Hopedale | 5,985 | 1 | 0 | 0 | 0 | 1 | 13 | 2 | 8 | 3 | 0 |
| Hopkinton | 19,192 | 13 | 0 | 0 | 0 | 13 | 28 | 2 | 24 | 2 | 0 |
| Hudson | 19,954 | 27 | 0 | 3 | 1 | 23 | 41 | 5 | 31 | 5 | 1 |
| Hull | 11,000 | 54 | 0 | 5 | 2 | 47 | 79 | 16 | 55 | 8 | 0 |
| Ipswich | 14,297 | 15 | 0 | 0 | 0 | 15 | 55 | 18 | 30 | 7 | 0 |
| Kingston | 14,843 | 19 | 0 | 5 | 1 | 13 | 69 | 3 | 62 | 4 | 0 |
| Lakeville | 12,360 | 15 | 0 | 4 | 1 | 10 | 51 | 12 | 32 | 7 | 0 |
| Lancaster | 7,900 | 13 | 0 | 0 | 0 | 13 | 29 | 13 | 15 | 1 | 0 |
| Lanesboro | 2,909 | 6 | 0 | 2 | 0 | 4 | 13 | 2 | 10 | 1 | 0 |
| Lawrence | 81,021 | 360 | 6 | 18 | 43 | 293 | 849 | 62 | 632 | 155 | 5 |
| Lee | 5,598 | 7 | 0 | 1 | 1 | 5 | 74 | 15 | 57 | 2 | 0 |
| Leicester | 11,401 | 16 | 0 | 4 | 0 | 12 | 77 | 7 | 66 | 4 | 1 |
| Lenox | 4,920 | 5 | 0 | 1 | 2 | 2 | 58 | 9 | 48 | 1 | 0 |
| Leominster | 41,965 | 169 | 0 | 18 | 19 | 132 | 676 | 90 | 536 | 50 | 4 |
| Leverett | 1,835 | 1 | 0 | 1 | 0 | 0 | 3 | 0 | 3 | 0 | 0 |
| Lexington | 33,427 | 23 | 0 | 2 | 1 | 20 | 101 | 19 | 78 | 4 | 0 |
| Lincoln | 7,114 | 1 | 0 | 1 | 0 | 0 | 24 | 1 | 20 | 3 | 0 |
| Littleton | 10,480 | 5 | 0 | 2 | 0 | 3 | 38 | 2 | 31 | 5 | 0 |
| Longmeadow | 15,764 | 4 | 0 | 0 | 1 | 3 | 97 | 19 | 65 | 13 | 0 |
| Lowell | 112,230 | 366 | 6 | 16 | 60 | 284 | 1,500 | 198 | 1,117 | 185 | 3 |
| Ludlow | 21,312 | 37 | 0 | 0 | 2 | 35 | 158 | 19 | 125 | 14 | 2 |
| Lunenburg | 12,098 | 9 | 0 | 1 | 0 | 8 | 102 | 17 | 75 | 10 | 0 |
| Lynn | 95,727 | 444 | 1 | 27 | 48 | 368 | 830 | 130 | 573 | 127 | 5 |
| Lynnfield | 13,300 | 11 | 0 | 1 | 0 | 10 | 70 | 2 | 62 | 6 | 0 |
| Malden | 60,433 | 155 | 3 | 10 | 25 | 117 | 714 | 100 | 521 | 93 | 2 |
| Manchester-by-the-Sea | 5,513 | 4 | 0 | 0 | 0 | 4 | 18 | 3 | 13 | 2 | 0 |
| Mansfield | 24,880 | 38 | 0 | 7 | 3 | 28 | 151 | 17 | 121 | 13 | 0 |
| Marblehead | 20,791 | 14 | 0 | 0 | 1 | 13 | 105 | 11 | 86 | 8 | 1 |
| Marion | 5,464 | 4 | 0 | 0 | 0 | 4 | 20 | 1 | 19 | 0 | 0 |
| Marlborough | 39,682 | 143 | 0 | 25 | 9 | 109 | 409 | 47 | 326 | 36 | 3 |
| Marshfield | 27,361 | 26 | 1 | 5 | 0 | 20 | 60 | 9 | 44 | 7 | 2 |
| Mashpee | 14,411 | 45 | 0 | 8 | 1 | 36 | 80 | 11 | 60 | 9 | 0 |
| Mattapoisett | 6,772 | 7 | 0 | 2 | 0 | 5 | 26 | 2 | 23 | 1 | 0 |
| Maynard | 11,508 | 22 | 0 | 4 | 0 | 18 | 38 | 6 | 28 | 4 | 0 |
| Medfield | 13,266 | 13 | 0 | 5 | 1 | 7 | 26 | 6 | 18 | 2 | 0 |
| Medford | 61,819 | 94 | 0 | 10 | 18 | 66 | 518 | 46 | 428 | 44 | 2 |
| Medway | 13,670 | 5 | 0 | 1 | 0 | 4 | 29 | 4 | 23 | 2 | 0 |
| Melrose | 28,094 | 30 | 0 | 1 | 3 | 26 | 147 | 23 | 105 | 19 | 1 |
| Mendon | 6,323 | 6 | 0 | 0 | 0 | 6 | 28 | 3 | 22 | 3 | 0 |
| Merrimac | 7,093 | 6 | 0 | 3 | 0 | 3 | 10 | 2 | 8 | 0 | 0 |
| Methuen | 51,691 | 87 | 0 | 9 | 11 | 67 | 425 | 29 | 355 | 41 | 1 |
| Middleboro | 27,228 | 84 | 1 | 15 | 2 | 66 | 150 | 25 | 105 | 20 | 1 |
| Middleton | 10,311 | 2 | 0 | 0 | 0 | 2 | 26 | 6 | 18 | 2 | 0 |
| Milford | 29,297 | 48 | 0 | 13 | 3 | 32 | 180 | 32 | 126 | 22 | 2 |
| Millbury | 14,160 | 19 | 0 | 1 | 3 | 15 | 98 | 15 | 76 | 7 | 0 |
| Millis | 8,683 | 7 | 0 | 1 | 0 | 6 | 20 | 4 | 16 | 0 | 0 |
| Millville | 3,267 | 0 | 0 | 0 | 0 | 0 | 15 | 3 | 12 | 0 | 0 |
| Milton | 27,911 | 10 | 1 | 2 | 2 | 5 | 111 | 11 | 93 | 7 | 0 |
| Monson | 8,857 | 25 | 0 | 4 | 2 | 19 | 33 | 13 | 14 | 6 | 0 |
| Montague | 8,178 | 65 | 0 | 0 | 4 | 61 | 87 | 25 | 58 | 4 | 0 |
| Monterey | 915 | 1 | 0 | 0 | 0 | 1 | 6 | 0 | 4 | 2 | 0 |
| Nahant | 3,544 | 6 | 0 | 1 | 0 | 5 | 10 | 0 | 9 | 1 | 0 |
| Nantucket | 11,600 | 24 | 0 | 4 | 0 | 20 | 184 | 27 | 143 | 14 | 0 |
| Natick | 36,340 | 47 | 0 | 9 | 6 | 32 | 432 | 24 | 389 | 19 | 2 |
| Needham | 32,159 | 14 | 0 | 1 | 1 | 12 | 123 | 21 | 97 | 5 | 1 |
| New Bedford | 96,346 | 615 | 4 | 51 | 84 | 476 | 1,658 | 254 | 1,228 | 176 | 10 |
| New Braintree | 1,030 | 4 | 0 | 0 | 0 | 4 | 3 | 0 | 1 | 2 | 0 |
| Newbury | 7,285 | 5 | 0 | 0 | 0 | 5 | 24 | 9 | 14 | 1 | 1 |
| Newburyport | 18,757 | 20 | 0 | 3 | 1 | 16 | 99 | 7 | 89 | 3 | 2 |
| Newton | 88,769 | 55 | 0 | 8 | 5 | 42 | 505 | 74 | 411 | 20 | 0 |
| Norfolk | 12,152 | 4 | 0 | 2 | 0 | 2 | 34 | 5 | 28 | 1 | 0 |
| North Adams | 12,638 | 137 | 0 | 7 | 10 | 120 | 305 | 61 | 228 | 16 | 0 |
| Northampton | 28,332 | 114 | 1 | 22 | 9 | 82 | 392 | 42 | 333 | 17 | 2 |
| North Andover | 32,040 | 18 | 0 | 2 | 2 | 14 | 116 | 15 | 93 | 8 | 2 |
| North Attleboro | 29,789 | 49 | 1 | 5 | 3 | 40 | 234 | 20 | 206 | 8 | 0 |
| Northborough | 15,223 | 5 | 0 | 0 | 2 | 3 | 32 | 2 | 23 | 7 | 0 |
| Northbridge | 16,850 | 26 | 0 | 3 | 2 | 21 | 63 | 11 | 48 | 4 | 2 |
| Northfield | 2,951 | 1 | 0 | 1 | 0 | 0 | 8 | 3 | 5 | 0 | 0 |

## Table 8. Offenses Known to Law Enforcement, by Selected State and City, 2021—Continued

(Number.)

| State/city | Population | Violent crime | Murder and nonnegligent manslaughter | Rape | Robbery | Aggravated assault | Property crime | Burglary | Larceny- theft | Motor vehicle theft | Arson |
|---|---|---|---|---|---|---|---|---|---|---|---|
| North Reading | 16,134 | 15 | 0 | 2 | 2 | 11 | 56 | 4 | 50 | 2 | 1 |
| Norton | 20,232 | 26 | 0 | 4 | 1 | 21 | 25 | 1 | 23 | 1 | 0 |
| Norwell | 11,770 | 14 | 0 | 2 | 1 | 11 | 43 | 6 | 33 | 4 | 0 |
| Norwood | 30,200 | 41 | 1 | 2 | 2 | 36 | 250 | 17 | 203 | 30 | 1 |
| Oak Bluffs | 4,772 | 24 | 0 | 2 | 0 | 22 | 31 | 6 | 25 | 0 | 0 |
| Oakham | 1,970 | 0 | 0 | 0 | 0 | 0 | 1 | 0 | 1 | 0 | 0 |
| Orange | 7,556 | 31 | 0 | 5 | 4 | 22 | 109 | 13 | 89 | 7 | 0 |
| Orleans | 5,841 | 15 | 0 | 3 | 1 | 11 | 62 | 4 | 56 | 2 | 0 |
| Oxford | 14,078 | 15 | 0 | 0 | 2 | 13 | 94 | 12 | 76 | 6 | 0 |
| Palmer | 12,300 | 39 | 1 | 4 | 0 | 34 | 80 | 16 | 59 | 5 | 1 |
| Paxton | 5,069 | 8 | 0 | 1 | 0 | 7 | 16 | 3 | 10 | 3 | 0 |
| Peabody | 53,669 | 145 | 0 | 16 | 14 | 115 | 418 | 47 | 336 | 35 | 2 |
| Pelham | 1,303 | 1 | 0 | 0 | 0 | 1 | 0 | 0 | 0 | 0 | 0 |
| Pembroke | 19,505 | 10 | 0 | 3 | 0 | 7 | 50 | 3 | 42 | 5 | 0 |
| Pepperell | 12,192 | 14 | 0 | 2 | 0 | 12 | 53 | 10 | 41 | 2 | 0 |
| Pittsfield | 41,556 | 276 | 1 | 37 | 28 | 210 | 658 | 226 | 368 | 64 | 10 |
| Plainville | 9,495 | 8 | 0 | 1 | 0 | 7 | 52 | 9 | 40 | 3 | 0 |
| Plymouth | 66,289 | 186 | 0 | 37 | 6 | 143 | 644 | 41 | 579 | 24 | 1 |
| Plympton | 3,157 | 2 | 0 | 0 | 0 | 2 | 21 | 2 | 18 | 1 | 1 |
| Princeton | 3,522 | 2 | 0 | 1 | 0 | 1 | 18 | 3 | 12 | 3 | 0 |
| Provincetown | 2,982 | 15 | 0 | 5 | 0 | 10 | 51 | 10 | 38 | 3 | 2 |
| Quincy | 95,737 | 303 | 0 | 27 | 25 | 251 | 1,166 | 221 | 806 | 139 | 4 |
| Randolph | 32,257 | 95 | 0 | 9 | 9 | 77 | 322 | 44 | 232 | 46 | 0 |
| Raynham | 14,799 | 31 | 0 | 5 | 4 | 22 | 112 | 11 | 94 | 7 | 0 |
| Reading | 25,900 | 9 | 0 | 0 | 1 | 8 | 121 | 10 | 108 | 3 | 2 |
| Rehoboth | 12,697 | 13 | 0 | 1 | 1 | 11 | 44 | 11 | 28 | 5 | 0 |
| Revere | 52,860 | 157 | 0 | 18 | 24 | 115 | 630 | 67 | 474 | 89 | 3 |
| Rockland | 18,898 | 45 | 0 | 8 | 1 | 36 | 39 | 8 | 26 | 5 | 1 |
| Rockport | 7,407 | 5 | 0 | 0 | 1 | 4 | 12 | 4 | 8 | 0 | 0 |
| Rowley | 6,501 | 6 | 0 | 0 | 0 | 6 | 23 | 6 | 16 | 1 | 0 |
| Royalston | 1,290 | 0 | 0 | 0 | 0 | 0 | 0 | 0 | 0 | 0 | 0 |
| Rutland | 9,208 | 28 | 0 | 7 | 0 | 21 | 21 | 9 | 9 | 3 | 0 |
| Salem | 44,120 | 100 | 0 | 7 | 15 | 78 | 590 | 80 | 470 | 40 | 0 |
| Salisbury | 9,811 | 19 | 0 | 8 | 1 | 10 | 92 | 16 | 64 | 12 | 0 |
| Sandwich | 20,266 | 40 | 0 | 8 | 0 | 32 | 69 | 6 | 56 | 7 | 1 |
| Saugus | 28,967 | 63 | 1 | 8 | 5 | 49 | 287 | 33 | 233 | 21 | 0 |
| Scituate | 20,046 | 15 | 0 | 2 | 0 | 13 | 34 | 11 | 23 | 0 | 0 |
| Seekonk | 16,212 | 36 | 1 | 8 | 3 | 24 | 257 | 44 | 196 | 17 | 1 |
| Sharon | 19,222 | 13 | 0 | 3 | 1 | 9 | 51 | 3 | 44 | 4 | 1 |
| Shelburne | 1,834 | 0 | 0 | 0 | 0 | 0 | 5 | 0 | 5 | 0 | 0 |
| Sherborn | 4,445 | 1 | 0 | 0 | 1 | 0 | 8 | 3 | 3 | 2 | 0 |
| Shirley | 7,641 | 17 | 1 | 2 | 0 | 14 | 23 | 6 | 13 | 4 | 0 |
| Shrewsbury | 39,602 | 10 | 1 | 2 | 3 | 4 | 240 | 23 | 199 | 18 | 1 |
| Shutesbury | 1,751 | 0 | 0 | 0 | 0 | 0 | 1 | 0 | 1 | 0 | 0 |
| Somerset | 18,286 | 40 | 0 | 7 | 2 | 31 | 117 | 9 | 100 | 8 | 1 |
| Somerville | 82,123 | 152 | 3 | 16 | 29 | 104 | 923 | 117 | 725 | 81 | 4 |
| Southampton | 6,199 | 3 | 0 | 1 | 0 | 2 | 27 | 3 | 24 | 0 | 0 |
| Southborough | 10,328 | 7 | 0 | 1 | 0 | 6 | 30 | 5 | 24 | 1 | 0 |
| Southbridge | 16,932 | 40 | 0 | 9 | 1 | 30 | 171 | 27 | 125 | 19 | 0 |
| South Hadley | 17,520 | 37 | 0 | 7 | 0 | 30 | 214 | 63 | 145 | 6 | 3 |
| Southwick | 9,835 | 8 | 0 | 1 | 0 | 7 | 53 | 16 | 35 | 2 | 0 |
| Spencer | 12,014 | 13 | 0 | 0 | 0 | 13 | 64 | 11 | 47 | 6 | 0 |
| Springfield | 154,098 | 1,445 | 18 | 57 | 306 | 1,064 | 3,602 | 580 | 2,514 | 508 | 23 |
| Sterling | 8,270 | 7 | 0 | 2 | 3 | 2 | 22 | 4 | 15 | 3 | 0 |
| Stockbridge | 1,877 | 1 | 0 | 0 | 0 | 1 | 20 | 5 | 13 | 2 | 0 |
| Stoneham | 24,439 | 29 | 0 | 3 | 4 | 22 | 143 | 40 | 97 | 6 | 2 |
| Stoughton | 29,418 | 80 | 0 | 14 | 12 | 54 | 238 | 34 | 160 | 44 | 1 |
| Stow | 7,294 | 3 | 0 | 0 | 1 | 2 | 14 | 3 | 11 | 0 | 0 |
| Sturbridge | 9,670 | 21 | 0 | 5 | 0 | 16 | 113 | 17 | 88 | 8 | 0 |
| Sudbury | 19,798 | 15 | 0 | 2 | 0 | 13 | 38 | 4 | 30 | 4 | 0 |
| Sunderland | 3,628 | 10 | 0 | 7 | 0 | 3 | 18 | 3 | 15 | 0 | 0 |
| Sutton | 9,716 | 14 | 0 | 2 | 2 | 10 | 51 | 16 | 33 | 2 | 0 |
| Swampscott | 15,766 | 6 | 0 | 0 | 2 | 4 | 110 | 12 | 94 | 4 | 1 |
| Swansea | 17,257 | 22 | 0 | 5 | 1 | 16 | 121 | 19 | 91 | 11 | 0 |
| Taunton | 58,333 | 226 | 2 | 27 | 19 | 178 | 561 | 69 | 404 | 88 | 1 |
| Templeton | 8,213 | 8 | 0 | 1 | 0 | 7 | 33 | 2 | 26 | 5 | 0 |
| Tewksbury | 31,407 | 93 | 0 | 17 | 4 | 72 | 354 | 26 | 308 | 20 | 1 |
| Tisbury | 4,198 | 25 | 0 | 1 | 0 | 24 | 44 | 8 | 34 | 2 | 1 |
| Topsfield | 6,774 | 6 | 0 | 0 | 0 | 6 | 7 | 0 | 7 | 0 | 0 |
| Townsend | 9,574 | 26 | 0 | 4 | 2 | 20 | 62 | 36 | 22 | 4 | 1 |
| Truro | 2,024 | 4 | 0 | 1 | 0 | 3 | 12 | 4 | 8 | 0 | 0 |
| Tyngsboro | 12,881 | 10 | 0 | 1 | 0 | 9 | 38 | 7 | 25 | 6 | 0 |
| Upton | 8,209 | 5 | 0 | 2 | 0 | 3 | 32 | 5 | 23 | 4 | 0 |
| Uxbridge | 14,561 | 15 | 0 | 2 | 0 | 13 | 72 | 12 | 54 | 6 | 0 |
| Wakefield | 27,470 | 31 | 1 | 6 | 0 | 24 | 92 | 13 | 70 | 9 | 2 |
| Walpole | 27,160 | 26 | 0 | 9 | 1 | 16 | 204 | 14 | 181 | 9 | 0 |
| Waltham | 62,693 | 75 | 0 | 9 | 8 | 58 | 291 | 39 | 236 | 16 | 2 |
| Ware | 9,900 | 51 | 0 | 4 | 2 | 45 | 41 | 3 | 36 | 2 | 0 |
| Wareham | 23,956 | 74 | 0 | 11 | 3 | 60 | 225 | 32 | 166 | 27 | 2 |
| Warren | 5,252 | 11 | 0 | 0 | 2 | 9 | 25 | 3 | 16 | 6 | 2 |
| Watertown | 36,858 | 36 | 0 | 6 | 4 | 26 | 263 | 26 | 215 | 22 | 1 |
| Wayland | 13,911 | 0 | 0 | 0 | 0 | 0 | 0 | 0 | 0 | 0 | 0 |
| Webster | 16,963 | 123 | 0 | 9 | 6 | 108 | 166 | 40 | 112 | 14 | 2 |

# Table 8. Offenses Known to Law Enforcement, by Selected State and City, 2021—Continued

(Number.)

| State/city | Population | Violent crime | Murder and nonnegligent manslaughter | Rape | Robbery | Aggravated assault | Property crime | Burglary | Larceny-theft | Motor vehicle theft | Arson |
|---|---|---|---|---|---|---|---|---|---|---|---|
| Wellesley | 29,088 | 5 | 0 | 1 | 0 | 4 | 121 | 14 | 95 | 12 | 1 |
| Wellfleet | 2,747 | 6 | 0 | 2 | 0 | 4 | 14 | 1 | 12 | 1 | 0 |
| Wenham | 5,236 | 0 | 0 | 0 | 0 | 0 | 13 | 1 | 12 | 0 | 0 |
| Westborough | 19,299 | 35 | 0 | 11 | 2 | 22 | 144 | 22 | 113 | 9 | 0 |
| West Boylston | 8,137 | 11 | 0 | 2 | 0 | 9 | 38 | 2 | 34 | 2 | 1 |
| West Bridgewater | 7,696 | 18 | 0 | 0 | 0 | 18 | 74 | 7 | 51 | 16 | 1 |
| West Brookfield | 3,749 | 4 | 0 | 0 | 0 | 4 | 8 | 0 | 5 | 3 | 0 |
| Westfield | 41,474 | 90 | 0 | 16 | 4 | 70 | 348 | 50 | 265 | 33 | 2 |
| Westford | 25,834 | 8 | 0 | 1 | 1 | 6 | 62 | 9 | 49 | 4 | 0 |
| Westminster | 8,244 | 9 | 0 | 3 | 0 | 6 | 48 | 4 | 40 | 4 | 0 |
| West Newbury | 4,878 | 3 | 0 | 0 | 0 | 3 | 17 | 1 | 15 | 1 | 0 |
| Weston | 12,195 | 7 | 0 | 4 | 0 | 3 | 27 | 9 | 17 | 1 | 0 |
| Westport | 16,286 | 29 | 0 | 7 | 0 | 22 | 75 | 10 | 53 | 12 | 1 |
| West Springfield | 28,688 | 167 | 0 | 29 | 23 | 115 | 864 | 66 | 719 | 79 | 4 |
| West Tisbury | 2,982 | 14 | 0 | 0 | 0 | 14 | 13 | 1 | 11 | 1 | 0 |
| Westwood | 16,767 | 7 | 0 | 1 | 1 | 5 | 123 | 5 | 113 | 5 | 0 |
| Weymouth | 59,242 | 141 | 1 | 9 | 11 | 120 | 515 | 33 | 447 | 35 | 0 |
| Whately | 1,591 | 1 | 0 | 0 | 0 | 1 | 9 | 1 | 6 | 2 | 0 |
| Whitman | 16,105 | 19 | 0 | 3 | 1 | 15 | 80 | 9 | 62 | 9 | 2 |
| Wilbraham | 14,864 | 28 | 0 | 1 | 3 | 24 | 133 | 15 | 106 | 12 | 0 |
| Williamsburg | 2,459 | 3 | 0 | 0 | 1 | 2 | 7 | 1 | 6 | 0 | 0 |
| Williamstown | 7,617 | 2 | 0 | 1 | 0 | 1 | 53 | 2 | 49 | 2 | 0 |
| Wilmington | 23,567 | 21 | 0 | 1 | 0 | 20 | 152 | 15 | 130 | 7 | 0 |
| Winchendon | 10,973 | 28 | 0 | 8 | 1 | 19 | 61 | 16 | 41 | 4 | 0 |
| Winchester | 22,988 | 7 | 0 | 1 | 1 | 5 | 82 | 13 | 66 | 3 | 0 |
| Winthrop | 18,692 | 23 | 0 | 4 | 1 | 16 | 119 | 13 | 95 | 11 | 0 |
| Woburn | 40,568 | 48 | 0 | 3 | 7 | 38 | 409 | 36 | 316 | 57 | 1 |
| Worcester | 186,365 | 1,199 | 6 | 46 | 191 | 956 | 3,538 | 713 | 2,445 | 380 | 12 |
| Worthington | 1,178 | 0 | 0 | 0 | 0 | 0 | 1 | 0 | 0 | 1 | 0 |
| Wrentham | 12,334 | 21 | 0 | 0 | 1 | 20 | 82 | 8 | 72 | 2 | 0 |
| Yarmouth | 23,295 | 78 | 0 | 15 | 6 | 57 | 216 | 41 | 167 | 8 | 2 |
| **MICHIGAN** | | | | | | | | | | | |
| Addison Township | 6,603 | 0 | 0 | 0 | 0 | 0 | 5 | 1 | 3 | 1 | 1 |
| Adrian | 20,371 | 131 | 2 | 33 | 11 | 85 | 405 | 82 | 283 | 40 | 0 |
| Adrian Township | 6,188 | 3 | 0 | 1 | 1 | 1 | 23 | 2 | 20 | 1 | 0 |
| Akron | 370 | 2 | 0 | 0 | 0 | 2 | 4 | 2 | 2 | 0 | 1 |
| Albion | 8,336 | 67 | 1 | 10 | 5 | 51 | 244 | 54 | 172 | 18 | 1 |
| Allegan | 5,018 | 4 | 0 | 1 | 0 | 3 | 22 | 2 | 18 | 2 | 0 |
| Allen Park | 26,615 | 47 | 0 | 6 | 6 | 35 | 336 | 24 | 246 | 66 | 0 |
| Alma | 8,754 | 38 | 0 | 17 | 2 | 19 | 87 | 9 | 72 | 6 | 0 |
| Almont | 2,830 | 12 | 0 | 3 | 0 | 9 | 21 | 3 | 16 | 2 | 1 |
| Alpena | 9,828 | 40 | 0 | 11 | 1 | 28 | 120 | 18 | 94 | 8 | 2 |
| Ann Arbor | 119,805 | 345 | 2 | 59 | 30 | 254 | 1,725 | 197 | 1,446 | 82 | 5 |
| Argentine Township | 6,439 | 1 | 0 | 0 | 0 | 1 | 8 | 4 | 3 | 1 | 0 |
| Armada | 1,695 | 8 | 0 | 0 | 0 | 8 | 6 | 0 | 5 | 1 | 0 |
| Auburn Hills | 25,256 | 111 | 1 | 21 | 11 | 78 | 413 | 31 | 322 | 60 | 2 |
| Au Gres | 828 | 2 | 0 | 0 | 0 | 2 | 1 | 0 | 1 | 0 | 0 |
| Augusta | 897 | 2 | 0 | 0 | 0 | 2 | 18 | 2 | 14 | 2 | 0 |
| Bad Axe | 2,868 | 3 | 0 | 0 | 0 | 3 | 31 | 2 | 27 | 2 | 0 |
| Bancroft | 491 | 0 | 0 | 0 | 0 | 0 | 1 | 0 | 1 | 0 | 0 |
| Bangor | 1,800 | 18 | 0 | 3 | 0 | 15 | 25 | 5 | 17 | 3 | 0 |
| Baroda-Lake Township | 3,891 | 3 | 0 | 1 | 0 | 2 | 44 | 8 | 31 | 5 | 0 |
| Barryton | 357 | 0 | 0 | 0 | 0 | 0 | 0 | 0 | 0 | 0 | 0 |
| Barry Township | 3,560 | 5 | 0 | 3 | 0 | 2 | 19 | 3 | 16 | 0 | 0 |
| Bath Township | 13,226 | 19 | 0 | 6 | 0 | 13 | 110 | 8 | 87 | 15 | 0 |
| Battle Creek | 60,134 | 614 | 7 | 53 | 38 | 516 | 1,556 | 337 | 1,052 | 167 | 14 |
| Bay City | 32,200 | 241 | 1 | 31 | 15 | 194 | 494 | 85 | 336 | 73 | 3 |
| Beaverton | 1,173 | 3 | 0 | 1 | 0 | 2 | 14 | 3 | 11 | 0 | 0 |
| Belding | 5,738 | 15 | 0 | 8 | 0 | 7 | 62 | 9 | 45 | 8 | 0 |
| Belleville | 3,854 | 16 | 0 | 1 | 2 | 13 | 49 | 9 | 31 | 9 | 0 |
| Benton Harbor | 9,660 | 240 | 7 | 11 | 16 | 206 | 216 | 40 | 127 | 49 | 5 |
| Benton Township | 14,230 | 307 | 3 | 17 | 22 | 265 | 672 | 87 | 514 | 71 | 5 |
| Berkley | 15,307 | 5 | 0 | 1 | 0 | 4 | 74 | 6 | 60 | 8 | 0 |
| Berrien Springs-Oronoko Township | 8,854 | 12 | 0 | 3 | 0 | 9 | 45 | 5 | 40 | 0 | 0 |
| Beverly Hills | 10,278 | 7 | 0 | 1 | 1 | 5 | 43 | 2 | 37 | 4 | 0 |
| Big Rapids | 10,406 | 14 | 0 | 3 | 0 | 11 | 15 | 4 | 8 | 3 | 0 |
| Birch Run | 1,461 | 2 | 0 | 0 | 0 | 2 | 69 | 2 | 61 | 6 | 0 |
| Birmingham | 21,436 | 9 | 0 | 0 | 2 | 7 | 131 | 8 | 106 | 17 | 0 |
| Blackman Township | 36,111 | 141 | 2 | 25 | 5 | 109 | 1,061 | 96 | 865 | 100 | 3 |
| Blissfield | 3,240 | 3 | 0 | 2 | 0 | 1 | 12 | 2 | 9 | 1 | 0 |
| Bloomfield Hills | 4,001 | 3 | 0 | 2 | 0 | 1 | 27 | 7 | 17 | 3 | 0 |
| Bloomfield Township | 41,809 | 25 | 0 | 7 | 2 | 16 | 215 | 26 | 172 | 17 | 0 |
| Boyne City | 3,717 | 8 | 0 | 5 | 0 | 3 | 22 | 0 | 22 | 0 | 0 |
| Brandon Township | 16,093 | 13 | 0 | 2 | 0 | 11 | 20 | 2 | 14 | 4 | 0 |
| Breckenridge | 1,259 | 1 | 0 | 0 | 0 | 1 | 8 | 0 | 6 | 2 | 0 |
| Bridgeport Township | 9,658 | 54 | 2 | 9 | 2 | 41 | 92 | 24 | 58 | 10 | 0 |
| Bridgman | 2,191 | 3 | 0 | 2 | 0 | 1 | 18 | 2 | 15 | 1 | 0 |
| Brighton | 7,654 | 9 | 1 | 2 | 2 | 4 | 119 | 3 | 110 | 6 | 0 |
| Bronson | 2,293 | 8 | 0 | 6 | 0 | 2 | 40 | 1 | 34 | 5 | 0 |
| Brown City | 1,230 | 2 | 0 | 2 | 0 | 0 | 8 | 0 | 7 | 1 | 0 |
| Brownstown Township | 32,300 | 83 | 1 | 8 | 2 | 72 | 266 | 63 | 177 | 26 | 2 |

## Table 8. Offenses Known to Law Enforcement, by Selected State and City, 2021—Continued

(Number.)

| State/city | Population | Violent crime | Murder and nonnegligent manslaughter | Rape | Robbery | Aggravated assault | Property crime | Burglary | Larceny-theft | Motor vehicle theft | Arson |
|---|---|---|---|---|---|---|---|---|---|---|---|
| Buchanan | 4,200 | 16 | 0 | 5 | 2 | 9 | 117 | 6 | 99 | 12 | 0 |
| Buena Vista Township | 8,035 | 76 | 2 | 6 | 3 | 65 | 134 | 39 | 70 | 25 | 1 |
| Burton | 28,319 | 208 | 1 | 18 | 14 | 175 | 721 | 110 | 534 | 77 | 5 |
| Cadillac | 10,536 | 25 | 0 | 11 | 0 | 14 | 248 | 35 | 199 | 14 | 2 |
| Cambridge Township | 5,663 | 2 | 0 | 0 | 0 | 2 | 14 | 4 | 9 | 1 | 0 |
| Canton Township | 94,777 | 202 | 1 | 18 | 15 | 168 | 848 | 49 | 712 | 87 | 13 |
| Capac | 1,842 | 9 | 0 | 0 | 0 | 9 | 22 | 4 | 18 | 0 | 0 |
| Caro | 3,967 | 21 | 0 | 7 | 1 | 13 | 82 | 8 | 71 | 3 | 0 |
| Carrollton Township | 5,560 | 31 | 0 | 2 | 3 | 26 | 40 | 15 | 24 | 1 | 2 |
| Carson City | 1,104 | 0 | 0 | 0 | 0 | 0 | 0 | 0 | 0 | 0 | 0 |
| Caseville | 720 | 0 | 0 | 0 | 0 | 0 | 9 | 2 | 7 | 0 | 0 |
| Caspian-Gaastra | 1,161 | 2 | 0 | 0 | 0 | 2 | 5 | 0 | 3 | 2 | 0 |
| Cass City | 2,259 | 9 | 0 | 1 | 0 | 8 | 20 | 0 | 18 | 2 | 0 |
| Cassopolis | 1,691 | 1 | 0 | 1 | 0 | 0 | 9 | 2 | 6 | 1 | 0 |
| Center Line | 8,074 | 21 | 1 | 8 | 3 | 9 | 98 | 18 | 60 | 20 | 2 |
| Charlevoix | 2,477 | 6 | 0 | 2 | 0 | 4 | 32 | 3 | 29 | 0 | 0 |
| Charlotte | 9,049 | 38 | 0 | 15 | 1 | 22 | 163 | 26 | 118 | 19 | 0 |
| Cheboygan | 4,682 | 10 | 0 | 7 | 0 | 3 | 61 | 5 | 54 | 2 | 0 |
| Chelsea | 5,422 | 5 | 0 | 1 | 0 | 4 | 30 | 4 | 22 | 4 | 0 |
| Chesaning | 2,204 | 16 | 0 | 2 | 0 | 14 | 17 | 1 | 14 | 2 | 0 |
| Chesterfield Township | 46,997 | 65 | 2 | 7 | 5 | 51 | 400 | 24 | 349 | 27 | 1 |
| Chikaming Township | 3,073 | 7 | 1 | 2 | 0 | 4 | 48 | 4 | 43 | 1 | 0 |
| Chocolay Township | 5,888 | 11 | 1 | 2 | 0 | 8 | 22 | 2 | 19 | 1 | 0 |
| Clare | 3,045 | 7 | 0 | 0 | 0 | 7 | 19 | 2 | 15 | 2 | 0 |
| Clarkston | 914 | 1 | 0 | 0 | 0 | 1 | 5 | 0 | 5 | 0 | 0 |
| Clawson | 11,720 | 12 | 2 | 2 | 0 | 8 | 38 | 6 | 29 | 3 | 0 |
| Clayton Township | 7,037 | 12 | 0 | 2 | 0 | 10 | 30 | 8 | 13 | 9 | 0 |
| Clay Township | 8,902 | 31 | 0 | 3 | 2 | 26 | 62 | 12 | 48 | 2 | 0 |
| Clinton | 2,283 | 6 | 0 | 0 | 1 | 5 | 9 | 1 | 8 | 0 | 0 |
| Clinton Township | 100,094 | 352 | 7 | 47 | 27 | 271 | 1,216 | 104 | 903 | 209 | 6 |
| Clio | 2,465 | 12 | 0 | 1 | 0 | 11 | 51 | 19 | 29 | 3 | 0 |
| Coldwater | 11,954 | 59 | 0 | 13 | 1 | 45 | 256 | 35 | 205 | 16 | 3 |
| Coleman | 1,202 | 1 | 0 | 1 | 0 | 0 | 13 | 0 | 12 | 1 | 0 |
| Coloma Township | 6,307 | 21 | 0 | 4 | 1 | 16 | 91 | 19 | 65 | 7 | 0 |
| Colon | 1,152 | 3 | 1 | 0 | 0 | 2 | 26 | 6 | 17 | 3 | 0 |
| Columbia Township | 7,312 | 17 | 0 | 6 | 0 | 11 | 49 | 4 | 38 | 7 | 0 |
| Commerce Township | 39,878 | 28 | 1 | 1 | 1 | 25 | 193 | 20 | 161 | 12 | 0 |
| Constantine | 2,106 | 13 | 0 | 5 | 0 | 8 | 28 | 6 | 19 | 3 | 3 |
| Corunna | 3,303 | 7 | 0 | 1 | 0 | 6 | 24 | 11 | 13 | 0 | 0 |
| Covert Township | 2,884 | 9 | 0 | 1 | 1 | 7 | 42 | 7 | 31 | 4 | 2 |
| Croswell | 2,235 | 10 | 0 | 3 | 0 | 7 | 49 | 9 | 39 | 1 | 0 |
| Davison | 4,828 | 4 | 0 | 1 | 2 | 1 | 65 | 7 | 38 | 20 | 0 |
| Davison Township | 19,226 | 33 | 0 | 5 | 4 | 24 | 130 | 10 | 108 | 12 | 1 |
| Dearborn | 92,930 | 350 | 4 | 26 | 45 | 275 | 1,744 | 143 | 1,319 | 282 | 6 |
| Dearborn Heights | 54,772 | 299 | 2 | 24 | 22 | 251 | 814 | 179 | 495 | 140 | 5 |
| Decatur | 1,707 | 14 | 0 | 1 | 0 | 13 | 53 | 11 | 39 | 3 | 0 |
| Denton Township | 5,412 | 6 | 0 | 0 | 0 | 6 | 39 | 1 | 38 | 0 | 0 |
| Detroit | 673,708 | 14,509 | 303 | 818 | 1,511 | 11,877 | 22,607 | 4,183 | 11,677 | 6,747 | 543 |
| DeWitt | 4,869 | 5 | 0 | 1 | 0 | 4 | 9 | 0 | 8 | 1 | 0 |
| DeWitt Township | 15,880 | 33 | 0 | 9 | 1 | 23 | 146 | 26 | 112 | 8 | 1 |
| Dowagiac | 5,536 | 40 | 1 | 8 | 3 | 28 | 177 | 11 | 144 | 22 | 2 |
| Dryden Township | 4,731 | 21 | 0 | 4 | 0 | 17 | 20 | 2 | 15 | 3 | 0 |
| Durand | 3,792 | 5 | 0 | 2 | 0 | 3 | 23 | 0 | 19 | 4 | 0 |
| East Grand Rapids | 12,129 | 9 | 0 | 7 | 0 | 2 | 179 | 12 | 157 | 10 | 0 |
| East Jordan | 2,338 | 1 | 0 | 1 | 0 | 0 | 20 | 4 | 16 | 0 | 0 |
| East Lansing | 47,548 | 119 | 1 | 21 | 12 | 85 | 841 | 84 | 550 | 207 | 28 |
| Eastpointe | 31,653 | 239 | 2 | 23 | 39 | 175 | 710 | 111 | 430 | 169 | 8 |
| Eaton Rapids | 5,223 | 30 | 0 | 3 | 0 | 27 | 58 | 9 | 43 | 6 | 1 |
| Eau Claire | 588 | 0 | 0 | 0 | 0 | 0 | 1 | 1 | 0 | 0 | 0 |
| Ecorse | 9,635 | 135 | 3 | 17 | 16 | 99 | 229 | 37 | 150 | 42 | 3 |
| Elkton | 735 | 0 | 0 | 0 | 0 | 0 | 12 | 0 | 12 | 0 | 0 |
| Elsie | 977 | 1 | 0 | 0 | 0 | 1 | 2 | 1 | 1 | 0 | 0 |
| Emmett Township | 11,531 | 40 | 0 | 3 | 4 | 33 | 650 | 44 | 577 | 29 | 0 |
| Escanaba | 12,052 | 45 | 0 | 14 | 4 | 27 | 220 | 10 | 201 | 9 | 2 |
| Essexville | 3,222 | 4 | 0 | 1 | 0 | 3 | 8 | 1 | 7 | 0 | 0 |
| Evart | 1,883 | 5 | 0 | 2 | 0 | 3 | 15 | 1 | 13 | 1 | 0 |
| Fair Haven Township | 1,029 | 0 | 0 | 0 | 0 | 0 | 2 | 0 | 1 | 1 | 0 |
| Farmington | 10,396 | 7 | 0 | 0 | 2 | 5 | 59 | 4 | 46 | 9 | 1 |
| Farmington Hills | 80,044 | 119 | 2 | 19 | 12 | 86 | 608 | 64 | 445 | 99 | 2 |
| Fennville | 1,438 | 4 | 0 | 1 | 0 | 3 | 2 | 0 | 2 | 0 | 0 |
| Fenton | 11,340 | 13 | 0 | 2 | 3 | 8 | 178 | 12 | 148 | 18 | 0 |
| Ferndale | 20,228 | 27 | 0 | 4 | 6 | 17 | 330 | 74 | 230 | 26 | 1 |
| Flat Rock | 9,968 | 27 | 1 | 4 | 2 | 20 | 110 | 9 | 81 | 20 | 0 |
| Flint | 94,290 | 982 | 37 | 57 | 44 | 844 | 875 | 162 | 608 | 105 | 5 |
| Flint Township | 30,015 | 320 | 5 | 16 | 28 | 271 | 1,056 | 141 | 776 | 139 | 6 |
| Flushing | 7,789 | 10 | 0 | 1 | 0 | 9 | 51 | 7 | 41 | 3 | 2 |
| Flushing Township | 10,096 | 17 | 0 | 2 | 0 | 15 | 55 | 12 | 39 | 4 | 1 |
| Forsyth Township | 6,160 | 20 | 0 | 10 | 0 | 10 | 31 | 1 | 30 | 0 | 0 |
| Fowlerville | 2,904 | 8 | 0 | 3 | 0 | 5 | 92 | 11 | 79 | 2 | 0 |
| Frankenmuth | 5,728 | 3 | 0 | 1 | 0 | 2 | 40 | 3 | 37 | 0 | 0 |
| Frankfort | 1,290 | 5 | 0 | 0 | 1 | 4 | 15 | 1 | 14 | 0 | 0 |
| Franklin | 3,228 | 3 | 0 | 0 | 0 | 3 | 15 | 2 | 11 | 2 | 0 |
| Fraser | 14,316 | 38 | 0 | 11 | 5 | 22 | 176 | 11 | 139 | 26 | 0 |

# Table 8. Offenses Known to Law Enforcement, by Selected State and City, 2021—Continued

(Number.)

| State/city | Population | Violent crime | Murder and nonnegligent manslaughter | Rape | Robbery | Aggravated assault | Property crime | Burglary | Larceny-theft | Motor vehicle theft | Arson |
|---|---|---|---|---|---|---|---|---|---|---|---|
| Fremont | 4,102 | 0 | 0 | 0 | 0 | 0 | 5 | 0 | 5 | 0 | 2 |
| Fruitport Township | 14,690 | 24 | 2 | 5 | 2 | 15 | 403 | 14 | 377 | 12 | 0 |
| Galien | 525 | 0 | 0 | 0 | 0 | 0 | 0 | 0 | 0 | 0 | 0 |
| Garden City | 26,084 | 74 | 1 | 5 | 6 | 62 | 239 | 49 | 167 | 23 | 3 |
| Garfield Township | 846 | 0 | 0 | 0 | 0 | 0 | 0 | 0 | 0 | 0 | 0 |
| Gaylord | 3,672 | 32 | 0 | 11 | 1 | 20 | 155 | 7 | 140 | 8 | 3 |
| Genesee Township | 20,258 | 109 | 0 | 8 | 6 | 95 | 235 | 84 | 120 | 31 | 5 |
| Gerrish Township | 2,946 | 4 | 0 | 1 | 0 | 3 | 13 | 2 | 11 | 0 | 0 |
| Gibraltar | 4,503 | 7 | 0 | 1 | 1 | 5 | 34 | 1 | 31 | 2 | 0 |
| Gladstone | 4,631 | 0 | 0 | 0 | 0 | 0 | 38 | 4 | 32 | 2 | 0 |
| Gladwin | 2,884 | 10 | 0 | 7 | 0 | 3 | 39 | 4 | 34 | 1 | 1 |
| Grand Beach/Michiana | 462 | 0 | 0 | 0 | 0 | 0 | 8 | 4 | 4 | 0 | 0 |
| Grand Blanc | 7,789 | 13 | 0 | 2 | 2 | 9 | 50 | 3 | 38 | 9 | 2 |
| Grand Blanc Township | 36,700 | 71 | 0 | 10 | 1 | 60 | 438 | 34 | 351 | 53 | 2 |
| Grand Haven | 11,110 | 23 | 0 | 10 | 3 | 10 | 142 | 8 | 123 | 11 | 2 |
| Grand Ledge | 7,891 | 4 | 0 | 3 | 0 | 1 | 67 | 7 | 55 | 5 | 0 |
| Grand Rapids | 201,280 | 1,929 | 17 | 150 | 295 | 1,467 | 5,060 | 569 | 3,563 | 928 | 52 |
| Grandville | 15,787 | 53 | 0 | 19 | 7 | 27 | 471 | 16 | 419 | 36 | 0 |
| Grant | 900 | 1 | 0 | 1 | 0 | 0 | 6 | 1 | 5 | 0 | 0 |
| Grayling | 1,841 | 5 | 0 | 4 | 0 | 1 | 85 | 3 | 77 | 5 | 0 |
| Green Oak Township | 19,155 | 4 | 0 | 1 | 0 | 3 | 83 | 9 | 69 | 5 | 0 |
| Greenville | 8,378 | 33 | 1 | 10 | 1 | 21 | 207 | 24 | 167 | 16 | 3 |
| Grosse Ile Township | 10,076 | 0 | 0 | 0 | 0 | 0 | 21 | 1 | 19 | 1 | 1 |
| Grosse Pointe | 5,094 | 10 | 0 | 0 | 0 | 10 | 58 | 3 | 50 | 5 | 1 |
| Grosse Pointe Farms | 9,012 | 4 | 0 | 0 | 1 | 3 | 68 | 7 | 54 | 7 | 0 |
| Grosse Pointe Park | 10,918 | 5 | 0 | 3 | 1 | 1 | 104 | 9 | 78 | 17 | 0 |
| Grosse Pointe Shores | 2,509 | 1 | 0 | 0 | 0 | 1 | 20 | 5 | 11 | 4 | 0 |
| Grosse Pointe Woods | 15,158 | 13 | 0 | 1 | 1 | 11 | 145 | 10 | 117 | 18 | 0 |
| Hamburg Township | 21,904 | 7 | 0 | 1 | 0 | 6 | 35 | 7 | 26 | 2 | 1 |
| Hampton Township | 9,282 | 17 | 0 | 7 | 0 | 10 | 98 | 15 | 75 | 8 | 1 |
| Hamtramck | 21,346 | 213 | 4 | 8 | 25 | 176 | 334 | 75 | 205 | 54 | 4 |
| Hancock | 4,426 | 7 | 0 | 1 | 0 | 6 | 30 | 5 | 24 | 1 | 0 |
| Harbor Beach | 1,557 | 7 | 0 | 6 | 0 | 1 | 16 | 1 | 15 | 0 | 0 |
| Harbor Springs | 1,204 | 1 | 0 | 1 | 0 | 0 | 6 | 0 | 6 | 0 | 0 |
| Harper Woods | 13,582 | 136 | 0 | 7 | 16 | 113 | 497 | 43 | 358 | 96 | 6 |
| Hart | 2,087 | 6 | 0 | 2 | 0 | 4 | 106 | 6 | 98 | 2 | 0 |
| Hartford | 2,561 | 18 | 0 | 3 | 0 | 15 | 22 | 1 | 17 | 4 | 1 |
| Hastings | 7,335 | 32 | 0 | 15 | 0 | 17 | 97 | 9 | 79 | 9 | 0 |
| Hazel Park | 16,189 | 47 | 0 | 7 | 6 | 34 | 220 | 27 | 160 | 33 | 3 |
| Hesperia | 935 | 1 | 0 | 0 | 0 | 1 | 12 | 0 | 10 | 2 | 0 |
| Highland Park | 10,620 | 220 | 9 | 13 | 14 | 184 | 362 | 55 | 220 | 87 | 12 |
| Highland Township | 20,151 | 17 | 0 | 2 | 0 | 15 | 58 | 9 | 32 | 17 | 4 |
| Hillsdale | 8,081 | 22 | 0 | 6 | 0 | 16 | 112 | 33 | 67 | 12 | 1 |
| Holland | 33,144 | 132 | 1 | 39 | 14 | 78 | 452 | 33 | 388 | 31 | 1 |
| Holly | 6,079 | 8 | 0 | 1 | 1 | 6 | 21 | 1 | 18 | 2 | 0 |
| Houghton | 7,524 | 1 | 0 | 0 | 0 | 1 | 67 | 3 | 64 | 0 | 0 |
| Howell | 9,667 | 12 | 0 | 4 | 0 | 8 | 59 | 9 | 47 | 3 | 2 |
| Hudson | 2,185 | 9 | 0 | 4 | 0 | 5 | 34 | 5 | 28 | 1 | 1 |
| Huntington Woods | 6,199 | 1 | 0 | 0 | 0 | 1 | 22 | 1 | 20 | 1 | 0 |
| Huron Township | 16,353 | 36 | 1 | 9 | 1 | 25 | 95 | 20 | 69 | 6 | 0 |
| Imlay City | 3,584 | 24 | 0 | 2 | 0 | 22 | 27 | 3 | 23 | 1 | 0 |
| Independence Township | 37,200 | 23 | 0 | 3 | 2 | 18 | 120 | 10 | 99 | 11 | 1 |
| Inkster | 23,999 | 362 | 9 | 28 | 28 | 297 | 426 | 85 | 239 | 102 | 12 |
| Ionia | 10,955 | 27 | 0 | 17 | 0 | 10 | 131 | 8 | 116 | 7 | 0 |
| Iron River | 2,808 | 8 | 0 | 0 | 0 | 8 | 23 | 6 | 14 | 3 | 0 |
| Ironwood | 4,760 | 3 | 0 | 0 | 0 | 3 | 64 | 7 | 52 | 5 | 1 |
| Ishpeming | 6,371 | 24 | 0 | 3 | 0 | 21 | 62 | 6 | 44 | 12 | 1 |
| Ishpeming Township | 3,496 | 1 | 0 | 0 | 0 | 1 | 1 | 0 | 0 | 1 | 0 |
| Jackson | 32,271 | 353 | 8 | 46 | 27 | 272 | 920 | 130 | 681 | 109 | 17 |
| Jonesville | 2,201 | 3 | 0 | 1 | 0 | 2 | 43 | 11 | 30 | 2 | 1 |
| Kalamazoo | 76,179 | 1,211 | 13 | 115 | 106 | 977 | 3,435 | 679 | 2,170 | 586 | 36 |
| Kalamazoo Township | 24,503 | 165 | 4 | 21 | 11 | 129 | 799 | 123 | 527 | 149 | 7 |
| Kalkaska | 2,090 | 4 | 0 | 2 | 0 | 2 | 26 | 2 | 21 | 3 | 0 |
| Keego Harbor | 3,396 | 14 | 0 | 0 | 1 | 13 | 13 | 0 | 11 | 2 | 0 |
| Kentwood | 52,028 | 180 | 1 | 37 | 22 | 120 | 1,275 | 143 | 890 | 242 | 11 |
| Kinde | 407 | 0 | 0 | 0 | 0 | 0 | 0 | 0 | 0 | 0 | 0 |
| Kingston | 404 | 0 | 0 | 0 | 0 | 0 | 4 | 0 | 4 | 0 | 0 |
| Kinross Township | 7,226 | 1 | 0 | 1 | 0 | 0 | 6 | 0 | 4 | 2 | 0 |
| Laingsburg | 1,283 | 1 | 0 | 0 | 0 | 1 | 7 | 1 | 6 | 0 | 1 |
| Lake Angelus | 309 | 0 | 0 | 0 | 0 | 0 | 6 | 0 | 5 | 1 | 0 |
| Lake Linden | 928 | 0 | 0 | 0 | 0 | 0 | 2 | 0 | 2 | 0 | 0 |
| Lake Odessa | 2,043 | 0 | 0 | 0 | 0 | 0 | 0 | 0 | 0 | 0 | 0 |
| Lake Orion | 3,207 | 5 | 0 | 4 | 1 | 0 | 14 | 2 | 12 | 0 | 0 |
| Lakeview | 993 | 4 | 0 | 3 | 0 | 1 | 15 | 2 | 13 | 0 | 0 |
| Lansing | 117,865 | 1,757 | 25 | 142 | 172 | 1,418 | 2,913 | 720 | 1,697 | 496 | 40 |
| Lansing Township | 8,158 | 55 | 1 | 7 | 9 | 38 | 387 | 64 | 276 | 47 | 0 |
| Lapeer | 8,416 | 19 | 0 | 4 | 2 | 13 | 153 | 18 | 123 | 12 | 0 |
| Lapeer Township | 5,017 | 0 | 0 | 0 | 0 | 0 | 4 | 1 | 3 | 0 | 0 |
| Lathrup Village | 4,046 | 5 | 0 | 0 | 1 | 4 | 28 | 2 | 24 | 2 | 0 |
| Laurium | 1,861 | 5 | 0 | 1 | 0 | 4 | 10 | 1 | 7 | 2 | 1 |
| Lawton | 1,791 | 3 | 0 | 0 | 0 | 3 | 35 | 4 | 24 | 7 | 0 |
| Lennon | 476 | 0 | 0 | 0 | 0 | 0 | 0 | 0 | 0 | 0 | 0 |
| Leslie | 1,886 | 4 | 0 | 2 | 0 | 2 | 37 | 5 | 24 | 8 | 0 |

## Table 8. Offenses Known to Law Enforcement, by Selected State and City, 2021—Continued

(Number.)

| State/city | Population | Violent crime | Murder and nonnegligent manslaughter | Rape | Robbery | Aggravated assault | Property crime | Burglary | Larceny-theft | Motor vehicle theft | Arson |
|---|---|---|---|---|---|---|---|---|---|---|---|
| Lexington | 1,114 | 2 | 0 | 0 | 0 | 2 | 3 | 0 | 3 | 0 | 0 |
| Lincoln Park | 35,879 | 269 | 3 | 21 | 23 | 222 | 726 | 107 | 512 | 107 | 10 |
| Lincoln Township | 14,590 | 15 | 0 | 7 | 0 | 8 | 188 | 18 | 158 | 12 | 0 |
| Linden | 3,950 | 5 | 0 | 2 | 0 | 3 | 10 | 0 | 9 | 1 | 0 |
| Litchfield | 1,324 | 0 | 0 | 0 | 0 | 0 | 8 | 0 | 8 | 0 | 0 |
| Livonia | 92,852 | 227 | 1 | 35 | 13 | 178 | 1,338 | 112 | 1,091 | 135 | 10 |
| Lowell | 4,239 | 14 | 0 | 4 | 2 | 8 | 64 | 15 | 44 | 5 | 2 |
| Ludington | 8,098 | 23 | 0 | 5 | 2 | 16 | 52 | 4 | 47 | 1 | 2 |
| Lyon Township | 22,098 | 16 | 0 | 2 | 2 | 12 | 83 | 9 | 70 | 4 | 0 |
| Mackinac Island | 477 | 5 | 0 | 5 | 0 | 0 | 62 | 3 | 59 | 0 | 0 |
| Mackinaw City | 792 | 10 | 0 | 1 | 0 | 9 | 19 | 0 | 18 | 1 | 0 |
| Madison Heights | 29,626 | 88 | 2 | 10 | 17 | 59 | 524 | 69 | 383 | 72 | 2 |
| Madison Township | 7,959 | 18 | 0 | 11 | 0 | 7 | 212 | 6 | 203 | 3 | 0 |
| Manistee | 6,158 | 16 | 0 | 9 | 0 | 7 | 62 | 9 | 44 | 9 | 2 |
| Manistique | 2,933 | 14 | 0 | 2 | 0 | 12 | 67 | 17 | 44 | 6 | 0 |
| Manton | 1,625 | 0 | 0 | 0 | 0 | 0 | 6 | 4 | 2 | 0 | 0 |
| Marenisco Township | 484 | 0 | 0 | 0 | 0 | 0 | 0 | 0 | 0 | 0 | 0 |
| Marine City | 4,015 | 5 | 1 | 1 | 0 | 3 | 25 | 7 | 14 | 4 | 1 |
| Marlette | 1,740 | 8 | 0 | 1 | 0 | 7 | 0 | 0 | 0 | 0 | 0 |
| Marquette | 20,208 | 31 | 1 | 11 | 0 | 19 | 139 | 10 | 116 | 13 | 0 |
| Marshall | 6,910 | 9 | 0 | 1 | 0 | 8 | 98 | 14 | 77 | 7 | 0 |
| Marysville | 9,621 | 14 | 0 | 2 | 0 | 12 | 61 | 10 | 46 | 5 | 0 |
| Mason | 8,402 | 17 | 0 | 4 | 0 | 13 | 47 | 4 | 40 | 3 | 1 |
| Mattawan | 1,972 | 15 | 0 | 0 | 1 | 14 | 34 | 7 | 23 | 4 | 0 |
| Mayville | 878 | 2 | 0 | 1 | 0 | 1 | 7 | 1 | 6 | 0 | 0 |
| Melvindale | 10,134 | 114 | 0 | 8 | 8 | 98 | 216 | 52 | 122 | 42 | 7 |
| Memphis | 1,167 | 2 | 0 | 0 | 0 | 2 | 2 | 0 | 2 | 0 | 0 |
| Mendon | 845 | 2 | 0 | 0 | 0 | 2 | 15 | 0 | 14 | 1 | 0 |
| Menominee | 7,909 | 35 | 0 | 11 | 0 | 24 | 127 | 20 | 97 | 10 | 0 |
| Meridian Township | 43,146 | 76 | 0 | 25 | 9 | 42 | 720 | 57 | 598 | 65 | 7 |
| Metamora Township | 4,323 | 6 | 1 | 2 | 0 | 3 | 14 | 2 | 12 | 0 | 0 |
| Metro Police Authority of Genesee County | 19,899 | 41 | 0 | 5 | 4 | 32 | 223 | 46 | 156 | 21 | 0 |
| Midland | 41,758 | 53 | 0 | 20 | 1 | 32 | 291 | 24 | 252 | 15 | 0 |
| Milan | 6,028 | 16 | 0 | 3 | 1 | 12 | 48 | 6 | 39 | 3 | 0 |
| Milford | 16,969 | 8 | 0 | 4 | 0 | 4 | 39 | 4 | 33 | 2 | 1 |
| Millington | 1,002 | 4 | 0 | 3 | 0 | 1 | 5 | 2 | 3 | 0 | 0 |
| Montague | 2,366 | 1 | 0 | 1 | 0 | 0 | 27 | 1 | 26 | 0 | 0 |
| Montrose Township | 7,420 | 8 | 0 | 3 | 0 | 5 | 50 | 6 | 37 | 7 | 0 |
| Morrice | 904 | 0 | 0 | 0 | 0 | 0 | 3 | 1 | 2 | 0 | 0 |
| Mount Morris | 2,803 | 18 | 0 | 4 | 0 | 14 | 70 | 23 | 39 | 8 | 0 |
| Mount Morris Township | 20,084 | 174 | 2 | 8 | 5 | 159 | 316 | 117 | 137 | 62 | 6 |
| Mount Pleasant | 24,109 | 49 | 1 | 10 | 3 | 35 | 253 | 21 | 216 | 16 | 4 |
| Munising | 2,171 | 3 | 0 | 0 | 0 | 3 | 15 | 1 | 12 | 2 | 0 |
| Muskegon | 36,296 | 278 | 4 | 16 | 22 | 236 | 895 | 125 | 694 | 76 | 17 |
| Muskegon Heights | 10,673 | 166 | 3 | 17 | 15 | 131 | 386 | 63 | 284 | 39 | 6 |
| Muskegon Township | 18,043 | 50 | 1 | 5 | 4 | 40 | 335 | 33 | 279 | 23 | 2 |
| Napoleon Township | 6,696 | 3 | 0 | 0 | 0 | 3 | 19 | 6 | 12 | 1 | 0 |
| Nashville | 1,704 | 4 | 0 | 2 | 0 | 2 | 14 | 2 | 10 | 2 | 0 |
| Negaunee | 4,494 | 2 | 0 | 2 | 0 | 0 | 48 | 1 | 43 | 4 | 0 |
| Newaygo | 2,110 | 3 | 0 | 1 | 0 | 2 | 52 | 10 | 40 | 2 | 0 |
| New Baltimore | 12,301 | 16 | 0 | 7 | 1 | 8 | 34 | 3 | 28 | 3 | 1 |
| New Buffalo | 1,863 | 1 | 0 | 0 | 0 | 1 | 22 | 2 | 20 | 0 | 0 |
| New Era | 439 | 1 | 0 | 0 | 0 | 1 | 1 | 0 | 1 | 0 | 0 |
| New Lothrop | 545 | 0 | 0 | 0 | 0 | 0 | 0 | 0 | 0 | 0 | 0 |
| Niles | 11,045 | 69 | 0 | 17 | 8 | 44 | 288 | 23 | 222 | 43 | 6 |
| Northfield Township | 8,679 | 10 | 0 | 2 | 0 | 8 | 56 | 6 | 40 | 10 | 0 |
| North Muskegon | 3,792 | 4 | 0 | 1 | 1 | 2 | 30 | 2 | 27 | 1 | 0 |
| Northville | 5,922 | 9 | 0 | 2 | 1 | 6 | 20 | 0 | 18 | 2 | 0 |
| Northville Township | 29,443 | 30 | 0 | 3 | 1 | 26 | 199 | 25 | 145 | 29 | 1 |
| Norton Shores | 24,689 | 46 | 1 | 10 | 5 | 30 | 506 | 43 | 440 | 23 | 2 |
| Novi | 61,440 | 48 | 0 | 6 | 8 | 34 | 448 | 24 | 369 | 55 | 1 |
| Oakland Township | 20,072 | 8 | 0 | 0 | 0 | 8 | 25 | 1 | 22 | 2 | 3 |
| Oakley | 269 | 0 | 0 | 0 | 0 | 0 | 0 | 0 | 0 | 0 | 0 |
| Oak Park | 29,280 | 87 | 1 | 11 | 15 | 60 | 372 | 52 | 248 | 72 | 0 |
| Olivet | 1,887 | 1 | 0 | 1 | 0 | 0 | 15 | 1 | 14 | 0 | 0 |
| Ontwa Township-Edwardsburg | 6,574 | 16 | 0 | 5 | 0 | 11 | 72 | 13 | 53 | 6 | 1 |
| Orchard Lake | 2,480 | 5 | 0 | 0 | 0 | 5 | 13 | 4 | 8 | 1 | 0 |
| Orion Township | 37,104 | 21 | 0 | 5 | 1 | 15 | 143 | 16 | 113 | 14 | 0 |
| Oscoda Township | 6,743 | 28 | 1 | 8 | 0 | 19 | 34 | 6 | 24 | 4 | 1 |
| Otisville | 821 | 0 | 0 | 0 | 0 | 0 | 7 | 0 | 7 | 0 | 0 |
| Otsego | 3,990 | 9 | 0 | 1 | 0 | 8 | 45 | 1 | 35 | 9 | 0 |
| Ovid | 1,609 | 2 | 0 | 1 | 0 | 1 | 4 | 0 | 4 | 0 | 0 |
| Owendale | 219 | 0 | 0 | 0 | 0 | 0 | 0 | 0 | 0 | 0 | 0 |
| Owosso | 14,258 | 102 | 0 | 21 | 3 | 78 | 245 | 47 | 178 | 20 | 4 |
| Oxford | 3,552 | 2 | 0 | 0 | 0 | 2 | 12 | 2 | 10 | 0 | 0 |
| Oxford Township | 19,529 | 23 | 4 | 3 | 0 | 16 | 37 | 6 | 24 | 7 | 0 |
| Paw Paw | 3,328 | 12 | 0 | 1 | 3 | 8 | 131 | 16 | 106 | 9 | 0 |
| Peck | 584 | 1 | 0 | 0 | 0 | 1 | 2 | 1 | 1 | 0 | 0 |
| Pentwater | 858 | 1 | 0 | 0 | 0 | 1 | 9 | 1 | 8 | 0 | 0 |
| Perry | 2,066 | 2 | 0 | 0 | 0 | 2 | 14 | 1 | 12 | 1 | 0 |
| Petoskey | 5,734 | 14 | 0 | 2 | 1 | 11 | 30 | 7 | 18 | 5 | 0 |
| Pigeon | 1,099 | 0 | 0 | 0 | 0 | 0 | 0 | 0 | 0 | 0 | 0 |

## Table 8. Offenses Known to Law Enforcement, by Selected State and City, 2021—Continued

(Number.)

| State/city | Population | Violent crime | Murder and nonnegligent manslaughter | Rape | Robbery | Aggravated assault | Property crime | Burglary | Larceny-theft | Motor vehicle theft | Arson |
|---|---|---|---|---|---|---|---|---|---|---|---|
| Pinckney | 2,425 | 4 | 0 | 2 | 0 | 2 | 16 | 4 | 12 | 0 | 0 |
| Pittsfield Township | 39,327 | 100 | 1 | 21 | 9 | 69 | 580 | 38 | 490 | 52 | 1 |
| Plainwell | 3,771 | 6 | 0 | 1 | 1 | 4 | 34 | 5 | 25 | 4 | 0 |
| Pleasant Ridge | 2,399 | 3 | 1 | 0 | 0 | 2 | 18 | 1 | 15 | 2 | 0 |
| Plymouth | 9,141 | 5 | 0 | 1 | 0 | 4 | 54 | 6 | 42 | 6 | 0 |
| Plymouth Township | 26,895 | 22 | 0 | 4 | 3 | 15 | 177 | 13 | 139 | 25 | 1 |
| Pontiac | 58,834 | 712 | 15 | 46 | 57 | 594 | 1,017 | 239 | 655 | 123 | 17 |
| Portage | 50,141 | 134 | 3 | 32 | 21 | 78 | 1,677 | 155 | 1,348 | 174 | 6 |
| Port Austin | 610 | 0 | 0 | 0 | 0 | 0 | 5 | 1 | 4 | 0 | 0 |
| Port Huron | 28,487 | 225 | 1 | 32 | 13 | 179 | 537 | 104 | 402 | 31 | 9 |
| Portland | 4,024 | 12 | 0 | 3 | 0 | 9 | 30 | 3 | 26 | 1 | 0 |
| Prairieville Township | 3,548 | 2 | 0 | 2 | 0 | 0 | 6 | 0 | 6 | 0 | 0 |
| Quincy | 1,614 | 5 | 0 | 1 | 0 | 4 | 34 | 7 | 26 | 1 | 1 |
| Raisin Township | 7,817 | 8 | 0 | 2 | 0 | 6 | 23 | 2 | 19 | 2 | 0 |
| Redford Township | 46,112 | 309 | 4 | 45 | 28 | 232 | 912 | 179 | 524 | 209 | 16 |
| Reed City | 2,372 | 16 | 0 | 2 | 0 | 14 | 33 | 6 | 25 | 2 | 2 |
| Reese | 1,358 | 2 | 0 | 1 | 1 | 0 | 8 | 0 | 8 | 0 | 0 |
| Richfield Township, Genesee County | 8,300 | 13 | 0 | 4 | 0 | 9 | 56 | 15 | 31 | 10 | 0 |
| Richfield Township, Roscommon County | 3,642 | 1 | 0 | 0 | 0 | 1 | 5 | 1 | 4 | 0 | 0 |
| Richland | 858 | 0 | 0 | 0 | 0 | 0 | 8 | 0 | 7 | 1 | 0 |
| Richland Township, Saginaw County | 3,891 | 11 | 0 | 1 | 0 | 10 | 9 | 3 | 6 | 0 | 0 |
| Richmond | 5,801 | 13 | 0 | 3 | 0 | 10 | 21 | 1 | 19 | 1 | 0 |
| River Rouge | 7,319 | 5 | 0 | 0 | 1 | 4 | 7 | 1 | 1 | 5 | 0 |
| Riverview | 11,920 | 24 | 0 | 3 | 2 | 19 | 87 | 5 | 73 | 9 | 3 |
| Rochester | 13,251 | 9 | 0 | 2 | 0 | 7 | 33 | 4 | 24 | 5 | 0 |
| Rochester Hills | 74,426 | 45 | 0 | 7 | 2 | 36 | 410 | 20 | 358 | 32 | 4 |
| Rockford | 6,468 | 10 | 0 | 5 | 1 | 4 | 39 | 1 | 35 | 3 | 2 |
| Rockwood | 3,133 | 0 | 0 | 0 | 0 | 0 | 11 | 3 | 7 | 1 | 0 |
| Rogers City | 2,651 | 4 | 0 | 3 | 0 | 1 | 4 | 1 | 3 | 0 | 0 |
| Romeo | 3,569 | 3 | 0 | 1 | 0 | 2 | 12 | 0 | 9 | 3 | 0 |
| Romulus | 23,488 | 214 | 7 | 22 | 12 | 173 | 653 | 86 | 437 | 130 | 1 |
| Roosevelt Park | 3,781 | 3 | 0 | 0 | 1 | 2 | 260 | 6 | 249 | 5 | 0 |
| Rose City | 627 | 0 | 0 | 0 | 0 | 0 | 0 | 0 | 0 | 0 | 0 |
| Roseville | 46,456 | 255 | 1 | 39 | 34 | 181 | 1,193 | 113 | 924 | 156 | 5 |
| Rothbury | 457 | 1 | 0 | 0 | 0 | 1 | 3 | 0 | 3 | 0 | 0 |
| Royal Oak | 59,137 | 60 | 0 | 8 | 9 | 43 | 406 | 29 | 340 | 37 | 2 |
| Saginaw | 47,480 | 1,080 | 14 | 36 | 52 | 978 | 737 | 222 | 406 | 109 | 24 |
| Saginaw Township | 38,836 | 84 | 2 | 8 | 14 | 60 | 499 | 49 | 410 | 40 | 2 |
| Saline | 9,402 | 10 | 0 | 1 | 0 | 9 | 68 | 4 | 51 | 13 | 1 |
| Sandusky | 2,477 | 5 | 0 | 3 | 0 | 2 | 25 | 5 | 19 | 1 | 1 |
| Saugatuck-Douglas | 2,337 | 1 | 0 | 0 | 0 | 1 | 19 | 0 | 19 | 0 | 0 |
| Sault Ste. Marie | 13,282 | 32 | 1 | 14 | 0 | 17 | 135 | 8 | 124 | 3 | 0 |
| Schoolcraft | 1,550 | 2 | 0 | 0 | 0 | 2 | 24 | 4 | 17 | 3 | 0 |
| Scottville | 1,209 | 1 | 0 | 0 | 0 | 1 | 4 | 0 | 4 | 0 | 0 |
| Sebewaing | 1,597 | 0 | 0 | 0 | 0 | 0 | 6 | 1 | 5 | 0 | 0 |
| Shelby | 2,042 | 8 | 0 | 1 | 0 | 7 | 33 | 2 | 29 | 2 | 0 |
| Shelby Township | 82,164 | 113 | 1 | 34 | 2 | 76 | 379 | 41 | 306 | 32 | 1 |
| Shepherd | 1,488 | 0 | 0 | 0 | 0 | 0 | 13 | 3 | 9 | 1 | 0 |
| Somerset Township | 4,520 | 5 | 0 | 1 | 1 | 3 | 26 | 10 | 12 | 4 | 0 |
| Southfield | 72,216 | 365 | 4 | 49 | 57 | 255 | 1,521 | 237 | 935 | 349 | 8 |
| Southgate | 29,052 | 103 | 2 | 11 | 14 | 76 | 584 | 79 | 441 | 64 | 5 |
| South Haven | 4,320 | 26 | 3 | 0 | 7 | 16 | 206 | 20 | 177 | 9 | 1 |
| South Lyon | 11,899 | 7 | 0 | 3 | 0 | 4 | 38 | 3 | 32 | 3 | 0 |
| Sparta | 4,437 | 4 | 0 | 2 | 1 | 1 | 33 | 2 | 26 | 5 | 0 |
| Spring Arbor Township | 7,684 | 4 | 0 | 0 | 0 | 4 | 10 | 2 | 5 | 3 | 0 |
| Springfield Township | 14,495 | 8 | 0 | 1 | 0 | 7 | 54 | 3 | 45 | 6 | 0 |
| Springport Township | 2,134 | 5 | 1 | 1 | 0 | 3 | 18 | 5 | 11 | 2 | 0 |
| Stanton | 1,421 | 0 | 0 | 0 | 0 | 0 | 2 | 0 | 2 | 0 | 0 |
| St. Charles | 1,871 | 4 | 0 | 0 | 0 | 4 | 18 | 0 | 18 | 0 | 0 |
| St. Clair | 5,500 | 9 | 0 | 1 | 0 | 8 | 35 | 8 | 24 | 3 | 0 |
| St. Clair Shores | 58,254 | 104 | 0 | 17 | 13 | 74 | 458 | 72 | 337 | 49 | 3 |
| Sterling Heights | 131,911 | 240 | 2 | 35 | 21 | 182 | 1,115 | 87 | 842 | 186 | 5 |
| St. Ignace | 2,315 | 4 | 0 | 1 | 0 | 3 | 27 | 4 | 22 | 1 | 0 |
| St. Johns | 7,908 | 16 | 0 | 7 | 0 | 9 | 34 | 8 | 25 | 1 | 0 |
| St. Joseph | 8,283 | 18 | 0 | 5 | 2 | 11 | 72 | 7 | 61 | 4 | 0 |
| St. Joseph Township | 9,602 | 27 | 0 | 5 | 1 | 21 | 73 | 8 | 60 | 5 | 1 |
| St. Louis | 7,051 | 6 | 0 | 1 | 0 | 5 | 46 | 4 | 36 | 6 | 1 |
| Stockbridge | 1,243 | 2 | 0 | 1 | 0 | 1 | 9 | 1 | 7 | 1 | 0 |
| Sturgis | 10,771 | 40 | 0 | 8 | 2 | 30 | 211 | 28 | 141 | 42 | 0 |
| Sumpter Township | 9,337 | 16 | 0 | 0 | 0 | 16 | 44 | 3 | 31 | 10 | 0 |
| Sylvan Lake | 1,848 | 2 | 0 | 0 | 0 | 2 | 17 | 0 | 17 | 0 | 0 |
| Tawas City | 1,777 | 5 | 0 | 0 | 0 | 5 | 44 | 1 | 42 | 1 | 0 |
| Taylor | 60,341 | 324 | 2 | 35 | 28 | 259 | 1,212 | 188 | 833 | 191 | 10 |
| Tecumseh | 8,369 | 11 | 0 | 5 | 0 | 6 | 40 | 4 | 31 | 5 | 0 |
| Thomas Township | 11,366 | 25 | 0 | 0 | 0 | 25 | 69 | 2 | 61 | 6 | 0 |
| Three Oaks | 1,533 | 3 | 0 | 3 | 0 | 0 | 28 | 0 | 24 | 4 | 0 |
| Three Rivers | 7,579 | 73 | 0 | 13 | 4 | 56 | 253 | 30 | 208 | 15 | 0 |
| Tittabawassee Township | 10,031 | 9 | 0 | 0 | 0 | 9 | 50 | 5 | 43 | 2 | 0 |
| Traverse City | 15,840 | 63 | 0 | 14 | 2 | 47 | 189 | 17 | 162 | 10 | 0 |
| Trenton | 17,954 | 14 | 0 | 2 | 5 | 7 | 84 | 7 | 68 | 9 | 0 |

## Table 8. Offenses Known to Law Enforcement, by Selected State and City, 2021—Continued

(Number.)

| State/city | Population | Violent crime | Murder and nonnegligent manslaughter | Rape | Robbery | Aggravated assault | Property crime | Burglary | Larceny-theft | Motor vehicle theft | Arson |
|---|---|---|---|---|---|---|---|---|---|---|---|
| Troy | 83,851 | 98 | 3 | 15 | 20 | 60 | 871 | 53 | 712 | 106 | 4 |
| Tuscarora Township | 2,918 | 2 | 0 | 1 | 0 | 1 | 57 | 2 | 55 | 0 | 0 |
| Ubly | 771 | 3 | 0 | 2 | 0 | 1 | 6 | 0 | 6 | 0 | 0 |
| Unadilla Township | 3,483 | 5 | 0 | 2 | 0 | 3 | 13 | 2 | 11 | 0 | 0 |
| Union City | 1,561 | 4 | 0 | 1 | 0 | 3 | 60 | 5 | 53 | 2 | 0 |
| Utica | 5,094 | 14 | 0 | 5 | 0 | 9 | 170 | 11 | 148 | 11 | 1 |
| Van Buren Township | 28,390 | 94 | 1 | 21 | 5 | 67 | 583 | 37 | 469 | 77 | 4 |
| Vassar | 2,521 | 11 | 0 | 3 | 0 | 8 | 15 | 6 | 9 | 0 | 0 |
| Vernon | 762 | 1 | 0 | 0 | 0 | 1 | 1 | 0 | 1 | 0 | 0 |
| Vicksburg | 3,657 | 7 | 0 | 5 | 0 | 2 | 60 | 3 | 49 | 8 | 0 |
| Walker | 25,443 | 38 | 1 | 9 | 9 | 19 | 635 | 58 | 538 | 39 | 1 |
| Walled Lake | 7,082 | 3 | 0 | 1 | 0 | 2 | 31 | 5 | 22 | 4 | 0 |
| Warren | 132,758 | 716 | 5 | 110 | 95 | 506 | 2,140 | 361 | 1,349 | 430 | 14 |
| Waterford Township | 72,213 | 152 | 0 | 17 | 6 | 129 | 558 | 143 | 360 | 55 | 5 |
| Watersmeet Township | 1,346 | 0 | 0 | 0 | 0 | 0 | 1 | 0 | 1 | 0 | 0 |
| Watervliet | 1,627 | 6 | 0 | 5 | 0 | 1 | 16 | 2 | 13 | 1 | 0 |
| Wayland | 4,253 | 10 | 0 | 2 | 0 | 8 | 49 | 4 | 40 | 5 | 1 |
| Wayne | 16,616 | 146 | 0 | 16 | 18 | 112 | 263 | 59 | 159 | 45 | 4 |
| West Bloomfield Township | 65,720 | 70 | 0 | 11 | 6 | 53 | 236 | 19 | 197 | 20 | 1 |
| West Branch | 2,037 | 5 | 0 | 1 | 0 | 4 | 24 | 2 | 21 | 1 | 0 |
| Westland | 80,837 | 348 | 1 | 50 | 27 | 270 | 1,038 | 182 | 712 | 144 | 11 |
| White Cloud | 1,381 | 1 | 0 | 0 | 0 | 1 | 3 | 0 | 3 | 0 | 0 |
| Whitehall | 2,879 | 8 | 0 | 4 | 1 | 3 | 31 | 1 | 28 | 2 | 0 |
| White Lake Township | 31,747 | 19 | 0 | 1 | 1 | 17 | 107 | 8 | 92 | 7 | 0 |
| White Pigeon | 1,520 | 3 | 0 | 1 | 0 | 2 | 23 | 1 | 16 | 6 | 0 |
| Williamston | 3,935 | 8 | 0 | 0 | 1 | 7 | 19 | 1 | 17 | 1 | 0 |
| Wixom | 14,145 | 35 | 0 | 5 | 3 | 27 | 215 | 18 | 168 | 29 | 2 |
| Wolverine Lake | 4,788 | 5 | 0 | 1 | 0 | 4 | 8 | 1 | 6 | 1 | 0 |
| Woodhaven | 12,388 | 21 | 0 | 2 | 5 | 14 | 146 | 10 | 117 | 19 | 0 |
| Wyandotte | 24,600 | 86 | 0 | 9 | 4 | 73 | 278 | 33 | 205 | 40 | 1 |
| Wyoming | 77,094 | 419 | 2 | 80 | 57 | 280 | 1,122 | 137 | 604 | 381 | 13 |
| Yale | 1,853 | 14 | 0 | 0 | 0 | 14 | 5 | 1 | 4 | 0 | 0 |
| Ypsilanti | 19,986 | 323 | 4 | 55 | 35 | 229 | 470 | 110 | 303 | 57 | 4 |
| Zeeland | 5,524 | 20 | 0 | 5 | 0 | 15 | 42 | 4 | 38 | 0 | 0 |
| Zilwaukee | 1,504 | 2 | 1 | 0 | 0 | 1 | 11 | 1 | 9 | 1 | 0 |
| **MINNESOTA** | | | | | | | | | | | |
| Aitkin | 1,954 | 3 | 0 | 2 | 0 | 1 | 55 | 10 | 39 | 6 | 0 |
| Akeley | 450 | 2 | 0 | 2 | 0 | 0 | 10 | 2 | 7 | 1 | 0 |
| Albert Lea | 17,686 | 28 | 0 | 3 | 3 | 22 | 461 | 88 | 338 | 35 | 0 |
| Alexandria | 14,032 | 47 | 0 | 3 | 1 | 43 | 262 | 20 | 231 | 11 | 1 |
| Annandale | 3,579 | 7 | 0 | 1 | 0 | 6 | 15 | 0 | 13 | 2 | 0 |
| Anoka | 17,553 | 35 | 0 | 13 | 5 | 17 | 246 | 25 | 218 | 3 | 3 |
| Appleton | 1,301 | 6 | 0 | 0 | 0 | 6 | 24 | 2 | 22 | 0 | 0 |
| Apple Valley | 55,455 | 97 | 0 | 20 | 8 | 69 | 1,110 | 76 | 979 | 55 | 2 |
| Atwater | 1,111 | 0 | 0 | 0 | 0 | 0 | 6 | 0 | 5 | 1 | 0 |
| Austin | 25,382 | 91 | 2 | 11 | 13 | 65 | 544 | 78 | 426 | 40 | 8 |
| Avon | 1,680 | 1 | 0 | 0 | 0 | 1 | 11 | 0 | 8 | 3 | 0 |
| Barnesville | 2,628 | 1 | 0 | 0 | 0 | 1 | 2 | 1 | 1 | 0 | 0 |
| Baxter | 8,571 | 11 | 0 | 2 | 0 | 9 | 308 | 18 | 278 | 12 | 1 |
| Bayport | 3,822 | 0 | 0 | 0 | 0 | 0 | 18 | 0 | 16 | 2 | 0 |
| Becker | 5,080 | 2 | 0 | 1 | 0 | 1 | 32 | 1 | 30 | 1 | 2 |
| Belgrade/Brooten | 1,543 | 0 | 0 | 0 | 0 | 0 | 14 | 1 | 13 | 0 | 0 |
| Belle Plaine | 7,166 | 10 | 0 | 3 | 0 | 7 | 76 | 9 | 62 | 5 | 0 |
| Bemidji | 15,574 | 86 | 0 | 15 | 12 | 59 | 1,206 | 89 | 1,075 | 42 | 5 |
| Benson | 2,977 | 9 | 0 | 1 | 0 | 8 | 0 | 0 | 0 | 0 | 0 |
| Big Lake | 11,721 | 5 | 0 | 2 | 1 | 2 | 57 | 5 | 48 | 4 | 0 |
| Blackduck | 838 | 0 | 0 | 0 | 0 | 0 | 2 | 0 | 2 | 0 | 0 |
| Blaine | 67,705 | 81 | 0 | 17 | 17 | 47 | 1,411 | 136 | 1,186 | 89 | 5 |
| Blooming Prairie | 1,921 | 2 | 0 | 0 | 0 | 2 | 4 | 0 | 4 | 0 | 0 |
| Bloomington | 84,740 | 263 | 1 | 41 | 74 | 147 | 3,098 | 256 | 2,543 | 299 | 16 |
| Blue Earth | 3,078 | 4 | 0 | 3 | 0 | 1 | 5 | 1 | 3 | 1 | 0 |
| Braham | 1,856 | 1 | 0 | 0 | 0 | 1 | 12 | 0 | 10 | 2 | 0 |
| Brainerd | 13,436 | 72 | 0 | 16 | 4 | 52 | 360 | 41 | 282 | 37 | 0 |
| Breckenridge | 3,111 | 8 | 0 | 1 | 0 | 7 | 29 | 5 | 23 | 1 | 0 |
| Breezy Point | 2,447 | 1 | 0 | 0 | 0 | 1 | 6 | 1 | 5 | 0 | 0 |
| Brooklyn Center | 30,258 | 178 | 4 | 19 | 65 | 90 | 1,105 | 183 | 721 | 201 | 5 |
| Brooklyn Park | 79,946 | 352 | 6 | 35 | 104 | 207 | 2,569 | 356 | 1,870 | 343 | 9 |
| Brownton | 706 | 1 | 0 | 0 | 0 | 1 | 4 | 1 | 3 | 0 | 0 |
| Buffalo | 16,994 | 6 | 0 | 0 | 0 | 6 | 131 | 13 | 114 | 4 | 0 |
| Buffalo Lake | 672 | 1 | 0 | 0 | 0 | 1 | 1 | 0 | 1 | 0 | 0 |
| Burnsville | 62,351 | 132 | 1 | 23 | 22 | 86 | 1,587 | 111 | 1,339 | 137 | 2 |
| Caledonia | 2,743 | 0 | 0 | 0 | 0 | 0 | 0 | 0 | 0 | 0 | 0 |
| Cambridge | 9,540 | 12 | 0 | 0 | 1 | 11 | 388 | 21 | 348 | 19 | 0 |
| Canby | 1,631 | 2 | 0 | 1 | 0 | 1 | 24 | 2 | 22 | 0 | 0 |
| Cannon Falls | 4,016 | 2 | 0 | 1 | 0 | 1 | 64 | 3 | 53 | 8 | 2 |
| Centennial Lakes | 11,721 | 18 | 0 | 0 | 1 | 17 | 128 | 8 | 115 | 5 | 0 |
| Champlin | 25,249 | 22 | 0 | 6 | 1 | 15 | 242 | 29 | 202 | 11 | 0 |
| Chisholm | 4,786 | 14 | 0 | 4 | 0 | 10 | 167 | 21 | 137 | 9 | 0 |
| Clara City | 1,265 | 2 | 0 | 0 | 0 | 2 | 1 | 0 | 1 | 0 | 0 |
| Cleveland | 733 | 0 | 0 | 0 | 0 | 0 | 9 | 1 | 6 | 2 | 0 |
| Cloquet | 12,002 | 27 | 0 | 1 | 0 | 26 | 210 | 5 | 196 | 9 | 0 |
| Cold Spring/Richmond | 5,869 | 4 | 0 | 1 | 0 | 3 | 27 | 2 | 25 | 0 | 1 |

# Table 8. Offenses Known to Law Enforcement, by Selected State and City, 2021—Continued

(Number.)

| State/city | Population | Violent crime | Murder and nonnegligent manslaughter | Rape | Robbery | Aggravated assault | Property crime | Burglary | Larceny-theft | Motor vehicle theft | Arson |
|---|---|---|---|---|---|---|---|---|---|---|---|
| Columbia Heights | 21,238 | 83 | 0 | 11 | 12 | 60 | 440 | 33 | 337 | 70 | 4 |
| Comfrey | 349 | 0 | 0 | 0 | 0 | 0 | 0 | 0 | 0 | 0 | 0 |
| Coon Rapids | 63,076 | 124 | 0 | 21 | 20 | 83 | 1,180 | 149 | 933 | 98 | 14 |
| Corcoran | 6,742 | 1 | 0 | 0 | 0 | 1 | 37 | 2 | 34 | 1 | 0 |
| Cottage Grove | 38,534 | 37 | 0 | 7 | 6 | 24 | 446 | 66 | 349 | 31 | 1 |
| Crookston | 7,605 | 25 | 0 | 10 | 0 | 15 | 81 | 16 | 59 | 6 | 1 |
| Crosby | 2,308 | 5 | 0 | 0 | 0 | 5 | 2 | 0 | 2 | 0 | 0 |
| Crosslake | 2,399 | 1 | 0 | 0 | 0 | 1 | 27 | 6 | 21 | 0 | 0 |
| Crystal | 22,628 | 87 | 0 | 11 | 23 | 53 | 439 | 41 | 322 | 76 | 1 |
| Cuyuna | 370 | 0 | 0 | 0 | 0 | 0 | 0 | 0 | 0 | 0 | 0 |
| Dayton | 7,754 | 4 | 0 | 0 | 0 | 4 | 38 | 1 | 30 | 7 | 0 |
| Deephaven | 3,926 | 0 | 0 | 0 | 0 | 0 | 26 | 3 | 19 | 4 | 0 |
| Deer River | 929 | 2 | 0 | 1 | 0 | 1 | 5 | 0 | 5 | 0 | 0 |
| Deerwood | 752 | 0 | 0 | 0 | 0 | 0 | 5 | 1 | 4 | 0 | 0 |
| Detroit Lakes | 9,310 | 26 | 0 | 5 | 1 | 20 | 260 | 23 | 217 | 20 | 0 |
| Dilworth | 4,497 | 15 | 0 | 2 | 2 | 11 | 276 | 34 | 224 | 18 | 1 |
| Duluth | 85,731 | 318 | 1 | 74 | 23 | 220 | 3,273 | 382 | 2,613 | 278 | 21 |
| Dundas | 1,682 | 1 | 0 | 1 | 0 | 0 | 27 | 3 | 24 | 0 | 1 |
| Eagan | 66,155 | 66 | 1 | 10 | 12 | 43 | 1,660 | 151 | 1,393 | 116 | 2 |
| Eagle Lake | 3,204 | 6 | 0 | 2 | 0 | 4 | 16 | 7 | 8 | 1 | 0 |
| East Grand Forks | 8,379 | 8 | 0 | 0 | 0 | 8 | 37 | 4 | 31 | 2 | 0 |
| Eden Prairie | 65,308 | 42 | 1 | 17 | 8 | 16 | 948 | 78 | 804 | 66 | 2 |
| Eden Valley | 1,037 | 1 | 0 | 0 | 0 | 1 | 1 | 0 | 1 | 0 | 0 |
| Edina | 52,943 | 37 | 0 | 9 | 15 | 13 | 1,037 | 231 | 732 | 74 | 1 |
| Elko New Market | 4,800 | 1 | 0 | 0 | 1 | 0 | 20 | 2 | 17 | 1 | 0 |
| Elk River | 25,873 | 28 | 0 | 19 | 0 | 9 | 414 | 31 | 367 | 16 | 0 |
| Elmore | 608 | 0 | 0 | 0 | 0 | 0 | 3 | 0 | 2 | 1 | 0 |
| Ely | 3,313 | 6 | 0 | 1 | 0 | 5 | 36 | 2 | 29 | 5 | 0 |
| Emily | 844 | 0 | 0 | 0 | 0 | 0 | 0 | 0 | 0 | 0 | 0 |
| Eveleth | 3,519 | 10 | 0 | 2 | 0 | 8 | 106 | 14 | 82 | 10 | 1 |
| Fairfax | 1,108 | 1 | 0 | 1 | 0 | 0 | 12 | 1 | 10 | 1 | 0 |
| Fairmont | 9,852 | 31 | 0 | 11 | 0 | 20 | 129 | 15 | 103 | 11 | 1 |
| Faribault | 23,960 | 70 | 1 | 33 | 3 | 33 | 371 | 47 | 295 | 29 | 3 |
| Farmington | 23,235 | 29 | 3 | 8 | 0 | 18 | 132 | 12 | 108 | 12 | 0 |
| Fergus Falls | 13,791 | 24 | 0 | 6 | 4 | 14 | 369 | 42 | 306 | 21 | 1 |
| Floodwood | 524 | 0 | 0 | 0 | 0 | 0 | 0 | 0 | 0 | 0 | 0 |
| Foley | 2,678 | 9 | 0 | 2 | 0 | 7 | 92 | 4 | 87 | 1 | 0 |
| Forest Lake | 21,592 | 26 | 0 | 13 | 1 | 12 | 547 | 92 | 416 | 39 | 2 |
| Fridley | 27,919 | 112 | 1 | 9 | 24 | 78 | 1,212 | 75 | 1,014 | 123 | 6 |
| Fulda | 1,196 | 5 | 0 | 0 | 0 | 5 | 6 | 0 | 6 | 0 | 0 |
| Gaylord | 2,237 | 2 | 0 | 0 | 0 | 2 | 18 | 2 | 14 | 2 | 0 |
| Gilbert | 1,758 | 9 | 0 | 1 | 0 | 8 | 62 | 11 | 51 | 0 | 0 |
| Glencoe | 5,484 | 11 | 0 | 1 | 0 | 10 | 66 | 1 | 62 | 3 | 0 |
| Glenwood | 2,610 | 4 | 0 | 0 | 0 | 4 | 31 | 0 | 29 | 2 | 0 |
| Glyndon | 1,384 | 1 | 0 | 1 | 0 | 0 | 23 | 5 | 16 | 2 | 0 |
| Golden Valley | 21,740 | 39 | 0 | 6 | 9 | 24 | 497 | 104 | 317 | 76 | 2 |
| Goodhue | 1,163 | 0 | 0 | 0 | 0 | 0 | 10 | 0 | 9 | 1 | 0 |
| Goodview | 4,138 | 2 | 0 | 0 | 0 | 2 | 5 | 1 | 3 | 1 | 0 |
| Grand Rapids | 11,255 | 12 | 0 | 3 | 0 | 9 | 75 | 0 | 65 | 10 | 1 |
| Granite Falls | 2,648 | 1 | 0 | 1 | 0 | 0 | 30 | 9 | 19 | 2 | 0 |
| Hallock | 896 | 0 | 0 | 0 | 0 | 0 | 1 | 0 | 1 | 0 | 0 |
| Hastings | 22,955 | 22 | 1 | 11 | 1 | 9 | 329 | 43 | 263 | 23 | 2 |
| Hawley | 2,225 | 0 | 0 | 0 | 0 | 0 | 19 | 2 | 15 | 2 | 1 |
| Hector | 1,031 | 2 | 0 | 0 | 0 | 2 | 7 | 0 | 5 | 2 | 0 |
| Hermantown | 9,512 | 11 | 0 | 0 | 0 | 11 | 530 | 33 | 478 | 19 | 0 |
| Heron Lake | 638 | 0 | 0 | 0 | 0 | 0 | 1 | 0 | 1 | 0 | 0 |
| Hibbing | 15,655 | 4 | 0 | 0 | 0 | 4 | 97 | 1 | 80 | 16 | 0 |
| Hill City | 575 | 1 | 0 | 0 | 0 | 1 | 8 | 1 | 7 | 0 | 0 |
| Hokah | 545 | 0 | 0 | 0 | 0 | 0 | 0 | 0 | 0 | 0 | 0 |
| Hopkins | 18,272 | 51 | 1 | 6 | 11 | 33 | 479 | 68 | 359 | 52 | 2 |
| Hutchinson | 13,961 | 39 | 0 | 13 | 2 | 24 | 188 | 13 | 165 | 10 | 0 |
| International Falls | 5,648 | 33 | 0 | 1 | 0 | 32 | 65 | 6 | 55 | 4 | 0 |
| Inver Grove Heights | 35,957 | 101 | 1 | 18 | 9 | 73 | 835 | 69 | 662 | 104 | 2 |
| Isanti | 6,576 | 9 | 0 | 1 | 0 | 8 | 93 | 8 | 79 | 6 | 0 |
| Isle | 793 | 6 | 0 | 0 | 0 | 6 | 34 | 7 | 25 | 2 | 0 |
| Janesville | 2,246 | 4 | 0 | 1 | 0 | 3 | 26 | 5 | 21 | 0 | 1 |
| Jordan | 6,523 | 10 | 0 | 2 | 0 | 8 | 53 | 10 | 38 | 5 | 1 |
| Kasson | 6,585 | 10 | 0 | 3 | 0 | 7 | 36 | 7 | 28 | 1 | 0 |
| Kenyon | 1,785 | 0 | 0 | 0 | 0 | 0 | 5 | 2 | 3 | 0 | 0 |
| La Crescent | 5,027 | 0 | 0 | 0 | 0 | 0 | 44 | 5 | 37 | 2 | 0 |
| Lake City | 5,119 | 4 | 0 | 0 | 0 | 4 | 75 | 11 | 61 | 3 | 0 |
| Lake Crystal | 2,508 | 3 | 0 | 3 | 0 | 0 | 12 | 2 | 10 | 0 | 0 |
| Lakes Area | 10,026 | 13 | 0 | 5 | 0 | 8 | 133 | 14 | 106 | 13 | 2 |
| Lake Shore | 1,076 | 0 | 0 | 0 | 0 | 0 | 2 | 0 | 2 | 0 | 0 |
| Lakeville | 71,092 | 97 | 1 | 34 | 6 | 56 | 634 | 55 | 528 | 51 | 1 |
| Lamberton | 753 | 0 | 0 | 0 | 0 | 0 | 3 | 1 | 1 | 1 | 0 |
| Le Center | 2,480 | 0 | 0 | 0 | 0 | 0 | 21 | 0 | 18 | 3 | 0 |
| Lester Prairie | 1,720 | 4 | 0 | 0 | 0 | 4 | 4 | 0 | 4 | 0 | 0 |
| Le Sueur | 4,029 | 3 | 0 | 2 | 0 | 1 | 31 | 2 | 28 | 1 | 0 |
| Lewiston | 1,536 | 1 | 0 | 1 | 0 | 0 | 14 | 0 | 14 | 0 | 0 |
| Lino Lakes | 22,657 | 23 | 0 | 6 | 0 | 17 | 233 | 24 | 188 | 21 | 0 |
| Litchfield | 6,656 | 13 | 0 | 4 | 0 | 9 | 93 | 9 | 79 | 5 | 0 |
| Little Falls | 8,597 | 16 | 1 | 1 | 0 | 14 | 166 | 19 | 131 | 16 | 0 |

## Table 8. Offenses Known to Law Enforcement, by Selected State and City, 2021—Continued

(Number.)

| State/city | Population | Violent crime | Murder and nonnegligent manslaughter | Rape | Robbery | Aggravated assault | Property crime | Burglary | Larceny-theft | Motor vehicle theft | Arson |
|---|---|---|---|---|---|---|---|---|---|---|---|
| Long Prairie | 3,282 | 2 | 1 | 0 | 0 | 1 | 27 | 0 | 27 | 0 | 0 |
| Lonsdale | 4,366 | 0 | 0 | 0 | 0 | 0 | 15 | 3 | 11 | 1 | 0 |
| Madelia | 2,217 | 2 | 0 | 1 | 0 | 1 | 16 | 3 | 12 | 1 | 0 |
| Madison Lake | 1,215 | 2 | 0 | 0 | 0 | 2 | 6 | 1 | 5 | 0 | 0 |
| Mankato | 43,802 | 152 | 2 | 31 | 21 | 98 | 1,103 | 167 | 873 | 63 | 5 |
| Maple Grove | 74,097 | 95 | 0 | 21 | 19 | 55 | 1,311 | 127 | 1,136 | 48 | 2 |
| Mapleton | 2,178 | 6 | 0 | 2 | 0 | 4 | 20 | 6 | 12 | 2 | 0 |
| Maplewood | 41,057 | 147 | 1 | 9 | 37 | 100 | 2,065 | 284 | 1,541 | 240 | 13 |
| Marshall | 13,391 | 37 | 0 | 15 | 2 | 20 | 121 | 14 | 101 | 6 | 3 |
| McGregor | 357 | 0 | 0 | 0 | 0 | 0 | 0 | 0 | 0 | 0 | 0 |
| Medina | 6,969 | 1 | 0 | 0 | 0 | 1 | 64 | 5 | 55 | 4 | 0 |
| Melrose | 3,680 | 9 | 0 | 0 | 0 | 9 | 21 | 9 | 11 | 1 | 0 |
| Mendota Heights | 11,469 | 24 | 0 | 3 | 2 | 19 | 234 | 36 | 186 | 12 | 1 |
| Milaca | 2,894 | 10 | 0 | 1 | 1 | 8 | 82 | 4 | 73 | 5 | 1 |
| Minneapolis | 438,463 | 5,616 | 94 | 345 | 2,215 | 2,962 | 18,369 | 2,531 | 11,648 | 4,190 | 116 |
| Minneota | 1,334 | 0 | 0 | 0 | 0 | 0 | 0 | 0 | 0 | 0 | 0 |
| Minnesota Lake | 630 | 0 | 0 | 0 | 0 | 0 | 0 | 0 | 0 | 0 | 0 |
| Minnetonka | 55,960 | 44 | 0 | 15 | 7 | 22 | 959 | 182 | 705 | 72 | 2 |
| Minnetrista | 11,095 | 3 | 0 | 2 | 0 | 1 | 89 | 11 | 72 | 6 | 0 |
| Montevideo | 4,995 | 2 | 0 | 0 | 0 | 2 | 0 | 0 | 0 | 0 | 0 |
| Moorhead | 44,488 | 231 | 2 | 28 | 20 | 181 | 1,324 | 270 | 903 | 151 | 8 |
| Moose Lake | 2,788 | 3 | 0 | 1 | 0 | 2 | 15 | 2 | 12 | 1 | 0 |
| Morgan | 826 | 1 | 0 | 0 | 0 | 1 | 4 | 0 | 2 | 2 | 0 |
| Morris | 5,319 | 11 | 0 | 2 | 0 | 9 | 73 | 7 | 65 | 1 | 0 |
| Motley | 651 | 0 | 0 | 0 | 0 | 0 | 41 | 2 | 37 | 2 | 0 |
| Mounds View | 13,625 | 39 | 1 | 6 | 7 | 25 | 370 | 25 | 299 | 46 | 0 |
| Mountain Lake | 2,037 | 10 | 0 | 1 | 0 | 9 | 8 | 0 | 5 | 3 | 0 |
| Nashwauk | 947 | 1 | 0 | 0 | 0 | 1 | 1 | 0 | 1 | 0 | 0 |
| New Brighton | 23,012 | 25 | 0 | 4 | 5 | 16 | 686 | 74 | 557 | 55 | 2 |
| New Hope | 20,671 | 64 | 1 | 6 | 21 | 36 | 593 | 61 | 448 | 84 | 1 |
| New Prague | 8,293 | 5 | 0 | 3 | 0 | 2 | 41 | 3 | 34 | 4 | 0 |
| New Richland | 1,167 | 1 | 0 | 1 | 0 | 0 | 30 | 8 | 21 | 1 | 0 |
| New Ulm | 13,106 | 6 | 0 | 2 | 0 | 4 | 126 | 17 | 100 | 9 | 0 |
| New York Mills | 1,222 | 2 | 0 | 0 | 0 | 2 | 3 | 0 | 2 | 1 | 0 |
| Nisswa | 2,130 | 1 | 0 | 0 | 0 | 1 | 0 | 0 | 0 | 0 | 0 |
| North Branch | 10,908 | 29 | 0 | 12 | 1 | 16 | 152 | 15 | 127 | 10 | 0 |
| Northfield | 20,828 | 28 | 0 | 7 | 1 | 20 | 154 | 13 | 134 | 7 | 2 |
| North Mankato | 14,117 | 20 | 0 | 4 | 2 | 14 | 166 | 28 | 130 | 8 | 3 |
| North St. Paul | 12,557 | 24 | 0 | 5 | 5 | 14 | 306 | 23 | 244 | 39 | 1 |
| Oakdale | 27,808 | 62 | 0 | 14 | 15 | 33 | 795 | 67 | 648 | 80 | 1 |
| Oak Park Heights | 5,031 | 4 | 0 | 1 | 0 | 3 | 205 | 13 | 182 | 10 | 1 |
| Olivia | 2,291 | 6 | 0 | 0 | 0 | 6 | 31 | 3 | 26 | 2 | 1 |
| Onamia | 856 | 15 | 0 | 0 | 0 | 15 | 29 | 4 | 22 | 3 | 0 |
| Orono | 20,241 | 17 | 0 | 9 | 1 | 7 | 136 | 14 | 107 | 15 | 1 |
| Ortonville | 1,732 | 3 | 0 | 1 | 0 | 2 | 19 | 2 | 17 | 0 | 0 |
| Osakis | 1,742 | 1 | 0 | 1 | 0 | 0 | 9 | 2 | 6 | 1 | 1 |
| Osseo | 2,732 | 0 | 0 | 0 | 0 | 0 | 66 | 1 | 63 | 2 | 0 |
| Owatonna | 25,683 | 58 | 0 | 10 | 0 | 48 | 270 | 29 | 220 | 21 | 2 |
| Park Rapids | 4,387 | 9 | 0 | 4 | 0 | 5 | 111 | 15 | 87 | 9 | 1 |
| Paynesville | 2,542 | 3 | 0 | 1 | 0 | 2 | 4 | 2 | 2 | 0 | 1 |
| Pequot Lakes | 2,320 | 2 | 0 | 0 | 0 | 2 | 4 | 2 | 1 | 1 | 0 |
| Pierz | 1,361 | 1 | 0 | 0 | 0 | 1 | 29 | 2 | 27 | 0 | 1 |
| Pillager | 488 | 0 | 0 | 0 | 0 | 0 | 5 | 0 | 5 | 0 | 0 |
| Pine River | 932 | 2 | 0 | 0 | 0 | 2 | 11 | 2 | 9 | 0 | 1 |
| Plainview | 3,287 | 0 | 0 | 0 | 0 | 0 | 14 | 2 | 12 | 0 | 0 |
| Plymouth | 80,588 | 46 | 0 | 15 | 7 | 24 | 1,147 | 274 | 785 | 88 | 3 |
| Preston | 1,275 | 0 | 0 | 0 | 0 | 0 | 8 | 5 | 3 | 0 | 0 |
| Princeton | 4,738 | 6 | 0 | 3 | 0 | 3 | 141 | 10 | 123 | 8 | 1 |
| Prior Lake | 27,779 | 45 | 0 | 10 | 2 | 33 | 661 | 23 | 582 | 56 | 0 |
| Proctor | 3,001 | 1 | 0 | 0 | 0 | 1 | 27 | 0 | 23 | 4 | 0 |
| Ramsey | 29,053 | 22 | 0 | 9 | 1 | 12 | 244 | 31 | 195 | 18 | 0 |
| Red Wing | 16,411 | 38 | 0 | 10 | 1 | 27 | 509 | 49 | 427 | 33 | 1 |
| Redwood Falls | 4,914 | 21 | 0 | 8 | 1 | 12 | 84 | 8 | 73 | 3 | 0 |
| Renville | 1,151 | 2 | 1 | 1 | 0 | 0 | 7 | 0 | 6 | 1 | 0 |
| Rice | 1,413 | 0 | 0 | 0 | 0 | 0 | 8 | 0 | 6 | 2 | 0 |
| Richfield | 36,336 | 131 | 1 | 22 | 29 | 79 | 986 | 113 | 744 | 129 | 5 |
| Robbinsdale | 14,213 | 84 | 4 | 9 | 23 | 48 | 282 | 37 | 186 | 59 | 2 |
| Rochester | 121,225 | 356 | 1 | 67 | 42 | 246 | 2,353 | 303 | 1,883 | 167 | 6 |
| Rogers | 13,889 | 11 | 0 | 2 | 0 | 9 | 298 | 22 | 255 | 21 | 1 |
| Roseau | 2,662 | 18 | 0 | 1 | 0 | 17 | 32 | 1 | 29 | 2 | 0 |
| Rosemount | 26,218 | 25 | 0 | 7 | 1 | 17 | 181 | 29 | 135 | 17 | 0 |
| Roseville | 36,561 | 159 | 1 | 19 | 52 | 87 | 2,275 | 187 | 1,922 | 166 | 12 |
| Royalton | 1,227 | 0 | 0 | 0 | 0 | 0 | 57 | 0 | 57 | 0 | 0 |
| Rushford | 1,692 | 0 | 0 | 0 | 0 | 0 | 0 | 0 | 0 | 0 | 0 |
| Sartell | 19,398 | 25 | 0 | 3 | 1 | 21 | 316 | 16 | 292 | 8 | 0 |
| Sauk Centre | 4,556 | 3 | 0 | 1 | 1 | 1 | 77 | 4 | 66 | 7 | 0 |
| Sauk Rapids | 14,489 | 9 | 0 | 1 | 1 | 7 | 255 | 16 | 227 | 12 | 0 |
| Savage | 33,510 | 25 | 0 | 8 | 4 | 13 | 407 | 35 | 329 | 43 | 2 |
| Shakopee | 43,641 | 48 | 1 | 15 | 7 | 25 | 927 | 52 | 814 | 61 | 2 |
| Silver Bay | 1,739 | 2 | 0 | 1 | 0 | 1 | 13 | 2 | 10 | 1 | 0 |
| Sleepy Eye | 3,304 | 12 | 0 | 3 | 0 | 9 | 11 | 5 | 6 | 0 | 0 |
| South Lake Minnetonka | 12,833 | 8 | 0 | 0 | 0 | 8 | 81 | 11 | 67 | 3 | 0 |
| South St. Paul | 19,895 | 75 | 0 | 12 | 4 | 59 | 542 | 52 | 393 | 97 | 3 |

## Table 8. Offenses Known to Law Enforcement, by Selected State and City, 2021—Continued

(Number.)

| State/city | Population | Violent crime | Murder and nonnegligent manslaughter | Rape | Robbery | Aggravated assault | Property crime | Burglary | Larceny-theft | Motor vehicle theft | Arson |
|---|---|---|---|---|---|---|---|---|---|---|---|
| Springfield | 1,975 | 2 | 0 | 1 | 0 | 1 | 10 | 7 | 3 | 0 | 0 |
| Spring Grove | 1,255 | 0 | 0 | 0 | 0 | 0 | 29 | 2 | 27 | 0 | 0 |
| Spring Lake Park | 6,960 | 25 | 0 | 2 | 3 | 20 | 204 | 26 | 158 | 20 | 0 |
| St. Anthony | 11,490 | 32 | 1 | 2 | 16 | 13 | 429 | 63 | 327 | 39 | 1 |
| Staples | 3,074 | 4 | 0 | 0 | 0 | 4 | 35 | 8 | 25 | 2 | 0 |
| Starbuck | 1,264 | 1 | 0 | 0 | 0 | 1 | 4 | 0 | 3 | 1 | 0 |
| St. Cloud | 68,756 | 387 | 5 | 48 | 50 | 284 | 2,547 | 231 | 2,088 | 228 | 14 |
| St. Francis | 8,154 | 6 | 0 | 1 | 0 | 5 | 63 | 5 | 52 | 6 | 0 |
| Stillwater | 19,799 | 25 | 0 | 4 | 2 | 19 | 208 | 29 | 152 | 27 | 1 |
| St. James | 4,336 | 10 | 0 | 5 | 0 | 5 | 49 | 17 | 31 | 1 | 0 |
| St. Joseph | 7,864 | 5 | 0 | 2 | 0 | 3 | 46 | 5 | 39 | 2 | 0 |
| St. Louis Park | 49,196 | 90 | 0 | 17 | 27 | 46 | 1,471 | 132 | 1,195 | 144 | 3 |
| St. Paul | 309,957 | 2,417 | 38 | 285 | 519 | 1,575 | 12,486 | 1,700 | 8,151 | 2,635 | 221 |
| St. Paul Park | 5,359 | 10 | 0 | 1 | 1 | 8 | 65 | 4 | 49 | 12 | 0 |
| St. Peter | 12,121 | 17 | 0 | 6 | 0 | 11 | 130 | 12 | 112 | 6 | 0 |
| Thief River Falls | 8,693 | 8 | 0 | 0 | 0 | 8 | 153 | 16 | 131 | 6 | 0 |
| Tracy | 2,045 | 6 | 0 | 3 | 0 | 3 | 23 | 8 | 14 | 1 | 0 |
| Two Harbors | 3,486 | 6 | 0 | 0 | 0 | 6 | 3 | 0 | 3 | 0 | 0 |
| Virginia | 8,259 | 46 | 1 | 4 | 3 | 38 | 199 | 30 | 151 | 18 | 5 |
| Wabasha | 2,462 | 1 | 0 | 0 | 0 | 1 | 38 | 6 | 30 | 2 | 0 |
| Wadena | 4,126 | 6 | 0 | 2 | 0 | 4 | 90 | 7 | 81 | 2 | 0 |
| Waite Park | 7,839 | 59 | 0 | 8 | 10 | 41 | 723 | 38 | 660 | 25 | 1 |
| Walker | 926 | 0 | 0 | 0 | 0 | 0 | 15 | 0 | 14 | 1 | 0 |
| Walnut Grove | 791 | 0 | 0 | 0 | 0 | 0 | 3 | 0 | 3 | 0 | 0 |
| Warroad | 1,792 | 4 | 0 | 2 | 0 | 2 | 12 | 0 | 12 | 0 | 0 |
| Waseca | 8,779 | 14 | 0 | 3 | 2 | 9 | 139 | 23 | 110 | 6 | 2 |
| Wayzata | 6,519 | 0 | 0 | 0 | 0 | 0 | 98 | 18 | 74 | 6 | 0 |
| Wells | 2,141 | 2 | 0 | 0 | 0 | 2 | 2 | 0 | 0 | 2 | 0 |
| West Concord | 761 | 1 | 0 | 1 | 0 | 0 | 9 | 2 | 7 | 0 | 0 |
| West Hennepin | 5,955 | 1 | 0 | 1 | 0 | 0 | 35 | 7 | 26 | 2 | 0 |
| West St. Paul | 19,840 | 108 | 1 | 18 | 21 | 68 | 1,390 | 90 | 1,198 | 102 | 3 |
| Wheaton | 1,255 | 8 | 0 | 1 | 0 | 7 | 11 | 3 | 5 | 3 | 0 |
| White Bear Lake | 25,747 | 21 | 0 | 4 | 4 | 13 | 632 | 123 | 458 | 51 | 3 |
| Willmar | 19,922 | 78 | 0 | 14 | 2 | 62 | 493 | 52 | 391 | 50 | 6 |
| Windom | 4,380 | 20 | 0 | 4 | 0 | 16 | 52 | 11 | 40 | 1 | 0 |
| Winnebago | 1,324 | 2 | 0 | 1 | 0 | 1 | 2 | 0 | 2 | 0 | 0 |
| Winona | 26,446 | 74 | 1 | 17 | 4 | 52 | 615 | 61 | 529 | 25 | 1 |
| Winsted | 2,220 | 6 | 0 | 0 | 0 | 6 | 2 | 0 | 2 | 0 | 0 |
| Winthrop | 1,315 | 1 | 0 | 0 | 0 | 1 | 3 | 2 | 1 | 0 | 0 |
| Woodbury | 75,577 | 83 | 3 | 26 | 19 | 35 | 1,434 | 162 | 1,175 | 97 | 8 |
| Worthington | 12,983 | 48 | 0 | 17 | 1 | 30 | 112 | 14 | 85 | 13 | 0 |
| Wyoming | 8,112 | 8 | 0 | 5 | 0 | 3 | 82 | 7 | 69 | 6 | 0 |
| Zumbrota | 3,556 | 5 | 0 | 0 | 0 | 5 | 28 | 1 | 26 | 1 | 0 |
| **MISSISSIPPI** | | | | | | | | | | | |
| Ackerman | 1,407 | 1 | 0 | 1 | 0 | 0 | 13 | 4 | 9 | 0 | 0 |
| Amory | 6,660 | 14 | 2 | 2 | 2 | 8 | 233 | 40 | 189 | 4 | 0 |
| Batesville | 7,085 | 35 | 2 | 3 | 7 | 23 | 298 | 36 | 240 | 22 | 1 |
| Bay Springs | 1,638 | 5 | 0 | 1 | 0 | 4 | 15 | 5 | 9 | 1 | 0 |
| Bay St. Louis | 15,188 | 23 | 1 | 6 | 4 | 12 | 307 | 54 | 224 | 29 | 1 |
| Biloxi | 46,317 | 181 | 5 | 29 | 41 | 106 | 2,366 | 609 | 1,557 | 200 | 8 |
| Blue Springs | 245 | 3 | 0 | 0 | 0 | 3 | 2 | 1 | 1 | 0 | 0 |
| Booneville | 8,368 | 17 | 0 | 4 | 1 | 12 | 245 | 25 | 209 | 11 | 1 |
| Brandon | 24,639 | 13 | 0 | 5 | 2 | 6 | 123 | 14 | 101 | 8 | 0 |
| Brookhaven | 11,798 | 60 | 7 | 6 | 6 | 41 | 372 | 159 | 178 | 35 | 0 |
| Bruce | 1,784 | 4 | 0 | 1 | 0 | 3 | 6 | 4 | 2 | 0 | 1 |
| Byhalia | 1,204 | 3 | 0 | 0 | 1 | 2 | 43 | 12 | 22 | 9 | 0 |
| Byram | 11,240 | 28 | 0 | 2 | 6 | 20 | 202 | 30 | 134 | 38 | 1 |
| Calhoun City | 1,637 | 5 | 0 | 0 | 0 | 5 | 14 | 8 | 6 | 0 | 0 |
| Charleston | 1,854 | 44 | 0 | 3 | 4 | 37 | 61 | 15 | 40 | 6 | 0 |
| Cleveland | 10,710 | 99 | 4 | 3 | 7 | 85 | 501 | 43 | 400 | 58 | 4 |
| Clinton | 23,737 | 42 | 1 | 13 | 10 | 18 | 291 | 20 | 252 | 19 | 1 |
| Coldwater | 1,521 | 5 | 0 | 0 | 0 | 5 | 7 | 2 | 0 | 5 | 0 |
| Corinth | 14,421 | 66 | 2 | 13 | 11 | 40 | 544 | 140 | 379 | 25 | 6 |
| Derma | 955 | 0 | 0 | 0 | 0 | 0 | 2 | 0 | 2 | 0 | 0 |
| D'Iberville | 14,234 | 10 | 0 | 0 | 1 | 9 | 734 | 52 | 657 | 25 | 0 |
| Eupora | 1,980 | 4 | 0 | 0 | 0 | 4 | 22 | 3 | 16 | 3 | 0 |
| Florence | 4,573 | 4 | 0 | 1 | 1 | 2 | 6 | 0 | 6 | 0 | 0 |
| Flowood | 9,743 | 22 | 0 | 7 | 2 | 13 | 189 | 14 | 165 | 10 | 0 |
| Forest | 5,461 | 31 | 0 | 3 | 3 | 25 | 145 | 73 | 53 | 19 | 0 |
| Fulton | 3,839 | 2 | 0 | 0 | 0 | 2 | 98 | 12 | 80 | 6 | 0 |
| Gautier | 18,362 | 55 | 0 | 5 | 6 | 44 | 354 | 70 | 233 | 51 | 3 |
| Gulfport | 71,803 | 307 | 15 | 44 | 44 | 204 | 3,112 | 455 | 2,377 | 280 | 23 |
| Hattiesburg | 45,809 | 190 | 9 | 24 | 29 | 128 | 2,348 | 495 | 1,681 | 172 | 7 |
| Heidelberg | 646 | 3 | 0 | 0 | 0 | 3 | 16 | 3 | 12 | 1 | 0 |
| Hernando | 17,155 | 13 | 0 | 4 | 3 | 6 | 157 | 12 | 133 | 12 | 0 |
| Holly Springs | 7,674 | 16 | 1 | 2 | 0 | 13 | 25 | 9 | 11 | 5 | 0 |
| Horn Lake | 27,401 | 28 | 1 | 1 | 9 | 17 | 514 | 93 | 371 | 50 | 3 |
| Kosciusko | 6,545 | 8 | 2 | 1 | 1 | 4 | 74 | 28 | 44 | 2 | 0 |
| Laurel | 18,165 | 113 | 4 | 17 | 18 | 74 | 802 | 191 | 577 | 34 | 8 |
| Long Beach | 16,260 | 7 | 1 | 0 | 1 | 5 | 324 | 91 | 217 | 16 | 0 |
| Louisville | 5,861 | 83 | 4 | 5 | 3 | 71 | 130 | 16 | 101 | 13 | 1 |
| Lucedale | 3,140 | 18 | 0 | 2 | 1 | 15 | 113 | 41 | 56 | 16 | 1 |

## Table 8. Offenses Known to Law Enforcement, by Selected State and City, 2021—Continued

(Number.)

| State/city | Population | Violent crime | Murder and nonnegligent manslaughter | Rape | Robbery | Aggravated assault | Property crime | Burglary | Larceny-theft | Motor vehicle theft | Arson |
|---|---|---|---|---|---|---|---|---|---|---|---|
| Madison | 25,860 | 6 | 0 | 0 | 1 | 5 | 119 | 11 | 103 | 5 | 0 |
| Mathiston | 665 | 0 | 0 | 0 | 0 | 0 | 3 | 0 | 3 | 0 | 0 |
| Mendenhall | 2,382 | 5 | 0 | 2 | 0 | 3 | 18 | 7 | 10 | 1 | 0 |
| Morton | 3,505 | 24 | 0 | 4 | 3 | 17 | 29 | 7 | 17 | 5 | 0 |
| Myrtle | 504 | 0 | 0 | 0 | 0 | 0 | 1 | 0 | 1 | 0 | 0 |
| Oakland | 489 | 2 | 0 | 1 | 0 | 1 | 20 | 10 | 9 | 1 | 0 |
| Ocean Springs | 17,833 | 17 | 0 | 2 | 5 | 10 | 411 | 37 | 340 | 34 | 2 |
| Olive Branch | 40,308 | 128 | 4 | 16 | 16 | 92 | 697 | 85 | 518 | 94 | 2 |
| Oxford | 29,367 | 39 | 2 | 17 | 2 | 18 | 503 | 66 | 424 | 13 | 0 |
| Pascagoula | 21,468 | 65 | 3 | 14 | 14 | 34 | 1,036 | 138 | 825 | 73 | 7 |
| Pass Christian | 6,724 | 5 | 0 | 0 | 1 | 4 | 109 | 9 | 94 | 6 | 0 |
| Petal | 10,717 | 15 | 0 | 2 | 0 | 13 | 54 | 30 | 20 | 4 | 0 |
| Pontotoc | 6,297 | 24 | 0 | 4 | 2 | 18 | 139 | 23 | 106 | 10 | 0 |
| Poplarville | 2,771 | 2 | 0 | 1 | 0 | 1 | 65 | 18 | 38 | 9 | 0 |
| Port Gibson | 1,263 | 1 | 0 | 0 | 0 | 1 | 27 | 6 | 21 | 0 | 0 |
| Puckett | 349 | 0 | 0 | 0 | 0 | 0 | 0 | 0 | 0 | 0 | 0 |
| Raymond | 2,101 | 0 | 0 | 0 | 0 | 0 | 4 | 1 | 3 | 0 | 0 |
| Richland | 7,305 | 20 | 1 | 5 | 2 | 12 | 138 | 49 | 72 | 17 | 0 |
| Ridgeland | 23,901 | 102 | 2 | 5 | 21 | 74 | 400 | 54 | 319 | 27 | 0 |
| Sandersville | 720 | 1 | 0 | 0 | 1 | 0 | 25 | 7 | 17 | 1 | 0 |
| Seminary | 281 | 0 | 0 | 0 | 0 | 0 | 4 | 0 | 3 | 1 | 0 |
| Smithville | 722 | 0 | 0 | 0 | 0 | 0 | 15 | 2 | 11 | 2 | 0 |
| Southaven | 57,455 | 158 | 2 | 31 | 28 | 97 | 1,618 | 173 | 1,283 | 162 | 3 |
| Starkville | 25,711 | 43 | 5 | 0 | 1 | 37 | 532 | 215 | 283 | 34 | 0 |
| Sumner | 259 | 0 | 0 | 0 | 0 | 0 | 13 | 0 | 12 | 1 | 0 |
| Sumrall | 1,984 | 4 | 0 | 0 | 0 | 4 | 24 | 4 | 13 | 7 | 0 |
| Tunica | 805 | 6 | 2 | 0 | 1 | 3 | 20 | 2 | 15 | 3 | 0 |
| Union | 1,866 | 3 | 0 | 0 | 0 | 3 | 22 | 4 | 14 | 4 | 0 |
| Vardaman | 1,254 | 2 | 0 | 0 | 0 | 2 | 4 | 1 | 3 | 0 | 0 |
| Vicksburg | 21,114 | 139 | 1 | 10 | 18 | 110 | 746 | 123 | 513 | 110 | 2 |
| Walnut | 733 | 1 | 0 | 0 | 0 | 1 | 17 | 9 | 7 | 1 | 0 |
| Water Valley | 3,206 | 9 | 1 | 3 | 2 | 3 | 115 | 17 | 85 | 13 | 0 |
| Waveland | 6,303 | 7 | 0 | 1 | 0 | 6 | 217 | 14 | 189 | 14 | 3 |
| Waynesboro | 4,847 | 28 | 2 | 7 | 0 | 19 | 77 | 24 | 47 | 6 | 0 |
| West Point | 10,294 | 70 | 0 | 8 | 5 | 57 | 264 | 44 | 201 | 19 | 4 |
| Wiggins | 4,535 | 26 | 1 | 3 | 2 | 20 | 147 | 35 | 106 | 6 | 1 |
| **MISSOURI** | | | | | | | | | | | |
| Adrian | 1,594 | 2 | 0 | 1 | 0 | 1 | 20 | 6 | 13 | 1 | 0 |
| Arnold | 21,172 | 23 | 0 | 3 | 3 | 17 | 304 | 10 | 234 | 60 | 1 |
| Ash Grove | 1,440 | 8 | 0 | 0 | 0 | 8 | 62 | 38 | 20 | 4 | 0 |
| Ashland | 4,063 | 7 | 0 | 0 | 1 | 6 | 35 | 3 | 27 | 5 | 1 |
| Aurora | 7,422 | 60 | 0 | 13 | 2 | 45 | 260 | 80 | 148 | 32 | 2 |
| Auxvasse | 979 | 5 | 0 | 1 | 1 | 3 | 19 | 6 | 6 | 7 | 0 |
| Ballwin | 30,061 | 16 | 0 | 2 | 3 | 11 | 174 | 11 | 138 | 25 | 1 |
| Battlefield | 6,776 | 18 | 0 | 1 | 0 | 17 | 128 | 111 | 13 | 4 | 0 |
| Bellefontaine Neighbors | 10,251 | 165 | 1 | 3 | 17 | 144 | 313 | 50 | 186 | 77 | 2 |
| Bellflower | 353 | 4 | 0 | 0 | 0 | 4 | 0 | 0 | 0 | 0 | 0 |
| Bel-Nor | 1,385 | 7 | 0 | 1 | 3 | 3 | 9 | 2 | 5 | 2 | 1 |
| Belton | 23,860 | 74 | 3 | 17 | 14 | 40 | 600 | 43 | 463 | 94 | 6 |
| Berkeley | 8,868 | 173 | 6 | 2 | 15 | 150 | 463 | 68 | 286 | 109 | 11 |
| Bertrand | 739 | 1 | 0 | 0 | 0 | 1 | 18 | 7 | 11 | 0 | 0 |
| Bethany | 3,025 | 5 | 0 | 1 | 0 | 4 | 36 | 8 | 19 | 9 | 1 |
| Bloomfield | 1,808 | 1 | 0 | 1 | 0 | 0 | 11 | 4 | 5 | 2 | 0 |
| Blue Springs | 56,952 | 113 | 2 | 21 | 8 | 82 | 1,244 | 105 | 970 | 169 | 1 |
| Bolivar | 11,285 | 30 | 1 | 10 | 0 | 19 | 282 | 39 | 218 | 25 | 2 |
| Bonne Terre | 6,811 | 10 | 1 | 1 | 0 | 8 | 76 | 5 | 52 | 19 | 1 |
| Boonville | 7,833 | 22 | 0 | 12 | 1 | 9 | 204 | 24 | 158 | 22 | 2 |
| Bourbon | 1,558 | 0 | 0 | 0 | 0 | 0 | 22 | 3 | 18 | 1 | 0 |
| Branson | 11,797 | 60 | 2 | 17 | 6 | 35 | 675 | 43 | 586 | 46 | 1 |
| Branson West | 449 | 6 | 0 | 3 | 0 | 3 | 53 | 2 | 43 | 8 | 0 |
| Breckenridge Hills | 4,533 | 51 | 0 | 0 | 0 | 51 | 165 | 22 | 108 | 35 | 1 |
| Brentwood | 7,944 | 18 | 1 | 1 | 8 | 8 | 350 | 24 | 298 | 28 | 0 |
| Bridgeton | 11,497 | 67 | 1 | 11 | 15 | 40 | 658 | 48 | 532 | 78 | 0 |
| Butler | 3,981 | 37 | 0 | 5 | 1 | 31 | 106 | 19 | 74 | 13 | 0 |
| Cabool | 2,063 | 4 | 0 | 2 | 1 | 1 | 10 | 4 | 5 | 1 | 0 |
| Camdenton | 4,186 | 13 | 0 | 4 | 0 | 9 | 120 | 15 | 96 | 9 | 0 |
| Cameron | 7,986 | 19 | 0 | 3 | 0 | 16 | 116 | 23 | 81 | 12 | 1 |
| Campbell | 1,773 | 2 | 0 | 0 | 0 | 2 | 7 | 3 | 4 | 0 | 0 |
| Canton | 2,308 | 8 | 0 | 2 | 0 | 6 | 48 | 4 | 36 | 8 | 0 |
| Cape Girardeau | 41,957 | 267 | 2 | 42 | 20 | 203 | 1,220 | 255 | 860 | 105 | 19 |
| Carl Junction | 8,527 | 36 | 0 | 3 | 0 | 33 | 91 | 23 | 57 | 11 | 6 |
| Carrollton | 3,387 | 6 | 0 | 4 | 0 | 2 | 18 | 5 | 8 | 5 | 0 |
| Carterville | 1,972 | 9 | 0 | 0 | 0 | 9 | 45 | 5 | 33 | 7 | 0 |
| Carthage | 14,766 | 44 | 0 | 12 | 2 | 30 | 477 | 55 | 376 | 46 | 2 |
| Caruthersville | 5,212 | 124 | 1 | 4 | 9 | 110 | 186 | 52 | 115 | 19 | 8 |
| Cassville | 3,223 | 19 | 0 | 1 | 0 | 18 | 201 | 33 | 156 | 12 | 2 |
| Charleston | 4,936 | 56 | 1 | 1 | 2 | 52 | 99 | 15 | 75 | 9 | 5 |
| Chesterfield | 47,578 | 35 | 0 | 3 | 5 | 27 | 816 | 84 | 662 | 70 | 2 |
| Chillicothe | 8,865 | 22 | 0 | 4 | 0 | 18 | 132 | 33 | 78 | 21 | 2 |
| Clarkson Valley | 2,601 | 0 | 0 | 0 | 0 | 0 | 10 | 2 | 7 | 1 | 0 |
| Clayton | 16,859 | 12 | 0 | 3 | 2 | 7 | 205 | 24 | 150 | 31 | 0 |
| Columbia | 126,418 | 623 | 6 | 136 | 51 | 430 | 3,149 | 400 | 2,376 | 373 | 15 |

## Table 8. Offenses Known to Law Enforcement, by Selected State and City, 2021—Continued

(Number.)

| State/city | Population | Violent crime | Murder and nonnegligent manslaughter | Rape | Robbery | Aggravated assault | Property crime | Burglary | Larceny-theft | Motor vehicle theft | Arson |
|---|---|---|---|---|---|---|---|---|---|---|---|
| Corder | 406 | 0 | 0 | 0 | 0 | 0 | 2 | 0 | 0 | 2 | 0 |
| Cottleville | 6,333 | 2 | 0 | 0 | 2 | 0 | 14 | 1 | 12 | 1 | 0 |
| Country Club Hills | 1,243 | 12 | 0 | 0 | 0 | 12 | 18 | 1 | 9 | 8 | 0 |
| Crestwood | 11,828 | 5 | 0 | 1 | 2 | 2 | 209 | 13 | 170 | 26 | 1 |
| Creve Coeur | 18,708 | 29 | 0 | 1 | 6 | 22 | 350 | 31 | 276 | 43 | 0 |
| Crocker | 1,023 | 5 | 1 | 1 | 0 | 3 | 23 | 2 | 11 | 10 | 0 |
| Crystal City | 4,680 | 3 | 0 | 0 | 1 | 2 | 95 | 2 | 67 | 26 | 1 |
| Cuba | 3,270 | 7 | 0 | 2 | 0 | 5 | 173 | 13 | 144 | 16 | 1 |
| Delta | 419 | 0 | 0 | 0 | 0 | 0 | 0 | 0 | 0 | 0 | 0 |
| Desloge | 4,883 | 15 | 1 | 1 | 1 | 12 | 109 | 8 | 91 | 10 | 1 |
| Dexter | 7,833 | 33 | 1 | 11 | 1 | 20 | 194 | 25 | 156 | 13 | 2 |
| Dixon | 1,446 | 4 | 0 | 0 | 0 | 4 | 29 | 11 | 16 | 2 | 1 |
| Doniphan | 1,911 | 6 | 0 | 2 | 0 | 4 | 72 | 7 | 61 | 4 | 0 |
| Duquesne | 1,681 | 6 | 0 | 3 | 0 | 3 | 50 | 11 | 36 | 3 | 1 |
| East Lynne | 313 | 0 | 0 | 0 | 0 | 0 | 0 | 0 | 0 | 0 | 0 |
| Edmundson | 827 | 6 | 0 | 2 | 0 | 4 | 72 | 2 | 25 | 45 | 0 |
| Eldon | 4,764 | 14 | 0 | 2 | 0 | 12 | 71 | 4 | 57 | 10 | 0 |
| El Dorado Springs | 3,605 | 16 | 1 | 3 | 0 | 12 | 166 | 27 | 128 | 11 | 6 |
| Ellisville | 9,905 | 18 | 0 | 1 | 1 | 16 | 115 | 14 | 88 | 13 | 0 |
| Eureka | 11,442 | 16 | 0 | 2 | 0 | 14 | 140 | 8 | 106 | 26 | 0 |
| Excelsior Springs | 11,908 | 18 | 0 | 9 | 1 | 8 | 203 | 27 | 154 | 22 | 2 |
| Farber | 309 | 0 | 0 | 0 | 0 | 0 | 0 | 0 | 0 | 0 | 0 |
| Farmington | 18,926 | 42 | 0 | 12 | 1 | 29 | 756 | 20 | 685 | 51 | 2 |
| Fayette | 2,682 | 10 | 0 | 2 | 0 | 8 | 11 | 1 | 8 | 2 | 0 |
| Flordell Hills | 797 | 25 | 0 | 2 | 5 | 18 | 27 | 8 | 11 | 8 | 0 |
| Florissant | 50,653 | 164 | 5 | 13 | 24 | 122 | 981 | 85 | 596 | 300 | 7 |
| Foristell | 627 | 1 | 0 | 0 | 0 | 1 | 17 | 0 | 14 | 3 | 0 |
| Fredericktown | 4,008 | 8 | 0 | 0 | 1 | 7 | 66 | 10 | 51 | 5 | 0 |
| Frontenac | 3,899 | 5 | 0 | 0 | 1 | 4 | 119 | 6 | 98 | 15 | 0 |
| Fulton | 12,530 | 39 | 1 | 2 | 4 | 32 | 347 | 49 | 280 | 18 | 2 |
| Galena | 443 | 2 | 0 | 0 | 0 | 2 | 8 | 5 | 3 | 0 | 0 |
| Gerald | 1,324 | 3 | 0 | 2 | 0 | 1 | 12 | 1 | 9 | 2 | 0 |
| Gladstone | 27,905 | 88 | 0 | 7 | 7 | 74 | 554 | 64 | 389 | 101 | 4 |
| Grain Valley | 15,038 | 28 | 0 | 15 | 0 | 13 | 239 | 18 | 177 | 44 | 0 |
| Greenwood | 5,951 | 2 | 0 | 1 | 0 | 1 | 13 | 3 | 6 | 4 | 1 |
| Hamilton | 1,680 | 2 | 0 | 1 | 0 | 1 | 8 | 1 | 5 | 2 | 0 |
| Hannibal | 17,194 | 62 | 0 | 5 | 4 | 53 | 677 | 92 | 526 | 59 | 11 |
| Harrisonville | 10,091 | 43 | 0 | 8 | 2 | 33 | 223 | 28 | 171 | 24 | 0 |
| Hartville | 616 | 0 | 0 | 0 | 0 | 0 | 12 | 1 | 10 | 1 | 0 |
| Hayti | 2,425 | 37 | 1 | 5 | 5 | 26 | 86 | 20 | 61 | 5 | 3 |
| Hazelwood | 24,976 | 170 | 3 | 13 | 21 | 133 | 759 | 69 | 461 | 229 | 0 |
| Herculaneum | 4,346 | 15 | 0 | 5 | 0 | 10 | 87 | 4 | 77 | 6 | 0 |
| Hermann | 2,311 | 1 | 0 | 1 | 0 | 0 | 41 | 3 | 34 | 4 | 0 |
| Highlandville | 1,070 | 0 | 0 | 0 | 0 | 0 | 0 | 0 | 0 | 0 | 0 |
| Hillsboro | 3,404 | 23 | 0 | 2 | 1 | 20 | 51 | 6 | 31 | 14 | 1 |
| Hillsdale | 1,542 | 37 | 0 | 0 | 4 | 33 | 31 | 5 | 17 | 9 | 1 |
| Holden | 2,232 | 3 | 0 | 2 | 0 | 1 | 32 | 3 | 25 | 4 | 0 |
| Hollister | 4,626 | 5 | 0 | 2 | 1 | 2 | 51 | 4 | 41 | 6 | 0 |
| Holts Summit | 5,296 | 6 | 0 | 0 | 0 | 6 | 48 | 16 | 26 | 6 | 0 |
| Hornersville | 579 | 1 | 0 | 1 | 0 | 0 | 5 | 1 | 3 | 1 | 0 |
| Houston | 2,085 | 11 | 1 | 1 | 1 | 8 | 105 | 13 | 90 | 2 | 1 |
| Independence | 116,761 | 674 | 8 | 128 | 91 | 447 | 4,380 | 400 | 2,984 | 996 | 13 |
| Jackson | 14,792 | 24 | 1 | 6 | 0 | 17 | 184 | 18 | 139 | 27 | 2 |
| Jefferson City | 41,851 | 125 | 0 | 40 | 13 | 72 | 745 | 77 | 585 | 83 | 8 |
| Joplin | 50,970 | 271 | 6 | 47 | 47 | 171 | 3,467 | 541 | 2,572 | 354 | 37 |
| Kansas City | 500,965 | 7,398 | 156 | 415 | 1,213 | 5,614 | 21,461 | 2,827 | 13,987 | 4,647 | 154 |
| Kearney | 11,467 | 23 | 0 | 7 | 3 | 13 | 113 | 7 | 91 | 15 | 0 |
| Kennett | 9,946 | 77 | 3 | 6 | 1 | 67 | 593 | 124 | 431 | 38 | 10 |
| Kimberling City | 2,321 | 2 | 0 | 0 | 0 | 2 | 11 | 2 | 8 | 1 | 0 |
| Kirksville | 17,666 | 84 | 3 | 15 | 3 | 63 | 719 | 123 | 546 | 50 | 7 |
| Kirkwood | 27,897 | 48 | 0 | 5 | 7 | 36 | 430 | 33 | 325 | 72 | 0 |
| Knob Noster | 2,806 | 7 | 0 | 4 | 0 | 3 | 24 | 4 | 17 | 3 | 0 |
| Ladue | 8,624 | 9 | 0 | 1 | 0 | 8 | 108 | 13 | 80 | 15 | 0 |
| Lake Lotawana | 2,152 | 1 | 0 | 0 | 0 | 1 | 23 | 3 | 18 | 2 | 0 |
| Lakeshire | 1,380 | 2 | 0 | 0 | 0 | 2 | 23 | 8 | 10 | 5 | 1 |
| Lake St. Louis | 17,469 | 29 | 0 | 3 | 0 | 26 | 209 | 18 | 171 | 20 | 1 |
| Lamar | 4,204 | 17 | 0 | 3 | 2 | 12 | 166 | 37 | 121 | 8 | 0 |
| Lathrop | 2,012 | 4 | 0 | 2 | 0 | 2 | 20 | 0 | 15 | 5 | 0 |
| Laurie | 983 | 4 | 0 | 0 | 0 | 4 | 23 | 1 | 21 | 1 | 0 |
| Lawson | 2,394 | 2 | 0 | 0 | 0 | 2 | 21 | 2 | 14 | 5 | 2 |
| Lebanon | 14,917 | 67 | 2 | 10 | 3 | 52 | 514 | 53 | 397 | 64 | 2 |
| Lee's Summit | 102,519 | 155 | 2 | 23 | 15 | 115 | 1,814 | 164 | 1,394 | 256 | 4 |
| Licking | 2,848 | 0 | 0 | 0 | 0 | 0 | 12 | 3 | 8 | 1 | 0 |
| Lincoln | 1,198 | 8 | 0 | 0 | 0 | 8 | 12 | 0 | 9 | 3 | 1 |
| Lone Jack | 1,412 | 0 | 0 | 0 | 0 | 0 | 4 | 0 | 2 | 2 | 0 |
| Louisiana | 3,206 | 6 | 0 | 1 | 0 | 5 | 57 | 9 | 35 | 13 | 1 |
| Macon | 5,327 | 3 | 0 | 1 | 0 | 2 | 89 | 14 | 71 | 4 | 1 |
| Malden | 3,812 | 20 | 0 | 4 | 0 | 16 | 92 | 13 | 57 | 22 | 0 |
| Manchester | 18,081 | 12 | 0 | 4 | 2 | 6 | 234 | 7 | 207 | 20 | 0 |
| Mansfield | 1,240 | 5 | 0 | 0 | 0 | 5 | 29 | 1 | 28 | 0 | 0 |
| Maplewood | 8,076 | 30 | 0 | 2 | 3 | 25 | 393 | 40 | 296 | 57 | 0 |
| Marble Hill | 1,457 | 9 | 0 | 1 | 0 | 8 | 61 | 3 | 51 | 7 | 0 |
| Marceline | 2,047 | 0 | 0 | 0 | 0 | 0 | 13 | 2 | 10 | 1 | 0 |

## Table 8. Offenses Known to Law Enforcement, by Selected State and City, 2021—Continued

(Number.)

| State/city | Population | Violent crime | Murder and nonnegligent manslaughter | Rape | Robbery | Aggravated assault | Property crime | Burglary | Larceny-theft | Motor vehicle theft | Arson |
|---|---|---|---|---|---|---|---|---|---|---|---|
| Marionville | 2,157 | 11 | 1 | 3 | 0 | 7 | 13 | 5 | 4 | 4 | 0 |
| Marshall | 12,868 | 33 | 0 | 5 | 1 | 27 | 164 | 38 | 105 | 21 | 3 |
| Marshfield | 7,786 | 31 | 0 | 3 | 1 | 27 | 256 | 31 | 194 | 31 | 3 |
| Maryland Heights | 26,839 | 44 | 1 | 11 | 7 | 25 | 660 | 31 | 503 | 126 | 0 |
| Maryville | 11,479 | 25 | 0 | 8 | 0 | 17 | 171 | 18 | 140 | 13 | 3 |
| Matthews | 580 | 3 | 0 | 0 | 0 | 3 | 20 | 2 | 17 | 1 | 0 |
| Mexico | 11,531 | 21 | 0 | 10 | 3 | 8 | 275 | 32 | 220 | 23 | 1 |
| Milan | 1,744 | 4 | 1 | 0 | 0 | 3 | 13 | 4 | 8 | 1 | 0 |
| Miner | 935 | 10 | 0 | 5 | 1 | 4 | 31 | 8 | 18 | 5 | 0 |
| Moberly | 13,459 | 53 | 1 | 8 | 3 | 41 | 251 | 58 | 171 | 22 | 2 |
| Moline Acres | 2,331 | 20 | 0 | 0 | 2 | 18 | 26 | 2 | 12 | 12 | 0 |
| Monett | 9,188 | 19 | 0 | 2 | 0 | 17 | 284 | 36 | 217 | 31 | 0 |
| Monroe City | 2,433 | 3 | 0 | 1 | 0 | 2 | 21 | 7 | 11 | 3 | 0 |
| Mound City | 982 | 1 | 0 | 1 | 0 | 0 | 26 | 3 | 16 | 7 | 0 |
| Mountain Grove | 4,697 | 24 | 0 | 8 | 0 | 16 | 62 | 3 | 51 | 8 | 1 |
| Mountain View | 2,649 | 4 | 0 | 1 | 0 | 3 | 35 | 2 | 28 | 5 | 0 |
| Mount Vernon | 4,468 | 10 | 0 | 1 | 2 | 7 | 135 | 12 | 107 | 16 | 0 |
| Neosho | 12,143 | 40 | 1 | 9 | 3 | 27 | 347 | 67 | 263 | 17 | 6 |
| Nevada | 8,177 | 152 | 1 | 17 | 3 | 131 | 431 | 43 | 347 | 41 | 1 |
| New Florence | 698 | 6 | 0 | 0 | 0 | 6 | 6 | 2 | 4 | 0 | 0 |
| New Madrid | 2,730 | 17 | 1 | 1 | 0 | 15 | 26 | 4 | 21 | 1 | 0 |
| Niangua | 426 | 0 | 0 | 0 | 0 | 0 | 0 | 0 | 0 | 0 | 0 |
| Nixa | 23,795 | 10 | 1 | 0 | 2 | 7 | 183 | 14 | 158 | 11 | 0 |
| Noel | 1,806 | 7 | 0 | 1 | 0 | 6 | 13 | 2 | 9 | 2 | 1 |
| Normandy | 7,385 | 79 | 2 | 1 | 7 | 69 | 184 | 14 | 120 | 50 | 0 |
| North Kansas City | 5,110 | 58 | 0 | 8 | 10 | 40 | 565 | 28 | 402 | 135 | 0 |
| Oak Grove | 8,493 | 8 | 0 | 1 | 1 | 6 | 92 | 10 | 63 | 19 | 0 |
| Odessa | 5,293 | 6 | 0 | 2 | 0 | 4 | 48 | 11 | 31 | 6 | 0 |
| O'Fallon | 90,813 | 96 | 1 | 35 | 7 | 53 | 730 | 42 | 597 | 91 | 1 |
| Olivette | 7,850 | 14 | 0 | 0 | 2 | 12 | 106 | 8 | 82 | 16 | 0 |
| Osage Beach | 4,706 | 9 | 0 | 1 | 0 | 8 | 148 | 15 | 121 | 12 | 0 |
| Osceola | 934 | 3 | 0 | 1 | 0 | 2 | 10 | 2 | 7 | 1 | 0 |
| Overland | 15,449 | 73 | 2 | 4 | 17 | 50 | 455 | 38 | 315 | 102 | 2 |
| Pacific | 7,108 | 18 | 0 | 3 | 0 | 15 | 119 | 12 | 95 | 12 | 2 |
| Pagedale | 3,287 | 77 | 0 | 1 | 4 | 72 | 77 | 16 | 44 | 17 | 0 |
| Palmyra | 3,574 | 3 | 1 | 2 | 0 | 0 | 61 | 7 | 50 | 4 | 0 |
| Park Hills | 8,482 | 25 | 0 | 9 | 1 | 15 | 235 | 15 | 181 | 39 | 1 |
| Parkville | 8,680 | 10 | 2 | 2 | 2 | 4 | 92 | 18 | 59 | 15 | 0 |
| Peculiar | 5,774 | 7 | 0 | 1 | 1 | 5 | 91 | 8 | 65 | 18 | 0 |
| Perryville | 8,570 | 38 | 0 | 4 | 1 | 33 | 126 | 17 | 90 | 19 | 0 |
| Pevely | 6,042 | 22 | 0 | 6 | 1 | 15 | 194 | 29 | 135 | 30 | 0 |
| Piedmont | 1,868 | 8 | 0 | 0 | 1 | 7 | 20 | 4 | 12 | 4 | 0 |
| Platte City | 4,998 | 17 | 0 | 6 | 5 | 6 | 61 | 8 | 45 | 8 | 0 |
| Pleasant Hill | 8,801 | 11 | 0 | 6 | 0 | 5 | 63 | 4 | 50 | 9 | 0 |
| Pleasant Valley | 3,063 | 4 | 0 | 0 | 0 | 4 | 54 | 9 | 35 | 10 | 1 |
| Portageville | 2,838 | 9 | 0 | 2 | 0 | 7 | 50 | 18 | 23 | 9 | 1 |
| Potosi | 2,538 | 27 | 0 | 3 | 2 | 22 | 245 | 52 | 176 | 17 | 1 |
| Qulin | 459 | 0 | 0 | 0 | 0 | 0 | 0 | 0 | 0 | 0 | 0 |
| Raymore | 22,885 | 17 | 1 | 5 | 3 | 8 | 211 | 23 | 171 | 17 | 2 |
| Richland | 1,791 | 0 | 0 | 0 | 0 | 0 | 27 | 5 | 21 | 1 | 0 |
| Richmond Heights | 8,799 | 34 | 0 | 1 | 11 | 22 | 517 | 9 | 457 | 51 | 1 |
| Riverside | 3,592 | 27 | 1 | 5 | 1 | 20 | 261 | 24 | 193 | 44 | 0 |
| Riverview | 2,810 | 29 | 1 | 0 | 1 | 27 | 64 | 10 | 39 | 15 | 1 |
| Rock Hill | 4,610 | 6 | 0 | 0 | 0 | 6 | 62 | 1 | 49 | 12 | 0 |
| Rogersville | 4,051 | 15 | 0 | 1 | 0 | 14 | 51 | 8 | 39 | 4 | 0 |
| Rolla | 20,519 | 89 | 0 | 15 | 9 | 65 | 682 | 112 | 536 | 34 | 1 |
| Rosebud | 398 | 0 | 0 | 0 | 0 | 0 | 5 | 1 | 3 | 1 | 0 |
| Salem | 4,866 | 8 | 0 | 1 | 0 | 7 | 97 | 15 | 76 | 6 | 2 |
| Savannah | 5,177 | 5 | 0 | 4 | 0 | 1 | 49 | 4 | 38 | 7 | 0 |
| Scott City | 4,520 | 2 | 0 | 0 | 1 | 1 | 75 | 4 | 62 | 9 | 1 |
| Seligman | 835 | 1 | 0 | 1 | 0 | 0 | 10 | 1 | 9 | 0 | 0 |
| Seneca | 2,400 | 2 | 0 | 0 | 0 | 2 | 44 | 11 | 31 | 2 | 0 |
| Seymour | 2,033 | 8 | 0 | 1 | 0 | 7 | 32 | 13 | 17 | 2 | 1 |
| Shelbina | 1,571 | 8 | 0 | 2 | 0 | 6 | 13 | 0 | 10 | 3 | 0 |
| Shrewsbury | 6,046 | 15 | 0 | 1 | 5 | 9 | 250 | 10 | 219 | 21 | 0 |
| Sikeston | 15,931 | 196 | 3 | 17 | 6 | 170 | 477 | 61 | 386 | 30 | 6 |
| Smithville | 11,311 | 16 | 0 | 2 | 1 | 13 | 91 | 10 | 65 | 16 | 0 |
| Sparta | 2,101 | 4 | 0 | 1 | 0 | 3 | 14 | 3 | 10 | 1 | 0 |
| Springfield | 168,988 | 2,651 | 19 | 200 | 339 | 2,093 | 10,940 | 1,543 | 7,960 | 1,437 | 40 |
| St. Ann | 12,540 | 62 | 0 | 5 | 5 | 52 | 228 | 27 | 148 | 53 | 0 |
| St. Charles | 72,323 | 192 | 0 | 22 | 30 | 140 | 1,337 | 124 | 1,024 | 189 | 3 |
| St. Clair | 4,686 | 21 | 1 | 4 | 0 | 16 | 258 | 34 | 198 | 26 | 1 |
| Steele | 1,825 | 14 | 0 | 1 | 4 | 9 | 64 | 16 | 43 | 5 | 0 |
| St. James | 3,986 | 12 | 1 | 2 | 0 | 9 | 166 | 9 | 150 | 7 | 0 |
| St. John | 6,299 | 46 | 0 | 1 | 6 | 39 | 155 | 20 | 112 | 23 | 2 |
| St. Joseph | 73,821 | 472 | 7 | 141 | 33 | 291 | 3,084 | 386 | 2,268 | 430 | 19 |
| St. Louis | 295,536 | 4,387 | 189 | 146 | 808 | 3,244 | 16,146 | 1,835 | 10,802 | 3,509 | 149 |
| St. Peters | 58,597 | 147 | 4 | 14 | 6 | 123 | 956 | 70 | 775 | 111 | 7 |
| St. Robert | 6,558 | 15 | 0 | 5 | 1 | 9 | 234 | 26 | 199 | 9 | 0 |
| Sugar Creek | 3,225 | 9 | 0 | 0 | 1 | 8 | 49 | 14 | 30 | 5 | 0 |
| Sullivan | 7,118 | 32 | 0 | 3 | 3 | 26 | 392 | 36 | 308 | 48 | 4 |
| Sunset Hills | 8,447 | 14 | 0 | 1 | 4 | 9 | 155 | 15 | 102 | 38 | 0 |
| Town and Country | 11,173 | 14 | 0 | 1 | 5 | 8 | 200 | 20 | 167 | 13 | 0 |

## Table 8. Offenses Known to Law Enforcement, by Selected State and City, 2021—Continued

(Number.)

| State/city | Population | Violent crime | Murder and nonnegligent manslaughter | Rape | Robbery | Aggravated assault | Property crime | Burglary | Larceny-theft | Motor vehicle theft | Arson |
|---|---|---|---|---|---|---|---|---|---|---|---|
| Trenton | 5,584 | 12 | 0 | 3 | 0 | 9 | 53 | 8 | 40 | 5 | 1 |
| Union | 12,292 | 57 | 0 | 6 | 1 | 50 | 482 | 23 | 410 | 49 | 6 |
| University City | 33,930 | 71 | 4 | 5 | 21 | 41 | 710 | 64 | 519 | 127 | 3 |
| Velda City | 1,351 | 35 | 0 | 0 | 3 | 32 | 35 | 10 | 14 | 11 | 1 |
| Versailles | 2,479 | 3 | 0 | 0 | 0 | 3 | 31 | 4 | 27 | 0 | 0 |
| Vienna | 599 | 1 | 0 | 1 | 0 | 0 | 8 | 1 | 7 | 0 | 0 |
| Vinita Park | 10,910 | 114 | 5 | 6 | 21 | 82 | 427 | 71 | 228 | 128 | 5 |
| Walnut Grove | 794 | 0 | 0 | 0 | 0 | 0 | 5 | 2 | 2 | 1 | 0 |
| Warrensburg | 20,707 | 51 | 1 | 20 | 4 | 26 | 448 | 44 | 361 | 43 | 4 |
| Warrenton | 9,019 | 28 | 1 | 4 | 1 | 22 | 250 | 19 | 216 | 15 | 1 |
| Warsaw | 2,227 | 0 | 0 | 0 | 0 | 0 | 57 | 3 | 49 | 5 | 0 |
| Warson Woods | 1,890 | 0 | 0 | 0 | 0 | 0 | 23 | 1 | 17 | 5 | 0 |
| Washington | 14,270 | 64 | 2 | 8 | 5 | 49 | 384 | 19 | 338 | 27 | 4 |
| Waynesville | 5,348 | 32 | 0 | 18 | 0 | 14 | 78 | 16 | 54 | 8 | 0 |
| Webster Groves | 22,885 | 15 | 0 | 0 | 3 | 12 | 198 | 18 | 143 | 37 | 0 |
| Wentzville | 44,793 | 108 | 0 | 13 | 5 | 90 | 444 | 20 | 385 | 39 | 0 |
| Weston | 1,854 | 3 | 1 | 1 | 1 | 0 | 35 | 6 | 28 | 1 | 1 |
| West Plains | 12,417 | 76 | 0 | 19 | 1 | 56 | 475 | 69 | 367 | 39 | 0 |
| Willard | 5,781 | 12 | 0 | 0 | 0 | 12 | 25 | 3 | 18 | 4 | 0 |
| Willow Springs | 2,090 | 9 | 0 | 2 | 0 | 7 | 48 | 4 | 41 | 3 | 2 |
| Winona | 1,292 | 3 | 0 | 0 | 0 | 3 | 5 | 0 | 3 | 2 | 0 |
| Woodson Terrace | 4,028 | 22 | 0 | 0 | 2 | 20 | 123 | 10 | 37 | 76 | 0 |
| **MONTANA** | | | | | | | | | | | |
| Baker | 1,910 | 4 | 0 | 0 | 0 | 4 | 5 | 1 | 2 | 2 | 0 |
| Belgrade | 10,738 | 44 | 0 | 12 | 1 | 31 | 212 | 13 | 182 | 17 | 1 |
| Billings | 110,274 | 1,162 | 6 | 115 | 128 | 913 | 5,267 | 622 | 3,612 | 1,033 | 47 |
| Bozeman | 52,586 | 173 | 1 | 60 | 6 | 106 | 668 | 56 | 556 | 56 | 8 |
| Bridger | 775 | 0 | 0 | 0 | 0 | 0 | 4 | 1 | 3 | 0 | 0 |
| Chinook | 1,233 | 1 | 0 | 0 | 0 | 1 | 4 | 0 | 3 | 1 | 0 |
| Colstrip | 2,216 | 3 | 0 | 0 | 0 | 3 | 3 | 0 | 2 | 1 | 0 |
| Columbia Falls | 6,385 | 19 | 0 | 6 | 0 | 13 | 89 | 9 | 69 | 11 | 0 |
| Columbus | 2,141 | 7 | 0 | 1 | 0 | 6 | 32 | 5 | 27 | 0 | 0 |
| Conrad | 2,396 | 6 | 0 | 1 | 0 | 5 | 16 | 1 | 13 | 2 | 0 |
| Cut Bank | 3,028 | 25 | 1 | 2 | 0 | 22 | 65 | 11 | 45 | 9 | 1 |
| Deer Lodge | 2,772 | 11 | 0 | 0 | 0 | 11 | 16 | 2 | 7 | 7 | 1 |
| East Helena | 2,140 | 1 | 0 | 0 | 0 | 1 | 33 | 3 | 29 | 1 | 0 |
| Ennis | 1,065 | 0 | 0 | 0 | 0 | 0 | 3 | 0 | 2 | 1 | 0 |
| Eureka | 1,449 | 0 | 0 | 0 | 0 | 0 | 1 | 0 | 1 | 0 | 0 |
| Fort Benton | 1,440 | 7 | 0 | 1 | 0 | 6 | 10 | 1 | 8 | 1 | 0 |
| Glasgow | 3,318 | 35 | 0 | 4 | 0 | 31 | 35 | 1 | 29 | 5 | 0 |
| Glendive | 4,873 | 22 | 0 | 4 | 1 | 17 | 76 | 14 | 51 | 11 | 0 |
| Great Falls | 58,265 | 324 | 2 | 36 | 27 | 259 | 2,767 | 255 | 2,227 | 285 | 25 |
| Havre | 9,724 | 74 | 0 | 13 | 2 | 59 | 273 | 28 | 213 | 32 | 4 |
| Helena | 34,262 | 235 | 0 | 45 | 17 | 173 | 1,098 | 102 | 903 | 93 | 3 |
| Hot Springs | 592 | 0 | 0 | 0 | 0 | 0 | 1 | 0 | 1 | 0 | 0 |
| Kalispell | 25,926 | 107 | 2 | 17 | 2 | 86 | 628 | 32 | 528 | 68 | 1 |
| Laurel | 6,710 | 48 | 0 | 2 | 0 | 46 | 210 | 8 | 184 | 18 | 1 |
| Lewistown | 5,882 | 29 | 0 | 4 | 0 | 25 | 10 | 6 | 4 | 0 | 0 |
| Livingston | 7,991 | 27 | 1 | 1 | 0 | 25 | 182 | 15 | 150 | 17 | 2 |
| Manhattan | 1,963 | 0 | 0 | 0 | 0 | 0 | 10 | 0 | 10 | 0 | 0 |
| Miles City | 8,160 | 52 | 0 | 2 | 0 | 50 | 115 | 8 | 105 | 2 | 2 |
| Missoula | 77,852 | 490 | 1 | 58 | 39 | 392 | 2,522 | 252 | 2,095 | 175 | 20 |
| Polson | 5,242 | 63 | 0 | 5 | 5 | 53 | 207 | 26 | 157 | 24 | 2 |
| Red Lodge | 2,384 | 8 | 0 | 3 | 0 | 5 | 12 | 2 | 9 | 1 | 0 |
| Ronan City | 2,195 | 20 | 0 | 1 | 1 | 18 | 60 | 3 | 52 | 5 | 0 |
| Sidney | 6,407 | 33 | 0 | 5 | 0 | 28 | 69 | 8 | 54 | 7 | 1 |
| Stevensville | 2,171 | 12 | 0 | 1 | 0 | 11 | 19 | 1 | 17 | 1 | 0 |
| St. Ignatius | 846 | 10 | 0 | 1 | 0 | 9 | 2 | 0 | 2 | 0 | 0 |
| Thompson Falls | 1,443 | 6 | 0 | 1 | 0 | 5 | 19 | 1 | 17 | 1 | 2 |
| Troy | 986 | 2 | 0 | 0 | 0 | 2 | 14 | 3 | 11 | 0 | 0 |
| West Yellowstone | 1,383 | 1 | 0 | 0 | 0 | 1 | 23 | 2 | 16 | 5 | 0 |
| Whitefish | 8,972 | 15 | 0 | 3 | 0 | 12 | 100 | 5 | 88 | 7 | 1 |
| Wolf Point | 2,734 | 19 | 0 | 0 | 1 | 18 | 28 | 7 | 16 | 5 | 1 |
| **NEBRASKA** | | | | | | | | | | | |
| Alliance | 7,986 | 57 | 0 | 11 | 9 | 37 | 324 | 234 | 77 | 13 | 0 |
| Ashland | 2,752 | 2 | 0 | 0 | 0 | 2 | 5 | 0 | 4 | 1 | 0 |
| Aurora | 4,491 | 5 | 0 | 0 | 0 | 5 | 15 | 2 | 13 | 0 | 0 |
| Beatrice | 12,225 | 22 | 0 | 9 | 0 | 13 | 147 | 17 | 117 | 13 | 2 |
| Bellevue | 53,436 | 77 | 4 | 46 | 10 | 17 | 734 | 76 | 537 | 121 | 2 |
| Bennington | 1,524 | 1 | 0 | 0 | 0 | 1 | 15 | 1 | 12 | 2 | 0 |
| Blair | 7,979 | 12 | 0 | 6 | 0 | 6 | 63 | 4 | 49 | 10 | 0 |
| Boys Town | 306 | 3 | 0 | 3 | 0 | 0 | 1 | 0 | 1 | 0 | 0 |
| Broken Bow | 3,427 | 3 | 0 | 1 | 0 | 2 | 5 | 0 | 4 | 1 | 0 |
| Chadron | 5,194 | 10 | 1 | 2 | 1 | 6 | 49 | 5 | 36 | 8 | 0 |
| Columbus | 23,727 | 23 | 0 | 13 | 0 | 10 | 223 | 14 | 196 | 13 | 2 |
| Crete | 6,864 | 58 | 0 | 21 | 1 | 36 | 121 | 16 | 98 | 7 | 0 |
| Emerson | 784 | 1 | 0 | 1 | 0 | 0 | 4 | 4 | 0 | 0 | 0 |
| Falls City | 4,052 | 7 | 0 | 2 | 0 | 5 | 33 | 5 | 27 | 1 | 0 |
| Franklin | 889 | 0 | 0 | 0 | 0 | 0 | 8 | 2 | 5 | 1 | 0 |
| Fremont | 26,210 | 49 | 1 | 30 | 5 | 13 | 534 | 44 | 437 | 53 | 3 |
| Gering | 8,017 | 12 | 0 | 1 | 3 | 8 | 89 | 13 | 67 | 9 | 1 |

## Table 8. Offenses Known to Law Enforcement, by Selected State and City, 2021—Continued

(Number.)

| State/city | Population | Violent crime | Murder and nonnegligent manslaughter | Rape | Robbery | Aggravated assault | Property crime | Burglary | Larceny-theft | Motor vehicle theft | Arson |
|---|---|---|---|---|---|---|---|---|---|---|---|
| Gordon | 1,475 | 3 | 0 | 0 | 0 | 3 | 28 | 3 | 21 | 4 | 0 |
| Gothenburg | 3,408 | 2 | 0 | 0 | 1 | 1 | 35 | 3 | 31 | 1 | 0 |
| Grand Island | 51,226 | 172 | 1 | 19 | 15 | 137 | 1,061 | 145 | 833 | 83 | 12 |
| Hastings | 24,680 | 82 | 0 | 18 | 6 | 58 | 576 | 70 | 458 | 48 | 5 |
| Holdrege | 5,375 | 4 | 0 | 3 | 1 | 0 | 31 | 3 | 24 | 4 | 0 |
| Kearney | 34,576 | 87 | 0 | 25 | 6 | 56 | 405 | 33 | 356 | 16 | 3 |
| La Vista | 17,057 | 22 | 0 | 11 | 1 | 10 | 198 | 20 | 147 | 31 | 0 |
| Lexington | 10,099 | 16 | 2 | 2 | 1 | 11 | 141 | 20 | 113 | 8 | 0 |
| Lincoln | 293,808 | 1,236 | 8 | 275 | 138 | 815 | 8,004 | 915 | 6,466 | 623 | 61 |
| McCook | 7,478 | 11 | 0 | 2 | 1 | 8 | 82 | 7 | 70 | 5 | 0 |
| Milford | 2,006 | 2 | 0 | 1 | 0 | 1 | 1 | 0 | 1 | 0 | 0 |
| Minden | 3,031 | 1 | 0 | 1 | 0 | 0 | 22 | 6 | 15 | 1 | 0 |
| Mitchell | 1,599 | 0 | 0 | 0 | 0 | 0 | 13 | 3 | 7 | 3 | 0 |
| Morrill | 869 | 0 | 0 | 0 | 0 | 0 | 10 | 1 | 9 | 0 | 0 |
| Nebraska City | 7,248 | 25 | 1 | 15 | 0 | 9 | 117 | 15 | 93 | 9 | 2 |
| Norfolk | 24,370 | 25 | 0 | 12 | 2 | 11 | 207 | 18 | 166 | 23 | 6 |
| North Platte | 23,057 | 65 | 1 | 14 | 6 | 44 | 642 | 104 | 486 | 52 | 7 |
| Ogallala | 4,448 | 8 | 0 | 2 | 1 | 5 | 115 | 11 | 92 | 12 | 0 |
| O'Neill | 3,521 | 0 | 0 | 0 | 0 | 0 | 5 | 1 | 3 | 1 | 0 |
| Papillion | 20,313 | 15 | 0 | 7 | 1 | 7 | 228 | 12 | 192 | 24 | 1 |
| Plattsmouth | 6,409 | 10 | 0 | 6 | 0 | 4 | 107 | 19 | 80 | 8 | 0 |
| Ralston | 7,386 | 9 | 0 | 2 | 2 | 5 | 109 | 12 | 72 | 25 | 0 |
| Schuyler | 6,219 | 3 | 0 | 1 | 0 | 2 | 16 | 1 | 15 | 0 | 0 |
| Scotia | 281 | 0 | 0 | 0 | 0 | 0 | 0 | 0 | 0 | 0 | 0 |
| Scottsbluff | 15,463 | 77 | 2 | 23 | 2 | 50 | 388 | 54 | 308 | 26 | 7 |
| Seward | 7,402 | 10 | 0 | 8 | 0 | 2 | 55 | 5 | 46 | 4 | 0 |
| Sidney | 6,186 | 31 | 0 | 2 | 0 | 29 | 99 | 2 | 91 | 6 | 1 |
| South Sioux City | 12,780 | 37 | 0 | 6 | 4 | 27 | 356 | 15 | 313 | 28 | 0 |
| St. Paul | 2,336 | 2 | 0 | 1 | 0 | 1 | 7 | 1 | 5 | 1 | 0 |
| Tilden | 934 | 0 | 0 | 0 | 0 | 0 | 0 | 0 | 0 | 0 | 0 |
| Valentine | 2,747 | 19 | 0 | 3 | 0 | 16 | 20 | 0 | 18 | 2 | 0 |
| Wahoo | 4,611 | 4 | 0 | 2 | 0 | 2 | 44 | 12 | 30 | 2 | 0 |
| Wayne | 5,766 | 12 | 0 | 8 | 1 | 3 | 51 | 7 | 42 | 2 | 1 |
| West Point | 3,223 | 3 | 0 | 0 | 1 | 2 | 13 | 2 | 10 | 1 | 0 |
| Wymore | 1,311 | 7 | 0 | 1 | 0 | 6 | 7 | 1 | 3 | 3 | 0 |
| York | 7,784 | 23 | 0 | 6 | 1 | 16 | 96 | 12 | 81 | 3 | 0 |
| **NEVADA** | | | | | | | | | | | |
| Boulder City | 16,556 | 26 | 0 | 4 | 2 | 20 | 152 | 34 | 92 | 26 | 0 |
| Carlin | 2,273 | 15 | 0 | 3 | 0 | 12 | 62 | 27 | 28 | 7 | 1 |
| Elko | 20,760 | 91 | 3 | 17 | 16 | 55 | 585 | 104 | 406 | 75 | 5 |
| Henderson | 337,375 | 772 | 14 | 90 | 151 | 517 | 5,567 | 813 | 3,961 | 793 | 36 |
| Las Vegas Metropolitan Police Department | 1,685,021 | 7,890 | 152 | 994 | 1,388 | 5,356 | 42,857 | 7,951 | 26,048 | 8,858 | 171 |
| Mesquite | 21,038 | 32 | 0 | 14 | 1 | 17 | 402 | 72 | 280 | 50 | 0 |
| North Las Vegas | 264,877 | 995 | 27 | 94 | 319 | 555 | 4,412 | 922 | 2,200 | 1,290 | 30 |
| Reno | 262,919 | 1,513 | 17 | 286 | 273 | 937 | 7,513 | 1,204 | 4,944 | 1,365 | 21 |
| Sparks | 108,612 | 477 | 8 | 105 | 74 | 290 | 2,571 | 396 | 1,754 | 421 | 6 |
| Winnemucca | 7,835 | 48 | 0 | 16 | 1 | 31 | 199 | 60 | 112 | 27 | 9 |
| **NEW HAMPSHIRE** | | | | | | | | | | | |
| Alexandria | 1,629 | 2 | 0 | 2 | 0 | 0 | 5 | 2 | 3 | 0 | 0 |
| Allenstown | 4,505 | 4 | 0 | 2 | 0 | 2 | 15 | 1 | 14 | 0 | 0 |
| Alstead | 1,952 | 1 | 0 | 1 | 0 | 0 | 3 | 1 | 2 | 0 | 0 |
| Alton | 5,445 | 18 | 0 | 12 | 0 | 6 | 20 | 2 | 17 | 1 | 0 |
| Amherst | 11,440 | 5 | 0 | 1 | 2 | 2 | 110 | 3 | 106 | 1 | 0 |
| Andover | 2,392 | 0 | 0 | 0 | 0 | 0 | 9 | 1 | 8 | 0 | 0 |
| Antrim | 2,687 | 1 | 0 | 1 | 0 | 0 | 19 | 3 | 16 | 0 | 0 |
| Ashland | 2,066 | 1 | 0 | 0 | 0 | 1 | 43 | 3 | 38 | 2 | 0 |
| Atkinson | 7,296 | 0 | 0 | 0 | 0 | 0 | 10 | 0 | 8 | 2 | 0 |
| Auburn | 5,771 | 2 | 0 | 0 | 0 | 2 | 42 | 2 | 32 | 8 | 0 |
| Barnstead | 4,852 | 1 | 0 | 1 | 0 | 0 | 37 | 3 | 34 | 0 | 0 |
| Barrington | 9,423 | 10 | 0 | 5 | 0 | 5 | 60 | 16 | 40 | 4 | 0 |
| Bartlett | 2,818 | 1 | 0 | 1 | 0 | 0 | 26 | 7 | 16 | 3 | 0 |
| Bath | 1,110 | 0 | 0 | 0 | 0 | 0 | 11 | 0 | 11 | 0 | 0 |
| Bedford | 23,137 | 4 | 2 | 0 | 1 | 1 | 153 | 7 | 139 | 7 | 0 |
| Belmont | 7,406 | 8 | 0 | 2 | 0 | 6 | 95 | 8 | 80 | 7 | 0 |
| Bennington | 1,520 | 3 | 0 | 1 | 0 | 2 | 4 | 1 | 3 | 0 | 0 |
| Bethlehem | 2,669 | 5 | 0 | 2 | 0 | 3 | 24 | 1 | 20 | 3 | 0 |
| Bow | 8,119 | 5 | 0 | 2 | 0 | 3 | 42 | 1 | 38 | 3 | 0 |
| Bradford | 1,748 | 0 | 0 | 0 | 0 | 0 | 18 | 1 | 17 | 0 | 0 |
| Brentwood | 4,682 | 0 | 0 | 0 | 0 | 0 | 16 | 1 | 14 | 1 | 0 |
| Bristol | 3,168 | 1 | 0 | 0 | 1 | 0 | 36 | 4 | 28 | 4 | 0 |
| Brookline | 5,547 | 2 | 0 | 2 | 0 | 0 | 9 | 2 | 6 | 1 | 0 |
| Campton | 3,335 | 7 | 0 | 3 | 1 | 3 | 29 | 4 | 23 | 2 | 0 |
| Canaan | 3,914 | 10 | 0 | 7 | 0 | 3 | 7 | 0 | 5 | 2 | 0 |
| Candia | 4,016 | 1 | 0 | 0 | 0 | 1 | 24 | 0 | 24 | 0 | 0 |
| Canterbury | 2,510 | 0 | 0 | 0 | 0 | 0 | 13 | 0 | 11 | 2 | 1 |
| Carroll | 754 | 1 | 0 | 0 | 0 | 1 | 16 | 0 | 16 | 0 | 0 |
| Center Harbor | 1,112 | 2 | 0 | 1 | 0 | 1 | 5 | 0 | 5 | 0 | 0 |
| Charlestown | 5,023 | 1 | 0 | 0 | 0 | 1 | 21 | 4 | 15 | 2 | 0 |
| Chester | 5,399 | 1 | 0 | 0 | 0 | 1 | 31 | 4 | 24 | 3 | 0 |
| Chesterfield | 3,648 | 7 | 0 | 5 | 0 | 2 | 40 | 12 | 24 | 4 | 0 |

# Table 8. Offenses Known to Law Enforcement, by Selected State and City, 2021—Continued

(Number.)

| State/city | Population | Violent crime | Murder and nonnegligent manslaughter | Rape | Robbery | Aggravated assault | Property crime | Burglary | Larceny-theft | Motor vehicle theft | Arson |
|---|---|---|---|---|---|---|---|---|---|---|---|
| Chichester | 2,750 | 1 | 0 | 1 | 0 | 0 | 23 | 1 | 22 | 0 | 0 |
| Colebrook | 2,118 | 2 | 0 | 1 | 0 | 1 | 24 | 2 | 19 | 3 | 0 |
| Concord | 44,053 | 60 | 3 | 12 | 17 | 28 | 740 | 56 | 642 | 42 | 9 |
| Conway | 10,364 | 24 | 0 | 13 | 4 | 7 | 181 | 5 | 167 | 9 | 1 |
| Cornish | 1,614 | 0 | 0 | 0 | 0 | 0 | 11 | 0 | 11 | 0 | 0 |
| Deerfield | 4,652 | 0 | 0 | 0 | 0 | 0 | 21 | 1 | 18 | 2 | 0 |
| Deering | 1,974 | 4 | 0 | 1 | 0 | 3 | 5 | 1 | 3 | 1 | 0 |
| Derry | 33,892 | 28 | 1 | 21 | 1 | 5 | 257 | 19 | 217 | 21 | 4 |
| Dublin | 1,552 | 0 | 0 | 0 | 0 | 0 | 9 | 0 | 8 | 1 | 0 |
| Dunbarton | 2,934 | 2 | 0 | 2 | 0 | 0 | 8 | 1 | 7 | 0 | 0 |
| Durham | 16,848 | 17 | 0 | 15 | 0 | 2 | 43 | 5 | 36 | 2 | 0 |
| East Kingston | 2,446 | 1 | 0 | 1 | 0 | 0 | 1 | 0 | 0 | 1 | 0 |
| Enfield | 4,563 | 1 | 0 | 1 | 0 | 0 | 8 | 1 | 7 | 0 | 0 |
| Epping | 7,233 | 2 | 0 | 0 | 0 | 2 | 91 | 3 | 88 | 0 | 0 |
| Epsom | 4,848 | 5 | 0 | 4 | 0 | 1 | 23 | 0 | 23 | 0 | 0 |
| Exeter | 15,596 | 23 | 0 | 8 | 2 | 13 | 85 | 6 | 74 | 5 | 0 |
| Farmington | 7,058 | 15 | 0 | 9 | 2 | 4 | 79 | 11 | 62 | 6 | 2 |
| Fitzwilliam | 2,373 | 2 | 0 | 0 | 0 | 2 | 7 | 0 | 6 | 1 | 1 |
| Franconia | 1,117 | 0 | 0 | 0 | 0 | 0 | 14 | 0 | 14 | 0 | 0 |
| Franklin | 8,782 | 14 | 0 | 3 | 3 | 8 | 106 | 4 | 98 | 4 | 0 |
| Freedom | 1,603 | 0 | 0 | 0 | 0 | 0 | 11 | 3 | 8 | 0 | 0 |
| Fremont | 4,847 | 2 | 0 | 0 | 0 | 2 | 16 | 0 | 15 | 1 | 0 |
| Gilford | 7,391 | 10 | 0 | 8 | 0 | 2 | 92 | 10 | 74 | 8 | 2 |
| Gilmanton | 3,850 | 4 | 0 | 2 | 1 | 1 | 24 | 2 | 18 | 4 | 0 |
| Goffstown | 18,184 | 18 | 0 | 11 | 3 | 4 | 124 | 10 | 100 | 14 | 0 |
| Gorham | 2,569 | 2 | 0 | 2 | 0 | 0 | 64 | 4 | 57 | 3 | 0 |
| Goshen | 813 | 0 | 0 | 0 | 0 | 0 | 1 | 0 | 1 | 0 | 0 |
| Grantham | 2,953 | 1 | 0 | 1 | 0 | 0 | 12 | 0 | 10 | 2 | 0 |
| Greenfield | 1,855 | 1 | 0 | 1 | 0 | 0 | 11 | 0 | 10 | 1 | 0 |
| Greenland | 4,228 | 1 | 0 | 0 | 0 | 1 | 14 | 2 | 12 | 0 | 0 |
| Greenville | 2,111 | 3 | 0 | 1 | 0 | 2 | 0 | 0 | 0 | 0 | 1 |
| Groton | 611 | 1 | 0 | 1 | 0 | 0 | 6 | 0 | 6 | 0 | 0 |
| Hampstead | 8,733 | 7 | 0 | 3 | 0 | 4 | 35 | 2 | 29 | 4 | 0 |
| Hampton | 16,206 | 36 | 0 | 6 | 1 | 29 | 124 | 3 | 113 | 8 | 0 |
| Hampton Falls | 2,459 | 2 | 0 | 0 | 1 | 1 | 14 | 0 | 14 | 0 | 0 |
| Hancock | 1,650 | 2 | 0 | 0 | 0 | 2 | 3 | 1 | 2 | 0 | 0 |
| Hanover | 11,586 | 2 | 0 | 1 | 0 | 1 | 67 | 5 | 62 | 0 | 1 |
| Harrisville | 953 | 0 | 0 | 0 | 0 | 0 | 3 | 0 | 3 | 0 | 0 |
| Haverhill | 4,542 | 2 | 0 | 1 | 0 | 1 | 37 | 2 | 33 | 2 | 0 |
| Hebron | 635 | 0 | 0 | 0 | 0 | 0 | 2 | 0 | 2 | 0 | 0 |
| Henniker | 5,024 | 5 | 0 | 2 | 0 | 3 | 24 | 3 | 17 | 4 | 0 |
| Hinsdale | 3,894 | 12 | 1 | 3 | 0 | 8 | 68 | 2 | 64 | 2 | 1 |
| Holderness | 2,133 | 1 | 0 | 0 | 0 | 1 | 13 | 0 | 10 | 3 | 0 |
| Hollis | 8,166 | 0 | 0 | 0 | 0 | 0 | 27 | 1 | 25 | 1 | 0 |
| Hooksett | 14,834 | 17 | 0 | 12 | 1 | 4 | 156 | 3 | 140 | 13 | 1 |
| Hopkinton | 5,852 | 3 | 0 | 1 | 0 | 2 | 34 | 0 | 30 | 4 | 0 |
| Hudson | 25,736 | 23 | 0 | 12 | 3 | 8 | 199 | 21 | 159 | 19 | 1 |
| Jackson | 869 | 1 | 0 | 1 | 0 | 0 | 9 | 2 | 7 | 0 | 0 |
| Jaffrey | 5,271 | 8 | 0 | 3 | 0 | 5 | 21 | 1 | 16 | 4 | 0 |
| Keene | 22,619 | 28 | 0 | 16 | 4 | 8 | 388 | 28 | 346 | 14 | 2 |
| Kensington | 2,116 | 0 | 0 | 0 | 0 | 0 | 3 | 0 | 3 | 0 | 0 |
| Kingston | 6,549 | 3 | 0 | 2 | 1 | 0 | 12 | 0 | 5 | 7 | 0 |
| Laconia | 16,929 | 36 | 0 | 21 | 3 | 12 | 408 | 17 | 380 | 11 | 3 |
| Lancaster | 3,209 | 5 | 0 | 0 | 2 | 3 | 21 | 1 | 17 | 3 | 0 |
| Langdon | 688 | 0 | 0 | 0 | 0 | 0 | 0 | 0 | 0 | 0 | 0 |
| Lebanon | 13,877 | 20 | 0 | 11 | 3 | 6 | 262 | 14 | 237 | 11 | 1 |
| Lee | 4,684 | 1 | 0 | 0 | 0 | 1 | 21 | 0 | 20 | 1 | 0 |
| Lincoln | 1,787 | 3 | 0 | 3 | 0 | 0 | 33 | 2 | 31 | 0 | 1 |
| Litchfield | 8,696 | 1 | 0 | 0 | 1 | 0 | 17 | 0 | 15 | 2 | 0 |
| Littleton | 5,898 | 14 | 0 | 10 | 0 | 4 | 82 | 3 | 73 | 6 | 0 |
| Loudon | 5,740 | 4 | 0 | 2 | 0 | 2 | 27 | 1 | 20 | 6 | 1 |
| Lyndeborough | 1,735 | 0 | 0 | 0 | 0 | 0 | 2 | 0 | 2 | 0 | 0 |
| Madison | 2,646 | 3 | 0 | 0 | 0 | 3 | 14 | 2 | 12 | 0 | 0 |
| Manchester | 112,844 | 510 | 1 | 49 | 77 | 383 | 2,585 | 245 | 2,129 | 211 | 16 |
| Marlborough | 2,089 | 1 | 0 | 0 | 0 | 1 | 18 | 3 | 12 | 3 | 0 |
| Mason | 1,438 | 3 | 0 | 0 | 0 | 3 | 6 | 0 | 4 | 2 | 0 |
| Meredith | 6,579 | 9 | 0 | 7 | 1 | 1 | 54 | 10 | 42 | 2 | 0 |
| Merrimack | 27,656 | 6 | 0 | 2 | 2 | 2 | 151 | 7 | 137 | 7 | 0 |
| Middleton | 1,859 | 1 | 0 | 0 | 0 | 1 | 10 | 2 | 7 | 1 | 0 |
| Milford | 16,662 | 15 | 0 | 4 | 3 | 8 | 68 | 4 | 58 | 6 | 1 |
| Milton | 4,676 | 5 | 0 | 4 | 0 | 1 | 33 | 2 | 29 | 2 | 0 |
| Mont Vernon | 2,749 | 1 | 0 | 1 | 0 | 0 | 11 | 1 | 10 | 0 | 0 |
| Moultonborough | 4,227 | 2 | 0 | 0 | 0 | 2 | 26 | 0 | 25 | 1 | 0 |
| Nashua | 89,431 | 135 | 2 | 72 | 16 | 45 | 976 | 45 | 864 | 67 | 6 |
| New Boston | 6,006 | 4 | 0 | 1 | 0 | 3 | 9 | 0 | 7 | 2 | 0 |
| Newbury | 2,263 | 0 | 0 | 0 | 0 | 0 | 8 | 0 | 7 | 1 | 0 |
| New Durham | 2,771 | 3 | 0 | 0 | 0 | 3 | 18 | 1 | 14 | 3 | 1 |
| Newfields | 1,760 | 1 | 0 | 1 | 0 | 0 | 25 | 4 | 20 | 1 | 0 |
| New Hampton | 2,270 | 0 | 0 | 0 | 0 | 0 | 21 | 1 | 19 | 1 | 0 |
| Newington | 849 | 1 | 0 | 0 | 1 | 0 | 89 | 3 | 82 | 4 | 0 |
| New Ipswich | 5,462 | 3 | 0 | 3 | 0 | 0 | 25 | 2 | 22 | 1 | 1 |
| New London | 4,257 | 1 | 0 | 1 | 0 | 0 | 37 | 8 | 26 | 3 | 0 |
| Newmarket | 9,349 | 8 | 0 | 5 | 1 | 2 | 31 | 3 | 26 | 2 | 0 |

## Table 8. Offenses Known to Law Enforcement, by Selected State and City, 2021—Continued

(Number.)

| State/city | Population | Violent crime | Murder and nonnegligent manslaughter | Rape | Robbery | Aggravated assault | Property crime | Burglary | Larceny-theft | Motor vehicle theft | Arson |
|---|---|---|---|---|---|---|---|---|---|---|---|
| Newton | 5,030 | 1 | 0 | 0 | 0 | 1 | 10 | 2 | 7 | 1 | 0 |
| Northfield | 4,995 | 1 | 0 | 0 | 0 | 1 | 55 | 6 | 40 | 9 | 0 |
| Northumberland | 2,101 | 6 | 0 | 2 | 0 | 4 | 29 | 8 | 19 | 2 | 1 |
| Northwood | 4,385 | 1 | 0 | 0 | 0 | 1 | 18 | 4 | 12 | 2 | 0 |
| Nottingham | 5,281 | 0 | 0 | 0 | 0 | 0 | 19 | 0 | 16 | 3 | 0 |
| Orford | 1,323 | 1 | 1 | 0 | 0 | 0 | 13 | 1 | 12 | 0 | 0 |
| Ossipee | 4,387 | 4 | 0 | 2 | 0 | 2 | 50 | 2 | 47 | 1 | 1 |
| Pelham | 14,453 | 6 | 0 | 3 | 0 | 3 | 86 | 5 | 78 | 3 | 0 |
| Pembroke | 7,265 | 7 | 0 | 5 | 0 | 2 | 49 | 8 | 36 | 5 | 0 |
| Peterborough | 6,792 | 8 | 0 | 5 | 0 | 3 | 59 | 3 | 50 | 6 | 0 |
| Pittsfield | 4,146 | 16 | 0 | 5 | 0 | 11 | 25 | 1 | 20 | 4 | 0 |
| Plainfield | 2,425 | 1 | 0 | 1 | 0 | 0 | 19 | 3 | 15 | 1 | 0 |
| Plaistow | 7,847 | 3 | 0 | 1 | 1 | 1 | 36 | 5 | 28 | 3 | 0 |
| Plymouth | 6,911 | 10 | 0 | 1 | 1 | 8 | 109 | 4 | 97 | 8 | 1 |
| Portsmouth | 21,913 | 54 | 1 | 26 | 1 | 26 | 326 | 11 | 298 | 17 | 1 |
| Raymond | 10,752 | 8 | 0 | 5 | 0 | 3 | 86 | 5 | 73 | 8 | 0 |
| Rollinsford | 2,615 | 3 | 0 | 0 | 0 | 3 | 15 | 0 | 13 | 2 | 0 |
| Roxbury | 220 | 0 | 0 | 0 | 0 | 0 | 1 | 0 | 1 | 0 | 0 |
| Rumney | 1,585 | 0 | 0 | 0 | 0 | 0 | 30 | 8 | 21 | 1 | 0 |
| Rye | 5,566 | 2 | 0 | 1 | 0 | 1 | 23 | 1 | 20 | 2 | 0 |
| Salem | 31,231 | 16 | 0 | 7 | 2 | 7 | 336 | 16 | 299 | 21 | 0 |
| Sanbornton | 3,055 | 1 | 0 | 1 | 0 | 0 | 12 | 5 | 7 | 0 | 0 |
| Sandown | 6,693 | 3 | 0 | 2 | 0 | 1 | 19 | 1 | 16 | 2 | 0 |
| Sandwich | 1,371 | 0 | 0 | 0 | 0 | 0 | 10 | 3 | 7 | 0 | 0 |
| Seabrook | 8,974 | 11 | 0 | 2 | 2 | 7 | 198 | 4 | 179 | 15 | 0 |
| Somersworth | 12,498 | 18 | 0 | 12 | 4 | 2 | 307 | 11 | 283 | 13 | 4 |
| South Hampton | 835 | 0 | 0 | 0 | 0 | 0 | 3 | 1 | 2 | 0 | 0 |
| Springfield | 1,351 | 0 | 0 | 0 | 0 | 0 | 2 | 0 | 2 | 0 | 0 |
| Stoddard | 1,256 | 0 | 0 | 0 | 0 | 0 | 0 | 0 | 0 | 0 | 0 |
| Strafford | 4,314 | 0 | 0 | 0 | 0 | 0 | 9 | 0 | 6 | 3 | 0 |
| Stratham | 7,707 | 1 | 0 | 0 | 0 | 1 | 23 | 1 | 21 | 1 | 1 |
| Sunapee | 3,519 | 4 | 0 | 1 | 0 | 3 | 20 | 1 | 18 | 1 | 0 |
| Swanzey | 7,275 | 5 | 0 | 3 | 1 | 1 | 25 | 8 | 15 | 2 | 1 |
| Tamworth | 3,117 | 2 | 0 | 1 | 0 | 1 | 16 | 1 | 15 | 0 | 0 |
| Thornton | 2,559 | 4 | 0 | 3 | 0 | 1 | 12 | 3 | 8 | 1 | 0 |
| Tilton | 3,602 | 12 | 0 | 4 | 0 | 8 | 160 | 4 | 148 | 8 | 0 |
| Troy | 2,114 | 0 | 0 | 0 | 0 | 0 | 20 | 2 | 12 | 6 | 0 |
| Tuftonboro | 2,443 | 0 | 0 | 0 | 0 | 0 | 22 | 1 | 21 | 0 | 0 |
| Wakefield | 5,812 | 3 | 0 | 0 | 0 | 3 | 57 | 7 | 47 | 3 | 1 |
| Walpole | 4,064 | 3 | 0 | 2 | 0 | 1 | 5 | 1 | 2 | 2 | 0 |
| Warner | 2,964 | 1 | 0 | 1 | 0 | 0 | 35 | 1 | 32 | 2 | 0 |
| Warren | 952 | 0 | 0 | 0 | 0 | 0 | 0 | 0 | 0 | 0 | 0 |
| Washington | 1,102 | 1 | 0 | 0 | 0 | 1 | 4 | 0 | 3 | 1 | 0 |
| Waterville Valley | 242 | 0 | 0 | 0 | 0 | 0 | 7 | 0 | 7 | 0 | 0 |
| Weare | 9,130 | 5 | 0 | 5 | 0 | 0 | 21 | 2 | 11 | 8 | 0 |
| Whitefield | 2,186 | 2 | 0 | 0 | 0 | 2 | 5 | 1 | 4 | 0 | 0 |
| Wilmot | 1,412 | 0 | 0 | 0 | 0 | 0 | 2 | 0 | 2 | 0 | 0 |
| Winchester | 4,205 | 5 | 0 | 3 | 0 | 2 | 33 | 6 | 22 | 5 | 2 |
| Windham | 15,191 | 5 | 0 | 1 | 1 | 3 | 54 | 5 | 46 | 3 | 0 |
| Wolfeboro | 6,467 | 5 | 0 | 3 | 0 | 2 | 34 | 2 | 30 | 2 | 1 |
| Woodstock | 1,373 | 1 | 0 | 1 | 0 | 0 | 18 | 2 | 16 | 0 | 0 |
| | | | | | | | | | | | |
| **NEW JERSEY**[1] | | | | | | | | | | | |
| Absecon | 8,820 | 22 | 0 | 7 | 1 | 14 | 295 | 27 | 261 | 7 | 3 |
| Bernardsville | 7,883 | 0 | 0 | 0 | 0 | 0 | 48 | 3 | 32 | 13 | 0 |
| Bloomingdale | 8,415 | 13 | 0 | 1 | 0 | 12 | 26 | 3 | 22 | 1 | 0 |
| Cranford Township | 25,189 | 6 | 0 | 0 | 2 | 4 | 149 | 27 | 95 | 27 | 0 |
| Dumont | 18,340 | 5 | 0 | 0 | 0 | 5 | 56 | 1 | 51 | 4 | 0 |
| East Brunswick Township | 50,438 | 38 | 1 | 3 | 10 | 24 | 522 | 49 | 442 | 31 | 1 |
| Eatontown | 12,100 | 25 | 0 | 4 | 5 | 16 | 215 | 23 | 181 | 11 | 0 |
| Elizabeth | 134,131 | 644 | 10 | 68 | 246 | 320 | 2,976 | 294 | 1,964 | 718 | 12 |
| Elmwood Park | 20,738 | 24 | 1 | 1 | 5 | 17 | 211 | 20 | 172 | 19 | 0 |
| Emerson | 7,900 | 0 | 0 | 0 | 0 | 0 | 22 | 2 | 19 | 1 | 0 |
| Englewood | 29,592 | 49 | 0 | 6 | 5 | 38 | 261 | 45 | 179 | 37 | 1 |
| Franklin | 4,662 | 4 | 0 | 1 | 0 | 3 | 61 | 1 | 57 | 3 | 0 |
| Gloucester Township | 66,365 | 63 | 0 | 11 | 14 | 38 | 802 | 64 | 682 | 56 | 3 |
| Hackensack | 45,932 | 52 | 0 | 10 | 12 | 30 | 603 | 35 | 518 | 50 | 3 |
| Hamilton Township, Mercer County | 90,195 | 225 | 6 | 25 | 42 | 152 | 1,401 | 219 | 1,065 | 117 | 7 |
| Hanover Township | 14,814 | 7 | 0 | 1 | 3 | 3 | 155 | 9 | 134 | 12 | 1 |
| Hawthorne | 19,442 | 7 | 0 | 2 | 0 | 5 | 114 | 10 | 97 | 7 | 0 |
| Hillsborough Township | 42,116 | 15 | 2 | 3 | 4 | 6 | 143 | 15 | 113 | 15 | 0 |
| Hillside Township | 22,799 | 54 | 6 | 4 | 15 | 29 | 548 | 107 | 333 | 108 | 0 |
| Hoboken | 55,632 | 80 | 0 | 1 | 17 | 62 | 652 | 75 | 539 | 38 | 0 |
| Island Heights | 1,773 | 2 | 0 | 0 | 0 | 2 | 5 | 0 | 2 | 3 | 0 |
| Jefferson Township | 21,409 | 7 | 0 | 2 | 0 | 5 | 42 | 5 | 36 | 1 | 0 |
| Kenilworth | 8,520 | 7 | 0 | 4 | 1 | 2 | 93 | 3 | 72 | 18 | 0 |
| Lakehurst | 2,862 | 6 | 0 | 1 | 0 | 5 | 27 | 2 | 24 | 1 | 0 |
| Lawrence Township, Mercer County | 33,882 | 16 | 0 | 10 | 6 | 0 | 482 | 108 | 343 | 31 | 0 |
| Lodi | 25,235 | 27 | 1 | 5 | 5 | 16 | 268 | 35 | 206 | 27 | 0 |
| Lyndhurst Township | 23,987 | 11 | 0 | 1 | 2 | 8 | 184 | 12 | 145 | 27 | 0 |
| Madison | 18,563 | 2 | 0 | 0 | 1 | 1 | 83 | 3 | 64 | 16 | 0 |

## Table 8. Offenses Known to Law Enforcement, by Selected State and City, 2021—Continued

(Number.)

| State/city | Population | Violent crime | Murder and nonnegligent manslaughter | Rape | Robbery | Aggravated assault | Property crime | Burglary | Larceny-theft | Motor vehicle theft | Arson |
|---|---|---|---|---|---|---|---|---|---|---|---|
| Milltown | 7,203 | 3 | 0 | 0 | 0 | 3 | 49 | 2 | 46 | 1 | 0 |
| Mine Hill Township | 3,602 | 0 | 0 | 0 | 0 | 0 | 9 | 2 | 7 | 0 | 1 |
| Montclair | 40,224 | 29 | 0 | 1 | 5 | 23 | 298 | 37 | 205 | 56 | 0 |
| Morristown | 20,130 | 21 | 1 | 3 | 2 | 15 | 104 | 3 | 92 | 9 | 0 |
| Newark | 295,039 | 1,446 | 60 | 55 | 375 | 956 | 4,298 | 435 | 2,006 | 1,857 | 24 |
| North Plainfield | 22,160 | 63 | 0 | 3 | 42 | 18 | 279 | 18 | 228 | 33 | 2 |
| Oradell | 8,447 | 0 | 0 | 0 | 0 | 0 | 15 | 2 | 10 | 3 | 0 |
| Pompton Lakes | 11,374 | 8 | 0 | 1 | 1 | 6 | 40 | 3 | 32 | 5 | 0 |
| Princeton | 32,436 | 10 | 0 | 0 | 4 | 6 | 224 | 28 | 181 | 15 | 1 |
| Rahway | 31,362 | 48 | 1 | 7 | 7 | 33 | 190 | 18 | 131 | 41 | 2 |
| Rochelle Park Township | 5,775 | 10 | 0 | 0 | 4 | 6 | 93 | 2 | 83 | 8 | 0 |
| Rockaway Township | 27,360 | 8 | 0 | 2 | 2 | 4 | 142 | 19 | 121 | 2 | 0 |
| Roxbury Township | 23,676 | 4 | 0 | 0 | 0 | 4 | 142 | 19 | 121 | 2 | 0 |
| Saddle River | 3,287 | 0 | 0 | 0 | 0 | 0 | 31 | 18 | 6 | 7 | 0 |
| Seaside Park | 1,629 | 3 | 0 | 0 | 0 | 3 | 21 | 4 | 16 | 1 | 0 |
| Secaucus | 23,102 | 47 | 0 | 9 | 8 | 30 | 466 | 38 | 399 | 29 | 0 |
| Shrewsbury | 4,065 | 0 | 0 | 0 | 0 | 0 | 52 | 2 | 48 | 2 | 0 |
| South Amboy | 9,536 | 13 | 0 | 2 | 0 | 11 | 72 | 9 | 44 | 19 | 0 |
| South Brunswick Township | 47,479 | 33 | 0 | 6 | 5 | 22 | 322 | 28 | 262 | 32 | 0 |
| South River | 16,240 | 12 | 0 | 1 | 1 | 10 | 45 | 16 | 25 | 4 | 0 |
| Sparta Township | 18,503 | 3 | 0 | 0 | 0 | 3 | 70 | 7 | 63 | 0 | 0 |
| Springfield Township, Union County | 18,285 | 8 | 0 | 0 | 1 | 7 | 203 | 16 | 157 | 30 | 0 |
| Stafford Township | 30,025 | 18 | 0 | 1 | 0 | 17 | 194 | 6 | 177 | 11 | 0 |
| Stanhope | 3,258 | 9 | 0 | 1 | 1 | 7 | 8 | 4 | 4 | 0 | 0 |
| Verona | 14,233 | 3 | 0 | 0 | 0 | 3 | 90 | 10 | 62 | 18 | 0 |
| Wallington | 12,086 | 3 | 0 | 1 | 0 | 2 | 125 | 18 | 100 | 7 | 0 |
| Wanaque | 12,281 | 3 | 0 | 0 | 0 | 3 | 5 | 2 | 3 | 0 | 0 |
| Westfield | 30,361 | 6 | 0 | 3 | 1 | 2 | 271 | 10 | 229 | 32 | 0 |
| Westwood | 11,495 | 3 | 0 | 0 | 0 | 3 | 43 | 3 | 36 | 4 | 1 |
| Wharton | 6,728 | 3 | 0 | 0 | 0 | 3 | 24 | 4 | 17 | 3 | 0 |
| Woodcliff Lake | 6,094 | 1 | 0 | 1 | 0 | 0 | 25 | 1 | 21 | 3 | 0 |
| Woodland Park | 13,278 | 7 | 0 | 0 | 1 | 6 | 137 | 5 | 113 | 19 | 0 |
| Wyckoff Township | 17,589 | 3 | 0 | 0 | 1 | 2 | 65 | 16 | 45 | 4 | 0 |
| **NEW MEXICO[1]** | | | | | | | | | | | |
| Albuquerque | 564,147 | 7,831 | 120 | 497 | 1,689 | 5,525 | 24,551 | 4,328 | 15,340 | 4,883 | 126 |
| Artesia | 12,286 | 29 | 0 | 13 | 1 | 15 | 226 | 56 | 133 | 37 | 5 |
| Aztec | 6,289 | 22 | 0 | 6 | 0 | 16 | 76 | 28 | 38 | 10 | 0 |
| Carlsbad | 30,029 | 151 | 6 | 15 | 7 | 123 | 814 | 97 | 587 | 130 | 6 |
| Farmington | 43,973 | 497 | 0 | 53 | 45 | 399 | 1,097 | 175 | 792 | 130 | 18 |
| Sunland Park | 18,920 | 73 | 0 | 9 | 2 | 62 | 104 | 21 | 61 | 22 | 1 |
| **NEW YORK[1]** | | | | | | | | | | | |
| Arcade Village | 1,902 | 3 | 0 | 2 | 0 | 1 | 10 | 2 | 8 | 0 | 0 |
| Auburn | 25,746 | 72 | 1 | 28 | 7 | 36 | 591 | 61 | 499 | 31 | 4 |
| Batavia | 14,210 | 68 | 1 | 13 | 11 | 43 | 298 | 54 | 232 | 12 | 3 |
| Beacon | 13,940 | 11 | 0 | 0 | 2 | 9 | 64 | 5 | 56 | 3 | 2 |
| Bedford Town | 17,455 | 2 | 0 | 0 | 0 | 2 | 16 | 0 | 13 | 3 | 0 |
| Binghamton | 43,828 | 345 | 3 | 29 | 51 | 262 | 1,482 | 318 | 1,061 | 103 | 26 |
| Brighton Town | 35,689 | 24 | 1 | 6 | 4 | 13 | 662 | 69 | 559 | 34 | 1 |
| Brockport Village | 7,821 | 9 | 0 | 3 | 1 | 5 | 66 | 5 | 57 | 4 | 0 |
| Buffalo | 253,809 | 2,394 | 65 | 127 | 606 | 1,596 | 7,755 | 1,044 | 5,201 | 1,510 | 121 |
| Carmel Town | 34,351 | 13 | 0 | 1 | 0 | 12 | 149 | 11 | 129 | 9 | 1 |
| Clarkstown Town | 80,188 | 55 | 0 | 6 | 15 | 34 | 854 | 38 | 782 | 34 | 0 |
| Colonie Town | 78,364 | 51 | 1 | 4 | 18 | 28 | 2,108 | 138 | 1,892 | 78 | 3 |
| Deerpark Town | 7,667 | 5 | 0 | 1 | 0 | 4 | 38 | 8 | 25 | 5 | 0 |
| Dunkirk | 11,622 | 25 | 0 | 0 | 8 | 17 | 181 | 34 | 141 | 6 | 1 |
| East Rochester Village | 6,443 | 10 | 0 | 1 | 4 | 5 | 69 | 9 | 58 | 2 | 1 |
| Ellicott Town | 4,945 | 4 | 0 | 0 | 1 | 3 | 162 | 15 | 140 | 7 | 0 |
| Endicott Village | 12,335 | 66 | 0 | 6 | 8 | 52 | 311 | 59 | 248 | 4 | 4 |
| Fairport Village | 5,271 | 2 | 0 | 2 | 0 | 0 | 25 | 5 | 17 | 3 | 0 |
| Glens Falls | 14,116 | 12 | 0 | 7 | 0 | 5 | 138 | 10 | 119 | 9 | 0 |
| Goshen Town | 8,803 | 2 | 0 | 1 | 0 | 1 | 47 | 2 | 40 | 5 | 0 |
| Gouverneur Village | 3,615 | 17 | 0 | 8 | 0 | 9 | 117 | 11 | 104 | 2 | 0 |
| Greece Town | 95,202 | 124 | 0 | 9 | 34 | 81 | 1,770 | 170 | 1,443 | 157 | 7 |
| Greenburgh Town | 44,483 | 24 | 0 | 3 | 9 | 12 | 455 | 22 | 406 | 27 | 0 |
| Hempstead Village | 54,817 | 245 | 3 | 4 | 66 | 172 | 523 | 71 | 344 | 108 | 8 |
| Hudson | 5,952 | 23 | 0 | 4 | 2 | 17 | 71 | 6 | 62 | 3 | 1 |
| Hyde Park Town | 20,641 | 4 | 0 | 0 | 0 | 4 | 61 | 8 | 49 | 4 | 2 |
| Ilion Village | 7,562 | 19 | 0 | 2 | 3 | 14 | 179 | 11 | 160 | 8 | 3 |
| Irondequoit Town | 49,569 | 76 | 3 | 7 | 21 | 45 | 646 | 134 | 431 | 81 | 1 |
| Jamestown | 28,649 | 230 | 2 | 24 | 38 | 166 | 782 | 201 | 538 | 43 | 24 |
| Johnson City Village | 13,928 | 54 | 1 | 8 | 12 | 33 | 670 | 79 | 574 | 17 | 3 |
| Lakewood-Busti | 7,077 | 3 | 0 | 2 | 1 | 0 | 308 | 56 | 248 | 4 | 0 |
| Lloyd Town | 10,665 | 4 | 0 | 0 | 0 | 4 | 116 | 3 | 111 | 2 | 0 |
| Massena Village | 10,045 | 11 | 1 | 1 | 1 | 8 | 98 | 8 | 83 | 7 | 1 |
| Middletown | 28,010 | 76 | 0 | 7 | 18 | 51 | 304 | 29 | 261 | 14 | 3 |
| New Hartford Town and Village | 20,124 | 17 | 0 | 3 | 6 | 8 | 652 | 30 | 596 | 26 | 1 |
| New Rochelle | 81,367 | 127 | 3 | 3 | 38 | 83 | 771 | 55 | 675 | 41 | 4 |
| Niagara Falls | 47,139 | 366 | 9 | 28 | 64 | 265 | 1,368 | 197 | 1,011 | 160 | 27 |
| Niagara Town | 7,949 | 7 | 0 | 3 | 0 | 4 | 143 | 18 | 111 | 14 | 0 |
| North Tonawanda | 29,904 | 39 | 0 | 8 | 4 | 27 | 300 | 39 | 244 | 17 | 1 |

## Table 8. Offenses Known to Law Enforcement, by Selected State and City, 2021—Continued

(Number.)

| State/city | Population | Violent crime | Murder and nonnegligent manslaughter | Rape | Robbery | Aggravated assault | Property crime | Burglary | Larceny-theft | Motor vehicle theft | Arson |
|---|---|---|---|---|---|---|---|---|---|---|---|
| Ogdensburg | 10,319 | 49 | 0 | 11 | 4 | 34 | 330 | 54 | 270 | 6 | 3 |
| Ogden Town | 20,715 | 16 | 1 | 3 | 1 | 11 | 163 | 16 | 133 | 14 | 0 |
| Old Westbury Village | 4,052 | 0 | 0 | 0 | 0 | 0 | 33 | 4 | 26 | 3 | 0 |
| Olean | 13,272 | 46 | 0 | 2 | 1 | 43 | 359 | 33 | 305 | 21 | 6 |
| Orangetown Town | 37,135 | 31 | 1 | 4 | 5 | 21 | 220 | 17 | 187 | 16 | 0 |
| Oswego City | 17,132 | 39 | 0 | 3 | 2 | 34 | 549 | 52 | 477 | 20 | 0 |
| Plattekill Town | 10,158 | 0 | 0 | 0 | 0 | 0 | 25 | 1 | 24 | 0 | 1 |
| Port Jervis | 8,415 | 36 | 0 | 5 | 7 | 24 | 128 | 11 | 111 | 6 | 4 |
| Poughkeepsie Town | 38,808 | 91 | 0 | 11 | 15 | 65 | 894 | 60 | 789 | 45 | 5 |
| Rome | 31,991 | 99 | 0 | 5 | 14 | 80 | 596 | 63 | 496 | 37 | 3 |
| Saugerties Town | 18,954 | 21 | 0 | 3 | 2 | 16 | 133 | 20 | 105 | 8 | 0 |
| Scarsdale Village | 17,847 | 4 | 0 | 0 | 1 | 3 | 96 | 8 | 68 | 20 | 0 |
| Schenectady | 65,140 | 362 | 2 | 33 | 70 | 257 | 1,719 | 200 | 1,345 | 174 | 18 |
| Seneca Falls Town | 8,570 | 18 | 0 | 9 | 1 | 8 | 174 | 18 | 153 | 3 | 1 |
| Shawangunk Town | 13,751 | 3 | 0 | 0 | 0 | 3 | 22 | 0 | 22 | 0 | 0 |
| Southold Town | 20,045 | 17 | 0 | 3 | 3 | 11 | 184 | 12 | 165 | 7 | 0 |
| Spring Valley Village | 32,340 | 93 | 3 | 7 | 13 | 70 | 255 | 23 | 221 | 11 | 3 |
| Stony Point Town | 15,309 | 3 | 0 | 0 | 0 | 3 | 54 | 8 | 45 | 1 | 1 |
| Tarrytown Village | 11,287 | 3 | 0 | 0 | 2 | 1 | 39 | 4 | 29 | 6 | 1 |
| Ulster Town | 12,745 | 5 | 1 | 0 | 1 | 3 | 84 | 5 | 73 | 6 | 0 |
| Utica | 58,965 | 317 | 5 | 28 | 83 | 201 | 2,088 | 237 | 1,624 | 227 | 8 |
| Vestal Town | 28,843 | 25 | 0 | 7 | 1 | 17 | 557 | 33 | 514 | 10 | 2 |
| Walden Village | 6,593 | 2 | 0 | 0 | 1 | 1 | 39 | 3 | 35 | 1 | 0 |
| Waterloo Village | 4,837 | 14 | 0 | 4 | 1 | 9 | 69 | 6 | 59 | 4 | 0 |
| Watertown | 24,091 | 109 | 2 | 27 | 7 | 73 | 891 | 90 | 770 | 31 | 11 |
| Webster Town and Village | 45,651 | 24 | 0 | 2 | 4 | 18 | 356 | 41 | 292 | 23 | 1 |
| Westfield Village | 2,938 | 0 | 0 | 0 | 0 | 0 | 15 | 2 | 12 | 1 | 0 |
| Woodstock Town | 5,743 | 0 | 0 | 0 | 0 | 0 | 33 | 1 | 32 | 0 | 0 |
| Yonkers | 200,397 | 530 | 8 | 21 | 144 | 357 | 1,659 | 202 | 1,263 | 194 | 19 |
| Yorktown Town | 35,970 | 3 | 0 | 1 | 0 | 2 | 218 | 9 | 200 | 9 | 1 |
| Youngstown Village | 1,824 | 0 | 0 | 0 | 0 | 0 | 1 | 0 | 1 | 0 | 0 |
| **NORTH CAROLINA** | | | | | | | | | | | |
| Aberdeen | 8,576 | 31 | 1 | 4 | 4 | 22 | 196 | 19 | 172 | 5 | 1 |
| Ahoskie | 4,653 | 38 | 7 | 2 | 6 | 23 | 124 | 24 | 85 | 15 | 1 |
| Albemarle | 16,391 | 87 | 3 | 10 | 19 | 55 | 786 | 106 | 639 | 41 | 12 |
| Angier | 5,610 | 12 | 0 | 0 | 7 | 5 | 226 | 151 | 68 | 7 | 0 |
| Apex | 67,878 | 41 | 0 | 10 | 8 | 23 | 594 | 53 | 517 | 24 | 4 |
| Archdale | 11,572 | 28 | 2 | 2 | 0 | 24 | 190 | 36 | 141 | 13 | 1 |
| Asheboro | 26,082 | 88 | 8 | 8 | 11 | 61 | 892 | 160 | 663 | 69 | 4 |
| Asheville | 93,855 | 704 | 6 | 65 | 117 | 516 | 4,991 | 686 | 3,786 | 519 | 24 |
| Atlantic Beach | 1,516 | 4 | 0 | 1 | 1 | 2 | 69 | 19 | 47 | 3 | 1 |
| Ayden | 5,174 | 30 | 0 | 1 | 5 | 24 | 65 | 8 | 54 | 3 | 0 |
| Beaufort | 4,522 | 12 | 0 | 2 | 1 | 9 | 67 | 17 | 45 | 5 | 0 |
| Belhaven | 1,572 | 1 | 0 | 0 | 0 | 1 | 22 | 5 | 16 | 1 | 0 |
| Benson | 4,101 | 29 | 0 | 1 | 2 | 26 | 172 | 35 | 122 | 15 | 1 |
| Bessemer City | 5,677 | 25 | 0 | 2 | 2 | 21 | 107 | 32 | 59 | 16 | 0 |
| Beulaville | 1,295 | 5 | 0 | 0 | 0 | 5 | 45 | 12 | 33 | 0 | 0 |
| Biltmore Forest | 1,440 | 3 | 0 | 0 | 0 | 3 | 19 | 8 | 11 | 0 | 0 |
| Biscoe | 1,704 | 5 | 0 | 0 | 0 | 5 | 132 | 15 | 114 | 3 | 0 |
| Black Mountain | 8,297 | 10 | 0 | 6 | 0 | 4 | 171 | 24 | 135 | 12 | 1 |
| Blowing Rock | 1,324 | 2 | 0 | 1 | 1 | 0 | 22 | 2 | 20 | 0 | 0 |
| Boone | 20,321 | 33 | 0 | 7 | 2 | 24 | 278 | 38 | 226 | 14 | 1 |
| Brevard | 7,922 | 9 | 0 | 1 | 2 | 6 | 104 | 13 | 85 | 6 | 3 |
| Broadway | 1,304 | 6 | 0 | 0 | 2 | 4 | 21 | 2 | 15 | 4 | 0 |
| Bunn | 407 | 0 | 0 | 0 | 0 | 0 | 6 | 3 | 3 | 0 | 0 |
| Burgaw | 4,154 | 13 | 0 | 2 | 0 | 11 | 57 | 5 | 51 | 1 | 0 |
| Burlington | 56,065 | 493 | 8 | 32 | 38 | 415 | 2,647 | 402 | 2,037 | 208 | 9 |
| Butner | 7,902 | 24 | 0 | 3 | 1 | 20 | 147 | 24 | 117 | 6 | 2 |
| Cape Carteret | 2,068 | 1 | 0 | 0 | 0 | 1 | 22 | 5 | 16 | 1 | 0 |
| Carolina Beach | 6,437 | 25 | 0 | 4 | 2 | 19 | 131 | 23 | 96 | 12 | 0 |
| Carrboro | 21,413 | 69 | 2 | 3 | 10 | 54 | 411 | 95 | 293 | 23 | 2 |
| Carthage | 2,626 | 7 | 0 | 2 | 1 | 4 | 74 | 16 | 56 | 2 | 1 |
| Cary | 177,735 | 130 | 4 | 9 | 31 | 86 | 1,710 | 180 | 1,427 | 103 | 6 |
| Chadbourn | 1,686 | 8 | 3 | 1 | 0 | 4 | 65 | 14 | 45 | 6 | 0 |
| Chapel Hill | 64,388 | 110 | 1 | 7 | 24 | 78 | 1,237 | 188 | 996 | 53 | 2 |
| Charlotte-Mecklenburg | 956,282 | 7,480 | 98 | 315 | 1,345 | 5,722 | 30,013 | 3,704 | 23,173 | 3,136 | 131 |
| Cherryville | 6,180 | 19 | 1 | 1 | 3 | 14 | 149 | 40 | 96 | 13 | 0 |
| China Grove | 4,256 | 3 | 0 | 0 | 1 | 2 | 56 | 16 | 32 | 8 | 0 |
| Clayton | 27,775 | 44 | 2 | 1 | 6 | 35 | 490 | 44 | 412 | 34 | 4 |
| Clinton | 8,299 | 112 | 0 | 1 | 4 | 107 | 374 | 164 | 191 | 19 | 1 |
| Coats | 2,563 | 5 | 0 | 1 | 1 | 3 | 99 | 53 | 41 | 5 | 0 |
| Columbus | 1,008 | 0 | 0 | 0 | 0 | 0 | 40 | 0 | 33 | 7 | 0 |
| Concord | 100,631 | 82 | 4 | 5 | 24 | 49 | 1,203 | 118 | 941 | 144 | 4 |
| Conover | 8,601 | 48 | 2 | 5 | 5 | 36 | 319 | 51 | 229 | 39 | 0 |
| Cooleemee | 983 | 0 | 0 | 0 | 0 | 0 | 27 | 8 | 18 | 1 | 0 |
| Cornelius | 31,453 | 36 | 1 | 4 | 1 | 30 | 358 | 40 | 289 | 29 | 3 |
| Creedmoor | 4,670 | 12 | 0 | 2 | 1 | 9 | 39 | 10 | 26 | 3 | 0 |
| Dallas | 4,891 | 19 | 3 | 3 | 4 | 9 | 123 | 25 | 85 | 13 | 1 |
| Davidson | 13,457 | 10 | 0 | 3 | 1 | 6 | 81 | 13 | 62 | 6 | 0 |
| Dobson | 1,529 | 3 | 0 | 1 | 0 | 2 | 20 | 5 | 14 | 1 | 0 |
| Drexel | 1,859 | 0 | 0 | 0 | 0 | 0 | 0 | 0 | 0 | 0 | 0 |
| Duck | 396 | 0 | 0 | 0 | 0 | 0 | 21 | 1 | 20 | 0 | 0 |

# Table 8. Offenses Known to Law Enforcement, by Selected State and City, 2021—Continued

(Number.)

| State/city | Population | Violent crime | Murder and nonnegligent manslaughter | Rape | Robbery | Aggravated assault | Property crime | Burglary | Larceny-theft | Motor vehicle theft | Arson |
|---|---|---|---|---|---|---|---|---|---|---|---|
| Dunn | 9,721 | 78 | 0 | 6 | 16 | 56 | 617 | 195 | 401 | 21 | 9 |
| Durham | 291,962 | 2,160 | 47 | 125 | 546 | 1,442 | 9,674 | 1,494 | 7,417 | 763 | 36 |
| East Spencer | 1,557 | 12 | 9 | 1 | 0 | 2 | 20 | 3 | 11 | 6 | 1 |
| Eden | 14,786 | 63 | 1 | 4 | 7 | 51 | 367 | 104 | 252 | 11 | 1 |
| Edenton | 4,528 | 56 | 1 | 4 | 2 | 49 | 65 | 22 | 39 | 4 | 0 |
| Elizabeth City | 17,948 | 72 | 7 | 5 | 10 | 50 | 440 | 169 | 233 | 38 | 6 |
| Elizabethtown | 3,353 | 22 | 0 | 0 | 4 | 18 | 132 | 28 | 100 | 4 | 0 |
| Elkin | 3,998 | 10 | 0 | 3 | 0 | 7 | 215 | 33 | 171 | 11 | 1 |
| Elon | 12,521 | 9 | 0 | 3 | 1 | 5 | 52 | 15 | 35 | 2 | 0 |
| Emerald Isle | 3,677 | 6 | 0 | 0 | 0 | 6 | 104 | 34 | 69 | 1 | 0 |
| Enfield | 2,234 | 31 | 2 | 1 | 3 | 25 | 54 | 31 | 22 | 1 | 2 |
| Erwin | 5,270 | 17 | 4 | 4 | 4 | 5 | 111 | 30 | 75 | 6 | 0 |
| Fair Bluff | 872 | 1 | 0 | 1 | 0 | 0 | 11 | 1 | 10 | 0 | 1 |
| Fairmont | 2,568 | 32 | 2 | 2 | 7 | 21 | 78 | 22 | 53 | 3 | 1 |
| Farmville | 4,756 | 45 | 4 | 5 | 2 | 34 | 101 | 17 | 80 | 4 | 0 |
| Fayetteville | 212,047 | 2,026 | 47 | 81 | 242 | 1,656 | 6,058 | 929 | 4,669 | 460 | 58 |
| Fletcher | 8,573 | 7 | 1 | 0 | 1 | 5 | 160 | 48 | 91 | 21 | 0 |
| Forest City | 7,106 | 50 | 1 | 3 | 5 | 41 | 459 | 67 | 369 | 23 | 1 |
| Four Oaks | 2,436 | 3 | 0 | 1 | 1 | 1 | 38 | 17 | 18 | 3 | 0 |
| Franklin | 4,145 | 8 | 0 | 3 | 0 | 5 | 247 | 121 | 106 | 20 | 2 |
| Franklinton | 2,344 | 2 | 0 | 1 | 0 | 1 | 29 | 5 | 24 | 0 | 0 |
| Fuquay-Varina | 34,018 | 32 | 0 | 3 | 5 | 24 | 305 | 36 | 250 | 19 | 0 |
| Garner | 32,889 | 146 | 4 | 8 | 22 | 112 | 1,014 | 95 | 833 | 86 | 2 |
| Gastonia | 78,260 | 711 | 11 | 28 | 118 | 554 | 3,096 | 336 | 2,414 | 346 | 30 |
| Gibsonville | 7,492 | 19 | 0 | 2 | 1 | 16 | 93 | 41 | 42 | 10 | 0 |
| Goldsboro | 34,352 | 317 | 7 | 8 | 41 | 261 | 1,484 | 241 | 1,145 | 98 | 4 |
| Graham | 15,919 | 76 | 3 | 5 | 11 | 57 | 404 | 87 | 263 | 54 | 1 |
| Granite Falls | 4,652 | 7 | 0 | 3 | 1 | 3 | 169 | 42 | 113 | 14 | 1 |
| Greensboro | 300,865 | 2,629 | 51 | 77 | 545 | 1,956 | 10,590 | 1,919 | 7,549 | 1,122 | 111 |
| Greenville | 95,815 | 464 | 4 | 24 | 73 | 363 | 2,038 | 292 | 1,651 | 95 | 17 |
| Grifton | 2,717 | 6 | 0 | 1 | 0 | 5 | 17 | 9 | 8 | 0 | 0 |
| Havelock | 19,450 | 42 | 1 | 6 | 4 | 31 | 357 | 83 | 265 | 9 | 0 |
| Haw River | 2,558 | 9 | 0 | 1 | 0 | 8 | 53 | 13 | 38 | 2 | 0 |
| Henderson | 15,067 | 246 | 5 | 8 | 39 | 194 | 639 | 117 | 473 | 49 | 11 |
| Hendersonville | 14,351 | 61 | 1 | 7 | 6 | 47 | 758 | 197 | 490 | 71 | 2 |
| Hickory | 41,604 | 250 | 8 | 12 | 31 | 199 | 1,861 | 325 | 1,359 | 177 | 11 |
| Highlands | 989 | 3 | 0 | 0 | 1 | 2 | 29 | 5 | 23 | 1 | 0 |
| High Point | 114,492 | 595 | 19 | 31 | 107 | 438 | 3,174 | 488 | 2,361 | 325 | 26 |
| Hillsborough | 7,291 | 38 | 1 | 0 | 4 | 33 | 319 | 20 | 291 | 8 | 0 |
| Holden Beach | 686 | 3 | 0 | 0 | 1 | 2 | 36 | 14 | 20 | 2 | 0 |
| Holly Ridge | 3,365 | 4 | 1 | 0 | 0 | 3 | 29 | 6 | 18 | 5 | 0 |
| Holly Springs | 41,798 | 33 | 0 | 5 | 3 | 25 | 419 | 22 | 378 | 19 | 2 |
| Hope Mills | 15,914 | 106 | 0 | 7 | 20 | 79 | 636 | 93 | 507 | 36 | 6 |
| Hudson | 3,696 | 4 | 1 | 0 | 1 | 2 | 92 | 10 | 75 | 7 | 0 |
| Huntersville | 60,450 | 98 | 5 | 8 | 12 | 73 | 735 | 93 | 565 | 77 | 4 |
| Indian Beach | 119 | 1 | 0 | 0 | 0 | 1 | 9 | 2 | 6 | 1 | 0 |
| Jacksonville | 76,130 | 274 | 6 | 20 | 37 | 211 | 1,391 | 224 | 1,096 | 71 | 2 |
| Jefferson | 1,528 | 2 | 0 | 1 | 0 | 1 | 17 | 3 | 14 | 0 | 0 |
| Jonesville | 2,198 | 8 | 0 | 1 | 1 | 6 | 95 | 37 | 53 | 5 | 0 |
| Kannapolis | 53,044 | 136 | 3 | 18 | 28 | 87 | 1,223 | 188 | 896 | 139 | 7 |
| Kenansville | 849 | 1 | 0 | 0 | 0 | 1 | 8 | 1 | 7 | 0 | 0 |
| Kernersville | 25,074 | 79 | 1 | 6 | 16 | 56 | 871 | 130 | 689 | 52 | 3 |
| Kill Devil Hills | 7,488 | 23 | 0 | 3 | 1 | 19 | 200 | 42 | 155 | 3 | 0 |
| King | 6,916 | 8 | 0 | 1 | 2 | 5 | 145 | 8 | 125 | 12 | 1 |
| Kings Mountain | 11,162 | 51 | 2 | 7 | 3 | 39 | 262 | 38 | 176 | 48 | 1 |
| Kinston | 19,672 | 205 | 4 | 15 | 16 | 170 | 985 | 237 | 689 | 59 | 22 |
| Kitty Hawk | 3,632 | 10 | 0 | 0 | 2 | 8 | 69 | 6 | 61 | 2 | 0 |
| Knightdale | 18,970 | 38 | 0 | 3 | 8 | 27 | 407 | 33 | 350 | 24 | 1 |
| Laurinburg | 14,798 | 249 | 10 | 7 | 21 | 211 | 568 | 212 | 302 | 54 | 5 |
| Lenoir | 17,881 | 60 | 5 | 9 | 9 | 37 | 688 | 157 | 454 | 77 | 3 |
| Lexington | 19,162 | 99 | 1 | 6 | 7 | 85 | 596 | 115 | 434 | 47 | 4 |
| Lillington | 3,680 | 8 | 0 | 2 | 1 | 5 | 77 | 29 | 42 | 6 | 0 |
| Lincolnton | 11,641 | 53 | 1 | 5 | 3 | 44 | 515 | 70 | 393 | 52 | 1 |
| Long View | 4,959 | 7 | 0 | 1 | 0 | 6 | 143 | 32 | 88 | 23 | 0 |
| Louisburg | 3,722 | 24 | 1 | 0 | 8 | 15 | 83 | 9 | 68 | 6 | 4 |
| Lowell | 3,767 | 10 | 0 | 2 | 1 | 7 | 70 | 32 | 27 | 11 | 0 |
| Lumberton | 20,109 | 455 | 1 | 20 | 63 | 371 | 1,312 | 290 | 951 | 71 | 5 |
| Madison | 2,095 | 7 | 0 | 4 | 0 | 3 | 59 | 14 | 41 | 4 | 1 |
| Maggie Valley | 1,268 | 7 | 0 | 0 | 1 | 6 | 216 | 163 | 46 | 7 | 0 |
| Manteo | 1,483 | 7 | 0 | 3 | 2 | 2 | 30 | 10 | 19 | 1 | 0 |
| Marion | 7,916 | 9 | 0 | 3 | 1 | 5 | 657 | 432 | 197 | 28 | 0 |
| Marshville | 2,875 | 15 | 2 | 0 | 0 | 13 | 67 | 20 | 42 | 5 | 0 |
| Matthews | 34,438 | 77 | 0 | 2 | 17 | 58 | 1,033 | 226 | 767 | 40 | 2 |
| Maxton | 2,321 | 13 | 9 | 0 | 3 | 1 | 105 | 22 | 71 | 12 | 1 |
| Mayodan | 2,401 | 9 | 0 | 3 | 0 | 6 | 115 | 12 | 96 | 7 | 0 |
| Mebane | 17,365 | 54 | 1 | 1 | 11 | 41 | 590 | 47 | 506 | 37 | 2 |
| Mint Hill | 28,701 | 61 | 1 | 9 | 5 | 46 | 283 | 38 | 218 | 27 | 3 |
| Monroe | 35,948 | 292 | 7 | 42 | 29 | 214 | 1,296 | 207 | 1,016 | 73 | 10 |
| Mooresville | 40,560 | 123 | 1 | 15 | 8 | 99 | 991 | 96 | 828 | 67 | 5 |
| Morehead City | 9,774 | 34 | 2 | 8 | 1 | 23 | 261 | 27 | 224 | 10 | 0 |
| Morrisville | 32,018 | 28 | 0 | 3 | 6 | 19 | 568 | 90 | 458 | 20 | 1 |
| Mount Gilead | 1,137 | 3 | 0 | 1 | 1 | 1 | 40 | 9 | 26 | 5 | 1 |
| Mount Holly | 16,720 | 36 | 1 | 4 | 6 | 25 | 241 | 28 | 185 | 28 | 1 |

## Table 8. Offenses Known to Law Enforcement, by Selected State and City, 2021—Continued

(Number.)

| State/city | Population | Violent crime | Murder and nonnegligent manslaughter | Rape | Robbery | Aggravated assault | Property crime | Burglary | Larceny-theft | Motor vehicle theft | Arson |
|---|---|---|---|---|---|---|---|---|---|---|---|
| Mount Olive | 4,665 | 13 | 0 | 0 | 0 | 13 | 83 | 17 | 60 | 6 | 0 |
| Murfreesboro | 2,873 | 7 | 1 | 0 | 0 | 6 | 48 | 15 | 30 | 3 | 0 |
| Nags Head | 3,021 | 6 | 0 | 3 | 0 | 3 | 112 | 13 | 93 | 6 | 0 |
| New Bern | 29,985 | 153 | 7 | 11 | 21 | 114 | 803 | 159 | 614 | 30 | 4 |
| Newland | 693 | 2 | 0 | 1 | 0 | 1 | 11 | 2 | 6 | 3 | 0 |
| Newport | 4,691 | 8 | 0 | 1 | 1 | 6 | 80 | 26 | 50 | 4 | 0 |
| Newton | 13,253 | 55 | 3 | 3 | 3 | 46 | 411 | 85 | 284 | 42 | 2 |
| North Topsail Beach | 743 | 4 | 1 | 1 | 0 | 2 | 31 | 13 | 16 | 2 | 0 |
| North Wilkesboro | 4,069 | 10 | 0 | 1 | 1 | 8 | 141 | 38 | 86 | 17 | 0 |
| Oak Island | 8,955 | 14 | 0 | 4 | 1 | 9 | 116 | 36 | 74 | 6 | 0 |
| Oxford | 8,950 | 70 | 0 | 4 | 6 | 60 | 182 | 30 | 137 | 15 | 0 |
| Pinehurst | 17,253 | 10 | 0 | 4 | 1 | 5 | 107 | 29 | 71 | 7 | 0 |
| Pine Knoll Shores | 1,313 | 0 | 0 | 0 | 0 | 0 | 12 | 5 | 7 | 0 | 0 |
| Pine Level | 2,123 | 4 | 0 | 1 | 1 | 2 | 18 | 5 | 11 | 2 | 0 |
| Pineville | 9,371 | 83 | 0 | 6 | 14 | 63 | 1,087 | 160 | 859 | 68 | 3 |
| Pittsboro | 4,491 | 3 | 0 | 2 | 0 | 1 | 59 | 8 | 47 | 4 | 0 |
| Plymouth | 3,285 | 30 | 1 | 2 | 3 | 24 | 93 | 40 | 49 | 4 | 5 |
| Raeford | 4,987 | 12 | 0 | 1 | 0 | 11 | 101 | 16 | 81 | 4 | 0 |
| Raleigh | 481,823 | 2,236 | 26 | 165 | 489 | 1,556 | 10,295 | 1,332 | 7,896 | 1,067 | 41 |
| Ranlo | 3,736 | 2 | 0 | 0 | 1 | 1 | 41 | 20 | 16 | 5 | 1 |
| Red Springs | 3,218 | 34 | 1 | 1 | 5 | 27 | 157 | 31 | 115 | 11 | 2 |
| Reidsville | 13,948 | 124 | 1 | 8 | 13 | 102 | 547 | 66 | 433 | 48 | 6 |
| Richlands | 1,741 | 3 | 0 | 0 | 0 | 3 | 17 | 3 | 13 | 1 | 0 |
| Roanoke Rapids | 14,046 | 114 | 3 | 9 | 14 | 88 | 552 | 101 | 415 | 36 | 4 |
| Robbins | 1,254 | 3 | 0 | 0 | 1 | 2 | 133 | 104 | 26 | 3 | 0 |
| Robersonville | 1,307 | 3 | 0 | 0 | 0 | 3 | 17 | 6 | 7 | 4 | 0 |
| Rockingham | 8,424 | 90 | 11 | 5 | 8 | 66 | 627 | 137 | 455 | 35 | 2 |
| Rockwell | 2,170 | 2 | 0 | 1 | 1 | 0 | 32 | 1 | 28 | 3 | 0 |
| Rocky Mount | 53,305 | 503 | 12 | 13 | 63 | 415 | 1,313 | 329 | 884 | 100 | 18 |
| Rolesville | 9,679 | 4 | 0 | 0 | 0 | 4 | 50 | 9 | 38 | 3 | 0 |
| Rowland | 980 | 16 | 4 | 0 | 3 | 9 | 39 | 10 | 28 | 1 | 0 |
| Roxboro | 8,387 | 93 | 0 | 11 | 5 | 77 | 278 | 67 | 199 | 12 | 4 |
| Rutherfordton | 4,081 | 1 | 0 | 0 | 1 | 0 | 21 | 0 | 20 | 1 | 0 |
| Salisbury | 33,856 | 315 | 13 | 10 | 42 | 250 | 1,335 | 165 | 1,064 | 106 | 6 |
| Scotland Neck | 1,789 | 21 | 2 | 4 | 3 | 12 | 26 | 13 | 6 | 7 | 1 |
| Selma | 7,454 | 37 | 2 | 3 | 11 | 21 | 174 | 40 | 108 | 26 | 1 |
| Sharpsburg | 2,017 | 2 | 0 | 0 | 0 | 2 | 35 | 12 | 22 | 1 | 0 |
| Shelby | 20,128 | 181 | 1 | 16 | 16 | 148 | 601 | 109 | 421 | 71 | 4 |
| Smithfield | 13,581 | 65 | 1 | 3 | 10 | 51 | 497 | 68 | 382 | 47 | 2 |
| Snow Hill | 1,476 | 3 | 0 | 1 | 1 | 1 | 36 | 6 | 29 | 1 | 0 |
| Southern Pines | 15,358 | 76 | 0 | 12 | 3 | 61 | 296 | 105 | 180 | 11 | 1 |
| Southern Shores | 3,026 | 1 | 0 | 1 | 0 | 0 | 15 | 7 | 6 | 2 | 0 |
| Spencer | 3,260 | 11 | 0 | 2 | 2 | 7 | 75 | 15 | 56 | 4 | 2 |
| Spring Lake | 12,028 | 53 | 1 | 4 | 9 | 39 | 304 | 46 | 235 | 23 | 0 |
| Spruce Pine | 2,115 | 0 | 0 | 0 | 0 | 0 | 5 | 1 | 3 | 1 | 0 |
| Stallings | 16,746 | 20 | 0 | 9 | 1 | 10 | 162 | 24 | 126 | 12 | 0 |
| Stantonsburg | 780 | 0 | 0 | 0 | 0 | 0 | 11 | 5 | 5 | 1 | 0 |
| Statesville | 28,420 | 324 | 2 | 13 | 11 | 298 | 1,102 | 231 | 772 | 99 | 5 |
| Stoneville | 1,257 | 1 | 0 | 0 | 0 | 1 | 14 | 1 | 11 | 2 | 0 |
| Surf City | 2,602 | 9 | 0 | 1 | 1 | 7 | 77 | 14 | 61 | 2 | 0 |
| Swansboro | 3,472 | 6 | 0 | 3 | 0 | 3 | 86 | 14 | 70 | 2 | 0 |
| Sylva | 2,757 | 20 | 0 | 1 | 0 | 19 | 98 | 14 | 72 | 12 | 0 |
| Tabor City | 3,883 | 21 | 3 | 4 | 2 | 12 | 98 | 22 | 68 | 8 | 0 |
| Taylorsville | 2,145 | 2 | 0 | 0 | 1 | 1 | 55 | 13 | 40 | 2 | 0 |
| Taylortown | 891 | 0 | 0 | 0 | 0 | 0 | 12 | 4 | 8 | 0 | 0 |
| Thomasville | 26,704 | 106 | 2 | 7 | 16 | 81 | 686 | 172 | 449 | 65 | 8 |
| Trent Woods | 3,973 | 1 | 0 | 0 | 0 | 1 | 12 | 5 | 7 | 0 | 0 |
| Troutman | 2,856 | 11 | 0 | 4 | 1 | 6 | 52 | 7 | 37 | 8 | 0 |
| Troy | 3,274 | 28 | 3 | 1 | 1 | 23 | 107 | 33 | 65 | 9 | 0 |
| Tryon | 1,635 | 3 | 0 | 2 | 0 | 1 | 71 | 54 | 14 | 3 | 0 |
| Valdese | 4,402 | 9 | 0 | 1 | 0 | 8 | 73 | 22 | 39 | 12 | 0 |
| Wadesboro | 5,190 | 111 | 3 | 3 | 10 | 95 | 303 | 110 | 171 | 22 | 1 |
| Wake Forest | 49,457 | 69 | 0 | 5 | 11 | 53 | 462 | 39 | 398 | 25 | 3 |
| Wallace | 3,855 | 13 | 0 | 0 | 2 | 11 | 144 | 12 | 126 | 6 | 0 |
| Washington | 9,451 | 85 | 0 | 5 | 10 | 70 | 290 | 39 | 239 | 12 | 3 |
| Waxhaw | 19,089 | 16 | 0 | 5 | 1 | 10 | 146 | 21 | 117 | 8 | 1 |
| Waynesville | 10,632 | 51 | 1 | 5 | 4 | 41 | 750 | 178 | 552 | 20 | 3 |
| Weldon | 1,438 | 17 | 5 | 0 | 2 | 10 | 54 | 17 | 33 | 4 | 0 |
| Wendell | 9,841 | 12 | 1 | 1 | 2 | 8 | 101 | 21 | 68 | 12 | 0 |
| West Jefferson | 1,311 | 4 | 0 | 1 | 0 | 3 | 76 | 9 | 65 | 2 | 0 |
| Whispering Pines | 3,515 | 1 | 0 | 0 | 0 | 1 | 15 | 0 | 15 | 0 | 0 |
| White Lake | 738 | 6 | 0 | 1 | 0 | 5 | 18 | 6 | 12 | 0 | 0 |
| Whiteville | 5,231 | 50 | 1 | 5 | 6 | 38 | 341 | 79 | 241 | 21 | 1 |
| Wilkesboro | 3,419 | 22 | 0 | 3 | 2 | 17 | 320 | 62 | 236 | 22 | 0 |
| Williamston | 5,072 | 69 | 2 | 5 | 7 | 55 | 272 | 92 | 170 | 10 | 1 |
| Wilmington | 126,759 | 655 | 14 | 86 | 107 | 448 | 3,527 | 577 | 2,715 | 235 | 11 |
| Wilson | 49,507 | 283 | 8 | 10 | 40 | 225 | 1,227 | 211 | 923 | 93 | 8 |
| Windsor | 3,485 | 6 | 2 | 0 | 0 | 4 | 24 | 3 | 20 | 1 | 0 |
| Wingate | 4,873 | 13 | 0 | 5 | 2 | 6 | 73 | 18 | 50 | 5 | 1 |
| Winston-Salem | 249,998 | 2,875 | 38 | 95 | 239 | 2,503 | 10,103 | 1,755 | 7,529 | 819 | 64 |
| Winterville | 10,225 | 7 | 0 | 0 | 0 | 7 | 69 | 17 | 49 | 3 | 0 |
| Woodfin | 6,718 | 15 | 0 | 1 | 1 | 13 | 72 | 20 | 43 | 9 | 0 |
| Wrightsville Beach | 2,519 | 22 | 0 | 5 | 1 | 16 | 68 | 14 | 49 | 5 | 0 |

# Table 8. Offenses Known to Law Enforcement, by Selected State and City, 2021—Continued

(Number.)

| State/city | Population | Violent crime | Murder and nonnegligent manslaughter | Rape | Robbery | Aggravated assault | Property crime | Burglary | Larceny-theft | Motor vehicle theft | Arson |
|---|---|---|---|---|---|---|---|---|---|---|---|
| Yadkinville | 2,864 | 4 | 0 | 2 | 1 | 1 | 139 | 108 | 28 | 3 | 1 |
| Youngsville | 1,442 | 1 | 0 | 0 | 1 | 0 | 28 | 4 | 24 | 0 | 0 |
| Zebulon | 6,764 | 27 | 2 | 1 | 1 | 23 | 233 | 49 | 172 | 12 | 1 |
| **NORTH DAKOTA** | | | | | | | | | | | |
| Berthold | 494 | 1 | 0 | 0 | 0 | 1 | 3 | 0 | 3 | 0 | 0 |
| Beulah | 3,129 | 3 | 0 | 1 | 0 | 2 | 16 | 2 | 13 | 1 | 0 |
| Bismarck | 75,396 | 216 | 1 | 32 | 41 | 142 | 2,618 | 313 | 2,002 | 303 | 5 |
| Bowman | 1,571 | 1 | 0 | 0 | 1 | 0 | 13 | 1 | 12 | 0 | 0 |
| Burlington | 1,213 | 0 | 0 | 0 | 0 | 0 | 4 | 0 | 1 | 3 | 0 |
| Carrington | 1,940 | 0 | 0 | 0 | 0 | 0 | 9 | 2 | 6 | 1 | 0 |
| Cavalier | 1,190 | 1 | 0 | 1 | 0 | 0 | 13 | 6 | 6 | 1 | 0 |
| Devils Lake | 7,237 | 20 | 0 | 3 | 1 | 16 | 284 | 28 | 211 | 45 | 2 |
| Dickinson | 24,179 | 61 | 0 | 11 | 1 | 49 | 379 | 43 | 281 | 55 | 2 |
| Ellendale | 1,160 | 0 | 0 | 0 | 0 | 0 | 11 | 1 | 8 | 2 | 0 |
| Emerado | 464 | 2 | 0 | 1 | 0 | 1 | 9 | 4 | 4 | 1 | 0 |
| Fargo | 127,313 | 658 | 6 | 120 | 103 | 429 | 5,545 | 1,359 | 3,595 | 591 | 33 |
| Garrison | 1,458 | 1 | 0 | 1 | 0 | 0 | 11 | 2 | 7 | 2 | 0 |
| Grafton | 4,055 | 6 | 0 | 2 | 1 | 3 | 57 | 6 | 42 | 9 | 0 |
| Grand Forks | 56,253 | 170 | 1 | 42 | 12 | 115 | 1,425 | 218 | 1,078 | 129 | 2 |
| Harvey | 1,568 | 6 | 0 | 3 | 1 | 2 | 8 | 2 | 5 | 1 | 0 |
| Hazen | 2,322 | 0 | 0 | 0 | 0 | 0 | 5 | 1 | 2 | 2 | 0 |
| Jamestown | 14,879 | 46 | 0 | 9 | 0 | 37 | 344 | 50 | 274 | 20 | 3 |
| Kenmare | 1,019 | 2 | 0 | 1 | 0 | 1 | 3 | 0 | 1 | 2 | 0 |
| Killdeer | 1,209 | 7 | 0 | 5 | 0 | 2 | 8 | 2 | 6 | 0 | 0 |
| Lamoure | 884 | 2 | 0 | 0 | 0 | 2 | 5 | 2 | 3 | 0 | 0 |
| Lincoln | 4,052 | 5 | 0 | 0 | 0 | 5 | 24 | 4 | 17 | 3 | 0 |
| Lisbon | 2,002 | 2 | 0 | 0 | 0 | 2 | 11 | 0 | 10 | 1 | 0 |
| Mandan | 23,292 | 85 | 0 | 20 | 4 | 61 | 898 | 90 | 694 | 114 | 6 |
| Medora | 125 | 0 | 0 | 0 | 0 | 0 | 0 | 0 | 0 | 0 | 0 |
| Minot | 48,086 | 128 | 3 | 49 | 4 | 72 | 679 | 123 | 423 | 133 | 14 |
| Napoleon | 756 | 0 | 0 | 0 | 0 | 0 | 3 | 2 | 1 | 0 | 0 |
| New Town | 2,706 | 1 | 0 | 0 | 0 | 1 | 5 | 0 | 4 | 1 | 0 |
| Northwood | 879 | 0 | 0 | 0 | 0 | 0 | 1 | 0 | 1 | 0 | 0 |
| Oakes | 1,639 | 0 | 0 | 0 | 0 | 0 | 1 | 0 | 1 | 0 | 0 |
| Powers Lake | 284 | 0 | 0 | 0 | 0 | 0 | 0 | 0 | 0 | 0 | 0 |
| Ray | 989 | 0 | 0 | 0 | 0 | 0 | 2 | 1 | 0 | 1 | 0 |
| Rolette | 585 | 0 | 0 | 0 | 0 | 0 | 5 | 2 | 3 | 0 | 0 |
| Rolla | 1,271 | 1 | 0 | 0 | 1 | 0 | 11 | 5 | 1 | 5 | 0 |
| Rugby | 2,538 | 1 | 0 | 0 | 0 | 1 | 20 | 1 | 17 | 2 | 0 |
| Stanley | 2,885 | 0 | 0 | 0 | 0 | 0 | 11 | 1 | 6 | 4 | 0 |
| Steele | 701 | 0 | 0 | 0 | 0 | 0 | 4 | 0 | 4 | 0 | 0 |
| Surrey | 1,460 | 0 | 0 | 0 | 0 | 0 | 1 | 1 | 0 | 0 | 0 |
| Thompson | 1,031 | 0 | 0 | 0 | 0 | 0 | 4 | 0 | 4 | 0 | 0 |
| Tioga | 1,405 | 3 | 0 | 0 | 0 | 3 | 12 | 1 | 9 | 2 | 0 |
| Valley City | 6,268 | 13 | 0 | 2 | 0 | 11 | 137 | 24 | 99 | 14 | 0 |
| Wahpeton | 7,725 | 33 | 1 | 3 | 1 | 28 | 148 | 24 | 114 | 10 | 2 |
| Watford City | 9,301 | 21 | 0 | 6 | 0 | 15 | 113 | 4 | 97 | 12 | 0 |
| West Fargo | 39,704 | 65 | 1 | 15 | 4 | 45 | 595 | 141 | 403 | 51 | 2 |
| Williston | 31,680 | 93 | 0 | 14 | 1 | 78 | 426 | 78 | 301 | 47 | 1 |
| Wishek | 858 | 0 | 0 | 0 | 0 | 0 | 8 | 2 | 6 | 0 | 0 |
| **OHIO** | | | | | | | | | | | |
| Addyston | 936 | 2 | 0 | 0 | 0 | 2 | 10 | 2 | 8 | 0 | 0 |
| Akron | 195,701 | 1,633 | 36 | 178 | 175 | 1,244 | 6,476 | 1,209 | 4,264 | 1,003 | 69 |
| Alliance | 21,328 | 95 | 0 | 6 | 1 | 88 | 424 | 47 | 360 | 17 | 7 |
| Amberley Village | 3,538 | 1 | 0 | 0 | 0 | 1 | 28 | 6 | 19 | 3 | 0 |
| American Township | 11,989 | 3 | 0 | 0 | 0 | 3 | 72 | 7 | 62 | 3 | 0 |
| Amherst | 12,425 | 5 | 0 | 1 | 0 | 4 | 104 | 6 | 97 | 1 | 0 |
| Archbold | 4,286 | 4 | 0 | 0 | 0 | 4 | 61 | 9 | 50 | 2 | 0 |
| Ashland | 19,919 | 21 | 0 | 8 | 1 | 12 | 215 | 22 | 182 | 11 | 1 |
| Ashville | 4,510 | 3 | 0 | 1 | 0 | 2 | 30 | 4 | 22 | 4 | 0 |
| Athens | 24,638 | 27 | 0 | 4 | 2 | 21 | 514 | 85 | 407 | 22 | 1 |
| Aurora | 16,568 | 5 | 0 | 1 | 1 | 3 | 120 | 7 | 105 | 8 | 0 |
| Austintown | 34,472 | 47 | 1 | 11 | 6 | 29 | 623 | 84 | 512 | 27 | 0 |
| Avon Lake | 25,040 | 9 | 3 | 2 | 0 | 4 | 101 | 9 | 67 | 25 | 0 |
| Barberton | 25,746 | 75 | 0 | 23 | 12 | 40 | 674 | 102 | 533 | 39 | 6 |
| Barnesville | 3,925 | 1 | 0 | 0 | 0 | 1 | 3 | 0 | 3 | 0 | 0 |
| Batavia | 1,973 | 0 | 0 | 0 | 0 | 0 | 21 | 2 | 18 | 1 | 0 |
| Bath Township, Summit County | 9,606 | 4 | 0 | 1 | 2 | 1 | 137 | 4 | 131 | 2 | 0 |
| Bay Village | 15,154 | 5 | 0 | 1 | 0 | 4 | 74 | 3 | 60 | 11 | 0 |
| Bazetta Township | 5,454 | 6 | 0 | 1 | 0 | 5 | 195 | 3 | 188 | 4 | 0 |
| Beachwood | 11,580 | 22 | 1 | 0 | 7 | 14 | 247 | 7 | 229 | 11 | 0 |
| Beavercreek | 48,282 | 24 | 1 | 11 | 5 | 7 | 616 | 38 | 549 | 29 | 1 |
| Beaver Township | 6,321 | 4 | 1 | 2 | 0 | 1 | 79 | 14 | 58 | 7 | 0 |
| Bedford | 12,386 | 9 | 0 | 0 | 1 | 8 | 163 | 24 | 86 | 53 | 0 |
| Bedford Heights | 10,430 | 28 | 1 | 0 | 4 | 23 | 195 | 23 | 147 | 25 | 1 |
| Bellaire | 3,927 | 4 | 0 | 0 | 1 | 3 | 20 | 4 | 16 | 0 | 1 |
| Bellbrook | 7,426 | 0 | 0 | 0 | 0 | 0 | 39 | 6 | 33 | 0 | 1 |
| Bellefontaine | 13,131 | 20 | 0 | 6 | 2 | 12 | 168 | 11 | 149 | 8 | 4 |
| Bellville | 1,937 | 0 | 0 | 0 | 0 | 0 | 10 | 0 | 10 | 0 | 0 |
| Belpre | 6,348 | 3 | 1 | 0 | 0 | 2 | 85 | 6 | 74 | 5 | 0 |

## Table 8. Offenses Known to Law Enforcement, by Selected State and City, 2021—Continued

(Number.)

| State/city | Population | Violent crime | Murder and nonnegligent manslaughter | Rape | Robbery | Aggravated assault | Property crime | Burglary | Larceny-theft | Motor vehicle theft | Arson |
|---|---|---|---|---|---|---|---|---|---|---|---|
| Berea | 18,563 | 5 | 0 | 0 | 1 | 4 | 72 | 6 | 60 | 6 | 1 |
| Blanchester | 4,257 | 4 | 0 | 1 | 0 | 3 | 97 | 11 | 85 | 1 | 0 |
| Blue Ash | 12,525 | 20 | 0 | 5 | 2 | 13 | 183 | 16 | 152 | 15 | 1 |
| Boardman | 38,377 | 67 | 0 | 21 | 18 | 28 | 1,297 | 138 | 1,082 | 77 | 7 |
| Botkins | 1,159 | 3 | 0 | 0 | 0 | 3 | 10 | 1 | 9 | 0 | 0 |
| Bowling Green | 31,537 | 22 | 2 | 9 | 2 | 9 | 443 | 19 | 416 | 8 | 3 |
| Brecksville | 13,611 | 2 | 0 | 0 | 0 | 2 | 23 | 0 | 23 | 0 | 0 |
| Brewster | 2,141 | 3 | 0 | 1 | 0 | 2 | 13 | 2 | 10 | 1 | 0 |
| Brimfield Township | 10,328 | 5 | 0 | 4 | 0 | 1 | 332 | 5 | 314 | 13 | 0 |
| Brunswick Hills Township | 10,621 | 0 | 0 | 0 | 0 | 0 | 33 | 5 | 28 | 0 | 0 |
| Bucyrus | 11,676 | 14 | 0 | 4 | 3 | 7 | 261 | 34 | 216 | 11 | 0 |
| Butler Township | 7,835 | 26 | 0 | 6 | 1 | 19 | 472 | 17 | 436 | 19 | 0 |
| Cambridge | 10,279 | 10 | 0 | 4 | 0 | 6 | 85 | 13 | 72 | 0 | 2 |
| Canal Fulton | 5,396 | 2 | 0 | 1 | 1 | 0 | 70 | 26 | 43 | 1 | 1 |
| Canfield | 7,104 | 3 | 0 | 2 | 0 | 1 | 33 | 2 | 30 | 1 | 0 |
| Canton | 69,623 | 1,025 | 15 | 106 | 131 | 773 | 3,563 | 802 | 2,352 | 409 | 22 |
| Carlisle | 5,573 | 0 | 0 | 0 | 0 | 0 | 11 | 2 | 8 | 1 | 0 |
| Carroll Township | 2,067 | 0 | 0 | 0 | 0 | 0 | 18 | 3 | 14 | 1 | 0 |
| Cedarville | 4,364 | 3 | 0 | 0 | 0 | 3 | 11 | 1 | 9 | 1 | 0 |
| Centerville | 23,669 | 15 | 0 | 2 | 4 | 9 | 244 | 17 | 215 | 12 | 0 |
| Chagrin Falls | 3,921 | 3 | 0 | 0 | 0 | 3 | 34 | 2 | 27 | 5 | 0 |
| Chardon | 5,138 | 0 | 0 | 0 | 0 | 0 | 37 | 2 | 31 | 4 | 0 |
| Cheviot | 8,164 | 28 | 1 | 4 | 7 | 16 | 220 | 22 | 163 | 35 | 2 |
| Chillicothe | 21,622 | 43 | 0 | 16 | 9 | 18 | 1,004 | 84 | 877 | 43 | 6 |
| Cincinnati | 305,308 | 2,479 | 90 | 204 | 625 | 1,560 | 10,030 | 1,752 | 6,811 | 1,467 | 0 |
| Circleville | 14,226 | 28 | 1 | 7 | 4 | 16 | 456 | 78 | 355 | 23 | 2 |
| Clearcreek Township | 16,724 | 0 | 0 | 0 | 0 | 0 | 39 | 4 | 30 | 5 | 0 |
| Cleveland | 379,313 | 6,316 | 165 | 444 | 1,325 | 4,382 | 14,230 | 2,997 | 8,300 | 2,933 | 153 |
| Cleveland Heights | 43,608 | 123 | 2 | 10 | 33 | 78 | 523 | 79 | 364 | 80 | 4 |
| Coitsville Township | 1,306 | 0 | 0 | 0 | 0 | 0 | 8 | 4 | 4 | 0 | 0 |
| Coldwater | 4,577 | 1 | 0 | 1 | 0 | 0 | 14 | 2 | 12 | 0 | 0 |
| Colerain Township | 59,223 | 96 | 0 | 12 | 14 | 70 | 972 | 99 | 766 | 107 | 3 |
| Columbiana | 6,276 | 4 | 0 | 1 | 0 | 3 | 26 | 5 | 20 | 1 | 0 |
| Columbus | 916,001 | 5,382 | 203 | 779 | 1,997 | 2,403 | 29,589 | 4,844 | 20,407 | 4,338 | 12 |
| Commercial Point | 1,704 | 7 | 0 | 4 | 0 | 3 | 19 | 3 | 15 | 1 | 0 |
| Copley Township | 17,233 | 19 | 0 | 2 | 2 | 15 | 202 | 14 | 178 | 10 | 0 |
| Cortland | 6,702 | 1 | 0 | 0 | 0 | 1 | 37 | 4 | 33 | 0 | 1 |
| Covington | 2,730 | 0 | 0 | 0 | 0 | 0 | 2 | 1 | 1 | 0 | 0 |
| Dayton | 139,671 | 1,445 | 30 | 138 | 247 | 1,030 | 5,041 | 1,293 | 2,973 | 775 | 30 |
| Defiance | 16,415 | 37 | 0 | 16 | 5 | 16 | 208 | 21 | 187 | 0 | 0 |
| Delhi Township | 29,785 | 16 | 0 | 5 | 1 | 10 | 242 | 21 | 200 | 21 | 1 |
| Delphos | 6,873 | 13 | 0 | 2 | 1 | 10 | 39 | 7 | 31 | 1 | 1 |
| Delta | 3,085 | 5 | 0 | 2 | 0 | 3 | 11 | 2 | 9 | 0 | 0 |
| Dover | 12,676 | 15 | 0 | 4 | 0 | 11 | 65 | 7 | 53 | 5 | 0 |
| Dublin | 50,236 | 18 | 0 | 7 | 8 | 3 | 389 | 37 | 321 | 31 | 5 |
| East Palestine | 4,350 | 7 | 0 | 2 | 0 | 5 | 51 | 11 | 37 | 3 | 0 |
| Eaton | 8,098 | 11 | 0 | 3 | 0 | 8 | 105 | 10 | 90 | 5 | 1 |
| Elyria | 53,809 | 134 | 3 | 25 | 21 | 85 | 733 | 140 | 528 | 65 | 4 |
| Englewood | 13,507 | 14 | 0 | 4 | 2 | 8 | 276 | 17 | 253 | 6 | 1 |
| Fairborn | 34,076 | 71 | 0 | 14 | 7 | 50 | 452 | 82 | 332 | 38 | 6 |
| Fairfax | 1,702 | 3 | 0 | 0 | 1 | 2 | 119 | 3 | 113 | 3 | 0 |
| Fairfield Township | 23,206 | 10 | 0 | 1 | 1 | 8 | 208 | 11 | 188 | 9 | 0 |
| Findlay | 40,803 | 97 | 0 | 32 | 7 | 58 | 738 | 87 | 614 | 37 | 1 |
| Forest Park | 18,518 | 50 | 3 | 11 | 15 | 21 | 324 | 36 | 243 | 45 | 0 |
| Fremont | 15,764 | 42 | 1 | 8 | 1 | 32 | 479 | 67 | 398 | 14 | 1 |
| Gahanna | 35,765 | 84 | 3 | 18 | 11 | 52 | 673 | 63 | 568 | 42 | 2 |
| Gallipolis | 3,534 | 8 | 0 | 2 | 1 | 5 | 148 | 10 | 132 | 6 | 1 |
| Garfield Heights | 27,296 | 153 | 8 | 18 | 38 | 89 | 465 | 92 | 341 | 32 | 5 |
| Georgetown | 4,189 | 8 | 1 | 2 | 1 | 4 | 63 | 10 | 49 | 4 | 0 |
| Germantown | 5,570 | 9 | 0 | 5 | 0 | 4 | 30 | 2 | 27 | 1 | 0 |
| Goshen Township, Clermont County | 16,498 | 12 | 0 | 1 | 2 | 9 | 67 | 14 | 48 | 5 | 2 |
| Goshen Township, Mahoning County | 3,079 | 7 | 0 | 0 | 0 | 7 | 47 | 5 | 38 | 4 | 0 |
| Grafton | 5,920 | 1 | 0 | 0 | 0 | 1 | 18 | 0 | 16 | 2 | 0 |
| Grandview Heights | 9,395 | 6 | 0 | 0 | 2 | 4 | 150 | 18 | 118 | 14 | 0 |
| Granville | 5,842 | 8 | 0 | 6 | 0 | 2 | 45 | 5 | 40 | 0 | 0 |
| Greenfield | 4,556 | 2 | 0 | 0 | 0 | 2 | 9 | 3 | 5 | 1 | 0 |
| Greenhills | 3,548 | 5 | 0 | 2 | 1 | 2 | 16 | 0 | 14 | 2 | 0 |
| Green Township | 59,115 | 55 | 0 | 12 | 7 | 36 | 763 | 75 | 632 | 56 | 2 |
| Grove City | 42,992 | 38 | 2 | 10 | 15 | 11 | 1,009 | 77 | 865 | 67 | 1 |
| Groveport | 5,642 | 21 | 0 | 3 | 1 | 17 | 119 | 2 | 107 | 10 | 0 |
| Hamilton Township, Warren County | 24,711 | 7 | 0 | 3 | 0 | 4 | 56 | 4 | 49 | 3 | 1 |
| Heath | 11,111 | 18 | 0 | 6 | 3 | 9 | 449 | 75 | 356 | 18 | 1 |
| Hebron | 2,513 | 6 | 0 | 3 | 1 | 2 | 51 | 3 | 45 | 3 | 1 |
| Highland Heights | 8,389 | 0 | 0 | 0 | 0 | 0 | 70 | 10 | 60 | 0 | 0 |
| Hilliard | 37,776 | 24 | 0 | 5 | 7 | 12 | 281 | 16 | 241 | 24 | 1 |
| Hillsboro | 6,576 | 2 | 0 | 1 | 0 | 1 | 88 | 7 | 70 | 11 | 0 |
| Hinckley Township | 8,174 | 4 | 0 | 2 | 0 | 2 | 20 | 3 | 17 | 0 | 0 |
| Holland | 1,682 | 4 | 0 | 0 | 2 | 2 | 481 | 6 | 471 | 4 | 0 |
| Howland Township | 16,220 | 20 | 0 | 3 | 1 | 16 | 182 | 14 | 154 | 14 | 0 |
| Hubbard | 7,320 | 15 | 0 | 2 | 1 | 12 | 64 | 11 | 52 | 1 | 0 |

## Table 8. Offenses Known to Law Enforcement, by Selected State and City, 2021—Continued

(Number.)

| State/city | Population | Violent crime | Murder and nonnegligent manslaughter | Rape | Robbery | Aggravated assault | Property crime | Burglary | Larceny-theft | Motor vehicle theft | Arson |
|---|---|---|---|---|---|---|---|---|---|---|---|
| Huber Heights | 38,244 | 71 | 1 | 26 | 6 | 38 | 657 | 81 | 509 | 67 | 9 |
| Hudson | 22,170 | 5 | 0 | 3 | 0 | 2 | 129 | 4 | 119 | 6 | 0 |
| Huron | 6,794 | 1 | 0 | 0 | 0 | 1 | 52 | 5 | 44 | 3 | 1 |
| Independence | 7,244 | 15 | 0 | 1 | 6 | 8 | 157 | 8 | 136 | 13 | 0 |
| Ironton | 10,354 | 12 | 0 | 4 | 2 | 6 | 69 | 24 | 40 | 5 | 0 |
| Jackson | 6,224 | 8 | 0 | 3 | 0 | 5 | 152 | 51 | 92 | 9 | 0 |
| Jackson Township, Mahoning County | 1,993 | 1 | 0 | 0 | 1 | 0 | 15 | 1 | 14 | 0 | 0 |
| Jackson Township, Stark County | 40,215 | 85 | 2 | 23 | 20 | 40 | 845 | 152 | 649 | 44 | 1 |
| Jamestown | 2,157 | 1 | 0 | 0 | 0 | 1 | 43 | 14 | 27 | 2 | 0 |
| Kent | 29,364 | 21 | 0 | 0 | 4 | 17 | 333 | 51 | 262 | 20 | 1 |
| Lakemore | 3,060 | 8 | 0 | 1 | 4 | 3 | 91 | 16 | 67 | 8 | 2 |
| Lakewood | 49,404 | 64 | 1 | 2 | 35 | 26 | 547 | 80 | 414 | 53 | 0 |
| Lancaster | 41,152 | 100 | 3 | 28 | 10 | 59 | 645 | 73 | 534 | 38 | 8 |
| Lawrence Township | 8,275 | 4 | 0 | 0 | 0 | 4 | 36 | 14 | 18 | 4 | 0 |
| Lebanon | 20,826 | 34 | 0 | 10 | 5 | 19 | 293 | 28 | 248 | 17 | 4 |
| Lexington | 4,685 | 2 | 1 | 0 | 0 | 1 | 10 | 2 | 8 | 0 | 1 |
| Lima | 36,233 | 231 | 0 | 33 | 28 | 170 | 1,162 | 235 | 856 | 71 | 2 |
| Lisbon | 2,606 | 3 | 0 | 0 | 0 | 3 | 14 | 2 | 11 | 1 | 0 |
| Lithopolis | 2,022 | 4 | 0 | 2 | 0 | 2 | 13 | 2 | 8 | 3 | 0 |
| Lockland | 3,436 | 25 | 1 | 0 | 7 | 17 | 90 | 15 | 58 | 17 | 2 |
| Logan | 6,918 | 17 | 0 | 3 | 1 | 13 | 152 | 31 | 115 | 6 | 0 |
| London | 10,360 | 17 | 0 | 2 | 0 | 15 | 137 | 5 | 126 | 6 | 1 |
| Lorain | 63,859 | 340 | 7 | 24 | 62 | 247 | 1,217 | 265 | 866 | 86 | 5 |
| Lordstown | 3,227 | 7 | 0 | 0 | 0 | 7 | 26 | 5 | 19 | 2 | 0 |
| Loudonville | 2,620 | 2 | 0 | 1 | 0 | 1 | 13 | 2 | 11 | 0 | 1 |
| Louisville | 9,390 | 5 | 0 | 0 | 0 | 5 | 70 | 6 | 61 | 3 | 0 |
| Loveland | 13,253 | 8 | 0 | 4 | 0 | 4 | 80 | 5 | 73 | 2 | 1 |
| Lyndhurst | 13,258 | 16 | 0 | 1 | 5 | 10 | 155 | 11 | 134 | 10 | 0 |
| Macedonia | 12,120 | 3 | 0 | 0 | 0 | 3 | 112 | 4 | 107 | 1 | 0 |
| Madeira | 9,340 | 1 | 0 | 0 | 0 | 1 | 31 | 0 | 24 | 7 | 0 |
| Madison Township, Franklin County | 20,118 | 27 | 2 | 1 | 3 | 21 | 171 | 19 | 116 | 36 | 3 |
| Mansfield | 45,971 | 203 | 0 | 44 | 42 | 117 | 1,581 | 322 | 1,168 | 91 | 22 |
| Maple Heights | 21,888 | 49 | 5 | 5 | 26 | 13 | 202 | 38 | 87 | 77 | 4 |
| Marion | 35,391 | 77 | 2 | 25 | 21 | 29 | 639 | 139 | 451 | 49 | 5 |
| Martins Ferry | 6,380 | 14 | 0 | 2 | 2 | 10 | 41 | 5 | 35 | 1 | 0 |
| Mason | 34,660 | 5 | 0 | 2 | 2 | 1 | 177 | 13 | 159 | 5 | 0 |
| Massillon | 32,679 | 65 | 0 | 26 | 8 | 31 | 628 | 93 | 503 | 32 | 3 |
| Maumee | 13,541 | 22 | 0 | 4 | 4 | 14 | 359 | 13 | 333 | 13 | 1 |
| McConnelsville | 1,714 | 1 | 0 | 0 | 0 | 1 | 16 | 5 | 10 | 1 | 0 |
| Mechanicsburg | 1,610 | 2 | 0 | 2 | 0 | 0 | 17 | 0 | 16 | 1 | 0 |
| Medina | 25,905 | 16 | 1 | 6 | 2 | 7 | 240 | 55 | 175 | 10 | 3 |
| Mentor | 47,084 | 61 | 0 | 11 | 3 | 47 | 527 | 35 | 468 | 24 | 3 |
| Mentor-on-the-Lake | 7,372 | 8 | 0 | 4 | 0 | 4 | 38 | 3 | 33 | 2 | 0 |
| Miamisburg | 20,112 | 38 | 0 | 16 | 3 | 19 | 314 | 33 | 244 | 37 | 0 |
| Miami Township, Clermont County | 43,182 | 25 | 1 | 14 | 0 | 10 | 361 | 26 | 318 | 17 | 0 |
| Miami Township, Montgomery County | 29,213 | 49 | 0 | 20 | 3 | 26 | 678 | 63 | 566 | 49 | 0 |
| Middlefield | 2,690 | 2 | 0 | 0 | 0 | 2 | 15 | 1 | 14 | 0 | 0 |
| Middletown | 48,944 | 140 | 2 | 17 | 20 | 101 | 1,440 | 196 | 1,111 | 133 | 3 |
| Milford | 6,815 | 8 | 0 | 1 | 0 | 7 | 111 | 2 | 104 | 5 | 0 |
| Monroe | 16,858 | 20 | 0 | 7 | 3 | 10 | 255 | 10 | 227 | 18 | 0 |
| Montgomery | 10,943 | 9 | 0 | 2 | 1 | 6 | 93 | 5 | 75 | 13 | 0 |
| Montpelier | 3,893 | 17 | 0 | 7 | 0 | 10 | 122 | 16 | 100 | 6 | 1 |
| Moraine | 6,518 | 61 | 0 | 9 | 11 | 41 | 392 | 40 | 322 | 30 | 3 |
| Mount Orab | 3,397 | 6 | 0 | 0 | 0 | 6 | 72 | 2 | 66 | 4 | 0 |
| Mount Vernon | 16,625 | 10 | 0 | 2 | 1 | 7 | 132 | 19 | 109 | 4 | 1 |
| Napoleon | 8,088 | 13 | 0 | 6 | 0 | 7 | 145 | 27 | 113 | 5 | 0 |
| Navarre | 1,788 | 2 | 0 | 0 | 1 | 1 | 64 | 58 | 6 | 0 | 2 |
| Nelsonville | 5,094 | 6 | 0 | 1 | 1 | 4 | 62 | 30 | 30 | 2 | 1 |
| New Albany | 11,449 | 8 | 0 | 3 | 2 | 3 | 127 | 11 | 106 | 10 | 0 |
| Newark | 50,980 | 129 | 0 | 31 | 20 | 78 | 1,720 | 273 | 1,264 | 183 | 23 |
| New Boston | 2,103 | 6 | 0 | 1 | 1 | 4 | 43 | 10 | 31 | 2 | 0 |
| New Franklin | 14,090 | 13 | 0 | 1 | 0 | 12 | 93 | 18 | 67 | 8 | 0 |
| New Lebanon | 3,988 | 9 | 0 | 3 | 0 | 6 | 22 | 6 | 16 | 0 | 0 |
| New Lexington | 4,667 | 19 | 0 | 9 | 2 | 8 | 89 | 20 | 62 | 7 | 1 |
| New Philadelphia | 17,428 | 2 | 0 | 0 | 1 | 1 | 20 | 2 | 18 | 0 | 0 |
| North Baltimore | 3,569 | 0 | 0 | 0 | 0 | 0 | 23 | 4 | 19 | 0 | 0 |
| North Canton | 17,084 | 10 | 1 | 3 | 0 | 6 | 239 | 18 | 208 | 13 | 2 |
| Northfield | 3,647 | 0 | 0 | 0 | 0 | 0 | 38 | 2 | 35 | 1 | 0 |
| North Olmsted | 31,224 | 59 | 0 | 7 | 8 | 44 | 313 | 14 | 280 | 19 | 1 |
| Northwood | 5,481 | 12 | 1 | 6 | 1 | 4 | 145 | 15 | 113 | 17 | 0 |
| Norton | 11,894 | 12 | 0 | 1 | 1 | 10 | 216 | 36 | 160 | 20 | 0 |
| Norwalk | 16,752 | 16 | 0 | 4 | 1 | 11 | 181 | 15 | 160 | 6 | 0 |
| Oak Harbor | 2,685 | 0 | 0 | 0 | 0 | 0 | 20 | 6 | 13 | 1 | 0 |
| Oak Hill | 1,527 | 6 | 0 | 0 | 0 | 6 | 7 | 2 | 5 | 0 | 0 |
| Oberlin | 8,107 | 7 | 1 | 0 | 3 | 3 | 100 | 14 | 79 | 7 | 0 |
| Obetz | 5,479 | 10 | 0 | 3 | 1 | 6 | 202 | 12 | 152 | 38 | 1 |
| Olmsted Falls | 9,156 | 6 | 0 | 0 | 0 | 6 | 27 | 5 | 20 | 2 | 0 |
| Olmsted Township | 13,644 | 0 | 0 | 0 | 0 | 0 | 14 | 1 | 11 | 2 | 0 |

## Table 8. Offenses Known to Law Enforcement, by Selected State and City, 2021—Continued

(Number.)

| State/city | Population | Violent crime | Murder and nonnegligent manslaughter | Rape | Robbery | Aggravated assault | Property crime | Burglary | Larceny-theft | Motor vehicle theft | Arson |
|---|---|---|---|---|---|---|---|---|---|---|---|
| Ontario | 6,089 | 4 | 0 | 0 | 0 | 4 | 198 | 8 | 186 | 4 | 1 |
| Oregon | 19,986 | 38 | 1 | 10 | 3 | 24 | 579 | 54 | 500 | 25 | 0 |
| Orrville | 8,442 | 17 | 1 | 1 | 0 | 15 | 76 | 15 | 59 | 2 | 0 |
| Ottawa Hills | 4,541 | 2 | 0 | 0 | 0 | 2 | 30 | 2 | 23 | 5 | 0 |
| Oxford Township | 2,234 | 0 | 0 | 0 | 0 | 0 | 9 | 2 | 7 | 0 | 0 |
| Parma | 77,674 | 124 | 3 | 19 | 11 | 91 | 570 | 80 | 411 | 79 | 2 |
| Parma Heights | 19,669 | 4 | 0 | 0 | 0 | 4 | 73 | 10 | 58 | 5 | 0 |
| Pepper Pike | 6,525 | 1 | 0 | 0 | 0 | 1 | 33 | 4 | 26 | 3 | 0 |
| Perrysburg | 21,806 | 12 | 0 | 5 | 1 | 6 | 174 | 9 | 161 | 4 | 0 |
| Perrysburg Township | 13,072 | 3 | 0 | 0 | 1 | 2 | 96 | 14 | 80 | 2 | 0 |
| Perry Township, Franklin County | 3,756 | 1 | 0 | 0 | 1 | 0 | 37 | 5 | 31 | 1 | 0 |
| Perry Township, Stark County | 27,970 | 69 | 0 | 16 | 7 | 46 | 447 | 98 | 313 | 36 | 5 |
| Pickerington | 23,343 | 18 | 0 | 5 | 6 | 7 | 223 | 21 | 184 | 18 | 2 |
| Pierce Township | 15,178 | 14 | 1 | 5 | 2 | 6 | 142 | 15 | 121 | 6 | 0 |
| Pioneer | 1,398 | 0 | 0 | 0 | 0 | 0 | 11 | 2 | 9 | 0 | 0 |
| Piqua | 21,531 | 73 | 0 | 29 | 5 | 39 | 646 | 75 | 543 | 28 | 2 |
| Poland Township | 11,703 | 6 | 0 | 4 | 1 | 1 | 50 | 4 | 44 | 2 | 0 |
| Port Clinton | 6,113 | 8 | 0 | 2 | 1 | 5 | 73 | 8 | 59 | 6 | 0 |
| Portsmouth | 19,702 | 106 | 2 | 16 | 21 | 67 | 831 | 151 | 594 | 86 | 3 |
| Powell | 13,591 | 9 | 0 | 2 | 1 | 6 | 86 | 4 | 79 | 3 | 1 |
| Reading | 10,928 | 32 | 0 | 3 | 4 | 25 | 236 | 34 | 178 | 24 | 3 |
| Richmond Heights | 10,332 | 46 | 1 | 0 | 2 | 43 | 126 | 15 | 91 | 20 | 0 |
| Riverside | 25,168 | 44 | 3 | 12 | 3 | 26 | 344 | 37 | 237 | 70 | 6 |
| Rocky River | 20,007 | 9 | 0 | 2 | 1 | 6 | 85 | 8 | 63 | 14 | 0 |
| Ross Township | 9,050 | 13 | 0 | 2 | 2 | 9 | 66 | 2 | 57 | 7 | 0 |
| Russells Point | 1,377 | 3 | 0 | 2 | 0 | 1 | 11 | 2 | 9 | 0 | 0 |
| Sabina | 2,559 | 2 | 0 | 1 | 1 | 0 | 21 | 5 | 13 | 3 | 0 |
| Salem | 11,441 | 17 | 1 | 3 | 0 | 13 | 216 | 16 | 192 | 8 | 0 |
| Salineville | 1,203 | 4 | 0 | 0 | 0 | 4 | 12 | 2 | 9 | 1 | 0 |
| Sandusky | 24,172 | 21 | 3 | 11 | 5 | 2 | 424 | 96 | 308 | 20 | 1 |
| Sebring | 4,133 | 8 | 0 | 2 | 1 | 5 | 57 | 21 | 36 | 0 | 1 |
| Seven Hills | 11,600 | 4 | 0 | 0 | 0 | 4 | 73 | 6 | 58 | 9 | 0 |
| Shawnee Township | 12,072 | 10 | 0 | 4 | 0 | 6 | 104 | 15 | 82 | 7 | 0 |
| Sheffield Lake | 8,930 | 10 | 0 | 5 | 1 | 4 | 49 | 5 | 42 | 2 | 0 |
| Shelby | 9,042 | 28 | 1 | 13 | 3 | 11 | 115 | 19 | 94 | 2 | 1 |
| Sidney | 20,217 | 43 | 3 | 16 | 2 | 22 | 411 | 51 | 342 | 18 | 4 |
| Solon | 22,740 | 24 | 0 | 7 | 2 | 15 | 155 | 7 | 145 | 3 | 0 |
| South Euclid | 21,174 | 41 | 2 | 1 | 7 | 31 | 406 | 26 | 344 | 36 | 0 |
| South Zanesville | 2,106 | 0 | 0 | 0 | 0 | 0 | 5 | 2 | 3 | 0 | 1 |
| Springboro | 19,429 | 3 | 0 | 2 | 0 | 1 | 71 | 10 | 53 | 8 | 0 |
| Springfield | 58,253 | 649 | 5 | 42 | 128 | 474 | 2,266 | 439 | 1,555 | 272 | 63 |
| Springfield Township, Hamilton County | 35,873 | 72 | 0 | 1 | 14 | 57 | 414 | 55 | 315 | 44 | 0 |
| Springfield Township, Mahoning County | 6,310 | 5 | 0 | 2 | 0 | 3 | 52 | 12 | 39 | 1 | 0 |
| Springfield Township, Summit County | 14,459 | 52 | 0 | 8 | 4 | 40 | 615 | 56 | 525 | 34 | 5 |
| St. Clair Township | 7,365 | 5 | 0 | 0 | 0 | 5 | 115 | 0 | 115 | 0 | 0 |
| Steubenville | 17,482 | 31 | 2 | 2 | 5 | 22 | 598 | 46 | 538 | 14 | 3 |
| St. Marys | 8,094 | 3 | 0 | 0 | 0 | 3 | 58 | 12 | 42 | 4 | 0 |
| Strasburg | 2,697 | 2 | 0 | 0 | 0 | 2 | 18 | 2 | 16 | 0 | 0 |
| Streetsboro | 16,769 | 20 | 0 | 3 | 1 | 16 | 253 | 14 | 223 | 16 | 0 |
| Strongsville | 44,745 | 54 | 0 | 7 | 2 | 45 | 402 | 18 | 361 | 23 | 0 |
| Struthers | 9,976 | 16 | 0 | 0 | 2 | 14 | 35 | 14 | 18 | 3 | 0 |
| Sugarcreek Township | 8,536 | 4 | 0 | 2 | 0 | 2 | 99 | 9 | 83 | 7 | 0 |
| Swanton | 3,841 | 1 | 0 | 1 | 0 | 0 | 27 | 4 | 23 | 0 | 0 |
| Sylvania | 19,560 | 16 | 0 | 6 | 5 | 5 | 140 | 11 | 119 | 10 | 0 |
| Sylvania Township | 30,078 | 24 | 1 | 4 | 2 | 17 | 534 | 28 | 472 | 34 | 0 |
| Tiffin | 17,308 | 17 | 0 | 9 | 2 | 6 | 262 | 23 | 237 | 2 | 2 |
| Tipp City | 10,217 | 3 | 0 | 0 | 2 | 1 | 122 | 7 | 105 | 10 | 0 |
| Toledo | 269,941 | 2,908 | 66 | 191 | 447 | 2,204 | 7,579 | 1,405 | 5,046 | 1,128 | 133 |
| Toronto | 4,864 | 3 | 0 | 1 | 0 | 2 | 5 | 1 | 4 | 0 | 1 |
| Trotwood | 24,433 | 149 | 2 | 27 | 25 | 95 | 624 | 127 | 399 | 98 | 17 |
| Twinsburg | 18,956 | 5 | 0 | 2 | 0 | 3 | 106 | 8 | 92 | 6 | 0 |
| Uhrichsville | 5,287 | 8 | 0 | 2 | 0 | 6 | 46 | 20 | 22 | 4 | 0 |
| Uniontown | 3,306 | 4 | 0 | 0 | 0 | 4 | 89 | 10 | 77 | 2 | 1 |
| Union Township, Clermont County | 48,994 | 40 | 1 | 22 | 6 | 11 | 610 | 45 | 539 | 26 | 2 |
| University Heights | 12,638 | 37 | 1 | 2 | 4 | 30 | 112 | 12 | 98 | 2 | 0 |
| Upper Arlington | 35,540 | 13 | 1 | 1 | 8 | 3 | 275 | 28 | 226 | 21 | 1 |
| Upper Sandusky | 6,420 | 11 | 0 | 6 | 0 | 5 | 101 | 7 | 92 | 2 | 3 |
| Urbana | 11,368 | 26 | 0 | 8 | 2 | 16 | 202 | 16 | 183 | 3 | 1 |
| Utica | 2,293 | 7 | 0 | 1 | 0 | 6 | 4 | 2 | 2 | 0 | 0 |
| Vandalia | 14,960 | 19 | 0 | 12 | 3 | 4 | 250 | 39 | 171 | 40 | 3 |
| Van Wert | 10,594 | 38 | 0 | 12 | 1 | 25 | 293 | 55 | 235 | 3 | 1 |
| Vienna Township | 3,747 | 3 | 0 | 1 | 0 | 2 | 43 | 7 | 30 | 6 | 0 |
| Wadsworth | 24,656 | 36 | 0 | 8 | 3 | 25 | 310 | 26 | 279 | 5 | 1 |
| Wapakoneta | 9,664 | 9 | 0 | 1 | 1 | 7 | 106 | 6 | 97 | 3 | 0 |
| Warren | 38,193 | 171 | 5 | 25 | 30 | 111 | 1,009 | 232 | 703 | 74 | 13 |
| Warren Township | 5,113 | 14 | 0 | 1 | 2 | 11 | 46 | 8 | 32 | 6 | 0 |
| Washington Court House | 14,189 | 26 | 1 | 8 | 2 | 15 | 319 | 31 | 262 | 26 | 1 |
| Waterville | 5,605 | 2 | 0 | 0 | 0 | 2 | 27 | 2 | 24 | 1 | 0 |

# Table 8. Offenses Known to Law Enforcement, by Selected State and City, 2021—Continued

(Number.)

| State/city | Population | Violent crime | Murder and nonnegligent manslaughter | Rape | Robbery | Aggravated assault | Property crime | Burglary | Larceny-theft | Motor vehicle theft | Arson |
|---|---|---|---|---|---|---|---|---|---|---|---|
| Wauseon | 7,410 | 11 | 0 | 5 | 1 | 5 | 125 | 8 | 108 | 9 | 0 |
| Waverly | 4,115 | 4 | 0 | 0 | 0 | 4 | 40 | 9 | 31 | 0 | 0 |
| Weathersfield | 7,941 | 9 | 0 | 3 | 1 | 5 | 112 | 15 | 78 | 19 | 0 |
| Wellston | 5,519 | 17 | 0 | 2 | 0 | 15 | 129 | 21 | 97 | 11 | 1 |
| West Carrollton | 12,821 | 39 | 0 | 9 | 4 | 26 | 282 | 40 | 188 | 54 | 3 |
| West Chester Township | 63,211 | 82 | 1 | 27 | 14 | 40 | 1,091 | 93 | 928 | 70 | 3 |
| Westerville | 41,985 | 52 | 1 | 6 | 9 | 36 | 595 | 49 | 519 | 27 | 0 |
| Whitehall | 18,985 | 198 | 1 | 19 | 68 | 110 | 888 | 124 | 684 | 80 | 5 |
| Whitehouse | 5,020 | 5 | 0 | 2 | 0 | 3 | 14 | 2 | 12 | 0 | 0 |
| Wickliffe | 12,725 | 15 | 0 | 1 | 0 | 14 | 116 | 9 | 100 | 7 | 0 |
| Willard | 5,964 | 4 | 1 | 1 | 0 | 2 | 69 | 11 | 54 | 4 | 0 |
| Williamsburg | 2,584 | 9 | 0 | 1 | 0 | 8 | 13 | 3 | 10 | 0 | 0 |
| Willoughby Hills | 9,545 | 9 | 0 | 4 | 4 | 1 | 86 | 9 | 65 | 12 | 0 |
| Wintersville | 3,619 | 4 | 0 | 1 | 0 | 3 | 33 | 4 | 28 | 1 | 0 |
| Woodlawn | 3,402 | 4 | 0 | 1 | 1 | 2 | 84 | 9 | 66 | 9 | 0 |
| Wooster | 26,160 | 75 | 0 | 33 | 4 | 38 | 753 | 97 | 616 | 40 | 4 |
| Worthington | 14,884 | 10 | 0 | 1 | 6 | 3 | 313 | 27 | 272 | 14 | 0 |
| Xenia | 27,228 | 45 | 0 | 17 | 7 | 21 | 451 | 63 | 372 | 16 | 5 |
| Yellow Springs | 3,787 | 5 | 0 | 0 | 0 | 5 | 49 | 8 | 39 | 2 | 0 |
| Youngstown | 63,538 | 488 | 27 | 56 | 73 | 332 | 1,540 | 405 | 961 | 174 | 21 |
| Zanesville | 25,166 | 75 | 3 | 18 | 13 | 41 | 764 | 70 | 656 | 38 | 3 |
| **OKLAHOMA** | | | | | | | | | | | |
| Achille | 556 | 0 | 0 | 0 | 0 | 0 | 2 | 0 | 1 | 1 | 0 |
| Ada | 17,280 | 58 | 1 | 10 | 9 | 38 | 458 | 107 | 311 | 40 | 3 |
| Adair | 804 | 0 | 0 | 0 | 0 | 0 | 9 | 1 | 6 | 2 | 0 |
| Allen | 930 | 2 | 0 | 0 | 2 | 0 | 16 | 2 | 13 | 1 | 0 |
| Altus | 18,007 | 51 | 2 | 5 | 2 | 42 | 305 | 82 | 198 | 25 | 1 |
| Alva | 4,867 | 5 | 0 | 1 | 0 | 4 | 77 | 32 | 39 | 6 | 0 |
| Amber | 502 | 0 | 0 | 0 | 0 | 0 | 2 | 0 | 1 | 1 | 0 |
| Anadarko | 6,444 | 56 | 1 | 5 | 3 | 47 | 200 | 58 | 131 | 11 | 6 |
| Antlers | 2,286 | 2 | 0 | 0 | 0 | 2 | 63 | 18 | 34 | 11 | 1 |
| Apache | 1,385 | 1 | 0 | 0 | 0 | 1 | 24 | 12 | 10 | 2 | 0 |
| Arcadia | 280 | 0 | 0 | 0 | 0 | 0 | 2 | 0 | 2 | 0 | 0 |
| Ardmore | 24,795 | 164 | 3 | 25 | 12 | 124 | 998 | 251 | 640 | 107 | 4 |
| Arkoma | 1,885 | 2 | 0 | 0 | 0 | 2 | 11 | 1 | 2 | 8 | 0 |
| Atoka | 3,038 | 8 | 0 | 0 | 0 | 8 | 116 | 39 | 63 | 14 | 4 |
| Avant | 311 | 0 | 0 | 0 | 0 | 0 | 2 | 0 | 2 | 0 | 1 |
| Barnsdall | 1,123 | 1 | 0 | 0 | 0 | 1 | 8 | 3 | 5 | 0 | 0 |
| Bartlesville | 36,688 | 120 | 4 | 32 | 14 | 70 | 1,030 | 269 | 674 | 87 | 8 |
| Beaver | 1,350 | 1 | 0 | 1 | 0 | 0 | 16 | 4 | 11 | 1 | 0 |
| Beggs | 1,225 | 7 | 1 | 0 | 1 | 5 | 28 | 10 | 15 | 3 | 0 |
| Bennington | 378 | 1 | 0 | 0 | 0 | 1 | 2 | 0 | 2 | 0 | 0 |
| Bernice | 581 | 0 | 0 | 0 | 0 | 0 | 13 | 0 | 11 | 2 | 0 |
| Bethany | 19,209 | 63 | 0 | 14 | 6 | 43 | 550 | 227 | 241 | 82 | 5 |
| Big Cabin | 250 | 0 | 0 | 0 | 0 | 0 | 7 | 0 | 4 | 3 | 0 |
| Binger | 624 | 0 | 0 | 0 | 0 | 0 | 4 | 0 | 3 | 1 | 0 |
| Bixby | 29,327 | 34 | 1 | 13 | 3 | 17 | 398 | 73 | 273 | 52 | 2 |
| Blackwell | 6,474 | 17 | 0 | 2 | 1 | 14 | 105 | 31 | 63 | 11 | 4 |
| Blanchard | 9,303 | 11 | 1 | 1 | 0 | 9 | 75 | 10 | 48 | 17 | 1 |
| Boise City | 1,071 | 0 | 0 | 0 | 0 | 0 | 31 | 15 | 12 | 4 | 0 |
| Bokchito | 711 | 2 | 0 | 0 | 0 | 2 | 14 | 2 | 11 | 1 | 0 |
| Bokoshe | 495 | 0 | 0 | 0 | 0 | 0 | 2 | 1 | 1 | 0 | 0 |
| Boley | 1,165 | 2 | 0 | 0 | 0 | 2 | 2 | 0 | 2 | 0 | 0 |
| Boswell | 677 | 2 | 0 | 0 | 0 | 2 | 0 | 0 | 0 | 0 | 0 |
| Bristow | 4,174 | 9 | 0 | 1 | 0 | 8 | 151 | 35 | 86 | 30 | 0 |
| Broken Arrow | 112,990 | 177 | 5 | 33 | 21 | 118 | 2,156 | 294 | 1,598 | 264 | 5 |
| Broken Bow | 4,085 | 21 | 0 | 4 | 0 | 17 | 209 | 52 | 137 | 20 | 2 |
| Burns Flat | 1,865 | 5 | 0 | 0 | 0 | 5 | 6 | 0 | 3 | 3 | 1 |
| Butler | 289 | 0 | 0 | 0 | 0 | 0 | 0 | 0 | 0 | 0 | 0 |
| Cache | 2,824 | 9 | 0 | 0 | 1 | 8 | 31 | 7 | 22 | 2 | 0 |
| Caddo | 1,125 | 0 | 0 | 0 | 0 | 0 | 8 | 5 | 1 | 2 | 0 |
| Calera | 2,440 | 6 | 0 | 1 | 0 | 5 | 48 | 8 | 33 | 7 | 0 |
| Calvin | 267 | 1 | 0 | 0 | 0 | 1 | 2 | 0 | 2 | 0 | 0 |
| Caney | 202 | 2 | 0 | 1 | 0 | 1 | 4 | 2 | 0 | 2 | 0 |
| Canton | 583 | 0 | 0 | 0 | 0 | 0 | 1 | 0 | 1 | 0 | 0 |
| Carnegie | 1,634 | 10 | 0 | 0 | 0 | 10 | 11 | 4 | 5 | 2 | 0 |
| Cashion | 943 | 0 | 0 | 0 | 0 | 0 | 5 | 2 | 3 | 0 | 0 |
| Catoosa | 6,876 | 19 | 0 | 2 | 1 | 16 | 189 | 44 | 77 | 68 | 1 |
| Cement | 468 | 0 | 0 | 0 | 0 | 0 | 2 | 0 | 1 | 1 | 0 |
| Chandler | 3,080 | 9 | 0 | 3 | 0 | 6 | 49 | 13 | 32 | 4 | 1 |
| Chattanooga | 457 | 0 | 0 | 0 | 0 | 0 | 3 | 0 | 2 | 1 | 0 |
| Checotah | 3,051 | 5 | 0 | 1 | 0 | 4 | 69 | 22 | 40 | 7 | 1 |
| Chelsea | 1,868 | 4 | 0 | 2 | 0 | 2 | 30 | 2 | 20 | 8 | 1 |
| Cherokee | 1,492 | 6 | 0 | 1 | 0 | 5 | 35 | 12 | 20 | 3 | 0 |
| Choctaw | 12,938 | 18 | 0 | 4 | 1 | 13 | 128 | 29 | 88 | 11 | 1 |
| Chouteau | 2,111 | 7 | 0 | 0 | 1 | 6 | 73 | 11 | 47 | 15 | 0 |
| Claremore | 18,961 | 81 | 0 | 44 | 4 | 33 | 488 | 103 | 331 | 54 | 2 |
| Clayton | 771 | 1 | 0 | 0 | 0 | 1 | 9 | 5 | 4 | 0 | 0 |
| Cleveland | 3,101 | 10 | 0 | 1 | 1 | 8 | 59 | 15 | 33 | 11 | 0 |
| Clinton | 8,943 | 22 | 0 | 4 | 4 | 14 | 175 | 53 | 85 | 37 | 5 |
| Coalgate | 1,830 | 2 | 0 | 0 | 0 | 2 | 4 | 0 | 4 | 0 | 1 |
| Colbert | 1,281 | 6 | 0 | 0 | 0 | 6 | 8 | 1 | 2 | 5 | 0 |

## Table 8. Offenses Known to Law Enforcement, by Selected State and City, 2021—Continued

(Number.)

| State/city | Population | Violent crime | Murder and nonnegligent manslaughter | Rape | Robbery | Aggravated assault | Property crime | Burglary | Larceny- theft | Motor vehicle theft | Arson |
|---|---|---|---|---|---|---|---|---|---|---|---|
| Colcord | 854 | 8 | 0 | 1 | 0 | 7 | 12 | 1 | 5 | 6 | 0 |
| Collinsville | 7,765 | 14 | 0 | 6 | 2 | 6 | 92 | 21 | 66 | 5 | 0 |
| Comanche | 1,540 | 8 | 0 | 0 | 1 | 7 | 26 | 13 | 13 | 0 | 1 |
| Commerce | 2,482 | 12 | 2 | 1 | 0 | 9 | 32 | 14 | 10 | 8 | 0 |
| Cordell | 2,689 | 1 | 0 | 0 | 0 | 1 | 21 | 8 | 9 | 4 | 0 |
| Covington | 533 | 1 | 0 | 0 | 0 | 1 | 6 | 1 | 5 | 0 | 0 |
| Coweta | 10,297 | 46 | 0 | 6 | 1 | 39 | 132 | 32 | 90 | 10 | 1 |
| Crescent | 1,596 | 0 | 0 | 0 | 0 | 0 | 7 | 2 | 2 | 3 | 0 |
| Cushing | 7,558 | 28 | 0 | 3 | 1 | 24 | 176 | 49 | 109 | 18 | 1 |
| Cyril | 997 | 1 | 0 | 0 | 0 | 1 | 18 | 4 | 12 | 2 | 0 |
| Davenport | 808 | 2 | 0 | 0 | 0 | 2 | 7 | 3 | 4 | 0 | 0 |
| Davis | 2,874 | 16 | 0 | 2 | 0 | 14 | 100 | 15 | 78 | 7 | 0 |
| Del City | 21,665 | 169 | 5 | 10 | 18 | 136 | 633 | 118 | 434 | 81 | 5 |
| Depew | 476 | 0 | 0 | 0 | 0 | 0 | 1 | 1 | 0 | 0 | 0 |
| Dewar | 843 | 1 | 0 | 0 | 0 | 1 | 6 | 1 | 4 | 1 | 0 |
| Dewey | 3,411 | 9 | 0 | 0 | 0 | 9 | 93 | 33 | 56 | 4 | 1 |
| Dibble | 884 | 2 | 0 | 1 | 0 | 1 | 8 | 3 | 2 | 3 | 0 |
| Dickson | 1,260 | 4 | 0 | 1 | 0 | 3 | 21 | 7 | 10 | 4 | 0 |
| Disney | 302 | 0 | 0 | 0 | 0 | 0 | 0 | 0 | 0 | 0 | 0 |
| Drumright | 2,805 | 7 | 0 | 0 | 0 | 7 | 88 | 34 | 43 | 11 | 2 |
| Duncan | 22,145 | 54 | 2 | 7 | 8 | 37 | 674 | 188 | 442 | 44 | 4 |
| Durant | 19,518 | 53 | 0 | 7 | 2 | 44 | 593 | 142 | 388 | 63 | 1 |
| Earlsboro | 625 | 3 | 0 | 0 | 0 | 3 | 17 | 2 | 15 | 0 | 1 |
| Edmond | 96,861 | 135 | 1 | 40 | 9 | 85 | 1,450 | 259 | 1,134 | 57 | 3 |
| Eldorado | 397 | 0 | 0 | 0 | 0 | 0 | 2 | 2 | 0 | 0 | 0 |
| Elgin | 3,359 | 0 | 0 | 0 | 0 | 0 | 1 | 0 | 1 | 0 | 0 |
| Elk City | 11,326 | 17 | 1 | 2 | 0 | 14 | 217 | 38 | 146 | 33 | 1 |
| Elmore City | 753 | 0 | 0 | 0 | 0 | 0 | 9 | 2 | 5 | 2 | 0 |
| El Reno | 21,018 | 49 | 1 | 9 | 5 | 34 | 295 | 59 | 193 | 43 | 5 |
| Enid | 49,545 | 161 | 0 | 35 | 10 | 116 | 1,255 | 350 | 798 | 107 | 4 |
| Erick | 969 | 4 | 0 | 0 | 1 | 3 | 11 | 1 | 7 | 3 | 0 |
| Eufaula | 2,841 | 3 | 1 | 0 | 1 | 1 | 47 | 14 | 27 | 6 | 0 |
| Fairfax | 1,229 | 8 | 0 | 4 | 0 | 4 | 14 | 4 | 6 | 4 | 0 |
| Fairland | 1,021 | 2 | 0 | 0 | 0 | 2 | 12 | 1 | 10 | 1 | 0 |
| Fairview | 2,580 | 0 | 0 | 0 | 0 | 0 | 43 | 12 | 31 | 0 | 1 |
| Fletcher | 1,137 | 1 | 0 | 1 | 0 | 0 | 3 | 1 | 0 | 2 | 0 |
| Forest Park | 1,078 | 2 | 0 | 0 | 0 | 2 | 8 | 0 | 8 | 0 | 0 |
| Fort Cobb | 604 | 0 | 0 | 0 | 0 | 0 | 3 | 2 | 1 | 0 | 0 |
| Fort Gibson | 3,912 | 15 | 1 | 1 | 0 | 13 | 50 | 13 | 36 | 1 | 1 |
| Fort Towson | 485 | 0 | 0 | 0 | 0 | 0 | 0 | 0 | 0 | 0 | 1 |
| Frederick | 3,490 | 16 | 1 | 5 | 1 | 9 | 90 | 20 | 59 | 11 | 3 |
| Gans | 294 | 0 | 0 | 0 | 0 | 0 | 0 | 0 | 0 | 0 | 0 |
| Garber | 802 | 0 | 0 | 0 | 0 | 0 | 5 | 3 | 1 | 1 | 0 |
| Geary | 1,271 | 2 | 0 | 0 | 0 | 2 | 20 | 4 | 13 | 3 | 0 |
| Geronimo | 1,220 | 0 | 0 | 0 | 0 | 0 | 12 | 2 | 10 | 0 | 0 |
| Goodwell | 1,261 | 0 | 0 | 0 | 0 | 0 | 7 | 3 | 2 | 2 | 0 |
| Gore | 943 | 1 | 0 | 1 | 0 | 0 | 15 | 2 | 9 | 4 | 0 |
| Grandfield | 922 | 1 | 0 | 0 | 0 | 1 | 15 | 6 | 8 | 1 | 0 |
| Granite | 1,946 | 2 | 0 | 0 | 0 | 2 | 12 | 3 | 7 | 2 | 1 |
| Grove | 7,242 | 18 | 0 | 3 | 0 | 15 | 223 | 16 | 187 | 20 | 1 |
| Guthrie | 11,968 | 39 | 2 | 5 | 2 | 30 | 268 | 60 | 170 | 38 | 1 |
| Guymon | 10,960 | 32 | 0 | 9 | 0 | 23 | 163 | 39 | 107 | 17 | 4 |
| Haileyville | 740 | 0 | 0 | 0 | 0 | 0 | 0 | 0 | 0 | 0 | 0 |
| Harrah | 6,805 | 15 | 1 | 2 | 1 | 11 | 96 | 38 | 52 | 6 | 1 |
| Hartshorne | 1,928 | 2 | 0 | 0 | 0 | 2 | 31 | 12 | 13 | 6 | 0 |
| Haskell | 1,949 | 6 | 2 | 0 | 0 | 4 | 48 | 20 | 23 | 5 | 0 |
| Healdton | 2,684 | 8 | 0 | 3 | 0 | 5 | 28 | 11 | 14 | 3 | 0 |
| Heavener | 3,285 | 7 | 0 | 0 | 0 | 7 | 39 | 11 | 23 | 5 | 0 |
| Hennessey | 2,234 | 2 | 0 | 0 | 0 | 2 | 11 | 3 | 6 | 2 | 0 |
| Henryetta | 5,464 | 12 | 0 | 2 | 1 | 9 | 86 | 20 | 51 | 15 | 2 |
| Hinton | 3,221 | 2 | 0 | 1 | 0 | 1 | 27 | 4 | 19 | 4 | 0 |
| Hobart | 3,405 | 8 | 0 | 0 | 1 | 7 | 64 | 29 | 29 | 6 | 1 |
| Holdenville | 5,394 | 14 | 1 | 3 | 2 | 8 | 122 | 33 | 76 | 13 | 6 |
| Hollis | 1,794 | 5 | 0 | 1 | 0 | 4 | 33 | 15 | 14 | 4 | 0 |
| Hominy | 3,332 | 4 | 0 | 2 | 0 | 2 | 23 | 11 | 9 | 3 | 0 |
| Hooker | 1,834 | 3 | 0 | 0 | 0 | 3 | 13 | 2 | 8 | 3 | 0 |
| Howe | 786 | 0 | 0 | 0 | 0 | 0 | 6 | 2 | 3 | 1 | 0 |
| Hugo | 5,047 | 46 | 1 | 1 | 1 | 43 | 230 | 58 | 147 | 25 | 9 |
| Hulbert | 579 | 7 | 0 | 1 | 0 | 6 | 14 | 2 | 9 | 3 | 0 |
| Hydro | 933 | 0 | 0 | 0 | 0 | 0 | 4 | 1 | 1 | 2 | 0 |
| Inola | 1,793 | 3 | 0 | 0 | 0 | 3 | 18 | 8 | 10 | 0 | 0 |
| Jay | 2,536 | 11 | 1 | 3 | 0 | 7 | 84 | 21 | 52 | 11 | 15 |
| Jenks | 25,111 | 28 | 1 | 8 | 1 | 18 | 329 | 51 | 237 | 41 | 1 |
| Jennings | 355 | 0 | 0 | 0 | 0 | 0 | 14 | 4 | 7 | 3 | 0 |
| Jones | 3,280 | 10 | 0 | 2 | 0 | 8 | 62 | 13 | 37 | 12 | 1 |
| Kansas | 805 | 0 | 0 | 0 | 0 | 0 | 11 | 5 | 3 | 3 | 0 |
| Kellyville | 1,127 | 1 | 0 | 0 | 0 | 1 | 9 | 3 | 4 | 2 | 0 |
| Keota | 544 | 3 | 0 | 0 | 0 | 3 | 3 | 1 | 1 | 1 | 0 |
| Kiefer | 2,072 | 0 | 0 | 0 | 0 | 0 | 36 | 7 | 24 | 5 | 0 |
| Kingfisher | 4,919 | 10 | 0 | 4 | 1 | 5 | 79 | 10 | 55 | 14 | 0 |
| Kingston | 1,698 | 0 | 0 | 0 | 0 | 0 | 3 | 2 | 1 | 0 | 0 |
| Kiowa | 671 | 0 | 0 | 0 | 0 | 0 | 6 | 2 | 4 | 0 | 0 |
| Konawa | 1,184 | 1 | 0 | 0 | 0 | 1 | 30 | 6 | 18 | 6 | 1 |

# Table 8. Offenses Known to Law Enforcement, by Selected State and City, 2021—Continued

(Number.)

| State/city | Population | Violent crime | Murder and nonnegligent manslaughter | Rape | Robbery | Aggravated assault | Property crime | Burglary | Larceny- theft | Motor vehicle theft | Arson |
|---|---|---|---|---|---|---|---|---|---|---|---|
| Krebs | 1,995 | 4 | 0 | 1 | 0 | 3 | 63 | 16 | 39 | 8 | 1 |
| Lahoma | 610 | 1 | 0 | 1 | 0 | 0 | 5 | 4 | 1 | 0 | 0 |
| Lamont | 391 | 0 | 0 | 0 | 0 | 0 | 0 | 0 | 0 | 0 | 0 |
| Langley | 821 | 0 | 0 | 0 | 0 | 0 | 3 | 2 | 1 | 0 | 0 |
| Langston | 1,882 | 1 | 0 | 0 | 0 | 1 | 4 | 4 | 0 | 0 | 0 |
| Laverne | 1,293 | 0 | 0 | 0 | 0 | 0 | 1 | 0 | 0 | 1 | 0 |
| Lawton | 92,711 | 544 | 11 | 48 | 44 | 441 | 897 | 411 | 280 | 206 | 41 |
| Lexington | 2,190 | 6 | 0 | 0 | 0 | 6 | 37 | 7 | 22 | 8 | 1 |
| Lindsay | 2,767 | 10 | 1 | 2 | 0 | 7 | 117 | 41 | 60 | 16 | 0 |
| Locust Grove | 1,392 | 6 | 0 | 0 | 0 | 6 | 44 | 10 | 26 | 8 | 0 |
| Lone Grove | 5,225 | 11 | 0 | 2 | 1 | 8 | 94 | 26 | 62 | 6 | 1 |
| Luther | 1,842 | 2 | 0 | 0 | 0 | 2 | 10 | 2 | 6 | 2 | 0 |
| Madill | 4,096 | 2 | 0 | 0 | 0 | 2 | 111 | 10 | 89 | 12 | 1 |
| Mangum | 2,662 | 8 | 0 | 0 | 0 | 8 | 29 | 3 | 20 | 6 | 1 |
| Mannford | 3,191 | 2 | 0 | 0 | 0 | 2 | 29 | 9 | 11 | 9 | 0 |
| Marble City | 249 | 0 | 0 | 0 | 0 | 0 | 0 | 0 | 0 | 0 | 0 |
| Marietta | 2,764 | 6 | 0 | 0 | 0 | 6 | 78 | 11 | 49 | 18 | 0 |
| Marlow | 4,393 | 7 | 0 | 0 | 0 | 7 | 93 | 23 | 63 | 7 | 0 |
| Maud | 1,059 | 8 | 0 | 0 | 0 | 8 | 20 | 8 | 10 | 2 | 0 |
| Maysville | 1,199 | 6 | 0 | 2 | 0 | 4 | 39 | 9 | 27 | 3 | 0 |
| McAlester | 17,729 | 50 | 1 | 12 | 6 | 31 | 476 | 91 | 336 | 49 | 2 |
| McCurtain | 501 | 0 | 0 | 0 | 0 | 0 | 2 | 1 | 1 | 0 | 0 |
| McLoud | 4,828 | 10 | 2 | 1 | 0 | 7 | 50 | 14 | 27 | 9 | 2 |
| Medford | 939 | 1 | 0 | 0 | 0 | 1 | 7 | 1 | 5 | 1 | 0 |
| Medicine Park | 469 | 1 | 0 | 0 | 0 | 1 | 3 | 2 | 0 | 1 | 0 |
| Meeker | 1,139 | 3 | 0 | 0 | 0 | 3 | 16 | 1 | 15 | 0 | 0 |
| Miami | 12,885 | 67 | 1 | 7 | 5 | 54 | 408 | 84 | 282 | 42 | 12 |
| Minco | 1,646 | 4 | 0 | 0 | 0 | 4 | 11 | 3 | 6 | 2 | 0 |
| Mooreland | 1,135 | 1 | 0 | 0 | 0 | 1 | 8 | 4 | 3 | 1 | 0 |
| Morris | 1,404 | 0 | 0 | 0 | 0 | 0 | 2 | 1 | 1 | 0 | 0 |
| Mounds | 1,253 | 3 | 0 | 0 | 0 | 3 | 14 | 2 | 10 | 2 | 1 |
| Mountain View | 739 | 0 | 0 | 0 | 0 | 0 | 2 | 1 | 1 | 0 | 0 |
| Muldrow | 3,260 | 8 | 0 | 3 | 0 | 5 | 70 | 20 | 44 | 6 | 1 |
| Muskogee | 36,598 | 350 | 7 | 34 | 24 | 285 | 1,191 | 347 | 731 | 113 | 9 |
| Mustang | 24,822 | 32 | 0 | 8 | 1 | 23 | 240 | 48 | 177 | 15 | 1 |
| Nash | 195 | 0 | 0 | 0 | 0 | 0 | 0 | 0 | 0 | 0 | 0 |
| Newcastle | 11,788 | 11 | 0 | 6 | 0 | 5 | 179 | 40 | 105 | 34 | 1 |
| Newkirk | 2,147 | 3 | 0 | 0 | 0 | 3 | 32 | 7 | 21 | 4 | 0 |
| Nichols Hills | 3,982 | 0 | 0 | 0 | 0 | 0 | 70 | 13 | 41 | 16 | 0 |
| Nicoma Park | 2,486 | 11 | 0 | 2 | 1 | 8 | 41 | 14 | 22 | 5 | 0 |
| Ninnekah | 1,046 | 2 | 0 | 0 | 0 | 2 | 17 | 8 | 6 | 3 | 1 |
| Noble | 7,329 | 10 | 0 | 2 | 0 | 8 | 117 | 37 | 70 | 10 | 0 |
| Norman | 127,304 | 397 | 1 | 87 | 31 | 278 | 3,722 | 501 | 2,714 | 507 | 6 |
| North Enid | 923 | 2 | 0 | 0 | 0 | 2 | 10 | 1 | 9 | 0 | 0 |
| Nowata | 3,527 | 13 | 0 | 1 | 0 | 12 | 68 | 23 | 41 | 4 | 0 |
| Oilton | 1,011 | 1 | 0 | 0 | 0 | 1 | 17 | 3 | 8 | 6 | 0 |
| Okarche | 1,346 | 2 | 0 | 2 | 0 | 0 | 4 | 0 | 3 | 1 | 0 |
| Okeene | 1,130 | 1 | 0 | 1 | 0 | 0 | 13 | 1 | 9 | 3 | 0 |
| Okemah | 3,031 | 14 | 1 | 0 | 1 | 12 | 120 | 28 | 76 | 16 | 0 |
| Oklahoma City | 670,872 | 4,313 | 82 | 545 | 645 | 3,041 | 25,557 | 6,370 | 15,691 | 3,496 | 112 |
| Okmulgee | 11,531 | 41 | 1 | 4 | 4 | 32 | 284 | 57 | 201 | 26 | 0 |
| Olustee | 545 | 0 | 0 | 0 | 0 | 0 | 2 | 2 | 0 | 0 | 0 |
| Oologah | 1,182 | 0 | 0 | 0 | 0 | 0 | 14 | 5 | 9 | 0 | 0 |
| Owasso | 38,057 | 56 | 0 | 19 | 2 | 35 | 580 | 46 | 448 | 86 | 0 |
| Paoli | 612 | 2 | 0 | 0 | 0 | 2 | 2 | 0 | 1 | 1 | 0 |
| Pauls Valley | 6,101 | 47 | 0 | 8 | 4 | 35 | 246 | 58 | 164 | 24 | 2 |
| Pawhuska | 3,341 | 5 | 0 | 2 | 0 | 3 | 73 | 24 | 43 | 6 | 0 |
| Pawnee | 2,092 | 13 | 0 | 3 | 5 | 5 | 42 | 19 | 18 | 5 | 1 |
| Perkins | 2,798 | 11 | 0 | 4 | 0 | 7 | 40 | 6 | 31 | 3 | 1 |
| Perry | 4,804 | 15 | 0 | 1 | 1 | 13 | 96 | 21 | 68 | 7 | 1 |
| Piedmont | 9,385 | 7 | 0 | 4 | 0 | 3 | 30 | 6 | 20 | 4 | 1 |
| Pocola | 4,163 | 12 | 0 | 1 | 1 | 8 | 27 | 6 | 13 | 8 | 0 |
| Ponca City | 23,307 | 193 | 0 | 26 | 14 | 153 | 838 | 209 | 547 | 82 | 6 |
| Pond Creek | 848 | 2 | 0 | 2 | 0 | 0 | 8 | 3 | 5 | 0 | 0 |
| Porum | 696 | 2 | 0 | 1 | 0 | 1 | 7 | 2 | 3 | 2 | 0 |
| Poteau | 8,942 | 37 | 0 | 5 | 2 | 30 | 335 | 71 | 241 | 23 | 0 |
| Prague | 2,362 | 6 | 0 | 1 | 0 | 5 | 53 | 22 | 29 | 2 | 2 |
| Pryor Creek | 9,377 | 51 | 0 | 3 | 2 | 46 | 217 | 25 | 150 | 42 | 0 |
| Purcell | 6,409 | 13 | 0 | 2 | 3 | 8 | 180 | 29 | 124 | 27 | 3 |
| Quinton | 978 | 2 | 0 | 0 | 0 | 2 | 13 | 3 | 7 | 3 | 0 |
| Ramona | 557 | 0 | 0 | 0 | 0 | 0 | 12 | 2 | 10 | 0 | 0 |
| Rattan | 293 | 0 | 0 | 0 | 0 | 0 | 3 | 2 | 0 | 1 | 0 |
| Roland | 4,112 | 9 | 0 | 0 | 1 | 8 | 70 | 13 | 44 | 13 | 0 |
| Rush Springs | 1,254 | 9 | 0 | 0 | 0 | 9 | 28 | 5 | 18 | 5 | 1 |
| Salina | 1,396 | 8 | 0 | 1 | 1 | 6 | 34 | 6 | 17 | 11 | 1 |
| Sallisaw | 8,405 | 41 | 0 | 13 | 2 | 26 | 284 | 50 | 205 | 29 | 1 |
| Sand Springs | 20,139 | 35 | 5 | 7 | 6 | 17 | 821 | 103 | 604 | 114 | 1 |
| Sapulpa | 21,535 | 79 | 0 | 21 | 6 | 52 | 493 | 135 | 286 | 72 | 1 |
| Savanna | 646 | 1 | 0 | 0 | 0 | 1 | 14 | 3 | 7 | 4 | 0 |
| Sawyer | 326 | 2 | 0 | 1 | 0 | 1 | 2 | 0 | 2 | 0 | 0 |
| Sayre | 4,443 | 9 | 0 | 1 | 2 | 6 | 93 | 21 | 71 | 1 | 1 |
| Seiling | 838 | 0 | 0 | 0 | 0 | 0 | 3 | 3 | 0 | 0 | 0 |
| Seminole | 6,993 | 20 | 0 | 3 | 0 | 17 | 272 | 69 | 157 | 46 | 0 |

## Table 8. Offenses Known to Law Enforcement, by Selected State and City, 2021—Continued

(Number.)

| State/city | Population | Violent crime | Murder and nonnegligent manslaughter | Rape | Robbery | Aggravated assault | Property crime | Burglary | Larceny-theft | Motor vehicle theft | Arson |
|---|---|---|---|---|---|---|---|---|---|---|---|
| Shady Point | 994 | 1 | 0 | 0 | 0 | 1 | 0 | 0 | 0 | 0 | 1 |
| Shattuck | 1,234 | 0 | 0 | 0 | 0 | 0 | 5 | 4 | 1 | 0 | 0 |
| Shawnee | 31,724 | 168 | 0 | 28 | 11 | 129 | 1,160 | 248 | 762 | 150 | 3 |
| Skiatook | 8,189 | 31 | 0 | 5 | 0 | 26 | 185 | 36 | 137 | 12 | 3 |
| Snyder | 1,270 | 9 | 0 | 0 | 0 | 9 | 7 | 2 | 5 | 0 | 0 |
| South Coffeyville | 725 | 0 | 0 | 0 | 0 | 0 | 18 | 0 | 14 | 4 | 0 |
| Sparks | 172 | 0 | 0 | 0 | 0 | 0 | 0 | 0 | 0 | 0 | 1 |
| Spavinaw | 432 | 2 | 0 | 0 | 0 | 2 | 3 | 1 | 1 | 1 | 0 |
| Spencer | 3,962 | 10 | 0 | 1 | 0 | 9 | 91 | 28 | 49 | 14 | 1 |
| Sperry | 1,370 | 3 | 0 | 0 | 0 | 3 | 48 | 16 | 22 | 10 | 1 |
| Spiro | 2,153 | 8 | 0 | 0 | 0 | 8 | 13 | 0 | 11 | 2 | 1 |
| Sterling | 775 | 2 | 0 | 1 | 0 | 1 | 8 | 3 | 4 | 1 | 0 |
| Stigler | 2,698 | 2 | 0 | 1 | 0 | 1 | 26 | 6 | 19 | 1 | 0 |
| Stillwater | 50,786 | 139 | 0 | 26 | 15 | 98 | 1,012 | 224 | 716 | 72 | 18 |
| Stilwell | 4,014 | 30 | 1 | 2 | 2 | 25 | 167 | 39 | 103 | 25 | 5 |
| Stratford | 1,522 | 1 | 0 | 1 | 0 | 0 | 20 | 2 | 10 | 8 | 0 |
| Stringtown | 406 | 1 | 0 | 0 | 0 | 1 | 2 | 0 | 1 | 1 | 0 |
| Stroud | 2,705 | 7 | 0 | 1 | 0 | 6 | 72 | 25 | 38 | 9 | 1 |
| Sulphur | 4,995 | 19 | 0 | 0 | 0 | 19 | 87 | 16 | 62 | 9 | 0 |
| Tahlequah | 17,126 | 35 | 0 | 1 | 3 | 31 | 196 | 27 | 154 | 15 | 0 |
| Talala | 270 | 1 | 0 | 0 | 0 | 1 | 1 | 0 | 1 | 0 | 0 |
| Talihina | 1,074 | 1 | 0 | 0 | 0 | 1 | 29 | 16 | 12 | 1 | 1 |
| Tecumseh | 6,656 | 26 | 0 | 4 | 0 | 22 | 156 | 32 | 105 | 19 | 1 |
| Texhoma | 900 | 1 | 0 | 0 | 0 | 1 | 5 | 0 | 3 | 2 | 1 |
| Thackerville | 527 | 0 | 0 | 0 | 0 | 0 | 3 | 0 | 3 | 0 | 0 |
| The Village | 9,709 | 18 | 0 | 3 | 5 | 10 | 188 | 23 | 146 | 19 | 1 |
| Thomas | 1,178 | 0 | 0 | 0 | 0 | 0 | 4 | 1 | 3 | 0 | 0 |
| Tipton | 747 | 2 | 0 | 0 | 0 | 2 | 12 | 8 | 4 | 0 | 0 |
| Tishomingo | 2,992 | 6 | 0 | 0 | 0 | 6 | 40 | 17 | 16 | 7 | 0 |
| Tonkawa | 2,934 | 10 | 0 | 3 | 0 | 7 | 54 | 20 | 34 | 0 | 0 |
| Tulsa | 404,255 | 4,474 | 59 | 374 | 592 | 3,449 | 20,120 | 4,057 | 11,809 | 4,254 | 103 |
| Tupelo | 306 | 1 | 0 | 0 | 0 | 1 | 0 | 0 | 0 | 0 | 0 |
| Tushka | 395 | 3 | 0 | 3 | 0 | 0 | 7 | 2 | 5 | 0 | 0 |
| Tuttle | 7,796 | 8 | 0 | 3 | 1 | 4 | 69 | 7 | 49 | 13 | 2 |
| Tyrone | 741 | 1 | 0 | 0 | 0 | 1 | 5 | 5 | 0 | 0 | 0 |
| Union City | 2,273 | 3 | 0 | 1 | 0 | 2 | 21 | 6 | 12 | 3 | 1 |
| Valley Brook | 767 | 10 | 0 | 0 | 2 | 8 | 25 | 6 | 14 | 5 | 0 |
| Valliant | 740 | 0 | 0 | 0 | 0 | 0 | 6 | 1 | 5 | 0 | 0 |
| Velma | 593 | 1 | 0 | 1 | 0 | 0 | 3 | 1 | 0 | 2 | 0 |
| Verden | 537 | 2 | 0 | 0 | 0 | 2 | 13 | 6 | 4 | 3 | 0 |
| Verdigris | 4,810 | 5 | 0 | 2 | 1 | 2 | 42 | 3 | 29 | 10 | 0 |
| Vian | 1,345 | 4 | 0 | 0 | 1 | 3 | 34 | 7 | 25 | 2 | 1 |
| Vici | 685 | 0 | 0 | 0 | 0 | 0 | 2 | 0 | 2 | 0 | 0 |
| Vinita | 5,264 | 22 | 0 | 10 | 2 | 10 | 86 | 26 | 43 | 17 | 0 |
| Wagoner | 9,479 | 32 | 1 | 6 | 3 | 22 | 237 | 65 | 153 | 19 | 2 |
| Wakita | 326 | 0 | 0 | 0 | 0 | 0 | 0 | 0 | 0 | 0 | 0 |
| Walters | 2,336 | 1 | 0 | 0 | 0 | 1 | 39 | 12 | 21 | 6 | 1 |
| Warner | 1,570 | 1 | 0 | 0 | 0 | 1 | 24 | 6 | 14 | 4 | 1 |
| Washington | 605 | 0 | 0 | 0 | 0 | 0 | 3 | 1 | 1 | 1 | 0 |
| Watonga | 2,823 | 5 | 0 | 0 | 0 | 5 | 53 | 11 | 32 | 10 | 0 |
| Watts | 305 | 1 | 0 | 0 | 0 | 1 | 4 | 0 | 2 | 2 | 0 |
| Waukomis | 1,290 | 2 | 0 | 0 | 0 | 2 | 20 | 2 | 14 | 4 | 0 |
| Waurika | 1,847 | 13 | 0 | 0 | 0 | 13 | 30 | 13 | 15 | 2 | 0 |
| Waynoka | 899 | 0 | 0 | 0 | 0 | 0 | 8 | 0 | 6 | 2 | 0 |
| Weatherford | 12,013 | 10 | 0 | 5 | 0 | 5 | 143 | 24 | 108 | 11 | 0 |
| Webbers Falls | 588 | 1 | 0 | 0 | 0 | 1 | 7 | 2 | 4 | 1 | 0 |
| Weleetka | 931 | 5 | 0 | 0 | 1 | 4 | 13 | 3 | 7 | 3 | 0 |
| Wellston | 776 | 0 | 0 | 0 | 0 | 0 | 12 | 2 | 6 | 4 | 0 |
| West Siloam Springs | 861 | 1 | 0 | 0 | 0 | 1 | 54 | 4 | 40 | 10 | 0 |
| Westville | 1,523 | 3 | 0 | 0 | 0 | 3 | 34 | 4 | 22 | 8 | 0 |
| Wetumka | 1,177 | 8 | 0 | 2 | 1 | 5 | 42 | 13 | 23 | 6 | 4 |
| Wewoka | 3,198 | 3 | 0 | 1 | 0 | 2 | 73 | 17 | 36 | 20 | 1 |
| Wilburton | 2,542 | 4 | 0 | 1 | 0 | 3 | 45 | 9 | 29 | 7 | 1 |
| Wilson | 1,705 | 11 | 0 | 1 | 0 | 10 | 18 | 7 | 6 | 5 | 1 |
| Wister | 1,060 | 2 | 0 | 0 | 0 | 2 | 13 | 5 | 8 | 0 | 0 |
| Woodward | 11,871 | 26 | 1 | 7 | 2 | 16 | 387 | 138 | 225 | 24 | 5 |
| Wyandotte | 321 | 0 | 0 | 0 | 0 | 0 | 4 | 1 | 3 | 0 | 0 |
| Wynnewood | 2,203 | 7 | 0 | 0 | 0 | 7 | 13 | 2 | 10 | 1 | 0 |
| Wynona | 434 | 0 | 0 | 0 | 0 | 0 | 0 | 0 | 0 | 0 | 0 |
| Yale | 1,211 | 10 | 0 | 7 | 1 | 2 | 29 | 7 | 18 | 4 | 4 |
| Yukon | 29,467 | 53 | 0 | 10 | 0 | 43 | 662 | 175 | 463 | 24 | 0 |
| **OREGON** | | | | | | | | | | | |
| Albany | 56,746 | 99 | 2 | 10 | 28 | 59 | 1,293 | 119 | 1,048 | 126 | 31 |
| Ashland | 21,308 | 48 | 0 | 6 | 15 | 27 | 541 | 38 | 469 | 34 | 4 |
| Astoria | 10,086 | 61 | 0 | 13 | 9 | 39 | 297 | 70 | 207 | 20 | 5 |
| Baker City | 9,882 | 16 | 0 | 4 | 3 | 9 | 290 | 77 | 197 | 16 | 6 |
| Bandon | 3,181 | 2 | 0 | 0 | 0 | 2 | 35 | 3 | 27 | 5 | 0 |
| Banks | 2,058 | 4 | 0 | 1 | 1 | 2 | 25 | 3 | 18 | 4 | 2 |
| Beaverton | 99,886 | 249 | 1 | 51 | 55 | 142 | 2,359 | 287 | 1,713 | 359 | 22 |
| Bend | 104,833 | 182 | 2 | 23 | 27 | 130 | 1,629 | 157 | 1,327 | 145 | 28 |
| Boardman | 3,855 | 11 | 0 | 0 | 0 | 11 | 57 | 12 | 38 | 7 | 4 |
| Brookings | 6,583 | 21 | 0 | 8 | 1 | 12 | 63 | 6 | 49 | 8 | 2 |

# Table 8. Offenses Known to Law Enforcement, by Selected State and City, 2021—Continued

(Number.)

| State/city | Population | Violent crime | Murder and nonnegligent manslaughter | Rape | Robbery | Aggravated assault | Property crime | Burglary | Larceny-theft | Motor vehicle theft | Arson |
|---|---|---|---|---|---|---|---|---|---|---|---|
| Canby | 18,161 | 37 | 0 | 9 | 6 | 22 | 192 | 24 | 149 | 19 | 2 |
| Carlton | 2,204 | 3 | 0 | 3 | 0 | 0 | 29 | 5 | 21 | 3 | 0 |
| Central Point | 19,313 | 22 | 0 | 6 | 3 | 13 | 296 | 26 | 250 | 20 | 2 |
| Coos Bay | 16,378 | 82 | 0 | 8 | 8 | 66 | 727 | 142 | 527 | 58 | 6 |
| Cornelius | 13,241 | 44 | 2 | 9 | 6 | 27 | 216 | 21 | 177 | 18 | 6 |
| Corvallis | 59,585 | 130 | 0 | 22 | 35 | 73 | 2,195 | 265 | 1,815 | 115 | 26 |
| Cottage Grove | 10,606 | 28 | 1 | 4 | 4 | 19 | 103 | 5 | 78 | 20 | 1 |
| Dallas | 17,630 | 38 | 0 | 8 | 1 | 29 | 427 | 41 | 366 | 20 | 4 |
| Eagle Point | 9,782 | 12 | 0 | 2 | 2 | 8 | 112 | 10 | 95 | 7 | 0 |
| Enterprise | 1,999 | 0 | 0 | 0 | 0 | 0 | 15 | 3 | 11 | 1 | 0 |
| Eugene | 175,007 | 714 | 3 | 114 | 165 | 432 | 6,478 | 1,037 | 4,670 | 771 | 172 |
| Florence | 9,285 | 2 | 0 | 0 | 1 | 1 | 249 | 24 | 205 | 20 | 10 |
| Forest Grove | 25,890 | 76 | 0 | 15 | 7 | 54 | 380 | 50 | 265 | 65 | 7 |
| Gervais | 2,805 | 8 | 0 | 2 | 0 | 6 | 25 | 2 | 20 | 3 | 1 |
| Gladstone | 12,506 | 32 | 0 | 14 | 5 | 13 | 270 | 26 | 179 | 65 | 3 |
| Grants Pass | 38,672 | 130 | 1 | 15 | 32 | 82 | 1,167 | 117 | 860 | 190 | 20 |
| Gresham | 110,448 | 500 | 14 | 57 | 100 | 329 | 3,258 | 470 | 1,773 | 1,015 | 33 |
| Hermiston | 17,898 | 49 | 1 | 4 | 12 | 32 | 507 | 71 | 394 | 42 | 5 |
| Hillsboro | 113,053 | 274 | 6 | 38 | 57 | 173 | 2,266 | 216 | 1,786 | 264 | 38 |
| Hines | 1,534 | 1 | 0 | 0 | 0 | 1 | 21 | 0 | 21 | 0 | 0 |
| Hood River | 7,848 | 10 | 0 | 2 | 0 | 8 | 315 | 20 | 240 | 55 | 3 |
| Hubbard | 3,639 | 0 | 0 | 0 | 0 | 0 | 29 | 2 | 20 | 7 | 1 |
| Independence | 11,129 | 15 | 0 | 2 | 2 | 11 | 149 | 18 | 112 | 19 | 1 |
| Jacksonville | 2,875 | 1 | 0 | 0 | 0 | 1 | 27 | 3 | 22 | 2 | 1 |
| Junction City | 6,303 | 11 | 0 | 1 | 2 | 8 | 130 | 18 | 99 | 13 | 0 |
| Keizer | 39,913 | 93 | 0 | 12 | 13 | 68 | 704 | 62 | 566 | 76 | 6 |
| King City | 4,446 | 3 | 0 | 1 | 0 | 2 | 37 | 3 | 26 | 8 | 1 |
| Klamath Falls | 22,960 | 169 | 2 | 15 | 24 | 128 | 694 | 93 | 421 | 180 | 17 |
| La Grande | 13,431 | 34 | 0 | 9 | 3 | 22 | 308 | 67 | 215 | 26 | 1 |
| Lake Oswego | 40,138 | 36 | 0 | 10 | 8 | 18 | 634 | 93 | 478 | 63 | 4 |
| Lebanon | 17,772 | 32 | 1 | 3 | 3 | 25 | 272 | 9 | 222 | 41 | 4 |
| Lincoln City | 9,391 | 70 | 0 | 7 | 3 | 60 | 297 | 49 | 220 | 28 | 1 |
| Malin | 841 | 0 | 0 | 0 | 0 | 0 | 0 | 0 | 0 | 0 | 0 |
| McMinnville | 35,498 | 84 | 0 | 16 | 8 | 60 | 704 | 98 | 557 | 49 | 17 |
| Medford | 84,297 | 275 | 6 | 47 | 60 | 162 | 2,707 | 202 | 2,292 | 213 | 33 |
| Milton-Freewater | 7,050 | 20 | 0 | 3 | 2 | 15 | 77 | 8 | 56 | 13 | 2 |
| Milwaukie | 21,094 | 28 | 0 | 11 | 3 | 14 | 236 | 20 | 145 | 71 | 0 |
| Molalla | 9,383 | 14 | 0 | 3 | 1 | 10 | 97 | 13 | 76 | 8 | 2 |
| Monmouth | 10,728 | 13 | 2 | 1 | 0 | 10 | 113 | 9 | 97 | 7 | 2 |
| Mount Angel | 3,677 | 5 | 0 | 2 | 0 | 3 | 17 | 3 | 12 | 2 | 1 |
| Myrtle Creek | 3,495 | 7 | 0 | 0 | 0 | 7 | 65 | 7 | 47 | 11 | 0 |
| Newberg-Dundee | 24,168 | 50 | 0 | 11 | 4 | 35 | 334 | 27 | 281 | 26 | 7 |
| Newport | 11,247 | 44 | 0 | 6 | 4 | 34 | 364 | 43 | 297 | 24 | 8 |
| North Bend | 9,751 | 11 | 1 | 1 | 2 | 7 | 237 | 28 | 189 | 20 | 4 |
| North Plains | 2,219 | 1 | 0 | 0 | 0 | 1 | 43 | 8 | 26 | 9 | 0 |
| Oregon City | 38,602 | 87 | 0 | 11 | 9 | 67 | 695 | 81 | 516 | 98 | 13 |
| Philomath | 5,742 | 4 | 1 | 1 | 0 | 2 | 58 | 6 | 48 | 4 | 2 |
| Phoenix | 4,705 | 7 | 0 | 3 | 0 | 4 | 173 | 5 | 161 | 7 | 1 |
| Portland | 664,350 | 4,785 | 83 | 326 | 1,111 | 3,265 | 37,049 | 4,430 | 23,612 | 9,007 | 310 |
| Prineville | 11,541 | 40 | 0 | 7 | 0 | 33 | 127 | 8 | 111 | 8 | 0 |
| Rainier | 2,032 | 1 | 0 | 0 | 0 | 1 | 68 | 6 | 49 | 13 | 1 |
| Redmond | 35,230 | 78 | 1 | 18 | 10 | 49 | 865 | 63 | 695 | 107 | 12 |
| Reedsport | 4,101 | 13 | 0 | 1 | 0 | 12 | 109 | 8 | 94 | 7 | 0 |
| Rogue River | 2,363 | 0 | 0 | 0 | 0 | 0 | 40 | 4 | 33 | 3 | 2 |
| Roseburg | 23,564 | 100 | 4 | 16 | 14 | 66 | 1,196 | 118 | 973 | 105 | 18 |
| Salem | 178,106 | 814 | 8 | 28 | 167 | 611 | 6,408 | 705 | 4,643 | 1,060 | 135 |
| Scappoose | 7,715 | 18 | 0 | 1 | 1 | 16 | 119 | 10 | 88 | 21 | 0 |
| Sherwood | 19,882 | 23 | 0 | 8 | 2 | 13 | 335 | 16 | 300 | 19 | 0 |
| Silverton | 10,764 | 12 | 0 | 3 | 1 | 8 | 191 | 20 | 140 | 31 | 10 |
| Springfield | 63,599 | • 180 | 0 | 2 | 32 | 28 | 118 | 1,656 | 194 | 1,290 | 172 | 27 |
| Stanfield | 2,113 | 3 | 0 | 0 | 0 | 3 | 37 | 17 | 19 | 1 | 0 |
| Stayton | 8,314 | 15 | 1 | 2 | 2 | 10 | 207 | 20 | 157 | 30 | 2 |
| St. Helens | 14,178 | 40 | 0 | 8 | 3 | 29 | 180 | 35 | 109 | 36 | 0 |
| Sutherlin | 8,267 | 34 | 0 | 3 | 1 | 30 | 216 | 24 | 171 | 21 | 7 |
| Sweet Home | 10,136 | 32 | 0 | 5 | 1 | 26 | 311 | 33 | 255 | 23 | 7 |
| Talent | 6,767 | 6 | 0 | 1 | 0 | 5 | 63 | 4 | 55 | 4 | 0 |
| The Dalles | 15,643 | 42 | 0 | 12 | 8 | 22 | 555 | 83 | 401 | 71 | 4 |
| Tigard | 56,914 | 156 | 4 | 25 | 36 | 91 | 1,545 | 174 | 1,214 | 157 | 3 |
| Tillamook | 5,480 | 8 | 0 | 2 | 0 | 6 | 137 | 16 | 113 | 8 | 5 |
| Tualatin | 27,617 | 75 | 0 | 8 | 17 | 50 | 910 | 115 | 673 | 122 | 5 |
| Vernonia | 2,309 | 2 | 0 | 0 | 0 | 2 | 7 | 1 | 5 | 1 | 0 |
| Warrenton | 5,815 | 16 | 0 | 1 | 6 | 9 | 227 | 10 | 209 | 8 | 1 |
| West Linn | 26,908 | 19 | 0 | 4 | 3 | 12 | 339 | 45 | 263 | 31 | 1 |
| Winston | 5,558 | 7 | 0 | 1 | 0 | 6 | 118 | 25 | 83 | 10 | 2 |
| Woodburn | 26,386 | 111 | 0 | 21 | 23 | 67 | 785 | 87 | 534 | 164 | 5 |
| | | | | | | | | | | | |
| **PENNSYLVANIA[1]** | | | | | | | | | | | |
| Bellevue | 7,944 | 9 | 0 | 0 | 6 | 3 | 86 | 11 | 66 | 9 | 0 |
| Camp Hill | 7,921 | 3 | 0 | 0 | 0 | 3 | 42 | 0 | 39 | 3 | 0 |
| Carlisle | 19,260 | 27 | 2 | 5 | 5 | 15 | 350 | 24 | 322 | 4 | 5 |
| Carroll Valley | 3,935 | 2 | 0 | 1 | 1 | 0 | 27 | 2 | 23 | 2 | 0 |
| East Earl Township | 6,938 | 1 | 0 | 0 | 0 | 1 | 47 | 4 | 40 | 3 | 0 |
| East Pennsboro Township | 21,595 | 15 | 2 | 3 | 1 | 9 | 112 | 6 | 101 | 5 | 0 |

## Table 8. Offenses Known to Law Enforcement, by Selected State and City, 2021—Continued

(Number.)

| State/city | Population | Violent crime | Murder and nonnegligent manslaughter | Rape | Robbery | Aggravated assault | Property crime | Burglary | Larceny-theft | Motor vehicle theft | Arson |
|---|---|---|---|---|---|---|---|---|---|---|---|
| Economy | 9,024 | 2 | 0 | 0 | 1 | 1 | 25 | 0 | 25 | 0 | 0 |
| Hampden Township | 32,134 | 11 | 0 | 3 | 4 | 4 | 133 | 17 | 111 | 5 | 0 |
| Jamestown | 563 | 0 | 0 | 0 | 0 | 0 | 2 | 1 | 1 | 0 | 0 |
| Liberty Township, Adams County | 1,270 | 0 | 0 | 0 | 0 | 0 | 5 | 0 | 4 | 1 | 0 |
| Mercersburg | 1,525 | 0 | 0 | 0 | 0 | 0 | 6 | 2 | 4 | 0 | 0 |
| Newville | 1,353 | 0 | 0 | 0 | 0 | 0 | 1 | 0 | 1 | 0 | 0 |
| Penbrook | 2,974 | 8 | 1 | 2 | 0 | 5 | 32 | 9 | 16 | 7 | 0 |
| Ross Township | 30,289 | 19 | 0 | 8 | 5 | 6 | 325 | 9 | 306 | 10 | 0 |
| Scranton | 76,580 | 288 | 1 | 90 | 29 | 168 | 1,040 | 171 | 724 | 145 | 19 |
| Shaler Township | 27,412 | 11 | 0 | 1 | 5 | 5 | 207 | 16 | 177 | 14 | 0 |
| Shippensburg | 5,687 | 7 | 0 | 3 | 1 | 3 | 40 | 5 | 33 | 2 | 0 |
| Silver Spring Township | 19,326 | 11 | 0 | 6 | 2 | 3 | 96 | 5 | 86 | 5 | 0 |
| Upper Allen Township | 20,972 | 10 | 0 | 3 | 1 | 6 | 89 | 4 | 72 | 13 | 0 |
| Washington Township, Franklin County | 15,037 | 11 | 0 | 4 | 1 | 6 | 209 | 19 | 184 | 6 | 2 |
| Waynesboro | 10,939 | 16 | 1 | 2 | 1 | 12 | 120 | 14 | 100 | 6 | 1 |
| West Shore Regional | 7,707 | 7 | 1 | 0 | 2 | 4 | 43 | 8 | 27 | 8 | 0 |
| **RHODE ISLAND** | | | | | | | | | | | |
| Barrington | 16,566 | 9 | 0 | 6 | 0 | 3 | 125 | 8 | 113 | 4 | 0 |
| Bristol | 22,550 | 12 | 0 | 2 | 0 | 10 | 58 | 7 | 49 | 2 | 0 |
| Burrillville | 17,501 | 15 | 0 | 8 | 0 | 7 | 52 | 8 | 39 | 5 | 2 |
| Central Falls | 20,174 | 67 | 1 | 15 | 8 | 43 | 246 | 45 | 175 | 26 | 2 |
| Charlestown | 8,118 | 8 | 0 | 2 | 0 | 6 | 43 | 7 | 30 | 6 | 0 |
| Coventry | 36,216 | 41 | 0 | 8 | 3 | 30 | 294 | 33 | 245 | 16 | 7 |
| Cranston | 84,105 | 111 | 0 | 23 | 17 | 71 | 974 | 79 | 789 | 106 | 10 |
| Cumberland | 36,648 | 28 | 0 | 15 | 2 | 11 | 167 | 27 | 129 | 11 | 2 |
| East Greenwich | 13,617 | 7 | 0 | 4 | 1 | 2 | 90 | 7 | 76 | 7 | 0 |
| East Providence | 49,064 | 66 | 0 | 12 | 4 | 50 | 353 | 39 | 264 | 50 | 2 |
| Foster | 4,933 | 2 | 0 | 0 | 0 | 2 | 25 | 4 | 18 | 3 | 0 |
| Glocester | 10,788 | 5 | 0 | 0 | 0 | 5 | 16 | 4 | 12 | 0 | 0 |
| Hopkinton | 8,379 | 3 | 0 | 1 | 0 | 2 | 33 | 3 | 28 | 2 | 0 |
| Jamestown | 5,687 | 0 | 0 | 0 | 0 | 0 | 28 | 2 | 24 | 2 | 1 |
| Johnston | 30,476 | 26 | 0 | 13 | 4 | 9 | 372 | 44 | 285 | 43 | 4 |
| Lincoln | 22,823 | 34 | 2 | 4 | 2 | 26 | 224 | 26 | 181 | 17 | 1 |
| Little Compton | 3,584 | 6 | 0 | 0 | 0 | 6 | 22 | 2 | 20 | 0 | 0 |
| Middletown | 16,338 | 32 | 0 | 6 | 1 | 25 | 96 | 10 | 79 | 7 | 0 |
| Narragansett | 15,801 | 2 | 0 | 0 | 0 | 2 | 55 | 7 | 44 | 4 | 0 |
| Newport | 25,240 | 53 | 0 | 12 | 1 | 38 | 418 | 70 | 333 | 15 | 3 |
| North Kingstown | 27,192 | 12 | 0 | 5 | 0 | 7 | 154 | 17 | 132 | 5 | 1 |
| North Providence | 33,712 | 32 | 0 | 5 | 6 | 19 | 291 | 32 | 185 | 74 | 9 |
| North Smithfield | 13,093 | 4 | 0 | 0 | 0 | 4 | 115 | 3 | 104 | 8 | 0 |
| Pawtucket | 74,342 | 324 | 5 | 48 | 36 | 235 | 1,311 | 163 | 937 | 211 | 15 |
| Portsmouth | 17,696 | 13 | 0 | 4 | 0 | 9 | 60 | 14 | 41 | 5 | 3 |
| Providence | 185,868 | 745 | 22 | 77 | 145 | 501 | 4,693 | 510 | 3,489 | 694 | 6 |
| Richmond | 8,189 | 1 | 0 | 0 | 0 | 1 | 29 | 3 | 23 | 3 | 0 |
| Scituate | 11,148 | 5 | 0 | 0 | 1 | 4 | 16 | 2 | 11 | 3 | 0 |
| Smithfield | 22,676 | 8 | 0 | 5 | 2 | 1 | 163 | 8 | 133 | 22 | 0 |
| South Kingstown | 31,537 | 16 | 0 | 5 | 0 | 11 | 127 | 26 | 92 | 9 | 0 |
| Tiverton | 16,106 | 21 | 0 | 8 | 0 | 13 | 127 | 21 | 93 | 13 | 4 |
| Warren | 10,830 | 19 | 2 | 3 | 4 | 10 | 96 | 11 | 80 | 5 | 1 |
| Warwick | 83,968 | 66 | 0 | 33 | 4 | 29 | 1,012 | 69 | 867 | 76 | 9 |
| Westerly | 23,088 | 14 | 0 | 3 | 2 | 9 | 170 | 17 | 142 | 11 | 0 |
| West Greenwich | 6,680 | 2 | 0 | 0 | 0 | 2 | 33 | 1 | 27 | 5 | 0 |
| West Warwick | 29,964 | 58 | 1 | 16 | 7 | 34 | 208 | 45 | 139 | 24 | 2 |
| Woonsocket | 43,072 | 231 | 1 | 39 | 25 | 166 | 751 | 120 | 541 | 90 | 9 |
| **SOUTH CAROLINA** | | | | | | | | | | | |
| Abbeville | 4,932 | 36 | 0 | 2 | 3 | 31 | 135 | 50 | 75 | 10 | 0 |
| Aiken | 31,270 | 209 | 12 | 12 | 32 | 153 | 1,185 | 84 | 1,013 | 88 | 4 |
| Allendale | 2,773 | 47 | 2 | 1 | 6 | 38 | 71 | 19 | 45 | 7 | 0 |
| Anderson | 27,831 | 177 | 0 | 12 | 12 | 153 | 1,767 | 189 | 1,395 | 183 | 10 |
| Aynor | 1,036 | 1 | 0 | 1 | 0 | 0 | 9 | 0 | 8 | 1 | 0 |
| Bamberg | 3,120 | 36 | 0 | 2 | 1 | 33 | 150 | 22 | 123 | 5 | 1 |
| Barnwell | 4,213 | 27 | 0 | 2 | 0 | 25 | 165 | 35 | 120 | 10 | 0 |
| Batesburg-Leesville | 5,405 | 29 | 0 | 10 | 2 | 17 | 191 | 15 | 165 | 11 | 0 |
| Beaufort | 13,293 | 48 | 1 | 1 | 10 | 36 | 472 | 57 | 394 | 21 | 1 |
| Bennettsville | 7,301 | 69 | 1 | 5 | 8 | 55 | 189 | 26 | 156 | 7 | 2 |
| Bluffton | 30,519 | 24 | 1 | 3 | 4 | 16 | 223 | 37 | 163 | 23 | 0 |
| Branchville | 936 | 5 | 0 | 0 | 0 | 5 | 25 | 1 | 20 | 4 | 0 |
| Burnettown | 2,784 | 1 | 0 | 0 | 0 | 1 | 41 | 7 | 31 | 3 | 0 |
| Camden | 7,335 | 97 | 4 | 5 | 9 | 79 | 367 | 49 | 296 | 22 | 1 |
| Cayce | 14,088 | 135 | 2 | 8 | 9 | 116 | 623 | 92 | 469 | 62 | 1 |
| Charleston | 141,768 | 618 | 17 | 72 | 89 | 440 | 3,173 | 256 | 2,444 | 473 | 19 |
| Cheraw | 5,527 | 34 | 0 | 2 | 9 | 23 | 277 | 34 | 210 | 33 | 0 |
| Chesterfield | 1,394 | 8 | 2 | 1 | 1 | 4 | 28 | 6 | 19 | 3 | 0 |
| Clemson | 18,220 | 34 | 0 | 9 | 3 | 22 | 383 | 23 | 314 | 46 | 2 |
| Clinton | 8,288 | 95 | 1 | 11 | 6 | 77 | 379 | 52 | 303 | 24 | 2 |
| Clover | 6,992 | 13 | 0 | 2 | 2 | 9 | 72 | 5 | 58 | 9 | 1 |
| Columbia | 132,255 | 965 | 23 | 87 | 176 | 679 | 5,536 | 739 | 4,218 | 579 | 9 |
| Conway | 27,781 | 164 | 2 | 11 | 19 | 132 | 767 | 58 | 659 | 50 | 1 |
| Cowpens | 2,498 | 9 | 0 | 1 | 1 | 7 | 40 | 5 | 30 | 5 | 0 |

## Table 8. Offenses Known to Law Enforcement, by Selected State and City, 2021—Continued

(Number.)

| State/city | Population | Violent crime | Murder and nonnegligent manslaughter | Rape | Robbery | Aggravated assault | Property crime | Burglary | Larceny-theft | Motor vehicle theft | Arson |
|---|---|---|---|---|---|---|---|---|---|---|---|
| Darlington | 5,856 | 83 | 4 | 1 | 4 | 74 | 315 | 49 | 244 | 22 | 0 |
| Denmark | 2,847 | 36 | 2 | 0 | 6 | 28 | 66 | 22 | 41 | 3 | 1 |
| Duncan | 3,772 | 9 | 0 | 1 | 0 | 8 | 64 | 8 | 43 | 13 | 0 |
| Easley | 21,789 | 102 | 0 | 1 | 13 | 88 | 859 | 85 | 698 | 76 | 4 |
| Edisto Beach | 401 | 4 | 0 | 0 | 0 | 4 | 14 | 0 | 13 | 1 | 0 |
| Elgin | 1,613 | 11 | 0 | 0 | 1 | 10 | 76 | 2 | 72 | 2 | 0 |
| Florence | 38,521 | 526 | 5 | 25 | 41 | 455 | 2,073 | 235 | 1,680 | 158 | 8 |
| Forest Acres | 10,261 | 40 | 0 | 3 | 11 | 26 | 441 | 70 | 344 | 27 | 0 |
| Fort Mill | 26,923 | 19 | 0 | 3 | 1 | 15 | 166 | 11 | 139 | 16 | 2 |
| Fountain Inn | 11,306 | 40 | 0 | 5 | 7 | 28 | 252 | 39 | 181 | 32 | 1 |
| Gaston | 1,720 | 5 | 0 | 1 | 1 | 3 | 66 | 10 | 43 | 13 | 0 |
| Georgetown | 8,753 | 120 | 2 | 9 | 6 | 103 | 356 | 42 | 284 | 30 | 2 |
| Goose Creek | 45,901 | 128 | 5 | 20 | 20 | 83 | 783 | 89 | 623 | 71 | 4 |
| Greenville | 73,653 | 504 | 7 | 36 | 71 | 390 | 2,633 | 279 | 2,091 | 263 | 6 |
| Greenwood | 23,369 | 264 | 20 | 30 | 20 | 194 | 1,004 | 169 | 793 | 42 | 2 |
| Greer | 36,423 | 89 | 1 | 7 | 14 | 67 | 999 | 104 | 786 | 109 | 5 |
| Hampton | 2,459 | 22 | 1 | 0 | 0 | 21 | 94 | 25 | 63 | 6 | 0 |
| Hanahan | 29,582 | 76 | 1 | 10 | 16 | 49 | 381 | 27 | 304 | 50 | 1 |
| Hardeeville | 9,332 | 50 | 1 | 3 | 3 | 43 | 184 | 26 | 137 | 21 | 0 |
| Hartsville | 7,454 | 108 | 2 | 2 | 11 | 93 | 421 | 53 | 340 | 28 | 3 |
| Irmo | 12,902 | 37 | 0 | 3 | 2 | 32 | 385 | 71 | 285 | 29 | 1 |
| Isle of Palms | 4,395 | 12 | 0 | 5 | 0 | 7 | 85 | 4 | 68 | 13 | 1 |
| Iva | 1,352 | 6 | 0 | 2 | 0 | 4 | 45 | 13 | 29 | 3 | 0 |
| Jackson | 1,825 | 5 | 0 | 1 | 0 | 4 | 16 | 2 | 12 | 2 | 0 |
| Johnsonville | 1,470 | 3 | 1 | 0 | 0 | 2 | 20 | 2 | 14 | 4 | 0 |
| Kingstree | 2,958 | 15 | 0 | 0 | 2 | 13 | 116 | 19 | 89 | 8 | 0 |
| Latta | 1,263 | 7 | 0 | 0 | 1 | 6 | 48 | 5 | 39 | 4 | 0 |
| Laurens | 8,835 | 68 | 1 | 3 | 4 | 60 | 400 | 117 | 260 | 23 | 2 |
| Lexington | 23,161 | 64 | 0 | 7 | 7 | 50 | 560 | 63 | 463 | 34 | 2 |
| Liberty | 3,140 | 6 | 0 | 2 | 0 | 4 | 111 | 13 | 83 | 15 | 1 |
| Marion | 6,136 | 45 | 0 | 3 | 12 | 30 | 330 | 57 | 250 | 23 | 1 |
| Mauldin | 25,808 | 50 | 2 | 7 | 8 | 33 | 454 | 47 | 341 | 66 | 1 |
| McColl | 1,922 | 45 | 0 | 1 | 2 | 42 | 77 | 21 | 54 | 2 | 1 |
| McCormick | 2,279 | 11 | 0 | 0 | 1 | 10 | 40 | 4 | 33 | 3 | 0 |
| Moncks Corner | 13,108 | 69 | 4 | 4 | 6 | 55 | 343 | 28 | 290 | 25 | 0 |
| Mount Pleasant | 95,657 | 94 | 0 | 14 | 9 | 71 | 1,069 | 96 | 866 | 107 | 0 |
| Mullins | 4,092 | 41 | 1 | 0 | 3 | 37 | 113 | 25 | 81 | 7 | 2 |
| Myrtle Beach | 36,543 | 451 | 9 | 63 | 94 | 285 | 3,056 | 265 | 2,491 | 300 | 10 |
| Newberry | 10,119 | 75 | 1 | 10 | 5 | 59 | 292 | 52 | 224 | 16 | 0 |
| New Ellenton | 2,201 | 4 | 0 | 0 | 1 | 3 | 28 | 6 | 22 | 0 | 1 |
| Ninety Six | 2,043 | 9 | 0 | 1 | 0 | 8 | 39 | 8 | 30 | 1 | 1 |
| North Augusta | 24,435 | 48 | 4 | 9 | 12 | 23 | 564 | 54 | 469 | 41 | 0 |
| North Charleston | 121,060 | 1,227 | 35 | 74 | 256 | 862 | 6,068 | 568 | 4,752 | 748 | 14 |
| North Myrtle Beach | 17,648 | 101 | 1 | 17 | 6 | 77 | 1,020 | 115 | 813 | 92 | 4 |
| Orangeburg | 12,335 | 254 | 2 | 7 | 17 | 228 | 728 | 169 | 512 | 47 | 3 |
| Pamplico | 1,207 | 3 | 0 | 0 | 0 | 3 | 10 | 3 | 6 | 1 | 0 |
| Pelion | 714 | 6 | 0 | 0 | 2 | 4 | 32 | 6 | 25 | 1 | 0 |
| Pickens | 3,193 | 17 | 0 | 1 | 0 | 16 | 165 | 8 | 143 | 14 | 0 |
| Port Royal | 14,970 | 46 | 1 | 5 | 7 | 33 | 193 | 23 | 159 | 11 | 0 |
| Quinby | 912 | 0 | 0 | 0 | 0 | 0 | 3 | 0 | 1 | 2 | 0 |
| Ridgeland | 3,853 | 7 | 1 | 5 | 0 | 1 | 55 | 14 | 36 | 5 | 1 |
| Ridge Spring | 738 | 4 | 1 | 0 | 1 | 2 | 14 | 4 | 9 | 1 | 0 |
| Seneca | 8,611 | 51 | 0 | 5 | 3 | 43 | 187 | 24 | 144 | 19 | 1 |
| Simpsonville | 26,077 | 96 | 2 | 11 | 11 | 72 | 766 | 63 | 641 | 62 | 3 |
| Spartanburg | 37,375 | 584 | 8 | 26 | 77 | 473 | 2,348 | 520 | 1,624 | 204 | 8 |
| Springdale | 2,743 | 11 | 0 | 2 | 2 | 7 | 88 | 12 | 65 | 11 | 0 |
| Summerville | 54,438 | 133 | 0 | 15 | 12 | 106 | 1,068 | 100 | 870 | 98 | 0 |
| Sumter | 39,328 | 350 | 8 | 6 | 38 | 298 | 1,375 | 215 | 1,068 | 92 | 3 |
| Surfside Beach | 4,661 | 13 | 0 | 5 | 2 | 6 | 133 | 18 | 109 | 6 | 2 |
| Tega Cay | 12,178 | 7 | 0 | 0 | 1 | 6 | 170 | 11 | 155 | 4 | 0 |
| Timmonsville | 2,345 | 28 | 0 | 0 | 3 | 25 | 58 | 7 | 43 | 8 | 0 |
| Travelers Rest | 8,297 | 3 | 0 | 0 | 1 | 2 | 254 | 11 | 227 | 16 | 0 |
| Union | 7,458 | 55 | 1 | 8 | 2 | 44 | 399 | 65 | 311 | 23 | 3 |
| Walhalla | 4,484 | 3 | 0 | 0 | 0 | 3 | 49 | 5 | 42 | 2 | 0 |
| Walterboro | 5,303 | 67 | 5 | 2 | 4 | 56 | 346 | 22 | 299 | 25 | 2 |
| Ware Shoals | 2,150 | 25 | 0 | 1 | 4 | 20 | 112 | 24 | 79 | 9 | 1 |
| Wellford | 2,813 | 5 | 0 | 2 | 0 | 3 | 22 | 3 | 16 | 3 | 0 |
| West Columbia | 18,257 | 132 | 3 | 7 | 31 | 91 | 996 | 101 | 786 | 109 | 3 |
| Westminster | 2,614 | 21 | 1 | 0 | 2 | 18 | 82 | 17 | 63 | 2 | 0 |
| Williamston | 4,333 | 26 | 0 | 0 | 3 | 23 | 112 | 25 | 79 | 8 | 0 |
| Williston | 2,890 | 9 | 3 | 2 | 1 | 3 | 102 | 37 | 59 | 6 | 1 |
| York | 8,728 | 84 | 1 | 3 | 4 | 76 | 332 | 42 | 268 | 22 | 3 |
| **SOUTH DAKOTA** | | | | | | | | | | | |
| Alcester | 750 | 2 | 0 | 1 | 0 | 1 | 6 | 3 | 3 | 0 | 0 |
| Beresford | 2,046 | 4 | 0 | 1 | 0 | 3 | 17 | 2 | 14 | 1 | 0 |
| Box Elder | 10,876 | 63 | 1 | 12 | 7 | 43 | 231 | 45 | 159 | 27 | 1 |
| Brandon | 10,297 | 7 | 0 | 0 | 0 | 7 | 47 | 7 | 39 | 1 | 0 |
| Brookings | 25,088 | 27 | 0 | 5 | 2 | 20 | 169 | 26 | 135 | 8 | 0 |
| Canton | 3,635 | 6 | 0 | 0 | 0 | 6 | 35 | 7 | 24 | 4 | 0 |
| Deadwood | 1,294 | 6 | 0 | 0 | 0 | 6 | 31 | 2 | 29 | 0 | 0 |
| Flandreau | 2,288 | 14 | 0 | 2 | 0 | 12 | 35 | 4 | 28 | 3 | 0 |
| Hot Springs | 3,479 | 14 | 0 | 1 | 0 | 13 | 19 | 3 | 16 | 0 | 0 |

## Table 8. Offenses Known to Law Enforcement, by Selected State and City, 2021—Continued

(Number.)

| State/city | Population | Violent crime | Murder and nonnegligent manslaughter | Rape | Robbery | Aggravated assault | Property crime | Burglary | Larceny-theft | Motor vehicle theft | Arson |
|---|---|---|---|---|---|---|---|---|---|---|---|
| Huron | 13,504 | 48 | 0 | 5 | 0 | 43 | 169 | 13 | 144 | 12 | 0 |
| Lead | 2,929 | 11 | 0 | 0 | 0 | 11 | 38 | 9 | 23 | 6 | 0 |
| Madison | 7,120 | 8 | 0 | 0 | 0 | 8 | 29 | 5 | 22 | 2 | 1 |
| Martin | 1,057 | 14 | 0 | 4 | 0 | 10 | 34 | 14 | 16 | 4 | 1 |
| Mitchell | 15,741 | 70 | 0 | 28 | 1 | 41 | 335 | 56 | 250 | 29 | 0 |
| Mobridge | 3,364 | 7 | 0 | 0 | 0 | 7 | 17 | 6 | 10 | 1 | 0 |
| Pierre | 13,710 | 45 | 0 | 13 | 2 | 30 | 282 | 76 | 184 | 22 | 0 |
| Rapid City | 79,910 | 513 | 10 | 100 | 60 | 343 | 2,450 | 454 | 1,575 | 421 | 5 |
| Sioux Falls | 191,508 | 1,031 | 3 | 100 | 78 | 850 | 5,545 | 606 | 4,003 | 936 | 28 |
| Spearfish | 12,047 | 21 | 0 | 13 | 0 | 8 | 231 | 31 | 190 | 10 | 0 |
| Sturgis | 7,013 | 20 | 0 | 3 | 0 | 17 | 173 | 35 | 124 | 14 | 1 |
| Tea | 6,739 | 11 | 0 | 2 | 0 | 9 | 80 | 8 | 64 | 8 | 0 |
| Vermillion | 11,088 | 17 | 0 | 2 | 0 | 15 | 179 | 13 | 141 | 25 | 0 |
| Watertown | 22,383 | 50 | 0 | 17 | 1 | 32 | 301 | 35 | 243 | 23 | 0 |
| Winner | 2,773 | 7 | 0 | 1 | 0 | 6 | 45 | 4 | 34 | 7 | 0 |
| Yankton | 14,669 | 54 | 0 | 18 | 2 | 34 | 304 | 12 | 269 | 23 | 2 |
| **TENNESSEE** | | | | | | | | | | | |
| Adamsville | 2,159 | 5 | 0 | 0 | 0 | 5 | 5 | 0 | 4 | 1 | 0 |
| Alamo | 2,251 | 12 | 0 | 1 | 0 | 11 | 50 | 18 | 28 | 4 | 0 |
| Alcoa | 10,605 | 67 | 1 | 6 | 2 | 58 | 357 | 42 | 280 | 35 | 0 |
| Algood | 4,666 | 6 | 0 | 0 | 0 | 6 | 86 | 4 | 75 | 7 | 0 |
| Ashland City | 4,763 | 12 | 0 | 1 | 0 | 11 | 114 | 20 | 86 | 8 | 0 |
| Athens | 14,166 | 88 | 2 | 11 | 5 | 70 | 806 | 103 | 611 | 92 | 2 |
| Atoka | 9,859 | 14 | 0 | 0 | 0 | 14 | 68 | 13 | 52 | 3 | 2 |
| Baileyton | 459 | 1 | 0 | 0 | 0 | 1 | 8 | 1 | 4 | 3 | 0 |
| Bartlett | 59,562 | 191 | 0 | 17 | 21 | 153 | 870 | 97 | 694 | 79 | 5 |
| Baxter | 1,563 | 6 | 0 | 0 | 0 | 6 | 48 | 4 | 36 | 8 | 0 |
| Bean Station | 3,121 | 9 | 0 | 0 | 0 | 9 | 32 | 9 | 16 | 7 | 0 |
| Belle Meade | 2,777 | 1 | 0 | 0 | 0 | 1 | 13 | 1 | 11 | 1 | 0 |
| Bells | 2,431 | 9 | 0 | 1 | 0 | 8 | 12 | 4 | 6 | 2 | 0 |
| Benton | 1,235 | 4 | 0 | 0 | 0 | 4 | 27 | 4 | 19 | 4 | 0 |
| Berry Hill | 488 | 13 | 0 | 1 | 3 | 9 | 132 | 25 | 95 | 12 | 1 |
| Blaine | 1,871 | 2 | 0 | 0 | 0 | 2 | 21 | 5 | 16 | 0 | 0 |
| Bolivar | 4,798 | 97 | 1 | 2 | 3 | 91 | 99 | 21 | 69 | 9 | 1 |
| Brentwood | 43,490 | 31 | 1 | 3 | 5 | 22 | 384 | 78 | 282 | 24 | 1 |
| Bristol | 27,182 | 168 | 1 | 16 | 7 | 144 | 676 | 120 | 465 | 91 | 5 |
| Brownsville | 9,128 | 108 | 1 | 4 | 2 | 101 | 262 | 63 | 175 | 24 | 2 |
| Camden | 3,624 | 1 | 0 | 0 | 0 | 1 | 15 | 2 | 10 | 3 | 0 |
| Carthage | 2,335 | 15 | 0 | 0 | 0 | 15 | 23 | 1 | 21 | 1 | 0 |
| Centerville | 3,557 | 10 | 1 | 1 | 0 | 8 | 31 | 6 | 18 | 7 | 0 |
| Chapel Hill | 1,584 | 1 | 0 | 0 | 0 | 1 | 12 | 1 | 11 | 0 | 0 |
| Charleston | 712 | 1 | 0 | 0 | 0 | 1 | 10 | 2 | 7 | 1 | 0 |
| Chattanooga | 186,222 | 2,541 | 33 | 207 | 193 | 2,108 | 10,914 | 1,145 | 8,153 | 1,616 | 31 |
| Church Hill | 6,633 | 20 | 0 | 2 | 1 | 17 | 43 | 20 | 18 | 5 | 1 |
| Clarksville | 164,336 | 941 | 15 | 110 | 82 | 734 | 3,516 | 449 | 2,634 | 433 | 11 |
| Cleveland | 46,440 | 359 | 4 | 10 | 47 | 298 | 2,013 | 274 | 1,541 | 198 | 8 |
| Clinton | 10,157 | 44 | 0 | 0 | 6 | 38 | 198 | 28 | 152 | 18 | 0 |
| Collegedale | 11,737 | 13 | 0 | 0 | 0 | 13 | 185 | 19 | 155 | 11 | 0 |
| Collierville | 52,059 | 64 | 1 | 5 | 4 | 54 | 610 | 66 | 487 | 57 | 1 |
| Columbia | 42,613 | 290 | 2 | 15 | 20 | 253 | 1,088 | 166 | 779 | 143 | 4 |
| Cookeville | 35,471 | 128 | 0 | 19 | 10 | 99 | 976 | 90 | 764 | 122 | 3 |
| Coopertown | 4,647 | 5 | 0 | 1 | 0 | 4 | 30 | 8 | 20 | 2 | 0 |
| Covington | 8,791 | 95 | 2 | 4 | 4 | 85 | 228 | 56 | 151 | 21 | 2 |
| Cowan | 1,662 | 3 | 0 | 0 | 0 | 3 | 17 | 0 | 14 | 3 | 0 |
| Crossville | 12,007 | 71 | 0 | 7 | 4 | 60 | 458 | 82 | 340 | 36 | 3 |
| Dandridge | 3,204 | 16 | 0 | 0 | 1 | 15 | 71 | 8 | 50 | 13 | 1 |
| Dayton | 7,338 | 10 | 0 | 0 | 1 | 9 | 104 | 16 | 77 | 11 | 1 |
| Decatur | 1,665 | 7 | 0 | 1 | 0 | 6 | 37 | 3 | 25 | 9 | 0 |
| Decherd | 2,375 | 21 | 0 | 4 | 0 | 17 | 76 | 17 | 51 | 8 | 0 |
| Dickson | 15,634 | 123 | 0 | 16 | 0 | 107 | 409 | 45 | 332 | 32 | 0 |
| Dover | 1,596 | 2 | 0 | 0 | 0 | 2 | 7 | 2 | 4 | 1 | 0 |
| Dunlap | 5,278 | 16 | 0 | 2 | 0 | 14 | 86 | 15 | 59 | 12 | 2 |
| Dyer | 2,192 | 12 | 0 | 2 | 0 | 10 | 25 | 4 | 18 | 3 | 0 |
| Dyersburg | 15,981 | 210 | 4 | 12 | 15 | 179 | 809 | 210 | 527 | 72 | 4 |
| East Ridge | 21,225 | 139 | 0 | 8 | 11 | 120 | 505 | 69 | 373 | 63 | 2 |
| Elizabethton | 13,406 | 52 | 0 | 2 | 1 | 49 | 443 | 64 | 316 | 63 | 2 |
| Erin | 1,304 | 1 | 0 | 0 | 0 | 1 | 10 | 7 | 1 | 2 | 0 |
| Estill Springs | 2,042 | 12 | 0 | 0 | 0 | 12 | 19 | 4 | 12 | 3 | 1 |
| Etowah | 3,530 | 23 | 0 | 2 | 0 | 21 | 72 | 4 | 56 | 12 | 3 |
| Fairview | 9,794 | 25 | 0 | 7 | 3 | 15 | 104 | 10 | 86 | 8 | 0 |
| Fayetteville | 7,033 | 70 | 1 | 2 | 6 | 61 | 208 | 32 | 159 | 17 | 2 |
| Franklin | 87,969 | 145 | 1 | 14 | 5 | 125 | 673 | 45 | 575 | 53 | 2 |
| Gallatin | 46,031 | 129 | 2 | 14 | 11 | 102 | 313 | 34 | 237 | 42 | 1 |
| Gatlinburg | 3,759 | 25 | 0 | 1 | 0 | 24 | 129 | 8 | 106 | 15 | 0 |
| Germantown | 39,217 | 56 | 0 | 5 | 4 | 47 | 549 | 24 | 488 | 37 | 2 |
| Goodlettsville | 16,818 | 77 | 1 | 4 | 14 | 58 | 311 | 26 | 238 | 47 | 2 |
| Greenbrier | 6,949 | 23 | 0 | 2 | 0 | 21 | 69 | 31 | 32 | 6 | 1 |
| Greeneville | 14,930 | 63 | 0 | 4 | 4 | 55 | 470 | 46 | 356 | 68 | 0 |
| Halls | 2,021 | 13 | 0 | 0 | 0 | 13 | 40 | 16 | 23 | 1 | 1 |
| Harriman | 6,167 | 20 | 0 | 2 | 0 | 18 | 107 | 16 | 72 | 19 | 0 |
| Henderson | 6,427 | 23 | 1 | 3 | 0 | 19 | 68 | 17 | 50 | 1 | 0 |
| Hendersonville | 60,170 | 45 | 0 | 6 | 3 | 36 | 407 | 56 | 322 | 29 | 1 |

## Table 8. Offenses Known to Law Enforcement, by Selected State and City, 2021—Continued

(Number.)

| State/city | Population | Violent crime | Murder and nonnegligent manslaughter | Rape | Robbery | Aggravated assault | Property crime | Burglary | Larceny-theft | Motor vehicle theft | Arson |
|---|---|---|---|---|---|---|---|---|---|---|---|
| Hohenwald | 3,992 | 28 | 0 | 0 | 0 | 28 | 55 | 3 | 44 | 8 | 0 |
| Humboldt | 8,092 | 82 | 2 | 4 | 3 | 73 | 205 | 36 | 149 | 20 | 0 |
| Huntingdon | 3,820 | 6 | 0 | 0 | 0 | 6 | 75 | 20 | 55 | 0 | 0 |
| Jacksboro | 2,069 | 6 | 0 | 1 | 0 | 5 | 67 | 3 | 60 | 4 | 0 |
| Jackson | 67,462 | 647 | 11 | 41 | 50 | 545 | 1,951 | 248 | 1,475 | 228 | 10 |
| Jamestown | 2,149 | 4 | 0 | 0 | 0 | 4 | 26 | 5 | 18 | 3 | 0 |
| Jasper | 3,419 | 5 | 0 | 0 | 0 | 5 | 35 | 2 | 25 | 8 | 1 |
| Jefferson City | 8,234 | 22 | 0 | 2 | 2 | 18 | 142 | 23 | 108 | 11 | 0 |
| Johnson City | 67,515 | 249 | 5 | 28 | 37 | 179 | 2,237 | 245 | 1,774 | 218 | 12 |
| Jonesborough | 5,840 | 12 | 0 | 0 | 1 | 11 | 88 | 9 | 60 | 19 | 1 |
| Kenton | 1,181 | 5 | 0 | 1 | 0 | 4 | 23 | 4 | 19 | 0 | 1 |
| Kimball | 1,457 | 5 | 0 | 0 | 0 | 5 | 77 | 4 | 67 | 6 | 0 |
| Kingsport | 54,229 | 413 | 2 | 24 | 31 | 356 | 2,102 | 261 | 1,532 | 309 | 10 |
| Kingston | 5,956 | 4 | 0 | 1 | 2 | 1 | 25 | 3 | 16 | 6 | 0 |
| Knoxville | 191,463 | 1,587 | 35 | 138 | 171 | 1,243 | 7,737 | 969 | 5,644 | 1,124 | 13 |
| Lafayette | 5,351 | 15 | 0 | 0 | 0 | 15 | 102 | 16 | 79 | 7 | 0 |
| La Follette | 6,502 | 19 | 0 | 2 | 0 | 17 | 154 | 36 | 94 | 24 | 2 |
| La Vergne | 35,954 | 142 | 0 | 9 | 13 | 120 | 523 | 49 | 418 | 56 | 1 |
| Lawrenceburg | 11,122 | 40 | 1 | 4 | 0 | 35 | 241 | 55 | 163 | 23 | 1 |
| Lebanon | 39,524 | 176 | 4 | 21 | 16 | 135 | 727 | 115 | 541 | 71 | 4 |
| Lenoir City | 9,401 | 56 | 1 | 1 | 2 | 52 | 250 | 25 | 209 | 16 | 2 |
| Lewisburg | 12,712 | 94 | 1 | 5 | 3 | 85 | 197 | 29 | 145 | 23 | 0 |
| Lexington | 7,888 | 52 | 1 | 10 | 4 | 37 | 181 | 16 | 144 | 21 | 2 |
| Livingston | 4,135 | 17 | 0 | 2 | 1 | 14 | 63 | 10 | 43 | 10 | 1 |
| Loudon | 6,079 | 1 | 0 | 1 | 0 | 0 | 56 | 5 | 49 | 2 | 0 |
| Madisonville | 5,056 | 26 | 0 | 2 | 0 | 24 | 163 | 29 | 120 | 14 | 0 |
| Manchester | 11,383 | 81 | 0 | 3 | 2 | 76 | 356 | 77 | 253 | 26 | 0 |
| Martin | 10,480 | 39 | 1 | 1 | 4 | 33 | 179 | 16 | 144 | 19 | 0 |
| Maryville | 30,262 | 60 | 0 | 9 | 1 | 50 | 271 | 33 | 214 | 24 | 1 |
| McKenzie | 5,309 | 15 | 0 | 2 | 2 | 11 | 96 | 30 | 54 | 12 | 1 |
| McMinnville | 13,790 | 118 | 2 | 22 | 4 | 90 | 341 | 42 | 267 | 32 | 4 |
| Medina | 4,465 | 11 | 0 | 0 | 0 | 11 | 24 | 5 | 18 | 1 | 0 |
| Memphis | 649,444 | 15,785 | 306 | 403 | 2,056 | 13,020 | 34,284 | 5,294 | 24,020 | 4,970 | 367 |
| Metropolitan Nashville Police Department | 690,553 | 8,057 | 99 | 404 | 1,591 | 5,963 | 24,943 | 3,429 | 18,657 | 2,857 | 76 |
| Milan | 7,583 | 51 | 1 | 5 | 1 | 44 | 168 | 39 | 118 | 11 | 0 |
| Millersville | 6,839 | 8 | 0 | 3 | 0 | 5 | 28 | 2 | 18 | 8 | 1 |
| Millington | 10,621 | 125 | 3 | 7 | 9 | 106 | 461 | 59 | 335 | 67 | 3 |
| Monteagle | 1,236 | 5 | 0 | 0 | 0 | 5 | 40 | 6 | 28 | 6 | 0 |
| Monterey | 2,895 | 10 | 0 | 0 | 0 | 10 | 60 | 13 | 38 | 9 | 0 |
| Morristown | 30,413 | 227 | 1 | 16 | 19 | 191 | 1,078 | 110 | 858 | 110 | 2 |
| Mountain City | 2,437 | 8 | 0 | 0 | 0 | 8 | 24 | 4 | 17 | 3 | 0 |
| Mount Carmel | 5,242 | 3 | 0 | 0 | 0 | 3 | 30 | 4 | 24 | 2 | 0 |
| Mount Juliet | 40,233 | 43 | 0 | 3 | 1 | 39 | 378 | 28 | 331 | 19 | 0 |
| Mount Pleasant | 5,014 | 24 | 0 | 2 | 1 | 21 | 74 | 19 | 44 | 11 | 1 |
| Munford | 6,233 | 21 | 0 | 2 | 0 | 19 | 32 | 9 | 20 | 3 | 0 |
| Murfreesboro | 155,652 | 629 | 7 | 119 | 53 | 450 | 3,486 | 325 | 2,870 | 291 | 3 |
| Newbern | 3,222 | 14 | 0 | 1 | 1 | 12 | 79 | 11 | 60 | 8 | 1 |
| New Johnsonville | 1,866 | 2 | 0 | 1 | 0 | 1 | 7 | 0 | 7 | 0 | 0 |
| New Market | 1,385 | 2 | 0 | 0 | 1 | 1 | 7 | 1 | 4 | 2 | 0 |
| Newport | 6,894 | 78 | 1 | 8 | 3 | 66 | 431 | 27 | 370 | 34 | 1 |
| Nolensville | 11,866 | 10 | 0 | 2 | 0 | 8 | 36 | 9 | 27 | 0 | 0 |
| Oakland | 8,903 | 3 | 0 | 0 | 0 | 3 | 46 | 8 | 35 | 3 | 0 |
| Oak Ridge | 29,343 | 150 | 1 | 21 | 7 | 121 | 736 | 91 | 594 | 51 | 2 |
| Obion | 1,035 | 3 | 0 | 2 | 0 | 1 | 10 | 2 | 7 | 1 | 0 |
| Oliver Springs | 3,443 | 3 | 1 | 0 | 0 | 2 | 44 | 1 | 28 | 15 | 0 |
| Oneida | 3,696 | 27 | 1 | 0 | 0 | 26 | 106 | 14 | 80 | 12 | 0 |
| Paris | 9,934 | 33 | 0 | 0 | 0 | 33 | 189 | 27 | 152 | 10 | 1 |
| Parsons | 2,264 | 7 | 0 | 1 | 0 | 6 | 19 | 1 | 17 | 1 | 0 |
| Pigeon Forge | 6,276 | 61 | 1 | 8 | 2 | 50 | 320 | 42 | 235 | 43 | 1 |
| Portland | 13,493 | 42 | 0 | 5 | 0 | 37 | 124 | 13 | 96 | 15 | 3 |
| Pulaski | 7,494 | 43 | 0 | 4 | 1 | 38 | 277 | 52 | 209 | 16 | 1 |
| Red Bank | 11,904 | 38 | 0 | 6 | 1 | 31 | 174 | 27 | 125 | 22 | 0 |
| Ripley | 7,552 | 136 | 2 | 3 | 3 | 128 | 243 | 56 | 168 | 19 | 1 |
| Rockwood | 5,449 | 34 | 0 | 6 | 2 | 26 | 255 | 47 | 184 | 24 | 0 |
| Rogersville | 4,356 | 10 | 0 | 1 | 2 | 7 | 122 | 15 | 91 | 16 | 0 |
| Rutledge | 1,358 | 1 | 0 | 1 | 0 | 0 | 14 | 2 | 10 | 2 | 0 |
| Savannah | 6,907 | 64 | 1 | 3 | 2 | 58 | 292 | 47 | 223 | 22 | 1 |
| Selmer | 4,277 | 21 | 0 | 5 | 0 | 16 | 71 | 9 | 55 | 7 | 1 |
| Sevierville | 18,836 | 93 | 1 | 9 | 2 | 81 | 709 | 54 | 597 | 58 | 1 |
| Shelbyville | 22,534 | 150 | 3 | 9 | 8 | 130 | 578 | 77 | 439 | 62 | 4 |
| Smithville | 5,027 | 16 | 0 | 0 | 1 | 15 | 78 | 13 | 59 | 6 | 5 |
| Smyrna | 54,645 | 191 | 1 | 14 | 28 | 148 | 1,107 | 91 | 883 | 133 | 4 |
| Soddy-Daisy | 13,799 | 22 | 0 | 3 | 0 | 19 | 215 | 38 | 146 | 31 | 1 |
| Somerville | 3,262 | 35 | 1 | 1 | 0 | 33 | 58 | 17 | 40 | 1 | 0 |
| South Fulton | 2,193 | 6 | 0 | 1 | 0 | 5 | 43 | 15 | 19 | 9 | 0 |
| Sparta | 4,994 | 4 | 0 | 0 | 0 | 4 | 125 | 27 | 84 | 14 | 3 |
| Spencer | 1,720 | 4 | 0 | 0 | 0 | 4 | 5 | 1 | 4 | 0 | 0 |
| Spring City | 1,837 | 13 | 0 | 2 | 0 | 11 | 41 | 7 | 31 | 3 | 0 |
| Springfield | 17,374 | 90 | 5 | 4 | 2 | 79 | 264 | 40 | 189 | 35 | 0 |
| Spring Hill | 48,297 | 73 | 0 | 5 | 3 | 65 | 349 | 35 | 295 | 19 | 0 |
| Sweetwater | 5,971 | 41 | 0 | 0 | 2 | 39 | 170 | 32 | 122 | 16 | 0 |
| Tazewell | 2,279 | 19 | 1 | 0 | 2 | 16 | 46 | 12 | 27 | 7 | 0 |

## Table 8. Offenses Known to Law Enforcement, by Selected State and City, 2021—Continued

(Number.)

| State/city | Population | Violent crime | Murder and nonnegligent manslaughter | Rape | Robbery | Aggravated assault | Property crime | Burglary | Larceny-theft | Motor vehicle theft | Arson |
|---|---|---|---|---|---|---|---|---|---|---|---|
| Tiptonville | 3,939 | 8 | 0 | 0 | 1 | 7 | 25 | 5 | 17 | 3 | 0 |
| Tullahoma | 19,913 | 139 | 0 | 8 | 4 | 127 | 424 | 69 | 321 | 34 | 8 |
| Unicoi | 3,576 | 5 | 0 | 0 | 0 | 5 | 28 | 3 | 18 | 7 | 0 |
| Union City | 10,272 | 88 | 2 | 5 | 1 | 80 | 432 | 65 | 319 | 48 | 5 |
| Vonore | 1,589 | 2 | 0 | 0 | 0 | 2 | 44 | 6 | 32 | 6 | 0 |
| Waverly | 4,123 | 9 | 0 | 2 | 0 | 7 | 79 | 15 | 55 | 9 | 0 |
| Waynesboro | 2,365 | 12 | 0 | 2 | 0 | 10 | 7 | 0 | 6 | 1 | 0 |
| Westmoreland | 2,438 | 2 | 0 | 1 | 0 | 1 | 2 | 1 | 1 | 0 | 0 |
| White Bluff | 3,741 | 8 | 0 | 1 | 0 | 7 | 46 | 14 | 23 | 9 | 1 |
| White House | 13,282 | 25 | 0 | 5 | 0 | 20 | 98 | 8 | 81 | 9 | 0 |
| White Pine | 2,673 | 9 | 0 | 1 | 0 | 8 | 53 | 5 | 42 | 6 | 0 |
| Whiteville | 4,430 | 3 | 0 | 0 | 0 | 3 | 17 | 3 | 12 | 2 | 0 |
| Winchester | 9,151 | 57 | 1 | 3 | 3 | 50 | 267 | 50 | 198 | 19 | 1 |
| Woodbury | 3,007 | 5 | 0 | 0 | 0 | 5 | 24 | 5 | 18 | 1 | 0 |
| **TEXAS** | | | | | | | | | | | |
| Abernathy | 2,678 | 2 | 0 | 1 | 0 | 1 | 7 | 2 | 1 | 4 | 0 |
| Abilene | 125,088 | 598 | 7 | 120 | 81 | 390 | 2,583 | 455 | 1,921 | 207 | 9 |
| Addison | 16,540 | 101 | 3 | 20 | 24 | 54 | 1,137 | 128 | 796 | 213 | 0 |
| Alamo | 20,779 | 142 | 3 | 19 | 7 | 113 | 629 | 64 | 531 | 34 | 1 |
| Alamo Heights | 8,848 | 17 | 1 | 4 | 2 | 10 | 193 | 13 | 164 | 16 | 0 |
| Alba | 555 | 0 | 0 | 0 | 0 | 0 | 1 | 1 | 0 | 0 | 0 |
| Alice | 18,538 | 120 | 1 | 17 | 14 | 88 | 725 | 163 | 524 | 38 | 9 |
| Alpine | 6,037 | 6 | 1 | 1 | 0 | 4 | 24 | 11 | 10 | 3 | 1 |
| Alton | 19,344 | 88 | 0 | 6 | 9 | 73 | 199 | 32 | 144 | 23 | 1 |
| Alvarado | 4,722 | 29 | 2 | 6 | 3 | 18 | 80 | 8 | 55 | 17 | 1 |
| Alvin | 27,448 | 65 | 0 | 11 | 10 | 44 | 698 | 71 | 564 | 63 | 3 |
| Amarillo | 200,515 | 1,501 | 21 | 150 | 183 | 1,147 | 6,771 | 1,308 | 4,603 | 860 | 46 |
| Andrews | 14,699 | 54 | 0 | 8 | 2 | 44 | 229 | 36 | 164 | 29 | 0 |
| Angleton | 19,593 | 64 | 3 | 15 | 5 | 41 | 216 | 32 | 156 | 28 | 0 |
| Anna | 18,215 | 39 | 1 | 4 | 1 | 33 | 140 | 22 | 109 | 9 | 0 |
| Anthony | 5,279 | 13 | 0 | 5 | 2 | 6 | 35 | 3 | 25 | 7 | 0 |
| Aransas Pass | 8,531 | 55 | 3 | 7 | 3 | 42 | 261 | 53 | 176 | 32 | 1 |
| Archer City | 1,711 | 1 | 0 | 0 | 0 | 1 | 7 | 2 | 3 | 2 | 0 |
| Arcola | 2,925 | 5 | 0 | 0 | 0 | 5 | 28 | 6 | 18 | 4 | 0 |
| Argyle | 4,781 | 0 | 0 | 0 | 0 | 0 | 36 | 5 | 31 | 0 | 0 |
| Arlington | 402,323 | 2,270 | 19 | 355 | 262 | 1,634 | 10,285 | 1,252 | 7,700 | 1,333 | 17 |
| Arp | 1,054 | 2 | 0 | 0 | 0 | 2 | 9 | 5 | 2 | 2 | 0 |
| Athens | 12,778 | 50 | 0 | 9 | 6 | 35 | 192 | 45 | 124 | 23 | 0 |
| Atlanta | 5,402 | 23 | 0 | 2 | 0 | 21 | 87 | 16 | 63 | 8 | 0 |
| Aubrey | 7,080 | 17 | 0 | 0 | 2 | 15 | 74 | 30 | 36 | 8 | 1 |
| Austin | 1,016,721 | 4,996 | 79 | 557 | 991 | 3,369 | 33,989 | 4,758 | 24,662 | 4,569 | 186 |
| Azle | 13,917 | 38 | 0 | 8 | 4 | 26 | 253 | 42 | 175 | 36 | 0 |
| Baird | 1,497 | 2 | 0 | 0 | 0 | 2 | 18 | 3 | 9 | 6 | 0 |
| Balch Springs | 24,746 | 161 | 2 | 13 | 25 | 121 | 804 | 132 | 473 | 199 | 1 |
| Balcones Heights | 3,174 | 46 | 0 | 2 | 5 | 39 | 227 | 49 | 129 | 49 | 3 |
| Ballinger | 3,681 | 16 | 0 | 2 | 0 | 14 | 66 | 30 | 32 | 4 | 0 |
| Bartonville | 1,871 | 3 | 0 | 0 | 3 | 0 | 15 | 2 | 10 | 3 | 0 |
| Bastrop | 10,020 | 48 | 0 | 11 | 5 | 32 | 305 | 21 | 257 | 27 | 0 |
| Bay City | 17,441 | 77 | 1 | 25 | 5 | 46 | 520 | 98 | 385 | 37 | 6 |
| Baytown | 77,816 | 288 | 9 | 48 | 51 | 180 | 2,716 | 337 | 1,918 | 461 | 1 |
| Beaumont | 115,290 | 1,221 | 17 | 85 | 233 | 886 | 3,822 | 942 | 2,498 | 382 | 26 |
| Bedford | 48,483 | 140 | 1 | 25 | 13 | 101 | 1,016 | 77 | 824 | 115 | 1 |
| Bee Cave | 7,378 | 21 | 0 | 4 | 1 | 16 | 148 | 9 | 122 | 17 | 1 |
| Beeville | 14,160 | 78 | 0 | 4 | 6 | 68 | 400 | 110 | 256 | 34 | 2 |
| Bellaire | 19,114 | 5 | 0 | 1 | 1 | 3 | 113 | 19 | 81 | 13 | 0 |
| Bellmead | 10,927 | 58 | 0 | 14 | 5 | 39 | 337 | 42 | 249 | 46 | 3 |
| Bells | 1,528 | 2 | 0 | 0 | 0 | 2 | 5 | 1 | 3 | 1 | 0 |
| Bellville | 4,214 | 12 | 0 | 3 | 4 | 5 | 55 | 12 | 35 | 8 | 0 |
| Belton | 23,731 | 43 | 2 | 15 | 4 | 22 | 483 | 52 | 394 | 37 | 1 |
| Benbrook | 23,529 | 49 | 8 | 6 | 7 | 28 | 298 | 48 | 207 | 43 | 2 |
| Bertram | 1,539 | 2 | 0 | 1 | 0 | 1 | 21 | 6 | 13 | 2 | 0 |
| Big Sandy | 1,418 | 2 | 0 | 0 | 0 | 2 | 19 | 4 | 10 | 5 | 0 |
| Big Spring | 28,166 | 195 | 6 | 7 | 19 | 163 | 648 | 147 | 440 | 61 | 3 |
| Blanco | 2,194 | 10 | 0 | 0 | 2 | 8 | 26 | 11 | 13 | 2 | 1 |
| Blue Mound | 2,411 | 1 | 0 | 0 | 0 | 1 | 3 | 1 | 0 | 2 | 0 |
| Boerne | 20,209 | 19 | 0 | 5 | 0 | 14 | 252 | 56 | 156 | 40 | 0 |
| Bogata | 1,054 | 5 | 0 | 0 | 0 | 5 | 14 | 5 | 7 | 2 | 1 |
| Borger | 12,121 | 33 | 0 | 19 | 2 | 12 | 260 | 71 | 169 | 20 | 0 |
| Bovina | 1,744 | 1 | 0 | 1 | 0 | 0 | 0 | 0 | 0 | 0 | 0 |
| Bowie | 5,133 | 10 | 0 | 3 | 2 | 5 | 110 | 57 | 46 | 7 | 0 |
| Boyd | 1,594 | 7 | 0 | 0 | 0 | 7 | 11 | 3 | 5 | 3 | 0 |
| Brady | 5,147 | 13 | 2 | 1 | 0 | 10 | 103 | 55 | 38 | 10 | 2 |
| Brazoria | 3,066 | 8 | 0 | 0 | 0 | 8 | 54 | 3 | 44 | 7 | 0 |
| Breckenridge | 5,365 | 20 | 0 | 5 | 0 | 15 | 73 | 12 | 55 | 6 | 0 |
| Bremond | 966 | 2 | 0 | 1 | 0 | 1 | 6 | 4 | 2 | 0 | 0 |
| Brenham | 17,940 | 84 | 0 | 6 | 6 | 72 | 216 | 34 | 160 | 22 | 0 |
| Bridge City | 7,809 | 9 | 0 | 5 | 0 | 4 | 94 | 20 | 66 | 8 | 0 |
| Bridgeport | 6,711 | 9 | 0 | 3 | 0 | 6 | 51 | 8 | 36 | 7 | 0 |
| Brookshire | 6,248 | 29 | 1 | 1 | 3 | 24 | 53 | 5 | 35 | 13 | 0 |
| Brownfield | 9,194 | 32 | 0 | 5 | 1 | 26 | 81 | 20 | 44 | 17 | 0 |
| Brownsboro | 1,321 | 0 | 0 | 0 | 0 | 0 | 0 | 0 | 0 | 0 | 0 |
| Brownsville | 184,287 | 727 | 2 | 81 | 131 | 513 | 3,345 | 416 | 2,794 | 135 | 21 |

# Table 8. Offenses Known to Law Enforcement, by Selected State and City, 2021—Continued

(Number.)

| State/city | Population | Violent crime | Murder and nonnegligent manslaughter | Rape | Robbery | Aggravated assault | Property crime | Burglary | Larceny-theft | Motor vehicle theft | Arson |
|---|---|---|---|---|---|---|---|---|---|---|---|
| Brownwood | 18,105 | 102 | 0 | 29 | 4 | 69 | 496 | 94 | 373 | 29 | 2 |
| Bruceville-Eddy | 1,712 | 6 | 0 | 2 | 0 | 4 | 15 | 10 | 2 | 3 | 0 |
| Buda | 19,130 | 56 | 0 | 5 | 2 | 49 | 301 | 32 | 242 | 27 | 0 |
| Buffalo | 1,916 | 2 | 0 | 0 | 0 | 2 | 27 | 6 | 16 | 5 | 0 |
| Bullard | 4,071 | 8 | 0 | 0 | 0 | 8 | 23 | 13 | 10 | 0 | 0 |
| Bulverde | 5,593 | 9 | 0 | 3 | 0 | 6 | 131 | 12 | 110 | 9 | 0 |
| Burkburnett | 11,465 | 36 | 0 | 18 | 1 | 17 | 100 | 18 | 66 | 16 | 0 |
| Burleson | 51,167 | 126 | 2 | 29 | 8 | 87 | 813 | 55 | 670 | 88 | 5 |
| Burnet | 6,598 | 28 | 0 | 4 | 3 | 21 | 77 | 19 | 50 | 8 | 0 |
| Cactus | 3,239 | 10 | 0 | 0 | 0 | 10 | 46 | 6 | 36 | 4 | 0 |
| Caddo Mills | 1,749 | 4 | 0 | 1 | 0 | 3 | 28 | 14 | 5 | 9 | 0 |
| Caldwell | 4,535 | 7 | 0 | 2 | 0 | 5 | 25 | 9 | 12 | 4 | 0 |
| Calvert | 1,132 | 7 | 0 | 1 | 0 | 6 | 5 | 3 | 2 | 0 | 0 |
| Cameron | 5,399 | 9 | 0 | 0 | 0 | 9 | 44 | 19 | 20 | 5 | 1 |
| Canyon | 16,726 | 17 | 0 | 6 | 1 | 10 | 178 | 16 | 152 | 10 | 1 |
| Carrollton | 141,694 | 216 | 4 | 31 | 39 | 142 | 1,934 | 277 | 1,416 | 241 | 5 |
| Carthage | 6,314 | 37 | 1 | 1 | 2 | 33 | 195 | 19 | 164 | 12 | 1 |
| Castle Hills | 4,480 | 17 | 0 | 0 | 2 | 15 | 271 | 26 | 206 | 39 | 0 |
| Castroville | 3,243 | 2 | 0 | 1 | 0 | 1 | 51 | 16 | 30 | 5 | 0 |
| Cedar Hill | 47,764 | 83 | 2 | 11 | 21 | 49 | 793 | 62 | 616 | 115 | 0 |
| Cedar Park | 84,131 | 106 | 3 | 37 | 9 | 57 | 997 | 94 | 823 | 80 | 5 |
| Celina | 22,521 | 16 | 3 | 2 | 1 | 10 | 125 | 19 | 105 | 1 | 0 |
| Center | 5,014 | 12 | 1 | 0 | 2 | 9 | 125 | 28 | 93 | 4 | 0 |
| Chandler | 3,271 | 0 | 0 | 0 | 0 | 0 | 29 | 5 | 22 | 2 | 1 |
| Childress | 5,880 | 11 | 0 | 1 | 1 | 9 | 32 | 12 | 16 | 4 | 0 |
| China Grove | 1,329 | 1 | 0 | 0 | 0 | 1 | 19 | 2 | 16 | 1 | 0 |
| Cibolo | 35,139 | 26 | 0 | 11 | 2 | 13 | 281 | 46 | 195 | 40 | 3 |
| Cisco | 3,848 | 11 | 0 | 0 | 0 | 11 | 58 | 31 | 22 | 5 | 1 |
| Cleburne | 32,248 | 153 | 0 | 32 | 7 | 114 | 511 | 69 | 397 | 45 | 4 |
| Clifton | 3,406 | 4 | 0 | 0 | 0 | 4 | 28 | 14 | 12 | 2 | 1 |
| Clint | 1,138 | 0 | 0 | 0 | 0 | 0 | 0 | 0 | 0 | 0 | 0 |
| Clute | 11,774 | 32 | 0 | 6 | 4 | 22 | 226 | 32 | 164 | 30 | 0 |
| Cockrell Hill | 4,048 | 12 | 0 | 1 | 3 | 8 | 82 | 17 | 53 | 12 | 0 |
| Coleman | 4,159 | 5 | 0 | 0 | 0 | 5 | 46 | 26 | 15 | 5 | 1 |
| College Station | 122,051 | 228 | 3 | 64 | 31 | 130 | 2,150 | 297 | 1,664 | 189 | 2 |
| Colleyville | 27,544 | 19 | 0 | 4 | 1 | 14 | 106 | 14 | 89 | 3 | 0 |
| Collinsville | 2,023 | 0 | 0 | 0 | 0 | 0 | 5 | 3 | 1 | 1 | 0 |
| Columbus | 3,703 | 14 | 0 | 3 | 2 | 4 | 5 | 57 | 7 | 46 | 4 | 1 |
| Comanche | 4,209 | 13 | 1 | 4 | 0 | 8 | 78 | 16 | 55 | 7 | 1 |
| Combes | 3,055 | 14 | 0 | 4 | 0 | 10 | 36 | 5 | 29 | 2 | 0 |
| Commerce | 9,878 | 23 | 0 | 3 | 3 | 17 | 125 | 12 | 97 | 16 | 1 |
| Conroe | 99,965 | 217 | 5 | 44 | 31 | 137 | 2,190 | 286 | 1,651 | 253 | 4 |
| Converse | 29,635 | 148 | 3 | 9 | 7 | 129 | 454 | 61 | 351 | 42 | 1 |
| Coppell | 40,889 | 23 | 0 | 4 | 3 | 16 | 581 | 71 | 482 | 28 | 1 |
| Copperas Cove | 33,613 | 126 | 0 | 29 | 11 | 86 | 624 | 114 | 468 | 42 | 9 |
| Corinth | 22,635 | 19 | 0 | 5 | 1 | 13 | 181 | 32 | 132 | 17 | 0 |
| Corpus Christi | 329,538 | 2,792 | 19 | 247 | 466 | 2,060 | 10,375 | 1,758 | 7,599 | 1,018 | 80 |
| Corrigan | 1,708 | 2 | 0 | 1 | 0 | 1 | 9 | 1 | 7 | 1 | 0 |
| Corsicana | 23,808 | 137 | 1 | 23 | 11 | 102 | 542 | 71 | 414 | 57 | 2 |
| Crandall | 4,418 | 32 | 0 | 5 | 6 | 21 | 139 | 30 | 87 | 22 | 0 |
| Crane | 3,681 | 2 | 0 | 1 | 0 | 1 | 5 | 0 | 3 | 2 | 0 |
| Crockett | 6,295 | 27 | 0 | 6 | 1 | 20 | 145 | 32 | 97 | 16 | 0 |
| Crowley | 18,146 | 45 | 0 | 12 | 2 | 31 | 298 | 53 | 223 | 22 | 0 |
| Cuero | 8,225 | 69 | 1 | 4 | 1 | 63 | 140 | 18 | 105 | 17 | 2 |
| Cuney | 140 | 0 | 0 | 0 | 0 | 0 | 1 | 1 | 0 | 0 | 0 |
| Daingerfield | 2,377 | 10 | 0 | 0 | 3 | 7 | 48 | 9 | 31 | 8 | 0 |
| Dalhart | 8,279 | 27 | 1 | 4 | 0 | 22 | 133 | 29 | 75 | 29 | 2 |
| Dallas | 1,349,185 | 11,131 | 212 | 583 | 2,426 | 7,910 | 46,149 | 6,920 | 27,426 | 11,803 | 231 |
| Dalworthington Gardens | 2,367 | 1 | 0 | 0 | 0 | 1 | 17 | 2 | 13 | 2 | 0 |
| Dayton | 8,767 | 19 | 0 | 2 | 4 | 13 | 159 | 31 | 102 | 26 | 0 |
| Decatur | 7,747 | 21 | 0 | 6 | 1 | 14 | 265 | 12 | 242 | 11 | 0 |
| Deer Park | 32,998 | 50 | 0 | 21 | 5 | 24 | 455 | 54 | 354 | 47 | 1 |
| Denison | 26,119 | 91 | 1 | 22 | 5 | 63 | 469 | 75 | 306 | 88 | 2 |
| Denton | 150,975 | 419 | 3 | 103 | 54 | 259 | 3,083 | 306 | 2,426 | 351 | 9 |
| Denver City | 4,928 | 8 | 0 | 3 | 0 | 5 | 29 | 5 | 19 | 5 | 0 |
| DeSoto | 52,891 | 171 | 6 | 20 | 38 | 107 | 1,089 | 128 | 756 | 205 | 6 |
| Devine | 4,998 | 4 | 0 | 0 | 0 | 4 | 148 | 4 | 130 | 14 | 0 |
| Diboll | 5,096 | 7 | 0 | 0 | 0 | 7 | 24 | 7 | 14 | 3 | 0 |
| Dickinson | 21,442 | 55 | 2 | 18 | 8 | 27 | 388 | 71 | 270 | 47 | 0 |
| Dimmitt | 3,966 | 6 | 0 | 1 | 0 | 5 | 14 | 4 | 8 | 2 | 1 |
| Donna | 16,371 | 245 | 0 | 14 | 12 | 219 | 401 | 48 | 313 | 40 | 1 |
| Double Oak | 3,124 | 2 | 0 | 0 | 0 | 2 | 8 | 2 | 6 | 0 | 0 |
| Dublin | 3,546 | 3 | 0 | 1 | 0 | 2 | 15 | 9 | 5 | 1 | 0 |
| Dumas | 13,503 | 46 | 1 | 11 | 1 | 33 | 257 | 26 | 205 | 26 | 0 |
| Duncanville | 37,869 | 162 | 4 | 10 | 35 | 113 | 991 | 137 | 617 | 237 | 1 |
| Eagle Pass | 29,807 | 53 | 0 | 2 | 8 | 43 | 726 | 212 | 443 | 71 | 1 |
| Early | 3,353 | 12 | 0 | 2 | 0 | 10 | 33 | 6 | 26 | 1 | 0 |
| Earth | 940 | 2 | 0 | 0 | 0 | 2 | 5 | 4 | 0 | 1 | 0 |
| Eastland | 3,853 | 20 | 0 | 10 | 0 | 10 | 73 | 15 | 50 | 8 | 2 |
| Edinburg | 104,604 | 358 | 3 | 74 | 41 | 240 | 2,282 | 253 | 1,944 | 85 | 5 |
| Edna | 5,787 | 19 | 1 | 3 | 0 | 15 | 49 | 13 | 26 | 10 | 2 |
| El Campo | 11,484 | 69 | 2 | 4 | 4 | 59 | 371 | 35 | 312 | 24 | 0 |
| Electra | 2,732 | 3 | 0 | 0 | 0 | 3 | 17 | 3 | 7 | 7 | 0 |

## Table 8. Offenses Known to Law Enforcement, by Selected State and City, 2021—Continued

(Number.)

| State/city | Population | Violent crime | Murder and nonnegligent manslaughter | Rape | Robbery | Aggravated assault | Property crime | Burglary | Larceny-theft | Motor vehicle theft | Arson |
|---|---|---|---|---|---|---|---|---|---|---|---|
| Elgin | 11,040 | 13 | 0 | 3 | 4 | 6 | 141 | 41 | 89 | 11 | 0 |
| Elmendorf | 2,198 | 1 | 0 | 0 | 0 | 1 | 19 | 2 | 14 | 3 | 1 |
| El Paso | 684,737 | 1,698 | 30 | 323 | 219 | 1,126 | 8,539 | 1,139 | 6,491 | 909 | 37 |
| Elsa | 7,205 | 21 | 0 | 2 | 1 | 18 | 173 | 30 | 138 | 5 | 0 |
| Emory | 1,384 | 5 | 0 | 0 | 0 | 5 | 9 | 1 | 6 | 2 | 0 |
| Ennis | 20,893 | 29 | 0 | 1 | 8 | 20 | 424 | 51 | 338 | 35 | 1 |
| Euless | 57,963 | 139 | 1 | 35 | 32 | 71 | 1,316 | 180 | 995 | 141 | 3 |
| Everman | 6,136 | 21 | 0 | 6 | 5 | 10 | 61 | 6 | 45 | 10 | 0 |
| Fair Oaks Ranch | 10,798 | 4 | 0 | 0 | 0 | 4 | 56 | 7 | 47 | 2 | 0 |
| Fairview | 9,595 | 4 | 0 | 0 | 1 | 3 | 47 | 7 | 34 | 6 | 0 |
| Farmers Branch | 54,026 | 103 | 1 | 14 | 25 | 63 | 1,216 | 180 | 822 | 214 | 0 |
| Farmersville | 3,754 | 10 | 0 | 2 | 2 | 6 | 66 | 13 | 48 | 5 | 0 |
| Farwell | 1,267 | 0 | 0 | 0 | 0 | 0 | 5 | 0 | 2 | 3 | 0 |
| Fate | 18,907 | 14 | 0 | 6 | 0 | 8 | 86 | 20 | 61 | 5 | 1 |
| Ferris | 3,143 | 5 | 1 | 1 | 0 | 3 | 49 | 4 | 37 | 8 | 0 |
| Flatonia | 1,460 | 1 | 0 | 0 | 0 | 1 | 9 | 3 | 4 | 2 | 0 |
| Floresville | 8,339 | 26 | 0 | 3 | 3 | 20 | 103 | 33 | 59 | 11 | 1 |
| Flower Mound | 83,367 | 54 | 0 | 11 | 6 | 37 | 480 | 38 | 415 | 27 | 0 |
| Floydada | 2,621 | 16 | 0 | 4 | 0 | 12 | 33 | 15 | 12 | 6 | 0 |
| Forest Hill | 13,002 | 77 | 4 | 8 | 20 | 45 | 273 | 34 | 172 | 67 | 0 |
| Forney | 31,521 | 36 | 0 | 2 | 6 | 28 | 353 | 29 | 279 | 45 | 0 |
| Fort Stockton | 8,375 | 6 | 0 | 1 | 0 | 5 | 56 | 14 | 33 | 9 | 1 |
| Fort Worth | 947,862 | 5,294 | 118 | 552 | 712 | 3,912 | 24,847 | 3,540 | 17,637 | 3,670 | 116 |
| Franklin | 1,646 | 3 | 0 | 1 | 0 | 2 | 13 | 6 | 6 | 1 | 0 |
| Frankston | 1,150 | 1 | 0 | 0 | 0 | 1 | 19 | 1 | 17 | 1 | 0 |
| Fredericksburg | 11,620 | 15 | 0 | 10 | 2 | 3 | 121 | 32 | 85 | 4 | 0 |
| Freeport | 12,132 | 62 | 0 | 2 | 3 | 57 | 216 | 39 | 177 | 0 | 1 |
| Freer | 2,602 | 4 | 0 | 0 | 0 | 4 | 26 | 10 | 12 | 4 | 0 |
| Friendswood | 40,434 | 26 | 0 | 10 | 5 | 11 | 243 | 32 | 190 | 21 | 2 |
| Friona | 3,741 | 6 | 0 | 2 | 0 | 4 | 9 | 2 | 3 | 4 | 0 |
| Frisco | 222,416 | 211 | 4 | 61 | 11 | 135 | 2,005 | 173 | 1,710 | 122 | 4 |
| Fulshear | 17,318 | 5 | 0 | 1 | 0 | 4 | 81 | 5 | 66 | 10 | 0 |
| Gainesville | 16,967 | 67 | 0 | 7 | 6 | 54 | 424 | 64 | 315 | 45 | 1 |
| Galena Park | 10,525 | 33 | 1 | 1 | 8 | 23 | 166 | 32 | 104 | 30 | 0 |
| Galveston | 50,321 | 302 | 3 | 92 | 39 | 168 | 1,331 | 142 | 949 | 240 | 1 |
| Ganado | 2,094 | 7 | 2 | 0 | 1 | 4 | 21 | 11 | 5 | 5 | 1 |
| Garden Ridge | 4,379 | 2 | 0 | 2 | 0 | 0 | 31 | 3 | 24 | 4 | 0 |
| Garland | 237,510 | 612 | 21 | 71 | 205 | 315 | 5,665 | 779 | 3,960 | 926 | 10 |
| Garrison | 867 | 0 | 0 | 0 | 0 | 0 | 2 | 2 | 0 | 0 | 0 |
| Gatesville | 12,558 | 25 | 0 | 12 | 1 | 12 | 138 | 31 | 89 | 18 | 1 |
| Georgetown | 90,629 | 109 | 2 | 28 | 7 | 72 | 974 | 128 | 775 | 71 | 4 |
| Giddings | 5,175 | 15 | 0 | 5 | 3 | 7 | 71 | 3 | 58 | 10 | 0 |
| Gilmer | 5,217 | 27 | 0 | 4 | 4 | 19 | 137 | 20 | 110 | 7 | 0 |
| Gladewater | 6,347 | 21 | 0 | 3 | 1 | 17 | 103 | 11 | 64 | 28 | 0 |
| Glenn Heights | 14,610 | 54 | 0 | 3 | 5 | 46 | 162 | 24 | 121 | 17 | 1 |
| Godley | 1,809 | 6 | 0 | 1 | 0 | 5 | 16 | 7 | 9 | 0 | 0 |
| Gonzales | 7,633 | 122 | 0 | 6 | 2 | 114 | 95 | 21 | 66 | 8 | 1 |
| Graham | 8,536 | 12 | 0 | 2 | 3 | 7 | 61 | 9 | 43 | 9 | 0 |
| Granbury | 11,466 | 12 | 0 | 1 | 0 | 11 | 442 | 17 | 406 | 19 | 1 |
| Grand Prairie | 196,334 | 433 | 8 | 51 | 74 | 300 | 3,430 | 330 | 2,623 | 477 | 6 |
| Grand Saline | 3,223 | 5 | 0 | 0 | 1 | 4 | 14 | 7 | 7 | 0 | 0 |
| Granger | 1,523 | 1 | 0 | 0 | 0 | 1 | 9 | 3 | 5 | 1 | 0 |
| Grapeland | 1,423 | 2 | 0 | 0 | 0 | 2 | 2 | 1 | 1 | 0 | 0 |
| Grapevine | 56,795 | 99 | 0 | 18 | 16 | 65 | 1,228 | 131 | 947 | 150 | 3 |
| Greenville | 29,780 | 72 | 2 | 9 | 18 | 43 | 552 | 142 | 350 | 60 | 16 |
| Groesbeck | 4,162 | 8 | 0 | 4 | 0 | 4 | 59 | 20 | 36 | 3 | 1 |
| Groves | 15,187 | 83 | 0 | 9 | 11 | 63 | 206 | 41 | 135 | 30 | 1 |
| Gun Barrel City | 6,377 | 5 | 0 | 1 | 0 | 4 | 59 | 17 | 34 | 8 | 0 |
| Hallettsville | 2,651 | 8 | 0 | 0 | 0 | 8 | 38 | 12 | 25 | 1 | 0 |
| Hallsville | 4,496 | 1 | 0 | 1 | 0 | 0 | 17 | 8 | 9 | 0 | 0 |
| Haltom City | 43,840 | 168 | 1 | 32 | 37 | 98 | 1,244 | 202 | 808 | 234 | 5 |
| Hamilton | 3,019 | 4 | 0 | 0 | 0 | 4 | 28 | 7 | 19 | 2 | 1 |
| Hamlin | 1,984 | 3 | 0 | 0 | 0 | 3 | 7 | 2 | 5 | 0 | 0 |
| Harker Heights | 33,752 | 61 | 1 | 15 | 15 | 30 | 379 | 49 | 283 | 47 | 3 |
| Harlingen | 65,186 | 262 | 6 | 7 | 50 | 199 | 2,189 | 330 | 1,723 | 136 | 10 |
| Haskell | 3,194 | 4 | 0 | 1 | 0 | 3 | 20 | 7 | 11 | 2 | 0 |
| Hawkins | 1,353 | 2 | 0 | 0 | 0 | 2 | 2 | 1 | 1 | 0 | 0 |
| Hearne | 4,331 | 25 | 2 | 3 | 4 | 16 | 50 | 23 | 20 | 7 | 0 |
| Heath | 9,996 | 8 | 0 | 5 | 0 | 3 | 34 | 7 | 27 | 0 | 0 |
| Hedwig Village | 2,605 | 7 | 0 | 0 | 6 | 1 | 137 | 9 | 121 | 7 | 0 |
| Helotes | 10,627 | 6 | 0 | 1 | 1 | 4 | 103 | 22 | 77 | 4 | 0 |
| Hempstead | 9,214 | 64 | 0 | 8 | 7 | 49 | 123 | 21 | 92 | 10 | 2 |
| Henderson | 12,989 | 87 | 2 | 6 | 9 | 70 | 358 | 40 | 282 | 36 | 5 |
| Hereford | 14,288 | 40 | 0 | 3 | 2 | 35 | 237 | 53 | 160 | 24 | 2 |
| Hewitt | 15,272 | 31 | 0 | 6 | 4 | 21 | 154 | 25 | 115 | 14 | 0 |
| Hickory Creek | 5,193 | 5 | 0 | 1 | 2 | 2 | 67 | 5 | 56 | 6 | 0 |
| Hico | 1,443 | 0 | 0 | 0 | 0 | 0 | 0 | 0 | 0 | 0 | 0 |
| Hidalgo | 14,488 | 29 | 1 | 7 | 1 | 20 | 131 | 19 | 99 | 13 | 1 |
| Highland Park | 9,032 | 9 | 0 | 3 | 1 | 5 | 207 | 35 | 162 | 10 | 0 |
| Highland Village | 17,071 | 4 | 0 | 4 | 0 | 0 | 93 | 4 | 80 | 9 | 0 |
| Hill Country Village | 1,122 | 0 | 0 | 0 | 0 | 0 | 40 | 4 | 31 | 5 | 0 |
| Hillsboro | 8,525 | 10 | 0 | 1 | 5 | 4 | 164 | 17 | 120 | 27 | 2 |
| Hollywood Park | 3,351 | 0 | 0 | 0 | 0 | 0 | 58 | 7 | 45 | 6 | 0 |

## Table 8. Offenses Known to Law Enforcement, by Selected State and City, 2021—Continued

(Number.)

| State/city | Population | Violent crime | Murder and nonnegligent manslaughter | Rape | Robbery | Aggravated assault | Property crime | Burglary | Larceny-theft | Motor vehicle theft | Arson |
|---|---|---|---|---|---|---|---|---|---|---|---|
| Hondo | 9,564 | 31 | 1 | 2 | 1 | 27 | 153 | 21 | 104 | 28 | 2 |
| Honey Grove | 1,746 | 5 | 0 | 0 | 1 | 4 | 15 | 7 | 6 | 2 | 0 |
| Hooks | 2,703 | 9 | 0 | 0 | 1 | 8 | 69 | 7 | 54 | 8 | 0 |
| Horizon City | 20,628 | 27 | 0 | 12 | 2 | 13 | 110 | 18 | 82 | 10 | 1 |
| Horseshoe Bay | 4,227 | 7 | 0 | 2 | 0 | 5 | 5 | 1 | 4 | 0 | 0 |
| Houston | 2,339,252 | 28,325 | 464 | 1,173 | 7,729 | 18,959 | 96,048 | 14,749 | 65,729 | 15,570 | 465 |
| Howe | 3,482 | 8 | 0 | 0 | 0 | 8 | 24 | 6 | 16 | 2 | 0 |
| Hudson Oaks | 3,857 | 5 | 0 | 1 | 0 | 4 | 79 | 6 | 66 | 7 | 0 |
| Hughes Springs | 1,664 | 0 | 0 | 0 | 0 | 0 | 6 | 4 | 1 | 1 | 0 |
| Humble | 15,579 | 163 | 3 | 35 | 39 | 86 | 1,591 | 124 | 1,275 | 192 | 4 |
| Huntington | 2,076 | 2 | 0 | 1 | 0 | 1 | 24 | 8 | 12 | 4 | 0 |
| Huntsville | 41,671 | 226 | 2 | 32 | 18 | 174 | 744 | 83 | 580 | 81 | 3 |
| Hurst | 38,250 | 76 | 1 | 15 | 16 | 44 | 934 | 67 | 763 | 104 | 1 |
| Hutchins | 6,048 | 35 | 1 | 7 | 7 | 20 | 312 | 52 | 182 | 78 | 0 |
| Hutto | 31,792 | 20 | 0 | 9 | 0 | 11 | 210 | 20 | 170 | 20 | 0 |
| Idalou | 2,314 | 2 | 0 | 2 | 0 | 0 | 13 | 1 | 6 | 6 | 1 |
| Ingleside | 10,188 | 23 | 0 | 3 | 3 | 17 | 131 | 32 | 89 | 10 | 1 |
| Ingram | 1,881 | 5 | 0 | 2 | 1 | 2 | 30 | 7 | 19 | 4 | 1 |
| Iowa Colony | 5,771 | 5 | 0 | 1 | 2 | 2 | 11 | 5 | 5 | 1 | 0 |
| Iowa Park | 6,435 | 18 | 0 | 8 | 0 | 10 | 29 | 7 | 18 | 4 | 1 |
| Irving | 241,692 | 807 | 12 | 162 | 186 | 447 | 5,897 | 611 | 4,334 | 952 | 7 |
| Italy | 1,972 | 7 | 0 | 1 | 0 | 6 | 16 | 5 | 10 | 1 | 0 |
| Jacinto City | 10,276 | 16 | 1 | 2 | 8 | 5 | 255 | 27 | 179 | 49 | 0 |
| Jacksboro | 4,443 | 10 | 0 | 5 | 0 | 5 | 17 | 3 | 11 | 3 | 2 |
| Jacksonville | 14,855 | 79 | 1 | 10 | 4 | 64 | 232 | 56 | 151 | 25 | 1 |
| Jamaica Beach | 1,085 | 1 | 0 | 1 | 0 | 0 | 4 | 0 | 3 | 1 | 0 |
| Jarrell | 2,228 | 3 | 0 | 0 | 0 | 3 | 16 | 3 | 5 | 8 | 0 |
| Jasper | 7,600 | 27 | 0 | 0 | 7 | 20 | 265 | 47 | 202 | 16 | 0 |
| Jersey Village | 7,782 | 22 | 0 | 4 | 6 | 12 | 408 | 36 | 188 | 184 | 2 |
| Jonestown | 2,207 | 1 | 0 | 0 | 0 | 1 | 39 | 13 | 23 | 3 | 0 |
| Joshua | 8,411 | 10 | 0 | 2 | 1 | 7 | 85 | 15 | 66 | 4 | 0 |
| Jourdanton | 4,495 | 30 | 1 | 0 | 0 | 29 | 61 | 5 | 45 | 11 | 0 |
| Junction | 2,421 | 3 | 0 | 0 | 0 | 3 | 5 | 2 | 2 | 1 | 0 |
| Karnes City | 3,441 | 14 | 0 | 0 | 0 | 14 | 30 | 7 | 21 | 2 | 0 |
| Katy | 25,183 | 65 | 0 | 19 | 13 | 33 | 738 | 62 | 606 | 70 | 1 |
| Kaufman | 8,804 | 16 | 0 | 2 | 0 | 14 | 96 | 10 | 76 | 10 | 1 |
| Keene | 6,637 | 8 | 0 | 3 | 0 | 5 | 58 | 9 | 40 | 9 | 1 |
| Keller | 47,721 | 42 | 0 | 14 | 5 | 23 | 244 | 20 | 214 | 10 | 1 |
| Kemah | 2,076 | 8 | 0 | 1 | 1 | 6 | 88 | 12 | 70 | 6 | 1 |
| Kemp | 1,273 | 5 | 0 | 0 | 0 | 5 | 11 | 0 | 10 | 1 | 0 |
| Kenedy | 3,396 | 13 | 0 | 2 | 1 | 10 | 69 | 16 | 50 | 3 | 1 |
| Kennedale | 8,829 | 14 | 0 | 2 | 2 | 10 | 113 | 15 | 78 | 20 | 0 |
| Kerens | 1,515 | 5 | 0 | 1 | 0 | 4 | 19 | 5 | 10 | 4 | 0 |
| Kermit | 6,441 | 7 | 0 | 1 | 1 | 5 | 59 | 33 | 21 | 5 | 1 |
| Kerrville | 23,982 | 77 | 0 | 11 | 2 | 64 | 287 | 27 | 231 | 29 | 3 |
| Kilgore | 15,004 | 45 | 2 | 8 | 4 | 31 | 288 | 58 | 195 | 35 | 0 |
| Killeen | 156,741 | 963 | 18 | 90 | 97 | 758 | 2,670 | 530 | 1,748 | 392 | 2 |
| Kingsville | 24,850 | 135 | 8 | 11 | 8 | 108 | 593 | 94 | 467 | 32 | 1 |
| Kirby | 8,792 | 106 | 0 | 2 | 3 | 101 | 114 | 9 | 76 | 29 | 3 |
| Knox City | 1,119 | 3 | 0 | 1 | 0 | 2 | 7 | 2 | 5 | 0 | 0 |
| Kountze | 2,106 | 4 | 0 | 0 | 0 | 4 | 34 | 7 | 24 | 3 | 0 |
| Kyle | 54,692 | 93 | 0 | 25 | 6 | 62 | 608 | 86 | 477 | 45 | 2 |
| Lacy-Lakeview | 6,836 | 26 | 0 | 4 | 4 | 18 | 168 | 29 | 124 | 15 | 0 |
| La Feria | 7,243 | 38 | 0 | 6 | 2 | 30 | 87 | 18 | 59 | 10 | 1 |
| Lago Vista | 8,158 | 3 | 0 | 1 | 0 | 2 | 64 | 1 | 57 | 6 | 0 |
| La Grange | 4,684 | 19 | 1 | 2 | 0 | 16 | 66 | 6 | 57 | 3 | 0 |
| La Grulla | 1,688 | 4 | 0 | 0 | 1 | 3 | 10 | 5 | 5 | 0 | 0 |
| Laguna Vista | 3,223 | 3 | 0 | 0 | 0 | 3 | 13 | 2 | 11 | 0 | 0 |
| La Joya | 4,638 | 19 | 0 | 4 | 0 | 15 | 14 | 4 | 10 | 0 | 0 |
| Lake Dallas | 8,230 | 22 | 2 | 2 | 2 | 16 | 91 | 18 | 60 | 13 | 1 |
| Lake Jackson | 27,088 | 89 | 0 | 16 | 8 | 65 | 472 | 61 | 379 | 32 | 0 |
| Lakeport | 999 | 2 | 1 | 1 | 0 | 0 | 0 | 0 | 0 | 0 | 0 |
| Lakeside | 1,594 | 2 | 0 | 1 | 0 | 1 | 13 | 3 | 9 | 1 | 0 |
| Lakeview, Harrison County | 6,214 | 9 | 0 | 3 | 2 | 4 | 44 | 11 | 30 | 3 | 0 |
| Lakeway | 16,747 | 11 | 0 | 4 | 0 | 7 | 169 | 22 | 137 | 10 | 0 |
| Lake Worth | 4,886 | 25 | 0 | 9 | 1 | 15 | 300 | 16 | 260 | 24 | 2 |
| La Marque | 17,984 | 110 | 4 | 20 | 12 | 74 | 681 | 111 | 509 | 61 | 0 |
| Lampasas | 8,269 | 23 | 0 | 4 | 0 | 19 | 151 | 18 | 129 | 4 | 0 |
| Lancaster | 39,235 | 223 | 3 | 18 | 41 | 161 | 1,039 | 85 | 762 | 192 | 2 |
| La Porte | 35,972 | 73 | 1 | 12 | 7 | 53 | 429 | 62 | 305 | 62 | 0 |
| Laredo | 266,489 | 801 | 13 | 100 | 94 | 594 | 3,165 | 398 | 2,551 | 216 | 59 |
| Lavon | 4,235 | 11 | 0 | 1 | 0 | 10 | 56 | 12 | 42 | 2 | 1 |
| League City | 111,279 | 93 | 3 | 21 | 15 | 54 | 1,221 | 142 | 956 | 123 | 0 |
| Leander | 77,457 | 60 | 1 | 24 | 8 | 27 | 595 | 56 | 499 | 40 | 1 |
| Leonard | 2,077 | 4 | 0 | 0 | 1 | 3 | 3 | 1 | 2 | 0 | 0 |
| Levelland | 13,495 | 112 | 0 | 11 | 3 | 98 | 267 | 81 | 160 | 26 | 1 |
| Lewisville | 113,998 | 318 | 2 | 65 | 42 | 209 | 2,050 | 242 | 1,496 | 312 | 15 |
| Liberty | 9,621 | 36 | 1 | 6 | 1 | 28 | 131 | 15 | 89 | 27 | 2 |
| Liberty Hill | 4,076 | 7 | 0 | 2 | 0 | 5 | 49 | 7 | 35 | 7 | 0 |
| Lindale | 6,956 | 10 | 0 | 4 | 0 | 6 | 93 | 14 | 61 | 18 | 0 |
| Linden | 1,880 | 1 | 0 | 0 | 0 | 1 | 13 | 3 | 10 | 0 | 0 |
| Little Elm | 61,181 | 88 | 1 | 26 | 16 | 45 | 196 | 23 | 147 | 26 | 0 |
| Littlefield | 5,696 | 12 | 0 | 3 | 0 | 9 | 64 | 16 | 38 | 10 | 0 |

## Table 8. Offenses Known to Law Enforcement, by Selected State and City, 2021—Continued

(Number.)

| State/city | Population | Violent crime | Murder and nonnegligent manslaughter | Rape | Robbery | Aggravated assault | Property crime | Burglary | Larceny-theft | Motor vehicle theft | Arson |
|---|---|---|---|---|---|---|---|---|---|---|---|
| Live Oak | 17,051 | 18 | 0 | 9 | 3 | 6 | 417 | 24 | 342 | 51 | 3 |
| Livingston | 5,533 | 25 | 2 | 5 | 3 | 15 | 220 | 12 | 190 | 18 | 2 |
| Llano | 3,535 | 3 | 0 | 0 | 2 | 1 | 33 | 11 | 18 | 4 | 0 |
| Lockhart | 14,209 | 9 | 1 | 2 | 0 | 6 | 93 | 13 | 59 | 21 | 1 |
| Log Cabin | 792 | 2 | 0 | 0 | 0 | 2 | 5 | 2 | 1 | 2 | 0 |
| Longview | 81,846 | 286 | 8 | 55 | 44 | 179 | 2,063 | 355 | 1,490 | 218 | 3 |
| Lorena | 1,762 | 7 | 0 | 2 | 0 | 5 | 30 | 5 | 24 | 1 | 0 |
| Los Fresnos | 7,908 | 36 | 0 | 2 | 2 | 32 | 86 | 8 | 75 | 3 | 0 |
| Lubbock | 265,990 | 2,826 | 26 | 272 | 377 | 2,151 | 9,759 | 2,152 | 6,524 | 1,083 | 93 |
| Lufkin | 34,934 | 240 | 5 | 32 | 22 | 181 | 1,413 | 275 | 1,013 | 125 | 9 |
| Luling | 5,874 | 21 | 1 | 2 | 0 | 18 | 91 | 10 | 63 | 18 | 0 |
| Lumberton | 13,528 | 12 | 0 | 5 | 0 | 7 | 28 | 5 | 17 | 6 | 0 |
| Lytle | 3,122 | 1 | 0 | 0 | 0 | 1 | 98 | 6 | 80 | 12 | 0 |
| Madisonville | 4,819 | 21 | 0 | 5 | 1 | 15 | 50 | 8 | 33 | 9 | 1 |
| Magnolia | 2,331 | 3 | 0 | 2 | 0 | 1 | 34 | 13 | 17 | 4 | 0 |
| Manor | 17,725 | 27 | 0 | 2 | 2 | 23 | 160 | 19 | 122 | 19 | 2 |
| Mansfield | 74,925 | 65 | 2 | 17 | 11 | 35 | 916 | 119 | 724 | 73 | 0 |
| Manvel | 15,262 | 28 | 0 | 3 | 2 | 23 | 100 | 20 | 76 | 4 | 0 |
| Marble Falls | 7,231 | 34 | 0 | 16 | 0 | 18 | 153 | 20 | 124 | 9 | 2 |
| Marfa | 1,555 | 1 | 0 | 0 | 0 | 1 | 2 | 0 | 2 | 0 | 0 |
| Marion | 1,305 | 0 | 0 | 0 | 0 | 0 | 3 | 0 | 2 | 1 | 0 |
| Marlin | 5,510 | 17 | 0 | 3 | 2 | 12 | 51 | 33 | 9 | 9 | 1 |
| Marshall | 22,425 | 95 | 3 | 8 | 16 | 68 | 468 | 118 | 299 | 51 | 2 |
| Maud | 1,062 | 0 | 0 | 0 | 0 | 0 | 18 | 2 | 10 | 6 | 0 |
| Maypearl | 1,060 | 0 | 0 | 0 | 0 | 0 | 3 | 2 | 0 | 1 | 0 |
| McAllen | 144,973 | 259 | 0 | 44 | 18 | 197 | 2,615 | 106 | 2,469 | 40 | 12 |
| McKinney | 217,841 | 277 | 5 | 53 | 21 | 198 | 1,933 | 202 | 1,530 | 201 | 6 |
| Meadows Place | 4,806 | 2 | 0 | 0 | 1 | 1 | 131 | 4 | 109 | 18 | 0 |
| Melissa | 15,322 | 10 | 0 | 0 | 0 | 10 | 100 | 16 | 76 | 8 | 0 |
| Memphis | 1,969 | 5 | 0 | 1 | 0 | 4 | 7 | 4 | 3 | 0 | 1 |
| Mercedes | 16,684 | 67 | 1 | 9 | 5 | 52 | 412 | 46 | 331 | 35 | 3 |
| Meridian | 1,501 | 0 | 0 | 0 | 0 | 0 | 7 | 0 | 5 | 2 | 0 |
| Merkel | 2,633 | 2 | 0 | 1 | 1 | 0 | 11 | 1 | 8 | 2 | 1 |
| Mesquite | 137,796 | 722 | 13 | 51 | 165 | 493 | 4,772 | 550 | 3,409 | 813 | 12 |
| Mexia | 7,269 | 24 | 0 | 3 | 2 | 19 | 122 | 24 | 89 | 9 | 0 |
| Midland | 151,243 | 594 | 12 | 132 | 38 | 412 | 2,253 | 289 | 1,707 | 257 | 5 |
| Midlothian | 36,655 | 38 | 0 | 11 | 4 | 23 | 378 | 33 | 318 | 27 | 0 |
| Miles | 898 | 1 | 0 | 0 | 1 | 0 | 13 | 7 | 4 | 2 | 0 |
| Mineola | 4,998 | 10 | 0 | 2 | 1 | 7 | 146 | 46 | 91 | 9 | 0 |
| Mineral Wells | 15,079 | 26 | 1 | 12 | 3 | 10 | 451 | 143 | 266 | 42 | 2 |
| Missouri City | 77,682 | 115 | 1 | 10 | 34 | 70 | 729 | 113 | 557 | 59 | 3 |
| Monahans | 7,959 | 28 | 0 | 14 | 2 | 12 | 127 | 21 | 95 | 11 | 0 |
| Mont Belvieu | 7,567 | 11 | 0 | 3 | 2 | 6 | 116 | 5 | 91 | 20 | 0 |
| Montgomery | 1,812 | 1 | 0 | 0 | 0 | 1 | 14 | 2 | 11 | 1 | 0 |
| Morgans Point Resort | 4,844 | 0 | 0 | 0 | 0 | 0 | 18 | 3 | 14 | 1 | 0 |
| Moulton | 905 | 0 | 0 | 0 | 0 | 0 | 6 | 3 | 3 | 0 | 0 |
| Mount Enterprise | 432 | 0 | 0 | 0 | 0 | 0 | 2 | 0 | 2 | 0 | 0 |
| Mount Pleasant | 16,023 | 92 | 0 | 19 | 6 | 67 | 345 | 61 | 256 | 28 | 1 |
| Mount Vernon | 2,765 | 10 | 0 | 4 | 0 | 6 | 42 | 17 | 21 | 4 | 0 |
| Muleshoe | 4,788 | 3 | 0 | 0 | 0 | 3 | 17 | 2 | 13 | 2 | 0 |
| Murphy | 21,147 | 5 | 0 | 1 | 2 | 2 | 213 | 18 | 193 | 2 | 1 |
| Mustang Ridge | 1,021 | 5 | 0 | 0 | 2 | 3 | 32 | 4 | 16 | 12 | 0 |
| Nacogdoches | 32,421 | 76 | 5 | 13 | 5 | 53 | 687 | 108 | 535 | 44 | 2 |
| Nash | 3,882 | 19 | 0 | 2 | 1 | 16 | 44 | 6 | 38 | 0 | 0 |
| Nassau Bay | 3,897 | 8 | 0 | 1 | 1 | 6 | 98 | 22 | 69 | 7 | 0 |
| Natalia | 1,643 | 2 | 0 | 1 | 0 | 1 | 5 | 3 | 2 | 0 | 0 |
| Navasota | 8,514 | 47 | 2 | 8 | 4 | 33 | 187 | 65 | 97 | 25 | 0 |
| Nederland | 17,205 | 73 | 0 | 17 | 5 | 51 | 233 | 43 | 163 | 27 | 1 |
| Needville | 3,150 | 6 | 0 | 0 | 1 | 5 | 9 | 1 | 8 | 0 | 0 |
| New Boston | 4,546 | 41 | 0 | 9 | 0 | 32 | 139 | 22 | 103 | 14 | 0 |
| New Braunfels | 100,427 | 245 | 1 | 16 | 31 | 197 | 1,226 | 184 | 882 | 160 | 0 |
| Newton | 2,315 | 1 | 0 | 0 | 1 | 0 | 17 | 5 | 12 | 0 | 0 |
| Nolanville | 6,335 | 6 | 0 | 0 | 1 | 5 | 49 | 10 | 34 | 5 | 0 |
| Northeast | 3,582 | 1 | 0 | 1 | 0 | 0 | 23 | 1 | 16 | 6 | 0 |
| Northlake | 4,751 | 17 | 0 | 4 | 1 | 12 | 78 | 7 | 63 | 8 | 0 |
| North Richland Hills | 72,881 | 158 | 1 | 50 | 21 | 86 | 1,565 | 141 | 1,283 | 141 | 1 |
| Oak Ridge North | 3,168 | 2 | 0 | 0 | 0 | 2 | 70 | 8 | 56 | 6 | 0 |
| Odem | 2,375 | 4 | 0 | 0 | 1 | 3 | 17 | 5 | 7 | 5 | 0 |
| Odessa | 128,328 | 654 | 10 | 62 | 101 | 481 | 2,884 | 512 | 1,998 | 374 | 16 |
| Olmos Park | 2,484 | 1 | 0 | 0 | 0 | 1 | 16 | 4 | 11 | 1 | 0 |
| Olney | 3,054 | 14 | 0 | 4 | 0 | 10 | 32 | 8 | 20 | 4 | 0 |
| Onalaska | 3,225 | 7 | 1 | 1 | 0 | 5 | 23 | 5 | 12 | 6 | 0 |
| Orange | 17,755 | 77 | 3 | 7 | 7 | 60 | 292 | 58 | 188 | 46 | 1 |
| Overton | 2,498 | 9 | 0 | 2 | 0 | 7 | 14 | 6 | 8 | 0 | 0 |
| Ovilla | 4,370 | 2 | 0 | 0 | 0 | 2 | 7 | 1 | 4 | 2 | 0 |
| Oyster Creek | 1,222 | 2 | 0 | 0 | 0 | 2 | 17 | 5 | 10 | 2 | 0 |
| Palacios | 4,529 | 24 | 0 | 5 | 0 | 19 | 88 | 9 | 71 | 8 | 2 |
| Palestine | 17,736 | 103 | 1 | 14 | 6 | 82 | 436 | 96 | 304 | 36 | 4 |
| Palmer | 2,185 | 4 | 0 | 1 | 0 | 3 | 15 | 5 | 3 | 7 | 0 |
| Palmhurst | 2,735 | 7 | 0 | 1 | 2 | 4 | 89 | 2 | 87 | 0 | 0 |
| Palmview | 5,875 | 84 | 3 | 10 | 6 | 65 | 217 | 50 | 147 | 20 | 0 |
| Pampa | 16,760 | 63 | 2 | 9 | 2 | 50 | 342 | 71 | 250 | 21 | 3 |
| Pantego | 2,505 | 11 | 0 | 0 | 4 | 7 | 101 | 28 | 67 | 6 | 0 |

## Table 8. Offenses Known to Law Enforcement, by Selected State and City, 2021—Continued

(Number.)

| State/city | Population | Violent crime | Murder and nonnegligent manslaughter | Rape | Robbery | Aggravated assault | Property crime | Burglary | Larceny-theft | Motor vehicle theft | Arson |
|---|---|---|---|---|---|---|---|---|---|---|---|
| Paris | 24,833 | 224 | 2 | 42 | 10 | 170 | 591 | 153 | 371 | 67 | 4 |
| Parker | 5,649 | 1 | 0 | 1 | 0 | 0 | 25 | 5 | 20 | 0 | 0 |
| Pasadena | 149,428 | 939 | 8 | 100 | 157 | 674 | 3,666 | 581 | 2,413 | 672 | 12 |
| Patton Village | 2,277 | 1 | 0 | 0 | 0 | 1 | 1 | 0 | 1 | 0 | 0 |
| Pearland | 126,983 | 136 | 1 | 24 | 24 | 87 | 1,838 | 186 | 1,510 | 142 | 0 |
| Pearsall | 10,776 | 26 | 1 | 3 | 2 | 20 | 154 | 69 | 65 | 20 | 2 |
| Pecos | 10,675 | 60 | 2 | 5 | 1 | 52 | 119 | 18 | 95 | 6 | 0 |
| Pelican Bay | 2,165 | 5 | 0 | 0 | 0 | 5 | 24 | 3 | 18 | 3 | 0 |
| Penitas | 4,625 | 10 | 0 | 2 | 1 | 7 | 49 | 10 | 29 | 10 | 0 |
| Perryton | 8,272 | 34 | 0 | 2 | 0 | 32 | 83 | 28 | 52 | 3 | 0 |
| Petersburg | 1,102 | 3 | 0 | 1 | 0 | 2 | 2 | 1 | 1 | 0 | 0 |
| Pflugerville | 68,978 | 98 | 1 | 24 | 10 | 63 | 935 | 84 | 756 | 95 | 0 |
| Pharr | 80,436 | 245 | 6 | 48 | 15 | 176 | 1,273 | 159 | 1,030 | 84 | 2 |
| Pilot Point | 4,741 | 2 | 0 | 0 | 0 | 2 | 35 | 5 | 21 | 9 | 0 |
| Pinehurst | 1,946 | 17 | 0 | 1 | 0 | 16 | 40 | 11 | 23 | 6 | 0 |
| Pineland | 789 | 2 | 0 | 2 | 0 | 0 | 1 | 0 | 1 | 0 | 0 |
| Pittsburg | 4,696 | 13 | 0 | 1 | 0 | 12 | 50 | 10 | 34 | 6 | 0 |
| Plainview | 19,436 | 119 | 0 | 7 | 10 | 102 | 523 | 134 | 335 | 54 | 2 |
| Plano | 294,496 | 463 | 5 | 118 | 84 | 256 | 4,809 | 569 | 3,764 | 476 | 13 |
| Pleasanton | 11,160 | 25 | 0 | 2 | 2 | 21 | 239 | 30 | 175 | 34 | 1 |
| Ponder | 2,555 | 1 | 0 | 1 | 0 | 0 | 2 | 0 | 2 | 0 | 0 |
| Port Aransas | 4,513 | 31 | 0 | 2 | 3 | 26 | 157 | 16 | 119 | 22 | 0 |
| Port Arthur | 53,865 | 412 | 6 | 37 | 77 | 292 | 923 | 199 | 571 | 153 | 1 |
| Port Isabel | 6,217 | 17 | 0 | 1 | 0 | 16 | 38 | 1 | 37 | 0 | 1 |
| Portland | 17,938 | 31 | 2 | 5 | 8 | 16 | 349 | 37 | 295 | 17 | 0 |
| Port Lavaca | 11,618 | 31 | 0 | 5 | 0 | 26 | 108 | 27 | 71 | 10 | 2 |
| Port Neches | 12,555 | 25 | 0 | 7 | 1 | 17 | 135 | 21 | 98 | 16 | 1 |
| Poteet | 3,571 | 5 | 1 | 0 | 1 | 3 | 68 | 24 | 41 | 3 | 0 |
| Prairie View | 7,174 | 14 | 0 | 0 | 2 | 12 | 49 | 23 | 20 | 6 | 1 |
| Primera | 5,394 | 2 | 0 | 0 | 0 | 2 | 2 | 0 | 2 | 0 | 0 |
| Princeton | 17,059 | 32 | 0 | 13 | 2 | 17 | 105 | 11 | 79 | 15 | 0 |
| Prosper | 29,848 | 8 | 0 | 2 | 0 | 6 | 212 | 29 | 178 | 5 | 0 |
| Queen City | 1,409 | 4 | 0 | 2 | 0 | 2 | 45 | 7 | 13 | 25 | 0 |
| Quitman | 1,866 | 6 | 0 | 1 | 1 | 4 | 16 | 8 | 6 | 2 | 0 |
| Rancho Viejo | 2,447 | 0 | 0 | 0 | 0 | 0 | 20 | 2 | 18 | 0 | 0 |
| Ranger | 2,343 | 9 | 0 | 4 | 0 | 5 | 55 | 28 | 21 | 6 | 1 |
| Raymondville | 10,714 | 103 | 0 | 8 | 5 | 90 | 186 | 36 | 137 | 13 | 4 |
| Red Oak | 14,483 | 30 | 1 | 5 | 8 | 16 | 188 | 29 | 139 | 20 | 0 |
| Refugio | 2,694 | 4 | 1 | 0 | 2 | 1 | 35 | 10 | 15 | 10 | 0 |
| Reno, Lamar County | 3,366 | 3 | 0 | 0 | 0 | 3 | 55 | 3 | 50 | 2 | 0 |
| Rice | 991 | 0 | 0 | 0 | 0 | 0 | 20 | 7 | 12 | 1 | 0 |
| Richardson | 122,872 | 182 | 5 | 20 | 55 | 102 | 2,502 | 285 | 1,960 | 257 | 10 |
| Richland Hills | 7,846 | 8 | 0 | 2 | 1 | 5 | 204 | 29 | 149 | 26 | 1 |
| Richmond | 12,520 | 50 | 3 | 9 | 16 | 22 | 177 | 29 | 135 | 13 | 0 |
| Richwood | 4,068 | 16 | 1 | 3 | 0 | 12 | 26 | 3 | 18 | 5 | 0 |
| Rio Grande City | 14,498 | 36 | 0 | 2 | 0 | 34 | 245 | 76 | 148 | 21 | 2 |
| Rio Hondo | 2,669 | 9 | 0 | 2 | 0 | 7 | 16 | 4 | 9 | 3 | 0 |
| River Oaks | 7,550 | 17 | 1 | 3 | 2 | 11 | 123 | 27 | 73 | 23 | 0 |
| Roanoke | 10,234 | 9 | 0 | 4 | 1 | 4 | 130 | 15 | 103 | 12 | 0 |
| Robinson | 12,254 | 14 | 1 | 4 | 0 | 9 | 225 | 26 | 184 | 15 | 1 |
| Rockdale | 5,444 | 22 | 0 | 4 | 1 | 17 | 196 | 54 | 114 | 28 | 1 |
| Rockport | 10,934 | 37 | 0 | 8 | 2 | 27 | 418 | 101 | 301 | 16 | 0 |
| Rockwall | 48,483 | 49 | 0 | 15 | 3 | 31 | 646 | 45 | 553 | 48 | 0 |
| Rogers | 1,255 | 0 | 0 | 0 | 0 | 0 | 2 | 0 | 1 | 1 | 0 |
| Rollingwood | 1,589 | 2 | 0 | 0 | 0 | 2 | 34 | 3 | 26 | 5 | 0 |
| Roma | 11,534 | 33 | 0 | 6 | 1 | 26 | 97 | 18 | 67 | 12 | 1 |
| Roman Forest | 2,086 | 1 | 0 | 1 | 0 | 0 | 20 | 3 | 16 | 1 | 0 |
| Roscoe | 1,302 | 3 | 0 | 1 | 1 | 1 | 10 | 3 | 5 | 2 | 0 |
| Rosenberg | 40,251 | 127 | 2 | 23 | 22 | 80 | 578 | 98 | 426 | 54 | 1 |
| Round Rock | 141,927 | 196 | 3 | 30 | 26 | 137 | 2,460 | 184 | 2,128 | 148 | 6 |
| Rowlett | 69,287 | 121 | 2 | 21 | 9 | 89 | 715 | 87 | 578 | 50 | 1 |
| Royse City | 16,013 | 27 | 0 | 8 | 2 | 17 | 249 | 34 | 190 | 25 | 0 |
| Runaway Bay | 1,665 | 0 | 0 | 0 | 0 | 0 | 2 | 0 | 2 | 0 | 0 |
| Rusk | 5,674 | 10 | 0 | 2 | 1 | 7 | 64 | 9 | 50 | 5 | 0 |
| Sabinal | 1,674 | 1 | 0 | 0 | 0 | 1 | 2 | 0 | 2 | 0 | 0 |
| Sachse | 26,463 | 15 | 1 | 6 | 0 | 8 | 195 | 20 | 159 | 16 | 1 |
| Saginaw | 25,387 | 62 | 1 | 14 | 10 | 37 | 358 | 31 | 269 | 58 | 0 |
| Salado | 2,401 | 0 | 0 | 0 | 0 | 0 | 18 | 5 | 12 | 1 | 0 |
| San Angelo | 102,448 | 342 | 5 | 60 | 43 | 234 | 2,617 | 478 | 1,918 | 221 | 15 |
| San Antonio | 1,592,693 | 10,881 | 168 | 1,090 | 1,716 | 7,907 | 60,745 | 7,553 | 44,306 | 8,886 | 275 |
| San Augustine | 1,842 | 2 | 0 | 0 | 1 | 1 | 103 | 74 | 27 | 2 | 1 |
| San Benito | 24,065 | 144 | 1 | 5 | 8 | 130 | 462 | 79 | 342 | 41 | 0 |
| San Elizario | 9,041 | 7 | 0 | 3 | 1 | 3 | 27 | 5 | 20 | 2 | 0 |
| Sanger | 9,383 | 19 | 0 | 6 | 1 | 12 | 132 | 27 | 77 | 28 | 1 |
| San Juan | 37,333 | 80 | 0 | 10 | 9 | 61 | 514 | 50 | 429 | 35 | 0 |
| San Marcos | 68,961 | 367 | 4 | 91 | 43 | 229 | 1,653 | 204 | 1,287 | 162 | 2 |
| San Saba | 3,135 | 5 | 0 | 0 | 0 | 5 | 22 | 2 | 14 | 6 | 0 |
| Sansom Park Village | 5,826 | 17 | 0 | 4 | 3 | 10 | 127 | 35 | 72 | 20 | 0 |
| Santa Fe | 13,583 | 23 | 0 | 12 | 0 | 11 | 94 | 27 | 56 | 11 | 2 |
| Schertz | 43,637 | 39 | 2 | 8 | 6 | 23 | 375 | 33 | 291 | 51 | 1 |
| Schulenburg | 2,944 | 13 | 0 | 2 | 0 | 11 | 57 | 8 | 46 | 3 | 0 |
| Seabrook | 14,102 | 40 | 1 | 12 | 7 | 20 | 240 | 70 | 146 | 24 | 1 |
| Seagoville | 17,291 | 27 | 0 | 11 | 4 | 12 | 331 | 53 | 184 | 94 | 0 |

## Table 8. Offenses Known to Law Enforcement, by Selected State and City, 2021—Continued

(Number.)

| State/city | Population | Violent crime | Murder and nonnegligent manslaughter | Rape | Robbery | Aggravated assault | Property crime | Burglary | Larceny-theft | Motor vehicle theft | Arson |
|---|---|---|---|---|---|---|---|---|---|---|---|
| Sealy | 6,478 | 9 | 0 | 2 | 0 | 7 | 66 | 17 | 42 | 7 | 0 |
| Seguin | 30,653 | 78 | 0 | 11 | 10 | 57 | 667 | 123 | 469 | 75 | 0 |
| Selma | 14,299 | 14 | 0 | 1 | 2 | 11 | 269 | 26 | 208 | 35 | 3 |
| Seminole | 8,115 | 9 | 0 | 0 | 1 | 8 | 61 | 8 | 49 | 4 | 1 |
| Seven Points | 1,571 | 5 | 1 | 0 | 1 | 3 | 33 | 2 | 22 | 9 | 0 |
| Seymour | 2,541 | 2 | 0 | 0 | 0 | 2 | 12 | 4 | 5 | 3 | 1 |
| Shallowater | 2,628 | 3 | 0 | 0 | 0 | 3 | 10 | 2 | 7 | 1 | 0 |
| Shavano Park | 4,137 | 4 | 1 | 0 | 2 | 1 | 57 | 8 | 44 | 5 | 0 |
| Shenandoah | 3,217 | 8 | 0 | 4 | 1 | 3 | 319 | 25 | 273 | 21 | 0 |
| Sherman | 45,814 | 193 | 0 | 40 | 14 | 139 | 843 | 242 | 514 | 87 | 5 |
| Silsbee | 6,604 | 11 | 1 | 0 | 1 | 9 | 75 | 11 | 51 | 13 | 0 |
| Sinton | 5,248 | 44 | 0 | 17 | 2 | 25 | 174 | 24 | 141 | 9 | 1 |
| Slaton | 5,960 | 8 | 0 | 1 | 0 | 7 | 116 | 36 | 71 | 9 | 2 |
| Snyder | 10,986 | 143 | 2 | 11 | 1 | 129 | 193 | 39 | 131 | 23 | 1 |
| Socorro | 36,282 | 74 | 1 | 16 | 6 | 51 | 283 | 49 | 182 | 52 | 4 |
| Somerset | 2,017 | 0 | 0 | 0 | 0 | 0 | 3 | 0 | 1 | 2 | 0 |
| Somerville | 1,450 | 3 | 0 | 1 | 0 | 2 | 8 | 1 | 4 | 3 | 0 |
| Sonora | 2,744 | 4 | 0 | 1 | 0 | 3 | 14 | 4 | 7 | 3 | 0 |
| Sour Lake | 1,962 | 2 | 0 | 1 | 0 | 1 | 19 | 4 | 13 | 2 | 2 |
| South Houston | 17,490 | 100 | 4 | 10 | 29 | 57 | 352 | 53 | 207 | 92 | 1 |
| Southlake | 32,905 | 6 | 0 | 0 | 2 | 4 | 306 | 37 | 257 | 12 | 1 |
| South Padre Island | 2,744 | 56 | 5 | 14 | 5 | 32 | 311 | 13 | 286 | 12 | 0 |
| Southside Place | 1,902 | 1 | 0 | 0 | 0 | 1 | 18 | 0 | 15 | 3 | 0 |
| Splendora | 2,371 | 5 | 0 | 1 | 0 | 4 | 30 | 7 | 18 | 5 | 0 |
| Spring Valley | 4,363 | 5 | 0 | 1 | 2 | 2 | 76 | 4 | 64 | 8 | 0 |
| Stafford | 17,102 | 140 | 0 | 25 | 30 | 85 | 830 | 79 | 657 | 94 | 1 |
| Stamford | 2,892 | 3 | 0 | 2 | 0 | 1 | 22 | 8 | 13 | 1 | 0 |
| Stanton | 3,114 | 11 | 0 | 3 | 0 | 8 | 52 | 24 | 28 | 0 | 0 |
| Stephenville | 22,221 | 53 | 0 | 27 | 2 | 24 | 222 | 49 | 159 | 14 | 0 |
| Stinnett | 1,742 | 2 | 0 | 0 | 0 | 2 | 3 | 1 | 1 | 1 | 0 |
| Sugar Land | 118,888 | 78 | 1 | 12 | 26 | 39 | 1,482 | 197 | 1,196 | 89 | 1 |
| Sulphur Springs | 16,357 | 21 | 0 | 9 | 1 | 11 | 128 | 29 | 79 | 20 | 0 |
| Sunnyvale | 7,232 | 10 | 0 | 2 | 1 | 7 | 95 | 11 | 74 | 10 | 0 |
| Sunrise Beach Village | 820 | 1 | 0 | 0 | 0 | 1 | 7 | 1 | 6 | 0 | 0 |
| Sunset Valley | 663 | 2 | 0 | 0 | 0 | 2 | 120 | 5 | 108 | 7 | 0 |
| Surfside Beach | 601 | 7 | 0 | 0 | 1 | 6 | 25 | 3 | 18 | 4 | 0 |
| Sweeny | 3,612 | 5 | 0 | 3 | 0 | 2 | 46 | 5 | 37 | 4 | 1 |
| Taft | 2,871 | 2 | 0 | 0 | 0 | 2 | 46 | 20 | 24 | 2 | 1 |
| Tahoka | 2,664 | 8 | 0 | 4 | 0 | 4 | 26 | 8 | 15 | 3 | 1 |
| Tatum | 1,417 | 0 | 0 | 0 | 0 | 0 | 8 | 2 | 5 | 1 | 0 |
| Taylor | 18,196 | 53 | 0 | 9 | 2 | 37 | 235 | 56 | 158 | 21 | 2 |
| Teague | 3,524 | 7 | 0 | 0 | 0 | 7 | 51 | 19 | 27 | 5 | 3 |
| Temple | 82,333 | 241 | 6 | 62 | 23 | 150 | 1,711 | 229 | 1,282 | 200 | 5 |
| Tenaha | 1,132 | 2 | 0 | 0 | 0 | 2 | 1 | 0 | 1 | 0 | 0 |
| Terrell | 20,092 | 66 | 0 | 13 | 9 | 44 | 312 | 30 | 255 | 27 | 0 |
| Terrell Hills | 5,510 | 6 | 0 | 1 | 1 | 4 | 71 | 13 | 53 | 5 | 0 |
| Texarkana | 36,208 | 278 | 20 | 36 | 36 | 186 | 1,187 | 117 | 951 | 119 | 5 |
| Texas City | 52,270 | 209 | 8 | 35 | 24 | 142 | 1,263 | 195 | 948 | 120 | 4 |
| The Colony | 46,510 | 196 | 2 | 111 | 9 | 74 | 1,093 | 43 | 972 | 78 | 2 |
| Thorndale | 1,303 | 0 | 0 | 0 | 0 | 0 | 8 | 2 | 5 | 1 | 0 |
| Tioga | 1,153 | 2 | 0 | 0 | 0 | 2 | 2 | 1 | 1 | 0 | 0 |
| Todd Mission | 113 | 0 | 0 | 0 | 0 | 0 | 0 | 0 | 0 | 0 | 0 |
| Tomball | 11,826 | 75 | 0 | 14 | 10 | 51 | 291 | 28 | 229 | 34 | 2 |
| Tool | 2,346 | 3 | 0 | 1 | 0 | 2 | 12 | 2 | 7 | 3 | 0 |
| Trophy Club | 13,205 | 1 | 0 | 0 | 1 | 0 | 61 | 6 | 53 | 2 | 0 |
| Tulia | 4,568 | 25 | 0 | 6 | 2 | 17 | 95 | 31 | 57 | 7 | 3 |
| Tye | 1,353 | 3 | 0 | 0 | 0 | 3 | 16 | 3 | 11 | 2 | 0 |
| Tyler | 109,408 | 476 | 5 | 57 | 50 | 364 | 2,789 | 343 | 2,225 | 221 | 1 |
| Universal City | 21,265 | 55 | 0 | 16 | 4 | 35 | 513 | 66 | 394 | 53 | 1 |
| University Park | 24,888 | 7 | 1 | 3 | 2 | 1 | 305 | 46 | 230 | 29 | 0 |
| Uvalde | 15,999 | 71 | 0 | 8 | 10 | 53 | 671 | 83 | 544 | 44 | 1 |
| Valley Mills | 1,168 | 2 | 0 | 0 | 0 | 2 | 18 | 5 | 12 | 1 | 0 |
| Van | 2,793 | 6 | 0 | 0 | 3 | 3 | 24 | 7 | 12 | 5 | 0 |
| Van Alstyne | 4,831 | 7 | 0 | 1 | 0 | 6 | 36 | 7 | 26 | 3 | 0 |
| Venus | 4,804 | 11 | 0 | 2 | 0 | 9 | 30 | 1 | 23 | 6 | 0 |
| Vernon | 10,057 | 40 | 0 | 4 | 6 | 30 | 138 | 29 | 94 | 15 | 4 |
| Victoria | 67,272 | 368 | 0 | 63 | 42 | 263 | 1,738 | 351 | 1,287 | 100 | 9 |
| Vidor | 10,267 | 15 | 0 | 2 | 2 | 11 | 232 | 78 | 125 | 29 | 0 |
| Waco | 143,089 | 1,031 | 15 | 112 | 147 | 757 | 4,774 | 932 | 3,419 | 423 | 9 |
| Wake Village | 5,538 | 10 | 0 | 5 | 0 | 5 | 54 | 14 | 35 | 5 | 0 |
| Waller | 3,732 | 12 | 0 | 1 | 1 | 10 | 39 | 16 | 10 | 13 | 0 |
| Wallis | 1,334 | 12 | 1 | 1 | 0 | 10 | 8 | 2 | 5 | 1 | 1 |
| Watauga | 24,254 | 50 | 0 | 8 | 8 | 34 | 292 | 46 | 216 | 30 | 0 |
| Waxahachie | 40,978 | 112 | 2 | 22 | 8 | 80 | 701 | 52 | 564 | 85 | 2 |
| Weatherford | 35,724 | 78 | 0 | 28 | 7 | 43 | 572 | 100 | 420 | 52 | 4 |
| Webster | 11,359 | 58 | 1 | 9 | 12 | 36 | 827 | 85 | 625 | 117 | 2 |
| Weimar | 2,238 | 3 | 0 | 1 | 0 | 2 | 20 | 7 | 12 | 1 | 0 |
| Weslaco | 43,954 | 193 | 1 | 42 | 32 | 118 | 1,142 | 128 | 982 | 32 | 0 |
| West Columbia | 3,823 | 22 | 0 | 8 | 0 | 14 | 46 | 4 | 38 | 4 | 1 |
| West Lake Hills | 3,272 | 6 | 0 | 1 | 4 | 1 | 78 | 5 | 67 | 6 | 0 |
| West Orange | 3,141 | 11 | 0 | 0 | 3 | 8 | 79 | 14 | 49 | 16 | 0 |
| Westover Hills | 683 | 0 | 0 | 0 | 0 | 0 | 3 | 1 | 2 | 0 | 0 |
| Westworth | 2,810 | 12 | 0 | 0 | 3 | 9 | 174 | 10 | 156 | 8 | 1 |

## Table 8. Offenses Known to Law Enforcement, by Selected State and City, 2021—Continued

(Number.)

| State/city | Population | Violent crime | Murder and nonnegligent manslaughter | Rape | Robbery | Aggravated assault | Property crime | Burglary | Larceny-theft | Motor vehicle theft | Arson |
|---|---|---|---|---|---|---|---|---|---|---|---|
| Wharton | 8,590 | 48 | 0 | 1 | 8 | 39 | 174 | 31 | 126 | 17 | 2 |
| Whitehouse | 9,260 | 15 | 0 | 7 | 0 | 8 | 57 | 7 | 48 | 2 | 0 |
| White Oak | 6,262 | 10 | 0 | 6 | 0 | 4 | 91 | 16 | 65 | 10 | 0 |
| White Settlement | 17,948 | 50 | 4 | 12 | 6 | 28 | 579 | 94 | 310 | 175 | 0 |
| Whitney | 2,151 | 1 | 0 | 0 | 1 | 0 | 38 | 17 | 18 | 3 | 0 |
| Wichita Falls | 105,468 | 599 | 11 | 122 | 55 | 411 | 3,232 | 642 | 2,195 | 395 | 2 |
| Willis | 7,258 | 44 | 0 | 5 | 6 | 33 | 179 | 29 | 132 | 18 | 0 |
| Willow Park | 6,244 | 5 | 0 | 2 | 2 | 1 | 79 | 3 | 71 | 5 | 0 |
| Wills Point | 3,723 | 5 | 0 | 0 | 0 | 5 | 35 | 16 | 16 | 3 | 0 |
| Wilmer | 5,620 | 10 | 0 | 0 | 1 | 9 | 86 | 18 | 46 | 22 | 0 |
| Windcrest | 5,901 | 16 | 0 | 1 | 5 | 10 | 296 | 12 | 248 | 36 | 1 |
| Wink | 1,022 | 1 | 0 | 0 | 0 | 1 | 6 | 5 | 1 | 0 | 0 |
| Winnsboro | 3,338 | 3 | 0 | 0 | 0 | 3 | 32 | 7 | 24 | 1 | 0 |
| Winters | 2,460 | 5 | 0 | 3 | 0 | 2 | 12 | 5 | 4 | 3 | 0 |
| Wolfforth | 5,973 | 7 | 0 | 2 | 1 | 4 | 35 | 4 | 24 | 7 | 1 |
| Woodsboro | 1,363 | 0 | 0 | 0 | 0 | 0 | 9 | 2 | 7 | 0 | 0 |
| Woodville | 2,428 | 5 | 1 | 0 | 0 | 4 | 43 | 18 | 25 | 0 | 0 |
| Woodway | 9,141 | 13 | 0 | 1 | 0 | 12 | 118 | 8 | 106 | 4 | 0 |
| Wylie | 55,889 | 45 | 1 | 16 | 3 | 25 | 305 | 23 | 255 | 27 | 0 |
| Yoakum | 5,949 | 11 | 0 | 1 | 0 | 10 | 23 | 7 | 12 | 4 | 0 |
| Zavalla | 712 | 3 | 0 | 0 | 0 | 3 | 16 | 5 | 11 | 0 | 0 |
| **UTAH** | | | | | | | | | | | |
| American Fork/Cedar Hills | 44,725 | 36 | 1 | 14 | 5 | 16 | 833 | 89 | 696 | 48 | 0 |
| Aurora | 1,065 | 0 | 0 | 0 | 0 | 0 | 0 | 0 | 0 | 0 | 0 |
| Bluffdale | 19,428 | 21 | 0 | 3 | 1 | 17 | 152 | 26 | 111 | 15 | 2 |
| Brian Head | 96 | 1 | 0 | 0 | 0 | 1 | 5 | 0 | 5 | 0 | 0 |
| Cedar City | 36,903 | 48 | 2 | 20 | 3 | 23 | 404 | 49 | 330 | 25 | 2 |
| Centerville | 17,765 | 31 | 0 | 18 | 2 | 11 | 390 | 38 | 339 | 13 | 1 |
| Clearfield | 32,375 | 51 | 0 | 13 | 5 | 33 | 449 | 59 | 341 | 49 | 3 |
| Cottonwood Heights | 33,301 | 47 | 0 | 10 | 8 | 29 | 755 | 66 | 610 | 79 | 3 |
| Draper | 49,671 | 63 | 0 | 26 | 8 | 29 | 1,097 | 142 | 829 | 126 | 5 |
| Enoch | 7,780 | 4 | 0 | 0 | 0 | 4 | 21 | 4 | 16 | 1 | 0 |
| Ephraim | 7,521 | 11 | 0 | 8 | 0 | 3 | 32 | 4 | 23 | 5 | 0 |
| Farmington | 26,218 | 26 | 0 | 16 | 2 | 8 | 319 | 33 | 261 | 25 | 1 |
| Grantsville | 12,819 | 26 | 0 | 11 | 0 | 15 | 109 | 14 | 82 | 13 | 0 |
| Harrisville | 6,983 | 4 | 0 | 1 | 1 | 2 | 242 | 25 | 215 | 2 | 0 |
| Heber | 18,336 | 9 | 0 | 3 | 0 | 6 | 226 | 125 | 98 | 3 | 0 |
| Helper | 2,135 | 6 | 0 | 5 | 0 | 1 | 19 | 5 | 14 | 0 | 1 |
| Herriman | 61,086 | 44 | 0 | 17 | 3 | 24 | 541 | 75 | 410 | 56 | 2 |
| Hurricane | 20,594 | 71 | 0 | 6 | 0 | 65 | 219 | 24 | 174 | 21 | 1 |
| Kanab | 5,045 | 12 | 0 | 1 | 0 | 11 | 41 | 1 | 37 | 3 | 0 |
| Kaysville | 33,139 | 21 | 0 | 12 | 1 | 8 | 265 | 39 | 202 | 24 | 5 |
| La Verkin | 4,503 | 15 | 0 | 9 | 0 | 6 | 58 | 3 | 50 | 5 | 3 |
| Layton | 80,230 | 141 | 0 | 73 | 16 | 52 | 1,379 | 181 | 1,079 | 119 | 19 |
| Lindon | 11,609 | 6 | 0 | 4 | 1 | 1 | 368 | 35 | 312 | 21 | 1 |
| Logan | 52,015 | 79 | 1 | 31 | 1 | 46 | 712 | 82 | 564 | 66 | 4 |
| Lone Peak | 30,210 | 12 | 0 | 7 | 2 | 3 | 176 | 44 | 118 | 14 | 0 |
| Mapleton | 11,497 | 9 | 0 | 4 | 0 | 5 | 60 | 13 | 43 | 4 | 0 |
| Moab | 5,400 | 35 | 0 | 13 | 1 | 21 | 108 | 12 | 81 | 15 | 3 |
| Mount Pleasant | 3,613 | 14 | 1 | 5 | 0 | 8 | 22 | 3 | 18 | 1 | 0 |
| Murray | 48,524 | 191 | 2 | 37 | 40 | 112 | 2,834 | 328 | 2,051 | 455 | 8 |
| Naples | 2,150 | 3 | 0 | 0 | 0 | 3 | 16 | 2 | 13 | 1 | 0 |
| Nephi | 6,598 | 12 | 0 | 4 | 1 | 7 | 71 | 13 | 51 | 7 | 0 |
| North Ogden | 21,379 | 28 | 0 | 6 | 2 | 20 | 206 | 31 | 147 | 28 | 2 |
| North Salt Lake | 21,768 | 23 | 0 | 8 | 2 | 13 | 468 | 72 | 337 | 59 | 0 |
| Ogden | 87,828 | 485 | 5 | 84 | 71 | 325 | 2,698 | 324 | 2,025 | 349 | 16 |
| Orem | 100,060 | 176 | 6 | 77 | 9 | 84 | 1,641 | 160 | 1,335 | 146 | 2 |
| Park City | 8,679 | 37 | 0 | 22 | 1 | 14 | 164 | 17 | 133 | 14 | 1 |
| Payson | 21,291 | 18 | 0 | 8 | 4 | 6 | 229 | 34 | 177 | 18 | 1 |
| Perry | 5,471 | 6 | 0 | 3 | 0 | 3 | 81 | 14 | 59 | 8 | 2 |
| Pleasant Grove | 38,730 | 39 | 0 | 16 | 1 | 22 | 369 | 50 | 271 | 48 | 4 |
| Pleasant View | 11,139 | 14 | 0 | 4 | 1 | 9 | 81 | 11 | 56 | 14 | 0 |
| Provo | 116,642 | 137 | 0 | 42 | 18 | 77 | 1,568 | 115 | 1,336 | 117 | 4 |
| Richfield | 7,947 | 13 | 0 | 4 | 1 | 8 | 230 | 27 | 192 | 11 | 1 |
| Riverdale | 9,038 | 17 | 0 | 3 | 5 | 9 | 412 | 24 | 368 | 20 | 1 |
| Riverton | 44,951 | 27 | 0 | 9 | 4 | 14 | 548 | 56 | 436 | 56 | 3 |
| Roosevelt | 7,377 | 35 | 0 | 19 | 0 | 16 | 209 | 21 | 174 | 14 | 0 |
| Roy | 39,765 | 69 | 0 | 23 | 7 | 39 | 452 | 72 | 322 | 58 | 1 |
| Salem | 9,151 | 4 | 0 | 2 | 0 | 2 | 41 | 5 | 35 | 1 | 0 |
| Salina | 2,661 | 12 | 0 | 2 | 0 | 10 | 53 | 6 | 42 | 5 | 0 |
| Salt Lake City | 205,929 | 1,996 | 16 | 319 | 439 | 1,222 | 14,087 | 1,636 | 10,329 | 2,122 | 64 |
| Santa Clara/Ivins | 18,948 | 13 | 1 | 2 | 0 | 10 | 87 | 16 | 58 | 13 | 1 |
| Santaquin/Genola | 15,647 | 11 | 0 | 4 | 0 | 7 | 85 | 11 | 66 | 8 | 0 |
| Saratoga Springs | 37,985 | 60 | 0 | 29 | 0 | 31 | 274 | 29 | 236 | 9 | 2 |
| South Jordan | 81,919 | 77 | 1 | 30 | 11 | 35 | 1,190 | 148 | 913 | 129 | 1 |
| South Ogden | 17,187 | 28 | 0 | 9 | 2 | 17 | 284 | 50 | 207 | 27 | 0 |
| South Salt Lake | 25,422 | 261 | 3 | 44 | 54 | 160 | 1,936 | 146 | 1,359 | 431 | 3 |
| Spanish Fork | 41,931 | 27 | 0 | 16 | 1 | 10 | 436 | 35 | 363 | 38 | 0 |
| Springdale | 672 | 1 | 0 | 0 | 0 | 1 | 17 | 3 | 13 | 1 | 0 |
| Springville | 33,977 | 34 | 0 | 10 | 4 | 20 | 452 | 36 | 377 | 39 | 0 |
| St. George | 94,601 | 211 | 3 | 63 | 15 | 130 | 1,210 | 144 | 925 | 141 | 3 |
| Sunset | 5,354 | 11 | 0 | 0 | 1 | 10 | 110 | 26 | 58 | 26 | 0 |

## Table 8. Offenses Known to Law Enforcement, by Selected State and City, 2021—Continued

(Number.)

| State/city | Population | Violent crime | Murder and nonnegligent manslaughter | Rape | Robbery | Aggravated assault | Property crime | Burglary | Larceny-theft | Motor vehicle theft | Arson |
|---|---|---|---|---|---|---|---|---|---|---|---|
| Syracuse | 33,340 | 30 | 0 | 12 | 2 | 16 | 232 | 35 | 187 | 10 | 2 |
| Tooele | 37,626 | 151 | 0 | 44 | 7 | 100 | 816 | 137 | 591 | 88 | 6 |
| Washington | 33,668 | 44 | 1 | 9 | 0 | 34 | 328 | 35 | 263 | 30 | 1 |
| West Bountiful | 5,988 | 11 | 0 | 8 | 0 | 3 | 112 | 7 | 99 | 6 | 0 |
| West Jordan | 117,862 | 297 | 4 | 50 | 31 | 212 | 2,439 | 186 | 1,973 | 280 | 6 |
| West Valley | 134,329 | 730 | 5 | 92 | 85 | 548 | 4,161 | 536 | 2,857 | 768 | 10 |
| Woods Cross | 11,870 | 19 | 0 | 2 | 1 | 16 | 180 | 13 | 136 | 31 | 0 |
| **VERMONT** | | | | | | | | | | | |
| Barre | 8,418 | 57 | 0 | 23 | 3 | 31 | 166 | 9 | 154 | 3 | 1 |
| Barre Town | 7,722 | 9 | 0 | 2 | 0 | 7 | 68 | 3 | 62 | 3 | 1 |
| Bellows Falls | 2,950 | 2 | 0 | 0 | 0 | 2 | 25 | 4 | 21 | 0 | 1 |
| Bennington | 14,814 | 38 | 1 | 0 | 2 | 35 | 233 | 48 | 174 | 11 | 1 |
| Berlin | 2,773 | 16 | 0 | 0 | 1 | 15 | 123 | 7 | 113 | 3 | 1 |
| Bradford | 2,673 | 0 | 0 | 0 | 0 | 0 | 34 | 14 | 16 | 4 | 0 |
| Brandon | 3,680 | 4 | 0 | 2 | 2 | 0 | 31 | 0 | 29 | 2 | 0 |
| Brattleboro | 11,182 | 33 | 0 | 2 | 4 | 27 | 420 | 57 | 345 | 18 | 0 |
| Brighton | 1,153 | 0 | 0 | 0 | 0 | 0 | 5 | 0 | 5 | 0 | 0 |
| Bristol | 3,831 | 1 | 0 | 0 | 0 | 1 | 10 | 1 | 9 | 0 | 0 |
| Burlington | 42,946 | 153 | 0 | 17 | 8 | 128 | 1,516 | 197 | 1,219 | 100 | 4 |
| Castleton | 4,468 | 1 | 0 | 0 | 1 | 0 | 16 | 4 | 12 | 0 | 0 |
| Chester | 3,005 | 2 | 0 | 0 | 0 | 2 | 28 | 5 | 22 | 1 | 0 |
| Colchester | 17,101 | 27 | 0 | 3 | 0 | 24 | 236 | 15 | 219 | 2 | 1 |
| Dover | 1,051 | 1 | 0 | 0 | 0 | 1 | 28 | 1 | 26 | 1 | 0 |
| Essex | 22,073 | 39 | 0 | 11 | 0 | 28 | 362 | 55 | 299 | 8 | 0 |
| Fair Haven | 2,511 | 1 | 0 | 0 | 0 | 1 | 32 | 4 | 27 | 1 | 0 |
| Fairlee | 975 | 0 | 0 | 0 | 0 | 0 | 2 | 1 | 1 | 0 | 0 |
| Hardwick | 2,824 | 3 | 0 | 0 | 0 | 3 | 46 | 6 | 39 | 1 | 0 |
| Hartford | 9,530 | 40 | 0 | 6 | 1 | 33 | 152 | 23 | 114 | 15 | 0 |
| Hinesburg | 4,535 | 0 | 0 | 0 | 0 | 0 | 12 | 1 | 9 | 2 | 0 |
| Ludlow | 1,846 | 4 | 0 | 0 | 0 | 4 | 25 | 3 | 22 | 0 | 0 |
| Lyndonville | 1,158 | 3 | 0 | 0 | 0 | 3 | 35 | 3 | 31 | 1 | 0 |
| Manchester | 4,197 | 8 | 0 | 2 | 0 | 6 | 41 | 3 | 36 | 2 | 1 |
| Middlebury | 8,807 | 13 | 0 | 6 | 1 | 6 | 62 | 3 | 56 | 3 | 0 |
| Milton | 10,962 | 22 | 0 | 8 | 1 | 13 | 89 | 10 | 77 | 2 | 0 |
| Montpelier | 7,278 | 12 | 0 | 1 | 0 | 11 | 143 | 10 | 132 | 1 | 1 |
| Morristown | 5,582 | 11 | 0 | 3 | 1 | 7 | 90 | 8 | 82 | 0 | 0 |
| Newport | 4,181 | 25 | 0 | 7 | 1 | 17 | 68 | 8 | 58 | 2 | 0 |
| Northfield | 6,536 | 11 | 0 | 1 | 0 | 10 | 8 | 2 | 6 | 0 | 0 |
| Norwich | 3,400 | 2 | 0 | 1 | 0 | 1 | 27 | 1 | 24 | 2 | 0 |
| Richmond | 4,102 | 1 | 0 | 0 | 0 | 1 | 9 | 3 | 5 | 1 | 1 |
| Royalton | 2,892 | 1 | 0 | 0 | 0 | 1 | 17 | 4 | 13 | 0 | 0 |
| Rutland | 14,771 | 74 | 1 | 7 | 19 | 47 | 556 | 83 | 434 | 39 | 3 |
| Rutland Town | 4,107 | 5 | 0 | 0 | 0 | 5 | 87 | 2 | 85 | 0 | 0 |
| Shelburne | 7,702 | 5 | 0 | 0 | 0 | 5 | 90 | 7 | 79 | 4 | 0 |
| South Burlington | 19,748 | 43 | 0 | 5 | 2 | 36 | 453 | 27 | 420 | 6 | 2 |
| Springfield | 8,828 | 32 | 0 | 10 | 0 | 22 | 224 | 33 | 186 | 5 | 1 |
| St. Albans | 6,787 | 30 | 0 | 8 | 1 | 21 | 215 | 14 | 199 | 2 | 1 |
| St. Johnsbury | 7,021 | 24 | 0 | 6 | 0 | 18 | 174 | 21 | 150 | 3 | 1 |
| Stowe | 4,460 | 4 | 0 | 1 | 0 | 3 | 68 | 4 | 63 | 1 | 3 |
| Swanton | 6,590 | 5 | 0 | 0 | 0 | 5 | 50 | 3 | 43 | 4 | 0 |
| Thetford | 2,519 | 1 | 0 | 1 | 0 | 0 | 11 | 5 | 5 | 1 | 1 |
| Vergennes | 2,594 | 3 | 0 | 1 | 0 | 2 | 28 | 2 | 26 | 0 | 0 |
| Weathersfield | 2,718 | 0 | 0 | 0 | 0 | 0 | 31 | 5 | 25 | 1 | 0 |
| Williston | 10,434 | 7 | 0 | 2 | 0 | 5 | 274 | 25 | 239 | 10 | 0 |
| Wilmington | 1,777 | 1 | 0 | 0 | 0 | 1 | 14 | 1 | 10 | 3 | 0 |
| Windsor | 3,259 | 2 | 0 | 0 | 0 | 2 | 32 | 3 | 25 | 4 | 0 |
| Winhall | 722 | 0 | 0 | 0 | 0 | 0 | 8 | 1 | 6 | 1 | 0 |
| Winooski | 7,554 | 29 | 0 | 4 | 0 | 25 | 204 | 30 | 167 | 7 | 5 |
| Woodstock | 2,899 | 2 | 0 | 1 | 0 | 1 | 13 | 3 | 10 | 0 | 0 |
| **VIRGINIA** | | | | | | | | | | | |
| Abingdon | 7,820 | 7 | 0 | 3 | 1 | 3 | 121 | 5 | 108 | 8 | 1 |
| Alexandria | 160,457 | 332 | 2 | 13 | 84 | 233 | 2,681 | 187 | 2,237 | 257 | 4 |
| Altavista | 3,419 | 6 | 0 | 1 | 0 | 5 | 62 | 2 | 59 | 1 | 1 |
| Amherst | 2,177 | 4 | 0 | 0 | 0 | 4 | 8 | 2 | 6 | 0 | 0 |
| Ashland | 7,976 | 37 | 0 | 3 | 3 | 31 | 135 | 4 | 123 | 8 | 0 |
| Bedford | 6,652 | 7 | 1 | 2 | 0 | 4 | 57 | 4 | 52 | 1 | 0 |
| Berryville | 4,388 | 2 | 0 | 1 | 0 | 1 | 37 | 4 | 32 | 1 | 0 |
| Big Stone Gap | 5,055 | 3 | 0 | 2 | 0 | 1 | 71 | 10 | 53 | 8 | 0 |
| Blacksburg | 44,228 | 35 | 1 | 19 | 4 | 11 | 274 | 33 | 227 | 14 | 2 |
| Blackstone | 3,275 | 7 | 0 | 0 | 1 | 6 | 99 | 10 | 86 | 3 | 1 |
| Bluefield | 4,761 | 6 | 0 | 3 | 2 | 1 | 226 | 4 | 221 | 1 | 0 |
| Bridgewater | 6,218 | 1 | 0 | 0 | 1 | 0 | 16 | 5 | 8 | 3 | 0 |
| Bristol | 17,265 | 68 | 1 | 19 | 6 | 42 | 368 | 49 | 264 | 55 | 6 |
| Brookneal | 1,103 | 0 | 0 | 0 | 0 | 0 | 15 | 1 | 13 | 1 | 0 |
| Buena Vista | 6,374 | 10 | 0 | 1 | 0 | 9 | 42 | 2 | 39 | 1 | 0 |
| Cape Charles | 1,061 | 4 | 0 | 0 | 0 | 4 | 5 | 1 | 3 | 1 | 0 |
| Charlottesville | 47,257 | 229 | 0 | 33 | 34 | 162 | 1,218 | 125 | 944 | 149 | 2 |
| Chase City | 2,205 | 11 | 0 | 0 | 0 | 11 | 26 | 5 | 19 | 2 | 0 |
| Chesapeake | 249,188 | 1,153 | 25 | 103 | 82 | 943 | 4,233 | 321 | 3,529 | 383 | 8 |
| Chilhowie | 1,687 | 2 | 0 | 0 | 0 | 2 | 26 | 1 | 22 | 3 | 0 |
| Chincoteague | 2,859 | 4 | 0 | 3 | 0 | 1 | 30 | 3 | 23 | 4 | 0 |

## Table 8. Offenses Known to Law Enforcement, by Selected State and City, 2021—Continued

(Number.)

| State/city | Population | Violent crime | Murder and nonnegligent manslaughter | Rape | Robbery | Aggravated assault | Property crime | Burglary | Larceny-theft | Motor vehicle theft | Arson |
|---|---|---|---|---|---|---|---|---|---|---|---|
| Christiansburg | 22,544 | 54 | 0 | 15 | 4 | 35 | 528 | 32 | 485 | 11 | 0 |
| Clarksville | 1,163 | 0 | 0 | 0 | 0 | 0 | 13 | 4 | 8 | 1 | 0 |
| Clifton Forge | 3,404 | 16 | 1 | 5 | 1 | 9 | 38 | 4 | 32 | 2 | 0 |
| Clintwood | 1,247 | 2 | 0 | 0 | 0 | 2 | 12 | 2 | 9 | 1 | 0 |
| Coeburn | 1,816 | 3 | 0 | 0 | 0 | 3 | 28 | 2 | 21 | 5 | 0 |
| Colonial Beach | 3,655 | 6 | 0 | 3 | 2 | 1 | 41 | 11 | 15 | 15 | 0 |
| Colonial Heights | 17,171 | 74 | 3 | 10 | 5 | 56 | 738 | 32 | 683 | 23 | 1 |
| Covington | 5,603 | 18 | 0 | 2 | 0 | 16 | 77 | 8 | 64 | 5 | 3 |
| Crewe | 2,096 | 7 | 0 | 2 | 0 | 5 | 44 | 15 | 27 | 2 | 1 |
| Culpeper | 19,485 | 28 | 0 | 4 | 5 | 19 | 258 | 5 | 231 | 22 | 2 |
| Damascus | 772 | 1 | 0 | 0 | 0 | 1 | 37 | 5 | 31 | 1 | 0 |
| Danville | 39,528 | 161 | 6 | 18 | 30 | 107 | 1,245 | 110 | 1,048 | 87 | 7 |
| Dayton | 1,652 | 1 | 0 | 1 | 0 | 0 | 32 | 1 | 29 | 2 | 0 |
| Dublin | 2,583 | 4 | 0 | 3 | 0 | 1 | 32 | 6 | 20 | 6 | 0 |
| Dumfries | 6,233 | 4 | 0 | 2 | 0 | 2 | 62 | 2 | 52 | 8 | 0 |
| Elkton | 2,933 | 3 | 0 | 0 | 0 | 3 | 22 | 3 | 18 | 1 | 0 |
| Emporia | 5,189 | 22 | 1 | 4 | 1 | 16 | 144 | 15 | 119 | 10 | 2 |
| Exmore | 1,352 | 13 | 0 | 1 | 2 | 10 | 38 | 4 | 29 | 5 | 0 |
| Fairfax City | 23,484 | 22 | 0 | 6 | 10 | 6 | 414 | 24 | 359 | 31 | 1 |
| Falls Church | 14,856 | 15 | 0 | 2 | 7 | 6 | 186 | 21 | 147 | 18 | 0 |
| Farmville | 7,811 | 20 | 0 | 6 | 0 | 14 | 197 | 5 | 188 | 4 | 1 |
| Franklin | 7,753 | 48 | 2 | 12 | 4 | 30 | 246 | 22 | 204 | 20 | 1 |
| Fredericksburg | 30,031 | 153 | 3 | 12 | 17 | 121 | 793 | 44 | 719 | 30 | 0 |
| Front Royal | 15,499 | 26 | 0 | 15 | 2 | 9 | 252 | 32 | 199 | 21 | 1 |
| Galax | 6,223 | 17 | 0 | 8 | 0 | 9 | 234 | 25 | 187 | 22 | 3 |
| Gate City | 1,850 | 2 | 0 | 0 | 0 | 2 | 24 | 4 | 16 | 4 | 0 |
| Glade Spring | 1,396 | 1 | 0 | 0 | 0 | 1 | 9 | 2 | 5 | 2 | 0 |
| Gordonsville | 1,665 | 4 | 0 | 1 | 0 | 3 | 7 | 1 | 6 | 0 | 0 |
| Gretna | 1,170 | 0 | 0 | 0 | 0 | 0 | 5 | 0 | 5 | 0 | 0 |
| Grottoes | 2,885 | 1 | 0 | 1 | 0 | 0 | 28 | 0 | 28 | 0 | 0 |
| Grundy | 871 | 0 | 0 | 0 | 0 | 0 | 26 | 2 | 24 | 0 | 0 |
| Halifax | 1,192 | 4 | 0 | 0 | 0 | 4 | 16 | 1 | 13 | 2 | 0 |
| Hampton | 135,107 | 382 | 27 | 39 | 98 | 218 | 3,441 | 256 | 2,836 | 349 | 24 |
| Harrisonburg | 53,582 | 125 | 2 | 28 | 9 | 86 | 800 | 64 | 713 | 23 | 5 |
| Herndon | 24,694 | 49 | 4 | 7 | 20 | 18 | 299 | 16 | 259 | 24 | 3 |
| Hillsville | 2,682 | 2 | 0 | 0 | 0 | 2 | 48 | 13 | 29 | 6 | 0 |
| Honaker | 1,311 | 1 | 0 | 0 | 0 | 1 | 2 | 0 | 2 | 0 | 0 |
| Hopewell | 22,322 | 75 | 3 | 8 | 12 | 52 | 425 | 43 | 324 | 58 | 2 |
| Independence | 881 | 1 | 0 | 1 | 0 | 0 | 9 | 2 | 7 | 0 | 2 |
| Kenbridge | 1,189 | 4 | 0 | 1 | 0 | 3 | 13 | 3 | 6 | 4 | 0 |
| Kilmarnock | 1,392 | 0 | 0 | 0 | 0 | 0 | 29 | 0 | 29 | 0 | 0 |
| Lawrenceville | 969 | 1 | 0 | 1 | 0 | 0 | 7 | 4 | 2 | 1 | 0 |
| Lebanon | 3,158 | 5 | 0 | 3 | 0 | 2 | 116 | 22 | 89 | 5 | 0 |
| Leesburg | 55,794 | 109 | 0 | 14 | 17 | 78 | 589 | 30 | 528 | 31 | 2 |
| Lexington | 7,294 | 3 | 0 | 1 | 0 | 2 | 55 | 4 | 47 | 4 | 0 |
| Louisa | 1,786 | 0 | 0 | 0 | 0 | 0 | 37 | 0 | 33 | 4 | 0 |
| Luray | 4,844 | 15 | 0 | 1 | 1 | 13 | 77 | 4 | 71 | 2 | 1 |
| Lynchburg | 82,088 | 332 | 9 | 32 | 49 | 242 | 1,651 | 184 | 1,289 | 178 | 9 |
| Manassas | 41,098 | 112 | 1 | 20 | 21 | 70 | 744 | 59 | 626 | 59 | 8 |
| Manassas Park | 18,385 | 37 | 0 | 12 | 6 | 19 | 141 | 7 | 123 | 11 | 1 |
| Marion | 5,515 | 10 | 1 | 1 | 1 | 7 | 123 | 12 | 101 | 10 | 3 |
| Martinsville | 12,206 | 56 | 1 | 8 | 5 | 42 | 314 | 32 | 258 | 24 | 3 |
| Middletown | 1,440 | 0 | 0 | 0 | 0 | 0 | 5 | 0 | 5 | 0 | 0 |
| Mount Jackson | 2,153 | 6 | 0 | 0 | 2 | 4 | 31 | 2 | 29 | 0 | 0 |
| New Market | 2,276 | 2 | 0 | 0 | 0 | 2 | 23 | 2 | 21 | 0 | 0 |
| Newport News | 178,662 | 1,164 | 29 | 61 | 129 | 945 | 3,537 | 347 | 2,807 | 383 | 31 |
| Norfolk | 242,488 | 1,792 | 62 | 119 | 281 | 1,330 | 7,756 | 481 | 6,184 | 1,091 | 6 |
| Norton | 3,978 | 13 | 0 | 3 | 2 | 8 | 179 | 5 | 167 | 7 | 1 |
| Onancock | 1,200 | 0 | 0 | 0 | 0 | 0 | 35 | 7 | 28 | 0 | 0 |
| Onley | 497 | 1 | 0 | 0 | 0 | 1 | 18 | 1 | 16 | 1 | 0 |
| Orange | 5,213 | 7 | 0 | 1 | 1 | 5 | 58 | 6 | 49 | 3 | 1 |
| Pearisburg | 2,604 | 1 | 0 | 0 | 0 | 1 | 39 | 5 | 33 | 1 | 0 |
| Petersburg | 30,212 | 228 | 17 | 8 | 19 | 184 | 726 | 69 | 576 | 81 | 5 |
| Pocahontas | 343 | 1 | 0 | 0 | 1 | 0 | 1 | 1 | 0 | 0 | 0 |
| Poquoson | 12,253 | 17 | 0 | 4 | 0 | 13 | 48 | 13 | 33 | 2 | 1 |
| Portsmouth | 94,943 | 731 | 36 | 30 | 138 | 527 | 3,691 | 322 | 3,007 | 362 | 3 |
| Pulaski | 8,615 | 17 | 0 | 6 | 5 | 6 | 254 | 38 | 198 | 18 | 1 |
| Purcellville | 10,575 | 4 | 0 | 0 | 0 | 4 | 44 | 3 | 40 | 1 | 0 |
| Radford | 18,427 | 45 | 0 | 7 | 4 | 34 | 156 | 28 | 125 | 3 | 0 |
| Rich Creek | 735 | 1 | 0 | 1 | 0 | 0 | 9 | 1 | 8 | 0 | 0 |
| Richlands | 5,167 | 5 | 0 | 3 | 0 | 2 | 79 | 14 | 60 | 5 | 0 |
| Richmond | 234,928 | 879 | 89 | 19 | 264 | 507 | 6,427 | 696 | 5,171 | 560 | 26 |
| Roanoke | 99,175 | 483 | 16 | 88 | 68 | 311 | 3,828 | 621 | 2,850 | 357 | 26 |
| Rocky Mount | 4,707 | 4 | 0 | 0 | 0 | 4 | 141 | 0 | 139 | 2 | 0 |
| Rural Retreat | 1,445 | 0 | 0 | 0 | 0 | 0 | 3 | 0 | 3 | 0 | 0 |
| Salem | 25,354 | 23 | 0 | 10 | 6 | 7 | 476 | 40 | 378 | 58 | 2 |
| Saltville | 1,880 | 2 | 0 | 0 | 1 | 1 | 17 | 2 | 12 | 3 | 0 |
| Shenandoah | 2,330 | 5 | 0 | 1 | 1 | 3 | 12 | 0 | 11 | 1 | 0 |
| Smithfield | 8,668 | 10 | 0 | 0 | 2 | 8 | 117 | 5 | 105 | 7 | 0 |
| South Boston | 7,459 | 32 | 3 | 3 | 6 | 20 | 151 | 25 | 116 | 10 | 0 |
| South Hill | 4,332 | 14 | 0 | 2 | 0 | 12 | 175 | 8 | 154 | 13 | 0 |
| Stanley | 1,675 | 2 | 0 | 0 | 1 | 1 | 23 | 3 | 18 | 2 | 0 |
| Staunton | 25,310 | 56 | 0 | 9 | 2 | 45 | 498 | 36 | 438 | 24 | 5 |

## Table 8. Offenses Known to Law Enforcement, by Selected State and City, 2021—Continued

(Number.)

| State/city | Population | Violent crime | Murder and nonnegligent manslaughter | Rape | Robbery | Aggravated assault | Property crime | Burglary | Larceny-theft | Motor vehicle theft | Arson |
|---|---|---|---|---|---|---|---|---|---|---|---|
| Stephens City | 2,136 | 1 | 0 | 0 | 0 | 1 | 16 | 2 | 13 | 1 | 0 |
| St. Paul | 837 | 2 | 0 | 0 | 0 | 2 | 20 | 1 | 18 | 1 | 0 |
| Strasburg | 6,745 | 8 | 0 | 4 | 0 | 4 | 59 | 9 | 49 | 1 | 1 |
| Suffolk | 94,755 | 466 | 6 | 22 | 59 | 379 | 1,695 | 108 | 1,438 | 149 | 15 |
| Tappahannock | 2,395 | 5 | 1 | 0 | 1 | 3 | 29 | 1 | 26 | 2 | 0 |
| Tazewell | 4,065 | 9 | 0 | 2 | 2 | 5 | 168 | 123 | 37 | 8 | 1 |
| Timberville | 2,724 | 7 | 0 | 1 | 0 | 6 | 8 | 1 | 7 | 0 | 0 |
| Vienna | 16,598 | 10 | 0 | 2 | 2 | 6 | 118 | 8 | 103 | 7 | 0 |
| Vinton | 8,142 | 21 | 2 | 0 | 1 | 18 | 148 | 10 | 128 | 10 | 0 |
| Virginia Beach | 451,938 | 507 | 14 | 65 | 141 | 287 | 7,095 | 378 | 5,945 | 772 | 29 |
| Warrenton | 10,019 | 11 | 1 | 7 | 1 | 2 | 101 | 3 | 94 | 4 | 0 |
| Waynesboro | 22,896 | 56 | 0 | 17 | 4 | 35 | 408 | 41 | 325 | 42 | 7 |
| West Point | 3,309 | 4 | 0 | 0 | 0 | 4 | 20 | 1 | 18 | 1 | 0 |
| White Stone | 329 | 0 | 0 | 0 | 0 | 0 | 0 | 0 | 0 | 0 | 0 |
| Williamsburg | 15,406 | 47 | 2 | 5 | 8 | 32 | 197 | 3 | 188 | 6 | 2 |
| Winchester | 27,827 | 79 | 1 | 23 | 14 | 41 | 677 | 70 | 587 | 20 | 0 |
| Windsor | 2,819 | 9 | 0 | 0 | 0 | 9 | 27 | 5 | 20 | 2 | 2 |
| Wise | 2,852 | 6 | 0 | 2 | 1 | 3 | 34 | 3 | 23 | 8 | 0 |
| Woodstock | 5,316 | 9 | 0 | 3 | 1 | 5 | 94 | 0 | 91 | 3 | 0 |
| Wytheville | 7,847 | 7 | 0 | 5 | 0 | 2 | 221 | 24 | 183 | 14 | 2 |
| **WASHINGTON** | | | | | | | | | | | |
| Aberdeen | 16,824 | 51 | 1 | 17 | 9 | 24 | 623 | 123 | 407 | 93 | 6 |
| Airway Heights | 10,030 | 51 | 0 | 10 | 8 | 33 | 554 | 67 | 437 | 50 | 0 |
| Algona | 3,216 | 6 | 0 | 2 | 0 | 4 | 67 | 15 | 40 | 12 | 0 |
| Anacortes | 17,923 | 20 | 0 | 0 | 4 | 16 | 401 | 63 | 309 | 29 | 3 |
| Arlington | 21,405 | 43 | 0 | 8 | 6 | 29 | 693 | 133 | 490 | 70 | 3 |
| Auburn | 82,158 | 366 | 7 | 47 | 136 | 176 | 3,735 | 595 | 2,285 | 855 | 16 |
| Bainbridge Island | 25,601 | 14 | 0 | 6 | 3 | 5 | 215 | 56 | 148 | 11 | 0 |
| Battle Ground | 22,143 | 26 | 0 | 9 | 3 | 14 | 357 | 29 | 293 | 35 | 2 |
| Beaux Arts | 324 | 0 | 0 | 0 | 0 | 0 | 1 | 0 | 1 | 0 | 0 |
| Bellevue | 150,208 | 186 | 2 | 10 | 88 | 86 | 5,202 | 644 | 4,124 | 434 | 9 |
| Bellingham | 95,279 | 391 | 2 | 27 | 130 | 232 | 4,784 | 614 | 3,811 | 359 | 19 |
| Bingen | 751 | 1 | 0 | 0 | 1 | 0 | 6 | 1 | 5 | 0 | 0 |
| Black Diamond | 5,551 | 0 | 0 | 0 | 0 | 0 | 63 | 14 | 41 | 8 | 0 |
| Blaine | 5,741 | 11 | 1 | 0 | 0 | 10 | 118 | 42 | 71 | 5 | 0 |
| Bonney Lake | 23,142 | 46 | 0 | 6 | 12 | 28 | 669 | 78 | 523 | 68 | 0 |
| Bothell | 48,356 | 53 | 2 | 12 | 14 | 25 | 1,112 | 144 | 885 | 83 | 3 |
| Bremerton | 42,798 | 161 | 2 | 33 | 22 | 104 | 1,357 | 246 | 869 | 242 | 4 |
| Brier | 7,030 | 5 | 0 | 3 | 1 | 1 | 40 | 3 | 32 | 5 | 1 |
| Buckley | 5,914 | 14 | 0 | 1 | 1 | 12 | 68 | 16 | 38 | 14 | 0 |
| Burien | 51,584 | 258 | 4 | 23 | 89 | 142 | 2,453 | 464 | 1,434 | 555 | 33 |
| Burlington | 9,666 | 15 | 0 | 2 | 7 | 6 | 919 | 84 | 736 | 99 | 1 |
| Carnation | 2,366 | 0 | 0 | 0 | 0 | 0 | 22 | 1 | 17 | 4 | 0 |
| Centralia | 18,131 | 38 | 1 | 11 | 2 | 24 | 658 | 102 | 497 | 59 | 4 |
| Chehalis | 7,885 | 39 | 1 | 5 | 10 | 23 | 493 | 78 | 380 | 35 | 1 |
| Cheney | 13,175 | 26 | 0 | 6 | 1 | 19 | 220 | 20 | 181 | 19 | 0 |
| Cle Elum | 3,103 | 6 | 0 | 2 | 1 | 3 | 105 | 19 | 74 | 12 | 0 |
| Clyde Hill | 3,441 | 1 | 0 | 1 | 0 | 0 | 26 | 10 | 14 | 2 | 0 |
| College Place | 9,560 | 11 | 0 | 1 | 1 | 9 | 210 | 30 | 168 | 12 | 1 |
| Colville | 4,840 | 1 | 0 | 0 | 0 | 1 | 2 | 0 | 2 | 0 | 0 |
| Connell | 5,660 | 1 | 0 | 0 | 0 | 1 | 19 | 8 | 9 | 2 | 0 |
| Covington | 22,024 | 36 | 0 | 6 | 15 | 15 | 882 | 101 | 672 | 109 | 0 |
| Darrington | 1,430 | 9 | 0 | 0 | 0 | 9 | 18 | 6 | 11 | 1 | 0 |
| Des Moines | 32,664 | 108 | 2 | 12 | 37 | 57 | 1,179 | 130 | 784 | 265 | 6 |
| Dupont | 9,740 | 11 | 0 | 2 | 1 | 8 | 161 | 17 | 127 | 17 | 1 |
| Duvall | 8,319 | 0 | 0 | 0 | 0 | 0 | 41 | 5 | 30 | 6 | 1 |
| East Wenatchee | 14,096 | 12 | 0 | 2 | 3 | 7 | 266 | 17 | 232 | 17 | 1 |
| Eatonville | 3,055 | 12 | 0 | 3 | 0 | 9 | 35 | 10 | 22 | 3 | 0 |
| Edgewood | 13,909 | 13 | 0 | 1 | 3 | 9 | 395 | 85 | 261 | 49 | 2 |
| Edmonds | 42,803 | 112 | 0 | 10 | 43 | 59 | 1,117 | 168 | 844 | 105 | 6 |
| Ellensburg | 21,933 | 55 | 6 | 10 | 8 | 31 | 632 | 88 | 505 | 39 | 2 |
| Elma | 3,387 | 4 | 1 | 0 | 0 | 3 | 72 | 16 | 53 | 3 | 1 |
| Enumclaw | 12,700 | 12 | 0 | 5 | 2 | 5 | 255 | 28 | 190 | 37 | 5 |
| Ephrata | 8,268 | 24 | 0 | 3 | 5 | 16 | 479 | 115 | 312 | 52 | 1 |
| Everett | 113,469 | 355 | 4 | 37 | 84 | 230 | 4,553 | 721 | 3,143 | 689 | 23 |
| Everson | 4,624 | 5 | 0 | 1 | 0 | 4 | 25 | 1 | 22 | 2 | 0 |
| Federal Way | 97,017 | 493 | 11 | 46 | 163 | 273 | 4,739 | 789 | 3,018 | 932 | 31 |
| Ferndale | 16,006 | 23 | 0 | 1 | 2 | 20 | 348 | 52 | 272 | 24 | 0 |
| Fife | 10,577 | 196 | 1 | 10 | 63 | 122 | 1,264 | 145 | 732 | 387 | 10 |
| Fircrest | 6,920 | 11 | 0 | 1 | 1 | 9 | 180 | 37 | 122 | 21 | 0 |
| Gig Harbor | 11,345 | 18 | 0 | 1 | 8 | 9 | 461 | 50 | 370 | 41 | 0 |
| Gold Bar | 2,408 | 3 | 0 | 0 | 1 | 2 | 29 | 23 | 5 | 1 | 0 |
| Goldendale | 3,696 | 10 | 0 | 0 | 2 | 8 | 113 | 17 | 90 | 6 | 0 |
| Grand Coulee | 2,047 | 7 | 0 | 1 | 0 | 6 | 68 | 16 | 49 | 3 | 1 |
| Grandview | 11,043 | 20 | 0 | 4 | 1 | 15 | 311 | 74 | 165 | 72 | 1 |
| Granite Falls | 4,728 | 1 | 0 | 0 | 0 | 1 | 40 | 10 | 27 | 3 | 0 |
| Hoquiam | 8,696 | 17 | 0 | 3 | 3 | 11 | 175 | 36 | 117 | 22 | 2 |
| Index | 218 | 0 | 0 | 0 | 0 | 0 | 0 | 0 | 0 | 0 | 0 |
| Issaquah | 40,738 | 16 | 0 | 4 | 9 | 3 | 1,711 | 229 | 1,347 | 135 | 2 |
| Kalama | 2,898 | 0 | 0 | 0 | 0 | 0 | 76 | 10 | 57 | 9 | 1 |
| Kelso | 12,493 | 42 | 1 | 9 | 14 | 18 | 450 | 54 | 339 | 57 | 6 |
| Kenmore | 23,326 | 18 | 1 | 2 | 5 | 10 | 266 | 36 | 203 | 27 | 3 |

## Table 8. Offenses Known to Law Enforcement, by Selected State and City, 2021—Continued

(Number.)

| State/city | Population | Violent crime | Murder and nonnegligent manslaughter | Rape | Robbery | Aggravated assault | Property crime | Burglary | Larceny-theft | Motor vehicle theft | Arson |
|---|---|---|---|---|---|---|---|---|---|---|---|
| Kennewick | 85,595 | 277 | 5 | 49 | 61 | 162 | 3,035 | 522 | 2,241 | 272 | 30 |
| Kent | 131,899 | 524 | 12 | 92 | 188 | 232 | 6,620 | 1,364 | 3,781 | 1,475 | 29 |
| Kettle Falls | 1,647 | 4 | 0 | 2 | 0 | 2 | 32 | 10 | 18 | 4 | 0 |
| Kirkland | 97,027 | 81 | 0 | 25 | 23 | 33 | 2,141 | 280 | 1,664 | 197 | 4 |
| La Center | 3,674 | 2 | 0 | 0 | 1 | 1 | 92 | 9 | 63 | 20 | 1 |
| Lacey | 55,484 | 113 | 0 | 24 | 33 | 56 | 1,579 | 155 | 1,216 | 208 | 9 |
| Lake Forest Park | 13,514 | 2 | 0 | 1 | 0 | 1 | 189 | 26 | 138 | 25 | 0 |
| Lake Stevens | 35,500 | 36 | 1 | 9 | 3 | 23 | 233 | 38 | 156 | 39 | 2 |
| Lakewood | 61,325 | 462 | 6 | 28 | 107 | 321 | 2,969 | 440 | 1,890 | 639 | 20 |
| Liberty Lake | 11,905 | 14 | 0 | 3 | 3 | 8 | 249 | 50 | 182 | 17 | 1 |
| Long Beach | 1,534 | 0 | 0 | 0 | 0 | 0 | 18 | 4 | 12 | 2 | 0 |
| Longview | 38,693 | 127 | 3 | 30 | 19 | 75 | 1,232 | 166 | 888 | 178 | 14 |
| Lynden | 15,791 | 20 | 0 | 6 | 1 | 13 | 232 | 27 | 197 | 8 | 1 |
| Maple Valley | 28,065 | 28 | 0 | 9 | 9 | 10 | 401 | 60 | 300 | 41 | 5 |
| Marysville | 72,620 | 126 | 1 | 31 | 18 | 76 | 1,057 | 212 | 657 | 188 | 12 |
| Medina | 3,343 | 1 | 0 | 0 | 0 | 1 | 47 | 13 | 31 | 3 | 0 |
| Mercer Island | 26,251 | 8 | 0 | 1 | 3 | 4 | 435 | 78 | 328 | 29 | 2 |
| Mill Creek | 21,076 | 25 | 0 | 6 | 6 | 13 | 430 | 55 | 328 | 47 | 0 |
| Milton | 8,325 | 23 | 0 | 1 | 6 | 16 | 275 | 50 | 162 | 63 | 0 |
| Monroe | 21,047 | 43 | 0 | 3 | 5 | 35 | 427 | 42 | 362 | 23 | 6 |
| Montesano | 4,083 | 5 | 0 | 1 | 0 | 4 | 51 | 13 | 33 | 5 | 0 |
| Mountlake Terrace | 21,462 | 32 | 0 | 4 | 6 | 22 | 629 | 80 | 462 | 87 | 2 |
| Mount Vernon | 36,830 | 75 | 0 | 15 | 15 | 45 | 1,019 | 132 | 723 | 164 | 16 |
| Moxee | 4,499 | 0 | 0 | 0 | 0 | 0 | 38 | 4 | 27 | 7 | 0 |
| Mukilteo | 21,461 | 48 | 0 | 5 | 3 | 40 | 538 | 74 | 434 | 30 | 1 |
| Newcastle | 13,188 | 10 | 0 | 2 | 1 | 7 | 254 | 34 | 185 | 35 | 1 |
| Newport | 2,278 | 2 | 0 | 1 | 0 | 1 | 28 | 3 | 23 | 2 | 0 |
| Normandy Park | 6,587 | 6 | 0 | 0 | 1 | 5 | 121 | 15 | 82 | 24 | 0 |
| North Bend | 7,790 | 2 | 0 | 0 | 2 | 0 | 312 | 26 | 265 | 21 | 0 |
| Oak Harbor | 23,792 | 12 | 0 | 5 | 0 | 7 | 167 | 17 | 126 | 24 | 0 |
| Oakville | 698 | 1 | 0 | 0 | 0 | 1 | 10 | 4 | 6 | 0 | 0 |
| Olympia | 54,322 | 245 | 1 | 33 | 71 | 140 | 2,087 | 311 | 1,505 | 271 | 8 |
| Orting | 8,866 | 17 | 0 | 4 | 0 | 13 | 101 | 13 | 72 | 16 | 5 |
| Othello | 8,572 | 9 | 1 | 2 | 2 | 4 | 110 | 19 | 75 | 16 | 0 |
| Pacific | 7,225 | 8 | 0 | 4 | 2 | 2 | 204 | 47 | 118 | 39 | 0 |
| Pasco | 78,680 | 200 | 3 | 24 | 44 | 129 | 1,587 | 268 | 1,112 | 207 | 12 |
| Port Angeles | 20,519 | 114 | 0 | 25 | 15 | 74 | 489 | 91 | 348 | 50 | 16 |
| Port Orchard | 14,995 | 66 | 0 | 9 | 13 | 44 | 703 | 106 | 465 | 132 | 5 |
| Port Townsend | 10,063 | 15 | 0 | 2 | 2 | 11 | 129 | 24 | 92 | 13 | 0 |
| Poulsbo | 11,425 | 28 | 0 | 7 | 4 | 17 | 236 | 28 | 176 | 32 | 2 |
| Prosser | 6,463 | 10 | 0 | 0 | 2 | 8 | 128 | 18 | 92 | 18 | 0 |
| Puyallup | 43,144 | 142 | 3 | 11 | 41 | 87 | 2,813 | 401 | 1,979 | 433 | 22 |
| Quincy | 8,564 | 11 | 0 | 3 | 1 | 7 | 119 | 23 | 69 | 27 | 2 |
| Raymond | 3,076 | 9 | 0 | 3 | 2 | 4 | 29 | 5 | 22 | 2 | 1 |
| Redmond | 74,583 | 80 | 0 | 18 | 16 | 46 | 2,066 | 236 | 1,666 | 164 | 7 |
| Renton | 102,458 | 325 | 3 | 29 | 98 | 195 | 4,427 | 517 | 2,997 | 913 | 18 |
| Richland | 60,615 | 178 | 1 | 53 | 23 | 101 | 1,806 | 315 | 1,379 | 112 | 8 |
| Ridgefield | 12,295 | 5 | 0 | 2 | 0 | 3 | 222 | 39 | 161 | 22 | 0 |
| Ritzville | 1,637 | 0 | 0 | 0 | 0 | 0 | 78 | 31 | 43 | 4 | 0 |
| Royal City | 2,697 | 1 | 0 | 0 | 0 | 1 | 32 | 8 | 19 | 5 | 0 |
| Ruston | 859 | 4 | 0 | 0 | 2 | 2 | 46 | 7 | 33 | 6 | 0 |
| Sammamish | 66,855 | 19 | 0 | 6 | 2 | 11 | 561 | 82 | 453 | 26 | 2 |
| SeaTac | 29,103 | 159 | 3 | 20 | 50 | 86 | 1,722 | 223 | 1,060 | 439 | 5 |
| Seattle | 787,749 | 5,869 | 41 | 283 | 1,736 | 3,809 | 40,192 | 9,926 | 25,005 | 5,261 | 223 |
| Sedro Woolley | 12,301 | 16 | 0 | 6 | 3 | 7 | 301 | 37 | 217 | 47 | 1 |
| Selah | 8,220 | 7 | 0 | 2 | 2 | 3 | 194 | 32 | 142 | 20 | 0 |
| Sequim | 7,911 | 20 | 0 | 5 | 3 | 12 | 206 | 33 | 162 | 11 | 1 |
| Shelton | 11,073 | 53 | 1 | 12 | 3 | 37 | 378 | 34 | 301 | 43 | 1 |
| Shoreline | 58,725 | 106 | 0 | 20 | 27 | 59 | 1,606 | 348 | 1,016 | 242 | 18 |
| Skykomish | 221 | 0 | 0 | 0 | 0 | 0 | 1 | 0 | 1 | 0 | 0 |
| Snohomish | 10,489 | 20 | 0 | 4 | 4 | 12 | 273 | 48 | 195 | 30 | 0 |
| Snoqualmie | 13,875 | 5 | 0 | 0 | 0 | 5 | 287 | 32 | 221 | 34 | 1 |
| Soap Lake | 1,614 | 8 | 0 | 0 | 0 | 8 | 50 | 9 | 37 | 4 | 0 |
| Spokane | 223,344 | 1,454 | 14 | 212 | 261 | 967 | 10,686 | 1,540 | 7,974 | 1,172 | 111 |
| Spokane Valley | 104,276 | 305 | 9 | 37 | 71 | 188 | 3,978 | 523 | 3,059 | 396 | 18 |
| Stanwood | 7,716 | 18 | 0 | 7 | 0 | 11 | 126 | 21 | 92 | 13 | 0 |
| Steilacoom | 6,460 | 13 | 0 | 4 | 1 | 8 | 76 | 15 | 51 | 10 | 0 |
| Sultan | 5,786 | 11 | 0 | 0 | 2 | 9 | 95 | 34 | 52 | 9 | 1 |
| Sumas | 1,665 | 2 | 0 | 1 | 0 | 1 | 6 | 1 | 5 | 0 | 0 |
| Sumner | 10,670 | 15 | 0 | 0 | 7 | 8 | 622 | 114 | 392 | 116 | 7 |
| Tacoma | 222,235 | 2,626 | 30 | 144 | 518 | 1,934 | 14,961 | 2,199 | 9,006 | 3,756 | 242 |
| Toledo | 792 | 1 | 0 | 0 | 1 | 0 | 6 | 1 | 5 | 0 | 0 |
| Toppenish | 8,745 | 47 | 1 | 5 | 13 | 28 | 569 | 100 | 390 | 79 | 4 |
| Tukwila | 20,369 | 165 | 1 | 16 | 77 | 71 | 3,326 | 219 | 2,514 | 593 | 16 |
| Tumwater | 24,727 | 51 | 0 | 7 | 9 | 35 | 691 | 116 | 490 | 85 | 2 |
| Union Gap | 6,163 | 17 | 4 | 2 | 3 | 8 | 364 | 82 | 226 | 56 | 0 |
| University Place | 34,404 | 66 | 1 | 8 | 19 | 38 | 784 | 141 | 546 | 97 | 2 |
| Vancouver | 188,160 | 1,109 | 18 | 135 | 226 | 730 | 9,281 | 1,299 | 5,908 | 2,074 | 62 |
| Walla Walla | 33,154 | 90 | 1 | 24 | 7 | 58 | 615 | 87 | 478 | 50 | 6 |
| Warden | 2,848 | 8 | 0 | 1 | 0 | 7 | 43 | 12 | 24 | 7 | 1 |
| Washougal | 16,317 | 44 | 1 | 16 | 4 | 23 | 265 | 35 | 193 | 37 | 5 |
| Wenatchee | 34,349 | 59 | 1 | 14 | 11 | 33 | 872 | 109 | 666 | 97 | 9 |
| Westport | 2,123 | 3 | 0 | 1 | 0 | 2 | 65 | 8 | 56 | 1 | 1 |

## Table 8. Offenses Known to Law Enforcement, by Selected State and City, 2021—Continued

(Number.)

| State/city | Population | Violent crime | Murder and nonnegligent manslaughter | Rape | Robbery | Aggravated assault | Property crime | Burglary | Larceny-theft | Motor vehicle theft | Arson |
|---|---|---|---|---|---|---|---|---|---|---|---|
| West Richland | 15,817 | 17 | 0 | 4 | 2 | 11 | 137 | 40 | 89 | 8 | 2 |
| White Salmon | 2,764 | 2 | 0 | 0 | 0 | 2 | 38 | 3 | 34 | 1 | 0 |
| Woodinville | 15,462 | 16 | 0 | 7 | 4 | 5 | 426 | 68 | 322 | 36 | 1 |
| Woodland | 6,659 | 16 | 0 | 7 | 3 | 6 | 294 | 65 | 194 | 35 | 2 |
| Woodway | 1,399 | 1 | 0 | 0 | 0 | 1 | 7 | 3 | 3 | 1 | 0 |
| Yakima | 94,594 | 515 | 12 | 20 | 74 | 409 | 2,886 | 561 | 1,825 | 500 | 19 |
| **WEST VIRGINIA** | | | | | | | | | | | |
| Alderson | 1,104 | 7 | 0 | 1 | 0 | 6 | 32 | 9 | 22 | 1 | 1 |
| Barboursville | 4,258 | 3 | 0 | 1 | 0 | 2 | 52 | 0 | 52 | 0 | 0 |
| Beckley | 15,632 | 119 | 2 | 19 | 13 | 85 | 950 | 137 | 771 | 42 | 0 |
| Bluefield | 9,416 | 104 | 2 | 3 | 0 | 99 | 7 | 0 | 7 | 0 | 1 |
| Bridgeport | 8,853 | 17 | 1 | 4 | 0 | 12 | 109 | 4 | 96 | 9 | 2 |
| Buckhannon | 5,376 | 1 | 0 | 0 | 0 | 1 | 63 | 0 | 63 | 0 | 0 |
| Ceredo | 1,233 | 10 | 0 | 0 | 0 | 10 | 8 | 1 | 7 | 0 | 0 |
| Chapmanville | 1,064 | 1 | 0 | 0 | 0 | 1 | 11 | 5 | 6 | 0 | 1 |
| Charleston | 45,378 | 287 | 9 | 27 | 41 | 210 | 1,608 | 347 | 1,114 | 147 | 17 |
| Charles Town | 6,098 | 9 | 0 | 0 | 1 | 8 | 57 | 27 | 25 | 5 | 0 |
| Clearview | 477 | 2 | 0 | 1 | 0 | 1 | 0 | 0 | 0 | 0 | 0 |
| Dunbar | 6,868 | 39 | 0 | 5 | 2 | 32 | 209 | 59 | 126 | 24 | 3 |
| Fairmont | 18,335 | 103 | 1 | 20 | 2 | 80 | 291 | 81 | 177 | 33 | 10 |
| Fayetteville | 2,659 | 2 | 0 | 0 | 0 | 2 | 105 | 4 | 99 | 2 | 0 |
| Follansbee | 2,640 | 0 | 0 | 0 | 0 | 0 | 12 | 4 | 7 | 1 | 0 |
| Glen Dale | 1,332 | 0 | 0 | 0 | 0 | 0 | 8 | 2 | 6 | 0 | 0 |
| Grafton | 4,950 | 1 | 0 | 0 | 0 | 1 | 28 | 7 | 18 | 3 | 0 |
| Hinton | 2,289 | 3 | 1 | 0 | 0 | 2 | 11 | 0 | 11 | 0 | 0 |
| Huntington | 44,522 | 293 | 10 | 34 | 43 | 206 | 1,528 | 326 | 1,037 | 165 | 28 |
| Kenova | 2,914 | 0 | 0 | 0 | 0 | 0 | 30 | 3 | 22 | 5 | 0 |
| Keyser | 4,811 | 4 | 0 | 0 | 0 | 4 | 73 | 5 | 66 | 2 | 0 |
| Madison | 2,574 | 16 | 0 | 1 | 0 | 15 | 49 | 7 | 39 | 3 | 0 |
| Moorefield | 2,375 | 23 | 0 | 0 | 0 | 23 | 70 | 2 | 65 | 3 | 0 |
| Morgantown | 31,079 | 89 | 2 | 32 | 6 | 49 | 746 | 56 | 667 | 23 | 2 |
| Moundsville | 8,036 | 35 | 1 | 7 | 0 | 27 | 108 | 0 | 108 | 0 | 0 |
| Mullens | 1,263 | 2 | 0 | 0 | 0 | 2 | 20 | 7 | 12 | 1 | 0 |
| Nitro | 6,225 | 15 | 0 | 2 | 2 | 11 | 197 | 12 | 180 | 5 | 2 |
| Oak Hill | 7,948 | 4 | 0 | 2 | 0 | 2 | 14 | 0 | 14 | 0 | 0 |
| Parkersburg | 28,793 | 131 | 1 | 26 | 16 | 88 | 1,143 | 155 | 884 | 104 | 31 |
| Princeton | 5,551 | 23 | 0 | 1 | 0 | 22 | 20 | 0 | 20 | 0 | 0 |
| Ravenswood | 3,594 | 18 | 0 | 0 | 0 | 18 | 35 | 6 | 29 | 0 | 0 |
| Romney | 1,665 | 14 | 0 | 0 | 0 | 14 | 3 | 0 | 2 | 1 | 0 |
| Shepherdstown | 1,901 | 0 | 0 | 0 | 0 | 0 | 3 | 0 | 3 | 0 | 0 |
| South Charleston | 11,884 | 53 | 0 | 5 | 2 | 46 | 605 | 55 | 520 | 30 | 3 |
| Spencer | 1,962 | 7 | 0 | 1 | 0 | 6 | 41 | 7 | 33 | 1 | 0 |
| St. Albans | 9,646 | 33 | 0 | 4 | 1 | 28 | 279 | 55 | 202 | 22 | 0 |
| Summersville | 3,194 | 4 | 0 | 0 | 0 | 4 | 65 | 10 | 52 | 3 | 0 |
| Vienna | 9,952 | 16 | 0 | 3 | 0 | 13 | 391 | 11 | 375 | 5 | 0 |
| Weirton | 17,911 | 17 | 1 | 6 | 0 | 10 | 41 | 0 | 41 | 0 | 2 |
| Weston | 3,770 | 2 | 0 | 0 | 0 | 2 | 2 | 0 | 2 | 0 | 0 |
| Wheeling | 26,081 | 255 | 2 | 16 | 12 | 225 | 437 | 95 | 314 | 28 | 2 |
| **WISCONSIN** | | | | | | | | | | | |
| Adams | 1,898 | 5 | 0 | 3 | 0 | 2 | 58 | 3 | 53 | 2 | 0 |
| Albany | 973 | 3 | 1 | 1 | 1 | 0 | 7 | 2 | 5 | 0 | 0 |
| Algoma | 3,026 | 2 | 0 | 0 | 0 | 2 | 23 | 0 | 22 | 1 | 0 |
| Altoona | 8,210 | 5 | 0 | 0 | 0 | 5 | 172 | 13 | 151 | 8 | 0 |
| Amery | 2,786 | 11 | 0 | 6 | 0 | 5 | 27 | 5 | 15 | 7 | 0 |
| Antigo | 7,671 | 15 | 0 | 2 | 1 | 12 | 170 | 11 | 156 | 3 | 0 |
| Appleton | 74,204 | 230 | 0 | 43 | 19 | 168 | 966 | 111 | 809 | 46 | 6 |
| Ashwaubenon | 17,008 | 15 | 1 | 4 | 2 | 8 | 354 | 21 | 306 | 27 | 0 |
| Barron | 3,215 | 9 | 0 | 1 | 0 | 8 | 30 | 4 | 18 | 8 | 0 |
| Bayside | 4,353 | 4 | 0 | 0 | 2 | 2 | 16 | 1 | 14 | 1 | 0 |
| Beaver Dam | 16,314 | 37 | 0 | 15 | 1 | 21 | 133 | 6 | 123 | 4 | 0 |
| Beloit | 36,603 | 215 | 4 | 22 | 29 | 160 | 836 | 88 | 670 | 78 | 8 |
| Beloit Town | 7,724 | 12 | 0 | 2 | 0 | 10 | 81 | 12 | 60 | 9 | 1 |
| Berlin | 5,367 | 8 | 0 | 2 | 1 | 5 | 55 | 6 | 47 | 2 | 1 |
| Bloomer | 3,504 | 10 | 0 | 2 | 0 | 8 | 26 | 2 | 21 | 3 | 0 |
| Boscobel | 3,126 | 8 | 0 | 3 | 0 | 5 | 10 | 0 | 9 | 1 | 0 |
| Boyceville | 1,127 | 5 | 0 | 1 | 0 | 4 | 6 | 0 | 6 | 0 | 0 |
| Brillion | 3,071 | 2 | 0 | 2 | 0 | 0 | 21 | 2 | 12 | 7 | 0 |
| Brodhead | 3,195 | 4 | 0 | 4 | 0 | 0 | 22 | 1 | 21 | 0 | 0 |
| Brookfield | 39,292 | 15 | 0 | 6 | 5 | 4 | 559 | 35 | 480 | 44 | 0 |
| Brown Deer | 12,310 | 55 | 3 | 7 | 7 | 38 | 679 | 25 | 525 | 129 | 1 |
| Burlington | 10,938 | 19 | 0 | 3 | 1 | 15 | 74 | 6 | 66 | 2 | 0 |
| Butler | 1,790 | 0 | 0 | 0 | 0 | 0 | 66 | 5 | 53 | 8 | 0 |
| Caledonia | 25,272 | 33 | 1 | 4 | 5 | 23 | 141 | 31 | 91 | 19 | 0 |
| Campbell Township | 4,273 | 4 | 0 | 0 | 3 | 1 | 61 | 12 | 44 | 5 | 0 |
| Cashton | 1,112 | 3 | 0 | 0 | 0 | 3 | 7 | 1 | 6 | 0 | 0 |
| Cedarburg | 11,818 | 5 | 0 | 1 | 1 | 3 | 67 | 3 | 59 | 5 | 0 |
| Chetek | 2,083 | 1 | 0 | 0 | 0 | 1 | 7 | 1 | 5 | 1 | 0 |
| Chilton | 3,862 | 2 | 0 | 0 | 0 | 2 | 10 | 1 | 9 | 0 | 0 |
| Chippewa Falls | 14,475 | 33 | 1 | 5 | 0 | 27 | 105 | 9 | 80 | 16 | 1 |
| Cleveland | 1,452 | 0 | 0 | 0 | 0 | 0 | 7 | 0 | 6 | 1 | 0 |
| Clinton | 2,116 | 4 | 1 | 2 | 0 | 1 | 13 | 0 | 12 | 1 | 0 |

# Table 8. Offenses Known to Law Enforcement, by Selected State and City, 2021—Continued

(Number.)

| State/city | Population | Violent crime | Murder and nonnegligent manslaughter | Rape | Robbery | Aggravated assault | Property crime | Burglary | Larceny-theft | Motor vehicle theft | Arson |
|---|---|---|---|---|---|---|---|---|---|---|---|
| Columbus | 5,129 | 1 | 0 | 1 | 0 | 0 | 37 | 1 | 34 | 2 | 0 |
| Cottage Grove | 7,241 | 1 | 0 | 1 | 0 | 0 | 43 | 9 | 32 | 2 | 0 |
| Cross Plains | 4,348 | 5 | 0 | 2 | 0 | 3 | 29 | 5 | 22 | 2 | 1 |
| Cudahy | 18,201 | 25 | 0 | 8 | 5 | 12 | 227 | 33 | 165 | 29 | 0 |
| Darlington | 2,305 | 1 | 0 | 0 | 0 | 1 | 15 | 1 | 11 | 3 | 0 |
| Deforest | 11,130 | 13 | 0 | 4 | 1 | 8 | 214 | 9 | 197 | 8 | 1 |
| Delafield | 7,607 | 3 | 0 | 1 | 2 | 0 | 99 | 1 | 96 | 2 | 0 |
| Delavan | 9,813 | 22 | 0 | 4 | 5 | 13 | 128 | 8 | 109 | 11 | 1 |
| Delavan Town | 5,361 | 1 | 0 | 0 | 0 | 1 | 20 | 2 | 13 | 5 | 0 |
| De Pere | 25,122 | 15 | 1 | 4 | 1 | 9 | 162 | 22 | 135 | 5 | 1 |
| East Troy | 4,307 | 4 | 0 | 1 | 0 | 3 | 21 | 1 | 20 | 0 | 0 |
| Eau Claire | 69,372 | 119 | 1 | 42 | 13 | 63 | 1,749 | 219 | 1,444 | 86 | 12 |
| Edgerton | 5,613 | 0 | 0 | 0 | 0 | 0 | 35 | 2 | 31 | 2 | 0 |
| Elkhart Lake | 1,018 | 0 | 0 | 0 | 0 | 0 | 0 | 0 | 0 | 0 | 0 |
| Elkhorn | 10,016 | 14 | 0 | 0 | 1 | 13 | 156 | 93 | 58 | 5 | 1 |
| Elk Mound | 885 | 2 | 0 | 0 | 0 | 2 | 15 | 1 | 14 | 0 | 1 |
| Ellsworth | 3,270 | 3 | 0 | 1 | 0 | 2 | 33 | 5 | 27 | 1 | 1 |
| Elm Grove | 6,158 | 3 | 0 | 0 | 2 | 1 | 55 | 2 | 48 | 5 | 0 |
| Everest Metropolitan | 17,341 | 44 | 1 | 12 | 0 | 31 | 181 | 26 | 148 | 7 | 0 |
| Fennimore | 2,464 | 4 | 0 | 2 | 0 | 2 | 0 | 0 | 0 | 0 | 0 |
| Fitchburg | 31,498 | 104 | 1 | 10 | 11 | 82 | 511 | 88 | 350 | 73 | 1 |
| Fond du Lac | 43,195 | 121 | 2 | 19 | 9 | 91 | 682 | 47 | 602 | 33 | 2 |
| Fontana | 1,749 | 1 | 0 | 0 | 1 | 0 | 6 | 0 | 6 | 0 | 0 |
| Fort Atkinson | 12,370 | 15 | 1 | 3 | 0 | 11 | 107 | 11 | 86 | 10 | 1 |
| Fox Crossing | 19,200 | 20 | 1 | 4 | 1 | 14 | 156 | 18 | 130 | 8 | 0 |
| Fox Point | 6,678 | 2 | 0 | 0 | 0 | 2 | 49 | 5 | 39 | 5 | 0 |
| Franklin | 36,264 | 25 | 0 | 3 | 4 | 18 | 496 | 23 | 445 | 28 | 0 |
| Geneva Town | 5,052 | 4 | 0 | 2 | 0 | 2 | 12 | 0 | 6 | 6 | 0 |
| Germantown | 20,066 | 13 | 0 | 1 | 2 | 10 | 385 | 15 | 358 | 12 | 0 |
| Glendale | 12,843 | 33 | 0 | 1 | 11 | 21 | 617 | 24 | 464 | 129 | 1 |
| Grafton | 11,783 | 6 | 1 | 1 | 1 | 3 | 142 | 8 | 132 | 2 | 0 |
| Grand Chute | 23,739 | 44 | 2 | 11 | 5 | 26 | 989 | 45 | 914 | 30 | 0 |
| Green Bay | 103,826 | 486 | 3 | 73 | 40 | 370 | 1,629 | 251 | 1,239 | 139 | 13 |
| Greendale | 14,251 | 15 | 0 | 2 | 2 | 11 | 142 | 5 | 124 | 13 | 0 |
| Greenfield | 37,531 | 58 | 0 | 2 | 17 | 39 | 782 | 59 | 582 | 141 | 0 |
| Green Lake | 961 | 0 | 0 | 0 | 0 | 0 | 8 | 0 | 7 | 1 | 0 |
| Hartford | 15,815 | 18 | 0 | 11 | 0 | 7 | 74 | 8 | 64 | 2 | 1 |
| Hartland | 9,360 | 9 | 0 | 3 | 1 | 5 | 34 | 6 | 28 | 0 | 0 |
| Hobart-Lawrence | 16,712 | 2 | 0 | 2 | 0 | 0 | 120 | 80 | 37 | 3 | 0 |
| Holmen | 10,497 | 11 | 0 | 3 | 0 | 8 | 68 | 4 | 62 | 2 | 0 |
| Horicon | 3,683 | 2 | 0 | 0 | 0 | 2 | 23 | 2 | 19 | 2 | 0 |
| Hudson | 14,313 | 25 | 0 | 3 | 1 | 21 | 379 | 17 | 322 | 40 | 0 |
| Hurley | 1,413 | 4 | 0 | 1 | 0 | 3 | 10 | 0 | 10 | 0 | 0 |
| Janesville | 64,768 | 145 | 1 | 36 | 22 | 86 | 1,172 | 116 | 975 | 81 | 10 |
| Jefferson | 8,042 | 10 | 0 | 3 | 0 | 7 | 154 | 6 | 138 | 10 | 0 |
| Kaukauna | 16,444 | 16 | 1 | 5 | 0 | 10 | 140 | 10 | 120 | 10 | 0 |
| Kenosha | 99,588 | 357 | 13 | 63 | 30 | 251 | 1,101 | 145 | 798 | 158 | 14 |
| Kewaunee | 2,824 | 1 | 0 | 1 | 0 | 0 | 16 | 1 | 15 | 0 | 0 |
| Kiel | 3,807 | 3 | 0 | 0 | 0 | 3 | 27 | 2 | 25 | 0 | 0 |
| Kohler | 2,042 | 2 | 0 | 1 | 0 | 1 | 43 | 1 | 42 | 0 | 0 |
| Kronenwetter | 8,242 | 4 | 0 | 2 | 0 | 2 | 23 | 4 | 19 | 0 | 0 |
| La Crosse | 51,143 | 129 | 0 | 52 | 12 | 65 | 2,058 | 186 | 1,779 | 93 | 14 |
| Lake Geneva | 8,155 | 9 | 0 | 1 | 0 | 8 | 124 | 4 | 110 | 10 | 0 |
| Lake Hallie | 6,807 | 8 | 0 | 2 | 0 | 6 | 88 | 2 | 77 | 9 | 0 |
| Lake Mills | 6,044 | 14 | 0 | 0 | 0 | 14 | 11 | 0 | 9 | 2 | 0 |
| Lancaster | 3,683 | 24 | 0 | 5 | 0 | 19 | 62 | 20 | 40 | 2 | 0 |
| Linn Township | 2,409 | 0 | 0 | 0 | 0 | 0 | 103 | 96 | 6 | 1 | 0 |
| Lodi | 3,115 | 1 | 0 | 0 | 0 | 1 | 16 | 0 | 15 | 1 | 0 |
| Lomira | 2,457 | 2 | 0 | 2 | 0 | 0 | 15 | 3 | 10 | 2 | 0 |
| Madison | 266,199 | 821 | 10 | 105 | 141 | 565 | 6,709 | 974 | 5,023 | 712 | 14 |
| Manitowoc | 32,233 | 75 | 0 | 7 | 4 | 64 | 550 | 66 | 450 | 34 | 0 |
| Marinette | 10,421 | 46 | 0 | 17 | 0 | 29 | 194 | 13 | 172 | 9 | 1 |
| Marshall Village | 4,031 | 7 | 0 | 2 | 0 | 5 | 21 | 0 | 18 | 3 | 0 |
| Mauston | 4,352 | 12 | 0 | 3 | 1 | 8 | 147 | 3 | 140 | 4 | 2 |
| Mayville | 4,798 | 6 | 0 | 2 | 0 | 4 | 28 | 0 | 28 | 0 | 0 |
| McFarland | 9,437 | 11 | 0 | 0 | 1 | 10 | 66 | 10 | 47 | 9 | 0 |
| Medford | 4,258 | 2 | 0 | 1 | 0 | 1 | 63 | 4 | 57 | 2 | 0 |
| Menasha | 17,823 | 31 | 0 | 12 | 0 | 19 | 159 | 22 | 130 | 7 | 2 |
| Menomonee Falls | 38,516 | 32 | 1 | 5 | 10 | 16 | 387 | 20 | 321 | 46 | 0 |
| Menomonie | 16,633 | 36 | 1 | 6 | 0 | 29 | 262 | 16 | 221 | 25 | 0 |
| Mequon | 24,936 | 15 | 0 | 2 | 3 | 10 | 184 | 20 | 154 | 10 | 0 |
| Merrill | 8,927 | 21 | 0 | 2 | 0 | 19 | 204 | 33 | 165 | 6 | 0 |
| Middleton | 20,472 | 38 | 0 | 8 | 4 | 26 | 254 | 33 | 197 | 24 | 1 |
| Milton | 5,653 | 6 | 0 | 1 | 0 | 5 | 71 | 7 | 63 | 1 | 0 |
| Milwaukee | 593,337 | 9,413 | 195 | 444 | 1,873 | 6,901 | 24,848 | 2,868 | 9,702 | 12,278 | 240 |
| Minocqua | 4,453 | 4 | 0 | 1 | 0 | 3 | 21 | 1 | 20 | 0 | 0 |
| Mishicot | 1,384 | 4 | 0 | 4 | 0 | 0 | 13 | 2 | 10 | 1 | 0 |
| Monona | 8,226 | 18 | 1 | 2 | 3 | 12 | 378 | 17 | 341 | 20 | 0 |
| Monroe | 10,387 | 5 | 0 | 5 | 0 | 0 | 99 | 7 | 89 | 3 | 0 |
| Montello | 1,451 | 0 | 0 | 0 | 0 | 0 | 9 | 0 | 9 | 0 | 0 |
| Mount Horeb | 7,606 | 7 | 0 | 3 | 0 | 4 | 26 | 2 | 24 | 0 | 0 |
| Mount Pleasant | 27,084 | 36 | 1 | 4 | 8 | 23 | 442 | 40 | 366 | 36 | 0 |
| Mukwonago | 8,184 | 5 | 0 | 1 | 0 | 4 | 85 | 2 | 82 | 1 | 0 |

## Table 8. Offenses Known to Law Enforcement, by Selected State and City, 2021—Continued

(Number.)

| State/city | Population | Violent crime | Murder and nonnegligent manslaughter | Rape | Robbery | Aggravated assault | Property crime | Burglary | Larceny-theft | Motor vehicle theft | Arson |
|---|---|---|---|---|---|---|---|---|---|---|---|
| Mukwonago Town | 8,184 | 2 | 0 | 0 | 0 | 2 | 6 | 0 | 6 | 0 | 0 |
| Muscoda | 1,227 | 1 | 0 | 0 | 1 | 0 | 12 | 1 | 10 | 1 | 0 |
| Muskego | 25,436 | 8 | 0 | 1 | 2 | 5 | 87 | 12 | 71 | 4 | 0 |
| Neenah | 26,451 | 62 | 1 | 16 | 3 | 42 | 306 | 38 | 248 | 20 | 0 |
| New Berlin | 39,833 | 15 | 0 | 3 | 0 | 12 | 342 | 19 | 299 | 24 | 0 |
| New Glarus | 2,132 | 0 | 0 | 0 | 0 | 0 | 21 | 0 | 21 | 0 | 0 |
| New Holstein | 3,092 | 0 | 0 | 0 | 0 | 0 | 19 | 1 | 18 | 0 | 0 |
| New Lisbon | 2,547 | 1 | 0 | 0 | 0 | 1 | 4 | 1 | 3 | 0 | 0 |
| New London | 7,043 | 12 | 0 | 5 | 1 | 6 | 29 | 0 | 26 | 3 | 0 |
| New Richmond | 9,875 | 12 | 0 | 1 | 0 | 11 | 94 | 17 | 67 | 10 | 1 |
| Niagara | 1,526 | 3 | 0 | 0 | 0 | 3 | 7 | 1 | 6 | 0 | 0 |
| North Fond du Lac | 5,064 | 3 | 0 | 0 | 0 | 3 | 35 | 0 | 29 | 6 | 0 |
| Oak Creek | 36,975 | 54 | 1 | 10 | 13 | 30 | 655 | 35 | 559 | 61 | 0 |
| Oconomowoc | 17,301 | 11 | 2 | 2 | 2 | 5 | 85 | 1 | 82 | 2 | 0 |
| Oconto | 4,580 | 10 | 1 | 0 | 0 | 9 | 63 | 3 | 55 | 5 | 0 |
| Oconto Falls | 2,796 | 1 | 0 | 1 | 0 | 0 | 31 | 5 | 25 | 1 | 0 |
| Omro | 3,599 | 6 | 0 | 3 | 0 | 3 | 23 | 3 | 19 | 1 | 0 |
| Onalaska | 19,243 | 16 | 0 | 7 | 1 | 8 | 613 | 33 | 570 | 10 | 0 |
| Oregon | 10,881 | 9 | 0 | 5 | 1 | 3 | 74 | 21 | 49 | 4 | 0 |
| Orfordville | 1,490 | 0 | 0 | 0 | 0 | 0 | 7 | 1 | 5 | 1 | 0 |
| Oshkosh | 66,513 | 212 | 1 | 55 | 13 | 143 | 1,050 | 122 | 858 | 70 | 2 |
| Palmyra | 1,742 | 0 | 0 | 0 | 0 | 0 | 9 | 1 | 8 | 0 | 0 |
| Peshtigo | 3,310 | 1 | 0 | 1 | 0 | 0 | 15 | 5 | 8 | 2 | 0 |
| Pewaukee Village | 8,089 | 6 | 0 | 0 | 3 | 3 | 188 | 0 | 185 | 3 | 1 |
| Phillips | 1,306 | 6 | 0 | 0 | 0 | 6 | 15 | 1 | 14 | 0 | 0 |
| Platteville | 11,690 | 45 | 0 | 9 | 1 | 35 | 253 | 13 | 225 | 15 | 1 |
| Pleasant Prairie | 21,542 | 44 | 0 | 14 | 3 | 27 | 260 | 22 | 215 | 23 | 0 |
| Plover | 13,360 | 34 | 2 | 6 | 0 | 26 | 170 | 7 | 159 | 4 | 0 |
| Plymouth | 8,766 | 4 | 0 | 3 | 1 | 0 | 46 | 5 | 37 | 4 | 2 |
| Portage | 10,387 | 31 | 0 | 10 | 1 | 20 | 215 | 12 | 180 | 23 | 1 |
| Prairie du Chien | 5,496 | 12 | 0 | 8 | 0 | 4 | 64 | 9 | 55 | 0 | 0 |
| Prescott | 4,281 | 10 | 0 | 2 | 1 | 7 | 31 | 4 | 22 | 5 | 0 |
| Racine | 76,018 | 284 | 5 | 23 | 42 | 214 | 1,089 | 286 | 644 | 159 | 8 |
| Rhinelander | 7,624 | 14 | 0 | 4 | 0 | 10 | 112 | 11 | 100 | 1 | 0 |
| Rice Lake | 8,511 | 43 | 0 | 8 | 1 | 34 | 161 | 8 | 141 | 12 | 1 |
| Ripon | 7,856 | 10 | 0 | 6 | 0 | 4 | 58 | 12 | 44 | 2 | 0 |
| River Hills | 1,585 | 0 | 0 | 0 | 0 | 0 | 4 | 1 | 3 | 0 | 0 |
| Rome Town | 2,790 | 4 | 0 | 3 | 0 | 1 | 29 | 0 | 28 | 1 | 0 |
| Rothschild | 5,255 | 6 | 0 | 3 | 0 | 3 | 55 | 6 | 46 | 3 | 1 |
| Saukville | 4,436 | 4 | 0 | 3 | 0 | 1 | 58 | 1 | 52 | 5 | 0 |
| Seymour | 3,457 | 3 | 0 | 2 | 0 | 1 | 13 | 1 | 12 | 0 | 0 |
| Shawano | 8,845 | 25 | 0 | 7 | 1 | 17 | 215 | 22 | 179 | 14 | 0 |
| Sheboygan | 47,667 | 167 | 1 | 49 | 5 | 112 | 684 | 84 | 566 | 34 | 5 |
| Sheboygan Falls | 7,924 | 5 | 0 | 1 | 0 | 4 | 47 | 5 | 41 | 1 | 0 |
| Shorewood | 13,222 | 9 | 0 | 2 | 4 | 3 | 269 | 10 | 176 | 83 | 0 |
| Shorewood Hills | 2,050 | 1 | 0 | 0 | 0 | 1 | 50 | 11 | 37 | 2 | 0 |
| South Milwaukee | 20,795 | 38 | 0 | 5 | 6 | 27 | 232 | 12 | 209 | 11 | 0 |
| Sparta | 9,827 | 40 | 0 | 14 | 0 | 26 | 132 | 11 | 109 | 12 | 0 |
| Stanley | 3,714 | 8 | 0 | 3 | 0 | 5 | 31 | 0 | 28 | 3 | 0 |
| St. Croix Falls | 2,052 | 7 | 1 | 1 | 0 | 5 | 63 | 1 | 52 | 10 | 1 |
| Stevens Point | 25,875 | 26 | 0 | 4 | 1 | 21 | 306 | 45 | 243 | 18 | 1 |
| St. Francis | 9,846 | 7 | 0 | 2 | 1 | 4 | 140 | 9 | 108 | 23 | 0 |
| Sturtevant | 6,642 | 5 | 0 | 0 | 0 | 5 | 44 | 0 | 37 | 7 | 0 |
| Summit | 5,321 | 3 | 0 | 0 | 0 | 3 | 21 | 2 | 19 | 0 | 0 |
| Sun Prairie | 35,722 | 69 | 0 | 7 | 9 | 53 | 570 | 60 | 452 | 58 | 0 |
| Superior | 26,117 | 54 | 0 | 12 | 7 | 35 | 802 | 80 | 626 | 96 | 3 |
| Thiensville | 3,107 | 0 | 0 | 0 | 0 | 0 | 10 | 0 | 9 | 1 | 0 |
| Thorp | 1,602 | 3 | 0 | 1 | 0 | 2 | 48 | 0 | 46 | 2 | 0 |
| Tomahawk | 3,107 | 3 | 0 | 2 | 0 | 1 | 66 | 4 | 62 | 0 | 0 |
| Town of East Troy | 4,065 | 1 | 0 | 0 | 0 | 1 | 7 | 0 | 6 | 1 | 0 |
| Town of Madison | 6,713 | 26 | 0 | 5 | 3 | 18 | 163 | 11 | 121 | 31 | 0 |
| Two Rivers | 10,903 | 32 | 1 | 3 | 0 | 28 | 93 | 6 | 81 | 6 | 1 |
| Verona | 13,860 | 13 | 0 | 6 | 1 | 6 | 150 | 26 | 117 | 7 | 0 |
| Waterford Town | 6,509 | 5 | 0 | 0 | 2 | 3 | 25 | 3 | 22 | 0 | 0 |
| Waukesha | 72,493 | 74 | 0 | 26 | 5 | 43 | 631 | 53 | 548 | 30 | 4 |
| Waunakee | 14,410 | 8 | 0 | 0 | 1 | 7 | 80 | 13 | 57 | 10 | 0 |
| Waupaca | 5,833 | 10 | 0 | 4 | 0 | 6 | 77 | 8 | 62 | 7 | 0 |
| Waupun | 11,264 | 12 | 0 | 4 | 0 | 8 | 51 | 8 | 37 | 6 | 0 |
| Wausau | 38,435 | 158 | 2 | 35 | 8 | 113 | 626 | 81 | 488 | 57 | 6 |
| Wauwatosa | 48,650 | 69 | 1 | 2 | 29 | 37 | 1,296 | 80 | 847 | 369 | 1 |
| Webster | 618 | 7 | 0 | 1 | 0 | 6 | 18 | 2 | 14 | 2 | 0 |
| West Allis | 60,176 | 149 | 3 | 20 | 39 | 87 | 1,689 | 157 | 1,183 | 349 | 10 |
| West Bend | 31,506 | 40 | 0 | 9 | 3 | 28 | 442 | 18 | 406 | 18 | 2 |
| Westfield | 1,270 | 0 | 0 | 0 | 0 | 0 | 6 | 0 | 6 | 0 | 0 |
| West Milwaukee | 4,113 | 34 | 0 | 2 | 12 | 20 | 677 | 20 | 562 | 95 | 5 |
| West Salem | 5,032 | 4 | 0 | 0 | 0 | 4 | 53 | 2 | 47 | 4 | 1 |
| Whitefish Bay | 13,848 | 5 | 0 | 2 | 1 | 2 | 119 | 4 | 93 | 22 | 0 |
| Whitewater | 15,057 | 37 | 0 | 13 | 2 | 22 | 177 | 10 | 161 | 6 | 2 |
| Williams Bay | 2,666 | 0 | 0 | 0 | 0 | 0 | 6 | 0 | 6 | 0 | 0 |
| Winneconne | 2,491 | 0 | 0 | 0 | 0 | 0 | 16 | 0 | 15 | 1 | 0 |
| Wisconsin Dells | 3,099 | 24 | 1 | 12 | 0 | 11 | 138 | 8 | 127 | 3 | 0 |
| Woodruff | 1,990 | 0 | 0 | 0 | 0 | 0 | 8 | 0 | 7 | 1 | 0 |

## Table 8. Offenses Known to Law Enforcement, by Selected State and City, 2021—Continued

(Number.)

| State/city | Population | Violent crime | Murder and nonnegligent manslaughter | Rape | Robbery | Aggravated assault | Property crime | Burglary | Larceny-theft | Motor vehicle theft | Arson |
|---|---|---|---|---|---|---|---|---|---|---|---|
| **WYOMING** | | | | | | | | | | | |
| Buffalo | 4,666 | 6 | 0 | 2 | 1 | 3 | 34 | 5 | 26 | 3 | 0 |
| Cheyenne | 65,263 | 201 | 3 | 51 | 24 | 123 | 2,414 | 326 | 1,680 | 408 | 16 |
| Cody | 9,878 | 16 | 1 | 5 | 0 | 10 | 107 | 13 | 92 | 2 | 1 |
| Diamondville | 769 | 0 | 0 | 0 | 0 | 0 | 2 | 1 | 1 | 0 | 0 |
| Douglas | 6,404 | 9 | 0 | 1 | 1 | 7 | 60 | 14 | 44 | 2 | 2 |
| Evanston | 11,494 | 46 | 1 | 26 | 1 | 18 | 262 | 56 | 195 | 11 | 1 |
| Evansville | 3,046 | 3 | 0 | 0 | 0 | 3 | 89 | 18 | 61 | 10 | 0 |
| Gillette | 32,294 | 67 | 0 | 18 | 3 | 46 | 553 | 56 | 453 | 44 | 0 |
| Glenrock | 2,560 | 2 | 0 | 0 | 0 | 2 | 12 | 2 | 6 | 4 | 0 |
| Laramie | 32,841 | 73 | 0 | 34 | 1 | 38 | 452 | 98 | 346 | 8 | 2 |
| Lusk | 1,465 | 8 | 0 | 3 | 0 | 5 | 12 | 4 | 6 | 2 | 0 |
| Medicine Bow | 255 | 0 | 0 | 0 | 0 | 0 | 1 | 0 | 1 | 0 | 0 |
| Mills | 4,144 | 1 | 0 | 0 | 0 | 1 | 63 | 16 | 39 | 8 | 0 |
| Moorcroft | 1,091 | 1 | 0 | 0 | 0 | 1 | 10 | 3 | 4 | 3 | 1 |
| Newcastle | 3,293 | 4 | 0 | 1 | 0 | 3 | 43 | 8 | 33 | 2 | 1 |
| Pine Bluffs | 1,163 | 0 | 0 | 0 | 0 | 0 | 8 | 2 | 4 | 2 | 0 |
| Powell | 6,108 | 14 | 0 | 6 | 0 | 8 | 83 | 15 | 62 | 6 | 2 |
| Riverton | 10,823 | 69 | 0 | 17 | 6 | 46 | 351 | 26 | 274 | 51 | 1 |
| Rock Springs | 22,937 | 49 | 1 | 17 | 2 | 29 | 286 | 44 | 217 | 25 | 3 |
| Sheridan | 18,157 | 15 | 0 | 0 | 0 | 15 | 239 | 19 | 202 | 18 | 2 |
| Thermopolis | 2,747 | 2 | 0 | 0 | 0 | 2 | 25 | 2 | 23 | 0 | 0 |
| Torrington | 6,564 | 16 | 1 | 4 | 0 | 11 | 63 | 15 | 40 | 8 | 1 |
| Worland | 4,947 | 5 | 0 | 2 | 0 | 3 | 37 | 0 | 34 | 3 | 1 |

1 Limited data for 2021 were available for California, District of Columbia, Florida, Illinois, Maryland, New Jersey, New Mexico, New York, and Pennsylvania.

## Table 9. Offenses Known to Law Enforcement, by Selected State and University and College, 2021

(Number.)

| State and university/college | Student enrollment[1] | Violent crime | Murder and nonnegligent manslaughter | Rape | Robbery | Aggravated assault | Property crime | Burglary | Larceny-theft | Motor vehicle theft | Arson |
|---|---|---|---|---|---|---|---|---|---|---|---|
| **ALABAMA** | | | | | | | | | | | |
| University of Alabama | | | | | | | | | | | |
| Birmingham | 25,843 | 18 | 0 | 5 | 1 | 12 | 159 | 23 | 124 | 12 | 2 |
| Tuscaloosa | 42,096 | 17 | 0 | 5 | 2 | 10 | 175 | 22 | 148 | 5 | 0 |
| University of North Alabama | 9,185 | 5 | 0 | 1 | 0 | 4 | 25 | 5 | 20 | 0 | 1 |
| University of South Alabama | 16,398 | 12 | 0 | 6 | 2 | 4 | 35 | 4 | 30 | 1 | 1 |
| | | | | | | | | | | | |
| **ALASKA** | | | | | | | | | | | |
| University of Alaska | | | | | | | | | | | |
| Anchorage | 20,526 | 5 | 0 | 0 | 1 | 4 | 21 | 2 | 19 | 0 | 3 |
| Fairbanks | 11,413 | 5 | 0 | 0 | 1 | 4 | 30 | 3 | 27 | 0 | 0 |
| | | | | | | | | | | | |
| **ARIZONA** | | | | | | | | | | | |
| Arizona Western College | 11,646 | 1 | 0 | 1 | 0 | 0 | 2 | 0 | 2 | 0 | 0 |
| Central Arizona College | 8,093 | 0 | 0 | 0 | 0 | 0 | 3 | 0 | 2 | 1 | 0 |
| Maricopa Community College[2] | | 4 | 0 | 0 | 0 | 4 | 94 | 4 | 81 | 9 | 0 |
| Northern Arizona University | 34,290 | 11 | 0 | 6 | 0 | 5 | 160 | 16 | 140 | 4 | 0 |
| Pima Community College | 36,384 | 2 | 0 | 0 | 0 | 2 | 41 | 10 | 28 | 3 | 0 |
| | | | | | | | | | | | |
| **ARKANSAS** | | | | | | | | | | | |
| Arkansas State University | | | | | | | | | | | |
| Beebe | 4,427 | 0 | 0 | 0 | 0 | 0 | 3 | 0 | 3 | 0 | 0 |
| Jonesboro | 18,762 | 8 | 0 | 3 | 0 | 5 | 30 | 3 | 27 | 0 | 0 |
| Arkansas Tech University | 13,316 | 3 | 0 | 2 | 0 | 1 | 27 | 2 | 25 | 0 | 0 |
| Southern Arkansas University | 5,249 | 0 | 0 | 0 | 0 | 0 | 9 | 1 | 8 | 0 | 0 |
| Southern Arkansas University Tech | 1,725 | 0 | 0 | 0 | 0 | 0 | 1 | 0 | 1 | 0 | 0 |
| University of Arkansas | | | | | | | | | | | |
| Fayetteville | 30,137 | 17 | 0 | 8 | 2 | 7 | 138 | 14 | 112 | 12 | 0 |
| Medical Sciences | 3,015 | 5 | 0 | 0 | 0 | 5 | 62 | 5 | 53 | 4 | 0 |
| Monticello | 3,499 | 0 | 0 | 0 | 0 | 0 | 7 | 0 | 7 | 0 | 0 |
| Pine Bluff | 2,724 | 5 | 0 | 1 | 1 | 3 | 22 | 2 | 19 | 1 | 1 |
| University of Central Arkansas | 12,333 | 2 | 0 | 1 | 0 | 1 | 44 | 4 | 40 | 0 | 0 |
| | | | | | | | | | | | |
| **CALIFORNIA[3]** | | | | | | | | | | | |
| | | | | | | | | | | | |
| **COLORADO** | | | | | | | | | | | |
| Adams State University | 3,883 | 0 | 0 | 0 | 0 | 0 | 9 | 0 | 9 | 0 | 0 |
| Arapahoe Community College | 19,102 | 0 | 0 | 0 | 0 | 0 | 7 | 1 | 5 | 1 | 0 |
| Colorado School of Mines | 7,092 | 0 | 0 | 0 | 0 | 0 | 70 | 7 | 57 | 6 | 0 |
| Colorado State University, Fort Collins | 37,806 | 10 | 0 | 1 | 0 | 9 | 247 | 15 | 226 | 6 | 3 |
| Fort Lewis College | 3,766 | 5 | 0 | 3 | 0 | 2 | 13 | 6 | 7 | 0 | 0 |
| Red Rocks Community College | 11,486 | 0 | 0 | 0 | 0 | 0 | 7 | 0 | 7 | 0 | 0 |
| University of Colorado | | | | | | | | | | | |
| Boulder | 41,826 | 10 | 0 | 5 | 3 | 2 | 436 | 30 | 388 | 18 | 7 |
| Colorado Springs | 16,715 | 3 | 0 | 3 | 0 | 0 | 36 | 1 | 31 | 4 | 0 |
| Denver | 31,796 | 3 | 0 | 0 | 1 | 2 | 136 | 3 | 73 | 60 | 1 |
| University of Northern Colorado | 15,248 | 3 | 0 | 2 | 1 | 0 | 93 | 5 | 84 | 4 | 0 |
| | | | | | | | | | | | |
| **CONNECTICUT** | | | | | | | | | | | |
| Central Connecticut State University | 13,046 | 1 | 0 | 0 | 1 | 0 | 28 | 0 | 27 | 1 | 0 |
| Eastern Connecticut State University | 5,508 | 4 | 0 | 4 | 0 | 0 | 9 | 0 | 9 | 0 | 0 |
| Southern Connecticut State University | 11,273 | 0 | 0 | 0 | 0 | 0 | 6 | 1 | 5 | 0 | 0 |
| University of Connecticut, Storrs, Avery Point, and Hartford[2] | | 3 | 0 | 2 | 0 | 1 | 72 | 9 | 60 | 3 | 1 |
| Western Connecticut State University | 6,463 | 1 | 0 | 1 | 0 | 0 | 7 | 0 | 6 | 1 | 0 |
| Yale University | 14,910 | 2 | 0 | 0 | 2 | 0 | 171 | 13 | 155 | 3 | 0 |
| | | | | | | | | | | | |
| **DELAWARE** | | | | | | | | | | | |
| Delaware State University | 5,263 | 13 | 0 | 4 | 0 | 9 | 42 | 5 | 36 | 1 | 0 |
| University of Delaware | 26,527 | 7 | 0 | 3 | 2 | 2 | 85 | 1 | 84 | 0 | 0 |
| | | | | | | | | | | | |
| **FLORIDA[3]** | | | | | | | | | | | |
| | | | | | | | | | | | |
| **GEORGIA** | | | | | | | | | | | |
| Abraham Baldwin Agricultural College | 4,667 | 0 | 0 | 0 | 0 | 0 | 26 | 2 | 23 | 1 | 0 |
| Agnes Scott College | 1,166 | 0 | 0 | 0 | 0 | 0 | 9 | 0 | 9 | 0 | 0 |
| Albany Technical College | 4,635 | 0 | 0 | 0 | 0 | 0 | 0 | 0 | 0 | 0 | 0 |
| Athens Technical College | 6,598 | 0 | 0 | 0 | 0 | 0 | 0 | 0 | 0 | 0 | 0 |
| Atlanta Metropolitan State College | 2,676 | 0 | 0 | 0 | 0 | 0 | 2 | 2 | 0 | 0 | 0 |
| Atlanta Technical College | 6,106 | 0 | 0 | 0 | 0 | 0 | 2 | 0 | 2 | 0 | 0 |
| Augusta Technical College | 6,088 | 0 | 0 | 0 | 0 | 0 | 1 | 0 | 1 | 0 | 0 |
| Augusta University | 9,706 | 3 | 0 | 0 | 0 | 3 | 92 | 2 | 81 | 9 | 0 |
| Berry College | 2,228 | 0 | 0 | 0 | 0 | 0 | 17 | 4 | 13 | 0 | 1 |
| Clayton State University | 8,420 | 7 | 0 | 5 | 1 | 1 | 23 | 1 | 21 | 1 | 0 |
| College of Coastal Georgia | 4,355 | 0 | 0 | 0 | 0 | 0 | 11 | 1 | 9 | 1 | 1 |
| Columbus State University | 9,643 | 4 | 0 | 2 | 2 | 0 | 38 | 4 | 31 | 3 | 0 |
| Dalton State College | 5,734 | 1 | 0 | 1 | 0 | 0 | 0 | 0 | 0 | 0 | 0 |
| Emory University | 15,970 | 13 | 0 | 6 | 0 | 7 | 235 | 32 | 197 | 6 | 1 |
| Fort Valley State University | 2,892 | 2 | 0 | 1 | 0 | 1 | 7 | 1 | 6 | 0 | 0 |
| Georgia College and State University | 8,039 | 8 | 0 | 1 | 0 | 7 | 35 | 0 | 34 | 1 | 0 |
| Georgia Gwinnett College | 15,489 | 2 | 0 | 0 | 1 | 1 | 13 | 0 | 13 | 0 | 0 |
| Georgia Highlands College | 7,895 | 0 | 0 | 0 | 0 | 0 | 1 | 0 | 1 | 0 | 0 |
| Georgia Institute of Technology | 43,217 | 10 | 0 | 3 | 2 | 5 | 205 | 20 | 156 | 29 | 1 |

## Table 9. Offenses Known to Law Enforcement, by Selected State and University and College, 2021—Continued

(Number.)

| State and university/college | Student enrollment[1] | Violent crime | Murder and nonnegligent manslaughter | Rape | Robbery | Aggravated assault | Property crime | Burglary | Larceny-theft | Motor vehicle theft | Arson |
|---|---|---|---|---|---|---|---|---|---|---|---|
| Georgia Military College | 14,828 | 0 | 0 | 0 | 0 | 0 | 0 | 0 | 0 | 0 | 0 |
| Georgia Northwestern Technical College | 8,811 | 0 | 0 | 0 | 0 | 0 | 2 | 0 | 2 | 0 | 0 |
| Georgia Piedmont Technical College | 4,979 | 0 | 0 | 0 | 0 | 0 | 2 | 0 | 2 | 0 | 0 |
| Georgia Southern University | 30,231 | 9 | 0 | 7 | 1 | 1 | 83 | 5 | 75 | 3 | 1 |
| Georgia Southwestern State University | 3,725 | 1 | 0 | 1 | 0 | 0 | 1 | 0 | 1 | 0 | 0 |
| Georgia State University | 41,177 | 13 | 0 | 2 | 4 | 7 | 88 | 6 | 73 | 9 | 0 |
| Gordon State College | 4,114 | 1 | 0 | 1 | 0 | 0 | 0 | 0 | 0 | 0 | 0 |
| Gwinnett Technical College | 12,929 | 0 | 0 | 0 | 0 | 0 | 0 | 0 | 0 | 0 | 0 |
| Kennesaw State University | 44,088 | 11 | 0 | 3 | 5 | 3 | 58 | 4 | 50 | 4 | 0 |
| Mercer University | 9,933 | 2 | 0 | 1 | 0 | 1 | 41 | 4 | 32 | 5 | 0 |
| Middle Georgia State University | 10,155 | 3 | 0 | 1 | 1 | 1 | 28 | 5 | 21 | 2 | 0 |
| Piedmont College | 3,052 | 0 | 0 | 0 | 0 | 0 | 0 | 0 | 0 | 0 | 0 |
| Southern Regional Technical College | 6,804 | 0 | 0 | 0 | 0 | 0 | 0 | 0 | 0 | 0 | 0 |
| Spelman College | 2,190 | 0 | 0 | 0 | 0 | 0 | 0 | 0 | 0 | 0 | 0 |
| University of Georgia | 42,941 | 17 | 0 | 14 | 1 | 2 | 372 | 15 | 346 | 11 | 2 |
| University of North Georgia | 23,141 | 4 | 0 | 4 | 0 | 0 | 11 | 1 | 10 | 0 | 0 |
| University of West Georgia | 15,915 | 5 | 0 | 2 | 0 | 3 | 34 | 2 | 29 | 3 | 0 |
| West Georgia Technical College | 10,089 | 0 | 0 | 0 | 0 | 0 | 2 | 0 | 2 | 0 | 0 |
| Young Harris College | 1,650 | 0 | 0 | 0 | 0 | 0 | 3 | 0 | 3 | 0 | 0 |
| **ILLINOIS[3]** | | | | | | | | | | | |
| Illinois State University | 23,141 | 6 | 0 | 5 | 1 | 0 | 70 | 5 | 63 | 2 | 1 |
| University of Illinois | | | | | | | | | | | |
| Chicago | 35,210 | 18 | 0 | 3 | 4 | 11 | 119 | 2 | 116 | 1 | 0 |
| Urbana | 57,324 | 13 | 0 | 3 | 2 | 8 | 169 | 3 | 161 | 5 | 1 |
| **INDIANA** | | | | | | | | | | | |
| Indiana State University | 13,990 | 0 | 0 | 0 | 0 | 0 | 102 | 2 | 95 | 5 | 0 |
| University of Indianapolis | 6,320 | 8 | 0 | 1 | 4 | 3 | 111 | 14 | 86 | 11 | 0 |
| **IOWA** | | | | | | | | | | | |
| Iowa State University | 35,319 | 13 | 0 | 11 | 0 | 2 | 140 | 15 | 118 | 7 | 0 |
| University of Iowa | 34,495 | 63 | 0 | 33 | 2 | 28 | 247 | 23 | 213 | 11 | 2 |
| University of Northern Iowa | 12,137 | 4 | 0 | 4 | 0 | 0 | 53 | 2 | 46 | 5 | 0 |
| **KANSAS** | | | | | | | | | | | |
| Fort Hays State University | 18,862 | 2 | 0 | 2 | 0 | 0 | 12 | 0 | 12 | 0 | 0 |
| Kansas State University | 23,353 | 3 | 0 | 1 | 0 | 2 | 89 | 1 | 87 | 1 | 0 |
| University of Kansas | | | | | | | | | | | |
| Main Campus | 30,983 | 4 | 0 | 2 | 0 | 2 | 136 | 5 | 121 | 10 | 0 |
| Medical Center[2] | | 28 | 0 | 0 | 1 | 27 | 169 | 5 | 157 | 7 | 0 |
| Wichita State University | 17,817 | 9 | 0 | 2 | 2 | 5 | 60 | 5 | 53 | 2 | 0 |
| **KENTUCKY** | | | | | | | | | | | |
| Eastern Kentucky University | 17,345 | 5 | 0 | 4 | 1 | 0 | 96 | 13 | 81 | 2 | 0 |
| Kentucky State University | 3,044 | 0 | 0 | 0 | 0 | 0 | 2 | 1 | 1 | 0 | 0 |
| Morehead State University | 10,971 | 0 | 0 | 0 | 0 | 0 | 12 | 0 | 12 | 0 | 0 |
| Murray State University | 10,853 | 3 | 0 | 3 | 0 | 0 | 33 | 4 | 28 | 1 | 0 |
| Northern Kentucky University | 18,308 | 2 | 0 | 2 | 0 | 0 | 16 | 4 | 11 | 1 | 0 |
| University of Kentucky | 32,756 | 21 | 0 | 13 | 0 | 8 | 424 | 21 | 380 | 23 | 0 |
| University of Louisville | 25,451 | 13 | 0 | 4 | 7 | 2 | 253 | 23 | 219 | 11 | 1 |
| Western Kentucky University | 21,535 | 5 | 0 | 4 | 1 | 0 | 79 | 6 | 67 | 6 | 0 |
| **LOUISIANA** | | | | | | | | | | | |
| Louisiana State University | | | | | | | | | | | |
| Baton Rouge | 34,811 | 9 | 0 | 4 | 2 | 3 | 165 | 22 | 140 | 3 | 0 |
| Health Sciences Center, Shreveport | 1,084 | 10 | 0 | 0 | 1 | 9 | 15 | 1 | 12 | 2 | 1 |
| Louisiana Tech University | 12,768 | 2 | 0 | 1 | 0 | 1 | 64 | 3 | 60 | 1 | 0 |
| Southern University and A&M College, New Orleans | 2,946 | 0 | 0 | 0 | 0 | 0 | 0 | 0 | 0 | 0 | 0 |
| University of New Orleans | 9,736 | 1 | 0 | 0 | 0 | 1 | 9 | 2 | 7 | 0 | 0 |
| **MAINE** | | | | | | | | | | | |
| University of Maine | | | | | | | | | | | |
| Farmington | 2,397 | 1 | 0 | 1 | 0 | 0 | 3 | 0 | 3 | 0 | 0 |
| Orono | 13,426 | 2 | 0 | 1 | 0 | 1 | 40 | 2 | 38 | 0 | 2 |
| University of Southern Maine | 10,788 | 0 | 0 | 0 | 0 | 0 | 11 | 0 | 9 | 2 | 0 |
| **MARYLAND[3]** | | | | | | | | | | | |
| Frostburg State University | 5,850 | 2 | 0 | 2 | 0 | 0 | 12 | 4 | 8 | 0 | 0 |
| **MASSACHUSETTS** | | | | | | | | | | | |
| Amherst College | 1,940 | 0 | 0 | 0 | 0 | 0 | 0 | 0 | 0 | 0 | 0 |
| Assumption College | 2,701 | 2 | 0 | 2 | 0 | 0 | 9 | 1 | 8 | 0 | 0 |
| Babson College | 3,987 | 3 | 0 | 1 | 0 | 2 | 30 | 6 | 24 | 0 | 0 |
| Bentley University | 5,579 | 0 | 0 | 0 | 0 | 0 | 8 | 1 | 7 | 0 | 1 |
| Boston College | 16,502 | 2 | 0 | 1 | 1 | 0 | 45 | 4 | 40 | 1 | 0 |
| Boston University | 42,047 | 9 | 0 | 5 | 3 | 1 | 287 | 7 | 280 | 0 | 1 |
| Bridgewater State University | 13,150 | 4 | 0 | 4 | 0 | 0 | 4 | 0 | 3 | 1 | 0 |
| Bristol Community College | 9,702 | 0 | 0 | 0 | 0 | 0 | 5 | 0 | 5 | 0 | 0 |
| Bunker Hill Community College | 16,306 | 0 | 0 | 0 | 0 | 0 | 8 | 0 | 8 | 0 | 0 |
| Cape Cod Community College | 4,512 | 0 | 0 | 0 | 0 | 0 | 0 | 0 | 0 | 0 | 0 |
| Clark University | 3,880 | 2 | 0 | 0 | 1 | 1 | 13 | 4 | 8 | 1 | 0 |

## Table 9. Offenses Known to Law Enforcement, by Selected State and University and College, 2021—Continued

(Number.)

| State and university/college | Student enrollment[1] | Violent crime | Murder and nonnegligent manslaughter | Rape | Robbery | Aggravated assault | Property crime | Burglary | Larceny-theft | Motor vehicle theft | Arson |
|---|---|---|---|---|---|---|---|---|---|---|---|
| College of the Holy Cross | 3,098 | 0 | 0 | 0 | 0 | 0 | 1 | 1 | 0 | 0 | 0 |
| Dean College | 1,569 | 0 | 0 | 0 | 0 | 0 | 7 | 3 | 4 | 0 | 0 |
| Emerson College | 5,496 | 2 | 0 | 1 | 0 | 1 | 12 | 0 | 12 | 0 | 0 |
| Endicott College | 6,649 | 2 | 0 | 2 | 0 | 0 | 7 | 0 | 7 | 0 | 0 |
| Fitchburg State University | 10,793 | 1 | 0 | 0 | 0 | 1 | 10 | 5 | 5 | 0 | 0 |
| Framingham State University | 8,366 | 0 | 0 | 0 | 0 | 0 | 4 | 0 | 4 | 0 | 0 |
| Gordon College | 2,314 | 0 | 0 | 0 | 0 | 0 | 15 | 1 | 14 | 0 | 0 |
| Greenfield Community College | 2,420 | 0 | 0 | 0 | 0 | 0 | 0 | 0 | 0 | 0 | 0 |
| Harvard University | 41,024 | 2 | 0 | 1 | 0 | 1 | 252 | 16 | 216 | 20 | 0 |
| Holyoke Community College | 6,374 | 0 | 0 | 0 | 0 | 0 | 2 | 0 | 2 | 0 | 0 |
| Lasell College | 2,353 | 1 | 0 | 1 | 0 | 0 | 8 | 2 | 6 | 0 | 0 |
| Massachusetts Bay Community College | 6,644 | 0 | 0 | 0 | 0 | 0 | 0 | 0 | 0 | 0 | 0 |
| Massachusetts College of Art | 2,502 | 0 | 0 | 0 | 0 | 0 | 0 | 0 | 0 | 0 | 0 |
| Massachusetts College of Liberal Arts | 1,922 | 1 | 0 | 1 | 0 | 0 | 4 | 0 | 4 | 0 | 0 |
| Massachusetts Institute of Technology | 12,195 | 2 | 0 | 0 | 0 | 2 | 146 | 7 | 137 | 2 | 0 |
| Massasoit Community College | 9,466 | 0 | 0 | 0 | 0 | 0 | 3 | 2 | 1 | 0 | 0 |
| MCPHS University | 8,078 | 0 | 0 | 0 | 0 | 0 | 9 | 0 | 9 | 0 | 0 |
| Merrimack College | 6,600 | 3 | 0 | 0 | 0 | 3 | 24 | 5 | 19 | 0 | 0 |
| Mount Holyoke College | 2,504 | 1 | 0 | 1 | 0 | 0 | 4 | 0 | 4 | 0 | 0 |
| Mount Wachusett Community College | 4,818 | 0 | 0 | 0 | 0 | 0 | 1 | 0 | 1 | 0 | 0 |
| Northeastern University | 30,003 | 7 | 0 | 6 | 0 | 1 | 163 | 7 | 150 | 6 | 0 |
| North Shore Community College | 7,729 | 0 | 0 | 0 | 0 | 0 | 0 | 0 | 0 | 0 | 0 |
| Quinsigamond Community College | 9,897 | 0 | 0 | 0 | 0 | 0 | 1 | 0 | 1 | 0 | 0 |
| Salem State University | 9,343 | 3 | 0 | 3 | 0 | 0 | 4 | 0 | 4 | 0 | 0 |
| Simmons College | 7,562 | 0 | 0 | 0 | 0 | 0 | 12 | 0 | 12 | 0 | 0 |
| Springfield College | 3,288 | 1 | 0 | 1 | 0 | 0 | 8 | 3 | 5 | 0 | 0 |
| Springfield Technical Community College | 6,833 | 0 | 0 | 0 | 0 | 0 | 1 | 1 | 0 | 0 | 0 |
| Stonehill College | 2,618 | 2 | 0 | 2 | 0 | 0 | 9 | 0 | 8 | 1 | 1 |
| Tufts University | | | | | | | | | | | |
| Medford | 13,458 | 2 | 0 | 1 | 0 | 1 | 32 | 2 | 28 | 2 | 0 |
| Suffolk[2] | | 0 | 0 | 0 | 0 | 0 | 13 | 1 | 11 | 1 | 0 |
| Worcester[2] | | 0 | 0 | 0 | 0 | 0 | 1 | 0 | 1 | 0 | 0 |
| University of Massachusetts | | | | | | | | | | | |
| Amherst | 35,781 | 13 | 0 | 8 | 2 | 3 | 84 | 7 | 75 | 2 | 2 |
| Dartmouth | 9,491 | 8 | 0 | 6 | 0 | 2 | 30 | 2 | 28 | 0 | 0 |
| Harbor Campus, Boston | 19,107 | 0 | 0 | 0 | 0 | 0 | 23 | 1 | 21 | 1 | 0 |
| Lowell | 22,192 | 8 | 0 | 6 | 0 | 2 | 44 | 10 | 34 | 0 | 0 |
| Medical Center, Worcester | 1,278 | 8 | 0 | 0 | 0 | 8 | 16 | 0 | 15 | 1 | 0 |
| Wentworth Institute of Technology | 5,456 | 4 | 0 | 1 | 0 | 3 | 23 | 3 | 20 | 0 | 0 |
| Western New England University | 4,005 | 2 | 0 | 1 | 0 | 1 | 12 | 3 | 9 | 0 | 0 |
| Westfield State University | 7,104 | 2 | 0 | 2 | 0 | 0 | 6 | 1 | 5 | 0 | 0 |
| Wheaton College | 1,807 | 0 | 0 | 0 | 0 | 0 | 9 | 2 | 7 | 0 | 0 |
| Worcester Polytechnic Institute | 7,654 | 3 | 0 | 1 | 0 | 2 | 22 | 1 | 21 | 0 | 0 |
| Worcester State University | 8,694 | 0 | 0 | 0 | 0 | 0 | 5 | 0 | 5 | 0 | 0 |
| | | | | | | | | | | | |
| **MICHIGAN** | | | | | | | | | | | |
| Central Michigan University | 22,512 | 1 | 0 | 1 | 0 | 0 | 31 | 2 | 28 | 1 | 0 |
| Delta College | 10,408 | 0 | 0 | 0 | 0 | 0 | 0 | 0 | 0 | 0 | 0 |
| Eastern Michigan University | 20,982 | 9 | 0 | 8 | 0 | 1 | 52 | 8 | 41 | 3 | 2 |
| Ferris State University | 14,874 | 0 | 0 | 0 | 0 | 0 | 0 | 0 | 0 | 0 | 0 |
| Grand Rapids Community College | 18,960 | 0 | 0 | 0 | 0 | 0 | 12 | 0 | 12 | 0 | 0 |
| Grand Valley State University | 26,993 | 8 | 0 | 6 | 0 | 2 | 56 | 1 | 53 | 2 | 0 |
| Kalamazoo Valley Community College | 11,012 | 0 | 0 | 0 | 0 | 0 | 5 | 0 | 5 | 0 | 0 |
| Kellogg Community College | 6,853 | 0 | 0 | 0 | 0 | 0 | 5 | 1 | 4 | 0 | 0 |
| Kirtland Community College | 2,311 | 0 | 0 | 0 | 0 | 0 | 0 | 0 | 0 | 0 | 0 |
| Lansing Community College | 16,021 | 0 | 0 | 0 | 0 | 0 | 10 | 0 | 10 | 0 | 0 |
| Macomb Community College | 27,402 | 0 | 0 | 0 | 0 | 0 | 11 | 0 | 10 | 1 | 0 |
| Michigan State University | 55,406 | 28 | 0 | 19 | 3 | 6 | 282 | 16 | 234 | 32 | 1 |
| Michigan Technological University | 7,786 | 0 | 0 | 0 | 0 | 0 | 52 | 0 | 52 | 0 | 0 |
| Mott Community College | 9,668 | 0 | 0 | 0 | 0 | 0 | 2 | 0 | 2 | 0 | 0 |
| Northern Michigan University | 10,080 | 2 | 0 | 2 | 0 | 0 | 15 | 1 | 14 | 0 | 0 |
| Oakland Community College | 23,813 | 0 | 0 | 0 | 0 | 0 | 1 | 0 | 1 | 0 | 0 |
| Oakland University | 22,230 | 1 | 0 | 1 | 0 | 0 | 16 | 0 | 15 | 1 | 0 |
| Saginaw Valley State University | 9,205 | 3 | 0 | 2 | 0 | 1 | 20 | 0 | 20 | 0 | 0 |
| Schoolcraft College | 15,561 | 0 | 0 | 0 | 0 | 0 | 12 | 0 | 11 | 1 | 0 |
| University of Michigan | | | | | | | | | | | |
| Ann Arbor | 49,530 | 37 | 0 | 7 | 1 | 29 | 309 | 5 | 301 | 3 | 2 |
| Dearborn | 10,611 | 0 | 0 | 0 | 0 | 0 | 0 | 0 | 0 | 0 | 0 |
| Flint | 8,398 | 1 | 0 | 0 | 0 | 1 | 10 | 2 | 7 | 1 | 0 |
| Washtenaw Community College | 20,899 | 1 | 0 | 0 | 0 | 1 | 3 | 0 | 2 | 1 | 0 |
| Western Michigan University | 22,996 | 3 | 0 | 2 | 0 | 1 | 91 | 5 | 80 | 6 | 0 |
| | | | | | | | | | | | |
| **MINNESOTA** | | | | | | | | | | | |
| University of Minnesota | | | | | | | | | | | |
| Duluth | 11,557 | 0 | 0 | 0 | 0 | 0 | 20 | 0 | 19 | 1 | 0 |
| Morris | 1,637 | 1 | 0 | 1 | 0 | 0 | 7 | 0 | 7 | 0 | 0 |
| Twin Cities | 63,760 | 21 | 0 | 4 | 11 | 6 | 457 | 35 | 383 | 39 | 3 |
| | | | | | | | | | | | |
| **MISSISSIPPI** | | | | | | | | | | | |
| Holmes Community College | | | | | | | | | | | |
| Goodman | 8,142 | 0 | 0 | 0 | 0 | 0 | 2 | 1 | 1 | 0 | 0 |
| Grenada[2] | | 0 | 0 | 0 | 0 | 0 | 0 | 0 | 0 | 0 | 0 |
| Ridgeland[2] | | 0 | 0 | 0 | 0 | 0 | 0 | 0 | 0 | 0 | 0 |

## Table 9. Offenses Known to Law Enforcement, by Selected State and University and College, 2021—Continued

(Number.)

| State and university/college | Student enrollment[1] | Violent crime | Murder and nonnegligent manslaughter | Rape | Robbery | Aggravated assault | Property crime | Burglary | Larceny-theft | Motor vehicle theft | Arson |
|---|---|---|---|---|---|---|---|---|---|---|---|
| Jones County Junior College | 6,009 | 1 | 0 | 1 | 0 | 0 | 3 | 1 | 1 | 1 | 0 |
| Mississippi Delta Community College | 4,340 | 0 | 0 | 0 | 0 | 0 | 2 | 1 | 1 | 0 | 0 |
| Mississippi State University | 24,449 | 4 | 0 | 1 | 2 | 1 | 17 | 2 | 14 | 1 | 0 |
| Northeast Mississippi Community College | 4,303 | 2 | 0 | 1 | 1 | 0 | 6 | 0 | 6 | 0 | 0 |
| Northwest Mississippi Community College, Desoto | 10,336 | 0 | 0 | 0 | 0 | 0 | 0 | 0 | 0 | 0 | 0 |
| Pearl River Community College, Forrest | 6,657 | 1 | 0 | 0 | 0 | 1 | 1 | 1 | 0 | 0 | 0 |
| University of Mississippi, Oxford | 24,309 | 5 | 0 | 4 | 0 | 1 | 29 | 1 | 28 | 0 | 0 |
| **MISSOURI** | | | | | | | | | | | |
| Lincoln University | 2,947 | 4 | 0 | 3 | 0 | 1 | 24 | 3 | 20 | 1 | 0 |
| Metropolitan Community College | 21,040 | 0 | 0 | 0 | 0 | 0 | 29 | 0 | 26 | 3 | 1 |
| Missouri Southern State University | 6,617 | 1 | 0 | 1 | 0 | 0 | 21 | 3 | 16 | 2 | 0 |
| Missouri University of Science and Technology | 8,618 | 3 | 0 | 0 | 0 | 3 | 75 | 2 | 70 | 3 | 0 |
| Northwest Missouri State University | 8,383 | 2 | 0 | 2 | 0 | 0 | 22 | 1 | 20 | 1 | 0 |
| Southeast Missouri State University | 11,812 | 2 | 0 | 0 | 2 | 0 | 33 | 3 | 30 | 0 | 0 |
| St. Louis Community College, Meramec | 26,166 | 0 | 0 | 0 | 0 | 0 | 21 | 0 | 19 | 2 | 0 |
| Truman State University | 5,637 | 4 | 0 | 1 | 0 | 3 | 52 | 1 | 49 | 2 | 0 |
| University of Central Missouri | 15,315 | 5 | 0 | 5 | 0 | 0 | 63 | 8 | 51 | 4 | 2 |
| University of Missouri | | | | | | | | | | | |
| Columbia | 32,916 | 25 | 0 | 8 | 1 | 16 | 230 | 10 | 204 | 16 | 1 |
| Kansas City | 18,894 | 7 | 0 | 1 | 1 | 5 | 58 | 7 | 47 | 4 | 1 |
| Washington University | 17,893 | 0 | 0 | 0 | 0 | 0 | 38 | 1 | 36 | 1 | 0 |
| **MONTANA** | | | | | | | | | | | |
| Montana State University | 18,756 | 7 | 0 | 2 | 0 | 5 | 53 | 5 | 48 | 0 | 2 |
| Montana State University, Billings | 5,824 | 1 | 0 | 0 | 0 | 1 | 26 | 3 | 23 | 0 | 0 |
| University of Montana | 12,694 | 12 | 0 | 3 | 0 | 9 | 97 | 8 | 88 | 1 | 0 |
| **NEBRASKA** | | | | | | | | | | | |
| University of Nebraska | | | | | | | | | | | |
| Kearney | 7,564 | 3 | 0 | 3 | 0 | 0 | 20 | 5 | 15 | 0 | 0 |
| Lincoln | 32,498 | 12 | 0 | 9 | 0 | 3 | 202 | 4 | 192 | 6 | 2 |
| Omaha | 17,913 | 8 | 0 | 0 | 0 | 8 | 106 | 0 | 94 | 12 | 0 |
| **NEVADA** | | | | | | | | | | | |
| University of Nevada, Reno | 23,692 | 9 | 0 | 3 | 2 | 4 | 126 | 24 | 98 | 4 | 1 |
| **NEW HAMPSHIRE** | | | | | | | | | | | |
| Plymouth State University | 5,475 | 4 | 0 | 4 | 0 | 0 | 29 | 0 | 29 | 0 | 0 |
| University of New Hampshire | 16,001 | 8 | 0 | 7 | 0 | 1 | 68 | 6 | 62 | 0 | 0 |
| **NEW JERSEY[3]** | | | | | | | | | | | |
| Rutgers University | | | | | | | | | | | |
| Newark | 15,633 | 10 | 0 | 0 | 5 | 5 | 98 | 0 | 94 | 4 | 0 |
| New Brunswick | 56,178 | 16 | 0 | 6 | 3 | 7 | 142 | 36 | 101 | 5 | 0 |
| **NEW MEXICO[3]** | | | | | | | | | | | |
| Eastern New Mexico University | 7,246 | 5 | 0 | 0 | 0 | 5 | 19 | 1 | 18 | 0 | 0 |
| **NEW YORK[3]** | | | | | | | | | | | |
| Cornell University | 24,594 | 4 | 0 | 3 | 1 | 0 | 162 | 10 | 149 | 3 | 3 |
| State University of New York Police | | | | | | | | | | | |
| New Paltz | 8,902 | 1 | 0 | 0 | 1 | 0 | 20 | 0 | 20 | 0 | 0 |
| Oswego | 9,190 | 0 | 0 | 0 | 0 | 0 | 38 | 4 | 33 | 1 | 1 |
| Stony Brook | 34,115 | 1 | 0 | 0 | 0 | 1 | 61 | 3 | 57 | 1 | 3 |
| **NORTH CAROLINA** | | | | | | | | | | | |
| Duke University | 17,855 | 4 | 0 | 2 | 0 | 2 | 272 | 13 | 250 | 9 | 1 |
| East Carolina University | 31,962 | 8 | 0 | 5 | 1 | 2 | 71 | 7 | 64 | 0 | 1 |
| Elon University | 7,424 | 1 | 0 | 1 | 0 | 0 | 46 | 10 | 33 | 3 | 0 |
| Fayetteville State University | 8,376 | 1 | 0 | 0 | 0 | 1 | 36 | 9 | 27 | 0 | 0 |
| North Carolina Agricultural and Technical State University | 13,854 | 6 | 0 | 3 | 2 | 1 | 77 | 19 | 54 | 4 | 0 |
| North Carolina State University, Raleigh | 40,537 | 9 | 0 | 3 | 2 | 4 | 124 | 29 | 89 | 6 | 1 |
| University of North Carolina | | | | | | | | | | | |
| Asheville | 4,153 | 0 | 0 | 0 | 0 | 0 | 21 | 2 | 19 | 0 | 0 |
| Chapel Hill | 32,160 | 14 | 0 | 6 | 0 | 8 | 143 | 12 | 123 | 8 | 1 |
| Charlotte | 34,715 | 2 | 0 | 0 | 0 | 2 | 117 | 5 | 110 | 2 | 0 |
| Greensboro | 22,487 | 7 | 0 | 3 | 0 | 4 | 70 | 7 | 57 | 6 | 0 |
| Wilmington | 20,367 | 10 | 0 | 9 | 0 | 1 | 128 | 0 | 127 | 1 | 0 |
| Western Carolina University | 13,783 | 13 | 0 | 12 | 0 | 1 | 49 | 5 | 44 | 0 | 0 |
| **NORTH DAKOTA** | | | | | | | | | | | |
| Bismarck State College | 4,855 | 0 | 0 | 0 | 0 | 0 | 0 | 0 | 0 | 0 | 0 |
| North Dakota State College of Science | 3,669 | 0 | 0 | 0 | 0 | 0 | 16 | 1 | 15 | 0 | 0 |
| North Dakota State University | 14,384 | 1 | 0 | 1 | 0 | 0 | 109 | 6 | 100 | 3 | 0 |
| University of North Dakota | 17,182 | 2 | 0 | 1 | 1 | 0 | 97 | 7 | 89 | 1 | 0 |
| **OHIO** | | | | | | | | | | | |
| Bowling Green State University | 20,945 | 3 | 0 | 3 | 0 | 0 | 57 | 1 | 56 | 0 | 0 |
| Hocking College | 4,323 | 1 | 0 | 0 | 0 | 1 | 42 | 7 | 34 | 1 | 0 |
| Kent State University | 32,341 | 10 | 0 | 10 | 0 | 0 | 75 | 4 | 69 | 2 | 0 |

## Table 9. Offenses Known to Law Enforcement, by Selected State and University and College, 2021—Continued

(Number.)

| State and university/college | Student enrollment[1] | Violent crime | Murder and nonnegligent manslaughter | Rape | Robbery | Aggravated assault | Property crime | Burglary | Larceny-theft | Motor vehicle theft | Arson |
|---|---|---|---|---|---|---|---|---|---|---|---|
| Ohio State University, Columbus | 66,017 | 26 | 0 | 12 | 7 | 7 | 472 | 18 | 425 | 29 | 3 |
| Ohio University | 31,679 | 6 | 0 | 5 | 0 | 1 | 54 | 5 | 49 | 0 | 0 |
| University of Cincinnati | 46,140 | 7 | 0 | 4 | 1 | 2 | 97 | 3 | 86 | 8 | 1 |
| University of Toledo | 22,028 | 3 | 1 | 1 | 0 | 1 | 64 | 5 | 58 | 1 | 0 |
| **OKLAHOMA** | | | | | | | | | | | |
| Bacone College | 314 | 0 | 0 | 0 | 0 | 0 | 1 | 1 | 0 | 0 | 0 |
| Cameron University | 4,767 | 1 | 0 | 1 | 0 | 0 | 6 | 1 | 4 | 1 | 0 |
| East Central University | 4,413 | 1 | 0 | 1 | 0 | 0 | 10 | 1 | 7 | 2 | 1 |
| Eastern Oklahoma State College | 1,829 | 0 | 0 | 0 | 0 | 0 | 2 | 2 | 0 | 0 | 0 |
| Langston University | 2,614 | 7 | 0 | 5 | 0 | 2 | 30 | 6 | 22 | 2 | 2 |
| Mid-America Christian University | 2,382 | 0 | 0 | 0 | 0 | 0 | 3 | 0 | 3 | 0 | 0 |
| Northeastern Oklahoma A&M College | 2,285 | 1 | 0 | 0 | 0 | 1 | 6 | 0 | 5 | 1 | 0 |
| Northeastern State University, Tahlequah | 9,075 | 0 | 0 | 0 | 0 | 0 | 13 | 4 | 9 | 0 | 0 |
| Northwestern Oklahoma State University | 2,295 | 1 | 0 | 1 | 0 | 0 | 3 | 0 | 3 | 0 | 0 |
| Oklahoma City Community College | 17,240 | 1 | 0 | 0 | 0 | 1 | 0 | 0 | 0 | 0 | 0 |
| Oklahoma City University | 3,071 | 0 | 0 | 0 | 0 | 0 | 22 | 5 | 16 | 1 | 0 |
| Oklahoma State University | | | | | | | | | | | |
| Main Campus | 26,463 | 9 | 0 | 8 | 0 | 1 | 130 | 11 | 114 | 5 | 0 |
| Okmulgee | 3,024 | 2 | 0 | 2 | 0 | 0 | 6 | 0 | 6 | 0 | 0 |
| Tulsa | 1,265 | 0 | 0 | 0 | 0 | 0 | 5 | 1 | 2 | 2 | 0 |
| Rogers State University | 4,290 | 1 | 0 | 1 | 0 | 0 | 2 | 1 | 1 | 0 | 0 |
| Seminole State College | 1,925 | 1 | 0 | 0 | 0 | 1 | 5 | 1 | 4 | 0 | 0 |
| Southeastern Oklahoma State University | 6,534 | 0 | 0 | 0 | 0 | 0 | 8 | 2 | 5 | 1 | 0 |
| Southwestern Oklahoma State University | 5,768 | 0 | 0 | 0 | 0 | 0 | 12 | 2 | 10 | 0 | 0 |
| Tulsa Community College | 22,569 | 0 | 0 | 0 | 0 | 0 | 24 | 0 | 22 | 2 | 0 |
| University of Oklahoma | | | | | | | | | | | |
| Health Sciences Center | 3,722 | 4 | 0 | 0 | 1 | 3 | 91 | 4 | 80 | 7 | 0 |
| Norman | 31,445 | 8 | 0 | 4 | 0 | 4 | 272 | 5 | 256 | 11 | 0 |
| **OREGON** | | | | | | | | | | | |
| Oregon State University | 37,586 | 3 | 0 | 2 | 0 | 1 | 223 | 13 | 204 | 6 | 0 |
| Portland State University | 30,571 | 3 | 0 | 0 | 3 | 0 | 210 | 35 | 161 | 14 | 10 |
| **PENNSYLVANIA[3]** | | | | | | | | | | | |
| RHODE ISLAND | | | | | | | | | | | |
| Brown University | 10,807 | 1 | 0 | 1 | 0 | 0 | 75 | 6 | 60 | 9 | 0 |
| University of Rhode Island | 21,108 | 4 | 0 | 4 | 0 | 0 | 26 | 2 | 24 | 0 | 0 |
| **SOUTH CAROLINA** | | | | | | | | | | | |
| Bob Jones University | 3,750 | 0 | 0 | 0 | 0 | 0 | 0 | 0 | 0 | 0 | 0 |
| Clemson University | 28,933 | 7 | 0 | 4 | 0 | 3 | 110 | 4 | 94 | 12 | 0 |
| Coastal Carolina University | 11,870 | 5 | 0 | 1 | 0 | 4 | 63 | 3 | 58 | 2 | 0 |
| Medical University of South Carolina | 3,458 | 10 | 0 | 1 | 1 | 8 | 116 | 5 | 98 | 13 | 0 |
| The Citadel | 4,409 | 3 | 0 | 1 | 0 | 2 | 27 | 1 | 25 | 1 | 0 |
| University of South Carolina | | | | | | | | | | | |
| Beaufort | 2,480 | 1 | 0 | 1 | 0 | 0 | 12 | 1 | 11 | 0 | 0 |
| Columbia | 38,526 | 4 | 0 | 2 | 1 | 1 | 172 | 7 | 139 | 26 | 1 |
| Upstate | 7,421 | 1 | 0 | 1 | 0 | 0 | 5 | 0 | 4 | 1 | 0 |
| **SOUTH DAKOTA** | | | | | | | | | | | |
| South Dakota State University | 13,937 | 1 | 0 | 1 | 0 | 0 | 12 | 1 | 10 | 1 | 0 |
| **TENNESSEE** | | | | | | | | | | | |
| Austin Peay State University | 12,796 | 2 | 1 | 0 | 0 | 1 | 29 | 3 | 17 | 9 | 0 |
| East Tennessee State University | 15,939 | 6 | 0 | 4 | 1 | 1 | 45 | 6 | 39 | 0 | 0 |
| Middle Tennessee State University | 25,346 | 4 | 0 | 1 | 0 | 3 | 46 | 0 | 42 | 4 | 0 |
| Tennessee State University | 8,997 | 3 | 0 | 2 | 0 | 1 | 22 | 0 | 22 | 0 | 0 |
| Tennessee Technological University | 11,103 | 1 | 0 | 0 | 0 | 1 | 37 | 0 | 36 | 1 | 0 |
| University of Memphis | 25,128 | 9 | 0 | 1 | 0 | 8 | 60 | 9 | 44 | 7 | 0 |
| University of Tennessee | | | | | | | | | | | |
| Knoxville | 32,056 | 8 | 0 | 5 | 1 | 2 | 113 | 7 | 95 | 11 | 0 |
| Martin | 8,379 | 2 | 0 | 2 | 0 | 0 | 11 | 1 | 10 | 0 | 0 |
| University of the South | 1,957 | 4 | 0 | 4 | 0 | 0 | 41 | 4 | 36 | 1 | 0 |
| Vanderbilt University | 13,918 | 30 | 0 | 5 | 0 | 25 | 336 | 7 | 314 | 15 | 2 |
| **TEXAS** | | | | | | | | | | | |
| Alvin Community College | 8,414 | 0 | 0 | 0 | 0 | 0 | 0 | 0 | 0 | 0 | 0 |
| Amarillo College | 12,389 | 0 | 0 | 0 | 0 | 0 | 8 | 1 | 6 | 1 | 0 |
| Angelo State University | 12,030 | 0 | 0 | 0 | 0 | 0 | 18 | 0 | 18 | 0 | 0 |
| Austin College | 1,326 | 0 | 0 | 0 | 0 | 0 | 0 | 0 | 0 | 0 | 0 |
| Austin Community College District | 63,569 | 0 | 0 | 0 | 0 | 0 | 36 | 4 | 28 | 4 | 0 |
| Baylor Health Care System[2] | | 2 | 0 | 2 | 0 | 0 | 317 | 5 | 273 | 39 | 0 |
| Brazosport College | 5,805 | 0 | 0 | 0 | 0 | 0 | 1 | 0 | 1 | 0 | 0 |
| Cisco College | 4,876 | 0 | 0 | 0 | 0 | 0 | 3 | 0 | 3 | 0 | 0 |
| Concordia University | 3,338 | 0 | 0 | 0 | 0 | 0 | 0 | 0 | 0 | 0 | 0 |
| Dallas County Community College District | 125,613 | 2 | 0 | 1 | 1 | 0 | 26 | 3 | 21 | 2 | 1 |
| El Paso Community College | 37,636 | 0 | 0 | 0 | 0 | 0 | 2 | 1 | 1 | 0 | 0 |
| Hardin-Simmons University | 2,487 | 0 | 0 | 0 | 0 | 0 | 4 | 0 | 4 | 0 | 0 |
| Houston Community College | 81,256 | 1 | 0 | 0 | 0 | 1 | 59 | 4 | 51 | 4 | 0 |
| Lamar University, Beaumont | 21,621 | 5 | 0 | 4 | 0 | 1 | 25 | 1 | 20 | 4 | 0 |
| Lone Star College System District | 102,989 | 0 | 0 | 0 | 0 | 0 | 24 | 3 | 19 | 2 | 0 |

## Table 9. Offenses Known to Law Enforcement, by Selected State and University and College, 2021—Continued

(Number.)

| State and university/college | Student enrollment[1] | Violent crime | Murder and nonnegligent manslaughter | Rape | Robbery | Aggravated assault | Property crime | Burglary | Larceny-theft | Motor vehicle theft | Arson |
|---|---|---|---|---|---|---|---|---|---|---|---|
| Lubbock Christian University | 2,040 | 0 | 0 | 0 | 0 | 0 | 6 | 0 | 5 | 1 | 0 |
| Midwestern State University | 6,947 | 0 | 0 | 0 | 0 | 0 | 21 | 2 | 19 | 0 | 1 |
| Odessa College | 10,162 | 0 | 0 | 0 | 0 | 0 | 9 | 2 | 6 | 1 | 0 |
| Paris Junior College | 6,822 | 0 | 0 | 0 | 0 | 0 | 0 | 0 | 0 | 0 | 0 |
| Prairie View A&M University | 10,184 | 4 | 0 | 1 | 2 | 1 | 67 | 12 | 53 | 2 | 0 |
| Rice University | 8,005 | 3 | 0 | 2 | 0 | 1 | 130 | 8 | 109 | 13 | 0 |
| Sam Houston State University | 24,116 | 7 | 0 | 4 | 1 | 2 | 71 | 15 | 52 | 4 | 0 |
| San Jacinto College, Central Campus | 42,923 | 0 | 0 | 0 | 0 | 0 | 24 | 0 | 21 | 3 | 0 |
| Southern Methodist University | 12,963 | 1 | 0 | 0 | 0 | 1 | 125 | 17 | 93 | 15 | 1 |
| South Plains College | 12,258 | 0 | 0 | 0 | 0 | 0 | 3 | 0 | 3 | 0 | 0 |
| Southwestern Christian College | 117 | 0 | 0 | 0 | 0 | 0 | 0 | 0 | 0 | 0 | 0 |
| Southwestern University | 1,562 | 0 | 0 | 0 | 0 | 0 | 15 | 0 | 15 | 0 | 0 |
| St. Edwards University | 4,324 | 2 | 0 | 1 | 0 | 1 | 40 | 4 | 36 | 0 | 0 |
| Stephen F. Austin State University | 14,759 | 4 | 0 | 3 | 0 | 1 | 29 | 3 | 26 | 0 | 0 |
| St. Mary's University | 3,757 | 2 | 0 | 1 | 0 | 1 | 18 | 1 | 15 | 2 | 0 |
| St. Thomas University | 3,938 | 1 | 0 | 0 | 1 | 0 | 10 | 0 | 10 | 0 | 0 |
| Sul Ross State University | 2,949 | 0 | 0 | 0 | 0 | 0 | 2 | 0 | 2 | 0 | 0 |
| Tarleton State University | 15,196 | 6 | 0 | 5 | 1 | 0 | 53 | 5 | 46 | 2 | 0 |
| Texas A&M University | | | | | | | | | | | |
|   College Station | 73,308 | 9 | 0 | 7 | 1 | 1 | 335 | 25 | 294 | 16 | 0 |
|   Commerce | 15,517 | 5 | 0 | 5 | 0 | 0 | 28 | 3 | 24 | 1 | 0 |
|   San Antonio | 7,724 | 0 | 0 | 0 | 0 | 0 | 6 | 0 | 6 | 0 | 0 |
| Texas Christian University | 11,506 | 2 | 0 | 2 | 0 | 0 | 53 | 6 | 43 | 4 | 0 |
| Texas State Technical College | | | | | | | | | | | |
|   Harlingen[2] | | 1 | 0 | 1 | 0 | 0 | 3 | 0 | 3 | 0 | 0 |
|   Waco | 13,892 | 3 | 0 | 2 | 0 | 1 | 41 | 3 | 36 | 2 | 0 |
|   West Texas[2] | | 0 | 0 | 0 | 0 | 0 | 0 | 0 | 0 | 0 | 0 |
| Texas State University, San Marcos | 42,292 | 8 | 0 | 4 | 2 | 2 | 28 | 6 | 21 | 1 | 0 |
| Texas Tech University, Lubbock | 41,909 | 5 | 0 | 1 | 1 | 3 | 290 | 9 | 279 | 2 | 1 |
| Texas Woman's University | 19,733 | 2 | 0 | 1 | 0 | 1 | 26 | 2 | 23 | 1 | 0 |
| Trinity Valley Community College | 8,188 | 1 | 0 | 1 | 0 | 0 | 6 | 1 | 4 | 1 | 0 |
| Tyler Junior College | 16,990 | 4 | 0 | 3 | 0 | 1 | 21 | 3 | 17 | 1 | 0 |
| University of Houston | | | | | | | | | | | |
|   Central Campus | 51,217 | 16 | 0 | 8 | 2 | 6 | 301 | 34 | 256 | 11 | 1 |
|   Clearlake | 11,134 | 0 | 0 | 0 | 0 | 0 | 15 | 0 | 14 | 1 | 0 |
|   Downtown Campus | 18,096 | 0 | 0 | 0 | 0 | 0 | 0 | 0 | 0 | 0 | 0 |
| University of North Texas, Denton | 45,298 | 10 | 0 | 5 | 1 | 4 | 101 | 5 | 92 | 4 | 0 |
| University of Texas | | | | | | | | | | | |
|   Arlington | 61,457 | 15 | 0 | 8 | 1 | 6 | 105 | 5 | 94 | 6 | 0 |
|   Austin | 54,243 | 9 | 0 | 3 | 2 | 4 | 353 | 24 | 316 | 13 | 0 |
|   Dallas | 32,043 | 3 | 0 | 3 | 0 | 0 | 79 | 1 | 74 | 4 | 0 |
|   El Paso | 29,556 | 2 | 0 | 0 | 0 | 2 | 26 | 5 | 20 | 1 | 0 |
|   Health Science Center, San Antonio | 4,043 | 1 | 0 | 0 | 0 | 1 | 33 | 1 | 31 | 1 | 0 |
|   Health Science Center, Tyler | 136 | 1 | 0 | 0 | 0 | 1 | 12 | 1 | 9 | 2 | 0 |
|   Houston | 7,329 | 9 | 0 | 1 | 6 | 2 | 203 | 13 | 175 | 15 | 1 |
|   Medical Branch | 3,889 | 1 | 0 | 1 | 0 | 0 | 69 | 6 | 60 | 3 | 0 |
|   Permian Basin | 8,667 | 0 | 0 | 0 | 0 | 0 | 10 | 1 | 9 | 0 | 0 |
|   Rio Grande Valley | 41,681 | 3 | 0 | 2 | 0 | 1 | 33 | 2 | 31 | 0 | 0 |
|   San Antonio | 36,089 | 8 | 0 | 7 | 0 | 1 | 85 | 4 | 76 | 5 | 0 |
|   Southwestern Medical School | 2,535 | 3 | 0 | 0 | 1 | 2 | 151 | 8 | 116 | 27 | 0 |
|   Tyler | 11,525 | 1 | 0 | 0 | 0 | 1 | 12 | 0 | 12 | 0 | 0 |
| West Texas A&M University | 11,678 | 2 | 0 | 2 | 0 | 0 | 23 | 0 | 23 | 0 | 0 |
| **UTAH** | | | | | | | | | | | |
| Dixie State University | 13,446 | 1 | 0 | 1 | 0 | 0 | 19 | 2 | 17 | 0 | 0 |
| Snow College | 5,909 | 1 | 0 | 1 | 0 | 0 | 11 | 1 | 10 | 0 | 0 |
| Southern Utah University | 15,872 | 4 | 0 | 0 | 0 | 4 | 29 | 1 | 27 | 1 | 0 |
| Utah State University, Logan | 33,055 | 4 | 0 | 4 | 0 | 0 | 36 | 3 | 32 | 1 | 0 |
| Utah Valley University | 45,299 | 0 | 0 | 0 | 0 | 0 | 28 | 8 | 20 | 0 | 0 |
| Weber State University | 36,761 | 1 | 0 | 1 | 0 | 0 | 22 | 1 | 21 | 0 | 0 |
| **VERMONT** | | | | | | | | | | | |
| University of Vermont | 15,903 | 1 | 0 | 1 | 0 | 0 | 113 | 8 | 105 | 0 | 1 |
| **VIRGINIA** | | | | | | | | | | | |
| Christopher Newport University | 5,058 | 3 | 0 | 3 | 0 | 0 | 55 | 0 | 55 | 0 | 0 |
| College of William and Mary | 9,785 | 0 | 0 | 0 | 0 | 0 | 52 | 2 | 48 | 2 | 0 |
| Eastern Virginia Medical School | 1,436 | 1 | 0 | 0 | 0 | 1 | 26 | 0 | 25 | 1 | 0 |
| George Mason University | 49,755 | 1 | 0 | 0 | 0 | 1 | 54 | 1 | 53 | 0 | 0 |
| James Madison University | 24,039 | 2 | 0 | 2 | 0 | 0 | 70 | 4 | 65 | 1 | 0 |
| Longwood University | 5,852 | 3 | 0 | 3 | 0 | 0 | 20 | 1 | 18 | 1 | 0 |
| Norfolk State University | 6,075 | 1 | 0 | 1 | 0 | 0 | 42 | 0 | 40 | 2 | 0 |
| Old Dominion University | 28,042 | 13 | 0 | 3 | 4 | 6 | 141 | 4 | 129 | 8 | 0 |
| Radford University | 14,711 | 5 | 0 | 1 | 0 | 4 | 38 | 0 | 37 | 1 | 1 |
| Southwest Virginia Community College | 3,026 | 0 | 0 | 0 | 0 | 0 | 0 | 0 | 0 | 0 | 0 |
| University of Richmond | 4,534 | 2 | 0 | 2 | 0 | 0 | 35 | 3 | 32 | 0 | 0 |
| University of Virginia | 29,237 | 15 | 0 | 9 | 3 | 3 | 164 | 3 | 149 | 12 | 0 |
| Virginia Commonwealth University | 32,628 | 24 | 0 | 7 | 3 | 14 | 262 | 12 | 244 | 6 | 1 |
| Virginia Military Institute | 1,740 | 1 | 0 | 0 | 0 | 1 | 10 | 4 | 6 | 0 | 0 |
| Virginia Polytechnic Institute and State University | 38,350 | 16 | 0 | 10 | 0 | 6 | 287 | 9 | 276 | 2 | 1 |
| Virginia State University | 4,708 | 4 | 0 | 2 | 0 | 2 | 12 | 2 | 10 | 0 | 0 |
| Virginia Western Community College | 8,535 | 0 | 0 | 0 | 0 | 0 | 0 | 0 | 0 | 0 | 0 |

## Table 9. Offenses Known to Law Enforcement, by Selected State and University and College, 2021—Continued

(Number.)

| State and university/college | Student enrollment[1] | Violent crime | Murder and nonnegligent manslaughter | Rape | Robbery | Aggravated assault | Property crime | Burglary | Larceny-theft | Motor vehicle theft | Arson |
|---|---|---|---|---|---|---|---|---|---|---|---|
| **WASHINGTON** | | | | | | | | | | | |
| Central Washington University | 14,090 | 2 | 0 | 1 | 0 | 1 | 90 | 2 | 85 | 3 | 0 |
| Eastern Washington University | 16,280 | 3 | 0 | 0 | 0 | 3 | 10 | 3 | 7 | 0 | 0 |
| Evergreen State College | 3,439 | 0 | 0 | 0 | 0 | 0 | 2 | 0 | 1 | 1 | 0 |
| University of Washington | 56,554 | 14 | 0 | 2 | 5 | 7 | 504 | 64 | 412 | 28 | 3 |
| Washington State University | | | | | | | | | | | |
| Pullman | 35,394 | 5 | 0 | 5 | 0 | 0 | 36 | 2 | 34 | 0 | 0 |
| Vancouver[2] | | 0 | 0 | 0 | 0 | 0 | 0 | 0 | 0 | 0 | 0 |
| Western Washington University | 17,883 | 3 | 0 | 2 | 1 | 0 | 89 | 3 | 80 | 6 | 1 |
| **WISCONSIN** | | | | | | | | | | | |
| University of Wisconsin | | | | | | | | | | | |
| Eau Claire | 12,230 | 0 | 0 | 0 | 0 | 0 | 31 | 1 | 30 | 0 | 0 |
| Madison | 47,831 | 10 | 0 | 4 | 1 | 5 | 191 | 15 | 171 | 5 | 1 |
| Platteville | 9,403 | 0 | 0 | 0 | 0 | 0 | 23 | 0 | 23 | 0 | 0 |
| River Falls | 6,561 | 0 | 0 | 0 | 0 | 0 | 43 | 0 | 43 | 0 | 0 |
| Stout | 9,702 | 0 | 0 | 0 | 0 | 0 | 76 | 0 | 76 | 0 | 0 |
| **WYOMING** | | | | | | | | | | | |
| University of Wyoming | 13,616 | 0 | 0 | 0 | 0 | 0 | 40 | 6 | 34 | 0 | 0 |

NOTE: Caution should be exercised in making any intercampus comparisons or ranking schools because university/college crime statistics are affected by a variety of factors. These include demographic characteristics of the surrounding community, ratio of male to female students, number of on-campus residents, accessibility of the campus to outside visitors, size of enrollment, etc.    1 The student enrollment figures provided by the United States Department of Education are for the 2020 school year, the most recent available. The enrollment figures include full-time and part-time students.    2 Student enrollment figures were not available.    3 Limited data for 2021 were available for California, Florida, Illinois, Maryland, New Jersey, New Mexico, New York, and Pennsylvania.

# Table 10. Offenses Known to Law Enforcement, by Selected State Metropolitan and Nonmetropolitan Counties, 2021

(Number.)

| State/county | Violent crime | Murder and nonnegligent manslaughter | Rape | Robbery | Aggravated assault | Property crime | Burglary | Larceny-theft | Motor vehicle theft | Arson |
|---|---|---|---|---|---|---|---|---|---|---|
| **ALABAMA** | | | | | | | | | | |
| **Metropolitan Counties** | | | | | | | | | | |
| Autauga | 62 | 2 | 12 | 3 | 45 | 265 | 43 | 177 | 45 | 4 |
| Bibb | 26 | 0 | 1 | 0 | 25 | 104 | 30 | 50 | 24 | 0 |
| Blount | 66 | 1 | 13 | 1 | 51 | 259 | 63 | 140 | 56 | 3 |
| Colbert | 61 | 3 | 3 | 8 | 47 | 241 | 78 | 133 | 30 | 3 |
| Etowah | 27 | 0 | 5 | 0 | 22 | 121 | 37 | 61 | 23 | 1 |
| Geneva | 23 | 1 | 4 | 0 | 18 | 151 | 30 | 89 | 32 | 1 |
| Henry | 21 | 5 | 3 | 0 | 13 | 51 | 10 | 34 | 7 | 0 |
| Houston | 11 | 1 | 0 | 0 | 10 | 113 | 51 | 47 | 15 | 0 |
| Lauderdale | 44 | 0 | 4 | 2 | 38 | 428 | 77 | 306 | 45 | 5 |
| Lawrence | 22 | 2 | 3 | 0 | 17 | 76 | 24 | 30 | 22 | 1 |
| Lowndes | 64 | 9 | 3 | 5 | 47 | 224 | 49 | 122 | 53 | 4 |
| Mobile | 265 | 10 | 16 | 8 | 231 | 1,288 | 337 | 704 | 247 | 13 |
| Shelby | 5 | 0 | 2 | 0 | 3 | 24 | 8 | 12 | 4 | 0 |
| St. Clair | 42 | 0 | 5 | 2 | 35 | 121 | 47 | 54 | 20 | 3 |
| Washington | 21 | 0 | 3 | 0 | 18 | 99 | 18 | 61 | 20 | 5 |
| **Nonmetropolitan Counties** | | | | | | | | | | |
| Barbour | 19 | 0 | 1 | 0 | 18 | 55 | 11 | 29 | 15 | 0 |
| Cherokee | 71 | 1 | 8 | 0 | 62 | 339 | 74 | 169 | 96 | 6 |
| Clarke | 63 | 1 | 3 | 2 | 57 | 99 | 34 | 53 | 12 | 3 |
| Clay | 25 | 0 | 1 | 0 | 24 | 65 | 25 | 37 | 3 | 0 |
| Cleburne | 18 | 1 | 2 | 0 | 15 | 188 | 40 | 133 | 15 | 0 |
| Covington | 8 | 0 | 0 | 0 | 8 | 101 | 18 | 65 | 18 | 0 |
| Crenshaw | 15 | 1 | 2 | 0 | 12 | 74 | 14 | 39 | 21 | 1 |
| Cullman | 109 | 1 | 17 | 6 | 85 | 918 | 228 | 537 | 153 | 2 |
| Dallas | 81 | 3 | 4 | 9 | 65 | 302 | 58 | 182 | 62 | 5 |
| DeKalb | 56 | 1 | 6 | 0 | 49 | 169 | 41 | 91 | 37 | 5 |
| Fayette | 3 | 0 | 0 | 0 | 3 | 27 | 4 | 9 | 14 | 0 |
| Macon | 5 | 0 | 1 | 0 | 4 | 16 | 1 | 9 | 6 | 1 |
| Marengo | 7 | 1 | 0 | 0 | 6 | 38 | 14 | 15 | 9 | 0 |
| Marion | 2 | 0 | 0 | 0 | 2 | 34 | 6 | 15 | 13 | 0 |
| Marshall | 37 | 1 | 7 | 1 | 28 | 295 | 144 | 109 | 42 | 3 |
| Monroe | 18 | 1 | 1 | 1 | 15 | 39 | 7 | 28 | 4 | 0 |
| Randolph | 34 | 0 | 0 | 0 | 34 | 210 | 54 | 142 | 14 | 0 |
| Talladega | 90 | 2 | 10 | 6 | 72 | 406 | 101 | 231 | 74 | 1 |
| Tallapoosa | 34 | 5 | 4 | 3 | 22 | 83 | 24 | 51 | 8 | 1 |
| Winston | 9 | 0 | 3 | 0 | 6 | 88 | 25 | 58 | 5 | 0 |
| **ARIZONA** | | | | | | | | | | |
| **Metropolitan Counties** | | | | | | | | | | |
| Cochise | 86 | 7 | 3 | 4 | 72 | 296 | 85 | 162 | 49 | 4 |
| Coconino | 94 | 2 | 12 | 5 | 75 | 213 | 69 | 130 | 14 | 5 |
| Mohave | 246 | 11 | 81 | 16 | 138 | 1,649 | 469 | 971 | 209 | 16 |
| Pima | 910 | 23 | 74 | 113 | 700 | 7,024 | 1,094 | 5,445 | 485 | 51 |
| Pinal | 311 | 6 | 9 | 11 | 285 | 1,531 | 299 | 1,015 | 217 | 7 |
| Yavapai | 260 | 1 | 14 | 2 | 243 | 602 | 123 | 394 | 85 | 11 |
| Yuma | 176 | 0 | 29 | 8 | 139 | 937 | 248 | 568 | 121 | 17 |
| **ARKANSAS** | | | | | | | | | | |
| **Metropolitan Counties** | | | | | | | | | | |
| Benton | 175 | 9 | 28 | 5 | 133 | 400 | 99 | 226 | 75 | 5 |
| Cleveland | 17 | 0 | 1 | 0 | 16 | 130 | 53 | 65 | 12 | 4 |
| Craighead | 52 | 4 | 14 | 0 | 34 | 314 | 105 | 167 | 42 | 8 |
| Crawford | 56 | 0 | 7 | 0 | 49 | 308 | 44 | 199 | 65 | 1 |
| Crittenden | 188 | 9 | 17 | 11 | 151 | 263 | 64 | 157 | 42 | 3 |
| Faulkner | 152 | 0 | 18 | 6 | 128 | 786 | 160 | 494 | 132 | 7 |
| Franklin | 59 | 0 | 7 | 0 | 52 | 131 | 39 | 79 | 13 | 0 |
| Garland | 360 | 2 | 33 | 7 | 318 | 1,260 | 536 | 583 | 141 | 0 |
| Grant | 34 | 0 | 1 | 0 | 33 | 179 | 49 | 107 | 23 | 0 |
| Jefferson | 82 | 7 | 9 | 5 | 61 | 440 | 107 | 254 | 79 | 9 |
| Lincoln | 4 | 0 | 0 | 0 | 4 | 36 | 10 | 19 | 7 | 0 |
| Little River | 20 | 0 | 6 | 0 | 14 | 82 | 21 | 54 | 7 | 2 |
| Lonoke | 122 | 5 | 15 | 6 | 96 | 366 | 41 | 228 | 97 | 2 |
| Madison | 56 | 5 | 13 | 0 | 38 | 128 | 39 | 61 | 28 | 4 |
| Miller | 63 | 2 | 12 | 0 | 49 | 147 | 40 | 87 | 20 | 1 |
| Perry | 24 | 0 | 1 | 0 | 23 | 121 | 33 | 88 | 0 | 0 |
| Poinsett | 31 | 0 | 5 | 0 | 26 | 100 | 30 | 40 | 30 | 4 |
| Pulaski | 722 | 4 | 31 | 13 | 674 | 1,593 | 276 | 1,058 | 259 | 27 |
| Saline | 165 | 3 | 41 | 8 | 113 | 712 | 361 | 267 | 84 | 1 |
| Sebastian | 37 | 0 | 4 | 1 | 32 | 112 | 31 | 70 | 11 | 2 |
| Washington | 125 | 1 | 18 | 1 | 105 | 552 | 109 | 367 | 76 | 9 |
| **Nonmetropolitan Counties** | | | | | | | | | | |
| Arkansas | 28 | 0 | 2 | 0 | 26 | 62 | 13 | 46 | 3 | 3 |
| Ashley | 24 | 1 | 5 | 1 | 17 | 105 | 15 | 83 | 7 | 0 |
| Baxter | 43 | 1 | 11 | 0 | 31 | 402 | 78 | 281 | 43 | 7 |
| Boone | 108 | 4 | 29 | 1 | 74 | 134 | 39 | 74 | 21 | 5 |
| Bradley | 7 | 0 | 4 | 0 | 3 | 26 | 11 | 13 | 2 | 1 |
| Calhoun | 9 | 0 | 1 | 0 | 8 | 57 | 12 | 35 | 10 | 0 |
| Carroll | 37 | 1 | 2 | 0 | 34 | 91 | 19 | 48 | 24 | 2 |

## Table 10. Offenses Known to Law Enforcement, by Selected State Metropolitan and Nonmetropolitan Counties, 2021—Continued

(Number.)

| State/county | Violent crime | Murder and nonnegligent manslaughter | Rape | Robbery | Aggravated assault | Property crime | Burglary | Larceny-theft | Motor vehicle theft | Arson |
|---|---|---|---|---|---|---|---|---|---|---|
| Chicot | 13 | 1 | 3 | 0 | 9 | 80 | 21 | 59 | 0 | 0 |
| Clark | 24 | 0 | 5 | 0 | 19 | 69 | 19 | 34 | 16 | 2 |
| Cleburne | 188 | 0 | 23 | 1 | 164 | 288 | 84 | 179 | 25 | 7 |
| Columbia | 37 | 1 | 2 | 1 | 33 | 130 | 26 | 93 | 11 | 2 |
| Conway | 72 | 0 | 10 | 1 | 61 | 260 | 46 | 182 | 32 | 6 |
| Drew | 32 | 0 | 7 | 0 | 25 | 91 | 25 | 52 | 14 | 0 |
| Fulton | 39 | 1 | 7 | 0 | 31 | 64 | 0 | 54 | 10 | 0 |
| Hempstead | 38 | 0 | 7 | 0 | 31 | 100 | 24 | 67 | 9 | 3 |
| Hot Spring | 24 | 2 | 0 | 0 | 22 | 122 | 61 | 24 | 37 | 0 |
| Howard | 11 | 1 | 1 | 0 | 9 | 59 | 25 | 27 | 7 | 0 |
| Independence | 191 | 2 | 44 | 0 | 145 | 448 | 95 | 282 | 71 | 16 |
| Izard | 97 | 0 | 14 | 0 | 83 | 97 | 37 | 59 | 1 | 0 |
| Jackson | 44 | 0 | 10 | 2 | 32 | 107 | 7 | 77 | 23 | 0 |
| Johnson | 97 | 0 | 21 | 0 | 76 | 115 | 47 | 58 | 10 | 4 |
| Lawrence | 31 | 0 | 10 | 0 | 21 | 85 | 27 | 54 | 4 | 1 |
| Lee | 15 | 0 | 1 | 0 | 14 | 72 | 18 | 36 | 18 | 6 |
| Logan | 68 | 1 | 8 | 1 | 58 | 190 | 38 | 119 | 33 | 0 |
| Marion | 27 | 2 | 7 | 0 | 18 | 122 | 38 | 77 | 7 | 1 |
| Mississippi | 20 | 1 | 4 | 0 | 15 | 288 | 103 | 140 | 45 | 1 |
| Nevada | 14 | 0 | 3 | 0 | 11 | 33 | 10 | 13 | 10 | 0 |
| Newton | 28 | 2 | 10 | 0 | 16 | 47 | 14 | 28 | 5 | 1 |
| Pike | 1 | 0 | 1 | 0 | 0 | 32 | 10 | 19 | 3 | 0 |
| Polk | 75 | 0 | 6 | 1 | 68 | 72 | 24 | 45 | 3 | 0 |
| Pope | 87 | 2 | 8 | 0 | 77 | 181 | 60 | 97 | 24 | 4 |
| Prairie | 11 | 2 | 2 | 0 | 7 | 60 | 17 | 35 | 8 | 0 |
| Randolph | 30 | 0 | 7 | 1 | 22 | 129 | 29 | 86 | 14 | 1 |
| Scott | 18 | 1 | 2 | 0 | 15 | 70 | 26 | 29 | 15 | 1 |
| Searcy | 17 | 0 | 3 | 0 | 14 | 11 | 4 | 6 | 1 | 0 |
| Sevier | 44 | 0 | 7 | 2 | 35 | 42 | 11 | 22 | 9 | 3 |
| St. Francis | 53 | 1 | 5 | 2 | 45 | 64 | 55 | 5 | 4 | 4 |
| Stone | 27 | 2 | 9 | 0 | 16 | 56 | 11 | 41 | 4 | 3 |
| Union | 61 | 5 | 5 | 0 | 51 | 209 | 55 | 135 | 19 | 2 |
| Van Buren | 42 | 0 | 1 | 1 | 40 | 144 | 35 | 76 | 33 | 4 |
| White | 270 | 6 | 62 | 1 | 201 | 628 | 161 | 364 | 103 | 12 |
| Yell | 54 | 0 | 7 | 0 | 47 | 126 | 34 | 71 | 21 | 2 |
| **CALIFORNIA**[1] | | | | | | | | | | |
| **Metropolitan Counties** | | | | | | | | | | |
| San Diego | 2,559 | 31 | 124 | 404 | 2,000 | 9,313 | 1,625 | 5,627 | 2,061 | 56 |
| **COLORADO** | | | | | | | | | | |
| **Metropolitan Counties** | | | | | | | | | | |
| Adams | 657 | 11 | 79 | 95 | 472 | 3,448 | 406 | 1,737 | 1,305 | 44 |
| Arapahoe | 217 | 1 | 11 | 30 | 175 | 2,566 | 431 | 1,404 | 731 | 19 |
| Boulder | 114 | 0 | 21 | 3 | 90 | 819 | 152 | 562 | 105 | 11 |
| Clear Creek | 7 | 0 | 3 | 1 | 3 | 59 | 8 | 44 | 7 | 1 |
| Douglas | 390 | 5 | 89 | 30 | 266 | 2,775 | 440 | 1,928 | 407 | 20 |
| El Paso | 553 | 14 | 104 | 39 | 396 | 2,291 | 409 | 1,504 | 378 | 26 |
| Gilpin | 13 | 2 | 2 | 0 | 9 | 96 | 19 | 69 | 8 | 1 |
| Jefferson | 386 | 3 | 95 | 28 | 260 | 3,287 | 445 | 2,277 | 565 | 24 |
| Larimer | 187 | 3 | 32 | 9 | 143 | 883 | 155 | 563 | 165 | 8 |
| Mesa | 225 | 3 | 38 | 12 | 172 | 1,160 | 208 | 756 | 196 | 20 |
| Park | 45 | 0 | 4 | 0 | 41 | 53 | 13 | 23 | 17 | 2 |
| Pueblo | 41 | 1 | 3 | 9 | 28 | 1,152 | 290 | 661 | 201 | 0 |
| Teller | 24 | 0 | 4 | 0 | 20 | 71 | 20 | 37 | 14 | 0 |
| Weld | 161 | 2 | 23 | 11 | 125 | 797 | 155 | 477 | 165 | 11 |
| **Nonmetropolitan Counties** | | | | | | | | | | |
| Alamosa | 14 | 3 | 9 | 0 | 2 | 104 | 54 | 42 | 8 | 0 |
| Archuleta | 41 | 2 | 10 | 0 | 29 | 88 | 23 | 60 | 5 | 4 |
| Baca | 2 | 0 | 0 | 0 | 2 | 3 | 0 | 1 | 2 | 0 |
| Bent | 6 | 0 | 3 | 0 | 3 | 56 | 16 | 31 | 9 | 1 |
| Chaffee | 17 | 0 | 1 | 0 | 16 | 49 | 14 | 23 | 12 | 0 |
| Conejos | 16 | 0 | 4 | 0 | 12 | 20 | 14 | 5 | 1 | 0 |
| Crowley | 12 | 0 | 2 | 0 | 10 | 33 | 14 | 13 | 6 | 0 |
| Custer | 14 | 0 | 0 | 0 | 14 | 53 | 9 | 36 | 8 | 1 |
| Delta | 10 | 1 | 5 | 0 | 4 | 160 | 41 | 103 | 16 | 0 |
| Dolores | 0 | 0 | 0 | 0 | 0 | 20 | 3 | 9 | 8 | 2 |
| Eagle | 26 | 0 | 5 | 0 | 20 | 80 | 4 | 69 | 7 | 0 |
| Fremont | 27 | 1 | 11 | 1 | 14 | 178 | 47 | 96 | 35 | 1 |
| Garfield | 71 | 0 | 28 | 1 | 42 | 183 | 52 | 111 | 20 | 6 |
| Gunnison | 5 | 1 | 0 | 0 | 4 | 14 | 3 | 10 | 1 | 0 |
| Hinsdale | 0 | 0 | 0 | 0 | 0 | 4 | 0 | 3 | 1 | 0 |
| Huerfano | 24 | 0 | 6 | 1 | 17 | 179 | 67 | 87 | 25 | 1 |
| Kiowa | 5 | 0 | 1 | 0 | 4 | 18 | 0 | 16 | 2 | 0 |
| Kit Carson | 5 | 0 | 0 | 0 | 5 | 21 | 2 | 16 | 3 | 0 |
| Lake | 6 | 1 | 1 | 0 | 4 | 22 | 6 | 13 | 3 | 0 |
| La Plata | 38 | 0 | 13 | 0 | 25 | 192 | 34 | 147 | 11 | 2 |
| Las Animas | 12 | 1 | 1 | 0 | 10 | 167 | 119 | 40 | 8 | 1 |
| Logan | 20 | 0 | 2 | 0 | 18 | 73 | 23 | 35 | 15 | 0 |
| Moffat | 14 | 0 | 3 | 0 | 11 | 43 | 8 | 32 | 3 | 1 |

# Table 10. Offenses Known to Law Enforcement, by Selected State Metropolitan and Nonmetropolitan Counties, 2021—Continued

(Number.)

| State/county | Violent crime | Murder and nonnegligent manslaughter | Rape | Robbery | Aggravated assault | Property crime | Burglary | Larceny-theft | Motor vehicle theft | Arson |
|---|---|---|---|---|---|---|---|---|---|---|
| Montezuma | 36 | 0 | 5 | 1 | 30 | 164 | 38 | 94 | 32 | 2 |
| Montrose | 26 | 0 | 1 | 0 | 25 | 171 | 35 | 108 | 28 | 0 |
| Morgan | 15 | 0 | 2 | 0 | 13 | 121 | 24 | 70 | 27 | 1 |
| Otero | 9 | 0 | 4 | 1 | 4 | 82 | 28 | 24 | 30 | 0 |
| Ouray | 1 | 0 | 0 | 0 | 1 | 32 | 2 | 25 | 5 | 0 |
| Phillips | 0 | 0 | 0 | 0 | 0 | 0 | 0 | 0 | 0 | 0 |
| Pitkin | 4 | 0 | 3 | 0 | 1 | 18 | 4 | 9 | 5 | 0 |
| Prowers | 7 | 0 | 1 | 0 | 6 | 33 | 5 | 23 | 5 | 1 |
| Rio Blanco | 2 | 0 | 1 | 0 | 1 | 16 | 0 | 14 | 2 | 1 |
| Rio Grande | 4 | 0 | 3 | 0 | 1 | 71 | 36 | 31 | 4 | 0 |
| Routt | 3 | 0 | 1 | 0 | 2 | 32 | 7 | 23 | 2 | 2 |
| San Juan | 2 | 0 | 1 | 0 | 1 | 6 | 0 | 4 | 2 | 0 |
| San Miguel | 2 | 0 | 0 | 0 | 2 | 6 | 1 | 3 | 2 | 0 |
| Summit | 40 | 0 | 24 | 0 | 16 | 199 | 23 | 149 | 27 | 0 |
| Washington | 2 | 0 | 0 | 0 | 2 | 63 | 5 | 50 | 8 | 1 |
| Yuma | 4 | 0 | 2 | 0 | 2 | 37 | 4 | 25 | 8 | 0 |
| **DELAWARE** | | | | | | | | | | |
| **Metropolitan Counties** | | | | | | | | | | |
| New Castle County Police Department | 791 | 23 | 88 | 64 | 616 | 3,430 | 571 | 2,477 | 382 | 2 |
| **FLORIDA[1]** | | | | | | | | | | |
| **GEORGIA** | | | | | | | | | | |
| **Metropolitan Counties** | | | | | | | | | | |
| Barrow | 107 | 0 | 19 | 1 | 87 | 808 | 85 | 663 | 60 | 7 |
| Bartow | 103 | 1 | 17 | 9 | 76 | 1,054 | 127 | 799 | 128 | 14 |
| Bibb | 1,821 | 44 | 60 | 161 | 1,556 | 4,492 | 665 | 3,157 | 670 | 25 |
| Brantley | 48 | 0 | 4 | 0 | 44 | 330 | 53 | 236 | 41 | 2 |
| Brooks | 28 | 0 | 9 | 0 | 19 | 118 | 33 | 64 | 21 | 1 |
| Bryan | 33 | 1 | 9 | 3 | 20 | 196 | 47 | 131 | 18 | 0 |
| Burke | 18 | 1 | 4 | 1 | 12 | 245 | 52 | 134 | 59 | 3 |
| Butts | 38 | 2 | 5 | 2 | 29 | 179 | 20 | 117 | 42 | 1 |
| Carroll | 147 | 1 | 23 | 8 | 115 | 988 | 200 | 669 | 119 | 13 |
| Catoosa | 65 | 1 | 9 | 1 | 54 | 489 | 85 | 333 | 71 | 3 |
| Cherokee | 189 | 10 | 34 | 8 | 137 | 899 | 138 | 692 | 69 | 6 |
| Clarke | 0 | 0 | 0 | 0 | 0 | 0 | 0 | 0 | 0 | 0 |
| Cobb | 23 | 0 | 6 | 0 | 17 | 366 | 0 | 357 | 9 | 0 |
| Cobb County Police Department | 1,330 | 29 | 139 | 176 | 986 | 7,988 | 978 | 6,170 | 840 | 15 |
| Coweta | 679 | 6 | 52 | 4 | 617 | 895 | 172 | 616 | 107 | 3 |
| Crawford | 35 | 3 | 6 | 1 | 25 | 134 | 33 | 76 | 25 | 0 |
| Dawson | 52 | 0 | 8 | 2 | 42 | 314 | 32 | 271 | 11 | 4 |
| DeKalb | 25 | 0 | 0 | 0 | 25 | 0 | 0 | 0 | 0 | 5 |
| DeKalb County Police Department | 4,135 | 119 | 235 | 768 | 3,013 | 14,944 | 1,951 | 10,228 | 2,765 | 94 |
| Dougherty | 10 | 0 | 3 | 0 | 7 | 22 | 1 | 18 | 3 | 0 |
| Dougherty County Police Department | 32 | 2 | 2 | 4 | 24 | 207 | 50 | 117 | 40 | 1 |
| Douglas | 202 | 9 | 12 | 20 | 161 | 807 | 120 | 559 | 128 | 1 |
| Effingham | 48 | 0 | 8 | 3 | 37 | 292 | 73 | 182 | 37 | 2 |
| Fayette | 38 | 1 | 3 | 4 | 30 | 329 | 61 | 237 | 31 | 1 |
| Floyd | 5 | 0 | 0 | 0 | 5 | 4 | 0 | 3 | 1 | 0 |
| Floyd County Police Department | 151 | 1 | 15 | 9 | 126 | 769 | 123 | 559 | 87 | 7 |
| Forsyth | 136 | 1 | 26 | 7 | 102 | 1,172 | 169 | 911 | 92 | 2 |
| Fulton County Police Department | 97 | 2 | 8 | 16 | 71 | 235 | 14 | 158 | 63 | 1 |
| Glynn | 0 | 0 | 0 | 0 | 0 | 0 | 0 | 0 | 0 | 0 |
| Glynn County Police Department | 280 | 4 | 65 | 42 | 169 | 1,356 | 183 | 1,014 | 159 | 3 |
| Hall | 297 | 7 | 35 | 7 | 248 | 1,285 | 251 | 877 | 157 | 0 |
| Haralson | 66 | 2 | 6 | 3 | 55 | 300 | 67 | 171 | 62 | 2 |
| Harris | 8 | 0 | 1 | 2 | 5 | 123 | 21 | 85 | 17 | 0 |
| Heard | 17 | 2 | 1 | 0 | 14 | 119 | 20 | 78 | 21 | 3 |
| Henry County Police Department | 476 | 8 | 73 | 50 | 345 | 2,605 | 247 | 2,014 | 344 | 5 |
| Jasper | 55 | 1 | 6 | 1 | 47 | 166 | 19 | 125 | 22 | 3 |
| Jones | 60 | 2 | 3 | 2 | 53 | 167 | 47 | 102 | 18 | 1 |
| Lamar | 9 | 0 | 3 | 1 | 5 | 79 | 10 | 51 | 18 | 0 |
| Lanier | 13 | 0 | 0 | 2 | 11 | 108 | 31 | 72 | 5 | 0 |
| Lee | 51 | 0 | 15 | 2 | 34 | 447 | 81 | 313 | 53 | 0 |
| Long | 9 | 1 | 1 | 1 | 6 | 70 | 27 | 34 | 9 | 1 |
| Lowndes | 126 | 4 | 28 | 10 | 84 | 795 | 113 | 603 | 79 | 4 |
| Madison | 90 | 2 | 8 | 8 | 72 | 244 | 59 | 134 | 51 | 14 |
| Marion | 11 | 0 | 1 | 1 | 9 | 41 | 10 | 25 | 6 | 1 |
| McDuffie | 42 | 1 | 1 | 7 | 33 | 164 | 47 | 100 | 17 | 1 |
| McIntosh | 20 | 5 | 1 | 1 | 13 | 129 | 31 | 77 | 21 | 2 |
| Murray | 72 | 1 | 4 | 1 | 66 | 222 | 47 | 142 | 33 | 1 |
| Newton | 392 | 6 | 44 | 19 | 323 | 1,070 | 166 | 734 | 170 | 7 |
| Oconee | 42 | 2 | 6 | 3 | 31 | 518 | 49 | 451 | 18 | 0 |
| Oglethorpe | 33 | 1 | 3 | 1 | 28 | 150 | 28 | 101 | 21 | 4 |
| Paulding | 411 | 4 | 137 | 12 | 258 | 1,247 | 199 | 919 | 129 | 9 |
| Peach | 21 | 0 | 3 | 2 | 16 | 129 | 20 | 91 | 18 | 3 |
| Pickens | 54 | 0 | 11 | 1 | 42 | 148 | 33 | 95 | 20 | 1 |
| Pike | 15 | 0 | 4 | 1 | 10 | 100 | 21 | 63 | 16 | 4 |
| Rockdale | 59 | 6 | 16 | 1 | 36 | 17 | 14 | 2 | 1 | 0 |
| Spalding | 154 | 4 | 16 | 9 | 125 | 578 | 104 | 362 | 112 | 2 |

## Table 10. Offenses Known to Law Enforcement, by Selected State Metropolitan and Nonmetropolitan Counties, 2021—Continued

(Number.)

| State/county | Violent crime | Murder and nonnegligent manslaughter | Rape | Robbery | Aggravated assault | Property crime | Burglary | Larceny-theft | Motor vehicle theft | Arson |
|---|---|---|---|---|---|---|---|---|---|---|
| Twiggs | 15 | 3 | 0 | 1 | 11 | 83 | 30 | 43 | 10 | 0 |
| Walton | 34 | 0 | 11 | 3 | 20 | 240 | 37 | 172 | 31 | 1 |
| Whitfield | 305 | 0 | 40 | 6 | 259 | 897 | 155 | 608 | 134 | 4 |
| Worth | 46 | 0 | 1 | 1 | 44 | 163 | 45 | 100 | 18 | 0 |
| **Nonmetropolitan Counties** | | | | | | | | | | |
| Atkinson | 18 | 0 | 2 | 1 | 15 | 56 | 12 | 38 | 6 | 0 |
| Baldwin | 173 | 1 | 13 | 7 | 152 | 535 | 78 | 414 | 43 | 3 |
| Banks | 37 | 1 | 4 | 0 | 32 | 376 | 40 | 314 | 22 | 0 |
| Ben Hill | 27 | 0 | 5 | 1 | 21 | 155 | 44 | 95 | 16 | 2 |
| Berrien | 19 | 0 | 8 | 0 | 11 | 116 | 30 | 72 | 14 | 0 |
| Bleckley | 19 | 0 | 3 | 1 | 15 | 85 | 5 | 68 | 12 | 0 |
| Bulloch | 24 | 0 | 3 | 2 | 19 | 308 | 44 | 251 | 13 | 1 |
| Candler | 15 | 0 | 2 | 0 | 13 | 91 | 13 | 73 | 5 | 1 |
| Chattooga | 33 | 0 | 7 | 0 | 26 | 202 | 38 | 148 | 16 | 3 |
| Clay | 3 | 0 | 1 | 0 | 2 | 10 | 2 | 7 | 1 | 0 |
| Clinch | 1 | 0 | 0 | 0 | 1 | 33 | 9 | 21 | 3 | 0 |
| Coffee | 70 | 1 | 7 | 3 | 59 | 329 | 61 | 226 | 42 | 1 |
| Cook | 13 | 0 | 3 | 2 | 8 | 130 | 20 | 98 | 12 | 0 |
| Crisp | 32 | 0 | 6 | 0 | 26 | 260 | 43 | 200 | 17 | 4 |
| Decatur | 49 | 2 | 13 | 2 | 32 | 233 | 62 | 148 | 23 | 2 |
| Dodge | 30 | 0 | 1 | 3 | 26 | 170 | 58 | 92 | 20 | 5 |
| Early | 22 | 0 | 5 | 0 | 17 | 58 | 13 | 38 | 7 | 1 |
| Elbert | 20 | 0 | 1 | 0 | 19 | 102 | 27 | 70 | 5 | 2 |
| Fannin | 17 | 0 | 7 | 1 | 9 | 117 | 37 | 67 | 13 | 0 |
| Franklin | 40 | 0 | 4 | 3 | 33 | 160 | 49 | 90 | 21 | 0 |
| Gilmer | 56 | 1 | 13 | 3 | 39 | 233 | 51 | 139 | 43 | 1 |
| Glascock | 10 | 0 | 1 | 0 | 9 | 30 | 7 | 19 | 4 | 0 |
| Gordon | 74 | 2 | 11 | 5 | 56 | 355 | 68 | 239 | 48 | 0 |
| Grady | 29 | 1 | 6 | 2 | 20 | 151 | 43 | 69 | 39 | 1 |
| Greene | 25 | 2 | 0 | 1 | 22 | 149 | 31 | 100 | 18 | 0 |
| Habersham | 33 | 0 | 11 | 2 | 20 | 305 | 67 | 199 | 39 | 0 |
| Hancock | 10 | 0 | 1 | 1 | 8 | 57 | 8 | 43 | 6 | 0 |
| Hart | 74 | 0 | 12 | 2 | 60 | 206 | 46 | 123 | 37 | 1 |
| Irwin | 15 | 0 | 1 | 2 | 12 | 79 | 9 | 62 | 8 | 1 |
| Jackson | 77 | 1 | 13 | 3 | 60 | 537 | 68 | 422 | 47 | 3 |
| Jeff Davis | 23 | 1 | 2 | 0 | 20 | 32 | 5 | 16 | 11 | 2 |
| Jefferson | 34 | 0 | 4 | 0 | 30 | 116 | 17 | 80 | 19 | 0 |
| Jenkins | 11 | 0 | 6 | 0 | 5 | 48 | 11 | 30 | 7 | 0 |
| Laurens | 66 | 2 | 7 | 2 | 55 | 346 | 71 | 230 | 45 | 2 |
| Lumpkin | 46 | 0 | 3 | 0 | 43 | 246 | 43 | 187 | 16 | 2 |
| Mitchell | 28 | 0 | 4 | 0 | 24 | 198 | 31 | 143 | 24 | 1 |
| Pierce | 42 | 1 | 7 | 2 | 32 | 222 | 53 | 142 | 27 | 0 |
| Polk | 3 | 0 | 0 | 0 | 3 | 1 | 0 | 0 | 1 | 0 |
| Pulaski | 40 | 1 | 0 | 3 | 36 | 167 | 33 | 106 | 28 | 2 |
| Putnam | 37 | 0 | 3 | 1 | 33 | 159 | 25 | 124 | 10 | 2 |
| Rabun | 14 | 0 | 8 | 0 | 6 | 161 | 28 | 120 | 13 | 0 |
| Schley | 3 | 1 | 0 | 0 | 2 | 14 | 5 | 7 | 2 | 0 |
| Seminole | 19 | 3 | 1 | 0 | 15 | 63 | 14 | 44 | 5 | 1 |
| Sumter | 17 | 0 | 1 | 0 | 16 | 114 | 31 | 77 | 6 | 0 |
| Tattnall | 11 | 0 | 6 | 0 | 5 | 119 | 25 | 78 | 16 | 0 |
| Thomas | 59 | 1 | 9 | 3 | 46 | 449 | 129 | 266 | 54 | 7 |
| Tift | 138 | 2 | 8 | 16 | 112 | 529 | 100 | 357 | 72 | 0 |
| Towns | 10 | 0 | 3 | 0 | 7 | 43 | 6 | 30 | 7 | 0 |
| Treutlen | 12 | 0 | 5 | 0 | 7 | 40 | 7 | 26 | 7 | 1 |
| Troup | 65 | 3 | 10 | 6 | 46 | 436 | 70 | 309 | 57 | 0 |
| Turner | 10 | 0 | 5 | 0 | 5 | 48 | 11 | 30 | 7 | 0 |
| Union | 10 | 0 | 3 | 0 | 7 | 157 | 33 | 108 | 16 | 1 |
| Ware | 22 | 0 | 4 | 0 | 18 | 98 | 20 | 65 | 13 | 2 |
| Washington | 35 | 1 | 6 | 1 | 27 | 115 | 16 | 91 | 8 | 0 |
| Webster | 0 | 0 | 0 | 0 | 0 | 0 | 0 | 0 | 0 | 0 |
| Wheeler | 4 | 0 | 2 | 0 | 2 | 38 | 10 | 22 | 6 | 0 |
| White | 28 | 0 | 2 | 0 | 26 | 163 | 48 | 92 | 23 | 1 |
| Wilkes | 84 | 0 | 7 | 1 | 76 | 153 | 52 | 79 | 22 | 1 |
| Wilkinson | 9 | 1 | 0 | 0 | 8 | 26 | 6 | 16 | 4 | 1 |
| **HAWAII** | | | | | | | | | | |
| **Metropolitan Counties** | | | | | | | | | | |
| Kauai Police Department | 212 | 0 | 50 | 15 | 147 | 1,003 | 233 | 678 | 92 | 54 |
| **IDAHO** | | | | | | | | | | |
| **Metropolitan Counties** | | | | | | | | | | |
| Ada | 243 | 2 | 52 | 2 | 187 | 510 | 81 | 389 | 40 | 9 |
| Bannock | 13 | 0 | 2 | 0 | 11 | 73 | 22 | 44 | 7 | 0 |
| Boise | 21 | 0 | 3 | 0 | 18 | 51 | 10 | 34 | 7 | 1 |
| Bonneville | 130 | 3 | 27 | 4 | 96 | 642 | 178 | 397 | 67 | 4 |
| Butte | 5 | 0 | 3 | 0 | 2 | 5 | 1 | 2 | 2 | 0 |
| Canyon | 114 | 1 | 30 | 0 | 83 | 325 | 88 | 172 | 65 | 4 |
| Franklin | 4 | 0 | 4 | 0 | 0 | 22 | 1 | 18 | 3 | 0 |
| Gem | 10 | 1 | 3 | 0 | 6 | 23 | 7 | 12 | 4 | 0 |
| Jefferson | 24 | 1 | 2 | 1 | 20 | 131 | 17 | 87 | 27 | 0 |

# Table 10. Offenses Known to Law Enforcement, by Selected State Metropolitan and Nonmetropolitan Counties, 2021—Continued

(Number.)

| State/county | Violent crime | Murder and nonnegligent manslaughter | Rape | Robbery | Aggravated assault | Property crime | Burglary | Larceny-theft | Motor vehicle theft | Arson |
|---|---|---|---|---|---|---|---|---|---|---|
| Jerome | 43 | 0 | 3 | 0 | 40 | 122 | 35 | 65 | 22 | 2 |
| Kootenai | 162 | 2 | 41 | 1 | 118 | 694 | 153 | 495 | 46 | 5 |
| Nez Perce | 11 | 0 | 3 | 0 | 8 | 46 | 17 | 27 | 2 | 0 |
| Power | 5 | 0 | 1 | 0 | 4 | 31 | 6 | 22 | 3 | 0 |
| **Nonmetropolitan Counties** | | | | | | | | | | |
| Adams | 10 | 0 | 0 | 0 | 10 | 36 | 2 | 31 | 3 | 1 |
| Benewah | 28 | 0 | 3 | 0 | 25 | 77 | 3 | 67 | 7 | 2 |
| Bingham | 40 | 0 | 7 | 0 | 33 | 146 | 55 | 77 | 14 | 0 |
| Blaine | 10 | 0 | 1 | 0 | 9 | 16 | 3 | 12 | 1 | 0 |
| Bonner | 41 | 2 | 7 | 0 | 32 | 274 | 69 | 171 | 34 | 2 |
| Boundary | 6 | 0 | 3 | 0 | 3 | 30 | 11 | 14 | 5 | 0 |
| Caribou | 5 | 0 | 1 | 0 | 4 | 7 | 2 | 5 | 0 | 0 |
| Cassia | 37 | 0 | 2 | 2 | 33 | 257 | 5 | 229 | 23 | 0 |
| Custer | 9 | 0 | 5 | 0 | 4 | 15 | 2 | 13 | 0 | 0 |
| Elmore | 12 | 0 | 4 | 0 | 8 | 20 | 6 | 9 | 5 | 1 |
| Fremont | 12 | 1 | 1 | 0 | 10 | 44 | 5 | 35 | 4 | 2 |
| Gooding | 17 | 0 | 3 | 0 | 14 | 38 | 11 | 20 | 7 | 1 |
| Latah | 20 | 0 | 4 | 0 | 16 | 70 | 18 | 46 | 6 | 0 |
| Lewis | 9 | 2 | 1 | 0 | 6 | 15 | 4 | 8 | 3 | 1 |
| Lincoln | 10 | 0 | 0 | 0 | 10 | 38 | 9 | 26 | 3 | 0 |
| Madison | 14 | 0 | 4 | 0 | 10 | 13 | 1 | 10 | 2 | 0 |
| Minidoka | 13 | 0 | 3 | 0 | 10 | 78 | 10 | 57 | 11 | 0 |
| Oneida | 15 | 0 | 5 | 0 | 10 | 33 | 8 | 23 | 2 | 0 |
| Payette | 23 | 0 | 1 | 2 | 20 | 75 | 12 | 54 | 9 | 1 |
| Teton | 8 | 0 | 3 | 0 | 5 | 29 | 1 | 26 | 2 | 1 |
| Valley | 21 | 0 | 8 | 0 | 13 | 83 | 26 | 49 | 8 | 0 |
| **ILLINOIS**[1] | | | | | | | | | | |
| **Metropolitan Counties** | | | | | | | | | | |
| Champaign | 29 | 0 | 15 | 2 | 12 | 244 | 70 | 152 | 22 | 7 |
| Henry | 8 | 0 | 2 | 0 | 6 | 56 | 11 | 37 | 8 | 0 |
| Jackson | 55 | 0 | 31 | 2 | 22 | 198 | 92 | 86 | 20 | 4 |
| Jersey | 6 | 0 | 3 | 0 | 3 | 18 | 2 | 12 | 4 | 0 |
| Kendall | 33 | 0 | 21 | 0 | 12 | 178 | 39 | 124 | 15 | 0 |
| Macon | 27 | 1 | 9 | 3 | 14 | 230 | 74 | 143 | 13 | 2 |
| Madison | 140 | 3 | 37 | 5 | 95 | 1,038 | 265 | 664 | 109 | 16 |
| McLean | 30 | 0 | 12 | 0 | 18 | 186 | 105 | 66 | 15 | 4 |
| Sangamon | 157 | 4 | 18 | 19 | 116 | 569 | 181 | 309 | 79 | 9 |
| St. Clair | 89 | 2 | 16 | 4 | 67 | 363 | 92 | 209 | 62 | 3 |
| Tazewell | 21 | 2 | 10 | 0 | 9 | 169 | 51 | 100 | 18 | 0 |
| **Nonmetropolitan Counties** | | | | | | | | | | |
| Iroquois | 23 | 0 | 6 | 2 | 15 | 135 | 31 | 86 | 18 | 1 |
| **INDIANA** | | | | | | | | | | |
| **Metropolitan Counties** | | | | | | | | | | |
| Allen | 55 | 4 | 19 | 2 | 30 | 619 | 96 | 473 | 50 | 1 |
| Bartholomew | 2 | 0 | 0 | 2 | 0 | 31 | 31 | 0 | 0 | 4 |
| Clark | 59 | 2 | 4 | 3 | 50 | 305 | 56 | 184 | 65 | 2 |
| Delaware | 21 | 1 | 6 | 1 | 13 | 198 | 48 | 111 | 39 | 0 |
| Elkhart | 20 | 0 | 2 | 3 | 15 | 97 | 17 | 66 | 14 | 3 |
| Floyd | 21 | 0 | 6 | 0 | 15 | 251 | 25 | 169 | 57 | 0 |
| Hamilton | 21 | 0 | 7 | 1 | 13 | 144 | 37 | 93 | 14 | 2 |
| Hancock | 52 | 0 | 3 | 2 | 47 | 197 | 38 | 116 | 43 | 2 |
| Harrison | 63 | 0 | 5 | 0 | 58 | 287 | 39 | 205 | 43 | 3 |
| Hendricks | 60 | 0 | 20 | 6 | 34 | 420 | 46 | 325 | 49 | 0 |
| Howard | 60 | 1 | 4 | 1 | 54 | 88 | 15 | 60 | 13 | 1 |
| Johnson | 20 | 0 | 7 | 1 | 12 | 275 | 20 | 223 | 32 | 0 |
| La Porte | 46 | 1 | 1 | 0 | 44 | 351 | 121 | 190 | 40 | 0 |
| Madison | 27 | 0 | 0 | 2 | 25 | 185 | 41 | 131 | 13 | 1 |
| Monroe | 27 | 1 | 5 | 3 | 18 | 451 | 43 | 362 | 46 | 4 |
| Porter | 57 | 1 | 3 | 0 | 53 | 195 | 30 | 146 | 19 | 0 |
| Posey | 27 | 0 | 10 | 0 | 17 | 127 | 12 | 92 | 23 | 0 |
| St. Joseph | 129 | 0 | 24 | 18 | 87 | 1,107 | 204 | 754 | 149 | 8 |
| Tippecanoe | 84 | 0 | 11 | 2 | 71 | 397 | 88 | 256 | 53 | 3 |
| Vanderburgh | 142 | 0 | 11 | 0 | 131 | 361 | 56 | 262 | 43 | 1 |
| Vigo | 89 | 0 | 18 | 4 | 67 | 1,027 | 384 | 519 | 124 | 10 |
| Washington | 46 | 0 | 1 | 0 | 45 | 122 | 18 | 64 | 40 | 0 |
| **Nonmetropolitan Counties** | | | | | | | | | | |
| Clinton | 6 | 3 | 2 | 1 | 0 | 69 | 19 | 47 | 3 | 0 |
| Dubois | 9 | 0 | 1 | 0 | 8 | 62 | 25 | 25 | 12 | 0 |
| Fulton | 13 | 0 | 4 | 0 | 9 | 73 | 17 | 50 | 6 | 0 |
| Gibson | 26 | 2 | 4 | 0 | 20 | 111 | 21 | 74 | 16 | 0 |
| Greene | 16 | 2 | 5 | 1 | 8 | 128 | 20 | 86 | 22 | 1 |
| Henry | 11 | 1 | 0 | 1 | 9 | 145 | 34 | 88 | 23 | 0 |
| Jackson | 31 | 3 | 4 | 2 | 22 | 38 | 9 | 16 | 13 | 1 |
| Jennings | 20 | 0 | 4 | 0 | 16 | 137 | 35 | 72 | 30 | 1 |
| Kosciusko | 63 | 1 | 15 | 0 | 47 | 378 | 51 | 280 | 47 | 5 |
| Montgomery | 11 | 0 | 3 | 1 | 7 | 155 | 65 | 82 | 8 | 0 |

## Table 10. Offenses Known to Law Enforcement, by Selected State Metropolitan and Nonmetropolitan Counties, 2021—Continued

(Number.)

| State/county | Violent crime | Murder and nonnegligent manslaughter | Rape | Robbery | Aggravated assault | Property crime | Burglary | Larceny-theft | Motor vehicle theft | Arson |
|---|---|---|---|---|---|---|---|---|---|---|
| Noble | 18 | 0 | 8 | 1 | 9 | 152 | 33 | 81 | 38 | 1 |
| Starke | 63 | 0 | 7 | 0 | 56 | 164 | 49 | 87 | 28 | 2 |
| Steuben | 18 | 2 | 8 | 1 | 7 | 294 | 87 | 171 | 36 | 1 |
| Wells | 2 | 0 | 1 | 0 | 1 | 22 | 8 | 11 | 3 | 0 |
| **IOWA** | | | | | | | | | | |
| **Metropolitan Counties** | | | | | | | | | | |
| Benton | 20 | 1 | 10 | 0 | 9 | 99 | 37 | 47 | 15 | 4 |
| Black Hawk | 17 | 0 | 8 | 0 | 9 | 126 | 68 | 42 | 16 | 0 |
| Dallas | 66 | 0 | 8 | 0 | 58 | 97 | 22 | 66 | 9 | 2 |
| Dubuque | 27 | 0 | 11 | 0 | 16 | 146 | 40 | 84 | 22 | 0 |
| Grundy | 10 | 1 | 2 | 0 | 7 | 33 | 11 | 15 | 7 | 0 |
| Harrison | 10 | 0 | 3 | 0 | 7 | 42 | 5 | 29 | 8 | 0 |
| Jasper | 8 | 0 | 1 | 0 | 7 | 37 | 15 | 12 | 10 | 2 |
| Johnson | 74 | 0 | 15 | 0 | 59 | 201 | 53 | 124 | 24 | 1 |
| Jones | 18 | 2 | 0 | 0 | 16 | 45 | 19 | 17 | 9 | 1 |
| Linn | 38 | 0 | 19 | 2 | 17 | 159 | 46 | 87 | 26 | 0 |
| Mills | 7 | 0 | 0 | 0 | 7 | 98 | 16 | 62 | 20 | 0 |
| Polk | 99 | 1 | 5 | 9 | 84 | 814 | 197 | 493 | 124 | 4 |
| Pottawattamie | 54 | 1 | 21 | 3 | 29 | 197 | 44 | 136 | 17 | 1 |
| Scott | 35 | 0 | 3 | 1 | 31 | 137 | 43 | 61 | 33 | 3 |
| Story | 19 | 0 | 3 | 0 | 16 | 117 | 23 | 74 | 20 | 2 |
| Warren | 21 | 0 | 5 | 0 | 16 | 79 | 11 | 57 | 11 | 1 |
| Washington | 42 | 0 | 3 | 0 | 39 | 79 | 20 | 49 | 10 | 0 |
| Woodbury | 38 | 1 | 6 | 1 | 30 | 89 | 20 | 61 | 8 | 1 |
| **Nonmetropolitan Counties** | | | | | | | | | | |
| Adair | 4 | 1 | 1 | 0 | 2 | 27 | 9 | 8 | 10 | 0 |
| Adams | 7 | 0 | 1 | 1 | 5 | 18 | 10 | 6 | 2 | 1 |
| Allamakee | 14 | 0 | 0 | 0 | 14 | 8 | 5 | 2 | 1 | 0 |
| Appanoose | 5 | 0 | 1 | 0 | 4 | 79 | 15 | 45 | 19 | 2 |
| Buchanan | 13 | 0 | 3 | 1 | 9 | 43 | 11 | 25 | 7 | 3 |
| Buena Vista | 13 | 0 | 2 | 0 | 11 | 34 | 16 | 13 | 5 | 0 |
| Butler | 7 | 0 | 1 | 0 | 6 | 37 | 21 | 13 | 3 | 0 |
| Carroll | 3 | 0 | 0 | 0 | 3 | 12 | 2 | 7 | 3 | 0 |
| Cass | 10 | 0 | 1 | 0 | 9 | 43 | 15 | 25 | 3 | 3 |
| Cedar | 7 | 0 | 2 | 0 | 5 | 25 | 11 | 9 | 5 | 1 |
| Cerro Gordo | 8 | 0 | 1 | 0 | 7 | 91 | 26 | 41 | 24 | · 1 |
| Cherokee | 4 | 0 | 0 | 0 | 4 | 19 | 5 | 13 | 1 | 0 |
| Chickasaw | 13 | 0 | 2 | 0 | 11 | 27 | 9 | 12 | 6 | 0 |
| Clarke | 10 | 0 | 4 | 0 | 6 | 20 | 4 | 10 | 6 | 0 |
| Clay | 5 | 0 | 0 | 0 | 5 | 30 | 14 | 14 | 2 | 0 |
| Clinton | 21 | 0 | 4 | 1 | 16 | 129 | 33 | 75 | 21 | 0 |
| Crawford | 4 | 0 | 0 | 0 | 4 | 6 | 3 | 1 | 2 | 0 |
| Delaware | 10 | 1 | 5 | 0 | 4 | 15 | 6 | 7 | 2 | 0 |
| Des Moines | 18 | 0 | 2 | 0 | 16 | 97 | 35 | 46 | 16 | 0 |
| Emmet | 29 | 1 | 0 | 0 | 28 | 7 | 0 | 4 | 3 | 0 |
| Fayette | 30 | 0 | 2 | 1 | 27 | 27 | 9 | 8 | 10 | 1 |
| Floyd | 1 | 0 | 0 | 0 | 1 | 26 | 13 | 8 | 5 | 0 |
| Fremont | 12 | 0 | 4 | 0 | 8 | 61 | 17 | 31 | 13 | 1 |
| Hancock | 24 | 0 | 4 | 0 | 20 | 37 | 13 | 15 | 9 | 0 |
| Hardin | 19 | 1 | 4 | 3 | 11 | 79 | 23 | 47 | 9 | 0 |
| Henry | 17 | 0 | 3 | 0 | 14 | 59 | 23 | 32 | 4 | 1 |
| Ida | 8 | 0 | 1 | 0 | 7 | 24 | 5 | 17 | 2 | 0 |
| Iowa | 12 | 0 | 0 | 0 | 12 | 7 | 2 | 2 | 3 | 1 |
| Jackson | 15 | 0 | 2 | 0 | 13 | 74 | 18 | 49 | 7 | 1 |
| Jefferson | 3 | 0 | 2 | 0 | 1 | 19 | 5 | 14 | 0 | 0 |
| Keokuk | 16 | 0 | 3 | 1 | 12 | 51 | 22 | 19 | 10 | 1 |
| Kossuth | 11 | 1 | 0 | 0 | 10 | 8 | 4 | 3 | 1 | 0 |
| Lee | 27 | 0 | 5 | 0 | 22 | 70 | 23 | 38 | 9 | 0 |
| Louisa | 24 | 0 | 3 | 0 | 21 | 34 | 9 | 21 | 4 | 0 |
| Lucas | 12 | 0 | 6 | 0 | 6 | 77 | 19 | 44 | 14 | 0 |
| Lyon | 15 | 0 | 2 | 0 | 13 | 60 | 13 | 38 | 9 | 0 |
| Mahaska | 8 | 0 | 0 | 0 | 8 | 30 | 8 | 20 | 2 | 0 |
| Marion | 24 | 0 | 8 | 0 | 16 | 60 | 25 | 29 | 6 | 0 |
| Mitchell | 7 | 0 | 1 | 0 | 6 | 30 | 19 | 9 | 2 | 1 |
| Monona | 14 | 0 | 5 | 0 | 9 | 69 | 19 | 38 | 12 | 0 |
| Muscatine | 24 | 0 | 9 | 0 | 15 | 33 | 15 | 11 | 7 | 2 |
| O'Brien | 13 | 0 | 2 | 0 | 11 | 63 | 12 | 42 | 9 | 2 |
| Osceola | 22 | 0 | 6 | 0 | 16 | 60 | 10 | 42 | 8 | 0 |
| Palo Alto | 3 | 0 | 0 | 0 | 3 | 43 | 16 | 24 | 3 | 0 |
| Plymouth | 3 | 0 | 2 | 0 | 1 | 21 | 4 | 11 | 6 | 0 |
| Pocahontas | 5 | 0 | 0 | 0 | 5 | 21 | 5 | 13 | 3 | 0 |
| Poweshiek | 16 | 0 | 5 | 0 | 11 | 42 | 9 | 22 | 11 | 1 |
| Sac | 13 | 0 | 3 | 0 | 10 | 35 | 14 | 20 | 1 | 0 |
| Sioux | 17 | 0 | 6 | 0 | 11 | 41 | 9 | 21 | 11 | 0 |
| Tama | 39 | 1 | 3 | 1 | 34 | 41 | 17 | 17 | 7 | 2 |
| Union | 8 | 0 | 0 | 0 | 8 | 44 | 13 | 24 | 7 | 1 |
| Van Buren | 6 | 0 | 0 | 0 | 6 | 26 | 10 | 14 | 2 | 1 |
| Wapello | 21 | 0 | 1 | 0 | 20 | 73 | 23 | 44 | 6 | 1 |
| Wayne | 9 | 0 | 1 | 0 | 8 | 28 | 9 | 14 | 5 | 1 |

## Table 10. Offenses Known to Law Enforcement, by Selected State Metropolitan and Nonmetropolitan Counties, 2021—Continued

(Number.)

| State/county | Violent crime | Murder and nonnegligent manslaughter | Rape | Robbery | Aggravated assault | Property crime | Burglary | Larceny-theft | Motor vehicle theft | Arson |
|---|---|---|---|---|---|---|---|---|---|---|
| Webster | 27 | 1 | 9 | 2 | 15 | 98 | 18 | 64 | 16 | 1 |
| Worth | 2 | 0 | 0 | 0 | 2 | 43 | 15 | 22 | 6 | 0 |
| Wright | 8 | 2 | 1 | 0 | 5 | 24 | 8 | 15 | 1 | 0 |
| **KANSAS** | | | | | | | | | | |
| **Metropolitan Counties** | | | | | | | | | | |
| Butler | 52 | 0 | 5 | 2 | 45 | 218 | 39 | 146 | 33 | 3 |
| Douglas | 50 | 0 | 0 | 1 | 49 | 85 | 16 | 59 | 10 | 1 |
| Geary | 8 | 1 | 3 | 1 | 3 | 28 | 6 | 20 | 2 | 0 |
| Harvey | 17 | 0 | 1 | 0 | 16 | 56 | 19 | 27 | 10 | 0 |
| Jackson | 19 | 0 | 3 | 1 | 15 | 84 | 8 | 67 | 9 | 1 |
| Jefferson | 39 | 0 | 3 | 1 | 35 | 273 | 106 | 139 | 28 | 7 |
| Johnson | 67 | 0 | 8 | 2 | 57 | 352 | 117 | 204 | 31 | 2 |
| Leavenworth | 38 | 1 | 0 | 2 | 35 | 148 | 54 | 66 | 28 | 8 |
| Linn | 7 | 1 | 1 | 0 | 5 | 82 | 7 | 67 | 8 | 0 |
| Miami | 33 | 0 | 1 | 2 | 30 | 122 | 21 | 80 | 21 | 2 |
| Osage | 21 | 0 | 1 | 0 | 20 | 75 | 49 | 25 | 1 | 0 |
| Pottawatomie | 37 | 0 | 10 | 0 | 27 | 158 | 37 | 104 | 17 | 2 |
| Riley County Police Department | 210 | 1 | 34 | 15 | 160 | 1,171 | 157 | 926 | 88 | 15 |
| Sedgwick | 60 | 1 | 3 | 2 | 54 | 236 | 43 | 136 | 57 | 3 |
| Shawnee | 83 | 2 | 5 | 4 | 72 | 589 | 129 | 396 | 64 | 4 |
| Sumner | 24 | 1 | 1 | 3 | 19 | 157 | 55 | 81 | 21 | 5 |
| **Nonmetropolitan Counties** | | | | | | | | | | |
| Allen | 12 | 0 | 0 | 0 | 12 | 40 | 11 | 20 | 9 | 2 |
| Anderson | 13 | 0 | 1 | 0 | 12 | 14 | 6 | 8 | 0 | 0 |
| Atchison | 5 | 0 | 1 | 0 | 4 | 61 | 17 | 38 | 6 | 0 |
| Barber | 3 | 0 | 0 | 0 | 3 | 19 | 4 | 14 | 1 | 0 |
| Barton | 29 | 0 | 8 | 1 | 20 | 101 | 57 | 36 | 8 | 1 |
| Bourbon | 18 | 0 | 2 | 0 | 16 | 59 | 22 | 30 | 7 | 2 |
| Brown | 4 | 0 | 2 | 0 | 2 | 94 | 75 | 15 | 4 | 1 |
| Cherokee | 28 | 0 | 1 | 2 | 25 | 171 | 54 | 84 | 33 | 0 |
| Cheyenne | 1 | 0 | 0 | 0 | 1 | 33 | 2 | 21 | 10 | 1 |
| Clark | 3 | 0 | 0 | 0 | 3 | 11 | 3 | 7 | 1 | 1 |
| Clay | 4 | 0 | 1 | 0 | 3 | 20 | 6 | 13 | 1 | 0 |
| Cowley | 21 | 0 | 1 | 1 | 19 | 130 | 44 | 69 | 17 | 2 |
| Crawford | 36 | 0 | 1 | 2 | 33 | 126 | 0 | 104 | 22 | 2 |
| Dickinson | 13 | 0 | 0 | 0 | 13 | 70 | 22 | 40 | 8 | 3 |
| Edwards | 7 | 0 | 1 | 0 | 6 | 13 | 3 | 8 | 2 | 0 |
| Ellis | 16 | 0 | 1 | 1 | 14 | 35 | 6 | 27 | 2 | 0 |
| Ellsworth | 6 | 0 | 1 | 0 | 5 | 40 | 4 | 31 | 5 | 1 |
| Finney | 40 | 0 | 5 | 1 | 34 | 173 | 56 | 91 | 26 | 3 |
| Ford | 6 | 0 | 0 | 1 | 5 | 59 | 36 | 20 | 3 | 0 |
| Franklin | 30 | 0 | 3 | 1 | 26 | 73 | 16 | 44 | 13 | 0 |
| Gove | 2 | 0 | 0 | 0 | 2 | 8 | 1 | 5 | 2 | 0 |
| Gray | 4 | 0 | 0 | 0 | 4 | 28 | 7 | 19 | 2 | 2 |
| Greeley | 6 | 0 | 1 | 0 | 5 | 4 | 2 | 2 | 0 | 0 |
| Greenwood | 10 | 0 | 2 | 0 | 8 | 84 | 21 | 58 | 5 | 0 |
| Hamilton | 6 | 0 | 1 | 0 | 5 | 27 | 5 | 17 | 5 | 0 |
| Harper | 1 | 0 | 0 | 0 | 1 | 28 | 9 | 14 | 5 | 1 |
| Haskell | 4 | 0 | 1 | 0 | 3 | 16 | 6 | 7 | 3 | 0 |
| Jewell | 3 | 0 | 0 | 1 | 2 | 9 | 3 | 2 | 4 | 1 |
| Kearny | 6 | 1 | 0 | 0 | 5 | 56 | 7 | 47 | 2 | 3 |
| Kingman | 4 | 0 | 2 | 0 | 2 | 47 | 15 | 28 | 4 | 0 |
| Labette | 5 | 0 | 0 | 0 | 5 | 88 | 42 | 32 | 14 | 0 |
| Lane | 2 | 0 | 1 | 0 | 1 | 6 | 3 | 1 | 2 | 0 |
| Logan | 3 | 0 | 0 | 0 | 3 | 11 | 0 | 11 | 0 | 0 |
| Lyon | 18 | 0 | 4 | 0 | 14 | 67 | 10 | 52 | 5 | 6 |
| Marion | 4 | 0 | 1 | 0 | 3 | 47 | 18 | 23 | 6 | 0 |
| Marshall | 4 | 0 | 0 | 0 | 4 | 20 | 2 | 16 | 2 | 2 |
| Mitchell | 4 | 0 | 1 | 0 | 3 | 20 | 11 | 8 | 1 | 0 |
| Montgomery | 17 | 0 | 2 | 1 | 14 | 141 | 70 | 61 | 10 | 0 |
| Morris | 14 | 0 | 1 | 0 | 13 | 19 | 1 | 16 | 2 | 0 |
| Morton | 3 | 0 | 0 | 0 | 3 | 9 | 6 | 3 | 0 | 0 |
| Nemaha | 4 | 0 | 0 | 0 | 4 | 15 | 4 | 10 | 1 | 1 |
| Neosho | 12 | 0 | 2 | 0 | 10 | 107 | 51 | 40 | 16 | 2 |
| Norton | 5 | 0 | 1 | 0 | 4 | 10 | 4 | 6 | 0 | 0 |
| Ottawa | 1 | 0 | 0 | 0 | 1 | 42 | 17 | 24 | 1 | 0 |
| Pawnee | 4 | 0 | 0 | 1 | 3 | 29 | 28 | 1 | 0 | 1 |
| Pratt | 5 | 0 | 0 | 0 | 5 | 15 | 8 | 6 | 1 | 0 |
| Republic | 11 | 0 | 0 | 2 | 9 | 29 | 7 | 19 | 3 | 0 |
| Rice | 4 | 0 | 2 | 0 | 2 | 39 | 10 | 19 | 10 | 0 |
| Rooks | 11 | 0 | 3 | 0 | 8 | 37 | 5 | 27 | 5 | 0 |
| Rush | 10 | 0 | 1 | 0 | 9 | 40 | 10 | 26 | 4 | 1 |
| Russell | 13 | 0 | 2 | 0 | 11 | 20 | 5 | 11 | 4 | 0 |
| Saline | 35 | 1 | 1 | 3 | 30 | 152 | 27 | 110 | 15 | 3 |
| Seward | 9 | 0 | 2 | 0 | 7 | 11 | 1 | 10 | 0 | 1 |
| Sheridan | 1 | 0 | 1 | 0 | 0 | 6 | 2 | 4 | 0 | 0 |
| Thomas | 1 | 0 | 0 | 0 | 1 | 28 | 10 | 14 | 4 | 0 |
| Trego | 4 | 0 | 0 | 1 | 3 | 6 | 2 | 4 | 0 | 0 |
| Washington | 7 | 1 | 2 | 0 | 4 | 16 | 4 | 10 | 2 | 1 |
| Woodson | 2 | 0 | 0 | 0 | 2 | 38 | 11 | 25 | 2 | 1 |

## Table 10. Offenses Known to Law Enforcement, by Selected State Metropolitan and Nonmetropolitan Counties, 2021—Continued

(Number.)

| State/county | Violent crime | Murder and nonnegligent manslaughter | Rape | Robbery | Aggravated assault | Property crime | Burglary | Larceny-theft | Motor vehicle theft | Arson |
|---|---|---|---|---|---|---|---|---|---|---|
| **KENTUCKY** | | | | | | | | | | |
| **Metropolitan Counties** | | | | | | | | | | |
| Allen | 10 | 0 | 2 | 2 | 6 | 95 | 31 | 40 | 24 | 1 |
| Boone | 69 | 2 | 27 | 4 | 36 | 652 | 80 | 468 | 104 | 3 |
| Bourbon | 8 | 0 | 4 | 0 | 4 | 79 | 19 | 48 | 12 | 0 |
| Boyd | 17 | 0 | 1 | 2 | 14 | 190 | 67 | 85 | 38 | 2 |
| Bracken | 4 | 0 | 0 | 0 | 4 | 23 | 6 | 13 | 4 | 0 |
| Bullitt | 24 | 2 | 8 | 3 | 11 | 269 | 62 | 144 | 63 | 3 |
| Butler | 7 | 0 | 1 | 1 | 5 | 32 | 11 | 14 | 7 | 2 |
| Campbell | 0 | 0 | 0 | 0 | 0 | 0 | 0 | 0 | 0 | 0 |
| Campbell County Police Department | 8 | 0 | 3 | 0 | 5 | 81 | 15 | 48 | 18 | 0 |
| Carter | 5 | 0 | 0 | 1 | 4 | 32 | 8 | 17 | 7 | 0 |
| Christian | 28 | 2 | 7 | 1 | 18 | 229 | 77 | 123 | 29 | 1 |
| Clark | 7 | 0 | 3 | 0 | 4 | 161 | 34 | 110 | 17 | 0 |
| Daviess | 34 | 1 | 9 | 3 | 21 | 372 | 66 | 257 | 49 | 2 |
| Edmonson | 7 | 0 | 0 | 0 | 7 | 19 | 4 | 5 | 10 | 0 |
| Fayette | 0 | 0 | 0 | 0 | 0 | 1 | 1 | 0 | 0 | 0 |
| Gallatin | 3 | 0 | 0 | 0 | 3 | 11 | 2 | 8 | 1 | 0 |
| Grant | 9 | 0 | 3 | 2 | 4 | 92 | 21 | 54 | 17 | 1 |
| Greenup | 1 | 0 | 0 | 0 | 1 | 41 | 12 | 17 | 12 | 0 |
| Hancock | 2 | 0 | 1 | 0 | 1 | 27 | 4 | 14 | 9 | 0 |
| Hardin | 27 | 0 | 4 | 3 | 20 | 130 | 39 | 71 | 20 | 2 |
| Henderson | 15 | 0 | 5 | 1 | 9 | 126 | 49 | 62 | 15 | 1 |
| Henry | 1 | 0 | 1 | 0 | 0 | 29 | 9 | 16 | 4 | 2 |
| Jefferson | 0 | 0 | 0 | 0 | 0 | 5 | 0 | 2 | 3 | 0 |
| Jessamine | 15 | 0 | 6 | 5 | 4 | 203 | 37 | 142 | 24 | 4 |
| Kenton | 0 | 0 | 0 | 0 | 0 | 0 | 0 | 0 | 0 | 0 |
| Kenton County Police Department | 20 | 1 | 3 | 0 | 16 | 79 | 16 | 50 | 13 | 2 |
| Larue | 7 | 0 | 0 | 0 | 7 | 21 | 6 | 9 | 6 | 0 |
| McLean | 2 | 0 | 0 | 0 | 2 | 33 | 10 | 16 | 7 | 0 |
| Meade | 12 | 1 | 2 | 0 | 9 | 73 | 12 | 34 | 27 | 1 |
| Oldham | 2 | 0 | 0 | 0 | 2 | 7 | 1 | 6 | 0 | 0 |
| Oldham County Police Department | 26 | 1 | 5 | 5 | 15 | 364 | 52 | 271 | 41 | 2 |
| Pendleton | 2 | 0 | 0 | 0 | 2 | 40 | 12 | 20 | 8 | 1 |
| Scott | 16 | 0 | 4 | 5 | 7 | 113 | 12 | 80 | 21 | 0 |
| Shelby | 19 | 0 | 5 | 5 | 9 | 220 | 42 | 146 | 32 | 0 |
| Spencer | 5 | 0 | 2 | 0 | 3 | 46 | 13 | 25 | 8 | 0 |
| Trigg | 6 | 0 | 3 | 0 | 3 | 58 | 23 | 29 | 6 | 0 |
| Warren | 49 | 0 | 9 | 6 | 34 | 603 | 168 | 331 | 104 | 12 |
| Woodford | 0 | 0 | 0 | 0 | 0 | 12 | 2 | 9 | 1 | 0 |
| **Nonmetropolitan Counties** | | | | | | | | | | |
| Adair | 2 | 0 | 0 | 0 | 2 | 16 | 5 | 7 | 4 | 0 |
| Anderson | 5 | 0 | 1 | 0 | 4 | 31 | 7 | 17 | 7 | 0 |
| Ballard | 9 | 0 | 2 | 0 | 7 | 59 | 21 | 30 | 8 | 0 |
| Barren | 16 | 0 | 2 | 1 | 13 | 156 | 50 | 75 | 31 | 1 |
| Bath | 9 | 0 | 0 | 0 | 9 | 36 | 12 | 17 | 7 | 0 |
| Bell | 10 | 0 | 1 | 0 | 9 | 57 | 17 | 29 | 11 | 1 |
| Boyle | 1 | 0 | 0 | 0 | 1 | 9 | 3 | 4 | 2 | 0 |
| Breathitt | 2 | 1 | 0 | 0 | 1 | 20 | 7 | 12 | 1 | 0 |
| Breckinridge | 11 | 1 | 3 | 0 | 7 | 54 | 6 | 24 | 24 | 0 |
| Caldwell | 5 | 0 | 0 | 1 | 4 | 45 | 20 | 20 | 5 | 0 |
| Calloway | 5 | 1 | 1 | 0 | 3 | 182 | 58 | 105 | 19 | 3 |
| Carlisle | 2 | 0 | 1 | 0 | 1 | 5 | 2 | 3 | 0 | 0 |
| Carroll | 4 | 0 | 1 | 0 | 3 | 45 | 6 | 22 | 17 | 0 |
| Casey | 4 | 0 | 1 | 1 | 2 | 26 | 17 | 5 | 4 | 0 |
| Clay | 6 | 0 | 0 | 0 | 6 | 87 | 21 | 42 | 24 | 1 |
| Clinton | 2 | 0 | 0 | 1 | 1 | 9 | 2 | 3 | 4 | 0 |
| Crittenden | 2 | 0 | 1 | 0 | 1 | 27 | 14 | 8 | 5 | 0 |
| Cumberland | 1 | 0 | 0 | 0 | 1 | 17 | 5 | 7 | 5 | 0 |
| Elliott | 0 | 0 | 0 | 0 | 0 | 8 | 3 | 4 | 1 | 0 |
| Estill | 7 | 0 | 0 | 0 | 7 | 42 | 13 | 22 | 7 | 0 |
| Fleming | 4 | 0 | 0 | 0 | 4 | 18 | 2 | 6 | 10 | 0 |
| Floyd | 2 | 0 | 0 | 0 | 2 | 53 | 11 | 17 | 25 | 1 |
| Franklin | 19 | 1 | 2 | 1 | 15 | 195 | 40 | 110 | 45 | 0 |
| Fulton | 1 | 0 | 1 | 0 | 0 | 0 | 0 | 0 | 0 | 0 |
| Garrard | 0 | 0 | 0 | 0 | 0 | 0 | 0 | 0 | 0 | 0 |
| Garrard County Police Department | 4 | 0 | 1 | 0 | 3 | 42 | 11 | 23 | 8 | 0 |
| Graves | 17 | 0 | 6 | 2 | 9 | 188 | 69 | 97 | 22 | 0 |
| Grayson | 9 | 0 | 1 | 1 | 7 | 74 | 21 | 40 | 13 | 1 |
| Green | 1 | 0 | 1 | 0 | 0 | 8 | 2 | 3 | 3 | 1 |
| Harlan | 4 | 0 | 0 | 0 | 4 | 42 | 12 | 24 | 6 | 2 |
| Harrison | 2 | 0 | 0 | 0 | 2 | 44 | 13 | 21 | 10 | 0 |
| Hart | 6 | 0 | 0 | 0 | 6 | 42 | 12 | 22 | 8 | 1 |
| Hickman | 1 | 0 | 1 | 0 | 0 | 10 | 5 | 3 | 2 | 0 |
| Hopkins | 26 | 1 | 10 | 5 | 10 | 201 | 46 | 132 | 23 | 1 |
| Jackson | 6 | 0 | 0 | 0 | 6 | 56 | 20 | 23 | 13 | 1 |
| Johnson | 6 | 1 | 1 | 0 | 4 | 42 | 13 | 16 | 13 | 0 |
| Knott | 2 | 0 | 1 | 0 | 1 | 24 | 4 | 10 | 10 | 0 |
| Knox | 7 | 0 | 0 | 0 | 7 | 69 | 20 | 22 | 27 | 1 |
| Laurel | 43 | 2 | 9 | 4 | 28 | 425 | 57 | 228 | 140 | 3 |

## Table 10. Offenses Known to Law Enforcement, by Selected State Metropolitan and Nonmetropolitan Counties, 2021—Continued

(Number.)

| State/county | Violent crime | Murder and nonnegligent manslaughter | Rape | Robbery | Aggravated assault | Property crime | Burglary | Larceny-theft | Motor vehicle theft | Arson |
|---|---|---|---|---|---|---|---|---|---|---|
| Lawrence | 4 | 0 | 1 | 1 | 2 | 52 | 14 | 20 | 18 | 0 |
| Lee | 0 | 0 | 0 | 0 | 0 | 22 | 2 | 9 | 11 | 1 |
| Leslie | 2 | 0 | 0 | 0 | 2 | 19 | 5 | 8 | 6 | 2 |
| Letcher | 3 | 0 | 0 | 0 | 3 | 7 | 0 | 2 | 5 | 0 |
| Lewis | 0 | 0 | 0 | 0 | 0 | 23 | 6 | 7 | 10 | 0 |
| Lincoln | 3 | 0 | 1 | 0 | 2 | 84 | 46 | 25 | 13 | 0 |
| Livingston | 2 | 0 | 0 | 1 | 1 | 54 | 28 | 17 | 9 | 0 |
| Logan | 14 | 0 | 3 | 0 | 11 | 67 | 19 | 33 | 15 | 1 |
| Lyon | 5 | 1 | 0 | 0 | 4 | 32 | 13 | 18 | 1 | 0 |
| Madison | 21 | 0 | 5 | 0 | 16 | 220 | 54 | 122 | 44 | 0 |
| Magoffin | 1 | 0 | 0 | 0 | 1 | 18 | 2 | 9 | 7 | 1 |
| Marion | 5 | 0 | 0 | 0 | 5 | 37 | 8 | 25 | 4 | 0 |
| Marshall | 24 | 0 | 8 | 1 | 15 | 230 | 60 | 141 | 29 | 1 |
| Martin | 4 | 0 | 0 | 1 | 3 | 9 | 0 | 5 | 4 | 0 |
| Mason | 4 | 0 | 0 | 0 | 4 | 73 | 18 | 40 | 15 | 0 |
| McCracken | 34 | 1 | 13 | 9 | 11 | 310 | 93 | 189 | 28 | 1 |
| McCreary | 2 | 0 | 0 | 0 | 2 | 50 | 12 | 21 | 17 | 1 |
| Menifee | 2 | 0 | 0 | 0 | 2 | 10 | 3 | 1 | 6 | 0 |
| Mercer | 4 | 1 | 0 | 0 | 3 | 19 | 8 | 9 | 2 | 1 |
| Metcalfe | 4 | 0 | 0 | 1 | 3 | 21 | 12 | 8 | 1 | 1 |
| Monroe | 2 | 0 | 0 | 0 | 2 | 19 | 6 | 6 | 7 | 1 |
| Montgomery | 14 | 0 | 5 | 2 | 7 | 201 | 41 | 130 | 30 | 0 |
| Morgan | 3 | 0 | 0 | 1 | 2 | 41 | 9 | 24 | 8 | 0 |
| Muhlenberg | 14 | 0 | 0 | 1 | 13 | 63 | 27 | 27 | 9 | 0 |
| Nelson | 26 | 2 | 2 | 0 | 22 | 188 | 50 | 114 | 24 | 0 |
| Nicholas | 0 | 0 | 0 | 0 | 0 | 6 | 3 | 2 | 1 | 1 |
| Ohio | 12 | 0 | 6 | 0 | 6 | 107 | 47 | 42 | 18 | 2 |
| Owen | 2 | 0 | 0 | 0 | 2 | 31 | 13 | 15 | 3 | 0 |
| Owsley | 0 | 0 | 0 | 0 | 0 | 1 | 1 | 0 | 0 | 0 |
| Perry | 13 | 0 | 2 | 0 | 11 | 41 | 10 | 11 | 20 | 2 |
| Pike | 1 | 0 | 0 | 0 | 1 | 38 | 10 | 19 | 9 | 0 |
| Powell | 0 | 0 | 0 | 0 | 0 | 4 | 1 | 1 | 2 | 0 |
| Pulaski | 16 | 1 | 2 | 2 | 11 | 285 | 125 | 100 | 60 | 5 |
| Robertson | 0 | 0 | 0 | 0 | 0 | 4 | 3 | 1 | 0 | 0 |
| Rockcastle | 3 | 0 | 2 | 0 | 1 | 46 | 16 | 15 | 15 | 0 |
| Rowan | 8 | 0 | 0 | 0 | 8 | 45 | 8 | 31 | 6 | 0 |
| Russell | 0 | 0 | 0 | 0 | 0 | 10 | 3 | 6 | 1 | 0 |
| Simpson | 8 | 0 | 4 | 0 | 4 | 35 | 9 | 12 | 14 | 1 |
| Taylor | 10 | 0 | 5 | 1 | 4 | 179 | 79 | 83 | 17 | 1 |
| Todd | 6 | 0 | 1 | 0 | 5 | 41 | 22 | 17 | 2 | 0 |
| Trimble | 1 | 0 | 0 | 0 | 1 | 23 | 4 | 15 | 4 | 1 |
| Union | 3 | 0 | 2 | 1 | 0 | 55 | 20 | 24 | 11 | 1 |
| Washington | 1 | 1 | 0 | 0 | 0 | 11 | 3 | 5 | 3 | 0 |
| Wayne | 6 | 0 | 1 | 0 | 5 | 34 | 10 | 14 | 10 | 1 |
| Webster | 2 | 0 | 0 | 0 | 2 | 31 | 7 | 15 | 9 | 0 |
| Whitley | 13 | 0 | 0 | 2 | 11 | 143 | 53 | 66 | 24 | 0 |
| Wolfe | 6 | 0 | 2 | 0 | 4 | 19 | 6 | 7 | 6 | 0 |
| **LOUISIANA** | | | | | | | | | | |
| **Metropolitan Counties** | | | | | | | | | | |
| Acadia | 0 | 0 | 0 | 0 | 0 | 0 | 0 | 0 | 0 | 0 |
| Ascension | 402 | 7 | 24 | 18 | 353 | 1,915 | 289 | 1,418 | 208 | 6 |
| Bossier | 149 | 1 | 16 | 3 | 129 | 506 | 102 | 354 | 50 | 2 |
| Caddo | 54 | 0 | 1 | 2 | 51 | 632 | 153 | 420 | 59 | 3 |
| Calcasieu | 909 | 5 | 69 | 23 | 812 | 4,069 | 748 | 2,929 | 392 | 6 |
| East Baton Rouge | 652 | 11 | 17 | 55 | 569 | 5,002 | 744 | 3,824 | 434 | 3 |
| Grant | 64 | 8 | 5 | 3 | 48 | 245 | 72 | 148 | 25 | 1 |
| Iberville | 118 | 3 | 2 | 2 | 111 | 204 | 40 | 152 | 12 | 22 |
| Jefferson | 1,263 | 46 | 54 | 165 | 998 | 7,405 | 1,126 | 5,518 | 761 | 29 |
| Lafayette | 180 | 2 | 17 | 17 | 144 | 628 | 156 | 383 | 89 | 0 |
| Lafourche | 224 | 9 | 11 | 4 | 200 | 1,490 | 273 | 1,127 | 90 | 5 |
| Livingston | 504 | 1 | 71 | 20 | 412 | 2,062 | 513 | 1,329 | 220 | 7 |
| Morehouse | 28 | 2 | 2 | 0 | 24 | 111 | 21 | 82 | 8 | 0 |
| Ouachita | 741 | 4 | 39 | 37 | 661 | 2,343 | 582 | 1,514 | 247 | 10 |
| Plaquemines | 68 | 0 | 0 | 0 | 68 | 141 | 38 | 90 | 13 | 2 |
| Pointe Coupee | 81 | 3 | 7 | 1 | 70 | 208 | 40 | 139 | 29 | 2 |
| Rapides | 381 | 6 | 30 | 8 | 337 | 1,609 | 652 | 807 | 150 | 9 |
| St. Bernard | 108 | 1 | 3 | 7 | 97 | 482 | 82 | 350 | 50 | 1 |
| St. Charles | 150 | 6 | 12 | 19 | 113 | 633 | 138 | 439 | 56 | 8 |
| St. Helena | 42 | 2 | 1 | 0 | 39 | 68 | 13 | 46 | 9 | 0 |
| St. James | 107 | 5 | 0 | 2 | 100 | 292 | 62 | 202 | 28 | 3 |
| St. John the Baptist | 121 | 6 | 0 | 4 | 111 | 777 | 225 | 486 | 66 | 0 |
| St. Martin | 200 | 11 | 11 | 5 | 173 | 696 | 185 | 404 | 107 | 3 |
| Tangipahoa | 819 | 16 | 27 | 37 | 739 | 1,423 | 358 | 853 | 212 | 16 |
| Terrebonne | 284 | 8 | 3 | 11 | 262 | 1,962 | 438 | 1,379 | 145 | 10 |
| Vermilion | 99 | 2 | 7 | 5 | 85 | 503 | 223 | 241 | 39 | 5 |
| West Baton Rouge | 39 | 1 | 0 | 4 | 34 | 455 | 60 | 347 | 48 | 1 |
| West Feliciana | 53 | 0 | 6 | 1 | 46 | 16 | 10 | 2 | 4 | 1 |
| **Nonmetropolitan Counties** | | | | | | | | | | |
| Beauregard | 46 | 0 | 7 | 0 | 39 | 128 | 23 | 83 | 22 | 4 |

## Table 10. Offenses Known to Law Enforcement, by Selected State Metropolitan and Nonmetropolitan Counties, 2021—Continued

(Number.)

| State/county | Violent crime | Murder and nonnegligent manslaughter | Rape | Robbery | Aggravated assault | Property crime | Burglary | Larceny-theft | Motor vehicle theft | Arson |
|---|---|---|---|---|---|---|---|---|---|---|
| Bienville | 40 | 1 | 3 | 2 | 34 | 169 | 46 | 102 | 21 | 0 |
| Caldwell | 0 | 0 | 0 | 0 | 0 | 0 | 0 | 0 | 0 | 0 |
| Catahoula | 21 | 1 | 2 | 1 | 17 | 93 | 18 | 60 | 15 | 1 |
| Claiborne | 20 | 0 | 3 | 1 | 16 | 60 | 12 | 40 | 8 | 0 |
| Concordia | 41 | 2 | 3 | 2 | 34 | 65 | 22 | 33 | 10 | 0 |
| East Carroll | 25 | 4 | 0 | 0 | 21 | 28 | 7 | 18 | 3 | 0 |
| Franklin | 88 | 5 | 5 | 2 | 76 | 201 | 40 | 140 | 21 | 1 |
| Jackson | 15 | 0 | 4 | 0 | 11 | 93 | 12 | 62 | 19 | 1 |
| Lincoln | 63 | 3 | 2 | 1 | 57 | 222 | 66 | 140 | 16 | 0 |
| Richland | 59 | 0 | 0 | 1 | 58 | 77 | 12 | 56 | 9 | 1 |
| St. Landry | 172 | 13 | 3 | 9 | 147 | 641 | 165 | 415 | 61 | 3 |
| St. Mary | 138 | 6 | 11 | 4 | 117 | 410 | 105 | 268 | 37 | 3 |
| Tensas | 0 | 0 | 0 | 0 | 0 | 1 | 1 | 0 | 0 | 0 |
| Washington | 163 | 6 | 18 | 1 | 138 | 370 | 91 | 205 | 74 | 5 |
| Webster | 25 | 0 | 1 | 2 | 22 | 159 | 26 | 110 | 23 | 0 |
| West Carroll | 6 | 1 | 3 | 1 | 1 | 20 | 3 | 13 | 4 | 0 |
| Winn | 34 | 1 | 3 | 1 | 29 | 40 | 11 | 20 | 9 | 0 |
| **MAINE** | | | | | | | | | | |
| **Metropolitan Counties** | | | | | | | | | | |
| Androscoggin | 20 | 0 | 13 | 1 | 6 | 128 | 22 | 100 | 6 | 0 |
| Cumberland | 31 | 0 | 15 | 1 | 15 | 287 | 58 | 212 | 17 | 1 |
| Penobscot | 15 | 0 | 0 | 0 | 15 | 349 | 66 | 249 | 34 | 1 |
| Sagadahoc | 8 | 0 | 0 | 1 | 7 | 46 | 8 | 35 | 3 | 1 |
| York | 40 | 0 | 28 | 4 | 8 | 266 | 47 | 212 | 7 | 0 |
| **Nonmetropolitan Counties** | | | | | | | | | | |
| Aroostook | 7 | 0 | 2 | 0 | 5 | 139 | 43 | 91 | 5 | 0 |
| Franklin | 19 | 0 | 6 | 0 | 13 | 76 | 15 | 58 | 3 | 0 |
| Hancock | 17 | 0 | 8 | 0 | 9 | 92 | 9 | 78 | 5 | 0 |
| Kennebec | 26 | 0 | 12 | 1 | 13 | 294 | 105 | 166 | 23 | 1 |
| Knox | 4 | 0 | 0 | 0 | 4 | 110 | 9 | 97 | 4 | 0 |
| Lincoln | 27 | 0 | 16 | 0 | 11 | 79 | 20 | 50 | 9 | 0 |
| Oxford | 35 | 0 | 23 | 0 | 12 | 228 | 42 | 176 | 10 | 0 |
| Piscataquis | 2 | 0 | 0 | 0 | 2 | 74 | 8 | 58 | 8 | 0 |
| Somerset | 37 | 0 | 16 | 4 | 17 | 291 | 41 | 220 | 30 | 1 |
| Waldo | 6 | 0 | 3 | 0 | 3 | 101 | 18 | 75 | 8 | 0 |
| Washington | 20 | 0 | 4 | 2 | 14 | 78 | 15 | 50 | 13 | 1 |
| **MARYLAND[1]** | | | | | | | | | | |
| **Metropolitan Counties** | | | | | | | | | | |
| Allegany | 17 | 0 | 8 | 0 | 9 | 80 | 16 | 60 | 4 | 0 |
| Baltimore County Police Department | 3,333 | 52 | 371 | 705 | 2,205 | 14,059 | 1,462 | 11,454 | 1,143 | 127 |
| Montgomery County Police Department | 1,630 | 30 | 309 | 432 | 859 | 13,151 | 1,076 | 10,737 | 1,338 | 14 |
| St. Mary's | 285 | 3 | 27 | 25 | 230 | 1,162 | 202 | 893 | 67 | 16 |
| **Nonmetropolitan Counties** | | | | | | | | | | |
| Garrett | 15 | 1 | 3 | 0 | 11 | 122 | 43 | 59 | 20 | 1 |
| Talbot | 26 | 0 | 11 | 0 | 15 | 97 | 29 | 63 | 5 | 3 |
| **MICHIGAN** | | | | | | | | | | |
| **Metropolitan Counties** | | | | | | | | | | |
| Bay | 46 | 0 | 19 | 3 | 24 | 432 | 59 | 338 | 35 | 5 |
| Berrien | 174 | 0 | 44 | 7 | 123 | 709 | 123 | 505 | 81 | 3 |
| Calhoun | 123 | 1 | 15 | 6 | 101 | 567 | 117 | 396 | 54 | 5 |
| Cass | 54 | 0 | 10 | 2 | 42 | 322 | 74 | 205 | 43 | 2 |
| Clinton | 21 | 1 | 2 | 2 | 16 | 139 | 18 | 113 | 8 | 1 |
| Eaton | 165 | 7 | 26 | 10 | 122 | 751 | 79 | 600 | 72 | 1 |
| Genesee | 95 | 2 | 23 | 2 | 68 | 351 | 35 | 243 | 73 | 2 |
| Ingham | 173 | 1 | 28 | 15 | 129 | 558 | 85 | 402 | 71 | 3 |
| Ionia | 4 | 0 | 1 | 0 | 3 | 10 | 0 | 8 | 2 | 0 |
| Jackson | 304 | 5 | 29 | 3 | 267 | 386 | 60 | 280 | 46 | 4 |
| Kalamazoo | 371 | 7 | 51 | 33 | 280 | 2,333 | 287 | 1,640 | 406 | 14 |
| Kent | 458 | 4 | 121 | 44 | 289 | 2,770 | 392 | 2,078 | 300 | 12 |
| Lapeer | 54 | 0 | 27 | 0 | 27 | 152 | 37 | 100 | 15 | 3 |
| Livingston | 71 | 1 | 27 | 1 | 42 | 359 | 66 | 280 | 13 | 5 |
| Macomb | 345 | 1 | 58 | 18 | 268 | 772 | 98 | 526 | 148 | 4 |
| Midland | 77 | 0 | 25 | 0 | 52 | 277 | 51 | 205 | 21 | 2 |
| Montcalm | 56 | 0 | 12 | 0 | 44 | 237 | 37 | 183 | 17 | 3 |
| Muskegon | 15 | 0 | 6 | 1 | 8 | 53 | 6 | 45 | 2 | 0 |
| Oakland | 16 | 1 | 3 | 1 | 11 | 31 | 5 | 17 | 9 | 2 |
| Ottawa | 589 | 1 | 213 | 15 | 360 | 1,847 | 354 | 1,356 | 137 | 12 |
| Saginaw | 126 | 5 | 18 | 9 | 94 | 353 | 28 | 295 | 30 | 0 |
| Shiawassee | 19 | 0 | 2 | 1 | 16 | 124 | 28 | 86 | 10 | 0 |
| St. Clair | 157 | 0 | 28 | 3 | 126 | 497 | 85 | 360 | 52 | 5 |
| Washtenaw | 665 | 8 | 61 | 42 | 554 | 1,247 | 234 | 791 | 222 | 11 |
| Wayne | 11 | 0 | 6 | 0 | 5 | 1 | 0 | 1 | 0 | 0 |
| **Nonmetropolitan Counties** | | | | | | | | | | |
| Alcona | 11 | 0 | 1 | 1 | 9 | 66 | 10 | 48 | 8 | 0 |
| Alger | 3 | 0 | 0 | 0 | 3 | 7 | 1 | 6 | 0 | 0 |

# Table 10. Offenses Known to Law Enforcement, by Selected State Metropolitan and Nonmetropolitan Counties, 2021—Continued

(Number.)

| State/county | Violent crime | Murder and nonnegligent manslaughter | Rape | Robbery | Aggravated assault | Property crime | Burglary | Larceny-theft | Motor vehicle theft | Arson |
|---|---|---|---|---|---|---|---|---|---|---|
| Allegan | 91 | 0 | 13 | 2 | 76 | 573 | 117 | 380 | 76 | 3 |
| Alpena | 4 | 0 | 4 | 0 | 0 | 27 | 1 | 25 | 1 | 0 |
| Antrim | 26 | 0 | 10 | 0 | 16 | 90 | 17 | 66 | 7 | 0 |
| Arenac | 32 | 1 | 3 | 0 | 28 | 80 | 31 | 43 | 6 | 0 |
| Baraga | 3 | 0 | 0 | 0 | 3 | 4 | 3 | 1 | 0 | 0 |
| Barry | 76 | 1 | 43 | 2 | 30 | 315 | 59 | 215 | 41 | 5 |
| Benzie | 16 | 0 | 8 | 0 | 8 | 46 | 6 | 38 | 2 | 1 |
| Branch | 25 | 0 | 10 | 0 | 15 | 161 | 56 | 89 | 16 | 2 |
| Charlevoix | 18 | 0 | 6 | 0 | 12 | 60 | 7 | 49 | 4 | 1 |
| Cheboygan | 19 | 0 | 3 | 0 | 16 | 26 | 2 | 21 | 3 | 0 |
| Chippewa | 6 | 0 | 1 | 0 | 5 | 6 | 1 | 5 | 0 | 0 |
| Clare | 76 | 5 | 13 | 0 | 58 | 387 | 178 | 177 | 32 | 6 |
| Crawford | 35 | 0 | 9 | 1 | 25 | 62 | 11 | 44 | 7 | 2 |
| Delta | 15 | 0 | 4 | 0 | 11 | 38 | 4 | 31 | 3 | 0 |
| Emmet | 42 | 0 | 7 | 0 | 35 | 69 | 12 | 51 | 6 | 4 |
| Gladwin | 44 | 0 | 2 | 1 | 41 | 129 | 40 | 77 | 12 | 4 |
| Gogebic | 11 | 1 | 2 | 0 | 8 | 18 | 2 | 14 | 2 | 0 |
| Grand Traverse | 191 | 1 | 49 | 1 | 140 | 399 | 33 | 346 | 20 | 6 |
| Gratiot | 31 | 1 | 10 | 1 | 19 | 228 | 17 | 198 | 13 | 2 |
| Hillsdale | 61 | 0 | 16 | 0 | 45 | 136 | 27 | 91 | 18 | 1 |
| Houghton | 15 | 0 | 4 | 1 | 10 | 53 | 7 | 41 | 5 | 0 |
| Huron | 28 | 0 | 7 | 1 | 20 | 76 | 9 | 61 | 6 | 0 |
| Iosco | 0 | 0 | 0 | 0 | 0 | 0 | 0 | 0 | 0 | 0 |
| Isabella | 54 | 0 | 20 | 2 | 32 | 333 | 35 | 265 | 33 | 2 |
| Kalkaska | 31 | 0 | 2 | 1 | 28 | 85 | 10 | 69 | 6 | 1 |
| Keweenaw | 0 | 0 | 0 | 0 | 0 | 14 | 3 | 11 | 0 | 0 |
| Leelanau | 24 | 0 | 5 | 0 | 19 | 50 | 10 | 37 | 3 | 3 |
| Lenawee | 65 | 1 | 20 | 1 | 43 | 184 | 45 | 121 | 18 | 3 |
| Luce | 12 | 0 | 1 | 0 | 11 | 55 | 10 | 42 | 3 | 1 |
| Mackinac | 15 | 0 | 6 | 0 | 9 | 93 | 28 | 61 | 4 | 0 |
| Manistee | 16 | 0 | 8 | 0 | 8 | 138 | 14 | 119 | 5 | 1 |
| Marquette | 34 | 0 | 8 | 0 | 26 | 122 | 8 | 107 | 7 | 0 |
| Mason | 31 | 0 | 8 | 0 | 23 | 104 | 19 | 72 | 13 | 0 |
| Mecosta | 13 | 0 | 1 | 0 | 12 | 43 | 9 | 28 | 6 | 1 |
| Missaukee | 32 | 0 | 11 | 0 | 21 | 112 | 31 | 72 | 9 | 0 |
| Montmorency | 6 | 0 | 1 | 0 | 5 | 12 | 6 | 5 | 1 | 0 |
| Newaygo | 11 | 0 | 5 | 0 | 6 | 43 | 11 | 24 | 8 | 0 |
| Oceana | 62 | 0 | 11 | 0 | 51 | 184 | 38 | 128 | 18 | 1 |
| Ogemaw | 7 | 0 | 2 | 0 | 5 | 84 | 10 | 69 | 5 | 0 |
| Ontonagon | 7 | 0 | 1 | 0 | 6 | 17 | 2 | 14 | 1 | 0 |
| Oscoda | 12 | 0 | 3 | 0 | 9 | 51 | 9 | 25 | 17 | 0 |
| Otsego | 7 | 0 | 3 | 0 | 4 | 15 | 2 | 11 | 2 | 0 |
| Presque Isle | 5 | 0 | 1 | 0 | 4 | 15 | 3 | 10 | 2 | 0 |
| Sanilac | 25 | 1 | 13 | 0 | 11 | 76 | 16 | 46 | 14 | 4 |
| Schoolcraft | 0 | 0 | 0 | 0 | 0 | 1 | 0 | 1 | 0 | 0 |
| St. Joseph | 81 | 1 | 10 | 1 | 69 | 278 | 73 | 161 | 44 | 3 |
| Tuscola | 54 | 0 | 22 | 1 | 31 | 121 | 31 | 75 | 15 | 3 |
| Van Buren | 102 | 2 | 18 | 2 | 80 | 323 | 91 | 210 | 22 | 4 |
| Wexford | 3 | 0 | 0 | 1 | 2 | 51 | 17 | 31 | 3 | 0 |
| **MINNESOTA** | | | | | | | | | | |
| **Metropolitan Counties** | | | | | | | | | | |
| Anoka | 55 | 0 | 14 | 2 | 39 | 659 | 84 | 505 | 70 | 5 |
| Benton | 10 | 0 | 2 | 0 | 8 | 120 | 34 | 69 | 17 | 0 |
| Blue Earth | 30 | 0 | 6 | 0 | 24 | 128 | 40 | 77 | 11 | 0 |
| Carlton | 23 | 1 | 5 | 0 | 17 | 168 | 45 | 117 | 6 | 0 |
| Carver | 40 | 1 | 15 | 2 | 22 | 610 | 72 | 508 | 30 | 7 |
| Chisago | 43 | 1 | 12 | 0 | 30 | 264 | 118 | 120 | 26 | 2 |
| Clay | 14 | 0 | 4 | 2 | 8 | 75 | 33 | 31 | 11 | 1 |
| Dakota | 14 | 0 | 1 | 0 | 13 | 33 | 24 | 6 | 3 | 0 |
| Dodge | 13 | 0 | 1 | 0 | 12 | 124 | 33 | 83 | 8 | 0 |
| Fillmore | 4 | 0 | 1 | 0 | 3 | 94 | 21 | 70 | 3 | 0 |
| Hennepin | 36 | 0 | 1 | 0 | 35 | 31 | 1 | 29 | 1 | 0 |
| Houston | 4 | 0 | 0 | 0 | 4 | 30 | 7 | 18 | 5 | 0 |
| Isanti | 28 | 1 | 4 | 0 | 23 | 207 | 42 | 136 | 29 | 1 |
| Lake | 5 | 0 | 3 | 0 | 2 | 22 | 1 | 18 | 3 | 0 |
| Le Sueur | 3 | 1 | 0 | 0 | 2 | 114 | 37 | 69 | 8 | 2 |
| Mille Lacs | 47 | 0 | 5 | 0 | 42 | 288 | 61 | 188 | 39 | 8 |
| Nicollet | 6 | 0 | 4 | 0 | 2 | 67 | 6 | 52 | 9 | 1 |
| Olmsted | 55 | 0 | 10 | 1 | 44 | 274 | 49 | 198 | 27 | 3 |
| Polk | 18 | 0 | 6 | 0 | 12 | 104 | 15 | 79 | 10 | 0 |
| Ramsey | 215 | 0 | 27 | 22 | 166 | 1,622 | 169 | 1,268 | 185 | 2 |
| Scott | 8 | 0 | 3 | 0 | 5 | 180 | 15 | 156 | 9 | 1 |
| Sherburne | 28 | 0 | 9 | 0 | 19 | 263 | 29 | 213 | 21 | 1 |
| Stearns | 45 | 0 | 14 | 1 | 30 | 244 | 58 | 155 | 31 | 1 |
| St. Louis | 83 | 2 | 24 | 2 | 55 | 591 | 183 | 335 | 73 | 3 |
| Wabasha | 3 | 1 | 0 | 0 | 2 | 29 | 6 | 22 | 1 | 0 |
| Washington | 85 | 1 | 24 | 5 | 55 | 786 | 132 | 575 | 79 | 6 |
| Wright | 114 | 1 | 28 | 3 | 82 | 742 | 83 | 618 | 41 | 1 |

## Table 10. Offenses Known to Law Enforcement, by Selected State Metropolitan and Nonmetropolitan Counties, 2021—Continued

(Number.)

| State/county | Violent crime | Murder and nonnegligent manslaughter | Rape | Robbery | Aggravated assault | Property crime | Burglary | Larceny-theft | Motor vehicle theft | Arson |
|---|---|---|---|---|---|---|---|---|---|---|
| **Nonmetropolitan Counties** | | | | | | | | | | |
| Aitkin | 13 | 0 | 7 | 0 | 6 | 166 | 48 | 94 | 24 | 0 |
| Becker | 34 | 0 | 7 | 1 | 26 | 109 | 32 | 56 | 21 | 0 |
| Beltrami | 66 | 2 | 23 | 5 | 36 | 297 | 76 | 191 | 30 | 4 |
| Big Stone | 2 | 0 | 1 | 0 | 1 | 28 | 8 | 19 | 1 | 1 |
| Brown | 3 | 0 | 1 | 0 | 2 | 48 | 13 | 29 | 6 | 0 |
| Cass | 46 | 0 | 1 | 1 | 44 | 312 | 77 | 214 | 21 | 1 |
| Clearwater | 4 | 0 | 1 | 0 | 3 | 55 | 10 | 34 | 11 | 0 |
| Cook | 16 | 0 | 2 | 0 | 14 | 41 | 2 | 36 | 3 | 0 |
| Cottonwood | 1 | 0 | 0 | 0 | 1 | 10 | 4 | 5 | 1 | 0 |
| Crow Wing | 34 | 1 | 14 | 0 | 19 | 193 | 34 | 145 | 14 | 1 |
| Douglas | 17 | 0 | 3 | 0 | 14 | 151 | 5 | 129 | 17 | 0 |
| Freeborn | 12 | 0 | 3 | 0 | 9 | 197 | 54 | 134 | 9 | 0 |
| Goodhue | 4 | 0 | 1 | 0 | 3 | 144 | 19 | 102 | 23 | 1 |
| Grant | 3 | 0 | 0 | 0 | 3 | 1 | 0 | 1 | 0 | 0 |
| Hubbard | 30 | 0 | 7 | 0 | 23 | 137 | 35 | 93 | 9 | 0 |
| Itasca | 55 | 0 | 14 | 1 | 40 | 114 | 21 | 79 | 14 | 1 |
| Jackson | 7 | 0 | 0 | 1 | 6 | 22 | 5 | 10 | 7 | 0 |
| Kanabec | 12 | 0 | 3 | 0 | 9 | 69 | 15 | 47 | 7 | 1 |
| Kandiyohi | 29 | 0 | 11 | 1 | 17 | 201 | 25 | 143 | 33 | 1 |
| Kittson | 2 | 0 | 1 | 0 | 1 | 6 | 0 | 5 | 1 | 0 |
| Koochiching | 10 | 0 | 2 | 0 | 8 | 45 | 23 | 20 | 2 | 0 |
| Lac qui Parle | 2 | 0 | 0 | 0 | 2 | 16 | 1 | 13 | 2 | 0 |
| Lincoln | 5 | 0 | 0 | 0 | 5 | 9 | 3 | 5 | 1 | 0 |
| Lyon | 11 | 0 | 5 | 0 | 6 | 41 | 16 | 19 | 6 | 0 |
| Mahnomen | 19 | 0 | 0 | 1 | 18 | 46 | 13 | 22 | 11 | 0 |
| Marshall | 11 | 0 | 4 | 0 | 7 | 30 | 5 | 24 | 1 | 0 |
| Martin | 1 | 0 | 0 | 0 | 1 | 6 | 0 | 5 | 1 | 0 |
| McLeod | 18 | 0 | 1 | 1 | 16 | 75 | 17 | 53 | 5 | 1 |
| Meeker | 24 | 1 | 3 | 0 | 20 | 119 | 33 | 79 | • 7 | 1 |
| Morrison | 32 | 0 | 13 | 0 | 19 | 238 | 51 | 167 | 20 | 1 |
| Mower | 14 | 0 | 4 | 0 | 10 | 138 | 48 | 70 | 20 | 2 |
| Murray | 1 | 0 | 0 | 0 | 1 | 10 | 5 | 5 | 0 | 0 |
| Nobles | 5 | 0 | 2 | 0 | 3 | 22 | 7 | 10 | 5 | 0 |
| Norman | 2 | 0 | 1 | 0 | 1 | 52 | 15 | 31 | 6 | 0 |
| Otter Tail | 18 | 0 | 4 | 0 | 14 | 148 | 46 | 87 | 15 | 1 |
| Pennington | 3 | 0 | 0 | 0 | 3 | 40 | 8 | 28 | 4 | 0 |
| Pine | 90 | 0 | 21 | 2 | 67 | 539 | 149 | 313 | 77 | 3 |
| Pipestone | 13 | 0 | 3 | 0 | 10 | 32 | 2 | 29 | 1 | 1 |
| Pope | 3 | 0 | 0 | 0 | 3 | 39 | 7 | 25 | 7 | 0 |
| Redwood | 14 | 0 | 5 | 0 | 9 | 63 | 9 | 48 | 6 | 0 |
| Renville | 7 | 0 | 5 | 0 | 2 | 86 | 16 | 65 | 5 | 0 |
| Rice | 22 | 0 | 6 | 0 | 16 | 124 | 20 | 92 | 12 | 0 |
| Rock | 6 | 0 | 1 | 0 | 5 | 45 | 5 | 28 | 12 | 0 |
| Roseau | 7 | 0 | 2 | 0 | 5 | 37 | 10 | 21 | 6 | 1 |
| Sibley | 5 | 0 | 1 | 0 | 4 | 15 | 1 | 12 | 2 | 0 |
| Steele | 6 | 0 | 2 | 0 | 4 | 61 | 13 | 39 | 9 | 0 |
| Stevens | 7 | 0 | 0 | 0 | 7 | 9 | 2 | 7 | 0 | 0 |
| Swift | 1 | 0 | 0 | 0 | 1 | 1 | 0 | 1 | 0 | 0 |
| Todd | 22 | 0 | 8 | 0 | 14 | 116 | 29 | 82 | 5 | 1 |
| Traverse | 2 | 0 | 0 | 0 | 2 | 25 | 4 | 15 | 6 | 2 |
| Waseca | 11 | 0 | 8 | 0 | 3 | 129 | 46 | 79 | 4 | 0 |
| Watonwan | 7 | 0 | 1 | 0 | 6 | 32 | 18 | 13 | 1 | 0 |
| Wilkin | 2 | 0 | 0 | 0 | 2 | 16 | 2 | 14 | 0 | 0 |
| Winona | 19 | 0 | 6 | 0 | 13 | 99 | 26 | 62 | 11 | 0 |
| Yellow Medicine | 4 | 0 | 0 | 0 | 4 | 44 | 7 | 35 | 2 | 0 |
| **MISSISSIPPI** | | | | | | | | | | |
| **Metropolitan Counties** | | | | | | | | | | |
| DeSoto | 51 | 0 | 16 | 3 | 32 | 286 | 59 | 176 | 51 | 3 |
| Forrest | 51 | 1 | 14 | 4 | 32 | 328 | 88 | 190 | 50 | 1 |
| Hancock | 25 | 3 | 6 | 4 | 12 | 466 | 92 | 309 | 65 | 5 |
| Harrison | 52 | 4 | 7 | 11 | 30 | 797 | 127 | 537 | 133 | 6 |
| Lamar | 59 | 4 | 7 | 5 | 43 | 526 | 314 | 147 | 65 | 0 |
| Madison | 104 | 1 | 9 | 1 | 93 | 174 | 41 | 120 | 13 | 1 |
| Stone | 17 | 0 | 7 | 0 | 10 | 107 | 24 | 65 | 18 | 0 |
| Tate | 21 | 2 | 3 | 5 | 11 | 151 | 34 | 80 | 37 | 6 |
| Tunica | 67 | 2 | 12 | 7 | 46 | 436 | 56 | 319 | 61 | 3 |
| **Nonmetropolitan Counties** | | | | | | | | | | |
| Alcorn | 10 | 0 | 2 | 0 | 8 | 263 | 72 | 152 | 39 | 1 |
| Amite | 9 | 2 | 0 | 0 | 7 | 24 | 11 | 4 | 9 | 3 |
| Attala | 11 | 0 | 2 | 1 | 8 | 129 | 35 | 75 | 19 | 2 |
| Bolivar | 46 | 11 | 4 | 2 | 29 | 219 | 53 | 130 | 36 | 1 |
| Calhoun | 14 | 0 | 0 | 1 | 13 | 36 | 14 | 19 | 3 | 0 |
| Chickasaw | 11 | 0 | 0 | 0 | 11 | 23 | 10 | 10 | 3 | 3 |
| Choctaw | 27 | 1 | 6 | 0 | 20 | 62 | 20 | 26 | 16 | 0 |
| Claiborne | 24 | 9 | 0 | 0 | 15 | 42 | 22 | 12 | 8 | 0 |
| Clay | 17 | 1 | 1 | 0 | 15 | 77 | 26 | 40 | 11 | 0 |
| Coahoma | 4 | 0 | 0 | 0 | 4 | 22 | 7 | 11 | 4 | 0 |
| George | 37 | 0 | 14 | 2 | 21 | 319 | 74 | 194 | 51 | 3 |

## Table 10. Offenses Known to Law Enforcement, by Selected State Metropolitan and Nonmetropolitan Counties, 2021—Continued

(Number.)

| State/county | Violent crime | Murder and nonnegligent manslaughter | Rape | Robbery | Aggravated assault | Property crime | Burglary | Larceny-theft | Motor vehicle theft | Arson |
|---|---|---|---|---|---|---|---|---|---|---|
| Grenada | 46 | 0 | 11 | 2 | 33 | 189 | 50 | 121 | 18 | 1 |
| Jasper | 19 | 0 | 3 | 4 | 12 | 60 | 21 | 35 | 4 | 0 |
| Jefferson | 9 | 2 | 2 | 0 | 5 | 17 | 5 | 9 | 3 | 0 |
| Kemper | 9 | 0 | 3 | 2 | 4 | 15 | 0 | 11 | 4 | 1 |
| Lafayette | 21 | 1 | 5 | 2 | 13 | 157 | 45 | 92 | 20 | 0 |
| Leake | 56 | 0 | 9 | 1 | 46 | 155 | 59 | 78 | 18 | 2 |
| Lee | 91 | 3 | 29 | 4 | 55 | 611 | 159 | 377 | 75 | 6 |
| Lincoln | 39 | 0 | 16 | 1 | 22 | 247 | 64 | 139 | 44 | 7 |
| Lowndes | 55 | 4 | 10 | 13 | 28 | 537 | 184 | 298 | 55 | 5 |
| Marion | 45 | 3 | 1 | 6 | 35 | 176 | 69 | 88 | 19 | 2 |
| Monroe | 61 | 0 | 13 | 0 | 48 | 105 | 46 | 37 | 22 | 3 |
| Neshoba | 24 | 0 | 4 | 2 | 18 | 100 | 35 | 44 | 21 | 1 |
| Noxubee | 22 | 2 | 0 | 0 | 20 | 35 | 12 | 20 | 3 | 1 |
| Oktibbeha | 63 | 2 | 17 | 10 | 34 | 383 | 107 | 240 | 36 | 5 |
| Pike | 57 | 0 | 5 | 4 | 48 | 300 | 180 | 92 | 28 | 9 |
| Pontotoc | 71 | 0 | 27 | 3 | 41 | 146 | 38 | 76 | 32 | 1 |
| Prentiss | 23 | 1 | 2 | 0 | 20 | 116 | 37 | 63 | 16 | 1 |
| Smith | 6 | 1 | 0 | 0 | 5 | 67 | 17 | 33 | 17 | 0 |
| Sunflower | 6 | 0 | 0 | 1 | 5 | 72 | 29 | 35 | 8 | 3 |
| Tallahatchie | 28 | 0 | 3 | 2 | 23 | 96 | 16 | 55 | 25 | 0 |
| Tishomingo | 28 | 1 | 5 | 0 | 22 | 128 | 36 | 79 | 13 | 3 |
| Union | 26 | 1 | 7 | 2 | 16 | 162 | 41 | 107 | 14 | 1 |
| Wayne | 15 | 0 | 6 | 0 | 9 | 103 | 26 | 67 | 10 | 1 |
| Webster | 8 | 0 | 0 | 0 | 8 | 30 | 7 | 15 | 8 | 0 |
| Winston | 22 | 0 | 3 | 0 | 19 | 76 | 33 | 40 | 3 | 0 |
| **MISSOURI** | | | | | | | | | | |
| **Metropolitan Counties** | | | | | | | | | | |
| Andrew | 15 | 0 | 5 | 0 | 10 | 131 | 25 | 82 | 24 | 0 |
| Bollinger | 74 | 1 | 11 | 0 | 62 | 67 | 30 | 28 | 9 | 1 |
| Boone | 98 | 6 | 18 | 6 | 68 | 608 | 75 | 430 | 103 | 4 |
| Buchanan | 23 | 0 | 13 | 2 | 8 | 148 | 27 | 84 | 37 | 1 |
| Caldwell | 6 | 1 | 4 | 0 | 1 | 42 | 8 | 26 | 8 | 0 |
| Callaway | 70 | 0 | 12 | 2 | 56 | 256 | 72 | 151 | 33 | 0 |
| Cape Girardeau | 64 | 0 | 11 | 1 | 52 | 209 | 59 | 116 | 34 | 4 |
| Clay | 34 | 1 | 6 | 3 | 24 | 175 | 37 | 101 | 37 | 3 |
| Clinton | 18 | 0 | 7 | 0 | 11 | 84 | 28 | 49 | 7 | 1 |
| Cole | 33 | 0 | 2 | 2 | 29 | 205 | 34 | 149 | 22 | 1 |
| Cooper | 11 | 0 | 0 | 0 | 11 | 25 | 4 | 17 | 4 | 0 |
| Franklin | 49 | 0 | 4 | 0 | 45 | 304 | 58 | 180 | 66 | 2 |
| Greene | 144 | 5 | 22 | 10 | 107 | 926 | 229 | 578 | 119 | 2 |
| Jackson | 130 | 2 | 9 | 7 | 112 | 382 | 66 | 239 | 77 | 12 |
| Jasper | 49 | 3 | 14 | 2 | 30 | 482 | 62 | 314 | 106 | 2 |
| Jefferson | 525 | 6 | 38 | 10 | 471 | 2,059 | 389 | 1,216 | 454 | 24 |
| Lincoln | 428 | 1 | 31 | 0 | 396 | 236 | 61 | 121 | 54 | 3 |
| Newton | 116 | 2 | 23 | 4 | 87 | 585 | 131 | 362 | 92 | 2 |
| Polk | 99 | 2 | 7 | 1 | 89 | 263 | 76 | 166 | 21 | 1 |
| St. Charles | 2 | 0 | 0 | 0 | 2 | 1 | 1 | 0 | 0 | 0 |
| St. Charles County Police Department | 117 | 0 | 27 | 7 | 83 | 460 | 62 | 312 | 86 | 2 |
| St. Louis County Police Department | 1,995 | 40 | 105 | 289 | 1,561 | 7,861 | 982 | 5,265 | 1,614 | 61 |
| Warren | 43 | 0 | 12 | 0 | 31 | 210 | 51 | 111 | 48 | 3 |
| Webster | 63 | 0 | 9 | 0 | 54 | 208 | 40 | 149 | 19 | 5 |
| **Nonmetropolitan Counties** | | | | | | | | | | |
| Adair | 5 | 0 | 0 | 0 | 5 | 63 | 29 | 24 | 10 | 1 |
| Audrain | 44 | 0 | 2 | 2 | 40 | 123 | 35 | 74 | 14 | 1 |
| Barry | 64 | 0 | 3 | 1 | 60 | 248 | 42 | 157 | 49 | 2 |
| Benton | 27 | 1 | 2 | 0 | 24 | 155 | 47 | 75 | 33 | 1 |
| Butler | 71 | 0 | 14 | 1 | 56 | 505 | 96 | 302 | 107 | 2 |
| Carter | 33 | 1 | 2 | 0 | 30 | 47 | 10 | 31 | 6 | 0 |
| Chariton | 2 | 0 | 1 | 0 | 1 | 42 | 4 | 32 | 6 | 1 |
| Clark | 4 | 0 | 0 | 0 | 4 | 93 | 32 | 53 | 8 | 1 |
| Crawford | 33 | 0 | 3 | 0 | 30 | 64 | 12 | 47 | 5 | 2 |
| Dade | 45 | 1 | 3 | 1 | 40 | 96 | 32 | 45 | 19 | 2 |
| Daviess | 12 | 0 | 1 | 0 | 11 | 9 | 2 | 4 | 3 | 0 |
| Dent | 24 | 1 | 4 | 0 | 19 | 87 | 26 | 41 | 20 | 1 |
| Douglas | 15 | 0 | 0 | 0 | 15 | 24 | 6 | 15 | 3 | 2 |
| Dunklin | 22 | 0 | 2 | 0 | 20 | 82 | 24 | 39 | 19 | 3 |
| Grundy | 6 | 0 | 3 | 0 | 3 | 10 | 4 | 4 | 2 | 0 |
| Henry | 97 | 4 | 12 | 2 | 79 | 410 | 213 | 139 | 58 | 4 |
| Holt | 6 | 0 | 0 | 0 | 6 | 41 | 6 | 28 | 7 | 1 |
| Howell | 64 | 0 | 12 | 0 | 52 | 272 | 54 | 185 | 33 | 6 |
| Johnson | 21 | 1 | 5 | 1 | 14 | 238 | 65 | 122 | 51 | 1 |
| Laclede | 54 | 0 | 8 | 2 | 44 | 294 | 24 | 218 | 52 | 2 |
| Lawrence | 60 | 0 | 10 | 1 | 49 | 232 | 67 | 124 | 41 | 3 |
| Lewis | 0 | 0 | 0 | 0 | 0 | 35 | 7 | 24 | 4 | 0 |
| Linn | 17 | 0 | 3 | 0 | 14 | 29 | 3 | 20 | 6 | 1 |
| Livingston | 5 | 0 | 0 | 1 | 4 | 41 | 15 | 25 | 1 | 0 |
| Macon | 5 | 0 | 4 | 0 | 1 | 68 | 26 | 37 | 5 | 0 |
| Madison | 10 | 0 | 3 | 0 | 7 | 97 | 26 | 50 | 21 | 0 |
| Maries | 10 | 0 | 3 | 0 | 7 | 54 | 8 | 38 | 8 | 1 |

## Table 10. Offenses Known to Law Enforcement, by Selected State Metropolitan and Nonmetropolitan Counties, 2021—Continued

(Number.)

| State/county | Violent crime | Murder and nonnegligent manslaughter | Rape | Robbery | Aggravated assault | Property crime | Burglary | Larceny-theft | Motor vehicle theft | Arson |
|---|---|---|---|---|---|---|---|---|---|---|
| McDonald | 119 | 2 | 10 | 0 | 107 | 189 | 37 | 111 | 41 | 3 |
| Mississippi | 7 | 0 | 1 | 0 | 6 | 41 | 10 | 26 | 5 | 1 |
| Monroe | 30 | 0 | 4 | 0 | 26 | 36 | 11 | 22 | 3 | 1 |
| Montgomery | 14 | 0 | 3 | 0 | 11 | 49 | 9 | 28 | 12 | 2 |
| New Madrid | 57 | 1 | 5 | 0 | 51 | 170 | 35 | 103 | 32 | 8 |
| Nodaway | 19 | 0 | 8 | 0 | 11 | 71 | 17 | 45 | 9 | 3 |
| Oregon | 11 | 1 | 4 | 0 | 6 | 52 | 16 | 27 | 9 | 0 |
| Pemiscot | 25 | 0 | 6 | 0 | 19 | 77 | 17 | 45 | 15 | 2 |
| Perry | 38 | 0 | 2 | 0 | 36 | 33 | 10 | 16 | 7 | 0 |
| Phelps | 29 | 2 | 7 | 1 | 19 | 187 | 51 | 108 | 28 | 1 |
| Pike | 23 | 0 | 7 | 0 | 16 | 73 | 25 | 33 | 15 | 2 |
| Randolph | 65 | 0 | 2 | 0 | 63 | 46 | 8 | 27 | 11 | 0 |
| Ripley | 5 | 0 | 0 | 0 | 5 | 45 | 11 | 22 | 12 | 2 |
| Saline | 117 | 1 | 4 | 0 | 112 | 80 | 13 | 51 | 16 | 3 |
| Schuyler | 16 | 0 | 9 | 0 | 7 | 52 | 12 | 33 | 7 | 1 |
| Ste. Genevieve | 42 | 0 | 9 | 0 | 33 | 111 | 15 | 68 | 28 | 0 |
| Stoddard | 34 | 1 | 10 | 1 | 22 | 149 | 36 | 93 | 20 | 3 |
| Stone | 69 | 0 | 7 | 1 | 61 | 400 | 100 | 234 | 66 | 5 |
| Taney | 64 | 1 | 3 | 2 | 58 | 276 | 28 | 192 | 56 | 0 |
| Texas | 61 | 0 | 7 | 0 | 54 | 148 | 31 | 90 | 27 | 2 |
| Vernon | 50 | 0 | 8 | 1 | 41 | 116 | 21 | 64 | 31 | 3 |
| Washington | 47 | 0 | 12 | 0 | 35 | 132 | 34 | 73 | 25 | 1 |
| Wayne | 57 | 0 | 4 | 0 | 53 | 143 | 53 | 69 | 21 | 1 |
| Wright | 17 | 0 | 1 | 1 | 15 | 80 | 16 | 47 | 17 | 0 |
| **MONTANA** | | | | | | | | | | |
| **Metropolitan Counties** | | | | | | | | | | |
| Carbon | 10 | 0 | 2 | 0 | 8 | 49 | 12 | 29 | 8 | 0 |
| Cascade | 100 | 1 | 7 | 3 | 89 | 331 | 90 | 211 | 30 | 1 |
| Missoula | 129 | 4 | 16 | 3 | 106 | 297 | 63 | 199 | 35 | 4 |
| Stillwater | 19 | 0 | 3 | 0 | 16 | 82 | 23 | 52 | 7 | 3 |
| Yellowstone | 143 | 1 | 11 | 9 | 122 | 804 | 73 | 565 | 166 | 11 |
| **Nonmetropolitan Counties** | | | | | | | | | | |
| Big Horn | 82 | 0 | 5 | 4 | 73 | 315 | 58 | 159 | 98 | 1 |
| Blaine | 5 | 0 | 2 | 0 | 3 | 11 | 2 | 7 | 2 | 0 |
| Broadwater | 21 | 0 | 0 | 0 | 21 | 29 | 13 | 12 | 4 | 0 |
| Butte-Silver Bow | 121 | 2 | 8 | 16 | 95 | 1,569 | 214 | 1,158 | 197 | 10 |
| Carter | 0 | 0 | 0 | 0 | 0 | 0 | 0 | 0 | 0 | 0 |
| Chouteau | 4 | 0 | 0 | 0 | 4 | 3 | 1 | 1 | 1 | 0 |
| Custer | 15 | 0 | 4 | 0 | 11 | 14 | 2 | 10 | 2 | 0 |
| Dawson | 8 | 0 | 1 | 0 | 7 | 26 | 7 | 16 | 3 | 0 |
| Deer Lodge | 24 | 0 | 0 | 0 | 24 | 188 | 45 | 120 | 23 | 0 |
| Fallon | 1 | 0 | 1 | 0 | 0 | 0 | 0 | 0 | 0 | 0 |
| Fergus | 2 | 0 | 0 | 0 | 2 | 9 | 3 | 6 | 0 | 0 |
| Flathead | 216 | 1 | 32 | 4 | 179 | 652 | 115 | 437 | 100 | 5 |
| Gallatin | 137 | 0 | 35 | 1 | 101 | 369 | 24 | 303 | 42 | 2 |
| Garfield | 4 | 0 | 1 | 0 | 3 | 2 | 0 | 2 | 0 | 0 |
| Glacier | 2 | 0 | 1 | 0 | 1 | 26 | 0 | 17 | 9 | 0 |
| Golden Valley | 2 | 0 | 1 | 0 | 1 | 5 | 0 | 4 | 1 | 0 |
| Granite | 5 | 0 | 1 | 0 | 4 | 31 | 5 | 24 | 2 | 2 |
| Hill | 22 | 0 | 4 | 1 | 17 | 149 | 9 | 126 | 14 | 0 |
| Jefferson | 30 | 0 | 1 | 0 | 29 | 115 | 30 | 66 | 19 | 0 |
| Judith Basin | 0 | 0 | 0 | 0 | 0 | 0 | 0 | 0 | 0 | 0 |
| Lake | 136 | 1 | 20 | 2 | 113 | 295 | 50 | 194 | 51 | 1 |
| Lewis and Clark | 120 | 0 | 27 | 4 | 89 | 324 | 119 | 166 | 39 | 7 |
| Liberty | 0 | 0 | 0 | 0 | 0 | 3 | 0 | 2 | 1 | 0 |
| Lincoln | 24 | 0 | 1 | 0 | 23 | 51 | 6 | 41 | 4 | 1 |
| Madison | 14 | 0 | 3 | 0 | 11 | 23 | 2 | 20 | 1 | 0 |
| McCone | 2 | 0 | 1 | 0 | 1 | 1 | 0 | 1 | 0 | 0 |
| Meagher | 4 | 0 | 0 | 0 | 4 | 12 | 1 | 9 | 2 | 0 |
| Mineral | 18 | 0 | 0 | 1 | 17 | 35 | 9 | 22 | 4 | 0 |
| Musselshell | 13 | 0 | 0 | 0 | 13 | 45 | 2 | 39 | 4 | 4 |
| Park | 22 | 0 | 4 | 0 | 18 | 59 | 11 | 40 | 8 | 1 |
| Petroleum | 2 | 1 | 0 | 0 | 1 | 0 | 0 | 0 | 0 | 0 |
| Phillips | 23 | 0 | 2 | 0 | 21 | 37 | 11 | 20 | 6 | 0 |
| Pondera | 5 | 0 | 1 | 0 | 4 | 24 | 0 | 18 | 6 | 0 |
| Powder River | 2 | 0 | 0 | 0 | 2 | 0 | 0 | 0 | 0 | 0 |
| Powell | 15 | 0 | 5 | 0 | 10 | 17 | 6 | 9 | 2 | 0 |
| Prairie | 7 | 0 | 0 | 0 | 7 | 1 | 0 | 0 | 1 | 0 |
| Richland | 5 | 0 | 2 | 0 | 3 | 20 | 3 | 10 | 7 | 0 |
| Roosevelt | 22 | 2 | 1 | 0 | 19 | 29 | 7 | 10 | 12 | 1 |
| Rosebud | 8 | 0 | 3 | 0 | 5 | 3 | 0 | 2 | 1 | 0 |
| Sanders | 13 | 0 | 3 | 0 | 10 | 42 | 3 | 31 | 8 | 1 |
| Sheridan | 21 | 0 | 3 | 0 | 18 | 43 | 7 | 33 | 3 | 2 |
| Sweet Grass | 13 | 0 | 0 | 0 | 13 | 33 | 1 | 28 | 4 | 1 |
| Teton | 23 | 1 | 4 | 0 | 18 | 78 | 7 | 59 | 12 | 1 |
| Toole | 10 | 0 | 6 | 0 | 4 | 77 | 12 | 58 | 7 | 0 |
| Valley | 1 | 0 | 0 | 0 | 1 | 4 | 1 | 3 | 0 | 0 |
| Wheatland | 2 | 0 | 0 | 0 | 2 | 2 | 0 | 2 | 0 | 0 |
| Wibaux | 0 | 0 | 0 | 0 | 0 | 0 | 0 | 0 | 0 | 0 |

## Table 10. Offenses Known to Law Enforcement, by Selected State Metropolitan and Nonmetropolitan Counties, 2021—Continued

(Number.)

| State/county | Violent crime | Murder and nonnegligent manslaughter | Rape | Robbery | Aggravated assault | Property crime | Burglary | Larceny-theft | Motor vehicle theft | Arson |
|---|---|---|---|---|---|---|---|---|---|---|
| **NEBRASKA** | | | | | | | | | | |
| **Metropolitan Counties** | | | | | | | | | | |
| Cass | 12 | 0 | 3 | 0 | 9 | 154 | 17 | 110 | 27 | 0 |
| Dixon | 2 | 0 | 0 | 0 | 2 | 28 | 8 | 20 | 0 | 0 |
| Douglas | 92 | 0 | 28 | 6 | 58 | 675 | 144 | 459 | 72 | 4 |
| Hall | 24 | 1 | 5 | 3 | 15 | 103 | 24 | 71 | 8 | 1 |
| Lancaster | 17 | 0 | 10 | 2 | 5 | 233 | 58 | 152 | 23 | 4 |
| Merrick | 1 | 0 | 0 | 0 | 1 | 6 | 0 | 4 | 2 | 0 |
| Sarpy | 37 | 0 | 15 | 3 | 19 | 723 | 52 | 569 | 102 | 1 |
| Saunders | 3 | 0 | 0 | 0 | 3 | 62 | 10 | 49 | 3 | 0 |
| Seward | 8 | 0 | 1 | 0 | 7 | 21 | 4 | 13 | 4 | 1 |
| Washington | 3 | 0 | 1 | 0 | 2 | 68 | 10 | 48 | 10 | 0 |
| **Nonmetropolitan Counties** | | | | | | | | | | |
| Adams | 5 | 0 | 1 | 0 | 4 | 48 | 9 | 37 | 2 | 1 |
| Boyd | 0 | 0 | 0 | 0 | 0 | 6 | 4 | 2 | 0 | 0 |
| Brown | 0 | 0 | 0 | 0 | 0 | 6 | 2 | 1 | 3 | 0 |
| Buffalo | 14 | 0 | 7 | 1 | 6 | 93 | 8 | 75 | 10 | 1 |
| Butler | 8 | 0 | 6 | 0 | 2 | 13 | 2 | 8 | 3 | 0 |
| Cedar | 6 | 0 | 1 | 0 | 5 | 48 | 7 | 33 | 8 | 0 |
| Cherry | 1 | 1 | 0 | 0 | 0 | 4 | 2 | 2 | 0 | 0 |
| Cheyenne | 25 | 0 | 1 | 0 | 24 | 8 | 2 | 5 | 1 | 0 |
| Custer | 4 | 0 | 0 | 0 | 4 | 22 | 4 | 15 | 3 | 0 |
| Dawson | 6 | 0 | 0 | 1 | 5 | 35 | 11 | 19 | 5 | 0 |
| Dodge | 6 | 0 | 2 | 0 | 4 | 100 | 16 | 74 | 10 | 0 |
| Dundy | 1 | 0 | 1 | 0 | 0 | 13 | 6 | 6 | 1 | 0 |
| Fillmore | 2 | 0 | 0 | 0 | 2 | 11 | 1 | 8 | 2 | 1 |
| Furnas | 4 | 0 | 3 | 0 | 1 | 40 | 10 | 28 | 2 | 0 |
| Gage | 18 | 0 | 4 | 0 | 14 | 42 | 4 | 32 | 6 | 2 |
| Grant | 0 | 0 | 0 | 0 | 0 | 0 | 0 | 0 | 0 | 0 |
| Hamilton | 2 | 0 | 0 | 0 | 2 | 17 | 5 | 9 | 3 | 0 |
| Harlan | 0 | 0 | 0 | 0 | 0 | 0 | 0 | 0 | 0 | 0 |
| Hayes | 0 | 0 | 0 | 0 | 0 | 5 | 0 | 5 | 0 | 0 |
| Hitchcock | 1 | 0 | 1 | 0 | 0 | 16 | 5 | 8 | 3 | 0 |
| Jefferson | 5 | 1 | 0 | 0 | 4 | 115 | 16 | 90 | 9 | 1 |
| Johnson | 6 | 0 | 0 | 0 | 6 | 19 | 8 | 10 | 1 | 0 |
| Kearney | 6 | 0 | 5 | 0 | 1 | 14 | 2 | 11 | 1 | 0 |
| Keith | 2 | 0 | 0 | 0 | 2 | 4 | 2 | 2 | 0 | 0 |
| Lincoln | 8 | 0 | 2 | 0 | 6 | 64 | 11 | 45 | 8 | 0 |
| Madison | 5 | 0 | 1 | 1 | 3 | 25 | 6 | 15 | 4 | 1 |
| McPherson | 0 | 0 | 0 | 0 | 0 | 0 | 0 | 0 | 0 | 0 |
| Morrill | 1 | 0 | 0 | 0 | 1 | 18 | 1 | 17 | 0 | 1 |
| Nemaha | 9 | 0 | 4 | 0 | 5 | 22 | 7 | 9 | 6 | 0 |
| Otoe | 5 | 0 | 2 | 0 | 3 | 39 | 9 | 21 | 9 | 0 |
| Perkins | 0 | 0 | 0 | 0 | 0 | 13 | 4 | 8 | 1 | 0 |
| Phelps | 3 | 0 | 2 | 0 | 1 | 8 | 2 | 5 | 1 | 0 |
| Platte | 6 | 0 | 3 | 0 | 3 | 64 | 9 | 50 | 5 | 0 |
| Polk | 1 | 0 | 0 | 0 | 1 | 16 | 1 | 13 | 2 | 0 |
| Richardson | 1 | 0 | 0 | 0 | 1 | 24 | 2 | 18 | 4 | 0 |
| Rock | 0 | 0 | 0 | 0 | 0 | 0 | 0 | 0 | 0 | 0 |
| Scotts Bluff | 8 | 0 | 3 | 1 | 4 | 66 | 9 | 52 | 5 | 1 |
| Stanton | 0 | 0 | 0 | 0 | 0 | 2 | 1 | 1 | 0 | 0 |
| Valley | 1 | 0 | 0 | 0 | 1 | 3 | 3 | 0 | 0 | 0 |
| Wayne | 2 | 0 | 0 | 0 | 2 | 16 | 4 | 12 | 0 | 0 |
| Webster | 0 | 0 | 0 | 0 | 0 | 3 | 0 | 1 | 2 | 0 |
| **NEVADA** | | | | | | | | | | |
| **Metropolitan Counties** | | | | | | | | | | |
| Carson City | 210 | 1 | 55 | 12 | 142 | 631 | 105 | 440 | 86 | 7 |
| Washoe | 337 | 1 | 52 | 16 | 268 | 772 | 178 | 489 | 105 | 11 |
| **Nonmetropolitan Counties** | | | | | | | | | | |
| Churchill | 27 | 0 | 6 | 0 | 21 | 260 | 183 | 68 | 9 | 1 |
| Douglas | 68 | 2 | 27 | 4 | 35 | 559 | 60 | 463 | 36 | 5 |
| Elko | 58 | 1 | 13 | 0 | 44 | 213 | 58 | 114 | 41 | 3 |
| Humboldt | 22 | 1 | 7 | 1 | 13 | 138 | 60 | 52 | 26 | 2 |
| Lander | 18 | 0 | 3 | 0 | 15 | 78 | 31 | 38 | 9 | 1 |
| Lyon | 159 | 0 | 30 | 9 | 120 | 546 | 110 | 356 | 80 | 10 |
| Nye | 174 | 3 | 24 | 10 | 137 | 760 | 232 | 427 | 101 | 10 |
| **NEW HAMPSHIRE** | | | | | | | | | | |
| **Metropolitan Counties** | | | | | | | | | | |
| Strafford | 2 | 0 | 1 | 0 | 1 | 0 | 0 | 0 | 0 | 0 |
| **Nonmetropolitan Counties** | | | | | | | | | | |
| Belknap | 5 | 0 | 3 | 0 | 2 | 11 | 0 | 11 | 0 | 0 |
| Carroll | 3 | 0 | 2 | 0 | 1 | 41 | 4 | 34 | 3 | 0 |
| Cheshire | 4 | 0 | 3 | 0 | 1 | 10 | 1 | 8 | 1 | 0 |
| Grafton | 4 | 0 | 3 | 0 | 1 | 2 | 0 | 2 | 0 | 0 |
| Merrimack | 0 | 0 | 0 | 0 | 0 | 1 | 0 | 1 | 0 | 0 |
| Sullivan | 1 | 0 | 1 | 0 | 0 | 9 | 1 | 6 | 2 | 0 |

## Table 10. Offenses Known to Law Enforcement, by Selected State Metropolitan and Nonmetropolitan Counties, 2021—Continued

(Number.)

| State/county | Violent crime | Murder and nonnegligent manslaughter | Rape | Robbery | Aggravated assault | Property crime | Burglary | Larceny-theft | Motor vehicle theft | Arson |
|---|---|---|---|---|---|---|---|---|---|---|
| **NEW JERSEY**[1] | | | | | | | | | | |
| **Metropolitan Counties** | | | | | | | | | | |
| Atlantic | 0 | 0 | 0 | 0 | 0 | 0 | 0 | 0 | 0 | 0 |
| | | | | | | | | | | |
| **NEW MEXICO**[1] | | | | | | | | | | |
| **Metropolitan Counties** | | | | | | | | | | |
| Bernalillo | 753 | 10 | 57 | 87 | 599 | 1,974 | 435 | 1,017 | 522 | 9 |
| Dona Ana | 318 | 2 | 53 | 11 | 252 | 854 | 248 | 462 | 144 | 9 |
| Valencia | 213 | 0 | 15 | 9 | 189 | 677 | 264 | 284 | 129 | 8 |
| | | | | | | | | | | |
| **Nonmetropolitan Counties** | | | | | | | | | | |
| McKinley | 58 | 1 | 4 | 10 | 43 | 162 | 45 | 89 | 28 | 6 |
| Socorro | 22 | 0 | 2 | 1 | 19 | 71 | 25 | 30 | 16 | 0 |
| | | | | | | | | | | |
| **NEW YORK**[1] | | | | | | | | | | |
| **Metropolitan Counties** | | | | | | | | | | |
| Broome | 40 | 0 | 12 | 3 | 25 | 477 | 58 | 394 | 25 | 2 |
| Dutchess | 28 | 1 | 9 | 0 | 18 | 332 | 28 | 275 | 29 | 2 |
| Jefferson | 12 | 0 | 2 | 1 | 9 | 183 | 24 | 154 | 5 | 1 |
| Livingston | 12 | 0 | 1 | 0 | 11 | 252 | 44 | 192 | 16 | 2 |
| Monroe | 141 | 1 | 15 | 34 | 91 | 1,862 | 174 | 1,517 | 171 | 2 |
| Niagara | 44 | 1 | 3 | 2 | 38 | 516 | 57 | 407 | 52 | 2 |
| Oneida | 41 | 0 | 36 | 2 | 3 | 214 | 44 | 154 | 16 | 6 |
| Oswego | 28 | 0 | 12 | 2 | 14 | 259 | 121 | 122 | 16 | 0 |
| Saratoga | 73 | 0 | 27 | 10 | 36 | 1,011 | 100 | 893 | 18 | 1 |
| Ulster | 9 | 0 | 0 | 0 | 9 | 104 | 8 | 92 | 4 | 1 |
| Warren | 15 | 0 | 8 | 3 | 4 | 458 | 40 | 406 | 12 | 3 |
| | | | | | | | | | | |
| **Nonmetropolitan Counties** | | | | | | | | | | |
| Cattaraugus | 37 | 0 | 8 | 2 | 27 | 199 | 37 | 142 | 20 | 4 |
| Chautauqua | 47 | 0 | 15 | 3 | 29 | 295 | 76 | 197 | 22 | 7 |
| Genesee | 40 | 1 | 9 | 0 | 30 | 246 | 24 | 203 | 19 | 2 |
| Montgomery | 5 | 0 | 0 | 0 | 5 | 167 | 9 | 152 | 6 | 0 |
| Seneca | 6 | 1 | 0 | 1 | 4 | 397 | 317 | 75 | 5 | 0 |
| St. Lawrence | 7 | 1 | 1 | 0 | 5 | 22 | 2 | 18 | 2 | 0 |
| | | | | | | | | | | |
| **NORTH CAROLINA** | | | | | | | | | | |
| **Metropolitan Counties** | | | | | | | | | | |
| Alamance | 192 | 10 | 13 | 7 | 162 | 654 | 160 | 398 | 96 | 7 |
| Alexander | 79 | 1 | 6 | 2 | 70 | 388 | 137 | 205 | 46 | 3 |
| Buncombe | 159 | 3 | 19 | 16 | 121 | 1,666 | 420 | 983 | 263 | 18 |
| Burke | 117 | 3 | 23 | 8 | 83 | 751 | 216 | 418 | 117 | 7 |
| Cabarrus | 47 | 2 | 8 | 10 | 27 | 566 | 118 | 390 | 58 | 3 |
| Caldwell | 69 | 3 | 5 | 5 | 56 | 908 | 283 | 505 | 120 | 11 |
| Camden | 22 | 0 | 6 | 0 | 16 | 59 | 18 | 31 | 10 | 0 |
| Catawba | 189 | 1 | 47 | 17 | 124 | 1,052 | 300 | 625 | 127 | 13 |
| Chatham | 94 | 1 | 25 | 6 | 62 | 602 | 194 | 362 | 46 | 4 |
| Craven | 94 | 1 | 8 | 3 | 82 | 500 | 167 | 270 | 63 | 2 |
| Currituck | 57 | 0 | 8 | 1 | 48 | 316 | 65 | 237 | 14 | 2 |
| Davidson | 95 | 0 | 4 | 10 | 81 | 1,261 | 381 | 719 | 161 | 16 |
| Durham | 96 | 0 | 3 | 14 | 79 | 533 | 138 | 346 | 49 | 1 |
| Forsyth | 249 | 6 | 14 | 35 | 194 | 1,404 | 312 | 986 | 106 | 15 |
| Franklin | 113 | 5 | 19 | 6 | 83 | 600 | 145 | 415 | 40 | 2 |
| Gaston | 13 | 0 | 0 | 0 | 13 | 3 | 1 | 2 | 0 | 0 |
| Gaston County Police Department | 192 | 9 | 15 | 16 | 152 | 998 | 248 | 566 | 184 | 11 |
| Granville | 59 | 3 | 10 | 2 | 44 | 357 | 149 | 183 | 25 | 6 |
| Guilford | 215 | 5 | 16 | 28 | 166 | 938 | 194 | 655 | 89 | 8 |
| Harnett | 241 | 14 | 17 | 17 | 193 | 1,422 | 330 | 950 | 142 | 15 |
| Haywood | 97 | 1 | 21 | 3 | 72 | 917 | 346 | 485 | 86 | 5 |
| Henderson | 112 | 3 | 22 | 8 | 79 | 1,227 | 476 | 639 | 112 | 10 |
| Iredell | 133 | 5 | 6 | 4 | 118 | 735 | 234 | 428 | 73 | 5 |
| Johnston | 133 | 2 | 25 | 10 | 96 | 1,485 | 280 | 1,047 | 158 | 5 |
| Lincoln | 91 | 2 | 12 | 5 | 72 | 877 | 151 | 625 | 101 | 7 |
| Madison | 23 | 2 | 4 | 2 | 15 | 219 | 128 | 71 | 20 | 4 |
| New Hanover | 139 | 6 | 19 | 16 | 98 | 1,139 | 163 | 922 | 54 | 9 |
| Orange | 86 | 1 | 6 | 5 | 74 | 471 | 111 | 324 | 36 | 1 |
| Pamlico | 39 | 0 | 2 | 1 | 36 | 226 | 61 | 147 | 18 | 0 |
| Person | 36 | 4 | 9 | 3 | 20 | 419 | 226 | 170 | 23 | 2 |
| Pitt | 153 | 4 | 9 | 21 | 119 | 697 | 224 | 431 | 42 | 5 |
| Rockingham | 49 | 6 | 18 | 3 | 22 | 584 | 146 | 375 | 63 | 5 |
| Rowan | 162 | 6 | 10 | 11 | 135 | 947 | 230 | 596 | 121 | 4 |
| Union | 198 | 2 | 41 | 10 | 145 | 1,423 | 295 | 1,027 | 101 | 10 |
| Wake | 224 | 7 | 14 | 17 | 186 | 1,344 | 236 | 906 | 202 | 18 |
| Wayne | 201 | 6 | 12 | 14 | 169 | 1,073 | 317 | 570 | 186 | 8 |
| Yadkin | 43 | 6 | 8 | 1 | 28 | 357 | 96 | 212 | 49 | 1 |
| | | | | | | | | | | |
| **Nonmetropolitan Counties** | | | | | | | | | | |
| Ashe | 41 | 1 | 10 | 1 | 29 | 147 | 55 | 73 | 19 | 0 |
| Avery | 14 | 2 | 3 | 0 | 9 | 108 | 15 | 72 | 21 | 1 |
| Bertie | 36 | 3 | 7 | 0 | 26 | 200 | 69 | 115 | 16 | 4 |
| Bladen | 108 | 6 | 12 | 8 | 82 | 425 | 132 | 248 | 45 | 5 |

## Table 10. Offenses Known to Law Enforcement, by Selected State Metropolitan and Nonmetropolitan Counties, 2021—Continued

(Number.)

| State/county | Violent crime | Murder and nonnegligent manslaughter | Rape | Robbery | Aggravated assault | Property crime | Burglary | Larceny-theft | Motor vehicle theft | Arson |
|---|---|---|---|---|---|---|---|---|---|---|
| Carteret | 89 | 1 | 20 | 3 | 65 | 516 | 147 | 330 | 39 | 0 |
| Caswell | 12 | 0 | 6 | 0 | 6 | 60 | 10 | 45 | 5 | 0 |
| Cherokee | 92 | 0 | 7 | 6 | 79 | 755 | 175 | 524 | 56 | 10 |
| Chowan | 7 | 0 | 3 | 1 | 3 | 65 | 23 | 35 | 7 | 1 |
| Cleveland | 180 | 1 | 34 | 17 | 128 | 637 | 175 | 365 | 97 | 3 |
| Dare | 17 | 2 | 2 | 1 | 12 | 172 | 40 | 130 | 2 | 0 |
| Duplin | 72 | 4 | 17 | 8 | 43 | 886 | 435 | 361 | 90 | 6 |
| Greene | 54 | 7 | 20 | 6 | 21 | 242 | 99 | 118 | 25 | 2 |
| Halifax | 86 | 6 | 15 | 9 | 56 | 371 | 130 | 206 | 35 | 6 |
| Hertford | 24 | 8 | 4 | 1 | 11 | 211 | 131 | 70 | 10 | 1 |
| Macon | 29 | 2 | 8 | 1 | 18 | 457 | 124 | 293 | 40 | 6 |
| Martin | 41 | 1 | 8 | 4 | 28 | 197 | 64 | 111 | 22 | 1 |
| McDowell | 51 | 1 | 13 | 2 | 35 | 733 | 306 | 344 | 83 | 4 |
| Montgomery | 52 | 4 | 6 | 6 | 36 | 226 | 63 | 134 | 29 | 5 |
| Moore | 62 | 6 | 12 | 1 | 43 | 522 | 119 | 379 | 24 | 5 |
| Pasquotank | 106 | 1 | 16 | 1 | 88 | 199 | 81 | 98 | 20 | 3 |
| Polk | 13 | 1 | 4 | 0 | 8 | 177 | 63 | 90 | 24 | 1 |
| Richmond | 228 | 4 | 12 | 14 | 198 | 1,083 | 352 | 583 | 148 | 21 |
| Robeson | 1,041 | 22 | 18 | 76 | 925 | 2,331 | 824 | 1,209 | 298 | 68 |
| Rutherford | 76 | 6 | 16 | 8 | 46 | 471 | 185 | 223 | 63 | 6 |
| Sampson | 153 | 3 | 27 | 14 | 109 | 788 | 306 | 395 | 87 | 9 |
| Scotland | 68 | 3 | 6 | 3 | 56 | 274 | 111 | 131 | 32 | 7 |
| Surry | 66 | 2 | 28 | 7 | 29 | 577 | 106 | 356 | 115 | 9 |
| Swain | 23 | 0 | 6 | 0 | 17 | 289 | 147 | 122 | 20 | 4 |
| Transylvania | 35 | 0 | 3 | 3 | 29 | 173 | 72 | 83 | 18 | 4 |
| Tyrrell | 6 | 0 | 1 | 1 | 4 | 24 | 14 | 8 | 2 | 0 |
| Vance | 124 | 9 | 8 | 6 | 101 | 511 | 197 | 274 | 40 | 9 |
| Warren | 34 | 2 | 4 | 0 | 28 | 315 | 98 | 182 | 35 | 3 |
| Watauga | 35 | 6 | 7 | 1 | 21 | 218 | 77 | 132 | 9 | 3 |
| Wilkes | 99 | 7 | 17 | 3 | 72 | 650 | 260 | 315 | 75 | 6 |
| Wilson | 45 | 6 | 2 | 5 | 32 | 270 | 44 | 188 | 38 | 7 |
| Yancey | 12 | 1 | 1 | 0 | 10 | 70 | 34 | 31 | 5 | 1 |
| **NORTH DAKOTA** | | | | | | | | | | |
| **Metropolitan Counties** | | | | | | | | | | |
| Burleigh | 27 | 0 | 2 | 0 | 25 | 120 | 24 | 81 | 15 | 1 |
| Cass | 18 | 0 | 4 | 2 | 12 | 153 | 52 | 84 | 17 | 0 |
| Grand Forks | 20 | 0 | 1 | 0 | 19 | 56 | 17 | 25 | 14 | 0 |
| Morton | 7 | 0 | 3 | 0 | 4 | 72 | 9 | 50 | 13 | 0 |
| Oliver | 0 | 0 | 0 | 0 | 0 | 6 | 2 | 4 | 0 | 0 |
| **Nonmetropolitan Counties** | | | | | | | | | | |
| Adams | 2 | 0 | 0 | 0 | 2 | 11 | 4 | 6 | 1 | 0 |
| Barnes | 4 | 0 | 1 | 0 | 3 | 18 | 10 | 5 | 3 | 0 |
| Benson | 2 | 0 | 0 | 0 | 2 | 6 | 1 | 2 | 3 | 0 |
| Billings | 0 | 0 | 0 | 0 | 0 | 3 | 2 | 0 | 1 | 0 |
| Bottineau | 1 | 0 | 0 | 0 | 1 | 52 | 11 | 32 | 9 | 2 |
| Bowman | 1 | 0 | 0 | 0 | 1 | 0 | 0 | 0 | 0 | 0 |
| Burke | 1 | 0 | 1 | 0 | 0 | 5 | 2 | 2 | 1 | 0 |
| Cavalier | 3 | 0 | 1 | 0 | 2 | 5 | 1 | 2 | 2 | 0 |
| Divide | 0 | 0 | 0 | 0 | 0 | 12 | 0 | 12 | 0 | 0 |
| Dunn | 4 | 1 | 0 | 0 | 3 | 19 | 2 | 11 | 6 | 0 |
| Eddy | 4 | 0 | 1 | 1 | 2 | 15 | 5 | 8 | 2 | 0 |
| Emmons | 3 | 0 | 1 | 0 | 2 | 34 | 8 | 19 | 7 | 0 |
| Golden Valley | 0 | 0 | 0 | 0 | 0 | 10 | 1 | 9 | 0 | 0 |
| Grant | 2 | 0 | 2 | 0 | 0 | 11 | 3 | 3 | 5 | 0 |
| Griggs | 1 | 0 | 0 | 0 | 1 | 13 | 2 | 9 | 2 | 1 |
| Hettinger | 3 | 0 | 2 | 0 | 1 | 5 | 1 | 3 | 1 | 0 |
| Kidder | 0 | 0 | 0 | 0 | 0 | 7 | 2 | 5 | 0 | 0 |
| Lamoure | 1 | 0 | 0 | 0 | 1 | 9 | 0 | 8 | 1 | 0 |
| McHenry | 8 | 0 | 2 | 0 | 6 | 28 | 7 | 12 | 9 | 0 |
| McIntosh | 1 | 0 | 1 | 0 | 0 | 10 | 1 | 7 | 2 | 0 |
| McKenzie | 15 | 0 | 3 | 1 | 11 | 90 | 10 | 62 | 18 | 3 |
| McLean | 8 | 0 | 1 | 0 | 7 | 75 | 10 | 54 | 11 | 0 |
| Mercer | 5 | 0 | 1 | 0 | 4 | 34 | 6 | 20 | 8 | 0 |
| Mountrail | 1 | 0 | 0 | 0 | 1 | 61 | 6 | 49 | 6 | 0 |
| Nelson | 1 | 0 | 1 | 0 | 0 | 25 | 4 | 18 | 3 | 0 |
| Pembina | 7 | 0 | 3 | 0 | 4 | 27 | 9 | 10 | 8 | 0 |
| Pierce | 0 | 0 | 0 | 0 | 0 | 14 | 3 | 10 | 1 | 0 |
| Ramsey | 4 | 0 | 0 | 0 | 4 | 37 | 6 | 19 | 12 | 1 |
| Ransom | 2 | 0 | 0 | 0 | 2 | 20 | 3 | 14 | 3 | 0 |
| Renville | 3 | 0 | 1 | 0 | 2 | 17 | 2 | 12 | 3 | 0 |
| Richland | 4 | 0 | 0 | 1 | 3 | 73 | 12 | 50 | 11 | 1 |
| Rolette | 4 | 0 | 1 | 0 | 3 | 17 | 5 | 5 | 7 | 0 |
| Sargent | 4 | 0 | 1 | 0 | 3 | 6 | 1 | 3 | 2 | 1 |
| Sheridan | 0 | 0 | 0 | 0 | 0 | 10 | 0 | 10 | 0 | 0 |
| Sioux | 0 | 0 | 0 | 0 | 0 | 0 | 0 | 0 | 0 | 0 |
| Slope | 0 | 0 | 0 | 0 | 0 | 0 | 0 | 0 | 0 | 0 |
| Stark | 2 | 0 | 0 | 1 | 1 | 53 | 6 | 39 | 8 | 0 |
| Steele | 1 | 0 | 0 | 0 | 1 | 1 | 1 | 0 | 0 | 1 |
| Stutsman | 4 | 0 | 2 | 0 | 2 | 44 | 12 | 27 | 5 | 2 |

## Table 10. Offenses Known to Law Enforcement, by Selected State Metropolitan and Nonmetropolitan Counties, 2021—Continued

(Number.)

| State/county | Violent crime | Murder and nonnegligent manslaughter | Rape | Robbery | Aggravated assault | Property crime | Burglary | Larceny-theft | Motor vehicle theft | Arson |
|---|---|---|---|---|---|---|---|---|---|---|
| Towner | 3 | 0 | 1 | 0 | 2 | 19 | 3 | 10 | 6 | 0 |
| Traill | 5 | 0 | 1 | 0 | 4 | 56 | 9 | 36 | 11 | 0 |
| Walsh | 3 | 0 | 2 | 0 | 1 | 52 | 10 | 34 | 8 | 1 |
| Ward | 24 | 0 | 4 | 0 | 20 | 178 | 52 | 99 | 27 | 4 |
| Williams | 11 | 0 | 2 | 1 | 8 | 123 | 27 | 61 | 35 | 0 |
| **OHIO** | | | | | | | | | | |
| **Metropolitan Counties** | | | | | | | | | | |
| Allen | 111 | 1 | 34 | 13 | 63 | 496 | 112 | 345 | 39 | 4 |
| Belmont | 44 | 2 | 5 | 0 | 37 | 78 | 13 | 63 | 2 | 1 |
| Clark | 28 | 0 | 5 | 6 | 17 | 627 | 106 | 488 | 33 | 2 |
| Clermont | 85 | 0 | 25 | 3 | 57 | 763 | 160 | 540 | 63 | 0 |
| Fairfield | 69 | 0 | 24 | 5 | 40 | 978 | 82 | 822 | 74 | 4 |
| Franklin | 56 | 3 | 20 | 12 | 21 | 335 | 41 | 256 | 38 | 1 |
| Fulton | 18 | 0 | 4 | 0 | 14 | 180 | 33 | 145 | 2 | 1 |
| Greene | 30 | 0 | 6 | 2 | 22 | 277 | 67 | 188 | 22 | 0 |
| Hamilton | 172 | 6 | 49 | 26 | 91 | 1,418 | 131 | 1,163 | 124 | 8 |
| Hocking | 38 | 1 | 6 | 3 | 28 | 219 | 60 | 141 | 18 | 1 |
| Lorain | 51 | 1 | 12 | 5 | 33 | 373 | 135 | 229 | 9 | 4 |
| Lucas | 85 | 0 | 13 | 9 | 63 | 739 | 82 | 550 | 107 | 1 |
| Madison | 32 | 1 | 9 | 4 | 18 | 173 | 29 | 138 | 6 | 1 |
| Medina | 30 | 5 | 3 | 1 | 21 | 196 | 44 | 137 | 15 | 3 |
| Miami | 38 | 0 | 2 | 1 | 35 | 302 | 57 | 214 | 31 | 3 |
| Montgomery | 248 | 4 | 41 | 37 | 166 | 971 | 169 | 569 | 233 | 14 |
| Perry | 0 | 0 | 0 | 0 | 0 | 28 | 20 | 7 | 1 | 0 |
| Pickaway | 30 | 0 | 9 | 0 | 21 | 441 | 67 | 344 | 30 | 3 |
| Richland | 90 | 2 | 40 | 8 | 40 | 499 | 63 | 409 | 27 | 1 |
| Stark | 103 | 1 | 20 | 8 | 74 | 1,367 | 286 | 936 | 145 | 6 |
| Summit | 91 | 1 | 34 | 3 | 53 | 1,017 | 119 | 826 | 72 | 0 |
| Trumbull | 21 | 0 | 1 | 0 | 20 | 156 | 34 | 96 | 26 | 1 |
| Union | 24 | 0 | 12 | 0 | 12 | 211 | 20 | 184 | 7 | 1 |
| Warren | 35 | 0 | 3 | 7 | 25 | 726 | 70 | 585 | 71 | 4 |
| Wood | 24 | 0 | 6 | 1 | 17 | 244 | 34 | 196 | 14 | 0 |
| **Nonmetropolitan Counties** | | | | | | | | | | |
| Adams | 3 | 0 | 0 | 0 | 3 | 67 | 36 | 26 | 5 | 1 |
| Ashtabula | 50 | 0 | 8 | 3 | 39 | 457 | 89 | 349 | 19 | 1 |
| Athens | 25 | 1 | 2 | 3 | 19 | 281 | 68 | 190 | 23 | 1 |
| Auglaize | 1 | 0 | 1 | 0 | 0 | 25 | 3 | 21 | 1 | 0 |
| Champaign | 23 | 0 | 5 | 0 | 18 | 141 | 21 | 104 | 16 | 1 |
| Clinton | 16 | 0 | 4 | 0 | 12 | 68 | 21 | 31 | 16 | 0 |
| Columbiana | 39 | 1 | 11 | 0 | 27 | 163 | 42 | 95 | 26 | 0 |
| Coshocton | 72 | 4 | 19 | 3 | 46 | 399 | 55 | 323 | 21 | 1 |
| Crawford | 8 | 0 | 3 | 0 | 5 | 67 | 23 | 40 | 4 | 0 |
| Defiance | 9 | 0 | 4 | 1 | 4 | 139 | 26 | 110 | 3 | 2 |
| Erie | 5 | 0 | 0 | 1 | 4 | 96 | 12 | 82 | 2 | 0 |
| Fayette | 34 | 0 | 3 | 4 | 27 | 205 | 38 | 146 | 21 | 0 |
| Gallia | 17 | 0 | 9 | 0 | 8 | 110 | 47 | 55 | 8 | 2 |
| Hancock | 25 | 3 | 12 | 2 | 8 | 197 | 35 | 152 | 10 | 2 |
| Harrison | 10 | 0 | 4 | 0 | 6 | 79 | 28 | 44 | 7 | 2 |
| Henry | 9 | 0 | 4 | 0 | 5 | 136 | 26 | 99 | 11 | 1 |
| Highland | 26 | 0 | 10 | 0 | 16 | 332 | 95 | 202 | 35 | 3 |
| Jackson | 47 | 2 | 20 | 0 | 25 | 185 | 59 | 112 | 14 | 0 |
| Knox | 28 | 0 | 6 | 2 | 20 | 285 | 64 | 207 | 14 | 0 |
| Logan | 15 | 0 | 2 | 1 | 12 | 188 | 42 | 133 | 13 | 0 |
| Meigs | 18 | 0 | 2 | 0 | 16 | 168 | 60 | 77 | 31 | 1 |
| Monroe | 5 | 0 | 0 | 0 | 5 | 14 | 6 | 7 | 1 | 1 |
| Morgan | 21 | 2 | 2 | 0 | 17 | 91 | 31 | 53 | 7 | 1 |
| Pike | 43 | 1 | 4 | 4 | 34 | 227 | 73 | 118 | 36 | 6 |
| Preble | 17 | 0 | 7 | 0 | 10 | 136 | 19 | 100 | 17 | 2 |
| Ross | 109 | 1 | 37 | 5 | 66 | 941 | 190 | 650 | 101 | 15 |
| Scioto | 32 | 1 | 5 | 1 | 25 | 245 | 100 | 112 | 33 | 2 |
| Seneca | 8 | 0 | 5 | 0 | 3 | 142 | 11 | 126 | 5 | 0 |
| Shelby | 15 | 1 | 9 | 1 | 4 | 101 | 20 | 75 | 6 | 0 |
| Tuscarawas | 36 | 1 | 9 | 2 | 24 | 278 | 76 | 163 | 39 | 2 |
| Van Wert | 20 | 2 | 5 | 0 | 13 | 60 | 22 | 37 | 1 | 0 |
| Washington | 16 | 3 | 7 | 0 | 6 | 142 | 41 | 92 | 9 | 6 |
| Wayne | 43 | 1 | 15 | 5 | 22 | 628 | 232 | 335 | 61 | 1 |
| **OKLAHOMA** | | | | | | | | | | |
| **Metropolitan Counties** | | | | | | | | | | |
| Canadian | 20 | 0 | 3 | 0 | 17 | 168 | 40 | 94 | 34 | 1 |
| Cleveland | 40 | 0 | 12 | 2 | 26 | 204 | 68 | 109 | 27 | 1 |
| Comanche | 19 | 1 | 3 | 0 | 15 | 118 | 42 | 62 | 14 | 1 |
| Cotton | 6 | 0 | 1 | 0 | 5 | 29 | 6 | 16 | 7 | 3 |
| Creek | 48 | 1 | 2 | 1 | 44 | 362 | 102 | 158 | 102 | 4 |
| Garfield | 16 | 0 | 1 | 0 | 15 | 92 | 25 | 49 | 18 | 3 |
| Grady | 40 | 0 | 7 | 0 | 33 | 265 | 84 | 138 | 43 | 7 |
| Lincoln | 57 | 3 | 8 | 1 | 45 | 289 | 104 | 151 | 34 | 11 |
| Logan | 33 | 3 | 4 | 1 | 25 | 354 | 100 | 185 | 69 | 2 |
| McClain | 19 | 0 | 4 | 2 | 13 | 192 | 51 | 93 | 48 | 1 |

## Table 10. Offenses Known to Law Enforcement, by Selected State Metropolitan and Nonmetropolitan Counties, 2021—Continued

(Number.)

| State/county | Violent crime | Murder and nonnegligent manslaughter | Rape | Robbery | Aggravated assault | Property crime | Burglary | Larceny-theft | Motor vehicle theft | Arson |
|---|---|---|---|---|---|---|---|---|---|---|
| Oklahoma | 29 | 1 | 3 | 0 | 25 | 144 | 35 | 70 | 39 | 1 |
| Okmulgee | 24 | 0 | 2 | 4 | 18 | 182 | 49 | 99 | 34 | 3 |
| Osage | 77 | 1 | 14 | 3 | 59 | 438 | 149 | 229 | 60 | 4 |
| Pawnee | 8 | 0 | 1 | 0 | 7 | 96 | 27 | 35 | 34 | 1 |
| Rogers | 88 | 1 | 30 | 1 | 56 | 404 | 125 | 224 | 55 | 5 |
| Sequoyah | 77 | 3 | 19 | 2 | 53 | 254 | 90 | 118 | 46 | 8 |
| Tulsa | 194 | 7 | 23 | 11 | 153 | 782 | 207 | 415 | 160 | 11 |
| Wagoner | 65 | 1 | 16 | 1 | 47 | 324 | 91 | 184 | 49 | 12 |
| **Nonmetropolitan Counties** | | | | | | | | | | |
| Adair | 24 | 2 | 3 | 2 | 17 | 138 | 46 | 44 | 48 | 3 |
| Alfalfa | 4 | 0 | 1 | 0 | 3 | 56 | 1 | 47 | 8 | 1 |
| Atoka | 19 | 0 | 0 | 0 | 19 | 75 | 20 | 41 | 14 | 0 |
| Beaver | 2 | 0 | 0 | 0 | 2 | 16 | 7 | 7 | 2 | 0 |
| Beckham | 14 | 0 | 8 | 0 | 6 | 66 | 27 | 26 | 13 | 2 |
| Blaine | 12 | 0 | 1 | 0 | 11 | 72 | 14 | 48 | 10 | 1 |
| Bryan | 24 | 0 | 1 | 1 | 22 | 269 | 78 | 133 | 58 | 2 |
| Caddo | 28 | 0 | 5 | 0 | 23 | 149 | 58 | 73 | 18 | 3 |
| Carter | 17 | 0 | 4 | 0 | 13 | 140 | 56 | 68 | 16 | 3 |
| Cherokee | 76 | 1 | 18 | 3 | 54 | 431 | 127 | 206 | 98 | 8 |
| Choctaw | 30 | 1 | 3 | 1 | 25 | 141 | 45 | 58 | 38 | 8 |
| Cimarron | 0 | 0 | 0 | 0 | 0 | 10 | 4 | 4 | 2 | 0 |
| Coal | 2 | 0 | 1 | 0 | 1 | 13 | 5 | 5 | 3 | 0 |
| Craig | 24 | 1 | 2 | 2 | 19 | 143 | 63 | 60 | 20 | 7 |
| Custer | 13 | 1 | 1 | 1 | 10 | 84 | 22 | 49 | 13 | 1 |
| Delaware | 81 | 2 | 11 | 0 | 68 | 385 | 124 | 179 | 82 | 9 |
| Dewey | 6 | 2 | 1 | 0 | 3 | 50 | 12 | 28 | 10 | 1 |
| Ellis | 3 | 0 | 0 | 0 | 3 | 48 | 8 | 31 | 9 | 1 |
| Garvin | 49 | 0 | 1 | 1 | 47 | 206 | 46 | 129 | 31 | 5 |
| Grant | 2 | 0 | 1 | 0 | 1 | 27 | 5 | 18 | 4 | 3 |
| Greer | 0 | 0 | 0 | 0 | 0 | 4 | 0 | 3 | 1 | 0 |
| Harmon | 2 | 0 | 1 | 0 | 1 | 3 | 1 | 1 | 1 | 0 |
| Harper | 3 | 0 | 1 | 0 | 2 | 21 | 5 | 15 | 1 | 0 |
| Haskell | 8 | 0 | 2 | 0 | 6 | 58 | 18 | 31 | 9 | 0 |
| Hughes | 5 | 0 | 0 | 0 | 5 | 104 | 22 | 74 | 8 | 1 |
| Jackson | 3 | 0 | 1 | 0 | 2 | 31 | 10 | 18 | 3 | 1 |
| Jefferson | 4 | 0 | 0 | 0 | 4 | 18 | 5 | 8 | 5 | 0 |
| Johnston | 14 | 0 | 0 | 1 | 13 | 58 | 32 | 17 | 9 | 1 |
| Kay | 29 | 0 | 10 | 1 | 18 | 120 | 37 | 64 | 19 | 4 |
| Kingfisher | 7 | 0 | 1 | 0 | 6 | 83 | 9 | 67 | 7 | 3 |
| Kiowa | 6 | 0 | 0 | 0 | 6 | 17 | 3 | 14 | 0 | 0 |
| Latimer | 15 | 1 | 0 | 0 | 14 | 78 | 22 | 44 | 12 | 1 |
| Le Flore | 28 | 1 | 4 | 0 | 23 | 202 | 73 | 92 | 37 | 4 |
| Love | 16 | 0 | 2 | 1 | 13 | 95 | 25 | 48 | 22 | 1 |
| Major | 9 | 0 | 3 | 0 | 6 | 61 | 16 | 35 | 10 | 5 |
| Marshall | 19 | 1 | 4 | 0 | 14 | 163 | 45 | 80 | 38 | 2 |
| Mayes | 46 | 1 | 10 | 7 | 28 | 465 | 140 | 223 | 102 | 11 |
| McCurtain | 39 | 1 | 0 | 1 | 37 | 273 | 88 | 146 | 39 | 14 |
| McIntosh | 33 | 0 | 2 | 0 | 31 | 200 | 53 | 93 | 54 | 7 |
| Murray | 3 | 0 | 0 | 0 | 3 | 38 | 9 | 27 | 2 | 0 |
| Muskogee | 48 | 1 | 5 | 1 | 41 | 179 | 52 | 88 | 39 | 1 |
| Noble | 15 | 0 | 6 | 0 | 9 | 67 | 16 | 45 | 6 | 1 |
| Nowata | 12 | 0 | 0 | 0 | 12 | 57 | 15 | 33 | 9 | 3 |
| Okfuskee | 10 | 1 | 1 | 0 | 8 | 85 | 25 | 47 | 13 | 1 |
| Ottawa | 28 | 0 | 1 | 5 | 22 | 238 | 52 | 145 | 41 | 14 |
| Payne | 29 | 0 | 5 | 1 | 23 | 269 | 65 | 158 | 46 | 5 |
| Pittsburg | 51 | 0 | 9 | 0 | 42 | 334 | 139 | 144 | 51 | 6 |
| Pottawatomie | 52 | 2 | 15 | 0 | 35 | 426 | 102 | 243 | 81 | 7 |
| Pushmataha | 13 | 0 | 0 | 0 | 13 | 82 | 28 | 37 | 17 | 4 |
| Roger Mills | 3 | 0 | 2 | 0 | 1 | 25 | 5 | 19 | 1 | 1 |
| Seminole | 18 | 0 | 0 | 0 | 18 | 273 | 81 | 156 | 36 | 6 |
| Stephens | 33 | 1 | 6 | 3 | 23 | 131 | 34 | 80 | 17 | 1 |
| Texas | 8 | 0 | 2 | 0 | 6 | 56 | 21 | 24 | 11 | 3 |
| Tillman | 8 | 0 | 0 | 0 | 8 | 42 | 20 | 19 | 3 | 1 |
| Washington | 17 | 1 | 1 | 0 | 15 | 101 | 28 | 56 | 17 | 1 |
| Washita | 7 | 0 | 0 | 0 | 7 | 35 | 12 | 15 | 8 | 1 |
| Woods | 5 | 0 | 2 | 0 | 3 | 30 | 13 | 17 | 0 | 0 |
| Woodward | 10 | 0 | 2 | 0 | 8 | 106 | 59 | 41 | 6 | 1 |
| **OREGON** | | | | | | | | | | |
| **Metropolitan Counties** | | | | | | | | | | |
| Benton | 20 | 0 | 4 | 2 | 14 | 256 | 50 | 187 | 19 | 4 |
| Clackamas | 469 | 4 | 52 | 103 | 310 | 5,071 | 586 | 3,573 | 912 | 30 |
| Columbia | 52 | 1 | 9 | 2 | 40 | 109 | 17 | 60 | 32 | 6 |
| Deschutes | 88 | 0 | 15 | 4 | 69 | 642 | 114 | 438 | 90 | 16 |
| Jackson | 112 | 5 | 32 | 5 | 70 | 571 | 146 | 323 | 102 | 3 |
| Josephine | 101 | 4 | 11 | 7 | 79 | 325 | 44 | 156 | 125 | 10 |
| Linn | 65 | 1 | 18 | 3 | 43 | 883 | 159 | 611 | 113 | 11 |
| Multnomah | 245 | 0 | 25 | 57 | 163 | 1,713 | 156 | 1,177 | 380 | 17 |
| Polk | 67 | 2 | 5 | 4 | 56 | 292 | 62 | 208 | 22 | 7 |
| Washington | 568 | 4 | 122 | 51 | 391 | 2,776 | 320 | 2,034 | 422 | 40 |
| Yamhill | 78 | 2 | 12 | 7 | 57 | 544 | 212 | 281 | 51 | 8 |

## Table 10. Offenses Known to Law Enforcement, by Selected State Metropolitan and Nonmetropolitan Counties, 2021—Continued

(Number.)

| State/county | Violent crime | Murder and nonnegligent manslaughter | Rape | Robbery | Aggravated assault | Property crime | Burglary | Larceny-theft | Motor vehicle theft | Arson |
|---|---|---|---|---|---|---|---|---|---|---|
| **Nonmetropolitan Counties** | | | | | | | | | | |
| Clatsop | 34 | 0 | 7 | 2 | 25 | 156 | 42 | 103 | 11 | 3 |
| Crook | 27 | 0 | 3 | 1 | 23 | 101 | 29 | 63 | 9 | 0 |
| Douglas | 160 | 0 | 13 | 11 | 136 | 790 | 174 | 419 | 197 | 10 |
| Gilliam | 8 | 0 | 3 | 0 | 5 | 42 | 9 | 25 | 8 | 2 |
| Hood River | 17 | 0 | 3 | 1 | 13 | 129 | 22 | 90 | 17 | 1 |
| Jefferson | 12 | 0 | 1 | 1 | 10 | 148 | 31 | 90 | 27 | 2 |
| Klamath | 129 | 4 | 26 | 5 | 94 | 656 | 159 | 334 | 163 | 8 |
| Lake | 32 | 0 | 7 | 1 | 24 | 123 | 39 | 62 | 22 | 1 |
| Lincoln | 53 | 1 | 7 | 2 | 43 | 292 | 69 | 186 | 37 | 6 |
| Malheur | 35 | 1 | 4 | 6 | 24 | 167 | 41 | 94 | 32 | 3 |
| Morrow | 19 | 1 | 3 | 0 | 15 | 104 | 24 | 65 | 15 | 0 |
| Sherman | 2 | 0 | 0 | 0 | 2 | 69 | 1 | 60 | 8 | 3 |
| Tillamook | 24 | 1 | 1 | 2 | 20 | 236 | 54 | 156 | 26 | 3 |
| Umatilla | 53 | 0 | 16 | 1 | 36 | 344 | 101 | 180 | 63 | 17 |
| Union | 20 | 0 | 1 | 0 | 19 | 144 | 32 | 100 | 12 | 0 |
| Wasco | 18 | 0 | 2 | 0 | 16 | 158 | 24 | 99 | 35 | 0 |
| **PENNSYLVANIA**[1] | | | | | | | | | | |
| **SOUTH CAROLINA** | | | | | | | | | | |
| **Metropolitan Counties** | | | | | | | | | | |
| Anderson | 744 | 15 | 67 | 47 | 615 | 4,079 | 648 | 2,845 | 586 | 28 |
| Beaufort | 479 | 8 | 36 | 36 | 399 | 2,234 | 410 | 1,624 | 200 | 4 |
| Berkeley | 439 | 11 | 38 | 31 | 359 | 1,985 | 350 | 1,374 | 261 | 20 |
| Calhoun | 51 | 0 | 7 | 2 | 42 | 194 | 36 | 121 | 37 | 0 |
| Charleston | 249 | 14 | 10 | 25 | 200 | 1,435 | 241 | 971 | 223 | 8 |
| Chester | 101 | 2 | 14 | 7 | 78 | 301 | 56 | 210 | 35 | 4 |
| Clarendon | 174 | 4 | 15 | 7 | 148 | 593 | 172 | 364 | 57 | 5 |
| Darlington | 467 | 16 | 22 | 28 | 401 | 1,604 | 434 | 909 | 261 | 23 |
| Dorchester | 270 | 6 | 10 | 21 | 233 | 1,501 | 203 | 1,071 | 227 | 6 |
| Fairfield | 107 | 6 | 3 | 7 | 91 | 314 | 58 | 197 | 59 | 7 |
| Florence | 550 | 13 | 62 | 44 | 431 | 2,216 | 358 | 1,575 | 283 | 9 |
| Greenville | 1,595 | 20 | 154 | 211 | 1,210 | 7,411 | 1,261 | 5,139 | 1,011 | 45 |
| Horry | 6 | 0 | 1 | 0 | 5 | 2 | 0 | 2 | 0 | 0 |
| Horry County Police Department | 851 | 14 | 130 | 59 | 648 | 5,072 | 665 | 3,772 | 635 | 27 |
| Jasper | 80 | 3 | 9 | 12 | 56 | 380 | 56 | 263 | 61 | 6 |
| Kershaw | 196 | 2 | 25 | 7 | 162 | 930 | 156 | 692 | 82 | 5 |
| Lancaster | 368 | 4 | 63 | 14 | 287 | 1,329 | 233 | 985 | 111 | 12 |
| Laurens | 243 | 5 | 14 | 15 | 209 | 1,016 | 225 | 640 | 151 | 9 |
| Lexington | 649 | 11 | 70 | 66 | 502 | 5,133 | 1,029 | 3,457 | 647 | 21 |
| Pickens | 188 | 2 | 20 | 13 | 153 | 1,095 | 273 | 656 | 166 | 12 |
| Richland | 2,124 | 33 | 94 | 201 | 1,796 | 7,599 | 958 | 5,592 | 1,049 | 43 |
| Saluda | 22 | 1 | 6 | 2 | 13 | 137 | 34 | 85 | 18 | 1 |
| Spartanburg | 1,100 | 7 | 125 | 57 | 911 | 4,478 | 1,093 | 2,841 | 544 | 36 |
| Sumter | 422 | 6 | 18 | 23 | 375 | 1,383 | 287 | 923 | 173 | 10 |
| York | 399 | 11 | 42 | 28 | 318 | 2,314 | 346 | 1,784 | 184 | 21 |
| **Nonmetropolitan Counties** | | | | | | | | | | |
| Abbeville | 60 | 0 | 4 | 0 | 56 | 233 | 65 | 148 | 20 | 6 |
| Bamberg | 6 | 1 | 2 | 1 | 2 | 132 | 33 | 87 | 12 | 0 |
| Barnwell | 84 | 3 | 8 | 4 | 69 | 251 | 69 | 139 | 43 | 0 |
| Cherokee | 126 | 0 | 15 | 8 | 103 | 888 | 290 | 461 | 137 | 12 |
| Colleton | 194 | 10 | 9 | 11 | 164 | 719 | 164 | 455 | 100 | 8 |
| Dillon | 246 | 6 | 12 | 11 | 217 | 576 | 186 | 333 | 57 | 9 |
| Georgetown | 154 | 8 | 19 | 5 | 122 | 707 | 128 | 487 | 92 | 9 |
| Greenwood | 197 | 10 | 32 | 13 | 142 | 683 | 147 | 490 | 46 | 9 |
| Marion | 78 | 6 | 4 | 3 | 65 | 386 | 72 | 277 | 37 | 0 |
| Marlboro | 117 | 9 | 16 | 6 | 86 | 330 | 83 | 209 | 38 | 2 |
| Newberry | 99 | 4 | 9 | 2 | 84 | 256 | 46 | 185 | 25 | 3 |
| Oconee | 206 | 5 | 37 | 5 | 159 | 1,484 | 256 | 1,032 | 196 | 19 |
| Orangeburg | 892 | 25 | 8 | 50 | 809 | 2,369 | 547 | 1,480 | 342 | 5 |
| Williamsburg | 126 | 0 | 10 | 8 | 108 | 417 | 96 | 256 | 65 | 6 |
| **SOUTH DAKOTA** | | | | | | | | | | |
| **Metropolitan Counties** | | | | | | | | | | |
| Lincoln | 31 | 0 | 8 | 0 | 23 | 357 | 140 | 193 | 24 | 1 |
| McCook | 4 | 0 | 2 | 0 | 2 | 18 | 2 | 13 | 3 | 0 |
| Meade | 21 | 0 | 5 | 1 | 15 | 161 | 25 | 119 | 17 | 0 |
| Minnehaha | 65 | 0 | 12 | 2 | 51 | 347 | 86 | 206 | 55 | 4 |
| Pennington | 139 | 1 | 60 | 2 | 76 | 372 | 67 | 266 | 39 | 2 |
| Turner | 17 | 0 | 5 | 0 | 12 | 39 | 15 | 21 | 3 | 0 |
| Union | 9 | 0 | 0 | 0 | 9 | 51 | 8 | 42 | 1 | 0 |
| **Nonmetropolitan Counties** | | | | | | | | | | |
| Bennett | 1 | 0 | 1 | 0 | 0 | 1 | 0 | 1 | 0 | 0 |
| Brookings | 11 | 0 | 1 | 0 | 10 | 21 | 5 | 15 | 1 | 0 |
| Butte | 3 | 0 | 1 | 0 | 2 | 30 | 3 | 21 | 6 | 0 |
| Charles Mix | 10 | 0 | 0 | 1 | 9 | 40 | 10 | 20 | 10 | 3 |
| Clay | 0 | 0 | 0 | 0 | 0 | 57 | 23 | 27 | 7 | 0 |
| Codington | 8 | 0 | 2 | 0 | 6 | 39 | 7 | 19 | 13 | 0 |

## Table 10. Offenses Known to Law Enforcement, by Selected State Metropolitan and Nonmetropolitan Counties, 2021—Continued

(Number.)

| State/county | Violent crime | Murder and nonnegligent manslaughter | Rape | Robbery | Aggravated assault | Property crime | Burglary | Larceny-theft | Motor vehicle theft | Arson |
|---|---|---|---|---|---|---|---|---|---|---|
| Corson | 7 | 0 | 0 | 1 | 6 | 13 | 6 | 6 | 1 | 0 |
| Custer | 15 | 0 | 1 | 0 | 14 | 163 | 19 | 128 | 16 | 0 |
| Day | 2 | 0 | 1 | 0 | 1 | 35 | 8 | 18 | 9 | 1 |
| Deuel | 9 | 0 | 1 | 0 | 8 | 16 | 2 | 10 | 4 | 0 |
| Hamlin | 3 | 0 | 1 | 0 | 2 | 24 | 4 | 15 | 5 | 0 |
| Hughes | 4 | 0 | 0 | 0 | 4 | 12 | 2 | 8 | 2 | 1 |
| Jerauld | 1 | 1 | 0 | 0 | 0 | 6 | 0 | 6 | 0 | 0 |
| Lake | 1 | 0 | 0 | 0 | 1 | 10 | 2 | 8 | 0 | 0 |
| Lawrence | 6 | 0 | 1 | 0 | 5 | 26 | 9 | 17 | 0 | 0 |
| Moody | 1 | 0 | 0 | 0 | 1 | 1 | 1 | 0 | 0 | 0 |
| Spink | 15 | 0 | 4 | 0 | 11 | 29 | 6 | 20 | 3 | 0 |
| Tripp | 2 | 0 | 1 | 0 | 1 | 7 | 0 | 6 | 1 | 0 |
| Walworth | 2 | 0 | 0 | 0 | 2 | 1 | 0 | 1 | 0 | 0 |
| Yankton | 11 | 0 | 0 | 0 | 11 | 40 | 11 | 27 | 2 | 0 |
| | | | | | | | | | | |
| **TENNESSEE** | | | | | | | | | | |
| **Metropolitan Counties** | | | | | | | | | | |
| Anderson | 99 | 0 | 11 | 3 | 85 | 398 | 97 | 240 | 61 | 13 |
| Blount | 264 | 2 | 40 | 4 | 218 | 760 | 202 | 464 | 94 | 4 |
| Bradley | 200 | 0 | 10 | 3 | 187 | 684 | 132 | 452 | 100 | 0 |
| Campbell | 55 | 1 | 9 | 1 | 44 | 207 | 56 | 109 | 42 | 3 |
| Cheatham | 72 | 1 | 6 | 3 | 62 | 248 | 35 | 177 | 36 | 0 |
| Dickson | 123 | 2 | 18 | 3 | 100 | 246 | 70 | 127 | 49 | 1 |
| Fayette | 42 | 2 | 0 | 2 | 38 | 125 | 28 | 77 | 20 | 2 |
| Gibson | 52 | 0 | 3 | 2 | 47 | 169 | 29 | 103 | 37 | 1 |
| Grainger | 23 | 2 | 3 | 0 | 18 | 182 | 33 | 102 | 47 | 0 |
| Hamblen | 101 | 0 | 9 | 5 | 87 | 435 | 86 | 257 | 92 | 6 |
| Hamilton | 311 | 1 | 34 | 5 | 271 | 1,104 | 213 | 757 | 134 | 7 |
| Hartsville/Trousdale | 31 | 0 | 4 | 1 | 26 | 114 | 24 | 77 | 13 | 1 |
| Hawkins | 62 | 1 | 6 | 0 | 55 | 400 | 83 | 249 | 68 | 5 |
| Jefferson | 112 | 2 | 16 | 3 | 91 | 383 | 100 | 221 | 62 | 4 |
| Knox | 567 | 7 | 71 | 26 | 463 | 2,868 | 434 | 2,038 | 396 | 9 |
| Loudon | 82 | 1 | 6 | 2 | 73 | 334 | 83 | 202 | 49 | 4 |
| Macon | 70 | 0 | 4 | 0 | 66 | 48 | 25 | 8 | 15 | 6 |
| Madison | 70 | 3 | 3 | 4 | 60 | 202 | 43 | 130 | 29 | 1 |
| Marion | 47 | 0 | 1 | 1 | 45 | 114 | 24 | 59 | 31 | 1 |
| Maury | 139 | 4 | 29 | 1 | 105 | 327 | 51 | 199 | 77 | 4 |
| Montgomery | 75 | 0 | 6 | 2 | 67 | 455 | 104 | 286 | 65 | 0 |
| Morgan | 46 | 1 | 0 | 0 | 45 | 196 | 21 | 138 | 37 | 0 |
| Polk | 35 | 1 | 2 | 0 | 32 | 285 | 56 | 171 | 58 | 2 |
| Roane | 80 | 2 | 8 | 7 | 63 | 246 | 65 | 141 | 40 | 0 |
| Robertson | 105 | 0 | 4 | 5 | 96 | 223 | 54 | 132 | 37 | 4 |
| Rutherford | 241 | 0 | 29 | 4 | 208 | 517 | 84 | 362 | 71 | 5 |
| Sequatchie | 35 | 0 | 0 | 0 | 35 | 102 | 22 | 56 | 24 | 4 |
| Shelby | 640 | 9 | 28 | 53 | 550 | 2,390 | 453 | 1,628 | 309 | 4 |
| Smith | 21 | 0 | 4 | 0 | 17 | 107 | 30 | 67 | 10 | 0 |
| Stewart | 33 | 1 | 6 | 0 | 26 | 68 | 24 | 35 | 9 | 0 |
| Sullivan | 290 | 4 | 51 | 6 | 229 | 889 | 211 | 510 | 168 | 19 |
| Sumner | 130 | 2 | 12 | 6 | 110 | 332 | 75 | 212 | 45 | 4 |
| Tipton | 113 | 2 | 10 | 5 | 96 | 337 | 64 | 224 | 49 | 0 |
| Unicoi | 32 | 1 | 1 | 0 | 30 | 37 | 6 | 24 | 7 | 0 |
| Union | 32 | 1 | 2 | 0 | 29 | 192 | 58 | 108 | 26 | 3 |
| Washington | 129 | 1 | 15 | 1 | 112 | 548 | 144 | 292 | 112 | 5 |
| Williamson | 137 | 2 | 10 | 0 | 125 | 299 | 44 | 232 | 23 | 4 |
| Wilson | 66 | 1 | 0 | 6 | 59 | 442 | 99 | 280 | 63 | 0 |
| | | | | | | | | | | |
| **Nonmetropolitan Counties** | | | | | | | | | | |
| Bedford | 69 | 4 | 18 | 0 | 47 | 165 | 37 | 103 | 25 | 0 |
| Benton | 34 | 1 | 7 | 1 | 25 | 141 | 38 | 79 | 24 | 1 |
| Bledsoe | 20 | 1 | 2 | 0 | 17 | 76 | 9 | 48 | 19 | 0 |
| Carroll | 34 | 0 | 4 | 1 | 29 | 140 | 35 | 77 | 28 | 2 |
| Claiborne | 22 | 1 | 3 | 0 | 18 | 67 | 14 | 41 | 12 | 1 |
| Clay | 5 | 0 | 1 | 0 | 4 | 19 | 7 | 10 | 2 | 0 |
| Cocke | 159 | 2 | 16 | 2 | 139 | 456 | 104 | 239 | 113 | 5 |
| Coffee | 177 | 4 | 7 | 1 | 165 | 411 | 91 | 254 | 66 | 1 |
| Cumberland | 74 | 0 | 0 | 1 | 73 | 438 | 132 | 239 | 67 | 3 |
| Decatur | 34 | 0 | 2 | 1 | 31 | 117 | 52 | 48 | 17 | 1 |
| DeKalb | 13 | 0 | 2 | 0 | 11 | 103 | 29 | 57 | 17 | 3 |
| Dyer | 52 | 0 | 4 | 1 | 47 | 222 | 47 | 124 | 51 | 1 |
| Fentress | 36 | 1 | 6 | 1 | 28 | 239 | 48 | 159 | 32 | 3 |
| Franklin | 63 | 0 | 6 | 1 | 56 | 235 | 39 | 146 | 50 | 3 |
| Giles | 35 | 0 | 1 | 0 | 34 | 83 | 25 | 40 | 18 | 2 |
| Greene | 187 | 3 | 14 | 1 | 169 | 767 | 195 | 427 | 145 | 11 |
| Grundy | 68 | 0 | 10 | 1 | 57 | 221 | 37 | 136 | 48 | 3 |
| Hancock | 16 | 0 | 1 | 0 | 15 | 97 | 34 | 59 | 4 | 2 |
| Hardeman | 125 | 3 | 3 | 4 | 115 | 148 | 35 | 75 | 38 | 1 |
| Hardin | 61 | 2 | 8 | 1 | 50 | 337 | 106 | 176 | 55 | 3 |
| Haywood | 21 | 0 | 2 | 1 | 18 | 119 | 27 | 78 | 14 | 0 |
| Henderson | 82 | 0 | 15 | 5 | 62 | 216 | 89 | 109 | 18 | 1 |
| Henry | 64 | 0 | 4 | 1 | 59 | 239 | 62 | 134 | 43 | 5 |
| Hickman | 83 | 2 | 5 | 2 | 74 | 382 | 69 | 240 | 73 | 4 |

## Table 10. Offenses Known to Law Enforcement, by Selected State Metropolitan and Nonmetropolitan Counties, 2021—Continued

(Number.)

| State/county | Violent crime | Murder and nonnegligent manslaughter | Rape | Robbery | Aggravated assault | Property crime | Burglary | Larceny-theft | Motor vehicle theft | Arson |
|---|---|---|---|---|---|---|---|---|---|---|
| Houston | 13 | 0 | 0 | 0 | 13 | 76 | 10 | 59 | 7 | 1 |
| Humphreys | 33 | 0 | 2 | 1 | 30 | 115 | 36 | 59 | 20 | 1 |
| Johnson | 37 | 0 | 6 | 1 | 30 | 101 | 31 | 51 | 19 | 2 |
| Lauderdale | 62 | 0 | 2 | 1 | 59 | 167 | 57 | 90 | 20 | 3 |
| Lawrence | 35 | 0 | 6 | 1 | 28 | 218 | 96 | 92 | 30 | 6 |
| Lewis | 27 | 0 | 2 | 0 | 25 | 74 | 15 | 45 | 14 | 1 |
| Lincoln | 45 | 0 | 7 | 1 | 37 | 231 | 62 | 141 | 28 | 3 |
| Marshall | 37 | 0 | 4 | 0 | 33 | 91 | 10 | 56 | 25 | 2 |
| McMinn | 85 | 0 | 7 | 4 | 74 | 427 | 101 | 241 | 85 | 6 |
| McNairy | 45 | 0 | 2 | 1 | 42 | 168 | 39 | 100 | 29 | 1 |
| Monroe | 147 | 2 | 22 | 1 | 122 | 628 | 158 | 338 | 132 | 4 |
| Moore | 10 | 0 | 1 | 0 | 9 | 34 | 3 | 28 | 3 | 0 |
| Obion | 39 | 2 | 0 | 2 | 35 | 165 | 51 | 86 | 28 | 1 |
| Overton | 55 | 0 | 5 | 0 | 50 | 186 | 16 | 134 | 36 | 8 |
| Pickett | 5 | 0 | 0 | 0 | 5 | 23 | 6 | 13 | 4 | 0 |
| Putnam | 80 | 0 | 13 | 2 | 65 | 333 | 61 | 221 | 51 | 1 |
| Scott | 16 | 1 | 0 | 0 | 15 | 159 | 73 | 62 | 24 | 2 |
| Sevier | 158 | 0 | 18 | 3 | 137 | 708 | 133 | 445 | 130 | 3 |
| Warren | 119 | 1 | 9 | 3 | 106 | 285 | 62 | 169 | 54 | 4 |
| Wayne | 27 | 0 | 5 | 0 | 22 | 65 | 15 | 38 | 12 | 1 |
| Weakley | 23 | 0 | 2 | 0 | 21 | 82 | 31 | 41 | 10 | 1 |
| White | 69 | 0 | 2 | 1 | 66 | 198 | 25 | 117 | 56 | 6 |
| **TEXAS** | | | | | | | | | | |
| **Metropolitan Counties** | | | | | | | | | | |
| Atascosa | 78 | 7 | 0 | 5 | 66 | 466 | 96 | 300 | 70 | 3 |
| Bandera | 33 | 3 | 2 | 1 | 27 | 153 | 41 | 90 | 22 | 0 |
| Bell | 71 | 0 | 17 | 3 | 51 | 628 | 153 | 416 | 59 | 5 |
| Bexar | 818 | 10 | 97 | 72 | 639 | 5,240 | 989 | 3,559 | 692 | 13 |
| Bowie | 82 | 1 | 18 | 3 | 60 | 336 | 80 | 196 | 60 | 3 |
| Brazoria | 238 | 3 | 39 | 29 | 167 | 1,068 | 187 | 742 | 139 | 2 |
| Brazos | 53 | 0 | 19 | 6 | 28 | 305 | 79 | 191 | 35 | 2 |
| Burleson | 28 | 0 | 2 | 2 | 24 | 73 | 27 | 36 | 10 | 0 |
| Caldwell | 27 | 4 | 3 | 1 | 19 | 91 | 23 | 47 | 21 | 1 |
| Cameron | 297 | 4 | 60 | 15 | 218 | 712 | 177 | 455 | 80 | 3 |
| Chambers | 120 | 2 | 16 | 9 | 93 | 614 | 116 | 413 | 85 | 1 |
| Clay | 11 | 0 | 3 | 0 | 8 | 67 | 25 | 28 | 14 | 0 |
| Collin | 74 | 1 | 24 | 4 | 45 | 345 | 72 | 224 | 49 | 1 |
| Comal | 91 | 0 | 31 | 6 | 54 | 604 | 149 | 351 | 104 | 1 |
| Coryell | 13 | 0 | 6 | 0 | 7 | 69 | 19 | 36 | 14 | 1 |
| Crosby | 4 | 0 | 0 | 0 | 4 | 27 | 14 | 7 | 6 | 0 |
| Dallas | 36 | 0 | 17 | 1 | 18 | 137 | 21 | 57 | 59 | 2 |
| Denton | 73 | 0 | 17 | 2 | 54 | 379 | 62 | 276 | 41 | 1 |
| Ector | 64 | 3 | 11 | 4 | 46 | 120 | 17 | 47 | 56 | 0 |
| Ellis | 89 | 1 | 27 | 3 | 58 | 410 | 96 | 264 | 50 | 0 |
| El Paso | 246 | 5 | 59 | 21 | 161 | 697 | 121 | 468 | 108 | 7 |
| Fort Bend | 988 | 17 | 147 | 107 | 717 | 4,671 | 636 | 3,626 | 409 | 0 |
| Galveston | 145 | 8 | 36 | 11 | 90 | 620 | 121 | 394 | 105 | 10 |
| Goliad | 13 | 0 | 1 | 3 | 9 | 175 | 122 | 46 | 7 | 2 |
| Grayson | 110 | 1 | 25 | 2 | 82 | 412 | 114 | 234 | 64 | 3 |
| Gregg | 99 | 1 | 21 | 6 | 71 | 358 | 86 | 218 | 54 | 0 |
| Hardin | 44 | 0 | 21 | 3 | 20 | 244 | 71 | 114 | 59 | 1 |
| Harris | 9,487 | 136 | 1,111 | 1,713 | 6,527 | 44,391 | 6,539 | 31,463 | 6,389 | 339 |
| Harrison | 92 | 1 | 0 | 4 | 87 | 433 | 107 | 253 | 73 | 0 |
| Hays | 196 | 1 | 45 | 11 | 139 | 814 | 180 | 535 | 99 | 0 |
| Hidalgo | 539 | 10 | 116 | 81 | 332 | 2,740 | 537 | 1,834 | 369 | 10 |
| Hudspeth | 12 | 0 | 3 | 0 | 9 | 4 | 1 | 2 | 1 | 0 |
| Hunt | 410 | 1 | 24 | 18 | 367 | 608 | 134 | 343 | 131 | 0 |
| Irion | 1 | 0 | 0 | 0 | 1 | 19 | 8 | 8 | 3 | 0 |
| Jefferson | 105 | 0 | 18 | 9 | 78 | 313 | 60 | 192 | 61 | 3 |
| Johnson | 200 | 2 | 45 | 7 | 146 | 573 | 102 | 388 | 83 | 8 |
| Jones | 10 | 0 | 2 | 0 | 8 | 44 | 14 | 24 | 6 | 0 |
| Kaufman | 158 | 9 | 38 | 7 | 104 | 607 | 154 | 355 | 98 | 1 |
| Kendall | 23 | 1 | 7 | 1 | 14 | 141 | 20 | 103 | 18 | 0 |
| Lampasas | 18 | 0 | 1 | 0 | 17 | 81 | 16 | 53 | 12 | 1 |
| Lubbock | 127 | 1 | 28 | 14 | 84 | 528 | 134 | 268 | 126 | 6 |
| Lynn | 6 | 0 | 1 | 0 | 5 | 11 | 6 | 3 | 2 | 0 |
| Martin | 14 | 0 | 0 | 2 | 12 | 79 | 6 | 73 | 0 | 0 |
| McLennan | 92 | 3 | 45 | 1 | 43 | 487 | 118 | 303 | 66 | 7 |
| Medina | 44 | 1 | 7 | 1 | 35 | 194 | 38 | 125 | 31 | 1 |
| Midland | 159 | 6 | 26 | 5 | 122 | 645 | 73 | 410 | 162 | 1 |
| Montgomery | 918 | 11 | 99 | 76 | 732 | 4,863 | 786 | 3,442 | 635 | 12 |
| Nueces | 29 | 0 | 8 | 1 | 20 | 56 | 23 | 33 | 0 | 1 |
| Oldham | 1 | 0 | 0 | 1 | 0 | 4 | 2 | 2 | 0 | 0 |
| Orange | 67 | 2 | 19 | 5 | 41 | 424 | 136 | 225 | 63 | 1 |
| Parker | 150 | 5 | 39 | 7 | 99 | 1,033 | 287 | 630 | 116 | 0 |
| Potter | 60 | 0 | 7 | 2 | 51 | 171 | 32 | 108 | 31 | 0 |
| Randall | 55 | 1 | 13 | 4 | 37 | 225 | 63 | 117 | 45 | 3 |
| Robertson | 15 | 0 | 4 | 0 | 11 | 97 | 23 | 59 | 15 | 1 |
| Rockwall | 25 | 0 | 4 | 0 | 21 | 99 | 20 | 66 | 13 | 0 |
| Rusk | 82 | 3 | 13 | 1 | 65 | 439 | 127 | 252 | 60 | 5 |

## Table 10. Offenses Known to Law Enforcement, by Selected State Metropolitan and Nonmetropolitan Counties, 2021—Continued

(Number.)

| State/county | Violent crime | Murder and nonnegligent manslaughter | Rape | Robbery | Aggravated assault | Property crime | Burglary | Larceny-theft | Motor vehicle theft | Arson |
|---|---|---|---|---|---|---|---|---|---|---|
| Smith | 310 | 5 | 30 | 16 | 259 | 1,132 | 261 | 681 | 190 | 1 |
| Sterling | 0 | 0 | 0 | 0 | 0 | 8 | 5 | 1 | 2 | 0 |
| Tarrant | 129 | 4 | 42 | 13 | 70 | 788 | 153 | 488 | 147 | 3 |
| Taylor | 27 | 0 | 11 | 1 | 15 | 168 | 109 | 51 | 8 | 0 |
| Tom Green | 52 | 1 | 14 | 3 | 34 | 162 | 36 | 93 | 33 | 3 |
| Travis | 782 | 11 | 109 | 60 | 602 | 3,406 | 664 | 2,279 | 463 | 13 |
| Upshur | 66 | 5 | 24 | 1 | 36 | 280 | 131 | 118 | 31 | 3 |
| Victoria | 113 | 5 | 23 | 3 | 82 | 227 | 68 | 134 | 25 | 1 |
| Waller | 55 | 1 | 11 | 2 | 41 | 201 | 64 | 119 | 18 | 0 |
| Webb | 54 | 0 | 8 | 4 | 42 | 176 | 40 | 92 | 44 | 1 |
| Wichita | 16 | 2 | 3 | 0 | 11 | 80 | 22 | 53 | 5 | 0 |
| Williamson | 177 | 0 | 54 | 15 | 108 | 1,556 | 278 | 1,149 | 129 | 2 |
| Wilson | 40 | 0 | 17 | 0 | 23 | 252 | 57 | 162 | 33 | 3 |
| Wise | 79 | 5 | 25 | 5 | 44 | 44 | 9 | 34 | 1 | 1 |
| **Nonmetropolitan Counties** | | | | | | | | | | |
| Bailey | 3 | 0 | 0 | 0 | 3 | 12 | 4 | 8 | 0 | 0 |
| Baylor | 0 | 0 | 0 | 0 | 0 | 5 | 0 | 2 | 3 | 0 |
| Bee | 30 | 0 | 4 | 0 | 26 | 127 | 42 | 71 | 14 | 4 |
| Blanco | 18 | 1 | 4 | 2 | 11 | 85 | 27 | 55 | 3 | 2 |
| Borden | 1 | 0 | 0 | 0 | 1 | 13 | 4 | 7 | 2 | 0 |
| Bosque | 11 | 0 | 2 | 0 | 9 | 68 | 26 | 36 | 6 | 1 |
| Brewster | 5 | 0 | 1 | 0 | 4 | 32 | 14 | 8 | 10 | 0 |
| Briscoe | 0 | 0 | 0 | 0 | 0 | 9 | 2 | 7 | 0 | 0 |
| Brooks | 1 | 0 | 0 | 0 | 1 | 3 | 3 | 0 | 0 | 0 |
| Brown | 44 | 0 | 4 | 5 | 35 | 206 | 80 | 113 | 13 | 7 |
| Burnet | 53 | 2 | 14 | 1 | 36 | 213 | 60 | 117 | 36 | 2 |
| Calhoun | 24 | 0 | 5 | 1 | 18 | 77 | 23 | 47 | 7 | 0 |
| Camp | 15 | 1 | 5 | 2 | 7 | 83 | 28 | 51 | 4 | 0 |
| Cass | 27 | 1 | 9 | 1 | 16 | 152 | 57 | 70 | 25 | 0 |
| Castro | 3 | 0 | 1 | 0 | 2 | 19 | 4 | 7 | 8 | 0 |
| Cherokee | 79 | 4 | 11 | 3 | 61 | 354 | 88 | 229 | 37 | 0 |
| Childress | 2 | 0 | 0 | 0 | 2 | 2 | 1 | 1 | 0 | 0 |
| Cochran | 9 | 0 | 1 | 0 | 8 | 21 | 11 | 9 | 1 | 0 |
| Collingsworth | 2 | 0 | 0 | 0 | 2 | 8 | 2 | 4 | 2 | 0 |
| Colorado | 13 | 0 | 3 | 1 | 9 | 136 | 31 | 77 | 28 | 0 |
| Comanche | 14 | 0 | 5 | 2 | 7 | 63 | 10 | 48 | 5 | 0 |
| Cooke | 56 | 0 | 20 | 2 | 34 | 132 | 53 | 66 | 13 | 1 |
| Crane | 1 | 0 | 0 | 0 | 1 | 6 | 0 | 3 | 3 | 0 |
| Crockett | 3 | 0 | 1 | 0 | 2 | 33 | 25 | 7 | 1 | 0 |
| Dallam | 0 | 0 | 0 | 0 | 0 | 5 | 2 | 0 | 3 | 0 |
| Dawson | 3 | 0 | 2 | 0 | 1 | 53 | 20 | 25 | 8 | 0 |
| Deaf Smith | 12 | 0 | 0 | 0 | 12 | 27 | 6 | 19 | 2 | 1 |
| Delta | 3 | 0 | 1 | 0 | 2 | 19 | 11 | 7 | 1 | 1 |
| DeWitt | 32 | 0 | 6 | 1 | 25 | 53 | 9 | 29 | 15 | 3 |
| Donley | 4 | 0 | 0 | 0 | 4 | 31 | 15 | 10 | 6 | 0 |
| Duval | 13 | 0 | 2 | 0 | 11 | 96 | 21 | 41 | 34 | 1 |
| Eastland | 7 | 0 | 0 | 0 | 7 | 35 | 7 | 20 | 8 | 1 |
| Edwards | 0 | 0 | 0 | 0 | 0 | 15 | 7 | 3 | 5 | 0 |
| Erath | 7 | 1 | 1 | 0 | 5 | 68 | 26 | 42 | 0 | 0 |
| Fannin | 51 | 1 | 13 | 2 | 35 | 129 | 25 | 89 | 15 | 1 |
| Fayette | 17 | 1 | 8 | 0 | 8 | 92 | 22 | 54 | 16 | 0 |
| Floyd | 7 | 0 | 1 | 0 | 6 | 27 | 4 | 18 | 5 | 0 |
| Freestone | 25 | 1 | 2 | 0 | 22 | 76 | 21 | 50 | 5 | 3 |
| Gaines | 11 | 0 | 2 | 1 | 8 | 74 | 22 | 43 | 9 | 0 |
| Garza | 5 | 0 | 3 | 0 | 2 | 24 | 9 | 15 | 0 | 0 |
| Gillespie | 14 | 1 | 7 | 0 | 6 | 27 | 10 | 14 | 3 | 0 |
| Gonzales | 61 | 0 | 6 | 1 | 54 | 77 | 20 | 40 | 17 | 2 |
| Gray | 7 | 1 | 0 | 1 | 5 | 46 | 19 | 24 | 3 | 1 |
| Grimes | 26 | 0 | 7 | 4 | 15 | 98 | 43 | 43 | 12 | 1 |
| Hall | 1 | 0 | 0 | 0 | 1 | 14 | 5 | 5 | 4 | 0 |
| Hamilton | 3 | 0 | 0 | 0 | 3 | 13 | 7 | 2 | 4 | 1 |
| Hansford | 1 | 0 | 0 | 0 | 1 | 5 | 2 | 3 | 0 | 0 |
| Hardeman | 4 | 1 | 0 | 1 | 2 | 21 | 2 | 19 | 0 | 0 |
| Hartley | 1 | 0 | 0 | 0 | 1 | 12 | 5 | 3 | 4 | 0 |
| Haskell | 6 | 0 | 2 | 0 | 4 | 10 | 1 | 5 | 4 | 0 |
| Hemphill | 0 | 0 | 0 | 0 | 0 | 15 | 1 | 13 | 1 | 0 |
| Hill | 77 | 1 | 25 | 2 | 49 | 235 | 43 | 166 | 26 | 2 |
| Hockley | 16 | 0 | 2 | 1 | 13 | 71 | 24 | 40 | 7 | 0 |
| Hood | 53 | 0 | 8 | 4 | 41 | 279 | 66 | 179 | 34 | 4 |
| Hopkins | 34 | 2 | 2 | 1 | 29 | 36 | 10 | 11 | 15 | 0 |
| Houston | 9 | 0 | 3 | 0 | 6 | 77 | 34 | 36 | 7 | 0 |
| Howard | 36 | 0 | 1 | 2 | 33 | 265 | 67 | 160 | 38 | 4 |
| Hutchinson | 8 | 0 | 1 | 0 | 7 | 47 | 18 | 15 | 14 | 0 |
| Jack | 1 | 0 | 0 | 0 | 1 | 22 | 14 | 4 | 4 | 0 |
| Jackson | 12 | 0 | 2 | 1 | 9 | 52 | 14 | 30 | 8 | 0 |
| Jasper | 56 | 1 | 11 | 6 | 38 | 388 | 165 | 195 | 28 | 2 |
| Jeff Davis | 3 | 0 | 0 | 0 | 3 | 2 | 0 | 1 | 1 | 0 |
| Jim Hogg | 9 | 0 | 0 | 0 | 9 | 40 | 17 | 15 | 8 | 0 |
| Jim Wells | 65 | 1 | 11 | 0 | 53 | 207 | 83 | 98 | 26 | 6 |
| Karnes | 9 | 0 | 4 | 0 | 5 | 64 | 18 | 42 | 4 | 1 |
| Kerr | 50 | 1 | 17 | 0 | 32 | 183 | 61 | 103 | 19 | 1 |

## Table 10. Offenses Known to Law Enforcement, by Selected State Metropolitan and Nonmetropolitan Counties, 2021—Continued

(Number.)

| State/county | Violent crime | Murder and nonnegligent manslaughter | Rape | Robbery | Aggravated assault | Property crime | Burglary | Larceny-theft | Motor vehicle theft | Arson |
|---|---|---|---|---|---|---|---|---|---|---|
| King | 0 | 0 | 0 | 0 | 0 | 0 | 0 | 0 | 0 | 0 |
| Kleberg | 14 | 0 | 2 | 0 | 12 | 23 | 5 | 17 | 1 | 0 |
| Lamar | 33 | 2 | 2 | 0 | 29 | 167 | 39 | 103 | 25 | 0 |
| Lamb | 7 | 0 | 3 | 1 | 3 | 53 | 28 | 21 | 4 | 1 |
| La Salle | 16 | 0 | 0 | 1 | 15 | 44 | 17 | 22 | 5 | 0 |
| Lavaca | 9 | 1 | 2 | 0 | 6 | 59 | 15 | 32 | 12 | 2 |
| Lee | 20 | 1 | 6 | 2 | 11 | 103 | 32 | 58 | 13 | 2 |
| Leon | 14 | 0 | 1 | 0 | 13 | 105 | 36 | 58 | 11 | 1 |
| Limestone | 36 | 0 | 12 | 0 | 24 | 104 | 44 | 48 | 12 | 1 |
| Lipscomb | 1 | 0 | 0 | 0 | 1 | 25 | 6 | 17 | 2 | 0 |
| Llano | 23 | 0 | 5 | 1 | 17 | 193 | 55 | 115 | 23 | 1 |
| Loving | 3 | 0 | 1 | 0 | 2 | 17 | 1 | 16 | 0 | 0 |
| Madison | 8 | 0 | 1 | 1 | 6 | 48 | 15 | 24 | 9 | 0 |
| Marion | 35 | 1 | 1 | 0 | 33 | 99 | 40 | 49 | 10 | 0 |
| Mason | 4 | 0 | 0 | 0 | 4 | 11 | 3 | 7 | 1 | 0 |
| Matagorda | 97 | 1 | 13 | 2 | 81 | 292 | 63 | 186 | 43 | 4 |
| McCulloch | 2 | 0 | 0 | 0 | 2 | 42 | 22 | 9 | 11 | 0 |
| Milam | 21 | 1 | 1 | 1 | 18 | 42 | 10 | 28 | 4 | 0 |
| Mills | 11 | 0 | 4 | 0 | 7 | 41 | 33 | 8 | 0 | 0 |
| Montague | 22 | 0 | 6 | 1 | 15 | 97 | 24 | 69 | 4 | 2 |
| Moore | 8 | 1 | 1 | 0 | 6 | 32 | 14 | 12 | 6 | 1 |
| Nacogdoches | 34 | 1 | 2 | 0 | 31 | 186 | 41 | 121 | 24 | 1 |
| Navarro | 69 | 1 | 19 | 3 | 46 | 224 | 75 | 131 | 18 | 4 |
| Newton | 8 | 0 | 2 | 0 | 6 | 53 | 15 | 31 | 7 | 0 |
| Nolan | 7 | 0 | 0 | 0 | 7 | 42 | 13 | 29 | 0 | 0 |
| Palo Pinto | 21 | 0 | 4 | 0 | 17 | 97 | 27 | 54 | 16 | 0 |
| Panola | 35 | 1 | 2 | 0 | 32 | 207 | 60 | 120 | 27 | 0 |
| Parmer | 2 | 0 | 0 | 0 | 2 | 39 | 10 | 21 | 8 | 0 |
| Polk | 82 | 5 | 15 | 4 | 58 | 477 | 126 | 278 | 73 | 3 |
| Presidio | 0 | 0 | 0 | 0 | 0 | 0 | 0 | 0 | 0 | 0 |
| Reagan | 3 | 0 | 2 | 1 | 0 | 28 | 4 | 20 | 4 | 0 |
| Real | 5 | 0 | 1 | 0 | 4 | 119 | 93 | 21 | 5 | 0 |
| Red River | 18 | 0 | 5 | 0 | 13 | 49 | 22 | 20 | 7 | 0 |
| Refugio | 3 | 1 | 0 | 0 | 2 | 44 | 13 | 12 | 19 | 0 |
| Runnels | 2 | 0 | 0 | 0 | 2 | 12 | 9 | 2 | 1 | 0 |
| Sabine | 20 | 0 | 7 | 0 | 13 | 69 | 15 | 47 | 7 | 2 |
| San Augustine | 14 | 0 | 2 | 0 | 12 | 54 | 21 | 22 | 11 | 1 |
| Schleicher | 2 | 0 | 0 | 0 | 2 | 11 | 4 | 7 | 0 | 0 |
| Scurry | 6 | 0 | 1 | 0 | 5 | 90 | 37 | 51 | 2 | 1 |
| Shelby | 20 | 1 | 1 | 0 | 18 | 157 | 43 | 91 | 23 | 3 |
| Somervell | 4 | 0 | 0 | 0 | 4 | 66 | 26 | 40 | 0 | 0 |
| Starr | 34 | 0 | 6 | 1 | 27 | 138 | 73 | 50 | 15 | 4 |
| Stephens | 4 | 0 | 1 | 0 | 3 | 35 | 8 | 17 | 10 | 0 |
| Sutton | 3 | 0 | 1 | 0 | 2 | 6 | 5 | 0 | 1 | 0 |
| Swisher | 5 | 0 | 0 | 0 | 5 | 22 | 10 | 11 | 1 | 0 |
| Terrell | 0 | 0 | 0 | 0 | 0 | 0 | 0 | 0 | 0 | 0 |
| Terry | 7 | 0 | 0 | 4 | 3 | 42 | 16 | 26 | 0 | 0 |
| Throckmorton | 8 | 0 | 2 | 0 | 6 | 2 | 0 | 2 | 0 | 0 |
| Titus | 37 | 0 | 7 | 3 | 27 | 149 | 34 | 100 | 15 | 0 |
| Trinity | 14 | 0 | 1 | 1 | 12 | 108 | 47 | 44 | 17 | 0 |
| Tyler | 24 | 3 | 2 | 2 | 17 | 185 | 69 | 78 | 38 | 2 |
| Upton | 1 | 0 | 0 | 0 | 1 | 13 | 3 | 7 | 3 | 0 |
| Uvalde | 19 | 1 | 2 | 0 | 16 | 63 | 26 | 23 | 14 | 0 |
| Val Verde | 52 | 0 | 11 | 2 | 39 | 125 | 63 | 48 | 14 | 1 |
| Walker | 52 | 0 | 15 | 1 | 36 | 211 | 70 | 92 | 49 | 3 |
| Ward | 16 | 0 | 3 | 3 | 10 | 151 | 46 | 71 | 34 | 3 |
| Washington | 49 | 0 | 4 | 0 | 45 | 95 | 21 | 65 | 9 | 2 |
| Wharton | 80 | 3 | 8 | 4 | 65 | 255 | 71 | 152 | 32 | 3 |
| Wheeler | 7 | 0 | 2 | 0 | 5 | 13 | 6 | 6 | 1 | 0 |
| Wilbarger | 6 | 0 | 0 | 0 | 6 | 14 | 2 | 9 | 3 | 0 |
| Willacy | 12 | 0 | 0 | 0 | 12 | 24 | 7 | 14 | 3 | 0 |
| Winkler | 6 | 0 | 1 | 0 | 5 | 44 | 13 | 26 | 5 | 0 |
| Wood | 37 | 1 | 8 | 4 | 24 | 175 | 64 | 91 | 20 | 3 |
| Yoakum | 10 | 0 | 1 | 2 | 7 | 46 | 7 | 34 | 5 | 1 |
| Young | 16 | 0 | 4 | 0 | 12 | 21 | 8 | 11 | 2 | 0 |
| Zapata | 10 | 0 | 0 | 0 | 10 | 59 | 21 | 37 | 1 | 0 |
| Zavala | 34 | 0 | 12 | 0 | 22 | 44 | 14 | 20 | 10 | 0 |
| **UTAH** | | | | | | | | | | |
| **Metropolitan Counties** | | | | | | | | | | |
| Box Elder | 12 | 0 | 2 | 1 | 9 | 117 | 22 | 82 | 13 | 0 |
| Cache | 44 | 1 | 14 | 0 | 29 | 257 | 39 | 201 | 17 | 3 |
| Davis | 29 | 0 | 10 | 1 | 18 | 129 | 16 | 103 | 10 | 0 |
| Salt Lake County Unified Police Department | 600 | 17 | 141 | 95 | 347 | 6,901 | 665 | 5,241 | 995 | 5 |
| Tooele | 48 | 1 | 20 | 3 | 24 | 198 | 35 | 138 | 25 | 0 |
| Utah | 85 | 0 | 35 | 1 | 49 | 287 | 35 | 224 | 28 | 1 |
| Washington | 17 | 0 | 6 | 0 | 11 | 94 | 8 | 69 | 17 | 0 |
| Weber | 125 | 0 | 40 | 4 | 81 | 794 | 126 | 575 | 93 | 3 |
| **Nonmetropolitan Counties** | | | | | | | | | | |
| Beaver | 12 | 2 | 3 | 1 | 6 | 63 | 24 | 29 | 10 | 0 |
| Carbon | 31 | 0 | 4 | 2 | 25 | 54 | 18 | 30 | 6 | 1 |

## Table 10. Offenses Known to Law Enforcement, by Selected State Metropolitan and Nonmetropolitan Counties, 2021—Continued

(Number.)

| State/county | Violent crime | Murder and nonnegligent manslaughter | Rape | Robbery | Aggravated assault | Property crime | Burglary | Larceny-theft | Motor vehicle theft | Arson |
|---|---|---|---|---|---|---|---|---|---|---|
| Duchesne | 42 | 3 | 14 | 0 | 25 | 196 | 39 | 127 | 30 | 3 |
| Garfield | 3 | 0 | 1 | 0 | 2 | 41 | 8 | 28 | 5 | 0 |
| Iron | 23 | 0 | 7 | 2 | 14 | 83 | 28 | 47 | 8 | 1 |
| Kane | 28 | 0 | 2 | 0 | 26 | 21 | 3 | 16 | 2 | 0 |
| Millard | 34 | 0 | 12 | 0 | 22 | 153 | 26 | 112 | 15 | 0 |
| Sanpete | 37 | 0 | 19 | 1 | 17 | 96 | 11 | 78 | 7 | 1 |
| Sevier | 9 | 0 | 3 | 0 | 6 | 41 | 14 | 25 | 2 | 1 |
| Summit | 50 | 1 | 41 | 1 | 7 | 314 | 29 | 249 | 36 | 1 |
| Uintah | 46 | 0 | 8 | 0 | 38 | 174 | 31 | 119 | 24 | 1 |
| Wasatch | 19 | 1 | 4 | 0 | 14 | 113 | 19 | 85 | 9 | 0 |
| **VERMONT** | | | | | | | | | | |
| **Metropolitan Counties** | | | | | | | | | | |
| Franklin | 28 | 0 | 11 | 0 | 17 | 53 | 3 | 49 | 1 | 0 |
| Grand Isle | 0 | 0 | 0 | 0 | 0 | 39 | 11 | 28 | 0 | 0 |
| Nonmetropolitan Counties | | | | | | | | | | |
| Bennington | 0 | 0 | 0 | 0 | 0 | 7 | 1 | 5 | 1 | 0 |
| Essex | 4 | 0 | 1 | 1 | 2 | 17 | 4 | 10 | 3 | 0 |
| Lamoille | 6 | 0 | 1 | 0 | 5 | 46 | 4 | 42 | 0 | 1 |
| Orange | 3 | 0 | 3 | 0 | 0 | 7 | 1 | 5 | 1 | 0 |
| Orleans | 7 | 0 | 2 | 0 | 5 | 60 | 4 | 56 | 0 | 0 |
| Rutland | 5 | 0 | 0 | 0 | 5 | 21 | 0 | 21 | 0 | 0 |
| Windham | 1 | 0 | 0 | 0 | 1 | 36 | 2 | 32 | 2 | 0 |
| Windsor | 0 | 0 | 0 | 0 | 0 | 1 | 0 | 0 | 1 | 0 |
| **VIRGINIA** | | | | | | | | | | |
| **Metropolitan Counties** | | | | | | | | | | |
| Albemarle County Police Department | 106 | 0 | 22 | 8 | 76 | 1,701 | 103 | 1,496 | 102 | 6 |
| Amelia | 24 | 1 | 6 | 0 | 17 | 153 | 29 | 108 | 16 | 2 |
| Amherst | 66 | 1 | 10 | 5 | 50 | 358 | 26 | 303 | 29 | 3 |
| Appomattox | 26 | 1 | 3 | 0 | 22 | 90 | 9 | 81 | 0 | 1 |
| Arlington County Police Department | 469 | 0 | 60 | 154 | 255 | 3,267 | 210 | 2,757 | 300 | 11 |
| Augusta | 90 | 2 | 24 | 3 | 61 | 692 | 126 | 482 | 84 | 2 |
| Bedford | 81 | 1 | 15 | 6 | 59 | 475 | 98 | 334 | 43 | 3 |
| Botetourt | 25 | 0 | 10 | 3 | 12 | 245 | 25 | 196 | 24 | 3 |
| Campbell | 102 | 1 | 24 | 5 | 72 | 529 | 59 | 425 | 45 | 5 |
| Charles City | 12 | 0 | 0 | 0 | 12 | 24 | 3 | 19 | 2 | 0 |
| Chesterfield County Police Department | 536 | 12 | 96 | 125 | 303 | 4,840 | 512 | 3,981 | 347 | 24 |
| Clarke | 4 | 0 | 2 | 1 | 1 | 41 | 2 | 35 | 4 | 0 |
| Craig | 6 | 0 | 4 | 1 | 1 | 29 | 5 | 21 | 3 | 0 |
| Culpeper | 20 | 0 | 0 | 1 | 19 | 115 | 6 | 90 | 19 | 1 |
| Dinwiddie | 83 | 3 | 6 | 4 | 70 | 266 | 33 | 218 | 15 | 4 |
| Fairfax County Police Department | 948 | 26 | 172 | 318 | 432 | 13,059 | 561 | 11,302 | 1,196 | 16 |
| Fauquier | 51 | 3 | 21 | 2 | 25 | 196 | 17 | 167 | 12 | 0 |
| Fluvanna | 41 | 0 | 11 | 1 | 29 | 127 | 13 | 102 | 12 | 1 |
| Franklin | 61 | 6 | 19 | 1 | 35 | 445 | 55 | 316 | 74 | 0 |
| Frederick | 61 | 2 | 16 | 6 | 37 | 846 | 65 | 695 | 86 | 5 |
| Giles | 15 | 0 | 2 | 0 | 13 | 74 | 18 | 50 | 6 | 0 |
| Gloucester | 25 | 0 | 11 | 8 | 6 | 335 | 18 | 289 | 28 | 6 |
| Goochland | 23 | 0 | 6 | 0 | 17 | 235 | 14 | 201 | 20 | 1 |
| Greene | 26 | 0 | 4 | 2 | 20 | 172 | 12 | 147 | 13 | 0 |
| Hanover | 180 | 1 | 19 | 11 | 149 | 873 | 33 | 794 | 46 | 5 |
| Henrico County Police Department | 651 | 23 | 40 | 132 | 456 | 6,917 | 373 | 6,084 | 460 | 37 |
| Isle of Wight | 29 | 1 | 3 | 3 | 22 | 235 | 15 | 202 | 18 | 2 |
| James City County Police Department | 101 | 3 | 14 | 12 | 72 | 727 | 37 | 658 | 32 | 4 |
| King and Queen | 5 | 0 | 0 | 0 | 5 | 25 | 6 | 19 | 0 | 0 |
| King William | 24 | 0 | 5 | 0 | 19 | 85 | 6 | 76 | 3 | 0 |
| Loudoun | 271 | 3 | 127 | 26 | 115 | 1,937 | 132 | 1,667 | 138 | 25 |
| Madison | 23 | 1 | 11 | 0 | 11 | 74 | 9 | 52 | 13 | 1 |
| Mathews | 3 | 0 | 2 | 0 | 1 | 51 | 7 | 42 | 2 | 1 |
| Montgomery | 85 | 1 | 19 | 3 | 62 | 245 | 48 | 162 | 35 | 8 |
| Nelson | 36 | 0 | 8 | 2 | 26 | 212 | 48 | 147 | 17 | 3 |
| New Kent | 46 | 1 | 2 | 1 | 42 | 145 | 13 | 127 | 5 | 0 |
| Powhatan | 51 | 0 | 10 | 0 | 41 | 157 | 15 | 140 | 2 | 0 |
| Prince George County Police Department | 129 | 3 | 16 | 10 | 100 | 376 | 50 | 284 | 42 | 5 |
| Prince William County Police Department | 1,024 | 10 | 104 | 185 | 725 | 5,174 | 420 | 4,257 | 497 | 31 |
| Pulaski | 34 | 3 | 11 | 2 | 18 | 469 | 85 | 358 | 26 | 5 |
| Rappahannock | 11 | 0 | 1 | 0 | 10 | 26 | 2 | 21 | 3 | 0 |
| Roanoke County Police Department | 210 | 0 | 27 | 17 | 166 | 1,052 | 134 | 831 | 87 | 1 |
| Rockingham | 78 | 4 | 17 | 2 | 55 | 305 | 80 | 217 | 8 | 8 |
| Scott | 36 | 0 | 8 | 1 | 27 | 245 | 52 | 165 | 28 | 5 |
| Southampton | 9 | 0 | 9 | 0 | 0 | 136 | 18 | 100 | 18 | 1 |
| Spotsylvania | 134 | 3 | 18 | 13 | 100 | 696 | 44 | 588 | 64 | 0 |
| Stafford | 318 | 4 | 85 | 24 | 205 | 1,249 | 92 | 1,070 | 87 | 11 |
| Sussex | 15 | 0 | 2 | 3 | 10 | 87 | 18 | 60 | 9 | 1 |
| Warren | 21 | 0 | 11 | 0 | 10 | 191 | 12 | 160 | 19 | 2 |
| Washington | 46 | 0 | 18 | 2 | 26 | 577 | 92 | 435 | 50 | 4 |
| York | 112 | 1 | 17 | 9 | 85 | 779 | 41 | 707 | 31 | 4 |

## Table 10. Offenses Known to Law Enforcement, by Selected State Metropolitan and Nonmetropolitan Counties, 2021—Continued

(Number.)

| State/county | Violent crime | Murder and nonnegligent manslaughter | Rape | Robbery | Aggravated assault | Property crime | Burglary | Larceny-theft | Motor vehicle theft | Arson |
|---|---|---|---|---|---|---|---|---|---|---|
| **Nonmetropolitan Counties** | | | | | | | | | | |
| Accomack | 95 | 9 | 12 | 7 | 67 | 257 | 52 | 192 | 13 | 1 |
| Alleghany | 35 | 1 | 7 | 0 | 27 | 82 | 21 | 57 | 4 | 0 |
| Bath | 0 | 0 | 0 | 0 | 0 | 22 | 2 | 17 | 3 | 0 |
| Brunswick | 6 | 0 | 3 | 0 | 3 | 104 | 19 | 77 | 8 | 2 |
| Buchanan | 39 | 2 | 16 | 0 | 21 | 218 | 21 | 167 | 30 | 2 |
| Buckingham | 20 | 1 | 6 | 3 | 10 | 188 | 33 | 123 | 32 | 0 |
| Caroline | 56 | 2 | 13 | 3 | 38 | 159 | 30 | 126 | 3 | 2 |
| Carroll | 23 | 1 | 13 | 0 | 9 | 209 | 42 | 129 | 38 | 1 |
| Charlotte | 13 | 0 | 2 | 3 | 8 | 121 | 18 | 89 | 14 | 0 |
| Cumberland | 14 | 0 | 4 | 1 | 9 | 42 | 7 | 30 | 5 | 1 |
| Dickenson | 18 | 3 | 2 | 0 | 13 | 64 | 26 | 31 | 7 | 2 |
| Essex | 7 | 0 | 2 | 0 | 5 | 34 | 8 | 23 | 3 | 0 |
| Floyd | 11 | 0 | 6 | 1 | 4 | 64 | 10 | 50 | 4 | 0 |
| Grayson | 21 | 0 | 5 | 0 | 16 | 132 | 16 | 94 | 22 | 2 |
| Greensville | 23 | 4 | 3 | 3 | 13 | 98 | 13 | 73 | 12 | 2 |
| Halifax | 29 | 3 | 7 | 2 | 17 | 171 | 37 | 114 | 20 | 2 |
| Henry | 128 | 3 | 32 | 12 | 81 | 688 | 178 | 457 | 53 | 4 |
| Highland | 1 | 0 | 0 | 0 | 1 | 31 | 3 | 27 | 1 | 1 |
| King George | 46 | 1 | 5 | 3 | 37 | 228 | 32 | 179 | 17 | 3 |
| Lancaster | 27 | 0 | 3 | 3 | 21 | 58 | 13 | 45 | 0 | 2 |
| Lee | 29 | 0 | 10 | 1 | 18 | 252 | 50 | 195 | 7 | 2 |
| Louisa | 32 | 0 | 11 | 1 | 20 | 259 | 11 | 216 | 32 | 3 |
| Lunenburg | 25 | 0 | 3 | 1 | 21 | 37 | 10 | 21 | 6 | 2 |
| Mecklenburg | 47 | 0 | 4 | 2 | 41 | 185 | 36 | 117 | 32 | 0 |
| Middlesex | 14 | 0 | 7 | 1 | 6 | 96 | 16 | 71 | 9 | 0 |
| Northampton | 27 | 1 | 1 | 0 | 25 | 52 | 8 | 40 | 4 | 0 |
| Northumberland | 11 | 0 | 2 | 0 | 9 | 44 | 8 | 32 | 4 | 0 |
| Nottoway | 20 | 0 | 1 | 1 | 18 | 82 | 23 | 50 | 9 | 1 |
| Orange | 44 | 2 | 14 | 1 | 27 | 146 | 9 | 125 | 12 | 1 |
| Page | 7 | 0 | 5 | 0 | 2 | 161 | 12 | 136 | 13 | 2 |
| Patrick | 44 | 0 | 10 | 1 | 33 | 218 | 46 | 154 | 18 | 4 |
| Pittsylvania | 45 | 3 | 11 | 3 | 28 | 309 | 72 | 218 | 19 | 6 |
| Prince Edward | 18 | 1 | 3 | 0 | 14 | 72 | 10 | 55 | 7 | 1 |
| Rockbridge | 37 | 1 | 5 | 1 | 30 | 215 | 29 | 164 | 22 | 1 |
| Russell | 43 | 3 | 19 | 0 | 21 | 168 | 39 | 109 | 20 | 6 |
| Shenandoah | 32 | 0 | 11 | 2 | 19 | 206 | 22 | 182 | 2 | 0 |
| Smyth | 19 | 1 | 6 | 1 | 11 | 141 | 22 | 108 | 11 | 1 |
| Surry | 5 | 0 | 1 | 0 | 4 | 21 | 5 | 15 | 1 | 0 |
| Tazewell | 46 | 1 | 21 | 2 | 22 | 237 | 49 | 162 | 26 | 3 |
| Westmoreland | 19 | 0 | 6 | 1 | 12 | 74 | 10 | 54 | 10 | 1 |
| Wise | 38 | 0 | 10 | 1 | 27 | 371 | 48 | 283 | 40 | 6 |
| Wythe | 21 | 0 | 16 | 1 | 4 | 132 | 12 | 102 | 18 | 1 |
| **WASHINGTON** | | | | | | | | | | |
| **Metropolitan Counties** | | | | | | | | | | |
| Asotin | 15 | 0 | 4 | 1 | 10 | 138 | 33 | 85 | 20 | 0 |
| Benton | 76 | 2 | 9 | 3 | 62 | 488 | 94 | 328 | 66 | 6 |
| Chelan | 30 | 1 | 1 | 0 | 28 | 305 | 118 | 145 | 42 | 0 |
| Clark | 338 | 4 | 93 | 41 | 200 | 3,218 | 422 | 2,024 | 772 | 14 |
| Cowlitz | 64 | 2 | 22 | 9 | 31 | 419 | 126 | 214 | 79 | 9 |
| Douglas | 13 | 0 | 10 | 0 | 3 | 259 | 69 | 151 | 39 | 2 |
| Franklin | 14 | 1 | 3 | 0 | 10 | 136 | 44 | 72 | 20 | 3 |
| King | 603 | 21 | 65 | 108 | 409 | 3,914 | 710 | 2,466 | 738 | 97 |
| Kitsap | 459 | 4 | 84 | 38 | 333 | 2,879 | 603 | 1,888 | 388 | 18 |
| Pierce | 1,301 | 18 | 114 | 175 | 994 | 8,341 | 1,866 | 4,731 | 1,744 | 71 |
| Skagit | 82 | 2 | 2 | 20 | 58 | 968 | 228 | 628 | 112 | 10 |
| Skamania | 10 | 1 | 2 | 0 | 7 | 100 | 14 | 71 | 15 | 0 |
| Snohomish | 482 | 2 | 51 | 63 | 366 | 4,125 | 838 | 2,634 | 653 | 20 |
| Spokane | 193 | 2 | 29 | 21 | 141 | 3,072 | 544 | 2,209 | 319 | 15 |
| Stevens | 38 | 6 | 7 | 2 | 23 | 326 | 94 | 194 | 38 | 1 |
| Thurston | 253 | 3 | 22 | 21 | 207 | 1,462 | 332 | 909 | 221 | 6 |
| Walla Walla | 44 | 0 | 3 | 4 | 37 | 234 | 79 | 130 | 25 | 1 |
| Whatcom | 130 | 4 | 24 | 2 | 100 | 936 | 239 | 590 | 107 | 3 |
| Yakima | 114 | 1 | 14 | 12 | 87 | 1,182 | 358 | 586 | 238 | 4 |
| **Nonmetropolitan Counties** | | | | | | | | | | |
| Adams | 26 | 2 | 3 | 4 | 17 | 258 | 71 | 148 | 39 | 1 |
| Clallam | 61 | 0 | 9 | 7 | 45 | 470 | 115 | 314 | 41 | 4 |
| Columbia | 3 | 0 | 0 | 1 | 2 | 49 | 18 | 25 | 6 | 0 |
| Garfield | 21 | 0 | 1 | 0 | 20 | 21 | 7 | 12 | 2 | 0 |
| Grant | 91 | 4 | 22 | 8 | 57 | 850 | 189 | 496 | 165 | 7 |
| Grays Harbor | 39 | 1 | 13 | 6 | 19 | 264 | 94 | 142 | 28 | 5 |
| Island | 49 | 1 | 15 | 1 | 32 | 491 | 135 | 320 | 36 | 3 |
| Jefferson | 36 | 1 | 6 | 3 | 26 | 162 | 53 | 86 | 23 | 2 |
| Kittitas | 11 | 0 | 3 | 2 | 6 | 222 | 47 | 145 | 30 | 0 |
| Lewis | 83 | 0 | 24 | 1 | 58 | 655 | 220 | 367 | 68 | 3 |
| Lincoln | 5 | 0 | 4 | 0 | 1 | 169 | 85 | 64 | 20 | 5 |
| Mason | 86 | 1 | 15 | 14 | 56 | 786 | 239 | 453 | 94 | 2 |
| Okanogan | 34 | 0 | 5 | 4 | 25 | 356 | 108 | 209 | 39 | 0 |

## Table 10. Offenses Known to Law Enforcement, by Selected State Metropolitan and Nonmetropolitan Counties, 2021—Continued

(Number.)

| State/county | Violent crime | Murder and nonnegligent manslaughter | Rape | Robbery | Aggravated assault | Property crime | Burglary | Larceny-theft | Motor vehicle theft | Arson |
|---|---|---|---|---|---|---|---|---|---|---|
| Pend Oreille | 9 | 0 | 4 | 0 | 5 | 181 | 42 | 109 | 30 | 2 |
| San Juan | 9 | 0 | 0 | 0 | 9 | 97 | 22 | 72 | 3 | 0 |
| Whitman | 11 | 1 | 4 | 0 | 6 | 53 | 11 | 36 | 6 | 1 |
| **WEST VIRGINIA** | | | | | | | | | | |
| **Metropolitan Counties** | | | | | | | | | | |
| Berkeley | 95 | 8 | 21 | 1 | 65 | 174 | 11 | 154 | 9 | 2 |
| Brooke | 5 | 0 | 0 | 0 | 5 | 2 | 0 | 2 | 0 | 0 |
| Cabell | 50 | 0 | 6 | 4 | 40 | 439 | 58 | 341 | 40 | 2 |
| Fayette | 57 | 1 | 7 | 1 | 48 | 186 | 58 | 110 | 18 | 4 |
| Jackson | 34 | 1 | 4 | 0 | 29 | 26 | 4 | 12 | 10 | 0 |
| Jefferson | 22 | 1 | 9 | 0 | 12 | 199 | 26 | 154 | 19 | 2 |
| Kanawha | 383 | 7 | 52 | 11 | 313 | 1,231 | 256 | 756 | 219 | 17 |
| Marshall | 18 | 1 | 3 | 0 | 14 | 83 | 25 | 51 | 7 | 1 |
| Mineral | 15 | 0 | 2 | 1 | 12 | 33 | 7 | 26 | 0 | 0 |
| Monongalia | 47 | 0 | 9 | 0 | 38 | 428 | 26 | 381 | 21 | 1 |
| Preston | 5 | 3 | 0 | 0 | 2 | 55 | 0 | 41 | 14 | 0 |
| Raleigh | 114 | 4 | 26 | 8 | 76 | 756 | 228 | 473 | 55 | 1 |
| Wood | 39 | 0 | 8 | 4 | 27 | 287 | 22 | 235 | 30 | 1 |
| **Nonmetropolitan Counties** | | | | | | | | | | |
| Barbour | 26 | 0 | 0 | 0 | 26 | 8 | 2 | 5 | 1 | 1 |
| Doddridge | 15 | 0 | 2 | 0 | 13 | 42 | 11 | 21 | 10 | 2 |
| Hardy | 8 | 0 | 1 | 0 | 7 | 27 | 4 | 20 | 3 | 0 |
| Harrison | 45 | 2 | 4 | 0 | 39 | 227 | 46 | 136 | 45 | 4 |
| Lewis | 14 | 1 | 0 | 0 | 13 | 33 | 7 | 16 | 10 | 0 |
| Logan | 118 | 2 | 1 | 0 | 115 | 0 | 0 | 0 | 0 | 5 |
| Mason | 10 | 1 | 0 | 1 | 8 | 66 | 13 | 51 | 2 | 2 |
| Mingo | 4 | 1 | 0 | 0 | 3 | 13 | 9 | 0 | 4 | 0 |
| Monroe | 2 | 0 | 1 | 0 | 1 | 22 | 7 | 13 | 2 | 1 |
| Nicholas | 155 | 2 | 3 | 0 | 150 | 4 | 0 | 4 | 0 | 1 |
| Randolph | 61 | 0 | 1 | 0 | 60 | 88 | 21 | 65 | 2 | 2 |
| Ritchie | 6 | 0 | 2 | 0 | 4 | 27 | 6 | 21 | 0 | 1 |
| Roane | 10 | 0 | 0 | 0 | 10 | 0 | 0 | 0 | 0 | 1 |
| Summers | 13 | 0 | 1 | 0 | 12 | 25 | 9 | 11 | 5 | 0 |
| Upshur | 4 | 0 | 1 | 0 | 3 | 7 | 0 | 7 | 0 | 5 |
| Wetzel | 12 | 0 | 1 | 0 | 11 | 32 | 20 | 9 | 3 | 2 |
| Wyoming | 101 | 0 | 5 | 0 | 96 | 60 | 20 | 29 | 11 | 2 |
| **WISCONSIN** | | | | | | | | | | |
| **Metropolitan Counties** | | | | | | | | | | |
| Brown | 85 | 0 | 31 | 7 | 47 | 893 | 127 | 709 | 57 | 3 |
| Calumet | 12 | 0 | 5 | 0 | 7 | 94 | 11 | 81 | 2 | 0 |
| Chippewa | 40 | 0 | 19 | 1 | 20 | 258 | 51 | 188 | 19 | 1 |
| Columbia | 30 | 0 | 13 | 3 | 14 | 146 | 27 | 110 | 9 | 0 |
| Dane | 118 | 3 | 29 | 5 | 81 | 586 | 98 | 428 | 60 | 7 |
| Douglas | 23 | 0 | 1 | 0 | 22 | 184 | 65 | 100 | 19 | 0 |
| Eau Claire | 17 | 2 | 9 | 1 | 5 | 251 | 71 | 169 | 11 | 1 |
| Fond du Lac | 23 | 0 | 9 | 0 | 14 | 138 | 25 | 98 | 15 | 2 |
| Green | 4 | 0 | 2 | 0 | 2 | 77 | 14 | 56 | 7 | 0 |
| Iowa | 17 | 0 | 0 | 0 | 17 | 39 | 7 | 27 | 5 | 0 |
| Kenosha | 101 | 3 | 24 | 1 | 73 | 410 | 70 | 301 | 39 | 5 |
| Kewaunee | 14 | 0 | 5 | 0 | 9 | 49 | 13 | 33 | 3 | 0 |
| La Crosse | 23 | 3 | 2 | 1 | 17 | 145 | 48 | 79 | 18 | 0 |
| Lincoln | 40 | 0 | 1 | 0 | 39 | 125 | 41 | 65 | 19 | 1 |
| Marathon | 67 | 0 | 13 | 1 | 53 | 334 | 45 | 267 | 22 | 2 |
| Milwaukee | 132 | 2 | 7 | 15 | 108 | 166 | 8 | 69 | 89 | 0 |
| Oconto | 32 | 1 | 11 | 1 | 19 | 178 | 45 | 117 | 16 | 2 |
| Outagamie | 38 | 0 | 10 | 1 | 27 | 224 | 62 | 152 | 10 | 0 |
| Pierce | 13 | 0 | 1 | 0 | 12 | 122 | 35 | 62 | 25 | 1 |
| Racine | 42 | 2 | 6 | 1 | 33 | 121 | 21 | 78 | 22 | 2 |
| Rock | 53 | 1 | 9 | 3 | 40 | 197 | 47 | 137 | 13 | 2 |
| Sheboygan | 29 | 0 | 13 | 1 | 15 | 353 | 75 | 265 | 13 | 0 |
| St. Croix | 45 | 0 | 3 | 0 | 42 | 271 | 37 | 204 | 30 | 0 |
| Waukesha | 73 | 1 | 32 | 2 | 38 | 244 | 27 | 200 | 17 | 2 |
| Winnebago | 21 | 0 | 6 | 1 | 14 | 320 | 149 | 161 | 10 | 1 |
| **Nonmetropolitan Counties** | | | | | | | | | | |
| Adams | 26 | 0 | 5 | 0 | 21 | 138 | 47 | 85 | 6 | 0 |
| Barron | 16 | 0 | 3 | 0 | 13 | 109 | 34 | 66 | 9 | 2 |
| Buffalo | 9 | 1 | 5 | 0 | 3 | 8 | 0 | 8 | 0 | 1 |
| Burnett | 21 | 1 | 6 | 0 | 14 | 190 | 48 | 111 | 31 | 1 |
| Clark | 28 | 0 | 0 | 0 | 28 | 117 | 19 | 83 | 15 | 0 |
| Dodge | 37 | 0 | 5 | 1 | 31 | 136 | 22 | 98 | 16 | 1 |
| Door | 10 | 0 | 3 | 0 | 7 | 76 | 19 | 55 | 2 | 0 |
| Dunn | 25 | 0 | 6 | 0 | 19 | 115 | 41 | 62 | 12 | 1 |
| Grant | 22 | 2 | 5 | 0 | 15 | 101 | 15 | 78 | 8 | 0 |
| Iron | 2 | 0 | 0 | 0 | 2 | 28 | 2 | 20 | 6 | 0 |
| Jefferson | 41 | 0 | 14 | 1 | 26 | 113 | 28 | 64 | 21 | 0 |
| Juneau | 47 | 2 | 24 | 0 | 21 | 177 | 32 | 123 | 22 | 0 |
| Lafayette | 8 | 0 | 3 | 0 | 5 | 45 | 11 | 28 | 6 | 0 |

## Table 10. Offenses Known to Law Enforcement, by Selected State Metropolitan and Nonmetropolitan Counties, 2021—Continued

(Number.)

| State/county | Violent crime | Murder and nonnegligent manslaughter | Rape | Robbery | Aggravated assault | Property crime | Burglary | Larceny-theft | Motor vehicle theft | Arson |
|---|---|---|---|---|---|---|---|---|---|---|
| Langlade | 9 | 0 | 2 | 0 | 7 | 59 | 6 | 47 | 6 | 0 |
| Manitowoc | 30 | 0 | 2 | 1 | 27 | 111 | 28 | 75 | 8 | 0 |
| Marinette | 42 | 1 | 16 | 0 | 25 | 167 | 35 | 125 | 7 | 0 |
| Marquette | 3 | 0 | 1 | 0 | 2 | 40 | 5 | 33 | 2 | 0 |
| Menominee | 1 | 0 | 0 | 0 | 1 | 9 | 1 | 7 | 1 | 0 |
| Monroe | 24 | 2 | 4 | 0 | 18 | 78 | 22 | 50 | 6 | 0 |
| Oneida | 33 | 1 | 12 | 0 | 20 | 93 | 41 | 46 | 6 | 0 |
| Pepin | 8 | 0 | 4 | 0 | 4 | 11 | 1 | 9 | 1 | 0 |
| Polk | 48 | 3 | 6 | 1 | 38 | 102 | 24 | 69 | 9 | 2 |
| Portage | 22 | 0 | 10 | 0 | 12 | 131 | 31 | 92 | 8 | 0 |
| Richland | 14 | 0 | 4 | 0 | 10 | 25 | 2 | 21 | 2 | 0 |
| Rusk | 37 | 1 | 4 | 0 | 32 | 64 | 29 | 30 | 5 | 1 |
| Sauk | 34 | 0 | 9 | 1 | 24 | 230 | 34 | 180 | 16 | 1 |
| Sawyer | 39 | 1 | 11 | 2 | 25 | 197 | 51 | 131 | 15 | 1 |
| Shawano | 19 | 0 | 6 | 1 | 12 | 256 | 67 | 159 | 30 | 1 |
| Taylor | 10 | 1 | 5 | 0 | 4 | 68 | 9 | 54 | 5 | 0 |
| Vilas | 4 | 0 | 0 | 0 | 4 | 90 | 17 | 63 | 10 | 0 |
| Walworth | 12 | 0 | 6 | 0 | 6 | 66 | 12 | 49 | 5 | 0 |
| Washburn | 9 | 0 | 0 | 0 | 9 | 77 | 23 | 45 | 9 | 2 |
| Waupaca | 36 | 1 | 11 | 0 | 24 | 48 | 6 | 41 | 1 | 0 |
| Waushara | 20 | 0 | 5 | 1 | 14 | 90 | 16 | 65 | 9 | 2 |
| Wood | 51 | 0 | 29 | 1 | 21 | 110 | 13 | 87 | 10 | 1 |
| **WYOMING** | | | | | | | | | | |
| **Metropolitan Counties** | | | | | | | | | | |
| Laramie | 69 | 0 | 6 | 4 | 59 | 571 | 154 | 321 | 96 | 5 |
| Natrona | 21 | 0 | 10 | 0 | 11 | 134 | 24 | 90 | 20 | 2 |
| **Nonmetropolitan Counties** | | | | | | | | | | |
| Albany | 8 | 0 | 2 | 0 | 6 | 75 | 27 | 43 | 5 | 0 |
| Campbell | 19 | 0 | 10 | 0 | 9 | 149 | 25 | 110 | 14 | 0 |
| Converse | 9 | 0 | 5 | 1 | 3 | 57 | 15 | 34 | 8 | 2 |
| Crook | 6 | 0 | 1 | 0 | 5 | 28 | 3 | 19 | 6 | 0 |
| Goshen | 5 | 0 | 0 | 0 | 5 | 42 | 14 | 24 | 4 | 0 |
| Hot Springs | 2 | 0 | 0 | 0 | 2 | 10 | 1 | 8 | 1 | 2 |
| Johnson | 4 | 0 | 2 | 0 | 2 | 36 | 11 | 20 | 5 | 0 |
| Lincoln | 15 | 0 | 3 | 0 | 12 | 60 | 7 | 48 | 5 | 0 |
| Niobrara | 4 | 0 | 2 | 0 | 2 | 10 | 0 | 6 | 4 | 0 |
| Park | 16 | 1 | 5 | 0 | 10 | 80 | 14 | 58 | 8 | 1 |
| Sheridan | 14 | 2 | 2 | 0 | 10 | 45 | 4 | 39 | 2 | 0 |
| Sublette | 5 | 0 | 2 | 0 | 3 | 43 | 6 | 36 | 1 | 0 |
| Sweetwater | 17 | 0 | 10 | 1 | 6 | 98 | 12 | 68 | 18 | 0 |
| Teton | 9 | 1 | 1 | 1 | 6 | 21 | 1 | 18 | 2 | 1 |
| Uinta | 14 | 0 | 10 | 0 | 4 | 42 | 12 | 24 | 6 | 0 |
| Washakie | 4 | 0 | 3 | 0 | 1 | 7 | 1 | 6 | 0 | 0 |
| Weston | 9 | 1 | 2 | 0 | 6 | 26 | 12 | 11 | 3 | 0 |

NOTE: The data shown in this table do not reflect county totals but are the number of offenses reported by the sheriff's office or county police department.   1 Limited data for 2021 were available for California, Florida, Illinois, Maryland, New Jersey, New Mexico, New York, and Pennsylvania.

# Table 11. Offenses Known to Law Enforcement, by Selected State, Tribal, and Other Agencies, 2021

(Number.)

| State/other agency unit/office | Violent crime | Murder and nonnegligent manslaughter | Rape | Robbery | Aggravated assault | Property crime | Burglary | Larceny-theft | Motor vehicle theft | Arson |
|---|---|---|---|---|---|---|---|---|---|---|
| **ALABAMA** | | | | | | | | | | |
| **State Agencies** | | | | | | | | | | |
| Alabama Law Enforcement Agency | 5 | 3 | 1 | 0 | 1 | 21 | 2 | 13 | 6 | 0 |
| Department of Conservation, Montgomery | 0 | 0 | 0 | 0 | 0 | 1 | 0 | 1 | 0 | 0 |
| Department of Corrections Investigations and Intelligence Division | 123 | 2 | 24 | 0 | 97 | 1 | 1 | 0 | 0 | 0 |
| **Other Agencies** | | | | | | | | | | |
| Etowah County Drug Enforcement Unit | 0 | 0 | 0 | 0 | 0 | 0 | 0 | 0 | 0 | 0 |
| **ALASKA** | | | | | | | | | | |
| **State Agencies** | | | | | | | | | | |
| Alaska State Troopers | 1,454 | 12 | 356 | 32 | 1,054 | 2,251 | 544 | 1,328 | 379 | 44 |
| **Tribal Agencies** | | | | | | | | | | |
| Metlakatla Tribal | 0 | 0 | 0 | 0 | 0 | 0 | 0 | 0 | 0 | 0 |
| **Other Agencies** | | | | | | | | | | |
| Fairbanks International Airport | 0 | 0 | 0 | 0 | 0 | 19 | 0 | 17 | 2 | 0 |
| **ARIZONA** | | | | | | | | | | |
| **Tribal Agencies** | | | | | | | | | | |
| Ak-Chin Tribal | 2 | 0 | 0 | 0 | 2 | 1 | 1 | 0 | 0 | 0 |
| Cocopah Tribal | 6 | 0 | 0 | 0 | 6 | 19 | 0 | 13 | 6 | 0 |
| Fort McDowell Tribal | 5 | 0 | 0 | 0 | 5 | 36 | 8 | 15 | 13 | 3 |
| Gila River Indian Community | 336 | 15 | 49 | 13 | 259 | 532 | 52 | 377 | 103 | 25 |
| Hopi Resource Enforcement Agency | 52 | 2 | 1 | 2 | 47 | 56 | 37 | 12 | 7 | 0 |
| Kaibab Paiute Tribal | 0 | 0 | 0 | 0 | 0 | 0 | 0 | 0 | 0 | 0 |
| Navajo Nation | 52 | 5 | 6 | 1 | 40 | 178 | 87 | 29 | 62 | 2 |
| Pascua Yaqui Tribal | 37 | 2 | 2 | 0 | 33 | 181 | 25 | 140 | 16 | 0 |
| San Carlos Apache | 501 | 1 | 41 | 10 | 449 | 212 | 94 | 102 | 16 | 24 |
| White Mountain Apache Tribal | 461 | 0 | 49 | 2 | 410 | 190 | 89 | 80 | 21 | 15 |
| Yavapai-Apache Nation | 8 | 1 | 0 | 0 | 7 | 8 | 2 | 4 | 2 | 0 |
| Yavapai-Prescott Tribal | 4 | 0 | 0 | 0 | 4 | 25 | 4 | 20 | 1 | 0 |
| **Other Agencies** | | | | | | | | | | |
| Tucson Airport Authority | 3 | 0 | 0 | 1 | 2 | 46 | 4 | 32 | 10 | 0 |
| **ARKANSAS** | | | | | | | | | | |
| **State Agencies** | | | | | | | | | | |
| Camp Robinson | 1 | 0 | 1 | 0 | 0 | 1 | 0 | 1 | 0 | 0 |
| State Capitol Police | 3 | 0 | 0 | 0 | 3 | 12 | 2 | 10 | 0 | 0 |
| **Other Agencies** | | | | | | | | | | |
| Northwest Arkansas Regional Airport | 4 | 0 | 1 | 0 | 3 | 19 | 0 | 11 | 8 | 0 |
| Pottsville School District | 0 | 0 | 0 | 0 | 0 | 1 | 0 | 1 | 0 | 0 |
| **CALIFORNIA**[1] | | | | | | | | | | |
| **Tribal Agencies** | | | | | | | | | | |
| Bear River Band | 5 | 3 | 0 | 0 | 2 | 4 | 0 | 2 | 2 | 0 |
| San Pasqual Band of Mission Indians Tribal | 4 | 0 | 0 | 1 | 3 | 40 | 3 | 30 | 7 | 0 |
| Sycuan Tribal | 20 | 1 | 2 | 2 | 15 | 137 | 8 | 84 | 45 | 0 |
| Table Mountain Rancheria | 0 | 0 | 0 | 0 | 0 | 61 | 5 | 49 | 7 | 0 |
| **Other Agencies** | | | | | | | | | | |
| Port of San Diego Harbor | 108 | 0 | 9 | 11 | 88 | 512 | 63 | 429 | 20 | 5 |
| **COLORADO** | | | | | | | | | | |
| **State Agencies** | | | | | | | | | | |
| Colorado Bureau of Investigation | 0 | 0 | 0 | 0 | 0 | 0 | 0 | 0 | 0 | 0 |
| Division of Gaming Criminal Enforcement and Investigations Section, Golden | 0 | 0 | 0 | 0 | 0 | 0 | 0 | 0 | 0 | 0 |
| State Patrol | 16 | 0 | 0 | 0 | 16 | 25 | 0 | 3 | 22 | 0 |
| **Tribal Agencies** | | | | | | | | | | |
| Southern Ute Tribal | 42 | 0 | 7 | 0 | 35 | 31 | 7 | 21 | 3 | 1 |
| Ute Mountain Tribal | 21 | 0 | 3 | 0 | 18 | 15 | 2 | 8 | 5 | 2 |
| **Other Agencies** | | | | | | | | | | |
| All Crimes Enforcement Team | 0 | 0 | 0 | 0 | 0 | 0 | 0 | 0 | 0 | 0 |
| Delta Montrose Drug Task Force | 0 | 0 | 0 | 0 | 0 | 0 | 0 | 0 | 0 | 0 |
| Southwest Drug Task Force | 0 | 0 | 0 | 0 | 0 | 0 | 0 | 0 | 0 | 0 |
| **CONNECTICUT** | | | | | | | | | | |
| **State Agencies** | | | | | | | | | | |
| Connecticut State Police | 235 | 8 | 58 | 41 | 128 | 1,683 | 241 | 1,101 | 341 | 8 |
| Department of Energy and Environmental Protection | 6 | 0 | 1 | 1 | 4 | 29 | 7 | 21 | 1 | 0 |
| Department of Motor Vehicles | 0 | 0 | 0 | 0 | 0 | 0 | 0 | 0 | 0 | 0 |
| State Capitol Police | 0 | 0 | 0 | 0 | 0 | 1 | 0 | 1 | 0 | 0 |
| **Tribal Agencies** | | | | | | | | | | |
| Mashantucket Pequot Tribal | 13 | 0 | 5 | 1 | 7 | 117 | 9 | 97 | 11 | 1 |
| Mohegan Tribal | 8 | 0 | 1 | 4 | 3 | 157 | 2 | 151 | 4 | 0 |
| **Other Agencies** | | | | | | | | | | |
| Metropolitan Transportation Authority | 3 | 0 | 1 | 2 | 0 | 32 | 2 | 30 | 0 | 0 |
| **DELAWARE** | | | | | | | | | | |
| **State Agencies** | | | | | | | | | | |
| Alcohol and Tobacco Enforcement | 0 | 0 | 0 | 0 | 0 | 0 | 0 | 0 | 0 | 0 |
| Animal Welfare | | | | | | | | | | |
| Kent County | 0 | 0 | 0 | 0 | 0 | 0 | 0 | 0 | 0 | 0 |

## Table 11. Offenses Known to Law Enforcement, by Selected State, Tribal, and Other Agencies, 2021—Continued

(Number.)

| State/other agency unit/office | Violent crime | Murder and nonnegligent manslaughter | Rape | Robbery | Aggravated assault | Property crime | Burglary | Larceny-theft | Motor vehicle theft | Arson |
|---|---|---|---|---|---|---|---|---|---|---|
| New Castle County | 0 | 0 | 0 | 0 | 0 | 0 | 0 | 0 | 0 | 0 |
| Sussex County | 0 | 0 | 0 | 0 | 0 | 0 | 0 | 0 | 0 | 0 |
| Environmental Control | 0 | 0 | 0 | 0 | 0 | 12 | 0 | 12 | 0 | 1 |
| Fish and Wildlife | 1 | 0 | 0 | 0 | 1 | 19 | 0 | 19 | 0 | 0 |
| Park Rangers | 4 | 0 | 1 | 0 | 3 | 116 | 52 | 59 | 5 | 1 |
| River and Bay Authority | 4 | 0 | 0 | 0 | 4 | 40 | 1 | 36 | 3 | 0 |
| State Capitol Police | 0 | 0 | 0 | 0 | 0 | 14 | 1 | 13 | 0 | 0 |
| State Fire Marshal | 2 | 0 | 0 | 0 | 2 | 8 | 7 | 1 | 0 | 135 |
| State Police | | | | | | | | | | |
| Headquarters | 0 | 0 | 0 | 0 | 0 | 0 | 0 | 0 | 0 | 0 |
| Kent County | 234 | 6 | 35 | 11 | 182 | 808 | 157 | 556 | 95 | 1 |
| New Castle County | 457 | 8 | 26 | 107 | 316 | 4,407 | 400 | 3,714 | 293 | 0 |
| Sussex County | 484 | 5 | 27 | 26 | 426 | 1,804 | 287 | 1,385 | 132 | 0 |
| | | | | | | | | | | |
| **DISTRICT OF COLUMBIA** | | | | | | | | | | |
| **Other Agencies** | | | | | | | | | | |
| Metro Transit Police | 398 | 0 | 2 | 200 | 196 | 331 | 0 | 303 | 28 | 2 |
| | | | | | | | | | | |
| **FLORIDA**[1] | | | | | | | | | | |
| **Tribal Agencies** | | | | | | | | | | |
| Miccosukee Tribal | 1 | 0 | 0 | 0 | 1 | 123 | 2 | 119 | 2 | 0 |
| Seminole Tribal | 78 | 0 | 12 | 24 | 42 | 602 | 18 | 537 | 47 | 0 |
| | | | | | | | | | | |
| **GEORGIA** | | | | | | | | | | |
| **State Agencies** | | | | | | | | | | |
| Georgia Department of Transportation, Office of Investigations | 0 | 0 | 0 | 0 | 0 | 0 | 0 | 0 | 0 | 0 |
| Georgia Forestry Commission | 0 | 0 | 0 | 0 | 0 | 3 | 1 | 2 | 0 | 25 |
| Georgia Public Safety Training Center | 0 | 0 | 0 | 0 | 0 | 0 | 0 | 0 | 0 | 0 |
| Georgia World Congress | 1 | 0 | 0 | 0 | 1 | 45 | 5 | 39 | 1 | 0 |
| Ports Authority, Savannah | 0 | 0 | 0 | 0 | 0 | 6 | 1 | 4 | 1 | 0 |
| Roosevelt Institute Facility Police | 0 | 0 | 0 | 0 | 0 | 0 | 0 | 0 | 0 | 0 |
| **Other Agencies** | | | | | | | | | | |
| Atlanta Public Schools | 23 | 0 | 17 | 5 | 1 | 96 | 14 | 79 | 3 | 2 |
| Bibb County Board of Education | 2 | 0 | 0 | 0 | 2 | 6 | 1 | 5 | 0 | 0 |
| Cherokee County Board of Education | 5 | 0 | 3 | 0 | 2 | 25 | 3 | 22 | 0 | 0 |
| Cherokee County Marshal | 0 | 0 | 0 | 0 | 0 | 0 | 0 | 0 | 0 | 0 |
| Cobb County Board of Education | 6 | 0 | 2 | 1 | 3 | 100 | 6 | 94 | 0 | 0 |
| Decatur County Schools | 0 | 0 | 0 | 0 | 0 | 1 | 0 | 1 | 0 | 0 |
| DeKalb County School System | 14 | 0 | 5 | 4 | 5 | 39 | 8 | 30 | 1 | 3 |
| Dougherty County Board of Education | 6 | 0 | 3 | 0 | 3 | 24 | 7 | 16 | 1 | 1 |
| Fayette County Marshal | 0 | 0 | 0 | 0 | 0 | 0 | 0 | 0 | 0 | 0 |
| Forsyth County Fire Investigation Unit | 0 | 0 | 0 | 0 | 0 | 0 | 0 | 0 | 0 | 5 |
| Fulton County Marshal | 1 | 0 | 0 | 0 | 1 | 4 | 0 | 2 | 2 | 0 |
| Fulton County School System | 15 | 0 | 3 | 1 | 11 | 59 | 7 | 50 | 2 | 1 |
| Glynn County School System | 5 | 0 | 0 | 0 | 5 | 9 | 1 | 8 | 0 | 0 |
| Grady County Schools | 0 | 0 | 0 | 0 | 0 | 2 | 0 | 2 | 0 | 0 |
| Gwinnett County Public Schools | 50 | 0 | 29 | 2 | 19 | 82 | 6 | 76 | 0 | 3 |
| Hall County Marshal | 0 | 0 | 0 | 0 | 0 | 0 | 0 | 0 | 0 | 0 |
| Metropolitan Atlanta Rapid Transit Authority | 102 | 2 | 1 | 26 | 73 | 136 | 0 | 126 | 10 | 8 |
| Muscogee County Schools | 9 | 0 | 2 | 0 | 7 | 475 | 4 | 469 | 2 | 1 |
| Paulding County Marshal | 0 | 0 | 0 | 0 | 0 | 0 | 0 | 0 | 0 | 0 |
| Richmond County Marshal | 0 | 0 | 0 | 0 | 0 | 0 | 0 | 0 | 0 | 0 |
| Washington County Board of Education | 0 | 0 | 0 | 0 | 0 | 0 | 0 | 0 | 0 | 0 |
| | | | | | | | | | | |
| **IDAHO** | | | | | | | | | | |
| **State Agencies** | | | | | | | | | | |
| Idaho State Police | 34 | 2 | 9 | 0 | 23 | 13 | 2 | 11 | 0 | 0 |
| **Tribal Agencies** | | | | | | | | | | |
| Coeur d'Alene Tribal | 18 | 0 | 6 | 0 | 12 | 23 | 7 | 14 | 2 | 1 |
| Fort Hall Tribal | 88 | 0 | 2 | 1 | 85 | 83 | 10 | 47 | 26 | 1 |
| Kootenai Tribal | 0 | 0 | 0 | 0 | 0 | 1 | 0 | 1 | 0 | 0 |
| | | | | | | | | | | |
| **ILLINOIS**[1] | | | | | | | | | | |
| **Other Agencies** | | | | | | | | | | |
| Rockford Park District | 9 | 0 | 2 | 2 | 5 | 39 | 6 | 32 | 1 | 4 |
| Tri-County Drug Enforcement Narcotics Team | 0 | 0 | 0 | 0 | 0 | 2 | 1 | 1 | 0 | 0 |
| | | | | | | | | | | |
| **INDIANA** | | | | | | | | | | |
| **State Agencies** | | | | | | | | | | |
| Indiana Gaming Commission | 19 | 0 | 0 | 1 | 18 | 179 | 1 | 176 | 2 | 0 |
| Indiana State Excise Police | 2 | 0 | 0 | 0 | 2 | 1 | 0 | 1 | 0 | 0 |
| Indiana State Police | 498 | 21 | 84 | 12 | 381 | 770 | 57 | 505 | 208 | 7 |
| **Other Agencies** | | | | | | | | | | |
| Indianapolis International Airport | 1 | 0 | 0 | 0 | 1 | 93 | 3 | 70 | 20 | 0 |
| Indianapolis Public Schools | 16 | 0 | 11 | 1 | 4 | 16 | 2 | 10 | 4 | 1 |
| | | | | | | | | | | |
| **KANSAS** | | | | | | | | | | |
| **State Agencies** | | | | | | | | | | |
| Kansas Bureau of Investigation | 15 | 2 | 1 | 0 | 12 | 2 | 1 | 1 | 0 | 0 |
| Kansas Department of Wildlife and Parks | 23 | 0 | 0 | 0 | 23 | 19 | 0 | 19 | 0 | 0 |
| **Tribal Agencies** | | | | | | | | | | |

## Table 11. Offenses Known to Law Enforcement, by Selected State, Tribal, and Other Agencies, 2021—Continued

(Number.)

| State/other agency unit/office | Violent crime | Murder and nonnegligent manslaughter | Rape | Robbery | Aggravated assault | Property crime | Burglary | Larceny-theft | Motor vehicle theft | Arson |
|---|---|---|---|---|---|---|---|---|---|---|
| Kickapoo Tribal | 0 | 0 | 0 | 0 | 0 | 0 | 0 | 0 | 0 | 0 |
| Potawatomi Tribal | 6 | 1 | 2 | 0 | 3 | 41 | 10 | 28 | 3 | 1 |
| Sac and Fox Tribal | 0 | 0 | 0 | 0 | 0 | 17 | 0 | 16 | 1 | 0 |
| Other Agencies | | | | | | | | | | |
| Johnson County Park | 2 | 0 | 1 | 0 | 1 | 39 | 3 | 36 | 0 | 0 |
| Unified School District, Kansas City | 10 | 0 | 3 | 1 | 6 | 59 | 2 | 57 | 0 | 1 |
| **KENTUCKY** | | | | | | | | | | |
| **State Agencies** | | | | | | | | | | |
| Alcohol Beverage Control | | | | | | | | | | |
| Enforcement Division | 0 | 0 | 0 | 0 | 0 | 0 | 0 | 0 | 0 | 0 |
| Investigative Division | 0 | 0 | 0 | 0 | 0 | 0 | 0 | 0 | 0 | 0 |
| Department of Agriculture Animal Health | | | | | | | | | | |
|   Enforcement Division | 0 | 0 | 0 | 0 | 0 | 0 | 0 | 0 | 0 | 0 |
| Fish and Wildlife Enforcement | 1 | 0 | 0 | 0 | 1 | 9 | 1 | 7 | 1 | 0 |
| Kentucky Horse Park | 0 | 0 | 0 | 0 | 0 | 11 | 0 | 11 | 0 | 0 |
| Motor Vehicle Enforcement | 1 | 0 | 0 | 0 | 1 | 10 | 0 | 7 | 3 | 0 |
| Park Security | 0 | 0 | 0 | 0 | 0 | 20 | 9 | 10 | 1 | 0 |
| State Police | | | | | | | | | | |
| Ashland | 34 | 1 | 19 | 1 | 13 | 102 | 22 | 69 | 11 | 5 |
| Bowling Green | 50 | 5 | 18 | 1 | 26 | 63 | 17 | 29 | 17 | 1 |
| Campbellsburg | 38 | 0 | 21 | 0 | 17 | 121 | 30 | 68 | 23 | 1 |
| Cannabis Suppression Section | 0 | 0 | 0 | 0 | 0 | 0 | 0 | 0 | 0 | 0 |
| Columbia | 43 | 0 | 27 | 1 | 15 | 61 | 20 | 28 | 13 | 1 |
| Drug Enforcement Area 2 | 1 | 0 | 0 | 0 | 1 | 6 | 1 | 5 | 0 | 0 |
| Dry Ridge | 34 | 2 | 22 | 0 | 10 | 59 | 8 | 35 | 16 | 0 |
| Electronic Crimes | 0 | 0 | 0 | 0 | 0 | 0 | 0 | 0 | 0 | 0 |
| Elizabethtown | 51 | 7 | 13 | 4 | 27 | 116 | 21 | 55 | 40 | 0 |
| Frankfort | 20 | 0 | 8 | 0 | 12 | 70 | 11 | 28 | 31 | 0 |
| Harlan | 52 | 3 | 19 | 1 | 29 | 207 | 72 | 75 | 60 | 3 |
| Hazard | 38 | 5 | 12 | 0 | 21 | 104 | 35 | 34 | 35 | 4 |
| Headquarters | 0 | 0 | 0 | 0 | 0 | 0 | 0 | 0 | 0 | 0 |
| Henderson | 25 | 1 | 10 | 0 | 14 | 78 | 31 | 39 | 8 | 1 |
| London | 46 | 2 | 16 | 3 | 25 | 172 | 53 | 69 | 50 | 8 |
| Madisonville | 24 | 1 | 13 | 2 | 8 | 42 | 13 | 17 | 12 | 0 |
| Mayfield | 47 | 10 | 22 | 1 | 14 | 110 | 30 | 61 | 19 | 1 |
| Morehead | 49 | 2 | 22 | 0 | 25 | 129 | 30 | 68 | 31 | 2 |
| Pikeville | 77 | 4 | 19 | 4 | 50 | 260 | 84 | 86 | 90 | 2 |
| Richmond | 44 | 5 | 17 | 1 | 21 | 101 | 32 | 50 | 19 | 1 |
| Special Operations | 0 | 0 | 0 | 0 | 0 | 0 | 0 | 0 | 0 | 2 |
| Vehicle Investigations | 0 | 0 | 0 | 0 | 0 | 5 | 0 | 0 | 5 | 0 |
| West Drug Enforcement Branch | 0 | 0 | 0 | 0 | 0 | 3 | 0 | 3 | 0 | 0 |
| Unlawful Narcotics Investigation Treatment | | | | | | | | | | |
|   and Education | 0 | 0 | 0 | 0 | 0 | 0 | 0 | 0 | 0 | 0 |
| **Other Agencies** | | | | | | | | | | |
| Barren County Drug Task Force | 0 | 0 | 0 | 0 | 0 | 0 | 0 | 0 | 0 | 0 |
| Bluegrass Narcotics Task Force | 0 | 0 | 0 | 0 | 0 | 0 | 0 | 0 | 0 | 0 |
| Bourbon County Constable District 8 | 0 | 0 | 0 | 0 | 0 | 0 | 0 | 0 | 0 | 0 |
| Bourbon County Schools | 0 | 0 | 0 | 0 | 0 | 2 | 1 | 1 | 0 | 0 |
| Casey County Constable District 3 | 0 | 0 | 0 | 0 | 0 | 0 | 0 | 0 | 0 | 0 |
| Cincinnati-Northern Kentucky International | | | | | | | | | | |
|   Airport | 0 | 0 | 0 | 0 | 0 | 34 | 0 | 22 | 12 | 0 |
| Clark County Constable | 0 | 0 | 0 | 0 | 0 | 0 | 0 | 0 | 0 | 0 |
| Clark County School System | 0 | 0 | 0 | 0 | 0 | 6 | 1 | 5 | 0 | 0 |
| Fayette County Constable District 2 | 0 | 0 | 0 | 0 | 0 | 0 | 0 | 0 | 0 | 0 |
| Fayette County Schools | 10 | 0 | 0 | 0 | 10 | 43 | 4 | 38 | 1 | 0 |
| FIVCO Area Drug Task Force | 0 | 0 | 0 | 0 | 0 | 0 | 0 | 0 | 0 | 0 |
| Garrard County Constable District 3 | 0 | 0 | 0 | 0 | 0 | 0 | 0 | 0 | 0 | 0 |
| Gateway Area Drug Task Force | 0 | 0 | 0 | 0 | 0 | 0 | 0 | 0 | 0 | 0 |
| Graves County Schools | 0 | 0 | 0 | 0 | 0 | 1 | 0 | 1 | 0 | 0 |
| Greater Hardin County Narcotics Task Force | 0 | 0 | 0 | 0 | 0 | 4 | 1 | 3 | 0 | 0 |
| Jefferson County Constable District 1 | 0 | 0 | 0 | 0 | 0 | 0 | 0 | 0 | 0 | 0 |
| Jefferson County Constable District 2 | 0 | 0 | 0 | 0 | 0 | 0 | 0 | 0 | 0 | 0 |
| Jefferson County School District | 21 | 0 | 0 | 0 | 21 | 55 | 28 | 27 | 0 | 0 |
| Johnson County Constable District 3 | 0 | 0 | 0 | 0 | 0 | 0 | 0 | 0 | 0 | 0 |
| Lake Cumberland Area Drug Enforcement | | | | | | | | | | |
|   Task Force | 0 | 0 | 0 | 0 | 0 | 1 | 0 | 1 | 0 | 0 |
| Lawrence County Constable District 4 | 0 | 0 | 0 | 0 | 0 | 0 | 0 | 0 | 0 | 0 |
| Lexington Bluegrass Airport | 0 | 0 | 0 | 0 | 0 | 25 | 0 | 4 | 21 | 0 |
| Louisville Regional Airport Authority | 0 | 0 | 0 | 0 | 0 | 93 | 1 | 70 | 22 | 0 |
| McCracken County Public Schools | 0 | 0 | 0 | 0 | 0 | 1 | 1 | 0 | 0 | 0 |
| McCreary County Constable District 4 | 0 | 0 | 0 | 0 | 0 | 1 | 0 | 0 | 1 | 0 |
| Metcalfe County Schools | 0 | 0 | 0 | 0 | 0 | 0 | 0 | 0 | 0 | 0 |
| Montgomery County Constable District 3 | 0 | 0 | 0 | 0 | 0 | 0 | 0 | 0 | 0 | 0 |
| Montgomery County School District | 0 | 0 | 0 | 0 | 0 | 1 | 0 | 1 | 0 | 0 |
| Northeast Kentucky Drug Task Force | 0 | 0 | 0 | 0 | 0 | 0 | 0 | 0 | 0 | 0 |
| Northern Kentucky Drug Strike Force | 0 | 0 | 0 | 0 | 0 | 0 | 0 | 0 | 0 | 0 |
| Pennyrile Narcotics Task Force | 0 | 0 | 0 | 0 | 0 | 0 | 0 | 0 | 0 | 0 |
| Pulaski County Constable District 5 | 0 | 0 | 0 | 0 | 0 | 0 | 0 | 0 | 0 | 0 |
| Russell County Constable District 4 | 0 | 0 | 0 | 0 | 0 | 0 | 0 | 0 | 0 | 0 |
| South Central Kentucky Drug Task Force | 0 | 0 | 0 | 0 | 0 | 0 | 0 | 0 | 0 | 0 |
| Taylor County Schools | 0 | 0 | 0 | 0 | 0 | 1 | 0 | 1 | 0 | 0 |
| Woodford County Public Schools | 0 | 0 | 0 | 0 | 0 | 0 | 0 | 0 | 0 | 0 |

## Table 11. Offenses Known to Law Enforcement, by Selected State, Tribal, and Other Agencies, 2021—Continued

(Number.)

| State/other agency unit/office | Violent crime | Murder and nonnegligent manslaughter | Rape | Robbery | Aggravated assault | Property crime | Burglary | Larceny-theft | Motor vehicle theft | Arson |
|---|---|---|---|---|---|---|---|---|---|---|
| **LOUISIANA** | | | | | | | | | | |
| **Tribal Agencies** | | | | | | | | | | |
| Chitimacha Tribal | 3 | 1 | 0 | 0 | 2 | 25 | 2 | 23 | 0 | 0 |
| Coushatta Tribal | 2 | 0 | 0 | 0 | 2 | 103 | 3 | 93 | 7 | 0 |
| Tunica-Biloxi Tribal | 3 | 0 | 0 | 0 | 3 | 110 | 3 | 103 | 4 | 2 |
| **MAINE** | | | | | | | | | | |
| **State Agencies** | | | | | | | | | | |
| Bureau of Capitol Police | 1 | 0 | 1 | 0 | 0 | 4 | 0 | 4 | 0 | 0 |
| Drug Enforcement Agency | 0 | 0 | 0 | 0 | 0 | 2 | 0 | 2 | 0 | 0 |
| State Fire Marshal | 1 | 1 | 0 | 0 | 0 | 7 | 6 | 0 | 1 | 104 |
| State Police | 114 | 11 | 50 | 2 | 51 | 924 | 150 | 684 | 90 | 0 |
| **Tribal Agencies** | | | | | | | | | | |
| Passamaquoddy Indian Township | 1 | 0 | 1 | 0 | 0 | 14 | 4 | 9 | 1 | 1 |
| Penobscot Nation | 0 | 0 | 0 | 0 | 0 | 0 | 0 | 0 | 0 | 0 |
| **MARYLAND**[1] | | | | | | | | | | |
| **State Agencies** | | | | | | | | | | |
| Natural Resources Police | 5 | 0 | 2 | 0 | 3 | 112 | 9 | 103 | 0 | 1 |
| Transit Administration | 44 | 0 | 0 | 20 | 24 | 67 | 3 | 60 | 4 | 4 |
| Transportation Authority | 72 | 0 | 1 | 2 | 69 | 181 | 1 | 116 | 64 | 0 |
| Division of Law Enforcement, Environmental Police | 5 | 0 | 0 | 0 | 5 | 15 | 2 | 8 | 5 | 1 |
| **State Police** | | | | | | | | | | |
| Barnstable County | 2 | 0 | 1 | 0 | 1 | 0 | 0 | 0 | 0 | 0 |
| Berkshire County | 1 | 0 | 0 | 0 | 1 | 20 | 7 | 10 | 3 | 0 |
| Bristol County | 2 | 0 | 0 | 0 | 2 | 4 | 1 | 2 | 1 | 0 |
| Essex County | 13 | 0 | 0 | 0 | 13 | 6 | 1 | 2 | 3 | 1 |
| Franklin County | 8 | 0 | 0 | 0 | 8 | 1 | 0 | 0 | 1 | 0 |
| Hampden County | 29 | 0 | 0 | 1 | 28 | 3 | 1 | 1 | 1 | 0 |
| Hampshire County | 10 | 0 | 0 | 0 | 10 | 1 | 0 | 0 | 1 | 0 |
| Middlesex County | 29 | 0 | 0 | 2 | 27 | 17 | 4 | 8 | 5 | 0 |
| Norfolk County | 6 | 1 | 0 | 0 | 5 | 3 | 0 | 2 | 1 | 0 |
| Plymouth County | 2 | 0 | 0 | 0 | 2 | 2 | 0 | 0 | 2 | 0 |
| Suffolk County | 44 | 0 | 0 | 1 | 43 | 52 | 3 | 23 | 26 | 0 |
| Worcester County | 19 | 0 | 0 | 1 | 18 | 4 | 0 | 1 | 3 | 0 |
| **Tribal Agencies** | | | | | | | | | | |
| Wampanoag Tribe of Gay Head | 0 | 0 | 0 | 0 | 0 | 0 | 0 | 0 | 0 | 0 |
| **MICHIGAN** | | | | | | | | | | |
| **State Agencies** | | | | | | | | | | |
| Department of Natural Resources Law Enforcement Division | 6 | 0 | 0 | 1 | 5 | 8 | 0 | 6 | 2 | 0 |
| **State Police** | | | | | | | | | | |
| Alger County | 15 | 0 | 7 | 0 | 8 | 16 | 4 | 8 | 4 | 1 |
| Allegan County | 79 | 1 | 38 | 2 | 38 | 239 | 75 | 146 | 18 | 2 |
| Alpena County | 45 | 2 | 19 | 0 | 24 | 98 | 22 | 60 | 16 | 1 |
| Antrim County | 14 | 0 | 9 | 0 | 5 | 18 | 3 | 14 | 1 | 0 |
| Arenac County | 3 | 1 | 2 | 0 | 0 | 2 | 0 | 2 | 0 | 0 |
| Baraga County | 11 | 0 | 2 | 0 | 9 | 15 | 0 | 11 | 4 | 2 |
| Barry County | 35 | 2 | 15 | 2 | 16 | 89 | 19 | 50 | 20 | 0 |
| Bay County | 46 | 0 | 21 | 2 | 23 | 97 | 20 | 64 | 13 | 1 |
| Benzie County | 8 | 0 | 6 | 0 | 2 | 24 | 5 | 18 | 1 | 0 |
| Berrien County | 43 | 0 | 14 | 1 | 28 | 204 | 112 | 82 | 10 | 1 |
| Branch County | 46 | 1 | 7 | 0 | 38 | 90 | 36 | 34 | 20 | 1 |
| Calhoun County | 37 | 0 | 10 | 0 | 27 | 105 | 27 | 58 | 20 | 1 |
| Cass County | 5 | 0 | 2 | 0 | 3 | 100 | 91 | 7 | 2 | 0 |
| Charlevoix County | 11 | 0 | 9 | 1 | 1 | 2 | 1 | 1 | 0 | 0 |
| Cheboygan County | 15 | 0 | 8 | 0 | 7 | 18 | 5 | 10 | 3 | 0 |
| Chippewa County | 20 | 1 | 6 | 0 | 13 | 22 | 11 | 10 | 1 | 1 |
| Clare County | 16 | 0 | 10 | 1 | 5 | 20 | 4 | 10 | 6 | 0 |
| Clinton County | 12 | 0 | 3 | 0 | 9 | 30 | 4 | 22 | 4 | 1 |
| Crawford County | 11 | 0 | 6 | 0 | 5 | 10 | 1 | 5 | 4 | 0 |
| Delta County | 10 | 0 | 6 | 0 | 4 | 37 | 11 | 24 | 2 | 0 |
| Dickinson County | 10 | 0 | 7 | 0 | 3 | 36 | 8 | 25 | 3 | 1 |
| Eaton County | 38 | 0 | 22 | 3 | 13 | 69 | 18 | 41 | 10 | 1 |
| Emmet County | 13 | 0 | 6 | 0 | 7 | 37 | 9 | 26 | 2 | 1 |
| Genesee County | 140 | 19 | 40 | 4 | 77 | 117 | 46 | 45 | 26 | 1 |
| Gladwin County | 10 | 0 | 8 | 0 | 2 | 2 | 0 | 1 | 1 | 0 |
| Gogebic County | 7 | 0 | 2 | 0 | 5 | 8 | 1 | 5 | 2 | 1 |
| Grand Traverse County | 42 | 1 | 33 | 1 | 7 | 29 | 4 | 22 | 3 | 1 |
| Gratiot County | 23 | 0 | 15 | 0 | 8 | 4 | 2 | 1 | 1 | 0 |
| Hillsdale County | 78 | 0 | 30 | 0 | 48 | 177 | 68 | 88 | 21 | 0 |
| Houghton County | 21 | 0 | 5 | 0 | 16 | 75 | 19 | 48 | 8 | 3 |
| Huron County | 15 | 0 | 8 | 0 | 7 | 11 | 3 | 5 | 3 | 0 |
| Ingham County | 29 | 0 | 14 | 1 | 14 | 40 | 19 | 17 | 4 | 0 |
| Ionia County | 49 | 1 | 20 | 0 | 28 | 108 | 12 | 80 | 16 | 0 |
| Iosco County | 40 | 1 | 19 | 0 | 20 | 57 | 16 | 33 | 8 | 1 |
| Iron County | 8 | 0 | 2 | 0 | 6 | 19 | 11 | 6 | 2 | 0 |
| Isabella County | 45 | 2 | 22 | 0 | 21 | 68 | 19 | 44 | 5 | 1 |
| Jackson County | 103 | 2 | 31 | 0 | 70 | 108 | 25 | 55 | 28 | 3 |
| Kalamazoo County | 72 | 1 | 8 | 3 | 60 | 153 | 16 | 99 | 38 | 4 |

# Table 11. Offenses Known to Law Enforcement, by Selected State, Tribal, and Other Agencies, 2021—Continued

(Number.)

| State/other agency unit/office | Violent crime | Murder and nonnegligent manslaughter | Rape | Robbery | Aggravated assault | Property crime | Burglary | Larceny-theft | Motor vehicle theft | Arson |
|---|---|---|---|---|---|---|---|---|---|---|
| Kalkaska County | 13 | 0 | 9 | 0 | 4 | 20 | 5 | 12 | 3 | 0 |
| Kent County | 30 | 0 | 9 | 0 | 21 | 49 | 1 | 40 | 8 | 2 |
| Lake County | 7 | 0 | 5 | 0 | 2 | 10 | 1 | 7 | 2 | 0 |
| Lapeer County | 34 | 0 | 19 | 0 | 15 | 36 | 11 | 16 | 9 | 0 |
| Leelanau County | 2 | 0 | 1 | 0 | 1 | 4 | 1 | 2 | 1 | 0 |
| Lenawee County | 41 | 2 | 20 | 0 | 19 | 67 | 11 | 43 | 13 | 0 |
| Livingston County | 52 | 2 | 14 | 1 | 35 | 131 | 32 | 77 | 22 | 1 |
| Luce County | 15 | 1 | 1 | 0 | 13 | 24 | 7 | 11 | 6 | 1 |
| Mackinac County | 12 | 1 | 4 | 0 | 7 | 16 | 4 | 11 | 1 | 1 |
| Macomb County | 49 | 0 | 13 | 0 | 36 | 32 | 9 | 17 | 6 | 0 |
| Manistee County | 9 | 1 | 3 | 0 | 5 | 46 | 5 | 39 | 2 | 2 |
| Marquette County | 64 | 0 | 17 | 0 | 47 | 97 | 19 | 66 | 12 | 1 |
| Mason County | 13 | 0 | 8 | 0 | 5 | 21 | 4 | 15 | 2 | 0 |
| Mecosta County | 11 | 0 | 10 | 0 | 1 | 18 | 3 | 12 | 3 | 0 |
| Menominee County | 4 | 0 | 2 | 0 | 2 | 20 | 9 | 7 | 4 | 0 |
| Midland County | 17 | 0 | 11 | 0 | 6 | 38 | 5 | 28 | 5 | 0 |
| Missaukee County | 13 | 1 | 4 | 0 | 8 | 25 | 5 | 14 | 6 | 0 |
| Monroe County | 49 | 1 | 10 | 2 | 36 | 85 | 16 | 56 | 13 | 0 |
| Montcalm County | 116 | 4 | 37 | 1 | 74 | 299 | 97 | 164 | 38 | 3 |
| Muskegon County | 83 | 1 | 33 | 1 | 48 | 162 | 24 | 119 | 19 | 1 |
| Newaygo County | 104 | 0 | 28 | 0 | 76 | 145 | 74 | 58 | 13 | 2 |
| Oakland County | 98 | 6 | 15 | 4 | 73 | 189 | 42 | 108 | 39 | 1 |
| Oceana County | 40 | 0 | 15 | 0 | 25 | 59 | 9 | 42 | 8 | 0 |
| Ogemaw County | 36 | 0 | 21 | 0 | 15 | 38 | 16 | 16 | 6 | 1 |
| Ontonagon County | 1 | 0 | 0 | 0 | 1 | 8 | 2 | 5 | 1 | 0 |
| Osceola County | 16 | 0 | 10 | 1 | 5 | 22 | 6 | 9 | 7 | 0 |
| Oscoda County | 2 | 0 | 2 | 0 | 0 | 3 | 1 | 2 | 0 | 0 |
| Otsego County | 33 | 0 | 10 | 0 | 23 | 43 | 10 | 27 | 6 | 0 |
| Ottawa County | 5 | 0 | 5 | 0 | 0 | 0 | 0 | 0 | 0 | 0 |
| Roscommon County | 17 | 0 | 9 | 0 | 8 | 40 | 9 | 26 | 5 | 0 |
| Saginaw County | 93 | 1 | 35 | 3 | 54 | 65 | 11 | 37 | 17 | 1 |
| Sanilac County | 17 | 0 | 12 | 0 | 5 | 8 | 2 | 4 | 2 | 0 |
| Schoolcraft County | 11 | 0 | 8 | 0 | 3 | 31 | 13 | 16 | 2 | 0 |
| Shiawassee County | 78 | 0 | 26 | 0 | 52 | 150 | 43 | 87 | 20 | 2 |
| St. Clair County | 17 | 1 | 6 | 0 | 10 | 29 | 10 | 15 | 4 | 0 |
| St. Joseph County | 51 | 0 | 23 | 2 | 26 | 140 | 40 | 75 | 25 | 1 |
| Tuscola County | 67 | 1 | 27 | 1 | 38 | 56 | 23 | 22 | 11 | 1 |
| Van Buren County | 71 | 1 | 16 | 2 | 52 | 179 | 53 | 96 | 30 | 3 |
| Washtenaw County | 84 | 2 | 36 | 1 | 45 | 110 | 43 | 42 | 25 | 3 |
| Wayne County | 204 | 7 | 26 | 2 | 169 | 154 | 2 | 96 | 56 | 0 |
| Wexford County | 30 | 0 | 17 | 0 | 13 | 125 | 18 | 94 | 13 | 0 |
| **Tribal Agencies** | | | | | | | | | | |
| Bay Mills Tribal | 8 | 0 | 2 | 0 | 6 | 7 | 2 | 5 | 0 | 0 |
| Gun Lake Tribal | 0 | 0 | 0 | 0 | 0 | 132 | 0 | 131 | 1 | 0 |
| Hannahville Tribal | 27 | 0 | 5 | 0 | 22 | 64 | 6 | 50 | 8 | 0 |
| Keweenaw Bay Tribal | 0 | 0 | 0 | 0 | 0 | 1 | 0 | 1 | 0 | 0 |
| Lac Vieux Desert Tribal | 0 | 0 | 0 | 0 | 0 | 0 | 0 | 0 | 0 | 0 |
| Little River Band of Ottawa Indians | 5 | 0 | 2 | 0 | 3 | 20 | 1 | 18 | 1 | 0 |
| Little Traverse Bay Bands of Odawa Indians | 0 | 0 | 0 | 0 | 0 | 35 | 0 | 34 | 1 | 0 |
| Nottawaseppi Huron Band of Potawatomi | 11 | 0 | 1 | 1 | 9 | 87 | 2 | 77 | 8 | 0 |
| Pokagon Tribal | 4 | 0 | 0 | 1 | 3 | 194 | 1 | 185 | 8 | 0 |
| Saginaw Chippewa Tribal | 37 | 1 | 14 | 3 | 19 | 135 | 12 | 114 | 9 | 2 |
| **Other Agencies** | | | | | | | | | | |
| Bishop International Airport | 0 | 0 | 0 | 0 | 0 | 13 | 0 | 0 | 13 | 0 |
| Capitol Region Airport Authority | 0 | 0 | 0 | 0 | 0 | 1 | 0 | 0 | 1 | 0 |
| Genesee County Parks and Recreation | 0 | 0 | 0 | 0 | 0 | 15 | 1 | 13 | 1 | 0 |
| Gerald R. Ford International Airport | 1 | 0 | 0 | 0 | 1 | 31 | 0 | 11 | 20 | 0 |
| Huron-Clinton Metropolitan Authority | | | | | | | | | | |
| Hudson Mills Metropark | 0 | 0 | 0 | 0 | 0 | 1 | 0 | 1 | 0 | 0 |
| Kensington Metropark | 4 | 0 | 0 | 0 | 4 | 2 | 0 | 2 | 0 | 0 |
| Lower Huron Metropark | 1 | 0 | 0 | 0 | 1 | 10 | 1 | 9 | 0 | 0 |
| Stony Creek Metropark | 4 | 0 | 0 | 0 | 4 | 8 | 2 | 6 | 0 | 0 |
| Wayne County Airport | 12 | 0 | 0 | 0 | 12 | 193 | 2 | 115 | 76 | 0 |
| | | | | | | | | | | |
| **MINNESOTA** | | | | | | | | | | |
| **State Agencies** | | | | | | | | | | |
| Department of Natural Resources Enforcement Division | 0 | 0 | 0 | 0 | 0 | 3 | 0 | 3 | 0 | 1 |
| Minnesota Department of Public Safety Alcohol and Gambling Enforcement | 0 | 0 | 0 | 0 | 0 | 0 | 0 | 0 | 0 | 0 |
| Minnesota State Fair Police | 0 | 0 | 0 | 0 | 0 | 0 | 0 | 0 | 0 | 0 |
| **State Patrol** | | | | | | | | | | |
| Brainerd | 0 | 0 | 0 | 0 | 0 | 4 | 0 | 4 | 0 | 0 |
| Detroit Lakes | 0 | 0 | 0 | 0 | 0 | 1 | 0 | 1 | 0 | 0 |
| Duluth | 0 | 0 | 0 | 0 | 0 | 1 | 0 | 1 | 0 | 0 |
| Golden Valley | 0 | 0 | 0 | 0 | 0 | 8 | 0 | 6 | 2 | 0 |
| Mankato | 0 | 0 | 0 | 0 | 0 | 0 | 0 | 0 | 0 | 0 |
| Marshall | 0 | 0 | 0 | 0 | 0 | 1 | 0 | 1 | 0 | 0 |
| Oakdale | 0 | 0 | 0 | 0 | 0 | 5 | 0 | 4 | 1 | 0 |
| Rochester | 0 | 0 | 0 | 0 | 0 | 0 | 0 | 0 | 0 | 0 |
| St. Cloud | 0 | 0 | 0 | 0 | 0 | 0 | 0 | 0 | 0 | 0 |
| Thief River Falls | 0 | 0 | 0 | 0 | 0 | 0 | 0 | 0 | 0 | 0 |
| Virginia | 0 | 0 | 0 | 0 | 0 | 0 | 0 | 0 | 0 | 0 |

## Table 11. Offenses Known to Law Enforcement, by Selected State, Tribal, and Other Agencies, 2021—Continued

(Number.)

| State/other agency unit/office | Violent crime | Murder and nonnegligent manslaughter | Rape | Robbery | Aggravated assault | Property crime | Burglary | Larceny-theft | Motor vehicle theft | Arson |
|---|---|---|---|---|---|---|---|---|---|---|
| **Tribal Agencies** | | | | | | | | | | |
| Fond du Lac Tribal | 40 | 0 | 8 | 0 | 32 | 104 | 18 | 72 | 14 | 0 |
| Mille Lacs Tribal | 39 | 0 | 0 | 3 | 36 | 86 | 6 | 69 | 11 | 0 |
| Nett Lake Tribal | 0 | 0 | 0 | 0 | 0 | 1 | 0 | 1 | 0 | 1 |
| White Earth Tribal | 58 | 0 | 10 | 3 | 45 | 161 | 25 | 108 | 28 | 1 |
| **Other Agencies** | | | | | | | | | | |
| Metropolitan Transit Commission | 297 | 0 | 9 | 148 | 140 | 318 | 6 | 307 | 5 | 20 |
| Minneapolis-St. Paul International Airport | 5 | 0 | 1 | 0 | 4 | 216 | 2 | 177 | 37 | 0 |
| Three Rivers Park District | 1 | 0 | 0 | 0 | 1 | 171 | 0 | 171 | 0 | 1 |
| **MISSISSIPPI** | | | | | | | | | | |
| **State Agencies** | | | | | | | | | | |
| Reservoir Police Department | 1 | 0 | 0 | 0 | 1 | 0 | 0 | 0 | 0 | 0 |
| **MISSOURI** | | | | | | | | | | |
| **State Agencies** | | | | | | | | | | |
| Department of Revenue, Compliance and Investigation Bureau | 0 | 0 | 0 | 0 | 0 | 9 | 0 | 8 | 1 | 0 |
| Division of Alcohol and Tobacco Control | 0 | 0 | 0 | 0 | 0 | 0 | 0 | 0 | 0 | 0 |
| Missouri State Highway Patrol | 22 | 0 | 0 | 0 | 22 | 320 | 7 | 264 | 49 | 1 |
| State Fire Marshal | 1 | 0 | 0 | 0 | 1 | 3 | 3 | 0 | 0 | 150 |
| State Park Rangers | 1 | 0 | 1 | 0 | 0 | 17 | 1 | 15 | 1 | 0 |
| **Other Agencies** | | | | | | | | | | |
| Kansas City International Airport | 8 | 0 | 1 | 1 | 6 | 189 | 1 | 112 | 76 | 0 |
| **MONTANA** | | | | | | | | | | |
| **Tribal Agencies** | | | | | | | | | | |
| Blackfeet Agency | 59 | 0 | 4 | 0 | 55 | 46 | 15 | 13 | 18 | 3 |
| Fort Peck Assiniboine and Sioux Tribes | 25 | 1 | 2 | 0 | 22 | 6 | 4 | 1 | 1 | 5 |
| Rocky Boy's Tribal | 24 | 1 | 0 | 0 | 23 | 52 | 21 | 17 | 14 | 2 |
| **NEBRASKA** | | | | | | | | | | |
| **State Agencies** | | | | | | | | | | |
| State Patrol | | | | | | | | | | |
| Adams County | 0 | 0 | 0 | 0 | 0 | 0 | 0 | 0 | 0 | 0 |
| Buffalo County | 3 | 0 | 0 | 0 | 3 | 0 | 0 | 0 | 0 | 0 |
| Cheyenne County | 1 | 0 | 0 | 0 | 1 | 0 | 0 | 0 | 0 | 0 |
| Cuming County | 0 | 0 | 0 | 0 | 0 | 0 | 0 | 0 | 0 | 0 |
| Dakota County | 0 | 0 | 0 | 0 | 0 | 0 | 0 | 0 | 0 | 0 |
| Dawson County | 1 | 0 | 0 | 0 | 1 | 1 | 0 | 1 | 0 | 0 |
| Douglas County | 6 | 0 | 0 | 0 | 6 | 2 | 0 | 1 | 1 | 0 |
| Hall County | 0 | 0 | 0 | 0 | 0 | 1 | 0 | 1 | 0 | 0 |
| Hamilton County | 0 | 0 | 0 | 0 | 0 | 0 | 0 | 0 | 0 | 0 |
| Keith County | 4 | 0 | 0 | 0 | 4 | 0 | 0 | 0 | 0 | 0 |
| Kimball County | 0 | 0 | 0 | 0 | 0 | 0 | 0 | 0 | 0 | 0 |
| Lancaster County | 4 | 0 | 1 | 0 | 3 | 2 | 0 | 2 | 0 | 0 |
| Lincoln County | 1 | 0 | 0 | 0 | 1 | 0 | 0 | 0 | 0 | 1 |
| Madison County | 4 | 0 | 0 | 0 | 4 | 0 | 0 | 0 | 0 | 0 |
| Otoe County | 0 | 0 | 0 | 0 | 0 | 0 | 0 | 0 | 0 | 0 |
| Pierce County | 0 | 0 | 0 | 0 | 0 | 1 | 0 | 1 | 0 | 0 |
| Sarpy County | 0 | 0 | 0 | 0 | 0 | 1 | 0 | 1 | 0 | 0 |
| Saunders County | 1 | 0 | 0 | 0 | 1 | 0 | 0 | 0 | 0 | 0 |
| Scotts Bluff County | 1 | 0 | 0 | 0 | 1 | 0 | 0 | 0 | 0 | 0 |
| Sheridan County | 1 | 0 | 0 | 0 | 1 | 0 | 0 | 0 | 0 | 0 |
| York County | 4 | 0 | 0 | 0 | 4 | 2 | 0 | 1 | 1 | 0 |
| **Tribal Agencies** | | | | | | | | | | |
| Omaha Tribal | 14 | 0 | 0 | 0 | 14 | 1 | 1 | 0 | 0 | 0 |
| Santee Tribal | 4 | 0 | 2 | 0 | 2 | 11 | 0 | 5 | 6 | 0 |
| Winnebago Tribal | 8 | 0 | 1 | 0 | 7 | 2 | 1 | 1 | 0 | 0 |
| **NEVADA** | | | | | | | | | | |
| **State Agencies** | | | | | | | | | | |
| Attorney General Investigations Division | 0 | 0 | 0 | 0 | 0 | 0 | 0 | 0 | 0 | 0 |
| Highway Patrol | | | | | | | | | | |
| Northeastern Division | 6 | 0 | 0 | 0 | 6 | 2 | 0 | 1 | 1 | 0 |
| Northwestern Division | 15 | 0 | 0 | 0 | 15 | 4 | 0 | 0 | 4 | 1 |
| Southern Division | 41 | 0 | 0 | 0 | 41 | 16 | 1 | 6 | 9 | 0 |
| State Fire Marshal | 0 | 0 | 0 | 0 | 0 | 0 | 0 | 0 | 0 | 6 |
| **Tribal Agencies** | | | | | | | | | | |
| Eastern Nevada Agency | 1 | 0 | 0 | 1 | 0 | 4 | 0 | 2 | 2 | 0 |
| Lovelock Paiute Tribal | 1 | 0 | 0 | 0 | 1 | 1 | 0 | 1 | 0 | 0 |
| Moapa Tribal | 5 | 0 | 0 | 1 | 4 | 142 | 0 | 142 | 0 | 0 |
| Pyramid Lake Tribal | 10 | 0 | 3 | 0 | 7 | 28 | 4 | 12 | 12 | 0 |
| Reno-Sparks Indian Colony | 9 | 0 | 2 | 1 | 6 | 66 | 4 | 58 | 4 | 0 |
| Western Shoshone Tribal | 0 | 0 | 0 | 0 | 0 | 0 | 0 | 0 | 0 | 0 |
| Yomba Shoshone Tribal | 0 | 0 | 0 | 0 | 0 | 0 | 0 | 0 | 0 | 0 |
| **Other Agencies** | | | | | | | | | | |
| City of Las Vegas Department of Publilc Safety | 55 | 0 | 0 | 7 | 48 | 152 | 14 | 130 | 8 | 3 |
| Reno Tahoe Airport Authority | 1 | 0 | 1 | 0 | 0 | 52 | 0 | 44 | 8 | 0 |
| Washoe County School District | 25 | 0 | 2 | 5 | 18 | 55 | 15 | 40 | 0 | 3 |
| **NEW HAMPSHIRE** | | | | | | | | | | |
| **State Agencies** | | | | | | | | | | |

## Table 11. Offenses Known to Law Enforcement, by Selected State, Tribal, and Other Agencies, 2021—Continued

(Number.)

| State/other agency unit/office | Violent crime | Murder and nonnegligent manslaughter | Rape | Robbery | Aggravated assault | Property crime | Burglary | Larceny-theft | Motor vehicle theft | Arson |
|---|---|---|---|---|---|---|---|---|---|---|
| Liquor Commission | 2 | 0 | 0 | 2 | 0 | 18 | 0 | 18 | 0 | 0 |
| **State Police** | | | | | | | | | | |
| Cheshire County | 1 | 1 | 0 | 0 | 0 | 6 | 0 | 4 | 2 | 0 |
| Grafton County | 6 | 1 | 2 | 0 | 3 | 24 | 5 | 14 | 5 | 0 |
| Hillsborough County | 6 | 0 | 1 | 1 | 4 | 4 | 1 | 3 | 0 | 0 |
| Merrimack County | 6 | 0 | 2 | 0 | 4 | 17 | 2 | 13 | 2 | 0 |
| Rockingham County | 1 | 0 | 1 | 0 | 0 | 4 | 0 | 4 | 0 | 0 |
| **NEW JERSEY**[1] | | | | | | | | | | |
| **NEW MEXICO**[1] | | | | | | | | | | |
| **Tribal Agencies** | | | | | | | | | | |
| Acoma Tribal | 18 | 0 | 2 | 0 | 16 | 20 | 6 | 11 | 3 | 0 |
| Isleta Tribal | 14 | 0 | 0 | 0 | 14 | 87 | 20 | 46 | 21 | 1 |
| Jemez Pueblo | 4 | 0 | 0 | 0 | 4 | 11 | 7 | 1 | 3 | 0 |
| Northern Pueblos Agency | 2 | 0 | 0 | 0 | 2 | 4 | 3 | 0 | 1 | 0 |
| Pojoaque Tribal | 9 | 1 | 2 | 0 | 6 | 51 | 19 | 31 | 1 | 1 |
| Ramah Navajo Tribal | 10 | 0 | 0 | 0 | 10 | 5 | 4 | 1 | 0 | 1 |
| Santa Ana Tribal | 3 | 0 | 0 | 0 | 3 | 59 | 8 | 41 | 10 | 0 |
| Santa Clara Pueblo | 2 | 0 | 1 | 0 | 1 | 12 | 4 | 7 | 1 | 1 |
| Southern Pueblos Agency | 14 | 0 | 3 | 0 | 11 | 10 | 6 | 3 | 1 | 0 |
| Tesuque Pueblo | 0 | 0 | 0 | 0 | 0 | 1 | 0 | 1 | 0 | 0 |
| Zia Pueblo | 6 | 1 | 0 | 0 | 5 | 5 | 1 | 1 | 3 | 0 |
| Zuni Tribal | 17 | 1 | 0 | 0 | 16 | 1 | 0 | 0 | 1 | 0 |
| **NEW YORK**[1] | | | | | | | | | | |
| **Tribal Agencies** | | | | | | | | | | |
| Oneida Indian Nation | 4 | 0 | 2 | 1 | 1 | 67 | 0 | 63 | 4 | 0 |
| St. Regis Tribal | 1 | 0 | 0 | 0 | 1 | 10 | 0 | 10 | 0 | 0 |
| **NORTH CAROLINA** | | | | | | | | | | |
| **State Agencies** | | | | | | | | | | |
| State Capitol Police | 11 | 0 | 5 | 1 | 5 | 18 | 6 | 9 | 3 | 1 |
| **State Park Rangers** | | | | | | | | | | |
| Elk Knob | 0 | 0 | 0 | 0 | 0 | 0 | 0 | 0 | 0 | 0 |
| Lake Norman | 0 | 0 | 0 | 0 | 0 | 11 | 4 | 7 | 0 | 0 |
| Merchants Millpond | 0 | 0 | 0 | 0 | 0 | 0 | 0 | 0 | 0 | 0 |
| **Other Agencies** | | | | | | | | | | |
| Moore County Schools | 2 | 0 | 0 | 0 | 2 | 13 | 0 | 13 | 0 | 0 |
| Raleigh-Durham International Airport | 4 | 0 | 0 | 2 | 2 | 86 | 0 | 66 | 20 | 0 |
| University of North Carolina Hospitals | 1 | 0 | 0 | 0 | 1 | 34 | 0 | 32 | 2 | 0 |
| WakeMed Campus Police | 19 | 0 | 0 | 0 | 19 | 82 | 8 | 70 | 4 | 0 |
| **NORTH DAKOTA** | | | | | | | | | | |
| **State Agencies** | | | | | | | | | | |
| North Dakota Highway Patrol | 8 | 0 | 0 | 0 | 8 | 33 | 0 | 6 | 27 | 0 |
| **OHIO** | | | | | | | | | | |
| **State Agencies** | | | | | | | | | | |
| Ohio Department of Natural Resources | 34 | 2 | 7 | 1 | 24 | 342 | 17 | 321 | 4 | 2 |
| Ohio Investigative Unit | 0 | 0 | 0 | 0 | 0 | 0 | 0 | 0 | 0 | 0 |
| Ohio State Highway Patrol | 325 | 3 | 43 | 3 | 276 | 240 | 4 | 170 | 66 | 5 |
| **Other Agencies** | | | | | | | | | | |
| Hamilton County Park District | 4 | 0 | 1 | 1 | 2 | 51 | 4 | 46 | 1 | 1 |
| Lake Metroparks | 0 | 0 | 0 | 0 | 0 | 0 | 0 | 0 | 0 | 0 |
| **OKLAHOMA** | | | | | | | | | | |
| **State Agencies** | | | | | | | | | | |
| Capitol Park Police | 0 | 0 | 0 | 0 | 0 | 0 | 0 | 0 | 0 | 0 |
| Grand River Dam Authority Lake Patrol | 0 | 0 | 0 | 0 | 0 | 38 | 2 | 35 | 1 | 1 |
| Oklahoma Highway Patrol | 0 | 0 | 0 | 0 | 0 | 1 | 0 | 0 | 1 | 0 |
| State Bureau of Investigation | 0 | 0 | 0 | 0 | 0 | 0 | 0 | 0 | 0 | 0 |
| State Park Rangers | 6 | 0 | 1 | 0 | 5 | 87 | 12 | 72 | 3 | 1 |
| **Tribal Agencies** | | | | | | | | | | |
| Absentee Shawnee Tribal | 3 | 0 | 1 | 0 | 2 | 21 | 8 | 12 | 1 | 0 |
| Anadarko Agency | 3 | 0 | 1 | 0 | 2 | 33 | 5 | 23 | 5 | 2 |
| Cherokee Nation | 9 | 1 | 1 | 0 | 7 | 39 | 10 | 21 | 8 | 2 |
| Choctaw Nation | 46 | 2 | 18 | 0 | 26 | 490 | 54 | 351 | 85 | 14 |
| Citizen Potawatomi Nation | 7 | 0 | 0 | 0 | 7 | 138 | 4 | 125 | 9 | 0 |
| Comanche Nation | 2 | 0 | 1 | 0 | 1 | 85 | 8 | 72 | 5 | 1 |
| Concho Agency | 8 | 1 | 0 | 0 | 7 | 30 | 5 | 21 | 4 | 0 |
| Eastern Shawnee Tribal | 0 | 0 | 0 | 0 | 0 | 64 | 2 | 55 | 7 | 0 |
| Iowa Tribal | 1 | 0 | 0 | 0 | 1 | 25 | 1 | 21 | 3 | 0 |
| Kaw Tribal | 0 | 0 | 0 | 0 | 0 | 6 | 1 | 5 | 0 | 0 |
| Kickapoo Tribal | 7 | 0 | 1 | 1 | 5 | 20 | 4 | 16 | 0 | 1 |
| Miami Agency | 0 | 0 | 0 | 0 | 0 | 63 | 3 | 56 | 4 | 2 |
| Miami Tribal | 1 | 0 | 0 | 0 | 1 | 25 | 4 | 18 | 3 | 0 |
| Osage Nation | 6 | 1 | 0 | 1 | 4 | 516 | 51 | 293 | 172 | 0 |
| Otoe-Missouria Tribal | 0 | 0 | 0 | 0 | 0 | 5 | 3 | 1 | 1 | 0 |
| Ponca Tribal | 3 | 0 | 2 | 0 | 1 | 6 | 0 | 2 | 4 | 0 |
| Quapaw Tribal | 16 | 0 | 1 | 1 | 14 | 187 | 12 | 162 | 13 | 2 |
| Sac and Fox Tribal | 5 | 0 | 0 | 1 | 4 | 34 | 9 | 17 | 8 | 0 |
| Seminole Nation Lighthorse | 19 | 0 | 3 | 2 | 14 | 67 | 21 | 25 | 21 | 3 |

## Table 11. Offenses Known to Law Enforcement, by Selected State, Tribal, and Other Agencies, 2021—Continued

(Number.)

| State/other agency unit/office | Violent crime | Murder and nonnegligent manslaughter | Rape | Robbery | Aggravated assault | Property crime | Burglary | Larceny-theft | Motor vehicle theft | Arson |
|---|---|---|---|---|---|---|---|---|---|---|
| Tonkawa Tribal | 1 | 0 | 0 | 1 | 0 | 16 | 0 | 14 | 2 | 0 |
| Wyandotte Nation | 2 | 0 | 0 | 0 | 2 | 18 | 4 | 14 | 0 | 0 |
| Other Agencies | | | | | | | | | | |
| Beggs Public Schools | 0 | 0 | 0 | 0 | 0 | 0 | 0 | 0 | 0 | 0 |
| District 1 Narcotics Task Force | 2 | 1 | 1 | 0 | 0 | 0 | 0 | 0 | 0 | 0 |
| District 8 Narcotics Task Force | 0 | 0 | 0 | 0 | 0 | 1 | 0 | 1 | 0 | 0 |
| Jenks Public Schools | 2 | 0 | 1 | 0 | 1 | 5 | 3 | 1 | 1 | 0 |
| Lawton Public Schools | 3 | 0 | 1 | 0 | 2 | 12 | 2 | 10 | 0 | 1 |
| Muskogee City Schools | 4 | 0 | 0 | 0 | 4 | 5 | 0 | 5 | 0 | 0 |
| Putnam City Campus | 4 | 0 | 2 | 0 | 2 | 14 | 2 | 12 | 0 | 0 |
| Victory Life | 0 | 0 | 0 | 0 | 0 | 0 | 0 | 0 | 0 | 0 |
| **OREGON** | | | | | | | | | | |
| **State Agencies** | | | | | | | | | | |
| State Police | | | | | | | | | | |
| Baker County | 4 | 0 | 0 | 0 | 4 | 3 | 1 | 2 | 0 | 1 |
| Clackamas County | 45 | 0 | 0 | 1 | 44 | 39 | 0 | 27 | 12 | 1 |
| Clatsop County | 5 | 0 | 0 | 0 | 5 | 22 | 0 | 18 | 4 | 0 |
| Columbia County | 1 | 0 | 0 | 0 | 1 | 7 | 1 | 5 | 1 | 0 |
| Coos County | 2 | 0 | 0 | 1 | 1 | 34 | 2 | 27 | 5 | 2 |
| Curry County | 3 | 0 | 0 | 0 | 3 | 26 | 1 | 22 | 3 | 0 |
| Deschutes County | 4 | 0 | 1 | 0 | 3 | 6 | 0 | 4 | 2 | 1 |
| Douglas County | 20 | 0 | 0 | 1 | 19 | 31 | 1 | 23 | 7 | 4 |
| Grant County | 2 | 0 | 0 | 0 | 2 | 1 | 0 | 1 | 0 | 0 |
| Harney County | 0 | 0 | 0 | 0 | 0 | 0 | 0 | 0 | 0 | 0 |
| Hood River County | 1 | 0 | 0 | 0 | 1 | 10 | 0 | 9 | 1 | 0 |
| Jackson County | 34 | 0 | 1 | 1 | 32 | 32 | 1 | 22 | 9 | 0 |
| Jefferson County | 1 | 0 | 0 | 0 | 1 | 5 | 0 | 4 | 1 | 0 |
| Josephine County | 30 | 3 | 6 | 1 | 20 | 22 | 2 | 15 | 5 | 5 |
| Klamath County | 17 | 0 | 2 | 2 | 13 | 15 | 2 | 11 | 2 | 0 |
| Lane County | 23 | 1 | 0 | 0 | 22 | 98 | 5 | 80 | 13 | 0 |
| Lincoln County | 5 | 0 | 0 | 0 | 5 | 52 | 0 | 52 | 0 | 0 |
| Linn County | 9 | 0 | 0 | 1 | 8 | 32 | 1 | 29 | 2 | 0 |
| Malheur County | 15 | 0 | 0 | 0 | 15 | 6 | 1 | 4 | 1 | 0 |
| Marion County | 59 | 3 | 2 | 2 | 52 | 92 | 7 | 67 | 18 | 3 |
| Multnomah County | 5 | 0 | 0 | 0 | 5 | 17 | 0 | 14 | 3 | 0 |
| Polk County | 1 | 0 | 0 | 0 | 1 | 5 | 0 | 5 | 0 | 0 |
| Tillamook County | 5 | 0 | 0 | 0 | 5 | 34 | 2 | 31 | 1 | 1 |
| Umatilla County | 14 | 0 | 0 | 0 | 14 | 10 | 1 | 6 | 3 | 0 |
| Wallowa County | 0 | 0 | 0 | 0 | 0 | 2 | 0 | 2 | 0 | 0 |
| Wasco County | 10 | 0 | 1 | 0 | 9 | 20 | 2 | 15 | 3 | 0 |
| Washington County | 6 | 0 | 1 | 0 | 5 | 5 | 0 | 3 | 2 | 0 |
| Yamhill County | 1 | 0 | 0 | 0 | 1 | 4 | 0 | 0 | 4 | 1 |
| Tribal Agencies | | | | | | | | | | |
| Columbia River Inter-Tribal Fisheries Enforcement | 0 | 0 | 0 | 0 | 0 | 1 | 1 | 0 | 0 | 0 |
| Coos, Lower Umpqua, and Siuslaw Tribal | 1 | 0 | 0 | 0 | 1 | 16 | 1 | 14 | 1 | 0 |
| Coquille Tribal | 1 | 0 | 1 | 0 | 0 | 1 | 0 | 1 | 0 | 0 |
| Grand Ronde Tribal | 7 | 0 | 0 | 0 | 7 | 105 | 1 | 96 | 8 | 0 |
| Warm Springs Tribal | 17 | 0 | 2 | 0 | 15 | 94 | 27 | 51 | 16 | 9 |
| Other Agencies | | | | | | | | | | |
| Hillsboro School District | 0 | 0 | 0 | 0 | 0 | 0 | 0 | 0 | 0 | 0 |
| Port of Portland | 13 | 0 | 1 | 2 | 10 | 491 | 0 | 411 | 80 | 1 |
| **PENNSYLVANIA**[1] | | | | | | | | | | |
| **State Agencies** | | | | | | | | | | |
| State Police, York County | 73 | 1 | 15 | 9 | 48 | 268 | 60 | 188 | 20 | 10 |
| Other Agencies | | | | | | | | | | |
| Franklin County Drug Task Force | 0 | 0 | 0 | 0 | 0 | 0 | 0 | 0 | 0 | 0 |
| **RHODE ISLAND** | | | | | | | | | | |
| **State Agencies** | | | | | | | | | | |
| Department of Environmental Management | 2 | 0 | 0 | 0 | 2 | 17 | 1 | 16 | 0 | 0 |
| Rhode Island State Police Headquarters | 62 | 0 | 54 | 2 | 6 | 46 | 1 | 38 | 7 | 0 |
| State Police | | | | | | | | | | |
| Chepachet/Scituate | 1 | 0 | 1 | 0 | 0 | 24 | 0 | 12 | 12 | 0 |
| Hope Valley | 4 | 0 | 2 | 0 | 2 | 12 | 2 | 8 | 2 | 0 |
| Lincoln | 16 | 0 | 4 | 0 | 12 | 48 | 0 | 27 | 21 | 2 |
| Wickford | 6 | 0 | 4 | 0 | 2 | 23 | 1 | 19 | 3 | 0 |
| T.F. Green Airport | 2 | 0 | 0 | 0 | 2 | 29 | 0 | 21 | 8 | 0 |
| **SOUTH CAROLINA** | | | | | | | | | | |
| **State Agencies** | | | | | | | | | | |
| Department of Mental Health | 7 | 1 | 1 | 0 | 5 | 7 | 0 | 6 | 1 | 0 |
| Department of Natural Resources | | | | | | | | | | |
| Anderson County | 0 | 0 | 0 | 0 | 0 | 0 | 0 | 0 | 0 | 0 |
| Beaufort County | 0 | 0 | 0 | 0 | 0 | 0 | 0 | 0 | 0 | 0 |
| Berkeley County | 0 | 0 | 0 | 0 | 0 | 0 | 0 | 0 | 0 | 0 |
| Charleston County | 0 | 0 | 0 | 0 | 0 | 0 | 0 | 0 | 0 | 0 |
| Cherokee County | 0 | 0 | 0 | 0 | 0 | 0 | 0 | 0 | 0 | 0 |
| Colleton County | 0 | 0 | 0 | 0 | 0 | 0 | 0 | 0 | 0 | 0 |
| Dorchester County | 0 | 0 | 0 | 0 | 0 | 0 | 0 | 0 | 0 | 0 |
| Georgetown County | 0 | 0 | 0 | 0 | 0 | 0 | 0 | 0 | 0 | 0 |

# Table 11. Offenses Known to Law Enforcement, by Selected State, Tribal, and Other Agencies, 2021—Continued

(Number.)

| State/other agency unit/office | Violent crime | Murder and nonnegligent manslaughter | Rape | Robbery | Aggravated assault | Property crime | Burglary | Larceny-theft | Motor vehicle theft | Arson |
|---|---|---|---|---|---|---|---|---|---|---|
| Greenville County | 0 | 0 | 0 | 0 | 0 | 0 | 0 | 0 | 0 | 0 |
| Greenwood County | 0 | 0 | 0 | 0 | 0 | 0 | 0 | 0 | 0 | 0 |
| Horry County | 0 | 0 | 0 | 0 | 0 | 0 | 0 | 0 | 0 | 0 |
| Jasper County | 0 | 0 | 0 | 0 | 0 | 0 | 0 | 0 | 0 | 0 |
| Lancaster County | 0 | 0 | 0 | 0 | 0 | 0 | 0 | 0 | 0 | 0 |
| Lexington County | 0 | 0 | 0 | 0 | 0 | 0 | 0 | 0 | 0 | 0 |
| Marion County | 0 | 0 | 0 | 0 | 0 | 0 | 0 | 0 | 0 | 0 |
| McCormick County | 0 | 0 | 0 | 0 | 0 | 0 | 0 | 0 | 0 | 0 |
| Newberry County | 0 | 0 | 0 | 0 | 0 | 0 | 0 | 0 | 0 | 0 |
| Oconee County | 0 | 0 | 0 | 0 | 0 | 0 | 0 | 0 | 0 | 0 |
| Orangeburg County | 0 | 0 | 0 | 0 | 0 | 0 | 0 | 0 | 0 | 0 |
| Pickens County | 0 | 0 | 0 | 0 | 0 | 0 | 0 | 0 | 0 | 0 |
| Saluda County | 0 | 0 | 0 | 0 | 0 | 0 | 0 | 0 | 0 | 0 |
| Spartanburg County | 0 | 0 | 0 | 0 | 0 | 0 | 0 | 0 | 0 | 0 |
| Sumter County | 0 | 0 | 0 | 0 | 0 | 0 | 0 | 0 | 0 | 0 |
| Union County | 0 | 0 | 0 | 0 | 0 | 0 | 0 | 0 | 0 | 0 |
| York County | 0 | 0 | 0 | 0 | 0 | 0 | 0 | 0 | 0 | 0 |
| Highway Patrol | | | | | | | | | | |
| Cherokee County | 0 | 0 | 0 | 0 | 0 | 0 | 0 | 0 | 0 | 0 |
| Florence County | 0 | 0 | 0 | 0 | 0 | 0 | 0 | 0 | 0 | 0 |
| Greenville County | 0 | 0 | 0 | 0 | 0 | 0 | 0 | 0 | 0 | 0 |
| Lancaster County | 0 | 0 | 0 | 0 | 0 | 0 | 0 | 0 | 0 | 0 |
| Oconee County | 0 | 0 | 0 | 0 | 0 | 0 | 0 | 0 | 0 | 0 |
| Other Agencies | | | | | | | | | | |
| Charleston County Aviation Authority | 1 | 0 | 0 | 0 | 1 | 22 | 0 | 15 | 7 | 0 |
| Greenville Hospital, Greenville | 6 | 0 | 1 | 0 | 5 | 61 | 0 | 58 | 3 | 0 |
| Greenville-Spartanburg International Airport | 2 | 0 | 0 | 2 | 0 | 32 | 0 | 28 | 4 | 0 |
| Lexington County Medical Center | 3 | 0 | 1 | 0 | 2 | 38 | 0 | 36 | 2 | 0 |
| **SOUTH DAKOTA** | | | | | | | | | | |
| **State Agencies** | | | | | | | | | | |
| Highway Patrol | 15 | 0 | 0 | 0 | 15 | 12 | 0 | 10 | 2 | 0 |
| **Tribal Agencies** | | | | | | | | | | |
| Cheyenne River Tribal | 99 | 0 | 12 | 2 | 85 | 16 | 9 | 3 | 4 | 0 |
| Crow Creek Tribal | 42 | 1 | 3 | 0 | 38 | 9 | 2 | 4 | 3 | 0 |
| Flandreau Santee Sioux Tribal | 6 | 0 | 0 | 0 | 6 | 9 | 3 | 2 | 4 | 0 |
| Lower Brule Tribal | 30 | 2 | 5 | 1 | 22 | 72 | 21 | 26 | 25 | 8 |
| Pine Ridge Sioux Tribal | 32 | 1 | 7 | 0 | 24 | 29 | 8 | 12 | 9 | 2 |
| Rosebud Tribal | 242 | 3 | 34 | 1 | 204 | 168 | 59 | 67 | 42 | 4 |
| Sisseton-Wahpeton Tribal | 39 | 0 | 3 | 2 | 34 | 82 | 26 | 33 | 23 | 5 |
| **TENNESSEE** | | | | | | | | | | |
| **State Agencies** | | | | | | | | | | |
| Alcoholic Beverage Commission | 0 | 0 | 0 | 0 | 0 | 0 | 0 | 0 | 0 | 0 |
| Department of Safety | 131 | 0 | 0 | 0 | 131 | 103 | 1 | 17 | 85 | 0 |
| TennCare Office of Inspector General | 0 | 0 | 0 | 0 | 0 | 0 | 0 | 0 | 0 | 0 |
| Tennessee Bureau of Investigation | 5 | 0 | 0 | 0 | 5 | 2 | 0 | 2 | 0 | 2 |
| **Other Agencies** | | | | | | | | | | |
| 8th Judicial District Crime Task Force | 2 | 0 | 0 | 0 | 2 | 0 | 0 | 0 | 0 | 0 |
| Drug Task Force | | | | | | | | | | |
| 2nd Judicial District | 1 | 0 | 0 | 0 | 1 | 1 | 0 | 1 | 0 | 0 |
| 3rd Judicial District | 0 | 0 | 0 | 0 | 0 | 0 | 0 | 0 | 0 | 0 |
| 5th Judicial District | 0 | 0 | 0 | 0 | 0 | 0 | 0 | 0 | 0 | 0 |
| 10th Judicial District | 0 | 0 | 0 | 0 | 0 | 0 | 0 | 0 | 0 | 0 |
| 12th Judicial District | 0 | 0 | 0 | 0 | 0 | 0 | 0 | 0 | 0 | 0 |
| 19th Judicial District | 1 | 0 | 0 | 0 | 1 | 0 | 0 | 0 | 0 | 0 |
| 23rd Judicial District | 0 | 0 | 0 | 0 | 0 | 2 | 0 | 0 | 2 | 0 |
| 24th Judicial District | 3 | 0 | 0 | 0 | 3 | 0 | 0 | 0 | 0 | 0 |
| Knoxville Metropolitan Airport | 0 | 0 | 0 | 0 | 0 | 8 | 0 | 5 | 3 | 0 |
| Memphis-Shelby County Airport Authority | 4 | 0 | 0 | 0 | 4 | 424 | 116 | 246 | 62 | 0 |
| Metropolitan Nashville Park Police | 4 | 0 | 0 | 0 | 4 | 155 | 2 | 148 | 5 | 0 |
| Nashville International Airport | 0 | 0 | 0 | 0 | 0 | 70 | 2 | 47 | 21 | 0 |
| West Tennessee Violent Crime Task Force | 0 | 0 | 0 | 0 | 0 | 0 | 0 | 0 | 0 | 0 |
| **TEXAS** | | | | | | | | | | |
| **Tribal Agencies** | | | | | | | | | | |
| Ysleta del Sur Pueblo Tribal | 2 | 0 | 1 | 0 | 1 | 17 | 1 | 12 | 4 | 0 |
| **Other Agencies** | | | | | | | | | | |
| Amarillo International Airport | 0 | 0 | 0 | 0 | 0 | 5 | 0 | 5 | 0 | 0 |
| Dallas-Fort Worth International Airport | 21 | 0 | 0 | 6 | 15 | 524 | 9 | 450 | 65 | 0 |
| Denton County Water District | 20 | 0 | 9 | 2 | 9 | 90 | 28 | 57 | 5 | 0 |
| Hidalgo County Constable, Precinct 2 | 0 | 0 | 0 | 0 | 0 | 0 | 0 | 0 | 0 | 0 |
| Hospital District, Tarrant County | 4 | 0 | 0 | 1 | 3 | 65 | 0 | 61 | 4 | 0 |
| **Independent School District** | | | | | | | | | | |
| Aldine | 20 | 0 | 0 | 5 | 15 | 135 | 4 | 124 | 7 | 2 |
| Alvin | 3 | 0 | 1 | 1 | 1 | 50 | 0 | 50 | 0 | 0 |
| Angleton | 22 | 0 | 0 | 0 | 22 | 5 | 1 | 4 | 0 | 0 |
| Anna | 2 | 0 | 2 | 0 | 0 | 2 | 0 | 2 | 0 | 1 |
| Aubrey | 0 | 0 | 0 | 0 | 0 | 0 | 0 | 0 | 0 | 0 |
| Austin | 35 | 0 | 21 | 1 | 13 | 161 | 26 | 128 | 7 | 6 |
| Barbers Hill | 1 | 0 | 0 | 0 | 1 | 4 | 0 | 4 | 0 | 0 |
| Bay City | 13 | 0 | 0 | 0 | 13 | 12 | 3 | 9 | 0 | 0 |
| Brazosport | 10 | 0 | 0 | 0 | 10 | 7 | 1 | 6 | 0 | 0 |

## Table 11. Offenses Known to Law Enforcement, by Selected State, Tribal, and Other Agencies, 2021—Continued

(Number.)

| State/other agency unit/office | Violent crime | Murder and nonnegligent manslaughter | Rape | Robbery | Aggravated assault | Property crime | Burglary | Larceny-theft | Motor vehicle theft | Arson |
|---|---|---|---|---|---|---|---|---|---|---|
| Brownsboro | 1 | 0 | 0 | 0 | 1 | 1 | 0 | 0 | 1 | 0 |
| Brownsville | 14 | 0 | 2 | 0 | 12 | 45 | 6 | 39 | 0 | 0 |
| Calhoun County | 0 | 0 | 0 | 0 | 0 | 2 | 0 | 2 | 0 | 0 |
| Castleberry | 0 | 0 | 0 | 0 | 0 | 1 | 1 | 0 | 0 | 0 |
| Centerpoint | 0 | 0 | 0 | 0 | 0 | 0 | 0 | 0 | 0 | 0 |
| Columbia-Brazoria | 3 | 0 | 1 | 0 | 2 | 2 | 0 | 2 | 0 | 0 |
| Conroe | 11 | 0 | 6 | 0 | 5 | 39 | 1 | 35 | 3 | 2 |
| Corsicana | 1 | 0 | 1 | 0 | 0 | 0 | 0 | 0 | 0 | 0 |
| Ector County | 18 | 0 | 0 | 0 | 18 | 28 | 4 | 22 | 2 | 0 |
| Edinburg | 0 | 0 | 0 | 0 | 0 | 5 | 0 | 5 | 0 | 0 |
| El Paso | 24 | 0 | 6 | 3 | 15 | 71 | 18 | 49 | 4 | 0 |
| Floresville | 4 | 0 | 1 | 0 | 3 | 5 | 1 | 4 | 0 | 1 |
| Fort Bend | 60 | 0 | 4 | 3 | 53 | 113 | 14 | 98 | 1 | 0 |
| Gonzales | 1 | 0 | 0 | 0 | 1 | 1 | 0 | 1 | 0 | 0 |
| Hallsville | 0 | 0 | 0 | 0 | 0 | 1 | 0 | 1 | 0 | 0 |
| Humble | 11 | 0 | 6 | 0 | 5 | 48 | 1 | 41 | 6 | 2 |
| Hutto | 0 | 0 | 0 | 0 | 0 | 18 | 2 | 16 | 0 | 1 |
| Idalou | 0 | 0 | 0 | 0 | 0 | 0 | 0 | 0 | 0 | 0 |
| Jonesboro | 0 | 0 | 0 | 0 | 0 | 0 | 0 | 0 | 0 | 0 |
| Killeen | 4 | 0 | 1 | 2 | 1 | 15 | 2 | 13 | 0 | 1 |
| Klein | 5 | 0 | 3 | 0 | 2 | 128 | 6 | 121 | 1 | 3 |
| Lancaster | 1 | 0 | 0 | 0 | 1 | 20 | 1 | 19 | 0 | 0 |
| Laredo | 5 | 0 | 0 | 0 | 5 | 4 | 0 | 4 | 0 | 1 |
| Lufkin | 1 | 0 | 1 | 0 | 0 | 12 | 0 | 12 | 0 | 1 |
| Lyford | 0 | 0 | 0 | 0 | 0 | 1 | 0 | 1 | 0 | 1 |
| Mansfield | 3 | 0 | 1 | 0 | 2 | 10 | 1 | 9 | 0 | 0 |
| Marlin | 0 | 0 | 0 | 0 | 0 | 0 | 0 | 0 | 0 | 0 |
| McAllen | 3 | 0 | 0 | 0 | 3 | 15 | 2 | 13 | 0 | 0 |
| Midland | 5 | 0 | 0 | 0 | 5 | 16 | 7 | 8 | 1 | 2 |
| Montgomery County | 1 | 0 | 0 | 0 | 1 | 2 | 0 | 2 | 0 | 0 |
| Northside | 14 | 0 | 3 | 0 | 11 | 0 | 0 | 0 | 0 | 0 |
| Pasadena | 5 | 0 | 0 | 3 | 2 | 49 | 8 | 37 | 4 | 0 |
| Pecos Barstow Toyah | 1 | 0 | 1 | 0 | 0 | 9 | 6 | 0 | 3 | 0 |
| Pflugerville | 1 | 0 | 0 | 0 | 1 | 16 | 4 | 12 | 0 | 1 |
| Pleasanton | 1 | 0 | 0 | 0 | 1 | 0 | 0 | 0 | 0 | 0 |
| Rio Grande City | 1 | 0 | 1 | 0 | 0 | 8 | 0 | 8 | 0 | 0 |
| Roma | 0 | 0 | 0 | 0 | 0 | 5 | 0 | 5 | 0 | 0 |
| San Antonio | 6 | 0 | 1 | 5 | 0 | 154 | 40 | 101 | 13 | 0 |
| Santa Fe | 0 | 0 | 0 | 0 | 0 | 17 | 1 | 16 | 0 | 0 |
| Socorro | 9 | 0 | 4 | 0 | 5 | 18 | 2 | 16 | 0 | 0 |
| Spring | 0 | 0 | 0 | 0 | 0 | 7 | 2 | 5 | 0 | 0 |
| Spring Branch | 1 | 0 | 0 | 0 | 1 | 21 | 5 | 16 | 0 | 0 |
| Taft | 0 | 0 | 0 | 0 | 0 | 0 | 0 | 0 | 0 | 0 |
| Terrell | 2 | 0 | 0 | 0 | 2 | 2 | 1 | 1 | 0 | 0 |
| Trinity | 0 | 0 | 0 | 0 | 0 | 0 | 0 | 0 | 0 | 0 |
| United | 0 | 0 | 0 | 0 | 0 | 0 | 0 | 0 | 0 | 0 |
| Van Vleck | 0 | 0 | 0 | 0 | 0 | 8 | 2 | 6 | 0 | 0 |
| Vensus | 2 | 0 | 1 | 0 | 1 | 3 | 0 | 3 | 0 | 0 |
| Wharton | 0 | 0 | 0 | 0 | 0 | 0 | 0 | 0 | 0 | 0 |
| Whitesboro | 0 | 0 | 0 | 0 | 0 | 1 | 0 | 1 | 0 | 0 |
| Kaufman County Constable, Precinct 2 | 21 | 0 | 0 | 6 | 15 | 105 | 27 | 63 | 15 | 0 |
| Montgomery County Constable | | | | | | | | | | |
| Precinct 1 | 8 | 0 | 0 | 0 | 8 | 5 | 0 | 4 | 1 | 0 |
| Precinct 3 | 57 | 1 | 15 | 4 | 37 | 138 | 17 | 108 | 13 | 0 |
| Port of Brownsville | 1 | 0 | 0 | 0 | 1 | 8 | 3 | 4 | 1 | 1 |
| Port of Houston Authority | 0 | 0 | 0 | 0 | 0 | 17 | 0 | 15 | 2 | 0 |
| **UTAH** | | | | | | | | | | |
| **State Agencies** | | | | | | | | | | |
| Parks and Recreation | 3 | 0 | 2 | 0 | 1 | 22 | 3 | 16 | 3 | 1 |
| Utah Highway Patrol | 92 | 4 | 14 | 1 | 73 | 80 | 3 | 61 | 16 | 1 |
| Utah Tax Commission Motor Vehicle Division, Vehicle Investigation Section | 0 | 0 | 0 | 0 | 0 | 0 | 0 | 0 | 0 | 0 |
| Wildlife Resources | 1 | 0 | 1 | 0 | 0 | 10 | 0 | 6 | 4 | 0 |
| **Tribal Agencies** | | | | | | | | | | |
| Goshute Tribal | 0 | 0 | 0 | 0 | 0 | 0 | 0 | 0 | 0 | 0 |
| Uintah and Ouray Tribal | 21 | 3 | 5 | 0 | 13 | 44 | 21 | 18 | 5 | 18 |
| **Other Agencies** | | | | | | | | | | |
| Cache-Rich Drug Task Force | 0 | 0 | 0 | 0 | 0 | 3 | 0 | 3 | 0 | 0 |
| Davis Metropolitan Narcotics Strike Force | 0 | 0 | 0 | 0 | 0 | 0 | 0 | 0 | 0 | 0 |
| Utah County Attorney, Investigations Division | 0 | 0 | 0 | 0 | 0 | 1 | 0 | 1 | 0 | 0 |
| Utah County Major Crimes Task Force | 0 | 0 | 0 | 0 | 0 | 6 | 0 | 4 | 2 | 0 |
| Utah Transit Authority | 39 | 0 | 0 | 16 | 23 | 1,601 | 3 | 1,537 | 61 | 5 |
| Weber Morgan Narcotics Strike Force | 7 | 0 | 0 | 0 | 7 | 5 | 0 | 4 | 1 | 0 |
| **VERMONT** | | | | | | | | | | |
| **State Agencies** | | | | | | | | | | |
| Attorney General | 0 | 0 | 0 | 0 | 0 | 0 | 0 | 0 | 0 | 0 |
| Capitol Police | 0 | 0 | 0 | 0 | 0 | 0 | 0 | 0 | 0 | 0 |
| Department of Liquor Control, Division of Enforcement and Licensing | 0 | 0 | 0 | 0 | 0 | 0 | 0 | 0 | 0 | 0 |

## Table 11. Offenses Known to Law Enforcement, by Selected State, Tribal, and Other Agencies, 2021—Continued

(Number.)

| State/other agency unit/office | Violent crime | Murder and nonnegligent manslaughter | Rape | Robbery | Aggravated assault | Property crime | Burglary | Larceny-theft | Motor vehicle theft | Arson |
|---|---|---|---|---|---|---|---|---|---|---|
| Fish and Wildlife Department, Law Enforcement Division | 0 | 0 | 0 | 0 | 0 | 1 | 0 | 1 | 0 | 0 |
| Derby | 36 | 0 | 3 | 5 | 28 | 123 | 36 | 70 | 17 | 0 |
| Middlesex | 32 | 0 | 11 | 1 | 20 | 167 | 24 | 126 | 17 | 0 |
| New Haven | 10 | 0 | 2 | 0 | 8 | 82 | 15 | 52 | 15 | 0 |
| Royalton | 27 | 1 | 4 | 0 | 22 | 115 | 29 | 70 | 16 | 1 |
| Rutland | 46 | 0 | 9 | 6 | 31 | 169 | 40 | 106 | 23 | 0 |
| Shaftsbury | 26 | 0 | 11 | 1 | 14 | 59 | 15 | 39 | 5 | 0 |
| St. Albans | 51 | 2 | 24 | 1 | 24 | 139 | 32 | 83 | 24 | 1 |
| St. Johnsbury | 37 | 1 | 1 | 1 | 34 | 176 | 40 | 113 | 23 | 0 |
| Westminster | 16 | 0 | 2 | 0 | 14 | 241 | 45 | 180 | 16 | 1 |
| Williston | 19 | 0 | 4 | 1 | 14 | 87 | 23 | 58 | 6 | 8 |
| Vermont State Police | 2 | 2 | 0 | 0 | 0 | 0 | 0 | 0 | 0 | 0 |
| Vermont State Police Headquarters Bureau of Criminal Investigations | 0 | 0 | 0 | 0 | 0 | 1 | 0 | 1 | 0 | 0 |
| **VIRGINIA** | | | | | | | | | | |
| **State Agencies** | | | | | | | | | | |
| Department of Conservation and Recreation | 1 | 0 | 1 | 0 | 0 | 47 | 2 | 45 | 0 | 1 |
| Department of Game and Inland Fisheries, Enforcement Division | 2 | 0 | 0 | 0 | 2 | 29 | 0 | 29 | 0 | 0 |
| Department of Motor Vehicles | 0 | 0 | 0 | 0 | 0 | 88 | 0 | 10 | 78 | 0 |
| **State Police** | | | | | | | | | | |
| Accomack County | 9 | 2 | 3 | 0 | 4 | 11 | 0 | 10 | 1 | 3 |
| Albemarle County | 2 | 0 | 0 | 0 | 2 | 2 | 0 | 2 | 0 | 0 |
| Alexandria | 1 | 0 | 0 | 0 | 1 | 3 | 0 | 0 | 3 | 0 |
| Alleghany County | 7 | 1 | 2 | 0 | 4 | 6 | 1 | 1 | 4 | 0 |
| Amherst County | 4 | 1 | 0 | 0 | 3 | 3 | 0 | 3 | 0 | 0 |
| Appomattox County | 1 | 0 | 0 | 0 | 1 | 4 | 1 | 1 | 2 | 0 |
| Arlington County | 1 | 0 | 0 | 0 | 1 | 3 | 0 | 3 | 0 | 0 |
| Augusta County | 5 | 0 | 0 | 0 | 5 | 9 | 1 | 7 | 1 | 1 |
| Bedford County | 1 | 0 | 0 | 0 | 1 | 3 | 0 | 3 | 0 | 0 |
| Botetourt County | 3 | 0 | 1 | 0 | 2 | 5 | 0 | 2 | 3 | 0 |
| Brunswick County | 0 | 0 | 0 | 0 | 0 | 3 | 1 | 1 | 1 | 0 |
| Buchanan County | 5 | 0 | 1 | 0 | 4 | 3 | 0 | 3 | 0 | 3 |
| Buckingham County | 2 | 0 | 0 | 0 | 2 | 4 | 0 | 2 | 2 | 0 |
| Buena Vista | 0 | 0 | 0 | 0 | 0 | 0 | 0 | 0 | 0 | 0 |
| Campbell County | 5 | 0 | 0 | 0 | 5 | 0 | 0 | 0 | 0 | 0 |
| Caroline County | 8 | 0 | 0 | 1 | 7 | 28 | 2 | 10 | 16 | 1 |
| Carroll County | 7 | 0 | 0 | 0 | 7 | 11 | 1 | 9 | 1 | 1 |
| Charlotte County | 2 | 0 | 1 | 0 | 1 | 1 | 0 | 1 | 0 | 0 |
| Charlottesville | 0 | 0 | 0 | 0 | 0 | 0 | 0 | 0 | 0 | 0 |
| Chesapeake | 12 | 0 | 0 | 0 | 12 | 10 | 0 | 5 | 5 | 0 |
| Chesterfield County | 11 | 0 | 1 | 0 | 10 | 9 | 0 | 3 | 6 | 0 |
| Colonial Heights | 1 | 0 | 0 | 0 | 1 | 0 | 0 | 0 | 0 | 0 |
| Culpeper County | 7 | 1 | 1 | 0 | 5 | 2 | 0 | 1 | 1 | 1 |
| Danville | 0 | 0 | 0 | 0 | 0 | 0 | 0 | 0 | 0 | 0 |
| Dickenson County | 4 | 0 | 0 | 0 | 4 | 3 | 0 | 3 | 0 | 0 |
| Dinwiddie County | 4 | 0 | 0 | 1 | 3 | 3 | 0 | 2 | 1 | 0 |
| Fairfax County | 33 | 1 | 1 | 2 | 29 | 30 | 1 | 15 | 14 | 0 |
| Fauquier County | 4 | 0 | 0 | 1 | 3 | 3 | 0 | 2 | 1 | 0 |
| Franklin County | 4 | 1 | 0 | 0 | 3 | 4 | 0 | 3 | 1 | 0 |
| Frederick County | 11 | 1 | 0 | 0 | 10 | 4 | 0 | 2 | 2 | 0 |
| Fredericksburg | 0 | 0 | 0 | 0 | 0 | 1 | 0 | 1 | 0 | 0 |
| Giles County | 2 | 0 | 0 | 0 | 2 | 4 | 0 | 4 | 0 | 0 |
| Gloucester County | 2 | 0 | 0 | 0 | 2 | 1 | 0 | 1 | 0 | 2 |
| Goochland County | 4 | 0 | 1 | 0 | 3 | 1 | 0 | 0 | 1 | 0 |
| Grayson County | 3 | 0 | 0 | 0 | 3 | 5 | 0 | 4 | 1 | 0 |
| Greensville County | 5 | 1 | 0 | 0 | 4 | 2 | 0 | 1 | 1 | 0 |
| Halifax County | 5 | 0 | 0 | 0 | 5 | 1 | 0 | 1 | 0 | 0 |
| Hampton | 14 | 0 | 0 | 0 | 14 | 1 | 0 | 0 | 1 | 0 |
| Hanover County | 2 | 0 | 0 | 0 | 2 | 3 | 0 | 1 | 2 | 0 |
| Harrisonburg | 0 | 0 | 0 | 0 | 0 | 3 | 0 | 3 | 0 | 0 |
| Henrico County | 12 | 0 | 0 | 0 | 12 | 5 | 0 | 2 | 3 | 0 |
| Henry County | 7 | 0 | 1 | 0 | 6 | 20 | 0 | 8 | 12 | 0 |
| Hopewell | 0 | 0 | 0 | 0 | 0 | 0 | 0 | 0 | 0 | 0 |
| Isle of Wight County | 0 | 0 | 0 | 0 | 0 | 4 | 0 | 1 | 3 | 1 |
| James City County | 6 | 0 | 0 | 0 | 6 | 2 | 0 | 0 | 2 | 1 |
| King George County | 0 | 0 | 0 | 0 | 0 | 1 | 0 | 1 | 0 | 0 |
| Lee County | 2 | 1 | 1 | 0 | 0 | 7 | 0 | 4 | 3 | 0 |
| Loudoun County | 6 | 0 | 0 | 0 | 6 | 3 | 0 | 2 | 1 | 2 |
| Louisa County | 4 | 0 | 0 | 0 | 4 | 1 | 0 | 1 | 0 | 2 |
| Lunenburg County | 1 | 1 | 0 | 0 | 0 | 3 | 0 | 2 | 1 | 0 |
| Lynchburg | 0 | 0 | 0 | 0 | 0 | 0 | 0 | 0 | 0 | 0 |
| Martinsville | 3 | 3 | 0 | 0 | 0 | 0 | 0 | 0 | 0 | 0 |
| Mecklenburg County | 7 | 0 | 0 | 0 | 7 | 2 | 0 | 2 | 0 | 0 |
| Montgomery County | 5 | 0 | 1 | 0 | 4 | 3 | 0 | 1 | 2 | 0 |
| Nelson County | 0 | 0 | 0 | 0 | 0 | 4 | 0 | 3 | 1 | 0 |
| New Kent County | 9 | 0 | 0 | 0 | 9 | 3 | 0 | 3 | 0 | 0 |
| Newport News | 11 | 0 | 0 | 1 | 10 | 4 | 0 | 1 | 3 | 0 |
| Norfolk | 27 | 1 | 0 | 0 | 26 | 4 | 0 | 2 | 2 | 0 |
| Northampton County | 8 | 0 | 0 | 0 | 8 | 2 | 0 | 2 | 0 | 0 |
| Northumberland County | 1 | 0 | 0 | 0 | 1 | 1 | 0 | 1 | 0 | 0 |

## Table 11. Offenses Known to Law Enforcement, by Selected State, Tribal, and Other Agencies, 2021—Continued

(Number.)

| State/other agency unit/office | Violent crime | Murder and nonnegligent manslaughter | Rape | Robbery | Aggravated assault | Property crime | Burglary | Larceny-theft | Motor vehicle theft | Arson |
|---|---|---|---|---|---|---|---|---|---|---|
| Nottoway County | 0 | 0 | 0 | 0 | 0 | 5 | 0 | 2 | 3 | 0 |
| Orange County | 2 | 0 | 0 | 0 | 2 | 3 | 0 | 2 | 1 | 1 |
| Page County | 6 | 1 | 2 | 0 | 3 | 1 | 0 | 1 | 0 | 0 |
| Patrick County | 2 | 0 | 0 | 0 | 2 | 0 | 0 | 0 | 0 | 0 |
| Petersburg | 8 | 1 | 1 | 1 | 5 | 0 | 0 | 0 | 0 | 1 |
| Pittsylvania County | 4 | 0 | 0 | 0 | 4 | 24 | 0 | 5 | 19 | 0 |
| Portsmouth | 2 | 0 | 0 | 0 | 2 | 5 | 0 | 0 | 5 | 0 |
| Prince Edward County | 2 | 0 | 1 | 0 | 1 | 2 | 0 | 2 | 0 | 0 |
| Prince George County | 3 | 0 | 0 | 0 | 3 | 3 | 0 | 1 | 2 | 0 |
| Prince William County | 6 | 0 | 0 | 0 | 6 | 8 | 0 | 6 | 2 | 2 |
| Pulaski County | 4 | 0 | 2 | 0 | 2 | 4 | 1 | 3 | 0 | 0 |
| Rappahannock County | 0 | 0 | 0 | 0 | 0 | 0 | 0 | 0 | 0 | 0 |
| Richmond | 15 | 1 | 2 | 0 | 12 | 17 | 0 | 3 | 14 | 0 |
| Richmond County | 4 | 0 | 0 | 0 | 4 | 0 | 0 | 0 | 0 | 0 |
| Roanoke | 1 | 0 | 0 | 0 | 1 | 5 | 1 | 4 | 0 | 1 |
| Roanoke County | 2 | 0 | 0 | 0 | 2 | 3 | 0 | 0 | 3 | 0 |
| Rockbridge County | 6 | 0 | 0 | 0 | 6 | 3 | 0 | 2 | 1 | 0 |
| Rockingham County | 5 | 0 | 0 | 0 | 5 | 33 | 0 | 11 | 22 | 0 |
| Russell County | 2 | 0 | 0 | 0 | 2 | 3 | 0 | 2 | 1 | 0 |
| Salem | 0 | 0 | 0 | 0 | 0 | 1 | 0 | 1 | 0 | 0 |
| Scott County | 2 | 1 | 1 | 0 | 0 | 1 | 0 | 1 | 0 | 4 |
| Shenandoah County | 6 | 0 | 0 | 0 | 6 | 3 | 0 | 3 | 0 | 0 |
| Smyth County | 4 | 0 | 1 | 0 | 3 | 17 | 0 | 12 | 5 | 0 |
| Spotsylvania County | 4 | 0 | 0 | 0 | 4 | 5 | 0 | 0 | 5 | 0 |
| Stafford County | 3 | 0 | 0 | 0 | 3 | 5 | 0 | 3 | 2 | 0 |
| Staunton | 4 | 0 | 4 | 0 | 0 | 1 | 0 | 1 | 0 | 0 |
| Suffolk | 1 | 0 | 0 | 0 | 1 | 3 | 0 | 1 | 2 | 0 |
| Sussex County | 3 | 0 | 0 | 0 | 3 | 4 | 0 | 4 | 0 | 0 |
| Tazewell County | 8 | 0 | 1 | 0 | 7 | 21 | 3 | 18 | 0 | 4 |
| Virginia Beach | 5 | 0 | 0 | 0 | 5 | 4 | 0 | 1 | 3 | 0 |
| Warren County | 2 | 0 | 0 | 0 | 2 | 0 | 0 | 0 | 0 | 0 |
| Washington County | 6 | 0 | 1 | 0 | 5 | 3 | 0 | 2 | 1 | 1 |
| Westmoreland County | 0 | 0 | 0 | 0 | 0 | 0 | 0 | 0 | 0 | 0 |
| Winchester | 0 | 0 | 0 | 0 | 0 | 3 | 0 | 2 | 1 | 0 |
| Wise County | 1 | 1 | 0 | 0 | 0 | 5 | 0 | 5 | 0 | 0 |
| Wythe County | 4 | 0 | 1 | 1 | 2 | 21 | 2 | 15 | 4 | 1 |
| York County | 1 | 0 | 0 | 0 | 1 | 3 | 0 | 3 | 0 | 0 |
| Virginia Marine Resources Commission Law Enforcement Division | 0 | 0 | 0 | 0 | 0 | 1 | 0 | 1 | 0 | 0 |
| Virginia State Capitol | 1 | 0 | 0 | 0 | 1 | 14 | 0 | 14 | 0 | 0 |
| Other Agencies | | | | | | | | | | |
| Norfolk Airport Authority | 0 | 0 | 0 | 0 | 0 | 42 | 0 | 41 | 1 | 0 |
| Port Authority, Norfolk | 1 | 0 | 0 | 0 | 1 | 4 | 0 | 4 | 0 | 0 |
| Reagan National Airport | 6 | 0 | 0 | 3 | 3 | 186 | 1 | 132 | 53 | 0 |
| Richmond International Airport | 0 | 0 | 0 | 0 | 0 | 27 | 0 | 17 | 10 | 0 |
| **WASHINGTON** | | | | | | | | | | |
| **State Agencies** | | | | | | | | | | |
| State Insurance Commissioner, Special Investigations Unit | 0 | 0 | 0 | 0 | 0 | 1 | 0 | 1 | 0 | 0 |
| Washington State Parks and Recreation Law Enforcement | 10 | 0 | 0 | 1 | 9 | 276 | 131 | 135 | 10 | 5 |
| Washington State Patrol | 0 | 0 | 0 | 0 | 0 | 0 | 0 | 0 | 0 | 0 |
| **Tribal Agencies** | | | | | | | | | | |
| Chehalis Tribal | 5 | 0 | 0 | 1 | 4 | 101 | 14 | 64 | 23 | 1 |
| Hoh Tribal | 0 | 0 | 0 | 0 | 0 | 0 | 0 | 0 | 0 | 0 |
| Jamestown S'Klallam Tribal | 0 | 0 | 0 | 0 | 0 | 13 | 0 | 13 | 0 | 0 |
| Kalispel Tribal | 6 | 0 | 2 | 1 | 3 | 426 | 35 | 371 | 20 | 0 |
| La Push Tribal | 1 | 0 | 1 | 0 | 0 | 15 | 2 | 13 | 0 | 0 |
| Lummi Tribal | 55 | 0 | 8 | 1 | 46 | 295 | 75 | 196 | 24 | 1 |
| Muckleshoot Tribal | 12 | 0 | 2 | 0 | 10 | 55 | 9 | 38 | 8 | 0 |
| Nooksack Tribal | 0 | 0 | 0 | 0 | 0 | 1 | 0 | 1 | 0 | 0 |
| Puyallup Tribal | 17 | 2 | 4 | 10 | 1 | 486 | 5 | 265 | 216 | 1 |
| Shoalwater Bay Tribal | 0 | 0 | 0 | 0 | 0 | 4 | 0 | 3 | 1 | 0 |
| Skokomish Tribal | 1 | 0 | 0 | 0 | 1 | 37 | 7 | 28 | 2 | 0 |
| Snoqualmie Tribal | 0 | 0 | 0 | 0 | 0 | 0 | 0 | 0 | 0 | 0 |
| Squaxin Island Tribal | 0 | 0 | 0 | 0 | 0 | 38 | 1 | 33 | 4 | 0 |
| Suquamish Tribal | 1 | 0 | 1 | 0 | 0 | 51 | 12 | 37 | 2 | 0 |
| Swinomish Tribal | 1 | 0 | 0 | 0 | 1 | 14 | 3 | 9 | 2 | 0 |
| Upper Skagit Tribal | 0 | 0 | 0 | 0 | 0 | 2 | 0 | 2 | 0 | 0 |
| **WEST VIRGINIA** | | | | | | | | | | |
| **State Agencies** | | | | | | | | | | |
| Capitol Protective Services | 1 | 0 | 0 | 0 | 1 | 12 | 2 | 10 | 0 | 0 |
| State Police | | | | | | | | | | |
| Beckley | 43 | 0 | 8 | 1 | 34 | 234 | 30 | 179 | 25 | 0 |
| Berkeley Springs | 6 | 0 | 4 | 1 | 1 | 43 | 7 | 32 | 4 | 1 |
| Bridgeport | 8 | 0 | 7 | 0 | 1 | 116 | 23 | 80 | 13 | 1 |
| Buckhannon | 6 | 0 | 4 | 1 | 1 | 59 | 12 | 34 | 13 | 0 |
| Clay | 8 | 1 | 3 | 0 | 4 | 47 | 22 | 16 | 9 | 1 |
| Fairmont | 11 | 0 | 2 | 1 | 8 | 90 | 17 | 62 | 11 | 0 |
| Franklin | 8 | 1 | 2 | 0 | 5 | 12 | 5 | 4 | 3 | 3 |
| Glenville | 19 | 1 | 9 | 0 | 9 | 34 | 11 | 16 | 7 | 1 |

## Table 11. Offenses Known to Law Enforcement, by Selected State, Tribal, and Other Agencies, 2021—Continued

(Number.)

| State/other agency unit/office | Violent crime | Murder and nonnegligent manslaughter | Rape | Robbery | Aggravated assault | Property crime | Burglary | Larceny-theft | Motor vehicle theft | Arson |
|---|---|---|---|---|---|---|---|---|---|---|
| Grafton | 6 | 0 | 5 | 0 | 1 | 29 | 9 | 19 | 1 | 0 |
| Grantsville | 4 | 1 | 1 | 1 | 1 | 36 | 14 | 19 | 3 | 1 |
| Hamlin | 31 | 1 | 15 | 0 | 15 | 130 | 33 | 72 | 25 | 2 |
| Harrisville | 5 | 0 | 1 | 0 | 4 | 37 | 8 | 23 | 6 | 0 |
| Hinton | 4 | 1 | 1 | 0 | 2 | 17 | 3 | 9 | 5 | 0 |
| Huntington | 53 | 0 | 42 | 0 | 11 | 149 | 13 | 123 | 13 | 0 |
| Internet Crimes Against Children Unit | 5 | 0 | 4 | 0 | 1 | 3 | 0 | 3 | 0 | 0 |
| Jesse | 2 | 0 | 1 | 0 | 1 | 16 | 2 | 8 | 6 | 0 |
| Keyser | 8 | 0 | 3 | 0 | 5 | 86 | 15 | 65 | 6 | 0 |
| Lewisburg | 8 | 0 | 4 | 0 | 4 | 70 | 7 | 54 | 9 | 1 |
| Logan | 14 | 0 | 6 | 0 | 8 | 61 | 7 | 32 | 22 | 1 |
| Madison | 7 | 1 | 4 | 0 | 2 | 66 | 16 | 39 | 11 | 1 |
| Marlinton | 8 | 0 | 5 | 0 | 3 | 43 | 5 | 32 | 6 | 3 |
| Martinsburg | 61 | 0 | 51 | 1 | 9 | 166 | 16 | 137 | 13 | 3 |
| Moorefield | 28 | 0 | 5 | 0 | 23 | 84 | 17 | 59 | 8 | 0 |
| Morgantown | 20 | 0 | 8 | 1 | 11 | 190 | 37 | 135 | 18 | 0 |
| Moundsville | 20 | 0 | 8 | 0 | 12 | 17 | 2 | 14 | 1 | 0 |
| New Cumberland | 6 | 0 | 5 | 0 | 1 | 0 | 0 | 0 | 0 | 0 |
| Oak Hill | 5 | 0 | 1 | 0 | 4 | 34 | 5 | 26 | 3 | 1 |
| Paden City | 8 | 0 | 5 | 0 | 3 | 19 | 2 | 13 | 4 | 0 |
| Parkersburg | 15 | 0 | 13 | 0 | 2 | 34 | 9 | 21 | 4 | 1 |
| Parsons | 4 | 1 | 1 | 0 | 2 | 12 | 2 | 8 | 2 | 0 |
| Philippi | 8 | 1 | 3 | 0 | 4 | 39 | 18 | 19 | 2 | 0 |
| Princeton | 11 | 0 | 3 | 0 | 8 | 161 | 18 | 124 | 19 | 1 |
| Rainelle | 8 | 0 | 1 | 1 | 6 | 62 | 20 | 40 | 2 | 1 |
| Richwood | 4 | 0 | 1 | 0 | 3 | 18 | 1 | 14 | 3 | 0 |
| Ripley | 3 | 0 | 3 | 0 | 0 | 28 | 10 | 15 | 3 | 0 |
| Romney | 12 | 0 | 1 | 1 | 10 | 25 | 3 | 19 | 3 | 0 |
| South Charleston | 38 | 0 | 24 | 2 | 12 | 340 | 24 | 293 | 23 | 0 |
| Spencer | 14 | 1 | 5 | 0 | 8 | 24 | 4 | 15 | 5 | 0 |
| Summersville | 3 | 0 | 3 | 0 | 0 | 35 | 4 | 23 | 8 | 1 |
| Sutton | 17 | 2 | 9 | 0 | 6 | 59 | 12 | 35 | 12 | 2 |
| Union | 6 | 0 | 2 | 0 | 4 | 26 | 11 | 14 | 1 | 0 |
| Upperglade | 11 | 0 | 3 | 0 | 8 | 37 | 10 | 20 | 7 | 0 |
| Wayne | 25 | 1 | 7 | 1 | 16 | 175 | 40 | 97 | 38 | 0 |
| Welch | 15 | 0 | 3 | 1 | 11 | 48 | 9 | 28 | 11 | 0 |
| Weston | 13 | 1 | 5 | 1 | 6 | 81 | 16 | 51 | 14 | 2 |
| West Union | 8 | 1 | 4 | 0 | 3 | 16 | 8 | 4 | 4 | 2 |
| Wheeling | 3 | 0 | 2 | 0 | 1 | 6 | 0 | 4 | 2 | 0 |
| Williamson | 15 | 1 | 11 | 0 | 3 | 74 | 19 | 35 | 20 | 3 |
| Winfield | 21 | 0 | 12 | 0 | 9 | 86 | 12 | 67 | 7 | 1 |
| Other Agencies | | | | | | | | | | |
| Ohio Valley Drug and Violent Crime Task Force | 0 | 0 | 0 | 0 | 0 | 0 | 0 | 0 | 0 | 0 |
| **WISCONSIN** | | | | | | | | | | |
| **State Agencies** | | | | | | | | | | |
| Division of Criminal Investigation, Madison | 2 | 1 | 1 | 0 | 0 | 1 | 0 | 1 | 0 | 0 |
| Lac Courte Oreilles Tribal | 28 | 0 | 6 | 1 | 21 | 37 | 11 | 25 | 1 | 0 |
| Oneida Tribal | 36 | 2 | 9 | 0 | 25 | 100 | 6 | 88 | 6 | 1 |
| St. Croix Tribal | 0 | 0 | 0 | 0 | 0 | 32 | 1 | 23 | 8 | 0 |
| **Tribal Agencies** | | | | | | | | | | |
| Stockbridge Munsee Tribal | 2 | 0 | 1 | 0 | 1 | 23 | 4 | 14 | 5 | 0 |
| **WYOMING** | | | | | | | | | | |
| **State Agencies** | | | | | | | | | | |
| Wyoming Division of Criminal Investigation | 28 | 5 | 9 | 1 | 13 | 6 | 3 | 1 | 2 | 4 |

1 Limited data for 2021 were available for California, Florida, Illinois, Maryland, New Jersey, New Mexico, New York, and Pennsylvania.

## Table 12. Crime Trends, by Population Group, 2019–2020

(Number, percent change.)

| Population group | Violent crime | Murder and nonnegligent manslaughter | Rape[1] | Robbery | Aggravated assault | Property crime | Burglary | Larceny-theft | Motor vehicle theft | Arson | Number of agencies | Estimated population, 2020 |
|---|---|---|---|---|---|---|---|---|---|---|---|---|
| **Total, All Agencies** | | | | | | | | | | | | |
| 2019 | 1,099,647 | 14,440 | 127,821 | 238,036 | 719,350 | 5,977,531 | 968,856 | 4,327,744 | 650,351 | 30,580 | 13,827 | 294,203,623 |
| 2020 | 1,147,914 | 18,623 | 111,947 | 215,106 | 802,238 | 5,563,304 | 893,344 | 3,906,065 | 726,283 | 37,612 | | |
| Percent change | 4.4 | 29.0 | -12.4 | -9.6 | 11.5 | -6.9 | -7.8 | -9.7 | 11.7 | 23.0 | | |
| **Total, Cities** | | | | | | | | | | | | |
| 2019 | 882,969 | 11,195 | 95,780 | 209,835 | 566,159 | 4,799,777 | 727,290 | 3,528,095 | 520,810 | 23,582 | 9,985 | 200,688,039 |
| 2020 | 922,257 | 14,794 | 82,808 | 189,624 | 635,031 | 4,457,179 | 679,313 | 3,162,763 | 585,754 | 29,349 | | |
| Percent change | 4.4 | 32.1 | -13.5 | -9.6 | 12.2 | -7.1 | -6.6 | -10.4 | 12.5 | 24.5 | | |
| **Group I (250,000 and over)** | | | | | | | | | | | | |
| 2019 | 431,053 | 5,837 | 36,083 | 119,853 | 269,280 | 1,794,877 | 280,025 | 1,263,441 | 242,884 | 8,527 | 84 | 60,095,451 |
| 2020 | 454,913 | 7,833 | 30,592 | 109,133 | 307,355 | 1,672,010 | 268,045 | 1,122,909 | 270,136 | 10,920 | | |
| Percent change | 5.5 | 34.2 | -15.2 | -8.9 | 14.1 | -6.8 | -4.3 | -11.1 | 11.2 | 28.1 | | |
| 1,000,000 and over (Group I subset) | | | | | | | | | | | | |
| 2019 | 185,593 | 1,987 | 14,984 | 55,642 | 112,980 | 646,333 | 100,111 | 453,510 | 90,773 | 1,939 | 11 | 27,146,381 |
| 2020 | 192,910 | 2,779 | 12,140 | 51,754 | 126,237 | 611,719 | 96,553 | 409,536 | 102,979 | 2,651 | | |
| Percent change | 3.9 | 39.9 | -19.0 | -7.0 | 11.7 | -5.4 | -3.6 | -9.7 | 13.4 | 36.7 | | |
| 500,000 to 999,999 (Group I subset) | | | | | | | | | | | | |
| 2019 | 134,189 | 2,136 | 10,004 | 36,403 | 85,646 | 601,095 | 94,854 | 424,586 | 78,525 | 3,130 | 23 | 16,076,918 |
| 2020 | 143,079 | 2,764 | 8,408 | 31,758 | 100,149 | 552,774 | 91,945 | 373,324 | 83,597 | 3,908 | | |
| Percent change | 6.6 | 29.4 | -16.0 | -12.8 | 16.9 | -8.0 | -3.1 | -12.1 | 6.5 | 24.9 | | |
| 250,000 to 499,999 (Group I subset) | | | | | | | | | | | | |
| 2019 | 111,271 | 1,714 | 11,095 | 27,808 | 70,654 | 547,449 | 85,060 | 385,345 | 73,586 | 3,458 | 50 | 16,872,152 |
| 2020 | 118,924 | 2,290 | 10,044 | 25,621 | 80,969 | 507,517 | 79,547 | 340,049 | 83,560 | 4,361 | | |
| Percent change | 6.9 | 33.6 | -9.5 | -7.9 | 14.6 | -7.3 | -6.5 | -11.8 | 13.6 | 26.1 | | |
| **Group II (100,000 to 249,999)** | | | | | | | | | | | | |
| 2019 | 140,351 | 1,857 | 15,917 | 33,730 | 88,847 | 844,224 | 125,334 | 616,880 | 97,847 | 4,163 | 223 | 32,301,225 |
| 2020 | 148,026 | 2,502 | 14,018 | 30,139 | 101,367 | 793,009 | 117,723 | 559,645 | 110,199 | 5,442 | | |
| Percent change | 5.5 | 34.7 | -11.9 | -10.6 | 14.1 | -6.1 | -6.1 | -9.3 | 12.6 | 30.7 | | |
| **Group III (50,000 to 99,999)** | | | | | | | | | | | | |
| 2019 | 107,242 | 1,226 | 12,891 | 24,427 | 68,698 | 705,455 | 102,260 | 530,921 | 68,854 | 3,420 | 475 | 33,149,178 |
| 2020 | 111,601 | 1,551 | 11,562 | 21,473 | 77,015 | 662,747 | 93,319 | 485,558 | 79,762 | 4,108 | | |
| Percent change | 4.1 | 26.5 | -10.3 | -12.1 | 12.1 | -6.1 | -8.7 | -8.5 | 15.8 | 20.1 | | |
| **Group IV (25,000 to 49,999)** | | | | | | | | | | | | |
| 2019 | 76,663 | 906 | 10,933 | 14,756 | 50,068 | 549,474 | 80,610 | 420,821 | 45,423 | 2,620 | 831 | 28,909,214 |
| 2020 | 80,251 | 1,150 | 9,841 | 13,670 | 55,590 | 510,310 | 73,590 | 381,353 | 52,087 | 3,280 | | |
| Percent change | 4.7 | 26.9 | -10.0 | -7.4 | 11.0 | -7.1 | -8.7 | -9.4 | 14.7 | 25.2 | | |
| **Group V (10,000 to 24,999)** | | | | | | | | | | | | |
| 2019 | 66,763 | 782 | 10,273 | 10,292 | 45,416 | 491,918 | 75,598 | 376,751 | 37,260 | 2,309 | 1,645 | 26,337,532 |
| 2020 | 68,750 | 1,039 | 9,001 | 9,539 | 49,171 | 458,635 | 68,695 | 344,088 | 43,119 | 2,733 | | |
| Percent change | 3.0 | 32.9 | -12.4 | -7.3 | 8.3 | -6.8 | -9.1 | -8.7 | 15.7 | 18.4 | | |
| **Group VI (under 10,000)** | | | | | | | | | | | | |
| 2019 | 60,897 | 587 | 9,683 | 6,777 | 43,850 | 413,829 | 63,463 | 319,281 | 28,542 | 2,543 | 6,727 | 19,895,439 |
| 2020 | 58,716 | 719 | 7,794 | 5,670 | 44,533 | 360,468 | 57,941 | 269,210 | 30,451 | 2,866 | | |
| Percent change | -3.6 | 22.5 | -19.5 | -16.3 | 1.6 | -12.9 | -8.7 | -15.7 | 6.7 | 12.7 | | |
| **Metropolitan Counties** | | | | | | | | | | | | |
| 2019 | 170,794 | 2,391 | 23,214 | 26,110 | 119,079 | 955,842 | 177,543 | 668,556 | 104,641 | 5,102 | 1,697 | 71,020,687 |
| 2020 | 177,270 | 2,807 | 21,133 | 23,373 | 129,957 | 894,680 | 156,865 | 617,695 | 114,150 | 5,970 | | |
| Percent change | 3.8 | 17.4 | -9.0 | -10.5 | 9.1 | -6.4 | -11.6 | -7.6 | 9.1 | 17.0 | | |
| **Nonmetropolitan Counties[2]** | | | | | | | | | | | | |
| 2019 | 45,884 | 854 | 8,827 | 2,091 | 34,112 | 221,912 | 64,023 | 131,093 | 24,900 | 1,896 | 2,145 | 22,494,897 |
| 2020 | 48,387 | 1,022 | 8,006 | 2,109 | 37,250 | 211,445 | 57,166 | 125,607 | 26,379 | 2,293 | | |
| Percent change | 5.5 | 19.7 | -9.3 | 0.9 | 9.2 | -4.7 | -10.7 | -4.2 | 5.9 | 20.9 | | |
| **Suburban Areas[3]** | | | | | | | | | | | | |
| 2019 | 294,113 | 3,691 | 41,756 | 49,027 | 199,639 | 1,908,002 | 309,769 | 1,406,493 | 182,277 | 9,463 | 7,430 | 125,892,017 |
| 2020 | 300,262 | 4,429 | 37,220 | 43,886 | 214,727 | 1,765,243 | 277,444 | 1,273,709 | 202,906 | 11,184 | | |
| Percent change | 2.1 | 20.0 | -10.9 | -10.5 | 7.6 | -7.5 | -10.4 | -9.4 | 11.3 | 18.2 | | |

1 The figures shown in this column for the offense of rape were reported using only the revised Uniform Crime Reporting definition of rape. See chapter notes for more detail.   2 Includes state police agencies that report aggregately for the entire state.
3 Suburban areas include law enforcement agencies in cities with less than 50,000 inhabitants and county law enforcement agencies that are within a Metropolitan Statistical Area. Suburban areas exclude all metropolitan agencies associated with a principal city. The agencies associated with suburban areas also appear in other groups within this table.

# Table 13. Crime Trends, by Suburban and Nonsuburban Cities,[1] by Population Group, 2019–2020

(Number, percent change.)

| Population group | Violent crime | Murder and nonnegligent manslaughter | Rape[2] | Robbery | Aggravated assault | Property crime | Burglary | Larceny-theft | Motor vehicle theft | Arson | Number of agencies | Estimated population, 20120 |
|---|---|---|---|---|---|---|---|---|---|---|---|---|
| **Suburban Cities** | | | | | | | | | | | | |
| 2019 | 123,319 | 1,300 | 18,542 | 22,917 | 80,560 | 952,160 | 132,226 | 737,937 | 77,636 | 4,361 | | |
| 2020 | 122,992 | 1,622 | 16,087 | 20,513 | 84,770 | 870,563 | 120,579 | 656,014 | 88,756 | 5,214 | 5,733 | 54,871,330 |
| Percent change | -0.3 | 24.8 | -13.2 | -10.5 | 5.2 | -8.6 | -8.8 | -11.1 | 14.3 | 19.6 | | |
| Group IV (25,000 to 49,999) | | | | | | | | | | | | |
| 2019 | 47,813 | 526 | 7,085 | 10,232 | 29,970 | 376,273 | 51,409 | 290,403 | 32,919 | 1,542 | | |
| 2020 | 49,111 | 644 | 6,363 | 9,507 | 32,597 | 353,078 | 46,976 | 265,325 | 38,737 | 2,040 | 658 | 22,704,238 |
| Percent change | 2.7 | 22.4 | -10.2 | -7.1 | 8.8 | -6.2 | -8.6 | -8.6 | 17.7 | 32.3 | | |
| Group V (10,000 to 24,999) | | | | | | | | | | | | |
| 2019 | 42,603 | 470 | 6,306 | 7,579 | 28,248 | 322,339 | 46,279 | 247,732 | 26,927 | 1,401 | | |
| 2020 | 43,654 | 617 | 5,658 | 6,944 | 30,435 | 301,971 | 41,951 | 227,016 | 31,390 | 1,614 | 1,243 | 20,074,390 |
| Percent change | 2.5 | 31.3 | -10.3 | -8.4 | 7.7 | -6.3 | -9.4 | -8.4 | 16.6 | 15.2 | | |
| Group VI (under 10,000) | | | | | | | | | | | | |
| 2019 | 32,903 | 304 | 5,151 | 5,106 | 22,342 | 253,548 | 34,538 | 199,802 | 17,790 | 1,418 | | |
| 2020 | 30,227 | 361 | 4,066 | 4,062 | 21,738 | 215,514 | 31,652 | 163,673 | 18,629 | 1,560 | 3,832 | 12,092,702 |
| Percent change | -8.1 | 18.8 | -21.1 | -20.4 | -2.7 | -15.0 | -8.4 | -18.1 | 4.7 | 10.0 | | |
| **Nonsuburban Cities** | | | | | | | | | | | | |
| 2019 | 56,800 | 645 | 9,339 | 4,813 | 42,003 | 359,759 | 63,291 | 270,479 | 23,759 | 2,230 | | |
| 2020 | 58,454 | 839 | 7,902 | 4,648 | 45,065 | 330,379 | 58,617 | 242,957 | 26,140 | 2,665 | 3,315 | 15,290,958 |
| Percent change | 2.9 | 30.1 | -15.4 | -3.4 | 7.3 | -8.2 | -7.4 | -10.2 | 10.0 | 19.5 | | |
| Group IV (25,000 to 49,999) | | | | | | | | | | | | |
| 2019 | 7,244 | 86 | 1,237 | 858 | 5,063 | 49,422 | 8,351 | 37,051 | 3,759 | 261 | | |
| 2020 | 7,582 | 95 | 1,158 | 830 | 5,499 | 46,841 | 8,450 | 34,169 | 3,914 | 308 | 62 | 2,006,781 |
| Percent change | 4.7 | 10.5 | -6.4 | -3.3 | 8.6 | -5.2 | 1.2 | -7.8 | 4.1 | 18.0 | | |
| Group V (10,000 to 24,999) | | | | | | | | | | | | |
| 2019 | 21,600 | 276 | 3,571 | 2,286 | 15,467 | 150,094 | 26,016 | 113,985 | 9,248 | 845 | | |
| 2020 | 22,392 | 386 | 3,017 | 2,212 | 16,777 | 138,613 | 23,880 | 103,277 | 10,404 | 1,052 | 360 | 5,489,178 |
| Percent change | 3.7 | 39.9 | -15.5 | -3.2 | 8.5 | -7.6 | -8.2 | -9.4 | 12.5 | 24.5 | | |
| Group VI (under 10,000) | | | | | | | | | | | | |
| 2019 | 27,956 | 283 | 4,531 | 1,669 | 21,473 | 160,243 | 28,924 | 119,443 | 10,752 | 1,124 | | |
| 2020 | 28,480 | 358 | 3,727 | 1,606 | 22,789 | 144,925 | 26,287 | 105,511 | 11,822 | 1,305 | 2,893 | 7,794,999 |
| Percent change | 1.9 | 26.5 | -17.7 | -3.8 | 6.1 | -9.6 | -9.1 | -11.7 | 10.0 | 16.1 | | |

1 Suburban cities include law enforcement agencies in cities with less than 50,000 inhabitants that are within a Metropolitan Statistical Area. Suburban cities exclude all metropolitan agencies associated with a principal city. Nonsuburban cities include law enforcement agencies in cities with less than 50,000 inhabitants that are not associated with a Metropolitan Statistical Area.   2 The figures shown in this column for the offense of rape were reported using only the revised Uniform Crime Reporting definition of rape. See chapter notes for more detail.

## Table 14. Crime Trends, by Metropolitan and Nonmetropolitan Counties,[1] by Population Group, 2019–2020

(Number, percent change.)

| Population group and range | Violent crime | Murder and nonnegligent manslaughter | Rape[2] | Robbery | Aggravated assault | Property crime | Burglary | Larceny-theft | Motor vehicle theft | Arson | Number of agencies | Estimated population, 2020 |
|---|---|---|---|---|---|---|---|---|---|---|---|---|
| **Metropolitan Counties** | | | | | | | | | | | | |
| 100,000 and over | | | | | | | | | | | | |
| 2019 | 114,972 | 1,596 | 13,900 | 22,020 | 77,456 | 653,838 | 107,266 | 475,199 | 68,214 | 3,159 | | |
| 2020 | 119,994 | 1,889 | 12,217 | 19,687 | 86,201 | 605,084 | 93,419 | 433,699 | 74,288 | 3,678 | 167 | 45,379,252 |
| Percent change | 4.4 | 18.4 | -12.1 | -10.6 | 11.3 | -7.5 | -12.9 | -8.7 | 8.9 | 16.4 | | |
| 25,000 to 99,999 | | | | | | | | | | | | |
| 2019 | 37,615 | 591 | 6,039 | 3,021 | 27,964 | 219,896 | 52,630 | 143,266 | 22,789 | 1,211 | | |
| 2020 | 39,541 | 641 | 5,748 | 2,763 | 30,389 | 212,676 | 47,285 | 138,751 | 25,234 | 1,406 | 401 | 20,874,056 |
| Percent change | 5.1 | 8.5 | -4.8 | -8.5 | 8.7 | -3.3 | -10.2 | -3.2 | 10.7 | 16.1 | | |
| Under 25,000 | | | | | | | | | | | | |
| 2019 | 18,207 | 204 | 3,275 | 1,069 | 13,659 | 82,108 | 17,647 | 50,091 | 13,638 | 732 | | |
| 2020 | 17,735 | 277 | 3,168 | 923 | 13,367 | 76,920 | 16,161 | 45,245 | 14,628 | 886 | 1,129 | 4,767,379 |
| Percent change | -2.6 | 35.8 | -3.3 | -13.7 | -2.1 | -6.3 | -8.4 | -9.7 | 7.3 | 21.0 | | |
| **Nonmetropolitan Counties** | | | | | | | | | | | | |
| 25,000 and over | | | | | | | | | | | | |
| 2019 | 19,531 | 323 | 3,405 | 1,197 | 14,606 | 101,496 | 28,715 | 61,381 | 10,645 | 755 | | |
| 2020 | 20,335 | 409 | 3,050 | 1,158 | 15,718 | 96,100 | 25,067 | 58,884 | 11,217 | 932 | 239 | 9,876,646 |
| Percent change | 4.1 | 26.6 | -10.4 | -3.3 | 7.6 | -5.3 | -12.7 | -4.1 | 5.4 | 23.4 | | |
| 10,000 to 24,999 | | | | | | | | | | | | |
| 2019 | 14,396 | 274 | 2,491 | 623 | 11,008 | 74,060 | 22,500 | 43,102 | 7,802 | 656 | | |
| 2020 | 15,439 | 326 | 2,251 | 593 | 12,269 | 70,096 | 19,834 | 40,946 | 8,597 | 719 | 534 | 8,573,146 |
| Percent change | 7.2 | 19.0 | -9.6 | -4.8 | 11.5 | -5.4 | -11.8 | -5.0 | 10.2 | 9.6 | | |
| Under 10,000 | | | | | | | | | | | | |
| 2019 | 11,957 | 257 | 2,931 | 271 | 8,498 | 46,356 | 12,808 | 26,610 | 6,453 | 485 | | |
| 2020 | 12,613 | 287 | 2,705 | 358 | 9,263 | 45,249 | 12,265 | 25,777 | 6,565 | 642 | 1,372 | 4,045,105 |
| Percent change | 5.5 | 11.7 | -7.7 | 32.1 | 9.0 | -2.4 | -4.2 | -3.1 | 1.7 | 32.4 | | |

1 Metropolitan counties include sheriffs and county law enforcement agencies associated with a Metropolitan Statistical Area. Nonmetropolitan counties include sheriffs and county law enforcement agencies that are not associated with a Metropolitan Statistical Area.　2 The figures shown in this column for the offense of rape were reported using only the revised Uniform Crime Reporting definition of rape. See notes for further detail.

## Table 15. Crime Trends, Additional Information About Selected Offenses, by Population Group, 2019–2020

(Number, percent change.)

| Population group | Rape[1] Rape | Assault to rape-attempts | Robbery Firearm | Knife or cutting instrument | Other weapon | Strong-arm | Aggravated assault Firearm | Knife or cutting instrument | Other weapon | Hands, fists, feet, etc. |
|---|---|---|---|---|---|---|---|---|---|---|
| **Total, All Agencies** | | | | | | | | | | |
| 2019 | 117,345 | 4,936 | 83,657 | 19,207 | 23,515 | 99,753 | 190,338 | 120,133 | 207,621 | 171,965 |
| 2020 | 103,199 | 4,133 | 77,179 | 18,590 | 22,414 | 85,340 | 266,983 | 126,421 | 220,157 | 157,466 |
| Percent change | -12.1 | -16.3 | -7.7 | -3.2 | -4.7 | -14.4 | 40.3 | 5.2 | 6.0 | -8.4 |
| **Total, Cities** | | | | | | | | | | |
| 2019 | 87,085 | 3,771 | 71,542 | 17,081 | 20,626 | 88,897 | 152,908 | 98,256 | 160,304 | 127,259 |
| 2020 | 75,736 | 3,065 | 66,437 | 16,577 | 19,589 | 75,659 | 215,325 | 103,323 | 170,280 | 116,940 |
| Percent change | -13.0 | -18.7 | -7.1 | -3.0 | -5.0 | -14.9 | 40.8 | 5.2 | 6.2 | -8.1 |
| Group I (250,000 and over) | | | | | | | | | | |
| 2019 | 32,628 | 1,670 | 42,251 | 9,771 | 11,168 | 48,673 | 85,295 | 47,860 | 75,140 | 45,702 |
| 2020 | 27,947 | 1,299 | 39,092 | 9,634 | 10,472 | 42,066 | 119,576 | 49,977 | 79,824 | 41,381 |
| Percent change | -14.3 | -22.2 | -7.5 | -1.4 | -6.2 | -13.6 | 40.2 | 4.4 | 6.2 | -9.5 |
| 1,000,000 and over (Group I subset) | | | | | | | | | | |
| 2019 | 12,466 | 733 | 15,378 | 4,802 | 5,188 | 22,284 | 24,692 | 21,287 | 28,480 | 23,238 |
| 2020 | 10,313 | 481 | 14,649 | 5,005 | 5,035 | 19,196 | 34,892 | 22,639 | 30,390 | 21,719 |
| Percent change | -17.3 | -34.4 | -4.7 | 4.2 | -2.9 | -13.9 | 41.3 | 6.4 | 6.7 | -6.5 |
| 500,000 to 999,999 (Group I subset) | | | | | | | | | | |
| 2019 | 9,535 | 469 | 15,390 | 2,836 | 3,712 | 14,465 | 33,825 | 14,534 | 26,746 | 10,541 |
| 2020 | 8,001 | 407 | 14,025 | 2,622 | 3,176 | 11,935 | 47,726 | 15,066 | 27,669 | 9,688 |
| Percent change | -16.1 | -13.2 | -8.9 | -7.5 | -14.4 | -17.5 | 41.1 | 3.7 | 3.5 | -8.1 |
| 250,000 to 499,999 (Group I subset) | | | | | | | | | | |
| 2019 | 10,627 | 468 | 11,483 | 2,133 | 2,268 | 11,924 | 26,778 | 12,039 | 19,914 | 11,923 |
| 2020 | 9,633 | 411 | 10,418 | 2,007 | 2,261 | 10,935 | 36,958 | 12,272 | 21,765 | 9,974 |
| Percent change | -9.4 | -12.2 | -9.3 | -5.9 | -0.3 | -8.3 | 38.0 | 1.9 | 9.3 | -16.3 |
| Group II (100,000 to 249,999) | | | | | | | | | | |
| 2019 | 14,992 | 584 | 11,794 | 2,914 | 3,437 | 14,864 | 24,908 | 16,390 | 25,778 | 19,478 |
| 2020 | 13,145 | 533 | 10,944 | 2,673 | 3,447 | 12,472 | 35,472 | 17,497 | 27,803 | 17,879 |
| Percent change | -12.3 | -8.7 | -7.2 | -8.3 | 0.3 | -16.1 | 42.4 | 6.8 | 7.9 | -8.2 |
| Group III (50,000 to 99,999) | | | | | | | | | | |
| 2019 | 11,902 | 483 | 7,475 | 2,057 | 2,629 | 11,462 | 16,211 | 12,021 | 21,048 | 17,320 |
| 2020 | 10,788 | 346 | 6,766 | 1,911 | 2,407 | 9,572 | 22,930 | 12,751 | 21,566 | 17,530 |
| Percent change | -9.4 | -28.4 | -9.5 | -7.1 | -8.4 | -16.5 | 41.4 | 6.1 | 2.5 | 1.2 |
| Group IV (25,000 to 49,999) | | | | | | | | | | |
| 2019 | 9,838 | 300 | 4,695 | 1,078 | 1,548 | 6,522 | 11,127 | 8,540 | 14,250 | 13,336 |
| 2020 | 8,817 | 300 | 4,653 | 1,168 | 1,513 | 5,540 | 16,016 | 9,181 | 15,297 | 12,078 |
| Percent change | -10.4 | 0.0 | -0.9 | 8.3 | -2.3 | -15.1 | 43.9 | 7.5 | 7.3 | -9.4 |
| Group V (10,000 to 24,999) | | | | | | | | | | |
| 2019 | 9,074 | 289 | 3,341 | 803 | 1,139 | 4,097 | 8,675 | 7,189 | 12,776 | 13,565 |
| 2020 | 8,013 | 248 | 3,169 | 790 | 1,075 | 3,566 | 12,557 | 7,651 | 13,749 | 12,205 |
| Percent change | -11.7 | -14.2 | -5.1 | -1.6 | -5.6 | -13.0 | 44.7 | 6.4 | 7.6 | -10.0 |
| Group VI (under 10,000) | | | | | | | | | | |
| 2019 | 8,651 | 445 | 1,986 | 458 | 705 | 3,279 | 6,692 | 6,256 | 11,312 | 17,858 |
| 2020 | 7,026 | 339 | 1,813 | 401 | 675 | 2,443 | 8,774 | 6,266 | 12,041 | 15,867 |
| Percent change | -18.8 | -23.8 | -8.7 | -12.4 | -4.3 | -25.5 | 31.1 | 0.2 | 6.4 | -11.1 |
| **Metropolitan Counties** | | | | | | | | | | |
| 2019 | 21,984 | 846 | 11,183 | 1,970 | 2,602 | 10,165 | 29,991 | 17,718 | 37,203 | 32,973 |
| 2020 | 19,953 | 805 | 9,857 | 1,856 | 2,509 | 9,003 | 41,567 | 18,732 | 38,765 | 29,754 |
| Percent change | -9.2 | -4.8 | -11.9 | -5.8 | -3.6 | -11.4 | 38.6 | 5.7 | 4.2 | -9.8 |
| **Nonmetropolitan Counties** | | | | | | | | | | |
| 2019 | 8,276 | 319 | 932 | 156 | 287 | 691 | 7,439 | 4,159 | 10,114 | 11,733 |
| 2020 | 7,510 | 263 | 885 | 157 | 316 | 678 | 10,091 | 4,366 | 11,112 | 10,772 |
| Percent change | -9.3 | -17.6 | -5.0 | 0.6 | 10.1 | -1.9 | 35.6 | 5.0 | 9.9 | -8.2 |
| **Suburban Areas[2]** | | | | | | | | | | |
| 2019 | 38,302 | 1,450 | 18,128 | 3,567 | 5,061 | 20,315 | 44,578 | 30,269 | 60,235 | 58,209 |
| 2020 | 34,142 | 1,322 | 16,541 | 3,470 | 4,805 | 17,240 | 62,294 | 31,905 | 62,791 | 51,657 |
| Percent change | -10.9 | -8.8 | -8.8 | -2.7 | -5.1 | -15.1 | 39.7 | 5.4 | 4.2 | -11.3 |

## Table 15. Crime Trends, Additional Information About Selected Offenses, by Population Group, 2019–2020 —Continued

(Number, percent change.)

| Population group | Burglary | | | Motor vehicle theft | | | Arson | | | Number of agencies | Estimated population, 2020 |
|---|---|---|---|---|---|---|---|---|---|---|---|
| | Forcible entry | Unlawful entry | Attempted forcible entry | Autos | Trucks and buses | Other vehicles | Structure | Mobile | Other | | |
| **Total, All Agencies** | | | | | | | | | | | |
| 2019 | 523,839 | 354,613 | 60,161 | 472,576 | 102,281 | 58,038 | 12,586 | 6,832 | 10,018 | | |
| 2020 | 483,712 | 323,985 | 58,398 | 522,620 | 118,947 | 64,999 | 13,902 | 8,756 | 13,440 | 13,159 | 282,835,011 |
| Percent change | -7.7 | -8.6 | -2.9 | 10.6 | 16.3 | 12.0 | 10.5 | 28.2 | 34.2 | | |
| **Total, Cities** | | | | | | | | | | | |
| 2019 | 391,133 | 262,104 | 47,729 | 382,527 | 82,196 | 39,826 | 9,727 | 4,991 | 7,801 | | |
| 2020 | 368,504 | 241,299 | 45,866 | 425,349 | 95,985 | 45,951 | 10,845 | 6,519 | 10,583 | 9,405 | 190,858,629 |
| Percent change | -5.8 | -7.9 | -3.9 | 11.2 | 16.8 | 15.4 | 11.5 | 30.6 | 35.7 | | |
| Group I (250,000 and over) | | | | | | | | | | | |
| 2019 | 163,230 | 88,237 | 18,949 | 171,359 | 47,320 | 15,113 | 3,374 | 2,127 | 2,606 | | |
| 2020 | 157,068 | 83,221 | 19,113 | 186,940 | 55,128 | 18,015 | 3,796 | 2,985 | 3,503 | 83 | 57,401,853 |
| Percent change | -3.8 | -5.7 | 0.9 | 9.1 | 16.5 | 19.2 | 12.5 | 40.3 | 34.4 | | |
| 1,000,000 and over (Group I subset) | | | | | | | | | | | |
| 2019 | 57,824 | 26,256 | 6,422 | 49,105 | 26,901 | 5,675 | 610 | 431 | 478 | | |
| 2020 | 56,840 | 24,614 | 6,456 | 54,021 | 31,425 | 7,480 | 768 | 593 | 654 | 10 | 24,452,783 |
| Percent change | -1.7 | -6.3 | 0.5 | 10.0 | 16.8 | 31.8 | 25.9 | 37.6 | 36.8 | | |
| 500,000 to 999,999 (Group I subset) | | | | | | | | | | | |
| 2019 | 55,881 | 32,324 | 6,649 | 62,613 | 10,608 | 5,304 | 1,262 | 820 | 1,048 | | |
| 2020 | 52,875 | 31,958 | 7,112 | 66,024 | 11,855 | 5,718 | 1,373 | 1,175 | 1,360 | 23 | 16,076,918 |
| Percent change | -5.4 | -1.1 | 7.0 | 5.4 | 11.8 | 7.8 | 8.8 | 43.3 | 29.8 | | |
| 250,000 to 499,999 (Group I subset) | | | | | | | | | | | |
| 2019 | 49,525 | 29,657 | 5,878 | 59,641 | 9,811 | 4,134 | 1,502 | 876 | 1,080 | | |
| 2020 | 47,353 | 26,649 | 5,545 | 66,895 | 11,848 | 4,817 | 1,655 | 1,217 | 1,489 | 50 | 16,872,152 |
| Percent change | -4.4 | -10.1 | -5.7 | 12.2 | 20.8 | 16.5 | 10.2 | 38.9 | 37.9 | | |
| Group II (100,000 to 249,999) | | | | | | | | | | | |
| 2019 | 67,307 | 46,368 | 9,153 | 75,215 | 14,092 | 7,465 | 1,667 | 946 | 1,427 | | |
| 2020 | 64,463 | 42,600 | 8,377 | 83,800 | 16,182 | 9,070 | 1,862 | 1,176 | 2,204 | 217 | 31,472,092 |
| Percent change | -4.2 | -8.1 | -8.5 | 11.4 | 14.8 | 21.5 | 11.7 | 24.3 | 54.4 | | |
| Group III (50,000 to 99,999) | | | | | | | | | | | |
| 2019 | 53,589 | 38,934 | 6,667 | 52,233 | 9,341 | 6,079 | 1,320 | 688 | 1,287 | | |
| 2020 | 48,804 | 35,790 | 6,031 | 59,881 | 11,449 | 7,010 | 1,502 | 835 | 1,666 | 454 | 31,774,613 |
| Percent change | -8.9 | -8.1 | -9.5 | 14.6 | 22.6 | 15.3 | 13.8 | 21.4 | 29.4 | | |
| Group IV (25,000 to 49,999) | | | | | | | | | | | |
| 2019 | 39,437 | 31,685 | 5,170 | 34,583 | 4,769 | 4,286 | 1,114 | 443 | 926 | | |
| 2020 | 36,325 | 28,400 | 5,142 | 39,552 | 5,451 | 4,742 | 1,307 | 555 | 1,199 | 773 | 26,961,554 |
| Percent change | -7.9 | -10.4 | -0.5 | 14.4 | 14.3 | 10.6 | 17.3 | 25.3 | 29.5 | | |
| Group V (10,000 to 24,999) | | | | | | | | | | | |
| 2019 | 37,177 | 30,206 | 4,141 | 27,707 | 3,959 | 3,476 | 969 | 359 | 835 | | |
| 2020 | 33,837 | 27,547 | 3,709 | 32,414 | 4,617 | 3,683 | 1,094 | 456 | 1,035 | 1,533 | 24,492,869 |
| Percent change | -9.0 | -8.8 | -10.4 | 17.0 | 16.6 | 6.0 | 12.9 | 27.0 | 24.0 | | |
| Group VI (under 10,000) | | | | | | | | | | | |
| 2019 | 30,393 | 26,674 | 3,649 | 21,430 | 2,715 | 3,407 | 1,283 | 428 | 720 | | |
| 2020 | 28,007 | 23,741 | 3,494 | 22,762 | 3,158 | 3,431 | 1,284 | 512 | 976 | 6,345 | 18,755,648 |
| Percent change | -7.9 | -11.0 | -4.2 | 6.2 | 16.3 | 0.7 | 0.1 | 19.6 | 35.6 | | |
| **Metropolitan Counties** | | | | | | | | | | | |
| 2019 | 97,064 | 67,726 | 10,107 | 73,491 | 16,071 | 14,184 | 1,980 | 1,425 | 1,643 | | |
| 2020 | 83,929 | 59,948 | 10,520 | 79,594 | 18,528 | 15,084 | 2,098 | 1,672 | 2,118 | 1,657 | 70,005,809 |
| Percent change | -13.5 | -11.5 | 4.1 | 8.3 | 15.3 | 6.3 | 6.0 | 17.3 | 28.9 | | |
| **Nonmetropolitan Counties** | | | | | | | | | | | |
| 2019 | 35,642 | 24,783 | 2,325 | 16,558 | 4,014 | 4,028 | 879 | 416 | 574 | | |
| 2020 | 31,279 | 22,738 | 2,012 | 17,677 | 4,434 | 3,964 | 959 | 565 | 739 | 2,097 | 21,970,573 |
| Percent change | -12.2 | -8.3 | -13.5 | 6.8 | 10.5 | -1.6 | 9.1 | 35.8 | 28.7 | | |
| **Suburban Areas[2]** | | | | | | | | | | | |
| 2019 | 161,795 | 118,719 | 18,958 | 131,657 | 24,007 | 21,664 | 3,845 | 2,210 | 3,106 | | |
| 2020 | 143,243 | 105,982 | 18,990 | 146,306 | 27,949 | 22,901 | 4,180 | 2,627 | 4,017 | 6,983 | 120,808,272 |
| Percent change | -11.5 | -10.7 | 0.2 | 11.1 | 16.4 | 5.7 | 8.7 | 18.9 | 29.3 | | |

1 The figures shown in the rape column include only those reported by law enforcement agencies that used the revised Uniform Crime Reporting (UCR) definition of rape. See notes for more detail.   2 Suburban areas include law enforcement agencies in cities with less than 50,000 inhabitants and county law enforcement agencies that are within a Metropolitan Statistical Area. Suburban areas exclude all metropolitan agencies associated with a principal city.  The agencies associated with suburban areas also appear in other groups within this table.

# Table 16. Rate: Number of Crimes Per 100,000 Population, by Population Group, 2020

(Number, rate.)

| Population group | Violent crime | | Murder and nonnegligent manslaughter | | Rape[1] | | Robbery | | Aggravated assault | |
|---|---|---|---|---|---|---|---|---|---|---|
| | Number of offenses known | Rate | Number of offenses known | Rate | Number of offenses known | Rate | Number of offenses known | Rate | Number of offenses known | Rate |
| **Total, All Agencies** | 1,106,727 | 404.5 | 17,597 | 6.4 | 107,907 | 39.4 | 207,636 | 75.9 | 773,587 | 282.9 |
| **Total, Cities** | 894,132 | 469.4 | 14,108 | 7.4 | 80,176 | 42.1 | 185,379 | 97.4 | 614,469 | 322.7 |
| Group I (250,000 and over) | 444,979 | 753.7 | 7,575 | 12.8 | 30,208 | 51.2 | 108,259 | 183.4 | 298,937 | 506.3 |
| 1,000,000 and over (Group I subset) | 192,910 | 710.6 | 2,779 | 10.2 | 12,140 | 44.7 | 51,754 | 190.6 | 126,237 | 465.0 |
| 500,000 to 999,999 (Group I subset) | 137,376 | 874.7 | 2,556 | 16.3 | 8,593 | 54.7 | 29,848 | 190.1 | 96,379 | 613.7 |
| 250,000 to 499,999 (Group I subset) | 114,693 | 708.5 | 2,240 | 13.8 | 9,475 | 58.5 | 26,657 | 164.7 | 76,321 | 471.4 |
| Group II (100,000 to 249,999) | 146,782 | 471.6 | 2,384 | 7.7 | 13,803 | 44.3 | 29,435 | 94.6 | 101,160 | 325.0 |
| Group III (50,000 to 99,999) | 109,725 | 347.2 | 1,469 | 4.6 | 11,324 | 35.8 | 20,896 | 66.2 | 76,036 | 240.6 |
| Group IV (25,000 to 49,999) | 74,413 | 279.0 | 1,050 | 3.9 | 9,100 | 34.1 | 12,706 | 47.6 | 51,557 | 193.6 |
| Group V (10,000 to 24,999) | 65,196 | 266.8 | 993 | 4.1 | 8,597 | 35.2 | 8,998 | 36.9 | 46,608 | 191.1 |
| Group VI (under 10,000) | 53,037 | 301.4 | 637 | 3.6 | 7,144 | 40.6 | 5,085 | 28.9 | 40,171 | 228.3 |
| **Metropolitan Counties** | 166,369 | 265.0 | 2,516 | 4.0 | 19,838 | 31.6 | 20,189 | 32.2 | 123,826 | 197.2 |
| **Nonmetropolitan Counties[2]** | 46,226 | 227.5 | 973 | 4.8 | 7,893 | 38.9 | 2,068 | 10.2 | 35,292 | 173.7 |
| **Suburban Areas[3]** | 271,751 | 250.4 | 3,888 | 3.6 | 33,299 | 30.7 | 37,638 | 34.7 | 196,926 | 181.5 |

## Table 16. Rate: Number of Crimes Per 100,000 Population, by Population Group, 2020—Continued

(Number, rate.)

| Population group | Property crime | | Burglary | | Larceny-theft | | Motor vehicle theft | |
|---|---|---|---|---|---|---|---|---|
| | Number of offenses known | Rate | Number of offenses known | Rate | Number of offenses known | Rate | Number of offenses known | Rate |
| **Total, All Agencies** | 5,304,354 | 1,938.9 | 858,592 | 315.0 | 3,740,519 | 1,422.6 | 705,243 | 257.8 |
| **Total, Cities** | 4,293,456 | 2,254.0 | 658,718 | 347.1 | 3,059,998 | 1,686.7 | 574,740 | 301.8 |
| Group I (250,000 and over) | 1,635,354 | 2,769.9 | 264,458 | 447.9 | 1,103,756 | 1,958.9 | 267,140 | 452.5 |
| 1,000,000 and over (Group I subset) | 609,068 | 2,243.6 | 96,553 | 355.7 | 409,536 | 1,674.8 | 102,979 | 379.3 |
| 500,000 to 999,999 (Group I subset) | 547,124 | 3,483.7 | 91,506 | 582.6 | 372,525 | 2,372.0 | 83,093 | 529.1 |
| 250,000 to 499,999 (Group I subset) | 479,162 | 2,959.8 | 76,399 | 471.9 | 321,695 | 1,987.1 | 81,068 | 500.8 |
| Group II (100,000 to 249,999) | 772,260 | 2,481.1 | 114,538 | 371.4 | 547,196 | 1,797.4 | 110,526 | 355.1 |
| Group III (50,000 to 99,999) | 640,987 | 2,028.1 | 92,111 | 291.9 | 470,968 | 1,551.6 | 77,908 | 246.5 |
| Group IV (25,000 to 49,999) | 475,556 | 1,782.8 | 68,387 | 258.2 | 357,646 | 1,435.0 | 49,523 | 185.7 |
| Group V (10,000 to 24,999) | 435,899 | 1,784.1 | 65,472 | 269.2 | 329,152 | 1,448.8 | 41,275 | 169.0 |
| Group VI (under 10,000) | 333,400 | 1,894.4 | 53,752 | 306.3 | 251,280 | 1,510.9 | 28,368 | 161.2 |
| **Metropolitan Counties** | 809,432 | 1,289.1 | 144,818 | 231.6 | 559,531 | 906.9 | 105,083 | 167.4 |
| **Nonmetropolitan Counties[2]** | 201,466 | 991.7 | 55,056 | 272.2 | 120,990 | 610.5 | 25,420 | 125.2 |
| **Suburban Areas[3]** | 1,616,701 | 1,489.8 | 251,026 | 231.3 | 1,181,850 | 1,089.1 | 183,825 | 169.4 |

NOTE: Due to a system upgrade, the rates in this table are now caculated using aggregate population for each individual offense. The agency counts and population are provided for each individual offense.

1 The figures shown in this column for the offense of rape were reported using only the revised Uniform Crime Reporting definition of rape. See the chapter notes for further explanation.   2 Includes state police agencies that report aggregately for the entire state.   3 Suburban areas include law enforcement agencies in cities with less than 50,000 inhabitants and county law enforcement agencies that are within a Metropolitan Statistical Area.  Suburban areas exclude all metropolitan agencies associated with a principal city.  The agencies associated with suburban areas also appear in other groups within this table.

# Table 17. Rate: Number of Crimes Per 100,000 Inhabitants, by Suburban and Nonsuburban Cities,[1] by Population Group, 2020

(Number, rate.)

| Population group | Violent crime | | Murder and nonnegligent manslaughter | | Rape[2] | | Robbery | | Aggravated assault | |
|---|---|---|---|---|---|---|---|---|---|---|
| | Number of offenses known | Rate | Number of offenses known | Rate | Number of offenses known | Rate | Number of offenses known | Rate | Number of offenses known | Rate |
| **Total, Suburban Cities** | 107,531 | 228.6 | 1,398 | 3.0 | 13,885 | 29.5 | 17,645 | 37.5 | 74,603 | 158.6 |
| Group IV (25,000 to 49,999) | 43,159 | 218.8 | 560 | 2.8 | 5,469 | 27.7 | 8,400 | 42.6 | 28,730 | 145.6 |
| Group V (10,000 to 24,999) | 38,571 | 222.8 | 522 | 3.0 | 4,947 | 28.6 | 5,879 | 34.0 | 27,223 | 157.2 |
| Group VI (under 10,000) | 25,801 | 258.3 | 316 | 3.2 | 3,469 | 34.8 | 3,366 | 33.7 | 18,650 | 186.7 |
| **Total, Nonsuburban Cities** | 50,659 | 399.5 | 744 | 5.9 | 6,770 | 53.5 | 3,994 | 31.5 | 39,151 | 308.8 |
| Group IV (25,000 to 49,999) | 5,465 | 378.1 | 73 | 5.1 | 863 | 59.7 | 601 | 41.6 | 3,928 | 271.8 |
| Group V (10,000 to 24,999) | 20,324 | 436.4 | 366 | 7.9 | 2,643 | 56.9 | 2,004 | 43.0 | 15,311 | 328.8 |
| Group VI (under 10,000) | 24,870 | 378.1 | 305 | 4.6 | 3,264 | 49.6 | 1,389 | 21.1 | 19,912 | 302.7 |

| Population group | Property crime | | Burglary | | Larceny-theft | | Motor vehicle theft | |
|---|---|---|---|---|---|---|---|---|
| | Number of offenses known | Rate | Number of offenses known | Rate | Number of offenses known | Rate | Number of offenses known | Rate |
| **Total, Suburban Cities** | 813,590 | 1,729.8 | 108,784 | 231.3 | 624,467 | 1,327.7 | 80,339 | 170.8 |
| Group IV (25,000 to 49,999) | 330,574 | 1,675.5 | 43,107 | 218.5 | 252,082 | 1,277.7 | 35,385 | 179.4 |
| Group V (10,000 to 24,999) | 284,878 | 1,645.3 | 37,886 | 218.8 | 218,700 | 1,263.1 | 28,292 | 163.4 |
| Group VI (under 10,000) | 198,138 | 1,983.5 | 27,791 | 278.2 | 153,685 | 1,538.5 | 16,662 | 166.8 |
| **Total, Nonsuburban Cities** | 293,678 | 2,316.2 | 51,223 | 404.0 | 219,449 | 1,730.8 | 23,006 | 181.4 |
| Group IV (25,000 to 49,999) | 36,263 | 2,509.2 | 5,736 | 396.9 | 27,533 | 1,905.1 | 2,994 | 207.2 |
| Group V (10,000 to 24,999) | 126,954 | 2,726.1 | 21,999 | 472.4 | 95,592 | 2,052.7 | 9,363 | 201.1 |
| Group VI (under 10,000) | 130,461 | 1,983.5 | 23,488 | 357.1 | 96,324 | 1,464.5 | 10,649 | 161.9 |

NOTE: Due to a system upgrade, the rates in this table are now caculated using aggregate popualtion for each individual offense. The agency counts and population are provided for each individual offense.
1 Suburban cities include law enforcement agencies in cities with less than 50,000 inhabitants that are within a Metropolitan Statistical Area. Suburban cities exclude all metropolitan agencies associated with a principal city. Nonsuburban cities include law enforcement agencies in cities with less than 50,000 inhabitants that are not associated with a Metropolitan Statistical Area.   2 The figures shown in this column for the offense of rape were reported using only the revised Uniform Crime Reporting definition of rape. See chapter notes for more detail.

## Table 18. Rate: Number of Crimes Per 100,000 Inhabitants, by Metropolitan and Nonmetropolitan Counties,[1] by Population Group, 2020

(Number, rate.)

| Population group | Violent crime | | Murder and nonnegligent manslaughter | | Rape[2] | | Robbery | | Aggravated assault | |
|---|---|---|---|---|---|---|---|---|---|---|
| | Number of offenses known | Rate | Number of offenses known | Rate | Number of offenses known | Rate | Number of offenses known | Rate | Number of offenses known | Rate |
| **Metropolitan Counties** | | | | | | | | | | |
| 100,000 and over | 109,089 | 275.9 | 1,641 | 4.1 | 11,153 | 28.2 | 16,736 | 42.3 | 79,559 | 201.2 |
| 25,000 to 99,999 | 38,661 | 217.3 | 583 | 3.3 | 5,251 | 29.5 | 2,403 | 13.5 | 30,424 | 171.0 |
| Under 25,000 | 16,470 | 397.5 | 266 | 6.4 | 3,010 | 73.1 | 854 | 20.6 | 12,340 | 297.9 |
| Nonmetropolitan Counties | | | | | | | | | | |
| 25,000 and over | 19,438 | 220.0 | 381 | 4.3 | 2,968 | 33.6 | 1,140 | 12.9 | 14,949 | 169.2 |
| 10,000 to 24,999 | 14,345 | 189.7 | 304 | 4.0 | 2,130 | 28.2 | 530 | 7.0 | 11,381 | 150.5 |
| Under 10,000 | 10,944 | 329.1 | 250 | 7.5 | 2,533 | 76.2 | 306 | 9.2 | 7,855 | 236.2 |

## Table 18. Rate: Number of Crimes Per 100,000 Inhabitants, by Metropolitan and Nonmetropolitan Counties,[1] by Population Group, 2020—Continued

(Number, rate.)

| Population group | Property crime | | Burglary | | Larceny-theft | | Motor vehicle theft | |
|---|---|---|---|---|---|---|---|---|
| | Number of offenses known | Rate | Number of offenses known | Rate | Number of offenses known | Rate | Number of offenses known | Rate |
| **Metropolitan Counties** | | | | | | | | |
| 100,000 and over | 536,853 | 1,357.6 | 84,086 | 212.6 | 386,022 | 976.2 | 66,745 | 168.8 |
| 25,000 to 99,999 | 193,972 | 1,090.0 | 43,489 | 244.4 | 128,069 | 719.7 | 22,414 | 126.0 |
| Under 25,000 | 72,286 | 1,744.8 | 14,667 | 354.0 | 43,292 | 1,045.0 | 14,327 | 345.8 |
| **Nonmetropolitan Counties** | | | | | | | | |
| 25,000 and over | 90,805 | 1,027.8 | 24,347 | 275.6 | 55,809 | 631.7 | 10,649 | 120.5 |
| 10,000 to 24,999 | 65,995 | 872.8 | 18,540 | 245.2 | 39,440 | 521.6 | 8,015 | 106.0 |
| Under 10,000 | 41,403 | 1,244.9 | 10,955 | 329.4 | 24,305 | 730.8 | 6,143 | 184.7 |

NOTE: Due to a system upgrade, the rates in this table are now caculated using aggregate popualtion for each individual offense. The agency counts and population are provided for each individual offense.

1 Metropolitan counties include sheriffs and county law enforcement agencies associated with a Metropolitan Statistical Area. Nonmetropolitan counties include sheriffs and county law enforcement agencies that are not associated with a Metropolitan Statistical Area.    2 The figures shown in this column for the offense of rape were reported using only the revised Uniform Crime Reporting definition of rape. See the chapter notes for further explanation.

## Table 19. Rate: Number of Crimes Per 100,000 Inhabitants, Additional Information About Selected Offenses, by Population Group, 2020

(Number, rate.)

| Population group | Rape[1] Rape | Rape[1] Assault to rape-attempts | Robbery Firearm | Robbery Knife or cutting instrument | Robbery Other weapon | Robbery Strong-arm | Aggravated assault Firearm | Aggravated assault Knife or cutting instrument | Aggravated assault Other weapon |
|---|---|---|---|---|---|---|---|---|---|
| **Total, All Agencies** | | | | | | | | | |
| Number of offenses known | 99,247 | 3,967 | 73,084 | 17,796 | 21,778 | 83,485 | 259,215 | 121,624 | 211,483 |
| Rate | 37.9 | 1.5 | 27.9 | 6.8 | 8.3 | 31.8 | 98.8 | 46.4 | 80.6 |
| **Total, Cities** | | | | | | | | | |
| Number of offenses known | 73,194 | 2,976 | 63,948 | 16,078 | 19,228 | 74,920 | 209,633 | 100,206 | 163,747 |
| Rate | 40.4 | 1.6 | 35.3 | 8.9 | 10.6 | 41.4 | 115.8 | 55.3 | 90.4 |
| Group I (250,000 and over) | | | | | | | | | |
| Number of offenses known | 27,556 | 1,306 | 38,145 | 9,407 | 10,342 | 42,496 | 116,495 | 48,880 | 76,948 |
| Rate | 48.9 | 2.3 | 67.7 | 16.7 | 18.4 | 75.4 | 206.7 | 86.7 | 136.6 |
| 1,000,000 and over (Group I subset) | | | | | | | | | |
| Number of offenses known | 10,313 | 481 | 14,649 | 5,005 | 5,035 | 19,196 | 34,892 | 22,639 | 30,390 |
| Rate | 42.2 | 2.0 | 59.9 | 20.5 | 20.6 | 78.5 | 142.7 | 92.6 | 124.3 |
| 500,000 to 999,999 (Group I subset) | | | | | | | | | |
| Number of offenses known | 8,172 | 421 | 13,310 | 2,453 | 3,095 | 10,990 | 46,652 | 14,610 | 25,877 |
| Rate | 52.0 | 2.7 | 84.7 | 15.6 | 19.7 | 70.0 | 297.0 | 93.0 | 164.8 |
| 250,000 to 499,999 (Group I subset) | | | | | | | | | |
| Number of offenses known | 9,071 | 404 | 10,186 | 1,949 | 2,212 | 12,310 | 34,951 | 11,631 | 20,681 |
| Rate | 56.0 | 2.5 | 62.9 | 12.0 | 13.7 | 76.0 | 215.9 | 71.8 | 127.7 |
| Group II (100,000 to 249,999) | | | | | | | | | |
| Number of offenses known | 12,953 | 538 | 10,547 | 2,642 | 3,409 | 12,289 | 35,783 | 17,367 | 27,435 |
| Rate | 42.5 | 1.8 | 34.6 | 8.7 | 11.2 | 40.4 | 117.5 | 57.0 | 90.1 |
| Group III (50,000 to 99,999) | | | | | | | | | |
| Number of offenses known | 10,572 | 338 | 6,448 | 1,863 | 2,434 | 9,415 | 22,365 | 12,562 | 21,578 |
| Rate | 34.8 | 1.1 | 21.2 | 6.1 | 8.0 | 31.0 | 73.7 | 41.4 | 71.1 |
| Group IV (25,000 to 49,999) | | | | | | | | | |
| Number of offenses known | 8,076 | 261 | 4,248 | 1,067 | 1,409 | 5,109 | 14,662 | 8,426 | 14,113 |
| Rate | 32.6 | 1.1 | 17.1 | 4.3 | 5.7 | 20.6 | 59.2 | 34.0 | 57.0 |
| Group V (10,000 to 24,999) | | | | | | | | | |
| Number of offenses known | 7,600 | 236 | 2,994 | 745 | 1,008 | 3,402 | 12,388 | 7,293 | 12,718 |
| Rate | 33.7 | 1.0 | 13.3 | 3.3 | 4.5 | 15.1 | 54.9 | 32.3 | 56.4 |
| Group VI (under 10,000) | | | | | | | | | |
| Number of offenses known | 6,437 | 297 | 1,566 | 354 | 626 | 2,209 | 7,940 | 5,678 | 10,955 |
| Rate | 38.9 | 1.8 | 9.5 | 2.1 | 3.8 | 13.3 | 47.9 | 34.3 | 66.1 |
| **Metropolitan Counties** | | | | | | | | | |
| Number of offenses known | 18,672 | 742 | 8,292 | 1,566 | 2,216 | 7,919 | 39,950 | 17,312 | 37,079 |
| Rate | 30.4 | 1.2 | 13.5 | 2.5 | 3.6 | 12.9 | 65.0 | 28.2 | 60.3 |
| **Nonmetropolitan Counties** | | | | | | | | | |
| Number of offenses known | 7,381 | 249 | 844 | 152 | 334 | 646 | 9,632 | 4,106 | 10,657 |
| Rate | 37.4 | 1.3 | 4.3 | 0.8 | 1.7 | 3.3 | 48.8 | 20.8 | 54.0 |
| **Suburban Areas[2]** | | | | | | | | | |
| Number of offenses known | 32,080 | 1,219 | 14,500 | 3,068 | 4,395 | 15,675 | 59,564 | 29,569 | 59,571 |
| Rate | 29.6 | 1.1 | 13.4 | 2.8 | 4.1 | 14.4 | 54.9 | 27.2 | 54.9 |

## Table 19. Rate: Number of Crimes Per 100,000 Inhabitants, Additional Information About Selected Offenses, by Population Group, 2020—Continued

(Number, rate.)

| Population group | Hands, fists, feet, etc. | Burglary | | | Motor vehicle theft | | |
|---|---|---|---|---|---|---|---|
| | | Forcible entry | Unlawful entry | Attempted forcible entry | Autos | Trucks and buses | Other vehicles |
| **Total, All Agencies** | | | | | | | |
| Number of offenses known | 149,984 | 465,177 | 312,018 | 55,066 | 506,408 | 115,406 | 62,578 |
| Rate | 57.2 | 177.6 | 119.1 | 21.0 | 193.1 | 44.0 | 23.9 |
| **Total, Cities** | | | | | | | |
| Number of offenses known | 112,212 | 357,389 | 233,877 | 44,911 | 417,068 | 94,155 | 44,876 |
| Rate | 62.0 | 197.7 | 129.4 | 24.8 | 230.4 | 52.0 | 24.8 |
| Group I (250,000 and over) | | | | | | | |
| Number of offenses known | 40,017 | 154,830 | 81,911 | 19,074 | 185,120 | 54,252 | 17,715 |
| Rate | 71.0 | 274.8 | 145.4 | 33.9 | 328.5 | 96.3 | 31.4 |
| 1,000,000 and over (Group I subset) | | | | | | | |
| Number of offenses known | 21,719 | 56,840 | 24,614 | 6,456 | 54,021 | 31,425 | 7,480 |
| Rate | 88.8 | 232.4 | 100.7 | 26.4 | 220.9 | 128.5 | 30.6 |
| 500,000 to 999,999 (Group I subset) | | | | | | | |
| Number of offenses known | 9,240 | 52,818 | 31,537 | 7,151 | 65,990 | 11,510 | 5,593 |
| Rate | 58.8 | 336.3 | 200.8 | 45.5 | 420.2 | 73.3 | 35.6 |
| 250,000 to 499,999 (Group I subset) | | | | | | | |
| Number of offenses known | 9,058 | 45,172 | 25,760 | 5,467 | 65,109 | 11,317 | 4,642 |
| Rate | 56.0 | 279.0 | 159.1 | 33.8 | 402.2 | 69.9 | 28.7 |
| Group II (100,000 to 249,999) | | | | | | | |
| Number of offenses known | 18,293 | 62,205 | 42,045 | 8,168 | 84,359 | 16,047 | 9,079 |
| Rate | 60.1 | 206.3 | 139.4 | 27.1 | 277.1 | 52.7 | 29.8 |
| Group III (50,000 to 99,999) | | | | | | | |
| Number of offenses known | 17,399 | 48,447 | 35,352 | 5,951 | 58,475 | 11,202 | 6,890 |
| Rate | 57.3 | 159.6 | 116.5 | 19.6 | 192.6 | 36.9 | 22.7 |
| Group IV (25,000 to 49,999) | | | | | | | |
| Number of offenses known | 11,128 | 33,482 | 26,667 | 4,864 | 37,111 | 5,216 | 4,587 |
| Rate | 44.9 | 135.1 | 107.6 | 19.6 | 149.8 | 21.1 | 18.5 |
| Group V (10,000 to 24,999) | | | | | | | |
| Number of offenses known | 11,383 | 32,273 | 26,001 | 3,619 | 30,851 | 4,466 | 3,418 |
| Rate | 50.5 | 143.0 | 115.2 | 16.0 | 136.7 | 19.8 | 15.1 |
| Group VI (under 10,000) | | | | | | | |
| Number of offenses known | 13,992 | 26,152 | 21,901 | 3,235 | 21,152 | 2,972 | 3,187 |
| Rate | 84.5 | 157.9 | 132.2 | 19.5 | 127.7 | 17.9 | 19.2 |
| **Metropolitan Counties** | | | | | | | |
| Number of offenses known | 27,982 | 77,833 | 56,265 | 8,144 | 72,702 | 16,966 | 13,818 |
| Rate | 45.5 | 126.6 | 91.5 | 13.2 | 118.2 | 27.6 | 22.5 |
| **Nonmetropolitan Counties** | | | | | | | |
| Number of offenses known | 9,790 | 29,955 | 21,876 | 2,011 | 16,638 | 4,285 | 3,884 |
| Rate | 49.6 | 151.9 | 110.9 | 10.2 | 84.4 | 21.7 | 19.7 |
| **Suburban Areas[2]** | | | | | | | |
| Number of offenses known | 48,224 | 134,722 | 100,033 | 16,271 | 136,390 | 26,163 | 21,272 |
| Rate | 44.4 | 124.2 | 92.2 | 15.0 | 125.7 | 24.1 | 19.6 |

NOTE: Due to a system upgrade, the rates in this table are now caculated using aggregate popualtion for each individual offense. The agency counts and population are provided for each individual offense.
1 The figures shown in this column for the offense of rape were reported using only the revised Uniform Crime Reporting definition of rape. See the chapter notes for further explanation.   2 Suburban areas include law enforcement agencies in cities with less than 50,000 inhabitants and county law enforcement agencies that are within a Metropolitan Statistical Area. Suburban areas exclude all metropolitan agencies associated with a principal city. The agencies associated with suburban areas also appear in other groups within this table.

## Table 20. Murder, by Selected State and Type of Weapon, 2021

(Number.)

| State | Total murders | Total firearms | Handguns | Rifles | Shotguns | Firearms (type unknown) | Knives or cutting instruments | Other weapons | Hands, fists, feet, etc.[1] |
|---|---|---|---|---|---|---|---|---|---|
| Alabama | 370 | 291 | 145 | 17 | 1 | 128 | 11 | 67 | 1 |
| Alaska | 18 | 10 | 5 | 1 | 1 | 3 | 3 | 1 | 4 |
| Arizona | 190 | 119 | 67 | 5 | 2 | 45 | 21 | 40 | 10 |
| Arkansas | 321 | 250 | 109 | 15 | 9 | 117 | 27 | 39 | 5 |
| California[2] | 123 | 61 | 36 | 0 | 0 | 25 | 16 | 30 | 16 |
| Colorado | 358 | 267 | 193 | 5 | 2 | 67 | 46 | 25 | 20 |
| Connecticut | 148 | 114 | 47 | 0 | 0 | 67 | 20 | 10 | 4 |
| Delaware | 94 | 73 | 39 | 1 | 2 | 31 | 12 | 5 | 4 |
| District of Columbia[2] | 109 | 88 | 72 | 4 | 0 | 12 | 16 | 3 | 2 |
| Florida[2] | | | | | | | | | |
| Georgia | 728 | 613 | 386 | 35 | 3 | 189 | 32 | 57 | 26 |
| Hawaii | 6 | 1 | 1 | 0 | 0 | 0 | 2 | 2 | 1 |
| Idaho | 36 | 26 | 21 | 0 | 1 | 4 | 2 | 7 | 1 |
| Illinois[2] | 514 | 459 | 266 | 6 | 0 | 187 | 19 | 27 | 9 |
| Indiana | 438 | 355 | 221 | 18 | 3 | 113 | 34 | 32 | 17 |
| Iowa | 70 | 42 | 24 | 0 | 2 | 16 | 9 | 13 | 6 |
| Kansas | 87 | 60 | 36 | 2 | 2 | 20 | 6 | 18 | 3 |
| Kentucky | 365 | 313 | 177 | 14 | 1 | 121 | 14 | 30 | 8 |
| Louisiana | 447 | 332 | 159 | 38 | 9 | 126 | 29 | 74 | 12 |
| Maine | 18 | 12 | 8 | 0 | 0 | 4 | 1 | 4 | 1 |
| Maryland[2] | 138 | 104 | 76 | 0 | 0 | 28 | 19 | 11 | 4 |
| Massachusetts | 132 | 84 | 36 | 0 | 0 | 48 | 28 | 16 | 4 |
| Michigan | 747 | 604 | 241 | 32 | 7 | 324 | 44 | 77 | 22 |
| Minnesota | 203 | 152 | 76 | 6 | 1 | 69 | 21 | 19 | 11 |
| Mississippi | 149 | 123 | 66 | 4 | 5 | 48 | 8 | 10 | 8 |
| Missouri | 593 | 509 | 237 | 14 | 5 | 253 | 31 | 45 | 8 |
| Montana | 31 | 16 | 12 | 1 | 0 | 3 | 6 | 5 | 4 |
| Nebraska | 25 | 12 | 6 | 0 | 1 | 5 | 3 | 9 | 1 |
| Nevada | 232 | 162 | 59 | 2 | 5 | 96 | 17 | 43 | 10 |
| New Hampshire | 14 | 9 | 6 | 0 | 0 | 3 | 2 | 3 | 0 |
| New Jersey[2] | 137 | 96 | 73 | 0 | 0 | 23 | 16 | 18 | 7 |
| New Mexico[2] | 169 | 125 | 28 | 5 | 4 | 88 | 14 | 22 | 8 |
| New York[2] | 124 | 89 | 8 | 2 | 1 | 78 | 16 | 12 | 7 |
| North Carolina | 928 | 748 | 398 | 50 | 16 | 284 | 47 | 106 | 27 |
| North Dakota | 14 | 10 | 5 | 1 | 0 | 4 | 1 | 0 | 3 |
| Ohio | 824 | 660 | 295 | 22 | 2 | 341 | 29 | 113 | 22 |
| Oklahoma | 284 | 204 | 126 | 6 | 4 | 68 | 27 | 40 | 13 |
| Oregon | 188 | 125 | 64 | 0 | 2 | 59 | 24 | 28 | 11 |
| Pennsylvania[2] | 510 | 439 | 303 | 1 | 1 | 134 | 24 | 35 | 12 |
| Rhode Island | 38 | 27 | 8 | 0 | 0 | 19 | 5 | 5 | 1 |
| South Carolina | 548 | 478 | 254 | 14 | 5 | 205 | 25 | 36 | 9 |
| South Dakota | 26 | 13 | 10 | 1 | 1 | 1 | 6 | 6 | 1 |
| Tennessee | 672 | 586 | 232 | 17 | 13 | 324 | 34 | 40 | 12 |
| Texas | 2,064 | 1,668 | 818 | 75 | 19 | 756 | 157 | 173 | 66 |
| Utah | 85 | 58 | 39 | 4 | 0 | 15 | 4 | 20 | 3 |
| Vermont | 8 | 6 | 3 | 0 | 1 | 2 | 1 | 1 | 0 |
| Virginia | 562 | 446 | 219 | 15 | 7 | 205 | 32 | 71 | 13 |
| Washington | 325 | 227 | 133 | 6 | 10 | 78 | 34 | 51 | 13 |
| West Virginia | 95 | 64 | 32 | 2 | 0 | 30 | 7 | 21 | 3 |
| Wisconsin | 315 | 259 | 116 | 6 | 3 | 134 | 25 | 27 | 4 |
| Wyoming | 17 | 5 | 4 | 0 | 0 | 1 | 3 | 5 | 4 |

1 Pushed is included in hands, fists, feet, etc.  2 Limited data for 2021 were available for California, District of Columbia, Illinois, Maryland, New Jersey, New Mexico, New York, and Pennsylvania; data for Florida were not available at the time of publication.

# Table 21. Robbery, by State and Type of Weapon, 2021

(Number.)

| State | Total robberies | Firearms | Knives or cutting instruments | Other weapons | Strong-arm | Agency count | Population |
|---|---|---|---|---|---|---|---|
| Alabama | 897 | 478 | 55 | 82 | 282 | 186 | 2,265,220 |
| Alaska | 57 | 8 | 8 | 6 | 35 | 28 | 371,959 |
| Arizona | 1,089 | 322 | 136 | 154 | 477 | 67 | 3,568,504 |
| Arkansas | 1,259 | 648 | 78 | 132 | 401 | 252 | 2,857,932 |
| California[1] | 2,296 | 403 | 281 | 370 | 1,242 | 14 | 2,861,998 |
| Colorado | 4,295 | 1,597 | 433 | 686 | 1,579 | 203 | 5,678,716 |
| Connecticut | 1,924 | 716 | 197 | 208 | 803 | 107 | 3,605,597 |
| Delaware | 564 | 214 | 57 | 59 | 234 | 53 | 1,001,629 |
| District of Columbia[1,2] | 200 | 33 | 29 | 4 | 134 | 1 | |
| Florida[1,2] | 24 | 2 | 2 | 2 | 18 | 2 | |
| Georgia | 3,825 | 2,224 | 151 | 305 | 1,145 | 380 | 7,950,625 |
| Hawaii | 733 | 120 | 85 | 120 | 408 | 2 | 1,059,012 |
| Idaho | 148 | 42 | 16 | 19 | 71 | 80 | 1,661,136 |
| Illinois[1] | 1,017 | 455 | 59 | 142 | 361 | 118 | 2,407,151 |
| Indiana | 2,791 | 1,644 | 160 | 280 | 707 | 129 | 4,671,815 |
| Iowa | 681 | 275 | 60 | 85 | 261 | 178 | 2,825,401 |
| Kansas | 341 | 123 | 22 | 45 | 151 | 192 | 1,850,993 |
| Kentucky | 2,218 | 1,176 | 165 | 187 | 690 | 426 | 4,505,498 |
| Louisiana | 1,310 | 617 | 68 | 189 | 436 | 113 | 3,042,729 |
| Maine | 159 | 35 | 20 | 22 | 82 | 127 | 1,360,671 |
| Maryland[1] | 1,314 | 484 | 144 | 178 | 508 | 16 | 2,189,086 |
| Massachusetts | 2,605 | 612 | 478 | 340 | 1,175 | 368 | 6,929,534 |
| Michigan | 3,994 | 1,773 | 265 | 343 | 1,613 | 611 | 9,780,531 |
| Minnesota | 3,987 | 1,911 | 234 | 384 | 1,458 | 361 | 5,590,467 |
| Mississippi | 457 | 288 | 24 | 50 | 95 | 130 | 1,663,780 |
| Missouri | 3,501 | 1,904 | 196 | 383 | 1,018 | 326 | 5,208,452 |
| Montana | 278 | 67 | 31 | 48 | 132 | 98 | 1,043,486 |
| Nebraska | 238 | 63 | 27 | 35 | 113 | 131 | 1,315,324 |
| Nevada | 2,294 | 917 | 190 | 249 | 938 | 35 | 3,095,335 |
| New Hampshire | 175 | 32 | 21 | 25 | 97 | 181 | 1,204,875 |
| New Jersey[1] | 865 | 352 | 74 | 45 | 394 | 64 | 1,650,076 |
| New Mexico[1] | 1,862 | 961 | 254 | 248 | 399 | 24 | 985,537 |
| New York[1] | 1,502 | 380 | 185 | 140 | 797 | 93 | 3,453,145 |
| North Carolina | 5,707 | 2,968 | 446 | 498 | 1,795 | 312 | 9,268,170 |
| North Dakota | 184 | 38 | 22 | 26 | 98 | 100 | 766,153 |
| Ohio | 6,410 | 2,167 | 279 | 469 | 3,495 | 356 | 8,743,840 |
| Oklahoma | 1,684 | 743 | 152 | 208 | 581 | 428 | 3,789,679 |
| Oregon | 2,461 | 723 | 236 | 462 | 1,040 | 149 | 3,867,155 |
| Pennsylvania[1] | 74 | 16 | 8 | 11 | 39 | 24 | 408,819 |
| Rhode Island | 277 | 86 | 51 | 17 | 123 | 46 | 1,094,546 |
| South Carolina | 2,401 | 1,334 | 185 | 173 | 709 | 178 | 4,731,543 |
| South Dakota | 166 | 37 | 25 | 32 | 72 | 61 | 679,305 |
| Tennessee | 4,874 | 3,070 | 259 | 327 | 1,218 | 273 | 6,716,048 |
| Texas | 22,208 | 11,502 | 1,731 | 2,363 | 6,612 | 922 | 28,232,533 |
| Utah | 1,009 | 252 | 110 | 151 | 496 | 105 | 2,934,855 |
| Vermont | 65 | 11 | 21 | 7 | 26 | 78 | 641,185 |
| Virginia | 2,910 | 1,397 | 268 | 260 | 985 | 340 | 8,599,971 |
| Washington | 5,608 | 1,694 | 568 | 915 | 2,431 | 211 | 7,459,711 |
| West Virginia | 186 | 87 | 14 | 27 | 58 | 122 | 1,210,067 |
| Wisconsin | 2,613 | 1,397 | 124 | 224 | 868 | 267 | 5,238,884 |
| Wyoming | 47 | 20 | 4 | 11 | 12 | 44 | 427,908 |

1 Limited data for 2021 were available for California, District of Columbia, Florida, Illinois, Maryland, New Jersey, New Mexico, New York, and Pennsylvania.   2 Includes tribal or other agencies to which no population is attributed.

## Table 22. Aggravated Assault, by State and Type of Weapon, 2021

(Number.)

| State | Total aggravated assaults | Firearms | Knives or cutting instruments | Other weapons | Personal weapons | Agency count | Population |
|---|---|---|---|---|---|---|---|
| Alabama | 9,841 | 5,233 | 1,152 | 1,307 | 2,149 | 186 | 2,265,220 |
| Alaska | 1,481 | 407 | 281 | 461 | 332 | 28 | 371,959 |
| Arizona | 8,059 | 2,331 | 1,229 | 2,539 | 1,960 | 67 | 3,568,504 |
| Arkansas | 16,608 | 6,709 | 1,656 | 3,288 | 4,955 | 252 | 2,857,932 |
| California[1] | 8,357 | 1,392 | 1,664 | 2,825 | 2,476 | 14 | 2,861,998 |
| Colorado | 18,713 | 7,182 | 3,624 | 4,953 | 2,954 | 203 | 5,678,716 |
| Connecticut | 2,981 | 743 | 718 | 909 | 611 | 107 | 3,605,597 |
| Delaware | 3,182 | 1,363 | 560 | 979 | 280 | 53 | 1,001,629 |
| District of Columbia[1,2] | 196 | 24 | 106 | 49 | 17 | 1 | |
| Florida[1,2] | 43 | 8 | 9 | 13 | 13 | 2 | |
| Georgia | 24,396 | 13,370 | 2,493 | 4,261 | 4,272 | 380 | 7,950,625 |
| Hawaii | 1,407 | 217 | 383 | 542 | 265 | 2 | 1,059,012 |
| Idaho | 2,871 | 674 | 451 | 926 | 820 | 80 | 1,661,136 |
| Illinois[1] | 5,653 | 2,447 | 689 | 1,144 | 1,373 | 118 | 2,407,151 |
| Indiana | 11,011 | 3,959 | 1,127 | 2,515 | 3,410 | 129 | 4,671,815 |
| Iowa | 6,373 | 1,171 | 991 | 1,529 | 2,682 | 178 | 2,825,401 |
| Kansas | 4,283 | 1,062 | 690 | 1,310 | 1,221 | 192 | 1,850,993 |
| Kentucky | 7,690 | 3,716 | 638 | 2,740 | 596 | 426 | 4,505,498 |
| Louisiana | 15,144 | 5,943 | 1,748 | 5,792 | 1,661 | 113 | 3,042,729 |
| Maine | 846 | 95 | 177 | 358 | 216 | 127 | 1,360,671 |
| Maryland[1] | 3,746 | 840 | 906 | 1,354 | 646 | 16 | 2,189,086 |
| Massachusetts | 16,073 | 2,310 | 3,635 | 7,317 | 2,811 | 368 | 6,929,534 |
| Michigan | 37,398 | 14,655 | 5,816 | 10,460 | 6,467 | 611 | 9,780,531 |
| Minnesota | 10,796 | 3,637 | 2,034 | 2,620 | 2,505 | 361 | 5,590,467 |
| Mississippi | 2,787 | 1,453 | 237 | 736 | 361 | 130 | 1,663,780 |
| Missouri | 22,125 | 9,522 | 2,258 | 7,835 | 2,510 | 326 | 5,208,452 |
| Montana | 3,905 | 836 | 460 | 1,285 | 1,324 | 98 | 1,043,486 |
| Nebraska | 1,804 | 193 | 341 | 720 | 550 | 131 | 1,315,324 |
| Nevada | 8,735 | 3,110 | 2,106 | 1,878 | 1,641 | 35 | 3,095,335 |
| New Hampshire | 831 | 175 | 176 | 219 | 261 | 181 | 1,204,875 |
| New Jersey[1] | 2,037 | 552 | 466 | 605 | 414 | 64 | 1,650,076 |
| New Mexico[1] | 7,335 | 3,110 | 1,179 | 2,175 | 871 | 24 | 985,537 |
| New York[1] | 4,857 | 1,264 | 1,796 | 1,190 | 607 | 93 | 3,453,145 |
| North Carolina | 30,871 | 17,679 | 3,531 | 5,578 | 4,083 | 312 | 9,268,170 |
| North Dakota | 1,302 | 85 | 152 | 598 | 467 | 100 | 766,153 |
| Ohio | 20,560 | 10,562 | 3,042 | 5,380 | 1,576 | 356 | 8,743,840 |
| Oklahoma | 12,127 | 4,144 | 2,054 | 3,718 | 2,211 | 428 | 3,789,679 |
| Oregon | 9,277 | 1,908 | 1,425 | 3,273 | 2,671 | 149 | 3,867,155 |
| Pennsylvania[1] | 302 | 47 | 53 | 73 | 129 | 24 | 408,819 |
| Rhode Island | 1,429 | 333 | 331 | 390 | 375 | 46 | 1,094,546 |
| South Carolina | 19,231 | 10,372 | 2,492 | 3,840 | 2,527 | 178 | 4,731,543 |
| South Dakota | 2,285 | 386 | 474 | 685 | 740 | 61 | 679,305 |
| Tennessee | 37,128 | 21,412 | 4,761 | 9,183 | 1,772 | 273 | 6,716,048 |
| Texas | 89,954 | 43,048 | 15,349 | 23,596 | 7,961 | 922 | 28,232,533 |
| Utah | 4,714 | 1,006 | 998 | 1,396 | 1,314 | 105 | 2,934,855 |
| Vermont | 860 | 130 | 136 | 159 | 435 | 78 | 641,185 |
| Virginia | 13,076 | 5,850 | 1,522 | 3,333 | 2,371 | 340 | 8,599,971 |
| Washington | 16,316 | 4,761 | 2,325 | 5,197 | 4,033 | 211 | 7,459,711 |
| West Virginia | 2,926 | 833 | 314 | 654 | 1,125 | 122 | 1,210,067 |
| Wisconsin | 12,503 | 4,780 | 1,040 | 3,319 | 3,364 | 267 | 5,238,884 |
| Wyoming | 549 | 142 | 125 | 172 | 110 | 44 | 427,908 |

1 Limited data for 2021 were available for California, District of Columbia, Florida, Illinois, Maryland, New Jersey, New Mexico, New York, and Pennsylvania.   2 Includes tribal or other agencies to which no population is attributed.

## Table 23. Offense Analysis, Number and Percent Distritbution, 2020–2021

(Number, percent, dollars; 12,751 agencies in 2020; 2020 estimated population 277,124,125; 11,794 agencies in 2021; 2021 estimated population 212,416,063.)

| Classification | Number of offenses, 2021 | Percent distribution[1] | Average value (dollars) |
|---|---|---|---|
| **Murder** | 22,900 | 100.0% | X |
| **Rape**[2] | 144,300 | 100.0% | X |
| **Robbery for which location is known** | 142,749 | 100.0% | NA |
| By location | | | |
| Highway/alley/street/sidewalk | 37,852 | 26.5% | NA |
| Commercial house | 40,337 | 28.3% | NA |
| Gas or service station | 7,964 | 5.6% | NA |
| Convenience store | 14,529 | 10.2% | NA |
| Residence | 28,375 | 19.9% | NA |
| Bank | 3,353 | 2.3% | 4,745 |
| Miscellaneous | 10,339 | 7.2% | NA |
| **Burglary for which location is known** | 610,811 | 100.0% | NA |
| By location | | | |
| Residence (dwelling) | 357,270 | 58.5% | |
| Residence, night | 154,723 | 25.3% | NA |
| Residence, day | 196,684 | 32.2% | NA |
| Residence, unknown | 5,863 | 1.0% | 2,844 |
| Nonresidence (store, office, etc.) | 262,541 | 43.0% | |
| Nonresidence, night | 125,253 | 20.5% | NA |
| Nonresidence, day | 123,232 | 20.2% | NA |
| Nonresidence, unknown | 5,056 | 0.8% | 3,417 |
| **Larceny-theft (except motor vehicle theft)** | 4,627,000 | 100.0% | NA |
| By type | | | |
| Pocket-picking | 14,439 | 0.3% | NA |
| Purse-snatching | 8,728 | 0.2% | NA |
| Shoplifting | 548,591 | 11.9% | NA |
| From motor vehicles (except accessories) | 721,752 | 15.6% | NA |
| Motor vehicle accessories | 359,670 | 7.8% | NA |
| Bicycles | 72,419 | 1.6% | NA |
| From buildings | 221,407 | 4.8% | NA |
| From coin-operated machines | 4,763 | 0.1% | 1,210 |
| All others | 927,255 | 20.0% | NA |
| By value | | | |
| Over $200 | 1,516,357 | 32.8% | NA |
| $50 to $200 | 525,376 | 11.4% | 105 |
| Under $50 | 837,291 | 18.1% | 11 |
| **Motor Vehicle Theft** | 890,200 | 100.0% | 9,166 |

NOTE: Totals are rounded to the nearest 100 due to uncertainty in the estimates.
NA = Not available.
X = Not applicable.
1 Because of rounding, the percentages may not add to 100.0.   2 The figures shown in this column for the offense of rape were reported using only the revised Uniform Crime Reporting definition of rape. See the chapter notes for further explanation.

## Table 24. Property Stolen and Recovered, by Type and Value, 2021

(Dollars, percent; 11,794 agencies in 2021; 2021 estimated population 212,416,063.)

| Type of property | Value of property (dollars) | | Percent recovered |
| --- | --- | --- | --- |
| | Stolen | Recovered | |
| Total | $737,294,919,165 | $89,484,651,977 | 12.1 |
| Currency, notes, etc. | 81,140,890,252 | 6,021,921,342 | 7.4 |
| Jewelry and precious metals | 20,111,283,161 | 2,017,048,199 | 10.0 |
| Clothing and furs | 74,493,057,007 | 11,119,074,943 | 14.9 |
| Locally stolen motor vehicles | 81,915,997,169 | 12,671,347,120 | 15.5 |
| Office equipment | 30,204,852,279 | 3,015,993,085 | 10.0 |
| Televisions, radios, stereos, etc. | 14,133,875,022 | 3,005,583,762 | 21.3 |
| Firearms | 7,120,846,761 | 10,327,168 | 0.1 |
| Household goods | 39,148,634,770 | 3,007,404,447 | 7.7 |
| Consumable goods | 107,512,394,297 | 9,008,496,543 | 8.4 |
| Livestock | 1,010,672,460 | 845,180 | 0.1 |
| Miscellaneous | 280,502,415,987 | 39,606,610,188 | 14.1 |

# SECTION III

# OFFENSES CLEARED

Law enforcement agencies that report crime to the Federal Bureau of Investigation (FBI) can clear, or "close," offenses in one of two ways: by arrest or by exceptional means. However, the administrative closing of a case by a local law enforcement agency does not necessarily mean that the agency can clear an offense for Uniform Crime Reporting (UCR) purposes. To clear an offense within the program's guidelines, the reporting agency must adhere to certain criteria, which are outlined in this section. *(The UCR program does not distinguish between offenses cleared by arrest and those cleared by exceptional means in its data presentations. The distinction is made solely for the purpose of a definition and not for data collection and publication.) See Appendix I for information on the UCR program's statistical methodology.*

### Important Note: Transition to NIBRS

As of January 1, 2021, the FBI's National Incident-Based Reporting System (NIBRS) became the national standard for law enforcement crime data reporting in the United States. The 2021 data year will mark the first time that the FBI and BJS estimate reported crime in the United States based solely on NIBRS data.

Section III – clearances – has been impacted by this limited release. New data for 2021 is included in Table 25. Data from 2020 is included in Table 25A through Table 28. However, given the alterations to the categories present in the 2021 data, year-over-year comparison is not provided between 2020 and 2021.

As of June 2022, all 50 U.S. states and the District of Columbia were certified to report crime data to NIBRS. Just under two-thirds of the U.S. population is covered by NIBRS-reporting law enforcement agencies, and 62 NIBRS-certified agencies serve cities with a population of 250,000 or more; these agencies cover a total population of more than 37 million. However, data is extremely limited for several large states in 2021, including California (7 percent of the population represented), the District of Columbia (47 percent of the population represented), Florida (0 percent of the population represented), Maryland (47 percent of the population represented), New Jersey (42 percent of the population represented), New York (19 percent of the population represented), and Pennsylvania (17 percent of the population represented). Of the 18,806 NIBRS-eligible law enforcement agencies, 11,333 (60.3 percent) reported data for 2021. (Eligibility is determined by the agency submitting a minimum of 3 months of data.)

The absence of these large segments of population, an issue that is expected to be alleviated in future years, makes the 2021 data not comparable to previous years. Consequently,

5-year and 10-year trend tables do not include the 2021 data. The FBI has provided limited analysis of year-over-year trends, and these are included where possible in this edition.

Some data has been suppressed by NIBRS. This occurs as a result of high uncertainty for a generated estimate. This uncertainty then requires is the application of suppression rules found within the NIBRS estimation methodologies. Suppression refers to the withholding of estimates from release due to high levels of uncertainty to ensure an unbiased view of the available NIBRS data.

In most instances, differences in the comparison of 2021 data to 2020 do not meet the criteria for statistical significance. However, it should be noted that the main contributor to that finding is the large amount of variation—both random and systematic—that is measured in the 2020 data due to low coverage of participating agencies. As coverage increases, the FBI will be able to improve its ability to measure these critical metrics for the nation.

The FBI has provided some estimates for 2021 trends based on this limited data; more information, including a detailed breakdown on how the values were extrapolated through the use of a confidence interval, can be found at <https://cde.ucr. cjis.gov> in the *Transition to the National Incident-Based Reporting System (NIBRS): A Comparison of 2020 and 2021 NIBRS Estimates* report.

NIBRS had not released 2021 clearance data for population groups (cities, metropolitan/nonmetropolitan areas, and suburban areas) or age groups at the time this book went to press. The 2020 tables have been provided in this edition for historical context.

### CLEARED BY ARREST

In the UCR program, a law enforcement agency reports that an offense is cleared by arrest, or solved for crime reporting purposes, when at least one person is arrested, charged with the commission of the offense, and turned over to the court for prosecution (whether following arrest, court summons, or police notice). To qualify as a clearance, *all* of these conditions must be met.

In its calculations, the UCR program counts the number of offenses that are cleared, not the number of arrestees. Therefore, the arrest of one person may clear several crimes, and the arrest of many persons may clear only one offense. In addition, some clearances recorded by an agency during a particular calendar year, such as 2020, may pertain to offenses that occurred in previous years.

## CLEARED BY EXCEPTIONAL MEANS

In certain situations, elements beyond law enforcement's control prevent the agency from arresting and formally charging the offender. When this occurs, the agency can clear the offense *exceptionally*. There are four UCR program requirements that law enforcement must meet in order to clear an offense by exceptional means. The agency must have:

- Identified the offender

- Gathered enough evidence to support an arrest, make a charge, and turn over the offender to the court for prosecution

- Identified the offender's exact location so that the suspect could be taken into custody immediately

- Encountered a circumstance outside the control of law enforcement that prohibits the agency from arresting, charging, and prosecuting the offender

Examples of exceptional clearances include, but are not limited to, the death of the offender (e.g., suicide or justifiably killed by a law enforcement officer or a citizen), the victim's refusal to cooperate with the prosecution after the offender has been identified, or the denial of extradition because the offender committed a crime in another jurisdiction and is being prosecuted for that offense. In the UCR program, the recovery of property does not clear an offense.

## NATIONAL CLEARANCES

A review of the data for 2021 revealed law enforcement agencies in the United States cleared 41.2 percent of crimes against persons (murder, assault, human trafficking, kidnapping/abduction, and sexual offenses); 13.7 percent of crimes against property (arson, bribery, burglary/breaking and entering, counterfeiting/forgery, destruction/damage/vandalism, embezzlement, extortion/blackmail, fraud, robbery, stolen property, larceny-theft, and motor vehicle theft); and 72.4 percent of crimes against society (animal cruelty, drug/narcotic offenses, gambling offenses, pornography/obscene material, and prostitution offenses) brought to their attention. (Table 25)

As in most years, law enforcement agencies cleared a higher percentage of crimes against persons and society than crimes against property in 2021. As a rule, clearance rates generally rise due to the more vigorous investigative efforts put forth for these crimes. In addition, these crimes more often involve victims and/or witnesses who are able to identify the perpetrators.

A further breakdown of the clearances for 2021 revealed that the nation's law enforcement agencies cleared 47.8 percent of homicide offenses, 41.2 percent of assault offenses, and 23.6 percent of robbery offenses. (Table 25)

For property crime offenses in 2021, law enforcement agencies throughout the nation collectively 13.4 percent of burglary/breaking and entering offenses, 12.5 percent of larceny-theft offenses, and 10.8 percent of motor vehicle theft offenses. (Table 25)

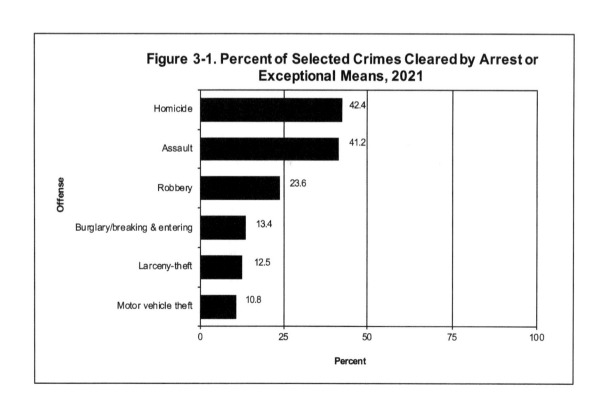

Figure 3-1. Percent of Selected Crimes Cleared by Arrest or Exceptional Means, 2021

# Table 25. Incidents Cleared, by Offense Category, 2021

(Number; percent.)

| Population group | Incidents cleared[1] | | | | | | |
| --- | --- | --- | --- | --- | --- | --- | --- |
| | Total incidents[2] | Total incidents cleared | Percent of incidents cleared | Cleared by arrest[3] | Percent cleared by arrest[3] | Cleared by exceptional means | Percent cleared by exceptional means |
| Total | 9,436,674 | 3,122,343 | 33.1 | 2,779,904 | 89.0 | 342,439 | 11.0 |
| **Crime Against Persons** | 2,552,446 | 1,052,525 | 41.2 | 844,719 | 80.3 | 207,806 | 19.7 |
| Assault offenses | 2,335,159 | 991,083 | 42.4 | 798,716 | 80.6 | 192,367 | 19.4 |
| Homicide offenses | 15,249 | 7,295 | 47.8 | 6,689 | 91.7 | 606 | 8.3 |
| Human trafficking offenses | 1,827 | 621 | 34.0 | 576 | 92.8 | 45 | 7.2 |
| Kidnapping/abduction | 33,429 | 17,303 | 51.8 | 15,701 | 90.7 | 1,602 | 9.3 |
| Sex offenses | 166,782 | 36,223 | 21.7 | 23,037 | 63.6 | 13,186 | 36.4 |
| **Crimes Against Property** | 6,531,976 | 896,238 | 13.7 | 789,450 | 88.1 | 106,788 | 11.9 |
| Arson | 26,491 | 6,265 | 23.6 | 5,744 | 91.7 | 521 | 8.3 |
| Bribery | 739 | 420 | 56.8 | 412 | 98.1 | 8 | 1.9 |
| Burglary/breaking & entering | 584,913 | 78,240 | 13.4 | 70,179 | 89.7 | 8,061 | 10.3 |
| Counterfeiting/forgery | 107,047 | 18,958 | 17.7 | 17,320 | 91.4 | 1,638 | 8.6 |
| Destruction/damage/vandalism | 1,283,633 | 199,497 | 15.5 | 166,291 | 83.4 | 33,206 | 16.6 |
| Embezzlement | 22,610 | 6,390 | 28.3 | 5,288 | 82.8 | 1,102 | 17.2 |
| Extortion/blackmail | 12,270 | 675 | 5.5 | 482 | 71.4 | 193 | 28.6 |
| Fraud offenses | 761,698 | 69,682 | 9.1 | 59,823 | 85.9 | 9,859 | 14.1 |
| Larceny-theft offenses | 2,967,229 | 370,822 | 12.5 | 332,792 | 89.7 | 38,030 | 10.3 |
| Motor vehicle theft | 554,618 | 59,779 | 10.8 | 49,582 | 82.9 | 10,197 | 17.1 |
| Robbery | 121,103 | 28,537 | 23.6 | 25,535 | 89.5 | 3,002 | 10.5 |
| Stolen property offenses | 89,625 | 56,973 | 63.6 | 56,002 | 98.3 | 971 | 1.7 |
| **Crime Against Society** | 1,620,563 | 1,173,580 | 72.4 | 1,145,735 | 97.6 | 27,845 | 2.4 |
| Animal cruelty | 16,497 | 3,777 | 22.9 | 3,445 | 91.2 | 332 | 8.8 |
| Drug/narcotic offenses | 1,290,858 | 987,166 | 76.5 | 965,713 | 97.8 | 21,453 | 2.2 |
| Gambling offenses | 1,815 | 570 | 31.4 | 499 | 87.5 | 71 | 12.5 |
| Pornography/obscene material | 31,873 | 6,163 | 19.3 | 4,553 | 73.9 | 1,610 | 26.1 |
| Prostitution offenses | 11,565 | 8,193 | 70.8 | 8,100 | 98.9 | 93 | 1.1 |

1 Clearance figures in this table represent the total number of incidents cleared and a breakdown of the clearance method for each offense category.   2 The total number of incidents is 9,436,674. However, the column figures and percentages will not add to the total because incidents may include more than one offense type, and one incident was counted for each offense type within each offense category in this table.   3 In the National Incident-Based Reporting System, the submission of arrestee data in connection with an incident automatically clears all offenses within the incident.

## Table 25A. Number and Percent of Offenses Cleared by Arrest or Exceptional Means, by Population Group, 2020

(Number, percent.)

| Population group | Violent crime | Murder and nonnegligent manslaughter | Rape[1] | Robbery | Aggravated assault | Property crime | Burglary | Larceny-theft | Motor vehicle theft | Arson[2] | Number of agencies | Estimated population, 2020 |
|---|---|---|---|---|---|---|---|---|---|---|---|---|
| **Total, All Agencies** | | | | | | | | | | | | |
| Offenses known | 1,137,525 | 18,109 | 110,095 | 209,643 | 799,678 | 5,670,244 | 898,176 | 4,004,124 | 727,045 | 40,899 | 13,804 | 288,224,102 |
| Percent cleared by arrest | 41.7 | 54.4 | 30.6 | 28.8 | 46.4 | 14.6 | 14.0 | 15.1 | 12.3 | 21.5 | | |
| **Total Cities** | | | | | | | | | | | | |
| Offenses known | 902,091 | 14,168 | 80,482 | 183,590 | 623,851 | 4,528,049 | 677,169 | 3,236,517 | 582,325 | 32,038 | 9,871 | 193,856,641 |
| Percent cleared by arrest | 39.5 | 52.3 | 28.5 | 27.8 | 44.0 | 14.4 | 13.5 | 15.1 | 11.2 | 20.7 | | |
| Group I (250,000 and over) | | | | | | | | | | | | |
| Offenses known | 438,385 | 7,303 | 29,775 | 105,215 | 296,092 | 1,693,877 | 267,123 | 1,146,402 | 266,470 | 13,882 | 84 | 58,292,525 |
| Percent cleared by arrest | 32.3 | 47.3 | 25.6 | 23.8 | 35.7 | 9.2 | 10.8 | 8.9 | 8.7 | 14.0 | | |
| 1,000,000 and over (Group I subset) | | | | | | | | | | | | |
| Offenses known | 166,327 | 2,008 | 10,794 | 43,885 | 109,640 | 595,381 | 87,910 | 409,536 | 92,926 | 5,009 | 10 | 24,452,783 |
| Percent cleared by arrest | 30.9 | 48.9 | 25.0 | 23.0 | 34.3 | 7.5 | 9.7 | 7.0 | 7.6 | 9.7 | | |
| 500,000 to 999,999 (Group I subset) | | | | | | | | | | | | |
| Offenses known | 151,635 | 3,005 | 9,031 | 34,116 | 105,483 | 590,900 | 99,666 | 396,817 | 89,984 | 4,433 | 24 | 16,967,590 |
| Percent cleared by arrest | 33.2 | 44.9 | 28.2 | 24.1 | 36.3 | 9.3 | 10.9 | 8.7 | 9.4 | 16.7 | | |
| 250,000 to 499,999 (Group I subset) | | | | | | | | | | | | |
| Offenses known | 120,423 | 2,290 | 9,950 | 27,214 | 80,969 | 507,596 | 79,547 | 340,049 | 83,560 | 4,440 | 50 | 16,872,152 |
| Percent cleared by arrest | 33.1 | 49.0 | 23.9 | 24.8 | 36.6 | 11.0 | 11.9 | 11.2 | 9.3 | 16.1 | | |
| Group II (100,000 to 249,999) | | | | | | | | | | | | |
| Offenses known | 147,671 | 2,482 | 13,834 | 29,726 | 101,629 | 799,322 | 117,152 | 564,511 | 112,380 | 5,279 | 218 | 31,572,750 |
| Percent cleared by arrest | 41.1 | 55.5 | 28.6 | 29.9 | 45.7 | 13.0 | 13.2 | 13.4 | 10.8 | 24.9 | | |
| Group III (50,000 to 99,999) | | | | | | | | | | | | |
| Offenses known | 111,246 | 1,534 | 11,399 | 21,076 | 77,237 | 674,088 | 93,809 | 496,226 | 79,971 | 4,082 | 459 | 32,114,069 |
| Percent cleared by arrest | 47.4 | 57.8 | 32.9 | 33.9 | 52.9 | 16.5 | 15.1 | 17.3 | 12.2 | 27.3 | | |
| Group IV (25,000 to 49,999) | | | | | | | | | | | | |
| Offenses known | 77,198 | 1,103 | 9,268 | 13,026 | 53,801 | 515,758 | 71,974 | 390,166 | 50,481 | 3,137 | 786 | 27,406,287 |
| Percent cleared by arrest | 46.3 | 58.0 | 29.8 | 34.2 | 51.9 | 18.9 | 15.3 | 20.2 | 13.7 | 24.2 | | |
| Group V (10,000 to 24,999) | | | | | | | | | | | | |
| Offenses known | 67,169 | 996 | 8,511 | 8,956 | 48,706 | 470,604 | 68,457 | 357,439 | 42,035 | 2,673 | 1,572 | 25,072,927 |
| Percent cleared by arrest | 49.4 | 62.3 | 29.6 | 35.9 | 55.1 | 21.8 | 16.8 | 23.4 | 16.3 | 26.4 | | |
| Group VI (under 10,000) | | | | | | | | | | | | |
| Offenses known | 60,422 | 750 | 7,695 | 5,591 | 46,386 | 374,400 | 58,654 | 281,773 | 30,988 | 2,985 | 6,752 | 19,398,083 |
| Percent cleared by arrest | 52.8 | 58.5 | 30.5 | 39.7 | 58.0 | 21.4 | 18.3 | 22.1 | 20.7 | 26.8 | | |
| **Metropolitan Counties** | | | | | | | | | | | | |
| Offenses known | 185,468 | 2,907 | 21,380 | 23,863 | 137,318 | 920,546 | 161,052 | 635,640 | 117,370 | 6,484 | 1,731 | 71,573,154 |
| Percent cleared by arrest | 50.3 | 61.8 | 37.2 | 35.4 | 54.6 | 15.5 | 15.6 | 15.3 | 15.7 | 23.7 | | |
| **Nonmetropolitan Counties** | | | | | | | | | | | | |
| Offenses known | 49,966 | 1,034 | 8,233 | 2,190 | 38,509 | 221,649 | 59,955 | 131,967 | 27,350 | 2,377 | 2,202 | 22,794,307 |
| Percent cleared by arrest | 50.8 | 62.1 | 34.3 | 37.8 | 54.8 | 15.1 | 15.2 | 13.6 | 20.7 | 26.2 | | |
| **Suburban Areas[3]** | | | | | | | | | | | | |
| Offenses known | 303,760 | 4,450 | 36,426 | 43,096 | 219,788 | 1,803,833 | 278,407 | 1,310,538 | 203,377 | 11,511 | 7,275 | 123,406,306 |
| Percent cleared by arrest | 50.1 | 60.7 | 34.4 | 35.7 | 55.3 | 17.5 | 15.9 | 18.2 | 15.1 | 24.2 | | |

1 The figures shown in this column for the offense of rape were reported using only the revised Uniform Crime Reporting definition of rape.   2 Not all agencies submit reports for arson to the FBI. As a result, the number of reports the FBI uses to compute the percent of offenses cleared for arson is less than the number it uses to compute the percent of offenses cleared for all other offenses.   3 Suburban area includes law enforcement agencies in cities with less than 50,000 inhabitants and county law enforcement agencies that are within a Metropolitan Statistical Area. Suburban area excludes all metropolitan agencies associated with a principal city. The agencies associated with suburban areas also appear in other groups within this table.

## Table 26. Number and Percent of Offenses Cleared by Arrest or Exceptional Means, by Region and Geographic Division, 2020

(Number, percent.)

| Geographic region/division | Violent crime | Murder and nonnegligent manslaughter | Rape[1] | Robbery | Aggravated assault | Property crime | Burglary | Larceny-theft | Motor vehicle theft | Arson[2] | Number of agencies | Estimated population, 2020 |
|---|---|---|---|---|---|---|---|---|---|---|---|---|
| **Total, All Agencies** | | | | | | | | | | | | |
| Offenses known | 1,137,525 | 18,109 | 110,095 | 209,643 | 799,678 | 5,670,244 | 898,176 | 4,004,124 | 727,045 | 40,899 | 13,804 | 288,224,102 |
| Percent cleared by arrest | 41.7 | 54.4 | 30.6 | 28.8 | 46.4 | 14.6 | 14.0 | 15.1 | 12.3 | 21.5 | | |
| **Northeast** | | | | | | | | | | | | |
| Offenses known | 123,273 | 1,565 | 10,848 | 27,926 | 82,934 | 558,820 | 68,059 | 439,212 | 48,870 | 2,679 | 2,292 | 43,704,953 |
| Percent cleared by arrest | 39.2 | 43.6 | 26.6 | 26.3 | 45.1 | 16.0 | 19.0 | 16.0 | 11.2 | 26.4 | | |
| New England | | | | | | | | | | | | |
| Offenses known | 34,377 | 379 | 4,043 | 5,857 | 24,098 | 179,469 | 22,908 | 136,619 | 18,811 | 1,131 | 931 | 14,743,475 |
| Percent cleared by arrest | 48.3 | 52.2 | 28.1 | 26.4 | 56.9 | 15.0 | 16.8 | 15.1 | 10.8 | 28.2 | | |
| Middle Atlantic | | | | | | | | | | | | |
| Offenses known | 88,896 | 1,186 | 6,805 | 22,069 | 58,836 | 379,351 | 45,151 | 302,593 | 30,059 | 1,548 | 1,361 | 28,961,478 |
| Percent cleared by arrest | 35.7 | 40.8 | 25.7 | 26.3 | 40.3 | 16.4 | 20.1 | 16.4 | 11.4 | 25.1 | | |
| **Midwest** | | | | | | | | | | | | |
| Offenses known | 201,425 | 3,576 | 23,421 | 29,893 | 144,535 | 952,938 | 152,605 | 675,934 | 116,919 | 7,480 | 3,690 | 51,461,147 |
| Percent cleared by arrest | 40.5 | 49.3 | 29.9 | 24.0 | 45.4 | 15.5 | 12.8 | 16.7 | 11.9 | 18.2 | | |
| East North Central | | | | | | | | | | | | |
| Offenses known | 121,108 | 2,330 | 14,355 | 18,701 | 85,722 | 509,744 | 83,724 | 363,241 | 58,443 | 4,336 | 1,755 | 30,943,029 |
| Percent cleared by arrest | 38.3 | 43.7 | 29.5 | 23.1 | 42.9 | 14.8 | 12.7 | 15.9 | 10.7 | 17.1 | | |
| West North Central | | | | | | | | | | | | |
| Offenses known | 80,317 | 1,246 | 9,066 | 11,192 | 58,813 | 443,194 | 68,881 | 312,693 | 58,476 | 3,144 | 1,935 | 20,518,118 |
| Percent cleared by arrest | 43.7 | 59.9 | 30.6 | 25.4 | 48.9 | 16.3 | 12.8 | 17.7 | 13.1 | 19.7 | | |
| **South** | | | | | | | | | | | | |
| Offenses known | 492,662 | 8,996 | 44,050 | 82,599 | 357,017 | 2,406,498 | 391,041 | 1,736,309 | 267,093 | 12,055 | 5,708 | 116,917,467 |
| Percent cleared by arrest | 40.2 | 55.9 | 32.4 | 28.1 | 43.6 | 15.6 | 14.6 | 15.9 | 15.0 | 22.4 | | |
| South Atlantic | | | | | | | | | | | | |
| Offenses known | 227,332 | 4,422 | 19,315 | 39,103 | 164,492 | 1,122,215 | 167,026 | 838,984 | 110,541 | 5,664 | 2,587 | 60,677,083 |
| Percent cleared by arrest | 45.0 | 59.3 | 40.7 | 35.0 | 47.5 | 17.9 | 18.7 | 17.8 | 17.4 | 27.2 | | |
| East South Central | | | | | | | | | | | | |
| Offenses known | 69,960 | 1,342 | 5,223 | 9,534 | 53,861 | 323,432 | 55,579 | 226,848 | 39,449 | 1,556 | 1,225 | 16,004,814 |
| Percent cleared by arrest | 41.0 | 48.4 | 38.0 | 26.1 | 43.7 | 18.7 | 16.2 | 19.0 | 20.6 | 23.4 | | |
| West South Central | | | | | | | | | | | | |
| Offenses known | 195,370 | 3,232 | 19,512 | 33,962 | 138,664 | 960,851 | 168,436 | 670,477 | 117,103 | 4,835 | 1,896 | 40,235,570 |
| Percent cleared by arrest | 34.5 | 54.5 | 22.6 | 20.6 | 39.0 | 11.9 | 9.9 | 12.5 | 10.9 | 16.4 | | |
| **West** | | | | | | | | | | | | |
| Offenses known | 320,165 | 3,972 | 31,776 | 69,225 | 215,192 | 1,751,988 | 286,471 | 1,152,669 | 294,163 | 18,685 | 2,114 | 76,140,535 |
| Percent cleared by arrest | 45.8 | 59.8 | 30.1 | 32.6 | 52.0 | 12.2 | 12.8 | 12.4 | 10.1 | 21.6 | | |
| Mountain | | | | | | | | | | | | |
| Offenses known | 104,878 | 1,289 | 12,872 | 16,426 | 74,291 | 555,272 | 83,777 | 387,633 | 79,898 | 3,964 | 891 | 23,944,023 |
| Percent cleared by arrest | 45.0 | 63.9 | 26.4 | 29.7 | 51.2 | 16.0 | 13.9 | 17.1 | 12.1 | 27.6 | | |
| Pacific | | | | | | | | | | | | |
| Offenses known | 215,287 | 2,683 | 18,904 | 52,799 | 140,901 | 1,196,716 | 202,694 | 765,036 | 214,265 | 14,721 | 1,223 | 52,196,512 |
| Percent cleared by arrest | 46.1 | 57.8 | 32.7 | 33.5 | 52.5 | 10.5 | 12.4 | 10.1 | 9.4 | 19.9 | | |

1 The figures shown in this column for the offense of rape were reported using only the revised Uniform Crime Reporting definition of rape.   2 Not all agencies submit reports for arson to the FBI. As a result, the number of reports the FBI uses to compute the percent of offenses cleared for arson is less than the number it uses to compute the percent of offenses cleared for all other offenses.

## Table 27. Number and Percent of Offenses Cleared by Arrest or Exceptional Means, Additional Information About Selected Offenses, by Population Group, 2020

(Number, percent.)

| Population group | Rape[1] Rape by force | Rape[1] Assault to rape-attempts | Robbery Firearm | Robbery Knife or cutting instrument | Robbery Other weapon | Robbery Strong-arm | Aggravated assault Firearm | Aggravated assault Knife or cutting instrument | Aggravated assault Other weapon | Aggravated assault Hands, fists, feet, etc. |
|---|---|---|---|---|---|---|---|---|---|---|
| **Total, All Agencies** | | | | | | | | | | |
| Offenses known | 105,827 | 4,267 | 79,628 | 18,871 | 23,024 | 88,120 | 277,820 | 129,643 | 228,271 | 163,946 |
| Percent cleared by arrest | 30.5 | 34.9 | 21.6 | 31.5 | 27.6 | 28.4 | 27.4 | 51.9 | 46.0 | 55.1 |
| **Total Cities** | | | | | | | | | | |
| Offenses known | 77,326 | 3,156 | 68,433 | 16,819 | 20,078 | 78,260 | 222,235 | 105,575 | 174,826 | 121,217 |
| Percent cleared by arrest | 28.3 | 34.6 | 21.6 | 31.4 | 27.3 | 28.4 | 25.8 | 51.6 | 45.5 | 55.0 |
| Group I (250,000 and over) | | | | | | | | | | |
| Offenses known | 28,450 | 1,325 | 40,525 | 9,770 | 10,722 | 44,198 | 122,444 | 50,748 | 81,056 | 41,844 |
| Percent cleared by arrest | 25.2 | 33.7 | 19.6 | 27.5 | 24.1 | 24.6 | 22.1 | 46.3 | 38.8 | 45.0 |
| 1,000,000 and over (Group I subset) | | | | | | | | | | |
| Offenses known | 10,313 | 481 | 14,649 | 5,005 | 5,035 | 19,196 | 34,892 | 22,639 | 30,390 | 21,719 |
| Percent cleared by arrest | 24.5 | 35.8 | 18.6 | 27.7 | 24.8 | 24.8 | 21.7 | 44.1 | 36.6 | 41.3 |
| 500,000 to 999,999 (Group I subset) | | | | | | | | | | |
| Offenses known | 8,584 | 447 | 15,458 | 2,758 | 3,426 | 12,474 | 50,594 | 15,837 | 28,901 | 10,151 |
| Percent cleared by arrest | 27.7 | 37.4 | 19.5 | 27.2 | 23.1 | 27.1 | 22.9 | 49.7 | 41.8 | 48.7 |
| 250,000 to 499,999 (Group I subset) | | | | | | | | | | |
| Offenses known | 9,553 | 397 | 10,418 | 2,007 | 2,261 | 12,528 | 36,958 | 12,272 | 21,765 | 9,974 |
| Percent cleared by arrest | 23.8 | 27.2 | 21.2 | 27.8 | 23.9 | 21.9 | 21.3 | 45.9 | 37.8 | 49.3 |
| Group II (100,000 to 249,999) | | | | | | | | | | |
| Offenses known | 13,286 | 548 | 11,049 | 2,688 | 3,472 | 12,517 | 36,981 | 17,794 | 28,299 | 18,555 |
| Percent cleared by arrest | 28.3 | 35.2 | 22.0 | 33.5 | 27.8 | 30.5 | 25.7 | 53.2 | 48.1 | 56.6 |
| Group III (50,000 to 99,999) | | | | | | | | | | |
| Offenses known | 11,045 | 354 | 6,884 | 1,938 | 2,537 | 9,717 | 23,402 | 12,983 | 22,454 | 18,398 |
| Percent cleared by arrest | 32.7 | 40.4 | 24.9 | 36.5 | 32.8 | 33.1 | 30.0 | 55.7 | 52.2 | 62.4 |
| Group IV (25,000 to 49,999) | | | | | | | | | | |
| Offenses known | 8,967 | 301 | 4,713 | 1,185 | 1,533 | 5,595 | 16,471 | 9,366 | 15,666 | 12,298 |
| Percent cleared by arrest | 29.7 | 32.6 | 25.6 | 38.2 | 29.0 | 34.9 | 31.4 | 56.3 | 51.6 | 57.1 |
| Group V (10,000 to 24,999) | | | | | | | | | | |
| Offenses known | 8,253 | 258 | 3,352 | 820 | 1,102 | 3,682 | 13,577 | 7,994 | 14,455 | 12,680 |
| Percent cleared by arrest | 29.3 | 38.0 | 28.1 | 40.6 | 33.9 | 35.5 | 36.0 | 59.8 | 54.0 | 62.1 |
| Group VI (under 10,000) | | | | | | | | | | |
| Offenses known | 7,325 | 370 | 1,910 | 418 | 712 | 2,551 | 9,360 | 6,690 | 12,896 | 17,442 |
| Percent cleared by arrest | 30.5 | 30.8 | 28.7 | 46.2 | 41.2 | 41.9 | 40.7 | 62.5 | 54.1 | 62.9 |
| **Metropolitan Counties** | | | | | | | | | | |
| Offenses known | 20,549 | 831 | 10,243 | 1,888 | 2,583 | 9,149 | 44,797 | 19,529 | 41,627 | 31,365 |
| Percent cleared by arrest | 37.2 | 37.7 | 20.9 | 32.2 | 29.9 | 28.0 | 31.0 | 52.1 | 46.0 | 55.3 |
| **Nonmetropolitan Counties** | | | | | | | | | | |
| Offenses known | 7,952 | 280 | 952 | 164 | 363 | 711 | 10,788 | 4,539 | 11,818 | 11,364 |
| Percent cleared by arrest | 34.4 | 30.4 | 30.3 | 40.9 | 27.5 | 36.8 | 44.3 | 59.2 | 52.9 | 55.5 |
| **Suburban Areas[3]** | | | | | | | | | | |
| Offenses known | 35,069 | 1,357 | 17,100 | 3,540 | 4,921 | 17,535 | 66,324 | 33,105 | 66,516 | 53,845 |
| Percent cleared by arrest | 34.3 | 35.7 | 22.8 | 35.8 | 31.8 | 32.4 | 32.5 | 55.5 | 48.7 | 57.7 |

## Table 27. Number and Percent of Offenses Cleared by Arrest or Exceptional Means, Additional Information About Selected Offenses, by Population Group, 2020—Continued

(Number, percent.)

| Population group | Burglary | | | Motor vehicle theft | | | Arson[2] | | | Number of agencies | Estimated population, 2020 |
|---|---|---|---|---|---|---|---|---|---|---|---|
| | Forcible entry | Unlawful entry | Attempted forcible entry | Autos | Trucks and buses | Other vehicles | Structure | Mobile | Other | | |
| **Total, All Agencies** | | | | | | | | | | | |
| Offenses known | 502,319 | 335,526 | 60,331 | 538,769 | 121,243 | 67,033 | 15,060 | 9,515 | 16,346 | 13,804 | 288,224,102 |
| Percent cleared by arrest | 12.9 | 15.8 | 13.9 | 13.1 | 10.3 | 9.4 | 25.6 | 10.6 | 24.0 | | |
| **Total Cities** | | | | | | | | | | | |
| Offenses known | 381,252 | 248,627 | 47,290 | 437,444 | 97,640 | 47,241 | 11,753 | 7,038 | 13,269 | 9,871 | 193,856,641 |
| Percent cleared by arrest | 12.4 | 15.3 | 13.7 | 12.0 | 8.9 | 8.4 | 24.2 | 9.9 | 23.3 | | |
| Group I (250,000 and over) | | | | | | | | | | | |
| Offenses known | 162,264 | 85,002 | 19,857 | 192,199 | 55,924 | 18,347 | 4,444 | 3,419 | 6,041 | 84 | 58,292,525 |
| Percent cleared by arrest | 10.1 | 12.0 | 11.7 | 9.5 | 7.0 | 6.2 | 17.6 | 6.8 | 15.4 | | |
| 1,000,000 and over (Group I subset) | | | | | | | | | | | |
| Offenses known | 56,840 | 24,614 | 6,456 | 54,021 | 31,425 | 7,480 | 1,138 | 834 | 3,037 | 10 | 24,452,783 |
| Percent cleared by arrest | 8.6 | 11.5 | 12.1 | 9.0 | 5.7 | 5.6 | 17.7 | 5.8 | 7.8 | | |
| 500,000 to 999,999 (Group I subset) | | | | | | | | | | | |
| Offenses known | 58,071 | 33,739 | 7,856 | 71,283 | 12,651 | 6,050 | 1,621 | 1,349 | 1,485 | 24 | 16,967,590 |
| Percent cleared by arrest | 10.4 | 11.7 | 11.1 | 9.7 | 9.3 | 6.2 | 17.4 | 7.9 | 23.9 | | |
| 250,000 to 499,999 (Group I subset) | | | | | | | | | | | |
| Offenses known | 47,353 | 26,649 | 5,545 | 66,895 | 11,848 | 4,817 | 1,685 | 1,236 | 1,519 | 50 | 16,872,152 |
| Percent cleared by arrest | 11.4 | 12.6 | 12.2 | 9.7 | 7.9 | 7.2 | 17.7 | 6.4 | 22.3 | | |
| Group II (100,000 to 249,999) | | | | | | | | | | | |
| Offenses known | 65,213 | 43,493 | 8,446 | 86,569 | 16,449 | 9,362 | 1,877 | 1,184 | 2,218 | 218 | 31,572,750 |
| Percent cleared by arrest | 12.1 | 14.5 | 14.6 | 11.4 | 9.4 | 7.5 | 26.3 | 10.4 | 31.4 | | |
| Group III (50,000 to 99,999) | | | | | | | | | | | |
| Offenses known | 50,788 | 36,841 | 6,180 | 61,181 | 11,614 | 7,176 | 1,531 | 844 | 1,707 | 459 | 32,114,069 |
| Percent cleared by arrest | 13.9 | 16.8 | 14.9 | 12.9 | 10.3 | 8.6 | 31.0 | 12.1 | 31.5 | | |
| Group IV (25,000 to 49,999) | | | | | | | | | | | |
| Offenses known | 37,330 | 29,428 | 5,216 | 40,007 | 5,537 | 4,937 | 1,343 | 565 | 1,229 | 786 | 27,406,287 |
| Percent cleared by arrest | 14.4 | 16.7 | 14.9 | 14.2 | 13.0 | 10.0 | 27.0 | 13.6 | 26.0 | | |
| Group V (10,000 to 24,999) | | | | | | | | | | | |
| Offenses known | 35,529 | 29,015 | 3,913 | 33,505 | 4,733 | 3,797 | 1,138 | 474 | 1,061 | 1,572 | 25,072,927 |
| Percent cleared by arrest | 15.4 | 18.6 | 15.9 | 17.1 | 13.8 | 12.1 | 30.2 | 15.2 | 27.4 | | |
| Group VI (under 10,000) | | | | | | | | | | | |
| Offenses known | 30,128 | 24,848 | 3,678 | 23,983 | 3,383 | 3,622 | 1,420 | 552 | 1,013 | 6,752 | 19,398,083 |
| Percent cleared by arrest | 16.6 | 20.6 | 16.4 | 21.7 | 19.2 | 15.3 | 27.7 | 16.5 | 31.2 | | |
| **Metropolitan Counties** | | | | | | | | | | | |
| Offenses known | 87,788 | 62,423 | 10,841 | 82,866 | 18,979 | 15,525 | 2,303 | 1,874 | 2,307 | 1,731 | 71,573,154 |
| Percent cleared by arrest | 14.3 | 17.6 | 14.9 | 16.5 | 15.7 | 11.2 | 30.1 | 11.4 | 27.4 | | |
| **Nonmetropolitan Counties** | | | | | | | | | | | |
| Offenses known | 33,279 | 24,476 | 2,200 | 18,459 | 4,624 | 4,267 | 1,004 | 603 | 770 | 2,202 | 22,794,307 |
| Percent cleared by arrest | 14.8 | 16.0 | 13.7 | 22.9 | 17.7 | 14.5 | 31.5 | 16.7 | 26.8 | | |
| **Suburban Areas[3]** | | | | | | | | | | | |
| Offenses known | 148,994 | 109,902 | 19,511 | 151,165 | 28,638 | 23,574 | 4,417 | 2,849 | 4,245 | 7,275 | 123,406,306 |
| Percent cleared by arrest | 14.6 | 17.9 | 14.8 | 15.7 | 14.8 | 11.1 | 29.5 | 12.1 | 26.8 | | |

1 The figures shown in the rape column include only those reported by law enforcement agencies that used the revised Uniform Crime Reporting definition of rape.   2 Not all agencies submit reports for arson to the FBI. As a result, the number of reports the FBI uses to compute the percent of offenses cleared for arson is less than the number it uses to compute the percent of offenses cleared for all other offenses. Agencies must report arson clearances by detailed property classification as specified on the Monthly Return of Arson Offenses Known to Law Enforcement to be included in this table; therefore, clearances in this table may differ from other clearance tables.   3 Suburban area includes law enforcement agencies in cities with less than 50,000 inhabitants and county law enforcement agencies that are within a Metropolitan Statistical Area. Suburban area excludes all metropolitan agencies associated with a principal city. The agencies associated with suburban areas also appear in other groups within this table.

## Table 28. Number of Offenses Cleared by Arrest or Exceptional Means and Percent Involving Persons Under 18 Years of Age, by Population Group, 2020

(Number, percent.)

| Population group | Violent crime | Murder and nonnegligent manslaughter | Rape[1] | Robbery | Aggravated assault | Property crime | Burglary | Larceny-theft | Motor vehicle theft | Arson[2] | Number of agencies | Estimated population, 2020 |
|---|---|---|---|---|---|---|---|---|---|---|---|---|
| **Total, All Agencies** | | | | | | | | | | | | |
| Total clearances | 474,611 | 9,855 | 33,738 | 60,287 | 370,731 | 826,856 | 126,029 | 602,711 | 89,322 | 8,794 | 13,804 | 288,224,102 |
| Percent under 18 years | 6.6 | 4.8 | 14.5 | 11.6 | 5.1 | 7.0 | 7.1 | 6.2 | 12.1 | 11.5 | | |
| **Total Cities** | | | | | | | | | | | | |
| Total clearances | 355,996 | 7,416 | 22,964 | 51,008 | 274,608 | 651,019 | 91,718 | 487,385 | 65,284 | 6,632 | 9,871 | 193,856,641 |
| Percent under 18 years | 6.6 | 5.0 | 13.5 | 11.7 | 5.2 | 6.7 | 6.8 | 5.9 | 12.3 | 11.0 | | |
| Group I (250,000 and over) | | | | | | | | | | | | |
| Total clearances | 141,721 | 3,453 | 7,622 | 25,075 | 105,571 | 155,565 | 28,830 | 101,489 | 23,305 | 1,941 | 84 | 58,292,525 |
| Percent under 18 years | 6.3 | 5.0 | 11.7 | 12.4 | 4.5 | 6.8 | 5.5 | 5.9 | 12.2 | 5.3 | | |
| 1,000,000 and over (Group I subset) | | | | | | | | | | | | |
| Total clearances | 51,435 | 981 | 2,695 | 10,115 | 37,644 | 44,864 | 8,488 | 28,837 | 7,052 | 487 | 10 | 24,452,783 |
| Percent under 18 years | 5.9 | 4.6 | 10.0 | 12.4 | 3.9 | 5.9 | 4.0 | 5.8 | 8.7 | 3.3 | | |
| 500,000 to 999,999 (Group I subset) | | | | | | | | | | | | |
| Total clearances | 50,379 | 1,350 | 2,546 | 8,222 | 38,261 | 54,732 | 10,890 | 34,614 | 8,489 | 739 | 24 | 16,967,590 |
| Percent under 18 years | 5.9 | 5.7 | 12.7 | 10.9 | 4.4 | 5.6 | 4.6 | 4.4 | 12.0 | 5.0 | | |
| 250,000 to 499,999 (Group I subset) | | | | | | | | | | | | |
| Total clearances | 39,907 | 1,122 | 2,381 | 6,738 | 29,666 | 55,969 | 9,452 | 38,038 | 7,764 | 715 | 50 | 16,872,152 |
| Percent under 18 years | 7.4 | 4.6 | 12.6 | 14.1 | 5.5 | 8.5 | 7.9 | 7.3 | 15.7 | 7.0 | | |
| Group II (100,000 to 249,999) | | | | | | | | | | | | |
| Total clearances | 60,720 | 1,377 | 3,951 | 8,898 | 46,494 | 104,296 | 15,444 | 75,453 | 12,087 | 1,312 | 218 | 31,572,750 |
| Percent under 18 years | 6.3 | 5.2 | 13.4 | 10.2 | 5.0 | 7.0 | 6.4 | 6.2 | 12.6 | 8.8 | | |
| Group III (50,000 to 99,999) | | | | | | | | | | | | |
| Total clearances | 52,677 | 886 | 3,755 | 7,141 | 40,895 | 110,985 | 14,178 | 85,959 | 9,735 | 1,113 | 459 | 32,114,069 |
| Percent under 18 years | 7.0 | 4.2 | 13.8 | 11.3 | 5.7 | 7.1 | 6.8 | 6.4 | 12.6 | 14.2 | | |
| Group IV (25,000 to 49,999) | | | | | | | | | | | | |
| Total clearances | 35,780 | 640 | 2,765 | 4,459 | 27,916 | 97,475 | 11,044 | 78,768 | 6,904 | 759 | 786 | 27,406,287 |
| Percent under 18 years | 7.1 | 6.1 | 15.8 | 11.1 | 5.7 | 6.5 | 7.5 | 5.7 | 13.4 | 11.9 | | |
| Group V (10,000 to 24,999) | | | | | | | | | | | | |
| Total clearances | 33,177 | 621 | 2,521 | 3,214 | 26,821 | 102,596 | 11,490 | 83,547 | 6,852 | 707 | 1,572 | 25,072,927 |
| Percent under 18 years | 6.8 | 5.0 | 15.6 | 10.3 | 5.5 | 6.5 | 8.3 | 5.6 | 12.7 | 17.4 | | |
| Group VI (under 10,000) | | | | | | | | | | | | |
| Total clearances | 31,921 | 439 | 2,350 | 2,221 | 26,911 | 80,102 | 10,732 | 62,169 | 6,401 | 800 | 6,752 | 19,398,083 |
| Percent under 18 years | 7.5 | 3.6 | 14.3 | 14.5 | 6.3 | 6.5 | 8.7 | 5.7 | 10.3 | 17.3 | | |
| **Metropolitan Counties** | | | | | | | | | | | | |
| Total clearances | 93,218 | 1,797 | 7,953 | 8,452 | 75,016 | 142,444 | 25,178 | 97,355 | 18,372 | 1,539 | 1,731 | 71,573,154 |
| Percent under 18 years | 6.9 | 4.7 | 16.5 | 12.1 | 5.3 | 8.6 | 8.3 | 7.8 | 12.4 | 14.4 | | |
| **Nonmetropolitan Counties** | | | | | | | | | | | | |
| Total clearances | 25,397 | 642 | 2,821 | 827 | 21,107 | 33,393 | 9,133 | 17,971 | 5,666 | 623 | 2,202 | 22,794,307 |
| Percent under 18 years | 5.6 | 3.3 | 17.0 | 4.5 | 4.2 | 6.3 | 6.0 | 5.6 | 8.5 | 9.5 | | |
| **Suburban Areas[3]** | | | | | | | | | | | | |
| Total clearances | 152,082 | 2,703 | 12,513 | 15,402 | 121,464 | 316,055 | 44,358 | 238,281 | 30,629 | 2,787 | 7,275 | 123,406,306 |
| Percent under 18 years | 7.1 | 4.8 | 16.3 | 12.3 | 5.6 | 7.5 | 8.3 | 6.6 | 12.3 | 15.0 | | |

1 The figures shown in this column for the offense of rape were reported using only the revised Uniform Crime Reporting definition of rape.   2 Not all agencies submit reports for arson to the FBI. As a result, the number of reports the FBI uses to compute the percent of offenses cleared for arson is less than the number it uses to compute the percent of offenses cleared for all other offenses.   3 Suburban area includes law enforcement agencies in cities with less than 50,000 inhabitants and county law enforcement agencies that are within a Metropolitan Statistical Area. Suburban area excludes all metropolitan agencies associated with a principal city. The agencies associated with suburban areas also appear in other groups within this table.

# SECTION IV

# PERSONS ARRESTED

# PERSONS ARRESTED

In the Uniform Crime Reporting (UCR) program, one arrest is counted for each separate instance in which an individual is arrested, cited, or summoned for criminal acts in Part I and Part II crimes. (See Appendix I for additional information concerning Part I and Part II crimes.) One person may be arrested multiple times during the year; as a result, the arrest figures in this section should not be taken as the total number of individuals arrested. Instead, it provides the number of *arrest occurrences* reported by law enforcement. Information regarding the UCR program's statistical methodology and table construction can be found in Appendix I.

### Important Note: Transition to NIBRS

As of January 1, 2021, the FBI's National Incident-Based Reporting System (NIBRS) became the national standard for law enforcement crime data reporting in the United States. The 2021 data year will mark the first time that the FBI and BJS estimate reported crime in the United States based solely on NIBRS data.

Section IV – arrests – has been impacted by this limited release. New data for 2021 is included in the limited areas in which availability was provided. Data from 2020 is included for context; however, given the alterations to the categories present in the 2021 data, year-over-year comparison and trend comparisons cannot be provided.

As of June 2022, all 50 U.S. states and the District of Columbia were certified to report crime data to NIBRS. Just under two-thirds of the U.S. population is covered by NIBRS-reporting law enforcement agencies, and 62 NIBRS-certified agencies serve cities with a population of 250,000 or more; these agencies cover a total population of more than 37 million. However, data is extremely limited for several large states in 2021, including California (7 percent of the population represented), the District of Columbia (47 percent of the population represented), Florida (0 percent of the population represented), Maryland (47 percent of the population represented), New Jersey (42 percent of the population represented), New York (19 percent of the population represented), and Pennsylvania (17 percent of the population represented). Of the 18,806 NIBRS-eligible law enforcement agencies, 11,333 (60.3 percent) reported data for 2021. (Eligibility is determined by the agency submitting a minimum of 3 months of data.)

The absence of these large segments of population, an issue that is expected to be alleviated in future years, makes the 2021 data not comparable to previous years. Consequently, 5-year and 10-year trend tables do not include the 2021 data. The FBI has provided limited analysis of year-over-year trends, and these are included where possible in this edition.

Some data has been suppressed by NIBRS. This occurs as a result of high uncertainty for a generated estimate. This uncertainty then requires is the application of suppression rules found within the NIBRS estimation methodologies. Suppression refers to the withholding of estimates from release due to high levels of uncertainty to ensure an unbiased view of the available NIBRS data.

In most instances, differences in the comparison of 2021 data to 2020 do not meet the criteria for statistical significance. However, it should be noted that the main contributor to that finding is the large amount of variation—both random and systematic—that is measured in the 2020 data due to low coverage of participating agencies. As coverage increases, the FBI will be able to improve its ability to measure these critical metrics for the nation.

NIBRS had not released 2021 data for population groups (cities, metropolitan/nonmetropolitan areas, and suburban areas) at the time this book went to press. The 2020 tables have been provided in this edition for historical context.

### Data Collection: Juveniles

The UCR Program considers a juvenile to be an individual under 18 years of age regardless of state definition.

## NATIONAL DATA

### *Volume*

The FBI reported an estimated 4,538,284 arrests occurred in 2021 for all offenses. Of these arrests, 816,942 were for crimes against persons, (assault, homicide, human trafficking, kidnapping/abduction, and sex offenses); 700,947 were for crimes against property (arson, bribery, burglary/breaking and entering, counterfeiting/forgery, destruction/damage/vandalism, embezzlement, extortion/blackmail, fraud, larceny-theft, motor vehicle theft, robbery, and stolen property offenses); 824,494 were for crimes against society (animal cruelty, drug/narcotic offenses, gambling offenses, pornography/obscene material, prostitution, and weapon law violations); and 2,195,901 were for Group B offenses (curfew/loitering/vagrancy violations, disorderly conduct, DWI/DUI, nonviolent family offenses, trespass of real property, and all other offenses). Assault offense arrests comprised 94.7 percent of the the crimes against persons total, while homicide accounted for 1.0 percent of the total. Robbery (categorized as a crime against property) represented 4.1 person of this category's total, while larceny-theft accounted for 48.5 percent of these arrests, burglary/breaking and entering accounted for 9.8 percent of arrests, motor vehicle theft accounted for

6.3 percent of arrests, and arson accounted for 0.7 percent of arrests. Outside of these categories, the most frequent identifiable arrests made in 2020 were for drug/narcotic offenses (estimated at 701,971 arrests). These arrests comprised 15.6 percent of the total number of all arrests. (Table 29)

## BY AGE, SEX, AND RACE

Law enforcement agencies that contributed arrest data to the UCR program reported information on the age, sex, and race of the persons they arrested. According to the data for 2021, adults accounted for 93.8 percent of arrestees nationally. The largest proportion of juvenile arrests occurred for disorderly conduct (39.7 percent). (Table 38)

By sex, males accounted for 72.7 percent of all persons arrested in 20201 Males represented 73.5 percent of arrestees for crimes against persons, 72.4 percent of arrestees for homicide, 96.4 percent of arrestees for sex offenses, and 73.5 percent for assault. Females accounted for 26.5 percent of crimes against persons arrestees, 27.6 percent of murder arrestees, 3.6 percent of sex offense arrestees, and 26.5 percent of assault arrestees. (Tables 39 and 40)

Most arrestees for crimes against property (a category that includes robbery in this section) in 2021 (91.0 percent) were over 18 years of age. By sex, males accounted for 69.0 percent of arrestees for crimes against property, 81.4 percent of arrestees for burglary/breaking and entering, 61.2 percent of arrestees for larceny-theft, 85.8 percent of robbery arrestees, 78.0 percent of arrestees for motor vehicle theft, and 76.6 percent of arrestees for arson. Females accounted for 31.0 percent of crimes against property arrestees, 18.6 percent of burglary/breaking and entering arrestees, 38.8 percent of larceny-theft arrestees, 22.0 percent of motor vehicle theft arrestees, 14.2 percent of robbery arrestees, and 23.4 percent of arson arrestees. (Tables 39 and 40)

In 2021, 66.4 percent of all persons arrested were White, 27.4 percent were Black or African American, and the remaining 6.2 percent were of other races (American Indian or Alaskan Native, Asian, and Native Hawaiian or Pacific Islander) or of unknown race. Of all arrestees crimes against persons, 60.3 percent were White, 34.0 percent were Black or African American, and 5.7 percent were of other races or of unknown race. For homicide, 39.3 percent of arrestees were White, 57.3 percent were Black or African American, and 3.4 percent were of other races or unknown race. For sex offenses, 68.8 percent of arrestees were White, 24.3 percent were Black or African American, and 6.9 percent of arrestees were of other races or unknown race. For assault, 60.2 percent of arrestees were White, 34.1 percent of arrestees were Black or African American, and 5.7 percent were of other races or of unknown race. (Table 43)

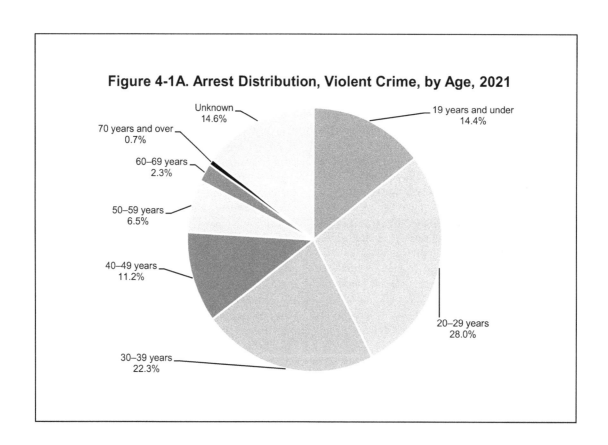

Figure 4-1A. Arrest Distribution, Violent Crime, by Age, 2021

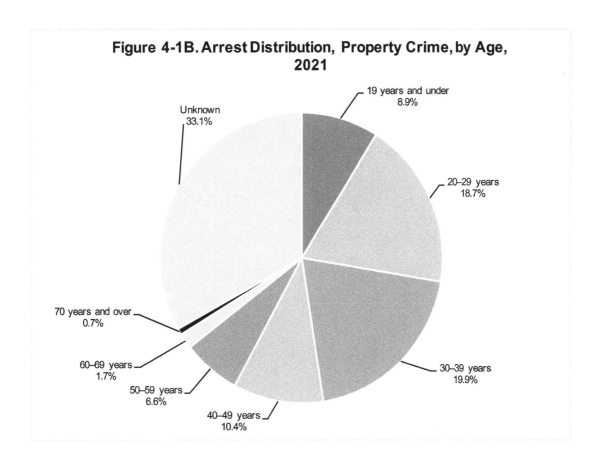

**Figure 4-1B. Arrest Distribution, Property Crime, by Age, 2021**

Unknown
33.1%

19 years and under
8.9%

20–29 years
18.7%

30–39 years
19.9%

40–49 years
10.4%

50–59 years
6.6%

60–69 years
1.7%

70 years and over
0.7%

Of all arrestees for crimes against property in 2021, 64.3 percent were White, 30.7 percent were Black or African American, and 5.1 percent were of other races or of unknown race. For robbery (included in this designation in this section), 38.9 percent of arrestees were White, 57.4 percent of arrestees were Black or African American, and 3.8 percent of arrestees were of other races or of unknown race. For burglary/breaking and entering, 67.3 percent of arrestees were White, 28.1 percent were Black or African American, and 4.6 percent were of other races or of unknown race. For larceny-theft, 66.7 percent of arrestees were White, 28.4 percent were Black or African American, and 4.9 percent were of other races or of unknown

race. For motor vehicle theft, 64.5 percent of arrestees were White, 30.8 percent of arrestees were Black or African American, and 4.7 percent were of other races or of unknown race. For arson, 70.6 percent of arrestees were White, 23.7 percent of arrestees were Black or African American, and 5.7 percent were of other races or of unknown race. (Table 43)

Outside of the scope of crimes against persons and property, White and Black or African American adults were most commonly arrested for drug/narcotic offenses (485,803 and 187,341 arrests, respectively) and driving under the influence (349,566 and 73,988 arrests, respectively). (Table 43)

## Table 29. Estimated Number of Arrests, 2021

(Number.)

| Offense | Arrests |
|---|---:|
| **Total** | 4,538,284 |
| | |
| **Crimes Against Persons** | 816,942 |
| Assault offenses | 773,342 |
| Homicide offenses | 8,365 |
| Human trafficking offenses | 378 |
| Kidnapping/abduction | 11,134 |
| Sex offenses | 23,723 |
| | |
| **Crimes Against Property** | 700,947 |
| Arson | 5,083 |
| Bribery | 278 |
| Burglary/breaking & entering | 68,440 |
| Counterfeiting/forgery | 15,499 |
| Destruction/damage/vandalism | 99309 |
| Embezzlement | 5,117 |
| Extortion/blackmail | 322 |
| Fraud offenses | 47,326 |
| Larceny-theft offenses | 340,053 |
| Motor vehicle theft | 44,435 |
| Robbery | 28,962 |
| Stolen property offenses | 46,123 |
| | |
| **Crimes Against Society** | 824,494 |
| Animal cruelty | 2,750 |
| Drug/narcotic offenses | 707,971 |
| Gambling offenses | 649 |
| Pornography/obscene material | 4,443 |
| Prostitution offenses | 7,928 |
| Weapon law violations | 100,753 |
| | |
| **Group B offenses** | 2,195,901 |
| Curfew/loitering/vagrancy violations | 14,659 |
| Disorderly conduct | 151,136 |
| Driving under the Influence | 463,100 |
| Family offenses, nonviolent | 34,251 |
| Liquor law violations | 72,753 |
| Trespass of real property | 149,769 |
| All other offenses | 1,310,233 |

# Table 30. Number and Rate of Arrests, by Geographic Region, 2020

(Number, rate per 100,000 inhabitants.)

| Offense charged | United States total (10,466 agencies; population 228,864,358) | | Northeast (2,015 agencies; population 32,300,146) | | Midwest (2,844 agencies; population 44,977,955) | | South (3,791 agencies; population 78,729,908) | | West (1,816 agencies; population 72,856,349) | |
|---|---|---|---|---|---|---|---|---|---|---|
| | Total | Rate | Total | Rate | Total | Rate | Total | Rate | Total | Rate |
| **Total[1]** | 5,291,886 | 2,312.2 | 565,777 | 1,751.6 | 1,052,926 | 2,341.0 | 1,895,649 | 2,407.8 | 1,777,534 | 2,439.8 |
| **Violent crime[2]** | 338,443 | 147.9 | 29,952 | 92.7 | 57,087 | 126.9 | 98,867 | 125.6 | 152,537 | 209.4 |
| Murder and nonnegligent manslaughter | 8,701 | 3.8 | 609 | 1.9 | 1,684 | 3.7 | 3,606 | 4.6 | 2,802 | 3.8 |
| Rape[3] | 14,462 | 6.3 | 1,739 | 5.4 | 3,452 | 7.7 | 4,574 | 5.8 | 4,697 | 6.4 |
| Robbery | 48,035 | 21.0 | 5,008 | 15.5 | 6,850 | 15.2 | 14,277 | 18.1 | 21,900 | 30.1 |
| Aggravated assault | 267,245 | 116.8 | 22,596 | 70.0 | 45,101 | 100.3 | 76,410 | 97.1 | 123,138 | 169.0 |
| **Property crime[2]** | 611,731 | 267.3 | 71,184 | 220.4 | 121,082 | 269.2 | 224,668 | 285.4 | 194,797 | 267.4 |
| Burglary | 104,535 | 45.7 | 10,424 | 32.3 | 15,139 | 33.7 | 34,876 | 44.3 | 44,096 | 60.5 |
| Larceny-theft | 442,016 | 193.1 | 55,952 | 173.2 | 95,879 | 213.2 | 170,187 | 216.2 | 119,998 | 164.7 |
| Motor vehicle theft | 58,326 | 25.5 | 4,156 | 12.9 | 9,078 | 20.2 | 17,945 | 22.8 | 27,147 | 37.3 |
| Arson | 6,854 | 3.0 | 652 | 2.0 | 986 | 2.2 | 1,660 | 2.1 | 3,556 | 4.9 |
| Other assaults | 633,704 | 276.9 | 81,111 | 251.1 | 134,078 | 298.1 | 230,240 | 292.4 | 188,275 | 258.4 |
| Forgery and counterfeiting | 22,559 | 9.9 | 2,903 | 9.0 | 4,406 | 9.8 | 9,278 | 11.8 | 5,972 | 8.2 |
| Fraud | 54,756 | 23.9 | 5,680 | 17.6 | 12,259 | 27.3 | 23,234 | 29.5 | 13,583 | 18.6 |
| Embezzlement | 6,592 | 2.9 | 411 | 1.3 | 1,411 | 3.1 | 3,192 | 4.1 | 1,578 | 2.2 |
| Stolen property; buying, receiving, possessing | 61,868 | 27.0 | 6,679 | 20.7 | 12,453 | 27.7 | 18,839 | 23.9 | 23,897 | 32.8 |
| Vandalism | 121,403 | 53.0 | 19,369 | 60.0 | 22,704 | 50.5 | 29,776 | 37.8 | 49,554 | 68.0 |
| Weapons; carrying, possessing, etc. | 115,832 | 50.6 | 8,927 | 27.6 | 27,124 | 60.3 | 36,955 | 46.9 | 42,826 | 58.8 |
| Prostitution and commercialized vice | 11,754 | 5.1 | 688 | 2.1 | 791 | 1.8 | 2,849 | 3.6 | 7,426 | 10.2 |
| Sex offenses (except forcible rape and prostitution) | 22,065 | 9.6 | 2,748 | 8.5 | 3,495 | 7.8 | 4,483 | 5.7 | 11,339 | 15.6 |
| Drug abuse violations | 801,546 | 350.2 | 91,969 | 284.7 | 131,965 | 293.4 | 302,931 | 384.8 | 274,681 | 377.0 |
| Gambling | 1,191 | 0.5 | 121 | 0.4 | 39 | 0.1 | 316 | 0.4 | 715 | 1.0 |
| Offenses against the family and children | 40,498 | 17.7 | 6,342 | 19.6 | 7,891 | 17.5 | 15,779 | 20.0 | 10,486 | 14.4 |
| Driving under the influence | 531,846 | 232.4 | 55,264 | 171.1 | 118,960 | 264.5 | 162,960 | 207.0 | 194,662 | 267.2 |
| Liquor laws | 70,875 | 31.0 | 4,657 | 14.4 | 28,061 | 62.4 | 16,554 | 21.0 | 21,603 | 29.7 |
| Drunkenness | 135,744 | 59.3 | 3,287 | 10.2 | 13,518 | 30.1 | 77,483 | 98.4 | 41,456 | 56.9 |
| Disorderly conduct | 156,502 | 68.4 | 24,078 | 74.5 | 55,086 | 122.5 | 41,543 | 52.8 | 35,795 | 49.1 |
| Vagrancy | 9,795 | 4.3 | 453 | 1.4 | 1,626 | 3.6 | 2,744 | 3.5 | 4,972 | 6.8 |
| All other offenses (except traffic) | 1,534,972 | 670.7 | 149,693 | 463.4 | 296,119 | 658.4 | 590,122 | 749.6 | 499,038 | 685.0 |
| Suspicion | 238 | 0.1 | 57 | 0.2 | 18 | * | 17 | * | 146 | 0.2 |
| Curfew and loitering law violations | 8,210 | 3.6 | 261 | 0.8 | 2,771 | 6.2 | 2,836 | 3.6 | 2,342 | 3.2 |

\* = Less than one-tenth of 1 percent.
1 Does not include suspicion.   2 Violent crimes are offenses of murder and nonnegligent manslaughter, rape, robbery, and aggravated assault. Property crimes are offenses of burglary, larceny-theft, motor vehicle theft, and arson.   3 The rape figures in this table are aggregate totals of the data submitted based on both the legacy and revised Uniform Crime Reporting definitions.

## Table 31. Number and Rate of Arrests, by Population Group, 2020

(Number, rate per 100,000 inhabitants.)

| Offense charged | Total (10,466 agencies; population 228,864,358) | | Total cities (7,634 cities; population 159,832,632) | | Group I (72 cities, 250,000 and over; population 44,271,326) | | Group II (189 cities, 100,000 to 249,999; population 27,356,047) | | Group III (398 cities, 50,000 to 99,999; population 27,901,884) | |
|---|---|---|---|---|---|---|---|---|---|---|
| | Total | Rate | Total | Rate | Total | Rate | Total | Rate | Total | Rate |
| Total[2] | 5,291,886 | 2,312.2 | 3,851,077 | 2,409.4 | 924,243 | 2,087.7 | 653,477 | 2,388.8 | 638,180 | 2,287.2 |
| Violent crime[3] | 338,443 | 147.9 | 267,047 | 167.1 | 99,537 | 224.8 | 52,274 | 191.1 | 43,245 | 155.0 |
| Murder and nonnegligent manslaughter | 8,701 | 3.8 | 6,510 | 4.1 | 2,877 | 6.5 | 1,354 | 4.9 | 828 | 3.0 |
| Rape[4] | 14,462 | 6.3 | 10,360 | 6.5 | 3,214 | 7.3 | 1,767 | 6.5 | 1,699 | 6.1 |
| Robbery | 48,035 | 21.0 | 41,569 | 26.0 | 18,541 | 41.9 | 7,707 | 28.2 | 6,468 | 23.2 |
| Aggravated assault | 267,245 | 116.8 | 208,608 | 130.5 | 74,905 | 169.2 | 41,446 | 151.5 | 34,250 | 122.8 |
| Property crime[3] | 611,731 | 267.3 | 506,199 | 316.7 | 114,060 | 257.6 | 85,923 | 314.1 | 87,236 | 312.7 |
| Burglary | 104,535 | 45.7 | 80,714 | 50.5 | 24,305 | 54.9 | 15,073 | 55.1 | 13,191 | 47.3 |
| Larceny-theft | 442,016 | 193.1 | 375,128 | 234.7 | 72,545 | 163.9 | 60,638 | 221.7 | 66,049 | 236.7 |
| Motor vehicle theft | 58,326 | 25.5 | 44,997 | 28.2 | 15,633 | 35.3 | 9,138 | 33.4 | 7,094 | 25.4 |
| Arson | 6,854 | 3.0 | 5,360 | 3.4 | 1,577 | 3.6 | 1,074 | 3.9 | 902 | 3.2 |
| Other assaults | 633,704 | 276.9 | 490,395 | 306.8 | 140,917 | 318.3 | 86,010 | 314.4 | 82,501 | 295.7 |
| Forgery and counterfeiting | 22,559 | 9.9 | 17,093 | 10.7 | 2,872 | 6.5 | 2,933 | 10.7 | 3,137 | 11.2 |
| Fraud | 54,756 | 23.9 | 40,644 | 25.4 | 7,754 | 17.5 | 5,888 | 21.5 | 6,964 | 25.0 |
| Embezzlement | 6,592 | 2.9 | 5,322 | 3.3 | 1,515 | 3.4 | 794 | 2.9 | 981 | 3.5 |
| Stolen property; buying, receiving, possessing | 61,868 | 27.0 | 46,638 | 29.2 | 14,083 | 31.8 | 8,560 | 31.3 | 8,596 | 30.8 |
| Vandalism | 121,403 | 53.0 | 96,164 | 60.2 | 27,373 | 61.8 | 16,463 | 60.2 | 16,242 | 58.2 |
| Weapons; carrying, possessing, etc. | 115,832 | 50.6 | 88,908 | 55.6 | 35,855 | 81.0 | 15,984 | 58.4 | 12,559 | 45.0 |
| Prostitution and commercialized vice | 11,754 | 5.1 | 10,617 | 6.6 | 7,381 | 16.7 | 1,651 | 6.0 | 712 | 2.6 |
| Sex offenses (except forcible rape and prostitution) | 22,065 | 9.6 | 16,162 | 10.1 | 5,040 | 11.4 | 2,780 | 10.2 | 2,818 | 10.1 |
| Drug abuse violations | 801,546 | 350.2 | 561,935 | 351.6 | 112,526 | 254.2 | 103,839 | 379.6 | 101,925 | 365.3 |
| Gambling | 1,191 | 0.5 | 861 | 0.5 | 322 | 0.7 | 236 | 0.9 | 177 | 0.6 |
| Offenses against the family and children | 40,498 | 17.7 | 26,519 | 16.6 | 6,291 | 14.2 | 3,527 | 12.9 | 3,386 | 12.1 |
| Driving under the influence | 531,846 | 232.4 | 311,168 | 194.7 | 66,656 | 150.6 | 46,421 | 169.7 | 48,732 | 174.7 |
| Liquor laws | 70,875 | 31.0 | 53,701 | 33.6 | 6,728 | 15.2 | 6,517 | 23.8 | 6,470 | 23.2 |
| Drunkenness | 135,744 | 59.3 | 115,065 | 72.0 | 16,215 | 36.6 | 23,564 | 86.1 | 19,891 | 71.3 |
| Disorderly conduct | 156,502 | 68.4 | 128,297 | 80.3 | 22,438 | 50.7 | 19,143 | 70.0 | 19,679 | 70.5 |
| Vagrancy | 9,795 | 4.3 | 8,813 | 5.5 | 2,742 | 6.2 | 2,705 | 9.9 | 1,188 | 4.3 |
| All other offenses (except traffic) | 1,534,972 | 670.7 | 1,052,267 | 658.4 | 232,421 | 525.0 | 167,283 | 611.5 | 170,432 | 610.8 |
| Suspicion | 238 | 0.1 | 200 | 0.1 | 3 | * | 0 | 0.0 | 12 | * |
| Curfew and loitering law violations | 8,210 | 3.6 | 7,262 | 4.5 | 1,517 | 3.4 | 982 | 3.6 | 1,309 | 4.7 |

## Table 31. Number and Rate of Arrests, by Population Group, 2020—Continued

(Number, rate per 100,000 inhabitants.)

| Offense charged | Group IV (664 cities, 25,000 to 49,999; population 23,023,304) | | Group V (1,351 cities, 10,000 to 24,999; population 21,468,840) | | Group VI (4,960 cities, under 10,000; population 15,811,231) | | Metropolitan counties (1,195 agencies; population 50,082,964) | | Nonmetropolitan counties (1,637 agencies; population 18,948,762) | | Suburban areas[1] (5,475 agencies; population 94,124,752) | |
|---|---|---|---|---|---|---|---|---|---|---|---|---|
| | Total | Rate | Total | Rate | Total | Rate | Total | Rate | Total | Rate | Total | Rate |
| Total[2] | 517,766 | 2,248.9 | 558,011 | 2,599.2 | 559,400 | 3,538.0 | 983,370 | 1,963.5 | 457,439 | 2,414.1 | 1,964,322 | 2,086.9 |
| **Violent crime[3]** | 26,233 | 113.9 | 24,695 | 115.0 | 21,063 | 133.2 | 54,143 | 108.1 | 17,253 | 91.1 | 97,976 | 104.1 |
| Murder and nonnegligent manslaughter | 537 | 2.3 | 532 | 2.5 | 382 | 2.4 | 1,554 | 3.1 | 637 | 3.4 | 2,282 | 2.4 |
| Rape[4] | 1,251 | 5.4 | 1,305 | 6.1 | 1,124 | 7.1 | 2,733 | 5.5 | 1,369 | 7.2 | 4,929 | 5.2 |
| Robbery | 3,936 | 17.1 | 2,902 | 13.5 | 2,015 | 12.7 | 5,390 | 10.8 | 1,076 | 5.7 | 11,687 | 12.4 |
| Aggravated assault | 20,509 | 89.1 | 19,956 | 93.0 | 17,542 | 110.9 | 44,466 | 88.8 | 14,171 | 74.8 | 79,078 | 84.0 |
| **Property crime[3]** | 76,071 | 330.4 | 82,959 | 386.4 | 59,950 | 379.2 | 81,314 | 162.4 | 24,218 | 127.8 | 218,927 | 232.6 |
| Burglary | 10,173 | 44.2 | 9,834 | 45.8 | 8,138 | 51.5 | 16,654 | 33.3 | 7,167 | 37.8 | 33,777 | 35.9 |
| Larceny-theft | 60,701 | 263.7 | 67,948 | 316.5 | 47,247 | 298.8 | 53,892 | 107.6 | 12,996 | 68.6 | 164,967 | 175.3 |
| Motor vehicle theft | 4,575 | 19.9 | 4,553 | 21.2 | 4,004 | 25.3 | 9,729 | 19.4 | 3,600 | 19.0 | 18,095 | 19.2 |
| Arson | 622 | 2.7 | 624 | 2.9 | 561 | 3.5 | 1,039 | 2.1 | 455 | 2.4 | 2,088 | 2.2 |
| Other assaults | 63,697 | 276.7 | 62,775 | 292.4 | 54,495 | 344.7 | 102,954 | 205.6 | 40,355 | 213.0 | 212,497 | 225.8 |
| Forgery and counterfeiting | 2,562 | 11.1 | 2,627 | 12.2 | 2,962 | 18.7 | 4,244 | 8.5 | 1,222 | 6.4 | 9,273 | 9.9 |
| Fraud | 6,085 | 26.4 | 6,056 | 28.2 | 7,897 | 49.9 | 10,675 | 21.3 | 3,437 | 18.1 | 23,240 | 24.7 |
| Embezzlement | 850 | 3.7 | 696 | 3.2 | 486 | 3.1 | 979 | 2.0 | 291 | 1.5 | 2,275 | 2.4 |
| Stolen property; buying, receiving, possessing | 6,018 | 26.1 | 5,412 | 25.2 | 3,969 | 25.1 | 11,739 | 23.4 | 3,491 | 18.4 | 22,898 | 24.3 |
| Vandalism | 12,267 | 53.3 | 12,616 | 58.8 | 11,203 | 70.9 | 19,020 | 38.0 | 6,219 | 32.8 | 39,983 | 42.5 |
| Weapons; carrying, possessing, etc. | 8,707 | 37.8 | 8,244 | 38.4 | 7,559 | 47.8 | 20,177 | 40.3 | 6,747 | 35.6 | 36,425 | 38.7 |
| Prostitution and commercialized vice | 468 | 2.0 | 284 | 1.3 | 121 | 0.8 | 1,054 | 2.1 | 83 | 0.4 | 1,689 | 1.8 |
| Sex offenses (except forcible rape and prostitution) | 1,974 | 8.6 | 1,840 | 8.6 | 1,710 | 10.8 | 4,333 | 8.7 | 1,570 | 8.3 | 7,889 | 8.4 |
| Drug abuse violations | 77,694 | 337.5 | 81,110 | 377.8 | 84,841 | 536.6 | 162,238 | 323.9 | 77,373 | 408.3 | 317,731 | 337.6 |
| Gambling | 32 | 0.1 | 59 | 0.3 | 35 | 0.2 | 273 | 0.5 | 57 | 0.3 | 359 | 0.4 |
| Offenses against the family and children | 3,781 | 16.4 | 4,064 | 18.9 | 5,470 | 34.6 | 8,915 | 17.8 | 5,064 | 26.7 | 15,426 | 16.4 |
| Driving under the influence | 44,414 | 192.9 | 51,461 | 239.7 | 53,484 | 338.3 | 140,244 | 280.0 | 80,434 | 424.5 | 235,930 | 250.7 |
| Liquor laws | 7,642 | 33.2 | 10,203 | 47.5 | 16,141 | 102.1 | 9,189 | 18.3 | 7,985 | 42.1 | 27,056 | 28.7 |
| Drunkenness | 14,789 | 64.2 | 15,990 | 74.5 | 24,616 | 155.7 | 14,141 | 28.2 | 6,538 | 34.5 | 39,762 | 42.2 |
| Disorderly conduct | 19,059 | 82.8 | 22,277 | 103.8 | 25,701 | 162.5 | 18,076 | 36.1 | 10,129 | 53.5 | 55,216 | 58.7 |
| Vagrancy | 892 | 3.9 | 659 | 3.1 | 627 | 4.0 | 803 | 1.6 | 179 | 0.9 | 2,126 | 2.3 |
| All other offenses (except traffic) | 143,434 | 623.0 | 162,716 | 757.9 | 175,981 | 1,113.0 | 318,146 | 635.2 | 164,559 | 868.4 | 594,985 | 632.1 |
| Suspicion | 16 | 0.1 | 54 | 0.3 | 115 | 0.7 | 3 | * | 35 | 0.2 | 122 | 0.1 |
| Curfew and loitering law violations | 1,097 | 4.8 | 1,268 | 5.9 | 1,089 | 6.9 | 713 | 1.4 | 235 | 1.2 | 2,659 | 2.8 |

* = Less than one-tenth of one percent.
1 Suburban areas include law enforcement agencies in cities with less than 50,000 inhabitants and county law enforcement agencies that are within a Metropolitan Statistical Area. Suburban areas exclude all metropolitan agencies associated with a principal city. The agencies associated with suburban areas also appear in other groups within this table.   2 Does not include suspicion.   3 Violent crimes are offenses of murder and nonnegligent manslaughter, forcible rape, robbery, and aggravated assault. Property crimes are offenses of burglary, larceny-theft, motor vehicle theft, and arson.   4 The rape figures in this table are aggregate totals of the data submitted based on both the legacy and revised Uniform Crime Reporting definitions.

## Table 32. Ten-Year Arrest Trends, 2011 and 2020

(Number, percent change; 8,708 agencies; 2020 estimated population 180,606,800; 2011 estimated population 170,682,854.)

| Offense charged | Number of persons arrested | | | | | | | | |
|---|---|---|---|---|---|---|---|---|---|
| | Total, all ages | | | Under 18 years of age | | | 18 years of age and over | | |
| | 2011 | 2020 | Percent change | 2011 | 2020 | Percent change | 2011 | 2020 | Percent change |
| Total[1] | 6,440,166 | 4,136,575 | -35.8 | 768,471 | 240,121 | -68.8 | 5,671,695 | 3,896,454 | -31.3 |
| Violent crime[2] | 267,941 | 247,966 | -7.5 | 31,103 | 17,730 | -43.0 | 236,838 | 230,236 | -2.8 |
| Murder and nonnegligent manslaughter | 5,095 | 6,135 | +20.4 | 376 | 456 | +21.3 | 4,719 | 5,679 | +20.3 |
| Rape[3] | 10,230 | 11,006 | NA | 1,557 | 1,661 | | 8,673 | 9,345 | NA |
| Robbery | 48,155 | 32,700 | -32.1 | 9,965 | 5,595 | -43.9 | 38,190 | 27,105 | -29.0 |
| Aggravated assault | 204,461 | 198,125 | -3.1 | 19,205 | 10,018 | -47.8 | 185,256 | 188,107 | +1.5 |
| Property crime[2] | 878,975 | 490,655 | -44.2 | 183,084 | 42,776 | -76.6 | 695,891 | 447,879 | -35.6 |
| Burglary | 160,004 | 81,350 | -49.2 | 33,098 | 8,251 | -75.1 | 126,906 | 73,099 | -42.4 |
| Larceny-theft | 680,688 | 359,412 | -47.2 | 140,780 | 27,417 | -80.5 | 539,908 | 331,995 | -38.5 |
| Motor vehicle theft | 32,157 | 44,419 | +38.1 | 6,454 | 6,387 | -1.0 | 25,703 | 38,032 | +48.0 |
| Arson | 6,126 | 5,474 | -10.6 | 2,752 | 721 | -73.8 | 3,374 | 4,753 | +40.9 |
| Other assaults | 650,128 | 484,992 | -25.4 | 98,892 | 39,639 | -59.9 | 551,236 | 445,353 | -19.2 |
| Forgery and counterfeiting | 36,910 | 18,761 | -49.2 | 848 | 285 | -66.4 | 36,062 | 18,476 | -48.8 |
| Fraud | 92,521 | 44,734 | -51.6 | 2,973 | 1,517 | -49.0 | 89,548 | 43,217 | -51.7 |
| Embezzlement | 9,016 | 5,358 | -40.6 | 224 | 270 | +20.5 | 8,792 | 5,088 | -42.1 |
| Stolen property; buying, receiving, possessing | 53,257 | 48,649 | -8.7 | 7,828 | 4,304 | -45.0 | 45,429 | 44,345 | -2.4 |
| Vandalism | 125,018 | 92,761 | -25.8 | 36,960 | 13,680 | -63.0 | 88,058 | 79,081 | -10.2 |
| Weapons; carrying, possessing, etc. | 75,788 | 82,728 | +9.2 | 14,392 | 5,666 | -60.6 | 61,396 | 77,062 | +25.5 |
| Prostitution and commercialized vice | 16,099 | 5,081 | -68.4 | 310 | 39 | -87.4 | 15,789 | 5,042 | -68.1 |
| Sex offenses (except forcible rape and prostitution) | 35,350 | 17,104 | -51.6 | 6,840 | 2,229 | -67.4 | 28,510 | 14,875 | -47.8 |
| Drug abuse violations | 759,311 | 645,454 | -15.0 | 77,623 | 24,723 | -68.1 | 681,688 | 620,731 | -8.9 |
| Gambling | 1,523 | 888 | -41.7 | 91 | 31 | -65.9 | 1,432 | 857 | -40.2 |
| Offenses against the family and children | 67,172 | 31,872 | -52.6 | 1,923 | 1,368 | -28.9 | 65,249 | 30,504 | -53.2 |
| Driving under the influence | 626,737 | 375,190 | -40.1 | 5,690 | 3,090 | -45.7 | 621,047 | 372,100 | -40.1 |
| Liquor laws | 257,232 | 58,057 | -77.4 | 52,527 | 10,732 | -79.6 | 204,705 | 47,325 | -76.9 |
| Drunkenness | 297,165 | 110,581 | -62.8 | 7,033 | 1,262 | -82.1 | 290,132 | 109,319 | -62.3 |
| Disorderly conduct | 277,249 | 127,096 | -54.2 | 67,460 | 14,470 | -78.6 | 209,789 | 112,626 | -46.3 |
| Vagrancy | 10,490 | 6,631 | -36.8 | 536 | 145 | -72.9 | 9,954 | 6,486 | -34.8 |
| All other offenses (except traffic) | 1,873,768 | 1,235,290 | -34.1 | 143,618 | 49,438 | -65.6 | 1,730,150 | 1,185,852 | -31.5 |
| Suspicion | 225 | 156 | -30.7 | 22 | 21 | -4.5 | 203 | 135 | -33.5 |
| Curfew and loitering law violations | 28,516 | 6,727 | -76.4 | 28,516 | 6,727 | -76.4 | NA | NA | NA |

NA = Not available.

1 Does not include suspicion.   2 Violent crimes are offenses of murder and nonnegligent manslaughter, rape, robbery, and aggravated assault.   Property crimes are offenses of burglary, larceny-theft, motor vehicle theft, and arson.   3 The 2011 rape figures are based on the legacy definition, and the 2020 rape figures are aggregate totals based on both the legacy and revised Uniform Crime Reporting definitions. For this reason, a percent change is not provided.

## Table 33. Ten-Year Arrest Trends, by Age and Sex, 2011 and 2020

(Number, percent change; 8,708 agencies; 2020 estimated population 180,606,800; 2011 estimated population 170,682,854.)

| Offense charged | Male | | | | | | Female | | | | | |
|---|---|---|---|---|---|---|---|---|---|---|---|---|
| | Total | | | Under 18 | | | Total | | | Under 18 | | |
| | 2011 | 2020 | Percent change | 2011 | 2020 | Percent change | 2011 | 2020 | Percent change | 2011 | 2020 | Percent change |
| **Total[1]** | 4,739,491 | 3,025,473 | -36.2 | 538,477 | 169,388 | -68.5 | 1,700,675 | 1,111,102 | -34.7 | 229,994 | 70,733 | -69.2 |
| **Violent crime[2]** | 215,616 | 196,651 | -8.8 | 25,625 | 14,343 | -44.0 | 52,325 | 51,315 | -1.9 | 5,478 | 3,387 | -38.2 |
| Murder and nonnegligent manslaughter | 4,474 | 5,364 | +19.9 | 347 | 418 | +20.5 | 621 | 771 | +24.2 | 29 | 38 | +31.0 |
| Rape[3] | 10,087 | 10,729 | | 1,518 | 1,593 | NA | 143 | 277 | | 39 | 68 | NA |
| Robbery | 42,033 | 27,658 | -34.2 | 9,047 | 4,911 | -45.7 | 6,122 | 5,042 | -17.6 | 918 | 684 | -25.5 |
| Aggravated assault | 159,022 | 152,900 | -3.8 | 14,713 | 7,421 | -49.6 | 45,439 | 45,225 | -0.5 | 4,492 | 2,597 | -42.2 |
| **Property crime[2]** | 544,261 | 318,610 | -41.5 | 115,101 | 30,237 | -73.7 | 334,714 | 172,045 | -48.6 | 67,983 | 12,539 | -81.6 |
| Burglary | 132,876 | 65,334 | -50.8 | 28,721 | 7,097 | -75.3 | 27,128 | 16,016 | -41.0 | 4,377 | 1,154 | -73.6 |
| Larceny-theft | 380,270 | 214,514 | -43.6 | 78,707 | 17,452 | -77.8 | 300,418 | 144,898 | -51.8 | 62,073 | 9,965 | -83.9 |
| Motor vehicle theft | 26,042 | 34,434 | +32.2 | 5,324 | 5,083 | -4.5 | 6,115 | 9,985 | +63.3 | 1,130 | 1,304 | +15.4 |
| Arson | 5,073 | 4,328 | -14.7 | 2,349 | 605 | -74.2 | 1,053 | 1,146 | +8.8 | 403 | 116 | -71.2 |
| Other assaults | 471,484 | 346,595 | -26.5 | 63,970 | 24,694 | -61.4 | 178,644 | 138,397 | -22.5 | 34,922 | 14,945 | -57.2 |
| Forgery and counterfeiting | 22,700 | 12,617 | -44.4 | 588 | 226 | -61.6 | 14,210 | 6,144 | -56.8 | 260 | 59 | -77.3 |
| Fraud | 53,577 | 28,563 | -46.7 | 1,959 | 997 | -49.1 | 38,944 | 16,171 | -58.5 | 1,014 | 520 | -48.7 |
| Embezzlement | 4,428 | 2,673 | -39.6 | 138 | 143 | +3.6 | 4,588 | 2,685 | -41.5 | 86 | 127 | +47.7 |
| Stolen property; buying, receiving, possession | 42,232 | 38,329 | -9.2 | 6,444 | 3,625 | -43.7 | 11,025 | 10,320 | -6.4 | 1,384 | 679 | -50.9 |
| Vandalism | 101,433 | 71,362 | -29.6 | 31,320 | 10,860 | -65.3 | 23,585 | 21,399 | -9.3 | 5,640 | 2,820 | -50.0 |
| Weapons; carrying, possessing, etc. | 69,583 | 74,689 | +7.3 | 12,986 | 5,197 | -60.0 | 6,205 | 8,039 | +29.6 | 1,406 | 469 | -66.6 |
| Prostitution and commercialized vice | 5,296 | 2,526 | -52.3 | 71 | 21 | -70.4 | 10,803 | 2,555 | -76.3 | 239 | 18 | -92.5 |
| Sex offenses (except forcible rape and prostitution) | 32,847 | 16,174 | -50.8 | 6,052 | 2,011 | -66.8 | 2,503 | 930 | -62.8 | 788 | 218 | -72.3 |
| Drug abuse violations | 599,260 | 481,073 | -19.7 | 63,672 | 18,413 | -71.1 | 160,051 | 164,381 | +2.7 | 13,951 | 6,310 | -54.8 |
| Gambling | 1,163 | 587 | -49.5 | 79 | 25 | -68.4 | 360 | 301 | -16.4 | 12 | 6 | -50.0 |
| Offenses against the family and children | 51,527 | 21,806 | -57.7 | 1,174 | 777 | -33.8 | 15,645 | 10,066 | -35.7 | 749 | 591 | -21.1 |
| Driving under the influence | 469,662 | 277,711 | -40.9 | 4,207 | 2,273 | -46.0 | 157,075 | 97,479 | -37.9 | 1,483 | 817 | -44.9 |
| Liquor laws | 178,929 | 40,560 | -77.3 | 31,330 | 6,282 | -79.9 | 78,303 | 17,497 | -77.7 | 21,197 | 4,450 | -79.0 |
| Drunkenness | 241,900 | 85,992 | -64.5 | 5,175 | 845 | -83.7 | 55,265 | 24,589 | -55.5 | 1,858 | 417 | -77.6 |
| Disorderly conduct | 199,498 | 89,536 | -55.1 | 44,100 | 9,167 | -79.2 | 77,751 | 37,560 | -51.7 | 23,360 | 5,303 | -77.3 |
| Vagrancy | 8,413 | 5,180 | -38.4 | 445 | 113 | -74.6 | 2,077 | 1,451 | -30.1 | 91 | 32 | -64.8 |
| All other offenses (except traffic) | 1,406,293 | 909,860 | -35.3 | 104,652 | 34,760 | -66.8 | 467,475 | 325,430 | -30.4 | 38,966 | 14,678 | -62.3 |
| Suspicion | 175 | 91 | -48.0 | 19 | 12 | -36.8 | 50 | 65 | +30.0 | 3 | 9 | +200.0 |
| Curfew and loitering law violations | 19,389 | 4,379 | -77.4 | 19,389 | 4,379 | -77.4 | 9,127 | 2,348 | -74.3 | 9,127 | 2,348 | -74.3 |

NA = Not available.

1 Does not include suspicion.   2 Violent crimes are offenses of murder and nonnegligent manslaughter, rape, robbery, and aggravated assault.  Property crimes are offenses of burglary, larceny-theft, motor vehicle theft, and arson.   3 The 2011 rape figures are based on the legacy definition, and the 2020 rape figures are aggregate totals based on both the legacy and revised Uniform Crime Reporting definitions. For this reason, a percent change is not provided.

## Table 34. Five-Year Arrest Trends, by Age, 2016 and 2020

(Number, percent change; 9,329 agencies; 2020 estimated population 200,962,238; 2016 estimated population 196,853,348.)

| Offense charged | Number of persons arrested | | | | | | | | |
|---|---|---|---|---|---|---|---|---|---|
| | Total, all ages | | | Under 18 years of age | | | 18 years of age and over | | |
| | 2016 | 2020 | Percent change | 2016 | 2020 | Percent change | 2016 | 2020 | Percent change |
| **Total[1]** | 6,479,915 | 4,768,317 | -26.4 | 512,375 | 267,338 | -47.8 | 5,967,540 | 4,500,979 | -24.6 |
| **Violent crime[2]** | 306,674 | 292,029 | -4.8 | 28,750 | 20,918 | -27.2 | 277,924 | 271,111 | -2.5 |
| Murder and nonnegligent manslaughter | 6,585 | 7,250 | +10.1 | 460 | 535 | +16.3 | 6,125 | 6,715 | +9.6 |
| Rape[3] | 13,839 | 12,609 | -8.9 | 2,152 | 1,812 | -15.8 | 11,687 | 10,797 | -7.6 |
| Robbery | 53,164 | 40,083 | -24.6 | 9,759 | 6,957 | -28.7 | 43,405 | 33,126 | -23.7 |
| Aggravated assault | 233,086 | 232,087 | -0.4 | 16,379 | 11,614 | -29.1 | 216,707 | 220,473 | +1.7 |
| **Property crime[2]** | 829,059 | 551,243 | -33.5 | 112,981 | 47,291 | -58.1 | 716,078 | 503,952 | -29.6 |
| Burglary | 128,847 | 93,195 | -27.7 | 19,778 | 9,433 | -52.3 | 109,069 | 83,762 | -23.2 |
| Larceny-theft | 644,576 | 401,887 | -37.7 | 83,553 | 29,845 | -64.3 | 561,023 | 372,042 | -33.7 |
| Motor vehicle theft | 50,192 | 49,965 | -0.5 | 8,174 | 7,237 | -11.5 | 42,018 | 42,728 | +1.7 |
| Arson | 5,444 | 6,196 | +13.8 | 1,476 | 776 | -47.4 | 3,968 | 5,420 | +36.6 |
| Other assaults | 654,284 | 563,102 | -13.9 | 76,185 | 44,961 | -41.0 | 578,099 | 518,141 | -10.4 |
| Forgery and counterfeiting | 34,923 | 20,762 | -40.5 | 737 | 304 | -58.8 | 34,186 | 20,458 | -40.2 |
| Fraud | 78,230 | 49,721 | -36.4 | 2,498 | 1,658 | -33.6 | 75,732 | 48,063 | -36.5 |
| Embezzlement | 10,236 | 6,166 | -39.8 | 333 | 285 | -14.4 | 9,903 | 5,881 | -40.6 |
| Stolen property; buying, receiving, possessing | 60,363 | 57,208 | -5.2 | 6,556 | 5,220 | -20.4 | 53,807 | 51,988 | -3.4 |
| Vandalism | 121,150 | 109,530 | -9.6 | 24,312 | 15,005 | -38.3 | 96,838 | 94,525 | -2.4 |
| Weapons; carrying, possessing, etc. | 91,760 | 99,827 | +8.8 | 11,092 | 6,630 | -40.2 | 80,668 | 93,197 | +15.5 |
| Prostitution and commercialized vice | 18,795 | 8,492 | -54.8 | 294 | 74 | -74.8 | 18,501 | 8,418 | -54.5 |
| Sex offenses (except forcible rape and prostitution) | 29,938 | 20,310 | -32.2 | 5,085 | 2,542 | -50.0 | 24,853 | 17,768 | -28.5 |
| Drug abuse violations | 956,732 | 726,791 | -24.0 | 60,401 | 26,608 | -55.9 | 896,331 | 700,183 | -21.9 |
| Gambling | 1,197 | 997 | -16.7 | 77 | 38 | -50.6 | 1,120 | 959 | -14.4 |
| Offenses against the family and children | 56,169 | 36,340 | -35.3 | 2,341 | 1,436 | -38.7 | 53,828 | 34,904 | -35.2 |
| Driving under the influence | 614,726 | 474,472 | -22.8 | 3,962 | 3,598 | -9.2 | 610,764 | 470,874 | -22.9 |
| Liquor laws | 142,435 | 65,069 | -54.3 | 23,444 | 11,435 | -51.2 | 118,991 | 53,634 | -54.9 |
| Drunkenness | 219,596 | 125,293 | -42.9 | 3,055 | 1,408 | -53.9 | 216,541 | 123,885 | -42.8 |
| Disorderly conduct | 207,631 | 143,595 | -30.8 | 36,665 | 15,961 | -56.5 | 170,966 | 127,634 | -25.3 |
| Vagrancy | 14,185 | 9,189 | -35.2 | 502 | 184 | -63.3 | 13,683 | 9,005 | -34.2 |
| All other offenses (except traffic) | 2,015,881 | 1,400,889 | -30.5 | 97,154 | 54,490 | -43.9 | 1,918,727 | 1,346,399 | -29.8 |
| Suspicion | 313 | 189 | -39.6 | 25 | 23 | -8.0 | 288 | 166 | -42.4 |
| Curfew and loitering law violations | 15,951 | 7,292 | -54.3 | 15,951 | 7,292 | -54.3 | NA | NA | NA |

NA = Not available.
1 Does not include suspicion.   2 Violent crimes are offenses of murder and nonnegligent manslaughter, rape, robbery, and aggravated assault.  Property crimes are offenses of burglary, larceny-theft, motor vehicle theft, and arson.   3 The rape figures in this table are aggregate totals of the data submitted based on both the legacy and revised Uniform Crime Reporting definitions.

## Table 35. Five-Year Arrest Trends, by Age and Sex, 2016 and 2020

(Number, percent change; 9,329 agencies; 2020 estimated population 200,962,238; 2016 estimated population 196,853,348.)

| Offense charged | Male | | | | | | Female | | | | | |
|---|---|---|---|---|---|---|---|---|---|---|---|---|
| | Total | | | Under 18 | | | Total | | | Under 18 | | |
| | 2016 | 2020 | Percent change | 2016 | 2020 | Percent change | 2016 | 2020 | Percent change | 2016 | 2020 | Percent change |
| **Total[1]** | 4,711,002 | 3,499,671 | -25.7 | 358,548 | 189,199 | -47.2 | 1,768,913 | 1,268,646 | -28.3 | 153,827 | 78,139 | -49.2 |
| **Violent crime[2]** | 243,347 | 231,354 | -4.9 | 23,328 | 16,993 | -27.2 | 63,327 | 60,675 | -4.2 | 5,422 | 3,925 | -27.6 |
| Murder and nonnegligent manslaughter | 5,766 | 6,316 | +9.5 | 407 | 490 | +20.4 | 819 | 934 | +14.0 | 53 | 45 | -15.1 |
| Rape[3] | 13,433 | 12,248 | -8.8 | 2,054 | 1,738 | -15.4 | 406 | 361 | -11.1 | 98 | 74 | -24.5 |
| Robbery | 45,253 | 33,984 | -24.9 | 8,651 | 6,130 | -29.1 | 7,911 | 6,099 | -22.9 | 1,108 | 827 | -25.4 |
| Aggravated assault | 178,895 | 178,806 | +0.0 | 12,216 | 8,635 | -29.3 | 54,191 | 53,281 | -1.7 | 4,163 | 2,979 | -28.4 |
| **Property crime[2]** | 517,879 | 361,275 | -30.2 | 74,286 | 33,716 | -54.6 | 311,180 | 189,968 | -39.0 | 38,695 | 13,575 | -64.9 |
| Burglary | 104,047 | 75,184 | -27.7 | 17,407 | 8,157 | -53.1 | 24,800 | 18,011 | -27.4 | 2,371 | 1,276 | -46.2 |
| Larceny-theft | 370,695 | 242,442 | -34.6 | 49,118 | 19,122 | -61.1 | 273,881 | 159,445 | -41.8 | 34,435 | 10,723 | -68.9 |
| Motor vehicle theft | 38,828 | 38,733 | -0.2 | 6,495 | 5,784 | -10.9 | 11,364 | 11,232 | -1.2 | 1,679 | 1,453 | -13.5 |
| Arson | 4,309 | 4,916 | +14.1 | 1,266 | 653 | -48.4 | 1,135 | 1,280 | +12.8 | 210 | 123 | -41.4 |
| Other assaults | 467,988 | 401,421 | -14.2 | 48,273 | 27,889 | -42.2 | 186,296 | 161,681 | -13.2 | 27,912 | 17,072 | -38.8 |
| Forgery and counterfeiting | 22,625 | 14,104 | -37.7 | 537 | 242 | -54.9 | 12,298 | 6,658 | -45.9 | 200 | 62 | -69.0 |
| Fraud | 48,435 | 32,154 | -33.6 | 1,676 | 1,087 | -35.1 | 29,795 | 17,567 | -41.0 | 822 | 571 | -30.5 |
| Embezzlement | 5,056 | 3,158 | -37.5 | 179 | 152 | -15.1 | 5,180 | 3,008 | -41.9 | 154 | 133 | -13.6 |
| Stolen property; buying, receiving, possessing | 47,255 | 45,254 | -4.2 | 5,483 | 4,433 | -19.2 | 13,108 | 11,954 | -8.8 | 1,073 | 787 | -26.7 |
| Vandalism | 95,001 | 84,079 | -11.5 | 20,205 | 11,890 | -41.2 | 26,149 | 25,451 | -2.7 | 4,107 | 3,115 | -24.2 |
| Weapons; carrying, possessing, etc. | 83,042 | 90,256 | +8.7 | 9,906 | 6,074 | -38.7 | 8,718 | 9,571 | +9.8 | 1,186 | 556 | -53.1 |
| Prostitution and commercialized vice | 7,101 | 3,613 | -49.1 | 71 | 28 | -60.6 | 11,694 | 4,879 | -58.3 | 223 | 46 | -79.4 |
| Sex offenses (except forcible rape and prostitution) | 27,698 | 19,113 | -31.0 | 4,451 | 2,295 | -48.4 | 2,240 | 1,197 | -46.6 | 634 | 247 | -61.0 |
| Drug abuse violations | 726,930 | 544,788 | -25.1 | 46,068 | 19,839 | -56.9 | 229,802 | 182,003 | -20.8 | 14,333 | 6,769 | -52.8 |
| Gambling | 958 | 679 | -29.1 | 70 | 32 | -54.3 | 239 | 318 | +33.1 | 7 | 6 | -14.3 |
| Offenses against the family and children | 40,138 | 24,698 | -38.5 | 1,417 | 825 | -41.8 | 16,031 | 11,642 | -27.4 | 924 | 611 | -33.9 |
| Driving under the influence | 456,806 | 352,972 | -22.7 | 2,930 | 2,657 | -9.3 | 157,920 | 121,500 | -23.1 | 1,032 | 941 | -8.8 |
| Liquor laws | 99,619 | 45,671 | -54.2 | 14,053 | 6,688 | -52.4 | 42,816 | 19,398 | -54.7 | 9,391 | 4,747 | -49.5 |
| Drunkenness | 175,006 | 97,346 | -44.4 | 2,144 | 939 | -56.2 | 44,590 | 27,947 | -37.3 | 911 | 469 | -48.5 |
| Disorderly conduct | 147,496 | 100,841 | -31.6 | 23,488 | 10,085 | -57.1 | 60,135 | 42,754 | -28.9 | 13,177 | 5,876 | -55.4 |
| Vagrancy | 10,843 | 7,036 | -35.1 | 370 | 135 | -63.5 | 3,342 | 2,153 | -35.6 | 132 | 49 | -62.9 |
| All other offenses (except traffic) | 1,477,228 | 1,035,073 | -29.9 | 69,062 | 38,414 | -44.4 | 538,653 | 365,816 | -32.1 | 28,092 | 16,076 | -42.8 |
| Suspicion | 246 | 122 | -50.4 | 18 | 13 | -27.8 | 67 | 67 | +0.0 | 7 | 10 | +42.9 |
| Curfew and loitering law violations | 10,551 | 4,786 | -54.6 | 10,551 | 4,786 | -54.6 | 5,400 | 2,506 | -53.6 | 5,400 | 2,506 | -53.6 |

1 Does not include suspicion.   2 Violent crimes are offenses of murder and nonnegligent manslaughter, rape, robbery, and aggravated assault.  Property crimes are offenses of burglary, larceny-theft, motor vehicle theft, and arson.   3 The rape figures in this table are aggregate totals of the data submitted based on both the legacy and revised Uniform Crime Reporting definitions.

## Table 36. Year Over Previous Year Arrest Trends, 2019–2020

(Number, percent change; 9,245 agencies; 2020 estimated population 199,329,726; 2019 estimated population 198,464,294.)

| Offense charged | Number of persons arrested | | | | | | | | | | | |
| --- | --- | --- | --- | --- | --- | --- | --- | --- | --- | --- | --- | --- |
| | Total, all ages | | | Under 15 years of age | | | Under 18 years of age | | | 18 years of age and over | | |
| | 2019 | 2020 | Percent change | 2019 | 2020 | Percent change | 2019 | 2020 | Percent change | 2019 | 2020 | Percent change |
| Total[1] | 5,945,932 | 4,620,603 | -22.3 | 133,506 | 76,275 | -42.9 | 415,981 | 263,317 | -36.7 | 5,529,951 | 4,357,286 | -21.2 |
| Violent crime[2] | 303,843 | 291,290 | -4.1 | 8,882 | 5,761 | -35.1 | 28,961 | 21,370 | -26.2 | 274,882 | 269,920 | -1.8 |
| Murder and nonnegligent manslaughter | 6,424 | 7,509 | +16.9 | 50 | 59 | +18.0 | 510 | 570 | +11.8 | 5,914 | 6,939 | +17.3 |
| Rape[3] | 14,601 | 12,742 | -12.7 | 1,122 | 784 | -30.1 | 2,524 | 1,832 | -27.4 | 12,077 | 10,910 | -9.7 |
| Robbery | 46,622 | 41,145 | -11.7 | 2,038 | 1,543 | -24.3 | 9,664 | 7,368 | -23.8 | 36,958 | 33,777 | -8.6 |
| Aggravated assault | 236,196 | 229,894 | -2.7 | 5,672 | 3,375 | -40.5 | 16,263 | 11,600 | -28.7 | 219,933 | 218,294 | -0.7 |
| Property crime[2] | 686,252 | 542,450 | -21.0 | 22,677 | 13,623 | -39.9 | 75,353 | 47,383 | -37.1 | 610,899 | 495,067 | -19.0 |
| Burglary | 103,980 | 91,817 | -11.7 | 4,119 | 3,041 | -26.2 | 12,807 | 9,561 | -25.3 | 91,173 | 82,256 | -9.8 |
| Larceny-theft | 527,116 | 394,234 | -25.2 | 15,731 | 8,007 | -49.1 | 53,216 | 29,599 | -44.4 | 473,900 | 364,635 | -23.1 |
| Motor vehicle theft | 49,783 | 50,257 | +1.0 | 2,240 | 2,146 | -4.2 | 8,281 | 7,430 | -10.3 | 41,502 | 42,827 | +3.2 |
| Arson | 5,373 | 6,142 | +14.3 | 587 | 429 | -26.9 | 1,049 | 793 | -24.4 | 4,324 | 5,349 | +23.7 |
| Other assaults | 613,181 | 553,284 | -9.8 | 31,927 | 17,000 | -46.8 | 73,463 | 43,819 | -40.4 | 539,718 | 509,465 | -5.6 |
| Forgery and counterfeiting | 28,784 | 20,156 | -30.0 | 89 | 47 | -47.2 | 557 | 305 | -45.2 | 28,227 | 19,851 | -29.7 |
| Fraud | 70,458 | 48,575 | -31.1 | 553 | 433 | -21.7 | 2,323 | 1,672 | -28.0 | 68,135 | 46,903 | -31.2 |
| Embezzlement | 9,056 | 5,928 | -34.5 | 17 | 9 | -47.1 | 365 | 287 | -21.4 | 8,691 | 5,641 | -35.1 |
| Stolen property; buying, receiving, possessing | 57,805 | 55,940 | -3.2 | 1,254 | 1,138 | -9.3 | 5,914 | 5,388 | -8.9 | 51,891 | 50,552 | -2.6 |
| Vandalism | 110,704 | 106,599 | -3.7 | 8,454 | 5,826 | -31.1 | 19,353 | 14,652 | -24.3 | 91,351 | 91,947 | +0.7 |
| Weapons; carrying, possessing, etc. | 94,199 | 99,430 | +5.6 | 2,844 | 1,298 | -54.4 | 9,830 | 6,774 | -31.1 | 84,369 | 92,656 | +9.8 |
| Prostitution and commercialized vice | 12,360 | 6,864 | -44.5 | 22 | 6 | -72.7 | 102 | 36 | -64.7 | 12,258 | 6,828 | -44.3 |
| Sex offenses (except forcible rape and prostitution) | 24,572 | 19,085 | -22.3 | 1,999 | 1,206 | -39.7 | 4,141 | 2,473 | -40.3 | 20,431 | 16,612 | -18.7 |
| Drug abuse violations | 927,890 | 709,607 | -23.5 | 9,337 | 3,978 | -57.4 | 47,811 | 25,971 | -45.7 | 880,079 | 683,636 | -22.3 |
| Gambling | 1,286 | 945 | -26.5 | 9 | 7 | -22.2 | 71 | 37 | -47.9 | 1,215 | 908 | -25.3 |
| Offenses against the family and children | 49,486 | 35,667 | -27.9 | 632 | 429 | -32.1 | 1,730 | 1,346 | -22.2 | 47,756 | 34,321 | -28.1 |
| Driving under the influence | 576,138 | 465,982 | -19.1 | 79 | 50 | -36.7 | 3,208 | 3,500 | +9.1 | 572,930 | 462,482 | -19.3 |
| Liquor laws | 95,438 | 62,473 | -34.5 | 2,296 | 1,355 | -41.0 | 14,824 | 10,998 | -25.8 | 80,614 | 51,475 | -36.1 |
| Drunkenness | 182,242 | 114,892 | -37.0 | 295 | 228 | -22.7 | 2,022 | 1,292 | -36.1 | 180,220 | 113,600 | -37.0 |
| Disorderly conduct | 180,812 | 138,200 | -23.6 | 13,856 | 6,076 | -56.1 | 31,733 | 15,310 | -51.8 | 149,079 | 122,890 | -17.6 |
| Vagrancy | 11,593 | 8,531 | -26.4 | 62 | 44 | -29.0 | 229 | 186 | -18.8 | 11,364 | 8,345 | -26.6 |
| All other offenses (except traffic) | 1,900,410 | 1,327,322 | -30.2 | 25,073 | 15,231 | -39.3 | 84,568 | 53,135 | -37.2 | 1,815,842 | 1,274,187 | -29.8 |
| Suspicion | 182 | 179 | -1.6 | 2 | 7 | +250.0 | 6 | 25 | +316.7 | 176 | 154 | -12.5 |
| Curfew and loitering law violations | 9,423 | 7,383 | -21.6 | 3,149 | 2,530 | -19.7 | 9,423 | 7,383 | -21.6 | NA | NA | NA |

NA = Not available.

1 Does not include suspicion.   2 Violent crimes are offenses of murder and nonnegligent manslaughter, rape, robbery, and aggravated assault.  Property crimes are offenses of burglary, larceny-theft, motor vehicle theft, and arson.   3 The rape figures in this table are aggregate totals of the data submitted based on both the legacy and revised Uniform Crime Reporting definitions.

## Table 37. Year Over Previous Year Arrest Trends, by Age and Sex, 2019–2020

(Number, percent change; 9,245 agencies; 2020 estimated population 199,329,726; 2019 estimated population 198,464,294.)

| Offense charged | Male Total 2019 | Male Total 2020 | Male Total Percent change | Male Under 18 2019 | Male Under 18 2020 | Male Under 18 Percent change | Female Total 2019 | Female Total 2020 | Female Total Percent change | Female Under 18 2019 | Female Under 18 2020 | Female Under 18 Percent change |
|---|---|---|---|---|---|---|---|---|---|---|---|---|
| **Total[1]** | 4,303,444 | 3,395,439 | -21.1 | 289,458 | 186,781 | -35.5 | 1,642,488 | 1,225,164 | -25.4 | 126,523 | 76,536 | -39.5 |
| **Violent crime[2]** | 239,598 | 230,675 | -3.7 | 23,423 | 17,318 | -26.1 | 64,245 | 60,615 | -5.7 | 5,538 | 4,052 | -26.8 |
| Murder and nonnegligent manslaughter | 5,672 | 6,583 | +16.1 | 469 | 522 | +11.3 | 752 | 926 | +23.1 | 41 | 48 | +17.1 |
| Rape[3] | 14,082 | 12,371 | -12.2 | 2,381 | 1,755 | -26.3 | 519 | 371 | -28.5 | 143 | 77 | -46.2 |
| Robbery | 39,183 | 34,870 | -11.0 | 8,550 | 6,470 | -24.3 | 7,439 | 6,275 | -15.6 | 1,114 | 898 | -19.4 |
| Aggravated assault | 180,661 | 176,851 | -2.1 | 12,023 | 8,571 | -28.7 | 55,535 | 53,043 | -4.5 | 4,240 | 3,029 | -28.6 |
| **Property crime[2]** | 427,303 | 356,342 | -16.6 | 50,309 | 33,831 | -32.8 | 258,949 | 186,108 | -28.1 | 25,044 | 13,552 | -45.9 |
| Burglary | 82,470 | 74,329 | -9.9 | 11,036 | 8,279 | -25.0 | 21,510 | 17,488 | -18.7 | 1,771 | 1,282 | -27.6 |
| Larceny-theft | 302,522 | 238,106 | -21.3 | 31,777 | 18,915 | -40.5 | 224,594 | 156,128 | -30.5 | 21,439 | 10,684 | -50.2 |
| Motor vehicle theft | 38,102 | 39,042 | +2.5 | 6,600 | 5,968 | -9.6 | 11,681 | 11,215 | -4.0 | 1,681 | 1,462 | -13.0 |
| Arson | 4,209 | 4,865 | +15.6 | 896 | 669 | -25.3 | 1,164 | 1,277 | +9.7 | 153 | 124 | -19.0 |
| Other assaults | 434,691 | 395,816 | -8.9 | 46,030 | 27,227 | -40.8 | 178,490 | 157,468 | -11.8 | 27,433 | 16,592 | -39.5 |
| Forgery and counterfeiting | 19,186 | 13,662 | -28.8 | 428 | 245 | -42.8 | 9,598 | 6,494 | -32.3 | 129 | 60 | -53.5 |
| Fraud | 45,083 | 31,410 | -30.3 | 1,577 | 1,106 | -29.9 | 25,375 | 17,165 | -32.4 | 746 | 566 | -24.1 |
| Embezzlement | 4,468 | 3,021 | -32.4 | 199 | 152 | -23.6 | 4,588 | 2,907 | -36.6 | 166 | 135 | -18.7 |
| Stolen property; buying, receiving, possessing | 44,860 | 44,288 | -1.3 | 4,874 | 4,554 | -6.6 | 12,945 | 11,652 | -10.0 | 1,040 | 834 | -19.8 |
| Vandalism | 85,067 | 81,859 | -3.8 | 15,614 | 11,609 | -25.7 | 25,637 | 24,740 | -3.5 | 3,739 | 3,043 | -18.6 |
| Weapons; carrying, possessing, etc. | 85,093 | 89,988 | +5.8 | 8,836 | 6,231 | -29.5 | 9,106 | 9,442 | +3.7 | 994 | 543 | -45.4 |
| Prostitution and commercialized vice | 5,175 | 3,322 | -35.8 | 59 | 19 | -67.8 | 7,185 | 3,542 | -50.7 | 43 | 17 | -60.5 |
| Sex offenses (except forcible rape and prostitution) | 22,936 | 18,015 | -21.5 | 3,685 | 2,233 | -39.4 | 1,636 | 1,070 | -34.6 | 456 | 240 | -47.4 |
| Drug abuse violations | 690,924 | 531,435 | -23.1 | 35,252 | 19,378 | -45.0 | 236,966 | 178,172 | -24.8 | 12,559 | 6,593 | -47.5 |
| Gambling | 944 | 646 | -31.6 | 62 | 31 | -50.0 | 342 | 299 | -12.6 | 9 | 6 | -33.3 |
| Offenses against the family and children | 34,711 | 24,351 | -29.8 | 1,023 | 778 | -23.9 | 14,775 | 11,316 | -23.4 | 707 | 568 | -19.7 |
| Driving under the influence | 425,867 | 347,070 | -18.5 | 2,418 | 2,586 | +6.9 | 150,271 | 118,912 | -20.9 | 790 | 914 | +15.7 |
| Liquor laws | 66,077 | 43,782 | -33.7 | 8,520 | 6,453 | -24.3 | 29,361 | 18,691 | -36.3 | 6,304 | 4,545 | -27.9 |
| Drunkenness | 142,728 | 89,503 | -37.3 | 1,371 | 857 | -37.5 | 39,514 | 25,389 | -35.7 | 651 | 435 | -33.2 |
| Disorderly conduct | 127,463 | 97,138 | -23.8 | 19,993 | 9,691 | -51.5 | 53,349 | 41,062 | -23.0 | 11,740 | 5,619 | -52.1 |
| Vagrancy | 8,927 | 6,532 | -26.8 | 167 | 135 | -19.2 | 2,666 | 1,999 | -25.0 | 62 | 51 | -17.7 |
| All other offenses (except traffic) | 1,386,107 | 981,786 | -29.2 | 59,382 | 37,549 | -36.8 | 514,303 | 345,536 | -32.8 | 25,186 | 15,586 | -38.1 |
| Suspicion | 121 | 111 | -8.3 | 6 | 15 | +150.0 | 61 | 68 | +11.5 | 0 | 10 | |
| Curfew and loitering law violations | 6,236 | 4,798 | -23.1 | 6,236 | 4,798 | -23.1 | 3,187 | 2,585 | -18.9 | 3,187 | 2,585 | -18.9 |

1 Does not include suspicion.   2 Violent crimes are offenses of murder and nonnegligent manslaughter, rape, robbery, and aggravated assault.   Property crimes are offenses of burglary, larceny-theft, motor vehicle theft, and arson.   3 The rape figures in this table are aggregate totals of the data submitted based on both the legacy and revised Uniform Crime Reporting definitions.

## Table 38. Arrests, Distribution by Age, by Arrest Offense Category, 2021

(Number; percent.)

| Offense charged | Total, all ages | 18 years and over | Percent adult | Under 18 years (juvenile) | Percent juvenile | 10 years and under | 11–15 | 16–20 | 21–25 |
|---|---|---|---|---|---|---|---|---|---|
| **Total** | 4,538,284 | 4,258,863 | 93.8 | 277,552 | 6.1 | 2,928 | 142,406 | 463,302 | 641,476 |
| **Crimes Against Persons** | 816,942 | 742,283 | 90.9 | 74,426 | 9.1 | 1,109 | 44,053 | 82,894 | 115,292 |
| Assault offenses | 773,342 | 703,753 | 91.0 | 69,379 | 9.0 | 1,028 | 41,252 | 76,118 | 108,857 |
| Homicide offenses | 8,365 | 7,606 | 90.9 | 755 | 9.0 | 3 | 211 | 1,818 | 1,717 |
| Human trafficking offenses | 378 | 370 | 97.9 | 8 | 2.1 | 0 | 3 | 44 | 73 |
| Kidnapping/abduction | 11,134 | 10,824 | 97.2 | 305 | 2.7 | 0 | 127 | 994 | 1,831 |
| Sex offenses | 23,723 | 19,730 | 83.2 | 3,979 | 16.8 | 78 | 2,460 | 3,920 | 2,814 |
| **Crimes Against Property** | 700,947 | 637,540 | 91.0 | 63,183 | 9.0 | 731 | 32,638 | 85,578 | 90,635 |
| Arson | 5,083 | 4,339 | 85.4 | 741 | 14.6 | 24 | 528 | 402 | 439 |
| Bribery | 278 | 269 | 96.8 | 9 | 3.2 | 0 | 3 | 26 | 46 |
| Burglary/breaking & entering | 68,440 | 62,290 | 91.0 | 6,129 | 9.0 | 101 | 3,583 | 7,129 | 8,347 |
| Counterfeiting/forgery | 15,499 | 15,218 | 98.2 | 273 | 1.8 | 0 | 63 | 1,872 | 1,997 |
| Destruction/damage/vandalism | 99,309 | 84,764 | 85.4 | 14,525 | 14.6 | 392 | 8,682 | 13,585 | 14,335 |
| Embezzlement | 5,117 | 4,854 | 94.9 | 259 | 5.1 | 1 | 20 | 1,066 | 935 |
| Extortion/blackmail | 322 | 301 | 93.5 | 21 | 6.5 | 1 | 8 | 43 | 33 |
| Fraud offenses | 47,326 | 45,739 | 96.6 | 1,570 | 3.3 | 11 | 623 | 4,736 | 6,253 |
| Larceny-theft offenses | 340,053 | 316,824 | 93.2 | 23,128 | 6.8 | 173 | 11,182 | 35,864 | 41,259 |
| Motor vehicle theft | 44,435 | 37,701 | 84.8 | 6,715 | 15.1 | 13 | 3,621 | 6,735 | 5,921 |
| Robbery | 28,962 | 23,662 | 81.7 | 5,282 | 18.2 | 10 | 2,298 | 7,234 | 4,562 |
| Stolen property offenses | 46,123 | 41,579 | 90.1 | 4,531 | 9.8 | 5 | 2,027 | 6,886 | 6,508 |
| **Crimes Against Society** | 824,494 | 783,114 | 95.0 | 41,183 | 5.0 | 120 | 15,748 | 105,157 | 134,700 |
| Animal cruelty | 2,750 | 2,657 | 96.6 | 89 | 3.2 | 4 | 53 | 175 | 371 |
| Drug/narcotic offenses | 707,971 | 676,035 | 95.5 | 31,770 | 4.5 | 40 | 11,617 | 86,916 | 110,128 |
| Gambling offenses | 649 | 637 | 98.2 | 12 | 1.8 | 0 | 3 | 95 | 78 |
| Pornography/obscene material | 4,443 | 3,395 | 76.4 | 1,048 | 23.6 | 3 | 737 | 653 | 593 |
| Prostitution offenses | 7,928 | 7,861 | 99.2 | 66 | 0.8 | 0 | 21 | 617 | 1,484 |
| Weapon law violations | 100,753 | 92,529 | 91.8 | 8,198 | 8.1 | 73 | 3,317 | 16,701 | 22,046 |
| **Group B offenses** | 2,195,901 | 2,095,926 | 95.4 | 98,760 | 4.5 | 968 | 49,967 | 189,673 | 300,849 |
| Curfew/loitering/vagrancy violations | 14,659 | 8,837 | 60.3 | 5,817 | 39.7 | 25 | 3,396 | 2,840 | 1,017 |
| Disorderly conduct | 151,136 | 130,648 | 86.4 | 20,384 | 13.5 | 227 | 12,935 | 17,290 | 19,970 |
| Driving under the Influence | 463,100 | 459,740 | 99.3 | 3,236 | 0.7 | 1 | 207 | 27,293 | 78,194 |
| Family offenses, nonviolent | 34,251 | 32,833 | 95.9 | 1,373 | 4.0 | 40 | 809 | 1,709 | 3,877 |
| Liquor law violations | 72,753 | 61,491 | 84.5 | 11,237 | 15.4 | 10 | 2,971 | 36,485 | 6,312 |
| Trespass of real property | 149,769 | 144,229 | 96.3 | 5,468 | 3.7 | 36 | 2,932 | 9,160 | 15,006 |
| All other offenses | 1,310,233 | 1,258,148 | 96.0 | 51,245 | 3.9 | 629 | 26,717 | 94,896 | 176,473 |

## Table 38. Arrests, Distribution by Age, by Arrest Offense Category, 2021—Continued

(Number; percent.)

| Offense charged | 26–30 | 31–35 | 36–40 | 41–45 | 46–50 | 51–55 | 56–60 | 61–64 | 65 and over | Unknown age |
|---|---|---|---|---|---|---|---|---|---|---|
| **Total** | 742,471 | 710,061 | 590,232 | 420,671 | 286,526 | 221,594 | 165,897 | 88,755 | 60,096 | 1,869 |
| **Crimes Against Persons** | 132,225 | 123,651 | 101,424 | 71,983 | 49,525 | 38,027 | 28,395 | 15,725 | 12,406 | 233 |
| Assault offenses | 126,039 | 117,748 | 96,642 | 68,676 | 47,209 | 36,268 | 27,014 | 14,858 | 11,423 | 210 |
| Homicide offenses | 1,454 | 1,044 | 736 | 481 | 270 | 238 | 178 | 102 | 109 | 4 |
| Human trafficking offenses | 59 | 53 | 43 | 39 | 21 | 18 | 16 | 7 | 2 | 0 |
| Kidnapping/abduction | 2,089 | 1,984 | 1,514 | 978 | 664 | 416 | 278 | 153 | 101 | 5 |
| Sex offenses | 2,584 | 2,822 | 2,489 | 1,809 | 1,361 | 1,087 | 909 | 605 | 771 | 14 |
| **Crimes Against Property** | 113,379 | 111,012 | 91,167 | 62,637 | 41,347 | 31,764 | 22,545 | 10,898 | 6,392 | 224 |
| Arson | 679 | 810 | 676 | 473 | 321 | 259 | 249 | 127 | 93 | 3 |
| Bribery | 55 | 47 | 37 | 28 | 13 | 7 | 8 | 6 | 2 | 0 |
| Burglary/breaking & entering | 11,347 | 11,889 | 9,742 | 6,479 | 3,840 | 2,851 | 1,936 | 818 | 357 | 21 |
| Counterfeiting/forgery | 2,662 | 2,579 | 2,256 | 1,655 | 967 | 659 | 465 | 195 | 121 | 8 |
| Destruction/damage/vandalism | 15,748 | 14,632 | 11,463 | 7,608 | 4,722 | 3,455 | 2,495 | 1,267 | 905 | 20 |
| Embezzlement | 730 | 630 | 533 | 392 | 304 | 238 | 153 | 68 | 43 | 4 |
| Extortion/blackmail | 49 | 43 | 46 | 34 | 28 | 19 | 9 | 7 | 2 | 0 |
| Fraud offenses | 8,388 | 7,930 | 6,729 | 4,601 | 3,092 | 2,268 | 1,513 | 728 | 437 | 17 |
| Larceny-theft offenses | 53,624 | 53,838 | 45,893 | 32,406 | 22,747 | 18,492 | 13,594 | 6,803 | 4,077 | 101 |
| Motor vehicle theft | 7,529 | 7,328 | 5,441 | 3,467 | 2,004 | 1,235 | 734 | 264 | 124 | 19 |
| Robbery | 4,562 | 3,701 | 2,485 | 1,670 | 919 | 732 | 494 | 212 | 65 | 18 |
| Stolen property offenses | 8,006 | 7,585 | 5,866 | 3,824 | 2,390 | 1,549 | 895 | 403 | 166 | 13 |
| **Crimes Against Society** | 143,157 | 130,165 | 106,483 | 73,124 | 45,870 | 32,480 | 22,168 | 10,436 | 4,689 | 197 |
| Animal cruelty | 403 | 344 | 301 | 246 | 196 | 180 | 154 | 121 | 198 | 4 |
| Drug/narcotic offenses | 122,075 | 114,321 | 95,035 | 65,544 | 40,980 | 29,092 | 19,551 | 8,990 | 3,516 | 166 |
| Gambling offenses | 69 | 69 | 68 | 56 | 61 | 51 | 42 | 24 | 33 | 0 |
| Pornography/obscene material | 519 | 485 | 477 | 282 | 205 | 161 | 140 | 94 | 94 | 0 |
| Prostitution offenses | 1,333 | 1,107 | 897 | 705 | 566 | 458 | 368 | 211 | 160 | 1 |
| Weapon law violations | 18,758 | 13,839 | 9,705 | 6,291 | 3,862 | 2,538 | 1,913 | 996 | 688 | 26 |
| **Group B offenses** | 353,710 | 345,233 | 291,158 | 212,927 | 149,784 | 119,323 | 92,789 | 51,696 | 36,609 | 1,215 |
| Curfew/loitering/vagrancy violations | 1,543 | 2,042 | 882 | 697 | 596 | 624 | 466 | 353 | 173 | 5 |
| Disorderly conduct | 20,972 | 20,610 | 17,322 | 12,663 | 9,016 | 7,425 | 6,332 | 3,652 | 2,618 | 104 |
| Driving under the Influence | 79,271 | 69,083 | 57,089 | 43,741 | 33,009 | 27,357 | 22,896 | 14,120 | 10,715 | 124 |
| Family offenses, nonviolent | 6,130 | 6,739 | 5,820 | 3,731 | 2,261 | 1,451 | 905 | 441 | 293 | 45 |
| Liquor law violations | 4,707 | 4,618 | 4,056 | 3,268 | 2,822 | 2,566 | 2,452 | 1,474 | 987 | 25 |
| Trespass of real property | 22,384 | 24,341 | 21,200 | 16,032 | 11,505 | 10,063 | 8,657 | 5,003 | 3,378 | 72 |
| All other offenses | 218,703 | 217,800 | 184,789 | 132,795 | 90,575 | 69,837 | 51,081 | 26,653 | 18,445 | 840 |

## Table 39. Male Arrests, 2021

(Number, percent.)

| Offense charged | Total arrested | Males arrested | Percent of males arrested |
|---|---:|---:|---:|
| **Total** | 4,538,284 | 3,301,434 | 72.7 |
| **Crimes Against Persons** | 816,942 | 600,342 | 73.5 |
| Assault offenses | 773,342 | 559,997 | 72.4 |
| Homicide offenses | 8,365 | 7,264 | 86.8 |
| Human trafficking offenses | 378 | 338 | 89.4 |
| Kidnapping/abduction | 11,134 | 9,881 | 88.7 |
| Sex offenses | 23,723 | 22,862 | 96.4 |
| **Crimes Against Property** | 700,947 | 483,840 | 69.0 |
| Arson | 5,083 | 3,893 | 76.6 |
| Bribery | 278 | 206 | 74.1 |
| Burglary/breaking & entering | 68,440 | 55,707 | 81.4 |
| Counterfeiting/forgery | 15,499 | 10,523 | 67.9 |
| Destruction/damage/vandalism | 99,309 | 75,798 | 76.3 |
| Embezzlement | 5,117 | 2,639 | 51.6 |
| Extortion/blackmail | 322 | 264 | 82.0 |
| Fraud offenses | 47,326 | 30,562 | 64.6 |
| Larceny-theft offenses | 340,053 | 208,038 | 61.2 |
| Motor vehicle theft | 44,435 | 34,669 | 78.0 |
| Robbery | 28,962 | 24,843 | 85.8 |
| Stolen property offenses | 46,123 | 36,698 | 79.6 |
| **Crimes Against Society** | 824,494 | 613,084 | 74.4 |
| Animal cruelty | 2,750 | 1,674 | 60.9 |
| Drug/narcotic offenses | 707,971 | 512,123 | 72.3 |
| Gambling offenses | 649 | 487 | 75.0 |
| Pornography/obscene material | 4,443 | 3,947 | 88.8 |
| Prostitution offenses | 7,928 | 3,969 | 50.1 |
| Weapon law violations | 100,753 | 90,884 | 90.2 |
| **Group B offenses** | 2,195,901 | 1,604,168 | 73.1 |
| Curfew/loitering/vagrancy violations | 14,659 | 10,341 | 70.5 |
| Disorderly conduct | 151,136 | 105,885 | 70.1 |
| Driving under the Influence | 463,100 | 342,069 | 73.9 |
| Family offenses, nonviolent | 34,251 | 22,440 | 65.5 |
| Liquor law violations | 72,753 | 50,010 | 68.7 |
| Trespass of real property | 149,769 | 111,431 | 74.4 |
| All other offenses | 1,310,233 | 961,992 | 73.4 |

## Table 40. Female Arrests, Distribution by Age, 2020

(Number, percent.)

| Offense charged | Total arrested | Females arrested | Percent of females arrested |
|---|---|---|---|
| **Total** | 4,538,284 | 1,236,850 | 27.3 |
| **Crimes Against Persons** | 816,942 | 216,600 | 26.5 |
| Assault offenses | 773,342 | 213,345 | 27.6 |
| Homicide offenses | 8,365 | 1,101 | 13.2 |
| Human trafficking offenses | 378 | 40 | 10.6 |
| Kidnapping/abduction | 11,134 | 1,253 | 11.3 |
| Sex offenses | 23,723 | 861 | 3.6 |
| **Crimes Against Property** | 700,947 | 217,107 | 31.0 |
| Arson | 5,083 | 1,190 | 23.4 |
| Bribery | 278 | 72 | 25.9 |
| Burglary/breaking & entering | 68,440 | 12,733 | 18.6 |
| Counterfeiting/forgery | 15,499 | 4,976 | 32.1 |
| Destruction/damage/vandalism | 99,309 | 23,511 | 23.7 |
| Embezzlement | 5,117 | 2,478 | 48.4 |
| Extortion/blackmail | 322 | 58 | 18.0 |
| Fraud offenses | 47,326 | 16,764 | 35.4 |
| Larceny-theft offenses | 340,053 | 132,015 | 38.8 |
| Motor vehicle theft | 44,435 | 9,766 | 22.0 |
| Robbery | 28,962 | 4,119 | 14.2 |
| Stolen property offenses | 46,123 | 9,425 | 20.4 |
| **Crimes Against Society** | 824,494 | 211,410 | 25.6 |
| Animal cruelty | 2,750 | 1,076 | 39.1 |
| Drug/narcotic offenses | 707,971 | 195,848 | 27.7 |
| Gambling offenses | 649 | 162 | 25.0 |
| Pornography/obscene material | 4,443 | 496 | 11.2 |
| Prostitution offenses | 7,928 | 3,959 | 49.9 |
| Weapon law violations | 100,753 | 9,869 | 9.8 |
| **Group B offenses** | 2,195,901 | 591,733 | 26.9 |
| Curfew/loitering/vagrancy violations | 14,659 | 4,318 | 29.5 |
| Disorderly conduct | 151,136 | 45,251 | 29.9 |
| Driving under the Influence | 463,100 | 121,031 | 26.1 |
| Family offenses, nonviolent | 34,251 | 11,811 | 34.5 |
| Liquor law violations | 72,753 | 22,743 | 31.3 |
| Trespass of real property | 149,769 | 38,338 | 25.6 |
| All other offenses | 1,310,233 | 348,241 | 26.6 |

## Table 41. Arrests of Persons Under 15, 18, 21, and 25 Years of Age, 2020

(Number, percent; 10,466 agencies; 2020 estimated population 228,864,358.)

| Offense charged | Total, all ages | Number of persons arrested | | | | Percent of total all ages | | | |
|---|---|---|---|---|---|---|---|---|---|
| | | Under 15 | Under 18 | Under 21 | Under 25 | Under 15 | Under 18 | Under 21 | Under 25 |
| **Total** | 5,292,124 | 85,931 | 297,074 | 708,176 | 1,328,320 | 1.6 | 5.6 | 13.4 | 25.1 |
| **Violent crime**[1] | 338,443 | 6,664 | 24,671 | 53,480 | 95,708 | 2.0 | 7.3 | 15.8 | 28.3 |
| Murder and nonnegligent manslaughter | 8,701 | 64 | 654 | 1,923 | 3,403 | 0.7 | 7.5 | 22.1 | 39.1 |
| Rape[2] | 14,462 | 885 | 2,065 | 3,613 | 5,295 | 6.1 | 14.3 | 25.0 | 36.6 |
| Robbery | 48,035 | 1,780 | 8,517 | 15,967 | 22,601 | 3.7 | 17.7 | 33.2 | 47.1 |
| Aggravated assault | 267,245 | 3,935 | 13,435 | 31,977 | 64,409 | 1.5 | 5.0 | 12.0 | 24.1 |
| **Property crime**[1] | 611,731 | 15,140 | 52,640 | 101,918 | 166,217 | 2.5 | 8.6 | 16.7 | 27.2 |
| Burglary | 104,535 | 3,362 | 10,563 | 19,147 | 30,452 | 3.2 | 10.1 | 18.3 | 29.1 |
| Larceny-theft | 442,016 | 8,918 | 32,948 | 68,272 | 114,011 | 2.0 | 7.5 | 15.4 | 25.8 |
| Motor vehicle theft | 58,326 | 2,387 | 8,273 | 13,324 | 20,019 | 4.1 | 14.2 | 22.8 | 34.3 |
| Arson | 6,854 | 473 | 856 | 1,175 | 1,735 | 6.9 | 12.5 | 17.1 | 25.3 |
| Other assaults | 633,704 | 19,459 | 50,129 | 91,703 | 164,093 | 3.1 | 7.9 | 14.5 | 25.9 |
| Forgery and counterfeiting | 22,559 | 47 | 333 | 2,609 | 5,051 | 0.2 | 1.5 | 11.6 | 22.4 |
| Fraud | 54,756 | 470 | 1,816 | 5,759 | 11,858 | 0.9 | 3.3 | 10.5 | 21.7 |
| Embezzlement | 6,592 | 9 | 302 | 1,295 | 2,241 | 0.1 | 4.6 | 19.6 | 34.0 |
| Stolen property; buying, receiving, possessing | 61,868 | 1,232 | 5,814 | 11,847 | 19,345 | 2.0 | 9.4 | 19.1 | 31.3 |
| Vandalism | 121,403 | 6,493 | 16,392 | 27,318 | 42,276 | 5.3 | 13.5 | 22.5 | 34.8 |
| Weapons; carrying, possessing, etc. | 115,832 | 1,478 | 7,809 | 21,727 | 42,045 | 1.3 | 6.7 | 18.8 | 36.3 |
| Prostitution and commercialized vice | 11,754 | 11 | 77 | 1,450 | 3,649 | 0.1 | 0.7 | 12.3 | 31.0 |
| Sex offenses (except forcible rape and prostitution) | 22,065 | 1,329 | 2,751 | 4,484 | 6,330 | 6.0 | 12.5 | 20.3 | 28.7 |
| Drug abuse violations | 801,546 | 4,539 | 29,368 | 106,854 | 212,021 | 0.6 | 3.7 | 13.3 | 26.5 |
| Gambling | 1,191 | 11 | 58 | 122 | 214 | 0.9 | 4.9 | 10.2 | 18.0 |
| Offenses against the family and children | 40,498 | 508 | 1,579 | 3,359 | 7,027 | 1.3 | 3.9 | 8.3 | 17.4 |
| Driving under the influence | 531,846 | 64 | 4,003 | 34,096 | 107,509 | * | 0.8 | 6.4 | 20.2 |
| Liquor laws | 70,875 | 1,525 | 12,372 | 39,512 | 44,230 | 2.2 | 17.5 | 55.7 | 62.4 |
| Drunkenness | 135,744 | 273 | 1,696 | 8,274 | 22,402 | 0.2 | 1.2 | 6.1 | 16.5 |
| Disorderly conduct | 156,502 | 6,767 | 17,041 | 29,164 | 47,356 | 4.3 | 10.9 | 18.6 | 30.3 |
| Vagrancy | 9,795 | 46 | 192 | 925 | 1,799 | 0.5 | 2.0 | 9.4 | 18.4 |
| All other offenses (except traffic) | 1,534,972 | 17,056 | 59,790 | 154,024 | 318,672 | 1.1 | 3.9 | 10.0 | 20.8 |
| Suspicion | 238 | 11 | 31 | 46 | 67 | 4.6 | 13.0 | 19.3 | 28.2 |
| Curfew and loitering law violations | 8,210 | 2,799 | 8,210 | 8,210 | 8,210 | 34.1 | 100.0 | 100.0 | 100.0 |

* = Less than one-tenth of one percent.
1 Violent crimes in this table are offenses of murder and nonnegligent manslaughter, rape, robbery, and aggravated assault.  Property crimes are offenses of burglary, larceny-theft, motor vehicle theft, and arson.
2 The rape figures in this table are aggregate totals of the data submitted based on both the legacy and revised Uniform Crime Reporting definitions.

# Table 42. Arrests, Distribution by Sex, 2020

(Number, percent; 10,466 agencies; 2020 estimated population 228,864,358.)

| Offense charged | Number of persons arrested | | | Percent male | Percent female | Percent distribution[1] | | |
|---|---|---|---|---|---|---|---|---|
| | Total | Male | Female | | | Total | Male | Female |
| **Total** | 5,292,124 | 3,891,282 | 1,400,842 | 73.5 | 26.5 | 100.0 | 100.0 | 100.0 |
| **Violent crime[2]** | 338,443 | 267,935 | 70,508 | 79.2 | 20.8 | 6.4 | 6.9 | 5.0 |
| Murder and nonnegligent manslaughter | 8,701 | 7,611 | 1,090 | 87.5 | 12.5 | 0.2 | 0.2 | 0.1 |
| Rape[3] | 14,462 | 14,050 | 412 | 97.2 | 2.8 | 0.3 | 0.4 | * |
| Robbery | 48,035 | 40,725 | 7,310 | 84.8 | 15.2 | 0.9 | 1.0 | 0.5 |
| Aggravated assault | 267,245 | 205,549 | 61,696 | 76.9 | 23.1 | 5.0 | 5.3 | 4.4 |
| **Property crime[2]** | 611,731 | 402,790 | 208,941 | 65.8 | 34.2 | 11.6 | 10.4 | 14.9 |
| Burglary | 104,535 | 84,454 | 20,081 | 80.8 | 19.2 | 2.0 | 2.2 | 1.4 |
| Larceny-theft | 442,016 | 267,564 | 174,452 | 60.5 | 39.5 | 8.4 | 6.9 | 12.5 |
| Motor vehicle theft | 58,326 | 45,359 | 12,967 | 77.8 | 22.2 | 1.1 | 1.2 | 0.9 |
| Arson | 6,854 | 5,413 | 1,441 | 79.0 | 21.0 | 0.1 | 0.1 | 0.1 |
| Other assaults | 633,704 | 452,374 | 181,330 | 71.4 | 28.6 | 12.0 | 11.6 | 12.9 |
| Forgery and counterfeiting | 22,559 | 15,318 | 7,241 | 67.9 | 32.1 | 0.4 | 0.4 | 0.5 |
| Fraud | 54,756 | 35,624 | 19,132 | 65.1 | 34.9 | 1.0 | 0.9 | 1.4 |
| Embezzlement | 6,592 | 3,387 | 3,205 | 51.4 | 48.6 | 0.1 | 0.1 | 0.2 |
| Stolen property; buying, receiving, possessing | 61,868 | 48,944 | 12,924 | 79.1 | 20.9 | 1.2 | 1.3 | 0.9 |
| Vandalism | 121,403 | 93,181 | 28,222 | 76.8 | 23.2 | 2.3 | 2.4 | 2.0 |
| Weapons; carrying, possessing, etc. | 115,832 | 104,992 | 10,840 | 90.6 | 9.4 | 2.2 | 2.7 | 0.8 |
| Prostitution and commercialized vice | 11,754 | 4,942 | 6,812 | 42.0 | 58.0 | 0.2 | 0.1 | 0.5 |
| Sex offenses (except forcible rape and prostitution) | 22,065 | 20,780 | 1,285 | 94.2 | 5.8 | 0.4 | 0.5 | 0.1 |
| Drug abuse violations | 801,546 | 600,966 | 200,580 | 75.0 | 25.0 | 15.1 | 15.4 | 14.3 |
| Gambling | 1,191 | 825 | 366 | 69.3 | 30.7 | * | * | * |
| Offenses against the family and children | 40,498 | 27,429 | 13,069 | 67.7 | 32.3 | 0.8 | 0.7 | 0.9 |
| Driving under the influence | 531,846 | 396,682 | 135,164 | 74.6 | 25.4 | 10.0 | 10.2 | 9.6 |
| Liquor laws | 70,875 | 49,833 | 21,042 | 70.3 | 29.7 | 1.3 | 1.3 | 1.5 |
| Drunkenness | 135,744 | 105,399 | 30,345 | 77.6 | 22.4 | 2.6 | 2.7 | 2.2 |
| Disorderly conduct | 156,502 | 109,929 | 46,573 | 70.2 | 29.8 | 3.0 | 2.8 | 3.3 |
| Vagrancy | 9,795 | 7,479 | 2,316 | 76.4 | 23.6 | 0.2 | 0.2 | 0.2 |
| All other offenses (except traffic) | 1,534,972 | 1,136,942 | 398,030 | 74.1 | 25.9 | 29.0 | 29.2 | 28.4 |
| Suspicion | 238 | 153 | 85 | 64.3 | 35.7 | * | * | * |
| Curfew and loitering law violations | 8,210 | 5,378 | 2,832 | 65.5 | 34.5 | 0.2 | 0.1 | 0.2 |

* = Less than one-tenth of 1 percent.
1 Because of rounding, the percentages may not sum to 100.   2 Violent crimes in this table are offenses of murder and nonnegligent manslaughter, rape, robbery, and aggravated assault.  Property crimes are offenses of burglary, larceny-theft, motor vehicle theft, and arson.   3 The rape figures in this table are aggregate totals of the data submitted based on both the legacy and revised Uniform Crime Reporting definitions.

## Table 43. Arrests, Distribution by Race, by Offense Category, 2021

(Number, percent.)

| Offense charged | Total arrests | | | | | | | Percent distribution[1] | | | | | | |
|---|---|---|---|---|---|---|---|---|---|---|---|---|---|---|
| | Total | White | Black or African American | American Indian or Alaskan Native | Asian | Native Hawaiian or Other Pacific Islander | Unknown race | Total | White | Black | American Indian or Alaskan Native | Asian | Native Hawaiian or Other Pacific Islander | Unknown race |
| **Total** | 4,538,284 | 3,011,660 | 1,244,006 | 115,435 | 50,969 | 15,781 | 100,433 | 100.0 | 66.4 | 27.4 | 2.5 | 1.1 | 0.3 | 2.2 |
| Crimes Against Persons | 816,942 | 492,348 | 278,162 | 18,737 | 10,538 | 2,894 | 14,263 | 100.0 | 60.3 | 34.0 | 2.3 | 1.3 | 0.4 | 1.7 |
| Assault offenses | 773,342 | 465,778 | 263,579 | 18,001 | 9,963 | 2,760 | 13,261 | 100.0 | 60.2 | 34.1 | 2.3 | 1.3 | 0.4 | 1.7 |
| Homicide offenses | 8,365 | 3,288 | 4,795 | 113 | 67 | 9 | 93 | 100.0 | 39.3 | 57.3 | 1.4 | 0.8 | 0.1 | 1.1 |
| Human trafficking offenses | 378 | 233 | 121 | 4 | 9 | 1 | 10 | 100.0 | 61.6 | 32.0 | 1.1 | 2.4 | 0.3 | 2.6 |
| Kidnapping/abduction | 11,134 | 6,730 | 3,903 | 181 | 124 | 29 | 167 | 100.0 | 60.4 | 35.1 | 1.6 | 1.1 | 0.3 | 1.5 |
| Sex offenses | 23,723 | 16,319 | 5,764 | 438 | 375 | 95 | 732 | 100.0 | 68.8 | 24.3 | 1.8 | 1.6 | 0.4 | 3.1 |
| **Crimes Against Property** | 700,947 | 450,420 | 215,309 | 13,788 | 7,136 | 2,015 | 12,279 | 100.0 | 64.3 | 30.7 | 2.0 | 1.0 | 0.3 | 1.8 |
| Arson | 5,083 | 3,589 | 1,206 | 126 | 71 | 22 | 69 | 100.0 | 70.6 | 23.7 | 2.5 | 1.4 | 0.4 | 1.4 |
| Bribery | 278 | 201 | 63 | 7 | 3 | 2 | 2 | 100.0 | 72.3 | 22.7 | 2.5 | 1.1 | 0.7 | 0.7 |
| Burglary/breaking & entering | 68,440 | 46,062 | 19,223 | 1,336 | 640 | 193 | 986 | 100.0 | 67.3 | 28.1 | 2.0 | 0.9 | 0.3 | 1.4 |
| Counterfeiting/forgery | 15499 | 10313 | 4418 | 192 | 217 | 41 | 318 | 100.0 | 66.5 | 28.5 | 1.2 | 1.4 | 0.3 | 2.1 |
| Destruction/damage/vandalism | 99,309 | 64,642 | 29,216 | 2,330 | 1,082 | 227 | 1,812 | 100.0 | 65.1 | 29.4 | 2.3 | 1.1 | 0.2 | 1.8 |
| Embezzlement | 5,117 | 2,940 | 1,951 | 30 | 77 | 2 | 117 | 100.0 | 57.5 | 38.1 | 0.6 | 1.5 | 0.0 | 2.3 |
| Extortion/blackmail | 322 | 234 | 76 | 4 | 2 | 0 | 6 | 100.0 | 72.7 | 23.6 | 1.2 | 0.6 | 0.0 | 1.9 |
| Fraud offenses | 47,326 | 29,726 | 14,980 | 1,008 | 459 | 97 | 1,056 | 100.0 | 62.8 | 31.7 | 2.1 | 1.0 | 0.2 | 2.2 |
| Larceny-theft offenses | 340,053 | 226,799 | 96,418 | 6,527 | 3,394 | 829 | 6,086 | 100.0 | 66.7 | 28.4 | 1.9 | 1.0 | 0.2 | 1.8 |
| Motor vehicle theft | 44,435 | 28,650 | 13,698 | 967 | 394 | 128 | 598 | 100.0 | 64.5 | 30.8 | 2.2 | 0.9 | 0.3 | 1.3 |
| Robbery | 28,962 | 11,264 | 16,620 | 399 | 197 | 136 | 346 | 100.0 | 38.9 | 57.4 | 1.4 | 0.7 | 0.5 | 1.2 |
| Stolen property offenses | 46,123 | 26,000 | 17,440 | 862 | 600 | 338 | 883 | 100.0 | 56.4 | 37.8 | 1.9 | 1.3 | 0.7 | 1.9 |
| **Crimes Against Society** | 824,494 | 536,905 | 247,971 | 14,824 | 7,057 | 1,318 | 16,419 | 100.0 | 65.1 | 30.1 | 1.8 | 0.9 | 0.2 | 2.0 |
| Animal cruelty | 2,750 | 1,970 | 613 | 41 | 47 | 7 | 72 | 100.0 | 71.6 | 22.3 | 1.5 | 1.7 | 0.3 | 2.6 |
| Drug/narcotic offenses | 707,971 | 485,803 | 187,341 | 13,668 | 5,422 | 1,118 | 14,619 | 100.0 | 68.6 | 26.5 | 1.9 | 0.8 | 0.2 | 2.1 |
| Gambling offenses | 649 | 277 | 247 | 6 | 87 | 4 | 28 | 100.0 | 42.7 | 38.1 | 0.9 | 13.4 | 0.6 | 4.3 |
| Pornography/obscene material | 4,443 | 3,439 | 787 | 23 | 78 | 9 | 107 | 100.0 | 77.4 | 17.7 | 0.5 | 1.8 | 0.2 | 2.4 |
| Prostitution offenses | 7,928 | 4,097 | 3,083 | 38 | 594 | 26 | 90 | 100.0 | 51.7 | 38.9 | 0.5 | 7.5 | 0.3 | 1.1 |
| Weapon law violations | 100,753 | 41,319 | 55,900 | 1,048 | 829 | 154 | 1,503 | 100.0 | 41.0 | 55.5 | 1.0 | 0.8 | 0.2 | 1.5 |
| **Group B offenses** | 2,195,901 | 1,531,987 | 502,564 | 68,086 | 26,238 | 9,554 | 57,472 | 100.0 | 69.8 | 22.9 | 3.1 | 1.2 | 0.4 | 2.6 |
| Curfew/loitering/vagrancy violations | 14,659 | 9,259 | 3,510 | 547 | 367 | 135 | 841 | 100.0 | 63.2 | 23.9 | 3.7 | 2.5 | 0.9 | 5.7 |
| Disorderly conduct | 151,136 | 94,082 | 43,313 | 8,429 | 1,346 | 424 | 3,542 | 100.0 | 62.2 | 28.7 | 5.6 | 0.9 | 0.3 | 2.3 |
| Driving under the Influence | 463,100 | 349,566 | 73,988 | 12,241 | 7,539 | 1,613 | 18,153 | 100.0 | 75.5 | 16.0 | 2.6 | 1.6 | 0.3 | 3.9 |
| Family offenses, nonviolent | 34,251 | 22,795 | 8,541 | 1,961 | 310 | 58 | 586 | 100.0 | 66.6 | 24.9 | 5.7 | 0.9 | 0.2 | 1.7 |
| Liquor law violations | 72,753 | 53,526 | 10,307 | 3,237 | 1,065 | 502 | 4,116 | 100.0 | 73.6 | 14.2 | 4.4 | 1.5 | 0.7 | 5.7 |
| Trespass of real property | 149,769 | 95,307 | 43,907 | 4,121 | 2,178 | 1,070 | 3,186 | 100.0 | 63.6 | 29.3 | 2.8 | 1.5 | 0.7 | 2.1 |
| All other offenses | 1,310,233 | 907,452 | 318,998 | 37,550 | 13,433 | 5,752 | 27,048 | 100.0 | 69.3 | 24.3 | 2.9 | 1.0 | 0.4 | 2.1 |

1 Because of rounding, the percentages may not sum to 100.

## Table 43A. Arrests, Distribution by Ethnicity, 2020

(Number, percent; 10,466 agencies; 2020 estimated population 228,864,358.)

| Offense charged | Total arrests | | | Percent distribution[1] | | | Arrests under 18 | | |
|---|---|---|---|---|---|---|---|---|---|
| | Total[2] | Hispanic or Latino | Not Hispanic or Latino | Total[2] | Hispanic or Latino | Not Hispanic or Latino | Total[2] | Hispanic or Latino | Not Hispanic or Latino |
| Total | 4,477,428 | 928,437 | 3,548,991 | 100.0 | 20.7 | 79.3 | 241,426 | 57,668 | 183,758 |
| Violent crime[3] | 294,088 | 78,577 | 215,511 | 100.0 | 26.7 | 73.3 | 20,987 | 5,792 | 15,195 |
| Murder and nonnegligent manslaughter | 7,269 | 1,633 | 5,636 | 100.0 | 22.5 | 77.5 | 543 | 154 | 389 |
| Rape[4] | 11,857 | 3,509 | 8,348 | 100.0 | 29.6 | 70.4 | 1,613 | 386 | 1,227 |
| Robbery | 41,970 | 10,887 | 31,083 | 100.0 | 25.9 | 74.1 | 7,514 | 2,049 | 5,465 |
| Aggravated assault | 232,992 | 62,548 | 170,444 | 100.0 | 26.8 | 73.2 | 11,317 | 3,203 | 8,114 |
| Property crime[3] | 515,672 | 91,320 | 424,352 | 100.0 | 17.7 | 82.3 | 42,868 | 9,314 | 33,554 |
| Burglary | 89,960 | 19,591 | 70,369 | 100.0 | 21.8 | 78.2 | 8,371 | 2,100 | 6,271 |
| Larceny-theft | 368,820 | 55,986 | 312,834 | 100.0 | 15.2 | 84.8 | 26,760 | 5,366 | 21,394 |
| Motor vehicle theft | 51,063 | 14,473 | 36,590 | 100.0 | 28.3 | 71.7 | 7,023 | 1,710 | 5,313 |
| Arson | 5,829 | 1,270 | 4,559 | 100.0 | 21.8 | 78.2 | 714 | 138 | 576 |
| Other assaults | 532,225 | 107,191 | 425,034 | 100.0 | 20.1 | 79.9 | 41,249 | 9,526 | 31,723 |
| Forgery and counterfeiting | 19,625 | 3,332 | 16,293 | 100.0 | 17.0 | 83.0 | 281 | 74 | 207 |
| Fraud | 46,491 | 6,896 | 39,595 | 100.0 | 14.8 | 85.2 | 1,430 | 307 | 1,123 |
| Embezzlement | 5,562 | 828 | 4,734 | 100.0 | 14.9 | 85.1 | 246 | 33 | 213 |
| Stolen property; buying, receiving, possessing | 52,652 | 10,875 | 41,777 | 100.0 | 20.7 | 79.3 | 4,745 | 989 | 3,756 |
| Vandalism | 102,777 | 21,209 | 81,568 | 100.0 | 20.6 | 79.4 | 13,422 | 2,971 | 10,451 |
| Weapons; carrying, possessing, etc. | 94,295 | 23,456 | 70,839 | 100.0 | 24.9 | 75.1 | 6,582 | 2,190 | 4,392 |
| Prostitution and commercialized vice | 10,949 | 2,725 | 8,224 | 100.0 | 24.9 | 75.1 | 63 | 12 | 51 |
| Sex offenses (except forcible rape and prostitution) | 18,924 | 5,754 | 13,170 | 100.0 | 30.4 | 69.6 | 2,201 | 588 | 1,613 |
| Drug abuse violations | 711,136 | 155,970 | 555,166 | 100.0 | 21.9 | 78.1 | 25,056 | 7,311 | 17,745 |
| Gambling | 1,111 | 468 | 643 | 100.0 | 42.1 | 57.9 | 49 | 29 | 20 |
| Offenses against the family and children | 34,157 | 5,542 | 28,615 | 100.0 | 16.2 | 83.8 | 1,271 | 272 | 999 |
| Driving under the influence | 435,235 | 123,406 | 311,829 | 100.0 | 28.4 | 71.6 | 3,124 | 999 | 2,125 |
| Liquor laws | 54,050 | 9,496 | 44,554 | 100.0 | 17.6 | 82.4 | 9,435 | 1,705 | 7,730 |
| Drunkenness | 128,105 | 31,408 | 96,697 | 100.0 | 24.5 | 75.5 | 1,433 | 467 | 966 |
| Disorderly conduct | 119,408 | 16,711 | 102,697 | 100.0 | 14.0 | 86.0 | 12,758 | 2,383 | 10,375 |
| Vagrancy | 8,832 | 1,608 | 7,224 | 100.0 | 18.2 | 81.8 | 124 | 32 | 92 |
| All other offenses (except traffic) | 1,285,377 | 229,968 | 1,055,409 | 100.0 | 17.9 | 82.1 | 47,522 | 10,998 | 36,524 |
| Suspicion | 205 | 22 | 183 | 100.0 | 10.7 | 89.3 | 28 | 1 | 27 |
| Curfew and loitering law violations | 6,552 | 1,675 | 4,877 | 100.0 | 25.6 | 74.4 | 6,552 | 1,675 | 4,877 |

## Table 43A. Arrests, Distribution by Ethnicity, 2020—Continued

(Number, percent; 10,466 agencies; 2020 estimated population 228,864,358.)

| Offense charged | Percent distribution[1] | | | Total[2] | Arrests 18 and over | | Total[2] | Percent distribution[1] | |
|---|---|---|---|---|---|---|---|---|---|
| | Total[2] | Hispanic or Latino | Not Hispanic or Latino | | Hispanic or Latino | Not Hispanic or Latino | | Hispanic or Latino | Not Hispanic or Latino |
| **Total** | 100.0 | 23.9 | 76.1 | 4,236,002 | 870,769 | 3,365,233 | 100.0 | 20.6 | 79.4 |
| **Violent crime[3]** | 100.0 | 27.6 | 72.4 | 273,101 | 72,785 | 200,316 | 100.0 | 26.7 | 73.3 |
| Murder and nonnegligent manslaughter | 100.0 | 28.4 | 71.6 | 6,726 | 1,479 | 5,247 | 100.0 | 22.0 | 78.0 |
| Rape[4] | 100.0 | 23.9 | 76.1 | 10,244 | 3,123 | 7,121 | 100.0 | 30.5 | 69.5 |
| Robbery | 100.0 | 27.3 | 72.7 | 34,456 | 8,838 | 25,618 | 100.0 | 25.7 | 74.3 |
| Aggravated assault | 100.0 | 28.3 | 71.7 | 221,675 | 59,345 | 162,330 | 100.0 | 26.8 | 73.2 |
| **Property crime[3]** | 100.0 | 21.7 | 78.3 | 472,804 | 82,006 | 390,798 | 100.0 | 17.3 | 82.7 |
| Burglary | 100.0 | 25.1 | 74.9 | 81,589 | 17,491 | 64,098 | 100.0 | 21.4 | 78.6 |
| Larceny-theft | 100.0 | 20.1 | 79.9 | 342,060 | 50,620 | 291,440 | 100.0 | 14.8 | 85.2 |
| Motor vehicle theft | 100.0 | 24.3 | 75.7 | 44,040 | 12,763 | 31,277 | 100.0 | 29.0 | 71.0 |
| Arson | 100.0 | 19.3 | 80.7 | 5,115 | 1,132 | 3,983 | 100.0 | 22.1 | 77.9 |
| Other assaults | 100.0 | 23.1 | 76.9 | 490,976 | 97,665 | 393,311 | 100.0 | 19.9 | 80.1 |
| Forgery and counterfeiting | 100.0 | 26.3 | 73.7 | 19,344 | 3,258 | 16,086 | 100.0 | 16.8 | 83.2 |
| Fraud | 100.0 | 21.5 | 78.5 | 45,061 | 6,589 | 38,472 | 100.0 | 14.6 | 85.4 |
| Embezzlement | 100.0 | 13.4 | 86.6 | 5,316 | 795 | 4,521 | 100.0 | 15.0 | 85.0 |
| Stolen property; buying, receiving, possessing | 100.0 | 20.8 | 79.2 | 47,907 | 9,886 | 38,021 | 100.0 | 20.6 | 79.4 |
| Vandalism | 100.0 | 22.1 | 77.9 | 89,355 | 18,238 | 71,117 | 100.0 | 20.4 | 79.6 |
| Weapons; carrying, possessing, etc. | 100.0 | 33.3 | 66.7 | 87,713 | 21,266 | 66,447 | 100.0 | 24.2 | 75.8 |
| Prostitution and commercialized vice | 100.0 | 19.0 | 81.0 | 10,886 | 2,713 | 8,173 | 100.0 | 24.9 | 75.1 |
| Sex offenses (except forcible rape and prostitution) | 100.0 | 26.7 | 73.3 | 16,723 | 5,166 | 11,557 | 100.0 | 30.9 | 69.1 |
| Drug abuse violations | 100.0 | 29.2 | 70.8 | 686,080 | 148,659 | 537,421 | 100.0 | 21.7 | 78.3 |
| Gambling | 100.0 | 59.2 | 40.8 | 1,062 | 439 | 623 | 100.0 | 41.3 | 58.7 |
| Offenses against the family and children | 100.0 | 21.4 | 78.6 | 32,886 | 5,270 | 27,616 | 100.0 | 16.0 | 84.0 |
| Driving under the influence | 100.0 | 32.0 | 68.0 | 432,111 | 122,407 | 309,704 | 100.0 | 28.3 | 71.7 |
| Liquor laws | 100.0 | 18.1 | 81.9 | 44,615 | 7,791 | 36,824 | 100.0 | 17.5 | 82.5 |
| Drunkenness | 100.0 | 32.6 | 67.4 | 126,672 | 30,941 | 95,731 | 100.0 | 24.4 | 75.6 |
| Disorderly conduct | 100.0 | 18.7 | 81.3 | 106,650 | 14,328 | 92,322 | 100.0 | 13.4 | 86.6 |
| Vagrancy | 100.0 | 25.8 | 74.2 | 8,708 | 1,576 | 7,132 | 100.0 | 18.1 | 81.9 |
| All other offenses (except traffic) | 100.0 | 23.1 | 76.9 | 1,237,855 | 218,970 | 1,018,885 | 100.0 | 17.7 | 82.3 |
| Suspicion | 100.0 | 3.6 | 96.4 | 177 | 21 | 156 | 100.0 | 11.9 | 88.1 |
| Curfew and loitering law violations | 100.0 | 25.6 | 74.4 | NA | NA | NA | NA | NA | NA |

NA = Not available.
1 Because of rounding, the percentages may not sum to 100.    2 The ethnicity totals are representative of those agencies that provided ethnicity breakdowns. Not all agencies provide ethnicity data; therefore, the race and ethnicity totals will not equal.
3 Violent crimes are offenses of murder and nonnegligent manslaughter, rape, robbery, and aggravated assault.  Property crimes are offenses of burglary, larceny-theft, motor vehicle theft, and arson.    4 The rape figures in this table are aggregate totals of the data submitted based on both the legacy and revised Uniform Crime Reporting definitions.

## Table 44. Arrest Trends, Cities, 2019–2020

(Number, percent change; 6,841 agencies; 2020 estimated population 140,331,250; 2019 estimated population 139,813,132.)

| Offense charged | Number of persons arrested | | | | | | | | |
|---|---|---|---|---|---|---|---|---|---|
| | Total, all ages | | | Under 18 years of age | | | 18 years of age and over | | |
| | 2019 | 2020 | Percent change | 2019 | 2020 | Percent change | 2019 | 2020 | Percent change |
| **Total[1]** | 4,348,178 | 3,384,987 | -22.2 | 339,874 | 213,227 | -37.3 | 4,008,304 | 3,171,760 | -20.9 |
| **Violent crime[2]** | 241,690 | 230,819 | -4.5 | 24,029 | 17,729 | -26.2 | 217,661 | 213,090 | -2.1 |
| Murder and nonnegligent manslaughter | 4,795 | 5,724 | +19.4 | 419 | 467 | +11.5 | 4,376 | 5,257 | +20.1 |
| Rape[3] | 10,513 | 9,134 | -13.1 | 1,736 | 1,257 | -27.6 | 8,777 | 7,877 | -10.3 |
| Robbery | 40,712 | 35,687 | -12.3 | 8,625 | 6,642 | -23.0 | 32,087 | 29,045 | -9.5 |
| Aggravated assault | 185,670 | 180,274 | -2.9 | 13,249 | 9,363 | -29.3 | 172,421 | 170,911 | -0.9 |
| **Property crime[2]** | 577,013 | 452,731 | -21.5 | 65,473 | 40,261 | -38.5 | 511,540 | 412,470 | -19.4 |
| Burglary | 80,581 | 71,371 | -11.4 | 10,420 | 7,633 | -26.7 | 70,161 | 63,738 | -9.2 |
| Larceny-theft | 453,761 | 337,188 | -25.7 | 47,242 | 25,809 | -45.4 | 406,519 | 311,379 | -23.4 |
| Motor vehicle theft | 38,465 | 39,317 | +2.2 | 6,959 | 6,194 | -11.0 | 31,506 | 33,123 | +5.1 |
| Arson | 4,206 | 4,855 | +15.4 | 852 | 625 | -26.6 | 3,354 | 4,230 | +26.1 |
| Other assaults | 478448 | 429714 | -10.2 | 57323 | 34111 | -40.5 | 421125 | 395603 | -6.1 |
| Forgery and counterfeiting | 22,303 | 15,404 | -30.9 | 471 | 251 | -46.7 | 21,832 | 15,153 | -30.6 |
| Fraud | 52,793 | 36,345 | -31.2 | 1,905 | 1,345 | -29.4 | 50,888 | 35,000 | -31.2 |
| Embezzlement | 7,445 | 4,838 | -35.0 | 320 | 253 | -20.9 | 7,125 | 4,585 | -35.6 |
| Stolen property; buying, receiving, possessing | 43,871 | 42,619 | -2.9 | 5,082 | 4,453 | -12.4 | 38,789 | 38,166 | -1.6 |
| Vandalism | 87,973 | 85,288 | -3.1 | 15,757 | 11,756 | -25.4 | 72,216 | 73,532 | +1.8 |
| Weapons; carrying, possessing, etc. | 72,333 | 76,850 | +6.2 | 8,295 | 5,789 | -30.2 | 64,038 | 71,061 | +11.0 |
| Prostitution and commercialized vice | 10,664 | 5,806 | -45.6 | 75 | 23 | -69.3 | 10,589 | 5,783 | -45.4 |
| Sex offenses (except forcible rape and prostitution) | 18,375 | 14,150 | -23.0 | 3,080 | 1,778 | -42.3 | 15,295 | 12,372 | -19.1 |
| Drug abuse violations | 670,131 | 507,824 | -24.2 | 38,034 | 20,414 | -46.3 | 632,097 | 487,410 | -22.9 |
| Gambling | 909 | 695 | -23.5 | 51 | 30 | -41.2 | 858 | 665 | -22.5 |
| Offenses against the family and children | 26,602 | 23,349 | -12.2 | 1,416 | 1,150 | -18.8 | 25,186 | 22,199 | -11.9 |
| Driving under the influence | 343,589 | 272,121 | -20.8 | 2,071 | 2,243 | +8.3 | 341,518 | 269,878 | -21.0 |
| Liquor laws | 75,137 | 47,184 | -37.2 | 10,728 | 7,772 | -27.6 | 64,409 | 39,412 | -38.8 |
| Drunkenness | 155,386 | 97,370 | -37.3 | 1,680 | 1,116 | -33.6 | 153,706 | 96,254 | -37.4 |
| Disorderly conduct | 150,583 | 114,127 | -24.2 | 26,724 | 12,842 | -51.9 | 123,859 | 101,285 | -18.2 |
| Vagrancy | 10,029 | 7,777 | -22.5 | 219 | 174 | -20.5 | 9,810 | 7,603 | -22.5 |
| All other offenses (except traffic) | 1,294,402 | 913,443 | -29.4 | 68,639 | 43,204 | -37.1 | 1,225,763 | 870,239 | -29.0 |
| Suspicion | 142 | 141 | -0.7 | 5 | 17 | +240.0 | 137 | 124 | -9.5 |
| Curfew and loitering law violations | 8,502 | 6,533 | -23.2 | 8,502 | 6,533 | -23.2 | NA | NA | NA |

NA = Not available.

1 Does not include suspicion.   2 Violent crimes are offenses of murder and nonnegligent manslaughter, rape, robbery, and aggravated assault.  Property crimes are offenses of burglary, larceny-theft, motor vehicle theft, and arson.   3 The rape figures in this table are aggregate totals of the data submitted based on both the legacy and revised Uniform Crime Reporting definitions.

## Table 45. Arrest Trends, Cities, by Age and Sex, 2019–2020

(Number, percent change; 6,841 agencies; 2020 estimated population 140,331,250; 2019 estimated population 139,813,132.)

| Offense charged | Male | | | | | | Female | | | | | |
| | Total | | | Under 18 | | | Total | | | Under 18 | | |
| | 2019 | 2020 | Percent change | 2019 | 2020 | Percent change | 2019 | 2020 | Percent change | 2019 | 2020 | Percent change |
|---|---|---|---|---|---|---|---|---|---|---|---|---|
| **Total[1]** | 3,135,642 | 2,481,028 | -20.9 | 235,198 | 150,844 | -35.9 | 1,212,536 | 903,959 | -25.4 | 104,676 | 62,383 | -40.4 |
| **Violent crime[2]** | 189,770 | 181,941 | -4.1 | 19,453 | 14,392 | -26.0 | 51,920 | 48,878 | -5.9 | 4,576 | 3,337 | -27.1 |
| Murder and nonnegligent manslaughter | 4,232 | 5,051 | +19.4 | 388 | 428 | +10.3 | 563 | 673 | +19.5 | 31 | 39 | +25.8 |
| Rape[3] | 10,181 | 8,864 | -12.9 | 1,652 | 1,208 | -26.9 | 332 | 270 | -18.7 | 84 | 49 | -41.7 |
| Robbery | 34,232 | 30,294 | -11.5 | 7,641 | 5,839 | -23.6 | 6,480 | 5,393 | -16.8 | 984 | 803 | -18.4 |
| Aggravated assault | 141,125 | 137,732 | -2.4 | 9,772 | 6,917 | -29.2 | 44,545 | 42,542 | -4.5 | 3,477 | 2,446 | -29.7 |
| **Property crime[2]** | 354,725 | 294,307 | -17.0 | 43,024 | 28,334 | -34.1 | 222,288 | 158,424 | -28.7 | 22,449 | 11,927 | -46.9 |
| Burglary | 63,786 | 57,900 | -9.2 | 8,968 | 6,569 | -26.8 | 16,795 | 13,471 | -19.8 | 1,452 | 1,064 | -26.7 |
| Larceny-theft | 258,149 | 202,076 | -21.7 | 27,751 | 16,252 | -41.4 | 195,612 | 135,112 | -30.9 | 19,491 | 9,557 | -51.0 |
| Motor vehicle theft | 29,523 | 30,498 | +3.3 | 5,582 | 4,979 | -10.8 | 8,942 | 8,819 | -1.4 | 1,377 | 1,215 | -11.8 |
| Arson | 3,267 | 3,833 | +17.3 | 723 | 534 | -26.1 | 939 | 1,022 | +8.8 | 129 | 91 | -29.5 |
| Other assaults | 337,622 | 306,007 | -9.4 | 35,579 | 21,041 | -40.9 | 140,826 | 123,707 | -12.2 | 21,744 | 13,070 | -39.9 |
| Forgery and counterfeiting | 14,814 | 10,387 | -29.9 | 358 | 203 | -43.3 | 7,489 | 5,017 | -33.0 | 113 | 48 | -57.5 |
| Fraud | 34,026 | 23,374 | -31.3 | 1,293 | 882 | -31.8 | 18,767 | 12,971 | -30.9 | 612 | 463 | -24.3 |
| Embezzlement | 3,641 | 2,478 | -31.9 | 177 | 129 | -27.1 | 3,804 | 2,360 | -38.0 | 143 | 124 | -13.3 |
| Stolen property; buying, receiving, possessing | 33,954 | 33,759 | -0.6 | 4,200 | 3,784 | -9.9 | 9,917 | 8,860 | -10.7 | 882 | 669 | -24.1 |
| Vandalism | 67,298 | 65,166 | -3.2 | 12,684 | 9,313 | -26.6 | 20,675 | 20,122 | -2.7 | 3,073 | 2,443 | -20.5 |
| Weapons; carrying, possessing, etc. | 65,554 | 69,689 | +6.3 | 7,486 | 5,347 | -28.6 | 6,779 | 7,161 | +5.6 | 809 | 442 | -45.4 |
| Prostitution and commercialized vice | 4,333 | 2,691 | -37.9 | 41 | 11 | -73.2 | 6,331 | 3,115 | -50.8 | 34 | 12 | -64.7 |
| Sex offenses (except forcible rape and prostitution) | 17,143 | 13,325 | -22.3 | 2,725 | 1,592 | -41.6 | 1,232 | 825 | -33.0 | 355 | 186 | -47.6 |
| Drug abuse violations | 504,455 | 384,947 | -23.7 | 27,998 | 15,288 | -45.4 | 165,676 | 122,877 | -25.8 | 10,036 | 5,126 | -48.9 |
| Gambling | 666 | 473 | -29.0 | 47 | 24 | -48.9 | 243 | 222 | -8.6 | 4 | 6 | +50.0 |
| Offenses against the family and children | 16,890 | 15,138 | -10.4 | 808 | 652 | -19.3 | 9,712 | 8,211 | -15.5 | 608 | 498 | -18.1 |
| Driving under the influence | 252,919 | 201,665 | -20.3 | 1,538 | 1,642 | +6.8 | 90,670 | 70,456 | -22.3 | 533 | 601 | +12.8 |
| Liquor laws | 52,149 | 33,247 | -36.2 | 6,173 | 4,546 | -26.4 | 22,988 | 13,937 | -39.4 | 4,555 | 3,226 | -29.2 |
| Drunkenness | 122,465 | 76,351 | -37.7 | 1,123 | 735 | -34.6 | 32,921 | 21,019 | -36.2 | 557 | 381 | -31.6 |
| Disorderly conduct | 106,038 | 80,056 | -24.5 | 16,645 | 8,083 | -51.4 | 44,545 | 34,071 | -23.5 | 10,079 | 4,759 | -52.8 |
| Vagrancy | 7,729 | 5,938 | -23.2 | 160 | 126 | -21.3 | 2,300 | 1,839 | -20.0 | 59 | 48 | -18.6 |
| All other offenses (except traffic) | 943,813 | 675,820 | -28.4 | 48,048 | 30,451 | -36.6 | 350,589 | 237,623 | -32.2 | 20,591 | 12,753 | -38.1 |
| Suspicion | 91 | 83 | -8.8 | 5 | 12 | +140.0 | 51 | 58 | +13.7 | 0 | 5 | |
| Curfew and loitering law violations | 5,638 | 4,269 | -24.3 | 5,638 | 4,269 | -24.3 | 2,864 | 2,264 | -20.9 | 2,864 | 2,264 | -20.9 |

1 Does not include suspicion.   2 Violent crimes are offenses of murder and nonnegligent manslaughter, rape, robbery, and aggravated assault.  Property crimes are offenses of burglary, larceny-theft, motor vehicle theft, and arson.   3 The rape figures in this table are aggregate totals of the data submitted based on both the legacy and revised Uniform Crime Reporting definitions.

## Table 46. Arrests, Cities, Distribution by Age, 2020

(Number, percent; 7,634 agencies; 2020 estimated population 159,832,632.)

| Offense charged | Total, all ages | Ages under 15 | Ages under 18 | Ages 18 and over | Under 10 | 10–12 | 13–14 | 15 | 16 | 17 | 18 | 19 |
|---|---|---|---|---|---|---|---|---|---|---|---|---|
| **Total** | 3,851,277 | 70,529 | 238,424 | 3,612,853 | 922 | 14,926 | 54,681 | 45,465 | 55,840 | 66,590 | 93,813 | 104,216 |
| Total percent distribution[1] | 100.0 | 1.8 | 6.2 | 93.8 | * | 0.4 | 1.4 | 1.2 | 1.4 | 1.7 | 2.4 | 2.7 |
| | | | | | | | | | | | | |
| **Violent crime[2]** | 267,047 | 5,486 | 20,454 | 246,593 | 60 | 1,139 | 4,287 | 3,928 | 5,028 | 6,012 | 7,443 | 7,674 |
| Violent crime percent distribution[1] | 100.0 | 2.1 | 7.7 | 92.3 | * | 0.4 | 1.6 | 1.5 | 1.9 | 2.3 | 2.8 | 2.9 |
| Murder and nonnegligent manslaughter | 6,510 | 48 | 520 | 5,990 | 1 | 3 | 44 | 78 | 161 | 233 | 340 | 338 |
| Rape[3] | 10,360 | 609 | 1,419 | 8,941 | 7 | 190 | 412 | 265 | 254 | 291 | 353 | 345 |
| Robbery | 41,569 | 1,631 | 7,679 | 33,890 | 2 | 185 | 1,444 | 1,575 | 2,092 | 2,381 | 2,560 | 2,067 |
| Aggravated assault | 208,608 | 3,198 | 10,836 | 197,772 | 50 | 761 | 2,387 | 2,010 | 2,521 | 3,107 | 4,190 | 4,924 |
| | | | | | | | | | | | | |
| **Property crime[2]** | 506,199 | 12,825 | 44,275 | 461,924 | 147 | 2,385 | 10,293 | 9,058 | 10,662 | 11,730 | 13,959 | 13,633 |
| Property crime percent distribution[1] | 100.0 | 2.5 | 8.7 | 91.3 | * | 0.5 | 2.0 | 1.8 | 2.1 | 2.3 | 2.8 | 2.7 |
| Burglary | 80,714 | 2,721 | 8,383 | 72,331 | 58 | 550 | 2,113 | 1,721 | 1,870 | 2,071 | 2,304 | 2,241 |
| Larceny-theft | 375,128 | 7,715 | 28,382 | 346,746 | 63 | 1,483 | 6,169 | 5,589 | 7,002 | 8,076 | 10,161 | 10,013 |
| Motor vehicle theft | 44,997 | 2,014 | 6,839 | 38,158 | 5 | 221 | 1,788 | 1,626 | 1,694 | 1,505 | 1,430 | 1,292 |
| Arson | 5,360 | 375 | 671 | 4,689 | 21 | 131 | 223 | 122 | 96 | 78 | 64 | 87 |
| | | | | | | | | | | | | |
| Other assaults | 490,395 | 15,347 | 38,945 | 451,450 | 184 | 4,026 | 11,137 | 7,427 | 7,917 | 8,254 | 9,520 | 10,711 |
| Forgery and counterfeiting | 17,093 | 43 | 269 | 16,824 | 0 | 6 | 37 | 44 | 66 | 116 | 489 | 699 |
| Fraud | 40,644 | 386 | 1,443 | 39,201 | 1 | 53 | 332 | 280 | 331 | 446 | 856 | 1,070 |
| Embezzlement | 5,322 | 6 | 265 | 5,057 | 0 | 1 | 5 | 5 | 83 | 171 | 297 | 290 |
| Stolen property; buying, receiving, possessing | 46,638 | 1,037 | 4,782 | 41,856 | 2 | 101 | 934 | 1,022 | 1,289 | 1,434 | 1,652 | 1,572 |
| | | | | | | | | | | | | |
| Vandalism | 96,164 | 5,267 | 13,019 | 83,145 | 132 | 1,365 | 3,770 | 2,573 | 2,635 | 2,544 | 2,821 | 2,918 |
| Weapons; carrying, possessing, etc. | 88,908 | 1,239 | 6,619 | 82,289 | 15 | 242 | 982 | 1,145 | 1,703 | 2,532 | 3,573 | 3,804 |
| Prostitution and commercialized vice | 10,617 | 5 | 57 | 10,560 | 0 | 0 | 5 | 7 | 19 | 26 | 308 | 445 |
| Sex offenses (except forcible rape and prostitution) | 16,162 | 962 | 1,959 | 14,203 | 24 | 277 | 661 | 309 | 356 | 332 | 405 | 443 |
| Drug abuse violations | 561,935 | 3,736 | 22,808 | 539,127 | 14 | 467 | 3,255 | 3,659 | 5,975 | 9,438 | 16,820 | 18,800 |
| | | | | | | | | | | | | |
| Gambling | 861 | 6 | 31 | 830 | 0 | 2 | 4 | 5 | 12 | 8 | 13 | 8 |
| Offenses against the family and children | 26,519 | 431 | 1,357 | 25,162 | 20 | 103 | 308 | 280 | 347 | 299 | 407 | 428 |
| Driving under the influence | 311,168 | 51 | 2,591 | 308,577 | 0 | 1 | 50 | 143 | 670 | 1,727 | 4,252 | 6,030 |
| Liquor laws | 53,701 | 1,178 | 8,746 | 44,955 | 4 | 132 | 1,042 | 1,501 | 2,451 | 3,616 | 7,117 | 7,236 |
| Drunkenness | 115,065 | 244 | 1,488 | 113,577 | 1 | 29 | 214 | 255 | 359 | 630 | 1,558 | 1,886 |
| | | | | | | | | | | | | |
| Disorderly conduct | 128,297 | 5,640 | 13,995 | 114,302 | 57 | 1,454 | 4,129 | 2,718 | 2,826 | 2,811 | 3,300 | 3,570 |
| Vagrancy | 8,813 | 42 | 179 | 8,634 | 2 | 5 | 35 | 33 | 51 | 53 | 238 | 233 |
| All other offenses (except traffic) | 1,052,267 | 14,046 | 47,857 | 1,004,410 | 246 | 2,738 | 11,062 | 9,436 | 11,224 | 13,151 | 18,779 | 22,760 |
| Suspicion | 200 | 9 | 23 | 177 | 2 | 3 | 4 | 2 | 5 | 7 | 6 | 6 |
| Curfew and loitering law violations | 7,262 | 2,543 | 7,262 | NA | 11 | 397 | 2,135 | 1,635 | 1,831 | 1,253 | NA | NA |

NA = Not available.
* = Less than one-tenth of one percent.
1 Because of rounding, the percentages may not sum to 100.   2 Violent crimes are offenses of murder and nonnegligent manslaughter, rape, robbery, and aggravated assault.  Property crimes are offenses of burglary, larceny-theft, motor vehicle theft, and arson.   3 The rape figures in this table are aggregate totals of the data submitted based on both the legacy and revised Uniform Crime Reporting definitions.

## Table 46. Arrests, Cities, Distribution by Age, 2020—Continued

(Number, percent; 7,634 agencies; 2020 estimated population 159,832,632.)

| Offense charged | 20 | 21 | 22 | 23 | 24 | 25–29 | 30–34 | 35–39 | 40–44 | 45–49 | 50–54 | 55–59 | 60–64 | 65 and over |
|---|---|---|---|---|---|---|---|---|---|---|---|---|---|---|
| **Total** | 109,401 | 110,690 | 112,363 | 113,333 | 117,043 | 648,064 | 609,848 | 499,479 | 358,009 | 245,376 | 198,840 | 153,008 | 84,099 | 55,271 |
| Total percent distribution[1] | 2.8 | 2.9 | 2.9 | 2.9 | 3.0 | 16.8 | 15.8 | 13.0 | 9.3 | 6.4 | 5.2 | 4.0 | 2.2 | 1.4 |
| | | | | | | | | | | | | | | |
| **Violent crime[2]** | 8,088 | 8,313 | 8,589 | 8,508 | 8,681 | 46,848 | 41,377 | 32,833 | 22,551 | 15,351 | 12,023 | 9,257 | 5,273 | 3,784 |
| Violent crime percent distribution[1] | 3.0 | 3.1 | 3.2 | 3.2 | 3.3 | 17.5 | 15.5 | 12.3 | 8.4 | 5.7 | 4.5 | 3.5 | 2.0 | 1.4 |
| Murder and nonnegligent manslaughter | 319 | 324 | 280 | 284 | 276 | 1,246 | 812 | 615 | 418 | 252 | 170 | 141 | 87 | 88 |
| Rape[3] | 333 | 334 | 296 | 277 | 303 | 1,336 | 1,354 | 1,192 | 861 | 642 | 478 | 383 | 233 | 221 |
| Robbery | 1,842 | 1,595 | 1,489 | 1,314 | 1,338 | 6,752 | 5,327 | 3,775 | 2,310 | 1,386 | 1,055 | 680 | 275 | 125 |
| Aggravated assault | 5,594 | 6,060 | 6,524 | 6,633 | 6,764 | 37,514 | 33,884 | 27,251 | 18,962 | 13,071 | 10,320 | 8,053 | 4,678 | 3,350 |
| | | | | | | | | | | | | | | |
| **Property crime[2]** | 13,124 | 12,863 | 13,059 | 13,342 | 13,979 | 82,039 | 82,163 | 66,783 | 46,980 | 31,278 | 25,725 | 18,340 | 9,235 | 5,422 |
| Property crime percent distribution[1] | 2.6 | 2.5 | 2.6 | 2.6 | 2.8 | 16.2 | 16.2 | 13.2 | 9.3 | 6.2 | 5.1 | 3.6 | 1.8 | 1.1 |
| Burglary | 2,163 | 2,005 | 2,154 | 2,221 | 2,440 | 13,868 | 13,546 | 10,545 | 7,101 | 4,405 | 3,460 | 2,343 | 1,051 | 484 |
| Larceny-theft | 9,677 | 9,502 | 9,495 | 9,740 | 10,068 | 59,204 | 60,136 | 50,052 | 35,827 | 24,645 | 20,685 | 15,041 | 7,758 | 4,742 |
| Motor vehicle theft | 1,197 | 1,254 | 1,312 | 1,283 | 1,341 | 8,133 | 7,659 | 5,450 | 3,514 | 1,863 | 1,286 | 752 | 289 | 103 |
| Arson | 87 | 102 | 98 | 98 | 130 | 834 | 822 | 736 | 538 | 365 | 294 | 204 | 137 | 93 |
| | | | | | | | | | | | | | | |
| Other assaults | 12,769 | 13,779 | 14,414 | 14,792 | 15,004 | 82,751 | 76,205 | 62,181 | 45,402 | 31,246 | 25,192 | 19,168 | 10,580 | 7,736 |
| Forgery and counterfeiting | 669 | 398 | 471 | 421 | 485 | 3,057 | 2,944 | 2,648 | 1,691 | 1,135 | 799 | 518 | 255 | 145 |
| Fraud | 1,180 | 1,075 | 1,152 | 1,182 | 1,268 | 7,123 | 7,209 | 5,928 | 4,089 | 2,606 | 1,920 | 1,409 | 709 | 425 |
| Embezzlement | 245 | 223 | 208 | 177 | 186 | 829 | 722 | 579 | 419 | 316 | 256 | 182 | 82 | 46 |
| Stolen property; buying, receiving, possessing | 1,494 | 1,379 | 1,407 | 1,322 | 1,518 | 8,358 | 8,025 | 6,033 | 3,881 | 2,263 | 1,467 | 922 | 399 | 164 |
| | | | | | | | | | | | | | | |
| Vandalism | 2,832 | 2,871 | 2,966 | 3,036 | 3,105 | 16,364 | 14,380 | 11,181 | 7,605 | 4,621 | 3,586 | 2,572 | 1,327 | 960 |
| Weapons; carrying, possessing, etc. | 3,915 | 4,310 | 4,134 | 3,930 | 3,658 | 17,555 | 13,141 | 9,228 | 5,929 | 3,458 | 2,383 | 1,718 | 933 | 620 |
| Prostitution and commercialized vice | 547 | 624 | 523 | 460 | 460 | 2,106 | 1,490 | 1,045 | 796 | 586 | 470 | 323 | 197 | 180 |
| Sex offenses (except forcible rape and prostitution) | 368 | 372 | 325 | 310 | 327 | 1,932 | 1,979 | 1,945 | 1,490 | 1,101 | 954 | 904 | 652 | 696 |
| Drug abuse violations | 19,325 | 18,108 | 18,011 | 18,004 | 18,671 | 103,384 | 94,234 | 75,934 | 51,966 | 32,821 | 24,515 | 17,156 | 8,029 | 3,349 |
| | | | | | | | | | | | | | | |
| Gambling | 29 | 14 | 21 | 21 | 16 | 109 | 120 | 124 | 98 | 89 | 71 | 47 | 20 | 30 |
| Offenses against the family and children | 577 | 628 | 626 | 721 | 775 | 4,720 | 4,987 | 4,071 | 2,811 | 1,753 | 1,174 | 759 | 429 | 296 |
| Driving under the influence | 7,615 | 10,448 | 10,822 | 11,043 | 11,191 | 55,648 | 47,694 | 38,321 | 29,271 | 22,509 | 18,893 | 16,230 | 10,396 | 8,214 |
| Liquor laws | 5,716 | 1,215 | 887 | 781 | 706 | 3,544 | 3,257 | 3,048 | 2,541 | 2,306 | 2,285 | 2,173 | 1,336 | 807 |
| Drunkenness | 2,098 | 2,925 | 2,962 | 2,971 | 3,153 | 17,113 | 17,039 | 15,997 | 12,131 | 9,794 | 9,180 | 8,040 | 4,375 | 2,355 |
| | | | | | | | | | | | | | | |
| Disorderly conduct | 3,556 | 4,109 | 3,918 | 3,675 | 3,723 | 18,838 | 17,490 | 14,800 | 11,180 | 7,948 | 6,801 | 5,637 | 3,313 | 2,444 |
| Vagrancy | 202 | 184 | 202 | 206 | 190 | 1,217 | 1,231 | 1,099 | 943 | 739 | 724 | 637 | 360 | 229 |
| All other offenses (except traffic) | 25,051 | 26,850 | 27,660 | 28,429 | 29,941 | 174,513 | 174,127 | 145,674 | 106,208 | 73,441 | 60,411 | 47,007 | 26,194 | 17,365 |
| Suspicion | 1 | 2 | 6 | 2 | 6 | 16 | 34 | 27 | 27 | 15 | 11 | 9 | 5 | 4 |
| Curfew and loitering law violations | NA | NA | NA | NA | NA | NA | NA | NA | NA | NA | NA | NA | NA | NA |

NA = Not available.

* = Less than one-tenth of one percent.

1 Because of rounding, the percentages may not sum to 100.   2 Violent crimes are offenses of murder and nonnegligent manslaughter, rape, robbery, and aggravated assault.  Property crimes are offenses of burglary, larceny-theft, motor vehicle theft, and arson.   3 The rape figures in this table are aggregate totals of the data submitted based on both the legacy and revised Uniform Crime Reporting definitions.

# Table 47. Arrests, Cities, Persons Under 15, 18, 21, and 25 Years of Age, 2020

(Number; percent; 7,634 agencies; 2020 estimated population 159,832,632.)

| Offense charged | Total, all ages | Number of persons arrested | | | | Percent of total of all ages | | | |
|---|---|---|---|---|---|---|---|---|---|
| | | Under 15 | Under 18 | Under 21 | Under 25 | Under 15 | Under 18 | Under 21 | Under 25 |
| **Total** | 3,851,277 | 70,529 | 238,424 | 545,854 | 999,283 | 1.8 | 6.2 | 14.2 | 25.9 |
| **Violent crime[1]** | 267,047 | 5,486 | 20,454 | 43,659 | 77,750 | 2.1 | 7.7 | 16.3 | 29.1 |
| Murder and nonnegligent manslaughter | 6,510 | 48 | 520 | 1,517 | 2,681 | 0.7 | 8.0 | 23.3 | 41.2 |
| Rape[2] | 10,360 | 609 | 1,419 | 2,450 | 3,660 | 5.9 | 13.7 | 23.6 | 35.3 |
| Robbery | 41,569 | 1,631 | 7,679 | 14,148 | 19,884 | 3.9 | 18.5 | 34.0 | 47.8 |
| Aggravated assault | 208,608 | 3,198 | 10,836 | 25,544 | 51,525 | 1.5 | 5.2 | 12.2 | 24.7 |
| **Property crime[1]** | 506,199 | 12,825 | 44,275 | 84,991 | 138,234 | 2.5 | 8.7 | 16.8 | 27.3 |
| Burglary | 80,714 | 2,721 | 8,383 | 15,091 | 23,911 | 3.4 | 10.4 | 18.7 | 29.6 |
| Larceny-theft | 375,128 | 7,715 | 28,382 | 58,233 | 97,038 | 2.1 | 7.6 | 15.5 | 25.9 |
| Motor vehicle theft | 44,997 | 2,014 | 6,839 | 10,758 | 15,948 | 4.5 | 15.2 | 23.9 | 35.4 |
| Arson | 5,360 | 375 | 671 | 909 | 1,337 | 7.0 | 12.5 | 17.0 | 24.9 |
| Other assaults | 490,395 | 15,347 | 38,945 | 71,945 | 129,934 | 3.1 | 7.9 | 14.7 | 26.5 |
| Forgery and counterfeiting | 17,093 | 43 | 269 | 2,126 | 3,901 | 0.3 | 1.6 | 12.4 | 22.8 |
| Fraud | 40,644 | 386 | 1,443 | 4,549 | 9,226 | 0.9 | 3.6 | 11.2 | 22.7 |
| Embezzlement | 5,322 | 6 | 265 | 1,097 | 1,891 | 0.1 | 5.0 | 20.6 | 35.5 |
| Stolen property; buying, receiving, possessing | 46,638 | 1,037 | 4,782 | 9,500 | 15,126 | 2.2 | 10.3 | 20.4 | 32.4 |
| Vandalism | 96,164 | 5,267 | 13,019 | 21,590 | 33,568 | 5.5 | 13.5 | 22.5 | 34.9 |
| Weapons; carrying, possessing, etc. | 88,908 | 1,239 | 6,619 | 17,911 | 33,943 | 1.4 | 7.4 | 20.1 | 38.2 |
| Prostitution and commercialized vice | 10,617 | 5 | 57 | 1,357 | 3,424 | * | 0.5 | 12.8 | 32.3 |
| Sex offenses (except forcible rape and prostitution) | 16,162 | 962 | 1,959 | 3,175 | 4,509 | 6.0 | 12.1 | 19.6 | 27.9 |
| Drug abuse violations | 561,935 | 3,736 | 22,808 | 77,753 | 150,547 | 0.7 | 4.1 | 13.8 | 26.8 |
| Gambling | 861 | 6 | 31 | 81 | 153 | 0.7 | 3.6 | 9.4 | 17.8 |
| Offenses against the family and children | 26,519 | 431 | 1,357 | 2,769 | 5,519 | 1.6 | 5.1 | 10.4 | 20.8 |
| Driving under the influence | 311,168 | 51 | 2,591 | 20,488 | 63,992 | * | 0.8 | 6.6 | 20.6 |
| Liquor laws | 53,701 | 1,178 | 8,746 | 28,815 | 32,404 | 2.2 | 16.3 | 53.7 | 60.3 |
| Drunkenness | 115,065 | 244 | 1,488 | 7,030 | 19,041 | 0.2 | 1.3 | 6.1 | 16.5 |
| Disorderly conduct | 128,297 | 5,640 | 13,995 | 24,421 | 39,846 | 4.4 | 10.9 | 19.0 | 31.1 |
| Vagrancy | 8,813 | 42 | 179 | 852 | 1,634 | 0.5 | 2.0 | 9.7 | 18.5 |
| All other offenses (except traffic) | 1,052,267 | 14,046 | 47,857 | 114,447 | 227,327 | 1.3 | 4.5 | 10.9 | 21.6 |
| Suspicion | 200 | 9 | 23 | 36 | 52 | 4.5 | 11.5 | 18.0 | 26.0 |
| Curfew and loitering law violations | 7,262 | 2,543 | 7,262 | 7,262 | 7,262 | 35.0 | 100.0 | 100.0 | 100.0 |

* = Less than one-tenth of one percent.
1 Violent crimes are offenses of murder and nonnegligent manslaughter, rape, robbery, and aggravated assault.  Property crimes are offenses of burglary, larceny-theft, motor vehicle theft, and arson.   2 The rape figures in this table are aggregate totals of the data submitted based on both the legacy and revised Uniform Crime Reporting definitions.

## Table 48. Arrests, Cities, Distribution by Sex, 2020

(Number, percent;7,634 agencies; 2020 estimated population 159,832,632.)

| Offense charged | Number of persons arrested | | | Percent male | Percent female | Percent distribution[1] | | |
|---|---|---|---|---|---|---|---|---|
| | Total | Male | Female | | | Total | Male | Female |
| **Total** | 3,851,277 | 2,822,740 | 1,028,537 | 73.3 | 26.7 | 100.0 | 100.0 | 100.0 |
| **Violent crime[2]** | 267,047 | 210,289 | 56,758 | 78.7 | 21.3 | 6.9 | 7.4 | 5.5 |
| Murder and nonnegligent manslaughter | 6,510 | 5,741 | 769 | 88.2 | 11.8 | 0.2 | 0.2 | 0.1 |
| Rape[3] | 10,360 | 10,062 | 298 | 97.1 | 2.9 | 0.3 | 0.4 | * |
| Robbery | 41,569 | 35,282 | 6,287 | 84.9 | 15.1 | 1.1 | 1.2 | 0.6 |
| Aggravated assault | 208,608 | 159,204 | 49,404 | 76.3 | 23.7 | 5.4 | 5.6 | 4.8 |
| **Property crime[2]** | 506,199 | 329,593 | 176,606 | 65.1 | 34.9 | 13.1 | 11.7 | 17.2 |
| Burglary | 80,714 | 65,245 | 15,469 | 80.8 | 19.2 | 2.1 | 2.3 | 1.5 |
| Larceny-theft | 375,128 | 225,192 | 149,936 | 60.0 | 40.0 | 9.7 | 8.0 | 14.6 |
| Motor vehicle theft | 44,997 | 34,942 | 10,055 | 77.7 | 22.3 | 1.2 | 1.2 | 1.0 |
| Arson | 5,360 | 4,214 | 1,146 | 78.6 | 21.4 | 0.1 | 0.1 | 0.1 |
| Other assaults | 490,395 | 348,226 | 142,169 | 71.0 | 29.0 | 12.7 | 12.3 | 13.8 |
| Forgery and counterfeiting | 17,093 | 11,526 | 5,567 | 67.4 | 32.6 | 0.4 | 0.4 | 0.5 |
| Fraud | 40,644 | 26,271 | 14,373 | 64.6 | 35.4 | 1.1 | 0.9 | 1.4 |
| Embezzlement | 5,322 | 2,740 | 2,582 | 51.5 | 48.5 | 0.1 | 0.1 | 0.3 |
| Stolen property; buying, receiving, possessing | 46,638 | 36,886 | 9,752 | 79.1 | 20.9 | 1.2 | 1.3 | 0.9 |
| Vandalism | 96,164 | 73,469 | 22,695 | 76.4 | 23.6 | 2.5 | 2.6 | 2.2 |
| Weapons; carrying, possessing, etc. | 88,908 | 80,740 | 8,168 | 90.8 | 9.2 | 2.3 | 2.9 | 0.8 |
| Prostitution and commercialized vice | 10,617 | 4,267 | 6,350 | 40.2 | 59.8 | 0.3 | 0.2 | 0.6 |
| Sex offenses (except forcible rape and prostitution) | 16,162 | 15,193 | 969 | 94.0 | 6.0 | 0.4 | 0.5 | 0.1 |
| Drug abuse violations | 561,935 | 426,272 | 135,663 | 75.9 | 24.1 | 14.6 | 15.1 | 13.2 |
| Gambling | 861 | 608 | 253 | 70.6 | 29.4 | * | * | * |
| Offenses against the family and children | 26,519 | 17,020 | 9,499 | 64.2 | 35.8 | 0.7 | 0.6 | 0.9 |
| Driving under the influence | 311,168 | 230,897 | 80,271 | 74.2 | 25.8 | 8.1 | 8.2 | 7.8 |
| Liquor laws | 53,701 | 37,960 | 15,741 | 70.7 | 29.3 | 1.4 | 1.3 | 1.5 |
| Drunkenness | 115,065 | 89,661 | 25,404 | 77.9 | 22.1 | 3.0 | 3.2 | 2.5 |
| Disorderly conduct | 128,297 | 89,935 | 38,362 | 70.1 | 29.9 | 3.3 | 3.2 | 3.7 |
| Vagrancy | 8,813 | 6,707 | 2,106 | 76.1 | 23.9 | 0.2 | 0.2 | 0.2 |
| All other offenses (except traffic) | 1,052,267 | 779,571 | 272,696 | 74.1 | 25.9 | 27.3 | 27.6 | 26.5 |
| Suspicion | 200 | 125 | 75 | 62.5 | 37.5 | * | * | * |
| Curfew and loitering law violations | 7,262 | 4,784 | 2,478 | 65.9 | 34.1 | 0.2 | 0.2 | 0.2 |

* = Less than one-tenth of 1 percent.
1 Because of rounding, the percentages may not sum to 100.    2 Violent crimes are offenses of murder and nonnegligent manslaughter, rape, robbery, and aggravated assault.  Property crimes are offenses of burglary, larceny-theft, motor vehicle theft, and arson.    3 The rape figures in this table are aggregate totals of the data submitted based on both the legacy and revised Uniform Crime Reporting definitions.

## Table 49. Arrests, Cities, Distribution by Race, 2020

(Number, percent; 7,634 agencies; 2020 estimated population 159,832,632.)

| Offense charged | Total arrests | | | | | | Percent distribution[1] | | | | | |
|---|---|---|---|---|---|---|---|---|---|---|---|---|
| | Total | White | Black | American Indian or Alaskan Native | Asian | Native Hawaiian or Other Pacific Islander | Total | White | Black | American Indian or Alaskan Native | Asian | Native Hawaiian or Other Pacific Islander |
| **Total** | 3,801,295 | 2,568,795 | 1,068,582 | 106,077 | 49,702 | 8,139 | 100.0 | 67.6 | 28.1 | 2.8 | 1.3 | 0.2 |
| **Violent crime[2]** | 264,244 | 150,319 | 101,962 | 6,664 | 4,423 | 876 | 100.0 | 56.9 | 38.6 | 2.5 | 1.7 | 0.3 |
| Murder and nonnegligent manslaughter | 6,447 | 2,680 | 3,595 | 73 | 85 | 14 | 100.0 | 41.6 | 55.8 | 1.1 | 1.3 | 0.2 |
| Rape[3] | 10,164 | 6,777 | 2,964 | 215 | 182 | 26 | 100.0 | 66.7 | 29.2 | 2.1 | 1.8 | 0.3 |
| Robbery | 41,265 | 19,146 | 20,970 | 629 | 399 | 121 | 100.0 | 46.4 | 50.8 | 1.5 | 1.0 | 0.3 |
| Aggravated assault | 206,368 | 121,716 | 74,433 | 5,747 | 3,757 | 715 | 100.0 | 59.0 | 36.1 | 2.8 | 1.8 | 0.3 |
| **Property crime[2]** | 499,491 | 336,712 | 145,099 | 11,208 | 5,623 | 849 | 100.0 | 67.4 | 29.0 | 2.2 | 1.1 | 0.2 |
| Burglary | 79,984 | 52,984 | 24,457 | 1,310 | 1,074 | 159 | 100.0 | 66.2 | 30.6 | 1.6 | 1.3 | 0.2 |
| Larceny-theft | 369,594 | 249,968 | 106,514 | 8,739 | 3,825 | 548 | 100.0 | 67.6 | 28.8 | 2.4 | 1.0 | 0.1 |
| Motor vehicle theft | 44,604 | 30,006 | 12,844 | 1,028 | 596 | 130 | 100.0 | 67.3 | 28.8 | 2.3 | 1.3 | 0.3 |
| Arson | 5,309 | 3,754 | 1,284 | 131 | 128 | 12 | 100.0 | 70.7 | 24.2 | 2.5 | 2.4 | 0.2 |
| Other assaults | 483,922 | 301,722 | 161,366 | 12,461 | 7,270 | 1,103 | 100.0 | 62.3 | 33.3 | 2.6 | 1.5 | 0.2 |
| Forgery and counterfeiting | 16,900 | 11,620 | 4,772 | 193 | 295 | 20 | 100.0 | 68.8 | 28.2 | 1.1 | 1.7 | 0.1 |
| Fraud | 40,104 | 25,781 | 12,770 | 887 | 613 | 53 | 100.0 | 64.3 | 31.8 | 2.2 | 1.5 | 0.1 |
| Embezzlement | 5,239 | 3,111 | 1,955 | 64 | 99 | 10 | 100.0 | 59.4 | 37.3 | 1.2 | 1.9 | 0.2 |
| Stolen property; buying, receiving, possessing | 46,053 | 27,588 | 16,861 | 796 | 691 | 117 | 100.0 | 59.9 | 36.6 | 1.7 | 1.5 | 0.3 |
| Vandalism | 94,762 | 63,073 | 27,608 | 2,596 | 1,276 | 209 | 100.0 | 66.6 | 29.1 | 2.7 | 1.3 | 0.2 |
| Weapons; carrying, possessing, etc. | 88,057 | 43,247 | 42,648 | 931 | 1,003 | 228 | 100.0 | 49.1 | 48.4 | 1.1 | 1.1 | 0.3 |
| Prostitution and commercialized vice | 10,560 | 5,529 | 4,442 | 47 | 491 | 51 | 100.0 | 52.4 | 42.1 | 0.4 | 4.6 | 0.5 |
| Sex offenses (except forcible rape and prostitution) | 15,959 | 11,259 | 3,830 | 406 | 424 | 40 | 100.0 | 70.5 | 24.0 | 2.5 | 2.7 | 0.3 |
| Drug abuse violations | 556,826 | 396,584 | 143,071 | 9,120 | 6,835 | 1,216 | 100.0 | 71.2 | 25.7 | 1.6 | 1.2 | 0.2 |
| Gambling | 852 | 535 | 196 | 2 | 110 | 9 | 100.0 | 62.8 | 23.0 | 0.2 | 12.9 | 1.1 |
| Offenses against the family and children | 25,711 | 17,038 | 5,856 | 2,495 | 282 | 40 | 100.0 | 66.3 | 22.8 | 9.7 | 1.1 | 0.2 |
| Driving under the influence | 306,030 | 242,551 | 48,889 | 8,356 | 5,152 | 1,082 | 100.0 | 79.3 | 16.0 | 2.7 | 1.7 | 0.4 |
| Liquor laws | 52,275 | 39,803 | 7,614 | 4,057 | 715 | 86 | 100.0 | 76.1 | 14.6 | 7.8 | 1.4 | 0.2 |
| Drunkenness | 114,038 | 84,776 | 16,531 | 11,336 | 1,162 | 233 | 100.0 | 74.3 | 14.5 | 9.9 | 1.0 | 0.2 |
| Disorderly conduct | 126,138 | 79,998 | 38,363 | 6,425 | 1,157 | 195 | 100.0 | 63.4 | 30.4 | 5.1 | 0.9 | 0.2 |
| Vagrancy | 8,743 | 5,682 | 2,550 | 375 | 121 | 15 | 100.0 | 65.0 | 29.2 | 4.3 | 1.4 | 0.2 |
| All other offenses (except traffic) | 1,038,048 | 716,685 | 280,353 | 27,412 | 11,900 | 1,698 | 100.0 | 69.0 | 27.0 | 2.6 | 1.1 | 0.2 |
| Suspicion | 216 | 121 | 41 | 51 | 2 | 1 | 100.0 | 56.0 | 19.0 | 23.6 | 0.9 | 0.5 |
| Curfew and loitering law violations | 7,127 | 5,061 | 1,805 | 195 | 58 | 8 | 100.0 | 71.0 | 25.3 | 2.7 | 0.8 | 0.1 |

## Table 49. Arrests, Cities, Distribution by Race, 2020—Continued

(Number, percent; 7,634 agencies; 2020 estimated population 159,832,632.)

| Offense charged | Arrests under 18 | | | | | | Percent distribution[1] | | | | | |
|---|---|---|---|---|---|---|---|---|---|---|---|---|
| | Total | White | Black | American Indian or Alaskan Native | Asian | Native Hawaiian or Other Pacific Islander | Total | White | Black | American Indian or Alaskan Native | Asian | Native Hawaiian or Other Pacific Islander |
| **Total** | 233,664 | 145,138 | 78,932 | 6,703 | 2,470 | 421 | 100.0 | 62.1 | 33.8 | 2.9 | 1.1 | 0.2 |
| **Violent crime[2]** | 20,133 | 9,867 | 9,533 | 489 | 193 | 51 | 100.0 | 49.0 | 47.4 | 2.4 | 1.0 | 0.3 |
| Murder and nonnegligent manslaughter | 513 | 196 | 301 | 7 | 6 | 3 | 100.0 | 38.2 | 58.7 | 1.4 | 1.2 | 0.6 |
| Rape[3] | 1,377 | 936 | 392 | 32 | 16 | 1 | 100.0 | 68.0 | 28.5 | 2.3 | 1.2 | 0.1 |
| Robbery | 7,614 | 2,803 | 4,671 | 57 | 55 | 28 | 100.0 | 36.8 | 61.3 | 0.7 | 0.7 | 0.4 |
| Aggravated assault | 10,629 | 5,932 | 4,169 | 393 | 116 | 19 | 100.0 | 55.8 | 39.2 | 3.7 | 1.1 | 0.2 |
| **Property crime[2]** | 43,440 | 23,809 | 18,011 | 969 | 544 | 107 | 100.0 | 54.8 | 41.5 | 2.2 | 1.3 | 0.2 |
| Burglary | 8,244 | 4,524 | 3,466 | 142 | 82 | 30 | 100.0 | 54.9 | 42.0 | 1.7 | 1.0 | 0.4 |
| Larceny-theft | 27,780 | 15,878 | 10,845 | 615 | 378 | 64 | 100.0 | 57.2 | 39.0 | 2.2 | 1.4 | 0.2 |
| Motor vehicle theft | 6,756 | 2,939 | 3,542 | 188 | 74 | 13 | 100.0 | 43.5 | 52.4 | 2.8 | 1.1 | 0.2 |
| Arson | 660 | 468 | 158 | 24 | 10 | 0 | 100.0 | 70.9 | 23.9 | 3.6 | 1.5 | 0.0 |
| Other assaults | 38,181 | 23,499 | 13,369 | 896 | 362 | 55 | 100.0 | 61.5 | 35.0 | 2.3 | 0.9 | 0.1 |
| Forgery and counterfeiting | 263 | 154 | 100 | 3 | 6 | 0 | 100.0 | 58.6 | 38.0 | 1.1 | 2.3 | 0.0 |
| Fraud | 1,425 | 763 | 593 | 42 | 24 | 3 | 100.0 | 53.5 | 41.6 | 2.9 | 1.7 | 0.2 |
| Embezzlement | 258 | 116 | 121 | 2 | 19 | 0 | 100.0 | 45.0 | 46.9 | 0.8 | 7.4 | 0.0 |
| Stolen property; buying, receiving, possessing | 4,700 | 1,406 | 3,159 | 84 | 36 | 15 | 100.0 | 29.9 | 67.2 | 1.8 | 0.8 | 0.3 |
| Vandalism | 12,718 | 9,100 | 3,131 | 364 | 109 | 14 | 100.0 | 71.6 | 24.6 | 2.9 | 0.9 | 0.1 |
| Weapons; carrying, possessing, etc. | 6,552 | 3,133 | 3,254 | 71 | 86 | 8 | 100.0 | 47.8 | 49.7 | 1.1 | 1.3 | 0.1 |
| Prostitution and commercialized vice | 56 | 22 | 30 | 2 | 1 | 1 | 100.0 | 39.3 | 53.6 | 3.6 | 1.8 | 1.8 |
| Sex offenses (except forcible rape and prostitution) | 1,905 | 1,423 | 410 | 38 | 32 | 2 | 100.0 | 74.7 | 21.5 | 2.0 | 1.7 | 0.1 |
| Drug abuse violations | 22,402 | 16,345 | 5,158 | 593 | 264 | 42 | 100.0 | 73.0 | 23.0 | 2.6 | 1.2 | 0.2 |
| Gambling | 29 | 14 | 13 | 1 | 1 | 0 | 100.0 | 48.3 | 44.8 | 3.4 | 3.4 | 0.0 |
| Offenses against the family and children | 1,298 | 880 | 212 | 201 | 5 | 0 | 100.0 | 67.8 | 16.3 | 15.5 | 0.4 | 0.0 |
| Driving under the influence | 2,483 | 2,144 | 175 | 120 | 39 | 5 | 100.0 | 86.3 | 7.0 | 4.8 | 1.6 | 0.2 |
| Liquor laws | 8,490 | 7,077 | 549 | 746 | 104 | 14 | 100.0 | 83.4 | 6.5 | 8.8 | 1.2 | 0.2 |
| Drunkenness | 1,340 | 913 | 209 | 198 | 18 | 2 | 100.0 | 68.1 | 15.6 | 14.8 | 1.3 | 0.1 |
| Disorderly conduct | 13,730 | 7,887 | 5,134 | 560 | 120 | 29 | 100.0 | 57.4 | 37.4 | 4.1 | 0.9 | 0.2 |
| Vagrancy | 178 | 127 | 43 | 3 | 5 | 0 | 100.0 | 71.3 | 24.2 | 1.7 | 2.8 | 0.0 |
| All other offenses (except traffic) | 46,931 | 31,387 | 13,918 | 1,117 | 444 | 65 | 100.0 | 66.9 | 29.7 | 2.4 | 0.9 | 0.1 |
| Suspicion | 25 | 11 | 5 | 9 | 0 | 0 | 100.0 | 44.0 | 20.0 | 36.0 | 0.0 | 0.0 |
| Curfew and loitering law violations | 7,127 | 5,061 | 1,805 | 195 | 58 | 8 | 100.0 | 71.0 | 25.3 | 2.7 | 0.8 | 0.1 |

## Table 49. Arrests, Cities, Distribution by Race, 2020—Continued

(Number, percent; 7,634 agencies; 2020 estimated population 159,832,632.)

| Offense charged | Arrests 18 and over | | | | | | Percent distribution[1] | | | | | |
|---|---|---|---|---|---|---|---|---|---|---|---|---|
| | Total | White | Black | American Indian or Alaskan Native | Asian | Native Hawaiian or Other Pacific Islander | Total | White | Black | American Indian or Alaskan Native | Asian | Native Hawaiian or Other Pacific Islander |
| **Total** | 3,567,631 | 2,423,657 | 989,650 | 99,374 | 47,232 | 7,718 | 100.0 | 67.9 | 27.7 | 2.8 | 1.3 | 0.2 |
| **Violent crime[2]** | 244,111 | 140,452 | 92,429 | 6,175 | 4,230 | 825 | 100.0 | 57.5 | 37.9 | 2.5 | 1.7 | 0.3 |
| Murder and nonnegligent manslaughter | 5,934 | 2,484 | 3,294 | 66 | 79 | 11 | 100.0 | 41.9 | 55.5 | 1.1 | 1.3 | 0.2 |
| Rape[3] | 8,787 | 5,841 | 2,572 | 183 | 166 | 25 | 100.0 | 66.5 | 29.3 | 2.1 | 1.9 | 0.3 |
| Robbery | 33,651 | 16,343 | 16,299 | 572 | 344 | 93 | 100.0 | 48.6 | 48.4 | 1.7 | 1.0 | 0.3 |
| Aggravated assault | 195,739 | 115,784 | 70,264 | 5,354 | 3,641 | 696 | 100.0 | 59.2 | 35.9 | 2.7 | 1.9 | 0.4 |
| **Property crime[2]** | 456,051 | 312,903 | 127,088 | 10,239 | 5,079 | 742 | 100.0 | 68.6 | 27.9 | 2.2 | 1.1 | 0.2 |
| Burglary | 71,740 | 48,460 | 20,991 | 1,168 | 992 | 129 | 100.0 | 67.5 | 29.3 | 1.6 | 1.4 | 0.2 |
| Larceny-theft | 341,814 | 234,090 | 95,669 | 8,124 | 3,447 | 484 | 100.0 | 68.5 | 28.0 | 2.4 | 1.0 | 0.1 |
| Motor vehicle theft | 37,848 | 27,067 | 9,302 | 840 | 522 | 117 | 100.0 | 71.5 | 24.6 | 2.2 | 1.4 | 0.3 |
| Arson | 4,649 | 3,286 | 1,126 | 107 | 118 | 12 | 100.0 | 70.7 | 24.2 | 2.3 | 2.5 | 0.3 |
| Other assaults | 445,741 | 278,223 | 147,997 | 11,565 | 6,908 | 1,048 | 100.0 | 62.4 | 33.2 | 2.6 | 1.5 | 0.2 |
| Forgery and counterfeiting | 16,637 | 11,466 | 4,672 | 190 | 289 | 20 | 100.0 | 68.9 | 28.1 | 1.1 | 1.7 | 0.1 |
| Fraud | 38,679 | 25,018 | 12,177 | 845 | 589 | 50 | 100.0 | 64.7 | 31.5 | 2.2 | 1.5 | 0.1 |
| Embezzlement | 4,981 | 2,995 | 1,834 | 62 | 80 | 10 | 100.0 | 60.1 | 36.8 | 1.2 | 1.6 | 0.2 |
| Stolen property; buying, receiving, possessing | 41,353 | 26,182 | 13,702 | 712 | 655 | 102 | 100.0 | 63.3 | 33.1 | 1.7 | 1.6 | 0.2 |
| Vandalism | 82,044 | 53,973 | 24,477 | 2,232 | 1,167 | 195 | 100.0 | 65.8 | 29.8 | 2.7 | 1.4 | 0.2 |
| Weapons; carrying, possessing, etc. | 81,505 | 40,114 | 39,394 | 860 | 917 | 220 | 100.0 | 49.2 | 48.3 | 1.1 | 1.1 | 0.3 |
| Prostitution and commercialized vice | 10,504 | 5,507 | 4,412 | 45 | 490 | 50 | 100.0 | 52.4 | 42.0 | 0.4 | 4.7 | 0.5 |
| Sex offenses (except forcible rape and prostitution) | 14,054 | 9,836 | 3,420 | 368 | 392 | 38 | 100.0 | 70.0 | 24.3 | 2.6 | 2.8 | 0.3 |
| Drug abuse violations | 534,424 | 380,239 | 137,913 | 8,527 | 6,571 | 1,174 | 100.0 | 71.1 | 25.8 | 1.6 | 1.2 | 0.2 |
| Gambling | 823 | 521 | 183 | 1 | 109 | 9 | 100.0 | 63.3 | 22.2 | 0.1 | 13.2 | 1.1 |
| Offenses against the family and children | 24,413 | 16,158 | 5,644 | 2,294 | 277 | 40 | 100.0 | 66.2 | 23.1 | 9.4 | 1.1 | 0.2 |
| Driving under the influence | 303,547 | 240,407 | 48,714 | 8,236 | 5,113 | 1,077 | 100.0 | 79.2 | 16.0 | 2.7 | 1.7 | 0.4 |
| Liquor laws | 43,785 | 32,726 | 7,065 | 3,311 | 611 | 72 | 100.0 | 74.7 | 16.1 | 7.6 | 1.4 | 0.2 |
| Drunkenness | 112,698 | 83,863 | 16,322 | 11,138 | 1,144 | 231 | 100.0 | 74.4 | 14.5 | 9.9 | 1.0 | 0.2 |
| Disorderly conduct | 112,408 | 72,111 | 33,229 | 5,865 | 1,037 | 166 | 100.0 | 64.2 | 29.6 | 5.2 | 0.9 | 0.1 |
| Vagrancy | 8,565 | 5,555 | 2,507 | 372 | 116 | 15 | 100.0 | 64.9 | 29.3 | 4.3 | 1.4 | 0.2 |
| All other offenses (except traffic) | 991,117 | 685,298 | 266,435 | 26,295 | 11,456 | 1,633 | 100.0 | 69.1 | 26.9 | 2.7 | 1.2 | 0.2 |
| Suspicion | 191 | 110 | 36 | 42 | 2 | 1 | 100.0 | 57.6 | 18.8 | 22.0 | 1.0 | 0.5 |
| Curfew and loitering law violations | NA | NA | NA | NA | NA | NA | NA | NA | NA | NA | NA | NA |

NA = Not available.
1 Because of rounding, the percentages may not sum to 100.    2 Violent crimes are offenses of murder and nonnegligent manslaughter, rape, robbery, and aggravated assault.    Property crimes are offenses of burglary, larceny-theft, motor vehicle theft, and arson.    3 The rape figures in this table are aggregate totals of the data submitted based on both the legacy and revised Uniform Crime Reporting definitions.

## Table 49A. Arrests, Cities, Distribution by Ethnicity, 2020

(Number, percent; 7,634 agencies; 2020 estimated population 159,832,632.)

| Offense charged | Total arrests | | | Percent distribution[1] | | | Arrests under 18 | | |
|---|---|---|---|---|---|---|---|---|---|
| | Total[2] | Hispanic or Latino | Not Hispanic or Latino | Total[2] | Hispanic or Latino | Not Hispanic or Latino | Total[2] | Hispanic or Latino | Not Hispanic or Latino |
| **Total** | 3,299,854 | 726,732 | 2,573,122 | 100.0 | 22.0 | 78.0 | 195,901 | 49,310 | 146,591 |
| **Violent crime[3]** | 233,818 | 65,793 | 168,025 | 100.0 | 28.1 | 71.9 | 17,595 | 5,046 | 12,549 |
| Murder and nonnegligent manslaughter | 5,447 | 1,286 | 4,161 | 100.0 | 23.6 | 76.4 | 444 | 137 | 307 |
| Rape[4] | 8,701 | 2,787 | 5,914 | 100.0 | 32.0 | 68.0 | 1,143 | 318 | 825 |
| Robbery | 36,611 | 9,676 | 26,935 | 100.0 | 26.4 | 73.6 | 6,782 | 1,857 | 4,925 |
| Aggravated assault | 183,059 | 52,044 | 131,015 | 100.0 | 28.4 | 71.6 | 9,226 | 2,734 | 6,492 |
| **Property crime[3]** | 427,403 | 79,467 | 347,936 | 100.0 | 18.6 | 81.4 | 36,222 | 8,122 | 28,100 |
| Burglary | 70,068 | 16,750 | 53,318 | 100.0 | 23.9 | 76.1 | 6,737 | 1,778 | 4,959 |
| Larceny-theft | 312,981 | 49,800 | 263,181 | 100.0 | 15.9 | 84.1 | 23,068 | 4,771 | 18,297 |
| Motor vehicle theft | 39,778 | 11,854 | 27,924 | 100.0 | 29.8 | 70.2 | 5,848 | 1,454 | 4,394 |
| Arson | 4,576 | 1,063 | 3,513 | 100.0 | 23.2 | 76.8 | 569 | 119 | 450 |
| Other assaults | 415,068 | 89,737 | 325,331 | 100.0 | 21.6 | 78.4 | 32,549 | 8,079 | 24,470 |
| Forgery and counterfeiting | 14,989 | 2,537 | 12,452 | 100.0 | 16.9 | 83.1 | 226 | 62 | 164 |
| Fraud | 34,644 | 5,266 | 29,378 | 100.0 | 15.2 | 84.8 | 1,114 | 237 | 877 |
| Embezzlement | 4,537 | 714 | 3,823 | 100.0 | 15.7 | 84.3 | 213 | 31 | 182 |
| Stolen property; buying, receiving, possessing | 39,664 | 8,862 | 30,802 | 100.0 | 22.3 | 77.7 | 3,883 | 844 | 3,039 |
| Vandalism | 81,879 | 18,017 | 63,862 | 100.0 | 22.0 | 78.0 | 10,759 | 2,588 | 8,171 |
| Weapons; carrying, possessing, etc. | 73,107 | 19,137 | 53,970 | 100.0 | 26.2 | 73.8 | 5,635 | 1,952 | 3,683 |
| Prostitution and commercialized vice | 9,968 | 2,535 | 7,433 | 100.0 | 25.4 | 74.6 | 53 | 12 | 41 |
| Sex offenses (except forcible rape and prostitution) | 13,976 | 4,442 | 9,534 | 100.0 | 31.8 | 68.2 | 1,623 | 502 | 1,121 |
| Drug abuse violations | 505,054 | 122,309 | 382,745 | 100.0 | 24.2 | 75.8 | 19,719 | 6,081 | 13,638 |
| Gambling | 820 | 360 | 460 | 100.0 | 43.9 | 56.1 | 23 | 13 | 10 |
| Offenses against the family and children | 21,993 | 4,422 | 17,571 | 100.0 | 20.1 | 79.9 | 1,103 | 240 | 863 |
| Driving under the influence | 264,457 | 77,007 | 187,450 | 100.0 | 29.1 | 70.9 | 2,064 | 710 | 1,354 |
| Liquor laws | 42,006 | 7,657 | 34,349 | 100.0 | 18.2 | 81.8 | 6,838 | 1,387 | 5,451 |
| Drunkenness | 108,742 | 26,696 | 82,046 | 100.0 | 24.5 | 75.5 | 1,265 | 423 | 842 |
| Disorderly conduct | 98,475 | 14,815 | 83,660 | 100.0 | 15.0 | 85.0 | 10,653 | 2,147 | 8,506 |
| Vagrancy | 7,993 | 1,454 | 6,539 | 100.0 | 18.2 | 81.8 | 114 | 29 | 85 |
| All other offenses (except traffic) | 895,248 | 173,904 | 721,344 | 100.0 | 19.4 | 80.6 | 38,382 | 9,215 | 29,167 |
| Suspicion | 163 | 11 | 152 | 100.0 | 6.7 | 93.3 | 18 | 0 | 18 |
| Curfew and loitering law violations | 5,850 | 1,590 | 4,260 | 100.0 | 27.2 | 72.8 | 5,850 | 1,590 | 4,260 |

## Table 49A. Arrests, Cities, Distribution by Ethnicity, 2020—Continued

(Number, percent; 7,634 agencies; 2020 estimated population 159,832,632.)

| Offense charged | Percent distribution[1] | | | | Arrests 18 and over | | | Percent distribution[1] | |
| --- | --- | --- | --- | --- | --- | --- | --- | --- | --- |
| | Total[2] | Hispanic or Latino | Not Hispanic or Latino | Total[2] | Hispanic or Latino | Not Hispanic or Latino | Total[2] | Hispanic or Latino | Not Hispanic or Latino |
| Total | 100.0 | 25.2 | 74.8 | 3,103,953 | 677,422 | 2,426,531 | 100.0 | 21.8 | 78.2 |
| Violent crime[3] | 100.0 | 28.7 | 71.3 | 216,223 | 60,747 | 155,476 | 100.0 | 28.1 | 71.9 |
| Murder and nonnegligent manslaughter | 100.0 | 30.9 | 69.1 | 5,003 | 1,149 | 3,854 | 100.0 | 23.0 | 77.0 |
| Rape[4] | 100.0 | 27.8 | 72.2 | 7,558 | 2,469 | 5,089 | 100.0 | 32.7 | 67.3 |
| Robbery | 100.0 | 27.4 | 72.6 | 29,829 | 7,819 | 22,010 | 100.0 | 26.2 | 73.8 |
| Aggravated assault | 100.0 | 29.6 | 70.4 | 173,833 | 49,310 | 124,523 | 100.0 | 28.4 | 71.6 |
| Property crime[3] | 100.0 | 22.4 | 77.6 | 391,181 | 71,345 | 319,836 | 100.0 | 18.2 | 81.8 |
| Burglary | 100.0 | 26.4 | 73.6 | 63,331 | 14,972 | 48,359 | 100.0 | 23.6 | 76.4 |
| Larceny-theft | 100.0 | 20.7 | 79.3 | 289,913 | 45,029 | 244,884 | 100.0 | 15.5 | 84.5 |
| Motor vehicle theft | 100.0 | 24.9 | 75.1 | 33,930 | 10,400 | 23,530 | 100.0 | 30.7 | 69.3 |
| Arson | 100.0 | 20.9 | 79.1 | 4,007 | 944 | 3,063 | 100.0 | 23.6 | 76.4 |
| Other assaults | 100.0 | 24.8 | 75.2 | 382,519 | 81,658 | 300,861 | 100.0 | 21.3 | 78.7 |
| Forgery and counterfeiting | 100.0 | 27.4 | 72.6 | 14,763 | 2,475 | 12,288 | 100.0 | 16.8 | 83.2 |
| Fraud | 100.0 | 21.3 | 78.7 | 33,530 | 5,029 | 28,501 | 100.0 | 15.0 | 85.0 |
| Embezzlement | 100.0 | 14.6 | 85.4 | 4,324 | 683 | 3,641 | 100.0 | 15.8 | 84.2 |
| Stolen property; buying, receiving, possessing | 100.0 | 21.7 | 78.3 | 35,781 | 8,018 | 27,763 | 100.0 | 22.4 | 77.6 |
| Vandalism | 100.0 | 24.1 | 75.9 | 71,120 | 15,429 | 55,691 | 100.0 | 21.7 | 78.3 |
| Weapons; carrying, possessing, etc. | 100.0 | 34.6 | 65.4 | 67,472 | 17,185 | 50,287 | 100.0 | 25.5 | 74.5 |
| Prostitution and commercialized vice | 100.0 | 22.6 | 77.4 | 9,915 | 2,523 | 7,392 | 100.0 | 25.4 | 74.6 |
| Sex offenses (except forcible rape and prostitution) | 100.0 | 30.9 | 69.1 | 12,353 | 3,940 | 8,413 | 100.0 | 31.9 | 68.1 |
| Drug abuse violations | 100.0 | 30.8 | 69.2 | 485,335 | 116,228 | 369,107 | 100.0 | 23.9 | 76.1 |
| Gambling | 100.0 | 56.5 | 43.5 | 797 | 347 | 450 | 100.0 | 43.5 | 56.5 |
| Offenses against the family and children | 100.0 | 21.8 | 78.2 | 20,890 | 4,182 | 16,708 | 100.0 | 20.0 | 80.0 |
| Driving under the influence | 100.0 | 34.4 | 65.6 | 262,393 | 76,297 | 186,096 | 100.0 | 29.1 | 70.9 |
| Liquor laws | 100.0 | 20.3 | 79.7 | 35,168 | 6,270 | 28,898 | 100.0 | 17.8 | 82.2 |
| Drunkenness | 100.0 | 33.4 | 66.6 | 107,477 | 26,273 | 81,204 | 100.0 | 24.4 | 75.6 |
| Disorderly conduct | 100.0 | 20.2 | 79.8 | 87,822 | 12,668 | 75,154 | 100.0 | 14.4 | 85.6 |
| Vagrancy | 100.0 | 25.4 | 74.6 | 7,879 | 1,425 | 6,454 | 100.0 | 18.1 | 81.9 |
| All other offenses (except traffic) | 100.0 | 24.0 | 76.0 | 856,866 | 164,689 | 692,177 | 100.0 | 19.2 | 80.8 |
| Suspicion | 100.0 | 0.0 | 100.0 | 145 | 11 | 134 | 100.0 | 7.6 | 92.4 |
| Curfew and loitering law violations | 100.0 | 27.2 | 72.8 | NA | NA | NA | NA | NA | NA |

NA = Not available.
1 Because of rounding, the percentages may not sum to 100.   2 The ethnicity totals are representative of those agencies that provided ethnicity breakdowns. Not all agencies provide ethnicity data; therefore, the race and ethnicity totals will not equal.
3 Violent crimes are offenses of murder and nonnegligent manslaughter, rape, robbery, and aggravated assault.  Property crimes are offenses of burglary, larceny-theft, motor vehicle theft, and arson.   4 The rape figures in this table are aggregate totals of the data submitted based on both the legacy and revised Uniform Crime Reporting definitions.

## Table 50. Arrest Trends, Metropolitan Counties, 2019–2020

(Number, percent change; 1,008 agencies; 2020 estimated population 42,367,070; 2019 estimated population 42,067,490.)

| Offense charged | Number of persons arrested | | | | | | | | |
|---|---|---|---|---|---|---|---|---|---|
| | Total, all ages | | | Under 18 years of age | | | 18 years of age and over | | |
| | 2019 | 2020 | Percent change | 2019 | 2020 | Percent change | 2019 | 2020 | Percent change |
| **Total[1]** | 1,089,827 | 838,935 | -23.0 | 57,377 | 36,871 | -35.7 | 1,032,450 | 802,064 | -22.3 |
| **Violent crime[2]** | 46,681 | 44,950 | -3.7 | 3,961 | 2,868 | -27.6 | 42,720 | 42,082 | -1.5 |
| Murder and nonnegligent manslaughter | 1,142 | 1,223 | +7.1 | 62 | 68 | +9.7 | 1,080 | 1,155 | +6.9 |
| Rape[3] | 2,753 | 2,375 | -13.7 | 541 | 385 | -28.8 | 2,212 | 1,990 | -10.0 |
| Robbery | 5,158 | 4,456 | -13.6 | 984 | 676 | -31.3 | 4,174 | 3,780 | -9.4 |
| Aggravated assault | 37,628 | 36,896 | -1.9 | 2,374 | 1,739 | -26.7 | 35,254 | 35,157 | -0.3 |
| **Property crime[2]** | 84,350 | 68,280 | -19.1 | 7,946 | 5,555 | -30.1 | 76,404 | 62,725 | -17.9 |
| Burglary | 16,290 | 14,127 | -13.3 | 1,782 | 1,391 | -21.9 | 14,508 | 12,736 | -12.2 |
| Larceny-theft | 59,163 | 45,514 | -23.1 | 5,034 | 3,099 | -38.4 | 54,129 | 42,415 | -21.6 |
| Motor vehicle theft | 8,090 | 7,782 | -3.8 | 981 | 947 | -3.5 | 7,109 | 6,835 | -3.9 |
| Arson | 807 | 857 | +6.2 | 149 | 118 | -20.8 | 658 | 739 | +12.3 |
| Other assaults | 95,315 | 87,802 | -7.9 | 12,749 | 7,633 | -40.1 | 82,566 | 80,169 | -2.9 |
| Forgery and counterfeiting | 4,858 | 3,671 | -24.4 | 76 | 45 | -40.8 | 4,782 | 3,626 | -24.2 |
| Fraud | 13,207 | 9,224 | -30.2 | 333 | 263 | -21.0 | 12,874 | 8,961 | -30.4 |
| Embezzlement | 1,257 | 832 | -33.8 | 42 | 31 | -26.2 | 1,215 | 801 | -34.1 |
| Stolen property; buying, receiving, possessing | 10,668 | 10,251 | -3.9 | 698 | 746 | +6.9 | 9,970 | 9,505 | -4.7 |
| Vandalism | 16,687 | 15,741 | -5.7 | 2,693 | 2,134 | -20.8 | 13,994 | 13,607 | -2.8 |
| Weapons; carrying, possessing, etc. | 16,128 | 16,756 | +3.9 | 1,301 | 822 | -36.8 | 14,827 | 15,934 | +7.5 |
| Prostitution and commercialized vice | 1,578 | 987 | -37.5 | 21 | 9 | -57.1 | 1,557 | 978 | -37.2 |
| Sex offenses (except forcible rape and prostitution) | 4,460 | 3,567 | -20.0 | 747 | 492 | -34.1 | 3,713 | 3,075 | -17.2 |
| Drug abuse violations | 176,117 | 135,876 | -22.8 | 7,456 | 4,018 | -46.1 | 168,661 | 131,858 | -21.8 |
| Gambling | 292 | 212 | -27.4 | 19 | 7 | -63.2 | 273 | 205 | -24.9 |
| Offenses against the family and children | 16,357 | 7,904 | -51.7 | 217 | 108 | -50.2 | 16,140 | 7,796 | -51.7 |
| Driving under the influence | 150,715 | 123,940 | -17.8 | 665 | 702 | +5.6 | 150,050 | 123,238 | -17.9 |
| Liquor laws | 12,065 | 7,957 | -34.0 | 2,412 | 1,627 | -32.5 | 9,653 | 6,330 | -34.4 |
| Drunkenness | 17,808 | 11,834 | -33.5 | 238 | 126 | -47.1 | 17,570 | 11,708 | -33.4 |
| Disorderly conduct | 19,673 | 15,311 | -22.2 | 3,642 | 1,766 | -51.5 | 16,031 | 13,545 | -15.5 |
| Vagrancy | 1,394 | 628 | -54.9 | 8 | 11 | +37.5 | 1,386 | 617 | -55.5 |
| All other offenses (except traffic) | 399,469 | 272,557 | -31.8 | 11,405 | 7,253 | -36.4 | 388,064 | 265,304 | -31.6 |
| Suspicion | 33 | 3 | -90.9 | 0 | 0 | | 33 | 3 | -90.9 |
| Curfew and loitering law violations | 748 | 655 | -12.4 | 748 | 655 | -12.4 | NA | NA | NA |

NA = Not available.
1 Does not include suspicion.   2 Violent crimes in this table are offenses of murder and nonnegligent manslaughter, rape, robbery, and aggravated assault.   Property crimes are offenses of burglary, larceny-theft, motor vehicle theft, and arson.   3 The rape figures in this table are aggregate totals of the data submitted based on both the legacy and revised Uniform Crime Reporting definitions.

# Table 51. Arrest Trends, Metropolitan Counties, by Age and Sex, 2019–2020

(Number, percent change; 1,008 agencies; 2020 estimated population 42,367,070; 2019 estimated population 42,067,490.)

| Offense charged | Male | | | | | | Female | | | | | |
| | Total | | | Under 18 | | | Total | | | Under 18 | | |
| | 2019 | 2020 | Percent change | 2019 | 2020 | Percent change | 2019 | 2020 | Percent change | 2019 | 2020 | Percent change |
|---|---|---|---|---|---|---|---|---|---|---|---|---|
| **Total[1]** | 797,943 | 621,599 | -22.1 | 40,906 | 26,507 | -35.2 | 291,884 | 217,336 | -25.5 | 16,471 | 10,364 | -37.1 |
| **Violent crime[2]** | 37,204 | 35,879 | -3.6 | 3,178 | 2,278 | -28.3 | 9,477 | 9,071 | -4.3 | 783 | 590 | -24.6 |
| Murder and nonnegligent manslaughter | 1,022 | 1,070 | +4.7 | 55 | 62 | +12.7 | 120 | 153 | +27.5 | 7 | 6 | -14.3 |
| Rape[3] | 2,637 | 2,320 | -12.0 | 505 | 367 | -27.3 | 116 | 55 | -52.6 | 36 | 18 | -50.0 |
| Robbery | 4,315 | 3,774 | -12.5 | 862 | 589 | -31.7 | 843 | 682 | -19.1 | 122 | 87 | -28.7 |
| Aggravated assault | 29,230 | 28,715 | -1.8 | 1,756 | 1,260 | -28.2 | 8,398 | 8,181 | -2.6 | 618 | 479 | -22.5 |
| **Property crime[2]** | 55,081 | 46,573 | -15.4 | 5,742 | 4,233 | -26.3 | 29,269 | 21,707 | -25.8 | 2,204 | 1,322 | -40.0 |
| Burglary | 12,975 | 11,355 | -12.5 | 1,528 | 1,223 | -20.0 | 3,315 | 2,772 | -16.4 | 254 | 168 | -33.9 |
| Larceny-theft | 35,303 | 28,403 | -19.5 | 3,317 | 2,143 | -35.4 | 23,860 | 17,111 | -28.3 | 1,717 | 956 | -44.3 |
| Motor vehicle theft | 6,154 | 6,133 | -0.3 | 764 | 771 | +0.9 | 1,936 | 1,649 | -14.8 | 217 | 176 | -18.9 |
| Arson | 649 | 682 | +5.1 | 133 | 96 | -27.8 | 158 | 175 | +10.8 | 16 | 22 | +37.5 |
| Other assaults | 67,972 | 63,394 | -6.7 | 8,169 | 4,830 | -40.9 | 27,343 | 24,408 | -10.7 | 4,580 | 2,803 | -38.8 |
| Forgery and counterfeiting | 3,311 | 2,568 | -22.4 | 64 | 34 | -46.9 | 1,547 | 1,103 | -28.7 | 12 | 11 | -8.3 |
| Fraud | 8,400 | 6,141 | -26.9 | 229 | 181 | -21.0 | 4,807 | 3,083 | -35.9 | 104 | 82 | -21.2 |
| Embezzlement | 650 | 432 | -33.5 | 20 | 21 | +5.0 | 607 | 400 | -34.1 | 22 | 10 | -54.5 |
| Stolen property; buying, receiving, possessing | 8,386 | 8,091 | -3.5 | 568 | 620 | +9.2 | 2,282 | 2,160 | -5.3 | 130 | 126 | -3.1 |
| Vandalism | 12,963 | 12,318 | -5.0 | 2,173 | 1,714 | -21.1 | 3,724 | 3,423 | -8.1 | 520 | 420 | -19.2 |
| Weapons; carrying, possessing, etc. | 14,436 | 15,087 | +4.5 | 1,134 | 731 | -35.5 | 1,692 | 1,669 | -1.4 | 167 | 91 | -45.5 |
| Prostitution and commercialized vice | 757 | 576 | -23.9 | 15 | 5 | -66.7 | 821 | 411 | -49.9 | 6 | 4 | -33.3 |
| Sex offenses (except forcible rape and prostitution) | 4,171 | 3,397 | -18.6 | 669 | 455 | -32.0 | 289 | 170 | -41.2 | 78 | 37 | -52.6 |
| Drug abuse violations | 128,927 | 99,913 | -22.5 | 5,572 | 2,991 | -46.3 | 47,190 | 35,963 | -23.8 | 1,884 | 1,027 | -45.5 |
| Gambling | 205 | 145 | -29.3 | 14 | 7 | -50.0 | 87 | 67 | -23.0 | 5 | 0 | -100.0 |
| Offenses against the family and children | 12,959 | 5,880 | -54.6 | 142 | 74 | -47.9 | 3,398 | 2,024 | -40.4 | 75 | 34 | -54.7 |
| Driving under the influence | 111,384 | 92,581 | -16.9 | 521 | 529 | +1.5 | 39,331 | 31,359 | -20.3 | 144 | 173 | +20.1 |
| Liquor laws | 8,337 | 5,497 | -34.1 | 1,386 | 954 | -31.2 | 3,728 | 2,460 | -34.0 | 1,026 | 673 | -34.4 |
| Drunkenness | 13,771 | 9,074 | -34.1 | 176 | 86 | -51.1 | 4,037 | 2,760 | -31.6 | 62 | 40 | -35.5 |
| Disorderly conduct | 13,924 | 10,909 | -21.7 | 2,421 | 1,133 | -53.2 | 5,749 | 4,402 | -23.4 | 1,221 | 633 | -48.2 |
| Vagrancy | 1,075 | 498 | -53.7 | 6 | 8 | +33.3 | 319 | 130 | -59.2 | 2 | 3 | +50.0 |
| All other offenses (except traffic) | 293,525 | 202,211 | -31.1 | 8,202 | 5,188 | -36.7 | 105,944 | 70,346 | -33.6 | 3,203 | 2,065 | -35.5 |
| Suspicion | 25 | 3 | -88.0 | 0 | 0 | | 8 | 0 | -100.0 | 0 | 0 | |
| Curfew and loitering law violations | 505 | 435 | -13.9 | 505 | 435 | -13.9 | 243 | 220 | -9.5 | 243 | 220 | -9.5 |

1 Does not include suspicion.   2 Violent crimes are offenses of murder and nonnegligent manslaughter, rape, robbery, and aggravated assault.   Property crimes are offenses of burglary, larceny-theft, motor vehicle theft, and arson.   3 The rape figures in this table are aggregate totals of the data submitted based on both the legacy and revised Uniform Crime Reporting definitions.

## Table 52. Arrests, Metropolitan Counties, Distribution by Age, 2020

(Number, percent; 1,195 agencies; 2020 estimated population 50,082,964.)

| Offense charged | Total, all ages | Ages under 15 | Ages under 18 | Ages 18 and over | Under 10 | 10–12 | 13–14 | 15 | 16 | 17 | 18 | 19 | 20 |
|---|---|---|---|---|---|---|---|---|---|---|---|---|---|
| **Total** | 983,373 | 11,711 | 43,670 | 939,703 | 167 | 2,504 | 9,040 | 8,261 | 10,689 | 13,009 | 20,806 | 24,079 | 25,980 |
| Total percent distribution[1] | 100.0 | 1.2 | 4.4 | 95.6 | * | 0.3 | 0.9 | 0.8 | 1.1 | 1.3 | 2.1 | 2.4 | 2.6 |
| | | | | | | | | | | | | | |
| **Violent crime[2]** | 54,143 | 908 | 3,372 | 50,771 | 7 | 201 | 700 | 631 | 847 | 986 | 1,433 | 1,514 | 1,468 |
| Violent crime percent distribution[1] | 100.0 | 1.7 | 6.2 | 93.8 | * | 0.4 | 1.3 | 1.2 | 1.6 | 1.8 | 2.6 | 2.8 | 2.7 |
| Murder and nonnegligent manslaughter | 1,554 | 7 | 95 | 1,459 | 0 | 2 | 5 | 12 | 28 | 48 | 57 | 84 | 75 |
| Rape[3] | 2,733 | 189 | 437 | 2,296 | 0 | 60 | 129 | 82 | 92 | 74 | 126 | 114 | 109 |
| Robbery | 5,390 | 142 | 784 | 4,606 | 0 | 7 | 135 | 155 | 193 | 294 | 357 | 281 | 236 |
| Aggravated assault | 44,466 | 570 | 2,056 | 42,410 | 7 | 132 | 431 | 382 | 534 | 570 | 893 | 1,035 | 1,048 |
| | | | | | | | | | | | | | |
| **Property crime[2]** | 81,314 | 1,769 | 6,644 | 74,670 | 8 | 331 | 1,430 | 1,433 | 1,722 | 1,720 | 2,420 | 2,144 | 2,131 |
| Property crime percent distribution[1] | 100.0 | 2.2 | 8.2 | 91.8 | * | 0.4 | 1.8 | 1.8 | 2.1 | 2.1 | 3.0 | 2.6 | 2.6 |
| Burglary | 16,654 | 439 | 1,604 | 15,050 | 1 | 77 | 361 | 379 | 405 | 381 | 454 | 406 | 433 |
| Larceny-theft | 53,892 | 992 | 3,799 | 50,093 | 4 | 200 | 788 | 769 | 1,006 | 1,032 | 1,664 | 1,475 | 1,412 |
| Motor vehicle theft | 9,729 | 270 | 1,108 | 8,621 | 1 | 29 | 240 | 253 | 292 | 293 | 283 | 242 | 269 |
| Arson | 1,039 | 68 | 133 | 906 | 2 | 25 | 41 | 32 | 19 | 14 | 19 | 21 | 17 |
| | | | | | | | | | | | | | |
| Other assaults | 102,954 | 3,295 | 8,847 | 94,107 | 40 | 846 | 2,409 | 1,804 | 1,955 | 1,793 | 1,886 | 2,124 | 2,320 |
| Forgery and counterfeiting | 4,244 | 4 | 53 | 4,191 | 0 | 0 | 4 | 7 | 14 | 28 | 93 | 103 | 153 |
| Fraud | 10,675 | 70 | 305 | 10,370 | 0 | 4 | 66 | 68 | 72 | 95 | 194 | 221 | 257 |
| Embezzlement | 979 | 1 | 34 | 945 | 0 | 0 | 1 | 1 | 13 | 19 | 55 | 53 | 31 |
| Stolen property; buying, receiving, possessing | 11,739 | 162 | 821 | 10,918 | 0 | 13 | 149 | 186 | 237 | 236 | 371 | 345 | 311 |
| | | | | | | | | | | | | | |
| Vandalism | 19,020 | 928 | 2,554 | 16,466 | 17 | 230 | 681 | 477 | 594 | 555 | 662 | 592 | 534 |
| Weapons; carrying, possessing, etc. | 20,177 | 193 | 1,000 | 19,177 | 3 | 53 | 137 | 155 | 254 | 398 | 650 | 758 | 804 |
| Prostitution and commercialized vice | 1,054 | 6 | 13 | 1,041 | 0 | 1 | 5 | 1 | 2 | 4 | 19 | 21 | 29 |
| Sex offenses (except forcible rape and prostitution) | 4,333 | 251 | 552 | 3,781 | 11 | 67 | 173 | 103 | 89 | 109 | 118 | 115 | 136 |
| Drug abuse violations | 162,238 | 615 | 4,808 | 157,430 | 4 | 69 | 542 | 717 | 1,271 | 2,205 | 4,483 | 5,383 | 5,445 |
| | | | | | | | | | | | | | |
| Gambling | 273 | 5 | 26 | 247 | 0 | 3 | 2 | 4 | 8 | 9 | 2 | 6 | 5 |
| Offenses against the family and children | 8,915 | 36 | 128 | 8,787 | 2 | 6 | 28 | 25 | 30 | 37 | 44 | 68 | 99 |
| Driving under the influence | 140,244 | 6 | 776 | 139,468 | 1 | 0 | 5 | 32 | 189 | 549 | 1,651 | 2,530 | 3,139 |
| Liquor laws | 9,189 | 185 | 1,902 | 7,287 | 0 | 12 | 173 | 288 | 533 | 896 | 1,345 | 1,253 | 1,021 |
| Drunkenness | 14,141 | 21 | 146 | 13,995 | 0 | 1 | 20 | 38 | 40 | 47 | 211 | 220 | 277 |
| | | | | | | | | | | | | | |
| Disorderly conduct | 18,076 | 845 | 2,229 | 15,847 | 25 | 224 | 596 | 450 | 471 | 463 | 381 | 378 | 380 |
| Vagrancy | 803 | 3 | 12 | 791 | 0 | 0 | 3 | 4 | 4 | 1 | 16 | 14 | 16 |
| All other offenses (except traffic) | 318,146 | 2,229 | 8,735 | 309,411 | 48 | 424 | 1,757 | 1,640 | 2,141 | 2,725 | 4,772 | 6,236 | 7,424 |
| Suspicion | 3 | 0 | 0 | 3 | 0 | 0 | 0 | 0 | 0 | 0 | 0 | 1 | 0 |
| Curfew and loitering law violations | 713 | 179 | 713 | NA | 1 | 19 | 159 | 197 | 203 | 134 | NA | NA | NA |

## Table 52. Arrests, Metropolitan Counties, Distribution by Age, 2020—Continued

(Number, percent; 1,195 agencies; 2020 estimated population 50,082,964.)

| Offense charged | 21 | 22 | 23 | 24 | 25–29 | 30–34 | 35–39 | 40–44 | 45–49 | 50–54 | 55–59 | 60–64 | 65 and over |
|---|---|---|---|---|---|---|---|---|---|---|---|---|---|
| **Total** | 27,610 | 28,298 | 28,878 | 30,583 | 169,211 | 160,391 | 134,849 | 97,332 | 66,780 | 51,910 | 38,604 | 20,555 | 13,837 |
| Total percent distribution[1] | 2.8 | 2.9 | 2.9 | 3.1 | 17.2 | 16.3 | 13.7 | 9.9 | 6.8 | 5.3 | 3.9 | 2.1 | 1.4 |
| **Violent crime[2]** | 1,495 | 1,628 | 1,507 | 1,685 | 8,910 | 8,261 | 7,141 | 5,040 | 3,437 | 2,796 | 2,223 | 1,203 | 1,030 |
| Violent crime percent distribution[1] | 2.8 | 3.0 | 2.8 | 3.1 | 16.5 | 15.3 | 13.2 | 9.3 | 6.3 | 5.2 | 4.1 | 2.2 | 1.9 |
| Murder and nonnegligent manslaughter | 58 | 68 | 70 | 39 | 326 | 202 | 149 | 121 | 62 | 47 | 46 | 29 | 26 |
| Rape[3] | 96 | 71 | 58 | 73 | 304 | 285 | 291 | 228 | 160 | 124 | 108 | 66 | 83 |
| Robbery | 214 | 212 | 173 | 195 | 856 | 734 | 502 | 346 | 183 | 160 | 101 | 37 | 19 |
| Aggravated assault | 1,127 | 1,277 | 1,206 | 1,378 | 7,424 | 7,040 | 6,199 | 4,345 | 3,032 | 2,465 | 1,968 | 1,071 | 902 |
| **Property crime[2]** | 2,184 | 2,109 | 2,033 | 2,238 | 13,160 | 13,273 | 10,979 | 7,587 | 5,129 | 4,103 | 2,980 | 1,436 | 764 |
| Property crime percent distribution[1] | 2.7 | 2.6 | 2.5 | 2.8 | 16.2 | 16.3 | 13.5 | 9.3 | 6.3 | 5.0 | 3.7 | 1.8 | 0.9 |
| Burglary | 409 | 417 | 455 | 441 | 2,813 | 2,975 | 2,326 | 1,626 | 987 | 634 | 445 | 152 | 77 |
| Larceny-theft | 1,487 | 1,410 | 1,295 | 1,468 | 8,366 | 8,385 | 7,178 | 5,042 | 3,628 | 3,107 | 2,339 | 1,196 | 641 |
| Motor vehicle theft | 266 | 263 | 260 | 302 | 1,855 | 1,741 | 1,328 | 809 | 447 | 302 | 158 | 63 | 33 |
| Arson | 22 | 19 | 23 | 27 | 126 | 172 | 147 | 110 | 67 | 60 | 38 | 25 | 13 |
| Other assaults | 2,612 | 2,619 | 2,572 | 2,837 | 16,007 | 15,476 | 13,572 | 10,140 | 7,367 | 5,941 | 4,300 | 2,413 | 1,921 |
| Forgery and counterfeiting | 122 | 134 | 134 | 146 | 801 | 761 | 595 | 431 | 263 | 217 | 136 | 70 | 32 |
| Fraud | 265 | 278 | 262 | 310 | 1,892 | 1,789 | 1,582 | 1,161 | 777 | 620 | 445 | 177 | 140 |
| Embezzlement | 40 | 24 | 38 | 29 | 140 | 130 | 122 | 101 | 74 | 45 | 43 | 16 | 4 |
| Stolen property; buying, receiving, possessing | 336 | 354 | 355 | 395 | 2,150 | 2,071 | 1,682 | 1,056 | 637 | 447 | 248 | 107 | 53 |
| Vandalism | 596 | 525 | 616 | 586 | 3,154 | 2,795 | 2,220 | 1,484 | 875 | 764 | 533 | 281 | 249 |
| Weapons; carrying, possessing, etc. | 861 | 834 | 876 | 830 | 3,958 | 3,041 | 2,353 | 1,554 | 998 | 688 | 505 | 268 | 199 |
| Prostitution and commercialized vice | 35 | 25 | 32 | 35 | 182 | 173 | 135 | 110 | 95 | 61 | 51 | 15 | 23 |
| Sex offenses (except forcible rape and prostitution) | 104 | 81 | 72 | 92 | 466 | 474 | 469 | 433 | 298 | 265 | 246 | 170 | 242 |
| Drug abuse violations | 5,441 | 5,448 | 5,386 | 5,557 | 29,505 | 27,186 | 22,360 | 15,502 | 10,008 | 7,323 | 4,978 | 2,390 | 1,035 |
| Gambling | 4 | 2 | 6 | 3 | 32 | 30 | 46 | 37 | 30 | 15 | 16 | 6 | 7 |
| Offenses against the family and children | 106 | 147 | 169 | 152 | 1,378 | 1,877 | 1,726 | 1,281 | 747 | 492 | 292 | 135 | 74 |
| Driving under the influence | 4,344 | 4,764 | 4,995 | 5,344 | 26,486 | 22,099 | 17,602 | 13,339 | 10,106 | 8,500 | 7,091 | 4,296 | 3,182 |
| Liquor laws | 174 | 153 | 134 | 127 | 610 | 572 | 490 | 378 | 295 | 294 | 211 | 134 | 96 |
| Drunkenness | 330 | 360 | 376 | 419 | 2,239 | 2,275 | 2,039 | 1,504 | 1,114 | 1,048 | 858 | 471 | 254 |
| Disorderly conduct | 434 | 403 | 428 | 476 | 2,505 | 2,475 | 2,192 | 1,606 | 1,258 | 1,098 | 901 | 537 | 395 |
| Vagrancy | 22 | 21 | 14 | 13 | 117 | 123 | 99 | 95 | 73 | 64 | 47 | 41 | 16 |
| All other offenses (except traffic) | 8,105 | 8,389 | 8,873 | 9,309 | 55,519 | 55,509 | 47,444 | 34,493 | 23,199 | 17,129 | 12,500 | 6,389 | 4,121 |
| Suspicion | 0 | 0 | 0 | 0 | 0 | 1 | 1 | 0 | 0 | 0 | 0 | 0 | 0 |
| Curfew and loitering law violations | NA | NA | NA | NA | NA | NA | NA | NA | NA | NA | NA | NA | NA |

NA = Not available.

* = Less than one-tenth of one percent.

1 Because of rounding, the percentages may not sum to 100.   2 Violent crimes are offenses of murder and nonnegligent manslaughter, rape, robbery, and aggravated assault.  Property crimes are offenses of burglary, larceny-theft, motor vehicle theft, and arson.   3 The rape figures in this table are aggregate totals of the data submitted based on both the legacy and revised Uniform Crime Reporting definitions.

## Table 53. Arrests, Metropolitan Counties, Persons Under 15, 18, 21, and 25 Years of Age, 2020

(Number, percent; 1,195 agencies; 2020 estimated population 50,082,964.)

| Offense charged | Total, all ages | Number of persons arrested | | | | Percent of total all ages | | | |
|---|---|---|---|---|---|---|---|---|---|
| | | Under 15 | Under 18 | Under 21 | Under 25 | Under 15 | Under 18 | Under 21 | Under 25 |
| **Total** | 983,373 | 11,711 | 43,670 | 114,535 | 229,904 | 1.2 | 4.4 | 11.6 | 23.4 |
| **Violent crime**[1] | 54,143 | 908 | 3,372 | 7,787 | 14,102 | 1.7 | 6.2 | 14.4 | 26.0 |
| Murder and nonnegligent manslaughter | 1,554 | 7 | 95 | 311 | 546 | 0.5 | 6.1 | 20.0 | 35.1 |
| Rape[2] | 2,733 | 189 | 437 | 786 | 1,084 | 6.9 | 16.0 | 28.8 | 39.7 |
| Robbery | 5,390 | 142 | 784 | 1,658 | 2,452 | 2.6 | 14.5 | 30.8 | 45.5 |
| Aggravated assault | 44,466 | 570 | 2,056 | 5,032 | 10,020 | 1.3 | 4.6 | 11.3 | 22.5 |
| **Property crime**[1] | 81,314 | 1,769 | 6,644 | 13,339 | 21,903 | 2.2 | 8.2 | 16.4 | 26.9 |
| Burglary | 16,654 | 439 | 1,604 | 2,897 | 4,619 | 2.6 | 9.6 | 17.4 | 27.7 |
| Larceny-theft | 53,892 | 992 | 3,799 | 8,350 | 14,010 | 1.8 | 7.0 | 15.5 | 26.0 |
| Motor vehicle theft | 9,729 | 270 | 1,108 | 1,902 | 2,993 | 2.8 | 11.4 | 19.5 | 30.8 |
| Arson | 1,039 | 68 | 133 | 190 | 281 | 6.5 | 12.8 | 18.3 | 27.0 |
| Other assaults | 102,954 | 3,295 | 8,847 | 15,177 | 25,817 | 3.2 | 8.6 | 14.7 | 25.1 |
| Forgery and counterfeiting | 4,244 | 4 | 53 | 402 | 938 | 0.1 | 1.2 | 9.5 | 22.1 |
| Fraud | 10,675 | 70 | 305 | 977 | 2,092 | 0.7 | 2.9 | 9.2 | 19.6 |
| Embezzlement | 979 | 1 | 34 | 173 | 304 | 0.1 | 3.5 | 17.7 | 31.1 |
| Stolen property; buying, receiving, possessing | 11,739 | 162 | 821 | 1,848 | 3,288 | 1.4 | 7.0 | 15.7 | 28.0 |
| Vandalism | 19,020 | 928 | 2,554 | 4,342 | 6,665 | 4.9 | 13.4 | 22.8 | 35.0 |
| Weapons; carrying, possessing, etc. | 20,177 | 193 | 1,000 | 3,212 | 6,613 | 1.0 | 5.0 | 15.9 | 32.8 |
| Prostitution and commercialized vice | 1,054 | 6 | 13 | 82 | 209 | 0.6 | 1.2 | 7.8 | 19.8 |
| Sex offenses (except forcible rape and prostitution) | 4,333 | 251 | 552 | 921 | 1,270 | 5.8 | 12.7 | 21.3 | 29.3 |
| Drug abuse violations | 162,238 | 615 | 4,808 | 20,119 | 41,951 | 0.4 | 3.0 | 12.4 | 25.9 |
| Gambling | 273 | 5 | 26 | 39 | 54 | 1.8 | 9.5 | 14.3 | 19.8 |
| Offenses against the family and children | 8,915 | 36 | 128 | 339 | 913 | 0.4 | 1.4 | 3.8 | 10.2 |
| Driving under the influence | 140,244 | 6 | 776 | 8,096 | 27,543 | * | 0.6 | 5.8 | 19.6 |
| Liquor laws | 9,189 | 185 | 1,902 | 5,521 | 6,109 | 2.0 | 20.7 | 60.1 | 66.5 |
| Drunkenness | 14,141 | 21 | 146 | 854 | 2,339 | 0.1 | 1.0 | 6.0 | 16.5 |
| Disorderly conduct | 18,076 | 845 | 2,229 | 3,368 | 5,109 | 4.7 | 12.3 | 18.6 | 28.3 |
| Vagrancy | 803 | 3 | 12 | 58 | 128 | 0.4 | 1.5 | 7.2 | 15.9 |
| All other offenses (except traffic) | 318,146 | 2,229 | 8,735 | 27,167 | 61,843 | 0.7 | 2.7 | 8.5 | 19.4 |
| Suspicion | 3 | 0 | 0 | 1 | 1 | 0.0 | 0.0 | 33.3 | 33.3 |
| Curfew and loitering law violations | 713 | 179 | 713 | 713 | 713 | 25.1 | 100.0 | 100.0 | 100.0 |

* = Less than one-tenth of one percent.
1 Violent crimes are offenses of murder and nonnegligent manslaughter, rape, robbery, and aggravated assault.   Property crimes are offenses of burglary, larceny-theft, motor vehicle theft, and arson.   2 The rape figures in this table are aggregate totals of the data submitted based on both the legacy and revised Uniform Crime Reporting definitions.

## Table 54. Arrests, Metropolitan Counties, Distribution by Sex, 2020

(Number, percent; 1,195 agencies; 2020 estimated population 50,082,964.)

| Offense charged | Number of persons arrested | | | Percent male | Percent female | Percent distribution[1] | | |
|---|---|---|---|---|---|---|---|---|
| | Total | Male | Female | | | Total | Male | Female |
| **Total** | 983,373 | 730,968 | 252,405 | 74.3 | 25.7 | 100.0 | 100.0 | 100.0 |
| **Violent crime[2]** | 54,143 | 43,344 | 10,799 | 80.1 | 19.9 | 5.5 | 5.9 | 4.3 |
| Murder and nonnegligent manslaughter | 1,554 | 1,342 | 212 | 86.4 | 13.6 | 0.2 | 0.2 | 0.1 |
| Rape[3] | 2,733 | 2,669 | 64 | 97.7 | 2.3 | 0.3 | 0.4 | * |
| Robbery | 5,390 | 4,579 | 811 | 85.0 | 15.0 | 0.5 | 0.6 | 0.3 |
| Aggravated assault | 44,466 | 34,754 | 9,712 | 78.2 | 21.8 | 4.5 | 4.8 | 3.8 |
| **Property crime[2]** | 81,314 | 55,706 | 25,608 | 68.5 | 31.5 | 8.3 | 7.6 | 10.1 |
| Burglary | 16,654 | 13,466 | 3,188 | 80.9 | 19.1 | 1.7 | 1.8 | 1.3 |
| Larceny-theft | 53,892 | 33,750 | 20,142 | 62.6 | 37.4 | 5.5 | 4.6 | 8.0 |
| Motor vehicle theft | 9,729 | 7,659 | 2,070 | 78.7 | 21.3 | 1.0 | 1.0 | 0.8 |
| Arson | 1,039 | 831 | 208 | 80.0 | 20.0 | 0.1 | 0.1 | 0.1 |
| Other assaults | 102,954 | 74,341 | 28,613 | 72.2 | 27.8 | 10.5 | 10.2 | 11.3 |
| Forgery and counterfeiting | 4,244 | 2,980 | 1,264 | 70.2 | 29.8 | 0.4 | 0.4 | 0.5 |
| Fraud | 10,675 | 7,167 | 3,508 | 67.1 | 32.9 | 1.1 | 1.0 | 1.4 |
| Embezzlement | 979 | 513 | 466 | 52.4 | 47.6 | 0.1 | 0.1 | 0.2 |
| Stolen property; buying, receiving, possessing | 11,739 | 9,292 | 2,447 | 79.2 | 20.8 | 1.2 | 1.3 | 1.0 |
| Vandalism | 19,020 | 14,817 | 4,203 | 77.9 | 22.1 | 1.9 | 2.0 | 1.7 |
| Weapons; carrying, possessing, etc. | 20,177 | 18,217 | 1,960 | 90.3 | 9.7 | 2.1 | 2.5 | 0.8 |
| Prostitution and commercialized vice | 1,054 | 613 | 441 | 58.2 | 41.8 | 0.1 | 0.1 | 0.2 |
| Sex offenses (except forcible rape and prostitution) | 4,333 | 4,103 | 230 | 94.7 | 5.3 | 0.4 | 0.6 | 0.1 |
| Drug abuse violations | 162,238 | 120,117 | 42,121 | 74.0 | 26.0 | 16.5 | 16.4 | 16.7 |
| Gambling | 273 | 177 | 96 | 64.8 | 35.2 | * | * | * |
| Offenses against the family and children | 8,915 | 6,604 | 2,311 | 74.1 | 25.9 | 0.9 | 0.9 | 0.9 |
| Driving under the influence | 140,244 | 104,994 | 35,250 | 74.9 | 25.1 | 14.3 | 14.4 | 14.0 |
| Liquor laws | 9,189 | 6,379 | 2,810 | 69.4 | 30.6 | 0.9 | 0.9 | 1.1 |
| Drunkenness | 14,141 | 11,030 | 3,111 | 78.0 | 22.0 | 1.4 | 1.5 | 1.2 |
| Disorderly conduct | 18,076 | 12,849 | 5,227 | 71.1 | 28.9 | 1.8 | 1.8 | 2.1 |
| Vagrancy | 803 | 633 | 170 | 78.8 | 21.2 | 0.1 | 0.1 | 0.1 |
| All other offenses (except traffic) | 318,146 | 236,614 | 81,532 | 74.4 | 25.6 | 32.4 | 32.4 | 32.3 |
| Suspicion | 3 | 3 | 0 | 100.0 | 0.0 | * | * | 0 |
| Curfew and loitering law violations | 713 | 475 | 238 | 66.6 | 33.4 | 0.1 | 0.1 | 0.1 |

* = Less than one-tenth of one percent.
1 Because of rounding, the percentages may not sum to 100.   2 Violent crimes are offenses of murder and nonnegligent manslaughter, rape, robbery, and aggravated assault.  Property crimes are offenses of burglary, larceny-theft, motor vehicle theft, and arson.   3 The rape figures in this table are aggregate totals of the data submitted based on both the legacy and revised Uniform Crime Reporting definitions.

## Table 55. Arrests, Metropolitan Counties, Distribution by Race, 2020

(Number, percent; 1,195 agencies; 2020 estimated population 50,082,964.)

| Offense charged | Total arrests | | | | | | Percent distribution[1] | | | | | |
|---|---|---|---|---|---|---|---|---|---|---|---|---|
| | Total | White | Black | American Indian or Alaskan Native | Asian | Native Hawaiian or Other Pacific Islander | Total | White | Black | American Indian or Alaskan Native | Asian | Native Hawaiian or Other Pacific Islander |
| **Total** | 969,062 | 715,694 | 232,718 | 8,591 | 10,863 | 1,196 | 100.0 | 73.9 | 24.0 | 0.9 | 1.1 | 0.1 |
| **Violent crime**[2] | 53,727 | 37,599 | 14,842 | 431 | 734 | 121 | 100.0 | 70.0 | 27.6 | 0.8 | 1.4 | 0.2 |
| Murder and nonnegligent manslaughter | 1,543 | 863 | 647 | 16 | 14 | 3 | 100.0 | 55.9 | 41.9 | 1.0 | 0.9 | 0.2 |
| Rape[3] | 2,684 | 2,123 | 509 | 13 | 36 | 3 | 100.0 | 79.1 | 19.0 | 0.5 | 1.3 | 0.1 |
| Robbery | 5,341 | 2,880 | 2,342 | 43 | 59 | 17 | 100.0 | 53.9 | 43.8 | 0.8 | 1.1 | 0.3 |
| Aggravated assault | 44,159 | 31,733 | 11,344 | 359 | 625 | 98 | 100.0 | 71.9 | 25.7 | 0.8 | 1.4 | 0.2 |
| **Property crime**[2] | 80,552 | 56,491 | 22,640 | 509 | 844 | 68 | 100.0 | 70.1 | 28.1 | 0.6 | 1.0 | 0.1 |
| Burglary | 16,521 | 12,835 | 3,449 | 98 | 126 | 13 | 100.0 | 77.7 | 20.9 | 0.6 | 0.8 | 0.1 |
| Larceny-theft | 53,335 | 35,381 | 16,971 | 326 | 616 | 41 | 100.0 | 66.3 | 31.8 | 0.6 | 1.2 | 0.1 |
| Motor vehicle theft | 9,665 | 7,464 | 2,027 | 75 | 86 | 13 | 100.0 | 77.2 | 21.0 | 0.8 | 0.9 | 0.1 |
| Arson | 1,031 | 811 | 193 | 10 | 16 | 1 | 100.0 | 78.7 | 18.7 | 1.0 | 1.6 | 0.1 |
| Other assaults | 101,788 | 74,374 | 25,059 | 968 | 1,267 | 120 | 100.0 | 73.1 | 24.6 | 1.0 | 1.2 | 0.1 |
| Forgery and counterfeiting | 4,205 | 2,707 | 1,399 | 19 | 76 | 4 | 100.0 | 64.4 | 33.3 | 0.5 | 1.8 | 0.1 |
| Fraud | 10,560 | 7,119 | 3,167 | 86 | 179 | 9 | 100.0 | 67.4 | 30.0 | 0.8 | 1.7 | 0.1 |
| Embezzlement | 965 | 575 | 368 | 5 | 16 | 1 | 100.0 | 59.6 | 38.1 | 0.5 | 1.7 | 0.1 |
| Stolen property; buying, receiving, possessing | 11,633 | 8,030 | 3,346 | 104 | 120 | 33 | 100.0 | 69.0 | 28.8 | 0.9 | 1.0 | 0.3 |
| Vandalism | 18,783 | 13,530 | 4,807 | 191 | 241 | 14 | 100.0 | 72.0 | 25.6 | 1.0 | 1.3 | 0.1 |
| Weapons; carrying, possessing, etc. | 20,032 | 11,748 | 7,984 | 106 | 168 | 26 | 100.0 | 58.6 | 39.9 | 0.5 | 0.8 | 0.1 |
| Prostitution and commercialized vice | 1,047 | 611 | 345 | 4 | 85 | 2 | 100.0 | 58.4 | 33.0 | 0.4 | 8.1 | 0.2 |
| Sex offenses (except forcible rape and prostitution) | 4,276 | 3,479 | 705 | 13 | 67 | 12 | 100.0 | 81.4 | 16.5 | 0.3 | 1.6 | 0.3 |
| Drug abuse violations | 160,647 | 117,080 | 40,784 | 970 | 1,628 | 185 | 100.0 | 72.9 | 25.4 | 0.6 | 1.0 | 0.1 |
| Gambling | 269 | 198 | 57 | 3 | 11 | 0 | 100.0 | 73.6 | 21.2 | 1.1 | 4.1 | 0.0 |
| Offenses against the family and children | 8,858 | 6,030 | 2,737 | 34 | 50 | 7 | 100.0 | 68.1 | 30.9 | 0.4 | 0.6 | 0.1 |
| Driving under the influence | 134,556 | 109,838 | 21,182 | 878 | 2,481 | 177 | 100.0 | 81.6 | 15.7 | 0.7 | 1.8 | 0.1 |
| Liquor laws | 8,949 | 7,413 | 1,247 | 159 | 121 | 9 | 100.0 | 82.8 | 13.9 | 1.8 | 1.4 | 0.1 |
| Drunkenness | 14,020 | 11,670 | 2,023 | 119 | 180 | 28 | 100.0 | 83.2 | 14.4 | 0.8 | 1.3 | 0.2 |
| Disorderly conduct | 17,886 | 12,739 | 4,765 | 263 | 107 | 12 | 100.0 | 71.2 | 26.6 | 1.5 | 0.6 | 0.1 |
| Vagrancy | 797 | 572 | 214 | 2 | 8 | 1 | 100.0 | 71.8 | 26.9 | 0.3 | 1.0 | 0.1 |
| All other offenses (except traffic) | 314,804 | 233,362 | 74,873 | 3,726 | 2,476 | 367 | 100.0 | 74.1 | 23.8 | 1.2 | 0.8 | 0.1 |
| Suspicion | 1 | 0 | 1 | 0 | 0 | 0 | 100.0 | 0.0 | 100.0 | 0.0 | 0.0 | 0.0 |
| Curfew and loitering law violations | 707 | 529 | 173 | 1 | 4 | 0 | 100.0 | 74.8 | 24.5 | 0.1 | 0.6 | 0.0 |

## Table 55. Arrests, Metropolitan Counties, Distribution by Race, 2020—Continued

(Number, percent; 1,195 agencies; 2020 estimated population 50,082,964.)

| Offense charged | Arrests under 18 | | | | | | Percent distribution[1] | | | | | |
|---|---|---|---|---|---|---|---|---|---|---|---|---|
| | Total | White | Black | American Indian or Alaskan Native | Asian | Native Hawaiian or Other Pacific Islander | Total | White | Black | American Indian or Alaskan Native | Asian | Native Hawaiian or Other Pacific Islander |
| Total | 42,877 | 28,661 | 13,214 | 516 | 433 | 53 | 100.0 | 66.8 | 30.8 | 1.2 | 1.0 | 0.1 |
| **Violent crime[2]** | 3,323 | 1,959 | 1,284 | 35 | 40 | 5 | 100.0 | 59.0 | 38.6 | 1.1 | 1.2 | 0.2 |
| Murder and nonnegligent manslaughter | 95 | 36 | 58 | 1 | 0 | 0 | 100.0 | 37.9 | 61.1 | 1.1 | 0.0 | 0.0 |
| Rape[3] | 427 | 334 | 86 | 1 | 6 | 0 | 100.0 | 78.2 | 20.1 | 0.2 | 1.4 | 0.0 |
| Robbery | 769 | 337 | 410 | 6 | 12 | 4 | 100.0 | 43.8 | 53.3 | 0.8 | 1.6 | 0.5 |
| Aggravated assault | 2,032 | 1,252 | 730 | 27 | 22 | 1 | 100.0 | 61.6 | 35.9 | 1.3 | 1.1 | * |
| **Property crime[2]** | 6,556 | 3,819 | 2,597 | 41 | 88 | 11 | 100.0 | 58.3 | 39.6 | 0.6 | 1.3 | 0.2 |
| Burglary | 1,585 | 1,001 | 550 | 15 | 17 | 2 | 100.0 | 63.2 | 34.7 | 0.9 | 1.1 | 0.1 |
| Larceny-theft | 3,740 | 2,110 | 1,538 | 18 | 65 | 9 | 100.0 | 56.4 | 41.1 | 0.5 | 1.7 | 0.2 |
| Motor vehicle theft | 1,101 | 612 | 476 | 8 | 5 | 0 | 100.0 | 55.6 | 43.2 | 0.7 | 0.5 | 0.0 |
| Arson | 130 | 96 | 33 | 0 | 1 | 0 | 100.0 | 73.8 | 25.4 | 0.0 | 0.8 | 0.0 |
| Other assaults | 8,701 | 5,499 | 2,979 | 121 | 94 | 8 | 100.0 | 63.2 | 34.2 | 1.4 | 1.1 | 0.1 |
| Forgery and counterfeiting | 52 | 31 | 19 | 1 | 1 | 0 | 100.0 | 59.6 | 36.5 | 1.9 | 1.9 | 0.0 |
| Fraud | 303 | 178 | 115 | 5 | 5 | 0 | 100.0 | 58.7 | 38.0 | 1.7 | 1.7 | 0.0 |
| Embezzlement | 33 | 18 | 15 | 0 | 0 | 0 | 100.0 | 54.5 | 45.5 | 0.0 | 0.0 | 0.0 |
| Stolen property; buying, receiving, possessing | 812 | 293 | 493 | 18 | 3 | 5 | 100.0 | 36.1 | 60.7 | 2.2 | 0.4 | 0.6 |
| Vandalism | 2,504 | 1,821 | 628 | 32 | 22 | 1 | 100.0 | 72.7 | 25.1 | 1.3 | 0.9 | * |
| Weapons; carrying, possessing, etc. | 987 | 505 | 467 | 5 | 8 | 2 | 100.0 | 51.2 | 47.3 | 0.5 | 0.8 | 0.2 |
| Prostitution and commercialized vice | 13 | 8 | 5 | 0 | 0 | 0 | 100.0 | 61.5 | 38.5 | 0.0 | 0.0 | 0.0 |
| Sex offenses (except forcible rape and prostitution) | 537 | 411 | 116 | 4 | 6 | 0 | 100.0 | 76.5 | 21.6 | 0.7 | 1.1 | 0.0 |
| Drug abuse violations | 4,707 | 3,514 | 1,116 | 41 | 32 | 4 | 100.0 | 74.7 | 23.7 | 0.9 | 0.7 | 0.1 |
| Gambling | 26 | 20 | 5 | 0 | 1 | 0 | 100.0 | 76.9 | 19.2 | 0.0 | 3.8 | 0.0 |
| Offenses against the family and children | 127 | 97 | 27 | 3 | 0 | 0 | 100.0 | 76.4 | 21.3 | 2.4 | 0.0 | 0.0 |
| Driving under the influence | 741 | 667 | 53 | 5 | 15 | 1 | 100.0 | 90.0 | 7.2 | 0.7 | 2.0 | 0.1 |
| Liquor laws | 1,847 | 1,692 | 104 | 30 | 19 | 2 | 100.0 | 91.6 | 5.6 | 1.6 | 1.0 | 0.1 |
| Drunkenness | 144 | 111 | 32 | 0 | 0 | 1 | 100.0 | 77.1 | 22.2 | 0.0 | 0.0 | 0.7 |
| Disorderly conduct | 2,194 | 1,268 | 874 | 34 | 15 | 3 | 100.0 | 57.8 | 39.8 | 1.5 | 0.7 | 0.1 |
| Vagrancy | 12 | 11 | 1 | 0 | 0 | 0 | 100.0 | 91.7 | 8.3 | 0.0 | 0.0 | 0.0 |
| All other offenses (except traffic) | 8,551 | 6,210 | 2,111 | 140 | 80 | 10 | 100.0 | 72.6 | 24.7 | 1.6 | 0.9 | 0.1 |
| Suspicion | 0 | 0 | 0 | 0 | 0 | 0 | | | | | | |
| Curfew and loitering law violations | 707 | 529 | 173 | 1 | 4 | 0 | 100.0 | 74.8 | 24.5 | 0.1 | 0.6 | 0.0 |

## Table 55. Arrests, Metropolitan Counties, Distribution by Race, 2020—Continued

(Number, percent; 1,195 agencies; 2020 estimated population 50,082,964.)

| Offense charged | Arrests 18 and over | | | | | | Percent distribution[1] | | | | | |
|---|---|---|---|---|---|---|---|---|---|---|---|---|
| | Total | White | Black | American Indian or Alaskan Native | Asian | Native Hawaiian or Other Pacific Islander | Total | White | Black | American Indian or Alaskan Native | Asian | Native Hawaiian or Other Pacific Islander |
| **Total** | 926,185 | 687,033 | 219,504 | 8,075 | 10,430 | 1,143 | 100.0 | 74.2 | 23.7 | 0.9 | 1.1 | 0.1 |
| **Violent crime[2]** | 50,404 | 35,640 | 13,558 | 396 | 694 | 116 | 100.0 | 70.7 | 26.9 | 0.8 | 1.4 | 0.2 |
| Murder and nonnegligent manslaughter | 1,448 | 827 | 589 | 15 | 14 | 3 | 100.0 | 57.1 | 40.7 | 1.0 | 1.0 | 0.2 |
| Rape[3] | 2,257 | 1,789 | 423 | 12 | 30 | 3 | 100.0 | 79.3 | 18.7 | 0.5 | 1.3 | 0.1 |
| Robbery | 4,572 | 2,543 | 1,932 | 37 | 47 | 13 | 100.0 | 55.6 | 42.3 | 0.8 | 1.0 | 0.3 |
| Aggravated assault | 42,127 | 30,481 | 10,614 | 332 | 603 | 97 | 100.0 | 72.4 | 25.2 | 0.8 | 1.4 | 0.2 |
| **Property crime[2]** | 73,996 | 52,672 | 20,043 | 468 | 756 | 57 | 100.0 | 71.2 | 27.1 | 0.6 | 1.0 | 0.1 |
| Burglary | 14,936 | 11,834 | 2,899 | 83 | 109 | 11 | 100.0 | 79.2 | 19.4 | 0.6 | 0.7 | 0.1 |
| Larceny-theft | 49,595 | 33,271 | 15,433 | 308 | 551 | 32 | 100.0 | 67.1 | 31.1 | 0.6 | 1.1 | 0.1 |
| Motor vehicle theft | 8,564 | 6,852 | 1,551 | 67 | 81 | 13 | 100.0 | 80.0 | 18.1 | 0.8 | 0.9 | 0.2 |
| Arson | 901 | 715 | 160 | 10 | 15 | 1 | 100.0 | 79.4 | 17.8 | 1.1 | 1.7 | 0.1 |
| Other assaults | 93,087 | 68,875 | 22,080 | 847 | 1,173 | 112 | 100.0 | 74.0 | 23.7 | 0.9 | 1.3 | 0.1 |
| Forgery and counterfeiting | 4,153 | 2,676 | 1,380 | 18 | 75 | 4 | 100.0 | 64.4 | 33.2 | 0.4 | 1.8 | 0.1 |
| Fraud | 10,257 | 6,941 | 3,052 | 81 | 174 | 9 | 100.0 | 67.7 | 29.8 | 0.8 | 1.7 | 0.1 |
| Embezzlement | 932 | 557 | 353 | 5 | 16 | 1 | 100.0 | 59.8 | 37.9 | 0.5 | 1.7 | 0.1 |
| Stolen property; buying, receiving, possessing | 10,821 | 7,737 | 2,853 | 86 | 117 | 28 | 100.0 | 71.5 | 26.4 | 0.8 | 1.1 | 0.3 |
| Vandalism | 16,279 | 11,709 | 4,179 | 159 | 219 | 13 | 100.0 | 71.9 | 25.7 | 1.0 | 1.3 | 0.1 |
| Weapons; carrying, possessing, etc. | 19,045 | 11,243 | 7,517 | 101 | 160 | 24 | 100.0 | 59.0 | 39.5 | 0.5 | 0.8 | 0.1 |
| Prostitution and commercialized vice | 1,034 | 603 | 340 | 4 | 85 | 2 | 100.0 | 58.3 | 32.9 | 0.4 | 8.2 | 0.2 |
| Sex offenses (except forcible rape and prostitution) | 3,739 | 3,068 | 589 | 9 | 61 | 12 | 100.0 | 82.1 | 15.8 | 0.2 | 1.6 | 0.3 |
| Drug abuse violations | 155,940 | 113,566 | 39,668 | 929 | 1,596 | 181 | 100.0 | 72.8 | 25.4 | 0.6 | 1.0 | 0.1 |
| Gambling | 243 | 178 | 52 | 3 | 10 | 0 | 100.0 | 73.3 | 21.4 | 1.2 | 4.1 | 0.0 |
| Offenses against the family and children | 8,731 | 5,933 | 2,710 | 31 | 50 | 7 | 100.0 | 68.0 | 31.0 | 0.4 | 0.6 | 0.1 |
| Driving under the influence | 133,815 | 109,171 | 21,129 | 873 | 2,466 | 176 | 100.0 | 81.6 | 15.8 | 0.7 | 1.8 | 0.1 |
| Liquor laws | 7,102 | 5,721 | 1,143 | 129 | 102 | 7 | 100.0 | 80.6 | 16.1 | 1.8 | 1.4 | 0.1 |
| Drunkenness | 13,876 | 11,559 | 1,991 | 119 | 180 | 27 | 100.0 | 83.3 | 14.3 | 0.9 | 1.3 | 0.2 |
| Disorderly conduct | 15,692 | 11,471 | 3,891 | 229 | 92 | 9 | 100.0 | 73.1 | 24.8 | 1.5 | 0.6 | 0.1 |
| Vagrancy | 785 | 561 | 213 | 2 | 8 | 1 | 100.0 | 71.5 | 27.1 | 0.3 | 1.0 | 0.1 |
| All other offenses (except traffic) | 306,253 | 227,152 | 72,762 | 3,586 | 2,396 | 357 | 100.0 | 74.2 | 23.8 | 1.2 | 0.8 | 0.1 |
| Suspicion | 1 | 0 | 1 | 0 | 0 | 0 | 100.0 | 0.0 | 100.0 | 0.0 | 0.0 | 0.0 |
| Curfew and loitering law violations | NA | NA | NA | NA | NA | NA | NA | NA | NA | NA | NA | NA |

NA = Not available.
* = Less than one-tenth of one percent.
1 Because of rounding, the percentages may not sum to 100.   2 Violent crimes are offenses of murder and nonnegligent manslaughter, rape, robbery, and aggravated assault.  Property crimes are offenses of burglary, larceny-theft, motor vehicle theft, and arson.   3 The rape figures in this table are an aggregate total of the data submitted using both the revised and legacy Uniform Crime Reporting definitions.

# Table 55A. Arrests, Metropolitan Counties, Distribution by Ethnicity, 2020

(Number, percent; 1,195 agencies; 2020 estimated population 50,082,964.)

| Offense charged | Total arrests | | | Percent distribution[1] | | | Arrests under 18 | | |
|---|---|---|---|---|---|---|---|---|---|
| | Total[2] | Hispanic or Latino | Not Hispanic or Latino | Total[2] | Hispanic or Latino | Not Hispanic or Latino | Total[2] | Hispanic or Latino | Not Hispanic or Latino |
| **Total** | 838,460 | 172,566 | 665,894 | 100.0 | 20.6 | 79.4 | 35,085 | 7,183 | 27,902 |
| **Violent crime[3]** | 47,819 | 11,721 | 36,098 | 100.0 | 24.5 | 75.5 | 2,807 | 671 | 2,136 |
| Murder and nonnegligent manslaughter | 1,322 | 313 | 1,009 | 100.0 | 23.7 | 76.3 | 71 | 16 | 55 |
| Rape[4] | 2,231 | 613 | 1,618 | 100.0 | 27.5 | 72.5 | 332 | 55 | 277 |
| Robbery | 4,827 | 1,171 | 3,656 | 100.0 | 24.3 | 75.7 | 691 | 186 | 505 |
| Aggravated assault | 39,439 | 9,624 | 29,815 | 100.0 | 24.4 | 75.6 | 1,713 | 414 | 1,299 |
| **Property crime[3]** | 70,282 | 10,729 | 59,553 | 100.0 | 15.3 | 84.7 | 5,466 | 1,096 | 4,370 |
| Burglary | 14,402 | 2,509 | 11,893 | 100.0 | 17.4 | 82.6 | 1,257 | 287 | 970 |
| Larceny-theft | 46,424 | 5,649 | 40,775 | 100.0 | 12.2 | 87.8 | 3,161 | 565 | 2,596 |
| Motor vehicle theft | 8,554 | 2,392 | 6,162 | 100.0 | 28.0 | 72.0 | 940 | 230 | 710 |
| Arson | 902 | 179 | 723 | 100.0 | 19.8 | 80.2 | 108 | 14 | 94 |
| Other assaults | 87,239 | 15,130 | 72,109 | 100.0 | 17.3 | 82.7 | 7,139 | 1,310 | 5,829 |
| Forgery and counterfeiting | 3,735 | 719 | 3,016 | 100.0 | 19.3 | 80.7 | 47 | 10 | 37 |
| Fraud | 9,310 | 1,424 | 7,886 | 100.0 | 15.3 | 84.7 | 268 | 66 | 202 |
| Embezzlement | 848 | 110 | 738 | 100.0 | 13.0 | 87.0 | 30 | 2 | 28 |
| Stolen property; buying, receiving, possessing | 10,204 | 1,845 | 8,359 | 100.0 | 18.1 | 81.9 | 691 | 125 | 566 |
| Vandalism | 16,151 | 2,859 | 13,292 | 100.0 | 17.7 | 82.3 | 2,053 | 330 | 1,723 |
| Weapons; carrying, possessing, etc. | 16,533 | 3,915 | 12,618 | 100.0 | 23.7 | 76.3 | 803 | 226 | 577 |
| Prostitution and commercialized vice | 938 | 183 | 755 | 100.0 | 19.5 | 80.5 | 9 | 0 | 9 |
| Sex offenses (except forcible rape and prostitution) | 3,791 | 1,206 | 2,585 | 100.0 | 31.8 | 68.2 | 418 | 79 | 339 |
| Drug abuse violations | 145,106 | 28,484 | 116,622 | 100.0 | 19.6 | 80.4 | 4,029 | 1,024 | 3,005 |
| Gambling | 259 | 94 | 165 | 100.0 | 36.3 | 63.7 | 25 | 15 | 10 |
| Offenses against the family and children | 7,794 | 827 | 6,967 | 100.0 | 10.6 | 89.4 | 87 | 22 | 65 |
| Driving under the influence | 119,809 | 39,670 | 80,139 | 100.0 | 33.1 | 66.9 | 622 | 207 | 415 |
| Liquor laws | 6,768 | 1,278 | 5,490 | 100.0 | 18.9 | 81.1 | 1,447 | 217 | 1,230 |
| Drunkenness | 13,516 | 4,084 | 9,432 | 100.0 | 30.2 | 69.8 | 115 | 37 | 78 |
| Disorderly conduct | 14,197 | 1,417 | 12,780 | 100.0 | 10.0 | 90.0 | 1,589 | 198 | 1,391 |
| Vagrancy | 692 | 131 | 561 | 100.0 | 18.9 | 81.1 | 9 | 3 | 6 |
| All other offenses (except traffic) | 262,901 | 46,664 | 216,237 | 100.0 | 17.7 | 82.3 | 6,863 | 1,469 | 5,394 |
| Suspicion | 0 | 0 | 0 | | | | 0 | 0 | 0 |
| Curfew and loitering law violations | 568 | 76 | 492 | 100.0 | 13.4 | 86.6 | 568 | 76 | 492 |

## Table 55A. Arrests, Metropolitan Counties, Distribution by Ethnicity, 2020—Continued

(Number, percent; 1,195 agencies; 2020 estimated population 50,082,964.)

| Offense charged | Percent distribution[1] | | | | Arrests 18 and over | | | Percent distribution[1] | |
| --- | --- | --- | --- | --- | --- | --- | --- | --- | --- |
| | Total[2] | Hispanic or Latino | Not Hispanic or Latino | Total[2] | Hispanic or Latino | Not Hispanic or Latino | Total[2] | Hispanic or Latino | Not Hispanic or Latino |
| **Total** | 100.0 | 20.5 | 79.5 | 803,375 | 165,383 | 637,992 | 100.0 | 20.6 | 79.4 |
| **Violent crime[3]** | 100.0 | 23.9 | 76.1 | 45,012 | 11,050 | 33,962 | 100.0 | 24.5 | 75.5 |
| Murder and nonnegligent manslaughter | 100.0 | 22.5 | 77.5 | 1,251 | 297 | 954 | 100.0 | 23.7 | 76.3 |
| Rape[4] | 100.0 | 16.6 | 83.4 | 1,899 | 558 | 1,341 | 100.0 | 29.4 | 70.6 |
| Robbery | 100.0 | 26.9 | 73.1 | 4,136 | 985 | 3,151 | 100.0 | 23.8 | 76.2 |
| Aggravated assault | 100.0 | 24.2 | 75.8 | 37,726 | 9,210 | 28,516 | 100.0 | 24.4 | 75.6 |
| **Property crime[3]** | 100.0 | 20.1 | 79.9 | 64,816 | 9,633 | 55,183 | 100.0 | 14.9 | 85.1 |
| Burglary | 100.0 | 22.8 | 77.2 | 13,145 | 2,222 | 10,923 | 100.0 | 16.9 | 83.1 |
| Larceny-theft | 100.0 | 17.9 | 82.1 | 43,263 | 5,084 | 38,179 | 100.0 | 11.8 | 88.2 |
| Motor vehicle theft | 100.0 | 24.5 | 75.5 | 7,614 | 2,162 | 5,452 | 100.0 | 28.4 | 71.6 |
| Arson | 100.0 | 13.0 | 87.0 | 794 | 165 | 629 | 100.0 | 20.8 | 79.2 |
| Other assaults | 100.0 | 18.3 | 81.7 | 80,100 | 13,820 | 66,280 | 100.0 | 17.3 | 82.7 |
| Forgery and counterfeiting | 100.0 | 21.3 | 78.7 | 3,688 | 709 | 2,979 | 100.0 | 19.2 | 80.8 |
| Fraud | 100.0 | 24.6 | 75.4 | 9,042 | 1,358 | 7,684 | 100.0 | 15.0 | 85.0 |
| Embezzlement | 100.0 | 6.7 | 93.3 | 818 | 108 | 710 | 100.0 | 13.2 | 86.8 |
| Stolen property; buying, receiving, possessing | 100.0 | 18.1 | 81.9 | 9,513 | 1,720 | 7,793 | 100.0 | 18.1 | 81.9 |
| Vandalism | 100.0 | 16.1 | 83.9 | 14,098 | 2,529 | 11,569 | 100.0 | 17.9 | 82.1 |
| Weapons; carrying, possessing, etc. | 100.0 | 28.1 | 71.9 | 15,730 | 3,689 | 12,041 | 100.0 | 23.5 | 76.5 |
| Prostitution and commercialized vice | 100.0 | 0.0 | 100.0 | 929 | 183 | 746 | 100.0 | 19.7 | 80.3 |
| Sex offenses (except forcible rape and prostitution) | 100.0 | 18.9 | 81.1 | 3,373 | 1,127 | 2,246 | 100.0 | 33.4 | 66.6 |
| Drug abuse violations | 100.0 | 25.4 | 74.6 | 141,077 | 27,460 | 113,617 | 100.0 | 19.5 | 80.5 |
| Gambling | 100.0 | 60.0 | 40.0 | 234 | 79 | 155 | 100.0 | 33.8 | 66.2 |
| Offenses against the family and children | 100.0 | 25.3 | 74.7 | 7,707 | 805 | 6,902 | 100.0 | 10.4 | 89.6 |
| Driving under the influence | 100.0 | 33.3 | 66.7 | 119,187 | 39,463 | 79,724 | 100.0 | 33.1 | 66.9 |
| Liquor laws | 100.0 | 15.0 | 85.0 | 5,321 | 1,061 | 4,260 | 100.0 | 19.9 | 80.1 |
| Drunkenness | 100.0 | 32.2 | 67.8 | 13,401 | 4,047 | 9,354 | 100.0 | 30.2 | 69.8 |
| Disorderly conduct | 100.0 | 12.5 | 87.5 | 12,608 | 1,219 | 11,389 | 100.0 | 9.7 | 90.3 |
| Vagrancy | 100.0 | 33.3 | 66.7 | 683 | 128 | 555 | 100.0 | 18.7 | 81.3 |
| All other offenses (except traffic) | 100.0 | 21.4 | 78.6 | 256,038 | 45,195 | 210,843 | 100.0 | 17.7 | 82.3 |
| Suspicion | | | | 0 | 0 | 0 | | | |
| Curfew and loitering law violations | 100.0 | 13.4 | 86.6 | NA | NA | NA | NA | NA | NA |

NA = Not available.
1 Because of rounding, the percentages may not sum to 100.　2 The ethnicity totals are representative of those agencies that provided ethnicity breakdowns. Not all agencies provide ethnicity data; therefore, the race and ethnicity totals will not be equal.
3 Violent crimes are offenses of murder and nonnegligent manslaughter, rape, robbery, and aggravated assault. Property crimes are offenses of burglary, larceny-theft, motor vehicle theft, and arson.　4 The rape figures in this table are an aggregate total of the data submitted using both the revised and legacy Uniform Crime Reporting definitions.

## Table 56. Arrest Trends, Nonmetropolitan Counties, 2019–2020

(Number, percent change; 1,396 agencies; 2020 estimated population 16,631,406; 2019 estimated population 16,583,672.)

| | Number of persons arrested | | | | | | | | |
| --- | --- | --- | --- | --- | --- | --- | --- | --- | --- |
| | Total, all ages | | | Under 18 years of age | | | 18 years of age and over | | |
| Offense charged | 2019 | 2020 | Percent change | 2019 | 2020 | Percent change | 2019 | 2020 | Percent change |
| **Total[1]** | 507,927 | 396,681 | -21.9 | 18,730 | 13,219 | -29.4 | 489,197 | 383,462 | -21.6 |
| **Violent crime[2]** | 15,472 | 15,521 | +0.3 | 971 | 773 | -20.4 | 14,501 | 14,748 | +1.7 |
| Murder and nonnegligent manslaughter | 487 | 562 | +15.4 | 29 | 35 | +20.7 | 458 | 527 | +15.1 |
| Rape[3] | 1,335 | 1,233 | -7.6 | 247 | 190 | (23.1) | 1,088 | 1,043 | -4.1 |
| Robbery | 752 | 1,002 | +33.2 | 55 | 50 | -9.1 | 697 | 952 | +36.6 |
| Aggravated assault | 12,898 | 12,724 | -1.3 | 640 | 498 | -22.2 | 12,258 | 12,226 | -0.3 |
| **Property crime[2]** | 24,889 | 21,439 | -13.9 | 1,934 | 1,567 | -19.0 | 22,955 | 19,872 | -13.4 |
| Burglary | 7,109 | 6,319 | -11.1 | 605 | 537 | -11.2 | 6,504 | 5,782 | -11.1 |
| Larceny-theft | 14,192 | 11,532 | -18.7 | 940 | 691 | -26.5 | 13,252 | 10,841 | -18.2 |
| Motor vehicle theft | 3,228 | 3,158 | -2.2 | 341 | 289 | -15.2 | 2,887 | 2,869 | -0.6 |
| Arson | 360 | 430 | +19.4 | 48 | 50 | +4.2 | 312 | 380 | +21.8 |
| Other assaults | 39,418 | 35,768 | -9.3 | 3,391 | 2,075 | -38.8 | 36,027 | 33,693 | -6.5 |
| Forgery and counterfeiting | 1,623 | 1,081 | -33.4 | 10 | 9 | -10.0 | 1,613 | 1,072 | -33.5 |
| Fraud | 4,458 | 3,006 | -32.6 | 85 | 64 | -24.7 | 4,373 | 2,942 | -32.7 |
| Embezzlement | 354 | 258 | -27.1 | 3 | 3 | +0.0 | 351 | 255 | -27.4 |
| Stolen property; buying, receiving, possessing | 3,266 | 3,070 | -6.0 | 134 | 189 | +41.0 | 3,132 | 2,881 | -8.0 |
| Vandalism | 6,044 | 5,570 | -7.8 | 903 | 762 | -15.6 | 5,141 | 4,808 | -6.5 |
| Weapons; carrying, possessing, etc. | 5,738 | 5,824 | +1.5 | 234 | 163 | -30.3 | 5,504 | 5,661 | +2.9 |
| Prostitution and commercialized vice | 118 | 71 | -39.8 | 6 | 4 | (33.3) | 112 | 67 | -40.2 |
| Sex offenses (except forcible rape and prostitution) | 1,737 | 1,368 | -21.2 | 314 | 203 | -35.4 | 1,423 | 1,165 | -18.1 |
| Drug abuse violations | 81,642 | 65,907 | -19.3 | 2,321 | 1,539 | -33.7 | 79,321 | 64,368 | -18.9 |
| Gambling | 85 | 38 | -55.3 | 1 | 0 | -100.0 | 84 | 38 | -54.8 |
| Offenses against the family and children | 6,527 | 4,414 | -32.4 | 97 | 88 | -9.3 | 6,430 | 4,326 | -32.7 |
| Driving under the influence | 81,834 | 69,921 | -14.6 | 472 | 555 | +17.6 | 81,362 | 69,366 | -14.7 |
| Liquor laws | 8,236 | 7,332 | -11.0 | 1,684 | 1,599 | -5.0 | 6,552 | 5,733 | -12.5 |
| Drunkenness | 9,048 | 5,688 | -37.1 | 104 | 50 | -51.9 | 8,944 | 5,638 | -37.0 |
| Disorderly conduct | 10,556 | 8,762 | -17.0 | 1,367 | 702 | -48.6 | 9,189 | 8,060 | -12.3 |
| Vagrancy | 170 | 126 | -25.9 | 2 | 1 | -50.0 | 168 | 125 | -25.6 |
| All other offenses (except traffic) | 206,539 | 141,322 | -31.6 | 4,524 | 2,678 | -40.8 | 202,015 | 138,644 | -31.4 |
| Suspicion | 7 | 35 | +400.0 | 1 | 8 | +700.0 | 6 | 27 | +350.0 |
| Curfew and loitering law violations | 173 | 195 | +12.7 | 173 | 195 | +12.7 | NA | NA | NA |

NA = Not available.
1 Does not include suspicion.   2 Violent crimes are offenses of murder and nonnegligent manslaughter, rape, robbery, and aggravated assault.   Property crimes are offenses of burglary, larceny-theft, motor vehicle theft, and arson.   3 The rape figures in this table are aggregate totals of the data submitted based on both the legacy and revised Uniform Crime Reporting definitions.

## Table 57. Arrest Trends, Nonmetropolitan Counties, by Age and Sex, 2019–2020

(Number, percent; 1,396 agencies; 2020 estimated population 16,631,406; 2019 estimated population 16,583,672.)

| Offense charged | Male | | | | | | Female | | | | | |
|---|---|---|---|---|---|---|---|---|---|---|---|---|
| | Total | | | Under 18 | | | Total | | | Under 18 | | |
| | 2019 | 2020 | Percent change | 2019 | 2020 | Percent change | 2019 | 2020 | Percent change | 2019 | 2020 | Percent change |
| **Total[1]** | 369,859 | 292,812 | -20.8 | 13,354 | 9,430 | -29.4 | 138,068 | 103,869 | -24.8 | 5,376 | 3,789 | -29.5 |
| **Violent crime[2]** | 12,624 | 12,855 | +1.8 | 792 | 648 | -18.2 | 2,848 | 2,666 | -6.4 | 179 | 125 | -30.2 |
| Murder and nonnegligent manslaughter | 418 | 462 | +10.5 | 26 | 32 | +23.1 | 69 | 100 | +44.9 | 3 | 3 | +0.0 |
| Rape[3] | 1,264 | 1,187 | -6.1 | 224 | 180 | -19.6 | 71 | 46 | -35.2 | 23 | 10 | -56.5 |
| Robbery | 636 | 802 | +26.1 | 47 | 42 | -10.6 | 116 | 200 | +72.4 | 8 | 8 | +0.0 |
| Aggravated assault | 10,306 | 10,404 | +1.0 | 495 | 394 | -20.4 | 2,592 | 2,320 | -10.5 | 145 | 104 | (28.3) |
| **Property crime[2]** | 17,497 | 15,462 | -11.6 | 1,543 | 1,264 | -18.1 | 7,392 | 5,977 | -19.1 | 391 | 303 | -22.5 |
| Burglary | 5,709 | 5,074 | -11.1 | 540 | 487 | -9.8 | 1,400 | 1,245 | -11.1 | 65 | 50 | -23.1 |
| Larceny-theft | 9,070 | 7,627 | -15.9 | 709 | 520 | -26.7 | 5,122 | 3,905 | -23.8 | 231 | 171 | -26.0 |
| Motor vehicle theft | 2,425 | 2,411 | -0.6 | 254 | 218 | -14.2 | 803 | 747 | -7.0 | 87 | 71 | -18.4 |
| Arson | 293 | 350 | +19.5 | 40 | 39 | -2.5 | 67 | 80 | +19.4 | 8 | 11 | +37.5 |
| Other assaults | 29,097 | 26,415 | -9.2 | 2,282 | 1,356 | -40.6 | 10,321 | 9,353 | -9.4 | 1,109 | 719 | -35.2 |
| Forgery and counterfeiting | 1,061 | 707 | -33.4 | 6 | 8 | +33.3 | 562 | 374 | -33.5 | 4 | 1 | -75.0 |
| Fraud | 2,657 | 1,895 | -28.7 | 55 | 43 | -21.8 | 1,801 | 1,111 | -38.3 | 30 | 21 | -30.0 |
| Embezzlement | 177 | 111 | -37.3 | 2 | 2 | +0.0 | 177 | 147 | -16.9 | 1 | 1 | 0.0 |
| Stolen property; buying, receiving, possessing | 2,520 | 2,438 | -3.3 | 106 | 150 | +41.5 | 746 | 632 | -15.3 | 28 | 39 | +39.3 |
| Vandalism | 4,806 | 4,375 | -9.0 | 757 | 582 | -23.1 | 1,238 | 1,195 | -3.5 | 146 | 180 | +23.3 |
| Weapons; carrying, possessing, etc. | 5,103 | 5,212 | +2.1 | 216 | 153 | -29.2 | 635 | 612 | -3.6 | 18 | 10 | -44.4 |
| Prostitution and commercialized vice | 85 | 55 | -35.3 | 3 | 3 | +0.0 | 33 | 16 | -51.5 | 3 | 1 | -66.7 |
| Sex offenses (except forcible rape and prostitution) | 1,622 | 1,293 | -20.3 | 291 | 186 | -36.1 | 115 | 75 | -34.8 | 23 | 17 | -26.1 |
| Drug abuse violations | 57,542 | 46,575 | -19.1 | 1,682 | 1,099 | -34.7 | 24,100 | 19,332 | -19.8 | 639 | 440 | -31.1 |
| Gambling | 73 | 28 | -61.6 | 1 | 0 | -100 | 12 | 10 | -16.7 | 0 | 0 | |
| Offenses against the family and children | 4,862 | 3,333 | -31.4 | 73 | 52 | -28.8 | 1,665 | 1,081 | -35.1 | 24 | 36 | +50.0 |
| Driving under the influence | 61,564 | 52,824 | -14.2 | 359 | 415 | 15.6 | 20,270 | 17,097 | -15.7 | 113 | 140 | +23.9 |
| Liquor laws | 5,591 | 5,038 | -9.9 | 961 | 953 | -0.8 | 2,645 | 2,294 | -13.3 | 723 | 646 | -10.7 |
| Drunkenness | 6,492 | 4,078 | -37.2 | 72 | 36 | -50.0 | 2,556 | 1,610 | -37.0 | 32 | 14 | -56.3 |
| Disorderly conduct | 7,501 | 6,173 | -17.7 | 927 | 475 | -48.8 | 3,055 | 2,589 | -15.3 | 440 | 227 | -48.4 |
| Vagrancy | 123 | 96 | -22.0 | 1 | 1 | +0.0 | 47 | 30 | -36.2 | 1 | 0 | -100.0 |
| All other offenses (except traffic) | 148,769 | 103,755 | -30.3 | 3,132 | 1,910 | -39.0 | 57,770 | 37,567 | -35.0 | 1,392 | 768 | -44.8 |
| Suspicion | 5 | 25 | +400.0 | 1 | 3 | +200.0 | 2 | 10 | +400.0 | 0 | 5 | |
| Curfew and loitering law violations | 93 | 94 | +1.1 | 93 | 94 | +1.1 | 80 | 101 | +26.3 | 80 | 101 | +26.3 |

1 Does not include suspicion.  2 Violent crimes are offenses of murder and nonnegligent manslaughter, rape, robbery, and aggravated assault. Property crimes are offenses of burglary, larceny-theft, motor vehicle theft, and arson.  3 The rape figures in this table are aggregate totals of the data submitted based on both the legacy and revised Uniform Crime Reporting definitions.

# Table 58. Arrests, Nonmetropolitan Counties, Distribution by Age, 2020

(Number, percent; 1,637 agencies; 2020 estimated population 18,948,762.)

| Offense charged | Total, all ages | Ages under 15 | Ages under 18 | Ages 18 and over | Under 10 | 10–12 | 13–14 | 15 | 16 | 17 | 18 | 19 | 20 |
|---|---|---|---|---|---|---|---|---|---|---|---|---|---|
| **Total** | 457,474 | 3,691 | 14,980 | 442,494 | 84 | 911 | 2,696 | 2,563 | 3,506 | 5,220 | 9,551 | 11,398 | 11,858 |
| Total percent distribution[1] | 100.0 | 0.8 | 3.3 | 96.7 | * | 0.2 | 0.6 | 0.6 | 0.8 | 1.1 | 2.1 | 2.5 | 2.6 |
| **Violent crime[2]** | 17,253 | 270 | 845 | 16,408 | 6 | 96 | 168 | 138 | 176 | 261 | 378 | 393 | 418 |
| Violent crime percent distribution[1] | 100.0 | 1.6 | 4.9 | 95.1 | * | 0.6 | 1.0 | 0.8 | 1.0 | 1.5 | 2.2 | 2.3 | 2.4 |
| Murder and nonnegligent manslaughter | 637 | 9 | 39 | 598 | 0 | 3 | 6 | 5 | 8 | 17 | 20 | 14 | 22 |
| Rape[3] | 1,369 | 87 | 209 | 1,160 | 0 | 34 | 53 | 37 | 33 | 52 | 64 | 58 | 46 |
| Robbery | 1,076 | 7 | 54 | 1,022 | 0 | 0 | 7 | 10 | 12 | 25 | 31 | 43 | 33 |
| Aggravated assault | 14,171 | 167 | 543 | 13,628 | 6 | 59 | 102 | 86 | 123 | 167 | 263 | 278 | 317 |
| **Property crime[2]** | 24,218 | 546 | 1,721 | 22,497 | 10 | 129 | 407 | 362 | 378 | 435 | 640 | 628 | 599 |
| Property crime percent distribution[1] | 100.0 | 2.3 | 7.1 | 92.9 | * | 0.5 | 1.7 | 1.5 | 1.6 | 1.8 | 2.6 | 2.6 | 2.5 |
| Burglary | 7,167 | 202 | 576 | 6,591 | 4 | 55 | 143 | 122 | 124 | 128 | 205 | 183 | 195 |
| Larceny-theft | 12,996 | 211 | 767 | 12,229 | 6 | 42 | 163 | 163 | 173 | 220 | 304 | 316 | 302 |
| Motor vehicle theft | 3,600 | 103 | 326 | 3,274 | 0 | 17 | 86 | 66 | 74 | 83 | 124 | 121 | 93 |
| Arson | 455 | 30 | 52 | 403 | 0 | 15 | 15 | 11 | 7 | 4 | 7 | 8 | 9 |
| Other assaults | 40,355 | 817 | 2,337 | 38,018 | 11 | 233 | 573 | 464 | 529 | 527 | 688 | 747 | 809 |
| Forgery and counterfeiting | 1,222 | 0 | 11 | 1,211 | 0 | 0 | 0 | 0 | 1 | 10 | 24 | 24 | 22 |
| Fraud | 3,437 | 14 | 68 | 3,369 | 0 | 2 | 12 | 11 | 12 | 31 | 43 | 59 | 63 |
| Embezzlement | 291 | 2 | 3 | 288 | 0 | 1 | 1 | 0 | 0 | 1 | 8 | 8 | 6 |
| Stolen property; buying, receiving, possessing | 3,491 | 33 | 211 | 3,280 | 0 | 6 | 27 | 52 | 55 | 71 | 92 | 116 | 80 |
| Vandalism | 6,219 | 298 | 819 | 5,400 | 12 | 91 | 195 | 153 | 175 | 193 | 192 | 202 | 173 |
| Weapons; carrying, possessing, etc. | 6,747 | 46 | 190 | 6,557 | 1 | 14 | 31 | 27 | 38 | 79 | 119 | 140 | 155 |
| Prostitution and commercialized vice | 83 | 0 | 7 | 76 | 0 | 0 | 0 | 4 | 1 | 2 | 0 | 3 | 1 |
| Sex offenses (except forcible rape and prostitution) | 1,570 | 116 | 240 | 1,330 | 4 | 35 | 77 | 36 | 45 | 43 | 62 | 46 | 40 |
| Drug abuse violations | 77,373 | 188 | 1,752 | 75,621 | 7 | 24 | 157 | 213 | 430 | 921 | 2,096 | 2,494 | 2,640 |
| Gambling | 57 | 0 | 1 | 56 | 0 | 0 | 0 | 1 | 0 | 0 | 0 | 0 | 1 |
| Offenses against the family and children | 5,064 | 41 | 94 | 4,970 | 0 | 2 | 39 | 26 | 15 | 12 | 49 | 43 | 65 |
| Driving under the influence | 80,434 | 7 | 636 | 79,798 | 0 | 2 | 5 | 41 | 171 | 417 | 1,242 | 1,710 | 1,924 |
| Liquor laws | 7,985 | 162 | 1,724 | 6,261 | 0 | 13 | 149 | 234 | 501 | 827 | 1,300 | 1,202 | 950 |
| Drunkenness | 6,538 | 8 | 62 | 6,476 | 0 | 2 | 6 | 5 | 19 | 30 | 100 | 112 | 116 |
| Disorderly conduct | 10,129 | 282 | 817 | 9,312 | 10 | 71 | 201 | 164 | 174 | 197 | 179 | 173 | 206 |
| Vagrancy | 179 | 1 | 1 | 178 | 0 | 0 | 1 | 0 | 0 | 0 | 3 | 5 | 6 |
| All other offenses (except traffic) | 164,559 | 781 | 3,198 | 161,361 | 21 | 169 | 591 | 574 | 734 | 1,109 | 2,336 | 3,293 | 3,583 |
| Suspicion | 35 | 2 | 8 | 27 | 0 | 2 | 0 | 3 | 0 | 3 | 0 | 0 | 1 |
| Curfew and loitering law violations | 235 | 77 | 235 | NA | 2 | 19 | 56 | 55 | 52 | 51 | NA | NA | NA |

NA = Not available.
* = Less than one-tenth of one percent.
1 Because of rounding, the percentages may not sum to 100.   2 Violent crimes are offenses of murder and nonnegligent manslaughter, rape, robbery, and aggravated assault.  Property crimes are offenses of burglary, larceny-theft, motor vehicle theft, and arson.   3 The rape figures in this table are aggregate totals of the data submitted based on both the legacy and revised Uniform Crime Reporting definitions.

## Table 58. Arrests, Nonmetropolitan Counties, Distribution by Age, 2020—Continued

(Number, percent; 1,637 agencies; 2020 estimated population 18,948,762.)

| Offense charged | 21 | 22 | 23 | 24 | 25–29 | 30–34 | 35–39 | 40–44 | 45–49 | 50–54 | 55–59 | 60–64 | 65 and over |
|---|---|---|---|---|---|---|---|---|---|---|---|---|---|
| **Total** | 12,575 | 12,727 | 12,898 | 13,146 | 74,177 | 73,425 | 64,925 | 48,475 | 33,554 | 25,345 | 19,440 | 10,812 | 8,188 |
| Total percent distribution[1] | 2.7 | 2.8 | 2.8 | 2.9 | 16.2 | 16.1 | 14.2 | 10.6 | 7.3 | 5.5 | 4.2 | 2.4 | 1.8 |
| | | | | | | | | | | | | | |
| **Violent crime[2]** | 491 | 461 | 452 | 418 | 2,539 | 2,575 | 2,366 | 1,747 | 1,303 | 1,021 | 875 | 519 | 452 |
| Violent crime percent distribution[1] | 2.8 | 2.7 | 2.6 | 2.4 | 14.7 | 14.9 | 13.7 | 10.1 | 7.6 | 5.9 | 5.1 | 3.0 | 2.6 |
| Murder and nonnegligent manslaughter | 29 | 17 | 23 | 12 | 90 | 83 | 73 | 51 | 39 | 40 | 31 | 28 | 26 |
| Rape[3] | 55 | 48 | 38 | 33 | 146 | 120 | 165 | 104 | 81 | 74 | 56 | 32 | 40 |
| Robbery | 32 | 24 | 19 | 29 | 173 | 161 | 134 | 125 | 88 | 54 | 30 | 17 | 29 |
| Aggravated assault | 375 | 372 | 372 | 344 | 2,130 | 2,211 | 1,994 | 1,467 | 1,095 | 853 | 758 | 442 | 357 |
| | | | | | | | | | | | | | |
| **Property crime[2]** | 651 | 614 | 603 | 624 | 3,941 | 4,163 | 3,501 | 2,429 | 1,599 | 1,113 | 752 | 383 | 257 |
| Property crime percent distribution[1] | 2.7 | 2.5 | 2.5 | 2.6 | 16.3 | 17.2 | 14.5 | 10.0 | 6.6 | 4.6 | 3.1 | 1.6 | 1.1 |
| Burglary | 207 | 183 | 181 | 192 | 1,219 | 1,270 | 1,035 | 727 | 424 | 269 | 178 | 82 | 41 |
| Larceny-theft | 329 | 321 | 315 | 309 | 2,036 | 2,205 | 1,863 | 1,322 | 955 | 734 | 488 | 250 | 180 |
| Motor vehicle theft | 104 | 103 | 98 | 109 | 638 | 614 | 533 | 342 | 184 | 95 | 67 | 28 | 21 |
| Arson | 11 | 7 | 9 | 14 | 48 | 74 | 70 | 38 | 36 | 15 | 19 | 23 | 15 |
| | | | | | | | | | | | | | |
| Other assaults | 935 | 886 | 952 | 988 | 5,941 | 6,375 | 5,579 | 4,321 | 3,214 | 2,521 | 1,949 | 1,122 | 991 |
| Forgery and counterfeiting | 31 | 34 | 38 | 28 | 202 | 205 | 200 | 135 | 124 | 63 | 46 | 21 | 14 |
| Fraud | 80 | 75 | 71 | 81 | 591 | 577 | 572 | 412 | 284 | 184 | 157 | 63 | 57 |
| Embezzlement | 5 | 5 | 5 | 6 | 37 | 46 | 46 | 44 | 18 | 21 | 19 | 9 | 5 |
| Stolen property; buying, receiving, possessing | 121 | 102 | 95 | 114 | 616 | 626 | 504 | 343 | 217 | 118 | 74 | 39 | 23 |
| | | | | | | | | | | | | | |
| Vandalism | 170 | 161 | 152 | 174 | 935 | 933 | 784 | 511 | 348 | 277 | 185 | 83 | 120 |
| Weapons; carrying, possessing, etc. | 217 | 211 | 215 | 242 | 1,147 | 1,064 | 957 | 693 | 473 | 316 | 281 | 190 | 137 |
| Prostitution and commercialized vice | 2 | 2 | 0 | 1 | 10 | 8 | 15 | 10 | 5 | 4 | 6 | 4 | 5 |
| Sex offenses (except forcible rape and prostitution) | 46 | 35 | 50 | 32 | 160 | 183 | 163 | 129 | 94 | 83 | 69 | 51 | 87 |
| Drug abuse violations | 2,664 | 2,674 | 2,685 | 2,518 | 13,748 | 12,686 | 10,829 | 7,852 | 4,872 | 3,500 | 2,588 | 1,224 | 551 |
| | | | | | | | | | | | | | |
| Gambling | 2 | 1 | 1 | 1 | 7 | 8 | 3 | 10 | 5 | 6 | 6 | 1 | 4 |
| Offenses against the family and children | 54 | 85 | 88 | 117 | 768 | 968 | 985 | 716 | 462 | 265 | 164 | 82 | 59 |
| Driving under the influence | 2,541 | 2,588 | 2,662 | 2,671 | 13,211 | 11,613 | 9,957 | 7,793 | 6,197 | 5,405 | 4,771 | 3,014 | 2,499 |
| Liquor laws | 176 | 150 | 114 | 101 | 476 | 418 | 336 | 267 | 238 | 181 | 153 | 122 | 77 |
| Drunkenness | 149 | 142 | 158 | 183 | 951 | 999 | 967 | 773 | 620 | 494 | 395 | 182 | 135 |
| | | | | | | | | | | | | | |
| Disorderly conduct | 247 | 260 | 269 | 250 | 1,349 | 1,460 | 1,321 | 1,070 | 743 | 687 | 527 | 291 | 280 |
| Vagrancy | 6 | 4 | 7 | 5 | 36 | 29 | 15 | 19 | 10 | 10 | 9 | 6 | 8 |
| All other offenses (except traffic) | 3,985 | 4,237 | 4,281 | 4,589 | 27,510 | 28,481 | 25,820 | 19,199 | 12,726 | 9,076 | 6,413 | 3,406 | 2,426 |
| Suspicion | 2 | 0 | 0 | 3 | 2 | 8 | 5 | 2 | 2 | 0 | 1 | 0 | 1 |
| Curfew and loitering law violations | NA | NA | NA | NA | NA | NA | NA | NA | NA | NA | NA | NA | NA |

NA = Not available.

* = Less than one-tenth of one percent.

1 Because of rounding, the percentages may not sum to 100.    2 Violent crimes are offenses of murder and nonnegligent manslaughter, rape, robbery, and aggravated assault.  Property crimes are offenses of burglary, larceny-theft, motor vehicle theft, and arson.    3 The rape figures in this table are aggregate totals of the data submitted based on both the legacy and revised Uniform Crime Reporting definitions.

## Table 59. Arrests, Nonmetropolitan Counties, Persons Under 15, 18, 21, and 25 Years of Age, 2020

(Number, percent; 1,637 agencies; 2020 estimated population 18,948,762.)

| Offense charged | Total, all ages | Number of persons arrested | | | | Percent of total all ages | | | |
|---|---|---|---|---|---|---|---|---|---|
| | | Under 15 | Under 18 | Under 21 | Under 25 | Under 15 | Under 18 | Under 21 | Under 25 |
| **Total** | 457,474 | 3,691 | 14,980 | 47,787 | 99,133 | 0.8 | 3.3 | 10.4 | 21.7 |
| **Violent crime**[1] | 17,253 | 270 | 845 | 2,034 | 3,856 | 1.6 | 4.9 | 11.8 | 22.3 |
| Murder and nonnegligent manslaughter | 637 | 9 | 39 | 95 | 176 | 1.4 | 6.1 | 14.9 | 27.6 |
| Rape[2] | 1,369 | 87 | 209 | 377 | 551 | 6.4 | 15.3 | 27.5 | 40.2 |
| Robbery | 1,076 | 7 | 54 | 161 | 265 | 0.7 | 5.0 | 15.0 | 24.6 |
| Aggravated assault | 14,171 | 167 | 543 | 1,401 | 2,864 | 1.2 | 3.8 | 9.9 | 20.2 |
| **Property crime**[1] | 24,218 | 546 | 1,721 | 3,588 | 6,080 | 2.3 | 7.1 | 14.8 | 25.1 |
| Burglary | 7,167 | 202 | 576 | 1,159 | 1,922 | 2.8 | 8.0 | 16.2 | 26.8 |
| Larceny-theft | 12,996 | 211 | 767 | 1,689 | 2,963 | 1.6 | 5.9 | 13.0 | 22.8 |
| Motor vehicle theft | 3,600 | 103 | 326 | 664 | 1,078 | 2.9 | 9.1 | 18.4 | 29.9 |
| Arson | 455 | 30 | 52 | 76 | 117 | 6.6 | 11.4 | 16.7 | 25.7 |
| Other assaults | 40,355 | 817 | 2,337 | 4,581 | 8,342 | 2.0 | 5.8 | 11.4 | 20.7 |
| Forgery and counterfeiting | 1,222 | 0 | 11 | 81 | 212 | 0.0 | 0.9 | 6.6 | 17.3 |
| Fraud | 3,437 | 14 | 68 | 233 | 540 | 0.4 | 2.0 | 6.8 | 15.7 |
| Embezzlement | 291 | 2 | 3 | 25 | 46 | 0.7 | 1.0 | 8.6 | 15.8 |
| Stolen property; buying, receiving, possessing | 3,491 | 33 | 211 | 499 | 931 | 0.9 | 6.0 | 14.3 | 26.7 |
| Vandalism | 6,219 | 298 | 819 | 1,386 | 2,043 | 4.8 | 13.2 | 22.3 | 32.9 |
| Weapons; carrying, possessing, etc. | 6,747 | 46 | 190 | 604 | 1,489 | 0.7 | 2.8 | 9.0 | 22.1 |
| Prostitution and commercialized vice | 83 | 0 | 7 | 11 | 16 | 0.0 | 8.4 | 13.3 | 19.3 |
| Sex offenses (except forcible rape and prostitution) | 1,570 | 116 | 240 | 388 | 551 | 7.4 | 15.3 | 24.7 | 35.1 |
| Drug abuse violations | 77,373 | 188 | 1,752 | 8,982 | 19,523 | 0.2 | 2.3 | 11.6 | 25.2 |
| Gambling | 57 | 0 | 1 | 2 | 7 | 0.0 | 1.8 | 3.5 | 12.3 |
| Offenses against the family and children | 5,064 | 41 | 94 | 251 | 595 | 0.8 | 1.9 | 5.0 | 11.7 |
| Driving under the influence | 80,434 | 7 | 636 | 5,512 | 15,974 | * | 0.8 | 6.9 | 19.9 |
| Liquor laws | 7,985 | 162 | 1,724 | 5,176 | 5,717 | 2.0 | 21.6 | 64.8 | 71.6 |
| Drunkenness | 6,538 | 8 | 62 | 390 | 1,022 | 0.1 | 0.9 | 6.0 | 15.6 |
| Disorderly conduct | 10,129 | 282 | 817 | 1,375 | 2,401 | 2.8 | 8.1 | 13.6 | 23.7 |
| Vagrancy | 179 | 1 | 1 | 15 | 37 | 0.6 | 0.6 | 8.4 | 20.7 |
| All other offenses (except traffic) | 164,559 | 781 | 3,198 | 12,410 | 29,502 | 0.5 | 1.9 | 7.5 | 17.9 |
| Suspicion | 35 | 2 | 8 | 9 | 14 | 5.7 | 22.9 | 25.7 | 40.0 |
| Curfew and loitering law violations | 235 | 77 | 235 | 235 | 235 | 32.8 | 100.0 | 100.0 | 100.0 |

* = Less than one-tenth of one percent.
1 Violent crimes are offenses of murder and nonnegligent manslaughter, rape, robbery, and aggravated assault. Property crimes are offenses of burglary, larceny-theft, motor vehicle theft, and arson.   2 The rape figures in this table are aggregate totals of the data submitted based on both the legacy and revised Uniform Crime Reporting definitions.

## Table 60. Arrests, Nonmetropolitan Counties, Distribution by Sex, 2020

(Number, percent; 1,637 agencies; 2020 estimated population 18,948,762.)

| Offense charged | Number of persons arrested | | | Percent male | Percent female | Percent distribution[1] | | |
|---|---|---|---|---|---|---|---|---|
| | Total | Male | Female | | | Total | Male | Female |
| **Total** | 457,474 | 337,574 | 119,900 | 73.8 | 26.2 | 100.0 | 100.0 | 100.0 |
| **Violent crime[2]** | 17,253 | 14,302 | 2,951 | 82.9 | 17.1 | 3.8 | 4.2 | 2.5 |
| Murder and nonnegligent manslaughter | 637 | 528 | 109 | 82.9 | 17.1 | 0.1 | 0.2 | 0.1 |
| Rape[3] | 1,369 | 1,319 | 50 | 96.3 | 3.7 | 0.3 | 0.4 | * |
| Robbery | 1,076 | 864 | 212 | 80.3 | 19.7 | 0.2 | 0.3 | 0.2 |
| Aggravated assault | 14,171 | 11,591 | 2,580 | 81.8 | 18.2 | 3.1 | 3.4 | 2.2 |
| **Property crime[2]** | 24,218 | 17,491 | 6,727 | 72.2 | 27.8 | 5.3 | 5.2 | 5.6 |
| Burglary | 7,167 | 5,743 | 1,424 | 80.1 | 19.9 | 1.6 | 1.7 | 1.2 |
| Larceny-theft | 12,996 | 8,622 | 4,374 | 66.3 | 33.7 | 2.8 | 2.6 | 3.6 |
| Motor vehicle theft | 3,600 | 2,758 | 842 | 76.6 | 23.4 | 0.8 | 0.8 | 0.7 |
| Arson | 455 | 368 | 87 | 80.9 | 19.1 | 0.1 | 0.1 | 0.1 |
| Other assaults | 40,355 | 29,807 | 10,548 | 73.9 | 26.1 | 8.8 | 8.8 | 8.8 |
| Forgery and counterfeiting | 1,222 | 812 | 410 | 66.4 | 33.6 | 0.3 | 0.2 | 0.3 |
| Fraud | 3,437 | 2,186 | 1,251 | 63.6 | 36.4 | 0.8 | 0.6 | 1.0 |
| Embezzlement | 291 | 134 | 157 | 46.0 | 54.0 | 0.1 | * | 0.1 |
| Stolen property; buying, receiving, possessing | 3,491 | 2,766 | 725 | 79.2 | 20.8 | 0.8 | 0.8 | 0.6 |
| Vandalism | 6,219 | 4,895 | 1,324 | 78.7 | 21.3 | 1.4 | 1.5 | 1.1 |
| Weapons; carrying, possessing, etc. | 6,747 | 6,035 | 712 | 89.4 | 10.6 | 1.5 | 1.8 | 0.6 |
| Prostitution and commercialized vice | 83 | 62 | 21 | 74.7 | 25.3 | * | * | * |
| Sex offenses (except forcible rape and prostitution) | 1,570 | 1,484 | 86 | 94.5 | 5.5 | 0.3 | 0.4 | 0.1 |
| Drug abuse violations | 77,373 | 54,577 | 22,796 | 70.5 | 29.5 | 16.9 | 16.2 | 19.0 |
| Gambling | 57 | 40 | 17 | 70.2 | 29.8 | * | * | * |
| Offenses against the family and children | 5,064 | 3,805 | 1,259 | 75.1 | 24.9 | 1.1 | 1.1 | 1.1 |
| Driving under the influence | 80,434 | 60,791 | 19,643 | 75.6 | 24.4 | 17.6 | 18.0 | 16.4 |
| Liquor laws | 7,985 | 5,494 | 2,491 | 68.8 | 31.2 | 1.7 | 1.6 | 2.1 |
| Drunkenness | 6,538 | 4,708 | 1,830 | 72.0 | 28.0 | 1.4 | 1.4 | 1.5 |
| Disorderly conduct | 10,129 | 7,145 | 2,984 | 70.5 | 29.5 | 2.2 | 2.1 | 2.5 |
| Vagrancy | 179 | 139 | 40 | 77.7 | 22.3 | * | * | * |
| All other offenses (except traffic) | 164,559 | 120,757 | 43,802 | 73.4 | 26.6 | 36.0 | 35.8 | 36.5 |
| Suspicion | 35 | 25 | 10 | 71.4 | 28.6 | * | * | * |
| Curfew and loitering law violations | 235 | 119 | 116 | 50.6 | 49.4 | 0.1 | * | 0.1 |

* = Less than one-tenth of 1 percent.
1 Because of rounding, the percentages may not sum to 100.   2 Violent crimes are offenses of murder and nonnegligent manslaughter, rape, robbery, and aggravated assault.  Property crimes are offenses of burglary, larceny-theft, motor vehicle theft, and arson.   3 The rape figures in this table are aggregate totals of the data submitted based on both the legacy and revised Uniform Crime Reporting definitions.

## Table 61A. Arrests, Nonmetropolitan Counties, Distribution by Ethnicity, 2020

(Number, percent; 1,637 agencies; 2020 estimated population 18,948,762.)

| Offense charged | Total arrests | | | Percent distribution[1] | | | Arrests under 18 | | |
|---|---|---|---|---|---|---|---|---|---|
| | Total[2] | Hispanic or Latino | Not Hispanic or Latino | Total[2] | Hispanic or Latino | Not Hispanic or Latino | Total[2] | Hispanic or Latino | Not Hispanic or Latino |
| **Total** | 339,114 | 29,139 | 309,975 | 100.0 | 8.6 | 91.4 | 10,440 | 1,175 | 9,265 |
| **Violent crime[3]** | 12,451 | 1,063 | 11,388 | 100.0 | 8.5 | 91.5 | 585 | 75 | 510 |
| Murder and nonnegligent manslaughter | 500 | 34 | 466 | 100.0 | 6.8 | 93.2 | 28 | 1 | 27 |
| Rape[4] | 925 | 109 | 816 | 100.0 | 11.8 | 88.2 | 138 | 13 | 125 |
| Robbery | 532 | 40 | 492 | 100.0 | 7.5 | 92.5 | 41 | 6 | 35 |
| Aggravated assault | 10,494 | 880 | 9,614 | 100.0 | 8.4 | 91.6 | 378 | 55 | 323 |
| **Property crime[3]** | 17,987 | 1,124 | 16,863 | 100.0 | 6.2 | 93.8 | 1,180 | 96 | 1,084 |
| Burglary | 5,490 | 332 | 5,158 | 100.0 | 6.0 | 94.0 | 377 | 35 | 342 |
| Larceny-theft | 9,415 | 537 | 8,878 | 100.0 | 5.7 | 94.3 | 531 | 30 | 501 |
| Motor vehicle theft | 2,731 | 227 | 2,504 | 100.0 | 8.3 | 91.7 | 235 | 26 | 209 |
| Arson | 351 | 28 | 323 | 100.0 | 8.0 | 92.0 | 37 | 5 | 32 |
| Other assaults | 29,918 | 2,324 | 27,594 | 100.0 | 7.8 | 92.2 | 1,561 | 137 | 1,424 |
| Forgery and counterfeiting | 901 | 76 | 825 | 100.0 | 8.4 | 91.6 | 8 | 2 | 6 |
| Fraud | 2,537 | 206 | 2,331 | 100.0 | 8.1 | 91.9 | 48 | 4 | 44 |
| Embezzlement | 177 | 4 | 173 | 100.0 | 2.3 | 97.7 | 3 | 0 | 3 |
| Stolen property; buying, receiving, possessing | 2,784 | 168 | 2,616 | 100.0 | 6.0 | 94.0 | 171 | 20 | 151 |
| Vandalism | 4,747 | 333 | 4,414 | 100.0 | 7.0 | 93.0 | 610 | 53 | 557 |
| Weapons; carrying, possessing, etc. | 4,655 | 404 | 4,251 | 100.0 | 8.7 | 91.3 | 144 | 12 | 132 |
| Prostitution and commercialized vice | 43 | 7 | 36 | 100.0 | 16.3 | 83.7 | 1 | 0 | 1 |
| Sex offenses (except forcible rape and prostitution) | 1,157 | 106 | 1,051 | 100.0 | 9.2 | 90.8 | 160 | 7 | 153 |
| Drug abuse violations | 60,976 | 5,177 | 55,799 | 100.0 | 8.5 | 91.5 | 1,308 | 206 | 1,102 |
| Gambling | 32 | 14 | 18 | 100.0 | 43.8 | 56.3 | 1 | 1 | 0 |
| Offenses against the family and children | 4,370 | 293 | 4,077 | 100.0 | 6.7 | 93.3 | 81 | 10 | 71 |
| Driving under the influence | 50,969 | 6,729 | 44,240 | 100.0 | 13.2 | 86.8 | 438 | 82 | 356 |
| Liquor laws | 5,276 | 561 | 4,715 | 100.0 | 10.6 | 89.4 | 1,150 | 101 | 1,049 |
| Drunkenness | 5,847 | 628 | 5,219 | 100.0 | 10.7 | 89.3 | 53 | 7 | 46 |
| Disorderly conduct | 6,736 | 479 | 6,257 | 100.0 | 7.1 | 92.9 | 516 | 38 | 478 |
| Vagrancy | 147 | 23 | 124 | 100.0 | 15.6 | 84.4 | 1 | 0 | 1 |
| All other offenses (except traffic) | 127,228 | 9,400 | 117,828 | 100.0 | 7.4 | 92.6 | 2,277 | 314 | 1,963 |
| Suspicion | 42 | 11 | 31 | 100.0 | 26.2 | 73.8 | 10 | 1 | 9 |
| Curfew and loitering law violations | 134 | 9 | 125 | 100.0 | 6.7 | 93.3 | 134 | 9 | 125 |

NA = Not available.
1 Because of rounding, the percentages may not sum to 100. 2 The ethnicity totals are representative of those agencies that provided ethnicity breakdowns. Not all agencies provide ethnicity data; therefore, the race and ethnicity totals will not equal.
3 Violent crimes are offenses of murder and nonnegligent manslaughter, rape, robbery, and aggravated assault. Property crimes are offenses of burglary, larceny-theft, motor vehicle theft, and arson. 4 The rape figures in this table are aggregate totals of the data submitted based on both the legacy and revised Uniform Crime Reporting definitions.

## Table 61A. Arrests, Nonmetropolitan Counties, Distribution by Ethnicity, 2020—Continued

(Number, percent; 1,637 agencies; 2020 estimated population 18,948,762.)

| Offense charged | Percent distribution[1] | | | Arrests 18 and over | | | Percent distribution[1] | | |
|---|---|---|---|---|---|---|---|---|---|
| | Total[2] | Hispanic or Latino | Not Hispanic or Latino | Total[2] | Hispanic or Latino | Not Hispanic or Latino | Total[2] | Hispanic or Latino | Not Hispanic or Latino |
| **Total** | 100.0 | 11.3 | 88.7 | 328,674 | 27,964 | 300,710 | 100.0 | 8.5 | 91.5 |
| **Violent crime[3]** | 100.0 | 12.8 | 87.2 | 11,866 | 988 | 10,878 | 100.0 | 8.3 | 91.7 |
| Murder and nonnegligent manslaughter | 100.0 | 3.6 | 96.4 | 472 | 33 | 439 | 100.0 | 7.0 | 93.0 |
| Rape[4] | 100.0 | 9.4 | 90.6 | 787 | 96 | 691 | 100.0 | 12.2 | 87.8 |
| Robbery | 100.0 | 14.6 | 85.4 | 491 | 34 | 457 | 100.0 | 6.9 | 93.1 |
| Aggravated assault | 100.0 | 14.6 | 85.4 | 10,116 | 825 | 9,291 | 100.0 | 8.2 | 91.8 |
| **Property crime[3]** | 100.0 | 8.1 | 91.9 | 16,807 | 1,028 | 15,779 | 100.0 | 6.1 | 93.9 |
| Burglary | 100.0 | 9.3 | 90.7 | 5,113 | 297 | 4,816 | 100.0 | 5.8 | 94.2 |
| Larceny-theft | 100.0 | 5.6 | 94.4 | 8,884 | 507 | 8,377 | 100.0 | 5.7 | 94.3 |
| Motor vehicle theft | 100.0 | 11.1 | 88.9 | 2,496 | 201 | 2,295 | 100.0 | 8.1 | 91.9 |
| Arson | 100.0 | 13.5 | 86.5 | 314 | 23 | 291 | 100.0 | 7.3 | 92.7 |
| Other assaults | 100.0 | 8.8 | 91.2 | 28,357 | 2,187 | 26,170 | 100.0 | 7.7 | 92.3 |
| Forgery and counterfeiting | 100.0 | 25.0 | 75.0 | 893 | 74 | 819 | 100.0 | 8.3 | 91.7 |
| Fraud | 100.0 | 8.3 | 91.7 | 2,489 | 202 | 2,287 | 100.0 | 8.1 | 91.9 |
| Embezzlement | 100.0 | 0.0 | 100.0 | 174 | 4 | 170 | 100.0 | 2.3 | 97.7 |
| Stolen property; buying, receiving, possessing | 100.0 | 11.7 | 88.3 | 2,613 | 148 | 2,465 | 100.0 | 5.7 | 94.3 |
| Vandalism | 100.0 | 8.7 | 91.3 | 4,137 | 280 | 3,857 | 100.0 | 6.8 | 93.2 |
| Weapons; carrying, possessing, etc. | 100.0 | 8.3 | 91.7 | 4,511 | 392 | 4,119 | 100.0 | 8.7 | 91.3 |
| Prostitution and commercialized vice | 100.0 | 0.0 | 100.0 | 42 | 7 | 35 | 100.0 | 16.7 | 83.3 |
| Sex offenses (except forcible rape and prostitution) | 100.0 | 4.4 | 95.6 | 997 | 99 | 898 | 100.0 | 9.9 | 90.1 |
| Drug abuse violations | 100.0 | 15.7 | 84.3 | 59,668 | 4,971 | 54,697 | 100.0 | 8.3 | 91.7 |
| Gambling | 100.0 | 100.0 | 0.0 | 31 | 13 | 18 | 100.0 | 41.9 | 58.1 |
| Offenses against the family and children | 100.0 | 12.3 | 87.7 | 4,289 | 283 | 4,006 | 100.0 | 6.6 | 93.4 |
| Driving under the influence | 100.0 | 18.7 | 81.3 | 50,531 | 6,647 | 43,884 | 100.0 | 13.2 | 86.8 |
| Liquor laws | 100.0 | 8.8 | 91.2 | 4,126 | 460 | 3,666 | 100.0 | 11.1 | 88.9 |
| Drunkenness | 100.0 | 13.2 | 86.8 | 5,794 | 621 | 5,173 | 100.0 | 10.7 | 89.3 |
| Disorderly conduct | 100.0 | 7.4 | 92.6 | 6,220 | 441 | 5,779 | 100.0 | 7.1 | 92.9 |
| Vagrancy | 100.0 | 0.0 | 100.0 | 146 | 23 | 123 | 100.0 | 15.8 | 84.2 |
| All other offenses (except traffic) | 100.0 | 13.8 | 86.2 | 124,951 | 9,086 | 115,865 | 100.0 | 7.3 | 92.7 |
| Suspicion | 100 | 10 | 90 | 32 | 10 | 22 | 100.0 | 31.3 | 68.8 |
| Curfew and loitering law violations | 100.0 | 6.7 | 93.3 | NA | NA | NA | NA | NA | NA |

NA = Not available.
1 Because of rounding, the percentages may not sum to 100.    2 The ethnicity totals are representative of those agencies that provided ethnicity breakdowns. Not all agencies provide ethnicity data; therefore, the race and ethnicity totals will not be equal.
3 Violent crimes are offenses of murder and nonnegligent manslaughter, rape, robbery, and aggravated assault.  Property crimes are offenses of burglary, larceny-theft, motor vehicle theft, and arson.    4 The rape figures in this table are aggregate totals of the data submitted based on both the legacy and revised Uniform Crime Reporting definitions.

## Table 61. Arrests, Nonmetropolitan Counties, Distribution by Race, 2020

(Number, percent; 1,637 agencies; 2020 estimated population 18,948,762.)

| Offense charged | Total arrests | | | | | | Percent distribution[1] | | | | | |
|---|---|---|---|---|---|---|---|---|---|---|---|---|
| | Total | White | Black | American Indian or Alaskan Native | Asian | Native Hawaiian or Other Pacific Islander | Total | White | Black | American Indian or Alaskan Native | Asian | Native Hawaiian or Other Pacific Islander |
| **Total** | 442,856 | 363,981 | 54,908 | 15,147 | 4,298 | 4,522 | 100.0 | 82.2 | 12.4 | 3.4 | 1.0 | 1.0 |
| **Violent crime[2]** | 16,952 | 13,404 | 2,167 | 973 | 132 | 276 | 100.0 | 79.1 | 12.8 | 5.7 | 0.8 | 1.6 |
| Murder and nonnegligent manslaughter | 628 | 425 | 152 | 34 | 11 | 6 | 100.0 | 67.7 | 24.2 | 5.4 | 1.8 | 1.0 |
| Rape[3] | 1,333 | 1,111 | 133 | 58 | 9 | 22 | 100.0 | 83.3 | 10.0 | 4.4 | 0.7 | 1.7 |
| Robbery | 1,068 | 662 | 207 | 40 | 43 | 116 | 100.0 | 62.0 | 19.4 | 3.7 | 4.0 | 10.9 |
| Aggravated assault | 13,923 | 11,206 | 1,675 | 841 | 69 | 132 | 100.0 | 80.5 | 12.0 | 6.0 | 0.5 | 0.9 |
| **Property crime[2]** | 23,767 | 19,893 | 2,479 | 746 | 238 | 411 | 100.0 | 83.7 | 10.4 | 3.1 | 1.0 | 1.7 |
| Burglary | 7,063 | 6,007 | 697 | 251 | 51 | 57 | 100.0 | 85.0 | 9.9 | 3.6 | 0.7 | 0.8 |
| Larceny-theft | 12,696 | 10,580 | 1,382 | 331 | 137 | 266 | 100.0 | 83.3 | 10.9 | 2.6 | 1.1 | 2.1 |
| Motor vehicle theft | 3,554 | 2,924 | 366 | 141 | 45 | 78 | 100.0 | 82.3 | 10.3 | 4.0 | 1.3 | 2.2 |
| Arson | 454 | 382 | 34 | 23 | 5 | 10 | 100.0 | 84.1 | 7.5 | 5.1 | 1.1 | 2.2 |
| Other assaults | 39,448 | 32,959 | 4,028 | 1,901 | 234 | 326 | 100.0 | 83.6 | 10.2 | 4.8 | 0.6 | 0.8 |
| Forgery and counterfeiting | 1,184 | 977 | 179 | 17 | 3 | 8 | 100.0 | 82.5 | 15.1 | 1.4 | 0.3 | 0.7 |
| Fraud | 3,304 | 2,668 | 448 | 138 | 24 | 26 | 100.0 | 80.8 | 13.6 | 4.2 | 0.7 | 0.8 |
| Embezzlement | 286 | 256 | 28 | 2 | 0 | 0 | 100.0 | 89.5 | 9.8 | 0.7 | 0.0 | 0.0 |
| Stolen property; buying, receiving, possessing | 3,400 | 2,649 | 649 | 88 | 14 | 0 | 100.0 | 77.9 | 19.1 | 2.6 | 0.4 | 0.0 |
| Vandalism | 6,110 | 5,053 | 716 | 233 | 56 | 52 | 100.0 | 82.7 | 11.7 | 3.8 | 0.9 | 0.9 |
| Weapons; carrying, possessing, etc. | 6,601 | 4,803 | 1,462 | 189 | 72 | 75 | 100.0 | 72.8 | 22.1 | 2.9 | 1.1 | 1.1 |
| Prostitution and commercialized vice | 85 | 69 | 5 | 1 | 6 | 4 | 100.0 | 81.2 | 5.9 | 1.2 | 7.1 | 4.7 |
| Sex offenses (except forcible rape and prostitution) | 1,539 | 1,352 | 129 | 38 | 13 | 7 | 100.0 | 87.8 | 8.4 | 2.5 | 0.8 | 0.5 |
| Drug abuse violations | 73,977 | 59,194 | 11,840 | 1,920 | 588 | 435 | 100.0 | 80.0 | 16.0 | 2.6 | 0.8 | 0.6 |
| Gambling | 53 | 44 | 5 | 1 | 2 | 1 | 100.0 | 83.0 | 9.4 | 1.9 | 3.8 | 1.9 |
| Offenses against the family and children | 5,014 | 3,932 | 725 | 341 | 10 | 6 | 100.0 | 78.4 | 14.5 | 6.8 | 0.2 | 0.1 |
| Driving under the influence | 76,379 | 65,204 | 7,295 | 2,185 | 1,265 | 430 | 100.0 | 85.4 | 9.6 | 2.9 | 1.7 | 0.6 |
| Liquor laws | 7,362 | 6,422 | 429 | 426 | 56 | 29 | 100.0 | 87.2 | 5.8 | 5.8 | 0.8 | 0.4 |
| Drunkenness | 6,450 | 5,759 | 403 | 251 | 29 | 8 | 100.0 | 89.3 | 6.2 | 3.9 | 0.4 | 0.1 |
| Disorderly conduct | 9,857 | 7,870 | 1,156 | 579 | 89 | 163 | 100.0 | 79.8 | 11.7 | 5.9 | 0.9 | 1.7 |
| Vagrancy | 170 | 140 | 11 | 19 | 0 | 0 | 100.0 | 82.4 | 6.5 | 11.2 | 0.0 | 0.0 |
| All other offenses (except traffic) | 160,638 | 131,116 | 20,751 | 5,081 | 1,454 | 2,236 | 100.0 | 81.6 | 12.9 | 3.2 | 0.9 | 1.4 |
| Suspicion | 47 | 45 | 0 | 2 | 0 | 0 | 100.0 | 95.7 | 0.0 | 4.3 | 0.0 | 0.0 |
| Curfew and loitering law violations | 233 | 172 | 3 | 16 | 13 | 29 | 100.0 | 73.8 | 1.3 | 6.9 | 5.6 | 12.4 |

## Table 61. Arrests, Nonmetropolitan Counties, Distribution by Race, 2020—Continued

(Number, percent; 1,637 agencies; 2020 estimated population 18,948,762.)

| Offense charged | Arrests under 18 | | | | | | Percent distribution[1] | | | | | |
|---|---|---|---|---|---|---|---|---|---|---|---|---|
| | Total | White | Black | American Indian or Alaskan Native | Asian | Native Hawaiian or Other Pacific Islander | Total | White | Black | American Indian or Alaskan Native | Asian | Native Hawaiian or Other Pacific Islander |
| **Total** | 14,307 | 11,525 | 1,808 | 693 | 106 | 175 | 100.0 | 80.6 | 12.6 | 4.8 | 0.7 | 1.2 |
| **Violent crime**[2] | 831 | 638 | 142 | 41 | 2 | 8 | 100.0 | 76.8 | 17.1 | 4.9 | 0.2 | 1.0 |
| Murder and nonnegligent manslaughter | 38 | 18 | 17 | 2 | 1 | 0 | 100.0 | 47.4 | 44.7 | 5.3 | 2.6 | 0.0 |
| Rape[3] | 205 | 179 | 16 | 8 | 0 | 2 | 100.0 | 87.3 | 7.8 | 3.9 | 0.0 | 1.0 |
| Robbery | 54 | 36 | 16 | 2 | 0 | 0 | 100.0 | 66.7 | 29.6 | 3.7 | 0.0 | 0.0 |
| Aggravated assault | 534 | 405 | 93 | 29 | 1 | 6 | 100.0 | 75.8 | 17.4 | 5.4 | 0.2 | 1.1 |
| **Property crime**[2] | 1,663 | 1,283 | 253 | 97 | 8 | 22 | 100.0 | 77.1 | 15.2 | 5.8 | 0.5 | 1.3 |
| Burglary | 563 | 428 | 83 | 44 | 3 | 5 | 100.0 | 76.0 | 14.7 | 7.8 | 0.5 | 0.9 |
| Larceny-theft | 734 | 579 | 118 | 21 | 5 | 11 | 100.0 | 78.9 | 16.1 | 2.9 | 0.7 | 1.5 |
| Motor vehicle theft | 316 | 238 | 47 | 27 | 0 | 4 | 100.0 | 75.3 | 14.9 | 8.5 | 0.0 | 1.3 |
| Arson | 50 | 38 | 5 | 5 | 0 | 2 | 100.0 | 76.0 | 10.0 | 10.0 | 0.0 | 4.0 |
| Other assaults | 2,277 | 1,794 | 334 | 116 | 11 | 22 | 100.0 | 78.8 | 14.7 | 5.1 | 0.5 | 1 |
| Forgery and counterfeiting | 9 | 7 | 2 | 0 | 0 | 0 | 100.0 | 77.8 | 22.2 | 0.0 | 0.0 | 0.0 |
| Fraud | 63 | 45 | 10 | 5 | 3 | 0 | 100.0 | 71.4 | 15.9 | 7.9 | 4.8 | 0.0 |
| Embezzlement | 3 | 2 | 1 | 0 | 0 | 0 | 100.0 | 66.7 | 33.3 | 0.0 | 0.0 | 0.0 |
| Stolen property; buying, receiving, possessing | 202 | 126 | 70 | 6 | 0 | 0 | 100.0 | 62.4 | 34.7 | 3.0 | 0.0 | 0.0 |
| Vandalism | 793 | 663 | 88 | 34 | 4 | 4 | 100.0 | 83.6 | 11.1 | 4.3 | 0.5 | 0.5 |
| Weapons; carrying, possessing, etc. | 186 | 112 | 70 | 2 | 2 | 0 | 100.0 | 60.2 | 37.6 | 1.1 | 1.1 | 0.0 |
| Prostitution and commercialized vice | 7 | 7 | 0 | 0 | 0 | 0 | 100.0 | 100.0 | 0.0 | 0.0 | 0.0 | 0.0 |
| Sex offenses (except forcible rape and prostitution) | 232 | 213 | 15 | 3 | 0 | 1 | 100.0 | 91.8 | 6.5 | 1.3 | 0.0 | 0.4 |
| Drug abuse violations | 1,633 | 1,334 | 205 | 68 | 11 | 15 | 100.0 | 81.7 | 12.6 | 4.2 | 0.7 | 0.9 |
| Gambling | 1 | 1 | 0 | 0 | 0 | 0 | 100.0 | 100.0 | 0.0 | 0.0 | 0.0 | 0.0 |
| Offenses against the family and children | 94 | 81 | 3 | 6 | 1 | 3 | 100.0 | 86.2 | 3.2 | 6.4 | 1.1 | 3.2 |
| Driving under the influence | 598 | 539 | 25 | 30 | 3 | 1 | 100.0 | 90.1 | 4.2 | 5.0 | 0.5 | 0.2 |
| Liquor laws | 1,567 | 1,410 | 25 | 110 | 13 | 9 | 100.0 | 90.0 | 1.6 | 7.0 | 0.8 | 0.6 |
| Drunkenness | 61 | 55 | 4 | 2 | 0 | 0 | 100.0 | 90.2 | 6.6 | 3.3 | 0.0 | 0.0 |
| Disorderly conduct | 784 | 571 | 156 | 54 | 2 | 1 | 100.0 | 72.8 | 19.9 | 6.9 | 0.3 | 0.1 |
| Vagrancy | 1 | 0 | 1 | 0 | 0 | 0 | 100.0 | 0.0 | 100.0 | 0.0 | 0.0 | 0.0 |
| All other offenses (except traffic) | 3,060 | 2,463 | 401 | 103 | 33 | 60 | 100.0 | 80.5 | 13.1 | 3.4 | 1.1 | 2 |
| Suspicion | 9 | 9 | 0 | 0 | 0 | 0 | 100.0 | 100.0 | 0.0 | 0.0 | 0.0 | 0.0 |
| Curfew and loitering law violations | 233 | 172 | 3 | 16 | 13 | 29 | 100.0 | 73.8 | 1.3 | 6.9 | 5.6 | 12.4 |

## Table 61. Arrests, Nonmetropolitan Counties, Distribution by Race, 2020—Continued

(Number, percent; 1,637 agencies; 2020 estimated population 18,948,762.)

| Offense charged | Arrests 18 and over | | | | | | Percent distribution[1] | | | | | |
|---|---|---|---|---|---|---|---|---|---|---|---|---|
| | Total | White | Black | American Indian or Alaskan Native | Asian | Native Hawaiian or Other Pacific Islander | Total | White | Black | American Indian or Alaskan Native | Asian | Native Hawaiian or Other Pacific Islander |
| **Total** | 428,549 | 352,456 | 53,100 | 14,454 | 4,192 | 4,347 | 100.0 | 82.2 | 12.4 | 3.4 | 1.0 | 1.0 |
| **Violent crime[2]** | 16,121 | 12,766 | 2,025 | 932 | 130 | 268 | 100.0 | 79.2 | 12.6 | 5.8 | 0.8 | 1.7 |
| Murder and nonnegligent manslaughter | 590 | 407 | 135 | 32 | 10 | 6 | 100.0 | 69.0 | 22.9 | 5.4 | 1.7 | 1.0 |
| Rape[3] | 1,128 | 932 | 117 | 50 | 9 | 20 | 100.0 | 82.6 | 10.4 | 4.4 | 0.8 | 1.8 |
| Robbery | 1,014 | 626 | 191 | 38 | 43 | 116 | 100.0 | 61.7 | 18.8 | 3.7 | 4.2 | 11.4 |
| Aggravated assault | 13,389 | 10,801 | 1,582 | 812 | 68 | 126 | 100.0 | 80.7 | 11.8 | 6.1 | 0.5 | 0.9 |
| **Property crime[2]** | 22,104 | 18,610 | 2,226 | 649 | 230 | 389 | 100.0 | 84.2 | 10.1 | 2.9 | 1.0 | 1.8 |
| Burglary | 6,500 | 5,579 | 614 | 207 | 48 | 52 | 100.0 | 85.8 | 9.4 | 3.2 | 0.7 | 0.8 |
| Larceny-theft | 11,962 | 10,001 | 1,264 | 310 | 132 | 255 | 100.0 | 83.6 | 10.6 | 2.6 | 1.1 | 2.1 |
| Motor vehicle theft | 3,238 | 2,686 | 319 | 114 | 45 | 74 | 100.0 | 83.0 | 9.9 | 3.5 | 1.4 | 2.3 |
| Arson | 404 | 344 | 29 | 18 | 5 | 8 | 100.0 | 85.1 | 7.2 | 4.5 | 1.2 | 2.0 |
| Other assaults | 37,171 | 31,165 | 3,694 | 1,785 | 223 | 304 | 100.0 | 83.8 | 9.9 | 4.8 | 0.6 | 0.8 |
| Forgery and counterfeiting | 1,175 | 970 | 177 | 17 | 3 | 8 | 100.0 | 82.6 | 15.1 | 1.4 | 0.3 | 0.7 |
| Fraud | 3,241 | 2,623 | 438 | 133 | 21 | 26 | 100.0 | 80.9 | 13.5 | 4.1 | 0.6 | 0.8 |
| Embezzlement | 283 | 254 | 27 | 2 | 0 | 0 | 100.0 | 89.8 | 9.5 | 0.7 | 0.0 | 0.0 |
| Stolen property; buying, receiving, possessing | 3,198 | 2,523 | 579 | 82 | 14 | 0 | 100.0 | 78.9 | 18.1 | 2.6 | 0.4 | 0.0 |
| Vandalism | 5,317 | 4,390 | 628 | 199 | 52 | 48 | 100.0 | 82.6 | 11.8 | 3.7 | 1.0 | 0.9 |
| Weapons; carrying, possessing, etc. | 6,415 | 4,691 | 1,392 | 187 | 70 | 75 | 100.0 | 73.1 | 21.7 | 2.9 | 1.1 | 1.2 |
| Prostitution and commercialized vice | 78 | 62 | 5 | 1 | 6 | 4 | 100.0 | 79.5 | 6.4 | 1.3 | 7.7 | 5.1 |
| Sex offenses (except forcible rape and prostitution) | 1,307 | 1,139 | 114 | 35 | 13 | 6 | 100.0 | 87.1 | 8.7 | 2.7 | 1.0 | 0.5 |
| Drug abuse violations | 72,344 | 57,860 | 11,635 | 1,852 | 577 | 420 | 100.0 | 80.0 | 16.1 | 2.6 | 0.8 | 0.6 |
| Gambling | 52 | 43 | 5 | 1 | 2 | 1 | 100.0 | 82.7 | 9.6 | 1.9 | 3.8 | 1.9 |
| Offenses against the family and children | 4,920 | 3,851 | 722 | 335 | 9 | 3 | 100.0 | 78.3 | 14.7 | 6.8 | 0.2 | 0.1 |
| Driving under the influence | 75,781 | 64,665 | 7,270 | 2,155 | 1,262 | 429 | 100.0 | 85.3 | 9.6 | 2.8 | 1.7 | 0.6 |
| Liquor laws | 5,795 | 5,012 | 404 | 316 | 43 | 20 | 100.0 | 86.5 | 7.0 | 5.5 | 0.7 | 0.3 |
| Drunkenness | 6,389 | 5,704 | 399 | 249 | 29 | 8 | 100.0 | 89.3 | 6.2 | 3.9 | 0.5 | 0.1 |
| Disorderly conduct | 9,073 | 7,299 | 1,000 | 525 | 87 | 162 | 100.0 | 80.4 | 11.0 | 5.8 | 1.0 | 1.8 |
| Vagrancy | 169 | 140 | 10 | 19 | 0 | 0 | 100.0 | 82.8 | 5.9 | 11.2 | 0.0 | 0.0 |
| All other offenses (except traffic) | 157,578 | 128,653 | 20,350 | 4,978 | 1,421 | 2,176 | 100.0 | 81.6 | 12.9 | 3.2 | 0.9 | 1.4 |
| Suspicion | 38 | 36 | 0 | 2 | 0 | 0 | 100.0 | 94.7 | 0.0 | 5.3 | 0.0 | 0.0 |
| Curfew and loitering law violations | NA | NA | NA | NA | NA | NA | NA | NA | NA | NA | NA | NA |

NA = Not available.
1 Because of rounding, the percentages may not sum to 100.   2 Violent crimes are offenses of murder and nonnegligent manslaughter, rape, robbery, and aggravated assault.  Property crimes are offenses of burglary, larceny-theft, motor vehicle theft, and arson.   3 The rape figures in this table are aggregate totals of the data submitted based on both the legacy and revised Uniform Crime Reporting definitions.

## Table 62. Arrest Trends, Suburban Areas,[1] 2019–2020

(Number, percent change; 4,908 agencies; 2020 estimated population 83,553,706; 2019 estimated population 83,105,781.)

| Offense charged | Number of persons arrested | | | | | | | | |
|---|---|---|---|---|---|---|---|---|---|
| | Total, all ages | | | Under 18 years of age | | | 18 years of age and over | | |
| | 2019 | 2020 | Percent change | 2019 | 2020 | Percent change | 2019 | 2020 | Percent change |
| Total[2] | 2,281,612 | 1,751,123 | -23.3 | 159,753 | 97,970 | -38.7 | 2,121,859 | 1,653,153 | -22.1 |
| **Violent crime[3]** | 90,368 | 85,991 | -4.8 | 9,264 | 6,366 | -31.3 | 81,104 | 79,625 | -1.8 |
| Murder and nonnegligent manslaughter | 1,806 | 1,897 | +5.0 | 127 | 127 | +0.0 | 1,679 | 1,770 | +5.4 |
| Rape[4] | 5,257 | 4,458 | -15.2 | 1,007 | 692 | -31.3 | 4,250 | 3,766 | -11.4 |
| Robbery | 11,740 | 10,303 | -12.2 | 2,449 | 1,835 | -25.1 | 9,291 | 8,468 | -8.9 |
| Aggravated assault | 71,565 | 69,333 | -3.1 | 5,681 | 3,712 | -34.7 | 65,884 | 65,621 | -0.4 |
| **Property crime[3]** | 246,826 | 196,499 | -20.4 | 26,041 | 16,515 | -36.6 | 220,785 | 179,984 | -18.5 |
| Burglary | 34,703 | 30,277 | -12.8 | 4,336 | 3,432 | -20.8 | 30,367 | 26,845 | -11.6 |
| Larceny-theft | 194,546 | 148,766 | -23.5 | 18,903 | 10,611 | -43.9 | 175,643 | 138,155 | -21.3 |
| Motor vehicle theft | 15,820 | 15,602 | -1.4 | 2,392 | 2,166 | -9.4 | 13,428 | 13,436 | +0.1 |
| Arson | 1,757 | 1,854 | +5.5 | 410 | 306 | -25.4 | 1,347 | 1,548 | +14.9 |
| Other assaults | 212,962 | 190,704 | -10.5 | 29,625 | 17,002 | -42.6 | 183,337 | 173,702 | -5.3 |
| Forgery and counterfeiting | 11,700 | 8,410 | -28.1 | 232 | 149 | -35.8 | 11,468 | 8,261 | -28.0 |
| Fraud | 29,502 | 21,154 | -28.3 | 1,020 | 720 | -29.4 | 28,482 | 20,434 | -28.3 |
| Embezzlement | 3,227 | 2,057 | -36.3 | 126 | 106 | -15.9 | 3,101 | 1,951 | -37.1 |
| Stolen property; buying, receiving, possessing | 21,242 | 20,795 | -2.1 | 1,927 | 1,746 | -9.4 | 19,315 | 19,049 | -1.4 |
| Vandalism | 37,592 | 35,484 | -5.6 | 7,368 | 5,719 | -22.4 | 30,224 | 29,765 | -1.5 |
| Weapons; carrying, possessing, etc. | 31,443 | 31,851 | +1.3 | 3,463 | 2,002 | -42.2 | 27,980 | 29,849 | +6.7 |
| Prostitution and commercialized vice | 2,667 | 1,572 | -41.1 | 36 | 14 | -61.1 | 2,631 | 1,558 | -40.8 |
| Sex offenses (except forcible rape and prostitution) | 9,032 | 6,935 | -23.2 | 1,675 | 1,007 | -39.9 | 7,357 | 5,928 | -19.4 |
| Drug abuse violations | 369,570 | 280,946 | -24.0 | 21,739 | 11,248 | -48.3 | 347,831 | 269,698 | -22.5 |
| Gambling | 464 | 291 | -37.3 | 50 | 16 | -68.0 | 414 | 275 | -33.6 |
| Offenses against the family and children | 23,203 | 13,864 | -40.2 | 514 | 446 | -13.2 | 22,689 | 13,418 | -40.9 |
| Driving under the influence | 265,340 | 211,629 | -20.2 | 1,312 | 1,351 | +3.0 | 264,028 | 210,278 | -20.4 |
| Liquor laws | 36,567 | 24,201 | -33.8 | 6,171 | 4,304 | -30.3 | 30,396 | 19,897 | -34.5 |
| Drunkenness | 56,533 | 35,422 | -37.3 | 908 | 621 | -31.6 | 55,625 | 34,801 | -37.4 |
| Disorderly conduct | 65,757 | 49,609 | -24.6 | 12,698 | 5,840 | -54.0 | 53,059 | 43,769 | -17.5 |
| Vagrancy | 2,765 | 1,790 | -35.3 | 42 | 70 | +66.7 | 2,723 | 1,720 | -36.8 |
| All other offenses (except traffic) | 761,688 | 529,439 | -30.5 | 32,378 | 20,248 | -37.5 | 729,310 | 509,191 | -30.2 |
| Suspicion | 136 | 98 | -27.9 | 3 | 7 | +133.3 | 133 | 91 | -31.6 |
| Curfew and loitering law violations | 3,164 | 2,480 | -21.6 | 3,164 | 2,480 | -21.6 | NA | NA | NA |

NA = Not available.
1 Suburban areas include law enforcement agencies in cities with less than 50,000 inhabitants and county law enforcement agencies that are within a Metropolitan Statistical Area. Suburban areas exclude all metropolitan agencies associated with a principal city.　2 Does not include suspicion.　3 Violent crimes are offenses of murder and nonnegligent manslaughter, rape, robbery, and aggravated assault.　Property crimes are offenses of burglary, larceny-theft, motor vehicle theft, and arson.　4 The rape figures in this table are aggregate totals of the data submitted based on both the legacy and revised Uniform Crime Reporting definitions.

## Table 63. Arrest Trends, Suburban Areas[1], by Age and Sex, 2019–2020

(Number, percent change; 4,908 agencies; 2020 estimated population 83,553,706; 2019 estimated population 83,105,781.)

| Offense charged | Male | | | | | | Female | | | | | |
|---|---|---|---|---|---|---|---|---|---|---|---|---|
| | Total | | | Under 18 | | | Total | | | Under 18 | | |
| | 2019 | 2020 | Percent change | 2019 | 2020 | Percent change | 2019 | 2020 | Percent change | 2019 | 2020 | Percent change |
| **Total[2]** | 1,645,958 | 1,280,649 | -22.2 | 111,893 | 69,945 | -37.5 | 635,654 | 470,474 | -26.0 | 47,860 | 28,025 | -41.4 |
| **Violent crime[3]** | 71,816 | 68,547 | -4.6 | 7,352 | 5,128 | -30.3 | 18,552 | 17,444 | -6.0 | 1,912 | 1,238 | -35.3 |
| Murder and nonnegligent manslaughter | 1,607 | 1,668 | +3.8 | 115 | 115 | +0.0 | 199 | 229 | +15.1 | 12 | 12 | +0.0 |
| Rape[4] | 5,065 | 4,358 | -14.0 | 939 | 666 | -29.1 | 192 | 100 | -47.9 | 68 | 26 | -61.8 |
| Robbery | 9,847 | 8,772 | -10.9 | 2,120 | 1,596 | -24.7 | 1,893 | 1,531 | -19.1 | 329 | 239 | -27.4 |
| Aggravated assault | 55,297 | 53,749 | -2.8 | 4,178 | 2,751 | -34.2 | 16,268 | 15,584 | -4.2 | 1,503 | 961 | -36.1 |
| **Property crime[3]** | 152,267 | 126,842 | -16.7 | 17,610 | 11,950 | -32.1 | 94,559 | 69,657 | -26.3 | 8,431 | 4,565 | -45.9 |
| Burglary | 27,643 | 24,450 | -11.6 | 3,745 | 2,985 | -20.3 | 7,060 | 5,827 | -17.5 | 591 | 447 | -24.4 |
| Larceny-theft | 111,110 | 88,746 | -20.1 | 11,614 | 6,968 | -40.0 | 83,436 | 60,020 | -28.1 | 7,289 | 3,643 | -50.0 |
| Motor vehicle theft | 12,102 | 12,159 | +0.5 | 1,894 | 1,738 | -8.2 | 3,718 | 3,443 | -7.4 | 498 | 428 | -14.1 |
| Arson | 1,412 | 1,487 | +5.3 | 357 | 259 | -27.5 | 345 | 367 | +6.4 | 53 | 47 | -11.3 |
| Other assaults | 150,855 | 136,545 | -9.5 | 18,929 | 10,748 | -43.2 | 62,107 | 54,159 | -12.8 | 10,696 | 6,254 | -41.5 |
| Forgery and counterfeiting | 7,950 | 5,750 | -27.7 | 184 | 120 | -34.8 | 3,750 | 2,660 | -29.1 | 48 | 29 | -39.6 |
| Fraud | 18,977 | 14,002 | -26.2 | 708 | 496 | -29.9 | 10,525 | 7,152 | -32.0 | 312 | 224 | -28.2 |
| Embezzlement | 1,560 | 1,037 | -33.5 | 64 | 55 | -14.1 | 1,667 | 1,020 | -38.8 | 62 | 51 | -17.7 |
| Stolen property; buying, receiving, possessing | 16,521 | 16,287 | -1.4 | 1,570 | 1,464 | -6.8 | 4,721 | 4,508 | -4.5 | 357 | 282 | -21.0 |
| Vandalism | 29,417 | 27,737 | -5.7 | 6,060 | 4,625 | -23.7 | 8,175 | 7,747 | -5.2 | 1,308 | 1,094 | -16.4 |
| Weapons; carrying, possessing, etc. | 28,122 | 28,559 | +1.6 | 3,039 | 1,789 | -41.1 | 3,321 | 3,292 | -0.9 | 424 | 213 | -49.8 |
| Prostitution and commercialized vice | 1,216 | 867 | -28.7 | 28 | 8 | -71.4 | 1,451 | 705 | -51.4 | 8 | 6 | -25.0 |
| Sex offenses (except forcible rape and prostitution) | 8,443 | 6,583 | -22.0 | 1,463 | 919 | -37.2 | 589 | 352 | -40.2 | 212 | 88 | -58.5 |
| Drug abuse violations | 271,506 | 207,388 | -23.6 | 15,943 | 8,345 | -47.7 | 98,064 | 73,558 | -25.0 | 5,796 | 2,903 | -49.9 |
| Gambling | 334 | 197 | -41.0 | 43 | 14 | -67.4 | 130 | 94 | -27.7 | 7 | 2 | -71.4 |
| Offenses against the family and children | 17,394 | 9,909 | -43.0 | 307 | 292 | -4.9 | 5,809 | 3,955 | -31.9 | 207 | 154 | -25.6 |
| Driving under the influence | 194,731 | 157,025 | -19.4 | 1,009 | 1,016 | +0.7 | 70,609 | 54,604 | -22.7 | 303 | 335 | +10.6 |
| Liquor laws | 24,947 | 16,654 | -33.2 | 3,560 | 2,588 | -27.3 | 11,620 | 7,547 | -35.1 | 2,611 | 1,716 | -34.3 |
| Drunkenness | 43,606 | 27,306 | -37.4 | 605 | 388 | -35.9 | 12,927 | 8,116 | -37.2 | 303 | 233 | -23.1 |
| Disorderly conduct | 46,637 | 35,213 | -24.5 | 8,210 | 3,814 | -53.5 | 19,120 | 14,396 | -24.7 | 4,488 | 2,026 | -54.9 |
| Vagrancy | 2,144 | 1,434 | -33.1 | 32 | 47 | +46.9 | 621 | 356 | -42.7 | 10 | 23 | +130.0 |
| All other offenses (except traffic) | 555,345 | 391,130 | -29.6 | 23,007 | 14,502 | -37.0 | 206,343 | 138,309 | -33.0 | 9,371 | 5,746 | -38.7 |
| Suspicion | 90 | 54 | -40.0 | 3 | 6 | +100.0 | 46 | 44 | -4.3 | 0 | 1 | |
| Curfew and loitering law violations | 2,170 | 1,637 | -24.6 | 2,170 | 1,637 | -24.6 | 994 | 843 | -15.2 | 994 | 843 | -15.2 |

1 Suburban areas include law enforcement agencies in cities with less than 50,000 inhabitants and county law enforcement agencies that are within a Metropolitan Statistical Area. Suburban areas exclude all metropolitan agencies associated with a principal city.   2 Does not include suspicion.   3 Violent crimes are offenses of murder and nonnegligent manslaughter, rape, robbery, and aggravated assault.  Property crimes are offenses of burglary, larceny-theft, motor vehicle theft, and arson.   4 The rape figures in this table are aggregate totals of the data submitted based on both the legacy and revised Uniform Crime Reporting definitions.

## Table 64. Arrests, Suburban Areas,[1] Distribution by Age, 2020

(Number, percent; 5,475 agencies; 2020 estimated population 94,124,752.)

| Offense charged | Total, all ages | Ages under 15 | Ages under 18 | Ages 18 and over | Under 10 | 10–12 | 13–14 | 15 | 16 | 17 | 18 | 19 | 20 |
|---|---|---|---|---|---|---|---|---|---|---|---|---|---|
| **Total** | 1,964,444 | 30,377 | 109,588 | 1,854,856 | 420 | 6,413 | 23,544 | 20,634 | 26,403 | 32,174 | 49,393 | 53,957 | 54,826 |
| Total percent distribution[2] | 100.0 | 1.5 | 5.6 | 94.4 | * | 0.3 | 1.2 | 1.1 | 1.3 | 1.6 | 2.5 | 2.7 | 2.8 |
| | | | | | | | | | | | | | |
| **Violent crime[3]** | 97,976 | 1,963 | 7,179 | 90,797 | 18 | 434 | 1,511 | 1,353 | 1,756 | 2,107 | 2,764 | 2,807 | 2,770 |
| Violent crime percent distribution[2] | 100.0 | 2.0 | 7.3 | 92.7 | * | 0.4 | 1.5 | 1.4 | 1.8 | 2.2 | 2.8 | 2.9 | 2.8 |
| Murder and nonnegligent manslaughter | 2,282 | 9 | 156 | 2,126 | 0 | 2 | 7 | 26 | 48 | 73 | 102 | 117 | 118 |
| Rape[4] | 4,929 | 314 | 762 | 4,167 | 2 | 83 | 229 | 138 | 161 | 149 | 227 | 208 | 179 |
| Robbery | 11,687 | 430 | 2,083 | 9,604 | 0 | 46 | 384 | 402 | 554 | 697 | 766 | 601 | 532 |
| Aggravated assault | 79,078 | 1,210 | 4,178 | 74,900 | 16 | 303 | 891 | 787 | 993 | 1,188 | 1,669 | 1,881 | 1,941 |
| | | | | | | | | | | | | | |
| **Property crime[3]** | 218,927 | 4,920 | 18,356 | 200,571 | 40 | 932 | 3,948 | 3,734 | 4,670 | 5,032 | 6,375 | 5,833 | 5,709 |
| Property crime percent distribution[2] | 100.0 | 2.2 | 8.4 | 91.6 | * | 0.4 | 1.8 | 1.7 | 2.1 | 2.3 | 2.9 | 2.7 | 2.6 |
| Burglary | 33,777 | 1,104 | 3,768 | 30,009 | 8 | 219 | 877 | 803 | 938 | 923 | 1,023 | 876 | 889 |
| Larceny-theft | 164,967 | 3,017 | 11,840 | 153,127 | 19 | 591 | 2,407 | 2,309 | 3,037 | 3,477 | 4,717 | 4,390 | 4,297 |
| Motor vehicle theft | 18,095 | 625 | 2,416 | 15,679 | 3 | 67 | 555 | 546 | 645 | 600 | 600 | 526 | 492 |
| Arson | 2,088 | 174 | 332 | 1,756 | 10 | 55 | 109 | 76 | 50 | 32 | 35 | 41 | 31 |
| | | | | | | | | | | | | | |
| Other assaults | 212,497 | 7,293 | 18,988 | 193,509 | 91 | 1,898 | 5,304 | 3,777 | 4,038 | 3,880 | 4,203 | 4,637 | 4,940 |
| Forgery and counterfeiting | 9,273 | 15 | 161 | 9,112 | 0 | 1 | 14 | 22 | 46 | 78 | 291 | 342 | 359 |
| Fraud | 23,240 | 171 | 784 | 22,456 | 1 | 21 | 149 | 170 | 184 | 259 | 481 | 558 | 617 |
| Embezzlement | 2,275 | 1 | 113 | 2,162 | 0 | 0 | 1 | 2 | 41 | 69 | 137 | 128 | 87 |
| Stolen property; buying, receiving, possessing | 22,898 | 407 | 1,898 | 21,000 | 0 | 33 | 374 | 408 | 537 | 546 | 791 | 733 | 686 |
| | | | | | | | | | | | | | |
| Vandalism | 39,983 | 2,450 | 6,340 | 33,643 | 53 | 598 | 1,799 | 1,217 | 1,359 | 1,314 | 1,466 | 1,356 | 1,179 |
| Weapons; carrying, possessing, etc. | 36,425 | 551 | 2,267 | 34,158 | 6 | 136 | 409 | 376 | 535 | 805 | 1,254 | 1,377 | 1,443 |
| Prostitution and commercialized vice | 1,689 | 7 | 23 | 1,666 | 0 | 1 | 6 | 5 | 6 | 5 | 29 | 31 | 42 |
| Sex offenses (except forcible rape and prostitution) | 7,889 | 504 | 1,102 | 6,787 | 22 | 136 | 346 | 203 | 188 | 207 | 232 | 239 | 217 |
| Drug abuse violations | 317,731 | 1,864 | 12,741 | 304,990 | 10 | 219 | 1,635 | 1,948 | 3,319 | 5,610 | 10,750 | 12,042 | 11,458 |
| | | | | | | | | | | | | | |
| Gambling | 359 | 6 | 35 | 324 | 0 | 3 | 3 | 5 | 13 | 11 | 5 | 8 | 13 |
| Offenses against the family and children | 15,426 | 127 | 480 | 14,946 | 7 | 27 | 93 | 103 | 121 | 129 | 159 | 162 | 219 |
| Driving under the influence | 235,930 | 18 | 1,487 | 234,443 | 1 | 0 | 17 | 58 | 374 | 1,037 | 2,885 | 4,226 | 5,164 |
| Liquor laws | 27,056 | 527 | 4,846 | 22,210 | 0 | 57 | 470 | 742 | 1,349 | 2,228 | 4,589 | 4,135 | 3,126 |
| Drunkenness | 39,762 | 141 | 665 | 39,097 | 1 | 18 | 122 | 124 | 168 | 232 | 674 | 706 | 809 |
| | | | | | | | | | | | | | |
| Disorderly conduct | 55,216 | 2,391 | 6,564 | 48,652 | 47 | 584 | 1,760 | 1,329 | 1,427 | 1,417 | 1,472 | 1,480 | 1,407 |
| Vagrancy | 2,126 | 12 | 71 | 2,055 | 0 | 0 | 12 | 13 | 24 | 22 | 69 | 60 | 42 |
| All other offenses (except traffic) | 594,985 | 6,148 | 22,822 | 572,163 | 118 | 1,202 | 4,828 | 4,427 | 5,527 | 6,720 | 10,762 | 13,092 | 14,538 |
| Suspicion | 122 | 0 | 7 | 115 | 0 | 0 | 0 | 0 | 2 | 5 | 5 | 5 | 1 |
| Curfew and loitering law violations | 2,659 | 861 | 2,659 | NA | 5 | 113 | 743 | 618 | 719 | 461 | NA | NA | NA |

# Table 64. Arrests, Suburban Areas,[1] Distribution by Age, 2020—Continued

(Number, percent; 5,475 agencies; 2020 estimated population 94,124,752.)

| Offense charged | 21 | 22 | 23 | 24 | 25–29 | 30–34 | 35–39 | 40–44 | 45–49 | 50–54 | 55–59 | 60–64 | 65 and over |
|---|---|---|---|---|---|---|---|---|---|---|---|---|---|
| **Total** | 56,503 | 57,121 | 57,325 | 59,732 | 327,941 | 311,205 | 259,392 | 187,384 | 129,349 | 102,544 | 77,502 | 42,122 | 28,560 |
| Total percent distribution[2] | 2.9 | 2.9 | 2.9 | 3.0 | 16.7 | 15.8 | 13.2 | 9.5 | 6.6 | 5.2 | 3.9 | 2.1 | 1.5 |
| | | | | | | | | | | | | | |
| **Violent crime[3]** | 2,870 | 3,008 | 2,808 | 2,978 | 16,202 | 14,827 | 12,489 | 8,744 | 6,095 | 4,819 | 3,783 | 2,099 | 1,734 |
| Violent crime percent distribution[2] | 2.9 | 3.1 | 2.9 | 3.0 | 16.5 | 15.1 | 12.7 | 8.9 | 6.2 | 4.9 | 3.9 | 2.1 | 1.8 |
| Murder and nonnegligent manslaughter | 93 | 89 | 103 | 57 | 466 | 286 | 221 | 160 | 96 | 69 | 59 | 44 | 46 |
| Rape[4] | 179 | 137 | 116 | 142 | 567 | 559 | 532 | 395 | 266 | 217 | 193 | 116 | 134 |
| Robbery | 459 | 446 | 366 | 382 | 1,803 | 1,542 | 1,029 | 670 | 378 | 298 | 206 | 84 | 42 |
| Aggravated assault | 2,139 | 2,336 | 2,223 | 2,397 | 13,366 | 12,440 | 10,707 | 7,519 | 5,355 | 4,235 | 3,325 | 1,855 | 1,512 |
| | | | | | | | | | | | | | |
| **Property crime[3]** | 5,618 | 5,474 | 5,512 | 5,814 | 34,533 | 35,506 | 29,208 | 20,461 | 14,061 | 11,591 | 8,289 | 4,236 | 2,351 |
| Property crime percent distribution[2] | 2.6 | 2.5 | 2.5 | 2.7 | 15.8 | 16.2 | 13.3 | 9.3 | 6.4 | 5.3 | 3.8 | 1.9 | 1.1 |
| Burglary | 833 | 844 | 920 | 902 | 5,593 | 5,746 | 4,535 | 3,024 | 1,931 | 1,360 | 949 | 399 | 185 |
| Larceny-theft | 4,264 | 4,107 | 4,055 | 4,325 | 25,334 | 26,326 | 22,021 | 15,770 | 11,243 | 9,587 | 6,968 | 3,657 | 2,066 |
| Motor vehicle theft | 478 | 493 | 493 | 541 | 3,329 | 3,103 | 2,362 | 1,463 | 765 | 538 | 305 | 127 | 64 |
| Arson | 43 | 30 | 44 | 46 | 277 | 331 | 290 | 204 | 122 | 106 | 67 | 53 | 36 |
| | | | | | | | | | | | | | |
| Other assaults | 5,569 | 5,563 | 5,697 | 6,030 | 33,308 | 31,591 | 27,436 | 20,389 | 14,676 | 11,962 | 8,690 | 4,920 | 3,898 |
| Forgery and counterfeiting | 233 | 271 | 242 | 276 | 1,671 | 1,563 | 1,373 | 923 | 588 | 441 | 308 | 154 | 77 |
| Fraud | 606 | 672 | 625 | 709 | 4,112 | 3,910 | 3,372 | 2,323 | 1,611 | 1,246 | 914 | 406 | 294 |
| Embezzlement | 108 | 74 | 82 | 77 | 325 | 282 | 243 | 216 | 142 | 112 | 97 | 38 | 14 |
| Stolen property; buying, receiving, possessing | 658 | 685 | 661 | 716 | 4,069 | 3,942 | 3,164 | 2,027 | 1,210 | 851 | 488 | 221 | 98 |
| | | | | | | | | | | | | | |
| Vandalism | 1,249 | 1,180 | 1,252 | 1,218 | 6,216 | 5,579 | 4,439 | 2,991 | 1,835 | 1,531 | 1,078 | 587 | 487 |
| Weapons; carrying, possessing, etc. | 1,588 | 1,563 | 1,539 | 1,497 | 6,932 | 5,330 | 4,102 | 2,737 | 1,717 | 1,261 | 941 | 490 | 387 |
| Prostitution and commercialized vice | 57 | 48 | 46 | 56 | 289 | 263 | 228 | 167 | 146 | 106 | 81 | 33 | 44 |
| Sex offenses (except forcible rape and prostitution) | 197 | 150 | 144 | 167 | 840 | 886 | 857 | 728 | 531 | 459 | 454 | 298 | 388 |
| Drug abuse violations | 11,164 | 10,980 | 10,780 | 10,890 | 57,266 | 51,885 | 42,030 | 29,024 | 18,315 | 13,318 | 9,068 | 4,188 | 1,832 |
| | | | | | | | | | | | | | |
| Gambling | 5 | 3 | 8 | 4 | 47 | 34 | 59 | 48 | 36 | 20 | 17 | 8 | 9 |
| Offenses against the family and children | 251 | 284 | 336 | 322 | 2,465 | 3,120 | 2,756 | 1,982 | 1,191 | 811 | 480 | 244 | 164 |
| Driving under the influence | 7,296 | 7,899 | 8,112 | 8,564 | 42,717 | 36,591 | 29,467 | 22,560 | 17,527 | 14,868 | 12,751 | 7,886 | 5,930 |
| Liquor laws | 531 | 440 | 357 | 339 | 1,654 | 1,457 | 1,271 | 1,028 | 846 | 892 | 757 | 481 | 307 |
| Drunkenness | 1,015 | 1,023 | 1,038 | 1,090 | 5,942 | 6,027 | 5,490 | 4,141 | 3,211 | 3,040 | 2,647 | 1,469 | 775 |
| | | | | | | | | | | | | | |
| Disorderly conduct | 1,684 | 1,544 | 1,473 | 1,540 | 7,620 | 7,265 | 6,319 | 4,753 | 3,625 | 3,128 | 2,600 | 1,586 | 1,156 |
| Vagrancy | 42 | 47 | 41 | 43 | 314 | 316 | 257 | 232 | 169 | 177 | 109 | 95 | 42 |
| All other offenses (except traffic) | 15,761 | 16,209 | 16,571 | 17,397 | 101,410 | 100,808 | 84,815 | 61,892 | 41,805 | 31,907 | 23,944 | 12,680 | 8,572 |
| Suspicion | 1 | 4 | 1 | 5 | 9 | 23 | 17 | 18 | 12 | 4 | 6 | 3 | 1 |
| Curfew and loitering law violations | NA | NA | NA | NA | NA | NA | NA | NA | NA | NA | NA | NA | NA |

NA = Not available.
\* = Less than one-tenth of one percent.
1 Suburban areas include law enforcement agencies in cities with less than 50,000 inhabitants and county law enforcement agencies that are within a Metropolitan Statistical Area. Suburban areas exclude all metropolitan agencies associated with a principal city.   2 Because of rounding, the percentages may not sum to 100.   3 Violent crimes are offenses of murder and nonnegligent manslaughter, rape, robbery, and aggravated assault.  Property crimes are offenses of burglary, larceny-theft, motor vehicle theft, and arson.   4 The rape figures in this table are aggregate totals of the data submitted based on both the legacy and revised Uniform Crime Reporting definitions.

## Table 65. Arrests, Suburban Areas,[1] Persons Under 15, 18, 21, and 25 Years of Age, 2020

(Number, percent; 5,475 agencies; 2020 estimated population 94,124,752.)

| Offense charged | Total, all ages | Number of persons arrested | | | | Percent of total all ages | | | |
|---|---|---|---|---|---|---|---|---|---|
| | | Under 15 | Under 18 | Under 21 | Under 25 | Under 15 | Under 18 | Under 21 | Under 25 |
| Total | 1,964,444 | 30,377 | 109,588 | 267,764 | 498,445 | 1.5 | 5.6 | 13.6 | 25.4 |
| **Violent crime**[2] | 97,976 | 1,963 | 7,179 | 15,520 | 27,184 | 2.0 | 7.3 | 15.8 | 27.7 |
| Murder and nonnegligent manslaughter | 2,282 | 9 | 156 | 493 | 835 | 0.4 | 6.8 | 21.6 | 36.6 |
| Rape[3] | 4,929 | 314 | 762 | 1,376 | 1,950 | 6.4 | 15.5 | 27.9 | 39.6 |
| Robbery | 11,687 | 430 | 2,083 | 3,982 | 5,635 | 3.7 | 17.8 | 34.1 | 48.2 |
| Aggravated assault | 79,078 | 1,210 | 4,178 | 9,669 | 18,764 | 1.5 | 5.3 | 12.2 | 23.7 |
| **Property crime**[2] | 218,927 | 4,920 | 18,356 | 36,273 | 58,691 | 2.2 | 8.4 | 16.6 | 26.8 |
| Burglary | 33,777 | 1,104 | 3,768 | 6,556 | 10,055 | 3.3 | 11.2 | 19.4 | 29.8 |
| Larceny-theft | 164,967 | 3,017 | 11,840 | 25,244 | 41,995 | 1.8 | 7.2 | 15.3 | 25.5 |
| Motor vehicle theft | 18,095 | 625 | 2,416 | 4,034 | 6,039 | 3.5 | 13.4 | 22.3 | 33.4 |
| Arson | 2,088 | 174 | 332 | 439 | 602 | 8.3 | 15.9 | 21.0 | 28.8 |
| Other assaults | 212,497 | 7,293 | 18,988 | 32,768 | 55,627 | 3.4 | 8.9 | 15.4 | 26.2 |
| Forgery and counterfeiting | 9,273 | 15 | 161 | 1,153 | 2,175 | 0.2 | 1.7 | 12.4 | 23.5 |
| Fraud | 23,240 | 171 | 784 | 2,440 | 5,052 | 0.7 | 3.4 | 10.5 | 21.7 |
| Embezzlement | 2,275 | 1 | 113 | 465 | 806 | * | 5.0 | 20.4 | 35.4 |
| Stolen property; buying, receiving, possessing | 22,898 | 407 | 1,898 | 4,108 | 6,828 | 1.8 | 8.3 | 17.9 | 29.8 |
| Vandalism | 39,983 | 2,450 | 6,340 | 10,341 | 15,240 | 6.1 | 15.9 | 25.9 | 38.1 |
| Weapons; carrying, possessing, etc. | 36,425 | 551 | 2,267 | 6,341 | 12,528 | 1.5 | 6.2 | 17.4 | 34.4 |
| Prostitution and commercialized vice | 1,689 | 7 | 23 | 125 | 332 | 0.4 | 1.4 | 7.4 | 19.7 |
| Sex offenses (except forcible rape and prostitution) | 7,889 | 504 | 1,102 | 1,790 | 2,448 | 6.4 | 14.0 | 22.7 | 31.0 |
| Drug abuse violations | 317,731 | 1,864 | 12,741 | 46,991 | 90,805 | 0.6 | 4.0 | 14.8 | 28.6 |
| Gambling | 359 | 6 | 35 | 61 | 81 | 1.7 | 9.7 | 17.0 | 22.6 |
| Offenses against the family and children | 15,426 | 127 | 480 | 1,020 | 2,213 | 0.8 | 3.1 | 6.6 | 14.3 |
| Driving under the influence | 235,930 | 18 | 1,487 | 13,762 | 45,633 | * | 0.6 | 5.8 | 19.3 |
| Liquor laws | 27,056 | 527 | 4,846 | 16,696 | 18,363 | 1.9 | 17.9 | 61.7 | 67.9 |
| Drunkenness | 39,762 | 141 | 665 | 2,854 | 7,020 | 0.4 | 1.7 | 7.2 | 17.7 |
| Disorderly conduct | 55,216 | 2,391 | 6,564 | 10,923 | 17,164 | 4.3 | 11.9 | 19.8 | 31.1 |
| Vagrancy | 2,126 | 12 | 71 | 242 | 415 | 0.6 | 3.3 | 11.4 | 19.5 |
| All other offenses (except traffic) | 594,985 | 6,148 | 22,822 | 61,214 | 127,152 | 1.0 | 3.8 | 10.3 | 21.4 |
| Suspicion | 122 | 0 | 7 | 18 | 29 | 0.0 | 5.7 | 14.8 | 23.8 |
| Curfew and loitering law violations | 2,659 | 861 | 2,659 | 2,659 | 2,659 | 32.4 | 100.0 | 100.0 | 100.0 |

* = Less than one-tenth of one percent.
1 Suburban areas include law enforcement agencies in cities with less than 50,000 inhabitants and county law enforcement agencies that are within a Metropolitan Statistical Area. Suburban areas exclude all metropolitan agencies associated with a principal city.   2 Violent crimes are offenses of murder and nonnegligent manslaughter, rape, robbery, and aggravated assault.   Property crimes are offenses of burglary, larceny-theft, motor vehicle theft, and arson.   3 The rape figures in this table are aggregate totals of the data submitted based on both the legacy and revised Uniform Crime Reporting definitions.

## Table 66. Arrests, Suburban Areas,[1] Distribution by Sex, 2020

(Number, percent; 5,475 agencies; 2020 estimated population 94,124,752.)

| Offense charged | Number of persons arrested | | | Percent male | Percent female | Percent distribution[2] | | |
|---|---|---|---|---|---|---|---|---|
| | Total | Male | Female | | | Total | Male | Female |
| **Total** | 1,964,444 | 1,439,254 | 525,190 | 73.3 | 26.7 | 100.0 | 100.0 | 100.0 |
| **Violent crime[3]** | 97,976 | 78,220 | 19,756 | 79.8 | 20.2 | 5.0 | 5.4 | 3.8 |
| Murder and nonnegligent manslaughter | 2,282 | 1,990 | 292 | 87.2 | 12.8 | 0.1 | 0.1 | 0.1 |
| Rape[4] | 4,929 | 4,817 | 112 | 97.7 | 2.3 | 0.3 | 0.3 | * |
| Robbery | 11,687 | 9,980 | 1,707 | 85.4 | 14.6 | 0.6 | 0.7 | 0.3 |
| Aggravated assault | 79,078 | 61,433 | 17,645 | 77.7 | 22.3 | 4.0 | 4.3 | 3.4 |
| **Property crime[3]** | 218,927 | 141,557 | 77,370 | 64.7 | 35.3 | 11.1 | 9.8 | 14.7 |
| Burglary | 33,777 | 27,317 | 6,460 | 80.9 | 19.1 | 1.7 | 1.9 | 1.2 |
| Larceny-theft | 164,967 | 98,438 | 66,529 | 59.7 | 40.3 | 8.4 | 6.8 | 12.7 |
| Motor vehicle theft | 18,095 | 14,129 | 3,966 | 78.1 | 21.9 | 0.9 | 1.0 | 0.8 |
| Arson | 2,088 | 1,673 | 415 | 80.1 | 19.9 | 0.1 | 0.1 | 0.1 |
| Other assaults | 212,497 | 152,171 | 60,326 | 71.6 | 28.4 | 10.8 | 10.6 | 11.5 |
| Forgery and counterfeiting | 9,273 | 6,351 | 2,922 | 68.5 | 31.5 | 0.5 | 0.4 | 0.6 |
| Fraud | 23,240 | 15,437 | 7,803 | 66.4 | 33.6 | 1.2 | 1.1 | 1.5 |
| Embezzlement | 2,275 | 1,159 | 1,116 | 50.9 | 49.1 | 0.1 | 0.1 | 0.2 |
| Stolen property; buying, receiving, possessing | 22,898 | 17,973 | 4,925 | 78.5 | 21.5 | 1.2 | 1.2 | 0.9 |
| Vandalism | 39,983 | 31,162 | 8,821 | 77.9 | 22.1 | 2.0 | 2.2 | 1.7 |
| Weapons; carrying, possessing, etc. | 36,425 | 32,714 | 3,711 | 89.8 | 10.2 | 1.9 | 2.3 | 0.7 |
| Prostitution and commercialized vice | 1,689 | 941 | 748 | 55.7 | 44.3 | 0.1 | 0.1 | 0.1 |
| Sex offenses (except forcible rape and prostitution) | 7,889 | 7,468 | 421 | 94.7 | 5.3 | 0.4 | 0.5 | 0.1 |
| Drug abuse violations | 317,731 | 235,268 | 82,463 | 74.0 | 26.0 | 16.2 | 16.3 | 15.7 |
| Gambling | 359 | 233 | 126 | 64.9 | 35.1 | * | * | * |
| Offenses against the family and children | 15,426 | 10,969 | 4,457 | 71.1 | 28.9 | 0.8 | 0.8 | 0.8 |
| Driving under the influence | 235,930 | 175,264 | 60,666 | 74.3 | 25.7 | 12.0 | 12.2 | 11.6 |
| Liquor laws | 27,056 | 18,774 | 8,282 | 69.4 | 30.6 | 1.4 | 1.3 | 1.6 |
| Drunkenness | 39,762 | 30,783 | 8,979 | 77.4 | 22.6 | 2.0 | 2.1 | 1.7 |
| Disorderly conduct | 55,216 | 39,108 | 16,108 | 70.8 | 29.2 | 2.8 | 2.7 | 3.1 |
| Vagrancy | 2,126 | 1,693 | 433 | 79.6 | 20.4 | 0.1 | 0.1 | 0.1 |
| All other offenses (except traffic) | 594,985 | 440,172 | 154,813 | 74.0 | 26.0 | 30.3 | 30.6 | 29.5 |
| Suspicion | 122 | 76 | 46 | 62.3 | 37.7 | * | * | * |
| Curfew and loitering law violations | 2,659 | 1,761 | 898 | 66.2 | 33.8 | 0.1 | 0.1 | 0.2 |

* = Less than one-tenth of one percent.
1 Suburban areas include law enforcement agencies in cities with less than 50,000 inhabitants and county law enforcement agencies that are within a Metropolitan Statistical Area. Suburban areas exclude all metropolitan agencies associated with a principal city.  2 Because of rounding, the percentages may not sum to 100.  3 Violent crimes are offenses of murder and nonnegligent manslaughter, rape, robbery, and aggravated assault. Property crimes are offenses of burglary, larceny-theft, motor vehicle theft, and arson.  4 The rape figures in this table are aggregate totals of the data submitted based on both the legacy and revised Uniform Crime Reporting definitions.

## Table 67. Arrests, Suburban Areas,[1] Distribution by Race, 2020

(Number, percent; 5,475 agencies; 2020 estimated population 94,124,752.)

| Offense charged | Total arrests | | | | | | Percent distribution[2] | | | | | |
|---|---|---|---|---|---|---|---|---|---|---|---|---|
| | Total | White | Black | American Indian or Alaskan Native | Asian | Native Hawaiian or Other Pacific Islander | Total | White | Black | American Indian or Alaskan Native | Asian | Native Hawaiian or Other Pacific Islander |
| **Total** | 1,935,105 | 1,421,302 | 469,053 | 20,638 | 21,307 | 2,805 | 100.0 | 73.4 | 24.2 | 1.1 | 1.1 | 0.1 |
| **Violent crime[3]** | 97,096 | 66,145 | 28,506 | 918 | 1,328 | 199 | 100.0 | 68.1 | 29.4 | 0.9 | 1.4 | 0.2 |
| Murder and nonnegligent manslaughter | 2,266 | 1,237 | 982 | 21 | 23 | 3 | 100.0 | 54.6 | 43.3 | 0.9 | 1.0 | 0.1 |
| Rape[4] | 4,827 | 3,716 | 1,001 | 37 | 69 | 4 | 100.0 | 77.0 | 20.7 | 0.8 | 1.4 | 0.1 |
| Robbery | 11,574 | 5,973 | 5,372 | 98 | 101 | 30 | 100.0 | 51.6 | 46.4 | 0.8 | 0.9 | 0.3 |
| Aggravated assault | 78,429 | 55,219 | 21,151 | 762 | 1,135 | 162 | 100.0 | 70.4 | 27.0 | 1.0 | 1.4 | 0.2 |
| **Property crime[3]** | 215,722 | 148,919 | 62,353 | 2,082 | 2,139 | 229 | 100.0 | 69.0 | 28.9 | 1.0 | 1.0 | 0.1 |
| Burglary | 33,452 | 25,025 | 7,845 | 230 | 304 | 48 | 100.0 | 74.8 | 23.5 | 0.7 | 0.9 | 0.1 |
| Larceny-theft | 162,260 | 108,901 | 49,892 | 1,677 | 1,643 | 147 | 100.0 | 67.1 | 30.7 | 1.0 | 1.0 | 0.1 |
| Motor vehicle theft | 17,945 | 13,366 | 4,234 | 155 | 158 | 32 | 100.0 | 74.5 | 23.6 | 0.9 | 0.9 | 0.2 |
| Arson | 2,065 | 1,627 | 382 | 20 | 34 | 2 | 100.0 | 78.8 | 18.5 | 1.0 | 1.6 | 0.1 |
| Other assaults | 209,629 | 150,864 | 53,379 | 2,397 | 2,643 | 346 | 100.0 | 72.0 | 25.5 | 1.1 | 1.3 | 0.2 |
| Forgery and counterfeiting | 9,165 | 6,116 | 2,841 | 48 | 152 | 8 | 100.0 | 66.7 | 31.0 | 0.5 | 1.7 | 0.1 |
| Fraud | 22,913 | 14,643 | 7,673 | 235 | 335 | 27 | 100.0 | 63.9 | 33.5 | 1.0 | 1.5 | 0.1 |
| Embezzlement | 2,233 | 1,383 | 810 | 7 | 31 | 2 | 100.0 | 61.9 | 36.3 | 0.3 | 1.4 | 0.1 |
| Stolen property; buying, receiving, possessing | 22,647 | 15,120 | 6,989 | 214 | 274 | 50 | 100.0 | 66.8 | 30.9 | 0.9 | 1.2 | 0.2 |
| Vandalism | 39,398 | 29,003 | 9,425 | 437 | 488 | 45 | 100.0 | 73.6 | 23.9 | 1.1 | 1.2 | 0.1 |
| Weapons; carrying, possessing, etc. | 36,080 | 21,448 | 14,012 | 223 | 340 | 57 | 100.0 | 59.4 | 38.8 | 0.6 | 0.9 | 0.2 |
| Prostitution and commercialized vice | 1,668 | 1,020 | 504 | 5 | 133 | 6 | 100.0 | 61.2 | 30.2 | 0.3 | 8.0 | 0.4 |
| Sex offenses (except forcible rape and prostitution) | 7,779 | 6,101 | 1,454 | 54 | 147 | 23 | 100.0 | 78.4 | 18.7 | 0.7 | 1.9 | 0.3 |
| Drug abuse violations | 314,259 | 231,813 | 76,477 | 2,401 | 3,095 | 473 | 100.0 | 73.8 | 24.3 | 0.8 | 1.0 | 0.2 |
| Gambling | 351 | 251 | 84 | 3 | 12 | 1 | 100.0 | 71.5 | 23.9 | 0.9 | 3.4 | 0.3 |
| Offenses against the family and children | 15,220 | 10,843 | 3,916 | 324 | 125 | 12 | 100.0 | 71.2 | 25.7 | 2.1 | 0.8 | 0.1 |
| Driving under the influence | 228,504 | 187,358 | 35,071 | 1,894 | 3,810 | 371 | 100.0 | 82.0 | 15.3 | 0.8 | 1.7 | 0.2 |
| Liquor laws | 26,390 | 21,411 | 4,076 | 481 | 383 | 39 | 100.0 | 81.1 | 15.4 | 1.8 | 1.5 | 0.1 |
| Drunkenness | 39,446 | 33,131 | 5,422 | 433 | 386 | 74 | 100.0 | 84.0 | 13.7 | 1.1 | 1.0 | 0.2 |
| Disorderly conduct | 54,506 | 37,652 | 14,917 | 1,461 | 425 | 51 | 100.0 | 69.1 | 27.4 | 2.7 | 0.8 | 0.1 |
| Vagrancy | 2,103 | 1,345 | 710 | 27 | 18 | 3 | 100.0 | 64.0 | 33.8 | 1.3 | 0.9 | 0.1 |
| All other offenses (except traffic) | 587,290 | 434,700 | 139,810 | 6,971 | 5,024 | 785 | 100.0 | 74.0 | 23.8 | 1.2 | 0.9 | 0.1 |
| Suspicion | 121 | 86 | 32 | 1 | 1 | 1 | 100.0 | 71.1 | 26.4 | 0.8 | 0.8 | 0.8 |
| Curfew and loitering law violations | 2,585 | 1,950 | 592 | 22 | 18 | 3 | 100.0 | 75.4 | 22.9 | 0.9 | 0.7 | 0.1 |

## Table 67. Arrests, Suburban Areas,[1] Distribution by Race, 2020—Continued

(Number, percent; 5,475 agencies; 2020 estimated population 94,124,752.)

| Offense charged | Arrests under 18 | | | | | | Percent distribution[2] | | | | | |
|---|---|---|---|---|---|---|---|---|---|---|---|---|
| | Total | White | Black | American Indian or Alaskan Native | Asian | Native Hawaiian or Other Pacific Islander | Total | White | Black | American Indian or Alaskan Native | Asian | Native Hawaiian or Other Pacific Islander |
| **Total** | 107,357 | 73,222 | 31,646 | 1,231 | 1,101 | 157 | 100.0 | 68.2 | 29.5 | 1.1 | 1.0 | 0.1 |
| **Violent crime[3]** | 7,079 | 4,100 | 2,823 | 73 | 69 | 14 | 100.0 | 57.9 | 39.9 | 1.0 | 1.0 | 0.2 |
| Murder and nonnegligent manslaughter | 155 | 66 | 87 | 1 | 1 | 0 | 100.0 | 42.6 | 56.1 | 0.6 | 0.6 | 0.0 |
| Rape[4] | 745 | 582 | 149 | 6 | 8 | 0 | 100.0 | 78.1 | 20.0 | 0.8 | 1.1 | 0.0 |
| Robbery | 2,052 | 824 | 1,190 | 9 | 19 | 10 | 100.0 | 40.2 | 58.0 | 0.4 | 0.9 | 0.5 |
| Aggravated assault | 4,127 | 2,628 | 1,397 | 57 | 41 | 4 | 100.0 | 63.7 | 33.9 | 1.4 | 1.0 | 0.1 |
| **Property crime[3]** | 18,008 | 10,371 | 7,199 | 165 | 236 | 37 | 100.0 | 57.6 | 40.0 | 0.9 | 1.3 | 0.2 |
| Burglary | 3,722 | 2,298 | 1,333 | 33 | 41 | 17 | 100.0 | 61.7 | 35.8 | 0.9 | 1.1 | 0.5 |
| Larceny-theft | 11,569 | 6,601 | 4,669 | 100 | 181 | 18 | 100.0 | 57.1 | 40.4 | 0.9 | 1.6 | 0.2 |
| Motor vehicle theft | 2,391 | 1,221 | 1,127 | 30 | 11 | 2 | 100.0 | 51.1 | 47.1 | 1.3 | 0.5 | 0.1 |
| Arson | 326 | 251 | 70 | 2 | 3 | 0 | 100.0 | 77.0 | 21.5 | 0.6 | 0.9 | 0.0 |
| Other assaults | 18,591 | 12,138 | 6,030 | 221 | 175 | 27 | 100.0 | 65.3 | 32.4 | 1.2 | 0.9 | 0.1 |
| Forgery and counterfeiting | 157 | 93 | 62 | 1 | 1 | 0 | 100.0 | 59.2 | 39.5 | 0.6 | 0.6 | 0.0 |
| Fraud | 774 | 428 | 325 | 6 | 13 | 2 | 100.0 | 55.3 | 42.0 | 0.8 | 1.7 | 0.3 |
| Embezzlement | 109 | 55 | 52 | 0 | 2 | 0 | 100.0 | 50.5 | 47.7 | 0.0 | 1.8 | 0.0 |
| Stolen property; buying, receiving, possessing | 1,868 | 658 | 1,166 | 20 | 17 | 7 | 100.0 | 35.2 | 62.4 | 1.1 | 0.9 | 0.4 |
| Vandalism | 6,191 | 4,727 | 1,332 | 75 | 55 | 2 | 100.0 | 76.4 | 21.5 | 1.2 | 0.9 | * |
| Weapons; carrying, possessing, etc. | 2,237 | 1,243 | 953 | 14 | 24 | 3 | 100.0 | 55.6 | 42.6 | 0.6 | 1.1 | 0.1 |
| Prostitution and commercialized vice | 22 | 11 | 10 | 0 | 0 | 1 | 100.0 | 50.0 | 45.5 | 0.0 | 0.0 | 4.5 |
| Sex offenses (except forcible rape and prostitution) | 1,070 | 817 | 227 | 13 | 12 | 1 | 100.0 | 76.4 | 21.2 | 1.2 | 1.1 | 0.1 |
| Drug abuse violations | 12,474 | 9,593 | 2,628 | 112 | 120 | 21 | 100.0 | 76.9 | 21.1 | 0.9 | 1.0 | 0.2 |
| Gambling | 33 | 23 | 9 | 0 | 1 | 0 | 100.0 | 69.7 | 27.3 | 0.0 | 3.0 | 0.0 |
| Offenses against the family and children | 471 | 351 | 96 | 23 | 1 | 0 | 100.0 | 74.5 | 20.4 | 4.9 | 0.2 | 0.0 |
| Driving under the influence | 1,430 | 1,289 | 99 | 19 | 21 | 2 | 100.0 | 90.1 | 6.9 | 1.3 | 1.5 | 0.1 |
| Liquor laws | 4,719 | 4,264 | 301 | 80 | 69 | 5 | 100.0 | 90.4 | 6.4 | 1.7 | 1.5 | 0.1 |
| Drunkenness | 657 | 450 | 189 | 9 | 7 | 2 | 100.0 | 68.5 | 28.8 | 1.4 | 1.1 | 0.3 |
| Disorderly conduct | 6,450 | 3,913 | 2,376 | 101 | 54 | 6 | 100.0 | 60.7 | 36.8 | 1.6 | 0.8 | 0.1 |
| Vagrancy | 71 | 60 | 8 | 1 | 2 | 0 | 100.0 | 84.5 | 11.3 | 1.4 | 2.8 | 0.0 |
| All other offenses (except traffic) | 22,352 | 16,684 | 5,164 | 276 | 204 | 24 | 100.0 | 74.6 | 23.1 | 1.2 | 0.9 | 0.1 |
| Suspicion | 9 | 4 | 5 | 0 | 0 | 0 | 100.0 | 44.4 | 55.6 | 0.0 | 0.0 | 0.0 |
| Curfew and loitering law violations | 2,585 | 1,950 | 592 | 22 | 18 | 3 | 100.0 | 75.4 | 22.9 | 0.9 | 0.7 | 0.1 |

## Table 67. Arrests, Suburban Areas,[1] Distribution by Race, 2020—Continued

(Number, percent; 5,475 agencies; 2020 estimated population 94,124,752.)

| Offense charged | Arrests 18 and over | | | | | | Percent distribution[2] | | | | | |
|---|---|---|---|---|---|---|---|---|---|---|---|---|
| | Total | White | Black | American Indian or Alaskan Native | Asian | Native Hawaiian or Other Pacific Islander | Total | White | Black | American Indian or Alaskan Native | Asian | Native Hawaiian or Other Pacific Islander |
| **Total** | 1,827,748 | 1,348,080 | 437,407 | 19,407 | 20,206 | 2,648 | 100.0 | 73.8 | 23.9 | 1.1 | 1.1 | 0.1 |
| **Violent crime[3]** | 90,017 | 62,045 | 25,683 | 845 | 1,259 | 185 | 100.0 | 68.9 | 28.5 | 0.9 | 1.4 | 0.2 |
| Murder and nonnegligent manslaughter | 2,111 | 1,171 | 895 | 20 | 22 | 3 | 100.0 | 55.5 | 42.4 | 0.9 | 1.0 | 0.1 |
| Rape[4] | 4,082 | 3,134 | 852 | 31 | 61 | 4 | 100.0 | 76.8 | 20.9 | 0.8 | 1.5 | 0.1 |
| Robbery | 9,522 | 5,149 | 4,182 | 89 | 82 | 20 | 100.0 | 54.1 | 43.9 | 0.9 | 0.9 | 0.2 |
| Aggravated assault | 74,302 | 52,591 | 19,754 | 705 | 1,094 | 158 | 100.0 | 70.8 | 26.6 | 0.9 | 1.5 | 0.2 |
| **Property crime[3]** | 197,714 | 138,548 | 55,154 | 1,917 | 1,903 | 192 | 100.0 | 70.1 | 27.9 | 1.0 | 1.0 | 0.1 |
| Burglary | 29,730 | 22,727 | 6,512 | 197 | 263 | 31 | 100.0 | 76.4 | 21.9 | 0.7 | 0.9 | 0.1 |
| Larceny-theft | 150,691 | 102,300 | 45,223 | 1,577 | 1,462 | 129 | 100.0 | 67.9 | 30.0 | 1.0 | 1.0 | 0.1 |
| Motor vehicle theft | 15,554 | 12,145 | 3,107 | 125 | 147 | 30 | 100.0 | 78.1 | 20.0 | 0.8 | 0.9 | 0.2 |
| Arson | 1,739 | 1,376 | 312 | 18 | 31 | 2 | 100.0 | 79.1 | 17.9 | 1.0 | 1.8 | 0.1 |
| Other assaults | 191,038 | 138,726 | 47,349 | 2,176 | 2,468 | 319 | 100.0 | 72.6 | 24.8 | 1.1 | 1.3 | 0.2 |
| Forgery and counterfeiting | 9,008 | 6,023 | 2,779 | 47 | 151 | 8 | 100.0 | 66.9 | 30.9 | 0.5 | 1.7 | 0.1 |
| Fraud | 22,139 | 14,215 | 7,348 | 229 | 322 | 25 | 100.0 | 64.2 | 33.2 | 1.0 | 1.5 | 0.1 |
| Embezzlement | 2,124 | 1,328 | 758 | 7 | 29 | 2 | 100.0 | 62.5 | 35.7 | 0.3 | 1.4 | 0.1 |
| Stolen property; buying, receiving, possessing | 20,779 | 14,462 | 5,823 | 194 | 257 | 43 | 100.0 | 69.6 | 28.0 | 0.9 | 1.2 | 0.2 |
| Vandalism | 33,207 | 24,276 | 8,093 | 362 | 433 | 43 | 100.0 | 73.1 | 24.4 | 1.1 | 1.3 | 0.1 |
| Weapons; carrying, possessing, etc. | 33,843 | 20,205 | 13,059 | 209 | 316 | 54 | 100.0 | 59.7 | 38.6 | 0.6 | 0.9 | 0.2 |
| Prostitution and commercialized vice | 1,646 | 1,009 | 494 | 5 | 133 | 5 | 100.0 | 61.3 | 30.0 | 0.3 | 8.1 | 0.3 |
| Sex offenses (except forcible rape and prostitution) | 6,709 | 5,284 | 1,227 | 41 | 135 | 22 | 100.0 | 78.8 | 18.3 | 0.6 | 2.0 | 0.3 |
| Drug abuse violations | 301,785 | 222,220 | 73,849 | 2,289 | 2,975 | 452 | 100.0 | 73.6 | 24.5 | 0.8 | 1.0 | 0.1 |
| Gambling | 318 | 228 | 75 | 3 | 11 | 1 | 100.0 | 71.7 | 23.6 | 0.9 | 3.5 | 0.3 |
| Offenses against the family and children | 14,749 | 10,492 | 3,820 | 301 | 124 | 12 | 100.0 | 71.1 | 25.9 | 2.0 | 0.8 | 0.1 |
| Driving under the influence | 227,074 | 186,069 | 34,972 | 1,875 | 3,789 | 369 | 100.0 | 81.9 | 15.4 | 0.8 | 1.7 | 0.2 |
| Liquor laws | 21,671 | 17,147 | 3,775 | 401 | 314 | 34 | 100.0 | 79.1 | 17.4 | 1.9 | 1.4 | 0.2 |
| Drunkenness | 38,789 | 32,681 | 5,233 | 424 | 379 | 72 | 100.0 | 84.3 | 13.5 | 1.1 | 1.0 | 0.2 |
| Disorderly conduct | 48,056 | 33,739 | 12,541 | 1,360 | 371 | 45 | 100.0 | 70.2 | 26.1 | 2.8 | 0.8 | 0.1 |
| Vagrancy | 2,032 | 1,285 | 702 | 26 | 16 | 3 | 100.0 | 63.2 | 34.5 | 1.3 | 0.8 | 0.1 |
| All other offenses (except traffic) | 564,938 | 418,016 | 134,646 | 6,695 | 4,820 | 761 | 100.0 | 74.0 | 23.8 | 1.2 | 0.9 | 0.1 |
| Suspicion | 112 | 82 | 27 | 1 | 1 | 1 | 100.0 | 73.2 | 24.1 | 0.9 | 0.9 | 0.9 |
| Curfew and loitering law violations | NA | NA | NA | NA | NA | NA | NA | NA | NA | NA | NA | NA |

NA = Not available.
* = Less than one-tenth of one percent.
1 Suburban areas include law enforcement agencies in cities with less than 50,000 inhabitants and county law enforcement agencies that are within a Metropolitan Statistical Area. Suburban areas exclude all metropolitan agencies associated with a principal city.   2 Because of rounding, the percentages may not sum to 100.   3 Violent crimes are offenses of murder and nonnegligent manslaughter, rape, robbery, and aggravated assault.  Property crimes are offenses of burglary, larceny-theft, motor vehicle theft, and arson.   4 The rape figures in this table are aggregate totals of the data submitted based on both the legacy and revised Uniform Crime Reporting definitions.

## Table 67A. Arrests, Suburban Areas,[1] Distribution by Ethnicity, 2020

(Number, percent; 5,475 agencies; 2020 estimated population 94,124,752.)

| Offense charged | Total arrests | | | Percent distribution[2] | | | Arrests under 18 | | |
|---|---|---|---|---|---|---|---|---|---|
| | Total[3] | Hispanic or Latino | Not Hispanic or Latino | Total[3] | Hispanic or Latino | Not Hispanic or Latino | Total[3] | Hispanic or Latino | Not Hispanic or Latino |
| Total | 1,665,752 | 323,978 | 1,341,774 | 100.0 | 19.4 | 80.6 | 87,945 | 18,693 | 69,252 |
| **Violent crime**[4] | 85,756 | 21,312 | 64,444 | 100.0 | 24.9 | 75.1 | 6,036 | 1,508 | 4,528 |
| Murder and nonnegligent manslaughter | 1,947 | 457 | 1,490 | 100.0 | 23.5 | 76.5 | 121 | 32 | 89 |
| Rape[5] | 4,026 | 1,077 | 2,949 | 100.0 | 26.8 | 73.2 | 577 | 118 | 459 |
| Robbery | 10,292 | 2,420 | 7,872 | 100.0 | 23.5 | 76.5 | 1,811 | 438 | 1,373 |
| Aggravated assault | 69,491 | 17,358 | 52,133 | 100.0 | 25.0 | 75.0 | 3,527 | 920 | 2,607 |
| **Property crime**[4] | 183,992 | 27,345 | 156,647 | 100.0 | 14.9 | 85.1 | 14,839 | 2,798 | 12,041 |
| Burglary | 29,307 | 5,714 | 23,593 | 100.0 | 19.5 | 80.5 | 3,000 | 694 | 2,306 |
| Larceny-theft | 137,046 | 16,945 | 120,101 | 100.0 | 12.4 | 87.6 | 9,544 | 1,596 | 7,948 |
| Motor vehicle theft | 15,838 | 4,319 | 11,519 | 100.0 | 27.3 | 72.7 | 2,010 | 466 | 1,544 |
| Arson | 1,801 | 367 | 1,434 | 100.0 | 20.4 | 79.6 | 285 | 42 | 243 |
| Other assaults | 178,141 | 31,177 | 146,964 | 100.0 | 17.5 | 82.5 | 15,377 | 3,223 | 12,154 |
| Forgery and counterfeiting | 8,105 | 1,354 | 6,751 | 100.0 | 16.7 | 83.3 | 136 | 28 | 108 |
| Fraud | 19,987 | 2,699 | 17,288 | 100.0 | 13.5 | 86.5 | 614 | 150 | 464 |
| Embezzlement | 1,912 | 253 | 1,659 | 100.0 | 13.2 | 86.8 | 96 | 11 | 85 |
| Stolen property; buying, receiving, possessing | 19,785 | 3,568 | 16,217 | 100.0 | 18.0 | 82.0 | 1,559 | 315 | 1,244 |
| Vandalism | 33,913 | 5,992 | 27,921 | 100.0 | 17.7 | 82.3 | 5,122 | 920 | 4,202 |
| Weapons; carrying, possessing, etc. | 30,125 | 7,086 | 23,039 | 100.0 | 23.5 | 76.5 | 1,890 | 576 | 1,314 |
| Prostitution and commercialized vice | 1,474 | 292 | 1,182 | 100.0 | 19.8 | 80.2 | 17 | 0 | 17 |
| Sex offenses (except forcible rape and prostitution) | 6,866 | 2,101 | 4,765 | 100.0 | 30.6 | 69.4 | 865 | 179 | 686 |
| Drug abuse violations | 282,288 | 57,039 | 225,249 | 100.0 | 20.2 | 79.8 | 10,868 | 2,905 | 7,963 |
| Gambling | 335 | 126 | 209 | 100.0 | 37.6 | 62.4 | 31 | 18 | 13 |
| Offenses against the family and children | 13,320 | 1,534 | 11,786 | 100.0 | 11.5 | 88.5 | 364 | 48 | 316 |
| Driving under the influence | 197,728 | 57,123 | 140,605 | 100.0 | 28.9 | 71.1 | 1,194 | 356 | 838 |
| Liquor laws | 20,376 | 3,116 | 17,260 | 100.0 | 15.3 | 84.7 | 3,666 | 571 | 3,095 |
| Drunkenness | 37,330 | 9,842 | 27,488 | 100.0 | 26.4 | 73.6 | 613 | 177 | 436 |
| Disorderly conduct | 43,149 | 5,040 | 38,109 | 100.0 | 11.7 | 88.3 | 4,880 | 789 | 4,091 |
| Vagrancy | 1,761 | 291 | 1,470 | 100.0 | 16.5 | 83.5 | 37 | 15 | 22 |
| All other offenses (except traffic) | 497,464 | 86,371 | 411,093 | 100.0 | 17.4 | 82.6 | 17,869 | 3,797 | 14,072 |
| Suspicion | 77 | 8 | 69 | 100.0 | 10.4 | 89.6 | 4 | 0 | 4 |
| Curfew and loitering law violations | 1,868 | 309 | 1,559 | 100.0 | 16.5 | 83.5 | 1,868 | 309 | 1,559 |

NA = Not available.

1 Suburban areas include law enforcement agencies in cities with less than 50,000 inhabitants and county law enforcement agencies that are within a Metropolitan Statistical Area. Suburban areas exclude all metropolitan agencies associated with a principal city.   2 Because of rounding, the percentages may not sum to 100.   3 The ethnicity totals are representative of those agencies that provided ethnicity breakdowns. Not all agencies provide ethnicity data; therefore, the race and ethnicity totals will not equal.   4 Violent crimes are offenses of murder and nonnegligent manslaughter, rape, robbery, and aggravated assault.  Property crimes are offenses of burglary, larceny-theft, motor vehicle theft, and arson.   5 The rape figures in this table are aggregate totals of the data submitted based on both the legacy and revised Uniform Crime Reporting definitions.

## Table 67A. Arrests, Suburban Areas,[1] Distribution by Ethnicity, 2020—Continued

(Number, percent; 5,475 agencies; 2020 estimated population 94,124,752.)

| Offense charged | Percent distribution[2] | | | Arrests 18 and over | | | Percent distribution[2] | | |
|---|---|---|---|---|---|---|---|---|---|
| | Total[3] | Hispanic or Latino | Not Hispanic or Latino | Total[3] | Hispanic or Latino | Not Hispanic or Latino | Total[3] | Hispanic or Latino | Not Hispanic or Latino |
| **Total** | 100.0 | 21.3 | 78.7 | 1,577,807 | 305,285 | 1,272,522 | 100.0 | 19.3 | 80.7 |
| **Violent crime[4]** | 100.0 | 25.0 | 75.0 | 79,720 | 19,804 | 59,916 | 100.0 | 24.8 | 75.2 |
| Murder and nonnegligent manslaughter | 100.0 | 26.4 | 73.6 | 1,826 | 425 | 1,401 | 100.0 | 23.3 | 76.7 |
| Rape[5] | 100.0 | 20.5 | 79.5 | 3,449 | 959 | 2,490 | 100.0 | 27.8 | 72.2 |
| Robbery | 100.0 | 24.2 | 75.8 | 8,481 | 1,982 | 6,499 | 100.0 | 23.4 | 76.6 |
| Aggravated assault | 100.0 | 26.1 | 73.9 | 65,964 | 16,438 | 49,526 | 100.0 | 24.9 | 75.1 |
| **Property crime[4]** | 100.0 | 18.9 | 81.1 | 169,153 | 24,547 | 144,606 | 100.0 | 14.5 | 85.5 |
| Burglary | 100.0 | 23.1 | 76.9 | 26,307 | 5,020 | 21,287 | 100.0 | 19.1 | 80.9 |
| Larceny-theft | 100.0 | 16.7 | 83.3 | 127,502 | 15,349 | 112,153 | 100.0 | 12.0 | 88.0 |
| Motor vehicle theft | 100.0 | 23.2 | 76.8 | 13,828 | 3,853 | 9,975 | 100.0 | 27.9 | 72.1 |
| Arson | 100.0 | 14.7 | 85.3 | 1,516 | 325 | 1,191 | 100.0 | 21.4 | 78.6 |
| Other assaults | 100.0 | 21.0 | 79.0 | 162,764 | 27,954 | 134,810 | 100.0 | 17.2 | 82.8 |
| Forgery and counterfeiting | 100.0 | 20.6 | 79.4 | 7,969 | 1,326 | 6,643 | 100.0 | 16.6 | 83.4 |
| Fraud | 100.0 | 24.4 | 75.6 | 19,373 | 2,549 | 16,824 | 100.0 | 13.2 | 86.8 |
| Embezzlement | 100.0 | 11.5 | 88.5 | 1,816 | 242 | 1,574 | 100.0 | 13.3 | 86.7 |
| Stolen property; buying, receiving, possessing | 100.0 | 20.2 | 79.8 | 18,226 | 3,253 | 14,973 | 100.0 | 17.8 | 82.2 |
| Vandalism | 100.0 | 18.0 | 82.0 | 28,791 | 5,072 | 23,719 | 100.0 | 17.6 | 82.4 |
| Weapons; carrying, possessing, etc. | 100.0 | 30.5 | 69.5 | 28,235 | 6,510 | 21,725 | 100.0 | 23.1 | 76.9 |
| Prostitution and commercialized vice | 100.0 | 0.0 | 100.0 | 1,457 | 292 | 1,165 | 100.0 | 20.0 | 80.0 |
| Sex offenses (except forcible rape and prostitution) | 100.0 | 20.7 | 79.3 | 6,001 | 1,922 | 4,079 | 100.0 | 32.0 | 68.0 |
| Drug abuse violations | 100.0 | 26.7 | 73.3 | 271,420 | 54,134 | 217,286 | 100.0 | 19.9 | 80.1 |
| Gambling | 100.0 | 58.1 | 41.9 | 304 | 108 | 196 | 100.0 | 35.5 | 64.5 |
| Offenses against the family and children | 100.0 | 13.2 | 86.8 | 12,956 | 1,486 | 11,470 | 100.0 | 11.5 | 88.5 |
| Driving under the influence | 100.0 | 29.8 | 70.2 | 196,534 | 56,767 | 139,767 | 100.0 | 28.9 | 71.1 |
| Liquor laws | 100.0 | 15.6 | 84.4 | 16,710 | 2,545 | 14,165 | 100.0 | 15.2 | 84.8 |
| Drunkenness | 100.0 | 28.9 | 71.1 | 36,717 | 9,665 | 27,052 | 100.0 | 26.3 | 73.7 |
| Disorderly conduct | 100.0 | 16.2 | 83.8 | 38,269 | 4,251 | 34,018 | 100.0 | 11.1 | 88.9 |
| Vagrancy | 100.0 | 40.5 | 59.5 | 1,724 | 276 | 1,448 | 100.0 | 16.0 | 84.0 |
| All other offenses (except traffic) | 100.0 | 21.2 | 78.8 | 479,595 | 82,574 | 397,021 | 100.0 | 17.2 | 82.8 |
| Suspicion | 100.0 | 0.0 | 100.0 | 73 | 8 | 65 | 100.0 | 11.0 | 89.0 |
| Curfew and loitering law violations | 100.0 | 16.5 | 83.5 | NA | NA | NA | NA | NA | NA |

NA = Not available.
1 Suburban areas include law enforcement agencies in cities with less than 50,000 inhabitants and county law enforcement agencies that are within a Metropolitan Statistical Area. Suburban areas exclude all metropolitan agencies associated with a principal city. 2 Because of rounding, the percentages may not sum to 100. 3 The ethnicity totals are representative of those agencies that provided ethnicity breakdowns. Not all agencies provide ethnicity data; therefore, the race and ethnicity totals will not equal. 4 Violent crimes are offenses of murder and nonnegligent manslaughter, rape, robbery, and aggravated assault. Property crimes are offenses of burglary, larceny-theft, motor vehicle theft, and arson. 5 The rape figures in this table are aggregate totals of the data submitted based on both the legacy and revised Uniform Crime Reporting definitions.

## Table 68. Police Disposition of Juvenile Offenders Taken into Custody, 2020

(Number, percent.)

| Population group | Total[1] | Handled within department and released | Referred to juvenile court jurisdiction | Referred to welfare agency | Referred to other police agency | Referred to criminal or adult court | Referred to other authorities not specified | Number of agencies | Estimated population, 2020 |
|---|---|---|---|---|---|---|---|---|---|
| **Total Agencies** | | | | | | | | | |
| Number | 315,048 | 58,393 | 141,313 | 1,643 | 4,965 | 2,953 | 105,781 | 10,466 | 228,864,358 |
| Percent[2] | 100.0 | 18.5 | 44.9 | 0.5 | 1.6 | 0.9 | 33.6 | | |
| **Total Cities** | | | | | | | | | |
| Number | 274,674 | 45,842 | 135,669 | 1,514 | 4,839 | 2,803 | 84,007 | 7,634 | 159,832,632 |
| Percent[2] | 100.0 | 16.7 | 49.4 | 0.6 | 1.8 | 1.0 | 30.6 | | |
| Group I (250,000 and over) | | | | | | | | | |
| Number | 35,953 | 9,280 | 8,685 | 33 | 352 | 261 | 17,342 | 72 | 44,271,326 |
| Percent[2] | 100.0 | 25.8 | 24.2 | 0.1 | 1.0 | 0.7 | 48.2 | | |
| Group II (100,000 to 249,999) | | | | | | | | | |
| Number | 27,917 | 6,842 | 6,780 | 0 | 75 | 50 | 14,170 | 189 | 27,356,047 |
| Percent[2] | 100.0 | 24.5 | 24.3 | 0.0 | 0.3 | 0.2 | 50.8 | | |
| Group III (50,000 to 99,999) | | | | | | | | | |
| Number | 32,679 | 7,154 | 8,488 | 117 | 191 | 99 | 16,630 | 398 | 27,901,884 |
| Percent[2] | 100.0 | 21.9 | 26.0 | 0.4 | 0.6 | 0.3 | 50.9 | | |
| Group IV (25,000 to 49,999) | | | | | | | | | |
| Number | 23,002 | 6,419 | 4,609 | 38 | 59 | 27 | 11,850 | 664 | 23,023,304 |
| Percent[2] | 100.0 | 27.9 | 20.0 | 0.2 | 0.3 | 0.1 | 51.5 | | |
| Group V (10,000 to 24,999) | | | | | | | | | |
| Number | 25,311 | 5,927 | 5,180 | 17 | 49 | 214 | 13,924 | 1,351 | 21,468,840 |
| Percent[2] | 100.0 | 23.4 | 20.5 | 0.1 | 0.2 | 0.8 | 55.0 | | |
| Group VI (under 10,000) | | | | | | | | | |
| Number | 129,812 | 10,220 | 101,927 | 1,309 | 4,113 | 2,152 | 10,091 | 4,960 | 15,811,231 |
| Percent[2] | 100.0 | 7.9 | 78.5 | 1.0 | 3.2 | 1.7 | 7.8 | | |
| **Metropolitan Counties** | | | | | | | | | |
| Number | 31,439 | 9,568 | 4,388 | 74 | 87 | 116 | 17,206 | 1,195 | 50,082,964 |
| Percent[2] | 100.0 | 30.4 | 14.0 | 0.2 | 0.3 | 0.4 | 54.7 | | |
| **Nonmetropolitan Counties** | | | | | | | | | |
| Number | 8,935 | 2,983 | 1,256 | 55 | 39 | 34 | 4,568 | 1,637 | 18,948,762 |
| Percent[2] | 100.0 | 33.4 | 14.1 | 0.6 | 0.4 | 0.4 | 51.1 | | |
| **Suburban Areas[3]** | | | | | | | | | |
| Number | 162,027 | 20,998 | 97,276 | 478 | 2,811 | 1,154 | 39,310 | 5,475 | 94,124,752 |
| Percent[2] | 100.0 | 13.0 | 60.0 | 0.3 | 1.7 | 0.7 | 24.3 | | |

1 Includes all offenses except traffic and neglect cases.   2 Because of rounding, the percentages may not sum to 100.   3 Suburban areas include law enforcement agencies in cities with less than 50,000 inhabitants and county law enforcement agencies that are within a Metropolitan Statistical Area. Suburban areas exclude all metropolitan agencies associated with a principal city. The agencies associated with suburban areas also appear in other groups within this table.

## Table 69. Arrests, by State, 2021

(Number.)

| State | Total, all classes[1] | Violent crime[2] | Property crime[2] | Murder and nonnegligent manslaughter | Rape | Robbery | Aggravated assault | Burglary | Larceny-theft | Motor vehicle theft | Arson | Other assaults | Forgery and counterfeiting | Fraud | Embezzlement | Stolen property; buying, receiving, possessing | Vandalism |
|---|---|---|---|---|---|---|---|---|---|---|---|---|---|---|---|---|---|
| **Alabama** | | | | | | | | | | | | | | | | | |
| Under 18 | 990 | 89 | 173 | 3 | 4 | 40 | 42 | 54 | 79 | 39 | 1 | 179 | 1 | 9 | 0 | 41 | 44 |
| Total, all ages | 48,349 | 1,192 | 4,058 | 82 | 68 | 166 | 876 | 782 | 2,898 | 354 | 24 | 3,539 | 207 | 471 | 4 | 694 | 683 |
| **Alaska** | | | | | | | | | | | | | | | | | |
| Under 18 | 416 | 60 | 78 | 0 | 21 | 4 | 35 | 45 | 23 | 8 | 2 | 114 | 1 | 0 | 0 | 0 | 43 |
| Total, all ages | 10,525 | 801 | 609 | 14 | 84 | 22 | 681 | 151 | 349 | 96 | 13 | 1,899 | 7 | 19 | 3 | 11 | 323 |
| **Arizona** | | | | | | | | | | | | | | | | | |
| Under 18 | 7,301 | 355 | 842 | 12 | 18 | 63 | 262 | 147 | 597 | 77 | 21 | 1,755 | 3 | 27 | 1 | 12 | 525 |
| Total, all ages | 90,161 | 3,619 | 9,573 | 103 | 126 | 363 | 3,027 | 1,153 | 7,622 | 697 | 101 | 11,505 | 194 | 610 | 54 | 314 | 3,285 |
| **Arkansas** | | | | | | | | | | | | | | | | | |
| Under 18 | 6,135 | 457 | 745 | 21 | 40 | 35 | 361 | 194 | 470 | 70 | 11 | 1,469 | 2 | 10 | 0 | 148 | 334 |
| Total, all ages | 104,439 | 5,660 | 9,342 | 196 | 285 | 348 | 4,831 | 1,653 | 6,961 | 660 | 68 | 11,540 | 499 | 505 | 26 | 1,663 | 1,688 |
| **California[5]** | | | | | | | | | | | | | | | | | |
| Under 18 | 5,267 | 283 | 207 | 5 | 5 | 72 | 201 | 33 | 126 | 41 | 7 | 285 | 0 | 6 | 0 | 29 | 88 |
| Total, all ages | 80,110 | 4,322 | 3,853 | 70 | 67 | 812 | 3,373 | 910 | 1,981 | 823 | 139 | 8,565 | 162 | 451 | 22 | 1,218 | 1,354 |
| **Colorado** | | | | | | | | | | | | | | | | | |
| Under 18 | 9,006 | 600 | 1,184 | 29 | 60 | 140 | 371 | 142 | 791 | 208 | 43 | 1,436 | 7 | 47 | 8 | 24 | 725 |
| Total, all ages | 154,110 | 8,403 | 19,517 | 229 | 437 | 1,164 | 6,573 | 2,430 | 12,741 | 4,044 | 302 | 15,902 | 369 | 1,638 | 72 | 981 | 5,469 |
| **Connecticut** | | | | | | | | | | | | | | | | | |
| Under 18 | 3,523 | 196 | 615 | 9 | 13 | 90 | 84 | 82 | 313 | 208 | 12 | 830 | 3 | 29 | 3 | 65 | 175 |
| Total, all ages | 69,831 | 2,346 | 7,356 | 111 | 129 | 517 | 1,589 | 986 | 5,654 | 669 | 47 | 14,977 | 212 | 450 | 66 | 245 | 1,602 |
| **Delaware** | | | | | | | | | | | | | | | | | |
| Under 18 | 1,651 | 230 | 244 | 4 | 8 | 80 | 138 | 71 | 115 | 52 | 6 | 469 | 1 | 26 | 2 | 95 | 68 |
| Total, all ages | 25,043 | 1,752 | 3,454 | 32 | 71 | 273 | 1,376 | 447 | 2,801 | 186 | 20 | 5,475 | 98 | 952 | 79 | 344 | 874 |
| **District of Columbia[5,6]** | | | | | | | | | | | | | | | | | |
| Under 18 | 148 | 45 | 11 | 0 | 0 | 35 | 10 | 0 | 8 | 3 | 0 | 36 | 0 | 0 | 0 | 1 | 4 |
| Total, all ages | 2,002 | 209 | 80 | 1 | 0 | 107 | 101 | 1 | 69 | 9 | 1 | 441 | 1 | 1 | 0 | 14 | 73 |
| **Florida[5,7]** | | | | | | | | | | | | | | | | | |
| Under 18 | 19 | 3 | 3 | 0 | 0 | 2 | 1 | 0 | 2 | 1 | 0 | 7 | 0 | 0 | 0 | 1 | 0 |
| Total, all ages | 927 | 49 | 115 | 0 | 5 | 17 | 27 | 10 | 92 | 13 | 0 | 199 | 5 | 16 | 1 | 21 | 13 |
| **Georgia** | | | | | | | | | | | | | | | | | |
| Under 18 | 9,286 | 768 | 1,580 | 40 | 57 | 168 | 503 | 170 | 1,055 | 338 | 17 | 1,985 | 26 | 98 | 1 | 196 | 375 |
| Total, all ages | 157,237 | 8,440 | 15,401 | 383 | 361 | 798 | 6,898 | 1,745 | 12,264 | 1,276 | 116 | 17,511 | 887 | 3,139 | 29 | 1,763 | 3,449 |
| **Hawaii** | | | | | | | | | | | | | | | | | |
| Under 18 | 971 | 78 | 77 | 0 | 18 | 27 | 33 | 15 | 52 | 9 | 1 | 319 | 0 | 0 | 0 | 19 | 3 |
| Total, all ages | 27,741 | 666 | 1,447 | 8 | 76 | 149 | 433 | 204 | 1,141 | 73 | 29 | 3,754 | 60 | 170 | 7 | 488 | 83 |
| **Idaho** | | | | | | | | | | | | | | | | | |
| Under 18 | 4,393 | 150 | 526 | 2 | 32 | 6 | 110 | 87 | 367 | 57 | 15 | 573 | 1 | 26 | 2 | 12 | 208 |
| Total, all ages | 46,857 | 1,621 | 2,859 | 25 | 127 | 62 | 1,407 | 565 | 2,078 | 181 | 35 | 3,442 | 75 | 390 | 34 | 166 | 710 |
| **Illinois[5]** | | | | | | | | | | | | | | | | | |
| Under 18 | 2,729 | 163 | 428 | 2 | 3 | 34 | 124 | 73 | 312 | 38 | 5 | 679 | 4 | 47 | 3 | 25 | 189 |
| Total, all ages | 38,027 | 1,761 | 4,208 | 43 | 72 | 184 | 1,462 | 568 | 3,423 | 164 | 53 | 7,414 | 104 | 712 | 35 | 141 | 1,649 |
| **Indiana** | | | | | | | | | | | | | | | | | |
| Under 18 | 6,641 | 538 | 889 | 20 | 28 | 173 | 317 | 107 | 563 | 208 | 11 | 1,466 | 7 | 23 | 2 | 47 | 162 |
| Total, all ages | 100,461 | 4,338 | 9,430 | 140 | 170 | 623 | 3,405 | 1,101 | 7,121 | 1,143 | 65 | 12,264 | 214 | 750 | 78 | 483 | 564 |
| **Iowa** | | | | | | | | | | | | | | | | | |
| Under 18 | 6,490 | 476 | 1,302 | 7 | 79 | 67 | 323 | 199 | 827 | 253 | 23 | 1,755 | 14 | 60 | 6 | 74 | 528 |
| Total, all ages | 68,342 | 4,868 | 7,780 | 41 | 263 | 218 | 4,346 | 1,046 | 5,824 | 824 | 86 | 8,587 | 275 | 756 | 62 | 288 | 1,951 |
| **Kansas** | | | | | | | | | | | | | | | | | |
| Under 18 | 3,629 | 152 | 522 | 6 | 22 | 12 | 112 | 64 | 386 | 51 | 21 | 850 | 4 | 11 | 0 | 24 | 247 |
| Total, all ages | 50,774 | 1,895 | 3,965 | 45 | 97 | 105 | 1,648 | 448 | 3,160 | 305 | 52 | 6,798 | 111 | 270 | 25 | 431 | 1,593 |
| **Kentucky** | | | | | | | | | | | | | | | | | |
| Under 18 | 2,520 | 282 | 429 | 26 | 27 | 120 | 109 | 125 | 199 | 98 | 7 | 610 | 6 | 14 | 1 | 351 | 100 |
| Total, all ages | 177,379 | 3,428 | 9,500 | 219 | 252 | 607 | 2,350 | 2,123 | 6,534 | 778 | 65 | 11,215 | 506 | 1,057 | 177 | 2,630 | 1,302 |
| **Louisiana** | | | | | | | | | | | | | | | | | |
| Under 18 | 8,115 | 466 | 1,207 | 36 | 16 | 52 | 362 | 344 | 688 | 166 | 9 | 1,712 | 3 | 12 | 0 | 160 | 289 |
| Total, all ages | 72,217 | 5,727 | 12,423 | 213 | 141 | 295 | 5,078 | 2,204 | 9,353 | 823 | 43 | 11,605 | 197 | 348 | 67 | 1,504 | 2,301 |
| **Maine** | | | | | | | | | | | | | | | | | |
| Under 18 | 1,556 | 57 | 325 | 3 | 17 | 15 | 22 | 69 | 192 | 43 | 21 | 363 | 0 | 6 | 1 | 5 | 185 |
| Total, all ages | 29,060 | 686 | 3,660 | 16 | 69 | 72 | 529 | 352 | 3,047 | 203 | 58 | 4,308 | 68 | 222 | 15 | 100 | 948 |
| **Maryland[5]** | | | | | | | | | | | | | | | | | |
| Under 18 | 2,488 | 291 | 447 | 8 | 31 | 128 | 124 | 79 | 241 | 121 | 6 | 812 | 2 | 7 | 3 | 18 | 197 |
| Total, all ages | 28,784 | 2,298 | 3,247 | 66 | 148 | 511 | 1,573 | 605 | 2,247 | 364 | 31 | 3,325 | 55 | 162 | 52 | 131 | 532 |
| **Massachusetts** | | | | | | | | | | | | | | | | | |
| Under 18 | 3,561 | 463 | 448 | 3 | 18 | 63 | 379 | 138 | 207 | 77 | 26 | 1,118 | 4 | 19 | 0 | 103 | 215 |
| Total, all ages | 81,377 | 7,168 | 6,189 | 61 | 283 | 582 | 6,242 | 1,242 | 4,347 | 523 | 77 | 16,333 | 201 | 648 | 35 | 681 | 1,980 |
| **Michigan** | | | | | | | | | | | | | | | | | |
| Under 18 | 7,136 | 740 | 1,061 | 15 | 114 | 112 | 499 | 234 | 574 | 226 | 27 | 1,955 | 1 | 62 | 26 | 207 | 443 |
| Total, all ages | 155,832 | 12,718 | 13,261 | 379 | 852 | 887 | 10,600 | 2,090 | 9,716 | 1,259 | 196 | 25,996 | 283 | 1,626 | 623 | 2,159 | 2,791 |
| **Minnesota** | | | | | | | | | | | | | | | | | |
| Under 18 | 11,084 | 689 | 1,223 | 9 | 91 | 256 | 333 | 149 | 901 | 153 | 20 | 1,426 | 11 | 83 | 14 | 207 | 311 |
| Total, all ages | 126,675 | 5,339 | 15,329 | 134 | 520 | 803 | 3,882 | 1,759 | 12,530 | 913 | 127 | 12,479 | 650 | 2,396 | 64 | 2,050 | 2,230 |
| **Mississippi** | | | | | | | | | | | | | | | | | |
| Under 18 | 2,083 | 113 | 284 | 12 | 13 | 46 | 42 | 63 | 184 | 37 | 0 | 303 | 2 | 10 | 8 | 44 | 146 |
| Total, all ages | 49,859 | 1,070 | 4,162 | 82 | 81 | 143 | 764 | 594 | 3,268 | 275 | 25 | 4,480 | 118 | 471 | 217 | 582 | 675 |
| **Missouri** | | | | | | | | | | | | | | | | | |
| Under 18 | 8,256 | 790 | 1,093 | 17 | 56 | 170 | 547 | 183 | 670 | 224 | 16 | 1,591 | 8 | 39 | 5 | 219 | 436 |
| Total, all ages | 133,059 | 8,104 | 15,138 | 254 | 344 | 860 | 6,646 | 2,204 | 10,829 | 1,965 | 140 | 14,790 | 738 | 1,276 | 173 | 2,076 | 3,267 |
| **Montana** | | | | | | | | | | | | | | | | | |
| Under 18 | 3,085 | 122 | 403 | 1 | 8 | 16 | 97 | 29 | 311 | 45 | 18 | 520 | 3 | 4 | 0 | 12 | 175 |
| Total, all ages | 26,923 | 1,762 | 3,734 | 22 | 69 | 103 | 1,568 | 298 | 3,067 | 318 | 51 | 4,820 | 92 | 147 | 28 | 230 | 848 |

# Table 69. Arrests, by State, 2021—Continued

(Number.)

| State | Weapons; carrying, possessing, etc. | Prostitution and commercial-ized vice | Sex offenses (except rape and prostitu-tion) | Drug abuse violations | Gam-bling | Offenses against the family and children | Driving under the influence | Liquor laws | Drunken-ness[3] | Disorderly conduct | Vagrancy | All other offenses (except traffic) | Suspi-cion[4] | Curfew and loitering law violations | Number of agencies | Estimated popula-tion, 2021 |
|---|---|---|---|---|---|---|---|---|---|---|---|---|---|---|---|---|
| **Alabama** | | | | | | | | | | | | | | | | |
| Under 18 | 54 | 0 | 2 | 137 | 0 | 2 | 3 | 39 | | 71 | 0 | 146 | | 0 | 186 | 2,265,220 |
| Total, all ages | 959 | 30 | 51 | 6,628 | 1 | 135 | 316 | 2,563 | | 891 | 0 | 25,927 | | 0 | | |
| **Alaska** | | | | | | | | | | | | | | | | |
| Under 18 | 3 | 0 | 8 | 26 | 0 | 0 | 16 | 18 | | 6 | 0 | 43 | | 0 | 28 | 371,959 |
| Total, all ages | 113 | 0 | 45 | 447 | 0 | 32 | 1,529 | 130 | | 405 | 1 | 4,151 | | 0 | | |
| **Arizona** | | | | | | | | | | | | | | | | |
| Under 18 | 100 | 0 | 41 | 538 | 0 | 18 | 124 | 406 | | 684 | 0 | 1,640 | | 230 | ⁸67 | 3,568,504 |
| Total, all ages | 982 | 64 | 178 | 9,457 | 0 | 351 | 11,932 | 1,909 | | 8,093 | 129 | 27,682 | | 230 | | |
| **Arkansas** | | | | | | | | | | | | | | | | |
| Under 18 | 118 | 1 | 15 | 719 | 0 | 3 | 43 | 99 | | 518 | 0 | 1,282 | | 172 | 252 | 2,857,932 |
| Total, all ages | 1,139 | 55 | 98 | 16,238 | 9 | 323 | 5,125 | 1,036 | | 2,311 | 214 | 46,796 | | 172 | | |
| **California**⁶ | | | | | | | | | | | | | | | | |
| Under 18 | 232 | 1 | 12 | 229 | 0 | 0 | 30 | 69 | | 3 | 0 | 3,737 | | 56 | 14 | 2,861,998 |
| Total, all ages | 2,103 | 363 | 125 | 11,629 | 11 | 6 | 4,858 | 166 | | 97 | 322 | 40,427 | | 56 | | |
| **Colorado** | | | | | | | | | | | | | | | | |
| Under 18 | 289 | 0 | 85 | 974 | 0 | 13 | 210 | 564 | | 747 | 0 | 1,937 | | 156 | 203 | 5,678,716 |
| Total, all ages | 2,535 | 205 | 385 | 10,203 | 2 | 2,149 | 17,037 | 3,000 | | 4,314 | 89 | 61,684 | | 156 | | |
| **Connecticut** | | | | | | | | | | | | | | | | |
| Under 18 | 158 | 0 | 26 | 125 | 0 | 13 | 25 | 9 | | 684 | 0 | 566 | | 1 | 107 | 3,605,597 |
| Total, all ages | 1,181 | 32 | 267 | 3,444 | 10 | 2,063 | 6,133 | 67 | | 8,489 | 109 | 20,781 | | 1 | | |
| **Delaware** | | | | | | | | | | | | | | | | |
| Under 18 | 68 | 0 | 18 | 113 | 0 | 1 | 0 | 12 | | 70 | 0 | 229 | | 4 | 53 | 1,001,629 |
| Total, all ages | 424 | 10 | 106 | 3,566 | 4 | 163 | 324 | 345 | | 936 | 105 | 6,026 | | 4 | | |
| **District of Columbia**⁵,⁸ | | | | | | | | | | | | | | | | |
| Under 18 | 17 | 0 | 0 | 2 | 0 | 0 | 0 | 0 | | 7 | 0 | 25 | | 0 | 1 | |
| Total, all ages | 60 | 0 | 30 | 103 | 0 | 3 | 5 | 233 | | 203 | 0 | 546 | | 0 | | |
| **Florida**⁵,⁷ | | | | | | | | | | | | | | | | |
| Under 18 | 0 | 0 | 0 | 0 | 0 | 0 | 0 | 0 | | 0 | 0 | 4 | | 1 | 2 | |
| Total, all ages | 21 | 0 | 0 | 104 | 0 | 11 | 30 | 1 | | 15 | 2 | 323 | | 1 | | |
| **Georgia** | | | | | | | | | | | | | | | | |
| Under 18 | 364 | 0 | 109 | 907 | 0 | 29 | 140 | 87 | | 638 | 0 | 1,854 | | 129 | 380 | 7,950,625 |
| Total, all ages | 2,753 | 175 | 548 | 27,358 | 8 | 972 | 18,504 | 1,531 | | 7,298 | 1,207 | 46,135 | | 129 | | |
| **Hawaii** | | | | | | | | | | | | | | | | |
| Under 18 | 4 | 0 | 19 | 69 | 0 | 0 | 17 | 24 | | 17 | 0 | 288 | | 37 | 2 | 1,059,012 |
| Total, all ages | 94 | 30 | 95 | 985 | 38 | 12 | 2,471 | 1,365 | | 593 | 337 | 15,009 | | 37 | | |
| **Idaho** | | | | | | | | | | | | | | | | |
| Under 18 | 75 | 0 | 46 | 663 | 0 | 10 | 88 | 162 | | 214 | 0 | 1,539 | | 98 | 80 | 1,661,136 |
| Total, all ages | 324 | 15 | 194 | 9,686 | 0 | 457 | 7,017 | 992 | | 1,283 | 5 | 17,489 | | 98 | | |
| **Illinois**⁶ | | | | | | | | | | | | | | | | |
| Under 18 | 133 | 0 | 5 | 319 | 0 | 3 | 25 | 77 | | 199 | 0 | 356 | | 74 | 118 | 2,407,151 |
| Total, all ages | 1,284 | 11 | 33 | 4,101 | 0 | 156 | 4,388 | 463 | | 1,144 | 1 | 10,348 | | 74 | | |
| **Indiana** | | | | | | | | | | | | | | | | |
| Under 18 | 244 | 0 | 48 | 640 | 0 | 4 | 38 | 248 | | 256 | 0 | 1,933 | | 96 | 129 | 4,671,815 |
| Total, all ages | 3,201 | 81 | 313 | 17,532 | 3 | 347 | 11,840 | 1,145 | | 2,308 | 3 | 35,471 | | 96 | | |
| **Iowa** | | | | | | | | | | | | | | | | |
| Under 18 | 96 | 1 | 18 | 726 | 0 | 3 | 78 | 357 | | 162 | 0 | 833 | | 1 | 178 | 2,825,401 |
| Total, all ages | 740 | 23 | 98 | 8,378 | 7 | 456 | 8,841 | 1,509 | | 662 | 6 | 23,054 | | 1 | | |
| **Kansas** | | | | | | | | | | | | | | | | |
| Under 18 | 19 | 1 | 17 | 623 | 0 | 10 | 92 | 254 | | 132 | 0 | 671 | | 0 | 192 | 1,850,993 |
| Total, all ages | 352 | 37 | 106 | 8,668 | 0 | 185 | 5,766 | 1,215 | | 1,118 | 0 | 18,239 | | 0 | | |
| **Kentucky** | | | | | | | | | | | | | | | | |
| Under 18 | 83 | 0 | 21 | 266 | 0 | 2 | 8 | 0 | | 23 | 0 | 324 | | 0 | 426 | 4,505,498 |
| Total, all ages | 704 | 15 | 214 | 20,758 | 8 | 3,990 | 12,426 | 20 | | 3,307 | 17 | 106,105 | | 0 | | |
| **Louisiana** | | | | | | | | | | | | | | | | |
| Under 18 | 285 | 1 | 34 | 675 | 2 | 1 | 6 | 55 | | 1,535 | 0 | 1,552 | | 120 | 113 | 3,042,729 |
| Total, all ages | 1,937 | 141 | 198 | 16,284 | 47 | 297 | 2,261 | 655 | | 3,249 | 7 | 12,849 | | 120 | | |
| **Maine** | | | | | | | | | | | | | | | | |
| Under 18 | 4 | 0 | 19 | 106 | 0 | 1 | 23 | 166 | | 49 | 0 | 235 | | 11 | 127 | 1,360,671 |
| Total, all ages | 127 | 5 | 70 | 2,807 | 1 | 87 | 4,318 | 623 | | 804 | 1 | 10,199 | | 11 | | |
| **Maryland**⁵ | | | | | | | | | | | | | | | | |
| Under 18 | 63 | 0 | 27 | 120 | 0 | 1 | 4 | 43 | | 56 | 0 | 395 | | 2 | 16 | 2,189,086 |
| Total, all ages | 624 | 45 | 100 | 2,557 | 0 | 178 | 3,312 | 305 | | 580 | 14 | 11,265 | | 2 | | |
| **Massachusetts** | | | | | | | | | | | | | | | | |
| Under 18 | 141 | 0 | 33 | 59 | 0 | 12 | 17 | 75 | | 103 | 0 | 751 | | 0 | 368 | 6,929,534 |
| Total, all ages | 1,298 | 151 | 294 | 5,361 | 38 | 835 | 7,422 | 679 | | 2,172 | 8 | 29,884 | | 0 | | |
| **Michigan** | | | | | | | | | | | | | | | | |
| Under 18 | 426 | 4 | 91 | 237 | 0 | 4 | 118 | 102 | | 208 | 0 | 1,339 | | 112 | 611 | 9,780,531 |
| Total, all ages | 10,148 | 104 | 561 | 12,411 | 43 | 774 | 21,397 | 2,803 | | 3,344 | 34 | 44,644 | | 112 | | |
| **Minnesota** | | | | | | | | | | | | | | | | |
| Under 18 | 240 | 0 | 60 | 652 | 3 | 1 | 192 | 2,299 | | 1,308 | 0 | 1,830 | | 535 | 361 | 5,590,467 |
| Total, all ages | 2,426 | 71 | 448 | 13,693 | 14 | 148 | 19,198 | 6,431 | | 6,631 | 2,401 | 34,140 | | 535 | | |
| **Mississippi** | | | | | | | | | | | | | | | | |
| Under 18 | 104 | 0 | 6 | 188 | 0 | 34 | 46 | 22 | | 301 | 0 | 446 | | 26 | 130 | 1,663,780 |
| Total, all ages | 869 | 17 | 53 | 8,271 | 8 | 559 | 6,928 | 288 | | 3,437 | 17 | 17,611 | | 26 | | |
| **Missouri** | | | | | | | | | | | | | | | | |
| Under 18 | 158 | 0 | 40 | 857 | 0 | 17 | 129 | 311 | | 690 | 0 | 1,553 | | 320 | 326 | 5,208,452 |
| Total, all ages | 2,224 | 71 | 213 | 23,624 | 13 | 820 | 14,567 | 2,240 | | 4,924 | 140 | 38,341 | | 320 | | |
| **Montana** | | | | | | | | | | | | | | | | |
| Under 18 | 8 | 0 | 18 | 63 | 0 | 67 | 90 | 390 | | 312 | 0 | 707 | | 191 | 98 | 1,043,486 |
| Total, all ages | 52 | 3 | 122 | 1,676 | 0 | 449 | 4,037 | 1,001 | | 2,177 | 22 | 5,532 | | 191 | | |

## Table 69. Arrests, by State, 2021—Continued

(Number.)

| State | Total, all classes[1] | Violent crime[2] | Property crime[2] | Murder and nonnegligent manslaughter | Rape | Robbery | Aggravated assault | Burglary | Larceny-theft | Motor vehicle theft | Arson | Other assaults | Forgery and counterfeiting | Fraud | Embezzlement | Stolen property; buying, receiving, possessing | Vandalism |
|---|---|---|---|---|---|---|---|---|---|---|---|---|---|---|---|---|---|
| **Nebraska** | | | | | | | | | | | | | | | | | |
| Under 18 | 4,424 | 121 | 588 | 2 | 16 | 29 | 74 | 68 | 409 | 94 | 17 | 1,007 | 1 | 43 | 9 | 16 | 424 |
| Total, all ages | 38,036 | 1,669 | 2,870 | 20 | 119 | 90 | 1,440 | 245 | 2,369 | 207 | 49 | 4,255 | 141 | 411 | 21 | 233 | 1,328 |
| **Nevada** | | | | | | | | | | | | | | | | | |
| Under 18 | 5,048 | 496 | 458 | 11 | 67 | 225 | 193 | 100 | 282 | 69 | 7 | 1,764 | 3 | 20 | 3 | 110 | 210 |
| Total, all ages | 102,790 | 5,701 | 7,283 | 159 | 315 | 1,147 | 4,080 | 1,751 | 4,704 | 702 | 126 | 20,439 | 263 | 955 | 164 | 1,837 | 2,120 |
| **New Hampshire** | | | | | | | | | | | | | | | | | |
| Under 18 | 1,915 | 35 | 115 | 0 | 12 | 3 | 20 | 25 | 82 | 8 | 0 | 359 | 0 | 10 | 3 | 13 | 138 |
| Total, all ages | 32,486 | 513 | 2,094 | 6 | 65 | 78 | 364 | 178 | 1,782 | 121 | 13 | 3,888 | 124 | 326 | 46 | 326 | 945 |
| **New Jersey[5]** | | | | | | | | | | | | | | | | | |
| Under 18 | 705 | 156 | 81 | 0 | 4 | 90 | 62 | 12 | 51 | 15 | 3 | 53 | 0 | 1 | 0 | 140 | 8 |
| Total, all ages | 15,032 | 1,346 | 1,616 | 39 | 37 | 274 | 996 | 262 | 1,237 | 102 | 15 | 2,532 | 54 | 90 | 22 | 428 | 367 |
| **New Mexico[5]** | | | | | | | | | | | | | | | | | |
| Under 18 | 459 | 63 | 40 | 2 | 1 | 7 | 53 | 11 | 19 | 10 | 0 | 128 | 1 | 0 | 1 | 8 | 15 |
| Total, all ages | 25,409 | 2,028 | 1,921 | 30 | 19 | 151 | 1,828 | 389 | 1,335 | 178 | 19 | 5,756 | 20 | 99 | 54 | 542 | 1,045 |
| **New York[5]** | | | | | | | | | | | | | | | | | |
| Under 18 | 1,610 | 185 | 392 | 2 | 22 | 63 | 98 | 65 | 216 | 99 | 12 | 291 | 2 | 5 | 1 | 50 | 300 |
| Total, all ages | 40,069 | 2,428 | 8,306 | 41 | 151 | 435 | 1,801 | 1,032 | 6,673 | 520 | 81 | 5,796 | 230 | 276 | 16 | 465 | 3,207 |
| **North Carolina** | | | | | | | | | | | | | | | | | |
| Under 18 | 7,249 | 619 | 1,376 | 40 | 32 | 233 | 314 | 358 | 739 | 262 | 17 | 1,593 | 6 | 65 | 19 | 328 | 318 |
| Total, all ages | 225,175 | 10,186 | 22,604 | 561 | 235 | 1,722 | 7,668 | 5,022 | 16,041 | 1,315 | 226 | 21,992 | 481 | 2,317 | 591 | 3,474 | 2,845 |
| **North Dakota** | | | | | | | | | | | | | | | | | |
| Under 18 | 4,047 | 68 | 396 | 0 | 14 | 2 | 52 | 42 | 301 | 50 | 3 | 625 | 0 | 26 | 1 | 36 | 194 |
| Total, all ages | 28,662 | 745 | 2,470 | 9 | 50 | 54 | 632 | 322 | 1,890 | 225 | 33 | 2,972 | 108 | 538 | 28 | 343 | 510 |
| **Ohio** | | | | | | | | | | | | | | | | | |
| Under 18 | 12,924 | 660 | 1,357 | 28 | 42 | 254 | 336 | 228 | 830 | 258 | 41 | 3,201 | 8 | 74 | 0 | 327 | 602 |
| Total, all ages | 136,529 | 6,265 | 16,645 | 268 | 298 | 1,116 | 4,583 | 2,348 | 13,234 | 935 | 128 | 27,807 | 156 | 973 | 4 | 1,546 | 3,017 |
| **Oklahoma** | | | | | | | | | | | | | | | | | |
| Under 18 | 4,423 | 296 | 689 | 21 | 16 | 50 | 209 | 162 | 357 | 162 | 8 | 657 | 2 | 14 | 6 | 91 | 199 |
| Total, all ages | 73,965 | 3,912 | 10,602 | 132 | 120 | 341 | 3,319 | 2,122 | 6,931 | 1,406 | 143 | 7,948 | 234 | 652 | 129 | 1,489 | 1,520 |
| **Oregon** | | | | | | | | | | | | | | | | | |
| Under 18 | 3,554 | 298 | 571 | 4 | 27 | 75 | 192 | 73 | 393 | 87 | 18 | 666 | 2 | 22 | 1 | 18 | 340 |
| Total, all ages | 91,146 | 5,239 | 13,488 | 73 | 210 | 884 | 4,072 | 1,832 | 9,033 | 2,168 | 455 | 9,638 | 343 | 1,137 | 40 | 792 | 4,010 |
| **Pennsylvania[5]** | | | | | | | | | | | | | | | | | |
| Under 18 | 404 | 12 | 56 | 0 | 2 | 6 | 4 | 15 | 36 | 3 | 2 | 110 | 2 | 3 | 0 | 5 | 39 |
| Total, all ages | 6,092 | 209 | 739 | 4 | 14 | 38 | 153 | 80 | 626 | 26 | 7 | 967 | 25 | 102 | 5 | 22 | 161 |
| **Rhode Island** | | | | | | | | | | | | | | | | | |
| Under 18 | 1,539 | 89 | 173 | 0 | 13 | 17 | 59 | 55 | 61 | 44 | 13 | 267 | 4 | 5 | 1 | 32 | 143 |
| Total, all ages | 21,800 | 873 | 1,550 | 14 | 80 | 86 | 693 | 350 | 1,007 | 164 | 29 | 3,366 | 117 | 252 | 49 | 264 | 879 |
| **South Carolina** | | | | | | | | | | | | | | | | | |
| Under 18 | 6,970 | 536 | 980 | 35 | 60 | 147 | 294 | 172 | 686 | 114 | 8 | 1,935 | 6 | 42 | 6 | 133 | 325 |
| Total, all ages | 119,278 | 6,834 | 15,932 | 444 | 424 | 812 | 5,154 | 2,346 | 12,389 | 1,082 | 115 | 14,954 | 737 | 2,086 | 187 | 2,214 | 2,836 |
| **South Dakota** | | | | | | | | | | | | | | | | | |
| Under 18 | 3,542 | 106 | 227 | 0 | 7 | 7 | 92 | 20 | 153 | 43 | 11 | 452 | 0 | 17 | 3 | 21 | 108 |
| Total, all ages | 44,544 | 1,175 | 1,194 | 9 | 37 | 44 | 1,085 | 191 | 733 | 248 | 22 | 3,969 | 128 | 550 | 11 | 152 | 352 |
| **Tennessee** | | | | | | | | | | | | | | | | | |
| Under 18 | 14,622 | 989 | 1,746 | 33 | 53 | 252 | 651 | 256 | 949 | 515 | 26 | 3,506 | 17 | 96 | 22 | 156 | 696 |
| Total, all ages | 255,863 | 13,174 | 25,096 | 380 | 361 | 1,190 | 11,243 | 3,748 | 17,586 | 3,587 | 175 | 27,343 | 1,376 | 3,434 | 399 | 1,931 | 4,117 |
| **Texas** | | | | | | | | | | | | | | | | | |
| Under 18 | 33,195 | 3,030 | 4,498 | 132 | 294 | 921 | 1,683 | 704 | 2,866 | 870 | 58 | 8,090 | 70 | 206 | 18 | 95 | 922 |
| Total, all ages | 524,958 | 30,998 | 51,046 | 1,108 | 1,758 | 4,616 | 23,516 | 7,241 | 36,586 | 6,681 | 538 | 80,235 | 2,045 | 5,486 | 211 | 1,015 | 7,216 |
| **Utah** | | | | | | | | | | | | | | | | | |
| Under 18 | 7,520 | 293 | 1,380 | 8 | 96 | 31 | 158 | 73 | 1,197 | 81 | 29 | 975 | 4 | 36 | 3 | 61 | 637 |
| Total, all ages | 82,552 | 2,710 | 10,266 | 55 | 358 | 319 | 1,978 | 723 | 9,083 | 374 | 86 | 8,459 | 402 | 644 | 17 | 938 | 2,907 |
| **Vermont** | | | | | | | | | | | | | | | | | |
| Under 18 | 523 | 40 | 45 | 0 | 9 | 0 | 31 | 5 | 24 | 11 | 5 | 136 | 3 | 8 | 0 | 2 | 153 |
| Total, all ages | 9,523 | 808 | 1,205 | 9 | 72 | 34 | 693 | 189 | 915 | 76 | 25 | 1,449 | 34 | 138 | 36 | 80 | 482 |
| **Virginia** | | | | | | | | | | | | | | | | | |
| Under 18 | 6,259 | 458 | 930 | 13 | 65 | 137 | 243 | 163 | 613 | 126 | 28 | 1,305 | 6 | 54 | 20 | 112 | 307 |
| Total, all ages | 186,270 | 6,693 | 17,681 | 379 | 483 | 957 | 4,874 | 1,583 | 14,925 | 1,010 | 163 | 27,361 | 810 | 3,699 | 627 | 734 | 3,166 |
| **Washington** | | | | | | | | | | | | | | | | | |
| Under 18 | 4,186 | 537 | 628 | 11 | 71 | 146 | 309 | 182 | 350 | 80 | 16 | 1,506 | 0 | 7 | 0 | 55 | 375 |
| Total, all ages | 117,132 | 7,935 | 16,892 | 165 | 463 | 1,429 | 5,878 | 4,208 | 11,299 | 1,124 | 261 | 21,887 | 287 | 634 | 16 | 2,839 | 4,407 |
| **West Virginia** | | | | | | | | | | | | | | | | | |
| Under 18 | 438 | 31 | 35 | 2 | 3 | 2 | 24 | 5 | 21 | 7 | 2 | 153 | 0 | 0 | 1 | 2 | 19 |
| Total, all ages | 26,845 | 1,196 | 3,109 | 32 | 77 | 41 | 1,046 | 526 | 2,362 | 176 | 45 | 3,156 | 107 | 156 | 13 | 321 | 357 |
| **Wisconsin** | | | | | | | | | | | | | | | | | |
| Under 18 | 19,852 | 769 | 1,921 | 21 | 209 | 159 | 380 | 200 | 1,248 | 442 | 31 | 1,793 | 13 | 91 | 46 | 454 | 1,091 |
| Total, all ages | 157,256 | 6,777 | 14,429 | 187 | 834 | 711 | 5,045 | 1,250 | 11,896 | 1,165 | 118 | 14,373 | 388 | 1,312 | 266 | 1,106 | 4,360 |
| **Wyoming** | | | | | | | | | | | | | | | | | |
| Under 18 | 1,746 | 28 | 175 | 1 | 4 | 1 | 22 | 13 | 130 | 29 | 3 | 274 | 1 | 4 | 0 | 0 | 85 |
| Total, all ages | 12,739 | 325 | 970 | 15 | 37 | 12 | 261 | 115 | 733 | 109 | 13 | 1,455 | 12 | 35 | 0 | 10 | 289 |

## Table 69. Arrests, by State, 2021—Continued

(Number.)

| State | Weapons; carrying, possessing, etc. | Prostitution and commercialized vice | Sex offenses (except rape and prostitution) | Drug abuse violations | Gambling | Offenses against the family and children | Driving under the influence | Liquor laws | Drunkenness[3] | Disorderly conduct | Vagrancy | All other offenses (except traffic) | Suspicion[4] | Curfew and loitering law violations | Number of agencies | Estimated population, 2021 |
|---|---|---|---|---|---|---|---|---|---|---|---|---|---|---|---|---|
| **Nebraska** | | | | | | | | | | | | | | | | |
| Under 18 | 35 | 0 | 40 | 610 | 0 | 218 | 60 | 298 | | 97 | 0 | 765 | | 92 | 131 | 1,315,324 |
| Total, all ages | 481 | 29 | 119 | 7,242 | 2 | 542 | 4,767 | 1,873 | | 1,530 | 620 | 9,811 | | 92 | | |
| **Nevada** | | | | | | | | | | | | | | | | |
| Under 18 | 137 | 42 | 49 | 428 | 4 | 3 | 60 | 251 | | 195 | 0 | 504 | | 311 | 35 | 3,095,335 |
| Total, all ages | 2,985 | 1,988 | 343 | 8,576 | 40 | 634 | 11,023 | 1,285 | | 1,971 | 327 | 34,545 | | 311 | | |
| **New Hampshire** | | | | | | | | | | | | | | | | |
| Under 18 | 4 | 0 | 17 | 145 | 0 | 5 | 24 | 198 | | 54 | 0 | 793 | | 2 | 181 | 1,204,875 |
| Total, all ages | 191 | 1 | 115 | 3,594 | 1 | 135 | 3,596 | 1,491 | | 732 | 98 | 14,268 | | 2 | | |
| **New Jersey[5]** | | | | | | | | | | | | | | | | |
| Under 18 | 101 | 1 | 2 | 33 | 0 | 0 | 6 | 2 | | 30 | 0 | 90 | | 1 | 64 | 1,650,076 |
| Total, all ages | 825 | 77 | 35 | 1,764 | 2 | 322 | 1,680 | 36 | | 423 | 24 | 3,388 | | 1 | | |
| **New Mexico[5]** | | | | | | | | | | | | | | | | |
| Under 18 | 13 | 0 | 2 | 38 | 0 | 5 | 19 | 18 | | 39 | 0 | 69 | | 0 | 24 | 985,537 |
| Total, all ages | 316 | 12 | 20 | 1,615 | 0 | 650 | 2,414 | 685 | | 673 | 45 | 7,514 | | 0 | | |
| **New York[6]** | | | | | | | | | | | | | | | | |
| Under 18 | 73 | 0 | 41 | 29 | 0 | 0 | 11 | 17 | | 17 | 0 | 196 | | 0 | 93 | 3,453,145 |
| Total, all ages | 829 | 14 | 214 | 3,502 | 7 | 39 | 3,589 | 72 | | 551 | 15 | 10,513 | | 0 | | |
| **North Carolina** | | | | | | | | | | | | | | | | |
| Under 18 | 299 | 0 | 19 | 570 | 0 | 4 | 101 | 55 | | 413 | 0 | 1,434 | | 30 | 312 | 9,268,170 |
| Total, all ages | 4,167 | 83 | 419 | 34,780 | 24 | 2,871 | 13,365 | 1,412 | | 2,957 | 214 | 100,363 | | 30 | | |
| **North Dakota** | | | | | | | | | | | | | | | | |
| Under 18 | 16 | 0 | 24 | 447 | 0 | 210 | 32 | 334 | | 654 | 0 | 905 | | 79 | 100 | 766,153 |
| Total, all ages | 247 | 6 | 86 | 4,120 | 2 | 330 | 4,014 | 2,068 | | 1,300 | 0 | 8,696 | | 79 | | |
| **Ohio** | | | | | | | | | | | | | | | | |
| Under 18 | 346 | 0 | 45 | 590 | 0 | 3 | 49 | 386 | | 1,145 | 0 | 3,928 | | 203 | 356 | 8,743,840 |
| Total, all ages | 5,353 | 337 | 291 | 17,839 | 6 | 412 | 9,891 | 3,305 | | 6,908 | 5 | 35,566 | | 203 | | |
| **Oklahoma** | | | | | | | | | | | | | | | | |
| Under 18 | 161 | 2 | 10 | 655 | 0 | 1 | 53 | 49 | | 363 | 0 | 964 | | 211 | 428 | 3,789,679 |
| Total, all ages | 2,653 | 180 | 131 | 11,357 | 6 | 291 | 8,526 | 645 | | 1,675 | 92 | 21,712 | | 211 | | |
| **Oregon** | | | | | | | | | | | | | | | | |
| Under 18 | 58 | 0 | 53 | 345 | 0 | 1 | 92 | 217 | | 262 | 0 | 538 | | 70 | 149 | 3,867,155 |
| Total, all ages | 2,140 | 213 | 343 | 4,110 | 1 | 191 | 11,527 | 868 | | 4,511 | 12 | 32,473 | | 70 | | |
| **Pennsylvania[5]** | | | | | | | | | | | | | | | | |
| Under 18 | 4 | 0 | 1 | 26 | 0 | 0 | 4 | 8 | | 68 | 0 | 59 | | 7 | 24 | 408,819 |
| Total, all ages | 100 | 1 | 12 | 820 | 1 | 28 | 1,144 | 40 | | 467 | 21 | 1,221 | | 7 | | |
| **Rhode Island** | | | | | | | | | | | | | | | | |
| Under 18 | 80 | 0 | 2 | 78 | 0 | 20 | 9 | 61 | | 259 | 0 | 304 | | 12 | 46 | 1,094,546 |
| Total, all ages | 477 | 4 | 62 | 1,637 | 1 | 91 | 2,799 | 402 | | 1,545 | 0 | 7,420 | | 12 | | |
| **South Carolina** | | | | | | | | | | | | | | | | |
| Under 18 | 425 | 0 | 41 | 987 | 0 | 16 | 25 | 151 | | 476 | 0 | 870 | | 16 | 178 | 4,731,543 |
| Total, all ages | 3,441 | 60 | 259 | 25,233 | 49 | 812 | 7,037 | 3,103 | | 6,472 | 375 | 26,641 | | 16 | | |
| **South Dakota** | | | | | | | | | | | | | | | | |
| Under 18 | 88 | 3 | 13 | 449 | 0 | 220 | 107 | 306 | | 559 | 0 | 843 | | 20 | 61 | 679,305 |
| Total, all ages | 321 | 8 | 41 | 5,402 | 3 | 812 | 6,143 | 1,405 | | 3,390 | 598 | 18,870 | | 20 | | |
| **Tennessee** | | | | | | | | | | | | | | | | |
| Under 18 | 466 | 0 | 98 | 1,792 | 1 | 18 | 100 | 221 | | 918 | 0 | 3,393 | | 387 | 273 | 6,716,048 |
| Total, all ages | 3,486 | 363 | 481 | 41,579 | 39 | 2,129 | 17,916 | 1,928 | | 4,379 | 4 | 106,302 | | 387 | | |
| **Texas** | | | | | | | | | | | | | | | | |
| Under 18 | 1,079 | 5 | 158 | 4,743 | 1 | 111 | 330 | 543 | | 707 | 0 | 8,133 | | 456 | 922 | 28,232,533 |
| Total, all ages | 16,960 | 1,918 | 865 | 83,839 | 152 | 2,140 | 62,233 | 4,992 | | 5,474 | 710 | 166,967 | | 456 | | |
| **Utah** | | | | | | | | | | | | | | | | |
| Under 18 | 80 | 1 | 118 | 1,358 | 0 | 21 | 89 | 403 | | 189 | 0 | 1,585 | | 287 | 105 | 2,934,855 |
| Total, all ages | 798 | 50 | 414 | 13,712 | 0 | 1,457 | 7,491 | 2,426 | | 2,068 | 13 | 27,493 | | 287 | | |
| **Vermont** | | | | | | | | | | | | | | | | |
| Under 18 | 2 | 0 | 3 | 15 | 0 | 4 | 8 | 20 | | 33 | 0 | 51 | | 0 | 78 | 641,185 |
| Total, all ages | 30 | 5 | 24 | 757 | 0 | 160 | 1,346 | 32 | | 445 | 0 | 2,492 | | 0 | | |
| **Virginia** | | | | | | | | | | | | | | | | |
| Under 18 | 248 | 0 | 54 | 308 | 0 | 40 | 56 | 139 | | 54 | 0 | 1,925 | | 243 | 340 | 8,599,971 |
| Total, all ages | 4,474 | 253 | 557 | 14,568 | 12 | 1,118 | 16,624 | 1,152 | | 2,358 | 8 | 84,132 | | 243 | | |
| **Washington** | | | | | | | | | | | | | | | | |
| Under 18 | 123 | 0 | 54 | 94 | 0 | 4 | 118 | 100 | | 54 | 0 | 528 | | 3 | 211 | 7,459,711 |
| Total, all ages | 1,438 | 133 | 409 | 1,921 | 2 | 127 | 20,399 | 439 | | 1,432 | 148 | 35,784 | | 3 | | |
| **West Virginia** | | | | | | | | | | | | | | | | |
| Under 18 | 6 | 0 | 3 | 57 | 0 | 0 | 6 | 7 | | 15 | 0 | 103 | | 0 | 122 | 1,210,067 |
| Total, all ages | 315 | 40 | 54 | 5,943 | 0 | 143 | 2,213 | 186 | | 545 | 17 | 8,974 | | 0 | | |
| **Wisconsin** | | | | | | | | | | | | | | | | |
| Under 18 | 322 | 3 | 288 | 1,613 | 0 | 172 | 144 | 912 | | 3,900 | 0 | 5,559 | | 761 | 267 | 5,238,884 |
| Total, all ages | 3,227 | 231 | 878 | 19,456 | 1 | 1,399 | 17,052 | 5,087 | | 20,713 | 207 | 45,232 | | 761 | | |
| **Wyoming** | | | | | | | | | | | | | | | | |
| Under 18 | 12 | 0 | 4 | 247 | 0 | 7 | 12 | 248 | | 112 | 0 | 475 | | 62 | 44 | 427,908 |
| Total, all ages | 40 | 4 | 26 | 2,460 | 0 | 81 | 1,969 | 890 | | 668 | 3 | 3,440 | | 62 | | |

NOTE: Because the number of agencies submitting arrest data varies from year to year, users are cautioned about making direct comparisons between 2021 arrest totals and those published in previous years' editions of Crime in the United States. Further, arrest figures may vary widely from state to state because some Part II crimes are not considered crimes in some states.
1 Does not include traffic arrests.   2 Violent crimes in this table are offenses of murder and nonnegligent manslaughter, rape, robbery, and aggravated assault. Property crimes are offenses of burglary, larceny-theft, motor vehicle theft, and arson.   3 Drunkenness was previously reported as a separate offense in NIBRS; however, starting in 2021, it is included with All Other Offenses (except traffic).   4 The offense of suspicion was previously collected in the Summary Reporting System; however, it is not collected in NIBRS.   5 Limited data for 2021 were available for California, the District of Columbia, Florida, Illinois, Maryland, New Jersey, New Mexico, New York, and Pennsylvania.   6 Includes arrests reported by the Metro Transit Police. This agency has no population associated with it.   7 Includes arrests reported by the Miccosukee and Seminole Tribes. These agencies have no population associated with them.

# SECTION V

# LAW ENFORCEMENT PERSONNEL

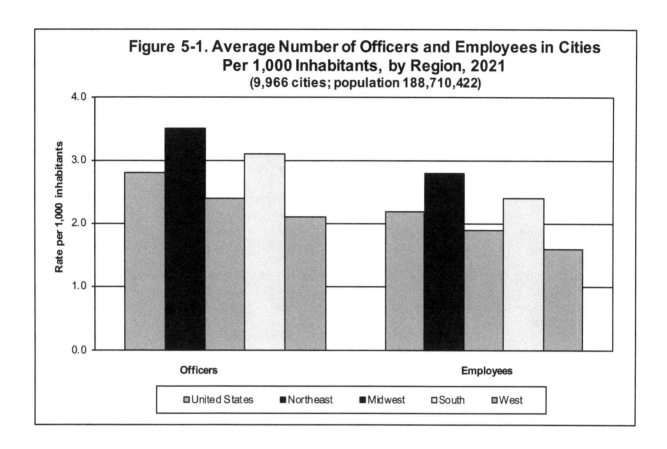

The Uniform Crime Reporting (UCR) program defines law enforcement officers as individuals who ordinarily carry a firearm and a badge, have full arrest powers, and are paid from government funds set aside specifically for sworn law enforcement representatives. Because of law enforcement's varied service requirements and functions, as well as the distinct demographic traits and characteristics of jurisdictions, readers should use caution when comparing staffing levels between agencies based on police employment data from the UCR program. In addition, the data presented here reflect existing staff levels and should not be interpreted as preferred officer strengths recommended by the Federal Bureau of Investigation (FBI). Also, readers should note that the totals given for sworn officers for any particular agency reflect both patrol officers on the street and officers assigned to various other duties, such as administrative and investigative positions and assignments to special teams.

Each year, law enforcement agencies across the United States report the total number of sworn law enforcement officers and civilians in their agencies as of October 31 to the UCR program. Civilian employees include personnel such as clerks, radio dispatchers, meter attendants, stenographers, jailers,

correctional officers, and mechanics, (provided that they are full-time employees of the agency).

Due to the varied service requirements and functions of law enforcement and the distinctive demographic traits and characteristics of each jurisdiction, caution should be exercised when comparing agencies' staffing levels based on the UCR Program's police employment data. The data presented here reflect existing staffing levels in locations reporting data and should not be interpreted as FBI-preferred or FBI-recommended officer strengths. The total number of sworn officers for any particular agency reflects patrol officers on the street and officers assigned to other duties, such as those in administrative, investigative, and special-teams roles. Care should also be taken with year-over-year and other timeline comparisons, as different numbers of agencies report data each year, and this has been compounded for 2021 by the FBI's data migration to its Crime Data Explorer.

This section of *Crime in the United States* presents those data as the number and rate of law enforcement officers and civilian employees throughout the United States. In 2021, among agencies reporting data, 660,288 sworn officers and 294,261 civilians provided law enforcement services to more than 282 million people nationwide. These law enforcement personnel were employed by 12,864 state, city, university/college, metropolitan/nonmetropolitan county, and other designated law enforcement agencies. Of the slightly more than 950,000 law enforcement employees, 72.2 percent were male. (Table 74)

The data in this section are broken down by geographic region and division, population group, state, city, university/college, metropolitan/nonmetropolitan county, and other law enforcement agency groups. (Information about geographic regions and divisions and population groups can be found in Appendix III.) UCR program staff compute the rate of sworn officers and law enforcement employees by taking the number of employees (sworn officers only or in combination with civilians), dividing by the population for which the agency provides law enforcement service, and multiplying by 1,000.

• Tables 70 and 71 present the number and rate of law enforcement personnel per 1,000 inhabitants collectively employed by agencies, broken down by geographic region and division by population group

• Tables 72 and 73 provide a count of law enforcement agencies by population group, based on the employment rate ranges for sworn officer and civilian employees per 1,000 inhabitants

• Table 74 provides the number of total officers, the percentage of male and female sworn officers, and the civilian employees by population group

• Table 75 lists the percentage of full-time civilian law enforcement employees by population group

• Table 76 breaks down by state the number of sworn law enforcement officers and civilians employed by state law enforcement agencies

• Table 77 provides the number of total officers, the percentage of male and female sworn officers, and the civilian employees by state

• Tables 78 to 80 list the number of law enforcement employees for cities, universities and colleges, and metropolitan and nonmetropolitan counties

• Table 81 supplies employee data for those law enforcement agencies that serve selected transit systems, parks and forests, schools and school districts, hospitals, etc., in the nation

The demographic traits and characteristics of a jurisdiction affect its requirements for law enforcement service. For instance, a village between two large cities may require more law enforcement than a community of the same size with no urban center nearby. A town with legal gambling may have different law enforcement needs than a town near a military base. A city largely made up of college students may have different law enforcement needs than a city whose residents are mainly retirees.

Similarly, the functions of law enforcement agencies are diverse. Employees of these agencies patrol local streets and major highways, protect citizens in the nation's smallest towns and largest cities, and conduct investigations on offenses at the local and state levels. State police in one area may enforce traffic laws on state highways and interstates; in another area, they may be responsible for investigating violent crimes. Sheriff's departments may collect tax monies, serve as the enforcement authority for local and state courts, administer jail facilities, or carry out some combination of these duties. This has an impact on an agency's staffing levels.

Because of the differing service requirements and functions, care should be taken when drawing comparisons between and among the staffing levels of law enforcement agencies. The data in this section are not intended as recommended or preferred officer strength; they should be used merely as guides. Adequate staffing levels can be determined only after careful study of the conditions that affect the service requirements in a particular jurisdiction.

### Rate

The UCR program computes these rates by taking the number of employees, dividing by the population of the agency's jurisdiction, and multiplying by 1,000.

An examination of the 2021 law enforcement employee data by population group  showed that the nation's participating cities (9,966 cities; population 188,710,422) had a collective rate of 2.8 law enforcement employees per 1,000 inhabitants. Cities with fewer than 10,000 inhabitants had the highest rate of law enforcement employees, with a rate of 5.7 per 1,000 inhabitants. Cities with 50,000 to 99,999 inhabitants had the lowest rate of law enforcement employees (2.0 per 1,000 in population). The nation's largest cities, those with 250,000 or more inhabitants, averaged 3.1 law enforcement employees for every 1,000 inhabitants. (Table 70)

### Sworn Personnel

An analysis of the 2021 data showed that participating law enforcement agencies (9,966 cities; population 188,710,422) in the cities in the Northeast had the highest rate of sworn officers—2.8 per 1,000 inhabitants, followed by the South (2.4), the Midwest (1.9), and the West (1.6). (Table 71)

By population group in 2021, there were 2.2 sworn officers for each 1,000 resident population. Cities with fewer than 10,000 inhabitants had the highest rate at 4.4 sworn officers per 1,000 inhabitants. The nation's largest cities, those with 250,000 or more inhabitants, averaged 2.3 officers per 1,000 inhabitants. The lowest rates were in cities with 50,000 to 99,999 inhabitants and 100,000 to 249,999 inhabitants (1.6 per 1,000 resident population for each). (Table 71)

Males accounted for 86.7 percent of all full-time sworn law enforcement officers in 2021. Cities with populations of 1 million and over employed the highest percentage (17.9 percent) of full-time female officers. Of the city population groups and subsets, cities with populations of 10,000 to 24,999 inhabitants employed the highest percentage (89.7 percent) of male officers. In metropolitan counties, 85.1 percent of officers were male; in nonmetropolitan counties, 91.5 percent of officers were male; and in suburban areas, 86.5 percent of officers were male. (Table 74) Among states, the District of Columbia and Louisiana had female sworn officer proportions of over 20 percent, while less than 5 percent of West Virginia's sworn officers and less than 6 percent of Kentucky's sworn officers were female. (Table 77)

**Civilian Employees**

Civilian employees provide a myriad of services to the nation's law enforcement and criminal justice agencies. Among other duties, they dispatch officers, provide administrative and record keeping support, and query local, state, and national databases.

In 2021, 30.8 percent of all law enforcement employees in the nation were civilians. Male employees accounted for 39.7 percent of all full-time civilian law enforcement employees in 2021. In cities, civilians made up 22.7 percent of law enforcement agency employees. Civilians made up 40.7 percent of law enforcement employees in metropolitan counties, 41.1 percent of law enforcement employees in nonmetropolitan counties, and 34.2 percent of law enforcement employees in suburban areas. (Table 75) More than half of the civilian employees in Illinois, the District of Columbia, and Indiana were male, while less than 30 percent of the civilian employees in Idaho, Virginia, and Nevada were male. (Table 77)

## Table 70. Full-Time Law Enforcement Employees,[1] by Region and Geographic Division and Population Group, 2021

(Number, rate per 1,000 inhabitants.)

| Region/geographic division | Total (9,966 cities; population 188,710,422) | Group I (79 cities, 250,000 and over; population 55,978,515) | Group II (215 cities, 100,000 to 249,999; population 31,542,073) | Group III (422 cities, 50,000 to 99,999; population 29,512,603) | Group IV (762 cities, 25,000 to 49,999; population 26,303,281) | Group V (1,590 cities, 10,000 to 24,999; population 25,267,743) | Group VI (6,898 cities, under 10,000; population 20,106,207) | Total city agencies | 2021 estimated city population | County[2] (2,898 agencies; population 94,272,796) | Total city and county agencies | 2021 estimated total agency population | Suburban areas[3] (6,804 agencies; population 123,731,502) |
|---|---|---|---|---|---|---|---|---|---|---|---|---|---|
| **Total, United States** | | | | | | | | | | | | | |
| Number of employees | 526,664 | 173,760 | 64,786 | 59,476 | 55,683 | 58,766 | 114,193 | 9,966 | 188,710,422 | 427,885 | 12,864 | 282,983,218 | 457,990 |
| Average number of employees per 1,000 inhabitants | 2.8 | 3.1 | 2.1 | 2.0 | 2.1 | 2.3 | 5.7 | | | 4.5 | | | 3.7 |
| **Northeast** | | | | | | | | | | | | | |
| Number of employees | 146,424 | 57,362 | 8,579 | 14,780 | 17,695 | 17,698 | 30,310 | 2,379 | 41,777,721 | | | | |
| Average number of employees per 1,000 inhabitants | 3.5 | 5.6 | 2.8 | 2.4 | 2.2 | 2.2 | 5.2 | | | | | | |
| New England | | | | | | | | | | | | | |
| Number of employees | 33,252 | 2,716 | 4,461 | 5,672 | 7,131 | 7,000 | 6,272 | 801 | 12,979,783 | | | | |
| Average number of employees per 1,000 inhabitants | 2.6 | 3.9 | 2.8 | 2.3 | 2.2 | 2.3 | 3.5 | | | | | | |
| Middle Atlantic | | | | | | | | | | | | | |
| Number of employees | 113,172 | 54,646 | 4,118 | 9,108 | 10,564 | 10,698 | 24,038 | 1,578 | 28,797,938 | | | | |
| Average number of employees per 1,000 inhabitants | 3.9 | 5.7 | 2.8 | 2.5 | 2.2 | 2.1 | 5.9 | | | | | | |
| **Midwest** | | | | | | | | | | | | | |
| Number of employees | 71,166 | 15,011 | 7,096 | 9,631 | 10,226 | 12,491 | 16,711 | 2,201 | 29,978,054 | | | | |
| Average number of employees per 1,000 inhabitants | 2.4 | 3.1 | 2.0 | 1.8 | 1.9 | 2.1 | 3.6 | | | | | | |
| East North Central | | | | | | | | | | | | | |
| Number of employees | 41,809 | 8,567 | 3,768 | 5,898 | 7,381 | 7,515 | 8,680 | 1,170 | 17,523,636 | | | | |
| Average number of employees per 1,000 inhabitants | 2.4 | 3.5 | 2.0 | 1.9 | 1.9 | 2.1 | 3.4 | | | | | | |
| West North Central | | | | | | | | | | | | | |
| Number of employees | 29,357 | 6,444 | 3,328 | 3,733 | 2,845 | 4,976 | 8,031 | 1,031 | 12,454,418 | | | | |
| Average number of employees per 1,000 inhabitants | 2.4 | 2.8 | 1.9 | 1.6 | 1.8 | 2.1 | 3.7 | | | | | | |
| **South** | | | | | | | | | | | | | |
| Number of employees | 191,872 | 49,560 | 28,934 | 20,356 | 19,134 | 21,658 | 52,230 | 3,992 | 62,433,053 | | | | |
| Average number of employees per 1,000 inhabitants | 3.1 | 2.7 | 2.3 | 2.4 | 2.5 | 2.8 | 7.1 | | | | | | |
| South Atlantic | | | | | | | | | | | | | |
| Number of employees | 85,648 | 19,179 | 13,560 | 11,007 | 10,148 | 9,443 | 22,311 | 1,595 | 25,634,262 | | | | |
| Average number of employees per 1,000 inhabitants | 3.3 | 3.4 | 2.4 | 2.5 | 2.6 | 3.0 | 7.9 | | | | | | |
| East South Central | | | | | | | | | | | | | |
| Number of employees | 35,256 | 6,251 | 5,014 | 2,731 | 4,167 | 4,836 | 12,257 | 957 | 10,284,731 | | | | |
| Average number of employees per 1,000 inhabitants | 3.4 | 2.7 | 2.8 | 2.5 | 2.7 | 2.9 | 6.6 | | | | | | |
| West South Central | | | | | | | | | | | | | |
| Number of employees | 70,968 | 24,130 | 10,360 | 6,618 | 4,819 | 7,379 | 17,662 | 1,440 | 26,514,060 | | | | |
| Average number of employees per 1,000 inhabitants | 2.7 | 2.3 | 2.0 | 2.1 | 2.2 | 2.6 | 6.6 | | | | | | |
| **West** | | | | | | | | | | | | | |
| Number of employees | 117,202 | 51,827 | 20,177 | 14,709 | 8,628 | 6,919 | 14,942 | 1,394 | 54,521,594 | | | | |
| Average number of employees per 1,000 inhabitants | 2.1 | 2.3 | 1.6 | 1.6 | 1.7 | 2.0 | 6.7 | | | | | | |
| Mountain | | | | | | | | | | | | | |
| Number of employees | 44,520 | 19,590 | 6,588 | 4,446 | 3,368 | 2,485 | 8,043 | 625 | 17,965,791 | | | | |
| Average number of employees per 1,000 inhabitants | 2.5 | 2.5 | 1.9 | 1.8 | 1.8 | 2.2 | 6.8 | | | | | | |
| Pacific | | | | | | | | | | | | | |
| Number of employees | 72,682 | 32,237 | 13,589 | 10,263 | 5,260 | 4,434 | 6,899 | 769 | 36,555,803 | | | | |
| Average number of employees per 1,000 inhabitants | 2.0 | 2.3 | 1.5 | 1.5 | 1.6 | 1.9 | 6.4 | | | | | | |

1 Full-time law enforcement employees include civilians.   2 The designation county is a combination of both metropolitan and nonmetropolitan counties.   3 Suburban areas include law enforcement agencies in cities with less than 50,000 inhabitants and county law enforcement agencies that are within a Metropolitan Statistical Area. Suburban areas exclude all metropolitan agencies associated with a principal city. The agencies associated with suburban areas also appear in other groups within this table.

## Table 71. Full-Time Law Enforcement Officers, by Region, Geographic Division, and Population Group, 2021

(Number, rate per 1,000 inhabitants.)

| Region/geographic division | Total (9,966 cities; population 188,710,422) | Group I (79 cities, 250,000 and over; population 55,978,515) | Group II (215 cities, 100,000 to 249,999; population 31,542,073) | Group III (422 cities, 50,000 to 99,999; population 29,512,603) | Group IV (762 cities, 25,000 to 49,999; population 26,303,281) | Group V (1,590 cities, 10,000 to 24,999; population 25,267,743) | Group VI (6,898 cities, under 10,000; population 20,106,207) | Total city agencies | 2021 estimated city population | County[1] (2,898 agencies; population 94,272,796) | Total city and county agencies | 2021 estimated total agency population | Suburban areas[2] (6,804 agencies; population 123,731,502) |
|---|---|---|---|---|---|---|---|---|---|---|---|---|---|
| **Total, United States** | | | | | | | | | | | | | |
| Number of officers | 406,918 | 131,238 | 49,746 | 46,073 | 44,516 | 47,639 | 87,706 | 9,966 | 188,710,422 | 253,370 | 12,864 | 282,983,218 | 301,482 |
| Average number of officers per 1,000 inhabitants | 2.2 | 2.3 | 1.6 | 1.6 | 1.7 | 1.9 | 4.4 | | | 2.7 | | | 2.4 |
| **Northeast** | | | | | | | | | | | | | |
| Number of officers | 115,152 | 40,826 | 7,312 | 12,330 | 14,866 | 15,101 | 24,717 | 2,379 | 41,777,721 | | | | |
| Average number of officers per 1,000 inhabitants | 2.8 | 4.0 | 2.4 | 2.0 | 1.8 | 1.8 | 4.2 | | | | | | |
| New England | | | | | | | | | | | | | |
| Number of officers | 27,332 | 2,184 | 3,849 | 4,831 | 5,923 | 5,634 | 4,911 | 801 | 12,979,783 | | | | |
| Average number of officers per 1,000 inhabitants | 2.1 | 3.1 | 2.4 | 1.9 | 1.8 | 1.8 | 2.7 | | | | | | |
| Middle Atlantic | | | | | | | | | | | | | |
| Number of officers | 87,820 | 38,642 | 3,463 | 7,499 | 8,943 | 9,467 | 19,806 | 1,578 | 28,797,938 | | | | |
| Average number of officers per 1,000 inhabitants | 3.0 | 4.0 | 2.3 | 2.0 | 1.8 | 1.9 | 4.9 | | | | | | |
| **Midwest** | | | | | | | | | | | | | |
| Number of officers | 57,791 | 12,059 | 5,841 | 7,683 | 8,214 | 10,194 | 13,800 | 2,201 | 29,978,054 | | | | |
| Average number of officers per 1,000 inhabitants | 1.9 | 2.5 | 1.6 | 1.4 | 1.5 | 1.7 | 3.0 | | | | | | |
| East North Central | | | | | | | | | | | | | |
| Number of officers | 34,287 | 7,130 | 3,187 | 4,651 | 5,924 | 6,184 | 7,211 | 1,170 | 17,523,636 | | | | |
| Average number of officers per 1,000 inhabitants | 2.0 | 2.9 | 1.7 | 1.5 | 1.5 | 1.7 | 2.9 | | | | | | |
| West North Central | | | | | | | | | | | | | |
| Number of officers | 23,504 | 4,929 | 2,654 | 3,032 | 2,290 | 4,010 | 6,589 | 1,031 | 12,454,418 | | | | |
| Average number of officers per 1,000 inhabitants | 1.9 | 2.1 | 1.5 | 1.3 | 1.4 | 1.7 | 3.1 | | | | | | |
| **South** | | | | | | | | | | | | | |
| Number of officers | 149,409 | 39,909 | 22,244 | 15,673 | 15,151 | 17,131 | 39,301 | 3,992 | 62,433,053 | | | | |
| Average number of officers per 1,000 inhabitants | 2.4 | 2.1 | 1.8 | 1.8 | 2.0 | 2.2 | 5.4 | | | | | | |
| South Atlantic | | | | | | | | | | | | | |
| Number of officers | 67,194 | 15,390 | 10,426 | 8,527 | 8,107 | 7,586 | 17,158 | 1,595 | 25,634,262 | | | | |
| Average number of officers per 1,000 inhabitants | 2.6 | 2.7 | 1.8 | 1.9 | 2.1 | 2.4 | 6.1 | | | | | | |
| East South Central | | | | | | | | | | | | | |
| Number of officers | 27,680 | 5,036 | 4,020 | 2,197 | 3,316 | 3,872 | 9,239 | 957 | 10,284,731 | | | | |
| Average number of officers per 1,000 inhabitants | 2.7 | 2.1 | 2.2 | 2.0 | 2.2 | 2.4 | 5.0 | | | | | | |
| West South Central | | | | | | | | | | | | | |
| Number of officers | 54,535 | 19,483 | 7,798 | 4,949 | 3,728 | 5,673 | 12,904 | 1,440 | 26,514,060 | | | | |
| Average number of officers per 1,000 inhabitants | 2.1 | 1.8 | 1.5 | 1.6 | 1.7 | 2.0 | 4.8 | | | | | | |
| **West** | | | | | | | | | | | | | |
| Number of officers | 84,566 | 38,444 | 14,349 | 10,387 | 6,285 | 5,213 | 9,888 | 1,394 | 54,521,594 | | | | |
| Average number of officers per 1,000 inhabitants | 1.6 | 1.7 | 1.2 | 1.1 | 1.2 | 1.5 | 4.4 | | | | | | |
| Mountain | | | | | | | | | | | | | |
| Number of officers | 31,769 | 14,121 | 4,734 | 3,191 | 2,561 | 1,892 | 5,270 | 625 | 17,965,791 | | | | |
| Average number of officers per 1,000 inhabitants | 1.8 | 1.8 | 1.4 | 1.3 | 1.4 | 1.7 | 4.5 | | | | | | |
| Pacific | | | | | | | | | | | | | |
| Number of officers | 52,797 | 24,323 | 9,615 | 7,196 | 3,724 | 3,321 | 4,618 | 769 | 36,555,803 | | | | |
| Average number of officers per 1,000 inhabitants | 1.4 | 1.7 | 1.1 | 1.1 | 1.2 | 1.4 | 4.3 | | | | | | |

1 The designation county is a combination of both metropolitan and nonmetropolitan counties.    2 Suburban areas include law enforcement agencies in cities with less than 50,000 inhabitants and county law enforcement agencies that are within a Metropolitan Statistical Area. Suburban areas exclude all metropolitan agencies associated with a principal city. The agencies associated with suburban areas also appear in other groups within this table.

## Table 72. Full-Time Law Enforcement Employees,[1] Range in Rate, by Population Group, 2021

(Number; percent.)

| Rate range | Total cities[2] (8,651 cities; population 188,710,422) | Group I (79 cities, 250,000 and over; population 55,978,515) | Group II (215 cities, 100,000 to 249,999; population 31,542,073) | Group III (422 cities, 50,000 to 99,999; population 29,512,603) | Group IV (762 cities, 25,000 to 49,999; population 26,303,281) | Group V (1,590 cities, 10,000 to 24,999; population 25,267,743) | Group VI (5,583 cities, under 10,000; population 20,106,207) |
|---|---|---|---|---|---|---|---|
| **Total Cities** | | | | | | | |
| Number | 8,651 | 79 | 215 | 422 | 762 | 1,590 | 5,583 |
| Percent[3] | 100.0 | 100.0 | 100.0 | 100.0 | 100.0 | 100.0 | 100.0 |
| **0.1–0.5** | | | | | | | |
| Number | 77 | 0 | 0 | 0 | 2 | 2 | 73 |
| Percent | 0.9 | 0.0 | 0.0 | 0.0 | 0.3 | 0.1 | 1.3 |
| **0.6–1.0** | | | | | | | |
| Number | 377 | 1 | 1 | 12 | 26 | 39 | 298 |
| Percent | 4.4 | 1.3 | 0.5 | 2.8 | 3.4 | 2.5 | 5.3 |
| **1.1–1.5** | | | | | | | |
| Number | 1,112 | 4 | 58 | 101 | 148 | 217 | 584 |
| Percent | 12.9 | 5.1 | 27.0 | 23.9 | 19.4 | 13.6 | 10.5 |
| **1.6–2.0** | | | | | | | |
| Number | 1,699 | 25 | 58 | 121 | 212 | 386 | 897 |
| Percent | 19.6 | 31.6 | 27.0 | 28.7 | 27.8 | 24.3 | 16.1 |
| **2.1–2.5** | | | | | | | |
| Number | 1,627 | 22 | 58 | 116 | 198 | 391 | 842 |
| Percent | 18.8 | 27.8 | 27.0 | 27.5 | 26.0 | 24.6 | 15.1 |
| **2.6–3.0** | | | | | | | |
| Number | 1,193 | 8 | 24 | 43 | 93 | 285 | 740 |
| Percent | 13.8 | 10.1 | 11.2 | 10.2 | 12.2 | 17.9 | 13.3 |
| **3.1–3.5** | | | | | | | |
| Number | 755 | 7 | 11 | 15 | 55 | 135 | 532 |
| Percent | 8.7 | 8.9 | 5.1 | 3.6 | 7.2 | 8.5 | 9.5 |
| **3.6–4.0** | | | | | | | |
| Number | 509 | 4 | 4 | 9 | 15 | 64 | 413 |
| Percent | 5.9 | 5.1 | 1.9 | 2.1 | 2.0 | 4.0 | 7.4 |
| **4.1–4.5** | | | | | | | |
| Number | 359 | 2 | 0 | 1 | 6 | 39 | 311 |
| Percent | 4.1 | 2.5 | 0.0 | 0.2 | 0.8 | 2.5 | 5.6 |
| **4.6–5.0** | | | | | | | |
| Number | 215 | 2 | 1 | 2 | 1 | 14 | 195 |
| Percent | 2.5 | 2.5 | 0.5 | 0.5 | 0.1 | 0.9 | 3.5 |
| **5.1 and over** | | | | | | | |
| Number | 728 | 4 | 0 | 2 | 6 | 18 | 698 |
| Percent | 8.4 | 5.1 | 0.0 | 0.5 | 0.8 | 1.1 | 12.5 |

1 Full-time law enforcement employees include civilians.   2 The number of agencies used to compile these figures differs from other tables that include data about law enforcement employees because agencies with no resident population are excluded from this table. Agencies not included in this table are associated with universities and colleges (see Table 79) and other agencies (see Table 81), as well as some state agencies that have concurrent jurisdiction with other local law enforcement.   3 Because of rounding, the percentages may not sum to 100.

## Table 73. Full-Time Law Enforcement Officers, Range in Rate, by Population Group, 2021

(Number, rate per 1,000 inhabitants.)

| Rate range | Total cities[1] (8,651 cities; population 188,710,422) | Group I (79 cities, 250,000 and over; population 55,978,515) | Group II (215 cities, 100,000 to 249,999; population 31,542,073) | Group III (422 cities, 50,000 to 99,999; population 29,512,603) | Group IV (762 cities, 25,000 to 49,999; population 26,303,281) | Group V (1,590 cities, 10,000 to 24,999; population 25,267,743) | Group VI (5,583 cities, under 10,000; population 20,106,207) |
|---|---|---|---|---|---|---|---|
| **Total Cities** | | | | | | | |
| Number | 8,651 | 79 | 215 | 422 | 762 | 1,590 | 5,583 |
| Percent[2] | 100.0 | 100.0 | 100.0 | 100.0 | 100.0 | 100.0 | 100.0 |
| **0.1–0.5** | | | | | | | |
| Number | 85 | 0 | 0 | 1 | 3 | 4 | 77 |
| Percent | 1.0 | 0.0 | 0.0 | 0.2 | 0.4 | 0.3 | 1.4 |
| **0.6–1.0** | | | | | | | |
| Number | 643 | 2 | 42 | 82 | 88 | 79 | 350 |
| Percent | 7.4 | 2.5 | 19.5 | 19.4 | 11.5 | 5.0 | 6.3 |
| **1.1–1.5** | | | | | | | |
| Number | 1,667 | 24 | 79 | 138 | 247 | 412 | 767 |
| Percent | 19.3 | 30.4 | 36.7 | 32.7 | 32.4 | 25.9 | 13.7 |
| **1.6–2.0** | | | | | | | |
| Number | 2,127 | 27 | 57 | 130 | 242 | 537 | 1,134 |
| Percent | 24.6 | 34.2 | 26.5 | 30.8 | 31.8 | 33.8 | 20.3 |
| **2.1–2.5** | | | | | | | |
| Number | 1,481 | 9 | 23 | 53 | 119 | 338 | 939 |
| Percent | 17.1 | 11.4 | 10.7 | 12.6 | 15.6 | 21.3 | 16.8 |
| **2.6–3.0** | | | | | | | |
| Number | 896 | 6 | 10 | 11 | 46 | 130 | 693 |
| Percent | 10.4 | 7.6 | 4.7 | 2.6 | 6.0 | 8.2 | 12.4 |
| **3.1–3.5** | | | | | | | |
| Number | 554 | 5 | 3 | 4 | 9 | 46 | 487 |
| Percent | 6.4 | 6.3 | 1.4 | 0.9 | 1.2 | 2.9 | 8.7 |
| **3.6–4.0** | | | | | | | |
| Number | 379 | 4 | 1 | 0 | 5 | 30 | 339 |
| Percent | 4.4 | 5.1 | 0.5 | 0.0 | 0.7 | 1.9 | 6.1 |
| **4.1–4.5** | | | | | | | |
| Number | 222 | 1 | 0 | 1 | 0 | 9 | 211 |
| Percent | 2.6 | 1.3 | 0.0 | 0.2 | 0.0 | 0.6 | 3.8 |
| **4.6–5.0** | | | | | | | |
| Number | 132 | 0 | 0 | 2 | 1 | 1 | 128 |
| Percent | 1.5 | 0.0 | 0.0 | 0.5 | 0.1 | 0.1 | 2.3 |
| **5.1 and over** | | | | | | | |
| Number | 465 | 1 | 0 | 0 | 2 | 4 | 458 |
| Percent | 5.4 | 1.3 | 0.0 | 0.0 | 0.3 | 0.3 | 8.2 |

1 The number of agencies used to compile these figures differs from other tables that include data about law enforcement officers because agencies with no resident population are excluded from this table. Agencies not included in this table are associated with universities and colleges (see Table 79) and other agencies (see Table 81), as well as some state agencies that have concurrent jurisdiction with other local law enforcement.    2 Because of rounding, the percentages may not sum to 100.

## Table 74. Full-Time Law Enforcement Employees, by Population Group, Percent Male and Female, 2021

(Number, percent.)

| Population group | Total law enforcement employees (number) | Law enforcement employees (percent) | | Total officers (number) | Officers (percent) | | Civilians (number) Total civilians | Civilians (percent) | | Agencies (number) | Population, 2021, estimated |
|---|---|---|---|---|---|---|---|---|---|---|---|
| | | Male | Female | | Male | Female | | Male | Female | | |
| **Total Agencies** | 954,549 | 72.2 | 27.8 | 660,288 | 86.7 | 13.3 | 294,261 | 39.7 | 60.3 | 12,864 | 282,983,218 |
| **Total Cities** | 526,664 | 74.4 | 25.6 | 406,918 | 86.6 | 13.4 | 119,746 | 32.9 | 67.1 | 9,966 | 188,710,422 |
| Group I  (250,000 and over) | 173,760 | 71.0 | 29.0 | 131,238 | 83.0 | 17.0 | 42,522 | 33.9 | 66.1 | 79 | 55,978,515 |
| 1,000,000 and over (Group I subset) | 90,824 | 69.5 | 30.5 | 66,710 | 82.1 | 17.9 | 24,114 | 34.6 | 65.4 | 10 | 24,539,177 |
| 500,000 to 999,999 (Group I subset) | 47,138 | 73.2 | 26.8 | 36,876 | 83.8 | 16.2 | 10,262 | 35.1 | 64.9 | 24 | 16,260,880 |
| 250,000 to 499,999 (Group I subset) | 35,798 | 71.8 | 28.2 | 27,652 | 84.1 | 15.9 | 8,146 | 30.0 | 70.0 | 45 | 15,178,458 |
| Group II (100,000 to 249,999) | 64,786 | 73.3 | 26.7 | 49,746 | 86.9 | 13.1 | 15,040 | 28.1 | 71.9 | 215 | 31,542,073 |
| Group III (50,000 to 99,999) | 59,476 | 74.4 | 25.6 | 46,073 | 87.5 | 12.5 | 13,403 | 29.6 | 70.4 | 422 | 29,512,603 |
| Group IV (25,000 to 49,999) | 55,683 | 76.6 | 23.4 | 44,516 | 88.9 | 11.1 | 11,167 | 27.9 | 72.1 | 762 | 26,303,281 |
| Group V (10,000 to 24,999) | 58,766 | 77.8 | 22.2 | 47,639 | 89.7 | 10.3 | 11,127 | 27.1 | 72.9 | 1,590 | 25,267,743 |
| Group VI (under 10,000) | 114,193 | 77.2 | 22.8 | 87,706 | 88.2 | 11.8 | 26,487 | 40.5 | 59.5 | 6,898 | 20,106,207 |
| **Metropolitan Counties** | 304,283 | 68.9 | 31.1 | 180,583 | 85.1 | 14.9 | 123,700 | 45.2 | 54.8 | 1,173 | 72,179,969 |
| **Nonmetropolitan Counties** | 123,602 | 71.2 | 28.8 | 72,787 | 91.5 | 8.5 | 50,815 | 42.1 | 57.9 | 1,725 | 22,092,827 |
| **Suburban Areas**[1] | 457,990 | 71.8 | 28.2 | 301,482 | 86.5 | 13.5 | 156,508 | 43.4 | 56.6 | 6,804 | 123,731,502 |

1 Suburban areas include law enforcement agencies in cities with less than 50,000 inhabitants and county law enforcement agencies that are within a Metropolitan Statistical Area. Suburban areas exclude all metropolitan agencies associated with a principal city. The agencies associated with suburban areas also appear in other groups within this table.

## Table 75. Full-Time Civilian Law Enforcement Employees, by Population Group, 2021

(Number, percent.)

| Population group | Civilian employees (percent) | Agencies (number) | Population, 2021, estimated |
|---|---|---|---|
| **Total Agencies** | 30.8 | 12,864 | 282,983,218 |
| **Total Cities** | 22.7 | 9,966 | 188,710,422 |
| Group I  (250,000 and over) | 24.5 | 79 | 55,978,515 |
| 1,000,000 and over (Group I subset) | 26.6 | 10 | 24,539,177 |
| 500,000 to 999,999 (Group I subset) | 21.8 | 24 | 16,260,880 |
| 250,000 to 499,999 (Group I subset) | 22.8 | 45 | 15,178,458 |
| Group II (100,000 to 249,999) | 23.2 | 215 | 31,542,073 |
| Group III (50,000 to 99,999) | 22.5 | 422 | 29,512,603 |
| Group IV (25,000 to 49,999) | 20.1 | 762 | 26,303,281 |
| Group V (10,000 to 24,999) | 18.9 | 1,590 | 25,267,743 |
| Group VI (under 10,000) | 23.2 | 6,898 | 20,106,207 |
| **Metropolitan Counties** | 40.7 | 1,173 | 72,179,969 |
| **Nonmetropolitan Counties** | 41.1 | 1,725 | 22,092,827 |
| **Suburban Areas**[1] | 34.2 | 6,804 | 123,731,502 |

[1]Suburban areas include law enforcement agencies in cities with less than 50,000 inhabitants and county law enforcement agencies that are within a Metropolitan Statistical Area. Suburban areas exclude all metropolitan agencies associated with a principal city. The agencies associated with suburban areas also appear in other groups within this table.

## Table 76. Full-Time State Law Enforcement Employees, by Selected State, 2021

(Number.)

| State/agency | Law enforcement employees | Officers | | Civilians | |
|---|---|---|---|---|---|
| | | Male | Female | Male | Female |
| **Alabama** | | | | | |
| Other state agencies | 1,717 | 1,032 | 46 | 157 | 482 |
| **Alaska** | | | | | |
| State Troopers | 566 | 344 | 23 | 80 | 119 |
| **Arizona** | | | | | |
| Department of Public Safety | 1,892 | 1,061 | 41 | 345 | 445 |
| **Arkansas** | | | | | |
| State Patrol | 911 | 509 | 24 | 114 | 264 |
| Other state agencies | 40 | 29 | 2 | 0 | 9 |
| **California** | | | | | |
| Highway Patrol | 9,870 | 6,316 | 420 | 1,325 | 1,809 |
| Other state agencies | 1,436 | 1,127 | 205 | 32 | 72 |
| **Colorado** | | | | | |
| State Patrol | 1,100 | 680 | 57 | 148 | 215 |
| Other state agencies | 408 | 72 | 13 | 103 | 220 |
| **Connecticut** | | | | | |
| State Police | 1,054 | 782 | 103 | 64 | 105 |
| Other state agencies | 151 | 109 | 17 | 16 | 9 |
| **Delaware** | | | | | |
| State Police | 988 | 655 | 100 | 83 | 150 |
| Other state agencies | 827 | 249 | 35 | 170 | 373 |
| **Florida** | | | | | |
| Highway Patrol | 2,213 | 1,623 | 172 | 131 | 287 |
| Other state agencies | 3,343 | 1,470 | 248 | 574 | 1,051 |
| **Georgia** | | | | | |
| Department of Public Safety | 1,482 | 992 | 30 | 200 | 260 |
| Other state agencies | 1,366 | 429 | 112 | 209 | 616 |
| **Idaho** | | | | | |
| State Police | 528 | 274 | 17 | 72 | 165 |
| **Illinois** | | | | | |
| State Police | 2,891 | 1,632 | 179 | 458 | 622 |
| Other state agencies | 29 | 21 | 8 | 0 | 0 |
| **Indiana** | | | | | |
| State Police | 1,702 | 1,135 | 66 | 209 | 292 |
| **Iowa** | | | | | |
| Department of Public Safety | 839 | 503 | 33 | 141 | 162 |
| **Kansas** | | | | | |
| Highway Patrol | 492 | 351 | 17 | 54 | 70 |
| Other state agencies | 307 | 244 | 16 | 18 | 29 |
| **Kentucky** | | | | | |
| State Police | 1,698 | 889 | 23 | 350 | 436 |
| Other state agencies | 194 | 176 | 9 | 1 | 8 |
| **Louisiana**[1] | | | | | |
| Other state agencies | 3 | 2 | 0 | 0 | 1 |
| **Maine** | | | | | |
| State Police | 465 | 280 | 31 | 64 | 90 |
| Other state agencies | 61 | 18 | 1 | 31 | 11 |
| **Maryland** | | | | | |
| State Police | 2,196 | 1,355 | 113 | 381 | 347 |
| Other state agencies | 1,458 | 914 | 137 | 179 | 228 |
| **Massachusetts** | | | | | |
| State Police | 2,771 | 2,076 | 129 | 209 | 357 |
| **Michigan** | | | | | |
| State Police | 2,982 | 1,747 | 179 | 419 | 637 |
| Other state agencies | 246 | 181 | 19 | 21 | 25 |
| **Minnesota** | | | | | |
| State Police | 678 | 499 | 57 | 39 | 83 |
| Other state agencies | 285 | 181 | 22 | 52 | 30 |
| **Mississippi** | | | | | |
| Highway Safety Patrol | 768 | 394 | 10 | 83 | 281 |

## Table 76. Full-Time State Law Enforcement Employees, by Selected State, 2021—Continued

(Number.)

| State/agency | Law enforcement employees | Officers | | Civilians | |
|---|---|---|---|---|---|
| | | Male | Female | Male | Female |
| **Missouri** | | | | | |
| State Highway Patrol | 2,313 | 1,154 | 58 | 514 | 587 |
| Other state agencies | 416 | 249 | 28 | 102 | 37 |
| **Montana** | | | | | |
| Highway Patrol | 308 | 226 | 19 | 23 | 40 |
| Other state agencies | 35 | 14 | 1 | 8 | 12 |
| **Nebraska** | | | | | |
| State Patrol | 775 | 466 | 34 | 90 | 185 |
| Other state agencies | 9 | 8 | 0 | 1 | 0 |
| **Nevada** | | | | | |
| Highway Patrol | 702 | 531 | 47 | 73 | 51 |
| Other state agencies | 470 | 129 | 29 | 110 | 202 |
| **New Hampshire** | | | | | |
| State Police | 517 | 308 | 30 | 67 | 112 |
| Other state agencies | 31 | 12 | 5 | 5 | 9 |
| **New Jersey** | | | | | |
| State Police | 4,126 | 2,770 | 161 | 565 | 630 |
| Other state agencies | 8,082 | 5,125 | 1,021 | 953 | 983 |
| Port Authority of New York and New Jersey[2] | 2,286 | 1,844 | 239 | 94 | 109 |
| **New Mexico[1]** | | | | | |
| State Police | | | | | |
| **New York** | | | | | |
| State Police | 5,540 | 4,261 | 558 | 269 | 452 |
| Other state agencies | 229 | 179 | 22 | 11 | 17 |
| **North Carolina** | | | | | |
| Highway Patrol | 2,108 | 1,573 | 53 | 262 | 220 |
| Other state agencies | 1,188 | 703 | 148 | 152 | 185 |
| **North Dakota** | | | | | |
| Highway Patrol | 189 | 148 | 7 | 10 | 24 |
| Other state agencies | 55 | 48 | 7 | 0 | 0 |
| **Ohio** | | | | | |
| State Highway Patrol | 2,312 | 1,333 | 120 | 415 | 444 |
| Other state agencies | 317 | 261 | 36 | 4 | 16 |
| **Oklahoma** | | | | | |
| Highway Patrol | 1,377 | 750 | 15 | 279 | 333 |
| Other state agencies | 550 | 218 | 31 | 113 | 188 |
| **Oregon** | | | | | |
| State Police | 1,186 | 625 | 55 | 163 | 343 |
| Other state agencies | 84 | 49 | 23 | 3 | 9 |
| **Pennsylvania** | | | | | |
| State Police | 6,381 | 4,283 | 329 | 794 | 975 |
| Other state agencies | 422 | 306 | 44 | 44 | 28 |
| **Rhode Island** | | | | | |
| State Police | 280 | 204 | 26 | 25 | 25 |
| Other state agencies | 69 | 50 | 3 | 10 | 6 |
| **South Carolina** | | | | | |
| Highway Patrol | 1,246 | 901 | 60 | 94 | 191 |
| Other State Agency | 258 | 122 | 36 | 42 | 58 |
| **South Dakota** | | | | | |
| Highway Patrol | 277 | 172 | 18 | 52 | 35 |
| Other state agencies | 189 | 49 | 3 | 50 | 87 |
| **Tennessee** | | | | | |
| Department of Safety | 1,657 | 811 | 52 | 214 | 580 |
| Other state agencies | 1,266 | 717 | 218 | 112 | 219 |
| **Texas** | | | | | |
| Department of Public Safety | 10,272 | 3,735 | 315 | 1,978 | 4,244 |
| **Utah** | | | | | |
| Highway Patrol | 581 | 461 | 25 | 26 | 69 |
| Other state agencies | 184 | 153 | 12 | 5 | 14 |
| **Vermont** | | | | | |
| State Police | 329 | 244 | 36 | 15 | 34 |
| Other state agencies | 110 | 78 | 13 | 11 | 8 |

## Table 76. Full-Time State Law Enforcement Employees, by Selected State, 2021—Continued

(Number.)

| State/agency | Law enforcement employees | Officers | | Civilians | |
|---|---|---|---|---|---|
| | | Male | Female | Male | Female |
| **Virginia** | | | | | |
| State Police | 2,665 | 1,752 | 134 | 260 | 519 |
| Other state agencies | 658 | 481 | 62 | 33 | 82 |
| **Washington** | | | | | |
| State Patrol | 1,999 | 843 | 93 | 505 | 558 |
| Other state agencies | 302 | 123 | 25 | 76 | 78 |
| **West Virginia** | | | | | |
| State Police | 604 | 485 | 21 | 18 | 80 |
| Other state agencies | 215 | 163 | 3 | 21 | 28 |
| **Wisconsin**[1] | | | | | |
| Other state agencies | 46 | 31 | 4 | 6 | 5 |
| **Wyoming** | | | | | |
| Highway Patrol | 318 | 171 | 7 | 61 | 79 |
| Other state agencies | 83 | 36 | 1 | 12 | 34 |

NOTE: Caution should be used when comparing data from one state to that of another. The responsibilities of the various state police, highway patrol, and department of public safety agencies range from full law enforcement duties to only traffic patrol, which can impact both the level of employment for agencies as well as the ratio of sworn officers to civilians employed. Any valid comparison must take these factors and the other identified variables affecting crime into consideration.

1 Police employee data were not received from the State Police/Highway Patrol for the state.    2 Data reported are the number of law enforcement employees for the state of New Jersey.

# Table 77. Full-Time Law Enforcement Employees, by State, 2021

(Number.)

| State | Total law enforcement employees | Total officers | | Total civilians | | Total agencies | Population, 2021, estimated |
|---|---|---|---|---|---|---|---|
| | | Male | Female | Male | Female | | |
| Alabama | 18,029 | 11,055 | 1,001 | 2,295 | 3,678 | 397 | 5,024,956 |
| Alaska | 1,948 | 1,181 | 116 | 219 | 432 | 38 | 732,673 |
| Arizona | 22,114 | 11,205 | 1,447 | 4,357 | 5,105 | 111 | 7,219,091 |
| Arkansas | 10,434 | 6,031 | 757 | 1,272 | 2,374 | 301 | 3,021,943 |
| California | 117,584 | 66,808 | 10,813 | 15,053 | 24,910 | 466 | 33,681,412 |
| Colorado | 19,069 | 10,581 | 1,835 | 2,570 | 4,083 | 240 | 5,801,890 |
| Connecticut | 9,041 | 6,624 | 933 | 601 | 883 | 107 | 3,605,597 |
| Delaware | 3,378 | 2,028 | 296 | 381 | 673 | 53 | 999,231 |
| District of Columbia | 5,101 | 3,095 | 930 | 601 | 475 | 2 | 670,050 |
| Florida | 76,233 | 40,198 | 7,795 | 10,506 | 17,734 | 344 | 20,581,447 |
| Georgia | 34,601 | 20,174 | 4,150 | 3,462 | 6,815 | 473 | 9,915,271 |
| Hawaii | 3,637 | 2,485 | 343 | 256 | 553 | 4 | 1,441,553 |
| Idaho | 4,742 | 2,759 | 236 | 397 | 1,350 | 102 | 1,884,072 |
| Illinois | 16,365 | 8,051 | 1,250 | 3,963 | 3,101 | 179 | 3,236,561 |
| Indiana | 6,878 | 4,271 | 335 | 1,177 | 1,095 | 75 | 2,136,079 |
| Iowa | 8,205 | 4,776 | 475 | 1,238 | 1,716 | 225 | 2,982,692 |
| Kansas | 7,941 | 5,050 | 627 | 902 | 1,362 | 309 | 2,104,783 |
| Kentucky | 9,839 | 6,980 | 514 | 906 | 1,439 | 289 | 3,971,950 |
| Louisiana | 12,976 | 7,981 | 2,230 | 886 | 1,879 | 160 | 2,983,699 |
| Maine | 2,954 | 2,146 | 202 | 238 | 368 | 129 | 1,370,436 |
| Maryland | 19,726 | 13,085 | 2,099 | 1,670 | 2,872 | 145 | 6,148,883 |
| Massachusetts | 19,353 | 14,333 | 1,590 | 1,394 | 2,036 | 300 | 6,294,191 |
| Michigan | 24,717 | 15,539 | 2,422 | 3,088 | 3,668 | 538 | 9,663,515 |
| Minnesota | 15,139 | 8,777 | 1,264 | 2,226 | 2,872 | 401 | 5,694,465 |
| Mississippi | 6,931 | 3,960 | 534 | 813 | 1,624 | 137 | 2,064,423 |
| Missouri | 13,540 | 8,399 | 1,067 | 1,612 | 2,462 | 220 | 3,637,629 |
| Montana | 3,391 | 1,873 | 159 | 633 | 726 | 112 | 1,104,271 |
| Nebraska | 5,370 | 3,386 | 412 | 515 | 1,057 | 157 | 1,888,040 |
| Nevada | 10,617 | 6,171 | 965 | 1,015 | 2,466 | 43 | 2,738,311 |
| New Hampshire | 3,763 | 2,571 | 300 | 275 | 617 | 193 | 1,339,962 |
| New Jersey | 49,472 | 33,807 | 4,416 | 4,600 | 6,649 | 529 | 8,882,067 |
| New Mexico | 4,500 | 2,788 | 393 | 462 | 857 | 94 | 1,650,825 |
| New York | 78,031 | 48,873 | 9,515 | 7,211 | 12,432 | 403 | 17,797,949 |
| North Carolina | 33,664 | 20,690 | 3,098 | 4,313 | 5,563 | 513 | 10,533,622 |
| North Dakota | 2,520 | 1,668 | 240 | 191 | 421 | 110 | 773,166 |
| Ohio | 14,765 | 9,681 | 1,241 | 1,447 | 2,396 | 224 | 4,722,587 |
| Oklahoma | 13,253 | 8,205 | 820 | 1,686 | 2,542 | 436 | 3,981,345 |
| Oregon | 10,632 | 5,571 | 715 | 1,967 | 2,379 | 197 | 4,246,155 |
| Pennsylvania | 19,399 | 14,949 | 1,253 | 1,223 | 1,974 | 792 | 6,272,968 |
| Rhode Island | 3,086 | 2,278 | 213 | 247 | 348 | 47 | 1,095,610 |
| South Carolina | 14,511 | 9,078 | 1,564 | 1,339 | 2,530 | 185 | 4,823,991 |
| South Dakota | 3,296 | 1,739 | 196 | 640 | 721 | 137 | 880,991 |
| Tennessee | 27,601 | 15,411 | 2,475 | 4,735 | 4,980 | 452 | 6,971,448 |
| Texas | 95,865 | 50,759 | 8,362 | 15,126 | 21,618 | 973 | 28,550,468 |
| Utah | 7,642 | 4,968 | 478 | 952 | 1,244 | 134 | 3,324,060 |
| Vermont | 1,383 | 969 | 120 | 97 | 197 | 85 | 644,595 |
| Virginia | 23,662 | 15,860 | 2,682 | 1,373 | 3,747 | 272 | 8,489,762 |
| Washington | 15,206 | 9,323 | 1,108 | 1,962 | 2,813 | 252 | 7,705,506 |
| West Virginia | 4,132 | 3,312 | 144 | 258 | 418 | 339 | 1,768,313 |
| Wisconsin | 15,651 | 9,515 | 1,590 | 1,934 | 2,612 | 381 | 5,370,316 |
| Wyoming | 2,662 | 1,372 | 179 | 444 | 667 | 59 | 558,398 |

## Table 78. Full-Time Law Enforcement Employees, by Selected State and City, 2020

(Number.)

| State/city | Population | Total law enforcement employees | Total officers | Total civilians |
|---|---|---|---|---|
| **ALABAMA** | | | | |
| Abbeville | 2,539 | 10 | 9 | 1 |
| Adamsville | 4,185 | 27 | 16 | 11 |
| Addison | 714 | 5 | 4 | 1 |
| Alabaster | 33,963 | 87 | 69 | 18 |
| Albertville | 21,837 | 67 | 45 | 22 |
| Alexander City | 14,066 | 64 | 50 | 14 |
| Aliceville | 2,208 | 7 | 6 | 1 |
| Altoona | 913 | 3 | 3 | 0 |
| Andalusia | 8,643 | 39 | 29 | 10 |
| Anniston | 20,913 | 82 | 76 | 6 |
| Arab | 8,437 | 35 | 26 | 9 |
| Ardmore | 1,548 | 11 | 7 | 4 |
| Argo | 4,306 | 7 | 7 | 0 |
| Arley | 338 | 2 | 2 | 0 |
| Ashford | 2,206 | 6 | 5 | 1 |
| Ashland | 1,857 | 15 | 10 | 5 |
| Ashville | 2,412 | 4 | 4 | 0 |
| Athens | 29,411 | 59 | 48 | 11 |
| Atmore | 8,837 | 37 | 26 | 11 |
| Attalla | 5,804 | 26 | 20 | 6 |
| Auburn | 70,003 | 135 | 127 | 8 |
| Autaugaville | 881 | 3 | 3 | 0 |
| Baker Hill | 227 | 4 | 4 | 0 |
| Bay Minette | 9,647 | 30 | 21 | 9 |
| Bayou La Batre | 2,444 | 18 | 13 | 5 |
| Bear Creek | 1,061 | 3 | 3 | 0 |
| Berry | 1,080 | 4 | 4 | 0 |
| Bessemer | 25,911 | 147 | 103 | 44 |
| Birmingham | 206,476 | 951 | 756 | 195 |
| Blountsville | 1,654 | 5 | 5 | 0 |
| Boaz | 9,731 | 36 | 25 | 11 |
| Brantley | 749 | 5 | 5 | 0 |
| Brent | 4,663 | 7 | 7 | 0 |
| Brewton | 5,116 | 26 | 19 | 7 |
| Bridgeport | 2,258 | 10 | 6 | 4 |
| Brighton | 2,805 | 9 | 5 | 4 |
| Brilliant | 859 | 1 | 1 | 0 |
| Brookside | 1,318 | 17 | 9 | 8 |
| Brookwood | 1,833 | 8 | 8 | 0 |
| Brundidge | 1,855 | 10 | 6 | 4 |
| Butler | 1,670 | 10 | 8 | 2 |
| Calera | 15,654 | 44 | 35 | 9 |
| Camden | 1,667 | 11 | 10 | 1 |
| Camp Hill | 927 | 4 | 4 | 0 |
| Carbon Hill | 1,872 | 11 | 5 | 6 |
| Carrollton | 927 | 3 | 3 | 0 |
| Cedar Bluff | 1,830 | 5 | 5 | 0 |
| Centre | 3,624 | 14 | 13 | 1 |
| Centreville | 2,538 | 5 | 5 | 0 |
| Chatom | 1,157 | 3 | 3 | 0 |
| Cherokee | 994 | 4 | 4 | 0 |
| Chickasaw | 5,618 | 20 | 20 | 0 |
| Childersburg | 4,747 | 14 | 13 | 1 |
| Citronelle | 3,867 | 29 | 13 | 16 |
| Clanton | 8,777 | 30 | 29 | 1 |
| Clayton | 2,814 | 2 | 2 | 0 |
| Cleveland | 1,316 | 2 | 2 | 0 |
| Clio | 1,258 | 5 | 5 | 0 |
| Coaling | 1,631 | 4 | 4 | 0 |
| Collinsville | 1,939 | 8 | 4 | 4 |
| Columbia | 743 | 2 | 2 | 0 |
| Columbiana | 4,738 | 15 | 11 | 4 |
| Coosada | 1,325 | 5 | 5 | 0 |
| Cordova | 1,795 | 6 | 4 | 2 |
| Cottonwood | 1,244 | 3 | 3 | 0 |
| Courtland | 579 | 1 | 1 | 0 |
| Creola | 2,043 | 8 | 7 | 1 |
| Crossville | 1,846 | 5 | 5 | 0 |
| Cuba | 282 | 2 | 2 | 0 |
| Cullman | 16,696 | 58 | 51 | 7 |
| Dadeville | 2,988 | 15 | 14 | 1 |
| Daleville | 5,075 | 21 | 15 | 6 |
| Daphne | 28,387 | 89 | 62 | 27 |
| Dauphin Island | 1,380 | 14 | 8 | 6 |
| Decatur | 54,240 | 137 | 116 | 21 |
| Demopolis | 6,455 | 27 | 23 | 4 |
| Dora | 1,963 | 12 | 7 | 5 |
| Dothan | 69,747 | 224 | 158 | 66 |
| Double Springs | 1,057 | 10 | 8 | 2 |
| Douglas | 784 | 5 | 5 | 0 |
| East Brewton | 2,311 | 9 | 5 | 4 |
| Eclectic | 1,011 | 9 | 9 | 0 |
| Elba | 3,916 | 15 | 7 | 8 |
| Elberta | 1,781 | 12 | 11 | 1 |

## Table 78. Full-Time Law Enforcement Employees, by Selected State and City, 2020—Continued

(Number.)

| State/city | Population | Total law enforcement employees | Total officers | Total civilians |
|---|---|---|---|---|
| Enterprise | 29,240 | 65 | 49 | 16 |
| Eufaula | 11,489 | 43 | 24 | 19 |
| Eutaw | 2,525 | 17 | 12 | 5 |
| Evergreen | 3,422 | 26 | 20 | 6 |
| Excel | 610 | 3 | 3 | 0 |
| Fairfield | 10,397 | 11 | 5 | 6 |
| Fairhope | 24,467 | 67 | 44 | 23 |
| Falkville | 1,253 | 6 | 6 | 0 |
| Fayette | 4,214 | 11 | 11 | 0 |
| Flomaton | 1,371 | 12 | 8 | 4 |
| Florala | 1,882 | 5 | 5 | 0 |
| Florence | 41,325 | 139 | 108 | 31 |
| Foley | 22,166 | 93 | 63 | 30 |
| Fort Deposit | 1,126 | 2 | 2 | 0 |
| Fort Payne | 14,038 | 32 | 27 | 5 |
| Franklin | 502 | 1 | 1 | 0 |
| Frisco City | 1,107 | 3 | 3 | 0 |
| Fultondale | 9,365 | 34 | 27 | 7 |
| Fyffe | 1,078 | 4 | 4 | 0 |
| Gadsden | 34,613 | 118 | 86 | 32 |
| Gantt | 214 | 1 | 1 | 0 |
| Gardendale | 14,128 | 41 | 31 | 10 |
| Geneva | 4,246 | 13 | 10 | 3 |
| Georgiana | 1,601 | 8 | 5 | 3 |
| Geraldine | 895 | 5 | 5 | 0 |
| Gilbertown | 195 | 3 | 2 | 1 |
| Glencoe | 5,074 | 10 | 10 | 0 |
| Goodwater | 1,271 | 8 | 4 | 4 |
| Gordo | 1,580 | 8 | 4 | 4 |
| Gordon | 328 | 1 | 1 | 0 |
| Grant | 904 | 1 | 1 | 0 |
| Greensboro | 2,245 | 9 | 9 | 0 |
| Greenville | 7,280 | 33 | 30 | 3 |
| Grove Hill | 1,688 | 8 | 8 | 0 |
| Guin | 2,238 | 6 | 6 | 0 |
| Gulf Shores | 13,421 | 75 | 52 | 23 |
| Guntersville | 8,720 | 47 | 37 | 10 |
| Gurley | 818 | 5 | 5 | 0 |
| Hackleburg | 1,227 | 2 | 2 | 0 |
| Haleyville | 4,077 | 16 | 11 | 5 |
| Hamilton | 6,621 | 16 | 14 | 2 |
| Hanceville | 3,571 | 24 | 15 | 9 |
| Harpersville | 1,757 | 6 | 6 | 0 |
| Hartford | 2,588 | 15 | 11 | 4 |
| Hartselle | 14,490 | 34 | 33 | 1 |
| Hayden | 1,359 | 3 | 3 | 0 |
| Hayneville | 814 | 3 | 3 | 0 |
| Headland | 4,770 | 27 | 12 | 15 |
| Heflin | 3,400 | 12 | 11 | 1 |
| Helena | 20,756 | 36 | 30 | 6 |
| Henagar | 2,367 | 6 | 6 | 0 |
| Hillsboro | 508 | 2 | 2 | 0 |
| Hokes Bluff | 4,237 | 9 | 7 | 2 |
| Hollywood | 981 | 4 | 3 | 1 |
| Homewood | 25,179 | 104 | 77 | 27 |
| Hoover | 86,514 | 211 | 175 | 36 |
| Hueytown | 15,109 | 52 | 35 | 17 |
| Huntsville | 205,307 | 529 | 435 | 94 |
| Ider | 737 | 7 | 4 | 3 |
| Irondale | 13,285 | 39 | 32 | 7 |
| Jackson | 4,523 | 31 | 24 | 7 |
| Jacksons Gap | 823 | 1 | 1 | 0 |
| Jacksonville | 12,949 | 43 | 33 | 10 |
| Jasper | 13,177 | 23 | 3 | 20 |
| Jemison | 2,700 | 13 | 13 | 0 |
| Killen | 958 | 4 | 4 | 0 |
| Kimberly | 3,688 | 7 | 7 | 0 |
| Kinsey | 2,302 | 2 | 2 | 0 |
| Kinston | 553 | 1 | 1 | 0 |
| LaFayette | 2,858 | 12 | 11 | 1 |
| Lake View | 2,816 | 5 | 4 | 1 |
| Lanett | 6,014 | 31 | 28 | 3 |
| Leeds | 12,050 | 30 | 29 | 1 |
| Leesburg | 1,017 | 4 | 4 | 0 |
| Leighton | 752 | 4 | 3 | 1 |
| Level Plains | 1,944 | 6 | 6 | 0 |
| Lexington | 709 | 4 | 4 | 0 |
| Lincoln | 7,058 | 21 | 19 | 2 |
| Linden | 1,829 | 7 | 7 | 0 |
| Lineville | 2,203 | 10 | 6 | 4 |
| Lipscomb | 2,101 | 9 | 5 | 4 |
| Littleville | 990 | 2 | 2 | 0 |
| Livingston | 3,106 | 9 | 6 | 3 |
| Louisville | 452 | 1 | 1 | 0 |
| Loxley | 3,544 | 24 | 17 | 7 |

## Table 78. Full-Time Law Enforcement Employees, by Selected State and City, 2020—Continued

(Number.)

| State/city | Population | Total law enforcement employees | Total officers | Total civilians |
|---|---|---|---|---|
| Luverne | 2,694 | 14 | 13 | 1 |
| Lynn | 630 | 1 | 1 | 0 |
| Madison | 53,663 | 107 | 79 | 28 |
| Maplesville | 694 | 6 | 6 | 0 |
| Margaret | 5,388 | 8 | 6 | 2 |
| Marion | 2,993 | 7 | 5 | 2 |
| McIntosh | 207 | 9 | 9 | 0 |
| Mentone | 333 | 2 | 2 | 0 |
| Midfield | 4,918 | 17 | 12 | 5 |
| Midland City | 2,396 | 9 | 5 | 4 |
| Millbrook | 16,226 | 48 | 34 | 14 |
| Millport | 963 | 2 | 2 | 0 |
| Mobile | 242,894 | 601 | 459 | 142 |
| Monroeville | 5,544 | 25 | 20 | 5 |
| Montevallo | 7,179 | 21 | 17 | 4 |
| Montgomery | 195,361 | 483 | 438 | 45 |
| Moody | 13,458 | 28 | 27 | 1 |
| Morris | 2,210 | 5 | 5 | 0 |
| Moulton | 3,177 | 11 | 11 | 0 |
| Moundville | 2,504 | 11 | 10 | 1 |
| Mountain Brook | 20,006 | 73 | 60 | 13 |
| Mount Vernon | 1,498 | 13 | 7 | 6 |
| Munford | 1,341 | 2 | 1 | 1 |
| Muscle Shoals | 15,051 | 48 | 38 | 10 |
| Napier Field | 343 | 1 | 1 | 0 |
| New Brockton | 1,301 | 2 | 2 | 0 |
| New Hope | 2,939 | 5 | 5 | 0 |
| New Site | 753 | 2 | 2 | 0 |
| Newton | 1,446 | 4 | 4 | 0 |
| North Courtland | 620 | 1 | 1 | 0 |
| Northport | 26,309 | 68 | 51 | 17 |
| Notasulga | 804 | 8 | 4 | 4 |
| Oakman | 706 | 1 | 1 | 0 |
| Odenville | 3,907 | 14 | 14 | 0 |
| Ohatchee | 1,149 | 5 | 5 | 0 |
| Oneonta | 6,603 | 24 | 23 | 1 |
| Opelika | 31,644 | 115 | 92 | 23 |
| Opp | 6,279 | 26 | 19 | 7 |
| Orange Beach | 6,440 | 88 | 58 | 30 |
| Owens Crossroads | 2,316 | 4 | 4 | 0 |
| Oxford | 21,182 | 82 | 68 | 14 |
| Ozark | 14,065 | 32 | 25 | 7 |
| Parrish | 923 | 2 | 2 | 0 |
| Pelham | 24,516 | 80 | 65 | 15 |
| Pell City | 14,461 | 40 | 37 | 3 |
| Phenix City | 36,744 | 98 | 77 | 21 |
| Phil Campbell | 1,067 | 5 | 1 | 4 |
| Pickensville | 569 | 1 | 1 | 0 |
| Piedmont | 4,436 | 21 | 14 | 7 |
| Pine Hill | 822 | 4 | 4 | 0 |
| Pleasant Grove | 9,528 | 20 | 15 | 5 |
| Powell | 910 | 2 | 2 | 0 |
| Prattville | 36,716 | 97 | 92 | 5 |
| Priceville | 4,137 | 6 | 6 | 0 |
| Prichard | 21,170 | 58 | 38 | 20 |
| Ragland | 1,727 | 4 | 4 | 0 |
| Rainbow City | 9,602 | 38 | 25 | 13 |
| Rainsville | 5,168 | 18 | 12 | 6 |
| Ranburne | 391 | 2 | 1 | 1 |
| Red Bay | 3,103 | 13 | 9 | 4 |
| Red Level | 473 | 2 | 2 | 0 |
| Reform | 1,531 | 5 | 5 | 0 |
| Repton | 252 | 2 | 1 | 1 |
| River Falls | 528 | 2 | 2 | 0 |
| Riverside | 2,393 | 5 | 5 | 0 |
| Roanoke | 5,926 | 28 | 23 | 5 |
| Robertsdale | 7,187 | 28 | 17 | 11 |
| Rogersville | 1,296 | 5 | 5 | 0 |
| Russellville | 9,751 | 25 | 21 | 4 |
| Samson | 1,845 | 7 | 7 | 0 |
| Saraland | 14,764 | 59 | 48 | 11 |
| Sardis City | 1,782 | 3 | 3 | 0 |
| Satsuma | 6,214 | 15 | 12 | 3 |
| Scottsboro | 14,333 | 71 | 44 | 27 |
| Selma | 16,309 | 44 | 26 | 18 |
| Sheffield | 8,820 | 30 | 24 | 6 |
| Shorter | 376 | 10 | 6 | 4 |
| Silverhill | 1,365 | 10 | 9 | 1 |
| Skyline | 834 | 1 | 1 | 0 |
| Slocomb | 1,924 | 10 | 10 | 0 |
| Snead | 837 | 6 | 6 | 0 |
| Somerville | 783 | 2 | 2 | 0 |
| Southside | 9,108 | 16 | 13 | 3 |
| Spanish Fort | 9,765 | 31 | 27 | 4 |
| Steele | 1,099 | 3 | 3 | 0 |

## Table 78. Full-Time Law Enforcement Employees, by Selected State and City, 2020—Continued

(Number.)

| State/city | Population | Total law enforcement employees | Total officers | Total civilians |
|---|---|---|---|---|
| Stevenson | 1,886 | 7 | 4 | 3 |
| St. Florian | 818 | 5 | 5 | 0 |
| Sulligent | 1,826 | 7 | 7 | 0 |
| Sumiton | 2,311 | 16 | 8 | 8 |
| Summerdale | 1,922 | 7 | 6 | 1 |
| Sylacauga | 11,859 | 36 | 34 | 2 |
| Sylvania | 1,863 | 3 | 3 | 0 |
| Talladega | 15,233 | 37 | 33 | 4 |
| Tallassee | 4,434 | 29 | 21 | 8 |
| Tarrant | 6,048 | 43 | 34 | 9 |
| Taylor | 2,449 | 4 | 3 | 1 |
| Thomaston | 379 | 1 | 1 | 0 |
| Thomasville | 3,726 | 27 | 21 | 6 |
| Thorsby | 2,081 | 6 | 6 | 0 |
| Town Creek | 1,040 | 3 | 3 | 0 |
| Trafford | 602 | 8 | 5 | 3 |
| Triana | 1,477 | 3 | 3 | 0 |
| Trinity | 2,477 | 8 | 8 | 0 |
| Troy | 18,822 | 51 | 40 | 11 |
| Trussville | 23,379 | 86 | 71 | 15 |
| Tuscaloosa | 104,151 | 344 | 273 | 71 |
| Tuscumbia | 8,449 | 28 | 21 | 7 |
| Tuskegee | 7,864 | 25 | 14 | 11 |
| Union Springs | 3,308 | 17 | 10 | 7 |
| Uniontown | 2,102 | 3 | 2 | 1 |
| Valley | 9,038 | 29 | 28 | 1 |
| Valley Head | 562 | 2 | 2 | 0 |
| Vance | 1,841 | 6 | 6 | 0 |
| Vernon | 1,828 | 9 | 9 | 0 |
| Vestavia Hills | 34,369 | 108 | 104 | 4 |
| Wadley | 706 | 4 | 4 | 0 |
| Warrior | 3,192 | 23 | 14 | 9 |
| Weaver | 3,027 | 11 | 8 | 3 |
| Wedowee | 800 | 10 | 9 | 1 |
| West Blocton | 1,222 | 1 | 1 | 0 |
| Wetumpka | 8,617 | 32 | 29 | 3 |
| White Hall | 726 | 3 | 1 | 2 |
| Winfield | 4,544 | 13 | 12 | 1 |
| Woodstock | 1,653 | 5 | 5 | 0 |
| York | 2,188 | 6 | 5 | 1 |
| | | | | |
| **ALASKA** | | | | |
| Anchorage | 286,238 | 574 | 413 | 161 |
| Bethel | 6,717 | 31 | 19 | 12 |
| Bristol Bay Borough | 769 | 10 | 4 | 6 |
| Cordova | 2,162 | 8 | 4 | 4 |
| Craig | 1,273 | 10 | 5 | 5 |
| Dillingham | 2,324 | 17 | 7 | 10 |
| Fairbanks | 30,598 | 41 | 36 | 5 |
| Haines | 2,624 | 8 | 4 | 4 |
| Homer | 6,143 | 21 | 11 | 10 |
| Hoonah | 801 | 7 | 4 | 3 |
| Juneau | 31,874 | 86 | 48 | 38 |
| Kenai | 7,970 | 25 | 16 | 9 |
| Ketchikan | 8,198 | 35 | 23 | 12 |
| Klawock | 781 | 2 | 2 | 0 |
| Kodiak | 5,776 | 39 | 16 | 23 |
| Kotzebue | 3,264 | 17 | 15 | 2 |
| Nome | 3,871 | 22 | 11 | 11 |
| North Pole | 2,106 | 15 | 13 | 2 |
| North Slope Borough | 9,310 | 75 | 43 | 32 |
| Palmer | 7,972 | 23 | 14 | 9 |
| Petersburg | 3,302 | 13 | 9 | 4 |
| Sand Point | 1,100 | 5 | 4 | 1 |
| Seldovia | 280 | 1 | 1 | 0 |
| Seward | 2,950 | 19 | 10 | 9 |
| Sitka | 8,353 | 29 | 14 | 15 |
| Skagway | 1,202 | 10 | 4 | 6 |
| Soldotna | 4,855 | 17 | 14 | 3 |
| St. Paul | 486 | 6 | 2 | 4 |
| Unalaska | 4,484 | 24 | 12 | 12 |
| Valdez | 3,842 | 12 | 12 | 0 |
| Wasilla | 11,485 | 28 | 25 | 3 |
| Whittier | 203 | 7 | 7 | 0 |
| Wrangell | 2,522 | 12 | 6 | 6 |
| | | | | |
| **ARIZONA** | | | | |
| Apache Junction | 44,607 | 96 | 65 | 31 |
| Avondale | 91,009 | 184 | 130 | 54 |
| Benson | 4,868 | 22 | 14 | 8 |
| Bisbee | 5,111 | 16 | 10 | 6 |
| Buckeye | 93,218 | 147 | 108 | 39 |
| Bullhead City | 41,958 | 111 | 70 | 41 |
| Camp Verde | 11,299 | 36 | 21 | 15 |
| Casa Grande | 62,566 | 101 | 79 | 22 |

## Table 78. Full-Time Law Enforcement Employees, by Selected State and City, 2020—Continued

(Number.)

| State/city | Population | Total law enforcement employees | Total officers | Total civilians |
|---|---|---|---|---|
| Chandler | 281,162 | 476 | 328 | 148 |
| Chino Valley | 13,039 | 32 | 25 | 7 |
| Clarkdale | 4,577 | 11 | 10 | 1 |
| Clifton | 3,675 | 8 | 3 | 5 |
| Coolidge | 13,973 | 48 | 34 | 14 |
| Cottonwood | 12,935 | 58 | 33 | 25 |
| Douglas | 16,349 | 42 | 29 | 13 |
| Eagar | 4,960 | 7 | 5 | 2 |
| El Mirage | 36,476 | 69 | 52 | 17 |
| Eloy | 17,347 | 40 | 31 | 9 |
| Flagstaff | 74,778 | 169 | 105 | 64 |
| Florence | 28,254 | 38 | 28 | 10 |
| Fredonia | 1,266 | 4 | 4 | 0 |
| Gilbert | 272,941 | 420 | 291 | 129 |
| Glendale | 252,981 | 540 | 409 | 131 |
| Globe | 7,368 | 23 | 19 | 4 |
| Goodyear | 97,081 | 168 | 118 | 50 |
| Hayden | 979 | 5 | 5 | 0 |
| Holbrook | 5,094 | 11 | 10 | 1 |
| Huachuca City | 1,722 | 7 | 4 | 3 |
| Jerome | 460 | 4 | 4 | 0 |
| Kearny | 2,233 | 12 | 7 | 5 |
| Kingman | 32,210 | 66 | 48 | 18 |
| Lake Havasu City | 57,735 | 105 | 72 | 33 |
| Mammoth | 1,740 | 4 | 3 | 1 |
| Marana | 53,347 | 127 | 97 | 30 |
| Maricopa | 55,768 | 81 | 69 | 12 |
| Mesa | 513,713 | 1,278 | 846 | 432 |
| Miami | 1,787 | 10 | 6 | 4 |
| Nogales | 20,039 | 60 | 40 | 20 |
| Oro Valley | 47,282 | 126 | 99 | 27 |
| Page | 7,530 | 30 | 16 | 14 |
| Paradise Valley | 12,895 | 48 | 34 | 14 |
| Parker | 3,304 | 14 | 11 | 3 |
| Payson | 16,011 | 48 | 27 | 21 |
| Peoria | 194,566 | 286 | 189 | 97 |
| Phoenix | 1,638,290 | 3,772 | 2,795 | 977 |
| Pima | 2,611 | 6 | 6 | 0 |
| Pinetop-Lakeside | 4,540 | 16 | 12 | 4 |
| Prescott | 45,391 | 89 | 74 | 15 |
| Prescott Valley | 48,921 | 105 | 74 | 31 |
| Quartzsite | 3,827 | 12 | 11 | 1 |
| Safford | 9,994 | 27 | 24 | 3 |
| Sahuarita | 33,005 | 63 | 51 | 12 |
| Scottsdale | 245,886 | 613 | 375 | 238 |
| Sedona | 10,358 | 43 | 24 | 19 |
| Show Low | 11,670 | 52 | 30 | 22 |
| Sierra Vista | 43,814 | 74 | 58 | 16 |
| Snowflake-Taylor | 10,559 | 15 | 12 | 3 |
| Somerton | 16,976 | 22 | 14 | 8 |
| South Tucson | 5,752 | 17 | 16 | 1 |
| Springerville | 1,987 | 6 | 4 | 2 |
| St. Johns | 3,529 | 11 | 8 | 3 |
| Superior | 3,270 | 15 | 14 | 1 |
| Surprise | 145,832 | 206 | 143 | 63 |
| Tempe | 183,973 | 460 | 326 | 134 |
| Thatcher | 5,310 | 13 | 12 | 1 |
| Tombstone | 1,302 | 11 | 8 | 3 |
| Tucson | 556,297 | 1,059 | 820 | 239 |
| Wellton | 3,187 | 7 | 6 | 1 |
| Wickenburg | 7,614 | 26 | 19 | 7 |
| Willcox | 3,485 | 17 | 9 | 8 |
| Williams | 3,349 | 23 | 13 | 10 |
| Winslow | 9,655 | 40 | 18 | 22 |
| Yuma | 100,710 | 242 | 132 | 110 |
| **ARKANSAS** | | | | |
| Alexander | 3,701 | 10 | 10 | 0 |
| Alma | 5,925 | 18 | 13 | 5 |
| Altus | 727 | 1 | 1 | 0 |
| Amity | 670 | 1 | 1 | 0 |
| Arkadelphia | 10,624 | 29 | 23 | 6 |
| Ashdown | 4,326 | 14 | 12 | 2 |
| Ash Flat | 1,101 | 6 | 6 | 0 |
| Atkins | 3,045 | 9 | 8 | 1 |
| Augusta | 1,900 | 5 | 5 | 0 |
| Austin | 4,874 | 4 | 4 | 0 |
| Bald Knob | 2,864 | 10 | 8 | 2 |
| Barling | 5,103 | 10 | 10 | 0 |
| Batesville | 10,880 | 25 | 24 | 1 |
| Bay | 1,817 | 5 | 5 | 0 |
| Bearden | 839 | 2 | 2 | 0 |
| Beebe | 8,299 | 23 | 18 | 5 |
| Bella Vista | 29,723 | 52 | 36 | 16 |
| Benton | 37,911 | 80 | 71 | 9 |

## Table 78. Full-Time Law Enforcement Employees, by Selected State and City, 2020—Continued

(Number.)

| State/city | Population | Total law enforcement employees | Total officers | Total civilians |
|---|---|---|---|---|
| Bentonville | 60,329 | 115 | 82 | 33 |
| Berryville | 5,537 | 14 | 13 | 1 |
| Blytheville | 13,003 | 54 | 33 | 21 |
| Bono | 2,637 | 4 | 4 | 0 |
| Booneville | 3,744 | 13 | 9 | 4 |
| Bradford | 735 | 3 | 3 | 0 |
| Brinkley | 2,480 | 15 | 7 | 8 |
| Brookland | 4,136 | 6 | 6 | 0 |
| Bryant | 21,902 | 58 | 47 | 11 |
| Bull Shoals | 1,951 | 4 | 4 | 0 |
| Cabot | 26,696 | 57 | 46 | 11 |
| Caddo Valley | 630 | 4 | 4 | 0 |
| Camden | 10,499 | 34 | 16 | 18 |
| Cammack Village | 706 | 5 | 4 | 1 |
| Caraway | 1,289 | 3 | 3 | 0 |
| Carlisle | 2,147 | 8 | 6 | 2 |
| Cave Springs | 6,386 | 11 | 11 | 0 |
| Cedarville | 1,411 | 2 | 2 | 0 |
| Centerton | 18,857 | 25 | 22 | 3 |
| Charleston | 2,499 | 5 | 5 | 0 |
| Cherokee Village | 4,650 | 7 | 6 | 1 |
| Cherry Valley | 565 | 1 | 1 | 0 |
| Clarendon | 1,303 | 4 | 4 | 0 |
| Clarksville | 9,775 | 22 | 19 | 3 |
| Clinton | 2,492 | 8 | 7 | 1 |
| Conway | 69,018 | 171 | 123 | 48 |
| Corning | 2,982 | 7 | 4 | 3 |
| Cotter | 956 | 3 | 3 | 0 |
| Crossett | 4,629 | 26 | 17 | 9 |
| Damascus | 383 | 1 | 1 | 0 |
| Danville | 2,361 | 7 | 6 | 1 |
| Dardanelle | 4,475 | 16 | 11 | 5 |
| Decatur | 1,800 | 7 | 7 | 0 |
| De Queen | 6,387 | 16 | 16 | 0 |
| Dermott | 2,385 | 8 | 4 | 4 |
| Des Arc | 1,553 | 6 | 6 | 0 |
| DeWitt | 2,941 | 12 | 8 | 4 |
| Diamond City | 803 | 1 | 1 | 0 |
| Diaz | 1,197 | 3 | 3 | 0 |
| Dierks | 1,071 | 4 | 4 | 0 |
| Dover | 1,451 | 5 | 5 | 0 |
| Dumas | 3,897 | 18 | 10 | 8 |
| Dyer | 891 | 1 | 1 | 0 |
| Earle | 2,142 | 3 | 3 | 0 |
| El Dorado | 17,263 | 61 | 45 | 16 |
| Elkins | 3,778 | 10 | 10 | 0 |
| England | 2,643 | 12 | 8 | 4 |
| Etowah | 308 | 1 | 1 | 0 |
| Eudora | 1,833 | 5 | 4 | 1 |
| Eureka Springs | 2,085 | 18 | 14 | 4 |
| Fairfield Bay | 2,164 | 17 | 7 | 10 |
| Farmington | 7,748 | 19 | 18 | 1 |
| Fayetteville | 91,309 | 168 | 123 | 45 |
| Flippin | 1,313 | 7 | 7 | 0 |
| Fordyce | 3,527 | 10 | 7 | 3 |
| Forrest City | 13,496 | 28 | 23 | 5 |
| Fort Smith | 87,912 | 184 | 138 | 46 |
| Gassville | 2,183 | 4 | 4 | 0 |
| Gentry | 4,323 | 11 | 9 | 2 |
| Gillett | 690 | 1 | 1 | 0 |
| Glenwood | 2,092 | 4 | 4 | 0 |
| Gosnell | 3,017 | 6 | 6 | 0 |
| Gravette | 3,660 | 15 | 14 | 1 |
| Greenbrier | 5,899 | 15 | 10 | 5 |
| Green Forest | 2,955 | 15 | 12 | 3 |
| Greenland | 1,408 | 4 | 4 | 0 |
| Greenwood | 9,426 | 21 | 20 | 1 |
| Greers Ferry | 857 | 5 | 4 | 1 |
| Gurdon | 2,050 | 6 | 4 | 2 |
| Guy | 796 | 2 | 2 | 0 |
| Hackett | 842 | 1 | 1 | 0 |
| Hamburg | 2,514 | 7 | 6 | 1 |
| Hampton | 1,230 | 4 | 3 | 1 |
| Hardy | 761 | 4 | 4 | 0 |
| Harrisburg | 2,287 | 8 | 6 | 2 |
| Harrison | 13,160 | 43 | 34 | 9 |
| Haskell | 4,700 | 7 | 7 | 0 |
| Hazen | 1,317 | 6 | 6 | 0 |
| Heber Springs | 6,872 | 19 | 18 | 1 |
| Helena-West Helena | 9,820 | 29 | 16 | 13 |
| Higginson | 749 | 1 | 1 | 0 |
| Highfill | 965 | 4 | 4 | 0 |
| Highland | 1,111 | 4 | 4 | 0 |
| Hope | 9,373 | 33 | 22 | 11 |
| Hot Springs | 39,040 | 145 | 109 | 36 |

## Table 78. Full-Time Law Enforcement Employees, by Selected State and City, 2020—Continued

(Number.)

| State/city | Population | Total law enforcement employees | Total officers | Total civilians |
|---|---|---|---|---|
| Hoxie | 2,559 | 4 | 4 | 0 |
| Hughes | 1,178 | 2 | 2 | 0 |
| Huntington | 613 | 1 | 1 | 0 |
| Huntsville | 2,617 | 10 | 8 | 2 |
| Jacksonville | 28,356 | 72 | 59 | 13 |
| Jericho | 98 | 2 | 2 | 0 |
| Johnson | 3,809 | 11 | 10 | 1 |
| Jonesboro | 81,208 | 195 | 166 | 29 |
| Judsonia | 1,989 | 4 | 3 | 1 |
| Kensett | 1,611 | 5 | 4 | 1 |
| Lake City | 2,810 | 4 | 4 | 0 |
| Lakeview | 723 | 2 | 2 | 0 |
| Lake Village | 2,113 | 16 | 10 | 6 |
| Lamar | 1,741 | 3 | 3 | 0 |
| Lavaca | 2,453 | 3 | 3 | 0 |
| Leachville | 1,816 | 5 | 4 | 1 |
| Lead Hill | 268 | 2 | 2 | 0 |
| Lepanto | 1,781 | 8 | 4 | 4 |
| Lewisville | 1,095 | 2 | 2 | 0 |
| Lincoln | 2,492 | 8 | 8 | 0 |
| Little Flock | 2,842 | 9 | 8 | 1 |
| Little Rock | 198,260 | 659 | 534 | 125 |
| Lonoke | 4,152 | 17 | 13 | 4 |
| Lowell | 10,171 | 29 | 23 | 6 |
| Luxora | 991 | 1 | 1 | 0 |
| Magnolia | 11,410 | 25 | 23 | 2 |
| Malvern | 10,805 | 25 | 23 | 2 |
| Mammoth Spring | 938 | 2 | 2 | 0 |
| Mansfield | 1,083 | 4 | 4 | 0 |
| Marianna | 3,219 | 22 | 10 | 12 |
| Marion | 12,266 | 35 | 30 | 5 |
| Marked Tree | 2,366 | 11 | 6 | 5 |
| Marmaduke | 1,262 | 3 | 3 | 0 |
| Marshall | 1,321 | 3 | 3 | 0 |
| Marvell | 860 | 7 | 4 | 3 |
| Maumelle | 18,343 | 42 | 32 | 10 |
| Mayflower | 2,437 | 10 | 9 | 1 |
| McCrory | 1,473 | 5 | 5 | 0 |
| McGehee | 3,545 | 20 | 8 | 12 |
| McRae | 670 | 4 | 1 | 3 |
| Mena | 5,377 | 14 | 13 | 1 |
| Menifee | 323 | 1 | 1 | 0 |
| Mineral Springs | 1,133 | 3 | 3 | 0 |
| Monette | 1,639 | 3 | 3 | 0 |
| Monticello | 9,145 | 29 | 21 | 8 |
| Morrilton | 6,672 | 28 | 25 | 3 |
| Mountainburg | 611 | 1 | 1 | 0 |
| Mountain Home | 12,657 | 41 | 33 | 8 |
| Mountain View | 2,917 | 11 | 10 | 1 |
| Mulberry | 1,699 | 4 | 4 | 0 |
| Murfreesboro | 1,565 | 3 | 3 | 0 |
| Nashville | 4,263 | 17 | 16 | 1 |
| Newport | 7,335 | 25 | 18 | 7 |
| North Little Rock | 66,677 | 200 | 170 | 30 |
| Ola | 1,190 | 4 | 3 | 1 |
| Osceola | 6,472 | 33 | 23 | 10 |
| Ozark | 3,618 | 12 | 10 | 2 |
| Paragould | 29,559 | 55 | 48 | 7 |
| Paris | 3,352 | 13 | 8 | 5 |
| Patterson | 382 | 1 | 1 | 0 |
| Pea Ridge | 6,652 | 14 | 13 | 1 |
| Perryville | 1,438 | 5 | 5 | 0 |
| Piggott | 3,464 | 8 | 8 | 0 |
| Pine Bluff | 39,670 | 124 | 102 | 22 |
| Plumerville | 773 | 1 | 1 | 0 |
| Pocahontas | 6,781 | 18 | 17 | 1 |
| Pottsville | 3,423 | 8 | 6 | 2 |
| Prairie Grove | 7,380 | 16 | 16 | 0 |
| Prescott | 2,892 | 8 | 7 | 1 |
| Quitman | 705 | 4 | 4 | 0 |
| Ravenden | 443 | 1 | 1 | 0 |
| Redfield | 1,513 | 7 | 6 | 1 |
| Rogers | 72,122 | 158 | 114 | 44 |
| Rose Bud | 493 | 4 | 3 | 1 |
| Russellville | 29,465 | 61 | 55 | 6 |
| Salem | 1,657 | 5 | 4 | 1 |
| Searcy | 23,604 | 71 | 53 | 18 |
| Shannon Hills | 4,196 | 4 | 4 | 0 |
| Sheridan | 5,075 | 29 | 15 | 14 |
| Sherwood | 31,857 | 96 | 77 | 19 |
| Siloam Springs | 17,877 | 54 | 39 | 15 |
| Springdale | 85,234 | 201 | 143 | 58 |
| Stamps | 1,446 | 4 | 3 | 1 |
| Star City | 1,989 | 6 | 5 | 1 |
| St. Charles | 210 | 3 | 1 | 2 |

## Table 78. Full-Time Law Enforcement Employees, by Selected State and City, 2020—Continued

(Number.)

| State/city | Population | Total law enforcement employees | Total officers | Total civilians |
|---|---|---|---|---|
| Stuttgart | 8,312 | 37 | 20 | 17 |
| Sulphur Springs | 532 | 13 | 13 | 0 |
| Swifton | 726 | 1 | 1 | 0 |
| Texarkana | 29,516 | 82 | 72 | 10 |
| Trumann | 6,869 | 26 | 18 | 8 |
| Tuckerman | 1,670 | 5 | 5 | 0 |
| Turrell | 543 | 1 | 1 | 0 |
| Tyronza | 707 | 2 | 1 | 1 |
| Van Buren | 23,912 | 63 | 53 | 10 |
| Vilonia | 4,824 | 9 | 9 | 0 |
| Waldron | 3,303 | 10 | 9 | 1 |
| Walnut Ridge | 5,137 | 9 | 9 | 0 |
| Ward | 5,649 | 13 | 12 | 1 |
| Warren | 5,458 | 22 | 14 | 8 |
| Weiner | 657 | 1 | 1 | 0 |
| West Fork | 2,649 | 7 | 6 | 1 |
| West Memphis | 23,959 | 86 | 69 | 17 |
| White Hall | 4,830 | 20 | 18 | 2 |
| Wilson | 793 | 1 | 1 | 0 |
| Wynne | 7,546 | 21 | 19 | 2 |
| **CALIFORNIA** | | | | |
| Alameda | 79,356 | 97 | 67 | 30 |
| Albany | 20,179 | 34 | 25 | 9 |
| Alhambra | 83,278 | 121 | 81 | 40 |
| Alturas | 2,514 | 9 | 8 | 1 |
| Anaheim | 355,301 | 550 | 390 | 160 |
| Anderson | 10,626 | 25 | 19 | 6 |
| Angels Camp | 3,981 | 8 | 7 | 1 |
| Antioch | 112,499 | 155 | 112 | 43 |
| Arcadia | 56,331 | 88 | 62 | 26 |
| Arcata | 18,081 | 33 | 20 | 13 |
| Arroyo Grande | 17,874 | 28 | 25 | 3 |
| Arvin | 22,011 | 27 | 20 | 7 |
| Atascadero | 30,444 | 40 | 27 | 13 |
| Atherton | 7,019 | 30 | 22 | 8 |
| Atwater | 30,470 | 35 | 25 | 10 |
| Auburn | 14,294 | 28 | 20 | 8 |
| Avenal | 13,194 | 20 | 18 | 2 |
| Azusa | 49,518 | 76 | 50 | 26 |
| Bakersfield | 389,632 | 636 | 422 | 214 |
| Baldwin Park | 74,389 | 79 | 56 | 23 |
| Banning | 30,543 | 49 | 32 | 17 |
| Barstow | 23,660 | 54 | 37 | 17 |
| Bear Valley | 120 | 6 | 5 | 1 |
| Beaumont | 53,116 | 63 | 48 | 15 |
| Bell | 34,662 | 39 | 27 | 12 |
| Bell Gardens | 40,846 | 67 | 47 | 20 |
| Belmont | 26,595 | 41 | 30 | 11 |
| Belvedere | 2,102 | 6 | 6 | 0 |
| Benicia | 28,083 | 48 | 29 | 19 |
| Berkeley | 123,754 | 239 | 149 | 90 |
| Beverly Hills | 32,911 | 211 | 125 | 86 |
| Bishop | 3,769 | 20 | 12 | 8 |
| Blythe | 19,588 | 28 | 19 | 9 |
| Brawley | 26,114 | 39 | 26 | 13 |
| Brea | 45,023 | 89 | 60 | 29 |
| Brentwood | 66,507 | 95 | 64 | 31 |
| Brisbane | 4,607 | 19 | 14 | 5 |
| Broadmoor | 4,148 | 18 | 17 | 1 |
| Buena Park | 81,342 | 121 | 83 | 38 |
| Burbank | 101,698 | 230 | 152 | 78 |
| Burlingame | 29,630 | 57 | 37 | 20 |
| Calexico | 39,637 | 38 | 22 | 16 |
| California City | 13,958 | 24 | 14 | 10 |
| Calipatria | 6,704 | 4 | 4 | 0 |
| Calistoga | 5,298 | 17 | 11 | 6 |
| Campbell | 42,608 | 69 | 44 | 25 |
| Capitola | 9,963 | 27 | 21 | 6 |
| Carlsbad | 116,633 | 160 | 123 | 37 |
| Carmel | 3,750 | 20 | 13 | 7 |
| Cathedral City | 56,122 | 64 | 46 | 18 |
| Central Marin | 34,691 | 56 | 42 | 14 |
| Ceres | 48,879 | 65 | 49 | 16 |
| Chico | 104,403 | 140 | 95 | 45 |
| Chino | 93,786 | 167 | 114 | 53 |
| Chowchilla | 18,103 | 31 | 20 | 11 |
| Chula Vista | 275,978 | 253 | 241 | 12 |
| Citrus Heights | 88,155 | 120 | 74 | 46 |
| Claremont | 35,119 | 66 | 41 | 25 |
| Clayton | 11,588 | 12 | 10 | 2 |
| Clearlake | 15,171 | 35 | 22 | 13 |
| Cloverdale | 8,823 | 21 | 13 | 8 |
| Clovis | 120,037 | 164 | 101 | 63 |
| Coalinga | 17,524 | 24 | 15 | 9 |

## Table 78. Full-Time Law Enforcement Employees, by Selected State and City, 2020—Continued

(Number.)

| State/city | Population | Total law enforcement employees | Total officers | Total civilians |
|---|---|---|---|---|
| Colma | 1,717 | 21 | 16 | 5 |
| Colton | 54,911 | 77 | 50 | 27 |
| Colusa | 6,085 | 9 | 9 | 0 |
| Concord | 129,173 | 169 | 131 | 38 |
| Corcoran | 21,524 | 31 | 17 | 14 |
| Corning | 7,621 | 20 | 12 | 8 |
| Corona | 172,922 | 222 | 151 | 71 |
| Coronado | 22,545 | 65 | 45 | 20 |
| Costa Mesa | 112,592 | 210 | 134 | 76 |
| Cotati | 7,470 | 18 | 12 | 6 |
| Covina | 47,207 | 82 | 54 | 28 |
| Crescent City | 6,767 | 13 | 12 | 1 |
| Culver City | 38,437 | 144 | 106 | 38 |
| Cypress | 49,094 | 67 | 52 | 15 |
| Daly City | 106,323 | 116 | 92 | 24 |
| Davis | 69,132 | 55 | 55 | 0 |
| Delano | 53,035 | 65 | 46 | 19 |
| Del Rey Oaks | 1,647 | 10 | 10 | 0 |
| Desert Hot Springs | 29,861 | 36 | 26 | 10 |
| Dinuba | 25,621 | 43 | 33 | 10 |
| Dixon | 20,655 | 36 | 30 | 6 |
| Dos Palos | 5,301 | 15 | 10 | 5 |
| Downey | 108,950 | 159 | 112 | 47 |
| East Palo Alto | 29,145 | 45 | 35 | 10 |
| El Cajon | 102,665 | 170 | 118 | 52 |
| El Centro | 43,684 | 67 | 43 | 24 |
| El Cerrito | 25,585 | 40 | 32 | 8 |
| Elk Grove | 179,887 | 230 | 139 | 91 |
| El Monte | 112,224 | 152 | 116 | 36 |
| El Segundo | 16,253 | 75 | 56 | 19 |
| Emeryville | 12,069 | 54 | 36 | 18 |
| Escalon | 7,626 | 13 | 12 | 1 |
| Escondido | 150,507 | 199 | 144 | 55 |
| Etna | 703 | 4 | 4 | 0 |
| Eureka | 26,598 | 58 | 38 | 20 |
| Exeter | 10,430 | 19 | 17 | 2 |
| Fairfax | 7,572 | 16 | 11 | 5 |
| Fairfield | 118,846 | 179 | 113 | 66 |
| Farmersville | 10,830 | 19 | 18 | 1 |
| Ferndale | 1,361 | 5 | 5 | 0 |
| Firebaugh | 7,775 | 18 | 13 | 5 |
| Folsom | 83,871 | 101 | 75 | 26 |
| Fontana | 218,167 | 288 | 191 | 97 |
| Fort Bragg | 7,213 | 19 | 15 | 4 |
| Fortuna | 12,115 | 26 | 18 | 8 |
| Foster City | 33,131 | 52 | 37 | 15 |
| Fountain Valley | 55,408 | 78 | 58 | 20 |
| Fowler | 6,678 | 13 | 12 | 1 |
| Fremont | 236,681 | 289 | 189 | 100 |
| Fresno | 533,633 | 1,070 | 769 | 301 |
| Fullerton | 140,399 | 169 | 114 | 55 |
| Galt | 26,849 | 39 | 28 | 11 |
| Gardena | 58,466 | 111 | 87 | 24 |
| Garden Grove | 171,397 | 237 | 172 | 65 |
| Gilroy | 55,438 | 87 | 59 | 28 |
| Glendale | 198,362 | 328 | 228 | 100 |
| Glendora | 50,543 | 81 | 50 | 31 |
| Gonzales | 8,245 | 13 | 10 | 3 |
| Grass Valley | 12,752 | 33 | 28 | 5 |
| Greenfield | 17,777 | 28 | 22 | 6 |
| Gridley | 7,481 | 17 | 12 | 5 |
| Grover Beach | 13,340 | 27 | 21 | 6 |
| Guadalupe | 8,255 | 17 | 15 | 2 |
| Gustine | 5,728 | 12 | 9 | 3 |
| Hanford | 58,751 | 85 | 59 | 26 |
| Hawthorne | 83,728 | 140 | 88 | 52 |
| Hayward | 159,368 | 282 | 170 | 112 |
| Healdsburg | 11,992 | 23 | 15 | 8 |
| Hemet | 85,792 | 99 | 70 | 29 |
| Hercules | 26,439 | 28 | 25 | 3 |
| Hermosa Beach | 18,734 | 65 | 38 | 27 |
| Hillsborough | 11,602 | 35 | 27 | 8 |
| Hollister | 42,505 | 40 | 31 | 9 |
| Huntington Beach | 198,980 | 289 | 183 | 106 |
| Huntington Park | 56,576 | 79 | 51 | 28 |
| Huron | 7,141 | 9 | 7 | 2 |
| Imperial | 20,228 | 22 | 19 | 3 |
| Indio | 93,242 | 105 | 64 | 41 |
| Inglewood | 106,967 | 233 | 180 | 53 |
| Ione | 8,397 | 8 | 8 | 0 |
| Irvine | 291,769 | 309 | 210 | 99 |
| Irwindale | 1,479 | 33 | 27 | 6 |
| Jackson | 5,006 | 11 | 9 | 2 |
| Kensington | 5,043 | 6 | 6 | 0 |
| Kerman | 15,523 | 26 | 22 | 4 |

## Table 78. Full-Time Law Enforcement Employees, by Selected State and City, 2020—Continued

(Number.)

| State/city | Population | Total law enforcement employees | Total officers | Total civilians |
|---|---|---|---|---|
| King City | 14,080 | 16 | 14 | 2 |
| Kingsburg | 12,484 | 25 | 21 | 4 |
| Laguna Beach | 22,680 | 88 | 52 | 36 |
| La Habra | 62,364 | 99 | 63 | 36 |
| Lakeport | 4,985 | 14 | 12 | 2 |
| Lake Shastina | 2,544 | 3 | 3 | 0 |
| La Mesa | 59,968 | 88 | 62 | 26 |
| La Palma | 15,402 | 26 | 20 | 6 |
| La Verne | 32,288 | 59 | 41 | 18 |
| Lemoore | 26,521 | 41 | 33 | 8 |
| Lincoln | 49,629 | 34 | 23 | 11 |
| Lindsay | 13,018 | 17 | 15 | 2 |
| Livermore | 92,677 | 128 | 90 | 38 |
| Livingston | 15,122 | 26 | 17 | 9 |
| Lodi | 68,811 | 100 | 70 | 30 |
| Lompoc | 42,251 | 67 | 40 | 27 |
| Long Beach | 453,931 | 1,023 | 772 | 251 |
| Los Alamitos | 11,389 | 23 | 19 | 4 |
| Los Altos | 30,400 | 43 | 29 | 14 |
| Los Angeles | 3,988,183 | 12,166 | 9,474 | 2,692 |
| Los Banos | 41,041 | 70 | 44 | 26 |
| Los Gatos | 30,315 | 53 | 36 | 17 |
| Madera | 67,215 | 91 | 65 | 26 |
| Mammoth Lakes | 8,326 | 19 | 14 | 5 |
| Manhattan Beach | 34,215 | 93 | 60 | 33 |
| Manteca | 86,327 | 103 | 73 | 30 |
| Marina | 22,060 | 36 | 29 | 7 |
| Martinez | 38,221 | 45 | 32 | 13 |
| Marysville | 12,648 | 27 | 18 | 9 |
| McFarland | 12,465 | 23 | 17 | 6 |
| Mendota | 12,545 | 22 | 16 | 6 |
| Menifee | 99,883 | 94 | 67 | 27 |
| Menlo Park | 35,235 | 58 | 42 | 16 |
| Merced | 89,210 | 132 | 96 | 36 |
| Mill Valley | 14,363 | 26 | 21 | 5 |
| Milpitas | 76,858 | 115 | 84 | 31 |
| Modesto | 216,946 | 275 | 184 | 91 |
| Monrovia | 37,892 | 72 | 46 | 26 |
| Montclair | 41,006 | 66 | 46 | 20 |
| Montebello | 61,435 | 94 | 71 | 23 |
| Monterey | 28,561 | 65 | 48 | 17 |
| Monterey Park | 59,255 | 102 | 72 | 30 |
| Moraga | 17,063 | 12 | 10 | 2 |
| Morgan Hill | 46,317 | 62 | 40 | 22 |
| Morro Bay | 10,591 | 18 | 16 | 2 |
| Mountain View | 80,688 | 128 | 88 | 40 |
| Mount Shasta | 3,218 | 14 | 8 | 6 |
| Murrieta | 117,835 | 159 | 102 | 57 |
| Napa | 77,018 | 103 | 61 | 42 |
| National City | 61,171 | 122 | 84 | 38 |
| Nevada City | 3,128 | 8 | 7 | 1 |
| Newark | 50,470 | 76 | 50 | 26 |
| Newman | 11,847 | 15 | 13 | 2 |
| Newport Beach | 86,993 | 227 | 144 | 83 |
| Novato | 53,493 | 75 | 55 | 20 |
| Oakdale | 23,487 | 34 | 22 | 12 |
| Oakland | 428,406 | 987 | 682 | 305 |
| Oceanside | 175,335 | 288 | 200 | 88 |
| Ontario | 185,414 | 339 | 261 | 78 |
| Orange | 138,312 | 218 | 150 | 68 |
| Orange Cove | 10,155 | 13 | 12 | 1 |
| Orland | 8,138 | 13 | 11 | 2 |
| Oroville | 20,405 | 34 | 21 | 13 |
| Oxnard | 208,911 | 317 | 227 | 90 |
| Pacifica | 38,077 | 33 | 31 | 2 |
| Pacific Grove | 15,322 | 31 | 19 | 12 |
| Palm Springs | 49,367 | 146 | 93 | 53 |
| Palo Alto | 67,266 | 114 | 70 | 44 |
| Palos Verdes Estates | 13,044 | 26 | 16 | 10 |
| Paradise | 3,986 | 24 | 17 | 7 |
| Parlier | 15,979 | 18 | 14 | 4 |
| Pasadena | 141,402 | 325 | 221 | 104 |
| Paso Robles | 31,700 | 50 | 33 | 17 |
| Petaluma | 60,898 | 101 | 65 | 36 |
| Piedmont | 11,400 | 30 | 20 | 10 |
| Pinole | 19,293 | 42 | 24 | 18 |
| Pismo Beach | 7,985 | 31 | 21 | 10 |
| Pittsburg | 73,607 | 102 | 81 | 21 |
| Placentia | 51,579 | 57 | 45 | 12 |
| Placerville | 11,140 | 26 | 18 | 8 |
| Pleasant Hill | 34,949 | 58 | 43 | 15 |
| Pleasanton | 81,313 | 112 | 78 | 34 |
| Pomona | 149,206 | 268 | 146 | 122 |
| Porterville | 59,022 | 94 | 64 | 30 |
| Port Hueneme | 21,748 | 31 | 20 | 11 |

## Table 78. Full-Time Law Enforcement Employees, by Selected State and City, 2020—Continued

(Number.)

| State/city | Population | Total law enforcement employees | Total officers | Total civilians |
|---|---|---|---|---|
| Red Bluff | 14,126 | 39 | 25 | 14 |
| Redding | 92,714 | 147 | 101 | 46 |
| Redlands | 72,623 | 110 | 76 | 34 |
| Redondo Beach | 65,401 | 139 | 88 | 51 |
| Redwood City | 85,250 | 115 | 83 | 32 |
| Reedley | 25,879 | 44 | 31 | 13 |
| Rialto | 104,600 | 146 | 111 | 35 |
| Richmond | 110,698 | 180 | 130 | 50 |
| Ridgecrest | 29,282 | 46 | 28 | 18 |
| Rio Dell | 3,446 | 6 | 5 | 1 |
| Rio Vista | 10,285 | 14 | 12 | 2 |
| Ripon | 17,028 | 33 | 24 | 9 |
| Riverside | 333,437 | 520 | 363 | 157 |
| Rocklin | 71,575 | 85 | 60 | 25 |
| Rohnert Park | 43,167 | 94 | 70 | 24 |
| Roseville | 147,468 | 197 | 135 | 62 |
| Ross | 2,485 | 8 | 8 | 0 |
| Sacramento | 517,637 | 997 | 716 | 281 |
| Salinas | 155,283 | 181 | 142 | 39 |
| San Bernardino | 218,205 | 345 | 245 | 100 |
| San Bruno | 44,336 | 55 | 42 | 13 |
| Sand City | 438 | 11 | 10 | 1 |
| San Diego | 1,434,673 | 2,394 | 1,877 | 517 |
| San Fernando | 24,369 | 41 | 28 | 13 |
| San Francisco | 865,393 | 2,857 | 2,129 | 728 |
| San Gabriel | 39,454 | 65 | 51 | 14 |
| Sanger | 26,881 | 42 | 36 | 6 |
| San Jose | 1,019,772 | 1,624 | 1,161 | 463 |
| San Leandro | 89,580 | 116 | 76 | 40 |
| San Luis Obispo | 47,837 | 86 | 57 | 29 |
| San Marino | 12,755 | 36 | 26 | 10 |
| San Mateo | 102,930 | 152 | 108 | 44 |
| San Pablo | 30,914 | 79 | 55 | 24 |
| San Rafael | 58,606 | 83 | 63 | 20 |
| San Ramon | 84,064 | 83 | 66 | 17 |
| Santa Ana | 331,934 | 588 | 361 | 227 |
| Santa Barbara | 90,428 | 181 | 121 | 60 |
| Santa Clara | 132,572 | 198 | 140 | 58 |
| Santa Cruz | 64,704 | 110 | 75 | 35 |
| Santa Maria | 106,495 | 164 | 120 | 44 |
| Santa Monica | 90,050 | 358 | 206 | 152 |
| Santa Paula | 30,297 | 41 | 30 | 11 |
| Santa Rosa | 174,562 | 240 | 164 | 76 |
| Sausalito | 7,107 | 25 | 19 | 6 |
| Scotts Valley | 12,038 | 26 | 17 | 9 |
| Seal Beach | 23,859 | 53 | 39 | 14 |
| Seaside | 34,211 | 39 | 28 | 11 |
| Sebastopol | 7,605 | 19 | 13 | 6 |
| Selma | 24,473 | 45 | 35 | 10 |
| Shafter | 21,136 | 43 | 30 | 13 |
| Sierra Madre | 10,592 | 21 | 16 | 5 |
| Signal Hill | 11,306 | 35 | 29 | 6 |
| Simi Valley | 125,243 | 173 | 119 | 54 |
| Soledad | 25,175 | 24 | 19 | 5 |
| Sonora | 4,828 | 19 | 13 | 6 |
| South Gate | 93,012 | 118 | 78 | 40 |
| South Lake Tahoe | 22,995 | 57 | 38 | 19 |
| South Pasadena | 24,935 | 49 | 33 | 16 |
| South San Francisco | 66,855 | 114 | 84 | 30 |
| Stallion Springs | 2,472 | 5 | 5 | 0 |
| St. Helena | 5,975 | 17 | 11 | 6 |
| Stockton | 314,764 | 615 | 432 | 183 |
| Suisun City | 29,425 | 33 | 22 | 11 |
| Sunnyvale | 152,893 | 282 | 205 | 77 |
| Susanville | 14,137 | 18 | 15 | 3 |
| Sutter Creek | 2,706 | 4 | 4 | 0 |
| Taft | 8,418 | 20 | 11 | 9 |
| Tehachapi | 12,596 | 28 | 19 | 9 |
| Tiburon | 9,099 | 17 | 13 | 4 |
| Torrance | 141,185 | 345 | 208 | 137 |
| Tracy | 96,252 | 146 | 93 | 53 |
| Truckee | 17,066 | 35 | 25 | 10 |
| Tulare | 67,583 | 106 | 73 | 33 |
| Tulelake | 950 | 3 | 3 | 0 |
| Turlock | 73,507 | 113 | 77 | 36 |
| Tustin | 80,277 | 161 | 95 | 66 |
| Ukiah | 15,870 | 41 | 26 | 15 |
| Union City | 75,009 | 88 | 70 | 18 |
| Upland | 78,260 | 94 | 65 | 29 |
| Vacaville | 102,258 | 167 | 104 | 63 |
| Vallejo | 121,221 | 143 | 98 | 45 |
| Ventura | 107,118 | 178 | 138 | 40 |
| Vernon | 318 | 55 | 41 | 14 |
| Visalia | 136,077 | 214 | 147 | 67 |
| Walnut Creek | 70,519 | 111 | 76 | 35 |

## Table 78. Full-Time Law Enforcement Employees, by Selected State and City, 2020—Continued

(Number.)

| State/city | Population | Total law enforcement employees | Total officers | Total civilians |
|---|---|---|---|---|
| Watsonville | 51,720 | 90 | 71 | 19 |
| Weed | 2,640 | 12 | 6 | 6 |
| West Covina | 103,417 | 134 | 87 | 47 |
| Westminster | 89,758 | 121 | 78 | 43 |
| Westmorland | 2,231 | 3 | 3 | 0 |
| West Sacramento | 54,187 | 99 | 71 | 28 |
| Wheatland | 3,682 | 9 | 8 | 1 |
| Whittier | 82,987 | 174 | 124 | 50 |
| Williams | 5,430 | 13 | 11 | 2 |
| Willits | 4,822 | 13 | 10 | 3 |
| Winters | 7,550 | 10 | 8 | 2 |
| Woodlake | 8,001 | 13 | 12 | 1 |
| Woodland | 60,958 | 82 | 67 | 15 |
| Yreka | 7,475 | 20 | 12 | 8 |
| Yuba City | 66,528 | 85 | 60 | 25 |
| | | | | |
| **COLORADO** | | | | |
| Alamosa | 9,414 | 30 | 25 | 5 |
| Arvada | 123,548 | 213 | 161 | 52 |
| Aspen | 7,750 | 35 | 26 | 9 |
| Ault | 2,197 | 7 | 6 | 1 |
| Aurora | 393,897 | 877 | 689 | 188 |
| Avon | 7,012 | 19 | 15 | 4 |
| Basalt | 4,226 | 12 | 11 | 1 |
| Bayfield | 2,614 | 9 | 8 | 1 |
| Black Hawk | 132 | 29 | 21 | 8 |
| Blue River | 936 | 5 | 3 | 2 |
| Boulder | 108,698 | 241 | 160 | 81 |
| Breckenridge | 4,996 | 24 | 20 | 4 |
| Brighton | 41,535 | 106 | 77 | 29 |
| Broomfield | 73,077 | 226 | 120 | 106 |
| Brush | 5,434 | 14 | 9 | 5 |
| Buena Vista | 3,175 | 11 | 9 | 2 |
| Burlington | 3,038 | 7 | 5 | 2 |
| Calhan | 831 | 5 | 4 | 1 |
| Canon City | 16,552 | 41 | 33 | 8 |
| Carbondale | 6,761 | 14 | 10 | 4 |
| Castle Rock | 73,221 | 111 | 80 | 31 |
| Cedaredge | 2,320 | 7 | 6 | 1 |
| Centennial | 111,199 | 191 | 138 | 53 |
| Center | 2,399 | 21 | 7 | 14 |
| Cherry Hills Village | 6,685 | 28 | 24 | 4 |
| Collbran | 731 | 2 | 2 | 0 |
| Colorado Springs | 488,747 | 1,055 | 766 | 289 |
| Columbine Valley | 1,537 | 5 | 5 | 0 |
| Commerce City | 60,845 | 139 | 111 | 28 |
| Cortez | 8,760 | 49 | 26 | 23 |
| Craig | 8,905 | 24 | 16 | 8 |
| Crested Butte | 1,703 | 9 | 8 | 1 |
| Cripple Creek | 1,270 | 15 | 8 | 7 |
| Dacono | 6,877 | 16 | 12 | 4 |
| De Beque | 551 | 5 | 5 | 0 |
| Del Norte | 1,528 | 4 | 3 | 1 |
| Delta | 9,047 | 24 | 18 | 6 |
| Denver | 740,209 | 1,784 | 1,447 | 337 |
| Dillon | 973 | 12 | 11 | 1 |
| Dinosaur | 334 | 3 | 3 | 0 |
| Durango | 19,995 | 66 | 52 | 14 |
| Eagle | 6,954 | 12 | 11 | 1 |
| Eaton | 6,191 | 13 | 9 | 4 |
| Edgewater | 5,415 | 22 | 18 | 4 |
| Elizabeth | 1,928 | 8 | 7 | 1 |
| Empire | 304 | 5 | 3 | 2 |
| Englewood | 35,630 | 111 | 74 | 37 |
| Erie | 31,873 | 47 | 40 | 7 |
| Estes Park | 6,617 | 34 | 21 | 13 |
| Evans | 23,698 | 36 | 31 | 5 |
| Fairplay | 814 | 3 | 3 | 0 |
| Federal Heights | 13,828 | 40 | 23 | 17 |
| Firestone | 15,932 | 33 | 30 | 3 |
| Florence | 3,993 | 14 | 12 | 2 |
| Fort Collins | 170,744 | 313 | 214 | 99 |
| Fort Lupton | 8,800 | 25 | 19 | 6 |
| Fort Morgan | 11,234 | 32 | 27 | 5 |
| Fountain | 31,557 | 65 | 57 | 8 |
| Fowler | 1,145 | 4 | 3 | 1 |
| Fraser/Winter Park | 2,478 | 12 | 10 | 2 |
| Frederick | 11,844 | 29 | 26 | 3 |
| Frisco | 2,892 | 13 | 11 | 2 |
| Fruita | 14,465 | 22 | 18 | 4 |
| Garden City | 282 | 4 | 4 | 0 |
| Georgetown | 1,109 | 2 | 2 | 0 |
| Glendale | 5,192 | 41 | 28 | 13 |
| Glenwood Springs | 10,297 | 24 | 20 | 4 |
| Golden | 20,498 | 65 | 50 | 15 |

## Table 78. Full-Time Law Enforcement Employees, by Selected State and City, 2020—Continued

(Number.)

| State/city | Population | Total law enforcement employees | Total officers | Total civilians |
|---|---|---|---|---|
| Granada | 508 | 2 | 1 | 1 |
| Granby | 2,209 | 12 | 9 | 3 |
| Grand Junction | 63,928 | 203 | 116 | 87 |
| Greeley | 110,660 | 208 | 149 | 59 |
| Green Mountain Falls | 737 | 2 | 2 | 0 |
| Greenwood Village | 15,012 | 83 | 62 | 21 |
| Gunnison | 6,950 | 20 | 15 | 5 |
| Haxtun | 936 | 1 | 1 | 0 |
| Hayden | 1,995 | 7 | 6 | 1 |
| Holyoke | 2,230 | 2 | 2 | 0 |
| Hotchkiss | 929 | 5 | 4 | 1 |
| Hudson | 2,812 | 12 | 10 | 2 |
| Hugo | 787 | 2 | 2 | 0 |
| Idaho Springs | 1,871 | 10 | 7 | 3 |
| Ignacio | 974 | 7 | 7 | 0 |
| Johnstown | 14,413 | 27 | 24 | 3 |
| Kersey | 1,833 | 5 | 4 | 1 |
| Kremmling | 1,532 | 4 | 3 | 1 |
| Lafayette | 29,027 | 46 | 34 | 12 |
| La Junta | 6,831 | 19 | 13 | 6 |
| Lakeside | 8 | 6 | 5 | 1 |
| Lakewood | 158,977 | 397 | 280 | 117 |
| Lamar | 7,612 | 21 | 15 | 6 |
| La Salle | 2,524 | 8 | 8 | 0 |
| La Veta | 810 | 1 | 1 | 0 |
| Leadville | 2,796 | 7 | 2 | 5 |
| Limon | 1,951 | 4 | 4 | 0 |
| Littleton | 46,466 | 104 | 74 | 30 |
| Lochbuie | 8,301 | 13 | 10 | 3 |
| Log Lane Village | 851 | 3 | 3 | 0 |
| Lone Tree | 14,007 | 62 | 50 | 12 |
| Longmont | 99,714 | 220 | 149 | 71 |
| Louisville | 19,127 | 35 | 28 | 7 |
| Loveland | 85,349 | 158 | 105 | 53 |
| Mancos | 1,404 | 5 | 5 | 0 |
| Manitou Springs | 5,509 | 15 | 14 | 1 |
| Manzanola | 408 | 1 | 1 | 0 |
| Mead | 5,190 | 10 | 8 | 2 |
| Meeker | 2,305 | 7 | 6 | 1 |
| Milliken | 9,074 | 15 | 12 | 3 |
| Monte Vista | 4,030 | 17 | 14 | 3 |
| Montrose | 19,984 | 60 | 43 | 17 |
| Monument | 8,397 | 23 | 20 | 3 |
| Morrison | 431 | 2 | 1 | 1 |
| Mountain View | 553 | 10 | 9 | 1 |
| Mountain Village | 1,486 | 10 | 7 | 3 |
| Mount Crested Butte | 901 | 9 | 8 | 1 |
| Nederland | 1,569 | 5 | 5 | 0 |
| New Castle | 5,012 | 12 | 10 | 2 |
| Northglenn | 39,162 | 82 | 64 | 18 |
| Nunn | 506 | 2 | 2 | 0 |
| Oak Creek | 966 | 3 | 3 | 0 |
| Olathe | 1,820 | 7 | 5 | 2 |
| Ouray | 1,050 | 5 | 5 | 0 |
| Pagosa Springs | 2,178 | 8 | 7 | 1 |
| Palisade | 2,812 | 11 | 9 | 2 |
| Palmer Lake | 3,092 | 2 | 2 | 0 |
| Paonia | 1,476 | 3 | 2 | 1 |
| Parachute | 1,118 | 6 | 5 | 1 |
| Parker | 60,178 | 109 | 68 | 41 |
| Platteville | 4,239 | 10 | 9 | 1 |
| Pueblo | 113,371 | 252 | 202 | 50 |
| Rangely | 2,295 | 11 | 5 | 6 |
| Ridgway | 1,055 | 3 | 3 | 0 |
| Rifle | 9,819 | 22 | 17 | 5 |
| Rocky Ford | 3,790 | 13 | 6 | 7 |
| Salida | 5,735 | 23 | 19 | 4 |
| Sanford | 901 | 1 | 1 | 0 |
| Severance | 8,343 | 11 | 8 | 3 |
| Sheridan | 6,070 | 35 | 33 | 2 |
| Silt | 3,129 | 8 | 6 | 2 |
| Silverthorne | 5,019 | 21 | 18 | 3 |
| Simla | 698 | 2 | 2 | 0 |
| Snowmass Village | 2,754 | 12 | 9 | 3 |
| South Fork | 422 | 2 | 2 | 0 |
| Springfield | 1,355 | 4 | 3 | 1 |
| Steamboat Springs | 13,282 | 33 | 19 | 14 |
| Sterling | 14,006 | 24 | 19 | 5 |
| Telluride | 2,436 | 14 | 10 | 4 |
| Thornton | 151,324 | 314 | 227 | 87 |
| Timnath | 3,801 | 15 | 13 | 2 |
| Trinidad | 8,045 | 37 | 21 | 16 |
| Vail | 5,507 | 57 | 28 | 29 |
| Westminster | 115,942 | 236 | 170 | 66 |
| Wheat Ridge | 32,027 | 96 | 79 | 17 |

## Table 78. Full-Time Law Enforcement Employees, by Selected State and City, 2020—Continued

(Number.)

| State/city | Population | Total law enforcement employees | Total officers | Total civilians |
|---|---|---|---|---|
| Wiggins | 1,184 | 2 | 2 | 0 |
| Windsor | 28,756 | 53 | 44 | 9 |
| Woodland Park | 8,257 | 30 | 20 | 10 |
| Wray | 2,352 | 7 | 6 | 1 |
| Yuma | 3,495 | 10 | 8 | 2 |
| **CONNECTICUT** | | | | |
| Ansonia | 18,452 | 48 | 38 | 10 |
| Avon | 18,226 | 43 | 33 | 10 |
| Berlin | 20,440 | 52 | 41 | 11 |
| Bethel | 20,066 | 52 | 39 | 13 |
| Bloomfield | 21,254 | 59 | 46 | 13 |
| Branford | 27,707 | 62 | 51 | 11 |
| Bridgeport | 143,394 | 378 | 330 | 48 |
| Bristol | 59,659 | 141 | 117 | 24 |
| Brookfield | 16,944 | 44 | 34 | 10 |
| Canton | 10,223 | 26 | 16 | 10 |
| Cheshire | 28,755 | 58 | 45 | 13 |
| Clinton | 12,846 | 37 | 27 | 10 |
| Coventry | 12,384 | 18 | 13 | 5 |
| Cromwell | 13,750 | 37 | 27 | 10 |
| Danbury | 84,631 | 146 | 141 | 5 |
| Darien | 21,790 | 67 | 49 | 18 |
| Derby | 12,197 | 36 | 34 | 2 |
| East Hampton | 12,726 | 19 | 17 | 2 |
| East Hartford | 49,470 | 156 | 118 | 38 |
| East Haven | 28,377 | 76 | 62 | 14 |
| East Lyme | 18,467 | 34 | 27 | 7 |
| Easton | 7,462 | 19 | 14 | 5 |
| East Windsor | 11,702 | 36 | 26 | 10 |
| Enfield | 43,452 | 119 | 96 | 23 |
| Fairfield | 62,473 | 129 | 106 | 23 |
| Farmington | 25,510 | 59 | 45 | 14 |
| Glastonbury | 34,424 | 72 | 54 | 18 |
| Granby | 11,585 | 21 | 16 | 5 |
| Greenwich | 62,917 | 172 | 146 | 26 |
| Groton | 8,823 | 33 | 26 | 7 |
| Groton Long Point | 504 | 5 | 5 | 0 |
| Groton Town | 28,753 | 73 | 58 | 15 |
| Guilford | 22,009 | 45 | 38 | 7 |
| Hamden | 60,165 | 116 | 90 | 26 |
| Hartford | 121,160 | 419 | 395 | 24 |
| Ledyard | 14,534 | 31 | 22 | 9 |
| Madison | 17,890 | 41 | 29 | 12 |
| Manchester | 57,274 | 143 | 107 | 36 |
| Meriden | 58,799 | 128 | 116 | 12 |
| Middlebury | 7,851 | 14 | 12 | 2 |
| Middletown | 45,852 | 120 | 106 | 14 |
| Milford | 54,984 | 121 | 110 | 11 |
| Monroe | 19,311 | 54 | 43 | 11 |
| Naugatuck | 30,810 | 86 | 68 | 18 |
| New Britain | 72,093 | 166 | 158 | 8 |
| New Canaan | 20,147 | 53 | 47 | 6 |
| New Haven | 130,903 | 361 | 315 | 46 |
| Newington | 29,803 | 62 | 49 | 13 |
| New London | 26,797 | 82 | 67 | 15 |
| New Milford | 26,548 | 61 | 48 | 13 |
| Newtown | 27,858 | 58 | 45 | 13 |
| North Branford | 14,031 | 30 | 23 | 7 |
| North Haven | 23,504 | 59 | 49 | 10 |
| Norwalk | 88,930 | 197 | 164 | 33 |
| Norwich | 38,431 | 96 | 82 | 14 |
| Old Saybrook | 10,007 | 33 | 22 | 11 |
| Orange | 13,874 | 51 | 42 | 9 |
| Plainfield | 15,053 | 23 | 18 | 5 |
| Plainville | 17,466 | 51 | 39 | 12 |
| Plymouth | 11,486 | 25 | 23 | 2 |
| Portland | 9,185 | 13 | 12 | 1 |
| Putnam | 9,354 | 20 | 15 | 5 |
| Redding | 9,042 | 22 | 16 | 6 |
| Ridgefield | 24,919 | 47 | 41 | 6 |
| Rocky Hill | 20,069 | 51 | 39 | 12 |
| Seymour | 16,306 | 39 | 37 | 2 |
| Shelton | 41,095 | 62 | 53 | 9 |
| Simsbury | 25,639 | 50 | 39 | 11 |
| Southington | 43,897 | 88 | 67 | 21 |
| South Windsor | 26,142 | 58 | 44 | 14 |
| Stamford | 132,292 | 282 | 260 | 22 |
| Stonington | 18,571 | 52 | 39 | 13 |
| Stratford | 51,683 | 109 | 103 | 6 |
| Suffield | 15,817 | 25 | 20 | 5 |
| Thomaston | 7,468 | 25 | 13 | 12 |
| Torrington | 33,631 | 83 | 73 | 10 |
| Trumbull | 35,378 | 82 | 73 | 9 |
| Vernon | 29,423 | 57 | 45 | 12 |

## Table 78. Full-Time Law Enforcement Employees, by Selected State and City, 2020—Continued

(Number.)

| State/city | Population | Total law enforcement employees | Total officers | Total civilians |
|---|---|---|---|---|
| Wallingford | 43,969 | 87 | 68 | 19 |
| Waterbury | 106,480 | 319 | 276 | 43 |
| Waterford | 18,803 | 60 | 44 | 16 |
| Watertown | 21,418 | 49 | 39 | 10 |
| West Hartford | 62,809 | 144 | 122 | 22 |
| West Haven | 54,248 | 126 | 118 | 8 |
| Weston | 10,204 | 18 | 17 | 1 |
| Westport | 28,652 | 71 | 61 | 10 |
| Wethersfield | 25,807 | 54 | 42 | 12 |
| Willimantic | 17,763 | 48 | 43 | 5 |
| Wilton | 18,236 | 45 | 41 | 4 |
| Winchester | 10,481 | 21 | 20 | 1 |
| Windsor | 28,601 | 57 | 45 | 12 |
| Windsor Locks | 12,828 | 34 | 26 | 8 |
| Wolcott | 16,550 | 37 | 26 | 11 |
| Woodbridge | 8,676 | 31 | 23 | 8 |
| **DELAWARE** | | | | |
| Bethany Beach | 1,308 | 11 | 10 | 1 |
| Blades | 1,526 | 2 | 2 | 0 |
| Bridgeville | 2,487 | 8 | 8 | 0 |
| Camden | 3,660 | 10 | 9 | 1 |
| Cheswold | 1,787 | 4 | 4 | 0 |
| Clayton | 3,707 | 10 | 9 | 1 |
| Dagsboro | 973 | 4 | 4 | 0 |
| Delaware City | 1,852 | 4 | 3 | 1 |
| Delmar | 1,911 | 12 | 11 | 1 |
| Dewey Beach | 419 | 13 | 10 | 3 |
| Dover | 38,439 | 133 | 102 | 31 |
| Ellendale | 457 | 1 | 1 | 0 |
| Elsmere | 5,741 | 13 | 12 | 1 |
| Felton | 1,447 | 4 | 4 | 0 |
| Fenwick Island | 468 | 8 | 7 | 1 |
| Frederica | 869 | 2 | 2 | 0 |
| Georgetown | 7,945 | 19 | 16 | 3 |
| Greenwood | 1,197 | 4 | 3 | 1 |
| Harrington | 3,672 | 13 | 12 | 1 |
| Laurel | 4,595 | 19 | 18 | 1 |
| Lewes | 3,479 | 12 | 11 | 1 |
| Middletown | 24,307 | 43 | 37 | 6 |
| Milford | 12,582 | 44 | 32 | 12 |
| Millsboro | 4,753 | 19 | 17 | 2 |
| Milton | 3,189 | 9 | 8 | 1 |
| Newark | 34,064 | 87 | 70 | 17 |
| New Castle | 5,419 | 17 | 16 | 1 |
| Newport | 871 | 6 | 6 | 0 |
| Ocean View | 2,290 | 14 | 13 | 1 |
| Rehoboth Beach | 1,622 | 33 | 19 | 14 |
| Seaford | 8,392 | 33 | 27 | 6 |
| Smyrna | 12,383 | 36 | 28 | 8 |
| South Bethany | 557 | 6 | 6 | 0 |
| Wilmington | 70,331 | 353 | 302 | 51 |
| Wyoming | 1,695 | 3 | 3 | 0 |
| **DISTRICT OF COLUMBIA** | | | | |
| Washington | 670,050 | 4,179 | 3,575 | 604 |
| **FLORIDA** | | | | |
| Alachua | 10,006 | 35 | 27 | 8 |
| Altamonte Springs | 44,030 | 111 | 95 | 16 |
| Apopka | 55,173 | 137 | 102 | 35 |
| Arcadia | 8,523 | 21 | 17 | 4 |
| Astatula | 2,156 | 8 | 8 | 0 |
| Atlantic Beach | 13,971 | 42 | 30 | 12 |
| Atlantis | 2,140 | 16 | 11 | 5 |
| Auburndale | 17,633 | 42 | 33 | 9 |
| Aventura | 36,621 | 125 | 93 | 32 |
| Bal Harbour Village | 2,946 | 36 | 25 | 11 |
| Bartow | 20,534 | 61 | 41 | 20 |
| Bay Harbor Islands | 5,731 | 30 | 24 | 6 |
| Belleair | 4,339 | 15 | 13 | 2 |
| Belle Isle | 7,437 | 20 | 17 | 3 |
| Belleview | 5,279 | 16 | 14 | 2 |
| Biscayne Park | 3,012 | 11 | 11 | 0 |
| Blountstown | 2,421 | 21 | 14 | 7 |
| Boca Raton | 101,504 | 303 | 207 | 96 |
| Bonifay | 2,685 | 6 | 5 | 1 |
| Bowling Green | 2,891 | 6 | 6 | 0 |
| Boynton Beach | 81,384 | 184 | 146 | 38 |
| Bradenton | 60,902 | 154 | 119 | 35 |
| Bradenton Beach | 1,284 | 9 | 9 | 0 |
| Cape Coral | 206,298 | 360 | 272 | 88 |
| Casselberry | 29,778 | 63 | 53 | 10 |
| Cedar Key | 726 | 4 | 4 | 0 |
| Clearwater | 117,336 | 329 | 237 | 92 |

## Table 78. Full-Time Law Enforcement Employees, by Selected State and City, 2020—Continued

(Number.)

| State/city | Population | Total law enforcement employees | Total officers | Total civilians |
|---|---|---|---|---|
| Clermont | 41,160 | 87 | 78 | 9 |
| Clewiston | 8,202 | 18 | 13 | 5 |
| Cocoa | 18,854 | 91 | 62 | 29 |
| Cocoa Beach | 11,695 | 51 | 34 | 17 |
| Coconut Creek | 58,166 | 145 | 107 | 38 |
| Cooper City | 34,599 | 72 | 56 | 16 |
| Coral Gables | 49,356 | 283 | 193 | 90 |
| Coral Springs | 135,168 | 313 | 215 | 98 |
| Crestview | 26,173 | 48 | 39 | 9 |
| Cross City | 1,743 | 4 | 4 | 0 |
| Dade City | 7,809 | 32 | 24 | 8 |
| Dania Beach | 31,906 | 82 | 76 | 6 |
| Davenport | 8,025 | 16 | 15 | 1 |
| Daytona Beach | 71,059 | 275 | 217 | 58 |
| Daytona Beach Shores | 4,681 | 35 | 27 | 8 |
| Deerfield Beach | 87,359 | 140 | 130 | 10 |
| DeFuniak Springs | 7,440 | 29 | 21 | 8 |
| DeLand | 37,089 | 83 | 67 | 16 |
| Delray Beach | 70,524 | 216 | 154 | 62 |
| Doral | 70,496 | 198 | 147 | 51 |
| Dunnellon | 1,881 | 11 | 10 | 1 |
| Eatonville | 2,196 | 15 | 13 | 2 |
| Edgewater | 24,403 | 34 | 29 | 5 |
| Edgewood | 3,095 | 16 | 13 | 3 |
| El Portal | 2,350 | 10 | 10 | 0 |
| Eustis | 21,636 | 51 | 38 | 13 |
| Fellsmere | 5,814 | 11 | 9 | 2 |
| Fernandina Beach | 13,499 | 42 | 37 | 5 |
| Flagler Beach | 5,220 | 18 | 15 | 3 |
| Florida City | 11,704 | 42 | 33 | 9 |
| Fort Lauderdale | 183,810 | 664 | 502 | 162 |
| Fort Myers | 94,586 | 324 | 238 | 86 |
| Fort Pierce | 46,794 | 141 | 113 | 28 |
| Fort Walton Beach | 22,713 | 76 | 51 | 25 |
| Fruitland Park | 12,226 | 22 | 21 | 1 |
| Gainesville | 136,085 | 333 | 247 | 86 |
| Golden Beach | 932 | 22 | 17 | 5 |
| Graceville | 2,090 | 8 | 8 | 0 |
| Green Cove Springs | 9,148 | 28 | 21 | 7 |
| Gretna | 1,407 | 4 | 4 | 0 |
| Groveland | 19,309 | 55 | 40 | 15 |
| Gulf Breeze | 7,219 | 23 | 23 | 0 |
| Gulfport | 12,311 | 33 | 29 | 4 |
| Gulf Stream | 998 | 13 | 13 | 0 |
| Haines City | 28,535 | 69 | 56 | 13 |
| Hallandale Beach | 41,454 | 119 | 86 | 33 |
| Hialeah | 232,699 | 353 | 288 | 65 |
| Hialeah Gardens | 23,348 | 60 | 45 | 15 |
| Highland Beach | 3,944 | 15 | 14 | 1 |
| Hillsboro Beach | 2,024 | 19 | 15 | 4 |
| Holly Hill | 12,477 | 26 | 22 | 4 |
| Hollywood | 153,948 | 407 | 314 | 93 |
| Holmes Beach | 4,353 | 25 | 18 | 7 |
| Homestead | 70,179 | 154 | 120 | 34 |
| Howey-in-the-Hills | 1,190 | 8 | 8 | 0 |
| Indialantic | 2,913 | 18 | 12 | 6 |
| Indian Creek Village | 88 | 14 | 10 | 4 |
| Indian Harbour Beach | 8,553 | 29 | 20 | 9 |
| Indian River Shores | 4,396 | 22 | 18 | 4 |
| Indian Shores | 3,774 | 14 | 13 | 1 |
| Interlachen | 1,478 | 3 | 3 | 0 |
| Jacksonville Beach | 23,846 | 85 | 65 | 20 |
| Juno Beach | 3,657 | 16 | 14 | 2 |
| Jupiter | 66,986 | 140 | 114 | 26 |
| Jupiter Inlet Colony | 456 | 4 | 4 | 0 |
| Jupiter Island | 954 | 23 | 18 | 5 |
| Kenneth City | 5,095 | 14 | 13 | 1 |
| Key Biscayne | 12,765 | 43 | 33 | 10 |
| Key Colony Beach | 795 | 4 | 4 | 0 |
| Kissimmee | 74,334 | 225 | 152 | 73 |
| Lady Lake | 16,410 | 34 | 29 | 5 |
| Lake Alfred | 6,492 | 14 | 10 | 4 |
| Lake City | 12,478 | 51 | 35 | 16 |
| Lake Clarke Shores | 3,641 | 9 | 8 | 1 |
| Lake Hamilton | 1,578 | 8 | 6 | 2 |
| Lake Helen | 2,846 | 7 | 6 | 1 |
| Lakeland | 117,214 | 355 | 248 | 107 |
| Lake Mary | 17,908 | 53 | 45 | 8 |
| Lake Placid | 2,514 | 8 | 6 | 2 |
| Lake Wales | 18,092 | 54 | 46 | 8 |
| Lantana | 12,775 | 39 | 29 | 10 |
| Largo | 85,244 | 188 | 155 | 33 |
| Lauderdale-by-the-Sea | 6,234 | 27 | 25 | 2 |
| Lauderdale Lakes | 36,161 | 46 | 38 | 8 |
| Lauderhill | 74,911 | 160 | 118 | 42 |

## Table 78. Full-Time Law Enforcement Employees, by Selected State and City, 2020—Continued

(Number.)

| State/city | Population | Total law enforcement employees | Total officers | Total civilians |
|---|---|---|---|---|
| Lawtey | 741 | 2 | 2 | 0 |
| Leesburg | 24,459 | 95 | 70 | 25 |
| Lighthouse Point | 10,546 | 42 | 31 | 11 |
| Live Oak | 7,004 | 20 | 17 | 3 |
| Longboat Key | 7,346 | 17 | 16 | 1 |
| Longwood | 17,245 | 45 | 41 | 4 |
| Lynn Haven | 20,390 | 48 | 37 | 11 |
| Madison | 2,766 | 17 | 16 | 1 |
| Maitland | 17,621 | 58 | 50 | 8 |
| Manalapan | 476 | 14 | 12 | 2 |
| Marco Island | 18,262 | 44 | 39 | 5 |
| Margate | 59,050 | 142 | 108 | 34 |
| Marianna | 5,564 | 23 | 17 | 6 |
| Mascotte | 7,030 | 15 | 13 | 2 |
| Melbourne | 84,112 | 232 | 162 | 70 |
| Melbourne Beach | 3,319 | 12 | 11 | 1 |
| Melbourne Village | 695 | 5 | 5 | 0 |
| Miami | 479,262 | 1,696 | 1,275 | 421 |
| Miami Beach | 87,729 | 504 | 414 | 90 |
| Miami Gardens | 109,296 | 252 | 206 | 46 |
| Miami Shores | 10,209 | 40 | 34 | 6 |
| Miami Springs | 13,716 | 55 | 45 | 10 |
| Midway | 2,948 | 6 | 5 | 1 |
| Milton | 11,001 | 20 | 15 | 5 |
| Miramar | 135,497 | 292 | 207 | 85 |
| Monticello | 2,447 | 13 | 9 | 4 |
| Mount Dora | 15,065 | 60 | 42 | 18 |
| Naples | 22,277 | 90 | 61 | 29 |
| Neptune Beach | 7,236 | 30 | 22 | 8 |
| New Port Richey | 17,259 | 61 | 43 | 18 |
| New Smyrna Beach | 29,314 | 62 | 49 | 13 |
| Niceville | 16,584 | 32 | 23 | 9 |
| North Bay Village | 8,044 | 34 | 28 | 6 |
| North Lauderdale | 45,052 | 64 | 57 | 7 |
| North Miami | 62,442 | 138 | 109 | 29 |
| North Miami Beach | 42,592 | 136 | 100 | 36 |
| North Palm Beach | 13,221 | 36 | 31 | 5 |
| North Port | 75,614 | 165 | 123 | 42 |
| Oakland | 3,218 | 15 | 13 | 2 |
| Oakland Park | 44,484 | 97 | 86 | 11 |
| Ocala | 62,206 | 309 | 186 | 123 |
| Ocean Ridge | 1,975 | 21 | 16 | 5 |
| Ocoee | 50,741 | 107 | 94 | 13 |
| Okeechobee | 5,681 | 32 | 23 | 9 |
| Opa Locka | 15,707 | 52 | 40 | 12 |
| Orange City | 12,803 | 28 | 24 | 4 |
| Orange Park | 8,808 | 35 | 26 | 9 |
| Orlando | 295,040 | 1,042 | 822 | 220 |
| Ormond Beach | 44,535 | 80 | 61 | 19 |
| Oviedo | 42,565 | 77 | 70 | 7 |
| Palatka | 10,445 | 29 | 27 | 2 |
| Palm Bay | 118,296 | 204 | 146 | 58 |
| Palm Beach | 8,905 | 90 | 66 | 24 |
| Palm Beach Gardens | 59,100 | 178 | 121 | 57 |
| Palmetto | 13,914 | 47 | 35 | 12 |
| Palm Springs | 25,583 | 62 | 43 | 19 |
| Panama City | 33,651 | 121 | 84 | 37 |
| Panama City Beach | 12,415 | 91 | 74 | 17 |
| Parker | 4,089 | 10 | 9 | 1 |
| Parkland | 34,870 | 55 | 50 | 5 |
| Pembroke Pines | 172,163 | 340 | 244 | 96 |
| Pensacola | 53,255 | 198 | 145 | 53 |
| Perry | 6,862 | 23 | 21 | 2 |
| Pinellas Park | 55,416 | 123 | 105 | 18 |
| Plantation | 92,278 | 252 | 166 | 86 |
| Plant City | 40,115 | 81 | 66 | 15 |
| Pompano Beach | 112,691 | 273 | 243 | 30 |
| Ponce Inlet | 3,367 | 15 | 13 | 2 |
| Port Orange | 66,380 | 116 | 82 | 34 |
| Port Richey | 3,080 | 24 | 17 | 7 |
| Port St. Joe | 3,517 | 10 | 8 | 2 |
| Port St. Lucie | 214,836 | 319 | 248 | 71 |
| Punta Gorda | 21,094 | 55 | 37 | 18 |
| Quincy | 6,689 | 33 | 23 | 10 |
| Riviera Beach | 35,981 | 148 | 104 | 44 |
| Rockledge | 28,605 | 66 | 49 | 17 |
| Sanford | 62,320 | 157 | 131 | 26 |
| Sanibel | 7,531 | 40 | 25 | 15 |
| Sarasota | 59,569 | 230 | 178 | 52 |
| Satellite Beach | 11,233 | 36 | 25 | 11 |
| Sea Ranch Lakes | 625 | 12 | 8 | 4 |
| Sebastian | 26,982 | 59 | 41 | 18 |
| Sebring | 10,645 | 44 | 39 | 5 |
| Sewall's Point | 2,265 | 9 | 8 | 1 |
| Shalimar | 854 | 3 | 3 | 0 |

## Table 78. Full-Time Law Enforcement Employees, by Selected State and City, 2020—Continued

(Number.)

| State/city | Population | Total law enforcement employees | Total officers | Total civilians |
|---|---|---|---|---|
| Sneads | 1,746 | 7 | 6 | 1 |
| South Daytona | 13,788 | 34 | 28 | 6 |
| South Miami | 11,816 | 53 | 48 | 5 |
| Springfield | 8,169 | 27 | 22 | 5 |
| Starke | 5,470 | 21 | 19 | 2 |
| St. Augustine Beach | 7,241 | 22 | 19 | 3 |
| St. Cloud | 58,896 | 127 | 89 | 38 |
| St. Petersburg | 270,175 | 750 | 551 | 199 |
| Stuart | 16,801 | 61 | 45 | 16 |
| Sunny Isles Beach | 21,709 | 62 | 51 | 11 |
| Sunrise | 97,895 | 236 | 177 | 59 |
| Surfside | 5,571 | 35 | 30 | 5 |
| Tallahassee | 197,883 | 445 | 367 | 78 |
| Tamarac | 72,311 | 99 | 82 | 17 |
| Tampa | 415,413 | 1,177 | 919 | 258 |
| Tavares | 18,266 | 30 | 28 | 2 |
| Temple Terrace | 27,035 | 68 | 51 | 17 |
| Tequesta | 6,178 | 21 | 20 | 1 |
| Titusville | 46,921 | 127 | 87 | 40 |
| Treasure Island | 6,911 | 21 | 17 | 4 |
| Trenton | 2,208 | 4 | 3 | 1 |
| Umatilla | 3,942 | 9 | 8 | 1 |
| Valparaiso | 5,941 | 15 | 10 | 5 |
| Vero Beach | 18,049 | 77 | 57 | 20 |
| Village of Pinecrest | 19,080 | 69 | 45 | 24 |
| Virginia Gardens | 2,342 | 8 | 7 | 1 |
| Wauchula | 4,757 | 18 | 15 | 3 |
| Welaka | 720 | 1 | 1 | 0 |
| West Melbourne | 27,796 | 50 | 43 | 7 |
| West Miami | 9,095 | 27 | 22 | 5 |
| West Palm Beach | 114,055 | 389 | 288 | 101 |
| West Park | 15,217 | 46 | 42 | 4 |
| Wildwood | 7,976 | 44 | 39 | 5 |
| Wilton Manors | 11,492 | 44 | 29 | 15 |
| Winter Garden | 48,011 | 110 | 82 | 28 |
| Winter Haven | 47,974 | 108 | 86 | 22 |
| Winter Park | 30,971 | 107 | 81 | 26 |
| Winter Springs | 37,864 | 59 | 51 | 8 |
| Zephyrhills | 17,368 | 47 | 33 | 14 |
| **GEORGIA** | | | | |
| Abbeville | 2,626 | 5 | 4 | 1 |
| Acworth | 22,956 | 68 | 45 | 23 |
| Adairsville | 5,094 | 18 | 16 | 2 |
| Alamo | 3,320 | 2 | 2 | 0 |
| Alapaha | 673 | 2 | 1 | 1 |
| Albany | 70,214 | 150 | 128 | 22 |
| Alma | 3,322 | 17 | 15 | 2 |
| Alpharetta | 68,954 | 132 | 100 | 32 |
| Alto | 1,209 | 5 | 2 | 3 |
| Americus | 14,798 | 41 | 31 | 10 |
| Arcade | 2,064 | 4 | 4 | 0 |
| Athens-Clarke County | 127,410 | 270 | 210 | 60 |
| Atlanta | 521,274 | 2,095 | 1,641 | 454 |
| Austell | 7,280 | 33 | 27 | 6 |
| Avondale Estates | 3,126 | 12 | 12 | 0 |
| Bainbridge | 12,074 | 55 | 47 | 8 |
| Ball Ground | 2,414 | 5 | 5 | 0 |
| Barnesville | 6,660 | 20 | 20 | 0 |
| Bartow | 246 | 3 | 3 | 0 |
| Baxley | 4,646 | 13 | 12 | 1 |
| Blackshear | 3,529 | 22 | 19 | 3 |
| Blairsville | 660 | 8 | 7 | 1 |
| Blakely | 4,439 | 18 | 14 | 4 |
| Bloomingdale | 3,194 | 16 | 14 | 2 |
| Blue Ridge | 1,486 | 8 | 8 | 0 |
| Blythe | 698 | 1 | 1 | 0 |
| Boston | 1,313 | 5 | 5 | 0 |
| Bowdon | 2,096 | 8 | 7 | 1 |
| Braselton | 14,568 | 20 | 19 | 1 |
| Braswell | 387 | 2 | 1 | 1 |
| Bremen | 6,880 | 19 | 18 | 1 |
| Brookhaven | 56,770 | 88 | 74 | 14 |
| Brooklet | 2,001 | 6 | 5 | 1 |
| Broxton | 1,198 | 6 | 5 | 1 |
| Brunswick | 16,387 | 46 | 40 | 6 |
| Butler | 1,797 | 4 | 4 | 0 |
| Byron | 5,350 | 28 | 25 | 3 |
| Cairo | 9,269 | 26 | 23 | 3 |
| Calhoun | 17,719 | 51 | 43 | 8 |
| Camilla | 4,907 | 22 | 19 | 3 |
| Canon | 791 | 1 | 1 | 0 |
| Canton | 33,386 | 56 | 48 | 8 |
| Carrollton | 27,786 | 87 | 73 | 14 |
| Cartersville | 22,276 | 51 | 44 | 7 |

## Table 78. Full-Time Law Enforcement Employees, by Selected State and City, 2020—Continued

(Number.)

| State/city | Population | Total law enforcement employees | Total officers | Total civilians |
|---|---|---|---|---|
| Cave Spring | 1,065 | 3 | 3 | 0 |
| Cecil | 285 | 4 | 3 | 1 |
| Cedartown | 9,999 | 35 | 31 | 4 |
| Centerville | 8,082 | 18 | 15 | 3 |
| Chamblee | 31,254 | 78 | 62 | 16 |
| Chatsworth | 4,246 | 18 | 17 | 1 |
| Chickamauga | 3,235 | 5 | 5 | 0 |
| Clarkston | 12,677 | 15 | 15 | 0 |
| Claxton | 2,200 | 17 | 10 | 7 |
| Clayton | 2,122 | 12 | 11 | 1 |
| Cleveland | 4,246 | 17 | 16 | 1 |
| Cochran | 5,013 | 10 | 9 | 1 |
| Cohutta | 644 | 3 | 3 | 0 |
| College Park | 15,241 | 105 | 77 | 28 |
| Columbus | 196,633 | 429 | 336 | 93 |
| Conyers | 16,235 | 92 | 66 | 26 |
| Coolidge | 523 | 2 | 2 | 0 |
| Cordele | 10,223 | 32 | 23 | 9 |
| Cornelia | 4,865 | 19 | 17 | 2 |
| Covington | 14,517 | 64 | 52 | 12 |
| Cumming | 6,765 | 23 | 20 | 3 |
| Dallas | 14,704 | 36 | 26 | 10 |
| Dalton | 33,389 | 93 | 82 | 11 |
| Danielsville | 605 | 4 | 4 | 0 |
| Darien | 1,848 | 11 | 10 | 1 |
| Davisboro | 1,952 | 3 | 3 | 0 |
| Dawson | 4,076 | 11 | 7 | 4 |
| Decatur | 26,350 | 50 | 39 | 11 |
| Demorest | 2,174 | 10 | 7 | 3 |
| Dillard | 374 | 4 | 3 | 1 |
| Doerun | 726 | 6 | 5 | 1 |
| Donalsonville | 2,471 | 12 | 9 | 3 |
| Doraville | 10,322 | 62 | 44 | 18 |
| Douglas | 11,606 | 40 | 36 | 4 |
| Douglasville | 34,475 | 104 | 88 | 16 |
| Dublin | 15,767 | 65 | 57 | 8 |
| Duluth | 29,986 | 76 | 59 | 17 |
| Dunwoody | 49,621 | 66 | 54 | 12 |
| East Ellijay | 573 | 14 | 6 | 8 |
| Eastman | 5,054 | 12 | 10 | 2 |
| East Point | 35,156 | 109 | 72 | 37 |
| Eatonton | 6,878 | 20 | 12 | 8 |
| Edison | 1,394 | 5 | 4 | 1 |
| Elberton | 4,328 | 23 | 20 | 3 |
| Ellaville | 1,835 | 5 | 5 | 0 |
| Ellijay | 1,736 | 10 | 9 | 1 |
| Emerson | 1,602 | 12 | 11 | 1 |
| Enigma | 1,354 | 3 | 2 | 1 |
| Eton | 890 | 4 | 4 | 0 |
| Euharlee | 4,450 | 12 | 10 | 2 |
| Fairburn | 17,583 | 50 | 41 | 9 |
| Fairmount | 745 | 7 | 7 | 0 |
| Fayetteville | 18,554 | 57 | 48 | 9 |
| Fitzgerald | 8,563 | 31 | 24 | 7 |
| Flowery Branch | 9,155 | 19 | 17 | 2 |
| Folkston | 5,074 | 7 | 7 | 0 |
| Forest Park | 20,015 | 78 | 48 | 30 |
| Forsyth | 4,346 | 19 | 17 | 2 |
| Fort Oglethorpe | 10,046 | 27 | 24 | 3 |
| Fort Valley | 8,906 | 33 | 24 | 9 |
| Franklin | 956 | 8 | 8 | 0 |
| Franklin Springs | 1,214 | 2 | 2 | 0 |
| Gainesville | 45,385 | 107 | 93 | 14 |
| Garden City | 9,268 | 41 | 32 | 9 |
| Gordon | 1,801 | 11 | 6 | 5 |
| Grantville | 3,369 | 14 | 13 | 1 |
| Gray | 3,240 | 14 | 13 | 1 |
| Greensboro | 3,262 | 21 | 17 | 4 |
| Greenville | 831 | 8 | 7 | 1 |
| Griffin | 22,617 | 86 | 69 | 17 |
| Grovetown | 17,293 | 23 | 17 | 6 |
| Guyton | 2,455 | 7 | 7 | 0 |
| Hagan | 950 | 5 | 3 | 2 |
| Hahira | 3,080 | 15 | 9 | 6 |
| Hampton | 8,313 | 19 | 17 | 2 |
| Hapeville | 6,601 | 37 | 26 | 11 |
| Harlem | 3,648 | 7 | 6 | 1 |
| Hartwell | 4,453 | 23 | 18 | 5 |
| Hazlehurst | 4,072 | 14 | 11 | 3 |
| Helen | 564 | 11 | 10 | 1 |
| Hephzibah | 3,926 | 10 | 10 | 0 |
| Hiawassee | 923 | 5 | 5 | 0 |
| Hinesville | 34,211 | 91 | 75 | 16 |
| Hiram | 4,315 | 20 | 17 | 3 |
| Hoboken | 542 | 3 | 1 | 2 |

## Table 78. Full-Time Law Enforcement Employees, by Selected State and City, 2020—Continued

(Number.)

| State/city | Population | Total law enforcement employees | Total officers | Total civilians |
|---|---|---|---|---|
| Hogansville | 3,155 | 17 | 12 | 5 |
| Holly Springs | 17,484 | 38 | 36 | 2 |
| Homerville | 2,335 | 7 | 5 | 2 |
| Jackson | 5,361 | 15 | 14 | 1 |
| Jacksonville | 125 | 3 | 2 | 1 |
| Jasper | 4,074 | 16 | 14 | 2 |
| Jefferson | 12,833 | 27 | 24 | 3 |
| Johns Creek | 85,974 | 85 | 75 | 10 |
| Jonesboro | 5,164 | 30 | 25 | 5 |
| Kennesaw | 35,145 | 72 | 62 | 10 |
| Kingsland | 18,556 | 39 | 34 | 5 |
| Kingston | 751 | 4 | 2 | 2 |
| LaFayette | 7,547 | 26 | 24 | 2 |
| LaGrange | 30,874 | 105 | 85 | 20 |
| Lake City | 2,818 | 12 | 11 | 1 |
| Lakeland | 3,339 | 9 | 7 | 2 |
| Lake Park | 1,464 | 4 | 3 | 1 |
| Lavonia | 2,191 | 14 | 13 | 1 |
| Lawrenceville | 31,223 | 96 | 73 | 23 |
| Leesburg | 3,098 | 13 | 13 | 0 |
| Lilburn | 13,199 | 37 | 31 | 6 |
| Locust Grove | 9,513 | 27 | 24 | 3 |
| Loganville | 13,633 | 30 | 28 | 2 |
| Lookout Mountain | 1,566 | 7 | 7 | 0 |
| Louisville | 2,162 | 5 | 5 | 0 |
| Lovejoy | 7,742 | 25 | 21 | 4 |
| Madison | 4,286 | 16 | 14 | 2 |
| Manchester | 3,890 | 18 | 12 | 6 |
| Marietta | 61,223 | 179 | 132 | 47 |
| Maysville | 2,212 | 4 | 4 | 0 |
| McDonough | 28,222 | 50 | 44 | 6 |
| McIntyre | 593 | 3 | 3 | 0 |
| McRae-Helena | 8,250 | 11 | 10 | 1 |
| Metter | 4,000 | 14 | 13 | 1 |
| Midville | 250 | 1 | 1 | 0 |
| Midway | 2,010 | 7 | 5 | 2 |
| Milledgeville | 18,551 | 55 | 39 | 16 |
| Millen | 2,730 | 12 | 12 | 0 |
| Milton | 40,781 | 45 | 41 | 4 |
| Monroe | 14,091 | 54 | 51 | 3 |
| Montezuma | 2,870 | 12 | 9 | 3 |
| Morrow | 7,254 | 26 | 25 | 1 |
| Moultrie | 14,133 | 40 | 36 | 4 |
| Mount Zion | 1,907 | 6 | 6 | 0 |
| Nahunta | 1,178 | 2 | 2 | 0 |
| Nashville | 4,797 | 21 | 17 | 4 |
| Newington | 263 | 1 | 1 | 0 |
| Newnan | 44,023 | 100 | 87 | 13 |
| Newton | 549 | 1 | 1 | 0 |
| Norcross | 18,337 | 56 | 40 | 16 |
| Oakwood | 4,342 | 25 | 23 | 2 |
| Ocilla | 3,746 | 14 | 13 | 1 |
| Oglethorpe | 1,109 | 4 | 3 | 1 |
| Omega | 1,222 | 6 | 6 | 0 |
| Oxford | 2,359 | 3 | 3 | 0 |
| Palmetto | 5,010 | 18 | 16 | 2 |
| Peachtree City | 36,994 | 68 | 63 | 5 |
| Pearson | 2,088 | 6 | 5 | 1 |
| Pelham | 3,362 | 14 | 12 | 2 |
| Pembroke | 2,743 | 13 | 11 | 2 |
| Pendergrass | 593 | 4 | 4 | 0 |
| Perry | 19,469 | 45 | 40 | 5 |
| Pine Mountain | 1,468 | 11 | 8 | 3 |
| Pooler | 26,911 | 70 | 59 | 11 |
| Port Wentworth | 10,416 | 46 | 41 | 5 |
| Poulan | 761 | 4 | 4 | 0 |
| Remerton | 1,054 | 9 | 8 | 1 |
| Reynolds | 942 | 7 | 7 | 0 |
| Richmond Hill | 15,025 | 42 | 34 | 8 |
| Rincon | 10,836 | 20 | 18 | 2 |
| Ringgold | 3,508 | 10 | 9 | 1 |
| Riverdale | 15,643 | 43 | 35 | 8 |
| Rochelle | 1,072 | 6 | 3 | 3 |
| Rockmart | 4,520 | 22 | 20 | 2 |
| Rome | 36,792 | 88 | 79 | 9 |
| Rossville | 3,986 | 12 | 11 | 1 |
| Roswell | 96,041 | 195 | 151 | 44 |
| Royston | 2,561 | 10 | 8 | 2 |
| Sandersville | 5,215 | 19 | 15 | 4 |
| Sandy Springs | 111,533 | 160 | 139 | 21 |
| Sardis | 967 | 1 | 1 | 0 |
| Senoia | 4,654 | 18 | 15 | 3 |
| Shiloh | 501 | 4 | 4 | 0 |
| Sky Valley | 273 | 5 | 5 | 0 |
| Smyrna | 57,024 | 131 | 83 | 48 |

## Table 78. Full-Time Law Enforcement Employees, by Selected State and City, 2020—Continued

(Number.)

| State/city | Population | Total law enforcement employees | Total officers | Total civilians |
|---|---|---|---|---|
| Snellville | 20,382 | 58 | 46 | 12 |
| Social Circle | 4,674 | 18 | 17 | 1 |
| South Fulton | 104,282 | 158 | 139 | 19 |
| Sparta | 1,205 | 11 | 4 | 7 |
| Springfield | 4,237 | 8 | 7 | 1 |
| Statesboro | 33,722 | 89 | 72 | 17 |
| Statham | 2,931 | 9 | 7 | 2 |
| St. Marys | 19,021 | 27 | 23 | 4 |
| Stone Mountain | 6,357 | 16 | 15 | 1 |
| Summerville | 4,213 | 17 | 15 | 2 |
| Suwanee | 22,579 | 45 | 33 | 12 |
| Swainsboro | 7,517 | 25 | 23 | 2 |
| Sylvania | 2,438 | 13 | 10 | 3 |
| Sylvester | 5,642 | 19 | 16 | 3 |
| Tallapoosa | 3,237 | 12 | 10 | 2 |
| Temple | 5,104 | 14 | 11 | 3 |
| Thomaston | 8,735 | 27 | 23 | 4 |
| Thomasville | 18,485 | 56 | 50 | 6 |
| Thunderbolt | 2,609 | 9 | 7 | 2 |
| Toccoa | 8,283 | 22 | 20 | 2 |
| Trenton | 2,139 | 8 | 8 | 0 |
| Tunnel Hill | 892 | 4 | 4 | 0 |
| Twin City | 1,693 | 3 | 3 | 0 |
| Tybee Island | 3,057 | 37 | 25 | 12 |
| Tyrone | 7,803 | 16 | 16 | 0 |
| Union City | 23,707 | 61 | 56 | 5 |
| Valdosta | 56,844 | 156 | 131 | 25 |
| Vidalia | 10,452 | 36 | 26 | 10 |
| Vienna | 3,436 | 4 | 3 | 1 |
| Villa Rica | 17,094 | 54 | 46 | 8 |
| Walthourville | 4,060 | 6 | 5 | 1 |
| Warm Springs | 400 | 2 | 2 | 0 |
| Warner Robins | 79,483 | 150 | 108 | 42 |
| Watkinsville | 2,973 | 8 | 7 | 1 |
| Waverly Hall | 830 | 4 | 3 | 1 |
| Waycross | 13,359 | 65 | 51 | 14 |
| Waynesboro | 5,340 | 25 | 22 | 3 |
| West Point | 3,750 | 31 | 20 | 11 |
| Whigham | 461 | 2 | 1 | 1 |
| Whitesburg | 617 | 6 | 6 | 0 |
| Willacoochee | 1,389 | 4 | 3 | 1 |
| Winder | 18,709 | 41 | 34 | 7 |
| Woodstock | 34,798 | 66 | 59 | 7 |
| Wrens | 1,900 | 10 | 9 | 1 |
| Zebulon | 1,229 | 7 | 7 | 0 |
| **HAWAII** | | | | |
| Honolulu | 985,138 | 2,437 | 1,942 | 495 |
| **IDAHO** | | | | |
| American Falls | 4,280 | 9 | 7 | 2 |
| Ashton | 1,034 | 2 | 2 | 0 |
| Bellevue | 2,519 | 5 | 5 | 0 |
| Blackfoot | 12,026 | 30 | 27 | 3 |
| Boise | 231,902 | 357 | 280 | 77 |
| Bonners Ferry | 2,712 | 7 | 7 | 0 |
| Buhl | 4,560 | 10 | 8 | 2 |
| Caldwell | 62,306 | 87 | 73 | 14 |
| Chubbuck | 16,168 | 35 | 21 | 14 |
| Coeur d'Alene | 54,358 | 112 | 90 | 22 |
| Cottonwood | 984 | 1 | 1 | 0 |
| Emmett | 7,346 | 15 | 13 | 2 |
| Filer | 2,984 | 5 | 5 | 0 |
| Fruitland | 5,655 | 18 | 14 | 4 |
| Garden City | 12,018 | 36 | 28 | 8 |
| Grangeville | 3,272 | 5 | 5 | 0 |
| Hailey | 8,988 | 12 | 11 | 1 |
| Heyburn | 3,496 | 6 | 5 | 1 |
| Homedale | 2,851 | 8 | 7 | 1 |
| Idaho City | 484 | 1 | 1 | 0 |
| Idaho Falls | 64,792 | 135 | 92 | 43 |
| Jerome | 12,231 | 21 | 19 | 2 |
| Kellogg | 2,130 | 9 | 8 | 1 |
| Ketchum | 2,932 | 8 | 7 | 1 |
| Kimberly | 4,257 | 10 | 9 | 1 |
| Lewiston | 33,153 | 68 | 44 | 24 |
| Meridian | 126,744 | 157 | 120 | 37 |
| Middleton | 9,359 | 11 | 10 | 1 |
| Montpelier | 2,523 | 5 | 4 | 1 |
| Moscow | 26,368 | 43 | 35 | 8 |
| Mountain Home | 14,555 | 31 | 27 | 4 |
| Nampa | 105,619 | 200 | 140 | 60 |
| Orofino | 3,112 | 6 | 5 | 1 |
| Osburn | 1,571 | 2 | 2 | 0 |
| Parma | 2,145 | 5 | 4 | 1 |

## Table 78. Full-Time Law Enforcement Employees, by Selected State and City, 2020—Continued

(Number.)

| State/city | Population | Total law enforcement employees | Total officers | Total civilians |
|---|---|---|---|---|
| Payette | 8,065 | 16 | 14 | 2 |
| Pinehurst | 1,621 | 2 | 2 | 0 |
| Pocatello | 57,306 | 140 | 96 | 44 |
| Post Falls | 40,252 | 73 | 51 | 22 |
| Preston | 5,724 | 9 | 8 | 1 |
| Priest River | 1,950 | 6 | 5 | 1 |
| Rathdrum | 9,723 | 18 | 15 | 3 |
| Rexburg | 30,105 | 43 | 34 | 9 |
| Rigby | 4,482 | 9 | 8 | 1 |
| Rupert | 5,981 | 14 | 13 | 1 |
| Salmon | 3,185 | 9 | 9 | 0 |
| Sandpoint | 9,476 | 25 | 20 | 5 |
| Shelley | 4,674 | 9 | 9 | 0 |
| Soda Springs | 2,998 | 7 | 7 | 0 |
| Spirit Lake | 2,632 | 9 | 7 | 2 |
| St. Anthony | 3,601 | 6 | 6 | 0 |
| Sun Valley | 1,513 | 11 | 10 | 1 |
| Twin Falls | 52,158 | 97 | 73 | 24 |
| Weiser | 5,461 | 15 | 12 | 3 |
| Wilder | 1,843 | 5 | 5 | 0 |
| | | | | |
| **ILLINOIS** | | | | |
| Addison | 36,149 | 127 | 67 | 60 |
| Albers | 1,109 | 2 | 1 | 1 |
| Algonquin | 30,796 | 54 | 46 | 8 |
| Alsip | 18,405 | 49 | 40 | 9 |
| Alton | 25,871 | 81 | 58 | 23 |
| Annawan | 839 | 1 | 1 | 0 |
| Arcola | 2,831 | 7 | 6 | 1 |
| Arthur | 2,183 | 4 | 4 | 0 |
| Assumption | 1,045 | 2 | 2 | 0 |
| Bartonville | 6,009 | 17 | 12 | 5 |
| Bedford Park | 608 | 39 | 37 | 2 |
| Blue Island | 22,509 | 47 | 38 | 9 |
| Bourbonnais | 19,442 | 27 | 25 | 2 |
| Bradley | 15,058 | 38 | 34 | 4 |
| Burbank | 27,836 | 58 | 40 | 18 |
| Campton Hills | 11,061 | 9 | 9 | 0 |
| Carbondale | 24,897 | 69 | 49 | 20 |
| Carlinville | 5,395 | 18 | 13 | 5 |
| Carlyle | 3,133 | 8 | 7 | 1 |
| Carthage | 2,401 | 4 | 4 | 0 |
| Charleston | 19,861 | 35 | 32 | 3 |
| Chenoa | 3,098 | 4 | 4 | 0 |
| Cherry Valley | 2,842 | 14 | 13 | 1 |
| Chicago Heights | 28,852 | 84 | 71 | 13 |
| Clarendon Hills | 8,745 | 13 | 12 | 1 |
| Colona | 5,039 | 14 | 12 | 2 |
| Countryside | 5,856 | 27 | 24 | 3 |
| Crete | 7,906 | 19 | 17 | 2 |
| Crystal Lake | 39,532 | 71 | 62 | 9 |
| Danville | 29,829 | 72 | 60 | 12 |
| Decatur | 69,426 | 149 | 138 | 11 |
| DeKalb | 42,475 | 78 | 61 | 17 |
| Des Plaines | 58,166 | 109 | 94 | 15 |
| Diamond | 2,479 | 4 | 4 | 0 |
| Downers Grove | 48,706 | 82 | 65 | 17 |
| East Hazel Crest | 1,472 | 11 | 9 | 2 |
| East Peoria | 22,235 | 47 | 43 | 4 |
| Evergreen Park | 18,813 | 72 | 54 | 18 |
| Farmer City | 1,895 | 4 | 4 | 0 |
| Flossmoor | 8,979 | 25 | 20 | 5 |
| Fox Lake | 10,386 | 32 | 26 | 6 |
| Galesburg | 29,576 | 75 | 49 | 26 |
| Geneseo | 6,494 | 20 | 14 | 6 |
| Geneva | 21,680 | 44 | 35 | 9 |
| Gibson City | 3,258 | 8 | 7 | 1 |
| Glen Carbon | 12,881 | 36 | 25 | 11 |
| Glendale Heights | 33,252 | 67 | 52 | 15 |
| Glenwood | 8,580 | 26 | 23 | 3 |
| Godley | 790 | 4 | 4 | 0 |
| Greenfield | 955 | 3 | 3 | 0 |
| Gurnee | 30,061 | 90 | 57 | 33 |
| Harvard | 8,935 | 18 | 16 | 2 |
| Havana | 2,912 | 15 | 9 | 6 |
| Hickory Hills | 13,506 | 39 | 28 | 11 |
| Highland | 10,022 | 26 | 20 | 6 |
| Highland Park | 29,392 | 65 | 55 | 10 |
| Homer Glen | 24,285 | 22 | 22 | 0 |
| Homewood | 18,393 | 46 | 41 | 5 |
| Hoopeston | 4,901 | 14 | 10 | 4 |
| Hudson | 1,807 | 2 | 2 | 0 |
| Itasca | 9,873 | 21 | 18 | 3 |
| Jacksonville | 18,398 | 45 | 41 | 4 |
| Joliet | 146,589 | 315 | 252 | 63 |

## Table 78. Full-Time Law Enforcement Employees, by Selected State and City, 2020—Continued

(Number.)

| State/city | Population | Total law enforcement employees | Total officers | Total civilians |
|---|---|---|---|---|
| Kankakee | 25,490 | 65 | 57 | 8 |
| Kenilworth | 2,436 | 9 | 8 | 1 |
| Kildeer | 4,002 | 10 | 8 | 2 |
| La Grange Park | 12,808 | 23 | 21 | 2 |
| Lake in the Hills | 28,284 | 47 | 39 | 8 |
| Lake Zurich | 19,764 | 50 | 31 | 19 |
| Lemont | 17,470 | 26 | 21 | 5 |
| Le Roy | 3,492 | 8 | 8 | 0 |
| Lincoln | 13,297 | 28 | 26 | 2 |
| Lisle | 23,208 | 45 | 35 | 10 |
| Livingston | 791 | 1 | 1 | 0 |
| Loves Park | 23,323 | 42 | 40 | 2 |
| Lovington | 1,000 | 2 | 2 | 0 |
| Mackinaw | 1,853 | 2 | 2 | 0 |
| Manito | 1,450 | 3 | 3 | 0 |
| Maple Park | 1,392 | 1 | 1 | 0 |
| Marseilles | 4,748 | 10 | 9 | 1 |
| Mascoutah | 8,119 | 16 | 15 | 1 |
| McHenry | 27,106 | 77 | 47 | 30 |
| McLeansboro | 2,716 | 5 | 5 | 0 |
| Metropolis | 5,821 | 19 | 14 | 5 |
| Milledgeville | 937 | 2 | 2 | 0 |
| Millstadt | 3,803 | 9 | 9 | 0 |
| Mokena | 20,194 | 34 | 31 | 3 |
| Morris | 15,321 | 29 | 25 | 4 |
| Morrison | 3,927 | 8 | 8 | 0 |
| Morton | 16,218 | 24 | 22 | 2 |
| Mount Carmel | 6,768 | 19 | 12 | 7 |
| Mount Prospect | 53,125 | 102 | 81 | 21 |
| Mount Pulaski | 1,438 | 2 | 2 | 0 |
| Mount Zion | 5,753 | 12 | 10 | 2 |
| New Lenox | 27,379 | 43 | 37 | 6 |
| Newman | 833 | 1 | 1 | 0 |
| Niles | 28,493 | 66 | 52 | 14 |
| Normal | 54,636 | 76 | 68 | 8 |
| North Aurora | 18,302 | 33 | 31 | 2 |
| Northlake | 11,994 | 48 | 35 | 13 |
| North Pekin | 1,524 | 6 | 6 | 0 |
| Oakwood | 1,447 | 2 | 2 | 0 |
| O'Fallon | 29,688 | 65 | 45 | 20 |
| Oswego | 37,362 | 62 | 51 | 11 |
| Ottawa | 18,017 | 50 | 35 | 15 |
| Palos Heights | 12,361 | 31 | 27 | 4 |
| Palos Hills | 16,813 | 32 | 29 | 3 |
| Palos Park | 4,704 | 12 | 11 | 1 |
| Pekin | 31,593 | 58 | 50 | 8 |
| Peoria | 108,891 | 216 | 196 | 20 |
| Pontiac | 11,106 | 21 | 19 | 2 |
| Princeton | 7,353 | 16 | 15 | 1 |
| Rantoul | 12,241 | 36 | 30 | 6 |
| Riverdale | 12,849 | 29 | 25 | 4 |
| River Forest | 10,647 | 26 | 24 | 2 |
| Rock Falls | 8,577 | 24 | 21 | 3 |
| Rockford | 144,027 | 325 | 282 | 43 |
| Rock Island | 36,666 | 108 | 81 | 27 |
| Rockton | 7,448 | 18 | 16 | 2 |
| Rossville | 1,189 | 3 | 3 | 0 |
| Roxana | 1,395 | 6 | 5 | 1 |
| Royalton | 1,106 | 3 | 3 | 0 |
| Salem | 6,904 | 26 | 18 | 8 |
| Sandwich | 7,381 | 18 | 15 | 3 |
| Skokie | 62,163 | 148 | 105 | 43 |
| Springfield | 113,331 | 239 | 216 | 23 |
| Spring Valley | 5,020 | 11 | 10 | 1 |
| St. Anne | 1,164 | 4 | 4 | 0 |
| Sugar Grove | 9,976 | 10 | 10 | 0 |
| Swansea | 13,245 | 23 | 21 | 2 |
| Sycamore | 18,399 | 33 | 30 | 3 |
| Thomson | 544 | 1 | 1 | 0 |
| Thornton | 2,365 | 11 | 10 | 1 |
| Tilton | 2,649 | 6 | 6 | 0 |
| Troy | 10,447 | 25 | 19 | 6 |
| Tuscola | 4,359 | 8 | 7 | 1 |
| Vernon Hills | 26,569 | 64 | 40 | 24 |
| Watseka | 4,639 | 12 | 11 | 1 |
| West Chicago | 26,526 | 49 | 45 | 4 |
| West Dundee | 8,938 | 22 | 19 | 3 |
| Westmont | 24,224 | 47 | 41 | 6 |
| Westville | 2,886 | 3 | 3 | 0 |
| Wheeling | 39,087 | 90 | 60 | 30 |
| Wilmette | 26,793 | 59 | 45 | 14 |
| Winnetka | 12,192 | 31 | 26 | 5 |
| Wood Dale | 13,455 | 41 | 32 | 9 |
| Worth | 10,289 | 28 | 26 | 2 |

# Table 78. Full-Time Law Enforcement Employees, by Selected State and City, 2020—Continued

(Number.)

| State/city | Population | Total law enforcement employees | Total officers | Total civilians |
|---|---|---|---|---|
| **INDIANA** | | | | |
| Albion | 2,372 | 6 | 6 | 0 |
| Auburn | 13,700 | 27 | 26 | 1 |
| Avon | 20,055 | 35 | 33 | 2 |
| Bargersville | 8,933 | 15 | 14 | 1 |
| Batesville | 6,773 | 18 | 13 | 5 |
| Bluffton | 10,113 | 33 | 21 | 12 |
| Brownsburg | 28,227 | 57 | 50 | 7 |
| Cannelton | 1,464 | 4 | 4 | 0 |
| Cedar Lake | 13,806 | 24 | 22 | 2 |
| Columbia City | 9,479 | 33 | 22 | 11 |
| Columbus | 48,902 | 91 | 83 | 8 |
| Danville | 10,364 | 20 | 18 | 2 |
| Dyer | 15,914 | 35 | 32 | 3 |
| Edinburgh | 4,629 | 13 | 12 | 1 |
| Elwood | 8,357 | 19 | 18 | 1 |
| Fishers | 99,184 | 131 | 117 | 14 |
| Fort Wayne | 274,295 | 529 | 462 | 67 |
| Frankfort | 15,692 | 39 | 34 | 5 |
| Franklin | 26,091 | 60 | 53 | 7 |
| Goshen | 34,336 | 71 | 60 | 11 |
| Greenwood | 61,277 | 75 | 67 | 8 |
| Highland | 22,144 | 46 | 41 | 5 |
| Hobart | 27,777 | 77 | 66 | 11 |
| Huntington | 17,006 | 38 | 35 | 3 |
| Kendallville | 9,895 | 27 | 18 | 9 |
| Kokomo | 58,248 | 106 | 87 | 19 |
| Leavenworth | 234 | 3 | 3 | 0 |
| Lebanon | 16,155 | 44 | 42 | 2 |
| Madison | 11,729 | 101 | 40 | 61 |
| Muncie | 67,262 | 102 | 94 | 8 |
| Munster | 22,377 | 45 | 40 | 5 |
| New Haven | 16,088 | 32 | 24 | 8 |
| New Whiteland | 6,443 | 8 | 7 | 1 |
| Noblesville | 67,290 | 106 | 96 | 10 |
| North Salem | 542 | 1 | 1 | 0 |
| North Vernon | 6,594 | 20 | 17 | 3 |
| Pendleton | 4,459 | 12 | 11 | 1 |
| Peru | 10,877 | 27 | 24 | 3 |
| Pittsboro | 3,913 | 9 | 8 | 1 |
| Plainfield | 37,257 | 68 | 61 | 7 |
| Seymour | 20,302 | 62 | 43 | 19 |
| Shirley | 911 | 2 | 2 | 0 |
| South Bend | 101,936 | 285 | 222 | 63 |
| St. John | 20,168 | 25 | 23 | 2 |
| Vincennes | 16,650 | 42 | 37 | 5 |
| Walkerton | 2,261 | 10 | 6 | 4 |
| West Lafayette | 52,675 | 60 | 40 | 20 |
| Westville | 5,840 | 5 | 5 | 0 |
| Whiteland | 4,753 | 13 | 12 | 1 |
| Whitestown | 10,738 | 30 | 28 | 2 |
| Whiting | 4,797 | 17 | 16 | 1 |
| **IOWA** | | | | |
| Adel | 5,845 | 11 | 10 | 1 |
| Albia | 3,706 | 7 | 6 | 1 |
| Algona | 5,340 | 14 | 10 | 4 |
| Altoona | 20,064 | 39 | 36 | 3 |
| Ames | 67,886 | 71 | 48 | 23 |
| Anamosa | 5,545 | 9 | 8 | 1 |
| Ankeny | 73,109 | 76 | 65 | 11 |
| Asbury | 5,999 | 6 | 6 | 0 |
| Atlantic | 6,457 | 13 | 12 | 1 |
| Audubon | 1,852 | 3 | 3 | 0 |
| Belle Plaine | 2,406 | 5 | 5 | 0 |
| Belmond | 2,222 | 5 | 5 | 0 |
| Bettendorf | 37,022 | 51 | 45 | 6 |
| Bloomfield | 2,699 | 7 | 6 | 1 |
| Boone | 12,383 | 18 | 17 | 1 |
| Burlington | 24,417 | 53 | 47 | 6 |
| Camanche | 4,360 | 9 | 9 | 0 |
| Carlisle | 4,369 | 9 | 8 | 1 |
| Carroll | 9,651 | 16 | 15 | 1 |
| Carter Lake | 3,793 | 11 | 10 | 1 |
| Cedar Rapids | 134,763 | 280 | 223 | 57 |
| Centerville | 5,394 | 14 | 9 | 5 |
| Charles City | 7,174 | 15 | 14 | 1 |
| Clarinda | 5,346 | 11 | 10 | 1 |
| Clarion | 2,662 | 7 | 6 | 1 |
| Clear Lake | 7,492 | 22 | 15 | 7 |
| Clinton | 24,865 | 52 | 46 | 6 |
| Clive | 17,652 | 33 | 28 | 5 |
| Colfax | 2,046 | 2 | 2 | 0 |
| Coralville | 22,874 | 37 | 33 | 4 |
| Council Bluffs | 62,202 | 141 | 119 | 22 |

## Table 78. Full-Time Law Enforcement Employees, by Selected State and City, 2020—Continued

(Number.)

| State/city | Population | Total law enforcement employees | Total officers | Total civilians |
|---|---|---|---|---|
| Creston | 7,644 | 16 | 12 | 4 |
| Davenport | 102,014 | 187 | 162 | 25 |
| Dayton | 776 | 1 | 1 | 0 |
| Decorah | 7,422 | 14 | 13 | 1 |
| Denison | 8,241 | 19 | 12 | 7 |
| Denver | 1,891 | 3 | 3 | 0 |
| Des Moines | 213,060 | 461 | 364 | 97 |
| DeWitt | 5,212 | 10 | 9 | 1 |
| Dubuque | 57,790 | 104 | 97 | 7 |
| Durant | 1,856 | 4 | 4 | 0 |
| Dyersville | 4,478 | 7 | 7 | 0 |
| Dysart | 1,305 | 2 | 2 | 0 |
| Eldora | 2,556 | 5 | 5 | 0 |
| Eldridge | 6,998 | 9 | 8 | 1 |
| Emmetsburg | 3,645 | 7 | 6 | 1 |
| Estherville | 5,516 | 12 | 12 | 0 |
| Evansdale | 4,732 | 9 | 8 | 1 |
| Fairfield | 10,608 | 18 | 12 | 6 |
| Fort Dodge | 23,788 | 42 | 39 | 3 |
| Fort Madison | 10,185 | 20 | 18 | 2 |
| Glenwood | 5,260 | 11 | 10 | 1 |
| Gowrie | 946 | 1 | 1 | 0 |
| Grinnell | 9,084 | 16 | 14 | 2 |
| Grundy Center | 2,666 | 5 | 5 | 0 |
| Hampton | 4,132 | 8 | 7 | 1 |
| Harlan | 4,767 | 9 | 8 | 1 |
| Hawarden | 2,434 | 4 | 4 | 0 |
| Hiawatha | 7,512 | 17 | 17 | 0 |
| Huxley | 4,379 | 6 | 6 | 0 |
| Independence | 6,227 | 12 | 11 | 1 |
| Indianola | 16,203 | 27 | 23 | 4 |
| Iowa City | 77,522 | 96 | 73 | 23 |
| Iowa Falls | 4,907 | 13 | 8 | 5 |
| Jefferson | 4,048 | 7 | 7 | 0 |
| Johnston | 23,759 | 35 | 30 | 5 |
| Keokuk | 10,025 | 25 | 22 | 3 |
| Knoxville | 7,062 | 16 | 14 | 2 |
| Lansing | 926 | 3 | 3 | 0 |
| Le Mars | 10,233 | 17 | 15 | 2 |
| Leon | 1,793 | 2 | 2 | 0 |
| Manchester | 4,987 | 17 | 10 | 7 |
| Maquoketa | 5,894 | 18 | 11 | 7 |
| Marengo | 2,460 | 3 | 3 | 0 |
| Marion | 41,370 | 58 | 45 | 13 |
| Mar-Mac | 1,268 | 2 | 2 | 0 |
| Marshalltown | 26,651 | 42 | 37 | 5 |
| Mason City | 26,550 | 47 | 40 | 7 |
| Mechanicsville | 1,113 | 1 | 1 | 0 |
| Monticello | 3,882 | 9 | 8 | 1 |
| Mount Pleasant | 8,494 | 16 | 14 | 2 |
| Mount Vernon-Lisbon | 6,794 | 9 | 8 | 1 |
| Muscatine | 23,499 | 42 | 38 | 4 |
| Nevada | 6,669 | 12 | 10 | 2 |
| New Hampton | 3,365 | 6 | 6 | 0 |
| Newton | 15,116 | 32 | 27 | 5 |
| North Liberty | 20,482 | 23 | 21 | 2 |
| Norwalk | 12,854 | 20 | 19 | 1 |
| Oelwein | 5,731 | 12 | 10 | 2 |
| Ogden | 1,980 | 3 | 3 | 0 |
| Orange City | 6,280 | 7 | 7 | 0 |
| Osage | 3,541 | 7 | 6 | 1 |
| Osceola | 5,320 | 12 | 11 | 1 |
| Oskaloosa | 11,832 | 17 | 15 | 2 |
| Ottumwa | 24,308 | 50 | 40 | 10 |
| Pella | 10,260 | 24 | 18 | 6 |
| Perry | 7,912 | 18 | 12 | 6 |
| Pleasant Hill | 10,153 | 22 | 20 | 2 |
| Polk City | 5,350 | 8 | 8 | 0 |
| Postville | 2,014 | 4 | 4 | 0 |
| Preston | 935 | 1 | 1 | 0 |
| Princeton | 962 | 1 | 1 | 0 |
| Red Oak | 5,229 | 12 | 10 | 2 |
| Rock Valley | 3,945 | 6 | 6 | 0 |
| Sabula | 541 | 1 | 1 | 0 |
| Sac City | 2,018 | 4 | 4 | 0 |
| Sergeant Bluff | 5,207 | 9 | 8 | 1 |
| Sheldon | 5,058 | 7 | 7 | 0 |
| Shenandoah | 4,749 | 9 | 8 | 1 |
| Sigourney | 1,972 | 2 | 1 | 1 |
| Sioux Center | 7,729 | 8 | 8 | 0 |
| Sioux City | 82,750 | 148 | 128 | 20 |
| Spencer | 10,966 | 28 | 20 | 8 |
| Spirit Lake | 5,292 | 10 | 9 | 1 |
| Storm Lake | 10,414 | 23 | 19 | 4 |
| Story City | 3,320 | 6 | 6 | 0 |

## Table 78. Full-Time Law Enforcement Employees, by Selected State and City, 2020—Continued

(Number.)

| State/city | Population | Total law enforcement employees | Total officers | Total civilians |
|---|---|---|---|---|
| Tama | 2,709 | 6 | 6 | 0 |
| Tipton | 3,174 | 7 | 6 | 1 |
| Toledo | 2,106 | 6 | 6 | 0 |
| University Heights | 1,024 | 5 | 5 | 0 |
| Urbandale | 45,201 | 61 | 52 | 9 |
| Vinton | 4,996 | 11 | 9 | 2 |
| Washington | 7,201 | 12 | 11 | 1 |
| Waterloo | 67,174 | 121 | 113 | 8 |
| Waukee | 27,858 | 32 | 29 | 3 |
| Waukon | 3,570 | 7 | 6 | 1 |
| Waverly | 10,340 | 17 | 16 | 1 |
| Webster City | 7,608 | 20 | 13 | 7 |
| West Branch | 2,539 | 4 | 4 | 0 |
| West Burlington | 2,863 | 10 | 10 | 0 |
| West Des Moines | 70,414 | 101 | 89 | 12 |
| West Union | 2,249 | 5 | 5 | 0 |
| Williamsburg | 3,191 | 6 | 6 | 0 |
| Windsor Heights | 4,717 | 14 | 13 | 1 |
| Winterset | 5,450 | 8 | 8 | 0 |
| **KANSAS** | | | | |
| Abilene | 6,055 | 16 | 13 | 3 |
| Andover | 13,871 | 32 | 24 | 8 |
| Anthony | 2,011 | 4 | 3 | 1 |
| Arkansas City | 11,531 | 42 | 22 | 20 |
| Arma | 1,405 | 6 | 6 | 0 |
| Atchison | 10,374 | 25 | 24 | 1 |
| Attica | 540 | 1 | 1 | 0 |
| Atwood | 1,210 | 3 | 3 | 0 |
| Augusta | 9,290 | 30 | 22 | 8 |
| Baldwin City | 4,706 | 12 | 10 | 2 |
| Baxter Springs | 3,859 | 11 | 9 | 2 |
| Bel Aire | 8,660 | 17 | 15 | 2 |
| Belle Plaine | 1,522 | 4 | 4 | 0 |
| Belleville | 1,828 | 5 | 5 | 0 |
| Beloit | 3,540 | 8 | 7 | 1 |
| Benton | 863 | 2 | 2 | 0 |
| Blue Rapids | 954 | 2 | 2 | 0 |
| Bonner Springs | 8,072 | 26 | 23 | 3 |
| Buhler | 1,263 | 3 | 3 | 0 |
| Burlingame | 879 | 2 | 2 | 0 |
| Burlington | 2,533 | 9 | 7 | 2 |
| Burrton | 849 | 6 | 2 | 4 |
| Caldwell | 963 | 3 | 3 | 0 |
| Caney | 1,924 | 11 | 6 | 5 |
| Canton | 682 | 1 | 1 | 0 |
| Carbondale | 1,339 | 3 | 3 | 0 |
| Chanute | 8,979 | 20 | 17 | 3 |
| Chapman | 1,314 | 2 | 2 | 0 |
| Cheney | 2,180 | 5 | 5 | 0 |
| Cherokee | 712 | 1 | 1 | 0 |
| Cherryvale | 2,098 | 7 | 6 | 1 |
| Claflin | 589 | 1 | 1 | 0 |
| Clay Center | 3,957 | 8 | 7 | 1 |
| Clearwater | 2,589 | 6 | 6 | 0 |
| Coffeyville | 9,066 | 32 | 23 | 9 |
| Colby | 5,305 | 12 | 11 | 1 |
| Coldwater | 725 | 1 | 1 | 0 |
| Columbus | 2,978 | 9 | 9 | 0 |
| Colwich | 1,509 | 3 | 3 | 0 |
| Conway Springs | 1,208 | 3 | 3 | 0 |
| Council Grove | 2,090 | 8 | 7 | 1 |
| Derby | 25,425 | 59 | 49 | 10 |
| Dodge City | 26,612 | 57 | 39 | 18 |
| Eastborough | 727 | 6 | 6 | 0 |
| Edwardsville | 4,540 | 19 | 18 | 1 |
| El Dorado | 12,819 | 28 | 25 | 3 |
| Elkhart | 1,685 | 2 | 2 | 0 |
| Ellis | 2,013 | 5 | 5 | 0 |
| Elwood | 1,171 | 3 | 3 | 0 |
| Emporia | 24,462 | 46 | 40 | 6 |
| Eudora | 6,418 | 14 | 14 | 0 |
| Fairway | 3,972 | 10 | 9 | 1 |
| Fort Scott | 7,607 | 21 | 20 | 1 |
| Fredonia | 2,154 | 7 | 6 | 1 |
| Frontenac | 3,387 | 10 | 7 | 3 |
| Galena | 2,798 | 9 | 7 | 2 |
| Garden City | 25,920 | 89 | 60 | 29 |
| Garden Plain | 919 | 2 | 2 | 0 |
| Gardner | 22,714 | 39 | 34 | 5 |
| Garnett | 3,243 | 7 | 7 | 0 |
| Girard | 2,644 | 8 | 6 | 2 |
| Goddard | 5,020 | 12 | 11 | 1 |
| Goodland | 4,283 | 11 | 9 | 2 |
| Grandview Plaza | 1,532 | 7 | 6 | 1 |

## Table 78. Full-Time Law Enforcement Employees, by Selected State and City, 2020—Continued

(Number.)

| State/city | Population | Total law enforcement employees | Total officers | Total civilians |
|---|---|---|---|---|
| Great Bend | 14,795 | 34 | 30 | 4 |
| Greensburg | 777 | 2 | 2 | 0 |
| Halstead | 2,022 | 6 | 5 | 1 |
| Haven | 1,178 | 3 | 3 | 0 |
| Hays | 20,861 | 49 | 31 | 18 |
| Haysville | 11,445 | 29 | 25 | 4 |
| Herington | 2,213 | 5 | 5 | 0 |
| Hesston | 3,738 | 7 | 6 | 1 |
| Hiawatha | 3,075 | 11 | 10 | 1 |
| Highland | 983 | 1 | 1 | 0 |
| Hill City | 1,343 | 4 | 4 | 0 |
| Hoisington | 2,429 | 7 | 6 | 1 |
| Holcomb | 2,037 | 3 | 3 | 0 |
| Holton | 3,193 | 11 | 7 | 4 |
| Horton | 1,659 | 8 | 4 | 4 |
| Hoxie | 1,191 | 2 | 2 | 0 |
| Hugoton | 3,653 | 7 | 6 | 1 |
| Humboldt | 1,762 | 7 | 5 | 2 |
| Hutchinson | 40,015 | 91 | 67 | 24 |
| Independence | 8,326 | 24 | 18 | 6 |
| Inman | 1,318 | 4 | 4 | 0 |
| Iola | 5,222 | 18 | 17 | 1 |
| Junction City | 21,680 | 67 | 47 | 20 |
| Kechi | 2,129 | 5 | 5 | 0 |
| Kingman | 2,727 | 19 | 8 | 11 |
| Kiowa | 907 | 1 | 1 | 0 |
| La Cygne | 1,104 | 2 | 2 | 0 |
| La Harpe | 527 | 1 | 1 | 0 |
| Lake Quivira | 932 | 1 | 1 | 0 |
| Lansing | 12,021 | 19 | 18 | 1 |
| Larned | 3,591 | 7 | 7 | 0 |
| Lawrence | 99,530 | 160 | 136 | 24 |
| Leavenworth | 35,990 | 73 | 53 | 20 |
| Leawood | 34,957 | 74 | 54 | 20 |
| Lebo | 878 | 4 | 4 | 0 |
| Lenexa | 57,012 | 130 | 81 | 49 |
| Liberal | 18,658 | 44 | 32 | 12 |
| Lindsborg | 3,259 | 8 | 7 | 1 |
| Louisburg | 4,619 | 11 | 10 | 1 |
| Lyndon | 1,009 | 1 | 1 | 0 |
| Lyons | 3,403 | 7 | 6 | 1 |
| Macksville | 515 | 1 | 1 | 0 |
| Maize | 5,491 | 14 | 13 | 1 |
| Marion | 1,721 | 5 | 5 | 0 |
| Marysville | 3,246 | 8 | 7 | 1 |
| McLouth | 833 | 2 | 2 | 0 |
| McPherson | 13,002 | 39 | 34 | 5 |
| Medicine Lodge | 1,784 | 5 | 5 | 0 |
| Merriam | 11,138 | 36 | 32 | 4 |
| Minneapolis | 1,883 | 4 | 4 | 0 |
| Mission | 9,931 | 30 | 26 | 4 |
| Moran | 504 | 1 | 1 | 0 |
| Mound City | 670 | 1 | 1 | 0 |
| Moundridge | 1,860 | 3 | 3 | 0 |
| Mount Hope | 805 | 2 | 2 | 0 |
| Mulberry | 521 | 1 | 1 | 0 |
| Mulvane | 6,610 | 14 | 14 | 0 |
| Neodesha | 2,186 | 9 | 7 | 2 |
| North Newton | 1,761 | 4 | 4 | 0 |
| Norton | 2,692 | 7 | 6 | 1 |
| Oakley | 2,028 | 10 | 6 | 4 |
| Oberlin | 1,658 | 4 | 4 | 0 |
| Onaga | 677 | 1 | 1 | 0 |
| Osage City | 2,748 | 7 | 7 | 0 |
| Osborne | 1,266 | 3 | 3 | 0 |
| Oswego | 1,668 | 5 | 5 | 0 |
| Ottawa | 12,303 | 36 | 31 | 5 |
| Overland Park | 199,881 | 318 | 251 | 67 |
| Paola | 5,668 | 19 | 14 | 5 |
| Park City | 8,006 | 18 | 16 | 2 |
| Parsons | 9,368 | 24 | 16 | 8 |
| Peabody | 1,067 | 5 | 3 | 2 |
| Pittsburg | 19,939 | 59 | 44 | 15 |
| Plainville | 1,755 | 5 | 5 | 0 |
| Pleasanton | 1,154 | 2 | 2 | 0 |
| Prairie Village | 22,402 | 51 | 41 | 10 |
| Pratt | 6,428 | 23 | 15 | 8 |
| Protection | 455 | 1 | 1 | 0 |
| Roeland Park | 6,644 | 14 | 12 | 2 |
| Rose Hill | 3,983 | 9 | 8 | 1 |
| Rossville | 1,110 | 2 | 2 | 0 |
| Russell | 4,369 | 14 | 8 | 6 |
| Sabetha | 2,552 | 9 | 5 | 4 |
| Salina | 46,112 | 97 | 76 | 21 |
| Scott City | 3,726 | 12 | 7 | 5 |

## Table 78. Full-Time Law Enforcement Employees, by Selected State and City, 2020—Continued

(Number.)

| State/city | Population | Total law enforcement employees | Total officers | Total civilians |
|---|---|---|---|---|
| Scranton | 667 | 1 | 1 | 0 |
| Sedan | 980 | 2 | 2 | 0 |
| Seneca | 2,087 | 4 | 4 | 0 |
| Shawnee | 66,710 | 112 | 90 | 22 |
| Smith Center | 1,542 | 2 | 2 | 0 |
| South Hutchinson | 2,498 | 6 | 6 | 0 |
| Spearville | 765 | 1 | 1 | 0 |
| Spring Hill | 8,167 | 15 | 14 | 1 |
| Stafford | 909 | 3 | 3 | 0 |
| Sterling | 2,160 | 5 | 5 | 0 |
| St. George | 1,066 | 2 | 1 | 1 |
| St. John | 1,125 | 3 | 3 | 0 |
| St. Marys | 2,649 | 6 | 6 | 0 |
| Tonganoxie | 5,761 | 14 | 13 | 1 |
| Topeka | 124,227 | 318 | 263 | 55 |
| Troy | 940 | 1 | 1 | 0 |
| Udall | 696 | 3 | 3 | 0 |
| Ulysses | 5,489 | 10 | 10 | 0 |
| Valley Center | 7,443 | 18 | 16 | 2 |
| Valley Falls | 1,149 | 3 | 3 | 0 |
| Victoria | 1,215 | 2 | 2 | 0 |
| WaKeeney | 1,724 | 5 | 5 | 0 |
| Wamego | 4,750 | 9 | 8 | 1 |
| Waterville | 628 | 1 | 1 | 0 |
| Wathena | 1,264 | 2 | 2 | 0 |
| Wellington | 7,491 | 20 | 17 | 3 |
| Wellsville | 1,777 | 6 | 5 | 1 |
| Westwood | 1,657 | 8 | 7 | 1 |
| Wilson | 707 | 7 | 6 | 1 |
| Winfield | 11,756 | 29 | 24 | 5 |
| Yates Center | 1,253 | 3 | 3 | 0 |
| | | | | |
| **KENTUCKY** | | | | |
| Adairville | 893 | 1 | 1 | 0 |
| Alexandria | 9,949 | 20 | 16 | 4 |
| Anchorage | 2,435 | 14 | 10 | 4 |
| Ashland | 19,913 | 50 | 46 | 4 |
| Bancroft | 513 | 1 | 1 | 0 |
| Bardstown | 13,378 | 32 | 29 | 3 |
| Beaver Dam | 3,558 | 7 | 7 | 0 |
| Bellevue | 5,748 | 12 | 11 | 1 |
| Benton | 4,461 | 8 | 8 | 0 |
| Berea | 16,576 | 37 | 34 | 3 |
| Bloomfield | 1,088 | 1 | 1 | 0 |
| Bowling Green | 71,826 | 160 | 121 | 39 |
| Brandenburg | 2,897 | 5 | 5 | 0 |
| Brownsville | 839 | 2 | 2 | 0 |
| Burgin | 997 | 1 | 1 | 0 |
| Burkesville | 1,427 | 6 | 6 | 0 |
| Burnside | 792 | 4 | 4 | 0 |
| Butler | 576 | 1 | 1 | 0 |
| Calvert City | 2,502 | 8 | 7 | 1 |
| Campbellsville | 11,500 | 15 | 13 | 2 |
| Carlisle | 2,056 | 10 | 6 | 4 |
| Carrollton | 3,794 | 14 | 13 | 1 |
| Catlettsburg | 1,724 | 5 | 5 | 0 |
| Cave City | 2,437 | 9 | 9 | 0 |
| Centertown | 429 | 1 | 1 | 0 |
| Central City | 5,664 | 11 | 11 | 0 |
| Clay | 1,083 | 1 | 1 | 0 |
| Cloverport | 1,151 | 1 | 1 | 0 |
| Coal Run Village | 1,475 | 6 | 3 | 3 |
| Cold Spring | 6,697 | 13 | 13 | 0 |
| Columbia | 4,937 | 14 | 14 | 0 |
| Corbin | 7,126 | 30 | 24 | 6 |
| Covington | 40,298 | 131 | 109 | 22 |
| Cynthiana | 6,294 | 19 | 18 | 1 |
| Danville | 17,042 | 38 | 36 | 2 |
| Dayton | 5,678 | 12 | 11 | 1 |
| Eddyville | 2,549 | 3 | 3 | 0 |
| Edgewood | 8,796 | 17 | 17 | 0 |
| Edmonton | 1,595 | 6 | 6 | 0 |
| Elizabethtown | 30,530 | 81 | 63 | 18 |
| Elkhorn City | 862 | 1 | 1 | 0 |
| Elkton | 2,158 | 8 | 7 | 1 |
| Elsmere | 8,672 | 15 | 15 | 0 |
| Eminence | 2,574 | 8 | 8 | 0 |
| Erlanger | 23,678 | 46 | 43 | 3 |
| Falmouth | 2,074 | 7 | 6 | 1 |
| Ferguson | 945 | 1 | 1 | 0 |
| Flatwoods | 7,019 | 5 | 5 | 0 |
| Fleming-Neon | 601 | 2 | 2 | 0 |
| Flemingsburg | 2,800 | 11 | 11 | 0 |
| Florence | 33,824 | 70 | 67 | 3 |
| Fort Mitchell | 8,273 | 13 | 13 | 0 |

## Table 78. Full-Time Law Enforcement Employees, by Selected State and City, 2020—Continued

(Number.)

| State/city | Population | Total law enforcement employees | Total officers | Total civilians |
|---|---|---|---|---|
| Fort Thomas | 16,269 | 23 | 22 | 1 |
| Fort Wright | 5,787 | 14 | 14 | 0 |
| Fountain Run | 207 | 1 | 1 | 0 |
| Frankfort | 27,753 | 77 | 59 | 18 |
| Franklin | 9,105 | 22 | 21 | 1 |
| Fulton | 2,077 | 9 | 9 | 0 |
| Georgetown | 36,590 | 91 | 64 | 27 |
| Glasgow | 14,452 | 42 | 34 | 8 |
| Graymoor-Devondale | 3,098 | 15 | 15 | 0 |
| Grayson | 3,808 | 13 | 12 | 1 |
| Greensburg | 2,048 | 6 | 6 | 0 |
| Greenville | 4,122 | 11 | 11 | 0 |
| Hardinsburg | 2,346 | 5 | 5 | 0 |
| Harlan | 1,447 | 12 | 10 | 2 |
| Harrodsburg | 8,560 | 21 | 18 | 3 |
| Hartford | 2,719 | 5 | 5 | 0 |
| Hazard | 4,721 | 26 | 18 | 8 |
| Highland Heights | 7,023 | 11 | 10 | 1 |
| Hillview | 9,274 | 20 | 20 | 0 |
| Hodgenville | 3,257 | 8 | 7 | 1 |
| Hopkinsville | 30,787 | 98 | 68 | 30 |
| Horse Cave | 2,422 | 7 | 7 | 0 |
| Hustonville | 367 | 1 | 1 | 0 |
| Hyden | 319 | 1 | 1 | 0 |
| Independence | 29,339 | 37 | 35 | 2 |
| Indian Hills | 2,980 | 8 | 8 | 0 |
| Irvine | 2,271 | 7 | 7 | 0 |
| Jackson | 1,892 | 12 | 7 | 5 |
| Jamestown | 1,802 | 6 | 6 | 0 |
| Jeffersontown | 27,533 | 65 | 54 | 11 |
| Jenkins | 1,865 | 7 | 7 | 0 |
| Junction City | 2,347 | 2 | 2 | 0 |
| La Grange | 9,186 | 17 | 15 | 2 |
| Lakeside Park-Crestview Hills | 6,110 | 13 | 12 | 1 |
| Lancaster | 3,845 | 12 | 12 | 0 |
| Lawrenceburg | 11,581 | 22 | 14 | 8 |
| Lebanon | 5,751 | 27 | 17 | 10 |
| Leitchfield | 6,838 | 19 | 18 | 1 |
| Lewisburg | 807 | 1 | 1 | 0 |
| Lexington | 328,965 | 635 | 521 | 114 |
| Louisa | 2,313 | 7 | 7 | 0 |
| Louisville Metro | 678,236 | 1,320 | 1,038 | 282 |
| Loyall | 576 | 2 | 2 | 0 |
| Ludlow | 4,502 | 11 | 10 | 1 |
| Manchester | 1,261 | 12 | 12 | 0 |
| Mayfield | 9,648 | 24 | 23 | 1 |
| Maysville | 8,650 | 36 | 26 | 10 |
| Middlesboro | 8,762 | 28 | 24 | 4 |
| Middletown | 7,930 | 18 | 17 | 1 |
| Millersburg | 785 | 2 | 2 | 0 |
| Monticello | 5,880 | 11 | 9 | 2 |
| Morehead | 7,673 | 27 | 19 | 8 |
| Mount Sterling | 7,281 | 23 | 21 | 2 |
| Mount Vernon | 2,366 | 7 | 7 | 0 |
| Mount Washington | 15,048 | 22 | 21 | 1 |
| Muldraugh | 985 | 3 | 3 | 0 |
| Munfordville | 1,665 | 5 | 5 | 0 |
| Murray | 19,605 | 43 | 36 | 7 |
| Newport | 14,851 | 47 | 43 | 4 |
| Nicholasville | 31,184 | 68 | 60 | 8 |
| Oak Grove | 7,355 | 16 | 16 | 0 |
| Olive Hill | 1,524 | 8 | 8 | 0 |
| Owensboro | 60,636 | 132 | 97 | 35 |
| Owenton | 1,546 | 5 | 3 | 2 |
| Owingsville | 1,569 | 5 | 5 | 0 |
| Paducah | 24,873 | 104 | 77 | 27 |
| Paintsville | 3,897 | 9 | 9 | 0 |
| Park Hills | 2,996 | 8 | 8 | 0 |
| Pewee Valley | 1,588 | 1 | 1 | 0 |
| Pikeville | 6,378 | 26 | 25 | 1 |
| Pineville | 1,670 | 7 | 7 | 0 |
| Pioneer Village | 3,003 | 5 | 5 | 0 |
| Pippa Passes | 611 | 1 | 1 | 0 |
| Powderly | 736 | 23 | 9 | 14 |
| Prestonsburg | 3,424 | 24 | 16 | 8 |
| Princeton | 6,036 | 15 | 14 | 1 |
| Prospect | 4,941 | 8 | 7 | 1 |
| Radcliff | 22,957 | 44 | 28 | 16 |
| Ravenna | 552 | 1 | 1 | 0 |
| Richmond | 37,354 | 68 | 58 | 10 |
| Russell Springs | 2,671 | 8 | 7 | 1 |
| Russellville | 7,190 | 19 | 18 | 1 |
| Science Hill | 693 | 3 | 3 | 0 |
| Scottsville | 4,579 | 29 | 19 | 10 |
| Shelbyville | 17,065 | 35 | 33 | 2 |

## Table 78. Full-Time Law Enforcement Employees, by Selected State and City, 2020—Continued

(Number.)

| State/city | Population | Total law enforcement employees | Total officers | Total civilians |
|---|---|---|---|---|
| Shepherdsville | 12,416 | 39 | 37 | 2 |
| Shively | 15,732 | 37 | 31 | 6 |
| Simpsonville | 3,014 | 9 | 9 | 0 |
| Smiths Grove | 827 | 2 | 2 | 0 |
| Somerset | 11,889 | 50 | 45 | 5 |
| Southgate | 4,073 | 8 | 8 | 0 |
| Springfield | 3,006 | 16 | 9 | 7 |
| Stanton | 2,660 | 8 | 8 | 0 |
| St. Matthews | 18,038 | 46 | 39 | 7 |
| Taylor Mill | 6,837 | 12 | 11 | 1 |
| Taylorsville | 1,335 | 3 | 3 | 0 |
| Tompkinsville | 2,217 | 12 | 8 | 4 |
| Trenton | 377 | 1 | 1 | 0 |
| Vanceburg | 1,392 | 6 | 6 | 0 |
| Versailles | 27,051 | 37 | 36 | 1 |
| Villa Hills | 7,498 | 14 | 14 | 0 |
| Vine Grove | 6,712 | 11 | 11 | 0 |
| Warsaw | 1,677 | 5 | 5 | 0 |
| West Buechel | 1,277 | 9 | 9 | 0 |
| West Point | 870 | 1 | 1 | 0 |
| Whitesburg | 1,784 | 8 | 7 | 1 |
| Wilder | 3,063 | 9 | 9 | 0 |
| Williamsburg | 5,408 | 18 | 17 | 1 |
| Williamstown | 3,941 | 8 | 7 | 1 |
| Wilmore | 6,388 | 10 | 9 | 1 |
| Winchester | 18,689 | 53 | 37 | 16 |
| Woodlawn Park | 970 | 1 | 1 | 0 |
| Worthington | 1,477 | 4 | 4 | 0 |
| **LOUISIANA** | | | | |
| Abbeville | 11,898 | 28 | 28 | 0 |
| Alexandria | 45,343 | 147 | 115 | 32 |
| Arnaudville | 1,040 | 7 | 3 | 4 |
| Baker | 12,931 | 33 | 26 | 7 |
| Baldwin | 2,124 | 1 | 1 | 0 |
| Ball | 3,896 | 14 | 12 | 2 |
| Basile | 1,788 | 8 | 7 | 1 |
| Bastrop | 9,543 | 18 | 18 | 0 |
| Baton Rouge | 218,060 | 575 | 575 | 0 |
| Bernice | 1,580 | 3 | 3 | 0 |
| Breaux Bridge | 8,038 | 15 | 14 | 1 |
| Broussard | 13,667 | 34 | 34 | 0 |
| Clinton | 1,472 | 8 | 8 | 0 |
| Coushatta | 1,691 | 7 | 6 | 1 |
| Covington | 10,746 | 40 | 36 | 4 |
| Crowley | 12,448 | 32 | 32 | 0 |
| Delcambre | 1,835 | 6 | 5 | 1 |
| De Quincy | 2,988 | 19 | 11 | 8 |
| De Ridder | 10,512 | 32 | 32 | 0 |
| Dixie Inn | 265 | 1 | 1 | 0 |
| Dubach | 895 | 2 | 2 | 0 |
| Epps | 805 | 1 | 1 | 0 |
| Erath | 2,022 | 11 | 7 | 4 |
| Evergreen | 285 | 1 | 1 | 0 |
| Farmerville | 3,621 | 14 | 14 | 0 |
| Ferriday | 3,159 | 12 | 12 | 0 |
| Fisher | 215 | 1 | 1 | 0 |
| Florien | 591 | 8 | 7 | 1 |
| Folsom | 888 | 5 | 4 | 1 |
| Franklin | 6,482 | 24 | 16 | 8 |
| Franklinton | 3,630 | 23 | 19 | 4 |
| French Settlement | 1,239 | 4 | 4 | 0 |
| Georgetown | 318 | 4 | 4 | 0 |
| Golden Meadow | 1,919 | 6 | 5 | 1 |
| Gonzales | 11,399 | 48 | 43 | 5 |
| Grambling | 5,125 | 16 | 10 | 6 |
| Gramercy | 3,160 | 8 | 8 | 0 |
| Greenwood | 3,074 | 4 | 2 | 2 |
| Harahan | 9,243 | 27 | 21 | 6 |
| Haughton | 3,222 | 13 | 13 | 0 |
| Haynesville | 1,970 | 6 | 5 | 1 |
| Heflin | 222 | 1 | 1 | 0 |
| Ida | 207 | 2 | 1 | 1 |
| Independence | 1,935 | 7 | 7 | 0 |
| Iowa | 3,121 | 21 | 19 | 2 |
| Jennings | 9,592 | 26 | 21 | 5 |
| Kaplan | 4,320 | 12 | 12 | 0 |
| Kenner | 66,250 | 203 | 140 | 63 |
| Kinder | 2,310 | 14 | 11 | 3 |
| Krotz Springs | 1,153 | 8 | 5 | 3 |
| Leesville | 5,430 | 22 | 21 | 1 |
| Livingston | 2,028 | 6 | 6 | 0 |
| Livonia | 1,394 | 7 | 5 | 2 |
| Lockport | 2,372 | 5 | 5 | 0 |
| Mamou | 3,059 | 19 | 11 | 8 |

## Table 78. Full-Time Law Enforcement Employees, by Selected State and City, 2020—Continued

(Number.)

| State/city | Population | Total law enforcement employees | Total officers | Total civilians |
|---|---|---|---|---|
| Mandeville | 12,602 | 53 | 40 | 13 |
| Marion | 737 | 2 | 2 | 0 |
| Marksville | 5,230 | 23 | 17 | 6 |
| Minden | 11,436 | 30 | 29 | 1 |
| Montgomery | 715 | 8 | 2 | 6 |
| Morgan City | 10,343 | 48 | 40 | 8 |
| Natchitoches | 17,063 | 48 | 48 | 0 |
| New Iberia | 27,788 | 67 | 54 | 13 |
| Oakdale | 7,474 | 14 | 14 | 0 |
| Oil City | 953 | 4 | 4 | 0 |
| Palmetto | 156 | 1 | 1 | 0 |
| Patterson | 5,616 | 27 | 27 | 0 |
| Plaquemine | 6,316 | 19 | 19 | 0 |
| Pollock | 482 | 5 | 4 | 1 |
| Ponchatoula | 7,648 | 32 | 28 | 4 |
| Port Barre | 2,091 | 14 | 9 | 5 |
| Port Vincent | 653 | 3 | 3 | 0 |
| Rayville | 3,411 | 13 | 9 | 4 |
| Richwood | 3,376 | 4 | 4 | 0 |
| Ruston | 21,888 | 47 | 34 | 13 |
| Springhill | 4,630 | 18 | 14 | 4 |
| St. Gabriel | 7,612 | 19 | 12 | 7 |
| St. Martinville | 5,635 | 20 | 16 | 4 |
| Tallulah | 6,382 | 13 | 9 | 4 |
| Thibodaux | 14,402 | 66 | 47 | 19 |
| Tickfaw | 788 | 5 | 5 | 0 |
| Vidalia | 3,611 | 25 | 25 | 0 |
| Ville Platte | 7,010 | 14 | 13 | 1 |
| Vinton | 3,192 | 15 | 10 | 5 |
| Welsh | 3,192 | 12 | 8 | 4 |
| Westlake | 4,906 | 15 | 10 | 5 |
| Westwego | 8,274 | 40 | 37 | 3 |
| White Castle | 1,618 | 34 | 29 | 5 |
| Winnfield | 4,224 | 16 | 12 | 4 |
| Youngsville | 16,208 | 35 | 31 | 4 |
| Zachary | 18,774 | 41 | 41 | 0 |
| **MAINE** | | | | |
| Ashland | 1,206 | 4 | 4 | 0 |
| Auburn | 23,446 | 59 | 53 | 6 |
| Augusta | 18,713 | 57 | 44 | 13 |
| Baileyville | 1,450 | 4 | 4 | 0 |
| Bangor | 31,898 | 93 | 81 | 12 |
| Bar Harbor | 7,752 | 28 | 19 | 9 |
| Bath | 8,320 | 23 | 18 | 5 |
| Belfast | 6,712 | 17 | 16 | 1 |
| Berwick | 8,074 | 11 | 10 | 1 |
| Biddeford | 21,523 | 81 | 55 | 26 |
| Boothbay Harbor | 2,232 | 6 | 5 | 1 |
| Brewer | 8,897 | 23 | 21 | 2 |
| Bridgton | 5,539 | 9 | 8 | 1 |
| Brunswick | 20,656 | 38 | 32 | 6 |
| Bucksport | 4,917 | 14 | 10 | 4 |
| Buxton | 8,402 | 14 | 8 | 6 |
| Calais | 3,017 | 3 | 3 | 0 |
| Camden | 4,802 | 13 | 11 | 2 |
| Cape Elizabeth | 9,356 | 13 | 12 | 1 |
| Caribou | 7,570 | 16 | 15 | 1 |
| Carrabassett Valley | 789 | 1 | 1 | 0 |
| Clinton | 3,358 | 3 | 3 | 0 |
| Cumberland | 8,415 | 15 | 13 | 2 |
| Damariscotta | 2,153 | 6 | 5 | 1 |
| Dexter | 3,685 | 6 | 6 | 0 |
| Dover-Foxcroft | 4,073 | 6 | 6 | 0 |
| East Millinocket | 7,139 | 9 | 9 | 0 |
| Eastport | 1,270 | 2 | 2 | 0 |
| Eliot | 7,212 | 8 | 7 | 1 |
| Ellsworth | 8,302 | 23 | 20 | 3 |
| Fairfield | 6,534 | 11 | 11 | 0 |
| Falmouth | 12,573 | 29 | 20 | 9 |
| Farmington | 7,621 | 10 | 9 | 1 |
| Fort Fairfield | 3,258 | 3 | 3 | 0 |
| Fort Kent | 3,778 | 9 | 5 | 4 |
| Freeport | 8,713 | 18 | 16 | 2 |
| Fryeburg | 3,435 | 3 | 3 | 0 |
| Gardiner | 5,675 | 11 | 10 | 1 |
| Gorham | 18,130 | 25 | 22 | 3 |
| Gouldsboro | 1,744 | 2 | 2 | 0 |
| Greenville | 1,626 | 3 | 3 | 0 |
| Hallowell | 2,386 | 5 | 5 | 0 |
| Hampden | 7,537 | 12 | 12 | 0 |
| Holden | 3,124 | 6 | 6 | 0 |
| Houlton | 5,732 | 17 | 12 | 5 |
| Islesboro | 562 | 1 | 1 | 0 |
| Jay | 4,575 | 9 | 8 | 1 |

## Table 78. Full-Time Law Enforcement Employees, by Selected State and City, 2020—Continued

(Number.)

| State/city | Population | Total law enforcement employees | Total officers | Total civilians |
|---|---|---|---|---|
| Kennebunk | 11,799 | 25 | 23 | 2 |
| Kennebunkport | 3,692 | 19 | 14 | 5 |
| Kittery | 9,915 | 29 | 23 | 6 |
| Lewiston | 36,191 | 92 | 79 | 13 |
| Limestone | 2,150 | 3 | 3 | 0 |
| Lincoln | 4,862 | 11 | 9 | 2 |
| Lisbon | 9,057 | 19 | 13 | 6 |
| Livermore Falls | 3,178 | 6 | 6 | 0 |
| Madawaska | 3,686 | 5 | 5 | 0 |
| Mechanic Falls | 2,977 | 2 | 2 | 0 |
| Mexico | 2,631 | 4 | 4 | 0 |
| Milbridge | 1,296 | 1 | 1 | 0 |
| Milo | 2,311 | 4 | 3 | 1 |
| Monmouth | 4,178 | 4 | 4 | 0 |
| Newport | 3,245 | 6 | 6 | 0 |
| North Berwick | 4,762 | 9 | 8 | 1 |
| Norway | 4,988 | 10 | 9 | 1 |
| Oakland | 6,351 | 10 | 9 | 1 |
| Ogunquit | 938 | 12 | 11 | 1 |
| Old Orchard Beach | 9,145 | 24 | 22 | 2 |
| Old Town | 7,362 | 15 | 14 | 1 |
| Orono | 10,666 | 13 | 12 | 1 |
| Oxford | 4,102 | 10 | 9 | 1 |
| Paris | 5,161 | 9 | 8 | 1 |
| Phippsburg | 2,281 | 1 | 1 | 0 |
| Pittsfield | 3,982 | 8 | 7 | 1 |
| Portland | 66,875 | 203 | 146 | 57 |
| Presque Isle | 8,882 | 21 | 16 | 5 |
| Rangeley | 1,149 | 2 | 2 | 0 |
| Richmond | 3,493 | 6 | 6 | 0 |
| Rockland | 7,172 | 17 | 15 | 2 |
| Rockport | 3,395 | 5 | 5 | 0 |
| Rumford | 5,726 | 15 | 13 | 2 |
| Sabattus | 5,077 | 6 | 5 | 1 |
| Saco | 20,290 | 46 | 33 | 13 |
| Sanford | 21,300 | 42 | 38 | 4 |
| Scarborough | 21,810 | 57 | 37 | 20 |
| Searsport | 2,635 | 4 | 4 | 0 |
| Skowhegan | 8,205 | 18 | 16 | 2 |
| South Berwick | 7,654 | 11 | 10 | 1 |
| South Portland | 26,048 | 57 | 49 | 8 |
| Southwest Harbor | 1,796 | 9 | 5 | 4 |
| Thomaston | 2,761 | 6 | 6 | 0 |
| Topsham | 8,960 | 17 | 15 | 2 |
| Veazie | 1,815 | 4 | 4 | 0 |
| Waldoboro | 5,079 | 6 | 6 | 0 |
| Washburn | 1,519 | 3 | 3 | 0 |
| Waterville | 16,667 | 40 | 30 | 10 |
| Wells | 10,950 | 33 | 24 | 9 |
| Westbrook | 19,451 | 45 | 40 | 5 |
| Wilton | 3,912 | 4 | 4 | 0 |
| Windham | 19,118 | 31 | 29 | 2 |
| Winslow | 7,641 | 12 | 11 | 1 |
| Winter Harbor | 510 | 1 | 1 | 0 |
| Winthrop | 6,023 | 13 | 8 | 5 |
| Wiscasset | 3,750 | 5 | 4 | 1 |
| Yarmouth | 8,628 | 14 | 13 | 1 |
| York | 13,413 | 36 | 25 | 11 |
| **MARYLAND** | | | | |
| Aberdeen | 16,067 | 50 | 35 | 15 |
| Annapolis | 39,638 | 143 | 112 | 31 |
| Baltimore | 590,536 | 2,843 | 2,360 | 483 |
| Baltimore City Sheriff | | 176 | 131 | 45 |
| Bel Air | 10,278 | 41 | 31 | 10 |
| Berlin | 4,993 | 18 | 13 | 5 |
| Berwyn Heights | 3,261 | 9 | 8 | 1 |
| Boonsboro | 3,676 | 5 | 4 | 1 |
| Bowie | 58,546 | 80 | 61 | 19 |
| Brentwood | 3,451 | 6 | 5 | 1 |
| Cambridge | 12,189 | 37 | 33 | 4 |
| Capitol Heights | 4,535 | 13 | 11 | 2 |
| Centreville | 5,025 | 15 | 13 | 2 |
| Chestertown | 4,974 | 9 | 8 | 1 |
| Cheverly | 6,441 | 13 | 11 | 2 |
| Chevy Chase Village | 2,060 | 17 | 11 | 6 |
| Colmar Manor | 1,463 | 4 | 3 | 1 |
| Cottage City | 1,360 | 5 | 5 | 0 |
| Crisfield | 2,517 | 14 | 11 | 3 |
| Cumberland | 18,971 | 54 | 49 | 5 |
| Delmar | 3,651 | 12 | 11 | 1 |
| Denton | 4,553 | 10 | 9 | 1 |
| District Heights | 6,002 | 11 | 7 | 4 |
| Easton | 16,644 | 51 | 36 | 15 |
| Edmonston | 1,496 | 4 | 3 | 1 |

## Table 78. Full-Time Law Enforcement Employees, by Selected State and City, 2020—Continued

(Number.)

| State/city | Population | Total law enforcement employees | Total officers | Total civilians |
|---|---|---|---|---|
| Elkton | 15,684 | 46 | 40 | 6 |
| Fairmount Heights | 1,530 | 1 | 1 | 0 |
| Federalsburg | 2,650 | 10 | 9 | 1 |
| Forest Heights | 2,566 | 16 | 12 | 4 |
| Frederick | 74,138 | 180 | 139 | 41 |
| Frostburg | 8,413 | 17 | 13 | 4 |
| Fruitland | 5,375 | 24 | 19 | 5 |
| Glenarden | 6,182 | 21 | 19 | 2 |
| Greenbelt | 23,336 | 65 | 46 | 19 |
| Greensboro | 1,875 | 4 | 4 | 0 |
| Hagerstown | 39,942 | 103 | 81 | 22 |
| Hampstead | 6,437 | 8 | 7 | 1 |
| Hancock | 1,518 | 4 | 3 | 1 |
| Havre de Grace | 14,263 | 42 | 32 | 10 |
| Hurlock | 1,999 | 11 | 10 | 1 |
| Hyattsville | 18,283 | 58 | 43 | 15 |
| Landover Hills | 1,641 | 6 | 5 | 1 |
| La Plata | 9,906 | 21 | 20 | 1 |
| Laurel | 25,604 | 86 | 66 | 20 |
| Manchester | 4,882 | 7 | 6 | 1 |
| Morningside | 1,285 | 8 | 7 | 1 |
| Mount Airy | 9,522 | 13 | 11 | 2 |
| Mount Rainier | 8,146 | 19 | 17 | 2 |
| New Carrollton | 12,965 | 27 | 20 | 7 |
| North East | 3,616 | 11 | 10 | 1 |
| Oakland | 1,794 | 2 | 2 | 0 |
| Ocean City | 6,894 | 141 | 115 | 26 |
| Ocean Pines | 11,696 | 18 | 14 | 4 |
| Oxford | 597 | 3 | 3 | 0 |
| Perryville | 4,460 | 13 | 12 | 1 |
| Pittsville | 1,481 | 1 | 1 | 0 |
| Pocomoke City | 4,086 | 20 | 13 | 7 |
| Princess Anne | 3,510 | 13 | 11 | 2 |
| Ridgely | 1,657 | 5 | 5 | 0 |
| Rising Sun | 2,783 | 4 | 4 | 0 |
| Riverdale Park | 7,217 | 30 | 23 | 7 |
| Rock Hall | 1,250 | 3 | 3 | 0 |
| Salisbury | 33,294 | 112 | 83 | 29 |
| Seat Pleasant | 4,757 | 39 | 31 | 8 |
| Smithsburg | 2,966 | 5 | 4 | 1 |
| Snow Hill | 2,039 | 7 | 7 | 0 |
| St. Michaels | 1,029 | 10 | 9 | 1 |
| Sykesville | 3,976 | 7 | 6 | 1 |
| Takoma Park | 17,788 | 60 | 41 | 19 |
| Taneytown | 6,855 | 16 | 14 | 2 |
| Thurmont | 7,163 | 14 | 11 | 3 |
| University Park | 2,635 | 8 | 7 | 1 |
| Upper Marlboro | 674 | 4 | 3 | 1 |
| Westminster | 18,731 | 50 | 40 | 10 |
| **MASSACHUSETTS** | | | | |
| Acton | 23,853 | 51 | 40 | 11 |
| Acushnet | 10,798 | 26 | 21 | 5 |
| Agawam | 28,757 | 60 | 47 | 13 |
| Amesbury | 17,809 | 39 | 33 | 6 |
| Amherst | 40,843 | 46 | 43 | 3 |
| Andover | 37,216 | 68 | 49 | 19 |
| Aquinnah | 328 | 4 | 4 | 0 |
| Arlington | 45,767 | 73 | 60 | 13 |
| Ashburnham | 6,429 | 17 | 12 | 5 |
| Ashby | 3,242 | 7 | 6 | 1 |
| Ashfield | 1,718 | 1 | 1 | 0 |
| Ashland | 18,160 | 29 | 23 | 6 |
| Attleboro | 46,007 | 85 | 70 | 15 |
| Auburn | 16,885 | 48 | 37 | 11 |
| Avon | 4,631 | 20 | 14 | 6 |
| Ayer | 8,357 | 31 | 19 | 12 |
| Barnstable | 44,841 | 130 | 106 | 24 |
| Barre | 5,637 | 10 | 9 | 1 |
| Becket | 1,700 | 5 | 5 | 0 |
| Belchertown | 15,148 | 29 | 23 | 6 |
| Bellingham | 17,634 | 39 | 30 | 9 |
| Belmont | 26,206 | 56 | 44 | 12 |
| Berkley | 7,007 | 9 | 9 | 0 |
| Bernardston | 2,085 | 3 | 3 | 0 |
| Beverly | 42,851 | 55 | 51 | 4 |
| Billerica | 43,644 | 75 | 61 | 14 |
| Blackstone | 9,304 | 22 | 18 | 4 |
| Bolton | 5,579 | 13 | 12 | 1 |
| Boston | 704,758 | 2,716 | 2,184 | 532 |
| Boxborough | 5,880 | 19 | 13 | 6 |
| Boxford | 8,436 | 12 | 12 | 0 |
| Boylston | 4,806 | 15 | 11 | 4 |
| Braintree | 37,643 | 102 | 84 | 18 |
| Brewster | 9,843 | 27 | 22 | 5 |

## Table 78. Full-Time Law Enforcement Employees, by Selected State and City, 2020—Continued

(Number.)

| State/city | Population | Total law enforcement employees | Total officers | Total civilians |
|---|---|---|---|---|
| Bridgewater | 8,446 | 44 | 40 | 4 |
| Brockton | 100,516 | 220 | 192 | 28 |
| Brookfield | 3,473 | 5 | 5 | 0 |
| Brookline | 59,748 | 152 | 114 | 38 |
| Buckland | 1,847 | 1 | 1 | 0 |
| Burlington | 29,087 | 73 | 66 | 7 |
| Cambridge | 121,699 | 303 | 262 | 41 |
| Canton | 24,570 | 45 | 45 | 0 |
| Carlisle | 5,312 | 15 | 10 | 5 |
| Carver | 12,347 | 22 | 17 | 5 |
| Charlton | 13,881 | 27 | 22 | 5 |
| Chatham | 6,031 | 27 | 21 | 6 |
| Chelmsford | 35,985 | 68 | 62 | 6 |
| Chelsea | 39,971 | 112 | 104 | 8 |
| Cheshire | 3,093 | 1 | 1 | 0 |
| Chester | 1,382 | 1 | 1 | 0 |
| Chicopee | 55,332 | 133 | 129 | 4 |
| Cohasset | 8,738 | 21 | 20 | 1 |
| Concord | 19,025 | 36 | 31 | 5 |
| Dalton | 6,452 | 13 | 12 | 1 |
| Danvers | 27,904 | 54 | 43 | 11 |
| Dedham | 25,699 | 60 | 55 | 5 |
| Deerfield | 5,041 | 12 | 11 | 1 |
| Dennis | 13,971 | 54 | 45 | 9 |
| Dighton | 8,207 | 21 | 16 | 5 |
| Douglas | 9,259 | 20 | 15 | 5 |
| Dover | 6,246 | 16 | 16 | 0 |
| Dracut | 31,879 | 46 | 42 | 4 |
| Dudley | 11,778 | 18 | 17 | 1 |
| Dunstable | 3,454 | 10 | 9 | 1 |
| Duxbury | 16,780 | 33 | 31 | 2 |
| East Bridgewater | 15,324 | 30 | 23 | 7 |
| Eastham | 4,937 | 22 | 17 | 5 |
| Easthampton | 15,720 | 35 | 29 | 6 |
| East Longmeadow | 16,286 | 29 | 26 | 3 |
| Easton | 25,509 | 36 | 33 | 3 |
| Edgartown | 4,470 | 21 | 19 | 2 |
| Erving | 1,744 | 5 | 5 | 0 |
| Essex | 3,888 | 10 | 9 | 1 |
| Everett | 46,959 | 114 | 105 | 9 |
| Fairhaven | 16,257 | 39 | 33 | 6 |
| Fall River | 90,618 | 269 | 222 | 47 |
| Falmouth | 31,320 | 58 | 54 | 4 |
| Fitchburg | 40,626 | 92 | 76 | 16 |
| Foxborough | 18,774 | 41 | 39 | 2 |
| Framingham | 75,042 | 143 | 123 | 20 |
| Franklin | 35,425 | 56 | 54 | 2 |
| Freetown | 9,567 | 21 | 20 | 1 |
| Gardner | 20,795 | 45 | 31 | 14 |
| Georgetown | 8,920 | 18 | 13 | 5 |
| Gill | 1,473 | 2 | 2 | 0 |
| Gloucester | 30,963 | 69 | 62 | 7 |
| Grafton | 19,347 | 24 | 20 | 4 |
| Granby | 6,264 | 14 | 10 | 4 |
| Great Barrington | 6,964 | 16 | 15 | 1 |
| Groton | 11,407 | 26 | 20 | 6 |
| Groveland | 6,967 | 12 | 10 | 2 |
| Hadley | 5,335 | 20 | 14 | 6 |
| Halifax | 8,275 | 13 | 12 | 1 |
| Hamilton | 8,165 | 18 | 14 | 4 |
| Hanover | 15,396 | 36 | 29 | 7 |
| Hanson | 11,550 | 24 | 23 | 1 |
| Hardwick | 3,077 | 6 | 6 | 0 |
| Harwich | 12,235 | 40 | 33 | 7 |
| Haverhill | 64,944 | 121 | 105 | 16 |
| Hingham | 26,172 | 55 | 53 | 2 |
| Hinsdale | 1,890 | 4 | 4 | 0 |
| Holbrook | 11,163 | 27 | 26 | 1 |
| Holden | 19,605 | 40 | 24 | 16 |
| Holland | 2,493 | 2 | 2 | 0 |
| Holliston | 15,138 | 30 | 25 | 5 |
| Holyoke | 40,326 | 131 | 107 | 24 |
| Hopedale | 5,985 | 17 | 13 | 4 |
| Hopkinton | 19,192 | 34 | 24 | 10 |
| Hudson | 19,954 | 45 | 34 | 11 |
| Hull | 11,000 | 27 | 25 | 2 |
| Ipswich | 14,297 | 29 | 25 | 4 |
| Kingston | 14,843 | 31 | 23 | 8 |
| Lakeville | 12,360 | 23 | 19 | 4 |
| Lancaster | 7,900 | 10 | 8 | 2 |
| Lanesboro | 2,909 | 6 | 6 | 0 |
| Lawrence | 81,021 | 185 | 162 | 23 |
| Leicester | 11,401 | 19 | 18 | 1 |
| Lenox | 4,920 | 11 | 11 | 0 |
| Leominster | 41,965 | 88 | 70 | 18 |

## Table 78. Full-Time Law Enforcement Employees, by Selected State and City, 2020—Continued

(Number.)

| State/city | Population | Total law enforcement employees | Total officers | Total civilians |
|---|---|---|---|---|
| Leverett | 1,835 | 3 | 3 | 0 |
| Lincoln | 7,114 | 19 | 13 | 6 |
| Littleton | 10,480 | 28 | 20 | 8 |
| Lowell | 112,230 | 306 | 236 | 70 |
| Ludlow | 21,312 | 48 | 39 | 9 |
| Lunenburg | 12,098 | 18 | 17 | 1 |
| Lynn | 95,727 | 202 | 184 | 18 |
| Lynnfield | 13,300 | 26 | 21 | 5 |
| Malden | 60,433 | 109 | 99 | 10 |
| Manchester-by-the-Sea | 5,513 | 32 | 26 | 6 |
| Mansfield | 24,880 | 48 | 38 | 10 |
| Marblehead | 20,791 | 40 | 30 | 10 |
| Marion | 5,464 | 15 | 15 | 0 |
| Marlborough | 39,682 | 81 | 70 | 11 |
| Mashpee | 14,411 | 46 | 38 | 8 |
| Mattapoisett | 6,772 | 21 | 21 | 0 |
| Maynard | 11,508 | 27 | 21 | 6 |
| Medfield | 13,266 | 24 | 18 | 6 |
| Medway | 13,670 | 27 | 26 | 1 |
| Melrose | 28,094 | 46 | 45 | 1 |
| Mendon | 6,323 | 14 | 13 | 1 |
| Methuen | 51,691 | 108 | 89 | 19 |
| Middleboro | 27,228 | 48 | 43 | 5 |
| Middleton | 10,311 | 18 | 17 | 1 |
| Millbury | 14,160 | 26 | 21 | 5 |
| Milton | 27,911 | 67 | 55 | 12 |
| Montague | 8,178 | 22 | 17 | 5 |
| Nahant | 3,544 | 13 | 12 | 1 |
| Nantucket | 11,600 | 51 | 34 | 17 |
| Natick | 36,340 | 73 | 57 | 16 |
| Needham | 32,159 | 54 | 45 | 9 |
| New Bedford | 96,346 | 271 | 234 | 37 |
| Newburyport | 18,757 | 39 | 32 | 7 |
| Newton | 88,769 | 171 | 140 | 31 |
| Norfolk | 12,152 | 23 | 21 | 2 |
| North Adams | 12,638 | 29 | 24 | 5 |
| Northampton | 28,332 | 67 | 60 | 7 |
| North Andover | 32,040 | 57 | 42 | 15 |
| North Attleboro | 29,789 | 54 | 38 | 16 |
| Northborough | 15,223 | 29 | 21 | 8 |
| Northbridge | 16,850 | 27 | 19 | 8 |
| Northfield | 2,951 | 3 | 3 | 0 |
| North Reading | 16,134 | 33 | 30 | 3 |
| Norton | 20,232 | 34 | 33 | 1 |
| Norwell | 11,770 | 26 | 23 | 3 |
| Norwood | 30,200 | 68 | 58 | 10 |
| Oak Bluffs | 4,772 | 20 | 18 | 2 |
| Oakham | 1,970 | 1 | 1 | 0 |
| Orleans | 5,841 | 24 | 19 | 5 |
| Oxford | 14,078 | 28 | 21 | 7 |
| Palmer | 12,300 | 29 | 22 | 7 |
| Paxton | 5,069 | 16 | 14 | 2 |
| Peabody | 53,669 | 106 | 88 | 18 |
| Pelham | 1,303 | 2 | 2 | 0 |
| Pembroke | 19,505 | 32 | 30 | 2 |
| Pepperell | 12,192 | 17 | 16 | 1 |
| Plainville | 9,495 | 18 | 18 | 0 |
| Plymouth | 66,289 | 131 | 109 | 22 |
| Plympton | 3,157 | 9 | 8 | 1 |
| Princeton | 3,522 | 7 | 6 | 1 |
| Provincetown | 2,982 | 23 | 16 | 7 |
| Quincy | 95,737 | 243 | 211 | 32 |
| Randolph | 32,257 | 65 | 59 | 6 |
| Raynham | 14,799 | 38 | 30 | 8 |
| Reading | 25,900 | 59 | 44 | 15 |
| Rehoboth | 12,697 | 35 | 29 | 6 |
| Revere | 52,860 | 116 | 106 | 10 |
| Rochester | 6,067 | 13 | 12 | 1 |
| Rockland | 18,898 | 36 | 33 | 3 |
| Rockport | 7,407 | 22 | 18 | 4 |
| Rowley | 6,501 | 16 | 12 | 4 |
| Salem | 44,120 | 95 | 85 | 10 |
| Salisbury | 9,811 | 25 | 16 | 9 |
| Sandwich | 20,266 | 44 | 34 | 10 |
| Saugus | 28,967 | 84 | 69 | 15 |
| Scituate | 20,046 | 38 | 36 | 2 |
| Seekonk | 16,212 | 40 | 38 | 2 |
| Sharon | 19,222 | 33 | 29 | 4 |
| Sheffield | 3,098 | 4 | 4 | 0 |
| Shelburne | 1,834 | 3 | 3 | 0 |
| Sherborn | 4,445 | 15 | 15 | 0 |
| Shirley | 7,641 | 14 | 12 | 2 |
| Shrewsbury | 39,602 | 62 | 45 | 17 |
| Somerset | 18,286 | 39 | 33 | 6 |
| Southampton | 6,199 | 13 | 9 | 4 |

# Table 78. Full-Time Law Enforcement Employees, by Selected State and City, 2020—Continued

(Number.)

| State/city | Population | Total law enforcement employees | Total officers | Total civilians |
|---|---|---|---|---|
| Southborough | 10,328 | 25 | 20 | 5 |
| Southbridge | 16,932 | 50 | 38 | 12 |
| South Hadley | 17,520 | 32 | 26 | 6 |
| Southwick | 9,835 | 23 | 18 | 5 |
| Spencer | 12,014 | 22 | 18 | 4 |
| Springfield | 154,098 | 574 | 465 | 109 |
| Sterling | 8,270 | 20 | 14 | 6 |
| Stockbridge | 1,877 | 8 | 7 | 1 |
| Stoneham | 24,439 | 47 | 39 | 8 |
| Stoughton | 29,418 | 75 | 62 | 13 |
| Stow | 7,294 | 13 | 11 | 2 |
| Sturbridge | 9,670 | 27 | 20 | 7 |
| Sudbury | 19,798 | 39 | 28 | 11 |
| Sunderland | 3,628 | 6 | 5 | 1 |
| Swampscott | 15,766 | 30 | 29 | 1 |
| Swansea | 17,257 | 39 | 33 | 6 |
| Taunton | 58,333 | 117 | 107 | 10 |
| Templeton | 8,213 | 14 | 9 | 5 |
| Tewksbury | 31,407 | 76 | 64 | 12 |
| Tisbury | 4,198 | 16 | 13 | 3 |
| Topsfield | 6,774 | 13 | 12 | 1 |
| Townsend | 9,574 | 13 | 12 | 1 |
| Truro | 2,024 | 17 | 12 | 5 |
| Uxbridge | 14,561 | 28 | 22 | 6 |
| Wakefield | 27,470 | 48 | 47 | 1 |
| Walpole | 27,160 | 56 | 45 | 11 |
| Waltham | 62,693 | 154 | 148 | 6 |
| Wareham | 23,956 | 55 | 45 | 10 |
| Warren | 5,252 | 9 | 8 | 1 |
| Watertown | 36,858 | 82 | 68 | 14 |
| Wayland | 13,911 | 24 | 23 | 1 |
| Webster | 16,963 | 34 | 32 | 2 |
| Wellesley | 29,088 | 57 | 43 | 14 |
| Wellfleet | 2,747 | 19 | 14 | 5 |
| Wenham | 5,236 | 11 | 10 | 1 |
| Westborough | 19,299 | 39 | 37 | 2 |
| West Brookfield | 3,749 | 7 | 6 | 1 |
| Westfield | 41,474 | 88 | 84 | 4 |
| Westford | 25,834 | 50 | 45 | 5 |
| Westminster | 8,244 | 19 | 15 | 4 |
| Weston | 12,195 | 35 | 26 | 9 |
| Westport | 16,286 | 36 | 31 | 5 |
| Westwood | 16,767 | 40 | 33 | 7 |
| Weymouth | 59,242 | 117 | 94 | 23 |
| Wilbraham | 14,864 | 28 | 27 | 1 |
| Williamsburg | 2,459 | 2 | 2 | 0 |
| Wilmington | 23,567 | 48 | 44 | 4 |
| Winchendon | 10,973 | 21 | 15 | 6 |
| Winchester | 22,988 | 51 | 40 | 11 |
| Winthrop | 18,692 | 33 | 32 | 1 |
| Woburn | 40,568 | 81 | 76 | 5 |
| Worcester | 186,365 | 497 | 447 | 50 |
| Worthington | 1,178 | 1 | 1 | 0 |
| Wrentham | 12,334 | 23 | 22 | 1 |
| Yarmouth | 23,295 | 75 | 61 | 14 |
| | | | | |
| **MICHIGAN** | | | | |
| Adrian | 20,371 | 31 | 29 | 2 |
| Adrian Township | 6,188 | 3 | 2 | 1 |
| Akron | 370 | 1 | 1 | 0 |
| Albion | 8,336 | 16 | 15 | 1 |
| Allegan | 5,018 | 9 | 8 | 1 |
| Allen Park | 26,615 | 40 | 37 | 3 |
| Alma | 8,754 | 16 | 14 | 2 |
| Almont | 2,830 | 7 | 7 | 0 |
| Alpena | 9,828 | 19 | 17 | 2 |
| Ann Arbor | 119,805 | 143 | 115 | 28 |
| Argentine Township | 6,439 | 5 | 5 | 0 |
| Armada | 1,695 | 2 | 2 | 0 |
| Auburn Hills | 25,256 | 50 | 45 | 5 |
| Augusta | 897 | 8 | 6 | 2 |
| Bad Axe | 2,868 | 7 | 7 | 0 |
| Bangor | 1,800 | 7 | 6 | 1 |
| Baraga | 1,927 | 2 | 2 | 0 |
| Baroda-Lake Township | 3,891 | 6 | 5 | 1 |
| Barryton | 357 | 1 | 1 | 0 |
| Barry Township | 3,560 | 4 | 4 | 0 |
| Bath Township | 13,226 | 13 | 12 | 1 |
| Battle Creek | 60,134 | 115 | 100 | 15 |
| Bay City | 32,200 | 50 | 47 | 3 |
| Beaverton | 1,173 | 4 | 4 | 0 |
| Belding | 5,738 | 8 | 8 | 0 |
| Bellaire | 1,067 | 2 | 2 | 0 |
| Belleville | 3,854 | 10 | 9 | 1 |
| Bellevue | 1,301 | 2 | 2 | 0 |

## Table 78. Full-Time Law Enforcement Employees, by Selected State and City, 2020—Continued

(Number.)

| State/city | Population | Total law enforcement employees | Total officers | Total civilians |
|---|---|---|---|---|
| Benton Harbor | 9,660 | 14 | 13 | 1 |
| Benton Township | 14,230 | 19 | 17 | 2 |
| Berkley | 15,307 | 40 | 30 | 10 |
| Berrien Springs-Oronoko Township | 8,854 | 9 | 8 | 1 |
| Beverly Hills | 10,278 | 27 | 25 | 2 |
| Big Rapids | 10,406 | 18 | 16 | 2 |
| Birch Run | 1,461 | 7 | 6 | 1 |
| Birmingham | 21,436 | 43 | 32 | 11 |
| Blackman Township | 36,111 | 42 | 41 | 1 |
| Blissfield | 3,240 | 7 | 6 | 1 |
| Bloomfield Hills | 4,001 | 28 | 24 | 4 |
| Bloomfield Township | 41,809 | 85 | 67 | 18 |
| Boyne City | 3,717 | 9 | 8 | 1 |
| Breckenridge | 1,259 | 1 | 1 | 0 |
| Bridgeport Township | 9,658 | 11 | 10 | 1 |
| Bridgman | 2,191 | 5 | 5 | 0 |
| Brighton | 7,654 | 19 | 17 | 2 |
| Bronson | 2,293 | 5 | 4 | 1 |
| Brown City | 1,230 | 2 | 2 | 0 |
| Brownstown Township | 32,300 | 38 | 30 | 8 |
| Buchanan | 4,200 | 10 | 9 | 1 |
| Buena Vista Township | 8,035 | 13 | 12 | 1 |
| Burton | 28,319 | 34 | 32 | 2 |
| Cadillac | 10,536 | 16 | 15 | 1 |
| Cambridge Township | 5,663 | 4 | 4 | 0 |
| Canton Township | 94,777 | 119 | 93 | 26 |
| Capac | 1,842 | 3 | 3 | 0 |
| Carleton | 2,358 | 4 | 3 | 1 |
| Caro | 3,967 | 7 | 7 | 0 |
| Carrollton Township | 5,560 | 6 | 6 | 0 |
| Carson City | 1,104 | 1 | 1 | 0 |
| Caseville | 720 | 2 | 2 | 0 |
| Caspian-Gaastra | 1,161 | 1 | 1 | 0 |
| Cass City | 2,259 | 4 | 4 | 0 |
| Cassopolis | 1,691 | 5 | 5 | 0 |
| Center Line | 8,074 | 20 | 15 | 5 |
| Central Lake | 941 | 1 | 1 | 0 |
| Charlevoix | 2,477 | 8 | 7 | 1 |
| Charlotte | 9,049 | 16 | 15 | 1 |
| Cheboygan | 4,682 | 9 | 9 | 0 |
| Chelsea | 5,422 | 14 | 10 | 4 |
| Chesaning | 2,204 | 2 | 2 | 0 |
| Chesterfield Township | 46,997 | 62 | 48 | 14 |
| Chikaming Township | 3,073 | 7 | 6 | 1 |
| Chocolay Township | 5,888 | 6 | 5 | 1 |
| Clare | 3,045 | 7 | 7 | 0 |
| Clawson | 11,720 | 15 | 14 | 1 |
| Clayton Township | 7,037 | 7 | 6 | 1 |
| Clay Township | 8,902 | 23 | 17 | 6 |
| Clinton | 2,283 | 4 | 4 | 0 |
| Clinton Township | 100,094 | 100 | 92 | 8 |
| Clio | 2,465 | 2 | 2 | 0 |
| Coldwater | 11,954 | 21 | 19 | 2 |
| Coleman | 1,202 | 2 | 2 | 0 |
| Coloma Township | 6,307 | 10 | 7 | 3 |
| Colon | 1,152 | 3 | 3 | 0 |
| Columbia Township | 7,312 | 6 | 6 | 0 |
| Constantine | 2,106 | 5 | 4 | 1 |
| Corunna | 3,303 | 3 | 3 | 0 |
| Covert Township | 2,884 | 9 | 9 | 0 |
| Croswell | 2,235 | 5 | 5 | 0 |
| Crystal Falls | 1,355 | 1 | 1 | 0 |
| Davison | 4,828 | 7 | 6 | 1 |
| Davison Township | 19,226 | 22 | 20 | 2 |
| Dearborn | 92,930 | 231 | 190 | 41 |
| Dearborn Heights | 54,772 | 100 | 79 | 21 |
| Decatur | 1,707 | 5 | 5 | 0 |
| Denton Township | 5,412 | 4 | 4 | 0 |
| Detroit | 673,708 | 3,100 | 2,475 | 625 |
| DeWitt | 4,869 | 7 | 6 | 1 |
| DeWitt Township | 15,880 | 17 | 16 | 1 |
| Dowagiac | 5,536 | 14 | 13 | 1 |
| Dryden Township | 4,731 | 4 | 4 | 0 |
| Dundee | 4,769 | 5 | 5 | 0 |
| Durand | 3,792 | 5 | 5 | 0 |
| East Grand Rapids | 12,129 | 29 | 27 | 2 |
| East Jordan | 2,338 | 5 | 5 | 0 |
| East Lansing | 47,548 | 58 | 46 | 12 |
| Eastpointe | 31,653 | 45 | 40 | 5 |
| Eaton Rapids | 5,223 | 10 | 9 | 1 |
| Eau Claire | 588 | 1 | 1 | 0 |
| Ecorse | 9,635 | 18 | 18 | 0 |
| Elk Rapids | 1,625 | 5 | 5 | 0 |
| Elkton | 735 | 1 | 1 | 0 |
| Emmett Township | 11,531 | 17 | 15 | 2 |

## Table 78. Full-Time Law Enforcement Employees, by Selected State and City, 2020—Continued

(Number.)

| State/city | Population | Total law enforcement employees | Total officers | Total civilians |
|---|---|---|---|---|
| Erie Township | 4,302 | 2 | 2 | 0 |
| Escanaba | 12,052 | 43 | 30 | 13 |
| Essexville | 3,222 | 8 | 8 | 0 |
| Evart | 1,883 | 3 | 3 | 0 |
| Fair Haven Township | 1,029 | 1 | 1 | 0 |
| Farmington | 10,396 | 23 | 22 | 1 |
| Farmington Hills | 80,044 | 137 | 101 | 36 |
| Fennville | 1,438 | 6 | 6 | 0 |
| Fenton | 11,340 | 15 | 12 | 3 |
| Ferndale | 20,228 | 51 | 40 | 11 |
| Flat Rock | 9,968 | 20 | 18 | 2 |
| Flint | 94,290 | 116 | 99 | 17 |
| Flint Township | 30,015 | 42 | 35 | 7 |
| Flushing | 7,789 | 11 | 10 | 1 |
| Flushing Township | 10,096 | 8 | 8 | 0 |
| Forsyth Township | 6,160 | 9 | 7 | 2 |
| Fowlerville | 2,904 | 7 | 6 | 1 |
| Frankenmuth | 5,728 | 9 | 7 | 2 |
| Frankfort | 1,290 | 4 | 4 | 0 |
| Franklin | 3,228 | 11 | 11 | 0 |
| Fraser | 14,316 | 29 | 28 | 1 |
| Fremont | 4,102 | 9 | 8 | 1 |
| Fruitport Township | 14,690 | 11 | 10 | 1 |
| Gagetown | 358 | 1 | 1 | 0 |
| Galien | 525 | 2 | 1 | 1 |
| Garden City | 26,084 | 37 | 34 | 3 |
| Garfield Township | 846 | 1 | 1 | 0 |
| Gaylord | 3,672 | 12 | 11 | 1 |
| Genesee Township | 20,258 | 19 | 17 | 2 |
| Gerrish Township | 2,946 | 7 | 6 | 1 |
| Gibraltar | 4,503 | 9 | 8 | 1 |
| Gladstone | 4,631 | 11 | 10 | 1 |
| Gladwin | 2,884 | 6 | 6 | 0 |
| Grand Beach/Michiana | 462 | 5 | 5 | 0 |
| Grand Blanc | 7,789 | 18 | 16 | 2 |
| Grand Blanc Township | 36,700 | 46 | 39 | 7 |
| Grand Haven | 11,110 | 36 | 29 | 7 |
| Grand Ledge | 7,891 | 15 | 15 | 0 |
| Grand Rapids | 201,280 | 385 | 283 | 102 |
| Grandville | 15,787 | 28 | 26 | 2 |
| Grant | 900 | 2 | 2 | 0 |
| Grayling | 1,841 | 6 | 6 | 0 |
| Green Oak Township | 19,155 | 18 | 16 | 2 |
| Greenville | 8,378 | 17 | 15 | 2 |
| Grosse Ile Township | 10,076 | 22 | 16 | 6 |
| Grosse Pointe | 5,094 | 23 | 23 | 0 |
| Grosse Pointe Farms | 9,012 | 37 | 32 | 5 |
| Grosse Pointe Park | 10,918 | 38 | 33 | 5 |
| Grosse Pointe Shores | 2,509 | 16 | 16 | 0 |
| Grosse Pointe Woods | 15,158 | 36 | 30 | 6 |
| Hamburg Township | 21,904 | 19 | 18 | 1 |
| Hampton Township | 9,282 | 10 | 10 | 0 |
| Hamtramck | 21,346 | 36 | 29 | 7 |
| Hancock | 4,426 | 9 | 9 | 0 |
| Harbor Beach | 1,557 | 4 | 4 | 0 |
| Harbor Springs | 1,204 | 7 | 6 | 1 |
| Harper Woods | 13,582 | 29 | 26 | 3 |
| Hart | 2,087 | 5 | 5 | 0 |
| Hartford | 2,561 | 4 | 4 | 0 |
| Hastings | 7,335 | 15 | 13 | 2 |
| Hazel Park | 16,189 | 38 | 33 | 5 |
| Hesperia | 935 | 2 | 2 | 0 |
| Highland Park | 10,620 | 12 | 8 | 4 |
| Hillsdale | 8,081 | 16 | 14 | 2 |
| Holland | 33,144 | 68 | 58 | 10 |
| Holly | 6,079 | 9 | 9 | 0 |
| Houghton | 7,524 | 11 | 10 | 1 |
| Howell | 9,667 | 17 | 15 | 2 |
| Hudson | 2,185 | 2 | 2 | 0 |
| Huntington Woods | 6,199 | 18 | 17 | 1 |
| Huron Township | 16,353 | 31 | 24 | 7 |
| Imlay City | 3,584 | 8 | 7 | 1 |
| Inkster | 23,999 | 39 | 29 | 10 |
| Ionia | 10,955 | 16 | 14 | 2 |
| Iron Mountain | 7,233 | 15 | 14 | 1 |
| Iron River | 2,808 | 3 | 3 | 0 |
| Ironwood | 4,760 | 13 | 13 | 0 |
| Ishpeming | 6,371 | 12 | 11 | 1 |
| Ishpeming Township | 3,496 | 1 | 1 | 0 |
| Jackson | 32,271 | 53 | 43 | 10 |
| Jonesville | 2,201 | 2 | 2 | 0 |
| Kalamazoo | 76,179 | 270 | 245 | 25 |
| Kalamazoo Township | 24,503 | 37 | 32 | 5 |
| Kalkaska | 2,090 | 8 | 7 | 1 |
| Keego Harbor | 3,396 | 5 | 5 | 0 |

## Table 78. Full-Time Law Enforcement Employees, by Selected State and City, 2020—Continued

(Number.)

| State/city | Population | Total law enforcement employees | Total officers | Total civilians |
|---|---|---|---|---|
| Kentwood | 52,028 | 82 | 69 | 13 |
| Kingsford | 4,903 | 19 | 19 | 0 |
| Kingston | 404 | 1 | 1 | 0 |
| Kinross Township | 7,226 | 2 | 2 | 0 |
| Laingsburg | 1,283 | 1 | 1 | 0 |
| Lake Angelus | 309 | 1 | 1 | 0 |
| Lake Linden | 928 | 1 | 1 | 0 |
| Lake Odessa | 2,043 | 4 | 4 | 0 |
| Lake Orion | 3,207 | 5 | 4 | 1 |
| Lakeview | 993 | 3 | 3 | 0 |
| L'Anse | 1,807 | 4 | 4 | 0 |
| Lansing | 117,865 | 242 | 190 | 52 |
| Lansing Township | 8,158 | 16 | 15 | 1 |
| Lapeer | 8,416 | 23 | 20 | 3 |
| Lathrup Village | 4,046 | 10 | 9 | 1 |
| Laurium | 1,861 | 4 | 4 | 0 |
| Lawton | 1,791 | 4 | 4 | 0 |
| Leslie | 1,886 | 4 | 4 | 0 |
| Lexington | 1,114 | 3 | 3 | 0 |
| Lincoln Park | 35,879 | 51 | 44 | 7 |
| Lincoln Township | 14,590 | 17 | 15 | 2 |
| Linden | 3,950 | 6 | 6 | 0 |
| Litchfield | 1,324 | 2 | 2 | 0 |
| Livonia | 92,852 | 157 | 120 | 37 |
| Lowell | 4,239 | 6 | 5 | 1 |
| Ludington | 8,098 | 16 | 14 | 2 |
| Luna Pier | 1,389 | 1 | 1 | 0 |
| Mackinac Island | 477 | 6 | 6 | 0 |
| Mackinaw City | 792 | 6 | 6 | 0 |
| Madison Heights | 29,626 | 68 | 51 | 17 |
| Madison Township | 7,959 | 5 | 5 | 0 |
| Mancelona | 1,374 | 1 | 1 | 0 |
| Manistee | 6,158 | 12 | 12 | 0 |
| Manistique | 2,933 | 8 | 8 | 0 |
| Manton | 1,625 | 1 | 1 | 0 |
| Marine City | 4,015 | 6 | 5 | 1 |
| Marlette | 1,740 | 4 | 4 | 0 |
| Marquette | 20,208 | 37 | 33 | 4 |
| Marshall | 6,910 | 15 | 15 | 0 |
| Marysville | 9,621 | 16 | 14 | 2 |
| Mason | 8,402 | 13 | 12 | 1 |
| Mattawan | 1,972 | 6 | 6 | 0 |
| Mayville | 878 | 3 | 3 | 0 |
| Melvindale | 10,134 | 23 | 23 | 0 |
| Memphis | 1,167 | 3 | 3 | 0 |
| Mendon | 845 | 1 | 1 | 0 |
| Menominee | 7,909 | 17 | 16 | 1 |
| Meridian Township | 43,146 | 40 | 37 | 3 |
| Metamora Township | 4,323 | 5 | 5 | 0 |
| Metro Police Authority of Genesee County | 19,899 | 27 | 24 | 3 |
| Midland | 41,758 | 52 | 50 | 2 |
| Milan | 6,028 | 17 | 12 | 5 |
| Milford | 16,969 | 21 | 19 | 2 |
| Millington | 1,002 | 2 | 2 | 0 |
| Monroe | 19,209 | 44 | 40 | 4 |
| Montague | 2,366 | 5 | 5 | 0 |
| Montrose Township | 7,420 | 8 | 8 | 0 |
| Morenci | 2,120 | 9 | 8 | 1 |
| Morrice | 904 | 1 | 1 | 0 |
| Mount Morris | 2,803 | 5 | 5 | 0 |
| Mount Morris Township | 20,084 | 31 | 28 | 3 |
| Mount Pleasant | 24,109 | 33 | 27 | 6 |
| Munising | 2,171 | 5 | 5 | 0 |
| Muskegon | 36,296 | 78 | 67 | 11 |
| Muskegon Heights | 10,673 | 27 | 24 | 3 |
| Muskegon Township | 18,043 | 16 | 16 | 0 |
| Napoleon Township | 6,696 | 5 | 5 | 0 |
| Nashville | 1,704 | 3 | 3 | 0 |
| Negaunee | 4,494 | 8 | 8 | 0 |
| Newaygo | 2,110 | 7 | 7 | 0 |
| New Baltimore | 12,301 | 18 | 16 | 2 |
| New Buffalo | 1,863 | 7 | 7 | 0 |
| New Era | 439 | 1 | 1 | 0 |
| Niles | 11,045 | 28 | 18 | 10 |
| Northfield Township | 8,679 | 13 | 11 | 2 |
| North Muskegon | 3,792 | 8 | 8 | 0 |
| Northville | 5,922 | 13 | 12 | 1 |
| Northville Township | 29,443 | 49 | 35 | 14 |
| Norton Shores | 24,689 | 41 | 38 | 3 |
| Norway | 2,702 | 6 | 6 | 0 |
| Novi | 61,440 | 90 | 68 | 22 |
| Oak Park | 29,280 | 63 | 50 | 13 |
| Olivet | 1,887 | 1 | 1 | 0 |
| Ontwa Township-Edwardsburg | 6,574 | 11 | 10 | 1 |
| Orchard Lake | 2,480 | 12 | 11 | 1 |

## Table 78. Full-Time Law Enforcement Employees, by Selected State and City, 2020—Continued

(Number.)

| State/city | Population | Total law enforcement employees | Total officers | Total civilians |
|---|---|---|---|---|
| Oscoda Township | 6,743 | 12 | 11 | 1 |
| Otsego | 3,990 | 8 | 7 | 1 |
| Ovid | 1,609 | 2 | 2 | 0 |
| Owosso | 14,258 | 20 | 18 | 2 |
| Oxford | 3,552 | 23 | 9 | 14 |
| Paw Paw | 3,328 | 9 | 8 | 1 |
| Pentwater | 858 | 2 | 2 | 0 |
| Perry | 2,066 | 4 | 4 | 0 |
| Petoskey | 5,734 | 20 | 19 | 1 |
| Pigeon | 1,099 | 2 | 2 | 0 |
| Pinckney | 2,425 | 6 | 6 | 0 |
| Pittsfield Township | 39,327 | 37 | 35 | 2 |
| Plainwell | 3,771 | 9 | 8 | 1 |
| Pleasant Ridge | 2,399 | 5 | 5 | 0 |
| Plymouth | 9,141 | 15 | 14 | 1 |
| Plymouth Township | 26,895 | 44 | 29 | 15 |
| Portage | 50,141 | 72 | 60 | 12 |
| Port Austin | 610 | 2 | 2 | 0 |
| Port Huron | 28,487 | 62 | 54 | 8 |
| Portland | 4,024 | 6 | 6 | 0 |
| Potterville | 2,778 | 2 | 2 | 0 |
| Prairieville Township | 3,548 | 2 | 2 | 0 |
| Quincy | 1,614 | 4 | 4 | 0 |
| Raisin Township | 7,817 | 4 | 4 | 0 |
| Reading | 1,039 | 2 | 2 | 0 |
| Redford Township | 46,112 | 62 | 54 | 8 |
| Reed City | 2,372 | 4 | 4 | 0 |
| Reese | 1,358 | 2 | 2 | 0 |
| Richfield Township, Genesee County | 8,300 | 11 | 9 | 2 |
| Richfield Township, Roscommon County | 3,642 | 5 | 5 | 0 |
| Richland | 858 | 3 | 3 | 0 |
| Richland Township, Saginaw County | 3,891 | 4 | 4 | 0 |
| Richmond | 5,801 | 14 | 11 | 3 |
| River Rouge | 7,319 | 27 | 19 | 8 |
| Riverview | 11,920 | 21 | 20 | 1 |
| Rochester | 13,251 | 30 | 22 | 8 |
| Rockford | 6,468 | 11 | 10 | 1 |
| Rockwood | 3,133 | 14 | 7 | 7 |
| Rogers City | 2,651 | 6 | 6 | 0 |
| Romeo | 3,569 | 9 | 6 | 3 |
| Romulus | 23,488 | 60 | 43 | 17 |
| Roosevelt Park | 3,781 | 5 | 5 | 0 |
| Roseville | 46,456 | 72 | 69 | 3 |
| Royal Oak | 59,137 | 107 | 75 | 32 |
| Saginaw | 47,480 | 60 | 51 | 9 |
| Saginaw Township | 38,836 | 48 | 43 | 5 |
| Saline | 9,402 | 19 | 15 | 4 |
| Sandusky | 2,477 | 6 | 5 | 1 |
| Saugatuck-Douglas | 2,337 | 5 | 4 | 1 |
| Sault Ste. Marie | 13,282 | 24 | 22 | 2 |
| Schoolcraft | 1,550 | 3 | 3 | 0 |
| Scottville | 1,209 | 3 | 3 | 0 |
| Sebewaing | 1,597 | 2 | 2 | 0 |
| Shelby | 2,042 | 2 | 2 | 0 |
| Shelby Township | 82,164 | 93 | 73 | 20 |
| Shepherd | 1,488 | 2 | 2 | 0 |
| Somerset Township | 4,520 | 3 | 3 | 0 |
| Southfield | 72,216 | 154 | 122 | 32 |
| Southgate | 29,052 | 43 | 37 | 6 |
| South Haven | 4,320 | 24 | 19 | 5 |
| South Lyon | 11,899 | 17 | 16 | 1 |
| South Rockwood | 1,646 | 2 | 2 | 0 |
| Sparta | 4,437 | 5 | 5 | 0 |
| Spring Arbor Township | 7,684 | 2 | 2 | 0 |
| Springport Township | 2,134 | 2 | 2 | 0 |
| Stanton | 1,421 | 1 | 1 | 0 |
| St. Charles | 1,871 | 2 | 2 | 0 |
| St. Clair | 5,500 | 7 | 7 | 0 |
| St. Clair Shores | 58,254 | 87 | 82 | 5 |
| Sterling Heights | 131,911 | 174 | 149 | 25 |
| St. Ignace | 2,315 | 5 | 5 | 0 |
| St. Johns | 7,908 | 13 | 11 | 2 |
| St. Joseph | 8,283 | 24 | 22 | 2 |
| St. Joseph Township | 9,602 | 13 | 12 | 1 |
| St. Louis | 7,051 | 10 | 7 | 3 |
| Stockbridge | 1,243 | 2 | 2 | 0 |
| Sturgis | 10,771 | 24 | 19 | 5 |
| Sumpter Township | 9,337 | 20 | 16 | 4 |
| Sylvan Lake | 1,848 | 5 | 5 | 0 |
| Tawas City | 1,777 | 3 | 3 | 0 |
| Taylor | 60,341 | 88 | 71 | 17 |
| Tecumseh | 8,369 | 14 | 13 | 1 |
| Thetford Township | 6,567 | 1 | 1 | 0 |
| Thomas Township | 11,366 | 9 | 8 | 1 |
| Three Oaks | 1,533 | 3 | 3 | 0 |

## Table 78. Full-Time Law Enforcement Employees, by Selected State and City, 2020—Continued

(Number.)

| State/city | Population | Total law enforcement employees | Total officers | Total civilians |
|---|---|---|---|---|
| Three Rivers | 7,579 | 18 | 16 | 2 |
| Tittabawassee Township | 10,031 | 8 | 7 | 1 |
| Traverse City | 15,840 | 32 | 30 | 2 |
| Trenton | 17,954 | 33 | 32 | 1 |
| Troy | 83,851 | 152 | 107 | 45 |
| Tuscarora Township | 2,918 | 9 | 8 | 1 |
| Ubly | 771 | 1 | 1 | 0 |
| Unadilla Township | 3,483 | 3 | 3 | 0 |
| Union City | 1,561 | 5 | 5 | 0 |
| Utica | 5,094 | 21 | 15 | 6 |
| Van Buren Township | 28,390 | 54 | 40 | 14 |
| Vassar | 2,521 | 5 | 5 | 0 |
| Vernon | 762 | 1 | 1 | 0 |
| Vicksburg | 3,657 | 6 | 6 | 0 |
| Walker | 25,443 | 42 | 38 | 4 |
| Walled Lake | 7,082 | 7 | 7 | 0 |
| Warren | 132,758 | 248 | 209 | 39 |
| Waterford Township | 72,213 | 81 | 62 | 19 |
| Watersmeet Township | 1,346 | 1 | 1 | 0 |
| Watervliet | 1,627 | 4 | 4 | 0 |
| Wayland | 4,253 | 7 | 6 | 1 |
| Wayne | 16,616 | 24 | 23 | 1 |
| West Bloomfield Township | 65,720 | 109 | 78 | 31 |
| West Branch | 2,037 | 6 | 6 | 0 |
| Westland | 80,837 | 99 | 74 | 25 |
| White Cloud | 1,381 | 3 | 3 | 0 |
| Whitehall | 2,879 | 8 | 8 | 0 |
| White Lake Township | 31,747 | 35 | 27 | 8 |
| White Pigeon | 1,520 | 4 | 4 | 0 |
| Williamston | 3,935 | 7 | 6 | 1 |
| Wixom | 14,145 | 23 | 20 | 3 |
| Wolverine Lake | 4,788 | 7 | 7 | 0 |
| Woodhaven | 12,388 | 31 | 29 | 2 |
| Wyandotte | 24,600 | 48 | 36 | 12 |
| Wyoming | 77,094 | 112 | 92 | 20 |
| Yale | 1,853 | 5 | 5 | 0 |
| Ypsilanti | 19,986 | 34 | 30 | 4 |
| Zeeland | 5,524 | 11 | 10 | 1 |
| Zilwaukee | 1,504 | 1 | 1 | 0 |
| **MINNESOTA** | | | | |
| Ada | 1,542 | 4 | 3 | 1 |
| Aitkin | 1,954 | 8 | 7 | 1 |
| Akeley | 450 | 1 | 1 | 0 |
| Albany | 2,813 | 5 | 4 | 1 |
| Albert Lea | 17,686 | 30 | 27 | 3 |
| Alexandria | 14,032 | 27 | 24 | 3 |
| Annandale | 3,579 | 6 | 5 | 1 |
| Anoka | 17,553 | 40 | 29 | 11 |
| Appleton | 1,301 | 3 | 3 | 0 |
| Apple Valley | 55,455 | 60 | 52 | 8 |
| Arlington | 2,102 | 3 | 2 | 1 |
| Atwater | 1,111 | 1 | 1 | 0 |
| Audubon | 517 | 1 | 1 | 0 |
| Austin | 25,382 | 35 | 32 | 3 |
| Avon | 1,680 | 4 | 3 | 1 |
| Babbitt | 1,471 | 5 | 5 | 0 |
| Bagley | 1,445 | 3 | 3 | 0 |
| Barnesville | 2,628 | 5 | 5 | 0 |
| Battle Lake | 935 | 3 | 3 | 0 |
| Baxter | 8,571 | 16 | 15 | 1 |
| Bayport | 3,822 | 6 | 6 | 0 |
| Becker | 5,080 | 8 | 7 | 1 |
| Belgrade/Brooten | 1,543 | 3 | 3 | 0 |
| Belle Plaine | 7,166 | 13 | 11 | 2 |
| Bemidji | 15,574 | 37 | 34 | 3 |
| Benson | 2,977 | 8 | 7 | 1 |
| Big Lake | 11,721 | 16 | 14 | 2 |
| Blaine | 67,705 | 81 | 70 | 11 |
| Blooming Prairie | 1,921 | 3 | 3 | 0 |
| Bloomington | 84,740 | 149 | 116 | 33 |
| Blue Earth | 3,078 | 5 | 5 | 0 |
| Bovey | 782 | 2 | 2 | 0 |
| Braham | 1,856 | 6 | 6 | 0 |
| Brainerd | 13,436 | 30 | 24 | 6 |
| Breckenridge | 3,111 | 8 | 8 | 0 |
| Breezy Point | 2,447 | 7 | 6 | 1 |
| Breitung Township | 613 | 1 | 1 | 0 |
| Brooklyn Center | 30,258 | 45 | 35 | 10 |
| Brooklyn Park | 79,946 | 147 | 98 | 49 |
| Brownton | 706 | 1 | 1 | 0 |
| Buffalo | 16,994 | 20 | 17 | 3 |
| Buffalo Lake | 672 | 2 | 2 | 0 |
| Burnsville | 62,351 | 87 | 76 | 11 |
| Caledonia | 2,743 | 6 | 5 | 1 |

## Table 78. Full-Time Law Enforcement Employees, by Selected State and City, 2020—Continued

(Number.)

| State/city | Population | Total law enforcement employees | Total officers | Total civilians |
|---|---|---|---|---|
| Callaway | 226 | 1 | 1 | 0 |
| Cambridge | 9,540 | 16 | 14 | 2 |
| Canby | 1,631 | 3 | 3 | 0 |
| Cannon Falls | 4,016 | 8 | 7 | 1 |
| Centennial Lakes | 11,721 | 18 | 16 | 2 |
| Champlin | 25,249 | 31 | 26 | 5 |
| Chaska | 27,632 | 31 | 26 | 5 |
| Chatfield | 2,831 | 5 | 5 | 0 |
| Chisholm | 4,786 | 12 | 11 | 1 |
| Clara City | 1,265 | 2 | 2 | 0 |
| Clearbrook | 537 | 1 | 1 | 0 |
| Cleveland | 733 | 1 | 1 | 0 |
| Cloquet | 12,002 | 24 | 22 | 2 |
| Cold Spring/Richmond | 5,869 | 11 | 10 | 1 |
| Coleraine | 1,972 | 2 | 2 | 0 |
| Columbia Heights | 21,238 | 33 | 26 | 7 |
| Coon Rapids | 63,076 | 79 | 69 | 10 |
| Corcoran | 6,742 | 12 | 11 | 1 |
| Cottage Grove | 38,534 | 50 | 42 | 8 |
| Crookston | 7,605 | 16 | 14 | 2 |
| Crosby | 2,308 | 9 | 8 | 1 |
| Crosslake | 2,399 | 6 | 6 | 0 |
| Crystal | 22,628 | 40 | 34 | 6 |
| Danube | 446 | 1 | 1 | 0 |
| Dawson/Boyd | 1,514 | 2 | 2 | 0 |
| Dayton | 7,754 | 11 | 9 | 2 |
| Deephaven | 3,926 | 9 | 8 | 1 |
| Deer River | 929 | 4 | 4 | 0 |
| Deerwood | 752 | 3 | 3 | 0 |
| Detroit Lakes | 9,310 | 19 | 17 | 2 |
| Dilworth | 4,497 | 8 | 7 | 1 |
| Duluth | 85,731 | 177 | 151 | 26 |
| Dundas | 1,682 | 3 | 3 | 0 |
| Eagan | 66,155 | 87 | 73 | 14 |
| Eagle Lake | 3,204 | 3 | 3 | 0 |
| East Grand Forks | 8,379 | 23 | 22 | 1 |
| East Range | 3,521 | 8 | 8 | 0 |
| Eden Prairie | 65,308 | 88 | 67 | 21 |
| Eden Valley | 1,037 | 1 | 1 | 0 |
| Edina | 52,943 | 84 | 57 | 27 |
| Elko New Market | 4,800 | 6 | 6 | 0 |
| Elk River | 25,873 | 44 | 35 | 9 |
| Ely | 3,313 | 6 | 5 | 1 |
| Emily | 844 | 2 | 2 | 0 |
| Eveleth | 3,519 | 11 | 10 | 1 |
| Fairfax | 1,108 | 7 | 7 | 0 |
| Fairmont | 9,852 | 20 | 18 | 2 |
| Faribault | 23,960 | 43 | 34 | 9 |
| Farmington | 23,235 | 28 | 25 | 3 |
| Fergus Falls | 13,791 | 29 | 24 | 5 |
| Foley | 2,678 | 4 | 4 | 0 |
| Forest Lake | 21,592 | 28 | 25 | 3 |
| Frazee | 1,384 | 3 | 3 | 0 |
| Fridley | 27,919 | 54 | 46 | 8 |
| Fulda | 1,196 | 2 | 2 | 0 |
| Gaylord | 2,237 | 4 | 4 | 0 |
| Gibbon | 735 | 1 | 1 | 0 |
| Gilbert | 1,758 | 8 | 7 | 1 |
| Glencoe | 5,484 | 9 | 8 | 1 |
| Glenwood | 2,610 | 63 | 25 | 38 |
| Glyndon | 1,384 | 4 | 4 | 0 |
| Golden Valley | 21,740 | 36 | 27 | 9 |
| Goodhue | 1,163 | 3 | 3 | 0 |
| Goodview | 4,138 | 6 | 5 | 1 |
| Grand Rapids | 11,255 | 23 | 20 | 3 |
| Granite Falls | 2,648 | 7 | 6 | 1 |
| Hallock | 896 | 1 | 1 | 0 |
| Hastings | 22,955 | 34 | 30 | 4 |
| Hawley | 2,225 | 5 | 5 | 0 |
| Hector | 1,031 | 1 | 1 | 0 |
| Henderson | 922 | 2 | 2 | 0 |
| Henning | 806 | 2 | 2 | 0 |
| Hermantown | 9,512 | 19 | 16 | 3 |
| Heron Lake | 638 | 1 | 1 | 0 |
| Hibbing | 15,655 | 31 | 28 | 3 |
| Hill City | 575 | 1 | 1 | 0 |
| Hokah | 545 | 1 | 1 | 0 |
| Hopkins | 18,272 | 37 | 30 | 7 |
| Houston | 970 | 2 | 2 | 0 |
| Howard Lake | 2,182 | 3 | 3 | 0 |
| Hutchinson | 13,961 | 32 | 23 | 9 |
| International Falls | 5,648 | 12 | 12 | 0 |
| Inver Grove Heights | 35,957 | 44 | 39 | 5 |
| Isanti | 6,576 | 11 | 10 | 1 |
| Isle | 793 | 4 | 4 | 0 |

## Table 78. Full-Time Law Enforcement Employees, by Selected State and City, 2020—Continued

(Number.)

| State/city | Population | Total law enforcement employees | Total officers | Total civilians |
|---|---|---|---|---|
| Janesville | 2,246 | 4 | 4 | 0 |
| Jordan | 6,523 | 9 | 7 | 2 |
| Kasson | 6,585 | 9 | 9 | 0 |
| Keewatin | 1,006 | 3 | 3 | 0 |
| La Crescent | 5,027 | 9 | 8 | 1 |
| Lake City | 5,119 | 11 | 10 | 1 |
| Lake Crystal | 2,508 | 3 | 3 | 0 |
| Lakefield | 1,591 | 3 | 3 | 0 |
| Lake Park | 788 | 2 | 2 | 0 |
| Lakes Area | 10,026 | 15 | 13 | 2 |
| Lake Shore | 1,076 | 2 | 2 | 0 |
| Lakeville | 71,092 | 71 | 61 | 10 |
| Le Center | 2,480 | 3 | 3 | 0 |
| Lester Prairie | 1,720 | 3 | 3 | 0 |
| Le Sueur | 4,029 | 8 | 7 | 1 |
| Lewiston | 1,536 | 2 | 2 | 0 |
| Lino Lakes | 22,657 | 30 | 26 | 4 |
| Litchfield | 6,656 | 11 | 10 | 1 |
| Little Falls | 8,597 | 16 | 14 | 2 |
| Long Prairie | 3,282 | 6 | 6 | 0 |
| Lonsdale | 4,366 | 8 | 7 | 1 |
| Madelia | 2,217 | 3 | 3 | 0 |
| Madison Lake | 1,215 | 2 | 2 | 0 |
| Mankato | 43,802 | 61 | 54 | 7 |
| Maple Grove | 74,097 | 82 | 69 | 13 |
| Mapleton | 2,178 | 3 | 3 | 0 |
| Maplewood | 41,057 | 55 | 50 | 5 |
| Marshall | 13,391 | 24 | 21 | 3 |
| Medina | 6,969 | 12 | 11 | 1 |
| Melrose | 3,680 | 6 | 5 | 1 |
| Menahga | 1,308 | 3 | 3 | 0 |
| Mendota Heights | 11,469 | 20 | 19 | 1 |
| Milaca | 2,894 | 8 | 7 | 1 |
| Minneapolis | 438,463 | 774 | 648 | 126 |
| Minneota | 1,334 | 1 | 1 | 0 |
| Minnesota Lake | 630 | 1 | 1 | 0 |
| Minnetonka | 55,960 | 65 | 55 | 10 |
| Minnetrista | 11,095 | 17 | 13 | 4 |
| Montevideo | 4,995 | 12 | 11 | 1 |
| Montgomery | 3,062 | 7 | 6 | 1 |
| Moorhead | 44,488 | 73 | 58 | 15 |
| Moose Lake | 2,788 | 5 | 5 | 0 |
| Morris | 5,319 | 10 | 8 | 2 |
| Motley | 651 | 1 | 1 | 0 |
| Mounds View | 13,625 | 23 | 21 | 2 |
| Mountain Lake | 2,037 | 4 | 4 | 0 |
| Nashwauk | 947 | 4 | 4 | 0 |
| New Brighton | 23,012 | 34 | 27 | 7 |
| New Hope | 20,671 | 42 | 33 | 9 |
| New Prague | 8,293 | 11 | 9 | 2 |
| New Richland | 1,167 | 2 | 2 | 0 |
| New Ulm | 13,106 | 22 | 22 | 0 |
| New York Mills | 1,222 | 3 | 3 | 0 |
| Nisswa | 2,130 | 6 | 6 | 0 |
| North Branch | 10,908 | 14 | 12 | 2 |
| Northfield | 20,828 | 29 | 24 | 5 |
| North Mankato | 14,117 | 16 | 15 | 1 |
| North St. Paul | 12,557 | 18 | 16 | 2 |
| Oakdale | 27,808 | 39 | 31 | 8 |
| Oak Park Heights | 5,031 | 11 | 10 | 1 |
| Olivia | 2,291 | 5 | 5 | 0 |
| Onamia | 856 | 3 | 3 | 0 |
| Orono | 20,241 | 31 | 27 | 4 |
| Ortonville | 1,732 | 4 | 4 | 0 |
| Osakis | 1,742 | 3 | 3 | 0 |
| Osseo | 2,732 | 8 | 7 | 1 |
| Owatonna | 25,683 | 40 | 36 | 4 |
| Parkers Prairie | 991 | 2 | 2 | 0 |
| Park Rapids | 4,387 | 12 | 11 | 1 |
| Paynesville | 2,542 | 4 | 4 | 0 |
| Pelican Rapids | 2,652 | 5 | 5 | 0 |
| Pequot Lakes | 2,320 | 7 | 6 | 1 |
| Perham | 3,708 | 8 | 7 | 1 |
| Pierz | 1,361 | 2 | 2 | 0 |
| Pillager | 488 | 2 | 2 | 0 |
| Pine River | 932 | 4 | 4 | 0 |
| Plainview | 3,287 | 9 | 8 | 1 |
| Plymouth | 80,588 | 94 | 78 | 16 |
| Preston | 1,275 | 3 | 3 | 0 |
| Princeton | 4,738 | 14 | 12 | 2 |
| Prior Lake | 27,779 | 34 | 30 | 4 |
| Proctor | 3,001 | 7 | 6 | 1 |
| Ramsey | 29,053 | 32 | 29 | 3 |
| Red Wing | 16,411 | 30 | 26 | 4 |
| Redwood Falls | 4,914 | 14 | 12 | 2 |

## Table 78. Full-Time Law Enforcement Employees, by Selected State and City, 2020—Continued

(Number.)

| State/city | Population | Total law enforcement employees | Total officers | Total civilians |
|---|---|---|---|---|
| Renville | 1,151 | 3 | 3 | 0 |
| Rice | 1,413 | 2 | 2 | 0 |
| Richfield | 36,336 | 54 | 44 | 10 |
| Robbinsdale | 14,213 | 29 | 25 | 4 |
| Rochester | 121,225 | 211 | 144 | 67 |
| Rogers | 13,889 | 25 | 21 | 4 |
| Roseau | 2,662 | 6 | 5 | 1 |
| Rosemount | 26,218 | 32 | 29 | 3 |
| Roseville | 36,561 | 61 | 53 | 8 |
| Rushford | 1,692 | 3 | 3 | 0 |
| Sartell | 19,398 | 24 | 21 | 3 |
| Sauk Centre | 4,556 | 9 | 8 | 1 |
| Sauk Rapids | 14,489 | 18 | 17 | 1 |
| Savage | 33,510 | 43 | 33 | 10 |
| Sebeka | 664 | 2 | 2 | 0 |
| Shakopee | 43,641 | 60 | 48 | 12 |
| Sherburn | 1,072 | 4 | 4 | 0 |
| Silver Bay | 1,739 | 4 | 4 | 0 |
| Slayton | 1,941 | 6 | 5 | 1 |
| Sleepy Eye | 3,304 | 7 | 7 | 0 |
| South Lake Minnetonka | 12,833 | 18 | 15 | 3 |
| South St. Paul | 19,895 | 36 | 32 | 4 |
| Springfield | 1,975 | 4 | 4 | 0 |
| Spring Grove | 1,255 | 3 | 3 | 0 |
| Spring Lake Park | 6,960 | 13 | 10 | 3 |
| St. Anthony | 11,490 | 23 | 20 | 3 |
| Staples | 3,074 | 8 | 7 | 1 |
| Starbuck | 1,264 | 4 | 4 | 0 |
| St. Charles | 3,771 | 7 | 7 | 0 |
| St. Cloud | 68,756 | 140 | 113 | 27 |
| St. Francis | 8,154 | 15 | 12 | 3 |
| Stillwater | 19,799 | 28 | 23 | 5 |
| St. James | 4,336 | 8 | 7 | 1 |
| St. Joseph | 7,864 | 13 | 11 | 2 |
| St. Louis Park | 49,196 | 73 | 58 | 15 |
| St. Paul | 309,957 | 760 | 627 | 133 |
| St. Paul Park | 5,359 | 8 | 8 | 0 |
| St. Peter | 12,121 | 20 | 14 | 6 |
| Thief River Falls | 8,693 | 18 | 16 | 2 |
| Tracy | 2,045 | 3 | 3 | 0 |
| Trimont | 686 | 1 | 1 | 0 |
| Truman | 1,020 | 2 | 2 | 0 |
| Twin Valley | 743 | 2 | 2 | 0 |
| Two Harbors | 3,486 | 9 | 8 | 1 |
| Tyler | 1,050 | 1 | 1 | 0 |
| Verndale | 574 | 2 | 2 | 0 |
| Virginia | 8,259 | 24 | 24 | 0 |
| Wabasha | 2,462 | 9 | 8 | 1 |
| Wadena | 4,126 | 10 | 9 | 1 |
| Waite Park | 7,839 | 23 | 20 | 3 |
| Walker | 926 | 3 | 3 | 0 |
| Walnut Grove | 791 | 1 | 1 | 0 |
| Warroad | 1,792 | 5 | 5 | 0 |
| Waseca | 8,779 | 19 | 17 | 2 |
| Waterville | 1,870 | 4 | 4 | 0 |
| Wayzata | 6,519 | 17 | 15 | 2 |
| Wells | 2,141 | 5 | 5 | 0 |
| Westbrook | 709 | 1 | 1 | 0 |
| West Concord | 761 | 1 | 1 | 0 |
| West Hennepin | 5,955 | 11 | 9 | 2 |
| West St. Paul | 19,840 | 38 | 34 | 4 |
| Wheaton | 1,255 | 3 | 3 | 0 |
| White Bear Lake | 25,747 | 35 | 31 | 4 |
| Willmar | 19,922 | 40 | 35 | 5 |
| Windom | 4,380 | 11 | 10 | 1 |
| Winnebago | 1,324 | 3 | 3 | 0 |
| Winona | 26,446 | 41 | 38 | 3 |
| Winsted | 2,220 | 4 | 4 | 0 |
| Winthrop | 1,315 | 3 | 3 | 0 |
| Woodbury | 75,577 | 87 | 68 | 19 |
| Worthington | 12,983 | 34 | 23 | 11 |
| Wyoming | 8,112 | 12 | 10 | 2 |
| Zumbrota | 3,556 | 6 | 6 | 0 |
| **MISSISSIPPI** | | | | |
| Aberdeen | 5,236 | 19 | 13 | 6 |
| Ackerman | 1,407 | 5 | 5 | 0 |
| Batesville | 7,085 | 50 | 37 | 13 |
| Bay Springs | 1,638 | 7 | 7 | 0 |
| Bay St. Louis | 15,188 | 28 | 26 | 2 |
| Biloxi | 46,317 | 181 | 128 | 53 |
| Brandon | 24,639 | 42 | 30 | 12 |
| Brookhaven | 11,798 | 41 | 29 | 12 |
| Bruce | 1,784 | 6 | 6 | 0 |
| Byhalia | 1,204 | 13 | 8 | 5 |

## Table 78. Full-Time Law Enforcement Employees, by Selected State and City, 2020—Continued

(Number.)

| State/city | Population | Total law enforcement employees | Total officers | Total civilians |
|---|---|---|---|---|
| Byram | 11,240 | 38 | 27 | 11 |
| Calhoun City | 1,637 | 5 | 5 | 0 |
| Canton | 11,801 | 35 | 23 | 12 |
| Clarksdale | 14,164 | 30 | 24 | 6 |
| Cleveland | 10,710 | 50 | 44 | 6 |
| Clinton | 23,737 | 76 | 59 | 17 |
| Columbus | 23,124 | 61 | 51 | 10 |
| Corinth | 14,421 | 43 | 38 | 5 |
| Derma | 955 | 1 | 1 | 0 |
| D'Iberville | 14,234 | 40 | 37 | 3 |
| Ellisville | 4,563 | 11 | 9 | 2 |
| Florence | 4,573 | 21 | 15 | 6 |
| Flowood | 9,743 | 63 | 50 | 13 |
| Gautier | 18,362 | 39 | 28 | 11 |
| Gloster | 843 | 8 | 2 | 6 |
| Greenwood | 13,215 | 50 | 33 | 17 |
| Gulfport | 71,803 | 201 | 148 | 53 |
| Hattiesburg | 45,809 | 164 | 104 | 60 |
| Hazlehurst | 3,656 | 20 | 12 | 8 |
| Holly Springs | 7,674 | 23 | 17 | 6 |
| Horn Lake | 27,401 | 64 | 47 | 17 |
| Houston | 3,351 | 10 | 10 | 0 |
| Iuka | 2,917 | 12 | 9 | 3 |
| Jackson | 156,320 | 416 | 278 | 138 |
| Kosciusko | 6,545 | 19 | 19 | 0 |
| Laurel | 18,165 | 66 | 47 | 19 |
| Leland | 3,587 | 20 | 13 | 7 |
| Long Beach | 16,260 | 43 | 30 | 13 |
| Louisville | 5,861 | 27 | 16 | 11 |
| Lucedale | 3,140 | 20 | 14 | 6 |
| Lumberton | 2,262 | 8 | 7 | 1 |
| Madison | 25,860 | 86 | 63 | 23 |
| Magee | 4,062 | 25 | 16 | 9 |
| Mathiston | 665 | 4 | 3 | 1 |
| McComb | 12,819 | 43 | 26 | 17 |
| Mendenhall | 2,382 | 8 | 5 | 3 |
| Morton | 3,505 | 12 | 6 | 6 |
| Moss Point | 13,182 | 39 | 27 | 12 |
| Oakland | 489 | 3 | 1 | 2 |
| Ocean Springs | 17,833 | 49 | 37 | 12 |
| Okolona | 2,563 | 6 | 6 | 0 |
| Olive Branch | 40,308 | 90 | 81 | 9 |
| Oxford | 29,367 | 94 | 75 | 19 |
| Pascagoula | 21,468 | 74 | 52 | 22 |
| Pass Christian | 6,724 | 29 | 21 | 8 |
| Pelahatchie | 1,393 | 10 | 7 | 3 |
| Philadelphia | 6,959 | 34 | 26 | 8 |
| Picayune | 10,814 | 35 | 30 | 5 |
| Pontotoc | 6,297 | 23 | 20 | 3 |
| Poplarville | 2,771 | 9 | 9 | 0 |
| Raymond | 2,101 | 5 | 5 | 0 |
| Richland | 7,305 | 28 | 14 | 14 |
| Ridgeland | 23,901 | 84 | 59 | 25 |
| Ripley | 5,168 | 16 | 15 | 1 |
| Ruleville | 2,466 | 15 | 15 | 0 |
| Saltillo | 5,105 | 14 | 14 | 0 |
| Seminary | 281 | 1 | 1 | 0 |
| Senatobia | 7,562 | 38 | 30 | 8 |
| Smithville | 722 | 1 | 1 | 0 |
| Southaven | 57,455 | 158 | 125 | 33 |
| Starkville | 25,711 | 72 | 58 | 14 |
| Summit | 1,533 | 8 | 7 | 1 |
| Sumrall | 1,984 | 7 | 6 | 1 |
| Union | 1,866 | 8 | 7 | 1 |
| Utica | 895 | 2 | 2 | 0 |
| Vardaman | 1,254 | 1 | 1 | 0 |
| Walnut | 733 | 4 | 4 | 0 |
| Waynesboro | 4,847 | 11 | 11 | 0 |
| West Point | 10,294 | 35 | 29 | 6 |
| Wiggins | 4,535 | 18 | 13 | 5 |
| **MISSOURI** | | | | |
| Adrian | 1,594 | 5 | 5 | 0 |
| Ashland | 4,063 | 9 | 8 | 1 |
| Ava | 2,897 | 12 | 7 | 5 |
| Bella Villa | 719 | 4 | 4 | 0 |
| Bellefontaine Neighbors | 10,251 | 30 | 28 | 2 |
| Belton | 23,860 | 67 | 49 | 18 |
| Berkeley | 8,868 | 33 | 25 | 8 |
| Bertrand | 739 | 1 | 1 | 0 |
| Bethany | 3,025 | 6 | 6 | 0 |
| Bonne Terre | 6,811 | 10 | 10 | 0 |
| Boonville | 7,833 | 28 | 21 | 7 |
| Bourbon | 1,558 | 8 | 8 | 0 |
| Branson | 11,797 | 65 | 45 | 20 |

## Table 78. Full-Time Law Enforcement Employees, by Selected State and City, 2020—Continued

(Number.)

| State/city | Population | Total law enforcement employees | Total officers | Total civilians |
|---|---|---|---|---|
| Brentwood | 7,944 | 30 | 29 | 1 |
| Buffalo | 3,214 | 7 | 6 | 1 |
| Butler | 3,981 | 19 | 12 | 7 |
| Cabool | 2,063 | 12 | 8 | 4 |
| Calverton Park | 1,265 | 7 | 7 | 0 |
| Camdenton | 4,186 | 17 | 15 | 2 |
| Campbell | 1,773 | 7 | 7 | 0 |
| Canton | 2,308 | 6 | 5 | 1 |
| Cape Girardeau | 41,957 | 102 | 70 | 32 |
| Caruthersville | 5,212 | 15 | 14 | 1 |
| Centralia | 4,376 | 16 | 11 | 5 |
| Chaffee | 2,895 | 12 | 7 | 5 |
| Charleston | 4,936 | 18 | 12 | 6 |
| Chillicothe | 8,865 | 27 | 17 | 10 |
| Cleveland | 669 | 2 | 2 | 0 |
| Clinton | 9,047 | 25 | 24 | 1 |
| Columbia | 126,418 | 208 | 162 | 46 |
| Concordia | 2,367 | 9 | 9 | 0 |
| Country Club Hills | 1,243 | 7 | 7 | 0 |
| Cuba | 3,270 | 16 | 15 | 1 |
| Des Peres | 8,757 | 48 | 42 | 6 |
| Dexter | 7,833 | 25 | 18 | 7 |
| Doniphan | 1,911 | 10 | 6 | 4 |
| Duquesne | 1,681 | 4 | 3 | 1 |
| East Prairie | 2,905 | 12 | 7 | 5 |
| Edmundson | 827 | 12 | 11 | 1 |
| Eldon | 4,764 | 13 | 12 | 1 |
| Ellisville | 9,905 | 33 | 32 | 1 |
| Ellsinore | 424 | 2 | 2 | 0 |
| Eureka | 11,442 | 30 | 26 | 4 |
| Excelsior Springs | 11,908 | 31 | 21 | 10 |
| Ferguson | 20,386 | 41 | 30 | 11 |
| Festus | 12,167 | 38 | 29 | 9 |
| Flordell Hills | 797 | 8 | 8 | 0 |
| Florissant | 50,653 | 120 | 89 | 31 |
| Fordland | 861 | 1 | 1 | 0 |
| Fredericktown | 4,008 | 14 | 13 | 1 |
| Frontenac | 3,899 | 22 | 21 | 1 |
| Fulton | 12,530 | 31 | 26 | 5 |
| Galena | 443 | 4 | 2 | 2 |
| Gerald | 1,324 | 4 | 4 | 0 |
| Gladstone | 27,905 | 55 | 38 | 17 |
| Glendale | 5,856 | 12 | 11 | 1 |
| Grain Valley | 15,038 | 29 | 24 | 5 |
| Grandview | 24,734 | 69 | 51 | 18 |
| Greenfield | 1,310 | 4 | 4 | 0 |
| Hamilton | 1,680 | 7 | 7 | 0 |
| Hannibal | 17,194 | 46 | 35 | 11 |
| Harrisonville | 10,091 | 28 | 20 | 8 |
| Hayti | 2,425 | 12 | 12 | 0 |
| Hazelwood | 24,976 | 72 | 57 | 15 |
| Higginsville | 4,639 | 22 | 10 | 12 |
| Holts Summit | 5,296 | 8 | 7 | 1 |
| Houston | 2,085 | 9 | 9 | 0 |
| Independence | 116,761 | 267 | 191 | 76 |
| Ironton | 1,378 | 7 | 7 | 0 |
| Jackson | 14,792 | 32 | 31 | 1 |
| Jefferson City | 41,851 | 122 | 87 | 35 |
| Jonesburg | 692 | 5 | 5 | 0 |
| Kansas City | 500,965 | 1,839 | 1,286 | 553 |
| Kearney | 11,467 | 20 | 18 | 2 |
| Kennett | 9,946 | 25 | 19 | 6 |
| Kimberling City | 2,321 | 4 | 4 | 0 |
| Kirksville | 17,666 | 29 | 26 | 3 |
| Ladue | 8,624 | 29 | 28 | 1 |
| Lakeshire | 1,380 | 3 | 3 | 0 |
| Lake St. Louis | 17,469 | 42 | 32 | 10 |
| Lake Tapawingo | 718 | 4 | 3 | 1 |
| La Plata | 1,297 | 4 | 4 | 0 |
| Laurie | 983 | 5 | 5 | 0 |
| Lebanon | 14,917 | 36 | 24 | 12 |
| Lee's Summit | 102,519 | 187 | 134 | 53 |
| Lexington | 4,526 | 10 | 8 | 2 |
| Lincoln | 1,198 | 4 | 4 | 0 |
| Lowry City | 629 | 6 | 1 | 5 |
| Macon | 5,327 | 11 | 9 | 2 |
| Malden | 3,812 | 15 | 10 | 5 |
| Manchester | 18,081 | 44 | 35 | 9 |
| Maplewood | 8,076 | 34 | 33 | 1 |
| Marionville | 2,157 | 4 | 4 | 0 |
| Marshall | 12,868 | 30 | 23 | 7 |
| Maryland Heights | 26,839 | 95 | 80 | 15 |
| Maryville | 11,479 | 27 | 19 | 8 |
| Merriam Woods | 1,870 | 1 | 1 | 0 |
| Mexico | 11,531 | 29 | 28 | 1 |

## Table 78. Full-Time Law Enforcement Employees, by Selected State and City, 2020—Continued

(Number.)

| State/city | Population | Total law enforcement employees | Total officers | Total civilians |
|---|---|---|---|---|
| Milan | 1,744 | 5 | 5 | 0 |
| Moberly | 13,459 | 35 | 25 | 10 |
| Monroe City | 2,433 | 6 | 5 | 1 |
| Moscow Mills | 3,784 | 8 | 8 | 0 |
| Mountain View | 2,649 | 7 | 5 | 2 |
| New Florence | 698 | 3 | 3 | 0 |
| Niangua | 426 | 1 | 1 | 0 |
| Northmoor | 364 | 10 | 10 | 0 |
| Odessa | 5,293 | 13 | 11 | 2 |
| Olivette | 7,850 | 22 | 21 | 1 |
| Oronogo | 2,696 | 6 | 6 | 0 |
| Osage Beach | 4,706 | 31 | 21 | 10 |
| Owensville | 2,551 | 8 | 7 | 1 |
| Palmyra | 3,574 | 9 | 8 | 1 |
| Peculiar | 5,774 | 11 | 10 | 1 |
| Perry | 703 | 1 | 1 | 0 |
| Perryville | 8,570 | 30 | 23 | 7 |
| Piedmont | 1,868 | 5 | 5 | 0 |
| Platte Woods | 408 | 4 | 4 | 0 |
| Pleasant Hill | 8,801 | 19 | 13 | 6 |
| Pleasant Valley | 3,063 | 21 | 9 | 12 |
| Poplar Bluff | 16,784 | 51 | 41 | 10 |
| Prairie Home | 280 | 1 | 1 | 0 |
| Raymore | 22,885 | 42 | 26 | 16 |
| Richland | 1,791 | 5 | 5 | 0 |
| Rock Hill | 4,610 | 11 | 10 | 1 |
| Rolla | 20,519 | 61 | 36 | 25 |
| Salem | 4,866 | 16 | 11 | 5 |
| Salisbury | 1,500 | 4 | 3 | 1 |
| Sarcoxie | 1,546 | 6 | 6 | 0 |
| Scott City | 4,520 | 17 | 12 | 5 |
| Seligman | 835 | 1 | 1 | 0 |
| Seymour | 2,033 | 8 | 8 | 0 |
| Sikeston | 15,931 | 68 | 50 | 18 |
| Springfield | 168,988 | 386 | 309 | 77 |
| St. Ann | 12,540 | 67 | 42 | 25 |
| Steele | 1,825 | 4 | 4 | 0 |
| Steelville | 1,636 | 6 | 6 | 0 |
| St. James | 3,986 | 11 | 10 | 1 |
| St. John | 6,299 | 18 | 17 | 1 |
| St. Louis | 295,536 | 1,537 | 1,119 | 418 |
| St. Peters | 58,597 | 123 | 96 | 27 |
| St. Robert | 6,558 | 25 | 19 | 6 |
| Sullivan | 7,118 | 26 | 19 | 7 |
| Summersville | 486 | 3 | 3 | 0 |
| Sunset Hills | 8,447 | 31 | 25 | 6 |
| Tarkio | 1,405 | 2 | 2 | 0 |
| Thayer | 2,092 | 12 | 8 | 4 |
| Trenton | 5,584 | 18 | 12 | 6 |
| Union | 12,292 | 27 | 25 | 2 |
| University City | 33,930 | 84 | 66 | 18 |
| Van Buren | 795 | 5 | 5 | 0 |
| Versailles | 2,479 | 10 | 9 | 1 |
| Viburnum | 645 | 2 | 2 | 0 |
| Vienna | 599 | 2 | 2 | 0 |
| Vinita Park | 10,910 | 48 | 46 | 2 |
| Warrensburg | 20,707 | 32 | 28 | 4 |
| Warson Woods | 1,890 | 8 | 8 | 0 |
| Washington | 14,270 | 31 | 29 | 2 |
| Waverly | 846 | 1 | 1 | 0 |
| Weatherby Lake | 2,125 | 12 | 12 | 0 |
| Wellsville | 1,125 | 12 | 12 | 0 |
| Weston | 1,854 | 9 | 9 | 0 |
| West Plains | 12,417 | 39 | 31 | 8 |
| Willard | 5,781 | 8 | 7 | 1 |
| Willow Springs | 2,090 | 9 | 6 | 3 |
| Winona | 1,292 | 2 | 2 | 0 |
| Woodson Terrace | 4,028 | 18 | 16 | 2 |
| Wright City | 4,654 | 17 | 15 | 2 |
| **MONTANA** | | | | |
| Baker | 1,910 | 4 | 4 | 0 |
| Belgrade | 10,738 | 21 | 17 | 4 |
| Billings | 110,274 | 185 | 154 | 31 |
| Bozeman | 52,586 | 73 | 64 | 9 |
| Bridger | 775 | 3 | 3 | 0 |
| Chinook | 1,233 | 4 | 4 | 0 |
| Colstrip | 2,216 | 11 | 7 | 4 |
| Columbia Falls | 6,385 | 11 | 10 | 1 |
| Columbus | 2,141 | 6 | 5 | 1 |
| Conrad | 2,396 | 5 | 5 | 0 |
| Cut Bank | 3,028 | 6 | 5 | 1 |
| Deer Lodge | 2,772 | 6 | 6 | 0 |
| Dillon | 4,352 | 11 | 10 | 1 |
| East Helena | 2,140 | 1 | 1 | 0 |

## Table 78. Full-Time Law Enforcement Employees, by Selected State and City, 2020—Continued

(Number.)

| State/city | Population | Total law enforcement employees | Total officers | Total civilians |
|---|---|---|---|---|
| Ennis | 1,065 | 2 | 2 | 0 |
| Eureka | 1,449 | 3 | 3 | 0 |
| Fairview | 886 | 3 | 3 | 0 |
| Fort Benton | 1,440 | 4 | 4 | 0 |
| Glasgow | 3,318 | 11 | 7 | 4 |
| Glendive | 4,873 | 11 | 6 | 5 |
| Great Falls | 58,265 | 125 | 87 | 38 |
| Hamilton | 5,140 | 15 | 14 | 1 |
| Havre | 9,724 | 23 | 17 | 6 |
| Helena | 34,262 | 71 | 47 | 24 |
| Hot Springs | 592 | 2 | 2 | 0 |
| Kalispell | 25,926 | 51 | 40 | 11 |
| Laurel | 6,710 | 19 | 13 | 6 |
| Lewistown | 5,882 | 18 | 13 | 5 |
| Libby | 2,867 | 6 | 6 | 0 |
| Livingston | 7,991 | 26 | 16 | 10 |
| Manhattan | 1,963 | 4 | 4 | 0 |
| Miles City | 8,160 | 17 | 17 | 0 |
| Missoula | 77,852 | 140 | 113 | 27 |
| Plains | 1,148 | 3 | 3 | 0 |
| Polson | 5,242 | 15 | 14 | 1 |
| Red Lodge | 2,384 | 5 | 5 | 0 |
| Ronan City | 2,195 | 6 | 6 | 0 |
| Sidney | 6,407 | 11 | 10 | 1 |
| Stevensville | 2,171 | 5 | 4 | 1 |
| St. Ignatius | 846 | 2 | 2 | 0 |
| Thompson Falls | 1,443 | 4 | 4 | 0 |
| Troy | 986 | 4 | 4 | 0 |
| West Yellowstone | 1,383 | 9 | 3 | 6 |
| Whitefish | 8,972 | 18 | 15 | 3 |
| Wolf Point | 2,734 | 8 | 6 | 2 |
| **NEBRASKA** | | | | |
| Alliance | 7,986 | 23 | 14 | 9 |
| Ashland | 2,752 | 5 | 4 | 1 |
| Aurora | 4,491 | 9 | 8 | 1 |
| Bayard | 1,069 | 4 | 4 | 0 |
| Beatrice | 12,225 | 37 | 21 | 16 |
| Bellevue | 53,436 | 116 | 104 | 12 |
| Bennington | 1,524 | 4 | 4 | 0 |
| Blair | 7,979 | 15 | 13 | 2 |
| Bloomfield | 936 | 2 | 2 | 0 |
| Boys Town | 306 | 10 | 10 | 0 |
| Broken Bow | 3,427 | 8 | 7 | 1 |
| Burwell | 1,158 | 1 | 1 | 0 |
| Central City | 2,887 | 6 | 5 | 1 |
| Chadron | 5,194 | 20 | 13 | 7 |
| Columbus | 23,727 | 42 | 36 | 6 |
| Cozad | 3,689 | 8 | 8 | 0 |
| Crete | 6,864 | 14 | 12 | 2 |
| Emerson | 784 | 1 | 1 | 0 |
| Falls City | 4,052 | 12 | 8 | 4 |
| Franklin | 889 | 2 | 2 | 0 |
| Fremont | 26,210 | 47 | 38 | 9 |
| Gering | 8,017 | 20 | 18 | 2 |
| Gordon | 1,475 | 8 | 6 | 2 |
| Gothenburg | 3,408 | 8 | 5 | 3 |
| Grand Island | 51,226 | 96 | 79 | 17 |
| Harvard | 961 | 2 | 2 | 0 |
| Hastings | 24,680 | 52 | 38 | 14 |
| Hemingford | 759 | 1 | 1 | 0 |
| Holdrege | 5,375 | 14 | 8 | 6 |
| Imperial | 2,005 | 3 | 3 | 0 |
| Kearney | 34,576 | 74 | 58 | 16 |
| Kimball | 2,261 | 5 | 4 | 1 |
| La Vista | 17,057 | 41 | 35 | 6 |
| Lexington | 10,099 | 22 | 20 | 2 |
| Lincoln | 293,808 | 490 | 354 | 136 |
| Madison | 2,337 | 3 | 3 | 0 |
| McCook | 7,478 | 22 | 15 | 7 |
| Milford | 2,006 | 3 | 3 | 0 |
| Minden | 3,031 | 6 | 6 | 0 |
| Morrill | 869 | 2 | 2 | 0 |
| Nebraska City | 7,248 | 14 | 13 | 1 |
| Neligh | 1,478 | 2 | 2 | 0 |
| Norfolk | 24,370 | 60 | 40 | 20 |
| North Platte | 23,057 | 62 | 40 | 22 |
| Omaha | 480,307 | 1,044 | 895 | 149 |
| O'Neill | 3,521 | 8 | 7 | 1 |
| Ord | 2,043 | 3 | 3 | 0 |
| Papillion | 20,313 | 49 | 45 | 4 |
| Pierce | 1,731 | 3 | 3 | 0 |
| Plattsmouth | 6,409 | 17 | 14 | 3 |
| Ralston | 7,386 | 15 | 14 | 1 |
| Ravenna | 1,361 | 2 | 2 | 0 |

## Table 78. Full-Time Law Enforcement Employees, by Selected State and City, 2020—Continued

(Number.)

| State/city | Population | Total law enforcement employees | Total officers | Total civilians |
|---|---|---|---|---|
| Scottsbluff | 15,463 | 34 | 29 | 5 |
| Scribner | 776 | 1 | 1 | 0 |
| Seward | 7,402 | 13 | 12 | 1 |
| Sidney | 6,186 | 12 | 10 | 2 |
| South Sioux City | 12,780 | 28 | 27 | 1 |
| St. Paul | 2,336 | 4 | 4 | 0 |
| Superior | 1,790 | 4 | 3 | 1 |
| Sutton | 1,441 | 3 | 3 | 0 |
| Tekamah | 1,703 | 5 | 5 | 0 |
| Tilden | 934 | 1 | 1 | 0 |
| Valentine | 2,747 | 6 | 5 | 1 |
| Valley | 2,985 | 5 | 5 | 0 |
| Wahoo | 4,611 | 6 | 6 | 0 |
| Waterloo | 921 | 4 | 4 | 0 |
| Wayne | 5,766 | 12 | 8 | 4 |
| West Point | 3,223 | 5 | 4 | 1 |
| Wymore | 1,311 | 4 | 4 | 0 |
| | | | | |
| **NEVADA** | | | | |
| Boulder City | 16,556 | 54 | 37 | 17 |
| Carlin | 2,273 | 7 | 5 | 2 |
| Elko | 20,760 | 46 | 39 | 7 |
| Fallon | 8,765 | 37 | 25 | 12 |
| Henderson | 337,375 | 642 | 469 | 173 |
| Las Vegas Metropolitan Police Department | 1,685,021 | 5,760 | 3,994 | 1,766 |
| Mesquite | 21,038 | 54 | 38 | 16 |
| Reno | 262,919 | 453 | 327 | 126 |
| Winnemucca | 7,835 | 29 | 24 | 5 |
| Yerington | 3,267 | 8 | 7 | 1 |
| | | | | |
| **NEW HAMPSHIRE** | | | | |
| Alexandria | 1,629 | 2 | 2 | 0 |
| Allenstown | 4,505 | 9 | 7 | 2 |
| Alstead | 1,952 | 2 | 2 | 0 |
| Alton | 5,445 | 14 | 12 | 2 |
| Amherst | 11,440 | 19 | 18 | 1 |
| Andover | 2,392 | 2 | 2 | 0 |
| Antrim | 2,687 | 5 | 5 | 0 |
| Ashland | 2,066 | 5 | 5 | 0 |
| Atkinson | 7,296 | 9 | 8 | 1 |
| Auburn | 5,771 | 12 | 10 | 2 |
| Barnstead | 4,852 | 7 | 7 | 0 |
| Barrington | 9,423 | 11 | 10 | 1 |
| Bartlett | 2,818 | 4 | 4 | 0 |
| Bedford | 23,137 | 48 | 36 | 12 |
| Belmont | 7,406 | 17 | 14 | 3 |
| Bennington | 1,520 | 2 | 2 | 0 |
| Berlin | 9,799 | 30 | 22 | 8 |
| Bethlehem | 2,669 | 6 | 6 | 0 |
| Boscawen | 4,110 | 7 | 6 | 1 |
| Bow | 8,119 | 12 | 11 | 1 |
| Bradford | 1,748 | 4 | 4 | 0 |
| Brentwood | 4,682 | 2 | 2 | 0 |
| Bristol | 3,168 | 10 | 9 | 1 |
| Brookline | 5,547 | 10 | 9 | 1 |
| Campton | 3,335 | 7 | 5 | 2 |
| Canaan | 3,914 | 6 | 5 | 1 |
| Candia | 4,016 | 8 | 7 | 1 |
| Canterbury | 2,510 | 3 | 3 | 0 |
| Carroll | 754 | 4 | 4 | 0 |
| Center Harbor | 1,112 | 4 | 4 | 0 |
| Charlestown | 5,023 | 9 | 5 | 4 |
| Chester | 5,399 | 9 | 8 | 1 |
| Chesterfield | 3,648 | 6 | 5 | 1 |
| Chichester | 2,750 | 5 | 5 | 0 |
| Claremont | 12,905 | 29 | 21 | 8 |
| Colebrook | 2,118 | 4 | 4 | 0 |
| Concord | 44,053 | 97 | 86 | 11 |
| Conway | 10,364 | 32 | 23 | 9 |
| Danville | 4,677 | 5 | 5 | 0 |
| Deerfield | 4,652 | 9 | 8 | 1 |
| Deering | 1,974 | 2 | 2 | 0 |
| Derry | 33,892 | 67 | 54 | 13 |
| Dover | 33,112 | 66 | 45 | 21 |
| Dublin | 1,552 | 3 | 2 | 1 |
| Dunbarton | 2,934 | 6 | 6 | 0 |
| Durham | 16,848 | 22 | 19 | 3 |
| East Kingston | 2,446 | 6 | 5 | 1 |
| Effingham | 1,483 | 2 | 2 | 0 |
| Enfield | 4,563 | 7 | 6 | 1 |
| Epping | 7,233 | 16 | 15 | 1 |
| Epsom | 4,848 | 7 | 6 | 1 |
| Exeter | 15,596 | 32 | 24 | 8 |
| Farmington | 7,058 | 12 | 11 | 1 |
| Fitzwilliam | 2,373 | 4 | 3 | 1 |

## Table 78. Full-Time Law Enforcement Employees, by Selected State and City, 2020—Continued

(Number.)

| State/city | Population | Total law enforcement employees | Total officers | Total civilians |
|---|---|---|---|---|
| Francestown | 1,584 | 1 | 1 | 0 |
| Franconia | 1,117 | 4 | 4 | 0 |
| Franklin | 8,782 | 25 | 17 | 8 |
| Freedom | 1,603 | 2 | 2 | 0 |
| Fremont | 4,847 | 7 | 6 | 1 |
| Gilford | 7,391 | 24 | 18 | 6 |
| Gilmanton | 3,850 | 6 | 5 | 1 |
| Goffstown | 18,184 | 45 | 31 | 14 |
| Gorham | 2,569 | 10 | 6 | 4 |
| Grafton | 1,337 | 1 | 1 | 0 |
| Grantham | 2,953 | 6 | 5 | 1 |
| Greenland | 4,228 | 10 | 9 | 1 |
| Greenville | 2,111 | 3 | 3 | 0 |
| Hampstead | 8,733 | 9 | 9 | 0 |
| Hampton | 16,206 | 42 | 35 | 7 |
| Hampton Falls | 2,459 | 5 | 5 | 0 |
| Hancock | 1,650 | 2 | 2 | 0 |
| Hanover | 11,586 | 28 | 18 | 10 |
| Harrisville | 953 | 1 | 1 | 0 |
| Haverhill | 4,542 | 7 | 5 | 2 |
| Hebron | 635 | 1 | 1 | 0 |
| Henniker | 5,024 | 9 | 8 | 1 |
| Hillsborough | 6,020 | 23 | 15 | 8 |
| Hinsdale | 3,894 | 7 | 6 | 1 |
| Holderness | 2,133 | 6 | 6 | 0 |
| Hollis | 8,166 | 18 | 16 | 2 |
| Hooksett | 14,834 | 41 | 30 | 11 |
| Hopkinton | 5,852 | 5 | 4 | 1 |
| Hudson | 25,736 | 67 | 50 | 17 |
| Jackson | 869 | 4 | 4 | 0 |
| Jaffrey | 5,271 | 11 | 10 | 1 |
| Keene | 22,619 | 49 | 39 | 10 |
| Kensington | 2,116 | 7 | 6 | 1 |
| Kingston | 6,549 | 7 | 6 | 1 |
| Laconia | 16,929 | 54 | 43 | 11 |
| Lancaster | 3,209 | 6 | 4 | 2 |
| Lebanon | 13,877 | 44 | 32 | 12 |
| Lee | 4,684 | 10 | 9 | 1 |
| Lincoln | 1,787 | 16 | 11 | 5 |
| Lisbon | 1,586 | 4 | 4 | 0 |
| Litchfield | 8,696 | 15 | 13 | 2 |
| Littleton | 5,898 | 16 | 13 | 3 |
| Londonderry | 27,268 | 73 | 58 | 15 |
| Loudon | 5,740 | 7 | 6 | 1 |
| Lyme | 1,682 | 2 | 2 | 0 |
| Madison | 2,646 | 4 | 4 | 0 |
| Manchester | 112,844 | 269 | 222 | 47 |
| Marlborough | 2,089 | 2 | 2 | 0 |
| Mason | 1,438 | 2 | 2 | 0 |
| Meredith | 6,579 | 17 | 13 | 4 |
| Merrimack | 27,656 | 52 | 39 | 13 |
| Middleton | 1,859 | 4 | 4 | 0 |
| Milford | 16,662 | 30 | 25 | 5 |
| Milton | 4,676 | 7 | 6 | 1 |
| Mont Vernon | 2,749 | 4 | 3 | 1 |
| Moultonborough | 4,227 | 9 | 8 | 1 |
| Nashua | 89,431 | 229 | 172 | 57 |
| New Boston | 6,006 | 8 | 7 | 1 |
| Newbury | 2,263 | 5 | 5 | 0 |
| New Castle | 985 | 4 | 4 | 0 |
| New Durham | 2,771 | 5 | 5 | 0 |
| Newfields | 1,760 | 2 | 2 | 0 |
| New Hampton | 2,270 | 5 | 4 | 1 |
| Newington | 849 | 11 | 10 | 1 |
| New Ipswich | 5,462 | 5 | 4 | 1 |
| New London | 4,257 | 14 | 9 | 5 |
| Newmarket | 9,349 | 20 | 13 | 7 |
| Newport | 6,366 | 16 | 11 | 5 |
| Newton | 5,030 | 8 | 7 | 1 |
| Northfield | 4,995 | 9 | 9 | 0 |
| North Hampton | 4,562 | 13 | 12 | 1 |
| Northumberland | 2,101 | 4 | 4 | 0 |
| Northwood | 4,385 | 8 | 7 | 1 |
| Nottingham | 5,281 | 9 | 8 | 1 |
| Orford | 1,323 | 1 | 1 | 0 |
| Ossipee | 4,387 | 9 | 8 | 1 |
| Pelham | 14,453 | 31 | 23 | 8 |
| Pembroke | 7,265 | 12 | 10 | 2 |
| Peterborough | 6,792 | 14 | 12 | 2 |
| Piermont | 821 | 1 | 1 | 0 |
| Pittsburg | 817 | 1 | 1 | 0 |
| Pittsfield | 4,146 | 7 | 7 | 0 |
| Plainfield | 2,425 | 3 | 3 | 0 |
| Plaistow | 7,847 | 22 | 15 | 7 |
| Plymouth | 6,911 | 18 | 11 | 7 |

## Table 78. Full-Time Law Enforcement Employees, by Selected State and City, 2020—Continued

(Number.)

| State/city | Population | Total law enforcement employees | Total officers | Total civilians |
|---|---|---|---|---|
| Portsmouth | 21,913 | 84 | 65 | 19 |
| Raymond | 10,752 | 25 | 17 | 8 |
| Rindge | 6,142 | 10 | 9 | 1 |
| Rochester | 32,327 | 65 | 51 | 14 |
| Rollinsford | 2,615 | 5 | 5 | 0 |
| Rumney | 1,585 | 1 | 1 | 0 |
| Rye | 5,566 | 11 | 10 | 1 |
| Salem | 31,231 | 79 | 64 | 15 |
| Sanbornton | 3,055 | 7 | 6 | 1 |
| Sandown | 6,693 | 9 | 8 | 1 |
| Sandwich | 1,371 | 2 | 2 | 0 |
| Seabrook | 8,974 | 34 | 28 | 6 |
| Somersworth | 12,498 | 32 | 25 | 7 |
| South Hampton | 835 | 3 | 3 | 0 |
| Springfield | 1,351 | 2 | 2 | 0 |
| Strafford | 4,314 | 5 | 5 | 0 |
| Stratham | 7,707 | 12 | 11 | 1 |
| Sugar Hill | 586 | 2 | 2 | 0 |
| Sunapee | 3,519 | 6 | 5 | 1 |
| Sutton | 1,945 | 2 | 2 | 0 |
| Swanzey | 7,275 | 11 | 10 | 1 |
| Tamworth | 3,117 | 2 | 2 | 0 |
| Thornton | 2,559 | 6 | 5 | 1 |
| Tilton | 3,602 | 18 | 13 | 5 |
| Troy | 2,114 | 2 | 2 | 0 |
| Tuftonboro | 2,443 | 4 | 4 | 0 |
| Wakefield | 5,812 | 13 | 11 | 2 |
| Walpole | 4,064 | 5 | 4 | 1 |
| Warner | 2,964 | 3 | 2 | 1 |
| Warren | 952 | 1 | 1 | 0 |
| Washington | 1,102 | 1 | 1 | 0 |
| Waterville Valley | 242 | 7 | 7 | 0 |
| Weare | 9,130 | 13 | 12 | 1 |
| Webster | 1,983 | 2 | 2 | 0 |
| Whitefield | 2,186 | 7 | 6 | 1 |
| Wilmot | 1,412 | 1 | 1 | 0 |
| Wilton | 3,854 | 9 | 8 | 1 |
| Winchester | 4,205 | 5 | 4 | 1 |
| Windham | 15,191 | 28 | 21 | 7 |
| Wolfeboro | 6,467 | 20 | 14 | 6 |
| Woodstock | 1,373 | 3 | 3 | 0 |
| | | | | |
| **NEW JERSEY** | | | | |
| Aberdeen Township | 19,475 | 49 | 42 | 7 |
| Absecon | 8,820 | 28 | 27 | 1 |
| Allendale | 7,003 | 21 | 16 | 5 |
| Allenhurst | 482 | 12 | 9 | 3 |
| Allentown | 1,756 | 7 | 6 | 1 |
| Alpine | 1,921 | 12 | 12 | 0 |
| Andover Township | 5,805 | 17 | 12 | 5 |
| Asbury Park | 15,305 | 90 | 86 | 4 |
| Atlantic City | 37,379 | 366 | 257 | 109 |
| Atlantic Highlands | 4,359 | 16 | 15 | 1 |
| Audubon | 8,959 | 18 | 17 | 1 |
| Avalon | 1,208 | 24 | 21 | 3 |
| Avon-by-the-Sea | 1,772 | 12 | 12 | 0 |
| Barnegat Township | 25,395 | 55 | 53 | 2 |
| Barrington | 6,849 | 18 | 16 | 2 |
| Bay Head | 1,028 | 10 | 9 | 1 |
| Bayonne | 68,121 | 230 | 178 | 52 |
| Beach Haven | 1,275 | 14 | 13 | 1 |
| Beachwood | 11,988 | 21 | 19 | 2 |
| Bedminster Township | 8,290 | 18 | 16 | 2 |
| Belleville | 38,053 | 111 | 106 | 5 |
| Bellmawr | 11,778 | 25 | 24 | 1 |
| Belmar | 5,514 | 31 | 25 | 6 |
| Belvidere | 2,552 | 6 | 5 | 1 |
| Bergenfield | 28,578 | 52 | 44 | 8 |
| Berkeley Heights Township | 13,892 | 32 | 29 | 3 |
| Berkeley Township | 44,366 | 99 | 77 | 22 |
| Berlin | 7,817 | 18 | 17 | 1 |
| Berlin Township | 6,152 | 19 | 18 | 1 |
| Bernards Township | 28,288 | 42 | 38 | 4 |
| Bernardsville | 7,883 | 30 | 24 | 6 |
| Beverly | 2,473 | 8 | 8 | 0 |
| Blairstown Township | 5,679 | 10 | 9 | 1 |
| Bloomfield | 52,181 | 147 | 123 | 24 |
| Bloomingdale | 8,415 | 19 | 18 | 1 |
| Bogota | 8,658 | 26 | 21 | 5 |
| Boonton | 9,312 | 23 | 22 | 1 |
| Boonton Township | 4,393 | 15 | 14 | 1 |
| Bordentown City | 3,782 | 14 | 14 | 0 |
| Bordentown Township | 12,134 | 31 | 27 | 4 |
| Bound Brook | 10,594 | 33 | 27 | 6 |
| Bradley Beach | 4,114 | 22 | 18 | 4 |

# Table 78. Full-Time Law Enforcement Employees, by Selected State and City, 2020—Continued

(Number.)

| State/city | Population | Total law enforcement employees | Total officers | Total civilians |
|---|---|---|---|---|
| Branchburg Township | 15,172 | 30 | 27 | 3 |
| Brick Township | 80,505 | 213 | 145 | 68 |
| Bridgeton | 23,472 | 77 | 64 | 13 |
| Bridgewater Township | 45,918 | 82 | 74 | 8 |
| Brielle | 4,652 | 19 | 18 | 1 |
| Brigantine | 8,495 | 45 | 35 | 10 |
| Brooklawn | 1,969 | 8 | 8 | 0 |
| Burlington City | 9,831 | 35 | 31 | 4 |
| Burlington Township | 22,635 | 53 | 44 | 9 |
| Butler | 7,965 | 17 | 16 | 1 |
| Byram Township | 7,839 | 15 | 15 | 0 |
| Caldwell | 8,284 | 18 | 18 | 0 |
| Camden County Police Department | 76,544 | 399 | 368 | 31 |
| Cape May | 3,384 | 23 | 22 | 1 |
| Carlstadt | 6,365 | 28 | 26 | 2 |
| Carney's Point Township | 7,656 | 21 | 20 | 1 |
| Carteret | 24,427 | 71 | 68 | 3 |
| Cedar Grove Township | 13,377 | 32 | 31 | 1 |
| Chatham | 8,924 | 26 | 22 | 4 |
| Chatham Township | 10,500 | 23 | 21 | 2 |
| Cherry Hill Township | 75,214 | 163 | 134 | 29 |
| Chesilhurst | 1,676 | 12 | 11 | 1 |
| Chesterfield Township | 7,570 | 11 | 10 | 1 |
| Chester Township | 7,917 | 24 | 23 | 1 |
| Cinnaminson Township | 16,708 | 27 | 27 | 0 |
| Clark Township | 16,622 | 56 | 45 | 11 |
| Clayton | 9,190 | 17 | 16 | 1 |
| Clementon | 5,157 | 14 | 13 | 1 |
| Cliffside Park | 27,363 | 44 | 42 | 2 |
| Clifton | 88,703 | 197 | 159 | 38 |
| Clinton | 2,671 | 12 | 12 | 0 |
| Clinton Township | 12,820 | 27 | 26 | 1 |
| Closter | 8,804 | 25 | 24 | 1 |
| Collingswood | 14,425 | 31 | 27 | 4 |
| Colts Neck Township | 9,811 | 29 | 27 | 2 |
| Cranbury Township | 4,361 | 20 | 19 | 1 |
| Cranford Township | 25,189 | 66 | 52 | 14 |
| Cresskill | 8,998 | 31 | 26 | 5 |
| Deal | 718 | 22 | 18 | 4 |
| Delanco Township | 4,441 | 14 | 13 | 1 |
| Delaware Township | 4,394 | 8 | 7 | 1 |
| Delran Township | 16,431 | 33 | 29 | 4 |
| Demarest | 5,033 | 15 | 15 | 0 |
| Denville Township | 17,019 | 41 | 33 | 8 |
| Deptford Township | 31,675 | 74 | 69 | 5 |
| Dover | 18,306 | 38 | 34 | 4 |
| Dumont | 18,340 | 40 | 31 | 9 |
| Dunellen | 7,434 | 19 | 19 | 0 |
| Eastampton Township | 6,145 | 21 | 20 | 1 |
| East Brunswick Township | 50,438 | 109 | 84 | 25 |
| East Greenwich Township | 11,587 | 24 | 22 | 2 |
| East Hanover Township | 11,296 | 38 | 34 | 4 |
| East Newark | 2,704 | 7 | 7 | 0 |
| East Orange | 67,392 | 267 | 205 | 62 |
| East Rutherford | 10,134 | 41 | 40 | 1 |
| East Windsor Township | 28,325 | 46 | 42 | 4 |
| Eatontown | 12,100 | 51 | 39 | 12 |
| Edgewater | 15,346 | 32 | 29 | 3 |
| Edgewater Park Township | 8,612 | 18 | 16 | 2 |
| Edison Township | 102,726 | 231 | 181 | 50 |
| Egg Harbor City | 4,038 | 14 | 13 | 1 |
| Egg Harbor Township | 41,966 | 125 | 92 | 33 |
| Elizabeth | 134,131 | 432 | 331 | 101 |
| Elk Township | 4,348 | 12 | 11 | 1 |
| Elmer | 1,304 | 2 | 2 | 0 |
| Elmwood Park | 20,738 | 54 | 48 | 6 |
| Emerson | 7,900 | 24 | 21 | 3 |
| Englewood | 29,592 | 103 | 75 | 28 |
| Englewood Cliffs | 5,544 | 26 | 25 | 1 |
| Englishtown | 1,916 | 7 | 7 | 0 |
| Essex Fells | 2,154 | 13 | 13 | 0 |
| Evesham Township | 45,137 | 103 | 93 | 10 |
| Ewing Township | 38,055 | 95 | 77 | 18 |
| Fairfield Township, Essex County | 7,775 | 47 | 43 | 4 |
| Fair Haven | 5,671 | 13 | 13 | 0 |
| Fair Lawn | 34,311 | 71 | 61 | 10 |
| Fairview | 14,747 | 36 | 33 | 3 |
| Fanwood | 8,092 | 18 | 16 | 2 |
| Far Hills | 940 | 7 | 6 | 1 |
| Flemington | 4,549 | 16 | 16 | 0 |
| Florence Township | 12,508 | 32 | 30 | 2 |
| Florham Park | 12,322 | 38 | 32 | 6 |
| Fort Lee | 40,285 | 117 | 96 | 21 |
| Franklin | 4,662 | 17 | 16 | 1 |
| Franklin Lakes | 11,744 | 29 | 24 | 5 |

## Table 78. Full-Time Law Enforcement Employees, by Selected State and City, 2020—Continued

(Number.)

| State/city | Population | Total law enforcement employees | Total officers | Total civilians |
|---|---|---|---|---|
| Franklin Township, Gloucester County | 16,980 | 42 | 38 | 4 |
| Franklin Township, Hunterdon County | 3,532 | 6 | 6 | 0 |
| Franklin Township, Somerset County | 69,423 | 124 | 103 | 21 |
| Freehold Borough | 11,621 | 34 | 30 | 4 |
| Freehold Township | 34,533 | 70 | 66 | 4 |
| Frenchtown | 1,345 | 4 | 3 | 1 |
| Galloway Township | 35,320 | 91 | 63 | 28 |
| Garfield | 33,092 | 71 | 60 | 11 |
| Garwood | 4,517 | 20 | 16 | 4 |
| Gibbsboro | 2,293 | 7 | 7 | 0 |
| Glassboro | 21,442 | 56 | 50 | 6 |
| Glen Ridge | 7,896 | 29 | 23 | 6 |
| Glen Rock | 12,153 | 26 | 24 | 2 |
| Gloucester City | 11,637 | 35 | 33 | 2 |
| Gloucester Township | 66,365 | 156 | 135 | 21 |
| Green Brook Township | 7,307 | 23 | 22 | 1 |
| Greenwich Township, Gloucester County | 5,006 | 22 | 20 | 2 |
| Greenwich Township, Warren County | 5,428 | 12 | 12 | 0 |
| Guttenberg | 11,458 | 32 | 26 | 6 |
| Hackensack | 45,932 | 119 | 102 | 17 |
| Hackettstown | 9,338 | 20 | 19 | 1 |
| Haddonfield | 11,772 | 25 | 22 | 3 |
| Haddon Heights | 7,829 | 18 | 17 | 1 |
| Haddon Township | 15,104 | 28 | 27 | 1 |
| Haledon | 8,604 | 21 | 21 | 0 |
| Hamburg | 3,101 | 12 | 11 | 1 |
| Hamilton Township, Atlantic County | 25,718 | 69 | 53 | 16 |
| Hamilton Township, Mercer County | 90,195 | 203 | 171 | 32 |
| Hammonton | 13,819 | 41 | 35 | 6 |
| Hanover Township | 14,814 | 38 | 31 | 7 |
| Harding Township | 3,904 | 18 | 17 | 1 |
| Hardyston Township | 7,718 | 26 | 20 | 6 |
| Harrington Park | 4,893 | 11 | 11 | 0 |
| Harrison | 22,252 | 54 | 45 | 9 |
| Harrison Township | 13,772 | 24 | 23 | 1 |
| Harvey Cedars | 365 | 9 | 9 | 0 |
| Hasbrouck Heights | 12,415 | 30 | 28 | 2 |
| Haworth | 3,516 | 13 | 12 | 1 |
| Hawthorne | 19,442 | 41 | 35 | 6 |
| Hazlet Township | 19,575 | 48 | 45 | 3 |
| High Bridge | 3,364 | 9 | 9 | 0 |
| Highland Park | 14,126 | 34 | 26 | 8 |
| Highlands | 4,662 | 16 | 14 | 2 |
| Hightstown | 5,473 | 14 | 13 | 1 |
| Hillsborough Township | 42,116 | 62 | 54 | 8 |
| Hillsdale | 10,692 | 19 | 18 | 1 |
| Hillside Township | 22,799 | 76 | 63 | 13 |
| Hi-Nella | 891 | 10 | 10 | 0 |
| Hoboken | 55,632 | 157 | 139 | 18 |
| Ho-Ho-Kus | 4,217 | 21 | 16 | 5 |
| Holland Township | 5,054 | 8 | 7 | 1 |
| Holmdel Township | 16,659 | 52 | 43 | 9 |
| Hopatcong | 14,051 | 47 | 39 | 8 |
| Hopewell Township | 18,348 | 39 | 30 | 9 |
| Howell Township | 52,098 | 108 | 93 | 15 |
| Independence Township | 5,391 | 11 | 10 | 1 |
| Irvington | 56,559 | 211 | 156 | 55 |
| Island Heights | 1,773 | 7 | 7 | 0 |
| Jackson Township | 61,350 | 124 | 106 | 18 |
| Jamesburg | 6,058 | 20 | 16 | 4 |
| Jefferson Township | 21,409 | 44 | 36 | 8 |
| Jersey City | 275,213 | 1,444 | 934 | 510 |
| Keansburg | 9,568 | 40 | 33 | 7 |
| Kearny | 42,183 | 111 | 105 | 6 |
| Kenilworth | 8,520 | 31 | 26 | 5 |
| Keyport | 6,925 | 24 | 22 | 2 |
| Kinnelon | 10,239 | 17 | 16 | 1 |
| Lacey Township | 31,324 | 59 | 44 | 15 |
| Lakehurst | 2,862 | 13 | 11 | 2 |
| Lakewood Township | 113,868 | 188 | 148 | 40 |
| Lambertville | 3,777 | 11 | 9 | 2 |
| Laurel Springs | 1,935 | 7 | 7 | 0 |
| Lavallette | 1,992 | 16 | 12 | 4 |
| Lawnside | 2,989 | 8 | 8 | 0 |
| Lawrence Township, Mercer County | 33,882 | 66 | 60 | 6 |
| Lebanon Township | 6,030 | 11 | 10 | 1 |
| Leonia | 9,370 | 24 | 21 | 3 |
| Lincoln Park | 10,439 | 30 | 24 | 6 |
| Linden | 44,010 | 180 | 136 | 44 |
| Lindenwold | 17,897 | 46 | 43 | 3 |
| Linwood | 6,592 | 22 | 20 | 2 |
| Little Egg Harbor Township | 23,203 | 58 | 45 | 13 |
| Little Falls Township | 15,019 | 38 | 29 | 9 |
| Little Ferry | 11,144 | 30 | 25 | 5 |
| Little Silver | 5,752 | 24 | 19 | 5 |

## Table 78. Full-Time Law Enforcement Employees, by Selected State and City, 2020—Continued

(Number.)

| State/city | Population | Total law enforcement employees | Total officers | Total civilians |
|---|---|---|---|---|
| Livingston Township | 31,787 | 85 | 70 | 15 |
| Lodi | 25,235 | 50 | 47 | 3 |
| Logan Township | 6,118 | 24 | 23 | 1 |
| Long Beach Township | 3,211 | 48 | 36 | 12 |
| Long Branch | 30,148 | 116 | 92 | 24 |
| Long Hill Township | 8,701 | 25 | 23 | 2 |
| Longport | 840 | 13 | 13 | 0 |
| Lopatcong Township | 8,561 | 17 | 16 | 1 |
| Lower Alloways Creek Township | 1,652 | 11 | 11 | 0 |
| Lower Township | 21,042 | 57 | 51 | 6 |
| Lumberton Township | 12,146 | 25 | 23 | 2 |
| Lyndhurst Township | 23,987 | 57 | 54 | 3 |
| Madison | 18,563 | 36 | 28 | 8 |
| Magnolia | 4,435 | 17 | 17 | 0 |
| Mahwah Township | 27,195 | 62 | 53 | 9 |
| Manalapan Township | 39,240 | 62 | 58 | 4 |
| Manasquan | 5,778 | 22 | 17 | 5 |
| Manchester Township | 46,188 | 122 | 70 | 52 |
| Mansfield Township, Burlington County | 8,523 | 14 | 13 | 1 |
| Mansfield Township, Warren County | 7,354 | 16 | 15 | 1 |
| Mantoloking | 258 | 10 | 9 | 1 |
| Mantua Township | 15,458 | 29 | 27 | 2 |
| Manville | 10,473 | 27 | 24 | 3 |
| Maple Shade Township | 18,395 | 41 | 37 | 4 |
| Maplewood Township | 27,320 | 75 | 63 | 12 |
| Margate City | 5,749 | 38 | 29 | 9 |
| Marlboro Township | 39,580 | 110 | 84 | 26 |
| Matawan | 8,579 | 25 | 24 | 1 |
| Maywood | 9,970 | 26 | 22 | 4 |
| Medford Lakes | 3,888 | 11 | 10 | 1 |
| Medford Township | 23,417 | 40 | 36 | 4 |
| Mendham | 5,023 | 13 | 12 | 1 |
| Mendham Township | 5,845 | 16 | 15 | 1 |
| Merchantville | 3,839 | 16 | 14 | 2 |
| Metuchen | 15,521 | 34 | 29 | 5 |
| Middlesex Borough | 14,101 | 28 | 25 | 3 |
| Middle Township | 18,041 | 70 | 57 | 13 |
| Middletown Township | 65,057 | 121 | 111 | 10 |
| Midland Park | 7,481 | 18 | 17 | 1 |
| Millburn Township | 20,949 | 64 | 58 | 6 |
| Milltown | 7,203 | 19 | 16 | 3 |
| Millville | 26,882 | 95 | 83 | 12 |
| Monmouth Beach | 3,261 | 13 | 12 | 1 |
| Monroe Township, Gloucester County | 38,685 | 69 | 64 | 5 |
| Monroe Township, Middlesex County | 47,391 | 86 | 67 | 19 |
| Montclair | 40,224 | 129 | 110 | 19 |
| Montgomery Township | 24,233 | 37 | 31 | 6 |
| Montvale | 9,021 | 27 | 25 | 2 |
| Montville Township | 21,797 | 44 | 39 | 5 |
| Moonachie | 2,802 | 24 | 21 | 3 |
| Moorestown Township | 20,593 | 38 | 33 | 5 |
| Morris Plains | 6,564 | 19 | 17 | 2 |
| Morristown | 20,130 | 60 | 55 | 5 |
| Morris Township | 23,286 | 55 | 49 | 6 |
| Mountain Lakes | 4,377 | 14 | 13 | 1 |
| Mountainside | 7,188 | 27 | 21 | 6 |
| Mount Arlington | 6,161 | 16 | 15 | 1 |
| Mount Ephraim | 4,759 | 14 | 13 | 1 |
| Mount Holly Township | 9,522 | 28 | 25 | 3 |
| Mount Laurel Township | 41,867 | 78 | 71 | 7 |
| Mount Olive Township | 30,093 | 58 | 49 | 9 |
| Mullica Township | 5,808 | 19 | 16 | 3 |
| Neptune City | 4,573 | 20 | 19 | 1 |
| Neptune Township | 27,283 | 87 | 75 | 12 |
| Netcong | 3,242 | 14 | 13 | 1 |
| Newark | 295,039 | 1,337 | 1,032 | 305 |
| New Brunswick | 58,691 | 164 | 146 | 18 |
| New Hanover Township | 8,121 | 3 | 3 | 0 |
| New Milford | 17,005 | 44 | 41 | 3 |
| New Providence | 14,785 | 27 | 25 | 2 |
| Newton | 7,963 | 27 | 22 | 5 |
| North Arlington | 16,288 | 39 | 31 | 8 |
| North Bergen Township | 62,275 | 141 | 123 | 18 |
| North Brunswick Township | 42,801 | 98 | 81 | 17 |
| North Caldwell | 6,973 | 21 | 16 | 5 |
| Northfield | 8,002 | 24 | 22 | 2 |
| North Haledon | 8,708 | 25 | 22 | 3 |
| North Hanover Township | 7,450 | 11 | 10 | 1 |
| North Plainfield | 22,160 | 53 | 45 | 8 |
| Northvale | 5,163 | 14 | 14 | 0 |
| North Wildwood | 3,710 | 36 | 27 | 9 |
| Norwood | 5,996 | 17 | 16 | 1 |
| Nutley Township | 29,666 | 84 | 72 | 12 |
| Oakland | 13,390 | 33 | 27 | 6 |
| Oaklyn | 4,102 | 13 | 12 | 1 |

## Table 78. Full-Time Law Enforcement Employees, by Selected State and City, 2020—Continued

(Number.)

| State/city | Population | Total law enforcement employees | Total officers | Total civilians |
|---|---|---|---|---|
| Ocean City | 10,825 | 83 | 70 | 13 |
| Ocean Gate | 2,154 | 12 | 11 | 1 |
| Oceanport | 5,693 | 16 | 15 | 1 |
| Ocean Township, Monmouth County | 26,776 | 78 | 63 | 15 |
| Ocean Township, Ocean County | 9,659 | 34 | 24 | 10 |
| Ogdensburg | 2,228 | 6 | 6 | 0 |
| Old Bridge Township | 68,177 | 121 | 100 | 21 |
| Old Tappan | 6,130 | 14 | 13 | 1 |
| Oradell | 8,447 | 23 | 22 | 1 |
| Orange City | 31,822 | 193 | 147 | 46 |
| Palisades Park | 21,969 | 41 | 40 | 1 |
| Palmyra | 7,111 | 14 | 13 | 1 |
| Paramus | 27,132 | 125 | 99 | 26 |
| Park Ridge | 8,994 | 21 | 20 | 1 |
| Parsippany-Troy Hills Township | 53,272 | 129 | 99 | 30 |
| Passaic | 72,223 | 247 | 164 | 83 |
| Paterson | 150,757 | 476 | 408 | 68 |
| Paulsboro | 6,090 | 23 | 21 | 2 |
| Peapack-Gladstone | 2,713 | 9 | 8 | 1 |
| Pemberton Borough | 1,315 | 6 | 6 | 0 |
| Pemberton Township | 26,829 | 55 | 50 | 5 |
| Pennington | 2,722 | 7 | 7 | 0 |
| Pennsauken Township | 37,212 | 90 | 86 | 4 |
| Penns Grove | 4,719 | 13 | 12 | 1 |
| Pennsville Township | 12,336 | 24 | 22 | 2 |
| Pequannock Township | 15,447 | 36 | 31 | 5 |
| Perth Amboy | 53,516 | 161 | 127 | 34 |
| Phillipsburg | 14,172 | 41 | 40 | 1 |
| Pine Beach | 2,307 | 7 | 6 | 1 |
| Pine Hill | 10,842 | 25 | 23 | 2 |
| Piscataway Township | 59,699 | 97 | 80 | 17 |
| Pitman | 9,095 | 22 | 20 | 2 |
| Plainfield | 52,163 | 146 | 122 | 24 |
| Plainsboro Township | 23,639 | 45 | 37 | 8 |
| Pleasantville | 20,038 | 60 | 55 | 5 |
| Plumsted Township | 9,038 | 15 | 14 | 1 |
| Pohatcong Township | 3,159 | 16 | 15 | 1 |
| Point Pleasant | 19,805 | 41 | 32 | 9 |
| Point Pleasant Beach | 4,794 | 30 | 24 | 6 |
| Pompton Lakes | 11,374 | 30 | 25 | 5 |
| Princeton | 32,436 | 60 | 51 | 9 |
| Prospect Park | 6,058 | 20 | 19 | 1 |
| Rahway | 31,362 | 93 | 81 | 12 |
| Ramsey | 15,463 | 41 | 35 | 6 |
| Randolph Township | 26,283 | 42 | 36 | 6 |
| Raritan | 8,199 | 22 | 21 | 1 |
| Raritan Township | 22,594 | 41 | 38 | 3 |
| Readington Township | 15,839 | 26 | 24 | 2 |
| Red Bank | 11,947 | 46 | 38 | 8 |
| Ridgefield | 11,599 | 31 | 29 | 2 |
| Ridgefield Park | 13,389 | 40 | 33 | 7 |
| Ridgewood | 25,959 | 49 | 45 | 4 |
| Ringwood | 12,659 | 26 | 21 | 5 |
| Riverdale | 4,348 | 22 | 17 | 5 |
| River Edge | 12,072 | 27 | 24 | 3 |
| Riverside Township | 7,844 | 18 | 18 | 0 |
| Riverton | 2,678 | 6 | 6 | 0 |
| River Vale Township | 10,394 | 27 | 26 | 1 |
| Robbinsville Township | 15,197 | 37 | 29 | 8 |
| Rochelle Park Township | 5,775 | 26 | 22 | 4 |
| Rockaway | 6,487 | 16 | 15 | 1 |
| Rockaway Township | 27,360 | 62 | 50 | 12 |
| Roseland | 6,066 | 22 | 21 | 1 |
| Roselle | 22,667 | 67 | 55 | 12 |
| Roselle Park | 14,101 | 36 | 34 | 2 |
| Roxbury Township | 23,676 | 43 | 42 | 1 |
| Rumson | 6,632 | 19 | 16 | 3 |
| Runnemede | 8,610 | 16 | 15 | 1 |
| Rutherford | 18,990 | 45 | 43 | 2 |
| Saddle Brook Township | 14,154 | 36 | 31 | 5 |
| Saddle River | 3,287 | 22 | 17 | 5 |
| Salem | 4,673 | 18 | 17 | 1 |
| Sayreville | 45,821 | 106 | 92 | 14 |
| Scotch Plains Township | 25,204 | 52 | 49 | 3 |
| Sea Bright | 1,323 | 21 | 11 | 10 |
| Sea Girt | 1,765 | 13 | 12 | 1 |
| Sea Isle City | 2,009 | 32 | 23 | 9 |
| Seaside Heights | 3,174 | 28 | 25 | 3 |
| Seaside Park | 1,629 | 14 | 13 | 1 |
| Secaucus | 23,102 | 94 | 79 | 15 |
| Ship Bottom | 1,223 | 15 | 13 | 2 |
| Shrewsbury | 4,065 | 20 | 16 | 4 |
| Somerdale | 5,751 | 18 | 17 | 1 |
| Somers Point | 10,091 | 34 | 27 | 7 |
| Somerville | 12,717 | 33 | 31 | 2 |

## Table 78. Full-Time Law Enforcement Employees, by Selected State and City, 2020—Continued

(Number.)

| State/city | Population | Total law enforcement employees | Total officers | Total civilians |
|---|---|---|---|---|
| South Amboy | 9,536 | 33 | 27 | 6 |
| South Bound Brook | 4,722 | 14 | 13 | 1 |
| South Brunswick Township | 47,479 | 113 | 88 | 25 |
| South Hackensack Township | 2,529 | 22 | 20 | 2 |
| South Orange Village | 17,420 | 45 | 39 | 6 |
| South Plainfield | 25,038 | 74 | 58 | 16 |
| South River | 16,240 | 41 | 31 | 10 |
| South Toms River | 3,892 | 13 | 12 | 1 |
| Sparta Township | 18,503 | 47 | 35 | 12 |
| Spotswood | 8,504 | 29 | 25 | 4 |
| Springfield Township, Burlington County | 3,236 | 11 | 10 | 1 |
| Springfield Township, Union County | 18,285 | 48 | 44 | 4 |
| Spring Lake | 2,881 | 14 | 14 | 0 |
| Spring Lake Heights | 4,478 | 15 | 15 | 0 |
| Stafford Township | 30,025 | 85 | 55 | 30 |
| Stanhope | 3,258 | 10 | 9 | 1 |
| Stone Harbor | 799 | 19 | 17 | 2 |
| Stratford | 7,219 | 15 | 15 | 0 |
| Summit | 22,766 | 52 | 48 | 4 |
| Surf City | 1,262 | 11 | 11 | 0 |
| Teaneck Township | 42,218 | 107 | 92 | 15 |
| Tenafly | 14,883 | 40 | 34 | 6 |
| Tewksbury Township | 5,723 | 13 | 12 | 1 |
| Tinton Falls | 17,345 | 45 | 43 | 2 |
| Toms River Township | 100,051 | 207 | 161 | 46 |
| Totowa | 11,251 | 32 | 29 | 3 |
| Trenton | 86,246 | 326 | 265 | 61 |
| Tuckerton | 3,586 | 14 | 13 | 1 |
| Union Beach | 5,209 | 21 | 17 | 4 |
| Union City | 70,023 | 208 | 174 | 34 |
| Union Township | 62,583 | 185 | 135 | 50 |
| Upper Saddle River | 8,498 | 21 | 17 | 4 |
| Ventnor City | 9,798 | 49 | 38 | 11 |
| Vernon Township | 21,715 | 42 | 33 | 9 |
| Verona | 14,233 | 36 | 30 | 6 |
| Vineland | 58,405 | 173 | 147 | 26 |
| Voorhees Township | 30,319 | 66 | 56 | 10 |
| Waldwick | 10,767 | 26 | 21 | 5 |
| Wallington | 12,086 | 22 | 22 | 0 |
| Wall Township | 25,455 | 87 | 68 | 19 |
| Wanaque | 12,281 | 30 | 25 | 5 |
| Warren Township | 16,378 | 38 | 31 | 7 |
| Washington Township, Bergen County | 9,530 | 26 | 21 | 5 |
| Washington Township, Gloucester County | 50,124 | 89 | 82 | 7 |
| Washington Township, Morris County | 18,746 | 35 | 32 | 3 |
| Washington Township, Warren County | 6,340 | 29 | 28 | 1 |
| Watchung | 6,280 | 35 | 29 | 6 |
| Waterford Township | 11,107 | 27 | 26 | 1 |
| Wayne Township | 55,249 | 149 | 121 | 28 |
| Weehawken Township | 15,266 | 70 | 61 | 9 |
| Westampton Township | 8,658 | 28 | 25 | 3 |
| West Caldwell Township | 11,299 | 33 | 27 | 6 |
| West Deptford Township | 21,835 | 46 | 43 | 3 |
| Westfield | 30,361 | 71 | 58 | 13 |
| West Long Branch | 7,855 | 23 | 22 | 1 |
| West Milford Township | 27,350 | 51 | 44 | 7 |
| West New York | 55,716 | 136 | 124 | 12 |
| West Orange | 49,619 | 109 | 96 | 13 |
| Westville | 4,315 | 14 | 13 | 1 |
| West Wildwood | 535 | 5 | 5 | 0 |
| West Windsor Township | 29,865 | 61 | 49 | 12 |
| Westwood | 11,495 | 33 | 27 | 6 |
| Wharton | 6,728 | 23 | 21 | 2 |
| Wildwood | 4,877 | 53 | 40 | 13 |
| Wildwood Crest | 3,011 | 29 | 26 | 3 |
| Willingboro Township | 32,053 | 71 | 61 | 10 |
| Winfield Township | 1,559 | 9 | 9 | 0 |
| Winslow Township | 40,044 | 83 | 77 | 6 |
| Woodbridge Township | 103,633 | 270 | 208 | 62 |
| Woodbury | 10,192 | 36 | 33 | 3 |
| Woodbury Heights | 3,085 | 8 | 7 | 1 |
| Woodcliff Lake | 6,094 | 20 | 20 | 0 |
| Woodland Park | 13,278 | 37 | 32 | 5 |
| Woodlynne | 3,022 | 7 | 5 | 2 |
| Wood-Ridge | 9,867 | 26 | 23 | 3 |
| Woodstown | 3,434 | 10 | 9 | 1 |
| Woolwich Township | 14,168 | 32 | 31 | 1 |
| Wyckoff Township | 17,589 | 27 | 26 | 1 |
| **NEW MEXICO** | | | | |
| Albuquerque | 564,147 | 1,474 | 940 | 534 |
| Angel Fire | 1,057 | 7 | 5 | 2 |
| Anthony | 9,258 | 11 | 10 | 1 |
| Artesia | 12,286 | 38 | 23 | 15 |
| Aztec | 6,289 | 16 | 14 | 2 |

## Table 78. Full-Time Law Enforcement Employees, by Selected State and City, 2020—Continued

(Number.)

| State/city | Population | Total law enforcement employees | Total officers | Total civilians |
|---|---|---|---|---|
| Bayard | 2,097 | 4 | 3 | 1 |
| Belen | 7,481 | 21 | 19 | 2 |
| Bosque Farms | 3,844 | 15 | 14 | 1 |
| Capitan | 1,454 | 4 | 3 | 1 |
| Carlsbad | 30,029 | 100 | 67 | 33 |
| Carrizozo | 946 | 2 | 1 | 1 |
| Clayton | 2,631 | 12 | 6 | 6 |
| Cloudcroft | 707 | 4 | 4 | 0 |
| Clovis | 38,073 | 64 | 45 | 19 |
| Corrales | 8,734 | 17 | 14 | 3 |
| Edgewood | 6,112 | 15 | 12 | 3 |
| Espanola | 9,950 | 39 | 28 | 11 |
| Eunice | 3,064 | 14 | 10 | 4 |
| Farmington | 43,973 | 164 | 118 | 46 |
| Gallup | 21,200 | 71 | 55 | 16 |
| Hatch | 1,680 | 10 | 9 | 1 |
| Hope | 104 | 1 | 1 | 0 |
| Jal | 2,126 | 16 | 7 | 9 |
| Las Cruces | 105,805 | 243 | 172 | 71 |
| Las Vegas | 12,711 | 42 | 29 | 13 |
| Logan | 967 | 4 | 4 | 0 |
| Lordsburg | 2,300 | 13 | 10 | 3 |
| Los Lunas | 16,405 | 43 | 39 | 4 |
| Lovington | 11,521 | 25 | 18 | 7 |
| Magdalena | 862 | 2 | 2 | 0 |
| Milan | 3,640 | 8 | 6 | 2 |
| Moriarty | 1,829 | 11 | 9 | 2 |
| Mountainair | 864 | 4 | 3 | 1 |
| Raton | 5,836 | 16 | 10 | 6 |
| Red River | 457 | 5 | 4 | 1 |
| Roswell | 47,510 | 101 | 81 | 20 |
| Ruidoso | 8,066 | 31 | 20 | 11 |
| Ruidoso Downs | 2,616 | 11 | 7 | 4 |
| Santa Clara | 1,748 | 4 | 2 | 2 |
| Santa Fe | 85,404 | 174 | 135 | 39 |
| Santa Rosa | 2,603 | 15 | 9 | 6 |
| San Ysidro | 205 | 2 | 2 | 0 |
| Silver City | 9,308 | 35 | 30 | 5 |
| Socorro | 8,248 | 14 | 11 | 3 |
| Springer | 898 | 3 | 3 | 0 |
| Sunland Park | 18,920 | 27 | 25 | 2 |
| Taos | 5,856 | 24 | 19 | 5 |
| Tatum | 833 | 3 | 2 | 1 |
| Texico | 1,056 | 1 | 1 | 0 |
| Truth or Consequences | 5,701 | 14 | 10 | 4 |
| Tucumcari | 4,775 | 14 | 12 | 2 |
| Tularosa | 3,058 | 11 | 6 | 5 |
| **NEW YORK** | | | | |
| Addison Town and Village | 2,437 | 3 | 3 | 0 |
| Akron Village | 2,840 | 1 | 1 | 0 |
| Albany | 95,201 | 359 | 283 | 76 |
| Albion Village | 5,712 | 12 | 12 | 0 |
| Alfred Village | 3,894 | 5 | 5 | 0 |
| Altamont Village | 1,651 | 1 | 1 | 0 |
| Amherst Town | 121,185 | 184 | 153 | 31 |
| Amityville Village | 9,366 | 25 | 24 | 1 |
| Amsterdam | 17,623 | 42 | 38 | 4 |
| Andover Village | 958 | 1 | 1 | 0 |
| Arcade Village | 1,902 | 6 | 6 | 0 |
| Ardsley Village | 4,510 | 19 | 19 | 0 |
| Asharoken Village | 635 | 3 | 3 | 0 |
| Attica Village | 2,371 | 5 | 5 | 0 |
| Auburn | 25,746 | 71 | 65 | 6 |
| Avon Village | 3,286 | 5 | 5 | 0 |
| Baldwinsville Village | 7,854 | 14 | 13 | 1 |
| Ballston Spa Village | 5,165 | 3 | 3 | 0 |
| Batavia | 14,210 | 32 | 29 | 3 |
| Beacon | 13,940 | 34 | 31 | 3 |
| Bedford Town | 17,455 | 41 | 36 | 5 |
| Binghamton | 43,828 | 145 | 133 | 12 |
| Blooming Grove Town | 11,694 | 20 | 18 | 2 |
| Boonville Village | 1,963 | 1 | 1 | 0 |
| Brant Town | 2,067 | 1 | 1 | 0 |
| Brighton Town | 35,689 | 44 | 39 | 5 |
| Brockport Village | 7,821 | 16 | 15 | 1 |
| Bronxville Village | 6,402 | 23 | 21 | 2 |
| Buchanan Village | 2,214 | 6 | 6 | 0 |
| Buffalo | 253,809 | 895 | 722 | 173 |
| Cairo Town | 6,398 | 2 | 2 | 0 |
| Cambridge Village | 1,788 | 3 | 3 | 0 |
| Camden Village | 2,133 | 2 | 2 | 0 |
| Camillus Town and Village | 24,267 | 26 | 24 | 2 |
| Canajoharie Village | 2,115 | 5 | 5 | 0 |
| Canandaigua | 10,112 | 27 | 25 | 2 |

## Table 78. Full-Time Law Enforcement Employees, by Selected State and City, 2020—Continued

(Number.)

| State/city | Population | Total law enforcement employees | Total officers | Total civilians |
|---|---|---|---|---|
| Canastota Village | 4,493 | 2 | 2 | 0 |
| Canisteo Village | 2,097 | 2 | 2 | 0 |
| Canton Village | 6,498 | 10 | 9 | 1 |
| Carmel Town | 34,351 | 42 | 34 | 8 |
| Carthage Village | 3,218 | 4 | 4 | 0 |
| Catskill Village | 3,791 | 16 | 14 | 2 |
| Cayuga Heights Village | 3,505 | 7 | 6 | 1 |
| Cazenovia Village | 2,844 | 6 | 5 | 1 |
| Central Square Village | 1,725 | 6 | 6 | 0 |
| Centre Island Village | 404 | 6 | 6 | 0 |
| Cheektowaga Town | 76,130 | 159 | 124 | 35 |
| Chester Town | 8,061 | 14 | 14 | 0 |
| Chester Village | 4,068 | 13 | 12 | 1 |
| Chittenango Village | 4,799 | 1 | 1 | 0 |
| Cicero Town | 28,743 | 17 | 16 | 1 |
| Clarkstown Town | 80,188 | 182 | 159 | 23 |
| Clayton Village | 1,755 | 2 | 2 | 0 |
| Clifton Springs Village | 2,003 | 1 | 1 | 0 |
| Cobleskill Village | 4,305 | 11 | 11 | 0 |
| Coeymans Town | 7,211 | 3 | 2 | 1 |
| Cohoes | 16,625 | 33 | 30 | 3 |
| Colchester Town | 1,944 | 2 | 2 | 0 |
| Colonie Town | 78,364 | 149 | 111 | 38 |
| Corning | 10,579 | 25 | 21 | 4 |
| Cornwall-on-Hudson Village | 2,887 | 2 | 2 | 0 |
| Cornwall Town | 9,449 | 12 | 10 | 2 |
| Crawford Town | 9,139 | 12 | 11 | 1 |
| Croton-on-Hudson Village | 8,011 | 21 | 19 | 2 |
| Cuba Town | 3,031 | 5 | 5 | 0 |
| Dansville Village | 4,301 | 5 | 5 | 0 |
| Deerpark Town | 7,667 | 6 | 6 | 0 |
| Delhi Village | 2,851 | 5 | 5 | 0 |
| Depew Village | 14,892 | 37 | 30 | 7 |
| Dobbs Ferry Village | 10,925 | 27 | 25 | 2 |
| Dolgeville Village | 2,031 | 2 | 2 | 0 |
| Dryden Village | 2,007 | 4 | 4 | 0 |
| Dunkirk | 11,622 | 36 | 35 | 1 |
| East Aurora-Aurora Town | 13,781 | 20 | 15 | 5 |
| Eastchester Town | 19,762 | 49 | 47 | 2 |
| East Fishkill Town | 29,547 | 37 | 29 | 8 |
| East Greenbush Town | 16,088 | 33 | 24 | 9 |
| East Hampton Town | 19,970 | 89 | 63 | 26 |
| East Hampton Village | 1,144 | 31 | 26 | 5 |
| Eden Town | 7,584 | 3 | 3 | 0 |
| Ellicott Town | 4,945 | 13 | 13 | 0 |
| Ellicottville | 1,564 | 4 | 4 | 0 |
| Elmira | 26,834 | 81 | 71 | 10 |
| Elmira Heights Village | 3,714 | 9 | 9 | 0 |
| Elmira Town | 5,447 | 5 | 5 | 0 |
| Elmsford Village | 5,245 | 25 | 22 | 3 |
| Endicott Village | 12,335 | 31 | 29 | 2 |
| Evans Town | 15,962 | 23 | 17 | 6 |
| Fairport Village | 5,271 | 11 | 10 | 1 |
| Fallsburg Town | 12,375 | 21 | 21 | 0 |
| Floral Park Village | 15,725 | 45 | 33 | 12 |
| Florida Village | 2,894 | 1 | 1 | 0 |
| Fort Edward Village | 3,223 | 6 | 6 | 0 |
| Fort Plain Village | 2,207 | 3 | 3 | 0 |
| Frankfort Town | 4,708 | 4 | 4 | 0 |
| Frankfort Village | 2,385 | 4 | 4 | 0 |
| Fredonia Village | 9,997 | 20 | 16 | 4 |
| Freeport Village | 42,686 | 111 | 99 | 12 |
| Fulton City | 10,936 | 37 | 36 | 1 |
| Garden City Village | 22,211 | 66 | 52 | 14 |
| Geddes Town | 9,945 | 20 | 17 | 3 |
| Geneseo Village | 7,960 | 8 | 8 | 0 |
| Geneva | 12,584 | 31 | 30 | 1 |
| Glen Cove | 27,007 | 56 | 52 | 4 |
| Glenville Town | 21,656 | 25 | 24 | 1 |
| Gloversville | 14,454 | 37 | 35 | 2 |
| Goshen Town | 8,803 | 6 | 6 | 0 |
| Goshen Village | 5,326 | 21 | 18 | 3 |
| Gouverneur Village | 3,615 | 9 | 6 | 3 |
| Granville Village | 2,404 | 4 | 4 | 0 |
| Great Neck Estates Village | 2,877 | 16 | 13 | 3 |
| Greece Town | 95,202 | 106 | 94 | 12 |
| Greene Village | 1,374 | 1 | 1 | 0 |
| Greenwich Village | 1,690 | 2 | 2 | 0 |
| Greenwood Lake Village | 3,044 | 6 | 5 | 1 |
| Groton Village | 2,137 | 1 | 1 | 0 |
| Guilderland Town | 34,129 | 53 | 38 | 15 |
| Hamburg Town | 46,555 | 66 | 63 | 3 |
| Hamburg Village | 9,756 | 13 | 12 | 1 |
| Hamilton Village | 4,064 | 4 | 4 | 0 |
| Harriman Village | 2,421 | 7 | 7 | 0 |

## Table 78. Full-Time Law Enforcement Employees, by Selected State and City, 2020—Continued

(Number.)

| State/city | Population | Total law enforcement employees | Total officers | Total civilians |
|---|---|---|---|---|
| Hastings-on-Hudson Village | 7,873 | 20 | 20 | 0 |
| Hempstead Village | 54,817 | 148 | 119 | 29 |
| Herkimer Village | 7,213 | 20 | 20 | 0 |
| Homer Village | 3,060 | 6 | 5 | 1 |
| Hornell | 8,181 | 22 | 21 | 1 |
| Horseheads Village | 6,225 | 10 | 10 | 0 |
| Hudson Falls Village | 6,957 | 12 | 12 | 0 |
| Hunter Town | 2,612 | 3 | 3 | 0 |
| Huntington Bay Village | 1,442 | 5 | 5 | 0 |
| Hyde Park Town | 20,641 | 20 | 16 | 4 |
| Ilion Village | 7,562 | 20 | 19 | 1 |
| Inlet Town | 298 | 2 | 2 | 0 |
| Irondequoit Town | 49,569 | 60 | 52 | 8 |
| Irvington Village | 6,424 | 25 | 23 | 2 |
| Ithaca | 31,076 | 67 | 59 | 8 |
| Jamestown | 28,649 | 66 | 59 | 7 |
| Johnson City Village | 13,928 | 43 | 39 | 4 |
| Johnstown | 8,045 | 26 | 25 | 1 |
| Kenmore Village | 14,893 | 29 | 25 | 4 |
| Kensington Village | 1,185 | 6 | 6 | 0 |
| Kent Town | 13,105 | 24 | 19 | 5 |
| Kings Point Village | 5,308 | 20 | 18 | 2 |
| Kingston | 22,631 | 70 | 65 | 5 |
| Kirkland Town | 8,317 | 2 | 2 | 0 |
| Lackawanna | 17,582 | 51 | 43 | 8 |
| Lake Placid Village | 2,340 | 15 | 12 | 3 |
| Lake Success Village | 3,146 | 23 | 23 | 0 |
| Lakewood-Busti | 7,077 | 11 | 10 | 1 |
| Lancaster Town | 37,644 | 66 | 51 | 15 |
| Larchmont Village | 6,132 | 22 | 21 | 1 |
| Le Roy Village | 4,218 | 7 | 7 | 0 |
| Lewisboro Town | 12,418 | 3 | 3 | 0 |
| Liberty Village | 4,315 | 20 | 18 | 2 |
| Little Falls | 4,562 | 13 | 12 | 1 |
| Liverpool Village | 2,401 | 5 | 5 | 0 |
| Lloyd Town | 10,665 | 13 | 11 | 2 |
| Lockport | 20,100 | 51 | 48 | 3 |
| Long Beach | 33,294 | 84 | 68 | 16 |
| Lowville Village | 3,277 | 6 | 6 | 0 |
| Lynbrook Village | 19,272 | 57 | 50 | 7 |
| Macedon Town and Village | 8,843 | 8 | 7 | 1 |
| Malone Village | 5,593 | 12 | 12 | 0 |
| Malverne Village | 8,452 | 21 | 21 | 0 |
| Mamaroneck Town | 11,807 | 38 | 37 | 1 |
| Mamaroneck Village | 19,090 | 58 | 50 | 8 |
| Manlius Town | 24,096 | 40 | 36 | 4 |
| Marlborough Town | 8,572 | 10 | 8 | 2 |
| Massena Village | 10,045 | 24 | 19 | 5 |
| Mechanicville | 4,987 | 9 | 9 | 0 |
| Medina Village | 5,539 | 13 | 12 | 1 |
| Menands Village | 3,817 | 16 | 13 | 3 |
| Middleport Village | 1,719 | 3 | 3 | 0 |
| Middletown | 28,010 | 77 | 64 | 13 |
| Mohawk Village | 2,487 | 4 | 4 | 0 |
| Monroe Village | 8,577 | 22 | 17 | 5 |
| Montgomery Town | 9,153 | 16 | 13 | 3 |
| Montgomery Village | 4,557 | 4 | 4 | 0 |
| Monticello Village | 6,361 | 22 | 20 | 2 |
| Mount Hope Town | 6,513 | 6 | 6 | 0 |
| Mount Pleasant Town | 26,564 | 54 | 48 | 6 |
| Mount Vernon | 66,713 | 212 | 151 | 61 |
| Newark Village | 8,696 | 15 | 14 | 1 |
| New Berlin Town | 1,500 | 1 | 1 | 0 |
| Newburgh | 27,801 | 75 | 63 | 12 |
| Newburgh Town | 31,705 | 60 | 48 | 12 |
| New Castle Town | 17,622 | 38 | 36 | 2 |
| New Hartford Town and Village | 20,124 | 23 | 20 | 3 |
| New Paltz Town and Village | 14,109 | 23 | 20 | 3 |
| New Rochelle | 81,367 | 197 | 167 | 30 |
| New Windsor Town | 27,702 | 58 | 47 | 11 |
| New York | 8,475,387 | 50,029 | 35,047 | 14,982 |
| New York Mills Village | 3,172 | 3 | 3 | 0 |
| Niagara Falls | 47,139 | 164 | 146 | 18 |
| Niagara Town | 7,949 | 8 | 7 | 1 |
| Niskayuna Town | 22,383 | 28 | 27 | 1 |
| North Greenbush Town | 12,306 | 20 | 18 | 2 |
| Northport Village | 7,245 | 22 | 17 | 5 |
| North Syracuse Village | 6,572 | 12 | 11 | 1 |
| Norwich | 6,370 | 21 | 20 | 1 |
| Ogdensburg | 10,319 | 22 | 19 | 3 |
| Ogden Town | 20,715 | 15 | 12 | 3 |
| Old Brookville Village | 2,181 | 30 | 24 | 6 |
| Old Westbury Village | 4,052 | 30 | 25 | 5 |
| Olean | 13,272 | 37 | 31 | 6 |
| Oneida | 10,776 | 29 | 25 | 4 |

## Table 78. Full-Time Law Enforcement Employees, by Selected State and City, 2020—Continued

(Number.)

| State/city | Population | Total law enforcement employees | Total officers | Total civilians |
|---|---|---|---|---|
| Oneonta City | 13,671 | 29 | 23 | 6 |
| Orangetown Town | 37,135 | 88 | 80 | 8 |
| Orchard Park Town | 29,778 | 48 | 36 | 12 |
| Ossining Village | 24,607 | 63 | 57 | 6 |
| Oswego City | 17,132 | 50 | 44 | 6 |
| Owego Village | 3,816 | 4 | 3 | 1 |
| Oxford Village | 1,362 | 2 | 2 | 0 |
| Oyster Bay Cove Village | 4,279 | 14 | 14 | 0 |
| Peekskill | 24,136 | 58 | 49 | 9 |
| Pelham Manor Village | 5,461 | 26 | 25 | 1 |
| Pelham Village | 6,920 | 27 | 24 | 3 |
| Penn Yan Village | 4,928 | 14 | 13 | 1 |
| Perry Village | 3,439 | 5 | 5 | 0 |
| Piermont Village | 2,528 | 8 | 8 | 0 |
| Plattsburgh City | 19,144 | 53 | 47 | 6 |
| Pleasantville Village | 7,239 | 26 | 23 | 3 |
| Port Chester Village | 28,847 | 59 | 58 | 1 |
| Port Dickinson Village | 1,497 | 5 | 4 | 1 |
| Port Jervis | 8,415 | 31 | 30 | 1 |
| Portville Village | 934 | 1 | 1 | 0 |
| Port Washington | 19,301 | 70 | 62 | 8 |
| Poughkeepsie | 30,409 | 112 | 85 | 27 |
| Poughkeepsie Town | 38,808 | 95 | 81 | 14 |
| Pound Ridge Town | 5,066 | 2 | 1 | 1 |
| Pulaski Village | 2,198 | 1 | 1 | 0 |
| Quogue Village | 1,019 | 14 | 13 | 1 |
| Ramapo Town | 96,160 | 118 | 101 | 17 |
| Red Hook Village | 1,933 | 4 | 4 | 0 |
| Rensselaer City | 9,119 | 31 | 25 | 6 |
| Riverhead Town | 33,424 | 106 | 90 | 16 |
| Rochester | 204,735 | 756 | 668 | 88 |
| Rockville Centre Village | 24,431 | 65 | 56 | 9 |
| Rome | 31,991 | 80 | 78 | 2 |
| Rosendale Town | 5,730 | 2 | 2 | 0 |
| Rotterdam Town | 30,179 | 42 | 40 | 2 |
| Rye | 15,625 | 39 | 34 | 5 |
| Rye Brook Village | 9,592 | 27 | 26 | 1 |
| Sag Harbor Village | 2,305 | 12 | 12 | 0 |
| Salamanca | 5,337 | 18 | 18 | 0 |
| Sands Point Village | 2,814 | 20 | 20 | 0 |
| Saranac Lake Village | 5,171 | 11 | 11 | 0 |
| Saratoga Springs | 28,461 | 88 | 72 | 16 |
| Saugerties Town | 18,954 | 28 | 24 | 4 |
| Scarsdale Village | 17,847 | 46 | 40 | 6 |
| Schenectady | 65,140 | 171 | 147 | 24 |
| Schodack Town | 11,594 | 11 | 10 | 1 |
| Scotia Village | 7,605 | 14 | 13 | 1 |
| Seneca Falls Town | 8,570 | 19 | 17 | 2 |
| Shandaken Town | 2,912 | 4 | 4 | 0 |
| Shawangunk Town | 13,751 | 6 | 6 | 0 |
| Shelter Island Town | 2,421 | 13 | 12 | 1 |
| Sherrill | 2,947 | 3 | 3 | 0 |
| Sidney Village | 3,525 | 8 | 8 | 0 |
| Skaneateles Village | 2,466 | 5 | 4 | 1 |
| Sleepy Hollow Village | 10,073 | 24 | 24 | 0 |
| Solvay Village | 6,219 | 15 | 14 | 1 |
| Southampton Town | 51,289 | 137 | 99 | 38 |
| Southampton Village | 3,334 | 45 | 31 | 14 |
| South Glens Falls Village | 3,627 | 6 | 6 | 0 |
| South Nyack Village | 3,284 | 3 | 3 | 0 |
| Southold Town | 20,045 | 71 | 55 | 16 |
| Spring Valley Village | 32,340 | 65 | 57 | 8 |
| Stony Point Town | 15,309 | 25 | 24 | 1 |
| Syracuse | 140,847 | 443 | 376 | 67 |
| Tarrytown Village | 11,287 | 38 | 34 | 4 |
| Ticonderoga Town | 4,698 | 7 | 7 | 0 |
| Tonawanda | 14,715 | 34 | 28 | 6 |
| Tonawanda Town | 56,178 | 142 | 98 | 44 |
| Troy | 48,678 | 143 | 134 | 9 |
| Trumansburg Village | 1,658 | 1 | 1 | 0 |
| Tuckahoe Village | 6,481 | 24 | 21 | 3 |
| Tupper Lake Village | 3,409 | 12 | 12 | 0 |
| Tuxedo Park Village | 591 | 4 | 3 | 1 |
| Ulster Town | 12,745 | 28 | 24 | 4 |
| Utica | 58,965 | 178 | 163 | 15 |
| Vestal Town | 28,843 | 43 | 39 | 4 |
| Walden Village | 6,593 | 15 | 12 | 3 |
| Wallkill Town | 29,523 | 51 | 49 | 2 |
| Walton Village | 2,747 | 5 | 5 | 0 |
| Warsaw Village | 3,141 | 5 | 5 | 0 |
| Warwick Town | 18,357 | 36 | 31 | 5 |
| Washingtonville Village | 5,713 | 15 | 13 | 2 |
| Waterford Town and Village | 8,420 | 10 | 8 | 2 |
| Waterloo Village | 4,837 | 9 | 8 | 1 |
| Watertown | 24,091 | 71 | 68 | 3 |

## Table 78. Full-Time Law Enforcement Employees, by Selected State and City, 2020—Continued

(Number.)

| State/city | Population | Total law enforcement employees | Total officers | Total civilians |
|---|---|---|---|---|
| Watervliet | 9,766 | 25 | 25 | 0 |
| Waverly Village | 4,081 | 11 | 10 | 1 |
| Webb Town | 1,773 | 8 | 7 | 1 |
| Webster Town and Village | 45,651 | 36 | 32 | 4 |
| Weedsport Village | 1,671 | 1 | 1 | 0 |
| Wellsville Village | 4,296 | 12 | 11 | 1 |
| Westfield Village | 2,938 | 7 | 7 | 0 |
| Westhampton Beach Village | 1,817 | 16 | 14 | 2 |
| West Seneca Town | 45,155 | 79 | 66 | 13 |
| Whitehall Village | 2,507 | 3 | 3 | 0 |
| White Plains | 58,426 | 198 | 187 | 11 |
| Whitesboro Village | 3,564 | 5 | 5 | 0 |
| Whitestown Town | 8,816 | 5 | 5 | 0 |
| Windham Town | 1,682 | 2 | 2 | 0 |
| Woodbury Town | 11,094 | 21 | 17 | 4 |
| Woodstock Town | 5,743 | 10 | 10 | 0 |
| Yonkers | 200,397 | 694 | 613 | 81 |
| Yorktown Town | 35,970 | 63 | 54 | 9 |
| | | | | |
| **NORTH CAROLINA** | | | | |
| Aberdeen | 8,576 | 30 | 28 | 2 |
| Ahoskie | 4,653 | 19 | 17 | 2 |
| Albemarle | 16,391 | 51 | 38 | 13 |
| Andrews | 1,863 | 5 | 4 | 1 |
| Angier | 5,610 | 15 | 15 | 0 |
| Apex | 67,878 | 111 | 93 | 18 |
| Archdale | 11,572 | 33 | 28 | 5 |
| Asheboro | 26,082 | 91 | 78 | 13 |
| Asheville | 93,855 | 211 | 162 | 49 |
| Atlantic Beach | 1,516 | 17 | 16 | 1 |
| Ayden | 5,174 | 20 | 16 | 4 |
| Badin | 1,930 | 4 | 4 | 0 |
| Bailey | 569 | 1 | 1 | 0 |
| Bakersville | 439 | 1 | 1 | 0 |
| Bald Head Island | 189 | 26 | 25 | 1 |
| Banner Elk | 1,088 | 9 | 8 | 1 |
| Beaufort | 4,522 | 19 | 18 | 1 |
| Beech Mountain | 320 | 14 | 10 | 4 |
| Belhaven | 1,572 | 7 | 6 | 1 |
| Belmont | 12,891 | 46 | 40 | 6 |
| Benson | 4,101 | 16 | 15 | 1 |
| Bessemer City | 5,677 | 13 | 13 | 0 |
| Bethel | 1,617 | 3 | 3 | 0 |
| Beulaville | 1,295 | 6 | 6 | 0 |
| Biltmore Forest | 1,440 | 16 | 12 | 4 |
| Biscoe | 1,704 | 10 | 9 | 1 |
| Black Creek | 768 | 1 | 1 | 0 |
| Black Mountain | 8,297 | 23 | 22 | 1 |
| Bladenboro | 1,684 | 6 | 6 | 0 |
| Blowing Rock | 1,324 | 15 | 13 | 2 |
| Boiling Spring Lakes | 6,545 | 14 | 12 | 2 |
| Boiling Springs | 4,614 | 11 | 10 | 1 |
| Boone | 20,321 | 38 | 30 | 8 |
| Boonville | 1,105 | 5 | 5 | 0 |
| Brevard | 7,922 | 27 | 24 | 3 |
| Bridgeton | 441 | 1 | 1 | 0 |
| Broadway | 1,304 | 4 | 4 | 0 |
| Bryson City | 1,445 | 8 | 7 | 1 |
| Bunn | 407 | 3 | 2 | 1 |
| Burgaw | 4,154 | 15 | 15 | 0 |
| Burlington | 56,065 | 171 | 123 | 48 |
| Burnsville | 1,638 | 8 | 8 | 0 |
| Butner | 7,902 | 38 | 32 | 6 |
| Canton | 4,387 | 18 | 13 | 5 |
| Cape Carteret | 2,068 | 7 | 7 | 0 |
| Carolina Beach | 6,437 | 27 | 25 | 2 |
| Carrboro | 21,413 | 34 | 31 | 3 |
| Carthage | 2,626 | 11 | 10 | 1 |
| Cary | 177,735 | 216 | 171 | 45 |
| Caswell Beach | 442 | 4 | 4 | 0 |
| Chadbourn | 1,686 | 8 | 7 | 1 |
| Chapel Hill | 64,388 | 105 | 86 | 19 |
| Charlotte-Mecklenburg[1] | 956,282 | 2,281 | 1,734 | 547 |
| Cherryville | 6,180 | 19 | 14 | 5 |
| China Grove | 4,256 | 12 | 12 | 0 |
| Chocowinity | 771 | 3 | 3 | 0 |
| Claremont | 1,420 | 8 | 8 | 0 |
| Clayton | 27,775 | 55 | 52 | 3 |
| Cleveland | 877 | 5 | 5 | 0 |
| Clinton | 8,299 | 29 | 24 | 5 |
| Coats | 2,563 | 7 | 7 | 0 |
| Columbus | 1,008 | 9 | 8 | 1 |
| Concord | 100,631 | 214 | 185 | 29 |
| Conover | 8,601 | 29 | 26 | 3 |
| Conway | 711 | 2 | 2 | 0 |

## Table 78. Full-Time Law Enforcement Employees, by Selected State and City, 2020—Continued

(Number.)

| State/city | Population | Total law enforcement employees | Total officers | Total civilians |
|---|---|---|---|---|
| Cooleemee | 983 | 1 | 1 | 0 |
| Cornelius | 31,453 | 73 | 57 | 16 |
| Cramerton | 4,546 | 16 | 16 | 0 |
| Creedmoor | 4,670 | 20 | 16 | 4 |
| Dallas | 4,891 | 17 | 15 | 2 |
| Davidson | 13,457 | 27 | 25 | 2 |
| Dobson | 1,529 | 8 | 8 | 0 |
| Drexel | 1,859 | 5 | 5 | 0 |
| Duck | 396 | 12 | 12 | 0 |
| Dunn | 9,721 | 47 | 42 | 5 |
| Durham | 291,962 | 634 | 460 | 174 |
| East Bend | 593 | 2 | 2 | 0 |
| East Spencer | 1,557 | 7 | 7 | 0 |
| Eden | 14,786 | 49 | 45 | 4 |
| Edenton | 4,528 | 16 | 14 | 2 |
| Elizabeth City | 17,948 | 67 | 60 | 7 |
| Elizabethtown | 3,353 | 15 | 14 | 1 |
| Elkin | 3,998 | 21 | 17 | 4 |
| Elon | 12,521 | 21 | 20 | 1 |
| Emerald Isle | 3,677 | 20 | 18 | 2 |
| Enfield | 2,234 | 8 | 7 | 1 |
| Erwin | 5,270 | 12 | 11 | 1 |
| Fair Bluff | 872 | 3 | 3 | 0 |
| Fairmont | 2,568 | 9 | 9 | 0 |
| Farmville | 4,756 | 22 | 18 | 4 |
| Fayetteville | 212,047 | 521 | 348 | 173 |
| Fletcher | 8,573 | 17 | 16 | 1 |
| Forest City | 7,106 | 35 | 33 | 2 |
| Four Oaks | 2,436 | 8 | 8 | 0 |
| Foxfire Village | 1,076 | 4 | 4 | 0 |
| Franklin | 4,145 | 18 | 17 | 1 |
| Franklinton | 2,344 | 10 | 9 | 1 |
| Fremont | 1,263 | 4 | 4 | 0 |
| Fuquay-Varina | 34,018 | 58 | 51 | 7 |
| Garner | 32,889 | 82 | 70 | 12 |
| Garysburg | 900 | 2 | 2 | 0 |
| Gaston | 1,010 | 2 | 2 | 0 |
| Gastonia | 78,260 | 185 | 163 | 22 |
| Gibsonville | 7,492 | 22 | 21 | 1 |
| Glen Alpine | 1,486 | 4 | 4 | 0 |
| Goldsboro | 34,352 | 92 | 80 | 12 |
| Graham | 15,919 | 42 | 38 | 4 |
| Granite Falls | 4,652 | 15 | 13 | 2 |
| Granite Quarry | 3,008 | 9 | 9 | 0 |
| Greensboro | 300,865 | 774 | 671 | 103 |
| Greenville | 95,815 | 223 | 178 | 45 |
| Grifton | 2,717 | 6 | 6 | 0 |
| Havelock | 19,450 | 36 | 26 | 10 |
| Haw River | 2,558 | 9 | 9 | 0 |
| Henderson | 15,067 | 49 | 41 | 8 |
| Hendersonville | 14,351 | 55 | 43 | 12 |
| Hickory | 41,604 | 143 | 110 | 33 |
| Highlands | 989 | 14 | 13 | 1 |
| High Point | 114,492 | 274 | 231 | 43 |
| Hillsborough | 7,291 | 32 | 28 | 4 |
| Holden Beach | 686 | 10 | 9 | 1 |
| Holly Ridge | 3,365 | 13 | 12 | 1 |
| Holly Springs | 41,798 | 86 | 68 | 18 |
| Hope Mills | 15,914 | 41 | 33 | 8 |
| Hot Springs | 576 | 1 | 1 | 0 |
| Hudson | 3,696 | 14 | 13 | 1 |
| Huntersville | 60,450 | 102 | 86 | 16 |
| Indian Beach | 119 | 5 | 5 | 0 |
| Jacksonville | 76,130 | 152 | 119 | 33 |
| Jefferson | 1,528 | 6 | 6 | 0 |
| Jonesville | 2,198 | 10 | 9 | 1 |
| Kannapolis | 53,044 | 105 | 76 | 29 |
| Kenansville | 849 | 3 | 3 | 0 |
| Kenly | 1,655 | 8 | 8 | 0 |
| Kernersville | 25,074 | 84 | 65 | 19 |
| Kill Devil Hills | 7,488 | 33 | 27 | 6 |
| King | 6,916 | 27 | 24 | 3 |
| Kings Mountain | 11,162 | 41 | 33 | 8 |
| Kinston | 19,672 | 68 | 61 | 7 |
| Kitty Hawk | 3,632 | 16 | 15 | 1 |
| Knightdale | 18,970 | 35 | 32 | 3 |
| Kure Beach | 2,083 | 14 | 13 | 1 |
| Lake Lure | 1,152 | 9 | 8 | 1 |
| Lake Royale | 2,529 | 8 | 8 | 0 |
| Lake Waccamaw | 1,385 | 4 | 4 | 0 |
| Landis | 3,155 | 11 | 11 | 0 |
| Laurel Park | 2,358 | 7 | 7 | 0 |
| Laurinburg | 14,798 | 39 | 37 | 2 |
| Leland | 27,271 | 42 | 39 | 3 |
| Lenoir | 17,881 | 69 | 52 | 17 |

## Table 78. Full-Time Law Enforcement Employees, by Selected State and City, 2020—Continued

(Number.)

| State/city | Population | Total law enforcement employees | Total officers | Total civilians |
|---|---|---|---|---|
| Lexington | 19,162 | 66 | 53 | 13 |
| Liberty | 2,672 | 11 | 10 | 1 |
| Lilesville | 478 | 1 | 1 | 0 |
| Lillington | 3,680 | 13 | 12 | 1 |
| Lincolnton | 11,641 | 34 | 31 | 3 |
| Littleton | 578 | 3 | 3 | 0 |
| Locust | 3,307 | 15 | 15 | 0 |
| Long View | 4,959 | 17 | 17 | 0 |
| Louisburg | 3,722 | 17 | 16 | 1 |
| Lowell | 3,767 | 10 | 10 | 0 |
| Lumberton | 20,109 | 95 | 86 | 9 |
| Madison | 2,095 | 17 | 17 | 0 |
| Maggie Valley | 1,268 | 10 | 9 | 1 |
| Magnolia | 951 | 1 | 1 | 0 |
| Maiden | 3,430 | 19 | 18 | 1 |
| Manteo | 1,483 | 8 | 7 | 1 |
| Marion | 7,916 | 28 | 26 | 2 |
| Marshall | 920 | 4 | 4 | 0 |
| Mars Hill | 1,884 | 5 | 5 | 0 |
| Marshville | 2,875 | 9 | 9 | 0 |
| Matthews | 34,438 | 80 | 64 | 16 |
| Maxton | 2,321 | 13 | 9 | 4 |
| Mayodan | 2,401 | 15 | 15 | 0 |
| Maysville | 908 | 3 | 3 | 0 |
| Mebane | 17,365 | 38 | 34 | 4 |
| Micro | 565 | 2 | 2 | 0 |
| Middlesex | 835 | 5 | 5 | 0 |
| Mint Hill | 28,701 | 39 | 36 | 3 |
| Misenheimer | 744 | 5 | 5 | 0 |
| Monroe | 35,948 | 100 | 90 | 10 |
| Montreat | 965 | 4 | 4 | 0 |
| Mooresville | 40,560 | 108 | 85 | 23 |
| Morehead City | 9,774 | 44 | 41 | 3 |
| Morganton | 16,605 | 90 | 56 | 34 |
| Morrisville | 32,018 | 41 | 39 | 2 |
| Mount Airy | 10,152 | 44 | 36 | 8 |
| Mount Gilead | 1,137 | 8 | 8 | 0 |
| Mount Holly | 16,720 | 41 | 33 | 8 |
| Mount Olive | 4,665 | 17 | 16 | 1 |
| Murfreesboro | 2,873 | 9 | 8 | 1 |
| Murphy | 1,672 | 12 | 10 | 2 |
| Nags Head | 3,021 | 24 | 22 | 2 |
| Nashville | 5,572 | 18 | 17 | 1 |
| Navassa | 2,675 | 1 | 1 | 0 |
| New Bern | 29,985 | 110 | 85 | 25 |
| Newland | 693 | 5 | 5 | 0 |
| Newport | 4,691 | 9 | 9 | 0 |
| Newton | 13,253 | 37 | 28 | 9 |
| Newton Grove | 562 | 2 | 2 | 0 |
| Norlina | 1,032 | 3 | 3 | 0 |
| North Topsail Beach | 743 | 15 | 13 | 2 |
| Northwest | 813 | 1 | 1 | 0 |
| North Wilkesboro | 4,069 | 21 | 20 | 1 |
| Norwood | 2,479 | 10 | 10 | 0 |
| Oakboro | 1,935 | 8 | 8 | 0 |
| Oak Island | 8,955 | 22 | 20 | 2 |
| Ocean Isle Beach | 726 | 13 | 12 | 1 |
| Old Fort | 926 | 3 | 3 | 0 |
| Oriental | 856 | 2 | 2 | 0 |
| Oxford | 8,950 | 29 | 25 | 4 |
| Parkton | 428 | 2 | 2 | 0 |
| Pembroke | 2,929 | 14 | 11 | 3 |
| Pikeville | 677 | 2 | 2 | 0 |
| Pilot Mountain | 1,402 | 9 | 8 | 1 |
| Pinebluff | 1,686 | 3 | 3 | 0 |
| Pinehurst | 17,253 | 28 | 23 | 5 |
| Pine Knoll Shores | 1,313 | 9 | 9 | 0 |
| Pine Level | 2,123 | 5 | 5 | 0 |
| Pinetops | 1,207 | 9 | 7 | 2 |
| Pineville | 9,371 | 43 | 39 | 4 |
| Pink Hill | 507 | 2 | 2 | 0 |
| Pittsboro | 4,491 | 11 | 11 | 0 |
| Plymouth | 3,285 | 6 | 5 | 1 |
| Polkton | 2,236 | 1 | 1 | 0 |
| Princeton | 1,451 | 4 | 4 | 0 |
| Raeford | 4,987 | 19 | 17 | 2 |
| Raleigh | 481,823 | 744 | 648 | 96 |
| Ramseur | 1,689 | 6 | 6 | 0 |
| Randleman | 4,138 | 16 | 16 | 0 |
| Ranlo | 3,736 | 13 | 12 | 1 |
| Red Springs | 3,218 | 15 | 14 | 1 |
| Reidsville | 13,948 | 55 | 47 | 8 |
| Richlands | 1,741 | 8 | 8 | 0 |
| Rich Square | 822 | 3 | 1 | 2 |
| River Bend | 2,995 | 6 | 6 | 0 |

# Table 78. Full-Time Law Enforcement Employees, by Selected State and City, 2020—Continued

(Number.)

| State/city | Population | Total law enforcement employees | Total officers | Total civilians |
|---|---|---|---|---|
| Roanoke Rapids | 14,046 | 38 | 34 | 4 |
| Robbins | 1,254 | 4 | 4 | 0 |
| Robersonville | 1,307 | 3 | 3 | 0 |
| Rockingham | 8,424 | 38 | 36 | 2 |
| Rockwell | 2,170 | 7 | 7 | 0 |
| Rocky Mount | 53,305 | 163 | 131 | 32 |
| Rolesville | 9,679 | 22 | 21 | 1 |
| Rose Hill | 1,620 | 5 | 5 | 0 |
| Rowland | 980 | 5 | 4 | 1 |
| Roxboro | 8,387 | 34 | 29 | 5 |
| Rutherfordton | 4,081 | 15 | 15 | 0 |
| Salisbury | 33,856 | 81 | 70 | 11 |
| Saluda | 702 | 3 | 3 | 0 |
| Sanford | 30,583 | 92 | 69 | 23 |
| Scotland Neck | 1,789 | 8 | 7 | 1 |
| Seagrove | 231 | 1 | 1 | 0 |
| Selma | 7,454 | 18 | 17 | 1 |
| Seven Devils | 204 | 6 | 6 | 0 |
| Shallotte | 4,511 | 18 | 17 | 1 |
| Sharpsburg | 2,017 | 9 | 8 | 1 |
| Shelby | 20,128 | 84 | 72 | 12 |
| Siler City | 8,473 | 23 | 17 | 6 |
| Smithfield | 13,581 | 42 | 38 | 4 |
| Snow Hill | 1,476 | 6 | 6 | 0 |
| Southern Pines | 15,358 | 48 | 39 | 9 |
| Southern Shores | 3,026 | 11 | 10 | 1 |
| Southport | 4,226 | 12 | 12 | 0 |
| Sparta | 1,721 | 6 | 6 | 0 |
| Spencer | 3,260 | 9 | 8 | 1 |
| Spring Hope | 1,319 | 7 | 7 | 0 |
| Spring Lake | 12,028 | 25 | 23 | 2 |
| Spruce Pine | 2,115 | 11 | 11 | 0 |
| Stallings | 16,746 | 23 | 21 | 2 |
| Stanfield | 1,559 | 5 | 5 | 0 |
| Stanley | 3,821 | 13 | 12 | 1 |
| Stantonsburg | 780 | 3 | 3 | 0 |
| Star | 846 | 4 | 4 | 0 |
| Statesville | 28,420 | 98 | 75 | 23 |
| Stoneville | 1,257 | 5 | 5 | 0 |
| St. Pauls | 2,279 | 17 | 12 | 5 |
| Sugar Mountain | 197 | 5 | 5 | 0 |
| Sunset Beach | 4,236 | 17 | 17 | 0 |
| Surf City | 2,602 | 23 | 22 | 1 |
| Swansboro | 3,472 | 14 | 13 | 1 |
| Sylva | 2,757 | 12 | 12 | 0 |
| Tabor City | 3,883 | 11 | 10 | 1 |
| Tarboro | 10,484 | 33 | 27 | 6 |
| Taylorsville | 2,145 | 13 | 13 | 0 |
| Taylortown | 891 | 3 | 3 | 0 |
| Thomasville | 26,704 | 70 | 64 | 6 |
| Topsail Beach | 446 | 8 | 7 | 1 |
| Trent Woods | 3,973 | 6 | 6 | 0 |
| Troutman | 2,856 | 15 | 14 | 1 |
| Troy | 3,274 | 10 | 9 | 1 |
| Tryon | 1,635 | 9 | 7 | 2 |
| Valdese | 4,402 | 14 | 13 | 1 |
| Vanceboro | 950 | 4 | 4 | 0 |
| Vass | 811 | 4 | 3 | 1 |
| Wadesboro | 5,190 | 24 | 19 | 5 |
| Wagram | 766 | 1 | 1 | 0 |
| Wake Forest | 49,457 | 99 | 83 | 16 |
| Wallace | 3,855 | 20 | 16 | 4 |
| Walnut Creek | 865 | 4 | 3 | 1 |
| Warrenton | 814 | 6 | 5 | 1 |
| Warsaw | 3,081 | 14 | 10 | 4 |
| Washington | 9,451 | 37 | 28 | 9 |
| Waxhaw | 19,089 | 32 | 30 | 2 |
| Waynesville | 10,632 | 43 | 32 | 11 |
| Weaverville | 4,077 | 17 | 16 | 1 |
| Weldon | 1,438 | 8 | 8 | 0 |
| Wendell | 9,841 | 21 | 19 | 2 |
| West Jefferson | 1,311 | 9 | 9 | 0 |
| Whispering Pines | 3,515 | 9 | 8 | 1 |
| Whitakers | 696 | 3 | 3 | 0 |
| White Lake | 738 | 5 | 5 | 0 |
| Whiteville | 5,231 | 21 | 17 | 4 |
| Wilkesboro | 3,419 | 22 | 20 | 2 |
| Williamston | 5,072 | 23 | 21 | 2 |
| Wilmington | 126,759 | 321 | 243 | 78 |
| Wilson | 49,507 | 123 | 108 | 15 |
| Wilson's Mills | 2,911 | 8 | 8 | 0 |
| Windsor | 3,485 | 9 | 9 | 0 |
| Winfall | 621 | 1 | 1 | 0 |
| Wingate | 4,873 | 8 | 7 | 1 |
| Winston-Salem | 249,998 | 626 | 456 | 170 |

## Table 78. Full-Time Law Enforcement Employees, by Selected State and City, 2020—Continued

(Number.)

| State/city | Population | Total law enforcement employees | Total officers | Total civilians |
|---|---|---|---|---|
| Winterville | 10,225 | 21 | 20 | 1 |
| Woodfin | 6,718 | 18 | 17 | 1 |
| Woodland | 691 | 1 | 1 | 0 |
| Wrightsville Beach | 2,519 | 27 | 25 | 2 |
| Yadkinville | 2,864 | 12 | 11 | 1 |
| Youngsville | 1,442 | 13 | 11 | 2 |
| Zebulon | 6,764 | 22 | 21 | 1 |
| | | | | |
| **NORTH DAKOTA** | | | | |
| Berthold | 494 | 1 | 1 | 0 |
| Beulah | 3,129 | 7 | 6 | 1 |
| Bismarck | 75,396 | 156 | 126 | 30 |
| Bowman | 1,571 | 4 | 4 | 0 |
| Burlington | 1,213 | 3 | 3 | 0 |
| Carrington | 1,940 | 5 | 5 | 0 |
| Cavalier | 1,190 | 3 | 3 | 0 |
| Devils Lake | 7,237 | 21 | 19 | 2 |
| Dickinson | 24,179 | 64 | 42 | 22 |
| Dunseith | 767 | 3 | 3 | 0 |
| Ellendale | 1,160 | 2 | 2 | 0 |
| Emerado | 464 | 1 | 1 | 0 |
| Fargo | 127,313 | 199 | 180 | 19 |
| Garrison | 1,458 | 3 | 3 | 0 |
| Grafton | 4,055 | 7 | 6 | 1 |
| Grand Forks | 56,253 | 114 | 94 | 20 |
| Harvey | 1,568 | 4 | 4 | 0 |
| Hazen | 2,322 | 5 | 5 | 0 |
| Jamestown | 14,879 | 31 | 27 | 4 |
| Kenmare | 1,019 | 2 | 2 | 0 |
| Killdeer | 1,209 | 5 | 5 | 0 |
| Lamoure | 884 | 1 | 1 | 0 |
| Lincoln | 4,052 | 8 | 8 | 0 |
| Lisbon | 2,002 | 4 | 4 | 0 |
| Mandan | 23,292 | 47 | 40 | 7 |
| Medora | 125 | 2 | 2 | 0 |
| Minot | 48,086 | 88 | 75 | 13 |
| Napoleon | 756 | 1 | 1 | 0 |
| New Town | 2,706 | 7 | 6 | 1 |
| Northwood | 879 | 2 | 2 | 0 |
| Oakes | 1,639 | 3 | 3 | 0 |
| Powers Lake | 284 | 2 | 2 | 0 |
| Ray | 989 | 1 | 1 | 0 |
| Rolette | 585 | 2 | 2 | 0 |
| Rolla | 1,271 | 4 | 4 | 0 |
| Rugby | 2,538 | 4 | 4 | 0 |
| Stanley | 2,885 | 4 | 4 | 0 |
| Steele | 701 | 1 | 1 | 0 |
| Surrey | 1,460 | 2 | 2 | 0 |
| Thompson | 1,031 | 1 | 1 | 0 |
| Tioga | 1,405 | 6 | 5 | 1 |
| Valley City | 6,268 | 17 | 15 | 2 |
| Wahpeton | 7,725 | 18 | 16 | 2 |
| Watford City | 9,301 | 27 | 21 | 6 |
| West Fargo | 39,704 | 81 | 68 | 13 |
| Williston | 31,680 | 91 | 75 | 16 |
| Wishek | 858 | 2 | 2 | 0 |
| | | | | |
| **OHIO** | | | | |
| Akron | 195,701 | 488 | 451 | 37 |
| Amberley Village | 3,538 | 23 | 18 | 5 |
| Amherst | 12,425 | 30 | 21 | 9 |
| Andover | 1,083 | 3 | 3 | 0 |
| Arcanum | 1,993 | 4 | 4 | 0 |
| Archbold | 4,286 | 11 | 11 | 0 |
| Ashland | 19,919 | 36 | 30 | 6 |
| Athens | 24,638 | 30 | 23 | 7 |
| Aurora | 16,568 | 37 | 29 | 8 |
| Avon Lake | 25,040 | 34 | 29 | 5 |
| Bainbridge Township | 11,395 | 27 | 23 | 4 |
| Bath Township, Summit County | 9,606 | 27 | 21 | 6 |
| Beachwood | 11,580 | 66 | 46 | 20 |
| Beavercreek | 48,282 | 63 | 47 | 16 |
| Beaver Township | 6,321 | 17 | 13 | 4 |
| Bedford Heights | 10,430 | 38 | 29 | 9 |
| Bellefontaine | 13,131 | 37 | 30 | 7 |
| Bellville | 1,937 | 6 | 6 | 0 |
| Belpre | 6,348 | 15 | 10 | 5 |
| Berea | 18,563 | 34 | 31 | 3 |
| Bethel | 2,837 | 5 | 4 | 1 |
| Blue Ash | 12,525 | 42 | 34 | 8 |
| Bluffton | 4,002 | 9 | 9 | 0 |
| Bowling Green | 31,537 | 50 | 38 | 12 |
| Brunswick | 35,132 | 49 | 40 | 9 |
| Butler Township | 7,835 | 21 | 20 | 1 |
| Canal Fulton | 5,396 | 10 | 9 | 1 |

## Table 78. Full-Time Law Enforcement Employees, by Selected State and City, 2020—Continued

(Number.)

| State/city | Population | Total law enforcement employees | Total officers | Total civilians |
|---|---|---|---|---|
| Canfield | 7,104 | 27 | 19 | 8 |
| Canton | 69,623 | 199 | 159 | 40 |
| Carey | 3,527 | 13 | 9 | 4 |
| Catawba Island Township | 3,495 | 5 | 5 | 0 |
| Celina | 10,440 | 23 | 18 | 5 |
| Centerville | 23,669 | 55 | 40 | 15 |
| Circleville | 14,226 | 30 | 22 | 8 |
| Cleveland | 379,313 | 1,696 | 1,475 | 221 |
| Cleveland Heights | 43,608 | 91 | 87 | 4 |
| Colerain Township | 59,223 | 58 | 49 | 9 |
| Columbiana | 6,276 | 18 | 14 | 4 |
| Copley Township | 17,233 | 23 | 22 | 1 |
| Dayton | 139,671 | 395 | 355 | 40 |
| Defiance | 16,415 | 34 | 29 | 5 |
| Delaware | 43,469 | 62 | 54 | 8 |
| Delhi Township | 29,785 | 40 | 31 | 9 |
| Dublin | 50,236 | 118 | 69 | 49 |
| East Cleveland | 16,810 | 51 | 40 | 11 |
| East Liverpool | 10,430 | 21 | 16 | 5 |
| Eaton | 8,098 | 17 | 16 | 1 |
| Elida | 1,803 | 2 | 2 | 0 |
| Elmore | 1,396 | 5 | 5 | 0 |
| Englewood | 13,507 | 27 | 21 | 6 |
| Evendale | 2,707 | 22 | 20 | 2 |
| Fairborn | 34,076 | 78 | 52 | 26 |
| Fairfax | 1,702 | 11 | 10 | 1 |
| Fairfield | 42,608 | 85 | 63 | 22 |
| Fairfield Township | 23,206 | 25 | 23 | 2 |
| Findlay | 40,803 | 80 | 61 | 19 |
| Forest Park | 18,518 | 43 | 36 | 7 |
| Fort Loramie | 1,541 | 2 | 2 | 0 |
| Fort Recovery | 1,471 | 3 | 3 | 0 |
| Fostoria | 13,172 | 26 | 22 | 4 |
| Galion | 9,865 | 23 | 19 | 4 |
| German Township, Montgomery County | 2,899 | 6 | 6 | 0 |
| Greenhills | 3,548 | 13 | 11 | 2 |
| Groveport | 5,642 | 26 | 25 | 1 |
| Hiram | 1,092 | 3 | 3 | 0 |
| Hubbard | 7,320 | 14 | 14 | 0 |
| Huber Heights | 38,244 | 72 | 53 | 19 |
| Hudson | 22,170 | 37 | 30 | 7 |
| Ironton | 10,354 | 17 | 16 | 1 |
| Jackson Township, Mahoning County | 1,993 | 8 | 8 | 0 |
| Jackson Township, Stark County | 40,215 | 56 | 48 | 8 |
| Jamestown | 2,157 | 5 | 5 | 0 |
| Kenton | 8,204 | 17 | 17 | 0 |
| Lake Township | 8,358 | 17 | 17 | 0 |
| Lancaster | 41,152 | 78 | 61 | 17 |
| Liberty Township | 11,291 | 20 | 19 | 1 |
| Logan | 6,918 | 23 | 19 | 4 |
| Lordstown | 3,227 | 14 | 10 | 4 |
| Lyndhurst | 13,258 | 37 | 29 | 8 |
| Macedonia | 12,120 | 32 | 24 | 8 |
| Madeira | 9,340 | 15 | 14 | 1 |
| Madison Township, Franklin County | 20,118 | 16 | 15 | 1 |
| Mansfield | 45,971 | 112 | 77 | 35 |
| Mariemont | 3,442 | 12 | 11 | 1 |
| Maumee | 13,541 | 38 | 36 | 2 |
| Medina | 25,905 | 48 | 39 | 9 |
| Medina Township | 9,176 | 9 | 9 | 0 |
| Mentor-on-the-Lake | 7,372 | 14 | 9 | 5 |
| Miamisburg | 20,112 | 40 | 38 | 2 |
| Miami Township, Clermont County | 43,182 | 44 | 41 | 3 |
| Middletown | 48,944 | 105 | 69 | 36 |
| Milan | 1,337 | 3 | 3 | 0 |
| Minerva Park | 1,322 | 10 | 9 | 1 |
| Monroeville | 1,333 | 5 | 5 | 0 |
| Montgomery | 10,943 | 24 | 21 | 3 |
| Montpelier | 3,893 | 10 | 9 | 1 |
| Munroe Falls | 5,054 | 9 | 8 | 1 |
| Napoleon | 8,088 | 23 | 18 | 5 |
| Navarre | 1,788 | 6 | 6 | 0 |
| New Albany | 11,449 | 37 | 26 | 11 |
| Newark | 50,980 | 87 | 76 | 11 |
| New Bremen | 2,944 | 8 | 8 | 0 |
| New Knoxville | 860 | 1 | 1 | 0 |
| New Lexington | 4,667 | 8 | 7 | 1 |
| Newton Falls | 4,413 | 6 | 6 | 0 |
| Niles | 17,943 | 42 | 36 | 6 |
| North Olmsted | 31,224 | 58 | 43 | 15 |
| North Randall | 984 | 11 | 11 | 0 |
| North Ridgeville | 35,708 | 49 | 42 | 7 |
| Norton | 11,894 | 17 | 16 | 1 |
| Norwalk | 16,752 | 32 | 25 | 7 |
| Oberlin | 8,107 | 25 | 17 | 8 |

## Table 78. Full-Time Law Enforcement Employees, by Selected State and City, 2020—Continued

(Number.)

| State/city | Population | Total law enforcement employees | Total officers | Total civilians |
|---|---|---|---|---|
| Orrville | 8,442 | 17 | 16 | 1 |
| Ottawa | 4,310 | 8 | 8 | 0 |
| Owensville | 836 | 4 | 4 | 0 |
| Pandora | 1,097 | 2 | 2 | 0 |
| Perkins Township | 11,552 | 21 | 20 | 1 |
| Perrysburg Township | 13,072 | 32 | 24 | 8 |
| Perry Township, Stark County | 27,970 | 27 | 24 | 3 |
| Pierce Township | 15,178 | 19 | 18 | 1 |
| Plain City | 4,820 | 12 | 11 | 1 |
| Poland Township | 11,703 | 13 | 13 | 0 |
| Port Clinton | 6,113 | 20 | 16 | 4 |
| Portsmouth | 19,702 | 40 | 37 | 3 |
| Powell | 13,591 | 21 | 19 | 2 |
| Rockford | 1,104 | 6 | 6 | 0 |
| Salem | 11,441 | 26 | 23 | 3 |
| Salineville | 1,203 | 2 | 2 | 0 |
| Seaman | 882 | 2 | 2 | 0 |
| Sebring | 4,133 | 13 | 8 | 5 |
| Seven Hills | 11,600 | 18 | 17 | 1 |
| Shaker Heights | 26,772 | 80 | 65 | 15 |
| Sharonville | 13,685 | 48 | 37 | 11 |
| Shawnee Hills | 852 | 5 | 5 | 0 |
| Shawnee Township | 12,072 | 19 | 13 | 6 |
| Sheffield Village | 4,634 | 21 | 14 | 7 |
| Sidney | 20,217 | 46 | 35 | 11 |
| Silver Lake | 2,480 | 9 | 8 | 1 |
| Solon | 22,740 | 84 | 48 | 36 |
| Springboro | 19,429 | 36 | 31 | 5 |
| Springfield Township, Hamilton County | 35,873 | 52 | 43 | 9 |
| Steubenville | 17,482 | 44 | 39 | 5 |
| St. Henry | 2,587 | 3 | 3 | 0 |
| Sugarcreek | 2,228 | 8 | 8 | 0 |
| Sugarcreek Township | 8,536 | 21 | 17 | 4 |
| Sylvania | 19,560 | 36 | 31 | 5 |
| Tallmadge | 17,532 | 27 | 23 | 4 |
| Toledo | 269,941 | 632 | 580 | 52 |
| Uhrichsville | 5,287 | 9 | 9 | 0 |
| Uniontown | 3,306 | 12 | 10 | 2 |
| Union Township, Clermont County | 48,994 | 65 | 51 | 14 |
| University Heights | 12,638 | 30 | 28 | 2 |
| Urbana | 11,368 | 17 | 17 | 0 |
| Valley View, Cuyahoga County | 1,992 | 18 | 16 | 2 |
| Vandalia | 14,960 | 42 | 31 | 11 |
| Van Wert | 10,594 | 27 | 21 | 6 |
| Wadsworth | 24,656 | 40 | 31 | 9 |
| Warren | 38,193 | 65 | 60 | 5 |
| Washington Court House | 14,189 | 27 | 21 | 6 |
| Wauseon | 7,410 | 19 | 14 | 5 |
| Westerville | 41,985 | 100 | 72 | 28 |
| West Salem | 1,531 | 1 | 1 | 0 |
| West Union | 3,137 | 4 | 3 | 1 |
| Whitehall | 18,985 | 64 | 51 | 13 |
| Whitehouse | 5,020 | 11 | 11 | 0 |
| Wickliffe | 12,725 | 39 | 30 | 9 |
| Willoughby Hills | 9,545 | 28 | 24 | 4 |
| Willowick | 14,056 | 30 | 22 | 8 |
| Wooster | 26,160 | 46 | 41 | 5 |
| Xenia | 27,228 | 69 | 43 | 26 |
| Youngstown | 63,538 | 173 | 133 | 40 |
| Zanesville | 25,166 | 95 | 55 | 40 |
| | | | | |
| **OKLAHOMA** | | | | |
| Achille | 556 | 5 | 4 | 1 |
| Ada | 17,280 | 36 | 33 | 3 |
| Adair | 804 | 4 | 4 | 0 |
| Allen | 930 | 1 | 1 | 0 |
| Altus | 18,007 | 54 | 41 | 13 |
| Alva | 4,867 | 12 | 10 | 2 |
| Amber | 502 | 1 | 1 | 0 |
| Anadarko | 6,444 | 22 | 21 | 1 |
| Antlers | 2,286 | 11 | 6 | 5 |
| Apache | 1,385 | 3 | 3 | 0 |
| Ardmore | 24,795 | 62 | 46 | 16 |
| Arkoma | 1,885 | 4 | 2 | 2 |
| Atoka | 3,038 | 19 | 17 | 2 |
| Avant | 311 | 1 | 1 | 0 |
| Barnsdall | 1,123 | 4 | 4 | 0 |
| Bartlesville | 36,688 | 85 | 61 | 24 |
| Beaver | 1,350 | 1 | 1 | 0 |
| Beggs | 1,225 | 7 | 1 | 6 |
| Bennington | 378 | 1 | 1 | 0 |
| Bernice | 581 | 1 | 1 | 0 |
| Bethany | 19,209 | 36 | 27 | 9 |
| Big Cabin | 250 | 3 | 2 | 1 |
| Binger | 624 | 1 | 1 | 0 |

## Table 78. Full-Time Law Enforcement Employees, by Selected State and City, 2020—Continued

(Number.)

| State/city | Population | Total law enforcement employees | Total officers | Total civilians |
|---|---|---|---|---|
| Bixby | 29,327 | 49 | 37 | 12 |
| Blackwell | 6,474 | 20 | 13 | 7 |
| Blair | 729 | 1 | 1 | 0 |
| Blanchard | 9,303 | 10 | 10 | 0 |
| Boise City | 1,071 | 1 | 1 | 0 |
| Bokchito | 711 | 7 | 6 | 1 |
| Bokoshe | 495 | 3 | 3 | 0 |
| Boley | 1,165 | 2 | 1 | 1 |
| Bristow | 4,174 | 16 | 11 | 5 |
| Broken Arrow | 112,990 | 213 | 151 | 62 |
| Broken Bow | 4,085 | 22 | 17 | 5 |
| Burns Flat | 1,865 | 4 | 4 | 0 |
| Cache | 2,824 | 8 | 6 | 2 |
| Caddo | 1,125 | 4 | 4 | 0 |
| Calera | 2,440 | 11 | 10 | 1 |
| Calumet | 623 | 1 | 1 | 0 |
| Calvin | 267 | 2 | 1 | 1 |
| Caney | 202 | 4 | 3 | 1 |
| Carnegie | 1,634 | 10 | 6 | 4 |
| Carney | 620 | 2 | 2 | 0 |
| Cashion | 943 | 3 | 3 | 0 |
| Catoosa | 6,876 | 19 | 16 | 3 |
| Cement | 468 | 1 | 1 | 0 |
| Chandler | 3,080 | 12 | 8 | 4 |
| Chattanooga | 457 | 2 | 1 | 1 |
| Checotah | 3,051 | 13 | 10 | 3 |
| Chelsea | 1,868 | 4 | 4 | 0 |
| Cherokee | 1,492 | 3 | 3 | 0 |
| Chickasha | 16,410 | 31 | 23 | 8 |
| Choctaw | 12,938 | 19 | 18 | 1 |
| Chouteau | 2,111 | 9 | 8 | 1 |
| Claremore | 18,961 | 47 | 39 | 8 |
| Clayton | 771 | 11 | 6 | 5 |
| Cleveland | 3,101 | 5 | 5 | 0 |
| Clinton | 8,943 | 23 | 14 | 9 |
| Coalgate | 1,830 | 6 | 6 | 0 |
| Colbert | 1,281 | 3 | 3 | 0 |
| Colcord | 854 | 6 | 6 | 0 |
| Collinsville | 7,765 | 23 | 14 | 9 |
| Comanche | 1,540 | 5 | 5 | 0 |
| Commerce | 2,482 | 5 | 5 | 0 |
| Cordell | 2,689 | 5 | 5 | 0 |
| Covington | 533 | 1 | 1 | 0 |
| Coweta | 10,297 | 23 | 16 | 7 |
| Crescent | 1,596 | 7 | 5 | 2 |
| Cushing | 7,558 | 23 | 16 | 7 |
| Cyril | 997 | 1 | 1 | 0 |
| Davenport | 808 | 1 | 1 | 0 |
| Davis | 2,874 | 13 | 12 | 1 |
| Del City | 21,665 | 48 | 38 | 10 |
| Dewar | 843 | 3 | 3 | 0 |
| Dewey | 3,411 | 12 | 10 | 2 |
| Dibble | 884 | 3 | 2 | 1 |
| Dickson | 1,260 | 4 | 3 | 1 |
| Disney | 302 | 1 | 1 | 0 |
| Drumright | 2,805 | 6 | 6 | 0 |
| Duncan | 22,145 | 62 | 45 | 17 |
| Durant | 19,518 | 41 | 37 | 4 |
| Earlsboro | 625 | 3 | 2 | 1 |
| Edmond | 96,861 | 158 | 121 | 37 |
| Eldorado | 397 | 1 | 1 | 0 |
| Elgin | 3,359 | 5 | 5 | 0 |
| Elk City | 11,326 | 39 | 26 | 13 |
| Elmore City | 753 | 5 | 4 | 1 |
| El Reno | 21,018 | 49 | 34 | 15 |
| Enid | 49,545 | 111 | 82 | 29 |
| Erick | 969 | 1 | 1 | 0 |
| Eufaula | 2,841 | 10 | 10 | 0 |
| Fairfax | 1,229 | 3 | 1 | 2 |
| Fairland | 1,021 | 3 | 2 | 1 |
| Fairview | 2,580 | 8 | 5 | 3 |
| Fletcher | 1,137 | 2 | 2 | 0 |
| Forest Park | 1,078 | 2 | 2 | 0 |
| Fort Cobb | 604 | 1 | 1 | 0 |
| Fort Gibson | 3,912 | 14 | 13 | 1 |
| Foyil | 388 | 1 | 1 | 0 |
| Frederick | 3,490 | 7 | 5 | 2 |
| Gans | 294 | 2 | 2 | 0 |
| Garber | 802 | 1 | 1 | 0 |
| Geary | 1,271 | 12 | 7 | 5 |
| Geronimo | 1,220 | 1 | 1 | 0 |
| Glenpool | 14,385 | 32 | 24 | 8 |
| Goodwell | 1,261 | 2 | 2 | 0 |
| Gore | 943 | 11 | 5 | 6 |
| Grandfield | 922 | 1 | 1 | 0 |

## Table 78. Full-Time Law Enforcement Employees, by Selected State and City, 2020—Continued

(Number.)

| State/city | Population | Total law enforcement employees | Total officers | Total civilians |
|---|---|---|---|---|
| Granite | 1,946 | 4 | 4 | 0 |
| Grove | 7,242 | 31 | 22 | 9 |
| Guthrie | 11,968 | 31 | 23 | 8 |
| Guymon | 10,960 | 18 | 16 | 2 |
| Haileyville | 740 | 4 | 3 | 1 |
| Hammon | 554 | 1 | 1 | 0 |
| Harrah | 6,805 | 11 | 10 | 1 |
| Hartshorne | 1,928 | 6 | 4 | 2 |
| Haskell | 1,949 | 7 | 7 | 0 |
| Haworth | 294 | 1 | 1 | 0 |
| Healdton | 2,684 | 4 | 4 | 0 |
| Heavener | 3,285 | 10 | 9 | 1 |
| Hennessey | 2,234 | 8 | 4 | 4 |
| Henryetta | 5,464 | 17 | 12 | 5 |
| Hinton | 3,221 | 5 | 5 | 0 |
| Hobart | 3,405 | 13 | 7 | 6 |
| Holdenville | 5,394 | 3 | 3 | 0 |
| Hollis | 1,794 | 8 | 5 | 3 |
| Hominy | 3,332 | 10 | 5 | 5 |
| Hooker | 1,834 | 2 | 2 | 0 |
| Howe | 786 | 1 | 1 | 0 |
| Hugo | 5,047 | 27 | 19 | 8 |
| Hulbert | 579 | 4 | 4 | 0 |
| Hydro | 933 | 3 | 3 | 0 |
| Idabel | 6,864 | 27 | 21 | 6 |
| Inola | 1,793 | 8 | 7 | 1 |
| Jay | 2,536 | 14 | 9 | 5 |
| Jenks | 25,111 | 32 | 24 | 8 |
| Jennings | 355 | 1 | 1 | 0 |
| Jones | 3,280 | 6 | 6 | 0 |
| Kansas | 805 | 5 | 5 | 0 |
| Kellyville | 1,127 | 2 | 2 | 0 |
| Keota | 544 | 2 | 2 | 0 |
| Kiefer | 2,072 | 5 | 5 | 0 |
| Kingfisher | 4,919 | 16 | 15 | 1 |
| Kingston | 1,698 | 6 | 6 | 0 |
| Kiowa | 671 | 4 | 4 | 0 |
| Konawa | 1,184 | 5 | 4 | 1 |
| Krebs | 1,995 | 9 | 7 | 2 |
| Langley | 821 | 4 | 4 | 0 |
| Langston | 1,882 | 2 | 1 | 1 |
| Laverne | 1,293 | 1 | 1 | 0 |
| Lawton | 92,711 | 209 | 165 | 44 |
| Lexington | 2,190 | 7 | 4 | 3 |
| Lindsay | 2,767 | 9 | 5 | 4 |
| Locust Grove | 1,392 | 7 | 6 | 1 |
| Lone Grove | 5,225 | 10 | 7 | 3 |
| Luther | 1,842 | 5 | 5 | 0 |
| Madill | 4,096 | 14 | 11 | 3 |
| Mangum | 2,662 | 10 | 5 | 5 |
| Mannford | 3,191 | 11 | 8 | 3 |
| Marble City | 249 | 2 | 1 | 1 |
| Marietta | 2,764 | 8 | 8 | 0 |
| Marlow | 4,393 | 9 | 9 | 0 |
| Maud | 1,059 | 4 | 3 | 1 |
| Maysville | 1,199 | 8 | 6 | 2 |
| McAlester | 17,729 | 43 | 40 | 3 |
| McLoud | 4,828 | 10 | 9 | 1 |
| Medford | 939 | 3 | 3 | 0 |
| Medicine Park | 469 | 2 | 2 | 0 |
| Meeker | 1,139 | 5 | 5 | 0 |
| Miami | 12,885 | 30 | 29 | 1 |
| Midwest City | 57,901 | 121 | 97 | 24 |
| Minco | 1,646 | 2 | 2 | 0 |
| Moore | 63,927 | 98 | 88 | 10 |
| Mooreland | 1,135 | 4 | 3 | 1 |
| Morris | 1,404 | 4 | 4 | 0 |
| Mounds | 1,253 | 2 | 2 | 0 |
| Mountain View | 739 | 1 | 1 | 0 |
| Muldrow | 3,260 | 13 | 8 | 5 |
| Muskogee | 36,598 | 91 | 83 | 8 |
| Mustang | 24,822 | 35 | 25 | 10 |
| Newcastle | 11,788 | 26 | 17 | 9 |
| Newkirk | 2,147 | 4 | 4 | 0 |
| Nichols Hills | 3,982 | 23 | 16 | 7 |
| Nicoma Park | 2,486 | 7 | 7 | 0 |
| Ninnekah | 1,046 | 4 | 3 | 1 |
| Noble | 7,329 | 19 | 13 | 6 |
| Norman | 127,304 | 225 | 162 | 63 |
| North Enid | 923 | 4 | 4 | 0 |
| Nowata | 3,527 | 9 | 6 | 3 |
| Oilton | 1,011 | 3 | 3 | 0 |
| Okarche | 1,346 | 5 | 5 | 0 |
| Okeene | 1,130 | 8 | 2 | 6 |
| Okemah | 3,031 | 15 | 10 | 5 |

## Table 78. Full-Time Law Enforcement Employees, by Selected State and City, 2020—Continued

(Number.)

| State/city | Population | Total law enforcement employees | Total officers | Total civilians |
|---|---|---|---|---|
| Oklahoma City | 670,872 | 1,378 | 1,105 | 273 |
| Okmulgee | 11,531 | 23 | 20 | 3 |
| Olustee | 545 | 1 | 1 | 0 |
| Oologah | 1,182 | 5 | 5 | 0 |
| Owasso | 38,057 | 82 | 63 | 19 |
| Panama | 1,353 | 3 | 3 | 0 |
| Paoli | 612 | 3 | 3 | 0 |
| Pauls Valley | 6,101 | 20 | 15 | 5 |
| Pawhuska | 3,341 | 12 | 7 | 5 |
| Pawnee | 2,092 | 6 | 6 | 0 |
| Perkins | 2,798 | 7 | 7 | 0 |
| Perry | 4,804 | 20 | 14 | 6 |
| Piedmont | 9,385 | 11 | 9 | 2 |
| Pocola | 4,163 | 14 | 9 | 5 |
| Ponca City | 23,307 | 71 | 50 | 21 |
| Pond Creek | 848 | 2 | 1 | 1 |
| Porum | 696 | 4 | 4 | 0 |
| Poteau | 8,942 | 33 | 26 | 7 |
| Prague | 2,362 | 13 | 8 | 5 |
| Pryor Creek | 9,377 | 34 | 29 | 5 |
| Purcell | 6,409 | 22 | 17 | 5 |
| Quinton | 978 | 8 | 6 | 2 |
| Ramona | 557 | 5 | 4 | 1 |
| Ratliff City | 117 | 2 | 2 | 0 |
| Rattan | 293 | 4 | 4 | 0 |
| Ringling | 937 | 1 | 1 | 0 |
| Roland | 4,112 | 11 | 7 | 4 |
| Rush Springs | 1,254 | 5 | 5 | 0 |
| Salina | 1,396 | 7 | 6 | 1 |
| Sallisaw | 8,405 | 31 | 23 | 8 |
| Sand Springs | 20,139 | 41 | 31 | 10 |
| Sapulpa | 21,535 | 60 | 45 | 15 |
| Savanna | 646 | 10 | 7 | 3 |
| Sawyer | 326 | 2 | 1 | 1 |
| Sayre | 4,443 | 11 | 6 | 5 |
| Seiling | 838 | 1 | 1 | 0 |
| Seminole | 6,993 | 13 | 12 | 1 |
| Shady Point | 994 | 2 | 2 | 0 |
| Shattuck | 1,234 | 1 | 1 | 0 |
| Shawnee | 31,724 | 86 | 73 | 13 |
| Skiatook | 8,189 | 27 | 21 | 6 |
| Snyder | 1,270 | 3 | 3 | 0 |
| South Coffeyville | 725 | 4 | 4 | 0 |
| Spavinaw | 432 | 1 | 1 | 0 |
| Spencer | 3,962 | 7 | 5 | 2 |
| Sperry | 1,370 | 4 | 4 | 0 |
| Spiro | 2,153 | 4 | 3 | 1 |
| Sterling | 775 | 2 | 2 | 0 |
| Stigler | 2,698 | 13 | 8 | 5 |
| Stillwater | 50,786 | 127 | 84 | 43 |
| Stilwell | 4,014 | 19 | 13 | 6 |
| Stratford | 1,522 | 4 | 4 | 0 |
| Stringtown | 406 | 6 | 5 | 1 |
| Stroud | 2,705 | 14 | 9 | 5 |
| Sulphur | 4,995 | 11 | 9 | 2 |
| Tahlequah | 17,126 | 44 | 39 | 5 |
| Talala | 270 | 1 | 1 | 0 |
| Talihina | 1,074 | 9 | 6 | 3 |
| Tecumseh | 6,656 | 10 | 10 | 0 |
| Texhoma | 900 | 2 | 2 | 0 |
| Thackerville | 527 | 1 | 1 | 0 |
| The Village | 9,709 | 29 | 23 | 6 |
| Thomas | 1,178 | 2 | 2 | 0 |
| Tipton | 747 | 1 | 1 | 0 |
| Tishomingo | 2,992 | 8 | 7 | 1 |
| Tonkawa | 2,934 | 13 | 8 | 5 |
| Tryon | 497 | 2 | 1 | 1 |
| Tulsa | 404,255 | 1,008 | 801 | 207 |
| Tupelo | 306 | 4 | 3 | 1 |
| Tushka | 395 | 2 | 2 | 0 |
| Tuttle | 7,796 | 21 | 15 | 6 |
| Tyrone | 741 | 2 | 1 | 1 |
| Union City | 2,273 | 12 | 8 | 4 |
| Valley Brook | 767 | 7 | 5 | 2 |
| Valliant | 740 | 4 | 3 | 1 |
| Velma | 593 | 1 | 1 | 0 |
| Verden | 537 | 3 | 3 | 0 |
| Verdigris | 4,810 | 8 | 7 | 1 |
| Vian | 1,345 | 5 | 5 | 0 |
| Vici | 685 | 1 | 1 | 0 |
| Vinita | 5,264 | 18 | 13 | 5 |
| Wagoner | 9,479 | 21 | 16 | 5 |
| Walters | 2,336 | 3 | 3 | 0 |
| Warner | 1,570 | 5 | 5 | 0 |
| Warr Acres | 10,105 | 30 | 25 | 5 |

## Table 78. Full-Time Law Enforcement Employees, by Selected State and City, 2020—Continued

(Number.)

| State/city | Population | Total law enforcement employees | Total officers | Total civilians |
|---|---|---|---|---|
| Washington | 605 | 2 | 1 | 1 |
| Watonga | 2,823 | 8 | 6 | 2 |
| Watts | 305 | 3 | 2 | 1 |
| Waukomis | 1,290 | 4 | 4 | 0 |
| Waurika | 1,847 | 1 | 1 | 0 |
| Waynoka | 899 | 4 | 4 | 0 |
| Weatherford | 12,013 | 42 | 27 | 15 |
| Webbers Falls | 588 | 6 | 5 | 1 |
| Weleetka | 931 | 7 | 5 | 2 |
| Wellston | 776 | 3 | 3 | 0 |
| West Siloam Springs | 861 | 12 | 11 | 1 |
| Westville | 1,523 | 9 | 6 | 3 |
| Wetumka | 1,177 | 14 | 2 | 12 |
| Wewoka | 3,198 | 5 | 5 | 0 |
| Wilburton | 2,542 | 7 | 6 | 1 |
| Wilson | 1,705 | 4 | 4 | 0 |
| Wister | 1,060 | 2 | 2 | 0 |
| Woodward | 11,871 | 26 | 22 | 4 |
| Wright City | 727 | 3 | 2 | 1 |
| Wyandotte | 321 | 10 | 9 | 1 |
| Wynnewood | 2,203 | 7 | 6 | 1 |
| Wynona | 434 | 1 | 1 | 0 |
| Yale | 1,211 | 7 | 4 | 3 |
| Yukon | 29,467 | 70 | 47 | 23 |
| | | | | |
| **OREGON** | | | | |
| Albany | 56,746 | 78 | 48 | 30 |
| Ashland | 21,308 | 30 | 24 | 6 |
| Astoria | 10,086 | 26 | 16 | 10 |
| Aumsville | 4,266 | 7 | 6 | 1 |
| Baker City | 9,882 | 13 | 12 | 1 |
| Bandon | 3,181 | 10 | 6 | 4 |
| Banks | 2,058 | 2 | 2 | 0 |
| Beaverton | 99,886 | 175 | 131 | 44 |
| Bend | 104,833 | 132 | 97 | 35 |
| Black Butte | | 9 | 7 | 2 |
| Boardman | 3,855 | 12 | 11 | 1 |
| Brookings | 6,583 | 23 | 16 | 7 |
| Burns | 2,791 | 6 | 4 | 2 |
| Canby | 18,161 | 29 | 25 | 4 |
| Cannon Beach | 1,788 | 10 | 8 | 2 |
| Carlton | 2,204 | 4 | 4 | 0 |
| Central Point | 19,313 | 34 | 27 | 7 |
| Coburg | 1,213 | 5 | 5 | 0 |
| Columbia City | 2,034 | 2 | 2 | 0 |
| Coos Bay | 16,378 | 39 | 25 | 14 |
| Coquille | 3,966 | 8 | 7 | 1 |
| Cornelius | 13,241 | 15 | 14 | 1 |
| Corvallis | 59,585 | 110 | 71 | 39 |
| Cottage Grove | 10,606 | 30 | 16 | 14 |
| Dallas | 17,630 | 26 | 21 | 5 |
| Eagle Point | 9,782 | 12 | 11 | 1 |
| Enterprise | 1,999 | 4 | 4 | 0 |
| Eugene | 175,007 | 302 | 187 | 115 |
| Florence | 9,285 | 23 | 16 | 7 |
| Forest Grove | 25,890 | 33 | 28 | 5 |
| Gaston | 723 | 1 | 1 | 0 |
| Gearhart | 1,672 | 2 | 2 | 0 |
| Gervais | 2,805 | 5 | 5 | 0 |
| Gladstone | 12,506 | 18 | 15 | 3 |
| Gold Beach | 2,355 | 7 | 6 | 1 |
| Grants Pass | 38,672 | 81 | 54 | 27 |
| Gresham | 110,448 | 141 | 115 | 26 |
| Hermiston | 17,898 | 32 | 28 | 4 |
| Hillsboro | 113,053 | 182 | 134 | 48 |
| Hines | 1,534 | 4 | 3 | 1 |
| Hood River | 7,848 | 16 | 14 | 2 |
| Hubbard | 3,639 | 7 | 6 | 1 |
| Independence | 11,129 | 19 | 14 | 5 |
| Jacksonville | 2,875 | 7 | 6 | 1 |
| John Day | 1,661 | 5 | 4 | 1 |
| Junction City | 6,303 | 13 | 7 | 6 |
| Keizer | 39,913 | 46 | 38 | 8 |
| King City | 4,446 | 7 | 6 | 1 |
| Klamath Falls | 22,960 | 38 | 34 | 4 |
| La Grande | 13,431 | 32 | 17 | 15 |
| Lake Oswego | 40,138 | 75 | 45 | 30 |
| Lebanon | 17,772 | 40 | 27 | 13 |
| Lincoln City | 9,391 | 42 | 25 | 17 |
| Madras | 7,191 | 12 | 11 | 1 |
| Malin | 841 | 1 | 1 | 0 |
| Manzanita | 678 | 4 | 4 | 0 |
| McMinnville | 35,498 | 46 | 40 | 6 |
| Medford | 84,297 | 143 | 108 | 35 |
| Milton-Freewater | 7,050 | 16 | 11 | 5 |

## Table 78. Full-Time Law Enforcement Employees, by Selected State and City, 2020—Continued

(Number.)

| State/city | Population | Total law enforcement employees | Total officers | Total civilians |
|---|---|---|---|---|
| Milwaukie | 21,094 | 42 | 37 | 5 |
| Molalla | 9,383 | 19 | 17 | 2 |
| Monmouth | 10,728 | 15 | 13 | 2 |
| Mount Angel | 3,677 | 7 | 6 | 1 |
| Myrtle Creek | 3,495 | 9 | 7 | 2 |
| Myrtle Point | 2,585 | 6 | 5 | 1 |
| Newberg-Dundee | 24,168 | 45 | 33 | 12 |
| Newport | 11,247 | 23 | 16 | 7 |
| North Bend | 9,751 | 23 | 16 | 7 |
| North Plains | 2,219 | 3 | 3 | 0 |
| Nyssa | 3,228 | 7 | 7 | 0 |
| Oakridge | 3,403 | 6 | 5 | 1 |
| Ontario | 11,117 | 28 | 24 | 4 |
| Oregon City | 38,602 | 52 | 44 | 8 |
| Pendleton | 16,587 | 28 | 24 | 4 |
| Philomath | 5,742 | 10 | 9 | 1 |
| Phoenix | 4,705 | 10 | 8 | 2 |
| Pilot Rock | 1,508 | 2 | 2 | 0 |
| Portland | 664,350 | 1,040 | 791 | 249 |
| Port Orford | 1,175 | 6 | 6 | 0 |
| Prineville | 11,541 | 34 | 23 | 11 |
| Rainier | 2,032 | 5 | 4 | 1 |
| Redmond | 35,230 | 62 | 48 | 14 |
| Reedsport | 4,101 | 14 | 9 | 5 |
| Rogue River | 2,363 | 6 | 5 | 1 |
| Roseburg | 23,564 | 41 | 37 | 4 |
| Salem | 178,106 | 245 | 180 | 65 |
| Sandy | 11,773 | 18 | 14 | 4 |
| Scappoose | 7,715 | 8 | 7 | 1 |
| Seaside | 6,971 | 29 | 20 | 9 |
| Sherwood | 19,882 | 28 | 24 | 4 |
| Silverton | 10,764 | 18 | 15 | 3 |
| Springfield | 63,599 | 86 | 56 | 30 |
| Stanfield | 2,113 | 5 | 5 | 0 |
| Stayton | 8,314 | 12 | 11 | 1 |
| St. Helens | 14,178 | 23 | 20 | 3 |
| Sunriver | 1,395 | 12 | 11 | 1 |
| Sutherlin | 8,267 | 18 | 14 | 4 |
| Sweet Home | 10,136 | 18 | 12 | 6 |
| Talent | 6,767 | 8 | 6 | 2 |
| The Dalles | 15,643 | 26 | 22 | 4 |
| Tigard | 56,914 | 84 | 69 | 15 |
| Tillamook | 5,480 | 12 | 10 | 2 |
| Toledo | 3,662 | 16 | 8 | 8 |
| Tualatin | 27,617 | 45 | 37 | 8 |
| Turner | 2,160 | 2 | 2 | 0 |
| Umatilla | 7,404 | 15 | 13 | 2 |
| Vernonia | 2,309 | 4 | 3 | 1 |
| Warrenton | 5,815 | 12 | 11 | 1 |
| West Linn | 26,908 | 27 | 23 | 4 |
| Winston | 5,558 | 12 | 11 | 1 |
| Woodburn | 26,386 | 40 | 31 | 9 |
| Yamhill | 1,188 | 6 | 3 | 3 |
| **PENNSYLVANIA** | | | | |
| Adams Township, Butler County | 14,234 | 17 | 17 | 0 |
| Adams Township, Cambria County | 5,425 | 5 | 5 | 0 |
| Alburtis | 2,674 | 4 | 4 | 0 |
| Aldan | 4,149 | 7 | 5 | 2 |
| Aliquippa | 8,678 | 13 | 12 | 1 |
| Allegheny Township, Blair County | 6,621 | 10 | 9 | 1 |
| Allegheny Valley Regional | 3,212 | 3 | 3 | 0 |
| Allentown | 121,819 | 237 | 216 | 21 |
| Altoona | 42,707 | 70 | 62 | 8 |
| Ambridge | 6,486 | 13 | 13 | 0 |
| Amity Township | 13,217 | 15 | 14 | 1 |
| Annville Township | 5,086 | 6 | 5 | 1 |
| Apollo | 1,494 | 1 | 1 | 0 |
| Archbald | 7,060 | 7 | 7 | 0 |
| Arnold | 4,756 | 10 | 10 | 0 |
| Ashland | 2,654 | 3 | 3 | 0 |
| Aspinwall | 2,641 | 6 | 6 | 0 |
| Aston Township | 16,762 | 22 | 20 | 2 |
| Athens | 3,162 | 7 | 6 | 1 |
| Athens Township | 5,028 | 10 | 10 | 0 |
| Avalon | 4,485 | 6 | 6 | 0 |
| Avoca | 2,600 | 3 | 3 | 0 |
| Baldwin Borough | 19,364 | 25 | 24 | 1 |
| Baldwin Township | 1,915 | 5 | 5 | 0 |
| Bally | 1,261 | 2 | 2 | 0 |
| Beaver | 4,193 | 13 | 12 | 1 |
| Beaver Falls | 9,329 | 21 | 19 | 2 |
| Beaver Meadows | 829 | 1 | 1 | 0 |
| Bedford | 2,651 | 5 | 5 | 0 |
| Bedminster Township | 7,286 | 8 | 7 | 1 |

## Table 78. Full-Time Law Enforcement Employees, by Selected State and City, 2020—Continued

(Number.)

| State/city | Population | Total law enforcement employees | Total officers | Total civilians |
|---|---|---|---|---|
| Bell Acres | 1,371 | 5 | 5 | 0 |
| Bellefonte | 6,188 | 11 | 10 | 1 |
| Bellevue | 7,944 | 14 | 13 | 1 |
| Bellwood | 1,741 | 3 | 3 | 0 |
| Bensalem Township | 60,496 | 129 | 102 | 27 |
| Bentleyville | 2,469 | 1 | 1 | 0 |
| Berlin | 1,916 | 1 | 1 | 0 |
| Bern Township | 6,897 | 12 | 12 | 0 |
| Bernville | 942 | 1 | 1 | 0 |
| Bethel Park | 32,195 | 35 | 33 | 2 |
| Bethel Township, Berks County | 4,163 | 6 | 5 | 1 |
| Biglerville | 1,215 | 1 | 1 | 0 |
| Birdsboro | 5,128 | 8 | 7 | 1 |
| Birmingham Township | 4,175 | 3 | 3 | 0 |
| Blairsville | 3,185 | 4 | 4 | 0 |
| Blair Township | 4,445 | 5 | 5 | 0 |
| Blakely | 6,138 | 15 | 15 | 0 |
| Blawnox | 1,373 | 3 | 3 | 0 |
| Bloomsburg Town | 13,643 | 23 | 18 | 5 |
| Bonneauville | 1,839 | 1 | 1 | 0 |
| Brackenridge | 3,099 | 6 | 6 | 0 |
| Braddock | 2,096 | 1 | 1 | 0 |
| Braddock Hills | 1,764 | 2 | 2 | 0 |
| Bradford Township | 4,541 | 5 | 5 | 0 |
| Branch Township | 1,718 | 2 | 2 | 0 |
| Brecknock Township, Berks County | 4,695 | 5 | 5 | 0 |
| Brentwood | 9,161 | 17 | 15 | 2 |
| Briar Creek Township | 2,952 | 5 | 5 | 0 |
| Bridgeville | 4,849 | 9 | 8 | 1 |
| Bridgewater | 829 | 4 | 3 | 1 |
| Brighton Township | 8,236 | 13 | 13 | 0 |
| Bristol | 9,558 | 14 | 12 | 2 |
| Bristol Township | 53,188 | 65 | 57 | 8 |
| Brockway | 2,011 | 2 | 2 | 0 |
| Brookhaven | 8,056 | 8 | 7 | 1 |
| Brookville | 3,746 | 8 | 7 | 1 |
| Brownsville | 2,190 | 3 | 3 | 0 |
| Buckingham Township | 20,301 | 22 | 20 | 2 |
| Buffalo Township | 7,529 | 9 | 9 | 0 |
| Buffalo Valley Regional | 12,613 | 15 | 14 | 1 |
| Bushkill Township | 8,704 | 16 | 15 | 1 |
| Butler | 12,760 | 24 | 23 | 1 |
| Butler Township, Butler County | 16,337 | 24 | 22 | 2 |
| Butler Township, Schuylkill County | 5,406 | 5 | 5 | 0 |
| Caernarvon Township, Berks County | 4,200 | 8 | 7 | 1 |
| California | 6,641 | 8 | 7 | 1 |
| Caln Township | 14,113 | 20 | 19 | 1 |
| Cambria Township | 5,698 | 4 | 4 | 0 |
| Cambridge Springs | 2,673 | 3 | 3 | 0 |
| Camp Hill | 7,921 | 14 | 12 | 2 |
| Canonsburg | 8,725 | 19 | 17 | 2 |
| Canton | 1,844 | 1 | 1 | 0 |
| Carlisle | 19,260 | 34 | 32 | 2 |
| Carnegie | 7,729 | 14 | 13 | 1 |
| Carrolltown | 773 | 2 | 2 | 0 |
| Carroll Valley | 3,935 | 4 | 3 | 1 |
| Castle Shannon | 8,377 | 14 | 13 | 1 |
| Catasauqua | 6,623 | 11 | 10 | 1 |
| Catawissa | 1,451 | 5 | 5 | 0 |
| Center Township | 11,401 | 19 | 18 | 1 |
| Centerville | 3,119 | 4 | 4 | 0 |
| Central Berks Regional | 13,695 | 21 | 20 | 1 |
| Central Bucks Regional | 15,532 | 30 | 26 | 4 |
| Chambersburg | 21,334 | 38 | 35 | 3 |
| Charleroi Regional | 6,397 | 10 | 10 | 0 |
| Chester Township | 4,083 | 13 | 13 | 0 |
| Chippewa Township | 7,840 | 9 | 8 | 1 |
| Christiana | 1,165 | 6 | 6 | 0 |
| Churchill | 2,889 | 9 | 9 | 0 |
| Clairton | 6,468 | 13 | 13 | 0 |
| Clarion | 5,744 | 10 | 9 | 1 |
| Clarks Summit | 6,186 | 5 | 5 | 0 |
| Clearfield | 5,744 | 7 | 7 | 0 |
| Cleona | 2,240 | 4 | 4 | 0 |
| Clifton Heights | 6,700 | 12 | 11 | 1 |
| Clymer | 1,253 | 2 | 2 | 0 |
| Coaldale | 2,117 | 3 | 3 | 0 |
| Coatesville | 12,999 | 30 | 26 | 4 |
| Cochranton | 1,056 | 2 | 2 | 0 |
| Collier Township | 8,368 | 19 | 18 | 1 |
| Collingdale | 8,782 | 14 | 13 | 1 |
| Columbia | 10,285 | 21 | 18 | 3 |
| Conemaugh Township, Cambria County | 1,785 | 1 | 1 | 0 |
| Conemaugh Township, Somerset County | 6,761 | 8 | 7 | 1 |
| Conewango Township | 3,293 | 4 | 4 | 0 |

## Table 78. Full-Time Law Enforcement Employees, by Selected State and City, 2020—Continued

(Number.)

| State/city | Population | Total law enforcement employees | Total officers | Total civilians |
|---|---|---|---|---|
| Conneaut Lake Regional | 4,697 | 4 | 4 | 0 |
| Connellsville | 7,244 | 18 | 17 | 1 |
| Conway | 2,034 | 5 | 5 | 0 |
| Coopersburg | 2,485 | 7 | 7 | 0 |
| Coplay | 3,225 | 5 | 4 | 1 |
| Coraopolis | 5,360 | 14 | 10 | 4 |
| Cornwall | 4,409 | 7 | 6 | 1 |
| Corry | 6,139 | 9 | 8 | 1 |
| Coudersport | 2,373 | 3 | 3 | 0 |
| Covington Township | 2,260 | 3 | 3 | 0 |
| Crafton | 6,114 | 10 | 9 | 1 |
| Cranberry Township | 32,563 | 34 | 31 | 3 |
| Crescent Township | 2,523 | 6 | 6 | 0 |
| Cresson | 1,515 | 1 | 1 | 0 |
| Cresson Township | 2,459 | 1 | 1 | 0 |
| Croyle Township | 2,177 | 1 | 1 | 0 |
| Cumberland Township, Adams County | 6,245 | 10 | 10 | 0 |
| Cumberland Township, Greene County | 6,041 | 5 | 4 | 1 |
| Cumru Township | 15,502 | 28 | 27 | 1 |
| Curwensville | 2,342 | 3 | 3 | 0 |
| Dallas | 2,757 | 6 | 6 | 0 |
| Dallas Township | 9,331 | 14 | 13 | 1 |
| Dalton | 1,185 | 3 | 3 | 0 |
| Danville | 4,584 | 9 | 8 | 1 |
| Darby | 10,705 | 11 | 10 | 1 |
| Darby Township | 9,275 | 15 | 14 | 1 |
| Darlington Township | 1,835 | 2 | 2 | 0 |
| Derry | 2,477 | 3 | 3 | 0 |
| Derry Township, Dauphin County | 25,388 | 40 | 38 | 2 |
| Donegal Township | 3,248 | 2 | 2 | 0 |
| Donora | 4,523 | 5 | 5 | 0 |
| Dormont | 8,187 | 14 | 13 | 1 |
| Douglass Township, Berks County | 3,625 | 6 | 6 | 0 |
| Downingtown | 8,475 | 23 | 19 | 4 |
| Doylestown Township | 17,335 | 23 | 21 | 2 |
| Dublin Borough | 2,113 | 2 | 2 | 0 |
| DuBois | 7,240 | 16 | 15 | 1 |
| Duncansville | 1,140 | 2 | 2 | 0 |
| Dunmore | 12,719 | 21 | 20 | 1 |
| Dupont | 2,689 | 2 | 2 | 0 |
| Duquesne | 5,528 | 13 | 13 | 0 |
| Duryea | 4,903 | 5 | 5 | 0 |
| East Berlin | 1,544 | 3 | 1 | 2 |
| East Brandywine Township | 9,434 | 16 | 14 | 2 |
| East Cocalico Township | 10,834 | 17 | 16 | 1 |
| East Coventry Township | 6,828 | 8 | 7 | 1 |
| East Earl Township | 6,938 | 6 | 6 | 0 |
| Eastern Adams Regional | 7,399 | 6 | 6 | 0 |
| East Fallowfield Township | 7,609 | 7 | 7 | 0 |
| East Hempfield Township | 24,835 | 38 | 34 | 4 |
| East Lampeter Township | 17,029 | 41 | 38 | 3 |
| East Lansdowne | 2,668 | 5 | 4 | 1 |
| East Marlborough Township | 7,673 | 2 | 2 | 0 |
| East McKeesport | 2,568 | 3 | 3 | 0 |
| East Pennsboro Township | 21,595 | 23 | 22 | 1 |
| East Pikeland Township | 7,692 | 11 | 11 | 0 |
| Easttown Township | 10,623 | 19 | 18 | 1 |
| East Union Township | 1,589 | 2 | 2 | 0 |
| East Vincent Township | 7,361 | 7 | 7 | 0 |
| East Whiteland Township | 13,412 | 25 | 24 | 1 |
| Ebensburg | 2,984 | 5 | 5 | 0 |
| Economy | 9,024 | 14 | 13 | 1 |
| Eddystone | 2,410 | 15 | 14 | 1 |
| Edgewood | 2,969 | 9 | 9 | 0 |
| Edgeworth | 1,643 | 5 | 4 | 1 |
| Edinboro | 5,312 | 8 | 8 | 0 |
| Edwardsville | 4,724 | 6 | 6 | 0 |
| Elizabeth | 1,965 | 1 | 1 | 0 |
| Elizabethtown | 11,491 | 19 | 17 | 2 |
| Elizabeth Township | 12,828 | 13 | 13 | 0 |
| Ellwood City | 7,168 | 12 | 11 | 1 |
| Emmaus | 11,524 | 20 | 19 | 1 |
| Emporium | 1,743 | 2 | 2 | 0 |
| Ephrata | 13,847 | 36 | 33 | 3 |
| Erie | 94,437 | 199 | 175 | 24 |
| Etna | 3,269 | 6 | 6 | 0 |
| Evans City-Seven Fields Regional | 4,424 | 5 | 5 | 0 |
| Everett | 1,706 | 3 | 3 | 0 |
| Exeter | 5,510 | 3 | 3 | 0 |
| Exeter Township, Berks County | 25,719 | 36 | 34 | 2 |
| Fairview Township, Luzerne County | 4,511 | 7 | 7 | 0 |
| Falls Township, Bucks County | 33,420 | 60 | 53 | 7 |
| Fawn Township | 2,247 | 2 | 2 | 0 |
| Ferguson Township | 19,818 | 23 | 21 | 2 |
| Ferndale | 1,458 | 1 | 1 | 0 |

## Table 78. Full-Time Law Enforcement Employees, by Selected State and City, 2020—Continued

(Number.)

| State/city | Population | Total law enforcement employees | Total officers | Total civilians |
|---|---|---|---|---|
| Findlay Township | 6,278 | 25 | 18 | 7 |
| Fleetwood | 4,095 | 10 | 9 | 1 |
| Folcroft | 6,635 | 13 | 12 | 1 |
| Ford City | 2,711 | 3 | 3 | 0 |
| Forest Hills | 6,228 | 9 | 9 | 0 |
| Fountain Hill | 4,722 | 11 | 10 | 1 |
| Fox Chapel | 5,042 | 11 | 11 | 0 |
| Franconia Township | 13,540 | 11 | 10 | 1 |
| Franklin Township, Beaver County | 3,785 | 4 | 4 | 0 |
| Franklin Township, Carbon County | 4,174 | 5 | 5 | 0 |
| Frazer Township | 1,107 | 2 | 2 | 0 |
| Freedom Township | 3,299 | 3 | 3 | 0 |
| Freeland | 3,402 | 3 | 3 | 0 |
| Freeport | 1,648 | 2 | 2 | 0 |
| Gallitzin | 1,715 | 2 | 2 | 0 |
| German Township | 4,701 | 2 | 2 | 0 |
| Gettysburg | 7,720 | 12 | 11 | 1 |
| Gilpin Township | 2,358 | 3 | 3 | 0 |
| Girard | 2,877 | 4 | 4 | 0 |
| Glassport | 4,265 | 11 | 11 | 0 |
| Glenolden | 7,099 | 9 | 8 | 1 |
| Greene County Regional Police Department | 3,296 | 1 | 1 | 0 |
| Greenfield Township | 1,998 | 1 | 1 | 0 |
| Greenfield Township, Blair County | 3,910 | 3 | 3 | 0 |
| Greensburg | 14,004 | 32 | 26 | 6 |
| Green Tree | 4,791 | 10 | 10 | 0 |
| Hamburg | 4,467 | 8 | 7 | 1 |
| Hampden Township | 32,134 | 27 | 25 | 2 |
| Hampton Township | 18,095 | 21 | 20 | 1 |
| Hanover Township, Luzerne County | 10,798 | 16 | 16 | 0 |
| Harmar Township | 2,989 | 8 | 8 | 0 |
| Harmony Township | 2,941 | 5 | 5 | 0 |
| Harrisburg | 49,303 | 171 | 130 | 41 |
| Harrison Township | 10,165 | 14 | 13 | 1 |
| Harveys Lake | 2,812 | 5 | 5 | 0 |
| Hastings | 1,133 | 2 | 2 | 0 |
| Hatboro | 7,526 | 19 | 16 | 3 |
| Haverford Township | 49,648 | 76 | 70 | 6 |
| Hazleton | 24,750 | 44 | 43 | 1 |
| Heidelberg | 1,195 | 4 | 4 | 0 |
| Hellam Township | 8,581 | 12 | 12 | 0 |
| Hemlock Township | 2,262 | 8 | 8 | 0 |
| Hempfield Township, Mercer County | 3,510 | 8 | 7 | 1 |
| Highspire | 2,366 | 5 | 5 | 0 |
| Hilltown Township | 16,134 | 19 | 17 | 2 |
| Hollidaysburg | 5,620 | 10 | 8 | 2 |
| Homer City | 1,573 | 1 | 1 | 0 |
| Homestead | 3,127 | 15 | 14 | 1 |
| Honey Brook | 1,759 | 1 | 1 | 0 |
| Hooversville | 584 | 1 | 1 | 0 |
| Hopewell Township | 12,541 | 17 | 16 | 1 |
| Horsham Township | 26,561 | 46 | 39 | 7 |
| Hughestown | 1,355 | 2 | 2 | 0 |
| Hughesville | 2,015 | 3 | 3 | 0 |
| Hummelstown | 4,844 | 8 | 7 | 1 |
| Huntingdon | 6,858 | 13 | 13 | 0 |
| Independence Township, Beaver County | 2,295 | 2 | 2 | 0 |
| Indiana | 13,041 | 20 | 19 | 1 |
| Indiana Township | 7,081 | 10 | 10 | 0 |
| Ingram | 3,161 | 4 | 4 | 0 |
| Jackson Township, Butler County | 4,674 | 11 | 10 | 1 |
| Jackson Township, Cambria County | 3,920 | 4 | 4 | 0 |
| Jefferson Hills Borough | 11,186 | 21 | 20 | 1 |
| Jefferson Township, Mercer County | 1,780 | 2 | 2 | 0 |
| Jenkins Township | 4,578 | 5 | 5 | 0 |
| Jermyn | 2,025 | 3 | 3 | 0 |
| Jessup | 4,343 | 6 | 6 | 0 |
| Jim Thorpe | 4,637 | 9 | 8 | 1 |
| Johnsonburg | 2,244 | 3 | 3 | 0 |
| Johnstown | 20,112 | 44 | 40 | 4 |
| Kane | 3,394 | 4 | 4 | 0 |
| Kennedy Township | 8,118 | 12 | 10 | 2 |
| Kennett Square | 6,218 | 14 | 12 | 2 |
| Kennett Township | 8,914 | 12 | 11 | 1 |
| Kidder Township | 1,933 | 8 | 8 | 0 |
| Kingston | 12,750 | 21 | 19 | 2 |
| Kiskiminetas Township | 4,394 | 3 | 3 | 0 |
| Kline Township | 1,350 | 1 | 1 | 0 |
| Knox | 1,059 | 2 | 2 | 0 |
| Kutztown | 5,078 | 14 | 12 | 2 |
| Lake City | 2,817 | 3 | 3 | 0 |
| Lancaster | 58,961 | 163 | 134 | 29 |
| Lancaster Township, Butler County | 2,898 | 4 | 4 | 0 |
| Langhorne Borough | 1,503 | 1 | 1 | 0 |
| Lansdowne | 10,643 | 18 | 16 | 2 |

## Table 78. Full-Time Law Enforcement Employees, by Selected State and City, 2020—Continued

(Number.)

| State/city | Population | Total law enforcement employees | Total officers | Total civilians |
|---|---|---|---|---|
| Lansford | 3,746 | 4 | 4 | 0 |
| Latrobe | 7,713 | 15 | 14 | 1 |
| Laureldale | 3,897 | 5 | 5 | 0 |
| Lawrence Park Township | 3,699 | 8 | 8 | 0 |
| Lawrence Township, Clearfield County | 7,477 | 12 | 11 | 1 |
| Lebanon | 25,751 | 41 | 38 | 3 |
| Leechburg | 1,952 | 2 | 2 | 0 |
| Leetsdale | 1,144 | 5 | 5 | 0 |
| Leet Township | 1,569 | 4 | 4 | 0 |
| Lehighton | 5,277 | 12 | 11 | 1 |
| Lehman Township | 3,432 | 7 | 7 | 0 |
| Liberty | 2,427 | 2 | 2 | 0 |
| Liberty Township, Adams County | 1,270 | 1 | 1 | 0 |
| Limerick Township | 19,645 | 31 | 28 | 3 |
| Lincoln | 1,008 | 3 | 2 | 1 |
| Linesville | 958 | 2 | 2 | 0 |
| Lititz | 10,113 | 17 | 15 | 2 |
| Littlestown | 4,504 | 9 | 9 | 0 |
| Lock Haven | 8,595 | 16 | 14 | 2 |
| Locust Township | 1,380 | 5 | 5 | 0 |
| Logan Township | 12,106 | 18 | 16 | 2 |
| Lower Allen Township | 20,470 | 29 | 26 | 3 |
| Lower Chichester Township | 3,479 | 5 | 5 | 0 |
| Lower Makefield Township | 32,840 | 41 | 37 | 4 |
| Lower Moreland Township | 13,192 | 32 | 25 | 7 |
| Lower Paxton Township | 51,097 | 65 | 57 | 8 |
| Lower Southampton Township | 19,168 | 35 | 32 | 3 |
| Lower Swatara Township | 9,339 | 14 | 14 | 0 |
| Luzerne | 2,798 | 4 | 4 | 0 |
| Lykens | 1,770 | 1 | 1 | 0 |
| Macungie | 3,194 | 4 | 4 | 0 |
| Mahanoy City | 3,905 | 5 | 5 | 0 |
| Mahanoy Township | 3,120 | 6 | 6 | 0 |
| Mahoning Township, Carbon County | 4,213 | 6 | 6 | 0 |
| Mahoning Township, Lawrence County | 2,820 | 2 | 2 | 0 |
| Malvern | 3,506 | 8 | 7 | 1 |
| Manheim | 4,812 | 18 | 17 | 1 |
| Manheim Township | 40,868 | 75 | 64 | 11 |
| Manor | 3,334 | 5 | 5 | 0 |
| Manor Township, Armstrong County | 3,978 | 4 | 4 | 0 |
| Manor Township, Lancaster County | 21,207 | 21 | 19 | 2 |
| Marcus Hook | 2,400 | 7 | 6 | 1 |
| Marion Township, Beaver County | 857 | 2 | 2 | 0 |
| Marlborough Township | 3,404 | 4 | 4 | 0 |
| Marple Township | 24,015 | 33 | 30 | 3 |
| Martinsburg | 1,846 | 3 | 3 | 0 |
| Masontown | 3,241 | 4 | 4 | 0 |
| McCandless | 27,934 | 31 | 29 | 2 |
| McKeesport | 20,551 | 41 | 39 | 2 |
| McKees Rocks | 5,789 | 12 | 11 | 1 |
| McSherrystown | 3,084 | 5 | 5 | 0 |
| Meadville | 12,292 | 24 | 19 | 5 |
| Mechanicsburg | 9,025 | 17 | 15 | 2 |
| Media | 5,825 | 13 | 12 | 1 |
| Mercer | 1,848 | 5 | 5 | 0 |
| Mercersburg | 1,525 | 2 | 2 | 0 |
| Meshoppen | 1,398 | 2 | 2 | 0 |
| Meyersdale | 2,070 | 3 | 3 | 0 |
| Middlesex Township, Butler County | 6,109 | 4 | 4 | 0 |
| Middlesex Township, Cumberland County | 7,637 | 13 | 12 | 1 |
| Middletown | 9,694 | 11 | 11 | 0 |
| Middletown Township | 44,854 | 66 | 59 | 7 |
| Midland | 2,421 | 4 | 4 | 0 |
| Mifflinburg | 3,438 | 8 | 7 | 1 |
| Millbourne | 1,160 | 1 | 1 | 0 |
| Millcreek Township, Erie County | 52,066 | 78 | 62 | 16 |
| Millcreek Township, Lebanon County | 5,847 | 2 | 2 | 0 |
| Millersburg | 2,513 | 3 | 2 | 1 |
| Millersville | 8,305 | 15 | 13 | 2 |
| Millvale | 3,619 | 7 | 7 | 0 |
| Milton | 6,518 | 8 | 8 | 0 |
| Mohnton | 3,012 | 3 | 3 | 0 |
| Monaca | 5,328 | 9 | 9 | 0 |
| Monessen | 7,125 | 14 | 13 | 1 |
| Monongahela | 9,720 | 9 | 8 | 1 |
| Monroeville | 27,299 | 52 | 43 | 9 |
| Montoursville | 4,371 | 7 | 6 | 1 |
| Montour Township | 1,278 | 3 | 3 | 0 |
| Montrose | 1,449 | 2 | 2 | 0 |
| Moon Township | 25,304 | 37 | 29 | 8 |
| Moosic | 5,822 | 8 | 8 | 0 |
| Morrisville | 8,467 | 9 | 9 | 0 |
| Morton | 2,669 | 4 | 3 | 1 |
| Moscow | 2,027 | 2 | 2 | 0 |
| Mount Holly Springs | 2,055 | 4 | 4 | 0 |

## Table 78. Full-Time Law Enforcement Employees, by Selected State and City, 2020—Continued

(Number.)

| State/city | Population | Total law enforcement employees | Total officers | Total civilians |
|---|---|---|---|---|
| Mount Joy | 8,352 | 13 | 12 | 1 |
| Mount Lebanon | 31,284 | 58 | 45 | 13 |
| Mount Oliver | 3,242 | 9 | 9 | 0 |
| Mount Pleasant | 4,163 | 4 | 4 | 0 |
| Mount Union | 2,299 | 5 | 5 | 0 |
| Muhlenberg Township | 20,395 | 31 | 29 | 2 |
| Munhall | 10,886 | 24 | 23 | 1 |
| Nanticoke | 10,260 | 13 | 12 | 1 |
| Nanty Glo | 2,411 | 1 | 1 | 0 |
| Narberth | 4,298 | 9 | 6 | 3 |
| Neshannock Township | 9,122 | 8 | 8 | 0 |
| Nether Providence Township | 13,782 | 17 | 16 | 1 |
| Newberry Township | 16,053 | 20 | 18 | 2 |
| New Bethlehem | 2,677 | 3 | 3 | 0 |
| New Brighton | 8,544 | 9 | 9 | 0 |
| New Britain Township | 11,582 | 15 | 14 | 1 |
| New Castle | 21,303 | 38 | 35 | 3 |
| New Cumberland | 7,302 | 9 | 8 | 1 |
| New Hanover Township | 13,739 | 11 | 10 | 1 |
| New Holland | 5,562 | 14 | 14 | 0 |
| New Hope | 2,531 | 9 | 8 | 1 |
| Newport Township | 5,325 | 4 | 4 | 0 |
| New Sewickley Township | 7,064 | 14 | 13 | 1 |
| Newtown | 2,228 | 6 | 6 | 0 |
| Newtown Township, Bucks County | 22,652 | 35 | 31 | 4 |
| Newtown Township, Delaware County | 14,412 | 22 | 20 | 2 |
| Newville | 1,353 | 4 | 4 | 0 |
| New Wilmington | 2,181 | 5 | 5 | 0 |
| Norristown | 34,319 | 80 | 65 | 15 |
| Northampton Township | 38,984 | 50 | 43 | 7 |
| North Braddock | 4,613 | 2 | 2 | 0 |
| North Buffalo | 2,860 | 1 | 1 | 0 |
| North Cornwall Township | 8,016 | 8 | 7 | 1 |
| North Coventry Township | 7,931 | 13 | 12 | 1 |
| North East, Erie County | 3,987 | 6 | 6 | 0 |
| Northern Berks Regional | 13,529 | 11 | 11 | 0 |
| Northern Cambria Borough | 3,421 | 4 | 4 | 0 |
| Northern Lancaster County Regional | 41,408 | 33 | 31 | 2 |
| Northern Regional | 36,880 | 41 | 39 | 2 |
| North Fayette Township | 15,015 | 32 | 25 | 7 |
| North Lebanon Township | 12,291 | 15 | 13 | 2 |
| North Londonderry Township | 8,673 | 10 | 9 | 1 |
| North Middleton Township | 12,128 | 12 | 11 | 1 |
| North Sewickley Township | 5,298 | 1 | 1 | 0 |
| North Versailles Township | 11,919 | 24 | 19 | 5 |
| Northwest Lancaster County Regional | 20,644 | 21 | 19 | 2 |
| North Woodbury | 2,548 | 1 | 1 | 0 |
| Norwood | 5,957 | 7 | 6 | 1 |
| Oakmont | 6,590 | 8 | 8 | 0 |
| O'Hara Township | 8,729 | 15 | 14 | 1 |
| Ohio Township | 7,171 | 20 | 18 | 2 |
| Ohioville | 3,242 | 2 | 2 | 0 |
| Oil City | 9,449 | 17 | 16 | 1 |
| Old Forge | 7,793 | 7 | 7 | 0 |
| Old Lycoming Township | 4,915 | 10 | 9 | 1 |
| Olyphant | 4,992 | 7 | 7 | 0 |
| Orangeville Area | 3,571 | 1 | 1 | 0 |
| Orwigsburg | 2,927 | 6 | 6 | 0 |
| Oxford | 5,647 | 12 | 11 | 1 |
| Palmerton | 5,311 | 10 | 9 | 1 |
| Palmer Township | 21,520 | 37 | 35 | 2 |
| Palmyra | 7,549 | 12 | 11 | 1 |
| Parkesburg | 4,106 | 8 | 7 | 1 |
| Parkside | 2,327 | 1 | 1 | 0 |
| Parks Township | 2,517 | 2 | 2 | 0 |
| Patterson Township | 4,085 | 4 | 4 | 0 |
| Patton | 1,559 | 2 | 2 | 0 |
| Patton Township | 15,766 | 22 | 20 | 2 |
| Penbrook | 2,974 | 9 | 9 | 0 |
| Penndel | 2,184 | 1 | 1 | 0 |
| Penn Hills | 40,335 | 53 | 50 | 3 |
| Pennridge Regional | 10,913 | 12 | 11 | 1 |
| Penn Township, Butler County | 4,891 | 4 | 4 | 0 |
| Penn Township, Westmoreland County | 19,418 | 23 | 21 | 2 |
| Penn Township, York County | 16,931 | 24 | 22 | 2 |
| Perkasie | 8,892 | 20 | 18 | 2 |
| Perryopolis | 1,622 | 2 | 2 | 0 |
| Phoenixville | 16,954 | 30 | 29 | 1 |
| Pine Creek Township | 3,181 | 1 | 1 | 0 |
| Pine Grove | 2,042 | 2 | 2 | 0 |
| Pittsburgh | 316,632 | 941 | 907 | 34 |
| Pleasant Hills | 7,940 | 20 | 18 | 2 |
| Plum | 26,979 | 28 | 26 | 2 |
| Plumstead Township | 14,701 | 18 | 16 | 2 |
| Plymouth | 5,735 | 10 | 10 | 0 |

## Table 78. Full-Time Law Enforcement Employees, by Selected State and City, 2020—Continued

(Number.)

| State/city | Population | Total law enforcement employees | Total officers | Total civilians |
|---|---|---|---|---|
| Pocono Mountain Regional | 43,315 | 47 | 42 | 5 |
| Point Township | 3,570 | 6 | 6 | 0 |
| Polk | 763 | 2 | 2 | 0 |
| Portage | 2,325 | 2 | 2 | 0 |
| Port Carbon | 1,758 | 3 | 3 | 0 |
| Port Vue | 3,606 | 3 | 3 | 0 |
| Prospect Park | 6,492 | 10 | 9 | 1 |
| Pulaski Township, Lawrence County | 3,196 | 2 | 2 | 0 |
| Punxsutawney | 5,638 | 9 | 8 | 1 |
| Pymatuning Township | 2,965 | 10 | 7 | 3 |
| Quakertown | 8,734 | 23 | 20 | 3 |
| Quarryville | 2,759 | 5 | 5 | 0 |
| Raccoon Township | 2,848 | 4 | 4 | 0 |
| Radnor Township | 31,936 | 49 | 45 | 4 |
| Ralpho Township | 4,175 | 6 | 6 | 0 |
| Rankin | 2,003 | 1 | 1 | 0 |
| Reading | 88,234 | 181 | 156 | 25 |
| Reading Township | 5,897 | 2 | 2 | 0 |
| Redstone Township | 4,115 | 2 | 2 | 0 |
| Richland Township, Bucks County | 13,375 | 18 | 16 | 2 |
| Richland Township, Cambria County | 11,527 | 23 | 22 | 1 |
| Ridgway | 3,674 | 8 | 7 | 1 |
| Ridley Park | 7,072 | 10 | 10 | 0 |
| Ridley Township | 31,227 | 35 | 31 | 4 |
| Riverside | 1,831 | 3 | 3 | 0 |
| Roaring Brook Township | 2,003 | 2 | 2 | 0 |
| Roaring Spring | 2,383 | 3 | 3 | 0 |
| Robeson Township | 7,441 | 6 | 6 | 0 |
| Robinson Township, Allegheny County | 13,927 | 30 | 29 | 1 |
| Rochester | 3,382 | 8 | 7 | 1 |
| Rochester Township | 2,589 | 4 | 4 | 0 |
| Ross Township | 30,289 | 43 | 42 | 1 |
| Rostraver Township | 10,916 | 17 | 16 | 1 |
| Royalton | 1,031 | 1 | 1 | 0 |
| Rural Valley | 799 | 1 | 1 | 0 |
| Sadsbury Township, Chester County | 4,234 | 4 | 4 | 0 |
| Salem Township, Luzerne County | 4,189 | 8 | 8 | 0 |
| Salisbury Township | 14,014 | 22 | 20 | 2 |
| Sandy Township | 10,331 | 13 | 12 | 1 |
| Saxton | 674 | 3 | 3 | 0 |
| Sayre | 6,311 | 15 | 13 | 2 |
| Schuylkill Township, Chester County | 8,578 | 13 | 11 | 2 |
| Scott Township, Allegheny County | 16,244 | 23 | 22 | 1 |
| Scott Township, Columbia County | 5,030 | 8 | 8 | 0 |
| Scott Township, Lackawanna County | 4,753 | 6 | 6 | 0 |
| Scranton | 76,580 | 159 | 144 | 15 |
| Sewickley Heights | 801 | 4 | 4 | 0 |
| Shaler Township | 27,412 | 26 | 26 | 0 |
| Shamokin Dam | 1,701 | 3 | 3 | 0 |
| Sharon Hill | 5,676 | 12 | 11 | 1 |
| Sharpsburg | 3,300 | 7 | 7 | 0 |
| Sharpsville | 4,006 | 7 | 7 | 0 |
| Shenandoah | 4,706 | 5 | 5 | 0 |
| Shenango Township, Lawrence County | 7,042 | 9 | 9 | 0 |
| Shillington | 5,301 | 9 | 8 | 1 |
| Shippensburg | 5,687 | 10 | 9 | 1 |
| Shippingport | 185 | 2 | 2 | 0 |
| Shiremanstown | 1,642 | 2 | 2 | 0 |
| Silver Spring Township | 19,326 | 23 | 22 | 1 |
| Sinking Spring | 4,106 | 7 | 6 | 1 |
| Slate Belt Regional | 12,522 | 20 | 19 | 1 |
| Slatington | 4,320 | 7 | 7 | 0 |
| Slippery Rock | 3,495 | 4 | 4 | 0 |
| Solebury Township | 8,505 | 18 | 16 | 2 |
| South Abington Township | 8,701 | 12 | 11 | 1 |
| South Beaver Township | 2,611 | 4 | 4 | 0 |
| South Buffalo Township | 2,520 | 2 | 2 | 0 |
| South Coatesville | 1,519 | 3 | 3 | 0 |
| Southern Chester County Regional | 16,500 | 20 | 18 | 2 |
| South Fayette Township | 16,098 | 22 | 21 | 1 |
| South Fork | 822 | 1 | 1 | 0 |
| South Heidelberg Township | 12,379 | 13 | 13 | 0 |
| South Lebanon Township | 10,101 | 9 | 8 | 1 |
| South Londonderry Township | 8,689 | 9 | 9 | 0 |
| South Park Township | 13,575 | 16 | 15 | 1 |
| South Pymatuning Township | 2,473 | 4 | 4 | 0 |
| South Strabane Township | 9,461 | 21 | 20 | 1 |
| Southwest Regional, Fayette County | 2,597 | 1 | 1 | 0 |
| South Whitehall Township | 20,117 | 42 | 40 | 2 |
| South Williamsport | 6,034 | 9 | 9 | 0 |
| Spring City | 3,281 | 3 | 3 | 0 |
| Springfield Township, Bucks County | 5,191 | 4 | 4 | 0 |
| Springfield Township, Delaware County | 24,268 | 37 | 34 | 3 |
| Springfield Township, Montgomery County | 19,898 | 30 | 29 | 1 |
| Spring Township, Berks County | 28,173 | 30 | 29 | 1 |

## Table 78. Full-Time Law Enforcement Employees, by Selected State and City, 2020—Continued

(Number.)

| State/city | Population | Total law enforcement employees | Total officers | Total civilians |
|---|---|---|---|---|
| Spring Township, Centre County | 8,193 | 8 | 7 | 1 |
| State College | 57,835 | 67 | 57 | 10 |
| St. Clair Boro | 2,805 | 6 | 6 | 0 |
| Steelton | 5,954 | 15 | 13 | 2 |
| St. Marys City | 12,072 | 16 | 15 | 1 |
| Stonycreek Township | 2,525 | 5 | 5 | 0 |
| Stowe Township | 6,051 | 10 | 10 | 0 |
| Strasburg | 3,035 | 4 | 4 | 0 |
| Stroud Area Regional | 35,086 | 51 | 43 | 8 |
| Sugarcreek | 4,826 | 3 | 3 | 0 |
| Sugarloaf Township, Luzerne County | 3,866 | 5 | 5 | 0 |
| Summerhill Township | 2,211 | 2 | 2 | 0 |
| Summit Hill | 2,966 | 5 | 5 | 0 |
| Sunbury | 9,268 | 10 | 9 | 1 |
| Susquehanna Township, Dauphin County | 25,280 | 44 | 40 | 4 |
| Swarthmore | 6,391 | 8 | 8 | 0 |
| Sweden Township | 810 | 1 | 1 | 0 |
| Swissvale | 8,550 | 17 | 17 | 0 |
| Swoyersville | 4,998 | 5 | 5 | 0 |
| Sykesville | 1,102 | 1 | 1 | 0 |
| Tarentum | 4,319 | 10 | 10 | 0 |
| Tatamy | 1,212 | 2 | 2 | 0 |
| Taylor | 5,842 | 8 | 8 | 0 |
| Telford | 4,884 | 7 | 6 | 1 |
| Throop | 3,867 | 7 | 7 | 0 |
| Tilden Township | 3,618 | 4 | 4 | 0 |
| Tinicum Township, Bucks County | 3,946 | 4 | 4 | 0 |
| Tinicum Township, Delaware County | 4,111 | 18 | 16 | 2 |
| Titusville | 5,059 | 11 | 11 | 0 |
| Trafford | 2,994 | 6 | 6 | 0 |
| Trainer | 1,824 | 16 | 16 | 0 |
| Tredyffrin Township | 29,234 | 47 | 42 | 5 |
| Troy | 1,221 | 2 | 2 | 0 |
| Tullytown | 2,171 | 4 | 4 | 0 |
| Tulpehocken Township | 3,534 | 3 | 3 | 0 |
| Tunkhannock | 1,660 | 3 | 3 | 0 |
| Tunkhannock Township, Wyoming County | 5,934 | 6 | 6 | 0 |
| Turtle Creek | 5,081 | 4 | 4 | 0 |
| Tyrone | 5,060 | 6 | 5 | 1 |
| Union City | 3,075 | 3 | 2 | 1 |
| Uniontown | 9,564 | 21 | 20 | 1 |
| Union Township, Lawrence County | 4,777 | 10 | 10 | 0 |
| Upland | 3,348 | 10 | 9 | 1 |
| Upper Allen Township | 20,972 | 25 | 24 | 1 |
| Upper Chichester Township | 16,979 | 23 | 22 | 1 |
| Upper Darby Township | 82,893 | 145 | 133 | 12 |
| Upper Macungie Township | 26,421 | 32 | 29 | 3 |
| Upper Makefield Township | 8,625 | 19 | 18 | 1 |
| Upper Providence Township, Delaware County | 10,366 | 16 | 15 | 1 |
| Upper Providence Township, Montgomery County | 24,889 | 28 | 25 | 3 |
| Upper Saucon Township | 17,725 | 22 | 20 | 2 |
| Upper Southampton Township | 14,868 | 25 | 22 | 3 |
| Upper St. Clair Township | 19,932 | 34 | 27 | 7 |
| Upper Uwchlan Township | 12,072 | 12 | 12 | 0 |
| Upper Yoder Township | 4,925 | 6 | 6 | 0 |
| Uwchlan Township | 18,807 | 25 | 23 | 2 |
| Valley Township | 7,829 | 8 | 8 | 0 |
| Vernon Township | 5,299 | 4 | 4 | 0 |
| Verona | 2,384 | 4 | 3 | 1 |
| Versailles | 1,445 | 2 | 2 | 0 |
| Warminster Township | 32,205 | 45 | 40 | 5 |
| Warrington Township | 24,747 | 36 | 35 | 1 |
| Warwick Township, Bucks County | 14,759 | 19 | 18 | 1 |
| Washington Township, Fayette County | 3,539 | 5 | 5 | 0 |
| Washington Township, Franklin County | 15,037 | 11 | 9 | 2 |
| Washington Township, Northampton County | 5,299 | 5 | 5 | 0 |
| Washington Township, Westmoreland County | 6,973 | 9 | 9 | 0 |
| Waverly Township | 1,668 | 3 | 3 | 0 |
| Waynesboro | 10,939 | 19 | 17 | 2 |
| Waynesburg | 3,825 | 8 | 8 | 0 |
| Weatherly | 2,445 | 5 | 5 | 0 |
| Wellsboro | 3,199 | 7 | 7 | 0 |
| Wesleyville | 3,069 | 8 | 7 | 1 |
| West Brandywine Township | 7,461 | 9 | 8 | 1 |
| West Caln Township | 9,079 | 4 | 4 | 0 |
| West Chester | 20,214 | 54 | 43 | 11 |
| West Deer Township | 12,046 | 15 | 14 | 1 |
| West Earl Township | 8,389 | 13 | 12 | 1 |
| West Fallowfield Township | 2,596 | 2 | 2 | 0 |
| Westfield | 1,022 | 2 | 2 | 0 |
| West Goshen Township | 23,089 | 35 | 32 | 3 |
| West Hempfield Township | 16,924 | 23 | 22 | 1 |
| West Hills Regional | 9,665 | 12 | 11 | 1 |
| West Homestead | 1,847 | 11 | 10 | 1 |
| West Kittanning | 1,069 | 2 | 2 | 0 |

## Table 78. Full-Time Law Enforcement Employees, by Selected State and City, 2020—Continued

(Number.)

| State/city | Population | Total law enforcement employees | Total officers | Total civilians |
|---|---|---|---|---|
| West Lampeter Township | 16,063 | 18 | 17 | 1 |
| West Mead Township | 4,930 | 2 | 2 | 0 |
| West Mifflin | 19,517 | 42 | 36 | 6 |
| West Penn Township | 4,280 | 1 | 1 | 0 |
| West Pittston | 4,730 | 3 | 3 | 0 |
| West Reading | 4,295 | 18 | 15 | 3 |
| West Sadsbury Township | 2,502 | 5 | 5 | 0 |
| West Shore Regional | 7,707 | 13 | 12 | 1 |
| Westtown-East Goshen Regional | 32,178 | 32 | 28 | 4 |
| West View | 6,441 | 11 | 10 | 1 |
| West Vincent Township | 6,181 | 8 | 7 | 1 |
| West Whiteland Township | 20,170 | 28 | 26 | 2 |
| Whitehall | 13,268 | 24 | 19 | 5 |
| Whitehall Township | 28,031 | 52 | 47 | 5 |
| White Haven Borough | 1,095 | 2 | 2 | 0 |
| White Oak | 7,354 | 13 | 12 | 1 |
| Wiconisco Township | 1,202 | 1 | 1 | 0 |
| Wilkinsburg | 15,120 | 24 | 21 | 3 |
| Wilkins Township | 6,065 | 10 | 10 | 0 |
| Williamsburg | 1,159 | 2 | 2 | 0 |
| Willistown Township | 11,031 | 21 | 19 | 2 |
| Woodward Township | 2,335 | 2 | 2 | 0 |
| Wyoming | 2,997 | 3 | 3 | 0 |
| Wyomissing | 10,622 | 23 | 22 | 1 |
| Yardley | 2,512 | 5 | 5 | 0 |
| Yeadon | 11,493 | 17 | 16 | 1 |
| Zelienople | 3,605 | 10 | 9 | 1 |
| Zerbe Township | 1,736 | 1 | 1 | 0 |
| **RHODE ISLAND** | | | | |
| Barrington | 16,566 | 29 | 23 | 6 |
| Bristol | 22,550 | 46 | 38 | 8 |
| Burrillville | 17,501 | 32 | 25 | 7 |
| Central Falls | 20,174 | 44 | 37 | 7 |
| Charlestown | 8,118 | 24 | 20 | 4 |
| Coventry | 36,216 | 72 | 57 | 15 |
| Cranston | 84,105 | 179 | 149 | 30 |
| Cumberland | 36,648 | 56 | 47 | 9 |
| East Greenwich | 13,617 | 38 | 31 | 7 |
| East Providence | 49,064 | 110 | 92 | 18 |
| Foster | 4,933 | 9 | 6 | 3 |
| Glocester | 10,788 | 22 | 16 | 6 |
| Hopkinton | 8,379 | 17 | 12 | 5 |
| Jamestown | 5,687 | 19 | 14 | 5 |
| Johnston | 30,476 | 77 | 64 | 13 |
| Lincoln | 22,823 | 38 | 30 | 8 |
| Little Compton | 3,584 | 14 | 10 | 4 |
| Middletown | 16,338 | 41 | 37 | 4 |
| Narragansett | 15,801 | 53 | 40 | 13 |
| Newport | 25,240 | 101 | 77 | 24 |
| New Shoreham | 1,064 | 12 | 6 | 6 |
| North Kingstown | 27,192 | 59 | 51 | 8 |
| North Providence | 33,712 | 69 | 62 | 7 |
| North Smithfield | 13,093 | 32 | 26 | 6 |
| Pawtucket | 74,342 | 171 | 140 | 31 |
| Portsmouth | 17,696 | 41 | 38 | 3 |
| Providence | 185,868 | 533 | 449 | 84 |
| Richmond | 8,189 | 18 | 14 | 4 |
| Scituate | 11,148 | 24 | 17 | 7 |
| Smithfield | 22,676 | 54 | 41 | 13 |
| South Kingstown | 31,537 | 69 | 54 | 15 |
| Tiverton | 16,106 | 40 | 28 | 12 |
| Warren | 10,830 | 29 | 22 | 7 |
| Warwick | 83,968 | 204 | 162 | 42 |
| Westerly | 23,088 | 59 | 45 | 14 |
| West Greenwich | 6,680 | 19 | 13 | 6 |
| West Warwick | 29,964 | 52 | 44 | 8 |
| Woonsocket | 43,072 | 115 | 96 | 19 |
| **SOUTH CAROLINA** | | | | |
| Abbeville | 4,932 | 20 | 19 | 1 |
| Aiken | 31,270 | 140 | 87 | 53 |
| Allendale | 2,773 | 5 | 5 | 0 |
| Anderson | 27,831 | 126 | 92 | 34 |
| Bamberg | 3,120 | 12 | 10 | 2 |
| Barnwell | 4,213 | 15 | 13 | 2 |
| Batesburg-Leesville | 5,405 | 27 | 23 | 4 |
| Beaufort | 13,293 | 50 | 46 | 4 |
| Belton | 4,517 | 14 | 12 | 2 |
| Bennettsville | 7,301 | 35 | 33 | 2 |
| Bethune | 356 | 1 | 1 | 0 |
| Blacksburg | 1,885 | 8 | 8 | 0 |
| Bluffton | 30,519 | 54 | 48 | 6 |
| Bonneau | 497 | 2 | 2 | 0 |
| Branchville | 936 | 3 | 2 | 1 |

## Table 78. Full-Time Law Enforcement Employees, by Selected State and City, 2020—Continued

(Number.)

| State/city | Population | Total law enforcement employees | Total officers | Total civilians |
|---|---|---|---|---|
| Briarcliffe Acres | 630 | 1 | 1 | 0 |
| Burnettown | 2,784 | 1 | 1 | 0 |
| Calhoun Falls | 1,873 | 3 | 3 | 0 |
| Camden | 7,335 | 37 | 34 | 3 |
| Cayce | 14,088 | 63 | 53 | 10 |
| Central | 5,478 | 12 | 11 | 1 |
| Charleston | 141,768 | 504 | 413 | 91 |
| Chester | 5,341 | 19 | 16 | 3 |
| Chesterfield | 1,394 | 5 | 5 | 0 |
| Clemson | 18,220 | 41 | 30 | 11 |
| Clinton | 8,288 | 28 | 25 | 3 |
| Columbia | 132,255 | 421 | 324 | 97 |
| Conway | 27,781 | 67 | 56 | 11 |
| Darlington | 5,856 | 29 | 27 | 2 |
| Denmark | 2,847 | 7 | 6 | 1 |
| Due West | 1,195 | 5 | 5 | 0 |
| Duncan | 3,772 | 17 | 16 | 1 |
| Easley | 21,789 | 63 | 52 | 11 |
| Edgefield | 4,831 | 9 | 9 | 0 |
| Ehrhardt | 471 | 2 | 1 | 1 |
| Elgin | 1,613 | 7 | 6 | 1 |
| Elloree | 626 | 4 | 3 | 1 |
| Florence | 38,521 | 99 | 75 | 24 |
| Folly Beach | 2,699 | 23 | 18 | 5 |
| Forest Acres | 10,261 | 34 | 26 | 8 |
| Fort Lawn | 888 | 3 | 2 | 1 |
| Fort Mill | 26,923 | 64 | 52 | 12 |
| Fountain Inn | 11,306 | 36 | 28 | 8 |
| Gifford | 259 | 3 | 1 | 2 |
| Goose Creek | 45,901 | 106 | 79 | 27 |
| Greenville | 73,653 | 247 | 205 | 42 |
| Greenwood | 23,369 | 61 | 53 | 8 |
| Greer | 36,423 | 84 | 60 | 24 |
| Hampton | 2,459 | 15 | 14 | 1 |
| Hanahan | 29,582 | 33 | 31 | 2 |
| Hardeeville | 9,332 | 28 | 25 | 3 |
| Hartsville | 7,454 | 40 | 37 | 3 |
| Holly Hill | 1,151 | 4 | 4 | 0 |
| Honea Path | 3,881 | 13 | 12 | 1 |
| Irmo | 12,902 | 28 | 25 | 3 |
| Isle of Palms | 4,395 | 24 | 17 | 7 |
| Iva | 1,352 | 10 | 9 | 1 |
| Jackson | 1,825 | 4 | 3 | 1 |
| Johnsonville | 1,470 | 7 | 6 | 1 |
| Johnston | 2,397 | 10 | 10 | 0 |
| Jonesville | 811 | 3 | 3 | 0 |
| Kingstree | 2,958 | 11 | 10 | 1 |
| Lake View | 773 | 3 | 3 | 0 |
| Landrum | 2,763 | 14 | 13 | 1 |
| Laurens | 8,835 | 36 | 31 | 5 |
| Lexington | 23,161 | 63 | 60 | 3 |
| Liberty | 3,140 | 16 | 11 | 5 |
| Loris | 2,855 | 14 | 11 | 3 |
| Lyman | 3,850 | 12 | 12 | 0 |
| Marion | 6,136 | 18 | 15 | 3 |
| Mauldin | 25,808 | 56 | 48 | 8 |
| McCormick | 2,279 | 6 | 6 | 0 |
| Mullins | 4,092 | 17 | 16 | 1 |
| Myrtle Beach | 36,543 | 283 | 207 | 76 |
| Newberry | 10,119 | 28 | 25 | 3 |
| New Ellenton | 2,201 | 5 | 4 | 1 |
| Ninety Six | 2,043 | 8 | 8 | 0 |
| North | 692 | 5 | 5 | 0 |
| North Augusta | 24,435 | 88 | 65 | 23 |
| North Charleston | 121,060 | 166 | 145 | 21 |
| North Myrtle Beach | 17,648 | 115 | 82 | 33 |
| Olanta | 550 | 2 | 1 | 1 |
| Pageland | 2,529 | 14 | 10 | 4 |
| Pamplico | 1,207 | 3 | 3 | 0 |
| Pawleys Island | 110 | 4 | 4 | 0 |
| Pelion | 714 | 3 | 2 | 1 |
| Port Royal | 14,970 | 24 | 23 | 1 |
| Quinby | 912 | 1 | 1 | 0 |
| Ridgeland | 3,853 | 15 | 14 | 1 |
| Ridge Spring | 738 | 2 | 2 | 0 |
| Ridgeville | 1,830 | 1 | 1 | 0 |
| Rock Hill | 77,334 | 183 | 137 | 46 |
| Salem | 154 | 1 | 1 | 0 |
| Seneca | 8,611 | 43 | 30 | 13 |
| Simpsonville | 26,077 | 52 | 42 | 10 |
| South Congaree | 2,504 | 7 | 6 | 1 |
| Spartanburg | 37,375 | 140 | 117 | 23 |
| Springdale | 2,743 | 13 | 12 | 1 |
| St. George | 2,206 | 10 | 9 | 1 |
| Sullivans Island | 1,953 | 11 | 10 | 1 |

## Table 78. Full-Time Law Enforcement Employees, by Selected State and City, 2020—Continued

(Number.)

| State/city | Population | Total law enforcement employees | Total officers | Total civilians |
|---|---|---|---|---|
| Summerville | 54,438 | 146 | 119 | 27 |
| Sumter | 39,328 | 137 | 104 | 33 |
| Surfside Beach | 4,661 | 23 | 18 | 5 |
| Swansea | 1,000 | 3 | 3 | 0 |
| Tega Cay | 12,178 | 33 | 25 | 8 |
| Travelers Rest | 8,297 | 21 | 15 | 6 |
| Trenton | 201 | 1 | 1 | 0 |
| Union | 7,458 | 27 | 25 | 2 |
| Wagener | 850 | 3 | 3 | 0 |
| Walhalla | 4,484 | 13 | 12 | 1 |
| Walterboro | 5,303 | 31 | 30 | 1 |
| Ware Shoals | 2,150 | 7 | 7 | 0 |
| Wellford | 2,813 | 11 | 9 | 2 |
| West Columbia | 18,257 | 56 | 46 | 10 |
| West Pelzer | 961 | 3 | 3 | 0 |
| West Union | 337 | 3 | 3 | 0 |
| Williston | 2,890 | 10 | 9 | 1 |
| Winnsboro | 3,091 | 18 | 17 | 1 |
| York | 8,728 | 43 | 37 | 6 |
| **SOUTH DAKOTA** | | | | |
| Aberdeen | 28,385 | 59 | 50 | 9 |
| Alcester | 750 | 2 | 2 | 0 |
| Belle Fourche | 5,755 | 13 | 11 | 2 |
| Beresford | 2,046 | 5 | 5 | 0 |
| Box Elder | 10,876 | 16 | 15 | 1 |
| Brandon | 10,297 | 15 | 14 | 1 |
| Brookings | 25,088 | 49 | 36 | 13 |
| Burke | 586 | 1 | 1 | 0 |
| Canton | 3,635 | 6 | 6 | 0 |
| Centerville | 868 | 2 | 2 | 0 |
| Chamberlain | 2,344 | 7 | 7 | 0 |
| Clark | 1,072 | 2 | 2 | 0 |
| Deadwood | 1,294 | 21 | 18 | 3 |
| Eagle Butte | 1,417 | 1 | 1 | 0 |
| Elk Point | 1,864 | 5 | 5 | 0 |
| Flandreau | 2,288 | 7 | 6 | 1 |
| Freeman | 1,250 | 2 | 2 | 0 |
| Gettysburg | 1,075 | 2 | 2 | 0 |
| Gregory | 1,246 | 2 | 2 | 0 |
| Groton | 1,477 | 4 | 4 | 0 |
| Hot Springs | 3,479 | 9 | 7 | 2 |
| Huron | 13,504 | 35 | 25 | 10 |
| Jefferson | 512 | 2 | 2 | 0 |
| Kadoka | 714 | 1 | 1 | 0 |
| Kimball | 663 | 1 | 1 | 0 |
| Lake Norden | 547 | 2 | 2 | 0 |
| Lead | 2,929 | 7 | 6 | 1 |
| Lennox | 2,540 | 5 | 5 | 0 |
| Madison | 7,120 | 14 | 13 | 1 |
| Martin | 1,057 | 3 | 3 | 0 |
| Menno | 616 | 1 | 1 | 0 |
| Milbank | 3,039 | 7 | 7 | 0 |
| Miller | 1,290 | 4 | 4 | 0 |
| Mitchell | 15,741 | 40 | 26 | 14 |
| Mobridge | 3,364 | 16 | 8 | 8 |
| Murdo | 456 | 1 | 1 | 0 |
| North Sioux City | 2,997 | 9 | 8 | 1 |
| Parkston | 1,450 | 3 | 3 | 0 |
| Philip | 751 | 2 | 2 | 0 |
| Pierre | 13,710 | 38 | 24 | 14 |
| Platte | 1,259 | 2 | 2 | 0 |
| Rapid City | 79,910 | 170 | 132 | 38 |
| Sioux Falls | 191,508 | 306 | 271 | 35 |
| Sisseton | 2,360 | 6 | 6 | 0 |
| Spearfish | 12,047 | 30 | 19 | 11 |
| Springfield | 1,909 | 2 | 2 | 0 |
| Sturgis | 7,013 | 20 | 17 | 3 |
| Summerset | 2,793 | 7 | 7 | 0 |
| Tea | 6,739 | 8 | 8 | 0 |
| Tripp | 611 | 1 | 1 | 0 |
| Tyndall | 1,010 | 2 | 2 | 0 |
| Vermillion | 11,088 | 17 | 16 | 1 |
| Viborg | 761 | 1 | 1 | 0 |
| Wagner | 1,534 | 3 | 3 | 0 |
| Watertown | 22,383 | 58 | 40 | 18 |
| Webster | 1,675 | 5 | 5 | 0 |
| Whitewood | 1,006 | 5 | 4 | 1 |
| Winner | 2,773 | 11 | 11 | 0 |
| Yankton | 14,669 | 39 | 30 | 9 |
| **TENNESSEE** | | | | |
| Adamsville | 2,159 | 7 | 6 | 1 |
| Alamo | 2,251 | 4 | 4 | 0 |
| Alcoa | 10,605 | 57 | 47 | 10 |

## Table 78. Full-Time Law Enforcement Employees, by Selected State and City, 2020—Continued

(Number.)

| State/city | Population | Total law enforcement employees | Total officers | Total civilians |
|---|---|---|---|---|
| Alexandria | 1,025 | 3 | 3 | 0 |
| Algood | 4,666 | 14 | 14 | 0 |
| Ardmore | 1,218 | 7 | 4 | 3 |
| Ashland City | 4,763 | 20 | 18 | 2 |
| Athens | 14,166 | 30 | 29 | 1 |
| Atoka | 9,859 | 23 | 22 | 1 |
| Baileyton | 459 | 3 | 3 | 0 |
| Bartlett | 59,562 | 161 | 124 | 37 |
| Baxter | 1,563 | 7 | 7 | 0 |
| Bean Station | 3,121 | 7 | 7 | 0 |
| Belle Meade | 2,777 | 20 | 14 | 6 |
| Bells | 2,431 | 4 | 4 | 0 |
| Benton | 1,235 | 7 | 6 | 1 |
| Berry Hill | 488 | 18 | 14 | 4 |
| Big Sandy | 515 | 1 | 1 | 0 |
| Blaine | 1,871 | 4 | 4 | 0 |
| Bluff City | 1,669 | 8 | 8 | 0 |
| Bolivar | 4,798 | 26 | 24 | 2 |
| Bradford | 967 | 5 | 5 | 0 |
| Brentwood | 43,490 | 84 | 67 | 17 |
| Brighton | 2,933 | 8 | 8 | 0 |
| Bristol | 27,182 | 96 | 76 | 20 |
| Brownsville | 9,128 | 40 | 34 | 6 |
| Bruceton | 1,383 | 5 | 5 | 0 |
| Burns | 1,570 | 1 | 1 | 0 |
| Calhoun | 504 | 3 | 3 | 0 |
| Camden | 3,624 | 19 | 14 | 5 |
| Carthage | 2,335 | 12 | 8 | 4 |
| Caryville | 2,103 | 7 | 6 | 1 |
| Celina | 1,398 | 6 | 2 | 4 |
| Centerville | 3,557 | 17 | 15 | 2 |
| Chapel Hill | 1,584 | 7 | 6 | 1 |
| Charleston | 712 | 3 | 3 | 0 |
| Chattanooga | 186,222 | 494 | 420 | 74 |
| Church Hill | 6,633 | 9 | 9 | 0 |
| Clarksville | 164,336 | 378 | 312 | 66 |
| Cleveland | 46,440 | 112 | 100 | 12 |
| Clifton | 2,651 | 5 | 5 | 0 |
| Clinton | 10,157 | 40 | 32 | 8 |
| Collegedale | 11,737 | 27 | 24 | 3 |
| Collierville | 52,059 | 145 | 110 | 35 |
| Collinwood | 927 | 4 | 4 | 0 |
| Columbia | 42,613 | 102 | 76 | 26 |
| Cookeville | 35,471 | 93 | 71 | 22 |
| Coopertown | 4,647 | 6 | 5 | 1 |
| Cornersville | 1,329 | 2 | 2 | 0 |
| Covington | 8,791 | 38 | 35 | 3 |
| Cowan | 1,662 | 3 | 3 | 0 |
| Cross Plains | 1,853 | 1 | 1 | 0 |
| Crossville | 12,007 | 45 | 42 | 3 |
| Cumberland City | 310 | 2 | 2 | 0 |
| Dandridge | 3,204 | 12 | 11 | 1 |
| Dayton | 7,338 | 17 | 15 | 2 |
| Decatur | 1,665 | 6 | 6 | 0 |
| Decaturville | 856 | 1 | 1 | 0 |
| Decherd | 2,375 | 15 | 13 | 2 |
| Dickson | 15,634 | 68 | 61 | 7 |
| Dover | 1,596 | 7 | 6 | 1 |
| Dresden | 2,890 | 8 | 7 | 1 |
| Dunlap | 5,278 | 15 | 13 | 2 |
| Dyer | 2,192 | 7 | 6 | 1 |
| Dyersburg | 15,981 | 64 | 57 | 7 |
| Eagleville | 824 | 3 | 3 | 0 |
| East Ridge | 21,225 | 52 | 47 | 5 |
| Elizabethton | 13,406 | 47 | 43 | 4 |
| Elkton | 520 | 2 | 2 | 0 |
| Englewood | 1,539 | 6 | 5 | 1 |
| Erin | 1,304 | 4 | 3 | 1 |
| Erwin | 5,832 | 17 | 16 | 1 |
| Estill Springs | 2,042 | 7 | 7 | 0 |
| Ethridge | 487 | 4 | 3 | 1 |
| Etowah | 3,530 | 12 | 11 | 1 |
| Fairview | 9,794 | 23 | 23 | 0 |
| Fayetteville | 7,033 | 26 | 25 | 1 |
| Franklin | 87,969 | 141 | 130 | 11 |
| Friendship | 658 | 1 | 1 | 0 |
| Gainesboro | 951 | 4 | 4 | 0 |
| Gallatin | 46,031 | 92 | 79 | 13 |
| Gallaway | 646 | 2 | 2 | 0 |
| Gatlinburg | 3,759 | 47 | 44 | 3 |
| Germantown | 39,217 | 134 | 106 | 28 |
| Gibson | 382 | 3 | 2 | 1 |
| Gleason | 1,361 | 5 | 5 | 0 |
| Goodlettsville | 16,818 | 52 | 38 | 14 |
| Gordonsville | 1,248 | 6 | 6 | 0 |

## Table 78. Full-Time Law Enforcement Employees, by Selected State and City, 2020—Continued

(Number.)

| State/city | Population | Total law enforcement employees | Total officers | Total civilians |
|---|---|---|---|---|
| Grand Junction | 261 | 4 | 4 | 0 |
| Graysville | 1,575 | 3 | 2 | 1 |
| Greenbrier | 6,949 | 17 | 14 | 3 |
| Greeneville | 14,930 | 58 | 56 | 2 |
| Greenfield | 2,058 | 7 | 6 | 1 |
| Halls | 2,021 | 10 | 10 | 0 |
| Harriman | 6,167 | 21 | 20 | 1 |
| Henderson | 6,427 | 17 | 16 | 1 |
| Hendersonville | 60,170 | 151 | 135 | 16 |
| Henry | 447 | 2 | 2 | 0 |
| Hohenwald | 3,992 | 18 | 16 | 2 |
| Hollow Rock | 677 | 1 | 1 | 0 |
| Hornbeak | 467 | 1 | 1 | 0 |
| Humboldt | 8,092 | 32 | 26 | 6 |
| Huntingdon | 3,820 | 19 | 15 | 4 |
| Huntland | 839 | 2 | 2 | 0 |
| Jacksboro | 2,069 | 7 | 6 | 1 |
| Jackson | 67,462 | 242 | 205 | 37 |
| Jamestown | 2,149 | 9 | 9 | 0 |
| Jasper | 3,419 | 9 | 9 | 0 |
| Jefferson City | 8,234 | 29 | 28 | 1 |
| Jellico | 2,114 | 6 | 5 | 1 |
| Johnson City | 67,515 | 172 | 148 | 24 |
| Jonesborough | 5,840 | 23 | 17 | 6 |
| Kenton | 1,181 | 4 | 4 | 0 |
| Kimball | 1,457 | 9 | 9 | 0 |
| Kingsport | 54,229 | 147 | 109 | 38 |
| Kingston | 5,956 | 13 | 13 | 0 |
| Kingston Springs | 2,712 | 8 | 7 | 1 |
| Knoxville | 191,463 | 492 | 382 | 110 |
| Lafayette | 5,351 | 25 | 16 | 9 |
| La Follette | 6,502 | 32 | 22 | 10 |
| La Vergne | 35,954 | 72 | 63 | 9 |
| Lawrenceburg | 11,122 | 40 | 36 | 4 |
| Lebanon | 39,524 | 135 | 103 | 32 |
| Lenoir City | 9,401 | 29 | 27 | 2 |
| Lewisburg | 12,712 | 29 | 28 | 1 |
| Lexington | 7,888 | 35 | 29 | 6 |
| Livingston | 4,135 | 23 | 18 | 5 |
| Lookout Mountain | 1,886 | 18 | 14 | 4 |
| Loretto | 1,790 | 5 | 5 | 0 |
| Loudon | 6,079 | 16 | 15 | 1 |
| Madisonville | 5,056 | 33 | 33 | 0 |
| Manchester | 11,383 | 38 | 35 | 3 |
| Martin | 10,480 | 39 | 29 | 10 |
| Maryville | 30,262 | 62 | 57 | 5 |
| Mason | 1,530 | 5 | 5 | 0 |
| Maynardville | 2,461 | 5 | 4 | 1 |
| McEwen | 1,744 | 4 | 4 | 0 |
| McKenzie | 5,309 | 19 | 14 | 5 |
| McMinnville | 13,790 | 40 | 37 | 3 |
| Medina | 4,465 | 10 | 10 | 0 |
| Memphis | 649,444 | 2,446 | 2,027 | 419 |
| Metropolitan Nashville Police Department | 690,553 | 1,850 | 1,450 | 400 |
| Middleton | 621 | 2 | 2 | 0 |
| Milan | 7,583 | 33 | 26 | 7 |
| Millersville | 6,839 | 16 | 14 | 2 |
| Millington | 10,621 | 37 | 29 | 8 |
| Minor Hill | 534 | 2 | 2 | 0 |
| Monteagle | 1,236 | 7 | 7 | 0 |
| Monterey | 2,895 | 10 | 9 | 1 |
| Morristown | 30,413 | 81 | 76 | 5 |
| Moscow | 544 | 7 | 7 | 0 |
| Mosheim | 2,355 | 2 | 2 | 0 |
| Mountain City | 2,437 | 9 | 9 | 0 |
| Mount Carmel | 5,242 | 7 | 7 | 0 |
| Mount Juliet | 40,233 | 83 | 65 | 18 |
| Mount Pleasant | 5,014 | 20 | 14 | 6 |
| Munford | 6,233 | 18 | 18 | 0 |
| Murfreesboro | 155,652 | 326 | 267 | 59 |
| Newbern | 3,222 | 11 | 11 | 0 |
| New Johnsonville | 1,866 | 6 | 5 | 1 |
| New Market | 1,385 | 5 | 4 | 1 |
| Newport | 6,894 | 30 | 26 | 4 |
| New Tazewell | 2,694 | 10 | 10 | 0 |
| Niota | 740 | 4 | 3 | 1 |
| Nolensville | 11,866 | 17 | 16 | 1 |
| Norris | 1,614 | 6 | 6 | 0 |
| Oakland | 8,903 | 19 | 17 | 2 |
| Oak Ridge | 29,343 | 82 | 63 | 19 |
| Obion | 1,035 | 2 | 2 | 0 |
| Oliver Springs | 3,443 | 12 | 12 | 0 |
| Oneida | 3,696 | 16 | 11 | 5 |
| Paris | 9,934 | 37 | 26 | 11 |
| Parsons | 2,264 | 7 | 7 | 0 |

## Table 78. Full-Time Law Enforcement Employees, by Selected State and City, 2020—Continued

(Number.)

| State/city | Population | Total law enforcement employees | Total officers | Total civilians |
|---|---|---|---|---|
| Petersburg | 579 | 1 | 1 | 0 |
| Pigeon Forge | 6,276 | 76 | 61 | 15 |
| Pikeville | 1,799 | 4 | 4 | 0 |
| Piperton | 2,212 | 5 | 5 | 0 |
| Pittman Center | 552 | 3 | 3 | 0 |
| Plainview | 2,191 | 2 | 2 | 0 |
| Pleasant View | 5,156 | 7 | 7 | 0 |
| Portland | 13,493 | 37 | 33 | 4 |
| Pulaski | 7,494 | 25 | 23 | 2 |
| Puryear | 651 | 2 | 1 | 1 |
| Red Bank | 11,904 | 26 | 24 | 2 |
| Red Boiling Springs | 1,125 | 5 | 5 | 0 |
| Ridgely | 1,586 | 3 | 3 | 0 |
| Ripley | 7,552 | 28 | 21 | 7 |
| Rockwood | 5,449 | 15 | 14 | 1 |
| Rocky Top | 1,776 | 7 | 6 | 1 |
| Rogersville | 4,356 | 20 | 14 | 6 |
| Rossville | 1,056 | 8 | 8 | 0 |
| Rutherford | 1,056 | 4 | 4 | 0 |
| Rutledge | 1,358 | 3 | 3 | 0 |
| Savannah | 6,907 | 23 | 21 | 2 |
| Scotts Hill | 972 | 3 | 3 | 0 |
| Selmer | 4,277 | 17 | 15 | 2 |
| Sevierville | 18,836 | 81 | 64 | 17 |
| Sharon | 900 | 3 | 2 | 1 |
| Shelbyville | 22,534 | 60 | 44 | 16 |
| Signal Mountain | 8,678 | 17 | 15 | 2 |
| Smithville | 5,027 | 14 | 13 | 1 |
| Smyrna | 54,645 | 107 | 90 | 17 |
| Soddy-Daisy | 13,799 | 35 | 28 | 7 |
| Somerville | 3,262 | 12 | 11 | 1 |
| South Carthage | 1,416 | 4 | 4 | 0 |
| South Fulton | 2,193 | 4 | 4 | 0 |
| South Pittsburg | 3,000 | 9 | 9 | 0 |
| Sparta | 4,994 | 16 | 15 | 1 |
| Spencer | 1,720 | 2 | 2 | 0 |
| Spring City | 1,837 | 10 | 8 | 2 |
| Springfield | 17,374 | 38 | 34 | 4 |
| Spring Hill | 48,297 | 71 | 67 | 4 |
| St. Joseph | 827 | 1 | 1 | 0 |
| Surgoinsville | 1,749 | 1 | 1 | 0 |
| Sweetwater | 5,971 | 20 | 19 | 1 |
| Tazewell | 2,279 | 9 | 9 | 0 |
| Tellico Plains | 915 | 7 | 7 | 0 |
| Tiptonville | 3,939 | 7 | 7 | 0 |
| Townsend | 483 | 5 | 5 | 0 |
| Tracy City | 1,398 | 1 | 1 | 0 |
| Trenton | 4,133 | 23 | 17 | 6 |
| Trimble | 599 | 1 | 1 | 0 |
| Troy | 1,321 | 5 | 5 | 0 |
| Tullahoma | 19,913 | 38 | 31 | 7 |
| Tusculum | 2,669 | 2 | 2 | 0 |
| Unicoi | 3,576 | 4 | 4 | 0 |
| Union City | 10,272 | 43 | 36 | 7 |
| Vonore | 1,589 | 11 | 10 | 1 |
| Wartburg | 899 | 6 | 6 | 0 |
| Wartrace | 726 | 1 | 1 | 0 |
| Watertown | 1,542 | 5 | 5 | 0 |
| Waverly | 4,123 | 11 | 10 | 1 |
| Waynesboro | 2,365 | 7 | 7 | 0 |
| Westmoreland | 2,438 | 10 | 9 | 1 |
| White Bluff | 3,741 | 6 | 6 | 0 |
| White House | 13,282 | 25 | 22 | 3 |
| White Pine | 2,673 | 11 | 10 | 1 |
| Whiteville | 4,430 | 7 | 7 | 0 |
| Whitwell | 1,718 | 6 | 5 | 1 |
| Winchester | 9,151 | 25 | 23 | 2 |
| Woodbury | 3,007 | 10 | 10 | 0 |
| **TEXAS** | | | | |
| Abernathy | 2,678 | 5 | 5 | 0 |
| Abilene | 125,088 | 285 | 210 | 75 |
| Addison | 16,540 | 76 | 66 | 10 |
| Alamo | 20,779 | 43 | 32 | 11 |
| Alamo Heights | 8,848 | 33 | 21 | 12 |
| Alba | 555 | 2 | 2 | 0 |
| Alice | 18,538 | 45 | 33 | 12 |
| Alpine | 6,037 | 15 | 9 | 6 |
| Alvarado | 4,722 | 18 | 16 | 2 |
| Alvin | 27,448 | 83 | 53 | 30 |
| Amarillo | 200,515 | 405 | 345 | 60 |
| Andrews | 14,699 | 24 | 19 | 5 |
| Angleton | 19,593 | 51 | 34 | 17 |
| Anna | 18,215 | 30 | 29 | 1 |
| Anthony | 5,279 | 19 | 19 | 0 |

## Table 78. Full-Time Law Enforcement Employees, by Selected State and City, 2020—Continued

(Number.)

| State/city | Population | Total law enforcement employees | Total officers | Total civilians |
|---|---|---|---|---|
| Aransas Pass | 8,531 | 43 | 29 | 14 |
| Archer City | 1,711 | 2 | 2 | 0 |
| Arcola | 2,925 | 9 | 9 | 0 |
| Argyle | 4,781 | 14 | 13 | 1 |
| Arlington | 402,323 | 860 | 674 | 186 |
| Arp | 1,054 | 8 | 7 | 1 |
| Athens | 12,778 | 33 | 25 | 8 |
| Atlanta | 5,402 | 16 | 10 | 6 |
| Aubrey | 7,080 | 22 | 21 | 1 |
| Austin | 1,016,721 | 2,087 | 1,613 | 474 |
| Azle | 13,917 | 39 | 29 | 10 |
| Baird | 1,497 | 3 | 3 | 0 |
| Balch Springs | 24,746 | 47 | 34 | 13 |
| Balcones Heights | 3,174 | 26 | 18 | 8 |
| Ballinger | 3,681 | 10 | 8 | 2 |
| Bartonville | 1,871 | 3 | 3 | 0 |
| Bastrop | 10,020 | 26 | 22 | 4 |
| Bay City | 17,441 | 55 | 36 | 19 |
| Baytown | 77,816 | 212 | 160 | 52 |
| Beaumont | 115,290 | 319 | 243 | 76 |
| Bedford | 48,483 | 116 | 75 | 41 |
| Beeville | 14,160 | 28 | 19 | 9 |
| Bellaire | 19,114 | 56 | 41 | 15 |
| Bellmead | 10,927 | 28 | 20 | 8 |
| Bells | 1,528 | 4 | 4 | 0 |
| Bellville | 4,214 | 12 | 11 | 1 |
| Belton | 23,731 | 56 | 43 | 13 |
| Benbrook | 23,529 | 48 | 37 | 11 |
| Bertram | 1,539 | 7 | 7 | 0 |
| Big Sandy | 1,418 | 5 | 5 | 0 |
| Big Spring | 28,166 | 46 | 35 | 11 |
| Blanco | 2,194 | 11 | 10 | 1 |
| Blue Mound | 2,411 | 12 | 7 | 5 |
| Boerne | 20,209 | 57 | 39 | 18 |
| Bogata | 1,054 | 5 | 5 | 0 |
| Bonham | 10,506 | 28 | 19 | 9 |
| Borger | 12,121 | 27 | 25 | 2 |
| Bovina | 1,744 | 3 | 3 | 0 |
| Bowie | 5,133 | 21 | 15 | 6 |
| Boyd | 1,594 | 7 | 6 | 1 |
| Brady | 5,147 | 14 | 13 | 1 |
| Brazoria | 3,066 | 11 | 8 | 3 |
| Breckenridge | 5,365 | 16 | 10 | 6 |
| Bremond | 966 | 3 | 3 | 0 |
| Brenham | 17,940 | 41 | 36 | 5 |
| Bridge City | 7,809 | 21 | 15 | 6 |
| Bridgeport | 6,711 | 23 | 15 | 8 |
| Brookshire | 6,248 | 22 | 17 | 5 |
| Brownfield | 9,194 | 25 | 18 | 7 |
| Brownsboro | 1,321 | 4 | 4 | 0 |
| Brownsville | 184,287 | 301 | 226 | 75 |
| Brownwood | 18,105 | 58 | 36 | 22 |
| Bruceville-Eddy | 1,712 | 3 | 3 | 0 |
| Bryan | 89,423 | 173 | 143 | 30 |
| Buda | 19,130 | 27 | 24 | 3 |
| Buffalo | 1,916 | 3 | 3 | 0 |
| Bullard | 4,071 | 14 | 12 | 2 |
| Bulverde | 5,593 | 18 | 17 | 1 |
| Burkburnett | 11,465 | 23 | 16 | 7 |
| Burleson | 51,167 | 94 | 82 | 12 |
| Burnet | 6,598 | 21 | 18 | 3 |
| Cactus | 3,239 | 12 | 9 | 3 |
| Caddo Mills | 1,749 | 9 | 9 | 0 |
| Caldwell | 4,535 | 11 | 10 | 1 |
| Calvert | 1,132 | 4 | 4 | 0 |
| Cameron | 5,399 | 15 | 11 | 4 |
| Canyon | 16,726 | 29 | 26 | 3 |
| Carrollton | 141,694 | 229 | 174 | 55 |
| Carthage | 6,314 | 22 | 17 | 5 |
| Castle Hills | 4,480 | 31 | 23 | 8 |
| Castroville | 3,243 | 10 | 9 | 1 |
| Cedar Hill | 47,764 | 86 | 70 | 16 |
| Cedar Park | 84,131 | 126 | 90 | 36 |
| Celina | 22,521 | 33 | 30 | 3 |
| Center | 5,014 | 25 | 18 | 7 |
| Chandler | 3,271 | 8 | 8 | 0 |
| Childress | 5,880 | 12 | 11 | 1 |
| China Grove | 1,329 | 6 | 6 | 0 |
| Cibolo | 35,139 | 46 | 41 | 5 |
| Cisco | 3,848 | 12 | 10 | 2 |
| Cleburne | 32,248 | 69 | 52 | 17 |
| Clifton | 3,406 | 8 | 7 | 1 |
| Clint | 1,138 | 4 | 4 | 0 |
| Clute | 11,774 | 37 | 25 | 12 |
| Cockrell Hill | 4,048 | 22 | 16 | 6 |

## Table 78. Full-Time Law Enforcement Employees, by Selected State and City, 2020—Continued

(Number.)

| State/city | Population | Total law enforcement employees | Total officers | Total civilians |
|---|---|---|---|---|
| Coffee City | 301 | 4 | 4 | 0 |
| Coleman | 4,159 | 6 | 6 | 0 |
| College Station | 122,051 | 201 | 146 | 55 |
| Colleyville | 27,544 | 44 | 39 | 5 |
| Collinsville | 2,023 | 4 | 4 | 0 |
| Columbus | 3,703 | 12 | 11 | 1 |
| Comanche | 4,209 | 13 | 10 | 3 |
| Combes | 3,055 | 7 | 7 | 0 |
| Commerce | 9,878 | 22 | 17 | 5 |
| Conroe | 99,965 | 193 | 151 | 42 |
| Converse | 29,635 | 51 | 46 | 5 |
| Coppell | 40,889 | 61 | 54 | 7 |
| Copperas Cove | 33,613 | 68 | 52 | 16 |
| Corinth | 22,635 | 37 | 32 | 5 |
| Corpus Christi | 329,538 | 594 | 425 | 169 |
| Corrigan | 1,708 | 15 | 10 | 5 |
| Corsicana | 23,808 | 53 | 39 | 14 |
| Crandall | 4,418 | 19 | 19 | 0 |
| Crane | 3,681 | 14 | 9 | 5 |
| Crockett | 6,295 | 14 | 12 | 2 |
| Crowley | 18,146 | 38 | 26 | 12 |
| Cuero | 8,225 | 16 | 15 | 1 |
| Cuney | 140 | 3 | 2 | 1 |
| Daingerfield | 2,377 | 6 | 5 | 1 |
| Dallas | 1,349,185 | 3,761 | 3,118 | 643 |
| Dawson | 797 | 1 | 1 | 0 |
| Dayton | 8,767 | 31 | 19 | 12 |
| Decatur | 7,747 | 31 | 24 | 7 |
| Deer Park | 32,998 | 89 | 60 | 29 |
| De Leon | 2,192 | 4 | 4 | 0 |
| Denison | 26,119 | 67 | 50 | 17 |
| Denton | 150,975 | 272 | 191 | 81 |
| Denver City | 4,928 | 15 | 9 | 6 |
| DeSoto | 52,891 | 115 | 79 | 36 |
| Devine | 4,998 | 15 | 11 | 4 |
| Diboll | 5,096 | 16 | 11 | 5 |
| Dickinson | 21,442 | 46 | 31 | 15 |
| Dimmitt | 3,966 | 9 | 7 | 2 |
| Donna | 16,371 | 50 | 36 | 14 |
| Double Oak | 3,124 | 8 | 8 | 0 |
| Driscoll | 740 | 2 | 2 | 0 |
| Dublin | 3,546 | 10 | 9 | 1 |
| Dumas | 13,503 | 28 | 23 | 5 |
| Duncanville | 37,869 | 66 | 58 | 8 |
| Earth | 940 | 1 | 1 | 0 |
| Eastland | 3,853 | 13 | 11 | 2 |
| Edgewood | 1,578 | 4 | 4 | 0 |
| Edinburg | 104,604 | 230 | 171 | 59 |
| Edna | 5,787 | 10 | 8 | 2 |
| El Campo | 11,484 | 39 | 27 | 12 |
| Electra | 2,732 | 13 | 8 | 5 |
| Elmendorf | 2,198 | 5 | 4 | 1 |
| El Paso | 684,737 | 1,395 | 1,138 | 257 |
| Elsa | 7,205 | 24 | 18 | 6 |
| Emory | 1,384 | 6 | 4 | 2 |
| Ennis | 20,893 | 44 | 35 | 9 |
| Euless | 57,963 | 136 | 88 | 48 |
| Everman | 6,136 | 23 | 17 | 6 |
| Fair Oaks Ranch | 10,798 | 24 | 21 | 3 |
| Fairview | 9,595 | 17 | 17 | 0 |
| Farmers Branch | 54,026 | 93 | 72 | 21 |
| Farmersville | 3,754 | 10 | 8 | 2 |
| Farwell | 1,267 | 2 | 2 | 0 |
| Fate | 18,907 | 22 | 20 | 2 |
| Ferris | 3,143 | 16 | 11 | 5 |
| Florence | 1,321 | 4 | 4 | 0 |
| Floresville | 8,339 | 19 | 18 | 1 |
| Flower Mound | 83,367 | 144 | 104 | 40 |
| Floydada | 2,621 | 6 | 6 | 0 |
| Forney | 31,521 | 40 | 27 | 13 |
| Fort Stockton | 8,375 | 29 | 19 | 10 |
| Fort Worth | 947,862 | 2,088 | 1,631 | 457 |
| Franklin | 1,646 | 5 | 5 | 0 |
| Frankston | 1,150 | 7 | 7 | 0 |
| Fredericksburg | 11,620 | 41 | 35 | 6 |
| Freeport | 12,132 | 46 | 32 | 14 |
| Friendswood | 40,434 | 78 | 59 | 19 |
| Friona | 3,741 | 9 | 5 | 4 |
| Frisco | 222,416 | 309 | 216 | 93 |
| Fulshear | 17,318 | 26 | 24 | 2 |
| Gainesville | 16,967 | 58 | 43 | 15 |
| Galena Park | 10,525 | 16 | 14 | 2 |
| Galveston | 50,321 | 171 | 141 | 30 |
| Ganado | 2,094 | 3 | 3 | 0 |
| Garden Ridge | 4,379 | 12 | 11 | 1 |

## Table 78. Full-Time Law Enforcement Employees, by Selected State and City, 2020—Continued

(Number.)

| State/city | Population | Total law enforcement employees | Total officers | Total civilians |
|---|---|---|---|---|
| Garland | 237,510 | 472 | 343 | 129 |
| Garrison | 867 | 1 | 1 | 0 |
| Gatesville | 12,558 | 33 | 21 | 12 |
| Georgetown | 90,629 | 115 | 84 | 31 |
| Giddings | 5,175 | 19 | 13 | 6 |
| Gilmer | 5,217 | 19 | 15 | 4 |
| Gladewater | 6,347 | 22 | 17 | 5 |
| Glenn Heights | 14,610 | 29 | 22 | 7 |
| Godley | 1,809 | 6 | 6 | 0 |
| Gonzales | 7,633 | 26 | 21 | 5 |
| Gorman | 1,028 | 2 | 2 | 0 |
| Graham | 8,536 | 19 | 17 | 2 |
| Granbury | 11,466 | 47 | 41 | 6 |
| Grand Prairie | 196,334 | 440 | 278 | 162 |
| Grand Saline | 3,223 | 11 | 10 | 1 |
| Granger | 1,523 | 3 | 3 | 0 |
| Grapeland | 1,423 | 4 | 4 | 0 |
| Grapevine | 56,795 | 148 | 92 | 56 |
| Greenville | 29,780 | 73 | 53 | 20 |
| Groesbeck | 4,162 | 9 | 9 | 0 |
| Groves | 15,187 | 25 | 21 | 4 |
| Gun Barrel City | 6,377 | 20 | 16 | 4 |
| Gunter | 1,776 | 6 | 6 | 0 |
| Hallettsville | 2,651 | 9 | 8 | 1 |
| Hallsville | 4,496 | 6 | 6 | 0 |
| Haltom City | 43,840 | 80 | 75 | 5 |
| Hamilton | 3,019 | 9 | 8 | 1 |
| Hamlin | 1,984 | 9 | 5 | 4 |
| Harker Heights | 33,752 | 61 | 45 | 16 |
| Harlingen | 65,186 | 180 | 134 | 46 |
| Haskell | 3,194 | 6 | 5 | 1 |
| Hawkins | 1,353 | 4 | 3 | 1 |
| Hearne | 4,331 | 19 | 13 | 6 |
| Heath | 9,996 | 26 | 25 | 1 |
| Hedwig Village | 2,605 | 23 | 17 | 6 |
| Helotes | 10,627 | 31 | 30 | 1 |
| Hempstead | 9,214 | 26 | 19 | 7 |
| Henderson | 12,989 | 45 | 36 | 9 |
| Hereford | 14,288 | 35 | 27 | 8 |
| Hewitt | 15,272 | 41 | 29 | 12 |
| Hickory Creek | 5,193 | 13 | 13 | 0 |
| Hico | 1,443 | 5 | 5 | 0 |
| Hidalgo | 14,488 | 43 | 33 | 10 |
| Highland Park | 9,032 | 75 | 61 | 14 |
| Highland Village | 17,071 | 41 | 29 | 12 |
| Hill Country Village | 1,122 | 15 | 11 | 4 |
| Hillsboro | 8,525 | 32 | 22 | 10 |
| Hitchcock | 7,983 | 18 | 17 | 1 |
| Hollywood Park | 3,351 | 16 | 15 | 1 |
| Hondo | 9,564 | 24 | 22 | 2 |
| Honey Grove | 1,746 | 6 | 6 | 0 |
| Hooks | 2,703 | 7 | 7 | 0 |
| Horseshoe Bay | 4,227 | 25 | 21 | 4 |
| Houston | 2,339,252 | 6,249 | 5,250 | 999 |
| Howe | 3,482 | 7 | 6 | 1 |
| Hudson Oaks | 3,857 | 12 | 11 | 1 |
| Hughes Springs | 1,664 | 5 | 5 | 0 |
| Humble | 15,579 | 77 | 61 | 16 |
| Huntington | 2,076 | 5 | 5 | 0 |
| Huntsville | 41,671 | 71 | 61 | 10 |
| Hutchins | 6,048 | 27 | 20 | 7 |
| Hutto | 31,792 | 48 | 44 | 4 |
| Idalou | 2,314 | 5 | 5 | 0 |
| Ingleside | 10,188 | 34 | 24 | 10 |
| Ingram | 1,881 | 8 | 7 | 1 |
| Iowa Colony | 5,771 | 9 | 8 | 1 |
| Iowa Park | 6,435 | 18 | 12 | 6 |
| Irving | 241,692 | 553 | 380 | 173 |
| Italy | 1,972 | 9 | 8 | 1 |
| Itasca | 1,797 | 6 | 6 | 0 |
| Jacinto City | 10,276 | 27 | 21 | 6 |
| Jacksboro | 4,443 | 8 | 7 | 1 |
| Jacksonville | 14,855 | 45 | 31 | 14 |
| Jamaica Beach | 1,085 | 7 | 7 | 0 |
| Jarrell | 2,228 | 9 | 8 | 1 |
| Jasper | 7,600 | 28 | 21 | 7 |
| Jefferson | 1,909 | 4 | 3 | 1 |
| Jersey Village | 7,782 | 27 | 24 | 3 |
| Jonestown | 2,207 | 12 | 11 | 1 |
| Joshua | 8,411 | 17 | 16 | 1 |
| Jourdanton | 4,495 | 7 | 6 | 1 |
| Junction | 2,421 | 9 | 7 | 2 |
| Karnes City | 3,441 | 8 | 7 | 1 |
| Katy | 25,183 | 110 | 91 | 19 |
| Kaufman | 8,804 | 19 | 16 | 3 |

## Table 78. Full-Time Law Enforcement Employees, by Selected State and City, 2020—Continued

(Number.)

| State/city | Population | Total law enforcement employees | Total officers | Total civilians |
|---|---|---|---|---|
| Keene | 6,637 | 13 | 12 | 1 |
| Keller | 47,721 | 84 | 47 | 37 |
| Kemah | 2,076 | 28 | 21 | 7 |
| Kemp | 1,273 | 5 | 4 | 1 |
| Kempner | 1,167 | 6 | 5 | 1 |
| Kenedy | 3,396 | 15 | 14 | 1 |
| Kennedale | 8,829 | 19 | 16 | 3 |
| Kerens | 1,515 | 4 | 4 | 0 |
| Kermit | 6,441 | 16 | 11 | 5 |
| Kerrville | 23,982 | 67 | 46 | 21 |
| Kilgore | 15,004 | 45 | 33 | 12 |
| Killeen | 156,741 | 284 | 230 | 54 |
| Kingsville | 24,850 | 61 | 42 | 19 |
| Kirby | 8,792 | 16 | 13 | 3 |
| Knox City | 1,119 | 2 | 2 | 0 |
| Kountze | 2,106 | 6 | 5 | 1 |
| Kyle | 54,692 | 87 | 51 | 36 |
| Lacy-Lakeview | 6,836 | 22 | 12 | 10 |
| La Feria | 7,243 | 15 | 12 | 3 |
| Lago Vista | 8,158 | 20 | 15 | 5 |
| La Grange | 4,684 | 12 | 11 | 1 |
| La Grulla | 1,688 | 8 | 6 | 2 |
| Laguna Vista | 3,223 | 8 | 8 | 0 |
| Lake Dallas | 8,230 | 14 | 11 | 3 |
| Lake Jackson | 27,088 | 65 | 48 | 17 |
| Lakeport | 999 | 3 | 3 | 0 |
| Lakeside | 1,594 | 7 | 7 | 0 |
| Lakeview, Harrison County | 6,214 | 14 | 13 | 1 |
| Lakeway | 16,747 | 51 | 35 | 16 |
| Lake Worth | 4,886 | 38 | 29 | 9 |
| La Marque | 17,984 | 43 | 35 | 8 |
| Lampasas | 8,269 | 32 | 21 | 11 |
| Lancaster | 39,235 | 61 | 56 | 5 |
| La Porte | 35,972 | 110 | 80 | 30 |
| Laredo | 266,489 | 602 | 510 | 92 |
| La Villa | 2,989 | 8 | 8 | 0 |
| Lavon | 4,235 | 13 | 13 | 0 |
| League City | 111,279 | 170 | 125 | 45 |
| Leander | 77,457 | 89 | 66 | 23 |
| Leonard | 2,077 | 5 | 5 | 0 |
| Leon Valley | 12,431 | 38 | 36 | 2 |
| Levelland | 13,495 | 33 | 24 | 9 |
| Lewisville | 113,998 | 247 | 171 | 76 |
| Liberty | 9,621 | 29 | 18 | 11 |
| Liberty Hill | 4,076 | 16 | 15 | 1 |
| Lindale | 6,956 | 25 | 18 | 7 |
| Linden | 1,880 | 6 | 5 | 1 |
| Little Elm | 61,181 | 86 | 79 | 7 |
| Littlefield | 5,696 | 20 | 13 | 7 |
| Live Oak | 17,051 | 46 | 34 | 12 |
| Livingston | 5,533 | 30 | 22 | 8 |
| Llano | 3,535 | 10 | 9 | 1 |
| Lockhart | 14,209 | 37 | 26 | 11 |
| Lockney | 1,600 | 4 | 3 | 1 |
| Log Cabin | 792 | 4 | 4 | 0 |
| Lone Star | 1,463 | 3 | 3 | 0 |
| Longview | 81,846 | 207 | 162 | 45 |
| Lorena | 1,762 | 8 | 7 | 1 |
| Los Fresnos | 7,908 | 25 | 25 | 0 |
| Lubbock | 265,990 | 535 | 421 | 114 |
| Lufkin | 34,934 | 86 | 69 | 17 |
| Luling | 5,874 | 20 | 11 | 9 |
| Lumberton | 13,528 | 21 | 18 | 3 |
| Lytle | 3,122 | 9 | 8 | 1 |
| Madisonville | 4,819 | 15 | 11 | 4 |
| Magnolia | 2,331 | 17 | 14 | 3 |
| Manor | 17,725 | 33 | 28 | 5 |
| Mansfield | 74,925 | 156 | 99 | 57 |
| Manvel | 15,262 | 30 | 22 | 8 |
| Marble Falls | 7,231 | 39 | 25 | 14 |
| Marfa | 1,555 | 4 | 4 | 0 |
| Marion | 1,305 | 3 | 3 | 0 |
| Marlin | 5,510 | 14 | 10 | 4 |
| Marshall | 22,425 | 65 | 50 | 15 |
| Maud | 1,062 | 1 | 1 | 0 |
| Maypearl | 1,060 | 4 | 4 | 0 |
| McAllen | 144,973 | 418 | 275 | 143 |
| McKinney | 217,841 | 295 | 225 | 70 |
| Meadows Place | 4,806 | 18 | 17 | 1 |
| Melissa | 15,322 | 16 | 16 | 0 |
| Memorial Villages | 12,243 | 43 | 30 | 13 |
| Memphis | 1,969 | 2 | 2 | 0 |
| Mercedes | 16,684 | 44 | 38 | 6 |
| Meridian | 1,501 | 3 | 3 | 0 |
| Merkel | 2,633 | 4 | 4 | 0 |

## Table 78. Full-Time Law Enforcement Employees, by Selected State and City, 2020—Continued

(Number.)

| State/city | Population | Total law enforcement employees | Total officers | Total civilians |
|---|---|---|---|---|
| Mesquite | 137,796 | 313 | 232 | 81 |
| Mexia | 7,269 | 16 | 14 | 2 |
| Midland | 151,243 | 251 | 164 | 87 |
| Midlothian | 36,655 | 102 | 68 | 34 |
| Miles | 898 | 2 | 2 | 0 |
| Mineola | 4,998 | 23 | 15 | 8 |
| Mineral Wells | 15,079 | 45 | 32 | 13 |
| Mission | 85,163 | 205 | 164 | 41 |
| Missouri City | 77,682 | 127 | 100 | 27 |
| Monahans | 7,959 | 21 | 14 | 7 |
| Mont Belvieu | 7,567 | 23 | 15 | 8 |
| Montgomery | 1,812 | 15 | 14 | 1 |
| Morgans Point Resort | 4,844 | 9 | 9 | 0 |
| Moulton | 905 | 4 | 4 | 0 |
| Mount Enterprise | 432 | 1 | 1 | 0 |
| Mount Pleasant | 16,023 | 46 | 33 | 13 |
| Mount Vernon | 2,765 | 8 | 8 | 0 |
| Muleshoe | 4,788 | 14 | 6 | 8 |
| Murphy | 21,147 | 29 | 21 | 8 |
| Mustang Ridge | 1,021 | 4 | 4 | 0 |
| Nacogdoches | 32,421 | 84 | 58 | 26 |
| Nash | 3,882 | 7 | 7 | 0 |
| Nassau Bay | 3,897 | 15 | 14 | 1 |
| Natalia | 1,643 | 4 | 4 | 0 |
| Navasota | 8,514 | 27 | 18 | 9 |
| Nederland | 17,205 | 43 | 28 | 15 |
| Needville | 3,150 | 8 | 8 | 0 |
| New Boston | 4,546 | 17 | 12 | 5 |
| New Braunfels | 100,427 | 172 | 139 | 33 |
| Newton | 2,315 | 4 | 4 | 0 |
| Nolanville | 6,335 | 12 | 11 | 1 |
| Northeast | 3,582 | 6 | 6 | 0 |
| Northlake | 4,751 | 23 | 21 | 2 |
| North Richland Hills | 72,881 | 206 | 112 | 94 |
| Oak Ridge, Kaufman County | 851 | 27 | 27 | 0 |
| Oak Ridge North | 3,168 | 16 | 16 | 0 |
| Odem | 2,375 | 6 | 6 | 0 |
| Odessa | 128,328 | 192 | 147 | 45 |
| Olmos Park | 2,484 | 14 | 13 | 1 |
| Olney | 3,054 | 10 | 8 | 2 |
| Onalaska | 3,225 | 9 | 9 | 0 |
| Orange | 17,755 | 60 | 44 | 16 |
| Overton | 2,498 | 7 | 6 | 1 |
| Ovilla | 4,370 | 12 | 11 | 1 |
| Oyster Creek | 1,222 | 13 | 9 | 4 |
| Palacios | 4,529 | 13 | 8 | 5 |
| Palestine | 17,736 | 50 | 33 | 17 |
| Palmer | 2,185 | 11 | 10 | 1 |
| Palmhurst | 2,735 | 17 | 12 | 5 |
| Pampa | 16,760 | 30 | 28 | 2 |
| Panhandle | 2,256 | 4 | 4 | 0 |
| Pantego | 2,505 | 18 | 13 | 5 |
| Paris | 24,833 | 68 | 43 | 25 |
| Parker | 5,649 | 11 | 10 | 1 |
| Pasadena | 149,428 | 367 | 274 | 93 |
| Patton Village | 2,277 | 10 | 10 | 0 |
| Payne Springs | 757 | 2 | 2 | 0 |
| Pearland | 126,983 | 230 | 169 | 61 |
| Pearsall | 10,776 | 19 | 15 | 4 |
| Pecos | 10,675 | 55 | 24 | 31 |
| Pelican Bay | 2,165 | 9 | 9 | 0 |
| Penitas | 4,625 | 16 | 15 | 1 |
| Perryton | 8,272 | 20 | 11 | 9 |
| Petersburg | 1,102 | 4 | 4 | 0 |
| Pflugerville | 68,978 | 127 | 86 | 41 |
| Pharr | 80,436 | 162 | 132 | 30 |
| Pilot Point | 4,741 | 10 | 10 | 0 |
| Pinehurst | 1,946 | 8 | 6 | 2 |
| Pineland | 789 | 3 | 3 | 0 |
| Pittsburg | 4,696 | 10 | 8 | 2 |
| Plainview | 19,436 | 37 | 30 | 7 |
| Plano | 294,496 | 591 | 416 | 175 |
| Pleasanton | 11,160 | 26 | 22 | 4 |
| Ponder | 2,555 | 7 | 6 | 1 |
| Port Aransas | 4,513 | 29 | 20 | 9 |
| Port Arthur | 53,865 | 151 | 113 | 38 |
| Portland | 17,938 | 50 | 35 | 15 |
| Port Lavaca | 11,618 | 24 | 18 | 6 |
| Port Neches | 12,555 | 25 | 21 | 4 |
| Poteet | 3,571 | 10 | 9 | 1 |
| Prairie View | 7,174 | 12 | 11 | 1 |
| Primera | 5,394 | 10 | 9 | 1 |
| Princeton | 17,059 | 28 | 26 | 2 |
| Prosper | 29,848 | 51 | 35 | 16 |
| Queen City | 1,409 | 5 | 5 | 0 |

## Table 78. Full-Time Law Enforcement Employees, by Selected State and City, 2020—Continued

(Number.)

| State/city | Population | Total law enforcement employees | Total officers | Total civilians |
|---|---|---|---|---|
| Rancho Viejo | 2,447 | 8 | 8 | 0 |
| Ranger | 2,343 | 4 | 4 | 0 |
| Raymondville | 10,714 | 21 | 12 | 9 |
| Red Oak | 14,483 | 29 | 26 | 3 |
| Refugio | 2,694 | 8 | 6 | 2 |
| Reno, Lamar County | 3,366 | 6 | 5 | 1 |
| Rice | 991 | 4 | 4 | 0 |
| Richardson | 122,872 | 254 | 164 | 90 |
| Richland | 274 | 3 | 2 | 1 |
| Richland Hills | 7,846 | 22 | 19 | 3 |
| Richmond | 12,520 | 40 | 29 | 11 |
| Richwood | 4,068 | 11 | 11 | 0 |
| Rio Grande City | 14,498 | 44 | 31 | 13 |
| Rio Hondo | 2,669 | 7 | 7 | 0 |
| River Oaks | 7,550 | 23 | 17 | 6 |
| Roanoke | 10,234 | 45 | 34 | 11 |
| Robinson | 12,254 | 32 | 22 | 10 |
| Robstown | 11,114 | 29 | 20 | 9 |
| Rockdale | 5,444 | 17 | 12 | 5 |
| Rockport | 10,934 | 34 | 27 | 7 |
| Rockwall | 48,483 | 102 | 84 | 18 |
| Rogers | 1,255 | 3 | 3 | 0 |
| Rollingwood | 1,589 | 8 | 7 | 1 |
| Roma | 11,534 | 32 | 24 | 8 |
| Roman Forest | 2,086 | 12 | 11 | 1 |
| Roscoe | 1,302 | 2 | 2 | 0 |
| Rosenberg | 40,251 | 97 | 72 | 25 |
| Round Rock | 141,927 | 239 | 168 | 71 |
| Rowlett | 69,287 | 142 | 93 | 49 |
| Royse City | 16,013 | 29 | 26 | 3 |
| Runaway Bay | 1,665 | 5 | 5 | 0 |
| Rusk | 5,674 | 10 | 9 | 1 |
| Sachse | 26,463 | 46 | 31 | 15 |
| Saginaw | 25,387 | 50 | 38 | 12 |
| Salado | 2,401 | 5 | 5 | 0 |
| San Angelo | 102,448 | 204 | 174 | 30 |
| San Antonio | 1,592,693 | 2,982 | 2,381 | 601 |
| San Augustine | 1,842 | 9 | 8 | 1 |
| San Benito | 24,065 | 49 | 40 | 9 |
| San Elizario | 9,041 | 3 | 3 | 0 |
| Sanger | 9,383 | 18 | 16 | 2 |
| San Marcos | 68,961 | 146 | 106 | 40 |
| San Saba | 3,135 | 5 | 5 | 0 |
| Sansom Park Village | 5,826 | 14 | 8 | 6 |
| Santa Anna | 995 | 4 | 4 | 0 |
| Santa Fe | 13,583 | 30 | 23 | 7 |
| Savoy | 867 | 2 | 2 | 0 |
| Schertz | 43,637 | 93 | 62 | 31 |
| Schulenburg | 2,944 | 9 | 8 | 1 |
| Seabrook | 14,102 | 39 | 30 | 9 |
| Seagoville | 17,291 | 38 | 25 | 13 |
| Sealy | 6,478 | 28 | 24 | 4 |
| Seguin | 30,653 | 73 | 52 | 21 |
| Selma | 14,299 | 34 | 30 | 4 |
| Seminole | 8,115 | 11 | 9 | 2 |
| Seymour | 2,541 | 4 | 2 | 2 |
| Shallowater | 2,628 | 5 | 5 | 0 |
| Shavano Park | 4,137 | 22 | 21 | 1 |
| Shenandoah | 3,217 | 27 | 26 | 1 |
| Sherman | 45,814 | 99 | 67 | 32 |
| Silsbee | 6,604 | 23 | 17 | 6 |
| Sinton | 5,248 | 13 | 12 | 1 |
| Slaton | 5,960 | 16 | 10 | 6 |
| Smithville | 4,759 | 19 | 12 | 7 |
| Snyder | 10,986 | 20 | 17 | 3 |
| Socorro | 36,282 | 60 | 44 | 16 |
| Somerset | 2,017 | 4 | 4 | 0 |
| Somerville | 1,450 | 3 | 3 | 0 |
| Sonora | 2,744 | 8 | 6 | 2 |
| Sour Lake | 1,962 | 10 | 8 | 2 |
| South Houston | 17,490 | 36 | 24 | 12 |
| Southlake | 32,905 | 68 | 60 | 8 |
| South Padre Island | 2,744 | 36 | 26 | 10 |
| Southside Place | 1,902 | 10 | 6 | 4 |
| Spearman | 3,161 | 4 | 4 | 0 |
| Splendora | 2,371 | 16 | 14 | 2 |
| Spring Valley | 4,363 | 26 | 20 | 6 |
| Stafford | 17,102 | 73 | 55 | 18 |
| Stamford | 2,892 | 7 | 6 | 1 |
| Stanton | 3,114 | 7 | 6 | 1 |
| Stephenville | 22,221 | 55 | 33 | 22 |
| Stinnett | 1,742 | 4 | 4 | 0 |
| Sudan | 871 | 1 | 1 | 0 |
| Sugar Land | 118,888 | 186 | 155 | 31 |
| Sulphur Springs | 16,357 | 38 | 28 | 10 |

# Table 78. Full-Time Law Enforcement Employees, by Selected State and City, 2020—Continued

(Number.)

| State/city | Population | Total law enforcement employees | Total officers | Total civilians |
|---|---|---|---|---|
| Sunnyvale | 7,232 | 22 | 21 | 1 |
| Sunrise Beach Village | 820 | 5 | 5 | 0 |
| Sunset Valley | 663 | 13 | 12 | 1 |
| Surfside Beach | 601 | 8 | 8 | 0 |
| Sweeny | 3,612 | 9 | 8 | 1 |
| Sweetwater | 10,497 | 33 | 24 | 9 |
| Taft | 2,871 | 9 | 7 | 2 |
| Tahoka | 2,664 | 4 | 4 | 0 |
| Tatum | 1,417 | 4 | 4 | 0 |
| Taylor | 18,196 | 40 | 28 | 12 |
| Teague | 3,524 | 6 | 6 | 0 |
| Temple | 82,333 | 176 | 142 | 34 |
| Tenaha | 1,132 | 2 | 2 | 0 |
| Terrell | 20,092 | 59 | 38 | 21 |
| Terrell Hills | 5,510 | 16 | 16 | 0 |
| Texarkana | 36,208 | 99 | 87 | 12 |
| Texas City | 52,270 | 112 | 86 | 26 |
| Thorndale | 1,303 | 3 | 3 | 0 |
| Tioga | 1,153 | 4 | 4 | 0 |
| Tomball | 11,826 | 64 | 46 | 18 |
| Tom Bean | 1,076 | 3 | 3 | 0 |
| Tool | 2,346 | 8 | 4 | 4 |
| Trophy Club | 13,205 | 22 | 18 | 4 |
| Tulia | 4,568 | 16 | 9 | 7 |
| Tye | 1,353 | 7 | 5 | 2 |
| Tyler | 109,408 | 236 | 191 | 45 |
| Universal City | 21,265 | 37 | 27 | 10 |
| University Park | 24,888 | 54 | 38 | 16 |
| Uvalde | 15,999 | 56 | 40 | 16 |
| Valley Mills | 1,168 | 4 | 4 | 0 |
| Van | 2,793 | 9 | 9 | 0 |
| Van Alstyne | 4,831 | 19 | 13 | 6 |
| Venus | 4,804 | 14 | 14 | 0 |
| Vernon | 10,057 | 29 | 20 | 9 |
| Victoria | 67,272 | 150 | 120 | 30 |
| Vidor | 10,267 | 33 | 31 | 2 |
| Waco | 143,089 | 349 | 253 | 96 |
| Waelder | 1,164 | 5 | 4 | 1 |
| Wake Village | 5,538 | 9 | 8 | 1 |
| Waller | 3,732 | 13 | 11 | 2 |
| Wallis | 1,334 | 7 | 7 | 0 |
| Watauga | 24,254 | 48 | 36 | 12 |
| Waxahachie | 40,978 | 106 | 79 | 27 |
| Weatherford | 35,724 | 82 | 58 | 24 |
| Webster | 11,359 | 67 | 48 | 19 |
| Weimar | 2,238 | 8 | 7 | 1 |
| Weslaco | 43,954 | 104 | 79 | 25 |
| West | 2,991 | 8 | 8 | 0 |
| West Columbia | 3,823 | 17 | 11 | 6 |
| West Lake Hills | 3,272 | 15 | 14 | 1 |
| West Orange | 3,141 | 12 | 10 | 2 |
| West University Place | 15,590 | 33 | 24 | 9 |
| Westworth | 2,810 | 18 | 13 | 5 |
| Wharton | 8,590 | 32 | 23 | 9 |
| Whitehouse | 9,260 | 15 | 14 | 1 |
| White Oak | 6,262 | 20 | 16 | 4 |
| White Settlement | 17,948 | 41 | 32 | 9 |
| Whitewright | 1,746 | 3 | 3 | 0 |
| Whitney | 2,151 | 6 | 6 | 0 |
| Wichita Falls | 105,468 | 265 | 197 | 68 |
| Willis | 7,258 | 17 | 15 | 2 |
| Willow Park | 6,244 | 19 | 18 | 1 |
| Wills Point | 3,723 | 10 | 9 | 1 |
| Wilmer | 5,620 | 26 | 21 | 5 |
| Windcrest | 5,901 | 39 | 27 | 12 |
| Wink | 1,022 | 2 | 2 | 0 |
| Winnsboro | 3,338 | 16 | 12 | 4 |
| Winters | 2,460 | 7 | 6 | 1 |
| Wolfforth | 5,973 | 14 | 13 | 1 |
| Woodsboro | 1,363 | 1 | 1 | 0 |
| Woodville | 2,428 | 11 | 10 | 1 |
| Woodway | 9,141 | 46 | 32 | 14 |
| Wortham | 1,000 | 4 | 4 | 0 |
| Wylie | 55,889 | 81 | 64 | 17 |
| Yoakum | 5,949 | 16 | 11 | 5 |
| Zavalla | 712 | 3 | 3 | 0 |
| **UTAH** | | | | |
| Alta | 376 | 8 | 4 | 4 |
| American Fork/Cedar Hills | 44,725 | 53 | 47 | 6 |
| Big Water | 510 | 1 | 1 | 0 |
| Blanding | 3,580 | 6 | 5 | 1 |
| Bluffdale | 19,428 | 14 | 14 | 0 |
| Bountiful | 44,048 | 57 | 37 | 20 |
| Brian Head | 96 | 15 | 7 | 8 |

## Table 78. Full-Time Law Enforcement Employees, by Selected State and City, 2020—Continued

(Number.)

| State/city | Population | Total law enforcement employees | Total officers | Total civilians |
|---|---|---|---|---|
| Brigham City | 19,901 | 29 | 24 | 5 |
| Cedar City | 36,903 | 46 | 39 | 7 |
| Centerville | 17,765 | 22 | 19 | 3 |
| Clearfield | 32,375 | 45 | 29 | 16 |
| Clinton | 22,957 | 22 | 21 | 1 |
| Cottonwood Heights | 33,301 | 48 | 39 | 9 |
| Draper | 49,671 | 54 | 44 | 10 |
| East Carbon | 1,601 | 4 | 4 | 0 |
| Enoch | 7,780 | 13 | 7 | 6 |
| Ephraim | 7,521 | 9 | 8 | 1 |
| Fairview | 1,395 | 1 | 1 | 0 |
| Farmington | 26,218 | 25 | 22 | 3 |
| Fountain Green | 1,194 | 1 | 1 | 0 |
| Grantsville | 12,819 | 19 | 16 | 3 |
| Harrisville | 6,983 | 9 | 8 | 1 |
| Heber | 18,336 | 26 | 20 | 6 |
| Helper | 2,135 | 5 | 4 | 1 |
| Herriman | 61,086 | 47 | 39 | 8 |
| Hildale | 2,962 | 11 | 9 | 2 |
| Hurricane | 20,594 | 28 | 25 | 3 |
| Kamas | 2,399 | 2 | 2 | 0 |
| Kanab | 5,045 | 9 | 8 | 1 |
| Kaysville | 33,139 | 35 | 32 | 3 |
| La Verkin | 4,503 | 6 | 5 | 1 |
| Layton | 80,230 | 106 | 71 | 35 |
| Lehi | 76,545 | 66 | 61 | 5 |
| Lindon | 11,609 | 17 | 15 | 2 |
| Logan | 52,015 | 83 | 54 | 29 |
| Lone Peak | 30,210 | 27 | 22 | 5 |
| Mapleton | 11,497 | 10 | 9 | 1 |
| Moab | 5,400 | 20 | 12 | 8 |
| Mount Pleasant | 3,613 | 5 | 5 | 0 |
| Murray | 48,524 | 84 | 73 | 11 |
| Naples | 2,150 | 7 | 7 | 0 |
| Nephi | 6,598 | 13 | 11 | 2 |
| North Ogden | 21,379 | 25 | 20 | 5 |
| North Park | 16,742 | 13 | 10 | 3 |
| North Salt Lake | 21,768 | 29 | 24 | 5 |
| Ogden | 87,828 | 165 | 125 | 40 |
| Orem | 100,060 | 134 | 96 | 38 |
| Park City | 8,679 | 37 | 32 | 5 |
| Parowan | 3,268 | 7 | 6 | 1 |
| Payson | 21,291 | 27 | 24 | 3 |
| Perry | 5,471 | 8 | 7 | 1 |
| Pleasant Grove | 38,730 | 32 | 28 | 4 |
| Pleasant View | 11,139 | 14 | 12 | 2 |
| Price | 8,399 | 19 | 16 | 3 |
| Provo | 116,642 | 127 | 98 | 29 |
| Richfield | 7,947 | 17 | 16 | 1 |
| Riverdale | 9,038 | 19 | 17 | 2 |
| Riverton | 44,951 | 39 | 35 | 4 |
| Roosevelt | 7,377 | 15 | 13 | 2 |
| Roy | 39,765 | 43 | 37 | 6 |
| Salem | 9,151 | 13 | 12 | 1 |
| Salina | 2,661 | 6 | 6 | 0 |
| Salt Lake City | 205,929 | 627 | 490 | 137 |
| Sandy | 95,353 | 143 | 110 | 33 |
| Santa Clara/Ivins | 18,948 | 18 | 14 | 4 |
| Santaquin/Genola | 15,647 | 15 | 13 | 2 |
| Saratoga Springs | 37,985 | 30 | 26 | 4 |
| Smithfield | 12,391 | 11 | 11 | 0 |
| South Jordan | 81,919 | 66 | 58 | 8 |
| South Ogden | 17,187 | 27 | 22 | 5 |
| South Salt Lake | 25,422 | 83 | 70 | 13 |
| Spanish Fork | 41,931 | 46 | 41 | 5 |
| Spring City | 1,111 | 1 | 1 | 0 |
| Springdale | 672 | 9 | 8 | 1 |
| Springville | 33,977 | 41 | 27 | 14 |
| St. George | 94,601 | 169 | 120 | 49 |
| Sunset | 5,354 | 10 | 8 | 2 |
| Syracuse | 33,340 | 26 | 24 | 2 |
| Tooele | 37,626 | 47 | 39 | 8 |
| Tremonton Garland | 12,280 | 17 | 15 | 2 |
| Vernal | 10,623 | 21 | 19 | 2 |
| Washington | 33,668 | 38 | 31 | 7 |
| Wellington | 1,642 | 2 | 2 | 0 |
| West Bountiful | 5,988 | 10 | 9 | 1 |
| West Jordan | 117,862 | 138 | 115 | 23 |
| West Valley | 134,329 | 248 | 203 | 45 |
| Willard | 2,022 | 5 | 4 | 1 |
| Woods Cross | 11,870 | 18 | 17 | 1 |
| **VERMONT** | | | | |
| Barre | 8,418 | 19 | 18 | 1 |
| Barre Town | 7,722 | 8 | 7 | 1 |

## Table 78. Full-Time Law Enforcement Employees, by Selected State and City, 2020—Continued

(Number.)

| State/city | Population | Total law enforcement employees | Total officers | Total civilians |
|---|---|---|---|---|
| Bellows Falls | 2,950 | 7 | 6 | 1 |
| Bennington | 14,814 | 31 | 24 | 7 |
| Berlin | 2,773 | 8 | 7 | 1 |
| Bradford | 2,673 | 2 | 2 | 0 |
| Brandon | 3,680 | 8 | 7 | 1 |
| Brattleboro | 11,182 | 31 | 18 | 13 |
| Brighton | 1,153 | 1 | 1 | 0 |
| Bristol | 3,831 | 3 | 3 | 0 |
| Burlington | 42,946 | 99 | 69 | 30 |
| Canaan | 906 | 1 | 1 | 0 |
| Castleton | 4,468 | 5 | 5 | 0 |
| Chester | 3,005 | 6 | 5 | 1 |
| Colchester | 17,101 | 33 | 25 | 8 |
| Dover | 1,051 | 7 | 6 | 1 |
| Essex | 22,073 | 34 | 28 | 6 |
| Fair Haven | 2,511 | 4 | 4 | 0 |
| Hardwick | 2,824 | 7 | 7 | 0 |
| Hartford | 9,530 | 27 | 17 | 10 |
| Hinesburg | 4,535 | 6 | 6 | 0 |
| Killington | 743 | 2 | 2 | 0 |
| Ludlow | 1,846 | 9 | 5 | 4 |
| Lyndonville | 1,158 | 2 | 2 | 0 |
| Manchester | 4,197 | 10 | 6 | 4 |
| Middlebury | 8,807 | 15 | 13 | 2 |
| Milton | 10,962 | 17 | 16 | 1 |
| Montpelier | 7,278 | 24 | 15 | 9 |
| Morristown | 5,582 | 9 | 9 | 0 |
| Newport | 4,181 | 16 | 12 | 4 |
| Northfield | 6,536 | 6 | 5 | 1 |
| Norwich | 3,400 | 4 | 3 | 1 |
| Pittsford | 2,736 | 1 | 1 | 0 |
| Richmond | 4,102 | 4 | 4 | 0 |
| Royalton | 2,892 | 3 | 3 | 0 |
| Rutland | 14,771 | 39 | 28 | 11 |
| Rutland Town | 4,107 | 4 | 4 | 0 |
| Shelburne | 7,702 | 15 | 7 | 8 |
| South Burlington | 19,748 | 49 | 35 | 14 |
| Springfield | 8,828 | 18 | 12 | 6 |
| St. Albans | 6,787 | 32 | 21 | 11 |
| St. Johnsbury | 7,021 | 16 | 10 | 6 |
| Stowe | 4,460 | 10 | 10 | 0 |
| Swanton | 6,590 | 9 | 9 | 0 |
| Thetford | 2,519 | 3 | 3 | 0 |
| Vergennes | 2,594 | 7 | 7 | 0 |
| Weathersfield | 2,718 | 2 | 2 | 0 |
| Williston | 10,434 | 21 | 15 | 6 |
| Wilmington | 1,777 | 7 | 5 | 2 |
| Windsor | 3,259 | 11 | 10 | 1 |
| Winhall | 722 | 8 | 7 | 1 |
| Winooski | 7,554 | 15 | 11 | 4 |
| Woodstock | 2,899 | 6 | 5 | 1 |
| | | | | |
| **VIRGINIA** | | | | |
| Abingdon | 7,820 | 28 | 25 | 3 |
| Alexandria | 160,457 | 379 | 295 | 84 |
| Altavista | 3,419 | 12 | 11 | 1 |
| Ashland | 7,976 | 28 | 25 | 3 |
| Bedford | 6,652 | 25 | 21 | 4 |
| Berryville | 4,388 | 9 | 8 | 1 |
| Big Stone Gap | 5,055 | 11 | 10 | 1 |
| Blacksburg | 44,228 | 15 | 12 | 3 |
| Blackstone | 3,275 | 15 | 12 | 3 |
| Bluefield | 4,761 | 23 | 20 | 3 |
| Bowling Green | 1,189 | 2 | 2 | 0 |
| Bridgewater | 6,218 | 9 | 9 | 0 |
| Bristol | 17,265 | 73 | 54 | 19 |
| Broadway | 4,026 | 7 | 6 | 1 |
| Brookneal | 1,103 | 2 | 2 | 0 |
| Buena Vista | 6,374 | 17 | 16 | 1 |
| Cedar Bluff | 986 | 3 | 3 | 0 |
| Charlottesville | 47,257 | 133 | 103 | 30 |
| Chase City | 2,205 | 10 | 9 | 1 |
| Chatham | 1,407 | 3 | 3 | 0 |
| Chesapeake | 249,188 | 517 | 378 | 139 |
| Chilhowie | 1,687 | 6 | 6 | 0 |
| Chincoteague | 2,859 | 14 | 10 | 4 |
| Christiansburg | 22,544 | 66 | 60 | 6 |
| Clarksville | 1,163 | 8 | 7 | 1 |
| Clifton Forge | 3,404 | 8 | 7 | 1 |
| Clintwood | 1,247 | 4 | 4 | 0 |
| Coeburn | 1,816 | 7 | 6 | 1 |
| Colonial Beach | 3,655 | 13 | 12 | 1 |
| Colonial Heights | 17,171 | 57 | 52 | 5 |
| Covington | 5,603 | 23 | 17 | 6 |
| Crewe | 2,096 | 4 | 3 | 1 |

## Table 78. Full-Time Law Enforcement Employees, by Selected State and City, 2020—Continued

(Number.)

| State/city | Population | Total law enforcement employees | Total officers | Total civilians |
|---|---|---|---|---|
| Culpeper | 19,485 | 51 | 42 | 9 |
| Damascus | 772 | 4 | 4 | 0 |
| Danville | 39,528 | 135 | 114 | 21 |
| Dayton | 1,652 | 5 | 5 | 0 |
| Dublin | 2,583 | 8 | 7 | 1 |
| Dumfries | 6,233 | 12 | 11 | 1 |
| Eastville | 344 | 6 | 6 | 0 |
| Elkton | 2,933 | 6 | 5 | 1 |
| Emporia | 5,189 | 37 | 26 | 11 |
| Exmore | 1,352 | 7 | 7 | 0 |
| Fairfax City | 23,484 | 89 | 67 | 22 |
| Falls Church | 14,856 | 56 | 45 | 11 |
| Farmville | 7,811 | 28 | 26 | 2 |
| Franklin | 7,753 | 33 | 24 | 9 |
| Fredericksburg | 30,031 | 93 | 68 | 25 |
| Front Royal | 15,499 | 44 | 33 | 11 |
| Galax | 6,223 | 26 | 24 | 2 |
| Gate City | 1,850 | 5 | 5 | 0 |
| Glade Spring | 1,396 | 3 | 3 | 0 |
| Glasgow | 1,107 | 1 | 1 | 0 |
| Gordonsville | 1,665 | 7 | 7 | 0 |
| Grottoes | 2,885 | 6 | 5 | 1 |
| Grundy | 871 | 4 | 4 | 0 |
| Halifax | 1,192 | 5 | 5 | 0 |
| Hampton | 135,107 | 396 | 297 | 99 |
| Harrisonburg | 53,582 | 122 | 99 | 23 |
| Haymarket | 1,709 | 6 | 6 | 0 |
| Haysi | 458 | 1 | 1 | 0 |
| Herndon | 24,694 | 64 | 49 | 15 |
| Hillsville | 2,682 | 12 | 11 | 1 |
| Honaker | 1,311 | 2 | 2 | 0 |
| Hopewell | 22,322 | 79 | 58 | 21 |
| Hurt | 1,203 | 2 | 2 | 0 |
| Independence | 881 | 2 | 2 | 0 |
| Jonesville | 911 | 2 | 2 | 0 |
| Kenbridge | 1,189 | 4 | 4 | 0 |
| Kilmarnock | 1,392 | 5 | 5 | 0 |
| La Crosse | 574 | 1 | 1 | 0 |
| Lawrenceville | 969 | 6 | 6 | 0 |
| Lebanon | 3,158 | 13 | 12 | 1 |
| Leesburg | 55,794 | 93 | 76 | 17 |
| Lexington | 7,294 | 18 | 14 | 4 |
| Louisa | 1,786 | 7 | 6 | 1 |
| Luray | 4,844 | 14 | 13 | 1 |
| Lynchburg | 82,088 | 184 | 150 | 34 |
| Manassas | 41,098 | 119 | 90 | 29 |
| Manassas Park | 18,385 | 41 | 30 | 11 |
| Marion | 5,515 | 20 | 19 | 1 |
| Martinsville | 12,206 | 49 | 45 | 4 |
| Middleburg | 853 | 7 | 6 | 1 |
| Middletown | 1,440 | 5 | 4 | 1 |
| Mount Jackson | 2,153 | 6 | 6 | 0 |
| Narrows | 1,940 | 5 | 5 | 0 |
| New Market | 2,276 | 6 | 6 | 0 |
| Newport News | 178,662 | 613 | 437 | 176 |
| Norfolk | 242,488 | 717 | 568 | 149 |
| Norton | 3,978 | 22 | 14 | 8 |
| Occoquan | 1,114 | 3 | 3 | 0 |
| Onancock | 1,200 | 4 | 4 | 0 |
| Onley | 497 | 4 | 4 | 0 |
| Orange | 5,213 | 15 | 13 | 2 |
| Parksley | 801 | 1 | 1 | 0 |
| Pearisburg | 2,604 | 8 | 8 | 0 |
| Pembroke | 1,073 | 2 | 2 | 0 |
| Pennington Gap | 1,692 | 5 | 5 | 0 |
| Petersburg | 30,212 | 100 | 76 | 24 |
| Pocahontas | 343 | 1 | 1 | 0 |
| Poquoson | 12,253 | 28 | 27 | 1 |
| Portsmouth | 94,943 | 219 | 175 | 44 |
| Pulaski | 8,615 | 30 | 26 | 4 |
| Purcellville | 10,575 | 17 | 15 | 2 |
| Radford | 18,427 | 52 | 37 | 15 |
| Remington | 667 | 1 | 1 | 0 |
| Rich Creek | 735 | 1 | 1 | 0 |
| Richlands | 5,167 | 21 | 16 | 5 |
| Richmond | 234,928 | 727 | 632 | 95 |
| Roanoke | 99,175 | 240 | 199 | 41 |
| Rocky Mount | 4,707 | 19 | 17 | 2 |
| Rural Retreat | 1,445 | 1 | 1 | 0 |
| Salem | 25,354 | 86 | 62 | 24 |
| Shenandoah | 2,330 | 8 | 7 | 1 |
| Smithfield | 8,668 | 6 | 2 | 4 |
| South Boston | 7,459 | 28 | 26 | 2 |
| South Hill | 4,332 | 23 | 21 | 2 |
| Stanley | 1,675 | 5 | 5 | 0 |

## Table 78. Full-Time Law Enforcement Employees, by Selected State and City, 2020—Continued

(Number.)

| State/city | Population | Total law enforcement employees | Total officers | Total civilians |
|---|---|---|---|---|
| Staunton | 25,310 | 61 | 46 | 15 |
| Stephens City | 2,136 | 4 | 4 | 0 |
| St. Paul | 837 | 7 | 7 | 0 |
| Strasburg | 6,745 | 19 | 17 | 2 |
| Suffolk | 94,755 | 213 | 175 | 38 |
| Tappahannock | 2,395 | 10 | 9 | 1 |
| Tazewell | 4,065 | 16 | 15 | 1 |
| Victoria | 1,623 | 4 | 4 | 0 |
| Vienna | 16,598 | 49 | 39 | 10 |
| Vinton | 8,142 | 23 | 22 | 1 |
| Virginia Beach | 451,938 | 964 | 734 | 230 |
| Warrenton | 10,019 | 31 | 29 | 2 |
| Warsaw | 1,490 | 4 | 4 | 0 |
| Waynesboro | 22,896 | 58 | 47 | 11 |
| West Point | 3,309 | 12 | 11 | 1 |
| Williamsburg | 15,406 | 41 | 40 | 1 |
| Winchester | 27,827 | 95 | 73 | 22 |
| Windsor | 2,819 | 7 | 7 | 0 |
| Wintergreen | 165 | 15 | 11 | 4 |
| Wise | 2,852 | 13 | 12 | 1 |
| Woodstock | 5,316 | 19 | 17 | 2 |
| Wytheville | 7,847 | 23 | 21 | 2 |
| | | | | |
| **WASHINGTON** | | | | |
| Aberdeen | 16,824 | 52 | 38 | 14 |
| Airway Heights | 10,030 | 22 | 20 | 2 |
| Algona | 3,216 | 9 | 8 | 1 |
| Anacortes | 17,923 | 30 | 24 | 6 |
| Arlington | 21,405 | 32 | 27 | 5 |
| Asotin | 1,296 | 1 | 1 | 0 |
| Auburn | 82,158 | 131 | 112 | 19 |
| Bainbridge Island | 25,601 | 25 | 21 | 4 |
| Battle Ground | 22,143 | 28 | 23 | 5 |
| Bellevue | 150,208 | 212 | 174 | 38 |
| Bellingham | 95,279 | 172 | 115 | 57 |
| Black Diamond | 5,551 | 11 | 9 | 2 |
| Blaine | 5,741 | 13 | 11 | 2 |
| Bonney Lake | 23,142 | 37 | 31 | 6 |
| Bothell | 48,356 | 93 | 63 | 30 |
| Bremerton | 42,798 | 70 | 54 | 16 |
| Brewster | 2,393 | 6 | 5 | 1 |
| Brier | 7,030 | 3 | 2 | 1 |
| Buckley | 5,914 | 13 | 11 | 2 |
| Burien | 51,584 | 69 | 47 | 22 |
| Burlington | 9,666 | 32 | 26 | 6 |
| Camas | 26,683 | 29 | 27 | 2 |
| Carnation | 2,366 | 2 | 2 | 0 |
| Castle Rock | 2,324 | 6 | 5 | 1 |
| Centralia | 18,131 | 32 | 24 | 8 |
| Chehalis | 7,885 | 19 | 15 | 4 |
| Cheney | 13,175 | 22 | 16 | 6 |
| Chewelah | 2,693 | 6 | 5 | 1 |
| Clarkston | 7,524 | 16 | 14 | 2 |
| Cle Elum | 3,103 | 9 | 7 | 2 |
| Clyde Hill | 3,441 | 10 | 9 | 1 |
| Colfax | 2,787 | 5 | 5 | 0 |
| College Place | 9,560 | 15 | 12 | 3 |
| Colville | 4,840 | 11 | 10 | 1 |
| Connell | 5,660 | 8 | 7 | 1 |
| Cosmopolis | 1,684 | 6 | 5 | 1 |
| Coulee Dam | 1,081 | 2 | 2 | 0 |
| Covington | 22,024 | 26 | 20 | 6 |
| Des Moines | 32,664 | 46 | 35 | 11 |
| Dupont | 9,740 | 15 | 13 | 2 |
| Duvall | 8,319 | 12 | 11 | 1 |
| East Wenatchee | 14,096 | 24 | 21 | 3 |
| Eatonville | 3,055 | 6 | 5 | 1 |
| Edgewood | 13,909 | 14 | 13 | 1 |
| Edmonds | 42,803 | 57 | 49 | 8 |
| Ellensburg | 21,933 | 39 | 29 | 10 |
| Elma | 3,387 | 10 | 8 | 2 |
| Enumclaw | 12,700 | 34 | 19 | 15 |
| Ephrata | 8,268 | 18 | 15 | 3 |
| Everett | 113,469 | 225 | 192 | 33 |
| Everson | 4,624 | 7 | 6 | 1 |
| Federal Way | 97,017 | 153 | 123 | 30 |
| Ferndale | 16,006 | 25 | 21 | 4 |
| Fife | 10,577 | 39 | 30 | 9 |
| Fircrest | 6,920 | 9 | 9 | 0 |
| Forks | 3,950 | 6 | 5 | 1 |
| Gig Harbor | 11,345 | 22 | 20 | 2 |
| Goldendale | 3,696 | 11 | 9 | 2 |
| Grand Coulee | 2,047 | 8 | 8 | 0 |
| Grandview | 11,043 | 22 | 18 | 4 |
| Granger | 3,950 | 8 | 8 | 0 |

## Table 78. Full-Time Law Enforcement Employees, by Selected State and City, 2020—Continued

(Number.)

| State/city | Population | Total law enforcement employees | Total officers | Total civilians |
|---|---|---|---|---|
| Hoquiam | 8,696 | 26 | 23 | 3 |
| Issaquah | 40,738 | 49 | 30 | 19 |
| Kalama | 2,898 | 7 | 6 | 1 |
| Kelso | 12,493 | 29 | 25 | 4 |
| Kenmore | 23,326 | 18 | 14 | 4 |
| Kennewick | 85,595 | 115 | 100 | 15 |
| Kent | 131,899 | 194 | 145 | 49 |
| Kettle Falls | 1,647 | 5 | 4 | 1 |
| Kirkland | 97,027 | 142 | 105 | 37 |
| Kittitas | 1,538 | 4 | 4 | 0 |
| La Center | 3,674 | 3 | 3 | 0 |
| Lacey | 55,484 | 63 | 49 | 14 |
| Lake Forest Park | 13,514 | 23 | 20 | 3 |
| Lake Stevens | 35,500 | 38 | 30 | 8 |
| Lakewood | 61,325 | 109 | 94 | 15 |
| Langley | 1,162 | 3 | 3 | 0 |
| Liberty Lake | 11,905 | 18 | 16 | 2 |
| Long Beach | 1,534 | 9 | 8 | 1 |
| Longview | 38,693 | 75 | 57 | 18 |
| Lynden | 15,791 | 21 | 17 | 4 |
| Lynnwood | 39,370 | 94 | 62 | 32 |
| Maple Valley | 28,065 | 27 | 21 | 6 |
| Marysville | 72,620 | 98 | 65 | 33 |
| Mattawa | 5,182 | 6 | 6 | 0 |
| McCleary | 1,849 | 5 | 5 | 0 |
| Medina | 3,343 | 11 | 9 | 2 |
| Mercer Island | 26,251 | 34 | 31 | 3 |
| Mill Creek | 21,076 | 23 | 20 | 3 |
| Milton | 8,325 | 12 | 12 | 0 |
| Monroe | 21,047 | 41 | 32 | 9 |
| Montesano | 4,083 | 9 | 8 | 1 |
| Morton | 1,227 | 3 | 3 | 0 |
| Moses Lake | 24,694 | 50 | 42 | 8 |
| Mountlake Terrace | 21,462 | 37 | 29 | 8 |
| Mount Vernon | 36,830 | 53 | 40 | 13 |
| Moxee | 4,499 | 8 | 7 | 1 |
| Mukilteo | 21,461 | 34 | 27 | 7 |
| Napavine | 2,069 | 3 | 2 | 1 |
| Newcastle | 13,188 | 15 | 12 | 3 |
| Newport | 2,278 | 5 | 4 | 1 |
| Normandy Park | 6,587 | 11 | 10 | 1 |
| Oak Harbor | 23,792 | 38 | 28 | 10 |
| Ocean Shores | 6,851 | 12 | 11 | 1 |
| Odessa | 899 | 1 | 1 | 0 |
| Olympia | 54,322 | 111 | 70 | 41 |
| Omak | 4,829 | 14 | 11 | 3 |
| Oroville | 1,686 | 5 | 4 | 1 |
| Orting | 8,866 | 9 | 8 | 1 |
| Othello | 8,572 | 24 | 17 | 7 |
| Pacific | 7,225 | 10 | 9 | 1 |
| Palouse | 1,061 | 2 | 2 | 0 |
| Pasco | 78,680 | 92 | 82 | 10 |
| Port Angeles | 20,519 | 54 | 32 | 22 |
| Port Orchard | 14,995 | 25 | 21 | 4 |
| Port Townsend | 10,063 | 12 | 10 | 2 |
| Poulsbo | 11,425 | 22 | 19 | 3 |
| Prosser | 6,463 | 13 | 11 | 2 |
| Pullman | 34,826 | 43 | 29 | 14 |
| Puyallup | 43,144 | 92 | 68 | 24 |
| Quincy | 8,564 | 29 | 21 | 8 |
| Raymond | 3,076 | 8 | 7 | 1 |
| Reardan | 626 | 1 | 1 | 0 |
| Redmond | 74,583 | 116 | 78 | 38 |
| Renton | 102,458 | 148 | 114 | 34 |
| Richland | 60,615 | 73 | 57 | 16 |
| Ridgefield | 12,295 | 14 | 12 | 2 |
| Ritzville | 1,637 | 3 | 3 | 0 |
| Roy | 828 | 2 | 2 | 0 |
| Royal City | 2,697 | 2 | 2 | 0 |
| Ruston | 859 | 4 | 4 | 0 |
| Sammamish | 66,855 | 40 | 32 | 8 |
| SeaTac | 29,103 | 64 | 46 | 18 |
| Seattle | 787,749 | 1,597 | 1,178 | 419 |
| Sedro Woolley | 12,301 | 25 | 20 | 5 |
| Selah | 8,220 | 19 | 16 | 3 |
| Sequim | 7,911 | 25 | 19 | 6 |
| Shelton | 11,073 | 22 | 19 | 3 |
| Shoreline | 58,725 | 66 | 47 | 19 |
| Snohomish | 10,489 | 19 | 17 | 2 |
| Snoqualmie | 13,875 | 24 | 20 | 4 |
| Soap Lake | 1,614 | 7 | 6 | 1 |
| South Bend | 1,741 | 5 | 4 | 1 |
| Spokane | 223,344 | 433 | 344 | 89 |
| Spokane Valley | 104,276 | 117 | 97 | 20 |
| Stanwood | 7,716 | 13 | 11 | 2 |

## Table 78. Full-Time Law Enforcement Employees, by Selected State and City, 2020—Continued

(Number.)

| State/city | Population | Total law enforcement employees | Total officers | Total civilians |
|---|---|---|---|---|
| Steilacoom | 6,460 | 10 | 9 | 1 |
| Sumas | 1,665 | 7 | 6 | 1 |
| Sumner | 10,670 | 25 | 20 | 5 |
| Sunnyside | 17,021 | 46 | 28 | 18 |
| Tacoma | 222,235 | 359 | 321 | 38 |
| Tenino | 1,886 | 5 | 4 | 1 |
| Tieton | 1,330 | 2 | 2 | 0 |
| Toledo | 792 | 2 | 1 | 1 |
| Toppenish | 8,745 | 15 | 12 | 3 |
| Tukwila | 20,369 | 86 | 65 | 21 |
| Tumwater | 24,727 | 38 | 31 | 7 |
| Twisp | 997 | 3 | 3 | 0 |
| Union Gap | 6,163 | 20 | 17 | 3 |
| University Place | 34,404 | 17 | 16 | 1 |
| Vancouver | 188,160 | 262 | 214 | 48 |
| Walla Walla | 33,154 | 77 | 48 | 29 |
| Wapato | 4,971 | 9 | 7 | 2 |
| Warden | 2,848 | 6 | 5 | 1 |
| Washougal | 16,317 | 24 | 21 | 3 |
| Wenatchee | 34,349 | 54 | 43 | 11 |
| Westport | 2,123 | 8 | 7 | 1 |
| West Richland | 15,817 | 23 | 19 | 4 |
| White Salmon | 2,764 | 7 | 6 | 1 |
| Winlock | 1,504 | 3 | 3 | 0 |
| Winthrop | 502 | 3 | 3 | 0 |
| Woodinville | 15,462 | 19 | 15 | 4 |
| Woodland | 6,659 | 13 | 11 | 2 |
| Yakima | 94,594 | 173 | 135 | 38 |
| Yelm | 9,913 | 18 | 16 | 2 |
| Zillah | 3,145 | 9 | 8 | 1 |
| | | | | |
| **WEST VIRGINIA** | | | | |
| Alderson | 1,104 | 4 | 4 | 0 |
| Anmoore | 728 | 3 | 3 | 0 |
| Ansted | 1,290 | 2 | 1 | 1 |
| Athens | 876 | 1 | 1 | 0 |
| Barboursville | 4,258 | 24 | 22 | 2 |
| Barrackville | 1,268 | 1 | 1 | 0 |
| Beckley | 15,632 | 72 | 56 | 16 |
| Belington | 1,896 | 3 | 3 | 0 |
| Belle | 1,094 | 2 | 2 | 0 |
| Benwood | 1,241 | 11 | 6 | 5 |
| Berkeley Springs | 584 | 3 | 2 | 1 |
| Bethlehem | 2,279 | 5 | 5 | 0 |
| Bluefield | 9,416 | 33 | 27 | 6 |
| Bradshaw | 251 | 1 | 1 | 0 |
| Bramwell | 331 | 2 | 2 | 0 |
| Bridgeport | 8,853 | 40 | 36 | 4 |
| Buckhannon | 5,376 | 12 | 11 | 1 |
| Burnsville | 461 | 2 | 2 | 0 |
| Cameron | 818 | 2 | 2 | 0 |
| Cedar Grove | 888 | 1 | 1 | 0 |
| Ceredo | 1,233 | 7 | 4 | 3 |
| Chapmanville | 1,064 | 5 | 5 | 0 |
| Charleston | 45,378 | 180 | 157 | 23 |
| Charles Town | 6,098 | 17 | 14 | 3 |
| Chesapeake | 1,378 | 1 | 1 | 0 |
| Chester | 2,291 | 6 | 5 | 1 |
| Clarksburg | 15,290 | 44 | 40 | 4 |
| Clendenin | 1,086 | 4 | 4 | 0 |
| Davy | 315 | 1 | 1 | 0 |
| Delbarton | 479 | 2 | 2 | 0 |
| Dunbar | 6,868 | 17 | 16 | 1 |
| East Bank | 847 | 1 | 1 | 0 |
| Eleanor | 1,585 | 1 | 1 | 0 |
| Elkins | 6,881 | 16 | 14 | 2 |
| Fairmont | 18,335 | 42 | 36 | 6 |
| Fairview | 402 | 1 | 1 | 0 |
| Fayetteville | 2,659 | 11 | 10 | 1 |
| Follansbee | 2,640 | 7 | 7 | 0 |
| Fort Gay | 677 | 3 | 3 | 0 |
| Gary | 741 | 1 | 1 | 0 |
| Gassaway | 808 | 1 | 1 | 0 |
| Gauley Bridge | 539 | 1 | 1 | 0 |
| Gilbert | 372 | 3 | 3 | 0 |
| Glen Dale | 1,332 | 5 | 5 | 0 |
| Glenville | 1,397 | 2 | 1 | 1 |
| Grafton | 4,950 | 9 | 8 | 1 |
| Grant Town | 587 | 1 | 1 | 0 |
| Granville | 3,727 | 14 | 14 | 0 |
| Hamlin | 995 | 4 | 3 | 1 |
| Harpers Ferry/Bolivar | 1,301 | 4 | 3 | 1 |
| Harrisville | 1,645 | 1 | 1 | 0 |
| Hartford City | 591 | 2 | 1 | 1 |
| Hinton | 2,289 | 4 | 3 | 1 |

## Table 78. Full-Time Law Enforcement Employees, by Selected State and City, 2020—Continued

(Number.)

| State/city | Population | Total law enforcement employees | Total officers | Total civilians |
|---|---|---|---|---|
| Huntington | 44,522 | 98 | 94 | 4 |
| Hurricane | 6,401 | 21 | 19 | 2 |
| Iaeger | 226 | 1 | 1 | 0 |
| Kenova | 2,914 | 14 | 10 | 4 |
| Keyser | 4,811 | 11 | 10 | 1 |
| Kingwood | 3,047 | 3 | 3 | 0 |
| Lewisburg | 3,759 | 15 | 13 | 2 |
| Logan | 1,418 | 11 | 8 | 3 |
| Lumberport | 831 | 2 | 2 | 0 |
| Mabscott | 1,236 | 2 | 2 | 0 |
| Madison | 2,574 | 7 | 7 | 0 |
| Man | 607 | 2 | 2 | 0 |
| Mannington | 2,004 | 4 | 4 | 0 |
| Marlinton | 947 | 1 | 1 | 0 |
| Marmet | 1,337 | 5 | 5 | 0 |
| Martinsburg | 17,542 | 54 | 43 | 11 |
| Mason | 915 | 6 | 5 | 1 |
| Masontown | 536 | 2 | 1 | 1 |
| Matewan | 407 | 1 | 1 | 0 |
| McMechen | 1,644 | 4 | 4 | 0 |
| Milton | 2,534 | 11 | 10 | 1 |
| Monongah | 1,173 | 1 | 1 | 0 |
| Montgomery | 1,478 | 8 | 6 | 2 |
| Moorefield | 2,375 | 9 | 8 | 1 |
| Morgantown | 31,079 | 83 | 71 | 12 |
| Moundsville | 8,036 | 20 | 16 | 4 |
| Mount Hope | 1,245 | 5 | 4 | 1 |
| Mullens | 1,263 | 3 | 3 | 0 |
| New Haven | 1,442 | 2 | 2 | 0 |
| New Martinsville | 5,088 | 13 | 9 | 4 |
| Nitro | 6,225 | 18 | 17 | 1 |
| Nutter Fort | 1,491 | 5 | 5 | 0 |
| Oak Hill | 7,948 | 22 | 18 | 4 |
| Oceana | 1,177 | 4 | 4 | 0 |
| Paden City | 2,266 | 5 | 4 | 1 |
| Parkersburg | 28,793 | 79 | 67 | 12 |
| Parsons | 1,387 | 1 | 1 | 0 |
| Pennsboro | 1,004 | 1 | 1 | 0 |
| Petersburg | 2,713 | 3 | 1 | 2 |
| Philippi | 3,271 | 6 | 6 | 0 |
| Piedmont | 784 | 1 | 1 | 0 |
| Pineville | 558 | 3 | 3 | 0 |
| Point Pleasant | 3,986 | 8 | 7 | 1 |
| Pratt | 547 | 2 | 1 | 1 |
| Princeton | 5,551 | 22 | 20 | 2 |
| Rainelle | 1,518 | 3 | 2 | 1 |
| Ranson | 5,466 | 18 | 17 | 1 |
| Ravenswood | 3,594 | 12 | 10 | 2 |
| Reedsville | 605 | 1 | 1 | 0 |
| Rhodell | 158 | 2 | 1 | 1 |
| Richwood | 1,822 | 3 | 3 | 0 |
| Ridgeley | 608 | 4 | 3 | 1 |
| Ripley | 3,130 | 11 | 10 | 1 |
| Rivesville | 893 | 1 | 1 | 0 |
| Romney | 1,665 | 7 | 6 | 1 |
| Rupert | 874 | 1 | 1 | 0 |
| Salem | 1,504 | 3 | 3 | 0 |
| Shepherdstown | 1,901 | 6 | 5 | 1 |
| Shinnston | 2,085 | 10 | 9 | 1 |
| Sistersville | 1,259 | 2 | 2 | 0 |
| Sophia | 1,208 | 6 | 6 | 0 |
| South Charleston | 11,884 | 49 | 45 | 4 |
| Spencer | 1,962 | 4 | 4 | 0 |
| St. Albans | 9,646 | 27 | 24 | 3 |
| Star City | 2,005 | 7 | 6 | 1 |
| St. Marys | 1,748 | 5 | 4 | 1 |
| Stonewood | 1,692 | 2 | 2 | 0 |
| Summersville | 3,194 | 17 | 16 | 1 |
| Sutton | 967 | 1 | 1 | 0 |
| Sylvester | 131 | 1 | 1 | 0 |
| Terra Alta | 1,505 | 1 | 1 | 0 |
| Triadelphia | 745 | 1 | 1 | 0 |
| Vienna | 9,952 | 23 | 19 | 4 |
| War | 642 | 3 | 3 | 0 |
| Wayne | 1,546 | 2 | 2 | 0 |
| Webster Springs | 649 | 4 | 3 | 1 |
| Weirton | 17,911 | 42 | 38 | 4 |
| Welch | 1,511 | 4 | 3 | 1 |
| Wellsburg | 2,468 | 6 | 6 | 0 |
| West Logan | 352 | 1 | 1 | 0 |
| West Milford | 607 | 2 | 2 | 0 |
| Weston | 3,770 | 8 | 6 | 2 |
| Westover | 4,243 | 14 | 14 | 0 |
| Wheeling | 26,081 | 87 | 71 | 16 |
| White Hall | 667 | 5 | 5 | 0 |

# Table 78. Full-Time Law Enforcement Employees, by Selected State and City, 2020—Continued

(Number.)

| State/city | Population | Total law enforcement employees | Total officers | Total civilians |
|---|---|---|---|---|
| White Sulphur Springs | 2,315 | 8 | 7 | 1 |
| Williamson | 2,565 | 7 | 6 | 1 |
| Williamstown | 2,855 | 8 | 7 | 1 |
| Winfield | 2,414 | 7 | 7 | 0 |
| **WISCONSIN** | | | | |
| Adams | 1,898 | 4 | 4 | 0 |
| Albany | 973 | 3 | 3 | 0 |
| Algoma | 3,026 | 10 | 5 | 5 |
| Altoona | 8,210 | 16 | 15 | 1 |
| Amery | 2,786 | 9 | 7 | 2 |
| Antigo | 7,671 | 18 | 15 | 3 |
| Appleton | 74,204 | 132 | 106 | 26 |
| Arcadia | 3,034 | 4 | 4 | 0 |
| Ashland | 7,723 | 21 | 19 | 2 |
| Ashwaubenon | 17,008 | 56 | 51 | 5 |
| Athens | 1,077 | 1 | 1 | 0 |
| Baraboo | 12,127 | 33 | 29 | 4 |
| Barneveld | 1,254 | 1 | 1 | 0 |
| Barron | 3,215 | 6 | 6 | 0 |
| Bayfield | 473 | 3 | 3 | 0 |
| Bayside | 4,353 | 12 | 12 | 0 |
| Beaver Dam | 16,314 | 35 | 31 | 4 |
| Belleville | 2,528 | 6 | 5 | 1 |
| Beloit | 36,603 | 83 | 71 | 12 |
| Beloit Town | 7,724 | 14 | 12 | 2 |
| Berlin | 5,367 | 13 | 12 | 1 |
| Big Bend | 1,511 | 3 | 3 | 0 |
| Birchwood | 424 | 1 | 1 | 0 |
| Black River Falls | 3,439 | 7 | 6 | 1 |
| Blair | 1,323 | 3 | 3 | 0 |
| Blanchardville | 784 | 3 | 3 | 0 |
| Bloomer | 3,504 | 8 | 7 | 1 |
| Bloomfield | 6,538 | 8 | 8 | 0 |
| Blue Mounds | 1,004 | 2 | 1 | 1 |
| Boscobel | 3,126 | 6 | 6 | 0 |
| Boyceville | 1,127 | 2 | 2 | 0 |
| Brillion | 3,071 | 8 | 8 | 0 |
| Brodhead | 3,195 | 11 | 7 | 4 |
| Brookfield | 39,292 | 95 | 80 | 15 |
| Brookfield Township | 6,561 | 16 | 15 | 1 |
| Brown Deer | 12,310 | 31 | 28 | 3 |
| Brownsville | 585 | 1 | 1 | 0 |
| Burlington | 10,938 | 23 | 22 | 1 |
| Butler | 1,790 | 9 | 8 | 1 |
| Caledonia | 25,272 | 39 | 37 | 2 |
| Campbellsport | 1,792 | 2 | 2 | 0 |
| Campbell Township | 4,273 | 5 | 5 | 0 |
| Cashton | 1,112 | 2 | 2 | 0 |
| Cedarburg | 11,818 | 29 | 21 | 8 |
| Chenequa | 610 | 8 | 8 | 0 |
| Chetek | 2,083 | 5 | 4 | 1 |
| Chilton | 3,862 | 8 | 7 | 1 |
| Cleveland | 1,452 | 1 | 1 | 0 |
| Clinton | 2,116 | 6 | 6 | 0 |
| Clintonville | 4,333 | 16 | 12 | 4 |
| Colby-Abbotsford | 4,165 | 9 | 8 | 1 |
| Coleman | 681 | 1 | 1 | 0 |
| Colfax | 1,150 | 2 | 2 | 0 |
| Columbus | 5,129 | 10 | 8 | 2 |
| Cornell | 1,394 | 3 | 3 | 0 |
| Cottage Grove | 7,241 | 15 | 13 | 2 |
| Crandon | 1,767 | 5 | 4 | 1 |
| Cross Plains | 4,348 | 7 | 6 | 1 |
| Cuba City | 2,043 | 8 | 4 | 4 |
| Cudahy | 18,201 | 39 | 30 | 9 |
| Cumberland | 2,090 | 7 | 7 | 0 |
| Darlington | 2,305 | 5 | 5 | 0 |
| Deforest | 11,130 | 23 | 20 | 3 |
| Delafield | 7,607 | 18 | 16 | 2 |
| Delavan | 9,813 | 27 | 25 | 2 |
| Delavan Town | 5,361 | 14 | 13 | 1 |
| Durand | 1,776 | 4 | 4 | 0 |
| Eagle River | 1,603 | 7 | 6 | 1 |
| Eagle Village | 2,213 | 2 | 2 | 0 |
| East Troy | 4,307 | 8 | 8 | 0 |
| Eau Claire | 69,372 | 128 | 94 | 34 |
| Edgar | 1,430 | 1 | 1 | 0 |
| Edgerton | 5,613 | 11 | 10 | 1 |
| Eleva | 659 | 1 | 1 | 0 |
| Elkhart Lake | 1,018 | 3 | 3 | 0 |
| Elkhorn | 10,016 | 16 | 15 | 1 |
| Elk Mound | 885 | 1 | 1 | 0 |
| Ellsworth | 3,270 | 6 | 6 | 0 |
| Elm Grove | 6,158 | 22 | 16 | 6 |

## Table 78. Full-Time Law Enforcement Employees, by Selected State and City, 2020—Continued

(Number.)

| State/city | Population | Total law enforcement employees | Total officers | Total civilians |
|---|---|---|---|---|
| Elroy | 1,293 | 3 | 3 | 0 |
| Evansville | 5,614 | 12 | 10 | 2 |
| Everest Metropolitan | 17,341 | 32 | 28 | 4 |
| Fall Creek | 1,289 | 2 | 2 | 0 |
| Fennimore | 2,464 | 6 | 6 | 0 |
| Fitchburg | 31,498 | 65 | 53 | 12 |
| Fond du Lac | 43,195 | 72 | 63 | 9 |
| Fontana | 1,749 | 8 | 7 | 1 |
| Fort Atkinson | 12,370 | 26 | 20 | 6 |
| Fox Crossing | 19,200 | 31 | 27 | 4 |
| Fox Lake | 1,432 | 3 | 3 | 0 |
| Fox Point | 6,678 | 18 | 17 | 1 |
| Fox Valley Metro | 22,891 | 28 | 26 | 2 |
| Franklin | 36,264 | 76 | 60 | 16 |
| Frederic | 1,075 | 4 | 2 | 2 |
| Galesville | 1,611 | 4 | 4 | 0 |
| Geneva Town | 5,052 | 8 | 7 | 1 |
| Germantown | 20,066 | 44 | 33 | 11 |
| Gillett | 1,298 | 4 | 4 | 0 |
| Glendale | 12,843 | 45 | 39 | 6 |
| Grafton | 11,783 | 50 | 22 | 28 |
| Grand Chute | 23,739 | 40 | 35 | 5 |
| Grand Rapids | 7,334 | 8 | 6 | 2 |
| Grantsburg | 1,292 | 4 | 3 | 1 |
| Green Bay | 103,826 | 213 | 175 | 38 |
| Greendale | 14,251 | 67 | 28 | 39 |
| Greenfield | 37,531 | 69 | 61 | 8 |
| Green Lake | 961 | 3 | 3 | 0 |
| Hales Corners | 7,603 | 17 | 16 | 1 |
| Hammond | 1,887 | 4 | 3 | 1 |
| Hartford | 15,815 | 33 | 27 | 6 |
| Hartford Township | 3,571 | 1 | 1 | 0 |
| Hartland | 9,360 | 18 | 16 | 2 |
| Hayward | 2,353 | 8 | 7 | 1 |
| Hazel Green | 1,215 | 2 | 2 | 0 |
| Highland | 824 | 1 | 1 | 0 |
| Hillsboro | 1,385 | 3 | 3 | 0 |
| Hobart-Lawrence | 16,712 | 13 | 12 | 1 |
| Holmen | 10,497 | 14 | 12 | 2 |
| Horicon | 3,683 | 9 | 8 | 1 |
| Hortonville | 3,005 | 7 | 6 | 1 |
| Hudson | 14,313 | 29 | 26 | 3 |
| Hurley | 1,413 | 7 | 6 | 1 |
| Independence | 1,286 | 3 | 3 | 0 |
| Iron Ridge | 880 | 1 | 1 | 0 |
| Iron River | 1,160 | 3 | 3 | 0 |
| Jackson | 7,304 | 14 | 13 | 1 |
| Janesville | 64,768 | 112 | 100 | 12 |
| Jefferson | 8,042 | 17 | 14 | 3 |
| Juneau | 2,506 | 5 | 4 | 1 |
| Kaukauna | 16,444 | 27 | 26 | 1 |
| Kenosha | 99,588 | 427 | 207 | 220 |
| Kewaskum | 4,323 | 8 | 8 | 0 |
| Kewaunee | 2,824 | 6 | 6 | 0 |
| Kiel | 3,807 | 9 | 8 | 1 |
| Kronenwetter | 8,242 | 9 | 8 | 1 |
| La Crosse | 51,143 | 115 | 96 | 19 |
| Ladysmith | 3,022 | 8 | 8 | 0 |
| La Farge | 765 | 1 | 1 | 0 |
| Lake Delton | 2,992 | 25 | 23 | 2 |
| Lake Geneva | 8,155 | 35 | 25 | 10 |
| Lake Hallie | 6,807 | 12 | 10 | 2 |
| Lake Mills | 6,044 | 12 | 10 | 2 |
| Lancaster | 3,683 | 8 | 7 | 1 |
| Lena | 538 | 1 | 1 | 0 |
| Linn Township | 2,409 | 7 | 7 | 0 |
| Lomira | 2,457 | 5 | 4 | 1 |
| Luxemburg | 2,582 | 1 | 1 | 0 |
| Madison | 266,199 | 595 | 484 | 111 |
| Manawa | 1,259 | 3 | 3 | 0 |
| Manitowoc | 32,233 | 71 | 60 | 11 |
| Maple Bluff | 1,306 | 14 | 6 | 8 |
| Marathon City | 1,513 | 3 | 3 | 0 |
| Marinette | 10,421 | 28 | 24 | 4 |
| Marion | 1,159 | 4 | 4 | 0 |
| Markesan | 1,382 | 4 | 4 | 0 |
| Marshfield | 18,347 | 44 | 38 | 6 |
| Mayville | 4,798 | 9 | 8 | 1 |
| Medford | 4,258 | 9 | 8 | 1 |
| Menasha | 17,823 | 38 | 31 | 7 |
| Menomonee Falls | 38,516 | 73 | 60 | 13 |
| Menomonie | 16,633 | 31 | 25 | 6 |
| Mequon | 24,936 | 49 | 40 | 9 |
| Merrill | 8,927 | 24 | 21 | 3 |
| Middleton | 20,472 | 47 | 38 | 9 |

## Table 78. Full-Time Law Enforcement Employees, by Selected State and City, 2020—Continued

(Number.)

| State/city | Population | Total law enforcement employees | Total officers | Total civilians |
|---|---|---|---|---|
| Milton | 5,653 | 13 | 11 | 2 |
| Milwaukee | 593,337 | 2,015 | 1,654 | 361 |
| Mineral Point | 2,449 | 6 | 6 | 0 |
| Minocqua | 4,453 | 15 | 10 | 5 |
| Mishicot | 1,384 | 3 | 3 | 0 |
| Mondovi | 2,542 | 4 | 4 | 0 |
| Monona | 8,226 | 26 | 21 | 5 |
| Monroe | 10,387 | 31 | 24 | 7 |
| Monticello | 1,182 | 3 | 3 | 0 |
| Mount Horeb | 7,606 | 14 | 14 | 0 |
| Mount Pleasant | 27,084 | 63 | 56 | 7 |
| Mukwonago | 8,184 | 21 | 15 | 6 |
| Mukwonago Town | 8,184 | 7 | 6 | 1 |
| Muscoda | 1,227 | 3 | 3 | 0 |
| Muskego | 25,436 | 49 | 39 | 10 |
| Neenah | 26,451 | 51 | 40 | 11 |
| Neillsville | 2,367 | 7 | 6 | 1 |
| Nekoosa | 2,373 | 7 | 7 | 0 |
| New Berlin | 39,833 | 83 | 70 | 13 |
| New Glarus | 2,132 | 4 | 4 | 0 |
| New Holstein | 3,092 | 6 | 5 | 1 |
| New Lisbon | 2,547 | 3 | 3 | 0 |
| New London | 7,043 | 19 | 17 | 2 |
| New Richmond | 9,875 | 19 | 18 | 1 |
| Niagara | 1,526 | 4 | 4 | 0 |
| North Fond du Lac | 5,064 | 8 | 7 | 1 |
| Norwalk | 631 | 1 | 1 | 0 |
| Oak Creek | 36,975 | 86 | 62 | 24 |
| Oakfield Village | 1,089 | 3 | 3 | 0 |
| Oconomowoc | 17,301 | 31 | 26 | 5 |
| Oconomowoc Lake | 611 | 6 | 6 | 0 |
| Oconomowoc Town | 8,801 | 11 | 10 | 1 |
| Omro | 3,599 | 8 | 7 | 1 |
| Onalaska | 19,243 | 32 | 30 | 2 |
| Oregon | 10,881 | 22 | 19 | 3 |
| Orfordville | 1,490 | 3 | 3 | 0 |
| Osceola | 2,582 | 6 | 5 | 1 |
| Oshkosh | 66,513 | 111 | 95 | 16 |
| Osseo | 1,668 | 4 | 4 | 0 |
| Palmyra | 1,742 | 12 | 6 | 6 |
| Park Falls | 2,168 | 7 | 7 | 0 |
| Pepin | 739 | 1 | 1 | 0 |
| Peshtigo | 3,310 | 6 | 6 | 0 |
| Pewaukee Village | 8,089 | 39 | 19 | 20 |
| Phillips | 1,306 | 5 | 5 | 0 |
| Pittsville | 815 | 2 | 2 | 0 |
| Plainfield | 829 | 2 | 1 | 1 |
| Platteville | 11,690 | 23 | 20 | 3 |
| Pleasant Prairie | 21,542 | 44 | 34 | 10 |
| Plover | 13,360 | 23 | 20 | 3 |
| Plymouth | 8,766 | 15 | 14 | 1 |
| Portage | 10,387 | 29 | 25 | 4 |
| Port Edwards | 1,746 | 3 | 3 | 0 |
| Port Washington | 12,147 | 24 | 19 | 5 |
| Prescott | 4,281 | 11 | 10 | 1 |
| Princeton | 1,162 | 4 | 4 | 0 |
| Pulaski | 3,789 | 8 | 7 | 1 |
| Racine | 76,018 | 201 | 175 | 26 |
| Reedsburg | 9,521 | 27 | 20 | 7 |
| Rhinelander | 7,624 | 18 | 16 | 2 |
| Rice Lake | 8,511 | 19 | 18 | 1 |
| Richland Center | 4,920 | 13 | 11 | 2 |
| Rio | 1,047 | 2 | 2 | 0 |
| Ripon | 7,856 | 16 | 14 | 2 |
| River Hills | 1,585 | 11 | 11 | 0 |
| Rome Town | 2,790 | 6 | 6 | 0 |
| Rosendale | 1,023 | 1 | 1 | 0 |
| Rothschild | 5,255 | 14 | 12 | 2 |
| Sauk Prairie | 4,666 | 15 | 13 | 2 |
| Saukville | 4,436 | 13 | 11 | 2 |
| Seymour | 3,457 | 6 | 6 | 0 |
| Sharon | 1,541 | 5 | 4 | 1 |
| Shawano | 8,845 | 23 | 21 | 2 |
| Sheboygan | 47,667 | 103 | 83 | 20 |
| Sheboygan Falls | 7,924 | 15 | 13 | 2 |
| Shiocton | 914 | 2 | 2 | 0 |
| Shorewood | 13,222 | 28 | 24 | 4 |
| Shorewood Hills | 2,050 | 8 | 7 | 1 |
| Shullsburg | 1,188 | 1 | 1 | 0 |
| Siren | 778 | 4 | 3 | 1 |
| Slinger | 5,770 | 13 | 12 | 1 |
| Somerset | 3,027 | 7 | 6 | 1 |
| South Milwaukee | 20,795 | 40 | 34 | 6 |
| Sparta | 9,827 | 22 | 20 | 2 |
| Spencer | 1,859 | 4 | 4 | 0 |

## Table 78. Full-Time Law Enforcement Employees, by Selected State and City, 2020—Continued

(Number.)

| State/city | Population | Total law enforcement employees | Total officers | Total civilians |
|---|---|---|---|---|
| Spooner | 2,539 | 8 | 7 | 1 |
| Spring Green | 1,631 | 4 | 3 | 1 |
| Spring Valley | 1,321 | 2 | 1 | 1 |
| Stanley | 3,714 | 5 | 5 | 0 |
| St. Croix Falls | 2,052 | 8 | 7 | 1 |
| Stevens Point | 25,875 | 49 | 45 | 4 |
| St. Francis | 9,846 | 22 | 21 | 1 |
| Stoughton | 13,274 | 28 | 22 | 6 |
| Strum | 1,068 | 2 | 2 | 0 |
| Sturgeon Bay | 8,970 | 24 | 22 | 2 |
| Sturtevant | 6,642 | 12 | 11 | 1 |
| Summit | 5,321 | 11 | 10 | 1 |
| Sun Prairie | 35,722 | 72 | 51 | 21 |
| Superior | 26,117 | 62 | 57 | 5 |
| Theresa | 1,193 | 2 | 2 | 0 |
| Thiensville | 3,107 | 9 | 8 | 1 |
| Thorp | 1,602 | 3 | 3 | 0 |
| Three Lakes | 2,126 | 5 | 5 | 0 |
| Tomah | 9,379 | 23 | 21 | 2 |
| Tomahawk | 3,107 | 10 | 9 | 1 |
| Town of East Troy | 4,065 | 6 | 5 | 1 |
| Town of Madison | 6,713 | 9 | 8 | 1 |
| Twin Lakes | 6,261 | 18 | 13 | 5 |
| Two Rivers | 10,903 | 29 | 25 | 4 |
| Verona | 13,860 | 28 | 25 | 3 |
| Viroqua | 4,398 | 12 | 10 | 2 |
| Walworth | 2,828 | 9 | 8 | 1 |
| Waterford Town | 6,509 | 10 | 9 | 1 |
| Waterloo | 3,320 | 8 | 7 | 1 |
| Watertown | 23,322 | 54 | 39 | 15 |
| Waukesha | 72,493 | 153 | 123 | 30 |
| Waupaca | 5,833 | 18 | 17 | 1 |
| Waupun | 11,264 | 16 | 14 | 2 |
| Wausau | 38,435 | 88 | 79 | 9 |
| Wautoma | 2,106 | 7 | 6 | 1 |
| Wauwatosa | 48,650 | 114 | 93 | 21 |
| Webster | 618 | 2 | 2 | 0 |
| West Allis | 60,176 | 149 | 122 | 27 |
| West Bend | 31,506 | 74 | 57 | 17 |
| Westfield | 1,270 | 1 | 1 | 0 |
| West Milwaukee | 4,113 | 23 | 19 | 4 |
| West Salem | 5,032 | 10 | 9 | 1 |
| Whitefish Bay | 13,848 | 22 | 21 | 1 |
| Whitewater | 15,057 | 54 | 23 | 31 |
| Wild Rose | 644 | 1 | 1 | 0 |
| Williams Bay | 2,666 | 8 | 8 | 0 |
| Winneconne | 2,491 | 6 | 5 | 1 |
| Wisconsin Dells | 3,099 | 19 | 15 | 4 |
| Woodruff | 1,990 | 6 | 5 | 1 |
| **WYOMING** | | | | |
| Afton | 2,086 | 4 | 4 | 0 |
| Buffalo | 4,666 | 16 | 9 | 7 |
| Casper | 58,840 | 150 | 101 | 49 |
| Cheyenne | 65,263 | 120 | 102 | 18 |
| Cody | 9,878 | 26 | 23 | 3 |
| Diamondville | 769 | 2 | 2 | 0 |
| Douglas | 6,404 | 18 | 15 | 3 |
| Evanston | 11,494 | 31 | 26 | 5 |
| Evansville | 3,046 | 14 | 12 | 2 |
| Gillette | 32,294 | 76 | 51 | 25 |
| Glenrock | 2,560 | 12 | 6 | 6 |
| Green River | 11,729 | 31 | 26 | 5 |
| Greybull | 1,792 | 7 | 6 | 1 |
| Hanna | 749 | 1 | 1 | 0 |
| Jackson | 10,672 | 39 | 31 | 8 |
| Kemmerer | 2,775 | 5 | 5 | 0 |
| Lander | 7,452 | 20 | 18 | 2 |
| Laramie | 32,841 | 68 | 44 | 24 |
| Lusk | 1,465 | 7 | 6 | 1 |
| Mills | 4,144 | 15 | 15 | 0 |
| Moorcroft | 1,091 | 4 | 3 | 1 |
| Newcastle | 3,293 | 16 | 7 | 9 |
| Pine Bluffs | 1,163 | 3 | 3 | 0 |
| Powell | 6,108 | 23 | 16 | 7 |
| Rawlins | 8,413 | 25 | 14 | 11 |
| Riverton | 10,823 | 40 | 29 | 11 |
| Rock Springs | 22,937 | 46 | 36 | 10 |
| Saratoga | 1,591 | 6 | 3 | 3 |
| Sheridan | 18,157 | 46 | 29 | 17 |
| Thermopolis | 2,747 | 11 | 6 | 5 |
| Torrington | 6,564 | 22 | 15 | 7 |
| Wheatland | 3,512 | 10 | 9 | 1 |
| Worland | 4,947 | 13 | 12 | 1 |

1 The employee data presented in this table for Charlotte-Mecklenburg represent only Charlotte-Mecklenburg Police Department and exclude Mecklenburg County Sheriff's Office.

# Table 79. Full-Time Law Enforcement Employees, by Selected State and University or College, 2021

(Number.)

| State and university/college | Student enrollment[1] | Law enforcement employees | Officers | Civilians |
|---|---|---|---|---|
| **ALABAMA** | | | | |
| Alabama A&M University | 6,560 | 31 | 15 | 16 |
| Auburn University, Montgomery | 6,199 | 27 | 17 | 10 |
| Bevill State Community College | 5,122 | 1 | 1 | 0 |
| Bishop State Community College | 4,242 | 5 | 5 | 0 |
| Calhoun Community College | 13,627 | 6 | 5 | 1 |
| Coastal Alabama Community College | 9,883 | 11 | 11 | 0 |
| Enterprise State Community College | 2,525 | 1 | 1 | 0 |
| Jacksonville State University | 10,561 | 27 | 15 | 12 |
| Jefferson State Community College | 12,361 | 16 | 14 | 2 |
| Lawson State Community College | 4,697 | 7 | 7 | 0 |
| Lurleen B. Wallace Community College | 2,286 | 1 | 1 | 0 |
| Samford University | 6,127 | 18 | 15 | 3 |
| Southern Union State Community College | 6,562 | 5 | 5 | 0 |
| Troy University | 20,854 | 16 | 13 | 3 |
| Tuskegee University | 3,195 | 22 | 8 | 14 |
| University of Alabama | | | | |
| Birmingham | 25,843 | 183 | 104 | 79 |
| Huntsville | 11,312 | 24 | 15 | 9 |
| Tuscaloosa | 42,096 | 137 | 76 | 61 |
| University of Montevallo | 2,829 | 18 | 9 | 9 |
| University of North Alabama | 9,185 | 15 | 9 | 6 |
| University of South Alabama | 16,398 | 27 | 20 | 7 |
| University of West Alabama | 8,506 | 13 | 8 | 5 |
| Wallace Community College | | | | |
| Dothan | 5,785 | 3 | 3 | 0 |
| Selma | 2,239 | 3 | 1 | 2 |
| Wallace State Community College | 6,944 | 8 | 8 | 0 |
| **ALASKA** | | | | |
| University of Alaska | | | | |
| Anchorage | 20,526 | 20 | 12 | 8 |
| Fairbanks | 11,413 | 14 | 8 | 6 |
| **ARIZONA** | | | | |
| Arizona State University, Main Campus | 152,488 | 152 | 83 | 69 |
| Arizona Western College | 11,646 | 12 | 7 | 5 |
| Central Arizona College | 8,093 | 15 | 13 | 2 |
| Northern Arizona University | 34,290 | 36 | 23 | 13 |
| Pima Community College | 36,384 | 44 | 25 | 19 |
| University of Arizona | 49,966 | 92 | 56 | 36 |
| **ARKANSAS** | | | | |
| Arkansas State University | | | | |
| Beebe | 4,427 | 6 | 5 | 1 |
| Jonesboro | 18,762 | 21 | 15 | 6 |
| Newport | 4,680 | 3 | 3 | 0 |
| Arkansas Tech University | 13,316 | 21 | 18 | 3 |
| Henderson State University | 4,562 | 9 | 8 | 1 |
| Southern Arkansas University | 5,249 | 9 | 8 | 1 |
| Southern Arkansas University Tech | 1,725 | 3 | 3 | 0 |
| University of Arkansas | | | | |
| Fayetteville | 30,137 | 50 | 33 | 17 |
| Little Rock | 11,826 | 29 | 20 | 9 |
| Medical Sciences | 3,015 | 45 | 30 | 15 |
| Monticello | 3,499 | 10 | 9 | 1 |
| Pine Bluff | 2,724 | 13 | 8 | 5 |
| University of Arkansas Community College at Morrilton | 2,343 | 3 | 3 | 0 |
| University of Central Arkansas | 12,333 | 31 | 23 | 8 |
| **CALIFORNIA** | | | | |
| Allan Hancock College | 16,689 | 13 | 6 | 7 |
| California State Polytechnic University | | | | |
| Pomona | 29,687 | 48 | 21 | 27 |
| San Luis Obispo | 22,817 | 21 | 17 | 4 |
| California State University | | | | |
| Bakersfield | 12,854 | 22 | 14 | 8 |
| Channel Islands | 8,436 | 27 | 14 | 13 |
| Chico | 18,664 | 23 | 15 | 8 |
| Dominguez Hills | 19,491 | 26 | 18 | 8 |
| East Bay | 18,717 | 19 | 11 | 8 |
| Fresno | 26,592 | 35 | 25 | 10 |
| Fullerton | 46,245 | 35 | 22 | 13 |
| Long Beach | 42,378 | 32 | 19 | 13 |
| Los Angeles | 28,607 | 31 | 18 | 13 |
| Monterey Bay | 8,493 | 24 | 16 | 8 |
| Northridge | 42,736 | 30 | 16 | 14 |
| Sacramento | 35,953 | 42 | 19 | 23 |
| San Bernardino | 22,157 | 27 | 16 | 11 |
| San Jose | 39,442 | 66 | 25 | 41 |
| San Marcos | 16,959 | 26 | 18 | 8 |
| Stanislaus | 12,213 | 20 | 12 | 8 |

## Table 79. Full-Time Law Enforcement Employees, by Selected State and University or College, 2021—Continued

(Number.)

| State and university/college | Student enrollment[1] | Law enforcement employees | Officers | Civilians |
|---|---|---|---|---|
| Chaffey College | 30,023 | 14 | 12 | 2 |
| College of the Sequoias | 16,379 | 7 | 6 | 1 |
| Contra Costa Community College | 53,641 | 32 | 20 | 12 |
| Cuesta College | 15,810 | 6 | 4 | 2 |
| El Camino College | 33,146 | 17 | 12 | 5 |
| Foothill-De Anza College | 57,996 | 17 | 10 | 7 |
| Humboldt State University | 7,813 | 19 | 12 | 7 |
| Irvine Valley College | 18,862 | 16 | 10 | 6 |
| Marin Community College | 7,395 | 7 | 5 | 2 |
| Pasadena Community College | 37,129 | 15 | 10 | 5 |
| Riverside Community College | 65,049 | 24 | 18 | 6 |
| San Bernardino Community College | 29,643 | 16 | 9 | 7 |
| San Diego State University | 38,336 | 54 | 27 | 27 |
| San Francisco State University | 32,541 | 41 | 19 | 22 |
| San Jose/Evergreen Community College | 29,222 | 18 | 7 | 11 |
| Sonoma County Junior College | 27,223 | 24 | 11 | 13 |
| Sonoma State University | 9,885 | 13 | 11 | 2 |
| State Center Community College District | 70,721 | 27 | 21 | 6 |
| University of California | | | | |
| Berkeley | 45,878 | 95 | 43 | 52 |
| Davis | 41,236 | 65 | 40 | 25 |
| Irvine | 39,059 | 105 | 46 | 59 |
| Los Angeles | 46,947 | 121 | 45 | 76 |
| Merced | 9,268 | 32 | 17 | 15 |
| Riverside | 27,507 | 35 | 26 | 9 |
| San Diego | 40,547 | 73 | 37 | 36 |
| San Francisco | 3,256 | 142 | 54 | 88 |
| Santa Barbara | 28,096 | 43 | 32 | 11 |
| Santa Cruz | 20,861 | 35 | 19 | 16 |
| Ventura County Community College District | 50,191 | 15 | 14 | 1 |
| West Valley-Mission College | 23,432 | 14 | 9 | 5 |
| | | | | |
| **COLORADO** | | | | |
| Adams State University | 3,883 | 6 | 5 | 1 |
| Arapahoe Community College | 19,102 | 12 | 9 | 3 |
| Auraria Higher Education Center[2] | | 45 | 28 | 17 |
| Colorado School of Mines | 7,092 | 16 | 15 | 1 |
| Colorado State University, Fort Collins | 37,806 | 41 | 27 | 14 |
| Fort Lewis College | 3,766 | 10 | 7 | 3 |
| Pikes Peak Community College | 17,357 | 15 | 15 | 0 |
| Red Rocks Community College | 11,486 | 9 | 6 | 3 |
| University of Colorado | | | | |
| Boulder | 41,826 | 73 | 40 | 33 |
| Colorado Springs | 16,715 | 32 | 18 | 14 |
| Denver | 31,796 | 60 | 24 | 36 |
| University of Northern Colorado | 15,248 | 19 | 13 | 6 |
| | | | | |
| **CONNECTICUT** | | | | |
| Central Connecticut State University | 13,046 | 23 | 15 | 8 |
| Eastern Connecticut State University | 5,508 | 22 | 13 | 9 |
| Southern Connecticut State University | 11,273 | 31 | 25 | 6 |
| University of Connecticut, Storrs, Avery Point, and Hartford[2] | | 115 | 84 | 31 |
| Western Connecticut State University | 6,463 | 18 | 12 | 6 |
| Yale University | 14,910 | 104 | 86 | 18 |
| | | | | |
| **DELAWARE** | | | | |
| Delaware State University | 5,263 | 34 | 8 | 26 |
| University of Delaware | 26,527 | 76 | 50 | 26 |
| | | | | |
| **FLORIDA** | | | | |
| Florida A&M University | 10,696 | 22 | 18 | 4 |
| Florida Atlantic University | 37,930 | 72 | 41 | 31 |
| Florida Gulf Coast University | 17,114 | 28 | 21 | 7 |
| Florida International University | 73,970 | 94 | 63 | 31 |
| Florida Polytechnic University | 1,376 | 12 | 10 | 2 |
| Florida SouthWestern State College | 21,947 | 27 | 15 | 12 |
| Florida State University | | | | |
| Panama City[2] | | 9 | 8 | 1 |
| Tallahassee | 47,836 | 78 | 63 | 15 |
| New College of Florida | 747 | 20 | 15 | 5 |
| Northwest Florida State College | 7,656 | 6 | 6 | 0 |
| Pensacola State College | 13,357 | 18 | 9 | 9 |
| Tallahassee Community College | 16,528 | 17 | 8 | 9 |
| University of Central Florida | 81,082 | 119 | 77 | 42 |
| University of Florida | 58,857 | 119 | 76 | 43 |
| University of North Florida | 20,515 | 44 | 32 | 12 |
| University of South Florida | | | | |
| St. Petersburg[2] | | 19 | 14 | 5 |
| Tampa | 60,343 | 64 | 43 | 21 |
| University of West Florida | 15,944 | 25 | 20 | 5 |

# Table 79. Full-Time Law Enforcement Employees, by Selected State and University or College, 2021—Continued

(Number.)

| State and university/college | Student enrollment[1] | Law enforcement employees | Officers | Civilians |
|---|---|---|---|---|
| **GEORGIA** | | | | |
| Abraham Baldwin Agricultural College | 4,667 | 16 | 15 | 1 |
| Agnes Scott College | 1,166 | 12 | 6 | 6 |
| Albany State University | 7,339 | 28 | 18 | 10 |
| Albany Technical College | 4,635 | 3 | 3 | 0 |
| Athens Technical College | 6,598 | 3 | 2 | 1 |
| Atlanta Metropolitan State College | 2,676 | 6 | 4 | 2 |
| Atlanta Technical College | 6,106 | 3 | 2 | 1 |
| Augusta Technical College | 6,088 | 7 | 5 | 2 |
| Augusta University | 9,706 | 53 | 39 | 14 |
| Berry College | 2,228 | 15 | 8 | 7 |
| Clark Atlanta University | 4,273 | 53 | 17 | 36 |
| College of Coastal Georgia | 4,355 | 14 | 14 | 0 |
| Columbus State University | 9,643 | 29 | 23 | 6 |
| Dalton State College | 5,734 | 13 | 10 | 3 |
| Emory University | 15,970 | 85 | 55 | 30 |
| Fort Valley State University | 2,892 | 21 | 9 | 12 |
| Georgia College and State University | 8,039 | 17 | 12 | 5 |
| Georgia Gwinnett College | 15,489 | 26 | 21 | 5 |
| Georgia Highlands College | 7,895 | 5 | 5 | 0 |
| Georgia Institute of Technology | 43,217 | 107 | 69 | 38 |
| Georgia Military College | 14,828 | 4 | 2 | 2 |
| Georgia Northwestern Technical College | 8,811 | 9 | 8 | 1 |
| Georgia Piedmont Technical College | 4,979 | 8 | 7 | 1 |
| Georgia Southern University | 30,231 | 66 | 51 | 15 |
| Georgia Southwestern State University | 3,725 | 8 | 7 | 1 |
| Georgia State University | 41,177 | 232 | 119 | 113 |
| Gordon State College | 4,114 | 14 | 12 | 2 |
| Gwinnett Technical College | 12,929 | 6 | 4 | 2 |
| Kennesaw State University | 44,088 | 85 | 56 | 29 |
| Mercer University | 9,933 | 30 | 22 | 8 |
| Middle Georgia State University | 10,155 | 26 | 21 | 5 |
| Morehouse College | 2,341 | 22 | 8 | 14 |
| Piedmont College | 3,052 | 8 | 5 | 3 |
| Savannah State University | 4,182 | 27 | 15 | 12 |
| Savannah Technical College | 6,049 | 9 | 7 | 2 |
| Southern Crescent Technical College | 7,829 | 8 | 8 | 0 |
| Southern Regional Technical College | 6,804 | 7 | 5 | 2 |
| South Georgia State College | 3,052 | 12 | 9 | 3 |
| Spelman College | 2,190 | 17 | 10 | 7 |
| University of Georgia | 42,941 | 90 | 70 | 20 |
| University of North Georgia | 23,141 | 46 | 35 | 11 |
| University of West Georgia | 15,915 | 38 | 28 | 10 |
| West Georgia Technical College | 10,089 | 11 | 11 | 0 |
| Young Harris College | 1,650 | 4 | 4 | 0 |
| | | | | |
| **ILLINOIS** | | | | |
| Chicago State University | 3,595 | 23 | 20 | 3 |
| Elgin Community College | 14,467 | 18 | 16 | 2 |
| Joliet Junior College | 22,871 | 24 | 15 | 9 |
| Lincoln Land Community College | 9,665 | 14 | 12 | 2 |
| McHenry County College | 11,434 | 7 | 6 | 1 |
| Millikin University | 2,333 | 16 | 4 | 12 |
| Morton College | 6,682 | 5 | 4 | 1 |
| Oakton Community College | 17,064 | 13 | 12 | 1 |
| University of Illinois | | | | |
| Chicago | 35,210 | 146 | 75 | 71 |
| Urbana | 57,324 | 101 | 61 | 40 |
| Waubonsee Community College | 15,423 | 9 | 8 | 1 |
| | | | | |
| **IOWA** | | | | |
| Iowa State University | 35,319 | 44 | 30 | 14 |
| University of Iowa | 34,495 | 65 | 32 | 33 |
| University of Northern Iowa | 12,137 | 20 | 17 | 3 |
| | | | | |
| **KANSAS** | | | | |
| Butler Community College | 11,237 | 7 | 7 | 0 |
| Emporia State University | 7,282 | 6 | 6 | 0 |
| Fort Hays State University | 18,862 | 11 | 9 | 2 |
| Garden City Community College | 2,584 | 3 | 2 | 1 |
| Kansas State University | 23,353 | 30 | 20 | 10 |
| Pittsburg State University | 8,065 | 15 | 12 | 3 |
| University of Kansas | | | | |
| Main Campus | 30,983 | 62 | 28 | 34 |
| Medical Center[2] | | 75 | 47 | 28 |
| Wichita State University | 17,817 | 40 | 28 | 12 |
| | | | | |
| **KENTUCKY** | | | | |
| Eastern Kentucky University | 17,345 | 29 | 22 | 7 |
| Kentucky State University | 3,044 | 7 | 3 | 4 |
| Murray State University | 10,853 | 21 | 14 | 7 |
| Northern Kentucky University | 18,308 | 22 | 15 | 7 |

## Table 79. Full-Time Law Enforcement Employees, by Selected State and University or College, 2021—Continued

(Number.)

| State and university/college | Student enrollment[1] | Law enforcement employees | Officers | Civilians |
|---|---|---|---|---|
| University of Kentucky | 32,756 | 157 | 47 | 110 |
| University of Louisville | 25,451 | 55 | 34 | 21 |
| Western Kentucky University | 21,535 | 32 | 23 | 9 |
| | | | | |
| **LOUISIANA** | | | | |
| Delgado Community College | 20,120 | 39 | 31 | 8 |
| Louisiana State University | | | | |
| Health Sciences Center, New Orleans | 3,004 | 14 | 14 | 0 |
| Health Sciences Center, Shreveport | 1,084 | 50 | 38 | 12 |
| Shreveport | 12,170 | 8 | 7 | 1 |
| Louisiana Tech University | 12,768 | 20 | 20 | 0 |
| McNeese State University | 8,134 | 10 | 8 | 2 |
| Southeastern Louisiana University | 17,053 | 27 | 20 | 7 |
| Southern University and A&M College | | | | |
| Baton Rouge | 8,050 | 35 | 19 | 16 |
| New Orleans | 2,946 | 14 | 14 | 0 |
| Shreveport | 4,506 | 10 | 9 | 1 |
| Tulane University | 14,652 | 70 | 70 | 0 |
| University of Louisiana | | | | |
| Lafayette | 18,796 | 37 | 35 | 2 |
| Monroe | 9,718 | 24 | 23 | 1 |
| University of New Orleans | 9,736 | 18 | 18 | 0 |
| | | | | |
| **MAINE** | | | | |
| University of Maine | | | | |
| Farmington | 2,397 | 6 | 5 | 1 |
| Orono | 13,426 | 19 | 11 | 8 |
| University of Southern Maine | 10,788 | 13 | 8 | 5 |
| | | | | |
| **MARYLAND** | | | | |
| Bowie State University | 7,010 | 22 | 10 | 12 |
| Coppin State University | 2,993 | 25 | 12 | 13 |
| Frostburg State University | 5,850 | 21 | 17 | 4 |
| Hagerstown Community College | 5,401 | 5 | 3 | 2 |
| Morgan State University | 8,432 | 44 | 30 | 14 |
| Prince George's County Community College | 16,876 | 17 | 10 | 7 |
| Salisbury University | 9,521 | 33 | 17 | 16 |
| Towson University | 25,370 | 46 | 33 | 13 |
| University of Baltimore | 5,198 | 26 | 12 | 14 |
| University of Maryland | | | | |
| Baltimore City | 24 | 163 | 58 | 105 |
| Baltimore County | 15,403 | 37 | 26 | 11 |
| College Park | 44,404 | 117 | 74 | 43 |
| Eastern Shore | 3,208 | 29 | 8 | 21 |
| | | | | |
| **MASSACHUSETTS** | | | | |
| Amherst College | 1,940 | 19 | 10 | 9 |
| Babson College | 3,987 | 25 | 16 | 9 |
| Bentley University | 5,579 | 31 | 21 | 10 |
| Boston College | 16,502 | 77 | 49 | 28 |
| Boston University | 42,047 | 58 | 46 | 12 |
| Brandeis University | 6,403 | 22 | 19 | 3 |
| Bridgewater State University | 13,150 | 24 | 20 | 4 |
| Bunker Hill Community College | 16,306 | 16 | 13 | 3 |
| Clark University | 3,880 | 15 | 12 | 3 |
| College of the Holy Cross | 3,098 | 20 | 17 | 3 |
| Emerson College | 5,496 | 22 | 18 | 4 |
| Endicott College | 6,649 | 18 | 15 | 3 |
| Fitchburg State University | 10,793 | 25 | 20 | 5 |
| Framingham State University | 8,366 | 15 | 11 | 4 |
| Gordon College | 2,314 | 10 | 7 | 3 |
| Harvard University | 41,024 | 91 | 66 | 25 |
| Holyoke Community College | 6,374 | 8 | 6 | 2 |
| Massachusetts College of Liberal Arts | 1,922 | 13 | 8 | 5 |
| Massasoit Community College | 9,466 | 15 | 14 | 1 |
| Merrimack College | 6,600 | 18 | 14 | 4 |
| Mount Wachusett Community College | 4,818 | 10 | 9 | 1 |
| Northeastern University | 30,003 | 102 | 64 | 38 |
| Quinsigamond Community College | 9,897 | 15 | 10 | 5 |
| Salem State University | 9,343 | 22 | 18 | 4 |
| Simmons College | 7,562 | 25 | 19 | 6 |
| Springfield College | 3,288 | 33 | 19 | 14 |
| Springfield Technical Community College | 6,833 | 17 | 14 | 3 |
| Stonehill College | 2,618 | 29 | 17 | 12 |
| Tufts University | 13,458 | 54 | 44 | 10 |
| University of Massachusetts | | | | |
| Amherst | 35,781 | 67 | 54 | 13 |
| Dartmouth | 9,491 | 24 | 17 | 7 |
| Medical Center, Worcester | 1,278 | 43 | 33 | 10 |
| Wellesley College | 2,735 | 14 | 10 | 4 |
| Wentworth Institute of Technology | 5,456 | 25 | 19 | 6 |
| Western New England University | 4,005 | 26 | 16 | 10 |

## Table 79. Full-Time Law Enforcement Employees, by Selected State and University or College, 2021—Continued

(Number.)

| State and university/college | Student enrollment[1] | Law enforcement employees | Officers | Civilians |
|---|---|---|---|---|
| Westfield State University | 7,104 | 20 | 16 | 4 |
| Worcester Polytechnic Institute | 7,654 | 24 | 17 | 7 |
| Worcester State University | 8,694 | 19 | 14 | 5 |
| **MICHIGAN** | | | | |
| Central Michigan University | 22,512 | 28 | 21 | 7 |
| Delta College | 10,408 | 9 | 6 | 3 |
| Eastern Michigan University | 20,982 | 45 | 32 | 13 |
| Ferris State University | 14,874 | 12 | 11 | 1 |
| Grand Rapids Community College | 18,960 | 18 | 14 | 4 |
| Grand Valley State University | 26,993 | 28 | 21 | 7 |
| Kalamazoo Valley Community College | 11,012 | 7 | 5 | 2 |
| Kellogg Community College | 6,853 | 3 | 3 | 0 |
| Kirtland Community College | 2,311 | 1 | 1 | 0 |
| Lansing Community College | 16,021 | 14 | 10 | 4 |
| Macomb Community College | 27,402 | 30 | 26 | 4 |
| Michigan State University | 55,406 | 108 | 74 | 34 |
| Michigan Technological University | 7,786 | 16 | 11 | 5 |
| Mott Community College | 9,668 | 14 | 9 | 5 |
| Northern Michigan University | 10,080 | 21 | 19 | 2 |
| Oakland Community College | 23,813 | 22 | 21 | 1 |
| Oakland University | 22,230 | 28 | 19 | 9 |
| Saginaw Valley State University | 9,205 | 9 | 9 | 0 |
| Schoolcraft College | 15,561 | 15 | 10 | 5 |
| University of Michigan | | | | |
| Ann Arbor | 49,530 | 76 | 63 | 13 |
| Dearborn | 10,611 | 28 | 14 | 14 |
| Flint | 8,398 | 33 | 18 | 15 |
| Washtenaw Community College | 20,899 | 12 | 5 | 7 |
| Western Michigan University | 22,996 | 47 | 33 | 14 |
| **MINNESOTA** | | | | |
| University of Minnesota | | | | |
| Duluth | 11,557 | 12 | 11 | 1 |
| Morris | 1,637 | 6 | 3 | 3 |
| Twin Cities | 63,760 | 83 | 53 | 30 |
| **MISSISSIPPI** | | | | |
| East Mississippi Community College | 5,166 | 3 | 3 | 0 |
| Holmes Community College | | | | |
| Goodman | 8,142 | 18 | 8 | 10 |
| Grenada[2] | | 4 | 4 | 0 |
| Ridgeland[2] | | 5 | 4 | 1 |
| Mississippi State University | 24,449 | 50 | 30 | 20 |
| Northeast Mississippi Community College | 4,303 | 8 | 7 | 1 |
| Pearl River Community College, Forrest | 6,657 | 5 | 4 | 1 |
| University of Mississippi, Oxford | 24,309 | 48 | 30 | 18 |
| **MISSOURI** | | | | |
| Metropolitan Community College | 21,040 | 36 | 29 | 7 |
| Missouri University of Science and Technology | 8,618 | 19 | 12 | 7 |
| Southeast Missouri State University | 11,812 | 19 | 12 | 7 |
| St. Louis Community College, Meramec | 26,166 | 33 | 27 | 6 |
| Truman State University | 5,637 | 9 | 7 | 2 |
| University of Central Missouri | 15,315 | 34 | 16 | 18 |
| University of Missouri | | | | |
| Columbia | 32,916 | 63 | 41 | 22 |
| Kansas City | 18,894 | 35 | 24 | 11 |
| St. Louis | 19,090 | 25 | 20 | 5 |
| **MONTANA** | | | | |
| Montana State University | 18,756 | 18 | 18 | 0 |
| Montana State University, Billings | 5,824 | 10 | 7 | 3 |
| University of Montana | 12,694 | 27 | 16 | 11 |
| **NEBRASKA** | | | | |
| Metropolitan Community College, Douglas County | 22,649 | 27 | 23 | 4 |
| University of Nebraska | | | | |
| Kearney | 7,564 | 10 | 8 | 2 |
| Lincoln | 32,498 | 59 | 24 | 35 |
| **NEVADA** | | | | |
| University of Nevada, Reno | 23,692 | 36 | 25 | 11 |
| University Police Services | 90,144 | 63 | 42 | 21 |
| **NEW HAMPSHIRE** | | | | |
| Plymouth State University | 5,475 | 8 | 8 | 0 |
| University of New Hampshire | 16,001 | 33 | 19 | 14 |
| **NEW JERSEY** | | | | |
| Brookdale Community College | 16,439 | 9 | 9 | 0 |
| Essex County College | 10,217 | 53 | 9 | 44 |

## Table 79. Full-Time Law Enforcement Employees, by Selected State and University or College, 2021—Continued

(Number.)

| State and university/college | Student enrollment[1] | Law enforcement employees | Officers | Civilians |
|---|---|---|---|---|
| Kean University | 16,991 | 41 | 19 | 22 |
| Middlesex County College | 16,466 | 20 | 12 | 8 |
| Monmouth University | 6,618 | 41 | 15 | 26 |
| Montclair State University | 24,101 | 44 | 33 | 11 |
| New Jersey Institute of Technology | 13,619 | 75 | 40 | 35 |
| Princeton University | 8,532 | 92 | 33 | 59 |
| Rowan University | 23,231 | 81 | 32 | 49 |
| Rutgers University | | | | |
| Camden | 8,113 | 52 | 14 | 38 |
| Newark | 15,633 | 140 | 55 | 85 |
| New Brunswick | 56,178 | 136 | 51 | 85 |
| Stevens Institute of Technology | 8,158 | 22 | 20 | 2 |
| Stockton University | 11,925 | 44 | 26 | 18 |
| The College of New Jersey | 8,943 | 28 | 16 | 12 |
| William Paterson University | 12,020 | 37 | 26 | 11 |
| **NEW MEXICO** | | | | |
| Eastern New Mexico University | 7,246 | 9 | 8 | 1 |
| New Mexico Military Institute | 576 | 6 | 6 | 0 |
| New Mexico State University | 16,064 | 47 | 23 | 24 |
| University of New Mexico | 25,420 | 65 | 43 | 22 |
| **NEW YORK** | | | | |
| Ithaca College | 6,780 | 34 | 15 | 19 |
| State University of New York Police | | | | |
| Albany | 20,099 | 54 | 35 | 19 |
| Alfred | 4,225 | 18 | 13 | 5 |
| Binghamton | 19,660 | 56 | 36 | 20 |
| Brockport | 9,194 | 20 | 15 | 5 |
| Buffalo | 35,509 | 74 | 61 | 13 |
| Buffalo State College | 9,955 | 35 | 30 | 5 |
| Canton | 4,756 | 11 | 10 | 1 |
| Cobleskill | 2,544 | 12 | 11 | 1 |
| Cortland | 7,657 | 27 | 19 | 8 |
| Delhi | 3,512 | 16 | 12 | 4 |
| Downstate Medical | 2,204 | 85 | 21 | 64 |
| Environmental Science | 2,385 | 13 | 8 | 5 |
| Farmingdale | 12,841 | 36 | 24 | 12 |
| Fredonia | 4,742 | 16 | 13 | 3 |
| Maritime | 1,860 | 14 | 10 | 4 |
| Morrisville | 3,127 | 15 | 13 | 2 |
| New Paltz | 8,902 | 24 | 20 | 4 |
| Old Westbury | 6,331 | 23 | 19 | 4 |
| Oneonta | 7,907 | 25 | 16 | 9 |
| Optometry | 410 | 17 | 6 | 11 |
| Oswego | 9,190 | 24 | 19 | 5 |
| Plattsburgh | 6,067 | 22 | 15 | 7 |
| Polytechnic Institute | 3,393 | 16 | 11 | 5 |
| Potsdam | 3,675 | 13 | 10 | 3 |
| Purchase | 4,677 | 31 | 23 | 8 |
| Stony Brook | 34,115 | 154 | 60 | 94 |
| Upstate Medical | 1,683 | 102 | 21 | 81 |
| **NORTH CAROLINA** | | | | |
| Appalachian State University | 20,799 | 42 | 26 | 16 |
| Beaufort County Community College | 2,076 | 4 | 4 | 0 |
| Belmont Abbey College | 1,600 | 8 | 8 | 0 |
| Davidson College | 2,022 | 10 | 8 | 2 |
| Duke University | 17,855 | 158 | 62 | 96 |
| East Carolina University | 31,962 | 63 | 50 | 13 |
| Elizabeth City State University | 2,027 | 9 | 9 | 0 |
| Elon University | 7,424 | 37 | 19 | 18 |
| Fayetteville State University | 8,376 | 30 | 15 | 15 |
| Meredith College | 1,972 | 14 | 3 | 11 |
| Methodist University | 2,109 | 19 | 8 | 11 |
| North Carolina Agricultural and Technical State University | 13,854 | 49 | 21 | 28 |
| North Carolina School of the Arts | 1,102 | 24 | 17 | 7 |
| North Carolina State University, Raleigh | 40,537 | 64 | 49 | 15 |
| Queens University | 2,873 | 7 | 5 | 2 |
| Saint Augustine's University | 1,108 | 14 | 3 | 11 |
| University of North Carolina | | | | |
| Asheville | 4,153 | 20 | 14 | 6 |
| Charlotte | 34,715 | 52 | 44 | 8 |
| Greensboro | 22,487 | 56 | 31 | 25 |
| Pembroke | 9,338 | 24 | 17 | 7 |
| Wilmington | 20,367 | 47 | 30 | 17 |
| Wake Forest University | 9,266 | 51 | 23 | 28 |
| Western Carolina University | 13,783 | 24 | 24 | 0 |
| Winston-Salem State University | 5,834 | 19 | 12 | 7 |
| **NORTH DAKOTA** | | | | |
| Bismarck State College | 4,855 | 3 | 3 | 0 |

## Table 79. Full-Time Law Enforcement Employees, by Selected State and University or College, 2021—Continued

(Number.)

| State and university/college | Student enrollment[1] | Law enforcement employees | Officers | Civilians |
|---|---|---|---|---|
| North Dakota State College of Science | 3,669 | 3 | 3 | 0 |
| North Dakota State University | 14,384 | 17 | 15 | 2 |
| University of North Dakota | 17,182 | 19 | 18 | 1 |
| **OHIO** | | | | |
| Bowling Green State University | 20,945 | 32 | 24 | 8 |
| Capital University | 3,735 | 14 | 9 | 5 |
| Columbus State Community College | 46,782 | 41 | 22 | 19 |
| Hocking College | 4,323 | 6 | 4 | 2 |
| Kent State University | 32,341 | 34 | 26 | 8 |
| Miami University | 21,667 | 30 | 22 | 8 |
| Muskingum University | 3,045 | 5 | 5 | 0 |
| Otterbein University | 3,298 | 10 | 10 | 0 |
| University of Akron | 19,819 | 32 | 27 | 5 |
| University of Cincinnati | 46,140 | 130 | 59 | 71 |
| University of Rio Grande | 2,594 | 7 | 6 | 1 |
| University of Toledo | 22,028 | 32 | 29 | 3 |
| **OKLAHOMA** | | | | |
| Bacone College | 314 | 4 | 4 | 0 |
| Cameron University | 4,767 | 13 | 13 | 0 |
| East Central University | 4,413 | 5 | 5 | 0 |
| Eastern Oklahoma State College | 1,829 | 5 | 5 | 0 |
| Langston University | 2,614 | 17 | 13 | 4 |
| Mid-America Christian University | 2,382 | 6 | 6 | 0 |
| Northeastern Oklahoma A&M College | 2,285 | 4 | 3 | 1 |
| Northeastern State University, Tahlequah | 9,075 | 19 | 14 | 5 |
| Northwestern Oklahoma State University | 2,295 | 3 | 3 | 0 |
| Oklahoma City Community College | 17,240 | 31 | 24 | 7 |
| Oklahoma City University | 3,071 | 13 | 9 | 4 |
| Oklahoma State University | | | | |
| Main Campus | 26,463 | 46 | 34 | 12 |
| Okmulgee | 3,024 | 6 | 6 | 0 |
| Tulsa | 1,265 | 6 | 5 | 1 |
| Rogers State University | 4,290 | 7 | 7 | 0 |
| Seminole State College | 1,925 | 3 | 3 | 0 |
| Southeastern Oklahoma State University | 6,534 | 8 | 7 | 1 |
| Southwestern Oklahoma State University | 5,768 | 7 | 6 | 1 |
| Tulsa Community College | 22,569 | 38 | 28 | 10 |
| University of Central Oklahoma | 17,440 | 20 | 13 | 7 |
| University of Oklahoma | | | | |
| Health Sciences Center | 3,722 | 66 | 38 | 28 |
| Norman | 31,445 | 61 | 33 | 28 |
| **OREGON** | | | | |
| Portland State University | 30,571 | 24 | 9 | 15 |
| University of Oregon | 24,381 | 40 | 17 | 23 |
| **PENNSYLVANIA** | | | | |
| Bloomsburg University | 9,568 | 18 | 15 | 3 |
| California University | 8,882 | 17 | 14 | 3 |
| Cheyney University | 674 | 11 | 7 | 4 |
| Clarion University | 5,496 | 10 | 7 | 3 |
| Edinboro University | 5,764 | 12 | 11 | 1 |
| Indiana University | 11,977 | 24 | 17 | 7 |
| Kutztown University | 9,105 | 14 | 13 | 1 |
| Lehigh University | 7,445 | 36 | 26 | 10 |
| Lock Haven University | 3,557 | 11 | 7 | 4 |
| Millersville University | 9,169 | 17 | 15 | 2 |
| Pennsylvania State University | | | | |
| Altoona[2] | | 9 | 9 | 0 |
| Beaver[2] | | 7 | 7 | 0 |
| Behrend[2] | | 12 | 10 | 2 |
| Berks[2] | | 9 | 8 | 1 |
| Brandywine[2] | | 7 | 7 | 0 |
| Dubois[2] | | 2 | 2 | 0 |
| Fayette[2] | | 3 | 3 | 0 |
| Greater Allegheny[2] | | 6 | 6 | 0 |
| Harrisburg[2] | | 6 | 6 | 0 |
| Lehigh Valley[2] | | 3 | 3 | 0 |
| Mont Alto[2] | | 6 | 6 | 0 |
| University Park[2] | | 108 | 53 | 55 |
| Worthington Scranton[2] | | 3 | 3 | 0 |
| Shippensburg University | 6,871 | 14 | 14 | 0 |
| Slippery Rock University | 10,238 | 13 | 12 | 1 |
| University of Pittsburgh | | | | |
| Johnstown | 2,581 | 12 | 9 | 3 |
| Pittsburgh | 35,563 | 123 | 71 | 52 |
| Titusville | 147 | 1 | 1 | 0 |
| West Chester University | 19,680 | 29 | 25 | 4 |
| Wilkes University | 6,482 | 25 | 15 | 10 |

## Table 79. Full-Time Law Enforcement Employees, by Selected State and University or College, 2021—Continued

(Number.)

| State and university/college | Student enrollment[1] | Law enforcement employees | Officers | Civilians |
|---|---|---|---|---|
| **RHODE ISLAND** | | | | |
| Brown University | 10,807 | 70 | 47 | 23 |
| University of Rhode Island | 21,108 | 46 | 28 | 18 |
| | | | | |
| **SOUTH CAROLINA** | | | | |
| Bob Jones University | 3,750 | 2 | 2 | 0 |
| Clemson University | 28,933 | 58 | 40 | 18 |
| Francis Marion University | 4,895 | 12 | 10 | 2 |
| Furman University | 2,919 | 21 | 14 | 7 |
| Greenville Technical College | 14,447 | 13 | 11 | 2 |
| Lander University | 3,489 | 22 | 12 | 10 |
| Medical University of South Carolina | 3,458 | 66 | 45 | 21 |
| Tri-County Technical College | 7,646 | 14 | 11 | 3 |
| University of South Carolina | | | | |
| Aiken | 4,450 | 9 | 8 | 1 |
| Columbia | 38,526 | 88 | 65 | 23 |
| Upstate | 7,421 | 16 | 14 | 2 |
| Winthrop University | 6,787 | 14 | 11 | 3 |
| York Technical College | 6,053 | 7 | 2 | 5 |
| | | | | |
| **SOUTH DAKOTA** | | | | |
| South Dakota School of Mines and Technology | 3,056 | 4 | 2 | 2 |
| South Dakota State University | 13,937 | 19 | 14 | 5 |
| University of South Dakota | 12,276 | 14 | 11 | 3 |
| | | | | |
| **TENNESSEE** | | | | |
| Austin Peay State University | 12,796 | 25 | 15 | 10 |
| Chattanooga State Community College | 10,425 | 13 | 6 | 7 |
| Christian Brothers University | 2,296 | 20 | 6 | 14 |
| Cleveland State Community College | 4,297 | 4 | 3 | 1 |
| Columbia State Community College | 8,381 | 6 | 2 | 4 |
| East Tennessee State University | 15,939 | 26 | 19 | 7 |
| Jackson State Community College | 6,851 | 3 | 3 | 0 |
| Lincoln Memorial University | 5,511 | 41 | 7 | 34 |
| Middle Tennessee State University | 25,346 | 41 | 32 | 9 |
| Motlow State Community College | 8,620 | 6 | 6 | 0 |
| Nashville State Community College | 10,670 | 20 | 4 | 16 |
| Northeast State Community College | 7,549 | 8 | 8 | 0 |
| Pellissippi State Community College | 14,651 | 17 | 14 | 3 |
| Roane State Community College | 7,241 | 8 | 8 | 0 |
| Southwest Tennessee Community College | 12,913 | 25 | 22 | 3 |
| Tennessee State University | 8,997 | 49 | 22 | 27 |
| Tennessee Technological University | 11,103 | 18 | 13 | 5 |
| University of Memphis | 25,128 | 44 | 35 | 9 |
| University of Tennessee | | | | |
| Chattanooga | 12,675 | 29 | 17 | 12 |
| Health Science Center | 3,379 | 64 | 33 | 31 |
| Knoxville | 32,056 | 90 | 58 | 32 |
| Martin | 8,379 | 13 | 10 | 3 |
| University of the South | 1,957 | 11 | 7 | 4 |
| Vanderbilt University | 13,918 | 248 | 104 | 144 |
| Volunteer State Community College | 11,761 | 12 | 9 | 3 |
| Walters State Community College | 7,726 | 11 | 10 | 1 |
| | | | | |
| **TEXAS** | | | | |
| Alvin Community College | 8,414 | 11 | 9 | 2 |
| Amarillo College | 12,389 | 12 | 10 | 2 |
| Angelo State University | 12,030 | 18 | 14 | 4 |
| Austin College | 1,326 | 9 | 8 | 1 |
| Austin Community College District | 63,569 | 115 | 94 | 21 |
| Baylor Health Care System[2] | | 133 | 46 | 87 |
| Brazosport College | 5,805 | 10 | 10 | 0 |
| Central Texas College | 22,886 | 8 | 7 | 1 |
| Cisco College | 4,876 | 2 | 1 | 1 |
| Concordia University | 3,338 | 6 | 6 | 0 |
| Dallas County Community College District | 125,613 | 144 | 115 | 29 |
| Hardin-Simmons University | 2,487 | 4 | 4 | 0 |
| Houston Community College | 81,256 | 101 | 65 | 36 |
| Kilgore College | 7,250 | 5 | 5 | 0 |
| Lamar University, Beaumont | 21,621 | 74 | 29 | 45 |
| Lone Star College System District | 102,989 | 175 | 105 | 70 |
| Lubbock Christian University | 2,040 | 7 | 2 | 5 |
| McLennan Community College | 13,631 | 18 | 11 | 7 |
| Midwestern State University | 6,947 | 16 | 11 | 5 |
| Odessa College | 10,162 | 7 | 7 | 0 |
| Panola College | 3,364 | 5 | 4 | 1 |
| Paris Junior College | 6,822 | 5 | 5 | 0 |
| Prairie View A&M University | 10,184 | 41 | 31 | 10 |
| Rice University | 8,005 | 49 | 26 | 23 |
| Sam Houston State University | 24,116 | 41 | 27 | 14 |
| San Jacinto College, Central Campus | 42,923 | 41 | 30 | 11 |
| Southern Methodist University | 12,963 | 35 | 27 | 8 |

## Table 79. Full-Time Law Enforcement Employees, by Selected State and University or College, 2021—Continued

(Number.)

| State and university/college | Student enrollment[1] | Law enforcement employees | Officers | Civilians |
|---|---|---|---|---|
| South Plains College | 12,258 | 7 | 6 | 1 |
| Southwestern Christian College | 117 | 2 | 2 | 0 |
| Southwestern University | 1,562 | 11 | 7 | 4 |
| St. Edwards University | 4,324 | 13 | 9 | 4 |
| Stephen F. Austin State University | 14,759 | 41 | 25 | 16 |
| St. Mary's University | 3,757 | 17 | 14 | 3 |
| St. Thomas University | 3,938 | 10 | 9 | 1 |
| Sul Ross State University | 2,949 | 5 | 4 | 1 |
| Tarleton State University | 15,196 | 18 | 18 | 0 |
| Texas A&M University | | | | |
| College Station | 73,308 | 136 | 69 | 67 |
| Commerce | 15,517 | 36 | 24 | 12 |
| San Antonio | 7,724 | 25 | 15 | 10 |
| Texas Christian University | 11,506 | 48 | 28 | 20 |
| Texas State Technical College | | | | |
| Harlingen[2] | | 12 | 10 | 2 |
| Waco | 13,892 | 7 | 5 | 2 |
| West Texas[2] | | 4 | 4 | 0 |
| Texas State University, San Marcos | 42,292 | 42 | 24 | 18 |
| Texas Tech University, Lubbock | 41,909 | 146 | 65 | 81 |
| Texas Woman's University | 19,733 | 40 | 18 | 22 |
| Trinity Valley Community College | 8,188 | 10 | 9 | 1 |
| Tyler Junior College | 16,990 | 26 | 16 | 10 |
| University of Houston | | | | |
| Central Campus | 51,217 | 142 | 54 | 88 |
| Clearlake | 11,134 | 27 | 16 | 11 |
| Downtown Campus | 18,096 | 47 | 21 | 26 |
| University of North Texas, Denton | 45,298 | 63 | 42 | 21 |
| University of Texas | | | | |
| Arlington | 61,457 | 89 | 40 | 49 |
| Austin | 54,243 | 134 | 84 | 50 |
| Dallas | 32,043 | 70 | 25 | 45 |
| El Paso | 29,556 | 45 | 21 | 24 |
| Health Science Center, San Antonio | 4,043 | 97 | 37 | 60 |
| Health Science Center, Tyler | 136 | 27 | 8 | 19 |
| Houston | 7,329 | 306 | 72 | 234 |
| Medical Branch | 3,889 | 128 | 67 | 61 |
| Permian Basin | 8,667 | 24 | 18 | 6 |
| Rio Grande Valley | 41,681 | 76 | 43 | 33 |
| San Antonio | 36,089 | 89 | 40 | 49 |
| Southwestern Medical School | 2,535 | 129 | 45 | 84 |
| Tyler | 11,525 | 32 | 9 | 23 |
| West Texas A&M University | 11,678 | 30 | 20 | 10 |
| | | | | |
| **UTAH** | | | | |
| Brigham Young University | 39,086 | 19 | 18 | 1 |
| Dixie State University | 13,446 | 9 | 8 | 1 |
| Snow College | 5,909 | 3 | 3 | 0 |
| Southern Utah University | 15,872 | 6 | 5 | 1 |
| University of Utah | 38,335 | 39 | 37 | 2 |
| Utah State University | | | | |
| Eastern[2] | | 2 | 2 | 0 |
| Logan | 33,055 | 28 | 18 | 10 |
| Utah Valley University | 45,299 | 17 | 13 | 4 |
| Weber State University | 36,761 | 12 | 10 | 2 |
| | | | | |
| **VERMONT** | | | | |
| University of Vermont | 15,903 | 29 | 18 | 11 |
| | | | | |
| **VIRGINIA** | | | | |
| Christopher Newport University | 5,058 | 27 | 19 | 8 |
| College of William and Mary | 9,785 | 28 | 21 | 7 |
| Eastern Virginia Medical School | 1,436 | 54 | 21 | 33 |
| Emory and Henry College | 1,376 | 7 | 4 | 3 |
| Ferrum College | 1,086 | 7 | 7 | 0 |
| George Mason University | 49,755 | 58 | 42 | 16 |
| Germanna Community College | 9,725 | 9 | 2 | 7 |
| Hampton University | 4,720 | 35 | 14 | 21 |
| James Madison University | 24,039 | 43 | 30 | 13 |
| J. Sargeant Reynolds Community College | 12,772 | 14 | 11 | 3 |
| Longwood University | 5,852 | 18 | 14 | 4 |
| Lord Fairfax Community College | 8,778 | 5 | 5 | 0 |
| Norfolk State University | 6,075 | 29 | 12 | 17 |
| Northern Virginia Community College | 71,294 | 52 | 39 | 13 |
| Old Dominion University | 28,042 | 59 | 39 | 20 |
| Radford University | 14,711 | 24 | 18 | 6 |
| Richard Bland College | 2,662 | 5 | 4 | 1 |
| Southwest Virginia Community College | 3,026 | 4 | 4 | 0 |
| Thomas Nelson Community College | 10,892 | 6 | 6 | 0 |
| University of Mary Washington | 5,098 | 19 | 15 | 4 |
| University of Richmond | 4,534 | 29 | 19 | 10 |
| University of Virginia | 29,237 | 128 | 53 | 75 |

## Table 79. Full-Time Law Enforcement Employees, by Selected State and University or College, 2021—Continued

(Number.)

| State and university/college | Student enrollment[1] | Law enforcement employees | Officers | Civilians |
|---|---|---|---|---|
| Virginia Commonwealth University | 32,628 | 106 | 77 | 29 |
| Virginia Highlands Community College | 2,892 | 1 | 1 | 0 |
| Virginia Military Institute | 1,740 | 12 | 11 | 1 |
| Virginia Polytechnic Institute and State University | 38,350 | 60 | 48 | 12 |
| Virginia State University | 4,708 | 30 | 18 | 12 |
| Virginia Western Community College | 8,535 | 8 | 8 | 0 |
| **WASHINGTON** | | | | |
| Central Washington University | 14,090 | 16 | 14 | 2 |
| Eastern Washington University | 16,280 | 12 | 11 | 1 |
| Evergreen State College | 3,439 | 12 | 6 | 6 |
| University of Washington | 56,554 | 62 | 29 | 33 |
| Washington State University | | | | |
| Pullman | 35,394 | 25 | 22 | 3 |
| Vancouver[2] | | 5 | 3 | 2 |
| Western Washington University | 17,883 | 21 | 13 | 8 |
| **WEST VIRGINIA** | | | | |
| Bluefield State College | 1,435 | 3 | 3 | 0 |
| Concord University | 2,319 | 8 | 6 | 2 |
| Fairmont State University | 4,358 | 15 | 8 | 7 |
| Glenville State College | 1,821 | 6 | 3 | 3 |
| Marshall University | 15,850 | 32 | 28 | 4 |
| Potomac State College | 1,514 | 5 | 4 | 1 |
| Shepherd University | 5,165 | 9 | 8 | 1 |
| West Liberty University | 2,966 | 7 | 7 | 0 |
| West Virginia State University | 5,808 | 6 | 5 | 1 |
| West Virginia University | | | | |
| Institute of Technology | 2,056 | 8 | 7 | 1 |
| Morgantown | 30,045 | 62 | 46 | 16 |
| **WISCONSIN** | | | | |
| University of Wisconsin | | | | |
| Eau Claire | 12,230 | 9 | 8 | 1 |
| Green Bay | 10,742 | 10 | 9 | 1 |
| La Crosse | 11,501 | 20 | 12 | 8 |
| Madison | 47,831 | 112 | 61 | 51 |
| Milwaukee | 30,081 | 43 | 34 | 9 |
| Oshkosh | 18,536 | 17 | 11 | 6 |
| Parkside | 5,317 | 13 | 9 | 4 |
| Platteville | 9,403 | 8 | 7 | 1 |
| River Falls | 6,561 | 5 | 5 | 0 |
| Stevens Point | 9,447 | 12 | 8 | 4 |
| Stout | 9,702 | 9 | 8 | 1 |
| Superior | 3,171 | 6 | 5 | 1 |
| Whitewater | 14,657 | 15 | 13 | 2 |
| **WYOMING** | | | | |
| University of Wyoming | 13,616 | 25 | 15 | 10 |

1 The student enrollment figures provided by the United States Department of Education are for the 2020 school year, the most recent available. The enrollment figures include full-time and part-time students.    2 Student enrollment figures were not available.

## Table 80. Full-Time Law Enforcement Employees, by Selected State Metropolitan and Nonmetropolitan Counties, 2021

(Number.)

| State/county | Law enforcement employees | Officers | Civilians |
|---|---|---|---|
| **ALABAMA** | | | |
| **Metropolitan Counties** | | | |
| Autauga | 46 | 35 | 11 |
| Baldwin | 327 | 140 | 187 |
| Bibb | 12 | 11 | 1 |
| Blount | 65 | 48 | 17 |
| Calhoun | 85 | 50 | 35 |
| Chilton | 37 | 34 | 3 |
| Colbert | 59 | 33 | 26 |
| Elmore | 125 | 57 | 68 |
| Etowah | 134 | 70 | 64 |
| Geneva | 30 | 12 | 18 |
| Greene | 31 | 11 | 20 |
| Hale | 32 | 11 | 21 |
| Henry | 40 | 24 | 16 |
| Houston | 175 | 83 | 92 |
| Jefferson | 785 | 581 | 204 |
| Lauderdale | 45 | 37 | 8 |
| Lawrence | 45 | 22 | 23 |
| Lee | 179 | 85 | 94 |
| Limestone | 119 | 50 | 69 |
| Lowndes | 40 | 19 | 21 |
| Madison | 323 | 132 | 191 |
| Mobile | 745 | 192 | 553 |
| Montgomery | 169 | 123 | 46 |
| Morgan | 164 | 49 | 115 |
| Pickens | 28 | 9 | 19 |
| Russell | 107 | 39 | 68 |
| Shelby | 223 | 139 | 84 |
| St. Clair | 114 | 51 | 63 |
| Tuscaloosa | 219 | 105 | 114 |
| Washington | 22 | 10 | 12 |
| **Nonmetropolitan Counties** | | | |
| Barbour | 32 | 17 | 15 |
| Bullock | 18 | 6 | 12 |
| Butler | 16 | 14 | 2 |
| Chambers | 56 | 23 | 33 |
| Cherokee | 55 | 31 | 24 |
| Choctaw | 10 | 8 | 2 |
| Clarke | 40 | 11 | 29 |
| Clay | 20 | 10 | 10 |
| Cleburne | 29 | 12 | 17 |
| Coffee | 60 | 30 | 30 |
| Conecuh | 35 | 10 | 25 |
| Coosa | 23 | 10 | 13 |
| Covington | 29 | 24 | 5 |
| Crenshaw | 12 | 10 | 2 |
| Cullman | 147 | 82 | 65 |
| Dale | 47 | 27 | 20 |
| Dallas | 61 | 28 | 33 |
| DeKalb | 100 | 44 | 56 |
| Escambia | 59 | 21 | 38 |
| Fayette | 19 | 10 | 9 |
| Franklin | 53 | 21 | 32 |
| Jackson | 81 | 33 | 48 |
| Lamar | 18 | 6 | 12 |
| Macon | 48 | 25 | 23 |
| Marengo | 23 | 9 | 14 |
| Marion | 31 | 15 | 16 |
| Marshall | 89 | 51 | 38 |
| Monroe | 44 | 18 | 26 |
| Perry | 19 | 7 | 12 |
| Pike | 37 | 24 | 13 |
| Randolph | 41 | 15 | 26 |
| Sumter | 16 | 6 | 10 |
| Talladega | 91 | 43 | 48 |
| Tallapoosa | 50 | 22 | 28 |
| Walker | 90 | 49 | 41 |
| Wilcox | 27 | 11 | 16 |
| Winston | 19 | 9 | 10 |
| **ARIZONA** | | | |
| **Metropolitan Counties** | | | |
| Cochise | 169 | 83 | 86 |
| Coconino | 221 | 66 | 155 |
| Maricopa | 3,147 | 628 | 2,519 |
| Mohave | 263 | 93 | 170 |
| Pima | 1,345 | 506 | 839 |
| Pinal | 476 | 205 | 271 |
| Yavapai | 177 | 117 | 60 |
| Yuma | 321 | 79 | 242 |
| **Nonmetropolitan Counties** | | | |

## Table 80. Full-Time Law Enforcement Employees, by Selected State Metropolitan and Nonmetropolitan Counties, 2021—Continued

(Number.)

| State/county | Law enforcement employees | Officers | Civilians |
|---|---|---|---|
| Apache | 31 | 21 | 10 |
| Gila | 111 | 42 | 69 |
| Graham | 73 | 20 | 53 |
| Greenlee | 41 | 15 | 26 |
| La Paz | 77 | 30 | 47 |
| Navajo | 139 | 58 | 81 |
| Santa Cruz | 82 | 36 | 46 |
| **ARKANSAS** | | | |
| **Metropolitan Counties** | | | |
| Benton | 251 | 159 | 92 |
| Cleveland | 13 | 8 | 5 |
| Craighead | 118 | 42 | 76 |
| Crawford | 73 | 33 | 40 |
| Crittenden | 121 | 36 | 85 |
| Faulkner | 142 | 47 | 95 |
| Franklin | 40 | 11 | 29 |
| Garland | 90 | 62 | 28 |
| Grant | 19 | 16 | 3 |
| Jefferson | 94 | 69 | 25 |
| Lincoln | 29 | 10 | 19 |
| Little River | 31 | 15 | 16 |
| Lonoke | 61 | 29 | 32 |
| Madison | 22 | 20 | 2 |
| Miller | 33 | 25 | 8 |
| Perry | 24 | 11 | 13 |
| Poinsett | 44 | 17 | 27 |
| Pulaski | 448 | 124 | 324 |
| Saline | 94 | 52 | 42 |
| Sebastian | 184 | 53 | 131 |
| Washington | 262 | 143 | 119 |
| **Nonmetropolitan Counties** | | | |
| Arkansas | 12 | 11 | 1 |
| Ashley | 40 | 19 | 21 |
| Baxter | 61 | 33 | 28 |
| Boone | 66 | 29 | 37 |
| Bradley | 10 | 6 | 4 |
| Calhoun | 12 | 6 | 6 |
| Carroll | 53 | 21 | 32 |
| Chicot | 8 | 7 | 1 |
| Clark | 25 | 16 | 9 |
| Clay | 16 | 10 | 6 |
| Cleburne | 49 | 26 | 23 |
| Columbia | 48 | 17 | 31 |
| Conway | 25 | 23 | 2 |
| Cross | 49 | 17 | 32 |
| Dallas | 6 | 5 | 1 |
| Desha | 10 | 9 | 1 |
| Drew | 14 | 13 | 1 |
| Fulton | 21 | 9 | 12 |
| Greene | 34 | 28 | 6 |
| Hempstead | 50 | 19 | 31 |
| Hot Spring | 31 | 29 | 2 |
| Howard | 23 | 11 | 12 |
| Independence | 54 | 34 | 20 |
| Izard | 38 | 22 | 16 |
| Jackson | 42 | 15 | 27 |
| Johnson | 37 | 21 | 16 |
| Lafayette | 10 | 9 | 1 |
| Lawrence | 38 | 17 | 21 |
| Lee | 15 | 7 | 8 |
| Logan | 49 | 14 | 35 |
| Marion | 14 | 12 | 2 |
| Mississippi | 87 | 43 | 44 |
| Monroe | 16 | 6 | 10 |
| Montgomery | 30 | 11 | 19 |
| Nevada | 11 | 5 | 6 |
| Newton | 19 | 9 | 10 |
| Ouachita | 50 | 22 | 28 |
| Phillips | 20 | 15 | 5 |
| Pike | 34 | 11 | 23 |
| Polk | 30 | 17 | 13 |
| Pope | 91 | 37 | 54 |
| Prairie | 28 | 8 | 20 |
| Randolph | 34 | 12 | 22 |
| Scott | 27 | 9 | 18 |
| Searcy | 19 | 8 | 11 |
| Sevier | 37 | 16 | 21 |
| Sharp | 35 | 14 | 21 |
| St. Francis | 46 | 40 | 6 |
| Stone | 25 | 12 | 13 |
| Union | 64 | 37 | 27 |

# Table 80. Full-Time Law Enforcement Employees, by Selected State Metropolitan and Nonmetropolitan Counties, 2021—Continued

(Number.)

| State/county | Law enforcement employees | Officers | Civilians |
|---|---|---|---|
| Van Buren | 39 | 19 | 20 |
| White | 87 | 52 | 35 |
| Woodruff | 11 | 6 | 5 |
| Yell | 24 | 16 | 8 |
| **CALIFORNIA** | | | |
| **Metropolitan Counties** | | | |
| Alameda | 1,597 | 1,035 | 562 |
| Butte | 263 | 95 | 168 |
| Contra Costa | 944 | 639 | 305 |
| El Dorado | 347 | 167 | 180 |
| Fresno | 1,136 | 408 | 728 |
| Imperial | 272 | 191 | 81 |
| Kern | 1,101 | 723 | 378 |
| Kings | 276 | 88 | 188 |
| Los Angeles | 15,286 | 9,522 | 5,764 |
| Madera | 245 | 105 | 140 |
| Marin | 289 | 196 | 93 |
| Merced | 272 | 203 | 69 |
| Monterey | 441 | 288 | 153 |
| Napa | 146 | 110 | 36 |
| Orange | 3,611 | 1,874 | 1,737 |
| Placer | 532 | 248 | 284 |
| Riverside | 3,799 | 1,663 | 2,136 |
| Sacramento | 1,937 | 1,271 | 666 |
| San Benito | 61 | 29 | 32 |
| San Bernardino | 3,312 | 1,940 | 1,372 |
| San Diego | 4,129 | 2,463 | 1,666 |
| San Francisco | 990 | 805 | 185 |
| San Joaquin | 751 | 314 | 437 |
| San Luis Obispo | 419 | 306 | 113 |
| San Mateo | 700 | 312 | 388 |
| Santa Barbara | 685 | 485 | 200 |
| Santa Clara | 1,533 | 1,189 | 344 |
| Santa Cruz | 314 | 147 | 167 |
| Shasta | 190 | 134 | 56 |
| Solano | 508 | 171 | 337 |
| Sonoma | 563 | 226 | 337 |
| Stanislaus | 732 | 514 | 218 |
| Sutter | 131 | 106 | 25 |
| Tulare | 735 | 511 | 224 |
| Ventura | 1,192 | 614 | 578 |
| Yolo | 252 | 72 | 180 |
| Yuba | 157 | 124 | 33 |
| **Nonmetropolitan Counties** | | | |
| Alpine | 16 | 13 | 3 |
| Amador | 85 | 49 | 36 |
| Calaveras | 119 | 64 | 55 |
| Colusa | 64 | 43 | 21 |
| Del Norte | 48 | 18 | 30 |
| Glenn | 62 | 29 | 33 |
| Humboldt | 261 | 183 | 78 |
| Inyo | 53 | 36 | 17 |
| Lake | 118 | 89 | 29 |
| Lassen | 83 | 62 | 21 |
| Mariposa | 74 | 58 | 16 |
| Mendocino | 173 | 139 | 34 |
| Modoc | 33 | 25 | 8 |
| Mono | 43 | 23 | 20 |
| Nevada | 159 | 60 | 99 |
| Plumas | 61 | 29 | 32 |
| Sierra | 15 | 10 | 5 |
| Siskiyou | 92 | 72 | 20 |
| Tehama | 94 | 70 | 24 |
| Trinity | 44 | 35 | 9 |
| Tuolumne | 130 | 59 | 71 |
| **COLORADO** | | | |
| **Metropolitan Counties** | | | |
| Adams | 605 | 417 | 188 |
| Arapahoe | 570 | 396 | 174 |
| Boulder | 403 | 110 | 293 |
| Clear Creek | 69 | 31 | 38 |
| Douglas | 543 | 361 | 182 |
| Elbert | 54 | 45 | 9 |
| El Paso | 783 | 501 | 282 |
| Gilpin | 56 | 30 | 26 |
| Jefferson | 739 | 381 | 358 |
| Larimer | 415 | 285 | 130 |
| Mesa | 245 | 132 | 113 |
| Park | 46 | 23 | 23 |
| Pueblo | 338 | 141 | 197 |

## Table 80. Full-Time Law Enforcement Employees, by Selected State Metropolitan and Nonmetropolitan Counties, 2021—Continued

(Number.)

| State/county | Law enforcement employees | Officers | Civilians |
|---|---|---|---|
| Teller | 71 | 41 | 30 |
| Weld | 437 | 101 | 336 |
| **Nonmetropolitan Counties** | | | |
| Alamosa | 51 | 25 | 26 |
| Archuleta | 50 | 20 | 30 |
| Baca | 14 | 5 | 9 |
| Bent | 41 | 13 | 28 |
| Chaffee | 61 | 22 | 39 |
| Cheyenne | 5 | 2 | 3 |
| Conejos | 26 | 10 | 16 |
| Costilla | 13 | 8 | 5 |
| Crowley | 15 | 7 | 8 |
| Custer | 19 | 12 | 7 |
| Delta | 74 | 38 | 36 |
| Dolores | 5 | 5 | 0 |
| Eagle | 80 | 48 | 32 |
| Fremont | 99 | 45 | 54 |
| Garfield | 128 | 50 | 78 |
| Grand | 50 | 22 | 28 |
| Gunnison | 30 | 16 | 14 |
| Hinsdale | 4 | 3 | 1 |
| Huerfano | 41 | 20 | 21 |
| Jackson | 6 | 4 | 2 |
| Kiowa | 6 | 4 | 2 |
| Kit Carson | 20 | 6 | 14 |
| Lake | 23 | 6 | 17 |
| La Plata | 117 | 101 | 16 |
| Las Animas | 28 | 10 | 18 |
| Lincoln | 28 | 12 | 16 |
| Logan | 39 | 15 | 24 |
| Mineral | 5 | 4 | 1 |
| Moffat | 37 | 18 | 19 |
| Montezuma | 74 | 29 | 45 |
| Montrose | 91 | 49 | 42 |
| Morgan | 51 | 22 | 29 |
| Otero | 22 | 11 | 11 |
| Ouray | 8 | 7 | 1 |
| Phillips | 3 | 3 | 0 |
| Pitkin | 56 | 27 | 29 |
| Prowers | 28 | 9 | 19 |
| Rio Blanco | 22 | 11 | 11 |
| Rio Grande | 39 | 18 | 21 |
| Routt | 48 | 24 | 24 |
| Saguache | 23 | 14 | 9 |
| San Juan | 3 | 3 | 0 |
| San Miguel | 34 | 12 | 22 |
| Sedgwick | 3 | 2 | 1 |
| Summit | 93 | 65 | 28 |
| Washington | 28 | 12 | 16 |
| Yuma | 23 | 20 | 3 |
| **DELAWARE** | | | |
| **Metropolitan Counties** | | | |
| New Castle County Police Department | 430 | 376 | 54 |
| **FLORIDA** | | | |
| **Metropolitan Counties** | | | |
| Alachua | 371 | 265 | 106 |
| Baker | 63 | 43 | 20 |
| Bay | 278 | 215 | 63 |
| Brevard | 973 | 540 | 433 |
| Broward | 2,571 | 1,531 | 1,040 |
| Charlotte | 431 | 286 | 145 |
| Citrus | 330 | 214 | 116 |
| Clay | 594 | 281 | 313 |
| Collier | 918 | 572 | 346 |
| Escambia | 662 | 393 | 269 |
| Flagler | 300 | 225 | 75 |
| Gilchrist | 58 | 44 | 14 |
| Hernando | 548 | 366 | 182 |
| Highlands | 343 | 157 | 186 |
| Hillsborough | 3,329 | 1,265 | 2,064 |
| Indian River | 487 | 189 | 298 |
| Jacksonville Sheriff's Office | 3,112 | 1,813 | 1,299 |
| Jefferson | 43 | 27 | 16 |
| Lake | 704 | 292 | 412 |
| Lee | 1,572 | 694 | 878 |
| Leon | 451 | 270 | 181 |
| Levy | 149 | 113 | 36 |
| Manatee | 1,297 | 598 | 699 |
| Marion | 808 | 569 | 239 |
| Martin | 395 | 264 | 131 |

## Table 80. Full-Time Law Enforcement Employees, by Selected State Metropolitan and Nonmetropolitan Counties, 2021—Continued

(Number.)

| State/county | Law enforcement employees | Officers | Civilians |
|---|---|---|---|
| Miami-Dade | 4,154 | 3,020 | 1,134 |
| Nassau | 257 | 141 | 116 |
| Okaloosa | 435 | 314 | 121 |
| Orange | 2,265 | 1,628 | 637 |
| Osceola | 684 | 448 | 236 |
| Palm Beach | 3,639 | 1,655 | 1,984 |
| Pasco | 941 | 609 | 332 |
| Pinellas | 2,316 | 810 | 1,506 |
| Polk | 1,181 | 671 | 510 |
| Santa Rosa | 336 | 239 | 97 |
| Sarasota | 959 | 408 | 551 |
| Seminole | 1,259 | 454 | 805 |
| St. Johns | 736 | 363 | 373 |
| St. Lucie | 766 | 331 | 435 |
| Volusia | 675 | 387 | 288 |
| Wakulla | 136 | 58 | 78 |
| Walton | 412 | 192 | 220 |
| **Nonmetropolitan Counties** | | | |
| Bradford | 87 | 34 | 53 |
| Calhoun | 22 | 19 | 3 |
| Columbia | 180 | 148 | 32 |
| DeSoto | 114 | 52 | 62 |
| Franklin | 50 | 29 | 21 |
| Glades | 103 | 24 | 79 |
| Gulf | 42 | 29 | 13 |
| Hamilton | 65 | 23 | 42 |
| Hardee | 72 | 49 | 23 |
| Hendry | 139 | 78 | 61 |
| Lafayette | 27 | 18 | 9 |
| Madison | 81 | 38 | 43 |
| Monroe | 516 | 204 | 312 |
| Okeechobee | 133 | 89 | 44 |
| Putnam | 223 | 122 | 101 |
| Suwannee | 114 | 85 | 29 |
| Union | 27 | 17 | 10 |
| Washington | 56 | 38 | 18 |
| **GEORGIA** | | | |
| **Metropolitan Counties** | | | |
| Augusta-Richmond | 606 | 345 | 261 |
| Barrow | 178 | 121 | 57 |
| Bartow | 202 | 163 | 39 |
| Bibb | 331 | 268 | 63 |
| Brantley | 47 | 19 | 28 |
| Brooks | 47 | 23 | 24 |
| Bryan | 83 | 50 | 33 |
| Burke | 123 | 71 | 52 |
| Butts | 100 | 61 | 39 |
| Carroll | 175 | 101 | 74 |
| Catoosa | 119 | 69 | 50 |
| Chatham County Police Department | 152 | 133 | 19 |
| Cherokee | 424 | 299 | 125 |
| Clarke | 129 | 94 | 35 |
| Clayton | 253 | 87 | 166 |
| Clayton County Police Department | 434 | 333 | 101 |
| Cobb | 764 | 480 | 284 |
| Cobb County Police Department | 712 | 647 | 65 |
| Coweta | 268 | 180 | 88 |
| Dawson | 120 | 76 | 44 |
| DeKalb | 541 | 176 | 365 |
| DeKalb County Police Department | 920 | 694 | 226 |
| Dougherty | 210 | 193 | 17 |
| Dougherty County Police Department | 39 | 28 | 11 |
| Douglas | 331 | 216 | 115 |
| Echols | 9 | 9 | 0 |
| Effingham | 138 | 77 | 61 |
| Fayette | 194 | 135 | 59 |
| Floyd County Police Department | 83 | 75 | 8 |
| Forsyth | 453 | 360 | 93 |
| Fulton | 880 | 642 | 238 |
| Fulton County Police Department | 74 | 35 | 39 |
| Glynn | 142 | 43 | 99 |
| Glynn County Police Department | 119 | 104 | 15 |
| Gwinnett County Police Department | 945 | 701 | 244 |
| Hall | 383 | 261 | 122 |
| Haralson | 67 | 36 | 31 |
| Harris | 75 | 54 | 21 |
| Heard | 37 | 19 | 18 |
| Henry | 299 | 232 | 67 |
| Henry County Police Department | 321 | 264 | 57 |
| Houston | 286 | 126 | 160 |
| Jasper | 50 | 36 | 14 |

## Table 80. Full-Time Law Enforcement Employees, by Selected State Metropolitan and Nonmetropolitan Counties, 2021—Continued

(Number.)

| State/county | Law enforcement employees | Officers | Civilians |
|---|---|---|---|
| Jones | 79 | 40 | 39 |
| Lamar | 56 | 34 | 22 |
| Lee | 73 | 48 | 25 |
| Liberty | 124 | 71 | 53 |
| Long | 30 | 26 | 4 |
| Lowndes | 207 | 176 | 31 |
| Madison | 81 | 43 | 38 |
| Marion | 16 | 8 | 8 |
| McIntosh | 114 | 50 | 64 |
| Meriwether | 40 | 25 | 15 |
| Monroe | 114 | 69 | 45 |
| Murray | 90 | 51 | 39 |
| Muscogee | 287 | 181 | 106 |
| Newton | 277 | 161 | 116 |
| Oconee | 96 | 62 | 34 |
| Oglethorpe | 41 | 24 | 17 |
| Paulding | 310 | 187 | 123 |
| Peach | 60 | 32 | 28 |
| Pickens | 74 | 64 | 10 |
| Pike | 43 | 26 | 17 |
| Rockdale | 263 | 238 | 25 |
| Spalding | 181 | 112 | 69 |
| Stewart | 9 | 6 | 3 |
| Talbot | 18 | 13 | 5 |
| Terrell | 23 | 10 | 13 |
| Twiggs | 48 | 21 | 27 |
| Walker | 109 | 67 | 42 |
| Walton | 176 | 150 | 26 |
| Whitfield | 216 | 185 | 31 |
| Worth | 40 | 28 | 12 |
| **Nonmetropolitan Counties** | | | |
| Atkinson | 20 | 9 | 11 |
| Baker | 9 | 7 | 2 |
| Banks | 71 | 51 | 20 |
| Ben Hill | 50 | 24 | 26 |
| Berrien | 46 | 27 | 19 |
| Bleckley | 41 | 18 | 23 |
| Bulloch | 134 | 122 | 12 |
| Candler | 29 | 19 | 10 |
| Chattooga | 43 | 26 | 17 |
| Clay | 8 | 7 | 1 |
| Clinch | 15 | 12 | 3 |
| Coffee | 126 | 60 | 66 |
| Cook | 49 | 28 | 21 |
| Crisp | 92 | 49 | 43 |
| Decatur | 65 | 31 | 34 |
| Dodge | 53 | 24 | 29 |
| Dooly | 69 | 34 | 35 |
| Early | 36 | 17 | 19 |
| Elbert | 57 | 33 | 24 |
| Emanuel | 50 | 30 | 20 |
| Fannin | 67 | 37 | 30 |
| Franklin | 63 | 38 | 25 |
| Gilmer | 98 | 57 | 41 |
| Glascock | 6 | 5 | 1 |
| Gordon | 115 | 73 | 42 |
| Grady | 24 | 21 | 3 |
| Greene | 48 | 43 | 5 |
| Habersham | 79 | 50 | 29 |
| Hancock | 37 | 11 | 26 |
| Hart | 54 | 30 | 24 |
| Irwin | 24 | 15 | 9 |
| Jackson | 142 | 93 | 49 |
| Jeff Davis | 42 | 19 | 23 |
| Jefferson | 50 | 24 | 26 |
| Jenkins | 21 | 12 | 9 |
| Laurens | 107 | 69 | 38 |
| Lumpkin | 79 | 45 | 34 |
| Mitchell | 51 | 25 | 26 |
| Pierce | 44 | 19 | 25 |
| Polk | 77 | 39 | 38 |
| Polk County Police Department | 40 | 35 | 5 |
| Pulaski | 22 | 14 | 8 |
| Quitman | 9 | 7 | 2 |
| Rabun | 56 | 51 | 5 |
| Randolph | 32 | 15 | 17 |
| Schley | 10 | 5 | 5 |
| Screven | 18 | 15 | 3 |
| Seminole | 33 | 25 | 8 |
| Sumter | 84 | 42 | 42 |
| Taylor | 20 | 10 | 10 |
| Tift | 92 | 48 | 44 |

## Table 80. Full-Time Law Enforcement Employees, by Selected State Metropolitan and Nonmetropolitan Counties, 2021—Continued

(Number.)

| State/county | Law enforcement employees | Officers | Civilians |
|---|---|---|---|
| Toombs | 76 | 23 | 53 |
| Towns | 40 | 19 | 21 |
| Treutlen | 21 | 12 | 9 |
| Troup | 141 | 78 | 63 |
| Turner | 45 | 22 | 23 |
| Union | 51 | 46 | 5 |
| Upson | 62 | 37 | 25 |
| Ware | 113 | 43 | 70 |
| Washington | 67 | 37 | 30 |
| Webster | 5 | 5 | 0 |
| White | 70 | 41 | 29 |
| Wilcox | 21 | 15 | 6 |
| Wilkes | 51 | 33 | 18 |
| Wilkinson | 28 | 16 | 12 |
| **HAWAII** | | | |
| **Metropolitan Counties** | | | |
| Maui Police Department | 412 | 310 | 102 |
| **Nonmetropolitan Counties** | | | |
| Hawaii Police Department | 587 | 431 | 156 |
| Kauai Police Department | 201 | 145 | 56 |
| **IDAHO** | | | |
| **Metropolitan Counties** | | | |
| Ada | 551 | 190 | 361 |
| Bannock | 68 | 45 | 23 |
| Boise | 21 | 13 | 8 |
| Bonneville | 107 | 71 | 36 |
| Butte | 10 | 4 | 6 |
| Canyon | 144 | 65 | 79 |
| Franklin | 20 | 13 | 7 |
| Gem | 26 | 14 | 12 |
| Jefferson | 39 | 23 | 16 |
| Jerome | 31 | 24 | 7 |
| Kootenai | 202 | 96 | 106 |
| Nez Perce | 41 | 22 | 19 |
| Owyhee | 22 | 12 | 10 |
| Power | 17 | 10 | 7 |
| Twin Falls | 75 | 44 | 31 |
| **Nonmetropolitan Counties** | | | |
| Adams | 15 | 8 | 7 |
| Bear Lake | 14 | 7 | 7 |
| Benewah | 20 | 10 | 10 |
| Bingham | 66 | 44 | 22 |
| Blaine | 49 | 37 | 12 |
| Bonner | 71 | 42 | 29 |
| Boundary | 25 | 12 | 13 |
| Camas | 6 | 4 | 2 |
| Caribou | 16 | 9 | 7 |
| Cassia | 74 | 31 | 43 |
| Clark | 7 | 3 | 4 |
| Clearwater | 23 | 15 | 8 |
| Custer | 16 | 10 | 6 |
| Elmore | 43 | 25 | 18 |
| Fremont | 31 | 23 | 8 |
| Gooding | 22 | 17 | 5 |
| Idaho | 30 | 18 | 12 |
| Latah | 39 | 28 | 11 |
| Lemhi | 10 | 8 | 2 |
| Lewis | 13 | 9 | 4 |
| Lincoln | 14 | 12 | 2 |
| Madison | 35 | 22 | 13 |
| Minidoka | 32 | 20 | 12 |
| Oneida | 13 | 8 | 5 |
| Payette | 27 | 14 | 13 |
| Shoshone | 31 | 19 | 12 |
| Teton | 22 | 14 | 8 |
| Valley | 31 | 20 | 11 |
| Washington | 21 | 13 | 8 |
| **ILLINOIS** | | | |
| **Metropolitan Counties** | | | |
| Cook | 5,170 | 1,588 | 3,582 |
| Grundy | 48 | 30 | 18 |
| Kane | 127 | 91 | 36 |
| Kendall | 106 | 51 | 55 |
| Madison | 166 | 84 | 82 |
| Marshall | 18 | 9 | 9 |
| McHenry | 361 | 104 | 257 |
| McLean | 140 | 52 | 88 |
| Rock Island | 178 | 64 | 114 |

## Table 80. Full-Time Law Enforcement Employees, by Selected State Metropolitan and Nonmetropolitan Counties, 2021—Continued

(Number.)

| State/county | Law enforcement employees | Officers | Civilians |
|---|---|---|---|
| Vermilion | 90 | 42 | 48 |
| Will | 567 | 229 | 338 |
| **Nonmetropolitan Counties** | | | |
| Fayette | 17 | 11 | 6 |
| Jefferson | 57 | 21 | 36 |
| Jo Daviess | 38 | 17 | 21 |
| Knox | 68 | 63 | 5 |
| Livingston | 63 | 30 | 33 |
| McDonough | 25 | 15 | 10 |
| Randolph | 46 | 10 | 36 |
| **INDIANA** | | | |
| **Metropolitan Counties** | | | |
| Boone | 81 | 36 | 45 |
| Hamilton | 181 | 59 | 122 |
| Hancock | 95 | 43 | 52 |
| Hendricks | 130 | 56 | 74 |
| Johnson | 150 | 134 | 16 |
| Lake | 439 | 161 | 278 |
| Madison | 111 | 40 | 71 |
| Monroe | 126 | 107 | 19 |
| St. Joseph | 270 | 117 | 153 |
| Whitley | 57 | 19 | 38 |
| **Nonmetropolitan Counties** | | | |
| Blackford | 32 | 10 | 22 |
| Decatur | 54 | 23 | 31 |
| DeKalb | 54 | 22 | 32 |
| Grant | 89 | 40 | 49 |
| Greene | 59 | 18 | 41 |
| Knox | 67 | 30 | 37 |
| Kosciusko | 111 | 40 | 71 |
| LaGrange | 62 | 20 | 42 |
| Montgomery | 75 | 26 | 49 |
| Noble | 75 | 20 | 55 |
| Steuben | 54 | 24 | 30 |
| **IOWA** | | | |
| **Metropolitan Counties** | | | |
| Benton | 39 | 14 | 25 |
| Black Hawk | 132 | 70 | 62 |
| Boone | 28 | 13 | 15 |
| Dallas | 72 | 30 | 42 |
| Dubuque | 103 | 76 | 27 |
| Grundy | 16 | 12 | 4 |
| Jasper | 52 | 18 | 34 |
| Johnson | 90 | 72 | 18 |
| Jones | 27 | 10 | 17 |
| Linn | 222 | 137 | 85 |
| Madison | 19 | 9 | 10 |
| Mills | 33 | 13 | 20 |
| Polk | 500 | 150 | 350 |
| Pottawattamie | 225 | 55 | 170 |
| Scott | 155 | 49 | 106 |
| Story | 90 | 32 | 58 |
| Warren | 40 | 20 | 20 |
| Washington | 22 | 19 | 3 |
| Woodbury | 124 | 42 | 82 |
| **Nonmetropolitan Counties** | | | |
| Adair | 15 | 6 | 9 |
| Adams | 13 | 8 | 5 |
| Allamakee | 20 | 10 | 10 |
| Appanoose | 17 | 10 | 7 |
| Buchanan | 31 | 13 | 18 |
| Buena Vista | 37 | 13 | 24 |
| Carroll | 12 | 10 | 2 |
| Cass | 11 | 9 | 2 |
| Cedar | 39 | 14 | 25 |
| Cerro Gordo | 72 | 20 | 52 |
| Cherokee | 20 | 8 | 12 |
| Chickasaw | 17 | 10 | 7 |
| Clay | 13 | 11 | 2 |
| Clinton | 46 | 26 | 20 |
| Crawford | 14 | 11 | 3 |
| Delaware | 26 | 13 | 13 |
| Des Moines | 29 | 24 | 5 |
| Emmet | 16 | 9 | 7 |
| Fayette | 36 | 12 | 24 |
| Floyd | 21 | 12 | 9 |
| Franklin | 10 | 7 | 3 |
| Fremont | 28 | 10 | 18 |

## Table 80. Full-Time Law Enforcement Employees, by Selected State Metropolitan and Nonmetropolitan Counties, 2021—Continued

(Number.)

| State/county | Law enforcement employees | Officers | Civilians |
|---|---|---|---|
| Hamilton | 31 | 11 | 20 |
| Hancock | 10 | 8 | 2 |
| Hardin | 14 | 9 | 5 |
| Henry | 37 | 12 | 25 |
| Howard | 17 | 9 | 8 |
| Humboldt | 18 | 9 | 9 |
| Ida | 17 | 9 | 8 |
| Iowa | 30 | 12 | 18 |
| Jackson | 21 | 11 | 10 |
| Jefferson | 30 | 11 | 19 |
| Keokuk | 14 | 7 | 7 |
| Kossuth | 24 | 10 | 14 |
| Lee | 46 | 18 | 28 |
| Louisa | 27 | 10 | 17 |
| Lucas | 13 | 6 | 7 |
| Lyon | 26 | 12 | 14 |
| Mahaska | 26 | 10 | 16 |
| Marion | 38 | 16 | 22 |
| Marshall | 53 | 19 | 34 |
| Mitchell | 17 | 7 | 10 |
| Monona | 23 | 8 | 15 |
| Monroe | 18 | 6 | 12 |
| Muscatine | 87 | 24 | 63 |
| O'Brien | 27 | 9 | 18 |
| Osceola | 14 | 9 | 5 |
| Page | 9 | 9 | 0 |
| Palo Alto | 17 | 8 | 9 |
| Plymouth | 35 | 12 | 23 |
| Pocahontas | 19 | 8 | 11 |
| Poweshiek | 22 | 11 | 11 |
| Ringgold | 12 | 6 | 6 |
| Sac | 22 | 10 | 12 |
| Shelby | 11 | 10 | 1 |
| Sioux | 40 | 14 | 26 |
| Tama | 23 | 14 | 9 |
| Union | 13 | 6 | 7 |
| Van Buren | 12 | 6 | 6 |
| Wapello | 47 | 14 | 33 |
| Wayne | 16 | 5 | 11 |
| Webster | 36 | 19 | 17 |
| Winnebago | 9 | 8 | 1 |
| Winneshiek | 28 | 13 | 15 |
| Worth | 24 | 13 | 11 |
| Wright | 23 | 10 | 13 |
| **KANSAS** | | | |
| **Metropolitan Counties** | | | |
| Butler | 54 | 51 | 3 |
| Geary | 91 | 38 | 53 |
| Harvey | 24 | 22 | 2 |
| Jackson | 42 | 22 | 20 |
| Jefferson | 42 | 23 | 19 |
| Johnson | 651 | 484 | 167 |
| Leavenworth | 78 | 52 | 26 |
| Linn | 38 | 21 | 17 |
| Miami | 60 | 32 | 28 |
| Osage | 43 | 29 | 14 |
| Pottawatomie | 41 | 28 | 13 |
| Riley County Police Department | 200 | 107 | 93 |
| Sedgwick | 256 | 192 | 64 |
| Shawnee | 186 | 114 | 72 |
| Sumner | 30 | 25 | 5 |
| Wabaunsee | 23 | 11 | 12 |
| **Nonmetropolitan Counties** | | | |
| Allen | 30 | 14 | 16 |
| Anderson | 31 | 9 | 22 |
| Atchison | 26 | 14 | 12 |
| Barber | 9 | 7 | 2 |
| Barton | 40 | 20 | 20 |
| Bourbon | 18 | 15 | 3 |
| Chase | 8 | 4 | 4 |
| Chautauqua | 15 | 6 | 9 |
| Cherokee | 52 | 25 | 27 |
| Cheyenne | 7 | 6 | 1 |
| Clark | 10 | 5 | 5 |
| Clay | 12 | 7 | 5 |
| Coffey | 41 | 14 | 27 |
| Comanche | 9 | 4 | 5 |
| Cowley | 43 | 23 | 20 |
| Crawford | 67 | 29 | 38 |
| Decatur | 4 | 4 | 0 |
| Dickinson | 43 | 21 | 22 |

## Table 80. Full-Time Law Enforcement Employees, by Selected State Metropolitan and Nonmetropolitan Counties, 2021—Continued

(Number.)

| State/county | Law enforcement employees | Officers | Civilians |
|---|---|---|---|
| Edwards | 7 | 6 | 1 |
| Elk | 5 | 5 | 0 |
| Ellis | 40 | 23 | 17 |
| Ellsworth | 23 | 9 | 14 |
| Finney | 93 | 37 | 56 |
| Franklin | 45 | 29 | 16 |
| Gove | 5 | 4 | 1 |
| Graham | 8 | 3 | 5 |
| Grant | 20 | 6 | 14 |
| Gray | 15 | 10 | 5 |
| Greenwood | 23 | 14 | 9 |
| Harper | 14 | 8 | 6 |
| Haskell | 15 | 10 | 5 |
| Hodgeman | 8 | 3 | 5 |
| Jewell | 10 | 6 | 4 |
| Kearny | 21 | 11 | 10 |
| Kiowa | 15 | 5 | 10 |
| Labette | 30 | 20 | 10 |
| Lane | 10 | 5 | 5 |
| Lincoln | 13 | 8 | 5 |
| Logan | 4 | 4 | 0 |
| Lyon | 30 | 24 | 6 |
| Marion | 12 | 11 | 1 |
| Marshall | 27 | 11 | 16 |
| McPherson | 22 | 19 | 3 |
| Meade | 7 | 7 | 0 |
| Mitchell | 11 | 10 | 1 |
| Morton | 11 | 5 | 6 |
| Nemaha | 28 | 10 | 18 |
| Neosho | 32 | 17 | 15 |
| Ness | 9 | 7 | 2 |
| Norton | 11 | 6 | 5 |
| Ottawa | 5 | 5 | 0 |
| Pawnee | 17 | 11 | 6 |
| Phillips | 14 | 9 | 5 |
| Pratt | 20 | 10 | 10 |
| Rawlins | 5 | 4 | 1 |
| Reno | 89 | 53 | 36 |
| Republic | 14 | 8 | 6 |
| Rice | 9 | 7 | 2 |
| Rooks | 20 | 9 | 11 |
| Rush | 12 | 7 | 5 |
| Russell | 16 | 10 | 6 |
| Saline | 52 | 39 | 13 |
| Scott | 7 | 4 | 3 |
| Seward | 29 | 17 | 12 |
| Smith | 6 | 6 | 0 |
| Stanton | 9 | 3 | 6 |
| Stevens | 17 | 6 | 11 |
| Trego | 6 | 4 | 2 |
| Wallace | 8 | 4 | 4 |
| Washington | 26 | 8 | 18 |
| Wichita | 9 | 4 | 5 |
| Wilson | 34 | 11 | 23 |
| Woodson | 13 | 8 | 5 |
| **KENTUCKY** | | | |
| **Metropolitan Counties** | | | |
| Boone | 164 | 159 | 5 |
| Bourbon | 10 | 9 | 1 |
| Boyd | 42 | 30 | 12 |
| Bullitt | 69 | 40 | 29 |
| Butler | 9 | 6 | 3 |
| Campbell | 24 | 17 | 7 |
| Campbell County Police Department | 33 | 31 | 2 |
| Carter | 16 | 13 | 3 |
| Christian | 48 | 43 | 5 |
| Clark | 17 | 13 | 4 |
| Daviess | 39 | 33 | 6 |
| Fayette | 79 | 56 | 23 |
| Grant | 22 | 20 | 2 |
| Greenup | 19 | 18 | 1 |
| Hancock | 7 | 6 | 1 |
| Hardin | 54 | 38 | 16 |
| Henderson | 25 | 19 | 6 |
| Jefferson | 242 | 192 | 50 |
| Jessamine | 34 | 30 | 4 |
| Kenton County Police Department | 39 | 37 | 2 |
| Larue | 7 | 6 | 1 |
| McLean | 20 | 10 | 10 |
| Meade | 16 | 13 | 3 |
| Oldham County Police Department | 45 | 42 | 3 |
| Pendleton | 7 | 6 | 1 |

## Table 80. Full-Time Law Enforcement Employees, by Selected State Metropolitan and Nonmetropolitan Counties, 2021—Continued

(Number.)

| State/county | Law enforcement employees | Officers | Civilians |
|---|---|---|---|
| Scott | 48 | 44 | 4 |
| Spencer | 9 | 8 | 1 |
| Trigg | 11 | 8 | 3 |
| Warren | 90 | 47 | 43 |
| Woodford | 11 | 9 | 2 |
| **Nonmetropolitan Counties** | | | |
| Adair | 8 | 6 | 2 |
| Anderson | 24 | 20 | 4 |
| Ballard | 12 | 10 | 2 |
| Barren | 23 | 18 | 5 |
| Bath | 7 | 4 | 3 |
| Bell | 31 | 19 | 12 |
| Boyle | 13 | 12 | 1 |
| Breckinridge | 9 | 7 | 2 |
| Caldwell | 10 | 8 | 2 |
| Calloway | 26 | 23 | 3 |
| Carlisle | 6 | 4 | 2 |
| Casey | 7 | 7 | 0 |
| Crittenden | 6 | 5 | 1 |
| Cumberland | 7 | 6 | 1 |
| Elliott | 2 | 2 | 0 |
| Estill | 8 | 5 | 3 |
| Fleming | 7 | 6 | 1 |
| Franklin | 32 | 29 | 3 |
| Garrard | 2 | 1 | 1 |
| Garrard County Police Department | 7 | 7 | 0 |
| Graves | 20 | 17 | 3 |
| Grayson | 16 | 12 | 4 |
| Green | 5 | 4 | 1 |
| Harlan | 18 | 14 | 4 |
| Harrison | 9 | 8 | 1 |
| Hart | 9 | 7 | 2 |
| Hickman | 3 | 2 | 1 |
| Hopkins | 40 | 31 | 9 |
| Johnson | 12 | 8 | 4 |
| Knott | 6 | 4 | 2 |
| Laurel | 48 | 33 | 15 |
| Lawrence | 11 | 9 | 2 |
| Lee | 1 | 1 | 0 |
| Leslie | 10 | 8 | 2 |
| Letcher | 8 | 4 | 4 |
| Lewis | 17 | 7 | 10 |
| Logan | 30 | 30 | 0 |
| Lyon | 11 | 7 | 4 |
| Madison | 38 | 35 | 3 |
| Marion | 11 | 8 | 3 |
| Marshall | 39 | 34 | 5 |
| Martin | 7 | 3 | 4 |
| McCracken | 45 | 40 | 5 |
| McCreary | 6 | 5 | 1 |
| Menifee | 5 | 5 | 0 |
| Mercer | 12 | 9 | 3 |
| Metcalfe | 5 | 3 | 2 |
| Monroe | 6 | 5 | 1 |
| Montgomery | 17 | 15 | 2 |
| Morgan | 8 | 7 | 1 |
| Muhlenberg | 17 | 15 | 2 |
| Nelson | 34 | 28 | 6 |
| Nicholas | 3 | 2 | 1 |
| Owen | 7 | 6 | 1 |
| Owsley | 3 | 1 | 2 |
| Perry | 26 | 24 | 2 |
| Pike | 22 | 10 | 12 |
| Powell | 5 | 3 | 2 |
| Robertson | 2 | 1 | 1 |
| Rowan | 17 | 14 | 3 |
| Russell | 13 | 10 | 3 |
| Simpson | 17 | 13 | 4 |
| Washington | 9 | 7 | 2 |
| Wayne | 15 | 13 | 2 |
| Whitley | 24 | 13 | 11 |
| **LOUISIANA** | | | |
| **Metropolitan Counties** | | | |
| Acadia | 106 | 106 | 0 |
| Ascension | 370 | 195 | 175 |
| Bossier | 393 | 315 | 78 |
| Caddo | 559 | 337 | 222 |
| Calcasieu | 795 | 593 | 202 |
| Cameron | 93 | 82 | 11 |
| De Soto | 157 | 111 | 46 |
| East Baton Rouge | 825 | 695 | 130 |

## Table 80. Full-Time Law Enforcement Employees, by Selected State Metropolitan and Nonmetropolitan Counties, 2021—Continued

(Number.)

| State/county | Law enforcement employees | Officers | Civilians |
|---|---|---|---|
| East Feliciana | 55 | 55 | 0 |
| Grant | 75 | 75 | 0 |
| Iberia | 166 | 95 | 71 |
| Jefferson | 1,273 | 858 | 415 |
| Lafayette | 392 | 392 | 0 |
| Lafourche | 360 | 260 | 100 |
| Livingston | 322 | 322 | 0 |
| Morehouse | 114 | 72 | 42 |
| Ouachita | 373 | 373 | 0 |
| Plaquemines | 287 | 287 | 0 |
| Pointe Coupee | 99 | 55 | 44 |
| Rapides | 6 | 5 | 1 |
| St. Charles | 235 | 235 | 0 |
| St. Helena | 46 | 28 | 18 |
| St. James | 105 | 57 | 48 |
| St. John the Baptist | 178 | 178 | 0 |
| St. Martin | 119 | 119 | 0 |
| Tangipahoa | 232 | 104 | 128 |
| Terrebonne | 233 | 233 | 0 |
| Vermilion | 132 | 108 | 24 |
| West Baton Rouge | 17 | 16 | 1 |
| West Feliciana | 78 | 23 | 55 |
| **Nonmetropolitan Counties** | | | |
| Allen | 114 | 31 | 83 |
| Bienville | 68 | 38 | 30 |
| Claiborne | 61 | 32 | 29 |
| Concordia | 32 | 32 | 0 |
| East Carroll | 47 | 16 | 31 |
| Evangeline | 55 | 31 | 24 |
| Franklin | 97 | 97 | 0 |
| Jackson | 106 | 106 | 0 |
| Jefferson Davis | 95 | 95 | 0 |
| Lincoln | 126 | 92 | 34 |
| Madison | 36 | 28 | 8 |
| Natchitoches | 147 | 69 | 78 |
| Red River | 72 | 48 | 24 |
| Richland | 132 | 106 | 26 |
| Sabine | 95 | 66 | 29 |
| St. Landry | 213 | 153 | 60 |
| Tensas | 36 | 22 | 14 |
| Vernon | 113 | 54 | 59 |
| Washington | 67 | 67 | 0 |
| Webster | 121 | 121 | 0 |
| West Carroll | 17 | 8 | 9 |
| Winn | 41 | 16 | 25 |
| **MAINE** | | | |
| **Metropolitan Counties** | | | |
| Androscoggin | 37 | 35 | 2 |
| Cumberland | 73 | 62 | 11 |
| Penobscot | 45 | 40 | 5 |
| Sagadahoc | 21 | 19 | 2 |
| York | 29 | 27 | 2 |
| **Nonmetropolitan Counties** | | | |
| Aroostook | 25 | 18 | 7 |
| Franklin | 16 | 15 | 1 |
| Hancock | 24 | 22 | 2 |
| Kennebec | 30 | 27 | 3 |
| Knox | 24 | 23 | 1 |
| Lincoln | 22 | 20 | 2 |
| Oxford | 34 | 31 | 3 |
| Piscataquis | 10 | 9 | 1 |
| Somerset | 30 | 26 | 4 |
| Waldo | 24 | 22 | 2 |
| Washington | 18 | 16 | 2 |
| **MARYLAND** | | | |
| **Metropolitan Counties** | | | |
| Allegany | 36 | 33 | 3 |
| Anne Arundel | 103 | 76 | 27 |
| Anne Arundel County Police Department | 999 | 784 | 215 |
| Baltimore County | 83 | 75 | 8 |
| Baltimore County Police Department | 2,047 | 1,832 | 215 |
| Calvert | 179 | 149 | 30 |
| Carroll | 256 | 126 | 130 |
| Cecil | 107 | 88 | 19 |
| Charles | 460 | 295 | 165 |
| Frederick | 250 | 185 | 65 |
| Harford | 407 | 311 | 96 |
| Howard | 77 | 55 | 22 |
| Howard County Police Department | 667 | 471 | 196 |

# Table 80. Full-Time Law Enforcement Employees, by Selected State Metropolitan and Nonmetropolitan Counties, 2021—Continued

(Number.)

| State/county | Law enforcement employees | Officers | Civilians |
|---|---|---|---|
| Montgomery | 194 | 157 | 37 |
| Montgomery County Police Department | 1,705 | 1,240 | 465 |
| Prince George's County Police Department | 1,707 | 1,471 | 236 |
| Queen Anne's | 72 | 61 | 11 |
| Somerset | 29 | 25 | 4 |
| St. Mary's | 313 | 206 | 107 |
| Washington | 124 | 105 | 19 |
| Wicomico | 108 | 86 | 22 |
| Worcester | 73 | 60 | 13 |
| **Nonmetropolitan Counties** | | | |
| Caroline | 44 | 40 | 4 |
| Dorchester | 44 | 39 | 5 |
| Garrett | 51 | 36 | 15 |
| Kent | 27 | 24 | 3 |
| Talbot | 40 | 37 | 3 |
| **MICHIGAN** | | | |
| **Metropolitan Counties** | | | |
| Bay | 86 | 43 | 43 |
| Berrien | 159 | 74 | 85 |
| Calhoun | 176 | 74 | 102 |
| Cass | 71 | 33 | 38 |
| Clinton | 61 | 26 | 35 |
| Eaton | 122 | 66 | 56 |
| Genesee | 274 | 269 | 5 |
| Ingham | 157 | 70 | 87 |
| Ionia | 49 | 22 | 27 |
| Jackson | 100 | 45 | 55 |
| Kalamazoo | 189 | 112 | 77 |
| Kent | 602 | 247 | 355 |
| Lapeer | 79 | 45 | 34 |
| Livingston | 130 | 60 | 70 |
| Macomb | 523 | 266 | 257 |
| Midland | 70 | 32 | 38 |
| Monroe | 154 | 77 | 77 |
| Montcalm | 50 | 24 | 26 |
| Muskegon | 108 | 48 | 60 |
| Oakland | 1,085 | 895 | 190 |
| Ottawa | 225 | 141 | 84 |
| Saginaw | 92 | 36 | 56 |
| Shiawassee | 51 | 19 | 32 |
| St. Clair | 192 | 81 | 111 |
| Washtenaw | 300 | 119 | 181 |
| Wayne | 713 | 620 | 93 |
| **Nonmetropolitan Counties** | | | |
| Alcona | 14 | 11 | 3 |
| Alger | 14 | 9 | 5 |
| Allegan | 105 | 60 | 45 |
| Alpena | 32 | 11 | 21 |
| Antrim | 46 | 16 | 30 |
| Arenac | 23 | 13 | 10 |
| Baraga | 6 | 6 | 0 |
| Barry | 55 | 30 | 25 |
| Benzie | 36 | 17 | 19 |
| Branch | 30 | 13 | 17 |
| Charlevoix | 39 | 23 | 16 |
| Cheboygan | 40 | 21 | 19 |
| Chippewa | 43 | 16 | 27 |
| Clare | 29 | 23 | 6 |
| Crawford | 33 | 26 | 7 |
| Delta | 46 | 18 | 28 |
| Dickinson | 29 | 12 | 17 |
| Emmet | 50 | 27 | 23 |
| Gladwin | 44 | 15 | 29 |
| Gogebic | 24 | 15 | 9 |
| Grand Traverse | 125 | 68 | 57 |
| Gratiot | 28 | 26 | 2 |
| Hillsdale | 34 | 20 | 14 |
| Houghton | 30 | 20 | 10 |
| Huron | 35 | 18 | 17 |
| Iosco | 31 | 4 | 27 |
| Iron | 20 | 9 | 11 |
| Isabella | 50 | 21 | 29 |
| Kalkaska | 35 | 17 | 18 |
| Keweenaw | 6 | 6 | 0 |
| Lake | 35 | 15 | 20 |
| Leelanau | 41 | 20 | 21 |
| Lenawee | 98 | 38 | 60 |
| Luce | 5 | 4 | 1 |
| Mackinac | 27 | 11 | 16 |
| Manistee | 29 | 15 | 14 |

## Table 80. Full-Time Law Enforcement Employees, by Selected State Metropolitan and Nonmetropolitan Counties, 2021—Continued

(Number.)

| State/county | Law enforcement employees | Officers | Civilians |
|---|---|---|---|
| Marquette | 65 | 23 | 42 |
| Mason | 51 | 23 | 28 |
| Mecosta | 19 | 18 | 1 |
| Menominee | 16 | 15 | 1 |
| Missaukee | 12 | 11 | 1 |
| Montmorency | 24 | 15 | 9 |
| Newaygo | 68 | 27 | 41 |
| Oceana | 35 | 21 | 14 |
| Ogemaw | 33 | 14 | 19 |
| Ontonagon | 11 | 5 | 6 |
| Osceola | 40 | 22 | 18 |
| Oscoda | 18 | 12 | 6 |
| Otsego | 29 | 12 | 17 |
| Presque Isle | 15 | 15 | 0 |
| Roscommon | 37 | 25 | 12 |
| Sanilac | 58 | 26 | 32 |
| Schoolcraft | 11 | 4 | 7 |
| St. Joseph | 56 | 27 | 29 |
| Tuscola | 48 | 20 | 28 |
| Van Buren | 88 | 48 | 40 |
| Wexford | 47 | 23 | 24 |
| **MINNESOTA** | | | |
| **Metropolitan Counties** | | | |
| Anoka | 263 | 127 | 136 |
| Benton | 70 | 25 | 45 |
| Blue Earth | 74 | 31 | 43 |
| Carlton | 57 | 24 | 33 |
| Carver | 135 | 61 | 74 |
| Chisago | 90 | 43 | 47 |
| Clay | 79 | 34 | 45 |
| Dakota | 170 | 81 | 89 |
| Dodge | 40 | 24 | 16 |
| Fillmore | 31 | 20 | 11 |
| Hennepin | 824 | 321 | 503 |
| Houston | 31 | 13 | 18 |
| Isanti | 56 | 21 | 35 |
| Lake | 29 | 17 | 12 |
| Le Sueur | 49 | 22 | 27 |
| Mille Lacs | 80 | 38 | 42 |
| Nicollet | 43 | 16 | 27 |
| Olmsted | 188 | 80 | 108 |
| Polk | 49 | 33 | 16 |
| Ramsey | 437 | 384 | 53 |
| Scott | 145 | 44 | 101 |
| Sherburne | 289 | 79 | 210 |
| Stearns | 202 | 74 | 128 |
| St. Louis | 244 | 100 | 144 |
| Wabasha | 46 | 18 | 28 |
| Washington | 269 | 120 | 149 |
| Wright | 270 | 157 | 113 |
| **Nonmetropolitan Counties** | | | |
| Aitkin | 50 | 20 | 30 |
| Becker | 66 | 21 | 45 |
| Beltrami | 83 | 30 | 53 |
| Big Stone | 7 | 5 | 2 |
| Brown | 36 | 13 | 23 |
| Cass | 76 | 44 | 32 |
| Chippewa | 21 | 9 | 12 |
| Clearwater | 18 | 10 | 8 |
| Cook | 19 | 11 | 8 |
| Cottonwood | 22 | 10 | 12 |
| Crow Wing | 128 | 40 | 88 |
| Douglas | 84 | 36 | 48 |
| Faribault | 30 | 13 | 17 |
| Freeborn | 70 | 24 | 46 |
| Goodhue | 99 | 43 | 56 |
| Grant | 16 | 11 | 5 |
| Hubbard | 48 | 19 | 29 |
| Itasca | 74 | 31 | 43 |
| Jackson | 27 | 14 | 13 |
| Kanabec | 50 | 21 | 29 |
| Kandiyohi | 104 | 32 | 72 |
| Kittson | 11 | 6 | 5 |
| Koochiching | 18 | 10 | 8 |
| Lac qui Parle | 13 | 8 | 5 |
| Lake of the Woods | 13 | 6 | 7 |
| Lincoln | 13 | 7 | 6 |
| Lyon | 52 | 17 | 35 |
| Mahnomen | 20 | 14 | 6 |
| Marshall | 24 | 13 | 11 |
| Martin | 35 | 14 | 21 |

## Table 80. Full-Time Law Enforcement Employees, by Selected State Metropolitan and Nonmetropolitan Counties, 2021—Continued

(Number.)

| State/county | Law enforcement employees | Officers | Civilians |
|---|---|---|---|
| McLeod | 63 | 25 | 38 |
| Meeker | 49 | 21 | 28 |
| Morrison | 56 | 22 | 34 |
| Mower | 81 | 28 | 53 |
| Murray | 17 | 11 | 6 |
| Nobles | 33 | 13 | 20 |
| Norman | 12 | 7 | 5 |
| Otter Tail | 86 | 38 | 48 |
| Pennington | 35 | 11 | 24 |
| Pine | 83 | 37 | 46 |
| Pipestone | 27 | 16 | 11 |
| Pope | 14 | 8 | 6 |
| Red Lake | 11 | 8 | 3 |
| Redwood | 35 | 17 | 18 |
| Renville | 43 | 16 | 27 |
| Rice | 62 | 34 | 28 |
| Rock | 17 | 12 | 5 |
| Roseau | 20 | 12 | 8 |
| Sibley | 27 | 15 | 12 |
| Steele | 29 | 23 | 6 |
| Stevens | 15 | 7 | 8 |
| Swift | 17 | 9 | 8 |
| Todd | 38 | 19 | 19 |
| Traverse | 15 | 6 | 9 |
| Wadena | 23 | 11 | 12 |
| Waseca | 31 | 14 | 17 |
| Watonwan | 20 | 8 | 12 |
| Wilkin | 18 | 8 | 10 |
| Winona | 61 | 21 | 40 |
| Yellow Medicine | 25 | 10 | 15 |
| | | | |
| **MISSISSIPPI** | | | |
| **Metropolitan Counties** | | | |
| Copiah | 34 | 16 | 18 |
| Covington | 46 | 16 | 30 |
| DeSoto | 304 | 155 | 149 |
| Forrest | 130 | 45 | 85 |
| Hancock | 117 | 100 | 17 |
| Harrison | 259 | 117 | 142 |
| Lamar | 94 | 48 | 46 |
| Madison | 161 | 74 | 87 |
| Rankin | 122 | 113 | 9 |
| Stone | 26 | 21 | 5 |
| Tate | 45 | 23 | 22 |
| Tunica | 97 | 49 | 48 |
| Yazoo | 14 | 12 | 2 |
| | | | |
| **Nonmetropolitan Counties** | | | |
| Adams | 64 | 36 | 28 |
| Alcorn | 25 | 23 | 2 |
| Amite | 15 | 6 | 9 |
| Bolivar | 34 | 26 | 8 |
| Calhoun | 5 | 5 | 0 |
| Chickasaw | 14 | 13 | 1 |
| Claiborne | 9 | 9 | 0 |
| Clay | 35 | 14 | 21 |
| Coahoma | 72 | 31 | 41 |
| George | 18 | 16 | 2 |
| Grenada | 11 | 9 | 2 |
| Jasper | 31 | 18 | 13 |
| Jones | 53 | 46 | 7 |
| Kemper | 20 | 15 | 5 |
| Lafayette | 49 | 47 | 2 |
| Lauderdale | 121 | 50 | 71 |
| Lee | 117 | 51 | 66 |
| Lincoln | 51 | 24 | 27 |
| Marion | 21 | 15 | 6 |
| Monroe | 57 | 34 | 23 |
| Neshoba | 17 | 16 | 1 |
| Newton | 17 | 14 | 3 |
| Noxubee | 14 | 8 | 6 |
| Oktibbeha | 34 | 32 | 2 |
| Pike | 60 | 32 | 28 |
| Pontotoc | 38 | 38 | 0 |
| Prentiss | 38 | 19 | 19 |
| Smith | 19 | 14 | 5 |
| Tallahatchie | 23 | 8 | 15 |
| Tishomingo | 30 | 14 | 16 |
| Union | 38 | 19 | 19 |
| Walthall | 28 | 13 | 15 |
| Washington | 51 | 37 | 14 |
| Wayne | 25 | 14 | 11 |
| Winston | 44 | 11 | 33 |
| **MISSOURI** | | | |

## Table 80. Full-Time Law Enforcement Employees, by Selected State Metropolitan and Nonmetropolitan Counties, 2021—Continued

(Number.)

| State/county | Law enforcement employees | Officers | Civilians |
|---|---|---|---|
| **Metropolitan Counties** | | | |
| Bollinger | 15 | 10 | 5 |
| Boone | 74 | 55 | 19 |
| Cape Girardeau | 99 | 55 | 44 |
| Cole | 101 | 60 | 41 |
| Cooper | 12 | 11 | 1 |
| Jackson | 146 | 110 | 36 |
| Jefferson | 236 | 165 | 71 |
| Ray | 37 | 25 | 12 |
| St. Charles | 47 | 32 | 15 |
| St. Charles County Police Department | 178 | 140 | 38 |
| St. Louis County Police Department | 1,252 | 907 | 345 |
| | | | |
| **Nonmetropolitan Counties** | | | |
| Adair | 10 | 10 | 0 |
| Atchison | 14 | 8 | 6 |
| Audrain | 62 | 50 | 12 |
| Butler | 52 | 32 | 20 |
| Carroll | 10 | 9 | 1 |
| Clark | 12 | 6 | 6 |
| Dade | 11 | 6 | 5 |
| Daviess | 15 | 12 | 3 |
| Dent | 37 | 15 | 22 |
| Douglas | 20 | 12 | 8 |
| Gasconade | 12 | 11 | 1 |
| Henry | 40 | 23 | 17 |
| Howell | 48 | 35 | 13 |
| Laclede | 67 | 26 | 41 |
| Marion | 41 | 18 | 23 |
| McDonald | 33 | 23 | 10 |
| Mississippi | 16 | 8 | 8 |
| Montgomery | 34 | 19 | 15 |
| Oregon | 11 | 7 | 4 |
| Phelps | 79 | 35 | 44 |
| Pulaski | 42 | 21 | 21 |
| Shelby | 27 | 11 | 16 |
| Stoddard | 34 | 18 | 16 |
| Wayne | 26 | 9 | 17 |
| | | | |
| **MONTANA** | | | |
| **Metropolitan Counties** | | | |
| Carbon | 20 | 13 | 7 |
| Cascade | 138 | 41 | 97 |
| Missoula | 182 | 56 | 126 |
| Stillwater | 22 | 13 | 9 |
| Yellowstone | 187 | 60 | 127 |
| | | | |
| **Nonmetropolitan Counties** | | | |
| Beaverhead | 19 | 7 | 12 |
| Big Horn | 31 | 12 | 19 |
| Blaine | 14 | 8 | 6 |
| Broadwater | 26 | 12 | 14 |
| Butte-Silver Bow | 94 | 48 | 46 |
| Carter | 5 | 4 | 1 |
| Chouteau | 22 | 9 | 13 |
| Custer | 18 | 7 | 11 |
| Daniels | 7 | 3 | 4 |
| Dawson | 55 | 8 | 47 |
| Deer Lodge | 19 | 19 | 0 |
| Fallon | 9 | 4 | 5 |
| Fergus | 22 | 16 | 6 |
| Flathead | 111 | 58 | 53 |
| Gallatin | 126 | 63 | 63 |
| Garfield | 4 | 3 | 1 |
| Glacier | 24 | 13 | 11 |
| Golden Valley | 2 | 2 | 0 |
| Granite | 6 | 6 | 0 |
| Hill | 25 | 12 | 13 |
| Jefferson | 30 | 15 | 15 |
| Judith Basin | 6 | 5 | 1 |
| Lake | 43 | 26 | 17 |
| Lewis and Clark | 116 | 49 | 67 |
| Liberty | 9 | 5 | 4 |
| Lincoln | 42 | 21 | 21 |
| Madison | 22 | 15 | 7 |
| McCone | 5 | 4 | 1 |
| Meagher | 9 | 4 | 5 |
| Mineral | 20 | 8 | 12 |
| Musselshell | 8 | 8 | 0 |
| Park | 26 | 17 | 9 |
| Petroleum | 2 | 2 | 0 |
| Phillips | 13 | 7 | 6 |
| Pondera | 9 | 8 | 1 |
| Powder River | 8 | 4 | 4 |
| Powell | 11 | 5 | 6 |

# Table 80. Full-Time Law Enforcement Employees, by Selected State Metropolitan and Nonmetropolitan Counties, 2021—Continued

(Number.)

| State/county | Law enforcement employees | Officers | Civilians |
|---|---|---|---|
| Prairie | 5 | 4 | 1 |
| Ravalli | 76 | 36 | 40 |
| Richland | 34 | 10 | 24 |
| Roosevelt | 40 | 13 | 27 |
| Rosebud | 27 | 14 | 13 |
| Sanders | 30 | 13 | 17 |
| Sheridan | 8 | 6 | 2 |
| Sweet Grass | 14 | 8 | 6 |
| Teton | 12 | 9 | 3 |
| Toole | 21 | 13 | 8 |
| Treasure | 2 | 2 | 0 |
| Valley | 21 | 9 | 12 |
| Wheatland | 13 | 7 | 6 |
| Wibaux | 3 | 3 | 0 |
| **NEBRASKA** | | | |
| **Metropolitan Counties** | | | |
| Cass | 38 | 20 | 18 |
| Dakota | 21 | 18 | 3 |
| Dixon | 11 | 8 | 3 |
| Douglas | 225 | 140 | 85 |
| Hall | 42 | 30 | 12 |
| Howard | 12 | 6 | 6 |
| Lancaster | 108 | 80 | 28 |
| Merrick | 16 | 9 | 7 |
| Sarpy | 194 | 119 | 75 |
| Saunders | 23 | 16 | 7 |
| Seward | 23 | 19 | 4 |
| Washington | 62 | 31 | 31 |
| **Nonmetropolitan Counties** | | | |
| Adams | 21 | 18 | 3 |
| Antelope | 13 | 4 | 9 |
| Arthur | 1 | 1 | 0 |
| Banner | 2 | 2 | 0 |
| Boone | 10 | 4 | 6 |
| Box Butte | 20 | 6 | 14 |
| Buffalo | 83 | 30 | 53 |
| Burt | 10 | 5 | 5 |
| Butler | 28 | 10 | 18 |
| Cedar | 6 | 6 | 0 |
| Chase | 8 | 5 | 3 |
| Cherry | 6 | 5 | 1 |
| Cheyenne | 22 | 10 | 12 |
| Clay | 12 | 7 | 5 |
| Colfax | 20 | 12 | 8 |
| Cuming | 6 | 5 | 1 |
| Custer | 10 | 9 | 1 |
| Dawes | 17 | 7 | 10 |
| Dawson | 65 | 27 | 38 |
| Deuel | 6 | 5 | 1 |
| Dodge | 24 | 20 | 4 |
| Dundy | 9 | 5 | 4 |
| Fillmore | 13 | 6 | 7 |
| Franklin | 8 | 4 | 4 |
| Frontier | 7 | 4 | 3 |
| Furnas | 11 | 5 | 6 |
| Gage | 19 | 16 | 3 |
| Garfield | 2 | 2 | 0 |
| Gosper | 5 | 4 | 1 |
| Grant | 2 | 2 | 0 |
| Harlan | 8 | 4 | 4 |
| Hayes | 1 | 1 | 0 |
| Hitchcock | 5 | 5 | 0 |
| Holt | 8 | 6 | 2 |
| Hooker | 2 | 2 | 0 |
| Jefferson | 29 | 15 | 14 |
| Johnson | 11 | 5 | 6 |
| Kearney | 11 | 6 | 5 |
| Keith | 19 | 9 | 10 |
| Keya Paha | 2 | 2 | 0 |
| Kimball | 10 | 4 | 6 |
| Lincoln | 71 | 26 | 45 |
| Logan | 2 | 2 | 0 |
| Loup | 1 | 1 | 0 |
| Madison | 58 | 33 | 25 |
| McPherson | 1 | 1 | 0 |
| Morrill | 13 | 9 | 4 |
| Nance | 8 | 7 | 1 |
| Nemaha | 12 | 12 | 0 |
| Nuckolls | 14 | 4 | 10 |
| Otoe | 35 | 17 | 18 |
| Pawnee | 5 | 4 | 1 |
| Perkins | 10 | 5 | 5 |
| Phelps | 24 | 7 | 17 |

## Table 80. Full-Time Law Enforcement Employees, by Selected State Metropolitan and Nonmetropolitan Counties, 2021—Continued

(Number.)

| State/county | Law enforcement employees | Officers | Civilians |
|---|---|---|---|
| Pierce | 5 | 5 | 0 |
| Platte | 25 | 22 | 3 |
| Polk | 7 | 6 | 1 |
| Red Willow | 16 | 2 | 14 |
| Richardson | 12 | 10 | 2 |
| Rock | 6 | 2 | 4 |
| Scotts Bluff | 25 | 19 | 6 |
| Sherman | 5 | 4 | 1 |
| Stanton | 10 | 9 | 1 |
| Thomas | 1 | 1 | 0 |
| Thurston | 30 | 8 | 22 |
| Valley | 10 | 5 | 5 |
| Wayne | 6 | 5 | 1 |
| Webster | 10 | 5 | 5 |
| **NEVADA** | | | |
| **Metropolitan Counties** | | | |
| Carson City | 145 | 100 | 45 |
| Washoe | 754 | 412 | 342 |
| **Nonmetropolitan Counties** | | | |
| Churchill | 51 | 42 | 9 |
| Douglas | 121 | 106 | 15 |
| Elko | 79 | 65 | 14 |
| Humboldt | 59 | 40 | 19 |
| Lander | 37 | 20 | 17 |
| Lyon | 115 | 81 | 34 |
| Mineral | 21 | 16 | 5 |
| Nye | 156 | 111 | 45 |
| **NEW HAMPSHIRE** | | | |
| **Metropolitan Counties** | | | |
| Hillsborough | 31 | 21 | 10 |
| Rockingham | 49 | 26 | 23 |
| Strafford | 39 | 22 | 17 |
| **Nonmetropolitan Counties** | | | |
| Belknap | 18 | 9 | 9 |
| Carroll | 24 | 11 | 13 |
| Cheshire | 22 | 10 | 12 |
| Grafton | 25 | 10 | 15 |
| Merrimack | 28 | 15 | 13 |
| Sullivan | 9 | 8 | 1 |
| **NEW JERSEY** | | | |
| **Metropolitan Counties** | | | |
| Atlantic | 132 | 102 | 30 |
| Bergen | 529 | 430 | 99 |
| Burlington | 104 | 86 | 18 |
| Camden | 218 | 188 | 30 |
| Cape May | 165 | 140 | 25 |
| Cumberland | 58 | 49 | 9 |
| Essex | 443 | 375 | 68 |
| Gloucester | 112 | 103 | 9 |
| Hudson | 415 | 284 | 131 |
| Hunterdon | 43 | 38 | 5 |
| Mercer | 187 | 141 | 46 |
| Middlesex | 213 | 176 | 37 |
| Monmouth | 569 | 367 | 202 |
| Morris | 120 | 91 | 29 |
| Ocean | 270 | 149 | 121 |
| Passaic | 696 | 562 | 134 |
| Salem | 234 | 187 | 47 |
| Somerset | 208 | 176 | 32 |
| Sussex | 109 | 78 | 31 |
| Union | 307 | 264 | 43 |
| Warren | 23 | 19 | 4 |
| **NEW MEXICO** | | | |
| **Metropolitan Counties** | | | |
| Dona Ana | 196 | 138 | 58 |
| Sandoval | 66 | 55 | 11 |
| San Juan | 91 | 69 | 22 |
| Santa Fe | 116 | 95 | 21 |
| Torrance | 23 | 18 | 5 |
| Valencia | 57 | 40 | 17 |
| **Nonmetropolitan Counties** | | | |
| Catron | 7 | 6 | 1 |
| Chaves | 48 | 38 | 10 |
| Cibola | 22 | 16 | 6 |
| Colfax | 12 | 11 | 1 |
| Curry | 26 | 14 | 12 |

## Table 80. Full-Time Law Enforcement Employees, by Selected State Metropolitan and Nonmetropolitan Counties, 2021—Continued

(Number.)

| State/county | Law enforcement employees | Officers | Civilians |
|---|---|---|---|
| Eddy | 82 | 63 | 19 |
| Grant | 35 | 31 | 4 |
| Guadalupe | 8 | 6 | 2 |
| Lea | 86 | 79 | 7 |
| Lincoln | 36 | 23 | 13 |
| Luna | 29 | 25 | 4 |
| McKinley | 40 | 34 | 6 |
| Mora | 9 | 6 | 3 |
| Rio Arriba | 28 | 24 | 4 |
| San Miguel | 11 | 7 | 4 |
| **NEW YORK** | | | |
| **Metropolitan Counties** | | | |
| Albany | 210 | 135 | 75 |
| Broome | 73 | 60 | 13 |
| Chemung | 49 | 43 | 6 |
| Dutchess | 124 | 101 | 23 |
| Erie | 294 | 148 | 146 |
| Herkimer | 18 | 11 | 7 |
| Jefferson | 58 | 41 | 17 |
| Livingston | 55 | 50 | 5 |
| Madison | 53 | 43 | 10 |
| Monroe | 331 | 283 | 48 |
| Niagara | 159 | 105 | 54 |
| Oneida | 137 | 100 | 37 |
| Onondaga | 255 | 217 | 38 |
| Ontario | 113 | 58 | 55 |
| Orleans | 40 | 26 | 14 |
| Putnam | 98 | 79 | 19 |
| Rensselaer | 48 | 41 | 7 |
| Rockland | 165 | 78 | 87 |
| Saratoga | 197 | 147 | 50 |
| Schenectady | 25 | 20 | 5 |
| Schoharie | 36 | 22 | 14 |
| Suffolk | 379 | 255 | 124 |
| Suffolk County Police Department | 2,812 | 2,331 | 481 |
| Tompkins | 42 | 39 | 3 |
| Ulster | 71 | 58 | 13 |
| Washington | 51 | 45 | 6 |
| Wayne | 92 | 84 | 8 |
| Westchester Public Safety | 357 | 287 | 70 |
| Yates | 45 | 24 | 21 |
| **Nonmetropolitan Counties** | | | |
| Allegany | 35 | 13 | 22 |
| Cattaraugus | 78 | 52 | 26 |
| Cayuga | 39 | 32 | 7 |
| Chautauqua | 103 | 62 | 41 |
| Chenango | 23 | 23 | 0 |
| Columbia | 71 | 56 | 15 |
| Cortland | 39 | 38 | 1 |
| Delaware | 25 | 19 | 6 |
| Essex | 25 | 24 | 1 |
| Fulton | 48 | 29 | 19 |
| Genesee | 78 | 50 | 28 |
| Greene | 36 | 32 | 4 |
| Hamilton | 7 | 6 | 1 |
| Lewis | 21 | 21 | 0 |
| Montgomery | 49 | 29 | 20 |
| Otsego | 18 | 16 | 2 |
| Steuben | 51 | 38 | 13 |
| St. Lawrence | 33 | 31 | 2 |
| Sullivan | 54 | 54 | 0 |
| Wyoming | 41 | 31 | 10 |
| **NORTH CAROLINA** | | | |
| **Metropolitan Counties** | | | |
| Alamance | 265 | 146 | 119 |
| Alexander | 77 | 38 | 39 |
| Anson | 58 | 31 | 27 |
| Brunswick | 332 | 191 | 141 |
| Buncombe | 359 | 227 | 132 |
| Burke | 133 | 78 | 55 |
| Cabarrus | 359 | 213 | 146 |
| Caldwell | 132 | 81 | 51 |
| Camden | 21 | 18 | 3 |
| Catawba | 225 | 149 | 76 |
| Chatham | 148 | 89 | 59 |
| Craven | 156 | 106 | 50 |
| Cumberland | 458 | 248 | 210 |
| Currituck | 100 | 66 | 34 |
| Davidson | 171 | 120 | 51 |
| Davie | 122 | 87 | 35 |

## Table 80. Full-Time Law Enforcement Employees, by Selected State Metropolitan and Nonmetropolitan Counties, 2021—Continued

(Number.)

| State/county | Law enforcement employees | Officers | Civilians |
|---|---|---|---|
| Durham | 403 | 190 | 213 |
| Edgecombe | 126 | 56 | 70 |
| Forsyth | 526 | 257 | 269 |
| Franklin | 104 | 93 | 11 |
| Gaston | 233 | 119 | 114 |
| Gaston County Police Department | 225 | 133 | 92 |
| Gates | 15 | 12 | 3 |
| Granville | 122 | 67 | 55 |
| Guilford | 601 | 259 | 342 |
| Harnett | 204 | 129 | 75 |
| Haywood | 133 | 70 | 63 |
| Henderson | 224 | 147 | 77 |
| Hoke | 98 | 57 | 41 |
| Iredell | 283 | 181 | 102 |
| Johnston | 186 | 126 | 60 |
| Jones | 29 | 19 | 10 |
| Lincoln | 179 | 124 | 55 |
| Madison | 48 | 26 | 22 |
| Mecklenburg[1] | 1,026 | 293 | 733 |
| Nash | 140 | 94 | 46 |
| New Hanover | 557 | 388 | 169 |
| Onslow | 267 | 147 | 120 |
| Orange | 155 | 104 | 51 |
| Pamlico | 50 | 22 | 28 |
| Pender | 119 | 76 | 43 |
| Person | 83 | 50 | 33 |
| Pitt | 350 | 120 | 230 |
| Randolph | 246 | 177 | 69 |
| Rockingham | 147 | 101 | 46 |
| Rowan | 187 | 119 | 68 |
| Stokes | 81 | 55 | 26 |
| Union | 316 | 227 | 89 |
| Wake | 830 | 327 | 503 |
| Wayne | 128 | 122 | 6 |
| Yadkin | 78 | 42 | 36 |
| **Nonmetropolitan Counties** | | | |
| Alleghany | 41 | 24 | 17 |
| Ashe | 75 | 36 | 39 |
| Avery | 51 | 27 | 24 |
| Beaufort | 81 | 49 | 32 |
| Bertie | 39 | 25 | 14 |
| Bladen | 87 | 44 | 43 |
| Carteret | 108 | 66 | 42 |
| Caswell | 55 | 34 | 21 |
| Cherokee | 67 | 33 | 34 |
| Chowan | 37 | 18 | 19 |
| Clay | 25 | 20 | 5 |
| Cleveland | 200 | 117 | 83 |
| Columbus | 137 | 95 | 42 |
| Dare | 138 | 69 | 69 |
| Duplin | 86 | 63 | 23 |
| Graham | 37 | 23 | 14 |
| Greene | 44 | 19 | 25 |
| Halifax | 83 | 60 | 23 |
| Hertford | 56 | 24 | 32 |
| Hyde | 17 | 16 | 1 |
| Jackson | 82 | 59 | 23 |
| Lee | 117 | 79 | 38 |
| Lenoir | 94 | 50 | 44 |
| Macon | 71 | 55 | 16 |
| Martin | 43 | 38 | 5 |
| McDowell | 85 | 58 | 27 |
| Mitchell | 21 | 20 | 1 |
| Montgomery | 57 | 31 | 26 |
| Moore | 168 | 83 | 85 |
| Northampton | 61 | 37 | 24 |
| Pasquotank | 57 | 50 | 7 |
| Perquimans | 26 | 22 | 4 |
| Polk | 51 | 30 | 21 |
| Richmond | 65 | 57 | 8 |
| Robeson | 151 | 137 | 14 |
| Rutherford | 127 | 77 | 50 |
| Sampson | 136 | 92 | 44 |
| Scotland | 63 | 36 | 27 |
| Stanly | 97 | 62 | 35 |
| Surry | 138 | 86 | 52 |
| Swain | 46 | 30 | 16 |
| Transylvania | 80 | 61 | 19 |
| Tyrrell | 12 | 11 | 1 |
| Vance | 85 | 46 | 39 |
| Warren | 57 | 26 | 31 |
| Washington | 36 | 17 | 19 |

## Table 80. Full-Time Law Enforcement Employees, by Selected State Metropolitan and Nonmetropolitan Counties, 2021—Continued

(Number.)

| State/county | Law enforcement employees | Officers | Civilians |
|---|---|---|---|
| Watauga | 76 | 46 | 30 |
| Wilkes | 137 | 76 | 61 |
| Wilson | 113 | 71 | 42 |
| Yancey | 44 | 22 | 22 |
| **NORTH DAKOTA** | | | |
| **Metropolitan Counties** | | | |
| Burleigh | 60 | 51 | 9 |
| Cass | 147 | 104 | 43 |
| Grand Forks | 40 | 33 | 7 |
| Morton | 39 | 39 | 0 |
| Oliver | 5 | 4 | 1 |
| **Nonmetropolitan Counties** | | | |
| Adams | 6 | 5 | 1 |
| Barnes | 10 | 8 | 2 |
| Benson | 4 | 4 | 0 |
| Billings | 6 | 6 | 0 |
| Bottineau | 20 | 11 | 9 |
| Bowman | 5 | 4 | 1 |
| Burke | 6 | 6 | 0 |
| Cavalier | 11 | 5 | 6 |
| Dickey | 5 | 4 | 1 |
| Divide | 6 | 5 | 1 |
| Dunn | 24 | 22 | 2 |
| Eddy | 6 | 5 | 1 |
| Emmons | 6 | 5 | 1 |
| Foster | 3 | 3 | 0 |
| Golden Valley | 5 | 4 | 1 |
| Grant | 5 | 5 | 0 |
| Griggs | 2 | 2 | 0 |
| Hettinger | 8 | 7 | 1 |
| Kidder | 3 | 3 | 0 |
| Lamoure | 6 | 5 | 1 |
| Logan | 3 | 3 | 0 |
| McHenry | 8 | 8 | 0 |
| McIntosh | 3 | 3 | 0 |
| McKenzie | 62 | 42 | 20 |
| McLean | 39 | 26 | 13 |
| Mercer | 28 | 16 | 12 |
| Mountrail | 23 | 11 | 12 |
| Nelson | 6 | 5 | 1 |
| Pembina | 14 | 9 | 5 |
| Pierce | 38 | 4 | 34 |
| Ramsey | 10 | 9 | 1 |
| Ransom | 6 | 5 | 1 |
| Renville | 8 | 7 | 1 |
| Richland | 35 | 15 | 20 |
| Rolette | 24 | 8 | 16 |
| Sargent | 6 | 5 | 1 |
| Sheridan | 3 | 3 | 0 |
| Sioux | 1 | 1 | 0 |
| Slope | 1 | 1 | 0 |
| Stark | 33 | 28 | 5 |
| Steele | 3 | 3 | 0 |
| Stutsman | 15 | 13 | 2 |
| Towner | 7 | 6 | 1 |
| Traill | 14 | 10 | 4 |
| Walsh | 20 | 12 | 8 |
| Ward | 104 | 42 | 62 |
| Wells | 5 | 4 | 1 |
| Williams | 89 | 40 | 49 |
| **OHIO** | | | |
| **Metropolitan Counties** | | | |
| Allen | 156 | 60 | 96 |
| Clermont | 205 | 79 | 126 |
| Delaware | 227 | 103 | 124 |
| Fairfield | 157 | 99 | 58 |
| Fulton | 25 | 23 | 2 |
| Greene | 149 | 63 | 86 |
| Hocking | 45 | 40 | 5 |
| Madison | 46 | 32 | 14 |
| Morrow | 49 | 25 | 24 |
| Pickaway | 94 | 39 | 55 |
| Portage | 170 | 78 | 92 |
| Richland | 119 | 49 | 70 |
| Summit | 389 | 312 | 77 |
| Union | 66 | 46 | 20 |
| **Nonmetropolitan Counties** | | | |
| Ashland | 90 | 52 | 38 |
| Ashtabula | 88 | 36 | 52 |

## Table 80. Full-Time Law Enforcement Employees, by Selected State Metropolitan and Nonmetropolitan Counties, 2021—Continued

(Number.)

| State/county | Law enforcement employees | Officers | Civilians |
|---|---|---|---|
| Athens | 36 | 31 | 5 |
| Champaign | 31 | 27 | 4 |
| Columbiana | 42 | 31 | 11 |
| Coshocton | 61 | 40 | 21 |
| Fayette | 50 | 23 | 27 |
| Hancock | 93 | 38 | 55 |
| Henry | 23 | 16 | 7 |
| Knox | 70 | 44 | 26 |
| Meigs | 19 | 17 | 2 |
| Mercer | 70 | 31 | 39 |
| Monroe | 53 | 25 | 28 |
| Muskingum | 131 | 80 | 51 |
| Paulding | 42 | 29 | 13 |
| Van Wert | 42 | 22 | 20 |
| Washington | 101 | 46 | 55 |
| Wayne | 73 | 52 | 21 |
| Wyandot | 34 | 18 | 16 |
| **OKLAHOMA** | | | |
| **Metropolitan Counties** | | | |
| Canadian | 129 | 92 | 37 |
| Cleveland | 171 | 86 | 85 |
| Comanche | 39 | 30 | 9 |
| Cotton | 13 | 6 | 7 |
| Creek | 82 | 39 | 43 |
| Garfield | 32 | 20 | 12 |
| Grady | 38 | 26 | 12 |
| Lincoln | 34 | 19 | 15 |
| Logan | 63 | 33 | 30 |
| McClain | 43 | 28 | 15 |
| Oklahoma | 209 | 151 | 58 |
| Okmulgee | 17 | 15 | 2 |
| Osage | 60 | 33 | 27 |
| Pawnee | 35 | 13 | 22 |
| Rogers | 42 | 38 | 4 |
| Sequoyah | 30 | 24 | 6 |
| Tulsa | 529 | 205 | 324 |
| Wagoner | 84 | 36 | 48 |
| **Nonmetropolitan Counties** | | | |
| Adair | 30 | 11 | 19 |
| Alfalfa | 10 | 5 | 5 |
| Atoka | 22 | 9 | 13 |
| Beaver | 13 | 7 | 6 |
| Beckham | 36 | 11 | 25 |
| Blaine | 26 | 15 | 11 |
| Bryan | 22 | 19 | 3 |
| Caddo | 16 | 14 | 2 |
| Carter | 58 | 21 | 37 |
| Cherokee | 31 | 25 | 6 |
| Choctaw | 14 | 5 | 9 |
| Cimarron | 8 | 2 | 6 |
| Coal | 13 | 8 | 5 |
| Craig | 28 | 13 | 15 |
| Custer | 33 | 12 | 21 |
| Delaware | 42 | 20 | 22 |
| Dewey | 18 | 5 | 13 |
| Ellis | 17 | 7 | 10 |
| Garvin | 31 | 15 | 16 |
| Grant | 10 | 5 | 5 |
| Greer | 7 | 2 | 5 |
| Harmon | 3 | 3 | 0 |
| Harper | 8 | 4 | 4 |
| Haskell | 22 | 9 | 13 |
| Hughes | 16 | 9 | 7 |
| Jackson | 39 | 11 | 28 |
| Jefferson | 14 | 6 | 8 |
| Johnston | 23 | 10 | 13 |
| Kay | 26 | 18 | 8 |
| Kingfisher | 32 | 12 | 20 |
| Kiowa | 11 | 10 | 1 |
| Latimer | 17 | 7 | 10 |
| Le Flore | 24 | 21 | 3 |
| Love | 12 | 11 | 1 |
| Major | 17 | 6 | 11 |
| Marshall | 35 | 10 | 25 |
| Mayes | 57 | 28 | 29 |
| McCurtain | 29 | 24 | 5 |
| McIntosh | 14 | 13 | 1 |
| Murray | 17 | 8 | 9 |
| Muskogee | 79 | 30 | 49 |
| Noble | 20 | 10 | 10 |
| Nowata | 14 | 5 | 9 |

## Table 80. Full-Time Law Enforcement Employees, by Selected State Metropolitan and Nonmetropolitan Counties, 2021—Continued

(Number.)

| State/county | Law enforcement employees | Officers | Civilians |
|---|---|---|---|
| Okfuskee | 26 | 9 | 17 |
| Ottawa | 26 | 11 | 15 |
| Payne | 83 | 40 | 43 |
| Pittsburg | 61 | 21 | 40 |
| Pontotoc | 19 | 17 | 2 |
| Pottawatomie | 32 | 28 | 4 |
| Pushmataha | 13 | 13 | 0 |
| Roger Mills | 12 | 7 | 5 |
| Seminole | 19 | 12 | 7 |
| Stephens | 25 | 21 | 4 |
| Texas | 27 | 10 | 17 |
| Tillman | 5 | 5 | 0 |
| Washington | 59 | 29 | 30 |
| Washita | 28 | 6 | 22 |
| Woods | 8 | 7 | 1 |
| Woodward | 12 | 11 | 1 |
| | | | |
| **OREGON** | | | |
| **Metropolitan Counties** | | | |
| Benton | 78 | 65 | 13 |
| Clackamas | 425 | 195 | 230 |
| Columbia | 56 | 18 | 38 |
| Deschutes | 240 | 181 | 59 |
| Jackson | 175 | 130 | 45 |
| Josephine | 95 | 33 | 62 |
| Lane | 291 | 68 | 223 |
| Linn | 184 | 73 | 111 |
| Marion | 327 | 95 | 232 |
| Multnomah | 740 | 121 | 619 |
| Polk | 63 | 27 | 36 |
| Washington | 589 | 257 | 332 |
| Yamhill | 97 | 44 | 53 |
| | | | |
| **Nonmetropolitan Counties** | | | |
| Baker | 41 | 31 | 10 |
| Clatsop | 85 | 58 | 27 |
| Coos | 87 | 59 | 28 |
| Crook | 68 | 41 | 27 |
| Curry | 48 | 19 | 29 |
| Douglas | 139 | 65 | 74 |
| Gilliam | 8 | 7 | 1 |
| Grant | 23 | 23 | 0 |
| Harney | 24 | 16 | 8 |
| Hood River | 46 | 25 | 21 |
| Jefferson | 40 | 18 | 22 |
| Klamath | 96 | 32 | 64 |
| Lake | 28 | 26 | 2 |
| Lincoln | 85 | 28 | 57 |
| Malheur | 57 | 24 | 33 |
| Morrow | 38 | 27 | 11 |
| Sherman | 7 | 6 | 1 |
| Tillamook | 53 | 45 | 8 |
| Umatilla | 104 | 25 | 79 |
| Union | 38 | 17 | 21 |
| Wallowa | 9 | 3 | 6 |
| Wasco | 29 | 15 | 14 |
| Wheeler | 5 | 4 | 1 |
| | | | |
| **PENNSYLVANIA** | | | |
| **Metropolitan Counties** | | | |
| Adams | 17 | 13 | 4 |
| Allegheny | 193 | 160 | 33 |
| Allegheny County Police Department | 232 | 215 | 17 |
| Beaver | 24 | 20 | 4 |
| Berks | 103 | 91 | 12 |
| Blair | 24 | 21 | 3 |
| Bucks | 77 | 63 | 14 |
| Butler | 30 | 27 | 3 |
| Centre | 26 | 22 | 4 |
| Chester | 80 | 65 | 15 |
| Cumberland | 37 | 31 | 6 |
| Erie | 50 | 43 | 7 |
| Franklin | 32 | 29 | 3 |
| Lancaster | 56 | 47 | 9 |
| Monroe | 45 | 20 | 25 |
| Northampton | 60 | 55 | 5 |
| Pike | 21 | 17 | 4 |
| | | | |
| **Nonmetropolitan Counties** | | | |
| Bedford | 12 | 10 | 2 |
| Bradford | 12 | 10 | 2 |
| Clarion | 9 | 6 | 3 |
| Elk | 8 | 7 | 1 |

## Table 80. Full-Time Law Enforcement Employees, by Selected State Metropolitan and Nonmetropolitan Counties, 2021—Continued

(Number.)

| State/county | Law enforcement employees | Officers | Civilians |
|---|---|---|---|
| Greene | 18 | 9 | 9 |
| Indiana | 25 | 22 | 3 |
| Jefferson | 10 | 8 | 2 |
| Lawrence | 22 | 17 | 5 |
| Northumberland | 11 | 9 | 2 |
| Union | 8 | 7 | 1 |
| Warren | 13 | 11 | 2 |
| | | | |
| **SOUTH CAROLINA** | | | |
| **Metropolitan Counties** | | | |
| Aiken | 235 | 127 | 108 |
| Anderson | 417 | 260 | 157 |
| Beaufort | 292 | 195 | 97 |
| Berkeley | 190 | 163 | 27 |
| Calhoun | 39 | 26 | 13 |
| Charleston | 651 | 271 | 380 |
| Chester | 125 | 58 | 67 |
| Clarendon | 74 | 65 | 9 |
| Darlington | 116 | 67 | 49 |
| Dorchester | 257 | 150 | 107 |
| Edgefield | 74 | 37 | 37 |
| Fairfield | 60 | 54 | 6 |
| Florence | 259 | 220 | 39 |
| Greenville | 617 | 500 | 117 |
| Horry | 87 | 63 | 24 |
| Horry County Police Department | 288 | 262 | 26 |
| Jasper | 51 | 41 | 10 |
| Kershaw | 72 | 70 | 2 |
| Lancaster | 186 | 127 | 59 |
| Laurens | 122 | 58 | 64 |
| Lexington | 412 | 288 | 124 |
| Pickens | 171 | 147 | 24 |
| Richland | 605 | 528 | 77 |
| Spartanburg | 365 | 334 | 31 |
| Sumter | 137 | 121 | 16 |
| York | 394 | 205 | 189 |
| | | | |
| **Nonmetropolitan Counties** | | | |
| Abbeville | 39 | 35 | 4 |
| Allendale | 11 | 9 | 2 |
| Barnwell | 98 | 36 | 62 |
| Cherokee | 118 | 67 | 51 |
| Colleton | 113 | 49 | 64 |
| Georgetown | 133 | 73 | 60 |
| Greenwood | 131 | 71 | 60 |
| Hampton | 46 | 36 | 10 |
| Lee | 20 | 16 | 4 |
| Marion | 40 | 38 | 2 |
| Marlboro | 32 | 32 | 0 |
| McCormick | 37 | 18 | 19 |
| Oconee | 183 | 101 | 82 |
| Orangeburg | 133 | 88 | 45 |
| Union | 35 | 30 | 5 |
| Williamsburg | 79 | 38 | 41 |
| | | | |
| **SOUTH DAKOTA** | | | |
| **Metropolitan Counties** | | | |
| Lincoln | 45 | 28 | 17 |
| McCook | 10 | 9 | 1 |
| Meade | 50 | 18 | 32 |
| Minnehaha | 249 | 84 | 165 |
| Pennington | 431 | 101 | 330 |
| Turner | 12 | 10 | 2 |
| Union | 19 | 9 | 10 |
| | | | |
| **Nonmetropolitan Counties** | | | |
| Aurora | 4 | 3 | 1 |
| Beadle | 24 | 5 | 19 |
| Bennett | 6 | 3 | 3 |
| Bon Homme | 8 | 3 | 5 |
| Brookings | 26 | 16 | 10 |
| Brown | 21 | 16 | 5 |
| Brule | 10 | 4 | 6 |
| Buffalo | 1 | 1 | 0 |
| Butte | 16 | 6 | 10 |
| Campbell | 3 | 3 | 0 |
| Charles Mix | 22 | 8 | 14 |
| Clark | 3 | 3 | 0 |
| Clay | 16 | 8 | 8 |
| Codington | 29 | 12 | 17 |
| Corson | 5 | 5 | 0 |
| Custer | 12 | 11 | 1 |
| Davison | 8 | 6 | 2 |

## Table 80. Full-Time Law Enforcement Employees, by Selected State Metropolitan and Nonmetropolitan Counties, 2021—Continued

(Number.)

| State/county | Law enforcement employees | Officers | Civilians |
|---|---|---|---|
| Day | 8 | 3 | 5 |
| Deuel | 6 | 5 | 1 |
| Dewey | 4 | 4 | 0 |
| Douglas | 4 | 4 | 0 |
| Edmunds | 9 | 4 | 5 |
| Fall River | 19 | 7 | 12 |
| Faulk | 22 | 4 | 18 |
| Grant | 11 | 5 | 6 |
| Gregory | 5 | 4 | 1 |
| Haakon | 2 | 2 | 0 |
| Hamlin | 6 | 6 | 0 |
| Hand | 3 | 2 | 1 |
| Hanson | 3 | 3 | 0 |
| Harding | 3 | 2 | 1 |
| Hughes | 47 | 8 | 39 |
| Hutchinson | 4 | 3 | 1 |
| Hyde | 1 | 1 | 0 |
| Jackson | 3 | 2 | 1 |
| Jerauld | 4 | 4 | 0 |
| Jones | 2 | 2 | 0 |
| Kingsbury | 6 | 5 | 1 |
| Lake | 18 | 8 | 10 |
| Lawrence | 45 | 20 | 25 |
| Lyman | 5 | 4 | 1 |
| Marshall | 12 | 6 | 6 |
| McPherson | 4 | 4 | 0 |
| Mellette | 4 | 3 | 1 |
| Miner | 4 | 3 | 1 |
| Moody | 11 | 7 | 4 |
| Oglala Lakota | 1 | 1 | 0 |
| Perkins | 8 | 7 | 1 |
| Potter | 4 | 3 | 1 |
| Roberts | 32 | 6 | 26 |
| Sanborn | 4 | 3 | 1 |
| Spink | 13 | 9 | 4 |
| Stanley | 6 | 5 | 1 |
| Sully | 3 | 3 | 0 |
| Tripp | 4 | 3 | 1 |
| Walworth | 9 | 3 | 6 |
| Yankton | 34 | 11 | 23 |
| Ziebach | 3 | 3 | 0 |
| **TENNESSEE** | | | |
| **Metropolitan Counties** | | | |
| Anderson | 160 | 68 | 92 |
| Blount | 302 | 175 | 127 |
| Bradley | 220 | 114 | 106 |
| Campbell | 77 | 42 | 35 |
| Cannon | 36 | 18 | 18 |
| Carter | 106 | 63 | 43 |
| Cheatham | 91 | 49 | 42 |
| Chester | 46 | 17 | 29 |
| Crockett | 36 | 15 | 21 |
| Dickson | 152 | 72 | 80 |
| Fayette | 85 | 47 | 38 |
| Gibson | 91 | 39 | 52 |
| Grainger | 45 | 24 | 21 |
| Hamblen | 102 | 48 | 54 |
| Hamilton | 436 | 173 | 263 |
| Hartsville/Trousdale | 48 | 22 | 26 |
| Hawkins | 115 | 67 | 48 |
| Jefferson | 99 | 53 | 46 |
| Knox | 932 | 400 | 532 |
| Loudon | 106 | 55 | 51 |
| Macon | 68 | 33 | 35 |
| Madison | 257 | 121 | 136 |
| Marion | 66 | 34 | 32 |
| Maury | 163 | 90 | 73 |
| Montgomery | 379 | 143 | 236 |
| Morgan | 28 | 24 | 4 |
| Polk | 62 | 27 | 35 |
| Roane | 80 | 43 | 37 |
| Robertson | 174 | 73 | 101 |
| Rutherford | 443 | 237 | 206 |
| Sequatchie | 26 | 23 | 3 |
| Shelby | 1,735 | 681 | 1,054 |
| Smith | 64 | 32 | 32 |
| Stewart | 58 | 24 | 34 |
| Sullivan | 316 | 140 | 176 |
| Sumner | 273 | 122 | 151 |
| Tipton | 96 | 59 | 37 |
| Unicoi | 58 | 26 | 32 |
| Union | 56 | 33 | 23 |

## Table 80. Full-Time Law Enforcement Employees, by Selected State Metropolitan and Nonmetropolitan Counties, 2021—Continued

(Number.)

| State/county | Law enforcement employees | Officers | Civilians |
|---|---|---|---|
| Washington | 195 | 87 | 108 |
| Williamson | 292 | 182 | 110 |
| Wilson | 268 | 138 | 130 |
| **Nonmetropolitan Counties** | | | |
| Bedford | 104 | 50 | 54 |
| Benton | 53 | 17 | 36 |
| Bledsoe | 37 | 13 | 24 |
| Carroll | 65 | 29 | 36 |
| Claiborne | 95 | 46 | 49 |
| Clay | 19 | 12 | 7 |
| Cocke | 93 | 50 | 43 |
| Coffee | 117 | 51 | 66 |
| Cumberland | 113 | 54 | 59 |
| Decatur | 40 | 18 | 22 |
| DeKalb | 27 | 27 | 0 |
| Dyer | 92 | 37 | 55 |
| Fentress | 27 | 21 | 6 |
| Franklin | 85 | 42 | 43 |
| Giles | 35 | 32 | 3 |
| Greene | 167 | 74 | 93 |
| Grundy | 28 | 17 | 11 |
| Hancock | 55 | 24 | 31 |
| Hardeman | 50 | 25 | 25 |
| Hardin | 59 | 29 | 30 |
| Haywood | 51 | 21 | 30 |
| Henderson | 72 | 33 | 39 |
| Henry | 67 | 32 | 35 |
| Hickman | 46 | 25 | 21 |
| Houston | 25 | 11 | 14 |
| Humphreys | 49 | 26 | 23 |
| Jackson | 32 | 16 | 16 |
| Johnson | 37 | 18 | 19 |
| Lake | 23 | 8 | 15 |
| Lauderdale | 58 | 19 | 39 |
| Lawrence | 70 | 52 | 18 |
| Lewis | 34 | 17 | 17 |
| Lincoln | 88 | 43 | 45 |
| Marshall | 53 | 30 | 23 |
| McMinn | 82 | 32 | 50 |
| McNairy | 39 | 19 | 20 |
| Meigs | 46 | 20 | 26 |
| Monroe | 53 | 47 | 6 |
| Moore | 26 | 15 | 11 |
| Obion | 70 | 35 | 35 |
| Overton | 58 | 28 | 30 |
| Perry | 32 | 18 | 14 |
| Pickett | 18 | 11 | 7 |
| Putnam | 161 | 79 | 82 |
| Rhea | 64 | 38 | 26 |
| Scott | 66 | 29 | 37 |
| Sevier | 211 | 109 | 102 |
| Van Buren | 21 | 8 | 13 |
| Warren | 114 | 55 | 59 |
| Wayne | 57 | 17 | 40 |
| Weakley | 51 | 28 | 23 |
| White | 81 | 38 | 43 |
| **TEXAS** | | | |
| **Metropolitan Counties** | | | |
| Atascosa | 107 | 42 | 65 |
| Austin | 70 | 35 | 35 |
| Bandera | 70 | 33 | 37 |
| Bastrop | 189 | 81 | 108 |
| Bell | 367 | 114 | 253 |
| Bexar | 1,623 | 578 | 1,045 |
| Bowie | 39 | 32 | 7 |
| Brazoria | 328 | 145 | 183 |
| Brazos | 243 | 98 | 145 |
| Burleson | 51 | 27 | 24 |
| Caldwell | 88 | 34 | 54 |
| Callahan | 19 | 6 | 13 |
| Cameron | 341 | 101 | 240 |
| Carson | 21 | 9 | 12 |
| Chambers | 73 | 67 | 6 |
| Clay | 31 | 16 | 15 |
| Collin | 470 | 139 | 331 |
| Comal | 344 | 162 | 182 |
| Coryell | 35 | 34 | 1 |
| Crosby | 19 | 10 | 9 |
| Dallas | 2,234 | 457 | 1,777 |
| Denton | 528 | 178 | 350 |
| Ector | 147 | 89 | 58 |

## Table 80. Full-Time Law Enforcement Employees, by Selected State Metropolitan and Nonmetropolitan Counties, 2021—Continued

(Number.)

| State/county | Law enforcement employees | Officers | Civilians |
|---|---|---|---|
| Ellis | 210 | 87 | 123 |
| El Paso | 410 | 255 | 155 |
| Fort Bend | 764 | 548 | 216 |
| Galveston | 475 | 325 | 150 |
| Goliad | 31 | 16 | 15 |
| Grayson | 181 | 63 | 118 |
| Gregg | 221 | 97 | 124 |
| Hardin | 77 | 37 | 40 |
| Harris | 5,009 | 2,327 | 2,682 |
| Harrison | 104 | 49 | 55 |
| Hays | 394 | 174 | 220 |
| Hidalgo | 822 | 274 | 548 |
| Hudspeth | 43 | 16 | 27 |
| Hunt | 137 | 46 | 91 |
| Irion | 11 | 6 | 5 |
| Jefferson | 390 | 134 | 256 |
| Johnson | 124 | 90 | 34 |
| Jones | 34 | 9 | 25 |
| Kaufman | 240 | 89 | 151 |
| Kendall | 97 | 50 | 47 |
| Lampasas | 41 | 14 | 27 |
| Liberty | 159 | 73 | 86 |
| Lubbock | 472 | 194 | 278 |
| Lynn | 21 | 7 | 14 |
| Martin | 19 | 9 | 10 |
| McLennan | 506 | 110 | 396 |
| Medina | 83 | 47 | 36 |
| Midland | 198 | 84 | 114 |
| Montgomery | 894 | 500 | 394 |
| Nueces | 278 | 40 | 238 |
| Oldham | 10 | 5 | 5 |
| Orange | 132 | 60 | 72 |
| Parker | 133 | 96 | 37 |
| Potter | 229 | 90 | 139 |
| Randall | 206 | 86 | 120 |
| Robertson | 42 | 15 | 27 |
| Rockwall | 136 | 54 | 82 |
| Rusk | 73 | 39 | 34 |
| Smith | 366 | 175 | 191 |
| Sterling | 5 | 5 | 0 |
| Tarrant | 1,414 | 1,230 | 184 |
| Taylor | 237 | 77 | 160 |
| Tom Green | 197 | 185 | 12 |
| Travis | 1,549 | 339 | 1,210 |
| Upshur | 86 | 50 | 36 |
| Victoria | 136 | 78 | 58 |
| Waller | 106 | 63 | 43 |
| Webb | 316 | 139 | 177 |
| Wichita | 188 | 61 | 127 |
| Williamson | 228 | 181 | 47 |
| Wilson | 75 | 34 | 41 |
| Wise | 135 | 64 | 71 |
| **Nonmetropolitan Counties** | | | |
| Angelina | 98 | 38 | 60 |
| Bailey | 23 | 8 | 15 |
| Baylor | 9 | 4 | 5 |
| Bee | 61 | 25 | 36 |
| Blanco | 34 | 15 | 19 |
| Borden | 4 | 3 | 1 |
| Bosque | 45 | 21 | 24 |
| Brewster | 33 | 18 | 15 |
| Briscoe | 4 | 4 | 0 |
| Brooks | 37 | 16 | 21 |
| Brown | 65 | 29 | 36 |
| Burnet | 139 | 53 | 86 |
| Calhoun | 70 | 28 | 42 |
| Camp | 21 | 10 | 11 |
| Cass | 48 | 19 | 29 |
| Castro | 23 | 6 | 17 |
| Cherokee | 68 | 34 | 34 |
| Childress | 19 | 4 | 15 |
| Cochran | 14 | 7 | 7 |
| Coke | 6 | 5 | 1 |
| Collingsworth | 3 | 3 | 0 |
| Colorado | 52 | 23 | 29 |
| Comanche | 29 | 20 | 9 |
| Concho | 15 | 8 | 7 |
| Cooke | 84 | 35 | 49 |
| Crane | 16 | 9 | 7 |
| Crockett | 17 | 10 | 7 |
| Dallam | 7 | 6 | 1 |
| Dawson | 21 | 9 | 12 |

## Table 80. Full-Time Law Enforcement Employees, by Selected State Metropolitan and Nonmetropolitan Counties, 2021—Continued

(Number.)

| State/county | Law enforcement employees | Officers | Civilians |
|---|---|---|---|
| Deaf Smith | 34 | 10 | 24 |
| Delta | 21 | 10 | 11 |
| DeWitt | 49 | 19 | 30 |
| Donley | 10 | 5 | 5 |
| Duval | 40 | 22 | 18 |
| Eastland | 32 | 13 | 19 |
| Edwards | 22 | 7 | 15 |
| Erath | 66 | 27 | 39 |
| Floyd | 10 | 6 | 4 |
| Foard | 3 | 2 | 1 |
| Franklin | 26 | 13 | 13 |
| Freestone | 35 | 16 | 19 |
| Gaines | 39 | 19 | 20 |
| Garza | 35 | 8 | 27 |
| Gillespie | 50 | 31 | 19 |
| Glasscock | 6 | 5 | 1 |
| Gonzales | 53 | 20 | 33 |
| Gray | 37 | 14 | 23 |
| Grimes | 57 | 30 | 27 |
| Hall | 8 | 4 | 4 |
| Hamilton | 20 | 11 | 9 |
| Hansford | 13 | 7 | 6 |
| Hardeman | 13 | 8 | 5 |
| Hartley | 6 | 6 | 0 |
| Haskell | 7 | 3 | 4 |
| Hemphill | 16 | 8 | 8 |
| Henderson | 139 | 49 | 90 |
| Hill | 64 | 30 | 34 |
| Hockley | 32 | 14 | 18 |
| Hood | 141 | 55 | 86 |
| Hopkins | 60 | 26 | 34 |
| Houston | 53 | 22 | 31 |
| Howard | 65 | 24 | 41 |
| Hutchinson | 36 | 14 | 22 |
| Jack | 33 | 15 | 18 |
| Jackson | 38 | 15 | 23 |
| Jasper | 47 | 20 | 27 |
| Jeff Davis | 5 | 4 | 1 |
| Jim Hogg | 35 | 11 | 24 |
| Jim Wells | 62 | 56 | 6 |
| Karnes | 64 | 31 | 33 |
| Kenedy | 19 | 12 | 7 |
| Kerr | 116 | 51 | 65 |
| Kimble | 11 | 6 | 5 |
| King | 2 | 2 | 0 |
| Kleberg | 59 | 27 | 32 |
| Lamar | 77 | 32 | 45 |
| Lamb | 26 | 9 | 17 |
| La Salle | 115 | 21 | 94 |
| Lavaca | 34 | 14 | 20 |
| Lee | 40 | 13 | 27 |
| Leon | 37 | 23 | 14 |
| Limestone | 62 | 18 | 44 |
| Lipscomb | 13 | 5 | 8 |
| Llano | 61 | 29 | 32 |
| Loving | 10 | 7 | 3 |
| Madison | 31 | 13 | 18 |
| Marion | 19 | 18 | 1 |
| Mason | 11 | 6 | 5 |
| Matagorda | 72 | 33 | 39 |
| McCulloch | 26 | 8 | 18 |
| Milam | 67 | 23 | 44 |
| Mills | 22 | 9 | 13 |
| Montague | 31 | 12 | 19 |
| Moore | 52 | 19 | 33 |
| Motley | 1 | 1 | 0 |
| Nacogdoches | 77 | 37 | 40 |
| Navarro | 121 | 44 | 77 |
| Newton | 15 | 15 | 0 |
| Nolan | 43 | 16 | 27 |
| Ochiltree | 25 | 8 | 17 |
| Palo Pinto | 63 | 25 | 38 |
| Panola | 67 | 40 | 27 |
| Parmer | 20 | 7 | 13 |
| Polk | 103 | 46 | 57 |
| Presidio | 28 | 6 | 22 |
| Rains | 29 | 13 | 16 |
| Reagan | 29 | 13 | 16 |
| Real | 11 | 5 | 6 |
| Red River | 33 | 11 | 22 |
| Refugio | 45 | 18 | 27 |
| Roberts | 6 | 5 | 1 |
| Runnels | 34 | 6 | 28 |

## Table 80. Full-Time Law Enforcement Employees, by Selected State Metropolitan and Nonmetropolitan Counties, 2021—Continued

(Number.)

| State/county | Law enforcement employees | Officers | Civilians |
|---|---|---|---|
| Sabine | 20 | 10 | 10 |
| San Augustine | 21 | 10 | 11 |
| Schleicher | 11 | 5 | 6 |
| Scurry | 50 | 10 | 40 |
| Shackelford | 16 | 6 | 10 |
| Shelby | 38 | 16 | 22 |
| Somervell | 42 | 22 | 20 |
| Starr | 110 | 46 | 64 |
| Sutton | 14 | 6 | 8 |
| Swisher | 16 | 5 | 11 |
| Terrell | 6 | 3 | 3 |
| Terry | 33 | 9 | 24 |
| Throckmorton | 7 | 2 | 5 |
| Titus | 58 | 23 | 35 |
| Trinity | 22 | 14 | 8 |
| Tyler | 29 | 15 | 14 |
| Upton | 24 | 11 | 13 |
| Uvalde | 70 | 25 | 45 |
| Val Verde | 72 | 47 | 25 |
| Van Zandt | 62 | 26 | 36 |
| Walker | 81 | 41 | 40 |
| Ward | 39 | 17 | 22 |
| Washington | 55 | 33 | 22 |
| Wharton | 75 | 39 | 36 |
| Wheeler | 24 | 10 | 14 |
| Wilbarger | 18 | 8 | 10 |
| Willacy | 40 | 21 | 19 |
| Winkler | 30 | 11 | 19 |
| Wood | 70 | 33 | 37 |
| Yoakum | 24 | 23 | 1 |
| Zapata | 82 | 75 | 7 |
| Zavala | 43 | 18 | 25 |
| | | | |
| **UTAH** | | | |
| **Metropolitan Counties** | | | |
| Box Elder | 79 | 27 | 52 |
| Cache | 151 | 133 | 18 |
| Davis | 285 | 86 | 199 |
| Juab | 26 | 16 | 10 |
| Morgan | 15 | 13 | 2 |
| Salt Lake County Unified Police Department | 407 | 323 | 84 |
| Tooele | 84 | 26 | 58 |
| Utah | 410 | 169 | 241 |
| Washington | 158 | 47 | 111 |
| Weber | 299 | 225 | 74 |
| | | | |
| **Nonmetropolitan Counties** | | | |
| Beaver | 76 | 22 | 54 |
| Carbon | 49 | 26 | 23 |
| Daggett | 5 | 4 | 1 |
| Duchesne | 39 | 24 | 15 |
| Emery | 36 | 23 | 13 |
| Garfield | 32 | 16 | 16 |
| Grand | 38 | 28 | 10 |
| Iron | 85 | 81 | 4 |
| Kane | 53 | 24 | 29 |
| Millard | 57 | 29 | 28 |
| Rich | 10 | 10 | 0 |
| San Juan | 32 | 16 | 16 |
| Sanpete | 61 | 23 | 38 |
| Sevier | 60 | 23 | 37 |
| Summit | 103 | 64 | 39 |
| Uintah | 95 | 29 | 66 |
| Wasatch | 72 | 36 | 36 |
| | | | |
| **VERMONT** | | | |
| **Metropolitan Counties** | | | |
| Chittenden | 15 | 13 | 2 |
| Franklin | 20 | 19 | 1 |
| Grand Isle | 4 | 4 | 0 |
| | | | |
| Nonetropolitan Counties | | | |
| Addison | 8 | 7 | 1 |
| Bennington | 15 | 12 | 3 |
| Caledonia | 4 | 3 | 1 |
| Essex | 3 | 3 | 0 |
| Lamoille | 21 | 9 | 12 |
| Orange | 10 | 10 | 0 |
| Orleans | 11 | 9 | 2 |
| Rutland | 24 | 19 | 5 |
| Washington | 6 | 4 | 2 |
| Windham | 18 | 12 | 6 |
| Windsor | 15 | 13 | 2 |
| **VIRGINIA** | | | |

## Table 80. Full-Time Law Enforcement Employees, by Selected State Metropolitan and Nonmetropolitan Counties, 2021—Continued

(Number.)

| State/county | Law enforcement employees | Officers | Civilians |
|---|---|---|---|
| **Metropolitan Counties** | | | |
| Albemarle County Police Department | 172 | 139 | 33 |
| Amelia | 29 | 19 | 10 |
| Amherst | 51 | 43 | 8 |
| Appomattox | 23 | 21 | 2 |
| Arlington County Police Department . | 434 | 332 | 102 |
| Augusta | 84 | 73 | 11 |
| Bedford | 87 | 79 | 8 |
| Botetourt | 117 | 97 | 20 |
| Campbell | 69 | 64 | 5 |
| Charles City | 21 | 14 | 7 |
| Chesterfield County Police Department | 668 | 542 | 126 |
| Clarke | 33 | 21 | 12 |
| Craig | 14 | 9 | 5 |
| Culpeper | 106 | 91 | 15 |
| Dinwiddie | 61 | 58 | 3 |
| Fairfax County Police Department | 1,768 | 1,430 | 338 |
| Fauquier | 170 | 131 | 39 |
| Fluvanna | 49 | 37 | 12 |
| Franklin | 101 | 80 | 21 |
| Frederick | 147 | 134 | 13 |
| Giles | 33 | 25 | 8 |
| Gloucester | 95 | 77 | 18 |
| Goochland | 63 | 46 | 17 |
| Greene | 43 | 26 | 17 |
| Hanover | 276 | 258 | 18 |
| Henrico County Police Department | 820 | 655 | 165 |
| Isle of Wight | 55 | 51 | 4 |
| James City County Police Department | 112 | 100 | 12 |
| King and Queen | 20 | 15 | 5 |
| King William | 35 | 23 | 12 |
| Loudoun | 702 | 571 | 131 |
| Madison | 37 | 23 | 14 |
| Mathews | 20 | 12 | 8 |
| Montgomery | 115 | 109 | 6 |
| Nelson | 25 | 20 | 5 |
| New Kent | 56 | 39 | 17 |
| Powhatan | 47 | 41 | 6 |
| Prince George County Police Department | 76 | 57 | 19 |
| Prince William County Police Department | 796 | 645 | 151 |
| Pulaski | 55 | 53 | 2 |
| Rappahannock | 21 | 15 | 6 |
| Roanoke County Police Department | 145 | 131 | 14 |
| Rockingham | 180 | 70 | 110 |
| Scott | 39 | 35 | 4 |
| Southampton | 73 | 58 | 15 |
| Stafford | 280 | 207 | 73 |
| Sussex | 51 | 45 | 6 |
| Warren | 76 | 59 | 17 |
| Washington | 86 | 68 | 18 |
| York | 126 | 114 | 12 |
| | | | |
| **Nonmetropolitan Counties** | | | |
| Accomack | 61 | 52 | 9 |
| Alleghany | 74 | 54 | 20 |
| Bath | 24 | 15 | 9 |
| Bland | 23 | 14 | 9 |
| Brunswick | 48 | 33 | 15 |
| Buchanan | 50 | 36 | 14 |
| Buckingham | 27 | 20 | 7 |
| Caroline | 70 | 50 | 20 |
| Carroll | 60 | 40 | 20 |
| Charlotte | 36 | 19 | 17 |
| Cumberland | 21 | 15 | 6 |
| Dickenson | 40 | 26 | 14 |
| Essex | 23 | 15 | 8 |
| Floyd | 37 | 27 | 10 |
| Grayson | 29 | 23 | 6 |
| Greensville | 36 | 25 | 11 |
| Halifax | 45 | 42 | 3 |
| Henry | 150 | 135 | 15 |
| Highland | 12 | 8 | 4 |
| King George | 57 | 42 | 15 |
| Lancaster | 41 | 31 | 10 |
| Lee | 42 | 29 | 13 |
| Louisa | 69 | 53 | 16 |
| Lunenburg | 16 | 11 | 5 |
| Mecklenburg | 50 | 48 | 2 |
| Middlesex | 29 | 21 | 8 |
| Northampton | 79 | 64 | 15 |
| Northumberland | 34 | 21 | 13 |
| Nottoway | 29 | 20 | 9 |
| Orange | 45 | 42 | 3 |

## Table 80. Full-Time Law Enforcement Employees, by Selected State Metropolitan and Nonmetropolitan Counties, 2021—Continued

(Number.)

| State/county | Law enforcement employees | Officers | Civilians |
|---|---|---|---|
| Page | 65 | 58 | 7 |
| Patrick | 70 | 55 | 15 |
| Pittsylvania | 115 | 102 | 13 |
| Prince Edward | 32 | 26 | 6 |
| Richmond | 23 | 15 | 8 |
| Rockbridge | 39 | 36 | 3 |
| Russell | 52 | 37 | 15 |
| Shenandoah | 68 | 61 | 7 |
| Smyth | 56 | 42 | 14 |
| Surry | 23 | 12 | 11 |
| Tazewell | 78 | 50 | 28 |
| Westmoreland | 47 | 30 | 17 |
| Wise | 73 | 57 | 16 |
| Wythe | 45 | 37 | 8 |
| **WASHINGTON** | | | |
| **Metropolitan Counties** | | | |
| Asotin | 29 | 13 | 16 |
| Benton | 72 | 60 | 12 |
| Chelan | 70 | 54 | 16 |
| Clark | 247 | 142 | 105 |
| Cowlitz | 61 | 41 | 20 |
| Douglas | 38 | 33 | 5 |
| Franklin | 84 | 31 | 53 |
| King | 244 | 185 | 59 |
| Kitsap | 245 | 120 | 125 |
| Pierce | 321 | 254 | 67 |
| Skagit | 137 | 56 | 81 |
| Skamania | 35 | 32 | 3 |
| Snohomish | 355 | 286 | 69 |
| Spokane | 133 | 113 | 20 |
| Stevens | 64 | 31 | 33 |
| Thurston | 244 | 93 | 151 |
| Walla Walla | 36 | 28 | 8 |
| Whatcom | 187 | 86 | 101 |
| Yakima | 86 | 57 | 29 |
| **Nonmetropolitan Counties** | | | |
| Adams | 36 | 16 | 20 |
| Clallam | 49 | 38 | 11 |
| Columbia | 8 | 8 | 0 |
| Ferry | 21 | 6 | 15 |
| Garfield | 14 | 7 | 7 |
| Grant | 123 | 56 | 67 |
| Grays Harbor | 78 | 56 | 22 |
| Island | 76 | 43 | 33 |
| Jefferson | 43 | 24 | 19 |
| Kittitas | 99 | 48 | 51 |
| Klickitat | 38 | 18 | 20 |
| Lewis | 106 | 38 | 68 |
| Lincoln | 27 | 15 | 12 |
| Mason | 88 | 48 | 40 |
| Okanogan | 82 | 28 | 54 |
| Pacific | 45 | 16 | 29 |
| Pend Oreille | 34 | 13 | 21 |
| San Juan | 36 | 22 | 14 |
| Wahkiakum | 20 | 9 | 11 |
| Whitman | 32 | 16 | 16 |
| **WEST VIRGINIA** | | | |
| **Metropolitan Counties** | | | |
| Berkeley | 70 | 61 | 9 |
| Boone | 20 | 18 | 2 |
| Brooke | 18 | 18 | 0 |
| Cabell | 56 | 44 | 12 |
| Clay | 3 | 3 | 0 |
| Fayette | 46 | 37 | 9 |
| Hampshire | 25 | 20 | 5 |
| Hancock | 34 | 31 | 3 |
| Jackson | 24 | 16 | 8 |
| Jefferson | 37 | 31 | 6 |
| Kanawha | 132 | 102 | 30 |
| Lincoln | 4 | 4 | 0 |
| Marshall | 34 | 31 | 3 |
| Mineral | 22 | 20 | 2 |
| Monongalia | 41 | 37 | 4 |
| Morgan | 14 | 13 | 1 |
| Ohio | 38 | 36 | 2 |
| Preston | 22 | 20 | 2 |
| Putnam | 50 | 38 | 12 |
| Raleigh | 68 | 54 | 14 |
| Wayne | 32 | 21 | 11 |
| Wirt | 5 | 3 | 2 |

## Table 80. Full-Time Law Enforcement Employees, by Selected State Metropolitan and Nonmetropolitan Counties, 2021—Continued

(Number.)

| State/county | Law enforcement employees | Officers | Civilians |
|---|---|---|---|
| Wood | 58 | 37 | 21 |
| **Nonmetropolitan Counties** | | | |
| Barbour | 19 | 11 | 8 |
| Braxton | 10 | 8 | 2 |
| Calhoun | 6 | 4 | 2 |
| Doddridge | 10 | 9 | 1 |
| Gilmer | 4 | 4 | 0 |
| Grant | 15 | 14 | 1 |
| Greenbrier | 29 | 28 | 1 |
| Hardy | 12 | 10 | 2 |
| Harrison | 59 | 54 | 5 |
| Lewis | 17 | 12 | 5 |
| Logan | 28 | 26 | 2 |
| Marion | 47 | 31 | 16 |
| Mason | 20 | 18 | 2 |
| McDowell | 11 | 11 | 0 |
| Mercer | 41 | 28 | 13 |
| Mingo | 21 | 19 | 2 |
| Monroe | 13 | 10 | 3 |
| Nicholas | 24 | 21 | 3 |
| Pendleton | 4 | 4 | 0 |
| Pleasants | 6 | 5 | 1 |
| Pocahontas | 12 | 7 | 5 |
| Randolph | 22 | 15 | 7 |
| Ritchie | 15 | 10 | 5 |
| Roane | 11 | 8 | 3 |
| Summers | 8 | 7 | 1 |
| Taylor | 17 | 9 | 8 |
| Tucker | 8 | 5 | 3 |
| Tyler | 15 | 13 | 2 |
| Upshur | 13 | 11 | 2 |
| Webster | 6 | 3 | 3 |
| Wetzel | 22 | 16 | 6 |
| Wyoming | 18 | 18 | 0 |
| **WISCONSIN** | | | |
| **Metropolitan Counties** | | | |
| Calumet | 60 | 30 | 30 |
| Chippewa | 74 | 32 | 42 |
| Columbia | 114 | 43 | 71 |
| Dane | 543 | 435 | 108 |
| Douglas | 75 | 30 | 45 |
| Eau Claire | 107 | 44 | 63 |
| Fond du Lac | 132 | 63 | 69 |
| Green | 57 | 28 | 29 |
| Kewaunee | 37 | 35 | 2 |
| La Crosse | 112 | 42 | 70 |
| Marathon | 178 | 74 | 104 |
| Milwaukee | 551 | 288 | 263 |
| Oconto | 68 | 30 | 38 |
| Ozaukee | 112 | 80 | 32 |
| Pierce | 48 | 45 | 3 |
| Rock | 128 | 100 | 28 |
| Sheboygan | 181 | 69 | 112 |
| St. Croix | 101 | 69 | 32 |
| Washington | 176 | 80 | 96 |
| Waukesha | 332 | 162 | 170 |
| Winnebago | 185 | 131 | 54 |
| **Nonmetropolitan Counties** | | | |
| Adams | 56 | 30 | 26 |
| Ashland | 45 | 23 | 22 |
| Barron | 75 | 35 | 40 |
| Bayfield | 41 | 19 | 22 |
| Buffalo | 22 | 12 | 10 |
| Burnett | 35 | 35 | 0 |
| Clark | 61 | 30 | 31 |
| Crawford | 31 | 26 | 5 |
| Dodge | 158 | 58 | 100 |
| Door | 59 | 48 | 11 |
| Dunn | 32 | 28 | 4 |
| Florence | 24 | 12 | 12 |
| Forest | 44 | 21 | 23 |
| Grant | 90 | 32 | 58 |
| Green Lake | 42 | 17 | 25 |
| Iron | 21 | 12 | 9 |
| Jackson | 45 | 23 | 22 |
| Jefferson | 119 | 94 | 25 |
| Lafayette | 29 | 28 | 1 |
| Langlade | 44 | 17 | 27 |
| Manitowoc | 100 | 63 | 37 |

## Table 80. Full-Time Law Enforcement Employees, by Selected State Metropolitan and Nonmetropolitan Counties, 2021—Continued

(Number.)

| State/county | Law enforcement employees | Officers | Civilians |
|---|---|---|---|
| Marinette | 63 | 35 | 28 |
| Menominee | 15 | 8 | 7 |
| Monroe | 51 | 26 | 25 |
| Oneida | 83 | 38 | 45 |
| Pepin | 19 | 18 | 1 |
| Portage | 100 | 46 | 54 |
| Price | 33 | 19 | 14 |
| Richland | 33 | 33 | 0 |
| Rusk | 34 | 31 | 3 |
| Sauk | 129 | 43 | 86 |
| Sawyer | 49 | 28 | 21 |
| Shawano | 102 | 37 | 65 |
| Taylor | 30 | 17 | 13 |
| Trempealeau | 61 | 29 | 32 |
| Vernon | 51 | 23 | 28 |
| Vilas | 100 | 37 | 63 |
| Walworth | 190 | 78 | 112 |
| Washburn | 35 | 17 | 18 |
| Waupaca | 103 | 50 | 53 |
| Waushara | 56 | 29 | 27 |
| Wood | 74 | 45 | 29 |
| | | | |
| **WYOMING** | | | |
| **Metropolitan Counties** | | | |
| Laramie | 175 | 43 | 132 |
| Natrona | 150 | 107 | 43 |
| | | | |
| **Nonmetropolitan Counties** | | | |
| Albany | 40 | 15 | 25 |
| Big Horn | 42 | 17 | 25 |
| Campbell | 147 | 58 | 89 |
| Carbon | 58 | 18 | 40 |
| Converse | 26 | 24 | 2 |
| Crook | 23 | 16 | 7 |
| Fremont | 95 | 33 | 62 |
| Goshen | 23 | 9 | 14 |
| Hot Springs | 14 | 4 | 10 |
| Johnson | 32 | 29 | 3 |
| Lincoln | 49 | 22 | 27 |
| Niobrara | 16 | 4 | 12 |
| Park | 61 | 21 | 40 |
| Platte | 38 | 25 | 13 |
| Sheridan | 56 | 18 | 38 |
| Sublette | 67 | 51 | 16 |
| Sweetwater | 88 | 67 | 21 |
| Uinta | 49 | 23 | 26 |
| Washakie | 21 | 7 | 14 |
| Weston | 17 | 8 | 9 |

1 The employee data presented in this table for Mecklenburg represent only Mecklenburg County Sheriff's Office employees and exclude Charlotte-Mecklenburg Police Department employees.

## Table 81. Full-Time Law Enforcement Employees, by Selected State and Agency, 2021

(Number.)

| State/agency | Law enforcement employees | Officers | Civilians |
|---|---|---|---|
| **ALABAMA** | | | |
| **State Agencies** | | | |
| Alabama Department of Mental Health | 4 | 3 | 1 |
| Alabama Law Enforcement Agency | 1,396 | 805 | 591 |
| Department of Conservation, Montgomery | 135 | 127 | 8 |
| Department of Corrections Investigations and Intelligence Division | 118 | 91 | 27 |
| State Fire Marshal | 42 | 34 | 8 |
| Tannehill Ironworks Historic State Park | 1 | 1 | 0 |
| Taylor Hardin Secure Medical Facility | 21 | 17 | 4 |
| | | | |
| **Tribal Agencies** | | | |
| Poarch Creek Tribal | 56 | 46 | 10 |
| | | | |
| **Other Agencies** | | | |
| Huntsville International Airport | 21 | 15 | 6 |
| Mobile Regional Airport | 20 | 14 | 6 |
| Trussville Fire Department Fire and Explosion Investigation Unit | 3 | 3 | 0 |
| | | | |
| **ALASKA** | | | |
| **Other Agencies** | | | |
| Fairbanks International Airport | 29 | 22 | 7 |
| Ted Stevens Anchorage International Airport | 70 | 60 | 10 |
| | | | |
| **ARIZONA** | | | |
| **Tribal Agencies** | | | |
| Ak-Chin Tribal | 48 | 14 | 34 |
| Cocopah Tribal | 22 | 15 | 7 |
| Colorado River Tribal | 25 | 15 | 10 |
| Fort McDowell Tribal | 25 | 17 | 8 |
| Gila River Indian Community | 179 | 139 | 40 |
| Hopi Resource Enforcement Agency | 30 | 16 | 14 |
| Hualapai Tribal | 13 | 12 | 1 |
| Kaibab Paiute Tribal | 1 | 1 | 0 |
| Navajo Nation | 271 | 186 | 85 |
| Salt River Tribal | 143 | 110 | 33 |
| San Carlos Apache | 56 | 29 | 27 |
| Tonto Apache Tribal | 8 | 8 | 0 |
| Truxton Canon Agency | 9 | 5 | 4 |
| White Mountain Apache Tribal | 51 | 28 | 23 |
| Yavapai-Prescott Tribal | 13 | 10 | 3 |
| | | | |
| **Other Agencies** | | | |
| Tucson Airport Authority | 54 | 23 | 31 |
| | | | |
| **ARKANSAS** | | | |
| **State Agencies** | | | |
| Camp Robinson | 8 | 2 | 6 |
| State Capitol Police | 32 | 29 | 3 |
| | | | |
| **Other Agencies** | | | |
| Northwest Arkansas Regional Airport | 19 | 12 | 7 |
| | | | |
| **CALIFORNIA** | | | |
| **State Agencies** | | | |
| Atascadero State Hospital | 169 | 156 | 13 |
| Coalinga State Hospital | 261 | 244 | 17 |
| Department of Parks and Recreation, Capital | 569 | 531 | 38 |
| Fairview Developmental Center | 5 | 4 | 1 |
| Metropolitan State Hospital | 134 | 125 | 9 |
| Napa State Hospital | 129 | 120 | 9 |
| Patton State Hospital | 112 | 100 | 12 |
| Porterville Developmental Center | 57 | 52 | 5 |
| | | | |
| **Tribal Agencies** | | | |
| Bear River Band | 8 | 8 | 0 |
| Blue Lake Tribal | 6 | 1 | 5 |
| La Jolla Tribal | 7 | 7 | 0 |
| San Pasqual Band of Mission Indians Tribal | 10 | 10 | 0 |
| Sycuan Tribal | 19 | 13 | 6 |
| Yurok Tribal | 11 | 9 | 2 |
| | | | |
| **Other Agencies** | | | |
| Clovis Unified School District | 17 | 16 | 1 |
| East Bay Regional Park District | 91 | 59 | 32 |
| Fontana Unified School District | 67 | 14 | 53 |
| Kern High School District | 36 | 31 | 5 |
| Port of San Diego Harbor | 155 | 123 | 32 |
| San Bernardino Unified School District | 88 | 28 | 60 |
| San Francisco Bay Area Rapid Transit, Contra County County | 355 | 221 | 134 |
| Shasta County Marshal | 27 | 21 | 6 |
| Stockton Unified School District | 39 | 27 | 12 |
| Twin Rivers Unified School District | 19 | 16 | 3 |
| Union Pacific Railroad | 21 | 21 | 0 |

# Table 81. Full-Time Law Enforcement Employees, by Selected State and Agency, 2021—Continued

(Number.)

| State/agency | Law enforcement employees | Officers | Civilians |
|---|---|---|---|
| **COLORADO** | | | |
| **State Agencies** | | | |
| Colorado Bureau of Investigation | 265 | 44 | 221 |
| Colorado Mental Health Institute | 74 | 14 | 60 |
| Division of Gaming Criminal Enforcement and Investigations Section | | | |
| Cripple Creek | 19 | 11 | 8 |
| Golden | 50 | 16 | 34 |
| | | | |
| **Tribal Agencies** | | | |
| Southern Ute Tribal | 35 | 17 | 18 |
| Ute Mountain Tribal | 9 | 3 | 6 |
| | | | |
| **Other Agencies** | | | |
| Southwest Drug Task Force | 4 | 3 | 1 |
| | | | |
| **CONNECTICUT** | | | |
| **State Agencies** | | | |
| Department of Energy and Environmental Protection | 57 | 49 | 8 |
| Department of Motor Vehicles | 57 | 51 | 6 |
| State Capitol Police | 37 | 26 | 11 |
| | | | |
| **Tribal Agencies** | | | |
| Mashantucket Pequot Tribal | 32 | 23 | 9 |
| Mohegan Tribal | 31 | 23 | 8 |
| | | | |
| **Other Agencies** | | | |
| Metropolitan Transportation Authority | 41 | 41 | 0 |
| | | | |
| **DELAWARE** | | | |
| **State Agencies** | | | |
| Alcohol and Tobacco Enforcement | 17 | 16 | 1 |
| Animal Welfare, New Castle County | 29 | 23 | 6 |
| Attorney General | | | |
| Kent County | 88 | 9 | 79 |
| New Castle County | 364 | 28 | 336 |
| Sussex County | 61 | 2 | 59 |
| Environmental Control | 16 | 14 | 2 |
| Fish and Wildlife | 30 | 26 | 4 |
| Park Rangers | 24 | 24 | 0 |
| River and Bay Authority | 62 | 52 | 10 |
| State Capitol Police | 88 | 70 | 18 |
| State Fire Marshal | 48 | 20 | 28 |
| | | | |
| **Other Agencies** | | | |
| Wilmington Fire Department | 14 | 9 | 5 |
| | | | |
| **DISTRICT OF COLUMBIA** | | | |
| **Other Agencies** | | | |
| Metro Transit Police | 922 | 450 | 472 |
| | | | |
| **FLORIDA** | | | |
| **State Agencies** | | | |
| Capitol Police | 79 | 66 | 13 |
| Department of Corrections, Office of the Inspector General, Leon County | 166 | 106 | 60 |
| Department of Law Enforcement | | | |
| Duval County, Jacksonville | 127 | 42 | 85 |
| Escambia County, Pensacola | 89 | 29 | 60 |
| Hillsborough County, Tampa | 167 | 56 | 111 |
| Lee County, Fort Myers | 75 | 32 | 43 |
| Leon County, Tallahassee | 915 | 113 | 802 |
| Miami-Dade County, Miami | 93 | 66 | 27 |
| Orange County, Orlando | 173 | 57 | 116 |
| Division of Alcoholic Beverages and Tobacco, Leon County | 131 | 73 | 58 |
| Department of Investigative and Forensic Services, Leon County | 307 | 250 | 57 |
| Fish and Wildlife Conservation Commission | | | |
| Leon County | 939 | 770 | 169 |
| Taylor County | 82 | 58 | 24 |
| | | | |
| **Tribal Agencies** | | | |
| Miccosukee Tribal | 60 | 46 | 14 |
| Seminole Tribal | 214 | 157 | 57 |
| | | | |
| **Other Agencies** | | | |
| Clay County School Board | 49 | 48 | 1 |
| Duval County Schools | 154 | 104 | 50 |
| Florida School for the Deaf and Blind | 17 | 8 | 9 |
| Fort Lauderdale Airport | 109 | 88 | 21 |
| Jacksonville Aviation Authority | 40 | 28 | 12 |
| Lee County Port Authority | 62 | 42 | 20 |
| Melbourne International Airport | 15 | 13 | 2 |
| Miami-Dade County Public Schools | 501 | 469 | 32 |
| Northwest Florida Beaches International Airport | 19 | 13 | 6 |
| Palm Beach County School District | 319 | 260 | 59 |
| Sarasota County Schools | 58 | 56 | 2 |

# Table 81. Full-Time Law Enforcement Employees, by Selected State and Agency, 2021—Continued

(Number.)

| State/agency | Law enforcement employees | Officers | Civilians |
|---|---|---|---|
| Sarasota-Manatee Airport Authority | 13 | 12 | 1 |
| Tampa International Airport | 131 | 74 | 57 |
| Volusia County Beach Safety | 73 | 56 | 17 |
| **GEORGIA** | | | |
| **State Agencies** | | | |
| Georgia Bureau of Investigation, Headquarters | 952 | 287 | 665 |
| Georgia Department of Transportation, Office of Investigations | 4 | 4 | 0 |
| Georgia Forestry Commission | 7 | 6 | 1 |
| Georgia Public Safety Training Center | 174 | 65 | 109 |
| Georgia World Congress | 29 | 15 | 14 |
| Ports Authority, Savannah | 184 | 151 | 33 |
| Roosevelt Institute Facility Police | 8 | 8 | 0 |
| State Board of Workers Compensation Fraud Investigation Division | 8 | 5 | 3 |
| **Other Agencies** | | | |
| Atlanta Public Schools | 91 | 90 | 1 |
| Augusta Board of Education | 31 | 28 | 3 |
| Bibb County Board of Education | 23 | 17 | 6 |
| Chatham County Board of Education | 93 | 55 | 38 |
| Cherokee County Board of Education | 25 | 21 | 4 |
| Cherokee County Marshal | 24 | 16 | 8 |
| Cobb County Board of Education | 70 | 67 | 3 |
| Decatur County Schools | 5 | 5 | 0 |
| DeKalb County School System | 174 | 61 | 113 |
| Dougherty County Board of Education | 19 | 18 | 1 |
| Fayette County Marshal | 5 | 3 | 2 |
| Forsyth County Fire Investigation Unit | 6 | 6 | 0 |
| Fulton County Marshal | 63 | 49 | 14 |
| Fulton County School System | 81 | 80 | 1 |
| Glynn County School System | 25 | 24 | 1 |
| Grady County Schools | 7 | 7 | 0 |
| Gwinnett County Public Schools | 101 | 92 | 9 |
| Hall County Marshal | 15 | 13 | 2 |
| Metropolitan Atlanta Rapid Transit Authority | 358 | 276 | 82 |
| Muscogee County Schools | 24 | 18 | 6 |
| Richmond County Marshal | 62 | 48 | 14 |
| Stone Mountain Park | 16 | 14 | 2 |
| Washington County Board of Education | 5 | 5 | 0 |
| **IDAHO** | | | |
| **Tribal Agencies** | | | |
| Fort Hall Tribal | 28 | 15 | 13 |
| Kootenai Tribal | 1 | 1 | 0 |
| **ILLINOIS** | | | |
| **State Agencies** | | | |
| Illinois Department of Revenue | 29 | 29 | 0 |
| **Other Agencies** | | | |
| Pekin Park District | 1 | 1 | 0 |
| **INDIANA** | | | |
| **Other Agencies** | | | |
| Brownsburg Community School | 5 | 5 | 0 |
| Indianapolis International Airport | 41 | 39 | 2 |
| **IOWA** | | | |
| Eastern Iowa Airport Public Safety | 13 | 13 | 0 |
| **KANSAS** | | | |
| **State Agencies** | | | |
| Kansas Alcoholic Beverage Control | 32 | 16 | 16 |
| Kansas Department of Wildlife and Parks | 174 | 172 | 2 |
| Kansas Lottery Security Division | 6 | 4 | 2 |
| Kansas Racing Commission, Security Division | 74 | 49 | 25 |
| Securities Office, Investigation Section | 9 | 8 | 1 |
| State Fire Marshal | 12 | 11 | 1 |
| **Tribal Agencies** | | | |
| Iowa Tribal | 4 | 3 | 1 |
| Kickapoo Tribal | 4 | 4 | 0 |
| Potawatomi Tribal | 30 | 20 | 10 |
| Sac and Fox Tribal | 5 | 4 | 1 |
| **Other Agencies** | | | |
| El Dorado School District | 2 | 2 | 0 |
| Johnson County Park | 26 | 25 | 1 |
| Metropolitan Topeka Airport Authority | 24 | 18 | 6 |
| Topeka Fire Department Arson Investigation | 7 | 3 | 4 |
| Unified School District | | | |
| Goddard | 5 | 5 | 0 |
| Nickerson/South Hutchinson | 1 | 1 | 0 |
| Seaman | 4 | 4 | 0 |
| Shawnee Heights | 1 | 1 | 0 |

## Table 81. Full-Time Law Enforcement Employees, by Selected State and Agency, 2021—Continued

(Number.)

| State/agency | Law enforcement employees | Officers | Civilians |
|---|---|---|---|
| **KENTUCKY** | | | |
| **State Agencies** | | | |
| Alcohol Beverage Control, Investigative Division | 13 | 8 | 5 |
| Department of Agriculture Animal Health Enforcement Division | 4 | 4 | 0 |
| Fish and Wildlife Enforcement | 120 | 117 | 3 |
| Kentucky Horse Park | 10 | 10 | 0 |
| Park Security | 47 | 46 | 1 |
| | | | |
| **Other Agencies** | | | |
| Barren County Drug Task Force | 4 | 3 | 1 |
| Bourbon County Schools | 2 | 2 | 0 |
| Cincinnati-Northern Kentucky International Airport | 50 | 46 | 4 |
| Clark County School System | 10 | 10 | 0 |
| Fayette County Constable District 1 | 10 | 6 | 4 |
| Fayette County Schools | 68 | 65 | 3 |
| Greater Hardin County Narcotics Task Force | 2 | 1 | 1 |
| Jefferson County School District | 28 | 19 | 9 |
| Lake Cumberland Area Drug Enforcement Task Force | 4 | 3 | 1 |
| Lexington Bluegrass Airport | 28 | 19 | 9 |
| Louisville Regional Airport Authority | 28 | 27 | 1 |
| McCracken County Public Schools | 7 | 7 | 0 |
| Montgomery County School District | 4 | 3 | 1 |
| Northern Kentucky Drug Strike Force | 3 | 2 | 1 |
| Pennyrile Narcotics Task Force | 3 | 2 | 1 |
| Warren County Drug Task Force | 3 | 2 | 1 |
| | | | |
| **LOUISIANA** | | | |
| **State Agencies** | | | |
| Tensas Basin Levee District | 3 | 2 | 1 |
| | | | |
| **Tribal Agencies** | | | |
| Chitimacha Tribal | 16 | 14 | 2 |
| Coushatta Tribal | 26 | 19 | 7 |
| | | | |
| **MAINE** | | | |
| **State Agencies** | | | |
| Bureau of Capitol Police | 19 | 12 | 7 |
| Drug Enforcement Agency | 3 | 1 | 2 |
| State Fire Marshal | 39 | 6 | 33 |
| | | | |
| **Tribal Agencies** | | | |
| Passamaquoddy Indian Township | 9 | 5 | 4 |
| | | | |
| **MARYLAND** | | | |
| **State Agencies** | | | |
| Comptroller of the Treasury, Field Enforcement Division | 27 | 9 | 18 |
| Department of Public Safety and Correctional Services, Internal Investigation Division | 125 | 72 | 53 |
| General Services | | | |
|   Annapolis, Anne Arundel County | 71 | 35 | 36 |
|   Baltimore City | 95 | 39 | 56 |
| Natural Resources Police | 308 | 251 | 57 |
| State Fire Marshal | 71 | 45 | 26 |
| Transit Administration | 212 | 160 | 52 |
| Transportation Authority | 549 | 440 | 109 |
| | | | |
| **Other Agencies** | | | |
| Maryland-National Capital Park Police | | | |
|   Montgomery County | 116 | 93 | 23 |
|   Prince George's County | 136 | 112 | 24 |
| | | | |
| **MASSACHUSETTS** | | | |
| **Tribal Agencies** | | | |
| Wampanoag Tribe of Gay Head | 3 | 3 | 0 |
| | | | |
| **Other Agencies** | | | |
| Massachusetts General Hospital | 154 | 51 | 103 |
| | | | |
| **MICHIGAN** | | | |
| **State Agencies** | | | |
| Department of Natural Resources Law Enforcement Division | 246 | 200 | 46 |
| | | | |
| **Tribal Agencies** | | | |
| Bay Mills Tribal | 7 | 6 | 1 |
| Grand Traverse Tribal | 11 | 6 | 5 |
| Gun Lake Tribal | 19 | 17 | 2 |
| Hannahville Tribal | 13 | 12 | 1 |
| Keweenaw Bay Tribal | 13 | 10 | 3 |
| Lac Vieux Desert Tribal | 5 | 5 | 0 |
| Little River Band of Ottawa Indians | 15 | 15 | 0 |
| Little Traverse Bay Bands of Odawa Indians | 14 | 9 | 5 |
| Nottawaseppi Huron Band of Potawatomi | 20 | 19 | 1 |
| Pokagon Tribal | 13 | 10 | 3 |
| Saginaw Chippewa Tribal | 38 | 29 | 9 |
| Sault Ste. Marie Tribal | 28 | 24 | 4 |

## Table 81. Full-Time Law Enforcement Employees, by Selected State and Agency, 2021—Continued

(Number.)

| State/agency | Law enforcement employees | Officers | Civilians |
|---|---|---|---|
| **Other Agencies** | | | |
| Bishop International Airport | 14 | 13 | 1 |
| Capitol Region Airport Authority | 14 | 7 | 7 |
| Genesee County Parks and Recreation | 8 | 8 | 0 |
| Gerald R. Ford International Airport | 20 | 18 | 2 |
| Huron-Clinton Metropolitan Authority | | | |
| Hudson Mills Metropark | 3 | 3 | 0 |
| Kensington Metropark | 11 | 11 | 0 |
| Lower Huron Metropark | 9 | 9 | 0 |
| Stony Creek Metropark | 9 | 9 | 0 |
| Wayne County Airport | 110 | 85 | 25 |
| | | | |
| **MINNESOTA** | | | |
| **State Agencies** | | | |
| Capitol Security, St. Paul | 78 | 21 | 57 |
| Department of Natural Resources Enforcement Division | 207 | 182 | 25 |
| | | | |
| **Tribal Agencies** | | | |
| Fond du Lac Tribal | 20 | 17 | 3 |
| Lower Sioux Tribal | 2 | 2 | 0 |
| Mille Lacs Tribal | 26 | 20 | 6 |
| Nett Lake Tribal | 5 | 4 | 1 |
| Red Lake Agency | 50 | 36 | 14 |
| Upper Sioux Community | 5 | 5 | 0 |
| White Earth Tribal | 29 | 22 | 7 |
| | | | |
| **Other Agencies** | | | |
| Metropolitan Transit Commission | 138 | 117 | 21 |
| Minneapolis-St. Paul International Airport | 151 | 87 | 64 |
| Three Rivers Park District | 12 | 11 | 1 |
| | | | |
| **MISSOURI** | | | |
| **State Agencies** | | | |
| Capitol Police | 31 | 29 | 2 |
| Department of Revenue, Compliance and Investigation Bureau | 17 | 14 | 3 |
| Department of Social Services, State Technical Assistance Team | 22 | 14 | 8 |
| Division of Alcohol and Tobacco Control | 34 | 22 | 12 |
| State Fire Marshal | 17 | 16 | 1 |
| State Park Rangers | 45 | 44 | 1 |
| | | | |
| **Other Agencies** | | | |
| Blue Spring Public Schools | 17 | 15 | 2 |
| Jackson County Drug Task Force | 22 | 20 | 2 |
| | | | |
| **MONTANA** | | | |
| **State Agencies** | | | |
| Gambling Investigations Bureau | 35 | 15 | 20 |
| | | | |
| **Tribal Agencies** | | | |
| Blackfeet Agency | 35 | 26 | 9 |
| Crow Agency | 14 | 11 | 3 |
| Fort Belknap Tribal | 12 | 7 | 5 |
| Fort Peck Assiniboine and Sioux Tribes | 31 | 29 | 2 |
| Northern Cheyenne Agency | 18 | 13 | 5 |
| Rocky Boy's Tribal | 22 | 13 | 9 |
| | | | |
| **NEBRASKA** | | | |
| **State Agencies** | | | |
| Nebraska State Fire Marshal | 9 | 8 | 1 |
| | | | |
| **Tribal Agencies** | | | |
| Omaha Tribal | 25 | 10 | 15 |
| Santee Tribal | 5 | 5 | 0 |
| Winnebago Tribal | 7 | 4 | 3 |
| | | | |
| **NEVADA** | | | |
| **State Agencies** | | | |
| Attorney General Investigations Division | 309 | 36 | 273 |
| Department of Wildlife, Law Enforcement Division | 46 | 31 | 15 |
| Nevada Gaming Control Board | | | |
| Clark County | 83 | 63 | 20 |
| Elko County | 5 | 4 | 1 |
| Carson City County | 5 | 4 | 1 |
| Washoe County | 16 | 15 | 1 |
| State Fire Marshal | 6 | 5 | 1 |
| | | | |
| **Tribal Agencies** | | | |
| Eastern Nevada Agency | 4 | 2 | 2 |
| Fallon Tribal | 7 | 6 | 1 |
| Las Vegas Paiute Tribal | 16 | 12 | 4 |
| Lovelock Paiute Tribal | 3 | 3 | 0 |
| Moapa Tribal | 16 | 11 | 5 |
| Pyramid Lake Tribal | 14 | 12 | 2 |
| Reno-Sparks Indian Colony | 14 | 12 | 2 |
| Western Nevada Agency | 4 | 3 | 1 |

## Table 81. Full-Time Law Enforcement Employees, by Selected State and Agency, 2021—Continued

(Number.)

| State/agency | Law enforcement employees | Officers | Civilians |
|---|---|---|---|
| **Other Agencies** | | | |
| City of Las Vegas Department of Publilc Safety | 393 | 100 | 293 |
| Clark County School District | 191 | 169 | 22 |
| Reno Municipal Court Marshal | 11 | 9 | 2 |
| Washoe County School District | 45 | 36 | 9 |
| | | | |
| **NEW HAMPSHIRE** | | | |
| **State Agencies** | | | |
| Liquor Commission | 31 | 17 | 14 |
| | | | |
| **NEW JERSEY** | | | |
| **State Agencies** | | | |
| Department of Corrections | 7,471 | 5,623 | 1,848 |
| Department of Human Services | 77 | 63 | 14 |
| Division of Fish and Wildlife | 51 | 48 | 3 |
| New Jersey Transit Police | 368 | 302 | 66 |
| Palisades Interstate Parkway | 35 | 31 | 4 |
| Port Authority of New York and New Jersey | 2,286 | 2,083 | 203 |
| State Park Police | 80 | 79 | 1 |
| | | | |
| **Other Agencies** | | | |
| Delaware River Port Authority Police Department | 159 | 132 | 27 |
| Park Police | | | |
|   Morris County | 22 | 21 | 1 |
|   Union County | 109 | 76 | 33 |
| Prosecutor | | | |
|   Atlantic County | 164 | 74 | 90 |
|   Bergen County | 213 | 106 | 107 |
|   Burlington County | 127 | 44 | 83 |
|   Camden County | 270 | 183 | 87 |
|   Cape May County | 88 | 40 | 48 |
|   Cumberland County | 114 | 41 | 73 |
|   Essex County | 238 | 118 | 120 |
|   Gloucester County | 105 | 34 | 71 |
|   Hudson County | 248 | 101 | 147 |
|   Hunterdon County | 50 | 25 | 25 |
|   Mercer County | 184 | 62 | 122 |
|   Middlesex County | 214 | 72 | 142 |
|   Monmouth County | 268 | 78 | 190 |
|   Morris County | 155 | 64 | 91 |
|   Ocean County | 172 | 66 | 106 |
|   Passaic County | 175 | 73 | 102 |
|   Salem County | 58 | 21 | 37 |
|   Somerset County | 127 | 53 | 74 |
|   Sussex County | 55 | 37 | 18 |
|   Union County | 170 | 77 | 93 |
|   Warren County | 60 | 20 | 40 |
| | | | |
| **NEW MEXICO** | | | |
| **Tribal Agencies** | | | |
| Acoma Tribal | 18 | 11 | 7 |
| Isleta Tribal | 48 | 27 | 21 |
| Jemez Pueblo | 13 | 11 | 2 |
| Jicarilla Apache Tribal | 29 | 18 | 11 |
| Laguna Tribal | 18 | 10 | 8 |
| Mescalero Tribal | 26 | 14 | 12 |
| Northern Pueblos Agency | 10 | 10 | 0 |
| Ohkay Owingeh Tribal | 10 | 7 | 3 |
| Pojoaque Tribal | 21 | 13 | 8 |
| Ramah Navajo Tribal | 17 | 8 | 9 |
| Santa Ana Tribal | 25 | 24 | 1 |
| Santa Clara Pueblo | 11 | 7 | 4 |
| Southern Pueblos Agency | 19 | 12 | 7 |
| Taos Pueblo | 12 | 11 | 1 |
| Tesuque Pueblo | 11 | 6 | 5 |
| Zia Pueblo | 6 | 5 | 1 |
| Zuni Tribal | 32 | 20 | 12 |
| | | | |
| **NEW YORK** | | | |
| **State Agencies** | | | |
| State Park | | | |
|   Allegany Region | 14 | 11 | 3 |
|   Central Region | 14 | 11 | 3 |
|   Finger Lakes Region | 13 | 10 | 3 |
|   Genesee Region | 16 | 14 | 2 |
|   Long Island Region | 51 | 47 | 4 |
|   New York City Region | 10 | 8 | 2 |
|   Niagara Region | 29 | 28 | 1 |
|   Palisades Region | 22 | 20 | 2 |
|   Saratoga/Capital Region | 36 | 30 | 6 |
|   Taconic Region | 11 | 10 | 1 |
|   Thousand Island Region | 13 | 12 | 1 |
| | | | |
| **Tribal Agencies** | | | |
| St. Regis Tribal | 31 | 24 | 7 |

## Table 81. Full-Time Law Enforcement Employees, by Selected State and Agency, 2021—Continued

(Number.)

| State/agency | Law enforcement employees | Officers | Civilians |
|---|---|---|---|
| **Other Agencies** | | | |
| New York City Department of Environmental Protection Police, Ashokan Precinct | 245 | 213 | 32 |
| New York City Metropolitan Transportation Authority | 1,056 | 1,000 | 56 |
| Niagara Frontier Transportation Authority | 83 | 80 | 3 |
| Onondaga County Parks | 1 | 1 | 0 |
| **NORTH CAROLINA** | | | |
| **State Agencies** | | | |
| Cherry Hospital | 18 | 12 | 6 |
| Department of Health and Human Resources | 7 | 7 | 0 |
| Department of Wildlife | 218 | 206 | 12 |
| Division of Alcohol Law Enforcement | 113 | 103 | 10 |
| Division of Marine Fisheries | 55 | 47 | 8 |
| North Carolina Arboretum | 4 | 4 | 0 |
| North Carolina State Bureau of Investigation | 410 | 236 | 174 |
| State Capitol Police | 96 | 59 | 37 |
| State Fairgrounds | 4 | 1 | 3 |
| State Park Rangers | | | |
| Carolina Beach | 5 | 4 | 1 |
| Carvers Creek | 3 | 3 | 0 |
| Chimney Rock | 9 | 5 | 4 |
| Cliffs of the Neuse | 6 | 3 | 3 |
| Crowders Mountain | 11 | 7 | 4 |
| Dismal Swamp | 6 | 3 | 3 |
| Elk Knob | 3 | 3 | 0 |
| Eno River | 10 | 6 | 4 |
| Falls Lake Recreation Area | 11 | 11 | 0 |
| Fort Fisher | 4 | 4 | 0 |
| Fort Macon | 5 | 4 | 1 |
| Goose Creek | 4 | 3 | 1 |
| Gorges | 7 | 4 | 3 |
| Grandfather Mountain | 2 | 2 | 0 |
| Hammocks Beach | 11 | 5 | 6 |
| Hanging Rock | 5 | 5 | 0 |
| Haw River | 2 | 2 | 0 |
| Jockey's Ridge | 6 | 5 | 1 |
| Jones Lake | 4 | 3 | 1 |
| Jordan Lake State Recreation Area | 18 | 16 | 2 |
| Kerr Lake | 23 | 9 | 14 |
| Lake James | 5 | 5 | 0 |
| Lake Norman | 9 | 4 | 5 |
| Lake Waccamaw | 7 | 3 | 4 |
| Lumber River | 7 | 3 | 4 |
| Mayo River | 4 | 2 | 2 |
| Medoc Mountain | 2 | 2 | 0 |
| Merchants Millpond | 4 | 3 | 1 |
| Morrow Mountain | 4 | 4 | 0 |
| Mount Mitchell | 3 | 3 | 0 |
| New River-Mount Jefferson | 7 | 7 | 0 |
| Pettigrew | 5 | 3 | 2 |
| Pilot Mountain | 11 | 5 | 6 |
| Raven Rock | 7 | 3 | 4 |
| Singletary Lake | 5 | 2 | 3 |
| South Mountains | 8 | 7 | 1 |
| Stone Mountain | 5 | 5 | 0 |
| Weymouth Woods/Sandhills Nature Preserve | 5 | 3 | 2 |
| William B. Umstead | 10 | 5 | 5 |
| **Tribal Agencies** | | | |
| Cherokee Tribal | 87 | 59 | 28 |
| **Other Agencies** | | | |
| Asheville Regional Airport | 18 | 16 | 2 |
| Beaufort County Alcoholic Beverage Control Enforcement | 1 | 1 | 0 |
| Moore County Schools | 11 | 11 | 0 |
| Nash County Alcoholic Beverage Control Enforcement | 1 | 1 | 0 |
| North Carolina General Assembly | 38 | 20 | 18 |
| North Carolina Museum of Art Park Police | 2 | 2 | 0 |
| North Carolina State Port Authority, Division 1 | 13 | 12 | 1 |
| Piedmont Triad International Airport | 36 | 22 | 14 |
| Raleigh-Durham International Airport | 36 | 35 | 1 |
| Triad Municipal Alcoholic Beverage Control Law Enforcement | 5 | 5 | 0 |
| University of North Carolina Hospitals | 123 | 36 | 87 |
| WakeMed Campus Police | 90 | 34 | 56 |
| **NORTH DAKOTA** | | | |
| **State Agencies** | | | |
| North Dakota Bureau of Criminal Investigation | 55 | 55 | 0 |
| **Tribal Agencies** | | | |
| Fort Totten Agency | 12 | 5 | 7 |
| Standing Rock Agency | 38 | 18 | 20 |
| Three Affiliated Tribes | 41 | 29 | 12 |
| Turtle Mountain Agency | 31 | 12 | 19 |

## Table 81. Full-Time Law Enforcement Employees, by Selected State and Agency, 2021—Continued

(Number.)

| State/agency | Law enforcement employees | Officers | Civilians |
|---|---|---|---|
| **OHIO** | | | |
| **State Agencies** | | | |
| Ohio Department of Natural Resources | 317 | 297 | 20 |
| | | | |
| **Other Agencies** | | | |
| Clark County Park District | 1 | 1 | 0 |
| Columbus and Franklin County Metropolitan Park District | 118 | 45 | 73 |
| Hamilton County Park District | 42 | 37 | 5 |
| Johnny Appleseed Metropolitan Park District | 7 | 7 | 0 |
| Sandusky County Park District | 5 | 5 | 0 |
| | | | |
| **OKLAHOMA** | | | |
| **State Agencies** | | | |
| Capitol Park Police | 59 | 13 | 46 |
| Grand River Dam Authority Lake Patrol | 48 | 38 | 10 |
| Oklahoma Department of Corrections | 86 | 69 | 17 |
| State Bureau of Investigation | 319 | 91 | 228 |
| State Park Rangers | 38 | 38 | 0 |
| | | | |
| **Tribal Agencies** | | | |
| Absentee Shawnee Tribal | 12 | 11 | 1 |
| Anadarko Agency | 15 | 9 | 6 |
| Cherokee Nation | 54 | 44 | 10 |
| Chickasaw Nation | 92 | 78 | 14 |
| Choctaw Nation | 95 | 89 | 6 |
| Citizen Potawatomi Nation | 43 | 30 | 13 |
| Comanche Nation | 32 | 22 | 10 |
| Eastern Shawnee Tribal | 16 | 15 | 1 |
| Iowa Tribal | 13 | 7 | 6 |
| Kickapoo Tribal | 16 | 15 | 1 |
| Miami Agency | 6 | 6 | 0 |
| Miami Tribal | 5 | 5 | 0 |
| Muscogee Nation Tribal | 86 | 73 | 13 |
| Osage Nation | 18 | 16 | 2 |
| Ponca Tribal | 6 | 6 | 0 |
| Quapaw Tribal | 17 | 16 | 1 |
| Sac and Fox Tribal | 10 | 10 | 0 |
| Seminole Nation Lighthorse | 11 | 10 | 1 |
| Tonkawa Tribal | 8 | 5 | 3 |
| Wyandotte Nation | 11 | 9 | 2 |
| | | | |
| **Other Agencies** | | | |
| Beggs Public Schools | 1 | 1 | 0 |
| District 1 Narcotics Task Force | 6 | 5 | 1 |
| District 8 Narcotics Task Force | 3 | 3 | 0 |
| Jenks Public Schools | 8 | 7 | 1 |
| Lawton Public Schools | 16 | 15 | 1 |
| Muskogee City Schools | 5 | 4 | 1 |
| Okmulgee County Criminal Justice Authority | 89 | 22 | 67 |
| Putnam City Campus | 19 | 12 | 7 |
| Victory Life | 1 | 1 | 0 |
| | | | |
| **OREGON** | | | |
| **State Agencies** | | | |
| Liquor Commission | | | |
| Benton County | 3 | 3 | 0 |
| Coos County | 1 | 1 | 0 |
| Deschutes County | 10 | 7 | 3 |
| Douglas County | 1 | 1 | 0 |
| Jackson County | 17 | 16 | 1 |
| Lane County | 13 | 9 | 4 |
| Lincoln County | 2 | 1 | 1 |
| Marion County | 8 | 6 | 2 |
| Multnomah County | 27 | 26 | 1 |
| Umatilla County | 2 | 2 | 0 |
| | | | |
| **Tribal Agencies** | | | |
| Columbia River Inter-Tribal Fisheries Enforcement | 20 | 12 | 8 |
| Coquille Tribal | 3 | 3 | 0 |
| Cow Creek Tribal | 4 | 3 | 1 |
| Grand Ronde Tribal | 14 | 13 | 1 |
| Umatilla Tribal | 25 | 19 | 6 |
| Warm Springs Tribal | 25 | 21 | 4 |
| | | | |
| **Other Agencies** | | | |
| Hillsboro School District | 1 | 1 | 0 |
| Port of Portland | 65 | 46 | 19 |
| | | | |
| **PENNSYLVANIA** | | | |
| **State Agencies** | | | |
| Pennsylvania Fish and Boat Commission | 122 | 114 | 8 |
| State Capitol Police | 104 | 95 | 9 |
| State Park Rangers | | | |
| Bald Eagle | 4 | 4 | 0 |

## Table 81. Full-Time Law Enforcement Employees, by Selected State and Agency, 2021—Continued

(Number.)

| State/agency | Law enforcement employees | Officers | Civilians |
|---|---|---|---|
| Beltzville | 2 | 2 | 0 |
| Bendigo | 2 | 2 | 0 |
| Ben Rush | 5 | 1 | 4 |
| Black Moshannon | 2 | 2 | 0 |
| Caledonia | 1 | 1 | 0 |
| Canoe Creek | 1 | 1 | 0 |
| Chapman | 1 | 1 | 0 |
| Clear Creek | 6 | 6 | 0 |
| Colonel Denning | 4 | 1 | 3 |
| Cook Forest | 6 | 6 | 0 |
| Cowans Gap | 2 | 2 | 0 |
| Delaware Canal | 4 | 4 | 0 |
| Evansburg | 3 | 3 | 0 |
| Fort Washington | 2 | 2 | 0 |
| Frances Slocum | 3 | 3 | 0 |
| French Creek | 10 | 10 | 0 |
| Greenwood Furnace | 6 | 3 | 3 |
| Hickory Run | 12 | 8 | 4 |
| Hills Creek | 3 | 3 | 0 |
| Jacobsburg Environmental Education Center | 1 | 1 | 0 |
| Jennings Environmental Education Center | 1 | 1 | 0 |
| Kettle Creek | 1 | 1 | 0 |
| Kings Gap Environmental Education Center | 1 | 1 | 0 |
| Lackawanna | 3 | 3 | 0 |
| Lyman Run | 2 | 2 | 0 |
| Marsh Creek | 3 | 3 | 0 |
| Memorial Lake | 3 | 1 | 2 |
| Moraine | 3 | 3 | 0 |
| Mount Pisgah | 3 | 1 | 2 |
| Neshaminy | 5 | 1 | 4 |
| Nockamixon | 2 | 2 | 0 |
| Ohiopyle | 6 | 6 | 0 |
| Parker Dam | 2 | 2 | 0 |
| Pine Grove Furnace | 1 | 1 | 0 |
| Point | 3 | 3 | 0 |
| Presque Isle | 12 | 10 | 2 |
| Prince Gallitzin | 2 | 2 | 0 |
| Pymatuning | 9 | 4 | 5 |
| Raccoon Creek | 15 | 5 | 10 |
| Ridley Creek | 3 | 3 | 0 |
| Ryerson Station | 4 | 1 | 3 |
| Shawnee | 3 | 2 | 1 |
| Shikellamy | 1 | 1 | 0 |
| Sinnemahoning | 7 | 1 | 6 |
| Sizerville | 1 | 1 | 0 |
| Susquehannock | 5 | 5 | 0 |
| Trough Creek | 1 | 1 | 0 |
| Tuscarora | 1 | 1 | 0 |
| Tyler | 2 | 1 | 1 |
| White Clay | 3 | 3 | 0 |
| Worlds End | 7 | 2 | 5 |
| Yellow Creek | 1 | 1 | 0 |
| **Other Agencies** | | | |
| Allegheny County Port Authority | 54 | 42 | 12 |
| County Detective | | | |
| Beaver County | 8 | 8 | 0 |
| Berks County | 37 | 33 | 4 |
| Bucks County | 29 | 23 | 6 |
| Butler County | 5 | 5 | 0 |
| Chester County | 24 | 22 | 2 |
| Dauphin County | 10 | 9 | 1 |
| Erie County | 11 | 9 | 2 |
| Lackawanna County | 14 | 14 | 0 |
| Lawrence County | 12 | 11 | 1 |
| Lebanon County | 5 | 5 | 0 |
| Luzerne County | 14 | 14 | 0 |
| McKean County | 7 | 2 | 5 |
| Pike County | 5 | 5 | 0 |
| Schuylkill County | 24 | 5 | 19 |
| Warren County | 1 | 1 | 0 |
| Wayne County | 3 | 3 | 0 |
| Westmoreland County | 56 | 14 | 42 |
| Wyoming County | 4 | 4 | 0 |
| Delaware County Park | 57 | 55 | 2 |
| Erie Municipal Airport Authority | 3 | 3 | 0 |
| Fort Indiantown Gap | 25 | 18 | 7 |
| Harrisburg International Airport | 12 | 9 | 3 |
| Lehigh Valley International Airport | 11 | 11 | 0 |
| Wyoming Area School District | 1 | 1 | 0 |
| **RHODE ISLAND** | | | |
| **State Agencies** | | | |
| Department of Environmental Management | 37 | 28 | 9 |
| T.F. Green Airport | 32 | 25 | 7 |

## Table 81. Full-Time Law Enforcement Employees, by Selected State and Agency, 2021—Continued

(Number.)

| State/agency | Law enforcement employees | Officers | Civilians |
|---|---|---|---|
| **SOUTH CAROLINA** | | | |
| **State Agencies** | | | |
| Bureau of Protective Services | 64 | 60 | 4 |
| Department of Mental Health | 92 | 64 | 28 |
| State Museum | 4 | 1 | 3 |
| State Ports Authority | 98 | 33 | 65 |
| | | | |
| **Other Agencies** | | | |
| 15th Circuit Drug Enforcement Unit | 4 | 2 | 2 |
| Charleston County Aviation Authority | 70 | 36 | 34 |
| Florence Regional Airport | 7 | 7 | 0 |
| Greenville Hospital, Greenville | 34 | 34 | 0 |
| Greenville-Spartanburg International Airport | 18 | 17 | 1 |
| Lexington County Medical Center | 70 | 27 | 43 |
| | | | |
| **SOUTH DAKOTA** | | | |
| **State Agencies** | | | |
| Division of Criminal Investigation | 189 | 52 | 137 |
| | | | |
| **Tribal Agencies** | | | |
| Cheyenne River Tribal | 43 | 39 | 4 |
| Crow Creek Tribal | 8 | 6 | 2 |
| Flandreau Santee Sioux Tribal | 3 | 3 | 0 |
| Lower Brule Tribal | 24 | 7 | 17 |
| Pine Ridge Sioux Tribal | 96 | 69 | 27 |
| Rosebud Tribal | 42 | 36 | 6 |
| Sisseton-Wahpeton Tribal | 17 | 14 | 3 |
| Yankton Tribal | 20 | 11 | 9 |
| | | | |
| **TENNESSEE** | | | |
| **State Agencies** | | | |
| Alcoholic Beverage Commission | 72 | 44 | 28 |
| Department of Agriculture, Agricultural Crime Unit | 7 | 7 | 0 |
| Department of Correction, Internal Affairs | 62 | 34 | 28 |
| State Park Rangers | | | |
| Bicentennial Capitol Mall | 4 | 4 | 0 |
| Big Cypress Tree Natural Area | 1 | 1 | 0 |
| Big Hill Pond | 3 | 3 | 0 |
| Big Ridge | 4 | 4 | 0 |
| Bledsoe Creek | 3 | 3 | 0 |
| Booker T. Washington | 4 | 4 | 0 |
| Burgess Falls Natural Area | 5 | 5 | 0 |
| Cedars of Lebanon | 5 | 5 | 0 |
| Chickasaw | 4 | 4 | 0 |
| Cordell Hull Birthplace | 2 | 2 | 0 |
| Cove Lake | 4 | 4 | 0 |
| Cumberland Mountain | 4 | 4 | 0 |
| Cumberland Trail | 9 | 9 | 0 |
| Cummins Falls | 5 | 5 | 0 |
| David Crockett | 4 | 4 | 0 |
| Davy Crockett Birthplace | 3 | 3 | 0 |
| Dunbar Cave Natural Area | 4 | 4 | 0 |
| Edgar Evins | 4 | 4 | 0 |
| Fall Creek Falls | 9 | 9 | 0 |
| Fort Loudon State Historic Park | 4 | 4 | 0 |
| Fort Pillow State Historic Park | 2 | 2 | 0 |
| Frozen Head Natural Area | 5 | 5 | 0 |
| Harpeth Scenic Rivers | 4 | 4 | 0 |
| Harrison Bay | 4 | 4 | 0 |
| Henry Horton | 8 | 6 | 2 |
| Hiwassee/Ocoee State Scenic Rivers | 6 | 6 | 0 |
| Indian Mountain | 3 | 3 | 0 |
| Johnsonville State Historic Park | 3 | 3 | 0 |
| Long Hunter | 5 | 5 | 0 |
| Meeman-Shelby Forest | 3 | 3 | 0 |
| Montgomery Bell | 6 | 6 | 0 |
| Mousetail Landing | 2 | 2 | 0 |
| Natchez Trace | 5 | 5 | 0 |
| Nathan Bedford Forrest | 3 | 3 | 0 |
| Norris Dam | 4 | 3 | 1 |
| Old Stone Fort State Archaeological Park | 3 | 3 | 0 |
| Panther Creek | 3 | 3 | 0 |
| Paris Landing | 4 | 4 | 0 |
| Pickett | 5 | 5 | 0 |
| Pickwick Landing | 5 | 5 | 0 |
| Pinson Mounds State Archaeological Park | 2 | 2 | 0 |
| Radnor Lake Natural Area | 6 | 6 | 0 |
| Red Clay State Historic Park | 2 | 2 | 0 |
| Reelfoot Lake | 4 | 4 | 0 |
| Roan Mountain | 4 | 4 | 0 |
| Rock Island | 5 | 5 | 0 |
| Rocky Fork | 2 | 2 | 0 |
| Seven Islands Birding Park | 3 | 3 | 0 |
| Sgt. Alvin C. York | 3 | 3 | 0 |

## Table 81. Full-Time Law Enforcement Employees, by Selected State and Agency, 2021—Continued

(Number.)

| State/agency | Law enforcement employees | Officers | Civilians |
|---|---|---|---|
| South Cumberland Recreation Area | 10 | 10 | 0 |
| Standing Stone | 4 | 4 | 0 |
| Sycamore Shoals State Historic Park | 7 | 3 | 4 |
| Tim's Ford | 4 | 4 | 0 |
| T.O. Fuller | 3 | 3 | 0 |
| Warrior's Path | 5 | 5 | 0 |
| TennCare Office of Inspector General | 44 | 20 | 24 |
| Tennessee Board of Regents | 1 | 1 | 0 |
| Tennessee Bureau of Investigation | 592 | 383 | 209 |
| Tennessee Department of Revenue | 44 | 31 | 13 |
| Wildlife Resources Agency | | | |
| Region 1 | 45 | 40 | 5 |
| Region 2 | 66 | 58 | 8 |
| Region 3 | 47 | 43 | 4 |
| Region 4 | 54 | 49 | 5 |
| | | | |
| **Other Agencies** | | | |
| 7th Judicial District Crime Task Force | 7 | 7 | 0 |
| Chattanooga Housing Authority | 6 | 5 | 1 |
| Chattanooga Metropolitan Airport | 11 | 9 | 2 |
| Dickson City Park Ranger Division | 3 | 2 | 1 |
| Drug Task Force | 3 | 3 | 0 |
| 2nd Judicial District | 5 | 4 | 1 |
| 3rd Judicial District | 4 | 4 | 0 |
| 4th Judicial District | 1 | 1 | 0 |
| 9th Judicial District | 5 | 4 | 1 |
| 10th Judicial District | 23 | 21 | 2 |
| 12th Judicial District | 3 | 3 | 0 |
| 14th Judicial District | 2 | 2 | 0 |
| 18th Judicial District | 4 | 3 | 1 |
| 21st Judicial District | 2 | 2 | 0 |
| 22nd Judicial District | 1 | 1 | 0 |
| 23rd Judicial District | 7 | 7 | 0 |
| 24th Judicial District | 3 | 2 | 1 |
| 25th Judicial District | 1 | 1 | 0 |
| 31st Judicial District | 2 | 2 | 0 |
| Knoxville Metropolitan Airport | 42 | 25 | 17 |
| Memphis-Shelby County Airport Authority | 58 | 48 | 10 |
| Metropolitan Nashville Park Police | 15 | 15 | 0 |
| Nashville International Airport | 99 | 80 | 19 |
| Tri-Cities Regional Airport | 15 | 14 | 1 |
| West Tennessee Violent Crime Task Force | 7 | 6 | 1 |
| | | | |
| **TEXAS** | | | |
| **Tribal Agencies** | | | |
| Ysleta del Sur Pueblo Tribal | 16 | 16 | 0 |
| | | | |
| **Other Agencies** | | | |
| Amarillo International Airport | 12 | 12 | 0 |
| Dallas-Fort Worth International Airport | 217 | 200 | 17 |
| Denton County Water District | 17 | 15 | 2 |
| Ector County Hospital District | 20 | 12 | 8 |
| Hidalgo County Constable, Precinct 1 | 19 | 17 | 2 |
| Hospital District, Tarrant County | 74 | 47 | 27 |
| Houston Metropolitan Transit Authority | 271 | 193 | 78 |
| Independent School District | | | |
| Aldine | 81 | 65 | 16 |
| Alief | 48 | 42 | 6 |
| Alvin | 45 | 36 | 9 |
| Angleton | 12 | 11 | 1 |
| Anna | 4 | 4 | 0 |
| Aubrey | 3 | 3 | 0 |
| Austin | 103 | 74 | 29 |
| Barbers Hill | 8 | 7 | 1 |
| Bastrop | 15 | 12 | 3 |
| Bay City | 8 | 7 | 1 |
| Brazosport | 22 | 21 | 1 |
| Brownsboro | 2 | 2 | 0 |
| Brownsville | 156 | 55 | 101 |
| Burkburnett | 3 | 3 | 0 |
| Calhoun County | 2 | 2 | 0 |
| Castleberry | 3 | 3 | 0 |
| Centerpoint | 2 | 2 | 0 |
| Columbia-Brazoria | 6 | 6 | 0 |
| Conroe | 106 | 72 | 34 |
| Corsicana | 15 | 11 | 4 |
| Crowley | 16 | 14 | 2 |
| Ector County | 29 | 27 | 2 |
| Edinburg | 112 | 82 | 30 |
| El Paso | 45 | 37 | 8 |
| Floresville | 6 | 5 | 1 |
| Fort Bend | 104 | 75 | 29 |
| Gonzales | 1 | 1 | 0 |
| Hallsville | 8 | 5 | 3 |

## Table 81. Full-Time Law Enforcement Employees, by Selected State and Agency, 2021—Continued

(Number.)

| State/agency | Law enforcement employees | Officers | Civilians |
|---|---|---|---|
| Houston | 229 | 189 | 40 |
| Humble | 62 | 43 | 19 |
| Hutto | 8 | 8 | 0 |
| Idalou | 1 | 1 | 0 |
| Jonesboro | 1 | 1 | 0 |
| Judson | 24 | 23 | 1 |
| Killeen | 27 | 26 | 1 |
| Klein | 74 | 49 | 25 |
| Lamar Consolidated | 24 | 22 | 2 |
| Lancaster | 12 | 9 | 3 |
| Laredo | 110 | 40 | 70 |
| Lufkin | 18 | 13 | 5 |
| Lyford | 5 | 5 | 0 |
| Mansfield | 63 | 54 | 9 |
| Marlin | 1 | 1 | 0 |
| McAllen | 73 | 62 | 11 |
| Midland | 24 | 18 | 6 |
| Montgomery County | 14 | 13 | 1 |
| Northside | 122 | 102 | 20 |
| Pasadena | 40 | 33 | 7 |
| Pecos Barstow Toyah | 12 | 10 | 2 |
| Pflugerville | 27 | 25 | 2 |
| Pleasanton | 3 | 3 | 0 |
| Rio Grande City | 69 | 19 | 50 |
| Roma | 12 | 11 | 1 |
| Round Rock | 30 | 29 | 1 |
| Royal | 4 | 3 | 1 |
| San Antonio | 68 | 58 | 10 |
| Santa Fe | 19 | 11 | 8 |
| Sealy | 4 | 4 | 0 |
| Socorro | 56 | 48 | 8 |
| Spring | 68 | 52 | 16 |
| Spring Branch | 51 | 41 | 10 |
| Taft | 2 | 2 | 0 |
| Terrell | 6 | 6 | 0 |
| Trinity | 3 | 3 | 0 |
| United | 228 | 88 | 140 |
| Van Vleck | 1 | 1 | 0 |
| Vensus | 1 | 1 | 0 |
| Warren | 1 | 1 | 0 |
| Wharton | 5 | 3 | 2 |
| Whitesboro | 1 | 1 | 0 |
| Independent School System | | | |
| Huntington | 5 | 5 | 0 |
| Nacogdoches | 9 | 8 | 1 |
| Montgomery County Constable | | | |
| Precinct 1 | 56 | 51 | 5 |
| Precinct 3 | 65 | 60 | 5 |
| Port of Brownsville | 20 | 12 | 8 |
| Port of Houston Authority | 50 | 36 | 14 |
| Sabine County Constable, Precinct 2 | 1 | 1 | 0 |
| University Medical Center | 10 | 10 | 0 |
| **UTAH** | | | |
| **State Agencies** | | | |
| Parks and Recreation | 66 | 65 | 1 |
| Utah Tax Commission Motor Vehicle Division, Vehicle Investigation Section | 34 | 19 | 15 |
| Wildlife Resources | 84 | 81 | 3 |
| **Tribal Agencies** | | | |
| Uintah and Ouray Tribal | 24 | 12 | 12 |
| **Other Agencies** | | | |
| Cache-Rich Drug Task Force | 5 | 4 | 1 |
| Granite School District | 30 | 24 | 6 |
| Iron, Garfield, Beaver Task Force | 4 | 4 | 0 |
| Utah County Attorney, Investigations Division | 7 | 5 | 2 |
| Utah Transit Authority | 92 | 77 | 15 |
| **VERMONT** | | | |
| **State Agencies** | | | |
| Attorney General | 5 | 5 | 0 |
| Capitol Police | 5 | 5 | 0 |
| Department of Liquor Control, Division of Enforcement and Licensing | 13 | 12 | 1 |
| Department of Motor Vehicles | 39 | 26 | 13 |
| Fish and Wildlife Department, Law Enforcement Division | 40 | 38 | 2 |
| Secretary of State, Investigations Unit | 8 | 5 | 3 |
| **VIRGINIA** | | | |
| **State Agencies** | | | |
| Alcoholic Beverage Control Commission | 146 | 85 | 61 |
| Department of Conservation and Recreation | 93 | 93 | 0 |
| Department of Game and Inland Fisheries, Enforcement Division | 176 | 157 | 19 |
| Department of Motor Vehicles | 83 | 71 | 12 |

## Table 81. Full-Time Law Enforcement Employees, by Selected State and Agency, 2021—Continued

(Number.)

| State/agency | Law enforcement employees | Officers | Civilians |
|---|---|---|---|
| Virginia Marine Resources Commission Law Enforcement Division | 82 | 73 | 9 |
| Virginia State Capitol | 78 | 64 | 14 |
| **Other Agencies** | | | |
| Norfolk Airport Authority | 40 | 32 | 8 |
| Port Authority, Norfolk | 51 | 37 | 14 |
| Reagan National Airport | 261 | 225 | 36 |
| Richmond International Airport | 17 | 17 | 0 |
| **WASHINGTON** | | | |
| **State Agencies** | | | |
| State Gambling Commission, Enforcement Unit | 89 | 49 | 40 |
| State Insurance Commissioner, Special Investigations Unit | 10 | 8 | 2 |
| Washington State Parks and Recreation Law Enforcement | 203 | 91 | 112 |
| **Tribal Agencies** | | | |
| Chehalis Tribal | 30 | 13 | 17 |
| Colville Tribal | 38 | 29 | 9 |
| Elwha Klallam Tribal | 16 | 12 | 4 |
| Hoh Tribal | 2 | 2 | 0 |
| Jamestown S'Klallam Tribal | 4 | 3 | 1 |
| Kalispel Tribal | 24 | 21 | 3 |
| La Push Tribal | 5 | 5 | 0 |
| Lummi Tribal | 22 | 20 | 2 |
| Makah Tribal | 14 | 9 | 5 |
| Muckleshoot Tribal | 16 | 14 | 2 |
| Nisqually Tribal | 23 | 19 | 4 |
| Nooksack Tribal | 9 | 9 | 0 |
| Port Gamble S'Klallam Tribal | 12 | 12 | 0 |
| Puyallup Tribal | 45 | 24 | 21 |
| Quinault Indian Nation | 16 | 8 | 8 |
| Shoalwater Bay Tribal | 5 | 4 | 1 |
| Skokomish Tribal | 8 | 7 | 1 |
| Snoqualmie Tribal | 4 | 3 | 1 |
| Spokane Agency | 23 | 12 | 11 |
| Squaxin Island Tribal | 14 | 12 | 2 |
| Stillaguamish Tribal | 13 | 13 | 0 |
| Suquamish Tribal | 20 | 13 | 7 |
| Swinomish Tribal | 22 | 15 | 7 |
| Tulalip Tribal | 54 | 37 | 17 |
| Upper Skagit Tribal | 7 | 7 | 0 |
| **Other Agencies** | | | |
| Port of Seattle | 140 | 106 | 34 |
| **WEST VIRGINIA** | | | |
| **State Agencies** | | | |
| Capitol Protective Services | 49 | 27 | 22 |
| Department of Natural Resources | | | |
|   Barbour County | 1 | 1 | 0 |
|   Berkeley County | 2 | 2 | 0 |
|   Braxton County | 2 | 2 | 0 |
|   Brooke County | 1 | 1 | 0 |
|   Calhoun County | 2 | 2 | 0 |
|   Clay County | 1 | 1 | 0 |
|   Doddridge County | 2 | 2 | 0 |
|   Fayette County | 2 | 2 | 0 |
|   Gilmer County | 1 | 1 | 0 |
|   Grant County | 2 | 2 | 0 |
|   Greenbrier County | 3 | 3 | 0 |
|   Hampshire County | 5 | 4 | 1 |
|   Hancock County | 1 | 1 | 0 |
|   Hardy County | 2 | 2 | 0 |
|   Harrison County | 1 | 1 | 0 |
|   Jackson County | 2 | 2 | 0 |
|   Jefferson County | 1 | 1 | 0 |
|   Kanawha County | 19 | 13 | 6 |
|   Lewis County | 1 | 1 | 0 |
|   Lincoln County | 2 | 2 | 0 |
|   Logan County | 1 | 1 | 0 |
|   Marion County | 7 | 6 | 1 |
|   Marshall County | 1 | 1 | 0 |
|   Mason County | 1 | 1 | 0 |
|   McDowell County | 1 | 1 | 0 |
|   Mercer County | 2 | 2 | 0 |
|   Mineral County | 1 | 1 | 0 |
|   Mingo County | 1 | 1 | 0 |
|   Monongalia County | 2 | 2 | 0 |
|   Monroe County | 2 | 2 | 0 |
|   Morgan County | 1 | 1 | 0 |
|   Nicholas County | 1 | 1 | 0 |
|   Ohio County | 1 | 1 | 0 |
|   Pendleton County | 1 | 1 | 0 |
|   Pleasants County | 1 | 1 | 0 |

## Table 81. Full-Time Law Enforcement Employees, by Selected State and Agency, 2021—Continued

(Number.)

| State/agency | Law enforcement employees | Officers | Civilians |
|---|---|---|---|
| Pocahontas County | 1 | 1 | 0 |
| Preston County | 3 | 3 | 0 |
| Putnam County | 3 | 3 | 0 |
| Raleigh County | 6 | 5 | 1 |
| Randolph County | 2 | 2 | 0 |
| Ritchie County | 1 | 1 | 0 |
| Roane County | 2 | 2 | 0 |
| Summers County | 3 | 3 | 0 |
| Taylor County | 1 | 1 | 0 |
| Tucker County | 2 | 2 | 0 |
| Tyler County | 1 | 1 | 0 |
| Upshur County | 4 | 3 | 1 |
| Wayne County | 2 | 2 | 0 |
| Webster County | 2 | 2 | 0 |
| Wetzel County | 1 | 1 | 0 |
| Wirt County | 1 | 1 | 0 |
| Wood County | 6 | 5 | 1 |
| Wyoming County | 1 | 1 | 0 |
| State Fire Marshal, Kanawha County | 47 | 31 | 16 |
| **Other Agencies** | | | |
| Central West Virginia Drug Task Force | 3 | 2 | 1 |
| Greenbrier County Drug and Violent Crime Task Force | 4 | 3 | 1 |
| Harrison County Drug and Violent Crime Task Force | 7 | 7 | 0 |
| Huntington Drug and Violent Crime Task Force | 4 | 3 | 1 |
| Kanawha County Parks and Recreation | 3 | 3 | 0 |
| Logan County Drug and Violent Crime Task Force | 7 | 6 | 1 |
| Metropolitan Drug Enforcement Network Team | 3 | 3 | 0 |
| Mon Metro Drug Task Force | 9 | 8 | 1 |
| Ohio Valley Drug and Violent Crime Task Force | 4 | 4 | 0 |
| Potomac Highlands Drug and Violent Crime Task Force | 4 | 4 | 0 |
| Southern Regional Drug and Violent Crime Task Force | 9 | 8 | 1 |
| Three Rivers Drug and Violent Crime Task Force | 2 | 2 | 0 |
| **WISCONSIN** | | | |
| **State Agencies** | | | |
| Capitol Police | 46 | 35 | 11 |
| **Tribal Agencies** | | | |
| Lac Courte Oreilles Tribal | 11 | 8 | 3 |
| Menominee Tribal | 25 | 19 | 6 |
| Oneida Tribal | 25 | 20 | 5 |
| Red Cliff Tribal | 9 | 6 | 3 |
| St. Croix Tribal | 12 | 8 | 4 |
| Stockbridge Munsee Tribal | 2 | 2 | 0 |
| **WYOMING** | | | |
| **State Agencies** | | | |
| Wyoming Division of Criminal Investigation | 83 | 37 | 46 |
| **Tribal Agencies** | | | |
| Wind River Agency | 22 | 17 | 5 |
| **PUERTO RICO AND OTHER OUTLYING AREAS** | | | |
| Guam | 333 | 277 | 56 |
| Puerto Rico | 12,732 | 11,976 | 756 |

# SECTION VI

# HATE CRIMES

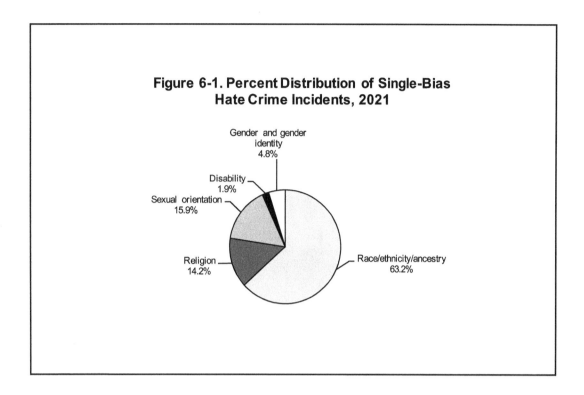

Figure 6-1. Percent Distribution of Single-Bias Hate Crime Incidents, 2021

The Federal Bureau of Investigation (FBI) began the procedures for implementing, collecting, and managing hate crime data after Congress passed the Hate Crime Statistics Act in 1990. This act required the collection of data "about crimes that manifest evidence of prejudice based on race, religion, sexual orientation, or ethnicity." Beginning in 2013, law enforcement agencies could submit hate crime data in accordance with a number of program modifications. In 1994, the Hate Crime Statistics Act was amended to include bias against persons with disabilities. The Church Arson Prevention Act, which was signed into law in July 1996, removed the sunset clause from the original statute and mandated that the collection of hate crime data become a permanent part of the UCR program. In 2009, Congress further amended the Hate Crime Statistics Act by passing the Matthew Shepard and James Byrd, Jr., Hate Crime Prevention Act. The amendment includes the collection of data for crimes motivated by bias against a particular gender and gender identity, as well as for crimes committed by, and crimes directed against, juveniles. In response to the Shepard/Byrd Act, the FBI modified its data collection so that reporting agencies could indicate whether hate crimes were committed by, or directed against, juveniles.

### Definitions

Hate crimes include any crime motivated by bias against race, religion, sexual orientation, ethnicity/national origin, and/or disability. Because motivation is subjective, it is sometimes difficult to know with certainty whether a crime resulted from the offender's bias. Moreover, the presence of bias alone does not necessarily mean that a crime can be considered a hate crime. Only when law enforcement investigation reveals sufficient evidence to lead a reasonable and prudent person to conclude that the offender's actions were motivated, in whole or in part, by his or her bias should an incident be reported as a hate crime.

### Data Collection

The UCR (Uniform Crime Reporting) program collects data about both single-bias and multiple-bias hate crimes. A single-bias incident is defined as an incident in which one or more offense types are motivated by the same bias. A multiple-bias incident is defined as an incident in which more than one offense type occurs and at least two offense types are motivated by different biases.

A table enumerating selected places in the United States that did not report hate crimes in 2021 is available on the FBI's Crime Data Explorer at https://cde.ucr.cjis.gov/LATEST/webapp/#/pages/explorer/crime/hate-crime.

### CRIMES AGAINST PERSONS, PROPERTY, OR SOCIETY

The UCR program's data collection guidelines stipulate that a hate crime may involve multiple offenses, victims, and offenders within one incident; therefore, the Hate Crime Statistics program is incident-based. According to UCR counting guidelines:

- One offense is counted for each victim in *crimes against persons*

- One offense is counted for each offense type in *crimes against property*

- One offense is counted for each offense type in *crimes against society*

## VICTIMS

In the UCR program, the victim of a hate crime may be an individual, a business, an institution, or society as a whole.

## OFFENDERS

According to the UCR program, the term *known offender* does not imply that the suspect's identity is known; rather, the term indicates that some aspect of the suspect was identified, thus distinguishing the suspect from an unknown offender. Law enforcement agencies specify the number of offenders, and when possible, the race of the offender or offenders as a group.

## RACE/ETHNICITY

The UCR program uses the following racial designations in its Hate Crime Statistics program: White; Black; American Indian or Alaskan Native; Asian; Native Hawaiian or Other Pacific Islander; and Multiple Races, Group. In addition, the UCR program uses the ethnic designations of Hispanic or Latino and Not Hispanic or Latino.

The law enforcement agencies that voluntarily participate in the Hate Crime Statistics program collect details about an offender's bias motivation associated with 11 offense types already being reported to the UCR program: murder and nonnegligent manslaughter, rape, aggravated assault, simple assault, and intimidation (crimes against persons); and robbery, burglary, larceny-theft, motor vehicle theft, arson, and destruction/damage/vandalism (crimes against property). The law enforcement agencies that participate in the UCR program via the National Incident-Based Reporting System (NIBRS) collect data about additional offenses for *crimes against persons* and *crimes against property*. These data appear in the category of other. These agencies also collect hate crime data for the category called *crimes against society*, which includes drug or narcotic offenses, gambling offenses, prostitution offenses, and weapon law violations.

### National Volume and Percent Distribution

In 2021, hate crime statistics were collected from 11,883 (of 18,812) law enforcement agencies. These law enforcement agencies reported 7,262 hate crime incidents involving 8,673 offenses. Of these, 7,074 were single-bias incidents. An analysis

of the single-bias incidents revealed that approximately 63.2 percent were racially/ethnically/ancestrally motivated, 15.9 percent resulted from sexual orientation bias, 14.2 percent were motivated by religious bias, 4.8 percent were motivated by gender and gender-identity bias, and 1.9 percent were prompted by a disability bias. (Table 82)

The largest proportion of the 4,470 single-bias hate crime incidents that were racially motivated resulted from an anti-Black or African American bias (49.6 percent) followed by an anti-White basis (21.2 percent). Bias against people of more than one race accounted for 2.9 percent of incidents, while anti-Asian bias accounted for an increased 6.8 percent of racially motivated incidents, anti-Arab bias accounted for 1.7 percent of these incidents, anti–Native Hawaiian and Other Pacific Islander accounted for 0.6 percent of these incidents, and anti–American Indian or Alaska Native bias accounted for 2.8 percent of these incidents. Approximately 9.7 percent of crimes were classified as an anti–Hispanic or Latino bias. (Table 82)

Hate crimes motivated by religious bias accounted for 1,005 incidents reported by law enforcement. A breakdown of these incidents revealed 31.2 percent were motivated by anti-Jewish bias, 21.3 percent were anti-Sikh, 9.5 percent by anti-Islamic (Muslim) bias, 6.5 percent were anti—Eastern Orthodox (Russian, Greek, or other), 6.1 percent were anti-Catholic, 4.0 percent were anti-Protestant, 3.8 percent were anti—other Christian, 3.3 percent were anti–multiple religions or groups, 2.8 percent were anti-Buddhist, 2.0 percent were anti-atheism/agnosticism/etc., 1.9 percent were anti-Mormon, 1.0 percent were anti-Hindu, 0.6 percent were anti—Jehovah's Witness, and the remainder, 5.5 percent, of offenses were based on a bias against other religions—those not specified. The 2021 numbers for incidents against Buddhists and Sikhs experienced a significant uptick from 2020, a pattern also seen from 2019 to 2020. (Table 82)

In 2021, 1,127 incidents were committed on the basis of sexual orientation bias. Of the offenses based on sexual orientation, 36.7 percent were classified as having an anti–lesbian, gay, bisexual, or transgender (mixed group) bias; 48.0 percent were classified as having an anti–gay (male) bias; 11.0 percent had an anti–lesbian basis; 3.0 percent had an anti-bisexual bias; and 1.2 percent had an anti-heterosexual bias. (Table 82)

Hate crime incidents committed based on disability totaled 134 incidents. The majority (65.7 percent) were classified as anti-mental disability, with the rest (34.3 percent) classified as anti–physical disability. (Table 82)

Of the 266 gender identity bias incidents reported, 176 (66.2 percent) were anti-transgender and 90 were anti–gender nonconforming. Of the 72 gender bias offenses reported, 55 were anti-female and 17 were anti-male. (Table 82)

### Crimes Against Persons

Law enforcement agencies reported 4,707 hate crime incidents against persons in 2021. Approximately 44.7 percent involved intimidation, 36.1 percent involved simple assault, and 17.5 percent involved aggravated assault. There were 8 murders and 13 rapes. (Table 83)

### Crimes Against Property

In 2021, hate crime incidents against property totaled 2,601. Approximately 64.4 percent of offenses involved destruction, damage, or vandalism. The remaining 35.6 percent of crimes against property consisted of robbery, burglary, larceny-theft, motor vehicle theft, arson, and other crimes. (Table 83)

### Offenders and Bias Motivation

Of the 8,673 total offenses committed in 2021, White (43.7 percent) and Black or African American (15.9 percent) represented the highest proportions of offenders, accounting for nearly 60 percent of this group. Persons of Hispanic or Latino ethnicity committed approximately 4.6 percent of offenses. Of the 9 murders committed, (one more is included when measuring offenses instead of incidents), 1 was motivated by anti–Black or African American bias; 2 were motivated by anti-Asian bias; and the remainder were motivated by anti–sexual orientation bias. Two of the murders encompassed multiple biases. The greatest proportions of destruction/damage/vandalism had an anti–Black or African American bias (33.3 percent) or an anti-Jewish bias (11.6 percent). Approximately four out of five known offenders were adults (18 years old or over). (Tables 84 and 85)

### Victims

Of the 8,673 reported offenses in 2021, the vast majority of victims were individuals (84.9 percent). Businesses and financial institutions represented 5.8 percent of the total, society/public represented 3.3 percent of the total, government represented 2.8 percent of the total, religious organizations represented 1.3 percent of the total, and other/unknown/multiple comprised the remaining 1.9 percent. The greatest number of adult and juvenile victims were the same for the race/ethnicity/ancestry (anti–Black or African American), sexual orientation (anti-gay [male]), and religion (anti-Jewish) categories. (Tables 87 and 88) Nearly half of all incidents occurred either in a residence/home (32.2 percent) or on a highway, road, alley, street, or sidewalk (16.9 percent). (Table 91)

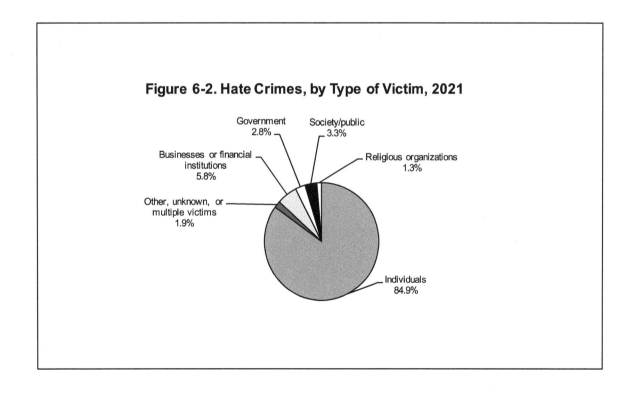

**Figure 6-2. Hate Crimes, by Type of Victim, 2021**

## Table 82. Incidents, Offenses, Victims, and Known Offenders, by Bias Motivation, 2021

(Number.)

| Bias motivation | Incidents | Offenses | Victims[1] | Known offenders[2] |
|---|---|---|---|---|
| **Total** | 7,262 | 8,673 | 9,024 | 6,312 |
| **Single-Bias Incidents** | 7,074 | 8,419 | 8,753 | 6,143 |
| Race/Ethnicity/Ancestry | 4,470 | 5,448 | 5,671 | 3,902 |
| Anti-White | 947 | 1,131 | 1,161 | 862 |
| Anti-Black or African American | 2,217 | 2,685 | 2,790 | 1,927 |
| Anti-American Indian or Alaska Native | 124 | 135 | 136 | 102 |
| Anti-Asian | 305 | 363 | 384 | 247 |
| Anti-Native Hawaiian or Other Pacific Islander | 26 | 29 | 29 | 20 |
| Anti-Multiple Races, Group | 130 | 150 | 177 | 87 |
| Anti-Arab | 75 | 99 | 100 | 66 |
| Anti-Hispanic or Latino | 432 | 588 | 612 | 422 |
| Anti-Other Race/Ethnicity/Ancestry | 214 | 268 | 282 | 169 |
| Religion | 1,005 | 1,112 | 1,164 | 741 |
| Anti-Jewish | 321 | 351 | 362 | 186 |
| Anti-Catholic | 61 | 71 | 73 | 42 |
| Anti-Protestant | 40 | 42 | 47 | 32 |
| Anti-Islamic (Muslim) | 95 | 121 | 134 | 81 |
| Anti-Other Religion | 55 | 62 | 69 | 35 |
| Anti-Multiple Religions, Group | 33 | 41 | 41 | 24 |
| Anti-Mormon | 19 | 22 | 22 | 13 |
| Anti-Jehovah's Witness | 6 | 6 | 6 | 3 |
| Anti-Eastern Orthodox (Russian, Greek, Other) | 65 | 74 | 76 | 75 |
| Anti-Other Christian | 38 | 42 | 43 | 24 |
| Anti-Buddhist | 28 | 28 | 28 | 27 |
| Anti-Hindu | 10 | 14 | 14 | 8 |
| Anti-Sikh | 214 | 218 | 229 | 175 |
| Anti-Atheism/Agnosticism/etc. | 20 | 20 | 20 | 16 |
| Sexual Orientation | 1,127 | 1,320 | 1,365 | 1,054 |
| Anti-Gay (Male) | 541 | 612 | 617 | 537 |
| Anti-Lesbian | 124 | 159 | 161 | 119 |
| Anti-Lesbian, Gay, Bisexual, or Transgender (Mixed Group) | 414 | 492 | 530 | 355 |
| Anti-Heterosexual | 14 | 15 | 15 | 10 |
| Anti-Bisexual | 34 | 42 | 42 | 33 |
| Disability | 134 | 150 | 153 | 122 |
| Anti-Physical | 46 | 53 | 54 | 39 |
| Anti-Mental | 88 | 97 | 99 | 83 |
| Gender | 72 | 82 | 88 | 66 |
| Anti-Male | 17 | 20 | 20 | 16 |
| Anti-Female | 55 | 62 | 68 | 50 |
| Gender Identity | 266 | 307 | 312 | 258 |
| Anti-Transgender | 176 | 200 | 205 | 168 |
| Anti-Gender Non-Conforming | 90 | 107 | 107 | 90 |
| **Multiple-Bias Incidents[3]** | 188 | 254 | 271 | 169 |

1 The term victim may refer to an individual, business/financial institution, government entity, religious organization, or society/public as a whole.   2 The term known offender does not imply the suspect's identity is known; rather, the term indicates some aspect of the suspect was identified, thus distinguishing the suspect from an unknown offender.   3 A multiple-bias incident is an incident in which one or more offense types are motivated by two or more biases.

## Table 83. Incidents, Offenses, Victims, and Known Offenders, by Offense Type, 2021

(Number.)

| Offense type | Incidents[1] | Offenses | Victims[2] | Known offenders[3] |
|---|---|---|---|---|
| **Total** | 7,262 | 8,673 | 9,024 | 6,312 |
| **Crimes Against Persons** | 4,707 | 5,781 | 5,781 | 4,730 |
| Murder and nonnegligent manslaughter | 8 | 9 | 9 | 4 |
| Rape | 13 | 13 | 13 | 15 |
| Aggravated assault | 822 | 1,058 | 1,058 | 914 |
| Simple assault | 1,700 | 2,074 | 2,074 | 1,888 |
| Intimidation | 2,104 | 2,558 | 2,558 | 1,841 |
| Other[4] | 60 | 69 | 69 | 68 |
| **Crimes Against Property** | 2,601 | 2,606 | 2,957 | 1,600 |
| Robbery | 104 | 104 | 123 | 141 |
| Burglary | 117 | 117 | 148 | 86 |
| Larceny-theft | 474 | 476 | 507 | 323 |
| Motor vehicle theft | 51 | 51 | 51 | 29 |
| Arson | 43 | 43 | 63 | 34 |
| Destruction/damage/vandalism | 1,674 | 1,674 | 1,914 | 899 |
| Other[4] | 138 | 141 | 151 | 88 |
| **Crimes Against Society[4]** | 276 | 286 | 286 | 311 |

1 The actual number of incidents is 7,262. However, the column figures will not add to the total because incidents may include more than one offense type, and these are counted in each appropriate offense type category.   2 The term victim may refer to an individual, business/financial institution, government entity, religious organization, or society/public as a whole.   3 The term known offender does not imply the suspect's identity is known; rather, the term indicates some aspect of the suspect was identified, thus distinguishing the suspect from an unknown offender. The actual number of known offenders is 6,312. However, the column figures will not add to the total because some offenders are responsible for more than one offense type, and are, therefore, counted more than once in this table.   4 The figures shown include additional offenses collected in the National Incident-Based Reporting System.

## Table 84. Offenses, Known Offender's Race and Ethnicity, by Offense Type, 2021

(Number.)

| | | Known offender's race | | | | | | | Known offender's ethnicity[1] | | | | |
| Bias motivation | Total offenses | White | Black or African American | American Indian or Alaska Native | Asian | Native Hawaiian or Other Pacific Islander | Group of multiple races | Unknown race | Hispanic or Latino | Not Hispanic or Latino | Group of multiple ethnicities | Unknown ethnicity | Unknown offender |
|---|---|---|---|---|---|---|---|---|---|---|---|---|---|
| **Total** | 8,673 | 3,791 | 1,382 | 107 | 78 | 25 | 270 | 755 | 400 | 2,896 | 229 | 1,445 | 2,265 |
| | | | | | | | | | | | | | |
| **Crimes Against Persons** | 5,781 | 3,000 | 1,111 | 89 | 63 | 23 | 242 | 369 | 322 | 2,347 | 174 | 998 | 884 |
| Murder and nonnegligent manslaughter | 9 | 4 | 1 | 0 | 0 | 0 | 0 | 0 | 0 | 4 | 0 | 1 | 4 |
| Rape | 13 | 8 | 4 | 0 | 0 | 0 | 0 | 0 | 0 | 4 | 0 | 2 | 1 |
| Aggravated assault | 1,058 | 612 | 235 | 12 | 11 | 3 | 32 | 45 | 77 | 461 | 30 | 221 | 108 |
| Simple assault | 2,074 | 1,020 | 493 | 40 | 21 | 7 | 166 | 112 | 132 | 932 | 87 | 335 | 215 |
| Intimidation | 2,558 | 1,316 | 367 | 37 | 30 | 13 | 43 | 207 | 109 | 924 | 54 | 432 | 545 |
| Other[2] | 69 | 40 | 11 | 0 | 1 | 0 | 1 | 5 | 4 | 22 | 3 | 7 | 11 |
| | | | | | | | | | | | | | |
| **Crimes Against Property** | 2,606 | 604 | 208 | 14 | 12 | 2 | 24 | 380 | 57 | 422 | 50 | 402 | 1,362 |
| Robbery | 104 | 35 | 31 | 1 | 5 | 1 | 6 | 7 | 7 | 37 | 5 | 21 | 18 |
| Burglary | 117 | 34 | 7 | 2 | 1 | 0 | 0 | 22 | 3 | 21 | 3 | 25 | 51 |
| Larceny-theft | 476 | 129 | 47 | 3 | 0 | 0 | 9 | 57 | 11 | 78 | 4 | 73 | 231 |
| Motor vehicle theft | 51 | 14 | 1 | 1 | 0 | 0 | 0 | 9 | 3 | 8 | 3 | 5 | 26 |
| Arson | 43 | 17 | 4 | 0 | 0 | 0 | 1 | 5 | 0 | 15 | 0 | 6 | 16 |
| Destruction/damage/ vandalism | 1,674 | 341 | 102 | 6 | 5 | 1 | 6 | 254 | 30 | 232 | 33 | 250 | 959 |
| Other[2] | 141 | 34 | 16 | 1 | 1 | 0 | 2 | 26 | 3 | 31 | 2 | 22 | 61 |
| | | | | | | | | | | | | | |
| **Crimes Against Society[2]** | 286 | 187 | 63 | 4 | 3 | 0 | 4 | 6 | 21 | 127 | 5 | 45 | 19 |

1 The sum of offenses by the known offender's ethnicity does not equal the sum of offenses by the known offender's race because not all law enforcement agencies that report offender race data also report offender ethnicity data.   2 The figures shown include additional offenses collected in the National Incident-Based Reporting System.

## Table 85. Offenses, Offense Type, by Bias Motivation, 2021

(Number.)

| Bias motivation | Total offenses | Crimes against persons | | | | | |
|---|---|---|---|---|---|---|---|
| | | Murder and nonnegligent manslaughter | Rape | Aggravated assault | Simple assault | Intimidation | Other[1] |
| **Total** | 8,673 | 9 | 13 | 1,058 | 2,074 | 2,558 | 69 |
| **Single-Bias Incidents** | 8,419 | 7 | 13 | 1,038 | 2,016 | 2,464 | 69 |
| Race/Ethnicity/Ancestry | 5,448 | 3 | 3 | 766 | 1,359 | 1,700 | 27 |
| Anti-White | 1,131 | 0 | 3 | 142 | 343 | 253 | 13 |
| Anti-Black or African American | 2,685 | 1 | 0 | 389 | 622 | 948 | 7 |
| Anti-American Indian or Alaska Native | 135 | 0 | 0 | 16 | 27 | 16 | 3 |
| Anti-Asian | 363 | 2 | 0 | 45 | 104 | 125 | 1 |
| Anti-Native Hawaiian or Other Pacific Islander | 29 | 0 | 0 | 3 | 4 | 2 | 0 |
| Anti-Multiple Races, Group | 150 | 0 | 0 | 6 | 27 | 26 | 0 |
| Anti-Arab | 99 | 0 | 0 | 20 | 20 | 42 | 0 |
| Anti-Hispanic or Latino | 588 | 0 | 0 | 118 | 154 | 202 | 3 |
| Anti-Other Race/Ethnicity/Ancestry | 268 | 0 | 0 | 27 | 58 | 86 | 0 |
| Religion | 1,112 | 0 | 5 | 50 | 111 | 240 | 11 |
| Anti-Jewish | 351 | 0 | 1 | 8 | 16 | 99 | 4 |
| Anti-Catholic | 71 | 0 | 1 | 3 | 1 | 16 | 1 |
| Anti-Protestant | 42 | 0 | 0 | 3 | 6 | 5 | 0 |
| Anti-Islamic (Muslim) | 121 | 0 | 0 | 10 | 29 | 48 | 2 |
| Anti-Other Religion | 62 | 0 | 0 | 3 | 7 | 20 | 0 |
| Anti-Multiple Religions, Group | 41 | 0 | 0 | 2 | 2 | 14 | 0 |
| Anti-Mormon | 22 | 0 | 0 | 0 | 3 | 2 | 0 |
| Anti-Jehovah's Witness | 6 | 0 | 0 | 0 | 0 | 0 | 0 |
| Anti-Eastern Orthodox (Russian, Greek, Other) | 74 | 0 | 1 | 2 | 17 | 12 | 1 |
| Anti-Other Christian | 42 | 0 | 0 | 2 | 3 | 10 | 0 |
| Anti-Buddhist | 28 | 0 | 0 | 3 | 5 | 0 | 0 |
| Anti-Hindu | 14 | 0 | 0 | 3 | 2 | 3 | 0 |
| Anti-Sikh | 218 | 0 | 2 | 11 | 19 | 11 | 3 |
| Anti-Atheism/Agnosticism/etc. | 20 | 0 | 0 | 0 | 1 | 0 | 0 |
| Sexual Orientation | 1,320 | 3 | 1 | 166 | 386 | 411 | 14 |
| Anti-Gay (Male) | 612 | 1 | 0 | 106 | 199 | 179 | 3 |
| Anti-Lesbian | 159 | 0 | 1 | 15 | 51 | 64 | 0 |
| Anti-Lesbian, Gay, Bisexual, or Transgender (Mixed Group) | 492 | 2 | 0 | 43 | 117 | 149 | 9 |
| Anti-Heterosexual | 15 | 0 | 0 | 1 | 2 | 3 | 2 |
| Anti-Bisexual | 42 | 0 | 0 | 1 | 17 | 16 | 0 |
| Disability | 150 | 0 | 0 | 10 | 42 | 24 | 7 |
| Anti-Physical | 53 | 0 | 0 | 2 | 18 | 9 | 0 |
| Anti-Mental | 97 | 0 | 0 | 8 | 24 | 15 | 7 |
| Gender | 82 | 0 | 2 | 6 | 22 | 25 | 2 |
| Anti-Male | 20 | 0 | 0 | 0 | 10 | 2 | 0 |
| Anti-Female | 62 | 0 | 2 | 6 | 12 | 23 | 2 |
| Gender Identity | 307 | 1 | 2 | 40 | 96 | 64 | 8 |
| Anti-Transgender | 200 | 1 | 1 | 26 | 62 | 53 | 5 |
| Anti-Gender Non-Conforming | 107 | 0 | 1 | 14 | 34 | 11 | 3 |
| **Multiple-Bias Incidents[2]** | 254 | 2 | 0 | 20 | 58 | 94 | 0 |

1 The figures shown include additional offenses collected in the National Incident-Based Reporting System.   2 A multiple-bias incident is an incident in which one or more offense types are motivated by two or more biases.

## Table 85. Offenses, Offense Type, by Bias Motivation, 2021—Continued

(Number.)

| Bias motivation | Crimes against property | | | | | | | Crimes against society[1] |
|---|---|---|---|---|---|---|---|---|
| | Robbery | Burglary | Larceny-theft | Motor vehicle theft | Arson | Destruction/damage/vandalism | Other[1] | |
| **Total** | 104 | 117 | 476 | 51 | 43 | 1,674 | 141 | 286 |
| **Single-Bias Incidents** | 103 | 113 | 471 | 51 | 41 | 1,609 | 141 | 283 |
| Race/Ethnicity/Ancestry | 70 | 64 | 226 | 29 | 11 | 954 | 65 | 171 |
| Anti-White | 18 | 23 | 116 | 16 | 3 | 108 | 30 | 63 |
| Anti-Black or African American | 17 | 14 | 47 | 3 | 4 | 557 | 19 | 57 |
| Anti-American Indian or Alaska Native | 0 | 5 | 20 | 6 | 0 | 15 | 6 | 21 |
| Anti-Asian | 11 | 6 | 8 | 1 | 1 | 55 | 1 | 3 |
| Anti-Native Hawaiian or Other Pacific Islander | 0 | 1 | 9 | 1 | 0 | 0 | 2 | 7 |
| Anti-Multiple Races, Group | 1 | 1 | 4 | 1 | 0 | 78 | 0 | 6 |
| Anti-Arab | 0 | 1 | 3 | 0 | 1 | 10 | 1 | 1 |
| Anti-Hispanic or Latino | 18 | 8 | 9 | 0 | 2 | 62 | 1 | 11 |
| Anti-Other Race/Ethnicity/Ancestry | 5 | 5 | 10 | 1 | 0 | 69 | 5 | 2 |
| Religion | 6 | 30 | 130 | 13 | 14 | 381 | 45 | 76 |
| Anti-Jewish | 5 | 7 | 10 | 0 | 2 | 193 | 3 | 3 |
| Anti-Catholic | 0 | 1 | 3 | 0 | 0 | 36 | 4 | 5 |
| Anti-Protestant | 0 | 3 | 10 | 1 | 0 | 13 | 1 | 0 |
| Anti-Islamic (Muslim) | 0 | 1 | 2 | 0 | 3 | 23 | 1 | 2 |
| Anti-Other Religion | 0 | 0 | 10 | 0 | 1 | 19 | 0 | 2 |
| Anti-Multiple Religions, Group | 0 | 1 | 2 | 0 | 2 | 12 | 1 | 5 |
| Anti-Mormon | 1 | 1 | 1 | 0 | 3 | 8 | 2 | 1 |
| Anti-Jehovah's Witness | 0 | 1 | 3 | 0 | 0 | 1 | 0 | 1 |
| Anti-Eastern Orthodox (Russian, Greek, Other) | 0 | 4 | 8 | 2 | 1 | 11 | 3 | 12 |
| Anti-Other Christian | 0 | 1 | 5 | 1 | 2 | 16 | 0 | 2 |
| Anti-Buddhist | 0 | 0 | 9 | 0 | 0 | 6 | 3 | 2 |
| Anti-Hindu | 0 | 0 | 3 | 0 | 0 | 3 | 0 | 0 |
| Anti-Sikh | 0 | 8 | 58 | 9 | 0 | 30 | 27 | 40 |
| Anti-Atheism/Agnosticism/etc. | 0 | 2 | 6 | 0 | 0 | 10 | 0 | 1 |
| Sexual Orientation | 21 | 8 | 66 | 3 | 16 | 204 | 10 | 11 |
| Anti-Gay (Male) | 15 | 2 | 17 | 1 | 4 | 73 | 4 | 8 |
| Anti-Lesbian | 0 | 1 | 4 | 1 | 1 | 21 | 0 | 0 |
| Anti-Lesbian, Gay, Bisexual, or Transgender (Mixed Group) | 6 | 4 | 41 | 0 | 11 | 106 | 2 | 2 |
| Anti-Heterosexual | 0 | 0 | 2 | 1 | 0 | 1 | 3 | 0 |
| Anti-Bisexual | 0 | 1 | 2 | 0 | 0 | 3 | 1 | 1 |
| Disability | 2 | 5 | 21 | 3 | 0 | 16 | 11 | 9 |
| Anti-Physical | 2 | 2 | 8 | 1 | 0 | 6 | 1 | 4 |
| Anti-Mental | 0 | 3 | 13 | 2 | 0 | 10 | 10 | 5 |
| Gender | 0 | 3 | 3 | 0 | 0 | 12 | 4 | 3 |
| Anti-Male | 0 | 1 | 1 | 0 | 0 | 4 | 0 | 2 |
| Anti-Female | 0 | 2 | 2 | 0 | 0 | 8 | 4 | 1 |
| Gender Identity | 4 | 3 | 25 | 3 | 0 | 42 | 6 | 13 |
| Anti-Transgender | 2 | 1 | 12 | 2 | 0 | 28 | 2 | 5 |
| Anti-Gender Non-Conforming | 2 | 2 | 13 | 1 | 0 | 14 | 4 | 8 |
| **Multiple-Bias Incidents[2]** | 1 | 4 | 5 | 0 | 2 | 65 | 0 | 3 |

1 The figures shown include additional offenses collected in the National Incident-Based Reporting System.
2 A multiple-bias incident is an incident in which one or more offense types are motivated by two or more biases.

# Table 86. Offenses, Known Offender's Race, by Bias Motivation, 2021

(Number.)

| Bias motivation | Total offenses | White | Black or African American | American Indian or Alaska Native | Asian | Native Hawaiian or Other Pacific Islander | Group of multiple races | Unknown race | Hispanic or Latino | Not Hispanic or Latino | Group of multiple ethnicities | Unknown ethnicity | Unknown offender |
|---|---|---|---|---|---|---|---|---|---|---|---|---|---|
| **Total** | 8,673 | 3,791 | 1,382 | 107 | 78 | 25 | 270 | 755 | 400 | 2,896 | 229 | 1,445 | 2,265 |
| **Single-Bias Incidents** | 8,419 | 3,680 | 1,355 | 105 | 73 | 23 | 263 | 726 | 391 | 2,819 | 222 | 1,388 | 2,194 |
| Race/Ethnicity/Ancestry | 5,448 | 2,553 | 872 | 86 | 53 | 13 | 195 | 381 | 275 | 1,930 | 131 | 881 | 1,295 |
| Anti-White | 1,131 | 283 | 473 | 39 | 4 | 9 | 31 | 54 | 56 | 440 | 20 | 162 | 238 |
| Anti-Black or African American | 2,685 | 1,511 | 168 | 17 | 25 | 2 | 122 | 193 | 121 | 929 | 56 | 441 | 647 |
| Anti-American Indian or Alaska Native | 135 | 43 | 18 | 21 | 0 | 0 | 5 | 9 | 13 | 38 | 3 | 13 | 39 |
| Anti-Asian | 363 | 140 | 76 | 1 | 5 | 1 | 8 | 23 | 17 | 116 | 11 | 65 | 109 |
| Anti-Native Hawaiian or Other Pacific Islander | 29 | 12 | 3 | 0 | 1 | 0 | 0 | 4 | 0 | 5 | 0 | 12 | 9 |
| Anti-Multiple Races, Group | 150 | 52 | 6 | 0 | 0 | 0 | 8 | 19 | 2 | 26 | 5 | 23 | 65 |
| Anti-Arab | 99 | 57 | 13 | 0 | 1 | 0 | 6 | 3 | 5 | 38 | 5 | 17 | 19 |
| Anti-Hispanic or Latino | 588 | 367 | 83 | 6 | 7 | 1 | 3 | 40 | 53 | 253 | 24 | 110 | 81 |
| Anti-Other Race/Ethnicity/Ancestry | 268 | 88 | 32 | 2 | 10 | 0 | 12 | 36 | 8 | 85 | 7 | 38 | 88 |
| Religion | 1,112 | 386 | 120 | 10 | 9 | 2 | 10 | 170 | 23 | 281 | 17 | 213 | 405 |
| Anti-Jewish | 351 | 77 | 15 | 2 | 5 | 1 | 2 | 58 | 4 | 51 | 8 | 60 | 191 |
| Anti-Catholic | 71 | 26 | 4 | 0 | 0 | 0 | 0 | 13 | 0 | 16 | 0 | 12 | 28 |
| Anti-Protestant | 42 | 18 | 4 | 1 | 0 | 0 | 0 | 3 | 4 | 8 | 1 | 4 | 16 |
| Anti-Islamic (Muslim) | 121 | 56 | 21 | 5 | 2 | 1 | 3 | 12 | 3 | 30 | 0 | 46 | 21 |
| Anti-Other Religion | 62 | 16 | 12 | 0 | 0 | 0 | 0 | 11 | 2 | 16 | 0 | 13 | 23 |
| Anti-Multiple Religions, Group | 41 | 10 | 6 | 2 | 0 | 0 | 0 | 11 | 0 | 7 | 0 | 13 | 12 |
| Anti-Mormon | 22 | 11 | 1 | 0 | 0 | 0 | 0 | 3 | 0 | 9 | 0 | 2 | 7 |
| Anti-Jehovah's Witness | 6 | 2 | 0 | 0 | 0 | 0 | 0 | 0 | 0 | 2 | 0 | 0 | 4 |
| Anti-Eastern Orthodox (Russian, Greek, Other) | 74 | 45 | 14 | 0 | 0 | 0 | 2 | 5 | 3 | 29 | 2 | 8 | 8 |
| Anti-Other Christian | 42 | 10 | 4 | 0 | 2 | 0 | 0 | 6 | 1 | 7 | 0 | 9 | 20 |
| Anti-Buddhist | 28 | 11 | 5 | 0 | 0 | 0 | 0 | 8 | 1 | 7 | 0 | 11 | 4 |
| Anti-Hindu | 14 | 11 | 1 | 0 | 0 | 0 | 0 | 0 | 0 | 7 | 0 | 2 | 2 |
| Anti-Sikh | 218 | 81 | 32 | 0 | 0 | 0 | 3 | 37 | 5 | 81 | 6 | 29 | 65 |
| Anti-Atheism/Agnosticism/etc. | 20 | 12 | 1 | 0 | 0 | 0 | 0 | 3 | 0 | 11 | 0 | 4 | 4 |
| Sexual Orientation | 1,320 | 506 | 266 | 8 | 6 | 4 | 40 | 131 | 64 | 432 | 58 | 214 | 359 |
| Anti-Gay (Male) | 612 | 241 | 148 | 3 | 3 | 2 | 22 | 50 | 31 | 227 | 31 | 98 | 143 |
| Anti-Lesbian | 159 | 54 | 38 | 0 | 0 | 2 | 4 | 19 | 8 | 56 | 7 | 24 | 42 |
| Anti-Lesbian, Gay, Bisexual, or Transgender (Mixed Group) | 492 | 185 | 72 | 5 | 1 | 0 | 14 | 53 | 22 | 134 | 20 | 82 | 162 |
| Anti-Heterosexual | 15 | 9 | 1 | 0 | 0 | 0 | 0 | 0 | 2 | 3 | 0 | 1 | 5 |
| Anti-Bisexual | 42 | 17 | 7 | 0 | 2 | 0 | 0 | 9 | 1 | 12 | 0 | 9 | 7 |
| Disability | 150 | 64 | 23 | 0 | 1 | 0 | 3 | 11 | 7 | 37 | 5 | 18 | 48 |
| Anti-Physical | 53 | 21 | 10 | 0 | 0 | 0 | 0 | 7 | 4 | 12 | 3 | 9 | 15 |
| Anti-Mental | 97 | 43 | 13 | 0 | 1 | 0 | 3 | 4 | 3 | 25 | 2 | 9 | 33 |
| Gender | 82 | 54 | 4 | 0 | 0 | 0 | 4 | 8 | 9 | 27 | 0 | 14 | 12 |
| Anti-Male | 20 | 14 | 2 | 0 | 0 | 0 | 0 | 3 | 1 | 12 | 0 | 3 | 1 |
| Anti-Female | 62 | 40 | 2 | 0 | 0 | 0 | 4 | 5 | 8 | 15 | 0 | 11 | 11 |
| Gender Identity | 307 | 117 | 70 | 1 | 4 | 4 | 11 | 25 | 13 | 112 | 11 | 48 | 75 |
| Anti-Transgender | 200 | 63 | 59 | 1 | 1 | 4 | 6 | 17 | 8 | 73 | 8 | 34 | 49 |
| Anti-Gender Non-Conforming | 107 | 54 | 11 | 0 | 3 | 0 | 5 | 8 | 5 | 39 | 3 | 14 | 26 |
| **Multiple-Bias Incidents[2]** | 254 | 111 | 27 | 2 | 5 | 2 | 7 | 29 | 9 | 77 | 7 | 57 | 71 |

1 The aggregate of offenses by the known offender's ethnicity does not equal the aggregate of offenses by the known offender's race because not all law enforcement agencies that report offender race data also report offender ethnicity data.   2 A multiple-bias incident is an incident in which one or more offense types are motivated by two or more biases.

## Table 87. Offenses, Victim Type, by Offense Type, 2021

(Number.)

| Offense type | Total offenses | Victim type | | | | | |
|---|---|---|---|---|---|---|---|
| | | Individual | Business/ financial institution | Government | Religious organization | Society/ public[1] | Other/ unknown/ multiple |
| **Total** | 8,673 | 7,353 | 502 | 247 | 117 | 286 | 168 |
| Crimes against persons[2] | 5,781 | 5,781 | NA | NA | NA | NA | NA |
| Crimes against property | 2,606 | 1,572 | 502 | 247 | 117 | 0 | 168 |
| Robbery | 104 | 98 | 0 | 0 | 0 | 0 | 6 |
| Burglary | 117 | 85 | 20 | 1 | 4 | 0 | 7 |
| Larceny-theft | 476 | 347 | 111 | 6 | 2 | 0 | 10 |
| Motor vehicle theft | 51 | 42 | 8 | 0 | 1 | 0 | 0 |
| Arson | 43 | 23 | 8 | 0 | 9 | 0 | 3 |
| Destruction/damage/vandalism | 1,674 | 862 | 337 | 237 | 100 | 0 | 138 |
| Other[2] | 141 | 115 | 18 | 3 | 1 | 0 | 4 |
| Crimes against society[2] | 286 | NA | NA | NA | NA | 286 | NA |

NA = Not available.
1 The victim type society/public is collected only in National Incident-Based Reporting System (NIBRS).    2 The figures shown include additional offenses collected in the NIBRS.

# Table 88. Victims, Offense Type, by Bias Motivation, 2021

(Number.)

| Bias motivation | Total victims[1] | Total number of adult victims[2] | Total number of juvenile victims[2] | Crimes against persons | | | | | |
|---|---|---|---|---|---|---|---|---|---|
| | | | | Murder and nonnegligent manslaughter | Rape | Aggravated assault | Simple assault | Intimidation | Other[3] |
| **Total** | 9,024 | 6,982 | 948 | 9 | 13 | 1,058 | 2,074 | 2,558 | 69 |
| **Single-Bias Incidents** | 8,753 | 6,776 | 921 | 7 | 13 | 1,038 | 2,016 | 2,464 | 69 |
| Race/Ethnicity/Ancestry | 5,671 | 4,582 | 563 | 3 | 3 | 766 | 1,359 | 1,700 | 27 |
| Anti-White | 1,161 | 950 | 87 | 0 | 3 | 142 | 343 | 253 | 13 |
| Anti-Black or African American | 2,790 | 2,195 | 344 | 1 | 0 | 389 | 622 | 948 | 7 |
| Anti-American Indian or Alaska Native | 136 | 93 | 12 | 0 | 0 | 16 | 27 | 16 | 3 |
| Anti-Asian | 384 | 347 | 29 | 2 | 0 | 45 | 104 | 125 | 1 |
| Anti-Native Hawaiian or Other Pacific Islander | 29 | 14 | 2 | 0 | 0 | 3 | 4 | 2 | 0 |
| Anti-Multiple Races, Group | 177 | 97 | 10 | 0 | 0 | 6 | 27 | 26 | 0 |
| Anti-Arab | 100 | 94 | 5 | 0 | 0 | 20 | 20 | 42 | 0 |
| Anti-Hispanic or Latino | 612 | 558 | 60 | 0 | 0 | 118 | 154 | 202 | 3 |
| Anti-Other Race/Ethnicity/Ancestry | 282 | 234 | 14 | 0 | 0 | 27 | 58 | 86 | 0 |
| Religion | 1,164 | 724 | 55 | 0 | 5 | 50 | 111 | 240 | 11 |
| Anti-Jewish | 362 | 206 | 14 | 0 | 1 | 8 | 16 | 99 | 4 |
| Anti-Catholic | 73 | 35 | 0 | 0 | 1 | 3 | 1 | 16 | 1 |
| Anti-Protestant | 47 | 33 | 1 | 0 | 0 | 3 | 6 | 5 | 0 |
| Anti-Islamic (Muslim) | 134 | 113 | 15 | 0 | 0 | 10 | 29 | 48 | 2 |
| Anti-Other Religion | 69 | 46 | 1 | 0 | 0 | 3 | 7 | 20 | 0 |
| Anti-Multiple Religions, Group | 41 | 22 | 1 | 0 | 0 | 2 | 2 | 14 | 0 |
| Anti-Mormon | 22 | 11 | 0 | 0 | 0 | 0 | 3 | 2 | 0 |
| Anti-Jehovah's Witness | 6 | 3 | 0 | 0 | 0 | 0 | 0 | 0 | 0 |
| Anti-Eastern Orthodox (Russian, Greek, Other) | 76 | 47 | 10 | 0 | 1 | 2 | 17 | 12 | 1 |
| Anti-Other Christian | 43 | 27 | 0 | 0 | 0 | 2 | 3 | 10 | 0 |
| Anti-Buddhist | 28 | 18 | 2 | 0 | 0 | 3 | 5 | 0 | 0 |
| Anti-Hindu | 14 | 13 | 0 | 0 | 0 | 3 | 2 | 3 | 0 |
| Anti-Sikh | 229 | 140 | 11 | 0 | 2 | 11 | 19 | 11 | 3 |
| Anti-Atheism/Agnosticism/etc. | 20 | 10 | 0 | 0 | 0 | 0 | 1 | 0 | 0 |
| Sexual Orientation | 1,365 | 1,074 | 208 | 3 | 1 | 166 | 386 | 411 | 14 |
| Anti-Gay (Male) | 617 | 524 | 68 | 1 | 0 | 106 | 199 | 179 | 3 |
| Anti-Lesbian | 161 | 130 | 30 | 0 | 1 | 15 | 51 | 64 | 0 |
| Anti-Lesbian, Gay, Bisexual, or Transgender (Mixed Group) | 530 | 384 | 93 | 2 | 0 | 43 | 117 | 149 | 9 |
| Anti-Heterosexual | 15 | 10 | 3 | 0 | 0 | 1 | 2 | 3 | 2 |
| Anti-Bisexual | 42 | 26 | 14 | 0 | 0 | 1 | 17 | 16 | 0 |
| Disability | 153 | 109 | 23 | 0 | 0 | 10 | 42 | 24 | 7 |
| Anti-Physical | 54 | 42 | 6 | 0 | 0 | 2 | 18 | 9 | 0 |
| Anti-Mental | 99 | 67 | 17 | 0 | 0 | 8 | 24 | 15 | 7 |
| Gender | 88 | 70 | 9 | 0 | 2 | 6 | 22 | 25 | 2 |
| Anti-Male | 20 | 11 | 6 | 0 | 0 | 0 | 10 | 2 | 0 |
| Anti-Female | 68 | 59 | 3 | 0 | 2 | 6 | 12 | 23 | 2 |
| Gender Identity | 312 | 217 | 63 | 1 | 2 | 40 | 96 | 64 | 8 |
| Anti-Transgender | 205 | 148 | 38 | 1 | 1 | 26 | 62 | 53 | 5 |
| Anti-Gender Non-Conforming | 107 | 69 | 25 | 0 | 1 | 14 | 34 | 11 | 3 |
| **Multiple-Bias Incidents[4]** | 271 | 206 | 27 | 2 | 0 | 20 | 58 | 94 | 0 |

## Table 88. Victims, Offense Type, by Bias Motivation, 2021—Continued

(Number.)

| Bias motivation | Crimes against property | | | | | | | Crimes against society[3] |
|---|---|---|---|---|---|---|---|---|
| | Robbery | Burglary | Larceny-theft | Motor vehicle theft | Arson | Destruction/ damage/ vandalism | Other[3] | |
| **Total** | 123 | 148 | 507 | 51 | 63 | 1,914 | 151 | 286 |
| **Single-Bias Incidents** | 122 | 143 | 502 | 51 | 61 | 1,833 | 151 | 283 |
| Race/Ethnicity/Ancestry | 86 | 90 | 235 | 29 | 12 | 1,118 | 72 | 171 |
| Anti-White | 20 | 29 | 120 | 16 | 3 | 125 | 31 | 63 |
| Anti-Black or African American | 17 | 21 | 48 | 3 | 5 | 650 | 22 | 57 |
| Anti-American Indian or Alaska Native | 0 | 5 | 20 | 6 | 0 | 16 | 6 | 21 |
| Anti-Asian | 14 | 14 | 8 | 1 | 1 | 65 | 1 | 3 |
| Anti-Native Hawaiian or Other Pacific Islander | 0 | 1 | 9 | 1 | 0 | 0 | 2 | 7 |
| Anti-Multiple Races, Group | 1 | 1 | 4 | 1 | 0 | 105 | 0 | 6 |
| Anti-Arab | 0 | 1 | 4 | 0 | 1 | 10 | 1 | 1 |
| Anti-Hispanic or Latino | 27 | 13 | 9 | 0 | 2 | 72 | 1 | 11 |
| Anti-Other Race/Ethnicity/Ancestry | 7 | 5 | 13 | 1 | 0 | 75 | 8 | 2 |
| Religion | 6 | 32 | 140 | 13 | 24 | 410 | 46 | 76 |
| Anti-Jewish | 5 | 7 | 10 | 0 | 2 | 204 | 3 | 3 |
| Anti-Catholic | 0 | 1 | 3 | 0 | 0 | 38 | 4 | 5 |
| Anti-Protestant | 0 | 4 | 11 | 1 | 0 | 16 | 1 | 0 |
| Anti-Islamic (Muslim) | 0 | 1 | 2 | 0 | 13 | 26 | 1 | 2 |
| Anti-Other Religion | 0 | 0 | 12 | 0 | 1 | 24 | 0 | 2 |
| Anti-Multiple Religions, Group | 0 | 1 | 2 | 0 | 2 | 12 | 1 | 5 |
| Anti-Mormon | 1 | 1 | 1 | 0 | 3 | 8 | 2 | 1 |
| Anti-Jehovah's Witness | 0 | 1 | 3 | 0 | 0 | 1 | 0 | 1 |
| Anti-Eastern Orthodox (Russian, Greek, Other) | 0 | 4 | 8 | 2 | 1 | 13 | 3 | 12 |
| Anti-Other Christian | 0 | 1 | 5 | 1 | 2 | 17 | 0 | 2 |
| Anti-Buddhist | 0 | 0 | 9 | 0 | 0 | 6 | 3 | 2 |
| Anti-Hindu | 0 | 0 | 3 | 0 | 0 | 3 | 0 | 0 |
| Anti-Sikh | 0 | 9 | 65 | 9 | 0 | 32 | 28 | 40 |
| Anti-Atheism/Agnosticism/etc. | 0 | 2 | 6 | 0 | 0 | 10 | 0 | 1 |
| Sexual Orientation | 24 | 9 | 74 | 3 | 25 | 228 | 10 | 11 |
| Anti-Gay (Male) | 16 | 2 | 17 | 1 | 4 | 77 | 4 | 8 |
| Anti-Lesbian | 0 | 1 | 5 | 1 | 1 | 22 | 0 | 0 |
| Anti-Lesbian, Gay, Bisexual, or Transgender (Mixed Group) | 8 | 5 | 48 | 0 | 20 | 125 | 2 | 2 |
| Anti-Heterosexual | 0 | 0 | 2 | 1 | 0 | 1 | 3 | 0 |
| Anti-Bisexual | 0 | 1 | 2 | 0 | 0 | 3 | 1 | 1 |
| Disability | 2 | 5 | 23 | 3 | 0 | 17 | 11 | 9 |
| Anti-Physical | 2 | 2 | 8 | 1 | 0 | 7 | 1 | 4 |
| Anti-Mental | 0 | 3 | 15 | 2 | 0 | 10 | 10 | 5 |
| Gender | 0 | 4 | 4 | 0 | 0 | 14 | 6 | 3 |
| Anti-Male | 0 | 1 | 1 | 0 | 0 | 4 | 0 | 2 |
| Anti-Female | 0 | 3 | 3 | 0 | 0 | 10 | 6 | 1 |
| Gender Identity | 4 | 3 | 26 | 3 | 0 | 46 | 6 | 13 |
| Anti-Transgender | 2 | 1 | 13 | 2 | 0 | 32 | 2 | 5 |
| Anti-Gender Non-Conforming | 2 | 2 | 13 | 1 | 0 | 14 | 4 | 8 |
| **Multiple-Bias Incidents[4]** | 1 | 5 | 5 | 0 | 2 | 81 | 0 | 3 |

NOTE: The aggregate of adult and juvenile individual victims does not equal the total number of victims because total victims include individuals, businesses/financial institutions, government entities, religious organizations, and society/public as a whole. In addition, the aggregate of adult and juvenile individual victims does not equal the aggregate of victims of crimes against persons because not all law enforcement agencies report the ages of individual victims.
1 The term victim may refer to an individual, business/financial institution, government entity, religious organization, or society/public as a whole.  2 The figures shown are individual victims only.  3 The figures shown include additional offenses collected in the National Incident-Based Reporting System.  4 A multiple-bias incident is an incident in which one or more offense types are motivated by two or more biases.

## Table 89. Incidents, Victim Type, by Bias Motivation, 2021

(Number.)

| Bias motivation | Total incidents | Victim type | | | | | |
|---|---|---|---|---|---|---|---|
| | | Individual | Business/ financial institution | Government | Religious organization | Society/ public[1] | Other/ unknown/ multiple |
| **Total** | 7,262 | 5,973 | 479 | 244 | 107 | 242 | 217 |
| **Single-Bias Incidents** | 7,074 | 5,837 | 459 | 229 | 104 | 241 | 204 |
| Race/Ethnicity/Ancestry | 4,470 | 3,790 | 256 | 146 | 12 | 135 | 131 |
| Religion | 1,005 | 612 | 130 | 59 | 86 | 73 | 45 |
| Sexual Orientation | 1,127 | 1,033 | 42 | 18 | 6 | 10 | 18 |
| Disability | 134 | 113 | 10 | 2 | 0 | 9 | 0 |
| Gender | 72 | 61 | 5 | 0 | 0 | 1 | 5 |
| Gender Identity | 266 | 228 | 16 | 4 | 0 | 13 | 5 |
| **Multiple-Bias Incidents[2]** | 188 | 136 | 20 | 15 | 3 | 1 | 13 |

1 The victim type society/public is collected only in the National Incident-Based Reporting System.   2 A multiple-bias incident is an incident in which one or more offense types are motivated by two or more biases.

## Table 90. Known Offenders,[1] by Known Offender's Race, Ethnicity, and Age, 2021

(Number.)

| Race/ethnicity/age | Total |
|---|---|
| **Race** | 6,312 |
| White | 3,541 |
| Black or African American | 1,345 |
| American Indian or Alaska Native | 85 |
| Asian | 63 |
| Native Hawaiian or Other Pacific Islander | 27 |
| Group of multiple races[2] | 400 |
| Unknown race | 851 |
| | |
| **Ethnicity[3]** | 4,884 |
| Hispanic or Latino | 372 |
| Not Hispanic or Latino | 2,704 |
| Group of multiple ethnicities[4] | 437 |
| Unknown ethnicity | 1,371 |
| | |
| **Age[3]** | 5,757 |
| Total known offenders 18 and over | 4,736 |
| Total known offenders under 18 | 1,021 |

1 The term known offender does not imply the suspect's identity is known; rather, the term indicates some aspect of the suspect was identified, thus distinguishing the suspect from an unknown offender.   2 The term group of multiple races is used to describe a group of offenders of varying races.   3 The total number of known offenders by age and the total number of known offenders by ethnicity do not equal the total number of known offenders by race because not all law enforcement agencies report the age and/or ethnicity of the known offenders.   4 The term group of multiple ethnicities is used to describe a group of offenders of varying ethnicities.

# Table 91. Incidents, Bias Motivation, by Location, 2021

(Number.)

| Location | Total incidents | Bias motivation | | | | | | Multiple-bias incidents[1] |
|---|---|---|---|---|---|---|---|---|
| | | Race/ethnicity/ ancestry | Religion | Sexual orientation | Disability | Gender | Gender identity | |
| Total | 7,262 | 4,470 | 1,005 | 1,127 | 134 | 72 | 266 | 188 |
| Abandoned/condemned structure | 9 | 7 | 2 | 0 | 0 | 0 | 0 | 0 |
| Air/bus/train terminal | 85 | 53 | 7 | 19 | 0 | 0 | 5 | 1 |
| Amusement park | 5 | 4 | 0 | 0 | 0 | 0 | 1 | 0 |
| Arena/stadium/fairgrounds/coliseum | 9 | 7 | 0 | 1 | 1 | 0 | 0 | 0 |
| ATM separate from bank | 1 | 1 | 0 | 0 | 0 | 0 | 0 | 0 |
| Auto dealership new/used | 13 | 8 | 1 | 3 | 1 | 0 | 0 | 0 |
| Bank/savings and loan | 20 | 11 | 2 | 3 | 1 | 1 | 0 | 2 |
| Bar/nightclub | 116 | 62 | 5 | 40 | 1 | 0 | 7 | 1 |
| Camp/campground | 11 | 4 | 1 | 4 | 0 | 1 | 1 | 0 |
| Church/synagogue/temple/mosque | 189 | 25 | 144 | 13 | 0 | 0 | 1 | 6 |
| Commercial office building | 163 | 106 | 19 | 19 | 0 | 5 | 6 | 8 |
| Community center | 20 | 10 | 5 | 5 | 0 | 0 | 0 | 0 |
| Construction site | 19 | 9 | 7 | 2 | 0 | 0 | 0 | 1 |
| Convenience store | 152 | 111 | 16 | 12 | 1 | 1 | 7 | 4 |
| Cyberspace | 107 | 60 | 17 | 18 | 1 | 2 | 6 | 3 |
| Daycare facility | 3 | 2 | 1 | 0 | 0 | 0 | 0 | 0 |
| Department/discount store | 87 | 58 | 16 | 6 | 2 | 0 | 1 | 4 |
| Dock/wharf/freight/modal terminal | 11 | 9 | 0 | 1 | 0 | 0 | 0 | 1 |
| Drug store/doctor's office/hospital | 94 | 74 | 7 | 6 | 1 | 2 | 3 | 1 |
| Farm facility | 4 | 2 | 0 | 0 | 0 | 1 | 0 | 1 |
| Field/woods | 43 | 30 | 5 | 3 | 0 | 0 | 4 | 1 |
| Gambling facility/casino/race track | 19 | 13 | 0 | 5 | 1 | 0 | 0 | 0 |
| Government/public building | 118 | 77 | 14 | 15 | 2 | 1 | 4 | 5 |
| Grocery/supermarket | 100 | 70 | 17 | 10 | 0 | 0 | 3 | 0 |
| Highway/road/alley/street/sidewalk | 1,224 | 835 | 135 | 159 | 17 | 9 | 44 | 25 |
| Hotel/motel/etc. | 90 | 62 | 7 | 14 | 1 | 3 | 3 | 0 |
| Industrial site | 14 | 7 | 3 | 2 | 1 | 0 | 1 | 0 |
| Jail/prison/penitentiary/corrections facility | 101 | 77 | 3 | 15 | 3 | 2 | 1 | 0 |
| Lake/waterway/beach | 13 | 11 | 1 | 1 | 0 | 0 | 0 | 0 |
| Liquor store | 12 | 10 | 2 | 0 | 0 | 0 | 0 | 0 |
| Military installation | 1 | 0 | 0 | 0 | 0 | 1 | 0 | 0 |
| Park/playground | 199 | 120 | 28 | 30 | 2 | 2 | 5 | 12 |
| Parking/drop lot/garage | 507 | 329 | 73 | 65 | 5 | 4 | 19 | 12 |
| Rental storage facility | 14 | 8 | 5 | 0 | 1 | 0 | 0 | 0 |
| Residence/home | 2,341 | 1,383 | 291 | 423 | 63 | 26 | 105 | 50 |
| Rest area | 3 | 2 | 0 | 1 | 0 | 0 | 0 | 0 |
| Restaurant | 205 | 136 | 18 | 42 | 0 | 0 | 5 | 4 |
| School/college[2] | 84 | 38 | 25 | 12 | 3 | 0 | 2 | 4 |
| School—college/university | 135 | 74 | 28 | 22 | 2 | 2 | 3 | 4 |
| School—elementary/secondary | 367 | 209 | 34 | 80 | 10 | 1 | 19 | 14 |
| Service/gas station | 84 | 65 | 11 | 4 | 1 | 1 | 0 | 2 |
| Shelter—mission/homeless | 17 | 6 | 1 | 6 | 1 | 0 | 2 | 1 |
| Shopping mall | 21 | 12 | 4 | 2 | 0 | 1 | 1 | 1 |
| Specialty store (TV, fur, etc.) | 99 | 73 | 6 | 15 | 3 | 1 | 1 | 0 |
| Tribal lands | 2 | 1 | 1 | 0 | 0 | 0 | 0 | 0 |
| Other/unknown | 307 | 184 | 42 | 47 | 8 | 4 | 5 | 17 |
| Multiple locations | 24 | 15 | 1 | 2 | 1 | 1 | 1 | 3 |

1 A multiple-bias incident is an incident in which one or more offense types are motivated by two or more biases.   2 The location designation School/college has been retained for agencies that have not updated their records management systems to include the new location designations of School—college/university and School—elementary/secondary, which allow for more specificity in reporting.

## Table 92. Offenses, Offense Type, by Participating State/Federal, 2021

(Number.)

| State | Total offenses | Crimes against persons | | | | | | Crimes against property | | | | | | | Crimes against society[1] |
|---|---|---|---|---|---|---|---|---|---|---|---|---|---|---|---|
| | | Murder and nonnegligent manslaughter | Rape | Aggravated assault | Simple assault | Intimidation | Other[1] | Robbery | Burglary | Larceny-theft | Motor vehicle theft | Arson | Destruction/ damage/ vandalism | Other[1] | |
| **Total** | 8,673 | 9 | 13 | 1,058 | 2,074 | 2,558 | 69 | 104 | 117 | 476 | 51 | 43 | 1,674 | 141 | 286 |
| Alabama | 263 | 0 | 1 | 35 | 60 | 51 | 2 | 1 | 7 | 28 | 10 | 2 | 46 | 10 | 10 |
| Alaska | 14 | 0 | 0 | 4 | 3 | 3 | 0 | 0 | 0 | 1 | 0 | 0 | 3 | 0 | 0 |
| Arizona | 106 | 0 | 0 | 18 | 25 | 21 | 0 | 1 | 2 | 11 | 2 | 0 | 24 | 1 | 1 |
| Arkansas | 47 | 0 | 0 | 11 | 4 | 15 | 1 | 0 | 3 | 5 | 0 | 0 | 3 | 2 | 3 |
| California[2] | 81 | 0 | 0 | 27 | 12 | 15 | 1 | 2 | 1 | 0 | 0 | 0 | 23 | 0 | 0 |
| Colorado | 375 | 0 | 0 | 54 | 89 | 113 | 3 | 7 | 6 | 15 | 1 | 1 | 79 | 5 | 2 |
| Connecticut | 102 | 0 | 0 | 7 | 12 | 39 | 0 | 2 | 0 | 3 | 3 | 1 | 34 | 1 | 0 |
| Delaware | 11 | 0 | 0 | 0 | 1 | 4 | 0 | 0 | 0 | 1 | 0 | 3 | 2 | 0 | 0 |
| District of Columbia[2] | 74 | 0 | 0 | 11 | 37 | 13 | 0 | 2 | 1 | 0 | 0 | 0 | 10 | 0 | 0 |
| Florida[3] | 1 | 0 | 0 | 0 | 1 | 0 | 0 | 0 | 0 | 0 | 0 | 0 | 0 | 0 | 0 |
| Georgia | 287 | 0 | 0 | 32 | 84 | 91 | 3 | 2 | 3 | 10 | 1 | 0 | 48 | 8 | 5 |
| Hawaii | 38 | 0 | 0 | 3 | 11 | 22 | 0 | 1 | 0 | 1 | 0 | 0 | 0 | 0 | 0 |
| Idaho | 62 | 0 | 1 | 9 | 27 | 14 | 0 | 0 | 0 | 3 | 0 | 0 | 5 | 0 | 3 |
| Illinois[2] | 112 | 0 | 0 | 12 | 29 | 37 | 0 | 1 | 1 | 7 | 0 | 0 | 21 | 1 | 3 |
| Indiana | 165 | 0 | 0 | 22 | 21 | 64 | 3 | 3 | 0 | 9 | 1 | 1 | 33 | 3 | 5 |
| Iowa | 117 | 0 | 0 | 7 | 28 | 36 | 2 | 0 | 5 | 14 | 4 | 0 | 12 | 3 | 6 |
| Kansas | 146 | 0 | 0 | 12 | 22 | 31 | 2 | 2 | 3 | 15 | 1 | 2 | 42 | 3 | 11 |
| Kentucky | 178 | 0 | 0 | 8 | 31 | 88 | 4 | 2 | 2 | 2 | 0 | 0 | 37 | 1 | 3 |
| Louisiana | 157 | 0 | 0 | 22 | 32 | 19 | 2 | 2 | 4 | 29 | 1 | 0 | 17 | 3 | 26 |
| Maine | 85 | 0 | 0 | 1 | 13 | 45 | 0 | 0 | 1 | 3 | 0 | 1 | 21 | 0 | 0 |
| Maryland[2] | 99 | 0 | 0 | 9 | 48 | 8 | 1 | 1 | 1 | 2 | 0 | 0 | 27 | 0 | 2 |
| Massachusetts | 489 | 3 | 0 | 56 | 97 | 174 | 1 | 3 | 1 | 8 | 1 | 0 | 140 | 1 | 4 |
| Michigan | 486 | 0 | 2 | 72 | 111 | 184 | 4 | 2 | 5 | 13 | 3 | 1 | 63 | 7 | 19 |
| Minnesota | 301 | 0 | 1 | 40 | 81 | 87 | 6 | 7 | 2 | 4 | 0 | 4 | 64 | 3 | 2 |
| Mississippi | 31 | 0 | 0 | 1 | 8 | 3 | 0 | 0 | 3 | 4 | 1 | 0 | 6 | 3 | 2 |
| Missouri | 238 | 0 | 1 | 39 | 76 | 45 | 1 | 2 | 2 | 10 | 3 | 0 | 50 | 1 | 8 |
| Montana | 18 | 0 | 0 | 2 | 7 | 1 | 0 | 0 | 0 | 2 | 0 | 2 | 4 | 0 | 0 |
| Nebraska | 56 | 0 | 0 | 3 | 13 | 12 | 0 | 0 | 0 | 4 | 0 | 1 | 19 | 1 | 3 |
| Nevada | 265 | 0 | 0 | 34 | 107 | 47 | 2 | 3 | 4 | 21 | 1 | 3 | 37 | 3 | 3 |
| New Hampshire | 36 | 0 | 0 | 1 | 6 | 13 | 0 | 0 | 0 | 0 | 0 | 0 | 16 | 0 | 0 |
| New Jersey[2] | 241 | 0 | 0 | 9 | 33 | 150 | 0 | 0 | 1 | 1 | 0 | 0 | 47 | 0 | 0 |
| New Mexico[2] | 60 | 0 | 0 | 13 | 19 | 6 | 0 | 2 | 0 | 6 | 1 | 1 | 9 | 3 | 0 |
| New York[2] | 71 | 0 | 0 | 4 | 4 | 39 | 1 | 0 | 1 | 3 | 0 | 0 | 17 | 0 | 2 |
| North Carolina | 358 | 0 | 0 | 56 | 65 | 112 | 1 | 4 | 5 | 24 | 2 | 1 | 58 | 10 | 20 |
| North Dakota | 49 | 0 | 0 | 4 | 13 | 22 | 0 | 1 | 0 | 0 | 1 | 0 | 7 | 0 | 1 |
| Ohio | 569 | 0 | 4 | 25 | 136 | 160 | 10 | 4 | 14 | 75 | 3 | 3 | 76 | 21 | 38 |
| Oklahoma | 82 | 0 | 0 | 6 | 20 | 31 | 1 | 2 | 1 | 8 | 2 | 0 | 4 | 4 | 3 |
| Oregon | 315 | 0 | 0 | 41 | 86 | 73 | 0 | 4 | 3 | 7 | 0 | 1 | 94 | 1 | 5 |
| Pennsylvania[2] | 161 | 0 | 0 | 25 | 30 | 56 | 2 | 8 | 3 | 4 | 0 | 2 | 18 | 6 | 7 |
| Rhode Island | 22 | 0 | 0 | 0 | 8 | 2 | 0 | 0 | 0 | 1 | 0 | 0 | 11 | 0 | 0 |
| South Carolina | 122 | 0 | 1 | 11 | 32 | 28 | 1 | 3 | 3 | 9 | 1 | 0 | 19 | 7 | 7 |
| South Dakota | 28 | 0 | 0 | 3 | 10 | 6 | 0 | 0 | 0 | 5 | 1 | 0 | 2 | 0 | 1 |
| Tennessee | 163 | 0 | 0 | 25 | 42 | 38 | 1 | 2 | 2 | 5 | 1 | 0 | 28 | 2 | 17 |
| Texas | 642 | 0 | 1 | 96 | 191 | 142 | 6 | 10 | 12 | 33 | 3 | 2 | 111 | 12 | 23 |
| Utah | 132 | 0 | 0 | 16 | 31 | 10 | 3 | 1 | 2 | 15 | 0 | 1 | 39 | 4 | 10 |
| Vermont | 45 | 0 | 0 | 5 | 12 | 5 | 0 | 0 | 0 | 7 | 0 | 0 | 16 | 0 | 0 |
| Virginia | 125 | 0 | 0 | 11 | 43 | 21 | 1 | 2 | 2 | 3 | 0 | 0 | 39 | 1 | 2 |
| Washington | 698 | 1 | 0 | 89 | 142 | 269 | 1 | 11 | 8 | 22 | 3 | 3 | 137 | 5 | 7 |
| West Virginia | 68 | 0 | 1 | 10 | 16 | 6 | 1 | 1 | 2 | 11 | 0 | 0 | 7 | 2 | 11 |
| Wisconsin | 118 | 0 | 0 | 12 | 27 | 25 | 1 | 0 | 1 | 10 | 0 | 0 | 28 | 3 | 11 |
| Wyoming | 21 | 0 | 0 | 3 | 4 | 10 | 0 | 0 | 0 | 2 | 0 | 0 | 2 | 0 | 0 |
| **Federal** | | | | | | | | | | | | | | | |
| Defense Intelligence Agency | 1 | 0 | 0 | 0 | 0 | 0 | 0 | 0 | 0 | 0 | 0 | 0 | 1 | 0 | 0 |
| Federal Bureau of Investigation | 134 | 5 | 0 | 42 | 13 | 46 | 1 | 3 | 0 | 0 | 0 | 7 | 17 | 0 | 0 |
| Pentagon Force Protection Agency | 2 | 0 | 0 | 0 | 0 | 2 | 0 | 0 | 0 | 0 | 0 | 0 | 0 | 0 | 0 |
| United States Air Force Security Police | 2 | 0 | 0 | 0 | 0 | 1 | 0 | 0 | 0 | 0 | 0 | 0 | 1 | 0 | 0 |
| United States Marine Corps Law Enforcement | 1 | 0 | 0 | 0 | 0 | 1 | 0 | 0 | 0 | 0 | 0 | 0 | 0 | 0 | 0 |
| United States Treasury Inspector General for Tax Administration | 3 | 0 | 0 | 0 | 1 | 2 | 0 | 0 | 0 | 0 | 0 | 0 | 0 | 0 | 0 |

[1]The figures shown include additional offenses collected in the National Incident-Based Reporting System.
[2]Limited data for 2021 were available for California, District of Columbia, Illinois, Maryland, New Jersey, New Mexico, New York, and Pennsylvania.
[3]Data submitted through the Bureau of Indian Affairs.

## Table 93. Agency Hate Crime Reporting, by Participating State and Federal, 2021

(Number.)

| State/federal | Number of participating agencies | Population covered | Agencies submitting incident reports | Total number of incidents reported |
|---|---|---|---|---|
| **Total** | 11,834 | 215,058,917 | 2,337 | 7,262 |
| Alabama | 356 | 3,734,077 | 77 | 242 |
| Alaska | 30 | 402,557 | 6 | 9 |
| Arizona | 79 | 3,949,562 | 26 | 93 |
| Arkansas | 285 | 2,916,168 | 23 | 42 |
| California[1] | 15 | 2,861,998 | 10 | 73 |
| Colorado | 235 | 5,766,585 | 68 | 285 |
| Connecticut | 107 | 3,605,597 | 44 | 89 |
| Delaware | 62 | 1,003,384 | 6 | 9 |
| District of Columbia | 2 | 670,050 | 2 | 64 |
| Florida[2] | 2 | | 1 | 1 |
| Georgia | 447 | 8,709,490 | 76 | 238 |
| Hawaii | 2 | 1,059,012 | 2 | 34 |
| Idaho | 110 | 1,889,225 | 21 | 42 |
| Illinois[1] | 328 | 7,845,636 | 53 | 91 |
| Indiana | 190 | 5,229,123 | 50 | 132 |
| Iowa | 205 | 2,927,835 | 43 | 101 |
| Kansas | 334 | 2,614,220 | 60 | 118 |
| Kentucky | 426 | 4,505,498 | 63 | 130 |
| Louisiana | 136 | 3,321,430 | 34 | 127 |
| Maine | 129 | 1,366,119 | 33 | 75 |
| Maryland[1] | 18 | 2,902,491 | 8 | 82 |
| Massachusetts | 376 | 6,937,375 | 101 | 407 |
| Michigan | 618 | 9,785,364 | 192 | 410 |
| Minnesota | 411 | 5,699,338 | 73 | 241 |
| Mississippi | 137 | 1,673,199 | 17 | 31 |
| Missouri | 477 | 5,885,677 | 85 | 194 |
| Montana | 106 | 1,098,323 | 11 | 17 |
| Nebraska | 267 | 1,471,365 | 20 | 44 |
| Nevada | 56 | 3,130,107 | 17 | 218 |
| New Hampshire | 208 | 1,355,329 | 21 | 34 |
| New Jersey[1] | 177 | 3,844,336 | 54 | 214 |
| New Mexico[1] | 42 | 1,285,483 | 7 | 48 |
| New York[1] | 124 | 3,719,239 | 33 | 61 |
| North Carolina | 387 | 9,859,219 | 100 | 273 |
| North Dakota | 112 | 774,948 | 11 | 37 |
| Ohio | 596 | 10,536,226 | 144 | 498 |
| Oklahoma | 452 | 3,965,482 | 45 | 73 |
| Oregon | 208 | 4,093,590 | 57 | 267 |
| Pennsylvania[1] | 40 | 2,173,050 | 8 | 151 |
| Rhode Island | 47 | 1,094,546 | 14 | 19 |
| South Carolina | 411 | 5,112,587 | 53 | 106 |
| South Dakota | 110 | 824,054 | 18 | 26 |
| Tennessee | 437 | 6,968,993 | 57 | 138 |
| Texas | 1,007 | 28,865,719 | 188 | 542 |
| Utah | 126 | 3,188,815 | 37 | 109 |
| Vermont | 88 | 645,570 | 25 | 39 |
| Virginia | 411 | 8,640,726 | 43 | 108 |
| Washington | 248 | 7,700,987 | 91 | 576 |
| West Virginia | 247 | 1,575,083 | 28 | 56 |
| Wisconsin | 323 | 5,423,821 | 64 | 111 |
| Wyoming | 47 | 450,309 | 11 | 18 |
| **Federal[3]** | | | | |
| Board of Governors of the Federal Reserve System and the Consumer Financial Protection Bureau, Office of Inspector General | 1 | | 0 | 0 |
| Central Intelligence Agency, Security Protective Service | 1 | | 0 | 0 |
| Commodity Futures Trading Commission, Office of Inspector General | 1 | | 0 | 0 |
| Corporation for National and Community Service, Office of Inspector General | 1 | | 0 | 0 |
| Defense Intelligence Agency | 1 | | 1 | 1 |
| Department of Veterans Affairs, Office of Inspector General | 1 | | 0 | 0 |
| Drug Enforcement Administration, Wilmington Resident Office | 1 | | 0 | 0 |
| Export-Import Bank of the United States, Office of Inspector General | 1 | | 0 | 0 |
| Federal Bureau of Investigation | 1 | | 1 | 110 |
| Federal Communications Commission, Office of Inspector General | 1 | | 0 | 0 |
| Federal Emergency Management Agency | 1 | | 0 | 0 |
| Federal Housing Finance Agency, Office of Inspector General | 1 | | 0 | 0 |
| Library of Congress, Office of Inspector General | 1 | | 0 | 0 |

## Table 93. Agency Hate Crime Reporting, by Participating State and Federal, 2021—Continued

(Number.)

| State/federal | Number of participating agencies | Population covered | Agencies submitting incident reports | Total number of incidents reported |
|---|---|---|---|---|
| National Institute of Health | 1 | | 0 | 0 |
| National Security Agency Police | 1 | | 0 | 0 |
| | | | | |
| Peace Corps, Office of Inspector General | 1 | | 0 | 0 |
| Pension Benefit Guaranty Corporation, Office of Inspector General | 1 | | 0 | 0 |
| Pentagon Force Protection Agency | 1 | | 1 | 2 |
| Smithsonian Institution, Office of Inspector General | 1 | | 0 | 0 |
| Tennessee Valley Authority, Office of Inspector General | 1 | | 0 | 0 |
| | | | | |
| United States Agency for International Development, Office of Inspector General | 1 | | 0 | 0 |
| United States Air Force, Office of Special Investigations | 1 | | 0 | 0 |
| United States Air Force Security Police | 1 | | 1 | 2 |
| United States Department of Agriculture, Office of Inspector General | 1 | | 0 | 0 |
| United States Department of Defense, Office of Inspector General | 1 | | 0 | 0 |
| | | | | |
| United States Department of Education, Office of Inspector General | 1 | | 0 | 0 |
| United States Department of Housing and Urban Development, Office of Inspector General | 1 | | 0 | 0 |
| United States Department of Justice, Office of Inspector General | 1 | | 0 | 0 |
| United States Department of State, Office of Inspector General | 1 | | 0 | 0 |
| United States Department of Transportation, Office of Inspector General | 1 | | 0 | 0 |
| | | | | |
| United States Environmental Protection Agency, Office of Inspector General | 1 | | 0 | 0 |
| United States Federal Deposit Insurance Corporation, Office of Inspector General | 1 | | 0 | 0 |
| United States General Services Administration, Office of Inspector General | 1 | | 0 | 0 |
| United States Marine Corps Law Enforcement | 1 | | 1 | 1 |
| United States National Archives and Records Administration, Office of Inspector General | 1 | | 0 | 0 |
| | | | | |
| United States Navy Law Enforcement | 1 | | 0 | 0 |
| United States Nuclear Regulatory Commission, Office of Inspector General | 1 | | 0 | 0 |
| United States Office of Personnel Management, Office of the Inspector General | 1 | | 0 | 0 |
| United States Securities and Exchange Commission, Office of Inspector General | 1 | | 0 | 0 |
| United States Treasury Inspector General for Tax Administration | 1 | | 1 | 3 |

1 Limited data for 2021 were available for California, Illinois, Maryland, New Jersey, New Mexico, New York, and Pennsylvania.    2 Data submitted through the Bureau of Indian Affairs. No population is attributed to tribal agencies.    3 Population estimates are not attributed to the federal agencies.

# Table 94. Hate Crime Incidents Per Bias Motivation and Quarter, by Selected State and  Agency and Federal, 2021

(Number.)

| State/agency | Number of incidents per bias motivation | | | | | | Number of incidents per quarter | | | | Population[1] |
|---|---|---|---|---|---|---|---|---|---|---|---|
| | Race/ Ethnicity/ Ancestry | Religion | Sexual orientation | Disability | Gender | Gender Identity | 1st quarter | 2nd quarter | 3rd quarter | 4th quarter | |
| **ALABAMA** | 137 | 72 | 32 | 5 | 5 | 4 | | | | | |
| **Cities** | 88 | 62 | 29 | 2 | 5 | 2 | | | | | |
| Abbeville | 1 | 0 | 0 | 0 | 0 | 0 | 0 | 1 | 0 | 0 | 2,539 |
| Alexander City | 1 | 0 | 1 | 0 | 0 | 0 | 0 | 0 | 1 | 1 | 14,066 |
| Altoona | 1 | 0 | 0 | 0 | 0 | 0 | 0 | 1 | 0 | 0 | 913 |
| Andalusia[2] | 4 | 1 | 0 | 0 | 0 | 0 | 0 | 2 | 1 | 1 | 8,643 |
| Anniston | 1 | 0 | 1 | 0 | 0 | 0 | 1 | 0 | 0 | 1 | 20,913 |
| Arab | 1 | 0 | 0 | 0 | 0 | 0 | 0 | 1 | 0 | 0 | 8,437 |
| Bay Minette | 0 | 0 | 1 | 0 | 0 | 0 | 0 | 0 | 0 | 1 | 9,647 |
| Birmingham[2] | 3 | 38 | 4 | 1 | 3 | 1 | 12 | 17 | 11 | 8 | 206,476 |
| Bridgeport | 1 | 0 | 0 | 0 | 0 | 0 | 0 | 0 | 1 | 0 | 2,258 |
| Camden | 1 | 0 | 0 | 0 | 0 | 0 | | 0 | 1 | 0 | 1,667 |
| Centre | 1 | 0 | 0 | 0 | 0 | 0 | 0 | 0 | 0 | 0 | 3,624 |
| Cullman | 2 | 0 | 0 | 0 | 0 | 0 | 1 | 0 | 0 | 1 | 16,696 |
| Daleville | 1 | 0 | 0 | 0 | 0 | 0 | 0 | 1 | 0 | 0 | 5,075 |
| Daphne | 0 | 1 | 1 | 0 | 0 | 0 | 0 | 2 | 0 | 0 | 28,387 |
| Decatur | 1 | 0 | 0 | 0 | 0 | 0 | 1 | | | | 54,240 |
| Enterprise[2] | 4 | 0 | 0 | 0 | 0 | 0 | 0 | 0 | 1 | 2 | 29,240 |
| Eufaula | 2 | 0 | 0 | 0 | 0 | 0 | 1 | 0 | 0 | 1 | 11,489 |
| Fairhope | 0 | 1 | 0 | 0 | 0 | 0 | 0 | 0 | 0 | 1 | 24,467 |
| Florala | 1 | 0 | 0 | 0 | 0 | 0 | 0 | 0 | 1 | 0 | 1,882 |
| Florence | 4 | 2 | 2 | 0 | 0 | 0 | 2 | 2 | 3 | 1 | 41,325 |
| Foley | 1 | 0 | 0 | 0 | 0 | 0 | 0 | 1 | 0 | 0 | 22,166 |
| Fultondale | 0 | 1 | 0 | 0 | 0 | 0 | 0 | 0 | 1 | 0 | 9,365 |
| Gadsden | 2 | 0 | 0 | 0 | 0 | 0 | 0 | 2 | 0 | 0 | 34,613 |
| Gulf Shores[2] | 8 | 0 | 1 | 0 | 0 | 1 | 1 | 4 | 2 | 1 | 13,421 |
| Hoover | 0 | 0 | 1 | 0 | 0 | 0 | 0 | 0 | 1 | | 86,514 |
| Jasper | 1 | 0 | 0 | 0 | 0 | 0 | 0 | 0 | 1 | 0 | 13,177 |
| Lanett | 1 | 0 | 0 | 0 | 0 | 0 | 0 | 1 | 0 | 0 | 6,014 |
| Level Plains | 1 | 0 | 0 | 0 | 0 | 0 | 0 | 1 | 0 | 0 | 1,944 |
| Lincoln | 0 | 1 | 0 | 0 | 0 | 0 | 0 | 1 | 0 | 0 | 7,058 |
| Luverne | 1 | 0 | 0 | 0 | 0 | 0 | 0 | 0 | 1 | 0 | 2,694 |
| Midfield[2] | 4 | 2 | 0 | 0 | 0 | 0 | 0 | 0 | 1 | 1 | 4,918 |
| Millbrook | 1 | 0 | 0 | 0 | 0 | 0 | 0 | 1 | 0 | 0 | 16,226 |
| Mobile | 8 | 0 | 14 | 0 | 0 | 0 | 6 | 5 | 4 | 7 | 242,894 |
| Moody | 1 | 0 | 0 | 0 | 0 | 0 | 0 | 0 | 1 | 0 | 13,458 |
| Muscle Shoals | 0 | 1 | 0 | 0 | 0 | 0 | 0 | 0 | 1 | 0 | 15,051 |
| Newton | 1 | 0 | 0 | 0 | 0 | 0 | 0 | 0 | 0 | 1 | 1,446 |
| Northport | 0 | 0 | 1 | 0 | 0 | 0 | 0 | 0 | 0 | 1 | 26,309 |
| Opelika | 3 | 1 | 0 | 0 | 0 | 0 | 1 | 1 | 1 | 1 | 31,644 |
| Opp | 2 | 0 | 0 | 0 | 0 | 0 | 1 | 1 | 0 | 0 | 6,279 |
| Ozark | 0 | 3 | 0 | 0 | 0 | 0 | 0 | 0 | 0 | 3 | 14,065 |
| Parrish | 1 | 0 | 0 | 0 | 0 | 0 | 0 | 0 | 0 | 1 | 923 |
| Pelham | 0 | 1 | 0 | 0 | 0 | 0 | 0 | 0 | 1 | 0 | 24,516 |
| Phenix City | 5 | 0 | 0 | 0 | 0 | 0 | 2 | 1 | 0 | 2 | 36,744 |
| Pleasant Grove | 1 | 0 | 0 | 0 | 0 | 0 | 0 | 1 | 0 | 0 | 9,528 |
| Priceville | 1 | 0 | 0 | 0 | 0 | 0 | 1 | 0 | 0 | 0 | 4,137 |
| Prichard | 2 | 0 | 0 | 1 | 0 | 0 | 2 | 0 | 1 | 0 | 21,170 |
| Rainbow City | 1 | 0 | 0 | 0 | 0 | 0 | 1 | 0 | 0 | 0 | 9,602 |
| Red Bay | 1 | 0 | 0 | 0 | 0 | 0 | 0 | 1 | 0 | 0 | 3,103 |
| Riverside | 2 | 0 | 0 | 0 | 0 | 0 | 0 | 1 | 1 | 0 | 2,393 |
| Saraland | 0 | 0 | 1 | 0 | 0 | 0 | 0 | 1 | 0 | 0 | 14,764 |
| Selma | 1 | 0 | 0 | 0 | 0 | 0 | 0 | 0 | 1 | 0 | 16,309 |
| Stevenson | 1 | 0 | 0 | 0 | 0 | 0 | 0 | 0 | 1 | 0 | 1,886 |
| Sylacauga | 1 | 1 | 0 | 0 | 1 | 0 | 0 | 1 | 0 | 2 | 11,859 |
| Troy | 1 | 4 | 0 | 0 | 0 | 0 | 0 | 0 | 1 | 4 | 18,822 |
| Trussville | 0 | 1 | 1 | 0 | 0 | 0 | 0 | 0 | 2 | 0 | 23,379 |
| Tuscaloosa | 0 | 2 | 0 | 0 | 1 | 0 | | | 0 | 3 | 104,151 |
| Valley Head | 1 | 0 | 0 | 0 | 0 | 0 | 1 | 0 | 0 | 0 | 562 |
| Vernon | 1 | 0 | 0 | 0 | 0 | 0 | 1 | 0 | 0 | 0 | 1,828 |
| Vestavia Hills | 2 | 1 | 0 | 0 | 0 | 0 | 0 | 1 | 1 | 1 | 34,369 |
| Woodstock | 1 | 0 | 0 | 0 | 0 | 0 | 1 | 0 | 0 | 0 | 1,653 |
| **Universities and Colleges** | 1 | 1 | 0 | 0 | 0 | 0 | | | | | |
| University of Alabama, Birmingham | 1 | 1 | 0 | 0 | 0 | 0 | 0 | 1 | 0 | 1 | 25,843 |
| **Metropolitan Counties** | 28 | 8 | 3 | 2 | 0 | 1 | | | | | |
| Blount | 0 | 1 | 0 | 0 | 0 | 0 | 0 | 1 | 0 | 0 | |
| Elmore | 1 | 2 | 0 | 0 | 0 | 0 | 0 | 0 | 2 | 1 | |
| Jefferson[2] | 20 | 4 | 3 | 0 | 0 | 0 | 2 | 9 | 10 | 5 | |
| Lee | 0 | 1 | 0 | 0 | 0 | 0 | 0 | 1 | 0 | 0 | |
| Lowndes | 1 | 0 | 0 | 0 | 0 | 0 | 0 | 0 | 1 | 0 | |
| Mobile | 5 | 0 | 0 | 0 | 0 | 1 | 1 | 1 | 0 | 4 | |
| St. Clair[2] | 0 | 0 | 0 | 2 | 0 | 0 | 0 | 0 | 0 | 1 | |
| Washington | 1 | 0 | 0 | 0 | 0 | 0 | 0 | 0 | 1 | 0 | |
| **Nonmetropolitan Counties** | 18 | 1 | 0 | 1 | 0 | 1 | | | | | |
| Cherokee | 1 | 0 | 0 | 0 | 0 | 0 | 0 | 1 | 0 | 0 | |
| Coffee | 1 | 0 | 0 | 0 | 0 | 0 | 0 | 0 | 1 | 0 | |

## Table 94. Hate Crime Incidents Per Bias Motivation and Quarter, by Selected State and Agency and Federal, 2021—Continued

(Number.)

| State/agency | Number of incidents per bias motivation | | | | | | Number of incidents per quarter | | | | Population[1] |
|---|---|---|---|---|---|---|---|---|---|---|---|
| | Race/ Ethnicity/ Ancestry | Religion | Sexual orientation | Disability | Gender | Gender Identity | 1st quarter | 2nd quarter | 3rd quarter | 4th quarter | |
| Cullman | 4 | 1 | 0 | 1 | 0 | 1 | 2 | 1 | 1 | 3 | |
| Dallas | 6 | 0 | 0 | 0 | 0 | 0 | 0 | 1 | 2 | 3 | |
| Fayette | 1 | 0 | 0 | 0 | 0 | 0 | 0 | 0 | 0 | 1 | |
| Franklin | 2 | 0 | 0 | 0 | 0 | 0 | 0 | 0 | 1 | 1 | |
| Marshall[2] | 3 | 0 | 0 | 0 | 0 | 0 | 0 | 0 | 2 | 0 | |
| **Other Agencies** | 2 | 0 | 0 | 0 | 0 | 0 | | | | | |
| Mobile Regional Airport | 2 | 0 | 0 | 0 | 0 | 0 | 2 | 0 | 0 | 0 | |
| **ALASKA** | 5 | 0 | 4 | 0 | 2 | 1 | | | | | |
| **Cities** | 2 | 0 | 4 | 0 | 2 | 1 | | | | | |
| Nome[2] | 0 | 0 | 2 | 0 | 0 | 0 | 0 | 0 | 1 | 0 | 3,871 |
| Palmer | 0 | 0 | 0 | 0 | 0 | 1 | 0 | 0 | 0 | 1 | 7,972 |
| Petersburg | 1 | 0 | 0 | 0 | 0 | 0 | 0 | 1 | 0 | 0 | 3,302 |
| Seward | 0 | 0 | 1 | 0 | 0 | 0 | 0 | 0 | 1 | 0 | 2,950 |
| Wasilla[2] | 1 | 0 | 1 | 0 | 2 | 0 | 0 | 0 | 2 | 0 | 11,485 |
| **State Police Agencies** | 3 | 0 | 0 | 0 | 0 | 0 | | | | | |
| Alaska State Troopers | 3 | 0 | 0 | 0 | 0 | 0 | 0 | 0 | 3 | 0 | |
| **ARIZONA** | 61 | 15 | 16 | 0 | 0 | 4 | | | | | |
| **Cities** | 31 | 10 | 9 | 0 | 0 | 3 | | | | | |
| Chandler | 3 | 0 | 0 | 0 | 0 | 0 | 0 | 3 | 0 | 0 | 281,162 |
| Clarkdale | 2 | 0 | 0 | 0 | 0 | 0 | 0 | 2 | 0 | 0 | 4,577 |
| Flagstaff | 0 | 1 | 0 | 0 | 0 | 0 | 1 | | | | 74,778 |
| Goodyear | 0 | 1 | 1 | 0 | 0 | 0 | 1 | 1 | 0 | | 97,081 |
| Maricopa | 1 | 1 | 0 | 0 | 0 | 0 | 1 | 0 | 0 | 1 | 55,768 |
| Mesa[2] | 17 | 0 | 0 | 0 | 0 | 1 | 3 | 4 | 5 | 4 | 513,713 |
| Payson[2] | 0 | 0 | 2 | 0 | 0 | 0 | 0 | 0 | 0 | 1 | 16,011 |
| Prescott | 1 | 1 | 1 | 0 | 0 | 0 | 3 | 0 | 0 | 0 | 45,391 |
| Prescott Valley | 0 | 0 | 1 | 0 | 0 | 1 | 2 | 0 | 0 | 0 | 48,921 |
| Quartzsite | 0 | 0 | 0 | 0 | 0 | 1 | 0 | 1 | 0 | 0 | 3,827 |
| Sahuarita | 0 | 1 | 0 | 0 | 0 | 0 | 1 | 0 | 0 | 0 | 33,005 |
| Show Low | 1 | 0 | 1 | 0 | 0 | 0 | 0 | 1 | 1 | 0 | 11,670 |
| Sierra Vista | 4 | 0 | 0 | 0 | 0 | 0 | 1 | 0 | 1 | 2 | 43,814 |
| Somerton | 0 | 2 | 0 | 0 | 0 | 0 | 0 | 1 | 1 | 0 | 16,976 |
| Surprise | 0 | 1 | 1 | 0 | 0 | 0 | 0 | 1 | 0 | 1 | 145,832 |
| Williams | 0 | 0 | 1 | 0 | 0 | 0 | 0 | 0 | 1 | 0 | 3,349 |
| Yuma | 2 | 2 | 1 | 0 | 0 | 0 | 1 | 1 | 1 | 2 | 100,710 |
| **Universities and Colleges** | 10 | 0 | 0 | 0 | 0 | 0 | | | | | |
| Maricopa Community College[3] | 9 | 0 | 0 | 0 | 0 | 0 | 8 | 1 | 0 | 0 | |
| Pima Community College | 1 | 0 | 0 | 0 | 0 | 0 | 0 | 0 | 1 | 0 | 36,384 |
| **Metropolitan Counties** | 20 | 4 | 6 | 0 | 0 | 1 | | | | | |
| Cochise | 0 | 0 | 1 | 0 | 0 | 0 | 0 | 0 | 0 | 1 | |
| Mohave | 1 | 1 | 0 | 0 | 0 | 0 | 1 | 1 | 0 | 0 | |
| Pima | 14 | 2 | 4 | 0 | 0 | 0 | 7 | 4 | 7 | 2 | |
| Pinal | 1 | 0 | 0 | 0 | 0 | 0 | 0 | 0 | 1 | 0 | |
| Yavapai | 4 | 1 | 1 | 0 | 0 | 1 | 0 | 3 | 4 | 0 | |
| **Nonmetropolitan Counties** | 0 | 0 | 1 | 0 | 0 | 0 | | | | | |
| La Paz | 0 | 0 | 1 | 0 | 0 | 0 | 0 | 0 | 1 | 0 | |
| **Tribal Agencies** | 0 | 1 | 0 | 0 | 0 | 0 | | | | | |
| Gila River Indian Community | 0 | 1 | 0 | 0 | 0 | 0 | 1 | 0 | 0 | 0 | |
| **ARKANSAS** | 31 | 3 | 9 | 0 | 3 | 2 | | | | | |
| **Cities** | 13 | 3 | 6 | 0 | 0 | 1 | | | | | |
| Bryant | 1 | 0 | 0 | 0 | 0 | 1 | 0 | 0 | 1 | 1 | 21,902 |
| Camden | 1 | 0 | 0 | 0 | 0 | 0 | 0 | 1 | 0 | 0 | 10,499 |
| El Dorado | 2 | 0 | 0 | 0 | 0 | 0 | 0 | 1 | 1 | 0 | 17,263 |
| Fort Smith[2] | 3 | 0 | 3 | 0 | 0 | 0 | 3 | 1 | 0 | 0 | 87,912 |
| Haskell | 0 | 1 | 0 | 0 | 0 | 0 | 0 | 0 | 0 | 1 | 4,700 |
| Jacksonville | 0 | 0 | 1 | 0 | 0 | 0 | 0 | 0 | 1 | 0 | 28,356 |
| Paragould | 1 | 0 | 0 | 0 | 0 | 0 | 0 | 0 | 1 | 0 | 29,559 |
| Rogers | 3 | 0 | 1 | 0 | 0 | 0 | 1 | 1 | 0 | 2 | 72,122 |
| Siloam Springs[2] | 1 | 1 | 0 | 0 | 0 | 0 | 0 | 0 | 0 | 1 | 17,877 |
| Springdale | 0 | 1 | 1 | 0 | 0 | 0 | 0 | 0 | 1 | 1 | 85,234 |
| Van Buren | 1 | 0 | 0 | 0 | 0 | 0 | 1 | 0 | 0 | 0 | 23,912 |
| **Universities and Colleges** | 1 | 0 | 0 | 0 | 0 | 0 | | | | | |
| University of Arkansas, Fayetteville | 1 | 0 | 0 | 0 | 0 | 0 | 0 | 1 | 0 | 0 | 30,137 |
| **Metropolitan Counties** | 13 | 0 | 3 | 0 | 1 | 1 | | | | | |
| Benton[2] | 3 | 0 | 1 | 0 | 0 | 1 | 1 | 2 | 1 | 0 | |
| Miller | 0 | 0 | 0 | 0 | 1 | 0 | 0 | 0 | 1 | 0 | |
| Perry | 2 | 0 | 0 | 0 | 0 | 0 | 0 | 1 | 0 | 1 | |
| Poinsett[2] | 2 | 0 | 0 | 0 | 0 | 0 | 0 | 0 | 0 | 1 | |

# Table 94. Hate Crime Incidents Per Bias Motivation and Quarter, by Selected State and Agency and Federal, 2021—Continued

(Number.)

| State/agency | Number of incidents per bias motivation | | | | | | Number of incidents per quarter | | | | Population[1] |
|---|---|---|---|---|---|---|---|---|---|---|---|
| | Race/ Ethnicity/ Ancestry | Religion | Sexual orientation | Disability | Gender | Gender Identity | 1st quarter | 2nd quarter | 3rd quarter | 4th quarter | |
| Pulaski | 3 | 0 | 2 | 0 | 0 | 0 | 0 | 3 | 0 | 2 | |
| Saline[2] | 3 | 0 | 0 | 0 | 0 | 0 | 1 | 1 | 0 | 0 | |
| **Nonmetropolitan Counties** | 4 | 0 | 0 | 0 | 2 | 0 | | | | | |
| Boone | 0 | 0 | 0 | 0 | 2 | 0 | 0 | 2 | 0 | 0 | |
| Hot Spring | 1 | 0 | 0 | 0 | 0 | 0 | 0 | 0 | 1 | 0 | |
| Mississippi | 1 | 0 | 0 | 0 | 0 | 0 | 0 | 0 | 1 | 0 | |
| Union | 1 | 0 | 0 | 0 | 0 | 0 | 0 | 0 | 0 | 1 | |
| Van Buren | 1 | 0 | 0 | 0 | 0 | 0 | 0 | 0 | 1 | 0 | |
| **CALIFORNIA** | 49 | 6 | 16 | 0 | 0 | 3 | | | | | |
| **Cities** | 37 | 4 | 13 | 0 | 0 | 3 | | | | | |
| Carlsbad | 1 | 0 | 1 | 0 | 0 | 1 | 1 | 2 | 0 | 0 | 116,633 |
| Chula Vista | 4 | 1 | 0 | 0 | 0 | 0 | 1 | 1 | 1 | 2 | 275,978 |
| El Cajon | 0 | 0 | 1 | 0 | 0 | 0 | 1 | 0 | 0 | 0 | 102,665 |
| Escondido | 3 | 0 | 0 | 0 | 0 | 0 | 2 | 1 | 0 | 0 | 150,507 |
| La Mesa | 2 | 0 | 1 | 0 | 0 | 0 | 1 | 2 | 0 | 0 | 59,968 |
| National City[2] | 2 | 0 | 1 | 0 | 0 | 0 | 2 | 0 | 0 | 0 | 61,171 |
| Oceanside | 3 | 0 | 0 | 0 | 0 | 1 | 1 | 1 | 1 | 1 | 175,335 |
| San Diego | 22 | 3 | 9 | 0 | 0 | 1 | 7 | 11 | 9 | 8 | 1,434,673 |
| **Metropolitan Counties** | 11 | 2 | 2 | 0 | 0 | 0 | | | | | |
| San Diego | 11 | 2 | 2 | 0 | 0 | 0 | 3 | 4 | 3 | 5 | |
| **Other Agencies** | 1 | 0 | 1 | 0 | 0 | 0 | | | | | |
| Port of San Diego Harbor | 1 | 0 | 1 | 0 | 0 | 0 | 1 | 0 | 1 | 0 | |
| **COLORADO** | 182 | 40 | 67 | 4 | 1 | 18 | | | | | |
| **Cities** | 154 | 28 | 52 | 2 | 1 | 13 | | | | | |
| Alamosa | 3 | 0 | 0 | 0 | 0 | 0 | 2 | 1 | 0 | 0 | 9,414 |
| Aurora[2] | 16 | 2 | 6 | 0 | 0 | 2 | 6 | 3 | 7 | 8 | 393,897 |
| Boulder | 1 | 0 | 1 | 0 | 0 | 0 | 0 | 1 | 0 | 1 | 108,698 |
| Brighton[2] | 2 | 0 | 0 | 0 | 0 | 0 | 1 | 0 | 0 | 0 | 41,535 |
| Broomfield | 0 | 0 | 0 | 0 | 0 | 1 | 0 | 0 | 1 | 0 | 73,077 |
| Canon City | 0 | 1 | 1 | 0 | 0 | 0 | 0 | 0 | 0 | 2 | 16,552 |
| Carbondale | 1 | 0 | 0 | 0 | 0 | 0 | 0 | 0 | 0 | 1 | 6,761 |
| Castle Rock | 1 | 0 | 0 | 0 | 0 | 0 | 0 | 1 | 0 | 0 | 73,221 |
| Centennial[2] | 5 | 0 | 3 | 0 | 0 | 1 | 1 | 1 | 6 | 0 | 111,199 |
| Colorado Springs | 12 | 3 | 1 | 0 | 0 | 0 | 3 | 5 | 4 | 4 | 488,747 |
| Commerce City[2] | 2 | 1 | 4 | 0 | 0 | 1 | 1 | 2 | 3 | 0 | 60,845 |
| Cortez | 1 | 0 | 0 | 0 | 0 | 0 | 0 | 0 | 0 | 1 | 8,760 |
| Denver[2] | 45 | 11 | 23 | 1 | 0 | 2 | 12 | 26 | 20 | 19 | 740,209 |
| Durango | 4 | 0 | 0 | 0 | 0 | 0 | 0 | 1 | 0 | 3 | 19,995 |
| Eagle | 1 | 0 | 0 | 0 | 0 | 0 | 0 | 0 | 0 | 1 | 6,954 |
| Englewood | 1 | 0 | 0 | 0 | 0 | 0 | 1 | 0 | 0 | 0 | 35,630 |
| Erie | 1 | 0 | 0 | 0 | 0 | 0 | 0 | 0 | 1 | 0 | 31,873 |
| Fort Collins | 1 | 1 | 2 | 0 | 0 | 1 | 2 | 3 | 0 | 0 | 170,744 |
| Fort Morgan | 0 | 0 | 1 | 0 | 0 | 0 | 0 | 0 | 1 | 0 | 11,234 |
| Fruita | 0 | 0 | 2 | 0 | 0 | 0 | 0 | 0 | 0 | 2 | 14,465 |
| Glendale | 1 | 0 | 0 | 0 | 0 | 0 | 0 | 0 | 1 | 0 | 5,192 |
| Golden | 1 | 0 | 0 | 0 | 0 | 0 | 0 | 1 | 0 | 0 | 20,498 |
| Grand Junction | 4 | 0 | 0 | 0 | 0 | 0 | 1 | 0 | 3 | 0 | 63,928 |
| Greeley | 1 | 0 | 0 | 0 | 0 | 0 | 1 | 0 | 0 | 0 | 110,660 |
| Gunnison | 0 | 1 | 0 | 0 | 0 | 0 | 0 | 0 | 1 | 0 | 6,950 |
| Johnstown | 1 | 0 | 0 | 0 | 0 | 0 | 0 | 0 | 1 | 0 | 14,413 |
| Lafayette | 2 | 0 | 0 | 0 | 0 | 0 | 0 | 0 | 2 | 0 | 29,027 |
| La Junta | 0 | 0 | 1 | 0 | 0 | 0 | 1 | 0 | 0 | 0 | 6,831 |
| Lakewood | 1 | 1 | 0 | 0 | 0 | 1 | 0 | 3 | 0 | 0 | 158,977 |
| Littleton | 1 | 0 | 0 | 0 | 0 | 0 | 0 | 1 | 0 | 0 | 46,466 |
| Lone Tree | 0 | 0 | 0 | 0 | 1 | 0 | 0 | 0 | 1 | 0 | 14,007 |
| Longmont[2] | 11 | 2 | 1 | 1 | 0 | 0 | 4 | 3 | 1 | 4 | 99,714 |
| Louisville[2] | 2 | 1 | 1 | 0 | 0 | 0 | 1 | 1 | 1 | 0 | 19,127 |
| Loveland | 1 | 0 | 0 | 0 | 0 | 0 | 1 | 0 | 0 | 0 | 85,349 |
| Montrose | 1 | 0 | 0 | 0 | 0 | 0 | 0 | 0 | 1 | 0 | 19,984 |
| Monument[2] | 2 | 0 | 0 | 0 | 0 | 3 | 2 | 0 | 0 | 2 | 8,397 |
| Parker | 1 | 0 | 0 | 0 | 0 | 0 | 0 | 0 | 1 | 0 | 60,178 |
| Platteville | 0 | 1 | 0 | 0 | 0 | 0 | 0 | 0 | 1 | 0 | 4,239 |
| Pueblo | 1 | 0 | 0 | 0 | 0 | 0 | 0 | 0 | 0 | 1 | 113,371 |
| Rifle | 1 | 0 | 0 | 0 | 0 | 0 | 0 | 1 | 0 | 0 | 9,819 |
| Severance | 1 | 0 | 0 | 0 | 0 | 0 | 1 | 0 | 0 | 0 | 8,343 |
| Sterling | 1 | 0 | 0 | 0 | 0 | 0 | 1 | 0 | 0 | 0 | 14,006 |
| Thornton | 14 | 3 | 3 | 0 | 0 | 0 | 3 | 5 | 4 | 8 | 151,324 |
| Timnath | 1 | 0 | 0 | 0 | 0 | 0 | 0 | 0 | 1 | 0 | 3,801 |
| Trinidad | 1 | 0 | 0 | 0 | 0 | 0 | 0 | 0 | 1 | 0 | 8,045 |
| Vail | 1 | 0 | 0 | 0 | 0 | 0 | 0 | 0 | 0 | 1 | 5,507 |
| Westminster | 2 | 0 | 2 | 0 | 0 | 1 | 0 | 4 | 0 | 1 | 115,942 |
| Wiggins | 1 | 0 | 0 | 0 | 0 | 0 | 0 | 1 | 0 | 0 | 1,184 |
| Windsor[2] | 3 | 0 | 0 | 0 | 0 | 0 | 0 | 0 | 1 | 1 | 28,756 |

## Table 94. Hate Crime Incidents Per Bias Motivation and Quarter, by Selected State and  Agency and Federal, 2021—Continued

(Number.)

| State/agency | Number of incidents per bias motivation | | | | | | Number of incidents per quarter | | | | Population[1] |
|---|---|---|---|---|---|---|---|---|---|---|---|
| | Race/ Ethnicity/ Ancestry | Religion | Sexual orientation | Disability | Gender | Gender Identity | 1st quarter | 2nd quarter | 3rd quarter | 4th quarter | |
| **Universities and Colleges** | 1 | 2 | 3 | 0 | 0 | 0 | | | | | |
| Fort Lewis College | 1 | 1 | 1 | 0 | 0 | 0 | 1 | 0 | 0 | 2 | 3,766 |
| University of Colorado | | | | | | | | | | | |
| Boulder[2] | 0 | 0 | 2 | 0 | 0 | 0 | 0 | 0 | 1 | 0 | 41,826 |
| Colorado Springs | 0 | 1 | 0 | 0 | 0 | 0 | 0 | 1 | 0 | 0 | 16,715 |
| **Metropolitan Counties** | 21 | 10 | 10 | 1 | 0 | 2 | | | | | |
| Adams | 1 | 0 | 0 | 0 | 0 | 0 | 1 | 0 | 0 | 0 | |
| Arapahoe[2] | 11 | 7 | 0 | 0 | 0 | 1 | 1 | 7 | 3 | 3 | |
| Boulder[2] | 1 | 1 | 2 | 0 | 0 | 0 | 0 | 1 | 2 | 0 | |
| Douglas[2] | 1 | 0 | 3 | 0 | 0 | 0 | 0 | 0 | 2 | 1 | |
| El Paso | 1 | 0 | 0 | 0 | 0 | 0 | 0 | 0 | 0 | 1 | |
| Jefferson[2] | 2 | 2 | 1 | 0 | 0 | 0 | 1 | 0 | 3 | 0 | |
| Larimer[2] | 2 | 0 | 4 | 1 | 0 | 1 | 0 | 1 | 5 | 1 | |
| Park | 1 | 0 | 0 | 0 | 0 | 0 | 1 | 0 | 0 | 0 | |
| Weld | 1 | 0 | 0 | 0 | 0 | 0 | 0 | 0 | 0 | 1 | |
| **Nonmetropolitan Counties** | 6 | 0 | 2 | 1 | 0 | 3 | | | | | |
| Bent | 0 | 0 | 1 | 0 | 0 | 0 | 0 | 0 | 0 | 1 | |
| Fremont | 1 | 0 | 0 | 0 | 0 | 0 | 0 | 1 | 0 | 0 | |
| Garfield | 0 | 0 | 0 | 0 | 0 | 1 | 0 | 0 | 1 | 0 | |
| Huerfano | 1 | 0 | 0 | 0 | 0 | 2 | 0 | 1 | 1 | 1 | |
| Montrose | 1 | 0 | 0 | 0 | 0 | 0 | 1 | 0 | 0 | 0 | |
| Routt | 0 | 0 | 1 | 1 | 0 | 0 | 0 | 0 | 2 | 0 | |
| Summit | 3 | 0 | 0 | 0 | 0 | 0 | 1 | 1 | 0 | 1 | |
| **CONNECTICUT** | 65 | 9 | 17 | 1 | 0 | 0 | | | | | |
| **Cities** | 59 | 7 | 16 | 1 | 0 | 0 | | | | | |
| Bethel | 0 | 0 | 1 | 0 | 0 | 0 | 0 | 1 | 0 | 0 | 20,066 |
| Bridgeport | 1 | 0 | 0 | 0 | 0 | 0 | 0 | 0 | 0 | 1 | 143,394 |
| Coventry | 1 | 0 | 0 | 0 | 0 | 0 | 0 | 1 | 0 | 0 | 12,384 |
| Danbury | 3 | 0 | 0 | 0 | 0 | 0 | 2 | 0 | 1 | 0 | 84,631 |
| Darien | 1 | 0 | 0 | 0 | 0 | 0 | 0 | 0 | 1 | 0 | 21,790 |
| East Hampton | 0 | 0 | 1 | 0 | 0 | 0 | 0 | 1 | 0 | 0 | 12,726 |
| Fairfield | 1 | 0 | 0 | 0 | 0 | 0 | 0 | 0 | 0 | 1 | 62,473 |
| Glastonbury | 2 | 0 | 0 | 0 | 0 | 0 | 1 | 1 | 0 | 0 | 34,424 |
| Hamden | 2 | 0 | 1 | 0 | 0 | 0 | 0 | 1 | 1 | 1 | 60,165 |
| Manchester | 2 | 0 | 1 | 0 | 0 | 0 | 2 | 0 | 1 | 0 | 57,274 |
| Meriden | 2 | 0 | 0 | 0 | 0 | 0 | 0 | 2 | 0 | 0 | 58,799 |
| Middletown | 2 | 0 | 1 | 0 | 0 | 0 | 0 | 0 | 0 | 3 | 45,852 |
| Milford | 1 | 1 | 0 | 0 | 0 | 0 | 1 | 0 | 1 | 0 | 54,984 |
| Naugatuck | 1 | 0 | 1 | 0 | 0 | 0 | 2 | 0 | 0 | 0 | 30,810 |
| New Britain[2] | 4 | 0 | 0 | 0 | 0 | 0 | 1 | 1 | 0 | 0 | 72,093 |
| New Haven | 3 | 1 | 1 | 1 | 0 | 0 | 1 | 2 | 2 | 1 | 130,903 |
| Newington | 1 | 0 | 0 | 0 | 0 | 0 | 0 | 0 | 0 | 1 | 29,803 |
| New London | 0 | 1 | 0 | 0 | 0 | 0 | 0 | 0 | 0 | 1 | 26,797 |
| Newtown | 1 | 0 | 0 | 0 | 0 | 0 | 0 | 1 | 0 | 0 | 27,858 |
| North Haven | 1 | 0 | 0 | 0 | 0 | 0 | 0 | 0 | 1 | 0 | 23,504 |
| Norwich | 1 | 0 | 0 | 0 | 0 | 0 | 0 | 1 | 0 | 0 | 38,431 |
| Old Saybrook | 1 | 0 | 0 | 0 | 0 | 0 | 0 | 1 | 0 | 0 | 10,007 |
| Orange | 1 | 1 | 0 | 0 | 0 | 0 | 0 | 1 | 1 | 0 | 13,874 |
| Plainfield | 2 | 0 | 0 | 0 | 0 | 0 | 0 | 1 | 0 | 1 | 15,053 |
| Plymouth | 3 | 0 | 0 | 0 | 0 | 0 | 1 | 1 | 1 | 0 | 11,486 |
| Ridgefield | 1 | 0 | 0 | 0 | 0 | 0 | 1 | 0 | 0 | 0 | 24,919 |
| Seymour | 1 | 0 | 1 | 0 | 0 | 0 | 0 | 1 | 0 | 1 | 16,306 |
| Shelton | 1 | 0 | 0 | 0 | 0 | 0 | 1 | 0 | 0 | 0 | 41,095 |
| Southington | 2 | 0 | 0 | 0 | 0 | 0 | 0 | 1 | 0 | 1 | 43,897 |
| South Windsor | 0 | 0 | 1 | 0 | 0 | 0 | 0 | 0 | 3 | 1 | 26,142 |
| Stamford | 10 | 2 | 4 | 0 | 0 | 0 | 6 | 3 | 3 | 4 | 132,292 |
| Stratford | 1 | 0 | 0 | 0 | 0 | 0 | 0 | 1 | 0 | 0 | 51,683 |
| Suffield | 1 | 0 | 0 | 0 | 0 | 0 | 0 | 1 | 0 | 0 | 15,817 |
| Thomaston | 1 | 0 | 0 | 0 | 0 | 0 | 0 | 0 | 0 | 1 | 7,468 |
| Torrington | 2 | 0 | 0 | 0 | 0 | 0 | 0 | 1 | 1 | 0 | 33,631 |
| Wallingford | 1 | 0 | 0 | 0 | 0 | 0 | 1 | 0 | 0 | 0 | 43,969 |
| Waterford | 0 | 1 | 0 | 0 | 0 | 0 | 0 | 0 | 1 | 0 | 18,803 |
| West Hartford | 1 | 0 | 0 | 0 | 0 | 0 | 1 | 0 | 0 | 0 | 62,809 |
| West Haven | 0 | 0 | 2 | 0 | 0 | 0 | 1 | 0 | 1 | 0 | 54,248 |
| Westport | 0 | 0 | 1 | 0 | 0 | 0 | 0 | 1 | 0 | 0 | 28,652 |
| **Universities and Colleges** | 2 | 2 | 0 | 0 | 0 | 0 | | | | | |
| University of Connecticut, Storrs, Avery Point, and Hartford[3] | 2 | 2 | 0 | 0 | 0 | 0 | 2 | 0 | 0 | 2 | |
| **State Police Agencies** | 1 | 0 | 1 | 0 | 0 | 0 | | | | | |
| Connecticut State Police[2] | 1 | 0 | 1 | 0 | 0 | 0 | 1 | 0 | 0 | 0 | |
| **Tribal Agencies** | 1 | 0 | 0 | 0 | 0 | 0 | | | | | |
| Mashantucket Pequot Tribal | 1 | 0 | 0 | 0 | 0 | 0 | 1 | 0 | 0 | 0 | |

# Table 94. Hate Crime Incidents Per Bias Motivation and Quarter, by Selected State and Agency and Federal, 2021—Continued

(Number.)

| | Number of incidents per bias motivation | | | | | | Number of incidents per quarter | | | | |
|---|---|---|---|---|---|---|---|---|---|---|---|
| State/agency | Race/ Ethnicity/ Ancestry | Religion | Sexual orientation | Disability | Gender | Gender Identity | 1st quarter | 2nd quarter | 3rd quarter | 4th quarter | Population[1] |
| **Other Agencies** | 2 | 0 | 0 | 0 | 0 | 0 | | | | | |
| Department of Energy and Environmental Protection[2] | 2 | 0 | 0 | 0 | 0 | 0 | 0 | 1 | 0 | 0 | |
| | | | | | | | | | | | |
| **DELAWARE** | 5 | 2 | 2 | 0 | 0 | 0 | | | | | |
| **Cities** | 2 | 0 | 0 | 0 | 0 | 0 | | | | | |
| Dover | 1 | 0 | 0 | 0 | 0 | 0 | 0 | 0 | 0 | 1 | 38,439 |
| Wilmington | 1 | 0 | 0 | 0 | 0 | 0 | 0 | 1 | 0 | 0 | 70,331 |
| | | | | | | | | | | | |
| **Universities and Colleges** | 1 | 1 | 0 | 0 | 0 | 0 | | | | | |
| University of Delaware | 1 | 1 | 0 | 0 | 0 | 0 | 0 | 0 | 0 | 2 | 26,527 |
| | | | | | | | | | | | |
| **Metropolitan Counties** | 1 | 0 | 0 | 0 | 0 | 0 | | | | | |
| New Castle County Police Department | 1 | 0 | 0 | 0 | 0 | 0 | 0 | 1 | 0 | 0 | |
| | | | | | | | | | | | |
| **Other Agencies** | 1 | 1 | 2 | 0 | 0 | 0 | | | | | |
| River and Bay Authority | 1 | 0 | 0 | 0 | 0 | 0 | 1 | 0 | 0 | 0 | |
| State Fire Marshal | 0 | 1 | 2 | 0 | 0 | 0 | 0 | 0 | 2 | 1 | |
| | | | | | | | | | | | |
| **DISTRICT OF COLUMBIA** | 35 | 3 | 17 | 0 | 0 | 12 | | | | | |
| **Cities** | 31 | 3 | 14 | 0 | 0 | 12 | | | | | |
| Washington[2] | 31 | 3 | 14 | 0 | 0 | 12 | | | 29 | 29 | 670,050 |
| | | | | | | | | | | | |
| **Other Agencies** | 4 | 0 | 3 | 0 | 0 | 0 | | | | | |
| Metro Transit Police[2] | 4 | 0 | 3 | 0 | 0 | 0 | 1 | 2 | 2 | 1 | |
| | | | | | | | | | | | |
| **FLORIDA** | 1 | 0 | 0 | 0 | 0 | 0 | | | | | |
| **Tribal Agencies** | 1 | 0 | 0 | 0 | 0 | 0 | | | | | |
| Seminole Tribal | 1 | 0 | 0 | 0 | 0 | 0 | 1 | 0 | 0 | 0 | |
| | | | | | | | | | | | |
| **GEORGIA** | 164 | 29 | 37 | 3 | 3 | 12 | | | | | |
| **Cities** | 81 | 13 | 24 | 2 | 1 | 4 | | | | | |
| Alpharetta | 0 | 2 | 0 | 0 | 0 | 0 | 1 | 0 | 0 | 1 | 68,954 |
| Athens-Clarke County | 2 | 0 | 0 | 0 | 0 | 0 | 1 | 0 | 1 | 0 | 127,410 |
| Atlanta | 4 | 0 | 3 | 0 | 0 | 3 | 1 | 5 | 3 | 1 | 521,274 |
| Bremen | 1 | 0 | 0 | 0 | 0 | 0 | 0 | 1 | 0 | 0 | 6,880 |
| Brookhaven[2] | 10 | 4 | 6 | 0 | 1 | 0 | 4 | 6 | 7 | 3 | 56,770 |
| Canton | 1 | 0 | 0 | 0 | 0 | 0 | 0 | 1 | 0 | 0 | 33,386 |
| Cartersville | 1 | 0 | 0 | 0 | 0 | 0 | 0 | 0 | 1 | 0 | 22,276 |
| Columbus | 0 | 0 | 1 | 1 | 0 | 1 | 3 | | | | 196,633 |
| Decatur | 1 | 0 | 0 | 0 | 0 | 0 | 1 | 0 | 0 | 0 | 26,350 |
| Douglasville | 4 | 0 | 0 | 0 | 0 | 0 | 4 | 0 | 0 | 0 | 34,475 |
| Duluth | 1 | 0 | 0 | 0 | 0 | 0 | 0 | 0 | 1 | 0 | 29,986 |
| Dunwoody | 2 | 0 | 0 | 0 | 0 | 0 | 1 | 1 | 0 | 0 | 49,621 |
| Fitzgerald | 0 | 0 | 1 | 0 | 0 | 0 | 0 | 0 | 1 | 0 | 8,563 |
| Forest Park | 1 | 0 | 0 | 0 | 0 | 0 | 1 | 0 | 0 | 0 | 20,015 |
| Gainesville | 4 | 1 | 1 | 0 | 0 | 0 | 1 | 1 | 2 | 2 | 45,385 |
| Griffin | 0 | 0 | 1 | 0 | 0 | 0 | 1 | 0 | 0 | 0 | 22,617 |
| Hartwell | 1 | 0 | 0 | 0 | 0 | 0 | 1 | 0 | 0 | 0 | 4,453 |
| Hiram | 1 | 0 | 0 | 0 | 0 | 0 | 0 | 1 | 0 | 0 | 4,315 |
| Jackson | 0 | 1 | 0 | 0 | 0 | 0 | 0 | 0 | 1 | 0 | 5,361 |
| Kennesaw | 1 | 0 | 1 | 0 | 0 | 0 | 2 | 0 | 0 | 0 | 35,145 |
| LaGrange | 1 | 0 | 0 | 0 | 0 | 0 | 0 | 0 | 1 | 0 | 30,874 |
| Lawrenceville | 2 | 0 | 0 | 0 | 0 | 0 | 0 | 0 | 0 | 2 | 31,223 |
| Madison | 0 | 0 | 1 | 0 | 0 | 0 | 0 | 0 | 0 | 1 | 4,286 |
| Marietta | 3 | 0 | 2 | 0 | 0 | 0 | 0 | 2 | 2 | 1 | 61,223 |
| Metter | 1 | 0 | 0 | 0 | 0 | 0 | 0 | 0 | 0 | 1 | 4,000 |
| Milton | 1 | 0 | 0 | 0 | 0 | 0 | 0 | 1 | 0 | 0 | 40,781 |
| Newnan | 2 | 1 | 1 | 0 | 0 | 0 | 2 | 1 | 1 | 0 | 44,023 |
| Norcross | 2 | 0 | 0 | 0 | 0 | 0 | 0 | 0 | 0 | 2 | 18,337 |
| Peachtree City | 0 | 1 | 0 | 0 | 0 | 0 | 0 | 0 | 1 | 0 | 36,994 |
| Rockmart | 1 | 0 | 0 | 0 | 0 | 0 | 1 | 0 | 0 | 0 | 4,520 |
| Rome | 3 | 0 | 0 | 0 | 0 | 0 | 1 | 0 | 0 | 2 | 36,792 |
| Sandy Springs | 3 | 0 | 0 | 0 | 0 | 0 | 0 | 0 | 1 | 2 | 111,533 |
| Smyrna[2] | 9 | 1 | 4 | 0 | 0 | 0 | 5 | 3 | 4 | 0 | 57,024 |
| South Fulton[2] | 3 | 0 | 2 | 0 | 0 | 0 | 2 | 2 | 0 | 0 | 104,282 |
| Suwanee | 2 | 0 | 0 | 0 | 0 | 0 | 1 | 0 | 0 | 1 | 22,579 |
| Temple | 1 | 0 | 0 | 0 | 0 | 0 | 0 | 1 | 0 | 0 | 5,104 |
| Thomasville | 11 | 1 | 0 | 1 | 0 | 0 | 4 | 5 | 3 | 1 | 18,485 |
| Toccoa | 0 | 1 | 0 | 0 | 0 | 0 | 0 | 0 | 1 | 0 | 8,283 |
| Woodstock | 1 | 0 | 0 | 0 | 0 | 0 | 0 | 1 | 0 | 0 | 34,798 |
| | | | | | | | | | | | |
| **Universities and Colleges** | 1 | 1 | 1 | 0 | 0 | 1 | | | | | |
| Emory University | 0 | 1 | 1 | 0 | 0 | 1 | 0 | 1 | 0 | 2 | 15,970 |
| University of North Georgia | 1 | 0 | 0 | 0 | 0 | 0 | 0 | 0 | 0 | 1 | 23,141 |
| | | | | | | | | | | | |
| **Metropolitan Counties** | 61 | 3 | 10 | 1 | 2 | 6 | | | | | |
| Carroll | 2 | 0 | 0 | 0 | 0 | 0 | 0 | 0 | 2 | 0 | |

## Table 94. Hate Crime Incidents Per Bias Motivation and Quarter, by Selected State and  Agency and Federal, 2021—Continued

(Number.)

| State/agency | Number of incidents per bias motivation | | | | | | Number of incidents per quarter | | | | Population[1] |
| --- | --- | --- | --- | --- | --- | --- | --- | --- | --- | --- | --- |
| | Race/ Ethnicity/ Ancestry | Religion | Sexual orientation | Disability | Gender | Gender Identity | 1st quarter | 2nd quarter | 3rd quarter | 4th quarter | |
| Cherokee | 1 | 0 | 1 | 0 | 0 | 0 | 0 | 1 | 1 | 0 | |
| Clayton County Police Department | 1 | 0 | 2 | 0 | 0 | 0 | 1 | 0 | 2 | 0 | |
| Cobb County Police Department | 7 | 2 | 2 | 0 | 0 | 1 | 3 | 4 | 2 | 3 | |
| Coweta | 6 | 0 | 1 | 0 | 0 | 0 | 1 | 1 | 4 | 1 | |
| DeKalb County Police Department | 0 | 0 | 1 | 0 | 0 | 0 | 0 | 0 | 0 | 1 | |
| Fayette | 1 | 0 | 0 | 0 | 0 | 0 | 0 | 1 | 0 | 0 | |
| Floyd County Police Department | 3 | 0 | 0 | 0 | 0 | 0 | 1 | 0 | 0 | 2 | |
| Forsyth | 7 | 0 | 0 | 0 | 0 | 0 | 4 | 1 | 1 | 1 | |
| Fulton | 0 | 0 | 0 | 1 | 0 | 0 | 0 | 0 | 1 | 0 | |
| Fulton County Police Department | 1 | 0 | 0 | 0 | 0 | 0 | 0 | 1 | 0 | 0 | |
| Glynn County Police Department | 4 | 0 | 1 | 0 | 0 | 1 | 2 | 0 | 0 | 4 | |
| Hall | 6 | 0 | 1 | 0 | 0 | 0 | 1 | 2 | 2 | 2 | |
| Lowndes | 1 | 0 | 0 | 0 | 0 | 0 | 0 | 0 | 0 | 1 | |
| McIntosh | 1 | 0 | 0 | 0 | 0 | 0 | 0 | 1 | 0 | 0 | |
| Newton[2] | 6 | 0 | 0 | 0 | 2 | 0 | 0 | 3 | 0 | 0 | |
| Oglethorpe | 2 | 0 | 0 | 0 | 0 | 0 | 2 | 0 | 0 | 0 | |
| Paulding[2] | 6 | 1 | 0 | 0 | 0 | 4 | 1 | 0 | 6 | 3 | |
| Rockdale | 1 | 0 | 0 | 0 | 0 | 0 | 1 | 0 | 0 | 0 | |
| Spalding | 2 | 0 | 0 | 0 | 0 | 0 | 1 | 0 | 1 | 0 | |
| Twiggs | 1 | 0 | 0 | 0 | 0 | 0 | 0 | 0 | 0 | 1 | |
| Whitfield | 2 | 0 | 1 | 0 | 0 | 0 | 1 | 2 | 0 | 0 | |
| **Nonmetropolitan Counties** | 15 | 10 | 2 | 0 | 0 | 0 | | | | | |
| Bulloch | 7 | 1 | 0 | 0 | 0 | 0 | 5 | 3 | 0 | 0 | |
| Crisp | 1 | 0 | 0 | 0 | 0 | 0 | 0 | 1 | 0 | 0 | |
| Elbert | 0 | 1 | 0 | 0 | 0 | 0 | 0 | 1 | 0 | 0 | |
| Gordon | 0 | 8 | 0 | 0 | 0 | 0 | 8 | 0 | 0 | 0 | |
| Lumpkin | 1 | 0 | 0 | 0 | 0 | 0 | 1 | 0 | 0 | 0 | |
| Pulaski | 3 | 0 | 0 | 0 | 0 | 0 | 0 | 0 | 0 | 3 | |
| Rabun | 0 | 0 | 1 | 0 | 0 | 0 | 0 | 0 | 1 | 0 | |
| Troup | 2 | 0 | 0 | 0 | 0 | 0 | 0 | 1 | 0 | 1 | |
| Union | 1 | 0 | 0 | 0 | 0 | 0 | 0 | 0 | 0 | 1 | |
| White | 0 | 0 | 1 | 0 | 0 | 0 | 0 | 0 | 0 | 1 | |
| **Other Agencies** | 6 | 2 | 0 | 0 | 0 | 1 | | | | | |
| Cherokee County Board of Education | 1 | 0 | 0 | 0 | 0 | 0 | 0 | 0 | 0 | 1 | |
| Cobb County Board of Education | 3 | 1 | 0 | 0 | 0 | 0 | 1 | 0 | 2 | 1 | |
| Fulton County School System | 2 | 1 | 0 | 0 | 0 | 1 | 1 | 0 | 2 | 1 | |
| **HAWAII** | 29 | 4 | 3 | 0 | 0 | 0 | | | | | |
| **Cities** | 20 | 3 | 3 | 0 | 0 | 0 | | | | | |
| Honolulu[2] | 20 | 3 | 3 | 0 | 0 | 0 | 9 | 4 | 10 | 2 | 985,138 |
| **Nonmetropolitan Counties** | 9 | 1 | 0 | 0 | 0 | 0 | | | | | |
| Kauai Police Department[2] | 9 | 1 | 0 | 0 | 0 | 0 | 4 | 3 | 0 | 2 | |
| **IDAHO** | 29 | 4 | 11 | 0 | 0 | 0 | | | | | |
| **Cities** | 24 | 4 | 10 | 0 | 0 | 0 | | | | | |
| Boise[2] | 8 | 1 | 5 | 0 | 0 | 0 | 0 | 5 | 5 | 3 | 231,902 |
| Chubbuck | 1 | 0 | 0 | 0 | 0 | 0 | 0 | 1 | 0 | 0 | 16,168 |
| Coeur d'Alene | 2 | 0 | 0 | 0 | 0 | 0 | 0 | 0 | 2 | 0 | 54,358 |
| Emmett | 0 | 0 | 1 | 0 | 0 | 0 | 0 | 0 | 1 | 0 | 7,346 |
| Fruitland | 0 | 0 | 1 | 0 | 0 | 0 | 0 | 0 | 1 | 0 | 5,655 |
| Garden City | 1 | 0 | 0 | 0 | 0 | 0 | 0 | 1 | 0 | 0 | 12,018 |
| Homedale | 2 | 1 | 0 | 0 | 0 | 0 | 0 | 0 | 1 | 2 | 2,851 |
| Idaho Falls | 0 | 0 | 2 | 0 | 0 | 0 | 1 | 0 | 1 | 0 | 64,792 |
| Jerome | 1 | 0 | 0 | 0 | 0 | 0 | 1 | 0 | 0 | 0 | 12,231 |
| Ketchum[2] | 2 | 0 | 0 | 0 | 0 | 0 | 0 | 0 | 1 | 0 | 2,932 |
| Moscow | 1 | 1 | 0 | 0 | 0 | 0 | 0 | 0 | 1 | 1 | 26,368 |
| Nampa | 2 | 0 | 0 | 0 | 0 | 0 | 0 | 0 | 2 | 0 | 105,619 |
| Payette | 1 | 0 | 0 | 0 | 0 | 0 | 0 | 0 | 1 | 0 | 8,065 |
| Pocatello | 1 | 0 | 0 | 0 | 0 | 0 | 0 | 1 | 0 | 0 | 57,306 |
| Twin Falls | 1 | 1 | 0 | 0 | 0 | 0 | 1 | 1 | 0 | 0 | 52,158 |
| Weiser | 1 | 0 | 1 | 0 | 0 | 0 | 2 | 0 | 0 | 0 | 5,461 |
| **Metropolitan Counties** | 1 | 0 | 0 | 0 | 0 | 0 | | | | | |
| Kootenai | 1 | 0 | 0 | 0 | 0 | 0 | 0 | 0 | 1 | 0 | |
| **Nonmetropolitan Counties** | 2 | 0 | 1 | 0 | 0 | 0 | | | | | |
| Blaine | 0 | 0 | 1 | 0 | 0 | 0 | 0 | 1 | 0 | 0 | |
| Oneida | 1 | 0 | 0 | 0 | 0 | 0 | 0 | 0 | 0 | 1 | |
| Valley | 1 | 0 | 0 | 0 | 0 | 0 | 0 | 0 | 1 | 0 | |
| **Tribal Agencies** | 2 | 0 | 0 | 0 | 0 | 0 | | | | | |
| Fort Hall Tribal | 2 | 0 | 0 | 0 | 0 | 0 | 0 | 2 | 0 | 0 | |
| **ILLINOIS** | 70 | 14 | 11 | 1 | 2 | 0 | | | | | |
| **Cities** | 53 | 12 | 8 | 1 | 1 | 0 | | | | | |
| Algonquin | 1 | 0 | 0 | 0 | 0 | 0 | 0 | 0 | 1 | 0 | 30,796 |
| Alton | 9 | 0 | 0 | 0 | 0 | 0 | 1 | 6 | 2 | 0 | 25,871 |

## Table 94. Hate Crime Incidents Per Bias Motivation and Quarter, by Selected State and Agency and Federal, 2021—Continued

(Number.)

| State/agency | Number of incidents per bias motivation | | | | | | Number of incidents per quarter | | | | Population[1] |
|---|---|---|---|---|---|---|---|---|---|---|---|
| | Race/ Ethnicity/ Ancestry | Religion | Sexual orientation | Disability | Gender | Gender Identity | 1st quarter | 2nd quarter | 3rd quarter | 4th quarter | |
| Belleville | 1 | 0 | 0 | 0 | 0 | 0 | 0 | 1 | 0 | 0 | 40,184 |
| Bloomington | 0 | 1 | 1 | 0 | 0 | 0 | 2 | 0 | 0 | 0 | 77,166 |
| Bolingbrook[2] | 2 | 0 | 0 | 0 | 0 | 0 | | 0 | 0 | 1 | 74,081 |
| Braidwood | 0 | 0 | 1 | 0 | 0 | 0 | | | 0 | 1 | 6,140 |
| Chicago Heights | 1 | 0 | 0 | 0 | 0 | 0 | | 1 | 0 | 0 | 28,852 |
| Crest Hill | 1 | 0 | 0 | 0 | 0 | 0 | | | 0 | 1 | 20,149 |
| Danville[2] | 4 | 0 | 0 | 0 | 0 | 0 | 0 | 1 | 2 | | 29,829 |
| Deerfield | 0 | 1 | 0 | 0 | 0 | 0 | 0 | 0 | 1 | 0 | 18,562 |
| DeKalb | 1 | 0 | 0 | 0 | 0 | 0 | 0 | 0 | 1 | 0 | 42,475 |
| Des Plaines | 0 | 0 | 1 | 0 | 0 | 0 | 0 | 0 | 1 | 0 | 58,166 |
| Edwardsville | 5 | 0 | 0 | 0 | 0 | 0 | 0 | 0 | 1 | 4 | 25,269 |
| Elmwood Park | 2 | 0 | 2 | 0 | 0 | 0 | | 0 | 3 | 1 | 23,699 |
| Evanston | 1 | 0 | 1 | 0 | 0 | 0 | 1 | 1 | 0 | 0 | 72,497 |
| Evergreen Park | 1 | 0 | 0 | 0 | 0 | 0 | 0 | 0 | 0 | 1 | 18,813 |
| Fox Lake[2] | 3 | 0 | 0 | 0 | 0 | 0 | 0 | 1 | 0 | 0 | 10,386 |
| Franklin Park | 1 | 0 | 0 | 0 | 1 | 0 | 2 | 0 | 0 | 0 | 17,313 |
| Freeport | 2 | 0 | 0 | 0 | 0 | 0 | 0 | 0 | 1 | 1 | 23,240 |
| Glenview | 1 | 0 | 0 | 0 | 0 | 0 | | 0 | 0 | 1 | 47,036 |
| Highland Park | 0 | 1 | 0 | 0 | 0 | 0 | 0 | 0 | 0 | 1 | 29,392 |
| Homewood | 1 | 0 | 0 | 0 | 0 | 0 | 0 | 0 | 0 | 1 | 18,393 |
| Lake Zurich | 0 | 1 | 1 | 0 | 0 | 0 | 0 | 1 | 1 | 0 | 19,764 |
| Maryville | 1 | 0 | 0 | 0 | 0 | 0 | 0 | 0 | 0 | 1 | 7,997 |
| Metropolis | 1 | 0 | 0 | 0 | 0 | 0 | 1 | 0 | 0 | 0 | 5,821 |
| Montgomery | 1 | 0 | 0 | 0 | 0 | 0 | 0 | 1 | 0 | 0 | 20,371 |
| Mount Prospect | 1 | 0 | 0 | 0 | 0 | 0 | | 1 | 0 | 0 | 53,125 |
| Normal | 0 | 0 | 1 | 0 | 0 | 0 | 0 | 0 | 0 | 1 | 54,636 |
| Palos Park | 1 | 0 | 0 | 0 | 0 | 0 | 1 | 0 | 0 | 0 | 4,704 |
| Pekin | 1 | 0 | 0 | 0 | 0 | 0 | 1 | 0 | 0 | 0 | 31,593 |
| Quincy | 2 | 2 | 0 | 0 | 0 | 0 | 0 | 4 | 0 | 0 | 39,473 |
| Rock Island | 1 | 0 | 0 | 0 | 0 | 0 | 1 | 0 | 0 | 0 | 36,666 |
| Rosemont | 0 | 1 | 0 | 0 | 0 | 0 | 0 | 0 | 0 | 1 | 4,128 |
| Schaumburg | 1 | 0 | 0 | 0 | 0 | 0 | | 0 | 0 | 1 | 71,829 |
| Skokie[2] | 0 | 3 | 0 | 0 | 0 | 0 | 1 | 1 | 0 | 0 | 62,163 |
| South Beloit | 0 | 1 | 0 | 0 | 0 | 0 | 0 | 0 | 1 | 0 | 7,509 |
| Southern View | 1 | 0 | 0 | 0 | 0 | 0 | 0 | 1 | 0 | 0 | 1,547 |
| Springfield | 2 | 0 | 0 | 0 | 0 | 0 | 0 | 2 | 0 | 0 | 113,331 |
| St. Charles | 1 | 0 | 0 | 1 | 0 | 0 | 0 | 2 | 0 | 0 | 32,748 |
| Stone Park | 0 | 1 | 0 | 0 | 0 | 0 | 0 | 0 | 0 | 1 | 4,746 |
| Worth | 1 | 0 | 0 | 0 | 0 | 0 | 0 | 0 | 0 | 1 | 10,289 |
| Yorkville | 1 | 0 | 0 | 0 | 0 | 0 | 0 | 0 | 1 | 0 | 21,622 |
| **Universities and Colleges** | 3 | 0 | 1 | 0 | 0 | 0 | | | | | |
| Parkland College | 0 | 0 | 1 | 0 | 0 | 0 | 0 | 0 | 1 | 0 | 10,349 |
| University of Illinois | | | | | | | | | | | |
| Chicago | 1 | 0 | 0 | 0 | 0 | 0 | 0 | 1 | 0 | 0 | 35,210 |
| Urbana | 2 | 0 | 0 | 0 | 0 | 0 | 0 | 1 | 1 | 0 | 57,324 |
| **Metropolitan Counties** | 14 | 2 | 2 | 0 | 0 | 0 | | | | | |
| Jackson | 2 | 0 | 0 | 0 | 0 | 0 | 2 | 0 | 0 | 0 | |
| Kendall[2] | 3 | 0 | 2 | 0 | 0 | 0 | 0 | 2 | 2 | 0 | |
| Madison | 1 | 0 | 0 | 0 | 0 | 0 | 0 | 1 | 0 | 0 | |
| Sangamon | 1 | 0 | 0 | 0 | 0 | 0 | 1 | 0 | 0 | 0 | |
| St. Clair[2] | 3 | 0 | 0 | 0 | 0 | 0 | 0 | 1 | 1 | 0 | |
| Will | 2 | 1 | 0 | 0 | 0 | 0 | | 0 | 1 | 2 | |
| Winnebago | 2 | 1 | 0 | 0 | 0 | 0 | 0 | 1 | 0 | 2 | |
| **Nonmetropolitan Counties** | 0 | 0 | 0 | 0 | 1 | 0 | | | | | |
| Stephenson | 0 | 0 | 0 | 0 | 1 | 0 | 0 | 1 | 0 | 0 | |
| **INDIANA** | 87 | 24 | 17 | 0 | 2 | 11 | | | | | |
| **Cities** | 71 | 16 | 12 | 0 | 2 | 10 | | | | | |
| Anderson | 4 | 1 | 0 | 0 | 0 | 1 | 3 | 0 | 3 | 0 | 54,490 |
| Bloomington | 1 | 3 | 1 | 0 | 0 | 1 | 1 | 1 | 4 | 0 | 86,118 |
| Bristol | 1 | 0 | 0 | 0 | 0 | 0 | 0 | 0 | 0 | 1 | 1,707 |
| Brownsburg[2] | 4 | 0 | 0 | 0 | 0 | 0 | 3 | 0 | 0 | 0 | 28,227 |
| Cedar Lake | 0 | 0 | 1 | 0 | 0 | 0 | 0 | 1 | 0 | 0 | 13,806 |
| Chesterton[2] | 0 | 0 | 1 | 0 | 0 | 1 | 0 | 1 | 0 | 0 | 14,351 |
| Clarksville | 1 | 0 | 0 | 0 | 0 | 0 | 0 | 0 | 1 | 0 | 21,434 |
| Columbus | 2 | 0 | 0 | 0 | 0 | 0 | 0 | 2 | 0 | 0 | 48,902 |
| Cumberland[2] | 2 | 0 | 0 | 0 | 0 | 0 | 0 | 0 | 0 | 1 | 6,197 |
| East Chicago | 1 | 0 | 0 | 0 | 0 | 0 | 0 | 1 | 0 | 0 | 27,554 |
| Elkhart | 1 | 0 | 0 | 0 | 0 | 0 | 0 | 1 | 0 | 0 | 52,205 |
| Evansville | 0 | 0 | 1 | 0 | 0 | 0 | 0 | 0 | 0 | 1 | 118,240 |
| Fishers | 1 | 0 | 0 | 0 | 0 | 0 | 0 | 0 | 1 | 0 | 99,184 |
| Fort Wayne | 0 | 0 | 0 | 0 | 0 | 1 | 0 | 0 | 0 | 1 | 274,295 |
| Franklin | 1 | 1 | 1 | 0 | 0 | 0 | 0 | 2 | 0 | 1 | 26,091 |
| Griffith | 3 | 0 | 0 | 0 | 0 | 0 | 1 | 2 | 0 | | 15,947 |
| Hammond[2] | 7 | 0 | 0 | 0 | 0 | 5 | 2 | 1 | 6 | 2 | 74,824 |
| Indianapolis[2] | 21 | 0 | 5 | 0 | 0 | 1 | 2 | 11 | 5 | 7 | 895,826 |
| Kokomo | 1 | 2 | 0 | 0 | 0 | 0 | 2 | 1 | 0 | 0 | 58,248 |

## Table 94. Hate Crime Incidents Per Bias Motivation and Quarter, by Selected State and Agency and Federal, 2021—Continued

(Number.)

| State/agency | Number of incidents per bias motivation | | | | | | Number of incidents per quarter | | | | Population[1] |
|---|---|---|---|---|---|---|---|---|---|---|---|
| | Race/ Ethnicity/ Ancestry | Religion | Sexual orientation | Disability | Gender | Gender Identity | 1st quarter | 2nd quarter | 3rd quarter | 4th quarter | |
| Lawrence | 1 | 1 | 0 | 0 | 0 | 0 | 0 | 0 | 1 | 1 | 49,916 |
| Michigan City | 1 | 0 | 0 | 0 | 0 | 0 | 0 | 1 | 0 | 0 | 31,008 |
| Mishawaka | 0 | 1 | 0 | 0 | 0 | 0 | 0 | 1 | 0 | 0 | 50,523 |
| Mount Vernon | 1 | 0 | 0 | 0 | 0 | 0 | 0 | 1 | 0 | 0 | 6,391 |
| New Albany | 2 | 0 | 0 | 0 | 0 | 0 | 1 | 0 | 0 | 1 | 36,921 |
| Plainfield[2] | 2 | 2 | 0 | 0 | 0 | 0 | 0 | 2 | 1 | 0 | 37,257 |
| Sheridan | 1 | 0 | 0 | 0 | 0 | 0 | 0 | 1 | 0 | 0 | 3,085 |
| South Bend[2] | 4 | 1 | 0 | 0 | 0 | 0 | 4 | 0 | 0 | 0 | 101,936 |
| Terre Haute | 0 | 2 | 0 | 0 | 0 | 0 | 0 | 1 | 0 | 1 | 60,372 |
| Vincennes | 0 | 0 | 0 | 0 | 1 | 0 | 0 | 0 | 1 | 0 | 16,650 |
| Warsaw | 2 | 0 | 0 | 0 | 0 | 0 | 0 | 0 | 1 | 1 | 15,353 |
| Washington | 1 | 1 | 0 | 0 | 1 | 0 | 0 | 3 | 0 | 0 | 12,722 |
| Westfield | 4 | 1 | 2 | 0 | 0 | 0 | 0 | 4 | 3 | 0 | 48,140 |
| Whitestown | 1 | 0 | 0 | 0 | 0 | 0 | 0 | 0 | 0 | 1 | 10,738 |
| **Metropolitan Counties** | 8 | 4 | 3 | 0 | 0 | 1 | | | | | |
| Floyd | 0 | 2 | 0 | 0 | 0 | 0 | 2 | 0 | 0 | 0 | |
| Hamilton | 1 | 0 | 0 | 0 | 0 | 0 | 0 | 1 | 0 | 0 | |
| Howard | 0 | 1 | 0 | 0 | 0 | 0 | 0 | 1 | 0 | 0 | |
| Johnson | 1 | 0 | 0 | 0 | 0 | 0 | 0 | 0 | 1 | 0 | |
| Madison | 0 | 0 | 0 | 0 | 0 | 1 | 0 | 0 | 1 | 0 | |
| Porter | 2 | 0 | 0 | 0 | 0 | 0 | 0 | 1 | 0 | 1 | |
| Posey[2] | 2 | 1 | 1 | 0 | 0 | 0 | 1 | 1 | 1 | 0 | |
| St. Joseph | 1 | 0 | 0 | 0 | 0 | 0 | 0 | 0 | 0 | 1 | |
| Tippecanoe | 1 | 0 | 1 | 0 | 0 | 0 | 1 | 0 | 1 | 0 | |
| Vanderburgh | 0 | 0 | 1 | 0 | 0 | 0 | 0 | 0 | 1 | 0 | |
| **Nonmetropolitan Counties** | 3 | 1 | 1 | 0 | 0 | 0 | | | | | |
| Henry | 0 | 1 | 0 | 0 | 0 | 0 | 0 | 0 | 0 | 1 | |
| Jackson | 1 | 0 | 0 | 0 | 0 | 0 | 1 | 0 | 0 | 0 | |
| Kosciusko | 0 | 0 | 1 | 0 | 0 | 0 | 0 | 0 | 0 | 1 | |
| Montgomery | 1 | 0 | 0 | 0 | 0 | 0 | 1 | 0 | 0 | 0 | |
| Wells | 1 | 0 | 0 | 0 | 0 | 0 | 0 | 1 | 0 | 0 | |
| **State Police Agencies** | 4 | 3 | 1 | 0 | 0 | 0 | | | | | |
| Indiana State Police | 4 | 3 | 1 | 0 | 0 | 0 | 3 | 2 | 0 | 3 | |
| **Other Agencies** | 1 | 0 | 0 | 0 | 0 | 0 | | | | | |
| Indianapolis Public Schools | 1 | 0 | 0 | 0 | 0 | 0 | 0 | 0 | 0 | 1 | |
| **IOWA** | 75 | 10 | 10 | 4 | 3 | 3 | | | | | |
| **Cities** | 49 | 9 | 9 | 0 | 2 | 3 | | | | | |
| Albia | 1 | 0 | 0 | 0 | 0 | 0 | 0 | 0 | 1 | 0 | 3,706 |
| Bettendorf | 1 | 0 | 0 | 0 | 0 | 0 | 0 | 0 | 1 | 0 | 37,022 |
| Cedar Rapids | 1 | 0 | 0 | 0 | 0 | 0 | 0 | 0 | 1 | 0 | 134,763 |
| Charles City | 2 | 0 | 0 | 0 | 0 | 0 | 1 | 0 | 1 | 0 | 7,174 |
| Clear Lake | 1 | 0 | 0 | 0 | 2 | 1 | 2 | 2 | 0 | 0 | 7,492 |
| Clinton | 4 | 2 | 0 | 0 | 0 | 0 | 0 | 3 | 2 | 1 | 24,865 |
| Clive | 1 | 0 | 0 | 0 | 0 | 0 | 0 | 1 | 0 | 0 | 17,652 |
| Coralville | 1 | 0 | 0 | 0 | 0 | 0 | 0 | 1 | 0 | 0 | 22,874 |
| Council Bluffs | 1 | 0 | 0 | 0 | 0 | 0 | 0 | 1 | 0 | 0 | 62,202 |
| Davenport | 2 | 0 | 0 | 0 | 0 | 0 | 0 | 2 | 0 | 0 | 102,014 |
| Dubuque | 0 | 0 | 0 | 0 | 0 | 1 | 0 | 0 | 0 | 1 | 57,790 |
| Fort Dodge | 1 | 0 | 0 | 0 | 0 | 0 | 0 | 0 | 1 | 0 | 23,788 |
| Grinnell[2] | 1 | 1 | 2 | 0 | 0 | 0 | 0 | 1 | 1 | 1 | 9,084 |
| Indianola | 4 | 1 | 2 | 0 | 0 | 1 | 4 | 0 | 3 | 1 | 16,203 |
| Iowa City | 5 | 1 | 1 | 0 | 0 | 0 | 2 | 2 | 2 | 1 | 77,522 |
| Marengo | 1 | 0 | 0 | 0 | 0 | 0 | 0 | 0 | 0 | 1 | 2,460 |
| Mason City | 3 | 0 | 0 | 0 | 0 | 0 | 0 | 3 | 0 | 0 | 26,550 |
| Muscatine | 0 | 0 | 1 | 0 | 0 | 0 | 0 | 0 | 1 | 0 | 23,499 |
| Oelwein | 10 | 0 | 0 | 0 | 0 | 0 | 6 | 4 | 0 | 0 | 5,731 |
| Ottumwa | 1 | 0 | 0 | 0 | 0 | 0 | 0 | 0 | 1 | 0 | 24,308 |
| Pella | 0 | 0 | 1 | 0 | 0 | 0 | 0 | 0 | 1 | 0 | 10,260 |
| Red Oak | 1 | 0 | 0 | 0 | 0 | 0 | 0 | 0 | 0 | 1 | 5,229 |
| Sac City | 1 | 0 | 0 | 0 | 0 | 0 | 0 | 1 | 0 | 0 | 2,018 |
| Storm Lake | 2 | 0 | 0 | 0 | 0 | 0 | 0 | 0 | 2 | 0 | 10,414 |
| Walcott | 1 | 0 | 0 | 0 | 0 | 0 | 0 | 1 | 0 | 0 | 1,628 |
| Waterloo | 0 | 3 | 0 | 0 | 0 | 0 | 0 | 0 | 0 | 3 | 67,174 |
| Waukee | 1 | 0 | 0 | 0 | 0 | 0 | 0 | 0 | 1 | 0 | 27,858 |
| West Des Moines | 2 | 1 | 2 | 0 | 0 | 0 | 0 | 3 | 2 | 0 | 70,414 |
| **Metropolitan Counties** | 4 | 0 | 0 | 0 | 0 | 0 | | | | | |
| Benton | 1 | 0 | 0 | 0 | 0 | 0 | 0 | 0 | 1 | 0 | |
| Harrison | 2 | 0 | 0 | 0 | 0 | 0 | 1 | 1 | 0 | 0 | |
| Johnson | 1 | 0 | 0 | 0 | 0 | 0 | 0 | 0 | 0 | 1 | |
| **Nonmetropolitan Counties** | 22 | 1 | 1 | 4 | 1 | 0 | | | | | |
| Clarke | 2 | 0 | 1 | 0 | 0 | 0 | 1 | 1 | 1 | 0 | |
| Clinton | 1 | 0 | 0 | 0 | 0 | 0 | 0 | 0 | 0 | 1 | |
| Floyd[2] | 3 | 0 | 0 | 0 | 0 | 0 | 1 | 1 | 0 | 0 | |

## Table 94. Hate Crime Incidents Per Bias Motivation and Quarter, by Selected State and Agency and Federal, 2021—Continued

(Number.)

| State/agency | Number of incidents per bias motivation | | | | | | Number of incidents per quarter | | | | Population[1] |
|---|---|---|---|---|---|---|---|---|---|---|---|
| | Race/ Ethnicity/ Ancestry | Religion | Sexual orientation | Disability | Gender | Gender Identity | 1st quarter | 2nd quarter | 3rd quarter | 4th quarter | |
| Henry | 2 | 0 | 0 | 0 | 0 | 0 | 0 | 0 | 0 | 2 | |
| Ida | 2 | 0 | 0 | 0 | 1 | 0 | 1 | 2 | 0 | 0 | |
| Louisa | 0 | 1 | 0 | 0 | 0 | 0 | 1 | 0 | 0 | 0 | |
| Muscatine | 5 | 0 | 0 | 0 | 0 | 0 | 0 | 3 | 1 | 1 | |
| Pocahontas | 1 | 0 | 0 | 0 | 0 | 0 | 1 | 0 | 0 | 0 | |
| Wapello[2] | 0 | 0 | 0 | 4 | 0 | 0 | 0 | 1 | 2 | 0 | |
| Wayne[2] | 3 | 0 | 0 | 0 | 0 | 0 | 1 | 1 | 0 | 0 | |
| Winneshiek | 1 | 0 | 0 | 0 | 0 | 0 | 1 | 1 | 0 | 0 | |
| Worth | 2 | 0 | 0 | 0 | 0 | 0 | 0 | 0 | 1 | 1 | |
| **KANSAS** | 72 | 35 | 16 | 5 | 1 | 1 | | | | | |
| **Cities** | 52 | 26 | 12 | 4 | 1 | 1 | | | | | |
| Atchison | 1 | 0 | 0 | 0 | 0 | 0 | 0 | 1 | 0 | 0 | 10,374 |
| Baxter Springs[2] | 2 | 0 | 0 | 0 | 0 | 0 | 1 | 0 | 0 | 0 | 3,859 |
| Bel Aire[2] | 2 | 0 | 0 | 0 | 0 | 0 | 0 | 0 | 0 | 1 | 8,660 |
| Bonner Springs | 0 | 1 | 1 | 0 | 0 | 0 | 0 | 2 | 0 | 0 | 8,072 |
| Coffeyville | 0 | 2 | 0 | 0 | 0 | 0 | 1 | 0 | 0 | 1 | 9,066 |
| Derby | 1 | 0 | 0 | 0 | 0 | 0 | 0 | 0 | 0 | 1 | 25,425 |
| Dodge City | 2 | 0 | 0 | 0 | 0 | 0 | 1 | 1 | 0 | 0 | 26,612 |
| Fort Scott | 1 | 0 | 0 | 0 | 0 | 0 | 0 | 0 | 1 | 0 | 7,607 |
| Frankfort | 1 | 0 | 0 | 0 | 0 | 0 | 0 | 1 | 0 | 0 | 686 |
| Garden City | 3 | 0 | 1 | 1 | 0 | 0 | 1 | 1 | 2 | 1 | 25,920 |
| Gardner | 0 | 0 | 1 | 0 | 0 | 1 | 0 | 0 | 1 | 1 | 22,714 |
| Garnett | 0 | 1 | 0 | 0 | 0 | 0 | 1 | 0 | 0 | 0 | 3,243 |
| Goddard | 1 | 0 | 0 | 0 | 0 | 0 | 0 | 0 | 0 | 1 | 5,020 |
| Goodland | 10 | 1 | 1 | 0 | 0 | 0 | 0 | 8 | 3 | 1 | 4,283 |
| Great Bend | 0 | 2 | 0 | 0 | 0 | 0 | 1 | 0 | 0 | 1 | 14,795 |
| Hays | 2 | 4 | 1 | 0 | 0 | 0 | 0 | 1 | 1 | 5 | 20,861 |
| Hoisington | 1 | 0 | 0 | 0 | 0 | 0 | 1 | 0 | 0 | 0 | 2,429 |
| Hutchinson[2] | 1 | 0 | 3 | 0 | 0 | 0 | 0 | 3 | 0 | 0 | 40,015 |
| Leawood | 0 | 0 | 1 | 0 | 0 | 0 | 0 | 0 | 1 | 0 | 34,957 |
| Liberal | 0 | 1 | 0 | 0 | 0 | 0 | 0 | 1 | 0 | 0 | 18,658 |
| Maize | 0 | 1 | 0 | 0 | 0 | 0 | 0 | 0 | 1 | 0 | 5,491 |
| McPherson | 1 | 0 | 1 | 0 | 0 | 0 | 0 | 2 | 0 | 0 | 13,002 |
| Newton[2] | 3 | 0 | 0 | 0 | 0 | 0 | 0 | 0 | 1 | 0 | 18,705 |
| Olathe | 3 | 0 | 0 | 0 | 0 | 0 | 1 | 1 | 1 | 0 | 143,307 |
| Ottawa | 2 | 0 | 0 | 0 | 0 | 0 | 0 | 1 | 0 | 1 | 12,303 |
| Overland Park[2] | 2 | 3 | 0 | 0 | 0 | 0 | 1 | 1 | 0 | 2 | 199,881 |
| Parsons | 0 | 1 | 0 | 0 | 0 | 0 | 1 | 0 | 0 | 0 | 9,368 |
| Pittsburg | 3 | 0 | 0 | 0 | 0 | 0 | 0 | 1 | 2 | 0 | 19,939 |
| Salina | 2 | 0 | 0 | 0 | 0 | 0 | 0 | 0 | 2 | 0 | 46,112 |
| Shawnee | 1 | 0 | 0 | 0 | 1 | 0 | 1 | 1 | 0 | 0 | 66,710 |
| Topeka[2] | 6 | 4 | 0 | 2 | 0 | 0 | 3 | 2 | 3 | | 124,227 |
| Valley Center | 0 | 2 | 1 | 0 | 0 | 0 | 0 | 2 | 0 | 1 | 7,443 |
| Wellington | 0 | 2 | 0 | 0 | 0 | 0 | 1 | 0 | 0 | 1 | 7,491 |
| Wichita | 1 | 0 | 1 | 0 | 0 | 0 | 0 | 2 | 0 | | 392,643 |
| Winfield | 0 | 1 | 0 | 1 | 0 | 0 | 0 | 2 | 0 | 0 | 11,756 |
| **Universities and Colleges** | 3 | 1 | 1 | 0 | 0 | 0 | | | | | |
| Fort Hays State University | 2 | 0 | 0 | 0 | 0 | 0 | 0 | 1 | 0 | 1 | 18,862 |
| University of Kansas, Main Campus | 0 | 1 | 1 | 0 | 0 | 0 | 0 | 2 | 0 | 0 | 30,983 |
| Washburn University | 1 | 0 | 0 | 0 | 0 | 0 | 0 | 1 | 0 | 0 | 7,222 |
| **Metropolitan Counties** | 5 | 4 | 0 | 0 | 0 | 0 | | | | | |
| Butler | 1 | 0 | 0 | 0 | 0 | 0 | 0 | 0 | 1 | 0 | |
| Douglas | 1 | 0 | 0 | 0 | 0 | 0 | 1 | 0 | 0 | 0 | |
| Jefferson[2] | 2 | 0 | 0 | 0 | 0 | 0 | 0 | 1 | 0 | 0 | |
| Johnson | 0 | 1 | 0 | 0 | 0 | 0 | 0 | 0 | 0 | 1 | |
| Pottawatomie | 0 | 1 | 0 | 0 | 0 | 0 | 0 | 0 | 0 | 1 | |
| Riley County Police Department | 1 | 0 | 0 | 0 | 0 | 0 | 0 | 0 | 1 | 0 | |
| Sedgwick | 0 | 1 | 0 | 0 | 0 | 0 | 1 | 0 | 0 | 0 | |
| Sumner | 0 | 1 | 0 | 0 | 0 | 0 | 0 | 0 | 0 | 1 | |
| **Nonmetropolitan Counties** | 7 | 1 | 2 | 1 | 0 | 0 | | | | | |
| Brown | 1 | 0 | 0 | 0 | 0 | 0 | 1 | 0 | 0 | 0 | |
| Crawford | 2 | 0 | 0 | 0 | 0 | 0 | 0 | 0 | 1 | 1 | |
| Ellis | 0 | 0 | 1 | 0 | 0 | 0 | 0 | 0 | 1 | 0 | |
| Hamilton | 0 | 1 | 0 | 0 | 0 | 0 | 0 | 0 | 0 | 1 | |
| Jewell | 1 | 0 | 0 | 0 | 0 | 0 | 0 | 0 | 1 | 0 | |
| Lyon | 0 | 0 | 1 | 0 | 0 | 0 | 1 | 0 | 0 | 0 | |
| Morris | 2 | 0 | 0 | 0 | 0 | 0 | 0 | 0 | 1 | 1 | |
| Reno | 0 | 0 | 0 | 1 | 0 | 0 | 0 | 1 | 0 | 0 | |
| Saline | 1 | 0 | 0 | 0 | 0 | 0 | 1 | 0 | 0 | 0 | |
| **State Police Agencies** | 0 | 3 | 0 | 0 | 0 | 0 | | | | | |
| Highway Patrol, Troop F[2] | 0 | 3 | 0 | 0 | 0 | 0 | 0 | 2 | 0 | 0 | |
| **Tribal Agencies** | 1 | 0 | 1 | 0 | 0 | 0 | | | | | |
| Potawatomi Tribal | 1 | 0 | 1 | 0 | 0 | 0 | 0 | 1 | 1 | 0 | |

## Table 94. Hate Crime Incidents Per Bias Motivation and Quarter, by Selected State and Agency and Federal, 2021—Continued

(Number.)

| State/agency | Number of incidents per bias motivation | | | | | | Number of incidents per quarter | | | | Population[1] |
|---|---|---|---|---|---|---|---|---|---|---|---|
| | Race/ Ethnicity/ Ancestry | Religion | Sexual orientation | Disability | Gender | Gender Identity | 1st quarter | 2nd quarter | 3rd quarter | 4th quarter | |
| **Other Agencies** | 4 | 0 | 0 | 0 | 0 | 0 | | | | | |
| Johnson County Park | 2 | 0 | 0 | 0 | 0 | 0 | 1 | 0 | 1 | 0 | |
| Kansas City Fire Department, Fire Investigation Division | 1 | 0 | 0 | 0 | 0 | 0 | 1 | 0 | 0 | 0 | |
| Unified School District, Kansas City | 1 | 0 | 0 | 0 | 0 | 0 | 0 | 0 | 0 | 1 | |
| | | | | | | | | | | | |
| **KENTUCKY** | 91 | 6 | 40 | 4 | 0 | 13 | | | | | |
| **Cities** | 72 | 5 | 26 | 3 | 0 | 7 | | | | | |
| Ashland[2] | 1 | 0 | 5 | 0 | 0 | 2 | 0 | 2 | 0 | 1 | 19,913 |
| Bardstown | 1 | 0 | 0 | 0 | 0 | 0 | 0 | 1 | 0 | 0 | 13,378 |
| Benton | 1 | 0 | 0 | 0 | 0 | 0 | 1 | 0 | 0 | 0 | 4,461 |
| Bowling Green | 2 | 0 | 1 | 0 | 0 | 1 | 0 | 2 | 1 | 1 | 71,826 |
| Carlisle | 1 | 0 | 0 | 0 | 0 | 0 | 1 | 0 | 0 | 0 | 2,056 |
| Covington[2] | 0 | 0 | 3 | 0 | 0 | 0 | 0 | 0 | 1 | 1 | 40,298 |
| Cynthiana | 1 | 0 | 0 | 0 | 0 | 0 | 0 | 0 | 1 | 0 | 6,294 |
| Dayton | 0 | 0 | 0 | 0 | 0 | 1 | 0 | 0 | 1 | 0 | 5,678 |
| Edgewood | 0 | 0 | 1 | 0 | 0 | 0 | 0 | 0 | 1 | 0 | 8,796 |
| Eminence | 1 | 0 | 0 | 0 | 0 | 0 | 0 | 1 | 0 | 0 | 2,574 |
| Erlanger | 1 | 0 | 0 | 0 | 0 | 0 | 0 | 0 | 0 | 1 | 23,678 |
| Falmouth | 0 | 1 | 0 | 0 | 0 | 0 | 1 | 0 | 0 | 0 | 2,074 |
| Florence | 1 | 0 | 0 | 0 | 0 | 0 | 0 | 0 | 0 | 1 | 33,824 |
| Fort Mitchell | 1 | 0 | 0 | 0 | 0 | 0 | 1 | 0 | 0 | 0 | 8,273 |
| Frankfort[2] | 3 | 0 | 1 | 0 | 0 | 0 | 0 | 1 | 0 | 2 | 27,753 |
| Georgetown | 3 | 0 | 0 | 0 | 0 | 0 | 0 | 1 | 2 | 0 | 36,590 |
| Glasgow | 1 | 0 | 0 | 0 | 0 | 0 | 0 | 0 | 0 | 1 | 14,452 |
| Greenville | 1 | 0 | 0 | 0 | 0 | 0 | 0 | 0 | 0 | 1 | 4,122 |
| Harrodsburg | 1 | 0 | 0 | 0 | 0 | 0 | 0 | 1 | 0 | 0 | 8,560 |
| Henderson | 3 | 0 | 1 | 1 | 0 | 0 | 0 | 3 | 2 | 0 | 27,878 |
| Hopkinsville | 2 | 0 | 0 | 0 | 0 | 0 | 1 | 1 | 0 | 0 | 30,787 |
| Lancaster[2] | 2 | 0 | 0 | 0 | 0 | 0 | 0 | 1 | 0 | 0 | 3,845 |
| Lawrenceburg | 0 | 0 | 1 | 0 | 0 | 0 | 0 | 0 | 1 | 0 | 11,581 |
| Lexington[2] | 10 | 0 | 2 | 0 | 0 | 0 | 1 | 5 | 3 | 1 | 328,965 |
| Liberty[2] | 2 | 0 | 0 | 0 | 0 | 0 | 1 | 0 | 0 | 0 | 2,136 |
| Louisville Metro | 15 | 3 | 5 | 0 | 0 | 3 | 8 | 8 | 5 | 5 | 678,236 |
| Madisonville | 0 | 0 | 1 | 0 | 0 | 0 | 0 | 0 | 1 | 0 | 18,546 |
| Middlesboro | 1 | 0 | 1 | 0 | 0 | 0 | 0 | 0 | 0 | 2 | 8,762 |
| Morehead | 1 | 0 | 0 | 0 | 0 | 0 | 0 | 0 | 1 | 0 | 7,673 |
| Murray[2] | 3 | 0 | 0 | 0 | 0 | 0 | 0 | 0 | 1 | 0 | 19,605 |
| Newport | 1 | 0 | 0 | 0 | 0 | 0 | 0 | 0 | 0 | 1 | 14,851 |
| Nicholasville | 1 | 0 | 0 | 0 | 0 | 0 | 0 | 1 | 0 | 0 | 31,184 |
| Northfield | 0 | 1 | 0 | 0 | 0 | 0 | 1 | 0 | 0 | 0 | 1,055 |
| Owensboro | 6 | 0 | 1 | 0 | 0 | 0 | 2 | 0 | 2 | 3 | 60,636 |
| Paducah | 0 | 0 | 1 | 0 | 0 | 0 | 1 | 0 | 0 | 0 | 24,873 |
| Paris | 0 | 0 | 1 | 0 | 0 | 0 | 1 | 0 | 0 | 0 | 9,710 |
| Pikeville | 1 | 0 | 0 | 1 | 0 | 0 | 0 | 0 | 1 | 1 | 6,378 |
| Radcliff | 0 | 0 | 0 | 1 | 0 | 0 | 0 | 1 | 0 | 0 | 22,957 |
| Scottsville | 1 | 0 | 0 | 0 | 0 | 0 | 0 | 0 | 1 | 0 | 4,579 |
| Simpsonville[2] | 2 | 0 | 0 | 0 | 0 | 0 | 1 | 0 | 0 | 0 | 3,014 |
| St. Matthews | 0 | 0 | 1 | 0 | 0 | 0 | 0 | 0 | 0 | 1 | 18,038 |
| West Buechel | 1 | 0 | 0 | 0 | 0 | 0 | 1 | 0 | 0 | 0 | 1,277 |
| | | | | | | | | | | | |
| **Universities and Colleges** | 1 | 0 | 7 | 0 | 0 | 5 | | | | | |
| Eastern Kentucky University | 0 | 0 | 1 | 0 | 0 | 0 | 0 | 1 | 0 | 0 | 17,345 |
| Murray State University | 0 | 0 | 0 | 0 | 0 | 1 | 0 | 0 | 0 | 1 | 10,853 |
| Northern Kentucky University[2] | 0 | 0 | 3 | 0 | 0 | 2 | 0 | 0 | 0 | 2 | 18,308 |
| University of Louisville[2] | 1 | 0 | 3 | 0 | 0 | 2 | 0 | 0 | 0 | 2 | 25,451 |
| | | | | | | | | | | | |
| **Metropolitan Counties** | 9 | 0 | 0 | 0 | 0 | 1 | | | | | |
| Bullitt | 1 | 0 | 0 | 0 | 0 | 0 | 0 | 1 | 0 | 0 | |
| Daviess | 0 | 0 | 0 | 0 | 0 | 1 | 0 | 0 | 0 | 1 | |
| Henry | 1 | 0 | 0 | 0 | 0 | 0 | 0 | 1 | 0 | 0 | |
| Kenton County Police Department | 1 | 0 | 0 | 0 | 0 | 0 | 0 | 0 | 0 | 1 | |
| Meade | 1 | 0 | 0 | 0 | 0 | 0 | 0 | 0 | 0 | 1 | |
| Oldham County Police Department[2] | 2 | 0 | 0 | 0 | 0 | 0 | 0 | 0 | 0 | 1 | |
| Trigg[2] | 3 | 0 | 0 | 0 | 0 | 0 | 0 | 1 | 0 | 0 | |
| | | | | | | | | | | | |
| **Nonmetropolitan Counties** | 2 | 1 | 2 | 0 | 0 | 0 | | | | | |
| Calloway | 0 | 1 | 1 | 0 | 0 | 0 | 0 | 1 | 1 | 0 | |
| Hart | 1 | 0 | 0 | 0 | 0 | 0 | 1 | 0 | 0 | 0 | |
| Simpson | 1 | 0 | 0 | 0 | 0 | 0 | 0 | 1 | 0 | 0 | |
| Trimble | 0 | 0 | 1 | 0 | 0 | 0 | 1 | 0 | 0 | 0 | |
| | | | | | | | | | | | |
| **State Police Agencies** | 3 | 0 | 1 | 1 | 0 | 0 | | | | | |
| State Police | | | | | | | | | | | |
|   Bowling Green | 2 | 0 | 0 | 0 | 0 | 0 | 1 | 0 | 1 | 0 | |
|   Dry Ridge | 1 | 0 | 0 | 0 | 0 | 0 | 0 | 0 | 1 | 0 | |
|   Elizabethtown | 0 | 0 | 0 | 1 | 0 | 0 | 0 | 0 | 1 | 0 | |
|   Mayfield | 0 | 0 | 1 | 0 | 0 | 0 | 1 | 0 | 0 | 0 | |

# Table 94. Hate Crime Incidents Per Bias Motivation and Quarter, by Selected State and Agency and Federal, 2021—Continued

(Number.)

| State/agency | Number of incidents per bias motivation | | | | | | Number of incidents per quarter | | | | Population[1] |
|---|---|---|---|---|---|---|---|---|---|---|---|
| | Race/ Ethnicity/ Ancestry | Religion | Sexual orientation | Disability | Gender | Gender Identity | 1st quarter | 2nd quarter | 3rd quarter | 4th quarter | |
| **Other Agencies** | 4 | 0 | 4 | 0 | 0 | 0 | | | | | |
| Fayette County Schools | 2 | 0 | 1 | 0 | 0 | 0 | 0 | 1 | 0 | 2 | |
| Jefferson County School District | 2 | 0 | 3 | 0 | 0 | 0 | 0 | 0 | 4 | 1 | |
| | | | | | | | | | | | |
| **LOUISIANA** | 109 | 30 | 7 | 3 | 1 | 0 | | | | | |
| **Cities** | 68 | 10 | 2 | 1 | 0 | 0 | | | | | |
| Arnaudville | 0 | 0 | 1 | 0 | 0 | 0 | 0 | 1 | 0 | 0 | 1,040 |
| Bastrop | 0 | 3 | 0 | 0 | 0 | 0 | 0 | 1 | 1 | 1 | 9,543 |
| Baton Rouge | 1 | 0 | 0 | 0 | 0 | 0 | 1 | 0 | 0 | 0 | 218,060 |
| Bossier City | 1 | 0 | 1 | 1 | 0 | 0 | 1 | 2 | 0 | 0 | 68,879 |
| Hammond | 1 | 0 | 0 | 0 | 0 | 0 | 0 | 1 | 0 | 0 | 21,544 |
| Houma[2] | 2 | 0 | 0 | 0 | 0 | 0 | 0 | 0 | 0 | 1 | 32,351 |
| Mansfield[2] | 3 | 0 | 0 | 0 | 0 | 0 | 1 | 1 | 0 | 0 | 4,544 |
| Marksville[2] | 50 | 0 | 0 | 0 | 0 | 0 | 11 | 11 | 13 | 6 | 5,230 |
| Monroe[2] | 0 | 2 | 0 | 0 | 0 | 0 | 0 | 0 | 1 | 0 | 46,808 |
| Opelousas[2] | 0 | 3 | 0 | 0 | 0 | 0 | 0 | 0 | 1 | 1 | 15,457 |
| Pearl River | 0 | 1 | 0 | 0 | 0 | 0 | 1 | 0 | 0 | 0 | 2,638 |
| Ponchatoula | 2 | 0 | 0 | 0 | 0 | 0 | 0 | 2 | 0 | 0 | 7,648 |
| Sulphur | 0 | 1 | 0 | 0 | 0 | 0 | 0 | 0 | 1 | 0 | 20,097 |
| Vidalia[2] | 8 | 0 | 0 | 0 | 0 | 0 | 1 | 1 | 3 | 1 | 3,611 |
| | | | | | | | | | | | |
| **Metropolitan Counties** | 30 | 19 | 3 | 2 | 0 | 0 | | | | | |
| Ascension | 0 | 4 | 0 | 0 | 0 | 0 | 0 | 1 | 1 | 2 | |
| Bossier | 0 | 0 | 0 | 1 | 0 | 0 | 0 | 1 | 0 | 0 | |
| Calcasieu[2] | 3 | 5 | 0 | 0 | 0 | 0 | 1 | 2 | 1 | 3 | |
| De Soto[2] | 2 | 0 | 0 | 0 | 0 | 0 | 0 | 1 | 0 | 0 | |
| East Baton Rouge | 1 | 1 | 1 | 0 | 0 | 0 | 0 | 2 | 0 | 1 | |
| Iberville | 0 | 1 | 0 | 0 | 0 | 0 | 0 | 0 | 0 | 1 | |
| Jefferson | 1 | 0 | 1 | 0 | 0 | 0 | 0 | 2 | 0 | 0 | |
| Lafourche | 0 | 1 | 0 | 0 | 0 | 0 | 0 | 1 | 0 | 0 | |
| Ouachita | 0 | 2 | 0 | 0 | 0 | 0 | 0 | 0 | 2 | 0 | |
| Rapides | 1 | 1 | 0 | 1 | 0 | 0 | 1 | 1 | 1 | 0 | |
| St. John the Baptist[2] | 3 | 0 | 0 | 0 | 0 | 0 | 1 | 0 | 0 | 1 | |
| Tangipahoa[2] | 14 | 3 | 1 | 0 | 0 | 0 | 3 | 2 | 3 | 7 | |
| Terrebonne[2] | 5 | 1 | 0 | 0 | 0 | 0 | 2 | 1 | 2 | 0 | |
| | | | | | | | | | | | |
| **Nonmetropolitan Counties** | 11 | 1 | 1 | 0 | 1 | 0 | | | | | |
| Catahoula[2] | 5 | 0 | 0 | 0 | 0 | 0 | 0 | 2 | 0 | 2 | |
| Madison | 3 | 0 | 0 | 0 | 0 | 0 | 1 | 2 | | | |
| Richland | 0 | 1 | 0 | 0 | 0 | 0 | 0 | 1 | 0 | 0 | |
| St. Mary | 1 | 0 | 0 | 0 | 0 | 0 | 0 | 0 | 1 | 0 | |
| Washington | 1 | 0 | 1 | 0 | 1 | 0 | 2 | 0 | 1 | 0 | |
| West Carroll | 1 | 0 | 0 | 0 | 0 | 0 | 0 | 0 | 0 | 1 | |
| | | | | | | | | | | | |
| **Tribal Agencies** | 0 | 0 | 1 | 0 | 0 | 0 | | | | | |
| Coushatta Tribal | 0 | 0 | 1 | 0 | 0 | 0 | 1 | 0 | 0 | 0 | |
| | | | | | | | | | | | |
| **MAINE** | 36 | 9 | 25 | 1 | 2 | 3 | | | | | |
| **Cities** | 27 | 8 | 19 | 1 | 2 | 2 | | | | | |
| Augusta | 0 | 0 | 1 | 0 | 0 | 0 | 0 | 1 | 0 | 0 | 18,713 |
| Bangor | 1 | 1 | 3 | 0 | 0 | 0 | 0 | 2 | 3 | 0 | 31,898 |
| Belfast | 0 | 0 | 1 | 0 | 0 | 0 | 0 | 1 | 0 | 0 | 6,712 |
| Biddeford | 3 | 1 | 1 | 0 | 2 | 0 | 2 | 1 | 4 | 0 | 21,523 |
| Brunswick | 0 | 1 | 0 | 0 | 0 | 0 | 0 | 1 | 0 | 0 | 20,656 |
| Camden | 0 | 0 | 1 | 0 | 0 | 0 | 0 | 0 | 0 | 1 | 4,802 |
| Cumberland | 0 | 0 | 0 | 1 | 0 | 0 | 0 | 0 | 1 | 0 | 8,415 |
| Fort Fairfield | 1 | 0 | 0 | 0 | 0 | 0 | 0 | 0 | 1 | 0 | 3,258 |
| Freeport | 1 | 0 | 0 | 0 | 0 | 0 | 0 | 0 | 0 | 1 | 8,713 |
| Lewiston | 1 | 1 | 1 | 0 | 0 | 0 | 0 | 2 | 1 | 0 | 36,191 |
| Lincoln | 0 | 0 | 1 | 0 | 0 | 0 | 0 | 1 | 0 | 0 | 4,862 |
| Old Orchard Beach | 0 | 1 | 0 | 0 | 0 | 0 | 0 | 0 | 1 | 0 | 9,145 |
| Portland | 10 | 2 | 8 | 0 | 0 | 1 | 10 | 3 | 6 | 2 | 66,875 |
| Rockland | 1 | 0 | 0 | 0 | 0 | 0 | 1 | 0 | 0 | 0 | 7,172 |
| Rumford | 1 | 0 | 0 | 0 | 0 | 0 | 0 | 0 | 1 | 0 | 5,726 |
| Sanford | 2 | 0 | 0 | 0 | 0 | 1 | 0 | 0 | 1 | 2 | 21,300 |
| Scarborough | 0 | 0 | 1 | 0 | 0 | 0 | 1 | 0 | 0 | 0 | 21,810 |
| Westbrook | 0 | 1 | 0 | 0 | 0 | 0 | 0 | 0 | 0 | 1 | 19,451 |
| Windham | 2 | 0 | 0 | 0 | 0 | 0 | 0 | 1 | 1 | 0 | 19,118 |
| Winslow | 1 | 0 | 1 | 0 | 0 | 0 | 0 | 1 | 0 | 1 | 7,641 |
| Yarmouth | 2 | 0 | 0 | 0 | 0 | 0 | 1 | 0 | 1 | 0 | 8,628 |
| York | 1 | 0 | 0 | 0 | 0 | 0 | 0 | 0 | 1 | 0 | 13,413 |
| | | | | | | | | | | | |
| **Metropolitan Counties** | 7 | 0 | 3 | 0 | 0 | 0 | | | | | |
| Androscoggin | 2 | 0 | 0 | 0 | 0 | 0 | 0 | 1 | 1 | 0 | |
| Cumberland[2] | 1 | 0 | 3 | 0 | 0 | 0 | 0 | 1 | 2 | 0 | |
| Penobscot | 1 | 0 | 0 | 0 | 0 | 0 | 0 | 0 | 0 | 1 | |
| Sagadahoc | 1 | 0 | 0 | 0 | 0 | 0 | 0 | 0 | 0 | 1 | |
| York | 2 | 0 | 0 | 0 | 0 | 0 | 1 | 1 | 0 | 0 | |

## Table 94. Hate Crime Incidents Per Bias Motivation and Quarter, by Selected State and  Agency and Federal, 2021—Continued

(Number.)

| State/agency | Number of incidents per bias motivation | | | | | | Number of incidents per quarter | | | | Population[1] |
|---|---|---|---|---|---|---|---|---|---|---|---|
| | Race/ Ethnicity/ Ancestry | Religion | Sexual orientation | Disability | Gender | Gender Identity | 1st quarter | 2nd quarter | 3rd quarter | 4th quarter | |
| **Nonmetropolitan Counties** | 1 | 0 | 2 | 0 | 0 | 1 | | | | | |
| Aroostook | 0 | 0 | 1 | 0 | 0 | 0 | 0 | 0 | 0 | 1 | |
| Knox | 0 | 0 | 1 | 0 | 0 | 0 | 0 | 0 | 0 | 1 | |
| Oxford | 0 | 0 | 0 | 0 | 0 | 1 | 0 | 0 | 0 | 1 | |
| Somerset | 1 | 0 | 0 | 0 | 0 | 0 | 0 | 1 | 0 | 0 | |
| **State Police Agencies** | 1 | 1 | 0 | 0 | 0 | 0 | | | | | |
| State Police | 1 | 1 | 0 | 0 | 0 | 0 | 0 | 1 | 0 | 1 | |
| **Other Agencies** | 0 | 0 | 1 | 0 | 0 | 0 | | | | | |
| State Fire Marshal | 0 | 0 | 1 | 0 | 0 | 0 | 0 | 0 | 1 | 0 | |
| **MARYLAND** | 56 | 14 | 12 | 2 | 1 | 4 | | | | | |
| **Cities** | 7 | 0 | 3 | 2 | 0 | 0 | | | | | |
| Cumberland | 2 | 0 | 1 | 1 | 0 | 0 | 2 | 0 | 0 | 2 | 18,971 |
| Hagerstown | 5 | 0 | 2 | 1 | 0 | 0 | 3 | 2 | 2 | 1 | 39,942 |
| **Universities and Colleges** | 0 | 1 | 0 | 0 | 0 | 0 | | | | | |
| University of Maryland, Baltimore County | 0 | 1 | 0 | 0 | 0 | 0 | 0 | 0 | 0 | 1 | 15,403 |
| **Metropolitan Counties** | 48 | 11 | 9 | 0 | 1 | 3 | | | | | |
| Baltimore County Police Department[2] | 42 | 9 | 5 | 0 | 0 | 2 | 9 | 16 | 19 | 8 | |
| Montgomery County Police Department[2] | 2 | 2 | 2 | 0 | 0 | 0 | 2 | 0 | 2 | 1 | |
| St. Mary's | 4 | 0 | 2 | 0 | 1 | 1 | 2 | 2 | 3 | 1 | |
| **Other Agencies** | 1 | 2 | 0 | 0 | 0 | 1 | | | | | |
| Natural Resources Police | 1 | 1 | 0 | 0 | 0 | 1 | 2 | 0 | 1 | 0 | |
| Transit Administration | 0 | 1 | 0 | 0 | 0 | 0 | 0 | 0 | 0 | 1 | |
| **MASSACHUSETTS** | 280 | 84 | 82 | 3 | 5 | 10 | | | | | |
| **Cities** | 268 | 74 | 80 | 3 | 5 | 10 | | | | | |
| Acton | 3 | 0 | 0 | 0 | 0 | 0 | 1 | 1 | 0 | 1 | 23,853 |
| Adams | 0 | 0 | 1 | 0 | 0 | 0 | 0 | 0 | 1 | 0 | 7,904 |
| Agawam | 1 | 0 | 0 | 0 | 0 | 0 | 0 | 0 | 1 | 0 | 28,757 |
| Andover[2] | 1 | 0 | 1 | 0 | 0 | 0 | 0 | 0 | 0 | 1 | 37,216 |
| Arlington | 5 | 4 | 0 | 0 | 0 | 0 | 0 | 5 | 2 | 2 | 45,767 |
| Auburn | 1 | 0 | 0 | 0 | 0 | 0 | 0 | 1 | 0 | 0 | 16,885 |
| Barnstable | 3 | 1 | 0 | 0 | 0 | 0 | 2 | 0 | 1 | 1 | 44,841 |
| Belmont[2] | 3 | 2 | 2 | 0 | 0 | 0 | 3 | 2 | 0 | 0 | 26,206 |
| Billerica | 1 | 0 | 0 | 0 | 0 | 0 | 0 | 1 | 0 | 0 | 43,644 |
| Boston[2] | 71 | 15 | 27 | 0 | 2 | 3 | 28 | 34 | 18 | 31 | 704,758 |
| Braintree[2] | 2 | 1 | 1 | 0 | 0 | 1 | 0 | 1 | 3 | 0 | 37,643 |
| Brookline[2] | 0 | 3 | 1 | 0 | 0 | 0 | 0 | 3 | 0 | 0 | 59,748 |
| Cambridge[2] | 25 | 4 | 7 | 1 | 0 | 1 | 7 | 6 | 14 | 8 | 121,699 |
| Chelsea | 1 | 0 | 0 | 0 | 0 | 0 | 1 | 0 | 0 | 0 | 39,971 |
| Concord | 2 | 0 | 0 | 0 | 0 | 0 | 0 | 1 | 0 | 1 | 19,025 |
| Danvers[2] | 5 | 5 | 1 | 0 | 0 | 0 | 0 | 4 | 1 | 2 | 27,904 |
| Dedham[2] | 2 | 0 | 0 | 0 | 0 | 0 | 0 | 1 | 0 | 0 | 25,699 |
| Dennis[2] | 3 | 0 | 0 | 0 | 0 | 0 | 0 | 0 | 1 | 0 | 13,971 |
| Dracut | 1 | 0 | 0 | 0 | 0 | 0 | 0 | 0 | 0 | 1 | 31,879 |
| Eastham[2] | 1 | 1 | 0 | 0 | 0 | 0 | 0 | 1 | 0 | 0 | 4,937 |
| East Longmeadow | 1 | 0 | 0 | 0 | 0 | 0 | 1 | 0 | 0 | 0 | 16,286 |
| Edgartown[2] | 2 | 0 | 0 | 0 | 0 | 0 | 1 | 0 | 0 | 0 | 4,470 |
| Everett | 1 | 0 | 0 | 0 | 0 | 0 | 0 | 0 | 1 | 0 | 46,959 |
| Falmouth[2] | 2 | 1 | 0 | 0 | 0 | 0 | 1 | 0 | 0 | 1 | 31,320 |
| Fitchburg | 1 | 0 | 0 | 0 | 0 | 0 | 0 | 1 | 0 | 0 | 40,626 |
| Framingham[2] | 1 | 3 | 0 | 0 | 0 | 0 | 0 | 0 | 1 | 2 | 75,042 |
| Franklin | 2 | 1 | 0 | 0 | 0 | 0 | 0 | 0 | 1 | 2 | 35,425 |
| Freetown | 0 | 0 | 1 | 0 | 0 | 0 | 0 | 1 | 0 | 0 | 9,567 |
| Gardner | 1 | 0 | 0 | 0 | 0 | 0 | 0 | 1 | 0 | 0 | 20,795 |
| Gloucester[2] | 2 | 0 | 0 | 0 | 0 | 0 | 0 | 1 | 0 | 0 | 30,963 |
| Groton | 5 | 3 | 0 | 0 | 0 | 0 | 0 | 1 | 0 | 7 | 11,407 |
| Hanover[2] | 0 | 0 | 2 | 0 | 0 | 0 | 0 | 1 | 0 | 0 | 15,396 |
| Hanson | 1 | 0 | 0 | 0 | 0 | 0 | 0 | 0 | 1 | 0 | 11,550 |
| Haverhill[2] | 11 | 3 | 1 | 0 | 0 | 3 | 4 | 2 | 3 | 5 | 64,944 |
| Hingham[2] | 1 | 0 | 0 | 1 | 0 | 0 | 0 | 0 | 0 | 1 | 26,172 |
| Holbrook[2] | 4 | 0 | 1 | 0 | 0 | 0 | 2 | 1 | 1 | 0 | 11,163 |
| Holyoke | 1 | 0 | 0 | 0 | 0 | 0 | 0 | 0 | 1 | 0 | 40,326 |
| Hull | 0 | 1 | 0 | 0 | 0 | 0 | 0 | 1 | 0 | 0 | 11,000 |
| Lakeville | 0 | 0 | 0 | 1 | 0 | 0 | 0 | 0 | 1 | 0 | 12,360 |
| Lawrence | 1 | 0 | 1 | 0 | 0 | 0 | 2 | 0 | 0 | 0 | 81,021 |
| Lee | 1 | 0 | 1 | 0 | 0 | 0 | 0 | 1 | 1 | 0 | 5,598 |
| Lexington | 2 | 1 | 0 | 0 | 0 | 0 | 0 | 0 | 2 | 1 | 33,427 |
| Lowell | 1 | 0 | 1 | 0 | 0 | 0 | 0 | 0 | 2 | 0 | 112,230 |
| Ludlow[2] | 0 | 1 | 1 | 0 | 0 | 0 | 0 | 1 | 0 | 0 | 21,312 |
| Lynn[2] | 11 | 0 | 1 | 0 | 0 | 0 | 3 | 3 | 1 | 4 | 95,727 |
| Marblehead[2] | 3 | 3 | 1 | 0 | 0 | 0 | 3 | 3 | 0 | 0 | 20,791 |
| Mashpee | 1 | 0 | 0 | 0 | 0 | 0 | 0 | 0 | 1 | 0 | 14,411 |
| Medford | 4 | 2 | 1 | 0 | 0 | 0 | 2 | 3 | 2 | 0 | 61,819 |

# Table 94. Hate Crime Incidents Per Bias Motivation and Quarter, by Selected State and Agency and Federal, 2021—Continued

(Number.)

| State/agency | Number of incidents per bias motivation | | | | | | Number of incidents per quarter | | | | Population[1] |
|---|---|---|---|---|---|---|---|---|---|---|---|
| | Race/ Ethnicity/ Ancestry | Religion | Sexual orientation | Disability | Gender | Gender Identity | 1st quarter | 2nd quarter | 3rd quarter | 4th quarter | |
| Natick | 1 | 0 | 0 | 0 | 0 | 0 | 1 | 0 | 0 | 0 | 36,340 |
| Needham | 1 | 0 | 0 | 0 | 0 | 0 | 0 | 0 | 1 | 0 | 32,159 |
| Newbury | 1 | 0 | 0 | 0 | 0 | 0 | 0 | 0 | 0 | 1 | 7,285 |
| Newburyport | 0 | 1 | 0 | 0 | 0 | 0 | 0 | 0 | 1 | 0 | 18,757 |
| Newton[2] | 8 | 1 | 0 | 0 | 0 | 0 | 2 | 3 | 1 | 1 | 88,769 |
| Northbridge | 1 | 0 | 0 | 0 | 0 | 0 | 0 | 1 | 0 | 0 | 16,850 |
| Pepperell | 1 | 0 | 0 | 0 | 0 | 0 | 0 | 0 | 0 | 1 | 12,192 |
| Pittsfield[2] | 4 | 0 | 1 | 0 | 0 | 0 | 0 | 2 | 2 | 0 | 41,556 |
| Plainville | 0 | 1 | 0 | 0 | 0 | 0 | 1 | 0 | 0 | 0 | 9,495 |
| Plymouth[2] | 1 | 0 | 1 | 0 | 0 | 0 | 0 | 1 | 0 | 0 | 66,289 |
| Provincetown[2] | 2 | 0 | 1 | 0 | 0 | 0 | 0 | 1 | 1 | 0 | 2,982 |
| Quincy | 6 | 1 | 2 | 0 | 0 | 0 | 1 | 4 | 1 | 3 | 95,737 |
| Randolph[2] | 6 | 0 | 0 | 0 | 0 | 0 | 1 | 1 | 1 | 2 | 32,257 |
| Revere | 2 | 0 | 0 | 0 | 0 | 0 | 0 | 1 | 0 | 1 | 52,860 |
| Rutland | 1 | 0 | 0 | 0 | 0 | 0 | 0 | 1 | 0 | 0 | 9,208 |
| Salem[2] | 7 | 6 | 9 | 0 | 1 | 0 | 7 | 12 | 1 | 2 | 44,120 |
| Sandwich[2] | 1 | 0 | 2 | 0 | 0 | 0 | 0 | 1 | 1 | 0 | 20,266 |
| Shrewsbury | 2 | 0 | 0 | 0 | 1 | 0 | 2 | 1 | 0 | 0 | 39,602 |
| Somerville[2] | 6 | 2 | 1 | 0 | 0 | 1 | 1 | 2 | 2 | 2 | 82,123 |
| Southborough | 1 | 0 | 0 | 0 | 0 | 0 | 0 | 0 | 0 | 1 | 10,328 |
| South Hadley[2] | 3 | 0 | 1 | 0 | 0 | 0 | 2 | 1 | 0 | 0 | 17,520 |
| Springfield | 1 | 1 | 0 | 0 | 0 | 0 | 1 | 0 | 0 | 1 | 154,098 |
| Stoneham[2] | 2 | 0 | 0 | 0 | 0 | 0 | 0 | 1 | 0 | 0 | 24,439 |
| Stoughton | 1 | 0 | 0 | 0 | 0 | 0 | 0 | 1 | 0 | 0 | 29,418 |
| Sudbury | 0 | 1 | 0 | 0 | 0 | 0 | 0 | 1 | 0 | 0 | 19,798 |
| Swansea[2] | 2 | 0 | 0 | 0 | 0 | 0 | 0 | 0 | 1 | 0 | 17,257 |
| Townsend | 0 | 0 | 1 | 0 | 0 | 0 | 0 | 0 | 0 | 1 | 9,574 |
| Wakefield | 1 | 0 | 0 | 0 | 0 | 0 | 0 | 1 | 0 | 0 | 27,470 |
| Waltham | 2 | 0 | 0 | 0 | 0 | 0 | 0 | 2 | 0 | 0 | 62,693 |
| Wenham[2] | 0 | 0 | 6 | 0 | 0 | 0 | 0 | 0 | 3 | 0 | 5,236 |
| West Boylston | 1 | 0 | 0 | 0 | 0 | 0 | 0 | 1 | 0 | 0 | 8,137 |
| Westwood | 1 | 1 | 0 | 0 | 0 | 0 | 0 | 0 | 2 | 0 | 16,767 |
| Wilmington | 0 | 0 | 1 | 0 | 0 | 0 | 0 | 0 | 1 | 0 | 23,567 |
| Winthrop[2] | 1 | 1 | 0 | 0 | 0 | 0 | 0 | 1 | 0 | 0 | 18,692 |
| Woburn | 1 | 0 | 1 | 0 | 0 | 0 | 0 | 1 | 0 | 1 | 40,568 |
| Worcester[2] | 9 | 2 | 0 | 0 | 0 | 1 | 3 | 7 | 0 | 1 | 186,365 |
| Yarmouth | 0 | 1 | 0 | 0 | 1 | 0 | 0 | 1 | 0 | 1 | 23,295 |
| | | | | | | | | | | | |
| **Universities and Colleges** | 9 | 9 | 2 | 0 | 0 | 0 | | | | | |
| Boston University | 2 | 0 | 0 | 0 | 0 | 0 | 0 | 1 | 1 | 0 | 42,047 |
| Bridgewater State University | 1 | 0 | 0 | 0 | 0 | 0 | 0 | 0 | 0 | 1 | 13,150 |
| Emerson College | 0 | 1 | 0 | 0 | 0 | 0 | 0 | 0 | 0 | 1 | 5,496 |
| Framingham State University | 1 | 0 | 0 | 0 | 0 | 0 | 0 | 0 | 0 | 1 | 8,366 |
| Harvard University | 0 | 1 | 0 | 0 | 0 | 0 | 0 | 1 | 0 | 0 | 41,024 |
| Massachusetts College of Liberal Arts | 0 | 2 | 1 | 0 | 0 | 0 | 0 | 2 | 0 | 1 | 1,922 |
| Massachusetts Institute of Technology | 2 | 0 | 0 | 0 | 0 | 0 | 0 | 1 | 0 | 1 | 12,195 |
| Mount Holyoke College | 0 | 3 | 0 | 0 | 0 | 0 | 0 | 0 | 0 | 3 | 2,504 |
| University of Massachusetts | | | | | | | | | | | |
| Amherst | 1 | 0 | 0 | 0 | 0 | 0 | 0 | 0 | 1 | 0 | 35,781 |
| Lowell | 1 | 0 | 0 | 0 | 0 | 0 | 0 | 1 | 0 | 0 | 22,192 |
| Western New England University | 0 | 1 | 0 | 0 | 0 | 0 | 0 | 0 | 0 | 1 | 4,005 |
| Westfield State University | 1 | 1 | 0 | 0 | 0 | 0 | 0 | 0 | 0 | 2 | 7,104 |
| Wheaton College | 0 | 0 | 1 | 0 | 0 | 0 | 0 | 1 | 0 | 0 | 1,807 |
| | | | | | | | | | | | |
| **State Police Agencies** | 2 | 0 | 0 | 0 | 0 | 0 | | | | | |
| State Police | | | | | | | | | | | |
| Norfolk County | 1 | 0 | 0 | 0 | 0 | 0 | 1 | 0 | 0 | 0 | |
| Suffolk County | 1 | 0 | 0 | 0 | 0 | 0 | 1 | 0 | 0 | 0 | |
| | | | | | | | | | | | |
| **Other Agencies** | 1 | 1 | 0 | 0 | 0 | 0 | | | | | |
| Division of Law Enforcement, Environmental Police[2] | 1 | 1 | 0 | 0 | 0 | 0 | 0 | 0 | 1 | 0 | |
| | | | | | | | | | | | |
| **MICHIGAN** | 294 | 52 | 60 | 4 | 7 | 13 | | | | | |
| **Cities** | 221 | 37 | 47 | 3 | 3 | 6 | | | | | |
| Adrian[2] | 2 | 0 | 0 | 0 | 0 | 0 | 0 | 0 | 1 | 0 | 20,371 |
| Albion | 6 | 1 | 0 | 0 | 0 | 0 | 1 | 4 | 0 | 2 | 8,336 |
| Allen Park | 0 | 2 | 0 | 0 | 0 | 0 | 0 | 0 | 0 | 2 | 26,615 |
| Ann Arbor[2] | 5 | 4 | 0 | 0 | 0 | 2 | 2 | 6 | 1 | 0 | 119,805 |
| Bath Township | 2 | 0 | 0 | 0 | 0 | 0 | 0 | 1 | 0 | 1 | 13,226 |
| Bay City | 4 | 0 | 0 | 0 | 0 | 0 | 1 | 0 | 1 | 2 | 32,200 |
| Benton Township | 1 | 0 | 1 | 0 | 0 | 0 | 0 | 1 | 1 | 0 | 14,230 |
| Birch Run[2] | 0 | 0 | 2 | 0 | 0 | 0 | 0 | 1 | 0 | 0 | 1,461 |
| Blissfield | 1 | 0 | 0 | 0 | 0 | 0 | 0 | 0 | 0 | 1 | 3,240 |
| Bloomfield Hills | 0 | 0 | 1 | 0 | 0 | 0 | 0 | 0 | 0 | 1 | 4,001 |
| Bloomfield Township | 1 | 0 | 0 | 0 | 0 | 0 | 0 | 0 | 0 | 1 | 41,809 |
| Boyne City | 1 | 0 | 0 | 0 | 0 | 0 | 0 | 0 | 0 | 1 | 3,717 |
| Brighton | 1 | 0 | 0 | 0 | 0 | 0 | 1 | 0 | 0 | 0 | 7,654 |
| Brownstown Township | 1 | 0 | 0 | 0 | 0 | 0 | 0 | 0 | 1 | 0 | 32,300 |
| Burton | 3 | 0 | 0 | 0 | 0 | 0 | 1 | 0 | 0 | 2 | 28,319 |

## Table 94. Hate Crime Incidents Per Bias Motivation and Quarter, by Selected State and Agency and Federal, 2021—Continued

(Number.)

| State/agency | Number of incidents per bias motivation | | | | | | Number of incidents per quarter | | | | Population[1] |
|---|---|---|---|---|---|---|---|---|---|---|---|
| | Race/ Ethnicity/ Ancestry | Religion | Sexual orientation | Disability | Gender | Gender Identity | 1st quarter | 2nd quarter | 3rd quarter | 4th quarter | |
| Cadillac | 0 | 0 | 0 | 0 | 0 | 1 | 0 | 0 | 0 | 1 | 10,536 |
| Canton Township[2] | 5 | 2 | 1 | 0 | 0 | 0 | 1 | 4 | 1 | 1 | 94,777 |
| Caro | 0 | 0 | 1 | 0 | 0 | 0 | 0 | 1 | 0 | 0 | 3,967 |
| Carrollton Township | 1 | 0 | 0 | 0 | 0 | 0 | 0 | 0 | 1 | 0 | 5,560 |
| Clinton | 0 | 0 | 1 | 0 | 0 | 0 | 0 | 0 | 0 | 1 | 2,283 |
| Clinton Township | 2 | 0 | 0 | 0 | 0 | 0 | 0 | 0 | 1 | 1 | 100,094 |
| Clio | 1 | 0 | 0 | 0 | 0 | 0 | 1 | 0 | 0 | 0 | 2,465 |
| Coldwater | 1 | 0 | 0 | 0 | 0 | 0 | 0 | 0 | 0 | 1 | 11,954 |
| Commerce Township | 0 | 1 | 0 | 0 | 0 | 0 | 0 | 1 | 0 | 0 | 39,878 |
| Croswell | 1 | 0 | 0 | 0 | 0 | 0 | 0 | 0 | 0 | 1 | 2,235 |
| Dearborn | 3 | 2 | 0 | 0 | 0 | 0 | 1 | 1 | 0 | 3 | 92,930 |
| Dearborn Heights | 1 | 1 | 0 | 0 | 0 | 0 | 1 | 0 | 0 | 1 | 54,772 |
| Decatur | 1 | 0 | 0 | 0 | 0 | 0 | 1 | 0 | 0 | 0 | 1,707 |
| Detroit[2] | 24 | 1 | 20 | 1 | 1 | 0 | 12 | 14 | 14 | 5 | 673,708 |
| Dowagiac | 0 | 0 | 2 | 0 | 0 | 0 | 0 | 1 | 0 | 1 | 5,536 |
| East Lansing[2] | 3 | 1 | 0 | 0 | 0 | 0 | 1 | 0 | 1 | 1 | 47,548 |
| Eastpointe | 2 | 0 | 0 | 0 | 0 | 0 | 0 | 2 | 0 | 0 | 31,653 |
| Eaton Rapids | 3 | 0 | 0 | 0 | 0 | 0 | 0 | 1 | 2 | 0 | 5,223 |
| Ecorse | 1 | 0 | 0 | 0 | 0 | 0 | 0 | 1 | 0 | 0 | 9,635 |
| Escanaba | 1 | 0 | 0 | 0 | 0 | 0 | 0 | 1 | 0 | 0 | 12,052 |
| Farmington Hills | 2 | 0 | 0 | 0 | 0 | 0 | 1 | 1 | 0 | 0 | 80,044 |
| Ferndale | 1 | 0 | 1 | 0 | 0 | 1 | 0 | 1 | 0 | 2 | 20,228 |
| Flint | 5 | 0 | 1 | 0 | 0 | 0 | 3 | 0 | 2 | 1 | 94,290 |
| Flint Township | 1 | 0 | 0 | 0 | 0 | 0 | 0 | 0 | 1 | 0 | 30,015 |
| Fraser | 1 | 0 | 0 | 0 | 0 | 0 | 1 | 0 | 0 | 0 | 14,316 |
| Garden City | 1 | 0 | 0 | 0 | 0 | 0 | 0 | 0 | 1 | 0 | 26,084 |
| Gaylord | 2 | 0 | 0 | 0 | 0 | 0 | 1 | 1 | 0 | 0 | 3,672 |
| Genesee Township | 2 | 0 | 0 | 0 | 0 | 0 | 1 | 0 | 1 | 0 | 20,258 |
| Grand Blanc Township | 1 | 0 | 0 | 0 | 0 | 0 | 0 | 1 | 0 | 0 | 36,700 |
| Grand Rapids[2] | 4 | 0 | 0 | 0 | 0 | 0 | 1 | 0 | 1 | 1 | 201,280 |
| Green Oak Township | 1 | 0 | 0 | 0 | 0 | 0 | 0 | 0 | 1 | 0 | 19,155 |
| Greenville | 2 | 0 | 0 | 0 | 0 | 0 | 0 | 0 | 1 | 1 | 8,378 |
| Grosse Pointe | 1 | 0 | 0 | 0 | 0 | 0 | 0 | 0 | 0 | 1 | 5,094 |
| Grosse Pointe Park | 1 | 0 | 0 | 0 | 0 | 0 | 1 | 0 | 0 | 0 | 10,918 |
| Hancock | 1 | 0 | 0 | 0 | 0 | 0 | 0 | 0 | 0 | 1 | 4,426 |
| Harbor Springs | 0 | 1 | 0 | 0 | 0 | 0 | 1 | 0 | 0 | 0 | 1,204 |
| Harper Woods | 1 | 1 | 0 | 0 | 0 | 0 | 2 | 0 | 0 | 0 | 13,582 |
| Hartford | 0 | 1 | 0 | 0 | 0 | 0 | 0 | 1 | 0 | 0 | 2,561 |
| Hastings | 1 | 0 | 1 | 0 | 0 | 0 | 2 | 0 | 0 | 0 | 7,335 |
| Highland Park | 8 | 0 | 0 | 0 | 0 | 1 | 2 | 2 | 1 | 4 | 10,620 |
| Hillsdale | 1 | 0 | 0 | 0 | 0 | 0 | 0 | 0 | 0 | 1 | 8,081 |
| Imlay City | 1 | 0 | 1 | 0 | 0 | 0 | 1 | 1 | 0 | 0 | 3,584 |
| Iron River | 2 | 0 | 0 | 0 | 0 | 0 | 0 | 1 | 1 | 0 | 2,808 |
| Kalamazoo Township | 1 | 0 | 0 | 0 | 0 | 0 | 0 | 1 | 0 | 0 | 24,503 |
| Kentwood | 1 | 0 | 1 | 0 | 0 | 0 | 1 | 0 | 1 | 0 | 52,028 |
| Lansing[2] | 11 | 3 | 1 | 0 | 0 | 0 | 2 | 4 | 5 | 1 | 117,865 |
| Lansing Township | 0 | 1 | 0 | 0 | 0 | 0 | 1 | 0 | 0 | 0 | 8,158 |
| Lincoln Park | 3 | 0 | 0 | 0 | 0 | 0 | 0 | 3 | 0 | 0 | 35,879 |
| Litchfield | 1 | 0 | 0 | 0 | 0 | 0 | 1 | 0 | 0 | 0 | 1,324 |
| Livonia | 2 | 0 | 0 | 0 | 0 | 0 | 0 | 1 | 1 | 0 | 92,852 |
| Lowell | 0 | 1 | 0 | 0 | 1 | 0 | 0 | 0 | 0 | 2 | 4,239 |
| Ludington | 1 | 0 | 0 | 0 | 0 | 0 | 0 | 1 | 0 | 0 | 8,098 |
| Madison Heights | 0 | 0 | 0 | 0 | 1 | 0 | 0 | 0 | 0 | 1 | 29,626 |
| Manistique | 1 | 0 | 0 | 0 | 0 | 0 | 0 | 0 | 1 | 0 | 2,933 |
| Marquette | 1 | 0 | 0 | 0 | 0 | 0 | 0 | 1 | 0 | 0 | 20,208 |
| Mason | 1 | 0 | 0 | 0 | 0 | 0 | 0 | 0 | 1 | 0 | 8,402 |
| Meridian Township | 2 | 0 | 0 | 0 | 0 | 0 | 0 | 0 | 2 | 0 | 43,146 |
| Milan | 0 | 1 | 0 | 0 | 0 | 0 | 0 | 1 | 0 | 0 | 6,028 |
| Montrose Township | 0 | 1 | 0 | 0 | 0 | 0 | 0 | 1 | 0 | 0 | 7,420 |
| Mount Morris[2] | 2 | 0 | 0 | 0 | 0 | 0 | 0 | 1 | 0 | 0 | 2,803 |
| Mount Pleasant | 1 | 0 | 1 | 0 | 0 | 0 | 0 | 1 | 1 | 0 | 24,109 |
| Muskegon | 0 | 0 | 0 | 1 | 0 | 0 | 0 | 1 | 0 | 0 | 36,296 |
| Muskegon Township | 1 | 0 | 0 | 0 | 0 | 0 | 0 | 0 | 1 | 0 | 18,043 |
| Niles | 0 | 0 | 1 | 0 | 0 | 0 | 0 | 0 | 1 | 0 | 11,045 |
| Norton Shores | 0 | 1 | 0 | 0 | 0 | 0 | 0 | 0 | 1 | 0 | 24,689 |
| Novi | 1 | 0 | 0 | 0 | 0 | 0 | 1 | 0 | 0 | 0 | 61,440 |
| Oscoda Township | 1 | 0 | 0 | 0 | 0 | 0 | 0 | 1 | 0 | 0 | 6,743 |
| Ovid | 1 | 0 | 0 | 0 | 0 | 0 | 1 | 0 | 0 | 0 | 1,609 |
| Owosso | 1 | 0 | 0 | 0 | 0 | 0 | 0 | 0 | 0 | 1 | 14,258 |
| Paw Paw | 1 | 0 | 0 | 0 | 0 | 0 | 0 | 1 | 0 | 0 | 3,328 |
| Pittsfield Township | 1 | 0 | 1 | 0 | 0 | 0 | 1 | 1 | 0 | 0 | 39,327 |
| Plymouth Township | 2 | 0 | 0 | 0 | 0 | 0 | 0 | 1 | 1 | 0 | 26,895 |
| Pontiac | 2 | 0 | 0 | 0 | 0 | 0 | 0 | 0 | 2 | 0 | 58,834 |
| Port Huron | 0 | 0 | 1 | 0 | 0 | 0 | 1 | 0 | 0 | 0 | 28,487 |
| Redford Township | 2 | 0 | 0 | 0 | 0 | 0 | 2 | 0 | 0 | 0 | 46,112 |
| Richfield Township, Roscommon County | 1 | 0 | 0 | 0 | 0 | 0 | 0 | 1 | 0 | 0 | 3,642 |
| Richmond | 1 | 0 | 0 | 0 | 0 | 0 | 1 | 0 | 0 | 0 | 5,801 |
| Rochester | 0 | 0 | 1 | 0 | 0 | 0 | 0 | 0 | 0 | 1 | 13,251 |
| Rockford | 1 | 0 | 0 | 0 | 0 | 0 | 0 | 0 | 1 | 0 | 6,468 |
| Roseville | 5 | 0 | 0 | 0 | 0 | 0 | 0 | 4 | 0 | 1 | 46,456 |

# Table 94. Hate Crime Incidents Per Bias Motivation and Quarter, by Selected State and Agency and Federal, 2021—Continued

(Number.)

| State/agency | Number of incidents per bias motivation | | | | | | Number of incidents per quarter | | | | Population[1] |
|---|---|---|---|---|---|---|---|---|---|---|---|
| | Race/Ethnicity/Ancestry | Religion | Sexual orientation | Disability | Gender | Gender Identity | 1st quarter | 2nd quarter | 3rd quarter | 4th quarter | |
| Royal Oak[2] | 0 | 2 | 0 | 0 | 0 | 0 | 0 | 0 | 1 | 0 | 59,137 |
| Saginaw | 2 | 0 | 0 | 0 | 0 | 0 | 1 | 0 | 1 | 0 | 47,480 |
| Saginaw Township | 2 | 0 | 0 | 0 | 0 | 0 | 0 | 1 | 1 | 0 | 38,836 |
| Sault Ste. Marie | 1 | 0 | 0 | 0 | 0 | 0 | 0 | 0 | 1 | 0 | 13,282 |
| Schoolcraft | 0 | 1 | 0 | 0 | 0 | 0 | 0 | 0 | 1 | 0 | 1,550 |
| Scottville | 1 | 0 | 0 | 0 | 0 | 0 | 1 | 0 | 0 | 0 | 1,209 |
| Shelby Township[2] | 2 | 0 | 0 | 0 | 0 | 0 | 0 | 1 | 0 | 0 | 82,164 |
| Southfield | 2 | 1 | 0 | 0 | 0 | 0 | 0 | 2 | 0 | 1 | 72,216 |
| Southgate | 3 | 0 | 0 | 0 | 0 | 0 | 0 | 1 | 2 | 0 | 29,052 |
| St. Charles | 0 | 0 | 1 | 0 | 0 | 0 | 0 | 0 | 1 | 0 | 1,871 |
| St. Clair Shores | 2 | 0 | 0 | 0 | 0 | 0 | 0 | 1 | 1 | 0 | 58,254 |
| Sterling Heights | 9 | 0 | 1 | 0 | 0 | 0 | 2 | 2 | 2 | 4 | 131,911 |
| St. Joseph | 1 | 0 | 0 | 0 | 0 | 0 | 0 | 0 | 0 | 1 | 8,283 |
| Sylvan Lake | 1 | 0 | 0 | 0 | 0 | 0 | 1 | 0 | 0 | 0 | 1,848 |
| Taylor | 0 | 0 | 1 | 0 | 0 | 0 | 0 | 1 | 0 | 0 | 60,341 |
| Traverse City | 1 | 0 | 1 | 0 | 0 | 0 | 1 | 1 | 0 | 0 | 15,840 |
| Troy | 1 | 0 | 0 | 0 | 0 | 0 | 0 | 0 | 0 | 1 | 83,851 |
| Van Buren Township | 2 | 0 | 1 | 0 | 0 | 0 | 0 | 1 | 2 | 0 | 28,390 |
| Walker | 1 | 0 | 1 | 0 | 0 | 0 | 0 | 0 | 2 | 0 | 25,443 |
| Walled Lake[2] | 3 | 1 | 0 | 1 | 0 | 0 | 0 | 1 | 2 | 0 | 7,082 |
| Warren | 2 | 0 | 1 | 0 | 0 | 0 | 0 | 1 | 0 | 2 | 132,758 |
| Waterford Township[2] | 4 | 0 | 0 | 0 | 0 | 1 | 0 | 0 | 2 | 2 | 72,213 |
| Wayland | 1 | 0 | 0 | 0 | 0 | 0 | 0 | 0 | 0 | 1 | 4,253 |
| Wayne | 1 | 0 | 0 | 0 | 0 | 0 | 0 | 0 | 1 | 0 | 16,616 |
| West Bloomfield Township[2] | 4 | 4 | 0 | 0 | 0 | 0 | 2 | 1 | 2 | 2 | 65,720 |
| Westland | 1 | 0 | 0 | 0 | 0 | 0 | 0 | 0 | 1 | 0 | 80,837 |
| White Pigeon | 1 | 0 | 0 | 0 | 0 | 0 | 0 | 0 | 0 | 1 | 1,520 |
| Wixom | 1 | 0 | 0 | 0 | 0 | 0 | 0 | 0 | 0 | 1 | 14,145 |
| Wolverine Lake | 1 | 0 | 0 | 0 | 0 | 0 | 0 | 0 | 1 | 0 | 4,788 |
| Wyandotte | 1 | 1 | 0 | 0 | 0 | 0 | 0 | 1 | 1 | 0 | 24,600 |
| Wyoming | 2 | 1 | 0 | 0 | 0 | 0 | 1 | 1 | 0 | 1 | 77,094 |
| Ypsilanti | 1 | 0 | 0 | 0 | 0 | 0 | 0 | 0 | 1 | 0 | 19,986 |
| **Universities and Colleges** | 8 | 3 | 2 | 0 | 1 | 0 | | | | | |
| Delta College | 2 | 0 | 0 | 0 | 0 | 0 | 0 | 1 | 0 | 1 | 10,408 |
| Ferris State University | 1 | 0 | 0 | 0 | 0 | 0 | 1 | 0 | 0 | 0 | 14,874 |
| Grand Rapids Community College | 1 | 0 | 0 | 0 | 0 | 0 | 0 | 1 | 0 | 0 | 18,960 |
| Michigan State University | 0 | 1 | 0 | 0 | 0 | 0 | 0 | 0 | 0 | 1 | 55,406 |
| University of Michigan, Ann Arbor | 2 | 1 | 2 | 0 | 1 | 0 | 2 | 0 | 3 | 1 | 49,530 |
| Washtenaw Community College | 2 | 0 | 0 | 0 | 0 | 0 | 1 | 1 | 0 | 0 | 20,899 |
| Western Michigan University | 0 | 1 | 0 | 0 | 0 | 0 | 0 | 0 | 0 | 1 | 22,996 |
| **Metropolitan Counties** | 20 | 5 | 3 | 0 | 0 | 0 | | | | | |
| Bay | 1 | 0 | 0 | 0 | 0 | 0 | 1 | 0 | 0 | 0 | |
| Calhoun | 1 | 0 | 0 | 0 | 0 | 0 | 0 | 0 | 1 | 0 | |
| Eaton | 1 | 0 | 1 | 0 | 0 | 0 | 0 | 0 | 2 | 0 | |
| Genesee | 0 | 0 | 1 | 0 | 0 | 0 | 0 | 0 | 1 | 0 | |
| Ingham | 2 | 2 | 0 | 0 | 0 | 0 | 1 | 2 | 0 | 1 | |
| Jackson | 1 | 0 | 0 | 0 | 0 | 0 | 0 | 0 | 1 | 0 | |
| Kent | 4 | 0 | 1 | 0 | 0 | 0 | 2 | 1 | 1 | 1 | |
| Macomb | 2 | 0 | 0 | 0 | 0 | 0 | 2 | 0 | 0 | 0 | |
| Montcalm | 2 | 0 | 0 | 0 | 0 | 0 | 0 | 1 | 1 | 0 | |
| Muskegon | 1 | 0 | 0 | 0 | 0 | 0 | 1 | 0 | 0 | 0 | |
| Oakland | 1 | 0 | 0 | 0 | 0 | 0 | 0 | 0 | 0 | 1 | |
| Ottawa | 1 | 2 | 0 | 0 | 0 | 0 | 0 | 2 | 1 | 0 | |
| Saginaw | 1 | 0 | 0 | 0 | 0 | 0 | 0 | 1 | 0 | 0 | |
| Washtenaw | 2 | 1 | 0 | 0 | 0 | 0 | 0 | 0 | 1 | 2 | |
| **Nonmetropolitan Counties** | 14 | 2 | 3 | 0 | 3 | 3 | | | | | |
| Barry | 2 | 0 | 0 | 0 | 0 | 0 | 0 | 2 | 0 | 0 | |
| Benzie | 1 | 0 | 1 | 0 | 0 | 0 | 2 | 0 | 0 | 0 | |
| Delta | 2 | 0 | 0 | 0 | 0 | 1 | 0 | 0 | 2 | 1 | |
| Gladwin | 0 | 1 | 0 | 0 | 0 | 0 | 0 | 0 | 1 | 0 | |
| Grand Traverse | 1 | 0 | 0 | 0 | 0 | 0 | 0 | 0 | 1 | 0 | |
| Gratiot | 1 | 0 | 0 | 0 | 0 | 0 | 0 | 1 | 0 | 0 | |
| Houghton | 0 | 0 | 0 | 0 | 1 | 0 | 0 | 0 | 0 | 1 | |
| Huron | 1 | 0 | 0 | 0 | 0 | 0 | 0 | 0 | 1 | 0 | |
| Kalkaska | 1 | 0 | 0 | 0 | 0 | 0 | 0 | 0 | 1 | 0 | |
| Leelanau[2] | 1 | 0 | 0 | 0 | 0 | 2 | 0 | 1 | 0 | 1 | |
| Lenawee | 1 | 0 | 0 | 0 | 0 | 0 | 1 | 0 | 0 | 0 | |
| Mackinac | 1 | 0 | 0 | 0 | 0 | 0 | 0 | 1 | 0 | 0 | |
| Marquette | 0 | 0 | 2 | 0 | 0 | 0 | 0 | 0 | 2 | 0 | |
| Ontonagon | 0 | 0 | 0 | 0 | 1 | 0 | 1 | 0 | 0 | 0 | |
| Oscoda | 1 | 0 | 0 | 0 | 0 | 0 | 0 | 0 | 1 | 0 | |
| Tuscola | 1 | 0 | 0 | 0 | 0 | 0 | 0 | 0 | 1 | 0 | |
| Van Buren | 0 | 1 | 0 | 0 | 1 | 0 | 0 | 0 | 1 | 1 | |
| **State Police Agencies** | 29 | 3 | 3 | 0 | 0 | 4 | | | | | |
| State Police | | | | | | | | | | | |

## Table 94. Hate Crime Incidents Per Bias Motivation and Quarter, by Selected State and  Agency and Federal, 2021—Continued

(Number.)

| State/agency | Number of incidents per bias motivation | | | | | | Number of incidents per quarter | | | | Population[1] |
|---|---|---|---|---|---|---|---|---|---|---|---|
| | Race/Ethnicity/Ancestry | Religion | Sexual orientation | Disability | Gender | Gender Identity | 1st quarter | 2nd quarter | 3rd quarter | 4th quarter | |
| Bay County | 1 | 0 | 0 | 0 | 0 | 1 | 0 | 0 | 2 | 0 | |
| Branch County | 2 | 0 | 0 | 0 | 0 | 0 | 1 | 1 | 0 | 0 | |
| Calhoun County | 2 | 1 | 0 | 0 | 0 | 0 | 1 | 1 | 1 | 0 | |
| Grand Traverse County | 1 | 0 | 0 | 0 | 0 | 0 | 1 | 0 | 0 | 0 | |
| Ingham County | 3 | 0 | 0 | 0 | 0 | 0 | 1 | 1 | 1 | 0 | |
| Isabella County | 0 | 1 | 0 | 0 | 0 | 0 | 0 | 1 | 0 | 0 | |
| Kalamazoo County | 1 | 0 | 0 | 0 | 0 | 1 | 0 | 2 | 0 | 0 | |
| Kent County | 1 | 0 | 0 | 0 | 0 | 0 | 1 | 0 | 0 | 0 | |
| Lenawee County | 1 | 0 | 0 | 0 | 0 | 0 | 1 | 0 | 0 | 0 | |
| Livingston County | 1 | 0 | 0 | 0 | 0 | 0 | 0 | 0 | 1 | 0 | |
| Macomb County | 1 | 0 | 0 | 0 | 0 | 0 | 1 | 0 | 0 | 0 | |
| Marquette County | 1 | 0 | 0 | 0 | 0 | 0 | 0 | 0 | 1 | 0 | |
| Midland County | 1 | 0 | 0 | 0 | 0 | 0 | 0 | 0 | 0 | 1 | |
| Montcalm County | 2 | 0 | 1 | 0 | 0 | 0 | 1 | 0 | 1 | 1 | |
| Newaygo County | 1 | 0 | 0 | 0 | 0 | 0 | 0 | 0 | 0 | 1 | |
| Osceola County | 1 | 0 | 0 | 0 | 0 | 0 | 0 | 1 | 0 | 0 | |
| Saginaw County | 1 | 0 | 0 | 0 | 0 | 2 | 0 | 2 | 0 | 1 | |
| Shiawassee County | 3 | 0 | 0 | 0 | 0 | 0 | 0 | 2 | 1 | 0 | |
| St. Joseph County | 2 | 1 | 1 | 0 | 0 | 0 | 3 | 0 | 0 | 1 | |
| Van Buren County | 0 | 0 | 1 | 0 | 0 | 0 | 0 | 0 | 0 | 1 | |
| Wayne County | 2 | 0 | 0 | 0 | 0 | 0 | 0 | 0 | 1 | 1 | |
| Wexford County | 1 | 0 | 0 | 0 | 0 | 0 | 0 | 1 | 0 | 0 | |
| | | | | | | | | | | | |
| Tribal Agencies | 2 | 2 | 1 | 1 | 0 | 0 | | | | | |
| Gun Lake Tribal | 0 | 1 | 0 | 0 | 0 | 0 | 0 | 0 | 0 | 1 | |
| Hannahville Tribal | 1 | 0 | 0 | 0 | 0 | 0 | 0 | 1 | 0 | 0 | |
| Nottawaseppi Huron Band of Potawatomi | 0 | 0 | 0 | 1 | 0 | 0 | 0 | 0 | 1 | 0 | |
| Saginaw Chippewa Tribal | 1 | 1 | 1 | 0 | 0 | 0 | 0 | 0 | 0 | 3 | |
| | | | | | | | | | | | |
| **Other Agencies** | 0 | 0 | 1 | 0 | 0 | 0 | | | | | |
| Wayne County Airport | 0 | 0 | 1 | 0 | 0 | 0 | 0 | 0 | 1 | 0 | |
| | | | | | | | | | | | |
| **MINNESOTA** | 175 | 44 | 44 | 2 | 2 | 7 | | | | | |
| **Cities** | 141 | 38 | 37 | 1 | 1 | 7 | | | | | |
| Bemidji | 1 | 0 | 1 | 0 | 0 | 0 | 0 | 0 | 0 | 2 | 15,574 |
| Blaine | 1 | 0 | 0 | 0 | 0 | 0 | 1 | 0 | 0 | 0 | 67,705 |
| Bloomington | 0 | 1 | 0 | 0 | 0 | 0 | 0 | 0 | 1 | 0 | 84,740 |
| Brainerd[2] | 4 | 0 | 0 | 0 | 0 | 0 | 1 | 0 | 0 | 0 | 13,436 |
| Brooklyn Park[2] | 7 | 0 | 2 | 0 | 1 | 0 | 2 | 3 | 3 | 0 | 79,946 |
| Buffalo | 1 | 0 | 0 | 0 | 0 | 0 | 1 | 0 | 0 | 0 | 16,994 |
| Burnsville | 5 | 0 | 0 | 0 | 0 | 0 | 0 | 2 | 3 | 0 | 62,351 |
| Cloquet | 0 | 1 | 0 | 0 | 0 | 0 | 0 | 1 | 0 | 0 | 12,002 |
| Cold Spring/Richmond[2] | 2 | 0 | 0 | 0 | 0 | 0 | 0 | 0 | 1 | 0 | 5,869 |
| Coon Rapids[2] | 2 | 0 | 0 | 0 | 0 | 0 | 0 | 1 | 0 | 0 | 63,076 |
| Deerwood | 0 | 0 | 1 | 0 | 0 | 0 | 0 | 0 | 1 | 0 | 752 |
| Detroit Lakes | 1 | 0 | 0 | 0 | 0 | 0 | 0 | 0 | 0 | 1 | 9,310 |
| Duluth | 0 | 0 | 1 | 0 | 0 | 0 | 0 | 0 | 1 | 0 | 85,731 |
| Eagan | 1 | 0 | 0 | 0 | 0 | 0 | 1 | 0 | 0 | 0 | 66,155 |
| Eden Prairie | 1 | 0 | 0 | 0 | 0 | 0 | 0 | 0 | 1 | 0 | 65,308 |
| Farmington | 2 | 0 | 0 | 0 | 0 | 0 | 1 | 1 | 0 | 0 | 23,235 |
| Foley | 1 | 0 | 0 | 0 | 0 | 0 | 0 | 1 | 0 | 0 | 2,678 |
| Forest Lake | 3 | 1 | 0 | 0 | 0 | 0 | 0 | 0 | 2 | 2 | 21,592 |
| Fridley | 3 | 0 | 0 | 0 | 0 | 0 | 1 | 0 | 2 | 0 | 27,919 |
| Glencoe | 0 | 1 | 0 | 0 | 0 | 0 | 0 | 1 | 0 | 0 | 5,484 |
| Hopkins[2] | 5 | 0 | 0 | 0 | 0 | 0 | 1 | 1 | 2 | 0 | 18,272 |
| Inver Grove Heights | 1 | 1 | 1 | 0 | 0 | 1 | 0 | 3 | 0 | 1 | 35,957 |
| Jordan | 0 | 1 | 0 | 0 | 0 | 0 | 0 | 0 | 0 | 1 | 6,523 |
| Lakes Area | 1 | 0 | 0 | 0 | 0 | 0 | 0 | 0 | 0 | 1 | 10,026 |
| Lakeville | 1 | 1 | 0 | 0 | 0 | 0 | 1 | 0 | 1 | 0 | 71,092 |
| Lino Lakes | 1 | 0 | 0 | 0 | 0 | 0 | 0 | 0 | 1 | 0 | 22,657 |
| Litchfield | 1 | 0 | 0 | 0 | 0 | 0 | 0 | 0 | 0 | 1 | 6,656 |
| Mankato | 4 | 1 | 1 | 0 | 0 | 0 | 2 | 2 | 1 | 1 | 43,802 |
| Maplewood[2] | 3 | 2 | 0 | 0 | 0 | 0 | 0 | 1 | 2 | 0 | 41,057 |
| Minneapolis[2] | 22 | 6 | 8 | 0 | 0 | 2 | 5 | 12 | 7 | 9 | 438,463 |
| Minnetonka | 1 | 2 | 0 | 0 | 0 | 1 | 1 | 0 | 0 | 3 | 55,960 |
| Morris | 1 | 0 | 0 | 0 | 0 | 0 | 1 | 0 | 0 | 0 | 5,319 |
| Mounds View | 1 | 0 | 0 | 0 | 0 | 0 | 0 | 1 | 0 | 0 | 13,625 |
| New Brighton | 1 | 0 | 0 | 0 | 0 | 0 | 0 | 0 | 1 | 0 | 23,012 |
| Plymouth | 2 | 1 | 0 | 0 | 0 | 0 | 0 | 2 | 1 | 0 | 80,588 |
| Princeton | 1 | 0 | 0 | 0 | 0 | 0 | 0 | 0 | 1 | 0 | 4,738 |
| Red Wing | 2 | 0 | 1 | 0 | 0 | 0 | 0 | 1 | 1 | 1 | 16,411 |
| Richfield | 2 | 0 | 0 | 0 | 0 | 0 | 1 | 0 | 1 | 0 | 36,336 |
| Rochester[2] | 4 | 2 | 1 | 1 | 0 | 0 | 0 | 5 | 0 | 2 | 121,225 |
| Rosemount | 2 | 0 | 0 | 0 | 0 | 0 | 0 | 1 | 1 | 0 | 26,218 |
| Roseville[2] | 8 | 1 | 2 | 0 | 0 | 0 | 2 | 1 | 0 | 4 | 36,561 |
| Sartell | 0 | 0 | 1 | 0 | 0 | 0 | 0 | 0 | 0 | 1 | 19,398 |
| Savage[2] | 3 | 2 | 0 | 0 | 0 | 0 | 2 | 0 | 1 | 1 | 33,510 |
| Shakopee | 0 | 0 | 1 | 0 | 0 | 0 | 1 | 0 | 0 | 0 | 43,641 |
| St. Anthony | 1 | 0 | 0 | 0 | 0 | 0 | 0 | 0 | 1 | 0 | 11,490 |

# Table 94. Hate Crime Incidents Per Bias Motivation and Quarter, by Selected State and Agency and Federal, 2021—Continued

(Number.)

| State/agency | Number of incidents per bias motivation | | | | | | Number of incidents per quarter | | | | Population[1] |
|---|---|---|---|---|---|---|---|---|---|---|---|
| | Race/ Ethnicity/ Ancestry | Religion | Sexual orientation | Disability | Gender | Gender Identity | 1st quarter | 2nd quarter | 3rd quarter | 4th quarter | |
| St. Cloud[2] | 7 | 4 | 3 | 0 | 0 | 0 | 3 | 4 | 1 | 2 | 68,756 |
| St. James | 0 | 0 | 1 | 0 | 0 | 0 | 0 | 0 | 0 | 1 | 4,336 |
| St. Louis Park[2] | 5 | 4 | 1 | 0 | 0 | 0 | 1 | 4 | 3 | 1 | 49,196 |
| St. Paul[2] | 18 | 6 | 10 | 0 | 0 | 3 | 5 | 9 | 13 | 6 | 309,957 |
| West St. Paul | 6 | 0 | 0 | 0 | 0 | 0 | 3 | 2 | 1 | 0 | 19,840 |
| Windom | 1 | 0 | 0 | 0 | 0 | 0 | 0 | 0 | 0 | 1 | 4,380 |
| Woodbury | 1 | 0 | 1 | 0 | 0 | 0 | 0 | 0 | 1 | 1 | 75,577 |
| **Universities and Colleges** | 0 | 0 | 1 | 0 | 0 | 0 | | | | | |
| University of Minnesota, Duluth | 0 | 0 | 1 | 0 | 0 | 0 | 1 | 0 | 0 | 0 | 11,557 |
| **Metropolitan Counties** | 25 | 4 | 6 | 0 | 1 | 0 | | | | | |
| Blue Earth | 1 | 0 | 0 | 0 | 0 | 0 | 0 | 0 | 1 | 0 | |
| Carver | 2 | 0 | 0 | 0 | 0 | 0 | 0 | 2 | 0 | 0 | |
| Lake | 0 | 1 | 0 | 0 | 0 | 0 | 1 | 0 | 0 | 0 | |
| Mille Lacs[2] | 6 | 0 | 0 | 0 | 0 | 0 | 0 | 2 | 1 | 2 | |
| Olmsted | 0 | 0 | 1 | 0 | 0 | 0 | 0 | 1 | 0 | 0 | |
| Ramsey | 6 | 0 | 0 | 0 | 0 | 0 | 0 | 5 | 1 | 0 | |
| Scott | 1 | 0 | 0 | 0 | 0 | 0 | 0 | 0 | 0 | 1 | |
| Sherburne | 2 | 1 | 0 | 0 | 0 | 0 | 1 | 0 | 1 | 1 | |
| Stearns | 1 | 0 | 1 | 0 | 0 | 0 | 0 | 2 | 0 | 0 | |
| St. Louis[2] | 0 | 0 | 3 | 0 | 0 | 0 | 0 | 0 | 1 | 0 | |
| Washington | 1 | 0 | 0 | 0 | 1 | 0 | 1 | 1 | 0 | 0 | |
| Wright | 5 | 2 | 1 | 0 | 0 | 0 | 3 | 4 | 0 | 1 | |
| **Nonmetropolitan Counties** | 4 | 2 | 0 | 1 | 0 | 0 | | | | | |
| Beltrami | 1 | 0 | 0 | 0 | 0 | 0 | 0 | 0 | 1 | 0 | |
| Cass | 1 | 0 | 0 | 0 | 0 | 0 | 0 | 1 | 0 | 0 | |
| Hubbard | 1 | 0 | 0 | 0 | 0 | 0 | 0 | 1 | 0 | 0 | |
| Koochiching | 0 | 1 | 0 | 0 | 0 | 0 | 0 | 1 | 0 | 0 | |
| Meeker | 0 | 0 | 0 | 1 | 0 | 0 | 0 | 1 | 0 | 0 | |
| Todd | 0 | 1 | 0 | 0 | 0 | 0 | 0 | 0 | 0 | 1 | |
| Waseca | 1 | 0 | 0 | 0 | 0 | 0 | 0 | 1 | 0 | 0 | |
| **Other Agencies** | 5 | 0 | 0 | 0 | 0 | 0 | | | | | |
| Metropolitan Transit Commission | 5 | 0 | 0 | 0 | 0 | 0 | 0 | 2 | 2 | 1 | |
| **MISSISSIPPI** | 26 | 0 | 2 | 0 | 3 | 0 | | | | | |
| **Cities** | 15 | 0 | 1 | 0 | 3 | 0 | | | | | |
| Booneville | 1 | 0 | 0 | 0 | 0 | 0 | 1 | 0 | 0 | 0 | 8,368 |
| Calhoun City | 0 | 0 | 1 | 0 | 0 | 0 | 0 | 0 | 1 | 0 | 1,637 |
| Forest | 2 | 0 | 0 | 0 | 2 | 0 | 0 | 2 | 1 | 1 | 5,461 |
| Morton | 0 | 0 | 0 | 0 | 1 | 0 | 0 | 1 | 0 | 0 | 3,505 |
| Southaven | 1 | 0 | 0 | 0 | 0 | 0 | 0 | 1 | 0 | 0 | 57,455 |
| Union | 10 | 0 | 0 | 0 | 0 | 0 | 0 | 0 | 0 | 10 | 1,866 |
| Water Valley | 1 | 0 | 0 | 0 | 0 | 0 | 0 | 1 | 0 | 0 | 3,206 |
| **Metropolitan Counties** | 3 | 0 | 0 | 0 | 0 | 0 | | | | | |
| DeSoto | 1 | 0 | 0 | 0 | 0 | 0 | 0 | 0 | 1 | 0 | |
| Lamar | 1 | 0 | 0 | 0 | 0 | 0 | 1 | 0 | 0 | 0 | |
| Stone | 1 | 0 | 0 | 0 | 0 | 0 | 0 | 0 | 1 | 0 | |
| **Nonmetropolitan Counties** | 8 | 0 | 1 | 0 | 0 | 0 | | | | | |
| Grenada | 3 | 0 | 0 | 0 | 0 | 0 | 1 | 0 | 2 | 0 | |
| Kemper | 1 | 0 | 0 | 0 | 0 | 0 | 0 | 0 | 0 | 1 | |
| Lafayette | 1 | 0 | 0 | 0 | 0 | 0 | 0 | 0 | 1 | 0 | |
| Monroe | 0 | 0 | 1 | 0 | 0 | 0 | 1 | 0 | 0 | 0 | |
| Oktibbeha | 1 | 0 | 0 | 0 | 0 | 0 | 0 | 0 | 0 | 1 | |
| Pontotoc | 1 | 0 | 0 | 0 | 0 | 0 | 0 | 1 | 0 | 0 | |
| Winston | 1 | 0 | 0 | 0 | 0 | 0 | 0 | 0 | 0 | 1 | |
| **MISSOURI** | 131 | 27 | 38 | 4 | 2 | 9 | | | | | |
| **Cities** | 107 | 17 | 31 | 4 | 1 | 7 | | | | | |
| Ash Grove | 0 | 0 | 0 | 0 | 0 | 1 | 0 | 0 | 1 | 0 | 1,440 |
| Aurora | 2 | 0 | 0 | 0 | 0 | 0 | 1 | 0 | 1 | 0 | 7,422 |
| Blue Springs | 4 | 1 | 1 | 0 | 0 | 0 | 0 | 4 | 0 | 2 | 56,952 |
| Bowling Green | 1 | 0 | 0 | 0 | 0 | 0 | 0 | 1 | 0 | 0 | 4,711 |
| Branson | 1 | 0 | 0 | 0 | 0 | 0 | 0 | 1 | 0 | 0 | 11,797 |
| Brookfield | 2 | 0 | 0 | 0 | 0 | 0 | 0 | 0 | 2 | 0 | 4,144 |
| Buckner | 1 | 0 | 0 | 0 | 0 | 0 | 1 | 0 | 0 | 0 | 3,004 |
| Cameron | 1 | 0 | 0 | 0 | 0 | 0 | 0 | 0 | 0 | 1 | 7,986 |
| Cape Girardeau | 0 | 0 | 1 | 0 | 0 | 0 | 0 | 0 | 0 | 1 | 41,957 |
| Charleston | 1 | 0 | 1 | 0 | 0 | 0 | 0 | 0 | 0 | 2 | 4,936 |
| Chesterfield | 1 | 0 | 0 | 0 | 0 | 0 | 0 | 0 | 1 | 0 | 47,578 |
| Clever | 2 | 0 | 0 | 0 | 0 | 0 | 2 | 0 | 0 | 0 | 2,907 |
| Florissant | 2 | 0 | 0 | 0 | 0 | 0 | 0 | 1 | 1 | 0 | 50,653 |
| Fredericktown | 1 | 0 | 0 | 0 | 0 | 0 | 0 | 1 | 0 | 0 | 4,008 |
| Gladstone | 1 | 0 | 1 | 0 | 0 | 0 | 1 | 1 | 0 | 0 | 27,905 |
| Glendale | 1 | 0 | 0 | 0 | 0 | 0 | 0 | 0 | 1 | 0 | 5,856 |

## Table 94. Hate Crime Incidents Per Bias Motivation and Quarter, by Selected State and Agency and Federal, 2021—Continued

(Number.)

| State/agency | Number of incidents per bias motivation | | | | | | Number of incidents per quarter | | | | Population[1] |
|---|---|---|---|---|---|---|---|---|---|---|---|
| | Race/ Ethnicity/ Ancestry | Religion | Sexual orientation | Disability | Gender | Gender Identity | 1st quarter | 2nd quarter | 3rd quarter | 4th quarter | |
| Grain Valley | 0 | 0 | 1 | 0 | 0 | 0 | 0 | 0 | 0 | 1 | 15,038 |
| Grandview | 1 | 0 | 0 | 0 | 0 | 0 | | | 0 | 1 | 24,734 |
| Greenwood | 1 | 0 | 0 | 0 | 0 | 1 | 0 | 0 | 1 | 1 | 5,951 |
| Hannibal | 2 | 0 | 1 | 0 | 0 | 0 | 1 | 0 | 0 | 2 | 17,194 |
| Independence | 7 | 2 | 0 | 0 | 0 | 0 | 2 | 3 | 2 | 2 | 116,761 |
| Kansas City[2] | 33 | 3 | 2 | 2 | 0 | 2 | 12 | 9 | 12 | 6 | 500,965 |
| Kimberling City | 2 | 0 | 0 | 0 | 0 | 0 | 0 | 0 | 2 | 0 | 2,321 |
| Kirksville | 0 | 0 | 1 | 0 | 0 | 0 | 0 | 0 | 1 | 0 | 17,666 |
| Lamar | 0 | 1 | 1 | 0 | 0 | 0 | 0 | 0 | 1 | 1 | 4,204 |
| Lebanon | 1 | 0 | 0 | 0 | 0 | 0 | 0 | 0 | 1 | 0 | 14,917 |
| Lee's Summit[2] | 5 | 5 | 2 | 0 | 0 | 0 | 1 | 1 | 5 | 3 | 102,519 |
| Maryville | 3 | 0 | 0 | 0 | 0 | 0 | 0 | 0 | 0 | 3 | 11,479 |
| Monroe City | 1 | 0 | 0 | 0 | 0 | 0 | 1 | 0 | 0 | 0 | 2,433 |
| Mountain Grove | 1 | 0 | 0 | 0 | 0 | 0 | 1 | 0 | 0 | 0 | 4,697 |
| Nevada | 1 | 0 | 0 | 0 | 0 | 0 | 0 | 0 | 1 | 0 | 8,177 |
| North Kansas City | 1 | 0 | 1 | 0 | 0 | 2 | 1 | 0 | 1 | 2 | 5,110 |
| Oak Grove | 0 | 0 | 1 | 0 | 0 | 0 | 0 | 0 | 1 | 0 | 8,493 |
| Overland | 0 | 0 | 1 | 0 | 0 | 0 | 0 | 0 | 0 | 1 | 15,449 |
| Peculiar | 0 | 0 | 1 | 0 | 0 | 0 | 0 | 0 | 0 | 1 | 5,774 |
| Perryville | 0 | 0 | 1 | 0 | 0 | 0 | 0 | 1 | 0 | 0 | 8,570 |
| Pevely | 0 | 1 | 0 | 0 | 0 | 0 | 1 | 0 | 0 | 0 | 6,042 |
| Raytown | 0 | 0 | 1 | 0 | 0 | 0 | 1 | 0 | 0 | 0 | 28,737 |
| Richmond[2] | 2 | 2 | 3 | 0 | 0 | 0 | 0 | 1 | 3 | 0 | 5,585 |
| Sedalia | 2 | 0 | 0 | 0 | 0 | 0 | 0 | 0 | 2 | 0 | 21,702 |
| Sikeston | 3 | 0 | 0 | 0 | 0 | 0 | 0 | 2 | 1 | 0 | 15,931 |
| Springfield[2] | 0 | 0 | 2 | 0 | 0 | 0 | 0 | 0 | 0 | 1 | 168,988 |
| St. Charles | 1 | 0 | 0 | 0 | 0 | 0 | 0 | 0 | 0 | 1 | 72,323 |
| St. Clair | 0 | 0 | 1 | 0 | 0 | 0 | 0 | 0 | 1 | 0 | 4,686 |
| St. James | 1 | 0 | 0 | 0 | 0 | 0 | 0 | 0 | 1 | 0 | 3,986 |
| St. Louis[2] | 10 | 0 | 1 | 0 | 1 | 1 | 0 | 2 | 5 | 2 | 295,536 |
| Strafford | 1 | 0 | 0 | 0 | 0 | 0 | 0 | 1 | 0 | 0 | 2,518 |
| St. Robert | 1 | 0 | 1 | 0 | 0 | 0 | 0 | 2 | 0 | 0 | 6,558 |
| Summersville | 1 | 0 | 0 | 0 | 0 | 0 | 0 | 1 | 0 | 0 | 486 |
| Sunset Hills | 1 | 0 | 0 | 0 | 0 | 0 | 0 | 0 | 1 | 0 | 8,447 |
| Tarkio | 0 | 0 | 1 | 0 | 0 | 0 | 0 | 0 | 1 | 0 | 1,405 |
| Town and Country | 1 | 0 | 0 | 0 | 0 | 0 | 1 | 0 | 0 | 0 | 11,173 |
| Trenton | 0 | 1 | 0 | 0 | 0 | 0 | 0 | 1 | 0 | 0 | 5,584 |
| Troy | 0 | 0 | 1 | 0 | 0 | 0 | 0 | 0 | 1 | 0 | 13,647 |
| Versailles | 1 | 0 | 1 | 0 | 0 | 0 | 0 | 0 | 1 | 1 | 2,479 |
| Warrensburg[2] | 1 | 0 | 2 | 0 | 0 | 0 | 0 | 0 | 0 | 2 | 20,707 |
| Webb City | 1 | 1 | 0 | 1 | 0 | 0 | 0 | 0 | 3 | 0 | 12,462 |
| Willard | 0 | 0 | 0 | 1 | 0 | 0 | 0 | 0 | 1 | 0 | 5,781 |
| **Universities and Colleges** | 2 | 0 | 0 | 0 | 0 | 0 | | | | | |
| Missouri University of Science and Technology | 1 | 0 | 0 | 0 | 0 | 0 | 0 | 0 | 1 | 0 | 8,618 |
| University of Missouri, Kansas City | 1 | 0 | 0 | 0 | 0 | 0 | 1 | 0 | 0 | 0 | 18,894 |
| **Metropolitan Counties** | 14 | 7 | 1 | 0 | 0 | 2 | | | | | |
| Bollinger | 0 | 0 | 1 | 0 | 0 | 0 | 1 | 0 | 0 | 0 | |
| Cape Girardeau | 0 | 1 | 0 | 0 | 0 | 0 | 0 | 1 | 0 | 0 | |
| Dallas | 0 | 1 | 0 | 0 | 0 | 0 | 0 | 0 | 1 | | |
| Franklin | 1 | 1 | 0 | 0 | 0 | 0 | 1 | 1 | 0 | 0 | |
| Greene | 3 | 0 | 0 | 0 | 0 | 0 | 2 | 1 | 0 | 0 | |
| Jackson | 1 | 1 | 0 | 0 | 0 | 0 | 0 | 1 | 1 | 0 | |
| Lincoln[2] | 2 | 0 | 0 | 0 | 0 | 0 | 0 | 0 | 1 | 0 | |
| Platte | 1 | 0 | 0 | 0 | 0 | 2 | 0 | 2 | 1 | 0 | |
| Polk | 1 | 0 | 0 | 0 | 0 | 0 | 1 | 0 | 0 | 0 | |
| St. Charles County Police Department[2] | 3 | 0 | 0 | 0 | 0 | 0 | 0 | 1 | 0 | 1 | |
| St. Louis County Police Department | 2 | 0 | 0 | 0 | 0 | 0 | 0 | 0 | 2 | 0 | |
| Webster | 0 | 3 | 0 | 0 | 0 | 0 | 2 | 0 | 0 | 1 | |
| **Nonmetropolitan Counties** | 7 | 3 | 5 | 0 | 1 | 0 | | | | | |
| Barry | 0 | 1 | 0 | 0 | 0 | 0 | 0 | 0 | 0 | 1 | |
| Benton | 2 | 0 | 0 | 0 | 0 | 0 | 0 | 2 | 0 | 0 | |
| Harrison | 1 | 0 | 0 | 0 | 0 | 0 | 1 | 0 | | | |
| Hickory | 1 | 0 | 1 | 0 | 0 | 0 | 0 | 1 | 1 | 0 | |
| Linn | 0 | 0 | 0 | 0 | 1 | 0 | 0 | 0 | 1 | 0 | |
| Montgomery | 0 | 1 | 0 | 0 | 0 | 0 | 0 | 1 | 0 | 0 | |
| Ozark | 0 | 0 | 1 | 0 | 0 | 0 | 0 | 0 | 1 | 0 | |
| Ste. Genevieve | 1 | 1 | 0 | 0 | 0 | 0 | 0 | 0 | 2 | 0 | |
| St. Francois | 1 | 0 | 0 | 0 | 0 | 0 | 0 | 1 | | | |
| Taney | 0 | 0 | 1 | 0 | 0 | 0 | 0 | 1 | 0 | 0 | |
| Wayne[2] | 1 | 0 | 2 | 0 | 0 | 0 | 1 | 0 | 0 | 2 | |
| | 1 | 0 | 0 | 0 | 0 | 0 | | | | | |
| Missouri State Highway Patrol | 1 | 0 | 0 | 0 | 0 | 0 | 1 | 0 | 0 | 0 | |
| | 0 | 0 | 1 | 0 | 0 | 0 | | | | | |
| Kansas City International Airport | 0 | 0 | 1 | 0 | 0 | 0 | 0 | 0 | 0 | 1 | |
| **MONTANA** | 10 | 0 | 6 | 0 | 0 | 1 | | | | | |
| **Cities** | 9 | 0 | 3 | 0 | 0 | 0 | | | | | |

## Table 94. Hate Crime Incidents Per Bias Motivation and Quarter, by Selected State and Agency and Federal, 2021—Continued

(Number.)

| State/agency | Number of incidents per bias motivation | | | | | | Number of incidents per quarter | | | | Population[1] |
|---|---|---|---|---|---|---|---|---|---|---|---|
| | Race/ Ethnicity/ Ancestry | Religion | Sexual orientation | Disability | Gender | Gender Identity | 1st quarter | 2nd quarter | 3rd quarter | 4th quarter | |
| Billings | 4 | 0 | 1 | 0 | 0 | 0 | 1 | 2 | 2 | 0 | 110,274 |
| Bozeman | 1 | 0 | 0 | 0 | 0 | 0 | 1 | 0 | 0 | 0 | 52,586 |
| Great Falls | 2 | 0 | 0 | 0 | 0 | 0 | 0 | 2 | 0 | 0 | 58,265 |
| Helena | 1 | 0 | 0 | 0 | 0 | 0 | 1 | 0 | 0 | 0 | 34,262 |
| Kalispell | 0 | 0 | 1 | 0 | 0 | 0 | 1 | 0 | 0 | 0 | 25,926 |
| Whitefish | 1 | 0 | 1 | 0 | 0 | 0 | 1 | 0 | 0 | 1 | 8,972 |
| **Metropolitan Counties** | 1 | 0 | 0 | 0 | 0 | 1 | | | | | |
| Cascade | 1 | 0 | 0 | 0 | 0 | 0 | 1 | 0 | 0 | 0 | |
| Missoula | 0 | 0 | 0 | 0 | 0 | 1 | 0 | 0 | 1 | 0 | |
| **Nonmetropolitan Counties** | 0 | 0 | 2 | 0 | 0 | 0 | | | | | |
| Lewis and Clark | 0 | 0 | 1 | 0 | 0 | 0 | 0 | 0 | 0 | 1 | |
| Sheridan | 0 | 0 | 1 | 0 | 0 | 0 | 0 | 1 | 0 | 0 | |
| **Tribal Agencies** | 0 | 0 | 1 | 0 | 0 | 0 | | | | | |
| Crow Agency | 0 | 0 | 1 | 0 | 0 | 0 | 0 | 1 | 0 | | |
| **NEBRASKA** | 32 | 4 | 7 | 2 | 0 | 2 | | | | | |
| **Cities** | 18 | 1 | 5 | 0 | 0 | 1 | | | | | |
| Crete[2] | 3 | 0 | 0 | 0 | 0 | 0 | 0 | 0 | 1 | 1 | 6,864 |
| Falls City | 1 | 0 | 0 | 0 | 0 | 0 | 0 | 0 | 0 | 1 | 4,052 |
| Fremont | 1 | 0 | 0 | 0 | 0 | 0 | 0 | 0 | 0 | 1 | 26,210 |
| Grand Island | 1 | 0 | 0 | 0 | 0 | 0 | 0 | 1 | 0 | 0 | 51,226 |
| Lincoln[2] | 8 | 0 | 5 | 0 | 0 | 0 | 1 | 3 | 5 | 3 | 293,808 |
| Madison | 1 | 0 | 0 | 0 | 0 | 0 | 0 | 1 | 0 | 0 | 2,337 |
| Norfolk | 0 | 0 | 0 | 0 | 0 | 1 | 0 | 1 | 0 | 0 | 24,370 |
| North Platte | 1 | 0 | 0 | 0 | 0 | 0 | 0 | 0 | 0 | 1 | 23,057 |
| Ralston | 1 | 0 | 0 | 0 | 0 | 0 | 0 | 0 | 0 | 1 | 7,386 |
| Scottsbluff | 1 | 0 | 0 | 0 | 0 | 0 | 0 | 1 | 0 | 0 | 15,463 |
| Valley | 0 | 1 | 0 | 0 | 0 | 0 | 0 | 1 | 0 | 0 | 2,985 |
| **Universities and Colleges** | 5 | 2 | 1 | 0 | 0 | 1 | | | | | |
| University of Nebraska, Lincoln[2] | 5 | 2 | 1 | 0 | 0 | 1 | 0 | 2 | 3 | 3 | 32,498 |
| **Metropolitan Counties** | 2 | 0 | 1 | 0 | 0 | 0 | | | | | |
| Douglas | 1 | 0 | 1 | 0 | 0 | 0 | 0 | 2 | 0 | 0 | |
| Hall | 1 | 0 | 0 | 0 | 0 | 0 | 0 | 0 | 1 | 0 | |
| **Nonmetropolitan Counties** | 7 | 1 | 0 | 2 | 0 | 0 | | | | | |
| Custer | 2 | 0 | 0 | 0 | 0 | 0 | 0 | 1 | 0 | 1 | |
| Dodge | 0 | 1 | 0 | 2 | 0 | 0 | 2 | 0 | 1 | 0 | |
| Fillmore | 1 | 0 | 0 | 0 | 0 | 0 | 0 | 1 | 0 | 0 | |
| Furnas | 1 | 0 | 0 | 0 | 0 | 0 | 0 | 1 | 0 | 0 | |
| Keith | 2 | 0 | 0 | 0 | 0 | 0 | 2 | 0 | 0 | 0 | |
| Thurston | 1 | 0 | 0 | 0 | 0 | 0 | 1 | 0 | 0 | 0 | |
| **NEVADA** | 174 | 19 | 30 | 1 | 2 | 6 | | | | | |
| **Cities** | 149 | 13 | 28 | 1 | 2 | 5 | | | | | |
| Elko | 1 | 0 | 0 | 0 | 0 | 0 | 0 | 0 | 1 | 0 | 20,760 |
| Henderson | 6 | 2 | 1 | 0 | 0 | 0 | 3 | 1 | 0 | 5 | 337,375 |
| Las Vegas Metropolitan Police Department[2] | 126 | 9 | 21 | 0 | 1 | 4 | 30 | 39 | 32 | 54 | 1,685,021 |
| North Las Vegas | 3 | 0 | 1 | 0 | 0 | 0 | 1 | 2 | 0 | 1 | 264,877 |
| Reno | 11 | 2 | 4 | 1 | 1 | 1 | 4 | 8 | 4 | 4 | 262,919 |
| Sparks | 2 | 0 | 1 | 0 | 0 | 0 | 0 | 2 | 0 | 1 | 108,612 |
| **Universities and Colleges** | 1 | 0 | 0 | 0 | 0 | 0 | | | | | |
| University of Nevada, Reno | 1 | 0 | 0 | 0 | 0 | 0 | 0 | 0 | 1 | 0 | 23,692 |
| **Metropolitan Counties** | 8 | 1 | 0 | 0 | 0 | 0 | | | | | |
| Storey | 1 | 0 | 0 | 0 | 0 | 0 | 0 | 0 | 0 | 1 | |
| Washoe[2] | 7 | 1 | 0 | 0 | 0 | 0 | 2 | 1 | 1 | 3 | |
| **Nonmetropolitan Counties** | 7 | 5 | 1 | 0 | 0 | 1 | | | | | |
| Douglas | 2 | 0 | 0 | 0 | 0 | 1 | 0 | 0 | 0 | 3 | |
| Elko | 0 | 0 | 1 | 0 | 0 | 0 | 0 | 1 | 0 | 0 | |
| Lander | 1 | 0 | 0 | 0 | 0 | 0 | 1 | 0 | 0 | 0 | |
| Nye[2] | 4 | 5 | 0 | 0 | 0 | 0 | 2 | 2 | 0 | 1 | |
| **State Police Agencies** | 7 | 0 | 0 | 0 | 0 | 0 | | | | | |
| Highway Patrol | | | | | | | | | | | |
| Northwestern Division[2] | 2 | 0 | 0 | 0 | 0 | 0 | 1 | 0 | 0 | 0 | |
| Southern Division[2] | 5 | 0 | 0 | 0 | 0 | 0 | 0 | 1 | 2 | 0 | |
| **Other Agencies** | 2 | 0 | 1 | 0 | 0 | 0 | | | | | |
| City of Las Vegas Department of Publilc Safety | 1 | 0 | 1 | 0 | 0 | 0 | 0 | 0 | 0 | 2 | |
| Reno Tahoe Airport Authority | 1 | 0 | 0 | 0 | 0 | 0 | 0 | 1 | 0 | 0 | |
| **NEW HAMPSHIRE** | 16 | 8 | 7 | 1 | 1 | 1 | | | | | |
| **Cities** | 15 | 7 | 7 | 1 | 1 | 1 | | | | | |

## Table 94. Hate Crime Incidents Per Bias Motivation and Quarter, by Selected State and  Agency and Federal, 2021—Continued

(Number.)

| State/agency | Number of incidents per bias motivation | | | | | | Number of incidents per quarter | | | | Population[1] |
| --- | --- | --- | --- | --- | --- | --- | --- | --- | --- | --- | --- |
| | Race/ Ethnicity/ Ancestry | Religion | Sexual orientation | Disability | Gender | Gender Identity | 1st quarter | 2nd quarter | 3rd quarter | 4th quarter | |
| Bedford | 0 | 0 | 1 | 0 | 0 | 0 | 0 | 0 | 0 | 1 | 23,137 |
| Bow | 1 | 0 | 0 | 0 | 0 | 0 | 1 | 0 | 0 | 0 | 8,119 |
| Concord | 1 | 0 | 0 | 0 | 0 | 0 | 0 | 1 | 0 | 0 | 44,053 |
| Dover | 1 | 1 | 1 | 1 | 0 | 0 | 0 | 2 | 2 | | 33,112 |
| Exeter | 3 | 0 | 1 | 0 | 0 | 0 | 0 | 4 | 0 | 0 | 15,596 |
| Hampton | 1 | 0 | 0 | 0 | 0 | 0 | 0 | 1 | 0 | 0 | 16,206 |
| Hollis | 0 | 1 | 0 | 0 | 0 | 0 | 1 | 0 | 0 | 0 | 8,166 |
| Kingston | 0 | 0 | 0 | 0 | 0 | 1 | 0 | 0 | 1 | 0 | 6,549 |
| Laconia | 2 | 0 | 0 | 0 | 0 | 0 | 0 | 0 | 1 | 1 | 16,929 |
| Manchester | 1 | 0 | 0 | 0 | 0 | 0 | 0 | 1 | 0 | 0 | 112,844 |
| Merrimack | 0 | 0 | 1 | 0 | 0 | 0 | 0 | 0 | 0 | 1 | 27,656 |
| Nashua | 0 | 1 | 0 | 0 | 0 | 0 | 0 | 1 | 0 | 0 | 89,431 |
| Newmarket | 2 | 1 | 0 | 0 | 0 | 0 | 0 | 0 | 1 | 2 | 9,349 |
| Pelham | 1 | 1 | 0 | 0 | 0 | 0 | 1 | 0 | 0 | 1 | 14,453 |
| Pittsfield | 0 | 0 | 0 | 0 | 1 | 0 | 0 | 1 | 0 | 0 | 4,146 |
| Portsmouth | 0 | 0 | 2 | 0 | 0 | 0 | 1 | 0 | 0 | 1 | 21,913 |
| Rochester | 1 | 1 | 0 | 0 | 0 | 0 | 0 | 2 | 0 | 0 | 32,327 |
| Rye | 0 | 1 | 0 | 0 | 0 | 0 | 1 | 0 | 0 | 0 | 5,566 |
| Seabrook | 1 | 0 | 1 | 0 | 0 | 0 | 0 | 1 | 1 | 0 | 8,974 |
| | | | | | | | | | | | |
| **Universities and Colleges** | 1 | 1 | 0 | 0 | 0 | 0 | | | | | |
| Plymouth State University | 1 | 0 | 0 | 0 | 0 | 0 | 1 | 0 | 0 | 0 | 5,475 |
| University of New Hampshire | 0 | 1 | 0 | 0 | 0 | 0 | 0 | 1 | 0 | 0 | 16,001 |
| | | | | | | | | | | | |
| **NEW JERSEY** | 148 | 40 | 23 | 0 | 0 | 15 | | | | | |
| **Cities** | 140 | 35 | 20 | 0 | 0 | 15 | | | | | |
| Belleville | 1 | 0 | 0 | 0 | 0 | 0 | 1 | | | 0 | 38,053 |
| Bloomfield | 1 | 0 | 0 | 0 | 0 | 0 | 0 | 0 | 0 | 1 | 52,181 |
| Bloomingdale | 2 | 1 | 0 | 0 | 0 | 2 | 0 | 0 | 4 | 1 | 8,415 |
| Closter | 2 | 0 | 0 | 0 | 0 | 0 | 0 | 0 | 0 | 2 | 8,804 |
| Cranford Township | 3 | 1 | 1 | 0 | 0 | 0 | 1 | 0 | 2 | 2 | 25,189 |
| Denville Township[2] | 5 | 1 | 0 | 0 | 0 | 0 | | | | 4 | 17,019 |
| Dumont | 1 | 0 | 0 | 0 | 0 | 0 | 0 | 1 | 0 | 0 | 18,340 |
| East Brunswick Township | 4 | 2 | 2 | 0 | 0 | 1 | 1 | 2 | 3 | 3 | 50,438 |
| Eatontown[2] | 1 | 4 | 0 | 0 | 0 | 0 | 1 | 0 | 2 | 1 | 12,100 |
| Elizabeth | 7 | 2 | 0 | 0 | 0 | 1 | 2 | 1 | 3 | 4 | 134,131 |
| Englewood | 0 | 0 | 0 | 0 | 0 | 1 | 1 | 0 | 0 | 0 | 29,592 |
| Ewing Township[2] | 3 | 1 | 0 | 0 | 0 | 0 | 0 | 1 | 2 | 0 | 38,055 |
| Fort Lee | 9 | 0 | 1 | 0 | 0 | 1 | 0 | 0 | 7 | 4 | 40,285 |
| Franklin | 1 | 0 | 0 | 0 | 0 | 0 | 0 | 1 | 0 | 0 | 4,662 |
| Franklin Lakes | 0 | 1 | 0 | 0 | 0 | 0 | 0 | 0 | 1 | 0 | 11,744 |
| Gloucester Township | 4 | 0 | 0 | 0 | 0 | 1 | 0 | 1 | 3 | 1 | 66,365 |
| Hackensack | 2 | 2 | 0 | 0 | 0 | 0 | 1 | 2 | 0 | 1 | 45,932 |
| Hamilton Township, Mercer County | 11 | 0 | 0 | 0 | 0 | 0 | 1 | 1 | 8 | 1 | 90,195 |
| Hanover Township | 1 | 0 | 0 | 0 | 0 | 0 | 0 | 0 | 1 | 0 | 14,814 |
| Hazlet Township | 0 | 0 | 1 | 0 | 0 | 0 | | | 0 | 1 | 19,575 |
| Hightstown | 4 | 0 | 0 | 0 | 0 | 3 | 4 | 2 | 0 | 1 | 5,473 |
| Hillsborough Township | 3 | 2 | 4 | 0 | 0 | 1 | 3 | 2 | 2 | 3 | 42,116 |
| Hillside Township | 0 | 2 | 0 | 0 | 0 | 0 | 1 | 0 | 0 | 1 | 22,799 |
| Jersey City | 0 | 1 | 0 | 0 | 0 | 0 | 0 | 1 | 0 | 0 | 275,213 |
| Lacey Township | 1 | 2 | 0 | 0 | 0 | 0 | 0 | 0 | 0 | 3 | 31,324 |
| Medford Township | 8 | 0 | 0 | 0 | 0 | 0 | | | | 8 | 23,417 |
| Middle Township | 6 | 0 | 1 | 0 | 0 | 0 | 2 | 1 | 2 | 2 | 18,041 |
| Montclair | 9 | 0 | 4 | 0 | 0 | 3 | 3 | 7 | 4 | 2 | 40,224 |
| Morristown[2] | 0 | 2 | 1 | 0 | 0 | 0 | 0 | 0 | 0 | 2 | 20,130 |
| Newark | 0 | 1 | 0 | 0 | 0 | 1 | 0 | 0 | 2 | 0 | 295,039 |
| New Brunswick | 6 | 1 | 1 | 0 | 0 | 0 | | | 3 | 5 | 58,691 |
| Newton | 2 | 0 | 0 | 0 | 0 | 0 | 0 | 0 | 2 | 0 | 7,963 |
| North Plainfield | 1 | 0 | 0 | 0 | 0 | 0 | 1 | 0 | 0 | 0 | 22,160 |
| Paramus | 3 | 1 | 0 | 0 | 0 | 0 | 1 | 0 | 0 | 3 | 27,132 |
| Passaic | 0 | 1 | 0 | 0 | 0 | 0 | 0 | | | 1 | 72,223 |
| Point Pleasant Beach | 2 | 0 | 0 | 0 | 0 | 0 | | 0 | 2 | 0 | 4,794 |
| Princeton[2] | 14 | 1 | 1 | 0 | 0 | 0 | 7 | 2 | 3 | 2 | 32,436 |
| Ringwood[2] | 2 | 0 | 1 | 0 | 0 | 0 | 0 | 0 | 0 | 2 | 12,659 |
| Roseland[2] | 1 | 1 | 0 | 0 | 0 | 0 | | | 0 | 1 | 6,066 |
| Roxbury Township | 1 | 0 | 0 | 0 | 0 | 0 | 0 | 0 | 0 | 1 | 23,676 |
| Secaucus | 4 | 3 | 0 | 0 | 0 | 0 | 2 | 1 | 4 | 0 | 23,102 |
| South Amboy[2] | 2 | 1 | 0 | 0 | 0 | 0 | 0 | 0 | 1 | 1 | 9,536 |
| South Brunswick Township | 4 | 0 | 0 | 0 | 0 | 0 | 2 | 1 | 1 | 0 | 47,479 |
| South Orange Village | 1 | 0 | 0 | 0 | 0 | 0 | | | | 1 | 17,420 |
| Sparta Township | 3 | 1 | 2 | 0 | 0 | 0 | 0 | 3 | 2 | 1 | 18,503 |
| Springfield Township, Union County | 1 | 0 | 0 | 0 | 0 | 0 | 1 | 0 | 0 | 0 | 18,285 |
| Vernon Township | 1 | 0 | 0 | 0 | 0 | 0 | 0 | 1 | 0 | 0 | 21,715 |
| Westwood | 1 | 0 | 0 | 0 | 0 | 0 | 0 | 0 | 1 | 0 | 11,495 |
| Woodland Park | 1 | 0 | 0 | 0 | 0 | 0 | 0 | 0 | 1 | 0 | 13,278 |
| Wyckoff Township | 1 | 0 | 0 | 0 | 0 | 0 | 1 | 0 | 0 | 0 | 17,589 |
| | | | | | | | | | | | |
| **Universities and Colleges** | 3 | 0 | 1 | 0 | 0 | 0 | | | | | |
| Rutgers University, New Brunswick | 3 | 0 | 0 | 0 | 0 | 0 | 1 | 0 | 0 | 2 | 56,178 |
| Stockton University | 0 | 0 | 1 | 0 | 0 | 0 | 0 | 0 | 0 | 1 | 11,925 |

# Table 94. Hate Crime Incidents Per Bias Motivation and Quarter, by Selected State and Agency and Federal, 2021—Continued

(Number.)

| State/agency | Number of incidents per bias motivation | | | | | | Number of incidents per quarter | | | | Population[1] |
|---|---|---|---|---|---|---|---|---|---|---|---|
| | Race/ Ethnicity/ Ancestry | Religion | Sexual orientation | Disability | Gender | Gender Identity | 1st quarter | 2nd quarter | 3rd quarter | 4th quarter | |
| **Other Agencies** | 5 | 5 | 2 | 0 | 0 | 0 | | | | | |
| New Jersey Transit Police[2] | 3 | 3 | 2 | 0 | 0 | 0 | | | 5 | 2 | |
| Port Authority of New York and New Jersey[2] | 2 | 2 | 0 | 0 | 0 | 0 | 0 | 2 | 1 | 0 | |
| **NEW MEXICO** | 33 | 11 | 7 | 2 | 0 | 1 | | | | | |
| **Cities** | 28 | 10 | 5 | 2 | 0 | 1 | | | | | |
| Albuquerque[2] | 23 | 6 | 4 | 2 | 0 | 1 | 4 | 11 | 8 | 8 | 564,147 |
| Carlsbad | 1 | 0 | 0 | 0 | 0 | 0 | 0 | 0 | 1 | 0 | 30,029 |
| Gallup | 0 | 1 | 0 | 0 | 0 | 0 | 1 | 0 | 0 | 0 | 21,200 |
| Las Cruces | 4 | 3 | 1 | 0 | 0 | 0 | 1 | 0 | 6 | 1 | 105,805 |
| **Universities and Colleges** | 1 | 0 | 0 | 0 | 0 | 0 | | | | | |
| New Mexico State University | 1 | 0 | 0 | 0 | 0 | 0 | 0 | 0 | 0 | 1 | 16,064 |
| **Metropolitan Counties** | 4 | 0 | 2 | 0 | 0 | 0 | | | | | |
| Bernalillo[2] | 4 | 0 | 2 | 0 | 0 | 0 | 0 | 3 | 1 | 1 | |
| **Nonmetropolitan Counties** | 0 | 1 | 0 | 0 | 0 | 0 | | | | | |
| Sierra | 0 | 1 | 0 | 0 | 0 | 0 | 1 | | | | |
| **NEW YORK** | 32 | 21 | 15 | 0 | 2 | 1 | | | | | |
| **Cities** | 27 | 20 | 10 | 0 | 2 | 1 | | | | | |
| Bethlehem Town[2] | 2 | 0 | 0 | 0 | 0 | 0 | | 0 | 0 | 1 | 34,928 |
| Brighton Town | 1 | 2 | 0 | 0 | 0 | 0 | 0 | 2 | 1 | 0 | 35,689 |
| Buffalo[2] | 4 | 2 | 5 | 0 | 2 | 0 | 3 | 3 | 2 | 3 | 253,809 |
| Clarkstown Town[2] | 0 | 5 | 0 | 0 | 0 | 0 | 0 | 1 | 1 | 1 | 80,188 |
| Colonie Town | 2 | 1 | 0 | 0 | 0 | 0 | 1 | 2 | 0 | 0 | 78,364 |
| Endicott Village | 0 | 1 | 0 | 0 | 0 | 0 | 1 | 0 | 0 | 0 | 12,335 |
| Fort Edward Village | 1 | 0 | 0 | 0 | 0 | 0 | | 1 | 0 | 0 | 3,223 |
| Greece Town | 0 | 0 | 2 | 0 | 0 | 0 | 0 | 0 | 2 | 0 | 95,202 |
| Greenburgh Town[2] | 3 | 1 | 0 | 0 | 0 | 0 | 0 | 0 | 2 | 1 | 44,483 |
| Hudson[2] | 2 | 0 | 0 | 0 | 0 | 0 | 1 | 0 | 0 | 0 | 5,952 |
| Jamestown | 2 | 0 | 0 | 0 | 0 | 0 | 0 | 0 | 2 | 0 | 28,649 |
| Lloyd Town | 1 | 0 | 0 | 0 | 0 | 0 | 0 | 0 | 0 | 0 | 10,665 |
| New Rochelle | 3 | 1 | 0 | 0 | 0 | 0 | 1 | 0 | 2 | 1 | 81,367 |
| Niagara Falls | 0 | 1 | 0 | 0 | 0 | 0 | 0 | 0 | 1 | 0 | 47,139 |
| Orangetown Town | 0 | 1 | 0 | 0 | 0 | 0 | 0 | 0 | 0 | 1 | 37,135 |
| Oswego City[2] | 2 | 0 | 0 | 0 | 0 | 0 | 0 | 1 | 0 | 0 | 17,132 |
| Poughkeepsie Town | 1 | 1 | 0 | 0 | 0 | 0 | 0 | 1 | 1 | 0 | 38,808 |
| Saugerties Town | 0 | 0 | 0 | 0 | 0 | 0 | 0 | 0 | 0 | 1 | 18,954 |
| Schenectady | 0 | 0 | 1 | 0 | 0 | 0 | 0 | 0 | 0 | 1 | 65,140 |
| Spring Valley Village | 0 | 1 | 0 | 0 | 0 | 1 | 0 | 1 | 1 | 0 | 32,340 |
| Utica | 0 | 0 | 1 | 0 | 0 | 0 | 0 | 1 | 0 | 0 | 58,965 |
| Vestal Town | 1 | 0 | 0 | 0 | 0 | 0 | 0 | 0 | 1 | 0 | 28,843 |
| Watertown | 1 | 0 | 0 | 0 | 0 | 0 | 1 | 0 | 0 | 0 | 24,091 |
| Yonkers[2] | 1 | 2 | 0 | 0 | 0 | 0 | 1 | 1 | 0 | 0 | 200,397 |
| Yorktown Town | 0 | 1 | 0 | 0 | 0 | 0 | 1 | 0 | 0 | 0 | 35,970 |
| **Universities and Colleges** | 1 | 0 | 1 | 0 | 0 | 0 | | | | | |
| Cornell University | 0 | 0 | 1 | 0 | 0 | 0 | 0 | 0 | 0 | 1 | 24,594 |
| State University of New York Police, Buffalo | 1 | 0 | 0 | 0 | 0 | 0 | | | | 1 | 35,509 |
| **Metropolitan Counties** | 4 | 0 | 3 | 0 | 0 | 0 | | | | | |
| Broome | 0 | 0 | 1 | 0 | 0 | 0 | 0 | 1 | 0 | 0 | |
| Jefferson[2] | 2 | 0 | 0 | 0 | 0 | 0 | 1 | 0 | 0 | 0 | |
| Monroe | 2 | 0 | 1 | 0 | 0 | 0 | 1 | 1 | 0 | 1 | |
| Rockland | 0 | 0 | 1 | 0 | 0 | 0 | 0 | 0 | 1 | 0 | |
| **Nonmetropolitan Counties** | 0 | 1 | 1 | 0 | 0 | 0 | | | | | |
| Chautauqua | 0 | 0 | 1 | 0 | 0 | 0 | 1 | 0 | 0 | 0 | |
| Genesee | 0 | 1 | 0 | 0 | 0 | 0 | 0 | 1 | 0 | 0 | |
| **NORTH CAROLINA** | 180 | 62 | 36 | 7 | 2 | 3 | | | | | |
| **Cities** | 130 | 29 | 24 | 3 | 1 | 2 | | | | | |
| Asheboro | 0 | 1 | 0 | 0 | 0 | 0 | 1 | 0 | 0 | 0 | 26,082 |
| Asheville | 5 | 0 | 3 | 0 | 0 | 0 | 0 | 3 | 2 | 3 | 93,855 |
| Boone[2] | 2 | 0 | 1 | 0 | 0 | 0 | 0 | 1 | 0 | 1 | 20,321 |
| Brevard | 1 | 0 | 0 | 0 | 0 | 0 | 1 | 0 | 0 | 0 | 7,922 |
| Bryson City | 1 | 0 | 0 | 0 | 0 | 0 | 0 | 0 | 1 | 0 | 1,445 |
| Burnsville | 0 | 1 | 0 | 0 | 0 | 0 | 1 | 0 | 0 | | 1,638 |
| Cary | 2 | 0 | 0 | 0 | 0 | 0 | 0 | 0 | 2 | 0 | 177,735 |
| Chapel Hill | 1 | 0 | 0 | 0 | 0 | 0 | 0 | 1 | 0 | 0 | 64,388 |
| Charlotte-Mecklenburg[2] | 12 | 1 | 5 | 0 | 0 | 0 | 4 | 4 | 3 | 5 | 956,282 |
| Concord | 2 | 0 | 0 | 1 | 0 | 0 | 1 | 0 | 2 | 0 | 100,631 |
| Cornelius | 1 | 0 | 0 | 0 | 0 | 0 | 0 | 0 | 0 | 1 | 31,453 |
| Dallas | 0 | 2 | 0 | 0 | 0 | 1 | 1 | 2 | 0 | 0 | 4,891 |
| Durham[2] | 8 | 0 | 0 | 0 | 0 | 1 | 3 | 2 | 3 | 0 | 291,962 |
| Elizabeth City | 1 | 0 | 0 | 0 | 0 | 0 | 0 | 1 | 0 | 0 | 17,948 |
| Erwin | 0 | 1 | 0 | 0 | 0 | 0 | 0 | 1 | 0 | 0 | 5,270 |

## Table 94. Hate Crime Incidents Per Bias Motivation and Quarter, by Selected State and  Agency and Federal, 2021—Continued

(Number.)

| State/agency | Number of incidents per bias motivation | | | | | | Number of incidents per quarter | | | | Population[1] |
|---|---|---|---|---|---|---|---|---|---|---|---|
| | Race/ Ethnicity/ Ancestry | Religion | Sexual orientation | Disability | Gender | Gender Identity | 1st quarter | 2nd quarter | 3rd quarter | 4th quarter | |
| Fayetteville[2] | 4 | 3 | 1 | 0 | 0 | 0 | 2 | 3 | 0 | 2 | 212,047 |
| Fletcher | 1 | 1 | 0 | 0 | 0 | 0 | 1 | 0 | 0 | 1 | 8,573 |
| Franklin | 0 | 1 | 0 | 0 | 0 | 0 | 0 | 0 | 0 | 1 | 4,145 |
| Gastonia | 4 | 1 | 0 | 0 | 0 | 0 | 1 | 2 | 2 | 0 | 78,260 |
| Greensboro | 9 | 2 | 2 | 1 | 0 | 0 | 0 | 9 | 3 | 2 | 300,865 |
| Greenville | 1 | 0 | 0 | 0 | 0 | 0 | 1 | 0 | 0 | 0 | 95,815 |
| Hendersonville | 2 | 0 | 0 | 0 | 0 | 0 | 0 | 1 | 1 | 0 | 14,351 |
| Hickory | 4 | 0 | 0 | 0 | 0 | 0 | 2 | 0 | 1 | 1 | 41,604 |
| High Point | 1 | 0 | 0 | 0 | 0 | 0 | 0 | 1 | 0 | 0 | 114,492 |
| Jacksonville | 0 | 0 | 2 | 0 | 0 | 0 | 0 | 0 | 2 | 0 | 76,130 |
| Kernersville | 2 | 0 | 0 | 0 | 0 | 0 | 0 | 0 | 1 | 1 | 25,074 |
| Long View | 0 | 0 | 1 | 0 | 0 | 0 | 1 | 0 | 0 | 0 | 4,959 |
| Lumberton | 0 | 7 | 0 | 0 | 0 | 0 | 1 | 0 | 3 | 3 | 20,109 |
| Matthews[2] | 2 | 0 | 1 | 0 | 0 | 0 | 1 | 0 | 1 | 0 | 34,438 |
| Mint Hill | 1 | 0 | 1 | 0 | 0 | 0 | 0 | 2 | 0 | 0 | 28,701 |
| Monroe | 1 | 0 | 0 | 0 | 0 | 0 | 1 | 0 | 0 | 0 | 35,948 |
| Mooresville | 2 | 0 | 1 | 0 | 0 | 0 | 0 | 0 | 2 | 1 | 40,560 |
| Morehead City | 1 | 0 | 0 | 0 | 0 | 0 | 0 | 1 | 0 | 0 | 9,774 |
| Murphy | 1 | 0 | 0 | 0 | 0 | 0 | 0 | 0 | 0 | 1 | 1,672 |
| Newport[2] | 3 | 0 | 0 | 0 | 0 | 0 | 0 | 2 | 0 | 0 | 4,691 |
| Oak Island | 1 | 0 | 0 | 0 | 0 | 0 | 0 | 1 | 0 | 0 | 8,955 |
| Pinebluff | 0 | 1 | 0 | 0 | 0 | 0 | 0 | 0 | 1 | 0 | 1,686 |
| Pinehurst[2] | 1 | 1 | 1 | 0 | 0 | 0 | 1 | 1 | 0 | 0 | 17,253 |
| Pineville | 0 | 1 | 0 | 0 | 0 | 0 | 0 | 0 | 0 | 1 | 9,371 |
| Pittsboro[2] | 2 | 0 | 0 | 0 | 0 | 0 | 1 | 0 | 0 | 0 | 4,491 |
| Raeford | 1 | 0 | 0 | 0 | 0 | 0 | 0 | 0 | 0 | 1 | 4,987 |
| Raleigh[2] | 30 | 0 | 3 | 0 | 1 | 0 | 6 | 9 | 5 | 12 | 481,823 |
| Reidsville | 4 | 0 | 0 | 0 | 0 | 0 | 3 | 0 | 1 | 0 | 13,948 |
| Sharpsburg | 0 | 1 | 0 | 0 | 0 | 0 | 0 | 1 | 0 | 0 | 2,017 |
| Shelby | 1 | 0 | 0 | 0 | 0 | 0 | 0 | 1 | 0 | 0 | 20,128 |
| Smithfield | 1 | 0 | 0 | 0 | 0 | 0 | 0 | 0 | 0 | 1 | 13,581 |
| Stallings | 2 | 0 | 0 | 0 | 0 | 0 | 0 | 1 | 1 | 0 | 16,746 |
| Statesville | 1 | 0 | 1 | 0 | 0 | 0 | 0 | 2 | 0 | 0 | 28,420 |
| Sylva | 0 | 2 | 0 | 0 | 0 | 0 | 0 | 0 | 0 | 2 | 2,757 |
| Thomasville | 1 | 0 | 0 | 0 | 0 | 0 | 0 | 0 | 0 | 1 | 26,704 |
| Valdese | 0 | 0 | 0 | 1 | 0 | 0 | 0 | 0 | 0 | 1 | 4,402 |
| Wake Forest | 1 | 0 | 0 | 0 | 0 | 0 | 0 | 0 | 0 | 1 | 49,457 |
| West Jefferson | 0 | 1 | 0 | 0 | 0 | 0 | 0 | 1 | 0 | 0 | 1,311 |
| Williamston | 0 | 1 | 0 | 0 | 0 | 0 | 0 | 0 | 0 | 1 | 5,072 |
| Wilmington[2] | 4 | 0 | 0 | 0 | 0 | 0 | 0 | 1 | 1 | 1 | 126,759 |
| Wilson | 1 | 0 | 0 | 0 | 0 | 0 | 0 | 1 | 0 | 0 | 49,507 |
| Winston-Salem | 4 | 0 | 1 | 0 | 0 | 0 | 2 | 2 | 1 | 0 | 249,998 |
| | | | | | | | | | | | |
| **Universities and Colleges** | 5 | 0 | 2 | 0 | 0 | 0 | | | | | |
| East Carolina University | 1 | 0 | 0 | 0 | 0 | 0 | 0 | 0 | 0 | 1 | 31,962 |
| Fayetteville State University | 0 | 0 | 2 | 0 | 0 | 0 | 0 | 0 | 1 | 1 | 8,376 |
| University of North Carolina | | | | | | | | | | | |
|    Chapel Hill | 2 | 0 | 0 | 0 | 0 | 0 | 0 | 0 | 1 | 1 | 32,160 |
|    Wilmington | 1 | 0 | 0 | 0 | 0 | 0 | 0 | 0 | 1 | 0 | 20,367 |
| Western Carolina University | 1 | 0 | 0 | 0 | 0 | 0 | 0 | 0 | 1 | 0 | 13,783 |
| | | | | | | | | | | | |
| **Metropolitan Counties** | 33 | 15 | 8 | 4 | 0 | 0 | | | | | |
| Buncombe | 3 | 1 | 1 | 0 | 0 | 0 | 0 | 1 | 1 | 3 | |
| Burke | 1 | 0 | 0 | 0 | 0 | 0 | 1 | 0 | 0 | 0 | |
| Caldwell | 1 | 0 | 0 | 0 | 0 | 0 | 0 | 1 | 0 | 0 | |
| Camden | 1 | 0 | 0 | 0 | 0 | 0 | 1 | 0 | 0 | 0 | |
| Chatham[2] | 2 | 0 | 0 | 3 | 0 | 0 | 1 | 0 | 0 | 2 | |
| Davidson | 1 | 0 | 0 | 0 | 0 | 0 | 0 | 0 | 1 | 0 | |
| Forsyth | 3 | 0 | 0 | 0 | 0 | 0 | 0 | 0 | 2 | 1 | |
| Gaston County Police Department | 2 | 0 | 0 | 0 | 0 | 0 | 0 | 1 | 0 | 1 | |
| Guilford | 2 | 0 | 2 | 0 | 0 | 0 | 0 | 2 | 1 | 1 | |
| Harnett[2] | 5 | 0 | 0 | 0 | 0 | 0 | 1 | 2 | 0 | 1 | |
| Haywood | 2 | 1 | 0 | 0 | 0 | 0 | 0 | 2 | 1 | 0 | |
| Henderson | 1 | 8 | 0 | 0 | 0 | 0 | 2 | 0 | 3 | 4 | |
| Johnston | 0 | 0 | 1 | 0 | 0 | 0 | 0 | 0 | 1 | 0 | |
| Madison | 0 | 1 | 0 | 0 | 0 | 0 | 0 | 1 | 0 | 0 | |
| New Hanover | 1 | 0 | 0 | 0 | 0 | 0 | 0 | 0 | 0 | 1 | |
| Onslow | 0 | 0 | 1 | 0 | 0 | 0 | 1 | 0 | | | |
| Orange | 1 | 0 | 0 | 0 | 0 | 0 | 1 | 0 | 0 | 0 | |
| Pamlico | 0 | 0 | 0 | 1 | 0 | 0 | 0 | 1 | 0 | 0 | |
| Person | 1 | 1 | 0 | 0 | 0 | 0 | 1 | 0 | 1 | 0 | |
| Pitt | 1 | 0 | 0 | 0 | 0 | 0 | 0 | 0 | 1 | 0 | |
| Randolph | 0 | 3 | 0 | 0 | 0 | 0 | 2 | 1 | 0 | 0 | |
| Union | 5 | 0 | 3 | 0 | 0 | 0 | 0 | 1 | 2 | 5 | |
| | | | | | | | | | | | |
| **Nonmetropolitan Counties** | 10 | 17 | 2 | 0 | 0 | 1 | | | | | |
| Carteret | 0 | 0 | 1 | 0 | 0 | 0 | 0 | 0 | 1 | 0 | |
| Caswell | 0 | 1 | 0 | 0 | 0 | 0 | 0 | 0 | 0 | 1 | |
| Cleveland | 1 | 0 | 0 | 0 | 0 | 0 | 0 | 0 | 0 | 1 | |
| Duplin | 0 | 2 | 0 | 0 | 0 | 0 | 0 | 0 | 0 | 2 | |

## Table 94. Hate Crime Incidents Per Bias Motivation and Quarter, by Selected State and Agency and Federal, 2021—Continued

(Number.)

| State/agency | Number of incidents per bias motivation | | | | | | Number of incidents per quarter | | | | Population[1] |
|---|---|---|---|---|---|---|---|---|---|---|---|
| | Race/ Ethnicity/ Ancestry | Religion | Sexual orientation | Disability | Gender | Gender Identity | 1st quarter | 2nd quarter | 3rd quarter | 4th quarter | |
| Halifax | 0 | 2 | 0 | 0 | 0 | 0 | 0 | 0 | 1 | 1 | |
| Montgomery | 0 | 1 | 0 | 0 | 0 | 0 | 0 | 0 | 1 | 0 | |
| Moore | 0 | 1 | 1 | 0 | 0 | 0 | 1 | 0 | 0 | 1 | |
| Richmond[2] | 6 | 6 | 0 | 0 | 0 | 0 | 5 | 5 | 0 | 1 | |
| Surry | 0 | 1 | 0 | 0 | 0 | 0 | 0 | 0 | 1 | 0 | |
| Swain | 1 | 1 | 0 | 0 | 0 | 1 | 0 | 2 | 0 | 1 | |
| Vance | 1 | 0 | 0 | 0 | 0 | 0 | 1 | 0 | 0 | 0 | |
| Warren | 0 | 1 | 0 | 0 | 0 | 0 | 1 | 0 | 0 | 0 | |
| Watauga[2] | 1 | 1 | 0 | 0 | 0 | 0 | 0 | 0 | 1 | 0 | |
| **Other Agencies** | 2 | 1 | 0 | 0 | 1 | 0 | | | | | |
| Moore County Schools | 1 | 0 | 0 | 0 | 0 | 0 | 0 | 0 | 0 | 1 | |
| State Capitol Police | 1 | 0 | 0 | 0 | 0 | 0 | 0 | 1 | 0 | 0 | |
| University of North Carolina Hospitals | 0 | 1 | 0 | 0 | 1 | 0 | 1 | 0 | 1 | 0 | |
| **NORTH DAKOTA** | 29 | 2 | 8 | 0 | 0 | 0 | | | | | |
| **Cities** | 15 | 1 | 8 | 0 | 0 | 0 | | | | | |
| Bismarck | 2 | 0 | 5 | 0 | 0 | 0 | 4 | 1 | 2 | 0 | 75,396 |
| Dickinson | 1 | 0 | 0 | 0 | 0 | 0 | 0 | 0 | 0 | 1 | 24,179 |
| Fargo[2] | 5 | 0 | 1 | 0 | 0 | 0 | 0 | 0 | 2 | 3 | 127,313 |
| Lincoln | 0 | 0 | 1 | 0 | 0 | 0 | 0 | 0 | 0 | 1 | 4,052 |
| Mandan | 4 | 0 | 1 | 0 | 0 | 0 | 2 | 1 | 0 | 2 | 23,292 |
| Valley City[2] | 3 | 0 | 0 | 0 | 0 | 0 | 1 | 1 | 0 | 0 | 6,268 |
| Williston | 0 | 1 | 0 | 0 | 0 | 0 | 0 | 1 | 0 | 0 | 31,680 |
| **Metropolitan Counties** | 1 | 0 | 0 | 0 | 0 | 0 | | | | | |
| Grand Forks | 1 | 0 | 0 | 0 | 0 | 0 | 0 | 0 | 0 | 1 | |
| **Nonmetropolitan Counties** | 2 | 1 | 0 | 0 | 0 | 0 | | | | | |
| Golden Valley | 0 | 1 | 0 | 0 | 0 | 0 | 0 | 0 | 1 | 0 | |
| Pembina | 2 | 0 | 0 | 0 | 0 | 0 | 1 | 1 | 0 | 0 | |
| **Tribal Agencies** | 11 | 0 | 0 | 0 | 0 | 0 | | | | | |
| Turtle Mountain Agency | 11 | 0 | 0 | 0 | 0 | 0 | 4 | 6 | 1 | 0 | |
| **OHIO** | 299 | 71 | 68 | 44 | 4 | 41 | | | | | |
| **Cities** | 245 | 54 | 55 | 40 | 1 | 37 | | | | | |
| Akron[2] | 8 | 5 | 1 | 2 | 0 | 7 | 0 | 7 | 9 | 6 | 195,701 |
| Amberley Village | 1 | 0 | 0 | 0 | 0 | 0 | 0 | 0 | 1 | 0 | 3,538 |
| Arcanum | 0 | 0 | 0 | 0 | 0 | 1 | 1 | 0 | 0 | 0 | 1,993 |
| Archbold | 0 | 0 | 0 | 1 | 0 | 0 | 1 | 0 | 0 | 0 | 4,286 |
| Ashland | 0 | 1 | 0 | 1 | 0 | 0 | 0 | 0 | 0 | 2 | 19,919 |
| Austintown | 2 | 0 | 0 | 0 | 0 | 0 | 1 | 1 | 0 | 0 | 34,472 |
| Barberton[2] | 4 | 0 | 0 | 0 | 0 | 0 | 0 | 1 | 1 | 0 | 25,746 |
| Bay Village | 1 | 0 | 0 | 0 | 0 | 0 | 0 | 0 | 0 | 1 | 15,154 |
| Beaver Township | 1 | 0 | 0 | 0 | 0 | 0 | 1 | 0 | 0 | 0 | 6,321 |
| Blue Ash | 2 | 0 | 0 | 0 | 0 | 0 | 0 | 1 | 1 | 0 | 12,525 |
| Boardman | 4 | 0 | 0 | 0 | 0 | 0 | 0 | 1 | 2 | 1 | 38,377 |
| Canton | 3 | 0 | 0 | 0 | 0 | 0 | 2 | 1 | 0 | 0 | 69,623 |
| Carrollton | 1 | 0 | 0 | 0 | 0 | 0 | 0 | 0 | 0 | 1 | 2,995 |
| Chillicothe[2] | 1 | 3 | 2 | 0 | 0 | 1 | 2 | 0 | 4 | 0 | 21,622 |
| Cincinnati[2] | 10 | 0 | 0 | 0 | 0 | 0 | 0 | 3 | 4 | 2 | 305,308 |
| Circleville | 2 | 0 | 0 | 0 | 0 | 0 | 0 | 1 | 1 | 0 | 14,226 |
| Clayton | 1 | 0 | 0 | 0 | 0 | 0 | 0 | 1 | 0 | 0 | 13,232 |
| Cleveland[2] | 40 | 11 | 6 | 5 | 0 | 18 | 25 | 22 | 21 | 6 | 379,313 |
| Colerain Township | 0 | 0 | 0 | 2 | 0 | 0 | 1 | 0 | 1 | 0 | 59,223 |
| Columbus[2] | 38 | 11 | 15 | 2 | 0 | 4 | 23 | 16 | 17 | 11 | 916,001 |
| Dayton | 1 | 0 | 0 | 0 | 0 | 0 | 0 | 1 | 0 | 0 | 139,671 |
| Defiance | 1 | 0 | 1 | 0 | 0 | 0 | 1 | 1 | 0 | 0 | 16,415 |
| Delaware | 0 | 0 | 0 | 0 | 0 | 1 | 0 | 0 | 1 | 0 | 43,469 |
| Delhi Township | 1 | 0 | 1 | 0 | 0 | 0 | 0 | 2 | 0 | 0 | 29,785 |
| Dover | 1 | 0 | 0 | 0 | 0 | 0 | 0 | 0 | 0 | 1 | 12,676 |
| East Cleveland | 15 | 1 | 0 | 0 | 0 | 0 | 0 | 3 | 1 | 12 | 16,810 |
| East Palestine | 1 | 0 | 1 | 0 | 0 | 0 | 1 | 1 | 0 | 0 | 4,350 |
| Elyria | 4 | 0 | 0 | 0 | 0 | 0 | 2 | 1 | 1 | 0 | 53,809 |
| Fairborn | 1 | 0 | 0 | 0 | 0 | 0 | 0 | 1 | 0 | 0 | 34,076 |
| Findlay | 0 | 0 | 0 | 1 | 0 | 0 | 1 | 0 | 0 | 0 | 40,803 |
| Gahanna | 4 | 0 | 0 | 0 | 0 | 0 | 2 | 0 | 2 | 0 | 35,765 |
| Garfield Heights[2] | 5 | 1 | 2 | 1 | 0 | 0 | 0 | 4 | 3 | 1 | 27,296 |
| Goshen Township, Clermont County | 1 | 0 | 0 | 0 | 0 | 0 | 0 | 0 | 0 | 1 | 16,498 |
| Grove City | 1 | 1 | 2 | 0 | 0 | 1 | 0 | 2 | 2 | 1 | 42,992 |
| Heath | 0 | 0 | 1 | 0 | 0 | 0 | 0 | 1 | 0 | 0 | 11,111 |
| Hilliard | 1 | 0 | 0 | 0 | 0 | 0 | 0 | 1 | 0 | 0 | 37,776 |
| Hillsboro | 0 | 0 | 1 | 0 | 1 | 0 | 0 | 1 | 1 | 0 | 6,576 |
| Holland | 0 | 1 | 1 | 0 | 0 | 0 | 1 | 1 | 0 | 0 | 1,682 |
| Hudson | 0 | 0 | 1 | 1 | 0 | 0 | 0 | 0 | 1 | 1 | 22,170 |
| Jackson Township, Stark County | 3 | 0 | 1 | 0 | 0 | 0 | 3 | 0 | 1 | 0 | 40,215 |
| Jamestown | 1 | 0 | 0 | 0 | 0 | 0 | 0 | 0 | 0 | 1 | 2,157 |
| Lakewood | 1 | 0 | 0 | 0 | 0 | 0 | 1 | 0 | 0 | 0 | 49,404 |
| Lancaster | 2 | 0 | 0 | 0 | 0 | 0 | 0 | 1 | 0 | 1 | 41,152 |

## Table 94. Hate Crime Incidents Per Bias Motivation and Quarter, by Selected State and Agency and Federal, 2021—Continued

(Number.)

| State/agency | Number of incidents per bias motivation | | | | | | Number of incidents per quarter | | | | Population[1] |
|---|---|---|---|---|---|---|---|---|---|---|---|
| | Race/Ethnicity/Ancestry | Religion | Sexual orientation | Disability | Gender | Gender Identity | 1st quarter | 2nd quarter | 3rd quarter | 4th quarter | |
| Lawrence Township[2] | 0 | 2 | 0 | 0 | 0 | 0 | 0 | 1 | 0 | 0 | 8,275 |
| Lima | 3 | 1 | 1 | 7 | 0 | 0 | 4 | 3 | 3 | 2 | 36,233 |
| Logan | 0 | 1 | 1 | 0 | 0 | 0 | 0 | 1 | 0 | 1 | 6,918 |
| Lorain | 1 | 0 | 0 | 0 | 0 | 0 | 0 | 0 | 0 | 1 | 63,859 |
| Lyndhurst | 1 | 0 | 0 | 0 | 0 | 0 | 0 | 1 | 0 | 0 | 13,258 |
| Mansfield[2] | 0 | 0 | 3 | 0 | 0 | 0 | 0 | 2 | 0 | 0 | 45,971 |
| Marietta | 2 | 0 | 0 | 0 | 0 | 0 | 0 | 0 | 2 | 0 | 13,295 |
| Mason | 0 | 1 | 0 | 0 | 0 | 2 | 1 | 1 | 0 | 1 | 34,660 |
| Massillon[2] | 1 | 0 | 1 | 0 | 0 | 0 | 0 | 0 | 0 | 1 | 32,679 |
| Maumee | 1 | 0 | 0 | 0 | 0 | 0 | 1 | 0 | 0 | 0 | 13,541 |
| Mayfield Heights | 2 | 0 | 0 | 0 | 0 | 0 | 0 | 1 | 1 | 0 | 18,421 |
| Mechanicsburg | 1 | 0 | 0 | 0 | 0 | 0 | 0 | 0 | 0 | 1 | 1,610 |
| Mentor | 0 | 0 | 0 | 1 | 0 | 0 | 0 | 0 | 0 | 1 | 47,084 |
| Miamisburg | 2 | 0 | 0 | 0 | 0 | 0 | 0 | 1 | 1 | 0 | 20,112 |
| Miami Township, Montgomery County | 1 | 1 | 1 | 0 | 0 | 0 | 0 | 1 | 0 | 2 | 29,213 |
| Middletown[2] | 9 | 1 | 2 | 0 | 0 | 0 | 0 | 6 | 3 | 1 | 48,944 |
| Monroe | 1 | 0 | 0 | 0 | 0 | 0 | 0 | 0 | 1 | 0 | 16,858 |
| Moraine | 2 | 3 | 0 | 0 | 0 | 0 | 1 | 0 | 3 | 1 | 6,518 |
| Mount Healthy | 0 | 0 | 0 | 1 | 0 | 0 | 1 | | | | 6,790 |
| Mount Vernon | 0 | 1 | 0 | 0 | 0 | 0 | 0 | 0 | 0 | 1 | 16,625 |
| Napoleon | 1 | 0 | 0 | 1 | 0 | 0 | 1 | 0 | 1 | 0 | 8,088 |
| Nelsonville | 1 | 0 | 0 | 0 | 0 | 0 | 0 | 1 | 0 | 0 | 5,094 |
| New Albany[2] | 3 | 0 | 0 | 0 | 0 | 0 | 0 | 2 | 0 | 0 | 11,449 |
| New Franklin | 0 | 1 | 0 | 0 | 0 | 0 | 0 | 0 | 1 | 0 | 14,090 |
| New Knoxville | 1 | 0 | 0 | 0 | 0 | 0 | 1 | 0 | 0 | 0 | 860 |
| North Canton | 1 | 0 | 0 | 0 | 0 | 0 | 0 | 0 | 0 | 1 | 17,084 |
| Norton | 0 | 0 | 0 | 1 | 0 | 0 | 0 | 0 | 0 | 1 | 11,894 |
| Norwood | 1 | 0 | 0 | 0 | 0 | 0 | 1 | 0 | 0 | | 19,749 |
| Oak Harbor | 2 | 0 | 0 | 0 | 0 | 0 | 0 | 2 | 0 | 0 | 2,685 |
| Obetz | 1 | 0 | 0 | 1 | 0 | 0 | 0 | 1 | 1 | 0 | 5,479 |
| Portsmouth | 0 | 0 | 2 | 2 | 0 | 0 | 1 | 0 | 0 | 3 | 19,702 |
| Powell | 1 | 0 | 0 | 0 | 0 | 0 | 1 | 0 | 0 | 0 | 13,591 |
| Riverside | 3 | 0 | 0 | 0 | 0 | 0 | 1 | 2 | 0 | 0 | 25,168 |
| Rocky River | 1 | 0 | 0 | 3 | 0 | 0 | 0 | 1 | 3 | 0 | 20,007 |
| Salineville | 0 | 0 | 0 | 0 | 0 | 1 | 0 | 0 | 1 | 0 | 1,203 |
| Shawnee Hills | 0 | 0 | 1 | 0 | 0 | 0 | 0 | 1 | 0 | | 852 |
| Sidney[2] | 3 | 0 | 0 | 0 | 0 | 0 | 0 | 2 | 0 | 0 | 20,217 |
| Springfield | 5 | 0 | 2 | 0 | 0 | 0 | 0 | 3 | 1 | 3 | 58,253 |
| Springfield Township, Summit County | 0 | 0 | 1 | 0 | 0 | 0 | 0 | 0 | 1 | 0 | 14,459 |
| St. Bernard | 0 | 1 | 0 | 0 | 0 | 0 | 0 | 1 | 0 | | 4,315 |
| Steubenville | 2 | 0 | 0 | 0 | 0 | 0 | 0 | 1 | 0 | 1 | 17,482 |
| Stow | 1 | 2 | 0 | 0 | 0 | 0 | 0 | 1 | 2 | 0 | 34,704 |
| Streetsboro | 0 | 0 | 0 | 1 | 0 | 0 | 1 | 0 | 0 | 0 | 16,769 |
| Struthers | 1 | 0 | 0 | 0 | 0 | 0 | 0 | 0 | 1 | 0 | 9,976 |
| Sylvania Township | 1 | 0 | 0 | 0 | 0 | 0 | 0 | 1 | 0 | 0 | 30,078 |
| Tallmadge | 0 | 0 | 0 | 0 | 0 | 1 | 0 | 0 | 0 | 0 | 17,532 |
| Toledo | 8 | 0 | 0 | 0 | 0 | 0 | 1 | 4 | 2 | 1 | 269,941 |
| Trotwood | 1 | 0 | 0 | 0 | 0 | 0 | 0 | 0 | 0 | 1 | 24,433 |
| Union | 1 | 0 | 0 | 0 | 0 | 0 | | | | | 6,958 |
| Union Township, Clermont County[2] | 2 | 0 | 0 | 0 | 0 | 0 | 0 | 0 | 1 | 0 | 48,994 |
| Upper Arlington | 1 | 0 | 0 | 0 | 0 | 0 | 0 | 0 | 1 | 0 | 35,540 |
| Van Wert | 1 | 0 | 0 | 0 | 0 | 0 | 0 | 1 | 0 | 0 | 10,594 |
| Wapakoneta | 0 | 2 | 0 | 0 | 0 | 0 | 0 | 0 | 1 | 1 | 9,664 |
| Washington Court House | 1 | 1 | 0 | 0 | 0 | 0 | 0 | 1 | 0 | 1 | 14,189 |
| Weathersfield | 1 | 0 | 0 | 0 | 0 | 0 | 0 | 0 | 1 | 0 | 7,941 |
| Wellston[2] | 1 | 0 | 2 | 0 | 0 | 0 | 1 | 1 | 0 | 0 | 5,519 |
| West Chester Township | 0 | 1 | 0 | 0 | 0 | 0 | 0 | 0 | 0 | 1 | 63,211 |
| Wooster | 1 | 0 | 0 | 5 | 0 | 0 | 0 | 3 | 2 | 1 | 26,160 |
| Worthington | 0 | 0 | 1 | 0 | 0 | 0 | 0 | 0 | 1 | 0 | 14,884 |
| Yellow Springs | 1 | 0 | 0 | 0 | 0 | 0 | 0 | 0 | 1 | 0 | 3,787 |
| Youngstown | 7 | 0 | 1 | 1 | 0 | 0 | 3 | 3 | 1 | 2 | 63,538 |
| **Universities and Colleges** | 11 | 3 | 2 | 1 | 0 | 1 | | | | | |
| Kent State University | 3 | 0 | 0 | 0 | 0 | 0 | 1 | 0 | 0 | 2 | 32,341 |
| Ohio State University, Columbus[2] | 8 | 1 | 2 | 1 | 0 | 1 | 4 | 2 | 2 | 4 | 66,017 |
| Ohio University | 0 | 2 | 0 | 0 | 0 | 0 | 0 | 0 | 1 | 1 | 31,679 |
| **Metropolitan Counties** | 27 | 5 | 5 | 0 | 2 | 1 | | | | | |
| Cuyahoga | 0 | 0 | 1 | 0 | 0 | 0 | 1 | 0 | 0 | | |
| Delaware | 1 | 0 | 0 | 0 | 0 | 0 | 0 | 1 | 0 | | |
| Fairfield | 0 | 0 | 1 | 0 | 0 | 0 | 0 | 0 | 1 | 0 | |
| Franklin | 1 | 0 | 0 | 0 | 0 | 0 | 0 | 0 | 0 | 1 | |
| Hamilton[2] | 6 | 0 | 0 | 0 | 1 | 0 | 2 | 0 | 2 | 2 | |
| Hocking | 0 | 0 | 1 | 0 | 0 | 0 | 1 | 0 | 0 | 0 | |
| Lorain | 1 | 0 | 0 | 0 | 0 | 0 | 0 | 1 | 0 | 0 | |
| Lucas | 1 | 1 | 0 | 0 | 0 | 0 | 0 | 0 | 1 | 1 | |
| Madison[2] | 3 | 0 | 0 | 0 | 0 | 0 | 0 | 1 | 1 | 0 | |
| Mahoning | 1 | 0 | 1 | 0 | 0 | 0 | 0 | 1 | 1 | | |
| Medina | 1 | 1 | 0 | 0 | 0 | 0 | 1 | 0 | 1 | 0 | |
| Montgomery | 2 | 1 | 0 | 0 | 0 | 0 | 1 | 1 | 0 | 1 | |

# Table 94. Hate Crime Incidents Per Bias Motivation and Quarter, by Selected State and Agency and Federal, 2021—Continued

(Number.)

| State/agency | Number of incidents per bias motivation | | | | | | Number of incidents per quarter | | | | Population[1] |
|---|---|---|---|---|---|---|---|---|---|---|---|
| | Race/ Ethnicity/ Ancestry | Religion | Sexual orientation | Disability | Gender | Gender Identity | 1st quarter | 2nd quarter | 3rd quarter | 4th quarter | |
| Pickaway | 1 | 0 | 0 | 0 | 0 | 0 | 1 | 0 | 0 | 0 | |
| Portage | 0 | 0 | 1 | 0 | 0 | 0 | 0 | 1 | 0 | 0 | |
| Richland | 2 | 0 | 0 | 0 | 0 | 0 | 0 | 1 | 0 | 1 | |
| Summit | 2 | 2 | 0 | 0 | 0 | 1 | 0 | 1 | 3 | 1 | |
| Union | 0 | 0 | 0 | 0 | 1 | 0 | 0 | 1 | 0 | 0 | |
| Warren[2] | 5 | 0 | 0 | 0 | 0 | 0 | 2 | 0 | 1 | 1 | |
| **Nonmetropolitan Counties** | 14 | 9 | 6 | 3 | 1 | 1 | | | | | |
| Ashtabula | 2 | 0 | 0 | 0 | 0 | 0 | 1 | 1 | 0 | 0 | |
| Athens | 0 | 0 | 0 | 1 | 0 | 0 | 0 | 0 | 1 | 0 | |
| Columbiana | 1 | 0 | 0 | 2 | 0 | 0 | 1 | 2 | 0 | 0 | |
| Coshocton | 1 | 0 | 1 | 0 | 0 | 0 | 1 | 0 | 1 | 0 | |
| Crawford | 1 | 0 | 0 | 0 | 0 | 0 | 0 | 0 | 0 | 1 | |
| Defiance | 0 | 1 | 0 | 0 | 0 | 0 | 1 | 0 | 0 | 0 | |
| Knox | 2 | 2 | 0 | 0 | 0 | 0 | 2 | 1 | 0 | 1 | |
| Logan | 2 | 1 | 0 | 0 | 0 | 0 | 2 | 0 | 1 | 0 | |
| Meigs | 1 | 0 | 0 | 0 | 0 | 0 | 0 | 0 | 0 | 1 | |
| Mercer | 0 | 0 | 1 | 0 | 0 | 0 | 1 | 0 | | | |
| Monroe | 0 | 0 | 0 | 0 | 1 | 0 | 0 | 1 | 0 | | |
| Morgan | 0 | 0 | 1 | 0 | 0 | 0 | 0 | 0 | 0 | 1 | |
| Muskingum | 1 | 0 | 0 | 0 | 0 | 0 | 0 | 1 | 0 | | |
| Pike[2] | 0 | 0 | 2 | 0 | 0 | 0 | 1 | 0 | 0 | 0 | |
| Preble | 0 | 5 | 0 | 0 | 0 | 0 | 0 | 2 | 1 | 2 | |
| Ross | 1 | 0 | 0 | 0 | 0 | 0 | 1 | 0 | 0 | 0 | |
| Tuscarawas | 0 | 0 | 0 | 0 | 0 | 1 | 0 | 1 | 0 | 0 | |
| Wayne | 2 | 0 | 1 | 0 | 0 | 0 | 1 | 1 | 0 | 1 | |
| **Other Agencies** | 2 | 0 | 0 | 0 | 0 | 1 | | | | | |
| Ohio Department of Natural Resources | 2 | 0 | 0 | 0 | 0 | 1 | 0 | 1 | 2 | 0 | |
| **OKLAHOMA** | 49 | 4 | 15 | 2 | 6 | 0 | | | | | |
| **Cities** | 35 | 3 | 11 | 2 | 6 | 0 | | | | | |
| Altus | 2 | 0 | 1 | 0 | 0 | 0 | 0 | 1 | 1 | 1 | 18,007 |
| Broken Arrow[2] | 0 | 0 | 0 | 0 | 5 | 0 | 0 | 1 | 1 | 0 | 112,990 |
| Catoosa | 1 | 0 | 0 | 0 | 0 | 0 | 0 | 1 | 0 | 0 | 6,876 |
| Chickasha | 1 | 0 | 0 | 0 | 0 | 0 | 0 | 0 | 0 | 1 | 16,410 |
| Choctaw | 0 | 0 | 0 | 1 | 0 | 0 | 0 | 0 | 1 | 0 | 12,938 |
| Chouteau | 1 | 0 | 0 | 0 | 0 | 0 | 0 | 0 | 0 | 1 | 2,111 |
| Coweta | 0 | 0 | 2 | 0 | 0 | 0 | 1 | 0 | 0 | 1 | 10,297 |
| Del City | 4 | 0 | 0 | 0 | 0 | 0 | 2 | 1 | 0 | 1 | 21,665 |
| Durant | 3 | 0 | 0 | 0 | 0 | 0 | 0 | 2 | 0 | 1 | 19,518 |
| Edmond | 1 | 0 | 0 | 0 | 0 | 0 | 0 | 0 | 1 | 0 | 96,861 |
| El Reno | 0 | 0 | 1 | 0 | 0 | 0 | 1 | 0 | 0 | 0 | 21,018 |
| Glenpool | 1 | 1 | 0 | 0 | 0 | 0 | 1 | 0 | 1 | 0 | 14,385 |
| Guthrie | 1 | 0 | 0 | 0 | 0 | 0 | 0 | 1 | 0 | 0 | 11,968 |
| Haskell | 1 | 0 | 0 | 0 | 0 | 0 | 0 | 1 | 0 | 0 | 1,949 |
| Healdton | 0 | 0 | 1 | 0 | 0 | 0 | 0 | 0 | 1 | 0 | 2,684 |
| Jones | 1 | 0 | 0 | 0 | 0 | 0 | 0 | 0 | 0 | 1 | 3,280 |
| Lawton | 1 | 0 | 0 | 0 | 0 | 0 | 0 | 0 | 1 | 0 | 92,711 |
| Miami | 0 | 0 | 1 | 1 | 0 | 0 | 0 | 1 | 0 | 1 | 12,885 |
| Muskogee | 1 | 0 | 1 | 0 | 0 | 0 | 0 | 1 | 1 | 0 | 36,598 |
| Norman | 1 | 0 | 0 | 0 | 0 | 0 | 0 | 0 | 0 | 1 | 127,304 |
| Oklahoma City | 1 | 0 | 0 | 0 | 1 | 0 | 1 | 0 | 0 | 1 | 670,872 |
| Okmulgee | 1 | 0 | 0 | 0 | 0 | 0 | 0 | 0 | 1 | 0 | 11,531 |
| Pawhuska | 1 | 0 | 0 | 0 | 0 | 0 | 0 | 0 | 1 | 0 | 3,341 |
| Piedmont | 1 | 0 | 1 | 0 | 0 | 0 | 0 | 0 | 0 | 2 | 9,385 |
| Pryor Creek | 5 | 0 | 0 | 0 | 0 | 0 | 2 | 1 | 1 | 1 | 9,377 |
| Sallisaw | 0 | 0 | 1 | 0 | 0 | 0 | 0 | 0 | 1 | 0 | 8,405 |
| Sapulpa | 1 | 0 | 0 | 0 | 0 | 0 | 0 | 0 | 0 | 1 | 21,535 |
| Shawnee | 1 | 0 | 0 | 0 | 0 | 0 | 1 | 0 | 0 | 0 | 31,724 |
| The Village | 0 | 1 | 0 | 0 | 0 | 0 | 0 | 0 | 1 | 0 | 9,709 |
| Tulsa | 2 | 1 | 2 | 0 | 0 | 0 | 1 | 3 | 0 | 1 | 404,255 |
| Vinita | 1 | 0 | 0 | 0 | 0 | 0 | 0 | 0 | 1 | 0 | 5,264 |
| Wilson | 1 | 0 | 0 | 0 | 0 | 0 | 1 | 0 | 0 | 0 | 1,705 |
| **Universities and Colleges** | 5 | 0 | 1 | 0 | 0 | 0 | | | | | |
| Southeastern Oklahoma State University | 1 | 0 | 0 | 0 | 0 | 0 | 1 | 0 | 0 | 0 | 6,534 |
| University of Central Oklahoma | 4 | 0 | 1 | 0 | 0 | 0 | 0 | 1 | 2 | 2 | 17,440 |
| **Metropolitan Counties** | 3 | 1 | 0 | 0 | 0 | 0 | | | | | |
| Canadian | 2 | 0 | 0 | 0 | 0 | 0 | 1 | 1 | 0 | 0 | |
| Logan | 0 | 1 | 0 | 0 | 0 | 0 | 0 | 0 | 1 | 0 | |
| Wagoner | 1 | 0 | 0 | 0 | 0 | 0 | 1 | 0 | 0 | 0 | |
| **Nonmetropolitan Counties** | 6 | 0 | 2 | 0 | 0 | 0 | | | | | |
| Alfalfa | 1 | 0 | 0 | 0 | 0 | 0 | 0 | 0 | 0 | 1 | |
| Atoka | 1 | 0 | 0 | 0 | 0 | 0 | 1 | 0 | 0 | 0 | |
| Craig | 1 | 0 | 0 | 0 | 0 | 0 | 0 | 0 | 1 | 0 | |
| Kingfisher | 1 | 0 | 0 | 0 | 0 | 0 | 0 | 0 | 0 | 1 | |
| Mayes | 1 | 0 | 1 | 0 | 0 | 0 | 0 | 1 | 1 | 0 | |

## Table 94. Hate Crime Incidents Per Bias Motivation and Quarter, by Selected State and Agency and Federal, 2021—Continued

(Number.)

| State/agency | Number of incidents per bias motivation | | | | | | Number of incidents per quarter | | | | Population[1] |
|---|---|---|---|---|---|---|---|---|---|---|---|
| | Race/ Ethnicity/ Ancestry | Religion | Sexual orientation | Disability | Gender | Gender Identity | 1st quarter | 2nd quarter | 3rd quarter | 4th quarter | |
| McCurtain | 1 | 0 | 0 | 0 | 0 | 0 | 0 | 1 | 0 | 0 | |
| McIntosh | 0 | 0 | 1 | 0 | 0 | 0 | 1 | 0 | 0 | 0 | |
| | | | | | | | | | | | |
| Tribal Agencies | 0 | 0 | 1 | 0 | 0 | 0 | | | | | |
| Wyandotte Nation | 0 | 0 | 1 | 0 | 0 | 0 | 0 | 0 | 0 | 1 | |
| | | | | | | | | | | | |
| **OREGON** | 201 | 27 | 51 | 2 | 1 | 13 | | | | | |
| **Cities** | 148 | 26 | 36 | 2 | 0 | 13 | | | | | |
| Albany[2] | 13 | 0 | 1 | 0 | 0 | 0 | 0 | 6 | 4 | 2 | 56,746 |
| Ashland | 1 | 0 | 0 | 0 | 0 | 0 | 0 | 1 | 0 | 0 | 21,308 |
| Astoria | 0 | 0 | 1 | 0 | 0 | 0 | 0 | 0 | 1 | 0 | 10,086 |
| Beaverton[2] | 5 | 0 | 0 | 0 | 0 | 0 | 1 | 1 | 2 | 0 | 99,886 |
| Bend | 12 | 2 | 1 | 0 | 0 | 0 | 5 | 5 | 2 | 3 | 104,833 |
| Boardman | 0 | 0 | 1 | 0 | 0 | 0 | 0 | 0 | 1 | 0 | 3,855 |
| Canby | 1 | 0 | 0 | 0 | 0 | 0 | 0 | 1 | 0 | 0 | 18,161 |
| Central Point[2] | 0 | 2 | 1 | 0 | 0 | 0 | 0 | 0 | 1 | 1 | 19,313 |
| Corvallis[2] | 6 | 0 | 1 | 0 | 0 | 1 | 1 | 2 | 2 | 2 | 59,585 |
| Eugene[2] | 15 | 5 | 1 | 2 | 0 | 1 | 8 | 10 | 2 | 3 | 175,007 |
| Gladstone[2] | 1 | 1 | 2 | 0 | 0 | 1 | 1 | 0 | 1 | 2 | 12,506 |
| Grants Pass | 2 | 1 | 1 | 0 | 0 | 0 | 1 | 2 | 1 | 0 | 38,672 |
| Gresham | 2 | 0 | 0 | 0 | 0 | 0 | 0 | 0 | 1 | 1 | 110,448 |
| Hillsboro[2] | 7 | 3 | 2 | 0 | 0 | 0 | 3 | 2 | 3 | 3 | 113,053 |
| Hood River | 1 | 0 | 0 | 0 | 0 | 0 | 0 | 1 | 0 | 0 | 7,848 |
| Klamath Falls | 1 | 1 | 2 | 0 | 0 | 0 | 0 | 1 | 2 | 1 | 22,960 |
| Lake Oswego | 0 | 0 | 0 | 0 | 0 | 1 | 0 | 1 | 0 | 0 | 40,138 |
| Lincoln City | 2 | 0 | 0 | 0 | 0 | 0 | 0 | 0 | 1 | 1 | 9,391 |
| McMinnville | 2 | 0 | 0 | 0 | 0 | 0 | 0 | 1 | 0 | 1 | 35,498 |
| Milwaukie[2] | 3 | 0 | 0 | 0 | 0 | 0 | 0 | 1 | 1 | 0 | 21,094 |
| Molalla | 1 | 0 | 0 | 0 | 0 | 0 | 0 | 0 | 1 | 0 | 9,383 |
| Oregon City | 5 | 0 | 1 | 0 | 0 | 0 | 2 | 1 | 3 | 0 | 38,602 |
| Pendleton | 0 | 0 | 0 | 0 | 0 | 1 | 0 | 0 | 0 | 1 | 16,587 |
| Portland[2] | 26 | 6 | 16 | 0 | 0 | 4 | 17 | 13 | 12 | 5 | 664,350 |
| Redmond | 2 | 0 | 0 | 0 | 0 | 0 | 1 | 0 | 0 | 1 | 35,230 |
| Salem[2] | 15 | 2 | 4 | 0 | 0 | 2 | 6 | 7 | 3 | 6 | 178,106 |
| Sherwood | 0 | 1 | 0 | 0 | 0 | 0 | 0 | 0 | 0 | 1 | 19,882 |
| Silverton | 1 | 0 | 0 | 0 | 0 | 0 | 0 | 1 | 0 | 0 | 10,764 |
| Springfield | 7 | 0 | 0 | 0 | 0 | 0 | 0 | 0 | 5 | 2 | 63,599 |
| Sutherlin | 1 | 0 | 0 | 0 | 0 | 0 | 0 | 1 | 0 | 0 | 8,267 |
| The Dalles | 1 | 0 | 0 | 0 | 0 | 0 | 1 | 0 | 0 | 0 | 15,643 |
| Tigard[2] | 8 | 1 | 1 | 0 | 0 | 2 | 1 | 3 | 5 | 2 | 56,914 |
| Tualatin | 4 | 0 | 0 | 0 | 0 | 0 | 2 | 1 | 0 | 1 | 27,617 |
| West Linn | 3 | 1 | 0 | 0 | 0 | 0 | 0 | 3 | 0 | 1 | 26,908 |
| | | | | | | | | | | | |
| **Universities and Colleges** | 5 | 0 | 2 | 0 | 1 | 0 | | | | | |
| Oregon State University | 2 | 0 | 0 | 0 | 1 | 0 | 1 | 0 | 2 | 0 | 37,586 |
| Portland State University[2] | 3 | 0 | 2 | 0 | 0 | 0 | 2 | 1 | 0 | 1 | 30,571 |
| | | | | | | | | | | | |
| **Metropolitan Counties** | 39 | 1 | 9 | 0 | 0 | 0 | | | | | |
| Benton | 1 | 0 | 0 | 0 | 0 | 0 | 0 | 0 | 1 | 0 | |
| Clackamas[2] | 21 | 0 | 1 | 0 | 0 | 0 | 3 | 7 | 2 | 2 | |
| Jackson | 0 | 0 | 1 | 0 | 0 | 0 | 0 | 0 | 0 | 1 | |
| Josephine | 1 | 0 | 0 | 0 | 0 | 0 | 0 | 0 | 1 | 0 | |
| Linn | 1 | 0 | 1 | 0 | 0 | 0 | 0 | 0 | 2 | 0 | |
| Multnomah | 3 | 0 | 2 | 0 | 0 | 0 | 0 | 1 | 1 | 3 | |
| Polk | 1 | 0 | 0 | 0 | 0 | 0 | 0 | 1 | 0 | 0 | |
| Washington[2] | 10 | 1 | 4 | 0 | 0 | 0 | 1 | 6 | 4 | 2 | |
| Yamhill | 1 | 0 | 0 | 0 | 0 | 0 | 0 | 1 | 0 | 0 | |
| | | | | | | | | | | | |
| **Nonmetropolitan Counties** | 7 | 0 | 1 | 0 | 0 | 0 | | | | | |
| Klamath | 1 | 0 | 0 | 0 | 0 | 0 | 0 | 0 | 0 | 1 | |
| Lake | 1 | 0 | 0 | 0 | 0 | 0 | 0 | 0 | 1 | 0 | |
| Lincoln[2] | 2 | 0 | 0 | 0 | 0 | 0 | 0 | 0 | 0 | 1 | |
| Malheur | 1 | 0 | 0 | 0 | 0 | 0 | 1 | 0 | 0 | 0 | |
| Tillamook | 1 | 0 | 0 | 0 | 0 | 0 | 0 | 0 | 1 | 0 | |
| Umatilla | 1 | 0 | 0 | 0 | 0 | 0 | 0 | 0 | 1 | 0 | |
| Union | 0 | 0 | 1 | 0 | 0 | 0 | 0 | 1 | 0 | 0 | |
| | | | | | | | | | | | |
| **State Police Agencies** | 2 | 0 | 2 | 0 | 0 | 0 | | | | | |
| State Police | | | | | | | | | | | |
| Clatsop County | 1 | 0 | 0 | 0 | 0 | 0 | 1 | 0 | 0 | 0 | |
| Coos County | 1 | 0 | 0 | 0 | 0 | 0 | 0 | 0 | 1 | 0 | |
| Douglas County | 0 | 0 | 1 | 0 | 0 | 0 | 1 | 0 | 0 | 0 | |
| Tillamook County | 0 | 0 | 1 | 0 | 0 | 0 | 0 | 1 | 0 | 0 | |
| | | | | | | | | | | | |
| **Other Agencies** | 0 | 0 | 1 | 0 | 0 | 0 | | | | | |
| Port of Portland | 0 | 0 | 1 | 0 | 0 | 0 | 0 | 1 | 0 | 0 | |
| | | | | | | | | | | | |
| **PENNSYLVANIA** | 117 | 19 | 25 | 1 | 1 | 0 | | | | | |
| **Cities** | 116 | 19 | 25 | 1 | 1 | 0 | | | | | |
| East Earl Township | 1 | 0 | 0 | 0 | 0 | 0 | 1 | 0 | 0 | 0 | 6,938 |

## Table 94. Hate Crime Incidents Per Bias Motivation and Quarter, by Selected State and  Agency and Federal, 2021—Continued

(Number.)

| State/agency | Number of incidents per bias motivation | | | | | | Number of incidents per quarter | | | | Population[1] |
|---|---|---|---|---|---|---|---|---|---|---|---|
| | Race/ Ethnicity/ Ancestry | Religion | Sexual orientation | Disability | Gender | Gender Identity | 1st quarter | 2nd quarter | 3rd quarter | 4th quarter | |
| East Pennsboro Township | 0 | 1 | 0 | 0 | 0 | 0 | 0 | 0 | 1 | 0 | 21,595 |
| Philadelphia[2] | 111 | 14 | 25 | 0 | 1 | 0 | 0 | 57 | 30 | 52 | 1,604,950 |
| Ross Township | 1 | 0 | 0 | 0 | 0 | 0 | 1 | 0 | 0 | 0 | 30,289 |
| Scranton | 2 | 1 | 0 | 1 | 0 | 0 | 0 | 1 | 3 | 0 | 76,580 |
| Southwest Regional, Fayette County | 0 | 1 | 0 | 0 | 0 | 0 | 0 | 0 | 1 | 0 | 2,597 |
| Washington Township, Franklin County | 1 | 2 | 0 | 0 | 0 | 0 | 1 | 0 | 2 | 0 | 15,037 |
| **State Police Agencies** | 1 | 0 | 0 | 0 | 0 | 0 | | | | | |
| State Police, York County | 1 | 0 | 0 | 0 | 0 | 0 | 0 | 1 | 0 | 0 | |
| **RHODE ISLAND** | 10 | 6 | 3 | 0 | 0 | 0 | | | | | |
| **Cities** | 8 | 3 | 2 | 0 | 0 | 0 | | | | | |
| Barrington | 1 | 0 | 0 | 0 | 0 | 0 | 1 | 0 | 0 | 0 | 16,566 |
| Bristol | 1 | 1 | 0 | 0 | 0 | 0 | 1 | 1 | 0 | 0 | 22,550 |
| Coventry | 1 | 0 | 0 | 0 | 0 | 0 | 0 | 0 | 1 | 0 | 36,216 |
| Cranston | 1 | 0 | 0 | 0 | 0 | 0 | 0 | 0 | 0 | 1 | 84,105 |
| Lincoln | 0 | 1 | 0 | 0 | 0 | 0 | 0 | 0 | 0 | 1 | 22,823 |
| Little Compton | 1 | 0 | 0 | 0 | 0 | 0 | 1 | 0 | 0 | 0 | 3,584 |
| Newport | 1 | 0 | 1 | 0 | 0 | 0 | 0 | 0 | 2 | 0 | 25,240 |
| North Providence | 0 | 1 | 0 | 0 | 0 | 0 | 0 | 0 | 0 | 1 | 33,712 |
| Smithfield | 1 | 0 | 0 | 0 | 0 | 0 | 1 | 0 | 0 | 0 | 22,676 |
| Tiverton | 0 | 0 | 1 | 0 | 0 | 0 | 0 | 1 | 0 | 0 | 16,106 |
| Warwick | 1 | 0 | 0 | 0 | 0 | 0 | 0 | 0 | 0 | 1 | 83,968 |
| **Universities and Colleges** | 1 | 3 | 1 | 0 | 0 | 0 | | | | | |
| Brown University | 1 | 1 | 0 | 0 | 0 | 0 | 1 | 0 | 0 | 1 | 10,807 |
| University of Rhode Island | 0 | 2 | 1 | 0 | 0 | 0 | 1 | 0 | 1 | 1 | 21,108 |
| **Other Agencies** | 1 | 0 | 0 | 0 | 0 | 0 | | | | | |
| Department of Environmental Management | 1 | 0 | 0 | 0 | 0 | 0 | 0 | 1 | 0 | 0 | |
| **SOUTH CAROLINA** | 49 | 32 | 21 | 2 | 0 | 3 | | | | | |
| **Cities** | 27 | 11 | 16 | 1 | 0 | 2 | | | | | |
| Andrews | 0 | 0 | 1 | 0 | 0 | 0 | 0 | | 1 | 0 | 2,866 |
| Beaufort | 1 | 0 | 0 | 0 | 0 | 0 | 0 | 0 | 1 | 0 | 13,293 |
| Calhoun Falls | 3 | 0 | 0 | 0 | 0 | 0 | 0 | 1 | 2 | 0 | 1,873 |
| Cayce[2] | 0 | 0 | 2 | 0 | 0 | 0 | 0 | 1 | 0 | 0 | 14,088 |
| Charleston | 1 | 2 | 5 | 0 | 0 | 1 | 1 | 2 | 4 | 2 | 141,768 |
| Clinton | 1 | 0 | 0 | 0 | 0 | 0 | 1 | 0 | 0 | 0 | 8,288 |
| Columbia | 0 | 0 | 1 | 0 | 0 | 0 | 0 | 1 | 0 | 0 | 132,255 |
| Easley | 1 | 0 | 0 | 0 | 0 | 0 | 1 | 0 | 0 | 0 | 21,789 |
| Edisto Beach | 0 | 0 | 1 | 0 | 0 | 0 | 0 | 0 | 1 | 0 | 401 |
| Fort Mill | 1 | 0 | 0 | 0 | 0 | 0 | 0 | 0 | 0 | 1 | 26,923 |
| Goose Creek | 3 | 2 | 0 | 0 | 0 | 0 | 1 | 0 | 0 | 4 | 45,901 |
| Hampton | 1 | 0 | 0 | 0 | 0 | 1 | 0 | 2 | 0 | 0 | 2,459 |
| Hardeeville | 1 | 0 | 0 | 0 | 0 | 0 | 1 | 0 | 0 | 0 | 9,332 |
| Hartsville | 0 | 1 | 0 | 0 | 0 | 0 | 1 | 0 | 0 | 0 | 7,454 |
| Kingstree | 0 | 1 | 0 | 0 | 0 | 0 | 1 | 0 | 0 | 0 | 2,958 |
| Laurens | 0 | 0 | 1 | 0 | 0 | 0 | 0 | 0 | 1 | 0 | 8,835 |
| Lexington | 0 | 0 | 1 | 0 | 0 | 0 | 0 | 1 | 0 | 0 | 23,161 |
| Mauldin | 2 | 0 | 1 | 0 | 0 | 0 | 0 | 2 | 0 | 1 | 25,808 |
| McColl | 0 | 0 | 1 | 0 | 0 | 0 | 0 | 1 | 0 | 0 | 1,922 |
| Moncks Corner | 1 | 2 | 0 | 0 | 0 | 0 | 1 | 1 | 0 | 1 | 13,108 |
| Mount Pleasant | 2 | 0 | 0 | 1 | 0 | 0 | 0 | 2 | 0 | 1 | 95,657 |
| North Augusta | 1 | 0 | 0 | 0 | 0 | 0 | 0 | 0 | 0 | 1 | 24,435 |
| North Myrtle Beach | 2 | 0 | 1 | 0 | 0 | 0 | 0 | 2 | 1 | 0 | 17,648 |
| Rock Hill | 1 | 3 | 0 | 0 | 0 | 0 | 1 | 0 | 0 | 3 | 77,334 |
| Tega Cay | 1 | 0 | 1 | 0 | 0 | 0 | 0 | 1 | 0 | 1 | 12,178 |
| Walterboro | 2 | 0 | 0 | 0 | 0 | 0 | 0 | 1 | 1 | 0 | 5,303 |
| Williamston | 2 | 0 | 0 | 0 | 0 | 0 | 0 | 2 | 0 | 0 | 4,333 |
| **Universities and Colleges** | 0 | 1 | 0 | 0 | 0 | 0 | | | | | |
| University of South Carolina, Beaufort | 0 | 1 | 0 | 0 | 0 | 0 | 1 | 0 | 0 | 0 | 2,480 |
| **Metropolitan Counties** | 10 | 11 | 4 | 1 | 0 | 0 | | | | | |
| Anderson | 0 | 2 | 0 | 0 | 0 | 0 | 0 | 1 | 1 | 0 | |
| Berkeley | 0 | 7 | 0 | 0 | 0 | 0 | 6 | 0 | 1 | 0 | |
| Charleston | 4 | 0 | 1 | 0 | 0 | 0 | 2 | 1 | 1 | 1 | |
| Clarendon | 1 | 0 | 0 | 0 | 0 | 0 | 0 | 1 | 0 | 0 | |
| Fairfield | 3 | 0 | 0 | 0 | 0 | 0 | 3 | 0 | 0 | 0 | |
| Horry County Police Department | 0 | 0 | 1 | 0 | 0 | 0 | 0 | 1 | 0 | 0 | |
| Kershaw | 0 | 1 | 0 | 0 | 0 | 0 | 1 | 0 | 0 | 0 | |
| Lexington | 1 | 0 | 1 | 0 | 0 | 0 | 0 | 0 | 1 | 1 | |
| Pickens | 0 | 0 | 1 | 0 | 0 | 0 | 1 | 0 | 0 | 0 | |
| Richland | 1 | 0 | 0 | 0 | 0 | 0 | 1 | 0 | 0 | 0 | |
| Saluda | 0 | 1 | 0 | 0 | 0 | 0 | 0 | 1 | 0 | 0 | |
| Sumter | 0 | 0 | 0 | 1 | 0 | 0 | 0 | 0 | 1 | 0 | |
| **Nonmetropolitan Counties** | 11 | 8 | 0 | 0 | 0 | 1 | | | | | |
| Bamberg | 0 | 1 | 0 | 0 | 0 | 0 | 0 | 0 | 1 | 0 | |

## Table 94. Hate Crime Incidents Per Bias Motivation and Quarter, by Selected State and Agency and Federal, 2021—Continued

(Number.)

| State/agency | Number of incidents per bias motivation | | | | | | Number of incidents per quarter | | | | Population[1] |
|---|---|---|---|---|---|---|---|---|---|---|---|
| | Race/ Ethnicity/ Ancestry | Religion | Sexual orientation | Disability | Gender | Gender Identity | 1st quarter | 2nd quarter | 3rd quarter | 4th quarter | |
| Barnwell | 1 | 0 | 0 | 0 | 0 | 0 | 0 | 0 | 1 | 0 | |
| Cherokee | 1 | 2 | 0 | 0 | 0 | 0 | 0 | 1 | 2 | 0 | |
| Chesterfield | 1 | 0 | 0 | 0 | 0 | 0 | 1 | 0 | 0 | 0 | |
| Colleton | 2 | 2 | 0 | 0 | 0 | 1 | 2 | 1 | 0 | 2 | |
| Georgetown | 1 | 1 | 0 | 0 | 0 | 0 | 0 | 0 | 1 | 1 | |
| Greenwood | 1 | 0 | 0 | 0 | 0 | 0 | 1 | 0 | 0 | 0 | |
| Hampton | 1 | 0 | 0 | 0 | 0 | 0 | 1 | 0 | 0 | | |
| Marlboro | 3 | 0 | 0 | 0 | 0 | 0 | 2 | 1 | 0 | 0 | |
| Oconee | 0 | 2 | 0 | 0 | 0 | 0 | 1 | 1 | 0 | 0 | |
| | | | | | | | | | | | |
| **State Police Agencies** | 1 | 1 | 0 | 0 | 0 | 0 | | | | | |
| Highway Patrol | | | | | | | | | | | |
| Edgefield County | 0 | 1 | 0 | 0 | 0 | 0 | 0 | 0 | 1 | 0 | |
| Lancaster County | 1 | 0 | 0 | 0 | 0 | 0 | 1 | 0 | 0 | 0 | |
| | | | | | | | | | | | |
| **Other Agencies** | 0 | 0 | 1 | 0 | 0 | 0 | | | | | |
| Charleston County Aviation Authority | 0 | 0 | 1 | 0 | 0 | 0 | 0 | 0 | 0 | 1 | |
| | | | | | | | | | | | |
| **SOUTH DAKOTA** | 15 | 2 | 9 | 0 | 2 | 0 | | | | | |
| **Cities** | 8 | 2 | 5 | 0 | 1 | 0 | | | | | |
| Alcester | 1 | 0 | 0 | 0 | 0 | 0 | 0 | 1 | 0 | 0 | 750 |
| Belle Fourche | 0 | 0 | 1 | 0 | 0 | 0 | 0 | 1 | 0 | 0 | 5,755 |
| Hot Springs | 1 | 0 | 0 | 0 | 0 | 0 | 1 | 0 | 0 | 0 | 3,479 |
| Huron | 0 | 0 | 1 | 0 | 0 | 0 | 0 | 0 | 1 | 0 | 13,504 |
| Lead | 0 | 1 | 0 | 0 | 0 | 0 | 1 | 0 | 0 | 0 | 2,929 |
| Martin | 0 | 0 | 1 | 0 | 0 | 0 | 0 | 0 | 0 | 1 | 1,057 |
| Mobridge | 1 | 0 | 0 | 0 | 0 | 0 | 0 | 0 | 1 | 0 | 3,364 |
| Rapid City | 4 | 0 | 0 | 0 | 0 | 0 | 0 | 1 | 2 | 1 | 79,910 |
| Sioux Falls | 1 | 1 | 1 | 0 | 0 | 0 | 0 | 0 | 2 | 1 | 191,508 |
| Sisseton | 0 | 0 | 1 | 0 | 0 | 0 | 0 | 1 | 0 | 0 | 2,360 |
| Sturgis | 0 | 0 | 0 | 0 | 1 | 0 | 0 | 1 | 0 | 0 | 7,013 |
| | | | | | | | | | | | |
| **Metropolitan Counties** | 0 | 0 | 2 | 0 | 0 | 0 | | | | | |
| Meade | 0 | 0 | 1 | 0 | 0 | 0 | 1 | 0 | 0 | 0 | |
| Minnehaha | 0 | 0 | 1 | 0 | 0 | 0 | 0 | 1 | 0 | 0 | |
| | | | | | | | | | | | |
| **Nonmetropolitan Counties** | 3 | 0 | 2 | 0 | 1 | 0 | | | | | |
| Charles Mix | 1 | 0 | 0 | 0 | 0 | 0 | 1 | 0 | 0 | 0 | |
| Custer | 2 | 0 | 0 | 0 | 0 | 0 | 0 | 0 | 1 | 1 | |
| Hamlin[2] | 0 | 0 | 2 | 0 | 1 | 0 | 0 | 1 | 1 | 0 | |
| | | | | | | | | | | | |
| Tribal Agencies | 4 | 0 | 0 | 0 | 0 | 0 | | | | | |
| Crow Creek Tribal[2] | 3 | 0 | 0 | 0 | 0 | 0 | 2 | 0 | 0 | 0 | |
| Pine Ridge Sioux Tribal | 1 | 0 | 0 | 0 | 0 | 0 | 0 | 1 | 0 | 0 | |
| | | | | | | | | | | | |
| **TENNESSEE** | 91 | 19 | 20 | 11 | 2 | 4 | | | | | |
| **Cities** | 55 | 8 | 15 | 9 | 2 | 2 | | | | | |
| Bartlett | 2 | 0 | 0 | 0 | 0 | 0 | 0 | 1 | 0 | 1 | 59,562 |
| Chattanooga | 0 | 1 | 0 | 0 | 0 | 0 | 1 | 0 | 0 | 0 | 186,222 |
| Clarksville | 1 | 0 | 1 | 0 | 0 | 0 | 0 | 0 | 1 | 1 | 164,336 |
| Cleveland[2] | 7 | 0 | 4 | 1 | 0 | 0 | 4 | 3 | 3 | 1 | 46,440 |
| Clinton | 1 | 0 | 0 | 0 | 0 | 0 | 0 | 0 | 1 | 0 | 10,157 |
| Collierville | 2 | 1 | 1 | 0 | 0 | 0 | 2 | 1 | 0 | 1 | 52,059 |
| Columbia | 0 | 0 | 1 | 0 | 0 | 0 | 0 | 1 | 0 | 0 | 42,613 |
| Covington | 0 | 0 | 1 | 1 | 0 | 0 | 0 | 1 | 1 | 0 | 8,791 |
| Cowan | 0 | 0 | 0 | 0 | 2 | 0 | 0 | 0 | 0 | 2 | 1,662 |
| Crossville | 1 | 0 | 0 | 0 | 0 | 0 | 0 | 0 | 0 | 1 | 12,007 |
| Dyersburg | 1 | 0 | 0 | 0 | 0 | 0 | 0 | 1 | 0 | 0 | 15,981 |
| Elizabethton | 1 | 0 | 0 | 0 | 0 | 0 | 0 | 0 | 1 | 0 | 13,406 |
| Elkton | 0 | 0 | 1 | 0 | 0 | 0 | 1 | 0 | 0 | 0 | 520 |
| Franklin | 3 | 1 | 0 | 0 | 0 | 2 | 0 | 0 | 2 | 4 | 87,969 |
| Germantown | 1 | 0 | 0 | 0 | 0 | 0 | 0 | 1 | 0 | 0 | 39,217 |
| Jackson | 2 | 0 | 0 | 0 | 0 | 0 | 0 | 0 | 1 | 1 | 67,462 |
| Jonesborough | 1 | 0 | 0 | 1 | 0 | 0 | 0 | 1 | 1 | 0 | 5,840 |
| Kingsport | 0 | 1 | 0 | 2 | 0 | 0 | 0 | 0 | 1 | 2 | 54,229 |
| Knoxville | 4 | 0 | 0 | 1 | 0 | 0 | 1 | 1 | 3 | 0 | 191,463 |
| La Vergne | 0 | 0 | 1 | 0 | 0 | 0 | 0 | 0 | 1 | 0 | 35,954 |
| Lebanon | 6 | 0 | 1 | 1 | 0 | 0 | 4 | 3 | 1 | 0 | 39,524 |
| Lenoir City | 1 | 1 | 0 | 0 | 0 | 0 | 0 | 1 | 0 | 1 | 9,401 |
| Lewisburg | 2 | 0 | 0 | 0 | 0 | 0 | 0 | 1 | 1 | 0 | 12,712 |
| Manchester | 1 | 0 | 0 | 0 | 0 | 0 | 0 | 1 | 0 | 0 | 11,383 |
| Martin | 1 | 0 | 0 | 0 | 0 | 0 | 0 | 0 | 0 | 1 | 10,480 |
| Memphis | 5 | 0 | 1 | 0 | 0 | 0 | 0 | 2 | 2 | 2 | 649,444 |
| Metropolitan Nashville Police Department | 2 | 0 | 0 | 0 | 0 | 0 | 0 | 0 | 1 | 1 | 690,553 |
| Millington | 0 | 0 | 1 | 0 | 0 | 0 | 0 | 1 | 0 | 0 | 10,621 |
| Murfreesboro | 0 | 0 | 1 | 0 | 0 | 0 | 0 | 1 | 0 | 0 | 155,652 |
| Oakland[2] | 3 | 2 | 1 | 2 | 0 | 0 | 0 | 0 | 1 | 2 | 8,903 |
| Pigeon Forge | 2 | 0 | 0 | 0 | 0 | 0 | 1 | 0 | 0 | 1 | 6,276 |
| Rockwood | 0 | 1 | 0 | 0 | 0 | 0 | 0 | 0 | 0 | 1 | 5,449 |
| Rogersville | 1 | 0 | 0 | 0 | 0 | 0 | 0 | 0 | 1 | 0 | 4,356 |

# Table 94. Hate Crime Incidents Per Bias Motivation and Quarter, by Selected State and Agency and Federal, 2021—Continued

(Number.)

| State/agency | Number of incidents per bias motivation | | | | | | Number of incidents per quarter | | | | Population[1] |
|---|---|---|---|---|---|---|---|---|---|---|---|
| | Race/ Ethnicity/ Ancestry | Religion | Sexual orientation | Disability | Gender | Gender Identity | 1st quarter | 2nd quarter | 3rd quarter | 4th quarter | |
| Sevierville | 1 | 0 | 0 | 0 | 0 | 0 | 1 | 0 | 0 | 0 | 18,836 |
| Spring Hill | 1 | 0 | 0 | 0 | 0 | 0 | 0 | 0 | 1 | 0 | 48,297 |
| Winchester[2] | 2 | 0 | 0 | 0 | 0 | 0 | 0 | 1 | 0 | 0 | 9,151 |
| **Universities and Colleges** | 3 | 1 | 1 | 0 | 0 | 0 | | | | | |
| Austin Peay State University | 1 | 0 | 0 | 0 | 0 | 0 | 1 | 0 | 0 | 0 | 12,796 |
| East Tennessee State University | 0 | 1 | 1 | 0 | 0 | 0 | 0 | 0 | 1 | 1 | 15,939 |
| Middle Tennessee State University | 2 | 0 | 0 | 0 | 0 | 0 | 0 | 2 | 0 | 0 | 25,346 |
| **Metropolitan Counties** | 13 | 5 | 1 | 0 | 0 | 2 | | | | | |
| Blount | 1 | 0 | 1 | 0 | 0 | 1 | 0 | 1 | 1 | 1 | |
| Bradley | 2 | 0 | 0 | 0 | 0 | 0 | 0 | 0 | 0 | 2 | |
| Carter | 0 | 2 | 0 | 0 | 0 | 0 | 0 | 0 | 0 | 2 | |
| Cheatham | 1 | 0 | 0 | 0 | 0 | 0 | 1 | 0 | 0 | 0 | |
| Jefferson | 0 | 1 | 0 | 0 | 0 | 0 | 0 | 1 | 0 | 0 | |
| Knox | 1 | 0 | 0 | 0 | 0 | 0 | 0 | 0 | 0 | 1 | |
| Robertson | 0 | 2 | 0 | 0 | 0 | 0 | 0 | 0 | 1 | 1 | |
| Rutherford | 3 | 0 | 0 | 0 | 0 | 1 | 0 | 1 | 3 | 0 | |
| Shelby | 4 | 0 | 0 | 0 | 0 | 0 | 0 | 1 | 1 | 2 | |
| Washington | 1 | 0 | 0 | 0 | 0 | 0 | 1 | 0 | 0 | 0 | |
| **Nonmetropolitan Counties** | 6 | 5 | 3 | 1 | 0 | 0 | | | | | |
| Greene | 0 | 0 | 0 | 1 | 0 | 0 | 0 | 0 | 0 | 1 | |
| Hardin | 0 | 1 | 0 | 0 | 0 | 0 | 0 | 1 | 0 | 0 | |
| Johnson[2] | 2 | 2 | 2 | 0 | 0 | 0 | 2 | 2 | 0 | 1 | |
| Meigs | 1 | 0 | 0 | 0 | 0 | 0 | 1 | 0 | 0 | 0 | |
| Monroe | 2 | 2 | 1 | 0 | 0 | 0 | 0 | 1 | 3 | 1 | |
| Warren | 1 | 0 | 0 | 0 | 0 | 0 | 0 | 0 | 1 | 0 | |
| **State Police Agencies** | 14 | 0 | 0 | 0 | 0 | 0 | | | | | |
| Department of Safety[2] | 14 | 0 | 0 | 0 | 0 | 0 | 6 | 1 | 4 | 2 | |
| **Other Agencies** | 0 | 0 | 0 | 1 | 0 | 0 | | | | | |
| Tennessee Bureau of Investigation | 0 | 0 | 0 | 1 | 0 | 0 | 1 | 0 | 0 | 0 | |
| **TEXAS** | 347 | 53 | 111 | 17 | 10 | 28 | | | | | |
| **Cities** | 281 | 38 | 88 | 9 | 5 | 23 | | | | | |
| Abilene | 5 | 0 | 1 | 0 | 0 | 0 | 0 | 1 | 2 | 3 | 125,088 |
| Alamo | 1 | 0 | 0 | 0 | 0 | 0 | 1 | 0 | 0 | 0 | 20,779 |
| Anna | 1 | 0 | 0 | 0 | 0 | 0 | 0 | 0 | 1 | 0 | 18,215 |
| Arlington | 6 | 0 | 1 | 0 | 0 | 0 | 2 | 1 | 1 | 3 | 402,323 |
| Austin | 13 | 6 | 7 | 0 | 0 | 2 | 2 | 6 | 8 | 12 | 1,016,721 |
| Balch Springs | 0 | 0 | 1 | 0 | 0 | 0 | 1 | 0 | 0 | 0 | 24,746 |
| Beaumont | 1 | 0 | 0 | 0 | 0 | 1 | 0 | 0 | 1 | 1 | 115,290 |
| Bedford | 2 | 0 | 0 | 0 | 0 | 0 | 0 | 1 | 1 | 0 | 48,483 |
| Beeville | 1 | 0 | 0 | 0 | 0 | 0 | 0 | 0 | 1 | 0 | 14,160 |
| Bellville | 0 | 1 | 0 | 0 | 0 | 0 | 1 | 0 | 0 | 0 | 4,214 |
| Boerne | 1 | 0 | 0 | 0 | 0 | 0 | 0 | 1 | 0 | 0 | 20,209 |
| Bonham | 4 | 0 | 1 | 0 | 0 | 0 | 4 | 0 | 1 | 0 | 10,506 |
| Brenham | 0 | 1 | 0 | 0 | 0 | 0 | 0 | 0 | 0 | 1 | 17,940 |
| Brownwood | 1 | 0 | 0 | 0 | 0 | 0 | 1 | 0 | 0 | 0 | 18,105 |
| Burleson | 1 | 0 | 1 | 0 | 0 | 0 | 0 | 0 | 1 | 1 | 51,167 |
| Burnet | 0 | 0 | 1 | 0 | 0 | 0 | 0 | 0 | 0 | 1 | 6,598 |
| Caldwell | 1 | 0 | 0 | 0 | 0 | 0 | 0 | 1 | 0 | 0 | 4,535 |
| Carrollton | 4 | 1 | 0 | 0 | 0 | 0 | 0 | 1 | 0 | 4 | 141,694 |
| Carthage | 1 | 0 | 0 | 0 | 0 | 0 | 1 | 0 | 0 | 0 | 6,314 |
| Cedar Park | 0 | 0 | 1 | 0 | 1 | 0 | 1 | 0 | 1 | 0 | 84,131 |
| Center | 1 | 0 | 0 | 0 | 0 | 0 | 0 | 1 | 0 | 0 | 5,014 |
| Childress | 2 | 0 | 0 | 0 | 0 | 0 | 1 | 1 | 0 | 0 | 5,880 |
| Cibolo | 0 | 1 | 0 | 0 | 0 | 0 | 1 | 0 | 0 | 0 | 35,139 |
| Clifton | 0 | 0 | 0 | 1 | 0 | 0 | 0 | 0 | 0 | 1 | 3,406 |
| College Station | 3 | 0 | 0 | 0 | 0 | 0 | 1 | 1 | 0 | 1 | 122,051 |
| Conroe | 2 | 0 | 1 | 0 | 0 | 0 | 0 | 2 | 1 | 0 | 99,965 |
| Coppell | 1 | 1 | 0 | 0 | 0 | 0 | 1 | 1 | 0 | 0 | 40,889 |
| Corpus Christi | 2 | 0 | 1 | 0 | 0 | 0 | 2 | 0 | 0 | 1 | 329,538 |
| Corsicana | 0 | 0 | 1 | 0 | 0 | 0 | 0 | 0 | 1 | 0 | 23,808 |
| Crowley | 1 | 0 | 0 | 0 | 0 | 0 | 1 | 0 | 0 | 0 | 18,146 |
| Dallas | 13 | 4 | 9 | 0 | 0 | 2 | 7 | 9 | 5 | 7 | 1,349,185 |
| Denton | 1 | 1 | 2 | 0 | 0 | 0 | 1 | 0 | 2 | 1 | 150,975 |
| Dublin | 0 | 2 | 0 | 0 | 0 | 0 | 1 | 0 | 0 | 1 | 3,546 |
| Dumas | 0 | 0 | 1 | 0 | 0 | 0 | 0 | 1 | 0 | 0 | 13,503 |
| Eagle Pass | 3 | 0 | 0 | 0 | 0 | 0 | 1 | 1 | 1 | 0 | 29,807 |
| Elgin | 1 | 2 | 0 | 0 | 0 | 0 | 0 | 2 | 0 | 1 | 11,040 |
| El Paso[2] | 1 | 0 | 2 | 0 | 2 | 0 | 1 | 2 | 0 | 1 | 684,737 |
| Elsa | 1 | 0 | 0 | 0 | 0 | 0 | 0 | 0 | 0 | 1 | 7,205 |
| Ennis | 0 | 0 | 1 | 0 | 0 | 0 | 0 | 0 | 1 | 0 | 20,893 |
| Euless | 2 | 0 | 0 | 0 | 0 | 0 | 1 | 0 | 1 | 0 | 57,963 |
| Forest Hill | 0 | 0 | 1 | 0 | 0 | 0 | 1 | 0 | 0 | 0 | 13,002 |
| Fort Worth[2] | 6 | 1 | 5 | 0 | 0 | 0 | 1 | 2 | 6 | 2 | 947,862 |
| Gainesville | 2 | 0 | 0 | 0 | 0 | 0 | 2 | 0 | 0 | 0 | 16,967 |

## Table 94. Hate Crime Incidents Per Bias Motivation and Quarter, by Selected State and Agency and Federal, 2021—Continued

(Number.)

| State/agency | Number of incidents per bias motivation | | | | | | Number of incidents per quarter | | | | Population[1] |
| | Race/ Ethnicity/ Ancestry | Religion | Sexual orientation | Disability | Gender | Gender Identity | 1st quarter | 2nd quarter | 3rd quarter | 4th quarter | |
|---|---|---|---|---|---|---|---|---|---|---|---|
| Galveston | 1 | 0 | 0 | 0 | 0 | 0 | 0 | 1 | 0 | 0 | 50,321 |
| Garland | 5 | 0 | 1 | 0 | 0 | 0 | 4 | 0 | 1 | 1 | 237,510 |
| Georgetown | 0 | 0 | 0 | 1 | 0 | 0 | 0 | 0 | 0 | 1 | 90,629 |
| Greenville | 2 | 0 | 0 | 0 | 0 | 0 | 1 | 1 | 0 | 0 | 29,780 |
| Gunter | 1 | 0 | 0 | 0 | 0 | 0 | 0 | 1 | 0 | 0 | 1,776 |
| Hamilton | 1 | 0 | 0 | 0 | 0 | 0 | 0 | 1 | 0 | 0 | 3,019 |
| Hamlin | 1 | 0 | 0 | 0 | 0 | 0 | 0 | 0 | 1 | 0 | 1,984 |
| Haskell | 0 | 0 | 0 | 1 | 0 | 0 | 0 | 0 | 0 | 1 | 3,194 |
| Henderson | 4 | 0 | 0 | 0 | 0 | 0 | 2 | 1 | 1 | 0 | 12,989 |
| Highland Village | 2 | 0 | 0 | 0 | 0 | 0 | 0 | 0 | 0 | 2 | 17,071 |
| Hillsboro | 1 | 0 | 0 | 0 | 0 | 0 | 0 | 1 | 0 | 0 | 8,525 |
| Horizon City | 1 | 0 | 0 | 0 | 0 | 0 | 1 | 0 | 0 | 0 | 20,628 |
| Houston[2] | 33 | 2 | 13 | 1 | 0 | 9 | 13 | 15 | 12 | 8 | 2,339,252 |
| Humble | 2 | 0 | 0 | 0 | 0 | 0 | 2 | 0 | 0 | 0 | 15,579 |
| Huntsville[2] | 0 | 0 | 2 | 0 | 0 | 0 | 0 | 0 | 0 | 1 | 41,671 |
| Hurst | 2 | 1 | 0 | 0 | 0 | 0 | 0 | 2 | 1 | 0 | 38,250 |
| Ingleside | 0 | 0 | 1 | 0 | 0 | 0 | 0 | 0 | 1 | 0 | 10,188 |
| Irving[2] | 2 | 0 | 2 | 0 | 0 | 0 | 0 | 2 | 1 | 0 | 241,692 |
| Kingsville | 1 | 0 | 0 | 1 | 0 | 0 | 0 | 1 | 1 | 0 | 24,850 |
| Kyle[2] | 3 | 0 | 1 | 0 | 0 | 0 | 0 | 0 | 1 | 2 | 54,692 |
| La Grange | 1 | 0 | 0 | 0 | 0 | 0 | 0 | 0 | 1 | 0 | 4,684 |
| Lake Jackson | 2 | 0 | 1 | 0 | 0 | 0 | 2 | 0 | 1 | 0 | 27,088 |
| Lampasas | 1 | 0 | 0 | 0 | 0 | 0 | 0 | 0 | 1 | 0 | 8,269 |
| La Porte | 0 | 0 | 0 | 0 | 0 | 1 | 0 | 0 | 0 | 1 | 35,972 |
| Laredo | 2 | 0 | 0 | 2 | 0 | 0 | 1 | 1 | 1 | 1 | 266,489 |
| League City | 2 | 0 | 1 | 0 | 0 | 0 | 0 | 2 | 0 | 1 | 111,279 |
| Leon Valley | 4 | 0 | 1 | 0 | 0 | 0 | 1 | 1 | 2 | 1 | 12,431 |
| Lewisville | 1 | 0 | 0 | 0 | 0 | 0 | 0 | 1 | 0 | 0 | 113,998 |
| Live Oak | 1 | 0 | 0 | 0 | 0 | 0 | 0 | 0 | 0 | 1 | 17,051 |
| Livingston | 1 | 0 | 0 | 0 | 0 | 0 | 0 | 1 | 0 | 0 | 5,533 |
| Longview | 1 | 0 | 0 | 0 | 0 | 0 | 0 | 1 | 0 | 0 | 81,846 |
| Lubbock | 4 | 0 | 3 | 0 | 0 | 0 | 3 | 1 | 3 | 0 | 265,990 |
| Lufkin | 1 | 0 | 1 | 0 | 0 | 0 | 1 | 0 | 0 | 1 | 34,934 |
| McAllen | 2 | 0 | 0 | 0 | 0 | 0 | 1 | 0 | 0 | 1 | 144,973 |
| McKinney[2] | 3 | 0 | 0 | 0 | 0 | 0 | 0 | 0 | 1 | 1 | 217,841 |
| Mercedes | 1 | 0 | 0 | 0 | 0 | 0 | 1 | 0 | 0 | 0 | 16,684 |
| Mesquite | 1 | 0 | 0 | 0 | 0 | 0 | 1 | 0 | 0 | 0 | 137,796 |
| Midland[2] | 2 | 0 | 0 | 0 | 0 | 0 | 1 | 0 | 0 | 0 | 151,243 |
| Missouri City | 1 | 0 | 1 | 0 | 0 | 1 | 3 | 0 | 0 | 0 | 77,682 |
| Mont Belvieu | 1 | 1 | 0 | 0 | 0 | 0 | 1 | 1 | 0 | 0 | 7,567 |
| Montgomery | 0 | 1 | 0 | 0 | 0 | 0 | 0 | 1 | 0 | 0 | 1,812 |
| New Braunfels | 0 | 0 | 1 | 0 | 0 | 0 | 0 | 1 | 0 | 0 | 100,427 |
| North Richland Hills | 1 | 0 | 0 | 0 | 0 | 0 | 0 | 0 | 1 | 0 | 72,881 |
| Oak Ridge North | 1 | 0 | 0 | 0 | 0 | 0 | 0 | 1 | 0 | 0 | 3,168 |
| Odessa | 2 | 0 | 1 | 0 | 0 | 0 | 2 | 0 | 1 | 0 | 128,328 |
| Olney | 1 | 0 | 0 | 0 | 0 | 0 | 0 | 0 | 1 | 0 | 3,054 |
| Orange | 0 | 2 | 0 | 0 | 0 | 0 | 0 | 0 | 1 | 1 | 17,755 |
| Palestine | 2 | 1 | 0 | 0 | 0 | 0 | 1 | 2 | 0 | 0 | 17,736 |
| Pampa | 2 | 0 | 0 | 0 | 0 | 0 | 0 | 2 | 0 | 0 | 16,760 |
| Pasadena[2] | 3 | 0 | 1 | 2 | 0 | 1 | 0 | 2 | 1 | 2 | 149,428 |
| Pflugerville | 1 | 0 | 0 | 0 | 0 | 0 | 0 | 1 | 0 | 0 | 68,978 |
| Pharr | 0 | 1 | 0 | 0 | 0 | 0 | 0 | 0 | 1 | 0 | 80,436 |
| Plainview | 1 | 0 | 0 | 0 | 0 | 1 | 0 | 0 | 1 | 1 | 19,436 |
| Plano | 1 | 0 | 0 | 0 | 0 | 0 | 1 | 0 | 0 | 0 | 294,496 |
| Pleasanton | 2 | 2 | 0 | 0 | 0 | 0 | 2 | 1 | 1 | 0 | 11,160 |
| Port Isabel | 1 | 0 | 0 | 0 | 0 | 0 | 0 | 1 | 0 | 0 | 6,217 |
| Refugio | 0 | 1 | 0 | 0 | 0 | 1 | 1 | 0 | 0 | 1 | 2,694 |
| Richwood | 0 | 0 | 1 | 0 | 0 | 0 | 1 | 0 | 0 | 0 | 4,068 |
| Rockdale | 2 | 0 | 0 | 0 | 0 | 0 | 0 | 0 | 0 | 2 | 5,444 |
| Round Rock | 6 | 1 | 0 | 0 | 1 | 0 | 1 | 3 | 3 | 1 | 141,927 |
| San Antonio[2] | 46 | 2 | 15 | 0 | 0 | 3 | 14 | 14 | 16 | 20 | 1,592,693 |
| Seagoville | 0 | 0 | 1 | 0 | 0 | 0 | 0 | 1 | 0 | 0 | 17,291 |
| Sherman | 1 | 0 | 1 | 0 | 0 | 0 | 0 | 1 | 1 | 0 | 45,814 |
| Socorro | 1 | 0 | 0 | 0 | 0 | 0 | 1 | 0 | 0 | 0 | 36,282 |
| Southlake | 1 | 0 | 0 | 0 | 0 | 0 | 0 | 1 | 0 | 0 | 32,905 |
| Stanton | 1 | 0 | 0 | 0 | 0 | 0 | 1 | 0 | 0 | 0 | 3,114 |
| Stephenville | 2 | 0 | 0 | 0 | 0 | 0 | 0 | 1 | 1 | 0 | 22,221 |
| Sugar Land | 1 | 0 | 0 | 0 | 0 | 0 | 0 | 0 | 1 | 0 | 118,888 |
| Taylor | 0 | 1 | 0 | 0 | 0 | 0 | 0 | 1 | 0 | 0 | 18,196 |
| Temple | 1 | 0 | 0 | 0 | 0 | 1 | 0 | 0 | 0 | 2 | 82,333 |
| The Colony | 1 | 0 | 0 | 0 | 0 | 0 | 0 | 1 | 0 | 0 | 46,510 |
| Trophy Club | 0 | 0 | 0 | 0 | 1 | 0 | 0 | 1 | 0 | 0 | 13,205 |
| Tyler | 1 | 0 | 0 | 0 | 0 | 0 | 1 | 0 | 0 | 0 | 109,408 |
| Uvalde | 5 | 0 | 0 | 0 | 0 | 0 | 0 | 3 | 0 | 2 | 15,999 |
| Van Alstyne | 1 | 0 | 0 | 0 | 0 | 0 | 0 | 0 | 1 | 0 | 4,831 |
| Vernon | 2 | 0 | 0 | 0 | 0 | 0 | 0 | 0 | 0 | 2 | 10,057 |
| Victoria | 0 | 0 | 1 | 0 | 0 | 0 | 0 | 0 | 1 | 0 | 67,272 |
| Vidor | 1 | 0 | 0 | 0 | 0 | 0 | 0 | 0 | 0 | 1 | 10,267 |
| Watauga[2] | 4 | 0 | 0 | 0 | 0 | 0 | 0 | 2 | 1 | 0 | 24,254 |
| Waxahachie[2] | 3 | 1 | 0 | 0 | 0 | 0 | 1 | 1 | 0 | 1 | 40,978 |

## Table 94. Hate Crime Incidents Per Bias Motivation and Quarter, by Selected State and Agency and Federal, 2021—Continued

(Number.)

| State/agency | Number of incidents per bias motivation | | | | | | Number of incidents per quarter | | | | Population[1] |
|---|---|---|---|---|---|---|---|---|---|---|---|
| | Race/ Ethnicity/ Ancestry | Religion | Sexual orientation | Disability | Gender | Gender Identity | 1st quarter | 2nd quarter | 3rd quarter | 4th quarter | |
| Webster | 1 | 0 | 0 | 0 | 0 | 0 | 1 | 0 | 0 | 0 | 11,359 |
| Weslaco | 1 | 0 | 0 | 0 | 0 | 0 | 0 | 0 | 1 | 0 | 43,954 |
| White Settlement | 2 | 0 | 0 | 0 | 0 | 0 | 2 | 0 | 0 | 0 | 17,948 |
| **Universities and Colleges** | 9 | 1 | 3 | 0 | 0 | 1 | | | | | |
| Angelo State University | 1 | 0 | 0 | 0 | 0 | 0 | 0 | 0 | 1 | 0 | 12,030 |
| Central Texas College | 2 | 0 | 0 | 0 | 0 | 0 | | | 2 | 0 | 22,886 |
| Rice University | 0 | 0 | 0 | 0 | 0 | 1 | 0 | 0 | 1 | 0 | 8,005 |
| St. Edwards University | 1 | 0 | 0 | 0 | 0 | 0 | 1 | 0 | 0 | 0 | 4,324 |
| Tarleton State University | 1 | 0 | 1 | 0 | 0 | 0 | 0 | 0 | 0 | 2 | 15,196 |
| Texas A&M University, Commerce | 1 | 1 | 0 | 0 | 0 | 0 | 1 | 0 | 1 | 0 | 15,517 |
| Texas State University, San Marcos | 1 | 0 | 0 | 0 | 0 | 0 | 1 | 0 | 0 | 0 | 42,292 |
| Tyler Junior College | 0 | 0 | 1 | 0 | 0 | 0 | 0 | 0 | 1 | 0 | 16,990 |
| University of Houston, Central Campus | 0 | 0 | 1 | 0 | 0 | 0 | 0 | 0 | 0 | 1 | 51,217 |
| University of Texas | | | | | | | | | | | |
| Austin | 1 | 0 | 0 | 0 | 0 | 0 | 0 | 0 | 0 | 1 | 54,243 |
| Houston | 1 | 0 | 0 | 0 | 0 | 0 | 0 | 1 | 0 | 0 | 7,329 |
| **Metropolitan Counties** | 32 | 7 | 15 | 8 | 5 | 3 | | | | | |
| Bexar | 1 | 0 | 0 | 1 | 0 | 0 | 0 | 1 | 0 | 1 | |
| Brazoria | 2 | 0 | 0 | 2 | 1 | 0 | 0 | 3 | 2 | 0 | |
| Cameron | 1 | 1 | 1 | 1 | 0 | 0 | 3 | 1 | 0 | 0 | |
| Chambers | 1 | 0 | 0 | 0 | 0 | 0 | 0 | 0 | 1 | 0 | |
| Denton | 1 | 0 | 0 | 0 | 0 | 0 | 1 | 0 | 0 | 0 | |
| Ellis | 2 | 0 | 0 | 0 | 0 | 0 | 1 | 0 | 1 | 0 | |
| El Paso | 0 | 0 | 0 | 1 | 0 | 0 | 0 | 0 | 0 | 1 | |
| Galveston | 1 | 0 | 0 | 1 | 2 | 0 | 1 | 1 | 0 | 2 | |
| Gregg | 2 | 0 | 0 | 0 | 2 | 0 | 1 | 3 | 0 | 0 | |
| Harris | 1 | 0 | 1 | 0 | 0 | 2 | 1 | 0 | 1 | 2 | |
| Hays | 7 | 1 | 2 | 0 | 0 | 0 | 2 | 1 | 2 | 5 | |
| Johnson | 0 | 0 | 1 | 0 | 0 | 0 | 0 | 0 | 0 | 1 | |
| Jones | 0 | 1 | 0 | 0 | 0 | 0 | 0 | 1 | 0 | 0 | |
| Kendall | 0 | 0 | 1 | 0 | 0 | 0 | 0 | 1 | 0 | 0 | |
| Lubbock | 2 | 2 | 0 | 1 | 0 | 0 | 1 | 1 | 1 | 2 | |
| McLennan | 0 | 1 | 0 | 0 | 0 | 0 | 0 | 1 | 0 | 0 | |
| Potter | 1 | 0 | 0 | 0 | 0 | 0 | 0 | 1 | 0 | 0 | |
| Randall | 1 | 0 | 0 | 0 | 0 | 0 | 0 | 1 | 0 | 0 | |
| Tarrant | 1 | 0 | 0 | 0 | 0 | 0 | 0 | 0 | 0 | 1 | |
| Tom Green | 0 | 0 | 0 | 1 | 0 | 0 | 0 | 1 | 0 | 0 | |
| Travis[2] | 4 | 1 | 8 | 0 | 0 | 0 | 1 | 2 | 4 | 5 | |
| Upshur | 0 | 0 | 1 | 0 | 0 | 0 | 0 | 1 | 0 | 0 | |
| Waller | 2 | 0 | 0 | 0 | 0 | 0 | 0 | 0 | 2 | 0 | |
| Webb | 2 | 0 | 0 | 0 | 0 | 0 | 1 | 1 | 0 | 0 | |
| Williamson | 0 | 0 | 0 | 0 | 0 | 1 | 0 | 0 | 1 | 0 | |
| **Nonmetropolitan Counties** | 10 | 6 | 2 | 0 | 0 | 1 | | | | | |
| Brown | 1 | 0 | 0 | 0 | 0 | 0 | 0 | 0 | 0 | 1 | |
| Colorado | 0 | 1 | 0 | 0 | 0 | 0 | 0 | 0 | 1 | 0 | |
| Donley | 1 | 0 | 0 | 0 | 0 | 0 | 1 | 0 | 0 | 0 | |
| Hemphill | 0 | 0 | 1 | 0 | 0 | 0 | 0 | 0 | 0 | 1 | |
| Hill | 0 | 0 | 0 | 0 | 0 | 1 | 0 | 0 | 0 | 1 | |
| Hood | 1 | 0 | 0 | 0 | 0 | 0 | 0 | 1 | 0 | 0 | |
| Houston | 1 | 0 | 0 | 0 | 0 | 0 | 0 | 0 | 1 | 0 | |
| Jasper | 1 | 0 | 1 | 0 | 0 | 0 | 2 | 0 | 0 | 0 | |
| Jim Wells | 0 | 1 | 0 | 0 | 0 | 0 | 1 | 0 | 0 | 0 | |
| Kerr | 2 | 0 | 0 | 0 | 0 | 0 | 0 | 2 | 0 | 0 | |
| Kleberg | 1 | 0 | 0 | 0 | 0 | 0 | 0 | 0 | 0 | 1 | |
| Leon | 1 | 2 | 0 | 0 | 0 | 0 | 0 | 2 | 0 | 1 | |
| Mason | 1 | 0 | 0 | 0 | 0 | 0 | 0 | 1 | 0 | 0 | |
| Nacogdoches | 0 | 1 | 0 | 0 | 0 | 0 | 0 | 1 | 0 | 0 | |
| Zavala | 0 | 1 | 0 | 0 | 0 | 0 | 0 | 0 | 0 | 1 | |
| **Other Agencies** | 15 | 1 | 3 | 0 | 0 | 0 | | | | | |
| Houston Metropolitan Transit Authority | 2 | 0 | 0 | 0 | 0 | 0 | | | 1 | 1 | |
| Independent School District | | | | | | | | | | | |
| Anna | 0 | 0 | 1 | 0 | 0 | 0 | 0 | 1 | 0 | 0 | |
| Austin | 2 | 0 | 0 | 0 | 0 | 0 | 1 | 0 | 1 | 0 | |
| Brownsville | 1 | 0 | 1 | 0 | 0 | 0 | 0 | 1 | 0 | 1 | |
| Burkburnett | 1 | 0 | 0 | 0 | 0 | 0 | | | 0 | 1 | |
| Castleberry | 1 | 0 | 0 | 0 | 0 | 0 | 0 | 0 | 0 | 1 | |
| Fort Bend | 1 | 0 | 0 | 0 | 0 | 0 | 1 | 0 | 0 | 0 | |
| Houston | 1 | 0 | 1 | 0 | 0 | 0 | 0 | 0 | 1 | 1 | |
| Humble | 2 | 1 | 0 | 0 | 0 | 0 | 0 | 1 | 1 | 1 | |
| Montgomery County Constable | | | | | | | | | | | |
| Precinct 1 | 1 | 0 | 0 | 0 | 0 | 0 | 1 | 0 | 0 | 0 | |
| Precinct 3 | 3 | 0 | 0 | 0 | 0 | 0 | 3 | 0 | 0 | 0 | |
| **UTAH** | 56 | 23 | 25 | 1 | 1 | 10 | | | | | |
| **Cities** | 37 | 21 | 19 | 0 | 0 | 6 | | | | | |
| American Fork/Cedar Hills | 0 | 2 | 0 | 0 | 0 | 1 | 0 | 1 | 1 | 1 | 44,725 |

## Table 94. Hate Crime Incidents Per Bias Motivation and Quarter, by Selected State and  Agency and Federal, 2021—Continued

(Number.)

| State/agency | Number of incidents per bias motivation | | | | | | Number of incidents per quarter | | | | Population[1] |
|---|---|---|---|---|---|---|---|---|---|---|---|
| | Race/ Ethnicity/ Ancestry | Religion | Sexual orientation | Disability | Gender | Gender Identity | 1st quarter | 2nd quarter | 3rd quarter | 4th quarter | |
| Bountiful | 1 | 0 | 0 | 0 | 0 | 0 | 1 | 0 | 0 | 0 | 44,048 |
| Cedar City | 2 | 0 | 1 | 0 | 0 | 0 | 2 | 1 | 0 | 0 | 36,903 |
| Centerville | 0 | 2 | 2 | 0 | 0 | 0 | 0 | 4 | 0 | 0 | 17,765 |
| Enoch | 0 | 1 | 0 | 0 | 0 | 0 | 0 | 1 | 0 | 0 | 7,780 |
| Farmington | 0 | 1 | 1 | 0 | 0 | 0 | 0 | 1 | 1 | 0 | 26,218 |
| Herriman | 0 | 1 | 0 | 0 | 0 | 0 | 0 | 1 | 0 | 0 | 61,086 |
| Kaysville | 0 | 0 | 1 | 0 | 0 | 0 | 0 | 1 | 0 | 0 | 33,139 |
| Layton | 4 | 0 | 1 | 0 | 0 | 1 | 2 | 2 | 1 | 1 | 80,230 |
| Logan | 0 | 1 | 1 | 0 | 0 | 1 | 1 | 0 | 1 | 1 | 52,015 |
| Lone Peak | 0 | 0 | 1 | 0 | 0 | 0 | 0 | 1 | 0 | 0 | 30,210 |
| Moab | 1 | 0 | 0 | 0 | 0 | 0 | 1 | 0 | 0 | 0 | 5,400 |
| Murray | 1 | 0 | 0 | 0 | 0 | 0 | 0 | 1 | 0 | 0 | 48,524 |
| North Ogden | 0 | 0 | 0 | 0 | 0 | 1 | 0 | 1 | 0 | 0 | 21,379 |
| Orem | 2 | 1 | 2 | 0 | 0 | 1 | 0 | 3 | 3 | 0 | 100,060 |
| Salt Lake City[2] | 3 | 2 | 1 | 0 | 0 | 0 | 0 | 2 | 1 | 1 | 205,929 |
| South Salt Lake | 0 | 0 | 3 | 0 | 0 | 0 | 0 | 2 | 1 | 0 | 25,422 |
| Springville[2] | 2 | 1 | 0 | 0 | 0 | 0 | 0 | 1 | 0 | 1 | 33,977 |
| St. George[2] | 10 | 1 | 2 | 0 | 0 | 0 | 5 | 1 | 0 | 6 | 94,601 |
| Sunset | 0 | 1 | 0 | 0 | 0 | 0 | 0 | 1 | 0 | 0 | 5,354 |
| Syracuse[2] | 0 | 3 | 1 | 0 | 0 | 0 | 1 | 0 | 0 | 1 | 33,340 |
| Tooele | 2 | 2 | 0 | 0 | 0 | 0 | 1 | 2 | 1 | 0 | 37,626 |
| Tremonton Garland | 0 | 1 | 0 | 0 | 0 | 0 | 0 | 0 | 1 | 0 | 12,280 |
| West Valley | 9 | 1 | 2 | 0 | 0 | 1 | 3 | 3 | 5 | 2 | 134,329 |
| **Universities and Colleges** | 2 | 0 | 0 | 0 | 0 | 0 | | | | | |
| Brigham Young University | 1 | 0 | 0 | 0 | 0 | 0 | 0 | 1 | 0 | | 39,086 |
| Southern Utah University | 1 | 0 | 0 | 0 | 0 | 0 | 0 | 0 | 0 | 1 | 15,872 |
| **Metropolitan Counties** | 4 | 1 | 3 | 0 | 0 | 3 | | | | | |
| Cache | 0 | 0 | 0 | 0 | 0 | 1 | 1 | 0 | 0 | 0 | |
| Salt Lake County Unified Police Department | 1 | 0 | 0 | 0 | 0 | 0 | 1 | 0 | 0 | 0 | |
| Tooele | 2 | 0 | 0 | 0 | 0 | 0 | 0 | 1 | 1 | 0 | |
| Washington | 0 | 1 | 0 | 0 | 0 | 0 | 0 | 1 | 0 | 0 | |
| Weber[2] | 1 | 0 | 3 | 0 | 0 | 2 | 1 | 1 | 1 | 2 | |
| **Nonmetropolitan Counties** | 5 | 1 | 0 | 1 | 1 | 0 | | | | | |
| Carbon | 4 | 0 | 0 | 0 | 0 | 0 | 0 | 2 | 1 | 1 | |
| Duchesne | 1 | 0 | 0 | 0 | 0 | 0 | 1 | 0 | 0 | 0 | |
| Iron | 0 | 1 | 0 | 1 | 1 | 0 | 0 | 1 | 0 | 2 | |
| **Tribal Agencies** | 5 | 0 | 0 | 0 | 0 | 0 | | | | | |
| Uintah and Ouray Tribal | 5 | 0 | 0 | 0 | 0 | 0 | 5 | 0 | 0 | 0 | |
| **Other Agencies** | 3 | 0 | 3 | 0 | 0 | 1 | | | | | |
| Granite School District | 1 | 0 | 1 | 0 | 0 | 0 | 0 | 1 | 0 | 1 | |
| Utah Transit Authority | 2 | 0 | 2 | 0 | 0 | 1 | 1 | 3 | 1 | 0 | |
| **VERMONT** | 30 | 5 | 6 | 0 | 0 | 0 | | | | | |
| **Cities** | 19 | 5 | 5 | 0 | 0 | 0 | | | | | |
| Burlington | 2 | 0 | 0 | 0 | 0 | 0 | 0 | 1 | 1 | 0 | 42,946 |
| Colchester | 2 | 0 | 0 | 0 | 0 | 0 | 1 | 0 | 1 | 0 | 17,101 |
| Essex | 2 | 0 | 0 | 0 | 0 | 0 | 0 | 1 | 1 | 0 | 22,073 |
| Hartford | 3 | 0 | 0 | 0 | 0 | 0 | 0 | 2 | 0 | 1 | 9,530 |
| Hinesburg | 0 | 0 | 1 | 0 | 0 | 0 | 0 | 1 | 0 | 0 | 4,535 |
| Middlebury[2] | 0 | 2 | 1 | 0 | 0 | 0 | 0 | 1 | 1 | 0 | 8,807 |
| Milton | 1 | 0 | 0 | 0 | 0 | 0 | 0 | 0 | 1 | 0 | 10,962 |
| Montpelier | 1 | 0 | 1 | 0 | 0 | 0 | 0 | 0 | 1 | 1 | 7,278 |
| Morristown | 0 | 1 | 0 | 0 | 0 | 0 | 0 | 0 | 0 | 1 | 5,582 |
| Rutland | 1 | 0 | 0 | 0 | 0 | 0 | 0 | 0 | 0 | 1 | 14,771 |
| Shelburne | 2 | 0 | 0 | 0 | 0 | 0 | 0 | 0 | 1 | 1 | 7,702 |
| South Burlington | 1 | 0 | 0 | 0 | 0 | 0 | 0 | 0 | 1 | 0 | 19,748 |
| Springfield | 0 | 0 | 1 | 0 | 0 | 0 | 0 | 0 | 0 | 1 | 8,828 |
| St. Albans | 1 | 0 | 1 | 0 | 0 | 0 | 0 | 1 | 0 | 1 | 6,787 |
| St. Johnsbury | 0 | 2 | 0 | 0 | 0 | 0 | 2 | 0 | 0 | 0 | 7,021 |
| Stowe | 1 | 0 | 0 | 0 | 0 | 0 | 0 | 1 | 0 | 0 | 4,460 |
| Winooski | 2 | 0 | 0 | 0 | 0 | 0 | 0 | 0 | 1 | 1 | 7,554 |
| **Nonmetropolitan Counties** | 3 | 0 | 0 | 0 | 0 | 0 | | | | | |
| Lamoille | 1 | 0 | 0 | 0 | 0 | 0 | 0 | 0 | 0 | 1 | |
| Orange | 1 | 0 | 0 | 0 | 0 | 0 | 0 | 0 | 0 | 1 | |
| Orleans | 1 | 0 | 0 | 0 | 0 | 0 | 0 | 0 | 1 | 0 | |
| **State Police Agencies** | 8 | 0 | 1 | 0 | 0 | 0 | | | | | |
| State Police | | | | | | | | | | | |
| Middlesex | 1 | 0 | 0 | 0 | 0 | 0 | 0 | 0 | 1 | 0 | |
| Royalton | 2 | 0 | 0 | 0 | 0 | 0 | 0 | 1 | 0 | 1 | |
| Rutland | 1 | 0 | 0 | 0 | 0 | 0 | 0 | 0 | 0 | 1 | |
| St. Albans[2] | 3 | 0 | 0 | 0 | 0 | 0 | 0 | 2 | 0 | 0 | |
| Williston | 1 | 0 | 1 | 0 | 0 | 0 | 0 | 2 | 0 | 0 | |

## Table 94. Hate Crime Incidents Per Bias Motivation and Quarter, by Selected State and Agency and Federal, 2021—Continued

(Number.)

| State/agency | Number of incidents per bias motivation | | | | | | Number of incidents per quarter | | | | Population[1] |
|---|---|---|---|---|---|---|---|---|---|---|---|
| | Race/ Ethnicity/ Ancestry | Religion | Sexual orientation | Disability | Gender | Gender Identity | 1st quarter | 2nd quarter | 3rd quarter | 4th quarter | |
| **VIRGINIA** | 76 | 11 | 23 | 0 | 0 | 1 | | | | | |
| **Cities** | 18 | 4 | 11 | 0 | 0 | 0 | | | | | |
| Alexandria | 0 | 1 | 0 | 0 | 0 | 0 | 1 | 0 | 0 | 0 | 160,457 |
| Blacksburg | 0 | 0 | 1 | 0 | 0 | 0 | 0 | 0 | 1 | 0 | 44,228 |
| Bristol | 0 | 0 | 1 | 0 | 0 | 0 | 0 | 0 | 0 | 1 | 17,265 |
| Charlottesville | 1 | 0 | 0 | 0 | 0 | 0 | 1 | 0 | 0 | 0 | 47,257 |
| Chesapeake | 0 | 0 | 1 | 0 | 0 | 0 | 0 | 0 | 0 | 1 | 249,188 |
| Clifton Forge | 0 | 0 | 1 | 0 | 0 | 0 | 1 | 0 | 0 | 0 | 3,404 |
| Dublin | 1 | 0 | 0 | 0 | 0 | 0 | 0 | 0 | 1 | 0 | 2,583 |
| Fairfax City | 2 | 0 | 0 | 0 | 0 | 0 | 0 | 1 | 1 | 0 | 23,484 |
| Hampton | 1 | 0 | 2 | 0 | 0 | 0 | 1 | 0 | 2 | 0 | 135,107 |
| Leesburg | 2 | 0 | 2 | 0 | 0 | 0 | 2 | 0 | 1 | 1 | 55,794 |
| Norfolk | 2 | 0 | 0 | 0 | 0 | 0 | 1 | 0 | 1 | 0 | 242,488 |
| Petersburg | 1 | 0 | 0 | 0 | 0 | 0 | 0 | 1 | 0 | 0 | 30,212 |
| Portsmouth[2] | 1 | 2 | 1 | 0 | 0 | 0 | 0 | 1 | 1 | 1 | 94,943 |
| Richmond | 1 | 0 | 1 | 0 | 0 | 0 | 0 | 0 | 2 | 0 | 234,928 |
| Strasburg | 2 | 0 | 0 | 0 | 0 | 0 | 0 | 0 | 1 | 1 | 6,745 |
| Suffolk | 2 | 1 | 0 | 0 | 0 | 0 | 1 | 0 | 2 | 0 | 94,755 |
| Virginia Beach | 2 | 0 | 0 | 0 | 0 | 0 | 0 | 0 | 1 | 1 | 451,938 |
| Waynesboro | 0 | 0 | 1 | 0 | 0 | 0 | 0 | 1 | 0 | 0 | 22,896 |
| | | | | | | | | | | | |
| **Universities and Colleges** | 2 | 0 | 3 | 0 | 0 | 0 | | | | | |
| George Mason University | 1 | 0 | 0 | 0 | 0 | 0 | 0 | 1 | 0 | 0 | 49,755 |
| University of Richmond | 0 | 0 | 1 | 0 | 0 | 0 | 0 | 0 | 1 | 0 | 4,534 |
| University of Virginia | 0 | 0 | 1 | 0 | 0 | 0 | 0 | 0 | 0 | 1 | 29,237 |
| Virginia Commonwealth University | 1 | 0 | 1 | 0 | 0 | 0 | 0 | 0 | 1 | 1 | 32,628 |
| | | | | | | | | | | | |
| **Metropolitan Counties** | 55 | 7 | 7 | 0 | 0 | 1 | | | | | |
| Albemarle County Police Department | 1 | 0 | 0 | 0 | 0 | 0 | 1 | 0 | 0 | 0 | |
| Appomattox | 1 | 0 | 0 | 0 | 0 | 0 | 0 | 1 | 0 | 0 | |
| Arlington County Police Department | 0 | 2 | 0 | 0 | 0 | 0 | 0 | 0 | 1 | 1 | |
| Bedford | 1 | 0 | 0 | 0 | 0 | 0 | 0 | 1 | 0 | 0 | |
| Botetourt | 0 | 0 | 0 | 0 | 0 | 1 | 1 | 0 | 0 | 0 | |
| Chesterfield County Police Department[2] | 6 | 0 | 1 | 0 | 0 | 0 | 1 | 0 | 3 | 2 | |
| Clarke | 1 | 0 | 0 | 0 | 0 | 0 | 1 | 0 | 0 | 0 | |
| Fairfax County Police Department | 27 | 1 | 2 | 0 | 0 | 0 | 8 | 9 | 4 | 9 | |
| Hanover | 1 | 0 | 0 | 0 | 0 | 0 | 0 | 0 | 0 | 1 | |
| Henrico County Police Department | 0 | 1 | 0 | 0 | 0 | 0 | 0 | 0 | 0 | 1 | |
| Loudoun | 4 | 2 | 2 | 0 | 0 | 0 | 0 | 2 | 1 | 5 | |
| Mathews | 1 | 0 | 0 | 0 | 0 | 0 | 0 | 0 | 0 | 1 | |
| Montgomery | 1 | 0 | 0 | 0 | 0 | 0 | 0 | 1 | 0 | 0 | |
| Powhatan | 1 | 0 | 1 | 0 | 0 | 0 | 0 | 0 | 0 | 2 | |
| Prince George County Police Department | 3 | 0 | 1 | 0 | 0 | 0 | 1 | 0 | 1 | 2 | |
| Prince William County Police Department | 1 | 1 | 0 | 0 | 0 | 0 | 0 | 2 | 0 | 0 | |
| Stafford | 3 | 0 | 0 | 0 | 0 | 0 | 1 | 0 | 0 | 2 | |
| Warren | 1 | 0 | 0 | 0 | 0 | 0 | 0 | 1 | 0 | 0 | |
| York | 2 | 0 | 0 | 0 | 0 | 0 | 2 | 0 | 0 | 0 | |
| | | | | | | | | | | | |
| **Nonmetropolitan Counties** | 0 | 0 | 2 | 0 | 0 | 0 | | | | | |
| Patrick[2] | 0 | 0 | 2 | 0 | 0 | 0 | 0 | 1 | 0 | 0 | |
| | | | | | | | | | | | |
| **Other Agencies** | 1 | 0 | 0 | 0 | 0 | 0 | | | | | |
| Reagan National Airport | 1 | 0 | 0 | 0 | 0 | 0 | 0 | 0 | 0 | 1 | |
| | | | | | | | | | | | |
| **WASHINGTON** | 449 | 67 | 105 | 7 | 4 | 19 | | | | | |
| **Cities** | 376 | 53 | 94 | 5 | 4 | 15 | | | | | |
| Aberdeen | 3 | 0 | 0 | 0 | 0 | 0 | 0 | 1 | 1 | 1 | 16,824 |
| Arlington | 0 | 1 | 0 | 0 | 0 | 0 | 1 | 0 | 0 | 0 | 21,405 |
| Auburn | 4 | 0 | 0 | 0 | 0 | 0 | 0 | 2 | 2 | 0 | 82,158 |
| Bainbridge Island | 1 | 0 | 0 | 0 | 0 | 0 | 0 | 0 | 0 | 1 | 25,601 |
| Bellevue | 6 | 4 | 1 | 0 | 0 | 0 | 7 | 3 | 1 | 0 | 150,208 |
| Bellingham | 6 | 1 | 2 | 0 | 0 | 0 | 1 | 4 | 0 | 4 | 95,279 |
| Black Diamond | 0 | 0 | 1 | 0 | 0 | 0 | 1 | 0 | 0 | 0 | 5,551 |
| Bothell | 1 | 0 | 1 | 0 | 0 | 0 | 1 | 0 | 1 | 0 | 48,356 |
| Bremerton | 1 | 0 | 0 | 0 | 0 | 0 | 0 | 0 | 1 | 0 | 42,798 |
| Brier[2] | 2 | 0 | 0 | 0 | 0 | 0 | 1 | 0 | 0 | 0 | 7,030 |
| Burien[2] | 5 | 1 | 3 | 0 | 0 | 0 | 2 | 2 | 3 | 1 | 51,584 |
| Burlington | 0 | 1 | 1 | 0 | 0 | 0 | 0 | 1 | 0 | 1 | 9,666 |
| Centralia | 1 | 0 | 0 | 0 | 0 | 0 | 1 | 0 | 0 | 0 | 18,131 |
| Cheney | 1 | 0 | 1 | 0 | 0 | 0 | 1 | 1 | 0 | 0 | 13,175 |
| College Place | 1 | 0 | 0 | 0 | 0 | 0 | 0 | 0 | 1 | 0 | 9,560 |
| Covington[2] | 5 | 0 | 0 | 0 | 0 | 0 | 2 | 1 | 0 | 1 | 22,024 |
| Des Moines | 2 | 0 | 0 | 0 | 0 | 1 | 0 | 1 | 1 | 1 | 32,664 |
| Edmonds | 4 | 0 | 1 | 0 | 0 | 0 | 1 | 1 | 2 | 1 | 42,803 |
| Everett[2] | 12 | 1 | 2 | 0 | 0 | 1 | 7 | 1 | 2 | 2 | 113,469 |
| Federal Way[2] | 5 | 0 | 3 | 0 | 0 | 0 | 1 | 3 | 3 | 0 | 97,017 |
| Fircrest | 1 | 0 | 0 | 0 | 0 | 0 | 0 | 0 | 1 | 0 | 6,920 |
| Gig Harbor | 1 | 1 | 0 | 0 | 0 | 0 | 0 | 0 | 1 | 1 | 11,345 |
| Grandview | 0 | 0 | 1 | 0 | 0 | 0 | 0 | 0 | 0 | 1 | 11,043 |

## Table 94. Hate Crime Incidents Per Bias Motivation and Quarter, by Selected State and  Agency and Federal, 2021—Continued

(Number.)

| State/agency | Number of incidents per bias motivation | | | | | | Number of incidents per quarter | | | | Population[1] |
|---|---|---|---|---|---|---|---|---|---|---|---|
| | Race/ Ethnicity/ Ancestry | Religion | Sexual orientation | Disability | Gender | Gender Identity | 1st quarter | 2nd quarter | 3rd quarter | 4th quarter | |
| Hoquiam | 0 | 2 | 0 | 0 | 0 | 0 | 0 | 0 | 1 | 1 | 8,696 |
| Issaquah[2] | 4 | 3 | 0 | 0 | 0 | 0 | 1 | 2 | 1 | 2 | 40,738 |
| Kenmore | 0 | 0 | 1 | 0 | 0 | 0 | 0 | 0 | 1 | 0 | 23,326 |
| Kent | 8 | 0 | 2 | 0 | 0 | 0 | 3 | 4 | 1 | 2 | 131,899 |
| Kirkland | 0 | 0 | 1 | 0 | 0 | 0 | 0 | 1 | 0 | 0 | 97,027 |
| Lake Stevens | 1 | 0 | 0 | 0 | 0 | 0 | 0 | 0 | 1 | 0 | 35,500 |
| Lakewood | 4 | 0 | 0 | 0 | 0 | 2 | 3 | 0 | 1 | 2 | 61,325 |
| Liberty Lake[2] | 0 | 0 | 2 | 0 | 0 | 1 | 1 | 0 | 1 | 0 | 11,905 |
| Longview | 2 | 0 | 0 | 0 | 0 | 0 | 0 | 0 | 1 | 1 | 38,693 |
| Lynden | 0 | 0 | 0 | 0 | 0 | 1 | 1 | 0 | 0 | 0 | 15,791 |
| Lynnwood | 0 | 1 | 0 | 0 | 0 | 0 | 0 | 1 | | | 39,370 |
| Marysville[2] | 2 | 2 | 2 | 0 | 0 | 0 | 0 | 3 | 2 | 0 | 72,620 |
| Mercer Island | 1 | 0 | 0 | 0 | 0 | 0 | 0 | 0 | 1 | 0 | 26,251 |
| Mill Creek | 2 | 0 | 0 | 0 | 0 | 0 | 2 | 0 | 0 | 0 | 21,076 |
| Monroe | 2 | 0 | 2 | 0 | 0 | 0 | 0 | 2 | 0 | 2 | 21,047 |
| Moses Lake | 0 | 0 | 1 | 0 | 0 | 1 | 2 | 0 | 0 | | 24,694 |
| Mountlake Terrace | 2 | 0 | 0 | 0 | 0 | 0 | 0 | 1 | 0 | 1 | 21,462 |
| Mukilteo[2] | 4 | 0 | 0 | 0 | 0 | 0 | 1 | 1 | 1 | 0 | 21,461 |
| North Bend | 0 | 0 | 1 | 0 | 0 | 0 | 0 | 1 | 0 | 0 | 7,790 |
| Oak Harbor | 0 | 0 | 2 | 0 | 0 | 0 | 0 | 2 | 0 | 0 | 23,792 |
| Olympia | 4 | 0 | 1 | 0 | 0 | 0 | 2 | 1 | 1 | 1 | 54,322 |
| Pasco | 1 | 0 | 0 | 0 | 0 | 0 | 1 | 0 | 0 | 0 | 78,680 |
| Port Angeles | 1 | 0 | 0 | 0 | 0 | 0 | 0 | 0 | 0 | 1 | 20,519 |
| Port Townsend | 1 | 1 | 0 | 0 | 0 | 0 | 0 | 2 | 0 | 0 | 10,063 |
| Pullman[2] | 3 | 0 | 0 | 0 | 1 | 0 | 0 | 0 | 2 | 0 | 34,826 |
| Puyallup | 4 | 1 | 0 | 0 | 0 | 0 | 1 | 1 | 1 | 2 | 43,144 |
| Redmond | 2 | 1 | 0 | 0 | 0 | 0 | 1 | 0 | 1 | 1 | 74,583 |
| Renton[2] | 4 | 0 | 0 | 0 | 0 | 0 | 0 | 1 | 0 | 2 | 102,458 |
| Richland | 1 | 0 | 0 | 0 | 0 | 0 | 0 | 1 | 0 | 0 | 60,615 |
| Sammamish | 1 | 0 | 1 | 0 | 0 | 1 | 0 | 1 | 2 | 0 | 66,855 |
| SeaTac | 1 | 0 | 0 | 0 | 0 | 0 | 0 | 1 | 0 | 0 | 29,103 |
| Seattle[2] | 132 | 15 | 34 | 0 | 2 | 3 | 26 | 38 | 51 | 48 | 787,749 |
| Sedro Woolley | 0 | 1 | 0 | 0 | 0 | 0 | 0 | 0 | 1 | 0 | 12,301 |
| Sequim | 1 | 0 | 0 | 0 | 0 | 0 | 0 | 0 | 1 | 0 | 7,911 |
| Shelton | 1 | 0 | 1 | 0 | 0 | 0 | 1 | 0 | 1 | 0 | 11,073 |
| Shoreline[2] | 7 | 1 | 0 | 0 | 0 | 0 | 1 | 1 | 2 | 3 | 58,725 |
| Soap Lake | 1 | 0 | 0 | 0 | 0 | 0 | 0 | 0 | 0 | 1 | 1,614 |
| Spokane | 10 | 1 | 1 | 1 | 0 | 0 | 3 | 2 | 6 | 2 | 223,344 |
| Spokane Valley[2] | 0 | 0 | 2 | 0 | 0 | 1 | 0 | 1 | 1 | 0 | 104,276 |
| Sumner | 1 | 0 | 0 | 0 | 0 | 0 | 0 | 0 | 1 | 0 | 10,670 |
| Tacoma[2] | 22 | 1 | 1 | 0 | 0 | 0 | 6 | 6 | 3 | 6 | 222,235 |
| Toppenish | 0 | 0 | 1 | 0 | 0 | 0 | 0 | 1 | 0 | 0 | 8,745 |
| Tukwila | 4 | 6 | 0 | 0 | 0 | 1 | 1 | 2 | 6 | 2 | 20,369 |
| University Place | 0 | 1 | 0 | 0 | 0 | 0 | 0 | 0 | 0 | 1 | 34,404 |
| Vancouver[2] | 76 | 5 | 18 | 4 | 1 | 2 | 13 | 27 | 28 | 19 | 188,160 |
| Walla Walla[2] | 2 | 0 | 1 | 0 | 0 | 0 | 0 | 0 | 1 | 1 | 33,154 |
| Woodinville | 1 | 0 | 0 | 0 | 0 | 0 | 1 | 0 | 0 | 0 | 15,462 |
| Yakima | 1 | 1 | 2 | 0 | 0 | 0 | 1 | 1 | 2 | 0 | 94,594 |
| | 4 | 4 | 1 | 0 | 0 | 1 | | | | | |
| University of Washington | 4 | 1 | 1 | 0 | 0 | 0 | 1 | 1 | 1 | 3 | 56,554 |
| Washington State University, Pullman | 0 | 1 | 0 | 0 | 0 | 1 | 1 | 0 | 0 | 1 | 35,394 |
| Western Washington University | 0 | 2 | 0 | 0 | 0 | 0 | 0 | 0 | 0 | 2 | 17,883 |
| **Metropolitan Counties** | 54 | 6 | 8 | 2 | 0 | 2 | | | | | |
| Clark | 4 | 0 | 0 | 0 | 0 | 0 | 1 | 0 | 1 | 2 | |
| Cowlitz | 1 | 0 | 0 | 0 | 0 | 0 | 0 | 0 | 1 | 0 | |
| King[2] | 30 | 3 | 7 | 2 | 0 | 0 | 7 | 12 | 8 | 7 | |
| Pierce | 4 | 1 | 0 | 0 | 0 | 1 | 2 | 1 | 2 | 1 | |
| Skagit | 1 | 0 | 0 | 0 | 0 | 1 | 1 | 1 | 0 | 0 | |
| Snohomish[2] | 11 | 1 | 1 | 0 | 0 | 0 | 0 | 2 | 4 | 5 | |
| Spokane | 2 | 1 | 0 | 0 | 0 | 0 | 0 | 2 | 1 | 0 | |
| Whatcom | 1 | 0 | 0 | 0 | 0 | 0 | 0 | 1 | 0 | 0 | |
| **Nonmetropolitan Counties** | 5 | 0 | 1 | 0 | 0 | 1 | | | | | |
| Adams | 1 | 0 | 0 | 0 | 0 | 0 | 0 | 0 | 1 | 0 | |
| Grant | 1 | 0 | 0 | 0 | 0 | 0 | 0 | 0 | 1 | 0 | |
| Island | 1 | 0 | 0 | 0 | 0 | 0 | 0 | 0 | 1 | 0 | |
| Lewis | 0 | 0 | 1 | 0 | 0 | 0 | 0 | 0 | 0 | 1 | |
| Okanogan | 2 | 0 | 0 | 0 | 0 | 1 | 0 | 1 | 0 | 2 | |
| **Tribal Agencies** | 1 | 0 | 1 | 0 | 0 | 0 | | | | | |
| Chehalis Tribal | 0 | 0 | 1 | 0 | 0 | 0 | 0 | 0 | 1 | 0 | |
| Squaxin Island Tribal | 1 | 0 | 0 | 0 | 0 | 0 | 0 | 0 | 1 | 0 | |
| **Other Agencies** | 9 | 4 | 0 | 0 | 0 | 0 | | | | | |
| Port of Seattle | 1 | 2 | 0 | 0 | 0 | 0 | 0 | 2 | 0 | 1 | |
| Washington State Parks and Recreation Law  Enforcement[2] | 8 | 2 | 0 | 0 | 0 | 0 | 1 | 2 | 3 | 2 | |

## Table 94. Hate Crime Incidents Per Bias Motivation and Quarter, by Selected State and Agency and Federal, 2021—Continued

(Number.)

| State/agency | Race/ Ethnicity/ Ancestry | Religion | Sexual orientation | Disability | Gender | Gender Identity | 1st quarter | 2nd quarter | 3rd quarter | 4th quarter | Population[1] |
|---|---|---|---|---|---|---|---|---|---|---|---|
| WEST VIRGINIA | 22 | 29 | 5 | 1 | 0 | 1 | | | | | |
| Cities | 13 | 20 | 4 | 0 | 0 | 1 | | | | | |
| Beckley | 1 | 0 | 0 | 0 | 0 | 0 | 1 | 0 | 0 | 0 | 15,632 |
| Bridgeport | 0 | 2 | 0 | 0 | 0 | 0 | 1 | 1 | 0 | 0 | 8,853 |
| Charleston | 3 | 1 | 1 | 0 | 0 | 0 | 2 | 0 | 0 | 3 | 45,378 |
| Clarksburg[2] | 0 | 4 | 0 | 0 | 0 | 0 | 0 | 0 | 0 | 2 | 15,290 |
| Fairmont | 1 | 0 | 0 | 0 | 0 | 0 | 0 | 0 | 0 | 1 | 18,335 |
| Huntington | 3 | 0 | 0 | 0 | 0 | 0 | 1 | 0 | 1 | 1 | 44,522 |
| Morgantown | 0 | 6 | 0 | 0 | 0 | 0 | 0 | 1 | 2 | 3 | 31,079 |
| Parkersburg | 0 | 7 | 1 | 0 | 0 | 1 | 5 | 2 | 1 | 1 | 28,793 |
| Pineville | 1 | 0 | 0 | 0 | 0 | 0 | 1 | | | | 558 |
| Ronceverte | 0 | 0 | 1 | 0 | 0 | 0 | 0 | 1 | 0 | 0 | 1,639 |
| South Charleston | 1 | 0 | 0 | 0 | 0 | 0 | 0 | 1 | 0 | 0 | 11,884 |
| Wheeling | 3 | 0 | 1 | 0 | 0 | 0 | 0 | 1 | 2 | 1 | 26,081 |
| **Universities and Colleges** | 1 | 0 | 0 | 0 | 0 | 0 | | | | | |
| Marshall University | 1 | 0 | 0 | 0 | 0 | 0 | 0 | 0 | 1 | 0 | 15,850 |
| **Metropolitan Counties** | 3 | 5 | 0 | 0 | 0 | 0 | | | | | |
| Cabell | 1 | 0 | 0 | 0 | 0 | 0 | 0 | 0 | 1 | 0 | |
| Hancock | 1 | 0 | 0 | 0 | 0 | 0 | 1 | 0 | 0 | 0 | |
| Monongalia | 0 | 1 | 0 | 0 | 0 | 0 | 1 | 0 | 0 | 0 | |
| Putnam | 0 | 2 | 0 | 0 | 0 | 0 | 0 | 1 | 0 | 1 | |
| Raleigh | 1 | 0 | 0 | 0 | 0 | 0 | 0 | 1 | 0 | 0 | |
| Wood | 0 | 2 | 0 | 0 | 0 | 0 | 1 | 0 | 1 | 0 | |
| **Nonmetropolitan Counties** | 4 | 1 | 1 | 1 | 0 | 0 | | | | | |
| Harrison | 1 | 0 | 1 | 1 | 0 | 0 | 0 | 0 | 3 | 0 | |
| Marion | 1 | 0 | 0 | 0 | 0 | 0 | 0 | 1 | 0 | 0 | |
| McDowell | 1 | 0 | 0 | 0 | 0 | 0 | 0 | 0 | 1 | 0 | |
| Mercer | 0 | 1 | 0 | 0 | 0 | 0 | 0 | 1 | 0 | 0 | |
| Randolph | 1 | 0 | 0 | 0 | 0 | 0 | 1 | 0 | 0 | 0 | |
| **State Police Agencies** | 1 | 2 | 0 | 0 | 0 | 0 | | | | | |
| State Police | | | | | | | | | | | |
| Huntington | 0 | 1 | 0 | 0 | 0 | 0 | 1 | 0 | 0 | 0 | |
| Internet Crimes Against Children Unit | 0 | 1 | 0 | 0 | 0 | 0 | 0 | 1 | 0 | 0 | |
| Rainelle | 1 | 0 | 0 | 0 | 0 | 0 | 0 | 0 | 0 | 1 | |
| **Other Agencies** | 0 | 1 | 0 | 0 | 0 | 0 | | | | | |
| Metropolitan Drug Enforcement Network Team | 0 | 1 | 0 | 0 | 0 | 0 | 0 | 0 | 1 | | |
| WISCONSIN | 69 | 14 | 16 | 3 | 3 | 11 | | | | | |
| Cities | 56 | 13 | 13 | 3 | 3 | 11 | | | | | |
| Altoona | 1 | 0 | 0 | 0 | 0 | 1 | 2 | 0 | 0 | 0 | 8,210 |
| Appleton[2] | 1 | 1 | 0 | 0 | 0 | 0 | 0 | 1 | 0 | 0 | 74,204 |
| Beaver Dam | 0 | 0 | 0 | 0 | 0 | 1 | 0 | 0 | 1 | 0 | 16,314 |
| Beloit | 1 | 0 | 0 | 0 | 2 | 0 | 0 | 1 | 2 | 0 | 36,603 |
| Boscobel | 1 | 0 | 0 | 0 | 0 | 0 | 0 | 0 | 1 | 0 | 3,126 |
| Brodhead | 1 | 0 | 0 | 0 | 0 | 0 | 1 | 0 | 0 | 0 | 3,195 |
| Brookfield | 1 | 0 | 0 | 0 | 0 | 0 | 0 | 0 | 0 | 1 | 39,292 |
| Darlington | 0 | 0 | 1 | 0 | 0 | 0 | 1 | 0 | 0 | 0 | 2,305 |
| De Pere | 0 | 0 | 0 | 1 | 0 | 0 | 0 | 1 | 0 | 0 | 25,122 |
| Eau Claire | 3 | 0 | 2 | 0 | 0 | 1 | 1 | 0 | 4 | 1 | 69,372 |
| Fall Creek | 1 | 0 | 0 | 0 | 0 | 0 | 0 | 0 | 0 | 1 | 1,289 |
| Fitchburg | 5 | 0 | 2 | 0 | 0 | 0 | 2 | 3 | 2 | 0 | 31,498 |
| Fond du Lac[2] | 2 | 0 | 0 | 0 | 0 | 0 | 1 | 0 | 0 | 0 | 43,195 |
| Green Bay | 0 | 0 | 1 | 1 | 0 | 1 | 0 | 2 | 1 | 0 | 103,826 |
| Hartland | 1 | 0 | 4 | 0 | 0 | 0 | 0 | 5 | 0 | 0 | 9,360 |
| Hayward | 2 | 0 | 0 | 0 | 0 | 0 | 0 | 1 | 1 | 0 | 2,353 |
| Hudson | 1 | 2 | 0 | 0 | 0 | 0 | 1 | 1 | 1 | 0 | 14,313 |
| Janesville | 1 | 0 | 0 | 0 | 0 | 0 | 0 | 1 | 0 | 0 | 64,768 |
| Kaukauna | 1 | 0 | 0 | 0 | 1 | 0 | 0 | 0 | 1 | 1 | 16,444 |
| Kenosha | 3 | 0 | 0 | 0 | 0 | 0 | 0 | 1 | 0 | 2 | 99,588 |
| La Crosse | 1 | 3 | 1 | 0 | 0 | 0 | 0 | 1 | 2 | 2 | 51,143 |
| Madison | 2 | 1 | 0 | 0 | 0 | 1 | 0 | 2 | 2 | 0 | 266,199 |
| Manitowoc[2] | 0 | 2 | 0 | 0 | 0 | 0 | 0 | 0 | 1 | 1 | 32,233 |
| Maple Bluff | 1 | 0 | 0 | 0 | 0 | 0 | 1 | 0 | 0 | 0 | 1,306 |
| Marinette | 2 | 0 | 0 | 0 | 0 | 1 | 0 | 1 | 2 | 0 | 10,421 |
| Menasha | 1 | 0 | 0 | 0 | 0 | 0 | 0 | 0 | 1 | 0 | 17,823 |
| Menomonie | 2 | 0 | 0 | 0 | 0 | 0 | 1 | 1 | 0 | 0 | 16,633 |
| Middleton | 1 | 0 | 0 | 0 | 0 | 0 | 0 | 0 | 1 | 0 | 20,472 |
| Milwaukee | 0 | 1 | 0 | 0 | 0 | 0 | 0 | 0 | 1 | 0 | 593,337 |
| Monona | 2 | 0 | 0 | 0 | 0 | 0 | 0 | 0 | 2 | 0 | 8,226 |
| Mount Horeb | 1 | 0 | 0 | 0 | 0 | 0 | 1 | 0 | 0 | 0 | 7,606 |
| Muscoda | 1 | 0 | 0 | 0 | 0 | 0 | 1 | 0 | 0 | 0 | 1,227 |
| Neenah | 0 | 0 | 1 | 0 | 0 | 0 | 0 | 0 | 0 | 1 | 26,451 |
| New Berlin | 1 | 0 | 0 | 0 | 0 | 0 | 1 | 0 | 0 | 0 | 39,833 |
| New Richmond | 1 | 0 | 0 | 0 | 0 | 0 | 0 | 0 | 0 | 1 | 9,875 |

## Table 94. Hate Crime Incidents Per Bias Motivation and Quarter, by Selected State and  Agency and Federal, 2021—Continued

(Number.)

| State/agency | Number of incidents per bias motivation | | | | | | Number of incidents per quarter | | | | Population[1] |
|---|---|---|---|---|---|---|---|---|---|---|---|
| | Race/ Ethnicity/ Ancestry | Religion | Sexual orientation | Disability | Gender | Gender Identity | 1st quarter | 2nd quarter | 3rd quarter | 4th quarter | |
| Oconto | 0 | 0 | 0 | 0 | 0 | 1 | 0 | 1 | 0 | 0 | 4,580 |
| Onalaska | 0 | 1 | 0 | 0 | 0 | 0 | 0 | 0 | 0 | 1 | 19,243 |
| Oregon | 1 | 0 | 0 | 0 | 0 | 0 | 0 | 0 | 0 | 1 | 10,881 |
| Oshkosh | 1 | 1 | 0 | 0 | 0 | 0 | 0 | 0 | 1 | 1 | 66,513 |
| Platteville | 1 | 0 | 1 | 0 | 0 | 0 | 0 | 1 | 1 | 0 | 11,690 |
| Portage | 1 | 0 | 0 | 0 | 0 | 0 | 1 | 0 | 0 | 0 | 10,387 |
| Rice Lake | 1 | 0 | 0 | 0 | 0 | 2 | 0 | 2 | 1 | 0 | 8,511 |
| Ripon | 2 | 0 | 0 | 0 | 0 | 0 | 0 | 1 | 1 | 0 | 7,856 |
| Shawano | 1 | 0 | 0 | 0 | 0 | 0 | 0 | 0 | 0 | 1 | 8,845 |
| Sparta | 0 | 1 | 0 | 0 | 0 | 2 | 1 | 0 | 2 | 0 | 9,827 |
| Stevens Point[2] | 3 | 0 | 0 | 0 | 0 | 0 | 0 | 0 | 0 | 1 | 25,875 |
| Two Rivers | 1 | 0 | 0 | 0 | 0 | 0 | 0 | 0 | 0 | 1 | 10,903 |
| Wausau | 2 | 0 | 0 | 1 | 0 | 0 | 1 | 2 | 0 | 0 | 38,435 |
| **Universities and Colleges** | 1 | 0 | 0 | 0 | 0 | 0 | | | | | |
| University of Wisconsin, Madison | 1 | 0 | 0 | 0 | 0 | 0 | 0 | 0 | 0 | 1 | 47,831 |
| **Metropolitan Counties** | 5 | 1 | 2 | 0 | 0 | 0 | | | | | |
| Columbia | 1 | 0 | 0 | 0 | 0 | 0 | 0 | 1 | 0 | 0 | |
| Douglas | 0 | 0 | 1 | 0 | 0 | 0 | 0 | 0 | 1 | 0 | |
| Eau Claire | 1 | 0 | 0 | 0 | 0 | 0 | 0 | 0 | 1 | 0 | |
| Lincoln | 1 | 0 | 0 | 0 | 0 | 0 | 0 | 0 | 1 | 0 | |
| Rock | 1 | 0 | 0 | 0 | 0 | 0 | 0 | 1 | 0 | 0 | |
| St. Croix | 0 | 1 | 0 | 0 | 0 | 0 | 0 | 0 | 1 | 0 | |
| Waukesha | 0 | 0 | 1 | 0 | 0 | 0 | 0 | 1 | 0 | 0 | |
| Winnebago | 1 | 0 | 0 | 0 | 0 | 0 | 0 | 0 | 1 | 0 | |
| **Nonmetropolitan Counties** | 7 | 0 | 1 | 0 | 0 | 0 | | | | | |
| Dodge[2] | 1 | 0 | 1 | 0 | 0 | 0 | 0 | 0 | 1 | 0 | |
| Florence | 1 | 0 | 0 | 0 | 0 | 0 | 0 | 1 | 0 | 0 | |
| Oneida | 1 | 0 | 0 | 0 | 0 | 0 | 1 | 0 | 0 | 0 | |
| Polk | 1 | 0 | 0 | 0 | 0 | 0 | 0 | 0 | 1 | 0 | |
| Sauk | 1 | 0 | 0 | 0 | 0 | 0 | 0 | 0 | 1 | 0 | |
| Shawano | 1 | 0 | 0 | 0 | 0 | 0 | 1 | 0 | 0 | 0 | |
| Taylor | 1 | 0 | 0 | 0 | 0 | 0 | 0 | 1 | 0 | 0 | |
| **WYOMING** | 11 | 2 | 4 | 1 | 1 | 0 | | | | | |
| **Cities** | 9 | 1 | 4 | 0 | 0 | 0 | | | | | |
| Cheyenne | 1 | 0 | 0 | 0 | 0 | 0 | 0 | 1 | 0 | 0 | 65,263 |
| Cody | 0 | 0 | 1 | 0 | 0 | 0 | 0 | 0 | 1 | 0 | 9,878 |
| Douglas | 0 | 1 | 0 | 0 | 0 | 0 | 1 | 0 | 0 | 0 | 6,404 |
| Newcastle | 2 | 0 | 0 | 0 | 0 | 0 | 2 | 0 | 0 | 0 | 3,293 |
| Riverton | 1 | 0 | 0 | 0 | 0 | 0 | 0 | 0 | 1 | 0 | 10,823 |
| Rock Springs | 1 | 0 | 1 | 0 | 0 | 0 | 0 | 2 | 0 | 0 | 22,937 |
| Sheridan[2] | 4 | 0 | 2 | 0 | 0 | 0 | 3 | 1 | 1 | 0 | 18,157 |
| **Universities and Colleges** | 1 | 1 | 0 | 0 | 0 | 0 | | | | | |
| University of Wyoming | 1 | 1 | 0 | 0 | 0 | 0 | 0 | 2 | 0 | 0 | 13,616 |
| **Nonmetropolitan Counties** | 1 | 0 | 0 | 1 | 1 | 0 | | | | | |
| Johnson | 0 | 0 | 0 | 0 | 1 | 0 | 1 | 0 | 0 | 0 | |
| Park | 0 | 0 | 0 | 1 | 0 | 0 | 0 | 0 | 0 | 1 | |
| Sheridan | 1 | 0 | 0 | 0 | 0 | 0 | 0 | 0 | 0 | 1 | |
| **FEDERAL AGENCIES** | 83 | 18 | 21 | 1 | 1 | 2 | | | | | |
| Defense Intelligence Agency | 1 | 0 | 0 | 0 | 0 | 0 | 1 | 0 | 0 | 0 | |
| Federal Bureau of Investigation[2] | 74 | 18 | 21 | 1 | 1 | 2 | 37 | 39 | 31 | 3 | |
| Pentagon Force Protection Agency | 2 | 0 | 0 | 0 | 0 | 0 | 2 | | | | |
| United States Air Force Security Police | 2 | 0 | 0 | 0 | 0 | 0 | 0 | 0 | 0 | 2 | |
| United States Marine Corps Law Enforcement | 1 | 0 | 0 | 0 | 0 | 0 | 1 | 0 | 0 | | |
| United States Treasury Inspector General for Tax Administration | 3 | 0 | 0 | 0 | 0 | 0 | 2 | 1 | 0 | 0 | |

1 Population figures are published only for the cities. The figures listed for the universities and colleges are student enrollment and were provided by the United States Department of Education for the 2020 school year, the most recent available. The enrollment figures include full-time and part-time students.   2 The figures shown include one incident reported with more than one bias motivation.   3 Student enrollment figures were not available.

## Table 95. Hate Crime Zero Data Submitted Per Quarter, by Federal Agency, State, and State Agency, 2021

(Number.)

| Agency name | Zero data per quarter[1] | | | | Population[2] |
|---|---|---|---|---|---|
| | 1st quarter | 2nd quarter | 3rd quarter | 4th quarter | |
| **ALABAMA** | | | | | |
| **Cities** | | | | | |
| Adamsville | 0 | 0 | 0 | | 4,185 |
| Addison | | 0 | 0 | 0 | 714 |
| Alabaster | 0 | 0 | 0 | 0 | 33,963 |
| Aliceville | 0 | 0 | 0 | 0 | 2,208 |
| Ardmore | 0 | 0 | 0 | 0 | 1,548 |
| Argo | 0 | 0 | 0 | 0 | 4,306 |
| Arley | 0 | 0 | 0 | 0 | 338 |
| Ashford | 0 | 0 | | | 2,206 |
| Ashland | 0 | 0 | 0 | 0 | 1,857 |
| Ashville | 0 | 0 | 0 | 0 | 2,412 |
| Athens | 0 | 0 | 0 | 0 | 29,411 |
| Atmore | 0 | 0 | 0 | | 8,837 |
| Attalla | 0 | 0 | 0 | 0 | 5,804 |
| Auburn | 0 | 0 | 0 | 0 | 70,003 |
| Autaugaville | 0 | 0 | 0 | | 881 |
| Bayou La Batre | 0 | 0 | 0 | 0 | 2,444 |
| Bear Creek | 0 | 0 | 0 | 0 | 1,061 |
| Berry | | 0 | 0 | 0 | 1,080 |
| Blountsville | 0 | 0 | 0 | 0 | 1,654 |
| Brantley | 0 | 0 | 0 | 0 | 749 |
| Brent | 0 | 0 | 0 | 0 | 4,663 |
| Brewton | 0 | 0 | 0 | 0 | 5,116 |
| Brilliant | 0 | 0 | 0 | 0 | 859 |
| Brookside | 0 | 0 | 0 | 0 | 1,318 |
| Brookwood | | 0 | 0 | 0 | 1,833 |
| Brundidge | | 0 | 0 | 0 | 1,855 |
| Butler | 0 | 0 | 0 | 0 | 1,670 |
| Camp Hill | 0 | 0 | 0 | 0 | 927 |
| Carbon Hill | 0 | 0 | 0 | 0 | 1,872 |
| Carrollton | 0 | 0 | 0 | 0 | 927 |
| Castleberry | 0 | 0 | 0 | | 521 |
| Cedar Bluff | 0 | 0 | 0 | 0 | 1,830 |
| Centreville | 0 | 0 | 0 | 0 | 2,538 |
| Chatom | 0 | 0 | 0 | 0 | 1,157 |
| Cherokee | 0 | 0 | 0 | 0 | 994 |
| Chickasaw | 0 | 0 | 0 | 0 | 5,618 |
| Childersburg | 0 | 0 | 0 | 0 | 4,747 |
| Citronelle | 0 | 0 | 0 | 0 | 3,867 |
| Clanton | 0 | 0 | 0 | 0 | 8,777 |
| Clayhatchee | | 0 | 0 | 0 | 579 |
| Clayton | 0 | 0 | 0 | 0 | 2,814 |
| Cleveland | 0 | 0 | 0 | 0 | 1,316 |
| Coaling | 0 | 0 | 0 | 0 | 1,631 |
| Coffeeville | 0 | | 0 | | 302 |
| Collinsville | 0 | 0 | 0 | 0 | 1,939 |
| Columbia | 0 | 0 | | | 743 |
| Columbiana | 0 | 0 | 0 | | 4,738 |
| Coosada | 0 | 0 | 0 | 0 | 1,325 |
| Cordova | | 0 | 0 | 0 | 1,795 |
| Cottonwood | 0 | 0 | 0 | 0 | 1,244 |
| Courtland | 0 | 0 | 0 | 0 | 579 |
| Creola | 0 | 0 | 0 | 0 | 2,043 |
| Crossville | 0 | 0 | | | 1,846 |
| Dadeville | 0 | 0 | 0 | 0 | 2,988 |
| Dauphin Island | 0 | 0 | 0 | 0 | 1,380 |
| Demopolis | | 0 | 0 | 0 | 6,455 |
| Dora | 0 | 0 | 0 | 0 | 1,963 |
| Dothan | 0 | 0 | 0 | 0 | 69,747 |
| Double Springs | 0 | 0 | 0 | 0 | 1,057 |
| Douglas | 0 | 0 | 0 | 0 | 784 |
| East Brewton | 0 | 0 | | | 2,311 |
| Eclectic | 0 | 0 | 0 | 0 | 1,011 |
| Elba | 0 | 0 | 0 | | 3,916 |
| Elberta | 0 | 0 | 0 | 0 | 1,781 |
| Eutaw | | 0 | 0 | 0 | 2,525 |
| Evergreen | 0 | 0 | 0 | 0 | 3,422 |
| Excel | 0 | 0 | 0 | 0 | 610 |
| Fayette | 0 | 0 | 0 | 0 | 4,214 |
| Flomaton | 0 | 0 | 0 | 0 | 1,371 |
| Fort Deposit | | 0 | 0 | 0 | 1,126 |
| Franklin | 0 | 0 | 0 | 0 | 502 |
| Frisco City | 0 | 0 | 0 | 0 | 1,107 |
| Fulton | 0 | 0 | | | 239 |
| Fyffe | 0 | 0 | 0 | 0 | 1,078 |
| Gantt | 0 | | 0 | 0 | 214 |
| Geneva | 0 | 0 | 0 | 0 | 4,246 |
| Georgiana | 0 | 0 | 0 | 0 | 1,601 |
| Geraldine | 0 | 0 | 0 | 0 | 895 |

## Table 95. Hate Crime Zero Data Submitted Per Quarter, by Federal Agency, State, and State Agency, 2021—Continued

(Number.)

| Agency name | Zero data per quarter[1] | | | | Population[2] |
|---|---|---|---|---|---|
| | 1st quarter | 2nd quarter | 3rd quarter | 4th quarter | |
| Gilbertown | 0 | 0 | 0 | 0 | 195 |
| Glencoe | 0 | 0 | 0 | 0 | 5,074 |
| Goodwater | 0 | 0 | 0 | 0 | 1,271 |
| Gordo | 0 | 0 | 0 | 0 | 1,580 |
| Gordon | 0 | 0 | 0 | 0 | 328 |
| Grant | 0 | 0 | 0 | 0 | 904 |
| Greensboro | 0 | 0 | 0 | 0 | 2,245 |
| Grove Hill | 0 | 0 | 0 | | 1,688 |
| Guin | 0 | 0 | 0 | 0 | 2,238 |
| Guntersville | 0 | 0 | 0 | 0 | 8,720 |
| Gurley | 0 | 0 | 0 | 0 | 818 |
| Hackleburg | 0 | 0 | 0 | 0 | 1,227 |
| Haleyville | 0 | 0 | 0 | 0 | 4,077 |
| Hamilton | 0 | 0 | 0 | 0 | 6,621 |
| Hammondville | | 0 | 0 | 0 | 485 |
| Hanceville | 0 | 0 | 0 | | 3,571 |
| Harpersville | 0 | 0 | 0 | 0 | 1,757 |
| Hartford | 0 | 0 | 0 | 0 | 2,588 |
| Hayden | 0 | 0 | 0 | 0 | 1,359 |
| Hayneville | 0 | 0 | 0 | | 814 |
| Headland | 0 | 0 | 0 | 0 | 4,770 |
| Heflin | 0 | 0 | 0 | 0 | 3,400 |
| Henagar | 0 | 0 | 0 | 0 | 2,367 |
| Highland Lake | 0 | 0 | 0 | | 410 |
| Hokes Bluff | 0 | 0 | 0 | 0 | 4,237 |
| Hollywood | 0 | 0 | 0 | 0 | 981 |
| Hueytown | 0 | 0 | 0 | 0 | 15,109 |
| Ider | 0 | 0 | 0 | 0 | 737 |
| Jackson | 0 | 0 | 0 | 0 | 4,523 |
| Jacksons Gap | 0 | 0 | 0 | 0 | 823 |
| Jacksonville | 0 | 0 | 0 | 0 | 12,949 |
| Killen | 0 | 0 | 0 | 0 | 958 |
| Kimberly | 0 | 0 | 0 | 0 | 3,688 |
| Kinsey | | 0 | | | 2,302 |
| Kinston | 0 | 0 | 0 | 0 | 553 |
| LaFayette | 0 | 0 | 0 | 0 | 2,858 |
| Lake View | 0 | 0 | 0 | 0 | 2,816 |
| Leesburg | 0 | 0 | 0 | 0 | 1,017 |
| Leighton | 0 | 0 | 0 | 0 | 752 |
| Lexington | 0 | 0 | 0 | 0 | 709 |
| Linden | 0 | 0 | 0 | 0 | 1,829 |
| Lineville | 0 | 0 | 0 | | 2,203 |
| Lipscomb | 0 | 0 | | 0 | 2,101 |
| Littleville | 0 | 0 | 0 | 0 | 990 |
| Lockhart | | | 0 | | 495 |
| Louisville | | 0 | 0 | 0 | 452 |
| Lynn | 0 | 0 | 0 | 0 | 630 |
| Maplesville | 0 | 0 | 0 | 0 | 694 |
| Margaret | 0 | 0 | 0 | 0 | 5,388 |
| Marion | 0 | 0 | 0 | 0 | 2,993 |
| McIntosh | 0 | 0 | 0 | 0 | 207 |
| Mentone | 0 | 0 | 0 | 0 | 333 |
| Midland City | 0 | 0 | 0 | 0 | 2,396 |
| Millport | 0 | 0 | 0 | 0 | 963 |
| Millry | 0 | 0 | 0 | 0 | 481 |
| Monroeville | 0 | 0 | 0 | 0 | 5,544 |
| Montevallo | 0 | 0 | 0 | 0 | 7,179 |
| Morris | 0 | 0 | 0 | 0 | 2,210 |
| Moulton | 0 | 0 | 0 | 0 | 3,177 |
| Mountain Brook | 0 | 0 | 0 | 0 | 20,006 |
| Mount Vernon | 0 | 0 | 0 | 0 | 1,498 |
| Napier Field | | 0 | 0 | 0 | 343 |
| New Brockton | | | 0 | 0 | 1,301 |
| New Hope | 0 | 0 | 0 | 0 | 2,939 |
| New Site | 0 | | 0 | 0 | 753 |
| North Courtland | | | 0 | | 620 |
| Notasulga | 0 | 0 | 0 | 0 | 804 |
| Odenville | 0 | 0 | 0 | 0 | 3,907 |
| Ohatchee | 0 | 0 | | | 1,149 |
| Oneonta | 0 | 0 | 0 | 0 | 6,603 |
| Orange Beach | 0 | 0 | 0 | 0 | 6,440 |
| Owens Crossroads | 0 | 0 | 0 | 0 | 2,316 |
| Oxford | 0 | 0 | 0 | 0 | 21,182 |
| Phil Campbell | 0 | 0 | 0 | 0 | 1,067 |
| Piedmont | 0 | 0 | 0 | 0 | 4,436 |
| Pinckard | | | | 0 | 625 |
| Pine Hill | 0 | 0 | 0 | 0 | 822 |
| Pisgah | 0 | 0 | 0 | 0 | 684 |
| Powell | 0 | 0 | 0 | 0 | 910 |
| Prattville | | 0 | 0 | | 36,716 |
| Ragland | 0 | 0 | 0 | 0 | 1,727 |

## Table 95. Hate Crime Zero Data Submitted Per Quarter, by Federal Agency, State, and State Agency, 2021—Continued

(Number.)

| Agency name | Zero data per quarter[1] | | | | Population[2] |
|---|---|---|---|---|---|
| | 1st quarter | 2nd quarter | 3rd quarter | 4th quarter | |
| Rainsville | 0 | 0 | 0 | 0 | 5,168 |
| Ranburne | 0 | 0 | 0 | 0 | 391 |
| Red Level | | | 0 | | 473 |
| Reform | 0 | 0 | 0 | 0 | 1,531 |
| Repton | | | 0 | 0 | 252 |
| River Falls | | 0 | 0 | 0 | 528 |
| Robertsdale | 0 | 0 | 0 | 0 | 7,187 |
| Rogersville | 0 | 0 | 0 | 0 | 1,296 |
| Russellville | | | 0 | | 9,751 |
| Samson | 0 | 0 | 0 | 0 | 1,845 |
| Sardis City | 0 | 0 | 0 | 0 | 1,782 |
| Satsuma | 0 | 0 | 0 | 0 | 6,214 |
| Sheffield | 0 | 0 | 0 | 0 | 8,820 |
| Silverhill | 0 | 0 | 0 | | 1,365 |
| Skyline | 0 | 0 | 0 | 0 | 834 |
| Slocomb | 0 | 0 | 0 | 0 | 1,924 |
| Snead | | | 0 | 0 | 837 |
| Somerville | 0 | 0 | 0 | 0 | 783 |
| Southside | 0 | 0 | 0 | 0 | 9,108 |
| Spanish Fort | 0 | 0 | 0 | 0 | 9,765 |
| Steele | | 0 | 0 | 0 | 1,099 |
| St. Florian | 0 | 0 | 0 | 0 | 818 |
| Sulligent | 0 | 0 | 0 | 0 | 1,826 |
| Sumiton | 0 | 0 | 0 | 0 | 2,311 |
| Sweet Water | | 0 | | | 240 |
| Sylvania | 0 | 0 | 0 | 0 | 1,863 |
| Tallassee | 0 | 0 | 0 | 0 | 4,434 |
| Tarrant | 0 | 0 | 0 | | 6,048 |
| Taylor | 0 | 0 | 0 | 0 | 2,449 |
| Thomaston | | 0 | 0 | | 379 |
| Thomasville | 0 | 0 | 0 | 0 | 3,726 |
| Thorsby | 0 | 0 | 0 | 0 | 2,081 |
| Town Creek | 0 | 0 | 0 | 0 | 1,040 |
| Trafford | 0 | 0 | 0 | 0 | 602 |
| Triana | 0 | 0 | 0 | 0 | 1,477 |
| Trinity | 0 | 0 | 0 | 0 | 2,477 |
| Tuscumbia | 0 | 0 | 0 | 0 | 8,449 |
| Tuskegee | 0 | 0 | 0 | 0 | 7,864 |
| Union Springs | 0 | 0 | 0 | 0 | 3,308 |
| Uniontown | 0 | 0 | 0 | 0 | 2,102 |
| Valley | 0 | 0 | 0 | 0 | 9,038 |
| Vance | 0 | 0 | 0 | 0 | 1,841 |
| Wadley | 0 | 0 | 0 | 0 | 706 |
| Walnut Grove | | 0 | | | 692 |
| Warrior | 0 | 0 | 0 | 0 | 3,192 |
| Weaver | 0 | 0 | 0 | 0 | 3,027 |
| Wedowee | 0 | 0 | 0 | 0 | 800 |
| West Blocton | 0 | 0 | 0 | | 1,222 |
| Wetumpka | 0 | 0 | 0 | 0 | 8,617 |
| White Hall | 0 | 0 | 0 | 0 | 726 |
| Winfield | 0 | 0 | 0 | 0 | 4,544 |
| York | 0 | 0 | | | 2,188 |
| **Universities and Colleges** | | | | | |
| Alabama A&M University | 0 | 0 | 0 | 0 | 6,560 |
| Auburn University, Montgomery | 0 | 0 | 0 | 0 | 6,199 |
| Calhoun Community College | 0 | 0 | | 0 | 13,627 |
| Coastal Alabama Community College | 0 | 0 | 0 | 0 | 9,883 |
| Enterprise State Community College | 0 | 0 | 0 | 0 | 2,525 |
| Jefferson State Community College | 0 | | | | 12,361 |
| Lawson State Community College | 0 | 0 | | | 4,697 |
| Troy University | 0 | 0 | 0 | | 20,854 |
| Tuskegee University | 0 | | | 0 | 3,195 |
| University of Alabama, Huntsville | | 0 | 0 | | 11,312 |
| Tuscaloosa | 0 | 0 | 0 | 0 | 42,096 |
| University of Montevallo | | 0 | | | 2,829 |
| University of North Alabama | 0 | 0 | 0 | 0 | 9,185 |
| University of South Alabama | 0 | 0 | 0 | 0 | 16,398 |
| University of West Alabama | | | 0 | 0 | 8,506 |
| Wallace State Community College | 0 | 0 | | | 6,944 |
| **Metropolitan Counties** | | | | | |
| Autauga | 0 | 0 | 0 | 0 | |
| Bibb | 0 | 0 | 0 | 0 | |
| Calhoun | 0 | 0 | 0 | 0 | |
| Colbert | 0 | 0 | 0 | 0 | |
| Etowah | 0 | 0 | 0 | 0 | |
| Geneva | 0 | 0 | 0 | 0 | |
| Greene | 0 | 0 | 0 | 0 | |
| Henry | 0 | 0 | 0 | 0 | |
| Houston | 0 | 0 | 0 | 0 | |

## Table 95. Hate Crime Zero Data Submitted Per Quarter, by Federal Agency, State, and State Agency, 2021—Continued

(Number.)

| Agency name | Zero data per quarter[1] | | | | Population[2] |
|---|---|---|---|---|---|
| | 1st quarter | 2nd quarter | 3rd quarter | 4th quarter | |
| Lauderdale | 0 | 0 | 0 | 0 | |
| Lawrence | 0 | 0 | 0 | 0 | |
| Montgomery | | 0 | 0 | 0 | |
| Pickens | 0 | 0 | | | |
| Russell | 0 | 0 | | | |
| Shelby | 0 | 0 | 0 | 0 | |
| **Nonmetropolitan Counties** | | | | | |
| Barbour | 0 | 0 | 0 | 0 | |
| Bullock | | 0 | 0 | 0 | |
| Chambers | 0 | 0 | 0 | | |
| Choctaw | 0 | 0 | 0 | 0 | |
| Clarke | 0 | 0 | 0 | 0 | |
| Clay | 0 | 0 | 0 | 0 | |
| Cleburne | 0 | 0 | 0 | 0 | |
| Conecuh | | | 0 | 0 | |
| Coosa | | | 0 | 0 | |
| Covington | 0 | 0 | 0 | 0 | |
| Crenshaw | 0 | 0 | 0 | 0 | |
| DeKalb | 0 | 0 | 0 | 0 | |
| Lamar | 0 | 0 | 0 | 0 | |
| Macon | 0 | 0 | 0 | 0 | |
| Marengo | 0 | 0 | 0 | 0 | |
| Marion | 0 | 0 | 0 | 0 | |
| Monroe | 0 | 0 | 0 | 0 | |
| Perry | | 0 | | | |
| Pike | | | 0 | 0 | |
| Randolph | 0 | 0 | 0 | 0 | |
| Sumter | 0 | 0 | 0 | 0 | |
| Talladega | 0 | 0 | 0 | 0 | |
| Tallapoosa | 0 | 0 | 0 | 0 | |
| Walker | 0 | 0 | 0 | 0 | |
| Winston | 0 | 0 | 0 | 0 | |
| **Other Agencies** | | | | | |
| 17th Judicial Circuit Drug Task Force | 0 | 0 | 0 | 0 | |
| 22nd Judicial Circuit Drug Task Force | 0 | 0 | | | |
| Alabama Department of Mental Health | 0 | | | | |
| Alabama Drug Enforcement Task Force | 0 | | 0 | 0 | |
| Alabama Law Enforcement Agency | 0 | 0 | 0 | 0 | |
| Department of Conservation, Montgomery | 0 | 0 | 0 | 0 | |
| Department of Corrections Investigations and Intelligence Division | 0 | 0 | 0 | 0 | |
| District Attorney, Hamilton | 0 | 0 | 0 | 0 | |
| Dothan-Houston County Airport Authority | 0 | 0 | 0 | | |
| Etowah County Drug Enforcement Unit | 0 | 0 | 0 | 0 | |
| Huntsville International Airport | 0 | | | | |
| Marshall County Drug Enforcement Unit | | 0 | | | |
| **ALASKA** | | | | | |
| **Cities** | | | | | |
| Bethel | 0 | 0 | 0 | 0 | 6,717 |
| Bristol Bay Borough | 0 | 0 | 0 | 0 | 769 |
| Cordova | 0 | 0 | 0 | 0 | 2,162 |
| Craig | 0 | 0 | 0 | 0 | 1,273 |
| Dillingham | 0 | 0 | 0 | 0 | 2,324 |
| Fairbanks | 0 | 0 | | | 30,598 |
| Haines | 0 | 0 | 0 | 0 | 2,624 |
| Homer | 0 | 0 | 0 | 0 | 6,143 |
| Kenai | 0 | 0 | 0 | 0 | 7,970 |
| Ketchikan | 0 | 0 | 0 | 0 | 8,198 |
| Kodiak | 0 | 0 | 0 | 0 | 5,776 |
| Kotzebue | 0 | 0 | 0 | 0 | 3,264 |
| North Pole | 0 | 0 | 0 | 0 | 2,106 |
| North Slope Borough | 0 | 0 | 0 | 0 | 9,310 |
| Skagway | 0 | 0 | 0 | 0 | 1,202 |
| Soldotna | 0 | 0 | 0 | 0 | 4,855 |
| Unalaska | 0 | 0 | 0 | 0 | 4,484 |
| Valdez | 0 | 0 | 0 | 0 | 3,842 |
| Wrangell | 0 | 0 | 0 | 0 | 2,522 |
| **Universities and Colleges** | | | | | |
| University of Alaska | | | | | |
| Anchorage | 0 | 0 | 0 | 0 | 20,526 |
| Fairbanks | 0 | 0 | 0 | 0 | 11,413 |
| **Tribal Agencies** | | | | | |
| Metlakatla Tribal | 0 | 0 | 0 | 0 | |
| **Other Agencies** | | | | | |
| Fairbanks International Airport | 0 | 0 | 0 | 0 | |
| Ted Stevens Anchorage International Airport | 0 | 0 | | 0 | |

## Table 95. Hate Crime Zero Data Submitted Per Quarter, by Federal Agency, State, and State Agency, 2021—Continued

(Number.)

| Agency name | Zero data per quarter[1] | | | | Population[2] |
|---|---|---|---|---|---|
| | 1st quarter | 2nd quarter | 3rd quarter | 4th quarter | |
| **ARIZONA** | | | | | |
| **Cities** | | | | | |
| Apache Junction | 0 | 0 | 0 | 0 | 44,607 |
| Avondale | 0 | 0 | 0 | 0 | 91,009 |
| Bisbee | 0 | 0 | 0 | 0 | 5,111 |
| Buckeye | 0 | 0 | 0 | 0 | 93,218 |
| Camp Verde | 0 | 0 | 0 | 0 | 11,299 |
| Casa Grande | 0 | 0 | 0 | 0 | 62,566 |
| Chino Valley | 0 | 0 | 0 | 0 | 13,039 |
| Coolidge | 0 | 0 | 0 | 0 | 13,973 |
| Douglas | 0 | 0 | 0 | 0 | 16,349 |
| Eagar | 0 | 0 | 0 | 0 | 4,960 |
| El Mirage | 0 | 0 | 0 | 0 | 36,476 |
| Fredonia | 0 | 0 | 0 | 0 | 1,266 |
| Gilbert | 0 | 0 | 0 | 0 | 272,941 |
| Huachuca City | 0 | 0 | 0 | 0 | 1,722 |
| Lake Havasu City | 0 | 0 | 0 | 0 | 57,735 |
| Litchfield Park | | | 0 | 0 | 6,941 |
| Marana | 0 | 0 | 0 | 0 | 53,347 |
| Oro Valley | 0 | 0 | 0 | 0 | 47,282 |
| Page | 0 | 0 | 0 | 0 | 7,530 |
| Paradise Valley | 0 | 0 | 0 | 0 | 12,895 |
| Parker | 0 | 0 | 0 | | 3,304 |
| Peoria | 0 | 0 | 0 | 0 | 194,566 |
| Pinetop-Lakeside | 0 | 0 | 0 | 0 | 4,540 |
| San Luis | 0 | 0 | 0 | 0 | 37,140 |
| Scottsdale | 0 | 0 | 0 | 0 | 245,886 |
| Springerville | 0 | 0 | 0 | 0 | 1,987 |
| Superior | 0 | 0 | 0 | 0 | 3,270 |
| Tempe | | | | 0 | 183,973 |
| Tolleson | 0 | 0 | 0 | 0 | 7,351 |
| Tombstone | 0 | 0 | 0 | 0 | 1,302 |
| Wellton | 0 | 0 | 0 | 0 | 3,187 |
| **Universities and Colleges** | | | | | |
| Arizona Western College | 0 | 0 | 0 | 0 | 11,646 |
| Central Arizona College | 0 | 0 | 0 | 0 | 8,093 |
| Northern Arizona University | 0 | 0 | 0 | 0 | 34,290 |
| **Metropolitan Counties** | | | | | |
| Coconino | 0 | 0 | 0 | 0 | |
| Yuma | 0 | 0 | 0 | 0 | |
| **Tribal Agencies** | | | | | |
| Ak-Chin Tribal | 0 | 0 | 0 | 0 | |
| Cocopah Tribal | 0 | 0 | 0 | 0 | |
| Colorado River Tribal | 0 | 0 | 0 | 0 | |
| Fort McDowell Tribal | 0 | 0 | 0 | 0 | |
| Fort Mojave Tribal | 0 | | | | |
| Hopi Resource Enforcement Agency | 0 | 0 | 0 | 0 | |
| Hualapai Tribal | | 0 | 0 | 0 | |
| Kaibab Paiute Tribal | 0 | 0 | 0 | 0 | |
| Navajo Nation | 0 | 0 | 0 | 0 | |
| Pascua Yaqui Tribal | 0 | 0 | 0 | 0 | |
| Salt River Tribal | 0 | | 0 | 0 | |
| San Carlos Apache | 0 | | 0 | 0 | |
| Truxton Canon Agency | 0 | 0 | 0 | 0 | |
| White Mountain Apache Tribal | 0 | 0 | 0 | 0 | |
| Yavapai-Apache Nation | 0 | 0 | 0 | 0 | |
| Yavapai-Prescott Tribal | 0 | 0 | 0 | 0 | |
| **Other Agencies** | | | | | |
| Tucson Airport Authority | 0 | 0 | 0 | 0 | |
| **ARKANSAS** | | | | | |
| **Cities** | | | | | |
| Alexander | 0 | 0 | 0 | 0 | 3,701 |
| Alma | 0 | 0 | 0 | 0 | 5,925 |
| Altus | 0 | 0 | | | 727 |
| Amity | 0 | 0 | 0 | 0 | 670 |
| Arkadelphia | 0 | 0 | 0 | 0 | 10,624 |
| Ashdown | 0 | 0 | 0 | 0 | 4,326 |
| Ash Flat | 0 | 0 | 0 | 0 | 1,101 |
| Atkins | 0 | 0 | 0 | | 3,045 |
| Augusta | 0 | 0 | 0 | 0 | 1,900 |
| Austin | 0 | 0 | 0 | 0 | 4,874 |
| Bald Knob | 0 | 0 | 0 | 0 | 2,864 |
| Barling | 0 | 0 | 0 | 0 | 5,103 |
| Batesville | 0 | 0 | 0 | 0 | 10,880 |

## Table 95. Hate Crime Zero Data Submitted Per Quarter, by Federal Agency, State, and State Agency, 2021—Continued

(Number.)

| Agency name | Zero data per quarter[1] | | | | Population[2] |
|---|---|---|---|---|---|
| | 1st quarter | 2nd quarter | 3rd quarter | 4th quarter | |
| Bay | 0 | 0 | 0 | 0 | 1,817 |
| Beebe | 0 | 0 | 0 | 0 | 8,299 |
| Bella Vista | 0 | 0 | 0 | 0 | 29,723 |
| Benton | 0 | 0 | 0 | 0 | 37,911 |
| Bentonville | 0 | 0 | 0 | 0 | 60,329 |
| Berryville | 0 | 0 | 0 | 0 | 5,537 |
| Blytheville | 0 | 0 | 0 | 0 | 13,003 |
| Bono | 0 | 0 | 0 | 0 | 2,637 |
| Booneville | 0 | 0 | 0 | 0 | 3,744 |
| Bradford | 0 | 0 | 0 | 0 | 735 |
| Brinkley | 0 | 0 | 0 | 0 | 2,480 |
| Brookland | 0 | 0 | 0 | 0 | 4,136 |
| Bull Shoals | 0 | 0 | 0 | 0 | 1,951 |
| Cabot | 0 | 0 | 0 | 0 | 26,696 |
| Caddo Valley | 0 | 0 | 0 | 0 | 630 |
| Cammack Village | 0 | 0 | 0 | 0 | 706 |
| Caraway | 0 | 0 | 0 | 0 | 1,289 |
| Carlisle | 0 | 0 | 0 | 0 | 2,147 |
| Cedarville | 0 | | | | 1,411 |
| Charleston | | 0 | 0 | 0 | 2,499 |
| Cherokee Village | 0 | 0 | 0 | 0 | 4,650 |
| Cherry Valley | 0 | 0 | 0 | 0 | 565 |
| Clarendon | 0 | 0 | 0 | 0 | 1,303 |
| Clarksville | 0 | 0 | 0 | 0 | 9,775 |
| Clinton | 0 | 0 | 0 | 0 | 2,492 |
| Conway | 0 | 0 | 0 | 0 | 69,018 |
| Corning | 0 | 0 | 0 | 0 | 2,982 |
| Cotter | 0 | 0 | 0 | 0 | 956 |
| Crossett | 0 | 0 | 0 | 0 | 4,629 |
| Damascus | 0 | 0 | 0 | 0 | 383 |
| Danville | 0 | 0 | 0 | 0 | 2,361 |
| Dardanelle | 0 | 0 | 0 | 0 | 4,475 |
| Decatur | 0 | 0 | 0 | 0 | 1,800 |
| De Queen | 0 | 0 | 0 | 0 | 6,387 |
| Des Arc | 0 | 0 | 0 | 0 | 1,553 |
| DeWitt | 0 | 0 | 0 | 0 | 2,941 |
| Diamond City | 0 | 0 | 0 | 0 | 803 |
| Diaz | 0 | 0 | 0 | | 1,197 |
| Dover | 0 | | 0 | 0 | 1,451 |
| Dumas | 0 | 0 | 0 | 0 | 3,897 |
| Dyer | 0 | | | | 891 |
| Earle | 0 | | | | 2,142 |
| Elkins | | 0 | 0 | 0 | 3,778 |
| England | 0 | 0 | 0 | 0 | 2,643 |
| Etowah | 0 | 0 | 0 | 0 | 308 |
| Eudora | 0 | 0 | 0 | | 1,833 |
| Eureka Springs | 0 | 0 | | | 2,085 |
| Fairfield Bay | | | 0 | 0 | 2,164 |
| Farmington | 0 | 0 | 0 | 0 | 7,748 |
| Fayetteville | 0 | 0 | 0 | 0 | 91,309 |
| Flippin | 0 | 0 | 0 | 0 | 1,313 |
| Fordyce | 0 | 0 | 0 | 0 | 3,527 |
| Forrest City | 0 | 0 | 0 | 0 | 13,496 |
| Gassville | 0 | 0 | 0 | 0 | 2,183 |
| Gentry | 0 | 0 | 0 | 0 | 4,323 |
| Gillett | 0 | | 0 | 0 | 690 |
| Glenwood | 0 | 0 | | | 2,092 |
| Goshen | | | 0 | 0 | 2,116 |
| Gosnell | 0 | | | | 3,017 |
| Gravette | 0 | 0 | 0 | 0 | 3,660 |
| Greenbrier | 0 | 0 | 0 | 0 | 5,899 |
| Green Forest | 0 | 0 | 0 | 0 | 2,955 |
| Greenland | 0 | 0 | 0 | 0 | 1,408 |
| Greenwood | 0 | 0 | 0 | 0 | 9,426 |
| Greers Ferry | 0 | 0 | 0 | 0 | 857 |
| Gurdon | 0 | 0 | 0 | 0 | 2,050 |
| Guy | 0 | 0 | 0 | 0 | 796 |
| Hackett | 0 | 0 | 0 | 0 | 842 |
| Hamburg | 0 | 0 | 0 | 0 | 2,514 |
| Hampton | 0 | 0 | 0 | 0 | 1,230 |
| Hardy | 0 | 0 | 0 | 0 | 761 |
| Harrisburg | 0 | 0 | 0 | 0 | 2,287 |
| Harrison | 0 | 0 | 0 | 0 | 13,160 |
| Hartford | | | 0 | 0 | 621 |
| Hazen | 0 | 0 | 0 | 0 | 1,317 |
| Heber Springs | 0 | 0 | 0 | 0 | 6,872 |
| Helena-West Helena | 0 | 0 | 0 | 0 | 9,820 |
| Higginson | 0 | 0 | 0 | 0 | 749 |
| Highfill | 0 | 0 | 0 | 0 | 965 |
| Highland | 0 | 0 | 0 | 0 | 1,111 |
| Hope | 0 | 0 | 0 | 0 | 9,373 |

## Table 95. Hate Crime Zero Data Submitted Per Quarter, by Federal Agency, State, and State Agency, 2021—Continued

(Number.)

| Agency name | Zero data per quarter[1] | | | | Population[2] |
|---|---|---|---|---|---|
| | 1st quarter | 2nd quarter | 3rd quarter | 4th quarter | |
| Hot Springs | 0 | 0 | 0 | 0 | 39,040 |
| Hoxie | 0 | 0 | 0 | 0 | 2,559 |
| Hughes | 0 | 0 | 0 | 0 | 1,178 |
| Huntington | 0 | | | | 613 |
| Johnson | 0 | 0 | 0 | 0 | 3,809 |
| Jonesboro | 0 | 0 | 0 | 0 | 81,208 |
| Judsonia | 0 | 0 | 0 | | 1,989 |
| Lake City | 0 | 0 | 0 | 0 | 2,810 |
| Lakeview | 0 | 0 | 0 | | 723 |
| Lake Village | 0 | 0 | | | 2,113 |
| Lamar | 0 | 0 | 0 | 0 | 1,741 |
| Lavaca | 0 | 0 | 0 | 0 | 2,453 |
| Leachville | 0 | 0 | 0 | 0 | 1,816 |
| Lead Hill | 0 | | | | 268 |
| Lewisville | 0 | 0 | | | 1,095 |
| Lincoln | 0 | 0 | 0 | 0 | 2,492 |
| Little Flock | 0 | 0 | 0 | 0 | 2,842 |
| Little Rock | 0 | 0 | 0 | 0 | 198,260 |
| Lonoke | 0 | 0 | 0 | 0 | 4,152 |
| Lowell | 0 | 0 | 0 | 0 | 10,171 |
| Luxora | 0 | 0 | 0 | 0 | 991 |
| Madison | 0 | | | | 668 |
| Magnolia | 0 | 0 | 0 | 0 | 11,410 |
| Malvern | 0 | 0 | 0 | 0 | 10,805 |
| Mammoth Spring | 0 | 0 | 0 | 0 | 938 |
| Mansfield | 0 | 0 | 0 | 0 | 1,083 |
| Marianna | 0 | 0 | 0 | 0 | 3,219 |
| Marion | 0 | 0 | 0 | 0 | 12,266 |
| Marked Tree | 0 | 0 | 0 | 0 | 2,366 |
| Marmaduke | 0 | 0 | 0 | 0 | 1,262 |
| Marshall | 0 | 0 | 0 | 0 | 1,321 |
| Maumelle | 0 | 0 | 0 | 0 | 18,343 |
| Mayflower | 0 | 0 | 0 | 0 | 2,437 |
| McCrory | 0 | 0 | 0 | 0 | 1,473 |
| McGehee | 0 | 0 | 0 | 0 | 3,545 |
| McRae | 0 | 0 | 0 | 0 | 670 |
| Mena | 0 | 0 | 0 | 0 | 5,377 |
| Menifee | 0 | 0 | 0 | 0 | 323 |
| Mineral Springs | 0 | 0 | 0 | 0 | 1,133 |
| Monette | 0 | 0 | 0 | 0 | 1,639 |
| Monticello | 0 | 0 | 0 | 0 | 9,145 |
| Morrilton | 0 | 0 | 0 | 0 | 6,672 |
| Mountain Home | 0 | 0 | 0 | 0 | 12,657 |
| Mountain View | 0 | 0 | 0 | 0 | 2,917 |
| Mulberry | 0 | 0 | 0 | 0 | 1,699 |
| Murfreesboro | 0 | 0 | 0 | 0 | 1,565 |
| Nashville | 0 | 0 | 0 | 0 | 4,263 |
| Newport | 0 | 0 | 0 | 0 | 7,335 |
| Norfork | 0 | 0 | 0 | 0 | 543 |
| North Little Rock | 0 | 0 | 0 | 0 | 66,677 |
| Ola | 0 | 0 | 0 | 0 | 1,190 |
| Osceola | 0 | 0 | 0 | 0 | 6,472 |
| Ozark | 0 | 0 | 0 | 0 | 3,618 |
| Paris | 0 | 0 | 0 | 0 | 3,352 |
| Patterson | 0 | 0 | 0 | 0 | 382 |
| Pea Ridge | 0 | 0 | 0 | 0 | 6,652 |
| Perryville | 0 | 0 | 0 | 0 | 1,438 |
| Piggott | 0 | 0 | 0 | 0 | 3,464 |
| Pine Bluff | 0 | 0 | 0 | 0 | 39,670 |
| Plumerville | 0 | 0 | 0 | 0 | 773 |
| Pocahontas | 0 | 0 | 0 | | 6,781 |
| Pottsville | 0 | 0 | 0 | 0 | 3,423 |
| Prairie Grove | 0 | 0 | 0 | 0 | 7,380 |
| Prescott | 0 | 0 | 0 | 0 | 2,892 |
| Quitman | 0 | 0 | 0 | 0 | 705 |
| Ravenden | 0 | 0 | 0 | 0 | 443 |
| Redfield | 0 | 0 | 0 | 0 | 1,513 |
| Rose Bud | 0 | 0 | 0 | 0 | 493 |
| Russellville | 0 | 0 | 0 | 0 | 29,465 |
| Salem | 0 | 0 | 0 | 0 | 1,657 |
| Searcy | 0 | 0 | 0 | 0 | 23,604 |
| Shannon Hills | 0 | 0 | 0 | 0 | 4,196 |
| Sheridan | 0 | 0 | 0 | 0 | 5,075 |
| Sherwood | 0 | 0 | 0 | 0 | 31,857 |
| Stamps | 0 | 0 | 0 | 0 | 1,446 |
| Star City | 0 | 0 | 0 | 0 | 1,989 |
| St. Charles | 0 | 0 | 0 | 0 | 210 |
| Stuttgart | 0 | 0 | 0 | 0 | 8,312 |
| Sulphur Springs | 0 | | | | 532 |
| Swifton | 0 | 0 | 0 | 0 | 726 |
| Texarkana | 0 | 0 | 0 | 0 | 29,516 |

## Table 95. Hate Crime Zero Data Submitted Per Quarter, by Federal Agency, State, and State Agency, 2021—Continued

(Number.)

| Agency name | Zero data per quarter[1] | | | | Population[2] |
|---|---|---|---|---|---|
| | 1st quarter | 2nd quarter | 3rd quarter | 4th quarter | |
| Trumann | 0 | 0 | 0 | 0 | 6,869 |
| Tuckerman | 0 | 0 | 0 | 0 | 1,670 |
| Turrell | 0 | 0 | 0 | | 543 |
| Tyronza | 0 | | | | 707 |
| Vilonia | 0 | 0 | 0 | 0 | 4,824 |
| Waldron | 0 | 0 | 0 | 0 | 3,303 |
| Walnut Ridge | 0 | 0 | 0 | 0 | 5,137 |
| Ward | 0 | 0 | 0 | 0 | 5,649 |
| Warren | 0 | 0 | 0 | 0 | 5,458 |
| Weiner | 0 | 0 | 0 | 0 | 657 |
| West Fork | 0 | 0 | 0 | 0 | 2,649 |
| West Memphis | 0 | 0 | 0 | 0 | 23,959 |
| White Hall | 0 | 0 | 0 | 0 | 4,830 |
| Wilson | 0 | 0 | 0 | 0 | 793 |
| Wynne | 0 | 0 | 0 | 0 | 7,546 |
| **Universities and Colleges** | | | | | |
| Arkansas State University | | | | | |
| Beebe | 0 | 0 | 0 | 0 | 4,427 |
| Jonesboro | 0 | 0 | 0 | 0 | 18,762 |
| Newport | 0 | 0 | 0 | | 4,680 |
| Arkansas Tech University | 0 | 0 | 0 | 0 | 13,316 |
| Henderson State University | 0 | 0 | 0 | | 4,562 |
| Southern Arkansas University | 0 | 0 | 0 | 0 | 5,249 |
| Southern Arkansas University Tech | 0 | 0 | 0 | 0 | 1,725 |
| University of Arkansas | | | | | |
| Little Rock | 0 | 0 | 0 | | 11,826 |
| Medical Sciences | 0 | 0 | 0 | 0 | 3,015 |
| Monticello | 0 | 0 | 0 | 0 | 3,499 |
| Pine Bluff | 0 | 0 | 0 | 0 | 2,724 |
| University of Arkansas Community College at Morrilton | 0 | 0 | 0 | 0 | 2,343 |
| University of Central Arkansas | 0 | 0 | 0 | 0 | 12,333 |
| **Metropolitan Counties** | | | | | |
| Cleveland | 0 | 0 | 0 | 0 | |
| Craighead | 0 | 0 | 0 | 0 | |
| Crawford | 0 | 0 | 0 | 0 | |
| Crittenden | 0 | 0 | 0 | 0 | |
| Faulkner | 0 | 0 | 0 | 0 | |
| Franklin | 0 | 0 | 0 | 0 | |
| Garland | 0 | 0 | 0 | 0 | |
| Grant | 0 | 0 | 0 | 0 | |
| Jefferson | 0 | 0 | 0 | 0 | |
| Lincoln | 0 | 0 | 0 | 0 | |
| Little River | 0 | 0 | 0 | 0 | |
| Lonoke | 0 | 0 | 0 | 0 | |
| Madison | 0 | 0 | 0 | 0 | |
| Sebastian | 0 | 0 | 0 | 0 | |
| Washington | 0 | 0 | 0 | 0 | |
| **Nonmetropolitan Counties** | | | | | |
| Arkansas | 0 | 0 | 0 | 0 | |
| Ashley | 0 | 0 | 0 | 0 | |
| Baxter | 0 | 0 | 0 | 0 | |
| Bradley | 0 | 0 | 0 | 0 | |
| Calhoun | 0 | 0 | 0 | 0 | |
| Carroll | 0 | 0 | 0 | 0 | |
| Chicot | 0 | 0 | 0 | 0 | |
| Clark | 0 | 0 | 0 | 0 | |
| Clay | 0 | 0 | | | |
| Cleburne | 0 | 0 | 0 | 0 | |
| Columbia | 0 | 0 | 0 | 0 | |
| Conway | 0 | 0 | 0 | 0 | |
| Drew | 0 | 0 | 0 | 0 | |
| Fulton | 0 | 0 | 0 | 0 | |
| Hempstead | 0 | 0 | 0 | 0 | |
| Howard | 0 | 0 | 0 | 0 | |
| Independence | 0 | 0 | 0 | 0 | |
| Izard | 0 | 0 | 0 | 0 | |
| Jackson | 0 | 0 | 0 | 0 | |
| Johnson | 0 | 0 | 0 | 0 | |
| Lawrence | 0 | 0 | 0 | 0 | |
| Lee | 0 | 0 | 0 | 0 | |
| Logan | 0 | 0 | 0 | 0 | |
| Marion | 0 | 0 | 0 | 0 | |
| Monroe | 0 | 0 | 0 | | |
| Nevada | 0 | 0 | 0 | 0 | |
| Newton | 0 | 0 | 0 | 0 | |
| Pike | 0 | 0 | 0 | 0 | |
| Polk | 0 | 0 | 0 | 0 | |
| Pope | 0 | 0 | 0 | 0 | |

## Table 95. Hate Crime Zero Data Submitted Per Quarter, by Federal Agency, State, and State Agency, 2021—Continued

(Number.)

| Agency name | Zero data per quarter[1] | | | | Population[2] |
|---|---|---|---|---|---|
| | 1st quarter | 2nd quarter | 3rd quarter | 4th quarter | |
| Prairie | 0 | 0 | 0 | 0 | |
| Randolph | 0 | 0 | 0 | 0 | |
| Scott | 0 | 0 | 0 | 0 | |
| Searcy | 0 | 0 | 0 | 0 | |
| Sevier | 0 | 0 | 0 | 0 | |
| St. Francis | 0 | 0 | 0 | 0 | |
| Stone | 0 | 0 | 0 | 0 | |
| White | 0 | 0 | 0 | 0 | |
| Yell | 0 | 0 | 0 | 0 | |
| **Other Agencies** | | | | | |
| Camp Robinson | 0 | 0 | 0 | 0 | |
| Fort Smith Public Schools | 0 | 0 | 0 | | |
| Northwest Arkansas Regional Airport | 0 | 0 | 0 | | |
| Pottsville School District | 0 | 0 | 0 | 0 | |
| State Capitol Police | 0 | 0 | 0 | 0 | |
| **CALIFORNIA** | | | | | |
| **Tribal Agencies** | | | | | |
| Bear River Band | 0 | 0 | 0 | 0 | |
| San Pasqual Band of Mission Indians Tribal | 0 | 0 | 0 | 0 | |
| Sycuan Tribal | 0 | 0 | 0 | 0 | |
| Table Mountain Rancheria | 0 | 0 | 0 | 0 | |
| Yurok Tribal | 0 | 0 | 0 | | |
| **COLORADO** | | | | | |
| **Cities** | | | | | |
| Arvada | 0 | 0 | 0 | 0 | 123,548 |
| Aspen | 0 | 0 | 0 | 0 | 7,750 |
| Ault | 0 | 0 | 0 | 0 | 2,197 |
| Avon | 0 | 0 | 0 | 0 | 7,012 |
| Basalt | 0 | 0 | 0 | 0 | 4,226 |
| Bayfield | 0 | 0 | 0 | 0 | 2,614 |
| Black Hawk | 0 | 0 | 0 | 0 | 132 |
| Blue River | 0 | | | 0 | 936 |
| Bow Mar | 0 | 0 | 0 | 0 | 958 |
| Breckenridge | 0 | 0 | 0 | 0 | 4,996 |
| Brush | 0 | 0 | 0 | 0 | 5,434 |
| Buena Vista | 0 | 0 | 0 | 0 | 3,175 |
| Burlington | 0 | 0 | 0 | 0 | 3,038 |
| Calhan | 0 | 0 | 0 | 0 | 831 |
| Cedaredge | 0 | 0 | 0 | 0 | 2,320 |
| Center | 0 | 0 | 0 | 0 | 2,399 |
| Cherry Hills Village | 0 | 0 | 0 | 0 | 6,685 |
| Collbran | 0 | 0 | 0 | 0 | 731 |
| Columbine Valley | 0 | 0 | 0 | 0 | 1,537 |
| Craig | 0 | 0 | 0 | 0 | 8,905 |
| Crested Butte | 0 | 0 | 0 | 0 | 1,703 |
| Cripple Creek | 0 | 0 | 0 | 0 | 1,270 |
| Dacono | 0 | 0 | 0 | 0 | 6,877 |
| Del Norte | 0 | 0 | 0 | 0 | 1,528 |
| Delta | 0 | 0 | 0 | 0 | 9,047 |
| Dillon | 0 | 0 | 0 | 0 | 973 |
| Dinosaur | 0 | 0 | 0 | 0 | 334 |
| Eaton | 0 | 0 | 0 | 0 | 6,191 |
| Edgewater | 0 | 0 | 0 | 0 | 5,415 |
| Elizabeth | 0 | 0 | 0 | 0 | 1,928 |
| Empire | 0 | 0 | 0 | 0 | 304 |
| Estes Park | 0 | 0 | 0 | 0 | 6,617 |
| Evans | 0 | 0 | 0 | 0 | 23,698 |
| Fairplay | 0 | 0 | 0 | 0 | 814 |
| Firestone | 0 | 0 | 0 | 0 | 15,932 |
| Florence | 0 | 0 | 0 | 0 | 3,993 |
| Fort Lupton | 0 | 0 | 0 | 0 | 8,800 |
| Fountain | 0 | 0 | 0 | 0 | 31,557 |
| Fowler | 0 | 0 | 0 | 0 | 1,145 |
| Fraser/Winter Park | 0 | 0 | 0 | 0 | 2,478 |
| Frederick | 0 | 0 | 0 | 0 | 11,844 |
| Frisco | 0 | 0 | 0 | 0 | 2,892 |
| Garden City | 0 | 0 | 0 | 0 | 282 |
| Georgetown | 0 | 0 | 0 | 0 | 1,109 |
| Glenwood Springs | 0 | 0 | 0 | 0 | 10,297 |
| Granada | 0 | 0 | 0 | 0 | 508 |
| Granby | 0 | 0 | 0 | 0 | 2,209 |
| Green Mountain Falls | 0 | 0 | 0 | 0 | 737 |
| Gypsum | 0 | 0 | 0 | 0 | 7,391 |
| Haxtun | 0 | 0 | 0 | 0 | 936 |
| Hayden | 0 | 0 | 0 | 0 | 1,995 |
| Holyoke | 0 | 0 | 0 | 0 | 2,230 |
| Hotchkiss | 0 | 0 | 0 | 0 | 929 |
| Hudson | 0 | 0 | 0 | 0 | 2,812 |

## Table 95. Hate Crime Zero Data Submitted Per Quarter, by Federal Agency, State, and State Agency, 2021—Continued

(Number.)

| Agency name | Zero data per quarter[1] | | | | Population[2] |
|---|---|---|---|---|---|
| | 1st quarter | 2nd quarter | 3rd quarter | 4th quarter | |
| Hugo | 0 | 0 | 0 | 0 | 787 |
| Idaho Springs | 0 | 0 | 0 | 0 | 1,871 |
| Ignacio | 0 | 0 | 0 | 0 | 974 |
| Keenesburg | 0 | 0 | 0 | | 1,320 |
| Kersey | 0 | 0 | 0 | 0 | 1,833 |
| Kremmling | | 0 | 0 | 0 | 1,532 |
| Lakeside | 0 | 0 | 0 | 0 | 8 |
| Lamar | 0 | 0 | 0 | 0 | 7,612 |
| La Salle | 0 | 0 | 0 | 0 | 2,524 |
| Leadville | 0 | 0 | 0 | 0 | 2,796 |
| Limon | 0 | 0 | 0 | 0 | 1,951 |
| Lochbuie | 0 | 0 | 0 | | 8,301 |
| Log Lane Village | 0 | 0 | | | 851 |
| Mancos | 0 | 0 | 0 | 0 | 1,404 |
| Manitou Springs | 0 | 0 | 0 | 0 | 5,509 |
| Mead | 0 | 0 | 0 | | 5,190 |
| Meeker | 0 | 0 | 0 | 0 | 2,305 |
| Milliken | 0 | 0 | 0 | 0 | 9,074 |
| Monte Vista | 0 | 0 | 0 | 0 | 4,030 |
| Morrison | 0 | 0 | 0 | | 431 |
| Mountain View | 0 | 0 | 0 | 0 | 553 |
| Mountain Village | 0 | 0 | 0 | 0 | 1,486 |
| Mount Crested Butte | 0 | 0 | 0 | 0 | 901 |
| Nederland | 0 | 0 | 0 | 0 | 1,569 |
| New Castle | 0 | 0 | 0 | 0 | 5,012 |
| Northglenn | 0 | 0 | 0 | 0 | 39,162 |
| Nunn | 0 | | | | 506 |
| Oak Creek | 0 | 0 | 0 | 0 | 966 |
| Olathe | 0 | | | | 1,820 |
| Ouray | 0 | 0 | 0 | 0 | 1,050 |
| Pagosa Springs | 0 | 0 | 0 | 0 | 2,178 |
| Palisade | 0 | 0 | 0 | 0 | 2,812 |
| Parachute | 0 | 0 | 0 | 0 | 1,118 |
| Rangely | 0 | 0 | 0 | 0 | 2,295 |
| Ridgway | 0 | 0 | 0 | 0 | 1,055 |
| Rocky Ford | 0 | 0 | 0 | 0 | 3,790 |
| Salida | 0 | 0 | 0 | 0 | 5,735 |
| Sheridan | 0 | 0 | 0 | 0 | 6,070 |
| Silt | 0 | 0 | 0 | 0 | 3,129 |
| Silverthorne | 0 | 0 | 0 | 0 | 5,019 |
| Simla | 0 | 0 | 0 | 0 | 698 |
| Snowmass Village | 0 | 0 | 0 | 0 | 2,754 |
| South Fork | 0 | 0 | 0 | 0 | 422 |
| Springfield | 0 | 0 | 0 | 0 | 1,355 |
| Steamboat Springs | 0 | 0 | 0 | 0 | 13,282 |
| Telluride | 0 | 0 | 0 | 0 | 2,436 |
| Walsh | 0 | 0 | 0 | 0 | 510 |
| Wheat Ridge | 0 | 0 | 0 | 0 | 32,027 |
| Woodland Park | 0 | 0 | 0 | 0 | 8,257 |
| Wray | 0 | 0 | 0 | 0 | 2,352 |
| Yuma | 0 | 0 | 0 | 0 | 3,495 |
| **Universities and Colleges** | | | | | |
| Adams State University | 0 | 0 | 0 | 0 | 3,883 |
| Aims Community College | 0 | 0 | 0 | 0 | 8,954 |
| Arapahoe Community College | 0 | 0 | 0 | 0 | 19,102 |
| Auraria Higher Education Center[3] | 0 | 0 | 0 | 0 | |
| Colorado School of Mines | 0 | 0 | 0 | 0 | 7,092 |
| Colorado State University, Fort Collins | 0 | 0 | 0 | 0 | 37,806 |
| Pikes Peak Community College | 0 | 0 | 0 | 0 | 17,357 |
| Red Rocks Community College | 0 | 0 | 0 | 0 | 11,486 |
| University of Colorado, Denver | 0 | 0 | 0 | 0 | 31,796 |
| University of Northern Colorado | 0 | 0 | 0 | 0 | 15,248 |
| **Metropolitan Counties** | | | | | |
| Clear Creek | 0 | 0 | 0 | 0 | |
| Elbert | 0 | 0 | 0 | 0 | |
| Gilpin | 0 | 0 | 0 | 0 | |
| Mesa | 0 | 0 | 0 | 0 | |
| Pueblo | 0 | 0 | 0 | 0 | |
| Teller | 0 | 0 | 0 | 0 | |
| **Nonmetropolitan Counties** | | | | | |
| Alamosa | 0 | 0 | 0 | 0 | |
| Archuleta | 0 | 0 | 0 | 0 | |
| Baca | 0 | 0 | 0 | 0 | |
| Chaffee | 0 | 0 | 0 | 0 | |
| Cheyenne | 0 | 0 | 0 | 0 | |
| Conejos | 0 | 0 | 0 | 0 | |
| Crowley | 0 | 0 | 0 | 0 | |
| Custer | 0 | 0 | 0 | 0 | |

## Table 95. Hate Crime Zero Data Submitted Per Quarter, by Federal Agency, State, and State Agency, 2021—Continued

(Number.)

| Agency name | Zero data per quarter[1] | | | | Population[2] |
|---|---|---|---|---|---|
| | 1st quarter | 2nd quarter | 3rd quarter | 4th quarter | |
| Delta | 0 | 0 | 0 | 0 | |
| Dolores | 0 | 0 | 0 | 0 | |
| Eagle | 0 | 0 | 0 | 0 | |
| Grand | 0 | 0 | 0 | 0 | |
| Gunnison | 0 | 0 | 0 | 0 | |
| Hinsdale | 0 | 0 | 0 | 0 | |
| Jackson | 0 | 0 | 0 | 0 | |
| Kiowa | 0 | 0 | 0 | 0 | |
| Kit Carson | 0 | 0 | 0 | 0 | |
| Lake | 0 | 0 | 0 | 0 | |
| La Plata | 0 | 0 | 0 | 0 | |
| Las Animas | 0 | 0 | 0 | 0 | |
| Lincoln | 0 | 0 | 0 | | |
| Logan | 0 | 0 | 0 | 0 | |
| Moffat | 0 | 0 | 0 | 0 | |
| Montezuma | 0 | 0 | 0 | 0 | |
| Morgan | 0 | 0 | 0 | 0 | |
| Otero | 0 | 0 | 0 | 0 | |
| Ouray | 0 | 0 | 0 | 0 | |
| Phillips | 0 | 0 | 0 | 0 | |
| Pitkin | 0 | 0 | 0 | 0 | |
| Prowers | 0 | 0 | 0 | 0 | |
| Rio Blanco | 0 | 0 | 0 | 0 | |
| Rio Grande | 0 | 0 | 0 | 0 | |
| San Juan | 0 | 0 | 0 | 0 | |
| San Miguel | 0 | 0 | 0 | 0 | |
| Sedgwick | 0 | 0 | 0 | | |
| Washington | 0 | 0 | 0 | 0 | |
| Yuma | 0 | 0 | 0 | 0 | |
| **State Police Agencies** | | | | | |
| Colorado State Patrol | 0 | 0 | 0 | 0 | |
| **Tribal Agencies** | | | | | |
| Southern Ute Tribal | 0 | 0 | 0 | 0 | |
| Ute Mountain Tribal | 0 | 0 | 0 | 0 | |
| **Other Agencies** | | | | | |
| All Crimes Enforcement Team | 0 | 0 | 0 | 0 | |
| Colorado Bureau of Investigation | 0 | 0 | 0 | 0 | |
| Colorado Mental Health Institute | 0 | 0 | 0 | 0 | |
| Delta Montrose Drug Task Force | 0 | 0 | 0 | 0 | |
| Division of Gaming Criminal Enforcement and Investigations Section, Golden | 0 | 0 | 0 | 0 | |
| Southwest Drug Task Force | 0 | 0 | 0 | 0 | |
| **CONNECTICUT** | | | | | |
| **Cities** | | | | | |
| Ansonia | 0 | 0 | 0 | 0 | 18,452 |
| Avon | 0 | 0 | 0 | 0 | 18,226 |
| Berlin | 0 | 0 | 0 | 0 | 20,440 |
| Bloomfield | 0 | 0 | 0 | 0 | 21,254 |
| Branford | 0 | 0 | 0 | 0 | 27,707 |
| Bristol | 0 | 0 | 0 | 0 | 59,659 |
| Brookfield | 0 | 0 | 0 | 0 | 16,944 |
| Canton | 0 | 0 | 0 | 0 | 10,223 |
| Cheshire | 0 | 0 | 0 | 0 | 28,755 |
| Clinton | 0 | 0 | 0 | 0 | 12,846 |
| Cromwell | 0 | 0 | 0 | 0 | 13,750 |
| Derby | 0 | 0 | 0 | 0 | 12,197 |
| East Hartford | 0 | 0 | 0 | 0 | 49,470 |
| East Haven | 0 | 0 | 0 | 0 | 28,377 |
| East Lyme | 0 | 0 | 0 | 0 | 18,467 |
| Easton | 0 | 0 | 0 | 0 | 7,462 |
| East Windsor | 0 | 0 | 0 | 0 | 11,702 |
| Enfield | 0 | 0 | 0 | 0 | 43,452 |
| Farmington | 0 | 0 | 0 | 0 | 25,510 |
| Granby | 0 | 0 | 0 | 0 | 11,585 |
| Greenwich | 0 | 0 | 0 | 0 | 62,917 |
| Groton | 0 | 0 | 0 | 0 | 8,823 |
| Groton Long Point | 0 | 0 | 0 | 0 | 504 |
| Groton Town | 0 | 0 | 0 | 0 | 28,753 |
| Guilford | 0 | 0 | 0 | 0 | 22,009 |
| Hartford | 0 | 0 | 0 | 0 | 121,160 |
| Ledyard | 0 | 0 | 0 | 0 | 14,534 |
| Madison | 0 | 0 | 0 | 0 | 17,890 |
| Middlebury | 0 | 0 | 0 | 0 | 7,851 |
| Monroe | 0 | 0 | 0 | 0 | 19,311 |
| New Canaan | 0 | 0 | 0 | 0 | 20,147 |
| New Milford | 0 | 0 | 0 | 0 | 26,548 |
| North Branford | 0 | 0 | 0 | 0 | 14,031 |
| Norwalk | 0 | 0 | 0 | 0 | 88,930 |

## Table 95. Hate Crime Zero Data Submitted Per Quarter, by Federal Agency, State, and State Agency, 2021—Continued

(Number.)

| Agency name | Zero data per quarter[1] | | | | Population[2] |
|---|---|---|---|---|---|
| | 1st quarter | 2nd quarter | 3rd quarter | 4th quarter | |
| Plainville | 0 | 0 | 0 | 0 | 17,466 |
| Portland | 0 | 0 | 0 | 0 | 9,185 |
| Putnam | 0 | 0 | 0 | 0 | 9,354 |
| Redding | 0 | 0 | 0 | 0 | 9,042 |
| Rocky Hill | 0 | 0 | 0 | 0 | 20,069 |
| Simsbury | 0 | 0 | 0 | 0 | 25,639 |
| Stonington | 0 | 0 | 0 | 0 | 18,571 |
| Trumbull | 0 | 0 | 0 | 0 | 35,378 |
| Vernon | 0 | 0 | 0 | 0 | 29,423 |
| Waterbury | 0 | 0 | 0 | 0 | 106,480 |
| Watertown | 0 | 0 | 0 | 0 | 21,418 |
| Weston | 0 | 0 | 0 | 0 | 10,204 |
| Wethersfield | 0 | 0 | 0 | 0 | 25,807 |
| Willimantic | 0 | 0 | 0 | 0 | 17,763 |
| Wilton | 0 | 0 | 0 | 0 | 18,236 |
| Winchester | 0 | 0 | 0 | 0 | 10,481 |
| Windsor | 0 | 0 | 0 | 0 | 28,601 |
| Windsor Locks | 0 | 0 | 0 | 0 | 12,828 |
| Wolcott | 0 | 0 | 0 | 0 | 16,550 |
| Woodbridge | 0 | 0 | 0 | 0 | 8,676 |
| **Universities and Colleges** | | | | | |
| Central Connecticut State University | 0 | 0 | 0 | 0 | 13,046 |
| Eastern Connecticut State University | 0 | 0 | 0 | 0 | 5,508 |
| Southern Connecticut State University | 0 | 0 | 0 | 0 | 11,273 |
| Western Connecticut State University | 0 | 0 | 0 | 0 | 6,463 |
| Yale University | 0 | 0 | 0 | 0 | 14,910 |
| **Tribal Agencies** | | | | | |
| Mohegan Tribal | 0 | 0 | 0 | 0 | |
| **Other Agencies** | | | | | |
| Department of Motor Vehicles | 0 | 0 | 0 | 0 | |
| Metropolitan Transportation Authority | 0 | 0 | 0 | 0 | |
| State Capitol Police | 0 | 0 | 0 | 0 | |
| **DELAWARE** | | | | | |
| **Cities** | | | | | |
| Bethany Beach | 0 | 0 | 0 | 0 | 1,308 |
| Blades | 0 | 0 | 0 | 0 | 1,526 |
| Bridgeville | 0 | 0 | 0 | 0 | 2,487 |
| Camden | 0 | 0 | 0 | 0 | 3,660 |
| Cheswold | 0 | 0 | 0 | 0 | 1,787 |
| Clayton | 0 | 0 | 0 | 0 | 3,707 |
| Dagsboro | 0 | 0 | 0 | 0 | 973 |
| Delaware City | 0 | 0 | 0 | 0 | 1,852 |
| Delmar | 0 | 0 | 0 | 0 | 1,911 |
| Dewey Beach | 0 | 0 | 0 | 0 | 419 |
| Ellendale | 0 | 0 | 0 | 0 | 457 |
| Elsmere | 0 | 0 | 0 | 0 | 5,741 |
| Felton | 0 | 0 | 0 | 0 | 1,447 |
| Fenwick Island | 0 | 0 | 0 | 0 | 468 |
| Frankford | 0 | 0 | 0 | 0 | 1,039 |
| Frederica | 0 | 0 | 0 | 0 | 869 |
| Georgetown | 0 | 0 | 0 | 0 | 7,945 |
| Greenwood | 0 | 0 | 0 | 0 | 1,197 |
| Harrington | 0 | 0 | 0 | 0 | 3,672 |
| Kenton | 0 | 0 | 0 | 0 | 278 |
| Laurel | 0 | 0 | 0 | 0 | 4,595 |
| Lewes | 0 | 0 | 0 | 0 | 3,479 |
| Middletown | 0 | 0 | 0 | 0 | 24,307 |
| Milford | 0 | 0 | 0 | 0 | 12,582 |
| Millsboro | 0 | 0 | 0 | 0 | 4,753 |
| Milton | 0 | 0 | 0 | 0 | 3,189 |
| Newark | 0 | 0 | 0 | 0 | 34,064 |
| New Castle | 0 | 0 | 0 | 0 | 5,419 |
| Newport | 0 | 0 | 0 | 0 | 871 |
| Ocean View | 0 | 0 | 0 | 0 | 2,290 |
| Rehoboth Beach | 0 | 0 | 0 | 0 | 1,622 |
| Seaford | 0 | 0 | 0 | 0 | 8,392 |
| Selbyville | 0 | 0 | 0 | 0 | 2,667 |
| Smyrna | 0 | 0 | 0 | 0 | 12,383 |
| South Bethany | 0 | 0 | 0 | 0 | 557 |
| Viola | 0 | 0 | 0 | 0 | 169 |
| Wyoming | 0 | 0 | 0 | 0 | 1,695 |
| Delaware State University | 0 | 0 | 0 | 0 | 5,263 |

## Table 95. Hate Crime Zero Data Submitted Per Quarter, by Federal Agency, State, and State Agency, 2021—Continued

(Number.)

| Agency name | Zero data per quarter[1] | | | | Population[2] |
|---|---|---|---|---|---|
| | 1st quarter | 2nd quarter | 3rd quarter | 4th quarter | |
| **State Police Agencies** | | | | | |
| State Police | | | | | |
| Headquarters | 0 | 0 | 0 | 0 | |
| Kent County | 0 | 0 | 0 | 0 | |
| New Castle County | 0 | 0 | 0 | 0 | |
| Sussex County | 0 | 0 | 0 | 0 | |
| **Other Agencies** | | | | | |
| Alcohol and Tobacco Enforcement | 0 | 0 | 0 | 0 | |
| Amtrak Police | 0 | 0 | 0 | 0 | |
| Animal Welfare | | | | | |
| Kent County | 0 | 0 | 0 | 0 | |
| New Castle County | 0 | 0 | 0 | 0 | |
| Sussex County | 0 | 0 | 0 | 0 | |
| Attorney General | | | | | |
| Kent County | 0 | 0 | 0 | 0 | |
| New Castle County | 0 | 0 | 0 | 0 | |
| Sussex County | 0 | 0 | 0 | 0 | |
| Dover Fire Marshal | 0 | 0 | 0 | 0 | |
| Environmental Control | 0 | 0 | 0 | 0 | |
| Fish and Wildlife | 0 | 0 | 0 | 0 | |
| Park Rangers | 0 | 0 | 0 | 0 | |
| State Capitol Police | 0 | 0 | 0 | 0 | |
| Wilmington Fire Department | 0 | 0 | 0 | 0 | |
| **FLORIDA** | | | | | |
| **Tribal Agencies** | | | | | |
| Miccosukee Tribal | 0 | 0 | 0 | 0 | |
| **GEORGIA** | | | | | |
| **Cities** | | | | | |
| Abbeville | 0 | 0 | 0 | 0 | 2,626 |
| Acworth | 0 | 0 | 0 | 0 | 22,956 |
| Adairsville | 0 | 0 | 0 | 0 | 5,094 |
| Alamo | 0 | 0 | 0 | | 3,320 |
| Alapaha | 0 | 0 | 0 | 0 | 673 |
| Albany | 0 | 0 | 0 | 0 | 70,214 |
| Alma | 0 | 0 | 0 | 0 | 3,322 |
| Alto | 0 | 0 | 0 | 0 | 1,209 |
| Americus | 0 | 0 | 0 | 0 | 14,798 |
| Arcade | 0 | 0 | 0 | 0 | 2,064 |
| Bainbridge | 0 | 0 | 0 | 0 | 12,074 |
| Ball Ground | 0 | 0 | 0 | 0 | 2,414 |
| Barnesville | 0 | 0 | 0 | 0 | 6,660 |
| Bartow | 0 | 0 | 0 | 0 | 246 |
| Baxley | 0 | 0 | 0 | 0 | 4,646 |
| Blackshear | 0 | 0 | 0 | 0 | 3,529 |
| Blairsville | 0 | 0 | 0 | 0 | 660 |
| Blakely | 0 | 0 | 0 | 0 | 4,439 |
| Bloomingdale | 0 | 0 | 0 | 0 | 3,194 |
| Blythe | 0 | 0 | 0 | 0 | 698 |
| Boston | 0 | 0 | 0 | 0 | 1,313 |
| Bowdon | 0 | 0 | 0 | 0 | 2,096 |
| Braselton | 0 | 0 | 0 | 0 | 14,568 |
| Braswell | 0 | 0 | 0 | 0 | 387 |
| Brooklet | 0 | | 0 | 0 | 2,001 |
| Broxton | 0 | 0 | 0 | 0 | 1,198 |
| Buchanan | 0 | 0 | 0 | | 1,205 |
| Buena Vista | 0 | | | | 2,053 |
| Butler | 0 | 0 | 0 | 0 | 1,797 |
| Byron | 0 | 0 | 0 | 0 | 5,350 |
| Cairo | 0 | 0 | 0 | 0 | 9,269 |
| Calhoun | 0 | 0 | 0 | 0 | 17,719 |
| Camilla | 0 | 0 | 0 | 0 | 4,907 |
| Canon | 0 | 0 | 0 | 0 | 791 |
| Carrollton | 0 | 0 | 0 | 0 | 27,786 |
| Cave Spring | 0 | 0 | 0 | 0 | 1,065 |
| Cecil | 0 | 0 | 0 | 0 | 285 |
| Cedartown | 0 | 0 | 0 | 0 | 9,999 |
| Centerville | 0 | 0 | 0 | 0 | 8,082 |
| Chamblee | 0 | 0 | 0 | 0 | 31,254 |
| Chatsworth | 0 | 0 | 0 | 0 | 4,246 |
| Chickamauga | 0 | 0 | 0 | 0 | 3,235 |
| Clarkston | 0 | 0 | 0 | 0 | 12,677 |
| Claxton | 0 | 0 | 0 | 0 | 2,200 |
| Clayton | 0 | 0 | 0 | 0 | 2,122 |
| Cleveland | 0 | 0 | 0 | 0 | 4,246 |
| Cochran | 0 | 0 | 0 | 0 | 5,013 |
| Cohutta | 0 | 0 | 0 | 0 | 644 |
| College Park | 0 | 0 | 0 | 0 | 15,241 |
| Coolidge | 0 | 0 | 0 | 0 | 523 |

## Table 95. Hate Crime Zero Data Submitted Per Quarter, by Federal Agency, State, and State Agency, 2021—Continued

(Number.)

| Agency name | Zero data per quarter[1] | | | | Population[2] |
|---|---|---|---|---|---|
| | 1st quarter | 2nd quarter | 3rd quarter | 4th quarter | |
| Cordele | 0 | 0 | 0 | 0 | 10,223 |
| Covington | 0 | 0 | 0 | 0 | 14,517 |
| Dallas | 0 | 0 | 0 | 0 | 14,704 |
| Dalton | 0 | 0 | 0 | 0 | 33,389 |
| Danielsville | 0 | 0 | 0 | 0 | 605 |
| Darien | 0 | 0 | 0 | 0 | 1,848 |
| Davisboro | | | | 0 | 1,952 |
| Dawson | 0 | 0 | 0 | 0 | 4,076 |
| Demorest | 0 | 0 | 0 | 0 | 2,174 |
| Dillard | 0 | 0 | 0 | 0 | 374 |
| Doerun | 0 | 0 | 0 | 0 | 726 |
| Donalsonville | 0 | 0 | 0 | 0 | 2,471 |
| Doraville | 0 | 0 | 0 | 0 | 10,322 |
| Douglas | 0 | 0 | 0 | 0 | 11,606 |
| Dublin | | 0 | 0 | 0 | 15,767 |
| East Ellijay | 0 | 0 | 0 | 0 | 573 |
| Eastman | 0 | 0 | 0 | 0 | 5,054 |
| East Point | 0 | 0 | 0 | 0 | 35,156 |
| Eatonton | 0 | 0 | 0 | 0 | 6,878 |
| Edison | 0 | 0 | 0 | 0 | 1,394 |
| Elberton | 0 | 0 | 0 | 0 | 4,328 |
| Ellaville | 0 | 0 | 0 | 0 | 1,835 |
| Ellijay | 0 | 0 | 0 | 0 | 1,736 |
| Emerson | 0 | 0 | 0 | 0 | 1,602 |
| Enigma | 0 | 0 | 0 | 0 | 1,354 |
| Eton | 0 | 0 | 0 | 0 | 890 |
| Euharlee | 0 | 0 | 0 | 0 | 4,450 |
| Fairburn | 0 | 0 | 0 | 0 | 17,583 |
| Fayetteville | 0 | 0 | 0 | 0 | 18,554 |
| Flowery Branch | 0 | 0 | 0 | 0 | 9,155 |
| Folkston | 0 | 0 | 0 | 0 | 5,074 |
| Forsyth | 0 | | | | 4,346 |
| Fort Valley | 0 | 0 | 0 | 0 | 8,906 |
| Franklin | 0 | 0 | 0 | 0 | 956 |
| Franklin Springs | 0 | 0 | 0 | 0 | 1,214 |
| Garden City | 0 | 0 | 0 | 0 | 9,268 |
| Glennville | 0 | 0 | | 0 | 4,999 |
| Gordon | 0 | 0 | 0 | 0 | 1,801 |
| Grantville | 0 | 0 | 0 | 0 | 3,369 |
| Gray | 0 | 0 | 0 | 0 | 3,240 |
| Greensboro | 0 | 0 | 0 | 0 | 3,262 |
| Greenville | 0 | | | | 831 |
| Grovetown | 0 | 0 | 0 | 0 | 17,293 |
| Guyton | 0 | 0 | 0 | 0 | 2,455 |
| Hagan | 0 | 0 | 0 | 0 | 950 |
| Hahira | 0 | 0 | 0 | 0 | 3,080 |
| Hampton | 0 | 0 | 0 | 0 | 8,313 |
| Hapeville | 0 | 0 | 0 | 0 | 6,601 |
| Harlem | 0 | 0 | 0 | 0 | 3,648 |
| Hazlehurst | 0 | 0 | 0 | 0 | 4,072 |
| Helen | 0 | 0 | 0 | 0 | 564 |
| Hephzibah | 0 | 0 | 0 | 0 | 3,926 |
| Hiawassee | 0 | 0 | 0 | 0 | 923 |
| Hinesville | 0 | | | | 34,211 |
| Hoboken | 0 | 0 | 0 | 0 | 542 |
| Hogansville | 0 | 0 | 0 | 0 | 3,155 |
| Holly Springs | 0 | 0 | 0 | 0 | 17,484 |
| Homerville | 0 | 0 | 0 | 0 | 2,335 |
| Jasper | 0 | 0 | 0 | 0 | 4,074 |
| Jefferson | 0 | 0 | 0 | 0 | 12,833 |
| Johns Creek | 0 | 0 | 0 | 0 | 85,974 |
| Kingsland | 0 | 0 | 0 | 0 | 18,556 |
| Kingston | 0 | 0 | 0 | 0 | 751 |
| Lake City | 0 | 0 | 0 | 0 | 2,818 |
| Lakeland | 0 | 0 | 0 | 0 | 3,339 |
| Lake Park | 0 | 0 | 0 | 0 | 1,464 |
| Lavonia | 0 | 0 | 0 | 0 | 2,191 |
| Leesburg | 0 | 0 | 0 | 0 | 3,098 |
| Leslie | 0 | 0 | 0 | 0 | 367 |
| Lilburn | 0 | 0 | 0 | 0 | 13,199 |
| Locust Grove | 0 | 0 | 0 | 0 | 9,513 |
| Loganville | 0 | 0 | 0 | 0 | 13,633 |
| Lookout Mountain | 0 | 0 | 0 | 0 | 1,566 |
| Louisville | 0 | 0 | 0 | 0 | 2,162 |
| Manchester | 0 | 0 | 0 | 0 | 3,890 |
| Marshallville | 0 | 0 | 0 | | 1,175 |
| Maysville | 0 | 0 | 0 | 0 | 2,212 |
| McDonough | 0 | 0 | 0 | 0 | 28,222 |
| McIntyre | 0 | 0 | 0 | 0 | 593 |
| McRae-Helena | 0 | 0 | 0 | 0 | 8,250 |
| Midville | 0 | 0 | 0 | 0 | 250 |

## Table 95. Hate Crime Zero Data Submitted Per Quarter, by Federal Agency, State, and State Agency, 2021—Continued

(Number.)

| Agency name | Zero data per quarter[1] | | | | Population[2] |
|---|---|---|---|---|---|
| | 1st quarter | 2nd quarter | 3rd quarter | 4th quarter | |
| Milledgeville | 0 | 0 | 0 | 0 | 18,551 |
| Millen | 0 | 0 | 0 | 0 | 2,730 |
| Monroe | 0 | 0 | 0 | 0 | 14,091 |
| Montezuma | 0 | 0 | 0 | 0 | 2,870 |
| Morrow | 0 | 0 | 0 | 0 | 7,254 |
| Moultrie | 0 | 0 | 0 | 0 | 14,133 |
| Mount Zion | 0 | 0 | 0 | 0 | 1,907 |
| Nahunta | 0 | 0 | 0 | 0 | 1,178 |
| Nashville | 0 | 0 | 0 | 0 | 4,797 |
| Newington | 0 | 0 | 0 | 0 | 263 |
| Newton | 0 | 0 | 0 | 0 | 549 |
| Norman Park | 0 | 0 | | | 957 |
| Oakwood | 0 | | | | 4,342 |
| Ocilla | 0 | 0 | 0 | 0 | 3,746 |
| Oglethorpe | 0 | 0 | 0 | 0 | 1,109 |
| Omega | 0 | 0 | 0 | 0 | 1,222 |
| Oxford | 0 | 0 | 0 | 0 | 2,359 |
| Palmetto | 0 | 0 | 0 | 0 | 5,010 |
| Pelham | 0 | 0 | 0 | 0 | 3,362 |
| Pembroke | 0 | 0 | 0 | 0 | 2,743 |
| Pendergrass | 0 | 0 | 0 | 0 | 593 |
| Perry | 0 | 0 | 0 | 0 | 19,469 |
| Pine Mountain | 0 | 0 | 0 | 0 | 1,468 |
| Pooler | 0 | 0 | 0 | 0 | 26,911 |
| Port Wentworth | 0 | 0 | 0 | 0 | 10,416 |
| Poulan | 0 | 0 | 0 | 0 | 761 |
| Remerton | 0 | 0 | 0 | 0 | 1,054 |
| Reynolds | 0 | 0 | 0 | 0 | 942 |
| Richmond Hill | 0 | 0 | 0 | 0 | 15,025 |
| Rincon | 0 | 0 | 0 | 0 | 10,836 |
| Ringgold | 0 | 0 | 0 | 0 | 3,508 |
| Riverdale | 0 | 0 | | | 15,643 |
| Rossville | 0 | 0 | 0 | 0 | 3,986 |
| Roswell | 0 | 0 | 0 | 0 | 96,041 |
| Sandersville | 0 | 0 | 0 | 0 | 5,215 |
| Sardis | 0 | 0 | 0 | 0 | 967 |
| Senoia | | | | 0 | 4,654 |
| Shiloh | 0 | 0 | 0 | 0 | 501 |
| Snellville | 0 | 0 | 0 | 0 | 20,382 |
| Social Circle | 0 | 0 | 0 | 0 | 4,674 |
| Sparta | 0 | 0 | 0 | 0 | 1,205 |
| Springfield | 0 | 0 | 0 | 0 | 4,237 |
| Stapleton | 0 | 0 | 0 | 0 | 389 |
| Statesboro | 0 | 0 | 0 | 0 | 33,722 |
| Stone Mountain | 0 | 0 | 0 | 0 | 6,357 |
| Swainsboro | 0 | 0 | 0 | 0 | 7,517 |
| Sylvania | 0 | 0 | 0 | 0 | 2,438 |
| Sylvester | 0 | 0 | 0 | 0 | 5,642 |
| Tallapoosa | 0 | 0 | 0 | 0 | 3,237 |
| Thomaston | | | | 0 | 8,735 |
| Thunderbolt | 0 | 0 | 0 | 0 | 2,609 |
| Tunnel Hill | 0 | 0 | 0 | 0 | 892 |
| Twin City | 0 | 0 | 0 | 0 | 1,693 |
| Tybee Island | 0 | 0 | 0 | 0 | 3,057 |
| Tyrone | 0 | 0 | 0 | 0 | 7,803 |
| Valdosta | 0 | 0 | 0 | 0 | 56,844 |
| Vidalia | 0 | 0 | 0 | 0 | 10,452 |
| Vienna | 0 | | | | 3,436 |
| Villa Rica | 0 | 0 | 0 | 0 | 17,094 |
| Warm Springs | 0 | 0 | 0 | 0 | 400 |
| Warner Robins | 0 | 0 | 0 | 0 | 79,483 |
| Warwick | 0 | 0 | 0 | 0 | 381 |
| Waycross | 0 | 0 | 0 | 0 | 13,359 |
| Waynesboro | 0 | 0 | 0 | 0 | 5,340 |
| Whitesburg | 0 | 0 | 0 | 0 | 617 |
| Winder | 0 | 0 | 0 | 0 | 18,709 |
| Zebulon | 0 | | | | 1,229 |
| **Universities and Colleges** | | | | | |
| Abraham Baldwin Agricultural College | 0 | 0 | 0 | 0 | 4,667 |
| Agnes Scott College | 0 | 0 | 0 | 0 | 1,166 |
| Albany Technical College | 0 | 0 | 0 | 0 | 4,635 |
| Athens Technical College | 0 | 0 | 0 | 0 | 6,598 |
| Atlanta Metropolitan State College | 0 | 0 | 0 | 0 | 2,676 |
| Atlanta Technical College | 0 | 0 | 0 | 0 | 6,106 |
| Augusta Technical College | 0 | 0 | 0 | 0 | 6,088 |
| Augusta University | 0 | 0 | 0 | 0 | 9,706 |
| Berry College | 0 | 0 | 0 | 0 | 2,228 |
| Chattahoochee Technical College | 0 | | | | 14,849 |
| Clayton State University | 0 | 0 | 0 | 0 | 8,420 |
| College of Coastal Georgia | 0 | 0 | 0 | 0 | 4,355 |

## Table 95. Hate Crime Zero Data Submitted Per Quarter, by Federal Agency, State, and State Agency, 2021—Continued

(Number.)

| Agency name | Zero data per quarter[1] | | | | Population[2] |
|---|---|---|---|---|---|
| | 1st quarter | 2nd quarter | 3rd quarter | 4th quarter | |
| Columbus State University | 0 | 0 | 0 | 0 | 9,643 |
| Dalton State College | 0 | 0 | 0 | 0 | 5,734 |
| Fort Valley State University | 0 | 0 | 0 | 0 | 2,892 |
| Georgia College and State University | 0 | 0 | 0 | 0 | 8,039 |
| Georgia Gwinnett College | 0 | 0 | 0 | 0 | 15,489 |
| Georgia Highlands College | 0 | 0 | 0 | 0 | 7,895 |
| Georgia Institute of Technology | 0 | 0 | 0 | 0 | 43,217 |
| Georgia Military College | 0 | 0 | 0 | 0 | 14,828 |
| Georgia Northwestern Technical College | 0 | 0 | 0 | 0 | 8,811 |
| Georgia Piedmont Technical College | 0 | 0 | 0 | 0 | 4,979 |
| Georgia Southern University | 0 | 0 | 0 | 0 | 30,231 |
| Georgia Southwestern State University | 0 | 0 | 0 | 0 | 3,725 |
| Georgia State University | 0 | 0 | 0 | 0 | 41,177 |
| Gordon State College | 0 | 0 | 0 | 0 | 4,114 |
| Gwinnett Technical College | 0 | 0 | 0 | 0 | 12,929 |
| Kennesaw State University | 0 | 0 | 0 | 0 | 44,088 |
| Mercer University | 0 | 0 | 0 | 0 | 9,933 |
| Middle Georgia State University | 0 | 0 | 0 | 0 | 10,155 |
| Morehouse College | 0 | 0 | 0 | 0 | 2,341 |
| Piedmont College | 0 | 0 | 0 | 0 | 3,052 |
| Savannah Technical College | 0 | 0 | 0 | 0 | 6,049 |
| Southern Crescent Technical College | 0 | | 0 | 0 | 7,829 |
| Southern Regional Technical College | 0 | 0 | 0 | 0 | 6,804 |
| South Georgia State College | 0 | 0 | 0 | 0 | 3,052 |
| Spelman College | 0 | 0 | 0 | 0 | 2,190 |
| University of Georgia | 0 | 0 | 0 | 0 | 42,941 |
| University of West Georgia | 0 | 0 | 0 | 0 | 15,915 |
| West Georgia Technical College | 0 | 0 | 0 | 0 | 10,089 |
| Young Harris College | 0 | 0 | 0 | 0 | 1,650 |
| **Metropolitan Counties** | | | | | |
| Barrow | 0 | 0 | 0 | 0 | |
| Bartow | 0 | 0 | 0 | 0 | |
| Bibb | 0 | 0 | 0 | 0 | |
| Brantley | 0 | 0 | 0 | 0 | |
| Brooks | 0 | 0 | 0 | 0 | |
| Bryan | 0 | 0 | 0 | 0 | |
| Burke | 0 | 0 | 0 | 0 | |
| Butts | 0 | 0 | 0 | 0 | |
| Catoosa | 0 | 0 | 0 | 0 | |
| Clarke | 0 | 0 | 0 | 0 | |
| Cobb | 0 | 0 | 0 | 0 | |
| Crawford | 0 | 0 | 0 | 0 | |
| Dawson | 0 | 0 | 0 | 0 | |
| DeKalb | 0 | 0 | 0 | 0 | |
| Dougherty | 0 | 0 | 0 | 0 | |
| Dougherty County Police Department | 0 | 0 | 0 | 0 | |
| Douglas | 0 | 0 | 0 | 0 | |
| Echols | 0 | | | | |
| Effingham | 0 | 0 | 0 | 0 | |
| Floyd | 0 | 0 | 0 | 0 | |
| Glynn | 0 | 0 | 0 | 0 | |
| Haralson | 0 | 0 | 0 | 0 | |
| Harris | 0 | 0 | 0 | 0 | |
| Heard | 0 | 0 | 0 | 0 | |
| Henry | 0 | 0 | 0 | 0 | |
| Henry County Police Department | 0 | 0 | 0 | 0 | |
| Jasper | 0 | 0 | 0 | 0 | |
| Jones | 0 | 0 | 0 | 0 | |
| Lamar | 0 | 0 | 0 | 0 | |
| Lanier | 0 | 0 | 0 | 0 | |
| Lee | 0 | 0 | 0 | 0 | |
| Liberty | 0 | | | | |
| Long | 0 | 0 | 0 | 0 | |
| Madison | 0 | 0 | 0 | 0 | |
| Marion | 0 | 0 | 0 | 0 | |
| McDuffie | 0 | 0 | 0 | 0 | |
| Meriwether | 0 | 0 | 0 | 0 | |
| Monroe | 0 | 0 | 0 | 0 | |
| Murray | 0 | 0 | 0 | 0 | |
| Muscogee | 0 | 0 | | | |
| Oconee | 0 | 0 | 0 | 0 | |
| Peach | 0 | 0 | 0 | 0 | |
| Pickens | 0 | 0 | 0 | 0 | |
| Pike | 0 | 0 | 0 | 0 | |
| Talbot | 0 | | | | |
| Walton | 0 | 0 | 0 | 0 | |
| Worth | 0 | 0 | 0 | 0 | |
| **Nonmetropolitan Counties** | | | | | |
| Atkinson | 0 | 0 | 0 | 0 | |

**Table 95. Hate Crime Zero Data Submitted Per Quarter, by Federal Agency, State, and State Agency, 2021—Continued**

(Number.)

| Agency name | Zero data per quarter[1] | | | | Population[2] |
|---|---|---|---|---|---|
| | 1st quarter | 2nd quarter | 3rd quarter | 4th quarter | |
| Baldwin | 0 | 0 | 0 | 0 | |
| Banks | 0 | 0 | 0 | 0 | |
| Ben Hill | 0 | 0 | 0 | 0 | |
| Berrien | 0 | 0 | 0 | 0 | |
| Bleckley | 0 | 0 | 0 | 0 | |
| Camden | | | 0 | 0 | |
| Candler | 0 | 0 | 0 | 0 | |
| Chattooga | 0 | 0 | 0 | 0 | |
| Clay | 0 | 0 | 0 | 0 | |
| Clinch | 0 | 0 | 0 | 0 | |
| Coffee | 0 | 0 | 0 | 0 | |
| Cook | 0 | 0 | 0 | 0 | |
| Decatur | 0 | 0 | 0 | 0 | |
| Dodge | 0 | 0 | 0 | 0 | |
| Early | 0 | 0 | 0 | 0 | |
| Fannin | 0 | 0 | 0 | 0 | |
| Franklin | 0 | 0 | 0 | 0 | |
| Gilmer | 0 | 0 | 0 | 0 | |
| Glascock | 0 | 0 | 0 | 0 | |
| Grady | 0 | 0 | 0 | 0 | |
| Greene | 0 | 0 | 0 | 0 | |
| Habersham | 0 | 0 | 0 | 0 | |
| Hancock | 0 | 0 | 0 | 0 | |
| Hart | 0 | 0 | 0 | 0 | |
| Irwin | 0 | 0 | 0 | 0 | |
| Jackson | 0 | 0 | 0 | 0 | |
| Jeff Davis | 0 | 0 | 0 | 0 | |
| Jefferson | 0 | 0 | 0 | 0 | |
| Jenkins | 0 | 0 | 0 | 0 | |
| Laurens | 0 | 0 | 0 | 0 | |
| Mitchell | 0 | 0 | 0 | 0 | |
| Pierce | 0 | 0 | 0 | 0 | |
| Polk | 0 | 0 | 0 | 0 | |
| Polk County Police Department | 0 | 0 | 0 | | |
| Putnam | 0 | 0 | 0 | 0 | |
| Schley | 0 | 0 | 0 | 0 | |
| Seminole | 0 | 0 | 0 | 0 | |
| Sumter | 0 | 0 | 0 | 0 | |
| Taliaferro | 0 | 0 | 0 | | |
| Tattnall | 0 | 0 | 0 | 0 | |
| Thomas | 0 | 0 | 0 | 0 | |
| Tift | 0 | 0 | 0 | 0 | |
| Towns | 0 | 0 | 0 | 0 | |
| Treutlen | 0 | 0 | 0 | 0 | |
| Turner | 0 | 0 | 0 | 0 | |
| Ware | 0 | 0 | 0 | 0 | |
| Washington | 0 | 0 | 0 | 0 | |
| Webster | 0 | 0 | 0 | 0 | |
| Wheeler | 0 | 0 | 0 | 0 | |
| Wilcox | 0 | 0 | 0 | 0 | |
| Wilkes | 0 | 0 | 0 | 0 | |
| Wilkinson | 0 | 0 | 0 | 0 | |
| **Other Agencies** | | | | | |
| Albany-Dougherty Metropolitan Drug Squad | 0 | | | | |
| Atlanta Public Schools | 0 | 0 | 0 | 0 | |
| Augusta Board of Education | 0 | 0 | 0 | 0 | |
| Bibb County Board of Education | 0 | 0 | 0 | 0 | |
| Chatham County Board of Education | 0 | | | | |
| Cherokee County Marshal | 0 | 0 | 0 | 0 | |
| Decatur County Schools | 0 | 0 | 0 | 0 | |
| DeKalb County School System | 0 | 0 | 0 | 0 | |
| Dougherty County Board of Education | 0 | 0 | 0 | 0 | |
| Fayette County Marshal | 0 | 0 | 0 | 0 | |
| Forsyth County Fire Investigation Unit | 0 | 0 | 0 | 0 | |
| Fulton County Marshal | 0 | 0 | 0 | 0 | |
| Georgia Bureau of Investigation, Headquarters | | 0 | | | |
| Georgia Department of Transportation, Office of Investigations | 0 | 0 | 0 | 0 | |
| Georgia Forestry Commission | 0 | 0 | 0 | 0 | |
| Georgia Public Safety Training Center | 0 | 0 | 0 | 0 | |
| Georgia World Congress | 0 | 0 | 0 | 0 | |
| Glynn County School System | 0 | 0 | 0 | 0 | |
| Grady County Schools | 0 | 0 | 0 | 0 | |
| Gwinnett County Public Schools | 0 | 0 | 0 | 0 | |
| Hall County Marshal | 0 | 0 | 0 | 0 | |
| Hartsfield-Jackson Atlanta International Airport | | 0 | 0 | 0 | |
| Metropolitan Atlanta Rapid Transit Authority | 0 | 0 | 0 | 0 | |
| Muscogee County Schools | 0 | 0 | 0 | 0 | |
| Paulding County Marshal | 0 | 0 | 0 | 0 | |
| Ports Authority, Savannah | 0 | 0 | 0 | 0 | |
| Richmond County Marshal | 0 | 0 | 0 | 0 | |

## Table 95. Hate Crime Zero Data Submitted Per Quarter, by Federal Agency, State, and State Agency, 2021—Continued

(Number.)

| Agency name | Zero data per quarter[1] | | | | Population[2] |
|---|---|---|---|---|---|
| | 1st quarter | 2nd quarter | 3rd quarter | 4th quarter | |
| Roosevelt Institute Facility Police | 0 | 0 | 0 | 0 | |
| State Board of Workers Compensation Fraud Investigation Division | 0 | 0 | 0 | 0 | |
| Stone Mountain Park | 0 | 0 | | 0 | |
| Twiggs County Board of Education | | | | 0 | |
| Washington County Board of Education | 0 | 0 | 0 | 0 | |
| | | | | | |
| **IDAHO** | | | | | |
| **Cities** | | | | | |
| Aberdeen | 0 | 0 | 0 | | 1,991 |
| American Falls | 0 | 0 | 0 | 0 | 4,280 |
| Ashton | 0 | 0 | 0 | | 1,034 |
| Bellevue | 0 | 0 | 0 | 0 | 2,519 |
| Blackfoot | 0 | 0 | 0 | 0 | 12,026 |
| Bonners Ferry | 0 | 0 | 0 | 0 | 2,712 |
| Buhl | 0 | 0 | 0 | 0 | 4,560 |
| Caldwell | 0 | 0 | 0 | 0 | 62,306 |
| Challis | 0 | 0 | 0 | 0 | 1,063 |
| Cottonwood | 0 | 0 | 0 | 0 | 984 |
| Filer | 0 | 0 | 0 | 0 | 2,984 |
| Gooding | 0 | 0 | 0 | 0 | 3,537 |
| Grangeville | 0 | 0 | 0 | 0 | 3,272 |
| Hagerman | 0 | 0 | 0 | 0 | 932 |
| Hailey | 0 | 0 | 0 | 0 | 8,988 |
| Heyburn | 0 | 0 | 0 | 0 | 3,496 |
| Kellogg | 0 | | 0 | 0 | 2,130 |
| Kimberly | 0 | 0 | 0 | 0 | 4,257 |
| Lewiston | 0 | 0 | 0 | 0 | 33,153 |
| McCall | 0 | 0 | 0 | 0 | 3,847 |
| Meridian | 0 | 0 | 0 | 0 | 126,744 |
| Middleton | 0 | 0 | 0 | 0 | 9,359 |
| Montpelier | 0 | 0 | 0 | 0 | 2,523 |
| Mountain Home | 0 | 0 | 0 | 0 | 14,555 |
| Orofino | 0 | | | | 3,112 |
| Osburn | 0 | 0 | 0 | 0 | 1,571 |
| Parma | 0 | | | | 2,145 |
| Pinehurst | 0 | 0 | 0 | 0 | 1,621 |
| Ponderay | 0 | 0 | 0 | 0 | 1,195 |
| Post Falls | 0 | 0 | 0 | | 40,252 |
| Preston | 0 | 0 | 0 | 0 | 5,724 |
| Priest River | 0 | 0 | 0 | 0 | 1,950 |
| Rexburg | 0 | 0 | 0 | 0 | 30,105 |
| Rigby | 0 | 0 | 0 | 0 | 4,482 |
| Rupert | 0 | 0 | 0 | 0 | 5,981 |
| Salmon | 0 | 0 | 0 | | 3,185 |
| Sandpoint | 0 | 0 | 0 | 0 | 9,476 |
| Shelley | 0 | 0 | 0 | 0 | 4,674 |
| Soda Springs | 0 | 0 | 0 | 0 | 2,998 |
| Spirit Lake | 0 | 0 | 0 | 0 | 2,632 |
| St. Anthony | 0 | 0 | 0 | 0 | 3,601 |
| Sun Valley | 0 | 0 | 0 | 0 | 1,513 |
| Wendell | 0 | 0 | 0 | 0 | 2,795 |
| Wilder | 0 | 0 | 0 | | 1,843 |
| | | | | | |
| **Metropolitan Counties** | | | | | |
| Ada | 0 | 0 | 0 | 0 | |
| Bannock | 0 | 0 | 0 | 0 | |
| Boise | 0 | 0 | 0 | 0 | |
| Bonneville | 0 | 0 | 0 | 0 | |
| Butte | 0 | 0 | 0 | 0 | |
| Canyon | 0 | 0 | 0 | 0 | |
| Franklin | 0 | 0 | 0 | 0 | |
| Gem | 0 | 0 | 0 | 0 | |
| Jefferson | 0 | 0 | 0 | 0 | |
| Jerome | 0 | 0 | 0 | 0 | |
| Nez Perce | 0 | 0 | 0 | 0 | |
| Owyhee | 0 | 0 | 0 | 0 | |
| Power | 0 | 0 | 0 | 0 | |
| Twin Falls | 0 | | | | |
| | | | | | |
| **Nonmetropolitan Counties** | | | | | |
| Adams | 0 | 0 | 0 | 0 | |
| Bear Lake | 0 | 0 | 0 | 0 | |
| Benewah | 0 | 0 | 0 | 0 | |
| Bingham | 0 | 0 | 0 | 0 | |
| Bonner | 0 | 0 | 0 | 0 | |
| Boundary | 0 | 0 | 0 | 0 | |
| Camas | 0 | 0 | 0 | 0 | |
| Caribou | 0 | 0 | 0 | 0 | |
| Cassia | 0 | 0 | 0 | 0 | |
| Clark | 0 | 0 | | | |
| Clearwater | 0 | 0 | 0 | 0 | |

# Table 95. Hate Crime Zero Data Submitted Per Quarter, by Federal Agency, State, and State Agency, 2021—Continued

(Number.)

| Agency name | Zero data per quarter[1] | | | | Population[2] |
|---|---|---|---|---|---|
| | 1st quarter | 2nd quarter | 3rd quarter | 4th quarter | |
| Custer | 0 | 0 | 0 | 0 | |
| Elmore | 0 | 0 | 0 | 0 | |
| Fremont | 0 | 0 | 0 | 0 | |
| Gooding | 0 | 0 | 0 | | |
| Idaho | 0 | 0 | | | |
| Latah | 0 | 0 | | 0 | |
| Lemhi | 0 | | | | |
| Lewis | 0 | | 0 | 0 | |
| Lincoln | 0 | 0 | 0 | 0 | |
| Madison | 0 | 0 | 0 | 0 | |
| Minidoka | 0 | 0 | 0 | 0 | |
| Payette | 0 | 0 | 0 | 0 | |
| Shoshone | 0 | 0 | | | |
| Teton | 0 | 0 | | 0 | |
| Washington | 0 | 0 | | 0 | |
| **State Police Agencies** | | | | | |
| Idaho State Police | 0 | 0 | 0 | 0 | |
| **Tribal Agencies** | | | | | |
| Coeur d'Alene Tribal | 0 | 0 | 0 | 0 | |
| Kootenai Tribal | 0 | 0 | 0 | 0 | |
| **Other Agencies** | | | | | |
| Attorney General | 0 | 0 | 0 | 0 | |
| Idaho State Lottery Security Division | 0 | 0 | 0 | | |
| **ILLINOIS** | | | | | |
| **Cities** | | | | | |
| Albers | | | 0 | | 1,109 |
| Aledo | | 0 | 0 | 0 | 3,358 |
| Alsip | 0 | 0 | 0 | 0 | 18,405 |
| Altamont | 0 | 0 | 0 | 0 | 2,351 |
| Annawan | | | 0 | 0 | 839 |
| Arlington Heights | | | 0 | 0 | 73,876 |
| Arthur | 0 | | 0 | 0 | 2,183 |
| Assumption | | | 0 | 0 | 1,045 |
| Auburn | | | 0 | 0 | 4,569 |
| Barrington | 0 | 0 | 0 | 0 | 10,163 |
| Barrington Hills | 0 | 0 | 0 | 0 | 4,144 |
| Batavia | 0 | 0 | 0 | 0 | 26,460 |
| Beecher | | | 0 | 0 | 4,388 |
| Bellwood | | | 0 | 0 | 18,375 |
| Bethalto | 0 | 0 | 0 | 0 | 9,170 |
| Bethany | 0 | 0 | 0 | 0 | 1,197 |
| Blue Island | | 0 | 0 | 0 | 22,509 |
| Breese | 0 | | | | 4,547 |
| Buffalo Grove | | | | 0 | 40,026 |
| Burbank | 0 | 0 | 0 | 0 | 27,836 |
| Carlinville | | | | 0 | 5,395 |
| Carlyle | 0 | 0 | 0 | 0 | 3,133 |
| Catlin | | | | 0 | 1,885 |
| Champaign | 0 | 0 | 0 | 0 | 90,231 |
| Channahon | 0 | 0 | 0 | 0 | 13,494 |
| Chatham | 0 | 0 | 0 | 0 | 13,306 |
| Chenoa | | | 0 | 0 | 3,098 |
| Cherry Valley | 0 | 0 | 0 | 0 | 2,842 |
| Chicago | | 0 | 0 | 0 | 2,721,948 |
| Chicago Ridge | 0 | 0 | 0 | 0 | 13,722 |
| Cicero | 0 | 0 | 0 | 0 | 79,288 |
| Coal City | 0 | 0 | 0 | 0 | 5,317 |
| Coal Valley | 0 | 0 | 0 | 0 | 3,717 |
| Colchester | | | 0 | 0 | 1,261 |
| Colfax | | | 0 | 0 | 1,004 |
| Colona | 0 | 0 | 0 | 0 | 5,039 |
| Cortland | | | 0 | 0 | 4,403 |
| Coulterville | 0 | 0 | 0 | 0 | 874 |
| Cowden | 0 | 0 | 0 | 0 | 568 |
| Crestwood | | | 0 | 0 | 10,569 |
| Crete | | 0 | 0 | 0 | 7,906 |
| Decatur | | | 0 | 0 | 69,426 |
| Diamond | | | | 0 | 2,479 |
| Durand | 0 | 0 | 0 | 0 | 1,380 |
| Dwight | 0 | 0 | 0 | 0 | 3,958 |
| East Hazel Crest | 0 | 0 | 0 | 0 | 1,472 |
| East Moline | 0 | 0 | | | 20,392 |
| East Peoria | 0 | 0 | 0 | 0 | 22,235 |
| Elburn | | 0 | 0 | 0 | 6,150 |
| Elk Grove Village | | | | 0 | 31,698 |
| El Paso | 0 | | | | 2,689 |
| Elwood | 0 | 0 | 0 | 0 | 2,200 |

## Table 95. Hate Crime Zero Data Submitted Per Quarter, by Federal Agency, State, and State Agency, 2021—Continued

(Number.)

| Agency name | Zero data per quarter[1] | | | | Population[2] |
|---|---|---|---|---|---|
| | 1st quarter | 2nd quarter | 3rd quarter | 4th quarter | |
| Fairbury | | | | 0 | 3,576 |
| Fairmount | 0 | | | | 582 |
| Fairview | | | | 0 | 453 |
| Fairview Heights | 0 | 0 | 0 | 0 | 16,034 |
| Farmer City | 0 | 0 | 0 | 0 | 1,895 |
| Findlay | | | | 0 | 623 |
| Fithian | | | | 0 | 440 |
| Flossmoor | 0 | 0 | 0 | 0 | 8,979 |
| Forest Park | 0 | | | | 13,472 |
| Fox River Grove | | | 0 | 0 | 4,494 |
| Frankfort | | | 0 | 0 | 19,577 |
| Freeburg | | 0 | 0 | 0 | 4,206 |
| Fulton | 0 | 0 | 0 | 0 | 3,266 |
| Geneseo | | | 0 | 0 | 6,494 |
| Geneva | 0 | 0 | 0 | 0 | 21,680 |
| Genoa | 0 | 0 | 0 | | 5,258 |
| Germantown | 0 | 0 | 0 | | 1,271 |
| Gilberts | | | | 0 | 8,198 |
| Glen Carbon | 0 | 0 | 0 | 0 | 12,881 |
| Glencoe | 0 | 0 | 0 | 0 | 8,749 |
| Glenwood | 0 | 0 | 0 | 0 | 8,580 |
| Godley | | | 0 | 0 | 790 |
| Golf | | | 0 | 0 | 488 |
| Grand Ridge | | | | 0 | 515 |
| Granite City | 0 | 0 | 0 | 0 | 27,787 |
| Grayslake | 0 | 0 | 0 | 0 | 24,076 |
| Grayville | 0 | 0 | 0 | 0 | 1,532 |
| Greenfield | | 0 | 0 | 0 | 955 |
| Hampshire | 0 | 0 | 0 | 0 | 6,275 |
| Harrisburg | | | 0 | 0 | 8,345 |
| Harvard | 0 | 0 | 0 | 0 | 8,935 |
| Havana | | | 0 | 0 | 2,912 |
| Henning | | | | 0 | 231 |
| Henry | 0 | 0 | 0 | 0 | 2,208 |
| Heyworth | 0 | 0 | 0 | | 2,871 |
| Highland | 0 | | | | 10,022 |
| Hodgkins | | 0 | 0 | 0 | 1,974 |
| Hoffman Estates | | 0 | 0 | 0 | 50,353 |
| Homer Glen | | | 0 | 0 | 24,285 |
| Hoopeston | | | 0 | 0 | 4,901 |
| Hopedale | 0 | 0 | 0 | 0 | 811 |
| Hudson | 0 | 0 | 0 | 0 | 1,807 |
| Indianola | | | | 0 | 252 |
| Inverness | | 0 | 0 | 0 | 7,293 |
| Jacksonville | 0 | 0 | 0 | 0 | 18,398 |
| Jerseyville | | | 0 | 0 | 8,077 |
| Johnsburg | 0 | 0 | 0 | 0 | 6,298 |
| Joliet | 0 | 0 | 0 | 0 | 146,589 |
| Kenilworth | | | 0 | 0 | 2,436 |
| Kildeer | 0 | 0 | 0 | 0 | 4,002 |
| Kincaid | 0 | | | | 1,349 |
| Kingston | | 0 | | 0 | 1,160 |
| Kirkland | 0 | | | | 1,714 |
| Lacon | | 0 | 0 | 0 | 1,692 |
| La Grange | 0 | 0 | 0 | 0 | 15,253 |
| La Grange Park | 0 | 0 | 0 | 0 | 12,808 |
| Lake Forest | 0 | 0 | 0 | 0 | 19,378 |
| Lake in the Hills | 0 | 0 | 0 | 0 | 28,284 |
| Lakemoor | 0 | 0 | 0 | 0 | 5,896 |
| La Salle | | | | 0 | 8,825 |
| Lemont | 0 | 0 | 0 | 0 | 17,470 |
| Le Roy | | | 0 | 0 | 3,492 |
| Lincoln | 0 | 0 | 0 | 0 | 13,297 |
| Lindenhurst | 0 | 0 | 0 | 0 | 14,070 |
| Lockport | 0 | 0 | 0 | 0 | 25,986 |
| Loves Park | 0 | 0 | 0 | 0 | 23,323 |
| Lovington | 0 | 0 | 0 | 0 | 1,000 |
| Machesney Park | 0 | 0 | 0 | 0 | 22,598 |
| Mackinaw | 0 | 0 | 0 | 0 | 1,853 |
| Mahomet | | | 0 | 0 | 9,151 |
| Manhattan | | | 0 | 0 | 8,991 |
| Manito | 0 | 0 | 0 | 0 | 1,450 |
| Maple Park | 0 | 0 | 0 | | 1,392 |
| Mark | | | | 0 | 544 |
| Mascoutah | | | | 0 | 8,119 |
| Mason City | 0 | 0 | 0 | 0 | 2,064 |
| McHenry | 0 | 0 | 0 | 0 | 27,106 |
| Midlothian | 0 | 0 | 0 | 0 | 14,116 |
| Milan | 0 | 0 | 0 | 0 | 4,922 |
| Millstadt | 0 | 0 | 0 | 0 | 3,803 |
| Minier | | 0 | | | 1,173 |

# Table 95. Hate Crime Zero Data Submitted Per Quarter, by Federal Agency, State, and State Agency, 2021—Continued

(Number.)

| Agency name | Zero data per quarter[1] | | | | Population[2] |
|---|---|---|---|---|---|
| | 1st quarter | 2nd quarter | 3rd quarter | 4th quarter | |
| Mokena | | | | 0 | 20,194 |
| Moline | 0 | 0 | 0 | 0 | 40,832 |
| Monee | | | 0 | 0 | 5,019 |
| Morris | 0 | 0 | 0 | 0 | 15,321 |
| Morrison | | | 0 | 0 | 3,927 |
| Morton | 0 | 0 | 0 | 0 | 16,218 |
| Morton Grove | 0 | 0 | 0 | | 22,495 |
| Mount Pulaski | 0 | 0 | 0 | 0 | 1,438 |
| Mount Zion | 0 | 0 | 0 | 0 | 5,753 |
| Mundelein | 0 | 0 | 0 | 0 | 30,936 |
| Naperville | | | | 0 | 148,556 |
| New Athens | | 0 | 0 | 0 | 1,846 |
| New Lenox | | | 0 | 0 | 27,379 |
| Newman | | | | 0 | 833 |
| Niles | 0 | 0 | 0 | 0 | 28,493 |
| Northfield | 0 | 0 | 0 | 0 | 5,380 |
| Oak Lawn | 0 | | | | 54,147 |
| Oakwood | 0 | 0 | | 0 | 1,447 |
| O'Fallon | 0 | 0 | 0 | 0 | 29,688 |
| Orion | 0 | 0 | 0 | 0 | 1,767 |
| Oswego | 0 | 0 | 0 | 0 | 37,362 |
| Ottawa | | | | 0 | 18,017 |
| Palatine | | 0 | 0 | 0 | 66,655 |
| Palos Heights | 0 | 0 | 0 | 0 | 12,361 |
| Palos Hills | 0 | 0 | 0 | 0 | 16,813 |
| Paris | | 0 | | | 8,076 |
| Pecatonica | 0 | 0 | | 0 | 2,052 |
| Peotone | | | | 0 | 4,094 |
| Phoenix | | 0 | 0 | 0 | 1,875 |
| Pingree Grove | 0 | 0 | 0 | 0 | 10,801 |
| Pittsfield | 0 | 0 | 0 | 0 | 4,126 |
| Plainfield | 0 | 0 | 0 | 0 | 45,026 |
| Plano | | | 0 | 0 | 11,983 |
| Polo | 0 | 0 | 0 | 0 | 2,140 |
| Potomac | | | | 0 | 674 |
| Princeton | | 0 | 0 | 0 | 7,353 |
| Prophetstown | 0 | 0 | 0 | 0 | 1,904 |
| Prospect Heights | | 0 | 0 | 0 | 15,647 |
| Rantoul | 0 | 0 | 0 | 0 | 12,241 |
| River Forest | 0 | 0 | 0 | 0 | 10,647 |
| River Grove | 0 | 0 | 0 | 0 | 9,724 |
| Riverwoods | 0 | 0 | 0 | 0 | 3,520 |
| Rochester | 0 | 0 | 0 | 0 | 3,714 |
| Rockford | 0 | 0 | 0 | 0 | 144,027 |
| Rockton | 0 | 0 | 0 | 0 | 7,448 |
| Rolling Meadows | | | | 0 | 23,162 |
| Romeoville | 0 | 0 | 0 | 0 | 39,777 |
| Roscoe | 0 | 0 | 0 | 0 | 10,368 |
| Rossville | 0 | 0 | | | 1,189 |
| Roxana | | | | 0 | 1,395 |
| Ruma | 0 | 0 | | 0 | 298 |
| Salem | 0 | 0 | 0 | 0 | 6,904 |
| Sandwich | 0 | 0 | 0 | 0 | 7,381 |
| Shiloh | 0 | 0 | 0 | 0 | 13,760 |
| Shorewood | 0 | 0 | 0 | 0 | 17,685 |
| Sidell | | | | 0 | 551 |
| Silvis | 0 | 0 | 0 | 0 | 7,467 |
| South Barrington | | | 0 | 0 | 5,017 |
| South Chicago Heights | 0 | 0 | 0 | 0 | 3,939 |
| Spring Valley | | | 0 | 0 | 5,020 |
| Steger | | | | 0 | 9,068 |
| Stickney | 0 | 0 | 0 | 0 | 6,462 |
| Streamwood | | | 0 | 0 | 38,666 |
| Streator | | | 0 | 0 | 12,833 |
| Swansea | 0 | 0 | 0 | 0 | 13,245 |
| Sycamore | 0 | 0 | 0 | 0 | 18,399 |
| Thornton | | | 0 | 0 | 2,365 |
| Tilton | 0 | 0 | 0 | | 2,649 |
| Tinley Park | 0 | 0 | 0 | 0 | 55,058 |
| Tolono | 0 | 0 | 0 | 0 | 3,337 |
| Toluca | 0 | 0 | 0 | 0 | 1,234 |
| Trenton | 0 | 0 | 0 | 0 | 2,551 |
| Troy | 0 | 0 | 0 | 0 | 10,447 |
| Tuscola | | | 0 | 0 | 4,359 |
| Union | | | | 0 | 545 |
| University Park | | | 0 | 0 | 6,787 |
| Urbana | 0 | 0 | 0 | 0 | 41,673 |
| Valmeyer | 0 | 0 | 0 | 0 | 1,237 |
| Villa Park | | 0 | 0 | 0 | 21,217 |
| Virden | | | 0 | 0 | 3,280 |
| Watseka | | | 0 | 0 | 4,639 |

## Table 95. Hate Crime Zero Data Submitted Per Quarter, by Federal Agency, State, and State Agency, 2021—Continued

(Number.)

| Agency name | Zero data per quarter[1] | | | | Population[2] |
|---|---|---|---|---|---|
| | 1st quarter | 2nd quarter | 3rd quarter | 4th quarter | |
| Wauconda | 0 | 0 | 0 | 0 | 13,410 |
| Wayne | | 0 | 0 | 0 | 2,443 |
| West Dundee | 0 | 0 | 0 | 0 | 8,938 |
| Westville | 0 | 0 | | | 2,886 |
| Wheeling | 0 | 0 | 0 | 0 | 39,087 |
| Willow Springs | 0 | 0 | 0 | 0 | 5,543 |
| Wilmette | 0 | 0 | 0 | 0 | 26,793 |
| Wilmington | | 0 | 0 | 0 | 5,579 |
| Winfield | 0 | 0 | 0 | 0 | 9,625 |
| Winnebago | 0 | 0 | 0 | 0 | 2,957 |
| Winnetka | | 0 | 0 | 0 | 12,192 |
| Woodstock | | 0 | 0 | 0 | 25,122 |
| **Universities and Colleges** | | | | | |
| Chicago State University | | | | 0 | 3,595 |
| Elgin Community College | | 0 | | 0 | 14,467 |
| Harper College | | | 0 | | 23,552 |
| Illinois Central College | 0 | 0 | 0 | 0 | 12,302 |
| Illinois State University | 0 | 0 | 0 | 0 | 23,141 |
| John Wood Community College | | | | 0 | 2,696 |
| Joliet Junior College | | | | 0 | 22,871 |
| Lewis University | 0 | 0 | 0 | 0 | 7,612 |
| McHenry County College | 0 | 0 | 0 | 0 | 11,434 |
| Millikin University | 0 | 0 | 0 | 0 | 2,333 |
| Morton College | 0 | 0 | 0 | 0 | 6,682 |
| Northeastern Illinois University | | | | 0 | 9,191 |
| Oakton Community College | | | 0 | 0 | 17,064 |
| Rock Valley College | | | 0 | 0 | 9,801 |
| Southern Illinois University Carbondale | 0 | | | | 13,129 |
| School of Medicine[3] | | | | 0 | |
| Southwestern Illinois College | 0 | 0 | 0 | 0 | 15,048 |
| University of Chicago, Cook County | 0 | 0 | 0 | 0 | 20,413 |
| Waubonsee Community College | | | 0 | 0 | 15,423 |
| **Metropolitan Counties** | | | | | |
| Champaign | 0 | 0 | 0 | 0 | |
| Clinton | 0 | 0 | 0 | 0 | |
| DeKalb | 0 | 0 | 0 | | |
| Henry | 0 | 0 | 0 | 0 | |
| Jersey | 0 | 0 | 0 | 0 | |
| Macon | 0 | 0 | 0 | 0 | |
| Marshall | | 0 | 0 | 0 | |
| McLean | 0 | 0 | 0 | 0 | |
| Monroe | | 0 | 0 | 0 | |
| Rock Island | 0 | 0 | 0 | 0 | |
| Tazewell | 0 | 0 | 0 | 0 | |
| Vermilion | 0 | 0 | | | |
| **Nonmetropolitan Counties** | | | | | |
| Cass | 0 | 0 | 0 | | |
| Christian | 0 | 0 | | | |
| Fayette | | | 0 | 0 | |
| Iroquois | 0 | 0 | 0 | 0 | |
| Jefferson | | | | 0 | |
| Logan | 0 | 0 | | | |
| Marion | 0 | 0 | 0 | 0 | |
| Mason | 0 | 0 | | 0 | |
| Massac | | 0 | 0 | 0 | |
| Pulaski | 0 | 0 | 0 | 0 | |
| Putnam | | | 0 | 0 | |
| **Other Agencies** | | | | | |
| Belt Railway | | | | 0 | |
| Canton Park District | | | | 0 | |
| Pekin Park District | 0 | 0 | 0 | 0 | |
| Rockford Park District | 0 | 0 | 0 | 0 | |
| Terminal Railroad Association | | | | 0 | |
| Tri-County Drug Enforcement Narcotics Team | 0 | 0 | 0 | 0 | |
| Will County Forest Preserve | | | | 0 | |
| **INDIANA** | | | | | |
| **Cities** | | | | | |
| Albion | 0 | 0 | 0 | 0 | 2,372 |
| Amo | | 0 | 0 | 0 | 435 |
| Angola | 0 | 0 | 0 | 0 | 8,851 |
| Arcadia | 0 | 0 | 0 | 0 | 1,647 |
| Argos | 0 | | | | 1,612 |
| Auburn | 0 | 0 | 0 | 0 | 13,700 |
| Avon | 0 | 0 | 0 | 0 | 20,055 |
| Bargersville | 0 | 0 | 0 | 0 | 8,933 |

## Table 95. Hate Crime Zero Data Submitted Per Quarter, by Federal Agency, State, and State Agency, 2021—Continued

(Number.)

| Agency name | Zero data per quarter[1] | | | | Population[2] |
|---|---|---|---|---|---|
| | 1st quarter | 2nd quarter | 3rd quarter | 4th quarter | |
| Batesville | 0 | 0 | 0 | 0 | 6,773 |
| Bedford | 0 | 0 | 0 | 0 | 13,217 |
| Beech Grove | 0 | 0 | 0 | 0 | 14,966 |
| Bluffton | 0 | 0 | 0 | 0 | 10,113 |
| Brookville | 0 | 0 | 0 | 0 | 2,522 |
| Burlington | 0 | 0 | 0 | 0 | 604 |
| Butler | 0 | 0 | 0 | 0 | 2,723 |
| Carmel | 0 | 0 | 0 | 0 | 103,540 |
| Charlestown | 0 | 0 | 0 | 0 | 8,645 |
| Cicero | 0 | 0 | 0 | 0 | 5,016 |
| Claypool | 0 | 0 | 0 | 0 | 430 |
| Clayton | | 0 | | | 1,043 |
| Clear Lake | 0 | 0 | 0 | 0 | 346 |
| Columbia City | 0 | 0 | 0 | 0 | 9,479 |
| Danville | 0 | 0 | 0 | 0 | 10,364 |
| Dayton | 0 | | 0 | | 1,694 |
| Dyer | 0 | 0 | 0 | 0 | 15,914 |
| Edinburgh | 0 | 0 | 0 | 0 | 4,629 |
| Fortville | 0 | | | | 4,251 |
| Frankfort | 0 | 0 | 0 | 0 | 15,692 |
| Fremont | 0 | 0 | 0 | 0 | 2,211 |
| Gaston | | 0 | 0 | 0 | 870 |
| Goshen | 0 | 0 | 0 | 0 | 34,336 |
| Greenfield | 0 | 0 | 0 | 0 | 23,650 |
| Greenwood | 0 | 0 | 0 | 0 | 61,277 |
| Hartford City | 0 | 0 | 0 | 0 | 5,620 |
| Highland | 0 | 0 | 0 | 0 | 22,144 |
| Hobart | 0 | 0 | 0 | 0 | 27,777 |
| Huntingburg | 0 | 0 | 0 | | 6,321 |
| Huntington | 0 | 0 | 0 | 0 | 17,006 |
| Jasper | 0 | 0 | 0 | 0 | 15,720 |
| Jeffersonville | 0 | 0 | 0 | 0 | 48,882 |
| Kendallville | 0 | 0 | 0 | 0 | 9,895 |
| Knightsville | 0 | 0 | | | 767 |
| Knox | 0 | 0 | 0 | 0 | 3,538 |
| La Porte | 0 | 0 | 0 | 0 | 21,391 |
| Lawrenceburg | 0 | 0 | 0 | | 5,045 |
| Leavenworth | 0 | 0 | 0 | | 234 |
| Lebanon | 0 | 0 | 0 | 0 | 16,155 |
| Linton | 0 | 0 | 0 | 0 | 5,286 |
| Logansport | 0 | 0 | 0 | 0 | 17,371 |
| Loogootee | 0 | 0 | 0 | 0 | 2,657 |
| Lowell | 0 | 0 | 0 | 0 | 10,223 |
| Markle | 0 | | | | 1,090 |
| McCordsville | 0 | 0 | 0 | 0 | 8,078 |
| Merrillville | 0 | 0 | | | 34,912 |
| Muncie | 0 | 0 | 0 | 0 | 67,262 |
| Munster | 0 | 0 | 0 | 0 | 22,377 |
| Nappanee | 0 | 0 | 0 | 0 | 6,864 |
| New Haven | 0 | 0 | 0 | 0 | 16,088 |
| New Palestine | 0 | 0 | | 0 | 2,718 |
| New Whiteland | 0 | 0 | 0 | 0 | 6,443 |
| Noblesville | 0 | 0 | 0 | 0 | 67,290 |
| North Vernon | 0 | 0 | 0 | 0 | 6,594 |
| North Webster | 0 | 0 | 0 | 0 | 1,162 |
| Ogden Dunes | 0 | 0 | 0 | 0 | 1,080 |
| Osceola | 0 | 0 | 0 | 0 | 2,488 |
| Pendleton | | | 0 | 0 | 4,459 |
| Pittsboro | 0 | 0 | 0 | 0 | 3,913 |
| Portage | 0 | 0 | 0 | 0 | 37,166 |
| Porter | 0 | 0 | 0 | 0 | 4,839 |
| Remington | 0 | 0 | | | 1,134 |
| Rockport | 0 | 0 | 0 | 0 | 2,123 |
| Roseland | 0 | 0 | 0 | 0 | 635 |
| Santa Claus | 0 | 0 | 0 | | 2,397 |
| Schererville | 0 | 0 | 0 | 0 | 28,533 |
| Sellersburg | 0 | 0 | 0 | 0 | 9,120 |
| Seymour | 0 | 0 | 0 | 0 | 20,302 |
| Shelburn | 0 | 0 | 0 | | 1,219 |
| Shelbyville | 0 | 0 | 0 | 0 | 19,557 |
| Shirley | 0 | 0 | 0 | | 911 |
| Silver Lake | 0 | 0 | 0 | 0 | 916 |
| Speedway | 0 | 0 | 0 | 0 | 12,264 |
| St. John | 0 | 0 | 0 | 0 | 20,168 |
| Syracuse | 0 | 0 | 0 | 0 | 2,856 |
| Trafalgar | 0 | 0 | 0 | 0 | 1,465 |
| Utica | | | 0 | 0 | 1,022 |
| Valparaiso | 0 | 0 | 0 | 0 | 34,167 |
| Vevay | 0 | | | | 1,637 |
| Walkerton | 0 | 0 | 0 | 0 | 2,261 |
| West Lafayette | 0 | 0 | 0 | 0 | 52,675 |

## Table 95. Hate Crime Zero Data Submitted Per Quarter, by Federal Agency, State, and State Agency, 2021—Continued

(Number.)

| Agency name | Zero data per quarter[1] | | | | Population[2] |
|---|---|---|---|---|---|
| | 1st quarter | 2nd quarter | 3rd quarter | 4th quarter | |
| Westville | 0 | | | | 5,840 |
| Whiteland | 0 | 0 | 0 | 0 | 4,753 |
| Whiting | 0 | 0 | 0 | 0 | 4,797 |
| Winona Lake | 0 | 0 | 0 | 0 | 4,888 |
| Zionsville | 0 | 0 | 0 | 0 | 29,876 |
| **Universities and Colleges** | | | | | |
| Indiana State University | 0 | 0 | 0 | 0 | 13,990 |
| Indiana University | | | | | |
| Bloomington | 0 | 0 | | | 46,441 |
| Columbus[3] | 0 | | | 0 | |
| East | | | 0 | | 5,451 |
| Evansville[3] | 0 | | | | |
| Kokomo | 0 | | 0 | | 3,748 |
| Northwest | 0 | | | | 4,858 |
| South Bend | 0 | | | | 5,943 |
| Southeast | | | 0 | | 5,985 |
| Marian University | 0 | 0 | 0 | 0 | 5,140 |
| Purdue University, Fort Wayne | 0 | 0 | 0 | 0 | 11,730 |
| University of Indianapolis | 0 | 0 | 0 | 0 | 6,320 |
| **Metropolitan Counties** | | | | | |
| Allen | 0 | 0 | 0 | 0 | |
| Bartholomew | 0 | 0 | 0 | 0 | |
| Clark | 0 | 0 | 0 | 0 | |
| Delaware | 0 | 0 | 0 | 0 | |
| Elkhart | 0 | 0 | 0 | 0 | |
| Hancock | 0 | 0 | 0 | 0 | |
| Harrison | 0 | 0 | 0 | 0 | |
| Hendricks | 0 | 0 | 0 | 0 | |
| Lake | 0 | 0 | 0 | | |
| La Porte | 0 | 0 | 0 | 0 | |
| Monroe | 0 | 0 | 0 | 0 | |
| Putnam | 0 | 0 | 0 | | |
| Vigo | 0 | 0 | 0 | 0 | |
| Washington | 0 | 0 | 0 | 0 | |
| **Nonmetropolitan Counties** | | | | | |
| Clinton | 0 | 0 | 0 | 0 | |
| Dubois | 0 | 0 | 0 | 0 | |
| Fulton | 0 | 0 | 0 | 0 | |
| Gibson | 0 | 0 | 0 | 0 | |
| Greene | 0 | 0 | 0 | 0 | |
| Jennings | 0 | 0 | 0 | 0 | |
| Miami | 0 | 0 | | | |
| Noble | 0 | 0 | 0 | 0 | |
| Pulaski | 0 | | | | |
| Starke | 0 | 0 | 0 | 0 | |
| Steuben | 0 | 0 | 0 | 0 | |
| **Other Agencies** | | | | | |
| Brownsburg Community School | 0 | 0 | 0 | 0 | |
| Hulman Regional Airport Authority | 0 | | | | |
| Indiana Gaming Commission | 0 | 0 | 0 | 0 | |
| Indiana Harbor Belt Railroad | 0 | 0 | | | |
| Indiana Office of Inspector General | | 0 | | | |
| Indianapolis International Airport | 0 | 0 | 0 | 0 | |
| Indiana State Excise Police | 0 | 0 | 0 | 0 | |
| Prairie Heights Community Schools Corporation | 0 | 0 | | | |
| Secretary of State, Securities Division | 0 | | | | |
| **IOWA** | | | | | |
| **Cities** | | | | | |
| Adel | 0 | 0 | 0 | 0 | 5,845 |
| Algona | 0 | 0 | 0 | 0 | 5,340 |
| Altoona | 0 | 0 | 0 | 0 | 20,064 |
| Ames | 0 | 0 | 0 | 0 | 67,886 |
| Ankeny | 0 | 0 | 0 | 0 | 73,109 |
| Asbury | 0 | 0 | 0 | 0 | 5,999 |
| Atlantic | 0 | 0 | 0 | 0 | 6,457 |
| Audubon | 0 | 0 | 0 | 0 | 1,852 |
| Belle Plaine | 0 | 0 | 0 | 0 | 2,406 |
| Bloomfield | 0 | 0 | 0 | 0 | 2,699 |
| Blue Grass | 0 | 0 | 0 | 0 | 1,682 |
| Buffalo | 0 | 0 | 0 | 0 | 1,256 |
| Burlington | 0 | 0 | 0 | 0 | 24,417 |
| Camanche | 0 | 0 | 0 | 0 | 4,360 |
| Carlisle | 0 | 0 | 0 | | 4,369 |
| Carroll | 0 | 0 | 0 | 0 | 9,651 |
| Carter Lake | 0 | 0 | 0 | 0 | 3,793 |
| Cedar Falls | 0 | 0 | 0 | 0 | 40,321 |

# Table 95. Hate Crime Zero Data Submitted Per Quarter, by Federal Agency, State, and State Agency, 2021—Continued

(Number.)

| Agency name | Zero data per quarter[1] | | | | Population[2] |
|---|---|---|---|---|---|
| | 1st quarter | 2nd quarter | 3rd quarter | 4th quarter | |
| Centerville | 0 | 0 | 0 | 0 | 5,394 |
| Cherokee | 0 | 0 | 0 | 0 | 4,800 |
| Clarinda | 0 | 0 | 0 | 0 | 5,346 |
| Clarion | 0 | 0 | 0 | 0 | 2,662 |
| Creston | 0 | 0 | 0 | 0 | 7,644 |
| Decorah | 0 | 0 | 0 | 0 | 7,422 |
| Denison | 0 | 0 | 0 | 0 | 8,241 |
| Des Moines | 0 | 0 | 0 | 0 | 213,060 |
| DeWitt | 0 | 0 | 0 | 0 | 5,212 |
| Durant | 0 | 0 | 0 | 0 | 1,856 |
| Dyersville | 0 | 0 | 0 | 0 | 4,478 |
| Dysart | 0 | 0 | 0 | 0 | 1,305 |
| Eldridge | 0 | 0 | 0 | 0 | 6,998 |
| Emmetsburg | 0 | 0 | 0 | 0 | 3,645 |
| Estherville | 0 | 0 | 0 | 0 | 5,516 |
| Evansdale | 0 | 0 | 0 | 0 | 4,732 |
| Fairfield | 0 | 0 | 0 | 0 | 10,608 |
| Fort Madison | 0 | 0 | 0 | 0 | 10,185 |
| Glenwood | 0 | 0 | 0 | 0 | 5,260 |
| Grundy Center | 0 | 0 | 0 | 0 | 2,666 |
| Harlan | 0 | 0 | 0 | 0 | 4,767 |
| Hiawatha | 0 | 0 | 0 | 0 | 7,512 |
| Huxley | 0 | 0 | 0 | 0 | 4,379 |
| Independence | 0 | 0 | 0 | 0 | 6,227 |
| Iowa Falls | 0 | 0 | 0 | | 4,907 |
| Johnston | 0 | 0 | 0 | 0 | 23,759 |
| Keokuk | 0 | 0 | 0 | 0 | 10,025 |
| Lansing | 0 | 0 | 0 | 0 | 926 |
| Le Claire | 0 | 0 | 0 | 0 | 3,977 |
| Le Mars | 0 | 0 | 0 | 0 | 10,233 |
| Leon | 0 | | | | 1,793 |
| Manchester | 0 | 0 | 0 | 0 | 4,987 |
| Maquoketa | 0 | 0 | 0 | 0 | 5,894 |
| Marion | 0 | 0 | 0 | 0 | 41,370 |
| Mar-Mac | 0 | 0 | 0 | 0 | 1,268 |
| Marshalltown | 0 | 0 | 0 | 0 | 26,651 |
| Mechanicsville | 0 | 0 | 0 | 0 | 1,113 |
| Monticello | 0 | 0 | 0 | 0 | 3,882 |
| Mount Pleasant | 0 | 0 | 0 | 0 | 8,494 |
| Mount Vernon-Lisbon | 0 | 0 | 0 | 0 | 6,794 |
| Newton | 0 | 0 | 0 | 0 | 15,116 |
| North Liberty | 0 | 0 | 0 | 0 | 20,482 |
| Norwalk | 0 | 0 | | | 12,854 |
| Osage | 0 | 0 | 0 | 0 | 3,541 |
| Osceola | 0 | 0 | 0 | 0 | 5,320 |
| Oskaloosa | 0 | 0 | 0 | 0 | 11,832 |
| Pleasant Hill | 0 | 0 | 0 | 0 | 10,153 |
| Polk City | 0 | 0 | 0 | 0 | 5,350 |
| Postville | 0 | 0 | | 0 | 2,014 |
| Prairie City | 0 | 0 | 0 | | 1,725 |
| Preston | 0 | 0 | 0 | | 935 |
| Rock Valley | 0 | 0 | 0 | 0 | 3,945 |
| Sabula | | 0 | 0 | 0 | 541 |
| Sheldon | 0 | 0 | 0 | 0 | 5,058 |
| Shenandoah | 0 | 0 | 0 | 0 | 4,749 |
| Sigourney | 0 | 0 | 0 | 0 | 1,972 |
| Sioux Center | 0 | 0 | 0 | 0 | 7,729 |
| Sioux City | 0 | 0 | 0 | 0 | 82,750 |
| Spencer | 0 | 0 | 0 | 0 | 10,966 |
| Spirit Lake | 0 | 0 | 0 | 0 | 5,292 |
| Story City | 0 | 0 | 0 | 0 | 3,320 |
| Tipton | 0 | 0 | 0 | 0 | 3,174 |
| Urbandale | 0 | 0 | 0 | 0 | 45,201 |
| Vinton | 0 | 0 | 0 | 0 | 4,996 |
| Washington | 0 | 0 | 0 | 0 | 7,201 |
| Waukon | 0 | 0 | 0 | 0 | 3,570 |
| Waverly | 0 | 0 | 0 | 0 | 10,340 |
| Webster City | 0 | 0 | 0 | 0 | 7,608 |
| West Branch | 0 | 0 | 0 | 0 | 2,539 |
| West Burlington | 0 | 0 | 0 | 0 | 2,863 |
| Williamsburg | 0 | 0 | 0 | 0 | 3,191 |
| Windsor Heights | 0 | 0 | 0 | 0 | 4,717 |
| **Universities and Colleges** | | | | | |
| Iowa State University | 0 | 0 | 0 | 0 | 35,319 |
| University of Iowa | 0 | 0 | 0 | 0 | 34,495 |
| University of Northern Iowa | 0 | 0 | 0 | 0 | 12,137 |
| **Metropolitan Counties** | | | | | |
| Black Hawk | 0 | 0 | 0 | 0 | |
| Bremer | 0 | 0 | 0 | | |

## Table 95. Hate Crime Zero Data Submitted Per Quarter, by Federal Agency, State, and State Agency, 2021—Continued

(Number.)

| Agency name | Zero data per quarter[1] | | | | Population[2] |
|---|---|---|---|---|---|
| | 1st quarter | 2nd quarter | 3rd quarter | 4th quarter | |
| Dallas | 0 | 0 | 0 | 0 | |
| Dubuque | 0 | 0 | 0 | 0 | |
| Grundy | 0 | 0 | 0 | 0 | |
| Jasper | 0 | 0 | 0 | 0 | |
| Jones | 0 | 0 | 0 | 0 | |
| Linn | 0 | 0 | 0 | 0 | |
| Mills | 0 | 0 | 0 | 0 | |
| Polk | 0 | 0 | 0 | 0 | |
| Pottawattamie | 0 | 0 | 0 | 0 | |
| Scott | 0 | 0 | 0 | 0 | |
| Story | 0 | 0 | 0 | 0 | |
| Warren | 0 | 0 | 0 | 0 | |
| Washington | 0 | 0 | 0 | 0 | |
| Woodbury | 0 | 0 | 0 | 0 | |
| **Nonmetropolitan Counties** | | | | | |
| Adair | 0 | | 0 | 0 | |
| Adams | 0 | 0 | 0 | 0 | |
| Allamakee | 0 | 0 | 0 | 0 | |
| Appanoose | 0 | 0 | 0 | 0 | |
| Buchanan | 0 | 0 | 0 | 0 | |
| Buena Vista | 0 | 0 | 0 | 0 | |
| Butler | 0 | 0 | 0 | 0 | |
| Carroll | 0 | 0 | 0 | 0 | |
| Cass | 0 | 0 | 0 | 0 | |
| Cedar | 0 | 0 | 0 | 0 | |
| Cerro Gordo | 0 | 0 | 0 | 0 | |
| Cherokee | 0 | 0 | 0 | 0 | |
| Chickasaw | 0 | 0 | 0 | 0 | |
| Clay | 0 | 0 | 0 | 0 | |
| Crawford | 0 | 0 | 0 | 0 | |
| Davis | 0 | 0 | 0 | 0 | |
| Delaware | 0 | 0 | 0 | 0 | |
| Des Moines | 0 | 0 | 0 | 0 | |
| Emmet | 0 | 0 | 0 | 0 | |
| Fayette | 0 | 0 | 0 | 0 | |
| Fremont | 0 | 0 | 0 | 0 | |
| Hancock | 0 | 0 | 0 | 0 | |
| Hardin | 0 | 0 | 0 | 0 | |
| Howard | 0 | 0 | 0 | 0 | |
| Humboldt | 0 | 0 | 0 | 0 | |
| Iowa | 0 | 0 | 0 | 0 | |
| Jackson | 0 | 0 | 0 | 0 | |
| Jefferson | 0 | 0 | 0 | 0 | |
| Keokuk | 0 | 0 | 0 | 0 | |
| Kossuth | 0 | 0 | 0 | 0 | |
| Lee | 0 | 0 | 0 | 0 | |
| Lucas | 0 | 0 | 0 | 0 | |
| Lyon | 0 | 0 | 0 | 0 | |
| Mahaska | 0 | 0 | 0 | 0 | |
| Marion | 0 | 0 | 0 | 0 | |
| Mitchell | 0 | 0 | 0 | 0 | |
| Monona | 0 | 0 | 0 | 0 | |
| Monroe | 0 | 0 | 0 | 0 | |
| O'Brien | 0 | 0 | 0 | 0 | |
| Osceola | 0 | 0 | 0 | 0 | |
| Palo Alto | 0 | 0 | 0 | 0 | |
| Plymouth | 0 | 0 | 0 | 0 | |
| Poweshiek | 0 | 0 | 0 | 0 | |
| Ringgold | 0 | 0 | 0 | 0 | |
| Sac | 0 | 0 | 0 | 0 | |
| Sioux | 0 | 0 | 0 | 0 | |
| Tama | 0 | 0 | 0 | 0 | |
| Union | 0 | 0 | 0 | 0 | |
| Van Buren | 0 | 0 | 0 | 0 | |
| Webster | 0 | 0 | 0 | 0 | |
| Wright | 0 | 0 | 0 | 0 | |
| **Other Agencies** | | | | | |
| Eastern Iowa Airport Public Safety | 0 | | 0 | 0 | |
| Southeast Iowa Interagency Drug Task Force | 0 | 0 | 0 | 0 | |
| **KANSAS** | | | | | |
| **Cities** | | | | | |
| Abilene | 0 | 0 | 0 | 0 | 6,055 |
| Alma | | 0 | 0 | | 771 |
| Americus | | 0 | | 0 | 870 |
| Andover | 0 | 0 | 0 | | 13,871 |
| Anthony | 0 | 0 | 0 | 0 | 2,011 |
| Arkansas City | 0 | 0 | 0 | 0 | 11,531 |
| Arma | 0 | 0 | 0 | 0 | 1,405 |

## Table 95. Hate Crime Zero Data Submitted Per Quarter, by Federal Agency, State, and State Agency, 2021—Continued

(Number.)

| Agency name | Zero data per quarter[1] | | | | Population[2] |
|---|---|---|---|---|---|
| | 1st quarter | 2nd quarter | 3rd quarter | 4th quarter | |
| Attica | 0 | 0 | 0 | 0 | 540 |
| Atwood | 0 | 0 | 0 | 0 | 1,210 |
| Augusta | 0 | 0 | 0 | 0 | 9,290 |
| Baldwin City | 0 | 0 | 0 | 0 | 4,706 |
| Basehor | 0 | 0 | 0 | 0 | 6,898 |
| Belle Plaine | 0 | 0 | 0 | | 1,522 |
| Belleville | 0 | 0 | 0 | 0 | 1,828 |
| Beloit | 0 | 0 | 0 | 0 | 3,540 |
| Benton | 0 | 0 | 0 | 0 | 863 |
| Blue Rapids | 0 | 0 | 0 | 0 | 954 |
| Bucklin | 0 | | | | 749 |
| Buhler | 0 | 0 | 0 | 0 | 1,263 |
| Burlington | 0 | 0 | 0 | 0 | 2,533 |
| Caldwell | 0 | 0 | 0 | 0 | 963 |
| Caney | 0 | 0 | 0 | 0 | 1,924 |
| Canton | 0 | | | | 682 |
| Carbondale | 0 | 0 | 0 | 0 | 1,339 |
| Cedar Vale | | | | 0 | 496 |
| Chanute | | 0 | 0 | | 8,979 |
| Chapman | | | 0 | | 1,314 |
| Cheney | 0 | 0 | 0 | 0 | 2,180 |
| Cherokee | 0 | | | | 712 |
| Cherryvale | 0 | 0 | 0 | 0 | 2,098 |
| Claflin | 0 | 0 | | | 589 |
| Clay Center | 0 | 0 | 0 | 0 | 3,957 |
| Clearwater | 0 | 0 | 0 | 0 | 2,589 |
| Colby | 0 | 0 | 0 | 0 | 5,305 |
| Coldwater | 0 | 0 | 0 | 0 | 725 |
| Colony | 0 | | 0 | | 425 |
| Columbus | 0 | 0 | 0 | 0 | 2,978 |
| Colwich | 0 | 0 | 0 | 0 | 1,509 |
| Concordia | 0 | 0 | 0 | 0 | 4,860 |
| Conway Springs | 0 | 0 | 0 | 0 | 1,208 |
| Council Grove | 0 | 0 | 0 | 0 | 2,090 |
| Edwardsville | 0 | 0 | 0 | 0 | 4,540 |
| El Dorado | 0 | 0 | 0 | 0 | 12,819 |
| Elkhart | 0 | 0 | 0 | 0 | 1,685 |
| Ellinwood | 0 | 0 | 0 | 0 | 1,913 |
| Ellis | 0 | 0 | 0 | 0 | 2,013 |
| Ellsworth | 0 | 0 | 0 | 0 | 2,917 |
| Emporia | 0 | 0 | 0 | 0 | 24,462 |
| Eudora | 0 | 0 | 0 | 0 | 6,418 |
| Fairway | 0 | 0 | 0 | 0 | 3,972 |
| Fredonia | | | | 0 | 2,154 |
| Frontenac | 0 | 0 | 0 | 0 | 3,387 |
| Galena | 0 | 0 | 0 | 0 | 2,798 |
| Garden Plain | 0 | 0 | 0 | 0 | 919 |
| Girard | 0 | 0 | 0 | 0 | 2,644 |
| Grandview Plaza | 0 | 0 | 0 | 0 | 1,532 |
| Greensburg | 0 | 0 | 0 | 0 | 777 |
| Halstead | 0 | 0 | 0 | 0 | 2,022 |
| Haysville | 0 | 0 | 0 | 0 | 11,445 |
| Hesston | 0 | 0 | 0 | 0 | 3,738 |
| Hiawatha | 0 | 0 | 0 | 0 | 3,075 |
| Highland | 0 | 0 | 0 | 0 | 983 |
| Hill City | 0 | 0 | 0 | 0 | 1,343 |
| Hillsboro | 0 | 0 | 0 | 0 | 2,739 |
| Holton | 0 | 0 | 0 | 0 | 3,193 |
| Horton | 0 | 0 | 0 | 0 | 1,659 |
| Hoyt | 0 | 0 | 0 | 0 | 626 |
| Hugoton | 0 | 0 | 0 | 0 | 3,653 |
| Humboldt | 0 | 0 | 0 | 0 | 1,762 |
| Independence | 0 | 0 | 0 | 0 | 8,326 |
| Iola | 0 | 0 | 0 | 0 | 5,222 |
| Junction City | 0 | 0 | 0 | 0 | 21,680 |
| Kechi | 0 | 0 | 0 | 0 | 2,129 |
| Kingman | 0 | 0 | 0 | 0 | 2,727 |
| La Cygne | | 0 | 0 | | 1,104 |
| La Harpe | | 0 | 0 | 0 | 527 |
| Lake Quivira | | 0 | 0 | 0 | 932 |
| Lansing | 0 | 0 | 0 | 0 | 12,021 |
| Larned | 0 | 0 | 0 | 0 | 3,591 |
| Leavenworth | 0 | 0 | 0 | 0 | 35,990 |
| Lebo | 0 | 0 | 0 | | 878 |
| Lenexa | 0 | 0 | 0 | 0 | 57,012 |
| Leon | | | 0 | | 729 |
| Le Roy | 0 | | | | 537 |
| Lindsborg | 0 | 0 | 0 | 0 | 3,259 |
| Louisburg | 0 | 0 | 0 | 0 | 4,619 |
| Lyndon | 0 | 0 | 0 | 0 | 1,009 |
| Lyons | 0 | 0 | 0 | 0 | 3,403 |

## Table 95. Hate Crime Zero Data Submitted Per Quarter, by Federal Agency, State, and State Agency, 2021—Continued

(Number.)

| Agency name | Zero data per quarter[1] | | | | Population[2] |
|---|---|---|---|---|---|
| | 1st quarter | 2nd quarter | 3rd quarter | 4th quarter | |
| Macksville | | 0 | 0 | 0 | 515 |
| Marion | 0 | 0 | 0 | 0 | 1,721 |
| Marysville | 0 | 0 | 0 | 0 | 3,246 |
| McLouth | 0 | 0 | 0 | 0 | 833 |
| Meade | 0 | | | | 1,500 |
| Medicine Lodge | 0 | 0 | 0 | 0 | 1,784 |
| Meriden | | | 0 | | 772 |
| Merriam | 0 | 0 | 0 | 0 | 11,138 |
| Minneapolis | 0 | 0 | 0 | 0 | 1,883 |
| Mission | 0 | 0 | 0 | 0 | 9,931 |
| Mission Hills | 0 | 0 | 0 | 0 | 3,539 |
| Mission Woods | 0 | 0 | | | 197 |
| Mulberry | 0 | 0 | 0 | 0 | 521 |
| Mulvane | 0 | 0 | 0 | 0 | 6,610 |
| Neodesha | 0 | 0 | 0 | 0 | 2,186 |
| North Newton | 0 | 0 | 0 | 0 | 1,761 |
| Norton | 0 | | | | 2,692 |
| Nortonville | 0 | 0 | 0 | 0 | 602 |
| Oakley | 0 | 0 | 0 | 0 | 2,028 |
| Oberlin | 0 | 0 | 0 | | 1,658 |
| Osage City | 0 | 0 | 0 | 0 | 2,748 |
| Osawatomie | 0 | | | | 4,202 |
| Osborne | 0 | 0 | 0 | | 1,266 |
| Oskaloosa | | 0 | 0 | 0 | 1,052 |
| Oswego | 0 | 0 | 0 | 0 | 1,668 |
| Overbrook | 0 | 0 | 0 | 0 | 1,000 |
| Oxford | 0 | 0 | 0 | 0 | 982 |
| Paola | 0 | 0 | 0 | 0 | 5,668 |
| Park City | 0 | 0 | 0 | 0 | 8,006 |
| Peabody | 0 | 0 | 0 | 0 | 1,067 |
| Perry | 0 | 0 | 0 | | 906 |
| Plainville | 0 | 0 | 0 | 0 | 1,755 |
| Pleasanton | 0 | 0 | 0 | 0 | 1,154 |
| Prairie Village | 0 | 0 | 0 | 0 | 22,402 |
| Pratt | | | 0 | | 6,428 |
| Protection | 0 | 0 | 0 | 0 | 455 |
| Roeland Park | 0 | 0 | 0 | 0 | 6,644 |
| Rose Hill | 0 | 0 | 0 | 0 | 3,983 |
| Russell | 0 | 0 | 0 | 0 | 4,369 |
| Sabetha | 0 | 0 | 0 | 0 | 2,552 |
| Scott City | 0 | 0 | 0 | 0 | 3,726 |
| Scranton | 0 | 0 | 0 | 0 | 667 |
| Sedan | 0 | | | | 980 |
| Seneca | 0 | 0 | 0 | 0 | 2,087 |
| South Hutchinson | | | | 0 | 2,498 |
| Spearville | 0 | 0 | 0 | | 765 |
| Spring Hill | 0 | 0 | 0 | 0 | 8,167 |
| Sterling | 0 | 0 | | | 2,160 |
| St. George | 0 | 0 | 0 | 0 | 1,066 |
| St. John | | | 0 | 0 | 1,125 |
| St. Marys | 0 | 0 | 0 | 0 | 2,649 |
| Tonganoxie | 0 | 0 | 0 | 0 | 5,761 |
| Troy | 0 | | 0 | 0 | 940 |
| Ulysses | 0 | 0 | 0 | 0 | 5,489 |
| Valley Falls | 0 | 0 | 0 | 0 | 1,149 |
| WaKeeney | 0 | 0 | 0 | 0 | 1,724 |
| Wakefield | | 0 | 0 | 0 | 915 |
| Wathena | 0 | | | | 1,264 |
| Waverly | 0 | | 0 | | 532 |
| Wellsville | 0 | 0 | 0 | 0 | 1,777 |
| Westwood | 0 | 0 | 0 | 0 | 1,657 |
| Westwood Hills | 0 | 0 | | | 393 |
| Winchester | 0 | 0 | 0 | 0 | 515 |
| **Universities and Colleges** | | | | | |
| Butler Community College | 0 | 0 | 0 | 0 | 11,237 |
| Emporia State University | 0 | 0 | 0 | 0 | 7,282 |
| Garden City Community College | 0 | 0 | 0 | 0 | 2,584 |
| Kansas City Kansas Community College | 0 | 0 | 0 | 0 | 8,213 |
| Kansas State University | 0 | 0 | 0 | 0 | 23,353 |
| Pittsburg State University | 0 | 0 | 0 | 0 | 8,065 |
| University of Kansas, Medical Center[3] | 0 | 0 | 0 | 0 | |
| Wichita State University | 0 | 0 | 0 | 0 | 17,817 |
| **Metropolitan Counties** | | | | | |
| Doniphan | 0 | 0 | 0 | 0 | |
| Geary | 0 | 0 | 0 | 0 | |
| Harvey | 0 | 0 | 0 | 0 | |
| Jackson | 0 | 0 | 0 | 0 | |
| Leavenworth | 0 | 0 | 0 | 0 | |
| Linn | 0 | 0 | 0 | 0 | |

## Table 95. Hate Crime Zero Data Submitted Per Quarter, by Federal Agency, State, and State Agency, 2021—Continued

(Number.)

| Agency name | Zero data per quarter[1] | | | | Population[2] |
|---|---|---|---|---|---|
| | 1st quarter | 2nd quarter | 3rd quarter | 4th quarter | |
| Miami | 0 | 0 | 0 | 0 | |
| Osage | 0 | 0 | 0 | 0 | |
| Shawnee | 0 | 0 | 0 | 0 | |
| Wabaunsee | 0 | 0 | 0 | | |
| Wyandotte | 0 | 0 | 0 | 0 | |
| **Nonmetropolitan Counties** | | | | | |
| Allen | 0 | 0 | 0 | 0 | |
| Anderson | 0 | 0 | 0 | 0 | |
| Atchison | 0 | 0 | 0 | 0 | |
| Barber | 0 | 0 | 0 | 0 | |
| Barton | 0 | 0 | 0 | 0 | |
| Bourbon | 0 | 0 | 0 | 0 | |
| Chautauqua | 0 | 0 | 0 | 0 | |
| Cherokee | 0 | 0 | 0 | 0 | |
| Cheyenne | 0 | 0 | 0 | 0 | |
| Clark | 0 | 0 | 0 | 0 | |
| Clay | 0 | 0 | 0 | 0 | |
| Cloud | 0 | | | | |
| Comanche | 0 | 0 | 0 | 0 | |
| Cowley | 0 | 0 | 0 | 0 | |
| Decatur | 0 | 0 | 0 | 0 | |
| Dickinson | 0 | 0 | 0 | 0 | |
| Edwards | 0 | 0 | 0 | 0 | |
| Ellsworth | 0 | 0 | 0 | 0 | |
| Finney | 0 | 0 | 0 | 0 | |
| Ford | 0 | 0 | 0 | 0 | |
| Franklin | 0 | 0 | 0 | 0 | |
| Gove | 0 | 0 | 0 | 0 | |
| Graham | | 0 | 0 | 0 | |
| Grant | 0 | 0 | 0 | 0 | |
| Gray | 0 | 0 | 0 | 0 | |
| Greeley | 0 | 0 | 0 | 0 | |
| Greenwood | 0 | 0 | 0 | 0 | |
| Harper | 0 | 0 | 0 | 0 | |
| Haskell | 0 | 0 | 0 | 0 | |
| Hodgeman | 0 | 0 | 0 | 0 | |
| Kearny | 0 | 0 | 0 | 0 | |
| Kingman | 0 | 0 | 0 | 0 | |
| Kiowa | 0 | 0 | 0 | 0 | |
| Labette | 0 | 0 | 0 | 0 | |
| Lane | 0 | 0 | 0 | 0 | |
| Lincoln | 0 | 0 | 0 | | |
| Logan | 0 | 0 | 0 | 0 | |
| Marion | 0 | 0 | 0 | 0 | |
| Marshall | 0 | 0 | 0 | 0 | |
| McPherson | 0 | 0 | 0 | 0 | |
| Meade | 0 | 0 | | | |
| Mitchell | 0 | | 0 | 0 | |
| Montgomery | 0 | 0 | 0 | 0 | |
| Morton | 0 | 0 | 0 | 0 | |
| Nemaha | 0 | 0 | 0 | 0 | |
| Neosho | 0 | 0 | 0 | 0 | |
| Ness | 0 | 0 | 0 | | |
| Norton | 0 | 0 | 0 | 0 | |
| Osborne | 0 | 0 | 0 | 0 | |
| Ottawa | 0 | 0 | 0 | 0 | |
| Pawnee | 0 | 0 | 0 | 0 | |
| Pratt | 0 | 0 | 0 | 0 | |
| Rawlins | 0 | 0 | 0 | 0 | |
| Republic | 0 | 0 | 0 | 0 | |
| Rice | 0 | 0 | 0 | 0 | |
| Rooks | 0 | 0 | 0 | 0 | |
| Rush | 0 | 0 | 0 | 0 | |
| Russell | 0 | 0 | 0 | 0 | |
| Scott | 0 | 0 | 0 | 0 | |
| Seward | 0 | 0 | 0 | 0 | |
| Sheridan | 0 | 0 | 0 | 0 | |
| Sherman | 0 | 0 | 0 | 0 | |
| Smith | 0 | 0 | 0 | 0 | |
| Stafford | 0 | 0 | 0 | 0 | |
| Thomas | 0 | 0 | 0 | 0 | |
| Trego | 0 | 0 | 0 | 0 | |
| Washington | 0 | 0 | 0 | 0 | |
| Wichita | | 0 | 0 | 0 | |
| Wilson | 0 | 0 | | | |
| Woodson | 0 | 0 | 0 | 0 | |
| **State Police Agencies** | | | | | |
| Highway Patrol | | | | | |
| Capitol | 0 | 0 | 0 | | |

## Table 95. Hate Crime Zero Data Submitted Per Quarter, by Federal Agency, State, and State Agency, 2021—Continued

(Number.)

| Agency name | Zero data per quarter[1] | | | | Population[2] |
|---|---|---|---|---|---|
| | 1st quarter | 2nd quarter | 3rd quarter | 4th quarter | |
| Headquarters | 0 | 0 | 0 | | |
| Troop A | 0 | 0 | 0 | | |
| Troop B | 0 | 0 | 0 | | |
| Troop C | 0 | 0 | 0 | | |
| Troop D | 0 | 0 | 0 | | |
| Troop E | 0 | 0 | 0 | 0 | |
| Troop G | 0 | 0 | 0 | 0 | |
| Troop H | 0 | 0 | 0 | | |
| Troop N | 0 | 0 | 0 | | |
| Troop S | 0 | 0 | 0 | | |
| Troop T | 0 | 0 | 0 | | |
| **Tribal Agencies** | | | | | |
| Iowa Tribal | 0 | 0 | 0 | 0 | |
| Kickapoo Tribal | 0 | 0 | 0 | 0 | |
| Sac and Fox Tribal | 0 | 0 | 0 | 0 | |
| **Other Agencies** | | | | | |
| Blue Valley School District | | 0 | 0 | 0 | |
| El Dorado School District | 0 | 0 | 0 | 0 | |
| Franklin County Drug Enforcement | 0 | | | | |
| Kansas Alcoholic Beverage Control | 0 | 0 | 0 | 0 | |
| Kansas Bureau of Investigation | 0 | 0 | 0 | 0 | |
| Kansas Department of Wildlife and Parks | 0 | 0 | 0 | 0 | |
| Kansas Racing and Gaming Commission | | | | | |
| Boothill Casino | | | 0 | | |
| Kansas Crossing Casino | 0 | 0 | | | |
| Kansas Racing Commission, Security Division | 0 | | | | |
| Metropolitan Topeka Airport Authority | 0 | 0 | 0 | 0 | |
| Reno County Drug Enforcement Unit | 0 | | | | |
| Shawnee Mission Public Schools | 0 | 0 | 0 | 0 | |
| State Fire Marshal | 0 | 0 | 0 | 0 | |
| Topeka Fire Department Arson Investigation | 0 | 0 | 0 | 0 | |
| Unified School District | | | | | |
| Auburn-Washburn | 0 | | 0 | 0 | |
| Goddard | 0 | 0 | 0 | 0 | |
| Nickerson/SouthHutchinson | 0 | 0 | 0 | 0 | |
| Seaman | | 0 | | 0 | |
| Shawnee Heights | | | 0 | 0 | |
| **KENTICKY** | | | | | |
| **Cities** | | | | | |
| Adairville | 0 | 0 | 0 | 0 | 893 |
| Albany | 0 | 0 | 0 | 0 | 1,974 |
| Alexandria | 0 | 0 | 0 | 0 | 9,949 |
| Anchorage | 0 | 0 | 0 | 0 | 2,435 |
| Auburn | 0 | 0 | 0 | 0 | 1,409 |
| Audubon Park | 0 | 0 | 0 | 0 | 1,489 |
| Augusta | 0 | 0 | 0 | 0 | 1,137 |
| Bancroft | 0 | 0 | 0 | 0 | 513 |
| Barbourville | 0 | 0 | 0 | 0 | 2,955 |
| Bardwell | 0 | 0 | 0 | 0 | 655 |
| Beattyville | 0 | 0 | 0 | 0 | 1,451 |
| Beaver Dam | 0 | 0 | 0 | 0 | 3,558 |
| Bellefonte | 0 | 0 | 0 | 0 | 803 |
| Bellevue | 0 | 0 | 0 | 0 | 5,748 |
| Berea | 0 | 0 | 0 | 0 | 16,576 |
| Bloomfield | 0 | 0 | 0 | 0 | 1,088 |
| Booneville | 0 | 0 | 0 | 0 | 153 |
| Brandenburg | 0 | 0 | 0 | 0 | 2,897 |
| Brodhead | 0 | 0 | 0 | 0 | 1,182 |
| Brooksville | 0 | 0 | 0 | 0 | 649 |
| Brownsville | 0 | 0 | 0 | 0 | 839 |
| Burgin | 0 | 0 | 0 | 0 | 997 |
| Burkesville | 0 | 0 | 0 | 0 | 1,427 |
| Burnside | 0 | 0 | 0 | 0 | 792 |
| Cadiz | 0 | 0 | 0 | 0 | 2,725 |
| Calvert City | 0 | 0 | 0 | 0 | 2,502 |
| Campbellsville | 0 | 0 | 0 | 0 | 11,500 |
| Carrollton | 0 | 0 | 0 | 0 | 3,794 |
| Catlettsburg | 0 | 0 | 0 | 0 | 1,724 |
| Cave City | 0 | 0 | 0 | 0 | 2,437 |
| Centertown | 0 | 0 | 0 | 0 | 429 |
| Central City | 0 | 0 | 0 | 0 | 5,664 |
| Clarkson | 0 | 0 | 0 | 0 | 889 |
| Clay | 0 | 0 | 0 | 0 | 1,083 |
| Clay City | 0 | 0 | 0 | 0 | 1,083 |
| Clinton | 0 | 0 | 0 | 0 | 1,231 |
| Cloverport | 0 | 0 | 0 | 0 | 1,151 |
| Coal Run Village | 0 | 0 | 0 | 0 | 1,475 |
| Cold Spring | 0 | 0 | 0 | 0 | 6,697 |

## Table 95. Hate Crime Zero Data Submitted Per Quarter, by Federal Agency, State, and State Agency, 2021—Continued

(Number.)

| Agency name | Zero data per quarter[1] | | | | Population[2] |
|---|---|---|---|---|---|
| | 1st quarter | 2nd quarter | 3rd quarter | 4th quarter | |
| Columbia | 0 | 0 | 0 | 0 | 4,937 |
| Corbin | 0 | 0 | 0 | 0 | 7,126 |
| Crab Orchard | 0 | 0 | 0 | 0 | 820 |
| Cumberland | 0 | 0 | 0 | 0 | 1,824 |
| Danville | 0 | 0 | 0 | 0 | 17,042 |
| Dawson Springs | 0 | 0 | 0 | 0 | 2,616 |
| Dry Ridge | 0 | 0 | 0 | 0 | 2,209 |
| Eddyville | 0 | 0 | 0 | 0 | 2,549 |
| Edmonton | 0 | 0 | 0 | 0 | 1,595 |
| Elizabethtown | 0 | 0 | 0 | 0 | 30,530 |
| Elkhorn City | 0 | 0 | 0 | 0 | 862 |
| Elkton | 0 | 0 | 0 | 0 | 2,158 |
| Elsmere | 0 | 0 | 0 | 0 | 8,672 |
| Eubank | 0 | 0 | 0 | 0 | 335 |
| Evarts | 0 | 0 | 0 | 0 | 783 |
| Ferguson | 0 | 0 | 0 | 0 | 945 |
| Flatwoods | 0 | 0 | 0 | 0 | 7,019 |
| Fleming-Neon | 0 | 0 | 0 | 0 | 601 |
| Flemingsburg | 0 | 0 | 0 | 0 | 2,800 |
| Fort Thomas | 0 | 0 | 0 | 0 | 16,269 |
| Fort Wright | 0 | 0 | 0 | 0 | 5,787 |
| Fountain Run | 0 | 0 | 0 | 0 | 207 |
| Franklin | 0 | 0 | 0 | 0 | 9,105 |
| Fulton | 0 | 0 | 0 | 0 | 2,077 |
| Graymoor-Devondale | 0 | 0 | 0 | 0 | 3,098 |
| Grayson | 0 | 0 | 0 | 0 | 3,808 |
| Greensburg | 0 | 0 | 0 | 0 | 2,048 |
| Greenup | 0 | 0 | 0 | 0 | 1,092 |
| Guthrie | 0 | 0 | 0 | 0 | 1,427 |
| Hardinsburg | 0 | 0 | 0 | 0 | 2,346 |
| Harlan | 0 | 0 | 0 | 0 | 1,447 |
| Hartford | 0 | 0 | 0 | 0 | 2,719 |
| Hawesville | 0 | 0 | 0 | 0 | 979 |
| Hazard | 0 | 0 | 0 | 0 | 4,721 |
| Heritage Creek | 0 | 0 | 0 | 0 | 1,146 |
| Hickman | 0 | 0 | 0 | 0 | 2,078 |
| Highland Heights | 0 | 0 | 0 | 0 | 7,023 |
| Hillview | 0 | 0 | 0 | 0 | 9,274 |
| Hodgenville | 0 | 0 | 0 | 0 | 3,257 |
| Horse Cave | 0 | 0 | 0 | 0 | 2,422 |
| Hurstbourne Acres | 0 | 0 | 0 | 0 | 1,902 |
| Hustonville | 0 | 0 | 0 | 0 | 367 |
| Hyden | 0 | 0 | 0 | 0 | 319 |
| Independence | 0 | 0 | 0 | 0 | 29,339 |
| Indian Hills | 0 | 0 | 0 | 0 | 2,980 |
| Irvine | 0 | 0 | 0 | 0 | 2,271 |
| Irvington | 0 | 0 | 0 | 0 | 1,194 |
| Jackson | 0 | 0 | 0 | 0 | 1,892 |
| Jamestown | 0 | 0 | 0 | 0 | 1,802 |
| Jeffersontown | 0 | 0 | 0 | 0 | 27,533 |
| Jenkins | 0 | 0 | 0 | 0 | 1,865 |
| Junction City | 0 | 0 | 0 | 0 | 2,347 |
| La Center | 0 | 0 | 0 | 0 | 936 |
| La Grange | 0 | 0 | 0 | 0 | 9,186 |
| Lakeside Park-Crestview Hills | 0 | 0 | 0 | 0 | 6,110 |
| Lebanon | 0 | 0 | 0 | 0 | 5,751 |
| Lebanon Junction | 0 | 0 | 0 | 0 | 1,986 |
| Leitchfield | 0 | 0 | 0 | 0 | 6,838 |
| Lewisburg | 0 | 0 | 0 | 0 | 807 |
| Lewisport | 0 | 0 | 0 | 0 | 1,683 |
| Livingston | 0 | 0 | 0 | 0 | 212 |
| London | 0 | 0 | 0 | 0 | 8,080 |
| Louisa | 0 | 0 | 0 | 0 | 2,313 |
| Loyall | 0 | 0 | 0 | 0 | 576 |
| Ludlow | 0 | 0 | 0 | 0 | 4,502 |
| Manchester | 0 | 0 | 0 | 0 | 1,261 |
| Marion | 0 | 0 | 0 | 0 | 2,833 |
| Martin | 0 | 0 | 0 | 0 | 533 |
| Mayfield | 0 | 0 | 0 | 0 | 9,648 |
| Maysville | 0 | 0 | 0 | 0 | 8,650 |
| McKee | 0 | 0 | 0 | 0 | 770 |
| Meadow Vale | 0 | 0 | 0 | 0 | 765 |
| Middletown | 0 | 0 | 0 | 0 | 7,930 |
| Millersburg | 0 | 0 | 0 | 0 | 785 |
| Monticello | 0 | 0 | 0 | 0 | 5,880 |
| Morganfield | 0 | 0 | 0 | 0 | 3,371 |
| Morgantown | 0 | 0 | 0 | 0 | 2,366 |
| Mount Sterling | 0 | 0 | 0 | 0 | 7,281 |
| Mount Vernon | 0 | 0 | 0 | 0 | 2,366 |
| Mount Washington | 0 | 0 | 0 | 0 | 15,048 |
| Muldraugh | 0 | 0 | 0 | 0 | 985 |

## Table 95. Hate Crime Zero Data Submitted Per Quarter, by Federal Agency, State, and State Agency, 2021—Continued

(Number.)

| Agency name | Zero data per quarter[1] | | | | Population[2] |
|---|---|---|---|---|---|
| | 1st quarter | 2nd quarter | 3rd quarter | 4th quarter | |
| Munfordville | 0 | 0 | 0 | 0 | 1,665 |
| New Haven | 0 | 0 | 0 | 0 | 904 |
| Oak Grove | 0 | 0 | 0 | 0 | 7,355 |
| Olive Hill | 0 | 0 | 0 | 0 | 1,524 |
| Owenton | 0 | 0 | 0 | 0 | 1,546 |
| Owingsville | 0 | 0 | 0 | 0 | 1,569 |
| Paintsville | 0 | 0 | 0 | 0 | 3,897 |
| Park Hills | 0 | 0 | 0 | 0 | 2,996 |
| Pembroke | 0 | 0 | 0 | 0 | 892 |
| Perryville | 0 | 0 | 0 | 0 | 763 |
| Pewee Valley | 0 | 0 | 0 | 0 | 1,588 |
| Pineville | 0 | 0 | 0 | 0 | 1,670 |
| Pioneer Village | 0 | 0 | 0 | 0 | 3,003 |
| Pippa Passes | 0 | 0 | 0 | 0 | 611 |
| Prestonsburg | 0 | 0 | 0 | 0 | 3,424 |
| Princeton | 0 | 0 | 0 | 0 | 6,036 |
| Prospect | 0 | 0 | 0 | 0 | 4,941 |
| Providence | 0 | 0 | 0 | 0 | 2,967 |
| Raceland | 0 | 0 | 0 | 0 | 2,331 |
| Ravenna | 0 | 0 | 0 | 0 | 552 |
| Richmond | 0 | 0 | 0 | 0 | 37,354 |
| Russell | 0 | 0 | 0 | 0 | 3,183 |
| Russell Springs | 0 | 0 | 0 | 0 | 2,671 |
| Russellville | 0 | 0 | 0 | 0 | 7,190 |
| Sadieville | 0 | 0 | 0 | 0 | 378 |
| Salyersville | 0 | 0 | 0 | 0 | 1,617 |
| Science Hill | 0 | 0 | 0 | 0 | 693 |
| Sebree | 0 | 0 | 0 | 0 | 1,516 |
| Shelbyville | 0 | 0 | 0 | 0 | 17,065 |
| Shepherdsville | 0 | 0 | 0 | 0 | 12,416 |
| Shively | 0 | 0 | 0 | 0 | 15,732 |
| Smiths Grove | 0 | 0 | 0 | 0 | 827 |
| Somerset | 0 | 0 | 0 | 0 | 11,889 |
| Southgate | 0 | 0 | 0 | 0 | 4,073 |
| South Shore | 0 | 0 | 0 | 0 | 1,042 |
| Springfield | 0 | 0 | 0 | 0 | 3,006 |
| Stamping Ground | 0 | 0 | 0 | 0 | 840 |
| Stanford | 0 | 0 | 0 | 0 | 3,634 |
| Stanton | 0 | 0 | 0 | 0 | 2,660 |
| Strathmoor Village | 0 | 0 | 0 | 0 | 662 |
| Sturgis | 0 | 0 | 0 | 0 | 1,782 |
| Taylor Mill | 0 | 0 | 0 | 0 | 6,837 |
| Taylorsville | 0 | 0 | 0 | 0 | 1,335 |
| Tompkinsville | 0 | 0 | 0 | 0 | 2,217 |
| Trenton | 0 | 0 | 0 | 0 | 377 |
| Uniontown | 0 | 0 | 0 | 0 | 923 |
| Vanceburg | 0 | 0 | 0 | 0 | 1,392 |
| Versailles | 0 | 0 | 0 | 0 | 27,051 |
| Villa Hills | 0 | 0 | 0 | 0 | 7,498 |
| Vine Grove | 0 | 0 | 0 | 0 | 6,712 |
| Warsaw | 0 | 0 | 0 | 0 | 1,677 |
| Wayland | 0 | 0 | 0 | 0 | 368 |
| West Liberty | 0 | 0 | 0 | 0 | 3,418 |
| West Point | 0 | 0 | 0 | 0 | 870 |
| Wheelwright | 0 | 0 | 0 | 0 | 450 |
| Whitesburg | 0 | 0 | 0 | 0 | 1,784 |
| Wilder | 0 | 0 | 0 | 0 | 3,063 |
| Williamsburg | 0 | 0 | 0 | 0 | 5,408 |
| Williamstown | 0 | 0 | 0 | 0 | 3,941 |
| Wilmore | 0 | 0 | 0 | 0 | 6,388 |
| Winchester | 0 | 0 | 0 | 0 | 18,689 |
| Windy Hills | 0 | 0 | 0 | 0 | 2,469 |
| Woodburn | 0 | 0 | 0 | 0 | 377 |
| Woodlawn Park | 0 | 0 | 0 | 0 | 970 |
| Worthington | 0 | 0 | 0 | 0 | 1,477 |
| **Universities and Colleges** | | | | | |
| Kentucky State University | 0 | 0 | 0 | 0 | 3,044 |
| Morehead State University | 0 | 0 | 0 | 0 | 10,971 |
| University of Kentucky | 0 | 0 | 0 | 0 | 32,756 |
| Western Kentucky University | 0 | 0 | 0 | 0 | 21,535 |
| **Metropolitan Counties** | | | | | |
| Allen | 0 | 0 | 0 | 0 | |
| Boone | 0 | 0 | 0 | 0 | |
| Bourbon | 0 | 0 | 0 | 0 | |
| Boyd | 0 | 0 | 0 | 0 | |
| Bracken | 0 | 0 | 0 | 0 | |
| Butler | 0 | 0 | 0 | 0 | |
| Campbell | 0 | 0 | 0 | 0 | |
| Campbell County Police Department | 0 | 0 | 0 | 0 | |

## Table 95. Hate Crime Zero Data Submitted Per Quarter, by Federal Agency, State, and State Agency, 2021—Continued

(Number.)

| Agency name | Zero data per quarter[1] | | | | Population[2] |
|---|---|---|---|---|---|
| | 1st quarter | 2nd quarter | 3rd quarter | 4th quarter | |
| Carter | 0 | 0 | 0 | 0 | |
| Christian | 0 | 0 | 0 | 0 | |
| Clark | 0 | 0 | 0 | 0 | |
| Edmonson | 0 | 0 | 0 | 0 | |
| Fayette | 0 | 0 | 0 | 0 | |
| Gallatin | 0 | 0 | 0 | 0 | |
| Grant | 0 | 0 | 0 | 0 | |
| Greenup | 0 | 0 | 0 | 0 | |
| Hancock | 0 | 0 | 0 | 0 | |
| Hardin | 0 | 0 | 0 | 0 | |
| Henderson | 0 | 0 | 0 | 0 | |
| Jefferson | 0 | 0 | 0 | 0 | |
| Jessamine | 0 | 0 | 0 | 0 | |
| Kenton | 0 | 0 | 0 | 0 | |
| Larue | 0 | 0 | 0 | 0 | |
| McLean | 0 | 0 | 0 | 0 | |
| Oldham | 0 | 0 | 0 | 0 | |
| Pendleton | 0 | 0 | 0 | 0 | |
| Scott | 0 | 0 | 0 | 0 | |
| Shelby | 0 | 0 | 0 | 0 | |
| Spencer | 0 | 0 | 0 | 0 | |
| Warren | 0 | 0 | 0 | 0 | |
| Woodford | 0 | 0 | 0 | 0 | |
| **Nonmetropolitan Counties** | | | | | |
| Adair | 0 | 0 | 0 | 0 | |
| Anderson | 0 | 0 | 0 | 0 | |
| Ballard | 0 | 0 | 0 | 0 | |
| Barren | 0 | 0 | 0 | 0 | |
| Bath | 0 | 0 | 0 | 0 | |
| Bell | 0 | 0 | 0 | 0 | |
| Boyle | 0 | 0 | 0 | 0 | |
| Breathitt | 0 | 0 | 0 | 0 | |
| Breckinridge | 0 | 0 | 0 | 0 | |
| Caldwell | 0 | 0 | 0 | 0 | |
| Carlisle | 0 | 0 | 0 | 0 | |
| Carroll | 0 | 0 | 0 | 0 | |
| Casey | 0 | 0 | 0 | 0 | |
| Clay | 0 | 0 | 0 | 0 | |
| Clinton | 0 | 0 | 0 | 0 | |
| Crittenden | 0 | 0 | 0 | 0 | |
| Cumberland | 0 | 0 | 0 | 0 | |
| Elliott | 0 | 0 | 0 | 0 | |
| Estill | 0 | 0 | 0 | 0 | |
| Fleming | 0 | 0 | 0 | 0 | |
| Floyd | 0 | 0 | 0 | 0 | |
| Franklin | 0 | 0 | 0 | 0 | |
| Fulton | 0 | 0 | 0 | 0 | |
| Garrard | 0 | 0 | 0 | 0 | |
| Garrard County Police Department | 0 | 0 | 0 | 0 | |
| Graves | 0 | 0 | 0 | 0 | |
| Grayson | 0 | 0 | 0 | 0 | |
| Green | 0 | 0 | 0 | 0 | |
| Harlan | 0 | 0 | 0 | 0 | |
| Harrison | 0 | 0 | 0 | 0 | |
| Hickman | 0 | 0 | 0 | 0 | |
| Hopkins | 0 | 0 | 0 | 0 | |
| Jackson | 0 | 0 | 0 | 0 | |
| Johnson | 0 | 0 | 0 | 0 | |
| Knott | 0 | 0 | 0 | 0 | |
| Knox | 0 | 0 | 0 | 0 | |
| Laurel | 0 | 0 | 0 | 0 | |
| Lawrence | 0 | 0 | 0 | 0 | |
| Lee | 0 | 0 | 0 | 0 | |
| Leslie | 0 | 0 | 0 | 0 | |
| Letcher | 0 | 0 | 0 | 0 | |
| Lewis | 0 | 0 | 0 | 0 | |
| Lincoln | 0 | 0 | 0 | 0 | |
| Livingston | 0 | 0 | 0 | 0 | |
| Logan | 0 | 0 | 0 | 0 | |
| Lyon | 0 | 0 | 0 | 0 | |
| Madison | 0 | 0 | 0 | 0 | |
| Magoffin | 0 | 0 | 0 | 0 | |
| Marion | 0 | 0 | 0 | 0 | |
| Marshall | 0 | 0 | 0 | 0 | |
| Martin | 0 | 0 | 0 | 0 | |
| Mason | 0 | 0 | 0 | 0 | |
| McCracken | 0 | 0 | 0 | 0 | |
| McCreary | 0 | 0 | 0 | 0 | |
| Menifee | 0 | 0 | 0 | 0 | |
| Mercer | 0 | 0 | 0 | 0 | |

## Table 95. Hate Crime Zero Data Submitted Per Quarter, by Federal Agency, State, and State Agency, 2021—Continued

(Number.)

| Agency name | Zero data per quarter[1] | | | | Population[2] |
|---|---|---|---|---|---|
| | 1st quarter | 2nd quarter | 3rd quarter | 4th quarter | |
| Metcalfe | 0 | 0 | 0 | 0 | |
| Monroe | 0 | 0 | 0 | 0 | |
| Montgomery | 0 | 0 | 0 | 0 | |
| Morgan | 0 | 0 | 0 | 0 | |
| Muhlenberg | 0 | 0 | 0 | 0 | |
| Nelson | 0 | 0 | 0 | 0 | |
| Nicholas | 0 | 0 | 0 | 0 | |
| Ohio | 0 | 0 | 0 | 0 | |
| Owen | 0 | 0 | 0 | 0 | |
| Owsley | 0 | 0 | 0 | 0 | |
| Perry | 0 | 0 | 0 | 0 | |
| Pike | 0 | 0 | 0 | 0 | |
| Powell | 0 | 0 | 0 | 0 | |
| Pulaski | 0 | 0 | 0 | 0 | |
| Robertson | 0 | 0 | 0 | 0 | |
| Rockcastle | 0 | 0 | 0 | 0 | |
| Rowan | 0 | 0 | 0 | 0 | |
| Russell | 0 | 0 | 0 | 0 | |
| Taylor | 0 | 0 | 0 | 0 | |
| Todd | 0 | 0 | 0 | 0 | |
| Union | 0 | 0 | 0 | 0 | |
| Washington | 0 | 0 | 0 | 0 | |
| Wayne | 0 | 0 | 0 | 0 | |
| Webster | 0 | 0 | 0 | 0 | |
| Whitley | 0 | 0 | 0 | 0 | |
| Wolfe | 0 | 0 | 0 | 0 | |
| **State Police Agencies** | | | | | |
| State Police | | | | | |
| Ashland | 0 | 0 | 0 | 0 | |
| Campbellsburg | 0 | 0 | 0 | 0 | |
| Cannabis Suppression Section | 0 | 0 | 0 | 0 | |
| Columbia | 0 | 0 | 0 | 0 | |
| Drug Enforcement Area [2] | 0 | 0 | 0 | 0 | |
| Electronic Crimes | 0 | 0 | 0 | 0 | |
| Frankfort | 0 | 0 | 0 | 0 | |
| Harlan | 0 | 0 | 0 | 0 | |
| Hazard | 0 | 0 | 0 | 0 | |
| Headquarters | 0 | 0 | 0 | 0 | |
| Henderson | 0 | 0 | 0 | 0 | |
| London | 0 | 0 | 0 | 0 | |
| Madisonville | 0 | 0 | 0 | 0 | |
| Morehead | 0 | 0 | 0 | 0* | |
| Pikeville | 0 | 0 | 0 | 0 | |
| Richmond | 0 | 0 | 0 | 0 | |
| Special Operations | 0 | 0 | 0 | 0 | |
| Vehicle Investigations | 0 | 0 | 0 | 0 | |
| West Drug Enforcement Branch | 0 | 0 | 0 | 0 | |
| **Other Agencies** | | | | | |
| Alcohol Beverage Control | | | | | |
| Enforcement Division | 0 | 0 | 0 | 0 | |
| Investigative Division | 0 | 0 | 0 | 0 | |
| Barren County Drug Task Force | 0 | 0 | 0 | 0 | |
| Bluegrass Narcotics Task Force | 0 | 0 | 0 | 0 | |
| Bourbon County Constable, District 7 | 0 | 0 | 0 | 0 | |
| Bourbon County Schools | 0 | 0 | 0 | 0 | |
| Casey County Constable, District 2 | 0 | 0 | 0 | 0 | |
| Cincinnati-Northern Kentucky International Airport | 0 | 0 | 0 | 0 | |
| Clark County Constable | 0 | 0 | 0 | 0 | |
| Clark County School System | 0 | 0 | 0 | 0 | |
| Department of Agriculture, Animal Health Enforcement Division | 0 | 0 | 0 | 0 | |
| Fayette County Constable, District 1 | 0 | 0 | 0 | 0 | |
| Fish and Wildlife Enforcement | 0 | 0 | 0 | 0 | |
| FIVCO Area Drug Task Force | 0 | 0 | 0 | 0 | |
| Garrard County Constable, District 2 | 0 | 0 | 0 | 0 | |
| Gateway Area Drug Task Force | 0 | 0 | 0 | 0 | |
| Graves County Schools | 0 | 0 | 0 | 0 | |
| Greater Hardin County Narcotics Task Force | 0 | 0 | 0 | 0 | |
| Jefferson County Constable, District 1 | 0 | 0 | 0 | 0 | |
| Jefferson County Constable, District 2 | 0 | 0 | 0 | 0 | |
| Johnson County Constable, District 2 | 0 | 0 | 0 | 0 | |
| Kentucky Horse Park | 0 | 0 | 0 | 0 | |
| Lake Cumberland Area Drug Enforcement Task Force | 0 | 0 | 0 | 0 | |
| Lawrence County Constable, District 3 | 0 | 0 | 0 | 0 | |
| Lexington Bluegrass Airport | 0 | 0 | 0 | 0 | |
| Louisville Regional Airport Authority | 0 | 0 | 0 | 0 | |
| McCracken County Public Schools | 0 | 0 | 0 | 0 | |
| McCreary County Constable, District 3 | 0 | 0 | 0 | 0 | |
| Metcalfe County Schools | 0 | 0 | 0 | 0 | |
| Montgomery County Constable, District 2 | 0 | 0 | 0 | 0 | |

# Table 95. Hate Crime Zero Data Submitted Per Quarter, by Federal Agency, State, and State Agency, 2021—Continued

(Number.)

| Agency name | 1st quarter | 2nd quarter | 3rd quarter | 4th quarter | Population[2] |
|---|---|---|---|---|---|
| Montgomery County School District | 0 | 0 | 0 | 0 | |
| Motor Vehicle Enforcement | 0 | 0 | 0 | 0 | |
| Northeast Kentucky Drug Task Force | 0 | 0 | 0 | 0 | |
| Northern Kentucky Drug Strike Force | 0 | 0 | 0 | 0 | |
| Park Security | 0 | 0 | 0 | 0 | |
| Pennyrile Narcotics Task Force | 0 | 0 | 0 | 0 | |
| Pulaski County Constable, District 4 | 0 | 0 | 0 | 0 | |
| Russell County Constable, District 3 | 0 | 0 | 0 | 0 | |
| South Central Kentucky Drug Task Force | 0 | 0 | 0 | 0 | |
| Taylor County Schools | 0 | 0 | 0 | 0 | |
| Unlawful Narcotics Investigation, Treatment and Education | 0 | 0 | 0 | 0 | |
| Woodford County Public Schools | 0 | 0 | 0 | 0 | |
| **LOUISIANA** | | | | | |
| **Cities** | | | | | |
| Abbeville | 0 | 0 | 0 | 0 | 11,898 |
| Addis | 0 | 0 | 0 | 0 | 6,850 |
| Alexandria | 0 | 0 | 0 | 0 | 45,343 |
| Baker | 0 | | | | 12,931 |
| Basile | 0 | 0 | 0 | 0 | 1,788 |
| Benton | 0 | 0 | 0 | 0 | 2,104 |
| Bernice | 0 | 0 | 0 | 0 | 1,580 |
| Berwick | 0 | 0 | 0 | 0 | 4,267 |
| Blanchard | 0 | 0 | 0 | 0 | 3,137 |
| Bogalusa | 0 | 0 | 0 | 0 | 11,334 |
| Broussard | 0 | 0 | 0 | 0 | 13,667 |
| Church Point | 0 | 0 | 0 | 0 | 4,344 |
| Clinton | 0 | 0 | 0 | 0 | 1,472 |
| Crowley | 0 | 0 | 0 | 0 | 12,448 |
| De Ridder | 0 | 0 | 0 | 0 | 10,512 |
| Dixie Inn | 0 | 0 | 0 | 0 | 265 |
| Epps | 0 | 0 | 0 | 0 | 805 |
| Erath | 0 | 0 | 0 | 0 | 2,022 |
| Evergreen | 0 | 0 | 0 | 0 | 285 |
| Fisher | 0 | 0 | 0 | 0 | 215 |
| Golden Meadow | 0 | 0 | 0 | 0 | 1,919 |
| Gonzales | 0 | 0 | 0 | 0 | 11,399 |
| Gramercy | 0 | 0 | 0 | 0 | 3,160 |
| Greensburg | 0 | 0 | 0 | | 637 |
| Greenwood | 0 | 0 | 0 | | 3,074 |
| Gretna | 0 | 0 | 0 | 0 | 17,603 |
| Harahan | 0 | 0 | 0 | 0 | 9,243 |
| Heflin | 0 | 0 | 0 | | 222 |
| Ida | | | | 0 | 207 |
| Iowa | 0 | 0 | 0 | 0 | 3,121 |
| Jennings | 0 | 0 | 0 | 0 | 9,592 |
| Kenner | 0 | 0 | 0 | 0 | 66,250 |
| Krotz Springs | 0 | 0 | 0 | 0 | 1,153 |
| Lake Charles | 0 | 0 | 0 | 0 | 79,053 |
| Lutcher | 0 | 0 | 0 | 0 | 3,088 |
| Marion | 0 | 0 | 0 | 0 | 737 |
| Morgan City | 0 | 0 | 0 | 0 | 10,343 |
| Norwood | | | | 0 | 278 |
| Patterson | 0 | 0 | 0 | 0 | 5,616 |
| Plain Dealing | 0 | 0 | 0 | 0 | 927 |
| Port Allen | 0 | 0 | 0 | | 4,676 |
| Rayne | 0 | 0 | 0 | 0 | 7,987 |
| Rayville | 0 | 0 | 0 | 0 | 3,411 |
| Ruston | 0 | 0 | 0 | 0 | 21,888 |
| Sibley | 0 | 0 | 0 | 0 | 1,149 |
| Slidell | 0 | 0 | 0 | 0 | 27,561 |
| Springhill | 0 | 0 | 0 | | 4,630 |
| St. Gabriel | 0 | 0 | 0 | 0 | 7,612 |
| Tallulah | 0 | 0 | 0 | 0 | 6,382 |
| Thibodaux | 0 | 0 | 0 | 0 | 14,402 |
| Tickfaw | 0 | 0 | 0 | 0 | 788 |
| Vinton | 0 | 0 | 0 | 0 | 3,192 |
| Walker | 0 | 0 | 0 | 0 | 6,325 |
| Westlake | 0 | 0 | 0 | 0 | 4,906 |
| West Monroe | 0 | 0 | 0 | 0 | 11,989 |
| Westwego | 0 | 0 | 0 | 0 | 8,274 |
| Wilson | 0 | 0 | 0 | | 542 |
| Zachary | 0 | 0 | 0 | 0 | 18,774 |
| **Universities and Colleges** | | | | | |
| Delgado Community College | | | | 0 | 20,120 |
| Louisiana State University | | | | | |
| Baton Rouge | 0 | 0 | 0 | | 34,811 |
| Eunice | 0 | 0 | 0 | 0 | 3,844 |
| Health Sciences Center, Shreveport | 0 | 0 | 0 | 0 | 1,084 |
| Shreveport | 0 | 0 | 0 | 0 | 12,170 |

## Table 95. Hate Crime Zero Data Submitted Per Quarter, by Federal Agency, State, and State Agency, 2021—Continued

(Number.)

| Agency name | Zero data per quarter[1] | | | | Population[2] |
|---|---|---|---|---|---|
| | 1st quarter | 2nd quarter | 3rd quarter | 4th quarter | |
| Louisiana Tech University | 0 | 0 | 0 | 0 | 12,768 |
| McNeese State University | 0 | 0 | 0 | 0 | 8,134 |
| Southeastern Louisiana University | 0 | 0 | | | 17,053 |
| Southern University and A&M College, New Orleans | 0 | 0 | 0 | 0 | 2,946 |
| University of Louisiana, Monroe | | | | 0 | 9,718 |
| University of New Orleans | 0 | 0 | 0 | 0 | 9,736 |
| **Metropolitan Counties** | | | | | |
| Acadia | 0 | 0 | 0 | 0 | |
| Caddo | 0 | 0 | 0 | 0 | |
| Grant | 0 | 0 | 0 | 0 | |
| Lafayette | 0 | 0 | 0 | 0 | |
| Livingston | 0 | 0 | 0 | 0 | |
| Morehouse | 0 | 0 | 0 | 0 | |
| Plaquemines | 0 | 0 | 0 | 0 | |
| Pointe Coupee | 0 | 0 | 0 | 0 | |
| St. Bernard | 0 | 0 | 0 | 0 | |
| St. Charles | 0 | 0 | 0 | 0 | |
| St. Helena | 0 | 0 | 0 | 0 | |
| St. James | 0 | 0 | 0 | 0 | |
| St. Martin | 0 | 0 | 0 | 0 | |
| St. Tammany | 0 | 0 | 0 | 0 | |
| Vermilion | 0 | 0 | 0 | 0 | |
| West Baton Rouge | 0 | 0 | 0 | 0 | |
| West Feliciana | 0 | 0 | 0 | 0 | |
| **Nonmetropolitan Counties** | | | | | |
| Beauregard | 0 | 0 | 0 | 0 | |
| Bienville | 0 | 0 | 0 | 0 | |
| Caldwell | | 0 | | 0 | |
| Claiborne | 0 | 0 | 0 | 0 | |
| Concordia | 0 | 0 | 0 | 0 | |
| East Carroll | 0 | 0 | 0 | 0 | |
| Franklin | 0 | 0 | 0 | 0 | |
| Jackson | 0 | 0 | 0 | 0 | |
| Lincoln | 0 | 0 | 0 | 0 | |
| St. Landry | 0 | 0 | 0 | 0 | |
| Tensas | 0 | | | | |
| Webster | | 0 | 0 | 0 | |
| Winn | 0 | 0 | 0 | 0 | |
| **Tribal Agencies** | | | | | |
| Chitimacha Tribal | 0 | 0 | 0 | 0 | |
| Tunica-Biloxi Tribal | 0 | 0 | 0 | 0 | |
| **Other Agencies** | | | | | |
| Tensas Basin Levee District | 0 | 0 | 0 | 0 | |
| **MAINE** | | | | | |
| **Cities** | | | | | |
| Ashland | 0 | 0 | 0 | 0 | 1,206 |
| Auburn | 0 | 0 | 0 | 0 | 23,446 |
| Baileyville | 0 | 0 | 0 | 0 | 1,450 |
| Bar Harbor | 0 | 0 | 0 | 0 | 7,752 |
| Bath | 0 | 0 | 0 | 0 | 8,320 |
| Berwick | 0 | 0 | 0 | 0 | 8,074 |
| Boothbay Harbor | 0 | 0 | 0 | 0 | 2,232 |
| Brewer | 0 | 0 | 0 | 0 | 8,897 |
| Bridgton | 0 | 0 | 0 | 0 | 5,539 |
| Bucksport | 0 | 0 | 0 | 0 | 4,917 |
| Buxton | 0 | 0 | 0 | 0 | 8,402 |
| Calais | 0 | 0 | 0 | 0 | 3,017 |
| Cape Elizabeth | 0 | 0 | 0 | 0 | 9,356 |
| Caribou | 0 | 0 | 0 | 0 | 7,570 |
| Carrabassett Valley | 0 | 0 | 0 | 0 | 789 |
| Clinton | 0 | 0 | 0 | 0 | 3,358 |
| Damariscotta | 0 | 0 | 0 | 0 | 2,153 |
| Dexter | 0 | 0 | 0 | 0 | 3,685 |
| Dover-Foxcroft | 0 | 0 | 0 | 0 | 4,073 |
| East Millinocket | 0 | 0 | 0 | | 7,139 |
| Eastport | 0 | 0 | | | 1,270 |
| Eliot | 0 | 0 | 0 | 0 | 7,212 |
| Ellsworth | 0 | 0 | 0 | 0 | 8,302 |
| Fairfield | 0 | 0 | 0 | 0 | 6,534 |
| Falmouth | 0 | 0 | 0 | 0 | 12,573 |
| Farmington | 0 | 0 | 0 | 0 | 7,621 |
| Fort Kent | 0 | 0 | 0 | 0 | 3,778 |
| Fryeburg | 0 | 0 | 0 | 0 | 3,435 |
| Gardiner | 0 | 0 | 0 | 0 | 5,675 |
| Gorham | 0 | 0 | 0 | 0 | 18,130 |
| Gouldsboro | 0 | 0 | 0 | 0 | 1,744 |

## Table 95. Hate Crime Zero Data Submitted Per Quarter, by Federal Agency, State, and State Agency, 2021—Continued

(Number.)

| Agency name | Zero data per quarter[1] | | | | Population[2] |
|---|---|---|---|---|---|
| | 1st quarter | 2nd quarter | 3rd quarter | 4th quarter | |
| Greenville | 0 | 0 | 0 | 0 | 1,626 |
| Hallowell | 0 | 0 | 0 | 0 | 2,386 |
| Hampden | 0 | 0 | 0 | 0 | 7,537 |
| Holden | 0 | 0 | 0 | 0 | 3,124 |
| Houlton | 0 | 0 | 0 | 0 | 5,732 |
| Islesboro | 0 | 0 | 0 | 0 | 562 |
| Jay | 0 | 0 | 0 | 0 | 4,575 |
| Kennebunk | 0 | 0 | 0 | 0 | 11,799 |
| Kennebunkport | 0 | 0 | 0 | 0 | 3,692 |
| Kittery | 0 | 0 | 0 | 0 | 9,915 |
| Limestone | 0 | 0 | 0 | 0 | 2,150 |
| Lisbon | 0 | 0 | 0 | 0 | 9,057 |
| Livermore Falls | 0 | 0 | 0 | 0 | 3,178 |
| Machias | 0 | 0 | 0 | 0 | 1,811 |
| Madawaska | 0 | 0 | 0 | 0 | 3,686 |
| Mechanic Falls | 0 | 0 | 0 | 0 | 2,977 |
| Mexico | 0 | 0 | 0 | 0 | 2,631 |
| Milbridge | 0 | 0 | 0 | 0 | 1,296 |
| Milo | 0 | 0 | 0 | 0 | 2,311 |
| Monmouth | 0 | 0 | 0 | 0 | 4,178 |
| Newport | 0 | 0 | 0 | 0 | 3,245 |
| North Berwick | 0 | 0 | 0 | 0 | 4,762 |
| Norway | 0 | 0 | 0 | 0 | 4,988 |
| Oakland | 0 | 0 | 0 | 0 | 6,351 |
| Ogunquit | 0 | 0 | 0 | 0 | 938 |
| Old Town | 0 | 0 | 0 | 0 | 7,362 |
| Orono | 0 | 0 | 0 | 0 | 10,666 |
| Oxford | 0 | 0 | 0 | 0 | 4,102 |
| Paris | 0 | 0 | 0 | 0 | 5,161 |
| Phippsburg | 0 | 0 | 0 | 0 | 2,281 |
| Pittsfield | 0 | 0 | 0 | 0 | 3,982 |
| Presque Isle | 0 | 0 | 0 | 0 | 8,882 |
| Rangeley | 0 | 0 | 0 | 0 | 1,149 |
| Rockport | 0 | 0 | 0 | 0 | 3,395 |
| Sabattus | 0 | 0 | 0 | 0 | 5,077 |
| Saco | 0 | 0 | 0 | 0 | 20,290 |
| Skowhegan | 0 | 0 | 0 | 0 | 8,205 |
| South Berwick | 0 | 0 | 0 | 0 | 7,654 |
| South Portland | 0 | 0 | 0 | 0 | 26,048 |
| Southwest Harbor | 0 | 0 | 0 | 0 | 1,796 |
| Thomaston | 0 | 0 | 0 | 0 | 2,761 |
| Topsham | 0 | 0 | 0 | 0 | 8,960 |
| Veazie | 0 | 0 | 0 | 0 | 1,815 |
| Waldoboro | 0 | 0 | 0 | 0 | 5,079 |
| Washburn | 0 | 0 | 0 | 0 | 1,519 |
| Waterville | 0 | 0 | 0 | 0 | 16,667 |
| Wells | 0 | 0 | 0 | 0 | 10,950 |
| Wilton | 0 | 0 | 0 | 0 | 3,912 |
| Winter Harbor | 0 | 0 | 0 | 0 | 510 |
| Winthrop | 0 | 0 | 0 | 0 | 6,023 |
| Wiscasset | 0 | 0 | 0 | 0 | 3,750 |
| **Universities and Colleges** | | | | | |
| University of Maine | | | | | |
| Farmington | 0 | 0 | 0 | 0 | 2,397 |
| Orono | 0 | 0 | 0 | 0 | 13,426 |
| University of Southern Maine | 0 | 0 | 0 | 0 | 10,788 |
| **Nonmetropolitan Counties** | | | | | |
| Franklin | 0 | 0 | 0 | 0 | |
| Hancock | 0 | 0 | 0 | 0 | |
| Kennebec | 0 | 0 | 0 | 0 | |
| Lincoln | 0 | 0 | 0 | 0 | |
| Piscataquis | 0 | 0 | 0 | 0 | |
| Waldo | 0 | 0 | 0 | 0 | |
| Washington | 0 | 0 | 0 | 0 | |
| **Tribal Agencies** | | | | | |
| Passamaquoddy Indian Township | 0 | 0 | 0 | 0 | |
| Penobscot Nation | 0 | 0 | 0 | 0 | |
| **Other Agencies** | | | | | |
| Bureau of Capitol Police | 0 | 0 | 0 | 0 | |
| Drug Enforcement Agency | 0 | 0 | 0 | 0 | |
| **MARYLAND** | | | | | |
| **Cities** | | | | | |
| Boonsboro | 0 | 0 | 0 | 0 | 3,676 |
| Bowie | 0 | 0 | 0 | 0 | 58,546 |
| Frostburg | 0 | 0 | 0 | 0 | 8,413 |
| Oakland | 0 | 0 | 0 | 0 | 1,794 |

## Table 95. Hate Crime Zero Data Submitted Per Quarter, by Federal Agency, State, and State Agency, 2021—Continued

(Number.)

| Agency name | Zero data per quarter[1] | | | | Population[2] |
|---|---|---|---|---|---|
| | 1st quarter | 2nd quarter | 3rd quarter | 4th quarter | |
| **Universities and Colleges** | | | | | |
| Frostburg State University | 0 | 0 | 0 | 0 | 5,850 |
| **Metropolitan Counties** | | | | | |
| Allegany | 0 | 0 | 0 | 0 | |
| Prince George's County Police Department | 0 | 0 | | | |
| **Nonmetropolitan Counties** | | | | | |
| Garrett | 0 | 0 | 0 | 0 | |
| Talbot | 0 | 0 | 0 | 0 | |
| **Other Agencies** | | | | | |
| Transportation Authority | 0 | 0 | 0 | 0 | |
| **MASSACHUSETTS** | | | | | |
| **Cities** | | | | | |
| Abington | 0 | 0 | 0 | 0 | 17,623 |
| Acushnet | 0 | 0 | 0 | 0 | 10,798 |
| Amesbury | 0 | 0 | 0 | 0 | 17,809 |
| Amherst | 0 | 0 | 0 | 0 | 40,843 |
| Aquinnah | 0 | 0 | 0 | 0 | 328 |
| Ashburnham | 0 | 0 | 0 | 0 | 6,429 |
| Ashby | 0 | 0 | 0 | 0 | 3,242 |
| Ashfield | 0 | 0 | 0 | 0 | 1,718 |
| Ashland | 0 | 0 | 0 | 0 | 18,160 |
| Athol | 0 | 0 | 0 | 0 | 11,802 |
| Attleboro | 0 | 0 | 0 | 0 | 46,007 |
| Avon | 0 | 0 | 0 | 0 | 4,631 |
| Ayer | 0 | 0 | 0 | 0 | 8,357 |
| Barre | 0 | 0 | 0 | 0 | 5,637 |
| Becket | 0 | 0 | 0 | 0 | 1,700 |
| Bedford | 0 | 0 | 0 | 0 | 14,241 |
| Belchertown | 0 | 0 | 0 | 0 | 15,148 |
| Bellingham | 0 | 0 | 0 | 0 | 17,634 |
| Berkley | 0 | 0 | 0 | 0 | 7,007 |
| Berlin | 0 | 0 | 0 | 0 | 3,864 |
| Bernardston | 0 | 0 | 0 | 0 | 2,085 |
| Beverly | 0 | 0 | 0 | 0 | 42,851 |
| Blackstone | 0 | 0 | 0 | 0 | 9,304 |
| Bolton | 0 | 0 | 0 | 0 | 5,579 |
| Bourne | 0 | 0 | 0 | 0 | 19,904 |
| Boxborough | 0 | 0 | 0 | 0 | 5,880 |
| Boxford | 0 | 0 | 0 | 0 | 8,436 |
| Boylston | 0 | 0 | 0 | 0 | 4,806 |
| Brewster | 0 | 0 | 0 | 0 | 9,843 |
| Bridgewater | 0 | 0 | 0 | 0 | 8,446 |
| Brimfield | 0 | 0 | 0 | 0 | 3,722 |
| Brockton | 0 | 0 | 0 | 0 | 100,516 |
| Brookfield | 0 | 0 | 0 | 0 | 3,473 |
| Burlington | 0 | 0 | 0 | 0 | 29,087 |
| Canton | 0 | 0 | 0 | 0 | 24,570 |
| Carlisle | 0 | 0 | 0 | 0 | 5,312 |
| Carver | 0 | 0 | 0 | 0 | 12,347 |
| Charlton | 0 | 0 | 0 | 0 | 13,881 |
| Chatham | 0 | 0 | 0 | 0 | 6,031 |
| Chelmsford | 0 | 0 | 0 | 0 | 35,985 |
| Cheshire | 0 | 0 | | | 3,093 |
| Chester | | | 0 | 0 | 1,382 |
| Chesterfield | 0 | | | | 1,252 |
| Chicopee | 0 | 0 | 0 | 0 | 55,332 |
| Chilmark | 0 | 0 | 0 | 0 | 948 |
| Clinton | 0 | 0 | 0 | 0 | 14,099 |
| Cohasset | 0 | 0 | 0 | 0 | 8,738 |
| Dalton | 0 | 0 | 0 | 0 | 6,452 |
| Dartmouth | 0 | 0 | 0 | 0 | 34,158 |
| Deerfield | 0 | 0 | 0 | 0 | 5,041 |
| Douglas | 0 | 0 | 0 | 0 | 9,259 |
| Dover | 0 | 0 | 0 | 0 | 6,246 |
| Dudley | 0 | 0 | 0 | 0 | 11,778 |
| Dunstable | 0 | 0 | 0 | 0 | 3,454 |
| Duxbury | 0 | 0 | 0 | 0 | 16,780 |
| East Bridgewater | 0 | 0 | 0 | 0 | 15,324 |
| East Brookfield | 0 | 0 | 0 | 0 | 2,215 |
| Easthampton | 0 | 0 | 0 | 0 | 15,720 |
| Easton | 0 | 0 | 0 | 0 | 25,509 |
| Erving | 0 | 0 | 0 | 0 | 1,744 |
| Essex | 0 | 0 | 0 | 0 | 3,888 |
| Fairhaven | 0 | 0 | 0 | 0 | 16,257 |
| Fall River | 0 | 0 | 0 | 0 | 90,618 |
| Foxborough | 0 | 0 | 0 | 0 | 18,774 |
| Georgetown | 0 | 0 | 0 | 0 | 8,920 |

## Table 95. Hate Crime Zero Data Submitted Per Quarter, by Federal Agency, State, and State Agency, 2021—Continued

(Number.)

| Agency name | Zero data per quarter[1] | | | | Population[2] |
|---|---|---|---|---|---|
| | 1st quarter | 2nd quarter | 3rd quarter | 4th quarter | |
| Gill | 0 | 0 | 0 | 0 | 1,473 |
| Goshen | 0 | 0 | 0 | 0 | 1,057 |
| Grafton | 0 | 0 | 0 | 0 | 19,347 |
| Granby | 0 | 0 | 0 | 0 | 6,264 |
| Granville | 0 | 0 | 0 | 0 | 1,626 |
| Great Barrington | 0 | 0 | 0 | 0 | 6,964 |
| Greenfield | 0 | 0 | 0 | 0 | 17,222 |
| Groveland | 0 | 0 | 0 | 0 | 6,967 |
| Hadley | 0 | 0 | 0 | 0 | 5,335 |
| Halifax | 0 | 0 | 0 | 0 | 8,275 |
| Hamilton | 0 | 0 | 0 | 0 | 8,165 |
| Hampden | 0 | 0 | 0 | 0 | 5,207 |
| Hardwick | 0 | 0 | 0 | 0 | 3,077 |
| Harvard | 0 | 0 | 0 | 0 | 6,681 |
| Harwich | 0 | 0 | 0 | 0 | 12,235 |
| Hatfield | 0 | 0 | 0 | 0 | 3,241 |
| Hinsdale | 0 | 0 | 0 | 0 | 1,890 |
| Holden | 0 | 0 | 0 | 0 | 19,605 |
| Holland | 0 | 0 | 0 | 0 | 2,493 |
| Holliston | 0 | 0 | 0 | 0 | 15,138 |
| Hopedale | 0 | 0 | 0 | 0 | 5,985 |
| Hopkinton | 0 | 0 | 0 | 0 | 19,192 |
| Hudson | 0 | 0 | 0 | 0 | 19,954 |
| Ipswich | 0 | 0 | 0 | 0 | 14,297 |
| Kingston | 0 | 0 | 0 | 0 | 14,843 |
| Lancaster | 0 | 0 | 0 | 0 | 7,900 |
| Lanesboro | 0 | 0 | 0 | 0 | 2,909 |
| Leicester | 0 | 0 | 0 | 0 | 11,401 |
| Lenox | 0 | 0 | 0 | 0 | 4,920 |
| Leominster | 0 | 0 | 0 | 0 | 41,965 |
| Leverett | 0 | 0 | 0 | 0 | 1,835 |
| Lincoln | 0 | 0 | 0 | 0 | 7,114 |
| Littleton | 0 | 0 | 0 | 0 | 10,480 |
| Longmeadow | 0 | 0 | 0 | 0 | 15,764 |
| Lunenburg | 0 | 0 | 0 | 0 | 12,098 |
| Lynnfield | 0 | 0 | 0 | 0 | 13,300 |
| Malden | 0 | 0 | 0 | 0 | 60,433 |
| Manchester-by-the-Sea | 0 | 0 | 0 | 0 | 5,513 |
| Mansfield | 0 | 0 | 0 | 0 | 24,880 |
| Marion | 0 | 0 | 0 | 0 | 5,464 |
| Marlborough | 0 | 0 | 0 | 0 | 39,682 |
| Marshfield | 0 | 0 | 0 | 0 | 27,361 |
| Mattapoisett | 0 | 0 | 0 | 0 | 6,772 |
| Maynard | 0 | 0 | 0 | 0 | 11,508 |
| Medfield | 0 | 0 | 0 | 0 | 13,266 |
| Medway | 0 | 0 | 0 | 0 | 13,670 |
| Melrose | 0 | 0 | 0 | 0 | 28,094 |
| Mendon | 0 | 0 | 0 | 0 | 6,323 |
| Merrimac | 0 | 0 | 0 | 0 | 7,093 |
| Methuen | 0 | 0 | 0 | 0 | 51,691 |
| Middleboro | 0 | 0 | 0 | 0 | 27,228 |
| Middleton | 0 | 0 | 0 | 0 | 10,311 |
| Milford | 0 | 0 | 0 | 0 | 29,297 |
| Millbury | 0 | 0 | 0 | 0 | 14,160 |
| Millis | 0 | 0 | 0 | 0 | 8,683 |
| Millville | 0 | 0 | 0 | 0 | 3,267 |
| Milton | 0 | 0 | 0 | 0 | 27,911 |
| Monson | 0 | 0 | 0 | 0 | 8,857 |
| Montague | 0 | 0 | 0 | 0 | 8,178 |
| Monterey | 0 | 0 | 0 | 0 | 915 |
| Nahant | 0 | 0 | 0 | 0 | 3,544 |
| Nantucket | 0 | 0 | 0 | 0 | 11,600 |
| New Bedford | 0 | 0 | 0 | 0 | 96,346 |
| New Braintree | 0 | 0 | 0 | 0 | 1,030 |
| Norfolk | 0 | 0 | 0 | 0 | 12,152 |
| North Adams | 0 | 0 | 0 | 0 | 12,638 |
| Northampton | 0 | 0 | 0 | 0 | 28,332 |
| North Andover | 0 | 0 | 0 | 0 | 32,040 |
| North Attleboro | 0 | 0 | 0 | 0 | 29,789 |
| Northborough | 0 | 0 | 0 | 0 | 15,223 |
| Northfield | 0 | 0 | 0 | 0 | 2,951 |
| North Reading | 0 | 0 | 0 | 0 | 16,134 |
| Norton | 0 | 0 | 0 | 0 | 20,232 |
| Norwell | 0 | 0 | 0 | 0 | 11,770 |
| Norwood | 0 | 0 | 0 | 0 | 30,200 |
| Oak Bluffs | 0 | 0 | 0 | 0 | 4,772 |
| Oakham | 0 | 0 | 0 | 0 | 1,970 |
| Orange | 0 | 0 | 0 | 0 | 7,556 |
| Orleans | 0 | 0 | 0 | 0 | 5,841 |
| Oxford | 0 | 0 | 0 | 0 | 14,078 |
| Palmer | 0 | 0 | 0 | 0 | 12,300 |

## Table 95. Hate Crime Zero Data Submitted Per Quarter, by Federal Agency, State, and State Agency, 2021—Continued

(Number.)

| Agency name | Zero data per quarter[1] | | | | Population[2] |
|---|---|---|---|---|---|
| | 1st quarter | 2nd quarter | 3rd quarter | 4th quarter | |
| Paxton | 0 | 0 | 0 | 0 | 5,069 |
| Peabody | 0 | 0 | 0 | 0 | 53,669 |
| Pelham | 0 | 0 | 0 | 0 | 1,303 |
| Pembroke | 0 | 0 | 0 | 0 | 19,505 |
| Plympton | 0 | 0 | 0 | 0 | 3,157 |
| Princeton | 0 | 0 | 0 | 0 | 3,522 |
| Raynham | 0 | 0 | 0 | 0 | 14,799 |
| Reading | 0 | 0 | 0 | 0 | 25,900 |
| Rehoboth | 0 | 0 | 0 | 0 | 12,697 |
| Rockland | 0 | 0 | 0 | 0 | 18,898 |
| Rockport | 0 | 0 | 0 | 0 | 7,407 |
| Rowley | 0 | 0 | 0 | 0 | 6,501 |
| Royalston | 0 | 0 | 0 | 0 | 1,290 |
| Salisbury | 0 | 0 | 0 | 0 | 9,811 |
| Saugus | 0 | 0 | 0 | 0 | 28,967 |
| Scituate | 0 | 0 | 0 | 0 | 20,046 |
| Seekonk | 0 | 0 | 0 | 0 | 16,212 |
| Sharon | 0 | 0 | 0 | 0 | 19,222 |
| Shelburne | 0 | 0 | 0 | 0 | 1,834 |
| Sherborn | 0 | 0 | 0 | 0 | 4,445 |
| Shirley | 0 | 0 | 0 | 0 | 7,641 |
| Shutesbury | 0 | 0 | 0 | 0 | 1,751 |
| Somerset | 0 | 0 | 0 | 0 | 18,286 |
| Southampton | 0 | 0 | 0 | 0 | 6,199 |
| Southbridge | 0 | 0 | 0 | 0 | 16,932 |
| Southwick | 0 | 0 | 0 | 0 | 9,835 |
| Spencer | 0 | 0 | 0 | 0 | 12,014 |
| Sterling | 0 | 0 | 0 | 0 | 8,270 |
| Stockbridge | 0 | 0 | 0 | 0 | 1,877 |
| Stow | 0 | 0 | 0 | 0 | 7,294 |
| Sturbridge | 0 | 0 | 0 | 0 | 9,670 |
| Sunderland | 0 | 0 | 0 | 0 | 3,628 |
| Sutton | 0 | 0 | 0 | 0 | 9,716 |
| Swampscott | 0 | 0 | 0 | 0 | 15,766 |
| Taunton | 0 | 0 | 0 | 0 | 58,333 |
| Templeton | 0 | 0 | 0 | 0 | 8,213 |
| Tewksbury | 0 | 0 | 0 | 0 | 31,407 |
| Tisbury | 0 | 0 | 0 | 0 | 4,198 |
| Topsfield | 0 | 0 | 0 | 0 | 6,774 |
| Truro | 0 | 0 | 0 | 0 | 2,024 |
| Tyngsboro | 0 | 0 | 0 | 0 | 12,881 |
| Upton | 0 | 0 | 0 | 0 | 8,209 |
| Uxbridge | 0 | 0 | 0 | 0 | 14,561 |
| Walpole | 0 | 0 | 0 | 0 | 27,160 |
| Ware | 0 | 0 | 0 | 0 | 9,900 |
| Wareham | 0 | 0 | 0 | 0 | 23,956 |
| Warren | 0 | 0 | 0 | 0 | 5,252 |
| Watertown | 0 | 0 | 0 | 0 | 36,858 |
| Wayland | 0 | 0 | 0 | 0 | 13,911 |
| Webster | 0 | 0 | 0 | 0 | 16,963 |
| Wellesley | 0 | 0 | 0 | 0 | 29,088 |
| Wellfleet | 0 | 0 | 0 | 0 | 2,747 |
| Westborough | 0 | 0 | 0 | 0 | 19,299 |
| West Bridgewater | 0 | 0 | 0 | 0 | 7,696 |
| West Brookfield | 0 | 0 | 0 | 0 | 3,749 |
| Westfield | 0 | 0 | 0 | 0 | 41,474 |
| Westford | 0 | 0 | 0 | 0 | 25,834 |
| Westminster | 0 | 0 | 0 | 0 | 8,244 |
| West Newbury | 0 | 0 | 0 | 0 | 4,878 |
| Weston | 0 | 0 | 0 | 0 | 12,195 |
| Westport | 0 | 0 | 0 | 0 | 16,286 |
| West Springfield | 0 | 0 | 0 | 0 | 28,688 |
| West Tisbury | 0 | 0 | 0 | 0 | 2,982 |
| Weymouth | 0 | 0 | 0 | 0 | 59,242 |
| Whately | 0 | 0 | 0 | 0 | 1,591 |
| Whitman | 0 | 0 | 0 | 0 | 16,105 |
| Wilbraham | 0 | 0 | 0 | 0 | 14,864 |
| Williamsburg | 0 | 0 | 0 | 0 | 2,459 |
| Williamstown | 0 | 0 | 0 | 0 | 7,617 |
| Winchendon | 0 | 0 | 0 | 0 | 10,973 |
| Winchester | 0 | 0 | 0 | 0 | 22,988 |
| Worthington | 0 | 0 | 0 | 0 | 1,178 |
| Wrentham | 0 | 0 | 0 | 0 | 12,334 |
| **Universities and Colleges** | | | | | |
| Amherst College | 0 | 0 | 0 | 0 | 1,940 |
| Assumption College | 0 | 0 | 0 | 0 | 2,701 |
| Babson College | 0 | 0 | 0 | 0 | 3,987 |
| Bentley University | 0 | 0 | 0 | 0 | 5,579 |
| Boston College | 0 | 0 | 0 | 0 | 16,502 |
| Bristol Community College | 0 | 0 | 0 | 0 | 9,702 |

## Table 95. Hate Crime Zero Data Submitted Per Quarter, by Federal Agency, State, and State Agency, 2021—Continued

(Number.)

| Agency name | Zero data per quarter[1] | | | | Population[2] |
|---|---|---|---|---|---|
| | 1st quarter | 2nd quarter | 3rd quarter | 4th quarter | |
| Bunker Hill Community College | 0 | 0 | 0 | 0 | 16,306 |
| Cape Cod Community College | 0 | 0 | 0 | 0 | 4,512 |
| Clark University | 0 | 0 | 0 | 0 | 3,880 |
| College of the Holy Cross | 0 | 0 | 0 | 0 | 3,098 |
| Dean College | 0 | 0 | 0 | 0 | 1,569 |
| Endicott College | 0 | 0 | 0 | 0 | 6,649 |
| Fisher College | 0 | | | | 2,950 |
| Fitchburg State University | 0 | 0 | 0 | 0 | 10,793 |
| Gordon College | 0 | 0 | 0 | 0 | 2,314 |
| Greenfield Community College | 0 | 0 | 0 | 0 | 2,420 |
| Holyoke Community College | 0 | 0 | 0 | 0 | 6,374 |
| Lasell College | 0 | 0 | 0 | 0 | 2,353 |
| Massachusetts Bay Community College | 0 | 0 | 0 | 0 | 6,644 |
| Massachusetts College of Art | 0 | 0 | 0 | 0 | 2,502 |
| Massasoit Community College | 0 | 0 | 0 | 0 | 9,466 |
| MCPHS University | 0 | 0 | 0 | 0 | 8,078 |
| Merrimack College | 0 | 0 | 0 | 0 | 6,600 |
| Mount Wachusett Community College | 0 | 0 | 0 | 0 | 4,818 |
| Northeastern University | 0 | 0 | 0 | 0 | 30,003 |
| North Shore Community College | 0 | 0 | 0 | 0 | 7,729 |
| Quinsigamond Community College | 0 | 0 | 0 | 0 | 9,897 |
| Salem State University | 0 | 0 | 0 | 0 | 9,343 |
| Simmons College | 0 | 0 | 0 | 0 | 7,562 |
| Springfield College | 0 | 0 | 0 | 0 | 3,288 |
| Springfield Technical Community College | 0 | 0 | 0 | 0 | 6,833 |
| Stonehill College | 0 | 0 | 0 | 0 | 2,618 |
| Tufts University | | | | | |
|   Medford | 0 | 0 | 0 | 0 | 13,458 |
|   Suffolk[3] | 0 | 0 | 0 | 0 | |
|   Worcester[3] | 0 | 0 | 0 | 0 | |
| University of Massachusetts | | | | | |
|   Dartmouth | 0 | 0 | 0 | 0 | 9,491 |
|   Harbor Campus, Boston | 0 | 0 | 0 | 0 | 19,107 |
|   Medical Center, Worcester | 0 | 0 | 0 | 0 | 1,278 |
| Wellesley College | 0 | 0 | 0 | 0 | 2,735 |
| Wentworth Institute of Technology | 0 | 0 | 0 | 0 | 5,456 |
| Worcester Polytechnic Institute | 0 | 0 | 0 | 0 | 7,654 |
| Worcester State University | 0 | 0 | 0 | 0 | 8,694 |
| **State Police Agencies** | | | | | |
| State Police | | | | | |
|   Barnstable County | 0 | 0 | 0 | 0 | |
|   Berkshire County | 0 | 0 | 0 | 0 | |
|   Bristol County | 0 | 0 | 0 | 0 | |
|   Essex County | 0 | 0 | 0 | 0 | |
|   Franklin County | 0 | 0 | 0 | 0 | |
|   Hampden County | 0 | 0 | 0 | 0 | |
|   Hampshire County | 0 | 0 | 0 | 0 | |
|   Middlesex County | 0 | 0 | 0 | 0 | |
|   Nantucket County | | 0 | 0 | | |
|   Plymouth County | 0 | 0 | 0 | 0 | |
|   Worcester County | 0 | 0 | 0 | 0 | |
| **Tribal Agencies** | | | | | |
| Mashpee Wampanoag Tribal Police | | 0 | 0 | 0 | |
| Wampanoag Tribe of Gay Head | 0 | 0 | 0 | 0 | |
| **Other Agencies** | | | | | |
| Massachusetts General Hospital | 0 | 0 | 0 | 0 | |
| **MICHIGAN** | | | | | |
| **Cities** | | | | | |
| Addison Township | 0 | 0 | 0 | 0 | 6,603 |
| Adrian Township | 0 | 0 | 0 | 0 | 6,188 |
| Akron | 0 | 0 | 0 | 0 | 370 |
| Allegan | 0 | 0 | 0 | 0 | 5,018 |
| Alma | 0 | 0 | 0 | 0 | 8,754 |
| Almont | 0 | 0 | 0 | 0 | 2,830 |
| Alpena | 0 | 0 | 0 | 0 | 9,828 |
| Argentine Township | 0 | 0 | 0 | 0 | 6,439 |
| Armada | 0 | 0 | 0 | 0 | 1,695 |
| Auburn Hills | 0 | 0 | 0 | 0 | 25,256 |
| Au Gres | 0 | 0 | 0 | 0 | 828 |
| Augusta | 0 | 0 | 0 | 0 | 897 |
| Bad Axe | 0 | 0 | 0 | 0 | 2,868 |
| Bancroft | 0 | 0 | 0 | 0 | 491 |
| Bangor | 0 | 0 | 0 | 0 | 1,800 |
| Baroda-Lake Township | 0 | 0 | 0 | 0 | 3,891 |
| Barryton | 0 | 0 | 0 | 0 | 357 |
| Barry Township | 0 | 0 | 0 | 0 | 3,560 |
| Battle Creek | 0 | 0 | 0 | 0 | 60,134 |

## Table 95. Hate Crime Zero Data Submitted Per Quarter, by Federal Agency, State, and State Agency, 2021—Continued

(Number.)

| Agency name | Zero data per quarter[1] | | | | Population[2] |
|---|---|---|---|---|---|
| | 1st quarter | 2nd quarter | 3rd quarter | 4th quarter | |
| Beaverton | 0 | 0 | 0 | 0 | 1,173 |
| Belding | 0 | 0 | 0 | 0 | 5,738 |
| Belleville | 0 | 0 | 0 | 0 | 3,854 |
| Benton Harbor | 0 | 0 | 0 | 0 | 9,660 |
| Berkley | 0 | 0 | 0 | 0 | 15,307 |
| Berrien Springs-Oronoko Township | 0 | 0 | 0 | 0 | 8,854 |
| Beverly Hills | 0 | 0 | 0 | 0 | 10,278 |
| Big Rapids | 0 | 0 | 0 | 0 | 10,406 |
| Birmingham | 0 | 0 | 0 | 0 | 21,436 |
| Blackman Township | 0 | 0 | 0 | 0 | 36,111 |
| Brandon Township | 0 | 0 | 0 | 0 | 16,093 |
| Breckenridge | 0 | 0 | 0 | 0 | 1,259 |
| Bridgeport Township | 0 | 0 | 0 | 0 | 9,658 |
| Bridgman | 0 | 0 | 0 | 0 | 2,191 |
| Bronson | 0 | 0 | 0 | 0 | 2,293 |
| Brown City | 0 | 0 | 0 | 0 | 1,230 |
| Buchanan | 0 | 0 | 0 | 0 | 4,200 |
| Buena Vista Township | 0 | 0 | 0 | 0 | 8,035 |
| Cambridge Township | 0 | 0 | 0 | 0 | 5,663 |
| Capac | 0 | 0 | 0 | 0 | 1,842 |
| Carson City | 0 | 0 | 0 | 0 | 1,104 |
| Caseville | 0 | 0 | 0 | 0 | 720 |
| Caspian-Gaastra | 0 | 0 | 0 | 0 | 1,161 |
| Cass City | 0 | 0 | 0 | 0 | 2,259 |
| Cassopolis | 0 | 0 | 0 | 0 | 1,691 |
| Center Line | 0 | 0 | 0 | 0 | 8,074 |
| Charlevoix | 0 | 0 | 0 | 0 | 2,477 |
| Charlotte | 0 | 0 | 0 | 0 | 9,049 |
| Cheboygan | 0 | 0 | 0 | 0 | 4,682 |
| Chelsea | 0 | 0 | 0 | 0 | 5,422 |
| Chesaning | 0 | 0 | 0 | 0 | 2,204 |
| Chesterfield Township | 0 | 0 | 0 | 0 | 46,997 |
| Chikaming Township | 0 | 0 | 0 | 0 | 3,073 |
| Chocolay Township | 0 | 0 | 0 | 0 | 5,888 |
| Clare | 0 | 0 | 0 | 0 | 3,045 |
| Clarkston | 0 | 0 | 0 | 0 | 914 |
| Clawson | 0 | 0 | 0 | 0 | 11,720 |
| Clayton Township | 0 | 0 | 0 | 0 | 7,037 |
| Clay Township | 0 | 0 | 0 | 0 | 8,902 |
| Coleman | 0 | 0 | 0 | 0 | 1,202 |
| Coloma Township | 0 | 0 | 0 | 0 | 6,307 |
| Colon | 0 | 0 | 0 | 0 | 1,152 |
| Columbia Township | 0 | 0 | 0 | 0 | 7,312 |
| Constantine | 0 | 0 | 0 | 0 | 2,106 |
| Corunna | 0 | 0 | 0 | 0 | 3,303 |
| Covert Township | 0 | 0 | 0 | 0 | 2,884 |
| Davison | 0 | 0 | 0 | 0 | 4,828 |
| Davison Township | 0 | 0 | 0 | 0 | 19,226 |
| Denton Township | 0 | 0 | 0 | 0 | 5,412 |
| DeWitt | 0 | 0 | 0 | 0 | 4,869 |
| DeWitt Township | 0 | 0 | 0 | 0 | 15,880 |
| Dryden Township | 0 | 0 | 0 | 0 | 4,731 |
| Durand | 0 | 0 | 0 | 0 | 3,792 |
| East Grand Rapids | 0 | 0 | 0 | 0 | 12,129 |
| East Jordan | 0 | 0 | 0 | 0 | 2,338 |
| East Tawas | 0 | 0 | 0 | 0 | 2,713 |
| Eau Claire | 0 | 0 | 0 | 0 | 588 |
| Elkton | 0 | 0 | 0 | 0 | 735 |
| Elsie | 0 | 0 | 0 | 0 | 977 |
| Emmett Township | 0 | 0 | 0 | 0 | 11,531 |
| Essexville | 0 | 0 | 0 | 0 | 3,222 |
| Evart | 0 | 0 | 0 | 0 | 1,883 |
| Fair Haven Township | 0 | 0 | 0 | 0 | 1,029 |
| Farmington | 0 | 0 | 0 | 0 | 10,396 |
| Fennville | 0 | 0 | 0 | 0 | 1,438 |
| Fenton | 0 | 0 | 0 | 0 | 11,340 |
| Flat Rock | 0 | 0 | 0 | 0 | 9,968 |
| Flushing | 0 | 0 | 0 | 0 | 7,789 |
| Flushing Township | 0 | 0 | 0 | 0 | 10,096 |
| Forsyth Township | 0 | 0 | 0 | 0 | 6,160 |
| Fowlerville | 0 | 0 | 0 | 0 | 2,904 |
| Frankenmuth | 0 | 0 | 0 | 0 | 5,728 |
| Frankfort | 0 | 0 | 0 | 0 | 1,290 |
| Franklin | 0 | 0 | 0 | 0 | 3,228 |
| Fremont | 0 | 0 | 0 | 0 | 4,102 |
| Fruitport Township | 0 | 0 | 0 | 0 | 14,690 |
| Galien | 0 | 0 | 0 | 0 | 525 |
| Garfield Township | 0 | 0 | 0 | 0 | 846 |
| Gerrish Township | 0 | 0 | 0 | 0 | 2,946 |
| Gibraltar | 0 | 0 | 0 | 0 | 4,503 |
| Gladstone | 0 | 0 | 0 | 0 | 4,631 |

## Table 95. Hate Crime Zero Data Submitted Per Quarter, by Federal Agency, State, and State Agency, 2021—Continued

(Number.)

| Agency name | Zero data per quarter[1] | | | | Population[2] |
|---|---|---|---|---|---|
| | 1st quarter | 2nd quarter | 3rd quarter | 4th quarter | |
| Gladwin | 0 | 0 | 0 | 0 | 2,884 |
| Grand Beach/Michiana | 0 | 0 | 0 | 0 | 462 |
| Grand Blanc | 0 | 0 | 0 | 0 | 7,789 |
| Grand Haven | 0 | 0 | 0 | 0 | 11,110 |
| Grand Ledge | 0 | 0 | 0 | 0 | 7,891 |
| Grandville | 0 | 0 | 0 | 0 | 15,787 |
| Grant | 0 | 0 | 0 | 0 | 900 |
| Grayling | 0 | 0 | 0 | 0 | 1,841 |
| Grosse Ile Township | 0 | 0 | 0 | 0 | 10,076 |
| Grosse Pointe Farms | 0 | 0 | 0 | 0 | 9,012 |
| Grosse Pointe Shores | 0 | 0 | 0 | 0 | 2,509 |
| Grosse Pointe Woods | 0 | 0 | 0 | 0 | 15,158 |
| Hamburg Township | 0 | 0 | 0 | 0 | 21,904 |
| Hampton Township | 0 | 0 | 0 | 0 | 9,282 |
| Hamtramck | 0 | 0 | 0 | 0 | 21,346 |
| Harbor Beach | 0 | 0 | 0 | 0 | 1,557 |
| Hart | 0 | 0 | 0 | 0 | 2,087 |
| Hazel Park | 0 | 0 | 0 | 0 | 16,189 |
| Hesperia | 0 | 0 | 0 | 0 | 935 |
| Highland Township | 0 | 0 | 0 | 0 | 20,151 |
| Holland | 0 | 0 | 0 | 0 | 33,144 |
| Holly | 0 | 0 | 0 | 0 | 6,079 |
| Houghton | 0 | 0 | 0 | 0 | 7,524 |
| Howell | 0 | 0 | 0 | 0 | 9,667 |
| Hudson | 0 | 0 | 0 | 0 | 2,185 |
| Huntington Woods | 0 | 0 | 0 | 0 | 6,199 |
| Huron Township | 0 | 0 | 0 | 0 | 16,353 |
| Independence Township | 0 | 0 | 0 | 0 | 37,200 |
| Inkster | 0 | 0 | 0 | 0 | 23,999 |
| Ionia | 0 | 0 | 0 | 0 | 10,955 |
| Ironwood | 0 | 0 | 0 | 0 | 4,760 |
| Ishpeming | 0 | 0 | 0 | 0 | 6,371 |
| Ishpeming Township | 0 | 0 | 0 | 0 | 3,496 |
| Jackson | 0 | 0 | 0 | 0 | 32,271 |
| Jonesville | 0 | 0 | 0 | 0 | 2,201 |
| Kalamazoo | 0 | 0 | 0 | 0 | 76,179 |
| Kalkaska | 0 | 0 | 0 | 0 | 2,090 |
| Keego Harbor | 0 | 0 | 0 | 0 | 3,396 |
| Kinde | 0 | 0 | 0 | 0 | 407 |
| Kingston | 0 | 0 | 0 | 0 | 404 |
| Kinross Township | 0 | 0 | 0 | 0 | 7,226 |
| Laingsburg | 0 | 0 | 0 | 0 | 1,283 |
| Lake Angelus | 0 | 0 | 0 | 0 | 309 |
| Lake Linden | 0 | 0 | 0 | 0 | 928 |
| Lake Odessa | 0 | 0 | 0 | 0 | 2,043 |
| Lake Orion | 0 | 0 | 0 | 0 | 3,207 |
| Lakeview | 0 | 0 | 0 | 0 | 993 |
| Lapeer | 0 | 0 | 0 | 0 | 8,416 |
| Lapeer Township | 0 | 0 | 0 | 0 | 5,017 |
| Lathrup Village | 0 | 0 | 0 | 0 | 4,046 |
| Laurium | 0 | 0 | 0 | 0 | 1,861 |
| Lawton | 0 | 0 | 0 | 0 | 1,791 |
| Lennon | 0 | 0 | 0 | 0 | 476 |
| Leslie | 0 | 0 | 0 | 0 | 1,886 |
| Lexington | 0 | 0 | 0 | 0 | 1,114 |
| Lincoln Township | 0 | 0 | 0 | 0 | 14,590 |
| Linden | 0 | 0 | 0 | 0 | 3,950 |
| Lyon Township | 0 | 0 | 0 | 0 | 22,098 |
| Mackinac Island | 0 | 0 | 0 | 0 | 477 |
| Mackinaw City | 0 | 0 | 0 | 0 | 792 |
| Madison Township | 0 | 0 | 0 | 0 | 7,959 |
| Manistee | 0 | 0 | 0 | 0 | 6,158 |
| Manton | 0 | 0 | 0 | 0 | 1,625 |
| Marenisco Township | 0 | 0 | 0 | 0 | 484 |
| Marine City | 0 | 0 | 0 | 0 | 4,015 |
| Marlette | 0 | 0 | 0 | 0 | 1,740 |
| Marshall | 0 | 0 | 0 | 0 | 6,910 |
| Marysville | 0 | 0 | 0 | 0 | 9,621 |
| Mattawan | 0 | 0 | 0 | 0 | 1,972 |
| Mayville | 0 | 0 | 0 | 0 | 878 |
| Melvindale | 0 | 0 | 0 | 0 | 10,134 |
| Memphis | 0 | 0 | 0 | 0 | 1,167 |
| Mendon | 0 | 0 | 0 | 0 | 845 |
| Menominee | 0 | 0 | 0 | 0 | 7,909 |
| Metamora Township | 0 | 0 | 0 | 0 | 4,323 |
| Metro Police Authority of Genesee County | 0 | 0 | 0 | 0 | 19,899 |
| Midland | 0 | 0 | 0 | 0 | 41,758 |
| Milford | 0 | 0 | 0 | 0 | 16,969 |
| Millington | 0 | 0 | 0 | 0 | 1,002 |
| Montague | 0 | 0 | 0 | 0 | 2,366 |
| Morenci | 0 | 0 | 0 | 0 | 2,120 |

## Table 95. Hate Crime Zero Data Submitted Per Quarter, by Federal Agency, State, and State Agency, 2021—Continued

(Number.)

| Agency name | Zero data per quarter[1] | | | | Population[2] |
|---|---|---|---|---|---|
| | 1st quarter | 2nd quarter | 3rd quarter | 4th quarter | |
| Morrice | 0 | 0 | 0 | 0 | 904 |
| Mount Morris Township | 0 | 0 | 0 | 0 | 20,084 |
| Munising | 0 | 0 | 0 | 0 | 2,171 |
| Muskegon Heights | 0 | 0 | 0 | 0 | 10,673 |
| Napoleon Township | 0 | 0 | 0 | 0 | 6,696 |
| Nashville | 0 | 0 | 0 | 0 | 1,704 |
| Negaunee | 0 | 0 | 0 | 0 | 4,494 |
| Newaygo | 0 | 0 | 0 | 0 | 2,110 |
| New Baltimore | 0 | 0 | 0 | 0 | 12,301 |
| New Buffalo | 0 | 0 | 0 | 0 | 1,863 |
| New Era | 0 | 0 | 0 | 0 | 439 |
| New Lothrop | 0 | 0 | 0 | 0 | 545 |
| Northfield Township | 0 | 0 | 0 | 0 | 8,679 |
| North Muskegon | 0 | 0 | 0 | 0 | 3,792 |
| Northville | 0 | 0 | 0 | 0 | 5,922 |
| Northville Township | 0 | 0 | 0 | 0 | 29,443 |
| Oakland Township | 0 | 0 | 0 | 0 | 20,072 |
| Oakley | 0 | 0 | 0 | 0 | 269 |
| Oak Park | 0 | 0 | 0 | 0 | 29,280 |
| Olivet | 0 | 0 | 0 | 0 | 1,887 |
| Ontwa Township-Edwardsburg | 0 | 0 | 0 | 0 | 6,574 |
| Orchard Lake | 0 | 0 | 0 | 0 | 2,480 |
| Orion Township | 0 | 0 | 0 | 0 | 37,104 |
| Otisville | 0 | 0 | 0 | 0 | 821 |
| Otsego | 0 | 0 | 0 | 0 | 3,990 |
| Owendale | 0 | 0 | 0 | 0 | 219 |
| Oxford | 0 | 0 | 0 | 0 | 3,552 |
| Oxford Township | 0 | 0 | 0 | 0 | 19,529 |
| Peck | 0 | 0 | 0 | 0 | 584 |
| Pentwater | 0 | 0 | 0 | 0 | 858 |
| Perry | 0 | 0 | 0 | 0 | 2,066 |
| Petoskey | 0 | 0 | 0 | 0 | 5,734 |
| Pigeon | 0 | 0 | 0 | 0 | 1,099 |
| Pinckney | 0 | 0 | 0 | 0 | 2,425 |
| Plainwell | 0 | 0 | 0 | 0 | 3,771 |
| Pleasant Ridge | 0 | 0 | 0 | 0 | 2,399 |
| Plymouth | 0 | 0 | 0 | 0 | 9,141 |
| Portage | 0 | 0 | 0 | 0 | 50,141 |
| Port Austin | 0 | 0 | 0 | 0 | 610 |
| Portland | 0 | 0 | 0 | 0 | 4,024 |
| Prairieville Township | 0 | 0 | 0 | 0 | 3,548 |
| Quincy | 0 | 0 | 0 | 0 | 1,614 |
| Raisin Township | 0 | 0 | 0 | 0 | 7,817 |
| Reed City | 0 | 0 | 0 | 0 | 2,372 |
| Reese | 0 | 0 | 0 | 0 | 1,358 |
| Richfield Township, Genesee County | 0 | 0 | 0 | 0 | 8,300 |
| Richland | 0 | 0 | 0 | 0 | 858 |
| Richland Township, Saginaw County | 0 | 0 | 0 | 0 | 3,891 |
| River Rouge | 0 | 0 | 0 | 0 | 7,319 |
| Riverview | 0 | 0 | 0 | 0 | 11,920 |
| Rochester Hills | 0 | 0 | 0 | 0 | 74,426 |
| Rockwood | 0 | 0 | 0 | 0 | 3,133 |
| Rogers City | 0 | 0 | 0 | 0 | 2,651 |
| Romeo | 0 | 0 | 0 | 0 | 3,569 |
| Romulus | 0 | 0 | 0 | 0 | 23,488 |
| Roosevelt Park | 0 | 0 | 0 | 0 | 3,781 |
| Rose City | 0 | 0 | 0 | 0 | 627 |
| Rothbury | 0 | 0 | 0 | 0 | 457 |
| Saline | 0 | 0 | 0 | 0 | 9,402 |
| Sandusky | 0 | 0 | 0 | 0 | 2,477 |
| Saugatuck-Douglas | 0 | 0 | 0 | 0 | 2,337 |
| Sebewaing | 0 | 0 | 0 | 0 | 1,597 |
| Shelby | 0 | 0 | 0 | 0 | 2,042 |
| Shepherd | 0 | 0 | 0 | 0 | 1,488 |
| Somerset Township | 0 | 0 | 0 | 0 | 4,520 |
| South Haven | 0 | 0 | 0 | 0 | 4,320 |
| South Lyon | 0 | 0 | 0 | 0 | 11,899 |
| Sparta | 0 | 0 | 0 | 0 | 4,437 |
| Spring Arbor Township | 0 | 0 | 0 | 0 | 7,684 |
| Springfield Township | 0 | 0 | 0 | 0 | 14,495 |
| Springport Township | 0 | 0 | 0 | 0 | 2,134 |
| Stanton | 0 | 0 | 0 | 0 | 1,421 |
| St. Clair | 0 | 0 | 0 | 0 | 5,500 |
| St. Ignace | 0 | 0 | 0 | 0 | 2,315 |
| St. Johns | 0 | 0 | 0 | 0 | 7,908 |
| St. Joseph Township | 0 | 0 | 0 | 0 | 9,602 |
| St. Louis | 0 | 0 | 0 | 0 | 7,051 |
| Stockbridge | 0 | 0 | 0 | 0 | 1,243 |
| Sturgis | 0 | 0 | 0 | 0 | 10,771 |
| Sumpter Township | 0 | 0 | 0 | 0 | 9,337 |
| Tawas City | 0 | 0 | 0 | 0 | 1,777 |

## Table 95. Hate Crime Zero Data Submitted Per Quarter, by Federal Agency, State, and State Agency, 2021—Continued

(Number.)

| Agency name | Zero data per quarter[1] | | | | Population[2] |
|---|---|---|---|---|---|
| | 1st quarter | 2nd quarter | 3rd quarter | 4th quarter | |
| Tecumseh | 0 | 0 | 0 | 0 | 8,369 |
| Thomas Township | 0 | 0 | 0 | 0 | 11,366 |
| Three Oaks | 0 | 0 | 0 | 0 | 1,533 |
| Three Rivers | 0 | 0 | 0 | 0 | 7,579 |
| Tittabawassee Township | 0 | 0 | 0 | 0 | 10,031 |
| Trenton | 0 | 0 | 0 | 0 | 17,954 |
| Tuscarora Township | 0 | 0 | 0 | 0 | 2,918 |
| Ubly | 0 | 0 | 0 | 0 | 771 |
| Unadilla Township | 0 | 0 | 0 | 0 | 3,483 |
| Union City | 0 | 0 | 0 | 0 | 1,561 |
| Utica | 0 | 0 | 0 | 0 | 5,094 |
| Vassar | 0 | 0 | 0 | 0 | 2,521 |
| Vernon | 0 | 0 | 0 | 0 | 762 |
| Vicksburg | 0 | 0 | 0 | 0 | 3,657 |
| Watersmeet Township | 0 | 0 | 0 | 0 | 1,346 |
| Watervliet | 0 | 0 | 0 | 0 | 1,627 |
| West Branch | 0 | 0 | 0 | 0 | 2,037 |
| White Cloud | 0 | 0 | 0 | 0 | 1,381 |
| Whitehall | 0 | 0 | 0 | 0 | 2,879 |
| White Lake Township | 0 | 0 | 0 | 0 | 31,747 |
| Williamston | 0 | 0 | 0 | 0 | 3,935 |
| Woodhaven | 0 | 0 | 0 | 0 | 12,388 |
| Yale | 0 | 0 | 0 | 0 | 1,853 |
| Zeeland | 0 | 0 | 0 | 0 | 5,524 |
| Zilwaukee | 0 | 0 | 0 | 0 | 1,504 |
| **Universities and Colleges** | | | | | |
| Central Michigan University | 0 | 0 | 0 | 0 | 22,512 |
| Eastern Michigan University | 0 | 0 | 0 | 0 | 20,982 |
| Grand Valley State University | 0 | 0 | 0 | 0 | 26,993 |
| Kalamazoo Valley Community College | 0 | 0 | 0 | 0 | 11,012 |
| Kellogg Community College | 0 | 0 | 0 | 0 | 6,853 |
| Kirtland Community College | 0 | 0 | 0 | 0 | 2,311 |
| Lansing Community College | 0 | 0 | 0 | 0 | 16,021 |
| Macomb Community College | 0 | 0 | 0 | 0 | 27,402 |
| Michigan Technological University | 0 | 0 | 0 | 0 | 7,786 |
| Mott Community College | 0 | 0 | 0 | 0 | 9,668 |
| Northern Michigan University | 0 | 0 | 0 | 0 | 10,080 |
| Oakland Community College | 0 | 0 | 0 | 0 | 23,813 |
| Oakland University | 0 | 0 | 0 | 0 | 22,230 |
| Saginaw Valley State University | 0 | 0 | 0 | 0 | 9,205 |
| Schoolcraft College | 0 | 0 | 0 | 0 | 15,561 |
| University of Michigan | | | | | |
| Dearborn | 0 | 0 | 0 | 0 | 10,611 |
| Flint | 0 | 0 | 0 | 0 | 8,398 |
| **Metropolitan Counties** | | | | | |
| Berrien | 0 | 0 | 0 | 0 | |
| Cass | 0 | 0 | 0 | 0 | |
| Clinton | 0 | 0 | 0 | 0 | |
| Ionia | 0 | 0 | 0 | 0 | |
| Kalamazoo | 0 | 0 | 0 | 0 | |
| Lapeer | 0 | 0 | 0 | 0 | |
| Livingston | 0 | 0 | 0 | 0 | |
| Midland | 0 | 0 | 0 | 0 | |
| Shiawassee | 0 | 0 | 0 | 0 | |
| St. Clair | 0 | 0 | 0 | 0 | |
| Wayne | 0 | 0 | 0 | 0 | |
| **Nonmetropolitan Counties** | | | | | |
| Alcona | 0 | 0 | 0 | 0 | |
| Alger | 0 | 0 | 0 | 0 | |
| Allegan | 0 | 0 | 0 | 0 | |
| Alpena | 0 | 0 | 0 | 0 | |
| Antrim | 0 | 0 | 0 | 0 | |
| Arenac | 0 | 0 | 0 | 0 | |
| Baraga | 0 | 0 | 0 | 0 | |
| Branch | 0 | 0 | 0 | 0 | |
| Charlevoix | 0 | 0 | 0 | 0 | |
| Cheboygan | 0 | 0 | 0 | 0 | |
| Chippewa | 0 | 0 | 0 | 0 | |
| Clare | 0 | 0 | 0 | 0 | |
| Crawford | 0 | 0 | 0 | 0 | |
| Emmet | 0 | 0 | 0 | 0 | |
| Gogebic | 0 | 0 | 0 | 0 | |
| Hillsdale | 0 | 0 | 0 | 0 | |
| Iosco | 0 | 0 | 0 | 0 | |
| Isabella | 0 | 0 | 0 | 0 | |
| Keweenaw | 0 | 0 | 0 | 0 | |
| Luce | 0 | 0 | 0 | 0 | |
| Manistee | 0 | 0 | 0 | 0 | |

## Table 95. Hate Crime Zero Data Submitted Per Quarter, by Federal Agency, State, and State Agency, 2021—Continued

(Number.)

| Agency name | Zero data per quarter[1] | | | | Population[2] |
|---|---|---|---|---|---|
| | 1st quarter | 2nd quarter | 3rd quarter | 4th quarter | |
| Mason | 0 | 0 | 0 | 0 | |
| Mecosta | 0 | 0 | 0 | 0 | |
| Missaukee | 0 | 0 | 0 | 0 | |
| Montmorency | 0 | 0 | 0 | 0 | |
| Newaygo | 0 | 0 | 0 | 0 | |
| Oceana | 0 | 0 | 0 | 0 | |
| Ogemaw | 0 | 0 | 0 | 0 | |
| Otsego | 0 | 0 | 0 | 0 | |
| Presque Isle | 0 | 0 | 0 | 0 | |
| Sanilac | 0 | 0 | 0 | 0 | |
| Schoolcraft | 0 | 0 | 0 | 0 | |
| St. Joseph | 0 | 0 | 0 | 0 | |
| Wexford | 0 | 0 | 0 | 0 | |
| **State Police Agencies** | | | | | |
| State Police | | | | | |
| Alcona County | 0 | 0 | 0 | 0 | |
| Alger County | 0 | 0 | 0 | 0 | |
| Allegan County | 0 | 0 | 0 | 0 | |
| Alpena County | 0 | 0 | 0 | 0 | |
| Antrim County | 0 | 0 | 0 | 0 | |
| Arenac County | 0 | 0 | 0 | 0 | |
| Baraga County | 0 | 0 | 0 | 0 | |
| Barry County | 0 | 0 | 0 | 0 | |
| Benzie County | 0 | 0 | 0 | 0 | |
| Berrien County | 0 | 0 | 0 | 0 | |
| Cass County | 0 | 0 | 0 | 0 | |
| Charlevoix County | 0 | 0 | 0 | 0 | |
| Cheboygan County | 0 | 0 | 0 | 0 | |
| Chippewa County | 0 | 0 | 0 | 0 | |
| Clare County | 0 | 0 | 0 | 0 | |
| Clinton County | 0 | 0 | 0 | 0 | |
| Crawford County | 0 | 0 | 0 | 0 | |
| Delta County | 0 | 0 | 0 | 0 | |
| Dickinson County | 0 | 0 | 0 | 0 | |
| Eaton County | 0 | 0 | 0 | 0 | |
| Emmet County | 0 | 0 | 0 | 0 | |
| Genesee County | 0 | 0 | 0 | 0 | |
| Gladwin County | 0 | 0 | 0 | 0 | |
| Gogebic County | 0 | 0 | 0 | 0 | |
| Gratiot County | 0 | 0 | 0 | 0 | |
| Hillsdale County | 0 | 0 | 0 | 0 | |
| Houghton County | 0 | 0 | 0 | 0 | |
| Huron County | 0 | 0 | 0 | 0 | |
| Ionia County | 0 | 0 | 0 | 0 | |
| Iosco County | 0 | 0 | 0 | 0 | |
| Iron County | 0 | 0 | 0 | 0 | |
| Jackson County | 0 | 0 | 0 | 0 | |
| Kalkaska County | 0 | 0 | 0 | 0 | |
| Keweenaw County | | 0 | 0 | 0 | |
| Lake County | 0 | 0 | 0 | 0 | |
| Lapeer County | 0 | 0 | 0 | 0 | |
| Leelanau County | 0 | 0 | 0 | 0 | |
| Luce County | 0 | 0 | 0 | 0 | |
| Mackinac County | 0 | 0 | 0 | 0 | |
| Manistee County | 0 | 0 | 0 | 0 | |
| Mason County | 0 | 0 | 0 | 0 | |
| Mecosta County | 0 | 0 | 0 | 0 | |
| Menominee County | 0 | 0 | 0 | 0 | |
| Missaukee County | 0 | 0 | 0 | 0 | |
| Monroe County | 0 | 0 | 0 | 0 | |
| Montmorency County | 0 | 0 | 0 | 0 | |
| Muskegon County | 0 | 0 | 0 | 0 | |
| Oakland County | 0 | 0 | 0 | 0 | |
| Oceana County | 0 | 0 | 0 | 0 | |
| Ogemaw County | 0 | 0 | 0 | 0 | |
| Ontonagon County | 0 | 0 | 0 | 0 | |
| Oscoda County | 0 | 0 | 0 | 0 | |
| Otsego County | 0 | 0 | 0 | 0 | |
| Ottawa County | 0 | 0 | 0 | 0 | |
| Presque Isle County | 0 | 0 | 0 | 0 | |
| Roscommon County | 0 | 0 | 0 | 0 | |
| Sanilac County | 0 | 0 | 0 | 0 | |
| Schoolcraft County | 0 | 0 | 0 | 0 | |
| St. Clair County | 0 | 0 | 0 | 0 | |
| Tuscola County | 0 | 0 | 0 | 0 | |
| Washtenaw County | 0 | 0 | 0 | 0 | |
| **Tribal Agencies** | | | | | |
| Bay Mills Tribal | 0 | 0 | 0 | 0 | |
| Keweenaw Bay Tribal | 0 | 0 | 0 | 0 | |

## Table 95. Hate Crime Zero Data Submitted Per Quarter, by Federal Agency, State, and State Agency, 2021—Continued

(Number.)

| Agency name | Zero data per quarter[1] | | | | Population[2] |
|---|---|---|---|---|---|
| | 1st quarter | 2nd quarter | 3rd quarter | 4th quarter | |
| Lac Vieux Desert Tribal | 0 | 0 | 0 | 0 | |
| Little River Band of Ottawa Indians | 0 | 0 | 0 | 0 | |
| Little Traverse Bay Bands of Odawa Indians | 0 | 0 | 0 | 0 | |
| Pokagon Tribal | 0 | 0 | 0 | 0 | |
| **Other Agencies** | | | | | |
| Bishop International Airport | 0 | 0 | 0 | 0 | |
| Capitol Region Airport Authority | 0 | 0 | 0 | 0 | |
| Department of Natural Resources Law Enforcement Division | 0 | 0 | 0 | 0 | |
| Genesee County Parks and Recreation | 0 | 0 | 0 | 0 | |
| Gerald R. Ford International Airport | 0 | 0 | 0 | 0 | |
| Great Lakes Central Railroad | | 0 | 0 | 0 | |
| Huron-Clinton Metropolitan Authority | | | | | |
| Hudson Mills Metropark | 0 | 0 | 0 | 0 | |
| Kensington Metropark | 0 | 0 | 0 | 0 | |
| Lower Huron Metropark | 0 | 0 | 0 | 0 | |
| Stony Creek Metropark | 0 | 0 | 0 | 0 | |
| **MINNESOTA** | | | | | |
| **Cities** | | | | | |
| Ada | 0 | 0 | 0 | 0 | 1,542 |
| Adrian | 0 | 0 | 0 | 0 | 1,206 |
| Aitkin | 0 | 0 | 0 | 0 | 1,954 |
| Akeley | 0 | 0 | 0 | 0 | 450 |
| Albany | 0 | 0 | 0 | | 2,813 |
| Albert Lea | 0 | 0 | 0 | 0 | 17,686 |
| Alexandria | 0 | 0 | 0 | 0 | 14,032 |
| Annandale | 0 | 0 | 0 | 0 | 3,579 |
| Anoka | 0 | 0 | 0 | 0 | 17,553 |
| Appleton | 0 | 0 | 0 | 0 | 1,301 |
| Apple Valley | 0 | 0 | 0 | 0 | 55,455 |
| Arlington | 0 | 0 | 0 | 0 | 2,102 |
| Atwater | 0 | 0 | 0 | 0 | 1,111 |
| Austin | 0 | 0 | 0 | 0 | 25,382 |
| Avon | 0 | 0 | 0 | 0 | 1,680 |
| Babbitt | 0 | 0 | 0 | 0 | 1,471 |
| Barnesville | 0 | 0 | 0 | 0 | 2,628 |
| Battle Lake | 0 | 0 | 0 | 0 | 935 |
| Baxter | 0 | 0 | 0 | 0 | 8,571 |
| Bayport | 0 | 0 | 0 | 0 | 3,822 |
| Becker | 0 | 0 | 0 | 0 | 5,080 |
| Belgrade/Brooten | 0 | 0 | 0 | 0 | 1,543 |
| Belle Plaine | 0 | 0 | 0 | 0 | 7,166 |
| Benson | 0 | 0 | 0 | 0 | 2,977 |
| Big Lake | 0 | 0 | 0 | 0 | 11,721 |
| Blackduck | 0 | 0 | 0 | 0 | 838 |
| Blooming Prairie | 0 | 0 | 0 | 0 | 1,921 |
| Blue Earth | 0 | 0 | 0 | 0 | 3,078 |
| Bovey | 0 | 0 | 0 | 0 | 782 |
| Braham | 0 | 0 | 0 | 0 | 1,856 |
| Breckenridge | 0 | 0 | 0 | 0 | 3,111 |
| Breezy Point | 0 | 0 | 0 | 0 | 2,447 |
| Breitung Township | 0 | | | 0 | 613 |
| Brooklyn Center | 0 | 0 | 0 | 0 | 30,258 |
| Brownton | 0 | 0 | 0 | 0 | 706 |
| Buffalo Lake | 0 | 0 | 0 | 0 | 672 |
| Caledonia | 0 | 0 | 0 | 0 | 2,743 |
| Callaway | 0 | 0 | 0 | 0 | 226 |
| Cambridge | 0 | 0 | 0 | 0 | 9,540 |
| Canby | 0 | 0 | 0 | 0 | 1,631 |
| Cannon Falls | 0 | 0 | 0 | 0 | 4,016 |
| Centennial Lakes | 0 | 0 | 0 | 0 | 11,721 |
| Champlin | 0 | 0 | 0 | 0 | 25,249 |
| Chaska | | 0 | 0 | 0 | 27,632 |
| Chatfield | 0 | 0 | 0 | 0 | 2,831 |
| Chisholm | 0 | 0 | 0 | 0 | 4,786 |
| Clara City | 0 | 0 | 0 | 0 | 1,265 |
| Clearbrook | 0 | | | | 537 |
| Cleveland | 0 | 0 | 0 | 0 | 733 |
| Coleraine | 0 | 0 | 0 | 0 | 1,972 |
| Columbia Heights | 0 | 0 | 0 | 0 | 21,238 |
| Comfrey | 0 | 0 | 0 | 0 | 349 |
| Corcoran | 0 | 0 | 0 | 0 | 6,742 |
| Cottage Grove | 0 | 0 | 0 | 0 | 38,534 |
| Crookston | 0 | 0 | 0 | 0 | 7,605 |
| Crosby | 0 | 0 | 0 | 0 | 2,308 |
| Crosslake | 0 | 0 | 0 | 0 | 2,399 |
| Crystal | 0 | 0 | 0 | 0 | 22,628 |
| Cuyuna | 0 | 0 | 0 | 0 | 370 |
| Dawson/Boyd | 0 | 0 | 0 | 0 | 1,514 |
| Dayton | 0 | 0 | 0 | 0 | 7,754 |

## Table 95. Hate Crime Zero Data Submitted Per Quarter, by Federal Agency, State, and State Agency, 2021—Continued

(Number.)

| Agency name | Zero data per quarter[1] | | | | Population[2] |
|---|---|---|---|---|---|
| | 1st quarter | 2nd quarter | 3rd quarter | 4th quarter | |
| Deephaven | 0 | 0 | 0 | 0 | 3,926 |
| Deer River | 0 | 0 | 0 | 0 | 929 |
| Dilworth | 0 | 0 | 0 | 0 | 4,497 |
| Dundas | 0 | 0 | 0 | 0 | 1,682 |
| Eagle Lake | 0 | 0 | 0 | 0 | 3,204 |
| East Grand Forks | 0 | 0 | 0 | 0 | 8,379 |
| East Range | 0 | 0 | 0 | 0 | 3,521 |
| Eden Valley | 0 | 0 | 0 | 0 | 1,037 |
| Edina | 0 | 0 | 0 | 0 | 52,943 |
| Elko New Market | 0 | 0 | 0 | 0 | 4,800 |
| Elk River | 0 | 0 | 0 | 0 | 25,873 |
| Elmore | 0 | 0 | 0 | 0 | 608 |
| Ely | 0 | 0 | 0 | 0 | 3,313 |
| Emily | 0 | 0 | 0 | 0 | 844 |
| Eveleth | 0 | 0 | 0 | 0 | 3,519 |
| Fairfax | 0 | 0 | 0 | 0 | 1,108 |
| Fairmont | 0 | 0 | 0 | 0 | 9,852 |
| Faribault | 0 | 0 | 0 | 0 | 23,960 |
| Fergus Falls | 0 | 0 | 0 | 0 | 13,791 |
| Floodwood | 0 | 0 | 0 | 0 | 524 |
| Frazee | 0 | 0 | 0 | 0 | 1,384 |
| Fulda | 0 | 0 | 0 | 0 | 1,196 |
| Gaylord | 0 | 0 | 0 | 0 | 2,237 |
| Gilbert | 0 | 0 | 0 | 0 | 1,758 |
| Glenwood | 0 | 0 | 0 | 0 | 2,610 |
| Glyndon | 0 | 0 | 0 | 0 | 1,384 |
| Golden Valley | 0 | 0 | 0 | 0 | 21,740 |
| Goodhue | 0 | 0 | 0 | 0 | 1,163 |
| Goodview | 0 | 0 | 0 | 0 | 4,138 |
| Grand Meadow | 0 | | 0 | | 1,198 |
| Grand Rapids | 0 | 0 | 0 | 0 | 11,255 |
| Granite Falls | 0 | 0 | 0 | 0 | 2,648 |
| Hallock | 0 | 0 | 0 | 0 | 896 |
| Hastings | 0 | 0 | 0 | 0 | 22,955 |
| Hawley | 0 | 0 | 0 | 0 | 2,225 |
| Hector | 0 | 0 | 0 | 0 | 1,031 |
| Henderson | 0 | 0 | 0 | 0 | 922 |
| Henning | | | | 0 | 806 |
| Hermantown | 0 | 0 | 0 | 0 | 9,512 |
| Heron Lake | 0 | 0 | 0 | 0 | 638 |
| Hibbing | 0 | 0 | 0 | 0 | 15,655 |
| Hill City | 0 | 0 | 0 | 0 | 575 |
| Hokah | 0 | 0 | 0 | 0 | 545 |
| Houston | 0 | 0 | 0 | 0 | 970 |
| Howard Lake | 0 | 0 | 0 | 0 | 2,182 |
| Hutchinson | 0 | 0 | 0 | 0 | 13,961 |
| International Falls | 0 | 0 | 0 | 0 | 5,648 |
| Isanti | 0 | 0 | 0 | 0 | 6,576 |
| Isle | 0 | 0 | 0 | 0 | 793 |
| Janesville | 0 | 0 | 0 | 0 | 2,246 |
| Kasson | 0 | 0 | 0 | 0 | 6,585 |
| Keewatin | 0 | 0 | 0 | 0 | 1,006 |
| Kenyon | 0 | 0 | 0 | 0 | 1,785 |
| La Crescent | 0 | 0 | 0 | 0 | 5,027 |
| Lake City | 0 | 0 | 0 | 0 | 5,119 |
| Lake Crystal | 0 | 0 | 0 | 0 | 2,508 |
| Lakefield | 0 | 0 | 0 | 0 | 1,591 |
| Lake Park | | 0 | | 0 | 788 |
| Lake Shore | 0 | 0 | 0 | 0 | 1,076 |
| Lamberton | 0 | 0 | 0 | 0 | 753 |
| Le Center | 0 | 0 | 0 | 0 | 2,480 |
| Lester Prairie | 0 | 0 | 0 | 0 | 1,720 |
| Le Sueur | 0 | 0 | 0 | 0 | 4,029 |
| Lewiston | 0 | 0 | 0 | 0 | 1,536 |
| Little Falls | 0 | 0 | 0 | 0 | 8,597 |
| Long Prairie | 0 | 0 | 0 | 0 | 3,282 |
| Lonsdale | 0 | 0 | 0 | 0 | 4,366 |
| Madelia | 0 | 0 | 0 | 0 | 2,217 |
| Madison Lake | 0 | 0 | 0 | 0 | 1,215 |
| Maple Grove | 0 | 0 | 0 | 0 | 74,097 |
| Mapleton | 0 | 0 | 0 | 0 | 2,178 |
| Marshall | 0 | 0 | 0 | 0 | 13,391 |
| McGregor | 0 | 0 | 0 | 0 | 357 |
| Medina | 0 | 0 | 0 | 0 | 6,969 |
| Melrose | 0 | 0 | 0 | 0 | 3,680 |
| Menahga | 0 | 0 | 0 | 0 | 1,308 |
| Mendota Heights | 0 | 0 | 0 | 0 | 11,469 |
| Milaca | 0 | 0 | 0 | 0 | 2,894 |
| Minneota | 0 | 0 | 0 | 0 | 1,334 |
| Minnesota Lake | 0 | 0 | 0 | 0 | 630 |
| Minnetrista | 0 | 0 | 0 | 0 | 11,095 |

## Table 95. Hate Crime Zero Data Submitted Per Quarter, by Federal Agency, State, and State Agency, 2021—Continued

(Number.)

| Agency name | Zero data per quarter[1] | | | | Population[2] |
|---|---|---|---|---|---|
| | 1st quarter | 2nd quarter | 3rd quarter | 4th quarter | |
| Montevideo | 0 | 0 | 0 | 0 | 4,995 |
| Montgomery | 0 | 0 | 0 | 0 | 3,062 |
| Moorhead | 0 | 0 | 0 | 0 | 44,488 |
| Moose Lake | 0 | 0 | 0 | 0 | 2,788 |
| Morgan | 0 | 0 | 0 | 0 | 826 |
| Motley | 0 | 0 | 0 | 0 | 651 |
| Mountain Lake | 0 | 0 | 0 | 0 | 2,037 |
| Nashwauk | 0 | 0 | 0 | 0 | 947 |
| New Hope | 0 | 0 | 0 | 0 | 20,671 |
| New Prague | 0 | 0 | 0 | 0 | 8,293 |
| New Richland | 0 | 0 | 0 | 0 | 1,167 |
| New Ulm | 0 | 0 | 0 | 0 | 13,106 |
| New York Mills | 0 | 0 | 0 | 0 | 1,222 |
| Nisswa | 0 | 0 | 0 | 0 | 2,130 |
| North Branch | 0 | 0 | 0 | 0 | 10,908 |
| Northfield | 0 | 0 | 0 | 0 | 20,828 |
| North Mankato | 0 | 0 | 0 | 0 | 14,117 |
| North St. Paul | 0 | 0 | 0 | 0 | 12,557 |
| Oakdale | 0 | 0 | 0 | 0 | 27,808 |
| Oak Park Heights | 0 | 0 | 0 | 0 | 5,031 |
| Olivia | 0 | 0 | 0 | 0 | 2,291 |
| Onamia | 0 | 0 | 0 | 0 | 856 |
| Orono | 0 | 0 | 0 | 0 | 20,241 |
| Ortonville | 0 | 0 | 0 | 0 | 1,732 |
| Osakis | 0 | 0 | 0 | 0 | 1,742 |
| Osseo | 0 | 0 | 0 | 0 | 2,732 |
| Owatonna | 0 | 0 | 0 | 0 | 25,683 |
| Parkers Prairie | 0 | 0 | 0 | 0 | 991 |
| Park Rapids | 0 | 0 | 0 | 0 | 4,387 |
| Paynesville | 0 | 0 | 0 | 0 | 2,542 |
| Pelican Rapids | 0 | 0 | 0 | 0 | 2,652 |
| Pequot Lakes | 0 | 0 | 0 | 0 | 2,320 |
| Perham | 0 | 0 | 0 | 0 | 3,708 |
| Pierz | 0 | 0 | 0 | 0 | 1,361 |
| Pike Bay | 0 | | | | 1,711 |
| Pillager | 0 | 0 | 0 | 0 | 488 |
| Pine River | 0 | 0 | 0 | 0 | 932 |
| Plainview | 0 | 0 | 0 | 0 | 3,287 |
| Preston | 0 | 0 | 0 | 0 | 1,275 |
| Prior Lake | 0 | 0 | 0 | 0 | 27,779 |
| Proctor | 0 | 0 | 0 | 0 | 3,001 |
| Ramsey | 0 | 0 | 0 | 0 | 29,053 |
| Redwood Falls | 0 | 0 | 0 | 0 | 4,914 |
| Renville | 0 | 0 | 0 | 0 | 1,151 |
| Rice | 0 | 0 | 0 | 0 | 1,413 |
| Robbinsdale | 0 | 0 | 0 | 0 | 14,213 |
| Rogers | 0 | 0 | 0 | 0 | 13,889 |
| Roseau | 0 | 0 | 0 | 0 | 2,662 |
| Royalton | 0 | 0 | 0 | 0 | 1,227 |
| Rushford | 0 | 0 | 0 | 0 | 1,692 |
| Sauk Centre | 0 | 0 | 0 | 0 | 4,556 |
| Sauk Rapids | 0 | 0 | 0 | 0 | 14,489 |
| Sebeka | 0 | 0 | 0 | 0 | 664 |
| Sherburn | 0 | 0 | 0 | 0 | 1,072 |
| Silver Bay | 0 | 0 | 0 | 0 | 1,739 |
| Slayton | 0 | 0 | 0 | 0 | 1,941 |
| Sleepy Eye | 0 | 0 | 0 | 0 | 3,304 |
| South Lake Minnetonka | 0 | 0 | 0 | 0 | 12,833 |
| South St. Paul | 0 | 0 | 0 | 0 | 19,895 |
| Springfield | 0 | 0 | 0 | 0 | 1,975 |
| Spring Grove | 0 | 0 | 0 | 0 | 1,255 |
| Spring Lake Park | 0 | 0 | 0 | 0 | 6,960 |
| Staples | 0 | 0 | 0 | 0 | 3,074 |
| Starbuck | 0 | 0 | 0 | 0 | 1,264 |
| St. Charles | 0 | 0 | 0 | 0 | 3,771 |
| St. Francis | 0 | 0 | 0 | 0 | 8,154 |
| Stillwater | 0 | 0 | 0 | 0 | 19,799 |
| St. Joseph | 0 | 0 | 0 | 0 | 7,864 |
| St. Paul Park | 0 | 0 | 0 | 0 | 5,359 |
| St. Peter | 0 | 0 | 0 | 0 | 12,121 |
| Thief River Falls | 0 | 0 | 0 | 0 | 8,693 |
| Tracy | 0 | 0 | 0 | 0 | 2,045 |
| Trimont | | 0 | 0 | 0 | 686 |
| Truman | 0 | 0 | 0 | 0 | 1,020 |
| Twin Valley | 0 | 0 | 0 | 0 | 743 |
| Two Harbors | 0 | 0 | 0 | 0 | 3,486 |
| Tyler | 0 | 0 | 0 | 0 | 1,050 |
| Verndale | 0 | 0 | 0 | 0 | 574 |
| Virginia | 0 | 0 | 0 | 0 | 8,259 |
| Wabasha | 0 | 0 | 0 | 0 | 2,462 |
| Wadena | 0 | 0 | 0 | 0 | 4,126 |

## Table 95. Hate Crime Zero Data Submitted Per Quarter, by Federal Agency, State, and State Agency, 2021—Continued

(Number.)

| Agency name | Zero data per quarter[1] | | | | Population[2] |
|---|---|---|---|---|---|
| | 1st quarter | 2nd quarter | 3rd quarter | 4th quarter | |
| Waite Park | 0 | 0 | 0 | 0 | 7,839 |
| Walker | 0 | 0 | 0 | 0 | 926 |
| Walnut Grove | 0 | 0 | 0 | 0 | 791 |
| Warroad | 0 | 0 | 0 | 0 | 1,792 |
| Waseca | 0 | 0 | 0 | 0 | 8,779 |
| Waterville | 0 | 0 | 0 | 0 | 1,870 |
| Wayzata | 0 | 0 | 0 | 0 | 6,519 |
| Wells | 0 | 0 | 0 | 0 | 2,141 |
| Westbrook | 0 | 0 | 0 | 0 | 709 |
| West Concord | 0 | 0 | 0 | 0 | 761 |
| West Hennepin | 0 | 0 | 0 | 0 | 5,955 |
| Wheaton | 0 | 0 | 0 | 0 | 1,255 |
| White Bear Lake | 0 | 0 | 0 | 0 | 25,747 |
| Willmar | 0 | 0 | 0 | 0 | 19,922 |
| Winnebago | 0 | 0 | 0 | 0 | 1,324 |
| Winona | 0 | 0 | 0 | 0 | 26,446 |
| Winsted | 0 | 0 | 0 | 0 | 2,220 |
| Winthrop | 0 | 0 | 0 | 0 | 1,315 |
| Worthington | 0 | 0 | 0 | 0 | 12,983 |
| Wyoming | 0 | 0 | 0 | 0 | 8,112 |
| Zumbrota | 0 | 0 | 0 | 0 | 3,556 |
| **Universities and Colleges** | | | | | |
| University of Minnesota | | | | | |
| Morris | 0 | 0 | 0 | 0 | 1,637 |
| Twin Cities | 0 | 0 | 0 | 0 | 63,760 |
| **Metropolitan Counties** | | | | | |
| Anoka | 0 | 0 | 0 | 0 | |
| Benton | 0 | 0 | 0 | 0 | |
| Carlton | 0 | 0 | 0 | 0 | |
| Chisago | 0 | 0 | 0 | 0 | |
| Clay | 0 | 0 | 0 | 0 | |
| Dakota | 0 | 0 | 0 | 0 | |
| Dodge | 0 | 0 | 0 | 0 | |
| Fillmore | 0 | 0 | 0 | 0 | |
| Hennepin | 0 | 0 | 0 | 0 | |
| Houston | 0 | 0 | 0 | 0 | |
| Isanti | 0 | 0 | 0 | 0 | |
| Le Sueur | 0 | 0 | 0 | 0 | |
| Nicollet | 0 | 0 | 0 | 0 | |
| Polk | 0 | 0 | 0 | 0 | |
| Wabasha | 0 | 0 | 0 | 0 | |
| **Nonmetropolitan Counties** | | | | | |
| Aitkin | 0 | 0 | 0 | 0 | |
| Becker | 0 | 0 | 0 | 0 | |
| Big Stone | 0 | 0 | 0 | 0 | |
| Brown | 0 | 0 | 0 | 0 | |
| Chippewa | 0 | | 0 | 0 | |
| Clearwater | 0 | 0 | 0 | 0 | |
| Cook | 0 | 0 | 0 | 0 | |
| Cottonwood | 0 | 0 | 0 | 0 | |
| Crow Wing | 0 | 0 | 0 | 0 | |
| Douglas | 0 | 0 | 0 | 0 | |
| Faribault | 0 | 0 | 0 | 0 | |
| Freeborn | 0 | 0 | 0 | 0 | |
| Goodhue | 0 | 0 | 0 | 0 | |
| Grant | 0 | 0 | 0 | 0 | |
| Itasca | 0 | 0 | 0 | 0 | |
| Jackson | 0 | 0 | 0 | 0 | |
| Kanabec | 0 | 0 | 0 | 0 | |
| Kandiyohi | 0 | 0 | 0 | 0 | |
| Kittson | 0 | 0 | 0 | 0 | |
| Lac qui Parle | 0 | 0 | 0 | 0 | |
| Lincoln | 0 | 0 | 0 | 0 | |
| Lyon | 0 | 0 | 0 | 0 | |
| Mahnomen | 0 | 0 | 0 | 0 | |
| Marshall | 0 | 0 | 0 | 0 | |
| Martin | 0 | 0 | 0 | 0 | |
| McLeod | 0 | 0 | 0 | 0 | |
| Morrison | 0 | 0 | 0 | 0 | |
| Mower | 0 | 0 | 0 | 0 | |
| Murray | 0 | 0 | 0 | 0 | |
| Nobles | 0 | 0 | 0 | 0 | |
| Norman | 0 | 0 | 0 | 0 | |
| Otter Tail | 0 | 0 | 0 | 0 | |
| Pennington | 0 | 0 | 0 | 0 | |
| Pine | 0 | 0 | 0 | 0 | |
| Pipestone | 0 | 0 | 0 | 0 | |
| Pope | 0 | 0 | 0 | 0 | |

**Table 95. Hate Crime Zero Data Submitted Per Quarter, by Federal Agency, State, and State Agency, 2021—Continued**

(Number.)

| Agency name | Zero data per quarter[1] | | | | Population[2] |
|---|---|---|---|---|---|
| | 1st quarter | 2nd quarter | 3rd quarter | 4th quarter | |
| Red Lake | 0 | 0 | 0 | 0 | |
| Redwood | 0 | 0 | 0 | 0 | |
| Renville | 0 | 0 | 0 | 0 | |
| Rice | 0 | 0 | 0 | 0 | |
| Rock | 0 | 0 | 0 | 0 | |
| Roseau | 0 | 0 | 0 | 0 | |
| Sibley | 0 | 0 | 0 | 0 | |
| Steele | 0 | 0 | 0 | 0 | |
| Stevens | 0 | 0 | 0 | 0 | |
| Swift | 0 | 0 | 0 | 0 | |
| Traverse | 0 | 0 | 0 | 0 | |
| Wadena | 0 | 0 | 0 | 0 | |
| Watonwan | 0 | 0 | 0 | 0 | |
| Wilkin | 0 | 0 | 0 | 0 | |
| Winona | 0 | 0 | 0 | 0 | |
| Yellow Medicine | 0 | 0 | 0 | 0 | |
| **State Police Agencies** | | | | | |
| Minnesota State Patrol | 0 | 0 | 0 | 0 | |
| State Patrol | | | | | |
| Brainerd | 0 | 0 | 0 | 0 | |
| Detroit Lakes | 0 | 0 | 0 | 0 | |
| Duluth | 0 | 0 | 0 | 0 | |
| Golden Valley | 0 | 0 | 0 | 0 | |
| Mankato | 0 | 0 | 0 | 0 | |
| Marshall | 0 | 0 | 0 | 0 | |
| Oakdale | 0 | 0 | 0 | 0 | |
| Rochester | 0 | 0 | 0 | 0 | |
| St. Cloud | 0 | 0 | 0 | 0 | |
| Thief River Falls | 0 | 0 | 0 | 0 | |
| Virginia | 0 | 0 | 0 | 0 | |
| **Tribal Agencies** | | | | | |
| Fond du Lac Tribal | 0 | 0 | 0 | 0 | |
| Lower Sioux Tribal | 0 | 0 | 0 | 0 | |
| Mille Lacs Tribal | 0 | 0 | 0 | 0 | |
| Nett Lake Tribal | 0 | 0 | 0 | 0 | |
| Red Lake Agency | 0 | 0 | 0 | 0 | |
| White Earth Tribal | 0 | 0 | 0 | 0 | |
| **Other Agencies** | | | | | |
| Bureau of Criminal Apprehension | 0 | 0 | 0 | 0 | |
| Capitol Security, St. Paul | 0 | 0 | 0 | 0 | |
| Department of Natural Resources Enforcement Division | 0 | 0 | 0 | 0 | |
| Minneapolis-St. Paul International Airport | 0 | 0 | 0 | 0 | |
| Minnesota Department of Public Safety Alcohol and Gambling Enforcement | 0 | 0 | 0 | 0 | |
| Minnesota State Fair Police | 0 | 0 | 0 | 0 | |
| Three Rivers Park District | 0 | 0 | 0 | 0 | |
| **MISSISSIPPI** | | | | | |
| **Cities** | | | | | |
| Ackerman | 0 | 0 | 0 | 0 | 1,407 |
| Amory | 0 | 0 | 0 | 0 | 6,660 |
| Batesville | 0 | 0 | 0 | 0 | 7,085 |
| Bay Springs | 0 | 0 | 0 | 0 | 1,638 |
| Bay St. Louis | 0 | 0 | 0 | 0 | 15,188 |
| Biloxi | 0 | 0 | 0 | 0 | 46,317 |
| Blue Springs | 0 | 0 | 0 | 0 | 245 |
| Brandon | 0 | 0 | 0 | 0 | 24,639 |
| Brookhaven | 0 | 0 | 0 | 0 | 11,798 |
| Bruce | 0 | 0 | 0 | 0 | 1,784 |
| Byhalia | 0 | 0 | 0 | 0 | 1,204 |
| Byram | 0 | 0 | 0 | 0 | 11,240 |
| Charleston | 0 | 0 | 0 | 0 | 1,854 |
| Cleveland | 0 | 0 | 0 | 0 | 10,710 |
| Clinton | 0 | 0 | 0 | 0 | 23,737 |
| Coffeeville | 0 | 0 | 0 | 0 | 803 |
| Coldwater | 0 | 0 | 0 | 0 | 1,521 |
| Collins | 0 | 0 | 0 | 0 | 2,402 |
| Corinth | 0 | 0 | 0 | 0 | 14,421 |
| Derma | 0 | 0 | 0 | 0 | 955 |
| D'Iberville | 0 | 0 | 0 | 0 | 14,234 |
| Eupora | 0 | 0 | 0 | 0 | 1,980 |
| Florence | 0 | 0 | 0 | 0 | 4,573 |
| Flowood | 0 | 0 | 0 | 0 | 9,743 |
| Fulton | 0 | 0 | 0 | 0 | 3,839 |
| Gautier | 0 | 0 | 0 | 0 | 18,362 |
| Gulfport | 0 | 0 | 0 | 0 | 71,803 |
| Hattiesburg | 0 | 0 | 0 | 0 | 45,809 |
| Heidelberg | 0 | 0 | 0 | 0 | 646 |
| Hernando | 0 | 0 | 0 | 0 | 17,155 |

## Table 95. Hate Crime Zero Data Submitted Per Quarter, by Federal Agency, State, and State Agency, 2021—Continued

(Number.)

| Agency name | Zero data per quarter[1] | | | | Population[2] |
|---|---|---|---|---|---|
| | 1st quarter | 2nd quarter | 3rd quarter | 4th quarter | |
| Holly Springs | 0 | 0 | 0 | 0 | 7,674 |
| Horn Lake | 0 | 0 | 0 | 0 | 27,401 |
| Kosciusko | 0 | 0 | 0 | 0 | 6,545 |
| Laurel | 0 | 0 | 0 | 0 | 18,165 |
| Long Beach | 0 | 0 | 0 | 0 | 16,260 |
| Louisville | 0 | 0 | 0 | 0 | 5,861 |
| Lucedale | 0 | 0 | 0 | 0 | 3,140 |
| Lumberton | 0 | 0 | 0 | 0 | 2,262 |
| Madison | 0 | 0 | 0 | 0 | 25,860 |
| Mathiston | 0 | 0 | 0 | 0 | 665 |
| Mendenhall | 0 | 0 | 0 | 0 | 2,382 |
| Myrtle | 0 | 0 | 0 | 0 | 504 |
| Oakland | 0 | 0 | 0 | 0 | 489 |
| Ocean Springs | 0 | 0 | 0 | 0 | 17,833 |
| Olive Branch | 0 | 0 | 0 | 0 | 40,308 |
| Oxford | 0 | 0 | 0 | 0 | 29,367 |
| Pascagoula | 0 | 0 | 0 | 0 | 21,468 |
| Pass Christian | 0 | 0 | 0 | 0 | 6,724 |
| Petal | 0 | 0 | 0 | 0 | 10,717 |
| Pontotoc | 0 | 0 | 0 | 0 | 6,297 |
| Poplarville | 0 | 0 | 0 | 0 | 2,771 |
| Port Gibson | 0 | 0 | 0 | 0 | 1,263 |
| Puckett | 0 | 0 | 0 | 0 | 349 |
| Quitman | | 0 | 0 | | 2,016 |
| Raymond | 0 | 0 | 0 | 0 | 2,101 |
| Richland | 0 | 0 | 0 | 0 | 7,305 |
| Ridgeland | 0 | 0 | 0 | 0 | 23,901 |
| Sandersville | 0 | 0 | 0 | 0 | 720 |
| Seminary | 0 | 0 | 0 | 0 | 281 |
| Smithville | 0 | 0 | 0 | 0 | 722 |
| Starkville | 0 | 0 | 0 | 0 | 25,711 |
| Sumner | 0 | 0 | 0 | 0 | 259 |
| Sumrall | 0 | 0 | 0 | 0 | 1,984 |
| Tunica | 0 | 0 | 0 | 0 | 805 |
| Vardaman | 0 | 0 | 0 | 0 | 1,254 |
| Vicksburg | 0 | 0 | 0 | 0 | 21,114 |
| Walls | 0 | 0 | | | 1,476 |
| Walnut | 0 | 0 | 0 | 0 | 733 |
| Waveland | 0 | 0 | 0 | 0 | 6,303 |
| Waynesboro | 0 | 0 | 0 | 0 | 4,847 |
| Webb | 0 | 0 | | | 460 |
| West Point | 0 | 0 | 0 | 0 | 10,294 |
| Wiggins | 0 | 0 | 0 | 0 | 4,535 |
| **Universities and Colleges** | | | | | |
| Holmes Community College | | | | | |
| Goodman | 0 | 0 | 0 | 0 | 8,142 |
| Grenada[3] | 0 | 0 | 0 | 0 | |
| Ridgeland[3] | 0 | 0 | 0 | 0 | |
| Jones County Junior College | 0 | 0 | 0 | 0 | 6,009 |
| Mississippi Delta Community College | 0 | 0 | 0 | 0 | 4,340 |
| Mississippi State University | 0 | 0 | 0 | 0 | 24,449 |
| Northeast Mississippi Community College | 0 | 0 | 0 | 0 | 4,303 |
| Northwest Mississippi Community College | | | | | |
| Desoto | 0 | 0 | 0 | 0 | 10,336 |
| Senatobia | 0 | 0 | 0 | 0 | 10,336 |
| Pearl River Community College, Forrest | 0 | 0 | 0 | 0 | 6,657 |
| University of Mississippi, Oxford | 0 | 0 | 0 | 0 | 24,309 |
| **Metropolitan Counties** | | | | | |
| Forrest | 0 | 0 | 0 | 0 | |
| Hancock | 0 | 0 | 0 | 0 | |
| Harrison | 0 | 0 | 0 | 0 | |
| Madison | 0 | 0 | 0 | 0 | |
| Tate | 0 | 0 | 0 | 0 | |
| Tunica | 0 | 0 | 0 | 0 | |
| **Nonmetropolitan Counties** | | | | | |
| Alcorn | 0 | 0 | 0 | 0 | |
| Amite | 0 | 0 | 0 | 0 | |
| Attala | 0 | 0 | 0 | 0 | |
| Bolivar | 0 | 0 | 0 | 0 | |
| Calhoun | 0 | 0 | 0 | 0 | |
| Chickasaw | 0 | 0 | 0 | 0 | |
| Choctaw | 0 | 0 | 0 | 0 | |
| Claiborne | 0 | 0 | 0 | 0 | |
| Clay | 0 | 0 | 0 | 0 | |
| Coahoma | 0 | 0 | 0 | 0 | |
| George | 0 | 0 | 0 | 0 | |
| Jasper | 0 | 0 | 0 | 0 | |
| Jefferson | 0 | 0 | 0 | 0 | |

## Table 95. Hate Crime Zero Data Submitted Per Quarter, by Federal Agency, State, and State Agency, 2021—Continued

(Number.)

| Agency name | Zero data per quarter[1] | | | | Population[2] |
|---|---|---|---|---|---|
| | 1st quarter | 2nd quarter | 3rd quarter | 4th quarter | |
| Leake | 0 | 0 | 0 | 0 | |
| Lee | 0 | 0 | 0 | 0 | |
| Lincoln | 0 | 0 | 0 | 0 | |
| Lowndes | 0 | 0 | 0 | 0 | |
| Marion | 0 | 0 | 0 | 0 | |
| Neshoba | 0 | 0 | 0 | 0 | |
| Noxubee | 0 | 0 | 0 | 0 | |
| Pike | 0 | 0 | 0 | 0 | |
| Prentiss | 0 | 0 | 0 | 0 | |
| Smith | 0 | 0 | 0 | 0 | |
| Sunflower | 0 | 0 | 0 | 0 | |
| Tallahatchie | 0 | 0 | 0 | 0 | |
| Tishomingo | 0 | 0 | 0 | 0 | |
| Union | 0 | 0 | 0 | 0 | |
| Wayne | 0 | 0 | 0 | 0 | |
| Webster | 0 | 0 | 0 | 0 | |
| **Other Agencies** | | | | | |
| Reservoir Police Department | 0 | 0 | 0 | 0 | |
| **MISSOURI** | | | | | |
| **Cities** | | | | | |
| Adrian | 0 | 0 | 0 | 0 | 1,594 |
| Alma | 0 | 0 | 0 | 0 | 383 |
| Annapolis | 0 | | | | 334 |
| Arbyrd | 0 | | 0 | 0 | 453 |
| Arcadia | 0 | 0 | 0 | | 549 |
| Arnold | 0 | 0 | 0 | 0 | 21,172 |
| Ashland | 0 | 0 | 0 | 0 | 4,063 |
| Auxvasse | 0 | 0 | 0 | 0 | 979 |
| Ava | 0 | 0 | 0 | 0 | 2,897 |
| Ballwin | 0 | 0 | 0 | 0 | 30,061 |
| Bates City | 0 | | | | 229 |
| Battlefield | 0 | 0 | 0 | 0 | 6,776 |
| Bella Villa | 0 | 0 | 0 | 0 | 719 |
| Bellefontaine Neighbors | 0 | 0 | 0 | 0 | 10,251 |
| Bellflower | 0 | 0 | 0 | 0 | 353 |
| Bel-Nor | 0 | 0 | 0 | 0 | 1,385 |
| Bel-Ridge | 0 | 0 | | | 2,660 |
| Belton | 0 | 0 | 0 | 0 | 23,860 |
| Berkeley | 0 | 0 | 0 | 0 | 8,868 |
| Bernie | 0 | | | | 1,867 |
| Bertrand | 0 | 0 | 0 | 0 | 739 |
| Bethany | 0 | 0 | 0 | 0 | 3,025 |
| Bloomfield | 0 | 0 | 0 | 0 | 1,808 |
| Bolivar | 0 | 0 | 0 | 0 | 11,285 |
| Bonne Terre | 0 | 0 | 0 | 0 | 6,811 |
| Boonville | 0 | 0 | 0 | 0 | 7,833 |
| Bourbon | 0 | 0 | 0 | 0 | 1,558 |
| Branson West | 0 | 0 | 0 | 0 | 449 |
| Breckenridge Hills | 0 | 0 | 0 | 0 | 4,533 |
| Brentwood | 0 | 0 | 0 | 0 | 7,944 |
| Bridgeton | 0 | 0 | 0 | 0 | 11,497 |
| Buffalo | 0 | 0 | 0 | 0 | 3,214 |
| Butler | 0 | 0 | 0 | 0 | 3,981 |
| Byrnes Mill | 0 | 0 | 0 | 0 | 3,040 |
| Cabool | 0 | 0 | 0 | 0 | 2,063 |
| Calverton Park | 0 | 0 | 0 | 0 | 1,265 |
| Camdenton | 0 | 0 | 0 | 0 | 4,186 |
| Campbell | 0 | 0 | 0 | 0 | 1,773 |
| Canalou | 0 | 0 | | | 282 |
| Canton | 0 | 0 | 0 | 0 | 2,308 |
| Carl Junction | 0 | 0 | 0 | 0 | 8,527 |
| Carrollton | 0 | 0 | 0 | 0 | 3,387 |
| Carterville | 0 | 0 | 0 | 0 | 1,972 |
| Carthage | 0 | 0 | 0 | 0 | 14,766 |
| Caruthersville | 0 | 0 | 0 | 0 | 5,212 |
| Cassville | 0 | 0 | 0 | 0 | 3,223 |
| Center | 0 | | | | 505 |
| Centralia | 0 | 0 | 0 | 0 | 4,376 |
| Chaffee | 0 | 0 | 0 | 0 | 2,895 |
| Chillicothe | 0 | 0 | 0 | 0 | 8,865 |
| Clarkson Valley | 0 | 0 | 0 | 0 | 2,601 |
| Clayton | 0 | 0 | 0 | 0 | 16,859 |
| Cleveland | 0 | 0 | 0 | 0 | 669 |
| Columbia | 0 | 0 | 0 | 0 | 126,418 |
| Concordia | 0 | 0 | 0 | 0 | 2,367 |
| Corder | 0 | 0 | 0 | 0 | 406 |
| Cottleville | 0 | 0 | 0 | 0 | 6,333 |
| Country Club Hills | 0 | 0 | 0 | 0 | 1,243 |
| Country Club Village | 0 | 0 | 0 | 0 | 2,537 |

## Table 95. Hate Crime Zero Data Submitted Per Quarter, by Federal Agency, State, and State Agency, 2021—Continued

(Number.)

| Agency name | Zero data per quarter[1] | | | | Population[2] |
|---|---|---|---|---|---|
| | 1st quarter | 2nd quarter | 3rd quarter | 4th quarter | |
| Crestwood | 0 | 0 | 0 | 0 | 11,828 |
| Creve Coeur | 0 | 0 | 0 | 0 | 18,708 |
| Crocker | 0 | 0 | 0 | 0 | 1,023 |
| Crystal City | 0 | 0 | 0 | 0 | 4,680 |
| Cuba | 0 | 0 | 0 | 0 | 3,270 |
| Delta | 0 | 0 | 0 | 0 | 419 |
| Desloge | 0 | 0 | 0 | 0 | 4,883 |
| Des Peres | 0 | 0 | 0 | 0 | 8,757 |
| Dexter | 0 | 0 | 0 | 0 | 7,833 |
| Dixon | 0 | 0 | 0 | 0 | 1,446 |
| Doniphan | 0 | 0 | 0 | 0 | 1,911 |
| Duquesne | 0 | 0 | 0 | 0 | 1,681 |
| East Lynne | 0 | | | | 313 |
| East Prairie | | 0 | 0 | 0 | 2,905 |
| Edgar Springs | 0 | 0 | 0 | | 194 |
| Edmundson | 0 | 0 | 0 | 0 | 827 |
| Eldon | 0 | 0 | 0 | 0 | 4,764 |
| El Dorado Springs | 0 | 0 | 0 | 0 | 3,605 |
| Ellisville | 0 | 0 | 0 | 0 | 9,905 |
| Ellsinore | 0 | 0 | 0 | 0 | 424 |
| Eureka | 0 | 0 | 0 | 0 | 11,442 |
| Excelsior Springs | 0 | 0 | 0 | 0 | 11,908 |
| Exeter | 0 | 0 | 0 | 0 | 770 |
| Farber | 0 | 0 | 0 | 0 | 309 |
| Farmington | 0 | 0 | 0 | 0 | 18,926 |
| Fayette | 0 | 0 | 0 | 0 | 2,682 |
| Ferguson | 0 | 0 | 0 | 0 | 20,386 |
| Festus | 0 | 0 | 0 | | 12,167 |
| Flordell Hills | 0 | 0 | 0 | 0 | 797 |
| Fordland | 0 | 0 | 0 | 0 | 861 |
| Foristell | 0 | 0 | 0 | 0 | 627 |
| Forsyth | 0 | 0 | 0 | 0 | 2,568 |
| Frontenac | 0 | 0 | 0 | 0 | 3,899 |
| Fulton | 0 | 0 | 0 | 0 | 12,530 |
| Galena | 0 | 0 | 0 | 0 | 443 |
| Gerald | 0 | 0 | 0 | 0 | 1,324 |
| Gideon | 0 | 0 | 0 | 0 | 939 |
| Gower | 0 | 0 | 0 | 0 | 1,446 |
| Granby | 0 | 0 | 0 | 0 | 2,096 |
| Greenfield | | 0 | 0 | 0 | 1,310 |
| Hamilton | 0 | 0 | | | 1,680 |
| Hardin | | | 0 | 0 | 527 |
| Harrisonville | 0 | 0 | 0 | 0 | 10,091 |
| Hartville | 0 | 0 | 0 | 0 | 616 |
| Hawk Point | 0 | 0 | 0 | | 723 |
| Hayti | 0 | 0 | 0 | 0 | 2,425 |
| Hazelwood | 0 | 0 | 0 | 0 | 24,976 |
| Herculaneum | 0 | 0 | 0 | 0 | 4,346 |
| Hermann | 0 | 0 | 0 | 0 | 2,311 |
| Higginsville | 0 | 0 | 0 | 0 | 4,639 |
| Highlandville | 0 | 0 | 0 | 0 | 1,070 |
| Hillsboro | 0 | 0 | 0 | 0 | 3,404 |
| Hillsdale | 0 | 0 | 0 | 0 | 1,542 |
| Holden | 0 | 0 | 0 | 0 | 2,232 |
| Hollister | 0 | 0 | 0 | 0 | 4,626 |
| Holts Summit | 0 | 0 | 0 | 0 | 5,296 |
| Hornersville | 0 | 0 | 0 | 0 | 579 |
| Houston | 0 | | 0 | 0 | 2,085 |
| Humansville | | 0 | 0 | 0 | 1,072 |
| Ironton | 0 | 0 | 0 | 0 | 1,378 |
| Jackson | 0 | 0 | 0 | 0 | 14,792 |
| Jefferson City | 0 | 0 | 0 | 0 | 41,851 |
| Jonesburg | 0 | 0 | 0 | 0 | 692 |
| Joplin | 0 | 0 | 0 | 0 | 50,970 |
| Kearney | 0 | 0 | 0 | 0 | 11,467 |
| Kennett | 0 | 0 | 0 | 0 | 9,946 |
| Kimmswick | | 0 | | 0 | 139 |
| Kirkwood | 0 | 0 | 0 | 0 | 27,897 |
| Knob Noster | 0 | 0 | 0 | 0 | 2,806 |
| Ladue | 0 | 0 | 0 | 0 | 8,624 |
| La Grange | 0 | 0 | 0 | | 889 |
| Lake Lafayette | 0 | 0 | 0 | 0 | 342 |
| Lake Lotawana | 0 | 0 | 0 | 0 | 2,152 |
| Lakeshire | 0 | 0 | 0 | 0 | 1,380 |
| Lake St. Louis | 0 | 0 | 0 | 0 | 17,469 |
| Lake Tapawingo | 0 | 0 | 0 | 0 | 718 |
| Lanagan | 0 | 0 | 0 | 0 | 403 |
| La Plata | 0 | 0 | 0 | 0 | 1,297 |
| Lathrop | 0 | 0 | 0 | 0 | 2,012 |
| Laurie | 0 | 0 | 0 | 0 | 983 |
| Lawson | 0 | 0 | 0 | 0 | 2,394 |

## Table 95. Hate Crime Zero Data Submitted Per Quarter, by Federal Agency, State, and State Agency, 2021—Continued

(Number.)

| Agency name | Zero data per quarter[1] | | | | Population[2] |
|---|---|---|---|---|---|
| | 1st quarter | 2nd quarter | 3rd quarter | 4th quarter | |
| Leadwood | 0 | 0 | 0 | 0 | 1,151 |
| Lexington | 0 | 0 | 0 | 0 | 4,526 |
| Licking | 0 | 0 | 0 | 0 | 2,848 |
| Lincoln | 0 | 0 | 0 | 0 | 1,198 |
| Linn Creek | 0 | 0 | 0 | 0 | 256 |
| Lone Jack | 0 | 0 | 0 | 0 | 1,412 |
| Louisiana | 0 | 0 | 0 | 0 | 3,206 |
| Lowry City | | | 0 | 0 | 629 |
| Macon | 0 | 0 | 0 | 0 | 5,327 |
| Malden | 0 | 0 | 0 | 0 | 3,812 |
| Manchester | 0 | 0 | 0 | 0 | 18,081 |
| Mansfield | 0 | 0 | 0 | 0 | 1,240 |
| Maplewood | 0 | 0 | 0 | 0 | 8,076 |
| Marble Hill | 0 | 0 | 0 | 0 | 1,457 |
| Marceline | 0 | 0 | 0 | 0 | 2,047 |
| Marionville | 0 | 0 | 0 | 0 | 2,157 |
| Marshall | 0 | 0 | 0 | 0 | 12,868 |
| Marshfield | 0 | 0 | 0 | 0 | 7,786 |
| Maryland Heights | 0 | 0 | 0 | 0 | 26,839 |
| Matthews | 0 | 0 | 0 | 0 | 580 |
| Merriam Woods | 0 | 0 | 0 | 0 | 1,870 |
| Mexico | 0 | 0 | 0 | 0 | 11,531 |
| Milan | 0 | 0 | 0 | 0 | 1,744 |
| Miner | 0 | 0 | 0 | 0 | 935 |
| Moberly | 0 | 0 | 0 | 0 | 13,459 |
| Moline Acres | 0 | 0 | 0 | 0 | 2,331 |
| Monett | 0 | 0 | 0 | 0 | 9,188 |
| Morehouse | 0 | 0 | | | 832 |
| Moscow Mills | 0 | 0 | 0 | 0 | 3,784 |
| Mound City | 0 | 0 | 0 | 0 | 982 |
| Mountain View | 0 | 0 | 0 | 0 | 2,649 |
| Mount Vernon | 0 | 0 | 0 | 0 | 4,468 |
| Neosho | 0 | 0 | 0 | 0 | 12,143 |
| New Florence | 0 | 0 | 0 | 0 | 698 |
| New Haven | 0 | 0 | | | 2,075 |
| New London | 0 | 0 | 0 | | 987 |
| New Madrid | 0 | 0 | 0 | 0 | 2,730 |
| Niangua | 0 | 0 | 0 | 0 | 426 |
| Nixa | 0 | 0 | 0 | 0 | 23,795 |
| Noel | 0 | 0 | 0 | 0 | 1,806 |
| Normandy | 0 | 0 | 0 | 0 | 7,385 |
| Northmoor | | 0 | 0 | 0 | 364 |
| Northwoods | 0 | 0 | 0 | 0 | 4,337 |
| Oakland | 0 | 0 | 0 | 0 | 1,375 |
| Oakview Village | 0 | 0 | 0 | | 395 |
| Odessa | 0 | 0 | 0 | 0 | 5,293 |
| O'Fallon | 0 | 0 | 0 | 0 | 90,813 |
| Old Monroe | 0 | 0 | 0 | 0 | 294 |
| Olivette | 0 | 0 | 0 | 0 | 7,850 |
| Oregon | 0 | 0 | 0 | 0 | 724 |
| Oronogo | 0 | 0 | 0 | 0 | 2,696 |
| Osage Beach | 0 | 0 | 0 | 0 | 4,706 |
| Osceola | 0 | 0 | 0 | 0 | 934 |
| Owensville | 0 | 0 | 0 | 0 | 2,551 |
| Ozark | | | 0 | 0 | 21,392 |
| Pacific | 0 | 0 | 0 | 0 | 7,108 |
| Pagedale | 0 | 0 | 0 | 0 | 3,287 |
| Palmyra | 0 | 0 | 0 | 0 | 3,574 |
| Park Hills | 0 | 0 | 0 | 0 | 8,482 |
| Parkville | 0 | 0 | 0 | 0 | 8,680 |
| Perry | 0 | 0 | 0 | 0 | 703 |
| Piedmont | 0 | 0 | 0 | 0 | 1,868 |
| Pierce City | 0 | 0 | 0 | 0 | 1,302 |
| Pilot Knob | 0 | 0 | 0 | 0 | 708 |
| Platte City | 0 | 0 | 0 | 0 | 4,998 |
| Pleasant Hill | 0 | 0 | 0 | 0 | 8,801 |
| Pleasant Hope | 0 | 0 | 0 | | 611 |
| Pleasant Valley | 0 | 0 | 0 | 0 | 3,063 |
| Poplar Bluff | 0 | 0 | 0 | 0 | 16,784 |
| Portageville | 0 | 0 | 0 | 0 | 2,838 |
| Potosi | 0 | 0 | 0 | 0 | 2,538 |
| Prairie Home | 0 | 0 | 0 | 0 | 280 |
| Puxico | 0 | 0 | 0 | | 843 |
| Qulin | 0 | 0 | 0 | 0 | 459 |
| Raymore | 0 | 0 | 0 | 0 | 22,885 |
| Reeds Spring | 0 | 0 | 0 | 0 | 873 |
| Republic | 0 | 0 | | | 17,757 |
| Rich Hill | 0 | 0 | 0 | | 1,315 |
| Richland | 0 | 0 | 0 | 0 | 1,791 |
| Richmond Heights | 0 | 0 | 0 | 0 | 8,799 |
| Riverside | 0 | 0 | 0 | 0 | 3,592 |

## Table 95. Hate Crime Zero Data Submitted Per Quarter, by Federal Agency, State, and State Agency, 2021—Continued

(Number.)

| Agency name | Zero data per quarter[1] | | | | Population[2] |
|---|---|---|---|---|---|
| | 1st quarter | 2nd quarter | 3rd quarter | 4th quarter | |
| Riverview | 0 | 0 | 0 | 0 | 2,810 |
| Rockaway Beach | 0 | 0 | 0 | 0 | 866 |
| Rock Hill | 0 | 0 | 0 | 0 | 4,610 |
| Rock Port | 0 | 0 | 0 | | 1,171 |
| Rogersville | 0 | 0 | 0 | 0 | 4,051 |
| Rolla | 0 | 0 | 0 | 0 | 20,519 |
| Rosebud | 0 | 0 | 0 | 0 | 398 |
| Salem | 0 | 0 | 0 | 0 | 4,866 |
| Salisbury | 0 | 0 | 0 | 0 | 1,500 |
| Sarcoxie | 0 | | | | 1,546 |
| Savannah | 0 | 0 | 0 | 0 | 5,177 |
| Scott City | 0 | 0 | 0 | 0 | 4,520 |
| Seligman | 0 | 0 | 0 | 0 | 835 |
| Senath | 0 | | 0 | | 1,580 |
| Seneca | 0 | 0 | 0 | 0 | 2,400 |
| Seymour | 0 | 0 | 0 | 0 | 2,033 |
| Shelbina | 0 | 0 | 0 | 0 | 1,571 |
| Shrewsbury | 0 | 0 | 0 | 0 | 6,046 |
| Smithville | 0 | 0 | 0 | 0 | 11,311 |
| Southwest City | | 0 | 0 | 0 | 954 |
| Sparta | 0 | 0 | 0 | 0 | 2,101 |
| St. Ann | 0 | 0 | 0 | 0 | 12,540 |
| Steele | 0 | 0 | 0 | 0 | 1,825 |
| Steelville | 0 | 0 | 0 | 0 | 1,636 |
| St. John | 0 | 0 | 0 | 0 | 6,299 |
| St. Joseph | 0 | 0 | . | 0 | 0 | 73,821 |
| St. Peters | 0 | 0 | 0 | 0 | 58,597 |
| Strasburg | 0 | 0 | 0 | | 140 |
| Sugar Creek | 0 | 0 | 0 | 0 | 3,225 |
| Sullivan | 0 | 0 | 0 | 0 | 7,118 |
| Sunrise Beach | 0 | 0 | 0 | 0 | 597 |
| Sweet Springs | 0 | 0 | 0 | 0 | 1,408 |
| Thayer | 0 | 0 | 0 | 0 | 2,092 |
| Truesdale | 0 | 0 | 0 | 0 | 944 |
| Union | 0 | 0 | 0 | 0 | 12,292 |
| University City | 0 | 0 | 0 | 0 | 33,930 |
| Van Buren | 0 | 0 | | 0 | 795 |
| Velda City | 0 | 0 | 0 | 0 | 1,351 |
| Verona | 0 | 0 | 0 | 0 | 605 |
| Viburnum | 0 | | | | 645 |
| Vienna | 0 | 0 | 0 | 0 | 599 |
| Vinita Park | 0 | 0 | 0 | 0 | 10,910 |
| Walnut Grove | 0 | 0 | 0 | 0 | 794 |
| Warrenton | 0 | 0 | 0 | 0 | 9,019 |
| Warsaw | 0 | 0 | 0 | 0 | 2,227 |
| Warson Woods | 0 | 0 | 0 | 0 | 1,890 |
| Washington | 0 | 0 | 0 | 0 | 14,270 |
| Waverly | 0 | 0 | 0 | 0 | 846 |
| Waynesville | 0 | 0 | 0 | 0 | 5,348 |
| Weatherby Lake | 0 | 0 | 0 | 0 | 2,125 |
| Webster Groves | 0 | 0 | 0 | 0 | 22,885 |
| Wellington | 0 | 0 | 0 | 0 | 812 |
| Wellsville | 0 | 0 | 0 | 0 | 1,125 |
| Wentzville | 0 | 0 | 0 | 0 | 44,793 |
| Weston | 0 | 0 | 0 | 0 | 1,854 |
| West Plains | 0 | 0 | 0 | 0 | 12,417 |
| Willow Springs | 0 | 0 | 0 | 0 | 2,090 |
| Winfield | 0 | 0 | 0 | 0 | 1,603 |
| Winona | 0 | 0 | 0 | 0 | 1,292 |
| Woodson Terrace | 0 | 0 | 0 | 0 | 4,028 |
| Wright City | 0 | 0 | | 0 | 4,654 |
| **Universities and Colleges** | | | | | |
| Jefferson College | 0 | 0 | 0 | 0 | 5,180 |
| Lincoln University | 0 | 0 | 0 | 0 | 2,947 |
| Metropolitan Community College | 0 | 0 | 0 | 0 | 21,040 |
| Missouri Southern State University | 0 | 0 | 0 | 0 | 6,617 |
| Missouri Western State University | 0 | 0 | 0 | 0 | 6,177 |
| Northwest Missouri State University | 0 | 0 | 0 | 0 | 8,383 |
| Southeast Missouri State University | 0 | 0 | 0 | 0 | 11,812 |
| St. Charles Community College | 0 | 0 | 0 | 0 | 9,056 |
| St. Louis Community College, Meramec | 0 | 0 | 0 | 0 | 26,166 |
| Truman State University | 0 | 0 | 0 | 0 | 5,637 |
| University of Central Missouri | 0 | 0 | 0 | 0 | 15,315 |
| University of Missouri, Columbia | 0 | 0 | 0 | 0 | 32,916 |
| Washington University | 0 | 0 | 0 | 0 | 17,893 |
| **Metropolitan Counties** | | | | | |
| Andrew | 0 | 0 | 0 | 0 | |
| Bates | 0 | 0 | 0 | 0 | |

## Table 95. Hate Crime Zero Data Submitted Per Quarter, by Federal Agency, State, and State Agency, 2021—Continued

(Number.)

| Agency name | Zero data per quarter[1] | | | | Population[2] |
|---|---|---|---|---|---|
| | 1st quarter | 2nd quarter | 3rd quarter | 4th quarter | |
| Boone | 0 | 0 | 0 | 0 | |
| Buchanan | 0 | 0 | 0 | 0 | |
| Caldwell | 0 | 0 | 0 | 0 | |
| Callaway | 0 | 0 | 0 | 0 | |
| Clay | 0 | 0 | 0 | 0 | |
| Clinton | 0 | 0 | 0 | 0 | |
| Cole | 0 | 0 | 0 | 0 | |
| Cooper | 0 | 0 | 0 | 0 | |
| DeKalb | 0 | 0 | 0 | 0 | |
| Howard | 0 | 0 | 0 | | |
| Jasper | 0 | 0 | 0 | 0 | |
| Jefferson | 0 | 0 | 0 | 0 | |
| Lafayette | 0 | 0 | 0 | 0 | |
| Newton | 0 | 0 | 0 | 0 | |
| Osage | 0 | 0 | 0 | 0 | |
| Ray | 0 | 0 | 0 | 0 | |
| St. Charles | 0 | 0 | 0 | 0 | |
| Warren | 0 | 0 | 0 | 0 | |
| **Nonmetropolitan Counties** | | | | | |
| Adair | 0 | 0 | 0 | 0 | |
| Audrain | 0 | 0 | 0 | 0 | |
| Butler | 0 | 0 | 0 | 0 | |
| Camden | 0 | 0 | 0 | 0 | |
| Carroll | 0 | 0 | 0 | 0 | |
| Carter | 0 | 0 | 0 | 0 | |
| Cedar | 0 | 0 | 0 | | |
| Chariton | 0 | 0 | 0 | 0 | |
| Clark | 0 | 0 | 0 | 0 | |
| Crawford | 0 | 0 | 0 | 0 | |
| Dade | 0 | 0 | 0 | 0 | |
| Daviess | 0 | 0 | 0 | 0 | |
| Dent | 0 | 0 | 0 | 0 | |
| Douglas | 0 | 0 | 0 | 0 | |
| Dunklin | 0 | 0 | 0 | 0 | |
| Gasconade | | | | 0 | |
| Grundy | 0 | 0 | 0 | 0 | |
| Henry | 0 | 0 | 0 | 0 | |
| Holt | 0 | 0 | 0 | 0 | |
| Howell | 0 | 0 | 0 | 0 | |
| Iron | 0 | 0 | | | |
| Johnson | 0 | | 0 | 0 | |
| Knox | | 0 | 0 | | |
| Laclede | 0 | 0 | 0 | 0 | |
| Lawrence | 0 | 0 | 0 | 0 | |
| Lewis | 0 | 0 | 0 | 0 | |
| Livingston | 0 | 0 | 0 | 0 | |
| Macon | 0 | 0 | 0 | 0 | |
| Madison | 0 | 0 | 0 | 0 | |
| Maries | 0 | 0 | 0 | 0 | |
| Marion | 0 | 0 | 0 | 0 | |
| McDonald | 0 | 0 | 0 | 0 | |
| Mercer | 0 | 0 | 0 | 0 | |
| Mississippi | 0 | 0 | 0 | 0 | |
| Monroe | 0 | 0 | 0 | 0 | |
| New Madrid | 0 | 0 | 0 | 0 | |
| Nodaway | 0 | 0 | 0 | 0 | |
| Oregon | 0 | 0 | 0 | 0 | |
| Pemiscot | 0 | 0 | 0 | 0 | |
| Perry | 0 | 0 | 0 | 0 | |
| Pettis | 0 | 0 | 0 | 0 | |
| Phelps | 0 | 0 | 0 | 0 | |
| Pike | 0 | 0 | 0 | 0 | |
| Pulaski | 0 | 0 | 0 | 0 | |
| Ralls | 0 | 0 | 0 | 0 | |
| Randolph | 0 | 0 | 0 | | |
| Reynolds | 0 | 0 | | | |
| Ripley | 0 | 0 | 0 | 0 | |
| Saline | 0 | 0 | 0 | 0 | |
| Schuyler | 0 | 0 | 0 | 0 | |
| Shannon | 0 | 0 | | | |
| Shelby | 0 | 0 | 0 | 0 | |
| St. Clair | 0 | 0 | 0 | 0 | |
| Stoddard | 0 | 0 | 0 | 0 | |
| Stone | 0 | 0 | 0 | 0 | |
| Sullivan | 0 | 0 | 0 | 0 | |
| Texas | 0 | 0 | 0 | 0 | |
| Vernon | 0 | 0 | 0 | 0 | |
| Washington | 0 | 0 | 0 | 0 | |
| Wright | 0 | 0 | 0 | 0 | |

## Table 95. Hate Crime Zero Data Submitted Per Quarter, by Federal Agency, State, and State Agency, 2021—Continued

(Number.)

| Agency name | Zero data per quarter[1] | | | | Population[2] |
|---|---|---|---|---|---|
| | 1st quarter | 2nd quarter | 3rd quarter | 4th quarter | |
| **Other Agencies** | | | | | |
| Blue Spring Public Schools | | 0 | 0 | 0 | |
| Capitol Police | 0 | 0 | 0 | 0 | |
| Department of Revenue, Compliance and Investigation Bureau | 0 | 0 | 0 | 0 | |
| Department of Social Services, State Technical Assistance Team | 0 | 0 | 0 | 0 | |
| Division of Alcohol and Tobacco Control | 0 | 0 | 0 | 0 | |
| Dunklin R-5 School District | 0 | 0 | 0 | 0 | |
| Jackson County Drug Task Force | | | | 0 | |
| Jackson County Park Rangers | | 0 | 0 | 0 | |
| Lambert-St. Louis International Airport | 0 | 0 | 0 | | |
| Logan-Rogersville School District | 0 | 0 | 0 | 0 | |
| Northwest Missouri Drug Task Force | 0 | 0 | 0 | 0 | |
| Springfield-Branson Airport | 0 | 0 | 0 | 0 | |
| State Fire Marshal | 0 | 0 | 0 | 0 | |
| State Park Rangers | 0 | 0 | 0 | 0 | |
| St. Louis County Park Rangers | 0 | 0 | 0 | 0 | |
| Terminal Railroad | 0 | 0 | 0 | 0 | |
| Willard Public Schools | | | 0 | 0 | |
| **MONTANA** | | | | | |
| **Cities** | | | | | |
| Baker | 0 | 0 | 0 | 0 | 1,910 |
| Belgrade | 0 | 0 | 0 | 0 | 10,738 |
| Boulder | 0 | 0 | 0 | 0 | 1,303 |
| Bridger | 0 | 0 | 0 | 0 | 775 |
| Chinook | 0 | 0 | 0 | 0 | 1,233 |
| Colstrip | 0 | 0 | 0 | 0 | 2,216 |
| Columbia Falls | 0 | 0 | 0 | 0 | 6,385 |
| Columbus | 0 | 0 | 0 | 0 | 2,141 |
| Conrad | 0 | 0 | 0 | 0 | 2,396 |
| Cut Bank | 0 | 0 | 0 | 0 | 3,028 |
| Deer Lodge | 0 | 0 | 0 | 0 | 2,772 |
| Dillon | 0 | 0 | 0 | 0 | 4,352 |
| East Helena | 0 | 0 | 0 | 0 | 2,140 |
| Ennis | 0 | 0 | 0 | 0 | 1,065 |
| Eureka | 0 | 0 | 0 | 0 | 1,449 |
| Fort Benton | 0 | 0 | 0 | 0 | 1,440 |
| Glasgow | 0 | 0 | 0 | 0 | 3,318 |
| Glendive | 0 | 0 | 0 | 0 | 4,873 |
| Hamilton | 0 | 0 | 0 | | 5,140 |
| Havre | 0 | 0 | 0 | 0 | 9,724 |
| Hot Springs | 0 | 0 | 0 | 0 | 592 |
| Laurel | 0 | 0 | 0 | 0 | 6,710 |
| Lewistown | 0 | 0 | 0 | 0 | 5,882 |
| Livingston | 0 | 0 | 0 | 0 | 7,991 |
| Manhattan | 0 | 0 | 0 | 0 | 1,963 |
| Miles City | 0 | 0 | 0 | 0 | 8,160 |
| Missoula | 0 | 0 | 0 | 0 | 77,852 |
| Polson | 0 | 0 | 0 | 0 | 5,242 |
| Red Lodge | 0 | 0 | 0 | 0 | 2,384 |
| Ronan City | 0 | 0 | 0 | 0 | 2,195 |
| Sidney | 0 | 0 | 0 | 0 | 6,407 |
| Stevensville | 0 | 0 | 0 | 0 | 2,171 |
| St. Ignatius | 0 | 0 | 0 | 0 | 846 |
| Thompson Falls | 0 | 0 | 0 | 0 | 1,443 |
| Troy | 0 | 0 | 0 | 0 | 986 |
| West Yellowstone | 0 | 0 | 0 | 0 | 1,383 |
| Wolf Point | 0 | 0 | 0 | 0 | 2,734 |
| **Universities and Colleges** | | | | | |
| Montana State University | 0 | 0 | 0 | 0 | 18,756 |
| Montana State University, Billings | 0 | 0 | 0 | 0 | 5,824 |
| University of Montana | 0 | 0 | 0 | 0 | 12,694 |
| **Metropolitan Counties** | | | | | |
| Carbon | 0 | 0 | 0 | 0 | |
| Stillwater | 0 | 0 | 0 | 0 | |
| Yellowstone | 0 | 0 | 0 | 0 | |
| **Nonmetropolitan Counties** | | | | | |
| Beaverhead | 0 | 0 | 0 | 0 | |
| Big Horn | 0 | 0 | 0 | 0 | |
| Blaine | 0 | 0 | 0 | 0 | |
| Broadwater | 0 | 0 | 0 | 0 | |
| Butte-Silver Bow | 0 | 0 | 0 | 0 | |
| Carter | 0 | 0 | 0 | 0 | |
| Chouteau | 0 | 0 | 0 | 0 | |
| Custer | 0 | 0 | 0 | 0 | |
| Dawson | 0 | 0 | 0 | 0 | |
| Deer Lodge | 0 | 0 | 0 | 0 | |
| Fallon | 0 | 0 | 0 | 0 | |

## Table 95. Hate Crime Zero Data Submitted Per Quarter, by Federal Agency, State, and State Agency, 2021—Continued

(Number.)

| Agency name | Zero data per quarter[1] | | | | Population[2] |
|---|---|---|---|---|---|
| | 1st quarter | 2nd quarter | 3rd quarter | 4th quarter | |
| Fergus | 0 | 0 | 0 | 0 | |
| Flathead | 0 | 0 | 0 | 0 | |
| Gallatin | 0 | 0 | 0 | 0 | |
| Garfield | 0 | 0 | 0 | 0 | |
| Glacier | 0 | 0 | 0 | 0 | |
| Golden Valley | 0 | 0 | 0 | 0 | |
| Granite | 0 | 0 | 0 | 0 | |
| Hill | 0 | 0 | 0 | 0 | |
| Jefferson | 0 | 0 | 0 | 0 | |
| Judith Basin | 0 | 0 | 0 | 0 | |
| Lake | 0 | 0 | 0 | 0 | |
| Liberty | 0 | 0 | 0 | 0 | |
| Lincoln | 0 | 0 | 0 | 0 | |
| Madison | 0 | 0 | 0 | 0 | |
| McCone | 0 | 0 | 0 | 0 | |
| Meagher | 0 | 0 | 0 | 0 | |
| Mineral | 0 | 0 | 0 | 0 | |
| Musselshell | 0 | 0 | 0 | 0 | |
| Park | 0 | 0 | 0 | 0 | |
| Petroleum | 0 | 0 | 0 | 0 | |
| Phillips | 0 | 0 | 0 | 0 | |
| Pondera | 0 | 0 | 0 | 0 | |
| Powder River | 0 | 0 | 0 | 0 | |
| Powell | 0 | 0 | 0 | 0 | |
| Prairie | 0 | 0 | 0 | 0 | |
| Ravalli | 0 | 0 | 0 | | |
| Richland | 0 | 0 | 0 | 0 | |
| Roosevelt | 0 | 0 | 0 | 0 | |
| Rosebud | 0 | 0 | 0 | 0 | |
| Sanders | 0 | 0 | 0 | 0 | |
| Sweet Grass | 0 | 0 | 0 | 0 | |
| Teton | 0 | 0 | 0 | 0 | |
| Toole | 0 | 0 | 0 | 0 | |
| Valley | 0 | 0 | 0 | 0 | |
| Wheatland | 0 | 0 | 0 | 0 | |
| Wibaux | 0 | 0 | 0 | 0 | |
| **Tribal Agencies** | | | | | |
| Blackfeet Agency | 0 | 0 | 0 | 0 | |
| Flathead Tribal | 0 | | | | |
| Fort Peck Assiniboine and Sioux Tribes | 0 | 0 | 0 | 0 | |
| Northern Cheyenne Agency | 0 | | | | |
| Rocky Boy's Tribal | 0 | 0 | 0 | 0 | |
| **NEBRASKA** | | | | | |
| **Cities** | | | | | |
| Albion | 0 | 0 | 0 | 0 | 1,547 |
| Alliance | 0 | 0 | 0 | 0 | 7,986 |
| Ashland | 0 | 0 | 0 | 0 | 2,752 |
| Aurora | 0 | 0 | 0 | 0 | 4,491 |
| Bayard | | 0 | 0 | 0 | 1,069 |
| Beatrice | 0 | 0 | 0 | 0 | 12,225 |
| Bellevue | 0 | 0 | 0 | 0 | 53,436 |
| Bennington | 0 | 0 | 0 | 0 | 1,524 |
| Blair | 0 | 0 | 0 | 0 | 7,979 |
| Bloomfield | | | | 0 | 936 |
| Boys Town | 0 | 0 | 0 | 0 | 306 |
| Broken Bow | 0 | 0 | 0 | 0 | 3,427 |
| Burwell | 0 | 0 | 0 | 0 | 1,158 |
| Central City | 0 | 0 | 0 | 0 | 2,887 |
| Chadron | 0 | 0 | 0 | 0 | 5,194 |
| Columbus | 0 | 0 | 0 | 0 | 23,727 |
| Cozad | 0 | 0 | 0 | 0 | 3,689 |
| Emerson | 0 | 0 | 0 | 0 | 784 |
| Franklin | 0 | 0 | 0 | 0 | 889 |
| Gering | 0 | 0 | 0 | 0 | 8,017 |
| Gordon | 0 | 0 | 0 | 0 | 1,475 |
| Gothenburg | 0 | 0 | 0 | 0 | 3,408 |
| Harvard | 0 | 0 | 0 | 0 | 961 |
| Hastings | 0 | 0 | 0 | 0 | 24,680 |
| Hemingford | | | 0 | 0 | 759 |
| Holdrege | 0 | 0 | 0 | 0 | 5,375 |
| Imperial | 0 | 0 | 0 | 0 | 2,005 |
| Kearney | 0 | 0 | 0 | 0 | 34,576 |
| Kimball | | 0 | 0 | 0 | 2,261 |
| Laurel | | 0 | 0 | 0 | 908 |
| La Vista | 0 | 0 | 0 | 0 | 17,057 |
| Lexington | 0 | 0 | 0 | 0 | 10,099 |
| McCook | 0 | 0 | 0 | 0 | 7,478 |
| Milford | 0 | 0 | 0 | 0 | 2,006 |
| Minatare | | | 0 | 0 | 780 |

## Table 95. Hate Crime Zero Data Submitted Per Quarter, by Federal Agency, State, and State Agency, 2021—Continued

(Number.)

| Agency name | Zero data per quarter[1] | | | | Population[2] |
|---|---|---|---|---|---|
| | 1st quarter | 2nd quarter | 3rd quarter | 4th quarter | |
| Minden | 0 | 0 | 0 | 0 | 3,031 |
| Mitchell | 0 | 0 | 0 | 0 | 1,599 |
| Morrill | 0 | 0 | 0 | 0 | 869 |
| Nebraska City | 0 | 0 | 0 | 0 | 7,248 |
| Ogallala | 0 | 0 | 0 | 0 | 4,448 |
| O'Neill | 0 | 0 | 0 | 0 | 3,521 |
| Ord | 0 | 0 | 0 | 0 | 2,043 |
| Papillion | 0 | 0 | 0 | | 20,313 |
| Pierce | 0 | 0 | | 0 | 1,731 |
| Plainview | | | | 0 | 1,192 |
| Plattsmouth | 0 | 0 | | 0 | 6,409 |
| Randolph | | | 0 | 0 | 884 |
| Ravenna | 0 | 0 | | | 1,361 |
| Schuyler | 0 | 0 | 0 | 0 | 6,219 |
| Scotia | 0 | 0 | 0 | 0 | 281 |
| Scribner | 0 | | | | 776 |
| Seward | 0 | 0 | 0 | 0 | 7,402 |
| Sidney | 0 | 0 | 0 | 0 | 6,186 |
| South Sioux City | 0 | 0 | 0 | 0 | 12,780 |
| Spalding | 0 | 0 | | | 427 |
| St. Paul | 0 | 0 | 0 | 0 | 2,336 |
| Superior | 0 | 0 | 0 | 0 | 1,790 |
| Sutton | 0 | 0 | 0 | | 1,441 |
| Tekamah | 0 | 0 | 0 | 0 | 1,703 |
| Tilden | 0 | 0 | 0 | 0 | 934 |
| Valentine | 0 | 0 | 0 | 0 | 2,747 |
| Wahoo | 0 | 0 | 0 | 0 | 4,611 |
| Wayne | 0 | 0 | 0 | 0 | 5,766 |
| West Point | 0 | 0 | 0 | 0 | 3,223 |
| Wisner | 0 | 0 | 0 | 0 | 1,164 |
| Wymore | 0 | 0 | 0 | 0 | 1,311 |
| York | 0 | 0 | 0 | 0 | 7,784 |
| **Universities and Colleges** | | | | | |
| Metropolitan Community College, Douglas County | 0 | 0 | 0 | 0 | 22,649 |
| University of Nebraska | | | | | |
|    Kearney | 0 | 0 | 0 | 0 | 7,564 |
|    Omaha | 0 | 0 | 0 | 0 | 17,913 |
| **Metropolitan Counties** | | | | | |
| Cass | 0 | 0 | 0 | 0 | |
| Dakota | 0 | 0 | 0 | | |
| Dixon | 0 | 0 | 0 | 0 | |
| Howard | 0 | 0 | 0 | 0 | |
| Lancaster | 0 | 0 | 0 | 0 | |
| Merrick | 0 | 0 | 0 | 0 | |
| Sarpy | 0 | 0 | 0 | 0 | |
| Saunders | 0 | 0 | 0 | 0 | |
| Seward | 0 | 0 | 0 | 0 | |
| Washington | 0 | 0 | 0 | 0 | |
| **Nonmetropolitan Counties** | | | | | |
| Adams | 0 | 0 | 0 | 0 | |
| Antelope | 0 | 0 | | | |
| Arthur | 0 | 0 | 0 | | |
| Banner | 0 | 0 | 0 | 0 | |
| Boone | 0 | 0 | 0 | 0 | |
| Box Butte | 0 | 0 | 0 | 0 | |
| Boyd | 0 | 0 | 0 | 0 | |
| Brown | 0 | 0 | 0 | 0 | |
| Buffalo | 0 | 0 | 0 | 0 | |
| Burt | 0 | 0 | 0 | 0 | |
| Butler | 0 | 0 | 0 | 0 | |
| Cedar | 0 | 0 | 0 | 0 | |
| Chase | 0 | 0 | 0 | | |
| Cherry | 0 | 0 | 0 | 0 | |
| Cheyenne | 0 | 0 | 0 | 0 | |
| Clay | 0 | 0 | | | |
| Colfax | 0 | 0 | | | |
| Cuming | 0 | 0 | 0 | 0 | |
| Dawes | 0 | 0 | 0 | 0 | |
| Dawson | 0 | 0 | 0 | 0 | |
| Deuel | 0 | 0 | 0 | | |
| Dundy | 0 | 0 | 0 | 0 | |
| Franklin | 0 | 0 | 0 | 0 | |
| Frontier | 0 | 0 | 0 | 0 | |
| Gage | 0 | 0 | 0 | 0 | |
| Garden | 0 | 0 | 0 | 0 | |
| Garfield | 0 | 0 | 0 | 0 | |
| Gosper | 0 | 0 | 0 | 0 | |
| Grant | 0 | 0 | 0 | 0 | |

# Table 95. Hate Crime Zero Data Submitted Per Quarter, by Federal Agency, State, and State Agency, 2021—Continued

(Number.)

| Agency name | Zero data per quarter[1] | | | | Population[2] |
|---|---|---|---|---|---|
| | 1st quarter | 2nd quarter | 3rd quarter | 4th quarter | |
| Greeley | 0 | 0 | 0 | 0 | |
| Hamilton | 0 | 0 | 0 | 0 | |
| Harlan | 0 | 0 | 0 | 0 | |
| Hayes | 0 | 0 | 0 | 0 | |
| Hitchcock | 0 | 0 | 0 | 0 | |
| Holt | 0 | 0 | 0 | 0 | |
| Hooker | 0 | 0 | 0 | 0 | |
| Jefferson | 0 | 0 | 0 | 0 | |
| Johnson | 0 | 0 | 0 | 0 | |
| Kearney | 0 | 0 | 0 | 0 | |
| Keya Paha | 0 | 0 | 0 | 0 | |
| Kimball | 0 | 0 | 0 | 0 | |
| Knox | 0 | | | | |
| Lincoln | 0 | 0 | 0 | 0 | |
| Logan | 0 | 0 | | | |
| Madison | 0 | | 0 | 0 | |
| McPherson | 0 | 0 | 0 | 0 | |
| Morrill | 0 | 0 | 0 | 0 | |
| Nance | 0 | 0 | 0 | 0 | |
| Nemaha | 0 | 0 | 0 | 0 | |
| Nuckolls | 0 | 0 | | | |
| Otoe | 0 | 0 | 0 | 0 | |
| Pawnee | 0 | 0 | | | |
| Perkins | 0 | 0 | 0 | 0 | |
| Phelps | 0 | 0 | 0 | 0 | |
| Platte | 0 | 0 | 0 | 0 | |
| Polk | 0 | 0 | 0 | 0 | |
| Red Willow | 0 | 0 | 0 | 0 | |
| Richardson | 0 | 0 | 0 | 0 | |
| Rock | 0 | 0 | 0 | 0 | |
| Saline | 0 | | | | |
| Scotts Bluff | 0 | 0 | 0 | 0 | |
| Sheridan | 0 | 0 | 0 | 0 | |
| Sherman | 0 | 0 | 0 | | |
| Sioux | 0 | 0 | 0 | | |
| Stanton | 0 | 0 | 0 | 0 | |
| Thayer | 0 | 0 | 0 | 0 | |
| Thomas | 0 | 0 | 0 | 0 | |
| Valley | 0 | 0 | 0 | 0 | |
| Wayne | 0 | 0 | 0 | 0 | |
| Webster | 0 | 0 | 0 | 0 | |
| Wheeler | 0 | 0 | 0 | 0 | |
| York | 0 | 0 | 0 | 0 | |
| **State Police Agencies** | | | | | |
| State Patrol | | | | | |
| Adams County | 0 | 0 | 0 | 0 | |
| Antelope County | 0 | 0 | 0 | 0 | |
| Arthur County | | 0 | | | |
| Banner County | 0 | 0 | 0 | 0 | |
| Blaine County | 0 | 0 | | 0 | |
| Boone County | 0 | | 0 | 0 | |
| Box Butte County | 0 | 0 | 0 | 0 | |
| Boyd County | | | | 0 | |
| Brown County | 0 | 0 | 0 | 0 | |
| Buffalo County | 0 | 0 | 0 | 0 | |
| Burt County | | | 0 | 0 | |
| Butler County | 0 | 0 | 0 | 0 | |
| Cass County | 0 | 0 | 0 | 0 | |
| Cedar County | 0 | 0 | 0 | 0 | |
| Chase County | | | | 0 | |
| Cherry County | 0 | 0 | 0 | 0 | |
| Cheyenne County | 0 | 0 | 0 | 0 | |
| Clay County | 0 | 0 | 0 | 0 | |
| Colfax County | 0 | | 0 | 0 | |
| Cuming County | 0 | 0 | 0 | 0 | |
| Custer County | 0 | 0 | 0 | 0 | |
| Dakota County | 0 | 0 | 0 | 0 | |
| Dawes County | 0 | 0 | 0 | 0 | |
| Dawson County | 0 | 0 | 0 | 0 | |
| Deuel County | 0 | 0 | 0 | 0 | |
| Dixon County | 0 | 0 | 0 | 0 | |
| Dodge County | 0 | 0 | 0 | 0 | |
| Douglas County | 0 | 0 | 0 | 0 | |
| Dundy County | | | 0 | 0 | |
| Fillmore County | 0 | | 0 | | |
| Franklin County | | | | 0 | |
| Frontier County | | 0 | 0 | 0 | |
| Furnas County | 0 | 0 | 0 | 0 | |
| Gage County | 0 | 0 | 0 | 0 | |
| Garden County | 0 | 0 | | | |

## Table 95. Hate Crime Zero Data Submitted Per Quarter, by Federal Agency, State, and State Agency, 2021—Continued

(Number.)

| Agency name | Zero data per quarter[1] | | | | Population[2] |
|---|---|---|---|---|---|
| | 1st quarter | 2nd quarter | 3rd quarter | 4th quarter | |
| Garfield County | 0 | 0 | 0 | 0 | |
| Gosper County | 0 | | | 0 | |
| Grant County | | 0 | | | |
| Greeley County | 0 | 0 | | 0 | |
| Hall County | 0 | 0 | | 0 | |
| Hamilton County | 0 | 0 | 0 | 0 | |
| Harlan County | 0 | 0 | 0 | | |
| Hayes County | 0 | | | 0 | |
| Hitchcock County | | 0 | 0 | 0 | |
| Holt County | 0 | 0 | 0 | 0 | |
| Hooker County | | 0 | 0 | | |
| Howard County | 0 | 0 | 0 | 0 | |
| Jefferson County | 0 | 0 | 0 | 0 | |
| Johnson County | | 0 | 0 | 0 | |
| Kearney County | 0 | 0 | 0 | 0 | |
| Keith County | 0 | 0 | 0 | 0 | |
| Kimball County | 0 | 0 | 0 | 0 | |
| Knox County | 0 | 0 | 0 | 0 | |
| Lancaster County | 0 | 0 | 0 | 0 | |
| Lincoln County | 0 | 0 | 0 | 0 | |
| Logan County | | 0 | 0 | 0 | |
| Loup County | | 0 | 0 | 0 | |
| Madison County | 0 | 0 | 0 | 0 | |
| McPherson County | | 0 | | | |
| Merrick County | 0 | 0 | 0 | 0 | |
| Morrill County | 0 | 0 | 0 | 0 | |
| Nance County | 0 | | 0 | 0 | |
| Nemaha County | 0 | 0 | 0 | 0 | |
| Nuckolls County | | 0 | | | |
| Otoe County | 0 | 0 | 0 | 0 | |
| Pawnee County | | | 0 | | |
| Perkins County | | | | 0 | |
| Phelps County | 0 | 0 | | 0 | |
| Pierce County | 0 | 0 | 0 | 0 | |
| Platte County | 0 | 0 | 0 | 0 | |
| Polk County | 0 | 0 | | 0 | |
| Red Willow County | 0 | 0 | 0 | 0 | |
| Richardson County | 0 | 0 | | 0 | |
| Saline County | 0 | 0 | 0 | | |
| Sarpy County | 0 | 0 | 0 | 0 | |
| Saunders County | 0 | 0 | 0 | 0 | |
| Scotts Bluff County | 0 | 0 | 0 | 0 | |
| Seward County | 0 | 0 | 0 | 0 | |
| Sheridan County | 0 | 0 | 0 | 0 | |
| Sherman County | | 0 | 0 | | |
| Sioux County | | 0 | 0 | 0 | |
| Stanton County | 0 | 0 | 0 | 0 | |
| Thayer County | | 0 | 0 | 0 | |
| Thomas County | 0 | 0 | 0 | 0 | |
| Thurston County | | 0 | | 0 | |
| Valley County | 0 | 0 | 0 | 0 | |
| Washington County | 0 | | 0 | | |
| Wayne County | 0 | 0 | 0 | 0 | |
| Webster County | | 0 | | | |
| Wheeler County | 0 | 0 | | | |
| York County | 0 | 0 | 0 | 0 | |
| **Tribal Agencies** | | | | | |
| Omaha Tribal | 0 | 0 | 0 | 0 | |
| Santee Tribal | 0 | 0 | 0 | 0 | |
| Winnebago Tribal | 0 | 0 | 0 | 0 | |
| **Other Agencies** | | | | | |
| Nebraska State Fire Marshal | 0 | 0 | 0 | 0 | |
| **NEVADA** | | | | | |
| **Cities** | | | | | |
| Boulder City | 0 | 0 | 0 | 0 | 16,556 |
| Carlin | 0 | 0 | 0 | 0 | 2,273 |
| Fallon | 0 | 0 | 0 | 0 | 8,765 |
| Lovelock | 0 | | | | 1,813 |
| Mesquite | 0 | | 0 | 0 | 21,038 |
| West Wendover | | 0 | 0 | 0 | 4,254 |
| Winnemucca | 0 | 0 | 0 | 0 | 7,835 |
| **Metropolitan Counties** | | | | | |
| Carson City | 0 | 0 | 0 | 0 | |
| Churchill | 0 | 0 | 0 | 0 | |
| Eureka | 0 | 0 | 0 | 0 | |
| Humboldt | 0 | 0 | 0 | 0 | |

**Table 95. Hate Crime Zero Data Submitted Per Quarter, by Federal Agency, State, and State Agency, 2021—Continued**

(Number.)

| Agency name | Zero data per quarter[1] | | | | Population[2] |
|---|---|---|---|---|---|
| | 1st quarter | 2nd quarter | 3rd quarter | 4th quarter | |
| Lyon | 0 | 0 | 0 | 0 | |
| Mineral | 0 | 0 | 0 | 0 | |
| **Nonmetropolitan Counties** | | | | | |
| White Pine | 0 | | | | |
| **State Police Agencies** | | | | | |
| Highway Patrol, Northeastern Division | 0 | 0 | 0 | 0 | |
| **Tribal Agencies** | | | | | |
| Eastern Nevada Agency | 0 | 0 | 0 | 0 | |
| Elko Band Tribal | | | 0 | | |
| Fallon Tribal | | 0 | 0 | 0 | |
| Las Vegas Paiute Tribal | 0 | 0 | 0 | 0 | |
| Lovelock Paiute Tribal | 0 | 0 | 0 | 0 | |
| Moapa Tribal | 0 | 0 | 0 | 0 | |
| Pyramid Lake Tribal | 0 | 0 | 0 | 0 | |
| Reno-Sparks Indian Colony | 0 | 0 | 0 | 0 | |
| Western Nevada Agency | 0 | | | | |
| Western Shoshone Tribal | 0 | 0 | 0 | 0 | |
| Yomba Shoshone Tribal | 0 | 0 | 0 | 0 | |
| **Other Agencies** | | | | | |
| Attorney General Investigations Division | 0 | 0 | 0 | 0 | |
| Capitol Police | 0 | | | | |
| Department of Public Safety, Investigative Division | 0 | 0 | 0 | 0 | |
| Department of Wildlife, Law Enforcement Division | 0 | 0 | 0 | 0 | |
| Las Vegas Fire and Rescue, Arson Bomb Unit | 0 | 0 | 0 | 0 | |
| Nevada Gaming Control Board | | | | | |
| Carson City County | | | | 0 | |
| Clark County | | | | 0 | |
| Elko County | | | | 0 | |
| Washoe County | | | | 0 | |
| Reno Municipal Court Marshal | 0 | 0 | 0 | 0 | |
| Secretary of State Securities Division, Enforcement Section | 0 | 0 | 0 | | |
| State Fire Marshal | 0 | 0 | 0 | 0 | |
| Washoe County School District | 0 | 0 | 0 | 0 | |
| **NEW HAMPSHIRE** | | | | | |
| **Cities** | | | | | |
| Alexandria | 0 | 0 | 0 | 0 | 1,629 |
| Allenstown | 0 | 0 | 0 | 0 | 4,505 |
| Alstead | 0 | 0 | 0 | 0 | 1,952 |
| Alton | 0 | 0 | 0 | 0 | 5,445 |
| Amherst | 0 | 0 | 0 | 0 | 11,440 |
| Andover | 0 | 0 | 0 | 0 | 2,392 |
| Antrim | 0 | 0 | 0 | 0 | 2,687 |
| Ashland | 0 | 0 | 0 | 0 | 2,066 |
| Atkinson | 0 | 0 | 0 | 0 | 7,296 |
| Auburn | 0 | 0 | 0 | 0 | 5,771 |
| Barnstead | 0 | 0 | 0 | 0 | 4,852 |
| Barrington | 0 | 0 | 0 | 0 | 9,423 |
| Bartlett | 0 | 0 | 0 | 0 | 2,818 |
| Bath | 0 | 0 | 0 | 0 | 1,110 |
| Belmont | 0 | 0 | 0 | 0 | 7,406 |
| Bennington | 0 | 0 | 0 | 0 | 1,520 |
| Berlin | 0 | 0 | 0 | 0 | 9,799 |
| Bethlehem | 0 | 0 | 0 | 0 | 2,669 |
| Bradford | 0 | 0 | 0 | 0 | 1,748 |
| Brentwood | 0 | 0 | 0 | 0 | 4,682 |
| Bristol | 0 | 0 | 0 | 0 | 3,168 |
| Brookline | 0 | 0 | 0 | 0 | 5,547 |
| Campton | 0 | 0 | 0 | 0 | 3,335 |
| Canaan | 0 | 0 | 0 | 0 | 3,914 |
| Candia | 0 | 0 | 0 | 0 | 4,016 |
| Canterbury | 0 | 0 | 0 | 0 | 2,510 |
| Carroll | 0 | 0 | 0 | 0 | 754 |
| Center Harbor | 0 | 0 | 0 | 0 | 1,112 |
| Charlestown | 0 | 0 | 0 | 0 | 5,023 |
| Chester | 0 | 0 | 0 | 0 | 5,399 |
| Chesterfield | 0 | 0 | 0 | 0 | 3,648 |
| Chichester | 0 | 0 | 0 | 0 | 2,750 |
| Colebrook | 0 | 0 | 0 | 0 | 2,118 |
| Conway | 0 | 0 | 0 | 0 | 10,364 |
| Cornish | 0 | 0 | 0 | 0 | 1,614 |
| Danbury | | | 0 | 0 | 1,243 |
| Danville | 0 | 0 | 0 | | 4,677 |
| Deerfield | 0 | 0 | 0 | 0 | 4,652 |
| Deering | 0 | 0 | 0 | 0 | 1,974 |
| Derry | 0 | 0 | 0 | 0 | 33,892 |

## Table 95. Hate Crime Zero Data Submitted Per Quarter, by Federal Agency, State, and State Agency, 2021—Continued

(Number.)

| Agency name | Zero data per quarter[1] | | | | Population[2] |
|---|---|---|---|---|---|
| | 1st quarter | 2nd quarter | 3rd quarter | 4th quarter | |
| Dublin | 0 | 0 | 0 | 0 | 1,552 |
| Dunbarton | 0 | 0 | 0 | 0 | 2,934 |
| Durham | 0 | 0 | 0 | 0 | 16,848 |
| East Kingston | 0 | 0 | 0 | 0 | 2,446 |
| Enfield | 0 | 0 | 0 | 0 | 4,563 |
| Epping | 0 | 0 | 0 | 0 | 7,233 |
| Epsom | 0 | 0 | 0 | 0 | 4,848 |
| Farmington | 0 | 0 | 0 | 0 | 7,058 |
| Fitzwilliam | 0 | 0 | 0 | 0 | 2,373 |
| Francestown | 0 | | | | 1,584 |
| Franconia | 0 | | 0 | 0 | 1,117 |
| Franklin | 0 | 0 | 0 | 0 | 8,782 |
| Freedom | 0 | 0 | 0 | 0 | 1,603 |
| Fremont | 0 | 0 | 0 | 0 | 4,847 |
| Gilford | 0 | 0 | 0 | 0 | 7,391 |
| Gilmanton | 0 | 0 | 0 | 0 | 3,850 |
| Goffstown | 0 | 0 | 0 | 0 | 18,184 |
| Gorham | 0 | 0 | 0 | 0 | 2,569 |
| Goshen | 0 | 0 | 0 | 0 | 813 |
| Grantham | 0 | 0 | 0 | 0 | 2,953 |
| Greenfield | 0 | 0 | 0 | 0 | 1,855 |
| Greenland | 0 | 0 | 0 | 0 | 4,228 |
| Greenville | 0 | 0 | 0 | 0 | 2,111 |
| Groton | 0 | 0 | 0 | 0 | 611 |
| Hampstead | 0 | 0 | 0 | 0 | 8,733 |
| Hampton Falls | 0 | 0 | 0 | 0 | 2,459 |
| Hancock | 0 | 0 | 0 | 0 | 1,650 |
| Hanover | 0 | 0 | 0 | 0 | 11,586 |
| Harrisville | 0 | 0 | 0 | 0 | 953 |
| Haverhill | 0 | 0 | 0 | 0 | 4,542 |
| Hebron | 0 | 0 | 0 | 0 | 635 |
| Henniker | 0 | 0 | 0 | 0 | 5,024 |
| Hinsdale | 0 | 0 | 0 | 0 | 3,894 |
| Holderness | 0 | 0 | 0 | 0 | 2,133 |
| Hooksett | 0 | 0 | 0 | 0 | 14,834 |
| Hopkinton | 0 | 0 | 0 | 0 | 5,852 |
| Hudson | 0 | 0 | 0 | 0 | 25,736 |
| Jackson | 0 | 0 | 0 | 0 | 869 |
| Jaffrey | 0 | 0 | 0 | 0 | 5,271 |
| Keene | 0 | 0 | 0 | 0 | 22,619 |
| Kensington | 0 | 0 | 0 | 0 | 2,116 |
| Lancaster | 0 | 0 | 0 | 0 | 3,209 |
| Langdon | 0 | 0 | 0 | 0 | 688 |
| Lebanon | 0 | 0 | 0 | 0 | 13,877 |
| Lee | 0 | 0 | 0 | 0 | 4,684 |
| Lincoln | 0 | 0 | 0 | | 1,787 |
| Lisbon | 0 | 0 | | | 1,586 |
| Litchfield | 0 | 0 | 0 | 0 | 8,696 |
| Littleton | 0 | 0 | 0 | 0 | 5,898 |
| Londonderry | 0 | 0 | 0 | 0 | 27,268 |
| Loudon | 0 | 0 | 0 | 0 | 5,740 |
| Lyme | 0 | 0 | 0 | 0 | 1,682 |
| Lyndeborough | 0 | 0 | 0 | 0 | 1,735 |
| Madbury | 0 | 0 | 0 | 0 | 1,913 |
| Madison | 0 | 0 | 0 | 0 | 2,646 |
| Marlborough | 0 | 0 | 0 | 0 | 2,089 |
| Mason | 0 | 0 | 0 | 0 | 1,438 |
| Meredith | 0 | 0 | 0 | 0 | 6,579 |
| Middleton | 0 | 0 | 0 | 0 | 1,859 |
| Milford | 0 | 0 | 0 | 0 | 16,662 |
| Milton | 0 | 0 | 0 | 0 | 4,676 |
| Mont Vernon | 0 | 0 | 0 | 0 | 2,749 |
| Moultonborough | 0 | 0 | 0 | 0 | 4,227 |
| New Boston | 0 | 0 | 0 | 0 | 6,006 |
| Newbury | 0 | 0 | 0 | | 2,263 |
| New Castle | 0 | | | | 985 |
| New Durham | 0 | 0 | 0 | 0 | 2,771 |
| Newfields | 0 | 0 | 0 | 0 | 1,760 |
| New Hampton | 0 | 0 | 0 | 0 | 2,270 |
| Newington | 0 | 0 | 0 | 0 | 849 |
| New Ipswich | 0 | 0 | 0 | 0 | 5,462 |
| New London | 0 | 0 | 0 | | 4,257 |
| Newport | 0 | 0 | | | 6,366 |
| Newton | 0 | 0 | 0 | 0 | 5,030 |
| Northfield | 0 | 0 | 0 | | 4,995 |
| North Hampton | 0 | | | | 4,562 |
| Northumberland | 0 | 0 | 0 | 0 | 2,101 |
| Northwood | 0 | 0 | 0 | 0 | 4,385 |
| Nottingham | 0 | 0 | 0 | 0 | 5,281 |
| Orford | 0 | 0 | 0 | 0 | 1,323 |
| Ossipee | 0 | 0 | 0 | 0 | 4,387 |

## Table 95. Hate Crime Zero Data Submitted Per Quarter, by Federal Agency, State, and State Agency, 2021—Continued

(Number.)

| Agency name | Zero data per quarter[1] | | | | Population[2] |
|---|---|---|---|---|---|
| | 1st quarter | 2nd quarter | 3rd quarter | 4th quarter | |
| Pembroke | 0 | 0 | 0 | 0 | 7,265 |
| Peterborough | 0 | 0 | 0 | 0 | 6,792 |
| Piermont | 0 | 0 | 0 | 0 | 821 |
| Pittsburg | 0 | 0 | 0 | 0 | 817 |
| Plainfield | 0 | 0 | 0 | 0 | 2,425 |
| Plaistow | 0 | 0 | 0 | 0 | 7,847 |
| Plymouth | 0 | 0 | 0 | 0 | 6,911 |
| Raymond | 0 | 0 | 0 | 0 | 10,752 |
| Rindge | 0 | 0 | 0 | 0 | 6,142 |
| Rollinsford | 0 | 0 | 0 | 0 | 2,615 |
| Roxbury | 0 | 0 | 0 | 0 | 220 |
| Rumney | 0 | 0 | 0 | 0 | 1,585 |
| Salem | 0 | 0 | 0 | 0 | 31,231 |
| Sanbornton | 0 | 0 | 0 | 0 | 3,055 |
| Sandown | 0 | 0 | 0 | 0 | 6,693 |
| Sandwich | 0 | 0 | 0 | 0 | 1,371 |
| Somersworth | 0 | 0 | 0 | 0 | 12,498 |
| South Hampton | 0 | 0 | 0 | 0 | 835 |
| Springfield | 0 | 0 | 0 | 0 | 1,351 |
| Stoddard | 0 | 0 | 0 | 0 | 1,256 |
| Strafford | 0 | 0 | 0 | 0 | 4,314 |
| Stratham | 0 | 0 | 0 | 0 | 7,707 |
| Sugar Hill | 0 | 0 | 0 | 0 | 586 |
| Sunapee | 0 | 0 | 0 | 0 | 3,519 |
| Sutton | 0 | | | | 1,945 |
| Swanzey | 0 | 0 | 0 | 0 | 7,275 |
| Tamworth | 0 | 0 | 0 | 0 | 3,117 |
| Thornton | 0 | 0 | 0 | 0 | 2,559 |
| Tilton | 0 | 0 | 0 | 0 | 3,602 |
| Troy | 0 | 0 | 0 | 0 | 2,114 |
| Tuftonboro | 0 | 0 | 0 | 0 | 2,443 |
| Wakefield | 0 | 0 | 0 | 0 | 5,812 |
| Walpole | 0 | 0 | 0 | 0 | 4,064 |
| Warner | 0 | 0 | 0 | 0 | 2,964 |
| Warren | 0 | 0 | 0 | 0 | 952 |
| Washington | 0 | 0 | 0 | 0 | 1,102 |
| Waterville Valley | 0 | 0 | 0 | 0 | 242 |
| Weare | 0 | 0 | 0 | 0 | 9,130 |
| Webster | 0 | 0 | 0 | | 1,983 |
| Wentworth | 0 | 0 | 0 | | 983 |
| Whitefield | 0 | 0 | 0 | 0 | 2,186 |
| Wilmot | 0 | 0 | 0 | 0 | 1,412 |
| Winchester | 0 | 0 | 0 | 0 | 4,205 |
| Windham | 0 | 0 | 0 | 0 | 15,191 |
| Wolfeboro | 0 | 0 | 0 | 0 | 6,467 |
| Woodstock | 0 | 0 | 0 | 0 | 1,373 |
| **Metropolitan Counties** | | | | | |
| Hillsborough | 0 | | | | |
| Rockingham | 0 | 0 | 0 | 0 | |
| Strafford | 0 | 0 | 0 | 0 | |
| **Nonmetropolitan Counties** | | | | | |
| Belknap | 0 | 0 | 0 | 0 | |
| Carroll | 0 | 0 | 0 | 0 | |
| Cheshire | 0 | 0 | 0 | 0 | |
| Grafton | 0 | 0 | 0 | 0 | |
| Merrimack | 0 | 0 | 0 | 0 | |
| Sullivan | 0 | 0 | 0 | 0 | |
| **State Police Agencies** | | | | | |
| State Police | | | | | |
| Belknap County | 0 | 0 | | 0 | |
| Carroll County | 0 | 0 | 0 | 0 | |
| Cheshire County | 0 | 0 | 0 | 0 | |
| Coos County | 0 | 0 | 0 | 0 | |
| Grafton County | 0 | 0 | 0 | 0 | |
| Hillsborough County | 0 | 0 | 0 | 0 | |
| Merrimack County | 0 | 0 | 0 | 0 | |
| Rockingham County | 0 | 0 | 0 | 0 | |
| Strafford County | 0 | 0 | 0 | 0 | |
| Sullivan County | 0 | 0 | 0 | 0 | |
| **Other Agencies** | | | | | |
| Liquor Commission | 0 | 0 | 0 | 0 | |
| **NEW JERSEY** | | | | | |
| **Cities** | | | | | |
| Aberdeen Township | 0 | 0 | 0 | | 19,475 |
| Absecon | 0 | 0 | 0 | 0 | 8,820 |
| Andover Township | 0 | 0 | 0 | 0 | 5,805 |

## Table 95. Hate Crime Zero Data Submitted Per Quarter, by Federal Agency, State, and State Agency, 2021—Continued

(Number.)

| Agency name | Zero data per quarter[1] | | | | Population[2] |
|---|---|---|---|---|---|
| | 1st quarter | 2nd quarter | 3rd quarter | 4th quarter | |
| Atlantic City | | 0 | 0 | 0 | 37,379 |
| Audubon | | 0 | 0 | 0 | 8,959 |
| Barnegat Township | | | 0 | 0 | 25,395 |
| Barrington | | | 0 | 0 | 6,849 |
| Bay Head | 0 | 0 | 0 | 0 | 1,028 |
| Berlin | | 0 | 0 | 0 | 7,817 |
| Bernards Township | 0 | | | 0 | 28,288 |
| Bernardsville | 0 | 0 | 0 | 0 | 7,883 |
| Boonton | | | 0 | 0 | 9,312 |
| Boonton Township | | | | 0 | 4,393 |
| Brigantine | 0 | | | | 8,495 |
| Brooklawn | | | 0 | 0 | 1,969 |
| Caldwell | 0 | 0 | 0 | 0 | 8,284 |
| Carlstadt | | 0 | 0 | 0 | 6,365 |
| Clark Township | 0 | | | 0 | 16,622 |
| Cresskill | 0 | 0 | 0 | 0 | 8,998 |
| East Hanover Township | | | | 0 | 11,296 |
| Egg Harbor City | | | | 0 | 4,038 |
| Egg Harbor Township | | 0 | 0 | 0 | 41,966 |
| Elmwood Park | 0 | 0 | 0 | 0 | 20,738 |
| Emerson | 0 | 0 | 0 | 0 | 7,900 |
| Fairfield Township, Essex County | 0 | 0 | 0 | 0 | 7,775 |
| Far Hills | 0 | 0 | 0 | 0 | 940 |
| Florham Park | 0 | 0 | 0 | 0 | 12,322 |
| Franklin Township, Gloucester County | | | 0 | 0 | 16,980 |
| Galloway Township | | 0 | 0 | 0 | 35,320 |
| Garfield | | 0 | 0 | 0 | 33,092 |
| Glen Ridge | | 0 | 0 | 0 | 7,896 |
| Hamburg | 0 | 0 | 0 | 0 | 3,101 |
| Hamilton Township, Atlantic County | | | | 0 | 25,718 |
| Hardyston Township | 0 | 0 | 0 | 0 | 7,718 |
| Harrison Township | | | | 0 | 13,772 |
| Hawthorne | 0 | 0 | 0 | 0 | 19,442 |
| Hoboken | 0 | 0 | 0 | 0 | 55,632 |
| Holland Township | | | | 0 | 5,054 |
| Island Heights | 0 | 0 | 0 | 0 | 1,773 |
| Jackson Township | | 0 | 0 | 0 | 61,350 |
| Jefferson Township | 0 | 0 | 0 | 0 | 21,409 |
| Kenilworth | 0 | 0 | 0 | 0 | 8,520 |
| Kinnelon | 0 | | 0 | 0 | 10,239 |
| Lakehurst | 0 | 0 | 0 | 0 | 2,862 |
| Lakewood Township | 0 | 0 | 0 | 0 | 113,868 |
| Lawrence Township, Mercer County | 0 | 0 | 0 | 0 | 33,882 |
| Leonia | | | | 0 | 9,370 |
| Lincoln Park | | 0 | 0 | 0 | 10,439 |
| Little Silver | 0 | | | | 5,752 |
| Lodi | 0 | 0 | 0 | 0 | 25,235 |
| Lower Alloways Creek Township | | | | 0 | 1,652 |
| Lyndhurst Township | 0 | 0 | 0 | 0 | 23,987 |
| Madison | 0 | 0 | 0 | 0 | 18,563 |
| Manchester Township | | | | 0 | 46,188 |
| Mantoloking | | | 0 | 0 | 258 |
| Maple Shade Township | | | | 0 | 18,395 |
| Metuchen | | | 0 | 0 | 15,521 |
| Middlesex Borough | | | 0 | 0 | 14,101 |
| Midland Park | | | 0 | 0 | 7,481 |
| Milltown | 0 | 0 | 0 | 0 | 7,203 |
| Millville | 0 | 0 | 0 | 0 | 26,882 |
| Mine Hill Township | 0 | 0 | 0 | 0 | 3,602 |
| Monroe Township, Gloucester County | | | | 0 | 38,685 |
| Montvale | 0 | 0 | 0 | 0 | 9,021 |
| Montville Township | | | | 0 | 21,797 |
| Mount Ephraim | | 0 | 0 | 0 | 4,759 |
| North Haledon | 0 | 0 | 0 | 0 | 8,708 |
| North Wildwood | 0 | 0 | 0 | 0 | 3,710 |
| Oakland | | | | 0 | 13,390 |
| Ocean Gate | | | 0 | 0 | 2,154 |
| Ocean Township, Ocean County | 0 | 0 | 0 | 0 | 9,659 |
| Ogdensburg | 0 | | | 0 | 2,228 |
| Oradell | 0 | 0 | 0 | 0 | 8,447 |
| Orange City | 0 | 0 | 0 | 0 | 31,822 |
| Parsippany-Troy Hills Township | | | | 0 | 53,272 |
| Pennsauken Township | | 0 | 0 | 0 | 37,212 |
| Pompton Lakes | 0 | 0 | 0 | 0 | 11,374 |
| Rahway | 0 | 0 | 0 | 0 | 31,362 |
| Riverdale | | | 0 | 0 | 4,348 |
| River Edge | | | 0 | 0 | 12,072 |
| Rochelle Park Township | 0 | 0 | 0 | 0 | 5,775 |
| Rockaway Township | 0 | 0 | 0 | 0 | 27,360 |
| Roselle Park | 0 | | | | 14,101 |
| Saddle River | 0 | 0 | 0 | 0 | 3,287 |

## Table 95. Hate Crime Zero Data Submitted Per Quarter, by Federal Agency, State, and State Agency, 2021—Continued

(Number.)

| Agency name | Zero data per quarter[1] | | | | Population[2] |
|---|---|---|---|---|---|
| | 1st quarter | 2nd quarter | 3rd quarter | 4th quarter | |
| Salem | | | | 0 | 4,673 |
| Seaside Park | 0 | 0 | 0 | 0 | 1,629 |
| Ship Bottom | | | | 0 | 1,223 |
| Shrewsbury | 0 | 0 | 0 | 0 | 4,065 |
| Somers Point | 0 | | 0 | | 10,091 |
| South Plainfield | 0 | 0 | 0 | 0 | 25,038 |
| South River | 0 | 0 | 0 | 0 | 16,240 |
| South Toms River | | 0 | 0 | 0 | 3,892 |
| Stafford Township | 0 | 0 | 0 | 0 | 30,025 |
| Stanhope | 0 | 0 | 0 | 0 | 3,258 |
| Stratford | 0 | 0 | 0 | 0 | 7,219 |
| Teaneck Township | 0 | | | | 42,218 |
| Toms River Township | | | | 0 | 100,051 |
| Ventnor City | | 0 | 0 | 0 | 9,798 |
| Verona | 0 | 0 | 0 | 0 | 14,233 |
| Waldwick | 0 | | 0 | 0 | 10,767 |
| Wallington | 0 | | 0 | 0 | 12,086 |
| Wanaque | 0 | 0 | 0 | 0 | 12,281 |
| Warren Township | 0 | 0 | 0 | 0 | 16,378 |
| Washington Township, Bergen County | 0 | 0 | 0 | 0 | 9,530 |
| Watchung | 0 | 0 | 0 | 0 | 6,280 |
| Wayne Township | | 0 | 0 | 0 | 55,249 |
| Weehawken Township | 0 | 0 | 0 | | 15,266 |
| Westfield | 0 | 0 | 0 | 0 | 30,361 |
| West Milford Township | 0 | 0 | 0 | 0 | 27,350 |
| West Wildwood | | | 0 | 0 | 535 |
| Wharton | 0 | 0 | 0 | 0 | 6,728 |
| Woodcliff Lake | 0 | 0 | 0 | 0 | 6,094 |
| **Universities and Colleges** | | | | | |
| Essex County College | | 0 | 0 | 0 | 10,217 |
| Kean University | | | | 0 | 16,991 |
| Montclair State University | | | | 0 | 24,101 |
| Rutgers University | | | | | |
| Camden | 0 | 0 | 0 | | 8,113 |
| Newark | 0 | 0 | 0 | 0 | 15,633 |
| The College of New Jersey | 0 | 0 | 0 | 0 | 8,943 |
| **Metropolitan Counties** | | | | | |
| Atlantic | 0 | 0 | 0 | 0 | |
| Camden | 0 | 0 | 0 | 0 | |
| Mercer | 0 | 0 | 0 | 0 | |
| **State Police Agencies** | | | | | |
| State Police | | | 0 | | |
| **Other Agencies** | | | | | |
| Delaware River Port Authority Police Department | | 0 | 0 | 0 | |
| **NEW MEXICO** | | | | | |
| **Cities** | | | | | |
| Angel Fire | 0 | 0 | 0 | 0 | 1,057 |
| Artesia | 0 | 0 | 0 | 0 | 12,286 |
| Aztec | 0 | 0 | 0 | 0 | 6,289 |
| Bloomfield | 0 | 0 | 0 | | 7,593 |
| Farmington | 0 | 0 | 0 | 0 | 43,973 |
| Hobbs | 0 | 0 | 0 | | 39,924 |
| Logan | 0 | 0 | 0 | 0 | 967 |
| Los Lunas | 0 | 0 | | | 16,405 |
| Sunland Park | 0 | | 0 | 0 | 18,920 |
| **Universities and Colleges** | | | | | |
| Eastern New Mexico University | 0 | 0 | 0 | 0 | 7,246 |
| University of New Mexico | 0 | 0 | 0 | 0 | 25,420 |
| **Metropolitan Counties** | | | | | |
| Dona Ana | 0 | 0 | 0 | 0 | |
| San Juan | 0 | 0 | | | |
| Valencia | 0 | | 0 | 0 | |
| **Nonmetropolitan Counties** | | | | | |
| Chaves | 0 | 0 | 0 | 0 | |
| Colfax | 0 | 0 | 0 | | |
| Lea | 0 | 0 | 0 | | |
| McKinley | 0 | 0 | 0 | 0 | |
| Quay | 0 | 0 | 0 | | |
| Socorro | 0 | 0 | 0 | 0 | |
| **Tribal Agencies** | | | | | |
| Acoma Tribal | 0 | 0 | 0 | 0 | |
| Isleta Tribal | 0 | 0 | 0 | 0 | |

## Table 95. Hate Crime Zero Data Submitted Per Quarter, by Federal Agency, State, and State Agency, 2021—Continued

(Number.)

| Agency name | Zero data per quarter[1] | | | | Population[2] |
|---|---|---|---|---|---|
| | 1st quarter | 2nd quarter | 3rd quarter | 4th quarter | |
| Jemez Pueblo | 0 | 0 | 0 | 0 | |
| Jicarilla Apache Tribal | 0 | 0 | | | |
| Laguna Tribal | 0 | | 0 | 0 | |
| Mescalero Tribal | 0 | | | 0 | |
| Northern Pueblos Agency | 0 | 0 | 0 | 0 | |
| Pojoaque Tribal | 0 | 0 | 0 | 0 | |
| Ramah Navajo Tribal | 0 | 0 | 0 | 0 | |
| Santa Ana Tribal | 0 | 0 | 0 | 0 | |
| Santa Clara Pueblo | 0 | 0 | 0 | 0 | |
| Southern Pueblos Agency | 0 | 0 | 0 | 0 | |
| Tesuque Pueblo | 0 | 0 | 0 | 0 | |
| Zia Pueblo | 0 | 0 | 0 | 0 | |
| Zuni Tribal | 0 | 0 | 0 | 0 | |
| **NEW YORK** | | | | | |
| **Cities** | | | | | |
| Arcade Village | 0 | 0 | 0 | 0 | 1,902 |
| Auburn | 0 | 0 | 0 | 0 | 25,746 |
| Batavia | 0 | 0 | 0 | 0 | 14,210 |
| Beacon | 0 | 0 | 0 | 0 | 13,940 |
| Bedford Town | 0 | 0 | 0 | 0 | 17,455 |
| Binghamton | 0 | 0 | 0 | 0 | 43,828 |
| Brockport Village | 0 | 0 | 0 | 0 | 7,821 |
| Canton Village | 0 | 0 | | | 6,498 |
| Carmel Town | | | 0 | 0 | 34,351 |
| Carroll Town | | | 0 | 0 | 3,291 |
| Deerpark Town | | | 0 | 0 | 7,667 |
| Dunkirk | 0 | 0 | 0 | 0 | 11,622 |
| East Fishkill Town | 0 | 0 | 0 | 0 | 29,547 |
| East Rochester Village | 0 | 0 | 0 | 0 | 6,443 |
| Ellicott Town | 0 | 0 | 0 | 0 | 4,945 |
| Fairport Village | 0 | 0 | 0 | 0 | 5,271 |
| Fredonia Village | 0 | 0 | 0 | 0 | 9,997 |
| Glens Falls | 0 | 0 | 0 | 0 | 14,116 |
| Goshen Town | 0 | 0 | 0 | 0 | 8,803 |
| Gouverneur Village | 0 | 0 | 0 | 0 | 3,615 |
| Hempstead Village | 0 | 0 | 0 | 0 | 54,817 |
| Hyde Park Town | 0 | 0 | 0 | 0 | 20,641 |
| Ilion Village | 0 | 0 | 0 | 0 | 7,562 |
| Irondequoit Town | 0 | 0 | 0 | 0 | 49,569 |
| Johnson City Village | 0 | 0 | 0 | 0 | 13,928 |
| Lakewood-Busti | 0 | 0 | 0 | 0 | 7,077 |
| Lewiston Town and Village | 0 | 0 | | | 15,647 |
| Marlborough Town | | | 0 | 0 | 8,572 |
| Massena Village | 0 | 0 | 0 | 0 | 10,045 |
| Maybrook Village | 0 | 0 | 0 | 0 | 3,730 |
| Middletown | 0 | 0 | 0 | 0 | 28,010 |
| New Hartford Town and Village | 0 | 0 | 0 | 0 | 20,124 |
| New Paltz Town and Village | 0 | 0 | 0 | | 14,109 |
| Niagara Town | 0 | 0 | 0 | 0 | 7,949 |
| North Tonawanda | 0 | 0 | 0 | 0 | 29,904 |
| Ogdensburg | 0 | 0 | 0 | 0 | 10,319 |
| Ogden Town | 0 | 0 | 0 | 0 | 20,715 |
| Old Westbury Village | 0 | 0 | 0 | 0 | 4,052 |
| Olean | 0 | 0 | 0 | 0 | 13,272 |
| Oneonta City | 0 | 0 | 0 | 0 | 13,671 |
| Piermont Village | 0 | 0 | 0 | 0 | 2,528 |
| Plattekill Town | 0 | 0 | 0 | 0 | 10,158 |
| Port Jervis | 0 | 0 | 0 | 0 | 8,415 |
| Potsdam Village | 0 | 0 | 0 | 0 | 8,735 |
| Rome | 0 | 0 | 0 | 0 | 31,991 |
| Rosendale Town | 0 | 0 | 0 | 0 | 5,730 |
| Scarsdale Village | 0 | 0 | 0 | 0 | 17,847 |
| Seneca Falls Town | 0 | 0 | 0 | 0 | 8,570 |
| Shandaken Town | 0 | 0 | 0 | | 2,912 |
| Shawangunk Town | 0 | 0 | | 0 | 13,751 |
| Sherrill | | | 0 | 0 | 2,947 |
| Somerset Town | 0 | 0 | 0 | | 2,027 |
| South Nyack Village | 0 | 0 | 0 | 0 | 3,284 |
| Southold Town | 0 | 0 | 0 | 0 | 20,045 |
| Stony Point Town | 0 | 0 | 0 | 0 | 15,309 |
| Tarrytown Village | 0 | 0 | 0 | 0 | 11,287 |
| Ulster Town | 0 | 0 | 0 | 0 | 12,745 |
| Walden Village | 0 | 0 | 0 | 0 | 6,593 |
| Waterloo Village | 0 | 0 | 0 | 0 | 4,837 |
| Webster Town and Village | 0 | 0 | 0 | 0 | 45,651 |
| Westfield Village | 0 | 0 | 0 | 0 | 2,938 |
| Woodstock Town | 0 | 0 | 0 | 0 | 5,743 |
| Youngstown Village | 0 | 0 | 0 | 0 | 1,824 |

# Table 95. Hate Crime Zero Data Submitted Per Quarter, by Federal Agency, State, and State Agency, 2021—Continued

(Number.)

| Agency name | Zero data per quarter[1] | | | | Population[2] |
|---|---|---|---|---|---|
| | 1st quarter | 2nd quarter | 3rd quarter | 4th quarter | |
| **Universities and Colleges** | | | | | |
| State University of New York Police | | | | | |
| Brockport | 0 | 0 | 0 | 0 | 9,194 |
| Buffalo State College | 0 | 0 | 0 | 0 | 9,955 |
| Farmingdale | 0 | 0 | 0 | 0 | 12,841 |
| Fredonia | 0 | 0 | 0 | 0 | 4,742 |
| Geneseo | 0 | 0 | 0 | | 5,724 |
| New Paltz | 0 | 0 | 0 | 0 | 8,902 |
| Optometry | | 0 | 0 | 0 | 410 |
| Oswego | 0 | 0 | 0 | 0 | 9,190 |
| Polytechnic Institute | | | 0 | 0 | 3,393 |
| Stony Brook | 0 | 0 | 0 | 0 | 34,115 |
| **Metropolitan Counties** | | | | | |
| Dutchess | 0 | 0 | 0 | 0 | |
| Livingston | 0 | 0 | 0 | 0 | |
| Niagara | 0 | 0 | 0 | 0 | |
| Oneida | 0 | 0 | 0 | 0 | |
| Oswego | 0 | 0 | 0 | 0 | |
| Saratoga | 0 | 0 | 0 | 0 | |
| Ulster | 0 | 0 | 0 | 0 | |
| Warren | 0 | 0 | 0 | 0 | |
| Yates | 0 | 0 | 0 | 0 | |
| **Nonmetropolitan Counties** | | | | | |
| Cattaraugus | 0 | 0 | 0 | 0 | |
| Lewis | 0 | 0 | 0 | 0 | |
| Montgomery | 0 | 0 | 0 | 0 | |
| Seneca | 0 | 0 | 0 | 0 | |
| St. Lawrence | 0 | 0 | 0 | 0 | |
| Wyoming | 0 | 0 | 0 | 0 | |
| **Tribal Agencies** | | | | | |
| Oneida Indian Nation | 0 | 0 | 0 | 0 | |
| St. Regis Tribal | 0 | 0 | 0 | 0 | |
| **Other Agencies** | | | | | |
| Ulster Regional Gang Enforcement Narcotics Team | 0 | 0 | 0 | 0 | |
| **NORTH CAROLINA** | | | | | |
| **Cities** | | | | | |
| Aberdeen | 0 | 0 | 0 | 0 | 8,576 |
| Ahoskie | 0 | 0 | 0 | 0 | 4,653 |
| Albemarle | 0 | 0 | 0 | 0 | 16,391 |
| Andrews | 0 | 0 | 0 | 0 | 1,863 |
| Angier | 0 | 0 | 0 | 0 | 5,610 |
| Apex | 0 | 0 | 0 | 0 | 67,878 |
| Archdale | 0 | 0 | 0 | 0 | 11,572 |
| Atlantic Beach | 0 | 0 | 0 | 0 | 1,516 |
| Ayden | 0 | 0 | 0 | 0 | 5,174 |
| Bailey | 0 | 0 | 0 | 0 | 569 |
| Bald Head Island | 0 | 0 | | | 189 |
| Banner Elk | 0 | 0 | 0 | 0 | 1,088 |
| Beaufort | 0 | 0 | 0 | 0 | 4,522 |
| Beech Mountain | 0 | 0 | 0 | 0 | 320 |
| Belhaven | 0 | 0 | 0 | 0 | 1,572 |
| Belmont | 0 | 0 | 0 | | 12,891 |
| Benson | 0 | 0 | 0 | 0 | 4,101 |
| Bessemer City | 0 | 0 | 0 | 0 | 5,677 |
| Beulaville | 0 | 0 | 0 | 0 | 1,295 |
| Biltmore Forest | 0 | 0 | 0 | 0 | 1,440 |
| Biscoe | 0 | 0 | 0 | 0 | 1,704 |
| Black Mountain | 0 | 0 | 0 | 0 | 8,297 |
| Bladenboro | 0 | 0 | 0 | 0 | 1,684 |
| Blowing Rock | 0 | 0 | 0 | 0 | 1,324 |
| Broadway | 0 | 0 | 0 | 0 | 1,304 |
| Bunn | 0 | 0 | 0 | 0 | 407 |
| Burgaw | 0 | 0 | 0 | 0 | 4,154 |
| Burlington | 0 | 0 | 0 | 0 | 56,065 |
| Butner | 0 | 0 | 0 | 0 | 7,902 |
| Candor | 0 | 0 | | | 815 |
| Canton | 0 | 0 | 0 | 0 | 4,387 |
| Cape Carteret | 0 | 0 | 0 | 0 | 2,068 |
| Carolina Beach | 0 | 0 | 0 | 0 | 6,437 |
| Carrboro | 0 | 0 | 0 | 0 | 21,413 |
| Carthage | 0 | 0 | 0 | 0 | 2,626 |
| Caswell Beach | 0 | 0 | 0 | 0 | 442 |
| Chadbourn | 0 | 0 | 0 | 0 | 1,686 |
| Cherryville | 0 | 0 | 0 | 0 | 6,180 |
| China Grove | 0 | 0 | 0 | 0 | 4,256 |

## Table 95. Hate Crime Zero Data Submitted Per Quarter, by Federal Agency, State, and State Agency, 2021—Continued

(Number.)

| Agency name | Zero data per quarter[1] | | | | Population[2] |
|---|---|---|---|---|---|
| | 1st quarter | 2nd quarter | 3rd quarter | 4th quarter | |
| Chocowinity | 0 | 0 | 0 | 0 | 771 |
| Clayton | 0 | 0 | 0 | 0 | 27,775 |
| Cleveland | 0 | 0 | 0 | 0 | 877 |
| Clinton | 0 | 0 | 0 | 0 | 8,299 |
| Coats | 0 | 0 | 0 | 0 | 2,563 |
| Columbus | 0 | 0 | 0 | 0 | 1,008 |
| Conover | 0 | 0 | 0 | 0 | 8,601 |
| Cooleemee | 0 | 0 | 0 | 0 | 983 |
| Creedmoor | 0 | 0 | 0 | 0 | 4,670 |
| Davidson | 0 | 0 | 0 | 0 | 13,457 |
| Dobson | 0 | 0 | 0 | 0 | 1,529 |
| Drexel | 0 | 0 | 0 | 0 | 1,859 |
| Duck | 0 | 0 | 0 | 0 | 396 |
| Dunn | 0 | 0 | 0 | 0 | 9,721 |
| East Spencer | 0 | 0 | 0 | 0 | 1,557 |
| Eden | 0 | 0 | 0 | 0 | 14,786 |
| Edenton | 0 | 0 | 0 | 0 | 4,528 |
| Elizabethtown | 0 | 0 | 0 | 0 | 3,353 |
| Elkin | 0 | 0 | 0 | 0 | 3,998 |
| Elon | 0 | 0 | 0 | 0 | 12,521 |
| Emerald Isle | 0 | 0 | 0 | 0 | 3,677 |
| Enfield | 0 | 0 | 0 | 0 | 2,234 |
| Fair Bluff | 0 | 0 | 0 | 0 | 872 |
| Fairmont | 0 | 0 | 0 | 0 | 2,568 |
| Farmville | 0 | 0 | 0 | 0 | 4,756 |
| Forest City | 0 | 0 | 0 | 0 | 7,106 |
| Four Oaks | 0 | 0 | 0 | 0 | 2,436 |
| Franklinton | 0 | 0 | 0 | 0 | 2,344 |
| Fuquay-Varina | 0 | 0 | 0 | 0 | 34,018 |
| Garner | 0 | 0 | 0 | 0 | 32,889 |
| Gibsonville | 0 | 0 | 0 | 0 | 7,492 |
| Goldsboro | 0 | 0 | 0 | 0 | 34,352 |
| Graham | 0 | 0 | 0 | 0 | 15,919 |
| Granite Falls | 0 | 0 | 0 | 0 | 4,652 |
| Grifton | 0 | 0 | 0 | 0 | 2,717 |
| Havelock | 0 | 0 | 0 | 0 | 19,450 |
| Haw River | 0 | 0 | 0 | 0 | 2,558 |
| Henderson | 0 | 0 | 0 | 0 | 15,067 |
| Highlands | 0 | 0 | 0 | 0 | 989 |
| Hillsborough | 0 | 0 | 0 | 0 | 7,291 |
| Holden Beach | 0 | 0 | 0 | 0 | 686 |
| Holly Ridge | 0 | 0 | 0 | 0 | 3,365 |
| Holly Springs | 0 | 0 | 0 | 0 | 41,798 |
| Hope Mills | 0 | 0 | 0 | 0 | 15,914 |
| Hudson | 0 | 0 | 0 | 0 | 3,696 |
| Huntersville | 0 | 0 | 0 | 0 | 60,450 |
| Indian Beach | 0 | 0 | 0 | 0 | 119 |
| Jefferson | 0 | 0 | 0 | 0 | 1,528 |
| Jonesville | 0 | 0 | 0 | 0 | 2,198 |
| Kannapolis | 0 | 0 | 0 | 0 | 53,044 |
| Kenansville | 0 | 0 | 0 | 0 | 849 |
| Kill Devil Hills | 0 | 0 | 0 | 0 | 7,488 |
| King | 0 | 0 | 0 | 0 | 6,916 |
| Kings Mountain | 0 | 0 | 0 | 0 | 11,162 |
| Kinston | 0 | 0 | 0 | 0 | 19,672 |
| Kitty Hawk | 0 | 0 | 0 | 0 | 3,632 |
| Knightdale | 0 | 0 | 0 | 0 | 18,970 |
| Laurinburg | 0 | 0 | 0 | 0 | 14,798 |
| Lenoir | 0 | 0 | 0 | 0 | 17,881 |
| Lexington | 0 | 0 | 0 | 0 | 19,162 |
| Lillington | 0 | 0 | 0 | 0 | 3,680 |
| Lincolnton | 0 | 0 | 0 | 0 | 11,641 |
| Louisburg | 0 | 0 | 0 | 0 | 3,722 |
| Lowell | 0 | 0 | 0 | 0 | 3,767 |
| Madison | 0 | 0 | 0 | 0 | 2,095 |
| Maggie Valley | 0 | 0 | 0 | 0 | 1,268 |
| Manteo | 0 | 0 | 0 | 0 | 1,483 |
| Marion | 0 | 0 | 0 | 0 | 7,916 |
| Mars Hill | 0 | 0 | 0 | | 1,884 |
| Marshville | 0 | 0 | 0 | 0 | 2,875 |
| Maxton | 0 | 0 | 0 | 0 | 2,321 |
| Mayodan | 0 | 0 | 0 | 0 | 2,401 |
| Maysville | 0 | 0 | 0 | 0 | 908 |
| Mebane | 0 | 0 | 0 | 0 | 17,365 |
| Middlesex | 0 | 0 | 0 | 0 | 835 |
| Morganton | 0 | 0 | | | 16,605 |
| Morrisville | 0 | 0 | 0 | 0 | 32,018 |
| Mount Gilead | 0 | 0 | 0 | 0 | 1,137 |
| Mount Holly | 0 | 0 | 0 | 0 | 16,720 |
| Mount Olive | 0 | 0 | 0 | 0 | 4,665 |
| Murfreesboro | 0 | 0 | 0 | 0 | 2,873 |

## Table 95. Hate Crime Zero Data Submitted Per Quarter, by Federal Agency, State, and State Agency, 2021—Continued

(Number.)

| Agency name | Zero data per quarter[1] | | | | Population[2] |
|---|---|---|---|---|---|
| | 1st quarter | 2nd quarter | 3rd quarter | 4th quarter | |
| Nags Head | 0 | 0 | 0 | 0 | 3,021 |
| New Bern | 0 | 0 | 0 | 0 | 29,985 |
| Newland | 0 | 0 | 0 | 0 | 693 |
| Newton | 0 | 0 | 0 | 0 | 13,253 |
| North Topsail Beach | 0 | 0 | 0 | 0 | 743 |
| North Wilkesboro | 0 | 0 | 0 | 0 | 4,069 |
| Oxford | 0 | 0 | 0 | 0 | 8,950 |
| Pembroke | 0 | | | | 2,929 |
| Pine Knoll Shores | 0 | 0 | | 0 | 1,313 |
| Pine Level | 0 | 0 | 0 | 0 | 2,123 |
| Plymouth | 0 | 0 | 0 | 0 | 3,285 |
| Princeton | 0 | 0 | 0 | 0 | 1,451 |
| Ramseur | 0 | 0 | | | 1,689 |
| Ranlo | 0 | 0 | 0 | 0 | 3,736 |
| Red Springs | 0 | 0 | 0 | 0 | 3,218 |
| Richlands | 0 | 0 | 0 | 0 | 1,741 |
| Roanoke Rapids | 0 | 0 | 0 | 0 | 14,046 |
| Robbins | 0 | 0 | 0 | 0 | 1,254 |
| Robersonville | 0 | 0 | 0 | 0 | 1,307 |
| Rockingham | 0 | 0 | 0 | 0 | 8,424 |
| Rockwell | 0 | 0 | 0 | 0 | 2,170 |
| Rocky Mount | 0 | 0 | 0 | 0 | 53,305 |
| Rolesville | 0 | 0 | 0 | 0 | 9,679 |
| Rowland | 0 | 0 | 0 | 0 | 980 |
| Roxboro | 0 | 0 | 0 | 0 | 8,387 |
| Rutherfordton | 0 | 0 | 0 | 0 | 4,081 |
| Salisbury | 0 | 0 | 0 | 0 | 33,856 |
| Saluda | 0 | 0 | 0 | 0 | 702 |
| Sanford | 0 | | | | 30,583 |
| Scotland Neck | 0 | | 0 | 0 | 1,789 |
| Selma | 0 | 0 | 0 | 0 | 7,454 |
| Seven Devils | 0 | | | | 204 |
| Siler City | 0 | 0 | 0 | | 8,473 |
| Snow Hill | 0 | 0 | 0 | 0 | 1,476 |
| Southern Pines | 0 | 0 | 0 | 0 | 15,358 |
| Southern Shores | 0 | 0 | 0 | 0 | 3,026 |
| Spencer | 0 | 0 | 0 | 0 | 3,260 |
| Spring Lake | 0 | 0 | 0 | 0 | 12,028 |
| Spruce Pine | 0 | 0 | 0 | 0 | 2,115 |
| Stantonsburg | 0 | 0 | 0 | 0 | 780 |
| Star | 0 | 0 | 0 | 0 | 846 |
| Stoneville | 0 | 0 | 0 | 0 | 1,257 |
| St. Pauls | 0 | 0 | 0 | 0 | 2,279 |
| Sugar Mountain | 0 | 0 | 0 | 0 | 197 |
| Surf City | 0 | 0 | 0 | 0 | 2,602 |
| Swansboro | 0 | 0 | 0 | 0 | 3,472 |
| Tabor City | 0 | 0 | 0 | 0 | 3,883 |
| Taylorsville | 0 | 0 | 0 | 0 | 2,145 |
| Taylortown | 0 | 0 | 0 | 0 | 891 |
| Trent Woods | 0 | 0 | 0 | 0 | 3,973 |
| Troutman | 0 | 0 | 0 | 0 | 2,856 |
| Troy | 0 | 0 | 0 | 0 | 3,274 |
| Tryon | 0 | 0 | 0 | 0 | 1,635 |
| Wadesboro | 0 | 0 | 0 | 0 | 5,190 |
| Wallace | 0 | 0 | 0 | 0 | 3,855 |
| Warrenton | 0 | 0 | 0 | 0 | 814 |
| Warsaw | 0 | 0 | 0 | 0 | 3,081 |
| Washington | 0 | 0 | 0 | 0 | 9,451 |
| Waxhaw | 0 | 0 | 0 | 0 | 19,089 |
| Waynesville | 0 | 0 | 0 | 0 | 10,632 |
| Weaverville | 0 | 0 | | | 4,077 |
| Weldon | 0 | 0 | 0 | 0 | 1,438 |
| Wendell | 0 | 0 | 0 | 0 | 9,841 |
| Whispering Pines | 0 | 0 | 0 | 0 | 3,515 |
| White Lake | 0 | 0 | 0 | 0 | 738 |
| Whiteville | 0 | 0 | 0 | 0 | 5,231 |
| Wilkesboro | 0 | 0 | 0 | 0 | 3,419 |
| Windsor | 0 | 0 | 0 | 0 | 3,485 |
| Wingate | 0 | 0 | 0 | 0 | 4,873 |
| Winterville | 0 | 0 | 0 | 0 | 10,225 |
| Woodfin | 0 | 0 | 0 | 0 | 6,718 |
| Woodland | 0 | 0 | 0 | 0 | 691 |
| Wrightsville Beach | 0 | 0 | 0 | 0 | 2,519 |
| Yadkinville | 0 | 0 | 0 | 0 | 2,864 |
| Youngsville | 0 | 0 | 0 | 0 | 1,442 |
| Zebulon | 0 | 0 | 0 | 0 | 6,764 |
| **Universities and Colleges** | | | | | |
| Appalachian State University | 0 | 0 | | 0 | 20,799 |
| Duke University | 0 | 0 | 0 | 0 | 17,855 |
| Elizabeth City State University | 0 | 0 | 0 | 0 | 2,027 |

## Table 95. Hate Crime Zero Data Submitted Per Quarter, by Federal Agency, State, and State Agency, 2021—Continued

(Number.)

| Agency name | Zero data per quarter[1] | | | | Population[2] |
|---|---|---|---|---|---|
| | 1st quarter | 2nd quarter | 3rd quarter | 4th quarter | |
| Elon University | 0 | 0 | 0 | 0 | 7,424 |
| Methodist University | 0 | 0 | 0 | 0 | 2,109 |
| North Carolina Agricultural and Technical State University | 0 | 0 | 0 | 0 | 13,854 |
| North Carolina Central University | 0 | 0 | | | 9,070 |
| North Carolina State University, Raleigh | 0 | 0 | 0 | 0 | 40,537 |
| University of North Carolina | | | | | |
|   Asheville | 0 | 0 | 0 | 0 | 4,153 |
|   Charlotte | 0 | 0 | 0 | 0 | 34,715 |
|   Greensboro | 0 | 0 | 0 | 0 | 22,487 |
| Wake Forest University | 0 | 0 | 0 | 0 | 9,266 |
| **Metropolitan Counties** | | | | | |
| Alamance | 0 | 0 | 0 | 0 | |
| Alexander | 0 | 0 | 0 | 0 | |
| Anson | 0 | 0 | 0 | 0 | |
| Cabarrus | 0 | 0 | 0 | 0 | |
| Catawba | 0 | 0 | 0 | 0 | |
| Craven | 0 | 0 | 0 | 0 | |
| Cumberland | 0 | 0 | 0 | 0 | |
| Currituck | 0 | 0 | 0 | 0 | |
| Durham | 0 | 0 | 0 | 0 | |
| Edgecombe | 0 | 0 | 0 | | |
| Franklin | 0 | 0 | 0 | 0 | |
| Gaston | 0 | 0 | 0 | 0 | |
| Gates | 0 | 0 | 0 | | |
| Granville | 0 | 0 | 0 | 0 | |
| Iredell | 0 | 0 | 0 | 0 | |
| Lincoln | 0 | 0 | 0 | 0 | |
| Rockingham | 0 | 0 | 0 | 0 | |
| Rowan | 0 | 0 | 0 | 0 | |
| Wake | 0 | 0 | 0 | 0 | |
| Wayne | 0 | 0 | 0 | 0 | |
| Yadkin | 0 | 0 | 0 | 0 | |
| **Nonmetropolitan Counties** | | | | | |
| Ashe | 0 | 0 | 0 | 0 | |
| Avery | 0 | 0 | 0 | 0 | |
| Bertie | 0 | 0 | 0 | 0 | |
| Bladen | 0 | 0 | 0 | 0 | |
| Cherokee | 0 | 0 | 0 | 0 | |
| Chowan | 0 | 0 | 0 | 0 | |
| Dare | 0 | 0 | 0 | 0 | |
| Graham | 0 | 0 | | | |
| Greene | 0 | 0 | 0 | 0 | |
| Hertford | 0 | 0 | 0 | 0 | |
| Jackson | 0 | | | | |
| Lee | 0 | 0 | | | |
| Macon | 0 | 0 | 0 | 0 | |
| Martin | 0 | 0 | 0 | 0 | |
| McDowell | 0 | 0 | 0 | 0 | |
| Pasquotank | 0 | 0 | 0 | 0 | |
| Perquimans | 0 | 0 | 0 | 0 | |
| Polk | 0 | 0 | 0 | 0 | |
| Robeson | 0 | 0 | 0 | 0 | |
| Rutherford | 0 | 0 | 0 | 0 | |
| Sampson | 0 | 0 | 0 | 0 | |
| Scotland | 0 | 0 | 0 | 0 | |
| Stanly | 0 | 0 | 0 | 0 | |
| Transylvania | 0 | 0 | 0 | 0 | |
| Tyrrell | 0 | 0 | 0 | 0 | |
| Wilkes | 0 | 0 | 0 | 0 | |
| Wilson | 0 | 0 | 0 | 0 | |
| Yancey | 0 | 0 | 0 | 0 | |
| **Tribal Agencies** | | | | | |
| Cherokee Tribal | | 0 | 0 | 0 | |
| **Other Agencies** | | | | | |
| North Carolina Arboretum | | 0 | 0 | 0 | |
| North Carolina Museum of Art Park Police | 0 | 0 | 0 | 0 | |
| North Carolina State Port Authority, Division [1] | 0 | 0 | 0 | 0 | |
| Raleigh-Durham International Airport | 0 | 0 | 0 | 0 | |
| State Park Rangers | | | | | |
|   Chimney Rock | 0 | 0 | 0 | | |
|   Crowders Mountain | 0 | 0 | 0 | 0 | |
|   Elk Knob | 0 | 0 | 0 | 0 | |
|   Eno River | 0 | 0 | 0 | 0 | |
|   Falls Lake Recreation Area | 0 | 0 | 0 | 0 | |
|   Gorges | 0 | 0 | 0 | 0 | |
|   Hammocks Beach | 0 | 0 | 0 | 0 | |

## Table 95. Hate Crime Zero Data Submitted Per Quarter, by Federal Agency, State, and State Agency, 2021—Continued

(Number.)

| Agency name | Zero data per quarter[1] | | | | Population[2] |
|---|---|---|---|---|---|
| | 1st quarter | 2nd quarter | 3rd quarter | 4th quarter | |
| Hanging Rock | 0 | 0 | | | |
| Haw River | 0 | 0 | 0 | 0 | |
| Jockey's Ridge | 0 | 0 | 0 | 0 | |
| Jordan Lake State Recreation Area | 0 | 0 | 0 | 0 | |
| Kerr Lake | 0 | 0 | 0 | 0 | |
| Lake James | 0 | | | | |
| Lake Norman | 0 | 0 | 0 | 0 | |
| Lumber River | 0 | 0 | | | |
| Merchants Millpond | 0 | 0 | 0 | 0 | |
| Morrow Mountain | | 0 | 0 | 0 | |
| Mount Mitchell | 0 | 0 | | | |
| New River-Mount Jefferson | 0 | 0 | 0 | 0 | |
| Pettigrew | 0 | | | | |
| Pilot Mountain | 0 | 0 | 0 | 0 | |
| Raven Rock | 0 | 0 | 0 | 0 | |
| Stone Mountain | 0 | 0 | 0 | 0 | |
| William B. Umstead | 0 | 0 | 0 | 0 | |
| WakeMed Campus Police | 0 | 0 | 0 | 0 | |
| **NORTH DAKOTA** | | | | | |
| **Cities** | | | | | |
| Belfield | 0 | 0 | 0 | | 1,063 |
| Berthold | 0 | 0 | 0 | 0 | 494 |
| Beulah | 0 | 0 | 0 | 0 | 3,129 |
| Bowman | 0 | 0 | 0 | 0 | 1,571 |
| Burlington | 0 | 0 | 0 | 0 | 1,213 |
| Carrington | 0 | 0 | 0 | 0 | 1,940 |
| Cavalier | 0 | 0 | 0 | 0 | 1,190 |
| Devils Lake | 0 | 0 | 0 | 0 | 7,237 |
| Drayton | | | | 0 | 719 |
| Dunseith | | 0 | 0 | 0 | 767 |
| Ellendale | 0 | 0 | 0 | 0 | 1,160 |
| Emerado | 0 | 0 | 0 | 0 | 464 |
| Garrison | 0 | 0 | 0 | 0 | 1,458 |
| Grafton | 0 | 0 | 0 | 0 | 4,055 |
| Grand Forks | 0 | 0 | 0 | 0 | 56,253 |
| Harvey | 0 | 0 | 0 | 0 | 1,568 |
| Hazen | 0 | 0 | 0 | 0 | 2,322 |
| Jamestown | 0 | 0 | 0 | 0 | 14,879 |
| Kenmare | 0 | 0 | 0 | 0 | 1,019 |
| Killdeer | 0 | 0 | 0 | 0 | 1,209 |
| Lamoure | 0 | 0 | 0 | 0 | 884 |
| Lisbon | 0 | 0 | 0 | 0 | 2,002 |
| Medora | 0 | 0 | 0 | 0 | 125 |
| Minot | 0 | 0 | 0 | 0 | 48,086 |
| Napoleon | 0 | 0 | 0 | 0 | 756 |
| New Town | 0 | 0 | 0 | 0 | 2,706 |
| Northwood | 0 | 0 | 0 | 0 | 879 |
| Oakes | 0 | 0 | 0 | 0 | 1,639 |
| Powers Lake | 0 | 0 | 0 | 0 | 284 |
| Ray | 0 | 0 | 0 | 0 | 989 |
| Rolette | 0 | 0 | 0 | 0 | 585 |
| Rolla | 0 | 0 | 0 | 0 | 1,271 |
| Rugby | 0 | 0 | 0 | 0 | 2,538 |
| Stanley | 0 | 0 | 0 | 0 | 2,885 |
| Steele | 0 | 0 | 0 | 0 | 701 |
| Surrey | 0 | 0 | 0 | 0 | 1,460 |
| Thompson | 0 | 0 | 0 | 0 | 1,031 |
| Tioga | 0 | 0 | 0 | 0 | 1,405 |
| Wahpeton | 0 | 0 | 0 | 0 | 7,725 |
| Watford City | 0 | 0 | 0 | 0 | 9,301 |
| West Fargo | 0 | 0 | 0 | 0 | 39,704 |
| Wishek | 0 | 0 | 0 | 0 | 858 |
| **Universities and Colleges** | | | | | |
| Bismarck State College | 0 | 0 | 0 | 0 | 4,855 |
| North Dakota State College of Science | 0 | 0 | 0 | 0 | 3,669 |
| North Dakota State University | 0 | 0 | 0 | 0 | 14,384 |
| University of North Dakota | 0 | 0 | 0 | 0 | 17,182 |
| **Metropolitan Counties** | | | | | |
| Burleigh | 0 | 0 | 0 | 0 | |
| Cass | 0 | 0 | 0 | 0 | |
| Morton | 0 | 0 | 0 | 0 | |
| Oliver | 0 | 0 | 0 | 0 | |
| **Nonmetropolitan Counties** | | | | | |
| Adams | 0 | 0 | 0 | 0 | |
| Barnes | 0 | 0 | 0 | 0 | |
| Benson | 0 | 0 | 0 | 0 | |

**Table 95. Hate Crime Zero Data Submitted Per Quarter, by Federal Agency, State, and State Agency, 2021—Continued**

(Number.)

| Agency name | Zero data per quarter[1] | | | | Population[2] |
|---|---|---|---|---|---|
| | 1st quarter | 2nd quarter | 3rd quarter | 4th quarter | |
| Billings | 0 | 0 | 0 | 0 | |
| Bottineau | 0 | 0 | 0 | 0 | |
| Bowman | 0 | 0 | 0 | 0 | |
| Burke | 0 | 0 | 0 | 0 | |
| Cavalier | 0 | 0 | 0 | 0 | |
| Dickey | 0 | 0 | 0 | 0 | |
| Divide | 0 | 0 | 0 | 0 | |
| Dunn | 0 | 0 | 0 | 0 | |
| Eddy | 0 | 0 | 0 | 0 | |
| Emmons | 0 | 0 | 0 | 0 | |
| Foster | 0 | 0 | 0 | 0 | |
| Grant | 0 | 0 | 0 | 0 | |
| Griggs | 0 | 0 | 0 | 0 | |
| Hettinger | 0 | 0 | 0 | 0 | |
| Kidder | 0 | 0 | 0 | 0 | |
| Lamoure | 0 | 0 | 0 | 0 | |
| Logan | 0 | 0 | 0 | 0 | |
| McHenry | 0 | 0 | 0 | 0 | |
| McIntosh | 0 | 0 | 0 | 0 | |
| McKenzie | 0 | 0 | 0 | 0 | |
| McLean | 0 | 0 | 0 | 0 | |
| Mercer | 0 | 0 | 0 | 0 | |
| Mountrail | 0 | 0 | 0 | 0 | |
| Nelson | 0 | 0 | 0 | 0 | |
| Pierce | 0 | 0 | 0 | 0 | |
| Ramsey | 0 | 0 | 0 | 0 | |
| Ransom | 0 | 0 | 0 | 0 | |
| Renville | 0 | 0 | 0 | 0 | |
| Richland | 0 | 0 | 0 | 0 | |
| Rolette | 0 | 0 | 0 | 0 | |
| Sargent | 0 | 0 | 0 | 0 | |
| Sheridan | 0 | 0 | 0 | 0 | |
| Sioux | 0 | 0 | 0 | 0 | |
| Slope | 0 | 0 | 0 | 0 | |
| Stark | 0 | 0 | 0 | 0 | |
| Steele | 0 | 0 | 0 | 0 | |
| Stutsman | 0 | 0 | 0 | 0 | |
| Towner | 0 | 0 | 0 | 0 | |
| Traill | 0 | 0 | 0 | 0 | |
| Walsh | 0 | 0 | 0 | 0 | |
| Ward | 0 | 0 | 0 | 0 | |
| Wells | 0 | 0 | 0 | 0 | |
| Williams | 0 | 0 | 0 | 0 | |
| **State Police Agencies** | | | | | |
| North Dakota Highway Patrol | 0 | 0 | 0 | 0 | |
| **Tribal Agencies** | | | | | |
| Fort Totten Agency | 0 | 0 | | | |
| Standing Rock Agency | 0 | 0 | | 0 | |
| Three Affiliated Tribes | 0 | | | | |
| **Other Agencies** | | | | | |
| North Dakota Bureau of Criminal Investigation | | 0 | 0 | 0 | |
| **OHIO** | | | | | |
| **Cities** | | | | | |
| Ada | 0 | 0 | 0 | 0 | 5,491 |
| Addyston | 0 | 0 | 0 | 0 | 936 |
| Albany | | | 0 | | 897 |
| Alliance | 0 | 0 | 0 | 0 | 21,328 |
| American Township | 0 | 0 | 0 | 0 | 11,989 |
| Amherst | 0 | 0 | 0 | 0 | 12,425 |
| Amsterdam | 0 | 0 | 0 | 0 | 465 |
| Andover | 0 | | | | 1,083 |
| Apple Creek | 0 | 0 | 0 | | 1,187 |
| Ashley | 0 | 0 | 0 | 0 | 1,674 |
| Ashville | 0 | 0 | 0 | 0 | 4,510 |
| Athens | 0 | 0 | 0 | 0 | 24,638 |
| Aurora | 0 | 0 | 0 | 0 | 16,568 |
| Avon Lake | 0 | 0 | 0 | 0 | 25,040 |
| Bainbridge Township | 0 | 0 | | | 11,395 |
| Baltimore | 0 | 0 | 0 | 0 | 3,030 |
| Barnesville | 0 | 0 | 0 | 0 | 3,925 |
| Batavia | 0 | 0 | 0 | 0 | 1,973 |
| Bath Township, Summit County | 0 | 0 | 0 | 0 | 9,606 |
| Bay View | 0 | 0 | | | 594 |
| Bazetta Township | 0 | 0 | 0 | 0 | 5,454 |
| Beach City | | 0 | | 0 | 973 |
| Beachwood | 0 | 0 | 0 | 0 | 11,580 |

## Table 95. Hate Crime Zero Data Submitted Per Quarter, by Federal Agency, State, and State Agency, 2021—Continued

(Number.)

| Agency name | Zero data per quarter[1] | | | | Population[2] |
| --- | --- | --- | --- | --- | --- |
| | 1st quarter | 2nd quarter | 3rd quarter | 4th quarter | |
| Beavercreek | 0 | 0 | 0 | 0 | 48,282 |
| Bedford | 0 | 0 | 0 | 0 | 12,386 |
| Bedford Heights | 0 | 0 | 0 | 0 | 10,430 |
| Bellaire | 0 | 0 | 0 | 0 | 3,927 |
| Bellbrook | 0 | 0 | 0 | 0 | 7,426 |
| Bellefontaine | 0 | 0 | 0 | 0 | 13,131 |
| Bellville | 0 | 0 | 0 | 0 | 1,937 |
| Belpre | 0 | 0 | 0 | 0 | 6,348 |
| Bentleyville Village | 0 | 0 | 0 | 0 | 844 |
| Berea | 0 | 0 | 0 | 0 | 18,563 |
| Bethel | 0 | 0 | 0 | 0 | 2,837 |
| Bexley | 0 | 0 | 0 | 0 | 13,822 |
| Blanchester | 0 | | | | 4,257 |
| Blendon Township | | 0 | 0 | 0 | 7,994 |
| Bluffton | 0 | 0 | 0 | | 4,002 |
| Bolivar | 0 | | | 0 | 962 |
| Boston Heights | 0 | | | | 1,311 |
| Botkins | 0 | 0 | 0 | 0 | 1,159 |
| Bowling Green | 0 | 0 | 0 | 0 | 31,537 |
| Bratenahl | 0 | 0 | 0 | 0 | 1,156 |
| Brecksville | 0 | 0 | 0 | 0 | 13,611 |
| Brewster | 0 | 0 | 0 | 0 | 2,141 |
| Bridgeport | 0 | 0 | 0 | 0 | 1,691 |
| Brimfield Township | 0 | 0 | 0 | 0 | 10,328 |
| Brookfield Township | 0 | 0 | | | 8,287 |
| Brooklyn | 0 | 0 | 0 | 0 | 10,648 |
| Brunswick | | 0 | 0 | | 35,132 |
| Brunswick Hills Township | 0 | 0 | 0 | 0 | 10,621 |
| Buckeye Lake | 0 | 0 | 0 | 0 | 2,908 |
| Bucyrus | 0 | 0 | 0 | 0 | 11,676 |
| Butler | 0 | 0 | 0 | | 894 |
| Butler Township ♦ | 0 | 0 | 0 | 0 | 7,835 |
| Byesville | 0 | 0 | 0 | 0 | 2,336 |
| Cambridge | 0 | 0 | 0 | 0 | 10,279 |
| Camden | 0 | | | | 1,968 |
| Canal Fulton | 0 | 0 | 0 | 0 | 5,396 |
| Canfield | 0 | 0 | 0 | 0 | 7,104 |
| Cardington | 0 | 0 | 0 | 0 | 2,079 |
| Carey | 0 | 0 | 0 | 0 | 3,527 |
| Carlisle | 0 | 0 | 0 | 0 | 5,573 |
| Carroll | 0 | | 0 | | 568 |
| Carroll Township | 0 | 0 | 0 | 0 | 2,067 |
| Catawba Island Township | 0 | 0 | 0 | 0 | 3,495 |
| Cedarville | 0 | 0 | 0 | 0 | 4,364 |
| Center Township | | 0 | | | 3,277 |
| Centerville | 0 | 0 | 0 | 0 | 23,669 |
| Chagrin Falls | 0 | 0 | 0 | 0 | 3,921 |
| Chardon | 0 | 0 | 0 | 0 | 5,138 |
| Cheviot | 0 | 0 | 0 | 0 | 8,164 |
| Clay Township, Montgomery County | 0 | 0 | 0 | 0 | 4,242 |
| Clearcreek Township | 0 | 0 | 0 | 0 | 16,724 |
| Cleveland Heights | 0 | 0 | 0 | 0 | 43,608 |
| Clinton Township | | 0 | 0 | 0 | 4,096 |
| Coal Grove | 0 | 0 | 0 | 0 | 2,038 |
| Coitsville Township | 0 | 0 | 0 | 0 | 1,306 |
| Coldwater | 0 | 0 | 0 | 0 | 4,577 |
| Columbiana | 0 | 0 | 0 | 0 | 6,276 |
| Commercial Point | 0 | 0 | 0 | 0 | 1,704 |
| Conneaut | 0 | | | | 12,180 |
| Copley Township | 0 | 0 | 0 | 0 | 17,233 |
| Cortland | 0 | 0 | 0 | 0 | 6,702 |
| Covington | 0 | 0 | 0 | | 2,730 |
| Craig Beach | 0 | 0 | | 0 | 1,103 |
| Creston | | 0 | | | 2,187 |
| Crooksville | 0 | 0 | 0 | | 2,470 |
| Cross Creek Township | 0 | 0 | 0 | 0 | 4,991 |
| Danville | 0 | 0 | 0 | 0 | 1,011 |
| Delphos | 0 | 0 | 0 | 0 | 6,873 |
| Delta | 0 | 0 | 0 | 0 | 3,085 |
| Dennison | 0 | 0 | 0 | 0 | 2,593 |
| Dillonvale | 0 | | 0 | 0 | 585 |
| Dresden | | 0 | | | 1,703 |
| Dublin | 0 | 0 | 0 | 0 | 50,236 |
| East Canton | 0 | 0 | | | 1,567 |
| Eastlake | 0 | 0 | | | 17,876 |
| East Liverpool | 0 | 0 | 0 | 0 | 10,430 |
| Eaton | 0 | 0 | 0 | 0 | 8,098 |
| Elida | 0 | 0 | 0 | 0 | 1,803 |
| Elmore | 0 | 0 | 0 | 0 | 1,396 |
| Elmwood Place | 0 | 0 | 0 | | 2,203 |

## Table 95. Hate Crime Zero Data Submitted Per Quarter, by Federal Agency, State, and State Agency, 2021—Continued

(Number.)

| Agency name | Zero data per quarter[1] | | | | Population[2] |
|---|---|---|---|---|---|
| | 1st quarter | 2nd quarter | 3rd quarter | 4th quarter | |
| Englewood | 0 | 0 | 0 | 0 | 13,507 |
| Enon | 0 | 0 | | 0 | 2,375 |
| Euclid | 0 | 0 | | | 46,248 |
| Evendale | | 0 | 0 | 0 | 2,707 |
| Fairfax | 0 | 0 | 0 | 0 | 1,702 |
| Fairfield Township | 0 | 0 | 0 | 0 | 23,206 |
| Fairlawn | 0 | 0 | 0 | 0 | 7,515 |
| Fairview Park | 0 | 0 | 0 | | 16,072 |
| Fayette | 0 | 0 | 0 | 0 | 1,227 |
| Felicity | 0 | 0 | 0 | 0 | 864 |
| Flushing | | 0 | | | 815 |
| Forest | 0 | 0 | 0 | 0 | 1,442 |
| Forest Park | 0 | 0 | 0 | 0 | 18,518 |
| Fort Loramie | | | 0 | 0 | 1,541 |
| Fort Recovery | 0 | 0 | 0 | 0 | 1,471 |
| Franklin Township | | | 0 | 0 | 9,741 |
| Frazeysburg | 0 | 0 | 0 | 0 | 1,316 |
| Fredericktown | 0 | 0 | 0 | 0 | 2,529 |
| Fremont | 0 | 0 | 0 | 0 | 15,764 |
| Galion | | 0 | | | 9,865 |
| Gallipolis | 0 | 0 | 0 | 0 | 3,534 |
| Garrettsville | 0 | 0 | 0 | 0 | 2,316 |
| Gates Mills | 0 | 0 | 0 | 0 | 2,213 |
| Genoa | | 0 | 0 | | 2,256 |
| Georgetown | 0 | 0 | 0 | 0 | 4,189 |
| Germantown | 0 | 0 | 0 | 0 | 5,570 |
| German Township, Montgomery County | 0 | 0 | 0 | 0 | 2,899 |
| Glendale | 0 | 0 | 0 | | 2,185 |
| Glouster | 0 | 0 | 0 | 0 | 1,778 |
| Goshen Township, Mahoning County | 0 | 0 | 0 | 0 | 3,079 |
| Grafton | 0 | 0 | 0 | 0 | 5,920 |
| Grandview Heights | 0 | 0 | 0 | 0 | 9,395 |
| Granville | 0 | 0 | 0 | 0 | 5,842 |
| Gratis | 0 | 0 | | | 844 |
| Greenfield | 0 | 0 | 0 | 0 | 4,556 |
| Greenhills | 0 | 0 | 0 | 0 | 3,548 |
| Green Township | 0 | 0 | 0 | 0 | 59,115 |
| Groveport | 0 | 0 | 0 | 0 | 5,642 |
| Hamilton Township, Warren County | 0 | 0 | 0 | 0 | 24,711 |
| Harveysburg | 0 | 0 | 0 | 0 | 571 |
| Hebron | 0 | 0 | 0 | 0 | 2,513 |
| Highland Heights | 0 | 0 | 0 | 0 | 8,389 |
| Highland Hills | 0 | | | | 900 |
| Hinckley Township | 0 | 0 | 0 | 0 | 8,174 |
| Hiram | 0 | 0 | 0 | | 1,092 |
| Howland Township | 0 | 0 | 0 | 0 | 16,220 |
| Hubbard | 0 | 0 | 0 | 0 | 7,320 |
| Huber Heights | 0 | 0 | 0 | 0 | 38,244 |
| Hunting Valley | 0 | 0 | 0 | | 722 |
| Huron | 0 | 0 | 0 | 0 | 6,794 |
| Independence | 0 | 0 | 0 | 0 | 7,244 |
| Ironton | 0 | 0 | 0 | 0 | 10,354 |
| Jackson | 0 | 0 | 0 | 0 | 6,224 |
| Jackson Township, Mahoning County | 0 | 0 | 0 | 0 | 1,993 |
| Jackson Township, Montgomery County | 0 | 0 | 0 | 0 | 3,685 |
| Kent | 0 | 0 | 0 | 0 | 29,364 |
| Kenton | 0 | 0 | 0 | 0 | 8,204 |
| Kipton | 0 | | | | 232 |
| Kirtland | | | 0 | 0 | 6,787 |
| Lakemore | 0 | 0 | 0 | 0 | 3,060 |
| Lebanon | 0 | 0 | 0 | 0 | 20,826 |
| Lexington | 0 | 0 | 0 | 0 | 4,685 |
| Linndale | | 0 | 0 | 0 | 144 |
| Lisbon | 0 | 0 | 0 | 0 | 2,606 |
| Lithopolis | 0 | 0 | 0 | 0 | 2,022 |
| Lockland | 0 | 0 | 0 | 0 | 3,436 |
| Lodi | 0 | 0 | 0 | 0 | 2,929 |
| London | 0 | 0 | 0 | 0 | 10,360 |
| Lordstown | 0 | 0 | 0 | 0 | 3,227 |
| Loudonville | 0 | 0 | 0 | 0 | 2,620 |
| Louisville | 0 | 0 | 0 | 0 | 9,390 |
| Loveland | 0 | 0 | 0 | 0 | 13,253 |
| Lowellville | | 0 | | 0 | 1,073 |
| Lynchburg | 0 | 0 | 0 | 0 | 1,493 |
| Macedonia | 0 | 0 | 0 | 0 | 12,120 |
| Madeira | 0 | 0 | 0 | 0 | 9,340 |
| Madison | | | | 0 | 3,157 |
| Madison Township, Franklin County | 0 | 0 | 0 | 0 | 20,118 |
| Magnolia | 0 | 0 | 0 | 0 | 963 |
| Maple Heights | 0 | 0 | 0 | 0 | 21,888 |

# Table 95. Hate Crime Zero Data Submitted Per Quarter, by Federal Agency, State, and State Agency, 2021—Continued

(Number.)

| Agency name | Zero data per quarter[1] | | | | Population[2] |
|---|---|---|---|---|---|
| | 1st quarter | 2nd quarter | 3rd quarter | 4th quarter | |
| Marion | 0 | 0 | 0 | 0 | 35,391 |
| Marlboro Township | 0 | 0 | 0 | 0 | 4,337 |
| Martins Ferry | 0 | 0 | 0 | 0 | 6,380 |
| McArthur | 0 | 0 | 0 | 0 | 1,612 |
| McConnelsville | 0 | 0 | 0 | 0 | 1,714 |
| Medina | 0 | 0 | 0 | 0 | 25,905 |
| Medina Township | 0 | 0 | 0 | | 9,176 |
| Mentor-on-the-Lake | 0 | 0 | 0 | 0 | 7,372 |
| Miami Township, Clermont County | 0 | 0 | 0 | 0 | 43,182 |
| Middleburg Heights | 0 | 0 | 0 | | 15,381 |
| Middlefield | 0 | 0 | 0 | 0 | 2,690 |
| Middleport | 0 | 0 | 0 | 0 | 2,378 |
| Mifflin Township | | 0 | 0 | 0 | 2,604 |
| Milan | 0 | 0 | 0 | 0 | 1,337 |
| Milford | 0 | 0 | 0 | 0 | 6,815 |
| Millersport | 0 | 0 | 0 | 0 | 1,084 |
| Minerva Park | 0 | 0 | 0 | 0 | 1,322 |
| Mogadore | | 0 | 0 | 0 | 3,794 |
| Monroeville | 0 | 0 | 0 | 0 | 1,333 |
| Montgomery | 0 | 0 | 0 | 0 | 10,943 |
| Montpelier | 0 | 0 | 0 | 0 | 3,893 |
| Montville Township | 0 | 0 | 0 | 0 | 12,073 |
| Moreland Hills | 0 | | | | 3,321 |
| Mount Gilead | | | 0 | 0 | 3,691 |
| Mount Orab | 0 | 0 | 0 | 0 | 3,397 |
| Munroe Falls | 0 | 0 | 0 | 0 | 5,054 |
| Navarre | 0 | 0 | 0 | 0 | 1,788 |
| Newark | 0 | 0 | 0 | 0 | 50,980 |
| New Boston | 0 | 0 | 0 | 0 | 2,103 |
| New Bremen | 0 | 0 | 0 | 0 | 2,944 |
| New Concord | 0 | 0 | 0 | 0 | 2,136 |
| New Lebanon | 0 | 0 | 0 | 0 | 3,988 |
| New Lexington | 0 | 0 | 0 | 0 | 4,667 |
| New Middletown | 0 | 0 | 0 | 0 | 1,538 |
| New Philadelphia | 0 | 0 | 0 | 0 | 17,428 |
| New Richmond | 0 | 0 | 0 | 0 | 2,717 |
| New Straitsville | 0 | 0 | 0 | 0 | 714 |
| Newton Falls | 0 | 0 | 0 | 0 | 4,413 |
| New Vienna | 0 | 0 | 0 | 0 | 1,202 |
| New Waterford | 0 | 0 | 0 | 0 | 1,157 |
| Niles | 0 | 0 | 0 | 0 | 17,943 |
| North Baltimore | 0 | 0 | 0 | 0 | 3,569 |
| North College Hill | 0 | 0 | 0 | 0 | 9,230 |
| Northfield | 0 | 0 | 0 | 0 | 3,647 |
| North Lewisburg | | 0 | 0 | 0 | 1,469 |
| North Olmsted | 0 | 0 | 0 | 0 | 31,224 |
| North Ridgeville | 0 | 0 | | | 35,708 |
| North Royalton | 0 | | | | 30,096 |
| Northwood | 0 | 0 | 0 | 0 | 5,481 |
| Norwalk | 0 | 0 | 0 | 0 | 16,752 |
| Oak Hill | 0 | 0 | 0 | 0 | 1,527 |
| Oberlin | 0 | 0 | 0 | 0 | 8,107 |
| Olmsted Falls | 0 | 0 | 0 | 0 | 9,156 |
| Olmsted Township | 0 | 0 | 0 | 0 | 13,644 |
| Ontario | 0 | 0 | 0 | 0 | 6,089 |
| Oregon | 0 | 0 | 0 | 0 | 19,986 |
| Orrville | 0 | 0 | 0 | 0 | 8,442 |
| Ottawa Hills | 0 | 0 | 0 | 0 | 4,541 |
| Oxford Township | 0 | 0 | 0 | 0 | 2,234 |
| Parma | 0 | 0 | 0 | 0 | 77,674 |
| Parma Heights | 0 | 0 | 0 | 0 | 19,669 |
| Paulding | 0 | 0 | 0 | 0 | 3,397 |
| Payne | | | | 0 | 1,126 |
| Peebles | 0 | 0 | 0 | 0 | 1,698 |
| Pemberville | | | 0 | 0 | 1,427 |
| Peninsula | 0 | 0 | 0 | 0 | 549 |
| Pepper Pike | 0 | 0 | 0 | 0 | 6,525 |
| Perkins Township | 0 | 0 | 0 | 0 | 11,552 |
| Perry | 0 | 0 | 0 | 0 | 1,622 |
| Perrysburg | 0 | 0 | 0 | 0 | 21,806 |
| Perrysburg Township | 0 | 0 | 0 | 0 | 13,072 |
| Perry Township, Columbiana County | 0 | 0 | 0 | 0 | 4,216 |
| Perry Township, Franklin County | 0 | 0 | 0 | 0 | 3,756 |
| Perry Township, Stark County | 0 | 0 | 0 | 0 | 27,970 |
| Pickerington | 0 | 0 | 0 | 0 | 23,343 |
| Pierce Township | 0 | 0 | 0 | 0 | 15,178 |
| Piketon | 0 | 0 | 0 | 0 | 2,164 |
| Pioneer | 0 | 0 | 0 | 0 | 1,398 |
| Piqua | 0 | 0 | 0 | 0 | 21,531 |
| Plain City | 0 | 0 | 0 | | 4,820 |

## Table 95. Hate Crime Zero Data Submitted Per Quarter, by Federal Agency, State, and State Agency, 2021—Continued

(Number.)

| Agency name | Zero data per quarter[1] | | | | Population[2] |
|---|---|---|---|---|---|
| | 1st quarter | 2nd quarter | 3rd quarter | 4th quarter | |
| Poland Township | 0 | 0 | 0 | 0 | 11,703 |
| Poland Village | 0 | 0 | 0 | 0 | 2,348 |
| Pomeroy | 0 | 0 | 0 | 0 | 1,730 |
| Port Clinton | 0 | 0 | 0 | 0 | 6,113 |
| Port Washington | | | | 0 | 564 |
| Powhatan Point | 0 | 0 | 0 | 0 | 1,493 |
| Put-In-Bay | | 0 | 0 | 0 | 141 |
| Racine | 0 | 0 | 0 | 0 | 651 |
| Ravenna | 0 | 0 | 0 | 0 | 11,288 |
| Reading | 0 | 0 | 0 | 0 | 10,928 |
| Reminderville | 0 | 0 | 0 | 0 | 4,786 |
| Reynoldsburg | 0 | 0 | 0 | | 38,623 |
| Richland Township | | | | 0 | 8,969 |
| Richmond Heights | 0 | 0 | 0 | 0 | 10,332 |
| Rio Grande | 0 | 0 | | | 763 |
| Risingsun | 0 | 0 | 0 | | 632 |
| Roaming Shores Village | | 0 | 0 | 0 | 1,437 |
| Rockford | 0 | 0 | 0 | 0 | 1,104 |
| Roseville | | | 0 | 0 | 1,830 |
| Ross Township | 0 | 0 | 0 | 0 | 9,050 |
| Russells Point | 0 | 0 | 0 | 0 | 1,377 |
| Russell Township | 0 | 0 | 0 | | 5,175 |
| Sabina | 0 | 0 | 0 | 0 | 2,559 |
| Sagamore Hills | 0 | 0 | 0 | 0 | 10,896 |
| Salem | 0 | 0 | 0 | 0 | 11,441 |
| Saline Township | | | | 0 | 1,255 |
| Sandusky | 0 | 0 | 0 | 0 | 24,172 |
| Seaman | 0 | 0 | 0 | 0 | 882 |
| Sebring | 0 | 0 | 0 | 0 | 4,133 |
| Seven Hills | 0 | 0 | 0 | 0 | 11,600 |
| Shadyside | 0 | 0 | 0 | 0 | 3,491 |
| Shaker Heights | 0 | | | | 26,772 |
| Sharon Township | 0 | 0 | 0 | 0 | 2,402 |
| Shawnee Township | 0 | 0 | 0 | 0 | 12,072 |
| Sheffield Lake | 0 | 0 | 0 | 0 | 8,930 |
| Sheffield Village | | | 0 | 0 | 4,634 |
| Shelby | 0 | 0 | 0 | 0 | 9,042 |
| Smithville | 0 | 0 | 0 | | 1,262 |
| Solon | 0 | 0 | 0 | 0 | 22,740 |
| Somerset | 0 | 0 | 0 | 0 | 1,462 |
| South Bloomfield | 0 | | | | 1,997 |
| South Charleston | 0 | 0 | 0 | 0 | 1,603 |
| South Euclid | 0 | 0 | 0 | 0 | 21,174 |
| South Russell | 0 | 0 | 0 | | 3,703 |
| South Vienna | | | | 0 | 395 |
| South Zanesville | 0 | 0 | 0 | 0 | 2,106 |
| Spencer | | | | 0 | 799 |
| Spencerville | 0 | 0 | 0 | 0 | 2,134 |
| Springboro | 0 | 0 | 0 | 0 | 19,429 |
| Springdale | 0 | 0 | | | 11,199 |
| Springfield Township, Hamilton County | 0 | 0 | 0 | 0 | 35,873 |
| Springfield Township, Mahoning County | 0 | 0 | 0 | 0 | 6,310 |
| St. Clair Township | 0 | 0 | 0 | 0 | 7,365 |
| St. Henry | 0 | 0 | 0 | 0 | 2,587 |
| St. Marys | 0 | 0 | 0 | 0 | 8,094 |
| St. Paris | | | 0 | 0 | 2,005 |
| Strasburg | 0 | 0 | 0 | 0 | 2,697 |
| Strongsville | 0 | 0 | 0 | 0 | 44,745 |
| Sugarcreek Township | 0 | 0 | 0 | 0 | 8,536 |
| Sugar Grove | 0 | 0 | | | 426 |
| Sunbury | 0 | 0 | | | 7,192 |
| Swanton | 0 | 0 | 0 | 0 | 3,841 |
| Sylvania | 0 | 0 | 0 | 0 | 19,560 |
| Thornville | | | | 0 | 1,008 |
| Tiffin | 0 | 0 | 0 | 0 | 17,308 |
| Tipp City | 0 | 0 | 0 | 0 | 10,217 |
| Toronto | 0 | 0 | 0 | 0 | 4,864 |
| Troy | 0 | | | | 26,601 |
| Twinsburg | 0 | 0 | 0 | 0 | 18,956 |
| Uhrichsville | 0 | 0 | 0 | 0 | 5,287 |
| Uniontown | 0 | 0 | 0 | 0 | 3,306 |
| University Heights | 0 | 0 | 0 | 0 | 12,638 |
| Upper Sandusky | 0 | 0 | 0 | 0 | 6,420 |
| Urbana | 0 | 0 | 0 | 0 | 11,368 |
| Utica | 0 | 0 | 0 | 0 | 2,293 |
| Valley View, Cuyahoga County | 0 | 0 | 0 | 0 | 1,992 |
| Vandalia | 0 | 0 | 0 | 0 | 14,960 |
| Vermilion | 0 | 0 | | | 10,454 |
| Vienna Township | 0 | 0 | 0 | 0 | 3,747 |
| Village of Leesburg | 0 | 0 | 0 | 0 | 1,322 |

## Table 95. Hate Crime Zero Data Submitted Per Quarter, by Federal Agency, State, and State Agency, 2021—Continued

(Number.)

| Agency name | Zero data per quarter[1] | | | | Population[2] |
|---|---|---|---|---|---|
| | 1st quarter | 2nd quarter | 3rd quarter | 4th quarter | |
| Wadsworth | 0 | 0 | 0 | 0 | 24,656 |
| Walbridge | 0 | 0 | | | 3,180 |
| Walton Hills | 0 | | 0 | 0 | 2,269 |
| Warren | 0 | 0 | 0 | 0 | 38,193 |
| Warren Township | 0 | 0 | 0 | 0 | 5,113 |
| Washingtonville | 0 | 0 | 0 | | 739 |
| Waterville | 0 | 0 | 0 | 0 | 5,605 |
| Wauseon | 0 | 0 | 0 | 0 | 7,410 |
| Waverly | 0 | 0 | 0 | 0 | 4,115 |
| Waynesville | 0 | 0 | 0 | 0 | 3,297 |
| Wellington | | | 0 | 0 | 4,960 |
| Wellsville | | | 0 | | 3,246 |
| West Carrollton | 0 | 0 | 0 | 0 | 12,821 |
| Westerville | 0 | 0 | 0 | 0 | 41,985 |
| West Liberty | 0 | 0 | 0 | 0 | 1,784 |
| West Milton | 0 | 0 | | | 4,876 |
| West Union | 0 | 0 | 0 | | 3,137 |
| Whitehall | 0 | 0 | 0 | 0 | 18,985 |
| Whitehouse | 0 | 0 | 0 | 0 | 5,020 |
| Wickliffe | 0 | 0 | 0 | 0 | 12,725 |
| Willard | 0 | 0 | 0 | 0 | 5,964 |
| Williamsburg | 0 | 0 | 0 | 0 | 2,584 |
| Willoughby | 0 | 0 | 0 | | 23,039 |
| Willoughby Hills | 0 | 0 | 0 | 0 | 9,545 |
| Willowick | 0 | 0 | 0 | 0 | 14,056 |
| Wilmington | 0 | 0 | 0 | 0 | 12,385 |
| Winchester | 0 | | | | 998 |
| Wintersville | 0 | 0 | 0 | 0 | 3,619 |
| Woodlawn | 0 | 0 | 0 | 0 | 3,402 |
| Woodsfield | 0 | 0 | 0 | 0 | 2,185 |
| Wyoming | 0 | 0 | 0 | 0 | 8,564 |
| Xenia | 0 | 0 | 0 | 0 | 27,228 |
| Zanesville | 0 | 0 | 0 | 0 | 25,166 |
| **Universities and Colleges** | | | | | |
| Bowling Green State University | 0 | 0 | 0 | 0 | 20,945 |
| Capital University | | | 0 | 0 | 3,735 |
| Central State University | 0 | 0 | 0 | 0 | 2,421 |
| Cuyahoga Community College | 0 | 0 | 0 | 0 | 34,407 |
| Hocking College | 0 | 0 | 0 | 0 | 4,323 |
| Lakeland Community College | 0 | 0 | | | 8,735 |
| Marietta College | 0 | | | | 1,459 |
| Miami University | | | | 0 | 21,667 |
| Mount St. Joseph University | 0 | 0 | | | 2,395 |
| Muskingum University | | | 0 | 0 | 3,045 |
| Notre Dame College | | | 0 | | 1,892 |
| Otterbein University | 0 | 0 | 0 | 0 | 3,298 |
| University of Akron | 0 | 0 | | | 19,819 |
| University of Cincinnati | 0 | 0 | 0 | 0 | 46,140 |
| University of Rio Grande | | | 0 | 0 | 2,594 |
| University of Toledo | 0 | 0 | 0 | 0 | 22,028 |
| **Metropolitan Counties** | | | | | |
| Allen | 0 | 0 | 0 | 0 | |
| Belmont | 0 | 0 | 0 | 0 | |
| Butler | 0 | 0 | | | |
| Carroll | 0 | 0 | 0 | | |
| Clark | 0 | 0 | 0 | 0 | |
| Clermont | 0 | 0 | 0 | 0 | |
| Fulton | 0 | 0 | 0 | 0 | |
| Geauga | 0 | 0 | 0 | 0 | |
| Greene | 0 | 0 | 0 | 0 | |
| Jefferson | 0 | 0 | 0 | 0 | |
| Lawrence | 0 | 0 | 0 | 0 | |
| Licking | 0 | 0 | | 0 | |
| Miami | 0 | 0 | 0 | 0 | |
| Morrow | 0 | | | | |
| Perry | 0 | 0 | 0 | 0 | |
| Stark | 0 | 0 | 0 | 0 | |
| Trumbull | 0 | 0 | 0 | 0 | |
| Wood | 0 | 0 | 0 | 0 | |
| **Nonmetropolitan Counties** | | | | | |
| Adams | 0 | 0 | 0 | 0 | |
| Ashland | 0 | 0 | 0 | 0 | |
| Auglaize | 0 | 0 | 0 | 0 | |
| Champaign | 0 | 0 | 0 | 0 | |
| Clinton | 0 | 0 | 0 | 0 | |
| Darke | 0 | 0 | 0 | | |
| Erie | 0 | 0 | 0 | 0 | |

## Table 95. Hate Crime Zero Data Submitted Per Quarter, by Federal Agency, State, and State Agency, 2021—Continued

(Number.)

| Agency name | Zero data per quarter[1] | | | | Population[2] |
|---|---|---|---|---|---|
| | 1st quarter | 2nd quarter | 3rd quarter | 4th quarter | |
| Fayette | 0 | 0 | 0 | 0 | |
| Gallia | 0 | 0 | 0 | 0 | |
| Hancock | 0 | 0 | 0 | 0 | |
| Hardin | 0 | 0 | | | |
| Harrison | 0 | 0 | 0 | 0 | |
| Henry | 0 | 0 | 0 | 0 | |
| Highland | 0 | 0 | 0 | 0 | |
| Jackson | 0 | 0 | 0 | 0 | |
| Noble | 0 | 0 | | | |
| Putnam | 0 | 0 | | | |
| Scioto | 0 | 0 | 0 | 0 | |
| Seneca | 0 | 0 | 0 | 0 | |
| Shelby | 0 | 0 | 0 | 0 | |
| Van Wert | 0 | 0 | 0 | 0 | |
| Vinton | 0 | 0 | 0 | 0 | |
| Washington | 0 | 0 | 0 | 0 | |
| Wyandot | 0 | 0 | 0 | 0 | |
| **State Police Agencies** | | | | | |
| Ohio State Highway Patrol | 0 | 0 | 0 | 0 | |
| **Other Agencies** | | | | | |
| Adena Health System | | 0 | 0 | 0 | |
| Belmont County Major Crimes Unit | 0 | 0 | 0 | 0 | |
| Butler County Metroparks | | | 0 | | |
| Cedar Point | | 0 | 0 | 0 | |
| Clark County Park District | | | 0 | | |
| Cleveland Metropolitan Park District | 0 | 0 | 0 | | |
| Columbus and Franklin County Metropolitan Park District | | 0 | 0 | | |
| Greater Cleveland Regional Transit Authority | 0 | 0 | 0 | | |
| Hamilton County Park District | 0 | 0 | 0 | 0 | |
| Johnny Appleseed Metropolitan Park District | 0 | 0 | | | |
| Lake Metroparks | 0 | 0 | 0 | 0 | |
| Lorain County Metropolitan Park District | | | | 0 | |
| Muskingum Watershed Conservancy District | 0 | 0 | 0 | 0 | |
| Ohio Investigative Unit | 0 | 0 | 0 | 0 | |
| Stark County Park District | | 0 | 0 | 0 | |
| Toledo Metropolitan Park District | | 0 | | | |
| Wood County Park District | 0 | 0 | 0 | 0 | |
| **OKLAHOMA** | | | | | |
| **Cities** | | | | | |
| Achille | 0 | 0 | 0 | 0 | 556 |
| Ada | 0 | 0 | 0 | 0 | 17,280 |
| Adair | 0 | 0 | 0 | 0 | 804 |
| Allen | 0 | 0 | 0 | 0 | 930 |
| Alva | 0 | 0 | 0 | 0 | 4,867 |
| Amber | 0 | 0 | 0 | 0 | 502 |
| Anadarko | 0 | 0 | 0 | 0 | 6,444 |
| Antlers | 0 | 0 | 0 | 0 | 2,286 |
| Apache | 0 | 0 | 0 | 0 | 1,385 |
| Arcadia | 0 | 0 | 0 | 0 | 280 |
| Ardmore | 0 | 0 | 0 | 0 | 24,795 |
| Arkoma | 0 | 0 | 0 | 0 | 1,885 |
| Atoka | 0 | 0 | 0 | 0 | 3,038 |
| Avant | 0 | 0 | 0 | 0 | 311 |
| Barnsdall | 0 | 0 | 0 | 0 | 1,123 |
| Bartlesville | 0 | 0 | 0 | 0 | 36,688 |
| Beaver | 0 | 0 | 0 | 0 | 1,350 |
| Beggs | 0 | 0 | 0 | 0 | 1,225 |
| Bennington | 0 | 0 | 0 | 0 | 378 |
| Bernice | 0 | 0 | 0 | 0 | 581 |
| Bethany | 0 | 0 | 0 | 0 | 19,209 |
| Big Cabin | 0 | 0 | 0 | 0 | 250 |
| Binger | 0 | 0 | 0 | 0 | 624 |
| Bixby | 0 | 0 | 0 | 0 | 29,327 |
| Blackwell | 0 | 0 | 0 | 0 | 6,474 |
| Blair | | | | 0 | 729 |
| Blanchard | 0 | 0 | 0 | 0 | 9,303 |
| Boise City | 0 | 0 | 0 | 0 | 1,071 |
| Bokchito | 0 | 0 | 0 | 0 | 711 |
| Bokoshe | 0 | 0 | 0 | 0 | 495 |
| Boley | 0 | 0 | 0 | 0 | 1,165 |
| Boswell | 0 | 0 | 0 | 0 | 677 |
| Bristow | 0 | 0 | 0 | 0 | 4,174 |
| Broken Bow | 0 | 0 | 0 | 0 | 4,085 |
| Burns Flat | 0 | 0 | 0 | 0 | 1,865 |
| Butler | 0 | 0 | 0 | 0 | 289 |
| Cache | 0 | 0 | 0 | 0 | 2,824 |
| Caddo | 0 | 0 | 0 | 0 | 1,125 |

**Table 95. Hate Crime Zero Data Submitted Per Quarter, by Federal Agency, State, and State Agency, 2021—Continued**

(Number.)

| Agency name | Zero data per quarter[1] | | | | Population[2] |
|---|---|---|---|---|---|
| | 1st quarter | 2nd quarter | 3rd quarter | 4th quarter | |
| Calera | 0 | 0 | 0 | 0 | 2,440 |
| Calumet | | | 0 | 0 | 623 |
| Calvin | 0 | 0 | 0 | 0 | 267 |
| Caney | 0 | 0 | 0 | 0 | 202 |
| Canton | 0 | 0 | 0 | 0 | 583 |
| Carnegie | 0 | 0 | 0 | 0 | 1,634 |
| Carney | 0 | 0 | 0 | 0 | 620 |
| Cashion | 0 | 0 | 0 | 0 | 943 |
| Cement | 0 | 0 | 0 | 0 | 468 |
| Chandler | 0 | 0 | 0 | 0 | 3,080 |
| Chattanooga | 0 | 0 | 0 | 0 | 457 |
| Checotah | 0 | 0 | 0 | 0 | 3,051 |
| Chelsea | 0 | 0 | 0 | 0 | 1,868 |
| Cherokee | 0 | 0 | 0 | 0 | 1,492 |
| Claremore | 0 | 0 | 0 | 0 | 18,961 |
| Clayton | 0 | 0 | 0 | 0 | 771 |
| Cleveland | 0 | 0 | 0 | 0 | 3,101 |
| Clinton | 0 | 0 | 0 | 0 | 8,943 |
| Coalgate | 0 | 0 | 0 | 0 | 1,830 |
| Colbert | 0 | 0 | 0 | 0 | 1,281 |
| Colcord | 0 | 0 | 0 | 0 | 854 |
| Collinsville | 0 | 0 | 0 | 0 | 7,765 |
| Comanche | 0 | 0 | 0 | 0 | 1,540 |
| Commerce | 0 | 0 | 0 | 0 | 2,482 |
| Cordell | 0 | 0 | 0 | 0 | 2,689 |
| Covington | 0 | 0 | 0 | 0 | 533 |
| Crescent | 0 | 0 | 0 | 0 | 1,596 |
| Cushing | 0 | 0 | 0 | 0 | 7,558 |
| Cyril | 0 | 0 | 0 | 0 | 997 |
| Davenport | 0 | 0 | 0 | 0 | 808 |
| Davis | 0 | 0 | 0 | 0 | 2,874 |
| Depew | 0 | 0 | 0 | 0 | 476 |
| Dewar | 0 | 0 | 0 | 0 | 843 |
| Dewey | 0 | 0 | 0 | 0 | 3,411 |
| Dibble | 0 | 0 | 0 | 0 | 884 |
| Dickson | 0 | 0 | 0 | 0 | 1,260 |
| Disney | 0 | 0 | 0 | 0 | 302 |
| Drumright | 0 | 0 | 0 | 0 | 2,805 |
| Duncan | 0 | 0 | 0 | 0 | 22,145 |
| Earlsboro | 0 | 0 | 0 | 0 | 625 |
| Eldorado | 0 | 0 | 0 | 0 | 397 |
| Elgin | 0 | 0 | 0 | 0 | 3,359 |
| Elk City | 0 | 0 | 0 | 0 | 11,326 |
| Elmore City | 0 | 0 | 0 | 0 | 753 |
| Enid | 0 | 0 | 0 | 0 | 49,545 |
| Erick | 0 | 0 | 0 | 0 | 969 |
| Eufaula | 0 | 0 | 0 | 0 | 2,841 |
| Fairfax | 0 | 0 | 0 | 0 | 1,229 |
| Fairland | 0 | 0 | 0 | 0 | 1,021 |
| Fairview | 0 | 0 | 0 | 0 | 2,580 |
| Fletcher | 0 | 0 | 0 | 0 | 1,137 |
| Forest Park | 0 | 0 | 0 | 0 | 1,078 |
| Fort Cobb | 0 | 0 | 0 | 0 | 604 |
| Fort Gibson | 0 | 0 | 0 | 0 | 3,912 |
| Fort Towson | 0 | 0 | 0 | 0 | 485 |
| Foyil | | 0 | 0 | 0 | 388 |
| Frederick | 0 | 0 | 0 | 0 | 3,490 |
| Gans | 0 | 0 | 0 | 0 | 294 |
| Garber | 0 | 0 | 0 | 0 | 802 |
| Geary | 0 | 0 | 0 | 0 | 1,271 |
| Geronimo | 0 | 0 | 0 | 0 | 1,220 |
| Goodwell | 0 | 0 | 0 | 0 | 1,261 |
| Gore | 0 | 0 | 0 | 0 | 943 |
| Grandfield | 0 | 0 | 0 | 0 | 922 |
| Granite | 0 | 0 | 0 | 0 | 1,946 |
| Grove | 0 | 0 | 0 | 0 | 7,242 |
| Guymon | 0 | 0 | 0 | 0 | 10,960 |
| Haileyville | 0 | 0 | 0 | 0 | 740 |
| Hammon | | | | 0 | 554 |
| Harrah | 0 | 0 | 0 | 0 | 6,805 |
| Hartshorne | 0 | 0 | 0 | 0 | 1,928 |
| Haworth | | | | 0 | 294 |
| Heavener | 0 | 0 | 0 | 0 | 3,285 |
| Hennessey | 0 | 0 | 0 | 0 | 2,234 |
| Henryetta | 0 | 0 | 0 | 0 | 5,464 |
| Hinton | 0 | 0 | 0 | 0 | 3,221 |
| Hobart | 0 | 0 | 0 | 0 | 3,405 |
| Holdenville | 0 | 0 | 0 | 0 | 5,394 |
| Hollis | 0 | 0 | 0 | 0 | 1,794 |
| Hominy | 0 | 0 | 0 | 0 | 3,332 |

## Table 95. Hate Crime Zero Data Submitted Per Quarter, by Federal Agency, State, and State Agency, 2021—Continued

(Number.)

| Agency name | Zero data per quarter[1] | | | | Population[2] |
|---|---|---|---|---|---|
| | 1st quarter | 2nd quarter | 3rd quarter | 4th quarter | |
| Hooker | 0 | 0 | 0 | 0 | 1,834 |
| Howe | 0 | 0 | 0 | 0 | 786 |
| Hugo | 0 | 0 | 0 | 0 | 5,047 |
| Hulbert | 0 | 0 | 0 | 0 | 579 |
| Hydro | 0 | 0 | 0 | 0 | 933 |
| Idabel | | | 0 | 0 | 6,864 |
| Inola | 0 | 0 | 0 | 0 | 1,793 |
| Jay | 0 | 0 | 0 | 0 | 2,536 |
| Jenks | 0 | 0 | 0 | 0 | 25,111 |
| Jennings | 0 | 0 | 0 | 0 | 355 |
| Kansas | 0 | 0 | 0 | 0 | 805 |
| Kellyville | 0 | 0 | 0 | 0 | 1,127 |
| Keota | 0 | 0 | 0 | 0 | 544 |
| Kiefer | 0 | 0 | 0 | 0 | 2,072 |
| Kingfisher | 0 | 0 | 0 | 0 | 4,919 |
| Kingston | 0 | 0 | 0 | 0 | 1,698 |
| Kiowa | 0 | 0 | 0 | 0 | 671 |
| Konawa | 0 | 0 | 0 | 0 | 1,184 |
| Krebs | 0 | 0 | 0 | 0 | 1,995 |
| Lahoma | 0 | 0 | 0 | 0 | 610 |
| Lamont | 0 | 0 | 0 | 0 | 391 |
| Langley | 0 | 0 | 0 | 0 | 821 |
| Langston | 0 | 0 | 0 | 0 | 1,882 |
| Laverne | 0 | 0 | 0 | 0 | 1,293 |
| Lexington | 0 | 0 | 0 | 0 | 2,190 |
| Lindsay | 0 | 0 | 0 | 0 | 2,767 |
| Locust Grove | 0 | 0 | 0 | 0 | 1,392 |
| Lone Grove | 0 | 0 | 0 | 0 | 5,225 |
| Luther | 0 | 0 | 0 | 0 | 1,842 |
| Madill | 0 | 0 | 0 | 0 | 4,096 |
| Mangum | 0 | 0 | 0 | 0 | 2,662 |
| Mannford | 0 | 0 | 0 | 0 | 3,191 |
| Marble City | 0 | 0 | 0 | 0 | 249 |
| Marietta | 0 | 0 | 0 | 0 | 2,764 |
| Marlow | 0 | 0 | 0 | 0 | 4,393 |
| Maud | 0 | 0 | 0 | 0 | 1,059 |
| Maysville | 0 | 0 | 0 | 0 | 1,199 |
| McAlester | 0 | 0 | 0 | 0 | 17,729 |
| McCurtain | 0 | 0 | 0 | 0 | 501 |
| McLoud | 0 | 0 | 0 | 0 | 4,828 |
| Medford | 0 | 0 | 0 | 0 | 939 |
| Medicine Park | 0 | 0 | 0 | 0 | 469 |
| Meeker | 0 | 0 | 0 | 0 | 1,139 |
| Midwest City | 0 | 0 | 0 | 0 | 57,901 |
| Minco | 0 | 0 | 0 | 0 | 1,646 |
| Moore | | 0 | 0 | 0 | 63,927 |
| Mooreland | 0 | 0 | 0 | 0 | 1,135 |
| Morris | 0 | 0 | 0 | 0 | 1,404 |
| Mounds | 0 | 0 | 0 | 0 | 1,253 |
| Mountain View | 0 | 0 | 0 | 0 | 739 |
| Muldrow | 0 | 0 | 0 | 0 | 3,260 |
| Mustang | 0 | 0 | 0 | 0 | 24,822 |
| Nash | 0 | 0 | 0 | 0 | 195 |
| Newcastle | 0 | 0 | 0 | 0 | 11,788 |
| Newkirk | 0 | 0 | 0 | 0 | 2,147 |
| Nichols Hills | 0 | 0 | 0 | 0 | 3,982 |
| Nicoma Park | 0 | 0 | 0 | 0 | 2,486 |
| Ninnekah | 0 | 0 | 0 | 0 | 1,046 |
| Noble | 0 | 0 | 0 | 0 | 7,329 |
| North Enid | 0 | 0 | 0 | 0 | 923 |
| Nowata | 0 | 0 | 0 | 0 | 3,527 |
| Oilton | 0 | 0 | 0 | 0 | 1,011 |
| Okarche | 0 | 0 | 0 | 0 | 1,346 |
| Okeene | 0 | 0 | 0 | 0 | 1,130 |
| Okemah | 0 | 0 | 0 | 0 | 3,031 |
| Olustee | 0 | 0 | 0 | 0 | 545 |
| Oologah | 0 | 0 | 0 | 0 | 1,182 |
| Owasso | 0 | 0 | 0 | 0 | 38,057 |
| Panama | | | | 0 | 1,353 |
| Paoli | 0 | 0 | 0 | 0 | 612 |
| Pauls Valley | 0 | 0 | 0 | 0 | 6,101 |
| Pawnee | 0 | 0 | 0 | 0 | 2,092 |
| Perkins | 0 | 0 | 0 | 0 | 2,798 |
| Perry | 0 | 0 | 0 | 0 | 4,804 |
| Pocola | 0 | 0 | 0 | 0 | 4,163 |
| Ponca City | 0 | 0 | 0 | 0 | 23,307 |
| Pond Creek | 0 | 0 | 0 | 0 | 848 |
| Porum | 0 | 0 | 0 | 0 | 696 |
| Poteau | 0 | 0 | 0 | 0 | 8,942 |
| Prague | 0 | 0 | 0 | 0 | 2,362 |

## Table 95. Hate Crime Zero Data Submitted Per Quarter, by Federal Agency, State, and State Agency, 2021—Continued

(Number.)

| Agency name | Zero data per quarter[1] | | | | Population[2] |
|---|---|---|---|---|---|
| | 1st quarter | 2nd quarter | 3rd quarter | 4th quarter | |
| Purcell | 0 | 0 | 0 | 0 | 6,409 |
| Quinton | 0 | 0 | 0 | 0 | 978 |
| Ramona | 0 | 0 | 0 | 0 | 557 |
| Ratliff City | | | | 0 | 117 |
| Rattan | 0 | 0 | 0 | 0 | 293 |
| Roland | 0 | 0 | 0 | 0 | 4,112 |
| Rush Springs | 0 | 0 | 0 | 0 | 1,254 |
| Salina | 0 | 0 | 0 | 0 | 1,396 |
| Sand Springs | 0 | 0 | 0 | 0 | 20,139 |
| Savanna | 0 | 0 | 0 | 0 | 646 |
| Sawyer | 0 | 0 | 0 | 0 | 326 |
| Sayre | 0 | 0 | 0 | 0 | 4,443 |
| Seiling | 0 | 0 | 0 | 0 | 838 |
| Seminole | 0 | 0 | 0 | 0 | 6,993 |
| Shady Point | 0 | 0 | 0 | 0 | 994 |
| Shattuck | 0 | 0 | 0 | 0 | 1,234 |
| Skiatook | 0 | 0 | 0 | 0 | 8,189 |
| Snyder | 0 | 0 | 0 | 0 | 1,270 |
| South Coffeyville | 0 | 0 | 0 | 0 | 725 |
| Sparks | 0 | 0 | 0 | 0 | 172 |
| Spavinaw | 0 | 0 | 0 | 0 | 432 |
| Spencer | 0 | 0 | 0 | 0 | 3,962 |
| Sperry | 0 | 0 | 0 | 0 | 1,370 |
| Spiro | 0 | 0 | 0 | 0 | 2,153 |
| Sportsmen Acres | 0 | | | | 309 |
| Sterling | 0 | 0 | 0 | 0 | 775 |
| Stigler | 0 | 0 | 0 | 0 | 2,698 |
| Stillwater | 0 | 0 | 0 | 0 | 50,786 |
| Stilwell | 0 | 0 | 0 | 0 | 4,014 |
| Stratford | 0 | 0 | 0 | 0 | 1,522 |
| Stringtown | 0 | 0 | 0 | 0 | 406 |
| Stroud | 0 | 0 | 0 | 0 | 2,705 |
| Sulphur | 0 | 0 | 0 | 0 | 4,995 |
| Tahlequah | 0 | 0 | 0 | 0 | 17,126 |
| Talala | 0 | 0 | 0 | 0 | 270 |
| Talihina | 0 | 0 | 0 | 0 | 1,074 |
| Tecumseh | 0 | 0 | 0 | 0 | 6,656 |
| Texhoma | 0 | 0 | 0 | 0 | 900 |
| Thackerville | 0 | 0 | 0 | 0 | 527 |
| Thomas | 0 | 0 | 0 | 0 | 1,178 |
| Tipton | 0 | 0 | 0 | 0 | 747 |
| Tishomingo | 0 | 0 | 0 | 0 | 2,992 |
| Tonkawa | 0 | 0 | 0 | 0 | 2,934 |
| Tryon | 0 | 0 | 0 | 0 | 497 |
| Tupelo | 0 | 0 | 0 | 0 | 306 |
| Tushka | 0 | 0 | 0 | 0 | 395 |
| Tuttle | 0 | 0 | 0 | 0 | 7,796 |
| Tyrone | 0 | 0 | 0 | 0 | 741 |
| Union City | 0 | 0 | 0 | 0 | 2,273 |
| Valley Brook | 0 | 0 | 0 | 0 | 767 |
| Valliant | 0 | 0 | 0 | 0 | 740 |
| Velma | 0 | 0 | 0 | 0 | 593 |
| Verden | 0 | 0 | 0 | 0 | 537 |
| Verdigris | 0 | 0 | 0 | 0 | 4,810 |
| Vian | 0 | 0 | 0 | 0 | 1,345 |
| Vici | 0 | 0 | 0 | 0 | 685 |
| Wagoner | 0 | 0 | 0 | 0 | 9,479 |
| Wakita | 0 | 0 | 0 | 0 | 326 |
| Walters | 0 | 0 | 0 | 0 | 2,336 |
| Warner | 0 | 0 | 0 | 0 | 1,570 |
| Warr Acres | 0 | 0 | 0 | 0 | 10,105 |
| Washington | 0 | 0 | 0 | 0 | 605 |
| Watonga | 0 | 0 | 0 | 0 | 2,823 |
| Watts | 0 | 0 | 0 | 0 | 305 |
| Waukomis | 0 | 0 | 0 | 0 | 1,290 |
| Waurika | 0 | 0 | 0 | 0 | 1,847 |
| Waynoka | 0 | 0 | 0 | 0 | 899 |
| Weatherford | 0 | 0 | 0 | 0 | 12,013 |
| Webbers Falls | 0 | 0 | 0 | 0 | 588 |
| Weleetka | 0 | 0 | 0 | 0 | 931 |
| Wellston | 0 | 0 | 0 | 0 | 776 |
| West Siloam Springs | 0 | 0 | 0 | 0 | 861 |
| Westville | 0 | 0 | 0 | 0 | 1,523 |
| Wetumka | 0 | 0 | 0 | 0 | 1,177 |
| Wewoka | 0 | 0 | 0 | 0 | 3,198 |
| Wilburton | 0 | 0 | 0 | 0 | 2,542 |
| Wister | 0 | 0 | 0 | 0 | 1,060 |
| Woodward | 0 | 0 | 0 | 0 | 11,871 |
| Wright City | 0 | 0 | | 0 | 727 |
| Wyandotte | 0 | 0 | 0 | 0 | 321 |

## Table 95. Hate Crime Zero Data Submitted Per Quarter, by Federal Agency, State, and State Agency, 2021—Continued

(Number.)

| Agency name | Zero data per quarter[1] | | | | Population[2] |
|---|---|---|---|---|---|
| | 1st quarter | 2nd quarter | 3rd quarter | 4th quarter | |
| Wynnewood | 0 | 0 | 0 | 0 | 2,203 |
| Wynona | 0 | 0 | 0 | 0 | 434 |
| Yale | 0 | 0 | 0 | 0 | 1,211 |
| Yukon | 0 | 0 | 0 | 0 | 29,467 |
| **Universities and Colleges** | | | | | |
| Bacone College | 0 | 0 | 0 | 0 | 314 |
| Cameron University | 0 | 0 | 0 | 0 | 4,767 |
| East Central University | 0 | 0 | 0 | 0 | 4,413 |
| Eastern Oklahoma State College | 0 | 0 | 0 | 0 | 1,829 |
| Langston University | 0 | 0 | 0 | 0 | 2,614 |
| Mid-America Christian University | 0 | 0 | 0 | 0 | 2,382 |
| Northeastern Oklahoma A&M College | 0 | 0 | 0 | 0 | 2,285 |
| Northeastern State University, Tahlequah | 0 | 0 | 0 | 0 | 9,075 |
| Northwestern Oklahoma State University | 0 | 0 | 0 | 0 | 2,295 |
| Oklahoma City Community College | 0 | 0 | 0 | 0 | 17,240 |
| Oklahoma City University | 0 | 0 | 0 | 0 | 3,071 |
| Oklahoma State University | | | | | |
|   Main Campus | 0 | 0 | 0 | 0 | 26,463 |
|   Okmulgee | 0 | 0 | 0 | 0 | 3,024 |
|   Tulsa | 0 | 0 | 0 | 0 | 1,265 |
| Rogers State University | 0 | 0 | 0 | 0 | 4,290 |
| Seminole State College | 0 | 0 | 0 | 0 | 1,925 |
| Southwestern Oklahoma State University | 0 | 0 | 0 | 0 | 5,768 |
| Tulsa Community College | 0 | 0 | 0 | 0 | 22,569 |
| University of Oklahoma | | | | | |
|   Health Sciences Center | 0 | 0 | 0 | 0 | 3,722 |
|   Norman | 0 | 0 | 0 | 0 | 31,445 |
| **Metropolitan Counties** | | | | | |
| Cleveland | 0 | 0 | 0 | 0 | |
| Comanche | 0 | 0 | 0 | 0 | |
| Cotton | 0 | 0 | 0 | 0 | |
| Creek | 0 | 0 | 0 | 0 | |
| Garfield | 0 | 0 | 0 | 0 | |
| Grady | 0 | 0 | 0 | 0 | |
| Lincoln | 0 | 0 | 0 | 0 | |
| McClain | 0 | 0 | 0 | 0 | |
| Oklahoma | 0 | 0 | 0 | 0 | |
| Okmulgee | 0 | 0 | 0 | 0 | |
| Osage | 0 | 0 | 0 | 0 | |
| Pawnee | 0 | 0 | 0 | 0 | |
| Rogers | 0 | 0 | 0 | 0 | |
| Sequoyah | 0 | 0 | 0 | 0 | |
| Tulsa | 0 | 0 | 0 | 0 | |
| **Nonmetropolitan Counties** | | | | | |
| Adair | 0 | 0 | 0 | 0 | |
| Beaver | 0 | 0 | 0 | 0 | |
| Beckham | 0 | 0 | 0 | 0 | |
| Blaine | 0 | 0 | 0 | 0 | |
| Bryan | 0 | 0 | 0 | 0 | |
| Caddo | 0 | 0 | 0 | 0 | |
| Carter | 0 | 0 | 0 | 0 | |
| Cherokee | 0 | 0 | 0 | 0 | |
| Choctaw | 0 | 0 | 0 | 0 | |
| Cimarron | 0 | 0 | 0 | 0 | |
| Coal | 0 | 0 | 0 | 0 | |
| Custer | 0 | 0 | 0 | 0 | |
| Delaware | 0 | 0 | 0 | 0 | |
| Dewey | 0 | 0 | 0 | 0 | |
| Ellis | 0 | 0 | 0 | 0 | |
| Garvin | 0 | 0 | 0 | 0 | |
| Grant | 0 | 0 | 0 | 0 | |
| Greer | 0 | 0 | 0 | 0 | |
| Harmon | 0 | 0 | 0 | 0 | |
| Harper | 0 | 0 | 0 | 0 | |
| Haskell | 0 | 0 | 0 | 0 | |
| Hughes | 0 | 0 | 0 | 0 | |
| Jackson | 0 | 0 | 0 | 0 | |
| Jefferson | 0 | 0 | 0 | 0 | |
| Johnston | 0 | 0 | 0 | 0 | |
| Kay | 0 | 0 | 0 | 0 | |
| Kiowa | 0 | 0 | 0 | 0 | |
| Latimer | 0 | 0 | 0 | 0 | |
| Le Flore | 0 | 0 | 0 | 0 | |
| Love | 0 | 0 | 0 | 0 | |
| Major | 0 | 0 | 0 | 0 | |
| Marshall | 0 | 0 | 0 | 0 | |
| Murray | 0 | 0 | 0 | 0 | |

# Table 95. Hate Crime Zero Data Submitted Per Quarter, by Federal Agency, State, and State Agency, 2021—Continued

(Number.)

| Agency name | Zero data per quarter[1] | | | | Population[2] |
|---|---|---|---|---|---|
| | 1st quarter | 2nd quarter | 3rd quarter | 4th quarter | |
| Muskogee | 0 | 0 | 0 | 0 | |
| Noble | 0 | 0 | 0 | 0 | |
| Nowata | 0 | 0 | 0 | 0 | |
| Okfuskee | 0 | 0 | 0 | 0 | |
| Ottawa | 0 | 0 | 0 | 0 | |
| Payne | 0 | 0 | 0 | 0 | |
| Pittsburg | 0 | 0 | 0 | 0 | |
| Pottawatomie | 0 | 0 | 0 | 0 | |
| Pushmataha | 0 | 0 | 0 | 0 | |
| Roger Mills | 0 | 0 | 0 | 0 | |
| Seminole | 0 | 0 | 0 | 0 | |
| Stephens | 0 | 0 | 0 | 0 | |
| Texas | 0 | 0 | 0 | 0 | |
| Tillman | 0 | 0 | 0 | 0 | |
| Washington | 0 | 0 | 0 | 0 | |
| Washita | 0 | 0 | 0 | 0 | |
| Woods | 0 | 0 | 0 | 0 | |
| Woodward | 0 | 0 | 0 | 0 | |
| **State Police Agencies** | | | | | |
| Oklahoma Highway Patrol | 0 | 0 | 0 | 0 | |
| **Tribal Agencies** | | | | | |
| Absentee Shawnee Tribal | 0 | 0 | 0 | 0 | |
| Anadarko Agency | 0 | 0 | 0 | 0 | |
| Cherokee Nation | 0 | 0 | 0 | 0 | |
| Chickasaw Nation | | 0 | 0 | 0 | |
| Choctaw Nation | 0 | 0 | 0 | 0 | |
| Citizen Potawatomi Nation | 0 | 0 | 0 | 0 | |
| Comanche Nation | 0 | 0 | 0 | 0 | |
| Concho Agency | 0 | 0 | 0 | 0 | |
| Eastern Shawnee Tribal | 0 | 0 | 0 | 0 | |
| Iowa Tribal | 0 | 0 | 0 | 0 | |
| Kaw Tribal | 0 | 0 | 0 | 0 | |
| Kickapoo Tribal | 0 | 0 | 0 | 0 | |
| Miami Agency | 0 | 0 | 0 | 0 | |
| Miami Tribal | 0 | 0 | 0 | 0 | |
| Muscogee Nation Tribal | 0 | 0 | 0 | | |
| Osage Nation | 0 | 0 | 0 | 0 | |
| Otoe-Missouria Tribal | 0 | 0 | 0 | 0 | |
| Pawnee Agency | 0 | 0 | | | |
| Pawnee Tribal | 0 | 0 | 0 | | |
| Ponca Tribal | 0 | 0 | 0 | 0 | |
| Quapaw Tribal | 0 | 0 | 0 | 0 | |
| Sac and Fox Tribal | 0 | 0 | 0 | 0 | |
| Seminole Nation Lighthorse | 0 | 0 | 0 | 0 | |
| Tonkawa Tribal | 0 | 0 | 0 | 0 | |
| **Other Agencies** | | | | | |
| Beggs Public Schools | 0 | 0 | 0 | 0 | |
| Capitol Park Police | 0 | 0 | 0 | 0 | |
| District 1 Narcotics Task Force | 0 | 0 | 0 | 0 | |
| District 8 Narcotics Task Force | 0 | 0 | 0 | 0 | |
| Grand River Dam Authority Lake Patrol | 0 | 0 | 0 | 0 | |
| Jenks Public Schools | 0 | 0 | 0 | 0 | |
| Lawton Public Schools | 0 | 0 | 0 | 0 | |
| Muskogee City Schools | 0 | 0 | 0 | 0 | |
| Oklahoma Department of Corrections | | | | 0 | |
| Okmulgee County Criminal Justice Authority | | 0 | | 0 | |
| Putnam City Campus | 0 | 0 | 0 | 0 | |
| State Bureau of Investigation | 0 | 0 | 0 | 0 | |
| State Park Rangers | 0 | 0 | 0 | 0 | |
| Victory Life | 0 | 0 | 0 | 0 | |
| **OREGON** | | | | | |
| **Cities** | | | | | |
| Baker City | 0 | 0 | 0 | 0 | 9,882 |
| Bandon | 0 | 0 | 0 | 0 | 3,181 |
| Banks | 0 | 0 | 0 | 0 | 2,058 |
| Black Butte | 0 | 0 | 0 | 0 | |
| Brookings | 0 | 0 | 0 | 0 | 6,583 |
| Burns | 0 | 0 | 0 | 0 | 2,791 |
| Cannon Beach | 0 | | | | 1,788 |
| Carlton | 0 | 0 | 0 | 0 | 2,204 |
| Columbia City | 0 | 0 | 0 | 0 | 2,034 |
| Coos Bay | 0 | 0 | 0 | 0 | 16,378 |
| Coquille | 0 | 0 | 0 | 0 | 3,966 |
| Cornelius | 0 | 0 | 0 | 0 | 13,241 |
| Cottage Grove | 0 | 0 | 0 | 0 | 10,606 |
| Dallas | 0 | 0 | 0 | 0 | 17,630 |

## Table 95. Hate Crime Zero Data Submitted Per Quarter, by Federal Agency, State, and State Agency, 2021—Continued

(Number.)

| Agency name | Zero data per quarter[1] | | | | Population[2] |
|---|---|---|---|---|---|
| | 1st quarter | 2nd quarter | 3rd quarter | 4th quarter | |
| Eagle Point | 0 | 0 | 0 | 0 | 9,782 |
| Enterprise | 0 | 0 | 0 | 0 | 1,999 |
| Florence | 0 | 0 | 0 | 0 | 9,285 |
| Forest Grove | 0 | 0 | 0 | 0 | 25,890 |
| Gaston | 0 | 0 | 0 | 0 | 723 |
| Gearhart | 0 | 0 | 0 | 0 | 1,672 |
| Gervais | 0 | 0 | 0 | 0 | 2,805 |
| Hermiston | 0 | 0 | 0 | 0 | 17,898 |
| Hines | 0 | 0 | 0 | 0 | 1,534 |
| Hubbard | 0 | 0 | 0 | 0 | 3,639 |
| Independence | 0 | 0 | 0 | 0 | 11,129 |
| Jacksonville | 0 | 0 | 0 | 0 | 2,875 |
| John Day | 0 | 0 | 0 | | 1,661 |
| Junction City | 0 | 0 | 0 | 0 | 6,303 |
| Keizer | 0 | 0 | 0 | 0 | 39,913 |
| King City | 0 | 0 | 0 | 0 | 4,446 |
| La Grande | 0 | 0 | 0 | 0 | 13,431 |
| Lebanon | 0 | 0 | 0 | 0 | 17,772 |
| Madras | 0 | 0 | 0 | 0 | 7,191 |
| Malin | 0 | 0 | 0 | 0 | 841 |
| Manzanita | 0 | 0 | 0 | 0 | 678 |
| Medford | 0 | 0 | 0 | 0 | 84,297 |
| Milton-Freewater | 0 | 0 | 0 | 0 | 7,050 |
| Monmouth | 0 | 0 | 0 | 0 | 10,728 |
| Mount Angel | 0 | 0 | 0 | 0 | 3,677 |
| Myrtle Creek | 0 | 0 | 0 | 0 | 3,495 |
| Newberg-Dundee | 0 | 0 | 0 | 0 | 24,168 |
| Newport | 0 | 0 | 0 | 0 | 11,247 |
| North Bend | 0 | 0 | 0 | 0 | 9,751 |
| North Plains | 0 | 0 | 0 | 0 | 2,219 |
| Oakridge | 0 | 0 | 0 | | 3,403 |
| Ontario | 0 | 0 | 0 | | 11,117 |
| Philomath | 0 | 0 | 0 | 0 | 5,742 |
| Phoenix | 0 | 0 | 0 | 0 | 4,705 |
| Pilot Rock | 0 | 0 | 0 | | 1,508 |
| Prineville | 0 | 0 | 0 | 0 | 11,541 |
| Rainier | 0 | 0 | 0 | 0 | 2,032 |
| Reedsport | 0 | 0 | 0 | 0 | 4,101 |
| Rogue River | 0 | 0 | 0 | 0 | 2,363 |
| Roseburg | 0 | 0 | 0 | 0 | 23,564 |
| Scappoose | 0 | 0 | 0 | 0 | 7,715 |
| Seaside | 0 | 0 | 0 | | 6,971 |
| Stanfield | 0 | 0 | 0 | 0 | 2,113 |
| Stayton | 0 | 0 | 0 | 0 | 8,314 |
| St. Helens | 0 | 0 | 0 | 0 | 14,178 |
| Sunriver | 0 | 0 | 0 | 0 | 1,395 |
| Sweet Home | 0 | 0 | 0 | 0 | 10,136 |
| Talent | 0 | 0 | 0 | 0 | 6,767 |
| Tillamook | 0 | 0 | 0 | 0 | 5,480 |
| Umatilla | 0 | 0 | 0 | | 7,404 |
| Vernonia | 0 | 0 | 0 | 0 | 2,309 |
| Warrenton | 0 | 0 | 0 | 0 | 5,815 |
| Winston | 0 | 0 | 0 | 0 | 5,558 |
| Woodburn | 0 | 0 | 0 | 0 | 26,386 |
| Yamhill | 0 | 0 | 0 | 0 | 1,188 |
| **Metropolitan Counties** | | | | | |
| Columbia | 0 | 0 | 0 | 0 | |
| Deschutes | 0 | 0 | 0 | 0 | |
| Marion | | | | 0 | |
| **Nonmetropolitan Counties** | | | | | |
| Baker | 0 | 0 | 0 | 0 | |
| Clatsop | 0 | 0 | 0 | 0 | |
| Coos | 0 | | | | |
| Crook | 0 | 0 | 0 | 0 | |
| Curry | 0 | 0 | 0 | 0 | |
| Douglas | 0 | 0 | 0 | 0 | |
| Gilliam | 0 | 0 | 0 | 0 | |
| Harney | 0 | 0 | 0 | | |
| Hood River | 0 | 0 | 0 | 0 | |
| Jefferson | 0 | 0 | 0 | 0 | |
| Morrow | 0 | 0 | 0 | 0 | |
| Sherman | 0 | 0 | 0 | 0 | |
| Wallowa | 0 | 0 | 0 | 0 | |
| Wasco | 0 | 0 | 0 | 0 | |
| **State Police Agencies** | | | | | |
| State Police | | | | | |
| Baker County | 0 | 0 | 0 | 0 | |

**Table 95. Hate Crime Zero Data Submitted Per Quarter, by Federal Agency, State, and State Agency, 2021—Continued**

(Number.)

| Agency name | Zero data per quarter[1] | | | | Population[2] |
|---|---|---|---|---|---|
| | 1st quarter | 2nd quarter | 3rd quarter | 4th quarter | |
| Benton County | 0 | 0 | 0 | 0 | |
| Clackamas County | 0 | 0 | 0 | 0 | |
| Columbia County | 0 | 0 | 0 | 0 | |
| Crook County | 0 | 0 | 0 | 0 | |
| Curry County | 0 | 0 | 0 | 0 | |
| Deschutes County | 0 | 0 | 0 | 0 | |
| Gilliam County | 0 | 0 | 0 | 0 | |
| Grant County | 0 | 0 | 0 | 0 | |
| Harney County | 0 | 0 | 0 | 0 | |
| Hood River County | 0 | 0 | 0 | 0 | |
| Jackson County | 0 | 0 | 0 | 0 | |
| Jefferson County | 0 | 0 | 0 | 0 | |
| Josephine County | 0 | 0 | 0 | 0 | |
| Klamath County | 0 | 0 | 0 | 0 | |
| Lake County | 0 | 0 | 0 | 0 | |
| Lane County | 0 | 0 | 0 | 0 | |
| Lincoln County | 0 | 0 | 0 | 0 | |
| Linn County | 0 | 0 | 0 | 0 | |
| Malheur County | 0 | 0 | 0 | 0 | |
| Marion County | 0 | 0 | 0 | 0 | |
| Morrow County | 0 | 0 | 0 | 0 | |
| Multnomah County | 0 | 0 | 0 | 0 | |
| Polk County | 0 | 0 | 0 | 0 | |
| Sherman County | 0 | 0 | 0 | 0 | |
| Umatilla County | 0 | 0 | 0 | 0 | |
| Union County | 0 | 0 | 0 | 0 | |
| Wallowa County | 0 | 0 | 0 | 0 | |
| Wasco County | 0 | 0 | 0 | 0 | |
| Washington County | 0 | 0 | 0 | 0 | |
| Wheeler County | 0 | 0 | 0 | 0 | |
| Yamhill County | 0 | 0 | 0 | 0 | |
| **Tribal Agencies** | | | | | |
| Columbia River Inter-Tribal Fisheries Enforcement | 0 | 0 | 0 | 0 | |
| Coos, Lower Umpqua, and Siuslaw Tribal | 0 | 0 | 0 | 0 | |
| Coquille Tribal | 0 | 0 | 0 | 0 | |
| Cow Creek Tribal | | 0 | 0 | 0 | |
| Grand Ronde Tribal | 0 | 0 | 0 | 0 | |
| Siletz Tribal | 0 | 0 | 0 | 0 | |
| Umatilla Tribal | 0 | 0 | 0 | 0 | |
| Warm Springs Tribal | 0 | 0 | 0 | 0 | |
| **Other Agencies** | | | | | |
| Hillsboro School District | 0 | 0 | 0 | 0 | |
| Liquor Commission | | | | | |
| Baker County | 0 | 0 | 0 | 0 | |
| Benton County | 0 | 0 | 0 | 0 | |
| Clackamas County | 0 | 0 | 0 | 0 | |
| Clatsop County | 0 | 0 | 0 | 0 | |
| Columbia County | 0 | 0 | 0 | 0 | |
| Coos County | 0 | 0 | 0 | 0 | |
| Crook County | 0 | 0 | 0 | 0 | |
| Deschutes County | 0 | 0 | 0 | 0 | |
| Douglas County | 0 | 0 | 0 | 0 | |
| Gilliam County | 0 | 0 | 0 | 0 | |
| Grant County | 0 | 0 | 0 | 0 | |
| Hood River County | 0 | 0 | 0 | 0 | |
| Jackson County | 0 | 0 | 0 | 0 | |
| Klamath County | 0 | 0 | 0 | 0 | |
| Lane County | 0 | 0 | 0 | 0 | |
| Lincoln County | 0 | 0 | 0 | 0 | |
| Marion County | 0 | 0 | 0 | 0 | |
| Multnomah County | 0 | 0 | 0 | 0 | |
| Polk County | 0 | 0 | 0 | 0 | |
| Sherman County | 0 | 0 | 0 | 0 | |
| Umatilla County | 0 | 0 | 0 | 0 | |
| Washington County | 0 | 0 | 0 | 0 | |
| Wheeler County | 0 | 0 | 0 | 0 | |
| Yamhill County | 0 | 0 | 0 | 0 | |
| **PENNSYLVANIA** | | | | | |
| **Cities** | | | | | |
| Bellevue | 0 | 0 | 0 | 0 | 7,944 |
| Bendersville | 0 | | | | 647 |
| Biglerville | 0 | 0 | 0 | 0 | 1,215 |
| Camp Hill | 0 | 0 | 0 | 0 | 7,921 |
| Carlisle | 0 | 0 | 0 | 0 | 19,260 |
| Carroll Valley | 0 | 0 | 0 | 0 | 3,935 |
| Conneaut Lake Regional | | | 0 | 0 | 4,697 |
| Derry Township, Dauphin County | | | | 0 | 25,388 |

## Table 95. Hate Crime Zero Data Submitted Per Quarter, by Federal Agency, State, and State Agency, 2021—Continued

(Number.)

| Agency name | Zero data per quarter[1] | | | | Population[2] |
|---|---|---|---|---|---|
| | 1st quarter | 2nd quarter | 3rd quarter | 4th quarter | |
| Economy | 0 | 0 | 0 | 0 | 9,024 |
| Erie | | | | 0 | 94,437 |
| Hampden Township | 0 | 0 | 0 | 0 | 32,134 |
| Jamestown | 0 | 0 | 0 | 0 | 563 |
| Liberty Township, Adams County | 0 | 0 | 0 | 0 | 1,270 |
| McDonald Borough | | | | 0 | 2,030 |
| Mercersburg | 0 | 0 | 0 | 0 | 1,525 |
| Mifflinburg | | | | 0 | 3,438 |
| New Cumberland | 0 | 0 | 0 | 0 | 7,302 |
| Newville | 0 | 0 | 0 | 0 | 1,353 |
| Palmyra | | | | 0 | 7,549 |
| Penbrook | 0 | 0 | 0 | 0 | 2,974 |
| Sandy Lake | | | | 0 | 618 |
| Saxton | 0 | 0 | 0 | 0 | 674 |
| Shaler Township | 0 | 0 | 0 | 0 | 27,412 |
| Shippensburg | 0 | 0 | 0 | 0 | 5,687 |
| Silver Spring Township | 0 | 0 | 0 | 0 | 19,326 |
| South Londonderry Township | | | | 0 | 8,689 |
| Upper Allen Township | 0 | 0 | 0 | 0 | 20,972 |
| Waynesboro | 0 | 0 | 0 | 0 | 10,939 |
| West Shore Regional | 0 | 0 | 0 | 0 | 7,707 |
| **Metropolitan Counties** | | | | | |
| Allegheny County Police Department | | 0 | 0 | 0 | |
| Franklin | 0 | 0 | 0 | 0 | |
| **Other Agencies** | | | | | |
| Franklin County Drug Task Force | 0 | 0 | 0 | 0 | |
| **RHODE ISLAND** | | | | | |
| **Cities** | | | | | |
| Burrillville | 0 | 0 | 0 | 0 | 17,501 |
| Central Falls | 0 | 0 | 0 | 0 | 20,174 |
| Charlestown | 0 | 0 | 0 | 0 | 8,118 |
| Cumberland | 0 | 0 | 0 | 0 | 36,648 |
| East Greenwich | 0 | 0 | 0 | 0 | 13,617 |
| East Providence | 0 | 0 | 0 | 0 | 49,064 |
| Foster | 0 | 0 | 0 | 0 | 4,933 |
| Glocester | 0 | 0 | 0 | 0 | 10,788 |
| Hopkinton | 0 | 0 | 0 | 0 | 8,379 |
| Jamestown | 0 | 0 | 0 | 0 | 5,687 |
| Johnston | 0 | 0 | 0 | 0 | 30,476 |
| Middletown | 0 | 0 | 0 | 0 | 16,338 |
| Narragansett | 0 | 0 | 0 | 0 | 15,801 |
| North Kingstown | 0 | 0 | 0 | 0 | 27,192 |
| North Smithfield | 0 | 0 | 0 | 0 | 13,093 |
| Pawtucket | 0 | 0 | 0 | 0 | 74,342 |
| Portsmouth | 0 | 0 | 0 | 0 | 17,696 |
| Providence | 0 | 0 | 0 | 0 | 185,868 |
| Richmond | 0 | 0 | 0 | 0 | 8,189 |
| Scituate | 0 | 0 | 0 | 0 | 11,148 |
| South Kingstown | 0 | 0 | 0 | 0 | 31,537 |
| Warren | 0 | 0 | 0 | 0 | 10,830 |
| Westerly | 0 | 0 | 0 | 0 | 23,088 |
| West Greenwich | 0 | 0 | 0 | 0 | 6,680 |
| West Warwick | 0 | 0 | 0 | 0 | 29,964 |
| Woonsocket | 0 | 0 | 0 | 0 | 43,072 |
| **State Police Agencies** | | | | | |
| Rhode Island State Police Headquarters | 0 | 0 | 0 | 0 | |
| State Police | | | | | |
|   Chepachet/Scituate | 0 | 0 | 0 | 0 | |
|   Hope Valley | 0 | 0 | 0 | 0 | |
|   Lincoln | 0 | 0 | 0 | 0 | |
|   Portsmouth | 0 | 0 | 0 | 0 | |
|   Wickford | 0 | 0 | 0 | 0 | |
| **Other Agencies** | | | | | |
| T.F. Green Airport | 0 | 0 | 0 | 0 | |
| **SOUTH CAROLINA** | | | | | |
| **Cities** | | | | | |
| Abbeville | 0 | 0 | 0 | 0 | 4,932 |
| Aiken | 0 | 0 | 0 | 0 | 31,270 |
| Allendale | 0 | 0 | 0 | 0 | 2,773 |
| Anderson | 0 | 0 | 0 | 0 | 27,831 |
| Atlantic Beach | 0 | 0 | 0 | | 501 |
| Aynor | 0 | 0 | 0 | 0 | 1,036 |
| Bamberg | 0 | 0 | 0 | 0 | 3,120 |
| Barnwell | 0 | 0 | 0 | 0 | 4,213 |

## Table 95. Hate Crime Zero Data Submitted Per Quarter, by Federal Agency, State, and State Agency, 2021—Continued

(Number.)

| Agency name | Zero data per quarter[1] | | | | Population[2] |
|---|---|---|---|---|---|
| | 1st quarter | 2nd quarter | 3rd quarter | 4th quarter | |
| Batesburg-Leesville | 0 | 0 | 0 | 0 | 5,405 |
| Belton | 0 | 0 | 0 | | 4,517 |
| Bennettsville | 0 | 0 | 0 | 0 | 7,301 |
| Bethune | 0 | 0 | 0 | 0 | 356 |
| Blackville | 0 | 0 | 0 | | 2,151 |
| Bluffton | 0 | 0 | 0 | 0 | 30,519 |
| Bowman | 0 | 0 | 0 | 0 | 870 |
| Branchville | 0 | 0 | 0 | 0 | 936 |
| Burnettown | 0 | 0 | 0 | 0 | 2,784 |
| Camden | 0 | 0 | 0 | 0 | 7,335 |
| Central | 0 | 0 | 0 | 0 | 5,478 |
| Chapin | 0 | 0 | 0 | 0 | 1,689 |
| Cheraw | 0 | 0 | 0 | 0 | 5,527 |
| Chesnee | 0 | 0 | 0 | 0 | 955 |
| Chester | 0 | 0 | | | 5,341 |
| Chesterfield | 0 | 0 | 0 | 0 | 1,394 |
| Clemson | 0 | 0 | 0 | 0 | 18,220 |
| Clio | 0 | 0 | 0 | 0 | 638 |
| Clover | 0 | 0 | 0 | 0 | 6,992 |
| Conway | 0 | 0 | 0 | 0 | 27,781 |
| Cottageville | 0 | | | | 745 |
| Coward | 0 | | | | 767 |
| Cowpens | 0 | 0 | 0 | 0 | 2,498 |
| Darlington | 0 | 0 | 0 | 0 | 5,856 |
| Denmark | 0 | 0 | 0 | 0 | 2,847 |
| Due West | 0 | | | | 1,195 |
| Duncan | 0 | 0 | 0 | 0 | 3,772 |
| Edgefield | 0 | 0 | 0 | 0 | 4,831 |
| Ehrhardt | 0 | 0 | 0 | 0 | 471 |
| Elgin | 0 | 0 | 0 | 0 | 1,613 |
| Elloree | 0 | | | | 626 |
| Eutawville | 0 | 0 | 0 | 0 | 281 |
| Florence | 0 | 0 | 0 | 0 | 38,521 |
| Forest Acres | 0 | 0 | 0 | 0 | 10,261 |
| Fountain Inn | 0 | 0 | 0 | 0 | 11,306 |
| Gaffney | 0 | | | | 12,707 |
| Gaston | 0 | 0 | 0 | 0 | 1,720 |
| Georgetown | 0 | 0 | 0 | 0 | 8,753 |
| Gifford | 0 | 0 | 0 | 0 | 259 |
| Greenville | 0 | 0 | 0 | 0 | 73,653 |
| Greenwood | 0 | 0 | 0 | 0 | 23,369 |
| Greer | 0 | 0 | 0 | 0 | 36,423 |
| Hanahan | 0 | 0 | 0 | 0 | 29,582 |
| Hemingway | 0 | 0 | 0 | 0 | 378 |
| Holly Hill | 0 | 0 | 0 | 0 | 1,151 |
| Honea Path | 0 | 0 | 0 | | 3,881 |
| Inman | 0 | 0 | | | 2,512 |
| Irmo | 0 | 0 | 0 | 0 | 12,902 |
| Isle of Palms | 0 | 0 | 0 | 0 | 4,395 |
| Iva | 0 | 0 | 0 | 0 | 1,352 |
| Jackson | 0 | 0 | 0 | 0 | 1,825 |
| Johnsonville | 0 | 0 | 0 | 0 | 1,470 |
| Jonesville | 0 | 0 | 0 | 0 | 811 |
| Lake View | 0 | 0 | | | 773 |
| Landrum | 0 | | 0 | 0 | 2,763 |
| Lane | 0 | 0 | 0 | 0 | 437 |
| Latta | 0 | 0 | 0 | 0 | 1,263 |
| Liberty | 0 | 0 | 0 | 0 | 3,140 |
| Loris | 0 | 0 | 0 | 0 | 2,855 |
| Lyman | 0 | 0 | 0 | 0 | 3,850 |
| Marion | 0 | 0 | 0 | 0 | 6,136 |
| McCormick | 0 | 0 | 0 | 0 | 2,279 |
| Mullins | 0 | 0 | 0 | 0 | 4,092 |
| Myrtle Beach | 0 | 0 | 0 | 0 | 36,543 |
| Newberry | 0 | 0 | 0 | 0 | 10,119 |
| New Ellenton | 0 | 0 | 0 | 0 | 2,201 |
| Ninety Six | 0 | 0 | 0 | 0 | 2,043 |
| North | 0 | 0 | 0 | 0 | 692 |
| North Charleston | 0 | 0 | 0 | 0 | 121,060 |
| Norway | 0 | 0 | 0 | | 301 |
| Olanta | 0 | 0 | 0 | 0 | 550 |
| Orangeburg | 0 | 0 | 0 | 0 | 12,335 |
| Pacolet | 0 | 0 | | | 2,639 |
| Pamplico | 0 | 0 | 0 | 0 | 1,207 |
| Pawleys Island | 0 | | | | 110 |
| Pelion | 0 | 0 | 0 | 0 | 714 |
| Pendleton | 0 | 0 | 0 | 0 | 3,343 |
| Pickens | 0 | 0 | 0 | 0 | 3,193 |
| Port Royal | 0 | 0 | 0 | 0 | 14,970 |
| Prosperity | 0 | 0 | 0 | 0 | 1,310 |

## Table 95. Hate Crime Zero Data Submitted Per Quarter, by Federal Agency, State, and State Agency, 2021—Continued

(Number.)

| Agency name | Zero data per quarter[1] | | | | Population[2] |
|---|---|---|---|---|---|
| | 1st quarter | 2nd quarter | 3rd quarter | 4th quarter | |
| Quinby | 0 | 0 | 0 | 0 | 912 |
| Ridgeland | 0 | 0 | 0 | 0 | 3,853 |
| Ridge Spring | 0 | 0 | 0 | 0 | 738 |
| Salem | 0 | 0 | 0 | 0 | 154 |
| Salley | 0 | 0 | 0 | | 421 |
| Scranton | 0 | 0 | | | 831 |
| Seneca | 0 | 0 | 0 | 0 | 8,611 |
| Simpsonville | 0 | 0 | 0 | 0 | 26,077 |
| Society Hill | 0 | 0 | 0 | 0 | 518 |
| Spartanburg | 0 | 0 | 0 | 0 | 37,375 |
| Springdale | 0 | 0 | 0 | 0 | 2,743 |
| Springfield | 0 | 0 | | | 472 |
| St. Matthews | 0 | 0 | 0 | 0 | 1,892 |
| Sullivans Island | 0 | 0 | 0 | | 1,953 |
| Summerville | 0 | 0 | 0 | 0 | 54,438 |
| Sumter | 0 | 0 | 0 | 0 | 39,328 |
| Surfside Beach | 0 | 0 | 0 | 0 | 4,661 |
| Swansea | 0 | 0 | 0 | 0 | 1,000 |
| Timmonsville | 0 | 0 | 0 | 0 | 2,345 |
| Travelers Rest | 0 | 0 | 0 | 0 | 8,297 |
| Union | 0 | 0 | 0 | 0 | 7,458 |
| Wagener | 0 | 0 | 0 | 0 | 850 |
| Walhalla | 0 | 0 | 0 | 0 | 4,484 |
| Ware Shoals | 0 | 0 | 0 | 0 | 2,150 |
| Wellford | 0 | 0 | 0 | 0 | 2,813 |
| West Columbia | 0 | 0 | 0 | 0 | 18,257 |
| Westminster | 0 | 0 | 0 | 0 | 2,614 |
| West Pelzer | 0 | 0 | 0 | 0 | 961 |
| Whitmire | 0 | 0 | 0 | 0 | 1,450 |
| Williston | 0 | 0 | 0 | 0 | 2,890 |
| Winnsboro | 0 | | | | 3,091 |
| York | 0 | 0 | 0 | 0 | 8,728 |
| **Universities and Colleges** | | | | | |
| Benedict College | | 0 | 0 | | 2,163 |
| Bob Jones University | 0 | 0 | 0 | 0 | 3,750 |
| Clemson University | 0 | 0 | 0 | 0 | 28,933 |
| Coastal Carolina University | 0 | 0 | 0 | 0 | 11,870 |
| College of Charleston | 0 | 0 | 0 | | 13,062 |
| Francis Marion University | 0 | 0 | 0 | 0 | 4,895 |
| Greenville Technical College | 0 | 0 | 0 | 0 | 14,447 |
| Lander University | 0 | 0 | 0 | 0 | 3,489 |
| Medical University of South Carolina | 0 | 0 | 0 | 0 | 3,458 |
| Orangeburg-Calhoun Technical College | 0 | | 0 | | 3,288 |
| Presbyterian College | 0 | 0 | | | 1,419 |
| South Carolina State University | 0 | 0 | 0 | 0 | 2,752 |
| The Citadel | 0 | 0 | 0 | 0 | 4,409 |
| Tri-County Technical College | 0 | 0 | 0 | 0 | 7,646 |
| Trident Technical College | 0 | 0 | 0 | 0 | 17,239 |
| University of South Carolina | | | | | |
| Columbia | 0 | 0 | 0 | 0 | 38,526 |
| Upstate | 0 | 0 | 0 | 0 | 7,421 |
| Winthrop University | 0 | 0 | | | 6,787 |
| York Technical College | | | | 0 | 6,053 |
| **Metropolitan Counties** | | | | | |
| Aiken | 0 | 0 | 0 | | |
| Beaufort | 0 | 0 | 0 | 0 | |
| Calhoun | 0 | 0 | 0 | 0 | |
| Chester | 0 | 0 | 0 | 0 | |
| Darlington | 0 | 0 | 0 | 0 | |
| Dorchester | 0 | 0 | 0 | 0 | |
| Edgefield | 0 | 0 | 0 | 0 | |
| Florence | 0 | 0 | 0 | 0 | |
| Greenville | 0 | 0 | 0 | 0 | |
| Horry | 0 | 0 | 0 | 0 | |
| Jasper | 0 | 0 | 0 | 0 | |
| Lancaster | 0 | 0 | 0 | 0 | |
| Laurens | 0 | 0 | 0 | 0 | |
| Spartanburg | 0 | 0 | 0 | 0 | |
| York | 0 | 0 | 0 | 0 | |
| **Nonmetropolitan Counties** | | | | | |
| Abbeville | 0 | 0 | 0 | 0 | |
| Allendale | 0 | 0 | 0 | 0 | |
| Dillon | 0 | 0 | 0 | 0 | |
| Lee | 0 | 0 | 0 | | |
| Marion | 0 | 0 | 0 | 0 | |
| McCormick | 0 | 0 | 0 | 0 | |
| Newberry | 0 | 0 | 0 | 0 | |

## Table 95. Hate Crime Zero Data Submitted Per Quarter, by Federal Agency, State, and State Agency, 2021—Continued

(Number.)

| Agency name | Zero data per quarter[1] | | | | Population[2] |
|---|---|---|---|---|---|
| | 1st quarter | 2nd quarter | 3rd quarter | 4th quarter | |
| Orangeburg | 0 | 0 | 0 | 0 | |
| Union | 0 | 0 | | | |
| Williamsburg | 0 | 0 | 0 | 0 | |
| **State Police Agencies** | | | | | |
| Highway Patrol | | | | | |
|   Abbeville County | 0 | 0 | 0 | 0 | |
|   Aiken County | 0 | 0 | 0 | 0 | |
|   Allendale County | 0 | 0 | 0 | 0 | |
|   Anderson County | 0 | 0 | 0 | 0 | |
|   Bamberg County | 0 | 0 | 0 | 0 | |
|   Barnwell County | 0 | 0 | 0 | 0 | |
|   Beaufort County | 0 | 0 | 0 | 0 | |
|   Berkeley County | 0 | 0 | 0 | 0 | |
|   Calhoun County | 0 | 0 | 0 | 0 | |
|   Charleston County | 0 | 0 | 0 | 0 | |
|   Cherokee County | 0 | 0 | 0 | 0 | |
|   Chester County | 0 | 0 | 0 | 0 | |
|   Chesterfield County | 0 | 0 | 0 | 0 | |
|   Clarendon County | 0 | 0 | 0 | 0 | |
|   Colleton County | 0 | 0 | 0 | 0 | |
|   Darlington County | 0 | 0 | 0 | 0 | |
|   Dillon County | 0 | 0 | 0 | 0 | |
|   Dorchester County | 0 | 0 | 0 | 0 | |
|   Fairfield County | 0 | 0 | 0 | 0 | |
|   Florence County | 0 | 0 | 0 | 0 | |
|   Georgetown County | 0 | 0 | 0 | 0 | |
|   Greenville County | 0 | 0 | 0 | 0 | |
|   Greenwood County | 0 | 0 | 0 | 0 | |
|   Hampton County | 0 | 0 | 0 | 0 | |
|   Horry County | 0 | 0 | 0 | 0 | |
|   Jasper County | 0 | 0 | 0 | 0 | |
|   Kershaw County | 0 | 0 | 0 | 0 | |
|   Laurens County | 0 | 0 | 0 | 0 | |
|   Lee County | 0 | 0 | 0 | 0 | |
|   Lexington County | 0 | 0 | 0 | 0 | |
|   Marion County | 0 | 0 | 0 | 0 | |
|   Marlboro County | 0 | 0 | 0 | 0 | |
|   McCormick County | 0 | 0 | 0 | 0 | |
|   Newberry County | 0 | 0 | 0 | 0 | |
|   Oconee County | 0 | 0 | 0 | 0 | |
|   Orangeburg County | 0 | 0 | 0 | 0 | |
|   Pickens County | 0 | 0 | 0 | 0 | |
|   Richland County | 0 | 0 | 0 | 0 | |
|   Saluda County | 0 | 0 | 0 | 0 | |
|   Spartanburg County | 0 | 0 | 0 | 0 | |
|   Sumter County | 0 | 0 | 0 | 0 | |
|   Union County | 0 | 0 | 0 | 0 | |
|   Williamsburg County | 0 | 0 | 0 | 0 | |
|   York County | 0 | 0 | 0 | 0 | |
| **Other Agencies** | | | | | |
| Bureau of Protective Services | 0 | | 0 | | |
| Columbia Metropolitan Airport | 0 | 0 | 0 | 0 | |
| Department of Mental Health | 0 | 0 | 0 | 0 | |
| Department of Natural Resources | | | | | |
|   Abbeville County | 0 | 0 | 0 | 0 | |
|   Aiken County | 0 | 0 | 0 | 0 | |
|   Allendale County | 0 | 0 | 0 | 0 | |
|   Anderson County | 0 | 0 | 0 | 0 | |
|   Bamberg County | 0 | 0 | 0 | 0 | |
|   Barnwell County | 0 | 0 | 0 | 0 | |
|   Beaufort County | 0 | 0 | 0 | 0 | |
|   Berkeley County | 0 | 0 | 0 | 0 | |
|   Calhoun County | | 0 | 0 | 0 | |
|   Charleston County | 0 | 0 | 0 | 0 | |
|   Cherokee County | 0 | 0 | 0 | 0 | |
|   Chester County | 0 | 0 | 0 | 0 | |
|   Chesterfield County | 0 | 0 | 0 | 0 | |
|   Clarendon County | 0 | 0 | 0 | 0 | |
|   Colleton County | 0 | 0 | 0 | 0 | |
|   Darlington County | 0 | 0 | 0 | 0 | |
|   Dillon County | 0 | 0 | 0 | 0 | |
|   Dorchester County | 0 | 0 | 0 | 0 | |
|   Edgefield County | 0 | 0 | 0 | 0 | |
|   Fairfield County | 0 | 0 | 0 | 0 | |
|   Florence County | 0 | 0 | 0 | 0 | |
|   Georgetown County | 0 | 0 | 0 | 0 | |
|   Greenville County | 0 | 0 | 0 | 0 | |
|   Greenwood County | 0 | 0 | 0 | 0 | |

## Table 95. Hate Crime Zero Data Submitted Per Quarter, by Federal Agency, State, and State Agency, 2021—Continued

(Number.)

| Agency name | Zero data per quarter[1] | | | | Population[2] |
|---|---|---|---|---|---|
| | 1st quarter | 2nd quarter | 3rd quarter | 4th quarter | |
| Hampton County | 0 | 0 | 0 | 0 | |
| Horry County | 0 | 0 | 0 | 0 | |
| Jasper County | 0 | 0 | 0 | 0 | |
| Kershaw County | 0 | 0 | 0 | 0 | |
| Lancaster County | 0 | 0 | 0 | 0 | |
| Laurens County | 0 | 0 | 0 | 0 | |
| Lee County | 0 | 0 | 0 | 0 | |
| Lexington County | 0 | 0 | 0 | 0 | |
| Marion County | 0 | | 0 | 0 | |
| Marlboro County | | 0 | | 0 | |
| McCormick County | 0 | 0 | 0 | 0 | |
| Newberry County | 0 | 0 | 0 | 0 | |
| Oconee County | 0 | 0 | 0 | 0 | |
| Orangeburg County | 0 | 0 | 0 | 0 | |
| Pickens County | 0 | 0 | 0 | 0 | |
| Richland County | 0 | 0 | 0 | 0 | |
| Saluda County | 0 | 0 | 0 | 0 | |
| Spartanburg County | 0 | 0 | 0 | 0 | |
| Sumter County | 0 | 0 | 0 | 0 | |
| Union County | 0 | 0 | 0 | 0 | |
| Williamsburg County | 0 | 0 | 0 | 0 | |
| York County | 0 | 0 | 0 | 0 | |
| Florence Regional Airport | 0 | 0 | 0 | 0 | |
| Forestry Commission | | | | | |
| Abbeville County | 0 | 0 | 0 | | |
| Aiken County | 0 | 0 | 0 | | |
| Allendale County | 0 | 0 | 0 | | |
| Anderson County | 0 | 0 | 0 | | |
| Bamberg County | 0 | 0 | 0 | | |
| Barnwell County | 0 | 0 | 0 | | |
| Beaufort County | 0 | 0 | 0 | | |
| Berkeley County | 0 | 0 | 0 | | |
| Calhoun County | 0 | 0 | 0 | | |
| Charleston County | 0 | 0 | 0 | | |
| Cherokee County | 0 | 0 | 0 | | |
| Chester County | 0 | 0 | 0 | | |
| Chesterfield County | 0 | 0 | 0 | | |
| Clarendon County | 0 | 0 | 0 | | |
| Colleton County | 0 | 0 | 0 | | |
| Darlington County | 0 | 0 | 0 | | |
| Dillon County | 0 | 0 | 0 | | |
| Dorchester County | 0 | 0 | 0 | | |
| Edgefield County | 0 | 0 | 0 | | |
| Fairfield County | 0 | 0 | 0 | | |
| Florence County | 0 | 0 | 0 | | |
| Georgetown County | 0 | 0 | 0 | | |
| Greenville County | 0 | 0 | 0 | | |
| Greenwood County | 0 | 0 | 0 | | |
| Hampton County | 0 | 0 | 0 | | |
| Horry County | 0 | 0 | 0 | | |
| Jasper County | 0 | 0 | 0 | | |
| Kershaw County | 0 | 0 | 0 | | |
| Lancaster County | 0 | 0 | 0 | | |
| Laurens County | 0 | 0 | 0 | | |
| Lee County | 0 | 0 | 0 | | |
| Lexington County | 0 | 0 | 0 | | |
| Marion County | 0 | 0 | 0 | | |
| Marlboro County | 0 | 0 | 0 | | |
| McCormick County | 0 | 0 | 0 | | |
| Newberry County | 0 | 0 | 0 | | |
| Oconee County | 0 | 0 | 0 | | |
| Orangeburg County | 0 | 0 | 0 | | |
| Pickens County | 0 | 0 | 0 | | |
| Richland County | 0 | 0 | 0 | | |
| Saluda County | 0 | 0 | 0 | | |
| Spartanburg County | 0 | 0 | 0 | | |
| Sumter County | 0 | 0 | 0 | | |
| Union County | 0 | 0 | 0 | | |
| Williamsburg County | 0 | 0 | 0 | | |
| York County | 0 | 0 | 0 | | |
| Greenville Hospital | | | | | |
| Greenville | 0 | 0 | 0 | 0 | |
| Laurens | 0 | 0 | 0 | | |
| Oconee | 0 | 0 | 0 | | |
| Greenville-Spartanburg International Airport | 0 | 0 | 0 | 0 | |
| Lexington County Medical Center | 0 | 0 | 0 | 0 | |
| South Carolina School for the Deaf and Blind | 0 | 0 | 0 | 0 | |
| State Museum | 0 | | 0 | 0 | |
| State Ports Authority | 0 | 0 | 0 | 0 | |
| State Transport Police | | | | | |

## Table 95. Hate Crime Zero Data Submitted Per Quarter, by Federal Agency, State, and State Agency, 2021—Continued

(Number.)

| Agency name | Zero data per quarter[1] | | | | Population[2] |
|---|---|---|---|---|---|
| | 1st quarter | 2nd quarter | 3rd quarter | 4th quarter | |
| Abbeville County | 0 | 0 | 0 | 0 | |
| Aiken County | 0 | 0 | 0 | 0 | |
| Allendale County | 0 | 0 | 0 | 0 | |
| Anderson County | 0 | 0 | 0 | 0 | |
| Bamberg County | 0 | 0 | 0 | 0 | |
| Barnwell County | 0 | 0 | 0 | 0 | |
| Beaufort County | 0 | 0 | 0 | 0 | |
| Berkeley County | 0 | 0 | 0 | 0 | |
| Calhoun County | 0 | 0 | 0 | 0 | |
| Charleston County | 0 | 0 | 0 | 0 | |
| Cherokee County | 0 | 0 | 0 | 0 | |
| Chester County | 0 | 0 | 0 | 0 | |
| Chesterfield County | 0 | 0 | 0 | 0 | |
| Clarendon County | 0 | 0 | 0 | 0 | |
| Colleton County | 0 | 0 | 0 | 0 | |
| Darlington County | 0 | 0 | 0 | 0 | |
| Dillon County | 0 | 0 | 0 | 0 | |
| Dorchester County | 0 | 0 | 0 | 0 | |
| Edgefield County | 0 | 0 | 0 | 0 | |
| Fairfield County | 0 | 0 | 0 | 0 | |
| Florence County | 0 | 0 | 0 | 0 | |
| Georgetown County | 0 | 0 | 0 | 0 | |
| Greenville County | 0 | 0 | 0 | 0 | |
| Greenwood County | 0 | 0 | 0 | 0 | |
| Hampton County | 0 | 0 | 0 | 0 | |
| Horry County | 0 | 0 | 0 | 0 | |
| Jasper County | 0 | 0 | 0 | 0 | |
| Kershaw County | 0 | 0 | 0 | 0 | |
| Lancaster County | 0 | 0 | 0 | 0 | |
| Laurens County | 0 | 0 | 0 | 0 | |
| Lee County | 0 | 0 | 0 | 0 | |
| Lexington County | 0 | 0 | 0 | 0 | |
| Marion County | 0 | 0 | 0 | 0 | |
| Marlboro County | 0 | 0 | 0 | 0 | |
| McCormick County | 0 | 0 | 0 | 0 | |
| Newberry County | 0 | 0 | 0 | 0 | |
| Oconee County | 0 | 0 | 0 | | |
| Orangeburg County | 0 | 0 | | 0 | |
| Pickens County | | | 0 | 0 | |
| Richland County | 0 | 0 | 0 | 0 | |
| Saluda County | 0 | 0 | 0 | 0 | |
| Spartanburg County | 0 | 0 | 0 | 0 | |
| Sumter County | 0 | 0 | 0 | 0 | |
| Union County | 0 | 0 | 0 | 0 | |
| Williamsburg County | 0 | 0 | 0 | 0 | |
| York County | 0 | 0 | 0 | 0 | |
| **SOUTH DAKOTA** | | | | | |
| **Cities** | | | | | |
| Aberdeen | 0 | 0 | | | 28,385 |
| Beresford | 0 | 0 | 0 | 0 | 2,046 |
| Box Elder | 0 | 0 | 0 | 0 | 10,876 |
| Brandon | 0 | 0 | 0 | 0 | 10,297 |
| Brookings | 0 | 0 | 0 | 0 | 25,088 |
| Burke | 0 | 0 | 0 | | 586 |
| Canton | 0 | 0 | 0 | 0 | 3,635 |
| Chamberlain | 0 | 0 | 0 | 0 | 2,344 |
| Clark | 0 | 0 | | | 1,072 |
| Deadwood | 0 | 0 | | 0 | 1,294 |
| Elk Point | 0 | 0 | 0 | 0 | 1,864 |
| Faith | 0 | | | | 409 |
| Flandreau | 0 | 0 | 0 | 0 | 2,288 |
| Freeman | 0 | 0 | 0 | | 1,250 |
| Gettysburg | 0 | 0 | 0 | 0 | 1,075 |
| Gregory | 0 | | | | 1,246 |
| Groton | 0 | | | | 1,477 |
| Jefferson | 0 | 0 | 0 | 0 | 512 |
| Lennox | 0 | 0 | | | 2,540 |
| Madison | 0 | 0 | 0 | 0 | 7,120 |
| Miller | 0 | 0 | | 0 | 1,290 |
| Mitchell | 0 | 0 | 0 | 0 | 15,741 |
| Murdo | 0 | 0 | 0 | 0 | 456 |
| North Sioux City | 0 | | | | 2,997 |
| Parkston | 0 | 0 | 0 | | 1,450 |
| Pierre | 0 | 0 | 0 | 0 | 13,710 |
| Spearfish | 0 | 0 | 0 | 0 | 12,047 |
| Tea | 0 | 0 | 0 | 0 | 6,739 |
| Tyndall | | 0 | 0 | | 1,010 |
| Vermillion | 0 | 0 | 0 | 0 | 11,088 |
| Wagner | 0 | 0 | 0 | 0 | 1,534 |

## Table 95. Hate Crime Zero Data Submitted Per Quarter, by Federal Agency, State, and State Agency, 2021—Continued

(Number.)

| Agency name | Zero data per quarter[1] | | | | Population[2] |
|---|---|---|---|---|---|
| | 1st quarter | 2nd quarter | 3rd quarter | 4th quarter | |
| Watertown | 0 | 0 | 0 | 0 | 22,383 |
| Webster | | 0 | | | 1,675 |
| Winner | 0 | 0 | 0 | 0 | 2,773 |
| Yankton | 0 | 0 | 0 | 0 | 14,669 |
| **Universities and Colleges** | | | | | |
| South Dakota School of Mines and Technology | | 0 | | 0 | 3,056 |
| South Dakota State University | 0 | 0 | 0 | 0 | 13,937 |
| University of South Dakota | 0 | 0 | 0 | 0 | 12,276 |
| **Metropolitan Counties** | | | | | |
| Lincoln | 0 | 0 | 0 | 0 | |
| McCook | 0 | 0 | 0 | 0 | |
| Pennington | 0 | 0 | 0 | 0 | |
| Turner | 0 | 0 | 0 | 0 | |
| Union | 0 | 0 | 0 | 0 | |
| **Nonmetropolitan Counties** | | | | | |
| Aurora | 0 | | | | |
| Bennett | 0 | 0 | 0 | 0 | |
| Bon Homme | 0 | 0 | 0 | 0 | |
| Brookings | 0 | 0 | 0 | | |
| Brown | 0 | 0 | | | |
| Brule | 0 | 0 | 0 | 0 | |
| Butte | 0 | 0 | 0 | 0 | |
| Clay | 0 | 0 | 0 | 0 | |
| Codington | 0 | 0 | 0 | 0 | |
| Corson | 0 | 0 | 0 | 0 | |
| Davison | | 0 | 0 | 0 | |
| Day | 0 | 0 | 0 | 0 | |
| Deuel | 0 | 0 | 0 | 0 | |
| Edmunds | 0 | 0 | 0 | 0 | |
| Faulk | 0 | 0 | 0 | 0 | |
| Gregory | 0 | 0 | 0 | 0 | |
| Hand | 0 | 0 | | | |
| Hanson | 0 | 0 | 0 | 0 | |
| Harding | 0 | 0 | 0 | | |
| Hughes | 0 | 0 | 0 | 0 | |
| Hutchinson | 0 | 0 | | | |
| Jerauld | 0 | 0 | 0 | 0 | |
| Jones | 0 | 0 | 0 | 0 | |
| Kingsbury | 0 | 0 | 0 | 0 | |
| Lake | 0 | 0 | 0 | 0 | |
| Lawrence | 0 | 0 | 0 | 0 | |
| Marshall | 0 | 0 | 0 | 0 | |
| McPherson | 0 | 0 | 0 | 0 | |
| Mellette | 0 | 0 | | | |
| Miner | 0 | 0 | 0 | 0 | |
| Moody | 0 | 0 | 0 | 0 | |
| Perkins | 0 | 0 | 0 | 0 | |
| Potter | 0 | 0 | 0 | 0 | |
| Roberts | 0 | | | | |
| Sanborn | 0 | 0 | 0 | 0 | |
| Spink | 0 | 0 | 0 | 0 | |
| Stanley | 0 | 0 | 0 | 0 | |
| Sully | 0 | 0 | 0 | 0 | |
| Todd | 0 | | | | |
| Tripp | 0 | 0 | 0 | 0 | |
| Walworth | 0 | 0 | 0 | 0 | |
| Yankton | 0 | 0 | 0 | 0 | |
| **State Police Agencies** | | | | | |
| Highway Patrol | 0 | 0 | 0 | 0 | |
| **Tribal Agencies** | | | | | |
| Cheyenne River Tribal | 0 | 0 | 0 | 0 | |
| Flandreau Santee Sioux Tribal | 0 | 0 | 0 | 0 | |
| Lower Brule Tribal | 0 | 0 | 0 | 0 | |
| Rosebud Tribal | 0 | 0 | 0 | 0 | |
| Sisseton-Wahpeton Tribal | 0 | 0 | 0 | 0 | |
| Yankton Tribal | 0 | 0 | 0 | 0 | |
| **TENNESSEE** | | | | | |
| **Cities** | | | | | |
| Adamsville | 0 | 0 | 0 | 0 | 2,159 |
| Alamo | 0 | 0 | 0 | 0 | 2,251 |
| Alcoa | 0 | 0 | 0 | | 10,605 |
| Alexandria | 0 | 0 | | | 1,025 |
| Algood | 0 | 0 | 0 | 0 | 4,666 |
| Ardmore | 0 | 0 | | 0 | 1,218 |

**Table 95. Hate Crime Zero Data Submitted Per Quarter, by Federal Agency, State, and State Agency, 2021—Continued**

(Number.)

| Agency name | Zero data per quarter[1] | | | | Population[2] |
|---|---|---|---|---|---|
| | 1st quarter | 2nd quarter | 3rd quarter | 4th quarter | |
| Ashland City | 0 | 0 | 0 | 0 | 4,763 |
| Athens | 0 | 0 | 0 | 0 | 14,166 |
| Atoka | 0 | 0 | 0 | 0 | 9,859 |
| Baileyton | 0 | 0 | 0 | 0 | 459 |
| Baxter | 0 | 0 | 0 | 0 | 1,563 |
| Bean Station | 0 | 0 | 0 | 0 | 3,121 |
| Belle Meade | 0 | 0 | 0 | 0 | 2,777 |
| Bells | 0 | 0 | 0 | 0 | 2,431 |
| Benton | 0 | 0 | 0 | 0 | 1,235 |
| Berry Hill | 0 | 0 | 0 | 0 | 488 |
| Big Sandy | 0 | 0 | 0 | 0 | 515 |
| Blaine | 0 | 0 | 0 | 0 | 1,871 |
| Bluff City | 0 | 0 | 0 | 0 | 1,669 |
| Bolivar | 0 | 0 | 0 | 0 | 4,798 |
| Bradford | 0 | 0 | 0 | 0 | 967 |
| Brentwood | 0 | 0 | 0 | 0 | 43,490 |
| Brighton | | 0 | | 0 | 2,933 |
| Bristol | 0 | 0 | 0 | 0 | 27,182 |
| Brownsville | 0 | 0 | 0 | 0 | 9,128 |
| Bruceton | 0 | 0 | | 0 | 1,383 |
| Burns | 0 | 0 | 0 | 0 | 1,570 |
| Calhoun | 0 | 0 | 0 | 0 | 504 |
| Camden | 0 | 0 | 0 | 0 | 3,624 |
| Carthage | 0 | 0 | 0 | 0 | 2,335 |
| Caryville | 0 | 0 | 0 | 0 | 2,103 |
| Celina | 0 | 0 | 0 | 0 | 1,398 |
| Centerville | 0 | 0 | 0 | 0 | 3,557 |
| Chapel Hill | 0 | 0 | 0 | 0 | 1,584 |
| Charleston | 0 | 0 | 0 | 0 | 712 |
| Church Hill | 0 | 0 | 0 | 0 | 6,633 |
| Clarksburg | | 0 | 0 | | 375 |
| Clifton | 0 | 0 | 0 | 0 | 2,651 |
| Collegedale | 0 | 0 | 0 | 0 | 11,737 |
| Cookeville | 0 | 0 | 0 | 0 | 35,471 |
| Coopertown | 0 | 0 | 0 | 0 | 4,647 |
| Cornersville | 0 | 0 | 0 | 0 | 1,329 |
| Cross Plains | 0 | 0 | | | 1,853 |
| Cumberland City | 0 | 0 | | | 310 |
| Dandridge | 0 | 0 | 0 | 0 | 3,204 |
| Dayton | 0 | 0 | 0 | 0 | 7,338 |
| Decatur | 0 | 0 | 0 | 0 | 1,665 |
| Decaturville | 0 | 0 | 0 | 0 | 856 |
| Decherd | 0 | 0 | 0 | 0 | 2,375 |
| Dickson | 0 | 0 | 0 | 0 | 15,634 |
| Dover | 0 | 0 | 0 | 0 | 1,596 |
| Dresden | 0 | 0 | 0 | 0 | 2,890 |
| Dunlap | 0 | 0 | 0 | 0 | 5,278 |
| Dyer | 0 | 0 | 0 | 0 | 2,192 |
| East Ridge | 0 | 0 | 0 | 0 | 21,225 |
| Englewood | 0 | 0 | 0 | 0 | 1,539 |
| Erin | 0 | 0 | 0 | 0 | 1,304 |
| Erwin | 0 | 0 | 0 | 0 | 5,832 |
| Estill Springs | 0 | 0 | 0 | 0 | 2,042 |
| Ethridge | 0 | 0 | 0 | 0 | 487 |
| Etowah | 0 | 0 | 0 | 0 | 3,530 |
| Fairview | 0 | 0 | 0 | 0 | 9,794 |
| Fayetteville | 0 | 0 | 0 | 0 | 7,033 |
| Friendship | 0 | 0 | 0 | 0 | 658 |
| Gainesboro | 0 | 0 | 0 | | 951 |
| Gallatin | 0 | 0 | 0 | 0 | 46,031 |
| Gallaway | 0 | 0 | 0 | 0 | 646 |
| Gates | 0 | 0 | 0 | 0 | 593 |
| Gatlinburg | 0 | 0 | 0 | 0 | 3,759 |
| Gibson | 0 | | 0 | | 382 |
| Gleason | 0 | 0 | 0 | 0 | 1,361 |
| Goodlettsville | 0 | 0 | 0 | 0 | 16,818 |
| Gordonsville | 0 | 0 | 0 | 0 | 1,248 |
| Grand Junction | | 0 | | 0 | 261 |
| Graysville | 0 | 0 | 0 | 0 | 1,575 |
| Greenbrier | 0 | 0 | 0 | 0 | 6,949 |
| Greeneville | 0 | 0 | 0 | 0 | 14,930 |
| Greenfield | 0 | 0 | 0 | 0 | 2,058 |
| Halls | 0 | 0 | 0 | 0 | 2,021 |
| Harriman | 0 | 0 | 0 | 0 | 6,167 |
| Henderson | 0 | 0 | 0 | 0 | 6,427 |
| Hendersonville | 0 | 0 | 0 | 0 | 60,170 |
| Henry | 0 | 0 | 0 | 0 | 447 |
| Hohenwald | 0 | 0 | 0 | 0 | 3,992 |
| Hollow Rock | 0 | | | | 677 |
| Humboldt | 0 | 0 | 0 | 0 | 8,092 |

## Table 95. Hate Crime Zero Data Submitted Per Quarter, by Federal Agency, State, and State Agency, 2021—Continued

(Number.)

| Agency name | Zero data per quarter[1] | | | | Population[2] |
|---|---|---|---|---|---|
| | 1st quarter | 2nd quarter | 3rd quarter | 4th quarter | |
| Huntingdon | 0 | 0 | 0 | 0 | 3,820 |
| Huntland | 0 | 0 | 0 | 0 | 839 |
| Jacksboro | 0 | 0 | 0 | 0 | 2,069 |
| Jamestown | 0 | 0 | 0 | 0 | 2,149 |
| Jasper | 0 | 0 | 0 | 0 | 3,419 |
| Jefferson City | 0 | 0 | 0 | 0 | 8,234 |
| Jellico | 0 | 0 | 0 | 0 | 2,114 |
| Johnson City | 0 | 0 | 0 | 0 | 67,515 |
| Kenton | 0 | 0 | 0 | 0 | 1,181 |
| Kimball | 0 | 0 | 0 | 0 | 1,457 |
| Kingston | 0 | 0 | 0 | 0 | 5,956 |
| Kingston Springs | 0 | 0 | 0 | 0 | 2,712 |
| Lafayette | 0 | 0 | 0 | 0 | 5,351 |
| La Follette | 0 | 0 | 0 | 0 | 6,502 |
| Lawrenceburg | 0 | 0 | 0 | 0 | 11,122 |
| Lexington | 0 | 0 | 0 | 0 | 7,888 |
| Livingston | 0 | 0 | 0 | 0 | 4,135 |
| Lookout Mountain | 0 | 0 | 0 | 0 | 1,886 |
| Loretto | 0 | 0 | 0 | 0 | 1,790 |
| Loudon | 0 | 0 | 0 | 0 | 6,079 |
| Madisonville | 0 | 0 | 0 | 0 | 5,056 |
| Maryville | 0 | 0 | 0 | 0 | 30,262 |
| Mason | 0 | 0 | 0 | 0 | 1,530 |
| Maynardville | 0 | 0 | 0 | 0 | 2,461 |
| McEwen | 0 | 0 | 0 | 0 | 1,744 |
| McKenzie | 0 | 0 | 0 | 0 | 5,309 |
| McMinnville | 0 | 0 | 0 | 0 | 13,790 |
| Medina | 0 | 0 | 0 | 0 | 4,465 |
| Milan | 0 | 0 | 0 | 0 | 7,583 |
| Millersville | 0 | 0 | 0 | 0 | 6,839 |
| Minor Hill | | | | 0 | 534 |
| Monteagle | 0 | 0 | 0 | 0 | 1,236 |
| Monterey | 0 | 0 | 0 | 0 | 2,895 |
| Morristown | 0 | 0 | 0 | 0 | 30,413 |
| Moscow | 0 | 0 | | | 544 |
| Mosheim | | | 0 | 0 | 2,355 |
| Mountain City | 0 | 0 | 0 | 0 | 2,437 |
| Mount Carmel | 0 | 0 | 0 | 0 | 5,242 |
| Mount Juliet | 0 | 0 | 0 | 0 | 40,233 |
| Mount Pleasant | 0 | 0 | 0 | 0 | 5,014 |
| Munford | 0 | 0 | 0 | 0 | 6,233 |
| Newbern | 0 | 0 | 0 | 0 | 3,222 |
| New Johnsonville | 0 | 0 | 0 | 0 | 1,866 |
| New Market | 0 | 0 | 0 | 0 | 1,385 |
| Newport | 0 | 0 | 0 | 0 | 6,894 |
| New Tazewell | 0 | 0 | 0 | 0 | 2,694 |
| Niota | 0 | 0 | 0 | 0 | 740 |
| Nolensville | 0 | 0 | 0 | 0 | 11,866 |
| Norris | | 0 | 0 | 0 | 1,614 |
| Oak Ridge | 0 | 0 | 0 | 0 | 29,343 |
| Obion | 0 | 0 | 0 | 0 | 1,035 |
| Oliver Springs | 0 | 0 | 0 | 0 | 3,443 |
| Oneida | 0 | 0 | 0 | 0 | 3,696 |
| Paris | 0 | 0 | 0 | 0 | 9,934 |
| Parsons | 0 | 0 | 0 | 0 | 2,264 |
| Petersburg | | 0 | 0 | 0 | 579 |
| Pikeville | 0 | 0 | 0 | 0 | 1,799 |
| Piperton | 0 | 0 | 0 | | 2,212 |
| Pittman Center | 0 | | | | 552 |
| Plainview | 0 | 0 | 0 | 0 | 2,191 |
| Pleasant View | 0 | 0 | 0 | 0 | 5,156 |
| Portland | 0 | 0 | 0 | 0 | 13,493 |
| Pulaski | 0 | 0 | 0 | 0 | 7,494 |
| Puryear | 0 | 0 | 0 | 0 | 651 |
| Red Bank | 0 | 0 | 0 | 0 | 11,904 |
| Red Boiling Springs | 0 | 0 | 0 | 0 | 1,125 |
| Ridgely | 0 | 0 | 0 | 0 | 1,586 |
| Ripley | 0 | 0 | 0 | 0 | 7,552 |
| Rocky Top | 0 | 0 | 0 | | 1,776 |
| Rossville | 0 | 0 | 0 | 0 | 1,056 |
| Rutherford | 0 | 0 | 0 | 0 | 1,056 |
| Rutledge | 0 | 0 | 0 | 0 | 1,358 |
| Saltillo | 0 | | | | 519 |
| Savannah | 0 | 0 | 0 | 0 | 6,907 |
| Scotts Hill | 0 | 0 | 0 | 0 | 972 |
| Selmer | 0 | 0 | 0 | 0 | 4,277 |
| Sharon | 0 | 0 | 0 | 0 | 900 |
| Shelbyville | 0 | 0 | 0 | 0 | 22,534 |
| Signal Mountain | 0 | 0 | 0 | 0 | 8,678 |
| Smithville | 0 | 0 | 0 | 0 | 5,027 |

## Table 95. Hate Crime Zero Data Submitted Per Quarter, by Federal Agency, State, and State Agency, 2021—Continued

(Number.)

| Agency name | Zero data per quarter[1] | | | | Population[2] |
|---|---|---|---|---|---|
| | 1st quarter | 2nd quarter | 3rd quarter | 4th quarter | |
| Smyrna | 0 | 0 | 0 | 0 | 54,645 |
| Soddy-Daisy | 0 | 0 | 0 | 0 | 13,799 |
| Somerville | 0 | 0 | 0 | 0 | 3,262 |
| South Carthage | 0 | 0 | | 0 | 1,416 |
| South Fulton | 0 | 0 | 0 | 0 | 2,193 |
| South Pittsburg | 0 | 0 | 0 | 0 | 3,000 |
| Sparta | 0 | 0 | 0 | 0 | 4,994 |
| Spencer | 0 | 0 | 0 | 0 | 1,720 |
| Spring City | 0 | 0 | 0 | 0 | 1,837 |
| Springfield | 0 | 0 | 0 | 0 | 17,374 |
| St. Joseph | 0 | 0 | 0 | 0 | 827 |
| Surgoinsville | 0 | | 0 | | 1,749 |
| Sweetwater | 0 | 0 | 0 | 0 | 5,971 |
| Tazewell | 0 | 0 | 0 | 0 | 2,279 |
| Tellico Plains | 0 | 0 | 0 | 0 | 915 |
| Tiptonville | 0 | 0 | 0 | 0 | 3,939 |
| Toone | 0 | 0 | | 0 | 333 |
| Townsend | 0 | 0 | 0 | 0 | 483 |
| Tracy City | 0 | 0 | 0 | 0 | 1,398 |
| Trenton | 0 | 0 | 0 | 0 | 4,133 |
| Trezevant | 0 | 0 | 0 | | 832 |
| Trimble | | 0 | | | 599 |
| Troy | 0 | 0 | 0 | 0 | 1,321 |
| Tullahoma | 0 | 0 | 0 | 0 | 19,913 |
| Tusculum | 0 | 0 | 0 | 0 | 2,669 |
| Unicoi | 0 | 0 | 0 | 0 | 3,576 |
| Union City | 0 | 0 | 0 | 0 | 10,272 |
| Vonore | 0 | 0 | 0 | 0 | 1,589 |
| Wartburg | 0 | 0 | 0 | 0 | 899 |
| Waverly | 0 | 0 | 0 | 0 | 4,123 |
| Waynesboro | 0 | 0 | 0 | 0 | 2,365 |
| Westmoreland | 0 | 0 | 0 | 0 | 2,438 |
| White Bluff | 0 | 0 | 0 | 0 | 3,741 |
| White House | 0 | 0 | 0 | 0 | 13,282 |
| White Pine | 0 | 0 | 0 | 0 | 2,673 |
| Whiteville | 0 | 0 | 0 | 0 | 4,430 |
| Whitwell | 0 | 0 | 0 | 0 | 1,718 |
| Woodbury | 0 | 0 | 0 | 0 | 3,007 |
| **Universities and Colleges** | | | | | |
| Chattanooga State Community College | 0 | 0 | 0 | 0 | 10,425 |
| Cleveland State Community College | 0 | 0 | | | 4,297 |
| Columbia State Community College | | | 0 | 0 | 8,381 |
| Jackson State Community College | | 0 | | | 6,851 |
| Lincoln Memorial University | 0 | 0 | 0 | 0 | 5,511 |
| Northeast State Community College | 0 | 0 | | 0 | 7,549 |
| Pellissippi State Community College | 0 | 0 | 0 | 0 | 14,651 |
| Roane State Community College | 0 | 0 | 0 | 0 | 7,241 |
| Southwest Tennessee Community College | | | 0 | 0 | 12,913 |
| Tennessee State University | 0 | 0 | 0 | 0 | 8,997 |
| Tennessee Technological University | 0 | 0 | 0 | 0 | 11,103 |
| University of Memphis | 0 | 0 | 0 | 0 | 25,128 |
| University of Tennessee | | | | | |
| Chattanooga | 0 | 0 | | | 12,675 |
| Health Science Center | 0 | 0 | 0 | 0 | 3,379 |
| Knoxville | 0 | 0 | 0 | 0 | 32,056 |
| Martin | 0 | 0 | 0 | 0 | 8,379 |
| University of the South | 0 | 0 | 0 | 0 | 1,957 |
| Vanderbilt University | 0 | 0 | 0 | 0 | 13,918 |
| Volunteer State Community College | 0 | | | 0 | 11,761 |
| Walters State Community College | 0 | | 0 | 0 | 7,726 |
| **Metropolitan Counties** | | | | | |
| Anderson | 0 | 0 | 0 | 0 | |
| Campbell | 0 | 0 | 0 | 0 | |
| Cannon | 0 | 0 | 0 | 0 | |
| Chester | 0 | 0 | | 0 | |
| Crockett | 0 | 0 | 0 | 0 | |
| Dickson | 0 | 0 | 0 | 0 | |
| Fayette | 0 | 0 | 0 | 0 | |
| Gibson | 0 | 0 | 0 | 0 | |
| Grainger | 0 | 0 | 0 | 0 | |
| Hamblen | 0 | 0 | 0 | 0 | |
| Hamilton | 0 | 0 | 0 | 0 | |
| Hartsville/Trousdale | 0 | 0 | 0 | 0 | |
| Hawkins | 0 | 0 | 0 | 0 | |
| Loudon | 0 | 0 | 0 | 0 | |
| Macon | 0 | 0 | 0 | 0 | |
| Madison | 0 | 0 | 0 | 0 | |
| Marion | 0 | 0 | 0 | 0 | |

## Table 95. Hate Crime Zero Data Submitted Per Quarter, by Federal Agency, State, and State Agency, 2021—Continued

(Number.)

| Agency name | Zero data per quarter[1] | | | | Population[2] |
|---|---|---|---|---|---|
| | 1st quarter | 2nd quarter | 3rd quarter | 4th quarter | |
| Maury | 0 | 0 | 0 | 0 | |
| Montgomery | 0 | 0 | 0 | 0 | |
| Morgan | 0 | 0 | 0 | 0 | |
| Polk | 0 | 0 | 0 | 0 | |
| Roane | 0 | 0 | 0 | 0 | |
| Sequatchie | 0 | 0 | 0 | 0 | |
| Smith | 0 | 0 | 0 | 0 | |
| Stewart | 0 | 0 | 0 | 0 | |
| Sullivan | 0 | 0 | 0 | 0 | |
| Sumner | 0 | 0 | 0 | 0 | |
| Tipton | 0 | 0 | 0 | 0 | |
| Unicoi | 0 | 0 | 0 | 0 | |
| Union | 0 | 0 | 0 | 0 | |
| Williamson | 0 | 0 | 0 | 0 | |
| Wilson | 0 | 0 | 0 | 0 | |
| **Nonmetropolitan Counties** | | | | | |
| Bedford | 0 | 0 | 0 | 0 | |
| Benton | 0 | 0 | 0 | 0 | |
| Bledsoe | 0 | 0 | 0 | 0 | |
| Carroll | 0 | 0 | 0 | 0 | |
| Claiborne | 0 | 0 | 0 | 0 | |
| Clay | 0 | 0 | 0 | 0 | |
| Cocke | 0 | 0 | 0 | 0 | |
| Coffee | 0 | 0 | 0 | 0 | |
| Cumberland | 0 | 0 | 0 | 0 | |
| Decatur | 0 | 0 | 0 | 0 | |
| DeKalb | 0 | 0 | 0 | 0 | |
| Dyer | 0 | 0 | 0 | 0 | |
| Fentress | 0 | 0 | 0 | 0 | |
| Franklin | 0 | 0 | 0 | 0 | |
| Giles | 0 | 0 | 0 | 0 | |
| Grundy | 0 | 0 | 0 | 0 | |
| Hancock | 0 | 0 | 0 | 0 | |
| Hardeman | 0 | 0 | 0 | 0 | |
| Haywood | 0 | 0 | 0 | 0 | |
| Henderson | 0 | 0 | 0 | 0 | |
| Henry | 0 | 0 | 0 | 0 | |
| Hickman | 0 | 0 | 0 | 0 | |
| Houston | 0 | 0 | 0 | 0 | |
| Humphreys | 0 | 0 | 0 | 0 | |
| Jackson | 0 | 0 | 0 | 0 | |
| Lake | 0 | 0 | 0 | | |
| Lauderdale | 0 | 0 | 0 | 0 | |
| Lawrence | 0 | 0 | 0 | 0 | |
| Lewis | 0 | 0 | 0 | 0 | |
| Lincoln | 0 | 0 | 0 | 0 | |
| Marshall | 0 | 0 | 0 | 0 | |
| McMinn | 0 | 0 | 0 | 0 | |
| McNairy | 0 | 0 | 0 | 0 | |
| Moore | 0 | 0 | 0 | 0 | |
| Obion | 0 | 0 | 0 | 0 | |
| Overton | 0 | 0 | 0 | 0 | |
| Perry | 0 | 0 | 0 | 0 | |
| Pickett | 0 | 0 | 0 | 0 | |
| Putnam | 0 | 0 | 0 | 0 | |
| Rhea | 0 | 0 | 0 | 0 | |
| Scott | 0 | 0 | 0 | 0 | |
| Sevier | 0 | 0 | 0 | 0 | |
| Van Buren | 0 | 0 | 0 | 0 | |
| Wayne | 0 | 0 | 0 | | |
| Weakley | 0 | 0 | 0 | 0 | |
| White | 0 | 0 | 0 | 0 | |
| **Other Agencies** | | | | | |
| 7th Judicial District Crime Task Force | 0 | 0 | 0 | 0 | |
| Alcoholic Beverage Commission | 0 | 0 | 0 | 0 | |
| Chattanooga Housing Authority | 0 | 0 | 0 | 0 | |
| Chattanooga Metropolitan Airport | 0 | 0 | 0 | 0 | |
| Department of Agriculture, Agricultural Crime Unit | 0 | 0 | 0 | 0 | |
| Department of Correction, Internal Affairs | 0 | 0 | 0 | | |
| Dickson City Park Ranger Division | 0 | 0 | 0 | 0 | |
| Drug Task Force | | | | | |
| 1st Judicial District | 0 | 0 | 0 | 0 | |
| 2nd Judicial District | 0 | 0 | 0 | 0 | |
| 3rd Judicial District | 0 | 0 | 0 | 0 | |
| 4th Judicial District | 0 | 0 | 0 | 0 | |
| 5th Judicial District | 0 | 0 | 0 | 0 | |
| 8th Judicial District | 0 | | | | |
| 9th Judicial District | 0 | 0 | 0 | 0 | |

## Table 95. Hate Crime Zero Data Submitted Per Quarter, by Federal Agency, State, and State Agency, 2021—Continued

(Number.)

| Agency name | Zero data per quarter[1] | | | | Population[2] |
|---|---|---|---|---|---|
| | 1st quarter | 2nd quarter | 3rd quarter | 4th quarter | |
| 10th Judicial District | 0 | 0 | 0 | 0 | |
| 12th Judicial District | 0 | 0 | 0 | 0 | |
| 15th Judicial District | 0 | 0 | 0 | 0 | |
| 17th Judicial District | 0 | 0 | 0 | 0 | |
| 18th Judicial District | 0 | 0 | 0 | 0 | |
| 19th Judicial District | 0 | 0 | 0 | 0 | |
| 21st Judicial District | 0 | | | | |
| 22nd Judicial District | 0 | 0 | 0 | 0 | |
| 23rd Judicial District | 0 | 0 | 0 | 0 | |
| 24th Judicial District | 0 | 0 | | | |
| 27th Judicial District | 0 | | 0 | 0 | |
| Knoxville Metropolitan Airport | 0 | 0 | 0 | 0 | |
| Memphis-Shelby County Airport Authority | 0 | 0 | 0 | 0 | |
| Metropolitan Nashville Park Police | 0 | 0 | 0 | 0 | |
| Nashville International Airport | 0 | 0 | 0 | 0 | |
| State Park Rangers | | | | | |
| Bicentennial Capitol Mall | 0 | 0 | 0 | 0 | |
| Bledsoe Creek | | | | 0 | |
| Booker T. Washington | 0 | 0 | | 0 | |
| Burgess Falls Natural Area | 0 | 0 | 0 | 0 | |
| Cedars of Lebanon | 0 | | 0 | | |
| Cove Lake | 0 | | 0 | 0 | |
| Cumberland Mountain | | 0 | | | |
| Cumberland Trail | | 0 | | | |
| Cummins Falls | 0 | 0 | 0 | 0 | |
| David Crockett | 0 | | | 0 | |
| Davy Crockett Birthplace | | 0 | | | |
| Dunbar Cave Natural Area | 0 | 0 | | 0 | |
| Edgar Evins | | | | 0 | |
| Fall Creek Falls | 0 | 0 | 0 | 0 | |
| Fort Loudon State Historic Park | | 0 | | | |
| Frozen Head Natural Area | 0 | 0 | 0 | | |
| Harpeth Scenic Rivers | 0 | 0 | | | |
| Harrison Bay | | 0 | 0 | | |
| Henry Horton | 0 | 0 | 0 | 0 | |
| Hiwassee/Ocoee State Scenic Rivers | 0 | 0 | 0 | 0 | |
| Long Hunter | 0 | 0 | 0 | | |
| Meeman-Shelby Forest | | 0 | | | |
| Montgomery Bell | | | 0 | 0 | |
| Natchez Trace | 0 | 0 | | | |
| Nathan Bedford Forrest | | 0 | | | |
| Norris Dam | 0 | | | | |
| Old Stone Fort State Archaeological Park | 0 | 0 | | 0 | |
| Panther Creek | 0 | 0 | | 0 | |
| Paris Landing | 0 | 0 | | | |
| Pickett | | | | 0 | |
| Pickwick Landing | 0 | 0 | 0 | | |
| Radnor Lake Natural Area | 0 | 0 | 0 | 0 | |
| Roan Mountain | | 0 | | | |
| Rock Island | 0 | 0 | 0 | 0 | |
| Seven Islands Birding Park | 0 | | 0 | | |
| South Cumberland Recreation Area | 0 | 0 | 0 | 0 | |
| Standing Stone | | 0 | 0 | 0 | |
| Sycamore Shoals State Historic Park | | 0 | | | |
| Tim's Ford | 0 | 0 | 0 | 0 | |
| T.O. Fuller | | 0 | | | |
| Warrior's Path | 0 | 0 | | | |
| TennCare Office of Inspector General | 0 | 0 | 0 | 0 | |
| Tennessee Department of Revenue, Special Investigations Unit | 0 | 0 | 0 | | |
| Tri-Cities Regional Airport | 0 | 0 | 0 | 0 | |
| West Tennessee Violent Crime Task Force | 0 | 0 | 0 | 0 | |
| Wildlife Resources Agency | | | | | |
| Region 1 | | 0 | | | |
| Region 2 | 0 | 0 | 0 | 0 | |
| Region 3 | 0 | 0 | 0 | | |
| Region 4 | 0 | 0 | 0 | 0 | |
| **TEXAS** | | | | | |
| **Cities** | | | | | |
| Abernathy | 0 | 0 | 0 | 0 | 2,678 |
| Addison | 0 | 0 | 0 | 0 | 16,540 |
| Alamo Heights | 0 | 0 | 0 | 0 | 8,848 |
| Alba | 0 | 0 | 0 | 0 | 555 |
| Alice | 0 | 0 | 0 | 0 | 18,538 |
| Alpine | 0 | 0 | 0 | 0 | 6,037 |
| Alton | 0 | 0 | 0 | 0 | 19,344 |
| Alvarado | 0 | 0 | 0 | 0 | 4,722 |
| Alvin | 0 | 0 | 0 | 0 | 27,448 |
| Amarillo | 0 | 0 | 0 | 0 | 200,515 |
| Andrews | 0 | 0 | 0 | 0 | 14,699 |

## Table 95. Hate Crime Zero Data Submitted Per Quarter, by Federal Agency, State, and State Agency, 2021—Continued

(Number.)

| Agency name | Zero data per quarter[1] | | | | Population[2] |
|---|---|---|---|---|---|
| | 1st quarter | 2nd quarter | 3rd quarter | 4th quarter | |
| Angleton | 0 | 0 | 0 | 0 | 19,593 |
| Anson | 0 | | | | 2,260 |
| Anthony | 0 | | 0 | 0 | 5,279 |
| Aransas Pass | 0 | 0 | 0 | 0 | 8,531 |
| Archer City | 0 | 0 | 0 | 0 | 1,711 |
| Arcola | 0 | 0 | 0 | 0 | 2,925 |
| Argyle | 0 | 0 | 0 | 0 | 4,781 |
| Arp | 0 | 0 | 0 | 0 | 1,054 |
| Athens | 0 | 0 | 0 | 0 | 12,778 |
| Atlanta | 0 | 0 | 0 | 0 | 5,402 |
| Aubrey | 0 | 0 | 0 | 0 | 7,080 |
| Azle | 0 | 0 | 0 | 0 | 13,917 |
| Baird | 0 | 0 | 0 | 0 | 1,497 |
| Balcones Heights | 0 | 0 | 0 | 0 | 3,174 |
| Ballinger | 0 | 0 | 0 | 0 | 3,681 |
| Bartonville | 0 | 0 | 0 | 0 | 1,871 |
| Bastrop | 0 | 0 | 0 | 0 | 10,020 |
| Bay City | 0 | 0 | 0 | 0 | 17,441 |
| Baytown | 0 | 0 | 0 | 0 | 77,816 |
| Bee Cave | 0 | 0 | 0 | 0 | 7,378 |
| Bellaire | 0 | 0 | 0 | 0 | 19,114 |
| Bellmead | 0 | 0 | 0 | 0 | 10,927 |
| Bells | 0 | 0 | 0 | 0 | 1,528 |
| Belton | 0 | 0 | 0 | 0 | 23,731 |
| Benbrook | 0 | 0 | 0 | 0 | 23,529 |
| Bertram | 0 | 0 | 0 | 0 | 1,539 |
| Big Sandy | 0 | 0 | 0 | 0 | 1,418 |
| Big Spring | 0 | 0 | 0 | 0 | 28,166 |
| Blanco | 0 | 0 | 0 | 0 | 2,194 |
| Blue Mound | 0 | 0 | 0 | 0 | 2,411 |
| Bogata | 0 | 0 | 0 | 0 | 1,054 |
| Borger | 0 | 0 | 0 | 0 | 12,121 |
| Bovina | 0 | 0 | 0 | 0 | 1,744 |
| Bowie | 0 | 0 | 0 | 0 | 5,133 |
| Boyd | 0 | 0 | 0 | 0 | 1,594 |
| Brady | 0 | 0 | 0 | 0 | 5,147 |
| Brazoria | 0 | 0 | 0 | 0 | 3,066 |
| Breckenridge | 0 | 0 | 0 | 0 | 5,365 |
| Bremond | 0 | 0 | 0 | 0 | 966 |
| Bridge City | 0 | 0 | 0 | 0 | 7,809 |
| Bridgeport | 0 | 0 | 0 | 0 | 6,711 |
| Brookshire | 0 | 0 | 0 | 0 | 6,248 |
| Brownfield | 0 | 0 | 0 | 0 | 9,194 |
| Brownsboro | 0 | 0 | 0 | 0 | 1,321 |
| Brownsville | 0 | 0 | 0 | 0 | 184,287 |
| Bruceville-Eddy | 0 | 0 | 0 | 0 | 1,712 |
| Bryan | 0 | 0 | 0 | 0 | 89,423 |
| Buda | 0 | 0 | 0 | 0 | 19,130 |
| Buffalo | 0 | 0 | 0 | 0 | 1,916 |
| Bullard | 0 | 0 | 0 | 0 | 4,071 |
| Bulverde | 0 | 0 | 0 | 0 | 5,593 |
| Burkburnett | 0 | 0 | 0 | 0 | 11,465 |
| Cactus | 0 | 0 | 0 | 0 | 3,239 |
| Caddo Mills | 0 | 0 | 0 | 0 | 1,749 |
| Calvert | 0 | 0 | 0 | 0 | 1,132 |
| Cameron | 0 | 0 | 0 | 0 | 5,399 |
| Canyon | 0 | 0 | 0 | 0 | 16,726 |
| Castle Hills | 0 | 0 | 0 | 0 | 4,480 |
| Castroville | 0 | 0 | 0 | 0 | 3,243 |
| Cedar Hill | 0 | 0 | 0 | 0 | 47,764 |
| Celina | 0 | 0 | 0 | 0 | 22,521 |
| Chandler | 0 | 0 | 0 | 0 | 3,271 |
| China Grove | 0 | 0 | 0 | 0 | 1,329 |
| Cisco | 0 | 0 | 0 | 0 | 3,848 |
| Clarksville | | 0 | 0 | 0 | 3,025 |
| Cleburne | 0 | 0 | 0 | 0 | 32,248 |
| Clint | 0 | 0 | 0 | 0 | 1,138 |
| Clute | 0 | 0 | 0 | 0 | 11,774 |
| Cockrell Hill | 0 | 0 | 0 | 0 | 4,048 |
| Coffee City | 0 | 0 | 0 | 0 | 301 |
| Coleman | 0 | 0 | 0 | 0 | 4,159 |
| Colleyville | 0 | 0 | 0 | 0 | 27,544 |
| Collinsville | 0 | 0 | 0 | 0 | 2,023 |
| Columbus | 0 | 0 | 0 | 0 | 3,703 |
| Comanche | 0 | 0 | 0 | 0 | 4,209 |
| Combes | 0 | 0 | 0 | 0 | 3,055 |
| Commerce | 0 | 0 | 0 | 0 | 9,878 |
| Converse | 0 | 0 | 0 | 0 | 29,635 |
| Copperas Cove | 0 | 0 | 0 | 0 | 33,613 |
| Corinth | 0 | 0 | 0 | 0 | 22,635 |

## Table 95. Hate Crime Zero Data Submitted Per Quarter, by Federal Agency, State, and State Agency, 2021—Continued

(Number.)

| Agency name | Zero data per quarter[1] | | | | Population[2] |
|---|---|---|---|---|---|
| | 1st quarter | 2nd quarter | 3rd quarter | 4th quarter | |
| Corrigan | 0 | 0 | 0 | 0 | 1,708 |
| Crandall | 0 | 0 | 0 | 0 | 4,418 |
| Crane | 0 | 0 | 0 | 0 | 3,681 |
| Crockett | 0 | 0 | 0 | 0 | 6,295 |
| Cuero | 0 | 0 | 0 | 0 | 8,225 |
| Cuney | 0 | 0 | 0 | 0 | 140 |
| Daingerfield | 0 | 0 | 0 | 0 | 2,377 |
| Dalhart | 0 | 0 | 0 | 0 | 8,279 |
| Dalworthington Gardens | 0 | 0 | 0 | 0 | 2,367 |
| Dawson | 0 | 0 | 0 | 0 | 797 |
| Dayton | 0 | 0 | 0 | 0 | 8,767 |
| Decatur | 0 | 0 | 0 | 0 | 7,747 |
| Deer Park | 0 | 0 | 0 | 0 | 32,998 |
| De Leon | | | 0 | 0 | 2,192 |
| Denison | 0 | 0 | 0 | 0 | 26,119 |
| Denver City | 0 | 0 | 0 | 0 | 4,928 |
| DeSoto | 0 | 0 | 0 | 0 | 52,891 |
| Devine | 0 | 0 | 0 | 0 | 4,998 |
| Diboll | 0 | 0 | 0 | 0 | 5,096 |
| Dickinson | 0 | 0 | 0 | 0 | 21,442 |
| Dimmitt | 0 | 0 | 0 | 0 | 3,966 |
| Donna | 0 | 0 | 0 | 0 | 16,371 |
| Double Oak | 0 | 0 | 0 | 0 | 3,124 |
| Duncanville | 0 | 0 | 0 | 0 | 37,869 |
| Early | 0 | 0 | 0 | 0 | 3,353 |
| Earth | 0 | 0 | 0 | 0 | 940 |
| Eastland | 0 | 0 | 0 | 0 | 3,853 |
| Edgewood | 0 | 0 | 0 | 0 | 1,578 |
| Edinburg | 0 | 0 | 0 | 0 | 104,604 |
| Edna | 0 | 0 | 0 | 0 | 5,787 |
| El Campo | 0 | 0 | 0 | 0 | 11,484 |
| Electra | 0 | 0 | 0 | 0 | 2,732 |
| Elmendorf | 0 | 0 | 0 | 0 | 2,198 |
| Emory | 0 | 0 | 0 | 0 | 1,384 |
| Everman | 0 | 0 | 0 | 0 | 6,136 |
| Fairfield | 0 | 0 | 0 | 0 | 2,867 |
| Fair Oaks Ranch | 0 | 0 | 0 | 0 | 10,798 |
| Fairview | 0 | 0 | 0 | 0 | 9,595 |
| Falfurrias | 0 | 0 | 0 | 0 | 4,695 |
| Farmers Branch | 0 | 0 | 0 | 0 | 54,026 |
| Farmersville | 0 | 0 | 0 | 0 | 3,754 |
| Farwell | 0 | 0 | 0 | 0 | 1,267 |
| Fate | 0 | 0 | 0 | 0 | 18,907 |
| Ferris | 0 | 0 | 0 | 0 | 3,143 |
| Flatonia | 0 | 0 | 0 | 0 | 1,460 |
| Florence | 0 | 0 | 0 | 0 | 1,321 |
| Floresville | 0 | 0 | 0 | 0 | 8,339 |
| Flower Mound | 0 | 0 | 0 | 0 | 83,367 |
| Floydada | 0 | 0 | 0 | 0 | 2,621 |
| Forney | 0 | 0 | 0 | 0 | 31,521 |
| Fort Stockton | 0 | 0 | 0 | 0 | 8,375 |
| Franklin | 0 | 0 | 0 | 0 | 1,646 |
| Frankston | 0 | 0 | 0 | 0 | 1,150 |
| Fredericksburg | 0 | 0 | 0 | 0 | 11,620 |
| Freeport | 0 | 0 | 0 | 0 | 12,132 |
| Freer | 0 | 0 | 0 | 0 | 2,602 |
| Friendswood | 0 | 0 | 0 | 0 | 40,434 |
| Friona | 0 | 0 | 0 | 0 | 3,741 |
| Frisco | 0 | 0 | 0 | 0 | 222,416 |
| Fulshear | 0 | 0 | 0 | 0 | 17,318 |
| Galena Park | 0 | 0 | 0 | 0 | 10,525 |
| Ganado | 0 | 0 | 0 | 0 | 2,094 |
| Garden Ridge | 0 | 0 | 0 | 0 | 4,379 |
| Garrison | 0 | 0 | 0 | 0 | 867 |
| Gatesville | 0 | 0 | 0 | 0 | 12,558 |
| Giddings | 0 | 0 | 0 | 0 | 5,175 |
| Gilmer | 0 | 0 | 0 | 0 | 5,217 |
| Gladewater | 0 | 0 | 0 | 0 | 6,347 |
| Glenn Heights | 0 | 0 | 0 | 0 | 14,610 |
| Godley | 0 | 0 | 0 | 0 | 1,809 |
| Gonzales | 0 | 0 | 0 | 0 | 7,633 |
| Graham | 0 | 0 | 0 | 0 | 8,536 |
| Granbury | 0 | 0 | 0 | 0 | 11,466 |
| Grand Prairie | 0 | 0 | 0 | 0 | 196,334 |
| Grand Saline | 0 | 0 | 0 | 0 | 3,223 |
| Granger | 0 | 0 | 0 | 0 | 1,523 |
| Grapeland | 0 | 0 | 0 | 0 | 1,423 |
| Grapevine | 0 | 0 | 0 | 0 | 56,795 |
| Groesbeck | 0 | 0 | 0 | 0 | 4,162 |
| Groves | 0 | 0 | 0 | 0 | 15,187 |

## Table 95. Hate Crime Zero Data Submitted Per Quarter, by Federal Agency, State, and State Agency, 2021—Continued

(Number.)

| Agency name | Zero data per quarter[1] | | | | Population[2] |
|---|---|---|---|---|---|
| | 1st quarter | 2nd quarter | 3rd quarter | 4th quarter | |
| Gun Barrel City | 0 | 0 | 0 | 0 | 6,377 |
| Hallettsville | 0 | 0 | 0 | 0 | 2,651 |
| Hallsville | 0 | 0 | 0 | 0 | 4,496 |
| Haltom City | 0 | 0 | 0 | 0 | 43,840 |
| Harker Heights | 0 | 0 | 0 | 0 | 33,752 |
| Harlingen | 0 | 0 | 0 | 0 | 65,186 |
| Hawkins | 0 | 0 | 0 | 0 | 1,353 |
| Hearne | 0 | 0 | 0 | 0 | 4,331 |
| Heath | 0 | 0 | 0 | 0 | 9,996 |
| Hedwig Village | 0 | 0 | 0 | 0 | 2,605 |
| Helotes | 0 | 0 | 0 | 0 | 10,627 |
| Hempstead | 0 | 0 | 0 | 0 | 9,214 |
| Hereford | 0 | 0 | 0 | 0 | 14,288 |
| Hewitt | 0 | 0 | 0 | 0 | 15,272 |
| Hickory Creek | 0 | 0 | 0 | 0 | 5,193 |
| Hico | 0 | 0 | 0 | 0 | 1,443 |
| Hidalgo | 0 | 0 | 0 | 0 | 14,488 |
| Highland Park | 0 | 0 | 0 | 0 | 9,032 |
| Hill Country Village | 0 | 0 | 0 | 0 | 1,122 |
| Hitchcock | | 0 | 0 | 0 | 7,983 |
| Hollywood Park | 0 | 0 | 0 | 0 | 3,351 |
| Hondo | 0 | 0 | 0 | 0 | 9,564 |
| Honey Grove | 0 | 0 | 0 | 0 | 1,746 |
| Hooks | 0 | 0 | 0 | 0 | 2,703 |
| Horseshoe Bay | 0 | 0 | 0 | 0 | 4,227 |
| Howe | 0 | 0 | 0 | 0 | 3,482 |
| Hudson Oaks | 0 | 0 | 0 | 0 | 3,857 |
| Hughes Springs | 0 | 0 | 0 | 0 | 1,664 |
| Huntington | 0 | 0 | 0 | 0 | 2,076 |
| Hutchins | 0 | 0 | 0 | 0 | 6,048 |
| Hutto | 0 | 0 | 0 | 0 | 31,792 |
| Idalou | 0 | 0 | 0 | 0 | 2,314 |
| Ingram | 0 | 0 | 0 | 0 | 1,881 |
| Iowa Colony | 0 | 0 | 0 | 0 | 5,771 |
| Iowa Park | 0 | 0 | 0 | 0 | 6,435 |
| Italy | 0 | 0 | 0 | 0 | 1,972 |
| Itasca | 0 | 0 | 0 | 0 | 1,797 |
| Jacinto City | 0 | 0 | 0 | 0 | 10,276 |
| Jacksboro | 0 | 0 | 0 | 0 | 4,443 |
| Jacksonville | 0 | 0 | 0 | 0 | 14,855 |
| Jamaica Beach | 0 | 0 | 0 | 0 | 1,085 |
| Jarrell | 0 | 0 | 0 | 0 | 2,228 |
| Jasper | 0 | 0 | 0 | 0 | 7,600 |
| Jersey Village | 0 | 0 | 0 | 0 | 7,782 |
| Jonestown | 0 | 0 | 0 | 0 | 2,207 |
| Josephine | 0 | 0 | 0 | | 2,673 |
| Joshua | 0 | 0 | 0 | 0 | 8,411 |
| Jourdanton | 0 | 0 | 0 | 0 | 4,495 |
| Junction | 0 | 0 | 0 | 0 | 2,421 |
| Karnes City | 0 | 0 | 0 | 0 | 3,441 |
| Katy | 0 | 0 | 0 | 0 | 25,183 |
| Kaufman | 0 | 0 | 0 | 0 | 8,804 |
| Keene | 0 | 0 | 0 | 0 | 6,637 |
| Keller | 0 | 0 | 0 | 0 | 47,721 |
| Kemah | 0 | 0 | 0 | 0 | 2,076 |
| Kemp | 0 | 0 | 0 | 0 | 1,273 |
| Kempner | 0 | 0 | 0 | 0 | 1,167 |
| Kenedy | 0 | 0 | 0 | 0 | 3,396 |
| Kennedale | 0 | 0 | 0 | 0 | 8,829 |
| Kerens | 0 | 0 | 0 | 0 | 1,515 |
| Kermit | 0 | 0 | 0 | 0 | 6,441 |
| Kerrville | 0 | 0 | 0 | 0 | 23,982 |
| Kilgore | 0 | 0 | 0 | 0 | 15,004 |
| Killeen | 0 | 0 | 0 | 0 | 156,741 |
| Kirby | 0 | 0 | 0 | 0 | 8,792 |
| Knox City | 0 | 0 | 0 | 0 | 1,119 |
| Kountze | 0 | 0 | 0 | 0 | 2,106 |
| Lacy-Lakeview | 0 | 0 | 0 | 0 | 6,836 |
| La Feria | 0 | 0 | 0 | 0 | 7,243 |
| Lago Vista | 0 | 0 | 0 | 0 | 8,158 |
| La Grulla | 0 | 0 | 0 | 0 | 1,688 |
| Laguna Vista | 0 | 0 | 0 | 0 | 3,223 |
| La Joya | 0 | 0 | 0 | 0 | 4,638 |
| Lake Dallas | 0 | 0 | 0 | 0 | 8,230 |
| Lakeport | 0 | 0 | 0 | 0 | 999 |
| Lakeside | 0 | 0 | 0 | 0 | 1,594 |
| Lakeview, Harrison County | 0 | 0 | 0 | 0 | 6,214 |
| Lakeway | 0 | 0 | 0 | 0 | 16,747 |
| Lake Worth | 0 | 0 | 0 | 0 | 4,886 |
| La Marque | 0 | 0 | 0 | 0 | 17,984 |

**Table 95. Hate Crime Zero Data Submitted Per Quarter, by Federal Agency, State, and State Agency, 2021—Continued**

(Number.)

| Agency name | Zero data per quarter[1] | | | | Population[2] |
|---|---|---|---|---|---|
| | 1st quarter | 2nd quarter | 3rd quarter | 4th quarter | |
| Lancaster | 0 | 0 | 0 | 0 | 39,235 |
| Lavon | 0 | 0 | 0 | 0 | 4,235 |
| Leander | 0 | 0 | 0 | 0 | 77,457 |
| Leonard | 0 | 0 | 0 | 0 | 2,077 |
| Levelland | 0 | 0 | 0 | 0 | 13,495 |
| Liberty | 0 | 0 | 0 | 0 | 9,621 |
| Liberty Hill | 0 | 0 | 0 | 0 | 4,076 |
| Lindale | 0 | 0 | 0 | 0 | 6,956 |
| Linden | 0 | 0 | 0 | 0 | 1,880 |
| Little Elm | 0 | 0 | 0 | 0 | 61,181 |
| Littlefield | 0 | 0 | 0 | 0 | 5,696 |
| Llano | 0 | 0 | 0 | 0 | 3,535 |
| Lockhart | 0 | 0 | 0 | 0 | 14,209 |
| Lockney | | | | 0 | 1,600 |
| Log Cabin | 0 | 0 | 0 | 0 | 792 |
| Lone Star | 0 | 0 | 0 | 0 | 1,463 |
| Lorena | 0 | 0 | 0 | 0 | 1,762 |
| Los Fresnos | 0 | 0 | 0 | 0 | 7,908 |
| Luling | 0 | 0 | 0 | 0 | 5,874 |
| Lumberton | 0 | 0 | 0 | 0 | 13,528 |
| Lytle | 0 | 0 | 0 | 0 | 3,122 |
| Madisonville | 0 | 0 | 0 | 0 | 4,819 |
| Magnolia | 0 | 0 | 0 | 0 | 2,331 |
| Manor | 0 | 0 | 0 | 0 | 17,725 |
| Mansfield | 0 | 0 | 0 | 0 | 74,925 |
| Manvel | 0 | 0 | 0 | 0 | 15,262 |
| Marble Falls | 0 | 0 | 0 | 0 | 7,231 |
| Marfa | 0 | 0 | 0 | 0 | 1,555 |
| Marion | 0 | 0 | 0 | 0 | 1,305 |
| Marlin | 0 | 0 | 0 | 0 | 5,510 |
| Marshall | 0 | 0 | 0 | 0 | 22,425 |
| Maud | 0 | 0 | 0 | 0 | 1,062 |
| Maypearl | 0 | 0 | 0 | 0 | 1,060 |
| Meadows Place | 0 | 0 | 0 | 0 | 4,806 |
| Melissa | 0 | 0 | 0 | 0 | 15,322 |
| Memorial Villages | 0 | 0 | 0 | 0 | 12,243 |
| Memphis | 0 | 0 | 0 | 0 | 1,969 |
| Meridian | 0 | 0 | 0 | 0 | 1,501 |
| Merkel | 0 | 0 | 0 | 0 | 2,633 |
| Mexia | 0 | 0 | 0 | 0 | 7,269 |
| Midlothian | 0 | 0 | 0 | 0 | 36,655 |
| Miles | 0 | 0 | 0 | 0 | 898 |
| Mineola | 0 | 0 | 0 | 0 | 4,998 |
| Mineral Wells | 0 | 0 | 0 | 0 | 15,079 |
| Mission | | | | 0 | 85,163 |
| Monahans | 0 | 0 | 0 | 0 | 7,959 |
| Morgans Point Resort | 0 | 0 | 0 | 0 | 4,844 |
| Moulton | 0 | 0 | 0 | 0 | 905 |
| Mount Enterprise | 0 | 0 | 0 | 0 | 432 |
| Mount Pleasant | 0 | 0 | 0 | 0 | 16,023 |
| Mount Vernon | 0 | 0 | 0 | 0 | 2,765 |
| Muleshoe | 0 | 0 | 0 | 0 | 4,788 |
| Murphy | 0 | 0 | 0 | 0 | 21,147 |
| Mustang Ridge | 0 | 0 | 0 | 0 | 1,021 |
| Nacogdoches | 0 | 0 | 0 | 0 | 32,421 |
| Naples | 0 | 0 | | | 1,298 |
| Nash | 0 | 0 | 0 | 0 | 3,882 |
| Nassau Bay | 0 | 0 | 0 | 0 | 3,897 |
| Natalia | 0 | 0 | 0 | 0 | 1,643 |
| Navasota | 0 | 0 | 0 | 0 | 8,514 |
| Nederland | 0 | 0 | 0 | 0 | 17,205 |
| Needville | 0 | 0 | 0 | 0 | 3,150 |
| New Boston | 0 | 0 | 0 | 0 | 4,546 |
| Newton | 0 | 0 | 0 | 0 | 2,315 |
| Nolanville | 0 | 0 | 0 | 0 | 6,335 |
| Northeast | 0 | 0 | 0 | 0 | 3,582 |
| Northlake | 0 | 0 | 0 | 0 | 4,751 |
| Oak Ridge, Kaufman County | 0 | 0 | 0 | 0 | 851 |
| Odem | 0 | 0 | 0 | 0 | 2,375 |
| Olmos Park | 0 | 0 | 0 | 0 | 2,484 |
| Onalaska | 0 | 0 | 0 | 0 | 3,225 |
| Ore City | 0 | 0 | | | 1,266 |
| Overton | 0 | 0 | 0 | 0 | 2,498 |
| Ovilla | 0 | 0 | 0 | 0 | 4,370 |
| Oyster Creek | 0 | 0 | 0 | 0 | 1,222 |
| Palacios | 0 | 0 | 0 | 0 | 4,529 |
| Palmer | 0 | 0 | 0 | 0 | 2,185 |
| Palmhurst | 0 | 0 | 0 | 0 | 2,735 |
| Palmview | 0 | 0 | 0 | 0 | 5,875 |
| Panhandle | 0 | 0 | 0 | 0 | 2,256 |

## Table 95. Hate Crime Zero Data Submitted Per Quarter, by Federal Agency, State, and State Agency, 2021—Continued

(Number.)

| Agency name | Zero data per quarter[1] | | | | Population[2] |
|---|---|---|---|---|---|
| | 1st quarter | 2nd quarter | 3rd quarter | 4th quarter | |
| Pantego | 0 | 0 | 0 | 0 | 2,505 |
| Paris | 0 | 0 | 0 | 0 | 24,833 |
| Parker | 0 | 0 | 0 | 0 | 5,649 |
| Patton Village | 0 | 0 | 0 | 0 | 2,277 |
| Payne Springs | 0 | 0 | 0 | 0 | 757 |
| Pearland | 0 | 0 | 0 | 0 | 126,983 |
| Pearsall | 0 | 0 | 0 | 0 | 10,776 |
| Pecos | 0 | 0 | 0 | 0 | 10,675 |
| Pelican Bay | 0 | 0 | 0 | 0 | 2,165 |
| Penitas | 0 | 0 | 0 | 0 | 4,625 |
| Perryton | 0 | 0 | 0 | 0 | 8,272 |
| Petersburg | 0 | 0 | 0 | 0 | 1,102 |
| Pilot Point | 0 | 0 | 0 | 0 | 4,741 |
| Pinehurst | 0 | 0 | 0 | 0 | 1,946 |
| Pineland | 0 | 0 | 0 | 0 | 789 |
| Pittsburg | 0 | 0 | 0 | 0 | 4,696 |
| Point Comfort | 0 | 0 | 0 | | 645 |
| Ponder | 0 | 0 | 0 | 0 | 2,555 |
| Port Aransas | 0 | 0 | 0 | 0 | 4,513 |
| Port Arthur | 0 | 0 | 0 | 0 | 53,865 |
| Portland | 0 | 0 | 0 | 0 | 17,938 |
| Port Lavaca | 0 | 0 | 0 | 0 | 11,618 |
| Port Neches | 0 | 0 | 0 | 0 | 12,555 |
| Poteet | 0 | 0 | 0 | 0 | 3,571 |
| Prairie View | 0 | 0 | 0 | 0 | 7,174 |
| Primera | 0 | 0 | 0 | 0 | 5,394 |
| Princeton | 0 | 0 | 0 | 0 | 17,059 |
| Prosper | 0 | 0 | 0 | 0 | 29,848 |
| Queen City | 0 | 0 | 0 | 0 | 1,409 |
| Quitman | 0 | 0 | 0 | 0 | 1,866 |
| Rancho Viejo | 0 | 0 | 0 | 0 | 2,447 |
| Ranger | 0 | 0 | 0 | 0 | 2,343 |
| Raymondville | 0 | 0 | 0 | 0 | 10,714 |
| Red Oak | 0 | 0 | 0 | 0 | 14,483 |
| Reno, Lamar County | 0 | 0 | 0 | 0 | 3,366 |
| Rice | 0 | 0 | 0 | 0 | 991 |
| Richardson | 0 | 0 | 0 | 0 | 122,872 |
| Richland | | 0 | | | 274 |
| Richland Hills | 0 | 0 | 0 | 0 | 7,846 |
| Richmond | 0 | 0 | 0 | 0 | 12,520 |
| Rio Grande City | 0 | 0 | 0 | 0 | 14,498 |
| Rio Hondo | 0 | 0 | 0 | 0 | 2,669 |
| River Oaks | 0 | 0 | 0 | 0 | 7,550 |
| Roanoke | 0 | 0 | 0 | 0 | 10,234 |
| Robinson | 0 | 0 | 0 | 0 | 12,254 |
| Robstown | 0 | 0 | 0 | 0 | 11,114 |
| Rockport | 0 | 0 | 0 | 0 | 10,934 |
| Rockwall | 0 | 0 | 0 | 0 | 48,483 |
| Rogers | 0 | 0 | 0 | 0 | 1,255 |
| Rollingwood | 0 | 0 | 0 | 0 | 1,589 |
| Roma | 0 | 0 | 0 | 0 | 11,534 |
| Roman Forest | 0 | 0 | 0 | 0 | 2,086 |
| Roscoe | 0 | 0 | 0 | 0 | 1,302 |
| Rosenberg | 0 | 0 | 0 | 0 | 40,251 |
| Rowlett | 0 | 0 | 0 | 0 | 69,287 |
| Royse City | 0 | 0 | 0 | 0 | 16,013 |
| Runaway Bay | 0 | 0 | 0 | 0 | 1,665 |
| Rusk | 0 | 0 | 0 | 0 | 5,674 |
| Sabinal | 0 | 0 | 0 | 0 | 1,674 |
| Sachse | 0 | 0 | 0 | 0 | 26,463 |
| Saginaw | 0 | 0 | 0 | 0 | 25,387 |
| Salado | 0 | 0 | 0 | 0 | 2,401 |
| San Angelo | 0 | 0 | 0 | 0 | 102,448 |
| San Augustine | 0 | 0 | 0 | 0 | 1,842 |
| San Benito | 0 | 0 | 0 | 0 | 24,065 |
| San Elizario | 0 | 0 | 0 | 0 | 9,041 |
| Sanger | 0 | 0 | 0 | 0 | 9,383 |
| San Juan | 0 | 0 | 0 | 0 | 37,333 |
| San Marcos | 0 | 0 | 0 | 0 | 68,961 |
| San Saba | 0 | 0 | 0 | 0 | 3,135 |
| Sansom Park Village | 0 | 0 | 0 | 0 | 5,826 |
| Santa Anna | 0 | 0 | 0 | 0 | 995 |
| Santa Fe | 0 | 0 | 0 | 0 | 13,583 |
| Savoy | 0 | 0 | 0 | 0 | 867 |
| Schertz | 0 | 0 | 0 | 0 | 43,637 |
| Schulenburg | 0 | 0 | 0 | 0 | 2,944 |
| Seabrook | 0 | 0 | 0 | 0 | 14,102 |
| Sealy | 0 | 0 | 0 | 0 | 6,478 |
| Seguin | 0 | 0 | 0 | 0 | 30,653 |
| Selma | 0 | 0 | 0 | 0 | 14,299 |

## Table 95. Hate Crime Zero Data Submitted Per Quarter, by Federal Agency, State, and State Agency, 2021—Continued

(Number.)

| Agency name | Zero data per quarter[1] | | | | Population[2] |
|---|---|---|---|---|---|
| | 1st quarter | 2nd quarter | 3rd quarter | 4th quarter | |
| Seminole | 0 | 0 | 0 | 0 | 8,115 |
| Seven Points | 0 | 0 | 0 | 0 | 1,571 |
| Seymour | 0 | 0 | 0 | 0 | 2,541 |
| Shallowater | 0 | 0 | 0 | 0 | 2,628 |
| Shavano Park | 0 | 0 | 0 | 0 | 4,137 |
| Shenandoah | 0 | 0 | 0 | 0 | 3,217 |
| Silsbee | 0 | 0 | 0 | 0 | 6,604 |
| Sinton | 0 | 0 | 0 | 0 | 5,248 |
| Slaton | 0 | 0 | 0 | 0 | 5,960 |
| Smithville | 0 | 0 | 0 | 0 | 4,759 |
| Snyder | 0 | 0 | 0 | 0 | 10,986 |
| Somerset | 0 | 0 | 0 | 0 | 2,017 |
| Somerville | 0 | 0 | 0 | 0 | 1,450 |
| Sonora | 0 | 0 | 0 | 0 | 2,744 |
| Sour Lake | 0 | 0 | 0 | 0 | 1,962 |
| South Houston | 0 | 0 | 0 | 0 | 17,490 |
| South Padre Island | 0 | 0 | 0 | 0 | 2,744 |
| Southside Place | 0 | 0 | 0 | 0 | 1,902 |
| Spearman | 0 | 0 | 0 | | 3,161 |
| Splendora | 0 | 0 | 0 | 0 | 2,371 |
| Spring Valley | 0 | 0 | 0 | 0 | 4,363 |
| Stafford | 0 | 0 | 0 | 0 | 17,102 |
| Stamford | 0 | 0 | 0 | 0 | 2,892 |
| Stinnett | 0 | 0 | 0 | 0 | 1,742 |
| Sudan | 0 | 0 | 0 | 0 | 871 |
| Sulphur Springs | 0 | 0 | 0 | 0 | 16,357 |
| Sunnyvale | 0 | 0 | 0 | 0 | 7,232 |
| Sunray | | | | 0 | 1,771 |
| Sunrise Beach Village | 0 | 0 | 0 | 0 | 820 |
| Sunset Valley | 0 | 0 | 0 | 0 | 663 |
| Surfside Beach | 0 | 0 | 0 | 0 | 601 |
| Sweeny | 0 | 0 | 0 | 0 | 3,612 |
| Taft | 0 | 0 | 0 | 0 | 2,871 |
| Tahoka | 0 | 0 | 0 | 0 | 2,664 |
| Tatum | 0 | 0 | 0 | 0 | 1,417 |
| Teague | 0 | 0 | 0 | 0 | 3,524 |
| Tenaha | 0 | 0 | 0 | 0 | 1,132 |
| Terrell | 0 | 0 | 0 | 0 | 20,092 |
| Terrell Hills | 0 | 0 | 0 | 0 | 5,510 |
| Texarkana | 0 | 0 | 0 | 0 | 36,208 |
| Texas City | 0 | 0 | 0 | 0 | 52,270 |
| Thorndale | 0 | 0 | 0 | 0 | 1,303 |
| Tioga | 0 | 0 | 0 | 0 | 1,153 |
| Todd Mission | 0 | 0 | 0 | 0 | 113 |
| Tomball | 0 | 0 | 0 | 0 | 11,826 |
| Tom Bean | 0 | 0 | 0 | 0 | 1,076 |
| Tool | 0 | 0 | 0 | 0 | 2,346 |
| Tulia | 0 | 0 | 0 | 0 | 4,568 |
| Tye | 0 | 0 | 0 | 0 | 1,353 |
| Universal City | 0 | 0 | 0 | 0 | 21,265 |
| University Park | 0 | 0 | 0 | 0 | 24,888 |
| Valley Mills | 0 | 0 | 0 | 0 | 1,168 |
| Van | 0 | 0 | 0 | 0 | 2,793 |
| Venus | 0 | 0 | 0 | 0 | 4,804 |
| Waco | 0 | 0 | 0 | 0 | 143,089 |
| Waelder | 0 | 0 | 0 | 0 | 1,164 |
| Wake Village | 0 | 0 | 0 | 0 | 5,538 |
| Waller | 0 | 0 | 0 | 0 | 3,732 |
| Wallis | 0 | 0 | 0 | 0 | 1,334 |
| Weatherford | 0 | 0 | 0 | 0 | 35,724 |
| Weimar | 0 | 0 | 0 | 0 | 2,238 |
| West | 0 | 0 | 0 | 0 | 2,991 |
| West Columbia | 0 | 0 | 0 | 0 | 3,823 |
| West Lake Hills | 0 | 0 | 0 | 0 | 3,272 |
| West Orange | 0 | 0 | 0 | 0 | 3,141 |
| Westover Hills | 0 | 0 | 0 | 0 | 683 |
| West University Place | | 0 | 0 | 0 | 15,590 |
| Westworth | 0 | 0 | 0 | 0 | 2,810 |
| Wharton | 0 | 0 | 0 | 0 | 8,590 |
| Whitehouse | 0 | 0 | 0 | 0 | 9,260 |
| White Oak | 0 | 0 | 0 | 0 | 6,262 |
| Whitewright | 0 | 0 | 0 | 0 | 1,746 |
| Whitney | 0 | 0 | 0 | 0 | 2,151 |
| Wichita Falls | 0 | 0 | 0 | 0 | 105,468 |
| Willis | 0 | 0 | 0 | 0 | 7,258 |
| Willow Park | 0 | 0 | 0 | 0 | 6,244 |
| Wills Point | 0 | 0 | 0 | 0 | 3,723 |
| Wilmer | 0 | 0 | 0 | 0 | 5,620 |
| Windcrest | 0 | 0 | 0 | 0 | 5,901 |
| Wink | 0 | 0 | 0 | 0 | 1,022 |

## Table 95. Hate Crime Zero Data Submitted Per Quarter, by Federal Agency, State, and State Agency, 2021—Continued

(Number.)

| Agency name | Zero data per quarter[1] | | | | Population[2] |
|---|---|---|---|---|---|
| | 1st quarter | 2nd quarter | 3rd quarter | 4th quarter | |
| Winnsboro | 0 | 0 | 0 | 0 | 3,338 |
| Winters | 0 | 0 | 0 | 0 | 2,460 |
| Wolfforth | 0 | 0 | 0 | 0 | 5,973 |
| Woodsboro | 0 | 0 | 0 | 0 | 1,363 |
| Woodville | 0 | 0 | 0 | 0 | 2,428 |
| Woodway | 0 | 0 | 0 | 0 | 9,141 |
| Wortham | 0 | 0 | 0 | 0 | 1,000 |
| Wylie | 0 | 0 | 0 | 0 | 55,889 |
| Yoakum | 0 | 0 | 0 | 0 | 5,949 |
| Zavalla | 0 | 0 | 0 | 0 | 712 |
| **Universities and Colleges** | | | | | |
| Alvin Community College | 0 | 0 | 0 | 0 | 8,414 |
| Amarillo College | 0 | 0 | 0 | 0 | 12,389 |
| Austin College | 0 | 0 | 0 | 0 | 1,326 |
| Austin Community College District | 0 | 0 | 0 | 0 | 63,569 |
| Baylor Health Care System[3] | 0 | 0 | 0 | 0 | |
| Brazosport College | 0 | 0 | 0 | 0 | 5,805 |
| Cisco College | 0 | 0 | 0 | 0 | 4,876 |
| Concordia University | 0 | 0 | 0 | 0 | 3,338 |
| Dallas County Community College District | 0 | 0 | 0 | 0 | 125,613 |
| El Paso Community College | 0 | 0 | 0 | 0 | 37,636 |
| Hardin-Simmons University | 0 | 0 | 0 | 0 | 2,487 |
| Houston Community College | 0 | 0 | 0 | 0 | 81,256 |
| Kilgore College | 0 | 0 | 0 | 0 | 7,250 |
| Lamar University, Beaumont | 0 | 0 | 0 | 0 | 21,621 |
| Lone Star College System District | 0 | 0 | 0 | 0 | 102,989 |
| Lubbock Christian University | 0 | 0 | 0 | 0 | 2,040 |
| McLennan Community College | 0 | 0 | 0 | 0 | 13,631 |
| Midwestern State University | 0 | 0 | 0 | 0 | 6,947 |
| Odessa College | 0 | 0 | 0 | 0 | 10,162 |
| Panola College | 0 | 0 | 0 | 0 | 3,364 |
| Paris Junior College | 0 | 0 | 0 | 0 | 6,822 |
| Prairie View A&M University | 0 | 0 | 0 | 0 | 10,184 |
| Sam Houston State University | 0 | 0 | 0 | 0 | 24,116 |
| San Jacinto College, Central Campus | 0 | 0 | 0 | 0 | 42,923 |
| Southern Methodist University | 0 | 0 | 0 | 0 | 12,963 |
| South Plains College | 0 | 0 | 0 | 0 | 12,258 |
| Southwestern Christian College | 0 | 0 | 0 | 0 | 117 |
| Southwestern University | 0 | 0 | 0 | 0 | 1,562 |
| Stephen F. Austin State University | 0 | 0 | 0 | 0 | 14,759 |
| St. Mary's University | 0 | 0 | 0 | 0 | 3,757 |
| St. Thomas University | 0 | 0 | 0 | 0 | 3,938 |
| Sul Ross State University | 0 | 0 | 0 | 0 | 2,949 |
| Texas A&M International University | 0 | 0 | 0 | 0 | 9,861 |
| Texas A&M University | | | | | |
| College Station | 0 | 0 | 0 | 0 | 73,308 |
| San Antonio | 0 | 0 | 0 | 0 | 7,724 |
| Texas Christian University | 0 | 0 | 0 | 0 | 11,506 |
| Texas State Technical College | | | | | |
| Harlingen[3] | 0 | 0 | 0 | 0 | |
| Waco | 0 | 0 | 0 | 0 | 13,892 |
| West Texas[3] | 0 | 0 | 0 | 0 | |
| Texas Tech University, Lubbock | 0 | 0 | 0 | 0 | 41,909 |
| Texas Woman's University | 0 | 0 | 0 | 0 | 19,733 |
| Trinity Valley Community College | 0 | 0 | 0 | 0 | 8,188 |
| University of Houston | | | | | |
| Clearlake | 0 | 0 | 0 | 0 | 11,134 |
| Downtown Campus | 0 | 0 | 0 | 0 | 18,096 |
| University of North Texas, Denton | 0 | 0 | 0 | 0 | 45,298 |
| University of Texas | | | | | |
| Arlington | 0 | 0 | 0 | 0 | 61,457 |
| Dallas | 0 | 0 | 0 | 0 | 32,043 |
| El Paso | 0 | 0 | 0 | 0 | 29,556 |
| Health Science Center, San Antonio | 0 | 0 | 0 | 0 | 4,043 |
| Health Science Center, Tyler | 0 | 0 | 0 | 0 | 136 |
| Medical Branch | 0 | 0 | 0 | 0 | 3,889 |
| Permian Basin | 0 | 0 | 0 | 0 | 8,667 |
| Rio Grande Valley | 0 | 0 | 0 | 0 | 41,681 |
| San Antonio | 0 | 0 | 0 | 0 | 36,089 |
| Southwestern Medical School | 0 | 0 | 0 | 0 | 2,535 |
| Tyler | 0 | 0 | 0 | 0 | 11,525 |
| West Texas A&M University | 0 | 0 | 0 | 0 | 11,678 |
| **Metropolitan Counties** | | | | | |
| Armstrong | 0 | 0 | 0 | 0 | |
| Atascosa | 0 | 0 | 0 | 0 | |
| Austin | 0 | 0 | 0 | 0 | |
| Bandera | 0 | 0 | 0 | 0 | |
| Bastrop | 0 | 0 | 0 | 0 | |

## Table 95. Hate Crime Zero Data Submitted Per Quarter, by Federal Agency, State, and State Agency, 2021—Continued

(Number.)

| Agency name | Zero data per quarter[1] | | | | Population[2] |
|---|---|---|---|---|---|
| | 1st quarter | 2nd quarter | 3rd quarter | 4th quarter | |
| Bell | 0 | 0 | 0 | 0 | |
| Bowie | 0 | 0 | 0 | 0 | |
| Brazos | 0 | 0 | 0 | 0 | |
| Burleson | 0 | 0 | 0 | 0 | |
| Caldwell | 0 | 0 | | | |
| Callahan | | | 0 | 0 | |
| Carson | | | 0 | 0 | |
| Clay | 0 | 0 | 0 | 0 | |
| Collin | 0 | 0 | 0 | 0 | |
| Comal | 0 | 0 | 0 | 0 | |
| Coryell | 0 | 0 | 0 | 0 | |
| Crosby | 0 | 0 | 0 | 0 | |
| Dallas | 0 | 0 | 0 | 0 | |
| Ector | 0 | 0 | 0 | 0 | |
| Fort Bend | 0 | 0 | 0 | 0 | |
| Goliad | 0 | 0 | 0 | 0 | |
| Grayson | 0 | 0 | 0 | 0 | |
| Hardin | 0 | 0 | 0 | 0 | |
| Harrison | 0 | 0 | 0 | 0 | |
| Hidalgo | 0 | 0 | 0 | 0 | |
| Hudspeth | 0 | 0 | 0 | 0 | |
| Hunt | 0 | 0 | 0 | 0 | |
| Irion | 0 | 0 | 0 | 0 | |
| Jefferson | 0 | 0 | 0 | 0 | |
| Kaufman | 0 | 0 | 0 | 0 | |
| Lampasas | 0 | 0 | 0 | 0 | |
| Liberty | 0 | 0 | 0 | | |
| Lynn | 0 | 0 | 0 | 0 | |
| Martin | 0 | 0 | 0 | 0 | |
| Medina | 0 | 0 | 0 | 0 | |
| Midland | 0 | 0 | 0 | 0 | |
| Montgomery | 0 | 0 | 0 | 0 | |
| Nueces | 0 | 0 | 0 | 0 | |
| Oldham | 0 | 0 | 0 | 0 | |
| Orange | 0 | 0 | 0 | 0 | |
| Parker | 0 | 0 | 0 | 0 | |
| Robertson | 0 | 0 | 0 | 0 | |
| Rockwall | 0 | 0 | 0 | 0 | |
| Rusk | 0 | 0 | 0 | 0 | |
| Smith | 0 | 0 | 0 | 0 | |
| Sterling | 0 | 0 | 0 | 0 | |
| Taylor | 0 | 0 | 0 | 0 | |
| Victoria | 0 | 0 | 0 | 0 | |
| Wichita | 0 | 0 | 0 | 0 | |
| Wilson | 0 | 0 | 0 | 0 | |
| Wise | 0 | 0 | 0 | 0 | |
| **Nonmetropolitan Counties** | | | | | |
| Angelina | | | | 0 | |
| Bailey | 0 | 0 | 0 | 0 | |
| Baylor | 0 | 0 | 0 | 0 | |
| Bee | 0 | 0 | 0 | 0 | |
| Blanco | 0 | 0 | 0 | 0 | |
| Borden | 0 | 0 | 0 | 0 | |
| Bosque | 0 | 0 | 0 | 0 | |
| Brewster | 0 | 0 | 0 | 0 | |
| Briscoe | 0 | 0 | 0 | 0 | |
| Brooks | 0 | 0 | 0 | 0 | |
| Burnet | 0 | 0 | 0 | 0 | |
| Calhoun | 0 | 0 | 0 | 0 | |
| Camp | 0 | 0 | 0 | 0 | |
| Cass | 0 | 0 | 0 | 0 | |
| Castro | 0 | 0 | 0 | 0 | |
| Cherokee | 0 | 0 | 0 | 0 | |
| Childress | 0 | 0 | 0 | 0 | |
| Cochran | 0 | 0 | 0 | 0 | |
| Coke | 0 | 0 | 0 | 0 | |
| Collingsworth | 0 | 0 | 0 | 0 | |
| Comanche | 0 | 0 | 0 | 0 | |
| Concho | 0 | 0 | 0 | 0 | |
| Cooke | 0 | 0 | 0 | 0 | |
| Crane | 0 | 0 | 0 | 0 | |
| Crockett | 0 | 0 | 0 | 0 | |
| Dallam | 0 | 0 | 0 | 0 | |
| Dawson | 0 | 0 | 0 | 0 | |
| Deaf Smith | 0 | 0 | 0 | 0 | |
| Delta | 0 | 0 | 0 | 0 | |
| DeWitt | 0 | 0 | 0 | 0 | |
| Duval | 0 | 0 | 0 | 0 | |
| Eastland | 0 | 0 | 0 | 0 | |

**Table 95. Hate Crime Zero Data Submitted Per Quarter, by Federal Agency, State, and State Agency, 2021—Continued**

(Number.)

| Agency name | Zero data per quarter[1] | | | | Population[2] |
|---|---|---|---|---|---|
| | 1st quarter | 2nd quarter | 3rd quarter | 4th quarter | |
| Edwards | 0 | 0 | 0 | 0 | |
| Erath | 0 | 0 | 0 | 0 | |
| Fannin | 0 | 0 | 0 | 0 | |
| Fayette | 0 | 0 | 0 | 0 | |
| Floyd | 0 | 0 | 0 | 0 | |
| Foard | 0 | 0 | 0 | 0 | |
| Franklin | 0 | 0 | 0 | 0 | |
| Freestone | 0 | 0 | 0 | 0 | |
| Gaines | 0 | 0 | 0 | 0 | |
| Garza | 0 | 0 | 0 | 0 | |
| Gillespie | 0 | 0 | 0 | 0 | |
| Glasscock | 0 | 0 | 0 | 0 | |
| Gonzales | 0 | 0 | 0 | 0 | |
| Gray | 0 | 0 | 0 | 0 | |
| Grimes | 0 | 0 | 0 | 0 | |
| Hall | 0 | 0 | 0 | 0 | |
| Hamilton | 0 | 0 | 0 | 0 | |
| Hansford | 0 | 0 | 0 | 0 | |
| Hardeman | 0 | 0 | 0 | 0 | |
| Hartley | 0 | 0 | 0 | 0 | |
| Haskell | 0 | 0 | 0 | 0 | |
| Henderson | | | 0 | 0 | |
| Hockley | 0 | 0 | 0 | 0 | |
| Hopkins | 0 | 0 | 0 | 0 | |
| Howard | 0 | 0 | 0 | 0 | |
| Hutchinson | 0 | 0 | 0 | 0 | |
| Jack | 0 | 0 | 0 | 0 | |
| Jackson | 0 | 0 | 0 | 0 | |
| Jeff Davis | 0 | 0 | 0 | 0 | |
| Jim Hogg | 0 | 0 | 0 | 0 | |
| Karnes | 0 | 0 | 0 | 0 | |
| Kenedy | 0 | 0 | 0 | 0 | |
| Kimble | 0 | 0 | 0 | 0 | |
| King | 0 | 0 | 0 | 0 | |
| Lamar | 0 | 0 | 0 | 0 | |
| Lamb | 0 | 0 | 0 | 0 | |
| La Salle | 0 | 0 | 0 | 0 | |
| Lavaca | 0 | 0 | 0 | 0 | |
| Lee | 0 | 0 | 0 | 0 | |
| Limestone | 0 | 0 | 0 | 0 | |
| Lipscomb | 0 | 0 | 0 | 0 | |
| Llano | 0 | 0 | 0 | 0 | |
| Loving | 0 | 0 | 0 | 0 | |
| Madison | 0 | 0 | 0 | 0 | |
| Marion | 0 | 0 | 0 | 0 | |
| Matagorda | 0 | 0 | 0 | 0 | |
| McCulloch | 0 | 0 | 0 | 0 | |
| Milam | 0 | 0 | 0 | 0 | |
| Mills | 0 | 0 | 0 | 0 | |
| Montague | 0 | 0 | 0 | 0 | |
| Moore | 0 | 0 | 0 | 0 | |
| Motley | 0 | 0 | 0 | 0 | |
| Navarro | 0 | 0 | 0 | 0 | |
| Newton | 0 | 0 | 0 | 0 | |
| Nolan | 0 | 0 | 0 | 0 | |
| Ochiltree | 0 | 0 | 0 | 0 | |
| Palo Pinto | 0 | 0 | 0 | 0 | |
| Panola | 0 | 0 | 0 | 0 | |
| Parmer | 0 | 0 | 0 | 0 | |
| Polk | 0 | 0 | 0 | 0 | |
| Presidio | 0 | 0 | 0 | 0 | |
| Rains | 0 | | | | |
| Reagan | 0 | 0 | 0 | 0 | |
| Real | 0 | 0 | 0 | 0 | |
| Red River | 0 | 0 | 0 | 0 | |
| Refugio | 0 | 0 | 0 | 0 | |
| Roberts | 0 | 0 | 0 | 0 | |
| Runnels | 0 | 0 | 0 | 0 | |
| Sabine | 0 | 0 | 0 | 0 | |
| San Augustine | 0 | 0 | 0 | 0 | |
| Schleicher | 0 | 0 | 0 | 0 | |
| Scurry | 0 | 0 | 0 | 0 | |
| Shackelford | 0 | 0 | 0 | 0 | |
| Shelby | 0 | 0 | 0 | 0 | |
| Somervell | 0 | 0 | 0 | 0 | |
| Starr | 0 | 0 | 0 | 0 | |
| Stephens | 0 | 0 | 0 | 0 | |
| Sutton | 0 | 0 | 0 | 0 | |
| Swisher | 0 | 0 | 0 | 0 | |
| Terrell | 0 | 0 | 0 | 0 | |

## Table 95. Hate Crime Zero Data Submitted Per Quarter, by Federal Agency, State, and State Agency, 2021—Continued

(Number.)

| Agency name | Zero data per quarter[1] | | | | Population[2] |
|---|---|---|---|---|---|
| | 1st quarter | 2nd quarter | 3rd quarter | 4th quarter | |
| Terry | 0 | 0 | 0 | 0 | |
| Throckmorton | 0 | 0 | 0 | 0 | |
| Titus | 0 | 0 | 0 | 0 | |
| Trinity | 0 | 0 | 0 | 0 | |
| Tyler | 0 | 0 | 0 | 0 | |
| Upton | 0 | 0 | 0 | 0 | |
| Uvalde | 0 | 0 | 0 | 0 | |
| Val Verde | 0 | 0 | 0 | 0 | |
| Van Zandt | 0 | 0 | 0 | | |
| Walker | 0 | 0 | 0 | 0 | |
| Ward | 0 | 0 | 0 | 0 | |
| Washington | 0 | 0 | 0 | 0 | |
| Wharton | 0 | 0 | 0 | 0 | |
| Wheeler | 0 | 0 | 0 | 0 | |
| Wilbarger | 0 | 0 | 0 | 0 | |
| Willacy | 0 | 0 | 0 | 0 | |
| Winkler | 0 | 0 | 0 | 0 | |
| Wood | 0 | 0 | 0 | 0 | |
| Yoakum | 0 | 0 | 0 | 0 | |
| Young | 0 | 0 | 0 | 0 | |
| Zapata | 0 | 0 | 0 | 0 | |
| **Tribal Agencies** | | | | | |
| Ysleta del Sur Pueblo Tribal | 0 | 0 | 0 | 0 | |
| **Other Agencies** | | | | | |
| Amarillo International Airport | 0 | 0 | 0 | 0 | |
| Dallas-Fort Worth International Airport | 0 | 0 | 0 | 0 | |
| Denton County Water District | 0 | 0 | 0 | 0 | |
| Ector County Hospital District | | | 0 | 0 | |
| Hidalgo County Constable, Precinct [1] | 0 | 0 | 0 | 0 | |
| Hospital District, Tarrant County | 0 | 0 | 0 | 0 | |
| Independent School District | | | | | |
| Aldine | 0 | | 0 | 0 | 0 |
| Alief | | 0 | 0 | 0 | |
| Alvin | 0 | 0 | 0 | 0 | |
| Angleton | 0 | 0 | 0 | 0 | |
| Aubrey | 0 | 0 | 0 | 0 | |
| Barbers Hill | 0 | 0 | 0 | 0 | |
| Bastrop | 0 | 0 | 0 | 0 | |
| Bay City | 0 | 0 | 0 | 0 | |
| Brazosport | 0 | 0 | 0 | 0 | |
| Brownsboro | 0 | 0 | 0 | 0 | |
| Calhoun County | 0 | 0 | 0 | 0 | |
| Centerpoint | 0 | 0 | 0 | 0 | |
| Columbia-Brazoria | 0 | 0 | 0 | 0 | |
| Conroe | 0 | 0 | 0 | 0 | |
| Corsicana | 0 | 0 | 0 | 0 | |
| Crowley | 0 | 0 | 0 | 0 | |
| Duncanville | 0 | 0 | 0 | | |
| Ector County | 0 | 0 | 0 | 0 | |
| Edinburg | 0 | 0 | 0 | 0 | |
| El Paso | 0 | 0 | 0 | 0 | |
| Floresville | 0 | 0 | 0 | 0 | |
| Gonzales | 0 | 0 | 0 | 0 | |
| Hallsville | 0 | 0 | 0 | 0 | |
| Hutto | 0 | 0 | 0 | 0 | |
| Idalou | 0 | 0 | 0 | 0 | |
| Jonesboro | 0 | 0 | 0 | 0 | |
| Judson | 0 | 0 | 0 | 0 | |
| Killeen | 0 | 0 | 0 | 0 | |
| Klein | 0 | 0 | 0 | 0 | |
| Lamar Consolidated | | 0 | 0 | 0 | |
| Lancaster | 0 | 0 | 0 | 0 | |
| Laredo | 0 | 0 | 0 | 0 | |
| Lufkin | 0 | 0 | 0 | 0 | |
| Lyford | 0 | 0 | 0 | 0 | |
| Mansfield | 0 | 0 | 0 | 0 | |
| Marlin | 0 | 0 | 0 | 0 | |
| McAllen | 0 | 0 | 0 | 0 | |
| Midland | 0 | 0 | 0 | 0 | |
| Montgomery County | 0 | 0 | 0 | 0 | |
| Northside | 0 | 0 | 0 | 0 | |
| Pasadena | 0 | 0 | 0 | 0 | |
| Pecos Barstow Toyah | 0 | 0 | 0 | 0 | |
| Pflugerville | 0 | 0 | 0 | 0 | |
| Pleasanton | 0 | 0 | 0 | 0 | |
| Rio Grande City | 0 | 0 | 0 | 0 | |
| Roma | 0 | 0 | 0 | 0 | |
| Round Rock | | 0 | 0 | 0 | |

## Table 95. Hate Crime Zero Data Submitted Per Quarter, by Federal Agency, State, and State Agency, 2021—Continued

(Number.)

| Agency name | Zero data per quarter[1] | | | | Population[2] |
|---|---|---|---|---|---|
| | 1st quarter | 2nd quarter | 3rd quarter | 4th quarter | |
| Royal | | | 0 | 0 | |
| San Antonio | 0 | 0 | 0 | 0 | |
| Santa Fe | 0 | 0 | 0 | 0 | |
| Sealy | 0 | 0 | 0 | 0 | |
| Socorro | 0 | 0 | 0 | 0 | |
| Spring | 0 | 0 | 0 | 0 | |
| Spring Branch | 0 | 0 | 0 | 0 | |
| Taft | 0 | 0 | 0 | 0 | |
| Terrell | 0 | 0 | 0 | 0 | |
| Trinity | 0 | 0 | 0 | 0 | |
| United | 0 | 0 | 0 | 0 | |
| Van Vleck | 0 | 0 | 0 | 0 | |
| Vensus | 0 | 0 | 0 | 0 | |
| Warren | 0 | 0 | 0 | 0 | |
| Wharton | 0 | 0 | 0 | 0 | |
| Whitesboro | 0 | 0 | 0 | 0 | |
| Independent School System | | | | | |
| Huntington | | 0 | 0 | 0 | |
| Nacogdoches | | 0 | 0 | 0 | |
| Kaufman County Constable, Precinct [2] | 0 | 0 | 0 | 0 | |
| Port of Brownsville | 0 | 0 | 0 | 0 | |
| Port of Houston Authority | 0 | 0 | 0 | 0 | |
| Sabine County Constable, Precinct [2] | 0 | 0 | 0 | 0 | |
| University Medical Center | | | 0 | 0 | |
| **UTAH** | | | | | |
| **Cities** | | | | | |
| Alta | | 0 | 0 | 0 | 376 |
| Aurora | 0 | 0 | 0 | 0 | 1,065 |
| Bluffdale | 0 | 0 | 0 | 0 | 19,428 |
| Brian Head | 0 | 0 | 0 | 0 | 96 |
| Brigham City | 0 | 0 | 0 | 0 | 19,901 |
| Clearfield | 0 | 0 | 0 | 0 | 32,375 |
| Clinton | 0 | 0 | 0 | 0 | 22,957 |
| Cottonwood Heights | 0 | 0 | 0 | 0 | 33,301 |
| Draper | 0 | 0 | 0 | 0 | 49,671 |
| Ephraim | 0 | 0 | 0 | 0 | 7,521 |
| Fairview | 0 | 0 | 0 | 0 | 1,395 |
| Grantsville | 0 | 0 | 0 | 0 | 12,819 |
| Harrisville | 0 | 0 | 0 | 0 | 6,983 |
| Heber | 0 | 0 | 0 | 0 | 18,336 |
| Helper | 0 | 0 | 0 | 0 | 2,135 |
| Hurricane | 0 | 0 | 0 | 0 | 20,594 |
| Kanab | 0 | 0 | 0 | 0 | 5,045 |
| La Verkin | 0 | 0 | 0 | 0 | 4,503 |
| Lindon | 0 | 0 | 0 | 0 | 11,609 |
| Mapleton | 0 | 0 | 0 | 0 | 11,497 |
| Mount Pleasant | 0 | 0 | 0 | 0 | 3,613 |
| Naples | 0 | 0 | 0 | 0 | 2,150 |
| Nephi | 0 | 0 | 0 | 0 | 6,598 |
| North Salt Lake | 0 | 0 | 0 | 0 | 21,768 |
| Ogden | 0 | 0 | 0 | 0 | 87,828 |
| Park City | 0 | 0 | 0 | 0 | 8,679 |
| Parowan | 0 | 0 | | | 3,268 |
| Payson | 0 | 0 | 0 | 0 | 21,291 |
| Perry | 0 | 0 | 0 | 0 | 5,471 |
| Pleasant Grove | 0 | 0 | 0 | 0 | 38,730 |
| Pleasant View | 0 | 0 | 0 | 0 | 11,139 |
| Price | 0 | 0 | | | 8,399 |
| Provo | 0 | 0 | 0 | 0 | 116,642 |
| Richfield | 0 | 0 | 0 | 0 | 7,947 |
| Riverdale | 0 | 0 | 0 | 0 | 9,038 |
| Riverton | 0 | 0 | 0 | 0 | 44,951 |
| Roosevelt | 0 | 0 | 0 | 0 | 7,377 |
| Roy | 0 | 0 | 0 | 0 | 39,765 |
| Salem | 0 | 0 | 0 | 0 | 9,151 |
| Salina | 0 | 0 | 0 | 0 | 2,661 |
| Sandy | 0 | | | | 95,353 |
| Santa Clara/Ivins | 0 | 0 | 0 | 0 | 18,948 |
| Santaquin/Genola | 0 | 0 | 0 | 0 | 15,647 |
| Saratoga Springs | 0 | 0 | 0 | 0 | 37,985 |
| Smithfield | 0 | 0 | 0 | 0 | 12,391 |
| South Jordan | 0 | 0 | 0 | 0 | 81,919 |
| South Ogden | 0 | 0 | 0 | 0 | 17,187 |
| Spanish Fork | 0 | 0 | 0 | 0 | 41,931 |
| Spring City | 0 | 0 | 0 | | 1,111 |
| Springdale | 0 | 0 | 0 | 0 | 672 |
| Vernal | 0 | 0 | 0 | | 10,623 |
| Washington | 0 | 0 | 0 | 0 | 33,668 |
| West Bountiful | 0 | 0 | 0 | 0 | 5,988 |

# Table 95. Hate Crime Zero Data Submitted Per Quarter, by Federal Agency, State, and State Agency, 2021—Continued

(Number.)

| Agency name | Zero data per quarter[1] | | | | Population[2] |
|---|---|---|---|---|---|
| | 1st quarter | 2nd quarter | 3rd quarter | 4th quarter | |
| West Jordan | 0 | 0 | 0 | 0 | 117,862 |
| Willard | 0 | 0 | 0 | 0 | 2,022 |
| Woods Cross | 0 | 0 | 0 | 0 | 11,870 |
| **Universities and Colleges** | | | | | |
| Dixie State University | 0 | 0 | 0 | 0 | 13,446 |
| Snow College | 0 | 0 | 0 | 0 | 5,909 |
| University of Utah | 0 | 0 | | 0 | 38,335 |
| Utah State University | | | | | |
|   Eastern[3] | 0 | 0 | 0 | | |
|   Logan | 0 | 0 | 0 | 0 | 33,055 |
| Utah Valley University | 0 | 0 | 0 | 0 | 45,299 |
| Weber State University | 0 | 0 | 0 | 0 | 36,761 |
| **Metropolitan Counties** | | | | | |
| Box Elder | 0 | 0 | 0 | 0 | |
| Davis | 0 | 0 | 0 | 0 | |
| Juab | 0 | 0 | 0 | | |
| Morgan | 0 | 0 | 0 | | |
| Utah | 0 | 0 | 0 | 0 | |
| **Nonmetropolitan Counties** | | | | | |
| Beaver | 0 | 0 | 0 | 0 | |
| Daggett | 0 | 0 | 0 | 0 | |
| Garfield | 0 | 0 | 0 | 0 | |
| Kane | 0 | 0 | 0 | 0 | |
| Millard | 0 | 0 | 0 | 0 | |
| Sanpete | 0 | 0 | 0 | 0 | |
| Sevier | 0 | 0 | 0 | 0 | |
| Summit | 0 | 0 | 0 | 0 | |
| Uintah | 0 | 0 | 0 | 0 | |
| Wasatch | 0 | 0 | 0 | 0 | |
| **State Police Agencies** | | | | | |
| Utah Highway Patrol | 0 | 0 | 0 | 0 | |
| **Tribal Agencies** | | | | | |
| Goshute Tribal | 0 | 0 | 0 | 0 | |
| **Other Agencies** | | | | | |
| Cache-Rich Drug Task Force | 0 | 0 | 0 | 0 | |
| Davis Metropolitan Narcotics Strike Force | 0 | 0 | 0 | 0 | |
| Iron, Garfield, Beaver Task Force | | 0 | 0 | 0 | |
| Parks and Recreation | | 0 | 0 | 0 | |
| Utah County Attorney, Investigations Division | 0 | 0 | 0 | 0 | |
| Utah County Major Crimes Task Force | 0 | 0 | 0 | 0 | |
| Utah Tax Commission Motor Vehicle Division, Vehicle Investigation Section | 0 | 0 | 0 | 0 | |
| Weber Morgan Narcotics Strike Force | 0 | 0 | 0 | 0 | |
| Wildlife Resources | 0 | 0 | 0 | 0 | |
| **VERMONT** | | | | | |
| **Cities** | | | | | |
| Barre | 0 | 0 | 0 | 0 | 8,418 |
| Barre Town | 0 | 0 | 0 | 0 | 7,722 |
| Bellows Falls | 0 | 0 | 0 | 0 | 2,950 |
| Bennington | 0 | 0 | 0 | 0 | 14,814 |
| Berlin | 0 | 0 | 0 | 0 | 2,773 |
| Bradford | 0 | 0 | 0 | 0 | 2,673 |
| Brandon | 0 | 0 | 0 | 0 | 3,680 |
| Brattleboro | 0 | 0 | 0 | 0 | 11,182 |
| Brighton | 0 | 0 | 0 | 0 | 1,153 |
| Bristol | 0 | 0 | 0 | 0 | 3,831 |
| Canaan | 0 | 0 | 0 | 0 | 906 |
| Castleton | 0 | 0 | 0 | 0 | 4,468 |
| Chester | 0 | 0 | 0 | 0 | 3,005 |
| Dover | 0 | 0 | 0 | 0 | 1,051 |
| Fair Haven | 0 | 0 | 0 | 0 | 2,511 |
| Fairlee | 0 | 0 | 0 | 0 | 975 |
| Hardwick | 0 | 0 | 0 | 0 | 2,824 |
| Killington | 0 | 0 | 0 | 0 | 743 |
| Ludlow | 0 | 0 | 0 | 0 | 1,846 |
| Lyndonville | 0 | 0 | 0 | 0 | 1,158 |
| Manchester | 0 | 0 | 0 | 0 | 4,197 |
| Newport | 0 | 0 | 0 | 0 | 4,181 |
| Northfield | 0 | 0 | 0 | 0 | 6,536 |
| Norwich | 0 | 0 | 0 | 0 | 3,400 |
| Pittsford | 0 | 0 | 0 | 0 | 2,736 |
| Richmond | 0 | 0 | 0 | 0 | 4,102 |
| Royalton | 0 | 0 | 0 | 0 | 2,892 |
| Rutland Town | 0 | 0 | 0 | 0 | 4,107 |

## Table 95. Hate Crime Zero Data Submitted Per Quarter, by Federal Agency, State, and State Agency, 2021—Continued

(Number.)

| Agency name | Zero data per quarter[1] | | | | Population[2] |
|---|---|---|---|---|---|
| | 1st quarter | 2nd quarter | 3rd quarter | 4th quarter | |
| Swanton | 0 | 0 | 0 | 0 | 6,590 |
| Thetford | 0 | 0 | 0 | 0 | 2,519 |
| Vergennes | 0 | 0 | 0 | 0 | 2,594 |
| Weathersfield | 0 | 0 | 0 | 0 | 2,718 |
| Williston | 0 | 0 | 0 | 0 | 10,434 |
| Wilmington | 0 | 0 | 0 | 0 | 1,777 |
| Windsor | 0 | 0 | 0 | 0 | 3,259 |
| Winhall | 0 | 0 | 0 | 0 | 722 |
| Woodstock | 0 | 0 | 0 | 0 | 2,899 |
| **Universities and Colleges** | | | | | |
| University of Vermont | 0 | 0 | 0 | 0 | 15,903 |
| **Metropolitan Counties** | | | | | |
| Chittenden | 0 | 0 | | 0 | |
| Franklin | 0 | 0 | 0 | 0 | |
| Grand Isle | 0 | 0 | 0 | 0 | |
| **Nonmetropolitan Counties** | | | | | |
| Addison | 0 | 0 | 0 | 0 | |
| Bennington | 0 | 0 | 0 | 0 | |
| Caledonia | 0 | 0 | 0 | 0 | |
| Essex | 0 | 0 | 0 | 0 | |
| Rutland | 0 | 0 | 0 | 0 | |
| Washington | 0 | 0 | 0 | 0 | |
| Windham | 0 | 0 | 0 | 0 | |
| Windsor | 0 | 0 | 0 | 0 | |
| **State Police Agencies** | | | | | |
| State Police | | | | | |
| Derby | 0 | 0 | 0 | 0 | |
| New Haven | 0 | 0 | 0 | 0 | |
| Shaftsbury | 0 | 0 | 0 | 0 | |
| St. Johnsbury | 0 | 0 | 0 | 0 | |
| Westminster | 0 | 0 | 0 | 0 | |
| Vermont State Police | 0 | 0 | 0 | 0 | |
| Vermont State Police Headquarters, Bureau of Criminal Investigations | 0 | 0 | 0 | 0 | |
| **Other Agencies** | | | | | |
| Attorney General | 0 | 0 | 0 | 0 | |
| Capitol Police | 0 | 0 | 0 | 0 | |
| Chittenden Unit for Special Investigations | 0 | 0 | 0 | 0 | |
| Department of Liquor Control, Division of Enforcement and Licensing | 0 | 0 | 0 | 0 | |
| Department of Motor Vehicles | 0 | 0 | 0 | 0 | |
| Fish and Wildlife Department, Law Enforcement Division | 0 | 0 | 0 | 0 | |
| Secretary of State, Investigations Unit | 0 | 0 | 0 | 0 | |
| **VIRGINIA** | | | | | |
| **Cities** | | | | | |
| Abingdon | 0 | 0 | 0 | 0 | 7,820 |
| Altavista | 0 | 0 | 0 | 0 | 3,419 |
| Amherst | 0 | 0 | 0 | 0 | 2,177 |
| Ashland | 0 | 0 | 0 | 0 | 7,976 |
| Bedford | 0 | 0 | 0 | 0 | 6,652 |
| Berryville | 0 | 0 | 0 | 0 | 4,388 |
| Big Stone Gap | 0 | 0 | 0 | 0 | 5,055 |
| Blackstone | 0 | 0 | 0 | 0 | 3,275 |
| Bluefield | 0 | 0 | 0 | 0 | 4,761 |
| Bowling Green | 0 | 0 | 0 | 0 | 1,189 |
| Bridgewater | 0 | 0 | 0 | 0 | 6,218 |
| Broadway | 0 | 0 | 0 | 0 | 4,026 |
| Brookneal | 0 | 0 | 0 | 0 | 1,103 |
| Buena Vista | 0 | 0 | 0 | 0 | 6,374 |
| Burkeville | 0 | 0 | 0 | | 395 |
| Cape Charles | 0 | 0 | 0 | 0 | 1,061 |
| Cedar Bluff | 0 | 0 | 0 | 0 | 986 |
| Chase City | 0 | 0 | 0 | 0 | 2,205 |
| Chatham | 0 | 0 | 0 | 0 | 1,407 |
| Chilhowie | 0 | 0 | 0 | 0 | 1,687 |
| Chincoteague | 0 | 0 | 0 | 0 | 2,859 |
| Christiansburg | 0 | 0 | 0 | 0 | 22,544 |
| Clarksville | 0 | 0 | 0 | 0 | 1,163 |
| Clintwood | 0 | 0 | 0 | 0 | 1,247 |
| Coeburn | 0 | 0 | 0 | 0 | 1,816 |
| Colonial Beach | 0 | 0 | 0 | 0 | 3,655 |
| Colonial Heights | 0 | 0 | 0 | 0 | 17,171 |
| Covington | 0 | 0 | 0 | 0 | 5,603 |
| Crewe | 0 | 0 | 0 | 0 | 2,096 |
| Culpeper | 0 | 0 | 0 | 0 | 19,485 |
| Damascus | 0 | 0 | 0 | 0 | 772 |

## Table 95. Hate Crime Zero Data Submitted Per Quarter, by Federal Agency, State, and State Agency, 2021—Continued

(Number.)

| Agency name | Zero data per quarter[1] | | | | Population[2] |
|---|---|---|---|---|---|
| | 1st quarter | 2nd quarter | 3rd quarter | 4th quarter | |
| Danville | 0 | 0 | 0 | 0 | 39,528 |
| Dayton | 0 | 0 | 0 | 0 | 1,652 |
| Dumfries | 0 | 0 | 0 | 0 | 6,233 |
| Eastville | 0 | 0 | 0 | 0 | 344 |
| Elkton | 0 | 0 | 0 | 0 | 2,933 |
| Emporia | 0 | 0 | 0 | 0 | 5,189 |
| Exmore | 0 | 0 | 0 | 0 | 1,352 |
| Falls Church | 0 | 0 | 0 | 0 | 14,856 |
| Farmville | 0 | 0 | 0 | 0 | 7,811 |
| Franklin | 0 | 0 | 0 | 0 | 7,753 |
| Fredericksburg | 0 | 0 | 0 | 0 | 30,031 |
| Front Royal | 0 | 0 | 0 | 0 | 15,499 |
| Galax | 0 | 0 | 0 | 0 | 6,223 |
| Gate City | 0 | 0 | 0 | 0 | 1,850 |
| Glade Spring | 0 | 0 | 0 | 0 | 1,396 |
| Glasgow | 0 | 0 | 0 | 0 | 1,107 |
| Glen Lyn | 0 | 0 | 0 | | 96 |
| Gordonsville | 0 | 0 | 0 | 0 | 1,665 |
| Gretna | 0 | 0 | 0 | 0 | 1,170 |
| Grottoes | 0 | 0 | 0 | 0 | 2,885 |
| Grundy | 0 | 0 | 0 | 0 | 871 |
| Halifax | 0 | 0 | 0 | 0 | 1,192 |
| Harrisonburg | 0 | 0 | 0 | 0 | 53,582 |
| Haymarket | 0 | 0 | 0 | 0 | 1,709 |
| Haysi | 0 | | 0 | 0 | 458 |
| Herndon | 0 | 0 | 0 | 0 | 24,694 |
| Hillsville | 0 | 0 | 0 | 0 | 2,682 |
| Honaker | 0 | 0 | 0 | 0 | 1,311 |
| Hopewell | 0 | 0 | 0 | 0 | 22,322 |
| Hurt | 0 | 0 | 0 | 0 | 1,203 |
| Independence | 0 | 0 | 0 | 0 | 881 |
| Jonesville | 0 | 0 | 0 | 0 | 911 |
| Kenbridge | 0 | 0 | 0 | 0 | 1,189 |
| Kilmarnock | 0 | 0 | 0 | 0 | 1,392 |
| La Crosse | 0 | 0 | 0 | 0 | 574 |
| Lawrenceville | 0 | 0 | 0 | 0 | 969 |
| Lebanon | 0 | 0 | 0 | 0 | 3,158 |
| Lexington | 0 | 0 | 0 | 0 | 7,294 |
| Louisa | 0 | 0 | 0 | 0 | 1,786 |
| Luray | 0 | 0 | 0 | 0 | 4,844 |
| Lynchburg | 0 | 0 | 0 | 0 | 82,088 |
| Manassas | 0 | 0 | 0 | 0 | 41,098 |
| Manassas Park | 0 | 0 | 0 | 0 | 18,385 |
| Marion | 0 | 0 | 0 | 0 | 5,515 |
| Martinsville | 0 | 0 | 0 | 0 | 12,206 |
| Middleburg | 0 | 0 | 0 | 0 | 853 |
| Middletown | 0 | 0 | 0 | 0 | 1,440 |
| Mount Jackson | 0 | 0 | 0 | 0 | 2,153 |
| Narrows | 0 | 0 | 0 | 0 | 1,940 |
| New Market | 0 | 0 | 0 | 0 | 2,276 |
| Newport News | 0 | 0 | 0 | 0 | 178,662 |
| Norton | 0 | 0 | 0 | 0 | 3,978 |
| Occoquan | 0 | 0 | 0 | 0 | 1,114 |
| Onancock | 0 | 0 | 0 | 0 | 1,200 |
| Onley | 0 | 0 | 0 | 0 | 497 |
| Orange | 0 | 0 | 0 | 0 | 5,213 |
| Parksley | 0 | 0 | 0 | 0 | 801 |
| Pearisburg | 0 | 0 | 0 | 0 | 2,604 |
| Pembroke | 0 | 0 | 0 | 0 | 1,073 |
| Pennington Gap | 0 | 0 | 0 | 0 | 1,692 |
| Pocahontas | 0 | 0 | 0 | 0 | 343 |
| Poquoson | 0 | 0 | 0 | 0 | 12,253 |
| Pulaski | 0 | 0 | 0 | 0 | 8,615 |
| Purcellville | 0 | 0 | 0 | 0 | 10,575 |
| Radford | 0 | 0 | 0 | 0 | 18,427 |
| Remington | 0 | | | | 667 |
| Rich Creek | 0 | 0 | 0 | 0 | 735 |
| Richlands | 0 | 0 | 0 | 0 | 5,167 |
| Roanoke | 0 | 0 | 0 | 0 | 99,175 |
| Rocky Mount | 0 | 0 | 0 | 0 | 4,707 |
| Rural Retreat | 0 | 0 | 0 | 0 | 1,445 |
| Salem | 0 | 0 | 0 | 0 | 25,354 |
| Saltville | 0 | 0 | 0 | 0 | 1,880 |
| Shenandoah | 0 | 0 | 0 | 0 | 2,330 |
| Smithfield | 0 | 0 | 0 | 0 | 8,668 |
| South Boston | 0 | 0 | 0 | 0 | 7,459 |
| South Hill | 0 | 0 | 0 | 0 | 4,332 |
| Stanley | 0 | 0 | 0 | 0 | 1,675 |
| Staunton | 0 | 0 | 0 | 0 | 25,310 |
| Stephens City | 0 | 0 | 0 | 0 | 2,136 |

## Table 95. Hate Crime Zero Data Submitted Per Quarter, by Federal Agency, State, and State Agency, 2021—Continued

(Number.)

| Agency name | Zero data per quarter[1] | | | | Population[2] |
|---|---|---|---|---|---|
| | 1st quarter | 2nd quarter | 3rd quarter | 4th quarter | |
| St. Paul | 0 | 0 | 0 | 0 | 837 |
| Tappahannock | 0 | 0 | 0 | 0 | 2,395 |
| Tazewell | 0 | 0 | 0 | 0 | 4,065 |
| Timberville | 0 | 0 | 0 | 0 | 2,724 |
| Victoria | 0 | 0 | 0 | 0 | 1,623 |
| Vienna | 0 | 0 | 0 | 0 | 16,598 |
| Vinton | 0 | 0 | 0 | 0 | 8,142 |
| Warrenton | 0 | 0 | 0 | 0 | 10,019 |
| Warsaw | 0 | 0 | 0 | 0 | 1,490 |
| Weber City | 0 | 0 | 0 | 0 | 1,204 |
| West Point | 0 | 0 | 0 | 0 | 3,309 |
| White Stone | 0 | 0 | 0 | 0 | 329 |
| Williamsburg | 0 | 0 | 0 | 0 | 15,406 |
| Winchester | 0 | 0 | 0 | 0 | 27,827 |
| Windsor | 0 | 0 | 0 | 0 | 2,819 |
| Wintergreen | 0 | 0 | 0 | 0 | 165 |
| Wise | 0 | 0 | 0 | 0 | 2,852 |
| Woodstock | 0 | 0 | 0 | 0 | 5,316 |
| Wytheville | 0 | 0 | 0 | 0 | 7,847 |
| **Universities and Colleges** | | | | | |
| Christopher Newport University | 0 | 0 | 0 | 0 | 5,058 |
| College of William and Mary | 0 | 0 | 0 | 0 | 9,785 |
| Eastern Virginia Medical School | 0 | 0 | 0 | 0 | 1,436 |
| Emory and Henry College | 0 | 0 | 0 | 0 | 1,376 |
| Hampton University | 0 | 0 | 0 | 0 | 4,720 |
| James Madison University | 0 | 0 | 0 | 0 | 24,039 |
| J. Sargeant Reynolds Community College | 0 | 0 | 0 | 0 | 12,772 |
| Longwood University | 0 | 0 | 0 | 0 | 5,852 |
| Lord Fairfax Community College | 0 | 0 | 0 | 0 | 8,778 |
| Norfolk State University | 0 | 0 | 0 | 0 | 6,075 |
| Northern Virginia Community College | 0 | 0 | 0 | 0 | 71,294 |
| Old Dominion University | 0 | 0 | 0 | 0 | 28,042 |
| Radford University | 0 | 0 | 0 | 0 | 14,711 |
| Richard Bland College | 0 | 0 | 0 | 0 | 2,662 |
| Southwest Virginia Community College | 0 | 0 | 0 | 0 | 3,026 |
| University of Mary Washington | 0 | 0 | 0 | 0 | 5,098 |
| University of Virginia's College at Wise | 0 | 0 | 0 | 0 | 3,174 |
| Virginia Military Institute | 0 | 0 | 0 | 0 | 1,740 |
| Virginia Polytechnic Institute and State University | 0 | 0 | 0 | 0 | 38,350 |
| Virginia State University | 0 | 0 | 0 | 0 | 4,708 |
| Virginia Western Community College | 0 | 0 | 0 | 0 | 8,535 |
| **Metropolitan Counties** | | | | | |
| Amelia | 0 | 0 | 0 | 0 | |
| Amherst | 0 | 0 | 0 | 0 | |
| Augusta | 0 | 0 | 0 | 0 | |
| Campbell | 0 | 0 | 0 | 0 | |
| Charles City | 0 | 0 | 0 | 0 | |
| Craig | 0 | 0 | 0 | 0 | |
| Culpeper | 0 | 0 | 0 | 0 | |
| Dinwiddie | 0 | 0 | 0 | 0 | |
| Fauquier | 0 | 0 | 0 | 0 | |
| Fluvanna | 0 | 0 | 0 | 0 | |
| Franklin | 0 | 0 | 0 | 0 | |
| Frederick | 0 | 0 | 0 | 0 | |
| Giles | 0 | 0 | 0 | 0 | |
| Gloucester | 0 | 0 | 0 | 0 | |
| Goochland | 0 | 0 | 0 | 0 | |
| Greene | 0 | 0 | 0 | 0 | |
| Isle of Wight | 0 | 0 | 0 | 0 | |
| James City County Police Department | 0 | 0 | 0 | 0 | |
| King and Queen | 0 | 0 | 0 | 0 | |
| King William | 0 | 0 | 0 | 0 | |
| Madison | 0 | 0 | 0 | 0 | |
| Nelson | 0 | 0 | 0 | 0 | |
| New Kent | 0 | 0 | 0 | 0 | |
| Pulaski | 0 | 0 | 0 | 0 | |
| Rappahannock | 0 | 0 | 0 | 0 | |
| Roanoke County Police Department | 0 | 0 | 0 | 0 | |
| Rockingham | 0 | 0 | 0 | 0 | |
| Scott | 0 | 0 | 0 | 0 | |
| Southampton | 0 | 0 | 0 | 0 | |
| Spotsylvania | 0 | 0 | 0 | 0 | |
| Sussex | 0 | 0 | 0 | 0 | |
| Washington | 0 | 0 | 0 | 0 | |
| **Nonmetropolitan Counties** | | | | | |
| Accomack | 0 | 0 | 0 | 0 | |
| Alleghany | 0 | 0 | 0 | 0 | |

## Table 95. Hate Crime Zero Data Submitted Per Quarter, by Federal Agency, State, and State Agency, 2021—Continued

(Number.)

| Agency name | Zero data per quarter[1] | | | | Population[2] |
|---|---|---|---|---|---|
| | 1st quarter | 2nd quarter | 3rd quarter | 4th quarter | |
| Bath | 0 | 0 | 0 | 0 | |
| Bland | 0 | 0 | 0 | 0 | |
| Brunswick | 0 | 0 | 0 | 0 | |
| Buchanan | 0 | 0 | 0 | 0 | |
| Buckingham | 0 | 0 | 0 | 0 | |
| Caroline | 0 | 0 | 0 | 0 | |
| Carroll | 0 | 0 | 0 | 0 | |
| Charlotte | 0 | 0 | 0 | 0 | |
| Cumberland | 0 | 0 | 0 | 0 | |
| Dickenson | 0 | 0 | 0 | 0 | |
| Essex | 0 | 0 | 0 | 0 | |
| Floyd | 0 | 0 | 0 | 0 | |
| Grayson | 0 | 0 | 0 | 0 | |
| Greensville | 0 | 0 | 0 | 0 | |
| Halifax | 0 | 0 | 0 | 0 | |
| Henry | 0 | 0 | 0 | 0 | |
| Highland | 0 | 0 | 0 | 0 | |
| King George | 0 | 0 | 0 | 0 | |
| Lancaster | 0 | 0 | 0 | 0 | |
| Lee | 0 | 0 | 0 | 0 | |
| Louisa | 0 | 0 | 0 | 0 | |
| Lunenburg | 0 | 0 | 0 | 0 | |
| Mecklenburg | 0 | 0 | 0 | 0 | |
| Middlesex | 0 | 0 | 0 | 0 | |
| Northampton | 0 | 0 | 0 | 0 | |
| Northumberland | 0 | 0 | 0 | 0 | |
| Nottoway | 0 | 0 | 0 | 0 | |
| Orange | 0 | 0 | 0 | 0 | |
| Page | 0 | 0 | 0 | 0 | |
| Pittsylvania | 0 | 0 | 0 | 0 | |
| Prince Edward | 0 | 0 | 0 | 0 | |
| Richmond | 0 | 0 | 0 | 0 | |
| Rockbridge | 0 | 0 | 0 | 0 | |
| Russell | 0 | 0 | 0 | 0 | |
| Shenandoah | 0 | 0 | 0 | 0 | |
| Smyth | 0 | 0 | 0 | 0 | |
| Surry | 0 | 0 | 0 | 0 | |
| Tazewell | 0 | 0 | 0 | 0 | |
| Westmoreland | 0 | 0 | 0 | 0 | |
| Wise | 0 | 0 | 0 | 0 | |
| Wythe | 0 | 0 | 0 | 0 | |
| **State Police Agencies** | | | | | |
| State Police | | | | | |
| Accomack County | 0 | 0 | 0 | 0 | |
| Albemarle County | 0 | 0 | 0 | 0 | |
| Alexandria | 0 | 0 | 0 | 0 | |
| Alleghany County | 0 | 0 | 0 | 0 | |
| Amelia County | 0 | 0 | 0 | 0 | |
| Amherst County | 0 | 0 | 0 | 0 | |
| Appomattox County | 0 | 0 | 0 | 0 | |
| Arlington County | 0 | 0 | 0 | 0 | |
| Augusta County | 0 | 0 | 0 | 0 | |
| Bath County | 0 | 0 | 0 | 0 | |
| Bedford County | 0 | 0 | 0 | 0 | |
| Bland County | 0 | 0 | 0 | 0 | |
| Botetourt County | 0 | 0 | 0 | 0 | |
| Bristol | 0 | 0 | 0 | 0 | |
| Brunswick County | 0 | 0 | 0 | 0 | |
| Buchanan County | 0 | 0 | 0 | 0 | |
| Buckingham County | 0 | 0 | 0 | 0 | |
| Buena Vista | 0 | 0 | 0 | 0 | |
| Campbell County | 0 | 0 | 0 | 0 | |
| Caroline County | 0 | 0 | 0 | 0 | |
| Carroll County | 0 | 0 | 0 | 0 | |
| Charles City County | 0 | 0 | 0 | 0 | |
| Charlotte County | 0 | 0 | 0 | 0 | |
| Charlottesville | 0 | 0 | 0 | 0 | |
| Chesapeake | 0 | 0 | 0 | 0 | |
| Chesterfield County | 0 | 0 | 0 | 0 | |
| Clarke County | 0 | 0 | 0 | 0 | |
| Colonial Heights | 0 | 0 | 0 | 0 | |
| Covington | 0 | 0 | 0 | 0 | |
| Craig County | 0 | 0 | 0 | 0 | |
| Culpeper County | 0 | 0 | 0 | 0 | |
| Cumberland County | 0 | 0 | 0 | 0 | |
| Danville | 0 | 0 | 0 | 0 | |
| Dickenson County | 0 | 0 | 0 | 0 | |
| Dinwiddie County | 0 | 0 | 0 | 0 | |
| Emporia | 0 | 0 | 0 | 0 | |

## Table 95. Hate Crime Zero Data Submitted Per Quarter, by Federal Agency, State, and State Agency, 2021—Continued

(Number.)

| Agency name | Zero data per quarter[1] | | | | Population[2] |
|---|---|---|---|---|---|
| | 1st quarter | 2nd quarter | 3rd quarter | 4th quarter | |
| Essex County | 0 | 0 | 0 | 0 | |
| Fairfax City | 0 | | 0 | 0 | |
| Fairfax County | 0 | 0 | 0 | 0 | |
| Falls Church | | 0 | 0 | | |
| Fauquier County | 0 | 0 | 0 | 0 | |
| Floyd County | 0 | 0 | 0 | 0 | |
| Fluvanna County | 0 | 0 | 0 | 0 | |
| Franklin | 0 | 0 | 0 | 0 | |
| Franklin County | 0 | 0 | 0 | 0 | |
| Frederick County | 0 | 0 | 0 | 0 | |
| Fredericksburg | 0 | 0 | 0 | 0 | |
| Galax | 0 | 0 | 0 | 0 | |
| Giles County | 0 | 0 | 0 | 0 | |
| Gloucester County | 0 | 0 | 0 | 0 | |
| Goochland County | 0 | 0 | 0 | 0 | |
| Grayson County | 0 | 0 | 0 | 0 | |
| Greene County | 0 | 0 | 0 | 0 | |
| Greensville County | 0 | 0 | 0 | 0 | |
| Halifax County | 0 | 0 | 0 | 0 | |
| Hampton | 0 | 0 | 0 | 0 | |
| Hanover County | 0 | 0 | 0 | 0 | |
| Harrisonburg | 0 | 0 | 0 | 0 | |
| Henrico County | 0 | 0 | 0 | 0 | |
| Henry County | 0 | 0 | 0 | 0 | |
| Highland County | 0 | 0 | 0 | | |
| Hopewell | 0 | 0 | 0 | 0 | |
| Isle of Wight County | 0 | 0 | 0 | 0 | |
| James City County | 0 | 0 | 0 | 0 | |
| King and Queen County | 0 | 0 | 0 | 0 | |
| King George County | 0 | 0 | 0 | 0 | |
| King William County | 0 | 0 | 0 | 0 | |
| Lancaster County | 0 | 0 | 0 | 0 | |
| Lee County | 0 | 0 | 0 | 0 | |
| Lexington | 0 | 0 | 0 | 0 | |
| Loudoun County | 0 | 0 | 0 | 0 | |
| Louisa County | 0 | 0 | 0 | 0 | |
| Lunenburg County | 0 | 0 | 0 | 0 | |
| Lynchburg | 0 | 0 | 0 | 0 | |
| Madison County | 0 | 0 | 0 | 0 | |
| Manassas | 0 | 0 | 0 | 0 | |
| Manassas Park | | | 0 | | |
| Martinsville | 0 | 0 | 0 | 0 | |
| Mathews County | 0 | 0 | 0 | | |
| Mecklenburg County | 0 | 0 | 0 | 0 | |
| Middlesex County | 0 | 0 | 0 | 0 | |
| Montgomery County | 0 | 0 | 0 | 0 | |
| Nelson County | 0 | 0 | 0 | 0 | |
| New Kent County | 0 | 0 | 0 | 0 | |
| Newport News | 0 | 0 | 0 | 0 | |
| Norfolk | 0 | 0 | 0 | 0 | |
| Northampton County | 0 | 0 | 0 | 0 | |
| Northumberland County | 0 | 0 | 0 | 0 | |
| Norton | 0 | 0 | 0 | | |
| Nottoway County | 0 | 0 | 0 | 0 | |
| Orange County | 0 | 0 | 0 | 0 | |
| Page County | 0 | 0 | 0 | 0 | |
| Patrick County | 0 | 0 | 0 | 0 | |
| Petersburg | 0 | 0 | 0 | 0 | |
| Pittsylvania County | 0 | 0 | 0 | 0 | |
| Poquoson | 0 | 0 | 0 | 0 | |
| Portsmouth | 0 | 0 | 0 | 0 | |
| Powhatan County | 0 | 0 | 0 | 0 | |
| Prince Edward County | 0 | 0 | 0 | 0 | |
| Prince George County | 0 | 0 | 0 | 0 | |
| Prince William County | 0 | 0 | 0 | 0 | |
| Pulaski County | 0 | 0 | 0 | 0 | |
| Radford | 0 | | 0 | 0 | |
| Rappahannock County | | 0 | 0 | 0 | |
| Richmond | 0 | 0 | 0 | 0 | |
| Richmond County | 0 | 0 | 0 | 0 | |
| Roanoke | 0 | 0 | 0 | 0 | |
| Roanoke County | 0 | 0 | 0 | 0 | |
| Rockbridge County | 0 | 0 | 0 | 0 | |
| Rockingham County | 0 | 0 | 0 | 0 | |
| Russell County | 0 | 0 | 0 | 0 | |
| Salem | 0 | 0 | 0 | 0 | |
| Scott County | 0 | 0 | 0 | 0 | |
| Shenandoah County | 0 | 0 | 0 | 0 | |
| Smyth County | 0 | 0 | 0 | 0 | |
| Southampton County | 0 | 0 | 0 | 0 | |

## Table 95. Hate Crime Zero Data Submitted Per Quarter, by Federal Agency, State, and State Agency, 2021—Continued

(Number.)

| Agency name | Zero data per quarter[1] | | | | Population[2] |
|---|---|---|---|---|---|
| | 1st quarter | 2nd quarter | 3rd quarter | 4th quarter | |
| Spotsylvania County | 0 | 0 | 0 | 0 | |
| Stafford County | 0 | 0 | 0 | 0 | |
| Staunton | 0 | 0 | 0 | 0 | |
| Suffolk | 0 | 0 | 0 | 0 | |
| Surry County | 0 | 0 | | 0 | |
| Sussex County | 0 | 0 | 0 | 0 | |
| Tazewell County | 0 | 0 | 0 | 0 | |
| Virginia Beach | 0 | 0 | 0 | 0 | |
| Warren County | 0 | 0 | 0 | 0 | |
| Washington County | 0 | 0 | 0 | 0 | |
| Waynesboro | 0 | 0 | 0 | 0 | |
| Westmoreland County | 0 | 0 | 0 | 0 | |
| Williamsburg | 0 | 0 | 0 | 0 | |
| Winchester | 0 | 0 | 0 | 0 | |
| Wise County | 0 | 0 | 0 | 0 | |
| Wythe County | 0 | 0 | 0 | 0 | |
| York County | 0 | 0 | 0 | 0 | |
| **Other Agencies** | | | | | |
| Alcoholic Beverage Control Commission | 0 | 0 | 0 | 0 | |
| Department of Conservation and Recreation | 0 | 0 | 0 | 0 | |
| Department of Game and Inland Fisheries, Enforcement Division | 0 | 0 | 0 | 0 | |
| Department of Motor Vehicles | 0 | 0 | 0 | 0 | |
| Norfolk Airport Authority | 0 | 0 | 0 | 0 | |
| Port Authority, Norfolk | 0 | 0 | 0 | 0 | |
| Richmond International Airport | 0 | 0 | 0 | 0 | |
| Virginia Marine Resources Commission, Law Enforcement Division | 0 | 0 | 0 | 0 | |
| Virginia State Capitol | 0 | 0 | 0 | 0 | |
| **WASHINGTON** | | | | | |
| **Cities** | | | | | |
| Airway Heights | 0 | 0 | 0 | 0 | 10,030 |
| Algona | 0 | 0 | 0 | 0 | 3,216 |
| Anacortes | 0 | 0 | | 0 | 17,923 |
| Asotin | 0 | | 0 | | 1,296 |
| Battle Ground | 0 | 0 | 0 | 0 | 22,143 |
| Beaux Arts | 0 | 0 | 0 | 0 | 324 |
| Bingen | 0 | 0 | 0 | 0 | 751 |
| Blaine | 0 | 0 | 0 | 0 | 5,741 |
| Bonney Lake | 0 | 0 | 0 | 0 | 23,142 |
| Brewster | 0 | 0 | 0 | 0 | 2,393 |
| Buckley | 0 | 0 | 0 | 0 | 5,914 |
| Camas | 0 | 0 | | | 26,683 |
| Carnation | 0 | 0 | 0 | 0 | 2,366 |
| Castle Rock | 0 | 0 | 0 | 0 | 2,324 |
| Chehalis | 0 | 0 | 0 | 0 | 7,885 |
| Chewelah | 0 | 0 | 0 | | 2,693 |
| Clarkston | 0 | 0 | | | 7,524 |
| Cle Elum | 0 | 0 | 0 | 0 | 3,103 |
| Clyde Hill | 0 | 0 | 0 | 0 | 3,441 |
| Colville | 0 | 0 | 0 | 0 | 4,840 |
| Connell | 0 | 0 | 0 | 0 | 5,660 |
| Coulee Dam | 0 | 0 | 0 | 0 | 1,081 |
| Darrington | 0 | 0 | 0 | 0 | 1,430 |
| Dupont | 0 | 0 | 0 | 0 | 9,740 |
| Duvall | 0 | 0 | 0 | 0 | 8,319 |
| East Wenatchee | 0 | 0 | 0 | 0 | 14,096 |
| Eatonville | 0 | 0 | 0 | 0 | 3,055 |
| Edgewood | 0 | 0 | 0 | 0 | 13,909 |
| Ellensburg | 0 | 0 | 0 | 0 | 21,933 |
| Elma | 0 | 0 | 0 | 0 | 3,387 |
| Enumclaw | 0 | 0 | 0 | 0 | 12,700 |
| Ephrata | 0 | 0 | 0 | 0 | 8,268 |
| Everson | 0 | 0 | 0 | 0 | 4,624 |
| Ferndale | 0 | 0 | 0 | 0 | 16,006 |
| Fife | 0 | 0 | 0 | 0 | 10,577 |
| Gold Bar | 0 | 0 | 0 | 0 | 2,408 |
| Goldendale | 0 | 0 | 0 | 0 | 3,696 |
| Grand Coulee | 0 | 0 | 0 | 0 | 2,047 |
| Granite Falls | 0 | 0 | 0 | 0 | 4,728 |
| Ilwaco | 0 | 0 | 0 | 0 | 1,014 |
| Index | 0 | 0 | 0 | 0 | 218 |
| Kalama | 0 | 0 | 0 | 0 | 2,898 |
| Kelso | 0 | 0 | 0 | 0 | 12,493 |
| Kennewick | 0 | 0 | 0 | 0 | 85,595 |
| Kettle Falls | 0 | 0 | 0 | 0 | 1,647 |
| La Center | 0 | 0 | 0 | 0 | 3,674 |
| Lacey | 0 | 0 | 0 | 0 | 55,484 |
| Lake Forest Park | 0 | 0 | 0 | 0 | 13,514 |
| Long Beach | 0 | 0 | 0 | 0 | 1,534 |

## Table 95. Hate Crime Zero Data Submitted Per Quarter, by Federal Agency, State, and State Agency, 2021—Continued

(Number.)

| Agency name | Zero data per quarter[1] | | | | Population[2] |
|---|---|---|---|---|---|
| | 1st quarter | 2nd quarter | 3rd quarter | 4th quarter | |
| Maple Valley | 0 | 0 | 0 | 0 | 28,065 |
| Mattawa | 0 | | | | 5,182 |
| Medina | 0 | 0 | 0 | 0 | 3,343 |
| Milton | 0 | 0 | 0 | 0 | 8,325 |
| Montesano | 0 | 0 | 0 | 0 | 4,083 |
| Mount Vernon | 0 | 0 | 0 | 0 | 36,830 |
| Moxee | 0 | 0 | 0 | 0 | 4,499 |
| Newcastle | 0 | 0 | 0 | 0 | 13,188 |
| Newport | 0 | 0 | 0 | 0 | 2,278 |
| Normandy Park | 0 | 0 | 0 | 0 | 6,587 |
| Oakville | 0 | 0 | 0 | 0 | 698 |
| Ocean Shores | 0 | 0 | 0 | 0 | 6,851 |
| Omak | 0 | 0 | 0 | | 4,829 |
| Oroville | 0 | 0 | | | 1,686 |
| Orting | 0 | 0 | 0 | 0 | 8,866 |
| Othello | 0 | 0 | 0 | 0 | 8,572 |
| Pacific | 0 | 0 | 0 | 0 | 7,225 |
| Palouse | 0 | | | | 1,061 |
| Port Orchard | 0 | 0 | 0 | 0 | 14,995 |
| Poulsbo | 0 | 0 | 0 | 0 | 11,425 |
| Prosser | 0 | 0 | 0 | 0 | 6,463 |
| Quincy | 0 | 0 | 0 | 0 | 8,564 |
| Raymond | 0 | 0 | 0 | 0 | 3,076 |
| Reardan | 0 | 0 | 0 | 0 | 626 |
| Ridgefield | 0 | 0 | 0 | 0 | 12,295 |
| Ritzville | 0 | 0 | 0 | 0 | 1,637 |
| Roy | 0 | 0 | 0 | 0 | 828 |
| Royal City | 0 | 0 | 0 | 0 | 2,697 |
| Ruston | 0 | 0 | 0 | 0 | 859 |
| Selah | 0 | 0 | 0 | 0 | 8,220 |
| Skykomish | 0 | 0 | 0 | 0 | 221 |
| Snohomish | 0 | 0 | 0 | 0 | 10,489 |
| Snoqualmie | 0 | 0 | 0 | 0 | 13,875 |
| South Bend | 0 | 0 | 0 | 0 | 1,741 |
| Stanwood | 0 | 0 | 0 | 0 | 7,716 |
| Steilacoom | 0 | 0 | 0 | 0 | 6,460 |
| Sultan | 0 | 0 | 0 | 0 | 5,786 |
| Sumas | 0 | 0 | 0 | 0 | 1,665 |
| Sunnyside | 0 | 0 | 0 | 0 | 17,021 |
| Toledo | 0 | 0 | 0 | 0 | 792 |
| Tumwater | 0 | 0 | 0 | 0 | 24,727 |
| Twisp | 0 | 0 | 0 | 0 | 997 |
| Union Gap | 0 | 0 | 0 | 0 | 6,163 |
| Warden | 0 | 0 | 0 | 0 | 2,848 |
| Washougal | 0 | 0 | 0 | 0 | 16,317 |
| Wenatchee | 0 | 0 | 0 | 0 | 34,349 |
| Westport | 0 | 0 | 0 | 0 | 2,123 |
| West Richland | 0 | 0 | 0 | 0 | 15,817 |
| White Salmon | 0 | 0 | 0 | 0 | 2,764 |
| Winlock | 0 | | | | 1,504 |
| Winthrop | 0 | 0 | 0 | 0 | 502 |
| Woodland | 0 | 0 | 0 | 0 | 6,659 |
| Woodway | 0 | 0 | 0 | 0 | 1,399 |
| Yarrow Point | 0 | 0 | 0 | 0 | 1,161 |
| Yelm | 0 | 0 | 0 | | 9,913 |
| **Universities and Colleges** | | | | | |
| Central Washington University | 0 | 0 | 0 | 0 | 14,090 |
| Eastern Washington University | 0 | 0 | 0 | 0 | 16,280 |
| Evergreen State College | 0 | 0 | 0 | 0 | 3,439 |
| Washington State University, Vancouver[3] | 0 | 0 | 0 | 0 | |
| **Metropolitan Counties** | | | | | |
| Asotin | 0 | 0 | 0 | 0 | |
| Benton | 0 | 0 | 0 | 0 | |
| Chelan | 0 | 0 | 0 | 0 | |
| Douglas | 0 | 0 | 0 | 0 | |
| Franklin | 0 | 0 | 0 | 0 | |
| Kitsap | 0 | 0 | 0 | 0 | |
| Skamania | 0 | 0 | 0 | 0 | |
| Stevens | 0 | 0 | 0 | 0 | |
| Thurston | 0 | 0 | 0 | 0 | |
| Walla Walla | 0 | 0 | 0 | 0 | |
| Yakima | 0 | 0 | 0 | 0 | |
| **Nonmetropolitan Counties** | | | | | |
| Clallam | 0 | 0 | 0 | 0 | |
| Columbia | 0 | 0 | 0 | 0 | |
| Ferry | 0 | 0 | 0 | 0 | |
| Garfield | 0 | 0 | 0 | 0 | |

## Table 95. Hate Crime Zero Data Submitted Per Quarter, by Federal Agency, State, and State Agency, 2021—Continued

(Number.)

| Agency name | Zero data per quarter[1] | | | | Population[2] |
|---|---|---|---|---|---|
| | 1st quarter | 2nd quarter | 3rd quarter | 4th quarter | |
| Grays Harbor | 0 | 0 | 0 | 0 | |
| Jefferson | 0 | 0 | 0 | 0 | |
| Kittitas | 0 | 0 | 0 | 0 | |
| Klickitat | 0 | 0 | 0 | | |
| Lincoln | 0 | 0 | 0 | 0 | |
| Mason | 0 | 0 | 0 | 0 | |
| Pacific | 0 | 0 | | 0 | |
| Pend Oreille | | | 0 | 0 | |
| San Juan | 0 | 0 | 0 | 0 | |
| Wahkiakum | 0 | 0 | 0 | 0 | |
| Whitman | 0 | 0 | 0 | 0 | |
| **State Police Agencies** | | | | | |
| Washington State Patrol | 0 | 0 | 0 | 0 | |
| **Tribal Agencies** | | | | | |
| Colville Tribal | 0 | 0 | 0 | | |
| Elwha Klallam Tribal | 0 | 0 | | 0 | |
| Hoh Tribal | 0 | | | 0 | |
| Jamestown S'Klallam Tribal | 0 | 0 | 0 | 0 | |
| Kalispel Tribal | 0 | 0 | 0 | 0 | |
| La Push Tribal | 0 | 0 | 0 | 0 | |
| Lummi Tribal | 0 | 0 | 0 | 0 | |
| Makah Tribal | 0 | | | | |
| Muckleshoot Tribal | 0 | 0 | 0 | 0 | |
| Nooksack Tribal | 0 | 0 | 0 | 0 | |
| Puyallup Tribal | 0 | 0 | 0 | 0 | |
| Shoalwater Bay Tribal | 0 | 0 | 0 | 0 | |
| Skokomish Tribal | 0 | 0 | 0 | 0 | |
| Snoqualmie Tribal | 0 | 0 | 0 | 0 | |
| Spokane Agency | 0 | 0 | | | |
| Stillaguamish Tribal | 0 | | | | |
| Suquamish Tribal | 0 | 0 | 0 | 0 | |
| Swinomish Tribal | 0 | 0 | 0 | 0 | |
| Tulalip Tribal | 0 | | | | |
| Upper Skagit Tribal | 0 | 0 | 0 | 0 | |
| **Other Agencies** | | | | | |
| State Gambling Commission, Enforcement Unit | 0 | 0 | 0 | 0 | |
| State Insurance Commissioner, Special Investigations Unit | 0 | 0 | 0 | 0 | |
| **WEST VIRGINIA** | | | | | |
| **Cities** | | | | | |
| Alderson | 0 | 0 | 0 | 0 | 1,104 |
| Ansted | 0 | 0 | 0 | 0 | 1,290 |
| Barboursville | 0 | 0 | 0 | 0 | 4,258 |
| Beech Bottom | | 0 | 0 | | 456 |
| Benwood | 0 | 0 | 0 | 0 | 1,241 |
| Bethlehem | 0 | 0 | 0 | 0 | 2,279 |
| Bluefield | 0 | 0 | 0 | 0 | 9,416 |
| Buckhannon | 0 | 0 | 0 | 0 | 5,376 |
| Cameron | 0 | 0 | 0 | 0 | 818 |
| Capon Bridge | | 0 | | | 372 |
| Ceredo | 0 | 0 | 0 | 0 | 1,233 |
| Chapmanville | 0 | 0 | 0 | 0 | 1,064 |
| Charles Town | 0 | 0 | 0 | 0 | 6,098 |
| Chester | 0 | 0 | 0 | | 2,291 |
| Clearview | 0 | 0 | 0 | 0 | 477 |
| Dunbar | 0 | 0 | 0 | 0 | 6,868 |
| Farmington | | | 0 | | 362 |
| Fayetteville | 0 | 0 | 0 | 0 | 2,659 |
| Follansbee | 0 | 0 | 0 | 0 | 2,640 |
| Gilbert | 0 | 0 | 0 | 0 | 372 |
| Glen Dale | 0 | 0 | 0 | 0 | 1,332 |
| Grafton | 0 | 0 | 0 | 0 | 4,950 |
| Grantsville | 0 | | | | 491 |
| Hamlin | | 0 | 0 | 0 | 995 |
| Hinton | 0 | 0 | 0 | 0 | 2,289 |
| Kenova | 0 | 0 | 0 | 0 | 2,914 |
| Keyser | 0 | 0 | 0 | 0 | 4,811 |
| Lewisburg | 0 | 0 | 0 | 0 | 3,759 |
| Madison | 0 | 0 | 0 | 0 | 2,574 |
| Marmet | 0 | 0 | 0 | | 1,337 |
| Mason | 0 | 0 | | | 915 |
| Milton | 0 | | | 0 | 2,534 |
| Moorefield | 0 | 0 | 0 | 0 | 2,375 |
| Moundsville | 0 | 0 | 0 | 0 | 8,036 |
| Mount Hope | 0 | 0 | 0 | 0 | 1,245 |
| Mullens | 0 | 0 | 0 | 0 | 1,263 |
| New Martinsville | 0 | 0 | 0 | 0 | 5,088 |

## Table 95. Hate Crime Zero Data Submitted Per Quarter, by Federal Agency, State, and State Agency, 2021—Continued

(Number.)

| Agency name | Zero data per quarter[1] | | | | Population[2] |
|---|---|---|---|---|---|
| | 1st quarter | 2nd quarter | 3rd quarter | 4th quarter | |
| Nitro | 0 | 0 | 0 | 0 | 6,225 |
| Oak Hill | 0 | 0 | 0 | 0 | 7,948 |
| Paden City | 0 | | | | 2,266 |
| Philippi | 0 | 0 | 0 | | 3,271 |
| Point Pleasant | 0 | 0 | 0 | 0 | 3,986 |
| Princeton | 0 | 0 | 0 | 0 | 5,551 |
| Ravenswood | 0 | 0 | 0 | 0 | 3,594 |
| Ripley | 0 | 0 | 0 | 0 | 3,130 |
| Romney | 0 | 0 | 0 | 0 | 1,665 |
| Shepherdstown | 0 | 0 | 0 | 0 | 1,901 |
| Sistersville | 0 | 0 | 0 | | 1,259 |
| Spencer | 0 | 0 | 0 | 0 | 1,962 |
| St. Albans | 0 | 0 | 0 | 0 | 9,646 |
| St. Marys | 0 | 0 | 0 | 0 | 1,748 |
| Summersville | 0 | 0 | 0 | 0 | 3,194 |
| Vienna | 0 | 0 | 0 | 0 | 9,952 |
| Weirton | 0 | 0 | 0 | 0 | 17,911 |
| Wellsburg | 0 | 0 | 0 | 0 | 2,468 |
| Weston | 0 | 0 | 0 | 0 | 3,770 |
| White Hall | 0 | 0 | 0 | 0 | 667 |
| White Sulphur Springs | 0 | 0 | 0 | 0 | 2,315 |
| Williamson | 0 | 0 | 0 | 0 | 2,565 |
| Williamstown | 0 | 0 | 0 | 0 | 2,855 |
| Winfield | 0 | 0 | 0 | 0 | 2,414 |
| **Universities and Colleges** | | | | | |
| Shepherd University | 0 | 0 | 0 | 0 | 5,165 |
| West Virginia State University | 0 | 0 | 0 | 0 | 5,808 |
| West Virginia University | | | | | |
| Institute of Technology | 0 | 0 | 0 | 0 | 2,056 |
| Morgantown | 0 | 0 | 0 | 0 | 30,045 |
| **Metropolitan Counties** | | | | | |
| Berkeley | 0 | 0 | 0 | 0 | |
| Boone | 0 | 0 | 0 | | |
| Brooke | 0 | 0 | 0 | 0 | |
| Fayette | 0 | 0 | 0 | 0 | |
| Hampshire | 0 | 0 | | | |
| Jackson | 0 | 0 | 0 | 0 | |
| Jefferson | 0 | 0 | 0 | 0 | |
| Kanawha | 0 | 0 | 0 | 0 | |
| Marshall | 0 | 0 | 0 | 0 | |
| Mineral | 0 | 0 | 0 | 0 | |
| Morgan | 0 | 0 | 0 | | |
| Ohio | 0 | 0 | | | |
| Preston | 0 | 0 | 0 | 0 | |
| Wirt | 0 | 0 | 0 | 0 | |
| **Nonmetropolitan Counties** | | | | | |
| Barbour | 0 | 0 | 0 | 0 | |
| Braxton | 0 | 0 | 0 | 0 | |
| Calhoun | 0 | 0 | 0 | 0 | |
| Doddridge | 0 | 0 | 0 | 0 | |
| Gilmer | 0 | 0 | | | |
| Grant | 0 | 0 | 0 | 0 | |
| Greenbrier | 0 | 0 | 0 | 0 | |
| Hardy | 0 | 0 | 0 | 0 | |
| Lewis | 0 | 0 | 0 | 0 | |
| Logan | 0 | 0 | 0 | 0 | |
| Mason | 0 | 0 | 0 | 0 | |
| Mingo | 0 | 0 | 0 | 0 | |
| Monroe | 0 | 0 | 0 | 0 | |
| Nicholas | 0 | 0 | 0 | 0 | |
| Pleasants | 0 | 0 | | | |
| Pocahontas | 0 | 0 | 0 | 0 | |
| Ritchie | 0 | 0 | 0 | 0 | |
| Roane | 0 | 0 | 0 | 0 | |
| Summers | 0 | 0 | 0 | 0 | |
| Tyler | 0 | 0 | 0 | 0 | |
| Upshur | 0 | 0 | 0 | 0 | |
| Webster | 0 | 0 | 0 | 0 | |
| Wetzel | 0 | 0 | 0 | 0 | |
| Wyoming | 0 | 0 | 0 | 0 | |
| **State Police Agencies** | | | | | |
| State Police | | | | | |
| Beckley | 0 | 0 | 0 | 0 | |
| Berkeley Springs | 0 | 0 | 0 | 0 | |
| Bridgeport | 0 | 0 | 0 | 0 | |
| Buckhannon | 0 | 0 | 0 | 0 | |

## Table 95. Hate Crime Zero Data Submitted Per Quarter, by Federal Agency, State, and State Agency, 2021—Continued

(Number.)

| Agency name | Zero data per quarter[1] | | | | Population[2] |
|---|---|---|---|---|---|
| | 1st quarter | 2nd quarter | 3rd quarter | 4th quarter | |
| Clay | 0 | 0 | 0 | 0 | |
| Elkins | 0 | 0 | 0 | | |
| Fairmont | 0 | 0 | 0 | 0 | |
| Franklin | 0 | 0 | 0 | 0 | |
| Gauley Bridge | 0 | 0 | 0 | 0 | |
| Glenville | 0 | 0 | 0 | 0 | |
| Grafton | 0 | 0 | 0 | 0 | |
| Grantsville | 0 | 0 | 0 | 0 | |
| Hamlin | 0 | 0 | 0 | 0 | |
| Harrisville | 0 | 0 | 0 | 0 | |
| Hinton | 0 | 0 | 0 | 0 | |
| Jesse | 0 | 0 | 0 | 0 | |
| Kearneysville | | 0 | 0 | 0 | |
| Keyser | 0 | 0 | 0 | 0 | |
| Kingwood | 0 | 0 | 0 | 0 | |
| Lewisburg | 0 | 0 | 0 | 0 | |
| Logan | 0 | 0 | 0 | 0 | |
| Madison | 0 | 0 | 0 | 0 | |
| Marlinton | 0 | 0 | 0 | 0 | |
| Martinsburg | 0 | 0 | 0 | 0 | |
| Moorefield | 0 | 0 | 0 | 0 | |
| Morgantown | 0 | 0 | 0 | 0 | |
| Moundsville | 0 | 0 | 0 | 0 | |
| New Cumberland | 0 | 0 | 0 | 0 | |
| Oak Hill | 0 | 0 | 0 | 0 | |
| Paden City | 0 | 0 | 0 | 0 | |
| Parkersburg | 0 | 0 | 0 | 0 | |
| Parsons | 0 | 0 | 0 | 0 | |
| Philippi | 0 | 0 | 0 | 0 | |
| Point Pleasant | 0 | 0 | 0 | 0 | |
| Princeton | 0 | 0 | 0 | 0 | |
| Quincy | 0 | 0 | 0 | 0 | |
| Richwood | 0 | 0 | 0 | 0 | |
| Ripley | 0 | 0 | 0 | 0 | |
| Romney | 0 | 0 | 0 | 0 | |
| South Charleston | 0 | 0 | 0 | 0 | |
| Spencer | 0 | 0 | 0 | 0 | |
| St. Marys | 0 | 0 | | 0 | |
| Summersville | 0 | 0 | 0 | 0 | |
| Sutton | 0 | 0 | 0 | 0 | |
| Union | 0 | 0 | 0 | 0 | |
| Upperglade | 0 | 0 | 0 | 0 | |
| Wayne | 0 | 0 | 0 | 0 | |
| Welch | 0 | 0 | 0 | 0 | |
| Wellsburg | 0 | 0 | 0 | 0 | |
| Weston | 0 | 0 | 0 | 0 | |
| West Union | 0 | 0 | 0 | 0 | |
| Wheeling | 0 | 0 | 0 | 0 | |
| Whitesville | 0 | 0 | 0 | 0 | |
| Williamson | 0 | 0 | 0 | 0 | |
| Winfield | 0 | 0 | 0 | 0 | |
| State Police, Bureau of Criminal Investigations | | | | | |
| Beckley | 0 | 0 | 0 | 0 | |
| Bluefield | 0 | 0 | 0 | 0 | |
| Charleston | 0 | 0 | 0 | 0 | |
| Martinsburg | 0 | 0 | 0 | 0 | |
| State Police, Parkway Authority, Raleigh County | 0 | 0 | 0 | | |
| **Other Agencies** | | | | | |
| Capitol Protective Services | 0 | 0 | 0 | 0 | |
| Central West Virginia Drug Task Force | 0 | | 0 | | |
| Department of Natural Resources | | | | | |
| Barbour County | 0 | 0 | 0 | 0 | |
| Berkeley County | 0 | 0 | 0 | | |
| Brooke County | 0 | 0 | 0 | 0 | |
| Calhoun County | 0 | 0 | 0 | | |
| Doddridge County | 0 | 0 | | | |
| Gilmer County | 0 | 0 | | | |
| Grant County | 0 | 0 | 0 | | |
| Hampshire County | 0 | 0 | 0 | | |
| Hancock County | 0 | 0 | 0 | 0 | |
| Hardy County | 0 | 0 | 0 | | |
| Harrison County | 0 | 0 | 0 | 0 | |
| Jackson County | 0 | 0 | | | |
| Jefferson County | 0 | 0 | 0 | | |
| Marion County | 0 | 0 | 0 | 0 | |
| Marshall County | 0 | 0 | 0 | 0 | |
| Mineral County | 0 | 0 | 0 | | |
| Monongalia County | | 0 | 0 | 0 | |
| Morgan County | 0 | 0 | 0 | | |

## Table 95. Hate Crime Zero Data Submitted Per Quarter, by Federal Agency, State, and State Agency, 2021—Continued

(Number.)

| Agency name | Zero data per quarter[1] | | | | Population[2] |
|---|---|---|---|---|---|
| | 1st quarter | 2nd quarter | 3rd quarter | 4th quarter | |
| Ohio County | 0 | 0 | 0 | 0 | |
| Pendleton County | 0 | 0 | 0 | | |
| Pleasants County | 0 | 0 | | | |
| Preston County | 0 | 0 | 0 | 0 | |
| Ritchie County | 0 | 0 | | | |
| Roane County | 0 | 0 | | | |
| Taylor County | 0 | 0 | 0 | 0 | |
| Tucker County | 0 | 0 | 0 | 0 | |
| Tyler County | 0 | 0 | | | |
| Wetzel County | 0 | 0 | 0 | 0 | |
| Wirt County | 0 | 0 | | | |
| Wood County | 0 | 0 | | | |
| Greenbrier County Drug and Violent Crime Task Force | 0 | | 0 | | |
| Hancock/Brooke/Weirton Drug Task Force | 0 | 0 | | 0 | |
| Logan County Drug and Violent Crime Task Force | 0 | 0 | 0 | 0 | |
| Marshall County Drug Task Force | 0 | 0 | 0 | 0 | |
| Mon Metro Drug Task Force | 0 | 0 | 0 | | |
| Morgantown Municipal Fire Marshal | 0 | 0 | | | |
| Ohio Valley Drug and Violent Crime Task Force | 0 | 0 | 0 | 0 | |
| State Fire Marshal | | | | | |
|   Barbour County | 0 | | | | |
|   Berkeley County | 0 | | 0 | | |
|   Cabell County | | 0 | | | |
|   Gilmer County | | 0 | | | |
|   Harrison County | 0 | | 0 | | |
|   Jackson County | | 0 | | | |
|   Jefferson County | 0 | | 0 | 0 | |
|   Kanawha County | | | | 0 | |
|   Marion County | 0 | | 0 | | |
|   Mineral County | | | 0 | | |
|   Pendleton County | 0 | | | | |
|   Preston County | | | 0 | | |
|   Raleigh County | | | | 0 | |
|   Randolph County | 0 | 0 | | 0 | |
|   Taylor County | 0 | | | 0 | |
|   Upshur County | | | 0 | | |
| Three Rivers Drug and Violent Crime Task Force | 0 | 0 | 0 | 0 | |
| **WISCONSIN** | | | | | |
| **Cities** | | | | | |
| Adams | 0 | 0 | 0 | 0 | 1,898 |
| Albany | 0 | 0 | 0 | 0 | 973 |
| Algoma | 0 | 0 | 0 | 0 | 3,026 |
| Amery | 0 | 0 | 0 | 0 | 2,786 |
| Antigo | 0 | 0 | 0 | 0 | 7,671 |
| Ashland | 0 | 0 | 0 | 0 | 7,723 |
| Ashwaubenon | 0 | 0 | 0 | 0 | 17,008 |
| Athens | 0 | 0 | 0 | 0 | 1,077 |
| Bangor | 0 | 0 | 0 | 0 | 1,441 |
| Barron | 0 | 0 | 0 | 0 | 3,215 |
| Bayside | 0 | 0 | 0 | 0 | 4,353 |
| Beaver Dam Township | 0 | 0 | 0 | 0 | 3,914 |
| Belleville | 0 | 0 | 0 | 0 | 2,528 |
| Beloit Town | 0 | 0 | 0 | 0 | 7,724 |
| Berlin | 0 | 0 | 0 | 0 | 5,367 |
| Blanchardville | 0 | | | 0 | 784 |
| Bloomer | 0 | 0 | 0 | 0 | 3,504 |
| Boyceville | 0 | 0 | 0 | 0 | 1,127 |
| Brillion | 0 | 0 | 0 | 0 | 3,071 |
| Brown Deer | 0 | 0 | 0 | 0 | 12,310 |
| Brownsville | 0 | 0 | 0 | 0 | 585 |
| Burlington | 0 | 0 | 0 | 0 | 10,938 |
| Butler | 0 | 0 | 0 | 0 | 1,790 |
| Caledonia | 0 | 0 | 0 | 0 | 25,272 |
| Campbell Township | 0 | 0 | 0 | 0 | 4,273 |
| Cascade | 0 | 0 | 0 | 0 | 691 |
| Cashton | 0 | 0 | 0 | 0 | 1,112 |
| Cedarburg | 0 | 0 | 0 | 0 | 11,818 |
| Chenequa | 0 | 0 | 0 | 0 | 610 |
| Chetek | 0 | 0 | 0 | 0 | 2,083 |
| Chilton | 0 | 0 | 0 | 0 | 3,862 |
| Chippewa Falls | 0 | 0 | 0 | 0 | 14,475 |
| Cleveland | 0 | 0 | 0 | 0 | 1,452 |
| Clinton | 0 | 0 | 0 | 0 | 2,116 |
| Coleman | 0 | | | | 681 |
| Columbus | 0 | 0 | 0 | 0 | 5,129 |
| Cornell | 0 | 0 | 0 | 0 | 1,394 |
| Cottage Grove | 0 | 0 | 0 | 0 | 7,241 |
| Crivitz | 0 | 0 | 0 | 0 | 934 |
| Cross Plains | 0 | 0 | 0 | 0 | 4,348 |

## Table 95. Hate Crime Zero Data Submitted Per Quarter, by Federal Agency, State, and State Agency, 2021—Continued

(Number.)

| Agency name | Zero data per quarter[1] | | | | Population[2] |
|---|---|---|---|---|---|
| | 1st quarter | 2nd quarter | 3rd quarter | 4th quarter | |
| Cuba City | 0 | 0 | | | 2,043 |
| Cudahy | 0 | 0 | 0 | 0 | 18,201 |
| Deforest | 0 | 0 | 0 | 0 | 11,130 |
| Delafield | 0 | 0 | 0 | 0 | 7,607 |
| Delavan | 0 | 0 | 0 | 0 | 9,813 |
| Delavan Town | 0 | 0 | 0 | 0 | 5,361 |
| East Troy | 0 | 0 | 0 | 0 | 4,307 |
| Edgerton | 0 | 0 | 0 | 0 | 5,613 |
| Elkhart Lake | 0 | 0 | 0 | 0 | 1,018 |
| Elkhorn | 0 | 0 | 0 | 0 | 10,016 |
| Elk Mound | 0 | 0 | 0 | 0 | 885 |
| Ellsworth | 0 | 0 | 0 | 0 | 3,270 |
| Elm Grove | 0 | 0 | 0 | 0 | 6,158 |
| Elroy | 0 | 0 | 0 | 0 | 1,293 |
| Endeavor | 0 | | | 0 | 464 |
| Evansville | 0 | 0 | 0 | 0 | 5,614 |
| Everest Metropolitan | 0 | 0 | 0 | 0 | 17,341 |
| Fennimore | 0 | 0 | 0 | 0 | 2,464 |
| Fontana | 0 | 0 | 0 | 0 | 1,749 |
| Fort Atkinson | 0 | 0 | 0 | 0 | 12,370 |
| Fox Crossing | 0 | 0 | 0 | 0 | 19,200 |
| Fox Lake | 0 | 0 | 0 | 0 | 1,432 |
| Fox Point | 0 | 0 | 0 | 0 | 6,678 |
| Fox Valley Metro | 0 | 0 | 0 | | 22,891 |
| Franklin | 0 | 0 | 0 | 0 | 36,264 |
| Geneva Town | 0 | 0 | 0 | 0 | 5,052 |
| Genoa City | 0 | 0 | 0 | 0 | 2,974 |
| Germantown | 0 | 0 | 0 | 0 | 20,066 |
| Gillett | 0 | 0 | 0 | | 1,298 |
| Gilman | 0 | 0 | 0 | 0 | 388 |
| Glendale | 0 | 0 | 0 | 0 | 12,843 |
| Grafton | 0 | 0 | 0 | 0 | 11,783 |
| Grand Chute | 0 | 0 | 0 | 0 | 23,739 |
| Greendale | 0 | 0 | 0 | 0 | 14,251 |
| Greenfield | 0 | 0 | 0 | 0 | 37,531 |
| Green Lake | 0 | 0 | 0 | 0 | 961 |
| Hammond | 0 | 0 | 0 | 0 | 1,887 |
| Hartford | 0 | 0 | 0 | 0 | 15,815 |
| Hazel Green | 0 | 0 | 0 | 0 | 1,215 |
| Hobart-Lawrence | 0 | 0 | 0 | 0 | 16,712 |
| Holmen | 0 | 0 | 0 | 0 | 10,497 |
| Horicon | 0 | 0 | 0 | 0 | 3,683 |
| Hortonville | 0 | 0 | 0 | 0 | 3,005 |
| Hurley | 0 | 0 | 0 | 0 | 1,413 |
| Jefferson | 0 | 0 | 0 | 0 | 8,042 |
| Juneau | 0 | 0 | 0 | 0 | 2,506 |
| Kewaunee | 0 | 0 | 0 | 0 | 2,824 |
| Kiel | 0 | 0 | 0 | 0 | 3,807 |
| Kohler | 0 | 0 | 0 | 0 | 2,042 |
| Kronenwetter | 0 | 0 | 0 | 0 | 8,242 |
| Lake Geneva | 0 | 0 | 0 | 0 | 8,155 |
| Lake Hallie | 0 | 0 | 0 | 0 | 6,807 |
| Lake Mills | 0 | 0 | 0 | 0 | 6,044 |
| Lancaster | 0 | 0 | 0 | 0 | 3,683 |
| Lena | 0 | 0 | 0 | 0 | 538 |
| Linn Township | 0 | 0 | 0 | 0 | 2,409 |
| Lodi | 0 | 0 | 0 | 0 | 3,115 |
| Lomira | 0 | 0 | 0 | 0 | 2,457 |
| Luxemburg | 0 | 0 | 0 | 0 | 2,582 |
| Manawa | 0 | 0 | 0 | 0 | 1,259 |
| Marathon City | 0 | 0 | 0 | 0 | 1,513 |
| Marshall Village | 0 | 0 | 0 | 0 | 4,031 |
| Mauston | 0 | 0 | 0 | 0 | 4,352 |
| Mayville | 0 | 0 | 0 | 0 | 4,798 |
| McFarland | 0 | 0 | 0 | 0 | 9,437 |
| Medford | 0 | 0 | 0 | 0 | 4,258 |
| Menomonee Falls | 0 | 0 | 0 | 0 | 38,516 |
| Mequon | 0 | 0 | 0 | 0 | 24,936 |
| Merrill | 0 | 0 | 0 | 0 | 8,927 |
| Milton | 0 | 0 | 0 | 0 | 5,653 |
| Minocqua | 0 | 0 | 0 | 0 | 4,453 |
| Mishicot | 0 | 0 | 0 | 0 | 1,384 |
| Mondovi | 0 | 0 | 0 | 0 | 2,542 |
| Monroe | 0 | 0 | 0 | 0 | 10,387 |
| Montello | 0 | 0 | 0 | 0 | 1,451 |
| Monticello | | | | 0 | 1,182 |
| Mount Pleasant | 0 | 0 | 0 | 0 | 27,084 |
| Mukwonago | 0 | 0 | 0 | 0 | 8,184 |
| Mukwonago Town | 0 | 0 | 0 | 0 | 8,184 |
| Muskego | 0 | 0 | 0 | 0 | 25,436 |

## Table 95. Hate Crime Zero Data Submitted Per Quarter, by Federal Agency, State, and State Agency, 2021—Continued

(Number.)

| Agency name | Zero data per quarter[1] | | | | Population[2] |
|---|---|---|---|---|---|
| | 1st quarter | 2nd quarter | 3rd quarter | 4th quarter | |
| Neshkoro | | 0 | 0 | 0 | 424 |
| New Glarus | 0 | 0 | 0 | 0 | 2,132 |
| New Holstein | 0 | 0 | 0 | 0 | 3,092 |
| New Lisbon | 0 | 0 | 0 | 0 | 2,547 |
| New London | 0 | 0 | 0 | 0 | 7,043 |
| Niagara | 0 | 0 | 0 | 0 | 1,526 |
| North Fond du Lac | 0 | 0 | 0 | 0 | 5,064 |
| Oak Creek | 0 | 0 | 0 | 0 | 36,975 |
| Oconomowoc | 0 | 0 | 0 | 0 | 17,301 |
| Oconto Falls | 0 | 0 | 0 | 0 | 2,796 |
| Omro | 0 | 0 | 0 | 0 | 3,599 |
| Orfordville | 0 | 0 | 0 | 0 | 1,490 |
| Oxford | 0 | 0 | 0 | 0 | 604 |
| Palmyra | 0 | 0 | 0 | 0 | 1,742 |
| Pepin | 0 | 0 | 0 | 0 | 739 |
| Peshtigo | 0 | 0 | 0 | 0 | 3,310 |
| Pewaukee Village | 0 | 0 | 0 | 0 | 8,089 |
| Phillips | 0 | 0 | 0 | 0 | 1,306 |
| Pleasant Prairie | 0 | 0 | 0 | 0 | 21,542 |
| Plover | 0 | 0 | 0 | 0 | 13,360 |
| Plymouth | 0 | 0 | 0 | 0 | 8,766 |
| Poynette | 0 | 0 | 0 | 0 | 2,506 |
| Prairie du Chien | 0 | 0 | 0 | 0 | 5,496 |
| Prescott | 0 | 0 | 0 | 0 | 4,281 |
| Racine | 0 | 0 | 0 | 0 | 76,018 |
| Rhinelander | 0 | 0 | 0 | 0 | 7,624 |
| Rib Lake | 0 | 0 | 0 | 0 | 857 |
| River Hills | 0 | 0 | 0 | 0 | 1,585 |
| Rome Town | 0 | 0 | 0 | 0 | 2,790 |
| Rothschild | 0 | 0 | 0 | 0 | 5,255 |
| Saukville | 0 | 0 | 0 | 0 | 4,436 |
| Seymour | 0 | 0 | 0 | 0 | 3,457 |
| Sheboygan | 0 | 0 | 0 | 0 | 47,667 |
| Sheboygan Falls | 0 | 0 | 0 | 0 | 7,924 |
| Shiocton | 0 | 0 | 0 | 0 | 914 |
| Shorewood | 0 | 0 | 0 | 0 | 13,222 |
| Shorewood Hills | 0 | 0 | 0 | 0 | 2,050 |
| Siren | 0 | 0 | 0 | 0 | 778 |
| South Milwaukee | 0 | 0 | 0 | 0 | 20,795 |
| Spencer | 0 | 0 | 0 | 0 | 1,859 |
| Spring Valley | 0 | 0 | | 0 | 1,321 |
| Stanley | 0 | 0 | 0 | 0 | 3,714 |
| St. Croix Falls | 0 | 0 | 0 | 0 | 2,052 |
| St. Francis | 0 | 0 | 0 | 0 | 9,846 |
| Stoughton | 0 | 0 | 0 | | 13,274 |
| Sturtevant | 0 | 0 | 0 | 0 | 6,642 |
| Summit | 0 | 0 | 0 | 0 | 5,321 |
| Sun Prairie | 0 | 0 | 0 | 0 | 35,722 |
| Superior | 0 | 0 | 0 | 0 | 26,117 |
| Thiensville | 0 | 0 | 0 | 0 | 3,107 |
| Thorp | 0 | 0 | 0 | 0 | 1,602 |
| Three Lakes | 0 | 0 | 0 | 0 | 2,126 |
| Tomahawk | 0 | 0 | 0 | 0 | 3,107 |
| Town of East Troy | 0 | 0 | 0 | 0 | 4,065 |
| Town of Madison | 0 | 0 | 0 | 0 | 6,713 |
| Verona | 0 | 0 | 0 | 0 | 13,860 |
| Waterford Town | 0 | 0 | 0 | 0 | 6,509 |
| Waterloo | 0 | 0 | 0 | 0 | 3,320 |
| Waukesha | 0 | 0 | 0 | 0 | 72,493 |
| Waunakee | 0 | 0 | 0 | 0 | 14,410 |
| Waupaca | 0 | 0 | 0 | 0 | 5,833 |
| Waupun | 0 | 0 | 0 | 0 | 11,264 |
| Wauwatosa | 0 | 0 | 0 | 0 | 48,650 |
| Webster | 0 | 0 | 0 | 0 | 618 |
| West Allis | 0 | 0 | 0 | 0 | 60,176 |
| West Bend | 0 | 0 | 0 | 0 | 31,506 |
| Westfield | 0 | 0 | 0 | 0 | 1,270 |
| West Milwaukee | 0 | 0 | 0 | 0 | 4,113 |
| West Salem | 0 | 0 | 0 | 0 | 5,032 |
| Whitefish Bay | 0 | 0 | 0 | 0 | 13,848 |
| Whitewater | 0 | 0 | 0 | 0 | 15,057 |
| Williams Bay | 0 | 0 | 0 | 0 | 2,666 |
| Wind Point | 0 | 0 | 0 | 0 | 1,681 |
| Winneconne | 0 | 0 | 0 | 0 | 2,491 |
| Wisconsin Dells | 0 | 0 | 0 | 0 | 3,099 |
| Woodruff | 0 | 0 | 0 | 0 | 1,990 |
| **Universities and Colleges** | | | | | |
| Marquette University | 0 | 0 | 0 | | 12,601 |
| University of Wisconsin | | | | | |

## Table 95. Hate Crime Zero Data Submitted Per Quarter, by Federal Agency, State, and State Agency, 2021—Continued

(Number.)

| Agency name | Zero data per quarter[1] | | | | Population[2] |
|---|---|---|---|---|---|
| | 1st quarter | 2nd quarter | 3rd quarter | 4th quarter | |
| Eau Claire | 0 | 0 | 0 | 0 | 12,230 |
| Platteville | 0 | 0 | 0 | 0 | 9,403 |
| River Falls | 0 | 0 | 0 | 0 | 6,561 |
| Stout | 0 | 0 | 0 | 0 | 9,702 |
| Superior | 0 | 0 | 0 | 0 | 3,171 |
| Whitewater | 0 | 0 | 0 | 0 | 14,657 |
| **Metropolitan Counties** | | | | | |
| Brown | 0 | 0 | 0 | 0 | |
| Calumet | 0 | 0 | 0 | 0 | |
| Chippewa | 0 | 0 | 0 | 0 | |
| Dane | 0 | 0 | 0 | 0 | |
| Fond du Lac | 0 | 0 | 0 | 0 | |
| Green | 0 | 0 | 0 | 0 | |
| Iowa | 0 | 0 | 0 | 0 | |
| Kenosha | 0 | 0 | 0 | 0 | |
| Kewaunee | 0 | 0 | 0 | 0 | |
| La Crosse | 0 | 0 | 0 | 0 | |
| Marathon | 0 | 0 | 0 | 0 | |
| Milwaukee | 0 | 0 | 0 | 0 | |
| Oconto | 0 | 0 | 0 | 0 | |
| Outagamie | 0 | 0 | 0 | 0 | |
| Pierce | 0 | 0 | 0 | 0 | |
| Racine | 0 | 0 | 0 | 0 | |
| Sheboygan | 0 | 0 | 0 | 0 | |
| **Nonmetropolitan Counties** | | | | | |
| Adams | 0 | 0 | 0 | 0 | |
| Ashland | 0 | 0 | 0 | | |
| Barron | 0 | 0 | 0 | 0 | |
| Buffalo | 0 | 0 | 0 | 0 | |
| Burnett | 0 | 0 | 0 | 0 | |
| Clark | 0 | 0 | 0 | 0 | |
| Crawford | 0 | 0 | 0 | 0 | |
| Door | 0 | 0 | 0 | 0 | |
| Dunn | 0 | 0 | 0 | 0 | |
| Grant | 0 | 0 | 0 | 0 | |
| Iron | 0 | 0 | 0 | 0 | |
| Jefferson | 0 | 0 | 0 | 0 | |
| Juneau | 0 | 0 | 0 | 0 | |
| Lafayette | 0 | 0 | 0 | 0 | |
| Langlade | 0 | 0 | 0 | 0 | |
| Manitowoc | 0 | 0 | 0 | 0 | |
| Marinette | 0 | 0 | 0 | 0 | |
| Marquette | 0 | 0 | 0 | 0 | |
| Menominee | 0 | 0 | 0 | 0 | |
| Monroe | 0 | 0 | 0 | 0 | |
| Pepin | 0 | 0 | 0 | 0 | |
| Portage | 0 | 0 | 0 | 0 | |
| Price | 0 | 0 | 0 | 0 | |
| Richland | 0 | 0 | 0 | 0 | |
| Rusk | 0 | 0 | 0 | 0 | |
| Sawyer | 0 | 0 | 0 | 0 | |
| Trempealeau | 0 | 0 | 0 | 0 | |
| Vernon | 0 | 0 | 0 | 0 | |
| Vilas | 0 | 0 | 0 | 0 | |
| Walworth | 0 | 0 | 0 | 0 | |
| Washburn | 0 | 0 | 0 | 0 | |
| Waupaca | 0 | 0 | 0 | 0 | |
| Waushara | 0 | 0 | 0 | 0 | |
| Wood | 0 | 0 | 0 | 0 | |
| **Tribal Agencies** | | | | | |
| Lac Courte Oreilles Tribal | 0 | 0 | 0 | 0 | |
| Oneida Tribal | 0 | 0 | 0 | 0 | |
| St. Croix Tribal | 0 | 0 | 0 | 0 | |
| Stockbridge Munsee Tribal | 0 | 0 | 0 | 0 | |
| **Other Agencies** | | | | | |
| Division of Criminal Investigation, Madison | 0 | 0 | 0 | 0 | |
| **WYOMING** | | | | | |
| **Cities** | | | | | |
| Buffalo | 0 | 0 | 0 | 0 | 4,666 |
| Diamondville | 0 | 0 | 0 | 0 | 769 |
| Evanston | 0 | 0 | 0 | 0 | 11,494 |
| Evansville | 0 | 0 | 0 | 0 | 3,046 |
| Gillette | 0 | 0 | 0 | 0 | 32,294 |
| Glenrock | 0 | 0 | 0 | 0 | 2,560 |
| Green River | | | 0 | 0 | 11,729 |

## Table 95. Hate Crime Zero Data Submitted Per Quarter, by Federal Agency, State, and State Agency, 2021—Continued

(Number.)

| Agency name | Zero data per quarter[1] | | | | Population[2] |
|---|---|---|---|---|---|
| | 1st quarter | 2nd quarter | 3rd quarter | 4th quarter | |
| Jackson | 0 | 0 | 0 | 0 | 10,672 |
| Laramie | 0 | 0 | 0 | 0 | 32,841 |
| Lusk | 0 | 0 | 0 | 0 | 1,465 |
| Medicine Bow | 0 | 0 | 0 | 0 | 255 |
| Mills | 0 | 0 | 0 | 0 | 4,144 |
| Moorcroft | 0 | 0 | 0 | 0 | 1,091 |
| Pine Bluffs | 0 | 0 | 0 | 0 | 1,163 |
| Powell | 0 | 0 | 0 | 0 | 6,108 |
| Thermopolis | 0 | 0 | 0 | 0 | 2,747 |
| Torrington | 0 | 0 | 0 | 0 | 6,564 |
| Worland | 0 | 0 | 0 | 0 | 4,947 |
| **Metropolitan Counties** | | | | | |
| Laramie | 0 | 0 | 0 | 0 | |
| Natrona | 0 | 0 | 0 | 0 | |
| **Nonmetropolitan Counties** | | | | | |
| Albany | 0 | 0 | 0 | 0 | |
| Campbell | 0 | 0 | 0 | 0 | |
| Converse | 0 | 0 | 0 | 0 | |
| Crook | 0 | 0 | 0 | 0 | |
| Goshen | 0 | 0 | 0 | 0 | |
| Hot Springs | 0 | 0 | 0 | 0 | |
| Lincoln | 0 | 0 | 0 | 0 | |
| Niobrara | 0 | 0 | 0 | 0 | |
| Sublette | 0 | 0 | 0 | 0 | |
| Sweetwater | 0 | 0 | 0 | 0 | |
| Teton | 0 | 0 | 0 | 0 | |
| Uinta | 0 | 0 | 0 | 0 | |
| Washakie | 0 | 0 | 0 | 0 | |
| Weston | 0 | 0 | 0 | 0 | |
| **Tribal Agencies** | | | | | |
| Wind River Agency | 0 | 0 | 0 | 0 | |
| **Other Agencies** | | | | | |
| Wyoming Division of Criminal Investigation | 0 | 0 | 0 | 0 | |
| **FEDERAL AGENCIES** | | | | | |
| Board of Governors of the Federal Reserve System and the Consumer Financial Protection Bureau, Office of Inspector General | 0 | 0 | 0 | 0 | |
| Central Intelligence Agency Security Protective Service | 0 | 0 | 0 | 0 | |
| Commodity Futures Trading Commission, Office of Inspector General | 0 | 0 | 0 | 0 | |
| Corporation for National and Community Service, Office of Inspector General | 0 | 0 | 0 | 0 | |
| Department of Veterans Affairs, Office of Inspector General | 0 | 0 | 0 | 0 | |
| Drug Enforcement Administration, Wilmington Resident Office | 0 | 0 | 0 | 0 | |
| Export-Import Bank of the United States, Office of Inspector General | 0 | 0 | 0 | 0 | |
| Federal Communications Commission, Office of Inspector General | 0 | 0 | 0 | 0 | |
| Federal Emergency Management Agency | 0 | 0 | 0 | 0 | |
| Federal Housing Finance Agency, Office of Inspector General | 0 | 0 | 0 | | |
| Library of Congress, Office of Inspector General | 0 | 0 | 0 | 0 | |
| National Institute of Health | 0 | 0 | 0 | 0 | |
| National Security Agency Police | 0 | 0 | 0 | 0 | |
| Peace Corps, Office of Inspector General | 0 | 0 | 0 | 0 | |
| Pension Benefit Guaranty Corporation, Office of Inspector General | 0 | 0 | 0 | 0 | |
| Smithsonian Institution, Office of Inspector General | 0 | 0 | 0 | 0 | |
| Tennessee Valley Authority, Office of Inspector General | 0 | 0 | 0 | 0 | |
| United States Agency for International Development, Office of Inspector General | | 0 | | | |
| United States Air Force, Office of Special Investigations | 0 | 0 | 0 | 0 | |
| United States Department of Agriculture, Office of Inspector General | 0 | 0 | 0 | 0 | |
| United States Department of Defense, Office of Inspector General | 0 | 0 | 0 | | |
| United States Department of Education, Office of Inspector General | 0 | 0 | 0 | | |
| United States Department of Housing and Urban Development, Office of Inspector General | 0 | 0 | 0 | 0 | |
| United States Department of Justice, Office of Inspector General | 0 | 0 | 0 | 0 | |
| United States Department of State, Office of Inspector General | 0 | 0 | 0 | 0 | |
| United States Department of Transportation, Office of Inspector General | 0 | 0 | 0 | 0 | |
| United States Environmental Protection Agency, Office of Inspector General | 0 | 0 | 0 | 0 | |
| United States Federal Deposit Insurance Corporation, Office of Inspector General | 0 | 0 | 0 | | |
| United States General Services Administration, Office of Inspector General | 0 | 0 | 0 | 0 | |
| United States National Archives and Records Administration, Office of Inspector General | 0 | 0 | 0 | | |
| United States Navy Law Enforcement | 0 | 0 | 0 | | |
| United States Nuclear Regulatory Commission, Office of Inspector General | 0 | 0 | 0 | 0 | |
| United States Office of Personnel Management, Office of the Inspector General | 0 | 0 | 0 | 0 | |
| United States Securities and Exchange Commission, Office of Inspector General | 0 | 0 | 0 | 0 | |

1 Agencies published in this table indicated that no hate crimes occurred in their jurisdictions during the quarters(s) for which they submitted reports to the Hate Crime Statistics Program. Blanks indicate quarters for which agencies did not submit reports.    2 Population figures are published only for the cities. The figures listed for the universities and colleges are student enrollment and were provided by the United States Department of Education for the 2020 school year, the most recent available. The enrollment figures include full-time and part-time students.

# SECTION VII

# COVID-19 AND THE INMATE POPULATION

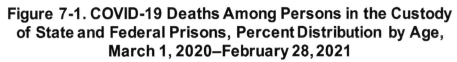

**Figure 7-1. COVID-19 Deaths Among Persons in the Custody
of State and Federal Prisons, Percent Distribution by Age,
March 1, 2020–February 28, 2021**

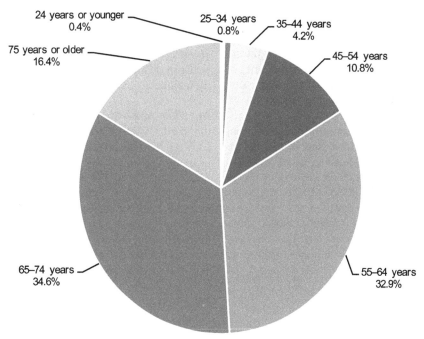

24 years or younger
0.4%

25–34 years
0.8%

35–44 years
4.2%

75 years or older
16.4%

45–54 years
10.8%

65–74 years
34.6%

55–64 years
32.9%

Tables 96–107 in Section VII are derived from the Bureau of Justice Statistics' *Impact of COVID-19 on State and Federal Prisons, March 2020–February 2021* report. This report is one of the only COVID-19 publications concentrating on correctional facilities. It includes data on COVID-19 tests and data on confirmed and suspected deaths due to COVID-19 among jail inmates and staff. State and federal prisons had a crude mortality rate (unadjusted for sex, race or ethnicity, or age) of 1.5 COVID-19–related deaths per 1,000 prisoners from the end of February 2020 to the end of February 2021, and 196 correction staff in state and federal prisons died due to COVID-19. The infection rate of state prisoners at risk of COVID-19 exposure was 219 per 1,000 prisoners, with White and Black prisoners accounting for two-thirds of infections. Less than 10 percent of prisoners who died from COVID-19 were under 44 years of age.

The impact of COVID-19 on local jails began in March 2020, with a drop of more than 16 percent in the inmate population in the timeframe studied. All states saw a drop in their inmate populations. The prison population declined by 157,500 persons during the first 6 months of the COVID-19 study period

through the end of August 2020, and by 58,300 in the 6 months through the end of February 2021. Twenty-four states released a total of 37,700 persons from prison on an expedited basis (earlier than scheduled) during the COVID-19 study period; however, fewer than 1 in 10 of these releases was earlier than scheduled.

Findings in this report are based on BJS's National Prisoner Statistics program – Coronavirus Pandemic Supplemental Survey, 2021 and the National Corrections Reporting Program, 2020. Respondents in state departments of corrections (DOCs) and the BOP were asked for information about their monthly populations of prisoners in custody, as well as their admissions and releases, from January 2020 to February 2021. BJS also requested counts and demographic distributions of prisoners who tested positive for and/or died from COVID-19. This 14-month survey period allowed BJS to track monthly trends in admissions and custody populations from just before the COVID-19 pandemic in the United States. The Missouri DOC did not participate in the NPS-CPan survey. The Oregon DOC attempted to participate but could not release its data due to ongoing litigation surrounding the state response to

COVID-19 in prisons. Data for Oregon were obtained from its DOC website <https://prod.oregon.gov/doc/covid19/Pages/default.aspx>.

The NPS-CPan also covered state and BOP policies and practices to mitigate transmission of the virus, to expedite release of prisoners, and to determine a process for vaccinating staff and prisoners in early 2021. State and federal prisons administered approximately 4.8 million viral COVID-19 tests to prisoners over the survey period, with a total of 396,300 positive tests (a rate of 8.2 positives per 100 tests). California, the BOP, and Texas had the most positive tests. At some point during the survey period (if not for the whole period), the majority of states attempted to mitigate the threat of COVID-19 by suspending family visitation and educational programming.

BJS augmented these data with prisoner information from the annual NPS and National Corrections Reporting Program (NCRP) data collections. Unless otherwise noted, statistics are based on the number of persons in the custody of prison facilities operated by states, the BOP, and private companies under contract with state or federal governments. The statistics presented in this report will differ from previously published statistics on U.S. prison populations based on the count of prisoners under jurisdiction or legal authority of state and federal governments.

### Definitions: COVID-19

*COVID-19*—Coronavirus disease and the virus causing the disease, i.e., severe acute respiratory syndrome coronavirus 2 (SARS-CoV-2).

*COVID-19 test*—A viral or polymerase chain reaction (PCR) test for COVID-19. Respondents were asked to exclude antibody or serology tests from their counts of COVID-19 tests and positive tests.

*Crude mortality rate*—The number of deaths per 1,000 U.S. residents, unadjusted for differences in sex, race or ethnicity, or age. (See *Methodology* for the Bureau of Justice Statistics' (BJS) calculation of crude mortality rate.)

*Custody*—The physical holding of a person in a prison operated by a state or the Federal Bureau of Prisons (BOP), regardless of sentence length or which authority has jurisdiction over the prisoner.

*Custody plus privates*—The physical holding of a person in a prison operated by a state, the BOP, or a private company under state or federal contract, regardless of sentence length or which authority has jurisdiction over the prisoner.

*Expedited release*—The release of a prisoner from the jurisdiction of a state department of corrections or the BOP at least 1 day before their scheduled or expected release date or post-custody community supervision eligibility date, to limit prisoner risk and exposure to COVID-19 or due to COVID-19-related understaffing, court orders, or legislative mandates.

*Federal prison system*—The system in which adult prisoners are held in the custody of the BOP in secure federal prison facilities, nonsecure community correctional facilities, and privately operated facilities. Persons convicted of a felony in the District of Columbia serve their sentence in federal prison.

*Home confinement*—When prisoners are in BOP custody but living in their residence or the residence of a designated family member.

*Infection rate*—The number of persons who tested positive for COVID-19 per 1,000 persons at risk of exposure to COVID-19. The infection rate is calculated as the number of unique prisoners who tested positive for COVID-19 from March 1, 2020 to February 28, 2021, divided by the total prison population. Infection rates among imprisoned and unimprisoned populations in the United States should not be compared because their demographic distributions differ significantly. The U.S. Centers for Disease Control and Prevention (CDC) has documented differences in infection rates by sex, race or ethnicity, and age.

*Prison/prison facility*—A long-term confinement facility that is operated by a state or federal government or private company under state or federal contract.

It includes prisons, penitentiaries, and correctional institutions; boot camps; prison farms; reception, diagnostic, and classification centers; release centers, halfway houses, and road camps; forestry and conservation camps; vocational training facilities; prison hospitals; and drug and alcohol treatment facilities. Prisons typically hold persons convicted of a felony, or those with a sentence of more than 1 year imposed by a state or federal court. Sentence length may vary by state. Alaska, Connecticut, Delaware, Hawaii, Rhode Island, and Vermont each operate an integrated system that combines prisons and jails, so their counts include prison and jail populations.

*Prisoner*—A person confined in a state or federal prison or privately operated prison under state or federal contract. Counts of prisoners exclude persons held in local jails under the legal authority of a state or federal correctional authority.

*Test positivity rate*—The number of COVID-19 tests with a positive result per 1,000 tests performed in a correctional jurisdiction. This is calculated by dividing the number of positive COVID-19 tests by the total number of tests given. The rate is per 1,000 tests administered. This measure does not correspond to the unique number of prisoners who tested positive for COVID-19 because prisoners could have multiple positive tests. This measure also does not indicate the severity of the outbreak in a particular jurisdiction because state DOCs that tested all or large subsets of their prison populations likely identified multiple infected individuals with no external symptoms of COVID-19. Jurisdictions that tested only symptomatic prisoners or staff would miss asymptomatic individuals and therefore have a higher test positivity rate.

### Jurisdiction Notes

**Alabama**—The state department of corrections (DOC) confirmed that no prisoner tested positive for COVID-19 more than once.

**Alaska**—Alaska runs an integrated prison-and-jail system for sentenced and unsentenced persons, with many entering and exiting each day. As such, there may be discrepancies in the flow of entries and exits calculated. Staff vaccinations were performed but not tracked, and the state DOC had no data on staff infections or deaths.

**Arizona**—The state DOC could not report on the number of positive COVID-19 tests, only the unique number of positive prisoners. Due to multiple sources for test data, the DOC used its local database systems to record strictly unique positive cases per prisoner. This was due to the mass testing the DOC initiated at the beginning of the pandemic with a different lab from the one normally used by its Health Services contractor.

**Arkansas**—No notes were reported.

**California**—Population counts included prisoners who had been temporarily absent for more than 30 days. California began its expedited release process in April 2020.

**Colorado**—There was a slight discrepancy between the February 29, 2020 prison population count and the sum of the January 31, 2020 prison population and all admissions minus all releases. Reported counts for the number of unique prisoners who tested positive and for staff who tested positive or died may differ slightly from those reported on other public websites.

**Connecticut**—If the deceased prisoner did not have an autopsy, the attending physician at the time of death pronounced the cause of death.

**Delaware**—Data on COVID-19 tests covered April 1, 2020 to April 1, 2021. The state DOC tracked the number of positive prisoners instead of the number of positive tests but confirmed that fewer than five prisoners tested positive more than once.

**Federal Bureau of Prisons**—All responses to the National Prisoner Statistics – Coronavirus Pandemic Supplemental Survey (NPS-CPan) covered facilities managed by the Federal Bureau of Prisons (BOP). Counts of admissions included prison-to-prison transfers and represented admissions rather than unique persons admitted. The total count of releases reflected the number of persons released at least once, including prison-to-prison transfers. The BOP did not report any expedited releases because sentencing is the purview of the courts. While some prisoners did receive a reduction in sentence during the NPS-CPan survey period, the reasons for court actions were not always provided and do not appear in the BOP's data systems.

**Florida**—Prisoners who tested positive for COVID-19 were rarely retested, so the number of positive tests and unique prisoners who tested positive were similar. Seven prisoners who tested positive had faulty identification information, so their sex and race or ethnicity data were not provided.

**Georgia**—Population counts reported to the NPS-CPan survey reflected persons who had a physical bed in a Georgia correctional facility, which differs from counts reported to the National Prisoner Statistics program (NPS-1B) collection. The state DOC could not access information on the number of prisoner deaths due to COVID-19 as determined by a medical examiner or coroner.

**Hawaii**—Counts of COVID-19 deaths excluded the coroner-evaluated deaths of two Native Hawaiian males (one in the 55–64 age group and the other 75 or older) that occurred at the private Saguaro Correctional Center in Arizona, which is contracted to multiple jurisdictions besides Hawaii. Staff vaccination counts were based on self-reports and excluded the 42 vaccinated staff at the Saguaro facility, where vaccinations began on March 9, 2021.

**Idaho**—No notes were reported.

**Illinois**—The state DOC tested prisoners frequently, resulting in a large number of reported tests. The DOC could not report the number of unique prisoners who tested positive. Illinois could not report the unique number of prisoners testing positive in the NPS-CPan. BJS used data scraped from state DOC websites at the time they were initially posted by the University of North Carolina Health and Justice Research Lab's COVID Prison Project, which is archived at <https://github.com/healthandjustice/covid-prison-project.>

**Indiana**—Indiana did not engage in expedited releases. Any releases due to court modifications were done at the court's behest and were not specifically identified as COVID-19-related. The state DOC confirmed that the number of positive tests represented the number of unique prisoners who tested positive. The number of prisoners vaccinated as of February 28, 2021 could not be determined. Vaccinations for newly admitted prisoners were prioritized at state facilities dedicated to prisoner intake. At other facilities, prisoners were prioritized for vaccination based on risk.

**Iowa**—Expedited releases were not solely based on the decision of the governor or state DOC and required parole board approval. Considerations were made to help release individuals early during the pandemic, and 4,700 persons were released on an expedited basis but not officially as a direct result of COVID-19.

**Kansas**—The state DOC had no data on the number of persons who received expedited release.

**Kentucky**—The state DOC reported the date that vaccines were made available to prisoners.

**Louisiana**—As a criteria for expedited release, age was considered not as a specific number but as a subjective variable reflecting health status.

**Maine**—No notes were reported.

**Maryland**—Population counts included committed detainees in the Baltimore City Detention Center or the Baltimore Central Booking and Intake Center.

**Massachusetts**—The criteria for expedited release included state DOC and court policies, although the DOC was unclear how the courts used particular policies in their decisions. Counts for vaccinated DOC staff included only persons who received the first dose from the DOC, not persons who were vaccinated in the community.

**Michigan**—The state DOC did not track staff vaccinations.

**Minnesota**—No notes were reported.

**Mississippi**—No notes were reported.

**Missouri**—The state DOC did not respond to the NPS-CPan survey.

**Montana**—The state DOC had no vaccination policies specifically for staff.

**Nebraska**—No notes were reported.

**Nevada**—The state DOC confirmed that the number of positive tests was equal to the number of unique prisoners who tested positive.

**New Hampshire**—The state DOC was unable to report the number of unique prisoners who tested positive. BJS allocated the number of positive tests to this count.

**New Jersey**—Prisoners given expedited release were placed on home confinement. The state DOC did not track the number of staff who died as a result of COVID-19.

**New Mexico**—No notes were reported.

**New York**—No notes were reported.

**North Carolina**—The number of expedited releases was an estimate. Small differences may exist in the population numbers reported to the NPS-CPan and NPS-1B.

**North Dakota**—The state DOC confirmed that the number of positive tests was equal to the number of unique prisoners who tested positive. The North Dakota Parole Board considered various factors when weighing release options, moving up parole review dates, or maintaining existing parole dates or review dates. Factors included, but were not limited to, time remaining on a sentence, case plan, risk classification scores, community placement options, release plan, medical risk factors, behavior in facility, and past community supervision instances. Counts of vaccinated prisoners and staff were estimates. The state DOC did not require staff to report their vaccination status. Staff could choose to voluntarily provide human resources with proof of vaccination.

**Ohio**—The state DOC did not report the number of expedited releases because the state used multiple legal mechanisms for early release and determined that it would be impossible to fully account for the range of judicial and agency responses that accelerated release for some prisoners in the context of the pandemic (e.g., judicial release, furlough approval, earned credit expansion, and emergency release). The DOC did not track whether COVID-19-related deaths were based on a medical examiner or coroner's report.

**Oklahoma**—The state approved criteria for expedited release but did not release anyone early due to the pandemic. The state DOC did not track staff vaccinations and was unable to report the number of COVID-19-related staff deaths. While the DOC reported the total number of employees who tested positive, it could not specify who did and did not work within a prison facility.

**Oregon**—BJS assigned data for Oregon based on its submission to the 2020 National Corrections Reporting Program and policy documents and statistics on the state DOC's website. Sex and age data were located for 30 of the 42 prisoners who died during the pandemic.

**Pennsylvania**—The state DOC did not have information on the number of COVID-19-related prisoner deaths confirmed by a medical examiner or coroner. Age was one factor for expedited release, with no minimum age limit.

**Rhode Island**—No notes were reported.

**South Carolina**—The state DOC did not track the vaccination status of staff.

**South Dakota**—Fewer than five prisoners tested positive more than once, so the number of unique prisoners who tested positive was similar to the number of positive tests. The state DOC did not track the vaccination status of staff.

**Tennessee**—No notes were reported.

**Texas**—The population and admission counts reported to the NPS-CPan and NPS-1B differ because treatment centers and halfway houses were excluded from the NPS-CPan survey.

**Utah**—No notes were reported.

**Vermont**—The state DOC did not track releases due to COVID-19. The first vaccine clinic for staff was on March 18, 2021, after the NPS-CPan survey period.

**Virginia**—The state DOC did not have any information on the demographics of prisoners who tested positive.

**Washington**—No notes were reported.

**West Virginia**—Changes to the February 28, 2021 population count that could not be explained by admissions and releases were due to increased use of regional jails by the state DOC during the pandemic. These facilities were not within the scope of the NPS- CPan survey. The DOC tracked only the number of positive tests. BJS assigned the number of unique prisoners who tested positive to represent as the total number of positive tests.

**Wisconsin**—The state DOC did not track staff deaths.

**Wyoming**—The numbers of unique prisoners and staff who tested positive for COVID-19 and COVID-19-related deaths reported by the Wyoming DOC to the NPS-CPan survey may differ from counts published by other media outlets. The state adopted a policy of repeatedly testing every new person admitted to prison during the first 10 days of confinement and 20% of staff and prisoners at least every other week. Following a positive result, 100% of staff and prisoners were tested in the following weeks until no tests returned a positive result.

## Table 96. Persons in the Custody of State and Federal Prisons, by Jurisdiction, February 29, 2020, August 31, 2020, and February 28, 2021

(Number; percent.)

| Jurisdiction | February 29, 2020 | August 31, 2020 | February 28, 2021 | Change, February 29, 2020–February 28, 2021 | Percent change, February 29, 2020–February 28, 2021 | Percent change, February 29, 2020–August 31, 2020 | Percent change, August 31, 2020–February 28, 2021 |
|---|---|---|---|---|---|---|---|
| Total[1] | 1,308,754 | 1,151,223 | 1,092,936 | -215,818 | -16.5 | -12.0 | -5.1 |
| Federal[2] | 157,218 | 141,520 | 138,744 | -18,474 | -11.8 | -10.0 | -2.0 |
| State[1] | 1,151,536 | 1,009,703 | 954,192 | -197,344 | -17.1 | -12.3 | -5.5 |
| Alabama | 22,004 | 19,328 | 17,553 | -4,451 | -20.2 | -12.2 | -9.2 |
| Alaska[3] | 4,769 | 4,413 | 4,517 | -252 | -5.3 | -7.5 | 2.4 |
| Arizona | 42,282 | 39,153 | 36,975 | -5,307 | -12.6 | -7.4 | -5.6 |
| Arkansas | 17,620 | 15,232 | 14,686 | -2,934 | -16.7 | -13.6 | -3.6 |
| California | 124,749 | 102,982 | 96,161 | -28,588 | -22.9 | -17.4 | -6.6 |
| Colorado | 18,880 | 15,807 | 14,385 | -4,495 | -23.8 | -16.3 | -9.0 |
| Connecticut[3] | 12,409 | 9,534 | 9,043 | -3,366 | -27.1 | -23.2 | -5.1 |
| Delaware[3] | 5,105 | 4,219 | 4,360 | -745 | -14.6 | -17.4 | 3.3 |
| Florida | 93,867 | 84,602 | 79,425 | -14,442 | -15.4 | -9.9 | -6.1 |
| Georgia | 53,424 | 47,863 | 44,285 | -9,139 | -17.1 | -10.4 | -7.5 |
| Hawaii[3] | 3,699 | 2,984 | 3,090 | -609 | -16.5 | -19.3 | 3.6 |
| Idaho | 7,815 | 6,818 | 7,531 | -284 | -3.6 | -12.8 | 10.5 |
| Illinois | 37,731 | 31,178 | 28,277 | -9,454 | -25.1 | -17.4 | -9.3 |
| Indiana | 26,871 | 24,508 | 23,707 | -3,164 | -11.8 | -8.8 | -3.3 |
| Iowa | 9,180 | 7,795 | 8,138 | -1,042 | -11.4 | -15.1 | 4.4 |
| Kansas | 9,799 | 8,580 | 8,714 | -1,085 | -11.1 | -12.4 | 1.6 |
| Kentucky | 23,188 | 19,533 | 18,627 | -4,561 | -19.7 | -15.8 | -4.6 |
| Louisiana | 14,841 | 14,107 | 13,560 | -1,281 | -8.6 | -4.9 | -3.9 |
| Maine | 2,164 | 1,790 | 1,672 | -492 | -22.7 | -17.3 | -6.6 |
| Maryland | 20,589 | 18,419 | 17,610 | -2,979 | -14.5 | -10.5 | -4.4 |
| Massachusetts | 7,940 | 6,969 | 6,452 | -1,488 | -18.7 | -12.2 | -7.4 |
| Michigan | 37,946 | 34,741 | 33,215 | -4,731 | -12.5 | -8.4 | -4.4 |
| Minnesota | 8,929 | 7,575 | 7,250 | -1,679 | -18.8 | -15.2 | -4.3 |
| Mississippi | 13,270 | 11,654 | 11,050 | -2,220 | -16.7 | -12.2 | -5.2 |
| Missouri | NR | NR | NR | NC | NC | NC | NC |
| Montana | 4,527 | 3,923 | 3,838 | -689 | -15.2 | -13.3 | -2.2 |
| Nebraska | 5,562 | 5,220 | 5,282 | -280 | -5.0 | -6.1 | 1.2 |
| Nevada | 12,371 | 11,505 | 10,891 | -1,480 | -12.0 | -7.0 | -5.3 |
| New Hampshire | 2,472 | 2,228 | 2,107 | -365 | -14.8 | -9.9 | -5.4 |
| New Jersey | 18,098 | 15,270 | 11,745 | -6,353 | -35.1 | -15.6 | -23.1 |
| New Mexico | 6,843 | 6,271 | 5,942 | -901 | -13.2 | -8.4 | -5.2 |
| New York | 43,786 | 37,016 | 32,376 | -11,410 | -26.1 | -15.5 | -12.5 |
| North Carolina | 35,176 | 31,830 | 29,484 | -5,692 | -16.2 | -9.5 | -7.4 |
| North Dakota | 1,750 | 1,279 | 1,458 | -292 | -16.7 | -26.9 | 14.0 |
| Ohio | 48,765 | 44,564 | 43,246 | -5,519 | -11.3 | -8.6 | -3.0 |
| Oklahoma | 24,979 | 21,985 | 21,676 | -3,303 | -13.2 | -12.0 | -1.4 |
| Oregon | 14,435 | 13,848 | 12,404 | -2,031 | -14.1 | -4.1 | -10.4 |
| Pennsylvania | 45,636 | 41,148 | 38,545 | -7,091 | -15.5 | -9.8 | -6.3 |
| Rhode Island[3] | 2,690 | 2,211 | 2,150 | -540 | -20.1 | -17.8 | -2.8 |
| South Carolina | 18,047 | 16,224 | 15,670 | -2,377 | -13.2 | -10.1 | -3.4 |
| South Dakota | 3,859 | 3,381 | 3,262 | -597 | -15.5 | -12.4 | -3.5 |
| Tennessee | 18,519 | 16,443 | 17,261 | -1,258 | -6.8 | -11.2 | 5.0 |
| Texas | 140,419 | 121,128 | 117,843 | -22,576 | -16.1 | -13.7 | -2.7 |
| Utah | 5,037 | 4,204 | 4,099 | -938 | -18.6 | -16.5 | -2.5 |
| Vermont[3] | 1,394 | 1,194 | 1,090 | -304 | -21.8 | -14.3 | -8.7 |
| Virginia | 29,232 | 25,919 | 23,486 | -5,746 | -19.7 | -11.3 | -9.4 |
| Washington | 17,311 | 15,446 | 14,518 | -2,793 | -16.1 | -10.8 | -6.0 |
| West Virginia | 5,927 | 4,381 | 3,970 | -1,957 | -33.0 | -26.1 | -9.4 |
| Wisconsin | 23,313 | 21,167 | 19,521 | -3,792 | -16.3 | -9.2 | -7.8 |
| Wyoming | 2,317 | 2,134 | 2,045 | -272 | -11.7 | -7.9 | -4.2 |

NC = Not calculated.
NR = Not reported.
1 Totals exclude Missouri, which did not submit data to the National Prisoner Statistics program – Coronavirus Pandemic Supplemental Survey. 2 The Federal Bureau of Prisons (BOP) did not report data for privately operated prisons under federal contract, so BOP counts include only persons in the custody of BOP-operated facilities. Persons convicted of a felony in the District of Columbia were in the custody of the BOP. 3 Prisons and jails form one integrated system. Data include both prison and jail populations.

## Table 97A. Admissions to the Custody of State and Federal Prisons, by Jurisdiction, January 1, 2020–February 28, 2021

(Number.)

| Jurisdiction | 2020 | | | | | | | | | | | | 2021 | | Total admissions, January 1, 2020– February 28, 2021 |
|---|---|---|---|---|---|---|---|---|---|---|---|---|---|---|---|
| | January | February | March | April | May | June | July | August | September | October | November | December | January | February | |
| Total[1] | 54,203 | 49,016 | 40,810 | 13,510 | 17,627 | 21,169 | 23,828 | 27,969 | 32,452 | 37,766 | 28,841 | 30,078 | 28,329 | 31,822 | 437,420 |
| Federal[2] | 3,670 | 2,976 | 2,969 | 37 | 1,135 | 287 | 1,399 | 1,884 | 2,937 | 2,753 | 1,683 | 2,351 | 2,503 | 4,144 | 30,728 |
| State[1] | 50,533 | 46,040 | 37,841 | 13,473 | 16,492 | 20,882 | 22,429 | 26,085 | 29,515 | 35,013 | 27,158 | 27,727 | 25,826 | 27,678 | 406,692 |
| Alabama | 794 | 645 | 443 | 123 | 121 | 222 | 127 | ^^ | 201 | 37 | 123 | 215 | ^ | 137 | 3,225 |
| Alaska[3] | 2,430 | 2,313 | 2,179 | 1,547 | 1,880 | 1,992 | 2,177 | 2,259 | 2,195 | 2,102 | 1,851 | 2,098 | 2,094 | 1,901 | 29,018 |
| Arizona | 1,438 | 1,201 | 1,182 | 938 | 1,065 | 635 | 557 | 1,117 | 996 | 975 | 892 | 959 | 886 | 864 | 13,705 |
| Arkansas | 879 | 668 | 1,062 | 631 | 594 | 489 | 139 | 233 | 364 | 378 | 609 | 568 | 86 | 607 | 7,307 |
| California | 2,781 | 2,429 | 2,269 | ^ | 37 | 194 | ^ | 104 | 536 | 1,560 | 1,748 | ^ | 593 | 1,743 | 14,003 |
| Colorado | 763 | 730 | 626 | 429 | 363 | 451 | 435 | 433 | 468 | 438 | 340 | 408 | 412 | 408 | 6,704 |
| Connecticut[3] | 1,753 | 1,516 | 1,042 | 368 | 609 | 600 | 744 | 735 | 844 | 970 | 833 | 834 | 902 | 832 | 12,582 |
| Delaware[3] | 1,235 | 1,035 | 712 | 349 | 508 | 550 | 678 | 696 | 724 | 866 | 671 | 590 | 691 | 613 | 9,918 |
| Florida | 2,342 | 2,196 | 1,467 | 552 | 438 | 864 | 518 | 1,059 | 623 | 1,361 | 826 | 916 | 1,797 | 1,993 | 16,952 |
| Georgia | 1,451 | 1,373 | 962 | ^ | 1,364 | 520 | 449 | 621 | 741 | 788 | 70 | 1,968 | ^^ | 791 | 11,140 |
| Hawaii[3] | 1,063 | 991 | 741 | 350 | 557 | 755 | 772 | 571 | 428 | 521 | 433 | 445 | 474 | 464 | 8,565 |
| Idaho | 589 | 486 | 426 | 249 | 531 | 499 | 288 | 340 | 379 | 395 | 389 | 454 | 372 | 423 | 5,820 |
| Illinois | 1,886 | 1,494 | 1,306 | 144 | 386 | 483 | 633 | 1,102 | 1,275 | 1,266 | 817 | 843 | 855 | 970 | 13,460 |
| Indiana | 868 | 754 | 744 | 321 | 271 | 450 | 485 | 444 | 527 | 544 | 479 | 483 | 489 | 504 | 7,363 |
| Iowa | 530 | 478 | 425 | 217 | 98 | 289 | 214 | 310 | 310 | 270 | 224 | 308 | 231 | 265 | 4,169 |
| Kansas | 440 | 449 | 414 | 149 | 110 | 160 | 147 | 172 | 235 | 317 | 282 | 407 | 376 | 317 | 3,975 |
| Kentucky | 1,668 | 1,587 | 1,223 | 659 | 744 | 893 | 900 | 938 | 1,091 | 1,041 | 975 | 835 | 1,001 | 950 | 14,505 |
| Louisiana | 380 | 388 | 266 | 145 | 95 | 61 | 98 | 89 | 535 | 700 | 103 | 87 | 74 | 92 | 3,113 |
| Maine | 89 | 86 | 59 | 12 | ^ | ^ | 67 | 87 | 56 | 61 | ^^ | 67 | 39 | 52 | 712 |
| Maryland | 1,625 | 1,525 | 110 | 580 | 822 | 678 | 880 | 1,008 | 1,041 | 1,154 | 923 | 900 | 865 | 775 | 12,886 |
| Massachu-setts | 458 | 437 | 254 | 96 | 140 | 172 | 315 | 270 | 289 | 320 | 241 | 205 | 214 | 245 | 3,656 |
| Michigan | 905 | 816 | 783 | 83 | 297 | 417 | 371 | 488 | 461 | 549 | 409 | 457 | 485 | 427 | 6,948 |
| Minnesota | 548 | 457 | 453 | 212 | 235 | 272 | 288 | 263 | 347 | 350 | 239 | 322 | 233 | 308 | 4,527 |
| Mississippi | 592 | 560 | 454 | 168 | 239 | 456 | 447 | 479 | 526 | 566 | 491 | 492 | 418 | 442 | 6,330 |
| Missouri | NR | NR | NR | NR | NR | NR | NR | NR | NR | NR | NR | NR | NR | NR | NC |
| Montana | 760 | 732 | 590 | 101 | 471 | 575 | 432 | 523 | 377 | 264 | 312 | 411 | 515 | 522 | 6,585 |
| Nebraska | 243 | 253 | 221 | 158 | 174 | 199 | 183 | 205 | 217 | 206 | 213 | 197 | 204 | 226 | 2,899 |
| Nevada | 467 | 490 | 448 | 372 | 301 | 319 | 320 | 341 | 363 | 333 | 281 | 328 | 326 | 324 | 5,013 |
| New Hamp-shire | 103 | 118 | 90 | 67 | 34 | 48 | 75 | 81 | 74 | 80 | 79 | 58 | 65 | 54 | 1,026 |
| New Jersey | 678 | 522 | 284 | 147 | 186 | 159 | 250 | 251 | 309 | 325 | 219 | 265 | 291 | 228 | 4,114 |
| New Mexico | 184 | 184 | 188 | 175 | 110 | 76 | 181 | 160 | 153 | 165 | 169 | 172 | 147 | 185 | 2,249 |
| New York | 1,643 | 1,587 | 920 | 78 | 51 | 323 | 607 | 735 | 851 | 746 | 505 | 356 | 56 | 41 | 8,499 |
| North Carolina | 2,077 | 1,849 | 2,003 | 567 | 287 | 1,940 | 1,577 | 1,362 | 854 | 1,111 | 1,280 | 1,360 | 1,056 | 1,261 | 18,584 |
| North Dakota | 125 | 115 | 61 | ^ | ^^ | 83 | 96 | 45 | 105 | 57 | 114 | 112 | 123 | 131 | 1,190 |
| Ohio | 1,775 | 1,632 | 1,731 | 517 | 566 | 918 | 1,013 | 1,061 | 1,407 | 1,243 | 954 | 1,205 | 1,146 | 1,158 | 16,326 |
| Oklahoma | 700 | 632 | 332 | ^ | ^ | 322 | 284 | 668 | 236 | 547 | 578 | 613 | 456 | 486 | 5,865 |
| Oregon | 432 | 391 | 429 | 285 | 208 | 236 | 278 | 227 | 274 | 291 | 258 | 333 | 269 | 236 | 4,147 |
| Pennsylvania | 1,385 | 1,309 | 1,101 | 413 | 484 | 554 | 804 | 846 | 711 | 891 | 938 | 788 | 796 | 830 | 11,850 |
| Rhode Island[3] | 1,065 | 1,084 | 707 | 279 | 478 | 626 | 736 | 716 | 756 | 830 | 673 | 612 | 769 | 734 | 10,065 |
| South Carolina | 530 | 595 | 506 | 101 | 265 | 285 | 35 | 33 | 665 | 414 | 361 | 367 | 206 | 244 | 4,607 |
| South Dakota | 424 | 376 | 391 | 249 | 210 | 291 | 281 | 297 | 285 | 231 | 209 | 283 | 286 | 290 | 4,103 |
| Tennessee | 1,778 | 1,718 | 732 | 71 | ^^ | 206 | ^^ | 1,280 | 912 | 1,948 | 1,238 | 792 | 999 | 813 | 12,531 |
| Texas | 4,724 | 4,468 | 4,954 | 625 | 41 | 100 | 1,565 | 1,659 | 3,835 | 5,713 | 3,416 | 3,099 | 2,587 | 2,068 | 38,854 |
| Utah | 363 | 301 | 312 | 182 | 189 | 200 | 265 | 217 | 247 | 249 | 96 | 324 | 237 | 292 | 3,474 |
| Vermont[3] | 618 | 435 | 283 | 162 | 168 | 232 | 237 | 227 | 209 | 183 | 141 | 142 | 139 | 115 | 3,291 |
| Virginia | 743 | 613 | 314 | 22 | 20 | ^^ | 59 | ^^ | 95 | 95 | 106 | ^^ | 253 | 205 | 2,591 |
| Washington | 626 | 600 | 602 | 293 | 293 | 264 | 314 | 337 | 383 | 497 | 398 | 236 | 411 | 341 | 5,595 |
| West Virginia | 362 | 361 | 206 | 113 | 146 | 225 | 146 | 143 | 226 | 284 | 224 | 242 | 305 | 255 | 3,238 |
| Wisconsin | 1,131 | 988 | 764 | 132 | 202 | 532 | 897 | 730 | 678 | 715 | 392 | 447 | 460 | 464 | 8,532 |
| Wyoming | 90 | 73 | 70 | ^^ | 49 | 50 | 45 | 59 | 101 | 66 | ^ | 94 | 95 | 52 | 881 |

NOTE: Includes persons admitted to government-operated or privately operated state and federal prisons, regardless of sentence status or length. Excludes persons admitted to local jails on behalf of state or federal correctional authorities. Estimates will differ from previously published statistics.
NC = Not calculated.
NR = Not reported.
^ = 10 or fewer admissions.
^^ = Estimate suppressed to protect confidentiality.
1 Totals exclude Missouri, which did not submit data to the National Prisoner Statistics program – Coronavirus Pandemic Supplemental Survey.   2 The Federal Bureau of Prisons (BOP) did not report data for privately operated prisons under federal contract, so BOP counts include only persons in the custody of BOP-operated facilities. Persons convicted of a felony in the District of Columbia were in the custody of the BOP.   3 Prisons and jails form one integrated system. Data include both prison and jail populations.

## Table 97B. Releases from the Custody of State and Federal Prisons, by Jurisdiction, January 1, 2020–February 28, 2021

(Number; percent.)

| Jurisdiction | Total releases | Expedited releases | |
|---|---|---|---|
| | | Number | Percent of total |
| Total[1] | 648,386 | 37,684 | 5.8 |
| Federal[2,3] | 46,993 | 0 | 0.0 |
| State[1] | 601,393 | 37,684 | 6.3 |
| Alabama | 7,160 | 0 | 0.0 |
| Alaska[4] | 29,164 | 0 | 0.0 |
| Arizona | 19,169 | 0 | 0.0 |
| Arkansas | 10,409 | 1,803 | 17.3 |
| California | 42,742 | 11,584 | 27.1 |
| Colorado | 10,643 | 611 | 5.7 |
| Connecticut[4] | 13,978 | 0 | 0.0 |
| Delaware[4] | 10,693 | 0 | 0.0 |
| Florida | 32,797 | 0 | 0.0 |
| Georgia | 20,895 | 918 | 4.4 |
| Hawaii[4] | 9,585 | 430 | 4.5 |
| Idaho | 6,034 | 293 | 4.9 |
| Illinois | 23,223 | 0 | 0.0 |
| Indiana | 11,294 | 0 | 0.0 |
| Iowa | 5,272 | 4,700 | 89.2 |
| Kansas | 5,278 | NR | NC |
| Kentucky | 18,414 | 1,717 | 9.3 |
| Louisiana | 4,515 | 68 | 1.5 |
| Maine | 1,297 | 0 | 0.0 |
| Maryland | 13,271 | 1,365 | 10.3 |
| Massachusetts | 4,266 | 73 | 1.7 |
| Michigan | 11,649 | 0 | 0.0 |
| Minnesota | 6,150 | 366 | 6.0 |
| Mississippi | 8,249 | 0 | 0.0 |
| Missouri | NR | NR | NC |
| Montana | 6,757 | 24 | 0.4 |
| Nebraska | 3,203 | 0 | 0.0 |
| Nevada | 6,621 | 0 | 0.0 |
| New Hampshire | 1,383 | 0 | 0.0 |
| New Jersey | 10,287 | 3,732 | 36.3 |
| New Mexico | 3,585 | 408 | 11.4 |
| New York | 20,400 | 2,106 | 10.3 |
| North Carolina | 24,287 | 3,500 | 14.4 |
| North Dakota | 1,393 | 191 | 13.7 |
| Ohio | 23,208 | NR | NC |
| Oklahoma | 9,815 | 0 | 0.0 |
| Oregon | 6,004 | 0 | 0.0 |
| Pennsylvania | 18,820 | 146 | 0.8 |
| Rhode Island[4] | 10,408 | 52 | 0.5 |
| South Carolina | 7,157 | 0 | 0.0 |
| South Dakota | 4,654 | 0 | 0.0 |
| Tennessee | 14,382 | 0 | 0.0 |
| Texas | 61,515 | 0 | 0.0 |
| Utah | 4,603 | 1,420 | 30.8 |
| Vermont[4] | 3,276 | NR | NC |
| Virginia | 7,933 | 1,597 | 20.1 |
| Washington | 8,405 | 422 | 5.0 |
| West Virginia | 3,550 | 158 | 4.5 |
| Wisconsin | 12,264 | 0 | 0.0 |
| Wyoming | 1,336 | 0 | 0.0 |

NOTE: Includes persons released from government-operated and privately operated state and federal prisons, regardless of sentence status or length. Excludes prisoners released from local jails on behalf of state or federal correctional authorities. Expedited release is the release of a person at least 1 day before their scheduled or expected release date or post-custody community supervision eligibility date, to limit prisoner risk and exposure to COVID-19 or due to COVID-19-related understaffing, court orders, or legislative mandates. Estimates will differ from previously published statistics.
NC = Not calculated.
NR = Not reported.
1 Totals exclude Missouri, which did not submit data to the National Prisoner Statistics program – Coronavirus Pandemic Supplemental Survey.   2 The Federal Bureau of Prisons (BOP) did not report data for privately operated prisons under federal contract, so BOP counts include only persons in the custody of BOP-operated facilities. Persons convicted of a felony in the District of Columbia were in the custody of the BOP.   3 The BOP had no expedited releases but moved almost 27,000 prisoners to home confinement in 2020. Prisoners on home confinement are still in BOP custody but living in their own residence or the residence of a designated family member.   4 Prisons and jails form one integrated system. Data include both prison and jail populations.

## Table 98. Number of Jurisdictions That Adopted Criteria for Expedited Release Due to the COVID-19 Pandemic, January 2020–February 2021

(Number.)

| Criterion | Number of jurisdictions |
|---|---:|
| No policy for expedited release | 22 |
| Time left on sentence | 25 |
| Nonviolent offenders only | 19 |
| Health status | 17 |
| Verified post-prison housing in community | 16 |
| Risk assessment score | 14 |
| Age | 12 |
| Only nonviolent offenders with no violent prior convictions | 10 |
| Positive viral test for COVID-19 | 3 |
| Prisoner was unsentenced | 1 |

NOTE: Expedited release is the release of a person at least 1 day before their scheduled or expected release date, or post-custody community supervision eligibility date, to limit prisoner risk and exposure to COVID-19 or due to COVID-19-related under-staffing, court orders, or legislative mandates. Jurisdictions could adopt criteria for expedited release at any time from January 2020 and February 2021.

## Table 99. Number of COVID-19 Tests and Test Positivity Rate Among Persons in the Custody of State and Federal Prisons, by Jurisdiction, March 1, 2020–February 28, 2021

(Number; percent.)

| Jurisdiction | Number of tests of prisoners, March 1, 2020–February 28, 2021[1] | Number of positive tests, March 1, 2020–February 28, 2021[1] | Test positivity rate per 100 tests | Number of unique prisoners with a positive test, March 1, 2020–February 28, 2021 |
|---|---|---|---|---|
| Total[2] | 4,816,411 | 396,320 | 8.2 | 374,437 |
| Federal[3,4] | 400,883 | 47,873 | NC | 54,029 |
| State[2] | 4,415,528 | 348,447 | 7.9 | 320,408 |
| | | | | |
| Alabama[5] | 15,129 | 1,527 | 10.1 | 1,527 |
| Alaska[6] | 27,197 | 2,650 | 9.7 | 2,330 |
| Arizona[7] | 70,112 | 12,058 | 17.2 | 12,058 |
| Arkansas | 57,706 | 11,436 | 19.8 | 11,428 |
| California | 1,116,763 | 58,857 | 5.3 | 49,325 |
| | | | | |
| Colorado | 174,029 | 8,998 | 5.2 | 8,657 |
| Connecticut[6] | 100,619 | 6,795 | 6.8 | 4,106 |
| Delaware[6,8] | 13,004 | 2,015 | 15.5 | 2,015 |
| Florida[5] | 87,694 | 17,334 | 19.8 | 17,208 |
| Georgia | 35,240 | 3,625 | 10.3 | 3,610 |
| | | | | |
| Hawaii[6,9] | 12,143 | 1,272 | 10.5 | 1,272 |
| Idaho | 25,510 | 4,198 | 16.5 | 3,961 |
| Illinois[10] | 326,538 | 10,714 | 3.3 | 10,700 |
| Indiana[5] | 16,639 | 3,289 | 19.8 | 3,289 |
| Iowa | 41,247 | 4,879 | 11.8 | 4,743 |
| | | | | |
| Kansas | 41,166 | 6,403 | 15.6 | 5,774 |
| Kentucky[9] | 32,171 | 7,145 | 22.2 | 7,145 |
| Louisiana | 22,140 | 3,376 | 15.2 | 3,168 |
| Maine | 7,216 | 284 | 3.9 | 156 |
| Maryland | 57,927 | 4,327 | 7.5 | 4,194 |
| | | | | |
| Massachusetts | 29,822 | 2,814 | 9.4 | 2,558 |
| Michigan | 563,241 | 29,049 | 5.2 | 25,018 |
| Minnesota | 97,874 | 4,122 | 4.2 | 3,852 |
| Mississippi | 3,861 | 1,399 | 36.2 | 1,358 |
| Missouri | NR | NR | NC | NR |
| | | | | |
| Montana | 10,071 | 1,460 | 14.5 | 1,445 |
| Nebraska | 6,719 | 1,510 | 22.5 | 584 |
| Nevada[5] | 30,681 | 4,510 | 14.7 | 4,510 |
| New Hampshire[9] | 1,485 | 449 | 30.2 | 449 |
| New Jersey | 252,052 | 4,340 | 1.7 | 3,055 |
| | | | | |
| New Mexico | 37,683 | 3,760 | 10.0 | 2,868 |
| New York | 74,209 | 5,994 | 8.1 | 5,885 |
| North Carolina | 109,974 | 10,508 | 9.6 | 9,691 |
| North Dakota | 27,062 | 608 | 2.2 | 608 |
| Ohio | 61,858 | 9,565 | 15.5 | 9,526 |
| | | | | |
| Oklahoma | 28,884 | 7,173 | 24.8 | 7,168 |
| Oregon[9] | 24,814 | 3,542 | 14.3 | 3,542 |
| Pennsylvania | 90,181 | 13,116 | 14.5 | 10,251 |
| Rhode Island[6] | NR | NR | NC | 1,147 |
| South Carolina | 32,282 | 4,568 | 14.2 | 3,161 |
| | | | | |
| South Dakota[5] | 7,488 | 2,339 | 31.2 | 2,336 |
| Tennessee | 38,659 | 6,587 | 17.0 | 6,113 |
| Texas | 308,194 | 30,128 | 9.8 | 29,367 |
| Utah | 22,416 | 1,100 | 4.9 | 1,047 |
| Vermont[6] | 14,871 | 196 | 1.3 | 114 |
| | | | | |
| Virginia[9] | 92,976 | 8,988 | 9.7 | 8,988 |
| Washington | 49,632 | 6,241 | 12.6 | 6,175 |
| West Virginia[9] | 9,661 | 1,553 | 16.1 | 1,553 |
| Wisconsin | 91,915 | 10,860 | 11.8 | 10,597 |
| Wyoming | 16,773 | 786 | 4.7 | 776 |

NOTE: Includes viral (polymerase chain reaction) COVID-19 tests among persons held for state or federal correctional authorities in government-operated and privately operated prisons, regardless of sentence status or length. Excludes antibody or serology tests and tests of prisoners held in local jails on behalf of state or federal correctional authorities. Individual prisoners could be tested more than once. Test positivity rates are per 100 tests administered and should not be compared between jurisdictions due to wide variation in testing practices. Jurisdictions that performed tests on most or all prisoners could identify asymptomatic and negative COVID-19 cases, while jurisdictions that tested persons only after the onset of symptoms could not.
NC = Not calculated.
NR = Not reported.
1 Counts do not represent the number of unique prisoners who tested positive for COVID-19, unless otherwise noted. Prisoners could have multiple tests or multiple positive tests.
2 Totals exclude Missouri, which did not submit data to the National Prisoner Statistics program - Coronavirus Pandemic Supplemental Survey.
3 Excludes counts from privately operated prisons under federal contract.
4 Federal Bureau of Prisons (BOP) counts for total tests administered and total positive tests exclude results from laboratories not under federal contract. The count of unique prisoners who tested positive for COVID-19 includes results from laboratories under and not under federal contract. The positivity rate was not calculated for the BOP due to the differences in populations for the numerator and denominator.
5 State department of corrections (DOC) confirmed that prisoners who tested positive for COVID-19 were tested only once.
6 Prisons and jails form one integrated system. Data include both prison and jail populations.
7 State could not report the total number of positive tests. Number of unique prisoners who tested positive for COVID-19 was allocated as the total number of positive tests.
8 Counts represent COVID-19 tests performed from April 1, 2020 to April 1, 2021. The state DOC confirmed that prisoners who tested positive for COVID-19 were tested only once.
9 State could not report the number of unique prisoners who tested positive for COVID-19. Total number of positive tests was allocated as the number of unique prisoners who tested positive for COVID-19.
10 State could not report the number of unique prisoners who tested positive for COVID-19. Data were taken from the February 28, 2021, entry in the University of North Carolina Health and Justice Research Lab's COVID Prison Project database, which scraped data posted on DOC websites and is archived at https://github.com/healthandjustice/covid-prison-project.

**Table 100. Number of Jurisdictions That Adopted Tactics to Mitigate COVID-19 Transmission in State and Federal Prisons, March 1, 2020–February 28, 2021**

(Number.)

| Mitigation tactic | Number of jurisdictions that implemented tactic | | | |
|---|---|---|---|---|
| | In all facilities | In some facilities | In no facilities | Not applicable/known/reported |
| All new prisoners tested at admission | 39 | 6 | 4 | 2 |
| Automatic quarantine of newly admitted prisoners | 40 | 9 | 0 | 2 |
| Lockdown of prisoners in cells | 25 | 16 | 7 | 3 |
| Daily temperature checks of prisoners | 26 | 11 | 9 | 5 |
| Staff temperature checks at start of shift | 49 | 1 | 0 | 1 |
| Isolation/quarantine of symptomatic prisoners | 50 | 0 | 0 | 1 |
| Enforced sick/administrative leave of symptomatic staff | 48 | 0 | 0 | 3 |
| Provision of hand sanitizer to prisoners | 41 | 3 | 4 | 3 |
| Provision of face masks to prisoners | 49 | 0 | 0 | 2 |
| Provision of face masks/gloves to staff | 50 | 0 | 0 | 1 |
| Viral testing of prisoners before release | 32 | 7 | 9 | 3 |
| Antibody/serology testing of staff | 8 | 5 | 29 | 9 |
| Antibody/serology testing of prisoners | 13 | 7 | 22 | 9 |
| Complete suspension of: | | | | |
| Transfers between prison and local jails | 43 | 6 | 0 | 2 |
| Educational programs | 38 | 7 | 4 | 2 |
| Drug/alcohol treatment programs | 31 | 9 | 6 | 5 |
| Prison labor programs | 39 | 9 | 1 | 2 |
| In-person family visitation | 49 | 1 | 0 | 1 |
| Legal visitation | 35 | 6 | 8 | 2 |
| Ministry/religious service programs | 37 | 6 | 5 | 3 |

NOTE: Tactics were adopted at any time from March 1, 2020 to February 28, 2021 in none, some (at least one), or all government-operated and privately operated prisons in each jurisdiction.

## Table 100A. Activities Completely Suspended to Mitigate COVID-19 Transmission in State and Federal Prisons, by Jurisdiction, March 1, 2020–February 28, 2021

| Jurisdiction | Transfers between prison and local facilities | Educational programs | Drug/alcohol treatment programs | Prison labor programs | In-person family visitation | Legal visitation | Ministry/religious service programs |
|---|---|---|---|---|---|---|---|
| Federal[1] | All | All | NA | All | All | All | Some |
| Alabama | All | All | All | All | All | All | All |
| Alaska[2] | All | All | All | All | All | All | All |
| Arizona | All | All | All | All | All | All | All |
| Arkansas | All | All | All | All | All | All | All |
| California | All | All | NA | All | All | NA | All |
| Colorado | All | All | All | All | All | Some | Some |
| Connecticut[2] | Some | All | All | All | All | None | All |
| Delaware[2] | All | All | Some | Some | All | All | All |
| Florida | All | All | All | All | All | None | All |
| Georgia | All | All | All | All | All | All | All |
| Hawaii[2] | Some | Some | Some | Some | All | Some | None |
| Idaho | All | All | All | All | All | None | All |
| Illinois | All | All | All | All | All | All | All |
| Indiana | All | All | All | All | All | All | All |
| Iowa | All | Some | Some | All | All | All | Some |
| Kansas | All | All | All | All | All | All | All |
| Kentucky | All | Some | Some | All | All | All | All |
| Louisiana | All | All | All | All | All | All | All |
| Maine | All | None | Some | All | All | All | Some |
| Maryland | All | All | NA | Some | All | None | UNK |
| Massachusetts | All | All | All | All | All | All | All |
| Michigan | All | All | All | All | All | All | All |
| Minnesota | Some | Some | Some | Some | Some | Some | Some |
| Mississippi | All | All | All | All | All | All | All |
| Missouri | NR | NR | NR | NR | NR | NR | NR |
| Montana | All | All | All | All | All | All | All |
| Nebraska | Some | None | None | None | All | None | None |
| Nevada | All | All | All | All | All | All | All |
| New Hampshire | All | All | All | All | All | All | All |
| New Jersey | All | All | All | Some | All | None | All |
| New Mexico | Some | Some | None | All | All | All | All |
| New York | All | All | All | Some | All | All | All |
| North Carolina | All | All | Some | All | All | None | All |
| North Dakota | All | All | All | All | All | All | All |
| Ohio | All | None | None | Some | All | None | None |
| Oklahoma | All | All | All | All | All | All | All |
| Oregon | UNK | UNK | NA | UNK | All | All | UNK |
| Pennsylvania | All | All | All | All | All | All | All |
| Rhode Island[2] | All | All | None | All | All | All | All |
| South Carolina | All | All | All | All | All | All | All |
| South Dakota | All | All | All | All | All | Some | All |
| Tennessee | Some | None | None | All | All | All | All |
| Texas | All | All | All | All | All | All | All |
| Utah | All | Some | All | All | All | All | All |
| Vermont[2] | All | All | None | Some | All | All | All |
| Virginia | All | All | All | All | All | All | None |
| Washington | All | Some | Some | Some | All | Some | None |
| West Virginia | All | All | Some | All | All | Some | Some |
| Wisconsin | All | All | All | All | All | All | All |
| Wyoming | All | All | All | All | All | All | All |

NOTE: Activities were suspended at any time from March 1, 2020 to February 28, 2021 in none, some (at least one), or all government-operated and privately operated prisons in each jurisdiction.
NA = Not applicable.
NR = Not reported.
UNK = Not known.
1 Excludes activities suspended in privately operated prisons under federal contract.    2 Prisons and jails form one integrated system. Data include both prison and jail populations.

## Table 101. COVID-19 Infection Rate Among Persons in the Custody of State and Federal Prisons, by Jurisdiction, March 1, 2020–February 28, 2021

(Number; rate.)

| Jurisdiction | Number of unique prisoners who tested positive | Rate of prisoners who tested positive per 1,000 prisoners at risk of exposure[1] | Rate of prisoners who tested positive per 100 prison-days of exposure risk[2] |
|---|---|---|---|
| **Total[3]** | 374,437 | 227.8 | NC |
| **Federal[4]** | 54,029 | 298.0 | NC |
| **State[3,5]** | 320,408 | 219.0 | 0.08 |
| | | | |
| Alabama | 1,527 | 64.2 | NC |
| Alaska[6] | 2,330 | 80.2 | NC |
| Arizona | 12,058 | 226.0 | NC |
| Arkansas | 11,428 | 488.8 | 0.21 |
| California | 49,325 | 369.4 | 0.13 |
| | | | |
| Colorado | 8,657 | 359.3 | 0.16 |
| Connecticut[6] | 4,106 | 189.0 | NC |
| Delaware[6,7] | 2,015 | 158.0 | NC |
| Florida | 17,208 | 161.9 | 0.06 |
| Georgia | 3,610 | 58.5 | 0.02 |
| | | | |
| Hawaii[6,8] | 1,272 | 112.6 | NC |
| Idaho | 3,961 | 315.4 | 0.15 |
| Illinois[9] | 10,700 | 223.8 | 0.09 |
| Indiana | 3,289 | 100.9 | 0.04 |
| Iowa | 4,743 | 384.3 | 0.17 |
| | | | |
| Kansas | 5,774 | 448.1 | 0.18 |
| Kentucky[6] | 7,145 | 207.5 | 0.10 |
| Louisiana | 3,168 | 184.3 | NC |
| Maine | 156 | 57.8 | 0.03 |
| Maryland | 4,194 | 138.3 | NC |
| | | | |
| Massachusetts | 2,558 | 239.0 | 0.09 |
| Michigan | 25,018 | 579.5 | NC |
| Minnesota | 3,852 | 309.4 | 0.14 |
| Mississippi | 1,358 | 73.6 | 0.03 |
| Missouri | NR | NC | NC |
| | | | |
| Montana | 1,445 | 150.2 | NC |
| Nebraska | 584 | 73.3 | 0.03 |
| Nevada | 4,510 | 274.5 | 0.13 |
| New Hampshire[6] | 449 | 137.0 | 0.06 |
| New Jersey | 3,055 | 145.4 | NC |
| | | | |
| New Mexico | 2,868 | 328.7 | NC |
| New York | 5,885 | 120.0 | 0.04 |
| North Carolina | 9,691 | 194.5 | 0.08 |
| North Dakota | 608 | 225.2 | 0.13 |
| Ohio | 9,526 | 154.4 | 0.06 |
| | | | |
| Oklahoma | 7,168 | 242.9 | 0.09 |
| Oregon | 3,542 | 199.4 | 0.07 |
| Pennsylvania | 10,251 | 187.1 | 0.07 |
| Rhode Island[6] | 1,147 | 108.1 | NC |
| South Carolina | 3,161 | 146.8 | 0.06 |
| | | | |
| South Dakota | 2,336 | 326.2 | 0.15 |
| Tennessee | 6,113 | 221.9 | 0.09 |
| Texas | 29,367 | 172.7 | 0.07 |
| Utah | 1,047 | 133.4 | 0.07 |
| Vermont[6] | 114 | 31.4 | 0.02 |
| | | | |
| Virginia[8] | 8,988 | 295.0 | 0.11 |
| Washington | 6,175 | 284.8 | 0.11 |
| West Virginia[8] | 1,553 | 184.0 | 0.11 |
| Wisconsin | 10,597 | 356.5 | 0.13 |
| Wyoming | 776 | 255.7 | 0.13 |

NOTE: Includes positive results of viral (polymerase chain reaction) COVID-19 tests among persons held for state or federal correctional authorities in government-operated and privately operated prisons, regardless of sentence status or length. Excludes results of antibody or serology tests and tests of prisoners held in local jails on behalf of state or federal correctional authorities.
NC = Not calculated.
NR = Not reported.
1 Denominator is the total number of persons in the custody of government-operated and privately operated prisons at any time from February 29, 2020 to February 28, 2021 (i.e., the sum of persons in custody on February 29, 2020 and persons admitted each month from March 2020 to February 2021).    2 Rate is per 100 days in prison custody. Denominator is the sum of the number of days of exposure risk for all persons in the custody of government-operated and privately operated prisons from their date of admission or from the date of the first documented positive COVID-19 test among prisoners in each jurisdiction (whichever is later), through their release date or through February 28, 2021 (whichever is earlier). Excludes states that either did not submit 2020 National Corrections Reporting Program (NCRP) data, or submitted 2020 NCRP admission and release data that were inconsistent with the aggregate counts provided by the same state in the National Prisoner Statistics program - Coronavirus Pandemic Supplemental Survey (NPS-CPan). A total of 256,205 unique prisoners tested positive for COVID-19 among the 36 states that submitted comparable NCRP and NPS-CPan data.    3 Totals exclude Missouri, which did not submit data to the NPS-CPan.    4 Excludes counts from privately operated prisons under federal contract.    5 Total for prison-days rates includes only the 36 states that submitted comparable 2020 NCRP and NPS-CPan data.    6 Prisons and jails form one integrated system. Data include both prison and jail populations.    7 Counts represent tests performed from April 1, 2020 to April 1, 2021.    8 State could not report the number of unique prisoners who tested positive for COVID-19. Total number of positive tests was imputed as the number of unique prisoners who tested positive for COVID-19.    9 State could not report the number of unique prisoners who tested positive for COVID-19. Data were taken from the February 28, 2021 entry in the COVID Prison Project database (https://github.com/healthandjustice/covid-prison-project).

## Table 102. COVID-19 Infections Among Persons in the Custody of State and Federal Prisons, by Demographic Characteristics, March 1, 2020–February 28, 2021

(Number; percent.)

| Demographic characteristics | Number of infections | Percent |
|---|---:|---:|
| **Sex** | 374,437 | 100.0 |
| Male | 321,315 | 85.8 |
| Female | 19,471 | 5.2 |
| Not reported | 33,651 | 9.0 |
| **Race/ethnicity** | 374,437 | 100.0 |
| White[1] | 137,757 | 36.8 |
| Black[1] | 113,603 | 30.3 |
| Hispanic | 69,754 | 18.6 |
| American Indian/Alaska Native[1] | 8,823 | 2.4 |
| Asian/Native Hawaiian/Other Pacific Islander[1] | 3,575 | 1.0 |
| Two or more races[1] | 316 | 0.1 |
| Other race[1] | 3,104 | 0.8 |
| Not reported | 37,505 | 10.0 |

NOTE: Includes positive results of viral (polymerase chain reaction) COVID-19 tests among persons held for state or federal correctional authorities in government-operated and privately operated prisons, regardless of sentence status or length. Excludes results of antibody or serology tests and tests of prisoners held in local jails on behalf of state or federal correctional authorities. Hawaii, Illinois, Kentucky, Missouri, New Hampshire, Oregon, West Virginia, and Virginia could not report sex for prisoners who tested positive. Those eight states and Alabama could not report race or ethnicity for prisoners who tested positive.
1 Excludes persons of Hispanic origin (e.g., "White" refers to non-Hispanic White persons and "Black" refers to non-Hispanic Black persons).

## Table 103. Number of COVID-19–Related Deaths and Crude Mortality Rate Among Persons in the Custody of State and Federal Prisons, by Sex and Jurisdiction, March 1, 2020–February 28, 2021

(Number; rate.)

| Jurisdiction | Total | Male | Female | Crude mortality rate per 1,000 prisoners[1,2] |
|---|---|---|---|---|
| **Total[3]** | 2,490 | 2,420 | 58 | 1.5 |
| **Federal[4]** | 212 | 205 | 7 | 1.2 |
| **State[3]** | 2,278 | 2,215 | 51 | 1.6 |
| Alabama | 61 | ^^ | ^^ | 2.6 |
| Alaska[5] | 5 | 5 | 0 | 0.2 |
| Arizona | 48 | 48 | 0 | 0.9 |
| Arkansas | 52 | ^^ | ^^ | 2.2 |
| California | 219 | ^^ | ^^ | 1.6 |
| Colorado | 29 | 29 | 0 | 1.2 |
| Connecticut[5] | 19 | 19 | 0 | 0.9 |
| Delaware[5] | 13 | 13 | 0 | 1.0 |
| Florida | 213 | 206 | 7 | 2.0 |
| Georgia | 90 | ^^ | ^^ | 1.5 |
| Hawaii[5] | 7 | 7 | 0 | 0.6 |
| Idaho | 5 | 5 | 0 | 0.4 |
| Illinois | 88 | ^^ | ^^ | 1.8 |
| Indiana | 30 | 30 | 0 | 0.9 |
| Iowa | 19 | 19 | 0 | 1.5 |
| Kansas | 15 | 15 | 0 | 1.2 |
| Kentucky | 48 | 48 | 0 | 1.4 |
| Louisiana | 35 | ^^ | ^^ | 2.0 |
| Maine | ^ | ^ | ^ | NC |
| Maryland | 28 | 28 | 0 | 0.9 |
| Massachusetts | 20 | 20 | 0 | 1.9 |
| Michigan | 136 | 132 | 4 | 3.2 |
| Minnesota | 11 | 11 | 0 | 0.9 |
| Mississippi | 23 | ^^ | ^^ | 1.2 |
| Missouri | NR | NR | NR | NC |
| Montana | 5 | 5 | 0 | 0.5 |
| Nebraska | 6 | 6 | 0 | 0.8 |
| Nevada | 49 | 49 | 0 | 3.0 |
| New Hampshire | ^ | ^ | ^ | 0.6 |
| New Jersey | 52 | ^^ | ^^ | 2.5 |
| New Mexico | 28 | 28 | 0 | 3.2 |
| New York | 33 | ^^ | ^^ | 0.7 |
| North Carolina | 53 | 48 | 5 | 1.1 |
| North Dakota | ^ | ^ | ^ | 0.4 |
| Ohio | 134 | 134 | 0 | 2.2 |
| Oklahoma | 48 | ^^ | ^^ | 1.6 |
| Oregon | 42 | NR | NR | 2.4 |
| Pennsylvania | 125 | ^^ | ^^ | 2.3 |
| Rhode Island[5] | ^ | ^ | ^ | NC |
| South Carolina | 40 | 40 | 0 | 1.9 |
| South Dakota | 7 | 7 | 0 | 1.0 |
| Tennessee | 42 | ^^ | ^^ | 1.5 |
| Texas | 255 | 245 | 10 | 1.5 |
| Utah | 18 | 18 | 0 | 2.3 |
| Vermont[5] | 0 | 0 | 0 | 0.0 |
| Virginia | 55 | ^^ | ^^ | 1.8 |
| Washington | 13 | 13 | 0 | 0.6 |
| West Virginia | 18 | 18 | 0 | 2.1 |
| Wisconsin | 32 | ^^ | ^^ | 1.1 |
| Wyoming | ^ | ^ | ^ | NC |

NOTE: Includes COVID-19-related deaths of persons held for state or federal correctional authorities in government-operated and privately operated prisons, regardless of sentence status or length. Excludes prisoners held in local jails on behalf of state or federal correctional authorities. Includes all deaths where COVID-19 was suspected or confirmed as the cause or a significant contributing factor. Estimates will differ from previously published statistics. Not all jurisdictions could report the sex of persons who died in their custody as a result of COVID-19.
NC = Not calculated.
NR = Not reported.
^ = Three or fewer deaths.
^^ = One of the sex-specific estimates includes three or fewer deaths. Both estimates were suppressed to protect confidentiality.
1 Per 1,000 prisoners at risk of exposure to COVID-19 from March 1, 2020 to February 28, 2021 while in custody.   2 Denominator is the total number of persons in the custody of government-operated and privately operated prisons at any time from February 29, 2020 to February 28, 2021 (i.e., the sum of persons in custody on February 29, 2020 and persons admitted each month from March 2020 to February 2021).   3 Totals exclude Missouri, which did not submit data to the National Prisoner Statistics program - Coronavirus Pandemic Supplemental Survey.   4 Excludes counts from privately operated prisons under federal contract.   5 Prisons and jails form one integrated system. Data include both prison and jail populations.

## Table 104. COVID-19–Related Deaths of Persons in the Custody of State and Federal Prisons, by Demographic Characteristics, March 1, 2020–February 28, 2021

(Number; percent.)

| Demographic characteristics | Number of deaths | Percent |
|---|---|---|
| **Sex** | 2,490 | 100.0 |
| Male | 2,420 | 97.2 |
| Female | 58 | 2.3 |
| Not reported | 12 | 0.5 |
| | | |
| **Race/ethnicity** | 2,490 | 100.0 |
| White[1] | 1,095 | 44.0 |
| Black[1] | 840 | 33.7 |
| Hispanic | 349 | 14.0 |
| American Indian/Alaska Native[1] | 53 | 2.1 |
| Asian/Native Hawaiian/Other Pacific Islander[1] | 19 | 0.8 |
| Two or more races[1] | 0 | 0.0 |
| Other race[1] | 17 | 0.7 |
| Not reported | 117 | 4.7 |
| | | |
| **Age at death** | 2,490 | 100.0 |
| 24 years or younger | ^ | NC |
| 25–34 years | 20 | 0.8 |
| 35–44 years | 104 | 4.2 |
| 45–54 years | 268 | 10.8 |
| 55–64 years | 815 | 32.7 |
| 65–74 years | 857 | 34.4 |
| 75 years or older | 406 | 16.3 |
| Not reported | ^^ | NC |

NOTE: Details may not sum to totals due to rounding. Includes COVID-19-related deaths of persons held for state or federal correctional authorities in government-operated and privately operated prisons, regardless of sentence status or length. Excludes prisoners held in local jails on behalf of state or federal correctional authorities. Includes all deaths where COVID-19 was suspected or confirmed as the cause or a significant contributing factor. Estimates will differ from previously published statistics. Missouri and Oregon did not report the sex, race or ethnicity, or age distribution of persons who died in their custody as a result of COVID-19. In addition, Hawaii did not report their decedents' race or ethnicity or age, and Alabama did not report decedents' race or ethnicity.
NC = Not calculated.
^ = 10 or fewer deaths.
^^ = Estimate suppressed to protect confidentiality.
1 Excludes persons of Hispanic origin (e.g., "White" refers to non-Hispanic White persons and "Black" refers to non-Hispanic Black persons).

## Table 105. COVID-19 Vaccine Availability and Administration to Staff and Persons in the Custody of State and Federal Prisons, by Jurisdiction, Through February 28, 2021

(Number.)

| Jurisdiction | Number of days vaccine was available[1] | Number of staff vaccinated[2] | Number of prisoners vaccinated[2] |
|---|---|---|---|
| Total[3] | NA | 119,217 | 126,299 |
| Federal[4] | 74 | 17,131 | 18,795 |
| State[3] | NA | 102,086 | 107,504 |
| | | | |
| Alabama[5] | 0 | NA | NA |
| Alaska[6] | 72 | 0 | 1,436 |
| Arizona | 43 | 2,610 | 0 |
| Arkansas | 54 | 207 | 0 |
| California | 67 | 26,270 | 39,476 |
| | | | |
| Colorado | 68 | 639 | 2,661 |
| Connecticut[6] | 51 | 2,476 | 1,031 |
| Delaware[6] | 54 | 1,056 | 137 |
| Florida[5] | 0 | NA | NA |
| Georgia | 44 | 680 | 14 |
| | | | |
| Hawaii[6] | 67 | 743 | 284 |
| Idaho | 26 | 297 | 103 |
| Illinois | 11 | 1,145 | 5,292 |
| Indiana | 10 | 2,036 | NR |
| Iowa | 52 | 1,208 | 206 |
| | | | |
| Kansas | 19 | 2,324 | 2,407 |
| Kentucky[5] | 0 | NA | NA |
| Louisiana | 54 | 676 | 621 |
| Maine | 39 | 578 | 0 |
| Maryland | 53 | 4,011 | 751 |
| | | | |
| Massachusetts | 41 | 2,885 | 4,379 |
| Michigan | 32 | 0 | 4,801 |
| Minnesota | 59 | 384 | 836 |
| Mississippi[5] | 0 | NA | NA |
| Missouri | NR | NR | NR |
| | | | |
| Montana | 54 | 203 | 570 |
| Nebraska | 51 | 428 | 291 |
| Nevada | 53 | 1,030 | ^ |
| New Hampshire | 67 | 468 | 385 |
| New Jersey | 62 | 2,985 | 3,545 |
| | | | |
| New Mexico | 74 | 1,527 | 601 |
| New York | 23 | 7,439 | 822 |
| North Carolina | 39 | 7,172 | 3,005 |
| North Dakota | 6 | 450 | 979 |
| Ohio | 60 | 5,922 | 8,910 |
| | | | |
| Oklahoma | 51 | 0 | 11 |
| Oregon | 62 | NR | NR |
| Pennsylvania | 12 | 609 | 1,300 |
| Rhode Island[6] | 64 | 909 | 1,408 |
| South Carolina[5] | 0 | NA | NA |
| | | | |
| South Dakota | 26 | 0 | 1,736 |
| Tennessee | 33 | 1,546 | 0 |
| Texas | 61 | 7,570 | 707 |
| Utah | 34 | 750 | 2,687 |
| Vermont[6] | 32 | NA | 17 |
| | | | |
| Virginia | 53 | 5,667 | 14,680 |
| Washington | 62 | 2,947 | 506 |
| West Virginia | 69 | 1,830 | 0 |
| Wisconsin | 46 | 2,235 | 599 |
| Wyoming | 53 | 174 | 300 |

NOTE: Includes persons held for state or federal correctional authorities in government-operated or privately operated prisons, regardless of sentence status or length, and staff working in those facilities. Excludes prisoners held in local jails on behalf of state or federal correctional authorities, and staff working in those facilities.
NA = Not applicable.
NR = Not reported.
1 Difference between the date a COVID-19 vaccine was made available to the state department of corrections (DOC) and February 28, 2021.   2 Number of unique persons who received at least one dose of the COVID-19 vaccine by February 28, 2021.
3 Totals exclude Missouri, which did not submit data to the National Prisoner Statistics program - Coronavirus Pandemic Supplemental Survey.   4 Excludes counts from privately operated prisons under federal contract.   5 State DOC did not receive the COVID-19 vaccine by February 28, 2021.   6 Prisons and jails form one integrated system. Data include both prison and jail populations.

## Table 106. Number of Jurisdictions That Adopted COVID-19 Vaccine Distribution Policies, Through February 28, 2021

(Number.)

| Vaccine distribution policy | Number of jurisdictions that adopted policy | Number of jurisdictions that did not adopt policy | Number of jurisdictions for which policy was not applicable/reported |
|---|---|---|---|
| All staff vaccinated before prisoners | 7 | 42 | 2 |
| All prisoners required to get vaccine | 0 | 49 | 2 |
| Prisoners allowed to opt out of vaccination | 49 | 0 | 2 |
| All staff required to get vaccine | 0 | 50 | 1 |
| Staff allowed to opt out of vaccination | 47 | 0 | 4 |
| Older prisoners prioritized over younger prisoners | 41 | 9 | 1 |
| Prisoners with chronic/other infectious diseases prioritized over healthy prisoners | 41 | 9 | 1 |
| Prisoners soon to be released prioritized for vaccination | 4 | 42 | 5 |
| Newly admitted prisoners prioritized for vaccination | 4 | 43 | 4 |
| Prisoners offered incentives to get vaccine | 15 | 32 | 4 |

NOTE: Includes COVID-19 vaccine distribution policies adopted by state and federal correctional authorities in government-operated and privately operated prisons.

## Table 107. Number of COVID-19 Infections, Test Positivity Rate, Number of COVID-19–Related Deaths, and Crude Mortality Rate Among Correctional Staff in State and Federal Prisons, by Jurisdiction, March 1, 2020–February 28, 2021

(Number; rate.)

| Jurisdiction | Total staff, February 28, 2021 | Number of staff who tested positive, Mar 1, 2020–Feb 28, 2021[1] | Test positivity rate per 1,000 staff | Number of staff deaths[2] | Crude mortality rate per 1,000 staff[2] |
|---|---|---|---|---|---|
| Total[3] | 360,314 | 94,122 | 261.2 | 196 | 0.5 |
| Federal | 34,979 | 6,574 | 187.9 | 4 | 0.1 |
| State[3] | 325,335 | 87,548 | 269.1 | 192 | 0.6 |
| Alabama | 3,179 | UNK | NC | ^ | 0.9 |
| Alaska[4] | 1,543 | NR | NC | NR | NC |
| Arizona | 8,000 | 2,535 | 316.9 | 6 | 0.8 |
| Arkansas | 5,215 | 952 | 182.6 | 4 | 0.8 |
| California | 55,207 | 14,977 | 271.3 | 26 | 0.5 |
| Colorado | 5,810 | 1,402 | 241.3 | 0 | 0.0 |
| Connecticut[4] | 6,010 | 1,541 | 256.4 | 0 | 0.0 |
| Delaware[4] | 1,705 | 765 | 448.7 | ^ | 0.6 |
| Florida | 17,597 | 5,167 | 293.6 | 6 | 0.3 |
| Georgia | 6,654 | 1,471 | 221.1 | 4 | 0.6 |
| Hawaii[4] | 1,269 | 208 | 163.9 | 0 | 0.0 |
| Idaho | 1,355 | 379 | 279.7 | 0 | 0.0 |
| Illinois | 11,398 | 4,130 | 362.3 | ^ | 0.1 |
| Indiana | 5,846 | 1,622 | 277.5 | 4 | 0.7 |
| Iowa | 2,435 | 698 | 286.7 | ^ | 0.8 |
| Kansas | 3,276 | 26 | 7.9 | 5 | 1.5 |
| Kentucky | 3,138 | 1,034 | 329.5 | 5 | 1.6 |
| Louisiana | 4,719 | 1,104 | 233.9 | 6 | 1.3 |
| Maine | 981 | 57 | 58.1 | 0 | 0.0 |
| Maryland | 6,191 | 1,769 | 285.7 | 4 | 0.6 |
| Massachusetts | 3,726 | 1,030 | 276.4 | 0 | 0.0 |
| Michigan | 9,120 | 3,298 | 361.6 | 5 | 0.5 |
| Minnesota | 3,657 | 1,077 | 294.5 | 0 | 0.0 |
| Mississippi | 995 | 205 | 206.0 | ^ | 2.0 |
| Missouri[5] | NR | 2,188 | NC | 6 | NC |
| Montana | 898 | 232 | 258.4 | 0 | 0.0 |
| Nebraska | 1,829 | 538 | 294.1 | 0 | 0.0 |
| Nevada | 2,571 | 969 | 376.9 | ^ | 1.2 |
| New Hampshire | 613 | 173 | 282.2 | 0 | 0.0 |
| New Jersey | 6,933 | 2,438 | 351.7 | NR | 0.0 |
| New Mexico | 1,434 | 928 | 647.1 | ^ | 1.4 |
| New York | 24,241 | 4,455 | 183.8 | 8 | 0.3 |
| North Carolina | 13,783 | 3,405 | 247.0 | 13 | 0.9 |
| North Dakota | 713 | 314 | 440.4 | ^ | 1.4 |
| Ohio | 13,799 | 4,917 | 356.3 | 10 | 0.7 |
| Oklahoma | 3,213 | NR | NC | NR | NC |
| Oregon | 4,500 | 830 | 184.4 | ^ | 0.4 |
| Pennsylvania | 13,840 | 3,399 | 245.6 | 6 | 0.4 |
| Rhode Island[4] | 1,048 | 324 | 309.2 | ^ | 1.0 |
| South Carolina | 3,558 | 1,048 | 294.5 | ^ | 0.6 |
| South Dakota | 812 | 186 | 229.1 | 0 | 0.0 |
| Tennessee | 6,042 | 1,858 | 307.5 | 10 | 1.7 |
| Texas | 27,183 | 9,375 | 344.9 | 41 | 1.5 |
| Utah | 840 | 399 | 475.0 | 0 | 0.0 |
| Vermont[4] | 591 | 62 | 104.9 | 0 | 0.0 |
| Virginia | 8,636 | 2,268 | 262.6 | 5 | 0.6 |
| Washington | 8,774 | 1,124 | 128.1 | ^ | 0.2 |
| West Virginia | 2,964 | 454 | 153.2 | ^ | 0.7 |
| Wisconsin | 6,647 | 2,104 | 316.5 | 0 | 0.0 |
| Wyoming | 847 | 301 | 355.4 | 0 | 0.0 |

NOTE: Includes correctional officers, health care workers, janitorial staff, and any other paid personnel who had contact with prisoners or worked inside a state-operated or federally operated correctional facility. Excludes staff employed in private prisons under state or federal contract and staff in state departments of corrections who did not enter a correctional facility as part of their employment. Estimates will differ from previously published statistics.
^ = Three or fewer deaths.
NC = Not calculated.
NR = Not reported.
UNK = Not known.
1 Includes staff who tested positive for COVID-19 through a viral (polymerase chain reaction) test at any point from March 1, 2020 to February 28, 2021, regardless of where the infection or testing occurred.    2 Includes all deaths of staff where COVID-19 was suspected or confirmed as the cause or a significant contributing factor, regardless of where the infection or death occurred.    3 Totals exclude Missouri, which did not submit data to the National Prisoner Statistics program - Coronavirus Pandemic Supplemental Survey.    4 Prisons and jails form one integrated system. Data include both prison and jail populations.    5 The Data on the total number of COVID-19-related deaths were taken from the March 1, 2021 entry in the COVID Prison Project database (https://github.com/healthandjustice/covid-prison-project).

# APPENDIXES

# APPENDIX I. METHODOLOGY

Submitting UCR data to the FBI is a collective effort on the part of city, university/college, county, state, tribal, and federal law enforcement agencies to present a nationwide view of crime. Participating agencies throughout the country voluntarily provide reports on crimes known to the police and on persons arrested. For the most part, agencies submit monthly crime reports, using uniform offense definitions, to a centralized repository within their state. The state UCR Program then forwards the data to the FBI's UCR Program. Agencies in states that do not have a state UCR Program submit their data directly to the FBI. Staff members review the information for accuracy and reasonableness. [The FBI distributes the data presentations, special studies, and other publications compiled from the data to all who are interested in knowing about crime in the nation.] The national UCR Program is housed in the Operational Programs (OP) Branch of the FBI's Criminal Justice Information Services (CJIS) Division. Within the OP Branch, four units (the Crime Statistics Management Unit [CSMU], the CJIS Audit Unit, the Multimedia Productions Group [MPG]), and the CJIS Training and Advisory Process [CTAP] Unit), are involved in the day-to-day administration of the program.

## Criteria for State UCR programs

The criteria established for state programs ensure consistency and comparability in the data submitted to the national program, as well as regular and timely reporting. These criteria are:

1. A UCR Program must conform to the FBI UCR Program's submission standards, definitions, specifications, and required deadlines.

2. A UCR Program must establish data integrity procedures and have personnel assigned to assist contributing agencies in quality assurance practices and crime reporting procedures. Data integrity procedures should include crime trend assessments, offense classification verification, and technical specification validation.

3. A UCR Program's submissions must cover more than 50 percent of the law enforcement agencies within its established reporting domain and be willing to cover any and all UCR-contributing agencies that wish to use the UCR Program from within its domain. (An agency wishing to become a UCR Program must be willing to report for all of the agencies within the state.)

4. A UCR Program must furnish the FBI UCR Program with all of the UCR data collected by the law enforcement agencies within its domain.

These requirements do not prohibit the state from gathering other statistical data beyond the national collection.

## Data Completeness and Quality

National program staff members contact the state UCR program in connection with crime-reporting matters and, when necessary and approved by the state, they contact individual contributors within the state. To fulfill its responsibilities in connection with the UCR program, the FBI reviews and edits individual agency reports for completeness and quality. Upon request, they conduct training programs within the state on law enforcement record-keeping and crime-reporting procedures. The FBI conducts an audit of each state's UCR data collection procedures once every three years, in accordance with audit standards established by the federal government. Should circumstances develop in which the state program does not comply with the aforementioned requirements, the national program may institute a direct collection of data from law enforcement agencies within the state.

During a review of publication processes, the UCR Program staff analyzed Web statistics from previous editions of *Crime in the United States* (*CIUS*) to determine the tables that users access the most. Based on these criteria, the UCR Program streamlined the 2016 edition by reducing the number of tables from 81 to 29. The publication, however, still presents the major topics (offenses known, clearances, and persons arrested) that readers have come to expect. On June 30, 2017, the UCR Program launched the Crime Data Explorer (CDE), which provides law enforcement and the general public with crime data at the agency, state, and national levels. Offering multiple pathways to reported crime data, the CDE provides data visualizations of high-level trends and incident data with more detailed perspectives through downloads and a system enabling developers to create software applications. Planned enhancements to the CDE include additional tools to create dynamic data presentations, progressing beyond the static data tables of *CIUS* and the National Incident-Based Reporting System (NIBRS).

Beginning January 1, 2017, the UCR Program discontinued collecting rape data via the SRS according to the legacy definition. Therefore, the 2016 editions of *CIUS* and *Hate Crime Statistics* are the final publications which include the legacy definition of rape. Only rape data submitted under the revised definition will be published for 2017 and subsequent years. This change did not affect agencies that submit rape data via NIBRS.

## Reporting Procedures

Offenses known and value of property–Law enforcement agencies tabulate the number of Part I offenses reported based on records of all reports of crime received from victims, officers who discover infractions, or other sources, and submit these reports each month to the FBI directly or through their

683

state UCR programs. Part I offenses include murder and non-negligent manslaughter, forcible rape, robbery, aggravated assault, burglary, larceny-theft, motor vehicle theft, and arson. Each month, law enforcement agencies also submit to the FBI the value of property stolen and recovered in connection with the offenses and detailed information pertaining to criminal homicide.

**Unfounded offenses and clearances**—When, through investigation, an agency determines that complaints of crimes are unfounded or false, the agency eliminates that offense from its crime tally through an entry on the monthly report. The report also provides the total number of actual Part I offenses, the number of offenses cleared, and the number of clearances that involve only offenders under the age of 18. (Law enforcement can clear crimes in one of two ways: by the arrest of at least one person who is charged and turned over to the court for prosecution or by exceptional means—when some element beyond law enforcement's control precludes the arrest of a known offender.)

**Persons arrested**—In addition to reporting Part I offenses each month, law enforcement agencies also provide data on the age, sex, and race of persons arrested for Part I and Part II offenses. Part II offenses encompass all crimes, except traffic violations, that are not classified as Part I offenses.

**Officers killed or assaulted**—Each month, law enforcement agencies also report information to the UCR program regarding law enforcement officers killed or assaulted, and each year they report the number of full-time sworn and civilian law enforcement personnel employed as of October 31.

**Hate crimes**—At the end of each quarter, law enforcement agencies report summarized data on hate crimes; that is specific offenses that were motivated by an offender's bias against the perceived race, religion, ethnic or national origin, sexual orientation, or physical or mental disability of the victim. Those agencies participating in the UCR program's National Incident-Based Reporting System (NIBRS) submit hate crime data monthly.

### Editing Procedures

The UCR program thoroughly examines each report it receives for arithmetical accuracy and for deviations in crime data from month to month and from present to past years that may indicate errors. UCR staff members compare an agency's monthly reports with its previous submissions and with reports from similar agencies to identify any unusual fluctuations in the agency's crime count. Considerable variations in crime levels may indicate modified records procedures, incomplete reporting, or changes in the jurisdiction's geopolitical structure.

**Evaluation of trends**—Data reliability is a high priority of the FBI, which brings any deviations or arithmetical adjustments to the attention of state UCR programs or the submitting agencies. Typically, FBI staff members study the monthly reports to evaluate periodic trends prepared for individual reporting units. Any significant increase or decrease becomes the subject of a special inquiry. Changes in crime reporting procedures or annexations that affect an agency's jurisdiction can influence the level of reported crime. When this occurs, the FBI excludes the figures for specific crime categories or totals, if necessary, from the trend tabulations.

**Training for contributors**—In addition to the evaluation of trends, the FBI provides training seminars and instructional materials on crime reporting procedures to assist contributors in complying with UCR standards. Throughout the country, representatives from the national program coordinate with representatives of state programs and law enforcement personnel and hold training sessions to explain the purpose of the program, the rules of uniform classification and scoring, and the methods of assembling the information for reporting. When an individual agency has specific problems with compiling its crime statistics and its remedial efforts are unsuccessful, personnel from the FBI's Criminal Justice Information Services Division may visit the contributor to aid in resolving the problems.

***UCR Handbook***—The national UCR program publishes the *Uniform Crime Reporting (UCR) Handbook*, which details procedures for classifying and scoring offenses and serves as the contributing agencies' basic resource for preparing reports. The national staff also produces letters to UCR contributors, state program bulletins, and UCR newsletters as needed. These publications provide policy updates and new information, as well as clarification of reporting issues.

The final responsibility for data submissions rests with the individual contributing law enforcement agency. Although the FBI makes every effort through its editing procedures, training practices, and correspondence to ensure the validity of the data it receives, the accuracy of the statistics depends primarily on the adherence of each contributor to the established standards of reporting. Deviations from these established standards that cannot be resolved by the national UCR program may be brought to the attention of the Criminal Justice Information Systems Committees of the International Association of Chiefs of Police and the National Sheriffs' Association.

### NIBRS Conversion

All state programs are certified to provide their UCR data in the expanded National Incident-Based Reporting System (NIBRS) format. The UCR program is currently in full transition/migration to NIBRS, as seen on the FBI's Crime Data Explorer.

## Crime Trends

By showing fluctuations from year to year, trend statistics offer the data user an added perspective from which to study crime. Percent change tabulations in this publication are computed only for reporting agencies that provided comparable data for the periods under consideration. The FBI excludes from the trend calculations all figures except those received for common months from common agencies. Also excluded are unusual fluctuations of data that the FBI determines are the result of such variables as improved records procedures, annexations, and so on.

## Caution to Users

Data users should exercise care in making any direct comparison between data in this publication and those in prior issues of *Crime in the United States*. Because of differing levels of participation from year to year and reporting problems that require the FBI to estimate crime counts for certain contributors, some data may not be comparable. In addition, this publication may contain updates to data provided in prior years' publications.

## Offense Estimation

Some tables in this publication contain statistics for the entire United States. Because not all law enforcement agencies provide data for complete reporting periods, the FBI includes estimated crime numbers in these presentations. The FBI estimates data for three areas: Metropolitan Statistical Areas (MSAs), cities outside MSAs, and nonmetropolitan counties; and computes estimates for participating agencies that do not provide 12 months of complete data. For agencies supplying 3 to 11 months of data, the national UCR program estimates for the missing data by following a standard estimation procedure using the data provided by the agency. If an agency has supplied less than 3 months of data, the FBI computes estimates by using the known crime figures of similar areas within a state and assigning the same proportion of crime volumes to nonreporting agencies. The estimation process considers the following: population size covered by the agency; type of jurisdiction; for example, police department versus sheriff's office; and geographic location.

## Estimation of State-Level Data

In response to various circumstances, the FBI calculates estimated offense totals for certain states. For example, some states do not provide forcible rape figures in accordance with UCR guidelines. In addition, problems at the state level have, at times, resulted in no useable data. Also, the conversion of the National Incident-Based Reporting System (NIBRS) data to Summary data has contributed to the need for unique estimation procedures.

# APPENDIX II. OFFENSE DEFINITIONS

The Uniform Crime Reporting (UCR) program divides offenses into two groups. Contributing agencies submit information on the number of Part I offenses known to law enforcement; those offenses cleared by arrest or exceptional means; and the age, sex, and race of persons arrested for each of these offenses. Contributors provide only arrest data for Part II offenses. These are definitions of offenses set forth by the UCR.

The UCR program collects data on Part I offenses to measure the level and scope of crime occurring throughout the nation. The program's founders chose these offenses because (1) they are serious crimes, (2) they occur with regularity in all areas of the country, and (3) they are likely to be reported to police.

**Part I** offenses include criminal homicide, forcible rape, robbery, aggravated assault, burglary, larceny-theft, motor vehicle theft, and arson.

**Criminal homicide**—a.) Murder and nonnegligent manslaughter: the willful (nonnegligent) killing of one human being by another. Deaths caused by negligence, attempts to kill, assaults to kill, suicides, and accidental deaths are excluded. The program classifies justifiable homicides separately and limits the definition to (1) the killing of a felon by a law enforcement officer in the line of duty; or (2) the killing of a felon, during the commission of a felony, by a private citizen. b. Manslaughter by negligence: the killing of another person through gross negligence. Deaths of persons due to their own negligence, accidental deaths not resulting from gross negligence, and traffic fatalities are excluded.

**Rape**—In 2013, the FBI UCR Program began collecting rape data under a revised definition within the Summary Reporting System. Previously, offense data for forcible rape were collected under the legacy UCR definition: the carnal knowledge of a female forcibly and against her will. Beginning with the 2013 data year, the term "forcible" was removed from the offense title, and the definition was changed. The revised UCR definition of rape is: penetration, no matter how slight, of the vagina or anus with any body part or object, or oral penetration by a sex organ of another person, without the consent of the victim. Attempts or assaults to commit rape are also included in the statistics presented here; however, statutory rape and incest are excluded. In 2016, the FBI director approved the recommendation to discontinue the reporting of rape data using the UCR legacy definition beginning in 2017. However, to maintain the 20-year trend in Table 1, national estimates for rape under the legacy definition are provided along with estimates under the revised definition for 2017. The UCR Program counts one offense for each victim of a rape, attempted rape, or assault with intent to rape, regardless of the victim's age. Non-consensual sexual relations involving a familial member is considered rape, not incest. All other crimes of a sexual nature are considered to be Part II offenses; as such, the UCR Program collects only arrest data for those crimes. The offense of statutory rape, in which no force is used but the female victim is under the age of consent, is included in the arrest total for the sex offenses category.

**Robbery**—The taking or attempted taking of anything of value from the care, custody, or control of a person or persons by force or threat of force or violence and/or by putting the victim in fear.

**Aggravated assault**—An unlawful attack by one person upon another for the purpose of inflicting severe or aggravated bodily injury. This type of assault usually is accompanied by the use of a weapon or by means likely to produce death or great bodily harm. Simple assaults are excluded.

**Burglary (breaking or entering)**—The unlawful entry of a structure to commit a felony or a theft. Attempted forcible entry is included.

**Larceny-theft (except motor vehicle theft)**—The unlawful taking, carrying, leading, or riding away of property from the possession or constructive possession of another. Examples are thefts of bicycles or automobile parts and accessories, shoplifting, pocket-picking, or the stealing of any property or article that is not taken by force and violence or by fraud. Attempted larcenies are included. Embezzlement, confidence games, forgery, worthless checks, and the like, are excluded.

**Motor vehicle theft**—The theft or attempted theft of a motor vehicle. A motor vehicle is self-propelled and runs on land surface and not on rails. Motorboats, construction equipment, airplanes, and farming equipment are specifically excluded from this category.

**Arson**—Any willful or malicious burning or attempt to burn, with or without intent to defraud, a dwelling house, public building, motor vehicle, aircraft, personal property of another, and the like.

# APPENDIX III. GEOGRAPHIC AREA DEFINITIONS

The program collects crime data and supplemental information that make it possible to generate a variety of statistical compilations, including data presented by reporting areas. These statistics enable data users to analyze local crime data in conjunction with those for areas of similar geographic location or population size. The reporting areas that the program uses in its data breakdowns include community types, population groups, and regions and divisions. For community types, the program considers proximity to metropolitan areas using the designations established by the U.S. Office of Management and Budget (OMB). (Generally, sheriffs, county police, and state police report crimes within counties but outside of cities; local police report crimes within city limits.) The number of inhabitants living in a locale (based on the U.S. Census Bureau's figures) determines the population group into which the program places it. For its geographic breakdowns, the program divides the United States into regions and divisions.

## Regions and Divisions

The map below illustrates the nine divisions that make up the four regions of the United States. The program uses this widely recognized geographic organization when compiling the nation's crime data. The regions and divisions are as follows:

NORTHEAST

*New England*—Connecticut, Maine, Massachusetts, New Hampshire, Rhode Island, and Vermont

*Middle Atlantic*—New York, New Jersey, and Pennsylvania

MIDWEST

*East North Central*—Illinois, Indiana, Michigan, Ohio, and Wisconsin

*West North Central*—Iowa, Kansas, Minnesota, Missouri, Nebraska, North Dakota, and South Dakota

SOUTH

*South Atlantic*—Delaware, District of Columbia, Florida, Georgia, Maryland, North Carolina, South Carolina, Virginia, and West Virginia

*East South Central*—Alabama, Kentucky, Mississippi, and Tennessee

*West South Central*—Arkansas, Louisiana, Oklahoma, and Texas

WEST

*Mountain*—Arizona, Colorado, Idaho, Montana, Nevada, New Mexico, Utah, and Wyoming

*Pacific*—Alaska, California, Hawaii, Oregon, and Washington

# APPENDIX IV. THE NATION'S TWO CRIME MEASURES

The Department of Justice administers two statistical programs to measure the magnitude, nature, and impact of crime in the nation: the Uniform Crime Reporting (UCR) program and the National Crime Victimization Survey (NCVS). Each of these programs produces valuable information about aspects of the nation's crime problem. Because the UCR and NCVS programs are conducted for different purposes, use different methods, and focus on somewhat different aspects of crime, the information they produce together provides a more comprehensive panorama of the nation's crime problem than either could produce alone.

## Uniform Crime Reporting (UCR) program

The UCR program, administered by the Federal Bureau of Investigation (FBI), was created in 1929 and collects information on the following crimes reported to law enforcement authorities: murder and nonnegligent manslaughter, forcible rape, robbery, aggravated assault, burglary, larceny-theft, motor vehicle theft, and arson. Law enforcement agencies also report arrest data for 20 additional crime categories.

The UCR program compiles data from monthly law enforcement reports and from individual crime incident records transmitted directly to the FBI or to centralized state agencies that report to the FBI. The program thoroughly examines each report it receives for reasonableness, accuracy, and deviations that may indicate errors. Large variations in crime levels may indicate modified records procedures, incomplete reporting, or changes in a jurisdiction's boundaries. To identify any unusual fluctuations in an agency's crime counts, the program compares monthly reports to previous submissions of the agency and to those for similar agencies.

The FBI annually publishes its findings in a preliminary release in the spring of the following calendar year, followed by a detailed annual report, *Crime in the United States*, issued in the fall. (The printed copy of *Crime in the United States* is now published by Bernan.) In addition to crime counts and trends, this report includes data on crimes cleared, persons arrested (age, sex, and race), law enforcement personnel (including the number of sworn officers killed or assaulted), and the characteristics of homicides (including age, sex, and race of victims and offenders; victim-offender relationships; weapons used; and circumstances surrounding the homicides). Other periodic reports are also available from the UCR program.

The state and local law enforcement agencies participating in the UCR program are continually converting to the more comprehensive and detailed National Incident-Based Reporting System (NIBRS).

The UCR program presents crime counts for the nation as a whole, as well as for regions, states, counties, cities, towns, tribal law enforcement areas, and colleges and universities. This allows for studies among neighboring jurisdictions and among those with similar populations and other common characteristics.

## National Crime Victimization Survey

The NCVS, conducted by the Bureau of Justice Statistics (BJS), began in 1973. It provides a detailed picture of crime incidents, victims, and trends. After a substantial period of research, the BJS completed an intensive methodological redesign of the survey in 1993. It conducted this redesign to improve the questions used to uncover crime, update the survey methods, and broaden the scope of crimes measured. The redesigned survey collects detailed information on the frequency and nature of the crimes of rape, sexual assault, personal robbery, aggravated and simple assault, household burglary, theft, and motor vehicle theft. It does not measure homicide or commercial crimes (such as burglaries of stores).

Twice a year, Census Bureau personnel interview household members in a nationally representative sample of approximately 90,000 households (about 160,000 people). Households stay in the sample for 3 years, and new households rotate into the sample on an ongoing basis.

The NCVS collects information on crimes suffered by individuals and households, whether or not those crimes were reported to law enforcement. It estimates the proportion of each crime type reported to law enforcement, and it summarizes the reasons that victims give for reporting or not reporting.

The survey provides information about victims (age, sex, race, ethnicity, marital status, income, and educational level); offenders (sex, race, approximate age, and victim-offender relationship); and crimes (time and place of occurrence, use of weapons, nature of injury, and economic consequences). Questions also cover victims' experiences with the criminal justice system, self-protective measures used by victims, and possible substance abuse by offenders. Supplements are added to the survey periodically to obtain detailed information on specific topics, such as school crime.

The BJS published the first data from the redesigned NCVS in a June 1995 bulletin. The publication of NCVS data includes *Criminal Victimization in the United States*, an annual report that covers the broad range of detailed information collected by the NCVS. The bureau also publishes detailed reports on topics such as crime against women, urban crime, and gun use in crime. The National Archive of Criminal Justice Data at the University of Michigan archives the NCVS data files to help researchers perform independent analyses.

### Comparing the UCR program and the NCVS

Because the BJS designed the NCVS to complement the UCR program, the two programs share many similarities. As much as their different collection methods permit, the two measure the same subset of serious crimes with the same definitions. Both programs cover rape, robbery, aggravated assault, burglary, theft, and motor vehicle theft; both define rape, robbery, theft, and motor vehicle theft virtually identically. (Although rape is defined analogously, the UCR program measures the crime against women only, and the NCVS measures it against both sexes.)

There are also significant differences between the two programs. First, the two programs were created to serve different purposes. The UCR program's primary objective is to provide a reliable set of criminal justice statistics for law enforcement administration, operation, and management. The BJS established the NCVS to provide previously unavailable information about crime (including crime not reported to police), victims, and offenders.

Second, the two programs measure an overlapping but non-identical set of crimes. The NCVS includes crimes both reported and not reported to law enforcement. The NCVS excludes—but the UCR program includes—homicide, arson, commercial crimes, and crimes committed against children under 12 years of age. The UCR program captures crimes reported to law enforcement but collects only arrest data for simple assaults and sexual assaults other than forcible rape.

Third, because of methodology, the NCVS and UCR have different definitions of some crimes. For example, the UCR defines burglary as the unlawful entry or attempted entry of a structure to commit a felony or theft. The NCVS, not wanting to ask victims to ascertain offender motives, defines burglary as the entry or attempted entry of a residence by a person who had no right to be there.

Fourth, for property crimes (burglary, theft, and motor vehicle theft), the two programs calculate crime rates using different bases. The UCR program rates for these crimes are per capita (number of crimes per 100,000 persons), whereas the NCVS rates for these crimes are per household (number of crimes per 1,000 households).

Because the number of households may not grow at the same annual rate as the total population, trend data for rates of property crimes measured by the two programs may not be comparable. In addition, some differences in the data from the two programs may result from sampling variation in the NCVS and from estimating for nonresponsiveness in the UCR program.

The BJS derives the NCVS estimates from interviewing a sample and are, therefore, subject to a margin of error. The bureau uses rigorous statistical methods to calculate confidence intervals around all survey estimates, and describes trend data in the NCVS reports as genuine only if there is at least a 90-percent certainty that the measured changes are not the result of sampling variation. The UCR program bases its data on the actual counts of offenses reported by law enforcement agencies. In some circumstances, the UCR program estimates its data for nonparticipating agencies or those reporting partial data. Apparent discrepancies between statistics from the two programs can usually be accounted for by their definitional and procedural differences, or resolved by comparing NCVS sampling variations (confidence intervals) of crimes said to have been reported to police with UCR program statistics.

For most types of crimes measured by both the UCR program and the NCVS, analysts familiar with the programs can exclude those aspects of crime not common to both from analysis. Resulting long-term trend lines can be brought into close concordance. The impact of such adjustments is most striking for robbery, burglary, and motor vehicle theft, whose definitions most closely coincide.

With robbery, the BJS bases the NCVS victimization rates on only those robberies reported to the police. It is also possible to remove UCR program robberies of commercial establishments, such as gas stations, convenience stores, and banks, from analysis. When users compare the resulting NCVS police-reported robbery rates and the UCR program noncommercial robbery rates, the results reveal closely corresponding long-term trends.

### Conclusion

Each program has unique strengths. The UCR program provides a measure of the number of crimes reported to law enforcement agencies throughout the country. The program's Supplementary Homicide Reports provide the most reliable, timely data on the extent and nature of homicides in the nation. The NCVS is the primary source of information on the characteristics of criminal victimization and on the number and types of crimes not reported to law enforcement authorities.

By understanding the strengths and limitations of each program, it is possible to use the UCR program and NCVS to achieve a greater understanding of crime trends and the nature of crime in the United States. For example, changes in police procedures, shifting attitudes towards crime and police, and other societal changes can affect the extent to which people report and law enforcement agencies record crime. NCVS and UCR program data can be used in concert to explore why trends in reported and police-recorded crime may differ.

# Index

CPSIA information can be obtained
at www.ICGtesting.com
Printed in the USA
BVHW021238210623
666188BV00001B/1